Über die Herausgeber

PROF. DR. MANFRED BRAUNECK, Jahrgang 1934, lehrt seit 1973 Neuere Deutsche Literaturwissenschaft und Theaterwissenschaft an der Universität Hamburg. Seit 1986 Leiter des Zentrums für Theaterforschung und seit 1988 Studienleiter im Fach Schauspiel-Regie am Institut für Theater, Musiktheater und Film. Seine Forschungsschwerpunkte sind: Theatergeschichte und -theorie, Grenzbereiche zwischen Theater und bildender Kunst.

Wichtigste Veröffentlichungen: Die Lieder Konrads von Würzburg, 1964/Wolfram von Eschenbachs ‹Parzifal›, 1967/Deutsche Literatur des 17. Jahrhunderts – Revision eines Epochenbildes. Forschungsbericht 1945–1970, 1971/Literatur und Öffentlichkeit im ausgehenden 19. Jahrhundert. Zur Rezeption des naturalistischen Theaters in Deutschland, 1974/Religiöse Volkskunst, 1978/Theater im 20. Jahrhundert. Programmschriften, Stilperioden, Reformmodelle, 1982 u. ö./Volkstümliche Hafnerkeramik im deutschsprachigen Raum, 1984/(mit Gérard Schneilin) Drama und Theater, 1987/Klassiker der Schauspielregie. Positionen und Kommentare zum Theater im 20. Jahrhundert, 1988 – *Herausgebertätigkeit:* Heinrich Julius von Braunschweig. Von einem Weibe. Von Vincentio Ladislao, 1967/Sixt Birck. Sämtliche Dramen. 3 Bde., 1969ff/Spieltexte der Wanderbühne des 17. Jahrhunderts. 4 Bde., 1979ff/Das deutsche Drama vom Expressionismus bis zur Gegenwart, 1979/Die Rote Fahne. Theorie, Kritik, Feuilleton 1918–1933, 1973/Der deutsche Roman im 20. Jahrhundert. 2 Bde., 1976/Film und Fernsehen. Materialien zur Theorie, Soziologie und Geschichte. 1980/Hanns Otto Münsterer. Mancher Mann. Gedichte, 1980/Weltliteratur im 20. Jahrhundert. 5 Bde., 1981/Autorenlexikon deutschsprachiger Literatur des 20. Jahrhunderts, 1984; 4. Aufl. 1991/(mit Christine Müller) Naturalismus. Manifeste und Dokumente zur deutschen Literatur 1880–1900, 1987/Theaterstadt Hamburg. Geschichte und Gegenwart. Hg. vom Zentrum für Theaterforschung der Universität Hamburg, 1989/Der deutsche Roman nach 1945, 1992.

PROF. DR. GÉRARD SCHNEILIN, Jahrgang 1934, lehrte seit 1968 Neuere Deutsche Literaturwissenschaft an der Universität Paris X – Nanterre; seit 1987 lehrt er an der Sorbonne, Paris IV, sowie Deutschlandkunde an der Hochschule für Wirtschaftswissenschaften Paris (CESA/HEC). Seine Forschungsschwerpunkte sind: Theatergeschichte und -theorie, Literatur des 19. und 20. Jahrhunderts, Literatur der Schweiz sowie Deutschlandkunde.

Wichtigste Veröffentlichungen: Der Nationalsozialismus, 1972/Die Wirtschaft der Bundesrepublik Deutschland, 1973, 1983/Das Theater Chr. D. Grabbes, 1976/Deutsche Rechtstexte, 1986/(mit Manfred Brauneck) Drama und Theater, 1986. – *Mitwirkung bei Sammelbänden:* Der amerikanische Süden zur Zeit vor dem Bürgerkrieg, 1969/Wien zur Zeit Franz Josephs, 1972/Person + Amt, 1980/Weltliteratur im 20. Jahrhundert (Hg. Manfred Brauneck), 1981/Das Bild des Schicksals in den Mythologien, 1983/Deutsch-französische Germanistik, 1984/Autorenlexikon deutschsprachiger Literatur des 20. Jahrhunderts (Hg. Manfred Brauneck), 1984.

Manfred Brauneck
Gérard Schneilin (Hg.)

Theaterlexikon

Begriffe und
Epochen, Bühnen
und Ensembles

rowohlts enzyklopädie

rowohlts enzyklopädie

Herausgegeben von Burghard König

Redaktionelle Mitarbeit Wolfgang Beck
und Ingeborg Janich
Übersetzungen aus dem Französischen
Horst Schumacher

3. vollständig überarbeitete und
erweiterte Neuausgabe
13.–22. Tausend, Dezember 1992

Originalausgabe
Umschlaggestaltung Jens Kreitmeyer
(Zeichnung von Fernand Léger)
Veröffentlicht im Rowohlt Taschenbuch Verlag GmbH,
Reinbek bei Hamburg, November 1986
Copyright © 1986 by Rowohlt Taschenbuch Verlag GmbH,
Reinbek bei Hamburg
Satz Times (Linotronic 500)
Gesamtherstellung Clausen & Bosse, Leck
Printed in Germany
3990-ISBN 3 499 55465 8

Verzeichnis der Stichwörter, Querverweise, Länder- und Städteübersichten

Stichwörter und Querverweise

Abbey Theatre   43
ABC   44
Abel Spel/Sotternie   44
Abenddienst   45
   Abendspielleiter → Betriebsorgani-
   sation des Theaters
Abonnement   46
   Abreaktionsspiele → Orgien
   Mysterien Theater
Abschiedsvorstellung   46
Absurdes Theater   46
   Académie Royale de danse → Ballet
   de l'Opéra de Paris
   Actor's Equity Association → Equity
Actor's Studio   49
   Actor's Studio Theatre → Actor's
   Studio
   ADA → Ind. Theater
Adaption   49
Admiral's Men   50
Afrikanisches Theater   50
Afterpiece   52
   Agitprop → Proletarisch-revolutio-
   näres Theater
Agon   53
Agora   53
AITA/IATA   53
   Akademie Ruchu (Warschau) → Stu-
   dententheater
Akt   54
   Aktionscollage → Happening
   Aktionskunst → Performance
   Aldwych Theatre → Royal Shake-
   speare Company
Alexandriner   55
Allegorie   55
   Alternative theatre → Fringe

Alternieren   56
Alt-Wiener Volksstück   56
   Amateur Dramatic Association
   (ADA) → Ind. Theater
Amateurtheater   60
Amoibaion   62
Amphitheater   62
Amsterdamsche Schouwburg   63
Angry Young Men   65
Angura   66
Animation   67
Ankara Devlet Tiyatrosu   68
   Ankoku Butôha → Butô
Ankündigung   68
Anstandsrolle   69
   Ante-masque → Masque
Antikenrezeption   69
Antikes Theater   74
Anti-Masque   92
antiteater   92
Aparte   93
Applaus   93
Arbeitertheater   94
Arbeiter-Theater-Bund Deutschland
   (ATBD)   94
Arbeitertheater (USA)   95
   Architekturtheater → Freilicht-
   theater
Arena Goldoni   97
   Arenatheater → Amphitheater
Argumentum   98
Aristotelisches Theater   98
   Arlecchino → Commedia dell'arte
Armes Theater   99
   Art et Action → Laboratoire de
   Théâtre Art et Action
Arte   100

▶▶▶

Artef → Jiddisches Theater
Art et Liberté → Laboratoire de
Théâtre Art et Action
Arte Nuevo de hacer Comedias en este
Tiempo   101
Art Theatre → Little Theatre Move-
ment
ASSITEJ   102
Association of Community Theatres
(TACT) → Community Theatre
Atellana   102
Aufführung   103
Aufklärung/Theater der Auf-
klärung   103
Auftritt   107
Aufzug → Akt
Ausdruckstanz   107
Ausstattungsstück   109
The Austrian Theatre (New York)
→ Österreichische Bühne
Auto Sacramental   110
Avantgarde   110
Bad Hersfelder Festspiele   111
BAG → Bundesarbeitsgemeinschaft
(BAG) Spiel und Theater e. V.
Balagan   111
Ballad Opera   111
Ballet Blanc   112
Ballet comique de la Reine   113
Ballet d'action   113
Ballet de Cour   115
Ballet de l'Opéra de Paris   115
Ballet du Roi   117
Ballet du XXe Siècle   117
Ballet héroïque-pantomime   119
Ballets de chevaux → Roßballett
Ballets Jooss   120
Ballets Russes → Compagnie des
Ballets Russes de Serge de Diaghilev
Ballets Suédois   121
Ballett   122
Ballett der Deutschen Oper Berlin   122
Ballett der Deutschen Staatsoper
Berlin   122
Ballettdramaturg   124
Ballett Frankfurt   124
Ballettintendant → Intendant

Ballett-Kompanie
(Ballettensemble)   125
Bänkelsang   125
banzuke → Kabuki
Barocktheater   127
La Barraca   130
Barrace → La Barraca
Basler Ballett → Stadttheater
Basel
Basoches   130
Bathsheva Dance Company   131
Bauhausbühne   131
Bauhaustänze   133
Bayerisches Staatsballett   134
Bayerisches Staatsschauspiel Mün-
chen   135
Bayreuther Festspielhaus → Theater-
bau
BDAT (Bund Deutscher Amateur-
theater)   136
«Bedingtes Theater» → Meyerhold-
Methode
Beifall → Applaus
Beiseitesprechen → Aparte
Béjart Ballet Lausanne → Ballet du
XXe Siècle
Benefizvorstellung   137
Berliner Ensemble   137
Berliner Festwochen   140
Berliner Theatertreffen   140
Berufstänze → Brauchtumstänze
Besetzung   141
Besserungsstück   141
Besucherorganisation   143
Besucherräte → Theatersystem
Betriebsorganisation des Theaters
(BRD)   144
Bewegungschor   146
Bhagavatam → Ind. Theater
Bharata Natyam   148
Bharata-Natyasastra → Ind. Theater
Bhavai → Ind. Theater
Bildungsanstalt Jacques-Dalcroze
(Hellerau)   149
Biomechanik   150
Birmingham → Repertory Theatre
BITEF   151

Black-Light-Theater Imaginace
→ Černé Divadlo (Prag)
Black Theatre → Schwarz-amerika-
nisches Theater
Blankvers 151
Die Blauen Blusen 152
Der Blaue Vogel 153
Blumensteg → Hanamichi
Body Art → Performance
Bolschoi-Ballett 153
Bolschoi-Theater 155
Bonner Bühnen 155
Bonvivant 156
Botenbericht 157
Boulevardtheater 157
Bowery Theatre → Broadway
Brauchtumstänze 158
Bread and Puppet Theatre 162
Brecht-Theater → Episches Theater,
→ Kleines Organon für das Theater,
→ Verfremdungseffekt
Bregenzer Festspiele 163
bremer shakespeare company 163
Bremer Tanztheater 164
Bremer Theaterlabor 165
Brighella → Commedia dell'arte
British Drama League → British
Theatre Association
British Theatre Association 166
Broadway 166
Bugaku → Mai-Tanzformen
Das Bügelbrett 171
Bühne 172
Bühnenbearbeitung 173
Bühnenbeleuchtung 173
Bühnenbild 176
Bühnenbildelemente 181
Bühnenbildner 182
Bühnenfall → Kulissenbühne
Bühnenkostüm 184
Bühnenmanuskript 190
Bühnenmaschinen → Bühnentechnik
Bühnenmusik 190
Bühnensprache 192
Bühnensynthese 193
Bühnentechnik 194
Bühnenturm → Bühnentechnik

Bühnenverein → Deutscher Bühnen-
verein
Bühnenverlag 197
Bühnenvertrieb 198
Bühnenwagen → Bühnentechnik
Bund der Theatergemeinden e. V.
→ Besucherorganisationen
Bund Deutscher Volksbühnen
→ BDAT (Bund Deutscher Ama-
teurtheater)
Bundesarbeitsgemeinschaft (BAG)
Spiel und Theater e. V. 199
Bundesverband der Deutschen
Volksbühne-Vereine e. V. → Besu-
cherorganisationen, → Volksbühne
Bunraku → Jôruri
Bürgerliches Trauerspiel 199
Burgtheater Wien 204
Burleske 205
BUSTA 205
Butô 206
Cabaret → Kabarett
Cabaret Federal → Cornichon
Cabaret Voltaire 207
Café La Mama → La Mama
Café-Theater 207
Caffe Cino → Off-Off-Broadway
Candomblé 208
Cantica 209
Capitano → Commedia dell'arte
Caranas → Ind. Theater
Carros → Auto Sacramental
Cartel (des quatre) 209
Cartoucherie 210
Center 68/70 → Angura
Centre International de la Création
Théâtrale / Centre International de
Recherches Théâtrales 210
Centre international de recherches
scéniques 212
Centre National de Création 213
Centres Dramatiques Nationaux 213
Centrum Sztuki «Studio» 214
Černé Divadlo 214
Chabildas-Movement → Ind. Thea-
ter
Chamberlain's Men 215

Chanson 216
Charakterdarsteller 217
Charakterkomödie 217
Charge 217
Chargieren 218
  Charivari → Brauchtumstänze,
  → Trionfi
Chat Noir 218
Chhao-Tänze 219
Chicano Theater 220
Children of Paul's 221
Chinesisches Sprechtheater 222
Chinesisches Theater 224
Chor 232
  Chorege → Antikes Theater
Choreodrama 233
Choreographie / Choreograph 234
Chorodidaskalos 235
Christmas Pantomime 235
Chuanqi 236
  Cinquecento → Rinascimento
  C.I.R.T. → Centre International de
  Recherches Théâtrales
Claque 236
  Clown → Narr, → Zirkus
Collage 237
  College Theatre → Little Theatre
  Movement, → Studententheater
  Colombina → Commedia dell'arte
  combination company → Broadway
Comedia / Siglo de Oro / Goldenes
  Zeitalter 238
Comédie-ballet 239
Comédie Française 240
Comédie Italienne 241
Comedy of Humours 242
Comedy of Manners 242
  Comic Opera → Ballad Opera
Commedia dell'arte 243
  Commedia erudita → Rinascimento
Community Theatre 247
Compagnia Dario Fo 247
Compagnia del Collettivo di
  Parma 248
Compagnie des Ballets Russes de Serge
  de Diaghilev 249
Compagnie Renaud-Barrault 250

Company 251
La Comune 251
  Concetti → Commedia dell'arte
Conférence 251
Conférencier 252
  Continental Players → Exiltheater
Cornichon 252
Corralbühne 253
  Cottesloe → National Theatre
Couplet 254
Covent Garden Theatre 254
Cricot 255
Cricot 2 (Krakau) 255
Csiky Gergely Szinház 256
Cullbergbaletten 256
Da capo 257
Dadaistisches Theater 257
Dance Theatre of Harlem (New
  York) 259
Darstellendes Spiel 259
  Daśāvatāra → Ind. Theater
  DBV → Deutscher Bühnenverein
Debüt 260
Deklamation 261
  Dengaku → Jap. Theater
Deus ex machina 261
  Deuteragonist → Protagonist
Deutsche Bühne 262
Deutscher Bühnenverein (DBV) 262
Deutsche Shakespeare-Gesell-
  schaft 264
Deutsches Nationaltheater
  Weimar 264
Deutsches Schauspielhaus
  (Hamburg) 265
Deutsches Theater (Berlin) 265
  Deutsches Theater Kolonne links
  → Exiltheater
Dialog 268
Diener 269
Difang xi (Lokales Theater) 272
  Dilettantentheater → Liebhaber-
  theater
Dionysien 274
Dionysostheater 274
Directeur / Director / Direktor 274
  Direktor → Intendant

Die Distel 275
Dithyrambos 276
Divadlo na Vinohradech 276
Divadlo Na zábradlí 277
Divertissement 278
Dokumentarisches Theater 278
Domestic Tragedy 279
  Dottore → Commedia dell'arte
Drama 279
Dramaten 280
Dramatic Workshop of the New School
  for Social Research (New York)
  281
Dramatisierung 282
Dramatis personae 282
Dramaturg 283
Dramaturgie 285
Dramaturgische Gesellschaft 290
  drame noir → Schicksalstragödie
Dramentheorie 290
Dramolett 298
  Drehbühne → Bühnentechnik
Drei Einheiten 298
Die Drei Tornados 299
Drottningholm 300
Drury Lane 301
  D 46 (Prag) → D 34 (Prag)
  The Duke's Men → Restaurations-
  theater
Dumb Show 301
Düsseldorfer Schauspielhaus 301
D 34 (Prag) 302
  Echo von links → Exiltheater
Ecole de Danse de l'Opéra de
  Paris 303
Edinburgh 303
Einakter 304
Einfühlung 305
Einnahmesoll 306
Eintrittspreis 306
Eiserner Vorhang 307
Ekkyklema 307
Die Elf Scharfrichter 308
Elisabethanisches Theater 309
Embolimon 310
Emigrantentheater / Migrantenthea-
  ter 310

Engagement 312
  Engels-Projekt → Exiltheater
Englische Komödianten 312
  English Stage Company → Royal
  Court Theatre
  Ennen → Mai-Tanzformen
Ensemble 314
en suite 314
Entfesseltes Theater 314
Entremés 316
Environmental Theatre 316
Epeisodion 317
Epilog 317
Episches Theater 318
Episode 320
Equity 320
  Erntetänze → Brauchtumstänze
Erotisches Theater 321
Erstaufführung 323
  Erzähltheater (türkisches) → Med-
  dah
Esperpento 324
Etagenbühne 324
Ethnikó Théatro 325
European Jewish Artists Society
  (EJAS) 326
Eurythmische Kunst / Eurythmie 327
Exiltheater 328
  Exodium → Nachspiel
Exodos 335
Experimentelles Theater 335
Exposition 336
Expressionistisches Theater 338
Extempore 341
Fabel 341
  Fächertänze → Candomblé, → Ritu-
  altänze
  Fackeltänze → Brauchtumstänze,
  → Ritualtänze, → Turniere
  Fahnentänze → Brauchtumstänze
Fahrendes Volk 342
Fallhöhe 345
Farce 346
  Farce → Afterpiece
Fastnachtsspiele 347
  Fastnachtstänze → Brauchtumstänze
La Fede 348

Federal Theatre Project 349
Féerie → Märchendrama
Felsenreitschule Salzburg 349
Feministisches Theater
→ Frauentheater
Fernsehen und Theater 350
Festival d'Avignon 355
Festival of Fools 356
Festspiele 357
Feuertänze → Brauchtumstänze,
→ Ritualtänze
Feuerwerkstheater 359
Figurentheater → Puppentheater
Figurine 360
Film und Theater 360
Fiolteatret 363
Die Fledermaus → Die Elf Scharf-
richter
Floh de Cologne 364
Fluter → Bühnenbeleuchtung
Fluxus → Happening
Folies-Bergère 365
Folkwang-Tanzstudio 365
Foolstheater → Festival of Fools,
→ Freies Theater, → Mimus
Fortune Theatre 366
Foyer 367
Frauentheater 368
Free Southern Theater 370
Freie Bühne 371
Freie Deutsche Bühne (Buenos
Aires) 371
Freier Tanz → Ausdruckstanz
Freies Deutsches Theater (New
York) → Exiltheater
Freies deutsches Theater (Theatre of
German Freemen) → Exiltheater
Freies Theater 372
Freie Volksbühne → Volksbühne
Freie Volksbühne Berlin 376
Freilichttheater 377
Friedrichstadt-Palast 378
Fringe 379
Fronleichnamsspiele 380
Fronttheater 381
Fruchtbarkeitstänze → Chhao-Tänze
(Chaitraparva), → Ritualtänze

Fundus 382
Furcht und Mitleid 382
Futuristisches Theater 383
Gaelic Theatre Organisation
→ Abbey Theatre
Gage 384
Gaiety Theatre (Manchester)
→ Repertory Theatre
Gala-Vorstellung 385
Gartentheater 385
Gassenbühne → Kulissenbühne
Gastspiel 385
Gauchotheater 386
GDBA → Genossenschaft Deutscher
Bühnenangehöriger
Geistliches Spiel → Mittelalter / Dra-
ma und Theater des Mittelalters
Generalintendanz 386
Generalprobe 386
Género Chico 387
Genossenschaft Deutscher Bühnen-
angehöriger (GDBA) 387
German Dance → Ausdruckstanz
Gesamtkunstwerk 388
Geschichtsdrama 390
Gestik → Nonverbale Kommuni-
kation
Gewandmeister 391
Ghettotheater 392
GITIS 393
The Globe → Shakespearebühne
Globe Theatre 393
Globusbühne → Segment-Globus-
Bühne
Glöcklerlaufen → Brauchtumstänze
Goethe-Theater Bad Lauchstädt 394
Goldenes Zeitalter → Comedia
Gorki-Theater 395
Gracioso 395
Grand Guignol 396
Le Grand Magic Circus (et ses animaux
tristes) 396
Grips Theater (Berlin) 397
Großes Schauspielhaus Berlin
→ Reinhardt-Bühnen
Groteske 397
Group Theatre 399

Gruppe junger Schauspieler 399
Guerilla Theatre 400
Guignol 400
Guthrie Theatre → Broadway
Habima 400
Halbmaske → Maske
Hamburg Ballett 402
Hamburger Kammerspiele 403
Hamburgische Dramaturgie 403
Hana 404
Hanamichi 404
Handlung 405
Handlungsballett → Ballet d'action
Handpuppe 406
Handwerkertänze → Brauchtums-
tänze
Hängestück → Versatzstück
Hansatheater 407
Hanswurst → Alt-Wiener Volks-
stück, → Hanswurstiade, → Komi-
sche Person
Hanswurstiade 408
Happening 408
Happy end(ing) 410
Harikatha → Ind. Theater
Haupt- und Staatsaktion 411
Hausbühne 411
Hebebühne → Bühnentechnik
Heckentheater 412
Heinrich-Heine-Klub (Mexiko) 412
Heinz-Bosl-Stiftung → Bayerisches
Staatsballett
Hellerau → Bildungsanstalt Jacques-
Dalcroze
Helsingin Kaupunginteatteri 412
Heroic Play / Heroic Drama → Hero-
ic Tragedy
Heroic Tragedy 413
Heroine 414
Hessisches Staatstheater Darm-
stadt 414
Historie 415
Histrio 415
Hofintendant → Hoftheater
Höfisches Theater 415
Hofschauspieler 419
Hoftheater 419

Horizonte / Festival der Welt-
kulturen 420
Horizontleuchte → Bühnenbeleuch-
tung
Hosenrolle 421
Hôtel de Bourgogne 421
The House 422
Humanismus / Drama und Theater
des Humanismus 423
Hyôbanki 425
Hypokrites 425
Hypothesis 426
Identifikation 426
Independent Theatre Council
→ Fringe
Iffland-Ring 427
Ikria 427
Illusionstheater 428
Impresario 428
Improvisation 429
Indian National Theatre (INT)
→ Ind. Theater
Indian Peoples' Theatre (IPT) → Ind.
Theater
Indisches Theater 429
Innamorati → Commedia dell'arte
Inspizient 441
Inszenierung 441
Inszenierungsanalyse 444
INT → Ind. Theater
Intendant 449
Interlude / Interludium → Zwischen-
spiel
Interludium → Intermezzo, → Zwi-
schenspiel
Intermezzo 451
Internationale Kulturfabrik Kamp-
nagel 451
Internationales Theaterinstitut → ITI
INTHEGA → Tourneetheater
Intimes Theater 452
Intrige 453
IPT → Ind. Theater
Iranisches Passionstheater → Taᶜziya
Irish Dramatic Movement 454
Irish National Dramatic Society
→ Abbey Theatre

Ironie 454
Isshin-denshin 455
İstanbul Şehir Tiyatrosu 456
ITI 456
Jahreszeitenspiele 457
Japanisches Theater 457
Jaunatnes Teātris Riga 461
Jaunimo Teatras Vilnius 461
Jedermann-Spiel → Moralitäten
Jesuitentheater 462
Jeune Premier 467
    jidaimono → Kabuki
Jiddisches Theater 467
    Jigs → Nachspiel
    John-Cranko-Schule → Staatstheater
    Stuttgart
    Jôkyô Gekijô → Angura
Jôruri (oder Bunraku) 471
    Joung Abbey → Abbey Theatre
Jüdisch-politisches Kabarett 473
Juese / lianpu (Chin. Rollenfächer /
    Masken) 473
    Jugendkulturring → Besucherorgani-
    sationen
    Jugendtheater → Kindertheater
Jugendtheater (in den Niederlanden)
    476
    Jugoslawien → BITEF
    Juvenile Theatre → Papiertheater
Kabarett (Cabaret) 476
Kabarett der Komiker 480
Kabuki 481
    Kagura → Mai-Tanzformen
    Kalambur (Wrocław) → Studenten-
    theater
Kamishibai 484
Kammerschauspieler 485
Kammerspiel 485
    Kammerspiele → (Münchner) Kam-
    merspiele
    Kammerspiele (La Paz) → Exil-
    theater
    Kammertheater (Moskau) → Mos-
    kauer Staatliches Kammertheater
Kampfbühne 486
    Kanevas → Commedia dell'arte
Karagiozis 486

Karagöz 487
    Kasperl → Alt-Wiener Volksstück
Kasperletheater 489
Kata 489
Die Katakombe 489
Katarimono-Rezitationskunst 490
Kathak 491
Kathakali 492
Katharsis 492
Katona József Szinház 493
Kindertheater / Jugendtheater 493
    Kindertruppen → Elisabethanisches
    Theater
    Kinetic Theatre → Happening
    King's Men → Chamberlain's Men,
    → Elisabethanisches Theater
    Kirchentänze → Mysterienspiele,
    → Ritualtänze
    Kirow-Ballett → St. Petersburger
    Ballett
Kirow-Theater 489
    Kīrtan → Ind. Theater
Klassik 498
    Klassizismus → Klassik
«Kleine Bühne» des Freien Deutschen
    Kulturbundes (London) 503
Die Kleine Freiheit 503
Kleines Dramatisches Theater 504
Kleines Organon für das Theater 505
    Klub-Theater → Exiltheater
    Klucht → Nachspiel
    Kneipentheater → Café-Theater
Kokette 506
    Kolonne links → Exiltheater
Komidylle (Komeidyllion) 507
Komiker 508
Komische Person 508
Komissarshewskaja-Theater 508
Das Kom(m)ödchen 510
Kommos 511
Komödie 511
    Die Komödie (Montevideo) → Exil-
    theater
    Komödie am Kurfürstendamm
    → Reinhardt-Bühnen
Komos 515
Komparse 516

Kom-Teatteri 516
Konflikt 516
Den Kongelige Ballet 517
Det Kongelige Teater 519
Konstruktivismus und Theater 521
Kontamination 523
Konversationsstück 523
Kordax 524
  Körpersprache → Nonverbale Kommunikation
Koryphaios 524
  Kosmologische Tänze → Brauchtumstänze
  Kostüm → Bühnenkostüm
Kostümbildner 524
Kothurn 525
  Kôwaka → Katarimono-Rezitationskunst
Kreolengroteske 525
Kriminalstück 526
Krippenspiel 526
  Kucipudi → Ind. Theater
  Küflertanz (Salzburger) → Brauchtumstänze
  Kugeltheater → Bauhausbühne
Kukla oyunu 526
Kulissenbühne 528
Kulturpolitik und Theater (BRD/DDR) 529
Kunqu 530
Kunstfach/Rollenfach 532
  Kutiyaṭṭam → Ind. Theater
Kyôgen 533
  KZ-Theater → Theater in den Konzentrationslagern
Labanschulen 534
Laboratoire de Théâtre Art et Action 536
  Labor Stage → Arbeitertheater (USA)
Lafayette Players 536
Laienspiel 537
Landesbühne 539
Landestheater Linz 540
  Lāsya → Ind. Theater
Lateinamerikanisches Theater 541
Laterna Magica 545

Das Laterndl (London) 546
Laufendes Band 546
  Laufsteg → Hanamichi
  Lazzi → Commedia dell'arte
League of Workers' Theatre 546
Lebende Bilder 547
Lehrstück 548
Leibeigenentheater 550
Leipziger Theater 551
Lesedrama 552
Libretto 552
  Lichtertanz → Brauchtumstänze
  Der liebe Augustin → Exiltheater
Lieber Augustin 553
Liebhaber 553
Liebhabertheater 554
  Lighting Designer → Bühnenbeleuchtung
Lilla Teatern 555
  Lille Grønnegadeteatret (Kopenhagen) → Det Kongelige Teater Linz → Landestheater Linz
Literatur am Naschmarkt 555
Little Theatre Movement 556
Living Newspaper 557
Living Theatre 558
Liyuan (Birnengarten) 559
Loa 560
Lokalposse 560
London Contemporary Dance School 561
Long-Run-System 561
Lord Chamberlain 562
Luisenburg-Festspiele 562
Lustige Person 563
Lustspiel 564
Lyceum Theatre 565
  Lyttelton → National Theatre
La Maddalena 566
  Magische Tänze → Candomblé, → Ritualtänze
Magyar Népi Szinház 566
Maison de la Culture 567
Mai-Tanzformen 568
Majakowski-Theater 570
Malersaal 571

Malyi dramatičeskij teatr → Kleines
Dramatisches Theater
Maly Theater   571
La Mama Experimental Theatre
Club   572
Manipuri   573
Mannheimer Nationaltheater
→ Nationaltheater
Mantel- und Degenstück   574
Marathi-Theatre → Ind. Theater
Märchendrama   574
Mariinski → Kirow-Theater
Marionette   575
Marionettentheater → Puppen-
theater
Marketing im Theater   576
Märtyrerdrama   577
Maschinenkomödie   579
The Mask   579
Maske / Maskentheater   580
Maskenbildner → Maske
Maskentänze   584
Maskeraden → Brauchtumstänze,
→ Maskentänze
Masque   586
Massenregie   586
Massentheater   587
Mauerschau → Teichoskopie
(Max Reinhardts) Workshop for
Stage, Screen and Radio → Exil-
theater
Maxim-Gorki-Theater (Berlin)   588
Max-Reinhardt-Seminar   588
MChAT   589
MChT → MChAT
Mechane   591
Mechanisches Ballett → Bauhaus-
bühne
Mechanisches Bühnenmodell
→ Bauhausbühne
Mechanisches Theater   592
Mecklenburgisches Staatstheater
Schwerin   593
Meddah   594
Die Meininger   595
Melodrama   596
Merzbühne   601

Meta Theater   603
The Method   604
Meyerhold-Methode   605
Mezzetino → Commedia dell'arte
michiyuki → Kabuki, → Nô
Mickerytheater   607
Migrantentheater → Emigranten-
theater
Mime   608
Mimesis   608
Mimik   609
Mimodrama   609
Mimus   609
Minimal Dance   610
Minstrel Show   611
Minutage   612
miracle plays → Mystery Play
Le Mirliton   612
Missionsschauspiel   613
Mitspiel(theater)   613
Mittelalter / Drama und Theater des
Mittelalters   614
Mittelstück   619
Modellaufführung   620
Modern Dance   621
Monodie   622
Monodrama   622
Monolog   623
Montage   626
Moralitäten   627
Moriske / Moreske / Moresca / Morris
dance   628
Moritat   629
Moskauer Dramentheater → Maja-
kowski-Theater
Moskauer Jiddisches Staatliches
Künstlertheater (GOSET) → Jiddi-
sches Theater
Moskauer Künstlertheater
→ MChAT
Moskauer Staatliches Kammerthea-
ter   629
Mudra   631
Mülheimer Theatertage   631
Mummers' Play   632
Münchener Künstlertheater   632
(Münchner) Kammerspiele   633

Münchner Lach- und Schießgesell-
schaft   634
(Münchner) Rationaltheater   635
Münchner Volkstheater GmbH   635
Muou xi / Kuilei xi (Chin. Puppen-
theater)   636
Musical → Broadway
Music Hall   637
Mysterienspiel   637
Mysterienspiel (Spanien)   638
Mystery Play   639
Mythologische Tänze → Ballet du
Roi, → Ballet comique de la Reine,
→ Ballet de Cour, → Ritualtänze,
→ Trionfi
Mythos   640
Nachspiel   641
Das Nachtlicht (Wien) → Die Elf
Scharfrichter
Naive   641
Nancy   642
Nanxi   643
Národní Divadlo   644
Narodnija teatar «Ivan Vazov»   645
Narr   646
Narrentänze → Brauchtumstänze,
→ Maskentänze, → Moriske, → My-
sterienspiel, → Narr, → Totentanz,
→ Trionfi
Het Nationale Ballet   650
Nationale Scene i Bergen   651
Nationaltheater   652
Nationaltheater «Iwan Wasow»
→ Narodnija teatar «Ivan Vazov»
National Theatre   653
Nationaltheatret i Oslo   654
Naturalistisches Theater   655
Naturtheater   659
Nederduytsche Academie   659
Nederlands Dans Theater   660
Negro Ensemble Company   661
Neidhartspiel → Jahreszeitenspiele
Nelson-Revue   662
Nemzeti Szinház   663
Neue Freie Volksbühne → Volks-
bühne
Neue Medien und Theater   664

Neue Sachlichkeit   668
Neues Theater Halle   669
Neutral-Maske → Maske
Neuzeit / Theater der Neuzeit   670
New Playwrights' Theatre   696
New Theatre League → League of
Worker's Theatre
New York City Ballet   697
Niederdeutsches Theater   698
Nô   700
Nonverbale Kommunikation / Körper-
kommunikation   703
Norddeutsches Theatertreffen   707
Normalvertrag-Solo → Schauspieler
Norske Teatret i Oslo   707
NSD → Ind. Theater
La Nuova Scena   708
Oberammergauer Passionsspiel   708
Oberlicht → Bühnenbeleuchtung
Odeion   710
Odéon → Théâtre National
de l'Odéon
Odin Teatret   710
Odissi   711
Off-Off-Broadway   712
Ojapali → Ind. Theater
Old Vic (Theatre)   714
Oliver Theatre → National Theatre
Onafhankelijk Toneel   715
Onkos   715
onnagata → Kabuki
Ontological-Hysteric Theatre   716
Open Theatre   716
Opéra-ballet   717
Orchestra → Antikes Theater
Orgien Mysterien Theater   717
Ortaoyunu   718
Österreichische Bühne (The Austrian
Theatre) (New York)   719
Osterspiele   719
Otto-Falckenberg-Schule   720
Outrieren   720
Oxford University Dramatic Society
(OUDS) → Studententheater
Pageant   721
Palliata   721
Pantalone → Commedia dell'arte

Pantomime 722
Pantomimentheater Warschau
→ Pantomime
Pantomimeteatret 724
Papiertheater 725
Parabase 725
Parabelstück 726
Parachoregema 727
Paraskenien 727
Paraszenien 728
Parkett 728
Park Theatre → Broadway
Parodie 728
Parodos 729
Passionsspiele 730
Pastorale → Schäferspiel
Paterson Pageant 730
Pathos 731
Pekingoper 732
Perchtenlaufen → Brauchtums-
tänze
Père noble 734
Performance 734
Performance Group 735
Periakten 736
Perioche 736
Persien → Ta^cziya
Person 737
Petruschka 739
Die Pfeffermühle 739
Pferdeballett → Roßballett
Phlyakenposse 740
Piaoyou (Laienschauspieler) 741
Piccolo Teatro di Milano 741
Pickelhering → Komische Person
Ping Pong → Exiltheater
Pip Simmons Theatre Group 742
Pirandellismus 742
Piscatorbühne 744
Plakat / Theaterplakat 746
Das Politische Kabarett 746
Politisches Theater 747
Politisches Volkstheater (USA)
750
Posse 751
Post Modern Dance 752
Praetexta 754

Prager Nationaltheater → Národní
Divadlo
Praktikabel → Bühnenbild
Premiere 754
Prinzipal 754
Privattheater 755
Proben 755
Programmheft 756
Projektionsapparate → Bühnen-
beleuchtung
Proletarisch-revolutionäres Theater
756
Prolog 757
Proskēnion / Proszenium 758
Prospekt → Kulissenbühne
Protagonist 758
Provincetown Players 759
Prozessionsspiel → Fronleichnams-
spiel
Psychodrama 759
Publikum 761
Pulcinella → Petruschka, → Comme-
dia dell'arte
Pulpitum 762
Puppentheater 762
Purana Qila Theatre → Ind. Theater
Pūrvaranga → Ind. Theater
Puschkin-Theater 765
Pyrrhiche → Brauchtumstänze,
→ Waffentänze
Quyi (Kleine Theaterformen des chin.
Theaters) 766
Rachetragödie 767
Radioteatret 768
Railwaytheater → Theaterausstel-
lungen
Rakugo → Katarimono-Rezitations-
kunst
Ranglogentheater → Rangtheater
Rangtheater 769
Rāsa → Ind. Theater
Raslila 770
Räsoneur 771
Rationaltheater → (Münchner)
Rationaltheater
Raumbühne → Bühne
Realistisches Theater 771

Rechts und links auf dem Theater 774
  Rederijkerdramen → Reformation/
  Drama und Theater der Reformation
Reduta 774
  Reflektorische Lichtspiele → Bauhausbühne
Reformation/Drama und Theater der
  Reformation 775
  Refugee Artists Group → Exiltheater
Regie 777
  Regiebetrieb → Theatersystem
Regietheater 780
Regisseur 781
Reichsdramaturg 781
Reichskabarett 782
  Reichstheatergesetz → Theatergesetz
Reichstheaterkammer 782
Reinhardt-Bühnen 783
  Reliefbühne → Bühne, → Theaterbau
  Religiöse Tänze → Mysterienspiele,
  → Ritualtänze
  Renaissance → Renaissancetheater
Renaissancetheater 784
Repertoire 784
Repertory Theatre 785
Replik 785
Reprise 786
Requisiten 786
Restaurationstheater 786
Revue 787
Rhetorik 789
Rinascimento/Cinquecento 791
  Ringtheater → Theaterausstellungen
Ritual 795
Ritualtänze 797
Rolle 800
  Rollenfach → Kunstfach
  romantic comedies → Comedy of
  Humours
  Romantik → Romantisches Theater
Romantisches Theater 801
  Roncalli → Zirkus
  The Rose → Shakespearebühne
Roßballett 806
Rote Grütze (Berlin) 807

Royal Academy of Dramatic Art 807
Royal Ballet 808
Royal Ballet School (London) 808
  Royal Coburg/Royal Victoria → Old
  Vic
Royal Court Theatre 809
Royal Shakespeare Company 810
  Rudra Béjart Lausanne → Ballet du
  XXe Siècle
Ruhrfestspiele 810
Rührstück 811
Sadir Natya 812
Sainete 812
  Saison → Spielzeit
Salondame 813
Salzburger Festspiele 813
San Francisco Mime Troupe 814
St. Petersburger Ballett 815
  Sanskrit-Drama → Ind. Theater
  Sarugaku → Nô
Satyrspiel 817
  Scapino → Commedia dell'arte
Schäferspiel 818
  Schäfflertanz (Münchener)
  → Brauchtumstänze
Schall und Rauch 820
Schattentheater/Schementheater/Silhouettentheater 821
Die Schaubude 822
Schaubühne am Lehniner Platz/Schaubühne am Halleschen Ufer 823
Schauspiel 825
Schauspieler 826
Schauspielhaus Bochum 829
Schauspielhaus Chemnitz 830
Schauspielhaus Köln/Oper der Stadt
  Köln 831
Schauspielschulen 831
Schausteller 833
Schautanz 834
  Scheinwerfer → Bühnenbeleuchtung
  Schemenlaufen → Brauchtumstänze
  Schementheater → Schattentheater
Schicksalstragödie 834
Schmidt Theater-Varieté-Kneipe 836
Die Schmiere 837
Schminke 838

Schminkmaske → Maske
Schnürboden → Bühnentechnik
Schönbrunner Schloßtheater
  → Reinhardt-Bühnen
School of American Ballet (New
  York) 838
Schuldrama 839
Schule der dramatischen Kunst
  → Škola dramatičeskogo iskusstva
Schulspiel 843
Schultheater 843
Schurke 845
Schwank 845
Schwarzamerikanisches Theater/Black
  Theatre 846
Schwarzes Theater Prag → Černé
  Divadlo
Schwerttänze → Brauchtumstänze,
  → Waffentänze
Scuola Teatro Dimitri → Pantomime
SDS im Exil → Exiltheater
Second Blackfriars → Elisabetha-
  nisches Theater
Segment-Globus-Bühne 848
Sentenz 849
Sentimental Comedy 849
Sentimentale 850
7 : 84 Theatre Company 850
sewamono → Kabuki
Shaffytheater 851
Shakespearebühne 852
Shakespeare Memorial Theatre
  → Stratford-upon-Avon
Shimpa 853
Shingeki 854
Shite → Kyôgen
shosagoto → Kabuki
Siglo de Oro → Comedia
Silhouettentheater → Schatten-
  theater
Simplicissimus 856
Simultanbühne 857
Simultantheater 857
Sinfonisches Ballett 858
Skēnographie 859
Sketch 860
Škola dramatičeskogo iskusstva 860

Skomorochen 860
Slovenské Narodné Divadlo 861
  SNA → Ind. Theater
Snake Theatre 861
Soffitten 861
  Sommertheater → Theatersystem
  Song → Chanson
Sotie 862
Soubrette 862
Souffleur 863
Souffleurkasten 863
Soufflierbuch 864
  Sozialistischer Realismus → Realisti-
  sches Theater
Spatz und Co 864
  Speertänze → Brauchtumstänze,
  → Waffentänze
  Spetodrama → Bauhausbühne
  Spezialitätentheater → Varieté
  Spiegeltänze → Candomblé,
  → Ritualtänze
Spiel 864
Spielpädagogik 866
Spielplan 868
Spielzeit 869
Sprechchor 869
Squat Theatre 870
  Staatliche Ballettschule Berlin → Bal
  lett der Deutschen Staatsoper Berlin
Staatliche Schauspielbühnen
  Berlin 870
Staatsschauspiel Dresden 871
  Staatsschauspieler → Hofschau-
  spieler
  Staatstheater → Theatersystem
Staatstheater Stuttgart 872
  Staberl → Alt-Wiener Volksstück,
  → Komische Person, → Lustige
  Person
Stabpuppe/Stockpuppe 873
  Stabtänze → Brauchtumstänze,
  → Waffentänze
Die Stachelschweine 874
  Städtebundtheater → Theatersystem
Städtische Bühnen Frankfurt 875
Stadttheater 875
Stadttheater Basel 876

Stadttheater in den Weinbergen
→ Divadlo na Vinohradech
Stagedoor Festival → Emigranten-
theater
Ständeklausel 877
Stanislawski-System 877
Stanze 879
Stasimon 880
Stationendrama 880
Statist 881
Stegreiftheater 881
Stehendes Theater 882
steirischer herbst 882
Stella Kultur Management 883
Stichomythie 883
Stilbühne 884
Stock company → Broadway
Stockpuppe → Stabpuppe
Stocktänze → Brauchtumstänze,
→ Waffentänze
Straßentheater 884
Stratford-upon-Avon 885
Striptease 886
Studententheater 886
Studio 890
Studio 1934 890
Studio-Theater-Bewegung 891
Stummes Spiel 891
Sturmbühne 892
Sturm und Drang / Theater des Sturm
und Drang 892
Stuttgarter Ballett → Staatstheater
Stuttgart
Sukzessionsbühne 895
Suomen Kansallisteatteri 895
Surrealistisches Theater 896
Sūtradhār → Ind. Theater
Symbolistisches Theater 897
The Swan → Shakespearebühne
«Synthetisches Theater» → Entfes-
seltes Theater, → Moskauer Staat-
liches Kammertheater
Szenographie 901
Tableau 903
tachiyaku → Kabuki
Tacziya 904
Taganka-Theater 905

Tairow-Theater → Moskauer Staat-
liches Kammertheater
Tamāśā → Ind. Theater
Tampereen Työväen Teatteri 906
Tanz 907
Tanzarchive / -museen / -biblio-
theken 917
Tanzfestspiele 918
Tanznotationen 819
Tanztheater 924
Tanztheater der Komischen Oper
Berlin 932
Tanztheorie → Tanz
TAT → Theater am Turm
Teatr Dramatyczny 933
Teatr im J. Słowackiego 934
Teatr Narodowy 934
Teatr Nowy 935
Teatro Arena 936
Teatro Campesino 936
Teatro Cooperativo 937
Teatro de Creación Colectiva 938
Teatro degli Independenti 938
Teatro de la Esperanza 939
Teatro dell'arti 940
Teatro Due → Compagnia del Collet-
tivo di Parma
Teatro Escambray 940
Teatro Experimental de Cali 941
Teatro Farnese 941
Teatro Farnese → Theaterbau
Teatro Goldoni 942
Teatro Immagine 942
Teatro Independiente 943
Teatro Olimpico 943
Teatr Osmego Dnia (Poznan)
→ Studententheater
Teatro San Ferdinando 944
Teatro stabile 944
Teatro Umoristico 944
Teatr Polski 945
Teatr Rapsodyczny 945
Teatr 77 → Studententheater
Teatr Stary 946
Teatr STU → Studententheater
Teatr Współczesny 946
Teichoskopie 947

Teichtheater 948
Telari-Bühne → Periakten
Tenjô Sajiki → Angura
Tenkei Gekijô → Angura
Terenzbühne 948
Tetralogie 949
Teufelstänze → Brauchtumstänze,
→ Moriske, → Mysterienspiele,
→ Ritualtänze
Thaddädl → Alt-Wiener Volksstück,
→ Komische Person, → Lustige
Person
Thalia Theater (Hamburg) 949
Theater 950
Theater am Geländer → Divadlo Na
zábradlí
Theater am Schiffbauerdamm
(Berlin) 952
Theater am Turm – TAT (Frank-
furt) 953
Theater an der Ruhr im Raffelberg-
Park 954
Theater auf dem Theater 955
Theaterausstellungen 955
Theaterbau 958
Theater der Freien Hansestadt
Bremen 978
Theater der Freien Volksbühne
→ Freie Volksbühne Berlin
Theater der Grausamkeit 978
Theater «Der Kreis» 979
Theater der Kunst (Athen)
→ Theatron Technis
Theater der Nationen (Théâtre des
Nations) 981
Theater der Neuzeit → Neuzeit /
Theater der Neuzeit
Theater der Prominenten 981
Theater der Revolution (Moskau)
→ Majakowski-Theater
Theater der Unterdrückten 982
Theater der Welt 982
Theatererhalterverband österreichi-
scher Bundesländer und Städte
→ Theatersystem
Theaterfilm → Fernsehen und
Theater

Theaterfotografie 983
Theater für Kinder im Reichs-
kabarett → Grips Theater Berlin
Theatergemeinde → Besucherorga-
nisationen
Theatergesetz 985
Theater in den Konzentrations-
lagern 986
Theater in der Josefstadt (Wien) 987
Theaterkritik 989
Theater-Manufaktur Berlin 991
Theatermuseum → Theatersamm-
lung
Theateroktober 991
Theaterpädagogik 992
Theaterreform um 1900 995
Theatersammlung / -museum / -archiv
997
Theaterskandal 998
Theatersystem (im deutschsprachigen
Raum) 1000
Theatertheorie 1011
Theatertherapie 1020
Theater und Philharmonie Essen
GmbH 1021
Theatervorhang 1022
theaterwerkstatt hannover 1024
Theaterwissenschaft 1024
Theaterzensur 1028
Theaterzettel 1031
Theatralisches Theater 1032
Theatralität 1032
The Theatre 1033
Théâtre Alfred Jarry 1034
Théâtre Antoine 1034
Théâtre de France → Théâtre Natio-
nal de l'Odéon
Théâtre de Gennevilliers 1035
Théâtre de la Foire 1035
Théâtre de la Mandragore 1036
Théâtre de l'Atelier 1036
Théâtre de l'Europe 1037
Théâtre de l'Œuvre 1038
Théâtre des Amandiers 1038
Théâtre des Bouffes du Nord 1039
Théâtre des Nations → Theater der
Nationen

Théâtre du Marais 1039
Théâtre du Quotidien 1040
   Théâtre du Rond-Point → Compagnie Renaud-Barrault
Théâtre du Soleil 1040
Théâtre du Vieux-Colombier 1041
Theatre Guild 1042
Theatre in Education (T.i.E.) 1043
   Théâtre Italien → Comédie Italienne
Théâtre-Libre 1043
Théâtre National de Chaillot (TNC) 1044
Théâtre National de l'Odéon 1045
Théâtre National Populaire (T.N.P.) 1046
Theatre of Images 1047
   Theatre Royal → Theatre Workshop
Theatre Union 1048
Theatre Workshop 1049
   Theatre Writers Union → Fringe
Theatromanie 1049
Théâtron Technis 1049
Theatrum mundi 1051
Theorikon 1052
Thespis 1052
Thingspiel 1052
   T.i.E. → Theatre in Education
   Tiertänze → Brauchtumstänze, → Maskentänze, → Ritualtänze, → Trionfi
Tirade 1053
   T.N.P. → Théâtre National Populaire
Togata 1054
Totaltheater 1054
Totentanz 1055
Tourneetheater 1056
Tragikomödie 1057
Tragödie 1061
TRAM 1065
Trauerspiel 1065
Traumspiel 1066
Travestie 1066
   Triadisches Ballett → Bauhausbühne, → Bauhaustänze
Tribüne für Freie Deutsche Literatur und Kunst in Amerika 1067

Trionfi 1067
   Tritagonist → Protagonist
   Trope → Drama und Theater des Mittelalters
Truppe 1068
   Truppe 31 → Exiltheater
   Tsure → Nô
Turniere 1069
Typenkomödie 1070
Überbrettl 1071
Über-Marionette 1071
Underground Theatre 1072
UNIMA 1073
Unity Theatre 1073
University Wits 1074
Unsichtbares Theater 1075
Unterhaltungstheater 1075
   Uraufführung → Aufführung
Urtheater 1075
   Uslovnyj → Meyerhold-Methode
   U-Theater → Bauhausbühne
Varieté 1076
   Varieté → Music Hall
Vaudeville 1078
   VDF → Verband Deutscher Freilichtbühnen
   Verband der deutschen Gemeinnützigen Theater → Deutscher Bühnenverein
Verband der Theaterschaffenden der DDR 1079
Verband Deutscher Freilichtbühnen e. V. (VDF) 1080
Vereinigte Bühnen Graz 1080
Verfremdung, Verfremdungseffekt (V-Effekt) 1080
Verismus 1082
Versatzstück 1083
Versdrama 1083
   Versenkung → Bühnentechnik
Vertooningen 1084
Vertrauter 1084
Videotanz 1085
   Vidūṣaka → Ind. Theater
Vierte Wand 1086
Vigszinház 1087
Viktorianisches Theater 1088

Viktor Kingissepa nim. Tallinna
Riiklik Akademiline Draama-
teater 1089
Villeurbanne → Théâtre National
Populaire
Virtuose 1089
Völkische Dramaturgie 1090
Volksbühne 1091
Volksbühne Berlin 1093
Volksschauspiel 1094
Volksstück 1096
Volkstheater Rostock 1099
Volkstheater Wien 1100
Vorhang → Theatervorhang
Vorspiel 1102
Vorstellung 1103
Wachtangow-Theater 1103
Waffentänze 1104
Waki → Nô
Wanderbühne 1104
Warschauer Jiddisches Künstler-
theater → Jiddisches Theater
Waseda-Shôgekijô → Angura
Washington Square Players 1107
weeping comedy → Sentimental
Comedy
Welttheater 1108
Werkstatt 1108
Het Werkteater 1108
West End 1109
Wiener Aktionismus → Happening
Wiener Bühnenverein → Theater-
system
Wiener Lokalposse → Alt-Wiener
Volksstück
Wiener Revue → Revue
Wiener Volksstück → Alt-Wiener
Volksstück
Wiener Werkl → Literatur am Nasch-
markt
Wilna-Truppe → Jiddisches Theater
Winkelrahmenbühne → Neuzeit/
Theater der Neuzeit

Wintergarten 1110
Wooster Group → Performance
Group
Workers' Laboratory Theatre 1111
Worker's Theatre Movement
→ Unity Theatre
Wuppertaler Bühnen 1111
Wuppertaler Tanztheater 1111
Wurstl → Alt-Wiener Volksstück
Württembergisches Staatstheater
→ Staatstheater Stuttgart
Yakṣagāna → Ind. Theater
Yātrā/Jātrā → Ind. Theater
Yiddish Art Theater → Jiddisches
Theater
Yingxi (Chin. Schattentheater) 1113
Yose → Katarimono-Rezitations-
kunst
Yûgen 1114
Zaju 1114
Zanni → Commedia dell'arte
Zarzuela 1116
Zauberstück 1116
Zeit 1117
Zeitstück 1119
Zeitungstheater 1120
Zensur → Theaterzensur
Zentrale Bühnen-, Fernseh- und
Filmvermittlung (ZBF) → Schau-
spieler
Zentralverband Schweizer Volks-
theater (ZSV) 1121
Zimmertheater 1121
Zirkus 1121
Zirkus Schumann → Reinhardt-
Bühnen
ZSV → Zentralverband Schweizer
Volkstheater
Zürcher Schauspielhaus 1124
20. Jahrhundert/Drama und Theater
im 20. Jahrhundert 1125
Zwischenakt 1130
Zwischenspiel 1131

Länderübersichten

Afrika

→ Afrikanisches Theater, → Candomblé

Belgien

→ Ballet du XXe Siècle, → Mudra

Bulgarien

→ Narodnija teatar «Ivan Vazov»

China

→ Chinesisches Sprechtheater, → Chinesisches Theater, → Chuanqi, → Difang xi, → Juese/lianpu, → Kunqu, → Liyuan, → Muou xi/Kuilei xi, → Nanxi, → Pekingoper, → Piaoyou, → Quyi, → Yingxi, → Zaju

Dänemark

→ ABC, → ARTE, → Fiolteatret, Den Kongelige Ballet, → Det Kongelige Teater, → Odin Teatret, → Pantomimeteatret, → Radioteatret

Deutschland / BRD / DDR

→ Amateurtheater, → antiteater, → Arbeiter-Theater-Bund Deutschland, → Bad Hersfeld, → Ballets Jooss, → Ballett der Deutschen Oper Berlin, → Ballett der Deutschen Staatsoper Berlin, → Ballett Frankfurt, → Bänkelsang, → Bauhausbühne, → Bauhaustänze, → Bayerisches Staatsballett, → Bayerisches Staatsschauspiel München, → Berliner Ensemble, → Berliner Festwochen, → Berliner Theatertreffen, Besucherorganisation, → Betriebsorganisation des Theaters (BRD), → Bildungsanstalt Jacques-Dalcroze (Hellerau), → Der Blaue Vogel,

→ Bonner Bühnen, → bremer shakespeare company, → Bremer Tanztheater, → Bremer Theaterlabor, → Das Bügelbrett, → Bund Deutscher Amateurtheater (BDAT), → Bundesarbeitsgemeinschaft (BAG) Spiel und Theater e. V., → BUSTA, → Chat Noir (Berlin), → Dadaistisches Theater, → Deutsche Bühne, → Deutscher Bühnenverein (DBV), Deutsche Shakespeare-Gesellschaft, → Deutsches Nationaltheater Weimar, → Deutsches Schauspielhaus Hamburg, → Deutsches Theater (Berlin), → Die Distel, → Dokumentarisches Theater, → Dramaturgische Gesellschaft, → Die Drei Tornados, → Düsseldorfer Schauspielhaus, → Die Elf Scharfrichter, → Episches Theater, → Eurythmische Kunst, → Exiltheater, → Expressionistisches Theater, → Fastnachtsspiele, → Floh de Cologne, → Folkwang-Tanzstudio, › Freie Bühne, → Freie Bühne (Stockholm), → Freie Deutsche Bühne (Buenos Aires), → Freie Volksbühne Berlin, → Friedrichstadt-Palast, → Fronttheater, → Genossenschaft Deutscher Bühnenangehöriger (GDBA), → Goethe-Theater Bad Lauchstädt, → Grips Theater (Berlin), → Gruppe junger Schauspieler, → Hamburg Ballett, → Hamburger Kammerspiele, → Hamburgische Dramaturgie, → Hansatheater, → Heinrich-Heine-Klub (Mexiko), → Hessisches Staatstheater Darmstadt, → Horizonte/Festival der Weltkulturen, → Humanismus/Drama und Theater des Humanismus, → Internationale Kulturfabrik Kampnagel, → Kabarett,

▶ ▶ ▶

→ Kabarett der Komiker, → Kampf-
bühne, → Die Katakombe, → Klassik,
→ «Kleine Bühne» des Freien Deut-
schen Kulturbundes, → Die Kleine
Freiheit, → Das Kom(m)ödchen,
→ Kulturpolitik und Theater (BRD/
DDR), → Labanschulen, → Leipziger
Theater, → Luisenburg-Festspiele,
→ Mannheimer Nationaltheater, → Ma-
xim-Gorki-Theater, → Mecklenburgi-
sches Staatstheater Schwerin, → Die
Meininger, → Merzbühne, → Meta
Theater, → Mittelalter/Drama und
Theater des Mittelalters, → Mülheimer
Theatertage, → Münchener Künstler-
theater, → Münchner Kammerspiele,
→ Münchner Lach- und Schießgesell-
schaft; → (Münchner) Rationaltheater,
→ Münchner Volkstheater GmbH,
→ Naturalistisches Theater, → Nelson-
Revue, → Neue Sachlichkeit, → Neues
Theater Halle, → Niederdeutsches
Theater, → Norddeutsches Thea-
tertreffen, → Oberammergau, → Otto-
Falckenberg-Schule, → Die Pfeffer-
mühle, → Piscatorbühne, → Politisches
Theater, → Proletarisch-revolutionäres
Theater, → Reformation/Drama und
Theater der Reformation, → Reichs-
dramaturg, → Reichskabarett,
→ Reichstheaterkammer, → Reinhardt-
Bühnen, → Romantisches Theater,
→ Rote Grütze Berlin, → Ruhrfest-
spiele, → Schall und Rauch, → Die
Schaubude, → Schaubühne am Lehni-
ner Platz/Schaubühne am Halleschen
Ufer, → Schauspielhaus Bochum,
→ Schauspielhaus Chemnitz, → Schau-
spiel Köln/Oper der Stadt Köln,
→ Schmidt Theater-Varieté-Kneipe,
→ Die Schmiere, → Simplicissimus,
→ Staatliche Schauspielbühnen Berlin,
→ Staatsschauspiel Dresden, → Staats-
theater Stuttgart, → Die Stachel-
schweine, → Städtische Bühnen Frank-
furt, → Stella Kultur Management,
→ Studio 1934, → Sturmbühne, → Sturm

und Drang, → Tanztheater, → Tanztheater der Komischen Oper Berlin,
→ Thalia Theater (Hamburg), → Theater am Turm (TAT)/Frankfurt,
→ Theater am Schiffbauerdamm (Berlin), → Theater an der Ruhr im Raffelbergpark, → Theater der Freien Hansestadt Bremen, → Theater der Freien
Volksbühne Berlin, → Neuzeit/Thea-
ter der Neuzeit, → Theater der Prominenten, → Theater der Welt, → Theatermanufaktur, → Theatersystem,
→ Theater und Philharmonie Essen
GmbH → theaterwerkstatt hannover,
→ Thingspiel, → Tribüne für Freie
Deutsche Literatur und Kunst in Amerika, → Überbrettl, → Verband Deutscher Freilichtbühnen e. V. (VDF),
→ Verband der Theaterschaffenden
der DDR, → Völkische Dramaturgie,
→ Volksbühne, → Volksbühne Berlin,
→ Volksstück, → Volkstheater Rostock, → Wintergarten, → Wuppertaler
Bühnen, → Wuppertaler Tanztheater,
→ 20. Jahrhundert/Drama und Theater
im 20. Jahrhundert

England
→ Admiral's Men, → Afterpiece,
→ Angry Young Men, → Anti-Masque,
→ Ballad Opera, → British Theatre
Association, → Chamberlain's Men,
→ Children of Paul's, → Christmas Pan-
tomime, → Comedy of Humours,
→ Comedy of Manners, → Community
Theatre, → Covent Garden Theatre,
→ Domestic Tragedy, → Drury Lane,
→ Dumb Show, → Edinburgh, → Elisa-
bethanisches Theater, → Englische
Komödianten, → Fortune Theatre,
→ Fringe, → Globe Theatre, → Heroic
Tragedy, → London Contemporary
Dance School, → Lord Chamberlain,
→ Lyceum Theatre, → The Mask,
→ Masque, → Mittelalter/Drama und
Theater des Mittelalters, → Moralitä-
ten, → Mummers' Play, → Music Hall,

→Mystery Play, →National Theatre, →Neuzeit/Theater der Neuzeit, →Old Vic (Theatre), →Pageant, →Pip Simmons Theatre Group, →Rachetragödie, →Repertory Theatre, →Restaurationstheater, →Royal Academy of Dramatic Art, →Royal Ballet, →Royal Ballet School, →Royal Court Theatre, →Royal Shakespeare Company, →Sentimental Comedy, →7:84 Theatre Company, →Shakespearebühne, →Stratford-upon-Avon, →The Theatre, →Theatre in Education, →Theatre Workshop, →Unity Theatre, →University Wits, →Viktorianisches Theater, →West End

Estland

→Viktor Kingissepa nim. Tallinna Riiklik Akademiline Draamateater

Exil

→European Jewish Artist Society (EJAS), →Freie Deutsche Bühne (Buenos Aires), →Heinrich-Heine-Klub (Mexiko), →«Kleine Bühne» des Freien Deutschen Kulturbundes (England), →Das Laterndl (London), →Österreichische Bühne (USA), →Studio 34 (Tschechoslowakei), →Theater der Prominenten (Niederlande), →Tribüne für Freie Deutsche Literatur und Kunst (USA)

Finnland

→Helsingin Kaupunginteatteri, →Kom-Teatteri, →Lilla Teatern, →Suomen Kansallisteatteri, →Tampereen Työväen Teatteri

Frankreich

→ABC, →Aufklärung/Theater der Aufklärung, →Ballet de l'Opéra de Paris, →Ballets Suédois, →Basoches, →Boulevardtheater, →Café-Theater, →Cartel (des quatre), →Cartoucherie, →Centre national de création, →Cen-

tres Dramatiques Nationaux, →Centre International de la Création Théâtrale, →Centre international de recherches scéniques, →Chat Noir, →Comédie-ballet, →Comédie Française, →Comédie Italienne, →Compagnie des Ballets Russes de Serge de Diaghilev, →Compagnie Renaud-Barrault, →Ecole de Danse de l'Opéra de Paris, →Festival d'Avignon, →Folies-Bergère, →Grand Guignol, →Le Grand Magic Circus, →Hôtel de Bourgogne, →Humanismus/Drama und Theater des Humanismus, →Laboratoire de Théâtre Art et Action, →Kabarett, →Klassik, →Maison de la Culture, →Le Mirliton, →Mittelalter/Drama und Theater des Mittelalters, →Nancy, →Naturalistisches Theater, →Neuzeit/Theater der Neuzeit, →Romantisches Theater, →Sotie, →Tanztheater, →Theater der Grausamkeit, →Theater der Nationen, →Théâtre Alfred Jarry, →Théâtre Antoine, →Théâtre de Gennevilliers, →Théâtre de la Foire, →Théâtre de la Mandragore, →Théâtre de l'Atelier, →Théâtre de l'Europe, →Théâtre de l'Œuvre, →Théâtre des Amandiers, →Théâtre des Bouffes du Nord, →Théâtre du Marais, →Théâtre du Quotidien, →Théâtre du Soleil, →Théâtre du Vieux-Colombier, →Théâtre-Libre, →Théâtre National de Chaillot, →Théâtre National de l'Odéon, →Théâtre National Populaire, →Vaudeville, →Videotanz, →20. Jahrhundert/Drama und Theater im 20. Jahrhundert

Griechenland

→Antikes Theater, →Dionysien, →Dionysostheater, →Ethnikó Théatro, →Karagiozis, →Komidylle (Komeidyllion), →Phlyakenposse, →Satyrspiel, →Théatron Technis

Indien
→ Bharata Natyam, → Chhao-Tanz, → Indisches Theater, → Kathak, → Kathakali, → Manipuri, → Odissi, → Raslila, → Sadir Natya

Iran
→ Ta^cziya

Irland
→ Abbey Theatre, → Irish Dramatic Movement

Israel
→ Bathsheva Dance Company, → Habima, → Jiddisches Theater

Italien
→ Antikes Theater, → Arena Goldoni, → Atellana, → Commedia dell'arte, → Compagnia Dario Fo, → Compagnia del Collettivo di Parma, → La Comune, → La Fede, → Futuristisches Theater, → Humanismus/Drama und Theater des Humanismus, → La Maddalena, → Mittelalter/Drama und Theater des Mittelalters, → Neuzeit/Theater der Neuzeit, → La Nuova Scena, → Piccolo Teatro di Milano, → Pirandellismus, → Rinascimento, → Teatro Cooperativo, → Teatro degli Independenti, → Teatro dell'arti, → Teatro Farnese, → Teatro Goldoni, → Teatro Immagine, → Teatro Olimpico, → Teatro San Ferdinando, → Teatro Stabile, → Teatro Umoristico, → Verismus, → 20. Jahrhundert/Drama und Theater im 20. Jahrhundert

Japan
→ Angura, → Butô, → Hana, → Hanamichi, → Hyôbanki, → Isshin-denshin, → Japanisches Theater, → Jôruri, → Kabuki, → Kamishibai, → Kata, → Katari-mono-Rezitationskunst, → Kyôgen,

→ Mai-Tanzformen, → Nô, → Shimpa, → Shingeki, → Yûgen

Kolumbien
→ Teatro Experimental de Cali

Kuba
→ Teatro Escambray

Lateinamerika
→ Gauchotheater, → Guerilla Theatre, → Kreolengroteske, → Lateinamerikanisches Theater, → Missionsschauspiel, → Teatro Arena (Brasilien), → Teatro de Creación Colectiva, → Teatro Escambray (Kuba), → Teatro Experimental de Cali (Kolumbien), → Theater der Unterdrückten

Lettland
→ Jaunatnes Teātris Riga

Litauen
→ Jaunimo Teatras Vilnius

Niederlande
→ ABC, → Abel Spel/Sotternie, → Amsterdamsche Schouwburg, → Emigrantentheater, → Festival of Fools, → Jugendtheater (in den Niederlanden), → Mickerytheater, → Mittelalter/Drama und Theater des Mittelalters, → Het Nationale Ballet, → Nederduytsche Academie, → Nederlands Dans Theater, → Neuzeit/Theater der Neuzeit, → Onafhankelijk Toneel, → Reformation/Drama und Theater der Reformation, → Shaffytheater, → Vertooningen, → Het Werkteater, → 20. Jahrhundert/Drama und Theater im 20. Jahrhundert

Norwegen
→ Chat Noir, → Nationale Scene i Bergen, → Nationalteatret Oslo, → Norske Teatret i Oslo, → Radioteatret

Österreich

→ ABC, → Alt-Wiener Volksstück, → Besserungsstück, → Bregenz, → Burgtheater Wien, → Exiltheater, → Felsenreitschule Salzburg, → Jüdisch-Politisches Kabarett, → Landestheater Linz, → Das Laterndl (London), → Lieber Augustin, → Literatur am Naschmarkt, → Maschinenkomödie, → Max-Reinhardt-Seminar, → Neuzeit/Theater der Neuzeit, → Orgien Mysterien Theater, → Österreichische Bühne (The Austrian Theatre), → Das politische Kabarett, → Salzburger Festspiele, → Simplicissimus, → Theater in der Josefstadt, → Theatersystem, → Vereinigte Bühnen Graz (Steiermark), → Volkstheater Wien, → Zauberstück, → 20. Jahrhundert/ Drama und Theater im 20. Jahrhundert

Polen

→ Armes Theater (Jerzy Grotowski), → Centrum Sztuki «Studio», → Cricot, → Cricot 2, → Jiddisches Theater, → Reduta, → Studententheater, → Teatr Dramatyczny, → Teatr im J. Słowackiego, → Teatr Narodowy, → Teatr Nowy, → Teatr Polski, → Teatr Rapsodyczny, → Teatr Stary, → Teatr Wspołczesny

Rußland/GUS

→ Balagan, → Biomechanik, → Die Blauen Blusen, → Bolschoi-Ballett, → Bolschoi-Theater, → Entfesseltes Theater, → GITIS, → Gorki-Theater Leningrad, → Habima, → Jiddisches Theater, → Kirow-Theater, → Kleines Dramatisches Theater (St. Petersburg), → Komissarshewskaja-Theater, → Leibeigenentheater, → Majakowski-Theater, → Maly Theater, → MChAT, → Meyerhold-Methode, → Moskauer Staatliches Kammertheater, → Petruschka, → Politisches Theater, → Puschkin-Theater, → St. Petersburger Ballett, → Škola dramatičeskogo iskusstva (Moskau), → Skomorochen, → Stanislawski-System, → Taganka-Theater/Theater an der Taganka, → Theateroktober, → TRAM, → Wachtangow-Theater, → 20. Jahrhundert/ Drama und Theater im 20. Jahrhundert

Schweden

→ Cullbergbaletten, → Dramaten, → Drottningholm, → Videotanz

Schweiz

→ Cabaret Voltaire, → Cornichon, → Intimes Theater, → Die Pfeffermühle, → Spatz und Co, → Stadttheater Basel, → Theatersystem, → Zentralverband Schweizer Volkstheater (ZSV), → Zürcher Schauspielhaus

Spanien

→ Arte Nuevo de hacer Comedias en este Tiempo, → Auto Sacramental, → La Barraca, → Comedia, → Corralbühne, → Entremés, → Esperpento, → Género Chico, → Gracioso, → Loa, → Mantel- und Degenstück, → Mysterienspiel, → Neuzeit/Theater der Neuzeit, → Sainete, → Teatro Independiente, → Zarzuela, → 20. Jahrhundert/ Drama und Theater im 20. Jahrhundert

Tschechoslowakei

→ ABC, → Divadlo na Vinohradech, → Divadlo Na zábradlí, → D 34, → Laterna Magica (Prag), → Národní Divadlo, → Slovenské Národné Divadlo (Bratislava)

Türkei

→ Ankara Devlet Tiyatrosu, → İstanbul Şehir Tiyatrosu, → Karagöz, → Kukla oyunu, → Meddah, → Ortaoyunu

Ungarn

→ Csiky Gergely Szinház, → Katona József Szinház, → Magyar Népi Szinház, → Nemzeti Szinház, → Vigszinház

USA

→ Actor's Studio, → Arbeitertheater (USA), → Bread and Puppet Theatre, → Broadway, → Chicano-Theater, → Dance Theatre of Harlem, → Dramatic Workshop of the New School for Social Research (New York), → Environmental Theatre, → Equity, → Federal Theatre Project, → Free Southern Theatre, → Group Theatre, → Guerilla Theatre, → The House, → Jiddisches Theater, → Lafayette Players, → League of Worker's Theatre, → Living Newspaper, → Living Theatre, → Little Theatre Movement, → La Mama Experimental Theatre Club, → The Method, → Minstrel Show, → Negro Ensemble Company, → New Playwrights' Theatre, → New York City Ballet, → Off-Off-Broadway, → Ontological-Hysteric Theatre, → Open Theatre, → Paterson Pageant, → Performance Group, → Politisches Volkstheater (USA), → Provincetown Players, → San Francisco Mime Troupe, → School of American Ballet, → Schwarzamerikanisches Theater/Black Theatre, → Snake Theatre, → Squat Theatre, → Teatro Campesino, → Teatro de la Esperanza, → Theatre Guild, → Theatre of Images, → Theatre Union, → Underground Theatre, → Videotanz, → Washington Square Players, → Worker's Laboratory Theatre

Städteübersichten

Amsterdam

→ Amsterdamsche Schouwburg, → Festival of Fools, → Mickerytheater, → Het Nationale Ballet, → Nederduytsche Academie, → Nelson-Revue *(s. a. Berlin)*, → Onafhankelijk Toneel, → Shaffytheater, → Het Werkteater

Ankara

→ Ankara Devlet Tiyatrosu

Athen

→ Ethnikó Théatro, → Théatron Technis

Avignon

→ Festival d'Avignon

Bad Hersfeld

→ Bad Hersfelder Festspiele

Bad Lauchstädt

→ Goethe-Theater Bad Lauchstädt

Basel

→ Stadttheater Basel

Belgrad

→ BITEF

Bergen

→ Nationale Scene i Bergen

Berlin

→ Ballett der Deutschen Oper Berlin, → Ballett der Deutschen Staatsoper Berlin, → Berliner Ensemble, → Berliner Festwochen, → Berliner Thea-

tertreffen, → Der Blaue Vogel, → Das
Bügelbrett *(s. a. Heidelberg)*, → Deutsche Bühne, → Deutsches Theater,
→ Die Distel, → Die Drei Tornados,
→ Freie Bühne *(s. a. Stockholm)*,
→ Freie Volksbühne Berlin, → Friedrichstadt-Palast, → Grips-Theater,
→ Gruppe junger Schauspieler,
→ Habima *(s. a. Moskau, Tel Aviv)*,
→ Horizonte/Festival der Weltkulturen, → Kabarett der Komiker *(s. a. New York)*, → Die Katakombe, → Maxim-Gorki-Theater, → Nelson-Revue
(s. a. Amsterdam), → Piscatorbühne,
→ Reichskabarett, → Reinhardt-Bühnen *(s. a. Wien)*, → Rote Grütze,
→ Schall und Rauch, → Schaubühne am
Lehniner Platz/Schaubühne am Halleschen Ufer, → Staatliche Schauspielbühnen Berlin, → Die Stachelschweine, → Sturmbühne, → Tanztheater der Komischen Oper Berlin,
→ Theater am Schiffbauerdamm,
→ Theater-Manufaktur Berlin,
→ Überbrettl, → Volksbühne, → Volksbühne Berlin, → Wintergarten

Bochum
→ Schauspielhaus Bochum

Bonn
→ Bonner Bühnen

Bratislava
→ Slovenské Narodné Divadlo

Bregenz
→ Bregenzer Festspiele

Bremen
→ bremer shakespeare company,
→ Bremer Tanztheater, → Bremer
Theaterlabor, → Theater der Freien
Hansestadt Bremen

Bremgarten
→ Spatz und Co

Brüssel
→ Ballet du XXe Siècle *(s. a. Lausanne)*

Budapest
→ Katona József Szinház, → Nemzeti
Szinház, → Squat Theatre *(s. a. New
York)*, → Vigszinház

Buenos Aires
→ Freie Deutsche Bühne

Chemnitz
→ Schauspielhaus Chemnitz

Darmstadt
→ Hessisches Staatstheater Darmstadt

Den Haag
→ Nederlands Dans Theater

Dresden
→ Staatsschauspiel Dresden

Dublin
→ Abbey Theatre

Düsseldorf
→ Düsseldorfer Schauspielhaus, → Das
Kom(m)ödchen

Edinburgh
→ Edinburgh

Essen
→ Ballets Jooss, → Folkwang-Tanzstudio, → Theater und Philharmonie
Essen GmbH

Florenz
→ Arena Goldoni, → Teatro Goldoni

Frankfurt am Main
→ Ballett Frankfurt, → Die Schmiere,
→ Städtische Bühnen Frankfurt,
→ Theater am Turm – TAT

Graz
→ steirischer herbst, → Vereinigte Bühnen Graz

Halle
→ Neues Theater Halle

Hamburg
→ Deutsches Schauspielhaus, → Ham-
burg Ballett, → Hamburger Kammer-
spiele, → Hansatheater, → Interna-
tionale Kulturfabrik Kampnagel,
→ Kampfbühne, → Schmidt Theater-
Varieté-Kneipe / Schmidts Tivoli,
→ Stella Kultur Management, → Thalia
Theater

Hannover
→ theaterwerkstatt hannover

Heidelberg
→ Das Bügelbrett *(s. a. Berlin)*

Hellerau
→ Bildungsanstalt Jacques-Dalcroze

Helsinki
→ Helsingin Kaupunginteatteri,
→ Kom-Teatteri, → Lilla Teatern,
→ Suomen Kansallisteatteri

Holstebro
→ Odin Teatret

Istanbul
→ İstanbul Şehir Tiyatrosu

Kaposvár
→ Csiky Gergely Szinház

Köln
→ Floh de Cologne, → Schauspiel Köln
/ Oper der Stadt Köln

Kopenhagen
→ Fiolteatret, → Den Kongelige Ballet,
→ Det Kongelige Teater, → Pantomi-
meteatret

Krakau
→ Cricot *(s. a. Warschau)*, → Cricot 2,
→ Teatr im J. Słowackiego, → Teatr
Rapsodyczny, → Teatr Stary

Lausanne
→ Ballet du XXe Siècle *(s. a. Brüssel)*

Leipzig
→ Leipziger Theater, → Die Pfeffermühle *(s. a. München, Zürich)*

Linz
→ Landestheater Linz

Łodz
→ Teatr Nowy

London
→ Admiral's Men, → Chamberlain's
Men, → Children of Paul's, → Covent
Garden Theatre, → Drury Lane,
→ Fortune Theatre, → Globe Theatre,
→ «Kleine Bühne» des Freien
Deutschen Kulturbundes, → Das
Laterndl, → London Contemporary
Dance School, → Lyceum Theatre,
→ National Theatre, → Old Vic
(Theatre), → Royal Academy of
Dramatic Art, → Royal Ballet, → Royal
Ballet School, → Royal Court Theatre,
→ Royal Shakespeare Company *(s. a.
Stratford-upon-Avon)*, → The Theatre,
→ Theatre Workshop, → Unity
Theatre, → West End

Los Angeles
→ Actor's Studio *(s. a. New York)*

Mailand
→ La Comune, → Piccolo Teatro di Milano

Meinigen
→ Die Meininger

Mexico City
→ Heinrich-Heine-Klub

Monte Carlo
→ Compagnie des Ballets Russes de Serge de Diaghilev *(s. a. Paris)*

Moskau
→ Bolschoi-Ballett, → Bolschoi-Theater, → GITIS, → Habima *(s. a. Berlin, Tel Aviv)*, → Majakowski-Theater, → Maly Theater, → MChatT, → Moskauer Staatliches Kammertheater, → Škola dramatičeskogo iskusstva, → Taganka-Theater / Theater an der Taganka, → Wachtangow-Theater

Mülheim
→ Mülheimer Theatertage, → Theater an der Ruhr im Raffelbergpark

München
→ antiteater, → Bayerisches Staatsballett, → Bayerisches Staatsschauspiel München, → Die Elf Scharfrichter, → Intimes Theater *(s. a. Stockholm)*, → Die Kleine Freiheit, → Meta Theater, → Münchener Künstlertheater, → Münchner Kammerspiele, → Münchner Lach- und Schießgesellschaft, → (Münchner) Rationaltheater, → Münchner Volkstheater GmbH, → Otto-Falckenberg-Schule, → Die Pfeffermühle *(s. a. Leipzig, Zürich)*, → Die Schaubude, → Simplicissimus *(s. a. Wien)*

Nancy
→ Nancy

Neapel
→ Teatro San Fernandino, → Teatro Umoristico

New Orleans
→ Free Southern Theater

New York
→ Actor's Studio *(s. a. Los Angeles)*, → Bread and Puppet Theatre, → Broadway, → Dance Theatre of Harlem, → Dramatic Workshop of the New School for Social Research, → The House, → Kabarett der Komiker *(s. a. Berlin)*, → Lafayette Players, → Living Theatre, → La Mama Experimental Theatre Club, → Negro Ensemble Company, → New York City Ballet, → Off-Off-Broadway, → Ontological-Hysteric Theatre, → Open Theatre, → Österreichische Bühne (The Austrian Theatre), → Paterson Pageant, → Performance Group, → Provincetown Players, → School of American Ballet, → Squat Theatre *(s. a. Budapest)*, → Tribüne für Freie Deutsche Literatur und Kunst in Amerika, → Washington Square Players

Oberammergau
→ Oberammergauer Passionsspiel

Oslo
→ Nationaltheatret i Oslo, → Norske Teatret i Oslo

Paris
→ Ballet de l'Opéra de Paris, → Ballets Suédois, → Basoches, → Cartoucherie, → Centre International de la Création Théâtrale / Centre International de Recherches Théâtrales, → Centre international de recherches scéniques, → Chat

Noir, → Comédie Française, → Comédie Italienne, → Compagnie des Ballets Russes de Serge de Diaghilev *(s. a. Monte Carlo)*, → Compagnie Renaud-Barrault, → Folies-Bergère, → Grand Guignol, → Hôtel de Bourgogne, → Laboratoire de Théâtre Art et Action, → Le Mirliton, → Théâtre Alfred Jarry, → Théâtre Antoine, → Théâtre de Gennevilliers, → Théâtre de la Foire, → Théâtre de la Mandragore, → Théâtre de l'Atelier, → Théâtre de l'Europe, → Théâtre de l'Œuvre, → Théâtre des Amandiers, → Théâtre des Bouffes du Nord, → Théâtre du Marais, → Théâtre du Soleil, → Théâtre du Vieux-Colombier, → Théâtre-Libre, → Théâtre National de Chaillot (TNC), → Théâtre National de l'Odéon, → Théâtre National Populaire (T.N.P.)

Parma
→ Compagnia del Collettivo di Parma, → Teatro Farnese

Prag
→ Černé Divadlo, → Divadlo na Vinohradech, → Divadlo Na zábradlí, → D 34, → Laterna Magica, → Národní Divadlo, → Studio 1934

Recklinghausen
→ Ruhrfestspiele

Riga
→ Jaunatnes Teātris Riga

Rom
→ La Maddalena, → Teatro dell'arti, → Teatro Immagine

Rostock
→ Volkstheater Rostock

Salzburg
→ Felsenreitschule Salzburg, → Salzburger Festspiele

San Francisco
→ San Francisco Mime Troupe

San Juan Bautista
→ Teatro Campesino

St. Petersburg
→ Gorki-Theater, → Kirow-Theater, → Kleines Dramatisches Theater, → Komissarshewskaja-Theater, → Puschkin-Theater, → St. Petersburger Ballett

Sao Paulo
→ Teatro Arena

Schwerin
→ Mecklenburgisches Staatstheater Schwerin

Shanghai
→ European Jewish Artists Society (EJAS)

Sofia
→ Narodnija teatar «Ivan Vazov»

Stockholm
→ Cullbergbaletten, → Dramaten, → Drottningholm, → Freie Bühne *(s. a. Berlin)*, → Intimes Theater *(s. a. München)*

Stratford-upon-Avon
→ Royal Shakespeare Company *(s. a. London)*, → Stratford-upon-Avon

Stuttgart
→ Staatstheater Stuttgart

Tallinn
→ Viktor Kingissepa nim. Tallinna Riiklik Akadeemiline Draamateater

Tampere
→ Tampereen Työväen Teatteri

Tel Aviv
→ Bathsheva Dance Company, → Habima *(s. a. Berlin, Moskau)*

Vicenza
→ Teatro Olimpico

Vilnius
→ Jaunimo Teatras

Warschau
→ Centrum Sztuki «Studio», → Cricot *(s. a. Krakau)*, → Reduta, → Teatr Dramatyczny, → Teatr Narodowy, → Teatr Polski, → Teatr Wspólczesny

Weimar
→ Deutsches Nationaltheater Weimar

Wien
→ ABC, → Burgtheater Wien, → Jüdisch-politisches Kabarett, → Lieber Augustin, → Literatur am Naschmarkt,

→ Max-Reinhardt-Seminar, → Das Politische Kabarett, → Reinhardt-Bühnen *(s. a. Berlin)*, → Simplicissimus *(s. a. München)*, → Theater Der Kreis, → Theater in der Josefstadt, → Volkstheater Wien

Wunsiedel
→ Luisenburg-Festspiele

Wuppertal
→ Wuppertaler Bühnen, → Wuppertaler Tanztheater

Zürich
→ Cabaret Voltaire, → Cornichon, → Die Pfeffermühle *(s. a. Leipzig, München)*, → Schauspielhaus Zürich

Vorwort	35
Verzeichnis der Mitarbeiter	41
Literaturhinweise	1133

Vorwort

> *«Die Schaubühne ist mehr als jede andere*
> *öffentliche Anstalt des Staats eine Schule*
> *der praktischen Weisheit...»*
> (Friedrich Schiller, 1784)

> *«Ein Theater ist ein Unternehmen,*
> *das Abendunterhaltung verkauft.»*
> (Bertolt Brecht, ca. 1926/27)

> *«Das Theater ist der seligste Schlupfwinkel für diejenigen,*
> *die ihre Kindheit heimlich in die Tasche gesteckt und sich*
> *damit auf und davon gemacht haben, um bis an ihr*
> *Lebensende weiterzuspielen.»*
> (Max Reinhardt, 1930)

> *«...daß das theatralische Spiel wie die Pest*
> *eine Raserei ist...»*
> (Antonin Artaud, 1933)

Die im Laufe der mehr als dreijährigen Vorbereitungen zu diesem Nachschlagewerk an die Herausgeber oft gestellte Frage, welche Bereiche dieses Theaterlexikon denn umfasse, ließ sich immer am besten so beantworten: eigentlich alles, von Abonnement bis Vorhang, von Afrikanisches Theater bis Zürcher Schauspielhaus – außer: Eigennamen, z. B. von Autoren, Schauspielern oder Regisseuren, und nationale Übersichten, z. B. über französisches oder koreanisches Theater. – Warum gerade diese Ausschließungen? Das vorliegende Nachschlagewerk legt seinen Schwerpunkt auf die Information über Sachbegriffe der Theaterästhetik, der Dramenliteratur, der Struktur des Theaterbetriebs, des Theaterbaus und der Bühnentechnik, über Stil- und Epochenentwicklungen des Theaters, Institutionen, Bühnen und Ensembles, den gesamten geschichtlichen Raum bis zur Gegenwart umfassend, unter Berücksichtigung auch der wichtigsten außereuropäischen Theaterkulturen. Es grenzt sich damit ab von bereits vorliegenden Theaterlexika, die gerade die Information über Bühnenautoren, Schauspieler, Regisseure etc. in den Mittelpunkt stellen. Nationale Übersichtsdarstellungen wurden nicht aufgenommen, weil sie den Rahmen des Buches gesprengt hätten. Dennoch bemüht sich auch dieses Nachschlagewerk um Zusammenschau und Verklammerung der Stichwörter und Querverweise.

Was an Darzustellendem und zu Berücksichtigendem bleibt, ist eine äußerst vielfältige, aber auch heterogene Daten- und Materialfülle, die die Herausgeber nur zu oft in die schwierige Entscheidung zwang, zwischen dem Anspruch des Buches auf umfassende Information und einer gegenüber dem Verlag noch vertretbaren Umfangsbegrenzung zu vermitteln. Ziel war ein Informationswerk, das sich an einen breiten Leserkreis wendet und den unterschiedlichsten Interessen, die ein so komplexer Bereich wie der des Theaters auf sich zieht, gerecht zu werden versucht. Es sollte ein Buch werden, das nicht nur auf gezielte Fragen Antwort gibt, sondern auch zum Lesen und zum Entdecken anreizt.

Es mußten neben den selbstverständlichen Standardinformationen Schwerpunkte gesetzt, aber auch Defizitbereiche der Theaterforschung angegangen werden, stets in Auseinandersetzung mit deutschsprachigen und außerdeutschen Theaterhandbüchern, Lexika und Enzyklopädien, deren Qualitäten zu einer Herausforderung wurden, deren Schwächen es nicht zu wiederholen galt. Die von den Herausgebern – mit Unterstützung von nahezu hundert weiteren Mitarbeitern – erarbeiteten Stichwortlisten blieben offen fast bis zum Redaktionsschluß; die Vielschichtigkeit des Gegenstandsbereichs vom Kindertheater bis zur Pekingoper zwang insbesondere in den Randbereichen immer wieder, die Aufnahme neuer Stichwörter zu überprüfen.

Gerade in diesem Zusammenhang haben die Herausgeber dem Rowohlt Verlag für ein weitgehendes Entgegenkommen in der Gestaltung der äußeren Rahmenbedingungen der Arbeit zu danken, insbesondere Herrn Dr. Burghard König, der als zuständiger Lektor und Herausgeber der Reihe *rowohlts enzyklopädie* das Unternehmen mit großem Engagement, ständiger Bereitschaft zu Diskussion und hilfreicher Kritik begleitet hat. Was nicht realisiert werden konnte, war die ursprünglich geplante Bebilderung des Buches, dafür wurde gegenüber der Anfangskalkulation der Gesamtumfang fast verdoppelt.

Der diesem Nachschlagewerk zugrunde liegende Theaterbegriff ist so weit gefaßt und so offen gehalten, wie es für eine noch überschaubare, an der gegenwärtigen Forschungslage orientierte Strukturierung der Daten und Sachbereiche möglich, wie es aber auch im Hinblick auf die Vielfalt an Theaterformen und -traditionen im europäischen und außereuropäischen Raum notwendig ist. Dabei steht das Schauspieltheater eindeutig im Mittelpunkt; das Musiktheater als ein Bereich eigener Prägung und Tradition bleibt ausgeschlossen. Dagegen ist der Tanz, wenngleich in geringerem Umfang als das Schauspieltheater, berücksichtigt, und dies aus folgenden Gründen: In vielen Formen des traditionellen Theaters Indiens, Japans oder Afrikas lassen sich Tanz und Theater ohnehin nicht im Sinne der westeuropäischen Trennung der Begriffe unterscheiden; aber auch im europäischen Bereich ist nicht nur der Ursprung des Theaters aufs engste mit dem Tanz verbunden, vielmehr ist auch in dieser Tradition die Synthese von Tanz und Theater, von den Mysterien des Mittelalters über die barocken Theaterfeste bis zu den Formen experimenteller Theaterarbeit im 20. Jahrhundert, ein äußerst produktives, die Theaterästhetik immer wieder vorantreibendes Moment, das nicht nur in der Entwicklung des modernen Tanztheaters seinen besonderen Ausdruck findet.

Berücksichtigt sind alle Theaterformen, die aus der Inszenierung der dramatischen Literatur heraus ihre Gestalt gewonnen haben, in den großen Gattungen von Tragödie und Komödie mit allen Sonderformen, Mischgattungen und auch jenen Entwicklungen, die sich im Auflösungsspektrum dieser Tradition herausgebildet haben. Aufgenommen wurden auch die einschlägigen Stichwörter aus den Bereichen der Poetologie, der Dramentheorie und der Dramaturgie. Damit wird der Tatsache Rechnung getragen, daß sich zumindest in der europäischen Tradition Theater überwiegend in der spannungsvollen Wechselbeziehung von Inszenierung und literarisch-dramatischem Werk entfaltet.

Aber auch jene Theaterformen, die von ihrem Ansatz her Inhalte und Formensprache nicht über die Auseinandersetzung mit einem vorgegebenen Text entwickeln, sind einbezogen: Pantomime, das barocke Garten- und Feuerwerkstheater, die Theaterexperimente des Bauhauses und der Konstruktivisten u. a. Dazu gehören auch Performance, Happening oder Aktionskunst, die sich im Grenzbereich von Theater und bildender Kunst entwickelt haben.

Einen erheblichen Raum nimmt die Darstellung der großen Stilentwicklungen (Renaissance, Klassik, Naturalismus, Symbolismus etc.) ein, ebenso bedeutende Sonderentwicklungen wie etwa das Jesuitentheater, das Arbeitertheater oder Theaterformen aus dem Umfeld pädagogischer Arbeit wie Kinder- und Jugendtheater, Schulspiel, Lehrstück, Psychodrama etc.

Eine ebenso große Breite ist bei der Darstellung der institutionellen Strukturen des Theaters angestrebt, vom höfischen Theater bis zu den Wandertruppen, von den Staats- und Stadttheatern bis zu den Amateurbühncn und den Freien Theatergruppen. Aus allen Bereichen sind – mit dem Schwerpunkt auf das 20. Jahrhundert und die Gegenwart – auch die wichtigsten Bühnen und Ensembles aufgenommen. Stichwörter, die sich auf Begriffe des Theatersystems beziehen, berücksichtigen in erster Linie den deutschsprachigen Raum. Da Artikel nicht aufgenommen sind, die nationale Entwicklungen als Zusammenhang darstellen, sind unter dem jeweiligen Landesstichwort Verweisungen auf sämtliche dazugehörigen Theaterinstitutionen und regionalspezifischen Theaterformen, die als Einzelstichwörter bearbeitet sind, verzeichnet.

Die weitestgehende Zusammenschau bieten Überblicksessays über das Theater der Antike, Afrikas, Chinas, Indiens, Japans, über lateinamerikanisches Theater, mittelalterliches Theater, über das Theater der Neuzeit und das Theater des 20. Jahrhunderts. Insbesondere diese Beiträge sind mit Verweisungen ausgestattet und binden eine große Anzahl weiterer zum Gegenstandsbereich gehöriger Artikel (in der Regel vom selben Autor geschrieben) ein.

Eine zweite Übersichtsebene bilden Stichwortgruppen über epochale bzw. stilistische Theaterentwicklungen, jeweils über die nationalen Grenzen hinweg; es sind Artikel zum Theater der Renaissance, der Klassik, des Symbolismus, des Expressionismus etc. oder soziologisch-programmatische Klassifizierungen wie Schuldrama/Schultheater, höfisches Theater, Jesuitentheater, Arbeitertheater, Amateurtheater, Kindertheater, Exiltheater etc.; hinzu kommen zusammenfassende Artikel über politisches Theater, experimentelles Theater, Kabarett etc. In gleicher Weise ist der Bereich Tanz angelegt.

Alle diese unter unterschiedlichen Perspektiven verfaßten Überblicksartikel verzeichnen die zugehörigen Stichwörter zu Einzelphänomenen als Querverweise. Der Leser kann sich also durch diese Stichwortvernetzung – seinem Interesse und diesen Verweisungen folgend – entsprechende Überblicke und Zusammenhänge selbst erschließen. Die Liste der Stichwörter und Querverweise, die den Artikeln als Inhaltsverzeichnis vorangestellt ist, bietet dabei eine hilfreiche Orientierung, die vom Leser genutzt werden sollte, die über das gesuchte Stichwort hinaus auch einen Überblick über den Gesamtbestand bietet.

Theaterbau, Bühnentechnik und Bühnenkostüm sind ebenso einbezogen wie Schauspielpädagogik, Rhetorik oder nonverbale Kommunikation als Grundlagen der Schauspielkunst, so daß Theater letztlich in der Vielfalt seiner Aspekte von Produktion und Rezeption unter strukturellen und historischen Gesichtspunkten umfassend repräsentiert ist.

Wenn im einzelnen dennoch manche Defizite bleiben, so hängt das nicht zuletzt vom Forschungsstand der Fachwissenschaften ab, an dem sich Nachschlagewerke grundsätzlich orientieren müssen; auch mögen bei der Auswahl der aufzunehmenden Stichwörter (besonders bei Bühnen und Ensembles) vor allem im Bereich der aktuellen Theaterentwicklungen sicherlich auch andere Entscheidungen vertretbar sein als die von den Herausgebern getroffenen.

Die Überblicksbibliographie am Ende des Bandes, von Wolfgang Beck zusammengestellt, systematisiert im wesentlichen einführende und auch weiterführende Forschungsliteratur in Ergänzung zu den bei den Artikeln angegebenen Literaturhinweisen. Ergänzend dazu sei ausdrücklich auch auf die Artikel, Theatersammlungen/-museen und Theaterausstellungen, ebenso Tanzzeitschriften, Tanzarchive, -museen und -bibliotheken hingewiesen.

Die Herausgeber haben allen Mitarbeitern für ihre Arbeit, oft auch für fachlichen Rat, zu danken, insbesondere jenen, die größere Bereiche selbständig strukturiert und auch weitgehend bearbeitet haben: Neeti Badwe für indisches Theater, Wolfgang Beck für Kabarett, Horst Birr für Theaterbau und Bühnentechnik, Annelore Engel-Braunschmidt für russisches Theater, Helga Ettl und Patricia Stöckemann für Tanz, Bernd Eberstein für chinesisches Theater, Martin Franzbach für lateinamerikanisches und spanisches Theater, Jan Hans für deutsches Exiltheater, Dieter Herms für US-amerikanisches Theater, Roswitha Körner für Theatersystem und Verbände im deutschsprachigen Raum, Bernd-Peter Lange für englisches Theater, Wolfgang F. Michael für mittelalterliches Theater, Hans-Wolfgang Nickel für Theater- und Spielpädagogik, Bernd Seidensticker für das Theater der Antike, Roland Schneider für japanisches Theater, Henri Schoenmakers für niederländisches Theater und Horst Schumacher für die Übersetzung zahlreicher Beiträge aus dem Französischen.

Hamburg und Paris, April 1986   *Manfred Brauneck*
                                                            Gérard Schneilin

Zur dritten revidierten Auflage

Die dritte Auflage dieses von einer breiten Leserschaft so erfreulich aufgenommenen Theaterlexikons wurde um ca. 30 Stichworte erweitert, weitaus die meisten Artikel auf den aktuellen Stand der Daten und Entwicklungen gebracht. Zur leichteren Auffindung der einzelnen Bühnen, die in der Regel als Stichworte unter ihrem offiziellen Namen, der den Ort vielfach nicht enthält, alphabetisiert sind, wurde ein Ortsverzeichnis angelegt. Einige osteuropäische Bühnen bzw. Ensembles erscheinen im Stichwort unter der im deutschsprachigen Raum gängigen Bezeichnung, da sie unter ihrem offiziellen Namen schwer auffindbar wären.

Vornehmlich die großen Übersichtsartikel erhielten eine reiche Bildausstattung. Die ausführliche Bibliographie der vorausgehenden Auflagen wurde zugunsten der Texterweiterungen gekürzt.

Schwerpunkte der Revision waren: der Bereich Tanz bzw. Tanztheater; die konzeptionelle Bearbeitung haben hier Patricia Stöckemann, Hamburg, und Horst Vollmer, Essen, geleistet. Aktualisiert und wesentlich ergänzt wurden alle Artikel zu den osteuropäischen Bühnen und Theaterverhältnissen. Die politischen Umwälzungen der letzten Jahre hatten insbesondere auch für den Kulturbetrieb dieser Länder einschneidende Auswirkungen, die es einzuarbeiten galt. Diesen osteuropäischen

Bereich hat Elke Wiegand, Berlin, bearbeitet. Aus den gleichen Gründen war eine umfassende Überprüfung aller Beiträge nötig, die die Theaterverhältnisse in der früheren DDR zum Gegenstand haben. Ergänzungen und kritische Durchsicht wurden hier von Roland Dreßler und Manfred Pauli, Leipzig, vorgenommen. Horst Schumacher, Paris, hat die Darstellung des zeitgenössischen französischen Theaters auf den neuesten Stand gebracht. Ingeborg Janich hat bei der kritischen Durchsicht des gesamten Artikelbestands und Wolfgang Beck bei den redaktionellen Aufgaben mitgearbeitet. Diesen Mitarbeitern vor allem, aber auch allen anderen Autoren, die zu dieser Neuauflage beigetragen haben, dankt der Herausgeber für ihre engagierte Arbeit.

Hamburg, im August 1992   *Manfred Brauneck*

Verzeichnis der Mitarbeiter

Wim J. M. Achten · Birgit Amlinger · Michel Autrand · Neeti A. Badwe · Uschi Bauer · Wolfgang Beck · Horst Birr · Werner Bleike · Frans Bosboom · Theo Buck · Thodoros Chatzipantazis · Diedrich Diederichsen · Dorothea Dieren · Roland Dreßler · Bernd Eberstein · Annelore Engel-Braunschmidt · Helga Ettl · Maren Fittschen · Martin Franzbach · Gérard Genot · Sándor Gulyás · J. Lawrence Guntner · Achim Haag · Ute Hagel · Jan Hans · Frédéric Hartweg · Adriana Hass · Dieter Herms · Knut Hickethier · Wil Hildebrand · Ingeborg Janich · Chiel Kattenbelt · Elke Kehr · Peter Kelting · Else Kjær · Martin Kolberg · Roswitha Körner · Rolf D. Krause · Erich Krieger · Uwe Krieger · Bernd-Peter Lange · Günter Langer · Paul Larrivaille · Sonja de Leeuw · Hans-Thies Lehmann · Ulf-Thomas Lesle · Gerhard Lohse · Wulf Lohse · Petra Lüdeke · Wolfgang F. Michael · François Moureau · Christine Müller · Barbara Müller-Wesemann · Alain Muzelle · Hans-Wolfgang Nickel · Manfred Pauli · Patrice Pavis · Hinnerk Peitmann · Bernard Poloni · Peter Pörtner · Carin van Rijswoudt · Hans Martin Ritter · Marjoke de Roos · Claudia Rosiny · Andreas Roßmann · Barbara Rüster · Sven Frederik Sager · Léon van der Sanden · Monika Sandhack · Jean-Pierre Sarrazac · Elisabeth Scherf · Ebba Schirmacher · Roland Schneider · Henri Schoenmakers · Johannes Lothar Schröder · Franzjosef Schuh · Werner Schulze-Reimpell · Horst Schumacher · Bernd Seidensticker · Peter Simhandl · Ulrich Stein · Georg Stenzaly · Patricia Stöckemann · Anneli Suur-Kujala · Slawomir Tryc · Jean-Marie Valentin · Horst Vollmer · Friedrich Wagner · Annette Waldmann · Carl Wege · Irene Wegner · Leonore Welzien · Elke Wiegand · Jean-Marie Winkler · Erna Wipplinger · Ellinor Woodworth · Jean-Marie Zemb · Roger Zuber

Abbey Theatre

Irisches → Nationaltheater; 1904 als ständige Spielstätte der Irish National Dramatic Society der Gebrüder Fay eröffnet. Zur Eröffnung im Mai 1899 wurden W. B. Yeats' (1865–1939) *On Baile's Strand* und Lady Gregorys (1882–1932) *Spreading the News* gezeigt. Yeats und Lady Gregory blieben, neben der Geldgeberin Annie Horniman (1860–1937), zunächst die bestimmenden Persönlichkeiten des Theaters, dessen Ziel es war, irische Stücke über irische Themen von irischen Schauspielern darstellen zu lassen. Mit der UA der Stücke von Dramatikern wie J. M. Synge (1871–1909), A. E. (George William Russell), Edward Martyn, G. B. Shaw (1856–1950) und das jungen O'Casey (1880–1964) leistete das A. T. einen bedeutenden Beitrag zur Irish Literary Renaissance, ohne Konflikten mit dem überkommenen Publikumsgeschmack immer ausweichen zu können. So führte die UA von Synges *The Playboy of the Western World* 1907 zu einem Theaterskandal (sog. Playboy Riots).

Seit 1924 als erstes Theater der englischsprachigen Länder staatlich subventioniert, wandte sich das A. T. bald dem → realistischen Theater zu und öffnete sich auch internationalen Autoren. Seit der Fusion mit der semi-professionellen Gaelic Theatre Organisation, An Comhar Drámúiochta, 1942, kommen zahlreiche Stücke in Gälisch auf die Bühne; es werden nur noch engl.- und gälischsprachige Schauspieler engagiert. Nachdem das alte A. T. 1951 einem Brand zum Opfer fiel, zog das Ensemble in das Queen's Theatre um, bis 1966 das neue A. T. mit einer Studiobühne, dem Peacock, fertiggestellt war. Die hohe internationale Reputation des A. T. manifestiert sich u. a. in Auftritten bei mehreren World Theatre Seasons, durch Gastspiele in den USA und in ganz Westeuropa.

Fay, G.: The Abbey Theatre. London 1958; Hunt, H.: The Abbey. Ireland's National Theatre 1904–1979. Dublin 1979; McCann, S. (ed.): The Story of the Abbey Theatre. London 1967; Robinson, L.: Ireland's Abbey Theatre, A History, 1899–1951. London 1951.

Werner Bleike

ABC

Kabarett der engagierten Linken in Wien. Am 25.3.1934 fand die erste Premiere des «Brettl am Alsergrund» im Café City statt. Als am 20.10.1934 ein neues Programm aus der Taufe gehoben wurde, hatte das Kabarett auch einen neuen Namen: A. (nach den Anfangsbuchstaben von: Alsergrund, Brettl, City). 1935 gab es kurze Zeit zwei A. Durchsetzen konnte sich aber nur das nun «ABC im Regenbogen» genannte, das sehr bald ein unverwechselbares Gesicht bekam. Anders als die meisten Wiener Kabaretts der Zwischenkriegszeit bezog das A. bzw. «Regenbogen», wie es sich nach Schwierigkeiten mit Behörden und Zensur nannte, stets eindeutig Stellung. Texte, an die sich andere Kabaretts nicht heranwagten, wurden hier gespielt, vor allem die →Mittelstücke des politisch profiliertesten Wiener Kabarettautors Jura Soyfer. Die Grenzen zwischen Kabarett und Theater waren auch im A. fließend. – Die Besetzung Österreichs beendete seine Tätigkeit abrupt. Ein Teil der Mitarbeiter ging ins Exil, andere (z. B. J. Soyfer) wurden im KZ umgebracht.

ABC war auch der Name anderer Kabaretts, Revue- und Musiktheater, so des 1936 von Wim Kan in Amsterdam gegründeten «ABC-kabaret», das 1954 noch einmal in veränderter Form auflebte. Zu nennen sind des weiteren das «ABC-Theater» in Kopenhagen, das aktuelle Revuen pflegt, das satirische «ABC-Theater» in Prag, das vor dem 2. Weltkrieg von Jiri Voskovec und Jan Werich gegründet und nach dem Krieg von Werich geleitet wurde, und das A. in Paris, eine «Music-Hall», in der zahlreiche Chansonniers ihre ersten Erfolge feierten.

Budzinski, K.: Pfeffer ins Getriebe. München 1982; Hakel, H.: Wiennärrische Welt. Wien 1961; ders. (Hg.): Wigl-Wogl. Wien 1962; Reisner, I.: Kabarett als Werkstatt des Theaters. 2 Bde. Diss. Wien 1961; Rösler, W. (Hg.): Geh ma halt a bisserl unter. Berlin 1991; Sallee, A./Chauveau, Ph.: Music-hall et café-concert. Paris 1985; Veigl, H.: Lachen im Keller. Wien 1986; Weys, R.: Cabaret und Kabarett in Wien. Wien 1970.

Wolfgang Beck

Abel Spel / Sotternie

Die Handschrift Van Hulthem (Hulthemse Handschrift), ein umfangreicher in Brüssel aufbewahrter Kodex aus dem Anfang des 15. Jh., umfaßt u. a. die Texte der vier ältesten bekannten weltlichen Dramen der Niederlande. Diese *abele spelen* (mittelniederl.: abel = schön, kunstreich, geschickt) datieren von ungefähr 1350; Ursprung: Ostbrabant; die Autoren sind nicht bekannt. Die Themen des A. S. sind nah verwandt mit der höfischen Ritterepik. Es handelt sich um romantische Liebesgeschichten. Titel: *Esmoreit, Gloriant, Lanseloet von Dänemark*. Das vierte Spiel *Vanden Winter ende vanden Somer* ist eine Allegorie über die Frage, wann die Liebe am besten gedeiht, im Winter oder im Sommer. Über die Inszenierungen gibt es nur wenige Daten. Vermutlich spielten stets mindestens zwei (bis acht) Darsteller (ghesellen van de spele) auf einer →Simultanbühne und trugen wahrscheinlich Masken. Als Nachspiel zu einem A. S. wurde eine *sotternie* (oder klucht/cluyte), →Posse, aufgeführt. Im Kodex folgt auf jedes der vier A. S der Text eines Possenspiels. Darüber hinaus gibt es noch zwei weitere *sotternien* in der Hulthemschen Handschrift. Titel der S.: *Lippijn, Die Buskenblaser, Die Hexe, Rubben, Truwanten* und *Drie daghen here*; Merkmale: schroffe Komik und witzige Szenen aus dem Alltagsleben des einfachen Volkes. Die S. wurden wohl auf einem Podium im Freien aufgeführt, ohne daß ein A. S. vorausging. Später (im Rederijker-Drama) werden die S. zumeist ‹esbattementen› genannt.

Hummelen, W. M. H.: Tekst en toneelinrichting in de abele spelen. In: De nieuwe taalgids 70 (1977), S. 229–249; Hunninger, B.: The Netherlandish abele spelen. In: Maske und Kothurn 10 (1964), S. 244–253; van Kammen, L. (Hg.): De abele spelen naar hat Hulthemse handschrift. Amsterdam 1968; Stellinga, G.: De abele spelen. Zinsvormen en zinsfuncties. Groningen 1955; Wijngaards, N. C. H.: De oorsprong der abele spelen en sotternieën. In: Handelingen van de Koninklijke Zuidnederlandse Maatschappij voor Taal-, Letterkunde en Geschiedenis 22 (1968), S. 411–423.

Marjoke de Roos

Abenddienst

Aufsichtsdienst des künstlerischen (→Regisseur) und technischen Personals (Theatermeister oder Vertreter des techn. Direktors) während der Abendvorstellung im Theater. Der Abendregisseur ist für den gesamten Ablauf der →Aufführung und für evtl. Ankündigungen an das Publikum (Erkrankung eines Schauspielers, Umbesetzung etc.) verantwortlich. Die Technik überwacht Auf- und Abbau der Dekoration sowie Bühnenumbauten im Verlauf der Vorstellung.

Monika Sandhack

Abonnement

Vertrag auf Abnahme einer Reihe gleicher oder einander ähnlicher Leistungen zu niedrigerem, in der Regel im voraus zu zahlenden Preis. Im Theater Gewährung eines Preisnachlasses von 20 bis 30 Prozent bei Verpflichtung der Zuschauer zur Abnahme von Eintrittskarten für eine bestimmte Anzahl von Aufführungen der Spielzeit (alle Neuinszenierungen oder nur Schauspiel, nur Musiktheater). Meist ein stets gleicher Platz im Theater. Im 19. Jh. zunächst Miete eines Platzes für jeden Aufführungstag. In den 80er Jahren am →Burgtheater Wien ein Premieren-A., um – ökonomisch abgesichert – das Publikum durch Vorzugspreise für Novitäten zu interessieren. Ökonomische Absicherung und Besuchergarantie für unbekannte, schwierige, wenig publikumswirksame Stücke bis heute Hauptgrund für Auflegen eines A. (auch Stammiete, Anrecht). Nachteil: vorgegebener Produktionszwang, geringe Flexibilität des Spielplans, Notwendigkeit, auch verfehlte Inszenierungen durchs A. zu ziehen. 1972 in Bochum Einführung eines Wahl-A. mit übertragbaren Gutscheinen zu beliebigem Theaterbesuch ohne vorherige Festlegung auf ein Stück oder einen Tag, so auch in Hamburg (Deutsches Schauspielhaus, Thalia). 25 bis 30 Prozent aller verkauften Theaterkarten in der Bundesrepublik gehen an Abonnenten.

Werner Schulze-Reimpell

Abschiedsvorstellung

Letzter Auftritt eines Schauspielers auf einer Bühne – vor dem Ende eines Engagements, eines Gastspiels oder am Ende seiner künstlerischen Laufbahn (Gegensatz: →Debüt). Speziell im 18. und 19. Jh. übliche Ehrung eines Schauspielers, häufig als →Benefizvorstellung durchgeführt.

Wolfgang Beck

Absurdes Theater

«Man will überall Schilder sehen», sagte Edward Albee (* 1928), als er zur selben Zeit wie Harold Pinter (* 1930) in England jenes ‹neue Theater› auf die Bühne brachte, das als a. T. in Paris Anfang der 50er Jahre Samuel Beckett (1906–89), Arthur Adamov (1908–70), Eugène Ionesco (* 1912), alle drei im Exil lebend, und Jean Genet (1910–1986), ein Außenseiter, geschaffen hatten. Ist die Bezeichnung ‹absurdes Theater› nicht eben ein solches Schild? Und ist fast 40 Jahre nach der Premiere von Stücken wie *Les Bonnes* (1946), *L'invasion* (1950), *La cantatrice chauve* (1950) und *Warten auf Godot* (1953) noch ein gemeinsamer Nenner zu finden für deren Autoren? Ist die von Kafka, Sartre und Camus abgeleitete philosophisch-literarische Kategorie des Absurden mehr als ein publizistisches Schlagwort? Der Pariser Regisseur solcher Stücke, Roger Blin (1907–84), behauptet: «Die Kritiker haben Bezüge zwischen vereinzelten Autoren erstellt, eine Konvergenz, die nicht vorhanden war… Es gab höchstens eine Beziehung zur Zeit.» Das war die Nachkriegszeit mit einer Art Trümmer- und Heimkehrertheater nach der Katastrophe. Das einzig Gemeinsame so verschiedenartiger Dramaturgien wie derjenigen Adamovs, Becketts, Genets und Ionescos war die Wiederherstellung der Intimität in den Ruinen des großen Welttheaters. Daher die Figuren der *Parodie* Adamovs (1947), des *Balkon* von Genet (1956) und des *Endspiels* Becketts (1957), die, eingesperrt, Gefangene von anonymen Kräften sind, daher die sich zerfleischenden Paare und Familien bei Ionesco (*La leçon*, 1951; *Les chaises*, 1952; *Victimes du devoir*, 1953, u. a.), Pinter (*The Caretaker*, 1960; *The Homecoming*, 1965; *Old Times*, 1971) oder Albee (*The American Dream*, 1961; *Who's afraid of Virginia Woolf*, 1962). Das Individuum träumt von seiner Größe, ist aber unter dem Druck einer feindlichen Außenwelt zur Regression gezwungen, in einem Niemandsland verloren. Pinter, der 1975 ein Stück mit dem Titel *No Man's land* schrieb, sagt über sein erstes Drama *The Room* (1959): «Selbstverständlich sind sie erschreckt vor dem, was außerhalb des Zimmers ist. Da ist eine schreckliche Welt, bereit zum Eindringen. Ich bin sicher, sie ist auch schrecklich für Sie und mich.» Im a. T. scheint die Menschheit gezwungen, an einer schwarzen Messe teilzunehmen, wo jeder seinen Teil des Nichts in sich aufnehmen muß. «Im Theater», so Genet, «gibt es kaum etwas Wirksameres als die Erhebung.» Daher bei ihm jene negativen Rituale als Gegenstücke zur Zeremonie der Werte in der → klassischen Tragödie.

Diese metaphysische Not gestalten die Autoren des Theaters des Absurden in der Konstruktion ihrer Fabeln und ihrer oft zu Ungeheuern überhöhten Figuren. Bei Adamov heißt der Protagonist von *La Grande et la petite manœuvre* (1950) der Verstümmelte; er verliert allmählich alle Glieder und wird zum Rumpf, zum Abfall. Becketts Winnie in *Oh les beaux jours* (1963) wird vom Sandhaufen verschluckt, auf dem sie stand. Die Figuren von Genets *Les bonnes, Le Balcon* oder *Les nègres* (1958) gehen in dem Spiegel auf, worin sie sich anstarren. Die Leiber der Figuren Ionescos werden vergrößert, verstümmelt, verwandelt in surrealistische Anatomien, so in *Jacques ou la soumission* (1950) Roberta I und II. Diese Unmenschlichkeit reflektiert die Ängste, aber auch die Mythen der Zeit, so etwa die ungeheuerlich ideale Körperlichkeit des «1. Zwillings» in Albees *The American Dream* (1961).

A. T. ist ein Theater des Unheimlichen im Freudschen Sinne, in ihm ist unsere Alltagswelt in erschreckenden Formen präsent. Das Unheimliche, so Freud, entsteht oft aus dem Überbetonen der psychischen Realität im Bezug zur materiellen Wirklichkeit. Solche Überbewertung des Psychischen ist einer der Schlüssel zum Theater der 50er Jahre: Die Personen nehmen die Außenwelt nur noch wahr durch das Prisma ihrer Ängste, Zwangsvorstellungen und Wahnbilder. Das Unsichtbare oder Unbewußte offenbart sich in diesem Theater am schärfsten in der Sprache. Sie ist jedoch nicht mehr Kommunikationsmittel, sondern Folterinstrument. Die Personen bei Ionesco, Beckett, Pinter, Kroetz, Martin Walser, Handke sind in eine Sprache verstrickt, die sie ganz durchdringt und übermannt. Sie reden nicht, es redet in ihnen: sie verlieren sich in Tiraden von Gemeinplätzen, Halbwahrheiten, Klischees und Stereotypen; äußerste Entfremdung der in einer ‹automatischen Sprache› (Ionesco), in uferlosem Jargon verlorenen Menschen. In dieser Enthumanisierung von Raum und Sprache bleibt diesen Figuren nichts anderes übrig als das Nachleben des Herr-Knecht-Rituals oder, wie bei Albee, das Ausleben eines endlosen Familienhappenings. Im Gegensatz zu Brechts dialektischem Geschichtstheater werden hier metaphysische Fragen verwandelt in antidialektisches Theater, parodistisch-zeremoniell, mit repetitiver, kreisförmiger →Handlung hinter verschlossenen Türen. Insofern ergeben sich auch thematische Überschneidungen mit dem Theater der Existenzphilosophen, vor allem bei Jean-Paul Sartre (1905–80) mit *Les mouches* (1943) und *Huis-clos* (dt. Bei geschlossenen Türen, 1944). In Deutschland vor allem bei Wolfgang Hildesheimer (1916–91).

Dramaturgisch wie ideologisch wird hier im Anschluß an Alfred Jarry (1873–1907) und die Surrealisten das aristotelische Theater parodiert. Eindeutig ist der Bruch mit Realismus und Naturalismus, mit jeder Form der Psychologisierung, mit der exklusiven Herrschaft einer sinnvermittelnden ‹literarischen› Sprache. Daher der häufige Einsatz von →Groteske und →Parodie, →Gestik, →Pantomime und nicht- bzw. außersprachlichen ‹Ersatzhandlungen›, zugleich der sinnbildhafte Gebrauch von Requisiten. Diese polysemische, stets provozierende Theatersprache, in der das Emotionale das Begriffliche vertreibt, das Körperliche die geistige Abstraktion zersprengt, erzeugt eine Kommunikationsstruktur (Bühne–Publikum), welche die Experimente des Theaters der 60er und 70er Jahre vorwegnimmt.

Viele der Autoren des a. T. haben sich später trotz Beibehaltung wesentlicher Bauformen dieses Theaters auch anderer theatralischer Mittel bedient: Adamov wandte sich dem →epischen, sogar dem Brechtschen Theater zu, Ionesco schrieb →Parabelstücke wie *Les Rhinocéros* (Die Nashörner, 1959). Ob in diesem Versuch einer Synthese ‹des Individuellen und Kollektiven› (Adamov) nicht die aggressive Originalität des a. T. verlorengegangen ist, steht zur Debatte.

Adamov, A.: Ici et maintenant. Paris 1964; Adorno, Th. W.: Versuch, das ‹Endspiel› zu verstehen. In: Noten zur Literatur II. Frankfurt/M. 1960; Gorvin, M.: Le théâtre nouveau en France. Paris 1963; Esslin, M.: Das Theater des Absurden. Reinbek bei Hamburg 1961 (1985); Daus, R.: Das Theater des Absurden. Stuttgart 1977; Hayman, R.: Theater and Anti-Theater. New York 1979; Hildesheimer, W.: Über das absurde Theater. In: Theaterstücke. Frankfurt/M. 1976; Ionesco, E.: Notes et contre-notes. Paris 1962; Jacquart, E.: Le théâtre de dérision. Paris 1974; Serreau, G.: Histoire du ‹Nouveau Théâtre›. Paris 1966; Styan, J. L.: The Dark Comedy. Cambridge 1962.

Jean-Pierre Sarrazac / Gérard Schneilin

Actor's Studio

1947 in New York von Cheryl Crawford, Elia Kazan und Robert Lewis gegr. Institut zur Fortbildung von Schauspielern. Bedeutendster Leiter (Regisseur, Schauspielpädagoge) war von 1952 bis 1982 Lee Strasberg (1901–82), der als einer der drei Direktoren des sozialkritischen →Group Theatre der 30er Jahre auch nach dem 2. Weltkrieg den Versuch machte, diese Tendenzen weiterzuführen. Strasberg entwickelte eine auf den Schauspieltheorien von Stanislawski und Meyerhold aufbauende Schauspielpädagogik (→The Method), die weit über das New Yorker Institut hinaus von Bedeutung wurde. – Die Arbeit des A. S. war und ist noch heute prägend für ganze Generationen von Film- und Theaterschauspielern der USA. 1964/65 betrieb das A. S. mit einer Subvention der Ford Foundation das Actor's Studio Theatre, das in der einzigen Saison seines Bestehens fünf Inszenierungen produzierte, darunter Tschechows *Drei Schwestern* und James Baldwins *Blues for Mr. Charley*. – Das A. S. hat eine Niederlassung in Los Angeles. Seit dem Tode von Strasberg (1982) leiten Ellen Burstyn und Al Pacino das A. S.

Garfield, D.: A Player's Place. New York 1980; Hetmon, R. H. (ed.): Strasberg at the Actor's Studio. New York 1965; Lee Strasberg – Schauspielerseminar. Hg. v. Schauspielhaus Bochum. Bochum 1979.

Dieter Herms / Red.

Adaption

(Lat. *adaptare* – anpassen) Bearbeitung eines literarischen Werks, um es den Gesetzmäßigkeiten einer anderen Gattung oder eines anderen Mediums anzupassen (z. B. Bühnenfassung eines Romans, Filmversion eines

Theaterstücks). Die A. kann durch den Autor selbst oder einen Adaptor erfolgen. →Bühnenbearbeitung, →Dramatisierung.

Rach, R.: Die filmische A. literarischer Werke. Diss. Köln 1964.

Monika Sandhack

Admiral's Men

Auch Lord Admiral's Men genannt, waren neben den →Chamberlain's Men die bekannteste Theatertruppe des →Elisabethanischen Theaters. Ihr Protektor, Lord Howard, führte von 1576–79 eine Schauspielertruppe, die den Namen Lord Howard's Men trug. Als Howard im Jahre 1585 Admiral wurde, wurde die Truppe umbenannt in A. M. und hatte an Weihnachten desselben Jahres ihr Debüt bei Hof. Der geschäftliche Leiter war ab 1594 Philip Henslowe (?–1616), dessen Bühnentagebücher eine der wichtigsten Quellen des Elisabethanischen Theaters darstellen. Star der acht bis zwölf Darsteller der Truppe war ab 1587 Edward Alleyn (1566–1626). Nach einem Bühnenunfall im November 1587 brechen die Nachrichten über die Truppe für mehr als ein Jahr ab. In den Jahren 1590–91 trat die Truppe in James Burbages Theatre zusammen mit den Strange's Men auf, später wechselten beide Truppen unter Henslowe ins Rose Theatre über. Als sich im Jahre 1594 die →Chamberlain's Men konstituierten, gingen etliche Mitglieder der Admiral's Men zu dieser neuen Truppe. Im Jahre 1621 verlor die Truppe beim Brand des →Fortune alle Kostüme und Rollenbücher. Es gelang zwar unter vielen Schwierigkeiten, das Fortune wieder aufzubauen (1623), an ihre alten Erfolge konnten die A. M. (inzwischen umbenannt in Palsgrave's Men) jedoch nicht wieder anknüpfen, und so wurde die Truppe im Jahre 1631 endgültig aufgelöst.

Chambers, E. K.: The Elizabethan Stage. [3] 1951; Frenzel, H. A.: Geschichte des Theaters. München 1979; Henslowe's Diary. Eb. by. W. W. Greg. 1904–08; Stamm, A.: Geschichte des engl. Theaters. 1951; The Oxford Companion to the Theatre. Ed. by Ph. Hartnell. London/New York/Toronto 1951.

Elke Kehr

Afrikanisches Theater

Die traditionellen Kulturen Schwarzafrikas, des südlich der Sahara gelegenen Teils von Afrika, sind aus klimatischen, geographischen, historischen, sozialen und ökonomischen Gründen verschiedenartig ausgeprägt. Keine weist ein Theater im modernen Sinne auf, nirgendwo fehlen jedoch theatralische Elemente. Da die Anzahl der schwarzafrikanischen

Kulturen 1000 übersteigt und in vielen Kulturen eine Vielfalt theatralischer Formen existiert, ist eine generalisierende Darstellung des A. T. schwierig.

Ansätze zu einem professionellen Theater sind im Westsudan, insbesondere in Mali, bereits im 19. Jh. beobachtet worden. Eine eingehende wissenschaftliche Erforschung der westsudanischen Schauspielertruppen, die auch mit →Stabpuppen arbeiten, fehlt bisher. In der Regel wird A. T. aber nicht berufsmäßig ausgeübt, sondern ist integrierender Bestandteil von Ritualen. Diese sind häufig Angelegenheit von Spezialisten wie Königen, Priestern, Heilkundigen und Wahrsagern, aber nicht von Theaterleuten. Die meisten Teilnehmer an Ritualen sind Laien. Ihr Ablauf ist durch die Überlieferung vorgegeben, aber trotzdem flexibel. Die aktuelle Situation erfordert immer wieder Abänderungen und Unterbrechungen. Idealtypische Darstellungen bestimmter Rituale sind Abstraktionen; sie fingieren eine Präzision, die üblicherweise nicht vorhanden ist. Wesentlicher Bestandteil von Ritualen ist die Wiederholung von Riten und Mythen, zum Beispiel Darstellungen des Schöpfungsaktes, Vergegenwärtigungen des in der Jugend durchgemachten Initiationsrituals. Anlaß für Rituale mit theatralischen Komponenten sind Übergangsriten aus Anlaß von Geburt, Initiation, Heirat oder Tod und Feste im bäuerlichen Jahreszyklus. Besondere Rituale sind in Krisensituationen (Epidemien, Krieg, Dürre, Überschwemmung) üblich. Für Einzelpersonen finden Heilungsrituale statt; oft wird die Wiedergeburt des Patienten als Drama dargestellt, besonders bei der Behandlung psychogener Krankheitsbilder.

Die Zentren traditioneller afrikanischer Kunst, d. h. der plastischen Kunst der Masken und Figuren, liegen in den tropischen Wald- und Savannengebieten. Hier finden sich auch die am weitesten theatralisch ausgestalteten Rituale Afrikas, die Maskenspiele. Die Kostüme der Maskenträger enthalten neben Faserblätter- und Textilgewändern von Schnitzern und Gießern gestaltete Gesichtsmasken, aber auch hölzerne, den ganzen Oberkörper bedeckende Masken, Helmmasken sowie Maskenaufsätze in Form von Figuren, Halbfiguren und Köpfen. Mechanisch bewegliche Teile verstärken gelegentlich die Maskenwirkung, zum Beispiel in Nigeria, in der Volksrepublik Benin oder in Mali. Auch einfache Masken aus Geflecht oder Stoff finden sich. Die Masken agieren vor allem als Tänzer, solo, in kleinen Gruppen und in Formation, als Akrobaten, als Sänger, als Rezitatoren. Die Maskierung ist unterschiedlich ausgeprägt; eine Grenze zum einfachen Tanz- und Festschmuck, wobei die Träger zu erkennen sind, läßt sich nicht allgemein festlegen. Männer treten häufiger maskiert auf als Frauen. Maskenspiele werden in der Regel von politisch, religiös oder verwandtschaftlich orientierten Gesellschaften veranstaltet. Es gibt aber auch reine Maskengesellschaften. Häufig üben diese strikte Geheimhaltung. Weitverbreitet ist die Fiktion, daß die Maskenträger

52 Afterpiece

nicht erkannt werden. In den Geheimbünden ist das Maskentragen meist an die Zugehörigkeit zu bestimmten Altersklassen gebunden, jedoch kommen auch Masken als Individualbesitz bestimmter Einzelmitglieder vor. Maskentragende Frauengeheimbünde sind selten. Puppenspiel ist in Schwarzafrika selten. Die Stabpuppen in Mali werden von Maskierten gespielt und können auch als Maskenaufputz interpretiert werden. Bei den westlichen Yoruba in Nigeria und der Volksrepublik Benin treten Gliederpuppen innerhalb von Darbietungen der gelede-Maskengesellschaft auf. Die Pangwe (Fang) in Äquatorialguinea und Kamerun verwendeten einmal jährlich Holzfiguren zum →Puppenspiel, die sonst als Wächter auf den Behältern für die Ahnenschädel steckten.

Unabhängig von Puppen- und Maskenspiel sind Tänze und Rezitationen in ganz Schwarzafrika verbreitet. Wo die Maskierung fehlt, sind Schmuck und Körperbemalung wichtig. – Alte Tanzformen werden in vielen modernen Staaten Schwarzafrikas zur Inszenierung pseudodemokratischer Akklamationen für die Politiker aufgeführt – eine Fortsetzung kolonialer Tradition. Auf nationaler Ebene wurden vielfach Ensembles gebildet, die mit bühnenwirksam arrangierten und standardisierten Programmen mit traditionellem Hintergrund auf Tournee gehen. In den städtischen Zentren Schwarzafrikas ist die wachsende Zahl moderner Hörfunk-, Fernseh-, Kino- und Theaterproduktionen kaum noch zu überblicken.

Barley, N.: The Innocent Anthropologist. Notes from a Mud Hut. London 1983; Huet, M.: Afrikanische Tänze. Köln 1979; Krieg, K.-H./Lohse, W.: Kunst und Religion bei den Gbato-Senufo. Hamburg 1981; Tessmann, G.: Die Pangwe. Berlin 1913; Zwernemann, J.:/Lohse, W.: Aus Afrika. Ahnen – Geister – Götter. Hamburg 1985.

Wulf Lohse

Afterpiece

Kurze →Komödie oder →Farce, fast immer Einakter, der in Londoner Theatern des 18. Jh. im Anschluß an eine klassische Tragödie aufgeführt wurde. Ihre Funktion bestand im komischen Kontrast und auch in der Integration bürgerlicher Zuschauerkreise, für die der frühe Beginn der Hauptaufführung (meist sechs Uhr abends) den Besuch des Theaters sonst unmöglich machte. Für das A. wurde nur das halbe Eintrittsgeld verlangt. Das A. war oft die Kurzform regulärer Komödien, daneben aber auch viele Originaltexte in diesem Format, z. T. von bekannten Autoren wie Henry Fielding (1707–54), David Garrick (1717–79), Samuel Foote (1720–77), Arthur Murphy (1727–1805) und George Colman d. Ä. (1732–94). Im 18. Jh. entstanden einige tausend Stücke dieser Art; das A. hatte seinen Höhepunkt um die Mitte des Jh. und verfiel als Form zeitgleich mit der Theaterinstitution der «double bill».

Bevis, R. W. (Hg.): Eighteenth Century Drama: Afterpieces. London 1970; Hughes, L.: A Century of English Farce. Princeton 1956.

Bernd-Peter Lange

Agon

Griech.: Streit, Wettstreit. Der Ausdruck bezeichnet: 1. die Dithyramben-, Dichter- und Schauspielerwettbewerbe (→ Antikes Theater); 2. ein konventionelles, strenggebautes Element der alten Komödie, das sich in den meisten erhaltenen Komödien des Aristophanes findet und neben Chorpartien vor allem die agonistische Diskussion des Plans des Helden zum Gegenstand hat; 3. die Streitszenen (v. a.) der griech. Tragödie, in deren Grundform auf zwei durch kurze Stellungnahmen des Chors getrennte lange Reden der Dialogpartner eine → Stichomythie folgt, in der Argument und Gegenargument, Vorwurf und Gegenvorwurf, Beleidigung und Replik Schlag auf Schlag aufeinander folgen.

Bernd Seidensticker

Agora

Griech.: Versammlungs-, Markplatz; religiöses, wirtschaftliches, politisches, juristisches, administratives und kulturelles Zentrum der Polis; in Athen unmittelbar nordwestlich der Akropolis. Vor der Verlegung der Dionysien in den heiligen Bezirk am Südosthang der Akropolis (wahrscheinlich am Ende des 6. Jh.) fanden die Theateraufführungen auf der A. statt.

Bernd Seidensticker

AITA/IATA

Internationaler → Amateurtheaterverband (Association International du Théâtre Amateur/International Amateur Theatre Association); Mitgliederländer vor allem in Europa, dann Amerika, neuerlich auch in Asien und Afrika; gibt regelmäßige Informationen heraus, organisiert Tagungen und Festivals; durch das Educational Drama Committee stark engagiert in der →Spiel- und Theaterpädagogik. – Sekretariat in Kopenhagen.

Hans-Wolfgang Nickel

Akt

Die dt. Bezeichnung ‹Aufzug› weist auf die urspr. Bedeutung des Worts, nämlich die bühnentechnische Unterbrechung des Handlungsablaufs zum Kulissenwechsel und das darauffolgende Aufziehen des Vorhangs, hin. Ein A. war somit ein rein räumliches Gliederungselement. Mit der Einführung des Zwischenvorhangs 1770 erlangte der A. eine mehr dramatische Funktion; jeder A. hat nun eine gewisse inhaltliche Einheit und Geschlossenheit und entspricht einer Stufe des Handlungsablaufs mit Unterteilungen in Szenen bzw. →Auftritte. Das griechische Drama kannte kein solches Einteilungsprinzip, sondern gliederte sich locker und ungleichmäßig in Handlungsphasen und Chorgesänge (epeisodion – stasima). Erst Horaz (65–8 v. Chr.) für die →Tragödie und Varro (116–27 v. Chr.) für die →Komödie verlangen die aus der aristotelischen Drei-Phasen-Handlung entwickelte, konsequente fünfteilige Gliederung, die von Seneca (4? v. Chr.–65) verwirklicht wird. Während dieses Prinzip weder im mittelalterlichen →Mysterienspiel noch im →Elisabethanischen Drama Beachtung findet, wird es über Italien mit der dreiaktigen →Commedia dell'arte und der fünfaktigen ‹commedia sostenuta› in das klassische Theater in Frankreich und Deutschland aufgenommen und bleibt bis auf einzelne Ausnahmen (*Faust 1*, 1797; *Penthesilea*, 1808; *Der zerbrochne Krug*, 1803) die obligate Norm bis Ende des 18. Jh. Dieses deduktiv-schematische Muster wird im 19. Jh. in Deutschland von Gustav Freytag (1816–95) in *Die Technik des Dramas* (1863) als eine Folge von Einleitung durch Exposition der Voraussetzungen (1. Akt), Steigerung der Verwirklichung (2. Akt), Höhepunkt mit entscheidendem Geschehen (3. Akt), Umschwung, Peripetie und Fallen (4. Akt) und Schluß mit Lösung (Katastrophe, 5. Akt) formuliert. Im 19. Jh. wird diese strenge Akteneinteilung aber schrittweise aufgegeben. Die Boulevardautoren ziehen die A. 1 und 2 bzw. 3 und 4 zusammen und schreiben Dreiakter; die Realisten des ausgehenden 19. Jh., Gerhart Hauptmann (1862–1946) oder Henrik Ibsen (1828–1906), bevorzugen den Drei- oder Vierakter, die Impressionisten und die Neuromantiker den →Einakter. Mit dem Stationenstück des Expressionismus erfolgt dann eine gänzliche Auflösung der Struktur in A. zugunsten einer Folge von einzelnen Szenen bzw. →Tableaus; historische Anregungen kamen dabei von William Shakespeare

(1564–1616), von Jacob Michael Reinhold Lenz (1751–92), Georg Büchner (1813–37), Christian Grabbe (1801–36) und Frank Wedekind (1864–1918); diese Entwicklung erreicht ihren Höhepunkt mit der offenen Form im →epischen Theater Bertolt Brechts (1898–1956) und in dem vom Hörspiel beeinflußten modernen Drama. Neuerdings werden sogar Stücke ohne jede Einteilung noch Pause geschrieben, etwa *Port Royal* (1954) von Henri de Montherlant (1896–1972) oder *Fin de partie* (1956) von Samuel Beckett (* 1906). *Warten auf Godot* (1953), ein ‹Stück in zwei Akten›, bestätigt parodistisch diese Tendenz, da der zweite A. nur eine variierte Wiederholung des ersten ist.

Klotz, V.: Geschlossene und offene Form im Drama. München 1969.

Bernard Poloni

Alexandriner

Sechshebiger gereimter Jambenvers mit Zäsur nach der dritten Hebung. «Auch unsre Tugend wird des Feindes Anstoß sein» (Lohenstein). In germ. Sprachen zählt der männliche A. 12 und der weibliche 13 Silben: ∪–∪ –∪–‖∪–∪–∪–(∪). In der frz. Sprache ist die Mittelzäsur nicht zwingend, was dem Vers eine größere Beweglichkeit und Musikalität verleiht. «Toujours aimer, toujours souffrir, toujours mourir» (Corneille). Der A. wurde von den dt. Dramatikern hauptsächlich in der Barockzeit verwendet, so von Andreas Gryphius (1616–64) und Caspar von Lohenstein (1635–83). Im frz. Theater hingegen ist er generell der gebräuchlichste Vers – vgl. Pierre Corneille (1606–84), Jean Racine (1639–99) und Molière (1622–73) im 17. Jh., Voltaire (1694–1778) im 18. Jh., Victor Hugo (1802–85) und Edmond Rostand (1868–1918) im 19. Jh. – Neuerdings wieder in klassizistischer Manier bei Peter Hacks (* 1928).

Barthes, R.: Sur Racine. Paris 1963; Cohen, J.: Structure du langage dramatique. Paris 1966; Pretzel, U.: Deutsche Verskunst. In: Stammler, W.: Deutsche Philosophie im Aufriß. Bd. 3. Berlin 1961; Storz, G.: Ein Versuch über den Alexandriner. In: Festschrift für Kluckhohn-Schneider. 1948.

Alain Muzelle

Allegorie

Sinnliche Darstellung eines abstrakten Begriffs. Die A. entsteht durch die Zusammensetzung verschiedener Elemente, die ein kohärentes Ganzes bilden, wobei jedes Element im dargestellten Begriff seine Entsprechung findet. So sind in der herkömmlichen A. der Zeit das hohe Alter der Gestalt, die graue Farbe ihrer Kleidung, die Sense, die sie in der Hand trägt, durchweg Zeichen, die zusammen eine Veranschaulichung des Zeitbegriffs ermöglichen. Die A. ist vom Symbol (Bild und Bedeutung sind eine nicht auffaßbare Einheit) streng zu unterscheiden. Der Bildzusammenhang der A. ist in allen seinen Details interpretierbar.

Blütezeit der A. in der dramatischen Dichtung ist die Renaissance und das Barock – vgl. das →Jesuitentheater, das →Schäferspiel und in Deutschland die Werke von Andreas Gryphius (1616–64: *Leo Armenius*, 1646; *Cardenio und Celinde*, 1657) und Caspar Daniel von Lohenstein (1635–83: *Sophonisbe*, 1666). In seinem Spätwerk greift J. W. von Goethe (1749–1832), der «zum Allgemeinen das Besondere sucht», auf die A. zurück (*Faust II*, 1831). Seitdem lebte die A. u. a. im Wiener Volksstück (vgl. besonders Ferdinand Raimund, 1790–1836: *Der Alpenkönig und der Menschenfeind*, 1828), im Spätwerk August Strindbergs (1849–1912: *Ein Traumspiel*, 1907) und im expressionistischen Theater (vgl. Frank Wedekind, 1864–1918: *Frühlings Erwachen*, 1891) wieder auf.

Benjamin, W.: Ursprung des dt. Trauerspiels. Frankfurt/M. 1963; Pfeffer, K. L.: Struktur und Funktionsprobleme der Allegorie. In: Dt. Vierteljahresschrift f. Literaturwiss. und Geistesgeschichte 51 (1977).

Alain Muzelle

Alternieren

(Lat. ‹alternare› = abwechseln) A. bedeutet die wechselnde Besetzung einer Rolle mit zwei verschiedenen Schauspielern in derselben Inszenierung. Früher vor allem benutzt, um die Rivalität im gleichen Rollenfach arbeitender Schauspieler auszuschalten, dient es in neuerer Zeit vorrangig als Attraktion für das Publikum, das so Gelegenheit erhält, verschiedene Interpretationen einer Rolle in einer Inszenierung zu vergleichen.

Wolfgang Beck

Alt-Wiener Volksstück

Als Emanzipation vom barocken Helden- und Hoftheater bildet das um 1710 in der Wiener Vorstadt entstandene A.-W. V. ein eng lokal gebundenes, volksnahes Pendant zum →bürgerlichen Trauerspiel, am Anfang der dt. Theatergeschichte überhaupt. Im Laufe seines nahezu 150jährigen

Alt-Wiener Volksstück 57

Bestehens bleibt es untrennbar mit der Donau-Metropole, der im 18. Jh.
bedeutendsten Stadt des dt. Sprachraums, deren politische und gesellschaftliche Schlüsselposition das Aufkommen neuer Schichten des
‹Volks› oder des ‹Mittelstands› neben dem etablierten Adel förderte,
verbunden. Dieses →Volkstheater bedarf des ‹Volks› in doppelter Hinsicht: als Personal und Adressaten zugleich. Diesem organischen Zusammenhang der volkstümlichen Bühne mit dem Volk verdankt die neue
Gattung wesentliche formale Konstanten: ein Bühnenpersonal von z. T.
bäuerlicher, meist aber handwerklich-kleinbürgerlicher Herkunft, das
sich von der bloßen komischen Nebenfigur zum heiteren, aber ernst
genommenen Träger der Handlung emporentwickelt und dabei naturgemäß den Durchbruch der wienerischen Mundart als Bühnensprache
ermöglicht; private, alltagsbezogene Handlungen mit komischem, versöhnlichem, oft moralisierendem Ausgang; häufig Einschübe mimischer,
musikalischer, tänzerischer oder märchenhafter Zwischenspiele; Stegreifspiel innerhalb des Stücks, das sog. →Extemporieren: Stoffe und
Themen entstammen zumeist als Adaptation der Barocktradition, der
Trivialliteratur oder der zeitgenössischen ital. Oper. Eigenständige dramatische Theorien werden nicht entwickelt; als gewachsenes, organisches Ganzes besteht das A.-W. V. nur in enger Verbindung mit seiner
Geschichte, mit deren Autoren und bedeutenden Schauspielerpersön-
lichkeiten. Mit seiner Figur des echt wienerischen Hanswurst leitet der
ehemalige Wanderkomödiant, Prinzipal eines Puppenspiel-Ensembles
und Zahnarzt Joseph Anton Stranitzky (1676–1726) eine reiche volkstümliche komische Theatertradition ein. In Hanswurst («Wurstl»), einem
derb-verschmitzten Bauerntölpel im Kostüm eines salzburgischen Bauern, führt Stranitzky als Parallelschaltung und mimischen Räsoneur eine
komische Figur aus dem Volk in die Haupt- und Staatsaktionen der ital.
Opernlibretti ein. Der ‹weltberühmte Kraut- und Sauschneider aus Salzburg› bleibt in seiner derben, oft mimischen Komik der romantischen
Tradition, dem ital. →Arlecchino der →Commedia dell'arte oder dem Pariser →Théâtre italien des Gherardi, verpflichtet; zudem schlägt er eine
Brücke zur Tradition des dt. →Narren aus den mittelalterlichen Fastnachtsspielen und zum →Pickelhering der wandernden →Engl. Komödianten. Im ‹Kärntnertor-Theater› (gegr. 1712) findet Hanswurst seine
echt wienerische Lebensstätte. Der ‹zweite wienerische Hanswurst› und
Verkleidungskönig Gottfried Prehauser (1699–1769), für den der ‹Vater
des Wiener V.› Philipp Hafner (1735–64) Lokalpossen und Singspiele
verfaßt, sichert das Fortleben Hanswursts auf den Wiener Vorstadtbühnen über den Tod Stranitzkys hinaus. Brisanz und Wirksamkeit dieses
neuen volkstümlichen Theaters, das zugleich eine Unterhaltungs- und
eine Emanzipationsfunktion erfüllt, unterstreichen a contrario die heftigen Bemühungen der Zensur im sog. ‹Hanswurststreit› (1747–83), ein Ver-

58 Alt-Wiener Volksstück

bot des V. oder zumindest des Stegreifspiels durchzusetzen. Dessenungeachtet lebt der Geist Hanswursts in der Bernadon-Figur des Joseph Felix
von Kurz (1717–84) weiter, allen Angriffen des ‹österr. Gottsched› und
Rationalisten Josef von Sonnenfels (1733–1817) zum Trotz. Ihren Höhepunkt erreicht die Hanswurst-Komik mit dem von Johann Laroche
(1745–1806) geschaffenen, an dem aufgenähten roten Herzen erkennbaren →Kasperl, der im 19. Jh. vor allem das volkstümliche Puppenspiel
oder ‹Kasperletheater› prägen wird. Mit den Erfolgen Kasperls und seiner Variante als Thaddädl klingt die Blütezeit der alten Volksnarren-
komik, die Stranitzky-Hanswurst eingeläutet hatte, endgültig aus. Die
seit Stranitzky parallel verlaufenden Gattungen des V. und des Puppenspiels gehen fortan getrennte Wege.

   Der Wandel in der gesellschaftlichen Struktur Wiens und eine aufkommende neue bürgerliche Mentalität machen eine Neugestaltung des Verhältnisses des A.-W. V. zur Wiener Wirklichkeit überfällig; diese Erneuerung wird zum Verdienst der ‹Großen Drei›: Gleich, Meisl und
Bäuerle. Eine feste Grundlage für ein reges volkstümliches Kulturleben
in Wien bilden dabei die wichtigsten Wiener Vorstadttheater: das Theater in der Leopoldstadt (gegr. 1781), das Theater an der Wien (gegr. 1786)
und das →Theater in der Josefstadt (gegr. 1788). Joseph Alois Gleich
(1772–1841) verfaßt nahezu 230 Stücke in Anlehnung an die volkstümliche Zauberspieltradition oder an die Ritter- und Geisterstücke mit hohen Ansprüchen an Bühnenbild und -maschinerie. Bezeichnend für die
Entwicklung des V. sind Gleichs parodierende Possen und komische Lo-
kalstücke (*Die Musikanten am Hohen Markt*, 1816), in denen Kasperl
zunehmend durch komische Volksgestalten ersetzt wird. Außerdem verdankt das Josefstädter Theater Gleich die Entdeckung des Schauspielers
Raimund. Als Hauptvertreter der Wiener Lokalposse erscheint Karl
Meisl (1775–1853), dessen →Besserungsstücke – wie diejenigen Gleichs –
komisches Unterhaltungstheater mit Belehrungs- und Erbauungsinten-
tionen verknüpfen. Der dritte im Bunde, Adolf Bäuerle (1786–1856),
eigensinniger Journalist, Theaterkritiker und Autor zugleich, gilt mit
über 80 Zauber- und Lustspielen als bedeutendster Vorläufer Raimunds,
in dessen Schatten sein Spätwerk geraten sollte. Im lokalkomischen
Lustspiel *Die Bürger in Wien* (1813) schafft Bäuerle mit dem Wiener
Parapluiemacher Chrysostomos Staberl, einem Vorstadt-Wiener der Un-
ter- und Mittelschicht, den würdigen Nachfolger Kasperls. Staberls wiederkehrende materialistische Sprüche («Wenn ich nur etwas davon
hätt'») zeichnen eine komische Figur aus, die erstmals im A.-W. V. eine
psychologische und gesellschaftliche Realität erlangt.

   Aus dieser Welt der ‹Großen Drei› spielen und schreiben sich zwei
Persönlichkeiten empor, welche dem A.-W. V. zu höchster Vollendung
und zu literarischem Wert verhelfen: Raimund und Nestroy. In seinen

‹Original-Zauberspielen› schafft Ferdinand Raimund (1790–1836) die bemerkenswerte Synthese von barockem Zaubertheater und Wiener Volksposse. Seine bekanntesten Weltanschauungs-Zauberspiele (*Das Mädchen aus der Feenwelt oder der Bauer als Millionär*, 1826; *Der Alpenkönig und der Menschenfeind*, 1828; *Der Verschwender*, 1834) veranschaulichen mittels naiv-ernster Allegorien oder ironisch-märchenhafter Zaubereffekte moralische Werte und bürgerliche Tugenden im Sinne des ‹Besserungsstücks›: Maß, Zufriedenheit, Liebe. Seine Figuren des Neureichen Fortunatus Wurzel oder des Tischlermeisters Valentin vermitteln zugleich ein lebendiges Bild Wiens in der Zeit des Biedermeier und der Ära Metternich. Einige Couplets (vgl. das «Hobellied» aus *Der Verschwender*) erlangen Berühmtheit über das Stück hinaus. Im Gegensatz zu Raimund kehrt Johann Nepomuk Nestroy (1801–62), der ‹Mephisto des Volksstücks›, die politische und kritische Brisanz der Gattung hervor. Neben Parodien auf Grillparzer, Hebbel, Wagner u. a. greift Nestroy die traditionell bestätigende Form des ‹Besserungsstücks› und des Zauberspiels auf, indem er sie durchgehend problematisiert. Das gute Ende der Zauberposse *Der böse Geist Lumpazivagabundus oder das liederliche Kleeblatt* (1833) stellt sich selbst als märchenhaft bloß: Das Theater strebt nach Desillusionierung. Das erfahrene Elend wird nicht mehr wie bei Raimund als rein menschlich relativiert, sondern als gesellschaftliche Wirklichkeit angeprangert. Nestroys Possen (*Zu ebener Erde und im ersten Stock*, 1835; *Das Mädl aus der Vorstadt*, 1841; *Einen Jux will er sich machen*, 1842) atmen den Geist des vormärzlichen Wiens. Mit unübertroffenem Sprachwitz und ätzender Satire verschmäht Nestroys Theater die Illusion der Identifikationsdramatik zugunsten einer z. T. zynischen, desillusionierenden Komik, die bis an das Groteske und Unheimliche vordringt. Mit Nestroy bewegt sich das A.-W. V. an der Grenze zur Parodie und zur eigenen Unmöglichkeit: Höhepunkt und Ende der Gattung fallen zusammen.

Sozioökonomische Ursachen wie die Massenzuwanderung und wachsende Überfremdung im Wien des ausklingenden 19. Jh., die zunehmende Aufsplitterung der Gesellschaft als Produkt der Industrialisierung entziehen fortan dem A.-W. V. seinen volkstümlichen Nährboden. Die aufkommende Gattung der Operette macht sich allmählich die Unterhaltungsfunktion des Volksstücks zu eigen, ohne jedoch denselben emanzipatorischen Gehalt aufzuweisen. Mit der Problematisierung der Form schafft Nestroy Ansätze zu einer Dramaturgie, die sich vom traditionsgeheiligten Rahmen absondert, den das A.-W. V. bedenkenlos übernommen und angewendet hat, ohne eine ‹Gegendramaturgie› zu erarbeiten. Die Entwicklung des A.-W. V. bleibt zugleich ein bedeutender Schritt in der Bewußtwerdung Wiener bzw. dt. ‹Mittelstands› und ein vollwertiger Abschnitt dt. Theatergeschichte.

Aust, H./Haida, P./Hein, J.: Volksstück. München 1989; Bauer, R.: La réalité, royaume de Dieu. München 1965; Gromes, H.: Vom Alt-Wiener Volksstück zur Wiener Operette. Diss. München 1967; Hein, J. (Hg.): Theater und Gesellschaft. Das Volksstück im 19. und 20. Jh. Düsseldorf 1973; ders.: Das Wiener Volkstheater. Darmstadt 1991; Klotz, V.: Dramaturgie des Publikums. München 1976; Rommel, O.: Die Altwiener Volkskomödie. Wien 1952; Schmitz, Th.: Das Volksstück. Stuttgart 1990.

Jean-Marie Winkler

Amateurtheater

Der Begriff A. bezeichnet eine konkret-historische Erscheinungsform des nichtprofessionellen Theaters im 19. und 20. Jh.; er sollte nicht verwendet werden als Sammelbegriff für das nichtprofessionelle Theater insgesamt.

A. in diesem Sinne sind bürgerlich-kleinstädtisch bestimmte Vereinstheater, die in der Nachfolge der →Liebhaber- und Dilettantentheater des 18. und 19. Jh. in Deutschland ab 1870 verstärkt gegründet werden. Soziologisch bestimmt durch wachsende Freizeit und Unterhaltungs- und Kontaktbedürfnis in Städten, orientieren sie sich an den Standards des traditionsorientierten professionellen Theaters, übernehmen von ihm das Ideal der autonomen, zweckfreien Kunst, die Bildung und Erbauung garantiert. Die Theatervereine werden also zum Autoren- und Literaturtheater, vervollständigen und trivialisieren freilich diesen hohen Anspruch durch das vielfach schon im Namen genannte Ziel der Geselligkeit und Unterhaltung («Theater- und Vergnügungsverein»). Die Aufführung wie der zumeist nachfolgende Tanzabend sind gekennzeichnet vom Streben nach repräsentativer Festlichkeit, ja möglichst nach pompösem Glanz. Anders als das →Arbeitertheater war also das Vereinstheater kaum jemals inhaltlich-politisch interessiert (Ausnahme: der Wiederbeginn nach 1945); es setzte sich vielmehr ab gegen Volksbrauch und Alltagskultur von Bauern und Handwerkern, gegen Tagesprobleme, Ideologie und ‹tendenzielle› Zeitfragen; es wollte nicht die eigenen Lebensumstände darstellen, nicht die eigenen Träume und Ängste formulieren und schon gar nicht kritisch untersuchen, sondern die ‹hohe Kunst› genießen, auch dann, wenn vor allem die Erfolgsstücke des wilhelminischen Schwanktheaters gespielt wurden. Es gab also kaum eine Fortführung von Traditionen des →Volksschauspiels (das ist anders im Alpengebiet, auch in Belgien, z. T. auch in Frankreich). Im Gegenteil, vielfach werden Volks- und Bauerntheater in Organisationsform und pseudoprofessionellen Theaterstil des Vereinstheaters hinübergeholt, auch ein großer Teil der Arbeitertheater wird vom Vereinstheater aufgesogen.

Das dörfliche Volksschauspiel setzt sich also im Bauern- und Mundarttheater fort; es wird, trotz anderslautender ideologischer Erklärungen, von der Praxis des Laienspiels nicht aufgenommen (evtl. noch in Spielstoffen oder Texten); auch die Vereins- und späteren Amateurtheater führen es nicht fort; in Deutschland findet es erst heute zögernd Anschluß an ein (verändertes) A.

Das kulturpolitisch akzentuierte Arbeitertheater entspricht im 19. Jh. weitgehend dem Vereinstheater; das politisch akzentuierte Arbeitertheater entwickelt insbesondere nach dem 1. Weltkrieg eine eigene Theaterkultur; viele Gruppen gleichen sich jedoch dem Vereins- und später Amateurtheater an. Laienspiel setzt sich bis 1933 stark ab gegen das Vereins- und ebenso stark gegen das Berufstheater; es nähert sich erst in den 50er Jahren unter dem Stichwort ‹A.› dem professionellen Theater (und dem A. der Theatervereine) an.

Der Begriff *Amateur* (aus dem Frz.) ist schon im 19. Jh. gebräuchlich, setzt sich aber erst nach dem 2. Weltkrieg in Deutschland durch. Vorher ist die Bezeichnung uneinheitlich: Vereins-, Dilettanten- (pejorativ vor allem von den Laienspielern gebraucht), Privat-, Liebhabertheater (eher für das höfisch-bürgerliche Theater bis zum 19. Jh.).

1892 schließen sich die Vereinstheater zum erstenmal zusammen; sie gründen in Berlin den «Verband der Privattheatervereine Deutschlands» anläßlich eines Festaktes im Königlichen Opernhaus (!) zur 100-Jahr-Feier der Privattheater-Gesellschaft Urania. Nach dem 1. Weltkrieg heißt der Zusammenschluß «Verband Deutscher Volksbühnen»; die Wiedergründung 1951 erfolgt unter dem Namen «Bund deutscher Volksbühnen», später umbenannt in «Bund Deutscher Amateurtheater», →BDAT. Zusammengefaßt werden hier die geselligkeits- und evtl. kunstinteressierten, kontinuierlich arbeitenden Erwachsenengruppen; die eher problembezogenen, meist kurzlebigen Schul- und Jugendgruppen trugen die Laienspielbewegung und sind jetzt, wenn überhaupt, in der →Bundesarbeitsgemeinschaft organisiert.

In der Gegenwart haben sich Stil und Spielplan der Gruppierungen angenähert: Die im BDAT zusammengeschlossenen A. sind zwar noch weithin der unterhaltenden Geselligkeit verpflichtet (meistgespielte Autoren: Curt Goetz, E. Kishon), bringen jedoch auch Klassiker und Experimentierstücke, machen Kindertheater (meistgespielt O. Preußler und Grimm), haben vielfach eigene Kinder- und Jugendabteilungen. Die freien Schul- und Jugendgruppen sind immer noch problem- und politiknäher, haben direktere Beziehungen zu den Freien Theatergruppen (→Freies Theater) (und nicht zum Stadttheater), sie setzen sich aber nicht mehr bewußt ab gegen die Vereinstheater, sondern betonen wie sie stärker die Handwerklichkeit der Kunst, haben also die dt. Sonderentwicklung des von einer besonderen Idee her bestimmten Laienspiels abgeschlossen und entsprechen wieder der allg. europ. Situation: A. definiert sich durch eine unideologische Abgrenzung vom Berufstheater, ist aber dem professionellen Theater in seinem Spielplan ähnlich. A. läßt sich also heute primär soziologisch unterteilen: →Studenten-, Schüler-, Lehrlingstheater usw. Ähnliches vollzog sich in der DDR wie in den anderen Volksdemokratien schon gleich nach 1945 mit starker staatlicher Unterstützung und straffer zentraler Leitung in Form von Pionier-, Arbeiter-, Bauern- und Studententheatern, die vom professionellen Theater vielfach unterstützt werden. Strukturell entwickeln alle A. immer stärker das Bedürfnis nach spielpädagogisch qualifizierten, professionell bezahlten Organisatoren und Spielleitern; von einer Realisierung dieser Vorstellungen ist das A. noch weit entfernt.

Bernhard, H. (Hg.): Theaterarbeit für Amateure. Wilhelmsfeld 1979 ff; Drenkow, Renate (Hg.): Handbuch für Laientheater. Berlin (DDR) 1968; Neue Gesellschaft für Bildende Kunst (Hg.): Theaterspielen nach Feierabend (Berliner Kulturplätze 1). Berlin 1984.

Hans-Wolfgang Nickel

Amoibaion

Griech. Wechselgesang; als Bauform der griech. Tragödie bezeichnet A. Dialogpartien zwischen Schauspielern oder zwischen Schauspielern und Chor, in denen beide oder wenigstens einer der Dialogpartner singt.

Popp, H. J.: Das Amoibaion. In: Jens, W. (Hg.): Die Bauformen der griech. Tragödie. Poetica Beiheft 6. München 1971, S. 221–275.

Bernd Seidensticker

Amphitheater

A. bezeichnet die Art von →Theaterbau, bei dem ansteigende Sitzplatzreihen im Halbrund oder Halboval um eine Szenenfläche angeordnet sind (→Antikes Theater). Der lat. Begriff Arenatheater geht in seiner Bedeutung von der urspr. aus Sand bestehenden Spielfläche für Zirkusdarbietungen, Tier- und Gladiatorenkämpfe aus. – Das A. hat sich aus der Ursituation des Theaters entwickelt, bei der der Schauspieler bzw. Sänger inmitten einer Menge direkt auf die Zuschauer hin agiert. Aus diesen kultischen Ursprüngen heraus hat sich das griech. A. als Darstellungsort der antiken Dramen entwickelt. Die kreisrunde →Orchestra wird im Dreiviertelrund von den ansteigenden Zuschauerplätzen umgeben. Die von den Römern übernommene Theaterbauform verändert sich durch eine andere zur Aufführung kommende Theaterliteratur (Unterhaltung) in der Art, daß die Zuschauer im Halbkreis vor einer reliefartigen Bühne sitzen. Das A. ist heute der Gegenpol zum perspektivisch orientierten barocken Guckkastentheater, bei dem Bühnen- und Zuschauerhaus zwei voneinander getrennte Räume bilden.

Das A. umfaßt Darsteller und Zuschauer in einer Raumeinheit. Das Licht hat keine dramatische Funktion, der Schauspieler kann nicht aus dem Dunkeln treten, der Gesamtraum wird gleichmäßig erhellt. In verschiedenen Theaterbaureformentwürfen, die sich gegen den dominierenden Bautyp des höfischen →Rangtheaters wenden, wird das antike A. in der Form zitiert, daß Logen, Ränge und Parkett ersetzt werden durch einen ansteigenden Zuschauerraum in der Grundrißform eines Kreissektors (Festspielhaus Bayreuth, 1871, Prinzregententheater München, 1901, Schiller-Theater Berlin, 1906). Die amphitheatralische Anordnung der Zuschauer ist Vorbild für alle Modelle, die im wahrsten Sinn des Wortes keine ‹Rangordnung› im Volkstheater des 20. Jh. zulassen wollen. – Da A. als eine Form des Einraumtheaters findet sich besonders wieder in den modernen Theaterbau-Utopien (Totaltheater von Walter Gropius, 1927). Realisiert jedoch ist wenig (Studios, Kleine Häuser und Freilichttheater), da offensichtlich die traditionelle axiale Zuordnung von Spieler und Zuschauer die gewohnte und auch einfachere Darstellungskunst ist.

August, E. C.: Zur Idee des Arenatheaterspiels. In: Schriften der Dramaturgischen Gesellschaft. Berlin 1979; Unruh, W.: ABC der Theatertechnik. Halle 1959.

Horst Birr

Amsterdamsche Schouwburg

Im Auftrag der Regenten des Altersheims und des Waisenhauses erbaute der holl. Baumeister Jacob van Campen im Jahre 1637 die «Schouwburg» an der Keizersgracht zu Amsterdam (→Barocktheater, →Theater der Neuzeit). Joost van den Vondel (1587–1679) schrieb das Spiel *Gijsbrecht van Aemstel*, mit dessen Uraufführung die A. S. am 3. Jan. 1638 feierlich eröffnet wurde. In den Aufführungen traten anfangs nur Männer auf, halbprofessionelle Schauspieler, die meistens noch eine Nebenbeschäftigung hatten. Im Jahre 1655 trat zum erstenmal eine Schauspielerin auf die Bühne, Ariana Noozemann (1635?–61); der große Erfolg ihres Auftretens stimulierte den starken Zuwachs von weiblichen Schauspielern auf der Bühne der A. S. Den Spielplan bestimmten die sog. Regenten, sechs von den Stadtbehörden angewiesene Männer. Sowohl die geschäftlichen als auch die künstlerischen Angelegenheiten wie Stückwahl und Besetzung der Rollen wurden von ihnen entschieden.

64 Amsterdamsche Schouwburg

Die architektonische Einheit von Bühne und Auditorium ergab einen fast hautnahen Kontakt zwischen Schauspielern und Zuschauern, die sich stehend im Parterre oder sitzend in den Logen und Galerien aufhielten. Die Bühne selbst war offen, ohne Vorhang. Sie war ungefähr 14 m breit und 6 m tief. Sie wurde vom Sonnenlicht (Aufführungen fanden nachmittags statt) beleuchtet, das von hinten durch ein großes Fenster hereinfiel; im Winter oder bei trübem Wetter spendete ein großer Kronleuchter Licht neben kleineren Leuchtern im Bühnenraum. Die Vorderbühne war links und rechts von auswechselbaren Schirmen umgeben. Die Hinterbühne konnte durch einen großen, von oben herunterfallenden Vorhang abgeschlossen werden. Die permanente Dekoration an der Hinterwand der Bühne bildeten Säulen und Pilaster mit bemalten Schirmen, die zu Kompartimenten zusammengeschlossen werden konnten. Über dem zentralen Kompartiment in der Mitte war ein Balkon, abgeschlossen durch ein zweiteiliges Gemälde mit dem Urteil des Paris. Wurden die beiden Hälften des Gemäldes geöffnet, erblickten die Zuschauer einen Wolkenhimmel, der in Wahrheit aber ein Lift war, auf dem Götter oder der Erzengel erschienen. Im Fond gab es Nischen, worin man unten Statuen von Herkules und Hermes, oben von Thalia und Melpomene postierte. Diese Dekoration war zwar sehr flexibel; aber da es noch kein Kulissensystem gab, muß man die Bühne der A. S. doch als entwickelte Form der → Simultanbühne bezeichnen.

Diese Bühne konnte die Ansprüche der barocken Dramaturgie und des schaulustigen Publikums nicht lange befriedigen. 1664 beschlossen die Regenten daher, die A. S. abzubrechen und an derselben Stelle eine neue Schauburg zu errichten, die mit einem Kulissensystem nach ‹venezianischer Art› ausgerüstet wurde. Die Bühne ist im typischen Barockstil ausgestattet: Gut 18 m tief und fast 10 m breit, hat sie eine große Versenkung, vier kleinere und eine sehr kleine; ein Teil des Bühnenbodens vor der fünften Kulisse läßt sich ganz entfernen. Links und rechts auf der Bühne befinden sich sieben Kulissenpaare. Hundert Jahre bestaunten die Zuschauer dieses Wunderwerk barocker Illusionstheaterkunst, bis es 1772 in Flammen aufging und total abbrannte. Schon zwei Jahre später erbaute man eine neue A. S., diesmal am Leidseplein, wiederum aus Holz. Mehr als hundert Jahre blieb sie erhalten, bis auch sie 1890 ein Opfer der Flammen wurde. Im Jahre 1894 wurde wiederum eine A. S. gebaut, die heute noch am Leidseplein steht, ein solides, aus Stein gebautes Theater.

Im 19. Jh. war die A. S. Mittelpunkt des holl. Theaterlebens. Viele berühmte Schauspieler/innen feierten dort ihre Triumphe, am bekanntesten Andries Snoek (1776–1829) und Johanna Cornelia Ziesenis-Wattier (1762–1827). Ungefähr bis 1840 bleibt die A. S. ein Unterhaltungsort für jedermann mit einem abwechslungsreichen Repertoire: klassizistische

Tragödien à la Racine, vaterländische historische Trauerspiele, moderne bürgerliche Schauspiele (Kotzebue), Lustspiele, Possen und reich ausgestattete Ballette. Es ist die Zeit der absoluten Dominanz der Schauspielkunst über die dramatische Literatur, die ‹Zeit des schönen Spiels›. Die Stadt hatte die Leitung der A. S. selbst in der Hand. Es dauert noch bis in die 80er Jahre des 19. Jh., ehe die Stadt die A. S. endgültig der Privatinitiative überließ.

Hummelen, W. W. H.: Inrichting en gebruik van het toneel in de Amsterdamse Schouwburg van 1637. Amsterdam 1967; Hunningher, B.: Het toneel in de Amsterdamse Schouwburg van 1637. Amsterdam 1957; De Leeuwe, Hans: «Amsterdam, 11. Mai 1772: Die Schauburg brennt!» In: Rolf Badenhausen, R./Zielske, H. (Hg.): Bühnenformen, Bühnenräume, Bühnendekorationen. Berlin 1974, S. 108–126; ders.: Stilepochen des holländischen Theaters im 19. Jahrhundert. In: Maske und Kothurn 3 (1957), Heft 4, S. 340–352; Worp, J. A.: Geschiedenis van den Amsterdamschen Schouwburg 1496–1772. Uitgegeven met aanvullingen tot 1872 door Dr. J. F. M. Sterck. Amsterdam 1920; Wybrands, C. N.: Het Amsterdamsche Tooneel 1617–1772. Utrecht 1873.

Wil Hildebrand

Angry Young Men

Aus dem Titel der Autobiographie Leslie Pauls *The Angry Young Man* (1951) hergeleitete Sammelbezeichnung für eine Anzahl von Bühnenautoren, die seit Mitte der 50er Jahre das engl. Theater stilistisch und inhaltlich maßgeblich beeinflußt haben. ‹Zornig› waren diese Autoren über die nach ihrer Meinung unbefriedigende Nachkriegsentwicklung, insbesondere in England. Ihren Ausdruck fand diese Bewegung in dem Bestreben, der herrschenden Unverbindlichkeit der meisten Bühnenstücke einen Perspektivenwechsel entgegenzusetzen. Die Protagonisten dieser Dramen waren ‹kleine Leute›, die dramatische Handlung wurde im Arbeiter- und Kleinbürgermilieu angesiedelt (daher der ebenfalls verwendete Begriff ‹kitchen-sink-drama›), dessen Leben kritisch und aus der Sicht der Betroffenen dargestellt wurde, jedoch ohne konkrete Alternativen ins Blickfeld zu rücken. Dennoch schienen hinter der meist konventionell-naturalistisch präsentierten Handlung ungelöste gesellschaftliche Widersprüche als das eigentliche Movens der Bühnenfiguren auf. John Osborne (* 1929) hat mit *Look back in Anger* (1956) und dem Protagonisten Jimmy Porter den Klassiker der A. Y. M. verfaßt, deren Hinwendung zu einer kritischen, aktuelle Probleme thematisierenden Dramatik als einer der Auslöser für die wenige Jahre später einsetzende Entwicklung des →fringe bzw. alternative theatre wirkte.

Zwei Theater verhalfen den A. Y. M. zum Durchbruch. Das →Royal

66 Angura

Court Theatre produzierte neben Osborne auch Arnold Weskers (* 1932) *Chicken Soup with Barley* (1958) und John Ardens (* 1930) *Sergeant Musgrave's Dance* (1959). Der →Theatre Workshop brachte Brendan Behans (1923–64) *The Quare Fellow* (1956) und Shelagh Delaneys (* 1939) *A Taste of Honey* (1958) heraus.

Mit A. Y. M. wird ebenfalls eine Gruppe von Prosa-Autoren bezeichnet, deren Werk im Bereich des Romans ähnliche Wirkung zeitigte (Kingsley Amis, * 1922; John Braine, * 1922; Alan Sillitoe, * 1928; John Wain, * 1925).

Anderson, M.: Anger and Detachment. London 1976; Klotz, G.: Alternativen im britischen Drama der Gegenwart. Berlin (DDR) 1978; Taylor, J. R.: Anger & After. A Guide to the New British Drama. London 1962.

Werner Bleike

Angura

Jap. Kürzel für ‹underground theatre›. A. umfaßt eine Reihe kleiner Theatergruppen, die Ende der 60er Jahre zur Zeit der Studentenrevolte entstanden. Jede Gruppe ist eine autonome Produktionsgemeinschaft, die sich durch Arbeit und Jobs ihrer Mitglieder außerhalb des Theaters finanziert. Wenngleich sich die Richtungen der einzelnen Gruppen voneinander unterscheiden, so gibt es dennoch gemeinsame Tendenzen, namentlich dem Theater des Bildungsbürgers (→*shingeki* = Neues Theater) eine Absage zu erteilen, um für ein junges Publikum radikale Gesellschaftskritik im Theater umzusetzen. Sie engagieren sich für Minderheiten wie Koreaner und Homosexuelle, spielen auf der Straße, in Kellern, Garagen, Diskotheken und Zelten. Beeinflußt sind sie vom Surrealismus und Dadaismus ebenso wie von Happening und Agitprop; als Vorlage dienen ihnen weniger literarische Texte als vielmehr →*kabuki* und Folklore, Unterhaltungs- und Trivialkunst wie →Striptease und Stegreif, *manzai* und *rakugo* (trad. Vortragskünste mit komischem Charakter). – In allen Gruppen herrscht – wie in Japan üblich – ein hierarchischer Führungsstil. An ihrer Spitze steht der Gründer der Gruppe, der zugleich die Funktion von Autor und Regisseur in Personalunion innehat. Er kann dank der engen, teilweise familiären Beziehung zu seinen Mitgliedern ihnen das jeweilige Stück auf den Leib schreiben. Die Stücke werden dann en suite gespielt.

Die wichtigsten Gruppen sind: Terayama Shûjis Tenjô Sajiki (Plätze des Paradieses; gemeint sind die Sitze im obersten Rang des kabuki-Theaters). Diese Gruppe erzählt Märchen und Träume, stellt groteske Ausschnitte der Wirklichkeit zur Schau und provoziert sein Publikum

Animation 67

aufs äußerste. Terayama gilt als Meister der Konzeptuierung theatralischer Räume. Seine Poesie stimuliert die Imaginationskraft seiner Schauspieler ebenso wie die der Zuschauer. – Kara Jurôs Jôkyô Gekijô (Theater der Situation). Anfangs spielte diese Gruppe auf der Straße. Weil das aber immer schwieriger wurde, kauften sie sich ein rotes Zelt, was zum Spitznamen *akatento* (Rotes Zelt) führte. In Karas Stücken überlagern sich mehrere Ereignisse, sind ineinander verschachtelt, und entsprechend komplex sind seine Texte. Beachtlich ist der vitale Spielstil, die Schauspieler sind pausenlos außer Rand und Band. – Suzuki Tadashis Waseda Shôgekijô (Waseda-Zimmertheater). Zunächst spielt diese Gruppe Stücke von Betsuyaku Minoru, später collagiert Suzuki Teile verschiedener kabuki-Stücke zu neuen Stücken. Er ist beständig auf der Suche nach dem Wesen des Dramatischen (*gekiteki naru mono o megutte*) und gelangt schließlich zum griechischen Drama (*Die Troerinnen* und *Die Bakchen*). Bekannt wurde die Gruppe durch die enorme Ausdruckskraft der Schauspielerin Shiraishi Kayoko und durch ihr hartes Training, das nach dem Leiter der Gruppe Suzuki-Methode genannt wird: Satô Makotos Center 68/70 (auch *kurotento* = schwarzes Zelt genannt). Im Gegensatz zu den anderen Gruppen arbeitet diese als Kollektiv. Ihr besonderes Interesse gilt Brecht, dessen Stücke häufig auf japanische Verhältnisse übertragen und umgeschrieben werden. Durch Gastspiele in Indonesien und auf den Philippinen wurden Elemente der dortigen Theaterkultur miteinbezogen. – Ôta Shôgôs Tenkei Gekijô (Theater der Veränderung). Diese Gruppe wurde mit dem Stück *Komachi Fuden* bekannt, einer gelungenen Verschmelzung des →Nô mit modernem Theater. Seitdem experimentiert die Gruppe mit Theater ohne Wortsprache, unterscheidet sich jedoch weitgehend vom →*butô*.

Leonore Welzien

Animation

Vor allem in Frankreich, Italien (animazione) und Österreich gebräuchlicher Begriff: Äquivalente in Deutschland sind Kindertheater (bei starker Betonung der Eigentätigkeit des Kindes bzw. der Zielgruppe), Spiel- und Theaterpädagogik (bei starker Betonung politischer und lokaler Inhalte), Zielgruppentheater (bei starker Betonung von Selbsttätigkeit und emanzipatorischen Zielen). Wesentlich weniger entspricht diesem Konzept der (unpolitische) A.-Begriff der dt. Freizeitpädagogik (Opaschowski); näher steht der Begriff A.-Theater, mit dem neuerdings intensive Formen von →Mitspieltheater bezeichnet werden (engl. →Theatre in Education = T. i. E.).

68   Ankara Devlet Tiyatrosu

Bartolucci, G. (ed.): Il Teatro Dei Ragazzi. Firenze 1972; Hanl, I./Schmidt-Greisenegger, I.: Animazione. Bericht über ein Experiment. Dramatisches Zentrum Wien 1975; Hanl, I. (Hg.): Kreatives Schulspiel. Wien/München 1977; Kulturpolitische Gesellschaft (Hg.): Kindertheater und Animation. Jahrestagung 1977, Dokumentation 2; Opaschowski, H. W.: Einführung in die freizeitkulturelle Breitenarbeit. Methoden und Modelle der Animation. Bad Heilbronn 1979; Passatore, F.: Animazione dopo. Firenze 1977; Scabia, G.; Das große Theater des Marco Cavallo. Frankfurt/M. – *Zeitschrift:* Animation (Fachzeitschrift Freizeit: Berufspraxis und Wissenschaft), seit 1979.

Hans-Wolfgang Nickel

Ankara Devlet Tiyatrosu

(Staatstheater Ankara) Es wurde 1949 gegr., nachdem die Gründung des Staatlichen Konservatoriums bereits im Jahre 1936 vorangegangen war; an dessen Aufbauarbeit hatten Paul Hindemith, Carl Ebert und Béla Bartók wesentlichen Anteil. Das A. D. T. führt Werke türk. und ausländischer Autoren auf: Theaterstücke, Opern, Musicals, Ballette. Ihm angeschlossen sind sechs Bühnen in Ankara und je eine in Izmir, Bursa und Adana. Die Zahl der Zuschauerplätze liegt zwischen 65 und 740. – Neben den staatlichen gibt es in der Türkei eine große Anzahl an privaten Bühnen.

Maren Fittschen

Ankündigung

Öffentliche Bekanntgabe von Theateraufführungen. – Im griech. Theater vollzog sich die A. des dramatischen Wettbewerbs (→ Agon) durch feierliche Einholung des Dionysos-Standbildes am Vortag sowie durch Aufmarsch der Dichter, Schauspieler, Chorführer und des Chores. Das röm. Theater kündigte Aufführungen durch Herolde und Anzeigen (auf dafür vorgesehenen Mauerwänden) in Volksbädern und auf Foren an. Zur Zeit Shakespeares wurden Vorstellungen durch Hissen einer Fahne auf dem Dach des Theaters bekanntgegeben. Im dt. Mittelalter verbreitete ein Ausrufer mit Klapper oder Trommel die Nachricht. 1626 lag die erste gedruckte A. einer Aufführung in Nürnberg vor. Heute erfolgen A. in Form von Zeitungsinseraten, Plakataushängen und hauseigenen Theaterzeitungen (→ Theaterzettel).

Monika Sandhack

Anstandsrolle

Eine Gattung von Rollen und Typen aus gehobenem Milieu, die sich vor allem durch äußere Repräsentation kennzeichnen wie der → Bonvivant, der → Liebhaber, der Intrigant oder die Gouvernante. Auch Könige, Fürsten, Minister und dergl. sind laut «Allgemeinem Theaterlexikon» (Leipzig, 1839 ff) A., soweit sie nur das Rettende, Belohnende oder Strafende verkörpern. Die A. erfordern elegantes Äußeres, sicheres Auftreten und vornehmes Benehmen und Sprechen.

Bernard Poloni

Antikenrezeption

Formen der Rezeption antiker Dramen und Stoffe. Grundlage einer Rezeption antiker Dramen auf der Bühne ist – soweit es sich nicht um originalsprachige Aufführungen für einen kleinen Kennerkreis handelt (z. B. → Humanismus) – das Vorhandensein brauchbarer Übersetzungen. Daran anschließen können sich 1. Bühnenbearbeitungen (z. B. A. Wilbrandt: *König Ödipus*), auch als Kompilation (z. B. die Zusammenfassung der beiden *Ödipus*-Dramen des Sophokles bei L. Jessner, Staatstheater Berlin 1929, Bearbeitung H. Lipmann); 2. zeitgemäße Adaptationen der Vorlage (z. B. F. Werfel: *Troerinnen*; J. Anouilh: *Antigone*); 3. Neudeutungen mit verändertem Fabelverlauf (z. B. P. Hacks: *Amphitryon*; J.-P. Sartre: *Die Fliegen*) sowie 4. eigene Gestaltungen auf der Grundlage des antiken Mythos (z. B. Hofmannsthal: *Ödipus und die Sphinx*; F. Dürrenmatt: *Herakles und der Stall des Augias*). Eine Sonderform ist 5. die Mythentravestie (z. B. J. Offenbach: *La belle Hélène*; P. Hacks: *Die schöne Helene*).

Davon zu trennen sind, insofern sie nicht unmittelbar in der Wirkungsgeschichte der antiken Dramen stehen, Stücke um historische Gestalten der Antike (z. B. Shakespeare: *Julius Caesar*), mit antikisierender Szenerie (z. B. Giraudoux: *Der trojanische Krieg findet nicht statt*), oder anderweitigen Antike-Anspielungen bis hin zum bloßen Zitat (Schönthan: *Raub der Sabinerinnen*).

Epochen der A.: Das Auffinden verschollener Dramentexte (12 Komödien des Plautus 1427), das Bekanntwerden des *Donat*-Kommentars zu Terenz und Vitruvs *De architectura* (V 3–9 über das Theater) sowie gelehrte Beschäftigung mit Senecas Tragödien löste im 15. Jh. ein neues Interesse am röm.-antiken Drama aus (das griech. wurde vernachlässigt). Es kam zur ‹Wiedergeburt› des antiken Theaters auf der ital. Renaissancebühne. Das Wirken des Pomponius Laetus (1427–97) an der Aka-

70 Antikenrezeption

demie in Rom führte 1473 bis 1475 zu ersten szenischen Darstellungen lat. Dramen (Terenz, Plautus, Seneca) in der Originalsprache (1486 folgte eine prächtige Aufführung von Senecas *Hippolytus* auf dem Forum; 1513 führte der Pomponius-Schüler Tommaso Inghirami auf dem Kapitol den *Poenulus* des Plautus auf). Einfluß auf die →Renaissance-Komödie hatten die Aufführungen von Plautus und Terenz in ital. Übersetzung, die am Hof von Hercole I. von Ferrara prunkvoll inszeniert wurden (Plautus: *Menaechmi*, 1486, vor 1000 Zuschauern aus allen Teilen Italiens). – Die ital. Entwicklung ist – auch in der Zweiteilung von gelehrter lat. und nationalsprachiger Rezeption – typisch für die szenische Wiederbelebung des röm.-antiken Dramas in Europa.

Lat. Einfluß bestimmt wesentlich das nationalsprachige Drama des Barock (→Barocktheater, →Jesuitentheater). Für die Entwicklung der Tragödie war Seneca wichtig (Opitz übersetzte 1625 Senecas *Troerinnen*). Die an den sog. Regeln des Aristoteles orientierte «haute tragédie» im Frankreich des 17. Jh. (→Tragödie) berücksichtigt neben der lat. Tradition auch die griech. Tragödie (Corneille: *Œdipe*, 1659, Seneca und Sophokles; Racine: *Andromaque*, 1667, Vergil: *Aen.* III. 291–332, und Euripides: *Troades; Iphigénie en Aulide*, 1674, Euripides; *Phèdre et Hippolyte*, 1677, Euripides: *Hippolytos* und Seneca: *Phaedra*). Molière führt 1668 seinen *Amphitryon* auf (nach Plautus: *Amphitruo*).

Während in Frankreich das Revolutionsdrama zum Teil lat. bestimmt ist (M.-J. Chénier, 1764–1811: *Caius Gracchus*, 1793), beginnt man im Deutschland des 18. Jh. neue Ideen von Freiheit an Hand der griech. Tradition zu formulieren. Damit wird eine neue Phase der A. eingeleitet. Der kritischen Auseinandersetzung mit der frz. Dramentheorie (Lessing) folgt eine betonte Hinwendung zu Shakespeare und den Griechen. Herder bahnt in seinem Aufsatz *Shakespeare* (1793) die Sonderstellung des Sophokles als Klassiker der antiken Tragödie an (Sophoklesübersetzung von Christian Graf zu Stolberg 1787). Diese Wertschätzung erfährt Sophokles über den Klassizismus des 19. Jh. (*Antigone* als Musterbeispiel der Tragödie, Hegel) hinaus bis ins 20. Jh. Während in der Zeit der dt. Klassik antike Dramen kaum im Spielplan standen (auch Goethe ließ in Weimar unter 601 aufgeführten Stücken nur *Antigone* und *König Ödipus* von Sophokles spielen), bewirkt die Aufführung der *Antigone* des Sophokles vor geladenem Publikum im Neuen Palais in Potsdam durch L. Tieck am 28. 10. 1841 (Übers. v. Donner, Musik v. Mendelssohn-Bartholdy), daß das Stück fortan häufiger im Repertoire erscheint (von Tiecks Aufführung angeregt wird 1844 die *Antigone* in frz. Sprache in Paris im Théâtre l'Odéon gespielt).

1852 kommt erstmals der *König Ödipus* in dt. Übersetzung in München auf die Bühne. A. Wilbrandt (Direktor des Burgtheaters 1881–87) erobert dem Stück durch Aufführungen in Wien und Berlin einen festen

Platz in deutschen Spielplänen und führt erstmals die *Elektra* auf. Auf lebendige Wirksamkeit bedacht, ersetzt er die Chöre durch selbstverfaßte Dialogpartien und Statistenrollen und problematisiert damit erstmals die Funktion des Chors auf der modernen Sprechbühne. Akademische Vereine des Berliner und Wiener Bildungsbürgertums der Jahrhundertwende setzen sich für eine verstärkte Rezeption der griech. Tragödien auf dem Theater ein. Mit erstklassigen Schauspielern werden auf kleineren Bühnen jetzt auch Aischylos (*Orestie*) und Euripides (*Herakles, Hippolytos, Medea*) in bewußter Absetzung vom vorherrschenden naturalistischen Stil aufgeführt (Übersetzung des klassischen Philologen U. v. Wilamowitz-Moellendorff).

Von besonderer Bedeutung waren Max Reinhardts Inszenierungen: 1903 *Elektra* (Hofmannsthal, frei nach Sophokles), 1906 *Antigone* (beide im Kleinen Theater, Berlin), vor allem aber die wirkungsgeschichtlich wichtigen Arena-Inszenierungen des *König Ödipus* (Sophokles/Hofmannsthal) 1910 (Münchener Musikfesthalle und Zirkus Schumann, Berlin) sowie die *Orestie*-Aufführungen 1911/12 (München und Berlin) und 1919 (Berlin). Die Monumentalität des Raums und der Bühnenbauten (bes. in der *Orestie*), die Masse der Statisten (in der *Orestie* 1000), die die Gemeinsamkeit zwischen Bühnengeschehen und Publikum herstellen sollte, Ton- und Lichteffekte ließen die Verbindung von archaischer Dramatik und neuzeitlicher Massenpsychologie als Wiedererweckung der griech. Tragödie erscheinen, das ‹klassenlose› Theater (keine Logen und Ränge) als utopisches Fest. Dabei nimmt Reinhardt inszenatorische Mittel der Arbeiterfestspiele wie auch der Massenveranstaltungen des Nationalsozialismus vorweg.

Anläßlich der Olympischen Spiele 1936 führt das Staatliche Schauspielhaus Berlin die *Orestie* des Aischylos auf (Inszenierung Lothar Müthel), in der die ‹Wiederherstellung› der Rechtsnormen durch den Nationalsozialismus gefeiert wird. Müthels Inszenierung der *Antigone* von Sophokles/Hölderlin am Wiener Burgtheater 1940 zeichnet sich neben nationalsozialistischer Hölderlin-Adaptation besonders durch die Verwendung ästhetischer Formen des →Thingspiels und nationalsozialistischer Massenveranstaltungen aus. Die fast gleichzeitige *Antigone*-Aufführung am Berliner Staatstheater (von Stroux inszeniert) zeigt demgegenüber widerständige Elemente.

In den Jahren nach 1945 wird der *König Ödipus*, die klassische Darstellung einer Vergangenheitsaufarbeitung, besonders häufig gespielt (zuerst im Dezember 1946 im Deutschen Theater, Berlin, mit G. Gründgens in der Titelrolle unter der Regie von Stroux). Die griech. Tragödie wird als ein Mittel zur Auseinandersetzung mit der jüngsten dt. Geschichte verstanden (so auch die *Antigone*, Hamburger Schauspielhaus 1946 und die *Troerinnen* des Euripides, Hamburger Kammerspiele 1947). Doch

72 Antikenrezeption

werden aufklärerische Bemühungen bald durch die politische Entwicklung überholt. In der Zeit der Entnazifizierung und des beginnenden ‹Kalten Krieges› wird *Ödipus* als der unschuldig Schuldige, als der vom Schicksal Geschlagene zur Identifikationsfigur Uneinsichtiger. 1948 kommt es zur Aufführung von Brechts *Antigone*-Bearbeitung (nach Hölderlin) in Chur/Schweiz. In Orffs Oper *Antigone* kündigen sich bereits 1949 die Re-Mythisierungstendenzen an, die dann die 50er Jahre beherrschen. Mit der Kreon-Gestalt, verstanden als die eines Tyrannen, wird allenfalls noch auf Stalin Bezug genommen (Berliner Festspielwochen 1953, Schillertheater Berlin).

Häufig gespielt wurden in der Nachkriegszeit Dramen frz. Autoren, in denen antike Stoffe behandelt oder zitiert wurden (Giraudoux: *Der trojanische Krieg findet nicht statt*, 1935, dt. Erstaufführung 1946; Anouilh: *Antigone*, entstanden 1942, aufgeführt Paris 1944, dt. Erstaufführung Darmstadt 1946; Sartre: *Die Fliegen*, Paris 1943, dt. Erstaufführung Düsseldorf 1947).

In der Restauration der 50er Jahre wird bei konservativ-historisierender Spielweise auf einer abstrakt stilisierten Bühne die zeitenthobene Unwandelbarkeit menschlichen Wesens betont (Seller: *Ödipus*, 1952, Übersetzung v. Schadewald; *Antigone*, 1957, Hölderlin, Darmstadt). Neue Impulse erhält die Rezeption antiker Dramen erst wieder durch die Autoren Heiner Müller und Peter Hacks, die in den 60er Jahren antike Stoffe aufgreifen. Hervorzuheben ist die Aufführung von *Ödipus Tyrannus* (Regie Benno Besson), einer Sophokles-Bearbeitung von Heiner Müller (nach Sophokles/Hölderlin), die historische gesellschaftliche Vorgänge (die Entwicklung zum Dualismus von Theorie und Praxis, von Individualbewußtsein und Gemeinschaft) in der alten Fabel aufzuspüren sucht. Die Bezüge zwischen Historischem und Aktuellem werden dabei als dialektische Zusammenhänge im historischen Prozeß verstanden, das Vergangene bleibt wichtig für die Formulierung des Zukünftigen.

Weiter geht die → Schaubühne am Halleschen Ufer im zweiten Teil ihres «Antiken Projekts», den *Bacchen* des Euripides (1974, Regie Klaus Michael Grüber). Nicht mehr die Interpretation des überlieferten Tragödientextes durch darstellerische Mittel ist das zentrale Anliegen, sondern es wird versucht, ‹die dramatischen Prozesse unterhalb ihrer Verbalisierung› aufzuspüren. In traumartiger Widersprüchlichkeit einander zugeordnete Zeichen, Bilder, Handlungselemente sollen das Mythisch-Unbewußte freilegen, das sich dem bewußtseinsgesteuerten Diskurs entzieht.

Beachtung fanden die Inszenierungen antiker Dramen des Italieners Luca Ronconi. Im März 1976 inszenierte er (wie schon 1972 in Venedig) die *Orestie* des Aischylos am Wiener Burgtheater. Auf der mit Stoffbahnen ausgestalteten Bühne entwarf Ronconi ein Bild der Menschheitsgeschichte, das aus archaischen Schrecknissen (*Agamemnon*) und einer viktorianisch kostümierten Gegenwart (*Choephoren*) im dritten Teil der Trilogie (*Eumeniden*) in eine zukünftige Zeit verwies, in der eine neue Vermittlung von Anarchie und Ordnung in einem neuen Recht vollzogen wird (eine Deutung, die gleichermaßen unterschieden ist von Sellners affirmativem *Orestie*-Verständnis, Hamburg 1951, wie P. Steins vorsichtiger Skepsis, Schaubühne, Berlin 1980).

In Griechenland werden seit Mitte der 30er Jahre antike Dramen aufgeführt, meist in Athen und Epidauros.

In den USA erscheinen die antiken Dramen wegen des Fehlens eines Repertoiretheaters weniger häufig auf der Bühne (meist handelt es sich um College-Aufführungen). Auseinandersetzungen mit den antiken Mythen und ihrer Gestaltung im attischen Drama erfolgten durch freie Gruppen vom Ansatz des Erfahrungstheaters her (z. B. R. Schechners *Dionysus in 69* nach Euripides' *Bacchen*; →Performance Group, New York 1968). In den letzten Jahren gab es auch Adaptationen an das jap. →Nô-Theater (Yuriko Doi, Theatre of Yugen, Wadsworth Theatre, Los Angeles 1984 – Sophokles: *Antigone*) sowie den Versuch, das zweite Ödipus-Drama des Sophokles, *Ödipus auf Kolonos*, als kathartisches Theater im Sinne der Blues- und Gospel-Tradition (Lee Bremer: *The Gospel of Colonus*, The Next Wave Festival 1984) zu interpretieren.

Anders als die Mythendramen der griech. Klassik hat die alte attische Komödie des Aristophanes keine kontinuierliche Wirkungsgeschichte. 1917 erschien von Lion Feuchtwanger *Friede* (nach *Acharnern und Eirene* des Aristophanes), 1962 inszenierte B. Besson *Der Frieden* von Peter Hacks. 1965 folgte die Aristophanes-Bearbeitung *Die Weibervolksversammlung* von Joachim Knauth. 1975 wurde in Wien *Utopia*, eine Bearbeitung der *Vögel* des Aristophanes unter der Regie von Ronconi aufgeführt.

Flashar, H.: Aufführung von griechischen Dramen in der Übersetzung von Wilamowitz. In: Wilamowitz nach 50 Jahren. Hg. von W. Calder u. a. Darmstadt 1985, S. 306–356; Lohse, G./Ohde, H.: Mitteilungen aus dem Land der Lotophagen. Zum Verhältnis von Antike und deutscher Nachkriegsliteratur. Teil II: G. Lohse: Der ‹König Ödipus› des Sophokles und die deutsche Vergangenheitsbewältigung nach 1945, Hephaistos 5/6 (1983/84), S. 163–226; Schadewald, W.: Antike Tragödie auf der modernen Bühne. Zur Geschichte der Rezeption der griechischen Tragödie auf der heutigen Bühne. Jahresheft der Heidelberger Akademie der Wissenschaften 1955–1956, S. 37–64 (= Hellas und Hesperien II: Antike und Gegenwart. Zürich ²1970, S. 622–650); Schirmer, L.: Theater und Antike. Probleme der Antikenrezeption auf Berliner Bühnen vom Ende des 18. Jahrhunderts bis zur Gegenwart. In: Berlin und die Antike. Ergänzungsband zum Katalog der Ausstellung «Berlin und die Antike». Berlin 1979, S. 303–349; Trilse, Ch.: Antike und Theater heute. Berlin 1979.

Gerhard Lohse

Antikes Theater

Das abendländische Theater ist in Griechenland entstanden und hat in Athen im 5. Jh. seine erste große Blütezeit erreicht, deren vielfältige Leistungen von ihrer ersten kreativen Rezeption in Rom über die Wiederentdeckung des antiken Dramas in der frühen Renaissance bis auf den heutigen Tag ihre nahezu kontinuierliche Wirkungskraft nachdrücklich bewiesen haben. Das klassische griech. Theater, das für uns vor allem durch die drei großen Tragiker Aischylos, Sophokles und Euripides sowie durch die Komödien des Aristophanes repräsentiert wird, ist durch eine Reihe von Wesensmerkmalen gekennzeichnet: Das a. T. ist seinen kultischen Ursprüngen getreu erstens *Festspieltheater*. Auch wenn sich die ursprünglichen formalen, inhaltlichen und organisatorischen Bindungen an den Dionysoskult und seine Feste bereits in Griechenland allmählich immer mehr lockern und in Rom dann ganz verlorengehen, so bleiben Spieltermine und Aufführungsorte trotz der schnell fortschreitenden Säkularisierung und Professionalisierung weitgehend an die großen Götter- und Staatsfeste gebunden. Daraus ergibt sich zweitens die Tatsache, daß das antike Theater ein →*Massentheater* war. Die Festtage waren heilig; der Besuch der Aufführungen war politisches Recht und religiös-moralische Pflicht des Bürgers. An den Großen →Dionysien strömten 14000 bis 17000 Zuschauer in das Theater am Fuß der Akropolis; ähnliche Zahlen lassen sich für viele griech. Theater und für die großen röm. Steintheater am Ausgang der röm. Republik errechnen. Daneben gab es allerdings auch kleinere Theater (und die Sonderform des ‹Theatrum tectum› →Odeion); die volkstümlichen Kleinformen des antiken Dramas (→Phlyakenposse und →Atellana, →Mimus und →Pantomimus) wurden sicher in der Regel vor weit weniger Zuschauern gespielt. Drittens war das a. T. ein *Freilichttheater* mit allen Möglichkeiten und Problemen, die diese Form des Theaters bietet. – Diese drei genannten Charakteristika erklären, wenn auch gewiß nicht allein, das vierte und letzte Wesensmerkmal des a. T., das zu Recht als *Theater der Konvention* aufgefaßt wird; das reicht von den festen Bauformen der griech. Tragödie und Komödie über konventionelle Handlungs- und Spielelemente bis zu geregelter Schauspielerzahl und obligatorischem Chor, zu Maske und ‹Einheitsbühne›.

Innerhalb des durch diese vier Konstanten gebildeten Rahmens ist die mehr als tausendjährige antike Theatergeschichte andererseits bestimmt durch den kontinuierlichen Wandel zahlloser Details in allen Bereichen. Die oft schwer zu deutenden archäologischen Funde und die wenigen erhaltenen literarischen Zeugnisse, zu denen als dritte ebenfalls selten eindeutige Gruppe von Quellen die erhaltenen dramatischen Texte kommen, erlauben oft nicht mehr als Hypothesen.

«Hephaistos». Maskentänzer. Korinthische Amphore, 600—575 v. Chr. (TS)

Tänzer und Flötenspieler. Campanarelief (TS)

Chor in Vogelmasken. Rotfigurige Vase (TS)

Reiterchor.
Rotfigurige attische Vase,
frühes 4. Jh. v. Chr. (TS)

Komödientänzer mit
Flötenspieler. Schwarzfigurige
attische Amphore, 550–540
v. Chr. (TS)

Theater von Pergamon (TS)

Theater von Epidauros. Gesamtansicht von Osten (TS)

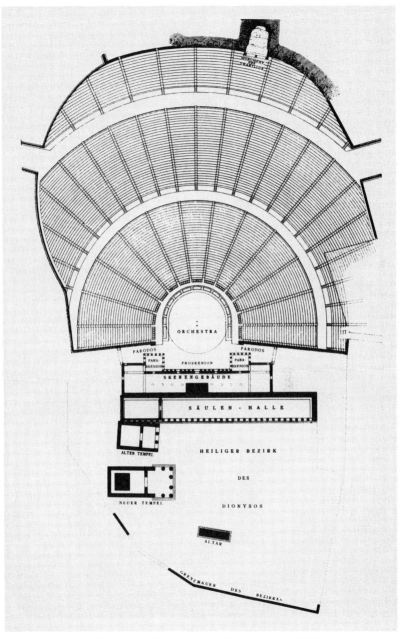

Dionysos-Theater in Athen. Grundrißrekonstruktion (Dorpfeld/Reisch) (TS)

«Kreon», Szene aus einem Phlyakenspiel. Apulisches Schallgefäß, 380–370 v. Chr. (TS)

Sophokles: «Antigone». Vasenmalerei, 380–370 v. Chr. (TS)

«Die Geburt der Helena». Szene aus einem Phlyakenspiel. Apulisches Schallgefäß. 2. Viertel 4. Jh. v. Chr. (TS)

«Chairon». Szene aus einem Phlyakenspiel. Apulisches Schallgefäß, 380–370 v. Chr. (TS)

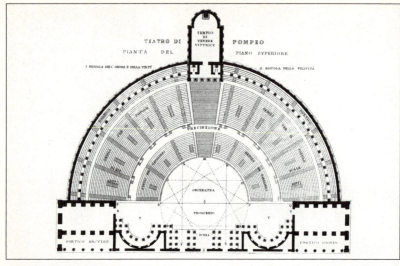

Pompeius-Theater in Rom. Rekonstruktion des Grundrisses (TS)

Rekonstruktion der Außenansicht des Pompeius-Theaters (TS)

Rekonstruktion der Innenansicht des Pompeius-Theaters (TS)

Rekonstruktion der Ansicht von Bühne und Orchestra eines römischen Theaters (TS)

Dosennus, der Philosoph.
Maske aus einer Atellane (TS)

Das griechische Theater

1. Organisation: Die Frühgeschichte des griech. Theaters liegt im dunkeln (zusammenfassende Darstellung der vielfältigen Ursprungsprobleme bei Lesky 1972, 17–48). Als gesichert gelten kann die Geburt des abendländischen Dramas aus primitiven Maskentänzen (→Maskentheater), die sich im Kontext des Dionysoskults über einfache chorische Vorstufen zu den drei dramatischen Genera Tragödie, Komödie, Satyrspiel entwickelt haben. Zumindest seit Mitte des 6. Jh. v. Chr. sind die engen Beziehungen von staatlich organisiertem Dionysoskult und Theater deutlich. Theateraufführungen gab es in Athen nur an zwei bedeutenden Dionysosfesten, d. h. zweimal im Jahr, an den zu Beginn des Jahres (Jan./Febr.) stattfindenden ‹Lenäen› und an den sog. ‹Städtischen› oder ‹Großen Dionysien›. Dieses Fest des Dionysos Eleuthereus (benannt nach der Herkunft des Kults aus Eleutherai, einem Dorf an der attisch-böotischen Grenze), das am Frühjahrsbeginn (März/April) gefeiert wurde, war neben den nur alle vier Jahre gefeierten ‹Panathenäen› das bedeutendste Staatsfest der Polis, in dem sich, wie bereits Organisationsform und Programm zeigten, religiöse, kulturelle und politische Aspekte unauflöslich miteinander verbinden. Die Verantwortung für die Durchführung des Festes lag in den Händen des obersten Beamten der Stadt, des ‹Archon Eponymos›. Das in klassischer Zeit fünf Tage dauernde Fest begann nach einer großen Opferprozession von Akteuren und Zuschauern zum Tempelbezirk des Gottes und nach einer Reihe von Staatsakten (z. B. Ehrung verdienter Bürger und Fremder; Präsentation der Tribute der Bundesgenossen) mit dem Dithyramben-Wettbewerb, in dem wahrscheinlich je zehn Männer- und Knabenchöre um den Sieg stritten (→Dithyrambos).

Den Höhepunkt des Fests bildeten die Tragödienaufführungen, zu denen seit 486 auch Komödien traten. Gespielt wurden an drei aufeinander folgenden Tagen drei →Tetralogien verschiedener Dichter und – in der Regel wohl an einem Tag hintereinander – fünf Komödien verschiedener Autoren. Wenn wir auch über das Tempo der Inszenierungen und die Pausen zwischen den vier bzw. fünf Stücken nichts wissen, kann die tägliche Aufführungsdauer doch kaum unter sieben bis acht Stunden gelegen haben. Es scheint, daß es in Ausnahmefällen (z. B. während des Peloponnesischen Kriegs) zu Kürzungen und Umstellungen des traditionellen Programms gekommen ist; wirkliche Veränderungen sind erst für das 4. Jh. bezeugt. An den insgesamt weniger bedeutungsvollen ‹Lenäen› trat die Tragödie deutlich hinter der Komödie zurück; hier umfaßte der Spielplan ebenfalls fünf Komödien, aber nur zwei Tragödien (und keine Satyrspiele).

Tragödien- wie Komödienaufführungen waren immer in der Form von Dichterwettbewerben (→Agon) organisiert (Tragödie seit dem Ende des 6 Jh.; Komödie seit 486; an den Lenäen seit ca. 440), zu denen seit 449 auch Schauspielerwettbewerbe hinzutraten, die in der Folgezeit immer bedeutungsvoller wurden. Die Auswahl der zu den Wettbewerben zugelassenen Dichter lag in den Händen des zuständigen Beamten, der jedem Dichter einen Choregen zur Verfügung stellte, der die Zusammenstellung und Ausstattung des →Chors sowie Verpflegung und Bezahlung der Choreuten während der nicht unbeträchtlichen Probenzeit übernahm. Der Chorege, der auch die gesamte Komparserie bezahlte, während die Schauspieler und die Bühnenausstattung aus der Staatskasse finanziert wurden, trug damit den wesentlichen Teil der Inszenierungskosten. Diese ebenso kostspielige wie ehrenvolle ‹Choregie› war Bürgerpflicht, zu der der Archon, wenn sich nicht genügend Freiwillige zur Verfügung stellten, reiche Bürger verpflichten konnte. Der finanzielle Aufwand, den ein Chorege – nicht zuletzt zum eigenen Ruhm – zu treiben bereit war, hatte maßgeblichen Anteil am Erfolg des Dichters. In den Urkunden der dramatischen Aufführungen wurde der Chorege an erster Stelle, noch vor dem Dichter, genannt. Das System, dem Dichter einen ‹Produzenten› an die Seite zu stellen, hat sich trotz gelegentlicher Schwierigkeiten lange Zeit bewährt. Es wurde erst am Ende des 4. Jh., in der Regierungszeit des Tyrannen Demetrios von Phaleron (317–306), aufgegeben. Nun übernahm ein jährlich gewählter ‹Agonothetes› (Wettkampfleiter) die Organisation der Dionysien. Die erforderlichen Mittel wurden aus der Staatskasse zur Verfügung gestellt.

Die Inszenierung lag in der Regel in den Händen des Autors, der, jedenfalls in der Frühzeit des attischen Theaters, nicht nur Regie führte, die Musik komponierte und die Chortänze arrangierte und einstudierte, sondern auch selber als Schauspieler auftrat. Die dadurch garantierte Einheit aller Aspekte der Inszenierung löste sich jedoch infolge der wachsenden Spezialisierung und Professionalisierung allmählich auf; die Dichter begannen, Choreographen und Komponisten zu beschäftigen: Sophokles soll als erster die Schauspielerei aufgegeben haben, und Aristophanes schließlich überließ sogar die Regie in einer Reihe von Fällen anderen. Es scheint, daß die Autoren sich – wie ihre modernen Kollegen – vom Ende des 5. Jh. an in zunehmendem Maß auf ihre Funktion als Stückeschreiber beschränkten und die szenische Umsetzung ihrer Texte den Theaterpraktikern (vor allem den →Protagonisten) überließen.

Kurze Zeit (wahrscheinlich zwei Tage) vor den Dionysien wurden die Theateraufführungen in einem sog. ‹Proagon› der interessierten Öffentlichkeit angekündigt. Dichter und Choregen, Chor und Schauspieler präsentierten sich, bekränzt, aber ohne Masken und Kostüme, dem Publikum. Ob und in welchem Umfang dabei auch die Stücke vorgestellt wurden, ist ebenso unklar wie der Zeitpunkt der Einführung des Proagons (vielleicht erst seit Mitte des 5. Jh.) und sein Ort (seit der Errichtung des →Odeions im Jahre 444 vermutlich dort).

Über die Reihenfolge der Tetralogien bzw. der Komödien im Wettbewerb entschied das Los; der Sieger wurde von einer Laienjury bestimmt, deren Wahl und Urteil, um Unparteilichkeit zu sichern, in einem komplizierten System geregelt war. Über die Kriterien, nach denen diese Bürgerjury, stellvertretend für die Zuschauer, urteilte, ist uns nichts bekannt. Gewiß haben die Popularität der Dichter und Zuschauerreaktionen, daneben wohl auch die gesellschaftliche und politische Bedeutung der verantwortlichen Choregen sowie der äußere Aufwand der Inszenierung eine Rolle gespielt.

In der Blütezeit des attischen Theaters wurde jedes Stück nur einmal gespielt. Wiederaufführungen sind für die ‹Großen Dionysien› nur in Form von Neubearbeitungen durchgefallener Stücke oder als Ausnahme bezeugt. So wurde nach dem Tod des Aischylos (456) durch einen Volksbeschluß die Wiederaufführung seiner Stücke (doch wohl außer Konkurrenz) erlaubt. Daß erfolgreiche Stücke außerhalb Athens (z. B. bei den überall in den Gemeinden gefeierten ‹Ländlichen Dionysien›) wiederaufgeführt worden sind, ist wahrscheinlich. Erst im 4. Jh. wurde als Zusatz zum normalen Programm der Dionysien eine alte Tragödie (zum erstenmal 386, regelmäßig vielleicht erst ab 341) und später auch eine alte Komödie (zum erstenmal 339, regelmäßig vielleicht erst ab 311) zugelassen. Im 3. Jh. (urkundlich bezeugt für 254) gab es an den Dionysien sogar Schauspielerwettbewerbe mit alten Dramen.

2. Das Theater: Wichtigste Spielstätte des klassischen griech. Dramas ist das →Dionysostheater am Südostabhang der Akropolis. Für dieses Theater sind so gut wie alle uns erhaltenen Dramen geschrieben worden; spätestens seit Ende des 6. Jh. wurden hier die ‹Großen Dionysien› gefeiert, seit Mitte des 5. Jh. (vermutlich im Zusammenhang mit dem Umbau des Theaters) auch die Lenäen, die ursprünglich ihren Platz im ‹Lenaion› hatten, dem heiligen Bezirk des ‹Dionysos Lenaios› (vermutlich) auf der Agora.

Die heute sichtbaren Überreste des Dionysostheaters, das auf Grund seiner zentralen Bedeutung über Jahrhunderte Modellcharakter besessen hat, stammen zum größten Teil aus hellenistischer und römischer Zeit; von der Bausubstanz des 5. Jh. sind nur minimale Reste erhalten. Wie das Theater damals ausgesehen hat und wann bzw. wie es im Verlauf seiner reichen Baugeschichte umgebaut worden ist, ist seit Beginn der wissenschaftlichen Grabungen in der zweiten Hälfte des 19. Jh. kontrovers und «nach den neuesten Ergebnissen der Bauforschung und Archäologie unsicherer denn je» (Newiger 1979, 447).

Das griech. Theater besteht aus drei Hauptbestandteilen: dem Platz, an dem der Chor singt und tanzt (Orchestra), dem Zuschauerraum (Theatron) und dem sich erst allmählich entwickelnden Bühnenhaus, vor dem die Schauspieler agieren (Skēnḗ).

(1) Die Orchestra: der gewöhnlich kreisrunde Platz (Durchmesser im Dionysostheater ca. 20 m), in dessen Mitte ursprünglich der Altar des Gottes stand, um den der Chor tanzte (Orchestra heißt ‹Tanzplatz›). Da das antike Drama aus Chortänzen entstanden ist, ist die Orchestra, die die Gestalt des griech. Theaters nachdrücklich prägt, der älteste Bestandteil.

(2) Das Theatron (Ort zum Schauen, Zuschauen): wie in Athen so liegt die Orchestra auch sonst gern auf einer natürlichen (oder geschaffenen) Terrasse direkt am Fuß eines Berghangs, der als Zuschauerraum genutzt wird. Ursprünglich standen die Zuschauer um die Orchestra herum und am Berghang; später legte man am Berghang konzentrische Sitzplatzreihen an, die die Orchestra zu ⅔ einschließen.

(3) Die Skēnē: die Entwicklung des Chortanzes und -lieds zum dramatischen Spiel führt zwangsläufig zur Entstehung des dritten Bestandteils des Theaters. Sobald Schauspieler zum Chor hinzutraten, wurde ein Ort gebraucht, wo diese sich während der Chorlieder ungesehen aufhalten und falls erforderlich (s. u.) umkleiden konnten. Es ist möglich, daß dafür (wie Melchinger 1974, 4ff vermutet) zunächst, im Dionysostheater und anderen Orts, Geländevorsprünge am Rand der Orchestra ausreichten, die von dem noch nicht weit den Hang hinaufsteigenden Theatron nicht eingesehen werden konnten; bald jedoch wurde zu diesem Zweck ein Zelt oder eine Holzhütte, die Skēnē (Grundbedeutung: Zelt, Hütte), errichtet, die sich zu einem breiten Bühnengebäude entwickelte, das auf der den Zuschauern gegenüberliegenden Seite die Orchestra begrenzte; es nahm gewiß neben Schauspielern, Statisten und technischem Personal auch Masken, Kostüme und die Requisiten auf. Die einzelnen Entwicklungsstufen der Skēnē des Dionysostheaters sind umstritten; sicher ist, daß wir spätestens im Jahr 458 mit einem stabilen, langgestreckten Bühnenhaus rechnen müssen, da Aischylos' *Orestie* ohne ein solches nicht vorstellbar ist; als sicher kann ferner gelten, daß seit dem grundlegenden Um- und Ausbau des Theaters in perikleischer Zeit vor der Skēnē eine flache Bühne lag, die mit der Orchestra durch zwei bis drei Stufen verbunden war. Sehr wahrscheinlich ist, daß das Bühnenhaus mehr als eine Tür besaß (wahrscheinlich drei); und immerhin als möglich erscheint es, daß wir nicht erst für das Steintheater des Lykurg (s. u.), sondern bereits für die perikleische Holzbühne mit vorspringenden Seitenflügeln, den sogenannten →Paraskenien, rechnen können, die die langgezogene, aber schmale Bühne optisch befriedigend abschlossen.

Das relativ niedrige, einstöckige Bühnenhaus hatte ein Flachdach, das ebenfalls in das dramatische Spiel einbezogen werden konnte, so daß die griech. Bühne seit Aischylos' *Orestie* drei Spielebenen besaß: die Orchestra für den Chor, die flache Bühne vor der Skēnē für die Schauspieler und das Dach der Skēnē, das vor allem für Götterauftritte genutzt wurde und daher ‹Theologeion› hieß. – Zwischen dem Bühnengebäude und dem

Antikes Theater 79

Zuschauerraum führten von beiden Seiten Zugänge in die Orchestra, die sogenannten →Parodoi, die sowohl vom Chor wie von Schauspielern zu Auf- und Abtritten benutzt werden konnten.

Lange Zeit wurden Bühne und Bühnengebäude in jedem Jahr neu aus Holz errichtet (seit dem perikleischen Umbau auf permanenten Steinfundamenten); erst beim zweiten großen Umbau des Theaters unter der Ägide des Lykurg (ca. 338–326), der auch Statuen der drei großen Tragiker aufstellen und ein Staatsexemplar ihrer Stücke herstellen ließ, wurden der gesamte Zuschauerraum und das Bühnengebäude aus Stein errichtet, ohne daß an der Grundkonzeption des perikleischen Theaters viel verändert wurde, so daß wir davon ausgehen können, daß auch die Stücke Menanders in einem Theater inszeniert wurden, das dem beschriebenen Theater des 5. Jh. in Form und technischen Möglichkeiten sehr ähnlich war. Eine grundlegende Veränderung vollzieht sich erst im 3. Jh. (der genaue Zeitpunkt ist umstritten), als infolge der stark reduzierten Rolle des Chors die Orchestra ihre Bedeutung als Spielstätte verliert und an Stelle der alten flachen Bühne eine drei bis vier Meter hohe Bühne entsteht, die mit Hilfe eines Säulenunterbaus vor der Skēnḗ gesetzt wird (und deswegen ‹Proskḗnion› heißt). Zugänglich war die neue Hochbühne sowohl von den Seiten (Parodoi) her, und zwar über Rampen, als auch von hinten aus dem Bühnengebäude (zur Veränderung des Bühnenhauses selbst, →Theaterbau).

3. Schauspieler (→Hypokritḗs): Das griech. Drama ist aus Chortänzen und -liedern entstanden, und der Chor prägt auch wesentlich die voll entwickelten dramatischen Genera (→Chor). – Thespis soll dem Chor einen ersten Schauspieler entgegengestellt haben, Aischylos den zweiten, Sophokles schließlich den dritten. In der Folgezeit ist es dann, jedenfalls in der Tragödie, immer bei der Dreizahl der Schauspieler geblieben; nur in Ausnahmefällen konnte ein vierter dazutreten. Daneben gab es natürlich, je nach Stück und Inszenierungsstil des Autors, eine mehr oder minder große Zahl von Statisten (→Parachorḗgēma).

Für die Komödie ist die Gültigkeit der Dreischauspieler-Regel umstritten. Es scheint, daß die größere Rollenvielfalt der aristophaneischen Komödie (Extrem: Aristophanes' *Vögel* mit 22 Rollen gegenüber Euripides' *Phoenissen* mit 11) mehr als drei Schauspieler verlangt, während vieles dafür spricht, daß für die ‹Neue Komödie› die strenge Regelung der Tragödie gegolten hat.

Die Begrenzung der zur Verfügung stehenden Schauspieler hat eine Reihe bedeutungsvoller Folgen: a) Jeder Schauspieler muß mehrere Rollen spielen; b) gelegentlich muß eine Rolle auf zwei oder gar alle drei Schauspieler aufgeteilt werden; c) es können nie mehr als drei sprechende Personen gleichzeitig agieren; das hat weitreichende Folgen für die dramatische Technik.

80 Antikes Theater

Die kleine Gruppe der Schauspieler ist hierarchisch gegliedert (→Prot-
agonist). Alle Schauspieler sind Männer; wir müssen uns also die großen
Frauenrollen des antiken Dramas (von Klytaimnestra, Antigone und Medea bis zu Lysistrata) von Männern gespielt denken.

Zunächst spielten die Dichter selbst (→Thespis) und wählten die weiteren Schauspieler selber aus. Nach Einführung der Schauspielerwettbewerbe wurden den Dichtern die →Protagonisten durch Los zugeteilt; der
Staat zahlte die Kosten für die Schauspieler.

Die rasche Entwicklung und Professionalisierung der Schauspielkunst
wird durch die Einführung der Schauspieler-Agone dokumentiert und
verstärkt; die Entwicklung des Dramas und des Theaterbetriebs läßt erkennen, daß die Bedeutung der Schauspieler ständig steigt und schließlich sogar, in Aristoteles' Urteil (*Rhet.* 1403b 33), die der Dichter übertrifft.

Von der zweiten Hälfte des 5. Jh. und dann zunehmend im 4. Jh. entwickelt sich auch außerhalb Athens (zunächst in Attika, dann überall in
Griechenland, schließlich in der gesamten griechischsprachigen Welt) ein
reiches Theaterleben, das bald zur Bildung von kleinen Wandertruppen
führt, die mit den in Athen uraufgeführten ‹Klassikern› auf Tournee gehen; schließlich entstehen am Ende des 3. Jh., zunächst in Athen, dann
auch anderenorts, gildenartige Künstlerorganisationen, die Verbände
der sogenannten Techniten des Dionysos (zur Entwicklung, sozialen Stellung und finanziellen Lage des Schauspielerberufs vgl. vor allem Blume
1978, 77–82, und Kob 1979, 527–30).

Der →Chor, dessen Bedeutung im Verlauf der Geschichte des griech.
Dramas immer mehr abnimmt, bis er in der ‹Neuen Komödie› auf Zwischenaktmusik reduziert ist (→Zwischenspiel), bleibt zwar, soweit wir sehen können, ein Bürgerchor, der also immer neu zusammengestellt und
einstudiert wurde, wird jedoch von der rasch fortschreitenden Professionalisierung des Theaterbetriebs nicht unberührt geblieben sein, d. h., es
werden sich auch in diesem Bereich ‹Spezialisten› herausgebildet haben,
die sich regelmäßig zur Verfügung stellten. Die Zahl der Choreuten betrug in Tragödie und Satyrspiel zunächst 12, dann 15; in der Komödie 24.

4. Inszenierung: Der knappe Überblick über Festprogramm (1), Elemente und Entwicklung des (Dionysos-)Theaters (2) und Schauspieler
(3) erlaubt den Schluß, daß die großen Werke des attischen Dramas von
Aischylos' *Orestie* bis Menander unter weitgehend gleichen organisatorischen und bühnentechnischen Bedingungen inszeniert worden sind. Die
Unterschiede der Inszenierungen waren dabei zweifellos von Autor zu
Autor, von Epoche zu Epoche, von Gattung zu Gattung erheblich. Leider wissen wir gerade über diesen für die Theatergeschichte besonders
interessanten Aspekt des griech. Theaters sehr wenig. Da die Stücke für
eine einzige Aufführung geschrieben wurden und die Autoren in der Re-

gel selber Regie führten, enthalten die Texte keine Regieanweisungen. Lange Zeit hat die moderne Forschung, nicht zuletzt infolge der aristotelischen Geringschätzung der ‹Opsis› (*Poet.* 1450b 18f; 1453b 3ff; 1462a 11), die Probleme der visuell-theatralischen Umsetzung der Dramentexte stark vernachlässigt (berühmte Ausnahme: Reinhardt, K.: Aischylos als Regisseur und Theologe. Bern 1949). Erst in den letzten Jahren dokumentieren zahlreiche gründliche Untersuchungen zur Bühnenkunst das ständig wachsende Interesse an diesem Aspekt des antiken Theaters (vgl. z. B. Steidle 1968; Taplin 1977; Seale 1982; Halleran 1984).

Leider sind uns wichtige Bereiche der Inszenierung antiker Dramen weitgehend verschlossen. Über die Schauspielkunst, die, wie die Einführung von Schauspielerwettbewerben zeigt, bereits früh hochentwickelt und populär war, wissen wir nur sehr wenig. Immerhin erlauben die Verwendung von Masken und die Größe des Theaters den Schluß, daß subtile mimische und gestische Effekte, wie sie für die moderne Bühne charakteristisch sind, nicht angestrebt werden konnten. Es ist sicher mit starker Stilisierung gearbeitet worden, mit einer klaren, wahrscheinlich konventionalisierten Körper- und Gebärdensprache. Besonders bedauerlich sind unsere mangelnden Kenntnisse in den Bereichen Choreographie und Musik, die beide die theatralische Wirkung der Stücke stark mitbestimmt haben. Wir können uns die Tänze des Chors, die sicher einen stark mimetischen Charakter hatten, nur schwer vorstellen. Auch hier wird es ein Grundrepertoire von Schritten und Figuren mit bestimmter Bedeutung gegeben haben; die Choreographie wurde aber für jedes Stück individuell entworfen und einstudiert. Angesichts der dramatischen und thematischen Bedeutung der Chorlieder dürfen wir davon ausgehen, daß der Text trotz Gesang und instrumentaler Begleitung verständlich blieb; der Chor hat wahrscheinlich unisono gesungen; die in der Regel den Gesang begleitende Flöte hatte eine dienende Funktion. Bedenkt man, daß im 5. Jh. zu den Chorliedern in zunehmendem Maße Wechselgesänge zwischen Chor und Schauspielern sowie Arien und Duette der Schauspieler (→Amoibaion und →Monodie) kamen, so wird die große Bedeutung des Gesangs im klassischen griech. Drama deutlich, das nicht zu Unrecht immer wieder mit der Oper und Operette verglichen wird. Im 4. Jh. treten Chorgesang und -tanz immer stärker zurück; die Komödie entwickelt sich zum reinen Sprechtheater, während in der Tragödie der Schauspielergesang, soweit wir sehen können, auch weiterhin eine bedeutungsvolle Rolle spielt.

Masken wurden in allen drei dramatischen Gattungen getragen. Der Gebrauch von →Masken reicht tief in primitives Brauchtum und religiöse Vorstellungen zurück, bietet aber auch wichtige praktische Vorteile. Die Maske ermöglicht es dem Schauspieler, in kürzester Zeit von einer Rolle in die andere zu schlüpfen; sie erleichtert die Darstellung von Frauenrol-

82 Antikes Theater

len durch Männer, und sie erlaubt die zeichenartige Visualisierung des Wesentlichen in einem Riesentheater, in dem individuelle Physiognomie und Mimik bedeutungslos waren. →Thespis soll zunächst mit einer Schminkmaske (genannt werden Bleiweiß oder Weinhefe), dann mit einer einfachen Leinenmaske gespielt haben. Originalmasken sind nicht erhalten, sie bestanden aus mit Gips oder Kleister gesteiftem Leinen, waren bemalt und bedeckten nicht nur das Gesicht, sondern wie ein Helm den gesamten Kopf. Die Perücken waren aus Wolle; unterschiedliche Farben markierten die verschiedenen Altersstufen.

In der klassischen Zeit wurden die Masken wahrscheinlich für jede Inszenierung individuell angefertigt. Aus Vasenbildern kann man schließen, daß die Masken (sc. der Tragödie) an der allgemeinen Kunstentwicklung ihrer Zeit teilhatten, daß sich ihr Stil von dem der gleichzeitigen Plastik nicht unterschied. Es ist wahrscheinlich, daß bald eine gewisse Typisierung (Alter, Stand, Charakter) entstanden ist, die in hellenistischer Zeit ihren Höhepunkt und Abschluß erreichte. In dem theatergeschichtlich bedeutungsvollen Lexikon des Pollux (2. Jh. n. Chr.) ist ein auf hellenistische Zeit zurückgehender Maskenkatalog erhalten, der 28 tragische, 44 komische und vier Satyrspiel-Masken verzeichnet.

Die ursprüngliche ‹natürliche› tragische Maske ist offenbar gegen Ende des 5. Jh. allmählich ‹theatralischer› geworden; die Mundöffnung ist deutlich größer; doch erst seit etwa 300 hat die Maske mit weit aufgerissenem Mund, pathetischem Ausdruck und hohem bogenförmigen Haaransatz (dem sogenannten Onkos) die expressive Form gefunden, die in der Neuzeit auf Grund der zahlreichen Abbildungen oft zu Unrecht als die typische antike Maske gilt.

In der →Komödie gab es wahrscheinlich von Anfang an eine größere Vielfalt. Zu der für das 5. Jh. bezeugten grotesken ‹Normalmaske› mit breitem Mund kommen phantastische Tiermasken (vor allem für die Chöre), parodierte Tragödienmasken und (vielleicht) Porträtmasken verspotteter Zeitgenossen. Die Satyrmaske hat eine stumpfe Nase, spitze Ohren, leicht hervortretende Augen und über einer hohen, meist gefurchten Stirn entweder üppiges Haar oder öfter eine weit nach hinten reichende Glatze.

Kostüme (→Bühnenkostüm): Wie die Maske dient auch das Kostüm ursprünglich der kultischen Vermummung und Verwandlung, hat jedoch später vor allem ästhetische und bühnentechnische Funktionen. In der →Tragödie tragen die Helden ein weites, bis auf die Füße fallendes buntgemustertes Prachtgewand mit langen Ärmeln; seine Herkunft ist ebenso umstritten wie der Zeitpunkt der Einführung, die Aischylos zugeschrieben wird, aber erst für das Ende des 5. Jh. sicher bezeugt ist. Das einteilige, den gesamten Körper bedeckende Kostüm verlieh nicht nur dem tragischen Helden Glanz und Würde, sondern ermöglichte schnelle Rollenwechsel und erleichterte die Darstellung von Frauenrollen durch Männer. Vor der Einführung dieses prachtvollen Schauspielergewands wurde wahrscheinlich eine stilisierte, reich differenzierte ‹Alltagskleidung› getragen, und auch das neue Theatergewand erlaubte zweifellos mit Hilfe von Farben, Schmuck, signifikanten Details und Requisiten die jeweils notwendige Differenzierung der Personen nach natürlichen (Geschlecht, Alter), geographischen und gesellschaftlichen Unterschieden.

Im →Satyrspiel trugen die Helden das gleiche Kostüm wie in den drei voraufgegangenen Tragödien; die Satyrn sind bis auf einen Schurz gewöhnlich nackt, d. h. nur mit einem enganliegenden fleischfarbenen Trikot bekleidet. Der Lendenschurz diente offenbar vor allem zur Befestigung eines Pferdeschwanzes und eines erigierten Phallus. – Während die Satyrn meist barfuß aufgetreten sind, trugen die Helden der Tragödie den →Kothurn.

Das Standardkostüm der →Komödie unterscheidet sich grundlegend von dem der Tragödie. Die Schauspieler trugen wie die Satyrn ein enganliegendes, fleischfarbenes (d. h. Haut symbolisierendes) Trikot, das an Bauch und Gesäß grotesk ausgestopft wurde (diese Ausstopfung heißt ‹Somation›). Darüber trugen die männlichen Personen ein kurzes Gewand oder einen kleinen Mantel, die das neben der Ausstopfung wichtigste Attribut des komischen Kostüms, den übergroßen erigierten Phallus, nicht verhüllte; die Frauen trugen stilisierte Alltagskleidung (knöchellanges, gelbes Gewand [Chitōn], Mantel, dazu Stirnband, Haarnetz, enge Schuhe), waren aber in derselben grotesken Weise ausgestopft wie die Männer. Natürlich müssen wir auch hier mit vielfältiger Variation dieses Standardkostüms und (besonders im Falle des →Chors) mit den verschiedensten phantastischen Spezialkostümen rechnen. Einen dem →Kothurn entsprechenden spezifischen Komödienschuh gab es nicht.

Im Verlauf des 4. Jh. veränderte sich das aristophaneische Komödienkostüm völlig. Somation und Phallus verschwanden ebenso wie das zu kurze Untergewand. Das Kostüm der Neuen Komödie ist die Alltagskleidung der Zeit. Dieser ‹Normalisierung› entspricht die Entwicklung der komischen Maske, die ihren grotesk-übertreibenden Charakter verliert und – allerdings nur für kurze Zeit am Ende des 4. Jh. – ‹natürlich› wird, bevor sich, wie bei der tragischen Maske, die expressive Form mit großen Augenhöhlen und extremer Mundöffnung endgültig durchsetzt.

Ein weiterer Bereich theatralischer Wirkung neben Masken und Kostümen ist die *Bühnenausstattung* mit Versatzstücken, Requisiten und Bühnenmalerei (→Bühnenbild).

In der Tragödie und im Satyrspiel sind Versatzstücke (z. B. Altäre, Gräber, Götterstatuen) und Requisiten wahrscheinlich nur sehr sparsam und immer dramatisch und thematisch funktional verwendet worden; in der Komödie haben dagegen Requisiten – daran lassen die Texte keinen

Zweifel – eine wesentlich größere Rolle gespielt. Die aristophaneische Komik lebt neben ihrem überwältigenden sprachlichen Witz in erheblichem Maße von dem, was sich auf der Bühne ereignet, und damit auch von der einfallsreichen und witzigen Verwendung der verschiedenartigsten alltäglichen und phantastischen Requisiten.

Im Zusammenhang mit der Entwicklung eines stabilen Bühnenhauses ist zwangsläufig die Bühnenmalerei entstanden. Bei der sog. →Skēnographie handelte es sich nicht darum, die von Stück zu Stück und nicht selten sogar innerhalb der Stücke wechselnden Schauplätze darzustellen, sondern um perspektivische Architekturmalerei, die der flächigen Holzfront der Skēnḗ, die den Hintergrund des Spiels bildet, Plastizität verleihen soll. Wirkliche Bühnenmalerei gibt es wohl erst seit hellenistischer Zeit (zu den Einzelheiten →Skēnographie). Im klassischen griech. Theater wurde also wie in anderen ‹Theatern der Konvention› vor einem weitgehend einheitlichen Bühnenhintergrund gespielt. Der Zuschauer war gewöhnt, sich den jeweiligen Schauplatz des Geschehens auf Grund der meist zu Beginn in den Text eingebauten Angaben vorzustellen (Wortregie).

Wichtig für Inszenierungsstil und Wirkung griech. Dramen sind schließlich die sog. Theatermaschinen, die spektakuläre Effekte ermöglichten: das →Ekkyklema. Der Zeitpunkt der Einführung dieser Theatermaschinen ist umstritten; vieles spricht dafür, daß sie bereits Aischylos zur Verfügung standen.

5. Zuschauer: Das griech. Theater war ein →Massentheater. Das Dionysostheater faßte ca. 17000 Zuschauer, die in jedem Frühjahr aus ganz Attika und in zunehmendem Maße auch aus anderen Städten der griech. Welt zusammenströmten. Angesichts des kultischen Festspielcharakters der Aufführungen besteht kaum Zweifel, daß jedermann Zutritt hatte, neben Bürgern auch Metöken und Sklaven und, was gelegentlich bezweifelt wird, auch Frauen. Der Eintritt war sicher zunächst frei, dann nicht hoch; ärmeren Bürgern wurde spätestens seit dem Ende des 5. Jh. ein Theatergeld (→Theorikon) gezahlt. Die Sitzordnung war zunächst wohl frei, später jedoch in zunehmendem Maße durch ein System von Sonderrechten (den sogenannten Prohedrien) hierarchisch geregelt. Priester und Amtsträger, Ratsmitglieder sowie verdiente Fremde und Metöken hatten Ehrenplätze. Die männlichen Bürger saßen, nach Phylen geordnet, in den besseren Reihen, d. h. näher zur Bühne als Nichtbürger und Sklaven, Frauen und Kinder (vgl. dazu Kob 1979, 530ff).

Das griech. Theaterpublikum war ausdauernd (die Aufführungen dauerten mehrere Tage und jeweils sieben bis neun Stunden) und sachverständig. Man besuchte regelmäßig die Aufführungen, und ein nicht unerheblicher Teil der Zuschauer war in irgendeiner Funktion (als Choreut, Statist, Bühnenarbeiter) selbst an Aufführungen beteiligt gewesen (allein für alle Chöre wurden beinahe 1200 Sänger gebraucht): ideale Voraussetzungen für die Entstehung eines interessierten und kunstverständigen Publikums, ohne das die literarische Qualität und thematische Komplexität des griech. Dramas nicht denkbar wären.

Das römische Theater

1. Entstehung: Die Geschichte des röm. Theaters beginnt im Jahr 240 v. Chr. In diesem Jahr erhält der Grieche Livius Andronicus den Auftrag, für die ‹Ludi Romani›, das bedeutendste Staatsfest der Römer, die lateinische Fassung je einer griech. Tragödie und Komödie herzustellen und zu inszenieren. Das Datum – ein Jahr nach Beendigung des ersten Kriegs gegen Karthago – ist aufschlußreich. Zwar bestanden bereits seit langer Zeit vielfältige wirtschaftliche, politische und kulturelle Kontakte mit den griech. Stadtstaaten Süditaliens und Siziliens; dennoch dürften erst während des langen Kriegs viele Römer in direkten Kontakt mit dem Theater der Magna Graecia (Hochburgen waren Tarent und Syrakus) gekommen sein und Gefallen daran gefunden haben. Es ist nicht unwahrscheinlich, daß in der röm. Oberschicht nach dem ersten großen Sieg über die Rivalen Karthago und der damit errungenen Vorherrschaft im westlichen Mittelmeerraum zugleich mit wachsendem politischen Selbstbewußtsein die Erkenntnis wuchs, daß die aufstrebende Weltmacht Rom kulturell Anschluß an die allesbeherrschende hellenistische Kultur finden müsse.

Das röm. Theater, das ca. 500 Jahre nach der mythischen Gründung der Stadt mit der Übersetzung und Inszenierung zweier griech. Stücke durch einen Griechen beginnt, ist also von Anfang an in entscheidendem Maße vom griech. Theater geprägt und bleibt diesem auch in der Folgezeit bei allen Unterschieden und Sonderentwicklungen eng verbunden.

Gewiß lassen sich auch auf ital. Boden primitive, im Kontext ländlichen Brauchtums entstandene dramatische Vorformen (mimetische Tänze, Lieder, Stegreifverse mit dialogischen, mimischen und gestischen Elementen) erschließen; gewiß waren den Römern seit langem etruskische Flötenspieler und Tänzer, Pantomimen und Masken vertraut (das römische Wort für Maske ‹persona› ist ebenso wie die Bezeichnung des Schauspielers ‹histrio› etruskischer Herkunft; zum etrusk. Einfluß auf das röm. Theater → histrio); gewiß hatte sich unter dem Einfluß der südital.-griech. → Phlyakenposse ein volkstümliches, derb komisches Maskenspiel entwickelt, die sog. → Atellana, die bereits im 3. Jh. v. Chr. über den oskischen Sprachraum, in dem es zu Hause war, hinaus bekannt geworden war, und gewiß sind alle diese vorliterarischen Formen nicht ohne Einfluß auf die Entwicklung des Dramas in Rom gewesen (vgl. dazu vor allem Blänsdorf 1978, 90–99); das röm. Theater ist jedoch nicht wie das griechische langsam aus eigenen Wurzeln gewachsen, sondern im Jahr 240 durch einen kultur- und religionspolitischen Willensakt geschaffen worden.

2. Organisation: Das röm. Theater ist nicht wie das griech. tief im Kult eines Gottes verwurzelt (der Theatergott Dionysos spielt in Rom keine Rolle), aber doch von Anfang an Festspieltheater. Tragödien- und Komödienaufführungen (ludi scaenici) gab es schon bald nach ihrer Aufnahme in das offizielle Festprogramm der ‹Ludi Romani› (240) und der ebenfalls dem Jupiter geweihten ‹Ludi plebeii› (seit 220) nicht nur zu Ehren des obersten Gottes, sondern auch an den ‹Ludi Apollinares› (seit 212), an den ‹Ludi Megalenses› (seit 194, zu Ehren der Magna Mater, der kleinasiatischen Göttermutter Kybele) und später auch an den ‹Ludi Cereales› (für die Fruchtbarkeitsgöttin Ceres).

Die Verantwortung für die ‹ludi scaenici› wie für das gesamte Festprogramm, zu dem neben den Theateraufführungen in der Regel Wagenrennen, Gladiatorenkämpfe und Tierhetzen gehörten, lag in der Hand von Beamten (meistens der Aedile). Diesen wurden für die Organisation der Spiele feste (im Verlauf der Zeit immer wieder erhöhte) Summen aus der Staatskasse zur Verfügung gestellt, die bei den ständig steigenden Ansprüchen und Kosten jedoch nicht ausreichten, so daß sie privat Riesensummen zuschießen mußten. Die Durchführung aufwendiger Spiele war ein wesentlicher Faktor für die weitere politische Karriere.

Zu den staatlich organisierten Theateraufführungen an den großen Götterfesten kamen private Inszenierungen (an ludi privati) anläßlich besonderer Ereignisse (Triumphe, Beerdigungen, Einweihungen), und die Zahl der Theatertage erhöhte sich noch durch die kuriose Möglichkeit, aus Anlaß jeder Art von Formfehler oder Störung des Festritus das gesamte Festprogramm zu wiederholen (instauratio), eine Möglichkeit, von der erstaunlich häufig Gebrauch gemacht wurde. Bereits am Beginn des 2. Jh. v. Chr. wurde in Rom folglich bereits an ca. 20 bis 30 Tagen Theater gespielt, eine Zahl, die sich in der Folge noch erhöhte. Wie viele Stücke jährlich inszeniert wurden, läßt sich allerdings nicht ermitteln, da es in Rom kein festes Programm gab, das die Zahl der Stücke wie in Griechenland im Rahmen eines oder mehrerer Theaterwettbewerbe festlegte.

Die eigentliche Inszenierung überließ der verantwortliche Beamte einem von ihm verpflichteten und bezahlten ‹Theaterdirektor› (dominus gregis), dem Leiter einer kleinen Schauspielertruppe (grex, caterva), der das Stück von einem Dichter (oder von anderen Wandertruppen) kaufte, die Musik für die Arien und Duette (→ Cantica) komponieren ließ sowie Kostüme und Requisiten bereitstellte (mit wachsendem Theaterbetrieb entstanden auch Kostümverleiher) und selber die Hauptrolle übernahm.

Die Theatergruppen, zu denen auch Musiker und Bühnenarbeiter gehörten, waren klein. Wie in Griechenland übernahm jeder Schauspieler mehrere Rollen, und wie dort wurden alle Frauenrollen von Männern gespielt; anders aber als in Griechenland waren die Schauspieler nicht Bürger, sondern meist Fremde (vor allem Griechen), Freigelassene und

Sklaven. Die Wahl des Schauspielerberufs wurde mit dem Verlust bürgerlicher Ehrenrechte (infamia) bezahlt; davon ausgenommen war nur der Auftritt in der volkstümlichen → Atellana.

3. Das Theater: Wo die offiziellen Theateraufführungen der großen Festspiele stattfanden, ist unsicher. Gespielt wurde offenbar an verschiedenen Orten in den großen Circus-Anlagen, auf dem Forum und vor allem im Tempelbezirk des jeweiligen Festgottes. Ein dem athenischen Dionysostheater vergleichbares zentrales Theater existierte nicht. Überhaupt gab es in Rom lange Zeit kein permanentes steinernes Theater; es sind zwar bereits für das 2. Jh. v. Chr. eine Reihe von Versuchen bezeugt, ein solches zu errichten, diese scheiterten jedoch alle. Erst ca. 200 Jahre nach den ersten Inszenierungen erhält Rom ein repräsentatives Steintheater, das Theater des Pompeius (55 v. Chr.), dem sehr bald das Theater des Marcellus (von Caesar begonnen, von Augustus vollendet) und das Theater des Balbus (13 v. Chr.) folgen. Wir wissen allerdings, daß bereits lange vor 55 eine Reihe großer und aufwendiger, temporärer Holztheater errichtet worden sind.

Das röm. Theater ist vom zeitgenössischen griech. Theaterbau beeinflußt, unterscheidet sich jedoch vom hell. Hochbühnen-Typ deutlich. Die röm. Theater sind nicht an einen natürlichen Hang gelegt; sie sind vielmehr auf ebenem Gelände (in Rom auf dem Marsfeld) errichtete, freistehende, geschlossene Baukomplexe. Der Zuschauerraum (cavea), der auf einem komplizierten System tragender Gewölbe ruht, ist mit dem Bühnenhaus verbunden; dadurch sind die seitlichen Zugänge (→ Parodos) überwölbt. Die halbkreisförmige Orchestra (s. o.) hat mit dem Zurücktreten des → Chors ihre Bedeutung als Spielfläche völlig verloren; sie wird zur Aufstellung von Ehrensitzen genutzt. Die breite und flache Bühne ist mit ein bis eineinhalb Meter deutlich niedriger als ihr drei bis vier Meter hohes hellenistisches Pendant. Dagegen ist die Front des Bühnenhauses (scaena) nun so hoch wie der direkt an sie heranreichende Zuschauerraum; ihre Stirnseite (die sog. scaenae frons) entwickelt sich zu einer mit Säulen, Nischen und kleinen Giebeln architektonisch reich gegliederten und mit kostbaren Materialien ausgestalteten Schmuckfassade. In der Kaiserzeit entstehen nach dem Modell des Pompeiustheaters überall im Imperium Romanum repräsentative Theaterbauten.

Es ist paradox, daß die Römer ihre prunkvollen permanenten Steintheater erst errichteten, als Tragödien- und Komödienaufführungen, die in Rom wohl immer hinter Wagenrennen und Gladiatorenkämpfen zurücktreten mußten, ihren Höhepunkt bereits hinter sich hatten. Die Blütezeit des republikanischen Dramas (mit den Komödien des Plautus und Terenz sowie den drei großen Tragikern Ennius, Pacuvius und Accius) war, als das Pompeiustheater (55 v. Ch.) eingeweiht wurde, längst vorbei.

Die Spielbedingungen des republikanischen Theaters müssen wir in erster Linie aus den erhaltenen Texten (vor allem des Plautus) erschließen, da die temporären Holzbühnen keine Spuren hinterlassen haben. Gespielt wurde auf einer einfachen Podiumsbühne (proscaenium oder pulpitum genannt), die von einer bemalten Rückwand (scaena) abgeschlossen wurde. Als Vorbild gelten die schnell zu errichtenden Holzbühnen fahrender Komödianten, wie sie uns am besten von den Phlyakenvasen bekannt sind (→Phlyakenposse). Die primitive Kleinform ist allerdings schon sehr bald unter dem Einfluß des hellenistischen Theaters weiterentwickelt worden. Die Analyse der dramatischen Technik (z. B. Auf- und Abtrittsmonologe, A-parte-Sprechen) sowie literarische Zeugnisse über die Errichtung von Theatern in Rom führen zu dem Schluß, daß wir bereits für Plautus und Terenz mit einer zwar flachen, aber außerordentlich langgestreckten Bühne (später 30 bis 60 m) rechnen müssen. Die lange Bühne stellte in der Regel einen Platz oder eine Straße dar, die – wie Türen und Bemalung (→Skēnographie) andeuteten – in der Tragödie vor einem Palast, in der Komödie vor ein bis drei Bürgerhäusern vorzustellen sind. Vor den (meist drei) Türen befanden sich (vielleicht) säulengeschmückte Vorbauten (vestibulum), die für Lauscherszenen und zur Darstellung von Innenszenen dienen konnten. Auch die Palast- bzw. Hausdächer konnten in das dramatische Spiel einbezogen werden.

4. Inszenierung: Über den Stil der Tragödien- bzw. Komödienaufführungen können wir (wie beim griech. Theater) nur wenig sagen; auch in den röm. Dramen gibt es keine Regieanmerkungen. ‹Theaterkritiken› sind nicht bekannt, und die theoretischen Schriften zum Theater sind verloren. Erlauben die zahlreichen erhaltenen Komödientexte immerhin einige Rückschlüsse auf Spiel und Requisiten, so müssen wir uns im Falle der republikanischen Tragödie, die nur in kümmerlichen Fragmenten erhalten ist, mit einigen wenigen, zufällig bezeugten Zuschauerreaktionen auf einzelne Aufführungen begnügen.

Von besonderer Bedeutung für die szenische Wirkung ist, daß das republikanische Drama in weit höherem Maße als seine griech. Vorbilder ‹Musiktheater› ist. Während es sich bei den griech. Vorlagen des Plautus und Terenz, von Chorintermezzi (→Zwischenspiel) und gelegentlicher Flötenbegleitung abgesehen, um Sprechdramen handelt, tritt in der röm. Komödie das musikalische Element in den Vordergrund. Nur etwa ein Drittel bis 50 Prozent aller Szenen sind in Sprechversen geschrieben; ein größerer Teil wird in einer Art von Rezitativ vorgetragen und dabei von der ‹Tibia› begleitet, einem vielfach paarweise gespielten, im Klang unserer Oboe ähnlichen Doppelblattinstrument. Dazu kommen die ebenfalls von der ‹Tibia› begleiteten Arien und Duette (→ Cantica) sowie rein instrumentale Vor- und Zwischenspiele, so daß wir uns die plautinischen Stücke als operettenartige Singspiele vorzustellen haben. Bei Terenz tritt das musikalische Element zwar wieder stärker zurück (vor allem die Cantica verschwinden fast ganz), bleibt jedoch wesentlich für Charakter und Aufführung der Stücke. Auch die röm. Tragiker haben einen Teil der Sprechpartien ihrer Vorlagen in Rezitative oder Arien verwandelt (dies übrigens, anders als in der Komödie, unter dem Einfluß der hellenistischen Tragödie). In der Tragödie kommen zu Schauspielerrezitativen, -arien und -duetten noch die Lieder des Chors, der jetzt neben den Schauspielern auf der Bühne agiert, hinzu. Größe des Chors und Vortragsform sind unklar. In der Komödie ist der Chor völlig eliminiert; auch seine letzte Funktion als musikalischer ‹Pausenfüller› (→ Zwischenspiel) hat er verloren; Plautus und Terenz kennen keine Aktpausen; das Spiel wird nicht unterbrochen (actio continua), wahrscheinlich, um das Publikum nicht an eine andere gleichzeitige Attraktion des Festprogramms zu verlieren. Leider ist uns die Musik, die das röm. Drama und seine Inszenierung in so hohem Maße geprägt hat, so gut wie verschlossen.

Ein zweiter, für die szenische Wirkung wichtiger Unterschied zwischen dem frühen röm. Drama und seinen griech. Vorbildern würde dann bestehen, wenn eine Reihe von allerdings nicht widerspruchsfreien Zeugnissen recht hat, die erklären bzw. zu implizieren scheinen, daß in Rom zunächst ohne Masken gespielt worden sei. Erst zur Zeit des Terenz oder sogar erst am Ende des 2. Jh. seien auch im röm. Theater Masken verwendet worden. Das Problem wird seit langem kontrovers diskutiert. Eine befriedigende Antwort auf die Frage, warum die Römer bei ihrer Rezeption des griech. Dramas und seines Theaters die dort obligatorischen Masken weggelassen haben sollten, ist allerdings bisher nicht gefunden worden. Die röm. Masken gleichen, wie die zahlreichen erhaltenen archäologischen Denkmäler beweisen, den expressiven hellenistischen Masken. Dasselbe gilt für die Kostüme, jedenfalls in den Adaptationen griech. Stücke. In diesen, also in allen plautinischen und terenzischen Komödien, wurde stilisierte, zeitgenössische griech. Kleidung getragen. Wahrscheinlich wurde ein Standardkostüm verwendet, das durch Farben und signifikante Details, durch Zusätze und Requisiten variiert werden konnte; bestimmte, häufig wiederkehrende Typen wurden mit denselben Requisiten gekennzeichnet (z. B. Löffel = Koch; Schwert = Soldat). Für die Tragödie dürfen wir das lange, reichgeschmückte griech. Kostüm voraussetzen. Dazu kommt als Charakteristikum des Tragödienkostüms der überhohe → Kothurn.

Neben den Bearbeitungen griech. Komödien und Tragödien entstand schon sehr bald (noch im 3. Jh.) ein eigenständiges ‹nationalröm.› Drama, dessen Stoffe das ital.-röm. Alltagsleben (Komödie) bzw. die röm. Geschichte (Tragödie) bildeten. In diesen Stücken wurde, wie nicht anders zu erwarten, röm. Kleidung getragen: in der Komödie die einfache Toga, in der Tragödie die Sonderform der ‹toga praetexta›, die mit einem Purpurstreifen besetzte Toga der hohen röm. Beamten. Für diese

90 Antikes Theater

Sonderform bildeten sich später die Gattungsbezeichnungen ‹fabula togata› bzw. ‹fabula praetexta›, während die Bearbeitungen griech. Komödien nach dem wichtigsten Kostümstück, dem pallium (griech.: himation), einem bequemen, weiten, mantelartigen Obergewand, ‹fabula palliata› genannt wurde. Die Bezeichnung für ihr tragisches Pendant (Bearbeitung einer griech. Tragödie) ist umstritten. Requisiten und Statisten wurden in der röm. Komödie wohl nur sparsam verwendet, während für die Tragödie aufwendige, ja pompöse Inszenierungen bezeugt sind.

Die wohl wichtigste Neuerung des röm. Theaters aus bühnentechnischer Sicht ist die Erfindung des Vorhangs, die natürlich erst mit der Wandlung der Orchestra vom Spielplatz des Chors zum Zuschauerraum möglich war. «Die gesamte Bühne konnte durch einen großen Vorhang (aulaeum) verdeckt werden. Zu Beginn des Stücks hob sich dieser Vorhang nicht, wie auf unseren Bühnen, sondern senkte sich, d. h. er wurde in eine Vertiefung im Boden hineingelassen. Diese Einlaßrille hat sich in vielen röm. Theatern erhalten» (Simon 1972, S. 52). Daneben gab es kleine markisenartige Vorhänge (sciparia), die zur Verhüllung einzelner Bühnenteile verwendet wurden und – vor allem im →Pantomimus – Scherwände.

5. Zuschauer: Zu den Spielen und damit zu den Theateraufführungen war in Rom jedermann zugelassen, der Eintritt war frei. Die plautinischen und terenzischen Prologe erlauben den Schluß, daß die republikanischen Dramatiker und Schauspieler mit einer bunten und lauten Menge aus Bürgern und Sklaven, Armen und Reichen, Frauen und Kindern rechnen mußten, einer Menge, die mehr an Spannung und Unterhaltung interessiert war als an Kunst, und die die Schauspieler schon einmal mitten im Stück im Stich ließen, wenn an anderer Stelle des Festplatzes Boxer oder Seiltänzer die Aufmerksamkeit auf sich lenkten oder sich das Gerücht verbreitete, daß die Gladiatorenkämpfe in Kürze beginnen würden (so geschehen bei den beiden ersten Versuchen, Terenz' *Hecyra* aufzuführen). Ein breites, fachkundiges Theaterpublikum wie in Athen hat sich in Rom auch in der Folgezeit nicht entwickelt, und es verwundert angesichts der rasch fortschreitenden Proletarisierung der Hauptstadt nicht, daß sich am Ende der Republik weniger anspruchsvolle Formen wachsender Beliebtheit erfreuten und in der Kaiserzeit die Tragödie und Komödie fast völlig von der Bühne verdrängten. Zwar sind Komödienaufführungen auch weiterhin bezeugt, zwar sind auch in augusteischer Zeit und in der frühen Kaiserzeit noch bedeutende Tragödien verfaßt worden; doch werden die beiden dramatischen Kunstformen jetzt eher gelesen, vor Freunden rezitiert, vielleicht auch einmal in einem ‹Privattheater› ganz oder szenenweise aufgeführt. Für die einzigen uns erhaltenen röm. Tragödien, die acht echten und zwei unechten

Stücke des L. A. Seneca, ist keine Aufführung bezeugt, ja es ist unsicher, ob Seneca sie überhaupt für eine Aufführung konzipiert hat.

Das Theater der Kaiserzeit wird beherrscht von →Mimus, einer volkstümlich derben, oft obszönen, komischen Kleinform, die weitgehend improvisiert wird und mit tänzerischen und akrobatischen Einlagen angereichert ist, und →Pantomimus, einer neuen ballettartigen, quasidramatischen Form, in der ein einziger Pantomime in wechselnden Kostümen und Masken die Höhepunkte einer Tragödie (oder weit seltener einer Komödie) mit Hilfe von Tanz, Gesten und Mimik darstellt, während ein Sänger oder ein Chor (dazu oder in den Pausen) den Text vortrug.

Arnott, P.: Greek Scenic Conventions in the Fifth Century B. C. Oxford 1962; Beare, W.: The Roman Stage. London ³1964; Bieber, M.: The History of the Greek and Roman Theater. Princeton ²1961; Blänsdorf, J.: Voraussetzungen und Entstehung der röm. Komödie. In: E. Lefèvre (Hg.): Das röm. Drama. Darmstadt 1978, S. 91–134; Blume, H.-D.: Einführung in das antike Theaterwesen. Darmstadt 1978; Brooke, I.: Costume in Greek Classical Drama. London 1962; Dingel, J.: Das Requisit in der griech. Tragödic. Tübingen 1967; Ghiron-Bistagne, P.: Recherches sur les acteurs dans la Grèce antique. Paris 1976; Hallerau, M. R.: Stagecraft in Euripides. London 1984; Hammond, N. G. L.: The Conditions of Dramatic Production to the Death of Aeschylus. In: Greek, Roman, and Byzantine Studies 13 (1972), p. 387–450; Jens, W. (Hg.): Die Bauformen der griech. Tragödie. Poetica Beiheft 6. München 1971; Kenner, H.: Das Theater und der Realismus in der griech. Kunst. Wien 1954; Kob, F.: Polis und Theater. In: G. A. Seeck (Hg.): Das griech. Drama. Darmstadt 1979, S. 504–545; Lawler, L. B.: The Dance of the Ancient Greek Theatre. Iowa 1964; Lefèvre, E. (Hg.): Das röm. Drama. Darmstadt 1978; Lesky, A.: Die tragische Dichtung der Hellenen. Göttingen ³1972; Melchinger, S.: Das Theater der Tragödie. Aischylos, Sophokles, Euripides auf der Bühne ihrer Zeit. München 1974; Newiger, H.-J.: Drama und Theater. In: G. A. Seeck (Hg.): Das griech. Drama. Darmstadt 1979, S. 434–503; Pickard-Cambridge, A. W.: The Theatre of Dionysos in Athens. Oxford 1946 (1966); ders.: Dithyramb, Tragedy, and Comedy. Oxford ²1962 (rev. T. B. L. Webster); ders.: The Dramatic Festivals of Athens. Oxford 1968 (rev. J. Gould, D. M. Lewis); Seale, D.: Vision and Stagecraft in Sophocles. London 1982; Seeck, G. A. (Hg.): Das griech. Drama. Darmstadt 1979; Sifakis, G. M.: Studies in the History of Hellenistic Drama. London 1967; Simon, E.: Das antike Theater. Heidelberg 1972; Steidle, W.: Studien zum antiken Drama. Unter besonderer Berücksichtigung des Bühnenspiels. München 1968; Taplin, O.: The Stagecraft of Aeschylus. Oxford 1977; ders.: Greek Tragedy in Action. Berkeley 1978; Trendall, A. D. / Webster, T. B. L.: Illustration of Greek Drama. London 1971; Webster, T. B. L.: Griech. Bühnenaltertümer. Göttingen 1963; ders.: Greek Theatre Production. London ²1970; Zwierlein, O.: Die Rezitationsdramen Senecas. Meisenheim 1966.

Bernd Seidensticker

Anti-Masque

Kontrapunktisches Gegenstück zum in England üblichen höfischen Maskenspiel, →‹masque›, in elisabethanischer Zeit. Ben Jonson (1573 bis 1637), der Autor eines runden Dutzends von ‹masques›, gilt als der Erfinder der A.-M., kürzeren, meistens den M. vorangehenden Stücken (daher auch *Ante-Masque* genannt, in denen negative Eigenschaften und das Böse schlechthin die Oberhand gewannen, meist in grotesker Form die abscheulichen Machenschaften der Sittenverderber geißelnd).

Brotanek, R.: Die englischen Maskenspiele. 1902; Reyher, P.: Les Masques anglais. Paris 1909.

Horst Schumacher

antiteater

Anfang 1968 gründen R. W. Fassbinder, P. Raben, H. Schygulla u. a. in der Nachfolge des «Action Theaters» (1967) in München das a. Das Ensemble, bestehend aus etwa zehn festen Mitgliedern, versteht sich als Kollektiv, das gemeinsam lebt und arbeitet, ohne den einzelnen auf eine bestimmte Funktion (Autor, Schauspieler, Regisseur etc.) festzulegen. Beeinflußt von Artauds →Theater der Grausamkeit und vor allem dem →Living Theatre, versteht sich das a. als Provokation gegenüber dem bürgerlichen Theaterverständnis: Auf aktuelles Zeitgeschehen wird direkt reagiert, die Bühnenklassiker werden – im Sinne des antiautoritären politischen Bewußtseins der Studentenbewegung – aktualisiert und politisiert. Extreme Stilisierungen und kulturrevolutionäre Verfremdungen sind kennzeichnend für Vorstellungen einer neuen Ästhetik. Dem Film entlehnte →Montage- und →Collageverfahren sowie Betonung des Choreographischen und Gestischen machen die a.-Inszenierungen zu Mischformen aus Theater und Film. Der politisch-aufklärerische Impetus der früheren Theaterarbeiten wird in dem Maße schwächer, in dem Fassbinder zur zentralen Figur aufsteigt; das Theater wird weitgehend zum Forum seiner Selbstdarstellung. Das a. als solches löst sich Anfang der 70er Jahre auf. Ein Großteil des Ensembles arbeitet aber weiterhin mit Fassbinder (bis zu dessen Tod 1982) zusammen.

Inszenierungen des Action Theaters: *Zum Beispiel Ingolstadt* (Fleißer/RWF, 1968); *Katzelmacher* (RWF, 1968); *Axel Caesar Haarmann* (Kollektiv, 1968). – Inszenierungen des antiteaters: *Wie dem Herrn Mockinpott das Leben ausgetrieben wird* (Weiss, 1968); *Orgie Ubuh* (Jarry/RWF/Raben u. a., 1968); *Iphigenie auf Tauris* (Goethe/RWF, 1968); *Ajax* (Sophokles/RWF, 1968); *Der amerikanische Soldat* (RWF, 1968); *Die Bettleroper* (Gay/RWF, 1969); *Pre-Paradise Sorry Now*

(RWF, 1969); *Anarchie in Bayern* (RWF, 1969); *Das Kaffeehaus* (Goldoni/RWF, 1969); *Werwolf* (Baer/RWF, 1969); *Das brennende Dorf* (Lope/RWF, 1970); *Das Blut am Hals der Katze* (RWF, 1971); *Die bitteren Tränen der Petra von Kant* (RWF, 1971); *Bremer Freiheit* (RWF, 1971).

Assenmacher, K. H.: Das engagierte Theater R. W. Fassbinders. In: C. Ch. Rump (Hg.), Sprachnetze. Hildesheim/New York 1976; Henrichs, B.: «Müder Wunderknabe. R. W. Fassbinder: Von der Theaterkommune zur Kunstfabrik». In: Zeit-Magazin Nr. 24/8. Juni 1973; Karsunke, Y.: anti-theatergeschichte. Die Anfänge; Iden, P.: Der Eindruck-Macher. R. W. Fassbinder und das Theater. Beide in: P. W. Jansen/W. Schütte (Hg.): R. W. Fassbinder. Reihe Film 2. München/Wien 1983.

Achim Haag

Aparte

Meist kurze Aussage einer Gestalt auf offener Bühne, die absichtlich beiseite formuliert wird, damit sie zwar das Publikum, jedoch nicht die anderen anwesenden Personen hören. Man unterscheidet das echte A. vom falschen: In diesem täuscht der Redende das Beiseitesprechen nur vor, in Wirklichkeit aber sorgt er dafür, daß die Anwesenden seine Worte doch vernehmen. Dadurch sollen sie glauben, daß sie seine heimlichen Gedanken und Gefühle zufällig erfahren. Das A. ist eine beliebte Technik der Komödie (vgl. u. a. Plautus, 254–184 v. Chr., und Pierre Corneille, 1606 bis 1684; *Der Lügner*, 1643), insbesondere des volkstümlichen Lustspiels. Es wird folgerichtig von den Naturalisten verworfen, da sie das Spielen ins Publikum vermeiden.

Scherer, J.: La Dramaturgie classique en France. Paris 1983; Schimmerling, E.: Das Beiseite im Drama des Sturm und Drang. Diss. Wien 1934.

Alain Muzelle

Applaus

Beifall meist durch Händeklatschen oder (seltener) Trampeln, Pfeifen oder Rufe (Bravo) für besonders gefallende Leistung auf der Bühne, vor allem für Darsteller, aber auch Bühnenbild und Kostüme sowie einen Satz des Autors. Mißbrauch durch käuflichen Beifall (→Claque), hauptsächlich im 19. Jh. Bezahlte Claqueure gab es bereits im röm. Theater (plausores) und span. Barocktheater (Mosqueteros). Im ganzen 19. Jh. in Theatermetropolen üblich, anfangs von Theaterdirektoren beauftragt (Freibillettinhaber). Systematisch organisiert (mit offiziellem Büro: Assurance des succès dramatiques) seit 1820 in Paris – feste Honorarsätze für Beifall (durch Tapageurs) und Ablehnung (durch Connaisseurs) sowie Mundpropaganda (durch Chatouilleurs und Chauffeurs). Zuweilen Parkettschlachten widerstreitender Claqueure. Im 20. Jh. freiwilliger Freundschaftsdienst.

Werner Schulze-Reimpell

Arbeitertheater

Jenseits des bürgerlichen Berufstheaters entwickeln sich Mitte des 19. Jh. Ansätze eines proletarischen Laientheaters. In Arbeiterbildungsvereinen und auf Volksfesten kamen eigens für ein proletarisches Publikum verfaßte Bühnenwerke zur Aufführung: Lustspiele, Schwänke, Satiren, ‹lebende Bilder› – überwiegend Einakter mit politisch-agitatorischem Charakter. Die in den 90er Jahren einsetzende Annäherung der Sozialdemokratie an bürgerliche Positionen sollte für das Arbeitertheater nicht ohne Folgen bleiben: Zunehmend orientierten sich die sozialistischen Dramatiker am ‹herrschenden› Theaterbetrieb und produzierten (dem naturalistischen Beispiel folgend) mehrere Akte umfassende Sozialtragödien, die zumeist von Berufsschauspielern aufgeführt wurden. Zugleich erfreuten sich bei den Laienbühnen unpolitische Unterhaltungsstücke wachsender Beliebtheit. Bei Kriegsbeginn (1914) auf dem Tiefpunkt angelangt, erlebte das politische A. nach der Novemberrevolution einen neuen Aufschwung; →proletarisch-revolutionäres Theater; →Arbeitertheater (USA).

Knilli, F./Münchow, U.: Frühes deutsches Arbeitertheater 1847–1918, eine Dokumentation. München 1970; Münchow, U. (Hg.): Aus den Anfängen der sozialistischen Dramatik, 2 Bde. Berlin 1964f; Rüden, P. v.: Sozialdemokratisches Arbeitertheater (1848–1914). Frankfurt/M. 1973.

Carl Wege

Arbeiter-Theater-Bund Deutschland (ATBD)

1906 schließen sich in Berlin mehrere Arbeiterlaienspiel-Bünde zum Bund der Theater- und Vergnügungsvereine Charlottenburgs zusammen. Nach Erweiterung 1908 in Bund der Arbeiter-Theater-Vereine Deutschland umbenannt (ab 1913: Dt. Arbeiter-Theater-Bund). Politisch eng verbunden mit den Zielen der dt. Sozialdemokratie, kamen klassische Dramen und Rührstücke zur Aufführung. Klassenkämpferische ‹Tendenzstücke› standen nicht auf dem Spielplan. Das sollte sich in der

2. Hälfte der 20er Jahre ändern, als die KPD begann, Einfluß auf die Entwicklung des Theater-Bunds zu nehmen: Aus einem Zusammenschluß sozialdemokratischer →Laienspiel-Bünde wurde ein Dachverband kommunistischer Agitprop-Truppen. 1928 erhielt die Organisation den Namen ATBD.

Knellessen, F. W.: Agitation auf der Bühne. Emsdetten 1970, S. 272–274; Rüden, P. v.: Sozialdemokratisches Arbeitertheater (1848–1914). Frankfurt/M. 1973, S. 176–209.

Carl Wege

Arbeitertheater (USA)

Abgesehen von punktuellen Einzelerscheinungen (z. B. dt. A. in Chicago 1880er/90er Jahre; →Paterson Pageant 1913) ist das amerik. proletarische Theater als kontinuierliche Praxis ein Produkt der 30er Jahre. Vorreiter waren auch in den 20er Jahren abermals Deutsche: John Bonn (Hans Bohn) gründete 1925 in New York die «Prolet-Bühne», die sich freilich erst in dem für A. günstigen Klima der ‹roten Dekade› nach der Weltwirtschaftskrise voll entfaltete. Die Agitprop-Sketche wie *Vote Communist, Miners are Striking, We Demand, 15 Minutes Red Revue* fußen auf Formen des sowj. wie des dt. Agitprop und kommen mit einfachsten Mitteln der Stilisierung aus. Immerhin gewann die Proletbühne 1932 den ersten Preis der ersten nationalen Arbeiter-Theater-Spartakiade der USA. Auch das linksintellektuelle →New Playwrights Theatre der späten 20er Jahre hatte – über den Verbindungsmann Michael Gold – seine Ursprünge im A., nämlich in der Workers' Drama League.

Ein durchgreifendes proletarisches →Massentheater entstand ab 1933 mit der →Theatre Union, das eingebunden war in eine von den Dramatikern A. Maltz und G. Sklar artikulierte Programmatik, wonach die Zukunft des amerik. Theaters in der Herausbildung eines A., bei den Arbeiterklubs, ethnischen Theatergruppen, beim Agitprop-Theater liege, weil nur in deren Inszenierungen das tatsächliche Leben der Menschen aussagekräftig behandelt werde. So erlebten die 30er Jahre die einmalige Blütezeit von Arbeiterlaienspielgruppen und halbprofessionellen Arbeiterschauspielkollektiven. Die Gruppen waren anfangs immer bewegliche Ensembles, gingen als Straßentheater vor die Fabriktore, in die Werkhallen und Versammlungen, zu den Streikpostenketten und in die Docks. In New York waren sie in der →League of Workers' Theatres zusammengefaßt oder arbeiteten direkt mit Gewerkschaften oder ethnisch-nationalen Vereinigungen zusammen. Innerhalb der Dachgewerkschaft American Federation of Labor (AFL) war es vor allem die International Ladies

96 Arbeitertheater (USA)

Garment Workers Union (ILGWU), die 1937 mit John Wexleys *Steel* (1931) die «Labor Stage» eröffnete. Die ILGWU verfügte bald über 63 Laienspielgruppen in 52 Städten. Der größte Erfolg der Labor Stage war die politische Revue *Pins and Needles*, die 1937 bis 1940 mit insgesamt 1105 Aufführungen ununterbrochen am Broadway lief – der Mangel an klassenkämpferischem Biß wurde durch humoristischen Schmiß, Tanz, Komik und Musikelemente aufgewogen.

Die Herausbildung der A.-Bewegung läßt sich nur hinreichend würdigen unter Berücksichtigung der fremdsprachigen Gruppen der nationalen Minderheiten. Es gab im ganzen Land verstreut die dramatischen Clubs der «foreign-born workers», die auf deutsch, italienisch, finnisch, schwedisch, litauisch, polnisch, russisch, ungarisch oder auch jiddisch soziale Dramen der naturalistischen Tradition am Leben erhielten, wenn diese aus der ‹Erstkultur› des kommerziellen Theaters längst verschwunden waren. In New York war es neben der Proletbühne vor allem das auf jiddisch spielende jüdische A. Artef, das seit 1926 zunehmend die Probleme der amerik. Arbeiterschaft aufnahm und halbprofessionell in abendfüllenden Stücken darstellte. Die Artef arbeitete eng mit der Kommunistischen Partei (CPUSA) und dem Gesangverein und Orchester ‹Freiheit› zusammen.

Das Repertoire des A. war um 1930 von einem Agitpropstil gekennzeichnet, der mit einem Minimum von Requisiten, roher Fabel und Charakterisierung, Tageslosungen und chorisch-rezitatorischem Sprechen (‹mass chant›) arbeitete, was alsbald zu Debatten über Ästhetik und Politik führte, die an die in den 20er Jahren in der Sowjetunion und Deutschland geführten Auseinandersetzungen um die Besonderheiten des proletarischen Theaters erinnerte. Doch in den USA wurden sektiererische und proletkultartige Tendenzen rasch überwunden, und im Verlauf der 30er Jahre läßt sich eine zunehmend künstlerische Qualität und Komplexität bei der Bewältigung sozialer und revolutionärer Inhalte feststellen. In Annäherung an die ‹Rote Revue› zeigt bereits 1934 die Montage des Workers' Laboratory Theatre, *Newsboy*, wie auf gekonnte Weise die Satire auf die kapitalistische Presse mit Musik, Tanz, Pantomime und Beleuchtungseffekten integriert wurde. Jazz, ‹mass chant› und Anklagen gegen Polizeiwillkür und Rassen-/Klassenjustiz verbinden sich wirkungsvoll im Drama *Scottsboro Limited* des Harlem Renaissance-Dichters Langston Hughes – damit ist auch eine sichtbare Verknüpfung des Theaters der Schwarzamerikaner mit den Klassenkämpfen der 30er Jahre aufgezeigt. In den →Living Newspapers verbinden sich schließlich die besten Formen des Agitprop mit Elementen des epischen Theaters zu einer höchst effektiven politischen Ästhetik.

Die Breite des klassenübergreifenden antifaschistischen Engagements hat zweifelsfrei dazu beigetragen, daß das A. in den 40er Jahren seine

Konturen verlor. Finanzprobleme führten zur Schließung vieler A., politische Zersplitterungen zur Auflösung mancher Gruppen des A. Ein auch in der Arbeiterbewegung sich ausbreitender Antistalinismus, der immer mehr und in neuerer Zeit zu einem hartnäckigen Antikommunismus und Antisowjetismus wurde, und die auf diesem Boden gedeihende Ideologie und Praxis des McCarthyismus sorgten dafür, daß die progressiven Theater-, Film- und Kulturschaffenden schlechthin zum Schweigen gebracht wurden. Daß sich auch in den 60er und 70er Jahren kein nennenswertes kontinuierliches A. neu entwickelte, hängt zu einem großen Teil mit der Erstarrung der amerik. Gewerkschaftsbewegung in den monolithischen Block AFL/CIO zusammen, innerhalb dessen der Antikommunismus fest verankert ist. Entsprechend versank die CPUSA seit den McCarthyistischen Razzien in völliger Bedeutungslosigkeit. Obgleich es punktuell zu Wiederbelebungen der ‹Labor Stage› gekommen ist, hat mit gewisser Kontinuität, wenn auch nicht massenhaft, das Straßentheater und →politische Volkstheater an das A. der 30er und frühen 40er Jahre angeknüpft. Vor allem wurden neben der tagespolitischen Agitation bestimmte Epochen und Themen der Geschichte der Arbeiterbewegung der USA dramatisch ausgeleuchtet, z. B. in *False Promises* (1976) und *Steeltown* (1984) der →San Francisco Mime Troupe oder in *Sacco and Vanzetti* und *Molly McGuires* des New York Street Theatre Caravan. Das konsequenteste A. der Jahre 1965 bis 1967 war dasjenige der mexikoamerik. Farmarbeiter in Kalifornien, →El Teatro Campesino.

Brüning, E.: Das amerik. Drama der dreißiger Jahre. Berling (DDR) 1966; Fröhlich, P.: Das nichtkommerzielle amerik. Theater. Rheinfelden 1974; Herms, D.: Agitprop USA. Zur Theorie und Strategie des politisch-emanzipatorischen Theaters in Amerika seit 1960. Kronberg 1973; Himelstein, M.: Drama Was a Weapon. The Left-Wing Theatre in New York, 1929–41. New Brunswick 1963; McDermott, D.: Agitprop: Production Practice in the Workers' Theatre, 1932 bis 42. In: Theatre Survey VII (1965), p. 115–124; Rabkin, G.: Drama and Commitment. Politics in the American Theatre of the Thirties. Bloomington 1964.

Dieter Herms

Arena Goldoni

Freilichttheater mit röm. Anklängen, erbaut im 19. Jh. in altem Kloster in Florenz. Von Edward Gordon Craig (1872–1966, engl. Schauspieler, Regisseur, Bühnenbildner und Theoretiker) zuerst als ‹Werkstatt› (Atelier, Theaterlaboratorium, Redaktion der Zeitschrift →«The Mask»), ab 1913–16 auch als Theaterschule genützt. Theaterforschung und -praxis aufs engste verbunden. Erprobung und Weiterentwicklung von Craigs

Theaterideen (Abkehr vom illusionistischen Theater; → Übermarionette; Kunst des Theaters: Gesamtheit aus Bewegung, Worten, Linie und Farben und aus dem Rhythmus).

Bablet, D.: Edward Gordon Craig. Paris 1962; dt.: Köln 1965; Craig, E. G.: A Living Theatre. The Gordon Craig School. The Arena Goldoni. The Mask. Setting forth the aims and objects of the movement and showing by many illustrations the city of Florence the Arena. Florenz 1913; ders: On the Art of the Theatre. London 1911; dt.: Über die Kunst des Theaters. Berlin 1969; Fiebach, J.: Von Craig bis Brecht. Studien zu Künstlertheorien des 20. Jhs. Berlin 1975; Fletcher, I. K./ Rood, A.: Edward Gordon Craig. A Bibliography. London 1967; Preißler-Lang, P.: Mensch und Material bei Edward Gordon Craig. Wien (Diss.) 1976.

Ingeborg Janich

Argumentum

Lat.: Gegenstand, Stoff, Inhalt; als Terminus bezeichnet A. den dramatisierten Stoff, die Fabel, über die der Zuschauer im antiken Drama oft im Prolog zusammenhängend und detailliert informiert wird (Hypothesis)

Bernd Seidensticker

Aristotelisches Theater

Im weiten Sinne: Die den Grundvorstellungen des Aristoteles *(Poetik)* folgende Tradition europäischen Theaters seit der Antike. Im engeren Sinne: In der Theatertheorie Brechts, der den Begriff a. T. geprägt hat, ein dem → epischen Theater entgegengesetzter Theatertypus. A. T. meint sowohl eine auf → Katharsis (Furcht und Mitleid) beruhende theatralische Wirkungsstrategie als auch eine auf Individualschicksale konzentrierte ‹geschlossene› Dramenform. Brechts Gegenüberstellung von aristotelischem und epischem Theater ist mehr polemische Zuspitzung als differenzierende theatergeschichtliche Wertung.

Brecht, B.: Schriften zum Theater (bes. *Der Messingkauf*, 1939/40, und *Kleines Organon für das Theater*, 1948). Berlin/Weimar 1964, und in: Gesammelte Werke, Bd. 15–17. Frankfurt/M. 1963; Rülicke-Weiler, K.: Die Dramaturgie Brechts. Berlin 1966; Klotz, V.: Geschlossene und offene Form im Drama. München 1969.

Manfred Pauli

Armes Theater

Dieser Begriff steht im Zentrum der Theaterkonzeption, die der poln. Theaterreformer Jerzy Grotowski (* 1933) im Zusammenhang mit der schauspielmethodischen Arbeit und den Inszenierungen des 1959 in Opole gegründeten und 1965 nach Wroclaw übersiedelten ‹Theater-Laboratoriums› entwickelt hat (Byrons *Kain, Kordian* nach Slowacky, Kalidasas *Shakuntala*, Adam Mickiewicz' *Totenfeier, Akropolis* nach Wyspanski, alle 1962; Marlowes *Doktor Faustus*, 1963; Calderóns *Standhafter Prinz*, 1965, und *Apokalypsis cum figuris* nach Motiven der Bibel, 1968). Im Gegensatz zum herrschenden ‹reichen Theater› mit seiner unvollkommenen Synthese der Einzelkünste und seiner wahllosen Anhäufung ihrer Zeichen, das mit seinem Versuch, in den technischen Mitteln Film und Fernsehen zu übertreffen, in die Sackgasse geraten ist, besinnt sich das A. T. auf die Grundstruktur, auf das, ‹was sich zwischen Schauspielern und Zuschauern abspielt›. Der Darsteller soll durch seine Ausdrucksmittel die übrigen Elemente des Theaters ersetzen; in seinem Körper soll das ‹totale Theater› entstehen.

Indem Grotowski sein Theater auf das beschränkt, ‹was aus dem Menschen selber kommt›, schafft er die Voraussetzung für die volle Entfaltung der schöpferischen Kräfte des Schauspielers. Ihm soll die Möglichkeit eröffnet werden, in einem ‹totalen Akt› sich selbst zu erkennen, zu offenbaren, zu befreien und dadurch auch den Zuschauer existentiell herauszufordern. In der Selbstoffenbarung des Schauspielers bietet sich die Möglichkeit, zu einer vom Publikum mitvollzogenen Erfahrung zu kommen, die in die psychischen Schichten unter der ‹Verhaltensmaske› dringt. In einer Zeit, in der die kollektiven Mythen ihre Gültigkeit verloren haben, kann allein das ‹Sensorium des menschlichen Organismus› seine ‹Entblößung bis zum äußersten Exzeß›, den Zugang zu universellen Wahrheiten eröffnen. Die überlieferten Mythen, die Grotowski in der dramatischen Weltliteratur aufgehoben sieht, können nur mehr als stoffliche Basis dienen, als ‹Trampolin› für die Selbstoffenbarung des Schauspielers. Die Fähigkeit dazu erwirbt der Darsteller durch die Überwindung von körperlichen Hindernissen, die einer direkten Umsetzung psychischer Impulse entgegenstehen (‹Via negativa›). Durch den Vollzug von Übungen, die der Schauspieler entsprechend seinen individuellen Schwierigkeiten aus einem Kanon auswählt, den Grotowski (zum Teil unter Rückgriff auf traditionelle europ. und asiat. Techniken) entwickelt hat, wird sein Körper von allen Widerständen befreit. Der Schauspieler wird ihn dann nicht exhibitionistisch ‹ausstellen›, nicht ‹verkaufen›, sondern ‹aufopfern›; er wird ein ‹Sühneopfer› vollziehen, der ‹Heiligkeit nahekommen›.

In der Begegnung mit dem Zuschauer muß der spontane Selbstausdruck des Schauspielers eine Disziplinierung erfahren; es müssen Zeichen gefunden werden. Im Gegensatz zu Antonin Artauds →Theater der Grausamkeit, dem Grotowskis Entwurf in seinem Rekurs auf den Mythos und das Unterbewußte nahesteht, orientiert sich das A. T. nicht an dem Vorbild der feststehenden Zeichen des fernöstlichen Theaters, sondern am Prinzip der ‹Ideogramme›, die ‹skelettierte Formen menschlicher Aktionen› sind. In den Inszenierungen Grotowskis sind diese Zeichen oft geprägt von denen der christlichen Heilsgeschichte; es sind die Gesten der Peinigung, des Leidens, der Verzweiflung und die Gesten der Verklärung und der Erlösung.

Die Konzeption des A. T. und die daraus resultierende Schauspielmethodik beeinflußten viele Theatergruppen in Westeuropa und in den USA (etwa Eugenio Barbas →Odin Teatret, das →Living Theatre und das →La Mama Theatre). Das →‹Theater-Laboratorium› wurde 1984 endgültig aufgelöst, nachdem es sich schon zehn Jahre vorher in Projektgruppen aufgespalten hatte, die sich vor allem ‹paratheatralen› Aktionen widmen, bei denen die Grundstruktur des Theaters aufgehoben ist. Grotowski selbst beschäftigte sich mit einem ‹Theater der Quellen› genannten Unternehmen, in dessen Rahmen Rituale und spirituelle Techniken in ihrer transkulturellen Bedeutung erforscht und praktisch erkundet werden. Nach längeren Reisen, u. a. durch Indien und Haiti, arbeitete Grotowski 1983–84 an der Universität von Irvine/Kalifornien an einem Projekt «Objektives Drama». Seit 1985 leitet er ein Theaterzentrum im Pontedera bei Florenz, wo er sich mit «Rituellen Künsten» beschäftigt. In beiden Fällen stehen erneut u. a. Voodoo-Praktiken, chassidische Tänze, nigerianische Yoruba-Riten, mexikanische Huichol-Bräuche und Meditationsübungen des Zen im Mittelpunkt.

Grotowski, J.: Das arme Theater. Velber 1969/1986; Schwerin von Krosigk, B.: Der nackte Schauspieler. Berlin 1985.

Peter Simhandl/Annette Waldmann

Arte

Ursprünglich eine dän. Theaterzentrale der Arbeiter, die 1946 in Anlehnung an die dt. →«Freie Volksbühne» gegründet wurde mit dem Ziel, das Interesse der Arbeiter für das Theater zu fördern und ihnen seriöse Theaterkunst zum günstigen Preis anzubieten. Vorstellungen wurden gekauft, so daß im Gegensatz zu heute die A. Einfluß auf das Repertoire hatte. Untersuchungen haben gezeigt, daß das Desinteresse der Arbeiter am Theater sowohl in einer kulturellen Stagnation (Arbejdernes Teater und Revolutionaert Teater hatten ihre Tätigkeit 1938 aufgeben müssen, und vielen anderen Privattheatern ging es schlecht) als auch in der Kostenfrage seine Ursache hatte. Am Anfang richteten sich die Angebote von der A. nur an Gewerkschaften und sozialdemokratische Verbände etc., aber allmählich wandte sich die Organisation auch an breitere Bevölkerungsschichten. Seit 1965 ist die A. ausschließlich eine Abonnement-Serviceorganisation, die durch eine 50prozentige öffentliche Unterstützung ermäßigte Karten an alle am Theater Interessierten vermittelt; seit 1973 als überregionale Institution, die jährlich über eine Mio. Karten verteilt. Diese Regelung bildet die finanzielle Grundlage vieler Privattheater und trägt zur Konjunktur des Theaterlebens in Dänemark bei (es gibt mehr als 80 professionelle Theater). Die A. veranstaltet auch Konzerte, Lesungen etc. und hat dadurch eine gewisse Monopolstellung für Kulturvermittlung im ganzen Land erworben.

Arte: Perspektiv og forslag. København 1979; Langsted, J.: Dansk teaterdebat omkring 1968. Gråsten 1978; ders.: Teaterlovgivning I–II. Gråsten 1981–82; ders.: Styr på teatret. Gråsten 1984; Nørgaard, U. u. a.: En demokratiseret teatergang? DSF-Tryk 1975; Observa: Undersøgelse blandt Arteabonnenter. København 1978; Theatre in Denmark: 1–15. København 1965–1980.

Else Kjær

Arte Nuevo de hacer Comedias en este Tiempo

Die *Neue Kunst, in dieser Zeit Schauspiele zu schreiben* von Lope Félix de Vega Carpio (1562–1635) ist die maßgebliche Poetik des → ‹Siglo de Oro› (Goldenes Zeitalter), der eine ähnlich normierende Funktion wie Nicolas Boileaus (1636–1711) *L'Art Poétique* (1674) zukam (→ Comedia). Im Gegensatz zu Boileau orientierte sich Lope de Vega in den 376 Elfsilblern seiner Poetik jedoch nicht an den humanistischen Gattungspoetiken im Gefolge Aristoteles' (384–322 v. Chr.) und Horaz' (65–8 v. Chr.), sondern entwickelte unter Berufung auf den Geschmack des Publikums und die Regeln der Natur eigene Kriterien: die Einteilung in drei statt fünf Akte, den Wechsel metrischer Formen, der dem jeweiligen Inhalt angepaßt war (Romanzenvers für beschreibende Partien, Sonette für Monologe, Décimas für Klagen usw.), die Mischung des → Tragisch-Komischen, Freiheit in der Anwendung der → drei Einheiten (Ort, Zeit, Handlung), Einführung der lustigen Person (→ Gracioso), die vorher nur als Tölpel vorgezeichnet war, Sprachdifferenzierung je nach sozialem Status, voll ausgeführte Nebenrollen, Handlungsstoff wichtiger als psychologische Durchfeilung der Charaktere u. a.

Neuschäfer, H.-J.: Lope de Vega und der Vulgo. In: Span. Lit. im Goldenen Zeitalter – Fritz Schalk zum 70. Geburtstag. Frankfurt/M. 1973, S. 338–356; Romera-

Navarro, M.: La preceptiva dramática de Lope de Vega y otros ensayos sobre el Fénix. Madrid 1935.

Martin Franzbach

ASSITEJ

Association internationale du Théâtre pour l'Enfance et la Jeunesse. – Die A. ist die internationale Vereinigung der →Kinder- und →Jugendtheater. Sie fördert die Entwicklung und Verbreitung des Kinder- und Jugendtheaters sowie deren Kontakte untereinander. Organisiert in 40 nationalen Zentren (Sektionen), hat die A.-Sektion Bundesrepublik e. V. ihren Sitz in Duisburg. Ordentliche Mitglieder sind 69 Theater, Gruppen und Verlage etc. sowie 123 assoziierte Mitglieder.

Genossenschaft Deutscher Bühnen-Angehöriger (Hg.): Deutsches Bühnen-Jahrbuch 1985. Hamburg 1984.

Ute Hagel

Atellana

Lat. Adjektiv, zu ergänzen ‹fabula›; unterital., im oskischen Sprachraum unter etruskischem und vor allem griech. Einfluß (→Phlyakenposse) entstandenes, derbkomisches, kurzes Stegreifspiel, das seinen Namen von der kampanischen Stadt Atella hat. Die A. wurde mit Masken gespielt und arbeitete mit einem festen Repertoire von Stoffen, Motiven und Typen: der gefräßige Dümmling (Maccus), der pausbäckige, kahlköpfige Hanswurst (Bucco), der einfältige Alte (Pappus) und der verfressene, bucklige Schlaumeier (Dossenus oder auch Manducus); die A. wurde bereits im 3. Jh. auch in Rom populär und hat auf die röm. Komödie, vor allem auf Plautus, stark gewirkt; ihre literarische Blüte erlebte sie zu Beginn des 1. Jh. v. Chr.; in Analogie zum Satyrspiel wurde die A. auch als komisches Nachspiel (Exodium) für Tragödienaufführungen verwendet.

Frassinetti, P.: Fabula Atellana, Saggio sul teatro populare latino. Genua 1953; Rieks, R.: Mimus und Atellane. In: E. Lefèvre (Hg.): Das römische Drama. Darmstadt 1978, S. 348–377.

Bernd Seidensticker

Aufführung

Szenisch-spielerische Darstellung vor Zuschauern durch Schauspieler auf der Grundlage eines dramatischen Textes oder einer freien (evtl. selbst erarbeiteten) Spielvorlage, meist unter Leitung des →Regisseurs nach einer Reihe von →Proben. Für den techn. einwandfreien Ablauf einer A. ist der →Inspizient verantwortlich. – Die erste öffentliche A. heißt →Premiere, der eine oder mehrere Vor-A. vorausgehen können, bei denen (im Gegensatz zur →Generalprobe) Publikum zugelassen, ein kritisches Echo durch Presse und andere Medien (im Gegensatz zur Premiere) nicht erwünscht wird. Vor-A. werden vor allem angesetzt, um den Übergang zwischen Arbeitsprozeß und A. zu erleichtern, evtl. den Zuschauern die Gelegenheit zur Diskussion und Kritik zu bieten und deren Resultate für Veränderungen an der →Inszenierung aufzunehmen. – Die erste A. eines zuvor nie gezeigten Werks heißt Ur-A. (abgekürzt: U oder UA), die erste Wiedergabe eines im Original bereits gespielten Stücks in der Übersetzung Erst-A. (abgekürzt mit Hinweis auf die jeweilige Sprache: DE oder DEA, auch dEA für dt. Erst-A.). Erst-A. (E) kann ebenso die erste Darbietung in einem best. Theater oder einer best. Stadt bedeuten. Wiederaufnahme (WA) meint die Darbietung einer nach zeitlicher Unterbrechung erneut vorgestellten A. in meist unveränderter Form, Neuinszenierung (NI) die A. eines an dem betreffenden Theater schon gespielten Stücks mit neuer Besetzung, Ausstattung und Regie. – A. wird z. T. synonym für die einzelne →Vorstellung einer Inszenierung sowie für die Inszenierung selbst verwendet.

Goldbaum, W.: Der A.-Vertrag. Berlin 1912; Henzel, N.: Das A.-Recht von Bühnen- und Tonkunstwerken. Diss. Würzburg 1920; Klemmig, R.: Möglichkeiten und Grenzen der Organisation einer Theater-A. Diss. Berlin 1956; Williams, R.: Drama in Performance. London ² 1968.

Monika Sandhack

Aufklärung / Theater der Aufklärung

Die Aufklärung ist die (kultur)politisch und sozioökonomisch wichtigste Strömung des 18. Jh. in Europa. Vereinfacht gesagt, ist sie der Versuch des wirtschaftlich erstarkenden Bürgertums, auch auf politischem und kulturellem Gebiet die herrschende Schicht zu werden und eigene Werte und Normen als verbindlich zu setzen. Es ist eine der wenigen Epochen, die sich selbst als Prozeß, als dynamische Entwicklung begriff. – Aufklärung als «Ausgang des Menschen aus seiner selbstverschuldeten Unmündigkeit» (Kant) war bereits bei den Zeitgenossen mit der Metaphorik des

Lichts, der Klarheit verbunden. Durch die unterschiedliche Entwicklung der europäischen Staaten fand dieser Prozeß nicht überall gleichzeitig statt, sondern begann in den ökonomisch am weitesten entwickelten Ländern Holland, England, Frankreich und breitete sich dann in Deutschland und dem übrigen Europa aus. Vorläufer reichen bis ins 17. Jh. zurück, Ausläufer bestimmen noch das frühe 19. Jh. Zumindest theoretisch umfaßte die Aufklärung alle Lebensbereiche. Überall sollte Vernunft an die Stelle unbefragter Traditionen treten, überall sollte Kritik, die Suche nach der ‹Wahrheit› die Menschen aufklären, besser und glücklicher machen. Daß die unbedingte Herrschaft des Verstandes immanent Probleme mit sich führte, daß die Verhältnisse Abstriche vom Ideal und Kompromisse mit den herrschenden Mächten verlangten, kann hier nur festgestellt werden.

Die Aufklärung war eine eminent pädagogische Zeit. So ist es kein Wunder, daß das Theater in der Aufklärung eine entscheidende Rolle spielte. Allerdings war auch die Lage des Theaters in den europ. Ländern unterschiedlich. Während in Italien der Kampf um die →Commedia dell'arte, ihre Improvisationen und typisierten Masken im Mittelpunkt von Auseinandersetzungen stand, setzte sich in Frankreich das klassizistische Theater durch, wenn sich daneben auch das von der Commedia dell'arte beeinflußte ‹Théâtre Italien› (→Comédie Italienne) lange Zeit noch zu behaupten wußte. Gab es in England längst ständige Theater und eine etablierte Schauspielkunst, sahen die Verhältnisse in den politisch zerrissenen, wirtschaftlich eher rückständigen dt. Einzelstaaten völlig anders aus. Neben Resten des →Jesuitentheaters und einer letzten Blüte des →Schultheaters sowie zumeist von frz. oder ital. Schauspielern und Sängern bespielten Hoftheatern gab es dt. Schauspieler bis weit ins 18. Jh. nur als Wandertruppen, deren wirtschaftliche und soziale Lage zumeist desolat war, die – von der Kirche diskriminiert und von großen Teilen der Bevölkerung mißachtet – lediglich kurzfristig die Erlaubnis zum Theaterspielen in den Städten erhielten. Die von ihnen aufgeführten Stücke waren zumeist →Haupt- und Staatsaktionen mit komischen Nachspielen.

Die Bemühungen dt. Aufklärer um das Theater begannen mit Versuchen, die dt. Schaubühne zu heben, ihre Stücke ‹regelmäßig› zu machen, die wirtschaftliche und soziale Lage der Schauspieler zu verbessern. Denn nur auf dieser Grundlage konnte das Theater die Funktion erfüllen, die ihm nun zugewiesen wurde. Gleichgültig, ob man es als «weltliche Kanzel» (Gottsched), als «Schule der moralischen Welt» (Lessing) oder als «moralische Anstalt» (Schiller) bezeichnete, gemeint war immer dasselbe: Theater sollte lehren, bilden, bessern. Über die Idee eines →«Nationaltheaters» sollte es schließlich zur Entwicklung einer kulturellen Identität und einer politischen Nation der Deutschen beitragen.

«Docere» – «delectare» – «movere» (lehren – erfreuen – rühren) wa-

Aufklärung / Theater der Aufklärung   105

ren seit der Antike immer wieder an das Theater gestellte Forderungen. Indem den bislang gespielten Theaterstücken die Fähigkeit dazu abgesprochen wurde und die Aufklärer sich bemühten, durch ein systematisches Regelwerk theoretische Grundlagen für neue Stücke zu entwickeln, versuchten sie im Rückgriff auf antike Dichtungstheorie ein zeitgemäßes Theater zu schaffen. In den verschiedenen Ländern geschah dies auf unterschiedliche Weise. Im zentralistisch organisierten Frankreich wurde Theater bereits im 17. Jh. von staatlicher Seite und im Interesse des Absolutismus gefördert. In dieser Zeit wurden die theoretischen Grundlagen für die klassizistische Tragödie gelegt (d'Aubignac, Boileau u. a.) und von Dramatikern umgesetzt. Hinzu trat mit Molière ein früher Höhepunkt in der Entwicklung der Komödie.

Bei den dt. Versuchen, dem Theater mehr Regelmäßigkeit zu geben, ist an erster Stelle der Leipziger Professor Gottsched zu nennen, dessen Bemühungen – unhistorisch betrachtet – bis heute gern unterschätzt werden. In der Dramentheorie, die sich in seiner *Critischen Dichtkunst* (1730 u. ö.) findet, ging er aus von der antiken Dichtungslehre und der darauf beruhenden frz. klassizistischen Dramatik. Um das ästhetische Urteil als ‹objektiv› erscheinen zu lassen, mußten die von ihm aufgestellten Regeln als «Aussprüche der gesunden Vernunft» aus der Sache selbst hervorgehen. Dann genügte es, die Befolgung der Regeln zu überprüfen, um über die Güte eines Dramas urteilen zu können. Zu diesen Regeln gehörte die Lehre von den →drei Einheiten (des Ortes, der Zeit und der Handlung) und die sog. →Ständeklausel. Gottsched verpflichtete die Tragödie auf einen moralischen Zweck. Daraus leitete er ab, wie eine regelrechte Tragödie zu verfertigen sei, die Schrecken und Mitleid erwecken und das Gemüt der Zuschauer «auf eine der Tugend gemäße Weise» erregen kann. Die Komödie hingegen ist, so Gottsched, «nichts anders als eine Nachahmung einer lasterhaften Handlung, die . . . den Zuschauer belustigen, aber auch zugleich erbauen kann». – Zum gereinigten Theater paßte weder das damals übliche Extemporieren noch die Figur, die für all das Unregelmäßige der traditionellen Bühne stand: der Hanswurst. Die theoretischen Interessen Gottscheds trafen sich mit praktischen der ‹Neuberin›, der bekanntesten Prinzipalin ihrer Zeit, die auf ihrer Bühne programmatisch beides abschaffte: Improvisation und Harlekin. Die weitere Entwicklung der Dramentheorie der Aufklärung zeigte in den meisten Ländern bei aller Verschiedenheit im Detail eine ähnliche Grundtendenz: die Annäherung der Genres. Die klassizistische Tragödie entwickelte sich zum «genre sérieux» (Diderot) und zur →Tragikomödie, die Komödie wurde zum «weinerlichen Lustspiel» (comédie larmoyante, sentimental comedy) und zum →bürgerlichen Trauerspiel.

In der Mitte des 18. Jh. hatte sich die Komödie so weit entfaltet, daß sie auch ernsthafte Stoffe mit dem bürgerlichen Personal behandeln konnte,

106 Aufklärung / Theater der Aufklärung

das die Ständeklausel von der Tragödie fernhielt. Entwickelten sich in England die →«sentimental comedy» und das bürgerliche Trauerspiel ohne vorhergehende systematische Theorie, so bedurfte in Ländern, in denen das (gehobene) Bürgertum nicht in gleichem Maße einflußreich war, die Entwicklung der neuen Genres theoretischer Grundlegung. Häufig waren es Dramatiker, die Theorien schrieben, bzw. Theoretiker, die zum Beleg ihrer Thesen Stücke verfaßten. Beispiele hierfür sind Denis Diderot, der den Abdruck seiner Dramen mit der Theorie des von ihm angestrebten «genre sérieux» verband, und Gotthold Ephraim Lessing, der das erste dt. bürgerliche Trauerspiel verfaßte und eine der ersten Komödien im modernen Sinn.

Diderots Einfluß auf die Entwicklung des Theaters war in Deutschland letztlich nachhaltiger als in Frankreich. Er lehnte die klassizistische Tragödie ab, weil sie keinen Bezug zur Wirklichkeit hatte; auch die Durchführung der drei Einheiten war für ihn nicht mehr entscheidend. Er wollte ein ernsthaftes Genre zwischen Tragödie und Komödie, das er als «genre sérieux», schließlich einfach als «drame» bezeichnete. Unter anderem auf Diderot berief sich Lessing bei seiner Dramentheorie. Er ging aus von der gesellschaftlichen Funktion des Theaters und zielte auf ein Drama, in dem die ständische Zugehörigkeit belanglos wird gegenüber der allgemeinen Menschlichkeit. Er untermauerte seine Ansichten durch eine Neuinterpretation der aristotelischen →Katharsis-Lehre. Im Gegensatz zu der von Gottsched geforderten Erregung von Furcht und Schrecken beim Zuschauer ging es Lessing in der Tragödie um die Verwandlung von Mitleid und Furcht in tugendhafte Fertigkeiten. Diese kollektive Katharsis gelingt jedoch nur, wenn sich der Zuschauer durch Illusion und Identifikation an die Stelle des leidenden Helden setzen kann. – Sollte die Tragödie die Fähigkeit, Mitleid zu fühlen, beim Zuschauer erweitern, so sah Lessing die Funktion der Komödie darin, daß durch sie das Publikum alles Lächerliche wahrnehmen kann und über dessen Vermeidung auf dem Wege zum ‹gesitteten› Menschen fortschreitet. Theater wird so «Schule der Menschlichkeit».

Die antizipatorisch-utopische Komponente der Lessingschen Theorie konnte in seiner Gegenwart nicht realisiert werden. Das bürgerliche Trauerspiel wie die neue Form der Komödie können deshalb auch verstanden werden als moralische Kompensation der sozialen und politischen Machtlosigkeit des Bürgertums.

Arntzen, H.: Die ernste Komödie. München 1968; Boeschenstein, H.: Dichtungstheorien der Aufklärung. Tübingen 1971; Burwick, F.: Illusion and the Drama. University Park 1991; Daunicht, R.: Die Entstehung des bürgerlichen Trauerspiels in Deutschland. Berlin 1963; Guthke, K. S.: Das bürgerliche Trauerspiel. Stuttgart 1972; Haider-Pregler, H.: Des sittlichen Bürgers Abendschule. Wien / München 1980; Hinck, W.: Das deutsche Lustspiel des 17. und 18. Jahrhunderts und die italienische Komödie. Stuttgart 1965; ders.: Theater der Hoffnung. Frankfurt/M. 1988; Koopmann, H.: Drama der Aufklärung. München 1979; Krauss, W.: Perspektiven und Probleme. Zur französischen und deutschen Aufklärung und andere Aufsätze. Neuwied, Berlin 1965; Krebs, R./Valentin, J.-M. (Hg.): Théâtre, Nation & Société en Allemagne au XVIIIe Siècle. Nancy 1990; Martino, A.: Geschichte der dramatischen Theorien in Deutschland im 18. Jahrhundert. Bd. 1: Die Dramaturgie der Aufklärung 1730–1780. Tübingen 1978; Michelsen, P.: Der unruhige Bürger. Würzburg 1990; Pütz, P.: Die deutsche Aufklärung. Darmstadt 1978; Schings, H.-J.: Der mitleidigste Mensch ist der beste Mensch. Poetik des Mitleids von Lessing bis Büchner. München 1980; Schulz, G.-M.: Tugend, Gewalt und Tod. Tübingen 1988; Steinmetz, H.: Das deutsche Drama von Gottsched bis Lessing. Stuttgart 1987; ders.: Die Komödie der Aufklärung. Stuttgart [2]1971; Szondi, P.: Die Theorie des bürgerlichen Trauerspiels im 18. Jahrhundert. Hg. von G. Mattenklott. Frankfurt/M. 1973; Wölfel, K.: Moralische Anstalt. Zur Dramaturgie von Gottsched bis Lessing. In: Grimm, R. (Hg.): Deutsche Dramentheorien. Bd. I. Wiesbaden [3]1980, S. 56–122.

Wolfgang Beck

Auftritt

Zunächst das Erscheinen eines Schauspielers auf dem Theater zu Beginn seiner Bühnenlaufbahn, seit dem 17. Jh. die durch Auf- und Abtreten der Darsteller gegliederten Abschnitte eines →Akts. Im deutschsprachigen Theater des 18. Jh. vielfach gleichbedeutend mit Szene als der kleinsten dramatischen Einheit innerhalb eines →Dramas oder →Aktes vom Erscheinen bis zum Abgehen einer oder mehrerer Figuren; damit Veränderung der dramatischen Situation, in der Regel aber kein Schauplatzwechsel. Die Gliederung der Akte in Szenen bzw. Auftritte bleibt bis ins 19. Jh. die typische Form des streng gebauten Dramas.

Monika Sandhack

Ausdruckstanz

Die Entwicklung des A., Freien Tanzes oder German Dance läuft in Deutschland parallel mit allgemeinen Reformbestrebungen zu Beginn des 20. Jh.: Jugendbewegung, Wandervogel, Bohème, Körperkultur. Gesucht wird nach neuen Lebensinhalten als Reaktion auf erstarrte bürgerliche Konventionen.

Die amerikanische Tänzerin Isadora Duncan (1877–1927; →Modern Dance), die 1902/03 in Berlin gastiert, gilt als Pionierin der deutschen Reformtanzbewegung. Sie lehnt die klassisch-akademische Ballett-Technik als Verfestigung ab. Die Duncan tritt barfuß in leicht wehendem Gewand vor das Publikum. Ihre Tänze drängen expressiv-vehement auf Emotionen und Stimmungen. Ihr Repertoire wirkt auf Zuschauer revolutionierend und befreiend. Sie nutzt expressionistische Stilmittel, glaubt aber, im Sinne des antiken Geistes- und Lebensgefühls zu gestalten.

Zentrum des A. ist der Monte Verità, eine Kolonie damaliger Lebensreformer und Avantgarde-Künstler im schweizerischen Ascona. Auf dem Monte Verità arbeiten u. a. Rudolf von Laban (1879–1958; →Labanschulen) und Mary Wigman (1886–1973). Labans Tanztechnik und die aus ihr sich entwickelnde Tanzlehre bauen auf einer vom Grunde aus ethischen Lebensführung des Menschen, seinen geistigen Haltungen und Vorstellungsbildern auf. Deshalb sucht Laban Tanzformen, die die Gestaltung eines einfachen harmonischen Lebens spiegeln, und ist bemüht, überdeckte rituelle Handlungen, die ehemals den Menschen in Natur und All einbanden (→Ritualtänze), wiederzubeleben. Laban erkennt, daß Technik und Industrialisierung die Verbundenheit des Menschen mit seiner Umwelt schmerzhaft zerstören. In seinen von →Bewegungschören gestalteten Freilicht- und Hallenaufführungen sucht er ein philosophisch-anthropologisches Programm zu verwirklichen. Eine dieser Freilichtaufführungen, *Der Sang an die Sonne*, ist z. B. ein zwölfstündiges Weihespiel.

Neben Laban bewährt sich in der phantasievollen und ausdrucksstarken choreographischen Realisation von Weihespielen seine Assistentin Mary Wigman. Sie setzt in Ascona und Zürich während der Kriegsjahre 1914–18 Labans Ideen einfühlsam in Tanzgebärden und Szenarien um. M. Wigman kommt aus →Hellerau, wo sie bei Dalcroze ihr Rhythmik-Examen absolviert hat. Weniger zur Musik, aber voll zum Tanz tendierend, hofft die Expressionistin, bei Laban ein erweitertes Ausdrucks- und Gestaltungsrepertoire zu finden. Auf Grund ihrer intensiven geistigen Auseinandersetzung mit Labans Tanzphilosophie gelangt M. Wigman zu einem eigenständigen dramatisch-expressiven Stil, der vor allem naturhafte Bewegungen: Stampfen, Knien, Fallen, bewußt akzentuiert und mit der Atemführung verbindet. M. Wigman greift über bloße Darstellungen von persönlichen Empfindungen weit hinaus und konstituiert kompromißlos das durchkomponierte Tanzkunstwerk ohne Handlung mit transzendenter Sinngebung und symbolistischen Tendenzen: *Die sieben Tänze des Lebens* (1921), *Tänze des Schweigens* (1920–23), *Raumgesänge* (1926), *Schwingende Landschaft* (1929); die Aufzüge «Wanderung», «Kreis», «Dreieck», «Chaos» des *Tanzdramas* (1923/24), *Das Opfer* (1931), *Der Weg* (1932). Zu ihren Schülern zählten u. a. Hanya Holm (*1893), Yvonne Georgi (1903–1975), Harald Kreutzberg (1902–1968), Gret Palucca (*1902), Max Terpis (1889–1958) und Margarete Wallmann (1904–92), die mit ihrem individuellen Stil den Aus-

H. Kreutzberg: «Gesang der Nacht» (TS)

Tanzbühne Laban Hamburg, 1922 (Th)

K. Joos: Szene aus «Der Grüne Tisch», 1932 (Die Schwarzen Herren) (RP)

M. Wigman in «Totentanz», 1926 (LR)

Bewegungschorische Studie. Lola Rogge, Hamburg um 1927 (LR)

D. Hoyer in «Frühlingsweihe», 1957. Inszenierung: M. Wigman (TS)

druckstanz in seinen vielfältigen, facettenreichen Erscheinungsformen maßgeblich mitbestimmten. In Dore Hoyer (1911–67), einer überragenden Tanzbegabung und ausgesprochenen Individualistin, deren Tänze durch formale Klarheit und Strenge überzeugten und vom emotionalen Pathos der ersten Ausdruckstanzgeneration abstrahierten, sah Mary Wigman ihr Erbe am adäquatesten weitergeführt. Dore Hoyer war nie Schülerin von Wigman gewesen, hat aber 1935 in deren Gruppe mitgetanzt und 1957 in Wigmans Inszenierung von *Sacre du Printemps* (Mus.: Strawinsky) den Part der Auserwählten gestaltet.

In gleichem Bestreben erweitert Kurt Jooss (1901–78; →Ballets Jooss) die Kreationen des deutschen A. und später des Modernen Tanzes. Auch er ist Laban-Schüler und -Assistent. Die Forderung nach der Verschmelzung von klassischer Technik und A., für die er mit einem Vortrag auf dem Tänzer-Kongreß 1928 in Essen eintrat, wird in der Gestaltungspraxis in eigenwilligen genialen choreographischen Entwürfen verwirklicht (→Tanztheater; →Choreodrama).

Boehn, M. v.: Der Tanz. Berlin 1925; Koegler, H.: Aus Rhythmus geboren, zum Tanzen bestellt – Hellerau-Laxenburg und die Anfänge des modernen Tanzes. In: Ballett (Jahrbuch) 1977, S. 40–51; Lämmel, R.: Der Moderne Tanz. Berlin-Schöneberg o. J.; Maack, R.: Tanz in Hamburg. Hamburg 1975; M. Müller/F.-M. Peter/G. Schuldt: Dore Hoyer. Berlin 1992; Schikowski, Geschichte des Tanzes. Berlin 1926.

Patricia Stöckemann

Ausstattungsstück

Bühnenwerk, das mehr durch prunkvolle Ausstattung als durch Handlungsgehalt wirken soll. Heute vor allem →Revuen, Operetten, →Musical. – Aufwendige, illusionserhöhende Ausstattung durch Bühnenbild, Kostüme, Theatermaschinerie vor allem im →Barocktheater: Gewitter, Regen, Blitz, Feuerwerk und Wasserspiele, Einsatz von Schiffen, Fluggeräten unterhalten das Publikum. Auch besondere Aufführungsorte (Parkanlagen, Schloßhöfe) betonen den aufwendigen ‹Festspiel›-Charakter. Die Haupt- und Staatsaktionen der dt. →Wanderbühnen des 17./18. Jh., die →Zauberposse und das Märchendrama sind weitere Beispiele. Film und Fernsehen haben im 20. Jh. das ‹Show-business› des A. weiter perfektioniert.

Horst Schumacher

Auto Sacramental

Meist einaktige (→Einakter) Stücke (1500 bis 2000 Verse) mit allegorischen Figuren, bei denen das Mysterium der Eucharistie oder der Erlösung im Mittelpunkt stand. Seit der Einrichtung des Fronleichnamfestes durch Papst Urban IV. (1263) gab es →Prozessionen, →Mysterienspiele und →Moralitäten an diesem Tage. Der Terminus ‹auto› (von actu = Handlung) existiert erst seit Anfang 16. Jh. Erstes Vorkommen bei Lucas Fernández (1474?–1542), Gil Vicente (1465?–1536?), Juan de Timoneda (?–1583). Blütezeit im 17. Jh. bei Lope Félix de Vega Carpio (1562–1635), Antonio Mira de Amescua (1574/77–1644), José de Valdivielso (1560?–1638), Pedro Calderón de la Barca (1600–81). Aufführungen unter Musikbegleitung auf Wagen (carros), die von Ochsen gezogen wurden. Das Verbot der ‹autos› am 11.6.1765 wegen ihrer vielen Unwahrscheinlichkeiten kurz vor dem Verbot des Jesuitenordens in Spanien (1767) spricht für die Beliebtheit der Gattung beim Volk noch im 18. Jh. Versuche der Wiederbelebung im 20. Jh. durch Rafael Alberti (*1902), Miguel Hernández (1910–42) u. a.

Dietz, D. Th.: The Auto sacramental and the Parable in Spanish Golden Age Literature. Chapel Hill 1973; Gewecke, F.: Themat. Untersuchungen zu dem vorcalderonianischen ‹Auto Sacramental›. Genève/Köln 1974.

Martin Franzbach

Avantgarde

(Frz. ‹Vorhut›) Ursprünglich militärischer Begriff, seit Ende des 19. Jh. Bezeichnung für jeweils neueste literarische und künstlerische Bewegung, die in Form und Inhalt in Opposition zu herrschenden und bestehenden Richtungen tritt. So wurden mit ihren radikalen Neuerungen zur A. gezählt: Expressionismus, Surrealismus, →Absurdes Theater, →Happening, →Living Theatre usw. Während im westlichen Sprachgebrauch A. eine positive Bewertung bedeutet, wird ‹Avantgardismus› von marxistischen Theaterkritikern als abwertende Charakterisierung für rein formalistische Neuerungssucht benutzt.

Bürger, P.: Theorie der Avantgarde. Frankfurt/M. 1974; Avantgarde. Geschichte und Krise einer Idee. Hg. v. d. Bayerischen Akademie der Schönen Künste. München 1966; Kofler, L.: Zur Theorie der modernen Literatur. Neuwied 1902; Lüdke, M. (Hg.): «Theorie der Avantgarde». Antworten auf Peter Bürgers Bestimmung von Kunst und bürgerlicher Gesellschaft. Frankfurt/M. 1976; Lukács, G.: Schriften zur Literatursoziologie. Neuwied 1961; Poggioli, R.: Teoria dell'arte d'avanguardia. Bologna 1962.

Horst Schumacher

Bad Hersfelder Festspiele

1951 wurden unter der Schirmherrschaft des damaligen Bundespräsidenten Theodor Heuss die «Hersfelder Festspiele» gegr. In einer der ältesten dt. romanischen Kirchenruinen, der Stiftskirche aus dem 11. Jh., finden alljährlich im Juli/August vor 2200 Plätzen Aufführungen modernen (Camus, Brecht, Dürrenmatt) und klassischen (Goethe, Shakespeare) Theaters statt, neben Sprechtheater neuerdings auch Musicals. Die über 3000 m^2 große Bühne bietet vielfältige Spielmöglichkeiten und verfügt über eine ausgezeichnete Akustik. Intendant: Dr. Peter Lotschak.

Ute Hagel/Red.

Balagan

(Russ. Schaubude) Seit Mitte des 18. Jh. in Rußland bekannt als temporäre Bühne für Theater- und Zirkusvorstellungen. Repertoire anfangs →Volksstücke, Inszenierungen von Ritterromanen; im 19. Jh. hauptsächlich mit starken Bühneneffekten ausgestattete Harlekinaden. Wichtig der in der Tradition der →Skomorochen stehende Ausrufer (djedrajoschnik), dessen gereimte Monologe nicht selten Ausfälle gegen die Herrschenden enthielt. 1880 in Petersburg Organisation eines B. neuer Art, der Unterhaltung und dem Nutzen (Volksbildung) dienend – neben →Harlekinaden und →Farcen Stücke russ. Dramatiker –, dessen künstlerische Leitung dem volksverbundenen A. J. Alexejew-Jakowlew (1850–1939) oblag. Der B. bestand bis in die 30er Jahre des 20. Jh.

Alekseev-Jakovlev, A.: Russkie narodnye guljanija. Leningrad/Moskva 1948; Lejfert, A. V.: Balagany. Petrograd 1922.

Annelore Engel-Braunschmidt

Ballad Opera

Populäre Form im engl. Theater des frühen 18. Jh., in der oft zeitgenössische Ereignisse behandelt wurden. Die B. O. mischte Dialoge mit zahlreichen Songs, meist zu bekannten Melodien, und hatte ein satirisches, oft auch parodistisches Gepräge. Zu ihren bekanntesten Autoren gehörten Henry Fielding (1707–54), David Garrick (1717–79) und Richard Brinsley Sheridan (1751–1816). Am einflußreichsten waren Charles Coffeys (?–1745) *The Devil to Pay* (1731), das das spätere dt. Singspiel anregte, Sheridans *The Duenna* (1775), das als frühe Operette gilt, und vor allem

John Gays (1685–1732) *The Beggar's Opera* (1728), das Brecht als Vorlage für seine *Dreigroschenoper* benutzte. Die B. O. wurde zu einer Vorläuferin der späteren comic opera.

Gagey, E.: Ballad Opera. New York 1937; Schultz, W. E.: Gay's Beggar's Opera: Its Content, History and Influence. New Haven 1923.

Bernd-Peter Lange

Ballet Blanc

Die Uraufführung von *La Sylphide* 1832 an der Pariser Oper markiert den Beginn der klassisch-romantischen Ära des Balletts mit einem Plot, in dem Realität und Phantasie konfrontiert werden. Der zweite Akt des Tanzdramas gibt dem romantischen Ballett insgesamt den Namen: ballet blanc; denn in ihm treten nicht nur die Protagonisten, sondern das gesamte Corps de ballet in Weiß auf. Marie Taglioni (1804–84) tanzt in enganliegendem Mieder und nur knielangem Gazerock die Sylphide, und sie wird zum Inbegriff aller romantisch-phantastischen Frauengestalten und Ballerinen, deren Wesen vorrangig durch ein hauchzartes, elfenhaft wirkendes, weißblendendes Kostüm charakterisiert wird. Doch nicht allein die Kostüme des ballet blanc, sondern auch der Bewegungsduktus, der Tanz auf den Spitzen und der danse volante, der fliegende Tanz (→ Ballet héroïque-pantomime, Didelot) und die Halte- und Hebefiguren des danseur étoile markieren das romantische Ballett als ballet blanc. Die Kostümrevolution, die den Charakter der Bühneninszenierung mit duftigen weißen Wolken vor blauen Szenenprospekten zu überziehen scheint, führt neben der Vervollkommnung der Spitzentanztechnik, der Hervorhebung der Primaballerina und ihrer Begleiterinnen zu einer neuen Ära in der Entwicklung des Tanztheaters. Der männliche Tänzer fungiert in diesem Tanzstil nur noch als Partner und unterstreicht in seiner Funktion die Dominanz, aber auch die ideale Phantasiebezogenheit eines feenhaft-ätherischen weiblichen Wesens, der zentralen Figur des Tanzdramas, der Primaballerina.

Balcar, A.: Das Ballett. München 1957; Liechtenhan, R.: Vom Tanz zum Ballett. Stuttgart/Zürich o. J.; Sorell, W.: Aspekte des Tanzes. Wilhelmshaven 1983.

Patricia Stöckemann

Ballet comique de la Reine

Sonderform des →Ballet de Cour, in dem die Königin als Protagonistin auftritt. «Comique», abzuleiten von «comédie» = dramatische Aktion mit heiterem Ausgang (→Comédie-ballet). – 1581: Höhepunkt des B. c. R. mit *Circe*. Plot von Beaujoyeux, Bühnenbilder und Kostüme: der Maler Jacques Patin. Das breitflächig angelegte, mit allen Mitteln der Barockdramaturgie aufgeführte Ballett dauert fünf Stunden. Feststehende, fahrende und sich herabsenkende Dekorationen. Nackte Sirenen mit Fischschwänzen; Arion auf einem wasserprustenden Delphin; bärtige Tritonen mit Dreizack, aber auch mit Blas- und Streichinstrumenten; drei Meerpferde ziehen Thetis; Gott Pan, Nymphen und Dryaden; Najaden mit Pfeil und Bogen; acht flötende Satyre; Minerva auf einem Triumphwagen; sechsstimmiger Chor; Circe und Jupiter; Scheingefechte, Ansprachen, Gesänge und das «Große Ballett» (Finale) als Huldigung an den König. Ein alle künstlerischen Mittel vereinendes Theater, in dem die Angesprochenen zugleich die Agierenden sind.

Biehn, H.: Feste und Feiern im alten Europa. München o. J.; Gregor, J.: Kulturgeschichte des Tanzes. Zürich o. J./Wien 1944; Lippe, R. zur: Naturbeherrschung am Menschen. Bd. II. Frankfurt/M. ²1981, S. 407–457; Schmidt-Garre, H.: Ballett. Vom Sonnenkönig bis Balanchine. Hannover 1966.

Helga Ettl

Ballet d'action

→Ballet héroïque-pantomime. – Ein nach dramatischen Gesichtspunkten aufgebautes Ballett, dessen Szenen auf die Darstellung einer *dramatischen Handlung* abgestimmt sind. Libretto, Musik, Choreographie, Dekoration und Kostüm stehen im Dienste pantomimisch-tänzerischer Mittel. Das B. d'a. (frz. Handlungsballett) tritt im 18. Jahrhundert in Gegensatz zum suitenhaften →Divertissement. Repräsentanten dieses Tanztheaters: J. Weaver (1673–1760), Franz Hilverding van Weven (1710–68), G. Angiolini (1723–96) und J. G. Noverre (1727–1810). 1719 kritisierte Abbé Dubois (*Réflexions critiques*), daß die Gesten des antiken Tanzes ehemals etwas auszudrücken vermocht hätten, und Cusuhač prophezeit, daß künftige Ballette, in Akte aufgeteilt, Handlungen, Charaktere und Leidenschaften ausdrücken würden. Gasparo Angiolini ereifert sich: «Das Publikum muß bei unseren Balletten *weinen* können!» 1757 mahnt Diderot (1713–84): «Der Tanz wartet noch auf sein Genie.» Noverre ersetzt den ‹stilisierten› Tanz des Barock durch den pantomimischen oder aktiven Tanz. Für diesen stellt er an Tänzer, Choreographen

114 Ballet d'action

und Musiker hohe Anforderungen. Voltaire nennt Noverres *Lettres sur la danse* (1760) das Werk eines Genies. Lessing und Bode haben die Briefe übersetzt. In ihnen wird ein dramatisches Tanzideal konzipiert, das in breiten Teilen bis heute gilt. Für Noverre ist jedes Ballett ein Gesamtkunstwerk aus Tanz, Musik, Dekor und Kostüm, eine «stumme Konversation», «ein lebendes Gemälde der Leidenschaften», «eine wahrheitsgetreue Nachbildung der Natur». Choreographisch meidet Noverre die barocke Symmetrie, wählt aufgelöste Formationen, wendet sich der Poesie, dem malerischen Duktus des Ausdrucks zu. «Körper und Tanz sind frei und unendlich.» In seine Reformen bezieht er auch das Corps de ballet ein. Es soll reden und malen, Seele und Physiognomie in Übereinstimmung bringen. Der Tanzpädagoge schickt seine Schüler auf Straßen, Marktplätze und in Werkstätten, damit sie vor Ort die Körperbewegungen des Lebens, der Zeitgenossen studieren können. Der Komponist hat auf ein Libretto zuzukomponieren. Außer Gluck (1714–87) vermag zu diesem Zeitpunkt kein anderer Komponist die Forderung zu erfüllen. Reformziele: 1. Abbau der üblen Routine; 2. Ausbildung des Geschmacks bei Tänzern und Publikum; Stärkung des Willens, Handlungen und Bewegungsoriginalität zu koordinieren und zu vertiefen; 3. die Einsicht, daß mechanistische Techniken den tänzerischen Geist ersticken. – Kreationen: 1749 *Les Fêtes chinoises*; 1754 *La Fontaine de jouvence*; 1755 *Les Réjouissances flamandes*. Als →Ballet héroïque-pantomime: *Der Tod des Ajax*; *Das Urteil des Paris, Orpheus*; *Rinaldo und Armida* (in Lyon) – ab 1760 in Stuttgart: *Admet und Alkestis, Amor und Psyche*; *Der Tod des Hercules*; *Medea und Jason* – ab 1767 in Wien: *Antonius und Kleopatra*; *Alexander, Die Danaiden*; *Agamemnon*; *Iphigenie auf Tauris*; *Die Horatier*; *Semiramis*; *Don Quichotte* u. a. – Mit Noverre wird der aus den Niederlanden stammende, in Wien geborene Franz Hilverding zum Mitstreiter für das B. d'a. Die Ballette Hilverdings betonen das der →Choreographie zugrunde liegende Drama. Hilverding choreographiert im Theater «nächst der Burg» französische ernste heroische Ballette, für das Kärntnertortheater deutsche und volkstümliche Stoffe. Der Terminus ballet d'action steht für das dramatische Handlungsballett des 18. Jh. Die dort proklamierte Einheit von dramaturgischer und choreographischer Struktur wird im 19. Jh. durch romantische Ballettproduktionen (→ballet blanc) wie *Giselle* (1841) vertieft. Das Handlungsballett des 20. Jh. gewinnt durch den tänzerisch-choreographischen Umgang mit unbewußten Beweggründen und psychologischen Gesetzmäßigkeiten (→Choreographie) eine neue Dimension seiner Darstellungsart hinzu. Fokin und Nijinsky (→Ballets Russes) stehen als Choreographen am Beginn dieser Entwicklung. Ihr Erbe wird u. a. von John Cranko (→Staatstheater Stuttgart) und John Neumeier (→Hamburg Ballett) mit psychologisch motivierten Handlungsballetten in selbständiger Weise fortgesetzt.

Bland, A.: L'Histoire du Ballet et de la Danse. Paris 1977; Dahms, S.: Choreographische Aspekte im Werk Jean-Georges Noverres und Gasparo Angiolinis. In: Klein, M. (Hg.): Tanzforschung. Bd. 2. Wilhelmshaven 1991, S. 93–110; Gregor, J.: Kulturgeschichte des Tanzes. Wien 1944; Jeschke, C.: Dramaturgie, Choreographie und Bühnentanz. In: Klein, M. (Hg.): Tanzforschung. Bd. 2. Wilhelmshaven 1991, S. 82–92; Krüger, M. J. G.: Noverre und das Ballet d'action. Emsdetten 1963.

Helga Ettl / Patricia Stöckemann

Ballet de Cour

Tanztheaterfestspiele der barocken Höfe. Hofballette entwachsen der Vielfalt höfischer Festlichkeiten in Spätgotik und Renaissance. Ihre Ursprünge liegen im → Turnier, der → Moriske, den → Trionfi, → Maskeraden und Prozessionsspielen, in griechischen Götter- und Heldenmythen. – Getanzt, gesungen und gespielt werden diese Großschauspiele vorrangig vom Adel und von wenigen hervorragenden professionellen Tänzern. Arrangeure sind die Tanzmeister (Balthazar de Beaujoyeux, gest. um 1587). Für Beaujoyeux bedeutet Choreographieren «das Entwerfen von geometrischen Figuren für mehrere Personen, die zum Klange von Instrumenten harmonisch tanzen». Er selbst bezeichnet sich als «erfindungsreichen Geometer». Beaujoyeux versucht, in seinen B. d. C. bereits alle Elemente des Spiels harmonisch miteinander zu verbinden. Beaujoyeux wird Ballettdirektor, Höfling und Vertrauter von Katharina di Medici (1519–89). Mit den B. d. C. wird eine neue Theatergattung geboren. *La défense du paradis* (1572) leitet, von Beaujoyeux unbeabsichtigt, die Bartholomäusnacht ein. 1573: B. d. C. zum Empfang einer polnischen Abordnung. Im Festsaal Aufbau eines riesigen silbernen Felsens mit 16 wolkenförmigen Nischen, 16 Damen des Adels verkörpern allegorisch 16 frz. Provinzen.

Biehn, H.: Feste und Feiern im alten Europa. München o. J.; Gregor, J.: Kulturgeschichte des Tanzes. Zürich o. J./Wien 1944; Prunières, H.: Le Ballet de cour en France avant Bensérade et Lully. Paris 1914; Walker, D. P.: Ballet de cour. In: Blume, F. (Hg.): Musik in Geschichte und Gegenwart. Bd. I. Sp. 1164–68.

Helga Ettl

Ballet de l'Opéra de Paris

Die Geschichte des B., das zu den bedeutendsten klassischen Ensembles der Welt zählt, beginnt 1661 mit der von Ludwig XIV. gegründeten Académie Royale de Danse, die den Tanz systematisieren, kodifizieren und

116 Ballet de l'Opéra de Paris

Berufstänzer trainieren soll. 1672 wird sie mit der Académie Royale de Musique (damaliger Name der seit 1669 bestehenden Pariser Oper) vereinigt. Durch die Zusammenarbeit von Jean-Baptiste Lully (1632–87), P. Beauchamp (1636–1705; →Ballet du Roi) und Molière (1622–73) gewinnt die Institution den Ruf, neue theatralische Genres auszubilden (→Comédie-ballet; →Choreodrama). 1713 nimmt die für das französische Tanzausbildungssystem maßgebliche →Ecole de Danse de l'Opéra de Paris den Betrieb auf. Das Ballettensemble und die Schule üben entscheidenden Einfluß auf die Entwicklung des klassischen Tanzes in Europa aus. Zu den zahlreichen bedeutenden Pädagogen, Choreographen und Tänzern, die aufgrund ihrer hier absolvierten Ausbildung und ihres Engagements beim B. daran Teil haben, gehören: Gaetano (1728–1808) und Auguste Vestris (1760–1842), zu dessen Schülern A. Bournonville (1805–79; →Den Kongelige Ballet) zählt, J.-G. Noverre (1727–1810; →Ballet d'action), J. Dauberval (1742–1806; →Comédie-ballet) und C.-L. Didelot (1767–1837; →Ballet héroïque-pantomime). Das romantische Ballett erlebt hier seine Höhepunkte mit *La Sylphide* (1832; →Ballet Blanc) von Filippo Taglioni (1777–1871; →Staatstheater Stuttgart) und *Giselle* (1841) von Jean Coralli (1779–1854) und Jules Perrot (1810–92). Als 1870 Arthur Saint-Léon (1821–70) *Coppélia* zur Uraufführung bringt, befindet sich das Ensemble bereits in einer Phase des Niedergangs, von dem es sich ab 1929 unter der Direktion Serge Lifars (1905–86), zuvor Solist in Diaghilews →Ballets Russes, wieder erholt. Bis 1944 sowie von 1947–58 prägen seine Choreographien das Repertoire des B. Gleichzeitig reorganisiert Lifar die Ballettschule, die zuvor an Bedeutung verloren hatte. Nach Lifar wechseln die Direktoren des B. in rascher Folge (u. a. 1958–62 George Skibine, 1920–81). Von 1983–89 leitet Rudolf Nurejew (*1938) die Kompanie, deren tänzerisches Niveau er – auch durch Verpflichtung ehemaliger Schüler der E. d. O. P., die unter Claude Bessy (*1932; Direktorin seit 1972) einen exzellenten Ruf genießt – wesentlich verbessert und ihr dadurch neue internationale Aufmerksamkeit verschafft. Seit 1990 ist Patrick Dupond (*1959) Direktor des B., das Werke nahezu aller wichtigen Choreographen des 20. Jahrhunderts tanzt.

Balcar, A.: Das Ballett. München 1957; Burian, K. v.: Das Ballett. Artia Praha 1963; Kunzle, R.: Beauchamp. In: Das Tanzarchiv, Sept. 1974, Febr. 1975, Mai 1975; Schmidt-Garre, H.: Ballett. Vom Sonnenkönig bis Balanchine. Hannover 1966.

Horst Vollmer

Ballet du Roi

Neben dem →Ballet comique de la Reine die zweite Sonderform des →Ballet de Cour. 1653 tritt der 15jährige Ludwig XIV. im «Ballet de la Nuit» als Sonne auf, eine Rolle, die ihm später den Titel «Roi Soleil» einbringt. Ludwig XIV. und Ludwig XV. tanzen als Könige mit dem Adel und lassen sich von großen Tänzern akkompagnieren, zum Beispiel vom Choreographen Pierre Beauchamps (1636–1705), später Direktor der Académie Royale de la Danse (→Ecole de Danse de l'Opéra). – Den Damen wird von 1653 bis 1681 Tanzen untersagt. Erst 1681, mit *Le triomphe de l'amour*, erhält die erste frz. Primaballerina, Mlle La Fontaine, offizielle Auftrittserlaubnis.

Christout, M.-F.: Le Ballet de cour de Louis XIV. 1643–72. Mises en scène. Paris 1967; Gregor, J.: Kulturgeschichte des Balletts. Zürich o. J./Wien 1944; Schmidt-Garre, H.: Ballett. Vom Sonnenkönig bis Balanchine. Hannover 1966.

Helga Ettl

Ballet du XXe Siècle

La Symphonie pour un homme seul, 1955 zur musique concrète von P. Henry und P. Schaeffer in Paris uraufgeführt, weist Maurice Béjart (*1924 oder 1927) bereits als revolutionären Ballettschöpfer aus. Den Händen eines Choreographen entwächst im Tanztheater das Urbild des einsamen Menschen, gestützt und gestellt in Ursituationen: hemmungslose, eindringliche, expressive, den Betrachter aufwühlende Gebärden; eine aus Klopfgeräuschen, undeutlichen Rufen, Lustseufzern und Explosionsdetonationen, neben anderen Alltagsgeräuschen, sich zu Verläufen und Collagen reihende und schichtende musique concrète, und nicht zuletzt die von nur fahlem Licht erhellte Bühne mit schwer lastend herabhängenden Seilen steigern die dramatisch-gespenstische Szenerie. *La Symphonie* eröffnet das vielschichtige Œuvre Béjarts. Die Wirkung der Choreographie gibt dennoch nur einen Vorgeschmack zu *der* Vorstellungsmagie, die Béjart 1959 mit Strawinskys *Sacre du Printemps* ausweist. Das Ballett ist eine Hymne an die Jugend, die Leidenschaft, die sexuelle Begeisterung. Die Polyrhythmik und -metrik Strawinskys, seine im Stile barbaro urtümlich hämmernden Orchesterschläge beantwortet Béjart mit kraftvollen, immer neu und variiert ausgelösten, plastisch pulsierenden Bewegungen der Kompanie. Er meidet jeden trügerisch geführten, färbenden Duktus, läßt geballte Kräfte kumulieren und einsinken.

Maurice Huisman, Intendant des «Monnaie-Theaters» in Brüssel,

118 Ballet du XXe Siècle

gründet mit Béjart als Direktor auf Grund des *Sacre*-Erfolges hin 1960 das
«Ballet du XXe Siècle». In der Kompanie sammeln sich Menschentypen
aller Kontinente und Völker mit unterschiedlichsten Physiognomien, differenten Fähigkeiten, Schwächen und Stärken. Béjart, stets von tiefer
Zuneigung zu Menschen erfüllt, pointiert die Individualität seiner Tänzer
auf der Bühne. «Das menschliche Abenteuer» zieht sich durch das choreographische Schaffen Béjarts, das selbst nicht Kunst, sondern Leben zu
sein beansprucht und das die Tänzer «alles umgreifende Ballette mit den
Ausmaßen der ganzen Welt, des ganzen Lebens» durchtanzen läßt: Fest –
Kampf – Zärtlichkeit – Sexualität – Leben in der Gesellschaft – Selbst-
sucht – Machtstreben – Liebe in verschiedenen Erscheinungsformen. Béjarts Sinnsuche treibt den geistigen Wanderer dazu, räumlich ferne Kulturen zu erforschen. Vom Abgestorbensein der westlichen Theaterpraxis
überzeugt, erkundet Béjart das Theater des Orients und stößt auf universale und lebendige Theatersprachen. Alle Künste vereinen sich in Ostasien zum → Totaltheater. Erfüllt von der Breite seiner Erfahrungen, bemüht sich Béjart um eine übergreifende Weltsprache, die die westliche
und östliche Vergangenheit verknüpft. 1967 gelingt die *Messe für die heutige Zeit*, deren Choreographie bewußt ohne dramatische Höhepunkte
verläuft. Zeremonie in mehreren Bildern: der Atem, der Körper, die
Welt, der Tanz, das Paar, *Mein Kampf*, die Stille, die Erwartung. Neben
diesen Bestrebungen um Kulturinterpretationen gelingen inspirative
Themengestaltungen aus dem buddhistischen und hinduistischen Indien,
dem taoistischen China, dem sufistischen Persien; Aufarbeitung literarischer Plots: Baudelaire, Balzac, Mallarmé, Molière und Goethe; Auseinandersetzungen mit Kompositionen von Bach, Beethoven, Berlioz, Bou-
lez, Debussy, Mahler und insbesondere Wagner.

1987 sieht sich die Stadt Brüssel nicht mehr in der Lage, Béjart die
Grundlage für seine Arbeit zu gewähren. Der dort seit 27 Jahren amtie-
rende, weltweit renommierte Choreograph muß sich nach einer neuen
Basis für sein Werk und seine Truppe umsehen. Er nimmt das Angebot
aus Lausanne an und läßt sich dort mit seinem Ballett des 20. Jahrhunderts nieder, das in «Béjart Ballet Lausanne» umgetauft wird. Fünf Jahre
später, 1992, finden die letzten Auftritte dieser «großen» Kompanie statt.
Béjart beabsichtigt, mit Beginn der Spielzeit 1992/93, das Ensemble stark
zu verkleinern und in «Rudra Béjart Lausanne» umzubenennen sowie
eine neue Ausbildungsstätte gleichen Namens zu gründen. Bewußt setzt
Béjart damit einer Periode seines Lebens ein Ende, um mit einer neuen
Truppe, einem neu zu erarbeitenden Repertoire und einer neuen Schule
wieder bei Null anzufangen.

Béjart. Antwerpen 1978; Interview Béjart/Gascard: Der Körper hat immer recht.
In: Ballett International 1 (1984), S. 25–27; Koegler, H.: Spectacle Total. In: Bal-

lett International 11 (1984), S. 25; Stuart, O.: Veni, vidi, vici. In: Ballett International 9 (1984), S. 5–9.

Patricia Stöckemann

Ballet héroïque-pantomime

→Ballettpantomime; →Ballet d'action. – Aus dem Comédie-ballet, in dem nur noch die Hauptfiguren rezitieren, wird die B. h.-p., in der alle Dialoge oder Monologe entfallen. Auch die Protagonisten tanzen. Hilverding van Wevens B. h.-p. entstehen in Wien: *Britannicus* (1740); *Idomeneus*; *Alzire*; *Ulysses und Circe*; *Acis und Galathea*; *Orpheus und Euridike*; *Ariadne und Bacchus*; *Amor und Psyche*; *Venus und Adonis*. Nach Hilverdings Tod choreographiert G. Angiolini (1723–96). Angiolini gilt als der große Neuerer der Ballettpantomime. Er hat als erster die tragisch-heroische Ballettpantomime vollendet, dank des genialen musikdramatischen Partners und Opernkomponisten W. Gluck (1714–87). Musik und Choreographie vereinen sich im *Don Juan* (1761) zu einem meisterhaften Gesamtkunstwerk. Angiolini beschwört abgrundtiefe tragische Gewalten. Seine Einleitung zum Szenarium des *Don Juan* weist Reformbestrebungen unmißverständlich aus. Bewegungen und Gebärden sollen zu einer Art Deklamation ausgestaltet werden. Die Ausdruckskraft der Musik unterstützt deutend. Ausgedehnte Stoffe müssen zu einer knappen Handlung von Minuten gerafft werden. Deshalb konzentrierte Bewegungen im Gegensatz zum poetischen Stil Noverres. Angiolini nutzt sein Corps de ballet als Träger von Interpretationen und Kommentaren im Sinne der griechischen Tragödienchöre. Der hochbegabte, vielseitige Künstler schreibt viele Libretti und Ballettmusiken selbst: *Solimano II* (1774); *La morte di Cleopatra* (1773); *L'orfano nella China* (1774); *Attila* (1781); *Amore e Psiche* (1789); *Tito* (1790). Musik Gluck: *Semiramis* (1765); *Iphigenie* (1765); *Alessandro* (1774). – Die vollendete Synthese zwischen Ballettpantomime und Tanz erreicht der in Stockholm geborene Choreograph Didelot, der Nachdruck auf virtuose Bewegungsbeherrschung legt. Seine Ballette nennt er dramatische Pantomimen. Didelot ist der Schöpfer der «ballets volants», Inszenierungen mit «Luftflügen». «Cupido» und der Luftgott «Zephire» schweben an Drähten über die Bühne. Diese Inszenierungen erinnern bereits an den Jugendstil. Dramatische Veränderungen der Kostüme: die Musselintunika und der fleischfarbene Trikot. Als Choreograph ist Didelot der Kreator der →Minutage. Höhepunkt des heroischen Ballettschaffens vor den sowjetischen →Choreodramen werden die expressiv-dramatischen Heldenballette Salvatore Viganos (1769–1821). Das Corps de ballet

120 Ballets Jooss

agiert dramatisch. 1801: Beethovens *Geschöpfe des Prometheus* (Wiener Burg). An der Mailänder Scala die heroisch-expressiven →Choreodramen: *Richard Löwenherz* (1795); *La Vestale* (1818) und *Othello* (1819); *Daedalus und Ikarus* (1819); *Titanen* (1819); *Jeanne d'Arc* (1820); *Dido* (1820). Nach Vigano baut Carlo Blasis (1797–1878) die B. h.-p. aus. Er sucht Urgründe für seelische Regungen in ungewöhnlichen Charakteren: Don Quichotte, Torquato Tasso, Faust. Blasis markiert die Moral eines Plots. Sein *Traité élémentaire, théoretique et pratique de l'art de la danse* (1820) kodifiziert verbindlich alle Tanztechniken der Zeit. Das Werk wird zur Basis für alle folgenden klassischen Tanztheorien.

Bland, A.: L'Histoire du Ballet et de la Danse. Paris 1977; Gregor, J.: Kulturgeschichte des Balletts. Zürich o. J./Wien 1944; Reyna, F.: Das Buch vom Ballett. Paris 1955; Schmidt-Garre, H.: Ballett. Vom Sonnenkönig bis Balanchine. Hannover 1966.

Helga Ettl

Ballets Jooss

Niemals ist ‹politischer Tanz› schlüssiger formuliert worden als im *Grünen Tisch*, eine auf dem Internationalen Choreographen-Wettbewerb zu Paris 1932 prämierte Choreographie – ein Totentanz in acht Bildern, in dem Kurt Jooss (1901–79; →Ausdruckstanz) die Schrecken des Krieges an vom Tod verfolgten Menschen unbarmherzig demonstriert. Die in expressiven, prägnanten Gebärden dargestellten Totentanzszenen werden von den ergebnislosen Verhandlungen der Diplomaten am grünen Tisch des Völkerbundes umrahmt. Das Konferieren der die Welt regierenden ‹Herren›, die Jooss mit stilisierten Masken und durch automatenhafte Bewegungen typisiert, mündet in ein Fiasko. Man zieht die Revolver – der Krieg wird aufs neue erklärt. Als Rad dreht sich das Wechselspiel machtgetriebener Kriegskonferenzen. Nach der Uraufführung des *Grünen Tisches*, der in die Tanzgeschichte als Plädoyer für Menschlichkeit eingegangen ist, gehört K. Jooss zur Elite der Weltchoreographen. Sein Antikriegsstück, das die Grauen des 2. Weltkriegs vorausahnt und die des 1. aufarbeitet, stellt choreographisch eine Synthese von klassisch-akademischem Stil und Ausdruckstanz dar. Es bleibt für die B. J. das nachhaltigste Repertoirestück und markiert insofern den Ausdruckswillen der Jooss-Kompanie, die sich 1924 als «Neue Tanzbühne» in Münster etabliert und 1928 unter der Bezeichnung «Folkwang-Tanztheater-Studio» nach Essen übersiedelt (→Folkwang-Tanzstudio). Ihr Leiter, K. Jooss, gründet 1927 gemeinsam mit R. Schulz-Dornburg die Folkwang-Schule Essen und übernimmt deren Tanzabteilung. Seine Kompanie wird 1930 als «Folkwang Tanzbühne Essen» dem Essener Theater angegliedert. Hitlers Machtübernahme zwingt die Truppe zur Emigration nach England; denn den unverhohlenen Pazifismus und den expressionistischen Stil des Ensembles lehnt der Nationalsozialismus ab. Eine neue Heimat- und Wirkungsstätte finden die B. J. bis zur Auflösung der Kompanie 1947 in Dartington Hall, später Cambridge/England. K. Jooss kehrt 1949 in die BRD an die Folkwang-Schule Essen zurück. Das dort neugegründete «Folkwang-Tanz-Theater/Ballets Jooss» ertanzt in den Jahren 1951 bis 1953 erneut internat. Erfolge, muß aber 1953 aus finanziellen Gründen seine Arbeit einstellen. Erst acht Jahre später, 1961, werden Meisterkurse für Tanz an der Folkwang-Hochschule eingerichtet, für die als Choreographen neben K. Jooss A. Tudor (* 1908), J. Cebron (* 1927) und P. Bausch (→ Wuppertaler Tanztheater, → Tanztheater) gewonnen werden. Aufführungen finden ab 1963 unter dem Namen «Folkwang-Ballett» statt. Als Choreograph und Lehrer gastiert der 1968 emeritierte K. Jooss im In- und Ausland. 1979 stirbt er an den Folgen eines Autounfalls.

Garske, R. (Hg.): Jooss – Dokumentation. Köln 1985; Regitz, H.: «Folkwang 1985». In: Ballett-Journal / Das Tanzarchiv 1 (1985), S. 56–57; Schmidt-Garre, H.: Ballett. Vom Sonnenkönig bis Balanchine. Hannover 1966.

Patricia Stöckemann

Ballets Suédois

Die B. S. wurden 1920 von dem schwed. Kunstsammler und Impresario Rolf de Maré (1888–1964) in Paris (Théâtre des Champs Élysées) gegründet. Marés Ziel war es, Tanz, Musik und Malerei im Gesamtkunstwerk gleichberechtigt nebeneinanderzustellen. Mittelmäßiges tänzerisches Können der Truppe (einzige positive Ausnahme: der Tänzer und Choreograph Jean Börlin) und herausragende bühnenbildnerische Leistungen verwandelten die Ballette jedoch eher in riesige Kunstausstellungen. *Les Mariés de la Tour Eiffel* (1921, Text: Cocteau, Musik: Honegger, Milhaud, Poulenc u. a., Dekoration: Hugo) verursachte einen Skandal durch seine antibürgerliche Botschaft, seine absurden und surrealistischen Stilmittel. Höhepunkt der B. S.: *Skating Rink* (1922, Text: Canudo, Musik: Honegger) und *La Création du Monde* (1923, Text: Cendrars, Musik: Milhaud), beide von Léger ausgestattet. Menschen und Tiere wurden reduziert zu sich mechanisch bewegenden Teilen des Bühnenbildes, Abstraktionen in Farben und geometrischen Formen. Das dadaistische Experiment *Relâche* (1924, Text und Dekoration: Picabia, Musik: Satie) war als Hymne auf das Leben ohne Konventionen gedacht. Für die Pause schuf René Clair sein erstes filmisches Meisterwerk: *Entr'acte*.

122 Ballett

Picabias Antikunst-Spektakel, an dem auch Man Ray mitwirkte, machte jede künstlerische Weiterentwicklung unmöglich. Die B. S. wurden aufgelöst.

de Maré, R. (ed.): Les Ballets Suédois dans l'art contemporain. Paris 1931.

Barbara Müller-Wesemann

Ballett

(Ital.: ballare = tanzen; ballo = Tanz) Zur Zeit des burgundisch-provençalischen Minnesanges unterscheiden die Quellen zwischen ballato = Paartanz und Reyhen, Reigen = Schreittanz in Ketten-, also Gruppenform; gesprungen = saltatio (saltare = tanzen). Ab 1550 treten die ersten Intermezzi, aus der →Moriske herausgebildet, an ital. Höfen als Balletti getanzt, in Frankreich als Ballets, in geschlossener dramatischer Tanzszenenabfolge mit Gesang und Rezitation auf. Aus diesen Balletti, später →Ballet de Cour (1572), entwickeln sich die varianten Erscheinungsformen des B. als Tanzgattung und Form des Schautanzes. Das Nomen B. bezeichnet außerdem die für Tanzbühnenwerke bestimmten Kompositionen (musikalische Gattung) sowie die Gesamtheit aller das Tanzbühnenwerk interpretierenden Akteure: Tänzer, Ballettdirektoren und -assistenten, Choreographen, Kinetographen. →Tanz, →Ballett-Kompanie.

Helga Ettl

Ballett der Deutschen Oper Berlin

Die Deutsche Oper Berlin steht in der Nachfolge des Charlottenburger Opernhauses von 1912, das später als Deutsches Opernhaus, schließlich als Städtische Oper Berlin firmiert. Ballettdirektor der Deutschen Oper ist seit der Eröffnung 1961–90 Gert Reinholm (* 1923). Bis 1966 fungiert Tatjana Gsovsky (* 1901), die zuvor das Ballett der Städtischen Oper leitete (seit 1954), als Chefchoreographin. Sie zählt zu den herausragenden Persönlichkeiten des Balletts in Deutschland (→Ballett der Deutschen Staatsoper Berlin, →Ballett Frankfurt) und gilt als Expressionistin des klassischen Tanzes. Wie bei ihren früheren Ensembles bringt T. Gsovsky beim B. neben Klassiker-Inszenierungen zahlreiche Choreographien zu zeitgenössischen Kompositionen u. a. von Boris Blacher, Hans Werner Henze und Luigi Nono heraus (z. T. Uraufführungen). Nach ihr prägen vorübergehend Werke des künstlerischen Leiters Kenneth MacMillan

(* 1929; 1966–69), später die von Valery Panov (* 1938) den ansonsten ausgesprochen eklektischen Spielplan. Unter der Direktion von Peter Schaufuss (* 1949; seit 1990) überwiegen dessen Klassiker-Produktionen, darunter Rekonstruktionen von Stücken August Bournonvilles (1805–79; →Den Kongelige Ballet). Gleichzeitig engagiert Schaufuss zeitgenössische Gastchoreographen wie Christopher Bruce (* 1945). Außerdem tanzt das B. Werke u. a. von George Balanchine (1904–83; →New York City Ballet), Maurice Béjart (* 1927; →Ballet du XXe Siècle) und John Neumeier (* 1942; →Hamburg Ballett).

Regitz, H. (Hg.): Tanz in Deutschland – Ballett seit 1945. Berlin 1984.

Horst Vollmer

Ballett der Deutschen Staatsoper Berlin

Das Opernhaus Unter den Linden (seit 1945 Deutsche Staatsoper) kann auf eine Bühnentanztradition seit seiner Eröffnung 1742 zurückblicken. Zu den Leitern des Balletts gehörten 1856–83 Paul Taglioni (1808–84), 1919–22 Heinrich Kröller (1880–1930), 1924–30 Max Terpis (1889 bis 1958), 1930–34 Rudolf von Laban (1879–1958; →Ausdruckstanz, Laban-schulen), 1945–52 Tatjana Gsovsky (* 1901; →Ballett der Deutschen Oper Berlin) und 1955–70 Lilo Gruber (1915–92). Seit 1974 leitet Egon Bischoff (* 1934) das Ensemble.

Bereits in der Amtszeit L. Grubers, die mit zahlreichen eigenen Arbeiten hervortrat, beginnt die Pflege des klassisch-romantischen Repertoires, das unter E. Bischoff den Spielplan des B. prägt. Außerdem stehen Gastchoreographien u. a. von George Balanchine (1904–83; →New York City Ballet), John Cranko (1927–73; →Staatstheater Stuttgart), William Forsythe (* 1949; →Ballett Frankfurt) und Maurice Béjart (* 1927; →Ballet du XXe Siècle) auf dem Spielplan.

Die nach dem Vorbild sowjetischer Tänzerausbildung arbeitende Staatliche Ballettschule Berlin, 1951 gegründet und maßgeblich geprägt von den Direktoren Albin Fritsch (1921–80) und Martin Puttke (* 1943; seit 1981), steht in enger Kooperation zum B.

Haedler, M.: Deutsche Staatsoper Berlin – Geschichte und Gegenwart. Berlin 1990; Helmstädter, I.: Terpsichore Unter den Linden. In: Quander, G.: Apollini et Musis. Berlin 1992.

Horst Vollmer

Ballettdramaturg

Vergleichsweise jung ist das Berufsbild des Ballettdramaturgen. Seine Aufgabengebiete entsprechen denen eines Musiktheater- oder Schauspieldramaturgen. In der Regel unterstützt er den Choreographen bei der Schöpfung neuer (Handlungs-)Ballette bzw. bei der inhaltlich-dramaturgischen Veränderung älterer, erzählender Werke des Ballettrepertoires. Mitunter fungiert er auch als Berater der Direktion in Fragen der Stückwahl, der Spielplangestaltung, der Besetzung und der Realisierung einer Produktion. Er übernimmt damit Aufgaben, die früher vom Choreograph bzw. Ballettdirektor erfüllt wurden. Neben fest angestellten und permanent für eine Kompanie tätigen Ballettdramaturgen, zu deren Aufgaben auch die Öffentlichkeitsarbeit zählt, ist die Verpflichtung von Ballettdramaturgen für bestimmte Inszenierungen üblich.

Horst Vollmer

Ballett Frankfurt

Die Tradition des Bühnentanzes in Frankfurt am Main reicht bis in das 18. Jh. zurück. Ballettdirektoren der Städtischen Bühnen nach dem 2. Weltkrieg waren u. a. 1959–66 Tatjana Gsovsky (* 1901; →Ballett der Deutschen Oper Berlin) und 1969–73 John Neumeier (* 1942; →Hamburg Ballett). Seit der Übernahme der Ballettdirektion durch William Forsythe (* 1949) 1984 entwickelt sich das Ensemble zu einer der wichtigsten zeitgenössischen Ballettkompanien. Forsythe, einst Mitglied des Joffrey Ballet in seiner Heimatstadt New York und des Stuttgarter Balletts (→Staatstheater Stuttgart), gilt als einer der bedeutendsten Choreographen der Gegenwart. Als Direktor des B. beginnt er umgehend mit dem Aufbau eines neuen Repertoires, in dem seine eigenen Arbeiten überwiegen. Daneben zeigt das Ballett Frankfurt Werke seiner ständigen Choreographin Amanda Miller (* 1961) und Gastchoreographien beispielsweise von Laura Dean (* 1945; →Minimal Dance), Susan Marshall (* 1959), Jan Fabre (* 1958), Ohad Naharin (* 1952; →Bathsheva Dance Company) und George Balanchine (1904–83; →New York City Ballet).

Forsythe sucht für seine Choreographien, die tänzerisch in der Nachfolge des Klassizismus George Balanchines anzusiedeln sind und gleichzeitig Aspekte des →Modern Dance und des →Post Modern Dance aufgreifen, bevorzugt die Zusammenarbeit mit zeitgenössischen Komponisten. Das Ballett selbst ist wiederholt Thema seiner Choreographien, wobei er mit den Elementen des Bühnentanzes – Bewegung, Musik, Raum, Lichtgestaltung, Requisiten – experimentiert und sie, oft unter

Einbeziehung von Stimmen und gesprochenen Texten, in neue Zusammenhänge stellt.

Wördehoff, T.: Ein möglicher Tatort: Ballett. In: Regitz, H./Koegler, H. (Hg.): Ballett 1983. Zürich 1983; van Schaik, E.: Neue Paradigmen für den Tanz? In: Ballett International 10 (1990).

Horst Vollmer

Ballett-Kompanie (Ballettensemble)

Die B. ist ein sozial organisiertes Gebilde von professionellen Tänzern, Choreographen, Ausstattern, Ballett- und Trainingsmeistern, das hierarchisch oder kollektiv-demokratisch gegliedert sein kann. Die B. ist eine privat oder staatlich geleitete und geförderte autonome oder einem Theater, Opernhaus, dem Fernsehunternehmen zugehörige Institution. Der Ballettdirektor prägt als künstlerischer Leiter und Choreograph das Image der Company vorrangig, das darüber hinaus von der Stilbreite und Anzahl der Repertoirestücke, dem geistigen Anliegen des Choreographen und der technischen Brillanz und Individualität der Tänzer bestimmt wird. →Ballet de l'Opéra de Paris, →Ballet du XXe Siècle, →Ballets Jooss, →Ballet Suédois, →Ballett der Deutschen Oper Berlin, →Ballett der Deutschen Staatsoper Berlin, →Ballett der Komischen Oper Berlin, →Ballett Frankfurt, →Bayerisches Staatsballett, →Bathsheva Dance Company, →Bolschoi-Ballett, →Bremer Tanztheater, →Cullbergballetten, →Dance Theatre of Harlem, →Folkwang-Tanzstudio, →Hamburg Ballett, →Het Nationale Ballet, →Den Kongelige Ballet, →Nederlands Dans Theater, →New York City Ballet, →Royal Ballet, →St. Petersburger Ballett (ehem. Kirow-Ballett), →Staatstheater Stuttgart, →Stadttheater Basel, →Wuppertaler Tanztheater.

Patricia Stöckemann

Bänkelsang

Etymologisch hergeleitet von ‹Bank›; B. bezeichnet von einer ‹Bank› (= erhöhtem Podium) herab vorgetragene Lieder. Ähnliche Bildungen in fast allen europ. Sprachen. – Der Begriff taucht als ‹Bänkleinsänger› zuerst 1709 auf. Auch in übertragener Bedeutung für schlechte Literatur ist B. bereits im 18. Jh. belegt. Eine genaue Definition und Abgrenzung von ähnlichen Erscheinungen ist schwierig und umstritten. Vereinfacht läßt sich der B. als frühes audiovisuelles Medium beschrieben, das durch die

126 Bänkelsang

Zusammenfassung von Musik, Bild, gesungenem (und verkauftem) Text charakterisiert ist. Seine Entstehung ist nicht völlig geklärt. Vorläufer und Einflüsse reichen wohl bis ins Mittelalter zurück, vor allem aber zu den Zeitungs- oder Avisensängern. Seit dem 16. Jh. wurden Flugblätter und ‹Avisen› (Frühformen der Zeitung) von Wanderhändlern verkauft. Da sie in der Regel neben mehreren Bildern auch einen gereimten Text enthielten, wurden sie wahrscheinlich durch öffentlichen (gesungenen) Vortrag angepriesen. Die Inhalte waren ‹aktuell› (= noch nicht bekannt) und enthielten Nachrichten über Katastrophen und Unglücksfälle wie über politische Ereignisse.

Der B. betont die reine Unterhaltung (nicht ohne auf eine mehr zeitlose Aktualität und eine didaktische Komponente zu rekurrieren). Zeitlich eingrenzen läßt sich der eigentliche B. auf die Zeit vom 17. Jh. bis zum Beginn des 2. Weltkriegs. Restformen des früher in ganz Europa verbreiteten B. sollen sich noch in den Pyrenäen und in Italien finden, wo die Bänkelsänger auch moderne Technik einbeziehen und eine eigene Zeitschrift besitzen («Il cantastorie»). Träger des B. waren seit Beginn vor allem Fahrende (→Fahrendes Volk), Schausteller, aber auch Kriegsinvaliden, deren Versorgung man auf diese Weise sicherstellen wollte. Die Nichtseßhaftigkeit in Verbindung mit dem Vorwurf zumindest latenter Kriminalität führte zur gesellschaftlichen Ächtung des Bänkelsängers, der starker obrigkeitlicher Kontrolle unterlag und allenfalls zur Unterhaltung der unteren Volksschichten geduldet wurde.

Die Autoren der Texte sind in der Regel unbekannt. Erst im 19. Jh. traten spezialisierte Verlage auf, darunter (im deutschsprachigen Raum) Kahlbrock in Hamburg und Reiche in Schwiebus. Folge dieser Entwicklung war u. a. die Standardisierung der Texte in Umfang und Format. Auch die Maler der zum B. gehörenden Bilder (‹Schilder›) sind zumeist unbekannt, nur die Namen weniger Spezialisten sind überliefert.

Der B. wurde immer auf ähnliche Art vorgetragen. Auf einem Podest stehend, erzählte der Sänger in Prosa vom Inhalt der Begebenheit, die daraufhin in gereimter Form auf eine der wenigen immer wieder benutzten Melodien gesungen wurde. Zur Illustrierung wies er dabei auf die verschiedenen Bilder des ‹Schildes› mit einem Zeigestab hin. Ziel des Vortrags war der Verkauf der gedruckten Texte. Thema des B. war neben Verbrechen, Unglücksfällen, Naturkatastrophen immer wieder die Liebe, zumeist verbunden mit tragischen Akzenten. Zeitgeschichtliche Themen blieben weitgehend ausgespart. Auffallend ist das Fehlen jeglicher Kritik an politischen und sozialen Verhältnissen, das Lob der Obrigkeit und die enge bürgerliche Moral der Texte. Es ist nicht immer leicht festzustellen, ob bereits vorhandene Vorstellungen des Publikums aus verkaufstechnischen Gründen aufgenommen und verstärkt wurden oder reglementierende Eingriffe der Zensur dafür verantwortlich waren. Seit dem Entstehen wurde der B. als unsittlich und der allgemeinen Moralität schädlich von Verboten der Obrigkeit begleitet.

B. ist keine Volksdichtung im Sinne romantischer Vorstellungen. Er ist massenhaft verbreitete Literatur für die Unterschicht. Entsprechend sind seine ästhetischen und stilistischen Mittel. Besondere Grausamkeit der Verbrechen, Häufung der Katastrophen und Unglücksfälle gehören ebenso hierzu wie eine ambitionierte, klischeehafte Sprache voll gesuchter Metaphorik. Bereits im 18. Jh. findet sich ernsthafte Aufnahme bänkelsängerischer Formen bei Dichtern wie Gleim und Bürger mit dem Ziel der ‹Volkstümlichkeit› ebenso wie das satirische Aufgreifen des B. (z. B. in den Parodien auf Goethes *Werther*). Der «stilisierte B.» (Sternitzke), die bewußte Aufnahme seiner Mittel in die Literatur vor allem in ironisch-parodistischer Absicht, aber auch zur politischen Agitation wurde seit Mitte des 19. Jh. ein beliebtes Kunstmittel, bei Heine und Hoffmann von Fallersleben wie bei F. Th. Vischer und W. Busch. Das frühe deutsche Kabarett wurde ebenso vom B. beeinflußt wie B. Brecht, der in Gedichten und Stücken bewußt Elemente des B. verwandte. Traditionslinien reichen bis zu Autoren wie H. C. Artmann, Ror Wolf und Christa Reinig, zu Liedermachern wie Degenhardt, Süverkrüp und Biermann (→Moritat).

Altamura, A.: I Cantastorie e la poesia populare Italiana. Neapel 1965; Braungart, W. (Hg.): Bänkelsang. Stuttgart 1985; Gugitz, G.: Lieder der Straße. Wien 1954; Janda, E./Nötzoldt, F.: Die Moritat vom Bänkelsang oder das Lied der Straße. München 1959; Oettich, G.: Der Bänkelsang in der Kunstdichtung des 20. Jahrhunderts. Diss. (masch.) Wien 1964; Petzoldt, L.: Bänkelsang. Stuttgart 1974; ders.: Die freudlose Muse. Stuttgart 1970; Rebiczek, F.: Der Wiener Volks- und Bänkelsang 1800–1840. Wien/Leipzig 1913; Riedel, K. V.: Der Bänkelsang. Hamburg 1963; Riha, K.: Moritat, Bänkelsang, Protestballade. Königstein/Ts. [2] 1979; Schilder Bilder Moritaten. Berlin 1987 (Katalog); Shepard, L.: The Broadside Ballad. London 1962; Zimmermann, H. D. (Hg.): Lechzend nach Tyrannenblut. Berlin 1972.

Wolfgang Beck

Barocktheater

Historisch gesehen ist das B. ein Element der Barockkultur, die sich in Kunst und Literatur von ca. Ende des 16. bis Ende des 17. Jh. erstreckt mit zeitlichen Verschiebungen und Akzentsetzungen je nach Land und Kultur. Gemeinsam ist das Anknüpfen an die Renaissance (→Renaissancetheater) und bes. die künstlerischen und literarischen Ansätze des ital. Cinquecento (→Rinascimento). Je nach Entwicklungslage mündet das B. ein in die →Klassik (Frankreich) oder die Aufklärung (Deutsch-

128 Barocktheater

land). Generell steht die gesamte Barockkultur im Zeichen einer Thea-
tralisierung (→Theatrum mundi), so daß dem Theater und dem Schau-
spiel eine zentrale Funktion im Selbstverständnis der Epoche zukommt.
Höhepunkte in der Entwicklung des B.: Goldenes Zeitalter (→Siglo de
Oro) in Spanien, →Elisabethanisches und Jakobinisches Theater in Eng-
land, Seicento in Italien, dt., frz. B.; Autoren: Shakespeare, Marlowe,
Jonson oder Ford, Calderón und Lope de Vega, in den Niederlanden
Joost van den Vondel, Gryphius und Lohenstein in Deutschland oder der
Franzose Pierre Corneille in seiner Frühphase.

Geistesgeschichtlich ist das B. noch dem heilsgeschichtlichen Denken
zuzuordnen: Im Bilde des Theatrum mundi erscheint Gott zugleich als
Regisseur und Zuschauer, die Figuren gehören jedoch nicht mehr dem
Mythos an, sondern der Geschichte. Diese erscheint im Sinne des →Welt-
theaters als Trauer- oder Lustspiel; jedenfalls ist dieses Theater vollstän-
diges Abbild und vollkommenes Sinnbild der Welt zugleich. In diesem
Kontext übernimmt das Theater die Grundmotive des barocken Denkens: Vanitas, Dialektik von Sein und Schein, Wahrheit und Maske,
Person und Rolle, Ewigkeit und Augenblick, Beständigkeit und Unbeständigkeit, Dauer und Vergänglichkeit, Illusion und Desillusion (span.:
engaño/desengaño). In der Folge der christlichen Lehre und des Absolutismus fungiert das B. auch als Fürstenspiegel, also nicht nur didaktisch
im Sinne des Religiös-Moralischen, sondern auch als ‹Schule der Politik›.

Dramaturgisch erstrebte dieses Welttheater Globalität, Totalität der
Gattungen bei aller Getrenntheit, der Formen, der Aufführung. Daraus
ergibt sich zuerst die Vielzahl und Vielfalt der Gattungen und Untergattungen, vom adaptierten →Mysterienspiel des span. →Auto Sacramental
und dem →Trauerspiel bis zum →Lustspiel und der →comedia über die
→Tragikomödie und das →Schäferspiel, von den Festen und →Balletts des
→höfischen Theaters bis zu den komischen Spielen der Volksspaßmacher
(vom Hanswurst und Pickelhering über die ital. Figuren der →Commedia
dell'arte bis zum engl. fool und clown); und wiederum innerhalb dieser
Hauptformen die Untergattungen des →Märtyrerdramas des →Jesuiten-
theaters oder des →Schuldramas, die engl. →masques und →anti-masques,
die →Historienspiele, →Haupt- und Staatsaktionen oder die vielen Formen des komischen →Volkstheaters. Es ist, als ob das B. das Auffangbek-
ken gewesen sei für die verschiedenen theatralischen Formen der Antike,
des Mittelalters und der Renaissance, die es im Sinne der damaligen Ideologie neugestaltet hat. Daher auch die Vielgestaltigkeit dieses Theaters.
Aus der Interpretation der Antike, auch bei ital. und frz. Theoretikern
der Renaissance, leitet sich im B. die Gattungshierarchie der Dreierstruk-
tur ab mit der Trias →Tragödie, Komödie sowie Tragikomödie/Schäfer-
spiel als gemischter Gattung. Die aristotelischen oder platonischen
Tendenzen jener Theoretiker bestimmen auch z. T. die dramatischen

Erstes Intermedio für «Veglia della liberatione di Tirreno» im Teatro Mediceo degli Uffizi 1617; Zeichnung: J. Callot (TS)

M. A. Cesti: «Il pomo d'oro». Akt II, Szene 6–7. Bühne: G. und L. Burnacini, 1666 (TS)

«Il pomo d'oro». Akt II, Szene 10–12 (TS)

«Nozze di Peleo e Teti». Ballett und Komödie, 1654. Bühne: G. Torelli (TS)

Prolog zu «La Monarchia latina Trionfante» von N. Minato, 1678. Bühne und Vorhang: L. Burnacini (TS)

Figurine von I. Jones: «Penthesilea», 1609 (TS)

Ludwig XIV. im Kostüm des «Sonnenkönigs» (TS)

Theater im Benediktinerkloster Ottobeuren, 1725 (TS)

Ruinentheater in der Eremitage von Bayreuth, 1743 (TS)

Innenraum des Markgräflichen Opernhauses zu Bayreuth; Entwurf: G. Galli-Bibiena, 1744/48 (TS)

Blatt aus dem Festbericht über das Feuerwerk zur Hochzeit Kaiser Leopolds I., Wien 1666 (TS)

Grundbegriffe der →Mimesis und der →Katharsis, freilich in religiös-moralischer Umdeutung. Insofern sind im Barock die drei Grundgattungen Träger der christlich-stoischen Morallehre, Aneiferung und Abschreckung durch tugend- und lasterhafte Charaktere oder moralisch-gesellschaftliches Normenspiel der Komödie. Angestrebt wird die Abschwächung der Affekte im Geiste der christlich-stoischen Ethik (christliche Tugendlehre vermischt mit der Morallehre des Seneca und eines Descartes), dies über den Trost (consolatio) der tragischen oder den Triumph der komischen/tragikomischen Form. Wesentlich in dieser Dramentheorie ist auch die in Anlehnung an die Antike oder die Renaissance adaptierte Form mit →Prolog und Exposition/Höhepunkt/Peripetie/Katastrophe und Anagnorisis sowie dem →Chor mit didaktisch-moralischer Funktion. Grundlegendes Strukturelement ist die Emblematik.

Theatertechnisch kennzeichnet das B. die Kongruenz von Lehre, Grundmotiven und Ausdrucksmitteln. →Theaterbau und -szenerie, →Bühnenbild und Bühnenspielraum stellten die Hauptgedanken des Barock dar und sind ebenfalls Komponenten der Theaterkultur als Innovation dieser Epoche. Der Anspruch auf die totale Wiedergabe der sinnlichen Welt führte zum Triumph der Maschinerie, der Kulissen, der Feuer- und Wassereffekte; insbesondere die Erfindung der Wechselkulisse und der Raumperspektive sind darauf bezogen. Der Renaissance-Spielraum repräsentierte in seinem horizontalen Bau die zwischenmenschliche Konfliktsphäre einer weltzugewandten Zeit. Im Barock wird alles ins Vertikale gewendet, mit Bezug nach oben hin auf Gott, nach unten hin auf den Gegenspieler, den Teufel; diesen beiden Kräften ausgeliefert, agiert im Zwischenreich der Mensch. Daher weicht die frühere Flächenstruktur der räumlichen Aufgliederung: oben, unten, Mitte erscheinen in der Kombination von Kulisse und Prospekt, Schauraum und Spielraum; alles in Bau, Kulissenmalerei und Maschineneffekten ist auf Perspektive und Augentäuschung angelegt im Sinne der Scheinhaftigkeit und Vergänglichkeit des Diesseitigen, zugleich aber auch seiner sinnlichen Reize und seines verführerischen Prunks. Dazu trugen auch bei das in diesem Bühnensystem der Illusion eingebaute Prinzip des →Theaters auf dem Theater, des Stücks im Stück sowie die dem Motiv der Täuschung entsprechenden Kostümverkleidungen und Masken.

Der Vielfalt dieser Formen und Mittel entsprach die Anzahl und Varietät der Mäzene, Truppen und Schauplätze: Fürstenhöfe, Ordensklöster, Schultheater, Marktplätze und →Wandertruppen aus England, den Niederlanden oder Italien, Schüler oder festangestellte Künstler.

Dramaturgisch und techn. hat das B. lange nachgewirkt. Die Formen dauern weiter an, wenn auch verändert; erst das 19. Jh. hat die Barocktechnik erneuert. Der Einfluß des span. Barock ist im österr. Theater bis Hofmannsthal (*Der Turm*, 1926) und bes. in der →Volksstücktradition

130   La Barraca

spürbar, im frz. Theater z. B. bei Paul Claudel (*Le soulier de satin*, 1930) oder Montherlant (*La reine morte*, 1942); das Don Juan-Thema bleibt weiterhin wirksam; thematisch und techn. finden sich sogar Einwirkungen auf das Theater Brechts.

Alewyn, R.: Schauspieler und Stegreifbühne des Barock. In: Mimus und Logos. Emsdetten 1952; ders./Sälzle, K.: Das große Welttheater. Reinbek bei Hamburg 1959; Alexander, R. J.: Das deutsche Barockdrama. Stuttgart 1984; Barner, W.: Barockrhetorik. Tübingen 1970; Baur-Heinhold, M.: Theater des Barock. München 1966; Benjamin, W.: Ursprung des dt. Trauerspiels. Frankfurt/M. 1963; Bircher, M. (Hg.): Inszenierung und Regie barocker Dramen. Stuttgart 1976; Catholy, E.: Das dt. Lustspiel. Vom Mittelalter bis zum Ende der Barockzeit. Stuttgart 1969; Hausenstein, W.: Vom Genie des Barock. München 1956; Rommel, O.: Die Alt-Wiener Volkskomödie. Wien 1952; Rousset, J.: La littérature de l'âge baroque en France. Paris 1953; ders.: L'intérieur et l'extérieur. Paris 1968; Schings, H.-J.: Consolatio Tragoediae. In: Grimm, R. (Hg.): Deutsche Dramentheorien I. Frankfurt/M. 1971; Schöne, A.: Das Zeitalter des Barock. München 1963; ders.: Emblematik und Drama im Zeitalter des Barock. München 1964; Schöne, G.: Die Entwicklung der Perspektivbühne von Serlio bis Galli-Bibiena nach den Perspektivbüchern. Leipzig 1933; Tintelnot, H.: Barocktheater und Barockkunst. Berlin 1937.

Gérard Schneilin

La Barraca

Span. studentisches Wandertheater (→Wanderbühne), mit dem Federico García Lorca (1898–1936) im Auftrag des span. Kulturministeriums zusammen mit seinem Freund Eduardo Ugarte 1932/33 die span. Provinzen durchstreifte, um seine Ideen des ‹Theaters der sozialen Aktion› und die kulturellen Reformbestrebungen der 2. span. Republik (1931–39) zu verwirklichen. Die Truppe brachte u. a. die span. Klassik des ‹Siglo de Oro› zum erstenmal einer größtenteils analphabetischen Landbevölkerung näher.

Byrd, S.: La Baraca and the Spanish National Theater. New York 1975; Sáenz de la Calzada, L.: La Barraca. Teatro universitario. Madrid 1976.

Martin Franzbach

Basoches

(Frz., möglicherweise von ‹basilique› als früherer Bezeichnung für das Gerichtsgebäude abgeleitet) Zu Beginn des 14. Jh. in Paris gegründete Gerichts- und Parlamentsschreiberzunft. Vereinigte vor allem die angehenden Juristen, deren Zusammenschluß in einer pädagogischen Zielsetzung analog zum Herrschaftssystem der Monarchie aufgebaut war; Leitung hatte ein von ‹Würdenträgern› (dignitaires) umgebener ‹König› mit eigener (Ehren-)Gerichtsbarkeit zur Schlichtung von Streitigkeiten unter den Schreibern. Die seit 1442 nachweisbaren Feste der B. (‹B. du Palais›, d. h. ‹B. des [Justiz-]Palastes› genannt) waren mit – die Justiz in Farcen, Sottien und Moralitäten aufs Korn nehmenden – Theateraufführungen verbunden. Gerichtsverhandlungen wurden nachgespielt, fiktive Prozesse aufgeführt, wobei oft in rüdem Ton und leicht erkennbaren Anspielungen hochgestellte Persönlichkeiten bloßgestellt wurden. Kritische Interventionen des frz. Königs waren die Folge. Ab 1538 wurden alle B. zensuriert, kurz danach waren Anspielungen auf Lebende grundsätzlich verboten. Ende des 16. Jh. ist die letzte B.-Aufführung feststellbar. Die Zunft der B. bestand in Paris und an frz. Provinzgerichten noch bis Ende des 18. Jh. weiter.

Harvey, H.: The theatre of the Basoches. Cambridge (Mass.) 1941.

Horst Schumacher

Bathsheva Dance Company

1963 gründet Bathsheva de Rothschild aus 16 hauptsächlich in der Graham-Technik ausgebildeten Tänzer/innen die Modern Dance Company Israels. Leitung bis 1970: Jane Dudley (*1912). Nachdem B. de Rothschild 1972 ihre Protektion zurückzog, wird die Kompanie vom Staat unterstützt. Verschiedene Gastchoreographen, u. a. G. Tetley, J. Cranko, R. Cohan, haben für das Ensemble gearbeitet, dessen künstlerische Direktion in den 70er Jahren häufig wechselte. Seit 1990 ist der Tänzer und Choreograph Ohad Naharin künstlerischer Direktor der Kompanie.

Koegler, H./Günther, H.: Reclams Ballettlexikon. Stuttgart 1984.

Helga Ettl / Patricia Stöckemann

Bauhausbühne

1921 wurde am Bauhaus (März 1919 in Weimar gegr.) eine B.-Werkstatt ins Leben gerufen. Unter der Leitung von Lothar Schreyer (1886–1966) stand die Theaterarbeit der frühen Jahre noch ganz im Zeichen des literarischen Expressionismus. Das sollte sich 1923 ändern, als Oskar Schlemmer (1888–1943) zum Werkstattleiter berufen wurde. Eingebunden in eine Gesamtkonzeption visueller Künste, eröffnete sich für die Thea-

132 Bauhausbühne

terarbeit am Bauhaus die Möglichkeit, eine von traditionellen literarischen Einflüssen weitgehend unabhängige B.-Kunst zu entwickeln.

Nicht das Sprechtheater und Erzähldrama als Sonderform abendländischer Hochkultur, sondern der Ort des theatralischen Geschehens – die B. – stand im Mittelpunkt der Bauhausexperimente. Die Schaubühne als ‹Aktionskonzentration von Ton, Licht (Farbe), Raum, Form und Bewegung› war in ihre Bestandteile zu zerlegen, um auf diese Weise zu einer ‹Grammatik der B.-Elemente› zu gelangen (vgl. dazu Kurt Schwerdtfeger, 1897–1966: *Reflektorische Lichtspiele*, Ludwig Hirschfeld-Mack, 1893–1965: *Farbenlichtspiele*, und Alexander Schawinsky, 1904–79: *Spektodrama*). Die Rückkehr zu den primären, theaterkonstituierenden Elementen bedeutete eine Abkehr von naturalistischer Imitationskunst: Scheinwerfer und Lichteffekte sollten nicht länger ‹der Erzeugung von Sonnen- und Mondschein dienen›, die B. war nicht mehr verurteilt, ‹Wald, Gebirge, ein Zimmer darzustellen›. Rückkehr zum Primären bedeutete Befreiung vom dekorativen Ballast und ‹elektizistischen Beiwerk aller Stile und Zeiten›.

Forderte die Bauhauswerkstatt eine umfassendere Einbeziehung des Publikums, so war zusammen mit dem B. auch der Zuschauerraum neu zu gestalten. Die Guckkastenbühne war durch Arena- und Rundbühne zu ersetzen – B.-Formen, die die Spielhandlung stärker in den Zuschauerraum hineinverlagerten und dem Publikum ein größeres Blickfeld eröffneten. In dem von Walter Gropius (1883–1969) konzipierten ‹Totaltheater› nahmen die Bauhausideen konkrete Gestalt an. Auch Heinz Loew (1903–81) mit seinem Entwurf eines ‹mechanischen B.-Modells› sowie Andreas Weininger (*1899) und Farkas Molnàr (1897–1945) mit ihren Plänen für ein ‹Kugeltheater› bzw. ‹U-Theater› arbeiteten an der Überwindung herkömmlicher B.-Formen. Das kommende Theater sollte gleichermaßen auf den präzisen Gesetzen der Mathematik wie auf den ‹unnennbaren› Hypothesen der Metaphysik fundiert sein. Walter Gropius forderte vom Theater Besinnung auf den übersinnlich kultischen ‹Urgrund› des Bühnenspiels – ein Gedanke, der trotz wissenschaftlich-experimenteller Ausrichtung der Theaterarbeit am Bauhaus Einlaß in die Gesamtkonzeption fand.

1925 erschien in der Reihe der Bauhausbücher der Band *Die Bühne im Bauhaus* mit einem Beitrag von Oskar Schlemmer (*Mensch und Kunstfigur*), in dem die Stellung des Menschen im kubischen (Bühnen-)Raum untersucht wird. Der Mensch als ‹Maß aller Dinge› war für Schlemmer zugleich Mechanismus aus Maß und Zahl. Zum einen entsprach der Mathematik des Raums eine Mathematik des menschlichen Körpers, zum anderen befand sich der Mensch als ‹mobile Raumplastik› zu den planimetrisch-stereometrischen Dimensionen des ihn umgebenden Bühnenraums in einem besonderen – von der bisherigen Theatertheorie noch nicht erfaßten – Spannungsverhältnis. An Hand des Tänzermenschen demonstrierte Schlemmer in seinem *Triadischen Ballett* (1922, vor seiner Bauhauszeit entstanden) die der Bühnensituation – ihrer Dynamik und Statik – zugrunde liegende Raum-Körper-Dialektik (‹Triade› meint hier die Dreiheit von Form, Farbe, Raum – die Dreidimensionalität des Raums: Höhe, Tiefe, Breite – die drei Grundformen der Geometrie: Kugel, Kegel, Kubus).

Entindividualisiert durch Maske und Kostüm trat der Mensch auf der Bauhausbühne nur noch als Träger mechanischer Körperfunktionen in Erscheinung. Er verlor seine zentrale Stellung im Theateruniversum und wurde zur Figurine – Bühnenelement in einer großen ‹Licht- und Raummaschinerie› –, ein auf Grund seiner unzulänglichen «Bewegungs- und Formorganisation» durchaus entbehrliches B.-Element, das durch wesentlich vollkommenere technische Apparate zu ersetzen war (so der Ungar Laszlo Moholy-Nagy, 1895–1946, über das kommende «Theater der Totalität»). Mit ihrem *Mechanischen Ballett* (1923) unternahmen Kurt Schmidt (*1901), Friedrich W. Bogler (1902–45) und Georg Teltscher (1904–83) einen ersten Schritt in die von Moholy-Nagy skizzierte Richtung.

Bossmann, A.: «Theater und Technik» – Theaterkonzeptionen des Bauhauses. Diss. Berlin 1988; Michaud, E.: Théâtre au Bauhaus (1919–29). Lausanne 1978; Scheper, D.: Oskar Schlemmer – Das Triadische Ballett und die Bauhausbühne. Diss. Wien 1970; Schlemmer, O. u. a.: Die Bühne im Bauhaus (1925, Bd. 4 der Bauhausbücher). Neuausgabe Mainz/Berlin 1965; Wingler, H. M.: Das Bauhaus. Bramsche [2]1968, bes. S. 350–361.

Carl Wege

Bauhaustänze

Mit der Gründung des ersten Bauhauses durch Gropius in Weimar 1919 ist zugleich die Bauhausbühne existent. Oskar Schlemmer (1888–1943) erkennt die Chance, Feste inszenieren, Masken erfinden, Kostüme bauen und Räume ausschmücken zu können. Die Vielfalt seiner Tätigkeiten vereint er bereits 1912 vor der Eröffnung des Bauhauses in seinem *Triadischen Ballett*. Kennzeichnend für dieses kubistische Ballett ist die Erzeugung theatralischer Wirkungen durch raumplastische Kostüme, die die Körper der Tänzer als geometrische Grundformen Kugel, Quadrat und Kubus umhüllen. Diese geometrischen Formen bewegen sich als Plastiken durch den Raum. Schlemmers *Triadisches Ballett*, eine dreiteilige Tanzfolge, wird von drei differenten Stimmungen durchzogen: einer heiter-burlesken, einer festlich-getragenen und einer mystisch-phantastischen. Das Bauhaus siedelt 1925/26 von Weimar nach Dessau über. Dort übernimmt Oskar Schlemmer den Aufbau einer Versuchsbühne. Seine Ansichten und Erkenntnisse über den Ursprung allen theatralischen Spiels entwickelt er im 1925 publizierten Bauhausbuch *Mensch und Kunstfigur*. Die Themen des Buches bilden zum Teil die Grundlage für die Konzeption der Bauhaustänze. Form, Farbe, Licht, Raum und Bewegung werden im Bauhaustanztheater in ihren Eigengesetzlichkeiten erforscht.

B.: 1. Im Raumtanz verfolgen drei Tänzer eine auf dem Boden markierte Liniengeometrie. Drei Gangarten – drei Farben – drei Formen – drei Charaktere werden verknüpft. 2. Aus dem Hantieren, Schwingen oder Sich-Bewegen mit Stäben, Stangen, Kugeln oder Keulen entfalten sich die Bewegungsmotive des Formentanzes. 3. Der Gestentanz spielt mit Fortbewegungsarten und menschlichen Gebärden. 4. Die Auseinandersetzung mit Materialien und Objekten und zugleich die Material-Mensch-Beziehungen führen zum Baukastenspiel und zu den Metall-, Reifen-, Glas-, Stab- und Kulissentänzen.

Günther, H.: Die Entstehungsgeschichte des Triadischen Balletts. In: Das Tanzarchiv, April 1978, S. 133–136; Maur, K. v.: Oskar Schlemmer. München 1982; Schlemmer, T.: Tut Schlemmer erinnert sich an das Bauhausfest und Bauhaustheater. In: Theater heute, Mai 1965, S. 37–39; Wingler, H. M.: Das Bauhaus. Bramsche [3] 1975.

Patricia Stöckemann

Bayerisches Staatsballett

Das Münchner Nationaltheater blickt auf eine lebendige Tanztradition seit seiner Eröffnung 1818 zurück. Zu seinen Ballettdirektoren gehören 1917–30 Heinrich Kröller (1880–1930), 1939–44 Pia (*1908) und Pino (*1907) Mlakar, 1945–48 Marcel Luipart (1912–89), 1950–52 Victor Gsovsky (1902–74), 1959–68 Heinz Rosen (1908–72) und kommissarisch 1968–70 John Cranko (1927–73; →Staatstheater Stuttgart). 1989 übernimmt die ehemalige Primaballerina des Staatsopernballetts Konstanze Vernon (*1939) die Leitung der zugleich in Bayerisches Staatsballett umbenannten Kompanie. Vernon baut das Ensemble neu auf und verpflichtet zahlreiche von der Heinz-Bosl-Stiftung (HBS) unterstützte Tänzer.

Die HBS, 1978 von Vernon und Fred Hoffmann (*1929) gegründet, wird rasch zu einer der bedeutendsten deutschen Institutionen zur Förderung junger Tänzer. Die Erfolge der Stiftung führen zur Kooperation mit der Ballett-Akademie der Münchner Hochschule für Musik, deren Direktorin Vernon seit 1975 ist. Das Staatsballett und die Akademie arbeiten eng zusammen.

Das B. hat keinen Chefchoreographen. Im Repertoire stehen u. a. Werke von Ulysses Dove (* 1950), Jiri Kylián (* 1947; → Nederlands Dans Theater), Ohad Naharin (* 1952; → Bathsheva Dance Company), Ray Barra (* 1930), George Balanchine (1904–83; → New York City Ballet), Peter Wright (* 1926), John Neumeier (* 1942; → Hamburg Ballett), Gerhard Bohner (1936–92; → Tanztheater), Hans van Manen (* 1932; → Nederlands Dans Theater, → Het Nationale Ballet), J. Cranko und dem stellvertretenden Ballettdirektor Riccardo Duse (* 1937).

Regitz, H. (Hg.): Tanz in Deutschland – Ballett seit 1945. Berlin 1984; Deutscher Berufsverband für Tanzpädagogik (Hg.): Festschrift Deutscher Tanzpreis 1991 – Konstanze Vernon. Essen 1991.

Horst Vollmer

Bayerisches Staatsschauspiel München

Residenztheater, Altes Residenztheater (Cuvilliés-Theater), Theater im Marstall. Vorgänger Hofbühne. 1778 Nationalschauspiel im alten Opernhaus. 1818 königliches Hof- und Nationaltheater. 1833 bis 1842 Intendant Karl Theodor von Küstner (1784–1864), 1851 bis 1857 Franz von Dingelstedt (1814–81), 1854 Einladungen der 30 besten Schauspieler des Reichs zu «Gesamtgastspielen» in zyklischen Klassiker-Aufführungen. 1894 bis 1905 Ernst von Possart (1841–1921). 1896 baute der technische Direktor Karl Lautenschläger (1843–1906) die erste → Drehbühne, Revolutionierung der Bühnentechnik. 1919 Bayerisches Staatstheater, organisatorisch von der Oper getrennt. – 1945 bis 1948 Intendant Paul Verhoeven (1901–75); 1948–1953 Alois Johannes Lippl (1903–1957), Inszenierungen von Jürgen Fehling; 1953 bis 1958 Kurt Horwitz (1887–1974), Inszenierungen von Kortner; 1958 bis 1972 Helmut Henrichs, 1972 bis 1983 Kurt Meisel (* 1912), zahlreiche Inszenierungen von Ingmar Bergman (* 1918). 1983 bis 1986 Frank Baumbauer; seit 1986 Günther Beelitz (* 1939). Stand in den letzten 60 Jahren meist im Schatten der Münchner Kammerspiele. Traditionelle Klassikerinszenierungen, bayerische Stücke – über 400 Aufführungen des *Brandner Kasper*. 1986 Renovierung des 1948 bis 1951 wiederhergestellten Hauses.

Wagner, H.: 200 Jahre Münchner Theaterchronik 1750–1950. München 1965. Verein d. Freunde d. Bayerischen Staatsschauspiels (Hg.): ... dann spielten sie wieder. München 1986.

Werner Schulze-Reimpell / Red.

BDAT (Bund Deutscher Amateurtheater)

Der BDAT ist die bundesweite Dachorganisation des organisierten → Amateurtheaters in Deutschland. Er wurde am 27.8.1892 in Berlin unter dem Namen «Verband der Privat-Theater-Vereine Deutschland e. V.» gegründet. Nach Zusammenschlüssen mit ähnlichen Organisationen und Gruppierungen (u. a. 1920 zum «Reichsbund für Volksbühnenspiele e. V.», 1951 zum «Bund deutscher Volksbühnenspieler e. V.») entstand 1971 der «Bund Deutscher Amateurtheater e. V.» (BdA, später BDAT).

Seit 1975 sind die Amateurtheaterverbände aller elf alten Bundesländer im BDAT zusammengeschlossen: Landesverband Amateurtheater Baden-Württemberg e. V.; Volksspielkunst-Verband Bayern e. V.; Landesverband Bremer Amateurtheater e. V.; Verband Hamburger Amateurtheater e. V.; Landesverband Hessischer Amateurbühnen e. V.; Landesverband Niedersächsischer Amateurbühnen e. V.; Amateurtheaterverband Nordrhein-Westfalen e. V.; Landesverband Amateurtheater Rheinland-Pfalz e. V.; Saarländischer Volksbühnenbund e. V.; Verband der Amateurtheater Schleswig-Holstein e. V. In den neuen Bundesländern (vormalige DDR) wurden folgende Amateurtheaterverbände gegründet: Landesverband Amateurtheater Sachsen e. V.; Landesverband Thüringer Amateurtheater e. V.; Brandenburgischer Amateurtheaterverband e. V.; Landesverband Amateurtheater Mecklenburg-Vorpommern e. V. Außerdem ist der «Verband Deutscher Freilichtbühnen e. V.» Vollmitglied.

Der BDAT vertritt «die Interessen aller Formen des darstellenden Spiels in der Bundesrepublik Deutschland». Die Bundesversammlung ist das oberste Organ. Mitglieder des Dachverbandes sind jeweils die autonomen Landesverbände mit ihren derzeit insgesamt ca. 1300 Mitgliedsbühnen. Diesen Mitgliedern werden u. a. folgende Dienste zur Verfügung gestellt: Schulungskurse für Darsteller, Spielleiter, Bühnenbildner, Kostümbildner und Techniker; Versicherungsschutz; GEMA-Rahmenvertrag; Vergünstigungsabkommen mit Bühnenverlagen; Werbung; Fachausschüsse für Erwachsenentheater, Theaterjugend, Öffentlichkeitsarbeit und Arbeitskreise für Senioren- und Figurentheater. Neben Partnerschaften mit Verbänden in Österreich, der Schweiz und Südtirol gibt es einen Spielgruppenaustausch mit Belgien, England, Finnland, Frankreich, Holland und Island. Der BDAT ist u. a. Mitglied der «Association Internationale du Théâtre Amateur» (AITA) und der «Association Internationale du Théâtre pour l'Enfance et la Jeunesse» (→ ASSITEJ). Für das «Central European Committee» der AITA verwaltet er das zentraleuropäische Sekretariat. Sitz der Bundesgeschäftsstelle ist Heidenheim/Br.; Publikationsorgan: *Spiel & Bühne* (erscheint dreimal jährlich). Die ca. 1300 Einzelbühnen haben annähernd 100000 Mitglieder und veranstalten im Jahr ca. 10600 Aufführungen, zu denen etwa 2,5 Millionen Zuschauer kommen.

Ute Hagel

Benefizvorstellung

(Lat. ‹beneficium› = Wohltat, Gefälligkeit) Heute vor allem eine Vorstellung, deren Reinerlös einem wohltätigen Zweck zugeführt wird. Im 18. und 19. Jh. übliche Einrichtung für einzelne Schauspieler – zur Aufbesserung des Gehalts (gelegentlich im Vertrag festgelegt), beim Wechsel des Engagements und beim Eintritt in den Ruhestand. Auch bei Gastspielen übliche Art der Entlohnung.

Wolfgang Beck

Berliner Ensemble

Am Bertolt-Brecht-Platz. Zwei Spielstätten (→Theater am Schiffbauerdamm, erbaut um 1890 mit 684 Plätzen, Probebühne mit ca. 100 Plätzen), Leitung seit 1991 ein Direktorium: Matthias Langhoff (* 1941), Fritz Marquardt (* 1928), Heiner Müller (* 1929), Peter Palitzsch (* 1918) und Peter Zadek (* 1926).

Gegründet 1949 von Helene Weigel (1900–71) und Bertolt Brecht (1898–1956) sowie Schauspielern und künstlerischen Mitarbeitern der Inszenierung von *Mutter Courage* (1949), Regie: Erich Engel (1891 bis 1966)/Brecht am →Deutschen Theater, dort zu Gast bis 1954, seitdem Theater am Schiffbauerdamm. Intendantin des B. E. war bis zu ihrem Tod (1971) Helene Weigel, Brecht ‹nur› künstlerischer Leiter, der hier zum erstenmal eine eigene Bühne und damit Arbeitsmöglichkeiten hatte, auf denen eine neue Epoche der Theaterkunst entstehen konnte. Folgende neun «Eigenarten des B. E.» nennt Brecht (1951):

«1. Die Gesellschaft als veränderbar darzustellen. 2. Die menschliche Natur als veränderbar darzustellen. 3. Die menschliche Natur als abhängig von der Klassenzugehörigkeit darzustellen. 4. Konflikte als gesellschaftliche Konflikte darzustellen. 5. Charaktere mit echten Widersprüchen darzustellen. 6. Entwicklungen von Charakteren, Zuständen und Ereignissen als diskontinuierlich (sprunghaft) darzustellen. 7. Die dialektische Betrachtungsweise zum Vergnügen zu machen. 8. Die Errungenschaften der Klassik im dialektischen Sinn ‹aufzuheben›. 9. Aus Realismus Poesie herzustellen.»

138 Berliner Ensemble

In den Modell-Inszenierungen seiner eigenen Werke *Mutter Courage* (1949); *Herr Puntila und sein Knecht Matti* (1949), Regie: Engel/Brecht; *Die Mutter* (1951), Regie: Brecht, Bühne: Caspar Neher (1897–1962); *Die Gewehre der Frau Carrar* (1952), Regie: Egon Monk (* 1927); *Der kaukasische Kreidekreis* (1954), Regie: Brecht; *Leben des Galilei* (1957), Regie: (nach Brechts Tod) Engel, entwickelt Brecht seine «Theaterarbeit», in der Textanalyse, ausprobierendes Bühnen- und Arrangementsentwerfen, diskursives Probenklima, sorgsamer Umgang mit den schauspielerischen Techniken sowie wissenschaftliche Begleitung (Modellbuch) ineinandergreifen. Weitere Inszenierungen u. a.: Brechts Bearbeitung des *Hofmeisters* (1950) von Lenz (1751–92), Regie: Brecht/Neher, in deren «Anmerkungen» (*Über das Poetische und Artistische*) er seine späte Theaterästhetik entwirft; *Wassa Schelesnowa* (1949) von Gorki, Regie: Berthold Viertel (1885–1953); *Biberpelz* und *Roter Hahn* (1951) von Hauptmann (1862–1946), Regie: Monk; *Der zerbrochne Krug* (1952) von Kleist (1777–1811), Regie: Therese Giehse (1898 bis 1975); *Urfaust* (1952) von Goethe (1749–1832), Regie: Monk; *Der Prozeß der Jeanne D'Arc zu Rouen 1431* (1952) von Anna Seghers (1900–83), Regie: Benno Besson (* 1922); *Katzgraben* (1953) von Erwin Strittmatter (* 1912), Regie: Brecht, Bühne: Karl von Appen (1900–81); *Don Juan* (1954) von Molière, Regie: Besson (zur Eröffnung am Schiffbauerdamm); *Winterschlacht* (1955) von Johannes R. Becher (1891–1958), Regie: Brecht; *Pauken und Trompeten* (1955) von Farquhar (1678–1707), Regie: Besson; *Die Ziehtochter oder Wohltaten tun weh* (1955) von Alexander N. Ostrowskij (1823–86), Regie: Angelika Hurwicz (* 1922); *Der Held der westlichen Welt* (1956) von Synge (1871–1909), Regie: Peter Palitzsch (* 1918)/Wekwerth (* 1929).

Nach Brechts Tod (1956) versuchten Erich Engel und die Schüler seine Arbeit fortzusetzen, was vor allem mit *Der gute Mensch von Sezuan* (1957), Regie: Besson, Titelrolle: Käthe Reichel (* 1926), und *Der aufhaltsame Aufstieg des Arturo Ui* (1959), Regie: Palitzsch/Wekwerth, Titelrolle: Brechts Schwiegersohn Ekkehard Schall (* 1930) gelang, doch wie Monk (1955) siedelten auch Hurwicz (1958) und Palitzsch (1961) in die Bundesrepublik über; mit Brechts Bearbeitung des *Coriolan* (1964), Regie: Wekwerth/Joachim Tenschert (* 1928), für die Ruth Berghaus (* 1927) furiose Schlachtszenen choreographierte, hatte das B. E. seinen vorerst letzten großen, auch international anerkannten Erfolg. Auch Besson (1960 ans →Deutsche Theater) und vorübergehend «Chefregisseur» Wekwerth (1968–77) verließen das B. E. Helene Weigel gab dem jungen Duo Manfred Karge (* 1938)/Matthias Langhoff (* 1941) erste Regiechancen (‹Schülerschüler›), holte Uta Birnbaum (* 1933), die eine vielbeachtete Inszenierung von *Mann ist Mann* (1967) herausbrachte. Gleichwohl nehmen Tendenzen zu Musealisierung und Akademismus zu, die erst nach Weigels Tod (1971) aufgehalten werden. Deren bisherige Stellvertreterin Berghaus übernahm die Intendanz des B. E. und machte es zu einem Theater, das sich Fragen der Zeit (wieder) öffnete: einmal, indem es sich dem Werk Brechts mit neuem, unvoreingenommenem Blick näherte (*Im Dickicht der Städte* und *Die Gewehre der Frau Carrar*, beide 1971, und *Die Mutter*, 1974), zum anderen, indem sie – durch Zusammenarbeit mit Heiner Müller (* 1929) und Karl Mickel (* 1935) – auf DDR-Dramatik setzte, schließlich, indem sie es zuließ, daß Werke der bürgerlichen Moderne auf die DDR-Gegenwart bezogen werden, vor allem *Frühlingserwachen* (1974) und *Fräulein Julie* (1975), Regie: B. K. Tragelehn (* 1936)/Einar Schleef (* 1944).

Im April 1977, wenige Monate nach der Ausbürgerung von Wolf Biermann (* 1936), mußte Berghaus zurücktreten und ihre Versuche «mit Brecht über Brecht hinaus» aufgeben; unterstützt von den konservativen Brecht-Erben, die bisher nur zwei Ostberliner Brecht-Inszenierungen außerhalb des B. E. zuließen (*Der gute Mensch von Sezuan*, 1971 an der Volksbühne, Regie: Besson; *Die Rundköpfe und die Spitzköpfe*, 1983 am Deutschen Theater, Regie: Alexander Lang, * 1941), wurde der Traditionalist Wekwerth neuer Intendant und blieb es bis zu seiner Ablösung 1990. Seine Inszenierungen – u. a. *Galileo Galilei*, 1978, *Jegor Bulytschow und andere* von Gorki, 1979, *Troilus und Cressida*, 1985, Brechts *Fatzer*-Fragment, 1987, und *Schweyk*, 1990 – konnten nicht annähernd an die Welterfolge der späten 50er und frühen 60er Jahre anknüpfen; auch von dem 1985 von der Volksbühne ans B. E. gekommenen Fritz Marquardt – u. a. *Bürger Schippel* von Sternheim, 1985, *Germania Tod in Berlin* von H. Müller, 1989 – gingen nicht die erhofften Impulse aus. Für das Ansehen des B. E. in den 80er Jahren bedeutsame Produktionen waren die Uraufführung von Volker Brauns (* 1939) *Großer Frieden*, Regie: Wekwerth, 1979, des Chilenen Carlos Medina Dramatisierung und Inszenierung des *Kleinen Prinzen*, 1981, Horst Sagerts (* 1934) Szenographie und Regie der *Faust-Szenen* nach Goethes Urfaust, 1984, und einige Inszenierungen des ehemals Schweriner Schauspieldirektors Christoph Schroth (* 1937): *Blaue Pferde auf rotem Gras* von Michail Schatrow, 1980, *Lenins Tod* von Volker Braun, 1988, und *Familie Schroffenstein*, 1991. Aus einem DDR-Staatstheater in ein privatrechtlich von einem Direktorium geführtes Unternehmen umgewandelt, geht das B. E. ohne erkennbare konzeptionelle Konturen einer ungewissen Zukunft entgegen.

Brecht, B.: Gesammelte Werke. Bde. 15 bis 17. Frankfurt/M. 1969 (Schriften zum Theater 1–3); ders.: Theaterarbeit. Dresden 1952; ders.: Aufbau einer Rolle. Berlin (DDR) 1956; ders.: Courage Modell 1949. Berlin (DDR) 1958; Dieckmann, F.: Karl von Appens Bühnenbilder am Berliner Ensemble. Berlin (DDR) 1971; Funke, Ch./Hoffmann-Ostwald, D./Otto, H.-G. (Hg.): Theater-Bilanz. Berlin (1971), S. 55–58; Funke, Ch./Kranz, D.: Theaterstadt Berlin.

Berlin (DDR) 1978, S. 81–97; Klunker, H.: Zeitstücke und Zeitgenossen: Gegenwartstheater in der DDR. München [2]1975, S. 114–163; Mittenzwei, W. (Hg.): Theater in der Zeitenwende. Berlin (DDR) 1972, S. 179–195 u. 287–312; Pietsch, J.: Werkstatt Theater. Berlin (DDR) 1975, S. 80–87 u. S. 129–140; Rühle, G.: Anarchie in der Regie? Theater in unserer Zeit 2. Frankfurt/M. 1982, S. 198–211; Schumacher, E.: Leben Brechts. Berlin (DDR) [3]1981, Kapitel IV; Tenschert, V.: Die Weigel. Berlin (DDR) 1981; Völker, K.: Bertolt Brecht. München 1975; Wekwerth, M.: Notate. Berlin (DDR) 1967; ders.: Theater in Diskussion: Notate, Gespräche, Polemiken. Berlin (DDR) 1982. Mittenzwei, W.: Das Leben des Bertolt Brecht, Bd. 2. Berlin 1986; Kranz, D.: Berliner Theater. Berlin 1990.

Andreas Roßmann / Manfred Pauli

Berliner Festwochen

Die B. F. werden seit 1951 jährlich im September veranstaltet. Konzertgastspiele und -reihen, Film, Ballett- und Theateraufführungen, letztere seit der Einrichtung des → Berliner Theatertreffens 1964 aber nicht mehr in erster Linie; dabei werden meist herausragende Produktionen des Welttheaters, oft als Werkschau eines Regisseurs vorgestellt: so 1979 Liviu Ciulei und das Teatrul Buladru (Bukarest), so 1984 Ariane Mnouchkine und das Théâtre du Soleil (Paris) mit ihrem Shakespeare-Zyklus, so 1985 Andrzej Wajda und das Stary Teatr Krakow mit ihren Dostojewski-Dramatisierungen. Manche Jahrgänge haben Schwerpunktthemen – z. B. «Naturalismus» (1979), «Strawinsky» (1980), «Preußen» (1981), «Symbolismus/Futurismus» (1983) oder «Berlin um 1900» (1984) –, doch werden diesen keineswegs alle (Theater-)Veranstaltungen zugeordnet. – Seit 1957 ‹Gegen›-Veranstaltung (Ost-)«Berliner Festtage der Musik und des Theaters» mit ausgesuchten Theatergastspielen aus der DDR und dem (auch westlichen) Ausland.

«Festwochen»-Magazine der Berliner Festspiele. Berlin 1951 ff.

Andreas Roßmann

Berliner Theatertreffen

Forum des deutschsprachigen Schauspieltheaters, das seit 1964 jährlich im Mai veranstaltet wird und bemerkenswerte Aufführungen (bis 1982: «b. Inszenierungen») aus der Bundesrepublik, Österreich und der Schweiz (Einladungen an DDR-Bühnen wurden nicht angenommen) versammelt und damit einen Mittelpunkt des Vergleichs, der Diskussion, des Meinungsaustauschs, der Information und der Orientierung schafft. Von einer ehrenamtlichen Jury, der sieben Theaterkritiker (bis 1982: zehn, darunter je einer aus der Schweiz und Österreich sowie zwei aus Berlin) angehören, werden etwa zehn Produktionen ausgesucht, die 64 bis 12 Wochen vor Beginn des Treffens Premiere hatten. «Maßgebend für die Auswahl ist das in einer Aufführung konzentrierte Zusammenwirken von Stück, Dramaturgie, Regie, schauspielerischen Leistungen und Bühnenbild. Darüber hinaus können Zusammenhänge von Theaterarbeit und ihren Bedingungen ebenso berücksichtigt werden wie besondere Leistungen in der Spielplangestaltung» (Theater-Magazin '83). Die Arbeit der Jury (und ihr Abstimmungsmodus) war oft umstritten, was die Auswahl angeht und auch deren Ausrichtung auf das Regietheater betrifft, das sie durchzusetzen half und deren Vertreter (Peter Stein, Peter Zadek, Claus Peymann) am häufigsten nominiert wurden. Auch die Vernachlässigung kleinerer Bühnen und Freier Gruppen wurde der Jury vorgeworfen. – Fürs Rahmenprogramm des B.T. werden Beiträge der beteiligten (und anderer) Bühnen, auch internationale Gastspiele eingeladen, parallel wird ein Seminar für junge Bühnenangehörige durchgeführt.

«Theatertreffen»-Magazine der Berliner Festspiele. Berlin 1964ff; Eckhardt, U., B. von Liebermann (Hg.): 25 Jahre Theatertreffen Berlin. 1964–1988. Berlin 1988.

Andreas Roßmann

Besetzung

Die von der Theaterleitung zusammen mit dem → Regisseur und ggf. auch nach Rücksprache mit den Mitgliedern des → Ensembles vorgenommene Verteilung der → Rollen. Neben den schauspielerischen Anforderungen mancher → Rollenfächer an die Darsteller können dabei auch Vertragsklauseln (Rollenansprüche, Ansehensrolle) oder die faktische Position eines Schauspielers (Beliebtheit beim Publikum, Starprinzip) ausschlaggebend sein.

Bernard Poloni

Besserungsstück

Das B. schafft als besondere Form des → Alt-Wiener Volksstücks eine äußerst publikumswirksame Synthese von Unterhaltungs- und Erbauungstheater, die während ihrer Blütezeit Anfang des 19. Jh. über 30 000 Aufführungen allein in Wien erfuhr. Die Intentionen der dramatischen

142 Besserungsstück

Gattung verbieten es, das B. als ‹Schaubühne ohne ideale Ansprüche› zu verkennen: Das B. erstrebt – zwar in mundartlicher, komisch-versöhnlicher Form – wie einst die hohe adelige Tragödie und das ernste bürgerliche Trauerspiel des aufgeklärten Bürgertums eine innere Läuterung und sittliche Besserung.

Dem B. liegt das typische Schema der Besserung eines Menschen zugrunde, der sich aus Torheit, Unzufriedenheit, Laster oder Vermessenheit der gesellschaftlichen Ordnung entzieht und durch Prüfungen und Schicksalsschläge zur Einsicht gebracht wird. Dem obligaten Happy-End entspricht die Eingliederung in gutbürgerliche Verhältnisse, die von einem volkstümlichen Publikum durch Identifikation mit ihm nahestehenden Figuren zugleich verinnerlicht wird. Insofern dient das B. dem Aufzeigen bürgerlicher Werte des Biedermeier und dem Preisen der bestehenden Ordnung in der Wiener Restaurationszeit, der Ära Metternich. Indem die erwünschte Besserung z. T. der größeren Bildhaftigkeit und Wirksamkeit halber durch das Eingreifen übernatürlicher Wesen wie Feen und Zauberer zustande kommt, fällt das B. häufig mit dem →Zauberstück gleich.

Herausragende Verfasser von B. sind die ‹Großen Drei› Joseph Alois Gleich (1772–1841), Karl Meisl (1775–1853), Adolf Bäuerle (1786 bis 1856). Seine literarisch vollendete Form erreicht das B. mit den ‹Original Zauberspiel› Ferdinand Raimunds (1790–1836), insbesondere mit *Der Bauer als Millionär* (1826), *Der Alpenkönig und der Menschenfeind* (1828), *Der Verschwender* (1834). Den moralischen Wert der Besserung und somit die Grundlage der bürgerlichen Gesellschaft im vormärzlichen Wien stellt Johann Nepomuk Nestroy (1801–62) in der Zauberposse *Der böse Geist Lumpazivagabundus oder das liederliche Kleeblatt* (1833) als künstlich und illusorisch bloß: Das Ende des B. und das Ausklingen eines bürgerlichen Zeitalters fallen zusammen. Im modernen Theater besiegelt der Österreicher Ödön von Horváth (1901–38) die Absage an das B., indem er die Besserung durch die zyklische, tragikomische Stagnation in *Geschichten aus dem Wiener Wald* (1931) ersetzt.

Dietze, W.: Tradition und Ursprünglichkeit in den Besserungsstücken des Wiener Volkstheaters. In: Weimarer Beiträge 12 (1966), S. 566–572; Rommel, O.: Die Altwiener Volkskomödie. Wien 1952.

Jean-Marie Winkler

Besucherorganisation

In der Bundesrepublik Deutschland werden rund 22 Prozent der Karten (Stand 1990/91) über Besucherorganisationen verkauft (→Abonnement).

Außer den lokalen Besucherringen sind insbesondere die Volksbühne und der Bund der Theatergemeinden von Bedeutung.

Volksbühne: Offizieller Titel ist Bundesverband der Dt. Volksbühnen-Vereine e. V., Sitz in Berlin (→Volksbühne). Der Bundesverband ist landesverbandschaftlich mit rechtlich selbständigen Vereinen organisiert (ca. 90 regionale Organisationen mit 240 000 Mitgliedern, Stand 1990). Historisch läßt er sich auf die 1890 in Berlin gegründete Freie Volksbühne Berlin zurückführen. Die Volksbühnenorganisation sah ihre Aufgabe zunächst in der Wahrung des Bildungsanspruchs des Theaters. Auf Grund hoher Mitgliederverluste wurde 1969 das Programm auch um den Unterhaltungsaspekt erweitert. «Der alte Auftrag, die Industrie-Arbeiter-Gesellschaft an die Inhalte der Kunst heranzuführen, hat sich zu der Aufgabe erweitert, breite Schichten für ein Theater zu gewinnen, das vorzüglich einem nur passiven Fernsehkonsum entgegenwirkt. Durch geistiges Miterleben und Bildung eines künstlerischen Geschmacks soll die Bereitschaft und Freiheit des eigenen Denkens und Entscheidens gefördert werden» (Arbeitspapier 1972). Verbandsorgan: Volksbühnenspiegel.

Bund der Theatergemeinden e. V., Sitz in Bonn, ist ebenfalls in Landesverbänden organisiert (47 örtliche Theatergemeinden incl. Junger Theatergemeinden mit rund 400 Zubringergruppen, Mitgliederstand 185 000, Stand 1991). Der Bund der Theatergemeinden ist der ideelle Nachfolger des früheren Bühnenvolksbundes, er richtet sich an alle Schichten der Bevölkerung, um Verständnis für alle Bereiche des künstlerischen und musischen Lebens zu fördern. Der Bund fühlt sich dem Gedanken einer christlichen Theatergemeinde verbunden. Verbandsorgan: «Theaterrundschau».

Von Bedeutung sind weiter die speziell für Schüler, Studenten und Auszubildende installierten Jugendkulturringe, die von den Kommunen getragen werden. Diese stellen z. T. feste Abonnementringe zusammen, z. T. verkaufen sie verbilligte Karten an ihre Abnehmerkreise.

Roswitha Körner / Red.

Betriebsorganisation des Theaters (BRD)

Die Theateraufführung ist das Ergebnis eines künstlerischen Schaffensprozesses, der im herkömmlichen Theaterwesen einen Unterbau aus Organisation und Technik hat. Im Idealfall haben Organisation und Technik dienende Funktion; in der alltäglichen Praxis zeigt sich jedoch, daß Organisation und Technik ein Eigenleben entwickeln und allzuoft dem künstlerischen Prozeß Kompromisse abverlangen. Im folgenden wird ein Überblick über den organisatorischen Aufbau des künstlerischen Bereichs, der Technik und der Verwaltung gegeben. Bei dieser Darstellung soll ferner berücksichtigt werden, daß der künstlerische Schaffensprozeß im Theater zugleich einen Arbeitsprozeß darstellt, der den allgemeinen Regeln des Arbeitsrechts und den besonderen Regeln des Bühnenarbeitsrechts unterworfen ist.

Der →*Intendant*, je nach rechtlicher Organisationsform allein oder zusammen mit einem kaufmännischen Direktor, steht dem gesamten Theaterbetrieb vor. Der *künstlerische Bereich* besteht aus Dramaturgie (wissenschaftliche und redaktionelle Vorbereitung der Stücke, Öffentlichkeitsarbeit, Programmheftgestaltung), künstlerischem Betriebsbüro (Spielplandispositionen, Proben- und Abstecherorganisation, z. T. Engagementvorbereitung des künstlerischen Personals). Je nach Größe des Hauses erfolgt eine weitere Untergliederung in die verschiedenen Sparten unter der Verantwortung jeweils eines Direktors: *Musikdirektor* bzw. *Generalmusikdirektor*, dem das Orchester untersteht, zum Teil auch der gesamte Musiktheaterbereich, sofern hierfür nicht ein eigener Oberspielleiter zuständig ist, *Schauspieldirektor, Ballettdirektor*. Dieses System ist nicht starr, sondern die Kompetenzverteilung hängt im einzelnen von den jeweiligen Verträgen, Betriebsordnungen etc. ab. Üblicherweise bilden die einzelnen Sparten (Schauspiel, Oper, Ballett) eigene Vorstände, die allerdings keine betrieblichen Funktionen haben, sondern eine Künstlervertretung darstellen. Diese Vorstände sind jedoch nicht zu verwechseln mit den sog. Bühnenvorständen, womit im dtspr. Theater Regisseure, Oberspielleiter, Chefbühnenbildner, Ausstattungsleiter, technische Direktoren und andere künstlerisch/technische Verantwortliche umschrieben werden.

Musiktheater: Solopersonal, Chormitglieder (die einen Chorvorstand wählen), Chorleiter/Chordirektor, Studienleiter, Repetitoren, Regisseure, Regieassistenten, Kapellmeister, Orchestermitglieder (die ebenfalls einen Orchestervorstand wählen, der insbesondere bei Besetzungsfragen beteiligt wird, ferner haben die einzelnen Stimmgruppen einen arbeitsvertraglich festgelegten Stimmführer). Die Orchester stellen teilweise eine rechtlich eigenständige Organisation dar, die auf Grund besonderer Verträge für ein Theater tätig werden. – *Ballett*: Solopersonal,

Betriebsorganisation des Theaters (BRD) 145

Corps de ballet. – *Schauspiel:* Solopersonal, Regisseure, Regieassistenten etc.

Jedes Theater verfügt ferner über eine Statistengruppe und Ersatzchormitglieder. Unabkömmlich für die abendliche Vorstellung ist der Mitarbeiterstab, der hinter der Bühne tätig wird: Abendspielleiter (der die Verantwortung für den abendlichen Ablauf hat), Inspizient (der dafür sorgt, daß niemand seinen Einsatz verpaßt).

Das Arbeitsverhältnis des künstlerischen Personals richtet sich nach dem zwischen dem Dt. Bühnenverein und der Genossenschaft Dt. Bühnenangehöriger ausgehandelten Tarifvertrag, dem sog. Normal-Vertrag Solo (zuzüglich der begleitenden Tarifverträge, → Schauspieler). Für das Ballettensemble sowie für die Chormitglieder gelten eigene Tarifverträge (NV-Tanz, NV-Chor).

Dem *techn. Bereich* steht der *techn. Direktor* vor. Dieser sorgt für die Umsetzung des Bühnen- bzw. Szenenbilds und trägt die Verantwortung dafür, daß die techn. Sicherheit gewährleistet wird (Arbeitsschutz, Unfallverhütung etc.). Je nach Größe der Bühne müssen während der Vorstellung und des sonstigen techn. Betriebs ein Bühnenmeister und ein Bühnenbeleuchtungsmeister anwesend sein (Versammlungsstättenverordnung). Üblicherweise untergliedert sich der techn. Bereich in folgende Abteilungen: Bühnentechnik (verschiedene Werkstätten mit Tischlern, Schlossern, Polsterern, Dekorateuren, Bühnenhandwerkern), Beleuchtungsabteilung, Malersaal (Vorstand des Malersaals), Bühnenmaler, Kascheure, Plastiker, Requisite, Kostümabteilung (Gewandmeister, Fundusverwalter, Schneider, Garderobiere), Maskenbildner (Chefmaskenbildner, Maskenbildner), Tontechnik (Tonmeister, Toningenieure), Wagenpark. In diesem Bereich sind die Beschäftigten z. T. überwiegend künstlerisch tätig, insoweit unterliegen sie dem Bühnentechnikertarifvertrag (mit Ausnahme der Mitarbeiter der Privattheater sowie der Landesbühnen, für letztere gilt der Bühnentechnikervertrag für Landesbühnen). Diese Tarifverträge enthalten spezielle Regelungen für die überwiegend künstlerisch tätigen Bühnentechniker, insbesondere läßt er befristete Arbeitsverhältnisse zu. Das Arbeitsverhältnis des nichtkünstlerischen techn. Personals richtet sich nach den üblichen Manteltarifverträgen. Für einige Berufe (Theatermeister, Beleuchtungsmeister) sind Zusatzausbildungen bzw. besondere Prüfungen erforderlich (vgl. Verordnung über techn. Bühnen – Studiofachkräfte).

Der *Verwaltungsabteilung* steht – je nach Rechtsform – ein Verwaltungsdirektor bzw. ein Verwaltungsleiter vor. Dieser Abteilung unterstehen: Personalabteilung (für künstlerisches und nichtkünstlerisches Personal), Vertragsabteilung (für Abschluß von Bühnenaufführungsverträgen, Tantiemenabwicklung etc.), Buchhaltung, Abonnement und Tageskasse, Archiv, Abendpersonal. Mit dem Verwaltungspersonal werden zeitlich unbefristete Arbeitsverträge abgeschlossen. In der Regel ist das Arbeitsverhältnis dem Bundesangestelltentarifvertrag angepaßt.

Es regeln sich also die Arbeitsverhältnisse der verschiedenen am theatralischen Arbeitsprozeß Beteiligten nach den unterschiedlichsten Bestimmungen. Während für die gewerblichen und techn. Arbeitnehmer, insbesondere die Verwaltungsangestellten die 38,5-Stunden-Wochenregelung gilt, gibt es eine derartige Regelung für den künstlerischen Bereich (NV-Solo-Personal, Chor, Ballett, Orchester) nicht. Hier wird vielmehr mittels tarifvertraglicher Ruhezeiten und Probenregelungen versucht, einen arbeitsrechtlichen Rahmen für die Inanspruchnahme vorzugeben. Probleme treten in der Praxis auf, wenn die unterschiedlichen Ruhezeitenregelungen miteinander kollidieren. Dem Betriebsrat steht im Rahmen der betriebsverfassungsrechtlichen Möglichkeiten ein Mitbestimmungsrecht beim Festlegen der Arbeitszeiten zu.

Für den Theaterbereich gibt es keine einheitliche Gewerkschaft, in der alle am Theater tätigen Mitglieder zusammengeschlossen sind; vielmehr sind sie ihrer Tätigkeit entsprechend organisiert: Dt. Orchestervereinigung, Vereinigung Dt. Opernchorsänger und Balletttänzer e. V., →Genossenschaft Dt. Bühnenangehöriger.

Die Personalausgaben für die am Theater Tätigen ergeben folgende durchschnittliche Verteilung: Solopersonal 19,3 %, Chor 6,3 %, Ballett 4,1 %, Bühnenleiter und Vorstände 11,5 %, Orchester 14 %, techn. und techn.-künstlerisches Personal 32 %, Verwaltungs- und Hauspersonal 8 % (insgesamt 78,2 % für Personalausgaben, Stand 1990). Dem steht folgende zahlenmäßige Aufteilung gegenüber: Bühnenleiter, Vorstände: 2325, Darsteller Musiktheater: 1115, Darsteller, Schauspieler: 1945, Ballett: 1247, Chor: 2094, Theaterorchester: 3065, künstlerisches Personal auf Gastspielvertrag: 6784, techn. Personal: 11206, Verwaltungspersonal: 1865 (davon teilzeitbeschäftigt 258), Hauspersonal: 316 (davon teilzeitbeschäftigt 1949) (Stand 1.1.1990).

Theaterstatistik 1989/90. Hg. vom Dt. Bühnenverein; Bühnen- und Musikrecht. Hg. vom Dt. Bühnenverein; Crisolli, J./Ramdolic, L.: Das Tarifrecht der Angestellten im öffentl. Dienst. Bd. 4.

Roswitha Körner/Red.

Bewegungschor

Die Bezeichnung B. für Großgruppen im Tanz-, Sprach- oder Musiktheater bürgert sich ein, als Rudolf von Laban (1879–1958) mit tanzbegeisterten, nach seiner Bewegungslehre geschulten Laien chorisches Tanztheater (Mysterien- und Weihespiele) einstudiert: *Der schwingende Tempel*

(1922); *Agamemnons Tod* (1924); *Dämmernde Rhythmen* (1925); *Titan*
(für Tänzerkongreß Magdeburg 1927, später im Zirkus Busch, Hamburg). Vor und neben Laban setzt Rudolf Steiner (1861–1925) im Rahmen seiner Erziehungskunst (→Eurythmische Kunst) in seinen Mysteriendramen 1910 bis 1913 und in den *Faust*-Inszenierungen der Jahre 1915
bis 1918 B. neben Sprechchören ein. – J. Dalcrozes *Orpheus*-Insze-
nierung 1913 in →Hellerau beeindruckt neben anderen szenischen Mitteln auch durch ‹rhythmisch› geführte Chöre. – 1927 eröffnet Lola Rogge
einen B. in Hamburg: Exzeptionelle «Chorische Tanzschauspiele» gelingen: *Thyll* (1933); *Die Amazonen* (1935); 1950: das szenische Oratorium
für Tanz, Chor und Orchester *Vita Nostra*. – Die Laientanzbewegungen,
in die B. einzugliedern sind, bilden einen Zweig der Volksbildungs- und
Jugendbewegung. Die theoretische Basis und Systematisierung des
Laientanzes leisten Künstler, Kunstpädagogen, Leibeserzieher und spezielle Vertreter der Gymnastik, des Volkstanzes und der Rhythmischen
Erziehung. Die →Labanschulen gehören zu den Reformschulen der 20er
Jahre. B. formieren sich an den Gymnastik- und Tanzschulen, in der
freien Jugend, in Arbeiterbildungsvereinen (erste «Arbeiterbildungs-
schule», Berlin, gegründet von Wilhelm Liebknecht) und in der sozialdemokratischen Arbeiterbewegung. Nach Laban sind B. ein Mittel, um
Laien für die Tanzkunst zu interessieren. Lola Rogge folgt dem sozialen
Gedanken, die gefährdeten Jugendlichen der Zeit durch musische Erziehung gesellschaftlich zu integrieren. Im Sinne der Reformgedanken soll
um der psychischen Stabilität willen Bewegungsfreude gestiftet und gefördert werden. Sich an die Katharsiserfahrung kultischer Rituale und
altgriech. Tragödien erinnernd, glaubt man, darüber hinaus im Bewe-
gungsakt kollektive Ausdrucksmöglichkeiten freilegen zu können. Kunst
und Erziehung suchen expressiv nach dem neuen und wahren Menschen,
der sich dem Druck seiner Zeit durch individuelle Gestaltung entziehen
kann. Demzufolge gehören zu den Themen der Chorgestaltungen die
Auseinandersetzung mit der Industrialisierung, der Verstädterung, der
Massengesellschaft und der Ausblick auf individuelle Welterfahrung. Die
geistigen Strömungen der Reformjahre stützen auf Grund der oft emotio-
nal unkritischen Euphorie die Ideen und Formationen des aufwachsenden NS-Regimes. Nach 1933 tanzen Gruppen der Frauenorganisation
«Glaube und Schönheit» in den B. Mary Wigmans (1886–1973; →Aus-
druckstanz). Laban und Wigman gestalten im Berliner Sportstadion 1936
die monumentalen Bewegungsspiele der olympischen Eröffnungs- und
Schlußfeiern.

B. als solche durchziehen tanzend die Zeiten: vom mythologischen
Drama (in Orissa: *Gita Govinda* [1200] 300 Tänzerinnen im Vishnu-Tem-
pel), über sakrale und profane Volksspiele und Schulspiele, Aufführungen der Höfe bis zu den Formen des Schau- und Tanztheaters. Im 18. Jh.

setzen sich die Ballettreformer Jean-Georges Noverre (1727–1810; →Ballett d'action) und Gaspero Angiolini (1723–1796; →Ballet héroïque-pantomime) für die Verselbständigung des Corps de ballet ein. Den entscheidenden Schritt zur Individualisierung des zu eigenen Funktionen vorstoßenden Corps de ballet, das als bewegter, aber tänzerisch eingesetzter ‹großer Chor› auftritt, wagt Salvatore Vigano (1769–1821; →Choreodrama). Diese Entwicklung wird jenseits und nach der dt. Laienchorbewegung durch die sowj. Ballettreform im großen Choreodrama der Jahre 1930 bis 1952 weitergeführt. Tänzerisch begabte Laien in allen Republiken der UdSSR erhalten eine sechsjährige intensive Volkstanzausbildung mit schauspielerischer und akrobatischer Schulung. Die Volkstanzensembles formen die bisherigen B. zu tänzerischen Charakterchören um. In den großen Tanzdramen sowj. Choreographen (Wainonen, Sacharow, Lawrowski) übernehmen sie, tanzend und pantomimisch-darstellend, tragende Handlungsfunktionen neben dem Corps de ballet (→Bolschoi-Ballett).

Laban, R. v.: Tanztheater und Bewegungschor. In: Laban. Die Tanzarchiv-Reihe 19/20, Köln 1979, S. 2–11; Lämmel, R.: Der Moderne Tanz. Berlin o. J.; Maack, R.: Tanz in Hamburg. Hamburg 1975, S. 26–27; Peters, K.: Lola Rogge – eine musische Insel der Tanzkultur. In: Die Tanzarchiv-Reihe. Bd. 3. Hamburg 1964.

Patricia Stöckemann

Bharata Natyam

Klassischer Tanzstil für Tanztheaterspiele im Südosten Vorderindiens (→Indisches Theater). Blütezeit 10. bis 13. Jh., Chola-Dynastie. Riesige Tempel mit prachtvollen Reliefs oder/und Skulpturen überliefern bis heute ca. 108 spezielle Tanzposen und Tanzpositionen, die Karanas. Der Begriff «Bharata» bezeichnet: 1. Aryastamm, 2. arische Herrscherdynastie, 3. Dynastie von Tänzern und Sängern; 4. *Bharata* heißt aber auch der legendäre Autor des Tanzspiels Natyashastra. Nach ihm soll letztendlich der klassische ind. Tanzstil B. N. benannt worden sein. Mit *Nata* werden seit dem 5. Jh. v. Chr. alle darstellenden Künstler Indiens bezeichnet. Jeder Nata ist Tänzer, Mime, Sänger und Schauspieler zugleich. B. N. ist ein erzählender pantomimischer Tanz, zu dem das gesprochene Wort und die instrumentale Begleitung hinzutreten. Das Nomen Natya bezeichnet das Werk eines Nata. Die Musik des B. N. ist ausschließlich südindisch-karnatisch. Das Bewegungsvokabular ist in theoretischen Schriften sehr früh schriftlich fixiert worden. Der Bewegungsduktus zeigt strenge Klarheit. – Die ind. Theaterkunst ist als Synkretismus bereits auf vorarische Bräuche zurückzuführen. Der B. N. lebte über Jahrhunderte hin von der

Stabilität der ind. Dorfgemeinden und dem Reichtum der Brahmanen. Vom 6. Jh. an wanderten Dschainisten, Hinduisten und Buddhisten in das Chola-Reich ein. Vom 12. Jh. an förderten die sozial-regionalen Bhakten-Bewegungen den natürlichen Differenzierungsprozeß Indiens und stützten zugleich die Weiterentwicklung aller regionalen Tanzstile, die Niederschriften theoretischer Abhandlungen zum Tanztheater, theatralische Spiele allgemein und die Renaissance des ind. Tempeltanzes. Nach dem Zerfall des Hindu-Reiches 1565 fliehen 500 Brahmanenfamilien nach Tanjore, der Haupt- und Tempelstadt der Tamilen, wo sie von den Nayaks aufgenommen werden. Im Nayak-Reich überlebt der B. N. in den Bhagavata-Mela-Tanzspielen bis ins 20. Jh. Im Zuge der ind. Nationalbewegung, etwa ab 1920, studiert der Advokat E. Krishna Jyer in einem Laienspiel-Theaterensemble zu Madras den B. N. Am 1.1.1933: erstes B. N.-Tanzspiel in der Musikakademie von Madras; 1934: in Benares allind. Musikkonferenz. Die Neuaufführung des Bhagavata-Mela-Tanztheaters leitet Bharatiye Natya Sangh. 1936 errichtet Rukmini Devi das Kunstzentrum Kalakshetra in Adyar/Madras (→ Ritualtänze).

Daniélou, A.: Bharata natyam. Der klassische Tanz Indiens. Hg.: vom Internationalen Institut für Vergleichende Musikstudien und Dokumentationen. Berlin 1970; Devi, R.: Dance Dialects of India. Delhi 1972; Rebling, E.: Die Tanzkunst Indiens. Wilhelmshaven 1982.

Helga Ettl

Bildungsanstalt Jacques-Dalcroze (Hellerau)

Nördlich von Dresden, «Am Heller», gründet Karl Schmidt (1872–1948), Tischler und Vertreter der Lebensreformbewegung, 1909 eine Fabrik und eine Gartenstadt für die Arbeiter seiner «Dresdner Werkstätten für Handwerkskunst». Die Reformsiedlung, die den Bauhausgedanken vorwegnimmt (→ Bauhaustänze), setzt sich zum Ziel, Künstler, Handwerker und Industrielle im Werkschaffen zu vereinen. Der Zusammenklang von Architektur und Dekor zielt auf die handwerkliche Erneuerung von Einrichtungsgegenständen. Ab 1911 wird H. zusätzlich zum Zentrum der musikpädagogischen Reformziele von Emile Jacques-Dalcroze (1865–1950). Dr. Dohrn (1878–1914) lernte 1910 das musikpädagogische System der Rhythmischen Gymnastik des Genfer Musikpädagogen Dalcroze kennen. Dohrn war von diesen zukunftweisenden musikpädagogischen Möglichkeiten überzeugt, die Beziehungen zwischen Körper und Musik pflegten und den Körper als Ausdrucksträger musikalischer Wahrnehmungen nutzen wollten. Dohrn richtet 1911 in Hellerau eine Musikreformschule ein. Der Unterricht beginnt in einem

150 Biomechanik

von Tessenow (1876–1950) entworfenen Festspiel- und Unterrichtshaus. Höhepunkte des Schulbetriebs werden alljährliche Schulfeste und Festspiele. Mit der Aufführung der Gluck-Oper *Orpheus* (1913) versucht Dalcroze, das Inszenierungswesen des Theaters zu reformieren. Das gesamte dramatische Geschehen des Werks von der Gebärde der Solisten bis zur Bewegung der Massenszenen soll aus dem Geiste der Musik erwachsen. Unter Vermeidung aller dekorativen Mittel und jedes naturalistischen Bühneneffekts gelingt Dalcroze eine vollendete szenische Wirkung auf Grund des Ineinandergreifens von Raum, Licht und Farbe. Die indirekte Beleuchtungsanlage setzt Lichtstrahlen und -bündel wie Klänge ein. Die Realisierung dankt Dalcroze dem Theaterreformer Adolphe Appia (1862–1928), der in H. erstmals eigene Inszenierungstheorien verwirklichen kann. H. besteht unter Dalcrozes persönlicher Leitung nur zweieinhalb Jahre. 1914 zieht sich Dalcroze nach Genf zurück. 1918 Wiedereröffnung H. als Neue Schule für Rhythmik, Musik und Körperbildung. 1925 Übersiedlung nach Laxenburg bei Wien. 1938 Schließung (Annexion Österreichs durch die Deutschen). – In H. studierten bedeutende Tänzer: Mary Wigman, die Vertreterin des dt. →Ausdruckstanzes, Marie Rambert (1888–1982), die Mitbegründerin des englischen Balletts 1926, und Rosalia Chladek (* 1905). H. ist in den Jahren pädagogisch-künstlerischer Reformen Auffangbecken und Umschlagplatz für nahezu jede soziale und künstlerische Strömung und Innovation gewesen.

Brauneck, M.: Theater im 20. Jahrhundert. Reinbek bei Hamburg 1982, S. 65–70; Feudel, E.: Rhythmisch-musikalische Erziehung. Wolfenbüttel 1956; Koegler, H.: Aus Rhythmus geboren, zum Tanzen bestellt. In: Ballett (Jahrbuch) 1977, S. 40–51; Landau, E. M.: Der Griff in die Geschichte, in: Rhythmik in der Erziehung 1 (1981), S. 11/12; 1 (1983), S. 7–13; 3 (1983), S. 2/3; 2 (1984), S. 6–11.

Patricia Stöckemann

Biomechanik

Von W. E. Meyerhold (→Meyerhold-Methode) eingeführtes System des Schauspielertrainings, die Gesamtheit der Verfahren und Verhaltensweisen (Gymnastik, Akrobatik, Tanz, Rhythmik, Fechten, Boxen), mit deren Hilfe der Schauspieler zu einem «ökonomischen Einsatz seiner Ausdrucksmittel» gelangt, Garantie für die «Genauigkeit der Bewegungen», wie sie der Regisseur verlangt. «Weil das Schaffen des Schauspielers im Schaffen plastischer Formen im Raum besteht, muß er die Mechanik seines Körpers studieren.» Die Kunst müsse auf wissenschaftlicher Grundlage basieren, das gesamte Schaffen des Künstlers ein bewußter Prozeß sein. Aufbauend auf Grundsätzen des Physiologen Pawlow, argumentiert

Meyerhold: «Jeder psychische Zustand wird durch bestimmte physiologische Prozesse hervorgerufen. Indem der Schauspieler die richtige Lösung seines physischen Zustands herausfindet, erreicht er die Ausgangsstellung, wo bei ihm die ‹Erregbarkeit› aufkommt, die die Zuschauer ansteckt.» Die kontrollierte Physis schafft also die Voraussetzung für das System des ‹Aufkommens von Gefühl›, für den Erfolg. – Von großer praktischer Bedeutung als pädagogische Methode (→Theaterpädagogik) barg das System die Gefahr bloßen Virtuosentums, der Vernachlässigung der inneren darstellerischen zugunsten der äußeren Technik.

Meyerhold, V.: Rezension des Buches «Aufzeichnungen eines Regisseurs» von A. J. Tairov (1921–22); ders.: Der Schauspieler der Zukunft und die Biomechanik. Vortrag vom 12.Juni 1922. Beide in: Tietze, R. (Hg.): Vsevolod Meyerhold. Theaterarbeit 1917–30. München 1974; Gordon, M.: Meyerhold's Biomechanics. In: The Drama Review 18 (1974), T. 63, 73–89; Rostockij, B.: O režisserskom tvorčestve V. È. Mejerchol'da. Moskva 1960.

Annelore Engel-Braunschmidt

BITEF

Beogradski Internacionalni TEatarski Festival. – Seit 1966 findet jährlich an drei Wochen im September in Belgrad das Internationale Theaterfest statt. Eingeladen werden Inszenierungen aus allen Kontinenten, die in ihren Ländern als avantgardistisch und bes. innovativ für die Theaterentwicklung gelten. Es werden zwei Preise vergeben: der eine von einer offiziellen Jury aus jugoslawischen Kritikern, der andere ist ein Preis, den das Publikum vergibt. Im Lauf der Entwicklung hat sich gezeigt, daß im Verhältnis mehr Stücke aus den westlichen Staaten, vor allem Europas, vorgestellt werden; entsprechend hoch ist die Anzahl der Preisnominierungen, bes. für bundesdt. Inszenierungen. 1976 richtete B. das «Theater der Nationen» aus.

Ute Hagel

Blankvers

Fünfhebiger ungereimter Jambenvers mit vollständigem letztem Fuß oder überzähliger letzter Silbe: $\cup – \cup – \cup – \cup – \cup – (\cup)$ «Mein Schwan sagt noch im Tod: Penthesilea» (Kleist). Der Gebrauch des B., der sich vom frz. vers commun herleitet, verbreitete sich in England im 16. Jh. (vgl. William Shakespeare, 1564–1616). G. E. Lessing (1729–81) übernahm ihn von der engl. Literatur, mit seinem Stück *Nathan der Weise* (1779) trug er entscheidend dazu bei, diesen Vers zum gebräuchlichsten des dt. Dramas zu machen. Goethe (1749–1832), Schiller (1759–1805), Kleist (1776–1811) und Hebbel (1813–63) schrieben ihre Versdramen in B. Seine Anwendung reicht bis ins 20. Jh. hinein – vgl. die *Atriden-Tetralogie* (1941) von Gerhart Hauptmann (1862–1946). Der B. wurde auch von russ. Dramatikern verwendet – vgl. Puschkin (1799–1837): *Boris Godunow* (1825).

Kayser, W.: Kleine deutsche Versschule. Bern/München [14]1969.

Alain Muzelle

Die Blauen Blusen

(*Sinjaja blusa*) Oberbegriff für eine erfolgreiche und weitverbreitete Laientheaterbewegung (→Laienspiele) der 20er und frühen 30er Jahre in der UdSSR; sie umfaßte etwa 100000 Mitglieder in mehr als 5000 Gruppen und arbeitete teilweise unter Anleitung von Berufskünstlern; verschmolz Ende der 20er Jahre mit der →TRAM-Bewegung. Ebenfalls Bezeichnung für eine Zeitschrift, die 1924 bis 1928 erschien und ein spezielles, von den zahlreichen Gruppen der B. B. aufzuführendes Repertoire druckte. Ihren Ursprung hatten die B. B. in der in Arbeiter-, Bauern- oder Soldatenklubs verbreiteten «Lebenden Zeitung», wie sie in verschiedenen Landesteilen fast gleichzeitig 1922/23 aus der Theatralisierung mündlicher Lesungen entstanden war, führend darunter die Gruppe des Staatlichen Instituts für Journalistik in Moskau B. B., die der Bewegung den Namen gab, ausgehend von der blauen Arbeitsbluse, getragen zur blauen langen Hose. Als «Lebende Zeitung» waren die B. B. überall und jederzeit einsatzbereit; sie hatten ein aktuelles Agitationsrepertoire, beteiligten sich an politischen Kampagnen, zogen Material aus dem lokalen Fabrikleben hinzu. Die Aufführungspraxis gründete auf dem Prinzip der Illustration eines Themas, die einzelnen Teile korrespondierten mit den Rubriken einer gedruckten Zeitung. Künstlerisch dominierten formalistische Elemente. Verlust an Aktualität, zunehmende Schematisierung und Ästhetisierung führten zum Niedergang. – Die Deutschlandtournee einer der professionellen Gruppen der B. B. 1927 hatte Vorbildwirkung für das dt. →Arbeitertheater.

Markov, P. A.: The Soviet Theatre. London 1934 (The New Soviet Library, 3); Zograf, N. G.: Teatral'naja samodejatel'nost'. In: Očerki istorii russkogo sovetskogo dramatičeskogo teatra. T. I. Moskva 1954, S. 467–478.

Annelore Engel-Braunschmidt

Der Blaue Vogel

Das russ. Emigrantenkabarett B. V. (Sinjaja ptica) in Berlin wurde stark beeinflußt vom ersten russ. Kabarett, der 1908 aus dem Moskauer Künstlertheater (→MChAT) Stanislawskis hervorgegangenen «Letučaja Myš» («Fledermaus»). In ihr wurden vor allem Literaturparodien gespielt, u. a. auf Maeterlincks damals beliebtes Stück *Der blaue Vogel*. Von ihm leitete sich auch der Name des von Duvan-Torzoff gegründeten, unter der Leitung J. Jushnijs berühmt gewordenen Emigrantenkabaretts ab. – Burlesken, Tänze, szenisch dargebotene Chansons und Parodien bildeten das Programm, das in ästhetisch einfallsreicher Dekoration ablief und schnell zum Markenzeichen des ‹Russenstils› in der theatralischen Kleinkunst wurde. Die exotisch anmutende poetische Darstellungsweise hatte internationalen Erfolg. Auf ausgedehnten Tourneen durch die ganze Welt zeigte der B. V. in über 3000 Vorstellungen bis 1931 sein Programm. Der Versuch, den B. V. nach 1945 durch russ. Künstler in München wiederzubeleben, blieb bei völlig veränderten historischen Bedingungen erfolglos.

Der blaue Vogel. Alben des russisch-deutschen Theaterkabaretts. Berlin 1922ff; Böhmig, M.: Das russische Theater in Berlin 1919–1931. München 1990; Budzinski, K.: Pfeffer ins Getriebe. München 1982; Greul, H.: Bretter, die die Zeit bedeuten. Köln/Berlin 1967 (erw. Ausg., 2 Bde., München 1971); Mierau, F. (Hg.): Russen in Berlin. 1928–1933. Leipzig 1987.

Wolfgang Beck

Bolschoi-Ballett

Vorrevolutionäre Epoche: Seit 1776 kann Moskau auf eine Kompanie verweisen. Bereits 1773 existierte eine Ballettklasse am Moskauer Waisenhaus, die Tänzer für das 1780 gebaute Petrowski-Theater ausbildete. Nach dem Brand von 1805 eröffnet Nikolaus I. 1825 das heutige Bolschoi-Theater. Das heute weitverzweigte Schulsystem des Choreographischen Instituts und das B. sind das Erbe der vor rund 200 Jahren begründeten Moskauer Ballett-Tradition. Im Gegensatz zum kosmopolitischen, alle westeuropäischen Strömungen auffangenden Petersburg ist das Moskau des 19. Jh. ausschließlich auf Tradierung bedacht. Mit Adam Gluschkowski gewinnt Moskau einen ersten bedeutenden Ballettmeister. Gluschkowski gleicht die tänzerischen Leistungen der Bolschoi-Kompanie denen des Petersburger Balletts an, studiert aber wegen des Publikumsgeschmacks nur Standardchoreographien ein. Die choreographische Situation bessert sich um 1900 mit Alexander Gorski (1871–1924). Seine von frührealistischen Kunstauffassungen geprägten dramatischen Ballette und seine das choreosinfonische Genre begründenden Experi-

154 Bolschoi-Ballett

mente (→Sinfonisches Ballett) tragen ihm nach der Oktoberrevolution den Ruf eines Vorkämpfers für das nachrevolutionäre sowj. Ballett ein. *Sowjetisches Ballett:* Gorski strukturiert nach 1917 die Bolschoi-Kompanie um. Anders als das Petersburger Ballettkollektiv, hält Gorski seine Kompanie in den Zeiten der Wirren nahezu geschlossen beieinander. Tschekrygin hatte bereits 1915 einen Brief veröffentlicht, in dem er die Unerläßlichkeit einer Ballett-Reform vorträgt. Notwendig seien: 1. ein einheitlicher Lehrstil, 2. die Fächer Tanz- und Kostümgeschichte, 3. das Studium des Charaktertanzes, 4. eine Ausbildung in Akrobatik und 5. die Ausweitung des musikalischen Grundstudiums. – 1918: «Petrograder Konferenz aller Ballettpädagogen der UdSSR.» Die Studienausweitung wird realisiert. Aus dem bisher dreijährigen Studium wird ein zunächst sieben-, dann 1934 zehnjähriges. Die Ballettschulen erhalten den Rang einer Kunstfachschule. Schirjajew, Lopuchow, Botscharow und Monachow erarbeiten in den 20er Jahren die *Grundlagen des Charaktertanzes* (Moskau). Agrippina Waganowa (1879–1951) systematisiert die *Grundlagen des Klassischen Tanzes* (Petersburg 1934). Ziel: Virtuosität und vitale dramatische Ausdruckskraft, der energiegeladene sowjetische Tänzer, der Einsatz des totalen Körpers. Der Volkskommissar für Bildung in der sowjetischen Regierung, Lunatscharski, gewährt volle Unterstützung. Die Choreographen und Tänzer gehen nach 1917 an die Arbeit (drei Entwicklungsphasen des sowjetischen Balletts →St. Petersburger Ballett). Die Bühne des Moskauer Tanztheaters wird bereits in den 20er Jahren zu einem stilistisch und künstlerisch Aufsehen erregenden Ort (→St. Petersburger Ballett). Nach Gorski führen ab 1924 Sacharow (1907–84) und Lawrowski (1905–67) das B., bevor 1964 Juri Grigorowitsch (*1927) mit seinen Konzeptionen vom tänzerischen Poem die Moskauer Kompanie übernimmt. Seine ausgeprägte tanztheoretische und choreographisch-praktische Befähigung lassen ihn zum international anerkannten Tanzpädagogen und Künstler aufsteigen. Grigorowitsch dringt auf einen kraftvollen, aber eleganten, mühelos erscheinenden, lyrisch ausdrucksstarken Bewegungsduktus und fordert die Verinnerlichung der Gebärdensprache. Mit der dritten *Spartacus*-Inszenierung erkämpft er für seine Kompanie ‹den› sowjetischen Nachkriegserfolg. Die spannungsgeladene Aussage im *Spartacus* erreicht er durch Zentrierung und psychologische Vertiefung. Er kürzt Libretto und Musik, nimmt Umstellungen vor, fügt Einschübe hinzu und kontrastiert so die bisherigen dominierenden und allzu massiven Chorszenen durch Monologe. – Auf Grund seiner rein tanzmusikalischen Raum- und Zeitgestaltungen gilt Grigorowitsch als Meister des →Sinfonischen Balletts. Er selbst umschreibt seinen Stil als tänzerisches Poem. – 1985 stellt Grigorowitsch auf dem Schostakowitsch-Festival in Duisburg *Das goldene Zeitalter* einem breiten Publikum vor.

Grigorowitsch, J.: Synthese der Traditionen. In: Die Welt des Tanzes in Selbst-
zeugnissen. Hg. von Wolgina, L./Pietzsch, U. Wilhelmshaven [2]1979, S. 310–321;
Koegler, H.: Bolschoi-Ballett. Berlin 1959; Lopuchow, F.: Nach dem großen Ok-
tober. In: Die Welt des Tanzes in Selbstzeugnissen. Hg. von Wolgina, L./Pietzsch,
U. Wilhelmshaven [2]1979, S. 93–125; Rebling, E.: Ballett – gestern und heute.
Berlin 1957; Programm des Hamburger Staatstheaters. Spartacus. Gastspiel des
Bolschoi-Balletts in Hamburg. 20. und 23. Mai 1983.

Helga Ettl

Bolschoi-Theater (Moskau)

(Bol'šoj teatr – das «Große» im Unterschied zum →Maly, dem «Kleinen» Theater) Das führende Musiktheater der GUS/ehem. UdSSR in
Moskau, auch für Repräsentationszwecke benutztes Haus. Gründung
1776, 1806 aus einem privaten in ein staatliches Theater umgewandelt.
Ende des 19. Jh. zahlreiche UA von Opern Mussorgskis, Borodins,
Rimski-Korsakows, von Opern und Balletten Tschaikowskis, mit denen
das gesamte Ensemble des B. zu einer künstlerischen Blüte gelangte, die
es erst nach der Jahrhundertwende dank der Bemühungen russ. Künstler um eine neue Inszenierungspraxis wiedererlangte. 1904–06 fruchtbare Tätigkeit S. W. Rachmaninows (Wiederherstellung der Original-
partituren russ. Opern, vertiefte Interpretation, Dirigate eigener Opern)
am B. In den 20er Jahren prägen hervorragende Sänger wie F. I. Schaljapin, L. V. Sobinowa, A. W. Neshdanowa eine neue Epoche in der
Geschichte der Opernkunst, indem sie höchste Gesangskultur mit ide-
eller Durchdringung der Darstellung und Psychologisierung der Gestalten vereinigen. Chefregisseur seit 1952 (mit Unterbrechungen) B. A.
Pokrowski (* 1912), der seine moderne Musiktheater-Auffassung gegen
den akademischen Stil nur bedingt durchsetzen konnte (gründet deshalb
1972 experimentelles Moskauer Kammermusik-Theater). Künstlerisch
1988 Wende mit Pokrowski, A. Lasarew (Dirigent), W. Lewental (Bühnenbild).

Annelore Engel-Braunschmidt/Elke Wiegand

Bonner Bühnen

Großes Haus, Kammerspiele Bad Godesberg, Werkstatt. Anfänge seit
1639 mit Schultheater der Minoriten, 1673 der Jesuiten (bis 1774). Ende
des 17. Jh. Hoftheater im Schloß, Prachtentfaltung unter Kurfürst Clemens August (1700–61), frz. und ital. Truppen. Mitte 18. Jh. bürgerliches

156 Bonvivant

Amateurtheater, Zusammenarbeit mit Hoftheater. 1778 Nationaltheater unter G. F. W. Großmann (1746–96). 20. Juli 1783 UA *Fiesko*. 1794 Ende des Kurfürstentums und Hoftheaters, zugeschüttet. 1826 Theaterbau auf Initiative Bonner Bürger, verpachtet an wechselnde Truppen, zeitweise Kooperation mit Köln. 1848 Neubau, seit 1859 in städtischer Regie, bespielt von Köln. 1902 eigenes Ensemble, nur Schauspiel, Operngastspiele. 1935 Opernensemble. 1944 Zerstörung des Theaters. Bis 1965 verschiedene Behelfstheater. 1951 bis 1970 Intendant Dr. Karl Pempelfort (1901 bis 75), Shakespearepflege, ‹junge Oper›. 1970 bis 1981 Intendant Hans-Joachim Heyse (* 1929), Fortsetzung der Shakespearepflege, ost-europ. Drama. 1981 Intendant Jean-Claude Riber (* 1934), Schauspieldirektor Peter Eschberg (* 1936). Aufwertung der Oper durch internationale Stars, Vernachlässigung der Regie. Im Schauspiel Pflege österreichischer Gegenwartsautoren. 1986 Trennung von Oper und Schauspiel, zwei Intendanzen. Schauspielintendant: Dr. Manfred Beilharz. – *Bonner Schauspiel-Biennale*: Zeitgenössische europäische Dramatik, zum ersten Mal Juni 1992, Festivalleitung Tankred Dorst.

Schulze-Reimpell, W.: Vom kurkölnischen Hoftheater zu den Bühnen der Bundeshauptstadt. Bonn 1983.

Werner Schulze-Reimpell / Red.

Bonvivant

Männliches →Rollenfach; das Wort B. wurde bereits gegen Anfang des 18. Jh. aus dem Frz. ins Dt. übernommen und bezeichnete urspr. den weltgewandten Intriganten; gegen Ende des 18. Jh. wurde B. mit Lebemann eingedeutscht. Laut dem «Allgemeinen Theaterlexikon» (Leipzig, 1839 ff) gehört gewöhnlich zum B. «ein Anzug nach der neuesten Mode und ein freies gewandtes Benehmen». Die literaturhistorische Entwicklung des 19. Jh. führt allerdings zu einer vorteilhafteren Bewertung des B. Aus dem intrigantischen Weltmann wird der elegante und redegewandte Gesellschaftsmensch und Herzensbrecher, so daß dem Begriff B. praktisch nichts Pejoratives mehr anhaftet.

Bernard Poloni

Botenbericht

Wenn ein für die Entwicklung der Handlung wichtiges Ereignis nicht auf der Bühne dargestellt werden kann, da dies zur Aufhebung der Ortseinheit führen würde; wenn die Darstellung eines Vorgangs als Verstoß gegen die Regeln des Anstands oder gegen die Wahrscheinlichkeit empfunden werden könnte oder ein Ereignis aus technischen Gründen einfach undarstellbar ist – dann wird es nachträglich durch einen Boten erzählt. Der B. dient zur Steigerung des Interesses, indem er entweder zur Peripetie beiträgt oder durch die Heraufbeschwörung der Katastrophe eine pathetische Wirkung auslöst. Er spielt auch in psychologischer Hinsicht eine Rolle: Die Persönlichkeit des Berichtenden kommt durch ihn zum Vorschein, und die Zuhörer entlarven sich selbst durch ihre Reaktionen. Schließlich soll er durch seine höchst rhetorische und bilderreiche Form dem Publikum ein besonderes ästhetisches Vergnügen bereiten. Als typisches Merkmal des geschlossenen Dramas wird der B. in der griech. Tragödie, im frz. Theater des 17. Jh. (vgl. *Phèdre* V, 6, 1677, von Jean Racine, 1639–99) und in der dt. Tragödie der Weimarer Zeit (vgl. *Wallensteins Tod* IV, 10, 1799, von Friedrich Schiller, 1759–1805) häufig verwendet (→ Teichoskopie).

Obmann, K.: Der Bericht im dt. Drama. Diss. Gießen 1925; Scherer, J.: La Dramaturgie classique en France. Paris 1983; Wanda, J.: Wesen und Form des Berichts im Drama. Berlin 1931.

Alain Muzelle

Boulevardtheater

B. entstanden nach der Pariser Stadterneuerung unter Baron Georges Haussmann im 19. Jh. an den neugeschaffenen Grands Boulevards. Goldenes Zeitalter des B. war la Belle Epoque, die frz. Gründerjahre 1860 bis 1914. Heute bezeichnet B. allgemein → Unterhaltungstheater auf kommerzieller Grundlage, oft mit Erfolgsstücken und Starbesetzung. Klassiker des B. sind: Eugène Labiche (1815–88) mit *Le Chapeau de Paille d'Italie* (Der Florentinerhut, 1851), *Ich werde den Major einladen* (1862) und insgesamt etwa 300 Stücken; Georges Feydeau (1862–1921) mit *La Dame de chez Maxim* (Die Dame vom Maxim, 1899), *La Puce à l'Oreille* (Floh im Ohr, 1907), *Occupe-toi d'Amélie* (Gib acht auf Amélie, 1908) u. a. Die besten Beispiele der comédie légère nehmen das Wohlstandsbürgertum aufs Korn, leben von Handlungsverwicklungen, Dreiecksgeschichten, Attacken auf die Standesmoral, die aber schließlich immer siegreich bleibt. Erste Formen des B. am Boulevard du Temple mit den

→Melodramen produktiver Autoren wie Pixérécourt und Bouchardy, gewissermaßen schon →Kriminalstücke, daher auch die Bezeichnung Boulevard du Crime (vgl. den Film von Marcel Carné mit Jean-Louis Barrault, *Les Enfants du Paradis*). In der dt. Literatur zählen Komödien von Axel von Ambesser (* 1910), Curt Goetz (1888–1960) u. a. zum B.

Huber, J.: Das deutsche Boulevardtheater. Diss. München 1986.

Horst Schumacher

Brauchtumstänze

Alle Rituale der magischen, mythischen oder religiösen Kulte erfahren im Laufe ihrer Existenzen Reduktionen. Sie werden in zum Teil noch sakral bestimmtes, dann schließlich rein profanes Brauchtum abgewandelt. Brauchtum ist traditionelles Handeln, das auf der Grenze zwischen sinnhaftem und bloß reaktivem Handeln steht (Max Weber). Die Aussage verweist darauf, daß in das Brauchtum jahrtausendealte, zutiefst sinnbezogene und aus den menschlichen Emotionen und Vorstellungen herausgewachsene, die Menschen bindende magisch-mythische und religiöse Bezüge eingegangen sind, die als archetypisches Bewußtseinsmaterial nach wie vor den Menschen bewegen und nach Ausdruck drängen, um sich im stetig wiederholenden Vollzug abzuschleifen. Brauchtum gehört zu den regelmäßigen Ausdrucksformen im sozialen Handeln. Es wird innerhalb sozialer Gruppen konkret praktiziert. Brauchtum bedeutet: 1. die akzentuierte Durchformung des Daseins. 2. Brauchtum zählt zu den bindenden Kräften sozialer Konfigurationen. 3. Es fordert die Kontaktnahme zwischen den Menschen und 4. die Kontaktnahme zum Übersinnlichen (Heilfurth). Alle markanten Einschnitte der sozialen Existenz drängen nach brauchtümlicher Ausgestaltung. Die «rites de passage» werden durch Brauchtum im Zeitverlauf verankert. Der Mensch kennt fünf sein Leben gliedernde und als rhythmisch empfundene Zyklen: A. Tageslauf, B. Wochenverlauf, C. Jahreszyklus, D. Lebensrhythmus des einzelnen Menschen, E. Zäsuren in der Geschichte der Sozietäten. Mit den Festen, welche die «rites de passage» aus dem Alltag herausheben, liegen auch die Brauchtumstänze fest. Klassifikation: I. Jahres- und lebenszeitlich bedingten Festen zugeordnete Tänze. II. Von ihrem Gehalt her bestimmte Tänze. (Der Gehalt wird sehr oft durch Tanzmedien: Reifen, Fahnen, Fackeln, Schwerter, Masken, Roßattrappen, Flaschen, Bänder, Stelzen etc. markiert oder/und zugleich durch Raumabgrenzungsformen wie Kreis, Acht, Schlange, Schnecke, Labyrinth, Front, Gassen, Lauben, das Rad, die Mühle u. a.) III. Von den Ausführenden her zu bestimmende Tänze: Männer, Frauen, Kinder, Berufe,

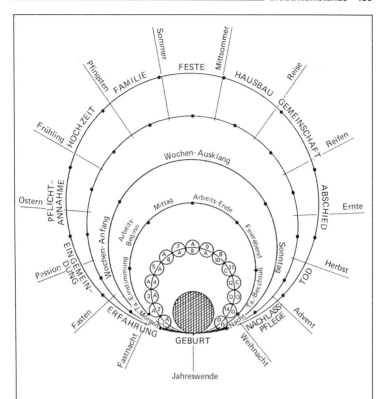

Mittel der Fest- und Feiergestaltung

A. Gestaltungsbereiche – Kunst
  1. Dichtung
  2. Malerei
  3. Architektur
  4. Musik
  5. Pantomime
  6. Tanz und Tanztheater
  7. Sprechtheater
  8. Musiktheater
  9. Film

B. Gestaltungsformen – Spiel
  10. Gesellschaftsspiele

C. Gestaltungsbereiche – Technik – Handwerk
  11. Raumgestaltungs- und Ausschmückungsbereiche
  12. Kulinarischer Gestaltungsbereich

D. Rhetorisch gestaltendes Mittel – Sprache
  13. Ansprachen
  14. Festvorträge
  15. Predigten

160 Brauchtumstänze

Volksschichten, einzelne, Paare, Gruppen. Jeder B. läßt sich in jede dieser drei Gruppen einordnen, und jeder B. vertritt wie der Ritualtanz eine Folge von pantomimischen und sinnbildlichen Tänzen, die zumeist auch in ein Spielgeschehen eingebettet sind, das Lied und Rezitation gleichermaßen nutzt.

Der B. tritt oft als Einzug, Umgang, Umzug etc. auf (→Trionfi). Die Aufzüge lassen sich alle, wenn nicht schon auf die Trionfi, dann auf die Charivari zurückführen, und sie bewahren noch immer liebevoll die Typen dieser Masken-, Gaukler-, Musikanten- und Bürgeraufzüge des Mittelalters und der Renaissance im profanen Raum des städtischen Lebens. Sie bilden das Wilde Heer ab und fußen im mittel- und nordeuropäischen Raum auf dem Mythos des Wilden Mannes oder Waldmannes. Mit ihm ziehen die Struwelfratze, der Harlekin, die Tiermasken der Wölfe, Widder, Löwen, Affen, der schwarze Sarazene (→Moresca), der Teufel, der Tod (→Totentanz), der Quacksalber (Medicus), die Gehörnten, die Mönche oder auch Nonnen, die Hexe, der Pferdemensch, das Lumpen- oder Lappenpaar. Stöcke, Riemen und Fackeln, Kuhglocken, Rasseln, Schellen, Tambourins, Trommeln und Maultierschellen beleben visuell und akustisch das «Straßentheater». Diese dem Volke bekannten Figuren und Insignien kehren zurück oder überleben in den großen Umgängen des *Jahresbrauchtums*. Die bekanntesten Aufzüge im abendländischen Raum sind: das Nikolaus- und Ruprechtslaufen (6. 12.); der Rauhnächtezug (ab 24. 12.) mit Schimmelreiter und Barbierspiel; der Dreikönigsauf-

---

Zäsuren menschlicher Lebens- und Welterfahrung:

A. Tag	*C. Jahr*	*D. Lebenslauf*
1. Morgen	1. Jahreswende	1. Geburt
2. Tageseinstimmung	2. Fastnacht	2. Erfahrung
3. Arbeitsbeginn	3. Fasten	3. Eingemeindung
4. Mittag	4. Passion	4. Pflichtannahme
5. Arbeitsende	5. Ostern	5. Hochzeit
6. Feierabend	6. Frühling	6. Familie
7. Tagesbeschluß	7. Pfingsten	7. Feste
8. Nacht	8. Sommer	8. Hausbau
	9. Mittsommer	9. Gemeinschaft
B. Woche	10. Reise	10. Abschied
1. Wochenanfang	11. Reifen	11. Tod
2. Wochenausklang	12. Ernte	12. Nachlaßpflege
3. Sonntag	13. Herbst	
	14. Advent	*E. Geschichte*
	15. Weihnacht	*der Sozietät*

Brauchtumstänze 161

zug (6.1.); die Fastnachtsumläufe (bis Aschermittwoch): vor allem das Perchten-, Glöckler-, Schellfaschen-, Schleicher- und Narrenlaufen. Feldbegehungen im Frühling kleiden das Laubmännchen ein, bevorzugen Fackeltänze und -läufe, den Siebensprung, Schwerttänze. Dem Jahr folgend begegnen wir Pfingstritten. Vielfältig ausgeschmückt und theatralisch aufgezogen werden Erntezüge, etwa durch Abschreckspiele, den Huck- und Kapuzinertanz. Zum Ende des Jahres folgen die Lambertusumzüge (phantasievoll ausgestaltete Lichterzüge), die St. Barbara- und Lucia-Aufzüge. Der Lebenskreis fügt den B. vor allem Hochzeitsspiele, Handwerkertänze und Leichenbegängnisse (→Totentänze) hinzu. Bedeutendster Festtag der Handwerker: der Dinzeltag, die Jahresversammlung der Zunft mit den Freisprechungen der Gesellen.

Beispiele: 1. *Perchtenlaufen:* Der Bercht ist als mythische Figur in Tirol seit dem 8. Jh. bekannt. Das 19. Jh. und die Gegenwart üben im Voralpen- und Alpenland den alten Brauch des Maskenlaufens. Der Perchtenlauf unterscheidet die schönen und die schiachn (bösen) Masken, den Vorpercht, den Wurstl, oft noch den Wilden Mann, einen Kaminkehrer, einen Teufel und ein Lumpenpaar. Der Perchtentanz oder Tresterer ist als sehr anstrengender, kunstvoller und eigenwilliger Tanz im Süden berühmt. Er differenziert Schweig- und Spieltänze. Die Tanzgruppe besteht aus acht bis zwölf Schönperchten und dem Wurstl. 2. *Glöcklerlaufen* im Advent: Beim Anglöckeln im Advent tragen die Masken hohe Lichtkappen in den Formen: Haus, Kirche, Schiff, Pyramiden, Stern, Sonne. Die Kappen werden von einer inwendig befestigten Kerze erleuchtet. Beim Glöckeln laufen das Brautpaar, der Scherenschleifer, die Ölträger (Teeröl zum Schwärzen), der Rauchfangkehrer, zwei schiach angezogene Hexen mit Besen. In den Glöcklerauftritt werden sogar Schwerttänze eingebaut (→Waffentänze). 3. *Münchener Schäfflertanz:* Aufführung alle drei Jahre im Februar auf dem Münchener Rathausmarkt. Teilnehmer: Träger der Zunftfahne, Reichsapfelträger, zwei Reifenschwinger, zwei Narren, eine Marketenderin (Gretl i. d. Buttn), der Vortänzer mit Stab, 24 Reifenschwinger. Die Narren schwingen akrobatisch Reifen in possenhafter Form und peitschen die Zuschauer aus. 4. *Schwerttanz der Kürschner in Hermannstadt:* zwölf Tänzer mit Vortänzer, ein Narr, 18 Tanzszenen.

Johannsmeier, R.: Spielmann, Schalk und Scharlatan. Reinbek bei Hamburg 1984; Oetke, H.: Der deutsche Volkstanz. Bd. I. Wilhelmshaven 1983; Sagan, C.: ... und werdet sein wie Götter. Das Wunder der menschlichen Intelligenz. München/Zürich 1978.

Helga Ettl

Bread and Puppet Theatre

Ehe Peter Schumann in New York 1961 das B. a. P. T. gründete, hatte er bereits in München mit Puppen und Masken in Tanzaufführungen gearbeitet (→Puppentheater). Der Name der Gruppe soll die Integration von Leben und Kunst signalisieren. Vor Aufführungen wird rituell selbstgebackenes Brot verteilt. In den Workshops wird neben der Puppenherstellung auch zum Brotbacken angeleitet. Das B. a. P. T. stellt wahrscheinlich den umfassendsten Ansatz im alternativen Theater der USA dar: Politisches →Volkstheater und →Environmental Theatre, →Guerilla Theatre und mittelalterliches→Pageant, Geschichte und Mythologie, Puppen und Brot. Das unvergeßliche Element der Inszenierungen des B. a. P. T. sind die Puppen, in allen Größen und Formen, versehen mit einer breiten Ausdrucksskala. Alle menschlichen Themen und Regungen, Geburt, Tod, Leiden, Freude, werden in den gestalteten Ausdruck der Puppen transportiert. Von 1961 bis 1970 arbeitete das B. a. P. T. in New York. Mit *The King's Story* (1963 ff), *A Man Says Goodbye to His Mother* (1968), *The Cry of the People for Meat* (1969) schaltete man sich aktiv in die oppositionellen Strömungen gegen den Krieg der USA in Südostasien ein. Seit 1970 leben Schumann, seine Familie und eine Kerngruppe von Puppenspielern auf einer Farm in Vermont, zunächst Plainfield, ab 1974 Glover, wo alljährlich im August der «Domestic Resurrection Circus» zur Aufführung gelangt: ein ein- bis zweitägiges Theaterereignis, das, harmonisch in die Landschaft eingepaßt, von den angereisten Gruppen aus dem verfügbaren Material an Puppen und Masken improvisierend entwickelt wird, ein rituelles Fest eher denn eine in sich geschlossene Theaterveranstaltung. In Davis, Kalifornien, ebenfalls in einer Freiluftszenerie, gab es im Mai 1975 als einmalige Vorstellung *The Monument for Ishi* ein ‹antibicentennial pageant›. Ishi ist der Name des letzten Mitglieds eines nordkalifornischen Indianerstamms. Die ideologische Gegenposition, daß Native Americans die eigentlichen Amerikaner seien, liegt dieser Zeremonie zugrunde. An der Aufführung war auch die Instrumentalgruppe →San Francisco Mime Troupe beteiligt. Es wird nunmehr projektbezogen gearbeitet, z. B. *Ave Maria Stella* (1978), wo neuerlich mythische Elemente aus verschiedenen Kulturen zusammengefügt werden oder *Columbus – The New World Order* (1992), der Beitrag des B. a. P. T. zu 500 Jahren Amerika. Das B. a. P. T. erzielt seine Wirkung durch die umfassende humanistische Weltsicht und die Originalität der Puppen, die überlebensgroß, auf Stelzen, an Stöcken vors Gesicht gehalten, oder auch Marionetten sein können. Die durch sie erzeugbaren Symbole und Bilder (Drachen, Clown, Madonna, Tierwelt, Politiker, Kapitalisten etc.) sind in einer universalen, grundsätzlichen Form ausdrucksstark und setzen durch ihre visuelle Intensität den verbalen Charakter von Theater teilweise außer Kraft.

Burger, G.: Die San Francisco Mime Troupe und Peter Schumanns Bread and Puppet Theatre: Zwei komplementäre Modelle aufklärerischen Theaters. Diss. Bremen 1992; Falk, F.: Bread and Puppet: Domestic Resurrection Circus. In: Performing Arts Journal II, 1 (1977), S. 19–30; Schumann, P.: Puppen und Masken. Das Bread and Puppet Theatre. Frankfurt/M. 1973; Shank, T.: The Bread and Puppet's AntiBicentennial: A Monument for Ishi. In: Theatre Quarterly V, 19 (1975), S. 73–88; ders.: American Alternative Theatre. London 1982.

Uschi Bauer/Dieter Herms

Bregenzer Festspiele

Österr. Festspielort. – Im Juli und August jeden Jahres wird an mehreren Aufführungsstätten ein vielfältiges Programm geboten: im «Theater am Kornmarkt» Oper und Schauspiel; im Festspielhaus (1980 eröffnet) große Oper; Orchesterkonzerte und Liederabende in den Kirchen und auf den Plätzen der Stadt; im Renaissanceschloßhof des benachbarten Hohenems Opern und Schauspielaufführungen. Neben Solistenkonzerten bestreiten die Wiener Symphoniker das Musik- und das →Burg- bzw. Josefstädter Theater das Theaterprogramm. Im Mittelpunkt steht das Spiel auf dem See, eine schwimmende Freilicht-Raumbühne mit einer 5000 Zuschauer fassenden Tribüne am Seeufer. 1946 eröffnet mit Mozarts Singspiel *Bastien und Bastienne*, wurden hier schwerpunktmäßig Operetten gespielt (Suppé, Millöcker, Zeller); ab 1970 kamen Operninszenierungen (Wagner, Weber u. ä.) und verstärkt Ballette hinzu. Die Umgebung des Sees und der angrenzenden Berghänge machen diese Bühne besonders geeignet für Einstudierungen mit großer Naturkulisse. Intendant: Dr. Alfred Wopmann.

Bär, E.: Welttheater auf dem Bodensee. Wien 1977; ders.: Spiel auf dem See. Wien 1984.

Ute Hagel/Red.

bremer shakespeare company

1983 als selbstverwaltetes Theaterensemble gegründet, seit 1984 zunächst in den Kammerspielen in der Böttcherstraße, ab 1988 im Theater am Leibnizplatz feste Spielstätte in Bremen; nicht subventioniert. – Kontinuierliche Beschäftigung mit Shakespeare und den Spielweisen des Volkstheaters: *König Lear, Othello, Komödie der Irrungen* (alle 1985); *König Heinrich IV/V* (1986); *Was ihr wollt, Das Wintermärchen* (1987); *Der Widerspenstigen Zähmung, Troilus und Cressida* (1988); *Macbeth* (1989);

164 Bremer Tanztheater

Antonius und Cleopatra (1990); *Die lustigen Weiber von Windsor, Der Sturm* (1991); *Titus Andronicus* (1992). Eigene Stücke u. a.: *Ich, Paula, Paula Becker, Paula Becker-Modersohn* (1985); *Kopfkrieg* (1985); *Rochade* (1987); *Wo ich die Welt anseh, möcht ich sie umdrehn* (1989); *Unter dem Glück* (1991) und *Bruderbande* (1991).

Die B. S. C. spielt Shakespeare als Volkstheater mit großer Nähe zum traditionellen historischen Verständnis Shakespeares und aktualisiert den Stil des elisabethanischen Volkstheaters: Weglassen der vierten Wand; eigene Übersetzungen, die gestische Spielweisen zulassen; Einbeziehen des Publikums; Aktualisierung besonders in den Passagen, die Shakespeare seinen Schauspielern zu Improvisationen offenließ; Betonung karnevalistischer und clownesker Elemente bei Shakespeare.

Bearbeitungen und Übersetzungen im Selbstverlag der B. S. C. Bremen 1985 ff; Herms, D./Th. Metscher (Hg.): Shakespeare als Volkstheater – Bremer Shakespeare Company. (Gulliver 24). Berlin 1988.

Uschi Bauer/Dieter Herms

Bremer Tanztheater

In der Spielzeit 1989/90 hat Johann Kresnik ein zweites Mal die Leitung des Tanztheaters in Bremen übernommen. Bereits 1968 hatte der Bremer Intendant Kurt Hübner den radikalen, gegen das klassische Ballett und seine Hierarchie sich auflehnenden Choreographen an sein Haus verpflichtet, an dem Kresnik bis 1978 mit seinen gesellschaftskritischen, politisch engagierten und auf aktuelle Ereignisse reagierenden Choreographien ein Tanztheater entwickelte, das er bis heute als Choreographisches Theater bezeichnet und das ihn als Wegbereiter des →Tanztheaters auszeichnet. Kresnik (* 1939), der eine Werkzeugschlosserlehre absolvierte, bevor er zum Tanz kam, begann 1967 zu choreographieren. Nach seinem zehnjährigen Engagement in Bremen wechselte er an die Städtischen Bühnen in Heidelberg und setzte dort seine Arbeit fort. Reinhild Hoffmann übernahm in seiner Nachfolge die Leitung des Bremer Tanztheaters 1978–86, 1978–81 gemeinsam mit Gerhard Bohner (→Tanztheater). Die damals noch fast unbekannte Choreographin gelangte mit ihren stark ikonographisch geprägten, symbolhaften Stücken, v. a. mit ihrer Produktion *Callas* (1983), zu nationalem und internationalem Erfolg. Nach ihrem Abschied von Bremen wurde die Fortführung der Bremer Tanztheatertradition zwei Frauen übertragen: der Schauspielerin und Regisseurin Rotraut de Neve und der Tänzerin und Choreographin Heidrun Vielhauer. Beider Ziel war es, eine Synthese von Tanz und Theater, Bewegung und Sprache zu schaffen. Mit seinen jüngsten Pro-

duktionen *Ulrike Meinhof* (1990), *Lear* (1991) und *Frida Kahlo* (1992) hat
Kresnik, nach zehn Jahren wieder an seine alte Wirkungsstätte in Bremen
zurückgekehrt, erneut Akzente gesetzt, die Variationsbreite seines Choreographischen Theaters erweitert und seinen immer noch engagiert kritischen Blick auf die politisch-historischen Ereignisse bewiesen.

Schlicher, S.: Tanztheater. Traditionen und Freiheiten. Reinbek 1987.

Patricia Stöckemann

Bremer Theaterlabor

1975–78 an den Bühnen der Freien Hansestadt Bremen unter Leitung
von George Tabori; Zusammenschluß einer Gruppe von zehn Ensemble-
Schauspielerinnen und -Schauspielern, regelmäßiges Sensitivitätstrai-
ning, erarbeiten mit Tabori und seinen von Lee Strasberg (→The Method)
inspirierten Methoden (Einfluß Stanislawskis, Living Theatre und Fritz
Perls' Gestalttherapie) Schauspielprojekte auf der Experimentierbühne
‹Concordia›: D. Rudkins *Vor der Nacht* und G. Taboris *Sigmunds Freude*
(1975), *Troerinnen* des Euripides und G. Taboris *Talk Show* (1976),
E. Bonds *Die Schaukel* und G. Taboris Kafka-Paraphrase *Hungerkünst-*
ler (1977) sowie Shakespeares *Hamlet* (1978). – George Tabori
(*24.5.1914 Budapest, ungarischer Romancier, Dramatiker und Regisseur, playmaker); Studium in Berlin, 1936 Emigration nach London, *Be-*
neath the Stone (Roman, 1943), *Companions of the Left Hand* (Roman,
1946), 1947 Übersiedlung in die USA, *Original Sin* (Roman, 1947), *The*
Caravan Passes (Roman, 1949), *The Good One* (Roman, 1952), Film-
drehbücher in Hollywood, Begegnung mit B. Brecht, Übersetzungen ins
Englische von *Der aufhaltsame Aufstieg des Arturo Ui, Die Gewehre der*
Frau Carrar und *Mutter Courage*; erstes Bühnenstück *Flight to Egypt*
(UA New York 1952, Regie: Elia Kazan), *The Emperor's Clothes* (Stück,
1953); erste Regiearbeit Strindbergs *Fräulein Julie* (Phoenix Theatre,
New York 1956), *Brouhaha* (politische Satire, UA Aldwych Theatre Lon-
don, Regie: Peter Hall, 1958); Gründung einer eigenen Gruppe ‹The
Strolling Players› 1966; Mitglied von Lee Strasbergs →Actor's Studio in
New York, *The Niggerlovers* (Stück 1968), *The Cannibals* (Auschwitz-
Stück, UA 1968 und DEA 1969 Schiller-Theater Berlin, Regie G. Tabori
und Martin Fried), *Pinkville* (Anti-Vietnam-Stück, DEA in Berliner Kirche, Regie G. Tabori, 1971); 1971 Rückkehr nach Berlin, seither ständiger Aufenthalt in der BRD, Regiearbeiten an verschiedenen dt. Bühnen: *Clowns* (Tübingen, UA 1972), J. Saunders' *Kohlhaas* und Mrozeks
Emigranten (Bonn 1974 und 75), *Verwandlungen* (München 1977),
1978–1981 hauptsächlich →Münchner Kammerspiele. Seit 1981 auch In-

szenierungen eigener und anderer Stücke in Bochum, Köln und Berlin: *Jubiläum* und *Peepshow*, Bochum, UA 1983 und 84; G. Stein: *Dr. Faustus Lichterloh*, Köln 1983; I. Eörsi: *Das Verhör*, Schaubühne 1984; 1986–90→Theater Der Kreis, Wien. – Auszeichnungen für Theaterarbeiten: Mülheimer Dramatikerpreise 1983 für *Jubiläum* und 1990 für *Weisman und Rotgesicht*, Filme (*Frohe Feste*) und Hörspiele (u. a. *Weißmann und Rotgesicht, Die 25. Stunde, Mutter Courage*): Prix Italia 1978, Großer Kunstpreis der Stadt Berlin 1981, Frankfurter Hörspielpreis 1985, Peter Weiss-Preis 1991. – Taboris Theaterarbeit ironisch, witzig bis grotesk, Lust am Schockieren, obszön, sentimental, manchmal grausam, Verbindung von Therapie und Theaterarbeit; Hauptthemen: Liebe und Tod, Bewältigung von Angst; kein Anstreben abgeschlossener Ergebnisse, Einblicke in den Arbeitsprozeß, Fortentwicklung der Aufführungen noch nach der Premiere.

Ohngemach, G.: George Tabori. Frankfurt/M. 1989; Gronius, J. W./W. Kässens: Tabori. Frankfurt/M. 1989; Tabori, G.: Betrachtungen über das Feigenblatt. Ein Handbuch für Verliebte und Verrückte. München/Wien 1991.

Ingeborg Janich

British Theatre Association

Die B. T. A. (London) wurde im Jahre 1919 von Geoffrey Whitworth unter dem Namen British Drama League gegründet. War der Zweck zunächst lediglich die Förderung der nichtkommerziellen Dramatik, so ist der Verein heute die offizielle Organisation der englischen Amateurtheater-Vereine (→Amateurtheater). Bereits seit seiner Gründung gibt der Verein die Vierteljahrsschrift «Drama» heraus. Die B. T. A. besitzt die umfassendste Bibliothek von Dramentexten im Vereinigten Königreich und verfügt über eine bedeutende Sammlung von Theaterkritiken. Die meisten der hier vorhandenen Dramentexte sind für Amateurtheatergruppen ausleihbar.

Elke Kehr

Broadway

Häufig synonym für amerik. Theater schlechthin, zumindest ‹nationaler Ausdruck› des US-Theaters, so wird der B. immer wieder apostrophiert. Insgesamt kaum gerechtfertigt, darf diese Einschätzung gleichwohl gelten für die privatwirtschaftliche Organisationsstruktur des B. und – im großen und ganzen – auch für seine ideologische Ausrichtung. Die Anfänge des B. gehen in die Kolonialzeit zurück. Aus dem Jahre 1699 ist ein Antrag beim Gouverneur New Yorks verbürgt, worin um eine Aufführungslizenz für Theater nachgesucht wird. Im Jahre 1716 wurde in Williamsburg, Virginia, das erste Theater gebaut. Eine Karte New Yorks von 1735 zeigt zwei Theaterhäuser. Als Folge der Theaterschließung in London orientierten sich die Theaterschaffenden auf die überseeischen Kolonien. Zwischen 1749 und 1751 gab es in Philadelphia, New York und Williamsburg mehrere Inszenierungen Shakespeares, Farquhars, Drydens und anderer Restaurationsdramen. Gruppen wie die Murray and Kean Company und die Londoner Company of Comedians (Hallam Company) rochierten zwischen den einzelnen kolonialen Kulturzentren (→Wanderbühnen). Lewis Hallam, David Douglas und Jacob Rickett gelten als die verantwortlichen Personen, wenn vom Bau von Theaterhäusern oder der Zusammensetzung der Schauspieltruppen in der vorrevolutionären Zeit die Rede ist.

Der ökonomische Boom nach der Unabhängigkeit, die zunehmende Bedeutung New Yorks als Hafen, das rasche Anwachsen der Bevölkerung, ein sich herausprägender Nationalstolz der herrschenden Schichten der neuen Republik waren Faktoren, die u. a. auch die Notwendigkeit des Theaters als Rekreation begründeten. 50 Jahre lang, von 1798 bis 1848 bestimmten die Inszenierungen des Park Theatre (erster Manager war William Dunlap, bedeutendster Schauspieler Thomas A. Cooper) die Theaterszene New Yorks. Hier wurden die ital. Oper eingeführt, die klangvollsten Namen der engl. Bühne verpflichtet, Grundsteine gelegt für den Aufstieg amerik. Stars. Das Bowery Theatre und Franklin Theatre waren seit den 1830er Jahren eine ernst zu nehmende Konkurrenz. Diese Gruppen waren Repertoireensembles, auch ‹stock companies› genannt. Die Bevölkerungsziffer hatte zu jener Zeit bereits eine Viertelmillion überschritten. Wurden bis zur Mitte des Jh. im wesentlichen importierte Dramen gespielt, etablierte sich seit 1847 (Christy Minstrels; Mechanics Hall) mit der nationalamerik. →Minstrel Show auch der Broadway im engeren Sinne. Die verschiedenen Minstrel-Gruppen konkurrierten in unmittelbarer geographischer Nachbarschaft um die Gunst des Publikums, eben an der Straße, die B. hieß. Bis in die 1870er Jahre hinein war Minstrelsy die dominierende Theatergattung New Yorks. Die zweite nationalamerik. Gattung war die des →Melodramas, deren erfolgreichste Beispiele häufig Dramatisierungen von Romanvorlagen waren, z. B. *Uncle Tom's Cabin*. Die Aufführungen der ‹stock companies› waren oft von mangelhafter Qualität, da der ständige Spielplanwechsel zu Premieren mit knappen Probenzeiten zwang, die Schauspieler zudem niedrige Gagen erhielten und ihre Kostüme selbst stellen mußten.

Neben New York als Theatermetropole des 19. Jh. ist auch in den rasch

168 Broadway

wachsenden, sich zunehmend industrialisierenden Städten des Ostens, zumal in Boston, Baltimore, Chicago und Philadelphia, im Süden etwa in Charleston, im Westen in San Francisco, ein immer regeres Theaterleben zu verzeichnen. Mit den Einwandererwellen aus Europa, die in den 1840er Jahren einsetzten, begann sich auch der europ. Einfluß auf das Theater der USA zu diversifizieren. Zwar blieben die Dramen der brit. Klassik dominant auf den Spielplänen, aber ein dt. Theater (in dt. Sprache) läßt sich beispielsweise in New York bis 1840 zurückverfolgen, wo in drei erfolgreichen Spielzeiten des Franklin Theatre z. B. neben den *Räubern, Käthchen von Heilbronn, Lumpazivagabundus* vor allem die Komödien Kotzebues populär waren. Von 1854 an hatte das dt. Theater eine feste Spielstätte im alten und im neuen ‹Stadttheater›, dem vormaligen Bowery Amphitheatre.

Geographisch hatten sich die B.-Theater im 19. Jh. noch eher um den Union Square angesiedelt, ab 1900 erstreckte sich der District vom Star Theatre an der 13. Straße bis zum New York Theatre an der 45. Straße, mit dem Times Square als Zentrum. Im Jahr 1900 gab es 16 B.-Theaterhäuser, die auch tatsächlich am Broadway lagen; 1950 waren es nur mehr drei. Das sog. ‹legitimate theater›, das sich mit der Idee des B. verbindet, realisiert sich in unserer Zeit in dessen Seitenstraßen. Obwohl heute der B. als Idee des nationalen Theaters selbst alternativ-oppositionelle Theaterschaffende wie den Chicano Luis Valdez (*Zoot Suit,* 1979) magisch anzieht, befindet sich der B. seit ca. 1930 in einer permanenten Krise. Brillantes Zentrum einer populären Massenkultur, die auch seriöse Versuche der Inszenierung des im 20. Jh. erst entstehenden literarischen Dramas der USA einschloß, war der B. nur in der Zeit zwischen den beiden Weltkriegen, wobei ab 1927 der Siegeszug des Tonfilms bereits den Niedergang des B. verursachte. Vor 1915 werden den → Vaudeville-Aufführungen und Burlesken, den Melodramen und gelegentlichen Klassikerinszenierungen des B. eher provinzielle Bedeutung zugeschrieben.

Die Etablierung des B. um 1900 markiert die vollzogene Zentralisierung des Theaters, dessen Kapital sich nunmehr in wenigen Großunternehmen konzentrierte. Damit wandelte sich das Bild von den ‹stock companies›, d. h. den Repertoiretheatern des 19. Jh., die bereits auf Grund der großen Mobilität, die der rapide Ausbau des Eisenbahnnetzes ermöglichte, immer mehr durch Wandertheater abgelöst worden waren, nunmehr zu einer Kombination von B. und → Tourneetheater (‹combination companies›), indem man in New York probte, ausstattete und eine erfolgreiche Laufzeit hatte, ehe die Inszenierung andernorts gezeigt wurde. Daß gelegentlich sog. ‹try-outs› in der ‹Provinz› stattfanden, war eher die Ausnahme als die Regel. Ähnlich wie andere Industriezweige hatte um 1900 auch das Theater seine ‹Räuberbarone›: A. L. Erlanger, Marc Klaw, Charles Frohman, Al Hayman, S. F. Nixon und J. F. Zimmerman als Bosse des Theatersyndikats kontrollierten das gesamte ‹booking system›, besaßen die größeren Anteile der Theaterhäuser und strichen die Profite ein. Die monopolistische Stellung des Syndikats, dem 1903 beispielsweise 53 Großstadttheater einverleibt waren, wirkte sich nachteilig auf die Entwicklung des US-Theaters aus, da nur ökonomisch ‹sichere› Projekte angefaßt wurden. Das Syndikat managte zwischen 1896 und 1916 ca. 600 Produktionen, seichte Unterhaltung, die vorwiegend aus Melodramen, Romanzen, leichten Komödien und einigen europ. Importen bestand.

Seit 1905 schlossen sich die mächtigsten Gegner des Syndikats, darunter der bekannteste Dramatiker der Jahrhundertwende, David Belasco, zu einer Gruppe von ‹Independents› zusammen, die sich rasch zu einem zweiten, in seinen Praktiken vom Syndikat kaum unterschiedenen Trust auswuchs, dem Shubert Incorporated. Erst 1929, im Börsenkrach, brachen beide Imperien zusammen. Zuerst der Rundfunk und Stummfilm, dann der Tonfilm und die größere Mobilität vermittels des Automobils, schließlich das größere Interesse an sozialer Dramatik, die das Theater der ‹roten Dekade› anbot, leiteten den Niedergang des B. ein. Die Zahl der Produktionen fiel von 264 in der Saison 1927/28 auf 69 in der Saison 1940/41. Dieser Stand hat sich in etwa bis heute erhalten. Die Zuschauerzahlen pro Woche gingen von rund 270000 (1926/27) auf 195000 (1965/66) zurück. Die Zahl der als Broadway-Theater eingestuften Häuser liegt heute bei etwa 30. Aber auch die Zahl der Regionaltheater und der ‹summer stock companies› ist seit 1930 kontinuierlich zurückgegangen. Werke der europ. Klassik wie auch die sog. ‹modern classics› der USA selbst haben am B. des 20. Jh. nur geringe Chancen gehabt; was zählt, ist die hochprofessionalisierte Sensationsshow mit klangvollen Namen, gleichsam der theatralische Bestseller. Profit und ‹künstlerische› Qualität sind sozusagen Synonyma. Entscheidenden Anteil daran, ob eine B.-Inszenierung zum ‹hit› oder ‹flop› wird, haben die Theaterkritiker der New Yorker Tageszeitungen. Starbesetzung, hoher techn. Standard, prunkvolle Ausstattung, Perfektionierung der Darbietung sind dafür oft die ausschließlichen Kriterien.

Die unter diesen Bedingungen dominierende Gattung des B. im 20. Jh. war das Musical. Geschickt nahm es Momente der →Minstrel Show, des →Melodramas, des →Vaudeville, der →Revue, des Balletts auf und verband diese Elemente mit der Eingängigkeit der Unterhaltungsmusik des 20. Jh. Indem die erfolgreichsten dieser Produktionen auch verfilmt wurden, erlangten die Komponisten weltweite Berühmtheit: Irving Berlin, George Gershwin (1898–1937), Jerome Kern (1885–1945), Frederick Loewe, Cole Porter, Richard Rodgers, Vincent Yourmans (1898–1946). Der bekannteste Librettist war Oscar Hammerstein (1895–1960). Neben seinem Musical *Oklahoma!* (1943) waren *My Fair Lady* (Lerner/Loewe),

Hello Dolly! (Stewart/Herman), *Fiddler on the Roof* (Bock/Harnick) und *The Fantasticks* (Jones/Schmidt) die Musicals mit der längsten Laufzeit und damit die erfolgreichsten, weil profitträchtigsten Produktionen des B. überhaupt. Seiner knappsten Definition nach besteht das Musical aus einer Reihe perfektionierter gesungener und/oder getanzter Musiknummern, die sich um eine dünngewebte Handlungsfabel mit komödiantischen Einlagen gruppieren. Das berühmteste Beispiel des Musiktheaters am B. in den 30er Jahren, *Porgy and Bess* (Gershwin, nach dem Roman von Dubose Heyward), ist der Form nach ein Musical mit opernhafter Tendenz, das inhaltlich sozialkritische Züge in sich aufgenommen hat, wenn freilich auch mit sentimentalen Zügen. Daß Sozialkritik und Protest, alternative oder ethnische Lebensstile auch am B. vermarktbar und kanalisierbar werden konnten, zeigen in jüngerer Zeit die außergewöhnlich erfolgreichen Beispiele *Westside Story* und *Hair*. Eine von manchen als abgeschmackt empfundene Verballhornung und populäre Vermarktung von Religiosität erfolgte mit *Jesus Christ Superstar*. Ganz vereinzelt gelang es, mit durchschnittlichem Kassenerfolg literarisch anerkannte Dramatik an den B. zu bringen. Als Beispiele aus den 60er Jahren mögen gelten: *After the Fall* von Arthur Miller (1964); *A Delicate Balance* von Edward Albee (1966); *Indians* von Arthur Kopit (1968). Diesen ‹kalkulierten Wagnissen› ging jeweils eine umfangreiche Werbekampagne voraus.

Versucht man, das Erscheinungsbild des modernen Theaters der USA seit etwa der Mitte der 60er Jahre grob zu skizzieren, ergeben sich fünf unterschiedliche Formen seiner Qualität und Organisation: 1. Profittheater am B., das im Fall seines kommerziellen Erfolgs auch als Tourneetheater in andere Großstädte der USA geht; 2. in New York als Off-Broadway oder → Off-Off-Broadway, mit ähnlicher Struktur jedoch auch in Dallas, Houston, San Francisco oder Washington D. C., seriöse professionelle Produktion des klassischen Repertoires, moderner amerik. und moderner europ. Dramatik (Genet, Ionesco, Beckett etc.) mit gemäßigt experimenteller Tendenz; 3. beginnend mit der Gründung des Guthrie Theatre in Minneapolis (1963) der Aufbau großer regionaler Repertoireensembles in den Großstädten des Landes mit Klassiker-Aufführungen und B.-Wiederaufnahmen. Zuerst privat und teilweise kommunal finanziert, mit der Einrichtung der National Endowment for the Arts 1965 auch Förderung durch Bundesmittel: seit der Schließung des → Federal Theatre 1939 zum erstenmal wieder Regierungsgelder für Theater; 4. College- und Universitätstheater als Teil und Produkt der Ausbildungsprogramme der meistens sehr gut ausgestatteten Drama Departments. Da große Staatsuniversitäten häufig in Kleinstädten untergebracht sind, bilden ihre Theater dort die zentralen kulturellen Einrichtungen; 5. ein breites Spektrum des Alternativtheaters, das, kaum oder gar nicht subventioniert, vom ethnischen und Protesttheater (→ San Francisco Mime

Troupe, →Teatro Campesino) über die Experimente des →Environmental Theatre bis zum →Ontological-Hysteric Theatre eines Foreman reicht. Das subventionierte Stadt- und Staatstheater europ. Provenienz ist in den USA in der Regel nicht vorhanden.

Atkinson, B.: Broadway. London 1970; Bloom, K.: Broadway. New York 1990; Brown, J.M.: Broadway in Review. Freeport 1940; Grabes, H. (Hg.): Das amerik. Drama der Gegenwart. Kronberg/Ts. 1976; Henderson, M.C.: The City and the Theatre. Clifton 1973; Lacombe, A.: Broadway. Paris 1987; Leuchs, F.A.: The Early German Theatre in New York. New York 1966; Poggi, J.: Theater in America. The Impact of Economic Forces, 1870–1967. Ithaca 1968; Schäfer, J.: Geschichte des amerik. Dramas im 20. Jh. Stuttgart 1982; Taubman, H.: The Making of the American Theatre. London 1965; Tompkins, E./Kilby, Q.: History of the Boston Theatre. New York ²1969; Wilson, A.H.: A History of the Philadelphia Theatre, 1835 to 1855. New York 1968.

Dieter Herms

Das Bügelbrett

Eines der bekanntesten und wichtigsten politischen Kabaretts in der BRD der 60er Jahre. 1959 wurde das B. von Studenten in Heidelberg gegründet. Seinen Ruf als eines der bissigsten und schärfsten Kabaretts bekam es, nachdem Hannelore Kaub 1961 die künstlerische Leitung übernommen hatte und als Hauptautorin, Regisseurin und Darstellerin fungierte.

Auf den «1. Berliner Kabarett-Tagen» an der FU Berlin (1961/62) zum besten Studentenkabarett gekürt, erlebte das B. 1962 seinen Durchbruch mit dem Programm «Trauer muß Europa tragen», das trotz künstlerischen Erfolgs ein finanzielles Fiasko war. 1964 zog das B. mit dem Programm «Millionen BILD-Leser fordern» nach West-Berlin um, wo es bis 1969 spielte. «Trotzdem... Rot ist die Hoffnung» war das letzte Programm des B., das sich im gleichen Jahr noch auflöste.

1982 erstand das B. neu. Mit «Keine Angst – wir kommen!» begann es wiederum in Heidelberg – zum Teil mit Mitgliedern der früheren Truppe, vor allem aber mit Hannelore Kaub. «Gemeinsam sind wir unausstehlich» war das letzte Programm vor dem erneuten Ende des B. im Frühjahr 1991.

Budzinski, K.: Das Kabarett. 100 Jahre literarische Zeitkritik – gesprochen – gesungen – gespielt. Düsseldorf 1985; ders.: Pfeffer ins Getriebe. München 1982; ders.: die öffentlichen Spaßmacher. München 1966; ders.: Wer lacht denn da? Braunschweig 1989; Greul, H.: Bretter, die die Zeit bedeuten. Köln/Berlin 1967 (erw. Ausg., 2 Bde. München 1971); Meyer, Ellen: Rot war die Hoffnung. Siegen 1988.

Wolfgang Beck

Bühne

Die B. bzw. der Bühnenraum ist neben dem Zuschauerraum das Kernstück des →Theaterbaus. Die Bühnenfläche umfaßt die vom Zuschauer einsehbare Spielfläche, die Umgangs- und Abstellflächen sowie die Bühnennebenflächen der Seiten- und Hinterbühne. In der Regel beträgt die Dimension der B. ohne Bühnennebenflächen 150 bis 300 m². Die Höhe des Raums über der Bühnenfläche (Bühnenturm) muß die doppelte Bühnenöffnungshöhe plus vier Meter betragen, um Prospekte und Hängestücke aus der Sicht der Zuschauer nach oben wegziehen zu können. Die Breite und Tiefe der B. sollte das Doppelte der Bühnenöffnungsbreite betragen. – Der Bühnenraum ist mit bühnentechn. Verwandlungseinrichtungen ausgestattet, die die horizontale und vertikale Bewegung von Dekorationsteilen ermöglichen. Elemente der Obermaschinerie sind vertikal verfahrbare Laststangen (Prospektzug), Beleuchtungsgestelle, →Vorhänge und der Feuerschutzvorhang. Die Elemente der Untermaschinerie wie Drehscheibe, Hebebühne, Wagen, Versenkung vereinfachen sowohl den Transport der plastischen Bühnenbilder als auch die topographische Gestaltung des Bühnenbodens. Das im modernen Theaterbau übliche Wagenbühnensystem schafft die Möglichkeit, Bühnenbilder auf den Seiten- und Hinterbühnenwagen vor der Vorstellung aufzubauen und dann nach Bedarf auf die Hauptbühne fahren zu lassen.

Die Guckkastenbühne öffnet sich zum Zuschauerraum mittels des Portalrahmens, der in der Höhe und Breite abhängig von der Geometrie des Zuschauerraums (Sichtlinien der Zuschauer) sich dem Bühnenbild anpassen kann. Allg. wird der Portalrahmen gestalterisch unauffällig und in seinem Ausschnitt veränderbar konzipiert. In historischen Bauten wird die Bühnenöffnung von einem Architekturbilderrahmen, dem →Proszenium, eingefaßt. Das Ausweiten der Bühnenfläche vor den Portalrahmen in der Art der Vorbühne ist einer der Versuche, die Abgeschlossenheit des Bühnenraums zum Zuschauer hin zu erweitern. Aus Gründen des Feuerschutzes ist dieser Übergang nur begrenzt möglich, da ein trennender Brandabschnitt mit Feuerschutzvorhang an dieser Übergangsstelle zwingend vorgeschrieben ist (→Eiserner Vorhang). Die B. liegt gegenüber dem Zuschauerraumfußboden 80 bis 120 cm höher.

Die Reliefbühne bezeichnet eine flache, aber in die Breite gehende Bühnenform, die zu Beginn des 20. Jh. als Überwindung der barocken Illusionsbühne den Schauspieler als wesentliches Wirkungsmittel des Theaters in den Mittelpunkt stellte (Münchner Künstlertheater, 1908, Max Littmann und Georg Fuchs).

B. und Zuschauerraum vereinigen sich in der Raumbühne zu einer Einheit. Dieses Theaterbaumodell stellt die weitestgehende Überwindung der gerichteten Barockbühne dar. Die Zuschauer umgeben oder werden umgeben von der im Raum veränderbaren Spielfläche. Die Technik (Licht, Projektion, Stahlbau) ist nicht mehr allein Hilfsmittel, sondern selbständiger Gestaltungsfaktor des Theaters (Andreas Weiningers → Kugeltheater, 1927; Walter Gropius' und Erwin Piscators → Totaltheater, 1927).

Gerhard, H./Kühnbaum, F.: Verordnung über Versammlungsstätten mit Erläuterungen. Berlin 1972; Graupner, G.: Theaterbau – Aufgabe und Planung. München 1970; Unruh, W.: ABC der Theatertechnik. Halle 1959.

Horst Birr

Bühnenbearbeitung

In Abgrenzung zu → Adaption und → Dramatisierung die Umgestaltung eines dramatischen Werks durch Streichungen oder Ergänzungen, durch Auswahl und Umstellung von Szenen im Hinblick auf best. Erfordernisse einer Aufführung. Gründe dafür sind die Regiekonzeption, theaterpraktische Zwänge (Reduzierung der Personenzahl, Zusammenlegung der Schauplätze, Kürzung der Aufführungsdauer), Beachtung gesellschaftlicher Konventionen (Streichung politisch oder moralisch anfechtbarer Stellen), bewußte Aktualisierung. – Werke von Shakespeare, Calderón, Racine, Molière wurden im 18. Jh. auf dt. Bühnen mit Hilfe umfassender B. durchgesetzt. Auch Dramen Lessings, Schillers, Goethes erlebten zahlreiche B. Bekannt ist die mißglückte B. Heinrich von Kleists *Der zerbrochne Krug* (Weimar, 1808) durch Goethe, ferner Goethes *Egmont* (Weimar, 1796) durch Schiller. Gegenwärtig sind B. (bes. klassischer Werke) als Voraussetzung für zeitgenössische Regie zur Regel geworden.

Gazdar, A.: Dt. Bearbeitungen der Shakespeare-Tragödien im 18. Jh. Diss. München 1979; Lutz, B. v.: Dramatische Hamlet-Bearbeitungen des 20. Jh. in England und aus den USA. Frankfurt/M. 1980; Dramenbearbeitungen. Zusammenstellung und Nachwort von H. Haffner. München/Oldenburg 1980.

Monika Sandhack

Bühnenbeleuchtung

Das Licht als Gestaltungsmittel hat das Theater in seiner Entwicklung ständig begleitet. Das Naturlicht in den antiken Amphitheatern war Zuschauern und Spielern gemeinsam, es erzeugte keine falschen Schatten, der Schauspieler konnte nicht aus dem Dunkeln hervortreten, Sonnenaufgang und Abendrot waren die einzigen Lichteffekte. Die Lage der Theater im Gelände hing vom Gang der Sonne bzw. dem Einfallswinkel

174 Bühnenbeleuchtung

des Lichts ab. Mit Verlegung der Theateraufführungen (16. Jh.) in geschlossene Säle der höfischen Paläste und später in eigenständige Theaterbauten nutzte man zur Erhellung der Bühne und des Zuschauerraums die zu der Zeit üblichen Kronleuchter, die gleichmäßig auf beide Räume verteilt waren. Der Zuschauerraum wurde während des Spiels nicht verdunkelt, ein bewegtes fahles Öl- oder Kerzenlicht erhellte das auf Leinwand oder Papier bemalte Kulissenbild (→Kulissenbühne). Das Beleuchtungssystem wurde in der Art verfeinert, daß in jede Gasse eine senkrecht stehende Lampenreihe, am vorderen Bühnenrand ein Fußlicht (Fußrampe) aufgestellt und hinter den →Soffitten und Wolken Oberlichtreihen gehängt wurden. Das Ergebnis war ein intensives, streuendes Allgemeinlicht, das durch farbiges Glas oder Ölpapier eingefärbt und durch Blechzylinder oder Klappen abgedunkelt werden konnte. Licht- und Schattenwirkungen wurden auf die Kulissen und Prospekte gemalt. Die Gesichter der Schauspieler erschienen im naturwidrigen Rampenlicht, das einen falschen Schatten nach oben und nicht auf die Erde warf, dämonisch. Schminke mußte diesen Fehler ausgleichen.

Eine Verbesserung der Beleuchtungsstärke brachte die Einführung des Gaslichts 1822 im →Covent Garden Theater in London. Das System der reihenweise angeordneten Flammen blieb, jedoch konnten die Brennstellen zentral gezündet und in ihrer Helligkeit reguliert werden. Die leicht brennbaren →Prospekte und →Kulissenteile, das offene Feuer der Lampen sowie pyrotechnische Effekte setzten im 19. Jh. etwa 1200 Theaterbauten in Brand. Das hatte in Preußen 1889 eine Polizeiverordnung zur Folge, die nichtbrennbare Baustoffe und die elektrische Beleuchtung vorschrieb. Die erste elektrische Beleuchtungsanlage wurde 1883 in das Stadttheater Brünn installiert. Das Prinzip der aneinandergereihten Einzellichter wurde beibehalten; an Stelle der Gasflamme traten Glühlampen, die im Mehrfarbensystem in den Grundfarben lasiert waren.

Das moderne Bühnenbeleuchtungsgerät, bestehend aus dem optischen System: Lampe, Spiegel, Linse und Blende in einem hitzebeständigen Gehäuse, hat sich seit 1910 nach den Kriterien hoher Lichtausbeute, Veränderung des Lichts in Farbe und Form, geringes Gewicht und Kosten ständig weiterentwickelt. Die Geräte lassen sich nach ihrem Einsatz bei der Lichtgestaltung und dem optischen Aufbau in Scheinwerfern für ein diffuses Allgemeinlicht oder gerichtetes, gebündeltes Effektlicht unterscheiden. Zu der ersten Gruppe (Fußrampe, Oberlicht, Horizontleuchte, Fluter) gehören einfache Gerätekonstruktionen, bestehend aus einer Lampe und einem Spiegel oder einer Leuchtstoffröhre, die allein oder in Reihenanordnung ein streuendes, konturloses, bei Bedarf farbiges Licht abgeben. Ihr Einsatz bewirkt eine allgemeine Grundbeleuchtung einer Spielfläche, eines Bühnenaufbaus oder Rundhorizonts. Die weitaus wichtigere Gruppe sind Gerätetypen (Linsen- und Stufenlinsenscheinwerfer, Ellipsenspiegel- und Profilscheinwerfer mit Kondensoroptik, Projektionsapparate), zusammengesetzt aus Lampe, Spiegel, Linse oder Linsensystem und einer Abblendvorrichtung, die das gebündelte Licht zu geometrischen Formen verändern kann. Diese Geräte werden eingesetzt zur Beleuchtung von Flächen, Personen und zur Gestaltung des Bühnenbildes durch Helligkeit, Farbe und Schattenbildung. Die Projektionsgeräte können mittels Großdias Hintergrundprospekte oder plastische Strukturen ersetzen und Naturerscheinungen wie Wolken, Nebel, Regen und Flammen vortäuschen. Zur Geräteausstattung gehören daneben Sonderleuchten wie Stroboskope, Blitze, elektrische Kerzen und Flammen.

Die Beleuchtungsgeräte sind im →Repertoiretheater in der Mehrzahl an festen Positionen je nach Wirkungsweise im Zuschauer- oder Bühnenraum aufgestellt. Die wesentlichen Positionen sind die Beleuchtungsbrücken in der Zuschauerraumdecke, Rinnen in der Zuschauerraumwand, Beleuchtungsbrücke und Türme im Portalrahmen, Arbeitsgalerien im Bühnenturm und Beleuchtungszüge. Zu diesen Positionen führen Stromkreise, die zentral aus einer Beleuchtungsloge an der hinteren Wand des Zuschauerraums geregelt werden können.

In einer Beleuchtungsprobe wird der Ablauf einer Aufführung in einzelne Lichtstimmungen geteilt. Die Lichtstimmung setzt sich aus verschiedenen Helligkeitswerten der in dieser Stimmung zum Einsatz gekommenen Beleuchtungsgeräte zusammen. Die Werte werden in einen elektronischen Speicher (Magnetband, Kassette, Diskette) gegeben und im Stückverlauf in chronologischer Folge durch den Stellwerksbeleuchter abgerufen. Auf einem Monitor werden die Schaltvorgänge sichtbar und können bei Bedarf korrigiert werden.

Die Beleuchtungsabteilung eines Theaters setzt sich zusammen aus den Stellwerksbeleuchtern, den Beleuchtern auf den verschiedenen Positionen, die die Scheinwerfer einrichten, Farben wechseln, den Darsteller verfolgen, sowie dem Beleuchtungsmeister, der neben dem Regisseur und Bühnenbildner wesentlich an der Lichtgestaltung beteiligt ist. In jüngster Zeit hat sich das neue Berufsbild des Lichtgestalters (Lighting Designer) entwickelt. Der Schwerpunkt seiner Tätigkeit liegt auf der konzeptionellen, künstlerischen und weniger auf der handwerklichen Ebene.

Die Gestaltung mit dem elektrischen Bühnenlicht ist neben der Tontechnik eine der jüngsten Theaterkünste. Der technologische Standard ist in der hundertjährigen Entwicklung derart verfeinert worden, daß heute ein Instrumentarium zur Verfügung steht, das alle spektralen Arten des Lichts, feinste Helligkeitsabstufungen, optische Sammlung oder Streuung und die elektronische Programmierung ermöglicht. Die unterschiedliche Handhabung des Lichts ist abhängig von der jeweiligen Konzeption, der ‹Handschrift› eines Bühnenbildners und der Theatertheorie, die verfochten wird. Richard Wagner forderte die Abschaffung der Beleuchtung des Zuschauerraums, um die Aufmerksamkeit des Publikums auf die Szene und die Musik zu lenken. Appia sieht in dem Licht und nicht in der Bühnenmalerei das einzige Mittel, die Plastik des abstrahierten Szenenraums und der Darstellerfigur plausibel herauszuarbeiten. Mit Hilfe der Sprache des ‹beweglichen Lichts› wird die prozeßhafte szenische Atmosphäre möglich. Brecht fordert die Sichtbarmachung der Lichtquellen, um unerwünschte Illussionen zu verhindern und das Theater als Arbeit erscheinen zu lassen. Auf der → Bauhausbühne wird Licht neben Farbe, Form, Bewegung und Ton zum gleichberechtigten Element. Lichtspiele avancieren zur eigenständigen Kunstform (Laszlo Moholy-Nagy), wie sie heute in den kommerzialisierten Lichtorgien der Rock-Konzerte und Diskotheken wieder auftauchen. – Die allgemeine physiologische Wirkung des Lichts auf den Menschen ist wissenschaftlich teilweise untersucht worden, und die Erkenntnisse finden im Alltag in der Lichtgestaltung von Wohnraum, Arbeitsplatz und des öffentlichen Raums ihren Niederschlag. Etwas Vergleichbares läßt sich für das Theater nicht entwickeln, da Kunst und der Einsatz ihrer Mittel individuell und zeitbezogen ist.

Bablet, D.: Licht und Ton im theatralischen Raum. Bühnentechnische Rundschau 3/74; Baumann, C.-F.: Licht im Theater. Stuttgart 1988; Bentham, F.: The Art of Stage Lighting. New York 1976; Bonnat, Y.: L'Éclairage des spectacles. Paris 1982; Feher, E.: Licht und Bühne. Toronto 1982; Keller, M.: Bühnenbeleuchtung. Köln 1985; McDandless, S.: A Method of Lighting the Stage. New York 1958; Pilbrow, R.: Stage Lighting. London 1973.

Horst Birr

Bühnenbild

Unter B. wird verstanden, was auf der Bühne den Handlungsrahmen durch Ausdrucksmittel der bildenden Künste und der Beleuchtung gestaltet (→ Bühne, → Bühnenbildelemente, → Bühnentechnik, → Szenographie, → Theaterbau). Schon die Grundbedeutung des Begriffs B. (Malerei, Ornament, Dekoration) deutet auf die mimetische und plastische Konzeption der bühnenbildnerischen Intention hin. Im naiven Bewußtsein ist das B. Hintergrundgemälde, meist perspektivisch und illusioniert, das den szenischen Raum auf ein bestimmtes Milieu fixiert. Diese Auffassung entspricht allerdings nur der Ästhetik des Naturalismus (→ Naturalistisches Theater) und stellt eine künstlerische Verengung dar. Daher die Versuche der Forschung, über den Begriff des B. hinauszugehen, zugunsten z. B. von Termini wie → Szenographie. Das B. von heute soll nützlich, wirksam, funktional sein: Werkzeug mehr als Bild, Instrument, nicht Ornament.

Das Beibehalten der Bezeichnung und der Praxis des B. kommt nicht von ungefähr. Die →Inszenierung hat sich lange auf Visualisierung und Illustrierung des Textes beschränkt in der Annahme, es obliege ihr, das, was im Text nur angedeutet ist, in die Anschauung zu übersetzen. Zola betont in diesem Sinne, das B. sei nur ‹ständige Beschreibung, die viel genauer und anschaulicher als die epische des Romans ist›. Und auch noch Copeau schreibt: «Symbolistisch oder realistisch, synthetisch oder anekdotisch, das B. bleibt ein Bild: Illustration.»

Seit Beginn des 20. Jh. ist im Bereich der B.-Gestaltung eine deutliche Reaktion gegen diese Tradition erkennbar. Das B. löst sich von seiner mimetischen Funktion und wird zum inneren Antrieb des Gesamtschauspiels. Es gestaltet den gesamten szenischen Raum in seiner Dreidimensionalität, aber auch durch die leeren Stellen, die es bewußt freiläßt. Es wird beweglich, vermag sich auszudehnen (→Bühnenbeleuchtung), fügt sich dem Spiel der Akteure, zwingt diese aber auch in spezifische Bewegungsrhythmen. Die Technik des Simultan-, des kontrapunktischen Spiels ist Anwendung der neuartigen szenographischen Prinzipien: Wahl einer Grundform oder eines Grundmaterials, Suche nach einer rhythmischen Tonart oder einem Strukturprinzip.

Die Ästhetik des →«Armen Theaters» (Brook, Grotowski) und die Tendenz zur Abstraktion seit dem Expressionismus (→Expressionistisches Theater) und dem Konstruktivismus (→Konstruktivismus und Theater) führen den Regisseur manchmal dazu, das B. vollständig auszuklammern, da ja die Bühne, auch wenn sie leer bleibt, immerhin als ‹ästhetisch entblößt› erscheint. Der Sinn liegt dann in der Leere, im Nicht-da-Seienden: Nicht-Vorhandensein eines Throns für den König, eines Orts für den Palast, eines genauen Raums für den Mythos. B. ist dann nur vorhanden als sprachlicher Kommentar, als Gestik, Mimik, Hinweis der Schauspieler (Rückkehr zur Bretterbühne des Volkstheaters und der Shakespeare-Zeit).

Bühnenmalerei gab es bereits im →antiken Theater, bes. im klassischen griech., dann aber auch im hellenistischen und im römischen Theater. Wesentliche Elemente sind für diese Zeit die →Proskenien, Drehprismen (Telari), →Periakten und Pinakten; dazu das grundlegende Werk des Vitruv (88–26 v. Chr.), *De architectura* (10 Bde.), das die ital. Renaissance im Cinquecento neu entdeckte und verwertete (→Renaissancetheater). Nach der Periode des mittelalterlichen Theaters (→Drama und Theater des Mittelalters), das ein B. im engeren Sinne nicht kannte, hat das →Rinascimento (Cinquecento) das neuzeitliche B. geschaffen, das bis ins 19. Jh. hinein vorherrschend und wegweisend bleiben sollte. Theoretiker, Architekten und Maler arbeiteten damals in Abhandlungen und Gestaltung die Grundprinzipien dieses modernen B. aus, vor allem die Darstel-

178 Bühnenbild

lung der von der Raumanlage her fehlenden Raumtiefe durch das illusionistisch-perspektivistische B. Im Anschluß an Baldassare Peruzzi (1481–1536) und Sebastiano Serlio (1475–1554) und deren Theorie der Perspektive entstanden in Ferrara und Vicenza die ersten großen ‹Winkelrahmen-Bühnen› mit je drei unveränderten B. für Tragödie, Komödie und Satyr-/Schäferspiel. In der Folge eroberte das B. durch die Drehbarkeit des Telari-Systems (1589), die mathematischen Grundlagen der Szenographie bei Guido Ubaldus (*De Scenis*, Pesaro 1600), die Maschinen- und Lichteffekte von Bernardo Buontalenti (1536–1609), Gian Lorenzo Bernini (1598–1680), Giacomo Torelli (1608–78), Jean-Nicolas Servandony (1695–1766) oder Nicola Sabbattini (dessen überlieferte Abhandlung *Practica di fabricar szene e macchine ne' teatri*, 1637–38, heute noch die Theaterleute fasziniert) den Tiefenraum. Die ‹feste teattrali› von Buontalenti in der Toskana und Torelli in Venedig wurden in ganz Europa nachgeahmt, u. a. in England und Frankreich: wichtig war dabei das Kulissensystem (→Kulissenbühne) zur schnellen Verwandlung, die Zentralisierung der Bühnenkontrolle, die Virtuosität des Illusionismus, beschrieben und eingeführt in Deutschland durch den Ulmer Josef Furttenbach (1591–1667: *Mannhafter Kunstspiegel*, 1663). Höhepunkt des barocken B. dann bei der Familie Galli-Bibiena: Ferdinando Galli-Bibiena (1657–1743: *La Prospettiva delle scene teatrali*, 1731) führt auf der Bühne den schräg über Eck gestellten Raum ein, sein Sohn Giuseppe (1696–1756) erweitert und vertieft die Effekte mit Hilfe polygonaler Raumsysteme. Das perspektivistische B. wird dann im Laufe des 19. Jh. durch die Übersteigerung des Illusionismus und falsche Augentäuschung ad absurdum geführt. Man griff z. T. auf die fast leere Bühne des →Elisabethanischen Theaters zurück oder bekannte sich mit den Regisseuren des Naturalismus, Antoine (1858–1943), Otto Brahm (1856–1912) oder K. S. Stanislawski (1863–1938) in seiner ersten Schaffensphase zur getreuen Wirklichkeitskopie.

Die zweite große Phase der B.-Entwicklung nach der ital. Illusionsbühne setzt ein nach der Jahrhundertwende (→Theaterreform, →Stilbühne) dank der großen Reformer Adolphe Appia (1862–1928) und Edward Gordon Craig (1872–1966) sowie dem Wiener Alfred Roller (1864–1935). Gewiß waren techn. Neuerungen wie die Einführung der Stahlkonstruktion, der Drehbühne, der Versenkung, des Rundhorizonts oder der elektrischen Bühnenbeleuchtung von großer Bedeutung; wesentlich aber war vor allem die Erkenntnis von der Einheit und Ganzheitlichkeit der Inszenierung als eigenwertigem Kunstwerk. A. Appia (*Die Musik und die Inszenierung*, 1899) schreibt: «Der Traum, dieser kostbare Zeuge, gibt uns mehr Aufschluß über die wesentlichen Wünsche unserer Persönlichkeit, als es die genaueste und feinste Analyse imstande wäre.» In Appias szenischem Anti-Illusionismus verhelfen Beleuchtung, Musik, massive, aber doch bewegliche Bauelemente wie Treppen, Podien, Pfeiler etc. zur Realisierung einer synthetischen Bühnenatmosphäre. Der Engländer G. Craig teilt diesen Glauben an die Autonomie und dynamische Synthese des B. in der Szenographie: Die Bedeutung der Geste, des Worts, des Rhythmus, der Linien und Farben verdichtet sich hier zu höchster Stilisierung (→Über-Marionette): «Mit seinen Screens, beweglichen Schirmen oder Tafeln als Teilen einer dadurch veränderten Dekoration, greift er auf barocke Szenenpraktiken zurück. Sein Ein-Mann-Theater hat eine Tendenz zum Puppenstil großen Stils, zur Ausklammerung der schauspielerischen Individualität, die ihm als naturalistische Zufälligkeit erscheint» (Rischbieter).

Nach dieser Eröffnung am Beginn des Jh. folgen unter dem Einfluß Appias und Craigs die vielfältigsten Experimente und Stile, insbesondere die Vorherrschaft der -ismen: die →Stilbühne des →Symbolistischen Theaters; das theatralische Theater eines Jacques Copeau (1879–1949) mit seiner Sehnsucht nach der Schlichtheit der nackten Bretter; die Bühnenabstraktionen des Futurismus, des Konstruktivismus und des Expressionismus mit seinen Groteskbildern und der expressiven Raumdynamik (Ludwig Sievert 1887–1968, Ernst Stern 1876–1954, Emil Pirchan 1884–1957), kulminierend in den diversen Konstruktionen der ‹Stufenbühne› Leopold Jessners (1878–1945).

Bedeutsam für das moderne Theater sind zwei Orientierungen: a) das ‹Maler-Theater›: Initiativen Diaghilews (‹Laßt die Maler tun, sie wissen, was sie wollen›) an den →Ballets Russes und →Ballets Suédois, die zu den Bühnenarbeiten von Picasso, Léger, Matisse, Miró, Braque, Dalí oder Sonia Delaunay führten; die Theaterexperimente von Wassily Kandinsky (*Über die abstrakte Bühnensynthese*, 1927, Theater als «Summe der abstrakten Klänge: 1. der Malerei – Farbe, 2. der Musik – Klang, 3. des Tanzes: Bewegung im gemeinsamen Klange der architektonischen Gestaltung»), von Piet Mondrian und von Marc Chagall für das →Jiddische Theater, schließlich die Experimente der →Bauhausbühne (Lothar Schreyer, Oskar Schlemmer); b) die Erneuerung des realistischen B. bei Piscator (1893–1966) und den Bühnenbildnern Brechts, Caspar Neher (1897–1962), Teo Otto (1904–68) und Karl von Appen (* 1900): Abkehr vom Dekorativen, Zweckhaftigkeit der Spielgerüste, Filmprojektion, Dokumentarmontage. Alle Theatermittel stehen im Dienst eines kritischen Realismus.

Zwischen Abstraktion und Realismus, Ausstellungsfülle und Armut neigt die heutige B.-Gestaltung im Rahmen der →Szenographie zur Kooperation innerhalb einer Gesamtkonzeption, totaler Schöpfungsakt oder wechselseitige Verfremdung. Immer mehr entwickeln sich Formen enger Zusammenarbeit eines Bühnenbildners mit einem Regisseur: Roger Allio/Roger Planchon, Georges Aillaud/K. M. Grüber, K.-G. Herrmann/Peter Stein, Wilfried Minks/Peter Zadek, Josef Svoboda/Otomar Krejča, Tadeusz Kantor/Jerzy Grotowski, Léon Gischia/Jean Vilar u. a. Die Zeit der großen Gesamtkonzeptionen und Einzelreformen ist vorbei; es geht um den je spezifisch definierten Gebrauch der Ausdrucksmittel, vor allem im Rahmen vielseitigster Kommunikation von Bühne und Publikum.

Eine Grundtendenz gegenwärtiger B.-Gestaltung ist die Neigung zum Bildhaften. Das Bild ist Ausdruck und Begriff in eins geworden und steht so in Opposition zu Text, Fabel oder Handlung. Weil das Theater den visuellen Charakter der Aufführung wieder ganz zurückgenommen hat, versteht es sich oft ganz als Folge von szenischen Bildern und behandelt Sprach- und Handlungsmaterialien wie Bilder. Dies gilt insbesondere für die Aufführungen von B. Wilson (→Theater of Images), M. Kirby, R. Foreman, C. Régy, D. Demarcy und – zeitlich näher – R. Planchon.

Die Inszenierung ist immer eine Ins-Bild-Setzung, aber sie ist mehr oder weniger bilderreich und ‹einfallsreich›: Das Thema der Bühnenrede, die dargestellte Welt werden in Bilderfolgen vorgetragen, mehr oder weniger nah an der Wirklichkeit, von der der Text spricht oder die er suggeriert. Die Nähe der Bühne zur Landschaft oder zum Gedankenbild ist jetzt viel größer, so als ginge es darum, die Nachahmung einer Sache oder ihre Versinnbildlichung zu überwinden. Nach Spielmaschine und Bild ist es nun die ‹Traummaschine›, wie A. Pierron feststellt: «Es ist an der Zeit, daß das Bühnenbild sich entintellektualisiert. Die weiße Fläche des abstrakten B. bietet in ihrer Schlichtheit oder ihrem Hermetismus die beste Entgiftungskur von einer zu sehr von Illustration und Zeichen befangenen Szenographie.» Diese Suche nach der entmaterialisierten Dimension des Bildes erneuert die Bedeutung des dramatischen Texts; dieser bietet sich durch seine Verbildlichung auf der Bühne zum Wiederlesen auf neue Art und Weise an. Das Bild bleibt trotz seiner Absicht, die Linearität und Logik des Texts zu brechen, eine Konstruktion der Theatermaschinerie und besitzt seine eigene Ordnung.

Alterdingen, J./Pöllner, H.: Handbuch für Theatermalerei und Bühnenbau. München o. J.; Badenhausen, R./Zielske, H. (Hg.): Bühnenformen, Bühnenräume, Bühnendekorationen. Berlin 1974; Bablet, D.: Le décor de théâtre de 1870 à 1914. Paris 1965; ders.: Le voies de la création théâtrale. Paris 1970–72; ders.: Les révolutions scéniques du XXe siècle. Paris 1975; Bellmann, W. F.: Scenography and Stage Technology. New York 1977; Boskovsky, K.: Die Entwicklung und Funktion des Bühnenbildes in Europa nach dem Zweiten Weltkrieg. Diss. Wien 1987; Brauneck, M.: Theater im 20. Jh. Reinbek bei Hamburg 1982; Frette, G.: Scenografia teatrale. Mailand 1955; Fuerst, W. R. u. Hume, S. J.: XXth Century Stage Decoration. London 1928/New York 1967; Hainaux, R.: Le décor de théâtre dans le monde. Brüssel 1956, 1964, 1973; Leclerc, H.: La scène d'illusion. In: Dumur, G. (ed.): Histoire des spectacles. Paris 1965; Mariani, V.: Storia della scenografia italiana. Florenz 1930; Pierron, A.: La scénographie: décor, masques, lumières.

In: Couty, D./Rey, A. (ed.): Le Théâtre. Paris 1980; Pirchan, E.: Zweitausend Jahre Bühnenbild. Wien 1949; Rischbieter, H./Storch, W. (Hg.): Bühne und bildende Kunst im XX. Jh. Velber 1968; Russel, D.: Theatrical Style. Palo Alto 1976; Schöne, G.: Die Entwicklung der Perspektivbühne von Serlio bis Galli Bibiena nach den Perspektivbüchern. Leipzig 1933; Schuberth, O.: Das Bühnenbild. München 1955; Simonson, L.: The Art of Scenic Design. New York 1950; Tintelnot, H.: Barocktheater und Barockkunst. Berlin 1937; Warre, M.: Designing and Making Stage Scenery. London 1966.

Patrice Pavis/Gérard Schneilin

Bühnenbildelemente

Das B. (→Szenographie) ist die künstlerisch bildnerische Umsetzung eines Stückkonzepts in den vorgegebenen dreidimensionalen Bühnenraum. Die historische Entwicklung der Bühnenbildkunst reicht von der Illusions-Perspektivbühne (→Kulissenbühne) über die Reformversuche Schinkels zu Beginn des 19. Jh. bis hin zu den Bestrebungen in den naturalistischen Dramen, Ausschnitte der Wirklichkeit auf der Bühne zu kopieren. Das moderne B. seit Adolphe Appia und Edward Gordon Craig definiert sich jedoch als szenischer Raum, dem eigene Gesetzmäßigkeiten unterliegen. Die Elemente des B. wie Material, Licht und Ton sind die wiederkehrenden Gestaltungsmittel, die künstlerischen Anregungen kommen aus der Bildgeschichte der Kultur und des Theaters, der Malerei, der Plastik, der Architektur und der Alltagskultur. Die Endlichkeit des vorgegebenen Bühnenhauses wird mittels eines Rundhorizonts aus Leinen zur Unendlichkeit des Himmels und der Nacht. Soll der Ort der Handlung in einem nebeligen Dunst erscheinen, so wird zwischen Bühne und Zuschauer ein Schleier aus feinem Tüll gespannt. Der ebene Bühnenboden wird über Praktikabel (Holz- und Stahlgerüste), Treppen, Schrägen, Versenkungen und Podien zur dreidimensionalen Topographie einer Natur- oder Stadtlandschaft.

Zweidimensionale Prospekte, Holzwände und Decken (Plafond) verbinden sich zu plastischen Architekturen. Die Gesetze der Schwerkraft scheinen in Leichtbaukonstruktion aus Holz, Stahl und Kunststoff aufgehoben zu sein. Flugmaschinen verhelfen dem Darsteller zu kühnen Bewegungen. Die Natur kann auf der Bühne durch die Prächtigkeit der Kunststofffarben noch in der Idealform erscheinen, die es real immer weniger oder noch nie gegeben hat. Zur bühnenwirksamen Erzeugung der elementaren Gewalten wie Feuer, Donner, Blitz, Schnee, Regen, Nebel und Sturm sind Spezialmaschinen entwickelt worden, die in ihren Effekten den Naturerscheinungen in nichts außer der Gefährlichkeit nachstehen. Orts- und Zeitwechsel werden durch den elektronisch gesteuerten und

182 Bühnenbildner

gespeicherten Einsatz der Bühnenmaschinerie und Beleuchtungstechnik (→Bühnentechnik, Beleuchtungstechnik) jederzeit möglich.

Mit der Erfindung der Glühlampe 1881 durch Edison verfügt der Bühnenbildner über die Gestaltungsmöglichkeit des Raums durch Licht, Schatten und Farbe. Imaginäre Räume werden durch Projektion von Großdias auf Leinwände oder durch plastisch erscheinende holographische Bilder zur scheinbaren Wirklichkeit. Zu den Möglichkeiten, Raumvorstellungen zu erwecken, gehört ebenso das gesprochene Wort, durch das Handlungsorte für die Vorstellungswelt der Zuschauer genauer beschrieben werden bzw. erst erscheinen. In die gleiche Richtung geht der Einsatz von Theatermusik und Geräuschen mittels Studio-Tonanlagen. – Die Mittel des Theaters, aber auch die Erwartungen der Zuschauer verfeinern sich in Konkurrenz zu Film, Fernsehen und Video-Clips. Die Faszination des Theatererlebnisses geht aber von dem sparsamen Gebrauch einfacher Bildelemente aus, die den Zuschauer zum Mitsehen, Mitfühlen und Mitdenken anregen.

Kranich, F.: Bühnentechnik der Gegenwart. München 1929; Mello, B.: Trattato di Scenotecnica. Mailand 1962; Sonrel, P.: Traîté de Scénographie. Paris 1944.

Horst Birr

Bühnenbildner

(Auch Szenograph oder Ausstatter) Beruf der bildenden Künste, freiberuflich oder in Vertragsverhältnis mit einzelnen Theatern. Aufgaben: Entwurf der Bühnenbilder für die einzelnen Szenen einer Neuinszenierung in Übereinstimmung mit dem Konzept des →Regisseurs; Anfertigung von maßgerechten, in allen Einzelheiten ausgearbeiteten Plänen und Modellen für die Bühnenwerkstätten unter Berücksichtigung des bühnentechnischen Apparats und der räumlichen Verhältnisse, der Auf- und Abbaumöglichkeiten, der Kapazität der Werkstätten und der Möglichkeit der Wiederverwendung von Bauten und Kostümen im Rahmen der vorgegebenen finanziellen Mittel; Erstellung von genauen Requisitenabbildungen und, falls für die Gesamtausstattung verantwortlich, auch von Kostümskizzen; Überwachung der Beleuchtungseinstellungen; Idealfall: Anwesenheit bei allen Proben. Ausbildung: sechs- bis achtsemestriges Studium an einer Kunstakademie oder -hochschule (Entwurfsübungen, Modellgestaltung, Maltechnik, Beleuchtungstechnik, Nebenfächer: Kunst- und Theatergeschichte, Stil- und Kostümkunde, dramaturgische Vorlesungen, Schriftzeichen, Perspektive, Architektur u. Körperzeichnen), danach Assistenz am Theater.

Bühnenbildner 183

→*Antikes Theater*: früheste bekannte Skenographen des abendländischen Theaters: Agatharchos von Samos (460–420 v. Chr., von Aischylos mitgebracht, Verfasser einer Schrift über die skene), Apollodoros (430–400 v. Chr.) u. Themokret aus Athen, Klesthenes und Sohn Menedemos aus Eretrien (4. Jh. v. Chr.). →*Renaissancetheater*: Maler und Architekten Baldassare Peruzzi (1481–1536), Sebastiano Serlio (1474–1554), Leonardo da Vinci (1452–1519), Raffaelo Santi (1483–1520), Bernardo Buontalenti (1536–1608, Verwendung von Periakten), Giulio Parigi († 1635), Joseph Furttenbach (1591–1667, Deutschland), Inigo Jones (1573–1652, England), →*Barocktheater*: Giovanni Battista Aleotti (1547–1636, Erfinder der Kulisse), Nicolà Sabbattini (um 1574–1654, Winkelrahmen), Giacomo Torelli (1608–78, 1. Berufsbühnenbildner), Ludovico Ottavio Burnacini (1636–1707, Wien), Familie Galli-Bibiena, Giovanni Nicolo Servandoni (Jean Nicolas Servandony, 1695–1766, Paris), Jean Bérain (1638–1711, Paris), Filippo Juvara (1676–1711, Rom). *Rokoko*: Frankreich: François Boucher (1700–70), Dominique François Slodtz († 1764). →*Klassik*: Italien: Brüder Galliari (Bernardino 1707–94, Fabrizio 1709–90, Giovanni Antonio 1718–83); England: Christopher Wren (1632–1723), William Capon (1757–1827).

19. Jh.: *Historismus und Romantik*: England: Philippe Jacques de Loutherbourg (1735–1812); Frankreich: Louis J. M. Daguerre (1787–1851). Pierre-Luc-Charles Cicéri (1782–1868), Charles-Antoine Cambon (1802–75); Deutschland und Österreich: Giorgio Fuentes (1756–1821, Frankfurt/M.), Friedrich Beuther (1777–1856, Weimar), Karl Friedrich Schinkel (1781–1841, Berlin), Familie Quaglio, Antonio de Pian (1784–1851), Carlo Brioschi (1826–95), Georg von Meiningen (1829–1914). *Reformbestrebungen* (→Theaterreform): Edward Gordon Craig (1872–1966, England), Adolphe Appia (1862–1928, Schweiz), Alfred Roller (1864–1935, Wien).

20. Jh.: Deutschland und Österreich: *Zusammenarbeit mit M. Reinhardt*: Lovis Corinth (1858–1925), Edvard Munch (1863–1944), Max Slevogt (1868–1932), Emil Orlik (1889–1932), Ernst Stern (1876–1954), Karl Walser (1877–1943), Oskar Strnad (1879–1935), John Heartfield (1891–1968, später mit Piscator); →*Expressionistisches Theater*: Ludwig Sievert (1887–1968), Emil Pirchan (1884–1957), César Klein (1876–1954); →*Bauhausbühne*: Wassily Kandinsky (1866–1944), Oskar Schlemmer (1888–1943), Laszlo Moholy-Nagy (1895–1946); Otto Reigbert (1890–1957, Zusammenarbeit mit Piscator und O. Falckenberg), George Grosz (1893–1959) und Traugott Müller (1895–1944), Zusammenarbeit mit E. Piscator; Caspar Neher (1897–1962, Zusammenarbeit mit B. Brecht), Theo Otto (1904–68), Rochus Gliese (1891–1978), Rudolf Heinrich (1926–75, Zusammenarbeit mit W. Felsenstein), Fritz Wotruba (1907–75), Oskar Kokoschka (1886–1980), Karl von Appen (1900–81, Berliner Ensemble), Wilhelm Reinking (1896–1985), Wolfgang Znamenacek (1913–53, München). *Italienische Futuristen* (→Futuristisches Theater): Enrico Prampolini (1894–1956), Giorgio de Chirico (1888–1978); *Russische Konstruktivisten* (→Konstruktivismus und Theater): Kasimir Malewitsch (1878–1935), El Lissitzky (1890–1959), Alexandra Exter (1882–1946), Natalia Gontscharowa (1881–1962), Michail Larionow (1881–1964). *USA*: Norman Bel Geddes (1893–1958, Zusammenarbeit mit Reinhardt), Alexander Calder (1898–1976), Barbara Hepworth (1903–1975).

Zeitgenössische B.: Achim Freyer (*1934), Rolf Glittenberg (*1945), Karl Ernst Herrmann (*1936), Hans Hoffer, Gerhard Jax, Herbert Kapplmüller, Bert Kistner, Matthias Kralj (*1933), Götz Loepelmann (*1930), Axel Manthey (*1945), Wilfried Minks (*1931), Andreas Reinhardt (*1937), Thomas Richter-Forgach

(* 1940), Jürgen Rose (* 1937), Horst Sagert (* 1934), Willi Schmidt (* 1910), Erich Wonder (* 1944), Jörg Zimmermann, Leni Bauer-Ecsy, Ita Maximowna, Susanne Thaler; Luciano Damiani (* 1923), Daniele Lievi (1954–1990), Pier Luigi Pizzi (* 1930), Ezio Toffolutti, Franco Zeffirelli (* 1923); Carl Toms, Josef Svoboda (* 1920), Tadeusz Kantor (1915–1990), David Borowski (* 1934); Waleri Lewental (* 1938), Eduard Kotschergin (* 1937), Ladislav Vychodil (* 1920).

Ingeborg Janich

Bühnenkostüm

1. Das B. ist – im Gegensatz zum Zeitkostüm – die Kleidung, die der Schauspieler während einer Vorführung trägt. Es unterstützt – aus dem Verständnis der Zeitläufte gesehen – Geist und Ziel der Inszenierung; es beeinflußt die Darstellungskraft des Schauspielers und trägt zur Wirkung auf das Publikum bei. Zeitgeist, Lebensverständnis und Weltkenntnis entscheiden weitgehend die Form des B.; in diesem Zusammenhang macht das B. durch Schnitt, Farbe, Dekor und Attribute dem Zuschauer den Dargestellten verständlich und erkennbar. Die Entwicklung des B. ist eng mit der Entwicklung des Theaters verbunden.

2. Urtümliche Lust und Angst, Schwanken zwischen Stabilisierung und Auflösung von Beziehungen und Abhängigkeiten in Natur und Umwelt lassen den Menschen frühzeitig zu Verkleidung und Verwandlung als Ausdrucksmittel greifen. Götterkulte, Totemismus, Schamanentum, Initiationsriten, Beschwörungen und Huldigungen, Fruchtbarkeits-, Sieges- und Freudentänze werden nicht nur in Abläufen und Handlungen bestimmt, sondern auch im Kostüm vorgegeben. Eine Trennung in Agierende und Betrachter ist noch nicht vollzogen.

Parallel zur Herausbildung der klassischen griech. Dramenformen (→Antikes Theater) läuft die Entwicklung des antiken B. Aischylos (525–456/55 v.Chr.) bestimmt für die Aufführung seiner Tragödien maßgebend Kostüm und Maske: der Schauspieler trägt Polster vor Brust und Unterleib, durch eine Art Trikot gehalten; darüber einen Ärmelchiton, bodenlang für Frauenrollen, kürzer für Männerrollen. An den Füßen weiche, kreuzweise geschnürte Kniestiefel (Kothurn; wird erst in der späten röm. Tragödie zum Stelzschuh). Als optische Verlängerung der Gestalt wird der Chiton unter der Brust breit gegürtet. Könige, Königinnen tragen purpurne Schleppkleider (Xystis), Seher über dem Chiton einen netzartigen Überwurf (Agrevon), Krieger über dem kurzen Chiton die Rüstung. Je nach Ort der Handlung wird als Obergewand eine Chlaina (rechteckig, dicke Wolle), ein Himation (rechteckig, feine Wolle), eine Chlamys (trapezförmig, kurzer Soldatenmantel) getragen. ‹Sprechende› Farben: helle, leuchtende, gemustert oder mit Ornamenten geschmückt für die Glücklichen; dunkle Farben für die Unglücklichen, schwarz für die Trauernden, zerfetzte Kleidung für die Verzweifelten. Kopfbedekkungen sind bis auf den Reisehut (Petasos) selten. Frauen fassen ihr Haar mit einem Band (Mitra) zusammen, Göttinnen und Königinnen mit einem Diadem. Herolde und vom Orakel Heimkehrende sind bekränzt, Götter und Helden mit ihren Attributen versehen (Herakles: Keule, Athene: Schild...). Die Masken werden durch Gesichtszüge, -farbe, Haarfarbe und Frisur dem Rollencharakter angepaßt. Der Chor ist schlicht gekleidet, ergänzende Merkmale nur, wenn die Handlung es erfordert (Eumeniden in schwarz, Schlangen in Händen und Haar).

Das B. der Komödie vermischt Reste aus dem Dionysoskult und der dorischen Posse. Ein ausgestopftes Wansttrikot mit aufgemalten Körperzeichen (Brustwarzen, Nabel...), Arm- und Beintrikots, mit Tätowierungen bemalt oder gestreift, und ein Phallos aus rotem Leder gehören zur ‹Grundausstattung› des Komödienspielers. Knöchelschuhe für Männerrollen, Kothurn für Frauenrollen. Karikierende oder typisierende Masken mit großen Augenlöchern und grinsenden Mündern, kennzeichnende Attribute. Die Choreuten tragen deutliche Masken (Wespen, Vögel, Frösche...). Der neuen Komödie (ab ca. 340 v. Chr.) fehlt der kritisch-politische Zug und die Bindung an Brauchtum und Mythos. Entsprechend verändert sich das B., Polsterung und Phallos verschwinden, das B. paßt sich der ‹Gesellschaftskomödie› an; die Länge des Chiton kennzeichnet die soziale Stellung, Farbe und Dekor geben Hinweis auf Alter, Beruf, Typ (Jüngling Purpurkleid, Greis weiß, Hetäre grellbunt...). Die Masken folgen der Charakterprofilierung, sie werden im Ausdruck differenzierter.

Die röm. Tragödie verwendet sowohl das griech. B. (fabula crepidata; Themen aus der griech. Mythologie) als auch röm. Kleidung (fabula praetexta; Themen aus der röm. Sage und Geschichte). Auch die Komödie unterscheidet im Kostüm griech. (fabula palliata) und röm. Themen (fabula togata). Im Mimus wird ohne Maske mit männlichen und weiblichen Darstellern gespielt; in der →Atellane sind die Darsteller maskiert (oft freie Bürger), Masken für vier Charaktertypen: der Narr (Maccus), der Tölpel (Bucco), der Alte (Pappus), der Scharlatan (Dossenus). In der Kaiserzeit wird das B. zum Luxus hin übertrieben, die Masken werden bis zur Häßlichkeit verzerrt.

3. Die christliche Kirche bekämpft das Theater grundsätzlich (Verherrlichung heidnischer Mythen, Unmoral). Die Verbindung zum antiken Theater verläuft über Byzanz. Dort begünstigen das politische Verhältnis Kaiser – Kirche, die Häufung von Reichtum und Luxus und das Hofzeremoniell die Entwicklung unterschiedlicher Theaterformen und die Ansammlung von Berufsschauspielern. Bei den Staatsfesten werden neben zirzensischen Darbietungen, Mimos und Pantomime auch Monologe aus

186 Bühnenkostüm

antiken Tragödien vorgetragen im Schleppgewand mit bodenlangen Hängeärmeln, Kothurn, Perücke und tragischer Maske. Vom 5./6. Jh. an tauchen dramatisierte christliche Inhalte bei Kirchenfesten auf. – Im weström. Reich behauptet sich bis ins 5. Jh. der Mimus (mit um den ‹Christen› erweitertem Typenrepertoire). Seine Tradition wird von Jokulatoren und Spielleuten fortgeführt. Karikierende Darstellungen in stark karikierenden Kostümen. Wiederholte kirchliche Verbote gegen die Darstellung von Geistlichen. Im 10. Jh. setzt die Entwicklung →geistlicher Spiele (→Mittelalterliches Theater) mit szenischen Darstellungen bei den Osterfeiern ein. Allmähliche szenische Erweiterung des Spiels, teilweise in der Landessprache; im 14. Jh. Abwandern der von der Liturgie getrennten Teile auf den Platz vor der Kirche. Kern des Spiels bleibt das Leben Christi, alle dazugehörigen Personen (Männer und Frauen) werden von Klerikern in dem entsprechenden geistlichen Gewand dargestellt. Die ‹angewachsenen› Legenden und Alltagsgeschichten beziehen die Gemeinde ein, bei der Rollenverteilung wird auf Stand und Ehrenhaftigkeit geachtet. Das B. der geistlichen Spiele ist voller symbolischer Aussagekraft. Es muß den Dargestellten erkennbar machen und die ‹unbegrenzte› Entfernung zum Betrachter berücksichtigen. Die Ausstattung bestimmt der Spielleiter (Geistlicher, Verfasser des Spiels, Stadtschreiber, Lehrer...), sie wird in der Dirigierrolle notiert.

In Italien (sacra rappresentazione) ist die Bildgestaltung bestimmend, in Frankreich (Mysterienspiel) das luxuriöse und modische B., in Deutschland die symbolische Phantasie. Die Kostüme werden vom Darsteller bezahlt; Zuschüsse von Städten und Zünften, Reiche für Arme. Bei allen anti- und nichtchristlichen Rollen wird das B. zuerst bereichert und übersteigert. Kostümwechsel im Spielverlauf ist üblich. So erscheint Christus im Gärtnergewand, im weißen oder blutroten (Karfreitag) Mantel, auferstanden im päpstlichen Ornat, Maria in der blauen oder schwarzen (Trauer) Cappa oder Dalmatika, Engel, Heilige und Propheten in Alben, kostbaren langen Mänteln, mit erklärenden Attributen. Könige in Purpur, Hermelin und mit Staatsinsignien; alle übrigen Personen, gleich aus welcher historischen Epoche, im Zeitkostüm des entsprechenden Stands, soweit vonnöten mit erläuternden Attributen. Krieger und Grabeswächter in voller Rüstung, Narren im bunten Schellenkleid, Teufel mit Schweifen, Krallen, entsetzlichen, oft feuerspeienden Masken. Bei Paradiesdarstellungen wird Nacktheit durch leinene Leibkleider vorgetäuscht.

Im 15. Jh. setzt eine zunehmende Verweltlichung der Spielanlässe ein (→Neuzeit/Theater der Neuzeit). Fürstenbesuche, fürstliche Hochzeiten, Geburten, Trauerfeiern sind Anlässe für mehrtägige Spiele und Prozessionen. Luxus und Pracht der Kostüme steigern sich.

4. Das 16. Jh. leitet die totale Veränderung der Theaterstruktur ein.

Bühnenkostüm 187

Passions- und Mysterienspiele wandern in bäuerliche Bereiche ab. Als Veranstalter treten Fürsten und Adel (weltliche Macht) und Berufsschauspielertruppen (‹Unternehmer›) auf. Laiengruppen (Confrérie de la Passion, Meistersinger, Schul- und Ordenstheater) spielen mit pädagogisch-sittlicher oder politisch-religiöser Zielsetzung. Es ändern sich die Inhalte und Formen der Aufführungen (antike Originale, historische Themen, Huldigungsspiele, höfisches Ballett, →Commedia dell'arte). Gewechselt wird von der Freilichtaufführung zum Innenraum-Theater, vom Simultan- zum Sukzessivspiel. Nicht mehr zu Gottes Ehre wird gespielt, sondern zur Verherrlichung der fürstlichen Macht oder, gegen Entgelt, zur Unterhaltung des Publikums. Für die höfischen Aufführungen werden Dichter, Musiker und bildende Künstler verpflichtet. Die veränderten Raum- und Lichtverhältnisse zwingen beim B. zu größerer Differenzierung in Detail, Requisit und Attribut. Ein Interesse am historisch richtigen B. macht sich in Ansätzen bemerkbar. Ausgangspunkt der Entwicklung ist Italien; Wiederaufführungen antiker Dramen in antikischem B., üppigste Prachtentfaltung und Hang zum exotischen Kostüm bei den →Trionfi und Huldigungsspielen. Im Volks-/Dialekttheater der →Commedia dell'arte festigen sich in Charakter und B. Typen des bürgerlichen Lebens (→Pantalone: rotes Wams, schwarzer Mantel, weißer Spitzbart; →Dottore: schwarze Robe, weiße Halskrause, anliegendes Käppchen, schwarzer Hut, Krempe hochgeschlagen; →Zanni: lederne Halbmaske, weites abgetragenes Gewand, Schlapphut, stumpfer Holzdolch; →Arlecchino, →Pulcinella, →Capitano...). Ital. Wandertruppen beeinflussen die Entwicklung in Frankreich und England. Am frz. Hof setzt sich vor allem das →ballet comique durch. Das Sprechtheater wird von Laiengruppen (Confrérie de la Passion) und von Schauspieltruppen bestritten. Die Ausstattung ist bei Hof-Aufführungen kostbar (königliche Kleiderkammer), sonst eher bescheiden.

England zeigt bei fast dekorationsloser Bühne die größte Prachtentfaltung im Kostüm. Die Theaterbesessenheit des Publikums und der wirtschaftliche Aufbau der Theatergruppen ermöglichen den hohen Kostenaufwand für die B. Der Kostümfundus ist wertvollster Besitz der Truppe. Das B. muß auch bei Bemühung um inhaltliche Echtheit optisch effektvoll sein. Antike Themen im nachempfundenen röm. Kostüm; Höflinge und Kavaliere in der farbenprächtigen Eleganz der Zeit; Bürger in bürgerlicher Festkleidung; niedrige Stände in Alltagstracht; Könige immer mit Krone auf dem Kopf. Daneben entwickeln sich bestimmte Kostümtypen: Orientalen in exotischen oder türk. Gewändern, mit Schmuck überladen; Juden (Shylock) im langen Rock, Maske mit großer Nase und rotem Bart; Dirnen in langen bauschigen Kleidern aus geflammtem Taft und Totenkopfring am Mittelfinger; ein die ganze Gestalt umhüllendes Tüllgewand als ‹the robe for to go invisible› (Oberon).

188 Bühnenkostüm

In Deutschland behält das Laientheater weitgehend seine Bedeutung bei (Meistersingerbühne, Schultheater). Das B. ist die bürgerliche Alltagstracht mit erläuternden Attributen (Wanderer: Stecken, Alchimist: Destillierglas...). Abgestuft nach sozialem Stand und Alter wird entsprechend den Kleiderordnungen. Trachtenbücher fördern das Interesse am historisch und ethnologisch richtigen B.

Das 17. Jh. ist bestimmt durch die Konsolidierung der Nationalstaaten, die Entwicklung des Absolutismus, die kulturelle Vorherrschaft Frankreichs, ungeachtet politischer Auseinandersetzungen. Rivalitäten zwischen Wien und Paris und der allgemeine Wunsch nach frz. Lebensstil bringen dem Theater Aufschwung. Kein Hof ohne Schauspieltruppe, keine Residenz ohne Theater. Die Revolution der Bühnentechnik und die Strenge des höfischen Zeremoniells führen zur Schwerpunktverschiebung vom dramatischen Inhalt zu Dekoration, Kostüm, Inszenierung. Bedeutende Künstler spezialisieren sich auf Theaterbau, Bühnen- und Kostümgestaltung und Prunkinszenierungen (Bernardo Buontalenti, 1536–1608; Lodovico Ottavio Burnacini, 1636–1707; Inigo Jones, 1573–1652; Jean Berain, 1637–1711...). Als barocke Theaterformen entwickeln sich die Oper, das →Ballet de Cour, die Comédie-ballet (Molière, Lully). Im Sprechtheater werden die ital. und frz. Komödie und die frz. Tragödie (Corneille, Racine) gepflegt. Das B. des 17. Jh. wird vom Zeitkostüm bestimmt. Die allgemeine Stilisierung der Hofkleidung und ihre Einbindung in das Hofzeremoniell sowie die Bedeutung von Festen und Theateraufführungen innerhalb des Hoflebens – Mitglieder des Hofs wirken bei den Aufführungen mit – führen zu Überschneidungen und gegenseitiger Beeinflussung von B. und Zeitmode. In der Regel ist das B. reicher und übersteigerter als das Hofkleid. Kostbarste Materialien, Stikkereien, Bänder, Juwelen werden bis zu den Kostümen der Komparserie verwandt. Farbsymbolik und Attribute deuten Zeit, Ort und Charakter der Rolle an. Daneben gibt es exotische und allegorische Kostüme. Für alle antiken Themen trägt der Mann ein brustpanzerähnliches Leibstück mit über einem Rock liegenden Schoßteilen. Rock und Schoß erweitern sich im Laufe des 18. Jh. zum reifrockähnlichen tonnelet, dazu Seidenstrümpfe und geschnürte Halbstiefel. Die ‹antike› Schauspielerin trägt eine anliegende, tiefdekolletierte Corsage mit weiten Schößen, Rock, langer Schleppe, Diadem oder Federbusch. Als Mantel tragen beide einen auf der Schulter geknöpften Umhang. Schauspielerinnen treten nie mit leeren Händen auf (Tragödie: Taschentuch, Komödie: Fächer). Bei den nicht vom Hof finanzierten Schauspieltruppen trägt der Schauspieler, oft von Gönnern unterstützt, die Kosten für sein Kostüm. Kostüm- und Schmuckverleihe kommen auf. Unter Ludwig XV. verändert das B. seine Form nur im Rahmen der veränderten Hofmode (Cäsar in Lockenperücke und Reifrock, Medea im Reifrockkleid). Dessinateur en titre de

Bühnenkostüm 189

l'Opéra ist Louis René Boquet (1717–1814). Die um die Jahrhundertmitte einsetzenden Versuche einer Kostümreform in Richtung Schlichtheit und historischer Echtheit gehen – gegen den Widerstand des Publikums – von einzelnen Schauspielern aus (Mlle Clairon, Lekain, Mme Favart, Talma), unterstützt aus dem Lager der Aufklärer von Johann Christoph Gottsched (1700–66), Denis Diderot (1713–84), Jean-François Marmontel (1723–79). David Garrick (1716–79), von 1747 bis 1776 Leiter des →Drury Lane-Theaters in London, suchte vor allem die psychologische Anpassung des B. an die Rolle. Die Auseinandersetzung zwischen Tradition und Fortschritt in Dekoration und B. zieht sich – über die Frz. Revolution hinweg – weit in das 19. Jh. hinein. Die grundlegende Änderung der Zeitkleidung zwischen Revolution und Restauration, eine neue Form des bürgerlichen Theaters und die Existenz herausragender Schauspieltruppen setzen allmählich das reale B. durch. Karl Moritz Graf von Brühl (1772–1837), von 1814 bis 1828 Generalintendant der königlichen Schauspiele in Berlin, fördert die Entwicklung. Herzog Georg II. von Meiningen (1826–1914) läßt seinen präzisen B.-Entwürfen genaue Studien vorangehen.

Das ausgehende 19. und vor allem das 20. Jh. bringen dem Theater eine neue Vielfältigkeit. Die wissenschaftlichen, techn., ökonomischen und gesellschaftlichen Veränderungen – im 19. Jh. eingeleitet – führen nun zum Nach- und Nebeneinander verschiedenster geistiger Strömungen. Alle suchen ihre theatralische Ausdrucksform (traditionelles Startheater, →Naturalistisches Theater, Symbolismus, Impressionismus, Expressionismus, politisches Theater...). Die Auseinandersetzung zwischen Dramatiker und Ausstatter wird in unserem Jh. um den Regisseur bereichert. Er versucht heute vielfach, Dichtung und Ausstattung seinem Werk- und Themenverständnis anzugleichen bis unterzuordnen. Das B. ist so facettenreich wie die Theaterlandschaft. Es kann historisch exakt, in eine andere Zeit versetzt, abstrahiert, verfremdet, symbolisch gedeutet oder auch ohne jede Beziehung frei erfunden sein, es muß nur in das Aufführungskonzept passen. Bedeutende Maler sind als Kostümbildner hervorgetreten: Juan Gris (1887–1927), George Grosz (1893–1959), Edvard Munch (1863–1944), Emil Orlik (1870–1932), Pablo Picasso (1881–1973).

Häufig liegt die Gestaltung von →Bühnenbild und B. in einer Hand. Die besonderen technischen Voraussetzungen von Film und Fernsehen fordern vom B. größte Genauigkeit. Frühere Abgrenzungen des B. in den Sparten Oper, Schauspiel, Operette, Revue, Kabarett, Zirkus sind heute fließend. Neben dem eigenen Kostümfundus werden, vor allem bei Film und Fernsehen, für die Ausstattung Kostümverleihfirmen in Anspruch genommen.

Fachbibliotheken/Sammlungen: Lipperheidesche Kostümbibliothek, Jebensstr. 2, 1000 Berlin 12; Institut für Theaterwissenschaft, Universität Köln; Schloß Wahn, 5000 Köln 90; Deutsches Theatermuseum, Galeriestr. 4 a und 6, 8000 München 22; Kostümforschungsinstitut von Parish, Kemnatenstr. 50, 8000 München 19; Bibliothèque – Musée de l'Opéra, Place Charles Garnier, Paris 9; Le Centre d' Enseignement et de Documentation du Costume, 105, bvd. Malesherbes, Paris 8; Musée de la Mode et du Costume, Palais Galliéra, Paris 16; Musée des Arts de la Mode, rue de Rivoli, Paris 1; Victoria & Albert Museum, South Kensington, London SW 7; Modesammlung im Schloß Hetzendorf, Hetzendorfer Str. 79, 1120 Wien.

Baur-Heinhold, M.: Theater des Barock. München 1966; Berckenhagen, E./ Wagner, G.: Bretter, die die Welt bedeuten. Berlin 1978; Berthold, M.: Weltgeschichte des Theaters. Stuttgart 1968; v. Boehn, M.: Das Bühnenkostüm in Altertum, Mittelalter und Neuzeit. Berlin 1921; Boucher, F.: Histoire du Costume. France 1965; Hadamowsky, F./Kindermann, H.: Europäische Theaterausstellung. Wien u. a. 1955; Kindermann, H.: Theatergeschichte Europas. Salzburg 1957–74; Laver, J.: Costume in the Theatre. London 1964; Rischbieter, H. (Hg.): Bühne und bildende Kunst im XX. Jahrhundert. Hannover 1968; Tilke, M.: Kostümschnitte und Gewandformen. Tübingen 1945.

Dorothea Dieren

Bühnenmanuskript

Hauptsächlich von Theaterverlagen hergestelltes hektographiertes oder gedrucktes Textbuch noch nicht gespielter Stücke oder Stückfassungen, -übersetzungen. Dient der Werbung für neue Stücke (Angebote für Theater) wie auch als Textheft für Proben, meist querformatig vervielfältigt. Als B. gedruckte Stücke gelten als noch nicht veröffentlicht, unterliegen aber auch als solche dem Urheberrecht.

Wolfgang Beck

Bühnenmusik

Im Musiktheater wird hierunter nur der Teil der Musik verstanden, der auf oder hinter der Bühne produziert wird und nicht aus dem Orchestergraben kommt. B. im Musiktheater ist als reine Inzidenzmusik zu bezeichnen (von lat. incidere = einfallen), die in die Szene ‹einfällt›. Inzidenzmusik kann entweder die Handlung unterstützen oder kontrapunktieren wie die Ballszene im 2. Akt von *Don Giovanni* von W. A. Mozart (1756 bis 91), die Militär- und Heurigenmusik in *Wozzeck* von A. Berg (1885 bis 1935). – Im Schauspiel wird, im Gegensatz zum Musiktheater, jeglicher Einsatz von Musik bei Aufführungen als B. bezeichnet. Generell

Bühnenmusik 191

sind drei Arten des Gebrauchs zu unterscheiden: 1. Inzidenzmusik, z. B. Fanfaren, Musik zu tänzerischen Szenen, Liedbegleitungen; 2. eine musikalische Ausgestaltung einzelner Szenen, die der Ausdeutung und psychologischen Vertiefung dient und/oder die Akte eines Dramas bzw. Szenen der Akte verbindet (Ouvertüre, Zwischenakts-, Verwandlungs- und Schlußmusik); 3. eine Form der B., die nur unterhaltende, Pausen ausfüllende oder verbindende Funktion hat und in keinem inneren Zusammenhang mit den Vorgängen auf der Bühne steht (vorwiegend im 19. Jh. eingesetzt).

Urformen der B. lassen sich in frühen Ritualen z. B. zur Gottesverehrung finden. Im chin. Schauspiel (→Chinesisches Theater) wurde bereits vor Jahrtausenden improvisierte Musik zur Betonung emotionaler Höhepunkte benutzt; im griech. Theater (→Antikes Theater) wurde der einstimmige Chor durch Instrumente unterstützt, und auch der Einzug der Schauspieler wurde instrumental begleitet. Musik gehörte zu den geistlichen und weltlichen Spielen des Mittelalters (→Drama und Theater des Mittelalters) ebenso wie zu den in Szene gesetzten →Trionfi der europäischen Renaissance. Für die Shakespeare-Zeit (→Elisabethanisches Theater) war die B. einer der wichtigsten Inszenierungsfaktoren. Shakespeare (1564–1616) schrieb instrumentale Musik präzise vor, u. a. zu Tänzen, Trinkszenen, Geistererscheinungen. In der zweiten Hälfte des 17. Jh. wurden in England Dramen Shakespeares und seiner Zeitgenossen mit Musik, Gesang und Balletteinlagen so angefüllt, daß eine Grenze zwischen Schauspiel mit Musik und Oper kaum zu ziehen ist. Für diese Zeit sind für Frankreich entstandene B. zu Dramen von Molière (1622–73), Corneille (1606–84) und Racine (1639–99) und für Spanien zu Dramen von Calderón (1600–81) und Lope de Vega (1562–1635) zu nennen. In Deutschland gab es B. als festen Bestandteil von Schauspielaufführungen seit den Wanderzügen der engl. Komödianten (→Wanderbühne); im 18. Jh. entwickelte sich eine anspruchsvolle, eher nach musikalischen Gesichtspunkten gestaltete, zum Schauspiel aber beziehungslose Rahmenmusik. Von den Romantikern gingen neue Bestrebungen aus, eine möglichst enge Verbindung von Musik und Drama zu schaffen, hier besonders E. T. A. Hoffmann (1776–1822), der selbst auch B. schrieb (*Braut von Messina* von Schiller). Bis zur Mitte des 19. Jh. war B. zu Schauspielaufführungen obligatorisch; bei Mangel an passender Musik wurden Repertoirestücke eingeschoben. F. Hiller (1811–85) und F. Liszt (1811–86) setzten sich Ende des Jh. dafür ein, für Schauspiele die nur eigens dafür komponierte Musik zu verwenden. Von ihrer ehemaligen Funktion losgelöst, werden u. a. folgende B. aus dem 19. Jh. heute noch konzertant aufgeführt: von F. Mendelssohn-Bartholdy (1809–47) *Ein Sommernachtstraum* und von E. Grieg (1843–1907) zu Ibsens *Peer Gynt*. Geprägt waren die B. des späten 19. Jh. bis um die Jahrhundertwende von psychologischer, ausdeutender, symbolistischer Musik. Seit Anfang des 20. Jh. arbeiten Regisseur / Autor und Komponist enger und experimentierfreudiger zusammen, z. B. Max Reinhardt (1873–1943) und E. Humperdinck (1854–1921). Besondere Bedeutung hatte die Zusammenarbeit von P. Dessau (1894–1979), K. Weill (1900–50), H. Eisler (1898–1962) mit B. Brecht (1898–1956), der im Sinne seines → epischen Theaters sogenannte ‹gestische Musik› einsetzte, die sich ‹rein kulinarischen Ambitionen› entziehen und statt dessen ‹bestimmte Haltungen beim Zuschauer organisieren› sollte.

So wie Brecht der B. eine eigenständige Funktion zuwies, hat die Frage nach der spezifischen Funktion der Musik im Schauspiel (dieses gilt heutzutage ebenso für den Film und das Fernsehspiel) immer wieder ästhetische Überlegungen mit sich gebracht: Dient sie der Textausdeutung, untermalt sie nur oder kommt ihr auch im Sinne Brechts die gleiche Bedeutung wie dem Wort und dem Bild zu?

Die heutige B.-Praxis: a) Kompositionen zeitgenössischer Musik für alte Theaterstücke wie auch neue Bühnenwerke; hier wird mit vielfältigen Mitteln gearbeitet: begleitende Songs, die Handlung unterstützende und auch relativ eigenständige Musiken werden entweder ‹live› oder als vorproduzierte Tonbandeinspielungen eingesetzt (durch synthetische Klangerzeugungs- und Mischtechniken ist der Hörbereich erweitert). b) Aneignung von Kompositionen, die nicht für das Theaterstück speziell geschrieben sind (hier auch aus dem Bereich der Jazz-/ Rock-/ Pop-Musik).

Adorno, Th. W./ Eisler, H.: Kompositionen für den Film. Bd. 15. Frankfurt/M. 1976; Bie, O.: Schauspiel mit Musik. In: Das deutsche Theater der Gegenwart. Hg. von M. Krell. München/Berlin 1923; Brecht, B.: Schriften zum Theater 1. Frankfurt/M. 1967; Hiller, F.: Aus dem Tonleben unserer Zeit. Bd. 1. Leipzig 1868; Hürlimann, M.: Das Atlantisbuch des Theaters. Zürich 1966; Liszt, F.: Keine Zwischenaktsmusiken mehr! In: Gesammelte Schriften. Hg. von L. Ramann. Bd. 3. Leipzig 1881.

Ebba Schirmacher

Bühnensprache

Die in jedem Land auf der Bühne übliche oder vorgeschriebene dialektfreie Aussprache. Sie lehnt sich an die Schriftsprache bzw. an die Hochsprache an und wird v. a. bei gehobenen Gattungen gepflegt (klassisches Theater, Rezitation, Oper). In Deutschland gehen die Versuche zur Regelung der Aussprache auf der Bühne v. a. auf Johann Wolfgang von Goethe (1749–1832) zurück, der 1803 in seinen *Regeln für Schauspieler* eine erste einheitliche, über allen Mundarten stehende und von jedem

Provinzialismus befreite sprachliche Norm vorschlägt. Für eine endgültige Regelung wurde dann Ende des 19. Jh. eine Kommission einberufen, die sich aus Vertretern des Dt. Bühnenvereins und Vertretern der Wissenschaft zusammensetzte. In ihrem Auftrag veröffentlichte Theodor Siebs (1862–1941) 1898 sein Werk *Deutsche Bühnenaussprache*. Die B. wurde für die ganze dt. Hochsprache, auch im Deutschunterricht in den Schulen, bestimmend. Sie kennzeichnet sich v. a. durch tadellose Aussprache der Vokale, Umlaute und Doppellaute, Beachtung der Kürze bzw. der Länge der Vokale, apikal artikuliertes ‹R› – auch ‹Zungen-R› genannt –, scharfe Unterscheidung zwischen stimmhaften (b, d, g) und stimmlosen (p, t, k) Konsonanten und richtige Verteilung des Zeitmaßes auf die einzelnen Stellen des Wortes – etwa nach der Regel: Stammsilbe eines Wortes doppelt so lang halten wie die Anfangs- und Schlußsilben. Dabei sollte jedoch das Wort Heinrich Laubes (1806–84) maßgebend sein: «In dem lobenswerten Streben nach einem deutlichen Aussprechen der Vokale und Konsonanten muß sich der Schauspieler vor der Gefahr hüten, ein sogenannter Buchstabensprecher zu werden. Fühlbare Absicht zerstört immer den Eindruck des Natürlichen.» Die B. erlaubte eine klare Typisierung der Personen im Lustspiel, etwa in der →Posse oder →Lokalposse: Der Wechsel zwischen B. und Dialekt bzw. dialektal gefärbter Sprache entspricht im Text dem Übergang von Typ zu Typ auf der Bühne. Allerdings geriet im 20. Jh. die B. in den meisten Ländern immer mehr ins Kreuzfeuer der Kritik und wurde immer weniger beachtet; sie widersprach nämlich dem im Theater vorherrschenden Hang zum Realismus bzw. zur Sprachverzerrung und wurde höchstens parodistisch benutzt. In jüngerer Zeit wird sie dagegen wieder verlangt, und zwar nicht nur bei Aufführungen klassischer Stücke, sondern auch bei modernen Dramen, in Reaktion auf Exzesse der letzten Jahrzehnte. Sie lehnt sich dabei immer mehr an die Hochlautung an, die als empfohlene moderne Aussprache der Hochsprache von Bühne, Film und Rundfunk getragen und verbreitet wird.

Bernard Poloni

Bühnensynthese

Der von Wassily Kandinsky (1866–1944) im Jahre 1923 zum erstenmal gebrauchte Begriff steht für die bereits im Zuge der →Theaterreform um 1900 von Adolphe Appia und Gordon Craig angestrebte Vereinigung der aus ihrem naturalistischen Verwendungszusammenhang gelösten, auf ihre Elemente reduzierten Einzelkünste des Theaters zu einem →Gesamtkunstwerk. Schon in seinem Szenarium *Der gelbe Klang*, das 1912 zusammen mit der Programmschrift *Über Bühnenkomposition* in dem Almanach *Der blaue Reiter* (Kandinsky/Marc, S. 189ff) erschienen ist, hat Kandinsky die Elemente Bewegung, Form und Farbe, Musik und Klang zu einer Einheit verbunden, die entsprechend seiner allgemeinen Kunsttheorie beim Zuschauer ähnliche ‹Seelenvibrationen› auslösen soll, wie sie den Künstler im Schöpfungsprozeß bewegt haben. In dem Manifest *Über die abstrakte Bühnensynthese* (S. 79ff) führt Kandinsky als übergreifendes Prinzip den Raum ein und erweitert das Spektrum der Elemente durch das der Dichtung. Allerdings insistiert er auf den ‹abstrakten› Einsatz des Wortes. Wie schon im *Gelben Klang* soll die Sprache ‹rein›, nur als Klangwort, nicht ‹verdunkelt durch den Sinn des Wortes› eingesetzt werden. Die einzelnen Elemente müssen ‹rücksichtslos› zerlegt und ‹unbewußt oder bewußt› auf der ‹inneren Waage› geprüft werden. So werden sie gleichsam gereinigt für ihre neue kompositorische Organisation in der ‹abstrakten B.›. Ein praktisches Beispiel dafür ist die zur Gattung des →Mechanischen Theaters zählende Produktion *Bilder einer Ausstellung*, die Kandinsky nach dem gleichnamigen Klavierstück von Modest Mussorgsky im Jahre 1928 für das Dessauer Friedrich-Theater erarbeitet hat. Es handelt sich dabei mit Ausnahme von zwei Bildern, in denen Tänzerinnen auftreten, um ein Spiel abstrakter Farbformen, die der Künstler beim Hören der Musik vor sich gesehen hat.

Kandinsky, W./Marc, F.: Der blaue Reiter. München 1912/1965; Kandinsky, W.: Essays über Kunst und Künstler. Bern 1955.

Peter Simhandl

Bühnentechnik

Die B. umfaßt alle Anlagen und Geräte auf der Bühne, die zur technischen Durchführung einer Vorstellung dienen. Es sind dies vor allem die Bühnenmaschinerie, die →Bühnenbeleuchtung, die Effektgeräte und die Sicherheitsanlagen. Bühnenmaschinen sind Geräte der Transporttechnik, die durch Anheben, Versenken, Drehen und Schieben den Aufbau bzw. die Veränderung eines Bühnenbilds ermöglichen. Die technische Verwandlung erfolgt entweder traditionell bei geschlossenem Spielvorhang (→Vorhang) oder für den Zuschauer sichtbar in der Form einer offenen Verwandlung als Teil der Inszenierung. Die Art und der Grad der Ausstattung eines modernen Theaters mit bühnentechnischen Anlagen hängt davon ab, für welche Theatersparte (Oper, Operette, Ballett, Schauspiel) das Haus konzipiert ist, ob abendlich wechselnde Vorstellungen (→Repertoirebetrieb) oder Wiederholungsvorstellungen (→En suite-Betrieb) geplant sind, welche Raumbedingungen durch die Bausubstanz gegeben

Bühnentechnik 195

sind und welche finanziellen Mittel zur Erstausstattung und zum Betrieb bereitstehen. Die Zahl der Theaterbauvarianten reicht aus den genannten Bedingungen vom monofunktionalen Opernhaus bis zum zahlenmäßig überwiegenden Typ des Mehrspartentheaters (→Theaterbau). Die entsprechenden bühnentechnischen Systeme unterscheiden sich im Aufwand und besonders in der Bewegungsrichtung der Verwandlungsart (Drehen, Heben, Schieben, Neigen).

Das Gesamtsystem wird zwischen der Obermaschinerie für die hängenden Bühnenbildteile und der Untermaschinerie für die stehenden Dekorationsaufbauten getrennt. Die Obermaschinerie hat sich aus dem barocken Dekorationssystem der →Kulissen- oder Gassenbühne entwickelt. Zum Absenken und Hochziehen von Prospekten und Vorhängen hat sich der Prospektzug als schnelles Verwandlungsmittel erhalten. Ein Prospektzug besteht aus einem parallel zur Rampe angeordneten Stahlrohr, das über mehrere Drahtseile und Umlenkrollen mit einem Gegengewicht ausgekontert ist und durch Menschenkraft bewegt werden kann. Der Luftraum über der Spielfläche (Bühnenturm) ist Magazin für hängende Dekorationsteile. Da die Ausstattung stetig gewichtiger geworden ist, setzen sich elektromotorisch oder hydraulisch angetriebene Maschinenzüge durch. Die Prospektzüge sind im Abstand von 25 bis 50 cm über die Spielfläche verteilt, der einzelne Zug hat eine Tragkraft von 250 bis 300 kg, Maschinenzüge bis 1000 kg. Das gesamte System nennt sich auch Schnürboden eines Theaters. Der Rollenboden ist ein begehbarer Zwischenboden im Bühnenturm, auf dem die Umlenkrollen der Züge montiert sind und von dem aus Spezialzüge herabgelassen werden können. Die Tendenz geht dahin, daß die von Hand bedienten Prospektzüge abgelöst werden von elektronisch vorprogrammierten und gesteuerten Elektrowinden, bei denen jedes einzelne Aufhängeseil von einem separaten Motor angetrieben wird (Punktzuganlage).

Teil der Obermaschinerie sind auch Aufhängevorrichtungen für Flugbewegungen der Darsteller (Flugwerk) und das Schienensystem für den die Spielfläche umfahrenden Rundhorizont aus Spezialleinen. An der Stahlkonstruktion des Bühnendachs hängen ferner die Portalanlage, bestehend aus der Beleuchterbrücke und den Beleuchtungstürmen, sowie die verschiedenen Vorhänge wie Schutz-, Spiel- und Schallvorhang. Während das System der Obermaschinerie in der Mehrzahl der Theater gleicher Art ist, unterscheiden sich die Systeme der Untermaschinerie je nach den örtlichen Bedingungen erheblich. Die Maschinen haben allgemein die Aufgabe, bisweilen mehrere Tonnen wiegende Bühnenaufbauten in den Verwandlungen zu bewegen, den Bühnenboden zu gliedern und Auftritte, Erscheinungen aus der Versenkung zu ermöglichen. Es werden nach Bewegungsrichtung folgende Systeme unterschieden: Hebebühne, Drehbühne und Schiebebühne.

196 Bühnentechnik

Bei der Hebebühne ist der Bühnenboden in zwei bis drei Meter breite Abschnitte (Podien) parallel zur Rampe geteilt, die über die Bühnenebene hebbar und in die Unterbühne senkbar sind. Sie dienen der Staffelung des Bühnenbodens, der Herstellung der Auftritte von oben oder aus der Tiefe und der Verwandlung von Bühnenaufbauten. In Sonderform können sie auch die Form einer Schrägen bilden. Eine Versenkung ist ein kleiner Ausschnitt im Bühnenboden, der durch Wegschieben einer Holztafel für z. B. Personenerscheinungen geöffnet wird.

Der Boden des Orchestergrabens ist ebenfalls in Podien gegliedert, die es im Mehrspartentheater erlauben, die Spielfläche durch eine Vorbühne zu erweitern. Die in den Bühnenboden eingelassene Drehbühne oder aufgelegte Drehscheibe ermöglicht zwei verschiedene Bühnenbild- und Verwandlungsformen. Einmal werden die Bilder in Segmenten auf der Kreisfläche nebeneinander aufgestellt und im Ablauf des Stücks vor die Portalöffnung gedreht. Im anderen Fall wird die Drehbühne als szenisches Mittel in der Form genutzt, daß das →Bühnenbild als begehbare Vollplastik sichtbar für den Zuschauer verschiedene Positionen im Verlauf des Stücks einnimmt. Die einfachste Verwendung ist beim Gehen des Darstellers auf der Stelle gegeben. Die Drehbühne wurde 1896 erstmalig im Münchner Residenztheater durch Karl Lautenschläger eingesetzt. Eine Verfeinerung der Verwendungsmöglichkeiten erfolgt durch den zusätzlichen Einbau von Hubpodien, Versenkungen oder der Teilung der Drehbühne in mehrere gegenläufig fahrbare Ringe. Die Durchmesser reichen von ca. 9 bis 38 Meter (Schauspielhaus Frankfurt). Die Drehbühne findet dort ihren Einsatz, wo aus Platzgründen das System der Schiebebühne nicht realisiert werden kann.

Im modernen Theaterbau wird in der Regel die zentrale Bühnenfläche um Seiten- und Hinterbühne ergänzt. Aus diesen Nebenbühnen fahren Wagen, auf denen Teile oder das ganze Szenenbild vormontiert sind, vor die Portalöffnung. Der Hinterbühnenwagen ist häufig mit einer eingelassenen Drehscheibe versehen. Er wird nach Bedarf dieser Verwandlungsmöglichkeit nach vorn gefahren.

Die bühnentechnische Ausstattung eines modernen Guckkasten-Repertoiretheaters besteht aus der Kombination einer Schiebebühne mit ein bis drei Bühnenwagen mit eingelassener Drehscheibe und mehreren Hubpodien im Spielflächenbereich. Die Unterkonstruktion der Bühnenmaschinerie ist aus Stahl gefertigt, der mit dauerhaften Holzbohlen (kanadische Kiefer) belegt ist. Die Antriebe sind elektromotorischer oder hydraulischer Art, die Bewegungen werden über Spindeln, Triebstöcke, hydraulische Zylinder, Seile und Ketten übertragen.

Die technische Ausstattung der Fabrik- und Mehrzweckhallen (z. B. →Schaubühne am Lehniner Platz, Berlin) als alternative Spielstätten haben aus konzeptionellen und finanziellen Gründen einen anderen technischen Schwerpunkt. Es wird für das jeweilige Theaterstück der besondere szenische Gesamtraum entwickelt. Der Spielraum und die Anordnung der Zuschauer verändert sich ständig. So liegt das Hauptgewicht der Technik in Systemen für mobile Zuschauertribünen und -podien, Gerüste für Bühnenaufbauten und einfache Aufhängevorrichtungen für Prospekte, Vorhänge und Beleuchtungskörper. Die Bilder eines Stückverlaufs werden seltener vor den Augen der Zuschauer bewegt, der Zuschauer selbst wird mobil und durchschreitet im Stückverlauf Environments. In anderen Konzepten wird der Gesamtraum zum Bild-Grund-Raum, der in sich durch geringe Veränderungen alle Spielorte simultan trägt. Die Gestaltungsmittel des Lichts haben in dieser Theaterform eine noch größere Bedeutung.

Die Hersteller bühnentechnischer Geräte sind mittlere und große Maschinenbaufirmen der Fördertechnik. Bühnenmaschinerie ist kein Serienprodukt, sondern in jedem Fall eine kostspielige Einzelanfertigung. Der Anteil der Bühnentechnik bei den Neubaukosten eines Theaters liegt bei 10 bis 30 Prozent. Bei den laufenden Kosten geht man davon aus, daß eine hinreichende technische Ausstattung die hohen Lohnkosten des technischen Personals einzusparen hilft.

Bühnentechnik. Stuttgart 1987; Hämer, H. W.: Stahlkonstruktion im Theaterbau. Merkblätter über sachgemäße Stahlverwendung Nr. 289. Düsseldorf; Kranich, F.: Bühnentechnik der Gegenwart. München 1929; Unruh, W.: Theatertechnik. Berlin 1969.

Horst Birr

Bühnenverlag

B. übernehmen den Vertrieb von literarischen Bühnenwerken (→Bühnenvertrieb). Neben eigenständigen Bühnenverlagen, von denen es rund 70 im deutschsprachigen Raum gibt, haben einige große Verlagshäuser Theaterabteilungen (z. B. Fischer, Suhrkamp und Rowohlt). Der B. tritt als Generalagent für best. Autoren (oder auch einzelne Werke) gegenüber den Theatern auf. Die grundlegenden Tätigkeiten sind Manuskriptvervielfältigung (→Bühnenmanuskript), Angebot der Werke an die Theater, Schutz der Werke vor tiefgreifenden Veränderungen und die Abrechnung der Urhebertantiemen. Mindestens 12, maximal 18 Prozent einer Tageseinnahme müssen von den Theatern als Urheberrechtsabgabe abgeführt werden. Die Höhe ist in sieben Gruppen gestaffelt und richtet sich nach den Aufwendungen eines Theaters für sein künstlerisches Personal. Wohl mit die wichtigste Aufgabe der B. ist die intensive Betreuung ihrer Autoren; sie arbeiten auch dramaturgisch an den Stücken mit, betreiben die aufwendige Werbung für Uraufführungen und helfen dabei, für die Stücke nicht nur passende Theater (auch Theater und Verlage im Ausland), sondern auch best. Regisseure und Darsteller zu finden. – Erfolgversprechende Nachwuchstalente werden durch Lektoratsbetreuung und die Herstellung von Kontakten zur Theaterpraxis gefördert. Das Profil eines B. wird nicht zuletzt geprägt durch seinen Inhaber oder Leiter: Die Spezialisierung auf best. Bereiche, z.B. moderne deutschsprachige Literatur, führt zur Entwicklung eines festen Verlagsprogramms, durch dessen jährlichen Ausbau, der Hinzunahme von neuen Stücken, eine programmatische Entwicklung deutlich wird. Ein weiteres Arbeitsgebiet ist die Übersetzung und Betreuung von ausländischen Werken für den deutschsprachigen Raum.

Preuss, J. W.: Theater immer in Reichweite. In: Theater 1967–1982. Berlin 1983.

Ute Hagel

Bühnenvertrieb

Unternehmung, die für den Autor eines Bühnenwerks (Drama, Musiktheater, Tanz, Pantomime) die Aufführungsrechte wahrnimmt. Der B. vervielfältigt das Manuskript und bietet es Theatern zum Kauf an. Regelung in der BRD: Der Autor erhält im Schnitt 10 Prozent der Kasseneinnahmen des Theaters als Tantieme, von denen der B. 20 bis 30 Prozent als Honorar einbehält. Nach dem Künstlersozialversicherungsgesetz muß der B. von seinem Anteil fünf Prozent des Künstlerhonorars an die Sozialkasse abführen.

Mitte des 19. Jh. begannen in Deutschland Theaterzeitschriften und Zeitungen mit der Vermittlung von Theaterengagements und Bühnenwerken; daraus entwickelten sich sog. Theateragenturen; daneben wurden Manuskripte oft nicht vom Autor, sondern vom «Manuskripthandel» verkauft. 1844 wird auf Betreiben des Berliner Generalintendanten Küstner der «Autorenanteil» festgelegt. 1870 regeln die Urhebergesetze die Aufführungsrechte genauer. B. und →Bühnenverlage treten an die Stelle der Agenten und befassen sich ausschließlich mit der Vermittlung von Bühnenwerken. – Die meisten heutigen B. in der BRD gehören dem Verband dt. Bühnenverleger e. V. an, der seinen Sitz in Berlin hat.

Beilharz, M.: Der Bühnenvertriebsvertrag als Beispiel eines urheberrechtlichen Wahrnehmungsvertrages. München 1970.

Ute Hagel

Bundesarbeitsgemeinschaft (BAG)
Spiel und Theater e. V.

1953/54 als Bundesarbeitsgemeinschaft Laienspiel und Laientheater wieder gegründet; jetzt BAG Spiel in der Jugend, BAG für das Darstellende Spiel in der Schule; gebildet aus Landesarbeitsgemeinschaften (LAG), der AGS (Arbeitsgemeinschaft Spiel in der Ev. Jugend), der KAST (der Kath. Arbeitsgemeinschaft Spiel und Theater) und den Spielzentren Korbach (Theatertreffen seit 1949), Remscheid (Akademie für Musische Bildung), Scheersberg (Intern. Theaterwerkstatt). Veranstaltung von Werkstätten, Regionaltagungen, Weiterbildungen, Theatertreffen; Herausgabe von Informationen, Arbeitsmaterialien.

Hans-Wolfgang Nickel

Bürgerliches Trauerspiel

Das b. T. ist eine historisch begrenzte Gattung, die nach früheren Vorstufen im 18. Jh. entstand und dort ihren Höhepunkt erreichte, sich auch noch im 19. Jh. mit Veränderungen behauptete.

Dieser zeitlichen Begrenzung entspricht eine räumliche und gesellschaftliche: Das b. T. geht in etwa einher mit der Verbürgerlichung der drei großen westeurop. Mächte in der historischen Folge des Emporkommens des Bürgertums in Großbritannien, Frankreich und Deutschland, vor allem im ökonomischen und kulturellen Bereich. Der mit dem b. T. verbundene literaturgeschichtliche und gattungstheoretische Fragenkreis ist komplex und die Wandlung des Genres im 18. und 19. Jh. erheblich.

Entstehungsland des b. T. ist Großbritannien; Vorstufen reichen zurück bis ins →Elisabethanische Theater mit der →‹domestic tragedy›: Im Gegensatz zur heroischen Tragödie und der →Haupt- und Staatsaktion werden Stoffe aus dem adligen und bürgerlichen Alltagsleben tragisch behandelt. Bes. die anonymen Stücke *The Tragedy of Mr. Arden of Feversham* (1592) und *A Yorkshire Tragedy* (1608) sowie die Werke von Thomas Heywood (1574?–1641: *The English Traveller*, 1633), Thomas Dekker (1570?–1632: *The Honest Whore*, 1604–30) und Thomas Middleton (1570?–1627: *Women beware Women*, 1657). Ausschlaggebend für die Gestaltung der Gattung wurde dann George Lillo (1693–1739: *The London Merchant, or the History of George Barnwell*, 1731) und Edward Moore (1712–57: *The Gamester*, 1753). Neben dem Bruch mit der Ständeklausel, vor allem in *The London Merchant*, Darstellung des Alltagsgeschehens eines Handelshauses mit tragischen Untertönen. Positiver Hinweis auf die Tugenden, die dem Kanon des frühkapitalistischen prote-

200 Bürgerliches Trauerspiel

stantischen Bürgertums entsprechen: Fleiß, Ehrlichkeit, Anständigkeit, Gottesfurcht, Nächstenliebe u. a. als Weg zu Ansehen, Erfolg, Reichtum und Macht, also zum religiös und wirtschaftlich begründeten Standesbewußtsein einer neuen Klasse.

Unter dem Einfluß Lillos und des Romanciers Samuel Richardson (1689–1761: *Pamela*, 1740–41; *Clarissa Harlowe*, 1747–48) griff das neue Genre zugleich auf Frankreich und Deutschland über. In Frankreich war die Bedeutung der theoretischen Abhandlungen größer als die der Bühnenwerke. Erster Gebrauch des Titels ‹tragédie bourgeoise› im Prosa-Einakter *Silvie* (1741–42) des Juristen Paul Landois. In der Folge Bühnenerfolge von Denis Diderot (1713–84: *Le Fils naturel*, 1757; *Le Père de famille*, 1758) und Michel-Jean Sedaine (1719–97: *Le Philosophe sans le savoir*, 1765); anschließend Pierre Caron de Beaumarchais (1732–99: *Les deux amis ou le Négociant de Lyon*, 1770) und Louis-Sébastien Mercier (1740–1814: *La Brouette du vinaigrier*, 1775). Grundlegend waren die Abhandlungen Diderots *Entretiens avec Dorval* (1757), *Discours sur la poésie dramatique* (1758) und *Paradoxe sur le comédien* (1773) sowie Beaumarchais' *Essai sur le genre dramatique sérieux* (1767) und Merciers *Du théâtre ou Nouvel essai sur l'art dramatique* (1773).

Philosophisch und politisch gründet dieses Trauerspiel auf zwei Grundsätzen: 1. Die menschliche Natur, ihrem Wesen nach gut, wird durch die Gesellschaft verdorben, was zu Unordnung und Unglück führt. 2. Die bürgerliche und kleinadlige Privatsphäre der Familie widersetzt sich als Zufluchtsort den moralischen Ausschweifungen der Großen und des Hofes. Natur, Bürgertum, Familie sind Hort der Tugend gegen das Laster; Funktion des Theaters ist es, diese Konflikte aufzuklären und aufzulösen. →Tragödie und Komödie werden abgelehnt, weil sie den Menschen verklären oder herabsetzen; nur die ‹ernste Gattung› (‹genre sérieux›) als ernste Komödie und das b. T. (‹tragédie domestique et bourgeoise›) stellen die Wahrheit des konkreten Alltagslebens dar. Moralität und Mitgefühl des Zuschauers können nicht durch die Repräsentation der Wandelbarkeit und Schicksalsschläge der Großen erregt werden, sondern nur durch die Darstellung des Bürgers in seinem Milieu: Mittelpunkt des Dramas ist der Widerspruch zwischen den drei Schlüsselbegriffen von ‹conditions› (Beruf, Stand), ‹relations› (Familienverhältnisse) und nebenbei Charakter. Auch hier wird eine gerechte, tugendhafte bürgerliche Ordnung angestrebt, aber verstanden als ein Privates im Widerstand gegen die Übergriffe der Gesellschaft. Zu diesem Zwecke erarbeitete bes. Diderot eine Poetik des b. T.:

– Die dramatische Rede soll lebensnah die Prosa dem Vers vorziehen;
– das Pathos der Empfindsamkeit soll lehrhaft das Publikum erregen;
– die Einfachheit der Handlung soll mit Hilfe einer modernen Szenographie unter Berücksichtigung des Dekors, der Gestik, der Stimme, der

Pantomime wiedergegeben werden – dadurch Vorherrschaft des → ‹tableau›, des szenischen Gemäldes über den Theaterstreich (‹coup de théâtre›): die gefühlvolle Ruhe und Vernunft des Bürgerhauses lieber als die Launen des Glücks bei Hofe.

– Als Gegeneffekt zur Empfindsamkeit sucht Diderot eine verfremdende Schauspielweise, worin die Urteilskraft die Emotionen zügelt; hier klingen Gedanken an, wie sie später bei Brecht ausgeführt werden.

Das dritte wichtige Land für die Entwicklung des b. T. im 18. Jh. war Deutschland. Nach Vorstufen bei Andreas Gryphius (1616–64: *Cardenio und Celinde*, 1657) und Christian Weise (1642–1708: *Trauerspiel von dem Neapolitanischen Hauptrebellen Masaniello*, 1683) bestimmt die Rezeption der engl. und frz. Vorbilder die zwei Grundphasen der Form im 18. Jh., das ‹empfindsame, private b. T.› bis in die 70er Jahre, sodann das Trauerspiel mit ständischem, gesellschaftskritischem Einschlag. Beide Phasen werden von Gotthold Ephraim Lessing entscheidend bestimmt (1729–81). Wesentlich für die erste Phase in Theorie Lessings *Briefwechsel mit Mendelssohn und Nicolaï über das Trauerspiel* (1756–57), seine *Hamburgische Dramaturgie* (1767–68) sowie in der Praxis das erste b. T. und Meisterwerk der Empfindsamkeit *Miss Sara Sampson* (1755). Betont wird die sozialbezogene Rührung als Fähigkeit, Mitleid mit den Menschen, mit den Ereignissen aus der bürgerlichen Erfahrungswelt zu empfinden. Zweck dieser Theatererziehung ist die Besserung des Menschen: «Der mitleidigste Mensch ist der beste Mensch ... Wer uns also mitleidig macht, macht uns besser und tugendhafter» (Lessing an Nicolaï, 13. 11. 1756): eine Dramaturgie der Privatsphäre mit Betonung des Moralisch-Seelischen; das Ständische bleibt hier noch zweitrangig. Interessant ist allerdings bei gewissen Theoretikern die strikte Begrenzung der ‹tragischen Denkungsart› auf den Mittelstand: Gottlob Benjamin Pfeil (*Vom bürgerlichen Trauerspiel*, in: *Neue Erweiterungen der Erkenntnis und des Vergnügens*, 1755) schließt Kleinbürgertum und ‹Pöbel› von der tragischen Rührung und Aufklärung aus; ihnen bleibt die Komik.

Nach dieser Tendenz zum ‹Mitmenschlich-Privat-Moralisch-Gefühlvollen› (Guthke) tritt das dt. b. T. in seine zweite Hauptphase ein, die der standesbewußten Gesellschaftskritik. Sie ist gekennzeichnet durch eine reichhaltige Produktion von Stücken. Auch sie wird eingeleitet durch ein epochemachendes Werk Lessings, *Emilia Galotti* (1772), worin die grundlegende Neuerung der dramatische Konflikt zwischen den Vertretern des Bürgertums (Familie Galotti) und des Adels (Prinz und Kammerherr) ist. Von da aus zieht sich der rote Faden der Sozialkritik durch die gesamte → Sturm und Drang-Dramatik, wenn auch mit anderen Formansätzen, so Heinrich Leopold Wagners (1747–79) *Kindermörderin* (1776), so vor allem Jakob Michael Reinhold Lenz (1751–92) in seinen zwei Stücken *Der Hofmeister* (1774) und *Die Soldaten* (1776): In der gro-

202 Bürgerliches Trauerspiel

tesken Entmannung des Hofmeisters und im tragikomischen Ende der Familie Wesener ist der Engpaß der Aggression des machtlosen Bürgers gegen sich selbst das Zeichen für die unmögliche Lösung des sozialen Konflikts. Kennzeichnend für dieses b. T. ist Schillers *Kabale und Liebe* (1784); die soziale und politische Herausforderung an Absolutismus und Adel erfolgt darin mit ungewöhnlicher Heftigkeit.

In der Folge verzerrt und verwässert sich die Form des b. T. in den bürgerlichen Tendenzdramen des Jungen Deuschland: Karl Gutzkows (1811–78) *Richard Savage* (UA 1839), *Werner* (UA 1840) und *Ottfried* (UA 1849), worin das bürgerliche Standesbewußtsein ein letztes Mal über die Aristokratie triumphiert. Das Endstadium des b. T. repräsentiert *Maria Magdalena* (1844) von Friedrich Hebbel (1813–63): Die Familie, vorher heiliges Gut, ist hier zur Hölle pervertiert. Der Konflikt entsteht nicht aus der Kollision der Stände, sondern «aus der bürgerlichen Welt selbst, aus ihrem zähen und in sich selbst begründeten Beharren auf den überlieferten patriarchalischen Anschauungen und ihrer Unfähigkeit, sich in verwickelten Lagen zu helfen» (Fr. Hebbel an A. Stich-Crelinger, 11. 12. 1843). Die erstrebte Versöhnung und Lösung bleiben im unklaren.

Überall weicht in der Folge das b. T. dem sozialen Drama, dem →Zeitstück oder dem →Melodrama, je mehr sich das Theater den Fragen des Proletariats und der Industriegesellschaft widmet. In Frankreich heißt es zwar noch ‹drame bourgeois›, wird aber zum Tendenzstück (pièce à thèse): so bei Alexandre Dumas Sohn (1824–95: *La Dame aux camélias*, 1852), Guillaume Augier (1820–86), Victorien Sardou (1831–1908: *La Tosca*, 1887), Henry Bataille (1872–1922: *La Femme nue*, 1908), Henry Bernstein (1876–1953: *Le Secret*, 1913; *Judith*, 1922). Seine letzte Umkehr erfährt es in der →Tragikomödie: z. B. bei Carl Sternheim (1878–1942: *Die Hose*, 1911; *Bürger Schippel*, 1913) oder in der →Parodie, so Adolf Muschg (* 1934: *Rumpelstilz,* 1968), Rainer Werner Fassbinder (1945–82: *Bremer Freiheit*, 1971).

Das b. T. war in Europa historisch und poetisch epochemachend: Die Machtergreifung des Bürgertums illustrierend, hilft es, die überlieferten hohen Gattungen der →Tragödie und z. T. der →Komödie zugunsten des →Dramas zu verdrängen, und trägt zu Innovationen in →Regie, →Bühnenbild und →Schauspielweise bei.

Daunicht, R.: Die Entstehung des b. T. in Deutschland. Berlin 1965; Guthke, K. S.: Das dt. b. T. Stuttgart 1980; Karl-Pantis, B.: Bauformen des b. T. 1977; Szondi, P.: Lektüren und Lektionen. Frankfurt/M. 1973; ders.: Die Theorie des b. T. im 18. Jh. Frankfurt/M. 1973; Wierlacher, A.: Das b. T. Seine theoretische Begründung im 18. Jh. München 1968; ders.: Das b. T. In: Hinck, W. (Hg.): Europ. Aufklärung I (Neues Handbuch der Literaturwissenschaft, Bd. XI). Wiesbaden 1974.

Gérard Schneilin

Burgtheater Wien

Größte und bedeutendste österr. Sprechbühne, Teil des staatlichen Österreichischen Bundestheaterverbandes, Spielstätten: B., Akademietheater (seit 1922) «Lusterboden» (seit 1979/80), 3. Raum am Schwarzenbergplatz (Kasino I und II, seit 1980/81) und Vestibül im B. (seit 1987/88). B., von Maria Theresia 1741 als «Königliches Theater nächst der Burg» im ehemaligen Ballhaus am Michaelerplatz gegr. (1. Direktor: Carl Joseph de Sellier); gemischtes Repertoire: frz. Schauspiel, dt. Komödie, ital. Singspiel, Oper und Ballett. 1776 von Kaiser Joseph II. zum «teutschen Nationaltheater» erklärt, Mitglieder der dt. Schauspielergesellschaft zu «k. k. National-Hofschauspielern» ernannt, fix besoldet. «Josephinisches Theatergesetz» (Statut) bis Anfang 20. Jh. verbindlich. Ökonomische Leitung und Verwaltung Hofämter, künstlerische Leitung: wechselnde Direktoren, bis 1789 «Künstlerrepublik» (Selbstverwaltung des Ensembles); 1789/90 Franz Brockmann (1745–1812); 1792–94 Regiekollegium; ab 1794 als «K. K. Hoftheater nächst der Burg» verpachtet, u. a. 1807–14 «Kavaliersdirektion», Repertoire: auch Oper, Singspiel und Ballett, ab 1810 Beschränkung auf Sprechtheater; 1814–32 Joseph Schreyvogel (1768–1832) artistischer Sekretär und Dramaturg, das B. wird die führende deutschsprachige Bühne, künstlerischer Spielplan: Franz Grillparzer (1791–1872) als Hoftheaterdichter, dt. Klassik, Shakespeare, span. Dramatik; dekretmäßig angestellte Hofschauspieler werden pensionsberechtigt; 1849–67 Heinrich Laube (1806–84) artistischer, ab 1855 auch Ökonomie-Direktor und Regisseur (Wortregie), umfangreichstes Repertoire (bis zu 164 Stücke pro Saison); 1870–81 Franz von Dingelstedt (1814–81); 1881–87 Adolf Wilbrandt (1837–1911); 1888 Übersiedlung des B. in ein neues Haus am Franzensring, erbaut von Gottfried Semper und Karl Frh. von Hasenauer. 1890–98 Max Burckhard (1854–1912); Spielplanerweiterung: H. Ibsen, G. Hauptmann, L. Anzengruber, A. Schnitzler, Gewinnung neuer Publikumsschichten durch verbilligte Sonntagnachmittagsvorstellungen. Das B. wird im 19. Jh. ‹geistiger Sammelpunkt Österreichs und bes. Ausdruck seiner Sonderart›, gesellschaftlicher Mittelpunkt des Bürgertums, bewahrende Bestrebungen im Repertoire und Ensemble, im Spielplan vorherrschend sind Klassik, zeitgenössische Dramatik zum Großteil Trival- und Gebrauchsliteratur, österr. Volkstheater wird sehr spät aufgenommen, kein Festlegen auf eine literarische Richtung, Hauptgewicht immer auf schauspielerischen Persönlichkeiten, trotz öfter wechselnder Direktoren bleibt das Schauspieler-Ensemble konstant; Mode und Konversationston der Hofburgschauspieler werden tonangebend.

Entwicklung im 20. Jh.: Hoftheaterintendanz nach 1918 von Staatstheaterverwaltung abgelöst, nach 1945 Bundestheaterverwaltung, seit

204 Burgtheater Wien

1971 Österreichischer Bundestheaterverband, oberste Instanz seit 1918 Bundesministerium für Unterricht. Direktoren: 1898–1910 Paul Schlenther (1854–1916); 1910–12 Alfred von Berger (1853–1912); 1912–17 Hugo Thimig (1854–1944); 1918–21 Alber Heine (1867–1949); 1912–22 und 1930–31 Anton Wildgans (1881–1932); 1923–30 Franz Herterich (1877–1966); 1932–1938 Hermann Röbbeling (1875–1949); 1939–45 Lothar Müthel (1896–1965); 1945 Brand des B., Spielbetrieb bis 1955 im Ronacher (ehemaliges Stadttheater). 1918 Bruch in der künstlerischen Tradition, unter A. Heine neue Dynamik in Klassikervorstellungen, revolutionäre Entwicklung im Bühnenbild, bes. Alfred Roller und später Remigius Geyling (bewegte Bühnenbildprojektion) während der Direktion F. Herterichs. Auffrischung des Ensembles: nach Rosa Albach-Retty (1874–1980), Hedwig Bleibtreu (1868–1958), Josef Kainz (1858–1910), Otto Tressler (1871–1965) neuengagiert: u. a. Raoul Aslan (1868–1958), Ewald Balser (1898–1978), Horst Caspar (1913–52), Ernst Deutsch (1890–1969), Käthe Dorsch (1890–1957), Maria Eis (1896 bis 1954), Paul Hartmann (1889–1972), Werner Krauss (1884–1959), Fred Liewehr (* 1909), Curd Jürgens (1906–82), Heinz Moog (1908–89), Susi Nicoletti (* 1918), Hans Thimig (1900–91), Hermann Thimig (1890 bis 1982), Hilde Wagener (* 1904), Oskar Werner (1922–84), Else Wohlgemuth (1881–1972), Liselotte Schreiner (1909–91). – Direktoren nach 1945: 1945–48 Raoul Aslan; 1948–54 Josef Gielen (1890–1968); 1954–59 Adolf Rott (1905–82); 1959–68 Ernst Haeussermann (1916–84); 1968–71 Paul Hoffmann (1902–90), 1971–76 Gerhard Klingenberg; 1976–86 Achim Benning, ab 1986 Claus Peymann zus. mit Hermann Beil, Uwe Jens Jensen und Alfred Kirchner (U. J. Jensen und A. Kirchner bis 1990). Beginn der 70er Jahre neue Tendenz in der Klassikerpflege: moderne Bühnenästhetik und gegenwartsbezogene Aussage, seit 1966 auch Brecht im Spielplan; seit den 80er Jahren UA von Herbert Achternbusch, Wolfgang Bauer, Thomas Bernhard, Achim Freyer, Rolf Hochhuth, George Tabori und Peter Turrini; wichtige Regisseure nach 1945: Berthold Viertel (1885–1953), Leopold Lindtberg (1902–84), Walter Felsenstein (1901–75), Fritz Kortner (1892–1970), Hans Schweikart (1895–1975), Gustav Rudolf Sellner (1905–90), Rudolf Steinboeck (* 1908), Giorgio Strehler (* 1921), ab den 70er Jahren auch: Ruth Berghaus, Harald Clemen, Dieter Dorn, Adolf Dresen, Achim Freyer, Hans Hollmann, Angelika Hurwicz, Manfred Karge, Cesare Lievi, Axel Manthey, Claus Peymann, Lore Stefanek, George Tabori, Peter Wood, Peter Zadek; im Ensemble nach 1945: Blanche Aubry (1921–86), Joachim Bißmeier, Sepp Bierbichler, Lore Brunner, Rolf Boysen, Kirsten Dene, Annemarie Düringer, O. W. Fischer, Adrienne Gessner (1896–1987), Boy Gobert (1925–86), Käthe Gold, Heidemarie Hatheyer (1918–90), Michael Heltau, Attila Hörbiger (1896–1987), Paul Hörbiger (1894–1981),

Judith Holzmeister, Marianne Hoppe, Gertraud Jesserer, Inge Konradi, Ignaz Kirchner, Hilde Krahl, Theo Lingen (1903–78), Helmut Lohner, Eva Mattes, Josef Meinrad, Robert Meyer, Elisabeth Orth, Erika Pluhar, Ilse Ritter, Heinrich Schweiger, Albin Skoda (1909–61), Sonja Sutter, Helene Thimig (1889–1974), Gert Voss, Gusti Wolf.

Alth, M. v.: Burgtheater 1776–1976. Aufführungen und Besetzungen von 200 Jahren. Wien 1979; Dietrich, M. (Hg.): Das Burgtheater und sein Publikum. Wien 1976; Haeussermann, E.: Das Wiener Burgtheater. Wien/München/Zürich 1975; Hennings, F.: Heimat Burgtheater. 3 Bde. Wien 1972–74; 175 Jahre Burgtheater 1776–1951. Fortgeführt bis Sommer 1954. Wien 1955; Österr. Bundestheaterverband: Berichte 1986/87 bis 1990/91.

Ingeborg Janich

Burleske

(Ital. burlesco = scherzhaft; →Parodie, →Travestie) Bauform des Komischen: derb-übertriebene Verspottung einer ernsten Gattung, die lächerlich degradiert wird, oder umgekehrt pseudo-feierliche Darstellung einer komischen Form. In Frankreich als antiklassische und antikensatirisierende Tendenz vor allem bei Paul Scarron (1610–60: *Virgile travesti*, 1648).

In England als Untergattung in Form von abendfüllenden Stücken, deren Merkmale sich mit denen der →Parodie und →Travestie überschneiden. So J. Buckinghams *The Rehearsal* (Die Probe, 1671) gegen die Heldendramen John Drydens (1631–1700); desgl. Henry Fielding (1707–54) mit *Tragedie of Tragedies, or the Life and Death of Tom Thumb the Great* (1730) oder John Gays *The Beggar's Opera* (1728), eine Travestie der ital. Oper und Brechts Modell für die Dreigroschenoper (1928).

Bar, F.: Le genre burlesque en France au 17e siècle. Paris 1960; Clinton-Baddeley, V. C.: The Burlesque Tradition in the Englisch Theatre after 1660. Oxford 1952; Werner, D.: Das Burleske. Diss. Berlin 1966.

Gérard Schneilin

BUSTA

Bundesverband Spiel Theater Animation, gegründet 1980 in Hannover; professionelles Diskussions- und Arbeitsforum insbesondere für Zielgruppentheater und soziokulturelle Animation. – Geschäftsstelle: Institut für Spiel- und Theaterpädagogik, Malteserstr. 100, 1000 Berlin 46.

Hans-Wolfgang Nickel

Butô

Tanzbewegung (→Tanztheater) der japanischen Avantgarde der 50er und 60er Jahre. Butô entsteht in der Subkultur und wendet sich gegen die erstarrten Formen des traditionellen Tanzes (*nihon buyô*) wie auch gegen westliche Tanzformen. Durch Rückgriffe auf archaische Ausdrucksmittel wie Nacktheit, Körperbemalung, Grimassierung, Meditation und Trance usw. sowie die Verwendung einer Fülle von Attributen und Requisiten aus Folklore und Alltag entwickelte sich experimentell eine authentische Tanzform. Thematisiert werden Erinnerungen, Unbewußtes, Tod und Erotik, um die Wurzeln menschlichen Daseins zu ergründen. Ziel ist ähnlich dem →Nô und früherer Formen des Sakraltanzes die Transformation der menschlichen Seele. Charakteristisch für butô sind u. a. die Entindividualisierung des Körpers, die Expressivität der Posen bis zur Groteske, die Langsamkeit der Bewegung, der Verzicht auf ein logisches Handlungsgerüst, die Entwicklung einer Metaphorik des Unbewußten.

Gründer und wichtigste Repräsentanten sind Hijikata Tatsumi (* 9. 3. 1928) und Kazuo Ôno, auch: Ohno (* 27. 10. 1906). Hijikatas Debüt als Tänzer und Choreograph 1959 mit *Kojiki* – nach dem gleichnamigen Stück von Mishima Yukio – ist spektakulär und bringt ihm den Ruf eines Tanzrevolutionärs; sein Auftritt gilt als die Geburtsstunde des butô (→Tanztheater). Kazuo Ôno, Altmeister und Virtuose des butô, verhilft der subkulturellen Tanzkunst 1977 zum Durchbruch. Mit seiner Widmung an die legendäre Flamencotänzerin *Hommage à La Argentina*, die der 23jährige Ôno 1929 in Tôkyô gesehen hatte, gewinnt er die Aufmerksamkeit eines breiten Publikums und den ersten Preis der Tanzkritik. Seit 1980 geht er mit dieser und neueren Solovorstellungen (*Watakushi no okâsan*; *Shikai*) auf Tournee. Hijikata Tatsumi prägt den Begriff *ankoku butô* (Tanz im Dunkel) und gründet die Gruppe Ankoku Butôha, später Asubestokan mit Ashikawa Yôko als Solistin. Aus der Zusammenarbeit lösen sich Ishii Mitsutaka und Kasai Akira, der durch →Eurythmiestudien butô zu erweitern bemüht ist. In den 70er Jahren trennen sich einige Tänzer von Hijikata, um ihre eigenen Gruppen zu bilden, zum Beispiel Maro Akaji, Amagatsu Ushio, Murobushi Kô und Carlotta Ikeda. Heute gibt es eine Vielzahl von butô-Solisten und -Gruppen, die alle jeweils ihren eigenen Stil entwickelt haben.

Leonore Welzien

Cabaret Voltaire

Der Name des C. V. ist untrennbar verknüpft mit der Begründung und Entwicklung des Dadaismus. Der ehemalige Dramaturg der Münchner Kammerspiele, Hugo Ball, vom Kriegsfreiwilligen zum Pazifisten geworden, emigrierte im Mai 1915 mit seiner späteren Frau, Emmy Hennings, in die Schweiz. Am 5.2.1916 eröffnete er in Zürich das C. V. Als Mitarbeiter kamen u. a. Richard Huelsenbeck, Hans Arp, Marcel und Georges Janco, Tristan Tzara und später Walter Serner hinzu. Das Programm umfaßte moderne Lyrik, aktuelle Klaviermusik und Chansons. Mit der Ankunft Richard Huelsenbecks aus Berlin änderte sich der Stil des C. V., der Begriff «Dada» entstand (bei umstrittener ‹Vaterschaft›). Man führte nun simultanistische Verse auf mit «bruitistischer» musikalischer Begleitung; «Chants nègres» und Hugo Balls «Klanggedichte» bestimmten die Programme. «Unser Kabarett ist eine Geste. Jedes Wort, das hier gesprochen und gesungen wird, besagt wenigstens das eine, daß es dieser erniedrigenden Zeit nicht gelungen ist, uns Respekt abzunötigen» (Ball). Am 15.5.1916 erschien die Zeitschrift C. V. als erste dadaistische Publikation, seit März 1917 wurde in der neuen «Galerie Dada» gespielt, bis sich im selben Jahr der Gründerkreis auflöste und den Dadaismus nach Berlin und Paris weitertrug (→ Dadaistisches Theater).

Ball, H.: Die Flucht aus der Zeit. München/Leipzig 1927 (Neuauflage Luzern 1946); Keiser, C.: Herrliche Zeiten – 1916–1976. 60 Jahre Cabaret in der Schweiz. Bern 1976; Kühn, V.: Das Kabarett der frühen Jahre. Berlin 1984; Schifferli, P.: Als Dada begann. Zürich 1957; ders. (Hg.): Die Geburt des Dada. Zürich 1957; Segel, H. B.: Turn-of-the-Century Cabaret. New York 1987.

Wolfgang Beck

Café-Theater

Entstand 1957 in New York, als der Kaffeehausbesitzer Joe Cino in Greenwich Village einer Gruppe junger Beatnik-Schauspieler erlaubte, vor seinen Gästen Theater zu spielen. 1966 das erste C.-T. (‹Café-théâtre›) im Pariser Montparnasse-Viertel: Der Wirt Michel Guiton wollte einem befreundeten jungen Autor Gelegenheit bieten, sein Stück aufzuführen (*Trio pour deux canaris*, Trio für zwei Kanarienvögel von Bernard Da Costa) und gab damit das Startzeichen für die Gründung zahlreicher C.-T., die oft nur kurze Lebensdauer hatten. In Paris überlebten die von der jeweiligen Truppe selbst bewirtschafteten C.-T., als bekanntestes das Café de la Gare mit 480 Sitzplätzen. Die Schauspieler erhalten in der Regel keine Gage und auch nicht immer eine Umsatzbeteiligung, sondern teilen die direkt beim Zuschauer (mit Klingelbeutel, Teller, Hut o. ä.) gesammelte Summe unter sich auf.

Die besonderen Aufführungsverhältnisse im C.-T. führen zu einer neueren Art der Beziehung zwischen ‹Zuschauerraum› und ‹Bühne›, einem sehr direkten Kontakt, der für die Schauspieler eine Herausforderung bildet und zu einem besonderen Stil geführt hat. Es handelt sich um kurze Stücke, direkte Dialoge, ‹Intimismus›, Schaffung einer Komplizenschaft zwischen Schauspielern und Zuschauern, Vorliebe für Humoristisches, äußerste Vereinfachung des Dekors und aller Bühneneffekte. In Deutschland hat sich für vergleichbare Aufführungen der Begriff «Kneipentheater» eingebürgert (→ Freies Theater). Das Publikum der C.-T. bestand zunächst aus jungen Intellektuellen, angehenden Schauspielern, Künstlern und hat sich erst mit dem Erfolg bestimmter Aufführungen das bürgerliche Theaterpublikum erobert. Eugène Ionesco, Bernard Pinget, René de Obaldia haben direkt für das C.-T. geschrieben. Etliche Autoren (Edward Albee) und Schauspieler (Bernard Haller, Coluche) begannen ihren Weg im C.-T.

Gripari, Pierre: Café-Théâtre. Paris 1980.

Horst Schumacher

Candomblé

Ein bis heute geübter Kult der Yoruba (Afrikaner aus Angola) und der Dahomey (aus dem Sudan). C. hießen ursprünglich die Orte auf Kaffeeplantagen oder Häusern in Städten, speziell Bahias und Afroamerikas allgemein, in denen die Afrikaner ihre Versammlungen, Feste und Kulte pflegten. Noch heute finden die Kulte im C.-Haus und in dessen heiliger, in freiem Gelände gelegener Umgebung statt. Verlauf: 1. Opferhandlung; 2. Tanz des Exu; 3. Anrufung der Orixas im Tanz bis zur Trance; 4. Zweiter Trancetanz; 5. gemeinsame Kommunion im C.-Haus. Alle Tänzer erscheinen im feierlich weißen Gewande der Orixas; 6. Fächer- und Spiegeltanz der Oshun (auch Oxun), der Göttin der Flüsse; 7. Tanz-Duett zwischen Oxun und Ogun, dem Gott des Krieges. Oxun wehrt den Herrn aller Kriege magisch und verzweifelt ab. Die Orixas verteilen mehrfach göttliche Energie an Außenstehende und Freunde (→ Ritualtänze; → Brauchtumstänze).

Berger, R.: African Dance. Wilhelmshaven 1984; Fichte, H.: «Xangô» – Die afroamerikanischen Religionen. Bahia, Haiti, Trinidad. Frankfurt/M. 1976; Simpson, G. E.: The Shango Cult in Trinidad. Institute of African Studies. Vol. 3. No. 1. Oct. 1965. Ibadan.

Helga Ettl

Cantica

Die Partien der röm. Tragödie und Komödie, die zu instrumentaler Begleitung gesungen oder rezitiert wurden; C. finden sich vor allem in den Komödien des Plautus, der vielfach Monologe und Dialoge seiner griech. Vorlagen in Arien und Duette umgesetzt hat. – Die antike Nachricht (Livius 7,2), daß die Lieder (wie im →Pantomimus) von einem hinter einer spanischen Wand verborgenen Sänger gesungen wurden, während der Schauspieler dazu stumm spielte und tanzte, verdient kein Vertrauen. – Die Ursprünge der C. sind umstritten; wahrscheinlich haben volkstümliche ital. und unterital.-griech. Formen ebenso dazu beigetragen wie (direkt oder über die röm. Tragödie vermittelt) die hell.-griech. Tragödie, in der Arien und Duette eine große Rolle spielten.

Blänsdorf, J.: Plautus. In: E. Lefèvre (Hg.): Das röm. Drama. Darmstadt 1978, S. 202–206.

Bernd Seidensticker

Cartel (des quatre)

1927 als Reaktion auf eine gegen das Theater gerichtete Pressekampagne gegründete Solidargemeinschaft der vier Schauspieler/Regisseure Gaston Baty (1885–1952), Charles Dullin (1885–1949), Louis Jouvet (1887–1951) und Georges Pitoeff (1887–1939). Neben dem finanziellen Zusammenschluß vor allem darum bemüht, die Reformarbeit Copeaus am Théâtre du Vieux-Colombier fortzuführen. Dem naturalistischen und dem akademischen Theater sollte eine Ästhetik im Dienst des Textes entgegengesetzt werden. Hierin teilweise inkonsequent war Baty mit auffallend üppigen Ausstattungen (Gantillons *Maya*, 1924; Dostojewskis *Schuld und Sühne*, 1932). Große Erfolge erzielten Dullin mit Aristophanes' *Die Vögel* (1928 und 1933), Shakespeares *Richard III.* (1933), Jouvet mit Giraudoux' *Siegfried et le Limousin* (1928), Pitoeff mit Shakespeares *Hamlet* (1922–29 mehrfach) und Pirandellos *Heinrich IV.* (1925). In der Herausstellung des Unbewußten und in dem Interesse für die Zusammenhänge von Realität und Imaginärem wird der Einfluß Freuds und Pirandellos auf die Mitglieder des C. und damit auf die Entwicklung des frz. Theaters nach 1920 deutlich sichtbar.

Anders, F.: Jacques Copeau et le cartel des quatre. Paris 1959.

Barbara Müller-Wesemann

Cartoucherie

Ehemals Munitionsfabrik und -lager am Rande des Waldparks Bois de Vincennes im Osten von Paris. Zwischen 1871 und 1881 errichtet, bestand aus einer Reihe von miteinander verbundenen Fabrikgebäuden in unmittelbarer Nähe einer Artilleriekaserne. Die lange ungenutzt gebliebene Anlage wurde 1969 von der frz. Heeresverwaltung an die Stadt Paris als Grundstückseigentümer zurückgegeben. 1971 etablierten sich in den baufälligen Gebäuden avantgardistische Theatergruppen. Die Fabrikhallen oder Schuppen («hangars») wurden mit sparsamsten Mitteln theatergerecht restauriert und umgebaut. Als Theaterstandort von Ariane Mnouchkine für ihre →Théâtre du Soleil entdeckt, bald gefolgt von den heute das Theaterzentrum C. bildenden Bühnen Théâtre de la Tempête («Sturm»), Théâtre du Chaudron («Wasserkessel»), Théâtre l'Aquarium und Théâtre de l'Epée du Bois («Holzschwert»).

Alle C.-Bühnen – mit vielen Uraufführungen und Eigenkreationen – arbeiten bewußt im Gegensatz zu den mondänen innerstädtischen Pariser Bühnen. Die Überlebensfähigkeit der verschiedenen C.-Theater wird inzwischen durch Subventionen der Stadt Paris und des frz. Kulturministeriums gesichert.

Horst Schumacher

Centre International de la Création Théâtrale / Centre International de Recherches Théâtrales

1968 wurde Peter Brook von Jean-Louis Barrault nach Paris eingeladen, eine Theaterwerkstatt mit Schauspielern, Autoren und Regisseuren unterschiedlichster Kultur und Ausgangsbasis zu schaffen. Es war ein kurzlebiges Experiment, das Brook aber durch die Möglichkeiten der internationalen Zusammenarbeit 1970 zur Gründung des Pariser Studienzentrums für Theaterforschung (C.I.R.T. – Centre International de Recherches Théâtrales) anregte; nach Interviews mit 155 Schauspielern und Theaterleitern wählte Brook Mitarbeiter aus: vier von →La Mama in New York (Andrei Serban, Andreas Katsulas, Michele Collison, Lou Zeldis), aus Deutschland Miriam Goldschmidt, aus Japan Yoshi Oida, aus Afrika Malick Bowens, aus England Bruce Myers und Natasha Parry, aus Frankreich François Marthouret. Später schlossen sich die Komponisten Richard Peaslee und Elizabeth Swados an. Das Zentrum erhielt Stiftungsmittel und vom frz. Kulturministerium in der Gobelinmanufaktur einen Raum. Das erste Experiment war der Versuch, zusammen mit dem britischen Dichter Ted Hughes Theater mittels einer Universalsprache zu entwickeln, die er Orghast nannte und die Sanskrit- und persische Wurzeln mit altgriech., lat. und Avesta-Elementen mischte. Das zweiteilige dramatische Epos *Orghast* stand thematisch neben dem zentralen Motiv der Prometheuslegende, jap. Samurailegenden, Sequenzen in Anlehnung an Calderóns *Das Leben ist ein Traum* sowie pers. Fabeln u. a. Aufführung während der Shiraz-Festspiele auf einem Berggipfel über den Ruinen von Persepolis.

Das zweite Experiment war eine Hundert-Tage-Reise durch West-Afrika, bei der Brooks Truppe in abgelegenen Orten spielte, wo noch nie ein europ. Illusionstheater aufgeführt worden war, die Theaterwirksamkeit in nicht theatergemäßen Raumverhältnissen getestet werden konnte. Nach Brook war dabei «Erfolg oder Mißerfolg nie ein Kriterium. Jede Begegnung war befriedigend, weil sie eine warme und reiche Erfahrung bildete und bewies, daß Unterschiede zwischen Völkern verschiedener Rassen ohne gemeinsame Sprache überbrückt werden konnten durch die Benutzung der Möglichkeiten einer erneuerten Form des Theaters.» Auf dieser Reise wurde außerdem das altpersische Stück von der *Versammlung der Vögel* von Farid Uddin Attar (1150–1220) einstudiert, das 1974 auf einer USA-Reise der Truppe und 1979 auch in →Avignon aufgeführt wurde.

1974 konnte Brooks Mitarbeiterin Micheline Rozan C.I.R.T. ein eigenes Haus sichern: Das zum Abriß bestimmte →Théâtre des Bouffes du Nord in einem Arbeiterviertel beim Nordbahnhof lag brach. Es hatte als Music-Hall Ende des 19. Jh. seine große Zeit gehabt und die ersten frz. Ibsen-Inszenierungen unter dem Avantgarde-Regisseur Lugné-Poë erlebt. Brook entfernte den Plüsch und Pomp der Gründerjahre aus dem Theaterraum, höhlte ihn sozusagen aus und kalkte die Wände, ostentativ bestreitend, daß aufwendige Bühnenmaschinerie und bequeme Einrichtung Voraussetzung für gutes Theater sein müßten.

1974 *Timon von Athen* von William Shakespeare in der Bearbeitung von Jean-Claude Carrière. 1975 *Les Iks*, ein Stück über die Vernichtung der Indianer (nach *The Mountain People* von Colin Turnbull). Aufenthalte von Brook in Warschau und Breslau auf Einladung von J. Grotowski für die Universität des Théâtre des Nations. 1976 *Iks*-Aufführung in London, bei den Festspielen von Caracas, auf Gastspielreisen in Lateinamerika und den Vereinigten Staaten. 1977 *Ubu aux Bouffes* nach *König Ubu* von Alfred Jarry. 1978 *Ubu*-Aufführung in London und Caracas. Shakespeare-Inszenierung *Antonius und Kleopatra* und *Maß für Maß*. 1979 Umbenennung des Studienzentrums in C.I.C.T. 1981 Tschechows *Kirschgarten* und *La Tragédie de Carmen* (nach Bizet, Mérimée, Meilhac und Halévy, bearbeitet von Jean-Claude Carrière, Marius Constant, Peter Brook). 1982 Gratisaufführung einer Musikkomödie *Ta–Da–Da*. 1985 nach zehnjähriger Vorbereitung Aufführung der neun

Stunden dauernden Dramatisierung des Sanskrit-Versepos *Mahabharata* beim →Festival d'Avignon, danach →Théâtre des Bouffes du Nord und auf Gastspielreise.

Brook, P.: Der leere Raum (The Empty Space). 1969; C.N.R.S.: Peter Brook. Paris 1985 (= Les voies de la création théâtrale).

Horst Schumacher

Centre international de recherches scéniques

1958 von Wolfram Mehring im Rahmen seines →Théâtre de la Mandragore zunächst unter dem Namen Centre franco-allemand de recherche théâtrale gegründetes experimentelles Theaterzentrum, das ähnlich bahnbrechend wirkte wie das kurz vorher von Jerzy Grotowski in Breslau und das 1968 ebenfalls in Paris von Peter Brook etablierte Zentrum. Mehrings Schüler arbeiten an vielen Plätzen v. a. Westeuropas, Asiens und Afrikas. Mehring hat mit seiner Auffassung von der magischen Dimension des Theaters und der kreativen Körper-Natur des Schauspielers nicht nur bei Gastspielen und Inszenierungen in Europa einflußreich gewirkt, um dem Theater «die Verbindung vom Kopf zum Körper und zum Boden» wiederzugeben, sondern besonders in der dritten Welt großes Echo gehabt. Er hat im Himalaya indische Regisseure unterrichtet, im thailändischen Cjeing-Mai die zehnte Inkarnation des Buddha für die Bühne inszeniert, in Kinshasa einen alten kongolesischen Mythos und in Khartum Büchners *Woyzeck* auf arabisch. Als Spezialist für asiatische Theaterformen hat M. die aus der Kabuki-Tradition fortentwickelte japanische Oper *Die Rache des Schauspielers* (1979) und Rabindranath Tagores *Das Postamt* (1992 in Indien auf Bengali, deutschsprachige Kreation Chur 1989) inszeniert. – Auf der Insel Malta beginnt Mehring mit der Einrichtung eines Theaterzentrums nach seiner Konzeption vom «totalen Schauspieler».

Mehring, W.: Die Möglichkeiten eines eigenständig-kreativen Darstellers im europäischen Theater. Paris o. J.; Masques brulées/Verbrannte Masken. Paris; Du rite au théâtre. Paris.

Horst Schumacher

Centre National de Création

Frz. Theater- und Filmwerkstatt, bis Ende 1985 als Atelier de Création Populaire mit Hauptsitz in Toulouse. Auf Initiative des frz. Kulturministers J. Lang gegründet und von dem Theatermann und Filmemacher Armand Gatti (* 1924) geleitet und entscheidend geprägt. Dieses mit audiovisuellen Mitteln gut ausgestattete Zentrum, das alle drei Jahre den Spielort wechseln soll, versteht sich als Forum der Begegnung und des Experimentierens mit politisch-ästhetischen Ausdrucksformen und wendet sich an professionelle Künstler und Amateure, an Immigranten und andere soziale Randgruppen. Bei der Umbesetzung historischer und gegenwartspolitischer Stoffe geht es Gatti vorrangig um das gemeinsame Erarbeiten einer Produktion im Sinne einer ‹création collective›. Seit Beginn 1986 befindet sich das Zentrum als La Parole Errante in dem Pariser Vorort Montreuil.

Barbara Müller-Wesemann

Centres Dramatiques Nationaux

(Frz., Sing. ‹Centre Dramatique National bzw. Centre National de Création et de Diffusion Dramatiques) Bezeichnung der staatlich geförderten Theaterensembles in der frz. Provinz außerhalb Paris und auch Pariser Randtheater oder Vorstadtbühnen (Théâtre de l'Est Parisien, T.E.P., und Théâtre Gérard Philipe in Saint-Denis). Die 1937 von Charles Dullin (1885–1949), einem der Begründer des modernen Regie-Theaters, geforderte Dezentralisierung des frz. Theaters führte erst nach dem 2. Weltkrieg zu Ergebnissen. 1946 Gründung von fünf C.D.N., deren Zahl sich später auf neun erhöhte: Comédie de Bourges, Comédie de l'Est, Comédie du Nord, Comédie de l'Ouest, Comédie de Provence, Comédie de St. Etienne, Grenier de Toulouse, T.E.P. Einige T.D.N. haben eigene Theaterschulen. Unter dem gaullistischen Kulturminister André Malraux (1901–76) wurden die C.D.N. teilweise in die Kulturhäuser (→ Maisons de la Culture) einbezogen.

Weitere Förderung der C.D.N. und Erhöhung ihrer Zahl unter dem sozialistischen Kulturminister Jack Lang, dem Begründer des Festivals von → Nancy und ehemaligen Leiter des → Théâtre National de Chaillot.

Horst Schumacher

Centrum Sztuki «Studio» im St. I. Witkiewicza (Warschau)

Kunstzentrum St. I. Witkiewicz-«Studio»-Theater: bis 1971 Teatr Klasyczny (Klassisches Theater), 1972 in eine experimentelle Studienbühne umgewandelt. Gründer und Intendant bis 1982 J. Szajna. Kunstgalerie und Museum für Gegenwartskunst; zwei Bühnen. J. Szajna (* 1922), ehemaliger Auschwitz-Häftling, Bühnenbildner, Regisseur, Kunstmaler, Mitarbeiter an einigen Theatern (u. a. →«Teatr Stary», 1966–71), entwickelt eigene Szenarien mit aufwendiger Bühnenausstattung; Illusionsbühnenbilder, abstrakte Formen bis hin zum plastischen Environment. Die Ästhetik seines Theaters wird durch das plastische Bild bestimmt, das jedes Element, auch den Schauspieler, integriert. Die Vorstellungskraft des Zuschauers soll dadurch besonders aktiviert und gefordert werden. Szajnas Theater zeigt das ‹Labyrinth der Welt und der Formen›, ‹die Welt, die aus der Bahn fiel›, ‹Kulturnekropolis›. Herausragende Inszenierungen: *Replika*, Uraufführung 1971 in Göteborg; *Dante*, Uraufführung 1974 in Florenz; *Cervantes*, 1976. Seit 1982 Intendant Jerzy Grzegorzewski (* 1939). In seinem Repertoire u. a. H. Müller, Beckett, Brecht (1986, *Dreigroschenoper*), Różewicz (1987, *Die Falle*), 1987 *Die sogenannte Menschheit im Wahnsinn* (Grzegorzewski nach Witkiewicz).

Slawomir Tryc / Elke Wiegand

Černé Divadlo (Prag)

(Schwarzes Theater). Das Č. D. wurde 1961 von Jiri Srnec (* 1931) gegründet und übernahm eine alte, ursprünglich aus China (→Chinesisches Theater) stammende Tradition der theatralischen Darstellung. Vor einem schwarzen Hintergrund bewegen ebenfalls schwarz gekleidete und schwarz maskierte Schauspieler helle Gegenstände. Durch komplizierte optische Verfahren und technische Tricks entsteht beim Zuschauer der Eindruck, daß diese Gegenstände schweben und sich verwandeln. Die Darstellungsform bewirkt, daß Schauspieler und Gegenstände als gleichwertige Partner erscheinen. – Seit 1991 nennt sich die Truppe «Black-Light-Theater Imaginace».

Elke Kehr / Red.

Chamberlain's Men

Das erste öffentliche Auftreten der C. M. ist für das Jahr 1594 verbürgt. Zu dieser Zeit beinhaltete das Repertoire bereits *Titus Andronicus, Der Widerspenstigen Zähmung* und eine *Hamlet*-Fassung, die aber nicht mit der Shakespeareschen Fassung identisch war. Die geschäftliche Basis der Truppe war ein Teilhabervertrag der Schauspieler; einer dieser Teilhaber war William Shakespeare (1564–1616), der der Truppe bis zu seinem Tod angehörte und die meisten seiner Stücke für die C. M. schrieb. Nach einer kurzen Zusammenarbeit mit den →Admiral's Men im Rose Theatre wechselte die Truppe in James Burbages ‹Theatre› über und spielte dort von 1594–99. Burbages Sohn Richard (ca. 1573–1619) war der Hauptschauspieler der Truppe. Später trat die Truppe im ‹Curtain› auf und spielte regelmäßig bei Hof, in der Regel mit Stücken von Shakespeare und Jonson. Es ist unwahrscheinlich, daß Jonson, der als mittelmäßiger Schauspieler galt, jemals bei den C. M. spielte; Shakespeare jedoch, der seine Schauspielerkarriere wahrscheinlich bei den Strange's Men oder den Pembroke's Men begonnen hatte, trat häufig auf, meist in kleineren Rollen. Sein letzter verbürgter Auftritt fand im Jahre 1603 statt.

Im Jahre 1599 zog die Truppe ins →‹Globe›, das aus dem Holz des abgerissenen ‹Theatre› erbaut worden war. *Heinrich V.* wurde vielleicht, *Julius Caesar* und Jonsons *Every Man out of his Humour* wurden mit Sicherheit dort uraufgeführt. Nach einem politischen Eklat im Jahre 1601 wurde die Truppe 1603 wieder bei Hof zugelassen und spielte als ‹King's Men› unter der Protektion James' I. Die Truppe galt nun als die erfolgreichste des →Elisabethanischen Theaters. Shakespeare zog sich jedoch ab 1608 immer mehr von der Truppe zurück, Beaumont und Fletcher traten als Autoren allmählich an seine Stelle. Zur selben Zeit übernahm die Truppe das ‹Blackfriars Theatre› und spielte dort bis 1642. Daneben wurde auch immer noch das ‹Globe› bespielt, das im Jahre 1613 während einer Aufführung von *Heinrich VIII.*, Shakespeares letztem Stück, völlig niederbrannte. – Nach dem Tod Shakespeares im Jahre 1616 und Burbages 1619 brach die Truppe auseinander, und etliche Mitglieder gingen zu anderen Truppen. Zur Zeit James' I. hatten die C. M. 35 feste Mitglieder sowie eine unbekannte Zahl von Knabenschauspielern, eine Ensemblegröße, die für die damalige Zeit äußerst ungewöhnlich war.

Frenzel, H. A.: Geschichte des Theaters. München 1979; The Oxford Companion to the Theatre. Ed. by Ph. Hartnell. London/New York/Toronto 1951.

Elke Kehr

Chanson

(Frz., von lat. ‹cantio› = Gesang) C. bezeichnete im Mittelalter jedes singbare Lied in frz. Sprache, vor allem das Liebeslied der nordfrz. Minnesänger (trouvères). Nach und nach Bedeutungseinengung auf das mehrstimmige Lied mit Kehrreim, z. B. im galanten C. des 17. und 18. Jh. Zur Zeit der Frz. Revolution wurde das C. politisch-satirisch.

Im modernen allgemeinen Wortsinn ist C. ein scharf pointiertes Lied der Kabarettisten (→Kabarett), mitunter lässig vorgetragen, ironisch-witzig, oft frech-frivol, auch sentimental und wehmütig-fatalistisch. Es entstand im 19. Jh. in Pariser Cafés, wo das von Pierre Jean Béranger (1780–1857) entwickelte zeitbezogene Gesellschaftslied vorgetragen wurde. Wichtiger Treffpunkt der Chansonniers war das in den 80er Jahren gegründete Cabaret artistique →Chat Noir auf dem Montmartre und Aristide Bruants Cabaret →Mirliton. Berühmte Chansonniers und Chansonnetten: Yvette Guilbert (für die Toulose-Lautrec Plakate entwarf), Jane Avril, La Goulue, die Mistinguett (eigentlich Jeanne-Marie Bourgeois, 1873–1956), Maurice Chevalier (1888–1984), Josephine Baker, Marianne Oswald, die im Nachtlokal Le Bœuf sur le Toit die ersten C. von Jacques Prévert (1900–77) vortrug, Edith Piaf, Juliette Gréco, Barbara, Georges Brassens, Yves Montand, Gilbert Bécaud, Charles Aznavour, Jacques Brel u. a.

In Deutschland wurde das C. durch die Kabaretts →Die Elf Scharfrichter und →Überbrettl heimisch. Seit den 60er Jahren verstärkte Entwicklung des politischen C., z. B. Wolf Biermann. Bei den ‹Liedermachern› der neuen Generation vorwiegend intellektuelle, oft von resigniert leisen Tönen geprägte Gesellschaftskritik.

Neben dem mehr lyrischen C. unterscheidet man das mondän-weltstädtische C., das sich vor dem 1. Weltkrieg in Berlin herausbildete mit Rudolf Nelson (1878–1960) und Friedrich H. Hollaender, der für Marlene Dietrich im *Blauen Engel* «Ich bin von Kopf bis Fuß auf Liebe eingestellt» schrieb. – Die C.-Einlagen im modernen Theater (etwa bei Bertolt Brecht, der die engl. Bezeichnung ‹Song› bevorzugte) kommen meist vom Kabarett her, seltener von Singspiel oder Posse.

Ruttkowski, W. V.: Das literar. Chanson in Deutschland. Bern/München 1966; Schmidt, Felix: Das Chanson. Herkunft, Entwicklung, Interpretation. Frankfurt/M. [2]1982; Schulz-Koehn, D.: Vive la chanson. Kunst zwischen Show und Poesie. Gütersloh 1969; La chanson d'aujourd'hui. Mythes et images du temps présent. Paris 1984, C.I.E.P. Dossiers de Sèvres.

Horst Schumacher

Charakterdarsteller

Schauspieler für Charakterrollen – z. B. Götz bei Johann Wolfgang von Goethe (1749–1832), Wallenstein bei Friedrich Schiller (1759–1805); im Komischen: Falstaff bei William Shakespeare (1564–1616) und der Dorfrichter Adam als sog. schwerer C. bei Heinrich von Kleist (1777–1811). Anders als in den Theaterformen, die eine strenge Rollenverteilung und -typisierung kennen, gewinnt der C. im psychologischen und realistischen Theater an Bedeutung. Dabei erfordert die Darstellung scharf betonter, individueller Charakterzüge, die in ihrer Eigenart vom Dramatiker oft nur angedeutet werden, vom C. ein ausgeprägtes Einfühlungs- und Gestaltungsvermögen.

Bernard Poloni

Charakterkomödie

Komödie, bei der die komische Wirkung nicht auf Verwicklungen in Situationen wie in der Situationskomödie, nicht auf der Zeichnung feststehender Typen wie in der → Typenkomödie liegt, sondern in der ein einziger, ausgeprägter Charakter oder Charakterzug zu lächerlicher Größe gesteigert wird.

Literatur: → Komödie.

Bernard Poloni

Charge

Aus dem Frz. entlehntes Wort zur Bezeichnung einer meist nur in wenigen Szenen auftretenden Nebenperson, der eine besondere dramaturgische Bedeutung zukommt und die deswegen vom Schauspieler oft überscharf charakterisiert wird und somit häufig komisch wirkt – z. B. Riccaut in Gotthold Ephraim Lessings (1727–81) *Minna von Barnhelm* (1767) oder der Kapuziner in Friedrich von Schillers (1759–1805) *Wallensteins Lager* (1799). Für Schauspieler, die sich nicht direkt für ein Typenfach eignen, bieten die C. abwechslungsreiche Spielmöglichkeiten. Dramaturgisch gesehen sind die C. Kontrastfiguren, die der Handlung und der Hauptfigur mehr Relief verleihen. Die Gefahr ist dabei, in eine karikaturistische Übertreibung und Effekthascherei zu verfallen, was die meist negative Konnotation des Verbs → ‹chargieren› dokumentiert.

Bernard Poloni

Chargieren

(Frz. ‹charger› = beladen, belasten, übertreiben) Charge ist die – ursprünglich neutrale – Bezeichnung einer Nebenrolle. Das Bemühen, dieser begrenzten Aufgabe mit darstellerischen Mitteln Bedeutung zu verleihen, führt häufig zur unangemessenen Überzeichnung, zum Spielen um des Effekts willen, zum ‹Ch.›. Diese Entwicklung führte zum negativen Bedeutungswandel des Ausdrucks. Im Theaterjargon werden solche Darsteller als «Knallchargen» bezeichnet.

Bab, J.: Nebenrollen. Berlin 1913; Schütz, J.: «Chargen» in der deutschen Theaterpraxis von Ekhof bis Reinhardt. Diss. Wien 1970.

Wolfgang Beck

Chat Noir

Der 18. 11. 1881, der Tag der Eröffnung des C. N. durch den Maler Rodolphe Salis, gilt als Beginn der Kabarettgeschichte. Die lebendige Chansontradition in Frankreich, die Fülle der «Café concerts» und der künstlerischen und literarischen Klubs bildeten den Nährboden für die neue theatralische Form. Salis plante ursprünglich die Gründung einer Künstlerkneipe, die er C. N. nannte (entweder nach einer eigenen Katze oder der bekannten Groteske E. A. Poes). Er hatte das Glück, die Künstlergruppe «Club des Hydropathes» in sein Lokal ziehen zu können, die sich bisher schon in geschlossenen Veranstaltungen eigene Produktionen vorgetragen hatte. Diese Tradition setzten sie im C. N. fort, nach einiger Zeit auch vor Publikum. Mit regelmäßigem Spielbetrieb begann Salis, als →Conférencier die auftretenden Autoren-Interpreten anzusagen. Die kostenlose Verteilung einer eigenen Zeitschrift seit dem 14. 1. 1882 verstärkte den Erfolg des neuen Etablissements. Nach gewaltsamen Versuchen der Anwohner, Salis zu vertreiben, zog er in ein größeres Domizil, wo weiterhin vor allem Chansons witziger, satirischer und sozialkritischer Art vorgetragen wurden. Sehr bald aber wurden die ursprünglich nur zur Illustrierung eines Chansons gedachten Schattenspiele der künstlerische Anziehungspunkt. Ausgedehnte Tourneen steigerten den Erfolg des C. N. Am 17. 3. 1897 starb Salis; der Conférencier Dominique Bonnaud führte das C. N. noch einige Zeit auf Tourneen weiter, bevor es endgültig geschlossen werden mußte.

Erfolg und Ruhm des ersten Cabarets veranlaßte weitere Gründungen unter diesem Namen. Im Herbst 1907 eröffnete Rudolf Nelson (→Nelson-Revue) in Berlin im ersten Stock von «Castans Panoptikum» sein C. N. von eher mondänem Charakter. 1914 verließ er das zu Kriegsbeginn patriotisch in «Schwarzer Kater» umgetaufte Etablissement, das unter neuer Leitung das bisherige Niveau nicht behalten konnte und schließlich «Kleinkunst und Ringkämpfe» bot, bevor es in den 20er Jahren schloß. – Auf dem Gelände des Tivoli von Oslo (damals noch Christiania) wurde am 1.3.1912 ein C. N. eröffnet, das bis in die Gegenwart existiert. Sein erfolgreicher Start gab den Anstoß für weitere Kabarettgründungen in Skandinavien. Ausgerichtet nach Berliner und Pariser Vorbildern, legte man zu Beginn vor allem Wert auf Literarisches, ging in den 20er Jahren aber zur aktuellen, politischen Revue über.

Bang-Hansen, O.: Chat Noir og Norsk Revy. Oslo 1961; Bordat, D., F. Boucrot: Les Théâtres d'ombres. Paris 1956; Casteras, R. de: Avant le Chat Noir – les Hydropathes. Paris 1945; Centenaire du Cabaret du Chat Noir. Paris 1981; Damianakos, S. (Hg.): Théâtres d'ombres. Charleville 1986; Donnay, M.: Autour du Chat Noir. Paris 1926; Goudeau, E. (ed.): Le Chat Noir (Zeitschrift). Paris 1882–95; Jameson, E.: Am Flügel: Rudolf Nelson. Berlin 1967; Nelson, R.: Nacht der Nächte – Revue meines Lebens. Berlin o.J.; Segel, H. B.: Turn-of-the-Century Cabaret. New York 1987.

Wolfgang Beck

Chhao-Tänze

Tanzspiele im Südosten (Westbengalen) und Nordosten (Orissa) Indiens (→Indisches Theater). Begriff: Chhadma (Sanskrit) = Maskierung, Verstellung; Chhaya = Masken, Schatten; Chhaumi (Orissa) = Kriegslager (Kriegstanz); Chhak (Mandari) = Geist; Chhata = von Geistern besessen. – In Purulia 1947 erstes Chhau-Tanztheater; Srikala Pitka/Bihar: Kulturzentrum zur Pflege des Ch.-Tanzes. Drei regionale C.-Stile: 1. Purulia, 2. Seraikella, 3. Mayurbhanj. Die ersten beiden sind →Maskentanzspiele. – Zu 1: Die Purulia führt auf urgesellschaftliche Bräuche zurück, liebt humoristische Einschübe, Tier- und Fruchtbarkeitsszenen. Führendes Tanzspiel: das *Ramayana*. Zu 2: Die Seraikella gehört zu den Palastspielen. Shiva ist Protagonist. Aufführungen zum Chaitraparva, dem Frühlingsfest. Zu 3: Der Mayurbhanj zeichnet sich aus durch Akrobatik und Waffentänze mit Stock und Schild. Szenenschwerpunkte: Säen, Ernten, Feuertanz, Dornenlauf (→Ritualtänze), die Liebe Krishnas und Radhas, Affenkönig Hanuman. Im Mayurbhanj erreicht der C.-Tanz äußerste Systematisierung und Stilisierung. Notiert wurden 250 Bewegungsarten (→Maskentänze; →Moresca).

Bhattacharyya, A.: Chhao-Dance of Purulia. Calcutta 1972; Rebling, E.: Die Tanzkunst Indiens. Wilhelmshaven 1982.

Helga Ettl

Chicano Theater

Chicanos (= aus Mexicanos) sind US-Amerikaner mexikan. Herkunft, in präziserem kulturhistorischen Verständnis Nachkommen mexikan. Mestizo, der sowohl europ. als auch indigene Vorfahren hat. Die frühesten Wurzeln des modernen C. T. sind Wandertheatertruppen der Azteken im 15. und 16. Jh., sog. *tlaquetzque* (‹diejenigen, welche die Dinge herausragen ließen›), die ähnlich der →Commedia dell'arte-Truppen Dörfer und Städte bereisten und auf öffentlichen Plätzen spielten. Ihre Spiele dramatisierten Mythen und Legenden, hielten Balance zwischen dem Heiligen und dem Profanen. Frühe Inszenierungen: *Los pastores* (1526), *El juicio final* (1533) und *El sacrificio de Isaac* (1539). Die ersten Theaterstücke aus der Region des heutigen Südwestens der USA (unter Hinweis auf die aztekischen Vorfahren von Chicanos häufig als Aztlán bezeichnet) datieren im Jahre 1598. Die Tradition dieser christlichen Passions- und Missionsspiele wurde durch die nachfolgenden Jh. bis in die Gegenwart hinein fortgesetzt und konzentrierte sich naturgemäß auf die Gemeinden um die Missionskirchen und die Jahreszeiten des christlichen Kalenders. Obgleich die modernen Gruppen des C. T. ihre Gründung wesentlich politischen Ursachen verdanken (→Teatro Campesino), hat man doch sehr bald die Notwendigkeit und die Möglichkeiten erkannt, durch das religiöse Drama breitere Publikumsschichten der Mexican American community zu erreichen.

Der politische Anlaß zur Gründung moderner C. T. war ein Streik philippinischer und mexikanischer Traubenpflücker in Delano, Kalifornien (1965), der sich zu einem Generalstreik der Campesinos und zur Formierung der United Farm Workers's Union ausweitete. Gegen Ende der 60er und zu Beginn der 70er Jahre kam es zu zahlreichen Gründungen von C. T.-Gruppen. Die wichtigsten, die heute noch bestehen, sind: Teatro Campesino, →Teatro de la Esperanza, Teatro de la Gente (San José), Teatro de los Barrios (San Antonio), Teatro Libertad (Tucson), Teatro Mestizo (San Diego), Teatro Quetzalcoatl (Seattle), Teatro Aguacero (Albuquerque). Mit der Gründung einer nationalen Vereinigung der C. T.-Gruppen in den USA, El Teatro Nacional de Aztlán (TENAZ, 1971), weiteten sich ihre Aktivitäten über die Staaten des Südwestens (Texas, New Mexico, Arizona, California) hinaus in alle jene Regionen der USA aus, wo Mexiko-Amerikaner oder solche, die aus anderen lateinamerik. spanischsprechenden Ländern stammten, lebten und arbeiteten. Eine wichtige Gruppe, die Chicanos, Puertoricaner und Weiße integrierte, war Teatro Desengaño del Pueblo, in Gary, Indiana (Nicolàs Kanellos, 1972). TENAZ veranstaltet jährlich an wechselnden Orten Festivals, Symposien und ‹summer workshops›.

Die Entwicklung des C. T. der 70er Jahre ist durch eine zunehmende

Professionalisierung gekennzeichnet. Der Stil des modernen C. T. ist durch vier Komponenten geprägt: Die Stücke sind im wesentlichen Eigenproduktionen, werden kollektiv produziert und meistens nicht durch Verlage publiziert. Erst seit 1983 gibt es die Publikation von Dramen individueller Autoren (Carlos Morton, Estela Portillo). Das C. T. ist politisch; Themen sind: Einwanderung, Arbeit, Erziehung, Krieg und Frieden, Chicanos auf dem Land und in der Stadt, Kollision der mexikan. Ausgangskultur und der imperialistischen Kultur der USA. Entsprechend ist die Sprache des C. T. engl., span. und zweisprachig, wobei den Varianten des ‹barrio›-Idioms, der gesprochenen Mischsprache der großen urbanen Gettos, spezifische Bedeutung zukommt.

Das C. T. ist wesentlich durch musikalische Elemente geprägt: Jede Inszenierung wird in der Regel durch eine Musikgruppe begleitet. Die wichtigsten Wurzeln sind die texanische ‹conjunto music› sowie ‹corridos›, die klassischen mexikan. Volksballaden der Grenzregionen. Häufig sind den Musikeinlagen Tänze zugeordnet, die der aztekischen Überlieferung entstammen. Das C. T. ist ferner mythologisch. Best. Versatzstücke der jahrhundertelangen Tradition werden in konkrete Bilder umgesetzt, z. B. ‹el diablo› und ‹el muerte›, die Teufelsmaske und das Skelettkostüm (‹calavera›); aztekische Götterfiguren wie Quetzalcoatl, Tonantzin oder Coatlique; die Jungfrau von Guadalupe. Die Darbietungsweise zeichnet sich durch eine enge Verklammerung politischer und mythologischer Themen und Stilmittel aus.

Brokaw, J. W.: Mexican American Drama. In: H. Bock/A. Wertheim (eds.): Essays on Contemporary American Drama. München 1981, p. 241–56; Campa, A. L.: Spanish Religious Folktheatre in the Southwest. Albuquerque 1934; R. Garza (ed.): Contemporary Chicano Theatre. Notre Dame 1976; Goldsmith, B.: Brecht and Chicano Theatre. In: J. Sommers/T. Ybarra-Frausto (eds.): Modern Chicano Writers. Englewood Cliffs 1979, p. 167–75; Herms, D.: Die zeitgenössische Literatur der Chicanos (1959–1988). Frankfurt/M. 1990, S. 50–117; Huerta, J. A.: Chicano Theater. Themes and Forms. Ypsilanti 1983.

Dieter Herms

Children of Paul's

Knabentruppe im England des 16. Jh. Neben den ‹Children of the Chapel Royal› und den ‹Children of Windsor› waren sie die bekannteste Knabentruppe ihrer Zeit. Sie spielten häufig bei Hofe und ab 1576 im Blackfriars, das lange Zeit ausschließlich den Vorstellungen der Knabentruppen vorbehalten blieb. Ihr Repertoire umfaßte Werke bedeutender Dramatiker wie Jonson, Lyly und Marston. So wurden etwa die beiden ersten Stücke Lylys, *Alexander and Campaspe* und *Sappho*, 1584 im Blackfriars von den

‹Children of Paul's and of the Chapel› uraufgeführt. – Die schauspielerischen Leistungen der Knabentruppen waren beachtlich und bildeten eine ernst zu nehmende Konkurrenz für die Berufsschauspieler.

Hillebrand, H. N.: The Child Actors. 1926.

Elke Kehr

Chinesisches Sprechtheater

Das C. S. (huaju) wurde im Zuge der allg. Kritik an der chin. kulturellen Tradition und der entsprechenden Bewunderung europ. Kultur zu Beginn des 20. Jh. in China eingeführt. Das hatte zur Folge, daß zunächst eine große Anzahl von Stücken übersetzt wurde; bis in die 30er Jahre waren 70–80 Prozent aller aufgeführten Stücke Übersetzungen oder Adaptionen. Aber auch viele Stücke chin. Autoren blieben formal und inhaltlich lange europ. Vorbildern verpflichtet. Es ist kein Zufall, daß bedeutende Dramatiker wie Cao Yu, Guo Moruo, Tian Han, Hong Shen u. a. sich auch als Übersetzer einen Namen machten. Diese europ. Prägung ist bei einer Theaterform, die auf keine Tradition in China selbst zurückgreifen konnte, nur natürlich. Dennoch konnte das C. S. schnell einen festen Platz im kulturellen Leben Chinas erobern. In einer Zeit des sozialen und kulturellen Umbruchs galt es vielen als willkommenes, ja notwendiges Medium eben dieses Umbruchs. Immer wieder wurde seine Funktion als Mittler neuer Ideen, als Promotor sozialen Wandels betont. Als Kunstform, die zumindest theoretisch in der Lage war, sich an die Masse des Volks zu wenden, welche zum großen Teil analphabetisch und damit durch kein anderes Kommunikationsmittel erreichbar war, wurde es von Anfang an getragen, aber auch belastet, durch den didaktischen Impuls der überwiegend reformerisch oder revolutionär eingestellten Intellektuellen und Literaten. Es stand stets – und steht bis heute – in einem Spannungsfeld zwischen literarischer Qualität und didaktischer Effektivität.

Als neue Theaterform hatte das C. S. sich mit der reichen Tradition des chin. Musiktheaters auseinanderzusetzen. Nachdem es sich zunächst radikal gegen das Musiktheater gestellt hatte, welches geradezu als konzentrierter Ausdruck aller Übel der alten Gesellschaft angesehen wurde, zeigte sich doch bald, daß dieses kaum aus der Gunst des Publikums zu verdrängen war. C. S. und Musiktheater konnten nur, unterschiedliche Bevölkerungskreise ansprechend, nebeneinander, nicht gegeneinander existieren. So kam es in den späten 30er und den 40er Jahren zu Berührungen zwischen beiden Theaterformen: Dramatiker des C. S. begannen, auch Stücke des Musiktheaters zu schreiben; es wurden für das C. S. zahlreiche historische Dramen geschrieben, bis dahin eine Domäne des Musiktheaters. Insgesamt indessen fand das C. S. sein Publikum vor allem in gebildeten Kreisen der großen Städte; der großen Masse der Landbevölkerung blieb es weitgehend fremd. Aus einer Statistik des Jahres 1958 ergibt sich, daß von den 3182 professionellen Theatergruppen nur 113 auf das C. S. entfielen.

Als bedeutendster Dramatiker des C. S. kann Cao Yu (* 1910) gelten, der bes. in seinen großen Dramen «Das Gewitter» (*Leiyu*, 1934) und «Der Pekingmensch» (*Beijingren,* 1941) am Beispiel zweier Familien den Niedergang der städtischen Oberschicht beschrieb. Tian Han (1898–1968) drückte in seinen lyrischen, oft auch sentimentalen Stücken der 20er Jahre die Gefühle junger Menschen aus, die sich, die eigene Individualität betonend, gegen die gesellschaftlichen Konventionen wandten. Überhaupt war der Konflikt zwischen Konvention und persönlicher Neigung eines der großen Themen des C. S. Später schrieb Tian Han zahlreiche Stücke zu politischen Zeitereignissen. Ding Xilin (1893–1974) tat sich in einem Genre hervor, welches sonst im C. S. nur wenig vertreten ist: der Komödie. Guo Moruo (1892–1978) machte sich vor allem mit seinen historischen Dramen (bes. *Qu Yuan*, 1942) einen Namen, in denen vielfach eine verschlüsselte Kritik an der Guomindang-Regierung und ihrer Haltung zu den Fragen des Krieges gegen Japan zum Ausdruck kam. Hong Shen (1894–1955), Li Jianwu (1906–82) und Xia Yan (* 1900) sind hervorzuheben, ebenso wie Xiong Foxi (1900–65), der es mit seinen burlesken und handlungsreichen Stücken vermochte, das C. S. wenigstens zeitweilig in einer ländlichen Region erfolgreich zu etablieren.

Nach 1949 wandten sich viele Dramatiker des C. S. von einer kritischen Darstellung der gesellschaftlichen und politischen Zustände ab oder hörten ganz auf zu schreiben. Nur noch wenige bedeutende Dramen entstanden, bes. Lao Shes (1899–1966) «Das Teehaus» (*Chaguan*, 1957), eine großangelegte Darstellung der ersten Hälfte des 20. Jh. am Beispiel der Wirte und Gäste eines Pekinger Teehauses. Auch Tian Hans *Guan Hanqing* (1958) ist zu nennen; es beschreibt Guan Hanqing (13. Jh.) bei der Arbeit an seinem bedeutendsten Drama *Dou E yuan* (→zaju) und handelt damit von den schwierigen Bedingungen schriftstellerischer Arbeit – auch in der Gegenwart. Eine Belebung und Weiterentwicklung des C. S. gab es erst wieder nach der Kulturrevolution. Erstmals gab es eine breite Auseinandersetzung mit dem epischen Theater Brechts, nachdem in den Jahrzehnten zuvor Stanislawski das Feld beherrscht hatte. Junge Autoren wie Sha Yexin (* 1930) und Gao Xingjian (* 1940) traten mit inhaltlich und formal beachtlichen, teilweise sogar experimentellen Stücken hervor. Gao Xingjians Hauptanliegen besteht in der Erweiterung der darstellerischen Möglichkeiten des Sprechtheaters. Er will durch ein «totales

Theater» vom einfachen Sprechtheater fortkommen und Elemente des traditionellen Musiktheaters, der Musik, der Pantomime, des Puppentheaters und des Tanztheaters bis hin zur griechischen Tragödie und zum absurden Theater integrieren. Er beruft sich vor allem auf Antonin Artaud, der in seinem Manifest *Das Theater der Grausamkeit* ebenfalls «die Unterwerfung des Theaters unter den Text» zu durchbrechen versuchte, sowie auf Jerzy Grotowski und dessen «armes Theater». Heute lebt Gao Xingjian im Exil in Paris.

Eberstein, B. (Hg.): Moderne Stücke aus China. Frankfurt/M. 1980; Eberstein, B.: Das chinesische Theater im 20. Jahrhundert. Wiesbaden 1983; Eberstein, B. (ed.): A Selective Guide to Chinese Literature 1900–1949, Vol. 4: The Drama, Leiden 1990; Gunn, E. M. (ed.): Twentieth Century Chinese Drama – An Anthology. Bloomington (Ind.) 1983; Mackerras, C.: The Performing Arts in Contemporary China. London 1981; Tatlow, A./Wong, Tak-Wai (eds.): Brecht and East Asian Theatre. Hongkong 1982; Wagner, R.: The Contemporary Chinese Historical Drama – Four Studies. Berkeley/Los Angeles/London 1990.

Bernd Eberstein

Chinesisches Theater

Figurative und lebendige Darstellung scheint zu den elementaren Äußerungsformen des Menschen zu gehören. Im religiösen wie im säkularen Leben spielte sie sicherlich seit frühester Zeit eine Rolle. Dabei war sie mit kultischem Tanz eng verbunden, hatte aber auch schon erzählende Funktion. Wann also Vorformen des Theaters als der darstellenden und unterhaltenden Kunst in China entstanden sind, ist kaum mit Sicherheit zu sagen. Auf jeden Fall lassen sich auch in China als Ursprünge des Theaters ganz allg. Lieder, Tänze, religiöse Rituale und akrobatisches Varieté nennen. So kann es als sicher gelten, daß viele Gesänge im «Buch der Lieder» (*Shijing*) zu Musik- und Tanzbegleitung vorgetragen wurden, z. T. sogar im Wechselgesang. Auch die «Neun Lieder» (*Jiu ge*) des Qu Yuan (ca. 340–ca. 278 v. Chr.) waren bei einem Vortrag offenbar durch Musik und Tanz zu begleiten.

Ein weiterer Ursprung waren die Tänze der Schamanen anläßlich religiöser Zeremonien, wie sie sich vor und während der Zhou-Zeit (11. Jh.–221 v. Chr.) nachweisen lassen. Aus ihren, der Medien zwischen Götter- und Menschenwelt, Tanzbewegungen wurde die Zukunft gedeutet. Auch die Darstellungen der Hofnarren der Zhou- und der Han-Zeit (206 v. Chr.–220 n. Chr.) waren Vorformen des Theaters. Die Rolle dieser Narren war nicht nur die des Unterhalters und Clowns, sondern auch die des Witze- und Geschichtenerzählers. Sie konnten sogar, den Freiraum einer Fertigkeit nutzend, die außerhalb der etablierten Ordnung stand, durch ihre Vorstellungen und Worte den Fürsten direkt, aber deutlich kritisieren. Geradezu als Ahnherr der Schauspieler wurde der Komiker Meng (You Meng) verehrt.

Regelrechte, wenn auch einfache theatralische Aufführungen – eine Geschichte, dargestellt durch schauspielerische Mittel – lassen sich seit der Han-Zeit nachweisen. Ihr Name «Hunderterlei Spiele» (bai xi) oder «Hornkampf-Spiele» (jiaodi xi) weist bereits auf ihre ausgeprägt varietéhafte Eigenart hin: Schwertschlucker, Seiltänzer, Kletterkünstler, Jongleure, Gewichtheber, Feuerspeier u. a. Schausteller prägten dieses Theater, welches eher einem Zirkus ähnelte. Auch aus den folgenden Jh. gibt es Berichte über Spiele und Aufführungen, akrobatische wie dramatische; vielfach hatten sie nur zwei Rollen und waren i. d. R. nicht mehr als kurze Sketche und Farcen. Erst zur Tang-Zeit (618–907) gab es eine weitere Entwicklung. Naben den populären Formen der Varieté-Unterhaltung erlangte das sog. Adjutanten-Spiel (canjun xi) Beliebtheit, welches meist in einer einfachen Komödie mit nur zwei oder drei Rollen bestand, vor allem der des Schurken, Grauer Falke (canggu) genannt, und der des Adjutanten (canjun), der des ersteren Streiche und Schläge einstecken muß. Hier findet sich zum erstenmal eine gewisse Typisierung der →Rollenfächer, die für das C. T. so charakteristisch werden sollte. Die Entstehung des Stilmittels der Rollentypisierung liegt im dunkeln. Eine komödienhafte oder burleske Darstellung, die über keinen festgelegten Text in Form eines Librettos verfügte, deren Verlauf daher weitgehend improvisiert war, mag eine Typisierung immerhin nahegelegt, wenn nicht gar erfordert haben. Sie gab den Darstellern einen Rahmen, den sie durch Dialoge auszufüllen hatten. Ihr Verhalten, ihre Handlungen und Sprache waren dabei durch die Rolle weitgehend bestimmt. Hier lassen sich deutliche Parallelen zur europ. Commedia dell'arte des 16. bis 19. Jh. ziehen, wenn auch die Rollentypen sehr unterschiedlich waren. Darüber hinaus erleichterte die Typisierung der Rollen es dem Publikum, der Aufführung zu folgen. Ein Typ läßt sich im Gegensatz zum individuellen Charakter auf Anhieb erkennen. Gut und Böse auf der Bühne sind sofort ersichtlich und ermöglichen eine unmittelbare Identifizierung oder Ablehnung.

Zur Tang-Zeit wurde von Kaiser Xuanzong (reg. 712–56), einem großen Mäzen der Künste, die legendäre Musik- und Gesangschule im Birnengarten (→liyuan) gegründet. Sie hatte zwar direkt nichts mit dem Theater zu tun, sondern mit Musik und Unterhaltung; das aber ist eine moderne Unterscheidung. Das Theater der Tang-Zeit war noch untrennbar mit Unterhaltung, Belustigung, höfischem Zeitvertreib und populärer Lust am Staunen verbunden. Theater galt weiterhin in erster Linie als Zurschaustellung sensationeller Effekte und Fertigkeiten, nicht als Darstellung der Welt auf der Bühne.

Einen großen Einfluß bes. auf die Stoffe und Sujets späterer Bühnenstücke hatte die Entwicklung volkstümlicher Erzählungen ebenfalls zur Tang-Zeit. Sowohl die säkularen «Wundergeschichten» (chuanqi, nicht zu verwechseln mit der gleichnamigen Theaterform) als auch die buddhistischen Erbauungsgeschichten (bianwen), popularisierte Sutren und andere buddhistische Erzählungen, geschrieben, um den Buddhismus im Volk zu verbreiten, waren in diesem Zusammenhang bedeutsam. Viele dieser Geschichten wurden in fast dramatischer Weise, jedenfalls unter ausgiebiger Verwendung von Dialogen vorgetragen und später von Geschichtenerzählern (vgl. Kleine Theaterformen, →Quyi) ebenso wie von Dramatikern adaptiert. Die enge Verbindung zwischen dem Geschichtenerzählen und dem Drama wurde auf diese Weise während der Tang-Zeit begründet und blieb während der gesamten weiteren Geschichte des C. T. von Bedeutung.

Alles bisher Genannte kann indessen nur als ein den Weg für ein Theater im eigentlichen Sinne Bereitendes angesehen werden. Nur sehr langsam schälte sich das Theater, neben diesen Formen und aus ihnen hervorgehend, sie miteinander verschmelzend und integrierend, heraus. Erst während der Song-Dynastie (960–1279) wurde die Kombination der verschiedenartigen Komponenten, die für sich bereits in einer langen Tradition existierten, zu einem Theater immer offenbarer. Die Ursache lag einerseits in einer Art naturwüchsiger Entwicklung in Richtung auf diese Kombination, auf der anderen Seite in dem Aufschwung urbaner Zentren während dieser Zeit infolge der Blüte des Handels und des Handwerks. Es entstanden neue städtische Mittelschichten, die nach eigenen Formen der Unterhaltung und des literarischen Ausdrucks suchten. In der Hauptstadt Kaifeng, in Hangzhou, der Hauptstadt der Süd-Song (1127–1279), in Peking und in anderen Großstädten vor allem Zentralchinas entstanden bedeutende Vergnügungsviertel (wazi oder washi: «Ziegel-Viertel»), in denen auch zahlreiche Theaterhäuser errichtet wurden. In Kaifeng allein soll es etwa 50 Theater gegeben haben, deren größte 1000 und mehr Menschen Platz boten.

Das Theater der Song wurde als →zaju oder yuanben («Texte der Unterhaltungsquartiere», «Bordelltexte») bezeichnet. Leider ist keines der Stücke erhalten, so daß wir uns kaum ein Bild über deren Inhalt machen können. Sicher ist jedoch, daß das Rollenspektrum weiter ausgebaut war – die Stücke hatten vier bis sechs Rollen – und daß viele der Stücke vier Akte hatten, einen kurzen Schwank als Prolog, zwei Akte, in denen die Handlung des Stücks entwickelt wurde, und einen gleichfalls komischen Epilog. Immer noch hatten die Stücke meist burlesken Charakter. Besonders die yuanben galten bis in die Ming-Zeit als kurze komische Einakter, die oft einem anderen Stück vorangestellt, zumindest mit anderen Stücken zusammen gespielt wurden.

Kanton-Oper: Akrobatischer Tanz aus «Die Mysteriöse aus dem neunten Himmel» (FM)

Peking-Oper: «Der König der Affen besiegt seine Angreifer» (TS)

Chao-Oper: Szene aus «Die entlaufene Dirne» (FM)

Getsai-Oper: Die Götter des Reichtums, der Hohen Ämter und des langen Lebens zu Beginn einer Aufführung bei einer Bühnenweihe (FM)

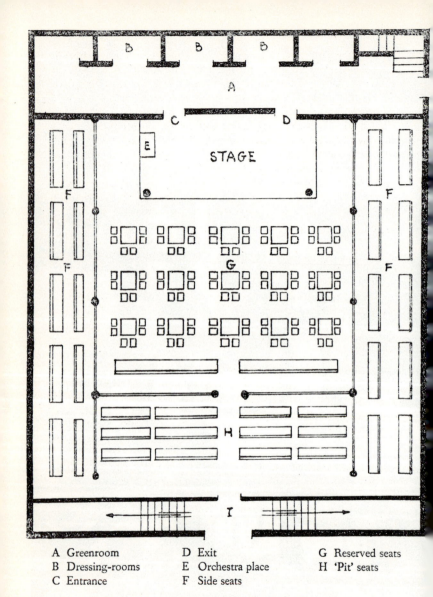

A Greenroom D Exit G Reserved seats
B Dressing-rooms E Orchestra place H 'Pit' seats
C Entrance F Side seats

Grundriß eines traditionellen chinesischen Theaters:
Zuschauerraum und Bühnenanlage (TS)

In der Song-Zeit tauchte außerdem ein Phänomen auf, welches die spätere Diversifizierung der Theaterstile einleitete: die Teilung der Theatertradition in eine nördliche und eine südliche. Diese Teilung hatte vielfältige Ursachen. Zunächst verlagerte sich mit dem rapiden wirtschaftlichen Aufschwung der Region im Einzugsbereich des unteren Yangzijiang das wirtschaftliche und damit auch das kulturelle Zentrum Chinas nach Süden. Der Norden blieb allerdings meistens Sitz der Hauptstadt und damit politisches Zentrum. Aber auch der außenpolitische Konflikt der Song-Dynastie trug dazu bei: Wegen des Vordringens nomadischer Völker im Norden Chinas mußte sich die Dynastie nach Süden zurückziehen, wo sie in Hangzhou ihre zeitweilige Residenz errichtete. Auch das gab dem südlichen Theater (→ nanxi) sicherlich Impulse.

Als klassische Zeit des C. T. gilt mit einigem Recht die der mongolischen Yuan-Dynastie (1280–1368). In dem knappen Jh. ihrer Herrschaft versuchten die Yuan, in China einen Gesellschaftsaufbau durchzusetzen, welcher die Chinesen selbst diskriminierte. Für die Gebildeten wurden jahrzehntelang keine Staatsprüfungen abgehalten, die den einzigen Weg zu sozialem Ansehen und politischem Einfluß darstellten. Also zogen sie sich vom Getriebe der Welt zurück und wandten sich anderen Tätigkeiten zu. Nicht wenige Gebildete widmeten sich erstmals ernsthaft dem Theater, so daß die politische Katastrophe zu einem Glücksfall für das Theater wurde. Manche sahen im Schreiben von Dramen sogar eine Möglichkeit, ihre Opposition gegen die Herrschaft der Yuan auszudrücken. In diesem aktiven Interesse der Gebildeten mag der Hauptgrund gesucht werden, warum das Theater so plötzlich im → zaju der Yuan-Zeit einen literarischen Höhepunkt erreichte, warum es in dieser Zeit seine ganze thematische Vielfalt und Besonderheit entfaltete. Einige der größten chin. Dramatiker wie Guan Hanqing, Ma Zhiyuan, Bai Pu und Wang Shifu lebten zu dieser Zeit.

Überraschend und einzigartig für China ist also der sehr jähe Übergang von dem noch sehr in der Burleske verhafteten Song-Drama zur literarischen Breite und Tiefe des Yuan zaju, aber auch das sehr späte Auftauchen des Dramas als reife literarische Form in der chin. Literaturgeschichte, bes. wenn man diese Entwicklung mit der europ. vergleicht. In der europ. Literatur und Literaturtheorie spielten das Theater und Drama bereits sehr früh eine bedeutende Rolle – Aristoteles' *Poetik* handelt hauptsächlich vom Drama –, während es sich in China erst spät entwickelte und auch dann von der orthodoxen Literaturkritik bis ins 20. Jh. kaum als Literatur angesehen wurde. Nur verhältnismäßig wenige unorthodoxe Persönlichkeiten wagten es, dieser Bewertung entgegenzutreten und dem Drama den gleichen Rang zuzuweisen wie dem Gedicht, den philosophischen Klassikern, dem Essay oder der Geschichtsschreibung. Thomas Mann sagte in seiner «Rede über das Theater»: «Ich glaube, daß das Theater die Urheimat ist aller sinnlichen Geistigkeit und geistigen Sinnlichkeit; daß das Theater immer und jedenfalls den Anfang der künstlerischen Regung bildet.» Das mag eine zutreffende Beobachtung für Europa gewesen sein. Sie trifft aber nicht für das C. T. zu, welches vielmehr am Ende der dortigen künstlerischen Regungen stand. Gewiß können einige zeremonielle lyrische Dialoge, wie sie im «Buch der Lieder» (*Shijing*) zu finden sind, sowie die Tatsache, daß diese Gesänge zur Instrumentenbegleitung gesungen und sogar durch rituelle und festliche Tänze begleitet wurden, als mögliche Vorformen des Theaters angesehen werden. Anders aber als in Europa, wo es ähnliche Erscheinungen gab, hatte sich daraus kein Theater entwickelt. In genauem Gegensatz zur griech. Poetik, welche nur das narrative epische Gedicht und das mimetische Drama als wirklich literarische Genres ansah und dem lyrischen Gedicht höchstens einen Platz am Rande einräumte, galt in China das lyrische Gedicht seit dem *Shijing* und den Gedichten Qu Yuans, seit dem Beginn der Literatur also, als eigentliche und höchste literarische Form. Beide Haltungen hatten einen tiefen Eindruck auf die jeweilige Literatur insgesamt.

Als die großen Persönlichkeiten der chin. Literatur galten die Dichter und die Schriftsteller nichterzählender Prosa, die Verfasser von Essays, nicht aber die Dramatiker. Guan Hanqing, Ma Zhiyuan und Tang Xianzu lagen in der literarischen Wertschätzung weit unter den Dichtern Li Bo und Du Fu; tatsächlich galten sie kaum als Literaten. Und den Dramen der Yuan-Zeit wurde bei weitem nicht der literarische Rang zuerkannt wie den Gedichten der Tang-Zeit. Zur Zeit der Blüte des chin. Dramas, während der Yuan- und frühen Ming-Dynastie, hatte es Tendenzen gegeben, dem Drama einen gewissen literarischen Wert zuzuerkennen. Die «Große Enzyklopädie der Yongle-Zeit» (*Yongle dadian*) aus dem Jahr 1408, in der über 2000 Gelehrte versucht hatten, alle bedeutenden literarischen Werke festzuhalten, hatte immerhin 33 Dramen enthalten (von denen allerdings nur drei erhalten sind). Diese Tendenz konnte sich aber nicht durchsetzen. Nicht ein einziges Theaterstück wurde drei Jh. später in die mit ähnlichem Anspruch konzipierte kaiserliche Bibliothek *Siku quanshu* aufgenommen, welche 1771 bis 1782 zusammengestellt wurde und 3450 Werke enthielt. Der letzte Abschnitt des Katalogs, welcher für dieses Sammelwerk verfaßt wurde, nennt Sammlungen von ci-Gedichten und dramatischen Liedern (qu); in einer Vorbemerkung aber heißt es, daß diese von sehr geringem literarischen Wert seien. Seit den Tang-Gedichten, auf dem Weg über die ci-Gedichte der Song- und die Lieder der Yuan-Zeit habe die Literatur sich in einem dauernden Niedergang befunden. Daher war es nicht überraschend, daß die Dramen, die als literarisches Genre auf die Lieder folgten, nicht für wert erachtet wurden, in die kaiserliche Sammlung aufgenommen zu werden. Für den Literaten und

Gelehrten in China also stand das Theater und Drama außerhalb und unterhalb der Literatur. Weder galt es ihm als Teil der traditionellen noch der überlieferungswürdigen Literatur, in der alles, was er als Kultur ansah, so eindrucksvoll zum Ausdruck kam. Theater war «wertloses Gerede» (xiaoshuo), bestenfalls zu dulden als triviale Unterhaltung und Spielerei. – So gesehen entsprang das Drama der Yuan-Zeit einer historischen und kulturellen Ausnahmesituation. Es gab auch später immer wieder große Dramatiker, nie wieder aber in so großer Anzahl wie im späten 13. und frühen 14. Jh.

Das zaju spielte auch nach der Yuan-Zeit eine wichtige Rolle im chin. Theaterleben. Aber es wurde während der Ming-Zeit (1368–1644) vom →chuanqi als populärer Theaterform verdrängt, welches in seiner sehr viel freieren formalen Gestaltung der freien Entfaltung der Phantasie und des Handlungsablaufs entgegenkam. Wie das zaju war auch das chuanqi eine literarische Theaterform. Auf literarischen Stil und gebildete Sprache war bei seiner Abfassung mindestens ebenso zu achten wie auf Bühnenwirksamkeit. Seine höchste Entwicklung fand das chuanqi als südliche Theaterform im →kunqu, welches seit dem 16. Jh. an Bedeutung gewann. Alle großen Dramatiker des 16. bis 18. Jh. schrieben ihre Dramen in dieser Form, vor allem Tang Xianzu, Kong Shangren und Hong Sheng. Das kunqu hatte sich aber als hochverfeinerte, sprachlich und formal sehr schwierige Theaterform der Gebildeten sehr weit von den populären Ursprüngen des Theaters entfernt. Das war ein wesentlicher Grund dafür, daß in der Ming-Zeit eine Entwicklung einsetzte, welche im 19. Jh. ihren Höhepunkt fand und den volkstümlichen Aspekten des Theaters Rechnung trug: die Auffächerung in viele verschiedene Stile des Lokalen Theaters (→difang xi).

Auch die →Pekingoper war zunächst lediglich einer dieser lokalen Theaterstile. Da sie aber, vom Hof direkt gefördert, seit dem frühen 19. Jh. in der Hauptstadt florierte, konnte sie sich im Laufe der Zeit in ganz China als «nationales Theater» (guoju) ausbreiten. In einer wichtigen Hinsicht indessen blieb sie den anderen Lokaltheater-Stilen stets gleich: Im eklatanten Unterschied zum zaju, chuanqi und kunqu war und blieb sie vor allem Bühnentheater. In der Pekingoper traten keine bedeutenden Dramatiker hervor, sehr wohl aber große Schauspieler. Durch deren Darstellungskunst allein wurde sie getragen, nicht durch die Qualität des Textes, sprachliche und formale Raffinesse. Ohnehin wurden die Texte der Pekingoper in den seltensten Fällen aufgeschrieben. Dementsprechend sah das 19. Jh. die ersten wirklichen Stars des C. T. Vor allem einige Darsteller des Rollenfachs (→juese) laosheng, «älterer Mann», gewannen eine vorher undenkbare Berühmtheit. Da durch dieses Rollenfach meist große Kaiser, Staatsmänner und Heerführer der chin. Geschichte dargestellt wurden, erwies sich das Theater einmal mehr als Seismograph politischer Entwicklungen und kollektiver Empfindungen. Die Bedrohung durch den Imperialismus europ. Staaten, welche auf Kosten der chin. Souveränität und des Selbstbewußtseins als kulturelles Zentrum der Welt im Laufe des 19. Jh. immer mehr Vorrechte erzwangen, führte dazu, daß sich die Chinesen im Theater der großen Persönlichkeiten der eigenen Geschichte entsannen.

Die Blüte des zaju zur Yuan-Zeit, die Verfeinerung der Ausdrucksformen im chuanqi und kunqu gegen Ende der Ming-Zeit, der Siegeszug der Pekingoper im 19. und das Aufkommen des →chinesischen Sprechtheaters im 20. Jh. zeigen, daß das Theater und Drama in China gerade in seinen Blütezeiten stets auch Ausdruck politischer und geistiger Krisen war.

Das chin. Musiktheater – das zeigt sich in der heutigen Pekingoper und in den lokalen Theaterformen besonders deutlich – ist Gesamtkunstwerk. Dem Publikum stellt es sich dar als eine organische Verschmelzung von visuellen und akustischen Eindrücken, von sinnlichen und intellektuellen Herausforderungen, von Musik, Gesang, verschiedenen Formen des sprachlichen Ausdrucks, von Bewegung des Körpers in Tanz, Gestik und Akrobatik, von mimischem Gesichtsausdruck und von Elementen der bildenden Kunst auf der Bühne, in den Kostümen und den Masken. Hierbei wird zu jedem Zeitpunkt streng darauf geachtet, daß keines der konstitutiven Elemente dieser Synthese, die anderen Elemente in den Hintergrund drängend, zu stark betont hervortritt. Wesentlich ist also das harmonische Zusammenwirken dieser Elemente. Damit ist dem chin. Musiktheater seit jeher eine Eigenschaft ganz wesentlich zu eigen, um die sich das europ. Musiktheater in Erinnerung an das klassische griech. Theater erst seit der Mitte des 19. Jh. bemüht, die indes nur selten erreicht wurde: die Einheit von Bühnengeschehen und Musik.

Als Gesamtkunstwerk bedient sich das C. T. einer stark typisierten, stilisierten und symbolhaften Weise des Ausdrucks. Eine solche Ausdrucksform setzt beim Publikum selbstverständlich Kenntnisse voraus. Die vielen stilisierten Bewegungsabläufe können – jenseits der unmittelbar ins Auge springenden Schönheit und Harmonie der Bewegungen – erst dann richtig beurteilt und genossen werden, wenn man ihren Sinn kennt, die Realität hinter der Abstraktion versteht. Diese Fähigkeit auf seiten des Publikums konnte offenbar immer in hinreichender Weise vorausgesetzt werden.

Das Theater ist wohl überall die sinnlichste aller Künste. Das tritt gerade in China so deutlich hervor, wo die Kunst – Literatur und bildende Kunst – durch einen hohen Grad der Abstraktion geprägt war. Auch dem Theater ist die Abstraktion selbstverständlich nicht fremd; zu ihm als Gesamtkunstwerk gehört notwendig eine Synthese von Sinnlichkeit und Abstraktion in der Darstellung. Wie jedes Theater ist auch das chin. Darstel-

Chinesisches Theater   231

lung der Welt auf der Bühne, Kunstwelt also. Aber in einem bestimmten Sinne ist die so dargestellte Welt wohl realistischer als die reale Welt; denn diese ist im chin. Kunstverständnis durch eine Fülle von Er-Scheinungen verstellt. In der Kunst fällt der Schein, und die dahinterstehende innere Realität tritt hervor. Das chin. Musiktheater, welches auf den ersten – und bei dem nicht Kundigen gewiß auch zweiten – Blick so weit entfernt von der Realität und extrem gekünstelt erscheint, ist tatsächlich zutiefst realistisch. Es ist Darstellung der nicht unmittelbar sichtbaren Welt, der Innenwelt der dargestellten Charaktere, der Idealwelt des Autors oder auch des Publikums, der Idealwelt aber im urspr. Wortsinn als innerer Bildwelt. Zusammenfassend kann man sagen: Das C. T. zeigt die Welt, wie sie ist, nicht wie sie erscheint.

In der Form, wie sich das chin. Musiktheater im 19. und frühen 20. Jh. entwickelt hatte, wird es im wesentlichen auch heute noch gespielt. Eine grundsätzlich neue Entwicklung hat es lediglich durch die Einführung des Sprechtheaters nach europ. Vorbild gegeben. Auch das Musiktheater hat einige Entwicklungen durchgemacht. So traten im 20. Jh. vor allem in der Pekingoper anstatt der Darsteller «älterer Männer» (laosheng) diejenigen von Frauenrollen (dan) in den Vordergrund, deren bedeutendster Repräsentant, Mei Lanfang (1894–1961), zum bekanntesten Schauspieler überhaupt wurde (s. a. →Juese: «Rollenfächer»). Auch wurde unter dem Einfluß des europ. Theaters mit neuen Aufführungsformen, bes. der Verwendung von Kulissen, experimentiert, ohne überzeugenden Erfolg allerdings. Neue Themen fanden Eingang in das Repertoire der Stücke, wobei insbesondere wiederholt die Möglichkeit diskutiert wurde, Gegenwartsthemen auf die Bühne des traditionellen Musiktheaters zu bringen. Bis heute ist diese Frage nicht entschieden. Hinsichtlich der Pekingoper ist die Ansicht am weitesten verbreitet, welche das moderne Sprechtheater als alleiniges Mittel ansieht, die Gegenwart mit ihren Problemen auf der Bühne darzustellen; die Pekingoper dagegen solle bei den traditionellen historischen Themen bleiben. Auch mit diesen läßt sich ja, wenn beabsichtigt, eine Meinung zu Gegenwartsfragen vorbringen, verschlüsselt zwar, aber deswegen für chin. Augen und Ohren nicht weniger deutlich.

Trotz dieser Versuche der Anpassung an unsere Zeit befindet sich das chin. Musiktheater heute in einer Krise. Diese macht sich – neben der vielfach beklagten mangelhaften Ausbildung und Qualität der Schauspieler, aber mit dieser wohl auch zusammenhängend – am deutlichsten in einer wachsenden Distanz des Publikums zu dieser Form des Theaters bemerkbar. Besonders jüngere Menschen stehen dem Musiktheater heute fern. Vielfach sind sie so wenig vertraut mit ihm, daß sie die Symbolik der Ausdrucksmittel nicht verstehen und die Qualität des Vortrags nicht mehr beurteilen können. Sie wenden sich daher dem einfacheren Sprechtheater oder noch eher dem Kino zu. Will das Musiktheater als verbreitete und lebendige Kunstform weiter bestehenbleiben, muß ein Weg gefunden werden, das Publikum erneut an diese Kunstform heranzuführen. S. a. →Piaoyou (Laienschauspieler); →Quyi (Kleine Theaterformen); →Muou xi, Kuilei xi (Puppentheater); →Yingxi (Chin. Schattentheater).

Dolby, W.: A History of Chinese Drama. London 1976; Eberstein, B.: Das chinesische Theater im 20. Jahrhundert. Wiesbaden 1983; Hsu Tao-ching: The Chinese Conception of the Theatre. Seattle/Wash. 1985; Scott, A. C.: The Classical Theatre of China. New York 1957; Zhang Geng/Guo Hancheng: Zhongguo xiqu tongshi. 3 vols. Peking 1980–81; Zhou Yibai: Zhongguo xiqu fazhan shi gangyao. Shanghai 1979.

Bernd Eberstein

Chor

Wichtiger Bestandteil des antiken Dramas; das Wort bezeichnet ursprünglich eine Gruppe von Tänzern bzw. den mit Gesang verbundenen Tanz. Der C. ist die Keimzelle des antiken Dramas, in dessen entwickelten Formen, Tragödie, Satyrspiel und Komödie, der C. und seine Lieder weiterhin eine bedeutungsvolle dramatische und thematische Rolle spielen; in Tragödie und Satyrspiel besteht der C. zunächst aus 12, seit Sophokles aus 15 Chorleuten; in der Komödie aus 24. Leiter und Sprecher des C. im Dialog mit den Schauspielern ist der Chorführer (→Koryphaios); der Platz des C. ist in der →Orchestra, in die er zu Beginn des Spiels (meist nach dem Schauspielerprolog) einzieht (→Parodos), wo er zwischen den →Epeisodia seine Chorlieder singt und tanzt und die er in der Regel vor seinem Auszug am Ende des Stücks nicht verläßt. Der C. fungiert als Betrachter und Kommentator des Bühnengeschehens, an dem er aber zugleich immer, wenn auch in unterschiedlichem Maße, als Akteur beteiligt ist; in der aristophaneischen Komödie spricht er in der →Parabase außerdem im Namen des Dichters direkt zum Publikum. Im Verlaufe des 5. Jh. verringerte sich die thematische Bedeutung des C. und der Umfang seiner dramatischen Rolle immer mehr; in der Tragödie führte diese Entwicklung zum →Embolimon, in der Komödie noch einen Schritt weiter zur reinen Zwischenaktmusik. Die römische Tragödie übernimmt den C. der von ihr bearbeiteten griech. Tragödien; die Komödie behält ihn dagegen nicht einmal in der reduzierten Form als ‹Pausenfüller› bei. Seit der Erfindung der hellenistischen →Proskenion-Bühne agiert der auch zahlenmäßig reduzierte C. nicht mehr in der Orchestra, sondern steht neben den Schauspielern auf der Bühne. Abgesehen von den stark von der antiken (zunächst der senecanischen, dann auch der griech.) Tragödie geprägten Anfängen des europ. ernsten Dramas spielt der C. im Sprechtheater der Neuzeit nur eine geringe Rolle. Großartige einzelne Wiederaufnahmen des antiken C. von Miltons *Samson Agonistes*, über Shelleys *Prometheus Unbound*, Manzonis *Aldechi* und Goethes *Faust II* bis zu T. S. Eliots *Murder in the Cathedral* haben daran ebenso wenig geändert wie die theoretischen Wiederbelebungsversuche am Anfang des 19. Jh. (z. B. Schiller, Vorwort zur *Braut von Messina*).

Dale, A. M.: Words, Music, and Dance (1960). In: A. M. Dale: Collected Paper. Cambridge 1969, p. 156–169; Kaimio, M.: The Chorus of Greek Drama. Helsinki 1970; Kranz, W.: Stasimon. Berlin 1933; Webster, T. B. L.: The Greek Chorus. London 1970.

Bernd Seidensticker

Choreodrama

Im Gegensatz zum vorwiegend geschrittenen, die untänzerischen mimischen und gestischen Ausdrucksformen des Körpers nutzenden Dramma pantomimico will das C. durchgetanzt werden. Der totale Körper wird zum Instrument allen tänzerischen Ausdrucksvermögens. Das Corps de ballet verselbständigt sich und erhält dramaturgisch eigenständige Aufgaben. Einerseits erlebt es prägnante Individualisierung (z. B. Fokins *Petruschka*, Paris 1911), andererseits dient es als Masse der Symbolisierung, etwa in der Bedeutung Anklage, Aufbruch oder Widerstand etc.

Geschichte: Geboren aus den Zielsetzungen des Ballettheaters ab 1800. Noverre (1727–1810), Hilverding (1710–68), Angiolini (1723–96) und Didelot (1767–1836/37) treten theoretisch und in ihrer künstlerischen Arbeit für das geschlossene Ballett-Kunstwerk ein (→Ballet héroïque-pantomime). Vigano (1769–1821) nennt seine heroisch-expressiven Choreographien (*Prometeo; Giovanna d'Arco*) erstmalig C. – Carlo Blasis (1797–1878) erweitert den Weg zum Tanzdrama, indem er feinsinnig die Charaktere der Figuren durchgestaltet. Mittel der Charakterisierung: Gebärden und Musikformen, z. B. Volkstänze. – Die Russen Fokin (1880–1942) und Gorski (1871–1924) vertreten die weitestgehende Individualisierung des Corps de ballet. Geschlossene Chorformationen werden aufgelöst (exzellente Lösung in der Jahrmarktsszene zu *Petruschka*). Dem →Ausdruckstanz dient das C. als Ansatz. 1913: *Orpheus*-Inszenierung von Dalcroze in →Hellerau. Chorische Reigenführung. Laban: Weihedramen, Mysterienspiele in Freilicht- und Hallenaufführungen (→Labanschulen: *Agamemnon*, 1924; Lola Rogge: *Lübecker Totentanz*, 1956). Rudolf Steiner inszeniert von 1910 bis 1913 vier «Mysteriendramen» und ab 1915 den *Faust* mit aufgelockerter Chorführung, Musik und Sprache (→Eurythmische Kunst). – 1930 bis 1950: Ära der großen sowj.

234 Choreographie/Choreograph

Sujetaufführungen. In dieser Epoche des C. treten reale durchgestaltete Charaktere auf, szenische Zeichnungen werden exakt ausgefeilt. Historischer Stil, konkrete Details, Integration aller Solisten in die Tanzgruppe, soziale Aussagen.

Gregor, J.: Kulturgeschichte des Balletts. Zürich o. J./Wien 1944; Grigorowitsch, J.: Synthese der Traditionen. In: Die Welt des Tanzes in Selbstzeugnissen. Hg. von Wolgina, L., Pietzsch, U. Wilhelmshaven [2]1979, S. 310–312; Reyna, F.: Das Buch vom Ballett. Paris 1955; Schmidt-Garre, H.: Ballett. Vom Sonnenkönig bis Balanchine. Hannover 1966.

Helga Ettl

Choreographie/Choreograph

Der Begriff läßt sich von «choros» (= Reigentanz, Tanzplatz, Tanzschar) und «graph» (= schreiben) ableiten. Im wörtlichen Sinn ist darunter die Aufzeichnung, die schriftliche Fixierung von Tanzschritten in ihrer räumlichen Anordnung zu verstehen. Versuche, Tänze zu notieren, soll es bereits bei den Ägyptern und Römern gegeben haben. Die älteste bekannte Notation stammt aus dem 15. Jh. Seitdem sind parallel zur Entwicklung der Choreographie immer wieder neue Aufzeichnungsmethoden entworfen worden (→ Tanznotation). Auf die Bühne bezogen versteht man unter Choreographie die gesamte Komposition eines Tanzwerks, das eine Idee mit den Mitteln der Bewegung auf der Grundlage einer Musik und unter Einbeziehung von Licht, Bühnenbild, Kostüm, Maske darstellt. Der Choreograph ist der Gestalter, der Schöpfer einer Tanzkomposition.

Bedeutet Choreographie im 16. Jh. noch das Arrangieren eines Hofrituals, eines sogenannten Hofballetts (→ Ballet de Cour), das sich in stark geometrischen Formen ereignet, so erweitert sich der choreographische Spielraum in dem Moment, wo sich Bewegung nicht nur als zeremonielle Funktion auf ihre formalen Eigenheiten beruft, sondern Ausdruck dramatischen Geschehens wird und als Handlungsträger fungiert. Dieser Schritt vollzieht sich im 17. Jh. und wird durch Jean-Georges Noverre und Gasparo Angiolini im 18. Jh. theoretisch fundiert. Beide fordern die Einheit der Handlung innerhalb eines Balletts mit Hilfe der Pantomime und der Ausdrucksbewegungen. Tanzformen werden dabei mit pantomimischen Sequenzen, die sich z. T. auf ganze Akte konzentrieren, verbunden. Im 19. Jh. (→ ballet blanc) kommt es verstärkt zu einer Verschmelzung der dramaturgisch aus dem Handlungsverlauf bestimmten Ausdrucksbewegungen bzw. pantomimischen Bewegungen mit den aus der Choreographie, dem Tanz selbst bezogenen. Eine Emanzipation der Choreographie, und das heißt die Befreiung von einer literarisch verstandenen

Dramaturgie, vollzieht sich im 20. Jh. durch Choreographen wie Michail Fokine, Vaslav Nijinsky (→Ballets Russes) und die Vertreter des →Ausdruckstanzes wie Isadora Duncan, Rudolf von Laban oder Mary Wigman. Die Bewegung selbst wird zur Schlüsselposition, d. h., sie muß aus dem Bewegungskontext bzw. aus der psychologischen Konstellation der Situation heraus motiviert sein. Die Choreographie bezeichnet nicht länger eine narrative Struktur, konzentriert sich nicht auf eine literarische Vorlage, sondern steht für das, was den Tänzer bewegt. Körperbewegungen spiegeln die Person, gewinnen ihre Impulse aus der Konfrontation von Individuum und Umwelt. Für die nachfolgende Generation des →Post Modern Dance, zu deren wegweisenden Vertretern Merce Cunnigham zählt, wird die Bewegung schließlich zum Ausdruck ihrer selbst, zum reinen Selbstzweck. Sie fungiert nicht mehr als Vehikel beispielsweise emotionaler Repräsentation.

Jeschke, C.: Dramaturgie, Choreographie und Bühnentanz. In: Klein, M. (Hg.): Tanzforschung. Jahrbuch Bd. 2. Wilhelmshaven 1991; Schneider, O.: Tanzlexikon. Wien/Main 1985.

Patricia Stöckemann

Chorodidaskalos

Bezeichnung für (professionellen) Chorleiter, der (an Stelle des Dichters) die Chorlieder choreographierte und einstudierte.

Bernd Seidensticker

Christmas Pantomime

In Großbritannien bis in die Gegenwart beliebte Form der Weihnachtsunterhaltung, bestehend aus einer Mischung von →Burleske, musikalischer Komödie, →Féerie und →Revue, verbunden mit einer Harlekinade, deren Hauptfiguren aus der →Commedia dell'arte stammen. Verwandlungen und Lichteffekte, musikalische und akrobatische Einlagen sind eingearbeitet in Stücke, in denen sich Märchen-, Sagen- und historische Motive häufig mischen. Im Gegensatz zur eigentlichen →Pantomime verzichtet die C. P. keineswegs auf Benutzung von Sprache. Entstanden in der ersten Hälfte des 18. Jh. als übliches Nachspiel im Theater, wurden im Lauf des 19. Jh. die sich ausweitenden und verändernden Harlekinaden zur beliebten Form familiärer Unterhaltung.

Kindermann, H.: Theatergeschichte Europas, Bd. IV. Salzburg 1961; Wilson, A. E.: Christmas Pantomime. London 1934.

Wolfgang Beck

Chuanqi

Im Bereiche des Theaters ist chuanqi (wörtlich: «Bericht über Merkwürdiges») die Bezeichnung für das südliche Theater der Ming- und Qing-Dynastie. Es ging aus dem →nanxi der Song- und Yuan-Zeit hervor, war literarisch aber sehr viel verfeinerter als dieses. Nichts am chuanqi erinnert mehr an die inhaltliche und sprachliche Derbheit, aber auch erfrischende Direktheit seiner Ursprünge. Ein chuanqi war meist sehr lang, nicht selten hatte es 40 bis 50 Akte oder Bilder. Es konnte daher kaum an einem Tag aufgeführt werden; oft wurde es an mehreren Abenden oder Tagen hintereinander gespielt. In der Qing-Zeit ging man wegen der Länge der Stücke dazu über, nur einzelne bes. eindrucksvolle Episoden und Szenen aus einem Stück zu spielen. – Das chuanqi ging in das →kunqu über, beeinflußte aber auch zahlreiche andere lokale Theaterstile (→difang xi).

Als chuanqi werden auch die Novellen der Tang-Zeit bezeichnet; sogar für das →zaju der Yuan-Zeit wurde dieser Begriff zuweilen verwendet. Diese begrifflichen Probleme, die auch im Falle des nanxi zu beobachten sind, können als eine Folge der relativen Geringschätzung volkstümlicher literarischer Formen durch die orthodox-konfuzianischen Gebildeten gewertet werden.

Bernd Eberstein

Claque

(Frz. = klatschen) Dieses Wort zur Bezeichnung bestellter und bezahlter Beifallklatscher (Claqueure) ist um die Mitte des 19. Jh. in Paris aufgekommen und bald darauf auch in Deutschland benutzt worden. Die Claqueure sollen den allgemeinen Beifall (→ Applaus) anregen und somit den Erfolg eines Theaterstücks oder einer Oper bzw. eines Schauspielers oder Sängers sichern. Schon in der Antike war die C. üblich und gut bezahlt, z. B. bei Bühnenauftritten Neros. Im römischen Volkstheater wurden ‹favorites› verpflichtet, die durch vorher abgesprochenen Beifall das Publikum in Stimmung bringen sollten, während die sog. ‹conquisitores› durch die Sitzreihen gingen, um solches bestelltes Beifallklatschen zu unterbinden. Die C. war ebenfalls im Mittelalter, in der Renaissance, in der elisabethanischen Zeit und im spanischen Barocktheater (die ‹mosqueteros›) bekannt. Im 19. Jh., der Zeit ihrer Hochblüte, ist die C. in allen großen Theaterstädten üblich und in Paris besonders entwickelt; hier übernahm die 1820 von Lanton gegründete ‹Assurance de succès dramatique› gegen festes Honorar Aufträge für alle Arten des Beifalls bzw. der Ablehnung: Klatschen, Trampeln, Beifallsmurmeln, Nebenbemerkungen, Ausrufe, Lachen bzw. Schluchzen, Dacaporufe bis hin zur Empfehlung des Stücks an Anschlagsäulen, in Cafés und Restaurants. Heute beschränkt sich die C. auf die Opernwelt.

Bernard Poloni

Collage

(Frz.: Aufkleben) Bezeichnung für ein künstlerisches Verfahren einer zitierenden Kombination von vorgefertigtem Material sowie für derartig entstandene künstlerische Produkte (→ Montage). – Alle Materialien sind für die C. prinzipiell gleichwertig, erfahrbar wird die Außenstruktur, da kein übergeordnetes, formales Konstruktionsprinzip einen integrierenden Zusammenhang bildet. Daher bekommt die Produktion wie die Rezeption einen prozessualen Charakter, zu realisieren ist die Spannung zwischen den zwei Ebenen des Materials: seiner Physis (Signifikant) und seiner Bedeutung (Signifikat). Das Grundverfahren der C., das addierende ‹Aufkleben› von ‹gefundenem› Material auf eine durch Rahmung definierte Fläche, wandte erstmals Gertrude Stein (1874–1946) in ihren Landschaftsstücken (*Four Saints in Three Acts*, 1927; *Listen to me*, 1936) an. Der dramatische Diskurs erscheint als C. von Stimmen, die als theatralische Figuren erkennbar werden, die Handlung wird zu einer Bewegung der Syntax. Wortbündel, ein reduktiv prädikatloser Satzbau und emblematischen Wert bekommende Wortwiederholungen funktionieren wie kubistische papier collé als syntaktische cut-outs, als ironische Reflexionen über das Verhältnis von Illusion und Authentizität, Faktischem und Fiktivem, dem ästhetischen Schein und dem empirisch Gegebenen. Stein kreiert so einen kaleidoskopischen Effekt durch eine Zersplitterung der Sprache, deren Fragmente sich verschiedenen Darstellungskonstellationen anpassen lassen. Steins Konstruktionsprinzip der Aufhebung der dramatischen Figur durch additive Multiplizierung wurde zur Standardmethode der Theateravantgarde der 70er Jahre. Es antizipierte die formal-informale Struktur der Stücke von Robert Wilson (*1941), die erkenntnistheoretische Tendenz der Arbeiten Richard Foremans und die opernhaften Mischformen des Tanztheaters von Pina Bausch (*1940).

Wescher, H.: Geschichte der Collage. Köln 1974; Hage, V. (Hg.): Literarische Collagen. Texte, Quellen, Theorie. Stuttgart 1981; Stein, G.: How Writing is Written. Ed. by R. B. Haas. Vol. II. Los Angeles 1974.

Ulrich Stein

Comedia / Siglo de Oro / Goldenes Zeitalter

Sammelbegriff für das span. Theater des ‹Siglo de Oro› (16./17. Jh.), der Komödie, Tragödie und Tragikomödie umfaßte (→ Arte Nuevo de hacer Comedias en este Tiempo). Merkmalskriterien nach der Poetik von Lope Félix de Vega Carpio (1609). Die große Zahl der auf 30000 geschätzten C. erklärt sich aus den geringen Wiederholungen, meist nur drei Aufführungen je Stück. Veröffentlichung der erfolgreichen C. in Sammlungen von zwölf Titeln (Partes) oder Einzeldrucken (Sueltas). Gattungseinteilung meist nach Inhalten: Mythologie, Geschichte, Sitten und Gebräuche, Bibelstoffe, Schäfer- und Ritterdramen. Am beliebtesten waren die Mantel- und Degenstücke (comedia de capa y espada). Unter den Symbolen dieser Requisiten höherer Stände entfaltete sich eine dramatische Handlung, die nach mancherlei Wechselfällen im Duell um Liebesaffären gipfelte, wobei der Ehrbegriff die Hauptrolle spielte. Die Stücke wurden auf der Volks-(→Corral-)bühne im Innenhof eines Häuserblocks oder auf den Palast-(Hof-)bühnen aufgeführt. – Ab 1621 sorgten hochdotierte ital. Bühnendekorateure für die raffiniertesten Perspektiven und Prospekte, um Schiffbrüche, Erdbeben, fliegende und im Meer versinkende Gottheiten innerhalb weniger Stunden darzustellen. Bekannteste Vorläufer der C. im 15. und 16. Jh.: Gil Vicente (1465?–1536, zweispr. port./span.), Juan del Encina (1469?–1529?), Bartolomé de Torres Naharro (zw. 1480/ 90–1524?), Lope de Rueda (1505?–65), Juan de la Cueva (1543–1610) u. a. Das span. →Barocktheater im 17. Jh. bewegte sich um die Schule von Lope de Vega (meist Volkstheater), Hauptvertreter: Guillén de Castro y Bellvís (1569–1631), Tirso de Molina (d. i. Fray Gabriel Téllez, 1584?–1648), Juan Ruiz de Alarcón y Mendoza (1581?–1639), Luis Vélez de Guevara (1579–1644), Antonio Mira de Amescua (1574/77–1644) u.a. und um die Schule von Pedro Calderón de la Barca (1600–81), Hauptvertreter: Francisco de Rojas Zorrilla (1607–48), Agustín Moreto y Cavana (1618–69) u. a. Stofflich variierten die Dramatiker häufig die drei Elementarkräfte Liebe, Ehre, Sieg des Guten über das Böse (mit religiöser Intention).

Die Rezeption des span. Theaters des ‹Siglo de Oro› in Europa wurde durch die Anerkennung in Gotthold Ephraim Lessings (1729–81) *Hamburgischer Dramaturgie* (bes. 69. und 70. Stück, 1767/68) und durch die dt. Romantiker, vor allem August Wilhelm von Schlegels (1767–1845) Wiener *Vorlesungen über dramatische Kunst und Literatur* (1809), vorbereitet. Obwohl die Geschichte dieser Rezeption in den europäischen Literaturen gelegentlich die Geschichte von Mißverständnissen ist, so läßt sich doch eine eindrucksvolle Fülle von Übersetzungen, Bearbeitungen, Nachahmungen und Adaptationen nachweisen. Im deutschsprachigen Raum fand aus kunsttheoretischen, kulturpolitischen, publikumssoziologischen u. a. Gründen besonders das Theater von Lope de Vega (1562 bis 1635) und Calderón de la Barca (1600–81) Interesse. Nach der fast kultischen Verehrung der dt. Romantiker (besonders Brüder Schlegel, Tieck, Eichendorff) für die span. Dramatiker machte sich in der nachgoethischen Zeit eine nüchternere Art der Betrachtung breit, die im Münchner Dichterkreis um König Maximilian II. (1848–64) und bei Franz Grillparzer (1791–1872) in dessen Märchendrama *Der Traum ein Leben* (1817 bis 1831, Aufführung 1834) kulminierte. – Im 20. Jh. versuchte Hugo von Hofmannsthal (1874–1929) in der Tradition des span.-habsburgischen kulturellen Erbes das span. Theater des ‹Siglo de Oro› wiederzubeleben.

Aubrun, Ch. V.: La comedia española 1600–80. Madrid 1968; Díez Borque, J. M.: Sociología de la comedia española del siglo XVII. Madrid 1976; Gerstinger, H.: Span. Komödie. Lope de Vega und seine Zeitgenossen. München 1976 (dtv 6848); Gregor, J.: Das span. Welttheater. Politik und Kunst der großen Epoche Spaniens. München 1943; Neumeister, S.: Die Differenzierung des Publikums im Theater des Siglo de Oro und die Interpretation der ‹comedia›. In: Kloepfer, R. (Hg.): Bildung und Ausbildung in der Romania. Bd. 3. München 1979, S. 66–81; Valbuena Prat, A.: El teatro español en su Siglo de Oro. Barcelona 1969.

Martin Franzbach

Comédie-ballet

Gattung des frz. Theaters, entworfen für die Hoffeste Ludwigs XIV. Molière (1622–73) gestaltet von ihm verfaßte Komödien in C. um (1664). Der Komponist Lully (1632–87) verbündet sich mit Molière. Ab 1664 *Les Fâcheux, Die erzwungene Heirat, Die Prinzessin von Elis, George Dandin, Monsieur de Pourceaugnac, Der Bürger als Edelmann, Die prachtliebenden Freier.* Gefühle und Leidenschaften, die sich verbal nicht fassen lassen, werden im C. dem Tanz zugewiesen. Aus dem C. wachsen → Ballet d'action und → Ballet héroïque-pantomime.

Gregor, J.: Kulturgeschichte des Balletts. Zürich o. J. / Wien 1944; Schmidt-Garre, H.: Ballett. Vom Sonnenkönig bis Balanchine. Hannover 1966; Sorell, W.: Der Tanz als Spiegel der Zeit. Wilhelmshaven [2]1985.

Helga Ettl

Comédie Française

Auch Théâtre Français. Am 18.8.1680 durch ein Dekret Ludwigs XIV. Fusion der Truppen des →Hôtel de Bourgogne und des Théâtre Guénégaud, das seinerseits aus dem Zusammenschluß der Schauspieler des →Théâtre du Marais und der früheren Truppe Molières entstanden war, zu C. F. Frz. Nationalbühne, ältestes Staatstheater überhaupt. – Die C. F. war zunächst im Théâtre Guénégaud untergebracht; ab 1687 im Palais des Quatre Nations; am 30.4.1783 Umzug ins von den Architekten Peyre und de Wailly in den Gärten des Hôtel de Condé gegenüber dem Palais du Luxembourg neuerbaute Theater, das später den Namen Odéon erhielt; Teilung der C. F. während der Revolutionszeit ins Théâtre de la République (Leitung: François-Joseph Talma) und Théâtre de la Nation (auch Odéon National genannt). 1799 wurde das Odéon durch Feuer zerstört, der amtliche Sitz der C. F. als Théâtre Français wurde der 1786 vom Architekten Victor Louis, der auch das neue Theater von Bordeaux gebaut hatte, errichtete Saal in der rue Richelieu, heute Salle Richelieu.

Der Moskauer Erlaß (décret de Moscou) Napoleons von 1812 regelt auch z. Z. noch die Beziehungen zwischen Staat und D. F.: Organisation als Schauspielergenossenschaft (association coopérative) mit 30 ständigen Mitgliedern als Teilhabern (sociétaires) und den pensionnaires genannten provisorischen Mitgliedern, die erst nach Ausscheiden eines sociétaire fest aufgenommen werden können. Ein vom Staat eingesetzter administrateur général mit Beamtenstatus bestimmt in allen technischen und künstlerischen Fragen; daher gewisse Immobilität, die im 20. Jh. immer wieder zu radikalen Erneuerungsversuchen Anlaß gab. – Konservativ in Spielplan und Aufführungsstil. Repertoire vornehmlich klassische frz. Komödien (Molière, Marivaux) und Tragödien (Corneille, Racine). Inszenierung vorzugsweise im Stil der Entstehungszeit des jeweiligen Stücks, perfekter Deklamationsstil, Verzicht auf psychologische und gesellschaftliche Deutung der Charaktere. Antikes Theater, ausländische Klassiker nehmen, wenn überhaupt, einen sehr bescheidenen Platz ein. Auch das romantische Theater mit Victor Hugo, Alfred de Musset wird gepflegt, außerdem Rostand, Feydeau, Claudel, Audiberti.

Zeitgenössische Stücke wurden eine Weile im →Odéon aufgeführt, das 1959 bis 68 unter dem Namen Théâtre de France als Zweites Haus (deuxième salle) der C. F. von Jean-Louis Barrault und Madeleine Renaud geleitet wurde. Die großen Theaterereignisse Frankreichs finden seit langem außerhalb der C. F. statt, auch wenn Regisseure wie Copeau, Dullin, Jouvet, Baty, Barrault vorübergehend dem Staatstheater angehörten. Dagegen vermochte die C. F. erste Schauspieler auf Dauer an sich zu binden. Heutzutage wird versucht, die Tendenz zum Musealen aufzulockern.

In der Spielzeit 1990/91 realisierte die Comédie Française ż. B. 599 Aufführungen: 399 im eigenen Haus Salle Richelieu, 198 Gastspiele im Raum Paris und in der frz. Provinz, zwei im Ausland; 20 Stücke wurden für den Hörfunk und vier für das Fernsehen aufgezeichnet.

Ricord, A.: Les fastes de la Comédie Française. Paris 1921–22; Touchard, P.-A.: Histoire sentimentale de la Comédie Française. Paris 1955; Valmy-Baysse, J.: Naissance et vie de la Comédie Française. Paris 1945.

Horst Schumacher

Comédie Italienne

Auch Théâtre Italien. Ab Ende des 16. Jh. (erste Erwähnung 1571) Auftreten von ital. →Commedia dell'arte-Truppen in Frankreich. Unter D. Locatelli, T. Fiorilli und G. D. Biancolelli ließ sich die später sog. Ancienne Troupe de la C. I. 1660 in Paris nieder, spielte in ital. Sprache im dem Louvre benachbarten Saal Petit-Bourbon abwechselnd mit der Truppe Molières, schließlich nach dem Abriß des Petit-Bourbon im von Richelieu erbauten Theater des *Palais Royal*. Die ital. Schauspieler standen unter dem Schutz des frz. Königs und trugen den Titel comédiens du roi. Nach Molières Tod 1673 zieht die C. I. auf Wunsch Lullis und um der gerade gegründeten Académie Royale de Musique Platz zu schaffen ins Théâtre Guénégaud, mit der frz. Truppe bis 1680 alternierend. Nach der Gründung der →Comédie Française durch Fusion der Truppen des →Théâtre du Marais und des →Hôtel de Bourgogne durch Ludwig XIV. 1680 erhält die C. I. den ehemaligen Sitz der Confrèrie de la Passion, das Hôtel de Bourgogne, zur alleinigen Nutzung. Die C. I. wurde weiter vom König begünstigt und spielte eine große Rolle im Pariser Theaterleben. Das ausgebildete Stegreifspiel hatte nachhaltigen Einfluß auf Entwicklung des frz. Theaters. Ab 1682 Einflechtung frz. Szenen, nach und nach Aufführung frz. Stücke. Verbannung der C. I. von 1697 bis 1716, weil Ludwig XIV. die angekündigte Komödie *La Fausse Prude* als beleidigende Anspielung auf seine Geliebte Mme. de Maintenon empfand. Mitte des 18. Jh. mehr und mehr Musiktheater geworden mit verschwenderischer Ausstattung und opernhaftem Stil. Nach dem Sieg der opéra-buffo über das genre italien Auflösung der Gesellschaft der comédiens italiens am 25. 12. 1779. – Die C. I. ging in der am 28. 4. 1783 eingeweihten Opéra Comique auf (das baufällig gewordene Hôtel de Bourgogne blieb ungenutzt).

Attinger, G.: L'Esprit de la Commedia dell'arte dans le théâtre français. Neuchâtel 1950; Campardon, E.: Les Comédiens du Roi de la troupe italienne pendant les deux derniers siècles. Paris 1880; Duchartre, P.-L.: La Commedia dell'arte et ses enfants. Paris 1955.

Horst Schumacher

Comedy of Humours

Eine satirische, sozialkritische →Komödie, entwickelt am Ende des 16. Jh. von Ben Jonson (1572–1637) und George Chapman (1559–1634). Ein Versuch, die klassische Komödie von Plautus und Terenz nachzuahmen als Reaktion auf die zahlreichen volkstümlichen ‹romantic comedies›; →University Wits. Wurzeln auch in den →Moralitäten. Die C. o. H. leitet ihre Komik von den übertriebenen und deshalb abnormen Verhaltensweisen der Figuren ab. Sie stellen psycho-physiologische Verkörperungen eines ‹humours› dar, d. h. eine eigensinnige Laune oder Einbildung, die durch die Unausgeglichenheit der vier Körperflüssigkeiten (Blut, Phlegma, Galle, Choler) verursacht wird. Die Zusammensetzung dieser Flüssigkeiten bestimmt die Persönlichkeit und das Verhalten des Menschen. George Chapman schreibt mit *An Humorous Day's Mirth* (1597) die erste C. o. H., aber erst Ben Jonson leitete eine Theorie des Komischen von der Theorie der Humours ab, um mit ihrer dramatischen Umsetzung irrationale und unmoralische Verhaltensweisen anzuprangern (siehe Einleitung zu *Everyman in His Humour*, 1600). Weitere bekannte Stücke des Genres *Everyman Out of His Humour* (1600) und *Eastward Ho!* (1605) (geschrieben zusammen mit Chapman und John Marston, 1575–1634). Elemente der C. o. H. auch in Jonsons *Volpone* (1606) und *The Alchemist* (1610). Die C. o. H. ist eine Vorläuferin der späteren Sittenkomödie.

Kernan, A.: Alchemy and Acting: The Plays of Ben Jonson. In: The Revels History of English Drama. Vol. 3. London 1975, pp. 326–345; Knights, L. C.: Society and Drama in the Age of Jonson. London 1937; Lyons, B.: Voices of Melancholy. Studies in Literary Treatments of Melancholy in Renaissance England. London 1971.

J. Lawrence Guntner

Comedy of Manners

Die C. o. M. ist eine brit. Variante der Sittenkomödie, die sich zuerst im engl. Theater der Restaurationszeit nach 1660, vor allem unter dem Einfluß Molières und der satirischen Komödientradition Englands, entwickelte. Sie stellte auf variantenreiche, im Handlungsmuster aber stereotype Weise das gesellschaftliche Verhalten von Charakteren aus den oberen sozialen Schichten dar. Die C. o. M. folgte einem hedonistischen, speziell antipuritanischen Verhaltenskodex, in dessen Antibürgerlichkeit sich jedoch bürgerlicher Individualismus entfaltete. Hauptautoren in der Blütezeit der C. o. M. waren Sir George Etherege (1635–91), William

Wycherley (1640–1716) und William Congreve (1670–1729), daneben Sir John Vanbrugh (1664–1726) und George Farquhar (1678–1707). Die C. o. M. behauptete sich, z. T. unter Tilgung ihrer Indezenz, auch im 18. Jh. neben empfindsamen Komödiengenres wie der →Sentimental Comedy, indem sie deren Verinnerlichungstendenz die komischen Aspekte gesellschaftlichen Verhaltens entgegenstellte, z. B. bei Richard Brinsley Sheridan (1751–1816). Danach verschwand die C. o. M. weitgehend aus dem originären Theaterschaffen und lebte kurzfristig im Fin de siècle bei Oscar Wilde (1856–1900) und in den Konversationskomödien Noel Cowards (1899–1973) wieder auf. Ihre besten Stücke bilden einen festen Bestandteil des brit. Theaterrepertoires, bes. Congreves *The Way of the World* (1700) und Wildes *The Importance of Being Earnest* (1895).

Hirst, D. L.: Comedy of Manners. London 1979; Muir, K.: The Comedy of Manners. London 1970; Palmer, J.: The Comedy of Manners. London 1913.

Bernd-Peter Lange

Commedia dell'arte

Die im 18. Jh. – vermutlich von Carlo Goldoni (1707–93) – geprägte Bezeichnung C. d. a. hat sich durchgesetzt für eine Theaterform, welche die Italiener ursprünglich ‹commedia improvisa, all'improviso› oder ‹asogetto› bzw. ‹commedia mercenaria› und die Franzosen →‹comédie italienne› oder ‹à l'italienne› genannt hatten. Diese Art Stegreifkomödie (im Gegensatz zur ‹commedia sostenuta›, der mehr literarischen Komödie), die auch heute noch Regisseure und Schauspieler immer wieder inspiriert, hat sich in ganz Europa, besonders in Frankreich, ausgebreitet und dauerhaft auf die Theaterkunst eingewirkt.

Die C. d. a. kam in Italien im 16. Jh. auf; ihre Ursprünge sind jedoch unklar, u. a. wird auf die röm. →Atellanes verwiesen. Goldoni (*Memoiren* II, XXIV) vermutet die Entstehung in der Zeit nach dem Verfall des Römischen Reiches. Demnach standen 1. am Anfang grobe Kanevas (Handlungsmuster mit wichtigen Dreh- und Wendepunkten des Spiels) als Erinnerungsstützen für Schauspieler; hinzu kam 2. die Übernahme von Typen aus den Komödien von Plautus (um 250–184 v. Chr.) und Terenz (um 190–159 v. Chr.) durch lesekundige Akteure; etwa geprellte Väter und verlumpte Söhne, verliebte schlaue Diener und liederliche Zofen; 3. schließlich im Zusammenhang mit Aufführungen in den verschiedenen ital. Städten und Regionen die Ergänzung durch Typen aus der zeitgenössischen Gesellschaft: Väter aus Venedig und Bologna, Diener aus Bergamo, Innamorati und Zofen aus der Toskana und den Vatikanstaaten. Dieser an sich unbewiesenen These Goldonis liegt die Hypothese

244 Commedia dell'arte

zugrunde, daß sich die C. d. a. zugleich aus volkstümlichen und professionellen bzw. halbprofessionellen Traditionen entwickelt hat. Andere Forscher sehen in der C. d. a. nur eine heruntergekommene Form der commedia erudita des →Rinascimento, die ihre Typen an den Volksgeschmack (das Volk war von den Aufführungen bei Hof ausgeschlossen) angepaßt hat. Die neueste Forschung setzt die Herkunft der Masken bei den Fastnachtsbräuchen an (Karneval); die C. d. a. soll sich vom Mittelalter zum →Rinascimento durch Spezialisierung und Spezifizierung gewisser Masken und Karnevalsriten (Satire, Mimik, Akrobatien etc.) entwickelt haben. Hinzu kommt die wohl ausschlaggebende Rolle der Gaukler und anderer Marktschreier, welche auch zu den Vorstellungen für die höfische Gesellschaft zugelassen waren: Sie waren fähiger als andere, die Typen und Motive der commedia erudita zu assimilieren und sie dann vereinfacht und karikiert zuerst einzeln, dann in Truppen weiterzuverwenden. Nach Zeugnissen aus dem 16. und 17. Jh. unterschieden sich die Berufsschauspieler zunächst nur wenig von diesen mit ihren Vorstellungen hausierenden Marktschreiern, die möglicherweise gar deren Vorbilder sind.

Wenngleich die Entstehungsgeschichte der C. d. a. in mancher Hinsicht noch nicht ganz geklärt ist, haben sich doch seit der 2. Hälfte des 16. Jh. für diese Theaterform einige Grundmerkmale herausgebildet, die in der Folgezeit kaum merklich verändert wurden: 1. Sie wird von Wandertruppen aus Berufsschauspielern praktiziert, wobei Schauspielerinnen die Frauenrollen innehaben (wichtige Truppen: Accesi, 1590 gegr.; Confidenti, 1574–1640; Desiosi, um 1600; Fedeli, Anfang 17. Jh.; Compagnia dei Gelosi, ab 1576). – Bedeutende Schauspieler: Andrea Calmo (1509–71, senex); Ganassa (1540–84?); die Familie Andreini: Francesco (1548–1624, capitano), Isabella (1562–1604, Innamorata), Giovan Battista (1576–1654, Innamorato), Virginia (1583–1628); Giulio Pasquati (1535–?, Pantalone); Familie Gabrielli, Giovanni (?–1611?, genannt Sivello), Francesco (1588–1636?, Scapino); Pier Maria Cecchini (1563–1645, 2. Zanno); Tristano Martinelli (1556–1630, Arlecchino); Fam. Biancolelli, Isabella Franchini B. (ca. 1650, Isabella), Giuseppe Domenico, gen. Dominique (1636–88, Arlecchino), Caterina (16?–1716, Colombina, in Stichen von Watteau porträtiert); Flaminio Scala (?–1620, Innamorato), Carlo Cantu (1609–76, 1. Zanno); Tiberio Fiorilli (16?–1694, gen. Scaramuccia, Scaramouche); Fam. Gherardi, Giovanni (16?–1675, Musikkomiker); Luigi A. Riccoboni, gen. Lelio (1676–1753) und Antonio R. (1707–72, Autor von *L'Art du théâtre*, 1750, von Lessing übersetzt). 2. Im Spiel werden feste Maskentypen verwendet. 3. Keine passive Unterwerfung der literarischen Vorlage gegenüber. 4. Die Bedeutung von Gestik, Akrobatik und Mimik ist z. T. streng geregelt. 5. Vereinfachte Handlungen, Fabeln, Intrigen, mit vielen Möglichkei-

Harlequin.

Harlekin, eine Maske in der Hand haltend (TS)

Figuren der Commedia dell'arte; in der Mitte Evaristo Gherardi als Harlekin.
Zeichnung von C. Gillot (TS)

Szene einer Commedia dell'arte-Aufführung von J. Fabbri für «La Famille Arlequins»
von C. Santelli, 1955 (TS)

ten zu skurriler Ausgelassenheit. 6. Alle Ausdrucksmittel sind auf Effekte der Natürlichkeit und Spontaneität konzentriert (nach R. Tessari).

Von den Literaten der Regellosigkeit und Unanständigkeit bezichtigt, von den Priestern als Werkzeuge des Satans verschrien, haben die ital. Truppen dennoch einen immer größeren Erfolg sowohl im Heimatland wie auch in Frankreich und bald in ganz Europa, und zwar selbst an den Höfen. Ihre Erfolge reichen bis ins 18. Jh. hinein (in Wien Einfluß auf das →Alt-Wiener Volksstück). Selbst die Zensur der Gegenreformation kommt nicht auf gegen die Stegreifrepliken und die Beliebtheit der C. d. a. Die Vermehrung der Truppen und Aufführungen führt zwar zu einer Verfeinerung der Technik und Gestik, jedoch ebenfalls zur Entwicklung eines stets wiederholten Repertoires. Die anfangs hochgelobte Improvisationskunst der C. d. a. ist bald begrenzt und auf eine Anzahl von Bühnenrezepten, Konventionen, Abmachungen und Formeln, die anwendbar sind auf alle Typen und Situationen. So wird die ursprünglich regelstörende Commedia allmählich im 17./18. Jh. zur ‹Schauspielmaschine› (Tessari), die an der Mittelmäßigkeit allzu vieler Schauspieler und der Veralterung der Technik und Effekte scheitert.

Die Masken sind nicht sehr zahlreich und verändern sich im Laufe der Zeit kaum; denn üblicherweise ist ein Komödiant sehr früh spezialisiert und spielt sein Leben lang dieselbe Rolle, wobei er sich mit der Figur (wenn auch kritisch, ironisch) identifiziert. Diese Grundbeständigkeit ist besonders bemerkenswert in den vier wichtigsten Masken, die ihrem Profil nach durchgehend bindend geblieben sind für alle Aufführungen der C. d. a.: die beiden Alten (Pantalone, Kaufmann aus Venedig, düpierter Vater und Ehemann, und der Dottore, Jurist, Arzt oder Philosoph aus Bologna, der geschwätzig-lächerliche Gelehrte) und die beiden Diener, die Zanni aus Bergamo (der dumme Arlecchino mit rhombisch geschecktem Kostüm, breitkrempigem Hut, schwarzer Leder-Halbmaske und Holzpritsche und der schlaue Brighella). Viele spätere Masken sind nur Varianten der beiden Urzanni: so Tortellino, Naccherino, Truffaldino, Pedrolino (frz. Pierrot) in der Nachfolge Arlecchinos und Scapino, Mezzetino oder der frz. Turlupin, eher Brighella vergleichbar; der interessanteste ist wohl Pulcinella, der neapolitanische Zanno, ein Vorgänger des →Hanswurst. Zu diesen ursprünglichen vier Grundtypen kamen anschließend einige andere, ebenfalls zum festen Bestand gehörige: Capitano/Il Capitan, der span. soldatische Liebhaber und Maulheld, Nachfolger des lat. miles gloriosus, die üblich nichtmaskierten Innamorati, die Verliebten (meist Florindo und Isabella) und die Dienerinnen, Colombina und Corallina. Die Truppen bestehen also gewöhnlich aus neun bis zwölf Schauspielern: Pantalone (Il Magnifico), Il Dottore und die beiden Zanni – als komische Rollen; zwei Liebespaare (ernste Rollen); eine Dienerin und eventuell ein Capitano sowie eine Kurtisane (bewegliche Rollen).

246 Commedia dell'arte

Zur Aufführung verfügen die Komödianten über feste Konventionen, die oft differenziert sind und, da schriftlich festgehalten, leicht tradierbar: 1. die Szenarien oder Kanevas (canovacci, soggetti, scenari), kurze Fabel- und Handlungsmuster mit Aufteilung in Akte und Szenen sowie Angaben zum Bühnenspiel und den komischen Situationen; 2. die Repertoires (repertori, centoni, zibaldoni, generici), Sammlungen von Bravourstücken, Monologen und Dialogen, anwendbar auf alle Situationstypen je nach den Rollen: concetti, rhetorisch-geistreiche Einfälle, und battute, schlagfertige Antworten; 3. die lazzi, fast ausschließlich den beiden Zanni vorbehalten: kleine Zwischennummern zum Aufpeitschen der Dialoge und Lachen der Zuschauer, manchmal rein sprachliche Gags, doch auch Pirouetten, Mimiken und obszöne Possen.

So ist es verständlich, daß die Schauspieler des C. d. a., in so viele Konventionen und Stereotypen eingezwängt, im 18. Jh. kaum mehr spontan zu improvisieren vermochten. Daher kommt Goldoni zu dem Urteil, daß die meisten Komödianten unfähig seien, sich anzupassen, in eine andere Theaterform umzusteigen. Die C. d. a. hatte ihre ursprünglichen Kraftquellen versiegen lassen und den regen Erfindungsgeist verloren. In Frankreich Molière im 17. Jh. und in Italien Goldoni im 18. Jh. schaffen die erstarrten Maskenfiguren ab und erneuern die Typen im Sinne realistischer Gestaltung bis hin zur Charakterkomödie.

Als Gegenreaktion zum naturalistischen Illusionstheater wird auch im frühen 20. Jh. im Zuge der ‹Retheatralisierung des Theaters› auf die C. d. a. zurückgegriffen: so von Max Reinhardt, Jacques Copeau, Charles Dullin. Das Erbe der C. d. a. ist heute noch in der Arbeit von Giorgio Strehler und Jean-Louis Barrault spürbar. Trotz ihrer späteren Erstarrung hat die C. d. a. wie kaum eine andere Theaterform ihr historisches Ende überlebt, wirkt weiter in neueren Theaterformen, insbesondere in den diversen Richtungen des komischen Theaters und der antiillusionistischen Theaterbewegung des 20. Jh.

Apollonio, M.: Storia della Commedia dell'arte. Rom/Mailand 1930; Attinger, G.: L'esprit de la Commedia dell'arte dans le théâtre français. Paris/Neuchâtel 1950; Heck, Th. F.: Commedia Dell'Arte. New York 1988; Hinck, W.: Das dt. Lustspiel des 17. bis 18. Jh. und die ital. Komödie. Stuttgart 1965; Jonard, N.: La Commedia dell'arte. Lyon 1982; Pandolfi, V.: La Commedia dell'arte. Storia e testo. 6 Bde. Florenz 1957–61; Spoerri, R. (Hg.): Die Commedia dell'arte und ihre Figuren. 1977; Tessari, R.: Commedia dell'arte – La maschera e l'ombra. Mailand 1981; Toschi, P.: Le origini del teatro italiano. Turin 1955.

Paul Larivaille

Community Theatre

Seit Mitte der 60er Jahre auch in Großbritannien existierende Bewegung (→ Volksbühne/Arbeitertheater), die es sich, in Anknüpfung an die Ideen der → repertory theatre movement, zum Ziel gesetzt hat, Theaterarbeit in die kommunalen Strukturen einer Stadt oder Region einzubringen und inhaltlich an den Problemen ihrer Bewohner anzuknüpfen, was häufig zu einer Ausweitung der herkömmlichen Theateraktivitäten in Richtung Sozialarbeit führt. Vorbildwirkung für die Bewegung hatte Ed Bermans Inter-Action in Nord-London, eine Dachorganisation für unterschiedliche Aktivitäten wie Selbsthilfeprojekte, Kinderbetreuung, Videoarbeit und Theaterspiel (The Other Company).

Das Bestreben, kulturelle Hemmschwellen des anvisierten Arbeiterpublikums abzubauen und dessen Lebens- und Arbeitsbedingungen zu thematisieren, führte zur Nutzung urspr. theaterfremder Spielstätten wie pubs, Werkskantinen oder picket lines sowie zur Entwicklung der Form der documentary plays, in der realhistorische Ereignisse der Region mit Hilfe multimedialer Techniken, mit Songs und Balladen und mit populären → Music-Hall-Elementen aufgearbeitet werden. Auf der Produktionsseite sind kollektive Erarbeitung des Stoffs, rasches Improvisieren und Aktualisieren kennzeichnend für diese Theaterform.

International bekannt wurde u. a. die Arbeit Peter Cheesemans am Victoria Theatre, Stoke-on-Trent (*The Fight for Shelton Bar*, 1975), Alan Platers am University Theatre, Newcastle (*Close the Coalhouse Door*, 1968) und John McGraths (* 1935) → 7 : 84 Company in Schottland (*The Cheviot, the Stag, and the Black, Black Oil*, 1973). Seit 1973 sind die C. T. in einem Dachverband, The Association of Community Theatres (TACT), organisiert.

Craig, S.: Reflexes of the Future. In: ders.: (ed.): Dreams and Deconstructions. Alternative Theatre in Britain. Ambergate 1980, p. 9–29; Gooch, S.: All Together Now. An Alternative View of Theatre and the Community. London 1984; Itzin, C.: Stages in the Revolution. London 1980.

Werner Bleike

Compagnia Dario Fo

Im Jahre 1959 gründete der 1926 in Leggiuno, Varese, geborene Dario Fo (→ La Nuova Scena, → la Comune) zusammen mit seiner Frau Franca Rame die C. D. F. – Mit der C. D. F. arbeitete er an subventionierten bürgerlichen Theatern für ein bürgerliches Publikum. In dieser Zeit entstanden sieben Komödien: 1959/60 *Gli arcangeli non giocano a flipper*;

1960/61 *Aveva due pistole con gli occhi bianchi e neri*; 1961/62 *Chi ruba un piede à fortunato in amore*; 1963/64 *Isabella, tre caravelle e un cacciaballe*; 1964/65 *Settimo: ruba un po' meno*; 1965/66 *La colpa à sempre del diavolo*; 1967/68 *La signora da buttare*.

Im Zuge der Regierungskoalition von Zentrum und Linken bekommt Fo eine eigene Fernsehshow. Eine Reportage über Grundstücksspekulationen in Mailand führt jedoch zum Eklat, er und Franca Rame werden fristlos entlassen und bis 1977 nicht mehr für Fernsehsendungen zugelassen. – Beeinflußt von der chinesischen Kulturrevolution und den Maiunruhen in Frankreich und Italien im Jahre 1968 verlassen Dario Fo und Franca Rame das subventionierte Theater und arbeiten von nun an für die PCI, die Kommunistische Partei Italiens.

Fo, D.: Dario Fo parla di Dario Fo. Cosenza 1977; Jungblut, H.: Das politische Theater Dario Fos. Frankfurt/M. 1978.

Elke Kehr

Compagnia del Collettivo di Parma

Aus dem Studententheater der 60er Jahre ging – zunächst unter dem Regisseur Bogdan Jankovic – 1971 die C.C.P., auch ‹Teatro Due› genannt, hervor. Später wurden die Produktionen in kollektiver Verantwortung erarbeitet. Die C.C.P. machte zunächst mit einer Shakespeare-Trilogie von sich reden (*Hamlet, Macbeth* und *Heinrich IV.*), mit der sie 1983 auch in Deutschland gastierte. 1984 folgte eine Büchner-Collage (*Dantons Tod, Leonce und Lena, Woyzeck* sowie aktuelles Material) und 1985 eine Pasolini-Adaption (*Uccellacci e Uccellini*). Charakteristisch sind die schnellen Rollen-, Gesten- und Tonwechsel sowie das Bestreben, die Relation zur heutigen Wirklichkeit herzustellen. Zu den umfassenden Darstellungsmöglichkeiten der Truppe gehören neben Musik und Gesang auch Tanz, Pantomime und Improvisation. Zur C.C.P. gehört auch ein Kinder- und Puppentheater; zudem organisiert das Kollektiv ein Theaterfestival.

Quadri, F.: L'avanguardia teatrale in Italia (Materiali 1960–1976). Turin 1977.

Elke Kehr

Compagnie des Ballets Russes de Serge de Diaghilev

1909 bis 1929, mit Hauptsitz in Paris, ab 1922 auch Monte Carlo. Leitung hatte der russ. Kunstmäzen und Impresario Serge de Diaghilew (1872–1929). Diaghilew begleitete 1909 Mitglieder des St. Petersburger und Moskauer Balletts für eine erste Saison nach Paris, u. a. die Tänzer T. Karsavina, W. Nijinsky, A. Pavlova, I. Rubinstein, die Maler L. Bakst, A. Benois und den Choreographen M. Fokine. Auf dem Programm standen kurze melodramatische und lyrische Stücke. *Les Sylphides* (Musik: Chopin), *Prince Igor* (Musik: Borodin), *Cléopâtre* (Musik: Arenskij, Rimsky-Korssakow, Mussorgski u. a.). Im erweiterten Repertoire der nun jährlich wiederholten Tourneen (ab 1911 auch in London) 1910: *Shéhérazade* (Musik: Rimsky-Korssakow), *L'Oiseau de Feu* (Musik: Strawinsky), 1911: *Pétrouchka* (Musik: Strawinsky), *Le Spectre de la Rose* (Musik: Weber/Berlioz), 1912: *L'Après-midi d'un faune* (Musik: Débussy, Choreographie: Nijinsky), *Sacre du printemps* (Musik: Strawinsky, Choreographie Nijinsky), 1913: *Le Coq d'or* (Musik: Rimsky-Korssakow). 1914 trennten sich die B. R. vom Petersburger Ballett, die klassisch-zeitlosen Tanzkonventionen wurden aufgegeben, ebenso die folkloristische, historisierende bzw. vom Jugendstil geprägte Dekoration. Hinwendung zur zeitgenössischen Kunst (schon ab 1912 Kubismus, Futurismus, Konstruktivismus sichtbar). Diaghilew engagierte neben Larionow und Gontscharowa Maler der Pariser Schule, förderte Zusammenarbeit der Künstler. Ergebnis: Experimente mit Raum-Farb-Ton-Konstellationen, Synthesen mit deutlichem Akzent auf dem Bühnenbild. Der Choreograph L. Massine schuf die «ballets d'action» mit komischen, satirischen und grotesken Elementen. Tanz verband sich mit Mimik und marionettenhaft-eckigen Bewegungen, das Corps de ballet wurde in die Handlung einbezogen. 1914 bis 1918 zahlreiche Gastspiele in Europa und Amerika. *Feu d'artifice* (1917, Musik: Strawinsky, Dekoration: Balla), ein plastisches Farblichtspiel, gilt als wichtigste futuristische Theaterarbeit. Mit *Parade* (1917, Musik: Satie, Dekoration: Picasso, Text: Cocteau) gelang dem Kubismus trotz empörter Öffentlichkeit der entscheidende Durchbruch auf der Bühne. Man verwendete Ganzmasken, der Körper wurde in eckige Einzelteile zerlegt. Weitere bedeutende Ballette: *La Tricorne* (1919, Musik: de Falla, Dekoration: Picasso), *Le Chout* (1921, Musik: Prokofiew, Dekoration/Choreographie: Larionow), *Les Fâcheux* (1924, Musik: Auric, Dekoration: Braque), *Jack in the Box* (1926, Musik: Satie, Dekoration: Derain), *Romeo and Juliet* (1926, Musik: Lambert, Dekoration: Ernst/Miró), *Pas d'acier* (1927, Musik: Prokofiew, Dekoration: Jakulow). Nach dem Tod ihres Leiters wurden die B. R. aufgelöst. Diaghilew gilt bis heute als ‹der› Initiator des modernen Tanzes. 1931 Gründung zweier Compagnien in der Nachfolge der B. R.: Ballet de l'Opéra de Monte Carlo (Leitung R. Blum), L'Opéra Russe Paris (Leitung W. de Basil).

Bertrand, A.: Les Ballets Russes. Paris 1990; Buckle, R.: Diaghilev. London 1979; Kochno, B.: Diaghilev and the Ballets Russes. New York, 1970; Lifar, S.: Serge de Diaghilev. Paris 1954.

Barbara Müller-Wesemann

Compagnie Renaud-Barrault

Pariser Theatertruppe seit 1946, Leitung hat das Ehepaar Madeleine Renaud (*1900), Schauspielerin, und Jean-Louis Barrault (*1910), Schauspieler und Regisseur. Beginn am Théâtre Marigny (1946–56), seit 1981 an ihrer 10. Pariser Spielstätte (Théâtre du Rond-Point). Zahlreiche Welttourneen. Erste herausragende Inszenierungen: Shakespeares *Hamlet* (1946, Bearbeitung A. Gide), Préverts/Kosmas *Baptiste* (1946, Ballett-Pantomime), Kafkas *Der Prozeß* (1947, Bearbeitung A. Gide/ J.-L. Barrault), Claudels *Partage de Midi* (1948) und *Christophe Colomb* (1953), Cervantes' *Numance* (1954). Intensive Zusammenarbeit mit zeitgenössischen Autoren (Anouilh, Camus, Claudel, Duras, Sarraute, Shéhadé), seit Anfang der 60er Jahre bes. auch mit Dramatikern der Avantgarde: Ionescos *Rhinocéros* (1960), Becketts *Oh, les Beaux Jours* (1963), Genets *Les Paravents* (1966). Regie führt i. d. R. Barrault, daneben als Gäste u. a. Maurice Béjart, Roger Blin, Claude Régy. Neben dem festen Ensemble Schauspieler wie Pierre Brasseur, Maria Casarès, Edwige Feuillère, Geneviève Page, Laurent Terzieff. Berühmte Dekorationen von Balthus, Masson, Bérard. Nach den Maiunruhen 1968 mußte die C. R. B. das TN Odéon auf Drängen des Kulturministers Malraux verlassen. Heute regelmäßige Zusammenarbeit mit dem Théâtre de la Criée, Marseille (Leitung Marcel Maréchal). Seit 1953 erscheinen die «Cahiers de la Compagnie Renaud-Barrault», ausführliche Begleithefte zu den jeweiligen Produktionen. In seiner schauspielerischen Arbeit wie auch in der Regie beruft sich Barrault auf seine geistigen Vorbilder Artaud und Claudel sowie auf das Prinzip des ‹théâtre total›, das Dekoration, Licht, Geräusche, Musik zum Bestandteil der theatralischen Handlung werden läßt. Wesentlicher Faktor für das Zusammenspiel von Mensch und Objekt: die Körpersprache.

Baurrault, J.-L.: Souvenirs pour demain. Paris 1972; ders.: Saisir le présent. Paris 1984; Le Bon, J. (ed.): Renaud-Barrault. Paris, notre siècle. Paris 1982.

Barbara Müller-Wesemann

Company

(Engl.) Bezeichnet zunächst jegliche Art von Personengruppierung. Im Theater und Ballett: Truppe, Ensemble, Compagnie; z. B. C. of actors = Schauspielertruppe, etwa die 1961 gegründete →Royal Shakespeare C. in Stratford bzw. London.

Horst Schumacher

La Comune

Die dritte Truppe Dario Fos (→Compagnia Dario Fo, →La Nuova Scena), gegründet im Jahre 1970, ist ein Theaterkollektiv, dessen Stücke für ein Arbeiterpublikum bestimmt sind. Zusammen mit der revolutionären Linken soll ein Kulturprogramm entwickelt werden als Alternative nicht nur zur bürgerlichen, sondern auch zur revisionistischen Kulturpolitik. Einige der wichtigsten Stücke, die L. C. aufführte, sind *Zufälliger Tod eines Anarchisten* (1970), *Einer für alle, alle für einen! Verzeihung, wer ist hier eigentlich der Boß?* (1971), *Tod und Auferstehung eines Popanz* (Fortsetzung der *Großen Pantomime*), *Fedayn* (1972), *Pum, pum. Wer ist das? Die Polizei.* (1972) ist die Fortsetzung des Pinelli-Stücks. Es bringt Fo einen politischen Prozeß und immer heftigere Angriffe durch neofaschistische Organisationen ein. Weiter entstehen *Bezahlt wird nicht* (1974), *Mama hat den besten Shit* (1976) und *Nur Kinder, Küche, Kirche* (1977), zusammen mit Franca Rame.

1974 erhält L. C. nach langen Verhandlungen das Palazzina Liberty in Mailand. Es wird konzipiert als Stadtteilzentrum mit Bibliothek, Kindergarten und Versammlungsräumen und ist seither ein Kulturzentrum mit autonomer Verwaltung.

Fo, D.: Dario Fo parla di Dario Fo, Cosenza 1977; Jungblut, H.: Das politische Theater Dario Fos. Frankfurt/M. 1978.

Elke Kehr

Conférence

Ansage eines →Conférenciers, im Kabarett und der Revue ebenso wie im Varieté oder einem «Bunten Abend», kann von bloßer Ankündigung der Programmnummer bis zur ausgefeilten literarischen Plauderei oder der satirischen Behandlung aktueller Probleme reichen. Eine im Wiener Kabarett →«Simplicissimus» in den 20er Jahren von Fritz Grünbaum und

Karl Farkas erfundene besondere Form ist die dialogische «Doppelconférence», die von anderen Kabaretts aufgenommen und bis in die Gegenwart hinein kultiviert wurde.

Wolfgang Beck

Conférencier

(Frz. ‹Vortragender›) Besonders in Kabarett, Revue, Varieté und verwandten theatralischen Formen üblicher Ansager, dessen Aufgabe von einleitenden und verbindenden Worten bis zu ausführlichen Plaudereien und zur Gestaltung des Programms reichen kann. – Seine Herkunft ist umstritten, verschiedene Traditionen laufen hier wohl zusammen. Einer der möglichen ‹Ahnherren› des C. war der «Mr. Interlocutor» der amerikanischen →Minstrel Show, der die einzelnen Nummern ansagte und dabei mit aktuellen Anspielungen ebensowenig sparte wie der «Mr. Chairman» der englischen →Music-Hall. Die Entwicklung des Kabaretts hat der C. von Anfang an begleitet, je nach eigener Fähigkeit und Stil des Kabaretts als bloßer Ansager und Witzeerzähler oder als mehr oder weniger den Programmablauf bestimmende eigene ‹Nummer›. Höhepunkt der Entwicklung waren die 20er und 30er Jahre, in denen eine Vielzahl bedeutender C. Programm und Stil vieler Kabaretts und Varietés prägten. Damals wie heute selten ist der weibliche C. Was die besondere Kunst der C. ausmacht, ihr Improvisationstalent, die Fähigkeit, auf Aktuelles zu reagieren, verhindert andererseits ihre internationale Bekanntheit. Sie sind an die Sprache gebunden und kaum übersetzbar, zudem veralten ihre Texte schnell. Mit dem Verschwinden zahlreicher Varietés, der Verdrängung des reinen Nummernkabaretts, verliert auch der C. an Bedeutung. Häufig ist er selbst bereits zur ‹humoristischen› Nummer geworden oder wurde durch den «Entertainer» verdrängt.

Wolfgang Beck

Cornichon

Das Züricher C. (benannt nach der Gewürzgurke) war das erste Schweizer Kabarett von internationalem Rang. Der Beginn der faschistischen Herrschaft in Deutschland und ähnliche Tendenzen in der Schweiz ließen den Gründern des C., dem Autor Walter Lesch, dem Konditor und Schauspieler Emil Hegetschweiler und dem Graphiker Alois Carigiet die

Eröffnung eines Kabaretts notwendig erscheinen, um «den Kampf zu führen gegen Unzulänglichkeit und Verstocktheit des schlechteren Teils des helvetischen Publikums» (Lesch). Nachdem der als Organisator und Komponist fungierende Otto Weissert das benötigte Geld aufgebracht hatte, begann das C. am 1.5.1934 seine Existenz. Schon nach kurzer Zeit konnte es sich durchsetzen. Als neuer Autor kam Max Werner Lenz hinzu. – Neu war die Behandlung eidgenössischer Themen auf schwyzerdütsch in einem Schweizer Kabarett. Seine Bedeutung jedoch erhielt das C. durch seine satirischen Angriffe auf die Entwicklungen in den faschistischen Nachbarstaaten. Welche Bedeutung man ihm beimaß, zeigen die beständigen Versuche Italiens und vor allem Deutschlands, das C. auf diplomatischem Wege verbieten zu lassen. Nachdem das dt. und österr. Kabarett mundtot gemacht worden war, übernahm das C. de facto so etwas wie eine Stellvertreterrolle.

Im C. arbeiteten neben einer Reihe von Emigranten zahlreiche bekannte Schauspieler, Musiker sowie als Bühnenbildner fast alle bedeutenden schw. Graphiker der Zeit. Arthur Honegger und Paul Burkhard schrieben Musik für das C., C. F. Vaucher und Friedrich Dürrenmatt (nach 1945) steuerten Texte bei. Nach Kriegsende führten Unstimmigkeiten im Ensemble und das Fehlen großer Themen zum Ausscheiden einiger Mitglieder (Weissert, Lenz) und zum langsamen Niedergang des C., das 1951 schloß. – Die ausgeschiedenen Mitglieder gründeten 1949 das «Cabaret Federal», das mit ähnlichen Problemen wie das C. zu kämpfen hatte und 1960 aufgab.

Attenhofer, E.: Cornichon – Erinnerungen an ein Cabaret. Bern 1975; Keiser, C.: Herrliche Zeiten – 1916–1976. 60 Jahre Cabaret in der Schweiz. Bern 1976; Lesch, W./Lenz, M. W.: Cornichons, Ellg o. J.; Weissert, O. (Hg.): Das Cornichon-Buch 1933–44. Basel 1945; ders (Hg.): Das Cornichon-Buch. Zürich 1950; ders.: Hinter dem eigenen Vorhang – Das Buch vom Cabaret Federal. Zürich 1954; Zwanzig Jahre Schweizer Cabaret. Sondernr. des «Nebelspalter». Bern, 18.3.1954.

Wolfgang Beck

Corralbühne

Bühnenform (→ Bühne) des span. Theaters im → ‹Siglo de Oro› im Innenhof eines Häuserblocks. Die breiten, meist vergitterten Fenster waren die Logen (aposentos). Hinter den Bänken vor der Bretterbühne waren die Stehplätze für die gefürchteten Buhrufer (mosqueteros). Die Frauen saßen auf dem ‹Olymp› (cazuela, eigtl. Pfanne). Aufführungen fanden an Sonn- und Festtagen statt, außer in der Fastenzeit. Einfach dekorierter Bühnenraum. Bemalter Vorhang seit 1610. Abgänge links und rechts,

Pappmaschinerie. Erste Aufführung 1568 in Madrid. Bekannte C. Teatro de la Cruz (seit 1579), Teatro del Príncipe (seit 1582), später als Berufstheater architektonisch umgestaltet.

Rennert, H. A.: The Spanish Stage in the Time of Lope de Vega. New York 1909.

Martin Franzbach

Couplet

(Frz. Diminutiv zu ‹couple› = Paar, Verbindung, von lat. ‹copula›) Ursprünglich Zwischenstrophe. Kurzes, pointiertes, witzig-satirisches und oft auch zweideutig-schlüpfriges Lied mit einer Vielzahl von stets auf den gleichen Kehrreim endenden Strophen. Häufig in → Vaudeville, Operette, komischer Oper, → Posse, Singspiel. Durch winzige Veränderungen oder Wortumstellungen im Schlußkehrreim werden oft zusätzliche Pointen geschaffen. Im Dialog-C. singen zwei (oder mehr) Schauspieler abwechselnd den Kehrreim. Zahlreiche berühmte C. bei Johann Nepomuk Nestroy (1801–62): z. B. Knieriems Kometenlied im *Lumpazivagabundus* (1833) und Lied des Lips in *Der Zerrissene* (1844).

Horst Schumacher

Covent Garden Theatre

Das C. G. T. wurde von John Rich in London gegründet und am 7. 12. 1732 mit *The Way of the World* eröffnet. Der Spielplan der Anfangszeit umfaßte Dramen, Pantomimen und Spektakelstücke. In den Jahren 1734–37 wurden dort von Händel Opern und Oratorien aufgeführt. Im Jahre 1761 starb Rich, der sich unter dem Künstlernamen Lun vor allem als Harlekin einen Namen gemacht hatte. Sein Schwiegersohn John Beard führte das Theater vorwiegend als Opernhaus, bis es 1767 an George Colman verkauft wurde, der das Haus äußerst erfolgreich führte. Nach einem Brand 1808 von Smirke neu errichtet, wurde das Haus von vielen berühmten englischen Schauspielern bespielt, u. a. von Madame Vestris. Nach einem erneuten Brand im Jahre 1856 wurde 1858 schließlich das heutige, 2800 Plätze umfassende Gebäude errichtet. Das Haus, das bereits ab 1847 vorwiegend als Opernhaus benutzt worden war, beherbergt seit 1948 endgültig die Oper und erhält staatliche Zuschüsse. Es ist gleichzeitig die Spielstätte des Royal Ballets.

The Oxford Companion to the Theatre. Ed. by Ph. Hartnell. London/New York/Toronto 951.

Elke Kehr

Cricot

1933 bis 1938 in Krakau, 1938 bis 1939 in Warschau. Kleines avantgardistisches Amateurtheater, das vor allem die Idee des ‹plastischen Theaters› realisierte. Ästhetische Einflüsse vom →Konstruktivismus, →Expressionismus und der Figurmalerei, 30 Premieren, u. a. von S. Wyspiański und S. I. Witkiewicz. Deutlicher Einfluß auf das Nachkriegsschaffen von T. Kantor (→Cricot 2), indirekt auch auf J. Szajna, K. Dejmek, A. Hanuszkiewicz.

Slawomir Tryc

Cricot 2 (Krakau)

Gegründet 1956 von T. Kantor (1915–90), Maler, Graphiker, Bühnenbildner und Regisseur. Knüpft an die Erfahrung von →Cricot an, Fortsetzung der im Untergrundtheater Teatr Niezależny (Unabhängiges Theater; 1942–44) begonnenen Arbeit. Hermetisches, autonomes Theater mit musikalischen und rituellen Elementen, geprägt von der künstlerischen Ideologie Kantors, seiner Entwicklung von metaphysischen Kompositionen bis hin zur abstrakten Kunst: Tachismus, Informel, geometrische Abstraktion, Pop-art. Das erste Happening in Polen (1965, bis 1970 aufgeführt); zahlreiche Theatermanifeste unter der Devise: «Die errungene Form überschreiten, auf die schon einmal gewonnenen Positionen verzichten, keinen Stil pflegen.» Autoren: S. T. Witkiewicz, W. Gombrowicz, B. Schulz; Tadeusz Kantors wichtigste Arbeiten (Szenarium und Regie): 1975 *Die tote Klasse* (Umarła klasa) – erste Aufführung des «Theaters des Todes» (Alles ist Sterben); 1979 Cricotage *Wo ist der Schnee vom vergangenen Jahr* (Gdzie są niegdysiejsze śniegi), UA in Rom; 1980 *Wielopole, Wielopole*, UA in Florenz; 1985 *Die Künstler sollen krepieren* (Niech zdechą artyści), UA in Nürnberg; 1988 *Ich kehre hierher nie mehr zurück* (Nigdy tu już ne powroze), UA in Mailand, 1990 *Heute ist mein Geburtstag*.

Slawomir Tryc/Elke Wiegand

Csiky Gergely Szinház (Kaposvár)

Csiky-Gergely-Theater. Gegr. 1911 als Stadttheater (eklektischer Jugendstilbau). Erhält sich mit Operettengastspielen. 1955 verstaatlicht, erstmals auch Schauspiel. Als 1968 Gábor Zsámbéki (*1943) das Ensemble reorganisiert, 1971–74 Chefregisseur und 1974–78 Intendant ist, wird es zum Ausgangspunkt neuen Theaterdenkens in Ungarn (Ensemblespiel, Wahrhaftigkeit der Darstellung, Unbefangenheit gegenüber Texten, Historie und politischen Ideen; alternative Formen). Durch kluge Spielplanpolitik (Kinderstück, Musical/Operette, Klassiker, Moderne) gewinnt man neues Publikum. Durchbruch mit G. Zsámbékis *Möwe*-Aufführung. Profilprägend auch der avantgardistische Bühnenbildner Gyula Pauer, Péter Gothár (1978–81), János Acs, Tamás Ascher (1971–78, ab 1981 Chefregisseur; 1983 *Hamlet*, 1986 *Meister und Margarita* nach M. Bulgakow, 1990 *Farm der Tiere*, Musical nach Orwell) und László Babarczy (1974–78 Chefregisseur, ab 1978 Intendant), der das Ensemble stabilisiert, unterschiedliche Regieinteressen (absurdes Theater, Brecht, Tschechow, engl. Naturalisten, zeitgenössische ungar. Autoren) fördert und die Spitzenposition des Ensembles vielseitiger Schauspieler (R. Koltai, J. Pogány u. a.) sichert. International aufsehenerregende Inzenierung *Marat-Sade* von P. Weiss durch J. Acs 1981.

Elke Wiegand

Cullbergbaletten

Das Ensemble wurde 1967 in Stockholm gegründet, um der bedeutenden schwedischen Choreographin Birgit Cullberg (*1908) eine Plattform für ihre Arbeiten zu bieten. Cullberg – von 1952–57 Choreographin des Königlichen Schwedischen Balletts – hatte 1950 mit *Fräulein Julie* (nach Strindberg) einen ‹Klassiker› des modernen Repertoires geschaffen und mit *Mondrentier* 1957 (beim Königlich Dänischen Ballett) den internationalen Durchbruch erzielt. Neben ihren und Werken schwedischer Choreographen (bspw. Elsa-Marianne von Rosen, *1927; Ulf Gadd, *1943) präsentiert das C. Gastchoreographien u. a. von Merce Cunningham (*1919; →Post Modern Dance), Fleming Flindt (*1936), Kurt Jooss (1901–79; →Ballets Jooss), Tom Schilling (*1928; →Tanztheater der Komischen Oper Berlin), Alvin Ailey (1931–89), Jiri Kylián; (1947; →Nederlands Dans Theater) und Maurice Béjart (*1927; →Ballet du XXᵉ Siècle). Cullberg, die vor ihrer Tanzausbildung (an der Jooss-Leeder-Schule in Dartington/England) ein Literaturstudium absolvierte, bevorzugt stark dramatische und literarische Stoffe.

1985 (bis 1993) wird Mats Ek (*1945), der Sohn Cullbergs und des Schauspielers Anders Ek, künstlerischer Leiter des C., dessen Choreograph er bereits seit Ende der 70er Jahre ist. Durch Eks Inszenierungen und Werke u. a. von J. Kylián, Nacho Duato (*1957), Christopher Bruce (*1945) und William Forsythe (*1949; →Ballett Frankfurt) wird das Repertoire erneuert. Neben meist erzählenden Kurzballetten schafft Ek, der vor seiner Tanz- eine Schauspielausbildung absolviert und als Theaterregisseur gearbeitet hat, eigenwillige moderne Interpretationen der Klassiker *Giselle* und *Schwanensee*, die dem Ensemble zu neuer internationaler Beachtung verhelfen.

Näslund, E.: Birgit Cullberg. Stockholm 1978; ders.: Mats Ek und sein Versuch, für das Ballett eine neue Form zu finden. In: Regitz, H./Koegler, H.: Ballett 1983. Zürich 1983; Rolf Garske: Interview mit Mats Ek. In: Ballett International 3 (1989).

Horst Vollmer

Da capo

(Ital. ‹noch einmal von vorn›, ‹von Anfang›) Beifallszuruf aus dem Publikum; Aufforderung an den Darsteller (Sänger, Schauspieler), das Vorgetragene noch einmal zu wiederholen.

Horst Schumacher

Dadaistisches Theater

Obwohl nur in Zusammenhang mit ‹Dada Paris› und in Kurt Schwitters' →Merzbühne ein eigentliches D. T. entstanden ist, spielen doch auch in der Zürcher Phase des Dadaismus, zentriert im →Cabaret Voltaire, sowie in der Berliner Erscheinungsform theatrale Elemente eine wesentliche Rolle: Der dadaistische Protest gegen die herrschende Realität und die traditionelle Kunst entfaltet sich in hohem Maße in direkter Kommunikation mit dem Publikum, das durch kalkulierte Provokation zum ‹Mitspiel› aufgefordert werden soll. Das geschieht einerseits in Veranstaltungen, zu denen man (oft mit falschen Ankündigungen) eigens einlädt, andererseits in realen Situationen, die man überraschend umfunktioniert. Berühmt für die vor allem von Raoul Hausmann (1900–71), Richard Huelsenbeck (1892–1974) und Johannes Baader (1875–1956) getragene Berliner Dada-Bewegung der Zeit nach dem 1. Weltkrieg mit ihrem stark politisch-anarchistischen Grundzug waren die Vortragsabende und Mati-

258 Dadaistisches Theater

neen, bei denen Manifeste, ‹Simultan-Gedichte› und Publikumsbeschimpfungen mit dem Ziel der Verhöhnung und Entlarvung des ‹Spießbürgers› vorgetragen wurden. Das markanteste Beispiel für eine Aktion in der Öffentlichkeit ist Johannes Baaders Auftritt 1918 im Berliner Dom: «Als der Hofprediger Dryander seine Predigt beginnen wollte, rief Baader mit lauter Stimme: ‹Einen Augenblick! Ich frage Sie, was ist Ihnen Jesus Christus? Er ist Ihnen Wurst.› Natürlich gab es einen fürchterlichen Tumult, Baader wurde verhaftet und wegen Gotteslästerei angeklagt» (Hausmann, S. 56).

Im Rahmen von ‹Dada-Soirée› oder ‹Dada-Festival› genannten Veranstaltungen wurden in Paris zwischen 1920 und 1922 die wichtigsten Stücke des D. T. aufgeführt, wobei die Autoren als ihre eigenen Darsteller auftraten, sich also existentiell mit ihrem Werk identifizierten, so daß ein neues Verhältnis zu ihrem Publikum entstand. Von Tristan Tzara (1896–1963), mit dessen Übersiedlung nach Zürich zu Beginn des Jahres 1920 ‹Paris Dada› erst seine revolutionäre Potenz erhielt, stammen *Die himmlischen Abenteuer des Monsieur Antipyrine* (1920/21), zwei ohne erkennbare Logik aus sinnlosen Wortgebilden aufgebaute Szenenfolgen. In Tzaras Dada-Stück *Das Gasherz* (1922) treten ‹Auge›, ‹Ohr›, ‹Nase›, ‹Hals›, ‹Mund› und ‹Augenbraue› als Figuren auf; es werden Tänze in phantastischen Kostümen gezeigt; die Konventionen des traditionellen Theaters erscheinen in parodierter Form. – Der zweite wichtige Dramatiker des D. T. ist Georges Ribemont-Dessaignes (1884–1974) mit seinen Stücken *Der Kaiser von China, Der Stumme Kanarienvogel* und *Zizi de Dada*, alle um 1920 entstanden. Zusammen mit Philippe Soupault (1897–1973) hat André Breton (1896–1966) die Komödie *Bitte sehr* und den Sketch *Sie werden mich vergessen* (beide 1920) geschrieben, die ebenfalls dem D. T. zuzurechnen sind, obwohl sie in Ansätzen schon Prinzipien des ‹automatischen Schreibens› vorwegnehmen, das dann mit seinem Rekurs auf das Unbewußte wesentlich wird für den Surrealismus (→ Surrealistisches Theater).

Sein äußeres Zeichen fand die Ablösung der Surrealisten von dem ihrer Meinung nach unproduktiv in der Destruktion verharrenden Dadaismus in einer Saalschlacht zwischen den Anhängern Bretons und den Gefolgsleuten von Tzara (1923), der den Dadaismus vergeblich am Leben zu halten versuchte. Nur einmal noch kam es zu einer Manifestation des D. T. in der Aufführung des von Francis Picabia und Marcel Duchamp entworfenen, von Erik Satie komponierten Balletts *Relâche* durch die «Ballets Suédois» (Paris 1924). Die Bühne bestand aus drei hintereinander aufgestellten Portalen und einer Rückwand, bedeckt von runden Metallscheiben mit Glühbirnen in der Mitte, so daß die Zuschauer geblendet wurden. Alltagsszenen waren aneinandergereiht und durchsetzt mit quasirealen Szenen: ein Feuerwehrmann, der eine Zigarette nach der anderen rauchte, ein Unbeschäftigter am Rand der Bühne, der von Zeit zu Zeit aufstand, um den Bühnenboden auszumessen. Zwischen den beiden Akten lief ein von Picabia und Duchamp zusammen mit dem noch unbekannten René Clair gedrehter Film *Entr'acte*. Am Schluß fuhren die Autoren mit einem Auto über die Bühne – und wurden ausgepfiffen. Mit der Provokation als Wirkungsabsicht, dem persönlichen Auftreten der Autoren als Zielscheibe der Zuschaueraggression und der tendenziellen Auflösung des Bühnengeschehens in Realität kamen in dieser Aufführung nochmals die wichtigsten Strukturmerkmale des D. T. zum Ausdruck, die im →Happening der 60er Jahre wiederaufgenommen wurden.

Ericson, J. D.: Dada. Boston 1984; Grimm, J.: Das avantgardistische Theater Frankreichs 1895–1930. München 1982; Hausmann, R.: Am Anfang war Dada. Gießen 1980; Rischbieter, H./Storch, W.: Theater und bildende Kunst im XX. Jh. Velber 1968.

Peter Simhandl

Dance Theatre of Harlem (New York)

Der erste farbige Solist in Balanchines →New York City Ballet, Arthur Mitchell (* 1934), gründet 1969 eine nur aus farbigen Tänzern bestehende Kompanie. Mitchell versucht zu zeigen, daß an afrikanischen Tanzstil gewohnte Tänzer die klassisch-akademische Tanztechnik erwerben können. Ausbildung erhalten die Tänzer des D. T. o. H. an einer zur Kompanie gehörigen und von Mitchell gegründeten Schule. Basis der Ausbildung: klassischer Tanz, Modern Dance, Jazz Dance, ethnischer Tanz, Step u. a. Weites Stilrepertoire: Agon, Bugaku, Concerto Barocco (Balanchine, Neoklassizismus); Greening (Tetley); Holberg Suite, Rhythmetron, Fête Noire, Giselle (Mitchell). Afrikanische Themen: *Forces of Rhythm* (L. Johnson). Die Entwicklung des afrikanischen Tanzes und seine Integration in die USA wird problematisiert.

Interview mit A. Mitchell von Rolf Garske. In: Ballett International 11 (1983), S. 21–23.

Patricia Stöckemann

Darstellendes Spiel

Der Begriff d. S. bezieht sich auf theatrale Tätigkeiten, bei denen die Spieler ihre eigene Lebenswirklichkeit bewältigen, indem sie sie in fiktiven Situationen ‹ausprobieren›. Ohne das Risiko realer Entscheidung tragen zu müssen, können sie sich selbst alternatives Verhalten realitätsnah vorführen. Zuschauer, die das Spielgeschehen passiv beobachten, sind nicht zwingend erforderlich. Wichtige Anregungen erhielt das d. S. durch Brechts Lehrstück-Theorie (um 1930): «Das Lehrstück lehrt dadurch, daß es gespielt, nicht dadurch, daß es gesehen wird... Es liegt dem Lehrstück die Erwartung zugrunde, daß der Spielende durch die Durchführung bestimmter Handlungsweisen, Einnahme bestimmter Haltungen, Wiedergabe bestimmter Reden und so weiter gesellschaftlich beeinflußt werden kann.» In der Gegenwart förderte das Beispiel des brasilianischen Theaterpädagogen, Regisseurs und Stückeschreibers Augusto Boal das d. S. Sein Modell des → «Theaters der Unterdrückten» orientiert sich auf Spieler, die ihnen bekannte Herrschaftsverhältnisse darstellen, sie dabei szenisch analysieren und mögliche Widerstandsformen entwickeln. Auch psychotherapeutische Übungen, in denen Spieler mittels übernommener → Rollen interpersonelle Konflikte erkennen und Aggressionen abbauen können, werden ebenso mit dem Dachbegriff d. S. bezeichnet wie schauspielerisch gestaltete Übungen im Fremdsprachen- oder Literaturunterricht der Schule. Hier sollte genauer zwischen → Schultheater, das auf eine öffentliche Vorstellung ausgerichtet ist, und d. S. unterschieden werden, bei dem der Lernprozeß wichtiger als das endgültige und fixierte Resultat ist. Im Kontext schulpädagogischer Reformen nach 1968 wurde das d. S. zunehmend in den Lehrplänen verankert, wenn auch in den einzelnen Bundesländern mit unterschiedlichem Gewicht und häufig als ‹dramatisches Gestalten› eingeschränkt. Die DDR-Schulpolitik ließ wenig Raum für d. S., weil es ihrem szientistischen Konzept widersprach. Gegenwärtig strebt die Bundesarbeitsgemeinschaft DARSTELLENDES SPIEL länderübergreifend eine noch stärkere Integration des d. S. in die Lehrpläne aller Klassenstufen an.

Bernd, Ch.: Bewegung und Theater. Lernen durch Verkörpern. Frankfurt/M. 1988; Ruping, B. (Hg.): Gebraucht das Theater. Die Vorschläge von Augusto Boal. Lingen-Remscheid 1991.

Roland Dreßler

Debüt

(Auch ‹Debut›, frz. ‹Anfang›) Erster öffentlicher Auftritt eines Schauspielers oder Sängers; auch Antrittsrolle an einem neuen Theater oder in neuem Engagement; bezeichnet in der Literatur das Erstlingswerk eines noch unbekannten Autors.

Horst Schumacher

Deklamation

(Lat. declamatio: Vortrag) Kunstmäßiger Vortrag einer Rede oder einer Rolle. Sie wurde bereits in der Antike gepflegt, als die Tragödie gesungen wurde. Seit der Mitte des 16. Jh. bezeichnet das Wort D. die kunstvolle Vortragsweise zunächst für die lateinischen Redeübungen in den Schulen der Reformationszeit, dann für alle Dichterwerke, v. a. der gehobenen Gattungen. Johann Wolfgang von Goethe (1749–1832) definiert sie folgendermaßen: «Ganz anders aber ist es bei der Deklamation oder gesteigerten Rezitation. Hier muß ich meinen angebornen Charakter verlassen, mein Naturell verleugnen und mich ganz in die Lage und Stimmung desjenigen versetzen, dessen Rolle ich deklamiere. Die Worte, welche ich ausspreche, müssen mit Energie und dem lebendigen Ausdruck hervorgebracht werden, so daß ich jede leidenschaftliche Regung als wirklich gegenwärtig mit zu empfinden scheine» (Bd. XII, S. 254. Hamburger Ausgabe in 14 Bdn. 6. Aufl. 1962). Mit der Zeit und v. a. seit Ende des 18. Jh., als das mit diesem Begriff verbundene schauspielerische Pathos nicht mehr geschätzt und als unnatürlich empfunden wurde, hat das Wort D. eine eher abwertende Konnotation angenommen, etwa ‹gekünstelter Vortrag›.

Bernard Poloni

Deus ex machina

In der griech. Tragödie Bezeichnung für den in der Regel mit der kranartigen Flugmaschine (→Mechane; lat. machina) inszenierten, überraschenden Auftritt eines Gottes, dessen Funktion darin besteht, dramatische Aporien zu lösen und das vom Mythos ‹geforderte› Ende herbeizuführen. Im weiteren Sinne kann der bereits in der Antike sprichwörtlich gewordene Ausdruck auch funktionsgleiche (oder doch verwandte) Auftritte von menschlichen Akteuren bezeichnen, die in einer restlos verfahrenen Situation Rettung und Aufklärung bringen.

Spira, A.: Untersuchungen zum Deus ex machina bei Sophokles und Euripides. Kallmütz 1960; Schmidt, W.: Der Deus ex machina bei Euripides. Diss. Tübingen 1964.

Bernd Seidensticker

Deutsche Bühne

Die D. B. entstand als Gegengründung zur →Freien Bühne 1890 in Berlin. Sie existierte nur knapp sieben Monate, vom 28. September 1890 bis zum 26. April 1891. An der Gründung waren maßgeblich beteiligt: M. G. Conrad, Karl Bleibtreu, Conrad Alberti, außerdem Wilhelm Walloth, Hermann Bahr und Detlev Freiherr v. Liliencron. Julius Hart unterstützte die D. B. zeitweilig. Die D. B. brachte insgesamt fünf Stücke zur Aufführung: K. Bleibtreus *Schicksal*; A. Müller-Guttenbrunns *Irma*; C. Albertis *Brot!*; H. Bahrs *Die neuen Menschen*; J. Harts *Sumpf*.

Christine Müller

Deutscher Bühnenverein (DBV)

Begriff: Der Deutsche Bühnenverein ist ein eingetragener Verein, in dem sich die öffentlichen und privaten Träger der Theater und Kulturorchester zusammengeschlossen haben. Er trägt den Namen «Deutscher Bühnenverein, Bundesverband deutscher Theater» und hat seinen Sitz in Köln.

Geschichte: Der D. B. wurde 1846 gegr. Er entwickelte insbesondere in der 2. Hälfte des vorigen Jh. seine Vorstellungen über die erforderlichen Reformen im dt. Theaterwesen. So forderte er die staatliche Aufsicht über das Ausbildungswesen, ferner versuchte er, Regelungen für das Bühnenarbeitsrecht zu finden. In dem neu errichteten Dt. Kaiserreich spielte der D. B. anfangs eine unwesentliche Rolle. Bemühungen, die Regierung zu bewegen, dringend notwendige Regelungen für das Theaterwesen zu erlassen, blieben zunächst erfolglos. Im Jahre 1871 wurde in Weimar auf dem ersten allgemeinen Bühnenkongreß die →Genossenschaft Deutscher Bühnenangehöriger (GDBA) gegr. D. B. und Bühnengenossenschaft nahmen sich in der Folgezeit der dringend zu regelnden Fragen an. In der Zeit zwischen 1873 und 1874 wurde der erste Normalvertrag vereinbart. 1905 errichtete sie eine paritätische Bühnenschiedsgerichtsbarkeit. Diese paritätische Einrichtung sah zwei Instanzen vor, in der beide Seiten paritätisch tätig waren. Wegen gravierender Meinungsverschiedenheiten über die Regelung eines Tarifvertrags berief die Genossenschaft 1909 ihre Schiedsrichter jedoch wieder ab. 1919 wurde im Zusammenhang mit der Verabschiedung eines neuen Normalvertrags die Bühnenschiedsgerichtsbarkeit als paritätische Einrichtung wieder eingesetzt.

Nach Zusammenbruch der kaiserlichen Ordnung stellte sich für die Länder und auch teilweise für die Städte die Frage nach ihrer Beteiligung am D. B. Auf einer Reichstheaterkonferenz im Oktober 1919 und Ende Februar 1920 wurde die Frage der Mitgliedschaft der Länder und Kommunen im D. B. und die Sicherung ihrer Rechte geregelt.

Während des sog. 3. Reiches teilte der B. das Schicksal aller Vereinigungen: Am 22. September 1933 wurde das Reichskulturkammergesetz (→Theatergesetz) erlassen. Dieses Gesetz sah eine sog. →Reichstheaterkammer vor. Der Präsident der Reichstheaterkammer löste am 6. September 1935 den D. B. auf. Nach dem Ende des 2. Weltkriegs gründeten sich zunächst in den verschiedenen Zonen Landesverbände. 1948 wurde der D. B. als Verband dt. Theater neu gegr. Seitdem hat er seinen Sitz in Köln.

Aufbau und Wirkungsweise: Neben der bundesverbandlichen Ordnung (Hauptversammlung, Verwaltungsrat, Präsidium, Tarifausschuß, Vorstand) verfügt der D. B. über eine regionale Struktur in Form der Landesverbände. Um den vielfältigen Interessen und Aufgaben seiner Mitglieder gerecht zu werden, bilden diese sechs Gruppen mit eigener Funktion: Staatstheatergruppe, Stadttheatergruppe, Landesbühnengruppe, Privattheatergruppe, Intendantengruppe, Gruppe der außerordentlichen Mitglieder (z. B. Rundfunk- oder Fernsehanstalten sowie sonstige Institutionen). – Der D. B. nimmt die Interessen der in ihm zusammengeschlossenen Theater und Kulturorchester auf kulturpolitischem und arbeitsrechtlichem Gebiet wahr. Er ist somit Tarifpartner auf Arbeitgeberseite und handelt mit den Arbeitnehmervereinigungen (→Genossenschaft Deutscher Bühnenangehöriger, Deutsche Orchestervereinigung, Vereinigung dt. Opernsänger und Balletttänzer e. V.) die für den Theaterbereich geltenden Tarifverträge aus. Zusammen mit der GDBA unterhält der D. B. sog. «Paritätische Einrichtungen»: die Versorgungsanstalt der deutschen Bühnen, die Versorgungsanstalt der deutschen Kulturorchester, die Paritätische Prüfungskommission (für Maskenbildner, Theatermaler und -plastiker; die Paritätische Prüfungskommission für Schauspieler, Sänger und Tänzer wird mit Ende 1993 aufgelöst) sowie Bühnenschiedsgerichte (zwei Instanzen mit Übergang in die Arbeitsgerichtsbarkeit).

Am 21. Okt. 1990 vereinigte sich der D. B. mit dem Deutschen Bühnenbund der DDR, der aufgelöst wurde.

Schöndienst, E.: Geschichte des Deutschen Bühnenvereins. 2 Bde. Frankfurt/M. 1979 und 1981; Bühnen- und Musikrecht. Hg. vom Deutschen Bühnenverein. Darmstadt (Loseblattsammlung); Deutsches Bühnenjahrbuch. Jährl. Erscheinungsweise. Hg. v. d. Genossenschaft Deutscher Bühnenangehöriger; Die Deutsche Bühne. Theatermagazin. Organ des Deutschen Bühnenvereins (monatl. Erscheinungsweise).

Roswitha Körner/Red.

Deutsche Shakespeare-Gesellschaft

Anläßlich des 300. Geburtstages von Shakespeare wurde am 23. April 1864 in Weimar eine literarische Gesellschaft – die älteste ihrer Art in Deutschland – gegründet. Initiatoren waren der Industrielle Wilhelm Oechelhäuser (später Präsident der Gesellschaft) und der Weimarer Intendant Franz Dingelstedt. Die Sh.-G. wollte durch Aufführungen, Ausstellungen, Vorträge und Colloquien zu jährlich im April stattfindenden Tagungen die dt. Shakespeare-Rezeption fördern; die seit 1865 erscheinenden Shakespeare-Jahrbücher (mit ausführlichen Bibliographien und Aufführungsverzeichnissen) und die in Weimar aufgebaute Shakespeare-Bibliothek sind Kompendien für Spezialisten und Interessenten. Zu den ersten Shakespeare-Tagen kam Dingelstedts berühmter Zyklus von sieben Historien zur Aufführung. Der zeitweise sehr fruchtbare Dialog zwischen Theaterleuten und Wissenschaftlern gehört zu den Qualitäten der Sh.-G.; nennenswert in dieser Hinsicht ist besonders das Wirken des Bochumer Intendanten Saladin Schmitt (Präsident der Sh.-G. 1943–51). Nach dem 2. Weltkrieg begannen Aktivitäten der Sh.-G. zunächst vorwiegend in Bochum; 1963 führte dann die von beiden Seiten ausgehende kulturpolitische Instrumentalisierung zur Spaltung der Gesellschaft (Dt. Sh.-G. Sitz Weimar und Dt. Sh.-G. West Sitz Bochum). Unter den Präsidenten Ulrich Suerbaum (West) und Robert Weimann (Ost) wird für 1993 die ‹Wiedervereinigung› vorbereitet. – Shakespeare-Jahrbücher seit 1865; 1964–92 getrennte Publikationsreihen in Weimar und Bochum.

Manfred Pauli

Deutsches Nationaltheater Weimar

Erbaut 1906–07 (mit 857 Plätzen), Intendant seit 1987: Fritz Wendrich (* 1934). – Gastspiele von Wandertruppen, erster Theaterbau 1696, 1769 bis 1771 Truppe von Gottfried Heinrich Koch (1703–75), 1771 bis 1774 von Abel Seyler (1730–1800, →Leipzig), Goethe (1749–1832), der 1775 nach Weimar kommt, eröffnet Liebhabertheater des Herzogs Karl Albert, leitet 1791 bis 1817 Hoftheater, Mitarbeiter: Schiller (1757–1805). 1857 bis 1867 ist Franz von Dingelstedt (1814–81) Intendant, der 1861 *Die Nibelungen* von Hebbel inszeniert, Wiedereröffnung des zerstörten Hauses 1948, 1949 bis 1952 ist Hans-Robert Bertfeldt (1906–55), 1952 bis 1958 Karl Kayser (* 1914), von 1958 bis 1973 Otto Lang (1906–78), von 1973–87 G. Beinemann (* 1918). – Die DDR-Kulturpolitik forderte das Theater der Klassikerstadt zu besonderer, affirmativer «Erbpflege» heraus. Dabei suchten immer wieder Regisseure – wie Fritz Bennewitz, Peter

Schroth/Volkmar Kleinert oder in jüngster Zeit Leander Hausmann – eigenwillige Inszenierungen durchzusetzen, die nicht auf sog. Werktreue, jedoch ganz auf gegenwärtig brennende Fragen zielten.

Abend, B.: Deutsches Nationaltheater. Weimar 1968; Satori-Neumann, B. Th.: Die Frühzeit des Weimarischen Hoftheaters unter Goethes Leitung (1791–1798). Berlin 1922.

Andreas Roßmann/Roland Dreßler

Deutsches Schauspielhaus (Hamburg)

Schauspielhaus, Malersaal. 1900 erbaut im Wiener Barockstil der Architekten Fellner (1847–1916) und Helmer (1849–1919) als «hanseatisch-republikanisches Hoftheater». Aktiengesellschaft Hamburger Bürger als «Bollwerk gegen die Herrschaft des schlechten Geschmacks». Künstlerisches Vorbild Wiener Burgtheater. Direktoren bzw. Intendanten: 1900 bis 1909 der Wiener Alfred von Berger (1853–1912), konservativ, Ablehnung des Naturalismus, Makartstil. 1910–1913 Carl Hagemann (1871 bis 1945). Hochqualifiziertes Ensemble, 1913 bis 1918 Max Grube, 1918 bis 1926 Paul Eger, 1926 bis 1928 Erich Ziegel (1876–1950) – zusätzlich zur Leitung der Hamburger Kammerspiele. 1928 bis 1932 Hermann Röbbeling. Seit 1933 verstaatlicht. 1932 bis 1945 Karl Wüstenhagen, 1945/46 Rolf Külüs, 1946 bis 1948 Arthur Hellmer, 1948–1955 Albert Lippert. 1955 bis 1963 Gustaf Gründgens (1899–1963) – glanzvolles, repräsentatives Schauspieltheater, vor allem Klassiker, 1959 UA *Heilige Johanna der Schlachthöfe* von Brecht. Gastspiele in New York und Moskau. 1963 bis 1968 Oscar Fritz Schuh (1904–85), 1968 Egon Monk, 1968/69 Gerhard Hirsch, 1969 bis 1970 Hans Lietzau (1913–91), 1970/71 Rolf Liebermann, 1972 bis 1979 Ivan Nagel (*1931) – radikale Vergegenwärtigung der Klassiker, zeitgenössische Stücke. Inszenierungen u. a. von Zadek, Noelte, Bondy, Flimm, Strehler. 1979/80 Günter König u. Rolf Mares (Geschäftsführer), 1980 bis 1985 Niels-Peter Rudolph (*1939), 1985 bis 1989 Peter Zadek (*1926). Risikobereites Theater. 1989–91 der Engländer Michael Bogdanov (*1938), 1992–93 Gerd Schlesselmann, ab 1993/94 Frank Baumbauer. Mit 1397 Plätzen größtes Schauspielhaus der Bundesrepublik. 1981 bis 1984 Restaurierung, Wiederherstellung des Originalzustands im Zuschauerraum, Verbesserung der Bühnentechnik.

75 Jahre Deutsches Schauspielhaus Hamburg. Hamburg 1975; Theaterstadt Hamburg. Hg. Zentrum f. Theaterforschung. Reinbek 1989.

Werner Schulze-Reimpell/Red.

Deutsches Theater (Berlin)

Schumannstraße 13 a/14, seit 1949 «Staatstheater der DDR». Zwei Spielstätten (D. T. mit 798 Plätzen, Kammerspiele mit 456 Plätzen). Intendant seit 1991: Thomas Langhoff (* 1938).

1850 Eröffnung als Friedrich-Wilhelmstädtisches Theater, 1872 Umbau, 1883 Gründung des D. T. durch den Direktor, Regisseur und Erfolgsdramatiker Adolph L'Arronge (1838–1908), der es kaufte und ausdekorieren ließ, sein Protagonist war Josef Kainz (1858–1910), Aufführungen im Stil der Meininger. Vor allem konservative Klassiker-Inszenierungen, aber auch Uraufführung von Gerhart Hauptmanns (1862 bis 1946) *Kollege Crampton* (1891). 1894 übernahm der Theaterkritiker Otto Brahm (1856–1912) die Intendanz, der vor allem Hauptmann, auch Ibsen (1828–1906) und Schnitzler (1862–1931) durchsetzte; 1904 folgte ihm Max Reinhardt (1873–1943), der 1906 Eigentümer des D. T. wurde und die benachbarten Kammerspiele eröffnete. Besonders mit seinen Shakespeare-Inszenierungen (darunter mehrmals *Sommernachtstraum*) führte Reinhardt, der «Theater als großes Fest» verstand, das D. T. zu Weltruhm (mehrere Tourneen in die USA), weitere Spielplanschwerpunkte: deutsche Klassik und Zeitgenossen wie Wedekind (1864–1918), Shaw (1856–1950), Werfel (1890–1945), Hofmannsthal (1874–1929). Reinhardt leitete das D. T. – mit Unterbrechungen – bis 1933; 1934 übernahm Heinz Hilpert (1890–1967), von 1926 bis 1932 schon Oberspielleiter, der Spielplanlinien (Shakespeare, Schiller, Goethe) fortführte und Erich Engel (1891–1966) als Spielleiter engagierte. Hilpert gelang bis 1944 ‹Bewahrung bürgerlich-humanistischer Traditionen› gegen nationalsozialistische Kulturfunktionäre.

Am 7. 10. 1945 Wiedereröffnung des D. T. mit Lessings (1729–81) *Nathan der Weise*, Regie: Fritz Wisten (1890–1962), Titelrolle Paul Wegener (1874–1948). Intendant zunächst (1945–46) Gustav von Wangenheim (1895–1975), ab August 1946 Wolfgang Langhoff (1901–66), der von 1949 bis 1954 dem → Berliner Ensemble Gastrecht bot. Sein Spielplan folgte seiner These, die Klassiker «zu wahren Zeitgenossen» zu machen, Inszenierungen meist mit dem Bühnenbildner Heinrich Kilger (1907–69), Bemühungen um Sowjet- und DDR-Dramatik, vor allem Peter Hacks (* 1928). Nach der politisch heftig angefeindeten UA von dessen *Sorgen um die Macht* (1962) kommt es zum Rücktritt Langhoffs. Ihm folgte Wolfgang Heinz (1900–84), der als Regisseur vor allem mit Gorki- (1868–1936), Tschechow- (1860–1904) und Shaw-Inszenierungen, als Schauspieler in der Titelrolle von Lessings *Nathan*, Regie: Friedo Solter (* 1933), reüssiert. In seine Amtszeit fallen die großen, weltbekannt gewordenen Inszenierungen des Brecht-Schülers Benno Besson (* 1922; → Berliner Ensemble, → Volksbühne): *Der Friede* (1962) von Hacks nach

Deutsches Theater (Berlin) **267**

Aristophanes (384–322 v. Chr.), *Der Drache* (1965) von Jewgenij Schwarz (1896–1958) und *Ödipus Tyrann* von Heiner Müller (*1929) nach Sophokles (497–406 v. Chr.)/Hölderlin (1770–1843). Adolf Dresens (*1935) Inszenierung von *Faust I* (1968), bei der Heinz als Ko-Regisseur verantwortlich zeichnete, wurde von der SED heftig attackiert und führte 1970 zu seinem Rücktritt als Intendant. Der Nachfolger Hans Anselm Perten (1917–85) – vorher und nachher Generalintendant in Rostock – scheiterte am Selbstbewußtsein des an bedeutenden Künstlerpersönlichkeiten reichen Ensembles. Gerhard Wolfram (1922–91), der das D. T. dann von 1972–82 leitete, schuf unter komplizierten Bedingungen Freiräume für sehr unterschiedliche Kunstinnovationen, wie sie bis 1978 von Dresen (u. a. 1975 Kleists *Prinz von Homburg* und *Der zerbrochene Krug* an einem Abend und 1978 die Adaption des *Michael Kohlhaas*), dem Team Klaus Erforth (*1936)/Alexander Stillmark (*1941) (u. a. 1973 *Die Kipper* von Volker Braun und 1976 Fugards *Insel*), Solters Klassiker-Inszenierungen und besonders von Alexander Lang (*1941) ausgingen. Lang wurde bis zu seinem Ausscheiden 1986 mit dem artifiziell-grotesken Stil seiner Inszenierungen – *Sommernachtstraum* (1980), *Dantons Tod* (1981), *Die Rundköpfe und die Spitzköpfe* (1983), *Die wahre Geschichte des Ah Q* von Christoph Hein (1983), *Iphigenie* und *Herzog Theodor von Gothland* als Doppelprojekt (1984), *Medea*, *Stella* und *Totentanz* zur *Trilogie der Leidenschaften* (1986) zusammengefaßt – zum wichtigsten Regisseur des D. T. Als Intendanten folgten Wolfram zunächst der Theaterwissenschaftler Rolf Rohmer (*1930), seit 1984 der Schauspieler Dieter Mann (*1941) und seit 1991 der Regisseur Thomas Langhoff (Sohn des früheren Intendanten Wolfgang Langhoff). Dessen gleichermaßen sensible wie komödiantische Inszenierungen (z. B. *Maria Stuart*, 1980; *Sturmgeselle Sokrates* von Sudermann, 1986; *Ein Monat auf dem Lande* von Turgenjew, 1987; Behans *Geisel*, 1989, oder *Der zerbrochne Krug*, 1990) wurden für das künstlerische Gesicht des D. T. ebenso wichtig wie Rolf Winkelgrunds (*1936) Barlach-Inszenierungen, die extremen Spiel-Versionen des Frank Castorf (*1951) (z. B. *John Gabriel Borkmann*, 1990) und die Regiearbeiten Heiner Müllers (dessen *Lohndrücker*, 1988, und *Hamlet*/*Hamletmaschine*, 1989, in gewisser Weise ein künstlerisches Fazit gescheiterter DDR-Entwicklung darstellten).

Boeser, K./Vatková, R. (Hg.): Max Reinhardt in Berlin. Berlin 1984; Dreifuss, A.: Deutsches Theater Berlin Schumannstraße 13a. Fünf Kapitel aus der Geschichte einer Schauspielbühne. Berlin (DDR) 1983; Funke, Ch./Kranz, D.: Theaterstadt Berlin. Berlin (DDR) 1978; Kuschnia, M. (Hg.): 100 Jahre Deutsches Theater Berlin 1883–1983. Berlin (DDR) 1983; Linzer, M. (Hg.): Alexander Lang: Abenteuer Theater. Berlin (DDR) 1983; Mittenzwei, W. (Hg.): Theater in der Zeitenwende. Berlin (DDR) 1972, S. 312–323; Müller, A.: Der Regisseur

Benno Besson. Berlin (DDR) 1967; Pietzsch, I.: Werkstatt Theater. Berlin (DDR) 1975, S. 9–16 u. 44–52; Seydel, R. (Hg.): Verweile doch…: Erinnerungen von Schauspielern des Deutschen Theaters Berlin. Berlin (DDR) 1984; Wardetzky, J.: Theaterpolitik im faschistischen Deutschland: Studien und Dokumente. Berlin (DDR) 1983, S. 114–137; Kranz, D.: Berliner Theater. Berlin 1990.

Andreas Roßmann / Manfred Pauli

Dialog

(Griech. dialogos = Unterredung) Im Gegensatz zum →Monolog das Wechsel- oder Zwiegespräch, genauer: die von zwei (Duolog) oder mehreren Personen (Polylog) abwechselnd geführte Rede und Gegenrede. Die Aussage des D. zielt vorrangig auf den Partner und auf die Zuhörerschaft, bezieht sich infolgedessen auf die Zuhörerbereitschaft und -situation. Sie kann sich simultan auf mehreren Referenzebenen entwickeln. Rein sprachlich betrachtet, charakterisiert sich die Aussage des D. durch das Vorhandensein metalinguistischer Elemente und die Häufigkeit der interrogativen Formen.

Der D. wird als grundlegende sprachliche Charakteristik des Dramas betrachtet, sogar als identisch mit der sprachlichen Struktur des Dramas: «Die vollständige dramatische Form ist der Dialog» (Hegel). Da aber Drama selbst Handlung bedeutet, wird der D. immer wieder aus diesem Bezugspunkt näher bestimmt und als aktional oder nichtaktional empfunden. Aktional ist jener D., in dem sich mit jeder Replik, jeder Rede und Gegenrede ein situationsveränderndes Handeln vollzieht, in dem das Wort also die Handlung trägt. In diesem Kontext erhält die theatergeschichtliche Tatsache, daß der D. nach bzw. aus dem Monolog entstanden ist, eine neue Bedeutung. Er entstand zwar im →antiken Theater aus der Wechselrede zwischen →Chor und →Protagonisten; aber erst die Einführung eines zweiten Schauspielers, die Aischylos, 524–426 v. Chr., zugesprochen wird, schuf die nötige Voraussetzung zum D. Die zeitgeschichtliche Entwicklung des D. wie auch die des Monologs hebt die Unmöglichkeit der Verabsolutierung dieser Begriffe hervor. Nach Mukarovsky (1967) sind die Übergänge von D. und Monolog fließend; ein D. beruhe auf der Polarität oder Spannung zwischen zwei (oder mehreren) Subjekten, die durch ein «Sich-Durchdringen und Sich-Lösen von mehrerlei, wenigstens zweierlei Kontexten bedingt wären».

Die durch Handlungsentwicklung gegebene Bedingtheit des aktionalen D. bringt auch eine wichtige Personenabhängigkeit mit sich. Redner und Gegenredner, Sprecher und Hörer stehen in einem bestimmten sozialen und menschlichen Verhältnis gegeneinander, führen mit persönlichen Mitteln und Zielen das Gespräch. Oft (besonders im klassischen Drama) nimmt es den Charakter einer kämpferischen Auseinandersetzung an, es ergibt sich eine stets wachsende Spannung, das Wort gewinnt an Dynamik, der Höhepunkt wird in der → Stichomythie (Streitgespräch) erreicht. Mit der Annahme einer «Krise des Dramas» (Szondi) folgt dementsprechend auch eine Krise des Dialogs. Die Vorherrschaft des offenen zum Nachteil des geschlossenen Dramas schiebt den nichtaktionalen D. in den Vordergrund; er verfällt dem Monologisierungsprozeß. Der durch das → Konversationsstück für das Drama gewagte «Rettungsversuch» (Szondi) führt bis auf seltene Ausnahmen (Hofmannsthals *Der Schwierige*, 1921, oder in ganz neu verdichteter Weise S. Becketts *Warten auf Godot*, 1953) zur weiteren Destruktion des D. wie des Dramas selbst. «...Was in dem Dialog ausgetragen wird, treibt die Handlung nicht vorwärts, verwirklicht nicht die Fabel in der Sprache, sondern ist Selbstaussage der Personen, verdeutlicht die Eigenart der Menschen...» (V. Klotz). Das ins Leere schwebende Konversationsstück, der zur Konversation an sich gewordene D. in der «pièce bien faite» wird von manchen Autoren der Moderne programmatisch bekämpft.

Da im modernen Theater das Problem gestörter Kommunikation oder gar der Sprachlosigkeit zu einem generellen Thema wurde, wird der Verfallsprozeß des D. im klassischen Sinne unaufhaltsam. Das Schweigen wird schließlich zum konsequenten Ausdruck der Dialog-Unmöglichkeit und manchmal sogar programmatisch thematisiert: «Das ausgeprägteste Verhalten meiner Figuren liegt im Schweigen; denn ihre Sprache funktioniert nicht... Ihre Probleme liegen so weit zurück und sind so weit fortgeschritten, daß sie nicht mehr in der Lage sind, sie wörtlich auszudrücken» (F. X. Kroetz, 1970). Der D. überlebt vielmehr im Dialogisierungsprozeß des Monologs.

Bauer, D.: Zur Poetik des Dialogs. Darmstadt 1969; Berohahn, K. L.: Formen der Dialogführung in Schillers klassischen Dramen. Münster 1970; Ducrot, O./Todorov, T.: Dictionnaire encyclopédique des Sciences du langage. Paris 1972; Klotz, V.: Geschlossene und offene Form im Drama. München 1980; Mukarovsky, J.: Dialog und Monolog. Frankfurt/M. 1967; Pfister, M.: Das Drama. München 1977; Szondi, P.: Theorie des modernen Dramas. Frankfurt/M. 1963.

Adriana Hass

Diener

Als Verkörperung der typischen Eigenschaften des Volkes – Witz, Schlagfertigkeit und Schlauheit – gehört der D. zur Tradition des komischen Theaters und ist hier eine Variante des Doubles. Er ist aber auch unter allen klassischen Bühnenrollen diejenige, die sich am grundlegendsten gewandelt hat: Urspr. nur eine quasi instrumentale, → lustige Person, gewinnt er nach und nach an moralischer Tiefe und wird schließlich bei manchen Autoren des 19. und 20. Jh. zur zentralen Person, die alle anderen an ‹Tugend› übertrifft und zum positiven Pol des Dramas wird. Der D. findet seinen Ursprung in den Sklavengestalten des antiken komischen Theaters, die abwechselnd verprügelt und belohnt werden, ihren Herren dienen, um sie dann wieder zu verraten. Der Weg führt dann über Aristophanes (445–386 v. Chr.), mit Xanthias, dem Diener des Dionysos in *Die Frösche* (405 v. Chr.), Plautus (250–184 v. Chr.) und in geringerem Maße Terenz (185?–160 v. Chr.), weiter zum ital. Theater (das Mittelalter kennt kaum D.-Figuren, höchstens als Narren- oder Knappengestalten). Hier herrscht Zani vor, ein als Clown verkleideter Mimus, dessen einziger präziser Wesenszug ist, daß er einem Herrn dient. Mit der →Commedia dell'arte entstehen aus Zani zwei zugleich entgegengesetzte und komplementäre Figuren: einerseits der schlaue und komische Intrigant – z. B. Truffaldino und Scapin; ersterer bei Carlo Gozzi (1720–1806: *Die Liebe zu den drei Orangen*, 1761) und Carlo Goldoni (1707–93: *Der Diener zweier Herren*, 1745) anzutreffen, letzterer die intelligenteste unter allen D.-Gestalten von Molière (1622–73: *Les fourberies de Scapin*, 1671). Andererseits der gefräßige Tölpel, so v. a. Arlequin, eine recht rätselhafte und vielseitige Figur; typisches Beispiel dafür ist wohl Dorantes Diener in Pierre de Marivaux' (1688–1763) *Das Spiel von Liebe und Zufall* (1730). Die klassische →Komödie, besonders in Frankreich, bietet außerdem eine ganze Reihe von D.-Gestalten auf halbem Wege zwischen diesen beiden Polen, v. a. bei Molière. Mit dem 18. Jh. wechseln Wesen und Rolle des D.; das Modell ist jetzt vielmehr der Crispin der Commedia dell'arte, der im Gracioso der spanischen Literatur und in den D.-Gestalten in *Le légataire universel* (1708) von Jean-François Regnard (1655–1709) oder *Crispin rival de son maître* (1707) von Alain René Lesage (1668–1747) fortlebt. Hier sind die D. ihren edlen Herren fast ebenbürtig. In einem Jh. des geistigen und sozialen Wandels entsteht außerdem eine andere, markante D.-Gestalt, die den Vergleich mit dem Herrn aushält: Jacques in Denis Diderots (1713–84) *Jacques le Fataliste et son maître* (1773–74). Diese Gradation vom Zynischen bei Lesage, über die gutmütige, bildungs- und nicht charakterbedingte Komik bei Marivaux und die materialistisch orientierte, zugleich aber auf Großzügigkeit ausgerichtete Intelligenz bei Diderot führt geradewegs zur hervorragendsten D.-Gestalt dieser Zeit, zum Figaro von Pierre Auguste Caron, alias Beaumarchais (1732–99). Figaro setzt zwar zuerst die Tradition des geschickten Intriganten fort; aber sein Charakter wechselt und vertieft sich von Stück zu Stück, vom *Barbier von Sevilla* (1775) bis zu *Figaros Hochzeit* (1784); nun verkörpert er zum erstenmal einen Diener mit menschlichen Wesens- und Charakterzügen, die bisher ausschließlich den anderen, ‹höheren› Personen zugeschrieben worden waren; mit ihm siegt die Intelligenz über den angeborenen sozialen Rang – die Frz. Revolution naht.

Mit dem 19. Jh. endet fürs erste die hohe Zeit des D. Die D.-Gestalt hat sozusagen ihre Schuldigkeit getan, die Funktion des Doubles wird von anderen Gestalten, in anderen durch die neue Gesellschaftshierarchie bedingten Schemen übernommen. Der D. lebt nur noch als fahler Typ weiter, z. B. als Kammerdiener (‹valet de chambre›) im → Boulevardtheater und im → Vaudeville oder im → Wiener Volkstheater, wo seine Rolle an die urspr. Tradition stark erinnert. Nur in einzelnen Werken wird der D. wieder zur echten, manchmal gar modellhaften Zentralfigur: wenn Jean in Johan August Strindbergs (1849–1912) *Fräulein Julie* (1888) noch eine zwiespältige D.-Figur ist, kommt die D.-Gestalt im 20. Jh. mit Theodor und Matti noch einmal voll zum Tragen, wobei allerdings die soziale Diener-Herr-Beziehung Einkleidung einer tiefer liegenden Herr-Knecht-Dialektik ist. In Hugo von Hofmannsthals (1874–1929) *Der Unbestechliche* verdankt man v. a. der Hauptfigur, dem D. Theodor, daß das Stück kein reines sentimentales Familiendrama ist, sondern vorwiegend eine Komödie. Dabei liegt das Neue an dieser D.-Komödie hauptsächlich im Charakter des Titelhelden, von dem Robert Musil (1880–1942) geschrieben hat, er sei «in einer erschütternden Weise komisch». Er handelt zwar aus der Position des sozial Schwachen, triumphiert aber über den Herrn und ermöglicht den Sieg des ‹Guten› über das ‹Schlechte›. – Systematischer und radikaler wird die Kritik und der Wandel in Rolle und Funktion des D. mit Bertolt Brechts (1898–1956) *Herr Puntila und sein Knecht Matti* (1940). Hier sind alle Figuren, und in erster Linie die beiden Hauptkontrahenten Herr = Puntila und Knecht = Matti, die «Mitglieder eines großen dialektischen Welttheaters, dessen Drahtzieher nicht mehr die himmlischen, sondern die politischen und ökonomischen Mächte sind» (Jost Hermand). Wir haben es also weder mit der herkömmlichen Herr-Diener-Komik antiker Tradition zu tun noch mit einer tragisch-rührenden Variation zum Thema D. Es ist ein distanziertes, kritisches Schauspiel, dessen Angelpunkt der vernünftige, wohl heitere, aber nie ins ‹Komische› alter Prägung abgleitende Matti ist, während der Herr und Großgrundbesitzer Puntila in seinem geschichtlichen Anachronismus komisch wirkt. Die alten sozialen Verhältnisse gelten hier als überholt; das traditionelle komische Schema und die althergebrachte D.-Gestalt ebenso. So kommt es nicht von ungefähr, wenn hier – symptomatisch für diese grundlegend geänderte Welt- und Komödienauffassung – der D. Matti zum Schluß nicht Prügel bekommt, nicht bestochen wird, sich nicht in sein Los fügt, sondern seinem Herrn kündigt. Der Wandel des D. ist somit vollkommen.

Aziza, C./Olivieri, C./Stick, R.: Dictonnaire des types et caractères littéraires. Paris 1978; Hermand, J.: Herr Puntila und sein Knecht Matti. In: Hinck, W. (Hg.): Die deutsche Komödie. Düsseldorf 1977; Leclerc, L.: Les valets au théâtre. Paris

1871 (reprint: Genève 1970); Ribaric/Demers, M.: Le valet et la soubrette de Molière à la Révolution. Paris 1970.

Bernard Poloni

Difang xi (Lokales Theater)

Im chin. Musiktheater (→Chin. Theater) gibt es neben der im ganzen Land verbreiteten →Pekingoper über 300 regionale und lokale Theaterstile. Es gehört damit gewiß zu den stilistisch vielfältigsten und reichsten Theatersystemen der Welt. Die einzelnen Stile unterscheiden sich zunächst hinsichtlich ihrer Entstehungszeit und Verbreitung stark voneinander. So gibt es Stile, die in mehreren Provinzen verbreitet sind wie das →kunqu und solche, deren Verbreitung nicht über einen Bezirk hinausgeht. Manche Stile sind schon mehrere Jh. alt, z. B. das Sichuan-Theater, das kunqu, das Jiangxi-Theater; andere entstanden erst vor wenigen Jahrzehnten. Die meisten lokalen Stile indessen entwickelten sich aus einer kleinen Anzahl von Grundstilen, die während der Ming-Dynastie (1368–1644) zuerst auftauchten. Die wichtigsten Grundstile waren: die «Musik aus Haiyan» (Haiyan qiang), nördliches Zhejiang, im 16. Jh. in weiten Teilen Zentralchinas, aber auch in Peking, verbreitet; die «Musik aus Yuyao» (Yuyao qiang), ebenfalls nördliches Zhejiang, wie das Haiyan qiang im 16. Jh. in Zentralchina verbreitet und im 17. Jh. verschwunden.

Der verbreitetste und für viele Lokaltheaterstile entscheidende Grundstil aber war die «Musik aus Yiyang» in Jiangxi (Yiyang qiang). Das Yiyang qiang hatte sich bereits im 16. Jh. in vielen Provinzen Chinas ausgebreitet. Dabei nahm es in den verschiedenen Regionen Einflüsse lokaler Musik auf, so daß sich ein regelrechtes Yiyang-System (auch Gaoqiang genannt) entwickelte. Ein Charakteristikum des Yiyang qiang war der Chorgesang, der von den Theaterstilen, die direkt aus dem Yiyang qiang hervorgingen (Sichuan-Theater, Jiangxi-Theater, Hunan-Theater, Chaozhou-Theater), übernommen wurde. Eine weitere Eigenart des Yiyang qiang war das gundiao («hervorsprudelnde Melodie»). Die Stücke des Yiyang qiang entstammten meist dem literarischen →chuanqi oder kunqu der Ming-Zeit. Dessen Texte waren in der Schriftsprache verfaßt und damit nur den Gebildeten verständlich. Für das populäre Yiyang qiang mußte also eine Form der Übertragung oder Erläuterung gefunden werden, ohne den urspr. Text zu sehr zu verändern. Das Problem wurde gelöst durch das Einfügen interpretierender Zusätze zum Text, gundiao genannt.

Die wichtigsten lokalen Theaterstile, neben dem Kunqu, sind: 1. Das

Difang xi (Lokales Theater)   **273**

«Klapper-Theater» (Bangzi qiang; so genannt, weil die Gesangspartien durch rhythmische Schläge einer Holzklapper begleitet werden), eine Form, die sich seit dem 18. Jh. in den meisten Provinzen ausgebreitet und in zahlreiche Unterstile aufgefächert hatte; dazu gehören das Shaanxi-Theater (Qinqiang), das Shanxi-Theater (Jinju, Shanxi bangzi), das Henan-Theater (Yuju, Henan bangzi), das Puzhou-Theater (Puju, Pu-zhou bangzi, Luantanxi) im Süden Shanxis und in Teilen der Provinzen Shaanxi, Gansu, Henan, das Hebei bangzi in Hebei, das Shandong bangzi in Shandong u. a. Formen; 2. das Han-Theater (Hanju) in der Gegend um Wuhan/Hubei; 3. das Hubei-Theater (Chuju); 4. das Hunan-Theater (Xiangju); 5. das Anhui-Theater (Huiju); 6. das Shanghai-Theater (Huju, Shenju); 7. das Jiangxi-Theater (Ganju); 8. das Sichuan-Theater (Chuanju); 9. das Zhejiang-Theater (Yueju); 10. das Fujian-Theater (Minju); 11. das Guangdong-Theater (Yueju); 12. das Guangxi-Theater (Guiju); 13. das Yunnan-Theater (Dianju); 14. das Blumentrommel-Theater (Huaguxi) mit vielen regionalen Unterstilen in Hunan, Hubei, Anhui; 15. das Teepflücker-Theater (Caichaxi), ebenfalls vielfach unter-gliedert, ebenso wie 16. die Pflanzgesänge (yangge) in Nordchina.

Die Hauptunterschiede zwischen den lokalen Theaterstilen betreffen die Musik (Melodien, Instrumente) und den Dialekt. Es gibt aber auch gewisse inhaltliche Unterschiede: Während die Behandlung der tradi-tionellen Stücke und Stoffe in den einzelnen Stilen kaum differiert, ist zu beobachten, daß diejenigen Stile, die nicht über eine sehr lange, prägende Tradition verfügen (z. B. Shanghai-Theater, Guangdong-Theater), leich-ter neue Stoffe und Themen aufnehmen als die alten, traditionsreichen Stile. Ein Gegenwartsstück des Shanghai-Theaters wird sehr viel leichter vom Publikum angenommen als eines des Sichuan-Theaters. Masken, Gestik, Rollenfächer unterscheiden sich nur geringfügig. Allerdings wird zwischen dem «Großen Theater» (daxi, difang daxi) mit der vollen Band-breite männlicher und weiblicher Rollenfächer und dem «Kleinen Thea-ter» (xiaoxi, difang xiaoxi, minjian xiaoxi) mit nur zwei oder drei Rollen (junge Frau, junger Mann und/oder lustige Figur, chou) unterschieden. (S. a. →juese: «Rollenfächer»). Beim «Kleinen Theater» gibt es Berüh-rungspunkte mit den sog. Kleinen Theaterformen (→Quyi).

Mackerras, C.: The Growth of the Chinese Regional Drama in the Ming and Ch'ing. In: Journal of Oriental Studies IX, 1 (Jan. 1971), 58–91; Tanaka Issei: Development of Chinese Local Plays in the 17th and 18th Centuries. In: Acta Asiatica 23 (1972), 42–62; Zhou Yibai: Zhongguo xiqu lunji. Beijing 1960; Zhong-guo da baike quanshu, xiqu quyi. Beijing/Shanghai 1983.

Bernd Eberstein

Dionysien

Sammelbezeichnung für alle Dionysosfeste; an drei der vier attischen D. wurde Theater gespielt; die bedeutendsten waren die ‹Großen D.› oder ‹Städtischen D.› (→ Antikes Theater); dazu kommen die dem Dionysos Lenaios geweihten ‹Lenäen› und die ‹Ländlichen D.› der attischen Landgemeinden; keine Theateraufführungen gab es lediglich an den ‹Anthesterien›.

Pickard-Cambridge, A.: The Dramatic Festivals of Athens. Oxford ²1968 (rev. by J. Gould and D. M. Lewis); Deubner, L.: Attische Feste (Berlin 1932). Darmstadt 1959.

Bernd Seidensticker

Dionysostheater

Das am Südosthang der Akropolis in Athen gelegene bedeutendste Theater der griech. Welt, in dem so gut wie alle uns erhaltenen griech. Tragödien und Komödien uraufgeführt worden sind (zu Struktur und Baugeschichte → Antikes Theater).

Newiger, H.-J.: Drama und Theater. In: G. A. Seeck (Hg.): Das griech. Theater. Darmstadt 1979, S. 434–503; Pickard-Cambridge, A. W.: The Theatre of Dionysos at Athens. Oxford 1966; Travlos, J.: Bildlexikon zur Topographie des antiken Athen. Tübingen 1971.

Bernd Seidensticker

Directeur / Director / Direktor

Das Wort *Directeur* bezeichnet, ähnlich wie das dt. Direktor, den Leiter eines Theaters. Der D. war einst zugleich Truppenleiter, Regisseur und nicht selten sogar Schauspieler. Heute bezeichnet das Wort oft nur den Eigentümer eines Theaters (→ Privattheater), der es einem ‹producteur› vermietet. Letzterer bringt die Geldmittel und übernimmt die entsprechenden Risiken.

Das engl. Wort *Director* bezeichnet den Verantwortlichen für die Leitung der Proben und die Inszenierung der Stücke; es entspricht dem dt. Begriff → Regisseur. Die in England bis 1956 gängige offizielle Bezeichnung ‹producer› wurde dann auch dort durch das in der amerik. Theater- und Kinowelt übliche Wort D. abgelöst.

Das Wort *Direktor* bezeichnete lange Zeit in Deutschland den Vorsteher einer Theatergruppe. Heute ist der D. der Leiter eines Privattheaters, verantwortlich für dessen geschäftliche Führung und künstlerische Arbeit – ähnlich dem frz. ‹directeur›, anders aber als der engl. ‹director›. An manchen Theatern amtiert auch neben dem D. ein Verwaltungs-D., der für Haushalt, Lohn- und Kassenwesen, Schriftverkehr usw. zuständig ist. Im 18. und 19. Jh. unterstand der D. oft einem Intendanten, v. a. an den →Hoftheatern. Heute sind diese beiden Begriffe gleichbedeutend. Nur heißen die Leiter der Privattheater D., während die Intendanten staatlichen oder städtischen Bühnen vorstehen (die Schweiz und Österreich kennen diese Unterscheidung nicht: hier heißen alle Theaterleiter D.).

Bernard Poloni

Die Distel

Am 2. 10. 1953 wurde in Berlin unter Leitung von Erich Brehm im «Haus der Presse» das erste professionelle Kabarett der DDR mit dem Programm «Hurra! Humor ist eingeplant!» eröffnet. Schon nach kurzer Zeit sehr erfolgreich, spielte man seit 1976 zusätzlich mit einem zweiten Ensemble in einem Berliner Randbezirk. Die D. schöpfte den tolerierten Rahmen für Satire aus, kritisierte bald nicht nur alltägliche Schwierigkeiten der Bürger, sondern auch grundsätzliche Probleme des Staates und der Politik. Die vorherige Abnahme der Programme machte Aktualisierungen schwierig. «Improvisationen» waren nur nach Genehmigung des Direktors möglich. Zwei Programme durften überhaupt nicht aufgeführt werden: 1965 *Kleine Geschichten vom großen Mucke-fuck*, 1988 *Keine Mündigkeit vorschützen*, von dem nur die Premiere (als «Probe») stattfand. In mehr als 80 Programmen und rund 14 000 Vorstellungen hat die D. ihre Stacheln gezeigt und sich – mit Autor/innen wie Inge Ristock und Peter Ensikat – um unbequeme Kritik auf hohem kaberettistischem Niveau bemüht. – Die D. hatte sich immer wieder zu wehren gegen Erwartungen von Funktionären, die Forderung nach «positiver Satire» und den Verdacht, ihre Kritik richte sich grundsätzlich gegen den Staat. «Wir sind das schlechte Gewissen einer guten Sache» – diese These von 1957 kennzeichnete das Selbstverständnis der D.

Nach E. Brehm, Hans Krause und Georg Honigmann wurde die D. seit 1968 von Otto Stark geleitet, der im Londoner Emigrantenkabarett →«Laterndl» mitgewirkt und in der DDR die Dresdener «Herkuleskeule» gegründet hatte. Seit dem 2. 2. 1990 ist Gisela Oechelhaeuser Intendantin, die Mitglied des Leipziger Kabaretts «academixer» war und Dozentin der Hochschule für Schauspielkunst Berlin. Ein Senatsbeschluß privatisierte 1991 die D. – Seit März 1989 produzierte die D. mit dem Fernsehen den «Scharfen Kanal», eigens geschriebene Programme, die

276 Dithyrambos

live übertragen wurden – bis auf die letzte Sendung am letzten Sendetag des Fernsehens der ehemaligen DDR. «Also ändert sich für uns an unserer Aufgabe gar nicht so viel, wie wir dachten» (Oechelhaeuser).

Brehm, E. (Hg.): «Die Distel blüht zum Spaße». Berlin o. J.; Disteleien. Berlin 1976; Hösch, R.: Kabarett von gestern und heute. 2 Bde. Berlin 1967–72; Gebhardt, H. (Hg.): Kabarett heute. Berlin 1987; Krause, H. H. (Hg.): «Das war distel(l)s Geschoß». Berlin 1961; ders. (Hg.): «Greif zur Frohkost, Kumpel». Berlin 1962; ders. (Hg.): Wir stoßen an. Zehn Jahre Distel. Berlin 1963; Oechelhaeuser, G. (Hg.): Von der Wende bis zum Ende. Wendejahr – die Distel im Scharfen Kanal. Berlin 1990; dies. (Hg.): Das letzte Ende. Berlin 1991; Otto, R./Rösler, W.: Kabarettgeschichte. Berlin ²1981.

Wolfgang Beck

Dithyrambos

Griech. Kultlied, speziell: das von einem Chor gesungene Lied zu Ehren des Dionysos; Herkunft und Bedeutung des nichtgriech. Namens sind ungeklärt. Laut Aristoteles (*Poetik* 1449 a 9 ff) ist die Tragödie aus dem D. entstanden; eine sichere Rekonstruktion der Entwicklungsstufen vom primitiven dionysischen Chorlied zur Tragödie des Aischylos erlauben die Quellen jedoch nicht. Der D. bleibt auch bei wachsender Bedeutung der dramatischen Aufführungen wichtiger Bestandteil vieler Feste, spätestens seit dem letzten Drittel des 6. Jh. v. Chr. gab es auch D.-Wettbewerbe; an den ‹Großen Dionysien› stritten (wahrscheinlich) je zehn Knaben- und Männerchöre um den Sieg; die Kosten wurden wie bei den dramatischen Wettbewerben von Choregen getragen (→ Antikes Theater). Die literarische Blütezeit des D. ist mit den Namen der großen griech. Chorlyriker Simonides, Pindar und Bakchylides verbunden; Ende des 5. Jh. entwickelt sich der sogenannte ‹Neue D.›, dessen virtuose Musik und manieristischer Sprachstil stark auf Euripides gewirkt haben.

Pickard-Cambridge, A. W.: Dithyramb, Tragedy, and Comedy. Oxford ²1962 (rev. T. B. L. Webster); Lesky, A.: Die tragische Dichtung der Hellenen. Göttingen ³1972, S. 24–26.

Bernd Seidensticker

Divadlo na Vinohradech (Prag)

(Stadttheater in den Weinbergen). 1907 auf Initiative der reichen Weinberger Gemeinde in Prag entstanden. Da das D. n. V. fast ausschließlich Operette spielte, verfügte es auf Grund dieses spezialisierten Repertoires sowohl über ein Schauspielensemble als auch über ein Ensemble und Orchester für das Musiktheater. Nachdem Schubert seinen Stuhl 1908 räumen mußte, sank das Theater auf Vorstadtbühnenniveau mit Operettenspielplan herab. Erst als 1914 Otakar Ostrčil neuer Opernchef wurde, änderten sich Spielplan und Organisation, und Ostrčil leitete eine neue Epoche des tschech. Musiktheaters ein. Er arbeitete eng mit K. H. Hilar, dem Wegbereiter des expressionistischen Theaters in der Tschechoslowakai, zusammen und verwertete dessen Ideen in der Spielplangestaltung und im Inszenierungsstil.

Kindermann, Heinz: Theatergeschichte Europas, X, Naturalismus und Impressionismus (3. Teil). Salzburg 1974.

Elke Kehr

Divadlo Na zábradlí (Prag)

Das staatliche Theater am Geländer hat sich seit seiner Gründung im Jahre 1958 vom literarischen Kabarett zu einem der wichtigsten Theater der Tschechoslowakei entwickelt. Schwerpunkte: Experimentiertheater, Pantomime. Der Theaterleiter Jan Grossmann (*1925), der Autor Václav Havel (*1936) und der Schauspieler/Pantomime Ladislav Fialka (1931–91) waren die Wegbereiter, die insbesondere das Theater des →Absurden in der Tschechoslowakei einführten. Grossmann spricht vom ‹appellativen Theater›, d. h., er will die Phantasie und das Urteilsvermögen des Publikums anregen und Entscheidungshilfen gegen Phrasen und Konventionen geben. – Neben Beckett, Ionesco und Kafka spielte man in den 60er Jahren vor allem die Stücke Havels (*Das Gartenfest, Die Benachrichtigung, Die entgleiste Turteltaube*), I. Vyskočils, M. Kunderas, B. Hrabals und Klassikerbearbeitungen. Nach der Niederschlagung des Prager Frühlings Repressalien durch die Zensur; Grossmann arbeitet im Ausland, kehrt erst 1989 an das D. N. z. zurück (1989 Molière: *Don Juan*; 1990 Havel: *Largo desolato*; 1991 *Gram, Gram, Angst, Strick und Grube* von Karel Steigerwald, der als Dramaturg dem D. N. z. angehört). Zahlreiche Auslandsgastspiele.

Elke Kehr/Elke Wiegand

Divertissement

(Divertire = sich unterhalten) D. entwickelten sich als Tanz- und Gesangseinlagen für Bühnenwerke zwischen den Akten, am Dramenende und als in die Akte eingeschobene Episoden, die an die Haupthandlung selten anknüpften. D. im →Opéra ballet, z. B. bei Campra (1660–1744).

Riemann, H./Gurlitt, W.: Divertissement. In: Riemann Musiklexikon. Sachteil. Mainz 1967, S. 235.

Helga Ettl

Dokumentarisches Theater

Die Anfänge des dokumentarischen Theaters reichen bis in die 20er Jahre zurück: Als Erwin Piscator (1893–1966; →Piscatorbühne) 1925 seine historische Revue über Krieg und Revolution (*Trotz alledem!*) aus «authentischen Reden, Aufsätzen, Zeitungsausschnitten, Aufrufen, Flugblättern, Fotografien und Filmen» zusammenmontierte, wurde er zum Wegbereiter einer neuen Theaterentwicklung. 40 Jahre später verhalf er durch seine Inszenierung von Rolf Hochhuths (*1931) *Der Stellvertreter* (1963) dem Dokumentartheater zum entscheidenden Durchbruch. Es folgten Aufführungen von Heinar Kipphardts (1922–82) *In der Sache J. Robert Oppenheimer* (1964) und Peter Weiss' (1916–82) *Die Ermittlung* (1965). – Anders als das gegenwartsbezogene →Zeitstück der 20er Jahre befaßte sich das Dokumentardrama der 60er Jahre zunächst vorwiegend mit Themen der jüngsten Vergangenheit (Naziherrschaft, Judenverfolgung, Kommunistenhetze). Das Dokumentartheater war die Antwort auf das apolitische Kunsttheater der Adenauerära. Grundlage des dokumentarischen Theaters bildete das authentische Geschichtsmaterial: Die durch journalistische Recherche zu ermittelnden historischen Fakten waren ohne ‹Beschädigung› des Inhalts in eine bühnengerechte Dramenform zu bringen. Das Publikum ‹zu stellen› betrachteten die Autoren als ihre Aufgabe: ‹Was ihr seht, ist belegt› – durch die Autorität des historischen Dokuments sollte in Erinnerung gerufen werden, was in der Zeit des Wirtschaftswunders verdrängt, verharmlost und verfälscht worden war. Das Dokument versperrte dem bürgerlichen Publikum den Fluchtweg in eine problemlose Vergangenheits‹bewältigung›. Die Autoren des Dokumentartheaters verstanden sich nicht als neutrale ‹objektive› Beobachter weltgeschichtlicher Prozesse, sondern ergriffen Partei für die «Unterdrückten und Verdammten dieser Erde», allen voran Peter Weiss in seinen Stücken gegen Imperialismus und Kolonialismus (*Gesang vom Lusitanischen Popanz*, 1966; *Vietnam-Diskurs*, 1967).

Barton, B.: Das Dokomentartheater. Stuttgart 1987; Blumer, A.: Das dokumentarische Theater der sechziger Jahre in der Bundesrepublik. Meisenheim 1977; Hilzinger, K. H.: Die Dramaturgie des dokumentarischen Theaters. Tübingen 1976; Ismayr, W.: Das politische Theater in Westdeutschland. Meisenheim 1977; Karasek, H. u. a., Dokumentartheater – und die Folgen. In: Akzente 3 (1966), S. 208–229; Rühle, G.: Das dokumentarische Drama und die deutsche Gesellschaft (1966). In: ders.: Theater in unserer Zeit. Frankfurt/M. ²1980; Weiss, P.: Notizen zum dokumentarischen Theater (1968). In: ders.: Rapporte 2. Frankfurt/M. 1971, S. 91–104.

Carl Wege

Domestic Tragedy

Engl. Form des →Bürgerlichen Trauerspiels, aber nicht auf die Aufklärungszeit beschränkt, sondern übergreifender typologischer Begriff. Die D. T. siedelt sich zwischen der Tragödie und der Komödie an. Zum Gegenstand hat sie die Lebensumstände, Probleme und Geschicke bürgerlicher Figuren. Gekennzeichnet durch sensationelle Motive (häufig Ehebruch und Mord), die zum Tod der Protagonisten führen, sowie Stoffe aus dem Bereich des Gegenwartlebens. Wurzeln in den →Moralitäten. Erstes Auftreten im späten 16. Jh. (anonym): *Arden of Faversham*, 1592; Thomas Heywood: *A Woman Killed With Kindness*, 1603; anonym:*The Yorkshire Tragedy*, 1608. Popularität schwand, aber D. T. erschienen wieder Mitte des 18. Jh. in sentimentalisierter Form (George Lillo: *The London Merchant*, 1731; Edward Moore: *The Gamester*, 1753). Nun werden Tugenden und Gefahren des bürgerlichen Privatlebens mit puritanisch-empfindsamer Moral thematisiert. Im angloamerik. Bereich wird D. T. häufig typologisch und ahistorisch verwendet, z. B. mit Bezug auf das amerik. Drama (Arthur Miller: *The Death of a Salesman*, 1949).

Clark, A.: Domestic Drama. A Survey of the Origins, Antecedents and Nature of the Domestic Play in England, 1500–1640. 2 Vols. Salzburg 1975; Szondi, P.: Die Theorie des bürgerlichen Trauerspiels im 18. Jh. Frankfurt/M. 1973.

J. Lawrence Guntner

Drama

(Griech. = Handlung, von griech. dran = tun) Textgattung, die sich vom narrativen (epischen) und lyrischen Text unterscheidet durch das Fehlen der Erzählfunktion. Dramatischer Text konstituiert sich durch Selbstaussagen der dramatis personae. Schon dieses Kriterium kann durchbrochen werden (z. B. im →epischen Theater); erst recht treffen alle weiteren Be-

280   Dramaten

stimmungen wie Fabel, dramatische Situation, Spannung, Charakter nur auf das klassische Modell-D. (→ D.-Theorie) zu und nicht generell. Das Merkmal «für die Bühne bestimmt» verfehlt Lese-D. sowie manche lyrischen D., die nur eine imaginierte Aufführung, keine reale implizieren. Der dramatische Text ist zu unterscheiden vom Inszenierungstext, der ohne linguistischen Text auskommen kann. Daher ist Gleichsetzung von dramatischem Text mit szenisch realisiertem Text (Inszenierungstext) problematisch. – Der dramatische Text kann (muß aber nicht) neben dem zu sprechenden Text (Dialog, Monolog) Regieanweisungen enthalten. Sie sind integraler Bestandteil des dramatischen Texts, manche, z. B. von Samuel Beckett (*1906), enthalten ausschließlich Regieanweisungen.

Generelle Definition des D. ist nach Auflösung der klassischen D.-Form zu offener Formenvielfalt nicht mehr sinnvoll. Man unterscheidet besser jeweils speziell zu beschreibende historisch gewordene D.-Typen. Nachdem jahrhundertelang D. Zentrum des Theaters war, spielt es im Theater des 20. Jh. eine eng umgrenzte Rolle. Theater betont eigene Qualität (→ Theatralität, → Theatertheorie), collagiert, zerstückt, ändert, streicht den Text, benutzt lyrisches und episches Textmaterial, das zum bloßen Teilmoment des Inszenierungstexts wird, einer eigenen Kunstform mit fließenden Übergängen zu → Performance, → Happening, Skulptur, Installation, → Tanztheater und allg. bildender Kunst.

Hamburger, K.: Die Logik der Dichtung. Frankfurt/M./Berlin/Wien 1977; Pfister, M.: Das Drama. München 1977.

Hans-Thies Lehmann

Dramaten

Kurzbezeichnung für eines der drei schwed. Staatstheater, das Kungliga Dramatiska Teatern Stockholm. Seine Vorgeschichte begann 1787 mit der Eröffnung eines Privattheaters durch A. F. Ristell. Als er ein Jahr später völlig verschuldet aufgeben mußte, assoziierte sich ein Teil der Schauspieler zu einer Stiftung, die sich dank eines königlichen Privilegs Kungliga Svenska Dramatiska Teatern nennen durfte und ihre Vorstellungen im Ballhaustheater mit G. F. Gyllenbergs Tragödie *Sine Jarl eller Sverkers död* (Jarl Sine oder Sverkers Tod) am 17.5.1788 begann.

Als das Ballhaus 1792 wegen Baufälligkeit abgerissen wurde, spielte die Truppe im Opernhaus, bis sie ein Jahr später das umgebaute Arsenal mit dem letzten Stück des «Theaterkönigs» Gustaf III. einweihen konnte. Historische Tragödien, später bürgerliche Schauspiele, Schwänke und Melodramen bestimmten den Spielplan. 1825 brannte das Arsenaltheater während einer Vorstellung ab, bis 1863 mußte das Schauspieltheater wieder im Opernhaus spielen. Die für das Sprechtheater ungünstigen Bühnen- und Akustikverhältnisse erschwerten erfolgreiche Aufführungen und trugen mit dazu bei, daß es lange Zeit hinter der Theaterentwicklung zurückblieb. Erst 1863 mit dem Bezug des Kleineren Theaters durch das sich nun Kungliga Dramatiska Teatern nennende Ensemble begann die kontinuierliche Pflege zeitgenössischer schwed. Dramatik und der Klassiker. 1871 wurde das D. verstaatlicht, 1888 die gemeinsame Verwaltung von Oper und Schauspiel aufgehoben; die Schauspieler organisierten sich nach dem Muster der →Comédie Française. Ausländische Gastspiele (u. a. Lugné-Poë) führten das D. an die moderne Theaterentwicklung heran. Am 18. 2. 1908 eröffnete es mit Strindbergs *Mäster Olof* sein neues Haus, in dem nun vor allem die europäische Gegenwartsdramatik gepflegt wurde.

Mit Strindbergs *Gespenstersonate* gastierte 1917 das Deutsche Theater Reinhardts (→Reinhardt-Bühnen), der 1921 am D. desselben Autors *Traumspiel* inszenierte. Im selben Jahr arbeitete auch Stanislawski am D., an dem 1923 eine lange Tradition mit Aufführungen der Dramen O'Neills begann.

Eine wichtige Phase der Entwicklung des D. begann 1963 mit der Intendanz Ingmar Bergmans, in dessen Amtszeit (bis 1966) u. a. Brecht, P. Weiss und Gombrowicz aufgeführt wurden. Sein Nachfolger wurde Erland Josephson, der 1975 von Jan-Olof Strandberg abgelöst wurde. Intendant ist seit 1985 Lars Löfgren.

Neben dem großen Haus wird heute ein kleines Haus bespielt, Tourneen führen das Ensemble durch ganz Schweden, eine angegliederte Schauspielschule fördert den Nachwuchs nicht nur des D.

Arpe, V.: Das schwedische Theater. Göteborg 1969; Bergmann, G. (Hg.): Dramaten 175 år. Stockholm 1963; Carlborg-Mannberg, E.: Gustaf IIIs skötebarn. Stockholm 1991; Marker, F. J. u. L.-L.: The Scandinavian Theatre. Oxford 1975; Sjögren, H.: Stage and Society in Sweden. Stockholm 1979; Svanberg, J.: Kungliga teatrarne under ett halft sekel 1860–1910. Stockholm 1918; Wieselgren, O.: Kungliga Dramatiska Teatern 25 år. Stockholm 1933.

Wolfgang Beck

Dramatic Workshop of the New School
for Social Research (New York)

Der 1940 von Erwin Piscator (→Piscatorbühne) gegr. und geleitete D. W. ist der bedeutendste Beitrag der deutschsprachigen Bühnenemigration zum amer. Theater. Er stellt einen für die damaligen amer. Verhältnisse völlig neuartigen Lehrbetrieb dar, in dem intensives theoretisches Studium und eine umfassende praktische Ausbildung («learning by doing»)

282 Dramatisierung

für ein gesellschaftlich orientiertes Theater miteinander verbunden wurden. Die Off-Broadway-Bewegung und das sozialkritische amer. Drama haben von dieser Arbeit wesentliche Impulse empfangen. Zu den Schülern gehörten die Begründer des → Living Theatre, Julian Beck und Judith Malina, die Dramatiker Tennessee Williams und Arthur Miller sowie die späteren Hollywood-Stars Marlon Brando, Tony Curtis, Paul Newman, Rod Steiger und Walter Matthau. Die Arbeit fand ein Ende, als Piscator 1951 vor den McCarthy-Ausschuß geladen wurde. Piscator verließ noch vor dem Verhör die USA.

Kirfel-Lenk, Th.: Erwin Piscator im Exil in den USA 1939–1951. Berlin 1984; Ley-Piscator, M.: The Piscator Experiment. Carbondale 1967.

Jan Hans

Dramatisierung

Bearbeitung eines epischen Stoffs oder anderer literarischer Texte für das Theater, d. h. Anpassung an die Gesetze der dramatischen Gattung und der Bühne durch Erstellen einer Dialog-Fassung. – Häufig dramatisiert wurden die Romane Fedor M. Dostojewskis (*Die Brüder Karamasow* 1910 am Moskauer Künstlertheater, 1911 bei Jacques Copeau in Paris; *Die Besessenen* von Albert Camus, Paris 1958), ferner die Romane Franz Kafkas (*Der Prozeß* von André Gide und Jean-Louis Barrault, Paris 1947; *Das Schloß* von Max Brod, Berlin 1953). Peter Zadek arbeitete Hans Falladas *Kleiner Mann, was nun* (Bochum, 1972) und *Jeder stirbt für sich allein* (Berlin, 1981) zu Revue-Spektakeln um. Als gelungene D. gilt Maxim Gorkis *Sommergäste* in der Fassung von Botho Strauß und Peter Stein an der → Schaubühne am Halleschen Ufer (Berlin, 1974).

Dieffenbacher, R. J.: Dramatisierung epischer Stoffe. Diss. Heidelberg 1935; Patsch, S. M.: Vom Buch zur Bühne. Dramatisierung engl. Romane durch ihre Autoren. Eine Studie zum Verhältnis zweier literarischer Gattungen. Innsbruck 1980; Sydow, U.: Dramatisierung epischer Vorlagen. Diss. Berlin 1973.

Monika Sandhack

Dramatis personae

(Lat.: die Personen eines Theaterstücks, Personenverzeichnis) → Person.

Adriana Hass

Dramaturg

(Griech. *dramaturgein* – ein Drama verfassen) Urspr. Autor und Aufführungsleiter von Dramen; seit Lessings →*Hamburgischer Dramaturgie* vollzog sich allmählich die Entwicklung zum literarisch-künstlerischen Berater und Mitarbeiter der Theaterleitung. – Das Tätigkeitsfeld des D. ist heute vielseitig, jedoch unscharf konturiert, zumal die Schwerpunkte in einzelnen Theatern unterschiedlich gewichtet sind. Zu den wesentlichen Aufgaben gehören – in Absprache mit der Bühnenleitung –: Lektüre und Auswahl von geeigneten Stücken, Gestaltung des →Spielplans, Suche nach →Regisseuren, Beschaffung, Bearbeitung und Übersetzung der Texte, Sichtung von Neuerscheinungen; in Zusammenarbeit mit dem Regisseur bei Aufführungsvorbereitungen (Produktionsdramaturgie): Erstellung der Spielfassung, Beratung bei Rollenbesetzungen, Auswahl von Hintergrundmaterial, Textanalyse, Vorschläge für Stückrealisation, Teilnahme an Proben, Redaktion des →Programmheftes, Weitergabe von Informationen an die Presse und andere Medien; ferner: Vertretung des Theaters nach außen durch Öffentlichkeitsarbeit (Vorträge, Publikationen, Diskussionen, Matineen u. ä.); rechtliche und terminliche Verhandlungen mit Bühnenverlagen; Gespräche mit Autoren, Autorenförderung.

Die Forderung nach dramaturgischer Mitarbeit wurde erstmals von Joh. Elias Schlegel (1719–49) formuliert (*Schreiben von Errichtung eines Theaters in Kopenhagen*, 1747). Gotthold Ephraim Lessing (1729–81) dagegen benannte in der *Hamburgischen Dramaturgie* nicht nur die Funktion eines D., sondern übte dieses Amt in seiner Tätigkeit als Theaterdichter und Kritiker des Hamburger →Nationaltheaters aus. Die Beschäftigung mit dramatischer Literatur und ästhetischen Theorien, der Entwurf eines an den Bedürfnissen der Gegenwart orientierten Spielplans sowie die Reflexion über die Bedeutung des Theaters standen im Zentrum seines Kompendiums angewandter →Dramaturgie. Dramaturgische Arbeit fiel ansonsten in den Bereich der →Regie, Theaterleitung und -dichtung; beschränkte sich auf Gestaltung des Spielplans, der neben dem Verfassen eigener Stücke durch Bearbeitungen, Einrichtungen und Übersetzungen erweitert wurde: Joseph Schreyvogel (1768–1832) nahm großen Einfluß auf das Repertoire und setzte Shakespeare, die Weimarer Klassik sowie Calderón am Wiener Hoftheater durch; der als D. ans Dresdener Hoftheater berufene Ludwig Tieck (1773–1853) bemühte sich um einen literarisch anspruchsvollen Spielplan und verfaßte richtungweisende dramaturgische Schriften; Tiecks Nachfolger Karl F. Gutzkow (1811–78) verlagerte das Aufführungsangebot vom Schauspiel auf das Konversationsstück; Karl L. Immermann (1796–1840), Autor und Theaterleiter, hob die Bedeutung der Dramaturgie für seine →Inszenierungen am Düsseldorfer Schauspielhaus hervor und schuf, angelehnt an Goethes Weimarer Theateraufführungen, mustergültige dramaturgische Bearbeitungen; der Theaterleiter und Regisseur Heinrich Laube (1806–84) schätzte das Lustspiel als Folie für das Drama des hohen Stils und trat für zeitgenössische Dramatik ein; Franz von Dingelstedt (1814–81) blieb in seinem Wirken als D. am Stuttgarter Hoftheater einflußlos. Otto Brahm (1856–1912) arbeitete neben seiner Theaterleitung als Regisseur weitgehend dramaturgisch durch überlegte Spielplan- und Ensemblebildung sowie Diskussion mit Schauspielern und Kritik nach den Proben. Im Zuge der Regieentwicklung nimmt das Berufsbild des D. zu Beginn des 20. Jh. eigene Gestalt an; seine Stellung gilt in dt. Staats- und Stadttheatern als selbstverständlich. Das Düsseldorfer Schauspielhaus unter Leitung von Luise Dumont (1862–1932) beschäftigte Autoren als D. (Paul Ernst, Herbert Eulenberg, Wilhelm Schmidtbonn, Albrecht Schaeffer u. a.), die die Zeitschrift *Die Masken* in Form eines Programmhefts herausgaben und literarische Matineen als feste Veranstaltungen einrichteten. Max Reinhardt (1873–1943) engagierte D. (Arthur Kahane, Felix Hollaender) in erster Linie für Öffentlichkeitsarbeit. Kleinere Theater verfügten über einen mit Disposition befaßten D. (Künstlerisches Betriebsbüro). Mit Bertolt Brechts (1898–1956) Arbeit am →Berliner Ensemble wurde durch Einbeziehung der Reflexion über Theater und Gesellschaft in den theatralischen Produktionsprozeß die Grundlage für die sich Ende der 60er Jahre in der BRD entfaltende Produktionsdramaturgie gelegt, damit ein neuer Maßstab für die Position des D. gesetzt: projektbezogene Arbeit durch Beteiligung am Entstehungsprozeß der Inszenierung, d. h. zusammen mit Regisseur, Bühnen- und Kostümbildner sowie Ensemble wurde ein Stück vorbereitet und zur Aufführung gebracht. Inhaltlich erfüllt wurde die Funktion des Produktions-D. erstmals an der →Schaubühne am Halleschen Ufer durch den Kritiker und späteren Autor Botho Strauß (*1944), der die Regiearbeit Peter Steins (*1937) maßgeblich beeinflußte. Diesem Beispiel folgten in den 70er Jahren die großen deutschsprachigen Theater; begleitende Stückdramaturgie gilt seitdem allgemeinhin als üblich. Daneben weitete sich der Planungssektor auf Grund höherer Komplexität von künstlerischen, personellen und dispositionellen Entscheidungen aus. Speziell eingerichtete Positionen für Öffentlichkeitsarbeit mit dem Schwerpunkt auf Publikumswerbung sind daher zur Regel geworden (s. auch →Ballettdramaturg).

Hausmann, W.: Der D.-Beruf. D.-Amt und -Persönlichkeit seit 1800. Diss. Köln 1955.

Monika Sandhack

Dramaturgie

(Griech. *dramaturgia* – Verfertigung und Aufführung eines Dramas)
1. Arbeitsbereich im Theater und die Tätigkeit des →Dramaturgen.
2. Das auf die praktisch-szenische Realisierung von Stücken bezogene Kompositionsprinzip des →Dramas, die Art seiner äußeren Bauform und inneren Struktur. 3. Die Theorie von der Kunst und Technik des Dramas als Teilgebiet der Poetik.

Gegenstand der D. sind die Regeln und Wirkungsgesetze für Wesen und Aufbau der dramatischen Dichtung. Meist werden diese an konkreten Einzelfällen aufgezeigt (z. B. die *Poetik* des Aristoteles), häufig auch in Form von Rezensionen und Theaterkritiken als D. zusammengefaßt (vorbildlich die →*Hamburgische D.* von Lessing, der den Begriff der D. einführte und prägte); seltener beschränkt sich die D. auf Festschreibung eines bloßen Katalogs von Regeln im Sinne der normativen Poetik (wie in Renaissance und Klassizismus).

Die Entfaltung des Dramas aus dem Mythos und den Dionysos geweihten Brauch- und Kultformen bestimmte weitgehend die Struktur des klassischen D. Das Theater formierte sich im 6. Jh. v. Chr. als Darstellung, nachdem die kultischen Zeremonien von der Polis als Festspiele organisiert wurden. In den eigens für den →Agon entworfenen und eingerichteten Stücken bildeten sich dramatische Formen heraus, die aufgenommen und weitergegeben werden konnten. Neben den überlieferten Texten der Dramatiker (bes. Aischylos, Sophokles, Euripides, Aristophanes) gilt die nur unvollständig erhaltene *Poetik* des Aristoteles als das wesentliche antike Zeugnis, dessen Inhalte in der Neuzeit in irrtümlichen Interpretationen aufgegriffen und zu einem Kodex verbindlicher Regeln umgestaltet wurden. In dieser ersten grundlegenden D. beschrieb Aristoteles die bis heute umstrittene Entstehung wie Entwicklung dramatischer Formen am Beispiel zeitgenössischer Werke und entwarf Regeln für die Bauform der →Tragödie. Als →Mimesis einer in sich geschlossenen Handlung mit Einheiten und Verlaufsskizzierung (Exposition, Höhepunkt, Verzögerung, Katastrophe) sollte die Tragödie durch Erweckung von Furcht und Mitleid eine Reinigung (→Katharsis) solcher Affekte bewirken. Die Charaktere blieben der Handlung untergeordnet. Die menschliche Verstrickung in das Schicksal war an die Darstellung hervorragender Persönlichkeiten geknüpft, durch welche die tragische →Fallhöhe offenbar wurde (→Ständeklausel). Figuren- und Dialoggestaltung waren stark eingeengt durch das Spiel nur eines Darstellers zunächst. Mit der Einführung eines zweiten Schauspielers (→Deuteragonist) durch Aischylos und eines dritten (→Tritagonist) durch Sophokles erweiterte sich der Handlungsspielraum und damit die Möglichkeit zu wirksamer Kontrastierung der Figuren. Die formale Struktur des antiken Dramas leitete sich aus der Span-

286 Dramaturgie

nung zwischen →Chor und Schauspieler, zwischen Gesang und dramatischer Rede her. Die D. war damit an Funktion und Stellung des Chors gebunden, der durch ständige Präsenz den Handlungsverlauf gliederte und die geschlossene Einheit des Aufbaus garantierte; eine feste Zahl der Einteilung in Akte gab es nicht. Die Verbindung zwischen Chor und Spiel lockerte sich in dem Maße, wie die Aktionen auf Einzeldarsteller übertragen und Gegenstand des Zusammenspiels wurden. Der Wechsel zwischen chorisch-musikalischen und dialogisch-gesprochenen Partien blieb als Grundstruktur durchgängig, wenn auch eingeschränkt erhalten.

Das röm. Drama bildete sich um 240 v. Chr. durch Übersetzung und freie Bearbeitung griech. Stoffe mit Livius Andronicus aus. Die Komödie (→Palliata) mit ihren Hauptvertretern Plautus und Terenz überwog. Daneben verbreiteten sich volkstümliche Formen im →Mimus, der →Atellane und im →Pantomimus. Die Tragödie löste sich von ihrem kultischen Hintergrund ab, blieb aber in der Struktur vom griech. Vorbild abhängig; erhalten sind die rhetorischen Bearbeitungen klassischer Stücke durch Seneca. Theoretisch spiegelte sich dies in der *Ars poetica* des Horaz wider. Eng an die aristotelische Lehre angelehnt, forderte Horaz jedoch den Aufbau der Tragödie in fünf Akten und befürwortete eine stärkere Charakterisierung der Personen an Stelle des griech. Schicksalsdramas.

Das mittelalterliche Drama, wie das Drama der Antike kulturellen Ursprungs, entwickelte sich seit dem 10. Jh. im Rahmen kirchlicher Liturgien. Strukturbestimmend wirkten sich biblische Inhalte aus, die den Gläubigen in dramatischer Gestaltung durch Wechsel von Gesang und Rede vorgetragen wurden (→Mittelalter/Drama und Theater des Mittelalters). Fortschreitende Dramatisierung und Verselbständigung des Spiels, wachsende Zuschauer- wie Darstellerzahlen, evtl. auch die Zunahme burlesker Szenen führten im 13. Jh. zur Verbannung des Spiels aus der Kirche auf Marktplätze und in weltliche Säle. Mit Durchsetzung der Volkssprache an Stelle des klerikalen Lateins kündigte sich im 15. Jh. die Entwicklung zum profanen Volksschauspiel (→Fastnachtsspiel) in unterschiedlichen nationalen Ausprägungen an. Realistische, oft drastische Darstellung löste die symbolische Vergegenwärtigung religiöser Wahrheiten in den Liturgien ab. Die Aufteilung in Massen- und Soloszenen mit wechselnden Schauplätzen (→Simultanbühne) diente der dramatischen Gliederung, Prolog und Epilog umrahmten das Spiel, die Gemeinde der Gläubigen wurde durch Chorgesang und Gebet in die Aufführung einbezogen.

An die D. der Antike knüpften im 16. Jh., von Italien ausgehend, der →Humanismus und das Renaissancedrama an. Die Auseinandersetzung mit der griech.-röm. Dichtung und Rhetorik führte zur Wiederentdeckung der Schriften des Aristoteles und Horaz. Diese bildeten mit neuen Kommentaren durch J. C. Scaliger (1561), S. A. Minturno (1559 und

1563), L. Castelvetro (1576) u. a. die Grundlage der ital. Renaissance-Poetiken. Zu ihren wesentlichen Kriterien zählten das normative Regelsystem und, als Ansatzpunkt einer einseitig ausgelegten Aristoteles-/Horaz-Interpretation, die Orientierung an der Rhetorik: Mimesis wurde als Nachahmung mißverstanden; die aristotelische Katharsislehre diente zur Rechtfertigung eines moralisch-ethischen Erziehungsprogramms; Dichtung hatte sich an Gebote der Vernunft, Wahrscheinlichkeit und Angemessenheit zu halten; →Fallhöhe und →Ständeklausel wurden als Strukturelemente der Tragödie verfestigt; Wahrung der drei Einheiten galt als verbindlich; Gliederung der fünf (seltener drei) Akte erfolgte durch allegorische Zwischenspiele oder Zwischenaktmusiken (später durch Vorhang). Vor diesem theoretischen Hintergrund entwickelte sich in Italien die Renaissancekomödie (Commedia erudita), neben ihr die volkstümliche Typenkomödie (→Commedia dell'arte) sowie die Renaissancetragödie, als weitere Form das →Schäferspiel. Ferner ging aus dem Versuch, die antike Tragödie wiederzubeleben, die Oper hervor, daneben Ballett und höfisches →Festspiel. Die Rezeption der sich in der ital. Renaissance ausprägenden D. verlief je nach gesellschaftlichen Situationen unterschiedlich in den einzelnen Nationalliteraturen. Am Anfang der dt. D. nach normativen Maßstäben stand in der Nachfolge des Niederländers D. Heinsius (1611) M. Opitz mit dem *Buch von der dt. Poeterey* (1624), das Anstöße zu zahlreichen Barock-Poetiken gab. In Frankreich bildete sich eine klassizistische D. mit P. de Ronsard (1565) u. a. heraus, deren Ansätze im 17. Jh. durch P. de Deimier (1610), Abbé d'Aubignac (1657) und vor allem durch N. Boileau (*Art poétique*, 1674) zu einem Kanon von Regeln mit der Tragödie als höchster Kunstform ausgebaut wurden. In der frz. *tragédie classique* durch Corneille und Racine erhielt die Renaissancetragödie ihre vollendete Gestalt: fünf Akte bei symmetrisch gebauter Handlung, Verzicht auf Zwischenakte u. ä., Beachtung der Einheiten, geringe Personenzahl, symmetrische Figurenkonstellation, Belichtung der Charaktere aus der dramatischen Situation, Verwendung des Verses. Sprache und Stoff fügten sich dem Gesetz der Wahrscheinlichkeit und Schicklichkeit. Die auf das Wesentliche beschränkte Handlung wurde ins Innere der Personen verlegt; äußere Geschehnisse tauchten in Berichten, nicht auf der Bühne selbst auf. Alles spielte sich allein in der Sprache ab und erschien nur darin faßbar.

Dieser dramatisch artifiziellen Form des frz. Nationaltheaters stand das von einer breiten Schicht getragene →Elisabethanische Drama Englands gegenüber. Trotz Aufnahme der Erneuerungstendenzen innerhalb der klassischen D. vollzog sich ein Formwandel zur →Historie mit Shakespeare als bedeutendstem Dramatiker. Die Forderungen der Renaissance-Poetiken wurden, abgesehen von der Einteilung in Akte, kaum beachtet. Der Wechsel von hohem und niederem Stil, Vers und Prosa,

288 Dramaturgie

von ernsten und komischen Szenen kennzeichnete Handlungsverlauf und D. Die oft mehrsträngige Handlungsführung mit lockerer Szenenfolge und einer Vielzahl ständisch gemischter Personen knüpfte formal an die Stationentechnik des mittelalterlichen Mysterienspiels an. Erste individualistische Menschen- und Charakterdarstellungen durch Shakespeare betonten zudem den Eigenwert der elisabethanischen D., die an Stelle äußerer Gesetzmäßigkeiten innere Gefühlswerte zum Maßstab erhob.

Die D. der offenen und geschlossenen Form, das Drama Shakespeares und die frz. Tragödie, bildeten den Ausgangspunkt für die Entwicklung im 18. Jh. In Deutschland schloß sich Gottsched als letzter Vertreter einer normativen Poetik dem dramatischen Formenmuster des frz. Klassizismus an. Erst mit Lessing vollzog sich schrittweise die Hinwendung zum historischen Denken, damit die Emanzipation des bürgerlichen Individuums und Neudefinition des Tragischen als innere, nicht soziale Bedingtheit. Für die D. bedeutete dies eine Ablösung von der normativen Poetik mit ihren Vorschriften für Stoff, Form und Stilhöhe der einzelnen Gattungen. Den entscheidenden Durchbruch leitete der →‹Sturm und Drang› mit der Rezeption Shakespeares ein. In den dramaturgischen Schriften von Herder (*Von dt. Art und Kunst*, 1773) und Lenz (*Anmerkungen über Theater*, 1774) wurde die offene Dramenform zum Vorbild für eine von Regeln befreite, allein durch Genie und Originalität des Dichters zu begründende Dramatik. Nur gelegentlich fanden sich formale Nachahmungen antiker Tragödien (Schillers *Die Braut von Messina*, 1803).

Die D. der Romantik (→Romantisches Theater) erweiterte mit A. W. Schlegels Vorlesungen über dramatische Kunst (1809–11) und Tiecks dramaturgischen Studien das Kunstverständnis nach dem Vorbild Herders, blieb in ihrer Formvielfalt jedoch auf den Bereich der Theorie beschränkt. Eine Annäherung an die Wirklichkeit vollzog die neuzeitliche D. im Realismus (→Realistisches Theater), daneben gewann die philosophische Weltdeutung an Einfluß. In der Theoriebildung beschränkte sich Gustav Freytag (*Die Technik des Dramas*, 1863) auf eine epigonale Auslegung der klassizistischen D.

Im Naturalismus (→Naturalistisches Theater) entfaltete sich das Milieudrama (Hauptmann, A. Holz) zur bestimmenden Gattung. Orientiert an der analytisch-konkreten Wiedergabe von sozialer Wirklichkeit, zeichnete sich die D. durch Übernahme naturwissenschaftlicher Methoden aus. Daraus erklärt sich neben der minuziösen Beschreibungstechnik (Sekundenstil) die Tendenz zur Auflösung der geschlossenen Dramenform in Stimmungsbilder, ferner die Vorliebe für geringe Personenzahl, analytischen Handlungsaufbau, präzise Regieanweisungen in Form von Prosaversatzstücken, Umgangssprache und Dialekt, Einhaltung der Orts- und Zeiteinheit aus Wahrscheinlichkeitsgründen.

Der materiellen Wirklichkeitsverwendung im Naturalismus stand die

Dramaturgie 289

D. des Expressionismus (→Expressionistisches Theater) als Ausdruck innerlich erfahrener Wahrheiten und seelischer Ich-Erlebnisse entgegen. Mit Auflösung der dramatischen Handlungsstruktur in die lose verknüpfte Bilderfolge (→Stationendrama) oder in das chorisch-oratorische Stimmungsspiel wurde, vorbereitet durch Dramen von Wedekind und Strindberg, der feste Handlungsrahmen aufgegeben. Als wesentliche Elemente prägten, ohne Bindung an reale Zeit- und Raumwerte, ausgiebige Monologe die D. ebenso wie Gebärde, Tanz und Pantomime. Die Sprache, in ihren unterschiedlichen Schattierungen bis hin zur gesteigerten Ekstase eingesetzt, drängte auf Ausdruck; auffallend daher verkürzte und grotesk verzerrte Satzformen. Die mit der Stationentechnik einsetzende Episierung des dramatischen Stoffes kulminierte im →epischen, nichtaristotelischen Theater Brechts. An die antike Wirkungsästhetik anknüpfend, verlangte die epische D. eine demonstrierend erzählende Form. Der Zuschauer sollte, durch Argumentation von Emotionen befreit und zum rationalen Betrachter gemacht, im Akt der Distanzierung zur kritischen Stellungnahme gezwungen und von der Veränderbarkeit gesellschaftlicher Verhältnisse überzeugt werden. Dieses durch →Verfremdungseffekt strukturierte erkenntniskritische Verfahren verzichtete auf Akteinteilung und bevorzugte die →Montage einzelner Szenen. Das Kriterium der Spannung fehlte auf Grund ständiger Kommentierung der szenischen Aktion durch Erzähler, eingeschobene Lieder, Spruchbänder u. ä. Der Schluß des Dramas blieb in einem dialektischen Sinne offen.

Den Versuch einer Abkehr von wirklichkeits- und gesellschaftsabbildenden Formen unternahm das →absurde Theater. Die Welt stellt sich als unveränderbar dar. Der inneren Leere und Sinnlosigkeit menschlicher Existenz entspricht die von etablierten D. abweichende Struktur. Konventionelle dramaturgische Techniken erscheinen parodistisch verzerrt (häufig Vermischung von tragischen und komischen Elementen). An Stelle einer überschaubaren, psychologisch motivierten Handlung werden sich steigernde, zum Höhepunkt drängende Vorgänge (Ionesco) oder kreisende Rituale mit sich weiter reduzierenden Abläufen (Beckett) vorgeführt. Mit der Entleerung des Handlungskonzepts ist die Aushöhlung der Zeit verbunden. Die Figuren erfahren keine Charakterzeichnungen, ihr Ich ist fragmentiert. Durch Verzicht auf vorantreibende Dialoge erfüllt die Sprache eine wesentliche Funktion: In ihrer Reduktion, Sinnentleerung wie in ihrem Verstummen gerät sie zum Ausdruck einer im ganzen entfremdeten Welt. Die Tendenz zur Auflösung des Dialogs zugunsten gesprächsferner Formen des dramatischen Diskurses (Monolog, Ansprache) schreitet gegenwärtig fort (Th. Bernhard, Botho Strauß). Die D. ist nicht mehr an den Dialog als Aussage- und Gesprächsform gebunden. Statt dessen bewegen häufig isolierte, sich kreuzende Sprechakte die Figuren. Realistische Formen mit Mimesis und stringenter Handlungs-

290 Dramaturgische Gesellschaft

führung (F. X. Kroetz) nehmen einen nur geringen Raum ein. Insgesamt hat sich der Schwerpunkt vom abgeschlossenen Werk auf den Prozeß, von der Mitteilung auf die Struktur der Stücke verschoben. Auffallend ist die Formenvielfalt, die sich einer literarischen Einordnung entzieht.

Bentley, E.: Das lebendige Drama. Eine elementare D. Velber 1967; Bulthaupt, H.: D. des Dt. Schauspiels. 4 Bde. Oldenburg/Leipzig 1893–1901; Dietrich, M.: Europ. D. im 19. Jh. Graz/Köln 1961; dies.: Europ. D. Der Wandel ihres Menschenbildes von der Antike bis zur Goethezeit. Graz/Wien/Köln ²1967; Ihering, H.: Aktuelle D. Berlin 1924; Perger, A.: Grundlagen der D. Graz/Köln 1952; Wendt, E.: Moderne D. Frankfurt/M. 1974; Wiese, Benno v.: Dt. D. 3 Bde. Tübingen 1956 (Vom Barock bis zur Klassik), 1969 (Dt. D. des 19. Jh.), 1970 (Vom Naturalismus bis zur Gegenwart).

Monika Sandhack

Dramaturgische Gesellschaft

Private Vereinigung von Persönlichkeiten und Institutionen im Bereich der darstellenden Künste (Theater) und Medien (Film, Funk, Fernsehen u. a.), die sich in Praxis oder Theorie, durch Beruf oder Interesse mit dramaturgischen Fragen beschäftigen. Gegründet 1956 mit Sitz in Berlin, setzt die D. G. die Tradition des 1953 gebildeten Dramaturgischen Arbeitskreises mit jährlichen Tagungen fort.

Schultze, F. (Hg.): Theater im Gespräch. Ein Forum der Dramaturgie (aus Tagungen 1953–1960 der Dt. D. G.). München/Wien 1963; Schulz, E.: 25 Jahre D. G. Berlin 1978.

Monika Sandhack

Dramentheorie

Während →Theatertheorie erst im 20. Jh. durch Besinnung auf Eigentümlichkeit des Theaters als Kunst (→Theatralität) Gewicht gewinnt, existiert D. als Poetik seit der Antike (→Antikes Theater). Ansätze zur Gattungspoetik finden sich bei Platon (429–347 v.Chr.). Er unterscheidet (*Politeia* 392d–398b) nachahmende Darstellung (Mimesis) von erzählender Darstellung (Dihegesis) sowie die Gattungen Komödie, Tragödie, Dithyrambos und Epos. Erste Dramaturgie ist die *Poetik* des Aristoteles (384–322 v. Chr.). Drama ist Nachahmung von Handlungen, Ziel der Tragödie (über sie die ausführlichste Darstellung in der fragmentarischen Schrift) ist Erregung von Furcht (Phobos) und Mitleid/Schauder (Eleos), dadurch die Reinigung (→Katharsis) von solchen Affekten (oder solcher Affekte). Alle Begriffe sind umstritten. Theater ist für Aristoteles nicht psychologisch; Fabel gilt ihm als Ursprung, Telos und ‹Seele› der Tragödie, diese soll nicht auf Charakter beruhen, der weder extrem gut noch schlecht sein soll. Unterscheidung von einfachen und komplexen Handlungen, Analyse dramaturgischer Grundmodelle wie Handlungsaufbau, Stoffwahl, Beschränkung, Peripetie (Umschlag von Glück in Unglück), Anagnorisis (Wiedererkennung). Motive der Handlung sind Hybris (Überhebung des Menschen, die Strafgericht der Götter herausfordert), Hamartia (tragischer Fehler) = Fehlverhalten oder Verblendung des Helden. Dichtung gilt in der D. des Aristoteles als philosophischer als die Geschichtsschreibung, weil sie das ‹Allgemeine› zeigt (das gemäß der Wahrscheinlichkeit Mögliche), Historie nur das ‹Besondere› (wirklich Geschehene). Aristoteles plädiert zugleich für das Staunenerregende (Thaumaston) im Drama und für innere Logik und Wahrscheinlichkeit, was im 16.–18. Jh. zu vielfältigem Streit über Legitimität des Unwahrscheinlichen und Phantastischen führte. Aristoteles kommt durch Beobachtung der antiken Theaterrealität zur Feststellung der Einheit von Zeit, Ort und Handlung. – Der Einfluß der *Poetik* reicht bis ins 19. Jh. Spätes Dokument ist Gustav Freytags (1816–95) *Technik des Dramas* (1863): Verabsolutierung der aristotelischen Dramaturgie, Fünfaktigkeit als überhistorisches Gesetz, demzufolge jedes Drama Pyramidenbau von Einleitung, Steigerung, Höhepunkt, Umkehr oder Fall und Katastrophe aufweisen soll. Die *Poetik* ist seit Auflösung der normativen Poetik und Ästhetik nur noch negativ wirksam, so als bekämpfte Position bei Bertolt Brecht (1898–1956).

In der Renaissance Umdeutung der deskriptiven Poetik des Aristoteles zu präskriptiven Regeln, z. B. Lodovico Castelvetro (1505–71) mit seinem bis ins 18. Jh. wirksamen Aristoteles-Kommentar. Daneben Paolo Beni (1552–1625), Francesco Buonamici u. a. Nachdem in der Renaissance zeitweise eine platonisierende Kunstauffassung Oberhand gewann, setzt sich Ende 16. Jh. die aristotelische Linie mit Akzent auf Nachahmung, Wahrscheinlichkeit, Rationalität durch, die in Klassizismus mündet. Für diesen wird zur wichtigsten Quelle Julius Caesar Scaligers (1484–1558) posthum publizierte *Poetices libri septem* (1561). Klassizistische Poetik will mit Wildwuchs der Renaissance-Spektakel aufräumen, statt caprice sollen Dichter den Regeln folgen. Die D. von Pierre Corneille (1606–84), dem Abbé Hédelin d'Aubignac (1604–76), Nicolas Boileau-Despréaux (1636–1711) behauptet Antike, im Sinn des Rationalismus umgedeutet, als unübertreffbare Norm. Das Postulat der Nachahmung (Mimesis) der Natur bleibt erhalten; da aber als Natur des Menschen Vernunft gilt, darf nur die der Ratio adäquate, idealisierte schöne Natur (belle nature) nachgeahmt werden. Oberstes Kriterium ist Wahrscheinlichkeit (vraisemblance), die das Drama verpflichtet, nur im Geist

292 Dramentheorie

der Schicklichkeit (bienséance, décence) zu schildern, Anstand, Maß und vor allem Religion nicht zu gefährden. Die von Aristoteles beobachteten Einheiten werden zur Vorschrift, scheint es doch z. B. ‹unwahrscheinlich›, daß ein und dieselbe Bühne verschiedene Räume darstellen könnte. Strenge Vorschriften regeln auch Wahl der Themen, Gattungen und Sprachbehandlung: Die → Tragödie behandelt historische (oder als solche geltende: mythische) Stoffe, zeigt Tugenden (Beständigkeit, Demut, Großmut), Sieg der Ratio und Pflicht über Leidenschaften. Fürsten, denen sie vor allem gilt, belehrt sie über Nichtigkeit des Irdischen, dramatis personae sind nur von hohem Stand (→ Ständeklausel). In der → Komödie tritt dagegen der bürgerliche Stand auf, sie ist definiert nicht in erster Linie durch Komik (starkes Lachen gilt vielmehr weithin als ungehörig; noch Molière, 1622–73, hat damit zu kämpfen), sondern durch bürgerliche Helden, andere Themen (Bestrafung und Verhöhnung der Laster und Schwächen) sowie durch den erfundenen statt historischen Charakter der Fabel. Katharsis wird von klassizistischer D. im Sinne neustoischchristlicher Lehre umgedeutet zu Mäßigung, ja Unterdrückung der Affekte. In der Praxis verstanden es die großen Autoren, dem Korsett der Regelpoetik sich so weit zu entziehen, daß sie die Vorzüge der Stilisierung nutzen, die Einengung mildern konnten. Rezeption des Dramas sollte nach Corneille durch Bewunderung (admiration) geprägt sein, der Zuschauer bewundert die übermenschliche Tugend des Helden. Jean Racine (1639–99) dagegen schafft psychologisch glaubhaftere, wenngleich nicht weniger stilisierte Figuren, die von ihren Leidenschaften beherrscht werden. – Parallelen zur klassizistischen D. finden sich in England (John Dryden 1631–1700) und verspätet in Deutschland (Johann Christoph Gottsched 1700–66).

Das geschlossene Regelsystem der klassischen D. zielt auf Ersetzung der Breitenperspektive der Renaissance durch Tiefenschärfe, Verinnerlichung, Konzentration auf seelischen Ausdruck, der der materiellen Fülle des Theaterapparats enträt. Die ästhetischen Chancen der artistischen hohen Stilisierung sind angesichts der seit dem 18. Jh. Topos gebliebenen Geringschätzung der tragédie classique in Deutschland bes. zu betonen.

Im 18. Jh. entwickeln vor allem Denis Diderot (1713–84) und Gotthold Ephraim Lessing (1729–81) die Theorie des → bürgerlichen Trauerspiels, auch drame, → domestic tragedy, comédie larmoyante (weinerliche Komödie). Die Trennwand zwischen Tragödie und Komödie wird eingerissen, die Forderung nach Mischgattung, Aufhebung der → Ständeklausel laut. An die Stelle konventionalisierter sollen natürliche Theaterzeichen treten, z. B. an die Stelle des barocken coup de théâtre Schlichtheit und Wahrscheinlichkeit der Handlungsführung, Stoffe aus dem Familienleben. An die Stelle von Bewunderung und Pathos (bzw. boshafter Komik)

Dramentheorie 293

tritt im Zeichen allg. Kultur der Empfindsamkeit die Rührung des Zuschauers.

Lessings Beitrag zur D. der bürgerlichen Epoche besteht vor allem in
der Privilegierung des Mitleids. In verengender Umdeutung der Furcht/
Mitleid-These des Aristoteles (Furcht wird als auf sich selbst gerichtetes
Mitleid interpretiert) macht Lessing das Drama zur Schule des Gefühls,
das ihm wiederum als Basis bürgerlicher Tugend gilt. Hatte die Spannung
zwischen Genie und Regeln (die Boileau ebenso wie Lessing anerkannt
hatte) die Geltung der Regel-Ästhetik wenig beeinträchtigt, so entscheiden sich die D. des →Sturm und Drang ganz für das Genie und seinen
‹Gesichtspunkt›. Im Drama ist jetzt die Fabel nur um des Charakters
willen da; offene Form, an der Zentralfigur orientierte Stationen treten
an die Stelle der klassischen Handlungseinheit. Die wichtigste dramen-
theoretische Schrift sind die *Anmerkungen übers Theater* (1774) von
Jakob Michael Reinhold Lenz (1751–92), der auch durch Verbindung
von Komik und Tragik zur Tragikomödie (*Der Hofmeister*) wirkt. Komödie soll nach Lenz an einer Begebenheit orientiert sein (nicht mehr am
komischen Typus wie in Molières Charakterkomödie).

Die gesamteurop. Entwicklung einer romantischen, dann realistischen
D. wird in Deutschland entscheidend modifiziert, sogar aufgehalten
durch das Zwischenspiel der Weimarer →Klassik. Ihre D. verlangt die
Wiederbelebung antiker, klassischer Stilisierung aus bürgerlich-humani-
stischem Geist. Kunst tritt neben Religion und Moral (Gesetzgebung) als
gleichberechtigte aufklärend-humanisierende Institution. Die Tragödie
zeigt das (kantische) Erhabene, den Sieg des moralischen Willens über
die physisch-natürlichen Zwecke der Leidenschaft. Die Beiträge Schillers
zur D. umfassen neben diesen Thesen und Reflexionen über den *Grund
des Vergnügens an tragischen Gegenständen* auch Überlegungen zum
Chor in der Tragödie (als ästhetisch distanzierendes Kunstmittel).
Goethes Beiträge zur D. bestehen vor allem in der Kontrastierung der
Grundtypen von Rhapsode (Epos) und Mime (Drama) sowie der Analyse
spezifisch dramatischer und epischer Motive. Er deutet zudem die aristotelische Katharsis neu als Ausgleich und ‹aussöhnende Abrundung› der
Tragödie.

Auch für die romantische D. ist Shakespeares Dramatik befreiender
Bezugspunkt, um die Legitimität der ‹modernen› Kunst gegen die Antike
zu behaupten. Ihr bedeutendstes Manifest ist Victor Hugos (1802–85)
Vorwort zu seinem historischen Drama *Cromwell* (1827). Die moderne
Zeit bevorzugt (im Gegensatz zur primitiven und zur antiken Epoche) das
‹Charakteristische› vor dem Schönen, läßt daher das Häßliche und Groteske zu, belebt die Bühne statt mit der abstrakten Schönheit und reduzierten Konstruktion der ‹alten Schule› mit bunter, konkreter, Einfühlung ermöglichender Lokalfarbe (couleur locale), die das Geschichtliche

294 Dramentheorie

erkennen läßt und zu ergreifender Versenkung in exotische und vergangene Realität führt statt zu bloßer Unterhaltung. Hugo setzt in dieser Polemik ebenfalls das Genie an oberste Stelle, das, vom Regelzwang befreit, im romantischen Drama eine «action vaste, vraie, et multiforme» schaffe.

Nachdem sich im 18. Jh. die Ästhetik als philosophische Disziplin entwickelt, kommt es in der Goethezeit zur Formulierung einer im Idealismus begründeten D. Neben Friedrich Hölderlin (1770–1843) und F. W. J. Schelling (1775–1854) hat vor allem die D. Georg Wilhelm Friedrich Hegels (1770–1831) nachgewirkt. Er bestimmt das Drama als Vermittlung von Objektivität (epische Poesie) und Subjektivität (lyrische Poesie), Drama ist somit höchste literarische Form. Es bringt in der Tragödie den objektiven Widerspruch zwischen feindlichen Positionen, zugleich aber auch deren höhere Einheit und Versöhnung der Gegensätze zur Erscheinung; insofern ist es wie alle Kunst «sinnliches Scheinen der Idee».

Die großen D. des 19. Jh. stammen von Friedrich Nietzsche (1844 bis 1900) und Richard Wagner (1813–83). Nietzsche deutet die antike Tragödie als widerspruchsvolle Einheit von Apollinischem und Dionysischem, Wagner entwickelt die Theorie des →«Gesamtkunstwerks» (Vereinigung aller Künste), die Theaterentwürfe und Kunstkonzeptionen von →Stilbühne über →Bauhaus bis zu Robert Wilson (*1941) beeinflußt hat.

Ende des 19. Jh. fordert der Naturalismus (→Naturalistisches Theater) ein Drama der experimentellen Analyse, Darstellung der Physiologie der Triebe und des Milieus mit soziologischer Präzision. Die naturalistisch perfektionierte Bühnenillusion soll fühlbar machen, wie der Mensch vom Milieu determiniert wird. Steigerung bürgerlicher Helden durch dramatische Kunst, Verzicht auf ‹Größe› durch klingende berühmte Namen. Emile Zola (1840–1907) sagt: «Kunst ist ein Stück Natur, gesehen durch ein Temperament»; der frühe Gerhart Hauptmann (1862–1946) vertritt das «soziale Drama».

Im 20. Jh. Problematisierung der für das Drama grundlegenden Kategorie des Subjekts: Ich, Identität, Person, Individualität werden fragwürdig durch Diskurs- und Sprachanalyse, Soziologie, Psychoanalyse sowie durch Erfahrungen wie Massengesellschaft, Maschinisierung, Großstadt, Verantwortungsverlust, mediale Manipulation. In Reaktion auf gesellschaftliche Veränderungen werden unterschiedliche neue Dramenkonzeptionen formuliert.

1. Bertolt Brechts (1898–1956) Theorie des epischen Dramas und Theaters (→Theatertheorie). Epische Elemente gab es schon früh, in griech. Tragödie (Chor-Erzählungen), mittelalterlichen Spielen, →elisabethanischem Drama, historischen Fresken von Christian Dietrich Grabbe (1801–36) und Georg Büchner (1813–37). Brecht: Bewußtheit des Zuschauers über den Theatervorgang soll erhalten bleiben, drama-

Dramentheorie 295

tische Illusion wird durchbrochen (Distanzierung des Zuschauers, Entdramatisierung, Episierung); keine dramatische Spannungskurve, sondern Reihung von Einzelsequenzen, in denen Aufmerksamkeit für Verhalten des Menschen in gesellschaftlich bestimmten Situationen (verdeutlicht durch «Gestus») erzeugt werden soll, nicht so sehr Spannung auf den dramatischen Ausgang. Unterbrechung der Handlung durch Erzähler, Chor, Lieder. Brechts D. geht von der lehrhaften Fabel aus. Episches Drama zeigt Veränderbarkeit des Menschen und der Welt. Statt Schicksal und Charakter Verhalten (behavioristischer Zug bei Brecht) und gesellschaftliche Implikationen dieses Verhaltens. Dieser D. entsprechen konsequent bestimmte Anweisungen für die Schauspieler, die durch Distanzierung, zitierendes Sprechen, Zeige-Gestus, Neben-sich-Treten, Verhinderung der Einfühlung Kritik an dem von ihnen dargestellten Verhalten ermöglichen. Eigene Erwähnung verdient Brechts Theorie des →Lehrstücks, die, in den späten 20er und 30er Jahren entwickelt, kurz vor Brechts Tod von ihm als Modell künftigen Theaters genannt wurde, nicht etwa das epische Theater, das er fast gleichzeitig mit Erwin Piscator (1893–1966) ebenfalls in den 20er Jahren aus der Taufe gehoben hatte. Die Lehrstücktheorie, die das Spiel nicht für Zuschauer vorsieht, sondern als Lernprozeß der Spielenden (in der Praxis gab es allerdings trotzdem Aufführungen) und die Bewußtwerdung über politische Konflikte zum Ziel hat, führte zu einer Reihe von Versuchen, Selbsterfahrung und politische Praxis mit Hilfe des Lehrstücks zu verbinden. Indessen geht die Bedeutung des Lehrstücks darüber hinaus: ästhetisches Modell eines Theaters, das als offen strukturiertes Dispositiv unterschiedlichen politischen Gebrauch ermöglicht.

2. In anderer Weise reagiert die Konzeption des →absurden Dramas (deutlich zu unterscheiden von früheren Formen wie Nonsensdichtung, Dada, Surrealismus) in den 50er Jahren auf Entsubjektivierung und Entfremdung: es zeigt Sinnverlust, Aushöhlung der Sprache, kommunikationslose Isolation des Menschen. Formen dieses Dramentyps sind Nichtbeachtung klassischer Dramaturgien, Stillstand, Wiederholung, scheinbare Inkohärenz der in sich nichtigen Handlungen, Autonomie der Sprachbewegung (Wortspiele) unabhängig von Intentionen der Figuren, so diese überhaupt erkennbar werden bei Abwesenheit oder äußerster Reduktion von Psychologie, Motivation, historischer Situierung. Häufig spielen die Dramen in einem Nirgendwo, surrealer Räumlichkeit, grotesk überzeichneten Alltagsorten. Das absurde Drama gibt die Tragödie wie die Komödie mit ihren metaphysischen Voraussetzungen preis, tendiert dafür zu Groteske, Satire, schwarzem Humor, →Tragikomödie. Verschiedene Akzentuierungen sind möglich: Absurdität als philosophische Position in den Thesendramen von Jean-Paul Sartre (1905–80) und Albert Camus (1913–60), keine absurden Dramen, da Absurdität hier nur

296 Dramentheorie

den existenzphilosophischen Gehalt, nicht die Form determiniert; als satirische Kritik an der «Verantwortungslosigkeit» des modernen Menschen (bei Friedrich Dürrenmatt, *1921, der Absurdismus und Groteske verbindet in der These «Uns kommt nur noch die Komödie bei»); satirisch-politische Kritik auch bei Eugène Ionesco (*1912), vor allem in der östlichen, bes. poln. Spielart des absurden Dramas; als ästhetisch-philosophische Mimesis an Negativität der Schmerz- und Leidenserfahrung ohne metaphysischen Trost bei Samuel Beckett (1906–89), dem mit Abstand bedeutendsten Vertreter des absurden Dramas: «(Die Subjekte) sind unvergleichlich mehr zu Objekten geworden als Brecht es sichtbar werden läßt. Unter diesem Aspekt sind die Beckettschen Menschenstümpfe realistischer als die Abbilder einer Realität, welche diese durch ihre Abbildlichkeit bereits sänftigen» (Adorno).

1950 benennt Ionesco sein Stück *Die kahle Sängerin* als «anti-pièce». Der danach schnell verbreitete Begriff Anti-Drama (Anti-Theater) weist seine Herkunft aus den radikal negierenden Kunstbewegungen Dada und Surrealismus aus. Peter Handke (*1942) z. B. läßt in seinen «Sprechstükken» Sprachformen, Systeme von Bühnengesten, Theaterkonventionen selbst zu Trägern des dramatischen Textes werden, macht die konsequente Ablehnung der Theaterkonventionen selbst zum Gegenstand, artikuliert die Wut auf die deformierende Mechanik der Sprache. In anderer Weise läßt Sam Shepard (*1943) ein Meta-Drama entstehen, indem Rede- und Selbstdarstellungsstile an Stelle der Personen die eigentlichen Subjekte der dramatischen Handlung werden.

Akademische D. steht heute vor dem Problem, daß modernes Theater weithin den dramatischen Text nicht mehr ins Zentrum stellt, ihn umschreibt, collagiert, zerstückelt, wegläßt. Es betont, wo es ihn benutzt, oft mehr Klangbild, Rhythmus, Buchstäblichkeit als Fabel und Handlung, greift immer öfter auch auf nichtdramatische Texte zurück. D., jahrhundertelang Zentrum der Theatertheorie, ist nur mehr ein begrenzter Teilaspekt davon. Der Kunstentwicklung folgt zudem die Abkehr vom Schema der triadischen Gattungspoetik (Epos, Lyrik, Drama oder Ableitungsformen davon). Das klassische Modelldrama überlebt nur als parodiert oder als well made play. D. müht sich weiter, die offene Formenvielfalt der Moderne wie episches Drama, absurdes Drama, dokumentarisches Drama, Meta-Drama, abstraktes Drama zu rastern. Aber die tradierten Kennzeichen wie Spannung, Gegenwärtigkeit, Ereignis, Handlung sind überholt.

Dualistische Kontrastbildungen wie aristotelisch–nichtaristotelisch, tektonisch–atektonisch, vor allem geschlossene und offene Form (Klotz) erfreuen sich großer Beliebtheit, leiden aber an schiefer Kontrastbildung: Offen verhält sich zu geschlossen wie unblau zu blau. Es bleibt meist unüberzeugend, warum die unterschiedlichen Weisen des Dramas, ‹nicht

Dramentheorie 297

geschlossen› zu sein, einen Formtypus bilden sollen. Andere in der Literaturwissenschaft geläufige Begriffe wie →Schicksalsdrama, →Geschichtsdrama, Entscheidungsdrama, Handlungsdrama, Figurendrama usw. bleiben wegen Überschneidungen ohne großen Erkenntniswert. Begrenzt ist auch der Erfolg der strukturalistischen D., durch linguistische Formalisierungen analog zur Narrativik Tiefenstrukturen (Aktantenmodelle) zu beschreiben. Das Repertoire des Dramas wird abstrahiert zu typischen Handlungsträgern (Aktanten wie Held, Übeltäter, Verbündeter und Handlungsmodelle wie Prüfung, Zweikampf, Vereinigung). Doch diese D. privilegiert unzulässig die Ebene der Fabel, findet nur schwer Zugang zur sprachlichen Eigendynamik, der Mikrostruktur des Texts, dessen Bildstrukturen, Lautmuster, metaphorische Verknüpfungen jedoch ebenso wichtig sind wie der Handlungsverlauf.

Erfolgreicher ist die historisierende D., die aus der «Krise des Dramas» (Szondi) Kriterien zur Beschreibung von Lösungs- und Rettungsversuchen entwickelt. Die Spannung zwischen überlieferter Form und neuen Inhalten erzeugt eine Dialektik, in der die tragenden Elemente des Dramas (Dialog, Gegenwärtigkeit, Zwischenmenschlichkeit) in Frage gestellt werden. Szondi (1963) unterscheidet neben den Rettungsversuchen durch Naturalismus, Konversationsstück, Einakter und Existentialismus (der durch dramaturgisch künstlich erzeugte «Enge» den ansonsten problematisch gewordenen Dialog erzwingt) die folgenden «Lösungsversuche»: expressionistische Ich-Dramatik, politische Revue, episches Theater, Montage, Spiel von der Unmöglichkeit des Dramas, Innerer Monolog, episches Ich als Spielleiter, Spiel von der Zeit, Erinnerung. Diese D. hat den Vorzug, unterschiedliche dramatische Gestaltungen aus der Zersetzung der dramatischen Form historisch zu verstehen, zugleich eine systematische Analyse nicht preiszugeben.

Insgesamt ist heute D. nur im Kontext von Theatertheorie möglich, so daß sich die Trennung von Theater- und Literaturwissenschaft hier besonders störend bemerkbar macht.

Abel, L.: Metatheatre. New York 1963; Adorno, T. W.: Offener Brief an Rolf Hochhuth. In: ders.: Noten zur Literatur IV. Frankfurt/M. 1974; Aristoteles: Poetik, Griech./Dt. Übers. u. hg. von M. Fuhrmann. Stuttgart 1982; Barthes, R.: Essais critiques. Paris 1964; Borie, M. u. a.: Esthétique théâtrale. Textes de Platon à Brecht. Paris 1982; Chabrol, C.: Sémiotique narrative et textuelle. Paris 1973; Else, G. F.: Aristotle's Poetics. The Argument. Cambridge (Mass.) 1957; Esslin, M.: Das Theater des Absurden. Reinbek bei Hamburg 1965 (u. ö.); Fischer-Lichte, E.: Semiotik des Theaters. Bd. 2. Tübingen 1983; Freytag, G.: Die Technik des Dramas. Darmstadt 1965; Grabes, H.: Metadrama and the History of Taste: Sam Shepard, The Tooth of Crime. In: C. W. Thomson (Hg.): Studien zur Ästhetik des Gegenwartstheaters. Heidelberg 1985; Grimm, R.: Deutsche Dramentheorie. 2 Bde. Frankfurt/M. 1971; Kayser, W.: Das sprachliche Kunstwerk. Bern 1968; Klotz, V.: Geschlossene und offene Form im Drama. München 1975;

298 Dramolett

Knopf, J.: Brecht-Handbuch Theater. Stuttgart 1980; Kommerell, M.: Lessing und Aristoteles. Frankfurt/M. 1957; Lehmann, H.-T./Lethen, H.: Ein Vorschlag zur Güte. Die doppelte Polarität des Lehrstücks. In: Steinweg, R. (Hg.): Auf Anregung Bertolt Brechts: Lehrstücke mit Schülern, Arbeitern, Theaterleuten. Frankfurt/M. 1978; Martini, F.: Die Poetik des Dramas im Sturm und Drang. In: Grimm 1971, Bd. I; Pfister, M.: Das Drama. München 1977; Scherer, J.: La Dramaturgie classique en France. Paris 1950; Staehle, U.: Theorie des Dramas. Stuttgart 1973; Staiger, E.: Grundbegriffe der Poetik. Zürich 1946; Szondi, P.: Theorie des modernen Dramas. Frankfurt/M. 1963; ders.: Die Theorie des bürgerlichen Trauerspiels im 18. Jh. Frankfurt/M. 1973; ders.: Poetik und Geschichtsphilosophie I. Frankfurt/M. 1974; Weinberg, B.: A History of Literary Criticism in the Italian Renaissance. University of Chicago Press 1961.

Hans-Thies Lehmann

Dramolett

(Frz. dramolet = kleines Drama) Kurzes dramatisches Theaterstück, z. B. Friedrich von Schillers (1759–1805) *Huldigung der Künste* (1804), Friedrich de la Motte Fouqués (1777–1843) *D. aus der Vorzeit*, Hugo von Hofmannsthals (1874–1929) frühe Versdramen oder Robert Walsers (1878–1956) Märchen-D.

Bernard Poloni

Drei Einheiten

Die Einheit der Handlung (eindeutige Haupthandlung, die ununterbrochen durchgeführt wird mit strenger Unterordnung der evtl. vorhandenen Nebenhandlungen), des Orts (kein Wechsel des Schauplatzes) und der Zeit (zeitliche Eingrenzung des Handlungsablaufs auf 24 Stunden). Ausgangspunkt der Theorie der d. E. ist die *Poetik* des Aristoteles (384–322), wo dieser sich auf die vorhandenen Werke der griech. Tragödie beruft, um dramatische Gesetze zu formulieren. Nur die Einheit der Handlung wird deutlich gefordert; die Gleichsetzung der Handlungsdauer mit der Aufführungszeit führt logisch zur Zeiteinheit, und die ständige Gegenwart des Chors auf der Bühne setzt die Einheit des Orts voraus, selbst wenn diese nicht ausdrücklich verlangt wird. Die moderne Auseinandersetzung um die d. E. setzt im 16. Jh. ein (vgl. Lodovico Castelvetro, 1505–71; Miguel Cervantes, 1547–1616; Lope de Vega, 1562–1635) und steht im 17. Jh. im Mittelpunkt der frz. theoretischen Diskussion über das Theater. Jean de Mairet (1604–86), Jean Chapelain (1595–1674), François d'Aubignac (1604–76) und Georges Scudéry (1601–77) fordern sie im Namen der Vernunft und der Wahrscheinlichkeit; sie werden von der Académie, später von Nicolas Boileau (1636–1711: *Art Poétique*, 1674) als Gesetz formuliert. Auf der Bühne aber behaupten sie sich erst allmählich: Pierre Corneille (1606-84), der 1660 eine *Rede über die Einheiten* schreibt, hält sich zuerst nur mit Mühe an sie (*Le Cid*, 1636); Jean Racine hingegen (1639–99) schreibt Tragödien, wo sie streng eingehalten werden (*Bérénice*, 1670). Im 18. Jh. zählen sie zu den Hauptmerkmalen des frz. klassizistischen Theaters; doch die Theoretiker des →Bürgerlichen Trauerspiels stehen ihnen kritisch gegenüber (vgl. Denis Diderot, 1713–84, und seine *Gespräche mit Dorval*, 1757, sowie G. E. Lessing, 1729–81, und seine *Hamburgische Dramaturgie*, 1767–69). Während die Stürmer und Dränger sie in Anlehnung an das elisabethanische Theater (Jakob M. Lenz, 1751–92: *Anmerkungen über das Theater*, 1771–74) verwerfen, greift die Weimarer Klassik auf sie zurück, wenn auch nicht systematisch (vgl. Goethes *Faust*). Am Anfang des 19. Jh. entwickeln die Romantiker eine die d. E. verstoßende Dramentheorie (vgl. A. W. Schlegel, 1767–1845; *Vorlesungen über dramatische Kunst und Literatur*, 1808, und Victor Hugo, 1802–85: Vorwort zu seinem Stück *Cromwell*, 1827); in der zweiten Hälfte des Jh. vollzieht sich mit dem zunehmenden Realismus jedoch wieder eine Annäherung an sie. Im 20. Jh. scheint die Debatte um die d. E. an Brisanz verloren zu haben: Während Expressionismus und absurdes Theater eher die ‹geschlossene› dramatische Form wählen, die zum Einhalten der d. E. führt, bevorzugen Dramatiker wie Brecht (1898–1956) die offene Form des Dramas. Das Einhalten bzw. Nicht-Einhalten der d. E. durch einen Dramatiker bleibt für die Kritik ein aufschlußreiches formales Merkmal, das ihr zwar nicht zur ästhetischen Beurteilung, jedoch zur Deutung des Werks verhilft.

Klotz, V.: Geschlossene und offene Form im Drama. München 1969; Scherer, J.: La Dramaturgie classique en France. Paris 1983.

Alain Muzelle

Die Drei Tornados

Eine der bekanntesten Kabarettgruppen der linken alternativen ‹Szene›, gegründet 1976 in West-Berlin. Aus einzelnen Sketchen, die sie auf studentischen Veranstaltungen und zur Unterstützung von Bürgerinitiativen usw. spielten, wuchsen abendfüllende Programme, die sie auf Veranstaltungen vor allem einer nicht parteipolitisch gebundenen linken ‹Gegenöffentlichkeit› vortragen. Ihre Abneigung gegen reine Kunstabende, ihr Bemühen um Unterstützung aktueller Initiativen haben sie bislang auf eine feste Spielstätte verzichten lassen. 1979 erhielten sie den Förderpreis der Stadt Mainz zum Deutschen Kleinkunstpreis.

Baumgarten, M./Schulz, W. (Hg.): Die Freiheit wächst auf keinem Baum... Theaterkollektive zwischen Volkstheater und Animation. Berlin 1979; Budzinski, K.: Das Kabarett. 100 Jahre literarische Zeitkritik – gesprochen – gesungen – gespielt. Düsseldorf 1985; ders.: Wer lacht denn da? Braunschweig 1989.

Wolfgang Beck

Drottningholm

Sommerresidenz der schwed. Könige auf der Insel Lovö im Mälarsee in der Nähe Stockholms. 1744 wurde hier von Angehörigen des Hofes erstmals Theater gespielt, zehn Jahre später das erste eigens gebaute Theater eingeweiht, das 1762 während einer Vorstellung abbrannte. Zwei Jahre später wurde nach Plänen C. F. Adelcrantz' mit dem Bau des noch heute erhaltenen Theaters begonnen, das 1766 eröffnet werden konnte. – D. hatte seine Blütezeit während der Herrschaft des «Theaterkönigs» Gustaf III. (1771–92), der die Entwicklung eines schwed. →Nationaltheaters als grundlegende Aufgabe zur Pflege schwed. Sprache und Kultur mit allen Mitteln förderte. Nach seinem Tode erlebte auch D. seinen Niedergang. Nach vereinzelten Aufführungen Ende des 18. und Mitte des 19. Jh. versank es in Vergessenheit. 1921 entdeckte der Bibliothekar A. Beijer das Theater durch Zufall wieder. Einschließlich der Bühnentechnik des Italieners Donato Stopani und rund 30 vollständiger Bühnenbilder aus der Zeit Gustafs III. stellte es sich als völlig erhalten heraus. Seit 1922 wird in D. wieder Theater gespielt, vor allem frz. und ital. Opern. In dem Theatergebäude befindet sich ebenfalls eine reiche theatergeschichtliche Sammlung.

Alm, G. (Hg.): Pictures from Drottningholm. Stockholm 1990; Beijer, A.: Slottsteatrarna på Drottningholm och Gripsholm. Stockholm 1937; ders.: Teatermuseet på Drottningholm. Uppsala 1940; Hilleström, G.: Drottningholmsföreställningar 1922–66. Stockholm 1966; ders.: Drottningholmteatern förr och nu. Stockholm 1956; ders.: Slottsteatern på Drottningholm. Stockholm 1960; Marker, F. J. u. L.-L.: The Scandinavian Theatre. Oxford 1975.

Wolfgang Beck

Drury Lane

Londons ältestes noch existierendes und berühmtestes Theater, das an der gleichen Stelle im Zentrum Londons mehrfach wiederaufgebaut wurde. Erste Gründung mit königlichem Patent 1663. Nach einem Brand 1674 von Christopher Wren (1632–1723) neu errichtet. In der Restaurationszeit (→Restaurationstheater) nach 1660 eins von nur zwei offiziell zugelassenen Theatern. Im 18. Jh. zählten zu seinen Intendanten David Garrick (1717–79) und Richard Brinsley Sheridan (1751–1816). Später verlor D. L. an künstlerischer Bedeutung und ist heute eines der zahlreichen Privattheater des Londoner →West End. Nach dem 2. Weltkrieg Ort zahlreicher Inszenierungen amerik. Musicals.

Macqueen-Pope, W.: Theatre Royal, Drury Lane. London 1945.

Bernd-Peter Lange

Dumb Show

Eine →pantomimische Einlage in Dramen, speziell des →Elisabethanischen Theaters. Häufig von Musik begleitet. Die D. S. griff manchmal auf allegorische Figuren wie in den Moralitäten und Maskenspielen zurück. Die D. S. kann eine Vorausdeutung oder einen Kommentar auf das Geschehen enthalten. Erscheint als Prolog, Zwischenspiel oder eingebettet ins Handlungsgeschehen. Erschien zuerst mit dem Einfluß Senecas in der Tragödie *Gorboduc* (1562) und setzte sich bis ins 17. Jh. fort, z. B. in John Websters *The Duchess of Malfi* (1614) und Thomas Middletons *The Changeling* (1623). Es existieren mehr als fünfzig Dramen der Shakespearezeit mit D. S. Die berühmteste ist die D. S. von der Mausefalle in *Hamlet*, III. ii.

Mehl, D.: Die Pantomime im Drama der Shakespearezeit. Ein Beitrag zur Geschichte der Dumb Show. Heidelberg 1964.

J. Lawrence Guntner

Düsseldorfer Schauspielhaus

Großes Haus, Kleines Haus. Gegründet 1905 durch Louise Dumont (1862–1932) und Dr. Gustav Lindemann (1872–1960) als Privattheater. Eine der führenden Bühnen in Deutschland, «reines Instrument der Schauspielkunst» (Dumont), karge Ausstattung. Tourneen durch Europa, Theaterakademie, Spielplanschwerpunkt: Naturalisten und nichtexpressionistische Gegenwartsautoren. 1933 aufgegangen in Städtischen Bühnen. 1945 bis 1946 Intendant Wolfgang Langhoff (1901–66). 1947 bis 1955 Gustaf Gründgens (1899–1963), großes Schauspielertheater bewahrenden Charakters, Klassiker, literarische Moderne. 1951 Trennung von Schauspiel und Oper, GmbH (Stadt und Land). 1955 bis 1972 Intendant Karl Heinz Stroux (1908–85), Einsatz für Ionesco (zahlreiche UA), Schauspielertheater. 1970 Neubau des Schauspielhauses. 1972 bis 1976 Ulrich Brecht, 1976 bis 1986 Günther Beelitz (* 1939), Einsatz für zeitgenössische Dramatik, vor allem deutsche Autoren in systematischer Pflege, teils durch UA. Dramaturgisch beziehungsvoller, bestimmte Themen reflektierender Spielplan mit langfristiger Zielsetzung (Antisemitismus, Faschismus). Als Kontrast intelligente literarische Unterhaltung. Gastspielreisen in die DDR, UdSSR, Israel u. a. Ensemble-Kontinuität. Ab 1986 Dr. Volker Canaris (* 1942).

Riemenschneider, H.: Theatergeschichte der Stadt Düsseldorf. 2 Bde. Düsseldorf 1987; Schwab-Felisch, H.: 75 Jahre Düsseldorfer Schauspielhaus. Düsseldorf 1980.

Werner Schulze-Reimpell

D 34 (Prag)

Das Theater D 34 wurde 1934 von Emil František Burian (1904–59) gegründet. Es entwickelte sich schnell zur führenden Avantgardebühne der Tschechoslowakei; bereits 1935 konnte eine internationale Tournee stattfinden. 1941 wurde das Theater von der dt. Besatzung verboten, Burian ins KZ verschleppt, er überlebte die Haft und konnte 1946 sein Theater als D 46 wiedereröffnen. Von 1956 bis zu seinem Tod 1959 wurde das Theater wieder unter dem Namen D 34 geführt. – Burian gelang es, mit einer Gruppe von Literaten, Musikern, Bühnenbildnern und Schauspielern seine progressiven Ideen und Ausdrucksmittel allgemeinverständlich darzubringen. Neben Filmprojektionen, Tänzen und Lichteffekten war die bereits vor 1934 von Burian entwickelte und erprobte «Voiceband» (Stimmorchester) ein spezifisches Ausdrucksmittel dieser Bühne, vokale und musikalische Elemente wurden durch Rhythmisierung der Dialoge und Sprechchöre zum selbständigen Bestandteil der Inszenierungen; gesprochenes Wort, Tanz und Musik bildeten in Burians Theater eine Einheit.

Otakar Fencl: Das Theater in der Tschechoslowakei. Prag 1963.

Elke Kehr

Ecole de Danse de l'Opéra de Paris

Seit über 200 Jahren bildet die E. d. O. P. den Tänzernachwuchs der Opéra und der französischen Provinztheater heran – 1661 von Ludwig XIV. gegründet, soll die Académie den Tanz systematisieren, kodifizieren und Berufstänzer trainieren. 1672 verschmilzt die Académie Royale de Danse mit der Académie Royale de Musique. Durch die Zusammenarbeit von Lully (1632–87), Beauchamp (1636–1705) und Molière (1622–73) gewinnt diese Institution im 17. Jh. den Ruf, europ. Tanzkunst zu bestimmen und neue theatralische Genres auszubilden (→Comédieballet; Ballettoper; Choreodrama). Zur Académie Royale gehören eine Ballett-Kompanie und ab 1713 eine Ballettschule, die E. d. O. P. Die Tradition der Schule hat, an Bedeutung verlierend, bis 1930 fortbestanden. Dann übernahm und reorganisierte sie Sergej Lifar (1905–86), ein ehemaliger Startänzer in Diaghilews →Ballets Russes und von 1929 bis 1945 danseur étoile de l'Opéra de Paris. Seine Erfolge führen die Kompanie vor dem Ausbruch des 2. Weltkriegs zu Spitzenleistungen (1935 *Icare*, 1941 *Le Chevalier et la Damoiselle*; 1942 *Joan von Zarissa* von Werner Egk). Nach 1947 nimmt Lifar zunächst mit sehr guten Kreationen seine Tätigkeit wieder auf (1947 *Les Mirages* von B. Sauguet; 1950 *Phèdre* von Auric), jedoch ohne die Schule durch Impulse erneut unter die Spitzenreiter der Nachkriegsproduktionen einreihen zu können.

Balcar, A.: Das Ballett. München 1957; Burian, K. v.: Das Ballett. Artia Praha 1963; Kunzle, R.: Beauchamp. In: Das Tanzarchiv, Sept. 1974, Febr. 1975, Mai 1975; Schmidt-Garre, H.: Ballett. Vom Sonnenkönig bis Balanchine. Hannover 1966.

Patricia Stöckemann

Edinburgh

Im Jahre 1947 wurde in Edinburgh, dessen Theatertradition bis ins Mittelalter zurückreicht, das international bedeutsame ‹Edinburgh Festival of Music and Drama› gegründet. Die Festspiele finden alljährlich im August/September statt. Der Schwerpunkt der Festivalaufführungen liegt beim Drama. 1960 wurde das Festivalprogramm um ein parallel zum Festival veranstaltetes Treffen der Amateur- und Studententheater erweitert.

Elke Kehr

Einakter

Bühnenstück geringeren Umfangs in einem → Akt. Tritt als selbständige Form erst seit der 2. Hälfte des 18. Jh. auf (vorher meist als Vor-, Nach- oder Zwischenspiel, oft improvisiert). Lessings (1729–81) Heldentragödie *Philotas* (1759) kann schon als Vorbote des modernen E. angesehen werden; die konzentrierte Spannung einer Grenzsituation ist hier schon gegeben. Nach 1880 führte die zunehmende Krise des Dramas viele Autoren zum E. August Strindberg (1849–1912) schreibt in dem Essay *Der Einakter* (1889): «Er ist vielleicht die Formel des kommenden Dramas.» Die Vielzahl der in dieser Periode entstehenden Stücke wie: Strindbergs *Elf Einakter* (1888–92, darunter *Fräulein Julie, Gläubiger, Die Stärkere, Rausch, Paria, Vom Tode*); Arthur Schnitzlers (1862–1931) Einakterzyklus *Anatol* (1893) und *Der grüne Kakadu* (1899); Frank Wedekinds (1864–1918) *Der Kammersänger* (1899), *Tod und Teufel* (1906), *Musik* und *Die Zensur* (1908); Hugo von Hofmannsthals (1874–1929) *Gestern, Theater in Versen, Der Tod des Tizian, Der Tor und der Tod* (1892–99); Maurice Maeterlincks (1862–1949) *Les Aveugles* (1890), *Intérieur* (1894), liefern einige allgemeine Kennzeichen des modernen E.: a) kein Drama im kleinen, sondern Teil eines Dramas, der sich verselbständigt hat zur Ganzheit mit offenem Anfang und Ende; b) Ausgangspunkt ist eine Situation; c) keine Handlung im traditionellen Sinne der agierenden → dramatis personae mit Exposition, Intrige, Höhepunkt und Ausgang; d) starke, intensive Spannung, die vor allem aus der Situation resultiert; e) stellt vornehmlich Menschen in Grenzsituationen dar.

Im 20. Jh. wird diese Form vor allem von existentialistischen Autoren aufgegriffen, gleichermaßen vom absurden Theater. Zahlreiche E. erscheinen, so z. B.: Luigi Pirandellos (1867–1936) *Der Mann mit einer Blume im Mund* (1923); Jean-Paul Sartres (1905–80) *Hinter geschlossenen Türen* (1944); Jean Genets (1910–86) *Die Zofen* (1947) und *Unter Aufsicht* (1949); Heinar Kipphardts (1922–84) *Entscheidungen* (1953); Wolfgang Hildesheimers (1916–91) *Nachtstück* (1963). Allerdings besteht die Gefahr einer möglichen Doppelfunktion. So ist Jean Cocteaus (1892–1963) *Die menschliche Stimme* (1930) ein E., aber gleichzeitig → ein Monodrama, ebenso Samuel Becketts (1906–89) *Das letzte Band* (1959). Andere Stücke, vorrangig die von Ionesco (*1912), sind E., aber auch Anti-Stücke (*Die kahle Sängerin*, 1950), komische Dramen (*Die Nachhilfestunde*, 1951) oder tragische Possen (*Die Stühle*, 1956), *Der neue Mieter* (1956/57), *Der König stirbt* (1962).

Schnetz, D.: Der moderne Einakter. Eine poetologische Untersuchung. Bern 1967; Szondi, P.: Theorie des modernen Dramas. Frankfurt/M. 1963.

Adriana Hass

Einfühlung

Aus dem Bereich der Ästhetik, der Kunst- und Literaturpsychologie übernommener Begriff (→Identifikation, →Verfremdung). Er bezeichnete das gefühlsmäßige, rein irrationale Verstehen und Erleben eines Kunstwerks, das ästhetische Sich-Wiederfinden, das Verschmelzen des eigenen Ichs im Kunstwerk über Stimmung, Emotion und Affekt, über das Sinnliche im Gegensatz zum Rationalen.

Im Theaterbereich wird der Begriff E. auf die beiden Hauptpole jeder Vorführung bezogen: Schauspieler und Zuschauer. Die Identifikation, das Einswerden des Schauspielers mit seiner Rolle, durch Verwandlungs- und Darstellungskunst, führt zur Illusionierung des Zuschauers, zu dessen E., zur Identifikation mit den Gestalten und den Vorgängen auf der Bühne. Eine der Hauptmethoden der Darstellungskunst war das ‹sich in die Rolle einfühlen›; diese Theaterpraxis wurde jahrhundertelang mehr oder weniger bewußt gepflegt. Als Arbeitsmethode für den Schauspieler wurde sie von Stanislawski (1863–1938) und seiner Schule systematisiert. In seinen theoretischen Schriften (*Mein Leben in der Kunst*, 1951; *Die Arbeit des Schauspielers an der Rolle*, 1955; *Die Arbeit des Schauspielers an sich selbst*, 1961/62) wie auch in seiner Theaterpraxis als Spielleiter und Direktor des Künstlertheaters in Moskau (→MChAT) forderte er in erster Hinsicht die «innere Wahrheit des Spiels», die der Schauspieler mit Hilfe von Improvisations- und Konzentrationsübungen erzielen sollte. Trotz großer Theatererfolge erkannten seine Schüler sehr bald die Grenzen dieses auf den Detailrealismus zu stark eingehenden Systems und suchten sie im →symbolischen Theater, besonders durch den Stanislawski-Schüler Meyerhold (1870–1940) zu überwinden.

Als erster wandte sich Diderot gegen die exklusive E. des Schauspielers in die Rolle in seinem *Paradox über den Schauspieler* (erschien 1830), in dem er ein bewußtes, kontrolliertes, nüchternes Spiel forderte. Nicht der Schauspieler sollte Emotionen empfinden, sondern sie beim Publikum hervorrufen. Viel radikaler argumentiert gegen die E. Bertolt Brecht. Er bekämpft sie sowohl in der Gestaltungskunst des Schauspielers als auch in der Rezeptionstätigkeit des Zuschauers. Als Gegensatz zur E. betont er die →Verfremdung. Bei aller Ablehnung der E. erkennt Brecht jedoch ihre Nützlichkeit beim Einstudieren einer Rolle: «Wenn auch beim Probieren Einfühlung in die Figur benutzt werden kann (was bei der Vorführung zu vermeiden ist), darf dies doch nur als eine unter mehreren Methoden der Beobachtung angewendet werden» (→*Kleines Organon für das Theater*). Weder die absolute Verwirklichung der E. noch der Verfremdung sind freilich möglich. Das Theater bleibt grundlegend angenommene Konvention, alles übrige nur Facetten, Modalitäten dieser komplexen Kunstform.

Brecht, B.: Schriften zum Theater. Frankfurt/M. 1981; Worringer, W.: Abstraktion und Einfühlung. Frankfurt/M. 1958.

Adriana Hass

Einnahmesoll

E. ist die Vorgabe des Rechtsträgers an das Theater, in welcher Höhe es sich durch eigene Einnahmen aus Kartenverkauf usw. selbst finanzieren soll. Derzeit werden die Theater der öffentlichen Hand in der BRD zwischen 70 und 80 Prozent subventioniert, während das Einnahmesoll in der Regel bei 20 bis 30 Prozent liegt. Im Bundesdurchschnitt spielen die Theater etwa 15,9 Prozent ihrer Ausgaben ein (1987/88).

Hohenemser, P.: Verteilungswirkungen staatlicher Theaterfinanzierung. Frankfurt/M. 1984.

Roswitha Körner

Eintrittspreis

(Auch ‹Entree› oder ‹Eintritt›) Erst seit dem 16. Jh. wird im europäischen Theater ein E. erhoben, und zwar meistens nicht als Einheits-E., sondern gestaffelt nach der Nähe der Sitzplätze zur Bühne oder auch dem Komfort (abgeschlossene Logen z. B.). E.-Ermäßigungen für sozial schwache Gruppen (Studenten, Kriegsversehrte, Soldaten, Arbeitslose, Rentner usw.) wurden erst nach dem 1. Weltkrieg allgemein eingeführt. Obwohl der E. heute im Theater aller Länder und Gesellschaftssysteme üblich ist, wird von Zeit zu Zeit die Forderung nach der ‹Kultur zum Nulltarif› (‹gratuité de la culture› programmierte der frz. Theatermann und zeitweilige Kulturminister Jack Lang) erhoben. – Schon im antiken Theater wurde – von der ältesten Zeit abgesehen – E. gefordert. Der erste Sozialtarif war die Gewährung von freiem E. für Minderbemittelte im Zeitalter des Perikles (6. Jh. v. Chr.). Im römischen Theater und im Mittelalter zahlten im allgemeinen nur auswärtige Besucher einen E. Im subventionierten Stadt- und Staats-Theater deckt der E. nur einen Bruchteil der Kosten von Aufführung und Theaterbetrieb als ganzem.

Horst Schumacher

Eiserner Vorhang

Feuerschutzwand, feuersicherer Verschluß, der im Theatergebäude die Bühne vom Zuschauerraum abschließt. Wird nach Schluß der Vorstellung nach dem Hauptvorhang herabgelassen. Besteht aus einer gegen den Zuschauerraum konvex gebogenen Stahlkonstruktion mit Wellblech verkleidet und ist meistens mit Asbest oder Kieselgur gefüllt; um ein Durchbrennen zu vermeiden, ist der e. V. oft mit einer Berieselungsanlage versehen. Er wird von elektrischen oder hydraulischen Anlagen bewegt; die Bedienung ist feuerpolizeilich geregelt.

Heutzutage ein nicht mehr wegzudenkender Bühnenbestandteil, wurde der e. V. erst ziemlich spät nach der Häufung von Theaterbränden im 19. Jh. verbindlich eingeführt; 1782 wurde er zum erstenmal in Lyon und nach dem Brand des Wiener Ringtheaters 1881 allgemein. An dt. Theatern ist er seit 1889 vorgeschrieben. Die ausgeprägte Experimentierlust, die das Theater der Nachkriegszeit kennzeichnet, führte zu einer Verlagerung des e. V. im modernen Theaterbau. Ausnahmefälle sind die 1953 erstmalig in Bochum, dann in Wuppertal, Trier u. a. m. durchgeführte Vorverlegung des e. V. über den überdachten Orchestergraben, unmittelbar vor dem Parkett.

Adriana Hass

Ekkyklema

Theatermaschine des griech. Theaters, mit deren Hilfe das Resultat hinterszenischer Ereignisse auf der Bühne präsentiert werden konnte; es handelt sich um eine Holzplattform, die aus der Haupttür des Bühnenhauses herausgerollt werden konnte. Der Zeitpunkt der Einführung des E. ist umstritten. Aischylos' *Orestie* setzt das E. wohl voraus; zwei aristophaneische Parodien der bühnenwirksamen Erfindung (*Archarner* 407 ff, *Thesmophoriazusen* 25 ff) lassen (wie der archäologische Befund) kaum einen Zweifel daran, daß das E. bereits im 5. Jh. verwendet worden ist.

Arnott, P.: Greek Scenic Conventions in the Fifth Century b. c. Oxford 1962, p. 78–88; Melchinger, S.: Das Theater der Tragödie. München 1974, S. 191–194; Newiger, H.-J.: Drama und Theater. In: G. A. Seeck (Hg.): Das griech. Drama. Darmstadt 1979, S. 451–454.

Bernd Seidensticker

Die Elf Scharfrichter

«Wir richten scharf und herzlich» – diese Zeile aus dem Eröffnungslied der Premiere am 13.4.1901 ist kennzeichnend für die Absichten des Münchener Kabaretts. Es ging hervor u. a. aus der Sektion des «Goethebundes zum Schutze freier Kunst und Wissenschaft», der (im Februar 1900 gegr.) sich gegen die geplante Einschränkung künstlerischer Freiheit durch die «Lex Heinze» wandte. Zu diesem Kreis gehörten u. a. Otto Falckenberg, Leo Greiner und der Franzose Achille Georges d'Ailly-Vaucheret, der sich Marc-Henry nannte und Erfahrungen aus Pariser Cabarets mitbrachte. Zuerst veranstaltete man kabarettistische Einzelabende. Nachdem man aber das nötige Geld geliehen hatte, wurde der Saal im Gasthof «Zum goldenen Hirschen» umgebaut und mit dem eher zufällig gefundenen Namen E. S. das künstlerisch wohl bedeutendste Kabarett der Jahrhundertwende begründet. Die elf männlichen Mitglieder des Beginns traten alle unter Pseudonym auf, Star des Programms wurde jedoch das anfangs einzige weibliche Mitglied, Marya Delvard (eigentlich Marie Biller). Sie kreierte einen neuen, vielfach nachgeahmten Stil des musikalischen Vortrags.

Schon bald gerieten die E. S. in Konflikt mit der Zensur. Ihre politisch-satirischen Puppenspiele wurden ebenso verboten wie jedes politische Couplet. So wurden literarische Chansons, eigene Gedichte und Literaturparodien Kernstücke der weiteren Programme. Weitere weibliche Mitglieder und «Henkersknechte» kamen hinzu. Neben der Delvard aber wurde Frank Wedekind zu einer Stütze des Programms. Er trug eigene Chansons vor, aber auch der 1. Akt seines Dramas *Der Erdgeist* und (in gekürzter Fassung) *Die Kaiserin von Neufundland* wurden hier aufgeführt.

Literarischer Anspruch und antibürgerliche Satire prägten ihre Programme. Der Erfolg rief zahlreiche – meist kurzlebige – Nachahmungen hervor. Die Zusammenarbeit mit bedeutenden Künstlern führte zur herausragenden Qualität ihrer Plakate, mit Ludwig Thoma, Hanns von Gumppenberg und Frank Wedekind bestimmten namhafte Autoren ihr literarisches Niveau. 1904 erzwangen erhebliche Schulden – trotz aller Erfolge – die Schließung der E. S. – Einzelne Mitglieder machten auch weiterhin Kabarett, in Soloauftritten, als Mitglieder anderer Ensembles oder durch Gründung eigener Gruppen. Marya Delvard und Marc-Henry gründeten mit dem «Nachtlicht» das erste wirkliche Kabarett Wiens (1906) und ein Jahr später die bis 1909 bestehende «Fledermaus», an der u. a. Oskar Kokoschka, Roda Roda, Egon Friedell und Alfred Polgar mitarbeiteten.

Delvard, M.: Meine ersten Münchner Jahre. München 1964; Die Elf Scharfrichter (Sondernr. der Zs. «Bühne und Brettl») 1903; Falckenberg, O.: Mein Leben – mein Theater. München 1944; Greul, Heinz: Die Elf Scharfrichter. Zürich 1962; Gumppenberg, H. von: Lebenserinnerungen. Berlin / Zürich 1929; ders.: Überdramen. 3 Bde. Berlin 1902; Kühn, V.: Das Kabarett der frühen Jahre. Berlin 1984; Segel, H. B.: Turn-of-the-Century Cabaret. New York 1987.

Wolfgang Beck

Elisabethanisches Theater

E. T. bezeichnet das Theater zur Zeit Elisabeths I. (1558–1603) und Jakobs I. (1603–25). Blütezeit ca. 1590 bis 1625. 1576 wurde die erste öffentliche Bühne, →The Theatre, von James Burbage eröffnet. Ab ca. 1574 wurden professionelle Schauspieltruppen unter dem Patronat eines Adligen gegr. und ließen sich in London nieder. Zu den bekanntesten gehörten William Shakespeares (1564–1616) und Richard Burbages (ca. 1567–1619), Lord Chamberlain's Men, später King's Men, und Edward Alleyns (1566–1626) Admiral's Men. Ein breites Publikum (15000 bis 21000) besuchte regelmäßig das Theater. Dadurch wurden auch die Voraussetzungen für professionelle Schriftsteller geschaffen. E. T. ist in öffentliche und private Bühnen zu unterscheiden. Diese Unterscheidung schlägt sich nieder in der Bühnenform, im Publikum, in den Schauspieltruppen und im Repertoire (für die öffentlichen Bühnen →Shakespearebühne). Die privaten Bühnen waren kleinere, rechteckige, künstlich beleuchtete Hallen in bereits bestehenden Häusern, z. B. das Kloster Blackfriars. Das Vorbild waren die great halls der großen Häuser und die Inns of Court. An einer Stirnseite wurde die Bühne aufgebaut, rechts und links befanden sich Eingänge, darüber eine Galerie. Rechts und links der Bühne waren Zuschauerlogen für die Adligen. Alle anderen Zuschauer saßen auf Bänken oder Stühlen vor der Bühne im pit oder auf den umlaufenden Galerien. Im Second Blackfriars soll Platz für ca. 700 Zuschauer gewesen sein. Die Eintrittspreise der privaten Bühnen lagen wesentlich höher als die der öffentlichen Bühnen. Dementsprechend war das Publikum der privaten Bühnen reicher und homogener als das der öffentlichen. Urspr. spielten nur Kindertruppen in den privaten Bühnen, aber ab 1609 spielten auch Shakespeares King's Men während des Winters im Second Blackfriars. Im Gegensatz zu den öffentlichen Bühnen lagen drei der vier privaten Bühnen innerhalb der Stadtgrenzen Londons.

Armstrong, W.: The Elizabethan Private Theatres: Facts and Problems. London 1958; Barroll, J. et al. (eds.): The Revels History of Drama in English. Vol. 3. London 1975; Beckerman, B.: Shakespeare at the Globe, 1599–1609. New York 1962; Castrop, H.: Das elisabethanische Theater. In: Schabert, I. (Hg.): Shake speare-Handbuch. Stuttgart 1972, S. 73–125; Chambers, E.: The Elizabethan Stage. 4 Vols., London 1923; Gurr, A.: The Shakespearean Stage, 1574–1642. Cambridge 1970; Southern, R.: The Open Stage. London 1953; Wickham, G.: Early English Stages 1300 to 1660. Rev. Ed. Vol. 2. London 1980.

Lawrence Guntner

Embolimon

Griech.: das eingeschobene (ergänze ‹Lied›); aristotelische Bezeichnung für ein Chorlied der griech. Tragödie, das keinen inneren Zusammenhang (dramatisch oder thematisch) mit dem Kontext hat (Aristoteles' *Poetik* 1456a 27–30). Die Entwicklung in Richtung auf chorische ‹Zwischenakt-Musik› beginnt bereits am Ende des 5. Jh. (→ Chor).

Neitzel, H.: Die dramatische Funktion des Chorliedes in den Tragödien des Euripides. Diss. Hamburg 1967.

Bernd Seidensticker

Emigrantentheater / Migrantentheater

Allgemeine Bezeichnung für alle Arten von Theater, das von Autoren geschrieben, Schauspielern aufgeführt und Zuschauern gesehen wird, die aus ihrer Heimat aus religiösen, politischen oder wirtschaftlichen Gründen vertrieben worden sind oder sie mehr oder weniger freiwillig verlassen haben. Bekanntestes Beispiel im 20. Jh. ist das deutschsprachige → Exiltheater. E. hat es auch in früheren Zeiten gegeben. Beispiele dafür sind die Bemühungen J. A. Komenskys (Comenius) und die Versuche der Böhmischen Brüder im 16. Jh., in der Emigration Theater zu spielen. Im 19. Jh. ist vor allem wichtig das poln. E.; Hauptwerke der poln. Romantik wurden im Ausland geschrieben und erlebten dort häufig auch ihre ersten Aufführungen.

Kennzeichnend für das E. ist zu allen Zeiten die festzustellende Konzentration auf Themen der eigenen Geschichte, aber auch auf Probleme, die durch den Zusammenstoß der eigenen Kultur mit einer andersartigen in den Ländern der Emigration entstehen. Die Themenwahl wird zumeist bestimmt durch die Funktion des E. Die Förderung nationalen Selbstbewußtseins gehört hierzu ebenso wie die Schaffung bzw. Erhaltung kultureller oder religiöser Identität in Zeiten der Unterdrückung und der politischen Ohnmacht. Dies gilt z. B. für das poln. E. im 19. Jh., als Polen zeitweise als selbständiger Staat nicht existierte und von anderen Mächten besetzt war.

Speziell in neuerer Zeit tritt zum eigentlichen E. das sog. Migrantentheater hinzu, das sich im Zuge der Entkolonialisierung und der Wirt-
schaftsmigration (Gastarbeiter) vor allem im westeurop. Raum entwikkelt hat.

In den Niederlanden ist diese Szene innerhalb Westeuropas sicherlich
am vielfältigsten entwickelt. Es sind drei Gruppen von Minderheiten, die
hier das Migrationstheater tragen: Emigranten aus den ehemaligen Kolonien (Surinamer, Antillianer, Molukker), ausländische Arbeitnehmer
(Türken, Marokkaner, Griechen, Spanier, Jugoslawen) und politische
Flüchtlinge (aus Uruguay, Argentinien, Chile, Südafrika u. a.). Eine endgültige Richtung der Entwicklung dieser Migrationskultur ist derzeit noch
nicht zu sehen: Vermittlung von allochthoner und autochthoner Kultur
oder Bewahrung der eigenen ethnischen Identität und gleichzeitige Isolation in der westeuropäischen Gesellschaft. Eine Organisation, die Projektarbeit in diesem Zusammenhang fördert, ist die «Stichting Intercul-
turele Projekten Theater» (STIPT) in Amsterdam. Eine besondere Rolle
spielen die Theatergruppen der Surinamer, deren kulturpolitische Ausrichtung durchweg auf Integration zielt; die Sprache ist in der Regel Nie-
derländisch. Älteste Gruppe ist «Bakuba» (gegründet 1975 in Amsterdam, ein Laienensemble unter Leitung von Hans Caprino). Unterstützt
wird diese Gruppe wie andere auch von staatlichen und kommunalen Behörden. Weitere Gruppen, die seit längerer Zeit arbeiten, sind «Djompo
Abra», «Gado Tjo», «Bruin Brood en spelen» (in Zusammenarbeit mit
der Schriftstellerin Astrid Roemer). – Theatergruppen, die von Gast-
arbeitern gegründet wurden, spielen im wesentlichen (in der jeweiligen Muttersprache) nur für ihre Landsleute. Ausnahmen sind die beiden professionellen Gruppen «Whalili» (Marokkaner) und «Öngören»
(Türken).

Ein internationales Forum für das Migrationstheater ist das in Amsterdam seit 1982 jährlich veranstaltete «Stagedoor Festival» (organisiert von
den Theatern De Balie, De Engelenbak, Polanentheater und Soeterijn),
dem seit 1984 ein vom Niederländischen Theaterinstitut veranstaltetes
«Stagedoor Colloquium» als Diskussionsforum für die Probleme der Migrationskultur angeschlossen ist.

Ca. 120 ausländische Theatergruppen gibt es in der Bundesrepublik
Deutschland und West-Berlin (ganz überwiegend Türken). Häufig reichen die kulturpolitischen Ambitionen dieser Gruppen über das Theater-
Spielen hinaus und umfassen generell die Pflege und Vermittlung der eigenen Kultur. Funktion und Thematik dieser Theaterarbeit ändern sich in
dem Maße, in dem es sich nicht mehr nur um einen vorübergehenden
Aufenthalt in einem anderen Land handelt, sondern um dauernde Niederlassung. Neben reinem Unterhaltungstheater (Folklore) spielt die Auseinandersetzung mit den Schwierigkeiten der Integration eine zentrale

312 Engagement

Rolle. – In der Bundesrepublik entstanden die meisten ausländischen Theatergruppen erst Ende der 70er Jahre, sie arbeiten überwiegend auf Amateurbasis, selten nur als halb-, wenige als professionelle Gruppen (zeitweilig ein «Türken-Ensemble» bei der Berliner →Schaubühne am Lehniner Platz). Mehr noch als dt. →Amateurtheater und →Freies Theater leiden sie unter ökonomischen Problemen und begrenzten Aufführungsmöglichkeiten.

Von ausschlaggebender Bedeutung für die Entfaltung des Migrationstheaters ist die Praxis der jeweiligen Ausländer- bzw. Minderheitenpolitik der Gastländer.

Bosboom, F./Hildebrand, W.: Bakuba speelt Oe'ma. Voorstellingsanalyse en Publieksonderzoek. Utrecht 1979; Brauneck, M. u. a.: Ausländertheater in der Bundesrepublik Deutschland und West-Berlin. Hamburg 1983; Brouwers, T. u. a. (Red.): Immigrantentheater (= Dramatisch Akkord 14, Utrecht 1981); Museum Bochum (Hg.): Dokumentation «Gastarbeiterkultur». Nr. 1 Musik, Tanz, Theater. Bochum 1980; Nederlands Theater Instituut (Hg.): Stagedoor Colloquium. Een internationale discussie over migrantentheater. Amsterdam 1985; Schumacher, P.: De minderheden. Amsterdam 1981; Migrantentheater (= Toneel Teatraal. Okt. 1980, Dez. 1984).

Wolfgang Beck / Frans Bosboom

Engagement

(Frz. ‹Verpflichtung›) Feste Bindung für eine Spielzeit oder mehrere Jahre an ein Theater, eine Theatertruppe oder auch für eine bestimmte Rolle, wie in den USA üblich. Dem Beamtenrecht entsprechende, nicht begrenzte Dienstverträge als ‹Staatsschauspieler› mit Unkündbarkeit, Pensionsberechtigung usw. sind im dt. Sprachraum nur an Staatstheatern zu finden, u. a. auch am Wiener →Burgtheater. Die →Comédie Française kennt das System des ‹sociétaire› (= ‹Teilhaber›), was eine beamtenähnliche Stellung bedeutet. – Dem E. liegt in der BRD in der Regel der sog. →Normalvertrag zwischen dem →Dt. Bühnenverein und der →Genossenschaft Dt. Bühnenangehöriger zugrunde, d. h. ein Rahmen(arbeits/dienst)vertrag mit genauer Beschreibung der Rechte und Pflichten der Vertragspartner: Vergütung, Arbeits- und Ruhezeiten, Urlaubsregelung, Altersversorgung, Kündigung usw.

Horst Schumacher

Englische Komödianten

E. K. ist der Sammelbegriff für jene engl. Wandertruppen, die vom Ende des 16. Jh. an – nachdem einige engl. Schauspieler, die sich 1585 am dän. Hof aufhielten, von Kurfürst Christian von Sachsen nach Deutschland geholt worden waren – bis etwa Mitte des 17. Jh. in Deutschland, Dänemark, den Niederlanden und auch in Osteuropa gastierten. Die Truppen wurden später von aus dt. Berufsschauspielern gebildeten Wandertruppen abgelöst, welche oft noch unter dem Namen ‹Englische Komödianten› auftraten, der zu einem Qualitätsbegriff geworden war. Die Truppen bestanden in der Regel aus rund 20 Schauspielern, Akrobaten und Musikern. Geleitet wurden sie zumeist vom Darsteller des →Narren (Pickelhering, Hanswurst), der in den kurzen musikalischen Sketchen, die zunächst weitgehend das Repertoire bildeten und erst später von dramatischen Bühnenstücken abgelöst wurden, die Hauptrolle spielte. Zu diesem Zeitpunkt bildeten dann Haupt- und Staatsaktionen, im Kern die Stücke Shakespeares und seiner Zeitgenossen, das Repertoire der E. K. Der Spielcharakter war geprägt durch eine naturalistische Spielweise, angereichert mit oft äußerst derben Zoten, so daß von einer originalorientierten Aufführungspraxis und einem vertretbaren künstlerischen Niveau in der Regel nicht die Rede sein konnte. In Deutschland wurde besonders Herzog Heinrich Julius von Braunschweig, selbst Verfasser zahlreicher Theaterstücke, Protektor der Wandertruppen. Andere von den E. K. aufgesuchte Spielorte waren zunächst Leipzig, Frankfurt/M., Köln, Nürnberg, Schmalkalden, Marburg, München, Augsburg. Einige der bekanntesten Prinzipale, die auf den Kontinent herüberkamen, waren Robert Browne, der Clown Sackville, John Green, John Spencer, Joris Joliphus. Letzterer ist aus zwei Gründen besonders erwähnenswert: Er war zum einen der erste Prinzipal, der mit der Tradition, Frauenrollen durch Männer oder Knaben zu besetzen, brach und ab 1653 Schauspielerinnen beschäftigte. Zum anderen war er es auch, der von Karl II. ein Patent erhielt, das ihm die Berufsausübung als Prinzipal in London ermöglichte. Dieses Privileg leitete in England die Sanktionierung des Schauspielerstandes ein. Die Spielfläche der E. K. war das sog. Gerüst, eine leicht auf- und abzubauende Vorrichtung, welche als Vorderbühne diente; der Handlungsort wurde nicht durch Dekorationen, sondern im gesprochenen Text angegeben. Es gab ferner einen Vorhang, unterteilt durch zwei Türen oder Schlitze, zwischen welchen sich die Hinterbühne befand, die als Spielfläche für örtlich festgelegte Szenen diente. Allgemein wurde den Kostümen eine größere Bedeutung beigemessen als der Dekoration. Darstellungsstil und szenische Ausstattung der einzelnen Truppen waren überaus unterschiedlich.

Baesecke, A.: Das Schauspiel der englischen Komödianten in Deutschland. Studien zur engl. Philologie, Heft 87. Halle 1937. Neuauflage 1974; Brauneck, M. (Hg.): Spieltexte der Wanderbühne I–IV. Berlin 1970; Cohn, A.: Shakespeare in Germany in the 16th and 17th centuries. London/Berlin 1865; Creizenach, W.: Die Schauspiele der engl. Komödianten (= Kürschners Deutsche Nationalliteratur, Bd. 23, Berlin, Stuttgart o. J.); Evans, M. B.: Traditions of the Elizabethan Stage in Germany. Phil. Quart. 2 (1923), p. 310–314; Heine, C.: Das Schauspiel der dt. Wanderbühne vor Gottsched. 1889; Herz, E.: Engl. Schauspieler und engl. Schauspiel zur Zeit Shakespeares in Deutschland. In: Theatergeschichtliche Forschungen, Bd. 18. Hamburg 1903.

Elke Kehr

Ensemble

(Frz. ‹zusammen›) Gesamtheit aller bei einem Theater oder einer Truppe engagierten Schauspieler, die eine künstlerische Gemeinschaft bilden, d. h., die nicht zufällig, sondern im Sinne bestimmter Stil- und Kunstprinzipien zusammenarbeiten. Berühmte Beispiele: →Berliner E.; Moskauer Künstlertheater (→MChAT) unter Stanislawski.

Horst Schumacher

en suite

(Frz. = ununterbrochen) In der Theatersprache Bezeichnung für eine Bühne, die Aufführungen eines und desselben Stückes in Serien (daher auch ‹Serientheater›), d. h. in ununterbrochener Folge über einen bestimmten Zeitraum spielt. Besonders verbreitet am →Broadway und bei den Boulevardtheatern (Gegensatz: Repertoiretheater).

Bernard Poloni

Entfesseltes Theater

E. T. meint die Befreiung des Theaters von der Gebundenheit an die Literatur, wie sie Alexander Tairow (1885–1950) gefordert hatte. In seiner programmatischen Schrift *Aufzeichnungen eines Regisseurs*, die 1921 in Moskau erschien und dem dt. Leser 1923 als *Das entfesselte Theater* vorgestellt wurde, legte Tairow sein Regiekonzept dar, das eine Synthese gegenüber dem «Naturalismus» Stanislawskis und der «Stilbühne» Meyerholds suchte und seine spezifische Ausprägung in dem 1914 von Tairow u. a. gegr. →Moskauer Kammertheater fand.

Tairow ersehnte ein Theater, das auf geschriebene Stücke verzichten und sich seine eigenen Szenarien schaffen würde, das damit ein wirklich theatralisches Theater sei, d. h. eine auf sich selbst gestellte, autonome Kunst. Die Aufgabe des Theaters sah er darin, unter Benutzung des Werks ein «neues und eigenartiges Kunstwerk zu schaffen». Die Kreation dieses neuen Kunstwerks bedarf eines Schauspielers, der in der Beherrschung der «inneren» wie der «äußeren» Technik ein Meister ist. Die «innere» Technik des Schauspielers besteht in der Fähigkeit, mit Hilfe des schöpferischen Willens und der schöpferischen Phantasie ein beliebiges szenisches Gebilde hervorzubringen und die notwendigen Emotionen zu beherrschen; die «äußere» Technik besteht in der Fähigkeit des Schauspielers, das von ihm erschaffene szenische Kunstwerk für den Zuschauer sichtbar zu machen, es in eine Form zu gießen und dazu das gesamte ihm zur Verfügung stehende Material – Körper, Atem, Stimme – auszuwerten. G. Craigs Vorstellungen von Marionette und → Über-Marionette lehnte Tairow ebenso ab wie die techn. Experimente Meyerholds: «Denn das Wesen des Theaters ist immer *die Handlung*, die einzig und allein vom *aktiv-handelnden* Menschen, d. h. vom Schauspieler getragen wird» (*Das entfesselte Theater*, S. 54).

Theater, verstanden als Kollektivkunstwerk, bedarf außerdem eines Spielleiters, der die Willensäußerungen aller Beteiligten konzentriert und der im Idealfall zugleich der Dramatiker ist, der gemeinsam mit den Schauspielern Werke schafft und szenisch verwirklicht.

Tairow propagierte ein → «synthetisches Theater», das alle Künste organisch miteinander verbinden sollte, eine «synthetische Konstruktion, die die heute noch getrennten Elemente der Harlekinade, der Tragödie, der Operette, der Pantomime und des Zirkus in ihrer Strahlenbrechung durch die Seele des heutigen Schauspielers und durch den ihm eigenen schöpferischen Rhythmus vereinigen würde» (*Das entfesselte Theater*, S. 105). Für dieses Theater blieb die traditionelle Rampe, blieb die Distanz zum Zuschauer notwendiger Bestandteil, wenn auch der Bühnenboden als wichtigster Teil des Bühnenbilds zu schiefen und unterschiedlich hohen Flächen durchbrochen werden durfte. Tairow wollte kein Theater für die Massen, sondern ein Studiotheater für Kenner. Die Sowjetdramatik stand lange außerhalb seines Aufführungsprogramms; 1929 geriet er in Konflikt mit der Partei, leitete das Kammertheater jedoch noch bis 1949.

Hoffmann, L./Wardetzky, D. (Hg.): Wsewolod E. Meyerhold. Alexander I. Tairow. Jewgeni B. Wachtangow. Theateroktober. Beiträge zur Entwicklung des sowj. Theaters. Frankfurt/M. 1972; Tairov, A. J.: Zapiski režissera. Moskva 1921; ders.: Das entfesselte Theater. Potsdam 1923 (ebf. Leipzig/Weimar 1980).

Annelore Engel-Braunschmidt

Entremés

(Span. = Einschiebsel) Als einaktige komische Spiele bei Festlichkeiten; als Zwischenspiele in vielaktigen Dramen des 17. Jh. Zunächst ohne Bezug zu deren Inhalt. Ausgeprägte Spielform des spanischen Theaters, z. B. bei Lope de Vega, Calderón, Cervantes. Calderóns possenhafte Einakter sind im Gegensatz zu den Pasos von Lope de Rueda unmittelbar mit dem Hauptwerk verknüpft.

Pirrotta, N.: Intermedium. In: Blume, F. (Hg.): Musik in Geschichte und Gegenwart. Band VI. Sp. 1310–1336. Kassel 1960; Rischbieter, H. (Hg.): Theater-Lexikon. Zürich/Schwäbisch Hall 1983, Sp. 396.

Helga Ettl

Environmental Theatre

Oberstes Prinzip des E. T. ist, daß Akteure und Publikum Raum und Umwelt gemeinsam teilen. In diesem allg. Sinn war alles Theater generell E. T., ehe mit Beginn der realistischen Traditionen die Guckkastenbühne eingeführt wurde. Es spielte entweder in keinem gesonderten Theaterraum, sondern in der Umwelt der Menschen (Straße, Markt, Burghof, Kneipe etc.), oder ragte als Proszeniumsbühne in den Zuschauerraum hinein. Das moderne E. T. der USA belebte beide Formen neu, indem es bes. ‹environments› schuf (die →Happenings; die Performing Garage der →Performance Group R. Schechners) oder die natürliche Umwelt (→Snake Theatre) als Rahmen und Funktion nutzte (Straßen, Parks, Strände etc.). Als wichtigster Theoretiker und Praktiker des modernen amerik. E. T. gilt der Professor für Theater und langjährige Herausgeber des Tulane Drama Review, Richard Schechner (* 1934), der sechs Prinzipien des E. T. entwickelte: 1. keine traditionelle Unterscheidung zwischen Leben und Kunst; 2. der ganze Raum für die Aufführung, der ganze Raum fürs Publikum; 3. das Theaterereignis findet im vorgefundenen oder im total verwandelten Raum statt; 4. das E. T. kann einen oder viele Brennpunkte haben; 5. der menschliche Darsteller ist nicht bedeutender als andere audiovisuelle Elemente der Aufführung; 6. das gesprochene Wort ist kein entscheidender Faktor der Inszenierung.

Schechner, R.: Environmental Theatre. New York 1973.

Dieter Herms

Epeisodion

Griech. (dazu) Auftritt; von Aristoteles (*Poetik* 1452 b 20 f) als «Teil der Tragödie zwischen zwei (→) Stasima» definiert; entspricht also etwa unserem Begriff ‹Akt›; daneben wird das Wort auch im Griech. in der Bedeutung von Episode verwendet.

Aichele, K.: Das Epeisodion. In: W. Jens (Hg.): Die Bauformen der Tragödie, Poetica Beiheft 6. München 1971, S. 47–83.

Bernd Seidensticker

Epilog

(Griech. ‹epilogos› = Nachwort, Schlußwort eines Stücks, getrennt vom Handlungsschluß wie der →Prolog von der →Exposition) Von Plautus in die röm. Komödie eingeführt als letzte Anrede des Epilogsprechers (‹epilogus›) ans Publikum über →Fabel, Darstellung und Sinn des Stücks mit Ankündigung eines folgenden. Im geistlichen Spiel des mittelalterlichen Theaters (→Mittelalter/Drama und Theater des Mittelalters) Kommentar der Heilsgeschichte für die Zuschauer; im →Fastnachtsspiel, bes. bei Hans Sachs (1494–1576), belehrende Erläuterungen zum Abschluß, bei den Humanisten dann Hinweise auf das historisch-politische Zeitgeschehen. Oft verwendet am Schluß der Barockstücke bei den Spaniern wie im →Elisabethanischen Theater (z. B. Puck in Shakespeares *Sommernachtstraum*, 1595–96, der auf den Alptraumcharakter des Spiels hinweist); im dt. und Wiener Barock- und →Volkstheater tritt oft der →Narr oder →Hanswurst als E.-Sprecher auf, das für den nächsten Abend vorgesehene Stück mit Titel und Inhalt ankündigend, aber auch zum komischen Schlußkommentar des Spiels. Heute ist der E. in der offenen Form und im →epischen Theater eine wesentliche Bauform, bes. bei Brecht oder den Volksstückautoren. Der E. kann auch wie das →Nachspiel als autonomer →Einakter mit satirischer Intention gebraucht werden, bes. im engl. Theater der Restaurationszeit mit großer Durchschlagskraft bei John Dryden (1631–1700).

Wie der →Prolog hat der E. wichtige kommunikationsbezogene, teils kritisch-verfremdende, teils spannungslösende, auf das Spiel und dessen Deutung ausgerichtete Funktionen. Er kann im dialektischen Beziehungsbogen zu Prolog und Handlungselementen stehen.

Jens, W. (Hg.): Die Bauformen der griechischen Tragödie. München 1971.

Gérard Schneilin

Episches Theater

1. Im weiten Sinne des Begriffs: das Einbauen nichtdramatischer Formen, vorwiegend episch-erzählerischer Art, jedoch auch lyrischer oder musikalischer Natur in die dialektische Auseinandersetzung zwischen Subjekt und Objekt, die lückenlose, lineare Zielstrebigkeit des Handlungsablaufs des Dramas zum Zweck der Unterbrechung der →Einfühlung. Historisch gesehen geht die Episierung auf die Ursprünge des griech. Theaters (→Antikes Theater) zurück mit dem Dialog zwischen dem Autor/Rhapsoden und dem Chor, in der späteren griech. Tragödie den Berichten und Chorkommentaren sowie bei Euripides der ‹epischen Vorschau und Hinausschau› von →Prolog und →Epilog. Dieselbe epische Grundhaltung ist in der Trennung von Aktions- und Sprachverlauf sowie der Erzählerfigur des mittelalterlichen →Mysterienspiels, dann des →Auto Sacramental und der →Fastnachtsspiele feststellbar. Nichtaristotelische Bauformen aus dem Bereich des Erzählerischen und des Lyrischen für Einführung einer kritischen Kommentarebene finden sich in den meisten Stücken der ‹offenen Form›, vom →Elisabethanischen Theater über den →Sturm und Drang bis zu den realistischen Dramen Christian Dietrich Grabbes (1801–36) und Georg Büchners (1803–37). Besonders wichtig sind in →Komödie und →Tragikomödie die Bauformen der Illusionsbrechung und Ironisierung als Momente der Reflexion und Aufklärung des Zuschauers; charakteristisch dafür das →romantische Lustspiel. Kulminationspunkt dieser epischen Tendenz ist am Ende des 19. Jh. das →naturalistische Theater, worin eine Vielzahl epischer Bauformen, Situationen und Motive das dramatische Gefüge zersplittert – so im Frühwerk Gerhart Hauptmanns (1862–1946) die Anhäufung von Elementen wie Revue, Bericht, Schilderung, Einbeziehung eines Milieu und Handlung von außen her betrachtenden Fremden als Vertreter des Autors etc.

Dies führt im Theater des 20. Jh. zur durchgehenden Episierung des Dramas. Margret Dietrich will vier Grundformen der epischen Technik feststellen: das Auftreten des epischen Ichs als auktorialen Erzählers in Form von Ansager, Schauspieler, Sänger, Spielleiter (Thornton Wilder 1897–1975: *Our Town*, 1938), Registrator (Max Frisch, *1911: *Biografie*, 1968); die Aufgliederung des Dramas in Bilderfolgen, die Guckkastentechnik oder die des Theaters im Theater; die Einbeziehung der epischen Rück- und Vorblendungstechnik (z. B. Arthur Miller, *1915: *Death of a Salesman*, 1949); die Unterbrechung der Handlungsfolge durch reflektiv-kontemplative Elemente.

2. Im engeren Sinne versteht man im 20. Jh. unter e. T. die von Erwin →Piscator (1893–1966) und Bertolt Brecht (1898–1956) wissenschaftlich und ideologisch ausgearbeitete Theatertheorie. Dieses marxistische Lehrtheater zielt ab auf «die Auslegung der Fabel und ihrer Vermittlung

Episches Theater **319**

durch geeignete Verfremdungen» (→*Kleines Organon*). In seinen Stükken und seinen Abhandlungen (u. a. *Über eine nichtaristotelische Dramatik*, 1933–41; *Der Messingkauf*, 1937–51; *Kleines Organon für das Theater*, 1948; *Arbeitsjournal*, 1938–55) hat es Brecht immer wieder in der Gegenüberstellung von dramatischer und epischer Form des Theaters (*Anmerkungen zur Oper Aufstieg und Fall der Stadt Mahagonny*, 1931) oder Karussell-/planetarisches Theater (*Arbeitsjournal*) letzten Endes als «Dialektik auf dem Theater» (1951–55) praktisch und theoretisch zu definieren versucht. Dieses verfremdende Zeigetheater mit ‹wissenschaftlichen› Merkmalen will dem belehrbaren Zuschauer «die Welt zum Zugriff vorlegen» und ihn dazu anregen, «in die Naturprozesse und die gesellschaftlichen Prozesse» verändernd einzugreifen. Dazu steht im Mittelpunkt der Brechtschen Theaterpraxis, wie im 1. Bild von *Leben des Galilei* (1938–55) exemplarisch dargestellt, der Perspektivismus als ständige Mobilität und Veränderung der Zuschauerperspektive.

In dieser «Technik des Dramenbaus, des Bühnenbaus und der Schauspielweise» (Brecht) werden zum Zweck einer parabolischen Paradigmatik und Dramatik sowohl nichtaristotelische epische als aristotelische dramatische Bauformen gebraucht, denn alle Theatermittel sollen verfügbar sein, ‹umfunktioniert› auf Zweck und Ziel des Theaters. Darin wird beabsichtigt, daß das dramatisch agierende und das episch-referierend-demonstrierende Theater eine dialektische Verbindung eingehen. Zum episch-auktorialen Kommentar der →Handlung und zur widersprüchlichen Darstellung der Figuren tragen nicht nur die üblichen epischen Bauformen bei, sondern lyrische, gestische, plastische, musikalische, kinematographische oder choreographische Ausdrucksmittel sowie die verfremdende Technik des Schauspielers im Sinne eines auktorialen Erzählers seiner Person. Alle Künste des Theaters werden zum Zweck der Verfremdung, des kritischen Mitgestaltens des Zuschauers in dialektisch-kontrapunktischem Widerspruch zueinander, nicht in einem illusionierenden Gesamtkunstwerk eingesetzt.

Im 20. Jh. wird diese Technik weitgehend angewendet im →dokumentarischen Theater bei den Nachahmern Brechts in der DDR, vor allem beim frühen Peter Hacks (* 1928) oder im frühen Werk von Heiner Müller (* 1929) sowie – ohne die ideologischen Intentionen – etwa in der Parabeldramatik von Max Frisch (1911–91) oder John Arden (* 1930) (→Theater im 20. Jh.). Wichtig auch der Einfluß der epischen Theorie auf →Regie, →Bühnenbild oder→Bühnenmusik.

Brecht, B.: Schriften zum Theater. In: Gesammelte Werke (Werkausgabe), Bd. 15–17. Frankfurt/M. 1963; Fischer, M.-J.: Brechts Theatertheorie. Frankfurt/M. u. a. 1989; Grimm, R. (Hg.): Episches Theater. Köln/Berlin 1966; Hinderer, W. (Hg.): Brechts Dramen. Stuttgart 1984; Hinck, W.: Die Dramaturgie des späten Brecht. Göttingen 1959; Kesting, M.: Das epische Theater. Stuttgart 1959;

320 Episode

Klotz, V.: Dramaturgie des Publikums. München 1976; Knopf, J.: Brecht-Handbuch: Theater. Stuttgart 1980; Piscator, E.: Das politische Theater. Reinbek bei Hamburg 1964; Rülicke-Weiler, K.: Die Dramaturgie Brechts. Berlin 1966; Sartre, J.-P.: Un théâtre de situations. Paris 1974; Sokel, W.: Figur-Handlung-Perspektive. In: Grimm, R. (Hg.): Deutsche Dramentheorien II. Frankfurt/M. 1971; Szondi, P.: Theorie des modernen Dramas. Frankfurt/M. 1981; Weigel, H./ Berliner Ensemble (Hg.): Theaterarbeit. Dresden 1952.

Gérard Schneilin

Episode

(Griech. ‹epeisodion› = Einschiebsel) Bei den Griechen bezeichneten die E. die zwischen den Chorgesängen eingegliederten Teile des Stücks, dem entsprechend, was später als →Akt oder Aufzug bezeichnet wird. Später, im 16. und 17. Jh., gilt die E. meist als mit der Haupthandlung mehr oder weniger lose verbundene Nebenhandlung. Ihre Bedeutung ging zurück unter dem Druck der Regelhaftigkeit, bes. der Einheit der Handlung (→Drei Einheiten). Für gewisse Theoretiker der frz. →Klassik waren die E. gleichbedeutend mit den verschiedenen Gliedern der →‹Intrige›. – Wichtig auch im Sinne eines E.-Stücks oder Films: Hierin sind Teile eines Stücks sehr lose oder ohne verbindende Handlung aneinandergereiht, wobei nur die Summe aller E. quantitativ ein Handlungsgeschehen bildet. Beispiele dafür sind einerseits die wiederholten E. der komischen Spiele, andererseits in der →Tragikomödie oft repetitiv aneinandergereihte Szenen im Sinne eines absurden Kreislaufs ohne Ende, so schon bei Arthur Schnitzler (1862–1931) im *Anatol* (UA 1893) und im *Reigen* (1912) als Anhäufung von Liebesaffären; heute oft als wesentliche Baustruktur des →absurden Theaters.

Jens, W. (Hg.): Die Bauformen der griech. Tragödie. München 1971; Scherer, J.: La dramaturgie classique en France. Paris 1966.

Gérard Schneilin

Equity

Eigtl.: ‹Actors Equity Association›, die 1913 gegr. amerik. Schauspielgenossenschaft, der von 1922 bis 1928 die nichtkommerzielle Schauspieltruppe ‹Equity Players› angeschlossen war. Die brit. Schauspielergewerkschaft trägt denselben Namen und ist mit ihrer Schwestervereinigung in den USA auf vielfältige Weise verbunden. E. der USA fiel mehrfach dadurch auf, daß sie der Gewerkschaftsbewegung zugetane ‹arme›

Theater-Einrichtungen (Off-Off Broadway, San Francisco Mime Troupe etc.) durch unerfüllbare ‹Gagenleitlinien› in ihrer Arbeit behinderte.

Dieter Herms

Erotisches Theater

Eine präzise Definition des e. T. ist schwierig und schon durch die Dehnbarkeit des Begriffs ‹Erotik› nur mit terminologischen Unschärfen zu erreichen. Aristophanes' Komödie *Lysistrata* ist zweifelsohne auch erotisch, ohne daß man sie deswegen ohne weiteres unter e. T. subsumieren könnte. Ähnliches gilt von Stücken wie Kleists *Penthesilea*, Shakespeares *Othello*, Wedekinds *Erdgeist*, die alle auch erotische Probleme thematisieren, ohne in diesem Aspekt aufzugehen. Um nicht große Teile der Weltdramatik als e. T. klassifizieren zu müssen und dadurch den Begriff so weit zu dehnen, daß er keinerlei Aussagekraft mehr hat, soll im folgenden e. T. verstanden werden als Form des Theaters, in dem die sexuelle Komponente der Liebe, das Sinnliche in allen seinen Äußerungen zum bestimmenden Inhalt wird und eine entsprechend ‹unverhüllte› Form erhält.

E. T. reicht dabei als Ausdruck der Sexualität der jeweiligen Zeit von künstlerisch bedeutenden Werken bis zu ‹obszönen› und ‹pornographischen› Stücken, deren wesentlicher Zweck in der geschlechtlichen Erregung des Publikums bestehen soll (I. Bloch), deren Wirkung allerdings umstritten ist. Da aber Sexualität wie ihre künstlerischen Ausdrucksformen nicht unabhängig vom Moralkodex der Entstehungszeit betrachtet werden können, müssen bei der Bestimmung des e. T. immer wieder der Zeitgeschmack, die Moralvorstellungen der Autoren wie ihres Publikums in Betracht gezogen werden. E. T. ist letztendlich das, was die jeweiligen Zeitgenossen dafür halten. Nur bei Beachtung all dieser Momente ist schließlich eine über allgemeine Feststellungen hinausgehende Analyse möglich.

Bei aller Eindeutigkeit des theatralisch zu gestaltenden Hauptinteresses verfolgen die Autoren des e. T. unterschiedliche Absichten. Soweit überhaupt feststellbar, reichen sie von programmatischer Darstellung der Sinnenfreude über Gesellschafts- und Moralkritik bis zu sozialer und politischer Satire. E. T. ist nicht auf eine theatralische Form festgelegt. Es reicht von erotischer Schauszenik bis zu mehraktigen Theaterstücken, von Tanz und Pantomime bis zu Schäferspielen. Nur reine Tragödien gibt es im e. T. so gut wie nicht. Die Vielfalt der Formen kennzeichnet das e. T. in jeder Epoche. Zu allen Zeiten griff man dabei gern auf die Revue zurück. Das gilt für die amerik. Burlesque-Show ebenso wie für die frz.

Revuen bereits des 19. Jh. Ausgehend von ‹lebenden Bildern› oder ‹plastischen Posen› erscheint dies Formprinzip voll ausgebildet in den ‹Nacktrevuen› von J. Klein im Berlin der 20er Jahre. Bis heute hat sich dieses Prinzip in den Programmen entsprechender Nachtklubs erhalten und weiterentwickelt (→Striptease).

Hier wird besonders deutlich, was – mit Einschränkungen – für das e. T. im ganzen gilt: Es ist Theater von und für Männer. Frauen spielen lediglich als Darstellerinnen eine wesentliche Rolle, eine wie auch immer künstlerisch sublimierte heterosexuelle Erotik ist bestimmend. Das hindert nicht, daß es auch homosexuelles e. T. gibt oder daß das in den letzten Jahren modisch gewordene Transvestitentheater mit den Unterschieden der Geschlechter spielt.

E. T. gibt es in seinen verschiedenen Formen seit der Antike. Der Mimus ist ebenso einzubeziehen wie die Atellanenspiele und Pantomimen der Spätantike, die Symposien wären dabei ebenso zu untersuchen wie die circensischen Darbietungen der römischen und byzantinischen Kaiserzeit. Die Dramen der Hrotswith von Gandersheim enthalten Elemente des e. T. ebenso wie die Fastnachtsspiele des 15. Jh. Größere Bedeutung erhält die erotische Literatur und damit das e. T. immer dann, wenn die gesellschaftliche Unterdrückung der Sexualität nach einem Ventil verlangt. Dann verstärkt sich auch das ‹pornographische› Element. Immer war und ist e. T. durch gesellschaftlichen Druck gezwungen, sich mit Geheimnis zu umgeben, immer stand und steht es in Gefahr, durch staatliche und kirchliche Zensur unterdrückt zu werden. Eine der Folgen dieser Entwicklung ist, daß Aufführungen speziell ‹pornographischer› Stücke nur selten belegbar sind. Genaues läßt sich heute nur in seltenen Fällen feststellen, gelegentlich kann eine inhaltliche Analyse ex negativo helfen: Das e. T. ist in seinen Stückvorlagen häufig derart unrealistisch und artifiziell, daß eine Aufführung sich schon aus physischen Gründen verbot. – Bereits durch den erzwungenen Geheimnischarakter ist e. T. zu einem nicht unwesentlichen Teil Liebhabertheater auf →Hausbühnen, in dem man auf professionelle Schauspieler verzichtete und die Grenzen zwischen Darstellern und Zuschauern sich verschoben.

Anders als das offizielle Theater kann sich das e. T. nur begrenzt auf durchgängige Traditionslinien berufen. E. T. wird zumeist von der jeweils gesellschaftlich herrschenden Schicht getragen. Waren das im 18. Jh. weitgehend Adlige, so trat im 19. Jh. das Bürgertum an ihre Stelle. War im vorrevolutionären 18. Jh. das e. T. zwar exklusiv, aber nicht in eine geheime Subkultur gedrängt, da gesellschaftlich akzeptiert, so änderte sich das im folgenden Jh. Das e. T. wurde Spiegelbild offizieller Doppelmoral, gesellschaftlicher Heuchelei. Weniger noch als im 18. Jh. war das e. T. Ausdruck natürlicher Sinnlichkeit, sondern erhielt ein verlogenlüsternes Moment.

Im Zuge der sog. sexuellen Revolution erlebte das e. T. in den 60er Jahren des 20. Jh. einen erneuten Aufschwung. Bühnen wie das Theatron Erotikon in München führten ‹erotische› Stücke von Picasso, McClure und anderen auf, inszenierten die *Hetärengespräche* Lukians und Novellen Maupassants, scheiterten letztendlich aber an einem Paradox: einerseits an den Grenzen, die die Moralvorstellungen der erotischen Darstellung auf der Bühne zogen, andererseits an der weitgehenden Freigabe der Pornographie in Wort und Bild. Mit den gewandelten Moralvorstellungen zeigte sich dann auch das kommerzielle Theater zunehmend der Erotik geneigt; revueartige Stücke wie *Oh, Calcutta* erlebten Serienerfolge; von erotischen Obsessionen handelnde Dramen von Genet oder Arrabal wurden auch in Stadttheatern aufgeführt. Ähnlich wie bereits Aristophanes' *Lysistrata* erotisches und politisches Theater miteinander verband, nahmen moderne Stücke wie T. Kupferbergs *Ficknam* beide Aspekte auf. Moralische Entrüstung über angebliche erotische Freizügigkeit verdeckte immer noch die Ablehnung der in den Stücken enthaltenen politischen Intentionen. Genuin e. T. verlor jedoch in dem Maße an Bedeutung und Reiz, in dem Sexualität zumindest offiziell weniger unterdrückt wurde.

D'Almeras, H./d'Estrée, P.: Les théâtres libertins aux XVIIIe siècle. Paris 1905; Gapin, G./Yve-Plessis, R.: Les théâtres clandestins. Paris 1905; Gorsen, P.: Sexualästhetik. Zur bürgerlichen Rezeption von Obszönität und Pornographie. Hamburg 1972; Grawert-May, E.: Theatrum eroticum. Tübingen 1981; Hayn, H./Gotendorf, A. N.: Bibliotheca Germanorum Erotica & Curiosa. 9 Bde. München 1910–29; Hanson, G.: Original Skin. London 1970; Hyde, H. M.: Geschichte der Pornographie. Stuttgart 1970; Marcuse, L.: Obszön – Geschichte einer Entrüstung. München 1962; Rabenalt, A. M.: Mimus eroticus. 5 Bde. Hamburg 1962–65; ders.: Theater der Lust. München 1982; ders.: Theater ohne Tabus. Voluptas ludens heute. Emsdetten 1970; ders.: Voluptas ludens. Erotisches Geheimtheater. 17., 18. und 19. Jahrhundert. München/Regensburg 1962; Schlaffer, H.: Musa iocosa. Gattungspoetik und Gattungsgeschichte der erotischen Dichtung in Deutschland. Stuttgart 1971; Toepfer, K.: Theatre, Aristocracy, and Pornocracy. Baltimore 1992; Wedeck, H. E.: Dictionary of Erotic Literature. New York 1962.

Wolfgang Beck

Erstaufführung

Im Gegensatz zur → Uraufführung (der ersten Aufführung eines Bühnenwerks überhaupt) die erste Aufführung eines an einer anderen Stelle, in einer anderen Sprache, in einem anderen Land, in anderer Übersetzung bereits uraufgeführten Stücks. Zur Unterscheidung von Wiederaufnahmen und Neuinszenierungen eines früher im betreffenden Theater oder Ort schon aufgeführten Stücks ist E. die überhaupt erste Aufführung an einer gegebenen Stelle.

324 Esperpento

Henzel, N.: Das Aufführungsrecht von Bühnen- und Tonkunstwerken. Diss. Würzburg 1920; Klemmig, R.: Möglichkeiten und Grenzen der Organisation einer Theater-Aufführung. Diss. Berlin 1956.

Horst Schumacher

Esperpento

Groteske Theaterform, die Ramón María del Valle-Inclán (1866–1936) in seinen sozialsatirischen Stücken vor allem zwischen 1920 und 1930 begründet hat, da sich «die Tragik des span. Lebens nur mittels einer systematisch verzerrten Ästhetik wiedergeben läßt» (*Lichter der Bohème*, 1920). Der Begriff wird auch auf seine Prosaschriften und Lyrik angewendet. Vorwegnahme von Elementen des →absurden Theaters Arthur Adamovs (1908–70), Eugène Ionescos (*1912) u. a. und der frühen Filme Luis Buñuels (1900–83), obwohl die Verwandtschaft mit dem ital. Futurismus, dem →Dadaismus, mit dem Theater Luigi Pirandellos (1867–1936) und Alfred Jarrys (1873–1907) neben der span. Tradition der Satiren Francisco de Quevedos (1580–1645) und der Malerei Francisco Goyas (1746–1828) nicht zu leugnen ist.

March, M. E.: Forma e idea de los ‹esperpentos› de Valle-Inclán. Madrid 1971; Risco, A.: La estética de Valle-Inclán en los esperpentos y en «El ruedo ibérico». Madrid 1966; Speratti Piñero, E. S.: De «Sonata de Otoño» al ‹esperpento›. Aspectos del arte de Valle-Inclán. London 1968; Zahareas, A. N./Cardona, R.: Visión del ‹esperpento›. Madrid 1970.

Martin Franzbach

Etagenbühne

Eine von Traugott Müller (1895–1944) für die →Piscatorbühne entworfene vierstöckige Bühnenkonstruktion, die es ermöglichte, alle Szenen von *Hoppla, wir leben* (1927) von Ernst Toller (1893–1939) ohne Umbau des Bühnenbilds zu spielen. «Ein Etagenbau mit vielen verschiedenen Spielplätzen über- und nebeneinander, der die gesellschaftliche Ordnung versinnbildlichen sollte» (Piscator). Ein ähnlicher Bühnenaufbau wurde bei der Uraufführung von Ferdinand Bruckners (1891–1958) *Die Verbrecher* (1928) verwendet, um die Vorgänge in einem Berliner Mietshaus simultan zur Darstellung zu bringen.

Knellessen, F. W.: Agitation auf der Bühne: Emsdetten 1970, S. 116–133; Piscator, E.: Das politische Theater (1929). Reinbek bei Hamburg 1963, S. 146–159.

Carl Wege

Ethnikó Théatro (Athen)

(Griechisches Nationaltheater). Die älteste subventionierte Theatereinrichtung Griechenlands, 1930 gegründet (→Nationaltheater). Die ersten Versuche zum Aufbau einer offiziellen staatlichen Bühne im Lande fielen in die Zeit der vormaligen Bewegung zur Organisation von Berufstheaterensembles im neugegründeten Königreich um die Mitte des 19. Jh. Doch erst 1901 gingen die Erwartungen der Gelehrten und Künstler in einer ersten Phase in Erfüllung, als das Königliche Theater gegründet und in einem klassizistischen, mit Spenden reicher Auslandsgriechen errichteten Bau untergebracht wurde. Diese Initiative hatte keinen Bestand; die konservative Kulturpolitik der Theaterleitung im Zusammenwirken mit denen Unwillen des breiteren Publikums, eine so aristokratische Auffassung der Theaterkunst zu unterstützen, war der Grund dafür, daß die Aufführungen aufhörten und der Versuch im Frühjahr 1908 aufgegeben wurde. Offenbar reiften die Voraussetzungen für eine dauerhaftere Lösung erst in den Jahren der ersten griechischen Republik (1924–36), in denen das Nationaltheater gegründet wurde, dessen Vorstellungen 1932 nach zweijähriger Vorbereitung begannen. Der Beginn seiner Tätigkeit bildet einen wichtigen Einschnitt in der Entwicklung der einheimischen Theaterkunst, zumal sich alle jungen, bisher zerstreuten Theaterkräfte zum erstenmal in einer Truppe vereinigten und Ensembleaufführungen, frei von den Beschränkungen der von Stars beherrschten kommerziellen Bühne, zustande zu bringen vermochten. Die parallele Tätigkeit einer Theaterschule legt den Grund zu systematischerem Üben junger begabter Schauspieler. Die einheimische Produktion von Theaterstücken wurde jedoch von den angeführten Entwicklungen nur unwesentlich beeinflußt, zumal der erste fest engagierte Regisseur des Theaters, Photos Politis (1890–1936), und auch sein Nachfolger, Dimitris Rondiris (1899–1981), mehr am klassischen und etablierten neueren westeuropäischen Repertoire (antike Tragödie, Shakespeare, Molière, Schiller, Bernard Shaw, Pirandello usw.) als an Originalstücken orientiert waren. Diese Politik verstärkte sich noch in den ersten Jahrzehnten nach dem 2. Weltkrieg, als das Repertoire entscheidend nach der Präferenz einer Gruppe von bereits altgedienten Hauptdarstellern des E. T., welche sich prinzipiell nur dafür interessierten, daß ihnen tragende Rollen gesichert würden, gestaltet wurde. Im Laufe der Zeit wurde die beharrliche Pflege des antiken Dramas, die bereits seit 1938 mit der Nutzung der Überreste der antiken Theater des Landes sporadisch verbunden wurde, zum wichtigsten Alibi für die Verdrängung der neueren nationalen Theaterproduktion. Im Sommer 1955 wird das alljährliche Festspiel von Epidauros im antiken Theater des argolischen Asklepios-Heiligtums eröffnet. Die Festspiele wurden vom E. T. bis zum Sommer 1975 monopolisiert; erst damals erweiterte man das Programm durch die Teilnahme auch anderer Theatergruppen. In diesen drei Jahrzehnten wird ein Stil szenischer Interpretation ausgestaltet und standardisiert, der die antike Tragödie und Komödie mehr als Fundgrube großer Rollen für die Schauspieler denn als poetische Konzeptionen betrachtet, die sich für phantasievolle Experimente schöpferischer Regisseure eigneten. In den letzten Jahren wird zwar beharrlich danach gesucht, neue Wege in der Kulturpolitik einzuschlagen; aber bis zur Mitte des Jahres 1985 war es noch nicht einmal möglich, das nach allgemeinem Bekenntnis überholte Reglement des Theaters zu revidieren.

Rosenthal-Kamarinea, I.: Hauptformen des griechischen Theaters und ihre Entwicklung. In: Kultur im Migrationsprozeß. Hg. von M. Fehr. Berlin 1982, S. 97–112; Valsa, M.: Le Théâtre grec moderne de 1453 à 1900. Berlin 1960.

Thodoros Chatzipantazis

European Jewish Artists Society (EJAS)

Die Tatsache, daß es in Shanghai ein vitales Exiltheater gegeben hat, und die Form, in der hier gearbeitet wurde, sind bezeichnend für die Bedeutung der Theater als Sozialisationszentren des Exils. Zwischen 1933 und 1947 haben hier rund 20000 deutschsprachige Emigranten überlebt. Da es in Shanghai keine kulturelle Tradition im westlichen Sinne gab und den Exilierten der Zugang zur chinesischen Kunst weitgehend versperrt blieb, lebten sie in einer Art kulturellem Vakuum. Der Mangel an Theatertexten führte zu einer Lösung, die diesen Aktivitäten ein ganz eigenes Gepräge gab: Man schrieb sich die Stücke, die man brauchte, selber. Rund 20 sind dem Titel nach überliefert, keines ist erhalten. Zur einen Hälfte waren es Schwänke und Boulevardkomödien, zur anderen Zeitstücke, die das jüdische Schicksal in Deutschland, die Flucht sowie Probleme behandelten, denen sich die Emigranten in China konfrontiert sahen. Mark Siegelberg und Hans Wiener, beide Journalisten an Shanghaier Exilzeitungen, waren die produktivsten Autoren. Die Aktivitäten der Gruppen fanden mit Beginn des Pazifischen Krieges im Dezember 1941 ein Ende.

Dreifuss, A.: Shanghai – Eine Emigration am Rande. In: Exil in den USA. Leipzig 1979; Wächter, H.-Ch.: Theater im Exil. München 1973.

Jan Hans

Eurythmische Kunst / Eurythmie

Rudolf Steiner (1861–1925) begründet nach langjähriger Mitarbeit in der theosophischen Gesellschaft eine eigene Geisteslehre, die Anthroposophie. 1912 entwirft er die eurythmische Kunst. In den folgenden Jahren vervollständigt und systematisiert er das Bewegungsvokabular. In der Praxis regt er an, kontrolliert und fördert (Vorträge; Inszenierungen von Aufführungen; Einstudierung: Marie Steiner). – Die E. darf weder als Gymnastik noch als Tanz verstanden werden. Sie erforscht den Eigenwert und die Breite der in den Wörtern schwingenden Ausdrucksqualitäten (Lauteurythmie) und folgt erlebend dem Wesen der Sprache, um diese sinnlich erfahrbar zu machen. Die Toneurythmie verkörperlicht die Klangverhältnisse in Gebärden und Formzeichnungen (sichtbare Sprache, sichtbare Musik). – Darstellende Mittel: neben Körperstellungen und -bewegungen vorrangig kodifizierte Gesten der Hände und Arme. Als dramaturgische Verstärkungen treten hinzu: schwingende oder gezackte Bodenlinien, fließende, zur Zeichendeutung geeignete Gewänder, Farbklangführungen der Bühnenbeleuchtung (Lichteurythmie). Festgelegtes Bedeutungsrepertoire für die Vokale: A = Staunen = sich öffnende Arme; E = Sich-Zurückhalten, Sich-Abschließen = Kreuzen der Arme oder Beine; I = Aufrechte Haltung = Strecken des rechten Arms nach oben, des linken nach unten; O = Liebe = sich rundende Arme (Kreis), umfassend; U = Sich-Zusammenziehen = parallele Arme im Schulterabstand. Die Vokale drücken innerseelisches Erleben aus, Konsonanten sind Ausdruck äußerer Erscheinungen: W = Wellenbewegung; R = rollendes Rad, durch Armbewegungen nachvollzogen. Zu den Ausdrucksgebärden findet der Gestaltende im konzentrierten Bewegungsfluß, nicht aber durch in den Raum projizierte statische Zeichen. Das Ineinanderfließen der Gesten findet sein Accompagnato im hochsensiblen dynamisch-symbolischen Farbenspiel (Gewänder und Lichtsetzung). Die Toneurythmie weckt und vertieft den Nachvollzug musikalischer Verlaufsgesetze. Ton- und Tonskalenspannungen erscheinen als Bewegungsgestalten sichtbar im Raum; denn Klänge oder Intervalle werden bestimmten Körpergliedern oder -stellungen zugeordnet. Die Tempowechsel nutzen die Bewegungsrichtungen vorwärts – rückwärts; dem Skandieren der Metren folgen eurythmisch geführte Bewegungen von rechts nach links etc. Schon die ersten szenisch-dramatischen Gestaltungen der Eurythmiegruppe Dornach in Steiners Mysteriendramen III und IV (1912 *Der Hüter der Schwelle* und 1913 *Der Seelen Erwachen*) beeindrucken (Aufführung: München). Erstaunliche Wirkungen erzielen *Faust*-Szenen 1915 bis 1924 und 1938 (u. a. *Der Prolog im Himmel*; *Mitternacht und Grablegung*). – Nach Steiners Tod entwickelt sich die E. als Bühnenkunst, Lehrfach an Waldorfschulen und Therapie.

Heute treten die anthroposophischen E.-Gruppen auf großen Bühnen und in Konzertsälen auf. Anerkannte Regisseure verpflichten sie für Operninszenierungen. August Everding: *Das verlorene Paradies* von Christof Penderecki (Stuttgart); Götz Friedrich: *Parsifal* von R. Wagner (Stuttgart); *Orpheus und Euridice* von Chr. W. Gluck (Stuttgart und Amsterdam, Holland-Festival). Höhepunkt der Theaterereignisse 1985: Else Klinks Choreographie zu Motiven aus *Peer Gynt* von H. Ibsen mit der Musik von E. Grieg in Bonn. Gastspiele führen die E.-Gruppen durch Europa, Nord- und Südamerika, Afrika und Japan. 21 E.-Schulen in elf Ländern bilden Eurythmisten mit Bühnenreife und Rhythmiklehrer aus. Grundstudium: vier Jahre. Abschluß: Diplom, Künstlerische Aufführung, Demonstrationen. Anschließend: ein- bis zweijähriges Aufbaustudium. Eurythmielehrer unterrichten an ca. 250 Waldorfschulen, ebenso vielen Kindergärten, heilpädagogischen und Seniorenheimen aller Erdteile.

Dauscher, E.: «Zart auf leisen Füßen naht es.» Die Eurythmie hat die Bühnen der Welt erobert. In: Ballett-Journal/Das Tanzarchiv, Nr. 2, April 1985; Froböse, E. (Hg.): Rudolf Steiner über Eurythmische Kunst. Köln 1983; Konrad, B.: Theatralische Glanzleistung. In: Ballett-Journal/Das Tanzarchiv, Nr. 3, Juni 1984; ders.: Eurythmie II. Einheit von Wort, Musik, Bild und Bewegung. In: Ballett-Journal/Das Tanzarchiv, Nr. 3, Juni 1985.

Helga Ettl

Exiltheater

Sammelbegriff für die vielfältigen Aktivitäten deutschsprachiger Bühnenkünstler und -autoren, die in den Jahren 1933 bis 1945 außerhalb der jeweiligen Grenzen des Deutschen Reiches mit den Mitteln des Theaters direkt oder indirekt gegen den dt. Faschismus Stellung bezogen haben (→Emigrantentheater). – Nach ihren jeweiligen institutionellen und strukturellen Voraussetzungen stellen ‹Exil› und ‹Theater› einander nahezu ausschließende Bereiche dar. Wenn die Forschung inzwischen dennoch auf annähernd 500 im Exil entstandene dramatische Werke und etwa 4000 Theaterpraktiker (Schauspieler, Regisseure, Bühnenbildner) verweisen kann, die in über 40 Asylländern mehr als 800 Inszenierungen zuwege gebracht haben, so ist das nur scheinbar ein Widerspruch: In diese Zahlen sind jene Theaterliebhaber und Laiendarsteller eingegangen, die jenseits ihres Brotberufs an einer jener zahlreichen Amateur- und Leseaufführungen beteiligt waren, deren organisierende Funktion und sozialtherapeutische Bedeutung für das Leben im Exil nicht hoch genug angesetzt werden können, die als Arbeits- und Verdienstmöglichkeit für Berufsschauspieler im Exil oder als Artikulationsakte einer dezidiert antifaschistischen Gesinnung jedoch nahezu bedeutungslos sind. Die Zahl der Bühnenkünstler, die sich auch im Exil dauerhaft oder auch nur annähernd ihren Lebensunterhalt durch Theaterarbeit verdienen konnten, ist ausgesprochen klein. Die (voraussehbar) schlechten Bedingungen für eine Fortsetzung des Theaterberufs unter Exilbedingungen hat das Fluchtverhalten der Bühnenpraktiker aus dem Einflußbereich der Nationalsozialisten geprägt: Schauspieler haben sich zögernder zum Exil entschlossen als Angehörige anderer Berufsgruppen, die in vergleichbarer Weise durch die faschistische Gleichschaltung in ihrer künstlerischen Identität bedroht waren. Die Gründe dafür sind neben den theaterfeindlichen Exilbedingungen in einer bes. Theaterpolitik der Nationalsozialisten zu suchen: Auf Grund des Stellenwerts, der dem Theater in einem auf ‹Ästhetisierung des Politischen› abzielenden faschistischen Kunstkonzept zukam (→ Völkische Dramaturgie), waren die daraus abgeleiteten hohen formalen Ansprüche offenbar nur dadurch zu erreichen, daß die Aussonderungskriterien hier weniger streng gehandhabt wurden als in anderen Bereichen. Eine besondere Spielplangestaltung (hoher Anteil von Klassikern und Unterhaltungsstücken) mag darüber hinaus dazu beigetragen haben, bei den unter nationalsozialistischer Leitung tätigen Schauspielern die Illusion von Unkorrumpierbarkeit zu nähren.

Die charakteristischen Formen von E. in einer ersten Phase des Exils, die bis Ende 1934 reicht und durch die Hoffnung auf eine baldige Rückkehr in ein von den Nazis befreites Deutschland gekennzeichnet ist, sind das Prominentengastspiel und der Tourneebetrieb. Mit Paraderollen und Erfolgsinszenierungen hatten prominente Schauspieler und Regisseure wie Bassermann, Bois, Deutsch, Durieux, Kortner, Kronacher, Massary, Mosheim, Ophüls, Pallenberg, Valetti, Viertel oder Werbezirk schon vor 1933 die an Deutschland angrenzenden Länder bereist. Ihre Tourneeaktivitäten waren daher nichts Ungewöhnliches und fanden nun nur häufiger statt. Sie wurden ergänzt durch Gastinszenierungen wie Reinhardts *Sommernachtstraum* (1934) in der Hollywood Bowl oder Jessners *Tell* (1936) an der Habimah in Tel Aviv. In dieser Zeit, in der das Exil als etwas Transitorisches betrachtet wurde, sah offenbar niemand die Notwendigkeit, Exilierten-Ensembles zu gründen, die an einem festen Ort spielten oder von diesem Ort aus operierten. Das gilt gleichermaßen für die westeuropäischen Asylländer wie für die Sowjetunion. Erst mit der Vereinigung des Agitpropensembles «Kolonne links» (das sich seit 1931 in der SU aufhielt und für ausländische Arbeiter in der SU spielte) mit dem Schauspielerkollektiv «Truppe 31» (das nahezu geschlossen ins Exil gegangen war und mit den Plänen, von Paris aus ein antifaschistisches Gastspieltheater zu betreiben, gescheitert war) zum «Deutschen Theater Kolonne Links» im Februar 1934 in Moskau wurden Bemühungen um eine längerfristige Sammlung und Beschäftigung exilierter Berufsschauspieler

330 Exiltheater

eingeleitet. Aus diesem Umkreis stammt auch das sogenannte «Engels-Projekt», der Versuch, in der Hauptstadt der Wolgarepublik eine Art sozialistisches dt. Nationaltheater zu gründen.

Die Hoffnungen, im Tourneebetrieb als Schauspieler zu leben und zu überleben, wurden sehr bald kleiner. An die Stelle der kollektiven traten nun die individuellen Überlebensstrategien. Die Integration in ein deutschsprachiges Ensemble des Gastlandes war häufig die einzige Form, in dem erlernten Beruf weiterzuarbeiten. Die theoretische Möglichkeit, daß sich auf diese Weise ein überwiegend von Exilierten getragenes Ensemble mit einem dezidiert antifaschistischen Spielplan herausbilden würde, ist nur ein einziges Mal Realität geworden: am → «Zürcher Schauspielhaus». Es gehört zur Tragik der exilierten Bühnenkünstler, daß die beiden Staaten, die noch am ehesten die sprachlichen und kulturellen Voraussetzungen für eine Fortsetzung ihrer Tätigkeit boten – Österreich und die Schweiz –, als Asylländer praktisch ausfielen: Der Einfluß der eigenen faschistischen Bewegung bzw. die Furcht vor Überfremdung schufen gerade in Österreich und der Schweiz ein Klima, das den Exilierten extrem unhold war. Zu solchen Tendenzen gesellten sich Rücksichtnahmen auf wirtschaftliche Verbindungen zum faschistischen Deutschland und schließlich – Ende der 30er Jahre – die Furcht vor einem faschistischen Überfall. Eine wichtige Rolle in diesem Beziehungsgeflecht spielten schließlich die mannigfaltigen Pressionsversuche, die die Nationalsozialisten über ihre verschiedenen auslandsdeutschen Organisationen unternahmen. Diese reichten von inszenierten Theaterskandalen, die automatisch die Fremdenpolizei auf den Plan riefen (was die Nichtverlängerung von Aufenthaltserlaubnissen zur Folge haben konnte), bis zur direkten Einflußnahme auf den Theaterbetrieb etwa über den «Kartellverband deutschsprachiger Bühnenkünstler».

Ähnlich war die Situation an den Bühnen in den deutschsprachigen Teilen der ČSR, an denen Exilierte in einem weit geringeren Umfang unterkamen, als es nach der Zahl der Bühnen möglich gewesen wäre. Vereinzelt führte eine Pattsituation zwischen nationalsozialistischen und antifaschistischen Interessengruppen bei der Vergabe von Spielkonzessionen zur völligen Paralysierung des Theaterlebens. Spieltrupps wie das → «Studio 1934» oder das in Agitprop-Manier agierende, von Louis Fürnberg geleitete «Echo von links» bildeten eine Ausnahme. In Österreich schließlich hat so gut wie kein bekannter Exilierter an einer der größeren Bühnen eine Anstellung bekommen. Lediglich an Kleinkunstbühnen wie → «Literatur am Naschmarkt», → «Der liebe Augustin» oder dem → «ABC» sind Exilierte beschäftigt worden. – Ansätze zu einer Selbstorganisation der Bühnenemigration – und damit zu einem Exiltheater im engeren Sinne – entwickelten sich parallel zu der Einsicht, daß an eine baldige Rückkehr in ein befreites Deutschland nicht zu denken war.

Wenn es in dieser zweiten Phase des europäischen Exils, die von Ende 1934 bis zum Beginn der dt. Annexionen ab 1938 reichte, nur bei Ansätzen blieb, so ist das – neben finanziellen Hindernissen – auf die Versprengtheit der Emigration zurückzuführen. Die Bühnenkünstler lebten auf eine Vielzahl europ. Zentren verstreut, von denen die bekanntesten – wie Amsterdam oder Paris – zudem eher Verlags- und Organisationszentren, seltener Wohnzentren waren.

Wenn es trotz solcher Schwierigkeiten tatsächlich einmal gelang, ein hinreichend qualifiziertes Ensemble an einem Ort für eine Exilinszenierung zusammenzubekommen – so etwa für die Erstaufführungen von *Die Gewehre der Frau Carrar* und *Furcht und Elend des Dritten Reiches*, die unter dem Patronat des «Schutzverbandes dt. Schriftsteller im Exil» im Oktober 1937 bzw. im Mai 1938 in Paris stattfanden –, so reichte die Publikumsnachfrage selten für mehr als zwei oder drei Aufführungen. Während sich die Bühnenkünstler – ähnlich wie die politisch-literarische Emigration – zunächst in den an Deutschland angrenzenden Ländern niedergelassen hatten, waren die europ. Asylländer für die jüdische Massenemigration, die gut 90 Prozent der Gesamtemigration ausmachte, nur Transitstationen gewesen. Da für sie die Vertreibung in der Regel den endgültigen Bruch mit Deutschland bedeutete, suchten sie Niederlassung in solchen Ländern, die die günstigsten Voraussetzungen für den Aufbau einer neuen wirtschaftlichen Existenz boten. Das größte Handicap des Exiltheaters dieser Phase bestand in der Trennung von seinem natürlichen Publikum. Jenseits der Emigration gab es kein als ökonomische Größe in die Planung einzubeziehendes Publikum. Für die Theaterinteressierten der jeweiligen Gastländer war deutschsprachiges Theater eben fremdsprachliches Theater.

Häufig blieb das E. den Besuchern der Gastländer auch nach seiner Dramaturgie und seinem Darstellungsstil fremd. Der Mangel an für Exilgruppen spielbaren Theatertexten kann im nachhinein als ein weiteres Hemmnis für die Entfaltung einer Exiltheaterkultur gelten. Die meisten Dramatiker waren nicht willens oder nicht fähig, sich auf die reduzierten Möglichkeiten von Exilensembles einzustellen. Viele der in diesen Jahren entstandenen Stücke waren wegen der Vielzahl der Rollen und Rollenfächer nicht oder nur unzureichend zu besetzen und wegen des Ausstattungsaufwandes schwer oder gar nicht zu realisieren. Gelegentlich haben Dramatiker Exilensembles auch die Aufführungsrechte verweigert, da sie befürchteten, sich durch eine unzureichende Inszenierung den Zugang zu den Bühnen des Gastlandes zu verbauen.

Doch auch dieser Zugang gelang nur in Ausnahmefällen. Der internationale Erfolg, den die Stücke der ersten Stunde – Bruckners *Rassen* und Wolfs *Professor Mamlock* (urspr. unter dem Titel «Professor Mannheim») – in nahezu allen Ländern gehabt hatten, darf nicht darüber hin-

332 Exiltheater

wegtäuschen, daß das stoffliche Interesse eines internationalen Publikums vielfach damit gesättigt war. Die Mehrzahl der Folgestücke über die Machtübergabe, das faschistische Deutschland oder das Leben im Exil sind häufig an den Theatertraditionen und den Sehgewohnheiten der Gastländer vorbeiproduziert. So scheiterte Kortner/Zuckmayers *Somewhere in France* in den Try-outs auf dem Weg nach New York und wurde Werfels *Jacobowsky* erst in einer Fassung ein Broadway-Hit, die der amerik. Erfolgsstück-Schreiber Sam Behrman erstellt hatte.

Auch unter diesem Aspekt bildet Brecht die löbliche Ausnahme, der mit der Szenenfolge *Furcht und Elend des Dritten Reiches* (Brecht hatte das Herauslösen einzelner Szenen ausdrücklich gestattet), dem Agitationsstück *Die Gewehre der Frau Carrar* sowie den Einaktern *Dansen* und *Was kostet das Eisen?* Spielvorlagen geliefert hatte, die den reduzierten personellen und apparativen Voraussetzungen der Exilensembles Rechnung trugen, ohne deren politisch-aufklärerischen Anspruch zu vernachlässigen. Die *Carrar* wurde schon im Exil zum meistgespielten Zeitstück. Vor allem die in verschiedenen Ländern zur Unterstützung des republikanischen Spanien gegr. Hilfskomitees haben das Stück – vielfach in Zusammenarbeit mit einheimischen Arbeiter-Amateurtruppen – nachgespielt.

Alle bislang gekennzeichneten Versuche, einen Exiltheaterbetrieb zu etablieren, waren an herkömmlichen Vorstellungen – und das bedeutete für die meisten Exilierten: Stadttheater – orientiert. Diese Organisationsform erwies sich unter den Bedingungen des europ. Exils als denkbar ungeeignet für die Theaterarbeit von Exilierten. Erfolgreicher waren demgegenüber die Versuche, die unterschiedlichen Kleinkunstformen für eine auf Aufklärung, Pflege des kulturellen Erbes und Selbstorganisation abzielende Theaterarbeit zu nutzen. Reine →Kabarett-Ensembles – wie Erika Manns →«Pfeffermühle» oder das kurzlebige «Ping-Pong», das bis zum Herbst 1934 in den Niederlanden aufgetreten ist – waren dabei relativ selten. Verbreiteter war die Kabarett-Revue, eine Mischform, die sich – neben dem für die dritte Phase des Exils charakteristischen Klub-Theater – als außerordentlich geeignet erwies, um die divergierenden Ansprüche innerhalb eines Ensembles auszubalancieren und mit den Möglichkeiten eines Exilbetriebs in Einklang zu bringen: Sie war unaufwendig in Hinblick auf Ausstattung und Probenaufwand; sie ermöglichte es, schnell und konkret auf Zeitereignisse zu reagieren, und sie erlaubte es, zwischen politischen Ansprüchen und ökonomischen Notwendigkeiten, zwischen Aufklärungs- und Unterhaltungswert eines Programms zu vermitteln. Die →«Nelson-Revue» und das von Willi Rosen geleitete →«Theater der Prominenten» sind die markantesten Exponenten dieser Form in den Jahren des europ. Exils; im USA-Exil sind es die «Refugee Artists Group» und das 1923 von Kurt Robitschek gegr. →«Kabarett der Komiker».

Einen kontinuierlichen, von Exilierten organisierten und getragenen Theaterbetrieb mit einem Spielplan, der sich an einer im faschistischen Deutschland unterdrückten Theaterkultur orientierte und den exilierten Bühnenkünstlern die Möglichkeit eröffnete, in ihrem erlernten Beruf zu arbeiten, gab es paradoxerweise erst in der dritten – der schlimmsten – Phase des Exils, als sich im Zuge der neuerlichen Vertreibung vor und während des 2. Weltkriegs in Schweden und Großbritannien (Asylländer, die zuvor kaum eine Rolle gespielt hatten), vor allem aber in den außereurop. Fluchtländern neue Exilzentren bildeten. Die neuerliche Vertreibung führte die zuvor auf Grund ihres unterschiedlichen Fluchtverhaltens geographisch voneinander getrennten Exilgruppen – die künstlerisch-literarische und die jüdische Massenemigration – wieder zusammen. Das schuf – kombiniert mit den kriegsbedingten Einschränkungen der Mobilität – die grundlegende soziologische Voraussetzung für Theaterunternehmungen. Die Chancen hierfür waren um so aussichtsreicher, je stärker das Gastland die Integration verweigerte oder die Exilierten aus anderen Gründen in diaspora-ähnlichen Formationen lebten: Bühnenkünstler und Publikum trafen sich in dem Bedürfnis, eine Kontinuität herzustellen zwischen einer verlorenen und einer erst noch zu gewinnenden Existenzform. Die Fortführung einer vertrauten bürgerlich-kulturbewußten Theaterpraxis in einer als fremd empfundenen (Kultur-)Umwelt war eine Möglichkeit, solche Bindungen und Identitätskontinuitäten zu gewährleisten. Unter solchen Rahmenbedingungen entstanden vor allem in Südamerika (→«Freie Deutsche Bühne», Buenos Aires; «Die Komödie», Montevideo; «Kammerspiele», La Paz) und Shanghai (→«European Jewish Artists Society») professionell arbeitende Gruppen, die ein bürgerliches Bildungs- und Unterhaltungstheater pflegten. Nicht ausschließlich auf einen kontinuierlichen Spielbetrieb orientiert war der von emigrierten Schriftstellern in Mexiko gegr. →«Heinrich-Heine-Klub». Wie bei den anderen Klub-Theatern auch, die sich in dieser Zeit in London (→«Kleine Bühne» des Freien Deutschen Kulturbundes, →«Das Laterndl») und Stockholm (→«Freie Bühne») bilden, gehören Vorträge, Lesungen, Rezitationen und musikalische Darbietungen neben Theateraufführungen zu einem den gesamten Kulturbedarf einer Emigrantenkolonie abdeckenden Programm. Der Ausbau des organisatorischen Zusammenhalts, die Gemeinsamkeit zu erhalten und zu stärken, den Exilalltag durch das Gemeinschaftserlebnis zu erleichtern, im individuellen Bereich Zuversicht und Selbstvertrauen zu wecken, waren wesentliche Aufgaben solcher Klub-Theater, die ‹mit dem Gesicht nach Deutschland› spielten.

Die Chancen für deutschsprachiges E. sanken, wenn ein Gastland einen starken Assimilationsdruck ausübte. Wenn sich etwa in New York, das bereits zu Beginn der 30er Jahre mehr als eine Million Bewohner

334 Exiltheater

zählte, die des Deutschen mächtig waren, alle Ansätze zu einem deutschsprachigen Theater als kurzlebig erwiesen, so hatte das vor allem mit der Haltung des Gastlandes zu tun, das von seinen Neubürgern eine rasche Assimilation und Integration erwartete und das Überleben der Künstler davon abhängig machte, wie schnell und wie weitreichend sie sich dem bestehenden Kulturbetrieb anpaßten. Daß dazu das Spielen in engl. Sprache nicht genügte, zeigte das Scheitern der «Continental Players»: Mit einer Art ‹German All Star›-Ensemble und einem bedeutenden Budget schuf Jessner 1940 in Hollywood eine *Tell*-Inszenierung, die beim amerik. Publikum Befremden und Verstörung hervorrief. Schillers Dramatik blieb dem amerik. Publikum ebenso unverständlich wie Jessners antirealistisches Regiekonzept. Die Vertrautheit der einzelnen Schauspieler mit der engl. Sprache war so unterschiedlich, daß der vorherrschende Eindruck, den die Inszenierung hinterließ, der des Chaotischen war. Der Mißerfolg einer vom künstlerischen Rang der Beteiligten so exponierten Gruppe verhalf der deutschsprachigen Theateremigration zu einer wesentlichen Einsicht: auf sich gestellte, die Eigengesetzlichkeiten des amerik. Theaters ignorierende Inszenierungen in engl. Sprache hatten so gut wie keinen Erfolg.

In New York ist es bis 1945 immer wieder zu Gründungen von Emigranten-Ensembles gekommen, deren Wirkungskreis jedoch in der Regel begrenzt, deren Existenz in den meisten Fällen von kurzer Dauer war. Ein «Freies dt. Theater» (Theatre of German Freemen), das 1941 mit einem eindrucksvollen Gründungsmanifest auftrat und Persönlichkeiten wie Bruckner, B. Frank, Kortner, Erika Mann, Werfel und Zuckmayer zu seinem künstlerischen Beirat zählte, ist nie realisiert worden. Mit einer gewissen Konstanz arbeiteten lediglich die → «Tribüne für Freie Deutsche Literatur und Kunst in Amerika» und die von Ernst Lothar gegr. → «Österreichische Bühne». – Auch den im Exil entstandenen Dramen ist am Broadway – sieht man von Werfels *Weg der Verheißung* und *Jacobowsky* ab – kein Erfolg beschieden gewesen. Den künstlerischen wie kommerziellen Mißerfolgen von Stücken wie Tollers *No More Peace* oder Brechts *The Private Life of the Master Race* (Furcht und Elend des Dritten Reichs) am Broadway stehen jedoch beachtliche Erfolge derselben Stücke bei den Drama Departments der amerik. Colleges und Universitäten gegenüber. Am einflußreichsten war der 1940 von Piscator gegr. → «Dramatic Workshop» an der «New School for Social Research» (der dt. Exil-Universität); weniger erfolgreich war Max Reinhardts «Workshop for Stage, Screen and Radio» in Hollywood.

Die Bedeutung des E. ist eine dreifache: Es hat den Berufsschauspielern eine bescheidene Möglichkeit eröffnet, in den Jahren ihrer Vertreibung in dem erlernten Beruf zu arbeiten. Es hat wesentlichen Anteil an der Zusammenführung der antifaschistischen Kräfte und am Ausbau des organisatorischen Zusammenhalts in den Zentren gehabt. Und es hat schließlich dazu beigetragen, die Tradition des zeit- und gesellschaftskritischen Theaters zu konservieren – sowohl in Hinblick auf das Repertoire als auch im Darstellungsstil. Eine Weiterentwicklung der Avantgarde, die im Ausgang der Weimarer Republik eine erstaunliche Formenvielfalt und ein nie wieder erreichtes Diskussionsniveau erreicht hatte, war unter Exilbedingungen nicht möglich. Wo dennoch Versuche gemacht wurden, konnten sie keiner Überprüfung in der Praxis unterzogen werden: Sie blieben Einsichten auf Vorrat.

Hans, J.: Dt. Theaterleute in Amerik. Exil (Katalog zur gleichnamigen Ausstellung). Hamburg 1976; Huder, W. (Hg.): Theater im Exil 1933–45 (Katalog zur gleichnamigen Ausstellung). Berlin 1973; Kunst und Literatur im antifaschistischen Exil 1933–45. 7 Bde. Leipzig 1979ff; Schirmer, L. (Hg.): Theater im Exil 1933–45. Ein Symposium der Akademie der Künste. Berlin 1979; Trepte, C.: Deutsches Theater im Exil der Welt. In: Protokoll des II. Internat. Symp. zur Erforschung des deutschspr. Exils nach 1933. Stockholm 1972; Wächter, H.-Ch.: Theater im Exil. München 1973.

Jan Hans

Exodos

Auszug (sc. des Chores im griech. Drama); ursprünglich Bezeichnung für das Auszugslied des Chors aus der Orchestra; dann, nach Aristoteles' *Poetik* (1452b 21f), der Teil des Stücks, auf den kein Chorlied mehr folgt, d. h. der gesamte Schlußteil der griech. Tragödie.

Kremer, G.: Die Struktur des Tragödienschlusses. In: W. Jens (Hg.): Die Bauformen der griech. Tragödie. Poetica Beiheft 6. München 1971, S. 117–141.

Bernd Seidensticker

Experimentelles Theater

Bevor es im 20. Jh. als vage, umstrittene, oft wegen Inhaltsleere abgelehnte Bezeichnung für etwas ‹Neues›, ‹Ungewohntes›, ‹Innovatives› in Zusammenhang mit Kunst gängig wurde, begegnet das Wort ‹experimentell› schon um 1880 in den naturalistischen Programmschriften von Émile Zola (1840–1902). Im Bemühen um Anpassung der Künste an die Wissenschaften, die zu seiner Zeit einen ungeheuren Aufschwung erlebt hatten (Positivismus, Vererbungslehre, Milieutheorie), orientiert sich Zola nicht nur an deren Inhalten, sondern auch an den Methoden: Von Claude Bernards *Experimenteller Physik* (1865) ausgehend, will er auch in der

Literatur die Methode des zielgerichteten Experiments einführen, um die Suche nach den ‹Naturgesetzen› des menschlichen Verhaltens und Zusammenlebens zu systematisieren. Seine für den Roman entwickelte Theorie überträgt Zola auch auf Drama und Theater, denen er die Aufgabe zuweist, auf der Bühne das psychologische und soziologische ‹Lebensexperiment› zu demonstrieren.

Auch Bertolt Brecht bezieht sich bei der Verwendung des Begriffs E. T. auf die Naturwissenschaften; den Unterschied zwischen dem ‹üblichen› Theater und dem von ihm konzipierten setzt er gleich mit dem zwischen ‹beschreibender und experimentierender Physik›. Sein →Episches Theater bezeichnet er mit einem gewissen Recht als ein experimentelles, denn es ist auf Erprobung von unerforschten Möglichkeiten, auf Theoriebildung, auf Veränderung aus. Mit dem Wort ‹experimentell› faßt Brecht aber auch das Faktum einer neuartigen Verwendung der Kunstmittel, wobei er auf deren gesellschaftlich progressive Funktion insistiert und in diesem Zusammenhang besonders auf das Theater von Erwin Piscator (→Politisches Theater) verweist.

Die radikale Infragestellung der überlieferten Formen und damit des Erwartungshorizonts der Zuschauer sowie das Erproben neuer Mittel und dadurch die Einübung neuer Sehweisen – das sind nach dem heute üblichen Sprachgebrauch, der sich erst in den 50er Jahren über die Fachkreise hinaus eingebürgert hat, die Hauptcharakteristika des E. T. Deutlich ausgeprägt begegnen sie zuerst in den Entwürfen der antinaturalistischen →Theaterreform um 1900. Vor allem Adolphe Appia und Gordon Craig vollziehen einen so radikalen Bruch mit herrschenden Konventionen, daß ihre Ideen erst Jahrzehnte später realisiert werden können. Aus ihren Gedanken speisen sich weitere Experimente, vor allem im Umkreis des →Expressionistischen Theaters und im →Futuristischen Theater sowie im Theater des →Konstruktivismus und an der →Bauhausbühne. Das →Dadaistische Theater macht die radikale Überschreitung des Horizonts seiner Zuschauer direkt zum Programmpunkt, wobei sich die Schöpfer selbst als Element ihres Kunstwerks ausstellen; spätere Formen des E. T., etwa das →Happening, die →Aktionskunst, die →Performance, nehmen dieses Prinzip wieder auf.

Einflüsse vor allem der modernen Musik, des Tanzes und der bildenden Kunst sind charakteristisch für das E. T. der Gegenwart. Dessen wichtigste Vertreter sind: Tadeusz Kantor (1915–90), der in seinem Theater ‹Cricot 2› in Krakau ein von der Realität autonomes, auf ein ‹Klima des Schocks› zielendes Kunstwerk zu realisieren suchte; Richard Foreman, der ab 1968 in seinem →«Ontological-Hysteric-Theatre» die klassische Erzählstruktur so veränderte, daß sie seinen Bewußtseinsprozeß beim Schreiben und Inszenieren spiegelt; Meredith Monk (*1942), die in ihren Arbeiten (→The House) musikalische, tänzerische und bildnerische Elemente zu fast sprachlosen Erzählungen mit oft mythischem Charakter verbindet; Robert Wilson (*1941), dessen Experimente in erster Linie durch die konsequente Reduktion der Handlung, durch die Konzentration auf die assoziative Aneinanderreihung präzise kalkulierter Bildfolgen gekennzeichnet sind; das 1976 aus Ungarn in die USA emigrierte →Squat Theatre, das mit ‹zeremoniellem Ernst› in teilweise kurzen und nur lose verbundenen Szenen Geschichten von Sex und Crime, Liebe und Tod erzählt; Pina Bausch (*1940) mit ihrem →Wuppertaler Tanztheater, dessen Produktionen in ihrer unkonventionellen Körpersprache als Beispiele für eine ‹weibliche Ästhetik› angesehen werden.

Brauneck, M.: Theater im 20. Jh. Reinbek bei Hamburg 1982; Pörtner, P.: Experiment Theater. Zürich 1960; Schmidt, S. J.: Das Experiment in Literatur und Kunst. München 1978.

Peter Simhandl

Exposition

(Lat. expositio = Darlegung) Die E. ist das erste Moment des dramatischen Baus, sei es in der geschlossenen oder der offenen Form. In ihr werden die Elemente der Vorgeschichte eingeführt, welche dem Zuschauer das Verständnis der Figurenkonstellation und des dramatischen Konflikts erleichtern.

1. Spielen in der Antike, im Mittelalter und auch noch in späteren Stücken der →Prolog oder das →Vorspiel diese Rolle, so besteht seit der Aufklärung bis zur Mitte des 20. Jh. kein Zweifel darüber, daß die E. als Teil der →Handlung in knappster Form eng auf das Geschehen bezogen am Anfang des Stücks stehen sollte. Noch für Gustav Freytag (1816–95) ist die E. «scharf bezeichnender Akkord, ausgeführte Szene, kurzer Übergang in das erste Moment der Bewegung» (*Die Technik des Dramas*, 1863). Abweichend von dieser Regel ist nur der Grenzfall der analytischen Technik, von Schiller im *Oedipus* des Sophokles bewundert und von Friedrich Hebbel (1813–63) und Henrik Ibsen (1828–1906) angewandt: Da ist am Anfang alles schon da, die notwendigen Elemente der Vorgeschichte werden progressiv fast bis zum Schluß dem Zuschauer enthüllt. Variabel sind im Allgemeinfall die genaue Länge der E. sowie die Form: Monolog des Helden, Dialog mit →Vertrauten, dynamische Szene.

2. Im Theater der offenen Form und bes. in den verschiedenen Ausdrucksformen des heutigen Theaters ist die E. weiterhin vorhanden, allerings in zahlreichen Varianten. Expositorische Hinweise sind im Gesamtrahmen der Aufführung zu finden, in den Szenenangaben des

Autors, bei den Ansagern des epischen Theaters, sogar a contrario in den Sprach- und Verstehensklischees der Figuren des absurden Theaters und des modernen Volksstücks.

Bickert, H.: Studien zum Problem der Exposition im Drama der tektonischen Bauform. Marburg 1969; Scherer, J.: La dramaturgie classique en France. Paris 1966.

Gérard Schneilin

Expressionistisches Theater

Der von 1910 bis in die 20er Jahre vor allem in Deutschland auf nahezu allen Gebieten der Kunst in Erscheinung tretende Expressionismus definiert das Theater als Ausdruck (Expression) des schöpferischen Individuums, stellt also insofern eine Fortsetzung der auf die Errichtung von Ersatzwirklichkeiten zielenden Strömungen der →Theaterreform um 1900 dar; mit seinem Selbstverständnis als ‹geistige Revolte› gegen die Gesamtheit der herrschenden Lebensverhältnisse und als Offenbarung einer ‹neuen Welt› setzt er sich aber gleichzeitig scharf davon ab. Das Drama und das sich in enger Beziehung dazu entwickelnde E. T. stehen in krassem Widerspruch zum Naturalismus und seiner positivistischen Grundhaltung: Im Theater soll das ‹Schattendasein› des Alltags vernichtet und durch die ‹Momente des wesenhaften Lebens› ersetzt werden; eine ‹höhere Wirklichkeit› soll dargestellt und als einzig gültige bekräftigt werden. Weil das Bild der Welt nur ‹im Menschen selbst› liegt, schafft der expressionistische Künstler ganz aus der Vision. Dieses Prinzip hat der nicht nur als Maler, sondern auch als Dramatiker bedeutende Oskar Kokoschka (1886–1980) in seinen Dramen (*Mörder, Hoffnung der Frauen*, 1907; *Sphinx und Strohmann*, 1908; *Orpheus und Eurydike*, 1910; *Der brennende Dornbusch*, 1917) sowie in seinen programmatischen Schriften als erster formuliert: Das Bewußtsein des Künstlers fängt die ‹Gesichte› auf, öffnet sich ihnen, ergießt sich in sie und bemächtigt sich dabei der geschauten Realität. Die Wirklichkeit löst sich also auf in Spiegelungen des schöpferischen Ichs; im eigenen Erlebnis und nicht in der objektiv gegebenen Realität liegt der Ansatzpunkt für die Gestaltung des ‹neuen Menschen›. Der wird natürlich nicht mehr – wie im Naturalismus – als das Produkt sozialer, biologischer, psychologischer Determinationen dargestellt, sondern geformt nach dem Ideal der absoluten Freiheit. In diesem ‹subjektiven Idealismus› und der Einsetzung des ‹abstrahierten› Menschen, der gleichsam als ‹Singular von Menschheit› (Bertolt Brecht) gedacht wird, liegt der Grund für die überspannte Pathetik und den Utopismus, der für das E. T. charakteristisch ist.

Als ‹Tribüne›, ‹Tribunal› und ‹Kultstätte› konzipiert, soll das Theater ‹der Menschheitsgemeinschaft dienen›, den ‹Kult des menschlichen Menschen feiern›, zur ‹weltverändernden Tat aufreizen› und den Anbruch des ‹Menschheitsparadieses› verkünden; als Ort der ‹Ekstase› und der ‹magischen Kommunikation› soll es seine Zuschauer zu einem ‹gemeinschaftlichen Gotteserlebnis führen›. Ausgangspunkt aller Veränderung ist die ‹Revolution des Geistes›. Aufgerüttelt durch die Kraft des Wortes vollzieht der einzelne Mensch die vielberufene ‹Wandlung› vom ‹Tier› und ‹bösen Feind› zur ‹reinen Lichtgestalt›, vom Egoisten zum ‹Mitmenschen›. Aus der Eskalation solcher individueller Wandlungen entsteht schließlich der Umschlag von der real existierenden Welt zum Menschheitsparadies. In dieser Programmatik ist schon angelegt, daß sich die ‹expressionistische Revolution› – entgegen ihrer Absicht – auf das Gebiet des Ideellen beschränkte.

In der Kunst des Theaters brachte der Expressionismus eine wesentliche Erweiterung der Ausdrucksmittel, die vor allem provoziert wurde durch die neue Gestalt des Dramas. Seine Dichter – Reinhard Johannes Sorge (1892–1916), Walter Hasenclever (1890–1940), Georg Kaiser (1878–1945), Arnolt Bronnen (1895–1959), Ernst Barlach (1870–1938), Paul Kornfeld (1889–1942), Ernst Toller (1893–1939) und Friedrich Wolf (1888–1953) sind die wichtigsten – geben alle Determinanten der Außenwelt auf, um eine Kunstwirklichkeit zu schaffen, in der sich die Idee ungehemmt entfalten kann. Es kommt nicht mehr auf Wahrscheinlichkeit, Glaubwürdigkeit und Psychologie an, sondern auf die Erschaffung einer ‹neuen Mythologie›. Im Sinne dieses Antinaturalismus wird die im Zuge der Theaterreform um 1900 von Gordon Craig und Adolphe Appia begonnene Herauslösung der Einzelkünste aus ihrem traditionellen Zusammenhang und die Reduktion auf ihre Elemente fortgesetzt und radikalisiert. Wassily Kandinsky (1866–1944), der seiner Kunst die Aufgabe zuweist, ‹Seelenvibrationen› hervorzurufen und damit ‹das Geistige› zu beschwören, hat mit dem Programm der →‹Bühnensynthese› eine Grundlage geschaffen, auf der dann Lothar Schreyer (1886–1966) mit der Sturmbühne und der →Kampfbühne Sonderformen des E. T. aufbaut. Der Tendenz zur Abstraktion vom Menschen als Träger des Bühnengeschehens, die in der Theaterarbeit am Bauhaus in Experimenten mit Formen des →Mechanischen Theaters ihren Höhepunkt findet, wirkt im Expressionismus die Überzeugung entgegen, daß eine menschliche Botschaft verkündet, einem neuen idealen Menschenbild der Weg gebahnt werden muß. So kommt es lediglich zu einer Entpsychologisierung der Figuren; statt durchindividualisierter Menschen begegnen oft bloße Ideenvertreter.

Die Konsequenz einer solchen Auffassung des Dramenpersonals für die Schauspielkunst liegt auf der Hand: Verzicht auf Nachahmung der Realität und psychologische Nuancen. An die Stelle der psychologisch zerlegenden Schauspielkunst soll eine rhythmisch aufbauende treten. Das bezieht sich auf die Sprechweise des expressionistischen Dramas mit seinen Übersteigerungen, Wortballungen, Verkürzungen, pathetischen Superlativen ebenso wie für die Körpersprache, die im Vergleich zum naturalistischen Theater eine ungeheure Aufwertung erfährt. Körperlichkeit als ‹Urgrund und Entblößung› ist die Zentralkategorie expressionistischer Schauspielkunst, wie sie vor allem von Werner Krauss (1884–1959), Fritz Kortner (1892–1970), Agnes Straub (1890–1941), Heinrich George (1893—1946) und Ernst Deutsch (1890–1969) realisiert worden ist.

Die rhythmisierte Darstellung findet ihre Entsprechung in der architektonisch gegliederten Bühne. Der Raum soll möglichst neutral sein, um die Handlung der Menschen nicht zu dominieren. Seine Bedeutung erhält er oft erst durch die Beleuchtung. Durch Veränderung des Lichts werden die raschen Schauplatzwechsel vollzogen, wie sie das expressionistische → Stationendrama fordert. Die Licht- und Raumwirkungen werden in den Szenenanweisungen meist detailliert beschrieben. Der Bühnenraum des E. T. ist ein nach außen gekehrter Innenraum, in dem auch die Dinge oft wie Lebewesen behandelt werden. Mit Hilfe verzerrter Perspektiven und magischer Lichtwirkungen versuchen die Bühnenbildner – die bedeutendsten sind Emil Pirchan (1894–1957), César Klein (1876–1954), Otto Reigbert (1890–1957), Ludwig Sievert (1887–1968) –, solche Wirkungen zu erzielen.

Während der Expressionismus im Drama allmählich durch die ‹Neue Sachlichkeit› abgelöst wurde, erreichte er im Theater erst seinen Höhepunkt. Vor Kriegsende nur in einigen Privattheatern erprobt, wurde er dann als exemplarischer Ausdruck der Weimarer Republik betrachtet und hielt Einzug in die Stadt- und Staatstheater. Regisseure wie Gustav Hartung (1887–1946), Karl-Heinz Martin (1888–1948), Richard Weichert (1880–1961), Otto Falckenberg (1873–1947) und vor allem Leopold Jessner (1878–1945) realisierten die in den Dramen schon zehn Jahre vorher entwickelte Konzeption und wandten sie auch auf Stücke der Klassiker an. Besonders Jessner hat als Intendant und Regisseur des Berliner Staatstheaters die Prinzipien der ideellen Konzentration, der szenischen Vereinfachung, der dynamischen Beschleunigung angewandt. Berühmt geworden ist vor allem seine Inszenierung von Schillers *Wilhelm Tell* (1919) als ‹Freiheitsschrei› auf einer (später ‹Jessner-Treppe› genannten) einfachen Stufenbühne, in der sein Grundsatz exemplarisch deutlich wurde: «Das Motiv absorbiert Detaildarstellung, in Konsequenz dessen auch die Details der Dekoration» (Jessner, S. 155).

Benson, R.: Deutsches expressionistisches Theater. Frankfurt/M. u. a. 1987; Denkler, H.: Drama des Expressionismus. München 1967; Jessner, L.: Schriften.

Berlin 1979; Rothe, W. (Hg.): Expressionismus als Literatur. Bern/München 1969.

Peter Simhandl

Extempore

(Lat. ‹ex tempora›, aus der Zeit, dem Augenblick) Aus dem Stegreif gefundener Text, entweder von der vorgeschriebenen Rolle abweichend oder auf Improvisation beruhend. Sowohl im Theater (→Commedia dell-'arte, →Alt-Wiener Volksstück) als auch im Kabarett und verwandten Formen beliebtes Stilmittel, das häufig zu Anspielungen auf aktuelle Zeitereignisse bzw. ein bestimmtes Publikum benutzt wurde. Zu beachten ist dabei immer die Möglichkeit nur scheinbaren Extemporierens, das als Mittel zur Verfremdung und zur Täuschung des Publikums genutzt werden kann. So waren etwa die Improvisationen und Extempores der Commedia dell'arte weit genauer festgelegt, als man dies lange Zeit hindurch annahm.

Wolfgang Beck

Fabel

(Lat.: fabula = Erzählung, griech.: Mythos) Die dramatische F. hat eine doppelte Begriffsbestimmung: 1. Als dem Zuschauer bekannter ‹Mythos› repräsentiert sie das Material des Stücks im Unterschied zu dessen Gegenstand: Die Gesamtheit der Themen und Motive, als logische und chronologische Ereignisfolge organisierbar, die Ursache des Geschehens, unabhängig von den Figuren, vor oder außerhalb der →Handlung. In der *Poetik* des Aristoteles ist die F. Imitation der →Handlung, ‹die Verkettung der Geschehnisse›, ‹Prinzip und Seele der Tragödie; erst nachher kommen die Charaktere›. Hier geht man von der F. als dramatischem Rohmaterial über zur F. als Handlungs- und Ereignisfolge. Die F. beschreibt ‹die Taten der Figuren, nicht die Figuren selbst. Taten und F. sind Ziel und Zweck der Tragödie.› Insofern lautet die klassische Definition der F.: «Der Gegenstand des Gedichts ist der Grundgedanke der Handlung: die Handlung ist also die Entwicklung des Geschehens; die F. ist dasselbe, nur von den Vorgängen der →Intrige her gesehen, welche die Handlung knüpfen und auflösen» (J. F. Marmontel).

2. Als Geschichtsperspektive ist dies bei Brecht (wie bei Aristoteles) ‹Herzstück der theatralischen Veranstaltung›, ‹Seele des Dramas›: «Das

große Unternehmen des Theaters ist die F., die Gesamtkomposition aller gestischen Vorgänge» (*Kleines Organon* § 65). Primat der F. bedeutet allerdings bei Brecht und im →epischen Theater nicht Kontinuität und Zielstrebigkeit einer geradlinigen Handlung, sondern Unterordnung der Teile in dialektischer Widersprüchlichkeit und ironischer Gebrochenheit. Die F. stellt die Personen als Konstellation in ihrer gesellschaftlichen Funktion und Interrelation dar: «es sind zurechtgemachte Vorgänge, in denen die Ideen des Fabelerfinders über das Zusammenleben der Menschen zum Ausdruck kommen» (*Nachträge zum Kleinen Organon*). Wesentlich sind also das Perspektivistische und Didaktische der Urteilsebene: «die Auslegung der Fabel und ihre Vermittlung durch geeignete Verfremdungen ist das Hauptgeschäft des Theaters. Die Fabel wird ausgelegt, hervorgebracht und ausgestellt vom Theater in seiner Gänze, von den Schauspielern, Bühnenbildnern, Maskenmachern, Kostümschneidern, Musikern und Choreographen. Sie alle vereinigen ihre Künste zu dem gemeinsamen Unternehmen» (*Kleines Organon* § 70). Auch die Auslegung ist verfremdend-dialektisch sowie veränderbar-historisch, also in ständiger Ausarbeitung: Die F. ist Geschichtsprozeß.

Brecht, B.: Kleines Organon für das Theater. In: Werkausgabe, Bd. 16. Frankfurt/M. 1968; Marmontel, J. F.: Eléments de littérature. Paris 1787; Olson, E.: The Elements of Drama: Plot. In: Calderwood, J. (ed.): Perspectives on Drama. Oxford 1968; Sokel, W. H.: Figur–Handlung–Perspektive. In: Grimm, R. (Hg.): Deutsche Dramentheorien, Bd. 2. Frankfurt/M. 1971.

Patrice Pavis

Fahrendes Volk

Spätestens seit dem Mittelalter wurden unter dieser Bezeichnung alle Arten von →Schaustellern, ambulanten Gewerbetreibenden, Landstreichern, Bettlern und Zigeunern zusammengefaßt. Spätantike ‹histriones› und ‹mimi› gehörten ebenso dazu wie die Vaganten, Goliarden, Spielleute, Gaukler, Joculatoren und Ménéstrels (Minstrels) des Mittelalters. Ihr einziges gemeinsames Kennzeichen war die Nichtseßhaftigkeit. Alle als f. V. zusammengefaßten Gruppen sind ‹randständig›, d. h. nicht oder nur teilweise gesellschaftlich integriert. Die Quellen über sie sind spärlich, lückenhaft und fast ausschließlich aus der Sicht der jeweils Herrschenden gesehen, die bestimmten, was der gesellschaftlichen Norm entsprach und was als ‹abweichend› anzusehen war. Erst dieses Definitionsmonopol ermöglichte die undifferenzierte, diskriminierende Zusammenfassung derart verschiedener Gruppierungen unter einem Oberbegriff, der nur durch ein einziges Merkmal – die Nichtseßhaftigkeit –

Fahrendes Volk 343

näher bestimmt ist. Gelehrte Vaganten und Landstreicher, Räuber und Akrobaten waren für die seßhafte Bevölkerung aller Zeiten gleichermaßen fremd. Demgegenüber war es nicht mehr wichtig, daß sie allen gesellschaftlichen Schichten entstammten, durch die unterschiedlichsten Gründe Fahrende geworden waren, verschiedenen Religionen und Bildungsschichten angehörten – und ganz verschiedene Tätigkeiten ausübten.

Fahrende gab und gibt es in der ganzen Welt, im alten China und Indien ebenso wie in den frühen vorderasiatischen Hochkulturen, in der antiken Welt, im Europa des Mittelalters und der Neuzeit. Einige ihrer Künste reichen bis in religiös-mythische Bereiche zurück, andere Tätigkeitsfelder haben sich erst im Lauf der Zeit entwickelt. Hierzu gehören u. a. Zeitungssänger, Bänkelsänger, wandernde Ärzte und Vorführer von Abnormitäten, →mechanischem Puppentheater und Wachsfiguren. Ihnen allen gemeinsam ist die unmittelbare Abhängigkeit vom Publikum. Um den Preis ihrer Existenz mußten sie ihm gefallen, Neues und Abwechslungsreiches bieten. Dies führte dazu, daß bereits in der Antike Sänger und Tänzer zugleich häufig auch Akrobaten waren, Schauspieler und Zauberer. Mit dem Zusammenbruch der spätantiken städtischen Kultur in der Völkerwanderungszeit wurden auch bislang weitgehend seßhafte Unterhaltungskünstler gezwungen, wandernd ihren Lebensunterhalt zu verdienen. Das Gebiet, das sie bereisen mußten, wurde immer größer, ihr Repertoire umfang- und einfallsreicher. Dennoch lassen sich auf Grund fehlender Quellen keine bruchlosen Übergänge von ihnen zum mittelalterlichen Spielmann oder Joculator ziehen.

‹Spilman› und ‹spilwîp› wanderten umher und führten an Höfen, in Klöstern, Dörfern und Städten ihre Künste vor, zu denen neben Gesang, Vortrag und Tanz auch Akrobatik und Taschenspielereien gehörten. Kleriker ohne Amt (Goliarden, Vaganten), wandernde Scholaren auf dem Weg zur nächsten Universität trugen ihre Gedichte und Lieder einem gebildeten Publikum vor, das in ganz Europa ihr Latein verstand. Vom späten Mittelalter bis ins 18. Jh. verkauften wandernde Ärzte und Quacksalber nicht nur ihre Wundermittel, zogen Zähne und operierten, sondern traten als Gaukler, ja als Seiltänzer auf, führten Spaßmacher mit sich, die Szenen vorführten und so das Publikum anzulocken suchten.

Seit der Antike war eine wichtige Funktion des f. V. die Übermittlung von Nachrichten. In einer Zeit, in der nur reiste, wer dazu gezwungen war, war die seßhafte Bevölkerung angewiesen auf die Fahrenden, die Neuigkeiten brachten, gelegentlich sogar als offizielle Boten benutzt wurden. Herausragendes Beispiel hierfür ist der Zeitungssänger, der seit der Erfindung des Buchdrucks Flugblätter und -schriften, später die ersten Zeitungen vertrieb, vorlas und vorsang (→Bänkelsang). Für die mittelalterlichen geistlichen und weltlichen Spiele brauchte man ebenso Spiel-

344 Fahrendes Volk

leute zur Begleitung wie an den Adelshöfen, wo sie die Langeweile vertreiben und das Lob des Fürsten verbreiten sollten (Minnesänger). Kein Jahrmarkt war ohne Gaukler und Musikanten denkbar, ebensowenig wie städtische Messen, Hochzeiten – aber auch Reichstage und Konzilien. Das f. V. war unentbehrlich, zugleich aber verachtet und vertrieben, weil es nicht seßhaft war, zu keiner Gemeinschaft gehörte, die ihm Schutz geboten hätte.

Über die Herkunft der Fahrenden im einzelnen ist wenig bekannt. ‹Künstlernamen› verdecken schon frühzeitig viele Spuren. Belegbar ist dennoch, daß keineswegs nur Kinder von Fahrenden das Leben ihrer Eltern fortsetzten. Daneben fanden sich arbeitslose Kleriker, durch Kriege und Teuerungen verarmte Bauern und Handwerker, Schüler und Studenten, aber auch Nachkommen von Adligen, deren Besitz nicht alle Kinder ernähren konnte. Die Art der Entlohnung war unterschiedlich. Wer Glück hatte, wurde von Adligen in die Dienerschaft aufgenommen oder wurde (seit dem 14. Jh.) Stadtmusikant. In der Regel aber speiste man sie mit Kleidungsstücken, kleinen Geldgeschenken oder bloßer Verpflegung ab.

Die juristische Stellung des f. V. war starken Beschränkungen unterworfen. Die byzantinische, die griech.-orthodoxe Kirche ebenso wie Judentum, Islam und die röm. Kirche eiferten gegen alle Fahrenden. Die Kirchenväter verdammten sie, das kirchliche Recht schloß sie von den Sakramenten aus. Die mittelalterlichen Theologen übernahmen diese Urteile und veranlaßten die weltlichen Mächte zum Erlaß und zur Durchführung entsprechender Gesetze. Im Heiligen Römischen Reich deutscher Nation verfuhr man besonders rigoros. Hier wurde jeder, der längere Zeit als Spielmann, als Vagant lebte, zum Verbrecher gestempelt, er verlor seine Ehre, konnte nicht mehr als Kläger oder Zeuge vor Gericht auftreten. Sie waren in jeder Hinsicht ehr- und rechtlos. Am schlechtesten war die Lage für weibliche Fahrende, die stärksten Einschränkungen unterlagen und grundsätzlich als Prostituierte galten. Im Mittelalter sicherte nur die Gemeinschaft, der man angehörte, die gesellschaftliche Existenz. Fahrende gehörten keiner Gruppe an, die sie beschützt hätte. Aber auch damals klafften Theorie und Praxis auseinander. Man war zu sehr auf das f. V. angewiesen, als daß die erdrückenden Einschränkungen völlig durchsetzbar gewesen wären.

Kirche und Staat hatten ein gemeinsames Interesse, nichtseßhafte Bevölkerungsgruppen in ihrer Freiheit einzuschränken, sie auszugrenzen aus der Gesellschaft. Kirche und Staat fürchteten ihre Unkontrollierbarkeit, das potentiell aufrührerische Element, das in ihren Darbietungen lag. Das Streben nach sozialer Disziplinierung des f. V. beherrschte die Gesetzgebung bis ins 19. Jh. hinein. Was alle Strafbestimmungen des Staats, alle Drohungen der Kirche nicht vermocht hatten, gelang letztendlich der Verwaltung. Einschränkungen von Feiertagen, Abschaffung von Jahrmärkten verminderten die Einnahmemöglichkeiten der Spielleute, Gaukler, Taschenspieler usw., die Einführung der Schulpflicht im 19. Jh. entzog ihnen wichtige Hilfskräfte und riß Familien auseinander, Legitimierungen aller Art (vom Leumundszeugnis bis zum Wandergewerbeschein) erschwerten ihr Leben und schufen neue ‹Klassen› von Fahrenden. Die Gruppensolidarität brach auseinander. Von den verschiedenen Arten wandernder Unterhaltungskünstler wurden die einen vom →Zirkus oder dem →Varieté aufgenommen, andere wurden →Schausteller im heutigen Sinn. Fabriken nahmen sie als Arbeiter auf. Wer nun noch Fahrender war, war endgültig diskriminiert und aus der Gesellschaft ausgeschlossen (→Schauspieler).

Arnold, H.: Fahrendes Volk. Landau [2] 1983; Becker, H. S.: Außenseiter. Frankfurt/M. 1971; Berthold, M.: Komödiantenfibel. München 1979; Burke, P.: Popular Culture in Early Modern Europe. New York 1978; Danckert, W.: Unehrliche Leute. Bern 1963; Fahrendes Volk. Recklinghausen 1981 (Katalog); Hampe, Th.: Die fahrenden Leute in der deutschen Vergangenheit. Leipzig [2] 1924; Hartung, W.: Die Spielleute. Wiesbaden 1982; Johannsmeier, R.: Spielmann, Schalk und Scharlatan. Reinbek bei Hamburg 1984; Kopečný, A.: Fahrende und Vagabunden. Berlin 1980; Nick, F.: Die Hofnarren, Lustigmacher, Possenreißer und Volksnarren älterer und neuerer Zeiten. 2 Bde. Stuttgart 1861; Salmen, W.: Der fahrende Musiker im europäischen Mittelalter. Kassel 1960; Saltarino (d. i. H.-W. Otto): Fahrend Volk. Leipzig 1895 (Nachdruck Bern 1978); Schwer, W.: Stand und Ständeordnung im Weltbild des Mittelalters. Paderborn [2] 1952; Wareman, P.: Spielmannsdichtung. Diss. Amsterdam 1951.

Wolfgang Beck

Fallhöhe

Dramaturgischer Begriff zur Begründung der →Ständeklausel, der gemäß den drei aristotelischen Grundprinzipien der →Tragödie ‹atrocitas› (bedingt den abschließenden Fall des Helden), ‹gravitas› (fordert erhabene Gegenstände und Personen) und ‹indignitas› (bedingt die richtige Spannung zwischen dem Charakter des Helden und seinem Unglück, damit die Tragödie ihr kathartisches Ziel erreicht) besagt, daß der tragische Fall eines Helden um so beispielhafter und um so tiefer empfunden werde, je höher sein sozialer Rang ist. Die höhere, meist fürstliche Stellung und Würde des Helden und dessen ausweglises, tragisches Scheitern lösten beim Zuschauer den Eindruck des Furchtbaren und eine tiefe Erschütterung aus. Der Fall des Helden wird dabei durch die Einheiten von Ort und Zeit noch beschleunigt, durch die ‹Fallgeschwindigkeit› noch eindrucksvoller. Personen niederen Rangs wie etwa im bürgerlichen Drama fehle dagegen die F., weil sich in der Regel ihre Not durch machtvolle Menschenhilfe beheben ließe. Diese Vorstellung der F. findet sich in Kommentaren der Renaissance zur Poetik des Aristoteles (384–322 v. Chr.) angedeutet, wird dann vom frz. Ästhetiker Charles Batteux (1713–80) geprägt und später in Deutschland von Johann Christoph Gottsched (1700–66) und Arthur Schopenhauer (1788–1860) übernommen. August Wilhelm Schlegel (1767–1845) und Gotthold Ephraim Lessing (1729–81) haben sie dagegen bei ihrer Rechtfertigung des bürgerlichen Trauerspiels zurückgewiesen.

Schings, H.-J.: Consolatio Tragoediae. In: Grimm, R. (Hg.): Deutsche Dramentheorien. Kronberg/Ts. 1971.

Bernard Poloni

Farce

Das aus dem Frz. entnommene Wort F. bezeichnet urspr. in Frankreich derb-komische Einlagen oder →Zwischenspiele in den geistlichen →Mysterien- und Mirakelspielen. Danach entwickelt sich die F. im 15./16. Jh. zu einem selbständigen, kurzen, possenhaften und meist anonymen Stück, das dem dt. →Fastnachtsspiel nahesteht. Die F., die 200 bis 500 Verse haben und in denen zwei bis sechs Personen auftreten, behandeln Themen und Typen aus dem familiären, sozialen oder beruflichen Leben – z. B. der betrogene Ehemann, der verliebte Jüngling und sein Nebenbuhler, der Tölpel, der Geizhals, der unfähige Medikus, der Jurist bzw. der Prozeß in den →basoches. Sie wurden bei öffentlichen Festlichkeiten, v. a. in der Fastnachtszeit, von fahrenden Schauspielern auf einem schlichten Podest von 2 mal 3 m vor einfacher Kulisse mitten unter den Zuschauern aufgeführt. Ziel der F. ist lediglich, mit Hilfe von stereotypen Gestalten und phantasievoll variierten schablonenhaften Situationen die Zuschauer zu belustigen. Man unterscheidet F. mit origineller Handlung, die auf Streitsituationen (Ehestreit, Weiberstreit, Streit in der Öffentlichkeit), Sprachspiel (Hauptfigur ist dabei ‹le badin›) beruhen, und Adaptations-F., bei denen eine aus Prosaerzählungen entnommene Handlung mit dem bekannten Dreiecksverhältnis Ehemann – Ehefrau – Nebenbuhler zur F. umgearbeitet wird. Mit der Zeit erfährt die F. einen Wesens- und Bedeutungswandel; der typische dumme Tölpel wird mit dem ausgehenden 15. Jh. und der Vorstellung der ‹verkehrten Welt› zum Narren, der sein wahres Wesen – Scharfsinn und Schlauheit – unter der Maske der scheinbaren Ahnungslosigkeit versteckt hält, dabei aber die Szene beherrscht und die Torheit der ‹normalen Welt› aufdeckt; die F. tendiert nun zur →sotie, die nicht nur spielerisch, sondern kritisch belustigt. – Besonders berühmt und langlebig war die *Farce de Maître Pathelin* (1464), mehrmals nachgeahmt (*Nouveau Pathelin*, 1474; *Testament de Pathelin*, 1490). Frei von jedem Grobianismus und den Weg zum späteren →Lustspiel weisend sind auch *La Farce de deux amoureux recreatis et fort joyeux* (1541) von Clément Marot (1496–1544) und die *Comédie* (1547) von Marguerite de Navarre (1492–1549), in denen die Thematik der Liebe und der Liebenden in raffinierterem, milderem Ton behandelt wird. Von Frankreich aus gewinnt die F. Einfluß auf die gesamte europ. Literatur: in Italien, wo sie zur Zeit der ital. Feldzüge der frz. Armee die →Commedia dell'arte beeinflußt haben mag, in Spanien, durch den Portugiesen Gil Vicente (1465?–1539?) eingeführt und durch die →Entremés von Miguel de Cervantes (1547–1616) vollendet, und in England (John Heywood, 1497?–1580). In Deutschland setzt sich die Bezeichnung F. im 18. Jh. durch; die F. wird hauptsächlich zu Zwecken der Literatursatire und -parodie in Knittelversen oder Prosa etwa bei Jacob Michael Reinhold Lenz (1751–92), Friedrich Maximilian von Klinger (1752–1831) oder Johann Wolfgang von Goethe (1749–1832) bzw. zu Zwecken der Polemik bei den Romantikern, etwa bei August Wilhelm von Schlegel (1767–1845) oder Ludwig Tieck (1773–1853), verwendet. Während der Begriff F. seit dem 19. Jh. zum Sammelbegriff für etliche Formen des komischen Theaters wurde, wird er mit dem →Absurden Theater in die Nähe der Groteske gedrückt, z. B. bei Arthur Adamov (1908–70), Eugène Ionesco (* 1909), Samuel Beckett (1906–89) oder bei Friedrich Dürrenmatt (* 1921) und Max Frisch (1911–91) (*Die chinesische Mauer – Eine Farce*, 1947).

Aubailly, J.-Cl.: Le théâtre médiéval profane et comique. Paris 1975; Hughes, L.: A Century of English Farce. London 1956; Levertin, O.: Studien zur Geschichte der Farce. 1970.

Bernard Poloni

Fastnachtsspiele

Zentrum der F. ist Nürnberg. Vor dem Ende des 15. Jh. wissen wir von F. sonst nur aus Lübeck und Eger. Aber von beiden Orten haben wir nur Archivmaterial, keine Texte. Das von Nürnberg nicht allzu ferne Eger mag seine Anregung aus der dt. Reichsstadt erhalten haben. Doch auch die norddt. Hansestadt könnte von dort her die Idee bekommen haben, zumal das Patriziat Lübecks, Träger der F., damals gerade dort in Verbannung lebte. Die Titel der frühen Lübecker Spiele widersprechen dem nicht, während allerdings spätere Titel mit Themen aus Allegorie oder Legende eher an holl. Einfluß denken lassen. Aus dem Südosten und vereinzelt auch von anderswo sind weitere weltliche, meist komische Spiele überliefert; insb. Dramatisierungen der Neidhart-Legende waren

348 La Fede

populär. Doch sind dies nicht Traditionen wie in Nürnberg. Dort beginnt die Tradition Anfang des 15. Jh., wenn nicht schon früher. Das *Spiel vom Tanawäschel*, seiner ganzen Art nach Nürnbergisch, entstand kurz nach 1414. Die einfachsten Nürnberger Texte bestehen nur aus groben sexuellen oder fäkalischen Witzen, die priamelhaft aneinandergereiht sind. Etwas mehr Struktur oder gar Handlung läßt dann später die Derbheit zurücktreten. Stoffe aus anderen Genres werden übernommen. Rosenplüt, Folz sind die einzigen bekannten Autoren von F. aus dem 15. Jh. Im späten 15. und 16. Jh. breitet sich das F. über den ganzen dt. Sprachraum aus; doch sind es dort traditionslose Eintagsfliegen, so anziehend sie auch in der Hand eines Manuel oder Wickram erscheinen mögen. Peter Probst und vor allem Hans Sachs wandeln die einfachen Formen in Nürnberg zu Perlen des deutschen Kurzspiels. In Nürnberg spielt man durchweg im Wirtshaus oder Privathaus. Erst mit den Handlungsspielen stellt sich ein Ortsempfinden ein. Doch begnügt man sich mit gesprochener Szenerie. Hans Sachs versteht es meisterhaft, die Einzelheiten der Umgebung mit ein paar Worten im Dialog vorzutäuschen.

Catholy, E.: Das Fastnachtspiel des Spätmittelalters. (Hermaea nF. 8) Tübingen 1961; Lenk, W.: Das Nürnberger Fastnachtspiel des 15. Jh. (Dt. Akademie der Wissenschaften zu Berlin 33, Reihe C). Berlin 1966; Michael, W. F.: Das dt. Drama des Mittelalters. (Grundriß der germanischen Philologie 20). Berlin 1971.

Wolfgang F. Michael

La Fede

1969 von dem Maler und Regisseur Giancarlo Nanni (*1941) gegründet. 1968 hatte Nanni zusammen mit Valentino Orfeo die Gruppo Space Re-(v)action (Azione e Rivoluzione nello spazio) gegründet. Diese Gruppe wurde später Teil von L. F., die experimentellen Charakter hat und sich der Suche nach neuen theatralischen Ausdrucksformen widmet. Die verschiedenen Aktivitäten des Malers, Schriftstellers und Schauspielers stehen gleichgewichtig nebeneinander. Hauptarbeitsgebiete der Gruppe sind der theatralische Raum, die theatralische Form, die Vorstellungskraft, Probleme der Gruppenstruktur, Entwicklung neuer Theaterformen unter der Fragestelllung ‹Theater und Revolution / Theater oder Revolution›. – Nach Nannis Vorstellung soll in der Gruppe ein Kollektiv entstehen, in dem bewußt nicht mehr für andere, sondern für sich selbst, d. h. für die Mitglieder des Kollektivs, gearbeitet wird.

Quadri, F.: L'avanguardia teatrale in Italia (Materiali 1960–76). Turin 1977.

Elke Kehr

Federal Theatre Project

Einziges staatlich subventioniertes Theaterunternehmen großen Stils (New York 1935–39). Es war Bestandteil der Arbeitsbeschaffungsmaßnahmen «Works Progress Administration» im Rahmen des New Deal-Programms Präsident Roosevelts. Unter der Projektleitung von Hallie Flanagan sahen in vier Jahren rund 30 Millionen Zuschauer ca. 1200 Inszenierungen von 830 klassischen und modernen Dramen in rund 63000 Vorstellungen. Das F. T. P. umschloß Straßentheater, Tourneetheater, Puppentheater, Kindertheater, Tanz, Musical, Operette und Passionsspiel. Neben allen wichtigen Theaterstücken der Dekade wurden vor allem Shakespeare und T. S. Eliot gespielt. Das F. T. P. entwickelte → Living Newspapers als neues Genre des → Agitproptheaters. Es sah sich starken politischen Anfeindungen ausgesetzt; 1938 wurde es zum ersten Opfer des Kongreßausschusses für ‹unamerik. Umtriebe› unter Martin Dies, der mehreren Künstlern auf Grund zweifelhafter Zeugenaussagen unterstellte, Mitglied oder Sympathisant der Kommunistischen Partei zu sein. Daraufhin strich 1939 der Kongreß den Etat des F. T. P., das danach unter landesweitem Protest von Autoren, Regisseuren und Kritikern eingestellt werden mußte.

Brüning, E.: Das amerik. Drama der dreißiger Jahre. Berlin (DDR) 1966; Fröhlich, P.: Das nichtkommerzielle amerik. Theater. Rheinfelden 1974; Mathews, J. D.: The Federal Theatre, 1935–39. New York 1980; Soceanu, M.: Das Federal Theatre Project und seine Dramen über amerikanische Geschichte. Frankfurt/M. 1987.

Dieter Herms

Felsenreitschule Salzburg

1693 wurden drei Galerien in die Steilwände des Mönchsbergs gebrochen, die eine Sommer- oder Felsenreitschule umrahmten. Seit 1926 als Bühne genutzt von den → Salzburger Festspielen. 1933 «Faust-Stadt» von Clemens Holzmeister (1873–1943). 1933–37 *Faust*-Inszenierung von Max Reinhardt (1873–1943). 1968–70 neugestaltet und überdacht. Seitdem ständige Spielstätte der Festspiele, Schauspiel und Oper.

Werner Schulze-Reimpell/Red.

Fernsehen und Theater

Theater im Fernsehen ist immer nur Fernsehen

‹Theater im Fernsehen› ist schon vom Begriff her ein Mißverständnis; denn er legt nahe, daß es so etwas wie eine Theateraufführung im Fernsehen geben könne. Theater im Fernsehen ist immer zuallererst Fernsehen, ist eine Fernsehsendung über eine Aufführung, nie die Aufführung selbst. So wie auch die Realitätsbereiche, die ein Feature oder eine Dokumentation im Fernsehen abbilden, durch das Fernsehen selbst nicht anwesend sind, sondern nur als Bilder von etwas gezeigt werden, so schafft auch die Theateraufzeichnung im Fernsehen kein Theatererlebnis, sondern immer nur ein, vielleicht besonderes, Fernseherlebnis (→ Film und Theater). Alle Debatten über die Defizite der Theateraufzeichnungen gegenüber dem Original und über die Verkürzungen, die das Theater im Fernsehen erfährt, sind deshalb fruchtlos, ja irreführend, weil sie implizit als Ideal die Möglichkeit eines ungebrochenen, ‹unverfälschten› Theatererlebnisses im Fernsehen voraussetzen. Wenn Georg Hensel, renommierter Theaterkritiker der FAZ (12.1.1984), anläßlich der Ausstrahlung von Peter Steins Schaubühnen-Inszenierung der *Orestie* im Fernsehen sich empört, auf dem Bildschirm verkomme «ein der Bühne angemessenes Ausdrucksmittel... zur Schmiere», erscheine alles «überlaut, pastos und plakativ» und werde «dem Zuschauer, der die Aufführung in Berlin nicht sehen konnte, nicht eine immerhin annähernde, sondern eine falsche Information geliefert», so steckt hinter seiner Argumentation, vielleicht ungewollt, immer noch dieses Ideal. Hensels Kritik ist zugleich Ausdruck einer kulturkritischen Angst, das hochstehende, für wertvoller gehaltene Medium Theater könnte durch die Berührung mit dem niederen Massenmedium Fernsehen Schaden nehmen, könne sich, gerade in der Form der Theateraufzeichnung, selbst verraten.

Theater im Fernsehen ist immer weniger als das Theater selbst, und es ist zugleich mehr als dieses, ist etwas anderes, ist Fernsehen. Der Theaterraum wird hier zu einer Folge unterschiedlicher, von der Kamera ausgewählter und dann in der Montage bzw. Bildmischung aneinandergefügter Raumsegmente, wird von einer Dreidimensionalität in ein zweidimensionales Bildformat überführt, dessen Kompositionsgesetze die Präsentation der Figuren und ihrer Bewegungen im theatralen Raum überformen und neu akzentuieren. Die Kamera läßt die Schauspieler, die auf der Bühne in aller Regel immer ganz zu sehen sind, oft nur im Ausschnitt erscheinen und gibt damit dem ausgewählten Segment eine besondere Bedeutung. Die zwischen Schauspieler und Zuschauer tretende Kamera weicht die doch relativ unveränderbare Distanz zwischen beiden im Theater kurzfristig durch Objektivveränderungen, Kamerabewegungen und auslassendem Schnitt auf, erlaubt blitzschnellen Perspektivwechsel

Fernsehen und Theater **351**

und kann dem Zuschauer durch Groß- und Nahaufnahmen eine größere Nähe und ‹Intimität› zum Schauspieler suggerieren. Sie kann den Zuschauer durch eine filmische Schnittechnik scheinbar in das Bühnengeschehen einbeziehen und ihn zugleich zum allgegenwärtigen Beobachter machen. Rhythmus und Ablauf der Darstellung werden nicht mehr wie auf der Bühne durch den Schauspieler, sondern durch Schnitt, Montage und Mischung bestimmt.

Grundlegendste Veränderung ist das Auseinandertreten von Produktion und Rezeption. Ist im Theater der Zuschauer in einer raumzeitlichen Einheit während des Schauspielens selbst anwesend und kann dieses durch seine Reaktionen (wenn auch innerhalb unserer Theaterkonventionen sehr begrenzt nur) beeinflussen, so ist im Fernsehen Spielen und Zuschauen räumlich und in aller Regel auch zeitlich voneinander getrennt. Kann der Fernsehzuschauer das Spiel in keiner Weise mehr beeinflussen, so erlaubt die Fixierung des Theaterspiels auf einen medialen Träger (Film oder Magnetband) seine jederzeitige Wiederholbarkeit, erlaubt so eine Konservierung dessen, was als transitorisch am Theater immer nur in der Erinnerung der Zeitgenossen bewahrbar schien: die Anschaulichkeit und Sinnlichkeit des gestischen und mimischen Ausdrucks der Schauspieler.

In der technisch bedingten Fixierung des Spiels auf einen medialen Träger steckt zugleich eine andere Differenz, die im ästhetischen Produkt nicht offenkundig wird, aber die die Produktion wesentlich beeinflußt und die Volker Canaris (Theater heute 1973/9) auf den Gegensatz vom Livecharakter des Theaters und der synthetischen Natur von Film und Fernsehen gebracht hat. Gemeint ist damit, daß die raumzeitliche Einheit des theatralen Spielens und Zuschauens auch das Darstellen im Kontinuum erfordert, während Film und Fernsehen ein diskontinuierliches und partikulares Darstellen ermöglichen und unter den gegebenen Produktionsbedingungen auch erfordern. Erst in der von den Schauspielern meist unabhängig vollzogenen Synthese der Aufnahmen am Schneidetisch bzw. in der elektronischen Bildmischung wird die endgültige Gestalt des Produkts festgelegt.

Die produktions- und rezeptionsästhetischen Differenzen zwischen Theater einerseits, Film und Fernsehen andererseits sind jedoch nicht statisch, sondern verändern sich in ihrer Bedeutung im historischen Prozeß. So wie sich die ästhetischen Gestaltungsmöglichkeiten von Film und Fernsehen erst langsam herausbildeten, veränderte sich umgekehrt auch das Theater selbst im Zeitalter seiner technischen Reproduzierbarkeit. Denn in Reaktion auf Film und Fernsehen bezog das Theater sich angleichend (z. B. in der Struktur der Bühnenliteratur, in der Beschleunigung des Spiels und der Technik ‹unterspielten› Darstellens auf der Bühne) als auch abwehrend (z. B. in der Überwindung der Guckkastenbühne, in den

352 Fernsehen und Theater

verschiedenen modernen und radikalen Theaterkonzepten) neue Positionen. Bei aller immer wieder behaupteten grundsätzlichen Gegensätzlichkeit der Medien wurden jedoch in allen historischen Phasen seit dem Aufkommen von Film und Fernsehen immer auch die ‹Zwischenformen› des Theaterfilms und dann des ‹Theaters im Fernsehen› gepflegt.

Programmgeschichte

Theater im Fernsehen entsteht in einem historischen Geflecht spezifischer Bedingungen. Gegenüber dem amerik. Fernsehvorbild sollte das bundesdeutsche Fernsehen kulturbewußter werden und war schon von den Rundfunkgesetzen und Programmrichtlinien her stärker als ein Instrument breit angelegter Volksbildung und Information und dann natürlich auch der Unterhaltung konzipiert. Nicht zufällig suchte man im kulturpolitischen Selbstverständnis eine Anlehnung an das Theater. Das Fernsehen des Nordwestdeutschen Rundfunks eröffnete seinen regulären Fernseh-Programmdienst am 25. 12. 1952 mit Goethes *Vorspiel auf dem Theater*, das ZDF zeigte es bei seiner Programmaufnahme am 1. 4. 1963 in anderer Inszenierung ebenfalls. Das gemeinsame ARD-Programm begann am 1. 11. 1954 mit Shakespeares *Was ihr wollt*, einer Inszenierung des Deutschen Theaters in Göttingen unter Heinz Hilpert, die im Hamburger NWDR-Studio neu eingerichtet worden war.

Den Kulturanspruch des neuen Mediums sollten besonders die Adaptionen der Weltliteratur in den Spielproduktionen und die Übertragungen von Theateraufführungen vertreten. Vor allem mit Klassiker-Inszenierungen sollte die ‹Kulturfähigkeit› des Mediums unter Beweis gestellt werden. Neben Goethe, Schiller, Shakespeare, Molière, Calderón kamen die ‹Klassiker der Moderne› ins Programm: Shaw, Priestley, Eliot, Fry, Giraudoux, Anouilh bestimmten in der zweiten Hälfte der 50er und der ersten Hälfte der 60er Jahre das Bild. Daß das Fernsehen an die Theatertradition und gerade nicht an die des Kinos anknüpfen sollte, wurde aus der Besonderheit der Technik abgeleitet. Denn die elektronische Kamera und Bildübertragung (bis 1957 gab es noch keine elektronische Aufzeichnungsmöglichkeit) schien über die Liveproduktion im Gegensatz zum Film ein theaterähnliches Zusammentreten von Produktion und Rezeption bei einer zugleich massenweisen Verbreitung zu ermöglichen. Im Fernsehen wurde auf Grund der noch unvollkommenen Technik zunächst nicht wie im Film einstellungs-(take-)weise produziert, sondern durchgehend wie auf der Bühne. Jeder Versprecher war wie im Theater nicht mehr zurückholbar bzw. eliminierbar, eine Eigenschaft, der der Regisseur Rudolf Noelte noch Mitte der 60er Jahre nachtrauerte, als er – längst hatten filmanaloge Produktionsweisen mit Magnetaufzeichnung (MAZ) die Liveproduktion verdrängt – noch einmal für den Nervenkitzel des Livespielens im Fernsehen plädierte.

Diese so verstandene Theaternähe des Mediums, die in der Überschätzung und Ideologisierung des Livebegriffs auch in anderen Programmbereichen eine Entsprechung hatte, führte in der fernseheigenen Spielproduktion, im Fernsehspiel dazu, daß zunächst fast ausschließlich dramatische Literatur aufgegriffen und adaptiert wurde, so daß Ende der 50er Jahre der Fernsehspieldramaturg Hans Gottschalk (Fernsehen 1955/59) vom «Kahlschlag im Zauberwald der Literatur» sprach. Gegenüber der Theaterübertragung hatte die Fernsehspielinszenierung von Bühnenstücken den Vorteil, daß diese zielgerichteter auf die Kamera hin eingerichtet und zugeschnitten werden konnte. Wesentlich veränderte sich auch das Schauspielen, das sich gegenüber der großen raumfüllenden Bühnengestik und der weittragenden theatralen Sprechweise verkleinern mußte, um glaubwürdig zu bleiben, das die Akzente hier auf die Mimik (‹das Gesicht als Landschaft›) und ein leises, zurückgenommenes Sprechen setzte.

Waren die 50er Jahre von einer weitgehenden Einheit von Fernsehspielproduktion und Theaterübertragungen bestimmt, so löst diese sich in den 60er Jahren auf: Das Fernsehspiel strebt von der Bühnenliteratur weg zum original geschriebenen und idealerweise filmisch produzierten Spiel, die Theaterübertragung (mit Ausnahme der seit Beginn der 50er Jahre gesendeten Schwankproduktionen des Ohnsorg- und Millowitsch-Theaters) dagegen wird zum Vermittlungsinstrument für ‹hohe› Kultur und Bildung. Das Zweite Deutsche Fernsehen richtet 1963, sicher auch aus dem Gefühl heraus, anders das Programm nicht füllen zu können, einen wöchentlichen Termin «Und heute ins Theater» ein, und die dort gesendeten Aufführungsübertragungen bildeten die bundesdeutsche Theaterlandschaft fast flächendeckend ab. Ziel war es, so der damalige ZDF-Intendant Karl Holzamer, «das deutsche Theater in seiner für Westeuropa einmaligen Vielfalt dem Fernsehpublikum vorzustellen» (Deutsche Bühne 1964/7–8).

Zwischen Boulevard- und Volksstücken und vermischt mit dem Musiktheater kamen in der Reihe auch wichtige Klassikeraufführungen auf den Bildschirm: Noeltes *Oedipus* vom Bayerischen Staatsschauspiel, Fleckensteins *Leonce und Lena* vom Landestheater Hannover, Schmidts *Clavigo* vom Berliner Schiller-Theater, *Don Gil* von Gründgens aus dem Schauspielhaus Hamburg und viele andere mehr. Die ARD-Sender hielten in ihren Dritten Programmen dagegen. Der NDR setzte z. B. ab 1964 mit seiner von Henning Rischbieter betreuten Reihe «Theater heute» ebenfalls auf eine systematische Präsentation von Theaterproduktionen. In der Debatte um das so präsentierte Theater im Fernsehen tauchte der von der zeitgenössischen Kulturproduktion hoch besetzte Begriff des «Dokuments» auf. Die Theateraufzeichnung galt bei Holzamer, Rischbieter und Kienzle als Dokumentation der Theaterkultur, die das transitorische Ereignis Theater in neuer Weise festhalte.

Nachdem sich jedoch herausstellte, daß die Theatervermittlung im

Fernsehen nicht zur insgeheim erhofften und oft auch laut ausgesprochenen Heranbildung eines neuen, breiteren Theaterpublikums führte, sondern daß das Fernsehen Ende der 60er Jahre mit als Ursache eines verstärkten Rückgangs an Theaterbesuchern verantwortlich zu machen war, setzte eine zunehmende und die 70er Jahre bestimmende Distanzierung zwischen Theater und Fernsehen ein. Denn zugleich erwiesen sich die Theaterübertragungen im Fernsehen gegenüber anderen Spielformen als Programme mit geringen Einschaltquoten. Die Zahl der Theaterübertragungen im Fernsehen ging ebenso wie die Zahl der Fernsehspiele nach Bühnenstücken drastisch zurück, die ‹Unverträglichkeit› von Theater und Fernsehen wurde zum festgefügten Topos der Debatte. Gleichwohl werden in dieser Zeit gerade auch die theatralisch ‹konsequenten› Aufführungen im Fernsehen gezeigt. Von der Schaubühne am Halleschen Ufer in Berlin kamen die wichtigsten Produktionen alle auch auf den Bildschirm, und bereits Mitte der 70er Jahre ging Peter Stein wie auch andere Theaterregisseure dazu über, bei den Aufzeichnungen und Verfilmungen seiner Aufführungen selbst Regie zu führen. In den 80er Jahren ist die Zahl der Theateraufzeichnungen im Fernsehen wieder im Steigen; vor allem dem Musiktheater wird nach Jahren der Vernachlässigung wieder mehr Aufmerksamkeit geschenkt. Programmkonzeptionell arbeitet ganz ausgeprägt das ZDF mit thematisch gebündelten Reihen («Shakespeare-Zyklus», «Neurosen der bürgerlichen Gesellschaft»), aber auch in den Programmen der ARD-Sender ist ein neues Interesse am Theater zu verzeichnen.

Theater, Fernsehen und neue Medien

Das erneute Aufeinander-zu-Gehen von Theater und Fernsehen in der Gegenwart der 80er Jahre ist doppelter und durchaus ambivalenter Natur (→ Neue Medien und Theater). Zum einen ist es ökonomisch und medienpolitisch bedingt. Viele Theater, vom → Deutschen Bühnenverein ermuntert, rechnen sich in einer Zeit wachsenden Programmbedarfs neue Chancen aus. Sie sind bestrebt, die Weiterverwertung ihrer Aufführungen durch Poolbildung und neu gegründete Verwertungsgesellschaften selbst in der Hand zu behalten. Da die Videotechnik in die Theaterproduktion bereits vielfach Eingang gefunden hat (in Form von hauseigenen Probenmitschnitten und Aufführungsdokumentationen), werden Zukunftsvisionen entwickelt von der Kassette der Aufführung, die der Theaterbesucher nach der Vorstellung erwerben kann, über die Liveübertragung aus dem Theater in die Stadt hinein bis zu eigenen Theaterkanälen und anderem mehr.

Zwar sind die privaten Programmanbieter an Aufführungsmitschnitten wegen der geringen Einschaltquoten solcher Programme noch wenig interessiert – der Münchener Theaterkanal im Kabelfernsehen ist die große

Ausnahme. Doch das öffentlich-rechtliche Fernsehen hat an Theater im Fernsehen nicht zuletzt wegen der geringen Produktionskosten einer Aufzeichnung im Vergleich zu den Kosten eines Fernsehspiels neues Interesse gefunden, können solche Sendungen doch immer noch als kulturelles Aushängeschild dienen, selbst wenn die Einschaltquoten unverändert niedrig (zwischen fünf und zehn Prozent) sind. Zum anderen ist das Interesse des öffentlich-rechtlichen Fernsehens am Theater auch unter dem Aspekt «mehr Phantasie ins Fernsehen», einer Forderung der Mainzer Tage der Fernsehkritik von 1978, zu sehen. Aus den Spielformen und Spielweisen des Theaters, aus dessen ungebrochener Imaginationskraft, aus diesem «Theater einer neuen Bildlichkeit» (Rühle) wollen Fernsehmacher Impulse für neue Ausdrucksweisen für eine ‹postrealistische› Spielproduktion gewinnen. Dem kommt das Interesse vieler Theaterregisseure am Filmemachen entgegen. Prototyp für diese ansatzweise erkennbare Tendenz ist Hans Neuenfels mit seinen Filmen *Heinrich Penthesilea von Kleist*, mit *Die Familie oder Schroffenstein* und der Verfilmung der *Schwärmer*. In diesen Theaterfilmen wird gegenüber den im Fernsehen konventionell gewordenen Spielen und einer allzu einfachen Fernsehnarrativik eine neue Verbindung von ‹theatralischer› Darstellungskunst und kinematographischer Mittel im Fernsehverbund gesucht. Hier wird gerade nicht auf ‹reinliche Scheidung› der Medien geachtet, sondern eine neue Melange der verschiedenen medialen Möglichkeiten erprobt.

Dübgen, V.: Theater im Fernsehen. Berlin 1977; Hickethier, K.: Das Fernsehspiel der Bundesrepublik. 1951–1977. Stuttgart 1980; Viedebantt, K.: Volkstheater im Fernsehen. Frankfurt/M. 1974.

Knut Hickethier

Festival d'Avignon

1947 Gründung der Theaterfestspiele von Avignon (F. d'A.), als auf Anregung des Lyrikers René Char und des Kunsthändlerehepaars Yvonne und Christian Zervos der Theaterregisseur Jean Vilar (1912–71) zur Mitwirkung an der ursprünglich nur als Kunstwoche (semaine d'art) mit Ausstellungen von Gemälden moderner Künstler stattfindenden Veranstaltung in der provençalischen Stadt eingeladen wurde. In dieser ersten Spielzeit (4.–10.9.1947) wurden Shakespeare, Claudel und Maurice Clavel aufgeführt, danach wurde der Juli Festspielmonat; Dauer anfangs zwei, später vier Wochen. Spielstätten neben dem Hauptort, dem Ehrenhof des Papstpalastes (cour d'honneur du Palais des Papes), der Garten Urban VI. (verger Urbain VI.), das Stadttheater von A., seit 1975 Karmeliterkloster (cloître des Carmes), Zölestinerkloster (cloître des Céle-

356 Festival d'Avignon

stins), Innenhof des erzbischöflichen Palasts, Kloster des Alten Palasts.
Vilar war bis 1971 Festspieldirektor, 1951 bis 1964 gleichzeitig Leiter des
Pariser →Théâtre National Populaire (TNP). 1951 triumphierte der ans
TNP verpflichtete Schauspieler Gérard Philipe (1922–59) in A. als Prinz
von Homburg. Die 50er Jahre gelten als die ruhmreichsten des Festivals.
In den 60er Jahren durch Musik-, Film-, Ballettvorführungen, Volksbelustigungen und Rundgespräche über Fragen der Zeit Ausweitung
(z. B. rencontres internationales, théâtre musical). Neben den in A. in
avant-première gezeigten Inszenierungen des TNP Gastspiele (Ballet du
XXe Siècle von Maurice Béjart, Théâtre de la Cité de Villeurbanne unter
Roger Planchon, Living Theatre, Comédie Française). Nach Vilars Tod
wurde sein langjähriger Mitarbeiter Paul Puaux neuer Leiter. Zunahme
der Veranstaltungen am Rande der Festspiele (spectacles «off»/hors festivals). Schon Mitte der 70er Jahre wurden dem Publikum täglich bis zu
60 Veranstaltungen geboten, etwa je zur Hälfte «in» und «off». Neue
Theaterformen wurden im Théâtre ouvert (seit 1971), im Gueuloir (seit
1974), in der Cellule de création (seit 1975) erprobt. Beinahe alle Inszenierungen werden in der anschließenden Saison in ganz Frankreich
gezeigt. In den 80er Jahren (Direktor Bernard Faivre-d'Arcier von
1980–85) weitere Entwicklung zum pluridisziplinären Mammutfestival
mit mehr als über 200 verschiedenen Darbietungen an über 70 Schauplätzen (etwa 60 Prozent Theater-Uraufführungen), um das Festival noch
stärker als Ort des Ideenaustauschs, als eine «opération de communication» zwischen Künstlern und Publikum zu profilieren. Seit 1. 1. 1985
Alain Crombecqué neuer Leiter, aus dessen erstem Amtsjahr Peter
Brooks neunstündige Dramatisierung des Sanskritepos *Mahabharata* in
einem Kalksteinbruch in Boulbon 10 km von A. herausragt; im gleichen
Jahr frz. Erstaufführung von Lessings *Emilia Galotti*.

Mit Beginn der 90er Jahre zunehmende Tendenz zur Internationalisierung, wobei nicht-französischsprachige Aufführungen allerdings die Ausnahme bleiben und v. a. bei den Rencontres de la Chartreuse (Centre
Acanthes) auftretende folkloristische Gruppen aus Ländern der dritten
Welt betreffen. Mit der Saison 1993 kehrt Bernard Faivre d'Arcier, der bis
dahin die Abteilung Theater im Kulturministerium unter Jack Lang geleitet hatte, als künstlerischer Leiter nach A. zurück und richtet in der umgebauten Chartreuse de Villeneuve-lès-Avignon eine ständige Werkstatt für
Bühnenautoren ein («Centre national des écritures du spectacle»).

Laube, H.: Der Trost der Vögel. Eindrücke in Avignon, vor allem von der neuen
Truppe Peter Brooks. In: Theater heute 20 (1979), H. 9; Stürzenegger: Theater für
ein neues Publikum. Diss. Wien 1961; Avignon, 20 ans de Festival. Paris 1966. 40
ans de festival. Paris 1986.

Horst Schumacher

Festival of Fools

Entstanden 1975, Organisation: De Melkweg und →Shaffy. Neben diesen beiden Theatern wurden das Paradiso, das Vondelpark Openlucht Theater und die Straße als Spielstätten benutzt; Gruppen aus zahlreichen Ländern beteiligten sich. Der Fool (→freies Theater, →Narr), der Spaßmacher steht im Mittelpunkt, kommentiert das Leben, ironisiert die Welt. Idee: Jango Edwards (*1950): «Seid klug, lacht einfach. Werdet Narren.» Das Festival sollte die Kommunikation von Spielern und Publikum fördern: «Zusammen lachen ist zusammen leben», unter diesem Motto zog 1975 bis 1978 alljährlich ein Jahrmarkt von Foolsgruppen und Solo-Artisten zwei Wochen lang durch Amsterdam, ab 1976 auch durch Delft, Nijmegen und Utrecht. Ca. 30000 Zuschauer sahen pro Jahr mehr als 50 Gruppen aus zehn verschiedenen Ländern, u. a. Jango Edwards and his Friends Roadshow (USA), Footsbarn Theatre (England), Dogtroep (Niederlande), Carlos Traffic (Argentinien), Philippe Duval (Frankreich), die Basisgruppen des F. Die Fools-Schule organisierte jedes Jahr während des F. Workshops (u. a. Mimik, Akrobatik, Tanz). Nach einer Pause von einem Jahr ging es 1980 weiter unter der Regie des sechsten Festivals →Théâtre des Nations. Man konzentrierte sich auf das Marge-Theater; nicht nur Fools, sondern auch freie Gruppen, die andere Formen alternativen Theaters zeigten, traten auf: 90 Gruppen aus 25 Ländern gaben 500 Vorstellungen für ca. 100000 Besucher. Neben den genannten Basisgruppen traten u. a. auf Gruppo →Teatro Escambray (Kuba), Mobiles Rhein Main Theater (BRD), Piccolo Teatro di Pontedera (Italien). Motto, dem Schauplatz (einer ehemaligen Schiffswerft) entsprechend: «Die Blüte des Verfalls». Fast ohne öffentliche finanzielle Unterstützung und deshalb mit vielen freiwilligen Mitarbeitern organisiert, findet das F. seit 1980 alle zwei Jahre statt.

1982: nur im Freien unter dem Motto «Die Straße ist eine einfache Bühne». Mehr als 50 Gruppen aus elf Ländern spielten auf fest installierten und improvisierten Schauplätzen in der Stadt mit freiem Zugang für jeden. Verschiedene Formen einer zukünftigen Straßen-Theater-Kultur wurden sichtbar: visuelles Theater, erzählendes Theater, Fools, Musik, Puppen und Masken. Basisgruppen waren u. a. Teatro Nucleo (Italien), Radeis (Belgien), Shusaku Dormu Dance Theater (Niederlande), Scherbentheater (BRD), Pigeon Drop (USA). Ca. 90000 Zuschauer. 1984: eine Kombination von Straßentheater und Vorstellungen u. a. im De Melkweg, Paradiso und anderen kleinen Theatern in Amsterdam. Das Programm zeigt einen Querschnitt von in der Marge operierenden autonomen Gruppen aus dem In- und Ausland. Ca. 80 Gruppen aus 14 Ländern gaben in zwei Wochen 500 Vorstellungen. Neben den bereits bekannten Gruppen der Debütanten, u. a. Théâtre des Falaises (Frankreich), Chrome (Australien). Der Einfluß des F. zeigt sich in der internationalen Anerkennung der Marge-Kultur. Das F. ist inzwischen internationales Zentrum der alternativen Theater-Szene.

De Boer, W./Schreirs, H.: Bericht Festival of Fools 1982. Amsterdam 1982; Bericht Festival of Fools 1984. Amsterdam 1984; Information: Wouter de Boer, Theater De Melkweg, Amsterdam o. J.; Knipselkrant Festival of Fools 1980; Knipselkrant Festival of Fools 1982; Pressebericht Festival of Fools 1984. Amsterdam 1984; Programm Festival of Fools 1978/1980/1982/1984. (Jeweils) Amsterdam.

Sonja de Leeuw

Festspiele

Im Ursprung standen fast alle Theateraufführungen im Zusammenhang mit Festen (→Dionysien) oder ähnlichen, vom Alltag abgehobenen Veranstaltungen. An den Höfen der Barockzeit (→Barocktheater) Entwicklung einer Repräsentationskultur mit enormem Aufwand an Technik und Kostümprunk, Feuerwerk und Wasserspielen, Tieren und Massenszenen. →Gesamtkunstwerke von großer Schauwirkung. Mit der Etablierung eines bürgerlichen Theaters und der ständigen oder doch regelmäßigen Präsenz von Aufführungen in allen großen Städten (Stadttheaterkultur) entstand im 19. Jh. der Wunsch nach herausgehobenen, künstlerisch überragenden Aufführungen besonderen Charakters (Mustervorstellungen in München 1854 mit 30 der besten Schauspieler aus Deutschland und Österreich) oder großbürgerlicher Adaption der höfischen F.-Tradition als eigene Einrichtung in einem kurzen, regelmäßig wiederkehrenden Zeitraum. 1876 gründete Richard Wagner (1813-83) in Bayreuth F., die ausschließlich für seine Werke reserviert sind und dort in exemplarischer Weise unter optimalen Bedingungen realisiert werden. Internationale Tendenz: seit 1879 Shakespeare-Festival in →Stratford-upon-Avon, 1896 Wiesbadener Maifestspiele, 1917 (1920) →Salzburger F. Idee der Überhöhung des Alltags, Kunst (Theater) als Steigerung des Lebens ins Festliche. Im 20. Jh. zunehmende Kommerzialisierung, «Festivalitis». Die Zahl der F. in Europa ist kaum noch zu überschauen.

Engler, B., G. Kreis (Hg.): Das Festspiel. Willisau 1988.

Werner Schulze-Reimpell

Feuerwerkstheater

F. charakteristischer Bestandteil höfischer Feste zwischen Mitte 16. und 18. Jh. Verbindung pyrotechnischer Effekte mit sinnbildhaften schauspielartigen Vorführungen, zuweilen volkstümliche Umzüge; publikumswirksames Ausdrucksmittel für den sozialen Rang oder Anspruch oder politische Ziele und Hoffnungen; theologische Gedankengänge und regionalgeschichtliche Auseinandersetzungen. Lange Handlungen in bis zu fünf Akte geteilt. Keine bürgerliche Tradition; städtische Feuerwerke durch kaiserliche oder fürstliche Persönlichkeiten veranlaßt, vor allem Schloßfeuerwerke (16./17. Jh. anläßlich der Kaiserbesuche) geprägt durch engen Rahmen der Zusammenstellung der Inventionen für die Arrangeure (Feuerwerksentwurf von Hans Hept: Plan eines pyrotechnischen Spiels). – 17. Jh.: Entfaltung der Sinnbildsprache des F. zur differenzierten emblematisch strukturierten Invention; später stehende Bilder durch Personen ersetzt. Ende des 17. Jh. zunehmend prachtvoller feuerwerkstechnischer Aufwand mit Vereinfachung der reichhaltigen sinnbildhaften Inventionen. Cartelle (zum Großteil von bürgerlichen Gelehrten verfaßte Texte): Erläuterungen der dargestellten Sinnbilder, Requisiten und Lichteffekte und deren spezielle Aussagen; Popularisierung der Pracht der Vorführungen, z. B. durch die Pegnitzschäfer in Nürnberg (Georg Philipp Harsdörfer, Johann Klaj, Sigmund von Birken). Erneuerungsversuche des F. durch André Heller (*1947): *Feuertheater mit Klangwolke*. Flammenrevuen und Pyroskulpturen 1983 in Lissabon und am Hallstätter See, 1984 in Berlin und Linz.

Berühmte Feuerwerke: Dresden 1547 und 1553 Feuerwerksgefechte, 1637 Kampf des hl. Georg, 1650 Argonautenzug, 1678 *Heldentaten des Herkules*; Nürnberg: 1665 *Historie vom reichen und armen Lazaro*; Wien 1666 anläßlich der Hochzeit Kaiser Leopold I., 1781: *Werthers Leiden*; München: 1662 Argonautensage; Grenoble: 1701 homerischer Apollonhymnus von der Gründung Delphis; Versailles 1664.

Alewyn, R./Sälzle, K.: Das große Welttheater. Die Epoche der höfischen Feste in Dokument und Deutung. Hamburg 1959; Baur-Heinhold, M.: Theater des Barock. Festliches Bühnenspiel im 17. und 18. Jh. München 1966; Fähler, E.: Feuerwerke des Barock. Studien zum öffentlichen Fest und seiner literarischen Deutung vom 16.–18. Jh. Stuttgart 1974; Heller, A.: Die Trilogie Der Möglichen Wunder. Roncalli Flic Flac Theater des Feuers. Wien/Berlin 1984; Wallbrecht, R. E.: Das Theater des Barockzeitalters an den welfischen Höfen Hannover und Celle. Hildesheim 1974.

Ingeborg Janich

Figurine

Im Bereich des Theaters Bezeichnung für die Entwurfsdarstellung des Kostümbildners. Die F. kann in unterschiedlichen Techniken ausgeführt sein, sollte aber immer für den Gewandmeister ‹lesbar› bleiben. In der Regel enthält die F. heute Ausführungsangaben über Schnitt, Farbe, Dekor, Verarbeitung und ist mit Materialproben ‹ausgemustert›.

Dorothea Dieren

Film und Theater

Historische und soziologische Aspekte
Béla Balázs charakterisiert 1938 den Film in seiner Anfangsperiode (von etwa 1895 bis etwa 1915) als «photographiertes Theater», eine Filmkunst gab es damals noch nicht: «Die Kinematographie war nichts weiter als Photoreportage, Jahrmarktssensation bewegter Bilder und eine durch die Reproduktionstechnik ermöglichte Herstellung des Schauspiels, als Massenartikel, als mechanisch wiederholbares, transportierbares, exportierbares Schauspiel.» Die Kinematographie hat in dieser Periode nur aus rein technischen Gründen die «Möglichkeiten des Theaters, seine Thematik, seine Objekte, seine Sujets, seine Wirkungen sehr erweitert». Balázs zielt dabei zum Beispiel auf die Konsequenzen der Tatsache, daß die Natur als Mit- oder Gegenspieler in der dramatischen Handlung des Films bewegt und lebendig dargestellt werden kann. In seiner Konkurrenz mit dem populären Theater richtete der Film sich besonders auf dasjenige, was das populäre Theater nicht darstellen konnte. Die anfänglichen Versuche des populären Theaters (zwischen 1899 und 1904), mit außergewöhnlichen, ‹superrealistischen› Spektakelinszenierungen der Konkurrenz des Films die Stirn zu bieten, waren von vornherein zum Scheitern verurteilt. Der Film konnte in seinen aufsehenerregenden, realistischen Effekten das populäre Theater leicht übertreffen. – Ein klassisches Genre in dieser Periode war die Filmgroteske, in der eine der ältesten Typen der Theatergeschichte, der Clown und Bewegungskomiker, neue Popularität gewann.

Im späten 19. Jh. und Anfang des 20. Jh. existierten neben dem populären →‹Unterhaltungstheater› (→Vaudeville, →Melodrama) das zwar florierende, aber weniger umfangreiche ‹Künstlertheater› (das →Théâtre Libre in Paris, die →Freie Bühne in Berlin, das Independent Theatre in London und das →Moskauer Künstler-Theater) und das ‹klassische› Repertoiretheater. Das Verhältnis zwischen dem Künstlertheater und dem ‹klassischen› Repertoiretheater und andererseits dem Unterhaltungs-

Film und Theater   361

theater hat sich seither hinsichtlich Umfang und Bedeutung unter dem Einfluß des Films wesentlich geändert. In der Periode 1915 bis 1920 wurden viele Schauspielhäuser in Kinos umgebaut, und seit 1920 ist das populäre Theater fast gänzlich in Verfall geraten, während vor allem das künstlerisch hochstehende Theater (‹Kulturtheater›) sein Prestige und seinen Einfluß behalten oder gar vergrößert hat.

Innerhalb von etwa fünfzehn Jahren hat der Film sich vom Theater völlig befreit und ist eine selbständige Kunst geworden. In den 20er Jahren findet eine sehr starke wechselseitige Beeinflussung zwischen Theater und Film statt. Viele Theaterregisseure versuchten in dieser Periode, in ihren Inszenierungen die Techniken des Films zu imitieren. In der Sowjetunion war Wsewolod Meyerhold (→Meyerhold-Theater) einer der ersten Regisseure, der mit der Kombination von Live- und Filmszenen in einer Aufführung experimentierte. So verwendete er in seiner Inszenierung von *Les Aubes* von dem symbolistischen Dichter Emile Verhaeren Filmbilder von den Kämpfen der Roten Armee, um damit die dramatische Handlung auf der Bühne direkt auf die aktuellen politischen Ereignisse zu beziehen. Meyerhold spricht von der «Filmisierung» des Theaters: Die Inflexibilität der konventionellen dramatischen Struktur sollte durch die Flexibilität einer episodischen Struktur, d. h. durch eine Reihe von mit ‹kinematographischer Geschwindigkeit› aufeinanderfolgenden Szenen, ersetzt werden.

In Deutschland war es vor allem Erwin Piscator, der die technischen Möglichkeiten des Theaterapparats erweitert hat. So benutzte er in vielen von seinen Inszenierungen (*Sturmflut, Gewitter über Gottland, Hoppla, wir leben, Rasputin, Der brave Soldat Schwejk*) Filmprojektionen und Tonaufzeichnungen als dokumentarisches Material zum Zwecke der politischen Aufklärung und Agitation. Charakteristisch für den dt. expressionistischen Film und das expressionistische Theater (von etwa 1915 bis etwa 1925) war, daß die wechselseitige Beeinflussung beider Medien in einem freien Austausch von Ausdrucksmitteln bestand. Das Theater entnahm dem Film dessen Tempo, strikte rhythmische Gliederung und starke Lichtwirkungen (z. B. in den Inszenierungen von Leopold Jessner), der Film übernahm seinerseits vom Theater dessen theatralische Raumdarstellung und Spielweise (zum Beispiel *Das Kabinett des Dr. Caligari*, 1919).

In Frankreich waren es vor allem die →surrealistischen Dramatiker (André Breton, Guillaume Apollinaire, Louis Aragon und Antonin Artaud) und Theaterregisseure, die durch die spezifischen Möglichkeiten des Films inspiriert wurden. Jean Cocteau war einer der bekanntesten Theatermacher, der das Theater verließ, um sich vor allem mit dem Film zu beschäftigen.

Mit der Einführung des Tonfilms Ende der 20er Jahre wurden die Beziehungen zwischen Theater und Film abrupt geändert. In erster Instanz ‹retheatralisierte› der Film sich, wurde der Film wieder «photographiertes Theater». Mit der Tonaufzeichnungsmöglichkeit sah der Film sich vor neue technische Probleme gestellt. Die Allgegenwärtigkeit von Stimmen und Geräuschen änderte die Produktionsbedingungen des Films völlig und entnahm teilweise dessen räumliche Flexibilität, die er so mühsam gewonnen hatte. Auch mußte der Film ‹sprechen› lernen; dafür wurden Dramatiker, Theaterregisseure und -schauspieler von der Filmindustrie engagiert. Seither folgen Film und Theater ihrer je eigenen Gesetzlichkeit (→Fernsehen und Theater, →Neue Medien und Theater).

Theoretische Abgrenzungen

Die russischen Formalisten haben in den 20er Jahren als erste versucht, Theater und Film auf systematische Weise miteinander zu vergleichen: dieser Ansatz ist bis heute noch nicht viel weiter ausgearbeitet worden. Er gilt jedenfalls noch immer als das theoretische Fundament, worauf spätere Vergleiche immer wieder zurückgeführt werden. Der von der formalistischen Schule unternommene Vergleich zwischen Theater und Film stand vor allem im Zeichen der Legitimation des Films als neuer Kunstform. Formale Unterschiede zwischen Theater und Film wurden unter diesem Aspekt herausgearbeitet:

1. Direkte versus indirekte Kommunikation: Charakteristisch für das Theater ist, daß die Schauspieler und die Zuschauer gleichzeitig in demselben Raum anwesend sind. In der Dialektik von Spielen und Zuschauen entsteht die Theatersituation. Kennzeichnend für den Film dagegen ist, daß Schauspieler und Zuschauer nicht gleichzeitig anwesend sind. Die Vorführung eines Films ist ein indirekter Kommunikationsprozeß, d. h., daß es keine unmittelbare Rückkopplungsmöglichkeit gibt; sie ist durch ihre Reproduzierbarkeit bestimmt – gegenüber der Authentizität und dem transitorischen Charakter der Theateraufführung.

2. Kollektiv versus Einzelbetrachter: Zuschauer im Theater bilden ein Kollektiv, während die Zuschauer im Kino Einzelbetrachter sind. Daß die Zuschauer im Dunkeln sitzen, ist für den Film eine Vorführungsbedingung. Durch die Dunkelheit werden die Zuschauer von ihrer Umgebung isoliert, und in der Dunkelheit ist jeder für sich den ‹eingleisigen› Informationsflüssen des Films ‹ausgeliefert›. Für das Theater ist die Dunkelheit im Zuschauerraum keine notwendige Aufführungsvoraussetzung; Theater kann im Prinzip überall aufgeführt werden. Wenn auch die Zuschauer im Theater voneinander getrennt werden, wird der direkte Kontakt zwischen Publikum und Schauspielern nicht zerstört, höchstens reduziert. Für die Interaktion zwischen Schauspielern und Zuschauern sind die geltenden Konventionen wichtiger als die Dunkelheit des Zuschauerraums. Das experimentelle Theater hat diese Verhältnisse vielfach variiert.

3. Raumzeitliche Immobilität versus Flexibilität: Die meistens gegenübergestellte ‹Immobilität› des Theaters und die Flexibilität des Films beziehen sich auf die Raum-Zeitlichkeit der theatralen und filmischen Fiktionalität. Die theatrale Fiktionalität findet im Theater statt, in einer physischen Wirklichkeit, in der auch die Zuschauer präsent sind. Demgegenüber steht die physische Abwesenheit der filmischen Fiktionalität. Was den Zuschauern vorgeführt wird, ist ihre Abbildung, eine Reihe von bewegten fotografischen Bildern. Die Flexibilität des Films äußert sich in der Beweglichkeit der Kamera und in den Montagemöglichkeiten des fotografischen Materials. Im Theater werden die dramatischen Handlungen und Geschehnisse überwiegend direkt wahrgenommen, d. h. ohne daß ein mediales System dazwischengeschaltet ist. Filmische Handlungen und Geschehnisse dagegen werden durch die Kamera als vermittelnde Erzählinstanz rezipiert.

Arnheim R.: Film als Kunst. München 1979 (urspr. Ausg. 1932); Balázs, B.: «Zur Kunstphilosophie des Films». In: Witte, K.: Theorie des Kinos. Ideologiekritik der Traumfabrik. Frankfurt/M. 1972 (urspr. Ausg. 1938); Bazin, A.: Theatre and Cinema – Part One/Theatre and Cinema – Part Two. In: ders.: What is Cinema? Vol. I. Berkeley/Los Angeles/London 1967, p. 76–94 und 95–124 (urspr. Ausg. 1959); Benjamin, W.: Das Kunstwerk im Zeitalter seiner technischen Reproduzierbarkeit. Drei Studien zur Kunstsoziologie. Frankfurt/M. 1963 (urspr. Ausg. 1936); Ejchenbaum, B.: Probleme der Filmstilistik. In: Beilenhoff, W. (Hg.): Poetik des Films. Deutsche Erstausgabe der filmtheoretischen Texte der russischen Formalisten mit einem Nachwort und Anmerkungen. München 1974, S. 12–39 (urspr. Ausg. 1927); Hurt, J. (ed.): Focus on Film and Theatre. Englewood Cliffs 1974; Kracauer, S.: Theory of Film. The Redemption of Physical Reality. London/Oxford/New York 1960; Mannvell, R.: Theatre and Film: a comparative Study of the two Forms of Dramatic Art, and the Problem of Adaptations of Stage Plays into Films. Rotherford 1979; Metz, Chr.: Le Signifiant Imaginaire. Psychanalyse et Cinéma. Paris 1977; Murray, E.: The Cinematic Imagination. New York 1972; Natew, W. A.: Die kinematographische Herausforderung. Diss. Berlin 1988; Nicoll, A.: Film und Theater. Köln 1989; Sontag, S.: Film and Theatre. In: Mast, G./Cohen, M. (ed.), Filmtheory and Criticism. Introductory Readings. New York 1974, p. 249–267.

Chiel Kattenbelt

Fiolteatret

Dän. Privattheater, gehörte bis 1985 zu Den storkøbenhavnske Landsdelsscene (zehn Kopenhagener Bühnen), die von Staat und Gemeinde subventioniert wird. Das F. wurde 1962 in Kopenhagen gegründet als erstes dän. professionelles Intim- und Avantgardetheater, das durch die Introduktion frz. und engl. absurder und dän. modernistischer Dramatik für dän. Theater sehr bedeutend war. 1963 schrieb das F. einen Wettbe-

364 Floh de Cologne

werb aus, um dän. Dramen zu fördern, und 1965 wurde eine experimentelle Werkstatt für Theaterarbeiter eröffnet, um eine alternative Ausbildung zu den etablierten Theaterschulen am Königlichen Theater und den Privattheatern anzubieten, die eine enge Zusammenarbeit zwischen Dramatiker, Schauspieler, Regisseur und Bühnenarbeiter voraussetzte. Als Ergebnis änderte das F. 1967 sein Repertoire und bewegte sich in Richtung eines gesellschaftskritischen Dokumentartheaters mit sozialistischer Tendenz. 1969 zog das F. aus den winzigen Räumen in der Innenstadt um in ein größeres Theatergebäude in einem Arbeiterviertel Kopenhagens und begann ‹vor Ort› im Anschluß an Arbeitskämpfe, Streiks und Demonstrationen zu spielen. – Das F. war nur eins von vielen Gruppentheatern (→Freies Theater), die in den 70er Jahren in ganz Dänemark mit politisch engagierten Stücken auftraten. Außer Eigenproduktionen, oft in enger Zusammenarbeit mit dän. Dramatikern, spielt das F. moderne, politisch engagierte Dramatiker. Während der 80er Jahre hat das F. seine Rolle als avantgardistisches politisches Theater allerdings völlig verloren. Mit seiner Existenz bereitete das F. jedoch den Weg für viele neue experimentierende dänische Theatergruppen.

Andersen, N. u. a.: 14 forfattere mod et rigere teater. København 1969; Dramatiker! En rapport om teaterarbejde. Kbh. 1981; Harsløv, O.: Kunst er våben. Kbh. 1976; Hind, T. u. a.: Teater/Fantasi/Klassekamp. Kbh. 1979; Jørgensen, A. u. a.: Det alternative teater i Danmark. Kbh. 1983; dies.: Gruppeteater i Norden. Kbh. 1981.

Else Kjær

Floh de Cologne

Das Kölner Studentenkabarett F. d. C. begann am 20. 1. 1966 seine Arbeit mit einem traditionellen Nummernprogramm: «Vor Gebrauch schütteln». Bereits mit dem dritten Programm «SimSAladimbambaSAladUSAladim» verließ die Gruppe den Bereich üblichen Kabaretts, mischte Musik- und optische Einlagen mit Kommentaren, Solonummern und Sprechchören. Mit Gerd Wollschon als Regisseur und Hauptautor entwickelte sich F. d. C. vom Kabarett gängiger Machart über die Aufführung von ‹Agitations-Revuen› zur Polit-Rock-Band. Mehr und mehr gewann dabei die Musik an Bedeutung. Spätestens mit «Fließbandbabys Beat-Show» (1969) verließ F. d. C. auch das traditionelle Kabarettpublikum zugunsten einer vorwiegend jugendlichen, Studenten wie Lehrlinge umfassenden, Zuhörerschaft. Ihre Texte wurden agitatorischer, so etwa in der ersten Rockoper in deutscher Sprache *Profitgeier* (1970) oder in *Geyer-Symphonie* (1973), in der sie aus den Trauerreden auf den wegen seiner Verbindung zur NSDAP belasteten Großindustriellen Friedrich Flick zitierten. 1980 erhielten sie den Deutschen Kleinkunstpreis. Mit dem Programm «F» (1981), einer Abschiedstournee im April 1983 und einem letzten Konzert am 14.5.1983 beendete F. d. C. nach mehr als 1500 Auftritten und mehr als 100000 verkauften Langspielplatten seine Existenz.

Budzinski, K.: Das Kabarett. 100 Jahre literarische Zeitkritik – gesprochen – gesungen – gespielt. Düsseldorf 1985; Ehnert, G./Kinsler, D.: Rock in Deutschland. Hamburg ³1984; Haring, H.: Rock aus Deutschland West. Reinbek bei Hamburg 1984.

Wolfgang Beck

Folies-Bergère

Pariser → Kabarett und Revuetheater, 1869 gegründet. Durch seine glanzvollen → Ausstattungsrevuen (erstes Auftreten von ‹girls› im kontinentaleuropäischen Unterhaltungstheater) neben den Londoner → Music Halls richtungweisend für die Entwicklung auch des dt. Revuetheaters (Metropoltheater und Admirals-Palast in Berlin, → Revue). Zwischen den Weltkriegen unter der Leitung von Paul Derval feierten hier Stars wie Josephine Baker u. a. Triumphe. Heute neben Paradis Latin, Moulin Rouge und Lido eines der meistbesuchten Pariser Revuetheater.

Horst Schumacher

Folkwang-Tanzstudio

Das Folkwang-Tanzstudio (FTS) gehört zur Staatlichen Hochschule für Musik Ruhr/Folkwang-Hochschule für Musik, Theater und Tanz in Essen-Werden. Es wird 1961 von Kurt Jooss (1901–79) als Meisterklassen für Tanz (dann Folkwang-Ballett) ins Leben gerufen (→ Ballets Jooss, → Ausdruckstanz). Jooss leitet das Ensemble bis Ende der 60er Jahre. Unter dem Nachfolger Hans Züllig (* 1914) Umbenennung in FTS. Nach ihm sind künstlerisch verantwortlich: 1969–73 Pina Bausch (* 1940), 1975–77 Susanne Linke (* 1944) und Reinhild Hoffmann (* 1943), bis 1985 Linke und seit 1987 wieder Bausch (zugleich auch Direktorin des → Wuppertaler Tanztheaters und der Tanzabteilung der Hochschule). Von 1985–88 ist Mitsuru Sasaki (* 1944) der ständige Choreograph des FTS.

Das Folkwang-Ballett unter Jooss pflegt den in der Tradition des → Ausdruckstanzes stehenden deutschen sowie den amerikanischen modernen Tanz (→ Modern Dance), bietet den Meisterklassen Gelegenheit für erste choreographische Versuche und wird zu einer der Geburtsstätten des neuen deutschen → Tanztheaters. Das Repertoire prägen Arbeiten von Jooss, Züllig, Antony Tudor (1908–87), Lucas Hoving (* 1912), Jean Cébron (* 1927) und P. Bausch. Als FTS wird die für ihre Produktionen jeweils neu zusammengestellte Kompanie zu einem bedeutenden Forum junger Choreographen des zeitgenössischen Tanzes in Deutschland. Bausch, Linke und Hoffmann, nach ihnen u. a. Marilen Breuker (* 1951) und Christine Brunel (* 1951) stellen hier ihre ersten Choreographien vor. – Unter der erneuten künstlerischen Leitung von Pina Bausch wird das FTS zu einer ‹ständigen› Kompanie, die zahlreiche (Auslands-) Gastspiele absolviert. Zum Repertoire gehören u. a. Arbeiten von S. Linke, Carolyn Carlson (* 1943) und Urs Dietrich (* 1958). ‹Junge Choreographen›-Programme sind fester Bestandteil des Spielplans.

Schlicher, S.: TanzTheater – Traditionen und Freiheiten. Reinbek 1987; Müller, H.: Kurt Jooss und die Folgen. In: Regitz, H./Koegler, H. (Hg.): Ballett 1985. Zürich 1985; Schulz, B.: Die Folkwang-Hochschule Essen. In: Tanz International 10 (1990).

Horst Vollmer

Fortune Theatre

Das F.T. wurde 1599 von Edward Alleyn und Philip Henslowe etwas nördlich der Stadtgrenzen Londons gebaut. Es diente von 1600 bis 1621 als Spielstätte für Alleyns Schauspieltruppe →The Admiral's Men (später Prince Henry's bzw. Elector Palatine's Men genannt), die Hauptrivalen von Shakespeares und Burbages →Lord Chamberlain's Men – King's Men. Obwohl die Plattformbühne und die Hinterbühne nach dem Vorbild des → Globe Theatre gebaut wurde, war die äußere Form des Hauses im Gegensatz zu allen anderen öffentlichen Bühnen quadratisch statt ‹rund›. Der Vertrag über den Bau des F.T. gehört zu den Hauptinformationsquellen über die Größe, Bauweise und Zuschauerkapazitäten der elisabethanischen Bühnen. Das F.T. hatte einen Durchmesser von ca. 25 Meter und einen Hof von ca. 15 Meter Durchmesser, in den die Plattformbühne (etwa 113 × 9 Meter) hineinragte. Es hatte drei Zuschauergalerien und Platz für ca. 2340 Menschen. 1621 brannte das F.T. ab.

Chambers, E.: The Elizabethan Stage. Vol. 2. Repr. London 1951; Hosley, R.: The Playhouse. In: J. Barroll et al. (eds.): The Revels History of Drama in English. Vol. 3. London 1975, pp. 119–236; King, T.: Shakespearean Staging 1599–1642. Cambridge, Mass., 1971.

J. Lawrence Guntner

Foyer

(Frz. ‹Feuer›, ‹Feuerstelle›, ‹Herd›, ‹Kamin›) Ursprünglich Raum im Theater, in dem sich Zuschauer und Schauspieler versammelten, um sich am Kamin aufzuwärmen. Heute Wandelhalle, Vorhalle, die dem Publikum vor Beginn der Aufführung und in den Pausen zugänglich ist, meist mit Buffet und Verkaufsstand für Bühnenliteratur, wie Programmheften, Textbüchern etc. Das erste F. im modernen Sinn befindet sich im 1753 erbauten Opernhaus des Versailler Schlosses.

Horst Schumacher

Frauentheater

F. ist ein relativ neuer Begriff in der Theaterpraxis und -theorie, dessen exakte Definition Probleme aufwirft, werden doch die verschiedensten Bereiche in ihm zusammengefaßt. Um begriffliche Unschärfe zu vermeiden, wird F. hier eingeengt auf Theater von, für und mit Frauen und über frauenspezifische Problemstellungen. Diese Art von Theater hat zunehmend erst seit dem Beginn der neuen Frauenbewegung Ende der 60er Jahre an Bedeutung gewonnen und kann ohne sie kaum gedacht werden. Inzwischen ist F. auch im kommerziellen Theaterbereich, am Stadttheater, möglich geworden, zumeist jedoch in gemäßigter Form, frei von feministischen Forderungen. Bisweilen spricht man schon von F., wenn das aufgeführte Stück von einer Frau geschrieben wurde. Gegenüber dieser Art wird F. im engeren Sinne neben wenigen professionellen vor allem von semi-professionellen und Amateurgruppen bestimmt. Besonders in diesem Bereich finden die wesentlichen Entwicklungen des F. statt. Neben Stücken von Dramatikerinnen führen diese Truppen zumeist selbstverfaßte und -entwickelte Stücke auf, häufig in Szenen aneinanderreihender Revue- und Kabarettform. Die Unterschiede der einzelnen Gruppen bedingen auch die divergierenden Inszenierungsweisen der Vorlagen. Z. T. programmatisch wird auf traditionelle Mittel des Theaters verzichtet, auch unter dem Aspekt der Entwicklung einer anderen, einer weiblichen Ästhetik. Dementsprechend lassen sich auf diesem Gebiet keine allgemeingültigen Übereinstimmungen herausarbeiten, keine Stilrichtungen oder ‹Schulen› bestimmen. Bei aller formalen Vielfalt ist F. jedoch gekennzeichnet durch inhaltliche Übereinstimmungen, die das weite Spektrum weiblicher Geschichte und Lebenszusammenhänge umfassen: die Unterdrückung der Frau in Vergangenheit und Gegenwart, die Aufarbeitung der häufig verschütteten weiblichen Geschichtstraditionen, politische und sozioökonomische Forderungen, Probleme weib-

368 Frauentheater _____

licher Sexualität und Homosexualität. Spielten am Beginn der Entwicklung Partnerprobleme im weitesten Sinne noch eine entscheidende Rolle, bedurfte es der Darstellung männlich-patriarchalischen Verhaltens als negativer Folie, vor der die eigene Forderungen und Entwicklungen dargestellt und gerechtfertigt werden konnten, so hat sich das F. inzwischen so weiterentwickelt und an innerer Stärke gewonnen, daß darauf verzichtet werden kann und selbstironische Reflexionen selbstverständlich geworden sind.

Wie vielfach im Bereich von Amateur- und →Freiem Theater hat auch das F. nicht nur die Funktion, eine Aufführung zu entwickeln, sondern dient in einem nicht unerheblichen Maße der Selbstfindung und Selbstverständigung. In kurzer Zeit hat sich hier ein beachtliches und in keiner Hinsicht mehr zu übersehendes Spektrum an Theaterarbeit entwickelt, das z. B. in den USA über den eigenen Bereich hinaus Einflüsse auf Avantgarde- und Off-Broadway-Theater ausübt. In den USA gibt es über das ganze Land verstreut eine Vielzahl von F.-Gruppen, deren bekannteste internationalen Ruf gewonnen haben: «The Women's Experimental Theatre», «Lilith» (San Francisco), «Spider Woman» (New York). Die wichtigeren engl. F.-Gruppen spielen zumeist in London, so etwa «Beryl & the Perils», «Monstrous Regiment», «The Cunning Stunts», «Gay Sweat-shop». In Italien gibt es mit →«La Maddalena», 1973 in Rom als Teil eines feministischen Kulturzentrums gegr., das einzige ausschließlich von Frauen betriebene und verwaltete Theater Europas. Auch dieses ist kollektiv organisiert und verzichtete zu Beginn seiner Tätigkeit programmatisch auf ein festes Ensemble. Für einzelne Projekte trafen sich interessierte Frauen aus allen Berufen, um gemeinsam ein Stück zu erarbeiten. Der dabei gelegentlich unvermeidliche Dilettantismus führte zum Aufbau einer professionellen Gruppe. Auch in den Niederlanden und den skandin. Ländern gibt es ein breites Spektrum von F., in Frankreich spielte das Frauenkabarett «Les Trois Jeannes» erfolgreich auch im Rahmen kommerziellen Theaters. In der BRD gibt es nur wenige über einen längeren Zeitraum spielende F.-Gruppen, von denen hier lediglich Kabarettgruppen (wegen ihrer Breitenwirkung) genannt werden sollen: das «Aachener Frauenkabarett» (1978–83), das Berliner Kabarett «Die Witwen» (1979–87) und die seit 1988 erfolgreichen «Missfits» aus Oberhausen.

Generell leiden gerade die vielen halbprofessionellen und Amateurgruppen des F. an dem Fehlen für sie aufführbarer Stücke. Gelegentlich entspringt das Entwickeln eigener Spielvorlagen auch diesem Mangel, häufiger jedoch steckt programmatische Intention hinter diesen Bemühungen. Das gemeinsame Erarbeiten von Text und Inszenierung – die meisten Gruppen sind kollektiv organisiert – steht in engem Zusammenhang mit den Versuchen, eigene ästhetische Vorstellungen zu entwickeln und zu erproben. Ein grundsätzliches Problem auch des F. ist der ökonomische Druck, der Zwang, wenigstens die Inszenierungskosten einzuspielen. Da Subventionen nur in den seltensten Fällen gezahlt werden, ist auch hier Selbstausbeutung die Regel, was eine kontinuierliche Entwicklung behindert, wenn nicht gar unmöglich macht. Dessenungeachtet finden inzwischen mehr und mehr F.-Treffen statt, nationale und internationale Festivals: 1980 zum erstenmal in der BRD, 1974 bereits in London, 1977 in Bologna, jährlich in Louisville in den USA, 1980 in Boston («First Women's Theatre Festival»). Im Zuge der Entfaltung des F. haben sich die am Theater beschäftigten Frauen zusammengeschlossen, um über Probleme, die sie als Frauen am Theater haben, nachzudenken und an der Weiterentwicklung des F. auch im kommerziellen Rahmen zu arbeiten. Zu nennen wären hier etwa die «National Conference for Women in Theatre» (USA, seit 1979) und der Arbeitskreis «Frauen im Theater (FiT)» im Rahmen der Dramaturgischen Gesellschaft der BRD.

Nicht nur im Theaterbetrieb sind Frauen vor allem in leitenden Positionen unterrepräsentiert; auch als Dramatikerinnen spielen sie eine eher untergeordnete Rolle. Erst seit der Jahrhundertwende konnten sich einzelne Frauen als Verfasserinnen von Theaterstücken durchsetzen (in den USA etwa Claire Boothe-Luce, Lillian Hellman; in Deutschland z. B. Marieluise Fleißer, Else Lasker-Schüler). Im Zuge der Frauenbewegung und der Entwicklung des F. hat sich hier etwas verändert; doch noch immer sind es vergleichsweise wenige Autorinnen, denen es gelungen ist, sich durchzusetzen: in der BRD etwa Gerlind Reinshagen, Elfriede Jelinek, Friederike Roth, Barbara Honigmann, Ria Endres, Kerstin Specht, in Frankreich Monique Wittig, Hélène Cixous, in Italien Dacia Mariani und Franca Rame. In den USA ist zu beobachten, daß sich hier auch ein überaus lebendiges schwarzes F. entwickelt hat, dessen bekannteste Autoren Marsha Norman, Ntozake Shange, Lorraine Hansberry Erfolge auch am Broadway aufzuweisen haben.

Barlow, J. E.: Plays by American Women. New York 1981; Bassnett, S.: Magdalena. International Women's Experimental Theatre. Oxford 1989; Brater, E.: The New Women Playwrights. New York 1989; Case, S.-E.: Feminism and Theatre. New York 1988; dies.: Performing Feminism. Baltimore 1990; Chinoy, H. K., L. Jenkins (Hg.): Women in American Theatre. New York 1980; Davis, T. C.: Actresses as Working Women. New York 1991; Dolan, J.: The Feminist Spectator as Critic. Ann Arbor 1988; Ferris, L.: Acting Women. London 1990; Frauen am Theater. TheaterZeitSchrift 9 u. 10. Berlin 1984; Fürle, B.: Theatermacherinnen. Diss. Wien 1987; Fürs Theater schreiben. Über zeitgenössische deutschsprachige Theaterautorinnen. (Schreiben, Nr. 29/30). Bremen 1986; Hoff, D. von: Dramen des Weiblichen. Opladen 1989; Kentrup, N. u. a. (Hg.): Frauentheater. Offenbach 1982; Leavitt, D. L.: Feminist Theatre Groups. Jefferson 1980; Miles, J.: Womenswork. New York 1989; Nichols, K. L.: Earlier American Women Dramatists. In: Theatre History Studies XI (1991), S. 129–150; Ohnmacht, S.: Dramen «weiblicher» und «männlicher» Subjektivität. Diss. Wien 1987; Perkins, K. A. (Hg.): Black Female Playwrights. An Anthology of Plays before 1950. Bloomington 1989; Redmond, J.: Women in Theatre. Cambridge 1989; Roeder, A. (Hg.): Autorinnen. Frankfurt/M. 1989; Stowell, S.: A Stage of their Own. Feminist Playwrights of the Suffrage Era. Ann Arbor 1992; Wurst, K. A. (Hg.): Frauen und Drama im 18. Jahrhundert. Köln/Wien 1991.

Wolfgang Beck

Free Southern Theater

Gegr. 1963, nahe Jackson, Mississippi; 1965 bis 1978 New Orleans. Hauptziele: Nachbarschafts-, d. h. Stadtteiltheater im Getto und Tourneetheater im ‹schwarzen Gürtel› des Südens der USA. Dichterlesungen, musikalische Unterhaltung, Workshops in ‹Creative Writing›, TV- und Radioprogramme kamen ergänzend hinzu. In der Geschichte des F. S. T. spiegeln sich die Positionen der afroamerik. Bewegung der 60er Jahre. Aus den Civil Rights-Kämpfen hervorgegangen, wurde 1965 bis 1970 der Black Power-Einfluß verstärkt deutlich. In den 70er Jahren wurde eine materialistische Theoriegrundlage mit antiimperialistischer Zielsetzung erarbeitet. Gespielt wurden neben Beckett, Brecht, Ionesco vor allem schwarzamerik. Dramen: Ossie Davies: *Purlie Victorious*; Douglas T. Ward: *Happy Ending*; Gilbert Moses: *Roots*; John O'Neal: *Hurricane Season*; *When the Opportunity Scratches Itch It*. Zur Überbrückung und Vertiefung der eigenen ethnischen Traditionslinien gab es z. B. 1975 *Langston and Company*, eine Montage aus Texten und Songs des wichtigsten Vertreters der Harlem Renaissance, Langston Hughes, von Chakula Cha Jua. Das F. S. T. verknüpfte musikalische, mimische und sprachliche Elemente des schwarzamerik. Lebenszusammenhangs mit relevanter politischer und pädagogischer Aufklärungsarbeit für die Gegenwart.

Dent, T. C./Schechner, R./Moses, G. (eds.): The Free Southern Theater by the Free Southern Theater. Indianapolis/New York 1969; Herms, D./Witzel, B.: Von James Baldwin zum Free Southern Theater. Bremen 1979.

Dieter Herms

Freie Bühne

Berlin: 1889 von den Kritikern und Literaten M. Harden, Th. Wolff, den Brüdern H. und J. Hart, L. Fulda, dem Verleger S. Fischer, P. Schlenther und O. Brahm gegr. Theaterverein zur Aufführung von Dramen zeitgenössischer Autoren nach dem Muster des →Théâtre Libre unter André Antoine in Paris. Vorstellungen in geschlossenen Mitgliederveranstaltungen in gemieteten Räumen zur Umgehung der Theaterzensur. Jeweils für eine Produktion wurden Ensemble und Regisseur engagiert. Präsident: Otto Brahm (1856–1912). Programmatisch der neuen naturalistischen Kunstrichtung verpflichtet, sollten «...in der Auswahl der dramatischen Werke, als auch in der schauspielerischen Darstellung... die Ziele einer der Schablone und dem Virtuosentum abgewandten lebendigen Kunst angestrebt werden» (Neuer Theater Almanach 1890). Gerhart Hauptmann (1862–1946), selbst Vereinsmitglied, avancierte zum Hausdichter. Wichtige Aufführungen: *Gespenster* (Henrik Ibsen, 1889), *Vor Sonnenaufgang* (Gerhart Hauptmann, 1889), *Das Vierte Gebot* (Ludwig Anzengruber, 1890), *Die Weber* (Gerhart Hauptmann, UA 1893). Die F. B. trug nachhaltig zur Entwicklung und Durchsetzung einer realistischen Dramatik und Schauspielkunst bei und wurde zum entscheidenden Vorläufer der Volksbühnenbewegung (→Volksbühne). – Publikationsorgan: «Freie Bühne für modernes Leben» (seit 1890); →Deutsche Bühne.

Stockholm: Das 1943 gegr. Emigranten-Ensemble brachte unter der Leitung seiner Regisseure Curt Trepte und Herman Greid in enger Zusammenarbeit mit dem Freien Deutschen Kulturbund in den drei Jahren seines Bestehens Texte von 23 Exilautoren, teils als Aufführung, teils als Lesung oder Rezitation. Wichtigste Uraufführung: H. Greids Widerstandsstück *Die andere Seite.*

Brahm, O. (mitget. v. Georg Hirschfeld): Briefe und Erinnerungen. Berlin 1925; Brauneck, M.: Literatur und Öffentlichkeit im ausgehenden 19. Jahrhundert. Stuttgart 1974; Genossenschaft Deutscher Bühnen Angehöriger (Hg.): Neuer Theater Almanach. Berlin 1890; Schley, G.: Die Freie Bühne in Berlin. Berlin 1967; Selo, H.: Die Freie Volksbühne in Berlin. Diss. phil. Erlangen 1930.

Erich Krieger / Jan Hans

Freie Deutsche Bühne (Buenos Aires)

Die 1941 von dem Multi-Talent P. Walter Jacob (Schauspieler, Regisseur, Dirigent, Theater- und Musikschriftsteller) gegr. (und von diesem auch bis 1950 geleitete) F. D. B. war das einzige ständig spielende deutschsprachige und völlig unabhängige Exiltheater in der ganzen Welt. In zehn

Spielzeiten brachte es die ausschließlich mit Berufsschauspielern arbeitende Bühne auf 215 Premieren mit 750 Aufführungen. Lillian Hellmans *Die Unbesiegten*, Werfels *Jacobowsky* und Zuckmayers *Des Teufels General* bilden die Glanzlichter in einem Spielplan, der durch Klassikeraufführungen, Konversations-Lustspiele und das demokratische Zeittheater der 20er Jahre gekennzeichnet ist. In geistig-künstlerischer Ausrichtung sowie hinsichtlich seiner Organisationsform hat das Ensemble konsequent die Tradition des dt. Stadttheaters weiterverfolgt. Die Bedeutung dieser Tradition für das dt. Nachkriegstheater verdeutlicht Jacobs Intendanz bei den Städtischen Bühnen in Dortmund von 1950 bis 1962.

Naumann, U. (Hg.): Ein Theatermann im Exil: P. Walter Jacob. Hamburg 1985.

Jan Hans

Freies Theater

→Fringe Theatre; →Politisches Volkstheater (USA); →Angura; →Studententheater; →Amateurtheater; →Straßentheater. Theatergruppen und Einzeldarsteller traten in den 60er Jahren dieses Jh. an die Öffentlichkeit und proklamierten ein neues Verständnis von Theaterarbeit; es betraf die Inhalte, die ästhetische Form, die soziale Sinngebung und die institutionelle Struktur des Theaters. Die Bewegung des F. T. sah sich im Widerspruch zu den etablierten Bühnen und der kommerzialisierten Theaterkultur, sie artikulierte in ihrer Kritik ein Aufbegehren gegen die gesellschaftlichen und kulturellen Verkrustungen dieser Zeit. F. T. organisierte sich außerhalb des Systems der Stadt- und Staatstheater sowie der kommerziellen Privatbühnen, die auf Grund festgefügter Hierarchien im künstlerischen und organisatorischen Apparat nicht mehr in der Lage zu sein schienen, der Forderung nach Entwicklungen einer modernen Theaterkunst gerecht zu werden.

Als geistiger Ahnherr der Bewegung kann der frz. Schriftsteller, Regisseur und Schauspieler Antonin Artaud (1896–1948) gelten, der 1933 in seinem Aufsatz *Schluß mit den Meisterwerken* schrieb: «Wenn die Menge nicht zu den literarischen Meisterwerken kommt, so deshalb, weil diese Meisterwerke literarisch, d. h. festgelegt sind; in Formen festgelegt, die nicht mehr den Bedürfnissen der Zeit entsprechen.» Im Sinne Artauds formuliert der Londoner Regisseur und Schauspieler Pip Simmons: «Seit das Theater literarisch wurde, ist es mit dem Theater rapide bergab gegangen. Es hat aufgehört, eine populäre Form der Unterhaltung und Kommunikation zu sein... Das Ausprobieren neuer Techniken, neuer Produktionsweisen – darum geht es allen Gruppen, die zum ‹fringe Theatre›, dem sogenannten Untergrund-Theater gehören, und all die Tricks,

Freies Theater 373

der ganze Dampf, der ganze Nebel, den heute Popgruppen benutzen, kommen vom ‹fringe›» (Programmheft Theater der Nationen, 1979). Insbesondere der poln. Regisseur Jerzy Grotowski (* 1933; →Armes Theater) bezog sich auf Artaud und entwickelte dramaturgische Praktiken, die weltweit Aufsehen erregten und dazu beitrugen, das Schwergewicht im Theater vom Autor und dem Text über den Regisseur auf den Schauspieler und die Darstellung zu verschieben. Richard Schechner, Gründer der →Performance Group, und Joseph Chaikin, Gründer des →Open Theatre in den USA; Peter Brook aus England und Eugenio Barba vom →Odin Teatret (Dänemark) wurden die markantesten Verfechter von Grotowskis neuen Theaterideen. Der radikale Versuch, zu den Wurzeln des Theaters vorzudringen, motivierte Peter Brook 1973 zu einer ‹Theatersafari› durch Afrika. In der Begegnung mit fremden Kulturen wurde die Tragfähigkeit der eigenen Theatererfahrung erprobt. Ähnliche Zielsetzungen leiteten die Reisen des Odin Teatret nach Sardinien und dem Amazonas. In Großbritannien formierte sich als erstes F.T. 1966 die People Show, es folgten in Edinburgh die Traverse Workshop Company und 1968 in London die →Pip Simmons Group. In Amsterdam gründete 1965 der Fernsehproduzent Ritsaert ten Cate das →Mickery Theater, in dem inzwischen fast alle bedeutenden F.T. aufgetreten sind.

Das Gründungsjahr des →Living Theatre 1951 kann in den USA als Beginn des →Off-Broadway begriffen werden. Im gleichen Jahr etablierte der Produzent und Regisseur Theodore Mann außerhalb des Broadway sein Theater Circle in the Square, in dem anspruchsvolle Stücke experimentell inszeniert wurden. Es folgten weitere Theatergründungen. 1954 veranstaltete Joseph Papp auf offener Straße das New York Shakespeare Festival, aus dem das alljährliche «Shakespeare in the Park» im Central Park entstand. Die Off-Broadway-Theater – konzentriert im New Yorker Stadtteil Greenwich Village – waren wesentlich kleiner als die etablierten Broadway-Häuser und damit auch flexibler in Produktionsweise und Spielplangestaltung. Der Off-Broadway erreichte um 1960 seinen Höhepunkt als ambitionierter Kontrast zum Broadway, wurde aber bald den gleichen Profitmechanismen unterworfen, die bereits am Broadway herrschten. In den 60er Jahren – mit Anfängen bereits in den 50ern, wie z. B. das Theater «La Mama» – entstanden schließlich in New York die →Off-Off-Broadway-Theater. In Kneipen, Cafés, Läden, leerstehenden Fabriken begannen Theaterbegeisterte ihrer Leidenschaft nachzugehen, oft am Rande des Existenzminimums lebend und zumeist nur von der Hoffnung, den Sprung in die etablierten Häuser zu schaffen, zum Weitermachen motiviert. Dennoch gingen von hier auch viele innovative Impulse auf die internationale und amerikanische Theaterszene aus. Im Umfeld des Off-Off-Broadway gründeten Joseph Chaikin und Peter Feldman vom Living Theatre 1963 das →Open Theatre, das Autoren wie

Terry (*Viet Rock*) und van Itallie (*American Hurrah*) inspirierte, in seiner Arbeit vor allem den Möglichkeiten der Improvisation und der wortlosen Kommunikation nachging und in den 60er und beginnenden 70er Jahren als vielversprechendste Freie Gruppe in den USA gelten konnte. Neben dem Living Theatre haben sich vor allem die →San Francisco Mime Troupe und →Bread and Puppet durch Auftritte in den USA und internationale Tourneen Popularität bei einem weltweiten Publikum verschafft.

In der zweiten Hälfte der 70er Jahre war das F.T. geprägt durch die Fools- und Clownspower-Bewegung. 1975 hatte der amerikanische Clown Jango Edwards ein Festival für F.T. angeregt, das im gleichen Jahr als →Festival of Fools in Amsterdam auch ausgerichtet wurde. In den größeren Amsterdamer Kommunikations- und Kulturzentren Paradiso, Melkway, →Shaffy-Theater, Vondelpark sowie auf Straßen und Plätzen trat eine kaum überschaubare Menge von Akteuren auf. Auf der Basis ihrer Erfahrungen mit frei arbeitenden Theatergruppen in den USA richteten Pea Fröhlich und Jens Heilmeyer 1970 nach dem Vorbild von «La Mama» aus New York in München einen gleichnamigen Theatertreffpunkt ein. Schüler der →Otto-Falckenberg-Schule nahmen am La Mama-Training und an den Übungen teil. Diese ersten Erfahrungen mit einer anderen freieren Form von Theaterarbeit zusammen mit der Ablehnung der konventionellen Schauspielerkarriere, der Ochsentour des Hochdienens über die Provinzbühne in die Großstadt, führten u.a. zur Gründung eines F.T. in München: Rote Rübe. Gleich mit ihrem zweiten Stück *Frauen-Power* – gegen den Paragraphen 218 – hatte die Gruppe großen Erfolg. Mit Agitationsstücken gegen den Terror in Chile, Italien und in der BRD entwickelte die Rote Rübe eine Politrevue- und Spektakelform, die sie erst 1977, kurz vor ihrer Auflösung, mit *Liebe, Tod und Hysterie* aufgab zugunsten des Emotions- und Psychodramatrends dieser Jahre. – Ähnliche Vorgänge waren in anderen Städten der BRD zu verzeichnen. Neben der Roten Rübe stellte in den 70er Jahren die Berliner →Theatermanufaktur das wichtigste F.T. in der BRD dar. Sich auf volkstümliche Art mit gesellschaftlichen Problemen auseinandersetzend, verknüpfte die Gruppe Brechtsche Erzählweise mit Comic- und →Commedia dell'arte-Elementen. Mit ihrem ersten Stück *1848* erregte die Theatermanufaktur im Jahre 1973 Begeisterung und Aufsehen. Mittlerweile produziert und spielt die Gruppe in den Räumen der alten Schaubühne am Halleschen Ufer, die sich auch anderen F.T. für Aufführungen zur Verfügung stellt. – Der lange Zeit am Württembergischen Staatstheater in Stuttgart unter Claus Peymann arbeitende Schauspieler Martin Lüttge gründete zusammen mit anderen Schauspielern den Theaterhof Priessenthal. Auf einem Bauernhof in Bayern leben die etwa 15 Mitglieder der Truppe, dort werden auch die Stücke erarbeitet, mit denen auf Tournee gegangen wird. Mit eigenen Lastwagen, Omnibussen, Wohnwagen und Zelt erin-

Freies Theater 375

nert der «Theaterhof» eher an einen kleinen Zirkus als an ein Theater. Volkstümliche historische Stoffe wie Nibelungen, Johanna von Orléans, Schildbürger werden mit Gegenwartsbezügen aktualisiert und zu derben Komödien verarbeitet. Wichtig ist den Mitgliedern die kollektive Erarbeitung der Stücke.

Die Frage nach dem Selbstverständnis und der Funktion von Kunst wurde seit Mitte der 60er Jahre auch dem Theater verstärkt gestellt. Insbesondere die Happening-Künstler versuchten, der Kunst einen neuen Wirkungsraum zu erschließen, das Leben als Kunst zu inszenieren. Die Erwartung an die Kunst verließ den Rahmen der Vermittlung über Schönheit, Illusion und Phantasie und kaprizierte sich auf das Erlebnis des Einmaligen und Authentischen. Dabei waren die Happening-Künstler bestrebt, die traditionellen Einzelkünste und neue Darstellungsmittel zu intermedialen Ereignissen zu verbinden (→ Performance, Happening, Aktionskunst).

Eine unmittelbare Inspiration für das F. T. ging von den Studentenbühnen aus. Aufgeschlossen für Neues, wurden aus zunächst eher dilettantischen Nachahmern der professionellen Theater experimentierfreudige Gruppen, die ihre Aufgabe im Ausprobieren neuer theatraler Formen und in der inhaltlichen Auseinandersetzung mit politischen Problemen ihrer Zeit sahen. Außer der «Studiobühne» in Erlangen wurde Anfang der 60er Jahre das interessanteste Studententheater in Berlin («die andere bühne») und in Frankfurt («neue bühne») produziert, in Städten also, die später zu Zentren der Studentenbewegung wurden. Ende der 60er Jahre betrieben manche Gruppen politisches →Straßentheater; andere lösten sich auf, ihre Mitglieder widmeten sich meist politischen Aufgaben; die Arbeit am Theater galt in dieser Phase politischer Unruhe eher als suspekt. Nach der 68er-Bewegung hatten die Studententheater ihre Bedeutung eingebüßt. Die Erlanger «Internationale Woche der Studentenbühnen» (seit 1949) fand 1968 ein letztes Mal statt. Fünf Jahre später veranstaltete Erlangen das erste Festival des F. T., ein Vorläufer des «Internationalen Freien Theater Festivals» in München.

Ende der 80er/Anfang der 90er Jahre hat sich F. T. in Deutschland von einer politisch und sozial engagierten, kritischen Gegenkultur zu einer eher formal interessierten Avantgarde gewandelt: Aus einem Protestgestus wurde ein alternativer Berufszweig. Mit der weitgehenden Abwendung von einer politischen Programmatik werden auch originäre Theaterformen des F. T. (Straßentheater, Betroffenentheater, engagiertes Volkstheater) immer seltener praktiziert. Schwerpunkte des F. T. liegen nun in den Bereichen Tanztheater, visuelle und multimediale Experimente, Kabarett und Kleinkunst sowie in der Wiederbelebung von Formen der Unterhaltungskunst der 20er Jahre (→Revue, →Kabarett, →Varieté), deren Tradition in Deutschland mit dem 3. Reich unterbrochen wurde. Mangels eigener Ausbildungsinstitutionen orientiert sich eine neue Generation freier Theatermacher nicht mehr an den traditionellen Vorbildern, sondern zunehmend an Staatstheatern, am Film und an der populären Massenkultur. Auch organisatorisch haben sich viele Gruppen den Staatsbühnen angenähert: Ihre Produktionen entstehen nun arbeitsteilig und nicht mehr in kollektiven Entwicklungsprozessen. Statt auf der Straße und an wechselnden, alternativen Auftrittsorten versuchen die Gruppen, sich durch staatlich geförderte Theaterzentren (→ Internationale Kulturfabrik Kampnagel/Hamburg, Mousonturm und → Theater am Turm [TaT]/Frankfurt, Theaterhaus Gessnerallee/Zürich) ein institutionelles Netz aus Probe- und Auftrittsmöglichkeiten, Technikpool, Werbung und Tourneemanagement aufzubauen. Die Ablehnung staatlicher Subventionen, einst Programmpunkt des F.T., wurde aufgegeben. Die Gruppen werden nun teilweise aus staatlichen Etats finanziert, die im allein auf die Staatstheater konzentrierten deutschen Subventionssystem allerdings gering ausfallen. Zum Wandel des F.T. hat nicht unwesentlich der Niedergang der neuen sozialen Bewegungen beigetragen, die früher hauptsächlich das Publikum des F.T. stellten. Vor einem breiteren Publikum stellt das F.T. nun eines von vielen künstlerischen Angeboten der großstädtischen Theaterlandschaft dar. Noch immer pflegt es vernachlässigte oder seltene Theatersparten (Kinder-, Masken-, Figurentheater) und bietet mehr als die Staatsbühnen Möglichkeiten zu innovativen, experimentellen Ansätzen.

Artaud, A.: Das Theater und sein Double. Frankfurt/M. 1979; Büscher, B.: Wirklichkeitstheater. Straßentheater. Freies Theater. Frankfurt/M. 1987; Freie Theater: Das lustvolle Chaos (Du. Themenheft Febr. 1992). Zürich 1992; Grotowski, J.: Das arme Theater. Velber 1970; Harjes, R.: Handbuch zur Praxis des Freien Theaters. Köln 1983; Heilmeyer, J./Fröhlich, P. (Hg.): Now. Theater der Erfahrung. Material zur neuen amerikanischen Theaterbewegung. Köln 1971; Roberg, D.: Theater muß wie Fußball sein. Freie Theatergruppen – eine Reise über Land. Berlin 1981; Waldmann, A.: Enfant terrible oder Sorgenkind der Kulturszene. Freies Theater in Hamburg 1989/90. Magisterarb. Hamburg 1991; Weihs, A.: Freies Theater. Reinbek 1981.

Georg Stenzaly/Annette Waldmann

Freie Volksbühne Berlin

Nach der Spaltung der Berliner → Volksbühne gründete die «Freie Volksbühne» in West-Berlin ein eigenes Theater, das bis 1963 im Theater am Kurfürstendamm spielte. Eröffnung am 1. Sept. 1949 mit *Hamlet*. Nach mühsamen Anfängen ohne deutliches Profil wurde das Haus unter dem Intendanten Oscar Fritz Schuh (1904–85) zwischen 1953 und 1958 zum zweiten wichtigen Theater in West-Berlin neben dem Schiller-Theater mit einem vorzüglichen Ensemble und renommierten Regisseuren. Zahlreiche UA. Die Kurz-Intendanzen Leonhard Steckel (1901–71) und Rudolf Noelte (*1921) vermochten an das erreichte Niveau anzuknüpfen, vor allem aber 1962 mit Erwin Piscator (1893–1966), unter dessen Leitung 1963 der Neubau des eigenen Theatergebäudes der «Freien Volksbühne» bezogen werden konnte. 1963 UA des *Stellvertreter* von Rolf Hochhuth (*1931), Regie Piscator. Politisches Theater, Einsatz für zeitgenössische Stücke. 1973 bis 1986 Intendant Kurt Hübner (*1916), risikofreudiger Spielplan, avantgardistische Inszenierungen wichtiger Regisseure (Peter Zadek, Klaus Michael Grüber, Hans Neuenfels). Ohne ständiges Ensemble. 1986–90 Intendant: Hans Neuenfels, Intendant Hermann Treusch 1990–92.

Werner Schulze-Reimpell

Freilichttheater

Eine Form des Theaterspiels im Freien (neben z. B. →Straßentheater), in der Spielfläche und Zuschauerraum nicht von einem festen Theaterhaus umgeben werden. Spiele vor landschaftlich bes. Hintergrund, z. B. an Seen oder in Bergschluchten, in der die Natur als dramaturgisches Mittel wirkt, werden auch als →Naturtheater bezeichnet, Spiele in Schloßanlagen, auf Marktplätzen oder Kirchentreppen als Architekturtheater.

Zur Abgrenzung von Theater im Freien in vergangenen Jh. (→Antikes Theater, mittelalterliche Marktplatzaufführungen, →Shakespearebühne, →Garten- und →Heckentheater) definiert E. Stadler das F. ab Mitte des 18. Jh. als ‹neueres Freilichttheater›. Denn erst in dieser Zeit bekam die einen Spielplatz umgebende ‹Natur› einen für die Aufführung eigenständig wirkenden Einfluß: Die ‹Naturstimmung› wurde bewußt wahrgenommen und erlebt. In Deutschland beginnt erst im 19. Jh., mit einer großen Zahl von Neugründungen, ein regelmäßiger Spielbetrieb im Freien. Mit Beginn des 20. Jh. wird das F. von der konservativen Heimatkunstbewegung vereinnahmt. In programmatischen Schriften von F. Lienhard, F. v. Wolzogen u. a. wird es unter Schlagwörtern wie ‹Einfachheit› und ‹Menschwerdung› dem vermeintlich dekadenten, naturalistischen professionellen Stadttheater entgegengestellt. Ernst Wachler gründet 1903 das Harzer Bergtheater bei Thale. Die von ihm eingeführten Neuerungen werden von vielen anderen F. übernommen: der Einsatz von Berufsschauspielern bei allen Aufführungen und der Aufbau eines Repertoiretheaters. 1933 werden die F. im «Reichsbund der dt. Freilicht- und Volksschauspiele» zusammengefaßt und dienen mit den neu eingerichteten

378 Friedrichstadt-Palast

→Thing-Spielen der Untermauerung der Blut-und-Boden-Propaganda. – Nach 1945 treten neben die National- und Heimatspiele und die →Passionsspiele verstärkt Stücke, wie sie auch in den festen Häusern gespielt werden: Klassiker des Welttheaters, Operetten, Schwänke und Opern. Viele F. heute sind, qualitativ sehr unterschiedlich, →Sommertheater mit professioneller Starbesetzung, die für den Spielort in der Regel auch eine Touristenattraktion darstellen.

Schöpel, B.: Naturtheater. Tübingen 1965; Stadler, E.: Das neuere Freilichttheater in Europa und Amerika. Bd. 1. Einsiedeln 1951.

Ute Hagel

Friedrichstadt-Palast

Varieté-Theater in Berlin. – Mit Unterstützung der sowj. Besatzungstruppen eröffnete die ehem. Artistin Marion Spadoni am 17. 8. 1945 das erste Varieté Berlins nach Kriegsende. Das Gebäude am Schiffbauerdamm war 1867 als Markthalle errichtet, später zu einem Zirkus umgewandelt (Renz, Schumann) und 1919 von Max Reinhardt zum Großen Schauspielhaus umgebaut worden (3000 Plätze, Arena-Bühne). Danach wurde es Spielstätte der berühmten Charell-Revuen und nach 1933 unter dem Namen «Theater des Volkes» Operettenbühne. In diesem – teilweise zerstörten – Haus eröffnete Spadoni den «Palast» und begann, Nummernprogramme von beachtenswertem Niveau aufzuführen. 1947 ging der «Palast» in kommunalen Besitz über (Direktor: Nicola Lupo) und erhielt den Namen F.-P. Er wurde das einzige institutionalisierte Varieté der DDR und das leistungsfähigste Haus Europas. Unter den folgenden Leitern wurde das Nummernvarieté verändert und weiterentwickelt, u. a. durch Einführung eines Balletts und Verstärkung der Show-Elemente. Gottfried Hermann als Direktor (1954–61) führte durchgestaltete, revueartige Programme ein und begründete das Kindervarieté des F.-P. Der langjährige Direktor Wolfgang E. Struck (1961–88) setzte die Entwicklung zu Revue und Show (dem sog. Palastical) fort. 1975 begann man mit der *Jugendrevue Nr. 1* neue Wege zu beschreiten, die auch ein junges Publikum für das Varieté gewinnen sollten. – Da eine Renovierung keinen Erfolg hatte, mußte das Haus am 29. 2. 1980 wegen Baufälligkeit geschlossen werden. Am 27. 6. 1981 begann man mit einem Neubau an der Friedrichstraße. Nach interimistischem Spielbetrieb in anderen Berliner Theatern (u. a. «Metropol-Theater») und auf Gastspielen konnte der F.-P. 1984 sein neues Haus beziehen, das als modernste Varietébühne der Welt gilt. Nach mehreren Wechseln in der Leitung des Hauses ist Julian Herrey seit 1992 Intendant. Vorgesehen ist die Überführung des F.-P. aus kommunaler Verwaltung (und Subventionierung) in privatwirtschaftliche Trägerschaft.

Carlé, W.: Das hat Berlin schon mal gesehn. Berlin 1975; ders./H. Martens: Kinder wie die Zeit vergeht. Berlin 1987; Günther, E.: Geschichte des Varietés. Berlin ²1981; Jansen, W.: Das Varieté. Berlin 1990; Moulin, J.-P./Kindler, E.: Eintritt frei – Varieté. Lausanne 1963; Winkler, G. (Hg.): Unterhaltungslexikon A–Z. Berlin 1978.

Wolfgang Beck/Manfred Pauli

Fringe

(→ Freies Theater) Sammelbezeichnung für Theatergruppen und Dramatiker in Großbritannien, die seit Ende der 60er Jahre bestrebt sind, dem etablierten brit. Theaterbetrieb inhaltliche und formale Alternativen entgegenzusetzen. Die Bezeichnung leitet sich her aus dem ‹fringe› des Edinburgh Festival; ‹am Rande› des eigentlichen Festivals wurden experimentelle und sozialkritische Stücke gezeigt. Als Geburtsstätte des F. gilt das 1968 von Jim Haynes gegr. Drury Lane Arts Lab, aus dem Gruppen wie Portable Theatre, The Freehold und → Pip Simmons Theatre Group hervorgingen. Bis Mitte der 70er Jahre gelang es nicht nur, für die damals weit über 100 F.-Gruppen, die überwiegend touring companies waren, ein Netzwerk alternativer Spielstätten wie workers clubs, Schulen, Werkskantinen, arts labs und kleinere Theater, zu denen auch die → Studiobühnen der subventionierten Londoner Theater gehörten, aufzubauen, sondern auch – durch die Gründung des Independent Theatre Council (ITC) 1974 und der Theatre Writers Union (TWU) 1976 – einen wirkungsvollen organisatorischen Rahmen zu schaffen. Seit Beginn der 70er Jahre erhalten viele der F.-Gruppen Subventionen des Arts Council, die jedoch, gemessen an den Summen, die die großen Londoner Theater und die Regionaltheater erhalten, sehr gering sind und zudem ein potentielles Zensurinstrument darstellen.

Inhaltlich und ästhetisch sind die Gruppen und Autoren durchaus heterogen; allen gemeinsam ist jedoch das Bestreben, dem Theater neue Publikumsschichten zu gewinnen und neue, meist sozialistisch geprägte Sichtweisen der Realität zu fördern. So sind Differenzierungen im Bereich des F.-Theaters notwendig, auch wenn sich deren Kategorien zum Teil überschneiden. Zu unterscheiden sind:

a) community theatre und → theatre-in-education
→ Community Theatre, z. B. Inter-Action, London, Bradford College of Art Theatre Group, → Victoria Theatre, Stoke-on-Trent.

b) → performance art-Gruppen

Kennzeichnend ist die Dominanz visueller Eindrücke, häufiges Rekurrieren auf rituelle und spirituale Formen, Mischung von Dadaismus und Happening. Herausragende Gruppen: The People Show und Welfare State.

c) →Politisches Theater

Propagierung einer sozialistischen Alternative, ästhetisch eine Mischung aus populären Unterhaltungsformen und →epischem Theater. Bekannteste Gruppen: CAST, Red Ladder, →7:84, Belt & Braces, Ken Campbell Road Show u. a. Hierher gehören auch feministische und homosexuelle Gruppen wie Monstrous Regiment, The Womens Theatre Group und Gay Sweatshop sowie die Gruppen und Autoren (Mustafa Matura, Hanif Kureishi u. a.) der ethnischen Minderheiten.

d) actor- und writer-based companies

actor-based companies: gekennzeichnet durch kollektive Arbeitsformen, Experimente mit theatralischen Ausdrucksmitteln. Gruppen: The Freehold, Joint Stock.

writer-based companies: Gruppen, deren feste Autoren das F.-Theater maßgeblich mitgeprägt haben, etwa das Portable Theatre mit den Autoren Howard Brenton, David Hare und Snoo Wilson.

Seit Mitte der 70er Jahre wechseln F.-Produktionen und -Autoren häufig in die subventionierten Londoner Theater und in das kommerzielle West End. Seit dieser Zeit hat sich für den F. der Begriff Alternative Theatre durchgesetzt, der die gewachsene Bedeutung dieses Bereichs bezeichnet.

Ansorge, P.: Disrupting the Spectacle: Five Years of Experimental and Fringe Theatre in Britain. London 1975; Bull, J.: New British Political Dramatists. London 1984; Craig, S. (ed.): Dreams and Deconstructions. Alternative Theatre in Britain. Ambergate 1980; Itzin, C.: Stages in the Revolution. Political Theatre in Britain since 1968. London 1980; Klotz, G.: Alternativen im britischen Drama der Gegenwart. Berlin (DDR) 1978; ders.: Britische Dramatiker der Gegenwart. Berlin (DDR) 1982.

Werner Bleike

Fronleichnamsspiele

F. (→ Mittelalter/Drama und Theater des Mittelalters) erscheinen vor allem in Spanien und England. Doch der älteste Text eines solchen Spiels, der zugleich der Urform dieses Phänomens am nächsten stehen mag, ist aus Deutschland überliefert: das *Schmalkaldener* (Innsbrucker) *Fronleichnamsspiel* (Handschrift 1391). Das Fronleichnamsfest wurde von der Kirche erst im 14. Jh. endgültig anerkannt und festgelegt, nachdem vorher bes. in Spanien und den Niederlanden im Volk impulsive Strömungen rege geworden waren gegen die frühe Leugnung der Transsubstantiation durch Berengar und im Glauben an die wirkliche Gegenwart von Christi Fleisch und Blut im Abendmahl-Sakrament. Die Betonung der wirklichen Gegenwart Gottes ist das Grundmotiv der Schmalkaldener Prozession von Propheten und Aposteln: «ich sehe en dort in des pristers henden.» Diese Urform übernahm das 100 Jahre jüngere *Künzelsauer Fronleichnamsspiel* Wort für Wort in seinem ganzen Umfang, weitete sie allerdings stark aus zu einem Zyklus kurzer bildartiger Monologe und Dialoge, woraus eine spätere *Zerbster Fronleichnamsfeier* eine Prozession lebender Bilder zu einer gesprochenen Erklärung machte. Doch können Fronleichnamsspiele auch in anderer Weise entstanden sein. Das *Bozener Fronleichnamsspiel* und sein Ableger, das *Freiburger Fronleichnamsspiel*, erklären sich als Textübernahme aus dem → Passionsspiel, das in Bozen eine lange Entwicklung durchgemacht hatte. So könnte man auch die span. Darbietungen als Übernahme aus älteren anderen Traditionen erklären. Der Ursprung der zahlreichen engl. Spiele bleibt dunkel. War auf dem Kontinent das F. seltene Ausnahme, so zeigt es sich in England als die fast ausschließliche Form. Bestand in Spanien, in den Niederlanden eine starke eucharistische Volksbewegung, so ist davon in England nichts bekannt. Auch dort werden die Spiele in prozessionaler Form dargebracht. Ob die religiös theophorische Prozession und die sehr ausgedehnten dramatischen Prozessionen wie auf dem Kontinent immer eine Einheit bildeten, ist umstritten.

Fricker, R.: Das ältere engl. Schauspiel. Bern 1975; Matern, G.: Zur Vorgeschichte und Geschichte der Fronleichnamsfeier bes. in Spanien (Spanische Forschungen der Görresgesellschaft II, 10). Münster 1962; Michael, W. F.: Die geistlichen Prozessionsspiele in Deutschland (Hesperia 22). Baltimore 1947.

Wolfgang F. Michael

Fronttheater

Zur «Erfüllung der kulturpolitischen Mission» und zur Gewährleistung der «Führungsrolle der dt. Nation» wurde auch das Medium Theater im Dritten Reich konsequent für den Bereich der Wehrmacht und später der Kampftruppen als Propagandamittel eingesetzt (Goebbels: «eine der wichtigsten Voraussetzungen für die Standhaftigkeit und Durchhaltekraft der ganzen Nation in ihrem Schicksalskampf»). Schon ab 1937 werden Soldatenbühnen gegr., die aus Berufsschauspielern bestehen und nur an Wehrmachtsstandorten und Truppenübungsplätzen auftreten; daneben werden auch Landes- und Stadttheater zur Wehrmachtsbetreuung verpflichtet. – Ab Oktober 1939 wird die Einsatzplanung der F. vom

Oberkommando der Wehrmacht (Abteilung Wehrmachtspropaganda), vom KdF, Amt Feierabend, und vom Reichspropagandaministerium übernommen. Letzteres kümmerte sich allerdings vornehmlich um die aufwendige Programmgestaltung bei bes. Anlässen: Für bes. hochrangige Politiker und Militärs wurden entsprechend bekannte und beliebte Künstler verpflichtet. Die einzelnen Armeegattungen hatten ihre eigenen F., z. B. die Kriegsmarine die im September 1939 gegr. «Front-Soldaten-Bühne, Sylt», die Luftwaffe die bes. erfolgreiche «Luftgaubühne Nord-West».

Kaufmann, E.: Medienmanipulation im Dritten Reich. Ziele und Wirkungsabsichten mit dem Einsatz von Theater und Fronttheater. Diss. Wien 1987; Murmann, G.: Komödianten für den Krieg. Deutsches und alliiertes Fronttheater. Düsseldorf 1992.

Ute Hagel / Red.

Fundus

(Lat. fundus = Grund, Boden) Gesamtheit des aufbewahrten Ausstattungsbestands (Kostüme, Requisiten, Dekorationsteile etc.) eines Theaters bzw. die dafür vorhandene Räumlichkeit. In früherer Zeit war der F. zumeist der wichtigste Besitzstand eines Theaterprinzipals. Noch bis zum Ende des 19. Jh. wurde die Ausstattung einer neuen Inszenierung weitgehend aus dem Bestand des F. zusammengestellt.

Manfred Brauneck

Furcht und Mitleid

Seit Lessing Übersetzung der Begriffe ‹Eleos› und ‹Phobos›, die in der aristotelischen Tragödiendefinition die Affekte bezeichnen, die bei der Betrachtung einer Tragödie im Zuschauer ausgelöst werden; es handelt sich dabei um seelisch-leibliche Elementaraffekte, die deshalb richtiger mit ‹Jammer, Ergriffenheit, Rührung› (für Eleos) bzw. ‹Schauder, Schrecken› (für Phobos) wiederzugeben sind.

Schadewaldt, W.: Furcht und Mitleid? (1955), in: ders.: Hellas und Hesperien. Zürich/Stuttgart 1970, S. 194–236.

Bernd Seidensticker

Futuristisches Theater

Mit der Veröffentlichung seines Manifests *Le Futurisme* (Brauneck, S. 178 f) im Jahre 1909 begründete Filippo Tommaso Marinetti (1876–1944) eine Kunstrichtung, die in Malerei und Dichtung, dann auch in der Musik (‹Brutuismus›), vor allem aber im Bereich des Theaters nach der Realitätsflucht der Jahrhundertwende-Kunst eine radikale Wende zur Wirklichkeit vollzog. Der Wortführer des Futurismus und die Künstler, die sich ihm anschlossen (Giacomo Balla, 1871–1958, Fortunato Depéro, 1892–1960, Enrico Prampolini, 1894–1956, u. a.), bejahten uneingeschränkt die Technisierung und Mechanisierung ihrer Welt ebenso wie den Gestus der Politik im Vorfeld des 1. Weltkriegs. In Opposition zur Erstarrung der Verhältnisse in ihrem Heimatland Italien propagierten sie in provokant angelegten theatralen Aktionen sowie in unzähligen Manifesten ein revolutionäres Lebensgefühl, verherrlichten die ‹Vernichtungstat des Anarchisten› und den Krieg, ‹diese einzige Hygiene der Welt›. Schon in seinem ersten Manifest schrieb Marinetti: «Nur im Kampf ist Schönheit. Kein Meisterstück ohne aggressives Moment» (Brauneck, S. 178). Diese Auffassung, die eine Reihe von Futuristen in die Nähe des Faschismus führte, drückt sich in einer ‹Dramatisierung› der Ästhetik aus. Die Simultanität, verstanden als Befreiung vom Verlauf der Zeit, also auch von der Geschichte, und die ‹Bewegung› werden zu beherrschenden Formelementen der künstlerischen Darstellung.

Das Theater entspricht dem simultanen wie dem dynamischen Grundsatz in hohem Maße und rückt deshalb in den Mittelpunkt des Interesses. Nach Auffassung der Futuristen muß allerdings die Wirklichkeitsnachahmung durch eine neuschöpferische Originalität, die historische Rekonstruktion durch die Darstellung des modernen Lebens, abgelöst werden. An die Stelle der ‹längst erschöpften Psychologie des Menschen› soll die ‹lyrische Besessenheit der Materie› treten. In den Entwürfen zu einem →Mechanischen Theater, in dem Gegenstände (Marinetti), mechanische Pflanzen (Depéro) oder ‹dynamische Lichtgestalten› (Prampolini) den Schauspieler ersetzen, erscheinen diese Forderungen am konsequentesten befolgt.

Die einzige Form bestehenden Theaters, die von den Futuristen akzeptiert und sogar als Vorbild genommen wird, ist das *Varieté*. In dem so betitelten Manifest von 1913 (Apollonio, S. 170 ff) betont Marinetti dessen von Konventionen unbelasteten, parodistischen, erheiternden, modern-technischen, körperlich-artistischen, auf Überraschung und Aktivierung des Publikums zielenden Charakter. Das →Varieté ist ein Alternativmodell zu der gesamten klassischen Theaterkultur. Auf eine grundsätzliche Neubestimmung des Bühnengeschehens zielt auch das 1915 von Marinetti zusammen mit Bruno Corra und Emilio Settimelli verfaßte Manifest *Das futuristische synthetische Theater* (Baumgart, S. 178ff). «Wir schaffen das futuristische Theater», verkünden recht selbstbewußt die Autoren; «synthetisch, also sehr kurz» müsse es sein, um im Einklang mit der «raschen und lakonischen futuristischen Sensibilität» zu stehen. An die Stelle von Exposition und Motivierung setzt das F. T. Überraschung und Improvisation. Entstanden durch einen ‹dynamischen Sprung ins Leere der totalen Schöpfung›, ist das Bühnengeschehen ‹alogisch› und ‹irreal› gestaltet. Mit Heftigkeit versetzt es seinen Zuschauer in Begeisterung und ‹schleudert ihn durch das Labyrinth der Sinneswahrnehmungen, die absolut originell und völlig unvorhergesehen zusammengefügt sind›. Zu diesem Zweck muß aber das Drama in allen seinen überlieferten Formen abgeschafft und durch das ‹befreite Wortgefecht›, die ‹extralogische Diskussion› ersetzt werden. Parallel dazu bedarf es einer Revolutionierung des Bühnenbildes. Enrico Prampolini fordert in seiner Programmschrift *Die futuristische Bühnenatmosphäre* (Brauneck, S. 98ff) die Ablösung der traditionellen Guckkastenbühne durch die ‹polydimensionale futuristische Raumbühne›, ausgestattet mit plastischen Leuchtelementen. Neben Prampolinis eigenen Experimenten sind vor allem die von Giacomo Balla bekannt geworden, der etwa bei der Realisierung von Strawinskys *Feuervogel* durch die Ballets Russes (Rom 1917) im Rhythmus der Musik dreidimensionale Körper bewegen ließ, die von innen wechselnd beleuchtet waren.

Apollonio, U.: Der Futurismus. Köln 1972; Baumgart, C.: Geschichte des Futurismus. Reinbek bei Hamburg 1966; Brauneck, M.: Theater im 20. Jh. Reinbek bei Hamburg 1982; Die Maler und das Theater im 20. Jahrhundert – Ausstellungskatalog. Frankfurt/M. 1986.

Peter Simhandl

Gage

(Frz. ‹Pfand›, ‹Lohn›) Entlohnung der Künstler, besonders der Schauspieler, Sänger, Musiker. Bei Spitzenkünstlern wird G. für jedes Auftreten vereinbart, sonst Tages-G., Wochen-G. usw. Die Interessenvertretung der Bühnenangehörigen hat im dtspr. Theater die Monats-G. als Regel durchsetzen können. Die Monats-G. wird für eine Spielzeit, u. U. länger fest vereinbart (vgl. →Engagement), entspricht also praktisch dem Gehalt (Lohn) eines gewöhnlichen Arbeitnehmers.

Horst Schumacher

Gala-Vorstellung

(Ital./span. *gala* – Festkleidung) Festliche →Vorstellung einer Theateraufführung aus besonderem Anlaß.

Monika Sandhack

Gartentheater

Höfische Theaterform des 17. und 18. Jh. Jeweils bei höfischen Festen Errichtung barocker Kulissentheater oder Bespielung von feststehenden Theatern (→Heckentheater und Theater mit steinernen antikisierenden Aufbauten) in Gärten (→Teichtheater). Aufführung von königlichen Pracht-Balletten, Ballett-Komödien, Opern. Beispiele: Steintheater Hellbrunn bei Salzburg (1617); kaiserliche Gärten um Wien (Laxenburg 1661, Schönbrunn 1673, Favorita 1673), Ausstattung von Ludovico Burnacini (1636–1707), später Francesco (1659–1739), Ferdinando (1657–1743) und Giuseppe Galli-Bibiena (1696–1757); Dresden (1664); ‹Römisches Theater›, Eremitage bei Bayreuth (1743); Sanspareil, Ruinentheater bei Burg Zwernitz (1745/48; ‹Lateinisches Theater› Wörlitz bei Dessau (um 1790); Spanien: Aranjuez (1623); Frankreich: Feste von Vaux-Le-Vicomte (1661), Fontainebleau (1661), Versailles (1664); Italien: Giardino Boboli, Florenz.

Baur-Heinhold, M.: Theater des Barock. Festliches Bühnenspiel im 17. und 18. Jh. München 1966; Meyer, R.: Hecken- und Gartentheater in Deutschland im 17. und 18. Jh. Emsdetten 1934.

Ingeborg Janich

Gastspiel

Auftreten eines Theaterensembles oder eines Bühnenkünstlers außerhalb seines Stammtheaters oder Orts. Mit der Entstehung des Berufsschauspielerstands und fester Bühnen mit eigenen Truppen (‹Ensembles›) wird durch Bespielung von Bühnenhäusern in der näheren oder weiteren Umgebung des Stammhauses die wirtschaftliche Basis verbessert und die künstlerische Ausstrahlung gefördert. Schon bei den →Meiningern üblich. Die →Comédie Française unterhält z. B. G.-Ensembles zur Aufführung von frz. Klassikern in Frankreich und außerhalb Frankreichs. Bedeutende Aufführungen werden heute meist durch G. auch auswärtigem (und internationalem) Publikum zugänglich gemacht. G.-

Theater sind einmal feste Häuser, die – vor allem in Mittelstädten – aus Haushaltsgründen kein eigenes Ensemble unterhalten und nur von verschiedenen auswärtigen Truppen (→Landesbühnen) bespielt werden; zum anderen Ensembles, die allenfalls einen Probenort, aber kein eigenes Theatergebäude haben und ausschließlich G. in einem mehr oder weniger großen geographischen Raum geben. – Der einzelne berühmte Schauspieler, der ein G. gibt, wird auf dem Theaterzettel ‹als Gast› (a. G.) vermerkt und integriert sich in der Regel in das am Ort vorgefundene Ensemble für die Dauer einer bestimmten Aufführung.

Horst Schumacher

Gauchotheater

Dramatische Gattung am La Plata Ende des 18. Jh., die ihre Stoffe Kolportageromanen entnahm und mit Gauchomilieu im Zirkusrahmen anreicherte. Unter Einbezug argentin. Tänze (Pericón, Milonga, Payada) und Pantomime wurde diese Gattung über die regionalen Grenzen hinaus in ganz Lateinamerika bekannt.

Sánchez Garrido, A.: Situación del teatro gauchesco en la historia del teatro argentino. In: Revista de la Univ. Nacional de La Plata 2 (1961), S. 9–27; 3 (1961), S. 29–44.

Martin Franzbach

Generalintendanz

(→Intendant) Dienstbezeichnung, dessen Träger mehrere Theater bzw. Theatersparten betreut. Die Bezeichnung wird z. T. auch als Titel von den Bundesländern vergeben.

Dünnwald, R.: Die Rechtsstellung des Intendanten. Köln, S. 33 ff.

Roswitha Körner

Generalprobe

Letzte Probe vor einer →Premiere, findet unter Aufführungsbedingungen meist am Vormittag der Premiere oder am Vortag (z. T. öffentlich) statt (→Proben).

Monika Sandhack

Género Chico

Sammelbegriff für meist musikalisch verbrämte dramatische Kleingattung (→Sainete, →Zarzuela usw.). Geburtshelfer war der Madrider Rechtsanwalt, Journalist und Stückeschreiber Tomás Luceño (1844 bis 1931), der seit 1869/70 gegen die aus Italien importierte Opera buffa und gegen die pompösen Singspiele und Operetten einfache Volkstypen in ihrer bildreichen und deftigen Sprache auf die Bühne brachte. Wegen der Zeitanspielungen auch heute noch kulturhistorisch interessant. Weite Verbreitung durch zündende Schlager in den Konzertcafés und später in eigenen Theatern.

Deleito Piñuela, J.: Origen y apogeo del ‹género chico›. Madrid 1949; Zurita, M.: Historia del género chico. Madrid 1920.

Martin Franzbach

Genossenschaft Deutscher Bühnenangehöriger (GDBA)

Die GDBA ist die gewerkschaftliche Vereinigung der Bühnenkünstler, Techniker und der Verwaltungsangehörigen. Sie ist Tarifpartner mit Hauptsitz in Hamburg.

Geschichte: Als Reaktion auf die bevorstehende Verabschiedung einer Hausordnung wurde auf Initiative des Schauspielers Ludwig Barney die GDBA im Juli 1871 in Weimar gegr. Das Gründungsprogramm forderte die Verwirklichung grundlegender sozialer Sicherungen des Schauspielerstands: die Schaffung eines Konzessionsgesetzes, das die Zulassung als Theaterleiter von bestimmten Eignungsvoraussetzungen abhängig machen sollte, die Schaffung eines Theatergesetzes, das die Bühnenangehörigen vor der Willkür der Bühnenleiter schützen sollte, ferner die Gründung einer Versorgungsinstitution, die Ausarbeitung eines «Contract-Formulars». Im Laufe der Zeit forderte die GDBA die vertragliche Regelung des Verhältnisses zwischen Bühnenmitglied und Bühnenunternehmer (insbes. die Regelung der Probleme wie Fachvertrag, Beschäftigungsanspruch, Saisonverträge, Schutz der Frauen etc.).

Der Kampf um die Verwirklichung der geforderten Rechte erforderte ein zähes Ringen mit dem Kontrahenten, dem →Deutschen Bühnenverein. So kam es 1909 zu einer schweren Auseinandersetzung mit dem DBV, nachdem die Delegiertenversammlung der GDBA dem Entwurf eines Bühnenvertrags nicht zustimmte, obwohl bereits der Zentralausschuß dem Entwurf zugestimmt hatte. Daraufhin wurden alle Verhandlungen abgebrochen. Nach dem 1. Weltkrieg nahmen Bühnengenossenschaft und Bühnenverein ihre Verhandlungen wieder auf. Am 14. März 1919 wurde ein Abkommen geschlossen, das die wichtigsten Vertragsfragen regelte (Kunstfach, Beschäftigungsanspruch, Lohnfortzahlung, Kostümregelung). Dieser Tarifvertrag gilt mit einigen Änderungen noch heute. Im 3. Reich wurde die GDBA aufgelöst (Sept. 1934). Nach dem am 15. Mai 1934 verkündeten Theatergesetz wurden alle Bühnenschaffende Zwangsmitglieder der →Reichstheaterkammer, der ebenfalls die übrigen Gewerkschaften und der Bühnenverein angehörte. Die Mitgliedschaft in der Reichstheaterkammer war Voraussetzung für die Tätigkeit als Schauspieler, Sänger etc. Nach Beendigung des 2. Weltkriegs erfolgte jedoch eine Neu- bzw. Wiedergründung. 1946 fand in Weimar eine erste Begegnung der Landesverbände statt.

Wirkungsweise: Die GDBA vertritt als Gewerkschaft die Interessen ihrer Mitglieder im Rahmen von Tarifverhandlungen und im Rahmen der gesetzlichen Mitbestimmungsregeln im Theateralltag. Für jedes Theater steht ein Obmann zur Verfügung. Zu den noch nicht verwirklichten Forderungen gehört insbes. eine Reform des für den künstlerischen Bereich geltenden Zeitvertragswesens, der Intendantenverfassung bzw. eine Verbesserung der Mitbestimmungsregelungen. Daneben unterhält sie mit der Arbeitgebervereinigung die Paritätische Prüfungskommission (→Deutscher Bühnenverein) und die Bühnenschiedsgerichtsbarkeit.

Barney, L.: Erinnerungen. 1903; Hochdorf, M.: Die Deutsche Bühnengenossenschaft. 1921; Rickert, G.: Direktoren und Schauspieler; Rübel, J.: Geschichte der Genossenschaft Deutscher Bühnen-Angehöriger. Hamburg 1992. Monatl. erscheinendes Verbandsorgan «Bühnengenossenschaft».

Roswitha Körner

Gesamtkunstwerk

Von Richard Wagner (1813–83) in seinen ‹Zürcher Schriften› von 1849/52 (*Kunst und Revolution, Das Kunstwerk der Zukunft, Oper und Drama*) als Signum für sein Kunstwollen entwickelt, hat der Begriff G. in der Theatertheorie und darüber hinaus weite Verbreitung gefunden. Sein Bedeutungsfeld hat sich vielfach gewandelt und ist diffus. Bei Wagner steht er als Leitwort für die angestrebte Wiedervereinigung der seit dem ‹großen Gesamtkunstwerk der griech. Tragödie› auseinandergefallenen Einzelkünste. Durch die Zusammenführung aller Kunstarten: der Tanzmusik, Tonkunst und Dichtkunst, unter Beihilfe der Baukunst, Bildhauerkunst und der Malerei zum ‹wahren Drama› soll das ‹große allgemeine Kunstwerk der Zukunft› entstehen, durch das ‹der Egoist Kommunist, der Eine Alle, der Mensch Gott, die Kunstarten Kunst› werden. Das G. entsteht in ‹freier Genossenschaft der Künstler›, zu der schließlich alle Menschen gehören, so daß das Drama wieder – wie in der griech. Antike – zum schöpferischen Ausdruck des Volks und seiner Religion wird. Im G. stellt sich ‹der Mythos›, dar, in dem sich das Volk ‹selber anschaut›; das G. ist die ‹lebendig dargestellte Religion›, die ‹Religion der Zukunft›.

Bei seinem Versuch, die Tragödie der Antike als Modell eines G. auszuweisen, steht Richard Wagner in der Tradition eines Denkens, das schon bei der Entstehung der Oper im Barock eine große Rolle gespielt hat. Allerdings geht er von der Überzeugung aus, daß sich die Oper auf einem Irrweg befindet, wenn sie eine der Künste, die Musik nämlich, absolut setzt und ihr alle anderen Elemente unterordnet; statt dessen müsse das G. die Künste als gleichrangige integrieren und an den inhaltlichen Zweck binden. Wagners konzeptionelle Überlegungen verdecken die Tatsache, daß auch in seinem Musikdrama ein hierarchisches Verhältnis der Künste herrscht. Auch da kommt der Musik die führende Rolle zu; dramatischer Vorgang und Bild werden zwar als Bestandteil des Ganzen verstanden, aber gleichzeitig nur als Anlaß und Rückhalt der Musik. Bei der Realisierung seiner Musikdramen verlangte Wagner von sich eine hohe Kompetenz und Spezialisierung auf möglichst vielen Gebieten, um so die Einheit der gerade zu seiner Zeit extrem voneinander isolierten, oft in Virtuosentum erstarrten Einzelkünste herstellen zu können. Gelang ihm dies in bezug auf das Sprachliche und Musikalische in einem hohen Maße, so blieb sein Verhältnis zu den visuellen Künsten unentwickelt. Wagner gesteht dem Bühnenbild im G. nur die Funktion eines dekorativen Rahmens zu, verlangt aber doch auch von ihm 'wie von den übrigen Einzelkünsten die Entfaltung zu seiner ‹höchsten Fülle›. Diese ist nach seiner Meinung in der zeitgenössischen Landschaftsmalerei erreicht. So benutzt er für die Inszenierung seiner Musikdramen realistisch gemalte Dekorationen.

Hier setzt die Kritik an, die Adolphe Appia an Wagners Konzept des G. geübt hat und die einen wichtigen Ausgangspunkt der →Theaterreform um 1900 bildet. Mit der Feststellung des Widerspruchs zwischen der Struktur der Musikdramen und den Prinzipien ihrer theatralen, vor allem bildnerischen Realisierung entsprechend den Konventionen der Zeit stellt Appia das von Richard Wagner konzipierte Modell des G. in Frage und schafft den Ansatz für dessen Revision. Diese beruht auf dem Grundsatz, daß die Inszenierung in allen ihren Teilen von den Ausdrucksgesetzen regiert wird, die im ‹Wort-Ton-Drama› durch den Schöpfungswillen des Autors festgesetzt sind. Nur so ist die Einheitlichkeit von Drama und Theater und damit die der Einzelkünste im G. garantiert. Voraussetzung dafür aber ist allerdings die Lösung der Inszenierungsmit-

390 Geschichtsdrama ─────────────────────────────

tel, vor allem der bildnerischen, aus ihren naturalistischen Zusammenhängen.

Während Adolphe Appia die Einheit des G. durch den funktionalen
Zusammenhang zwischen der Musik, der rhythmischen Bewegung des
Darstellers und der vom Prinzip der ‹Praktikabilität› bestimmten Raumgestaltung gewährleistet sieht, macht Gordon Craig das Gelingen der
Synthese von der ‹Genialität› des Regisseurs abhängig. Für Wassily Kan-
dinsky ist dann die Übereinstimmung des ‹inneren Klangs› der einzelnen
Elemente die entscheidende Bedingung ihrer Vereinigung in der →Büh-
nensynthese. Mit ihrer abstrakten Gestalt ist nun die Idee des G. in seiner
konsequentesten Form realisiert und die Voraussetzung geschaffen für
ihre Variation in den verschiedensten Erscheinungsformen wie etwa im
→Happening, in der →Performance und in anderen Phänomenen des
→Experimentellen Theaters.

Appia, A.: Die Musik und die Inscenierung. München 1899; Kunze, S.: Richard
Wagners Idee des Gesamtkunstwerks. In: Beiträge zur Theorie der Künste im
19. Jh. 2 (1972), S. 196–229; Szeemann, H. (Hg.): Der Hang zum Gesamtkunstwerk. Aarau/Frankfurt/M. 1983; Wagner, R.: Gesammelte Schriften und Dichtungen. Bd. 3 u. 4. Leipzig 1872.

Peter Simhandl

Geschichtsdrama

Das G. (auch: historisches Drama) kann nach Elfriede Neubuhr aus zwei-
facher Sicht definiert werden: 1. Vom Stoff ausgehend, «ein Drama mit
einem geschichtlichen, dokumentarisch-quellenmäßig verbürgten Stoff»;
2. vom Gehalt ausgehend, ein Drama, in dem Geschichte gedeutet wird,
wo nicht nur geschichtliche Bilder, ein historischer Bilderbogen dargeboten werden – wie etwa unter dem Einfluß des Historizismus in vielen epigonalen dt. Dramen des 19. Jh., z. B. des Erfolgsautors Ernst Raupach
(1784–1852). Diese beiden Begriffe des G. decken sich nicht immer mit
der dramatischen Produktion. Für viele Forscher ist aber nur das ein G.,
in dem explizit die Geschichtsauffassung des Autors thematisiert wird.
Ein Grenzfall sind Stücke, in denen der Autor eine Reflexion über die
Geschichte dramatisiert ohne ausgesprochenen Bezug auf eine historische Fabel/Begebenheit. So Goethes *Natürliche Tochter* (1803) oder
Hugo v. Hofmannsthals (1874–1929) *Der Turm* (UA 1928), beides fast
abstrakt geführte Reflexionen über den Sinn des Menschen in der Geschichte. Die meisten Forscher schließen auch Dramen mit mythischen
und vorgeschichtlichen Stoffen vom Bereich des G. aus.

Historisch gesehen gilt als das erste überlieferte G. *Die Perser* (UA 472

v. Chr.) des Aischylos (525/24–456/55 v. Chr.), aber aus dem →antiken Theater sind wenig G. tradiert. Im Theater des Mittelalters (→Mittelalter/Drama und Theater des Mittelalters) gehören die G. zur Heilsgeschichte. Einen ersten Höhepunkt erreichte das G. zur Zeit des →Barocktheaters, vor allem im →Elisabethanischen Theater: Shakespeare ist heute noch für viele das Modell des G. schlechthin, auf den man sich in der Theatergeschichte auch stets berufen hat. Im 17., 18. und bes. 19. Jh. war das G. vorherrschend im Vergleich zu Dramen, deren Stoff nur der dichterischen Erfindung zuzuschreiben sind. Trotz gewisser Widerstände im →symbolischen, →expressionistischen und im →absurden Theater hat sich das G. auch im 20. Jh. erhalten, vor allem im →epischen und im →Dokumentarischen Theater.

Nach Walter Hinck «gibt (es) keine für das G. konstitutiven Formen und Mittel, die es mit Notwendigkeit einem der dramaturgischen Systeme zuordneten, sei es der aristotelischen oder der nichtaristotelischen... Dramaturgie». Die eigentliche Problematik (ästhetisch, philosophisch) liegt in der «Umwandlung» (Hegel, *Ästhetik*) des historischen Stoffs durch den Autor. Die prinzipielle Notwendigkeit einer Bearbeitung des geschichtlichen Stoffs wird in der Forschungsdiskussion selbst für das →Dokumentarische Theater als unstrittig angesehen. Werner Keller spricht mit Hebbel (an A. Ruge, 15.9.1852) von dem ‹poetischen Logarithmus›: «das G. muß exemplarisch organisiert sein und typisierend verfahren.» Geschichte als das Typische, das Muster, die Konstante, das Parabolische. Wesentlich sind auch die Zeitbezüge: Die Vergangenheit wird aktualisiert oder die Gegenwart ‹historisiert› (Brecht), oft mit einer utopischen Vision der Zukunft.

Grimm, R./Hermand, J. (Hg.): Geschichte im Gegenwartsdrama. Stuttgart 1976; Hinck, W. (Hg.): Geschichte als Schauspiel. Frankfurt/M. 1981; Keller, W.: Drama und Geschichte. In: ders. (Hg.): Beiträge zur Poetik des Dramas. Darmstadt 1976; Lindenberger, H.: The Historical Drama. Chicago 1975; Martini, F.: Geschichte im Drama, Drama in der Geschichte. Stuttgart 1979; Neubuhr, E. (Hg.): Geschichtsdrama. Darmstadt 1980; Sengle, F.: Das historische Drama in Deutschland. Stuttgart 1974.

Gérard Schneilin

Gewandmeister

Der G. ist für die sach-, termin- und kostengerechte Fertigung der vom Kostümbildner entworfenen Ausstattung verantwortlich. Ihm unterliegt die Erhaltung und Verwahrung des Kostümfundus und – bei wechselndem Spielplan – die Bereitstellung der Kostüme für die jeweilige Aufführung. An kleineren Bühnen übernimmt der G. auch die Aufgaben des Kostümbildners. An den großen Institutionen wird unterhalb der Kostümdirektion das Arbeitsgebiet des G. meist in Männerkostüm, Frauenkostüm, Fundus aufgeteilt.

Dorothea Dieren

Ghettotheater

Einheitliche NS-Richtlinien zum Theaterleben in den osteuropäischen Ghettos gab es nicht. Im allgemeinen wurde ablenkende Unterhaltung gestattet (und gelegentlich sogar durch die Gestapo gefördert), während die Aufführung ‹arischer› Autoren verboten war; die Aufsicht blieb jedoch weitgehend den von der SS eingesetzten örtlichen Judenräten überlassen. Diese versuchten jede Provokation der SS zu verhindern; ihre Zensur konnte sich jedoch keineswegs überall durchsetzen. In den Ghettos Polens entwickelten sich unter diesen Bedingungen drei Grundtypen theatralischer Darbietungen: 1. Kleinbühnen, →Kabaretts, Nachtklubs und Kaffeehaus-Revuen, die dem Unterhaltungsbedürfnis nachkamen, sich zugleich aber durch Vielfalt und Spontaneität allen Zensureingriffen entzogen und so auch zum Ausdrucksort satirischer Kritik werden konnten; 2. die nichtkommerziellen Aufführungen der Selbsthilfeorganisationen, veranstaltet von Hauskomitees, in Freiküchen, als →Kindertheater, mit allgemein-erzieherischer Intention und meist jüdisch-nationalen Inhalten; 3. größere kommerzielle Privattheater, welche die Tradition der Vorkriegszeit fortsetzten, jedoch z. T. bewußt, z. T. gezwungen stärker auf jüdische Themen und Sprachwelt zurückgriffen und dabei auch die Ghettogegenwart nicht aussparten. Diese drei Formen lassen sich ebenfalls in dem deutsch-tschechischen Sonderghetto Theresienstadt nachweisen, wobei dort allerdings die bürgerlich-westeuropäische Kulturtradition eine stärkere Rolle spielte und die kommerzielle Funktion von geringer Bedeutung war.

Theaterarbeit in den Ghettos stand mehr noch als in den Konzentrationslagern vor einem doppelten Dilemma: zum einen, weil sie allein schon durch Kreativität, Geschichtsbezug und Organisationstalent Ausdruck der Selbstbehauptung war, dadurch zugleich aber gegen die SS-Politik der Demoralisierung und Dehumanisierung verstieß und deswegen immer unter der Drohung sofortiger Deportation und Ermordung stand; zum anderen, weil ungeachtet ihres Potentials an Widerstand jegliche kulturelle Tätigkeit sich propagandistisch zur Verschleierung des wahren Ausmaßes von Terror und Vernichtung einsetzen ließ – und zwar innerhalb wie außerhalb der Ghettomauern, nicht zuletzt auch gegenüber den Akteuren selbst.

Adler, H. G.: Theresienstadt 1941–1945. Das Antlitz einer Zwangsgemeinschaft. Tübingen [2]1960; M. Fass: Theatrical Activities in the Polish Ghettos During the Years 1939–1942. In: Jewish Social Studies 38 (1976), p. 54–72; Migdal, U.: Und die Musik spielt dazu. München 1986; Theresienstadt. Red.: R. Iltis u. a. Wien 1968.

Rolf D. Krause

GITIS

(Abk. für Gosudarstvennyj institut teatral'nogo iskusstva im. A. V. Lunačarskogo – Staatliches Lunatscharski-Theaterinstitut. Seit 1991: Theaterakademie GITIS [Teatral'naja akademija].) Moskau, älteste und bedeutendste Theaterhochschule der GUS/ehem. UdSSR, gegründet 1878; war und ist Wirkungsstätte renommierter Regisseure (K. S. Stanislawski, W. I. Nemirowitsch-Dantschenko, M. Knebel, A. Gontscharow, B. Pokrowski u. a.), Schauspieler und Theaterwissenschaftler. Verfügt über drei Fakultäten: Schauspiel, Regie (Drama, Musiktheater, Estrade, Zirkus), Theaterwissenschaft (Theatergeschichte, Kritik, Dramaturgie, Theaterverwaltung). 18 Lehrstühle, Promotionsmöglichkeit, Theaterbibliothek. Die Ausbildung basiert auf dem →Stanislawski-System. Der Schauspielfakultät sind nationale Studios angeschlossen, in denen Ensembles für kleinere Nationalitäten der GUS/ehem. UdSSR ausgebildet werden.

Annelore Engel-Braunschmidt / Red.

Globe Theatre

Das erste G. T. wurde 1599 am südlichen Ufer der Themse (Bankside), etwas westlich von der London Bridge, von der Schauspieltruppe →Lord Chamberlain's Men gebaut. Das G. T. diente als ihre einzige öffentliche Spielstätte bis 1608/09, als Burbage auch die Blackfriars, eine private Bühne innerhalb der Stadtgrenzen Londons, erwarb. In dieser Zeit (1599–1609) wurden 29 Stücke von den Chamberlain's Men – King's Men im G. T. uraufgeführt, davon 16 von Shakespeare, u. a. die großen Tragödien (*Hamlet, Othello, King Lear, Macbeth, Anthony and Cleopatra*), die späten Komödien (*As You Like It, Twelfth Night, Merry Wives of Windsor*) und die sog. Problemstücke (*Troilus and Cressida, All's Well That Ends Well, Measure for Measure*). Das G. T. wurde aus dem Holz von James Burbages Theater gebaut, das 1599 in Shoreditch abgerissen wurde. Aus diesem Tatbestand sowie aus dem Bauvertrag für das →Fortune Theatre (1599) und aus verschiedenen zeitgenössischen Stichen und Berichten können wir die äußere Form und die Größe des G. T. ableiten. Das G. T. war eine ‹runde› öffentliche Bühne, ca. 100 Fuß (= 30,48 Meter) im Durchmesser und ca. 10 Meter hoch mit einer rechteckigen Plattformbühne (ca. 13 × 8,5 Meter), die in den Hof (yard) hineinragte. Mit den drei umlaufenden Galerien und dem Hof war Platz für ca. 2700 Zuschauer (→Shakespearebühne). Im Jahre 1613 brannte das G. T. während einer Vorstellung von Shakespeares *Henry VIII.* bis auf die Grundmauern ab. Auf dem Fundament des ersten G. T. wurde im gleichen Jahr das ‹zweite› G. T. errichtet.

Beckerman, B.: Shakespeare at the Globe. 1599–1609. New York 1962; Hodges, C.: The Globe Restored: a Study of the Elizabethan Theatre. Rev. Ed. London 1968; ders.: The First Globe Playhouse (1599). In: J. Barroll et al. (eds.): The Revels History of Drama in English. Vol. 3. London 1975, pp. 175–196.

J. Lawrence Guntner

Goethe-Theater Bad Lauchstädt

Das einzige original erhaltene Theatergebäude der Goethezeit in Mitteleuropa ist Museum und lebendige Spielstätte zugleich. Seitdem das 1791 gegründete Weimarer Hoftheater unter Goethes Oberdirektion regelmäßig zur Sommersaison in Bad Lauchstädt, dem ‹sächsischen Pyrmont›, gastiert hatte, entstand der Plan für einen Theaterneubau. Goethe gab für die Innenausstattung im Sinne seiner Farbenlehre, für die Bühnengestaltung und die hölzerne Verwandlungsmaschinerie präzise Vorgaben. 1802 wurde das Haus programmatisch mit Goethes *Vorspiel* und mit Mozarts *Titus* eröffnet. Nicht nur die aristokratischen Kurgäste, sondern vor allem auch Akademiker aus Halle sahen in den regelmäßigen Gastspielen aus Weimar (mit Schillers Dramen!) eine «Nationalangelegenheit». Als der Napoleonische Krieg den Badebetrieb einschränkte, gastierten nur noch künstlerisch zweitrangige Gesellschaften in Bad Lauchstädt. – Heute ist das Haus (456 Plätze) von Mai bis Oktober Gastspielstätte für Ensembles, die meist Werke des 18. Jh. und dabei die noch funktionsfähige Bühnentechnik (Gassenbühne, sieben Versenkungen, drei Dekorationen, die auf offener Szene wechseln können) präsentieren.

Meyer, G.: Universität gegen Theater. Hallisches Theater im 18. Jh. Emsdetten 1950; Satori-Neumann, B. Th.: Die Frühzeit des Weimarischen Hoftheaters unter Goethes Leitung. Berlin 1922.

Roland Dreßler

Gorki-Theater (Sankt Petersburg)

(Bol'šoj dramatičeskij teatr im. Gor'kogo, BDT – Großes Gorki-Schauspielhaus, seit 1932 Name Gorkis, ab 1964 Akademisch). Eines der ersten nachrevolutionären Theater, unter unmittelbarer Beteiligung von A. M. Gorki, A. A. Blok und M. F. Andrejewa gegr., am 15. Febr. 1919 mit *Don Carlos* eröffnet, seit 1920 im Gebäude des ehem. Suworin-Theaters an der Fontanka beheimatet. War konzipiert als Pflegestätte des klassischen heroischen Schauspiels, hatte hervorragende Schauspieler, Regisseure und Künstler (unter den letzten M. W. Dobushinski, N. W. Petrow, A. N. Benois). Im Bereich der Tragödie wurden u. a. Werke von Schiller und Shakespeare gespielt (*Die Räuber*, 1919; *Macbeth*, 1919; *Othello*, 1920; *König Lear*, 1920), im Bereich der Komödie Shakespeare, Goldoni, Molière. 1922 Hinwendung zum dt. Expressionismus (Kaiser, 1922, Toller, 1924). 1925 wird mit B. A. Lawrenjows *Aufruhr* das erste Stück der sowj. Dramatik propagiert; später folgen Majakowskis *Wanze* (1929) und *Schwitzbad* (1930), in den 30er Jahren Dramen Gorkis, z. B. *Sommergäste* (1939). 1941 evakuiert, 1943 Rückkehr in das belagerte Leningrad. Entscheidender Aufschwung durch G. A. Towstonogow (1915–1989), der 1956 Künstlerischer Leiter des G. T. wurde. Ausgeprägtes Regietheater, Lakonismus der Ausdrucksmittel, Kraft der inneren Handlung; Inszenierungen klass. russ. Autoren wie Gribojedows *Verstand schafft Leiden* (1962), Gogol, Tschechows *Drei Schwestern* (1965); Werke der Weltliteratur (1969 *Heinrich IV.*), mehrfach Gorki (1959 *Barbaren*, 1966 *Kleinbürger*, 1976 *Sommergäste*) und sowjet. Autoren (A. Arbusow, V. Rosow, A. Wampilow, A. Gelman); erfolgreiche Dramatisierungen russ. Prosa: 1957 *Der Idiot* nach Dostojewski, 1975 *Geschichte eines Pferdes* nach Tolstoi. Seit 1989 Künstl. Leiter; Kirill Lawrow (*1925), Spitzenschauspieler am G. T. seit 1955.

Očerki istorii russkogo sovetskogo dramatičeskogo teatra. Bd. I–III. Moskva 1954–61; Tovstonogov, G. A.: Zerkalo sceny. Bd. I: O professii režissera. Bd. II: Stat'i, zapisi repeticij. Leningrad 1980; ders.: Besedy s kollegami. Moskva 1988.

Annelore Engel-Braunschmidt / Elke Wiegand

Gracioso

Typisch span. Ausprägung der →lustigen Person in der →Comedia des ‹Siglo de Oro›, die durch ihre Rolle Publikum und Bühne miteinander verband. Lope Félix de Vega Carpio (1562–1635) beanspruchte die Erfindung in *La Francesilla* (1598) für sich. Der Grundtyp hat als →Diener seines Herrn folgende Aufgaben: realistisches Gegengewicht zum (meist

Liebes-)Idealismus seines Herrn, Auflösung der Tragik durch Burleske, Spannungselement, Handlungsimitation auf niederer Ebene. Tirso de Molina (1548?–1648) nuancierte den Typ noch, aber bei Pedro Calderón de la Barca (1600–81) ließ sich schon eine gewisse Erstarrung feststellen. Der G. rückte seinem Herrn als Vertrauter näher und gab damit seinen Eigencharakter auf.

Kinter, B.: Die Figur des Gracioso im span. Theater des 17. Jh. München 1978; Ley, Ch. D.: El gracioso en el teatro de la Península (Siglos XVI–XVII). Madrid 1954.

Martin Franzbach

Grand Guignol

(Frz. ‹Großes Kasperle[theater]›) Name für Pariser Kabarett-Theater mit Bevorzugung kraß-veristischer Darstellung von Gewalt, Mord, Vergewaltigung, Geistererscheinungen. Théâtre du G. G. hieß ab 1899 das Pariser Théâtre Salon von Max Maurey. Bis 1962 – der Schließung des G. G. – standen Gruselstücke auf dem Spielplan. – G. G. wird auch die Gattung der Horror- und Schauerdramatik genannt, die mit Stücken wie *Le laboratoire des hallucinations* und *La mort lente* schon Elemente des →Theaters der Grausamkeit nach dem *Manifeste du théâtre de la cruauté* (1832) von Antonin Artaud (1896–1948) vorwegnimmt. Neben Edgar Allan Poe (1809–48) als Vorläufer sind Oscar Méténier und André de Lorde die klassischen Autoren des G. G.

Antona-Traversi, C.: Histoire du Grand Guignol. Paris 1933; Gordon, M.: The Grand Guignol. New York 1988.

Horst Schumacher

Le Grand Magic Circus (et ses animaux tristes)

Frz. Theatertruppe seit 1968, gegründet und geleitet von Jérôme Savary (*1942), besteht aus Artisten, Schauspielern, Musikern. Unter dem Einfluß des →Living Theatre zunächst als Straßentheater in der Provinz. Wichtigste Revuen: *Zartan* (1970), *Robinson Crusoe* (1971), *De Moïse à Mao* (1973), *Les Mélodies du Malheur* (1979). In Koproduktion mit dem Dt. Schauspielhaus Hamburg entstand 1981 das dt.-frz. Melodram über den 1. Weltkrieg: *Weihnachten an der Front.* Seit 1982 teilweise in Béziers (Nouveau Théâtre Populaire), zunehmend und mit großem Erfolg in Paris: Molières *Le Bourgeois Gentilhomme* (1981), Offenbachs *La Péri-*

chole (1984). Im Stil des G. M. C. verbinden sich Elemente aus →Commedia dell'arte, →Grand Guignol, →Zirkusartistik und Showbusiness zu einem musikalischen Spektakel. Alltägliche Trivialitäten, falsche Romantik, Klischees werden zur Schau gestellt, der Lächerlichkeit preisgegeben. Der Rahmen: stilisierte, farbenprächtige Bühnenbilder aus Pappmaché.

Savary, J.: Album du Grand Magic Circus. Paris 1974.

Barbara Müller-Wesemann

Grips Theater (Berlin)

Wichtigstes deutschsprachiges →Kinder- und Jugendtheater der Nachkriegszeit, gegründet als «Theater für Kinder im Reichskabarett» 1966, seit 1974 im eigenen Haus. Gründer, Leiter und Hauptautor ist Volker Ludwig (* 1937); mit *Stokkerlok und Millipilli* beginnt er 1969 das neue, politisch-pädagogisch verantwortliche, emanzipatorische Kindertheater der alltäglichen Erfahrung; 1975 wird das erste Jugendstück gespielt. – G. T. wurde durch seine auf Feld- und Zielgruppenforschungen beruhende Arbeitsmethode, seinen realitäts- und problemnahen Spielstil, seine selbstgeschriebenen Stücke und seine Nachbereitungshefte zur modellbildenden Theaterwerkstatt. Bis 1985 gab es bei 30 Uraufführungen über 500 Nachinszenierungen in 31 Sprachen. Mehrfach erhielten das Theater bzw. seine Autoren den Brüder-Grimm-Preis des Landes Berlin, 1977 den Kulturpreis des DGB. – Neuere Produktionen u. a. das (auch erfolgreich verfilmte) Musical *Linie 1* (1986), *Ab heute heißt du Sara* (1989) und *Himmel, Erde, Luft und Meer* (1991).

Kolneder, W.: Das G. T. Geschichte und Geschichten, Erfahrungen und Gespräche aus einem Kinder- und Jugendtheater. Berlin 1979.

Hans-Wolfgang Nickel

Groteske

(Ital. ‹grotesco›, evtl. von ‹grotta› = Grotte, mit bizarr-verschnörkelten Wandmalereien, in denen Pflanzen-, Tier- und Menschenformen spielerisch ineinander übergehen) Komischer Mischeffekt der Verzerrung des Realen bis zur Skurrilität, zum Alptraumhaften, zur Deformation, durch dessen Ambivalenz beim Zuschauer zugleich Lachen und Grauen erzielt werden. Wird oft durch Vermischung des Menschlichen und Tierischen, z. B. in Ödön v. Horváths (1901–38) Volksstück *Kasimir und Karoline*, 1931, die Zirkusmonster, die trotzdem menschlicher sind als die Men-

398 Groteske

schen, oder durch Erstarrung des Menschlichen im Wahnsinn, zum Mechanischen, z. B. E. T. A. Hoffmanns Figuren, Dürrenmatts Fräulein Dr. v. Zahnd und andere Insassen des Irrenhauses in *Die Physiker*, 1962, oder Claire Zachanassian im *Besuch der alten Dame*, 1956, erzielt.

Ästhetisch eine besondere Bauform, tendiert die G. dazu, in der Literatur- und Theatergeschichte oft zu einer bewegungs- oder gattungsorientierenden und -bestimmenden Form zu werden, so wohl zum erstenmal in der frz. Romantik (→ Romantisches Theater). Victor Hugo (1802–85) definiert das G. als «die reichhaltigste Quelle der Natur an die Kunst»; für Charles Baudelaire (1821–67) sollte die G. «absolute Komik, im Gegensatz zum Gemeinkomischen» sein (*Vom Wesen des Lachens*, 1855). In der Folgezeit hat das G. in Italien einer Autorengruppe ihren Namen gegeben, so dem «teatro grottesco» von u. a. Luigi Chiarelli (1884–1947) oder Pier Maria Rosso di San Secondo (1887–1956), welches z. T. Luigi Pirandello (1867–1936) und den → Pirandellismus beeinflußt hat.

Das G. wird vor allem auch als Totaleffekt in verschiedenen Theaterrichtungen zu diversen Formen der Verfremdung gebraucht, so bei Johann Nestroy (1801–62), Georg Büchner (1813–37), Frank Wedekind (1864–1918) oder Carl Sternheim (1878–1942) und dem jungen Brecht. Es ist aber vor allem im → absurden Theater und in der modernen → Tragikomödie die wohl charakteristische Bauform, so bei Eugène Ionesco (*1912), Samuel Beckett (1906–89) oder Friedrich Dürrenmatt (1921–90). Letzterer definiert das G. philosophisch als einzig mögliche Vision in einer chaotischen, fragwürdig gewordenen und rätselhaften Welt («unsere Welt hat ebenso zur G. geführt wie zur Atombombe») und ästhetisch als «sinnliches Paradox, die Gestalt einer Ungestalt, das Gesicht einer gesichtslosen Welt» (*Theaterprobleme*, 1955), als Mittel zur kritischen Genauigkeit, Erkenntnis und Darstellung.

Für Jàn Kott ist «die G. die alte Tragödie, neu und neuartig geschrieben». Von Shakespeare ausgehend im Hinblick auf Beckett, Ionesco und Dürrenmatt, will Kott in der G. eine ‹Philosophie›, ein ‹Theater› sehen, das der Tragödie entgegengesetzt ist: «Die Welt der Tragödie und die der G. besitzen eine ähnliche Struktur. Die G. übernimmt die dramatischen Schemata der Tragödie und wirft dieselben Grundfragen auf. Nur daß sie andere Antworten darauf gibt... Zwischen der Tragödie und der G. wird derselbe Streit ausgetragen, für oder wider die Eschatologie, den Glauben an das Absolute... Die Tragödie ist das Theater der Priester, die G. – das Theater der Narren» (1970).

Heidsieck, A.: Das Groteske und Absurde im modernen Drama. Stuttgart 1969; Kayser, W.: Das Groteske in Malerei und Dichtung. Reinbek bei Hamburg 1960; Kott, J.: Shakespeare heute. München 1970.

Gérard Schneilin

Group Theatre

Abspaltung (1931) von der →Theatre Guild unter Führung von Harold Clurman, Cheryl Crawford und Lee Strasberg (→The Method). Der Name sollte das kollektive Arbeitsprinzip signalisieren, dem man sich sogleich in einem ‹summer camp› verschrieb. Vorbild: die künstlerische Ensemblearbeit Stanislawskis (→Stanislawski-System). Im Vergleich zum →Broadway und zum proletarisch-revolutionären →Arbeitertheater wollte das G.T. einen ‹dritten Weg› gehen, den der Inszenierung einer radikaldemokratischen sozialen Dramatik. Mit nur mäßigen Inszenierungserfolgen und unter ökonomischen und ideologischen Schwierigkeiten (bei teilzeitlicher Schließung) schlug sich das G.T. bis 1935 durch. Dann erfolgte der Durchbruch mit den Dramen von Clifford Odets (1906–63) *Awake and Sing, Waiting for Lefty* und *Till the Day I Die*. Von den 23 Stücken, die bis zur Auflösung 1941 gespielt wurden, behandelten nur 13 eindeutig politisch-soziale Probleme. Intern scheiterte das G.T. an der Auseinandersetzung um den ‹dritten Weg› zwischen künstlerischem Anspruch und Propaganda, extern an den Finanzierungsproblemen; denn trotz der kurzfristigen New Deal-Konzeption der Kulturförderung blieb Theater in den USA eine privatwirtschaftliche Angelegenheit.

Brüning, E.: Das amerik. Drama der 30er Jahre. Berlin (DDR) 1966; Clurman, H.: The Fervent Years. New York 1945; Fröhlich, P.: Das nichtkommerzielle amerik. Theater. Rheinfelden 1974.

Dieter Herms

Gruppe junger Schauspieler

In Berlin im Herbst 1928 aus ökonomischen und geistig-künstlerischen Gründen gebildetes Kollektiv von weniger bekannten und bestätigten Berufsschauspielern, darunter Renée Stobrawa, Fritz Genschow, Gerhard Bienert, Werner Pledath. In Abgrenzung zur einseitigen Klassikerpflege spielte die G.j.S. ausschließlich politisches, realistisches Zeittheater. Große Erfolge mit *Revolte im Erziehungshaus* (Peter Martin Lampel, UA 1928) und *Cyankali* (Friedrich Wolf, UA 1928). Weitgehende politische Annäherung an die KPD und Gasttournee in der Sowjetunion 1930. Mitwirkung bei der Uraufführung von *Die Mutter* von Brecht (Regie: Emil Burri, 1932). Auflösung der G.j.S. im Jahre 1933.

Hoffmann, L. (Hg.): Theater der Kollektive. 2 Bde. Berlin 1980.

Erich Krieger

Guerilla Theatre

Radikale Form des politischen →Straßentheaters in den USA (1968–71). Der Begriff wurde von der Strategie des Befreiungskampfes des vietnamesischen Volkes auf das Theater übertragen. In seiner strengsten Form bedeutet G.T. zwar eine inszenierte Aktion, die sich aber als Theater nicht mehr zu erkennen gibt. G.T. enthüllt sich nicht, sondern geht schlicht in Realität über. Kennzeichnend ist die Nähe zur Manipulation, die freilich eine nur kurzfristige ist, um durch Aufklärung letztlich mehr Wahlmöglichkeiten einzuräumen. Das G.T. verstand sich als radikale Antwort auf die Gleichgültigkeit der US-Bevölkerung angesichts der Greuel des Vietnamkriegs.

Davis, R.G.: Guerillatheater. In: D. Herms (Hg.): Agitprop USA. Zur Theorie und Strategie des politisch-emanzipatorischen Theaters in Amerika seit 1960. Kronberg 1973; Kohtes, M.M.: Guerilla-Theater. Tübingen 1990.

Dieter Herms

Guignol

(Frz.) Kasperle, Hanswurst als Prototyp des frz. →Handpuppen- und Marionettenspiels. Wird auch für das →Puppenspiel allgemein und für ein einzelnes Stück mit der Hauptgestalt G. gebraucht. G. bezeichnet außerdem einen kleinen Nebenraum der Bühne mit Waschbecken und Spiegel, der sehr schnelles Umkleiden und Korrekturen an Kostüm, Schminkung usw. ermöglicht. Der Name G. geht zurück auf das 1795 nach ital. Vorbild (Polichinelle) von Laurent Mourquet (1769–1844) in Lyon errichtete Marionettentheater, das bald in ganz Frankreich bekannt und nachgeahmt wurde.

Purschke, Hans R.: Die Entwicklung des Puppenspiels in den klassischen Ursprungsländern Europas. Frankfurt/M. 1984/85; Rousset, P.: Théâtre lyonnais de Guignol. 2 Bde. Lyon 1892–95.

Horst Schumacher

Habima

(Hebr. ‹Szene›) Erstes ständiges hebr. Theater. Auf Initiative des Lehrers Nahum Zemach wurde die H. während der Revolution in Moskau gegründet. Nach ihrer Anerkennung als Studio des Moskauer Künstlertheaters (→MChAT) erhielt sie mit J.B. Wachtangow einen der bedeutendsten Schüler Stanislawskis als Leiter (→Wachtangow-Theater). Am

8. 10. 1918 fand die erste Vorstellung mit der Aufführung von vier Einaktern statt. Bestimmend für die endgültige Durchsetzung und für den Ruhm der H. war die Aufführung von An-Skis *Der Dibbuk* unter der Regie Wachtangows. Bis in die Gegenwart wird die H. mit dieser Inszenierung identifiziert. Seit dem 31. 1. 1922 wurde sie über tausendmal gespielt und steht bis in die Gegenwart im Repertoire.

Von Anfang an hatte H. mit existenzbedrohenden Schwierigkeiten zu kämpfen. Jüdisches Theater hatte keine Tradition, wurde von orthodoxen Kreisen grundsätzlich abgelehnt. Hebräisch war die Sprache der Religion, keine lebendige Alltagssprache; folgerichtig gab es in ihr auch keine Theaterstücke. Da nur der gebildete Teil der jüdischen Bevölkerung Hebräisch verstand, gab es kein Publikum, das längerfristig den Bestand des Theaters hätte sichern können. Auf die jiddisch bestimmte folkloristische Tradition griff H. programmatisch nicht zurück, wollte man doch die Kenntnis des Hebräischen verbreitern und ein neues jüdisches Selbstgefühl fördern.

Stanislawski, der selbst an der H. lehrte, und seine Schüler bestimmten lange Zeit den Stil der H. Am 26. 1. 1926 verließ das Ensemble Moskau für eine Europatournee, von der es nicht mehr zurückkehrte. Ende 1927 traf H. in den USA ein, wo ihr dort ungewohnter Theaterstil zu einem finanziellen Fiasko und zur Teilung der Truppe führte. Der größere Teil kehrte nach Berlin zurück, das für einige Zeit ihr Standquartier wurde. Im März 1928 gingen sie für anderthalb Jahre nach Palästina, kehrten noch einmal nach Europa zurück, bevor sie sich 1932 endgültig in Palästina niederließen. In den 30er und 40er Jahren entwickelte sich auch eine für das Theater und seine Bedürfnisse geschriebene hebr. Literatur, die H. ins Repertoire aufnahm. – 1945 wurde ein 1100 Plätze umfassendes Theater für H. in Tel Aviv fertiggestellt. Stagnation in der künstlerischen Entwicklung, mangelnder Nachwuchs, traditionell bestimmtes Repertoire und ständige finanzielle Probleme führten das H. immer wieder in schwere Krisen. 1958 wurde H. Nationaltheater des Staates Israel. Leiter des H. ist Omri Nitzan.

Habima (Einf. v. B. Diebold). Berlin 1928; Hannoch, G. (Hg.): Habima. 1945; Kohansky, M.: The Hebrew Theatre. New York 1969; Levy, E.: The Habima. New York 1979; Richetti, G.: Il Teatro Habima da Mosca a Tel-Aviv. Mailand o. J.; ders./Romano, G.: Teatro in Israele. Mailand 1960; Shakow, Z.: The Theatre in Israel. New York 1963; Le théâtre juif dans le monde. Paris 1930; Zum 25jährigen Bestehen des Habima. Tel Aviv 1945/46.

Wolfgang Beck

Hamburg Ballett

Seit Beginn dieses Jh. kann das Ballett an der Hamburgischen Staatsoper auf eine kontinuierliche Geschichte zurückblicken, die von Tänzer- und Choreographenpersönlichkeiten wie Olga Brandt-Knack, Helga Swedlund, Erika Hanka, Max Aust, Dore Hoyer, Isabel Vernici, Gustav Blank und Peter van Dyk geprägt wurde. Doch erst mit der Berufung John Neumeiers als Ballettdirektor an das Haus in der Dammtorstraße erlangte das Hamburger Ballett überregionale Anerkennung und internationale Bedeutung. 1942 in Milwaukee/Wisconsin, USA, geboren, wurde Neumeier 1963 Mitglied des Stuttgarter Balletts unter John Cranko, avancierte zum Solotänzer und schuf seine ersten Choreographien. 1969 folgte er einem Ruf als Ballettdirektor nach Frankfurt. Von dort holte ihn August Everding 1973 in die Hansestadt. Der Aufbau eines homogenen Ensembles und die Förderung des tänzerischen Nachwuchses gehörte zu Neumeiers erklärten Zielen. Die von ihm 1978 gegründete Ballettschule der Hamburgischen Staatsoper, eine professionelle Ausbildungsstätte, wurde 1989 zusammen mit dem Hamburger Ballett in dem eigens von der Stadt dafür eingerichteten Ballettzentrum untergebracht. In seinem choreographischen Schaffen fühlt sich Neumeier der Tradition verpflichtet. Bereits mit seinem ersten abendfüllenden Werk *Romeo und Julia* zeigte er, daß er darunter nicht Stagnation, sondern produktive Auseinandersetzung mit der gewachsenen Sprache des europäischen Tanzes versteht. Den Menschen in seinen vielschichtigen menschlichen Beziehungen zu erfassen, ihn in seiner Existenz, seinem physischen und metaphysischen Dasein zu begreifen, ist Neumeiers zentrales künstlerisches Anliegen. Häufig greift er auf literarische Vorlagen zurück, ohne den Stoff in seiner Gesamtheit nachzuzeichnen, sondern um die psychologische Motivation der handelnden Figuren herauszuarbeiten. Neben literarischen Balletten wie *Ein Sommernachtstraum*, *Die Kameliendame*, *Don Quichote* oder *Peer Gynt* kommt seinen dramaturgischen Neufassungen der Ballettklassiker *Dornröschen*, *Nußknacker* oder *Schwanensee* ein besonderer Stellenwert zu. Urbilder menschlichen Verhaltens, Archetypen, werden anhand dieser märchenhaften Sujets in einer zeitgemäßen choreographisch-tänzerischen Interpretation und Sichtweise aufgezeigt. In die Reihe der Choreographien, die sich auf die Grundlage einer Musik stützen, gehören u. a. die Mahler-Sinfonien Neumeiers. Die Musik wird für ihn, intuitiv, zum Auslöser von Handlungselementen. Einen ganz eigenen Raum nimmt die *Matthäus-Passion* ein, sein wohl persönlichstes Werk.

Patricia Stöckemann

Hamburger Kammerspiele

Privattheater, 1919 gegründet von Erich Ziegel (1876–1950) als literarisches Forum des Zeittheaters mit jungen Theaterleuten. Eröffnung mit Wedekind-Zyklus. Regisseure Erich Engel (1891–1966), Gustaf Gründgens (1899–1963, auch Schauspieler), Fritz Kortner (1892–1970), Werner Hinz (1903–85); 1926 bis 1928 leitete Ziegel zugleich das Deutsche Schauspielhaus Hamburg. – 1945 Neugründung durch Ida Ehre (1900 bis 1989). 1947 UA *Draußen vor der Tür* (Wolfgang Borchert). Anknüpfung an die Tradition des literarischen Zeittheaters; in den 60er Jahren Wendung zu Unterhaltungstheater. Intendantin 1990–91 Ursula Lingen. – Nach Konkurs 1991 Neugründung. Intendant ab 1992 Stephan Barbarino mit neuem Konzept: Eigenproduktionen und Gastspiele, Marionettentheater, Zusammenarbeit mit der Universität.

Theaterstadt Hamburg. Hg. Zentrum für Theaterforschung. Reinbek 1989.

Werner Schulze-Reimpell / Red.

Hamburgische Dramaturgie

Sammlung dramaturgisch-theoriekritischer Beiträge von Gotthold Ephraim Lessing (1729–81), veröff. von 1767 bis 1769 in bogenweise gedruckten Lieferungen (Buchausgabe in 2 Bden. zu je 52 Stück; neue, kritisch durchgesehene Gesamtausgabe 1958) anläßlich der Gründung des Hamburger Nationaltheaters, als dessen Dramaturg der Autor berufen wurde. Laut Ankündigung urspr. konzipiert als «kritisches Register» aller aufzuführenden Stücke, nach Differenzen mit Schauspielern Übergang zur Erörterung grundsätzlicher Probleme des Dramas und Theaters. Im Zentrum steht die scharfe Kritik am Führungsanspruch der frz. Klassizisten (Corneille, Voltaire, weniger Racine), die – gemessen an der *Poetik* des Aristoteles – mit Shakespeare als Gegenbild konfrontiert werden. Nur äußerlich an den Spielplan gebunden (die eigentliche Berichtszeit umfaßte kaum mehr als drei Monate), schuf Lessing durch Neuinterpretation der aristotelischen Tragödie die theoretischen Voraussetzungen für das bürgerliche Drama nach dem Vorbild Denis Diderots. Die H.D. stellte damit den Entwurf eines dt. →Nationaltheaters dar, das sein Publikum im Sinne des aufgeklärten Bürgertums erziehen sollte.

Berghahn, K. L.: Zur historischen Bedingung und Form von Lessings H. D. In: E. Bahr (Hg.): Humanität und Dialog. München/Detroit 1979, S. 155–164; Clivio, J.: Lessing und das Problem der Tragödie. Zürich 1928; Heitner, R. R.: The Effect of the H. D. In: Germanic Review XXXI (1956), pp. 23–34; Kommerell, M.: Lessing und Aristoteles. Frankfurt/M. 1940; Seeliger, W.: Lessings Kritik an der frz. Klassik. Diss. Kiel 1965; Steinmetz, H.: Der Kritiker Lessing. Zu Form und Methode der H. D. In: Neophilologus LII (1968), S. 30–48.

Monika Sandhack

Hana

Jap., wörtl. ‹Blüte›. – Von Zeami Motokiyo (1363–1443), dem Vollender des →Nô (vor allem in seinen Schriften Kadensho, *Das Buch von der Überlieferung der Blüte*; Kakyô, *Blumenspiegel*; Shikadôsho, *Das Buch vom Weg zur Erlangung der Blüte*) entwickelter theaterbezogener ästhetischer Begriff, der den Moment der durch Übung, Askese und selbstvergessene Hingabe erreichten Vollkommenheit bezeichnet; dabei mag die ‹zeitweilige› Blüte sich der Jugendschönheit (des Schauspielers) verdanken, die ‹wahre› Blüte eröffnet sich erst nach langen Jahren härtesten Trainings beim Durchbruch in die unaussprechlichen Tiefenbereiche der Psyche, der Natur und der Kunst. Aber die ‹Blüte› erblüht nicht ein für allemal, sie kann nur aufgehen in einem ‹Dazwischen›, einem imaginären und höchst gefährdeten Raum, den Schauspieler und Zuschauer gemeinsam schaffen, um in glücklichen Augenblicken der ‹Blüte› zu kurzer Erscheinung zu verhelfen.

Peter Pörtner

Hanamichi

Jap., wörtl. ‹Blumenweg›. – Ein Charakteristikum der →kabuki-Bühne, ein – vom Publikum aus gesehen – nach links versetzter durch den Zuschauerraum zur Bühne führender Laufsteg; wahrscheinlich hat sich das hanamichi aus den *shirasu-bashigo*, den drei Stufen an der Vorderseite der →Nô-Bühne entwickelt. Dem hanamichi (auf das die Zuschauer urspr. die ehemals üblichen Geldgeschenke an einem blühenden Zweig legten, daher ‹Blumenweg›) fällt eine wesentliche dramaturgische Funktion zu, insofern es den Schauspielern höchst spektakuläre Auf- und Abtritte erlaubt, die zudem – nach kabuki-Manier – bis zum Äußersten ausgespielt werden. Eine Versenkungsvorrichtung (*suppon, seri*) im hanamichi disponiert es für Überraschungsauftritte (vor allem von Dämonen und Kobolden). Zudem ermöglicht das hanamichi die Fortsetzung des Spiels, selbst wenn der Bühnenvorhang schon zugezogen ist, etwa in dem populären kabuki-Stück *Kanjinchô*: Am Ende bleibt der Held Benkei allein auf dem hanamichi zurück und tritt dann mit gravitätisch-stilisierten Tanzschritten, den ganzen Zuschauerraum durchquerend, ab.

Peter Pörtner

Handlung

(Griech.: praxis, engl.: story, frz.: action) Gesamtprozeß des auf der Bühne dargestellten Geschehens als Konzentration der Vorgänge, Dialektik zwischen inneren Geschehnissen und äußeren Ereignissen, Tiefenstruktur der dramatischen Entwicklung (→Intrige als oberflächliche Verknüpfung der Episoden).

In der ‹geschlossenen Form› (→Tragödie) kennzeichnet sich die H. durch Einheit (Regel der →drei Einheiten), Ganzheit, Geschlossenheit und Unersetzlichkeit der Teile. Sie ist ein Ausschnitt als Ganzes: Eine breitere Geschichte wird im Moment der Krise erfaßt, zur Auseinandersetzung zwischen Spiel und Gegenspiel konzentriert, zielstrebig steigend zum Höhepunkt (Kollision), dann fallend zur Katastrophe getrieben. Jedes Element der H. (→Akt, Szene) ist lückenlos auf das andere abgestimmt, die Spannung des Zuschauers auf den Ausgang richtend. Die H. widerspiegelt eine höhere, übergeordnete Idee; dadurch Tendenz zur Entstofflichung und Verinnerlichung. Das Prinzip der ‹verdeckten H.› ermöglicht durch Bauformen wie →Botenbericht, →Teichoskopie, Gespräch mit →Vertrauten die Verdrängung der äußeren Vorgänge, sprachliches Duell in →Stichomythien und →Sentenzen die Stilisierung der H. →Parodie dieser Form der H. in modernen Tragikomödien (Bekketts *Warten auf Godot*, 1953; Dürrenmatts *Besuch der alten Dame*, 1956).

In der ‹offenen Form› des Dramas (→tragikomisches Theater, →episches Theater) ist die H. charakterisiert durch Mehrsträngigkeit des Geschehens, ‹Offenheit› des Schlusses, ‹Spannung auf den Gang› (B. Brecht). Diese Momente sprengen das lineare, zielstrebige, pfeilförmige Vorwärtseilen, strukturelle Tendenzen zum Kaleidoskop (Grabbe), zur Kreis-, Kurvenform. Die äußeren Vorgänge sind in die H. einbezogen, dadurch Fülle der epischen Details. Die Gefahr des losen Nebeneinanders der Teile und Segmentierungseinheiten wird vermieden durch konzentrierende Bauformen: Kontrastierung zwischen den Bildern oder innerhalb der Einheiten, Variation oder Repetition derselben und der Motive, verklammernde Metaphorik (z. B. Messer in Büchners *Woyzeck*, 1836), ‹Integrationspunkt›, worin der Sinn des Ganzen in epischer oder lyrischer Kommentarform erscheint (Großmutterlied in Lenzens *Soldaten*, 1776; Großmuttermärchen in Büchners *Woyzeck*; ‹Finnische Erzählungen› in Brechts *Herr Puntila und sein Knecht Matti*, 1941). Zunehmender Hang zur Gestik und Pantomime als Ausdruck der H.

Im Theater des 20. Jh. oft auch Tendenz zur Auflösung des überlieferten Handlungsschemas, zur Ersatz-, Scheinhandlung und Handlungslosigkeit. Die Stücke sind ohne Spannung, Steigerung, Dialektik, die Figu-

406 Handpuppe

ren auf Sprachklischees oder Sprachlosigkeit reduziert: «was passiert, sind nur noch Wörter» (S. Beckett). Sprache als letzte Reduktion der H. – so Samuel Beckett (1906–89), Eugène Ionesco (*1912), Ödön von Horváth (1901–38), Martin Walser (*1927), Harold Pinter (*1930), Franz Xaver Kroetz (*1946) u. a.

Die komische H. weist im Vergleich zu den verschiedenen dramatischen H. spezifische Merkmale auf. Da der konventionelle Komödienschluß als Happy-End formelhaft und austauschbar wirkt, ist der Reiz mehr auf den Spielcharakter und -vollzug verlegt: H. als Kette oder assoziative Reihe von Verwicklungen, Auflösungen, Hindernissen und Umschlägen mit Betonung der Redundanzen, Reprisen und Umkehrsituationen. In der komischen H. der neueren Komödien dann eher Parodie oder Umfunktionierung des ‹guten› Schlusses zu einem offenen, kritischen Ende (wie Stücke von Lenzens *Hofmeister*, 1774, über Sternheims *Bürger Schippel*, 1913, bis zu den ‹Komödien› Ionescos und Dürrenmatts). Hier aber schlägt die komische H. wieder um in die ambivalente H. der modernen →Tragikomödie. Paradox bei Dürrenmatt: «Die schlimmstmögliche Wendung, die eine Geschichte nehmen kann, ist die Wendung in die Komödie» (*Dramaturgische Überlegungen zu den ‹Wiedertäufern›*).

Hinck, W.: Vom Ausgang der Komödie. In: Grimm, R./Hinck, W.: Zwischen Satire und Utopie. Frankfurt/M. 1982; Hübler, A.: Drama in der Vermittlung von Handlung, Sprache und Szene. Bonn 1973; Klotz, V.: Geschlossene und offene Form im Drama. München 1969; ders.: Dramaturgie des Publikums. München 1976; Pavis, P.: Dictionnaire du théâtre. Paris 1980; Pfister, M.: Das Drama. München 1977; Scherer, J.: La dramaturgie classique en France. Paris 1983; Stierle, K.-H.: Text als Handlung. München 1975.

Gérard Schneilin

Handpuppe

Nur aus Kopf, Armen und Kleid bestehende Figur des Puppentheaters, die vom Spieler von unten mit der Hand geführt wird. Die Einfachheit der Puppen, die unkomplizierte Bühnenausstattung und die wegen der begrenzten Größe der Puppen bedingte Nähe zum Publikum machen die H. bes. beliebt für (improvisiertes) Spiel auf Jahrmärkten und auf Straßen sowie als Kinderspielzeug. Sie wird auch als therapeutisches Mittel in der Kinderpsychiatrie, für Lern- und Rollenspiele eingesetzt. – Die Hauptfigur des Spiels mit der H. ist die komische Puppe, seit dem 18. Jh. im deutschsprachigen Raum als ‹Kasper› (→Kasperltheater), in Frankreich als →‹Guignol› bezeichnet. Sie wurzelt in Traditionen des Volksschauspiels, übt Kritik an Autorität und ihren Vertretern. Mehr als bei den übrigen Formen des Puppentheaters sind beim H.-Spiel wegen des unmittelbaren Publikumskontakts Improvisation und Einbeziehung der Zuschauer verbreitete Stilmittel.

Wie bei den meisten Formen des →Puppentheaters ist auch der Ursprung der H. umstritten. Übereinstimmungen in kennzeichnenden Merkmalen haben dazu geführt, eine gemeinsame Herkunft zu vermuten, möglicherweise aus Persien. Seit dem Mittelalter ist die H. in Europa bekannt. Die Beliebtheit der komischen Figur ließ im deutschsprachigen Raum «Kasperltheater» zum Synonym für das Spiel mit der H. werden und führte zugleich zur Abwertung als ‹bloßes› Kinderspiel. Im 20. Jh. gibt es zahlreiche Versuche bekannter Puppenspieler, es von diesem Vorurteil zu befreien und neu zu beleben.

Arndt, F.: Das Handpuppenspiel. Kassel/Basel [6]1976; Eichler, F.: Das Wesen des Handpuppen- und Marionettenspiels. Emsdetten 1937; Fettig, H.: Hand- und Stabpuppen. Stuttgart 1970; Jeanne, P.: Bibliographie des marionnettes. Paris 1926; Keller, Th.: Das Kasperspiel. o. O. 1954; Schreiner, K.: Puppen & Theater. Köln 1980; Technau, S. (Hg.): Zu Besuch in der Kasperbude. Frankfurt/M. 1992.

Wolfgang Beck

Hansatheater

Ältestes noch existierendes →Varieté Deutschlands in Hamburg. 1893 übernahm Paul W. Grell den 1878 erbauten Hansa-Concert-Saal und ließ ihn zu einem Varieté umbauen, dem am 5. 3. 1894 eröffneten H. Durch die Verpflichtung internationaler Stars und insgesamt qualitätvolle Programme wurde das H. zu einem der führenden dt. Varietés und erlangte in erstaunlich kurzer Zeit Weltgeltung. 1919 trat der Sohn des Gründers, Karl Grell, als Juniorchef, 1924 als Leiter an die Spitze des Unternehmens. Er ließ es 1927 zu einem Varieté ohne Gastronomie umbauen, das rund 1500 Personen Platz bot. 1943 bei der Bombardierung Hamburgs wurde auch das H. zerstört. – Als erstes Varieté in den westlichen Besatzungszonen erhielt das H. bereits im August 1945 die Erlaubnis zur Wiedereröffnung. Schon nach wenigen Jahren stand es an der Spitze der bundesrepublikanischen Varietés und überstand als einziges Unternehmen bislang alle ‹Varietékrisen›, die die gesamte Konkurrenz in der ehemaligen Bundesrepublik zum Aufgeben zwangen. Ein erneuter Umbau brachte 1953 das H. techn. auf den modernsten Stand. Es wurde zu einem Verzehr- und Rauchtheater mit 491 Plätzen. In monatlichem Wechsel bietet es heute in einem mehrstündigen Nummernprogramm bedeutende Varietékunst. Seit seiner Gründung fanden über 950 Monatsprogramme statt mit über 45000 Vorstellungen, die weit über 30 Millionen Zuschauer besuchten. Trotz möglichen Popularitätsgewinns verweigert sich das H. bis heute dem Medium Fernsehen.

Berg, R.: Varieté. Hannover 1988; Gedanken, Erinnerungen, Anerkennungen. März 1894–März 1964. 70 Jahre Hansa-Theater. Hamburg 1964; Günther, E.: Geschichte des Varietés. Berlin [2]1981; Jansen, W.: Das Varieté. Berlin 1990.

Wolfgang Beck

Hanswurstiade

Auch Hanswurstspiel. Komische Improvisationen zwischen und nach den Szenen der →Haupt- und Staatsaktionen, entstanden aus dem Pickelhering-Spiel der →engl. Komödianten; Einwirkungen des →Fastnachtsspiels und der →Commedia dell'arte (von Asper bestritten); Hauptfigur: Hanswurst, derb-komische Figur des dt. Volkstheaters und der Wanderbühnen; nachgewiesen seit Anfang des 16. Jh.; populär in Wien (→Alt-Wiener Volksstück) durch Joseph Stranitzky (1676–1726, Kostüm der Salzburger Bauern), Weiterentwicklung der H. durch Gottfried Prehauser (1699–1769) und Felix Kurz-Bernadon (1717–84), später Philip Hafner (1731–64), Fortleben bis 19. Jh. (Ferdinand Raimund 1790–1836; Johann Nestroy 1801–62). In Deutschland Kampf Johann Chr. Gottscheds (1700–66) und der Neuberin (1697–1760) gegen H.; Verbot des Stegreifspiels, Aussterben der H. im norddt. Raum trotz Verteidigung durch Gotthold E. Lessing (1729–81), Justus Möser (1720–94), Johann G. Herder (1744–1803) und des jungen Goethe.

Asper, H. G.: Hanswurst. Studien zum Lustigmacher auf der Berufsschauspielerbühne in Deutschland im 17. und 18. Jh. Emsdetten 1980; Hohenemser, H.: Pulcinella. Harlekin. Hanswurst. Ein Versuch über den zeitbeständigen Typus des Narren auf der Bühne. Emsdetten 1940 (Die Schaubühne, Bd. 33); Rommel, O.: Die Alt-Wiener Volkskomödie. Ihre Geschichte vom barocken Welt-Theater bis zum Tode Nestroys. Wien 1952; Ziltener, A.: Hanswursts lachende Erben. Bern u. a. 1989.

Ingeborg Janich

Happening

Seit Mitte der 50er Jahre entwickelten sich in Japan, USA und Europa gleichzeitig unter verschiedenen Voraussetzungen und Bezeichnungen interdisziplinäre Ausdrucksformen, für die der Oberbegriff H. eingeführt ist. Er geht auf einen Aufsatz des Kunsthistorikers und Malers Allan Ka-

Happening 409

prow (*1927) über Jackson Pollock zurück (veröff. 1958). H. wird von Kaprow aus der Aktionsmalerei und einem erweiterten Collagebegriff (Aktionscollage) abgeleitet. Weitere Anregungen gehen von der Wiederentdeckung des Brutismus (L. Russolo), des Dadaismus (Neo-Dada), des Informel, der Tanzgymnastik, der →Bauhausbühne, des Nouveau Réalisme, der Veröffentlichung der Schriften A. Artauds, der Antiatombewegung und der Beatliteratur (W. Burroughs) aus. – Beim H. beschränkt sich künstlerisches Handeln und Material nicht mehr auf traditionelle Ausstellungs- und Aufführungsorte, Bilder und Kunstobjekte, sondern erstreckt sich auf beliebige Innen- und Außenräume, Stoffe und Gegenstände aller Art (inkl. Nahrungsmittel und Lebewesen) (→Performance).

Seit 1955 fanden Aktionen der jap. Gutai-Gruppe (gegr. 1954) im Freien statt. Dabei wurden die Körper der Künstler zum aktiven Bestandteil von Installationen, die auch das Publikum einbezogen. In New York fanden in der Folge experimenteller Environments und ‹events› 1959 die ersten H. statt: Kaprows *18 Happenings in 6 Parts*, Reuben Gallery/Red Grooms (*1937) *The Burning Building*; *The Ray Gun Spex* (1960) mit H. von Robert Whitman (*1925), Jim Dine (*1935), Claes Oldenburg (*1929) und Al Hansen (*1927) u. a. Carolee Schneemann (*1939) entwickelte «Kinetic Theatre» als Sonderform (*Meat Joy*, 1964). Ab 1960 fanden in New York Festivals statt, in denen neben H. auch die parallele Fluxusbewegung maßgeblich beteiligt war und Musik, Theater, Tanz und bildende Kunst integriert wurden. Das «Festival of Avantgarde» fand z. B. 1963 bis 1969 jährlich statt. Ein Anreger und Lehrer der amerik. H.-Künstler war John Cage (1912–92), der durch seine vom Zen-Buddhismus und europ. Mystik (Meister Eckhart) beeinflußte Kompositionslehre der Unbestimmtheit (indeterminacy) und Zufallsoperationen und mit einem «theatrical event» 1952 am Black Mountain College erste Anstöße gab. In Europa gab es H. und H.-ähnliche Aktionen seit 1958. Das literarische Kabarett der Wiener Gruppe wird als Vorläufer des «Wiener Aktionismus» angesehen. Die Aktionisten Günter Brus (*1938), Otto Mühl (*1925), Hermann Nitsch (*1938) (→Orgien Mysterien Theater) und Rudolf Schwarzkogler (1940–69) veranstalteten von 1962 bis 1971 extreme, körperbezogene Selbstbemalungs-, Material- und Selbstverstümmelungsaktionen mit Simulation von Blutopfern und z. T. tatsächlichen Selbstverletzungen, führten diese als Film- oder Fotoaktionen ohne Publikum durch wie auch als öffentliche Aktionen, die von der Presse zum Skandal gesteigert wurden. – Als Künstler, Vermittler und Herausgeber hat Wolf Vostell (*1932) in Deutschland zur Entwicklung und Verbreitung des H. beigetragen (*Cityrama*, 1961; *In Ulm und um Ulm herum*, 1964). Der frz. Künstler Jean-Jacques Lebel begann aus Kundgebungen anläßlich von Malereiausstellungen (*Anti Process*, 1960) eine Theorie der Aktion zu entwickeln. H.: *Pour conjurer l'esprit de Catastrophe*, 1962; Organisation: Festival de la

Libre Expression, 1964 und 1965. Gustav Metzger (*1926) – Manifeste und Aktionen mit dem Titel «Auto-Destructive» seit 1959 – organisierte 1966 mit John Sharkey das internationale Destruction in Art Symposion (DIAS) in London, an dem über 20 Künstler teilnahmen. Weitere H., Aktionen und Festivals: Milan Knizak (*1940), Aktionen seit 1963, Gruppe «Aktual» gegründet 1964; Fluxusfestival 1966 in Prag; ZAJ-Festivals seit 1964 in Madrid; H. in Budapest, seit 1966.

Obwohl das H. schon mit Kurt Schwitters' →Merzbühne und den Tanz- und Theaterexperimenten Anfang des Jh. möglich war, blieben diese Experimente doch so weit in der Tradition, die nur Tänzern, Schauspielern und Sängern, nicht aber bildenden Künstlern und dem Publikum erlaubte, den Körper in das Werk einzubringen. Auf die komplexen historischen Zusammenhänge und die Umwälzungen in den Aufführungskünsten haben die amerik. Theaterwissenschaftler Michael Kirby und Richard Schechner hingewiesen. Das H. wird als ein wesentlicher Anreger des amerik. experimentellen Theaters angesehen: Trotz der historischen Affinität zum Theater und der Idee des Gesamtkunstwerks ist das H. wesentlich originär, ist eine integrale Aufführungsform, die die Demarkationslinien zwischen Kunst und Leben, Bühne und Publikum, Abbild und Wirklichkeit durchlässig hält. Ein H. ist überall möglich, wo akustische, visuelle und haptische Reize die Sinne ohne Vermittlung durch Sprache ansprechen. H. kennt keine Rollen; Künstler wie Zuschauer sind potentiell darstellerische Elemente (participation). Ein H. ist einmalig, Ort und Ablauf stehen zur Disposition, obwohl Partituren üblich sind. Durch diese formalen Merkmale wird eine «Faktizität» der zeichenhaften und unbestimmten Elemente erzielt, der den symbolischen, gleichnishaften und psychologischen Mechanismen traditioneller Ästhetiken zuwiderläuft.

Becker, J./Vostell, W.: H. Reinbek bei Hamburg 1965; dies.: Aktionen. Reinbek bei Hamburg 1970; H. und Fluxus. Kölnischer Kunstverein. Köln 1970; Kirby, M.: H. New York 1965; Kneubühler, T.: Das H. Geschichte, Theorie und Folgen. In: Werk. Febr. 1971.

Johannes Lothar Schröder

Happy end(ing)

(Engl.) Glückliches Ende, glücklicher Ausgang im Drama, Film, Roman usw., oft unerwartet und nach Überwindung vieler Widerwärtigkeiten und Schicksalsschläge, z. B. der traditionelle Märchenschluß: ‹Und wenn sie nicht gestorben sind, dann leben sie noch heute.›

Horst Schumacher

Haupt- und Staatsaktion

Von Johann Christoph Gottsched (1700–66; *Versuch einer kritischen Dichtkunst vor die Deutschen*, 1730) im Kampf um eine gereinigte, regelmäßige, der frz. → Klassik nachgeahmte Tragödie polemisch verwendete Bezeichnung für die Repertoirestücke der → ‹Englischen Komödianten› und dt. Wandertruppen von Ende 17. bis Anfang 18. Jh. ‹Hauptaktion› bezeichnet die ernsten Stücke im Gegensatz zum possenhaften Nachspiel, ‹Staatsaktion› den historischen oder politischen Stoff. Das Repertoire bestand meist aus Bearbeitungen ausländischer und dt. Barockstücke sowie frz. und span. Tragikomödien oder Opern. Die virtuos-effektbeladene Darstellung mischte, wie später das → Melodrama, das Grausige mit dem Rührenden, das Wunderbare mit dem Derb-Komischen. Von der Struktur her versuchte man, textlich fixierte ernst-höfische Szenen zu kontrastieren mit improvisierten komischen Einlagen satirischer Ausrichtung, worin → Hanswurst und Pickelhering die Hofgesellschaft verulkten und auch die pathetische Spannung aufhoben. Thematisch wurden z. B. gezeigt: Märtyrerleiden und Tyrannenwillkür, Gespensterszenen und Wahnsinnsausbrüche, Hinrichtungen und Hochzeiten. Der Darstellungsstil betonte Affekt- und Gebärdenspiel, Verkleidung und Demaskierung, Requisiteneffekte und Pomp von Szenerie und Kostüm. Anvisiert wurde durch vermeintlichen Einblick in die Affären der höfischen Welt das bürgerliche und plebejische Publikum.

Gérard Schneilin

Hausbühne

Private Bühne, die von Privatleuten für nichtöffentliche Aufführungen in ihren Häusern, Landsitzen und Schlössern eingebaut wurde. Vor allem im 18. Jh. beliebte Einrichtung (Frankreich, Rußland → Leibeigenentheater), die von Sälen ohne Bühneneinrichtung bis zu kleinen Theatern mit entsprechender technischer Ausstattung und Zuschauerräumen bis zu mehreren hundert Personen Fassungsvermögen reichte.

Wolfgang Beck

Heckentheater

Form des →Gartentheaters z. Z. des Rokoko. Das H. ist Teil des repräsentativen Gartens. Perspektivische →Kulissenbühne aus gewachsenen Materialien (Hecken, Baumalleen, Terrassen), amphitheatralischer Zuschauerraum. Aufführung von Komödien, Pastoralen, Singspielen. Ältestes H. in Collodi bei Lucca (1652), weitere H.: Schloß Herrenhausen bei Hannover (1693, noch heute Schauplatz sommerlicher Festspiele), Erlangen (1710), ‹Großer Garten› Dresden (1719), Schloß Mirabell Salzburg (um 1718), Schloß Nymphenburg München (um 1719), Schloß Favorita, Wien (um 1732), Schwetzingen (1770); Frankreich: Tuileriengarten Paris (1668); Schweden: Drottningholm (1785).

Meyer, R.: Hecken- und Gartentheater in Deutschland im 17. und 18. Jh. Emsdetten 1934.

Ingeborg Janich

Heinrich-Heine-Klub (Mexiko)

Mit seiner Theaterarbeit – die neben politischen und wissenschaftlichen Vorträgen, Lesungen sowie Musik- und Filmvorführungen nur einen Teil einer umfassenden Kulturarbeit ausmachte – ist der 1941 von exilierten Schriftstellern (u. a. Anna Seghers, Egon Erwin Kisch, Bodo Uhse) gegr. Klub eher als eine Liebhaberbühne zu bezeichnen. Seine bemerkenswertesten Inszenierungen waren Bechers *Winterschlacht* (1943 unter dem Titel «Hundert Kilometer vor Moskau») und Bruckners *Denn seine Zeit ist kurz*. Ein Kuriosum stellt die Aufführung von Kischs Tragikomödie *Der Fall des Generalstabschefs Redl* dar: unter dem Motto «Das Betreten der Bühne ist Schauspielern und Bühnentalenten strengstens verboten» spielten Alexander Abusch, Bruno Frei, Ludwig Renn, Anna Seghers und Bodo Uhse.

Kießling, W.: Alemania Libre in Mexico. 2 Bde. Berlin 1974.

Jan Hans

Helsingin Kaupunginteatteri

Die finnischen Stadttheater sind im allgemeinen das Ergebnis von kulturpolitischen Kompromissen. In den 40er Jahren dieses Jh. gab es in den meisten Städten eine Arbeiterbühne und ein sog. bürgerliches Theater. Aus wirtschaftlichen Gründen wurden diese beiden Bühnen jedoch zu

Stadttheatern vereinigt, die heutzutage bedeutende städtische Zuschüsse erhalten.

Das Stadttheater Helsinki geht auf das Volkstheater und die Arbeiterbühne zurück, die schon 1948 einen Vertrag über Zusammenarbeit unterzeichneten. Das Stadttheater wurde 1965 offiziell gegründet und zog 1967 in einen Theaterneubau um. Das Stadttheater und seine Vorgängertheater waren eher volkstümlich. Ihr Spielplan umfaßte neue und ältere finnische Dramen, leichte Stücke des Musiktheaters und Neuinszenierungen von Klassikern. In den letzten Jahrzehnten ist das Stadttheater durch seine eigenwilligen Regisseure hervorgetreten. Jouko Turkka (seit 1975 am Stadttheater) brachte umstrittene Klassiker-Inszenierungen auf die Bühne, die heftige Debatten mit dem Publikum, das an gängigere Interpretationen gewöhnt war, zur Folge hatten. In bezug auf die visuellen Lösungen orientierten sich Turkkas Arbeiten an dem sog. →«armen Theater» (Grotowski). Immer wieder hat er in seinen Inszenierungen die Simultantechnik verwendet.

Die Leitung des Theaters übernahm 1983 Ralf Långbacka, der zusammen mit Kalle Holmberg in den 70er Jahren das Stadttheater von Turku zur führenden künstlerischen Bühne des Landes gemacht hatte. Långbacka ist besonders als analytischer Interpret von Brecht und Tschechow hervorgetreten. Kalle Holmberg, den Ralf Långbacka dem Theater neben zwei anderen Regisseuren verpflichtete, hat beeindruckende Inszenierungen der Königsdramen von Shakespeare herausgebracht, in denen eine gnadenlose politische Analyse verbunden ist mit den mythischen Dimensionen der Stücke, Erörterungen der Fragen um Leben und Tod. Långbacka hat in seiner Intendantenzeit versucht, die Routine eines großen institutionellen Theaters aufzubrechen. Vorstellungen wurden auch außerhalb des Hauses gegeben, und neben dem Standardprogramm wird auch in spontan erarbeiteten Inszenierungen zu aktuellen Fragen Stellung bezogen.

Anneli Suur-Kujala

Heroic Tragedy

Auch als Heroic Play oder Heroic Drama bezeichnet, entstand nach der Restauration der brit. Monarchie 1660 und ist eins der für diese Epoche charakteristischen Tragödiengenres. Opernhafte engl. Imitation der frz. tragédie classique, behandelt in erhabenem Stil, meist in heroischen Reimpaaren, hohe, oft idealisierend stilisierte Motive wie Liebe, Ehre und Treue. Höhepunkt der kurzlebigen H. T. lag in John Drydens (1631–1700) Tragödienschaffen um 1670 (Aufführungen von *The Con-*

414 Heroine

quest of Granada). H.T. verband hocharistokratisches Szenarium mit wirkungsästhetischem Appell an ein sich immer mehr ins Bürgertum erweiterndes Londoner Theaterpublikum. Andere Hauptautoren sind Nathaniel Lee (1653–92), Thomas Otway (1652–85) und Elkanah Settle (1648–1724). Die Bühnenwirksamkeit der H.T. schwand bald nach dem immensen Erfolg ihrer Persiflage in des Herzogs von Buckingham (George Villiers, 1628–87) *The Rehearsal* (Aufführung 1671). Die Risiken des hohen Pathos der H.T. haben jeder Wiederbelebung bis heute im Wege gestanden.

Brunkhorst, M.: Drama und Theater der Restaurationszeit. Heidelberg 1985; Righter, A.: Heroic Tragedy. In: Brown, J. R./Harris, B. (ed.): Restoration Theatre. London 1965, p. 135–158; Waith, E. M.: Ideas of Greatness. Heroic Drama in England. New York 1971.

Bernd-Peter Lange

Heroine

(Von griech. ‹heros›) Darstellerin von Theaterheldinnen, der großen tragischen Rollen wie Antigone oder Iphigenie. Ursprünglich Rollenfach, heute als Begriff veraltet, ersetzt durch ‹Tragödin›. H. gilt auch als Spottname für übertrieben pathetische Schauspielerinnen.

Horst Schumacher

Hessisches Staatstheater Darmstadt

Großes Haus, Kleines Haus, Werkstattbühne. Hervorgegangen aus dem 1809 gegründeten hessisch-darmstädtischen Hoftheater. 1819 Theaterbau durch Georg Moller (1784–1852), im Krieg zerstört, Außenmauern erhalten. 1830 bis 1831 Intendant Karl Theodor (von) Küstner, Reorganisationsversuch, vorübergehend Auflösung des Hoftheaters. 1919 Staatstheater. 1920 bis 1924, 1931 bis 1933 Intendant Gustav Hartung (1887–1946), 1927 bis 1931 Carl Ebert (1887–1980), Dramaturg der expressionistische Dramatiker Paul Kornfeld (1889–1942). 1945 Schauspieldirektor Hans-J. Weitz (*1904), 1951 bis 1961 Intendant Gustav Rudolf Sellner (1905–90), 1961 bis 1971 Dr. Gerhard Hering (*1908), wichtigster Regisseur Hans Bauer (1914–70). 1971 bis 1976 Günther Beelitz (*1939), 1976 bis 1984 Kurt Horres (*1932), 1984–91 Dr. Peter Brenner (*1930), ab 1991 Dr. Peter Girth. 1973 Neubau einer Doppelanlage. – In den 20er Jahren wichtiges Theater für die expressionistische Dramatik.

Unter Sellner exemplarische Antiken-Inszenierungen und Einsatz für das absurde Drama.

Hensel, G.: Kritiken. Ein Jahrzehnt Sellner-Theater in Darmstadt. Darmstadt 1962; Kaiser, H.: Vom Zeittheater zur Sellner-Bühne. Darmstadt 1961.

Werner Schulze-Reimpell / Red.

Historie

Oft Historiendrama (→ Geschichtsdrama) genannt, engl. ‹history play› oder ‹history›, bezeichnet vor allem in der dt. Anglistik die Gruppe der historischen Dramen oder Königsdramen Shakespeares sowie allg. die des → Elisabethanischen Theaters. In Episodentechnik geschrieben, gelten sie als Muster für die offene Dramenform und z. T. das → epische Theater.

Kott, J.: Shakespeare heute. München 1970; Ribner, I.: The English History Play in the Age of Shakespeare. London 1957; Sen Gupta, S. C.: Shakespeare's Historical Plays. Oxford 1964.

Gérard Schneilin

Histrio

Lat. Wort für Schauspieler, das ebenso wie die Bezeichnungen für → Maske (persona), Tänzer (ludius) und für Flötenspieler (subulo) aus dem Etruskischen stammt. Der Historiker Livius (7, 2) sieht in seiner spekulativen Konstruktion der Entwicklung des röm. Dramas im ersten Auftreten etruskischer Kulttänzer in Rom (364 v. Chr.) den entscheidenden Anstoß zur Entstehung eines röm. Theaters. Allerdings sind weder ein etrusk. Drama noch ein etrusk. Theaterbetrieb bezeugt, so daß der etrusk. Einfluß auf Entstehung und Entwicklung des röm. Theaters nicht sehr groß gewesen sein kann (→ Antikes Theater).

Blänsdorf, J.: Voraussetzungen und Entstehung der röm. Komödie. In: E. Lefèvre (Hg.): Das röm. Drama. Darmstadt 1978, S. 92–94.

Bernd Seidensticker

Höfisches Theater

H. T. (frz.: théâtre de Cour; ital.: teatro di Corte; engl.: Court Stage) entsteht am Ende des feudalen Zeitalters und am Beginn des Absolutismus. In Frankreich sind die Anfänge am Hof von Burgund, Urbild der

416 Höfisches Theater

Verfeinerung im christlichen Abendland: Das große in Lille von Herzog Johann dem Guten 1453 gegebene Bankett-Schauspiel lieferte den Archetyp des höfischen Schauspiels. Man findet hier also seine konstituierenden Elemente vereinigt: politische Glorifizierung des Herrschers, Teilnahme der Zuschauer am szenischen Spiel: Allegorisierung der dramatischen Rede. Der der feudalen Ordnung nachtrauernde Hof führte sich selbst als Theater vor. Bis zum 18. Jh. setzten sich die allegorischen Vorführungen dieser sozialen Fiktion durch Turniere und Triumphzüge ununterbrochen fort. Schon bevor das Theater im eigentlichen Sinne sich am Hof etablierte, herrscht dort das Spektakulum uneingeschränkt. Man muß nämlich das h. T. (théâtre de Cour) vom Theater am Hof (théâtre à la Cour), dem Gastspiel einer in der Stadt produzierten Aufführung an der Residenz, unterscheiden. In Frankreich verwalteten z. B. die Menus Plaisirs, eine königliche Behörde von Ludwig XIV. bis zur Revolution, die ‹Gastspiele› der Pariser Truppen am Hof und später unter dem Kaiserreich: die frz. Komödianten (Comédiens-Français), die ital. Komödianten (Comédiens-Italiens) und die Oper, deren Schauspieler regelrechte Beamte sind und, was die Oper betrifft, ursprünglich dem Hof angegliedert, nun der Stadt zur Verfügung gestellt sind. Nach diesem ‹frz.› System arbeiteten in der Folgezeit verschiedene Versailles imitierende europ. Höfe, so in Dänemark das →Kongelige Danske Ballet und zahlreiche dt. Staaten. Im Kaiserreich spielt der große frz. Schauspieler Talma (von 1789 bis 1826 tätig) für Napoleon in Saint-Cloud oder in den Tuilerien. Napoleon III. beorderte die Schauspieler noch in seine Sommerresidenz Compiègne wie schon Ludwig XIV. ihre Vorgänger nach Fontainebleau (im Sommer) oder nach Versailles (im Winter). Eine andere Form des h. T. entwickelt sich zur gleichen Zeit, als der Adel nicht mehr an den Ringelspiel-Veranstaltungen teilnahm. Diese verschwanden Ende des 17. Jh. in Frankreich, etwas später in den anderen europ. Ländern: Das private Hoftheater tritt an seine Stelle. Man spielt Komödien im kleinen Kreis. Prinzen und Kurtisanen sind die Schauspieler und zugleich ihre eigenen Zuschauer. Als Ludwig XIV. am Ende seiner Regierungszeit aus Gründen der Frömmigkeit nicht mehr den offiziellen Schauspielen in Versailles beiwohnte, entdeckte man ihn als Zuschauer im Appartement seiner Geliebten Madame de Maintenon bei den von den Prinzen des Hofes gespielten Komödien. Marquise de Pompadour lud ihren königlichen Geliebten Ludwig XV. zu den Schauspielen der «Petits Cabinets» (1747–53), bei denen sie in Versailles oder Bellevue in Komödien oder Ballettopern selbst auftrat. Dasselbe taten später Marie-Antoinette und Königin Ulrike, Schwester Friedrichs II., in Schweden. Die Begeisterung für das Amateurtheater rüttelte die kleinen dt. Höfe auf, an denen man sich langweilte: In Weimar leitete Goethe mit der Herzogin Maria Amalia das ‹Liebhabertheater›, man spielte dort das moderne dt. Repertoirc (Lessing, Goethe), aber auch – Zeichen adliger Distinguiertheit – frz. Stücke in Übersetzung, oft im leichten Stil der komischen Oper, die der Vorstellung entsprach, die man sich zu jener Zeit von den Aufführungen am frz. Hof machte. Gerade Ende des 18. Jh. hatte ja das Schauspiel am Hof (*à la* Cour) fast ganz das höfische Schauspiel (*de* Cour) verdrängt.

Das Schauspiel am Hof hat als intime Zerstreuung des Monarchen fast keine politische Färbung. Anders verhält es sich mit dem höfischen Schauspiel, das vor allem ein Fest der Macht ist, das man seinen Untertanen gibt, um diesen die Größe des Monarchen vor Augen zu führen, und seinen Gästen bei Hochzeiten, Thronbesteigungen u. a., um sie von der Bedeutung des Herrschers zu überzeugen: mythologische Allegorien, in denen der Herrscher zugleich Mars (militärische Macht), Herkules (zivile Macht) und Apollon (kulturelle Macht) verkörpert. Das höfische Schauspiel ist zuallererst allegorisches Theater. Dieses kann dominierend sein wie in den in Whitehall Palace für die britischen Herrscher von Inigo Jones kreierten Aufführungen. *Neptune's Triumph* (1624) von Ben Jonson (1572–1637) ist ein perfektes Beispiel für politische Theaterallegorie, wo Schauspiel, Tanz, Musik und Ausstattung der Vorstellungswelt der Mächtigen schmeicheln.

Die gesamte Entwicklung nahm in Italien ihren Anfang, wo die kleinen, aber durch hochbegabte Künstler außerordentlich glänzenden Höfe seit einem Jh. Vorbild waren für Frankreich, das Deutsche Reich oder England. Nur Spanien entwickelte einen eigenen Stil. Inspiriert durch die Illustrationen zum *Traum des Poliphil* (1499) von Francesco Colonna, dem Werk *Triumphe* von Petrarca, den Zeichnungen von Giulio Romano oder Rosso für Fontainebleau, eroberte die Thematik des Turniers, des Ringelspiels oder des Hofballetts, auch der antikisierenden oder exotischen ‹königlichen Auftritte› die europäischen Höfe zwischen Mitte des 16. und Ende des 17. Jh. In Florenz gaben die Medici, in Rom die Barberini, zusammen mit Mailand, wo Leonardo da Vinci die *Festa del Paradiso* (1483) schuf, Ferrara, Mantua, Modena und Parma das Modell des höfischen Schauspiels ital. Art, das sich zum ‹dramma per musica› entwickelte und die europäische Hofkunst unbestritten bis Ende des 18. Jh. beherrschte. Man spielte ital. Oper am Hof Ladislaus' IV. von Polen (1635 bis 1648) wie in München oder am Wiener Hof, wo Marco Antonio Cesti *Il Pomo d'Oro* (1668) für die Hochzeitsfeier Leopolds I. kreierte und wo Ludovico Burnacini da Bibienna während des darauffolgenden Jh. mit der ital. Kunst des Dekors die Wiener Hofkunst monopolisierte. Paris sah die Geburtsstunde der Oper mit dem ital. Import *Ercole amante* (1662), geschaffen für die Hochzeit des Monarchen Ludwig XIV., und den Florentiner Jean-Baptiste Lully (1632–87), paradoxaler Erfinder des frz. Stils. Dagegen gab Frankreich in der Hofballettkunst Vorbilder für Europa, das an den Ufern der Seine vervollkommnete choreographische

418 Höfisches Theater

Spiel verbreitete sich im höfischen Europa und auf der bürgerlichen Bühne. In der Tat gehen unsere lyrischen und choreographischen Aufführungen unmittelbar auf die höfische Kunst zurück.

Sicher wurde die Sprechtheaterkunst manchmal von der höfischen Gesellschaft bevorzugt; Molière schuf mehrere Stücke für den Hof von Foucquet in Vaux-le-Vicomte oder von Ludwig XIV.: z. B. in den *Vergnügungen auf der Zauberinsel* (Les Plaisirs de l'Ile enchantée), wo man vom 8. bis 13. Mai 1664 in Versailles vier seiner Komödien sehen konnte, darunter die erste Fassung des *Tartuffe*. Das portugiesische Theater entstand am Hof von Johann III. mit *Auto da Visitacão* (1502) von Gil Vicente; Philipp IV. von Spanien ließ in seinem ‹salón de comedias› des Alcazar oder des Buen Retiro (ab 1632) zahlreiche Stücke von Lope de Vega und Calderón spielen; man gab 1611 *The Tempest* von Shakespeare vor Jakob I. in Whitehall und auf den dt. Hofbühnen – zwischen einem Ballett und einer Jagdpartie – *Zaïre* von Voltaire für den Kurfürsten Karl Eugen in Ludwigsburg 1763 oder den *Werther* von Goethe – als Feuerwerk (!) – 1781 in Wien. Das königliche und fürstliche Mäzenat war ein mächtiger Förderer der dramatischen Kunst in einer Zeit, in der die Bühne vom entstehenden modernen Staat kontrolliert, zensuriert und gleichgeschaltet wurde.

Die Oper hingegen entstand am Hof in Italien, und das Frankreich Ludwigs XIV. gab ihr nur eine offizielle Form als ‹tragédie en musique› mit Prolog, worin die Größe des Monarchen besungen wurde. Der Opernstreit (Querelle des Bouffons) 1752 führte in Frankreich zur Bildung zweier feindlicher Lager: nationale Kunst und italienische Oper, aber auch höfische Kunst und Kunst der aufsteigenden neuen Klassen: Lully und Rameau gegen Pergolèse. In Wien unterstützte Joseph II. Salieri stärker als Mozart, in Paris seine Schwester Marie-Antoinette denselben Salieri und Sacchini. Lange Zeit galt die Oper als die Kunst par excellence für die Aristokratie: ritterliche Ideologie, gesuchte Eleganz, eine überlegene Welt gegenüber dem bürgerlichen Geist, ‹opera seria› gegenüber ‹opera buffa›.

Geradewegs hervorgegangen aus dem Turnier oder den Karnevalsfesten, fügte sich das h. T. langsam in die Topographie des Palastes ein. Das erste spezialisierte Theater von Versailles datiert vom Ende der Herrschaft Ludwigs XV. (Théâtre Gabriel, 1770). Aber als das Theater sich in den Palästen einschloß, Hoftheater wurde, begann auch schon sein Niedergang, denn seine Aufgabe war, nach außen die Größe des Monarchen kundzutun. Das h. T. für das Volk wurde schlicht Propagandatheater: Feuerwerk für den gemeinen Mann, zu dem Händel die Musik komponierte (1748 an der Themse anläßlich des Aachener Friedens), königliche Einzüge. Mitte des 18. Jh. trennte sich diese Hofkunst fast ganz vom Theater, das bestenfalls eine Lieblingsbeschäftigung des Herrschers blieb. Schon 1640 hatte Philipp IV. von Spanien im Buen Retiro das ‹Coliseo› geschaffen, zur gleichen Zeit Richelieu in Paris das Theater im Kardinalspalast. Das folgende Jh. erlebte die Blüte von Theatereinrichtungen, deren eifrigste Intendanten die Fürsten selber waren: Friedrich der Große in Berlin, umsichtiger Direktor der Lindenoper (1742), vorher Kurfürst Wilhelm I., Begründer des Kasseler Hoftheaters und der Hofoper 1814. Der Fürst wurde Theaterunternehmer. Im brennenden Moskau unterzeichnete Napoleon die Reform der Comédie Française (1812). Mit dem Einbruch des Nationalismus verschwand das franco-italienische Europa des h. T.; im vorigen Jh. hatte man sogar am Hof von St. Petersburg in dt. Sprache gespielt. Die Nationen traten an die Stelle eines dynastischen Europa; der Kosmopolitismus des h. T. wurde eines der ersten Opfer dieser Entwicklung.

Alewyn, R./Sälzle, K.: Das große Welttheater. Die Epoche der höfischen Feste in Dokument und Deutung. Hamburg 1959; Boswell, E.: The Restoration of Court Stage 1660–1702. Cambridge 1932; Dickens, A. G. (ed.): The Courts of Europe: Politics, Patronage and Royalty. 1400–1800. London 1977; Elias, N.: Die höfische Gesellschaft. Darmstadt/Neuwied 1969; Fähler, E.: Feuerwerk des Barock: Studien zum öffentlichen Fest und reinen literarischen Deutung vom 16. bis 18. Jh. Stuttgart 1974; Mac Gowan, M.: L'art du ballet de Cour en France. 1581–1643. Paris 1963; Magne, E.: Les Fêtes en Europe au XVIIᵉ siècle. Paris 1930; Orgel, St.: The Illusion of Power. Political Theatre in the English Renaissance. Berkeley/London 1975; Sichardt, G.: Das Weimarer Liebhabertheater unter Goethes Leitung. Weimar 1957; Sondernummern Zeitschrift ›XVIIᵉ-Siècle‹: n⁰ 142, 1984 ‹Le théâtre dans les Cours d'Europe (1658–72)›; ‹Dix-Huitième Siècle›, n⁰ 17, 1985 ‹Les spectacles de Cour›.

François Moureau

Hofschauspieler

Ehrentitel, der an Schauspieler an Hoftheatern meist nach langjähriger Tätigkeit verliehen wird und mit einer Pension verbunden ist. Heute →Staatsschauspieler.

Bernard Poloni

Hoftheater

Unter der Bezeichnung H. bzw. Hofbühne wurde gegen Ende des 18. Jh. von den Landesherren Theater in eigener Regie eingerichtet (→Theatersystem). Dies geschah, indem eine →Prinzipalschaft an einem Hof unter Aufsicht eines Hofkavaliers, des sog. Hofintendanten, fest angestellt wurde. Der Intendant, der diese Stellung meist als Auszeichnung für Verdienste auf militärischem Gebiet o. a. erhielt, gehörte dem höheren Adel an (sog. Hofcharge). Ihm zur Seite stand ein artistischer Direktor, meist der ehemalige Prinzipal, der jedoch nur für die künstlerischen Fragen zuständig war. Über die Verantwortung für den Etat übten die Hofintendanten einen erheblichen Einfluß auch auf künstlerische Fragen aus, z. T. zogen sie sogar künstlerische Kompetenzen an sich. Der artistische Direktor sank damit zu einer Art Oberregisseur ab. In Einzelfällen (1865 in Kassel und 1867 in Wien) wurde die Stelle des artistischen Direktors bei dessen Ausscheiden nicht wieder besetzt, sondern dem Intendanten auch die künstlerischen Kompetenzen übertragen.

Bereits Anfang des 19. Jh. erfuhr dieses System eine heftige Kritik von seiten der Theaterleute. Auf Aufforderung des preußischen Kultusministers von Ladenberg im Jahre 1848 legte der Deutsche Bühnenverein die von Eduard Devrient ausgearbeitete Reformschrift «Das Nationaltheater des Neuen Deutschland» vor. Dieser forderte u. a.: Das Theater soll nicht mehr dem Hof, sondern der Staatsregierung bzw. dem Kultusministerium unterstellt sein; Selbstverwaltung des Theaters bzw. Wahl des künstlerischen Vorstands durch das Ensemble; künstlerische Fragen sollen allein in der Hand des Theaterdirektors liegen. Mit dem Mißlingen der 48er Revolution wurden diese Reformüberlegungen beiseite gelegt. Keine dieser Anregungen wurde aufgegriffen oder gar verwirklicht. Das Hoftheaterwesen dauerte bis zum Ende des 1. Weltkriegs und dem Zusammenbruch des Hof- und Adelwesens an. 1918 übernahmen die Länder als Rechtsnachfolger der Landesherren die Hoftheater. Für die Theater, die sich nunmehr Landestheater o. ä. nannten, war jedoch nicht mehr der Regierungschef, sondern der Kultusminister zuständig.

Devrient, E.: Das Nationaltheater des Neuen Deutschland. 1849; ders.: Geschichte der Deutschen Schauspielkunst. 2 Bde. 1848; Dünnwald, R.: Die Rechtsstellung des Theaterintendanten. Diss. 1964; Martersteig, M.: Das Deutsche Theater im 19. Jh. Leipzig.

Roswitha Körner

Horizonte / Festival der Weltkulturen

Triennale, die seit 1979 (im Juni) in Berlin veranstaltet wird. Großangelegter Versuch, die kulturellen Traditionen und Entwicklungen eines ganzen Kontinents in ihrer Vielfalt vorzustellen und den Dialog auf diesem Gebiet anzustoßen bzw. zu intensivieren. Schwerpunkte: 1979 «Afrika südlich der Sahara», 1982 Lateinamerika, 1985 Ost- und Südostasien. Gattungsübergreifender bzw. interdisziplinärer Ansatz: neben

Ausstellungen, Konzerten, Lesungen, Filmreihen, Vorträgen, Diskussionen und (wissenschaftlichen) Colloquien auch Theatergastspiele, so 1979 aus Ghana, Zaire, Kenia, Syrien, Frankreich (mit nigerianischem Stück), 1982 aus Mexiko, Venezuela, Kolumbien, Peru und Brasilien, 1985 aus China, Japan und Indonesien.

«Horizonte»-Magazine der Berliner Festspiele. Berlin 1979.

Andreas Roßmann

Hosenrolle

Darstellung einer Männer- oder Knabenrolle durch eine Schauspielerin (und umgekehrt auch einer Frauenrolle durch einen Schauspieler). Bis Mitte des 17. Jh. gab es nur männliche Schauspieler. Die ersten weiblichen Schauspielerinnen finden sich in Frankreich, Italien, Spanien und England, erst später in Deutschland (→Wanderbühne), bevorzugt in Verwechslungs- und Verkleidungskomödien. Die H. dient der Situationskomik und des Rollentauschs und ist für den Zuschauer als solche erkennbar. Bert Brecht hat die H. als Mittel der Verfremdung im *Guten Menschen von Sezuan* (1943) eingesetzt in der Doppelrolle Shen Te und Shui Ta. Berühmte H.: Juana in Tirso de Molinas *Don Gil von den grünen Hosen,* Rosalinde in Shakespeares *Wie es euch gefällt*; im Musiktheater: Beethovens *Fidelio*, Cherubin in Mozarts *Figaros Hochzeit*, Oktavian im *Rosenkavalier* von Richard Strauss.

Zerzawy, K.: Entwicklung, Wesen und Möglichkeiten der Hosenrolle. Diss. Wien 1951.

Horst Schumacher

Hôtel de Bourgogne

Das Théâtre de l'H. d. B. war das erste wichtige Theater in Paris und das einzige, das im 17. Jh. funktionsfähig war. Es war 1548 von der Confrérie de la Passion erbaut worden, konzipiert für die Aufführungen von Mysterienspielen (viele gleichzeitige Spielplätze für die Handlung, daher große, mit 18,27 m fast die ganze Breite des Saals einnehmende Bühne von 12 m Tiefe). 1598 durften Mysterienspiele nicht mehr aufgeführt werden, die Confrérie stellte das H. d. B. reisenden Schauspielertruppen zur Verfügung. Bevorzugte Spielstätte der comédiens du roi, der troupe royale bis 1680. Das 1634 eröffnete →Théâtre du Marais wurde unter Le Noir und Montdory ernsthafte Konkurrenz (Uraufführung von Dramen Cor-

422   The House

neilles). Auch Molière benutzte das H.d.B. ab 1658. 1680 Fusion zur
→Comédie Française. Bis 1783 wurde das H.d.B. von den ital. Schauspielern benutzt als Hôtel des Comédiens Italiens Ordinaires du Roi, entrete-
nus par sa Majesté (Fassadeninschrift 1716).

Deierkauf-Holsboer, S.W.: Le Théâtre de l'Hôtel de Bourgogne. 2 Bde. Paris
1968–70; Fransen, J.: Documents inédits sur l'Hôtel de Bourgogne. Paris 1927.

Horst Schumacher

The House

Theatergruppe und New Yorker Arbeitszentrum von Meredith Monk,
Tänzerin, Sängerin, Choreographin, Komponistin, Regisseurin und Filmemacherin; eine der bedeutendsten Repräsentantinnen der →Perfor-
mance Art seit Mitte der 60er Jahre. Ihre Wurzeln liegen im Tanz sowie in
der Musik. Ihre Ausbildung in beiden Bereichen begann sehr früh: bereits als Dreijährige nahm sie Tanzunterricht. Am Sarah Lawrence College studierte sie Choreographie, Vokalmusik und Komposition. Nach
Absolvierung des Studiums zog sie 1964 nach New York, wo sie im selben
Jahr ihre professionelle Laufbahn mit *Break* begann. Seitdem hat sie
mehr als 40 Tanz-, Theater- und Musikdarstellungen kreiert, die in etwa
fünf Kategorien eingeteilt werden können: frühe Tanzstücke; große
Stücke für spezifische Räumlichkeiten, z. B. *Juice: A Theatre Cantata* im
spiralförmigen Guggenheim Museum, 1969; Kammerwerke; Gemein-
schaftswerke, z. B. *The Games: Erinnerungen an heute* mit Ping Chong an
der →Schaubühne am Halleschen Ufer, Berlin, 1983, sowie rein musikalische Aufführungen. 1968 gründete sie ihre Gruppe «The House», die
aus einem kleinen Kern von Mitarbeitern besteht, der je nach Bedarf
eines Stücks durch Künstler aus verschiedenen Disziplinen erweitert
wird. Die gemeinschaftliche Erarbeitung von Aufführungen durch die gesamte Gruppe liefert einen wesentlichen Beitrag zu ihrer kreativen Entwicklung.

Meredith Monks Inszenierungen sind nicht am Wort orientiert, sondern zeichnen sich hauptsächlich durch ihren choreographischen und mu-
sikalischen Zusammenhang aus. In den letzten Jahren entwickelte sich
die vokal-musikalische Arbeit zum Schwerpunkt ihres künstlerischen
Schaffens, weil sie glaubt, durch die Stimme einen direkteren Zugang
zum Publikum zu finden. Sie betrachtet die Stimme als eigenständiges
Medium, als ‹eine Welt von immer neuen Entdeckungen›. Trillern,
Jauchzen, Atemstöße, Wiederholung von unvollständigen Wörtern und
Silben und Koloraturen mit ihrer dreieinhalb Oktaven umfassenden
Stimme sind ihre wesentlichen Ausdrucksmittel.

Banes, S.: The Art of Meredith Monk. In: Performing Art Journal 3 (1978), 1, p. 3ff; Koenig, C.: Meredith Monk. Performer-Creator. In: The Drama Review 20 (1976), 3, p. 51ff; Martins, K.: Interview mit Meredith Monk. In: Theater heute 25 (1984), 10, S. 29ff.

Ellinor Woodworth

Humanismus / Drama und Theater des Humanismus

Die Tradition des →Antiken Theaters war im Mittelalter völlig verschüttet. Von lat. Dramatikern kannte man zwar Terenz recht gut und begrenzt auch Plautus und Seneca; sie wurden jedoch nur gelesen. An eine Aufführung dachte man um so weniger, als sich die Auffassung gebildet hatte, Terenz sei nur vorgelesen worden von einem Freund namens Calliopius (er war in Wirklichkeit ein spätantiker Herausgeber von Terenz), die Darsteller hätten die Handlung nur gestikulierend zum Ausdruck gebracht. Erst als in der Renaissance der Terenz-Kommentar des Donatus, Vitruvs Buch über die Architektur entdeckt und gelesen wurden, gewann man ein besseres Verständnis. In Rom belebte man das röm. Theater wieder als die eigene glorreiche Vergangenheit. Der röm. Humanist Pomponius Laetus und sein Kreis veranstalteten die ersten, mehr oder weniger authentischen, zunächst anspruchslosen Aufführungen von Terenz und Plautus nach der Mitte des 15. Jh. Illustrationen in einer Lyoner Terenz-Ausgabe 1493 und ihr folgend Illustrationen in ital. Ausgaben zeigen einfache Türrahmen mit abschließenden Vorhängen. Aus diesen «Häusern» (Mansiones) kamen die Handelnden heraus, hier verschwanden sie wieder. Freilich mögen die Aufführungen später, unterstützt von hoher Geistlichkeit, weit besser ausgestattet worden sein.

Die ersten Versuche in eigenen Werken zeigen ein recht wirres Bild. Verardi aus dem Pomponius-Kreis behandelte in zwei Stücken zeitgeschichtliche Ereignisse, deren dialogisch monologischer Charakter an Rezitationsübungen denken läßt, ohne festes Ortsempfinden in der Szenenfolge. Doch bald lernt man auch, freilich nur sklavisch genau, das antike Lustspiel nachzuahmen. Gallus Aegidius in Rom, Harmonius Marsus und Bartholomaeus Zambertus in Venedig suchen mit meist primitiven Liebeshändeln auf der Einortbühne des Terenz, den antiken Geist lebendig zu machen.

Das stärkste Echo der ital. Stimmen kam aus dem dt. Sprachraum. Ortlosigkeit blieb aber auch hier grundlegend für das Drama der dt. Humanisten, die sowieso ihre Veranstaltungen gern in die Fastnachtszeit legten. Zudem war Verardi der Funke, der in Deutschland das dramatische Interesse entzündete. Frühe Anfänge wie Wimphelings *Stilpho* wurden vorgelesen, nicht dargestellt. Erst 1495 ist die erste Aufführung belegt.

Jacob Locher Philomusus, gerade zurück aus Italien, führte seine *Historia de Rege Francie* auf. Wie Verardi wählte er einen Stoff aus dem Zeitgeschehen und übernahm von Verardi auch den völligen Mangel an Ortsempfinden. Die Darsteller deklamierten Zeilen in einem Irgendwo Nirgendwo wie die Spieler der → Fastnachtsspiele. In der kurzen Zeit vor der Reformation setzt eine wahre Flut solcher Machwerke ein. Locher selbst schrieb noch ein halbes Dutzend weiterer Dramen; dazu kommen Werke von Bebel, Grünpeck, Pinician, Celtis, Vadian, Chelidonius, Sibutus, Stamler, Veus, Hegendorfinus, Kitzscher, verspätet Schottenius. Fast zwei Dutzend Dramen aus allen Teilen Deutschlands ergeben doch wesentlich nur ein Bild: Nie geht man vom reinen Deklamieren zu Handlung über. So bleibt die Bühne, besser der Platz, wo vorgetragen wird, ein Irgendwo Nirgendwo. Der undramatische Charakter zeigt sich auch darin, daß in mehreren Dramen Kaiser Maximilian oder ein anderer Fürst von der Zuschauerbank in die Handlung hineingezogen wird. Jeder Abstand durch die Theaterform fehlt. So muß man sich auch die Darbietungen von Terenz und Plautus mehr als Rezitationsübungen vorstellen denn als wirkliche Aufführungen. Sie setzten nämlich genau um die Jahrhundertwende 1500 ein. Das einzige wirkliche Drama der dt. Humanisten ist Reuchlins *Henno*.

Aus den leichten frz. → Farcen des Spätmittelalters ragt der *Maître Patelin* heraus, eine übermütige Parodie des Rechtslebens. Den Jurist Reuchlin beeindruckte auf seinem frz. Aufenthalt dieses leichtlebige Stück (es wird noch heute wirkungsreich aufgeführt). So wandelt er die mittelalterliche Form: → Simultanbühne, den frz. Text in ein lat. Drama in ganz neuer Bühnenform. Der Jurist wird zur Nebenfigur; der Fokus fällt auf den schlauen Knecht, der an den gerissenen Sklaven der → Palliata gemahnt. Die neue Bühnenform ist die → Sukzessionsbühne. Offensichtlich ist Reuchlin der erste, der diese Form anwendet.

In Frankreich kommt antiker humanistischer Geist weit weniger klar zum Ausdruck. Zwar werden auch dort in dem Jahrzehnt vor der Reformation Dramen von Plautus und bes. von Terenz aufgeführt. Eigene lat. Dramen, wenn man sie so nennen kann, gibt es die Fülle von Ravisius Textor. Sie haben Witz und Beweglichkeit. Aber auch sie bleiben wesentlich Rezitationsübungen. Interessanter scheinen die komischen Vorführungen der → Basoches und die → Soties. Parallel zu den dt. Fastnachtsspielen operieren auch diese Farcen mit den einfachsten szenischen Mitteln.

In England macht sich der Einfluß des Humanismus zunächst wenig bemerkbar. Erst ab 1510 werden Stücke der Palliata aufgeführt. Die eigentlich humanistische Welle von lat. oder engl. Stücken beginnt erst lange nach der Reformation.

Creizenach, W.: Geschichte des neueren Dramas I, II. Halle 1911, 1918; Frikker, R.: Das ältere engl. Schauspiel. München 1975; Michael, W. F.: Frühformen der dt. Bühne (Schriften der Gesellschaft für Theatergeschichte 62). Berlin 1963; ders.: Das dt. Drama des Mittelalters. Berlin 1971.

Wolfgang F. Michael

Hyôbanki

Jap., ‹Schauspielerkritiken›, ‹Schauspielerjournale›. – Erschienen zwischen 1656 und 1887. Auch kabukihyôbanki (‹Kabuki-Journale›), yakusha- oder yarôhyôbanki (‹Schauspielerjournale›), entstanden nach dem Modell der yûjôhôbanki (einer Art Führer durch die Freudenviertel, mit genauen kritischen Bewertungen – ‹hyôban› – der Qualitäten der Freudenmädchen), deren stereotypem Muster sie bis ca. 1680 folgen: literarisch verbrämte Charakterisierungen der (körperlichen) Reize der Kabuki-Schauspieler (z. B. Yakusha no uwasa, *Was man sich über die Schauspieler so erzählt*, 1656, und Yarômushi, *Diese Kerle!* (Schauspieler), 1659. Später werden auch künstlerische Fähigkeiten der Schauspieler kritisch unter die Lupe genommen; schließlich entwickelt sich ein rigides Zensuren- und Bewertungssystem. Mit seinen Klatschgeschichten aus Theaterkreisen und seinen qualitätsvollen Holzschnitt-Illustrationen ist etwa das *Yakusha kuchi jamisen* («Allerlei über Schauspieler», 1699–1735) des Hachimonjiya-Verlags in Kyôto eine theater- und kulturhistorische Fundgrube. Spätere hyôbanki haben den Charakter reiner Theaterreklame.

Peter Pörtner

Hypokrites

Griech. Bezeichnung für Schauspieler; die Bedeutung des Wortes ist umstritten. Neben ‹Antworten› (sc. ‹derjenige, der dem Chor antwortet›) ist auch ‹Deuter›, ‹Erklärer› (sc. der Ereignisse) erwogen worden.

Lesky, A.: Hypokrites (1955). In: ders.: Gesammelte Schriften. Bern 1966, S. 239–246; Patzer, H.: Die Anfänge der griech. Tragödie. Wiesbaden 1962, S. 127 und Anm. 4

Bernd Seidensticker

Hypothesis

Griech.: Grundlage; als dramentechnischer Begriff bezeichnet H. zunächst den Stoff, der dem Drama zugrunde liegt (lat. →argumentum), dann die knappen Einleitungen, die die antiken Philologen seit alexandrinischer Zeit in ihren Editionen dem Text voranstellten. Die H. bestand in der einfachsten Form nur aus einer knappen Inhaltsangabe; der bedeutungsvollere Typus enthielt außerdem Informationen über die Geschichte des Stoffs, zur Aufführung (z. B. Jahr, Erfolg im Theaterwettbewerb, Identität des Chors und des Prologsprechers) und literaturkritische Urteile.

Page, D. L.: Euripides Medea, The text ed. with introd. and comm. Oxford 1961, p. LIIIf.

Bernd Seidensticker

Identifikation

Einswerden des Schauspielers mit seiner →Rolle durch Verwandlung und dadurch Einführung des Zuschauers in den dramatischen Prozeß, in die Ereignisse und Figuren auf der Bühne. – Beruht bei Aristoteles auf der Theorie der →Mimesis und →Katharsis: Furcht- und mitleiderregende Vorgänge bewirken beim Zuschauer durch Anschauung und Einfühlung befreiende Gemütsbewegungen. Auch bei Gotthold Ephraim Lessing grundlegend im Sinne einer vernunftgeleiteten moralischen Besserung des Menschen (→Bürgerliches Trauerspiel). Bei Friedrich Nietzsche das grundlegende dramatische Phänomen (*Geburt der Tragödie*, 1872). Neuerdings bei H. R. Jauss fünf mögliche Modelle der I.: die assoziative, admirative, sympathisierende, kathartische und die ironische I.

Bes. im Theater des 20. Jh. entstand eine Gegenbewegung zur Dominanz der I. und somit auch der →Tragödie, die wesentlich auf I. beruht; so vor allem bei Brecht mit der Theorie der →Verfremdung zwecks Auslösung einer konstruktiven Kritik und Reflexion beim Zuschauer. Friedrich Dürrenmatt (1921–90) spricht von einem Theater der Nicht-I., bes. im Hinblick auf die →Komödie oder →Tragikomödie als «bewußte Theaterform» (1972). Allerdings war die Wirkung der Komödie seit jeher mehr auf Distanz denn auf Einfühlung aufgebaut; selbst bei Aristoteles war die I. schon verbunden mit Elementen der Ironie. Anderseits arbeitet auch der Verfremdungs-Theoretiker Brecht mit Elementen der Einfühlung, z. B. in *Furcht und Elend des Dritten Reiches* (1935–38) oder *Leben des Galilei* (1938–55). Bei einigen Theoretikern ist I. auch als Zuwendung des Bewußtseins des Zuschauers zur Ideologie von Autor und

Stück zu verstehen (Louis Althusser: *Notizen zu einem materialistischen Theater*, 1965). In der modernen Schauspieltheorie finden sich Positionen für und gegen die I. bei Stanislawski und Meyerhold.

Aristoteles: Poetik. Hg. von O. Gigon. Stuttgart 1961; Brecht, B.: Werke. Frankfurt/M. 1967; Dürrenmatt, F.: Dramaturgische Überlegungen zu den ‹Wiedertäufern›. In: Dramaturgisches und Kritisches. Zürich 1972; Jauss, H. R.: Ästhetische Erfahrung und literarische Hermeneutik. München 1977.

Gérard Schneilin

Iffland-Ring

Der Legende nach von August Wilhelm Iffland (1759–1814), dem größten dt. Schauspieler seiner Zeit, getragener Ring, den dieser wie jeder Träger nach ihm dem jeweils besten deutschsprachigen Schauspieler testamentarisch weitervermachen sollte. Der I.-R. dürfte aber nie im Besitz Ifflands gewesen sein. Der ab 1845 am Kgl. Schauspielhaus Berlin wirkende Schauspieler Theodor Döring (1803–78) hat ihn wahrscheinlich mit einem Bildnis Ifflands alt gekauft und die Herkunftsgeschichte erfunden. Döring gab den Ring an Friedrich Haase (1825–1911), Haase an Albert Bassermann (1867–1952), Bassermann an Werner Krauss (1884–1959), Krauss an Josef Meinrad (*1913). – Bassermann hatte den Ring zunächst dem Bundestheater-Museum Wien vermacht, bis der Kartellverband deutschsprachiger Bühnenangehöriger 1954 beschloß, ‹widmungsgemäß› den Ring an Werner Krauss zu verleihen.

Reimann, V.: Der Iffland-Ring. 1962.

Horst Schumacher

Ikria

Griech.: Bänke, Brettergerüste; Bezeichnung für die hölzernen Sitzbänke und Tribünen, die vor Errichtung steinerner Theater an der Orchestra bzw. auf in den Hang gelegten Terrassen aufgestellt wurden. Allgemeine Bedeutung: Sitzplätze im Theater.

Bernd Seidensticker

Illusionstheater

(Lat. ‹illudere› = täuschen) Die Illusion im Theater besteht darin, daß der Zuschauer unter dem Einfluß der Raumdarstellung, der Szenographie, der Regie oder der Figurenbehandlung (→Identifikation) für wahr und wirklich hält, was nur Imitation von Realität ist. Die Illusion ist Komponente jeder Theorie des Spiels und des Theaters.

Unter I. versteht man im engeren Sinne: 1. ein Theater, das durch naturgetreue Ausstattung den Eindruck von Realität erzeugt, so vor allem das →naturalistische Theater; 2. bühnentechn. Effekte zum Vortäuschen von unglaublichen Erscheinungen, z. B. →Barockbühne, →Alt-Wiener Volksstück, →Melodrama; 3. eine kritische Bezeichnung für das Theater des bürgerlichen Zeitalters (1750–1910), wo auf der Bühne (soziale, psychologische) Wirklichkeit vorgetäuscht wird. Der Begriff ist als solcher verallgemeinernd und anfechtbar, bes. was die Epochenabgrenzung betrifft; 4. den programmatischen Gegensatz zur Theorie des →epischen und des →tragikomischen Theaters, also der beiden wesentlichen Formen kritischen Theaters im 20. Jh. – Anti-I. heißt: betonte Erkennbarkeit des Theaters als Theater (Zeigen des Apparats), →Verfremdung, →Parabelform, distanzierende Schauspielweise etc.

Alewyn, R./Sälzle: Das große Welttheater. Reinbek bei Hamburg 1959; Bircher, M. (Hg.): Inszenierung und Regie barocker Dramen. Stuttgart 1976.

Gérard Schneilin

Impresario

Das Wort I. wurde in der zweiten Hälfte des 18. Jh., als feste Theater in den Großstädten entstanden, aus dem Ital. entlehnt. In Wien wurde um diese Zeit das verwandte Wort Theatral-Impresarius benutzt. Mit der zweiten Hälfte des 19. Jh. erfährt das Wort I. einen Bedeutungswandel und wird vorwiegend zur Bezeichnung des Geschäftsführers reisender →Virtuosen oder künstlerischer →Ensembles gebraucht. Heute versteht man unter I. – bzw. unter dem engl. Synonym ‹manager› – allgemein den Theater- und Konzertorganisator, der für einen Star bzw. eine Truppe Verträge vorbereitet und Gastspiele arrangiert.

Bernard Poloni

Improvisation

I. (von lat. improvisus = unvorhergesehen), das spontane, freie Spiel (ohne oder mit nur sehr umrißhaft skizzierter Vorgabe) charakterisiert spezifische Traditionen der Theatergeschichte; vor allem Formen wie →Commedia dell'arte, →Straßentheater, die Kunst der Gaukler, →Narren, Spaßmacher, Straßenverkäufer. Texterfindung, Handlungsgestaltung und Darstellung fallen dabei zusammen.

Zeitweilig zurückgedrängt wird I. durch das fixierte Literaturtheater (mit der Arbeitsteiligkeit Autor–Regisseur–Schauspieler), das über den Text hinaus den bewegungsmäßigen, mimisch-gestischen Ablauf mehr und mehr festlegen will (wenngleich in jeder Aufführung I.-Elemente erhalten bleiben), auch das Extemporieren nicht gestattet bzw. auf bestimmte Momente reduziert. – In jüngster Zeit tritt I. wieder verstärkt auf in Freien Theatergruppen (→Freies Theater) mit ihrem Wunsch nach Spontaneität und direktem Hier-und-Jetzt-Bezug, in Formen von Happening, Straßenaktion, Straßentheater, in Mitspielformen vor allem des Kindertheaters. – I. ist eine wichtige Zwischenform in der Rollenerarbeitung des Schauspielers, ein grundlegendes Mittel jeder Schauspielerausbildung und eine Basisform der Spiel- und Theaterpädagogik.

Ebert, G.: Improvisation und Schauspielkunst. Berlin (DDR) 1979.

Hans-Wolfgang Nickel

Indisches Theater

Die Entwicklung des ind. T. kann in vier Stufen eingeteilt werden: 1. das altind. und klassische Sanskrit-Drama, 2. die Entwicklung des Volkstheaters im Mittelalter, 3. das Theater unter dem Einfluß der Engländer, 4. die Entwicklung nach 1947.

Das altindische Theater
Der Ursprung des ind. T. ist nicht nachweisbar, seine Wurzeln reichen aber mindestens in die vedische Zeit. Der *Rgveda* (2000–1000 v. Chr.) enthält dramatische Dialoge, die wahrscheinlich szenisch aufgeführt wurden. Trotz der Vielfalt von Sprache und Religion ist die Einheitlichkeit des ind. T. durch die gemeinsame Kultur, Mythologie und Geschichte erhalten geblieben. Seine wesentlichen Züge sind Tanz und Musik; das spiegelt sich auch in dem sanskritischen Begriff für Drama: nāṭaka/nāṭya (naṭ = tanzen, eine Rolle spielen) wider. Die älteste ausgebildete Form dramatischer Kunst in Indien wollte religiöse und philosophische Lehren vermitteln. Die Aufführungen fanden hauptsächlich im Tempel und bei

430 Indisches Theater

religiösen Festen statt; die Themen stammten aus den Epen Rāmāyaṇa und Mahābhārata.

Das Wesen und ein Schlüsselbegriff der altind. Kunst ist eine komplexe geistige Aktion, der Rasā. Er besteht aus drei Phasen: 1. dargestellte Emotionen auf der Bühne; 2. ästhetischer Nachklang im Herzen der Zuschauer; 3. der Glückseligkeitszustand geistiger Befreiung. Emotionen wie Liebe und Haß gehen in diesem Prozeß in den Zustand der totalen Gemütsruhe über. Handlung und Charaktere sind nicht wichtig an sich, sondern sind nur Mittel, um einen bestimmten Rasā durch Kombination von Unterhaltung und Belehrung zu bewirken. Da das ind. T. im Religiösen wurzelt und nicht nur der Unterhaltung dient, unterscheidet es sich sowohl in der Absicht als auch in der Darstellungsform von dem neuzeitlichen europ. Theater. Die Rasātheorie ist auf Grund ihrer religiösen Begründung auch nicht vergleichbar mit der aristotelischen Theorie der Katharsis. Im Unterschied zum griech. Theater (→antikes Theater) gibt es im ind. keine Trennung von Tragödie und Komödie, noch gibt es formelle Regeln, die z. B. denen der drei Einheiten (von Handlung, Zeit und Ort) im europ. Theater vergleichbar sind.

Bharata-Nāṭyaśāstra: die erste bekannte Monographie über Dramaturgie in Sanskrit. Auf Bitte von Brahmā, dem Schöpfer der Welt, soll Bharata, der Asket (ca. 2 Jh.), die Form des Dramas vorgeschrieben haben. Bharata schuf den 5. Veda: *Bharata-Nāṭyaśāstra*, der auch den niedrigsten Kasten zugänglich war. *Bharata-Nāṭyaśāstra* schreibt vor, was auf der Bühne dargestellt werden darf: Eine Vorstellung soll dekorativ, unterhaltend, belehrend und erhebend sein. Jedes Drama muß harmonisch enden, was auch das Fehlen des Tragischen im Sanskrit-Theater erklärt. Die Darstellung von Essen, Schlafen und der sexuellen Vereinigung war verboten.

Bharata entwarf vier Formen der Vorstellung, in denen jeweils 1. Rede und Poesie, 2. Tanz und Musik, 3. Emotionen, 4. Handlung überwiegen, und zwei Typen der Vorstellung: 1. Sukumara (= sanft und empfindlich), 2. Aviddhā (= wühlend, kriegerisch), Frauen nehmen hier nicht teil. Er kennt zwei Tanztypen: 1. Lāsya (= zarter Liebestanz der Frauen), 2. Tāṇḍava (= gewaltsamer, rigoroser Tanz der Männer), und unterscheidet die dramatischen Formen nach der Handlung und nach der Herkunft der Helden sowie «vollständige» Dramen und Einakter. Es werden neun Typen von Heldinnen, drei Arten von Gestik und verschiedene Mudrās (= Gestik mit Fingern) festgelegt.

Das *Bharata-Nāṭyaśāstra* setzt bereits die Existenz vieler Dramen voraus. Als Themenkreise schreibt Bharata «Lokacarita» (= Verhaltensweise der Menschen) und Nachahmung der Welt vor, die dann nach den Regeln des Bharata gestaltet und dargestellt wurden. So kann ein Schauspieler auf der flachen Bühne einen Hügel hinaufklettern, mit leeren

Händen Blumen pflücken oder auf einem Pferd reiten, das es nicht gibt. Die Regeln des Bharata sind trotz politischer Umwälzungen einheitlich auf dem ganzen Subkontinent erhalten geblieben. So beginnt auch heute noch überall in Indien ein Volksdrama mit einem Prolog (Pūrvaraṅga), wie von Bharata vorgeschrieben. Das *Bharata-Nāṭyaśāstra* gab dem ind. Drama nicht nur Funktion und Form, sondern wies ihm auch eine bestimmte Stellung in der Geschichte und im kulturellen Leben Indiens zu.

Wichtige Elemente und Begriffe des altindischen Theaters

Sūtradhār: aus Sanskrit ‹sūtra› (= Faden) und ‹dhāra› (= Halter): der Fadenhalter, der beim Puppenspiel alle Figurenbewegungen kontrolliert, singt und mit Stimmveränderungen spricht. – Nāṭyācārya: Bezeichnung für Dichter, Regisseure, Bühnengestalter, Musiker, Maler und vor allem den Sūtradhār, der den Schauspielern Hinweise gibt, sie belehrt, die Gruppe organisiert und die Vorstellungen leitet. Er ist verantwortlich für den Erfolg der Darstellung, soll in allen Wissenschaften und Künsten bewandert sein, Länder und Gebräuche, Sprachen und Kleidung der Leute kennen und Dramaturgie, Musik und Astrologie studiert haben. Außerdem soll er intelligent, ein Dichter und ein rechtschaffener Mensch sein. Der Nāṭyācārya ist Hauptschauspieler und Leiter der Gruppe.

Vidūṣaka: →der Narr, der wichtigste Charakter im Sanskrit-Drama. Er ist Brāhmane und wird als kahlköpfig beschrieben, buckelig, zwergwüchsig, mit vorspringenden Zähnen, verzerrtem Gesicht, gelben Augenbrauen und schäbig gekleidet. Seine Erscheinung und sein Gang sollen Gelächter hervorrufen. Er ist der treue Freund und Begleiter des Helden, hilft ihm in schwierigen Situationen; er wirkt geschickt und flink.

Pūrvaraṅga: Vorspiel, eine Art Prolog. Der Zweck des Pūrvaraṅga ist die Einführung in das Thema, die Beseitigung aller kontemplativen Hindernisse durch Gebete, Erflehen der Gnade und des Segens Gottes, Lob des Königs und Danksagung, vor allem Erzeugung einer günstigen Stimmung im Publikum. Musik soll dem Zuschauer bei der Verwirklichung der Rasas helfen. Der Pūrvaraṅga ist aber kein Teil des eigentlichen Dramas und muß zeitlich begrenzt sein. Nach Bharata gibt es 20 wesentliche Elemente des Pūrvaraṅga; davon werden neun hinter dem Vorhang ausgeführt und elf auf der Bühne. Die ersten neun umfassen das Stimmen der Musikinstrumente und das Proben der Schauspieler. Auf der Bühne werden Lieder (Gīta) gesungen und Götter gepriesen. Der Sūtradhāra singt Dankgebet und Segensspruch (Nāndi). Darauf folgt ein rigoroser, männlicher Tanz (Tāṇḍava). Schließlich wird der Inhalt des Dramas angekündigt, manchmal in einem Gespräch zwischen dem Sūtradhāra und der Naṭī, seinem weiblichen Gegenbild.

432 Indisches Theater

Das klassische Sanskrit-Theater

Die Blütezeit des klassischen Sanskrit-Theaters dauert ungefähr vom 2. Jh. v. Chr. bis zum 9. Jh. n. Chr. Der älteste bekannte klassische Sanskrit-Dramatiker heißt Bhāsa (4. Jh. v. Chr.). Man schreibt ihm zehn Dramen zu, u. a. *Svapnavāsavadattam* und *Urubhaṅga*. Einige andere bekannte Sanskrit-Dramatiker mit ihren Hauptwerken sind: Śūdraka (?): *Mrchhakatika*; Kālīdāsa (ca. 1. Jh. v. Chr.): *Abhijñāna Śākuntalam*; Viśakhadatta (ca. 6. Jh.): *Mudrārākṣasa*; Bhavabhūti (ca. 8. Jh.): *Uttararāma-čarita*, *Mālati-Mādhava*; Baṭṭanārayaṇa (ca. 8. Jh.): *Venisaṃhār*; Rājasekhar (ca. 9 Jh.): *Karpūrmañjirí* (im Dialekt); Śriharṣa (?): *Ratnāvalī*.

Das Sanskrit-Drama strebt nicht nach Realismus, sondern drückt vor allem romantische Stimmungen aus, basiert auf Symbolen und strengen Konventionen der theatralen Zeichen. Der Dramatiker bemüht sich um eine ideelle Realität, die im Bereich der Vorstellung bleibt; das Geistige hat stets mehr Bedeutung als das Materielle. Thematisch geht es um den Weg des Menschen (und der Natur) zu seiner Wesensverwirklichung. Die Sprache der Dramen ist meistens lyrisch, von hohem Pathos. Wenn der Höhepunkt der Emotionen erreicht wird, wird die epische Darstellung von der lyrischen Sprechweise abgelöst. Je nach dem Status der Rollen in der damaligen Gesellschaft sprechen die Charaktere verschiedene Dialekte; Götter, Brahmanen, Könige und oft auch Königinnen und Asketinnen sprechen Sanskrit. Einige Autoren entnahmen ihre Themen der epischen Literatur, andere schrieben über die zeitgenössischen Könige oder ihre eigenen Mäzene. Sanskrit-Dramen gehören zum wesentlichen Bestand der traditionellen ind. Kultur.

Im *Arthaśāstra* und *Kāmasūtra* wird offensichtlich, daß spätestens 500 n. Chr. das Regelwerk des Theaters (Theorie, Formkanon) hoch entwickelt war. Die altind. Theater- und Konzerthallen waren den Palästen angeschlossen. Schauspieler und Schriftsteller standen im Dienst der Könige und hatten für deren Unterhaltung zu sorgen. Auch adelige Frauen wurden in den Künsten Tanz, Musik und Schauspiel unterwiesen.

Nach Bharata gab es zehn Haupttypen (Rūpakas) und viele Unterarten (Uparūpakas) des ind. Dramas, die wesentlich nach Körperbewegung, Gestik und Musik unterschieden werden. Uparūpakas sind Dramen im Dialekt, Formen des Tanztheaters. Sie stellen die älteste ind. Theaterform dar. Es werden davon 18 Typen in Nāṭyadarpaṇa (14. Jh.) erwähnt.

Soziale Stellung der Schauspieler: Nach Bharata gehörten Schauspieler zu den niedrigeren, nichtbrahmanischen Kasten. Im *Arthaśāstra* wie auch in der *Manusmṛti*, dem altind. Gesetzbuch, werden Schauspieler verachtet. Die Schauspielerinnen führten oft ein amoralisches Leben. Andererseits aber waren viele Schauspieler mit großen Königen und Dramatikern eng befreundet. Bhavabhūti (8. Jh.), Bāṇa (7. Jh.), Bhartṛhari (5. Jh.) er-

Charakteristische Odissi-Haltung (BM)

Kathakali: Rama und Hanuman (ITO)

Kuchipudi: Lichtertanz (SP)

Mamata Shankar. Tänzerin aus dem Tanzdrama «Sita Swayamavara» (BN)

Szene aus dem Volks-Tanztheater Ram Lila in Bihar: der Affenkönig Sugriva im Kampf mit seinem Halbbruder Bali (SNA)

Kathak (SP)

Jala Phyakja: Maskentänzer in Patan/Nepal (SNA)

wähnen ihre Freundschaft mit Schauspielern und Königen. Eine Schauspielerin war oft zugleich Kurtisane. Vielfach werden noch heute kleine Mädchen einem Gott als Opfergeschenk dargebracht. Diese Devadāsīs (Dienerinnen der Gottheit) wachsen im Tempel auf; sie tanzen und singen bei festlichen Anlässen. Oft war dies mit Tempelprostitution verbunden.

Das Volkstheater
Mit dem Ende des 10. Jh. verlor das Sanskrit-Theater mehr und mehr an Bedeutung. Sanskrit wurde nicht mehr gesprochen, und mit dem Verfall der hinduistischen Fürstentümer fanden sich keine Mäzene mehr. Im Zuge der politischen Veränderungen etablierte Śaṅkarācārya (ca. 8. Jh.) eine neue Lehre der monistischen Weltanschauung, die einen starken Einfluß auf das ind. T. ausübte.

Die folgenden mehr als 500 Jahre alten Formen des ind. Volkstheaters sind auch heute noch aktuell und deutlich von der damals aufkommenden Bhakti-Bewegung (deren religiöse Ziele in einer liebevollen Hingabe an die Gottheit bestanden) beeinflußt: Rāmalīlā, Kṛṣṇalīlā, Nauṭaṅki im Norden; Yātrā in Bengalen; Bhavāi in Gujarat; Bhāgavatam, Kudiyaṭṭam, Harikathā, Yakṣagāna, Kucipudi, Kathakali, Nalaṭaṅgi im Süden; Gondhaḷa, Lalit, Daśāvatāra, Tamāśā in Maharashtra; Bhāṇḍajaśan in Kashmir; Aṅkīya, Nāṭ in Assam; Kariyālā in Himachalpradesh.

Gemeinsame Züge des Volkstheaters sind: religiöser Ursprung, belehrende Darstellung, Episoden aus den Epen *Rāmāyaṇa* und *Mahābhārata*, Konflikt zwischen dem Guten und dem Bösen, Vortrag der mündlich überlieferten Sagen, Einfluß der Sanskrit-Literatur und des *Bharatanāṭyaśāstra*, vergleichbare Charaktere zu dem Sūtradhāra und Vidūṣaka, der Pūrvaraṅga mit Lobgesang und Gebet, Männer spielen Frauenrollen, Tanz und Musik machen den wesentlichen Teil der Vorstellung aus; wichtig sind Begleitinstrumente, besonders Schlaginstrumente; tänzerisch-rhythmische Körperbewegungen sowie bunt-attraktive Kostüme und Masken; keine Bühne, es wurde auf den Straßen gespielt.

Man kann drei Arten des Volkstheaters unterscheiden: 1. religiös-traditionelles Volkstheater mit Volkstänzen wie Yātrā, Rāsa, Bhavāi, Kīrtan; 2. entwickeltes klassisches Tanztheater wie → Kathakali, Bharata Nātyam; 3. unterhaltend-populäres volkstümliches Theater wie Tamāśā.

Religiös-traditionelles Volkstheater
Rāma und Kṛṣṇa sind beliebte Gottheiten in Nordindien (Uttarpradesh, Rajasthan, Punjab etc.). Das liebevolle Spiel zwischen ihnen und ihren Verehrern findet seinen Ausdruck in den Formen und Themen des Volkstheaters (z. B. Rāmalīlā, Kṛṣṇalīlā, Rāsalīlā). Bhavāi ist die traditionelle Volkstheaterform in Gujarat, eine Art Tanztheater, in dem sich Bhāva

434   Indisches Theater

(= irdisches Leben) widerspiegelt; Legenden, historische Ereignisse und Alltagsthemen werden in kurzen Szenen dargestellt, Dialoge werden improvisiert, eine Fackel gilt als Symbol der Göttin. Gaṇeśá, ein beliebter, elefantenköpfiger Gott, der alle Hindernisse beseitigt, ist eine der typischen Figuren.

Yātrā/Jatrā: Diese sehr alte Form des Volkstheaters wurde durch die Bhaktibewegung wiederbelebt. Das Wort ‹Yātrā/Jatrā› bedeutet religiösen Umzug oder Unterhaltung. In Bengalen gewann diese Darstellungsform der *Kṛṣṇa*-Geschichten durch den frommen Gelehrten und Schriftsteller Čaitanyaprabhū (1485–1533) mit seinem *Rukhmiṇīharaṇa* an Bedeutung; schon im 16. Jh. war diese Theaterform auch in Bihar und Orissa verbreitet. Der Dichter Jayadeva verfaßte im 14. Jh. das *Gītagovinda*, das heute noch – gewöhnlich im Freien – aufgeführt wird. Ojāpalī ist die alte dramatische Form der Aufführung mythischer Geschichten in Assam.

Harikatha: ‹Hari› (= Gott) und ‹Kathā› (= Erzählung), ähnliche Formen sind Kīrtan in Maharashtra, Bhomākalāpam in Andhra, Burrākatha in Karnataka. Dies sind Solo-Aufführungen eines Haridāsa, eines Dieners des Gottes. Sie umfassen Sagen und Episoden aus den Epen mit Kommentaren und Bezugnahme auf zeitgenössische weltpolitische Probleme. Haridāsas sind Gelehrte und Weise, die ungeschminkt, mit klimperndem Geklingel um die Fußspangen und mit einem Paar Zimbeln in der Hand auftreten. In einem Tempelhof oder im Hof eines Reichen unterhalten sie das einfache Publikum tanzend und singend mit ihren immer auch belehrenden Geschichten. Sie kennen die Mythen, sind gute Sänger und Tänzer, improvisieren Dialoge, tragen Sanskrit-Verse vor und legen diese an Hand von Beispielen aus dem alltäglichen Leben aus.

Čaraṇas: Haupterzähler oder Darsteller in einem Volkstheater; dem Sūtradhāra vergleichbar; sie heißen Bhāgavata in Yakṣagāna und Bhāgavatam, dagegen Naṭvar in einem Tanztheater. Im Punjab heißen sie Jogis und in Kashmir Bhānd. Sie waren Gelehrte wie die Haridāsas im Süden und wurden mit der Verbreitung des Bhakti-Kults nicht mehr zu den niedrigen Kasten gezählt. Die Čaraṇas rezitierten Sanskrit-Verse und erklärten sie durch Tanz, Gesang und Dialoge.

Yakṣagāna: Beliebte Theaterform in der Küstengegend von Karnataka. Auf dem Flachland heißen ähnliche Formen Mada-paya oder Bāyaṭal. Verehrer Viṣṇus etablierten dieses Tanztheater unter dem Einfluß der Bhakti-Bewegung. Vor der Zeit des Bharata war es bekannt als →Puppentheater oder Tableaux. Der Hauptcharakter heißt Bhāgavata, das Gegenstück zum Čaraṇa des ländlichen Theaters. Er ist Brahmane, ebenfalls ein guter Tänzer und Sänger. Der Bhāgavata trägt den Text deklamierend vor und singt ihn, andere Charaktere sind zweitrangig und reagieren nur auf seinen Text. Der Bhāgavata hat eine ähnliche Funktion wie Sūtradhāra. Ein anderer wichtiger Charakter in Yakṣagāna ist *Kodaṅgi*, ein zeitgenössisch gekleideter Vertreter der Zuschauer. Er heißt auch Hāsyāgāra (= der Gelächtermacher) und kann auf den klassischen Charakter des Vidūṣaka zurückgeführt werden.

Der Tanz, das Grundelement des Yakṣagāna, ist dramatisch und paßt zu den historischen Kampfthemen. Andere Gefühle kommen kaum zum Ausdruck; weibliche Charaktere treten nicht auf. Die Figuren tragen bunte, prächtige Kostüme, der Bösewicht trägt eine Maske. Es gibt keine Bühne, keine Vorhänge, es wird auf Innenhöfen, Plätzen und Straßen gespielt.

Im 16. Jh. wurde in Andhra Yakṣagāna frei komponiert, allerdings wurde sie beeinflußt durch das noch ältere Volkstheater Andhras-Vithināṭak. Bharata beschreibt Vithināṭak als Einakter mit zwei oder drei Charakteren, bei dem improvisierte Dialoge, Gesang und Tanz die zentrale Rolle spielen.

In Südindien haben die Staaten Tamilnadu, Andhra, Karnataka und Kerala eine sehr alte Tradition des Volkstheaters. Es gab einen Berufsstand, dessen Angehörige, die Bhāgavata, von Ort zu Ort zogen und Volkslieder über mythische Themen sangen. Die Volkstheaterform Bhāgavatam entwickelte sich zu einem Tanztheater, in dem Geschichten aus den großen Epen gespielt wurden. Heute sind Formen des Volkstheaters unter den Namen Yakṣagāna in Karnataka und Tamilnadu, Kucipudi-Bhāgavatam in Andhra und Kathakali in Kerala bekannt.

Kucipudi: Dieser Tanz ist eine andere Art der Manifestation von Yakṣagāna. Kucipudi hieß der Ort, aus dem die Tänzerfamilien stammten, die diese Kunst über Generationen hinweg pflegten und entwickelten. Früher spielten sie *Bhāgavatam* und andere mythische Dramen auf den Straßen und verdienten damit ihr tägliches Brot. Der mohammedanische Fürst Tānāśāha war ihr Mäzen, er schenkte ihnen Land und einen großen Tempel; so wurden sie seßhaft. Heute gehört der Kucipudi-Tanz zu den hochentwickelten klassischen ind. Tänzen.

Daśāvatāra: Darstellung der zehn Inkarnationen von Viṣṇu; dem Yakṣagāna vergleichbare Form des Volkstheaters in Maharashtra. In Yakṣagāna sowie in Daśāvatāra spielen Männer Frauenrollen. Alle Schauspieler treten tanzend auf. Vorstellungen an Festtagen, traditionelle Schauspielerfamilien; eine Maske des Gottes Brahmā mit vier Gesichtern und eine Gaṇeśamaske, Lobgesang des Gaṇeśa sind charakteristisch für den Daśāvatāra. Die Hauptfigur ähnelt dem Sūtradhāra, im Vorspiel werden Kṛṣṇa-Possen inszeniert, keine geschriebenen fixierten Texte, überwiegender Gebrauch von Schlaginstrumenten, Kampfthemen; den Höhepunkt bilden immer dramatische Kampfszenen mit Gebrüll, Trommeln, Geräuschen und viel Geschrei.

436 Indisches Theater

Das klassische Tanztheater

Die vier ind. klassischen Haupttanzformen sind → *Kathakali*, → *Kathak*, → *Bharata Nāṭyam* und → *Manipurī*. Sie bestehen aus drei Elementen: 1. Tanz (nṛtta), 2. Mimik (abhinaya), 3. Kombination der ersten beiden Elemente (nṛtya). Während reiner Tanz kein Thema hat und nur Emotionen vor rhythmischem Hintergrund ausdrückt, werden im sog. Abhinaya-Teil der Tänze Geschichten und Rollen mit Gesang, Gestik und Mimik dargestellt. – Die Technik des Bharatanāṭyam und Kathakali findet in heutigen Dramen und Balletts ihre Anwendung. → Odissi, → Chhao-Tänze, → Tanz, → Brauchtumstänze.

Unterhaltend-populäres volkstümliches Theater

Neben den erwähnten Formen des Unterhaltungstheaters gab es immer auch volkstümliche, meist erotisch-vulgäre Theaterformen, die mit dem Verfall des klassischen Sanskrit-Theaters an Bedeutung gewannen. Dies sind zum Teil Derivate zweier Uparūpakus: Prahasana und Bhāṇa – Formen eher primitiver Unterhaltung.

Tamāśā: beliebteste Unterhaltungsform auf dem Lande in Maharashtra wie *Nauṭaṅki* in Nordindien. Eine Gruppe von sechs bis acht Leuten mit einem Führer, einer Tänzerin und Begleitinstrumenten. Die erste Hälfte eines Tamāśā besteht aus Gebet an Gaṇeśa (Gaṇa), Kṛṣṇa-Possen (Gaulaṇa), einem erotischen Lied mit erotischem Tanz (Lāvaṇi), Liedern (Kavana), Danksagung und Verehrung der Götter, Fürsten, Helden und Dichter mit Powadas, einer Art Ballade. Die zweite Hälfte wird Vag genannt: eine kleine Szene mit Kṛṣṇa und seinen Liebhaberinnen. Das Tamāśā erlebte seinen Höhepunkt Anfang des 19. Jh. unter den Pesvas im Marathenreich. – Das Wort ‹Tamāśā› stammt wahrscheinlich aus dem Arabischen. Ein Junge (Nācyā), der die Tänzerin spielt, hat Ähnlichkeiten mit dem Saki, dem persischen Weinservierer.

Indisches Theater unter dem Einfluß der Engländer

Mit der Niederlassung der East Indian Company (18. Jh., Bengalen) und dem damit verbundenen wachsenden Einfluß der engl. Sprache, der europ. Kultur und Denkweise nahm die Entwicklung des ind. Theaters eine neue Richtung. Am 7. November 1795 wurde die erste nicht-ind. Komödie in Kalkutta aufgeführt. Dies bewirkte freilich sofort als Gegenreaktion ein wiedererwachendes Interesse an dem klassischen Sanskrit-Theater. Sanskrit-Dramen wurden in viele regionale Sprachen übersetzt, aber nie veröffentlicht.

Das erste Theater in der Folge dieser Entwicklung wurde 1831 in Bengalen gebaut, wo ind. Schauspieler engl. Dramen vor einem kleinen Publikum aufführten. Ein zweites bengalisches Theater wurde 1833 im Haus des Navin Candra Basū gegründet. Dort wurden bengalische Stücke inszeniert. Das gebildete städtische Publikum versuchte, im Zusammenhang einer umfassenden Reformbewegung, Tradition mit Modernität zu verbinden. Das erste eigenständige, bengalische Drama war *Kulinākula-Sarbasva* (UA 1857); das erste Urdu-Drama *Inder-Sabhā* (UA 1854) bestand nur aus Musik und Spektakel ohne Moral, hatte aber großen Erfolg beim Publikum. Das erste epische Marathi-Drama, *Thorle Māḍhurao Peśue* von Kirtane, behandelte politische Probleme. Der Hindi-Dramatiker Bharatendu Hariscandra (19. Jh.) bearbeitete viele Sanskrit- und bengalische Dramen und interpretierte sie neu im zeitgenössischen sozialpolitischen Kontext.

Eine Theatergruppe von Parsen, Parsi Nāṭak Maṇḍaḷi, wurde 1852 in Bombay gegründet; sie ließen dort viele neue Theaterhäuser bauen. Durch spektakuläre Szenen und reichliche Bühnenausstattung kommerzialisierten sie das Theater sehr schnell. Die Parsen führten ihre Stücke in Gujarati auf.

Angeregt vom Parsi-Theater bildeten sich gegen Ende des 19. Jh. neue Theatergruppen in Karnataka. Dort wurde 1877 das erste Berufstheater gegründet, dem noch zahlreiche weitere Theatergründungen folgten.

Den Beginn des Marathi-Theaters kann man in der Inszenierung des *Daśāvatāra* (1843) von Vishnudas Bhave sehen, gefördert durch den Rāja von Sangli. Gegen 1860 waren schon mehr als zwölf Gruppen in Maharashtra aktiv. Bedeutende kommerzielle Gruppen in der zweiten Hälfte des 19. Jh. waren das Pṛthvirāj-Theater in Bombay und die Gubbi Company in Karnataka.

Bis Mitte des 19. Jh. wurden öffentliche Vorstellungen von den reichen Bürgern finanziert und waren in der Regel eintrittsfrei. Der Beruf des Schauspielers, ursprünglich nur best. Kasten vorbehalten, wurde jetzt zunehmend auch anderen Kasten zugänglich. Mit der Entstehung neuer Gruppen erfolgte auch die Kommerzialisierung des Theaters (Eintrittsgeld).

Die Problematik dieser Theaterrichtung, schließlich ihr Ende waren bald absehbar: alter mythischer Inhalt, schwer verständliche Sprache mit vielen Zitaten aus dem Sanskrit und steigende Konkurrenz; schließlich verlor es mit dem Beginn der Filmindustrie das Interesse des Publikums. In Tamilnadu und Kerala wurde das kommerzielle Theater freilich von Anfang an nie hoch geschätzt.

Anfang des 20. Jh. wurden viele Dramen aus dem Englischen (bes. Stücke von Shakespeare) und dem Sanskrit in regionalen Sprachen aufgeführt. Besonders in Maharashtra und in Bengalen wurden historische Episoden im Licht der wachsenden Unabhängigkeitsbewegung neu interpretiert. Die Kirloskar Nāṭak Company (gegr. 1880) entwickelte eine neue Theaterform, das Saṅgīt-Nāṭaka, eine Art Operette: einfache Marathi-Lieder, wenige Dialoge, Darstellung von Emotionen und idealisier-

438 Indisches Theater

ten Inhalten in lyrischer Form. N. S. Rajhans, Bal Gandharva (1888 bis 1967) genannt, der begabteste und beliebteste Sänger seiner Zeit, faszinierte das Publikum mit seinen Frauenrollen und nimmt einen bes. Platz in der Geschichte des Marathi-Theaters ein.

Im Gegensatz zu anderen Regionen Indiens gab es in Maharashtra eine Reihe engagierter Dramatiker, z. B.: K. P. Khadilkar (1872–1948), ein Schüler von Tilak, dem Nationalhelden; er brachte die aktuelle ind. Politik auf die Bühne, N. C. Kelkar (1872–1947), Mitglied derselben politischen Gruppe, und R. G. Gadkari (1885–1919) – sie alle machten die sozialen Ungerechtigkeiten und die Sklaverei zu Hauptthemen ihrer Dramen. Deval (1855–1916) bearbeitete Stücke von Shakespeare, Molière und von Sanskrit-Autoren. Die Theatergruppe Nāṭyamanvantar (gegr. 1932) protestierte gegen die Formen des traditionellen Theaters, vor allem dagegen, daß Frauenrollen von Männern gespielt werden sollten.

Im bengalischen Theater stand die Prosa im Vordergrund. Neue Interpretationen mythischer Motive sowie zeitgenössische politische Protestthemen waren charakteristisch. Rabindranath Tagore (1861 bis 1941) war zugleich Künstler, Philosoph, Pädagoge, Dichter und Dramatiker. Seine Dramen sind der Form nach sehr lyrisch, mit sparsamer Handlung. Viele von ihnen wurden ins Englische übertragen, z. B. *The Cycle of Spring, Sacrifice*.

Realistische Elemente wurden auf der ind. Bühne erst in den 20er Jahren des 20. Jh. von Sisir Kumar Bhaduri, Naresh Mitra und Ahindra Chaudhari eingeführt. Sisir Kumar Bhaduri, selber ein ausgezeichneter Schauspieler, prägte das bengalische Theater fast 50 Jahre lang.

Das moderne Tamil-Theater begann 1904 mit Saṃbanda Mudaliar, einer Amateurorganisation. Ihre Mitglieder waren gebildete Leute aus angesehenen Familien. T. P. Kailasan gab 1920 dem Amateurtheater mit seinen sozialkritischen Satiren neue Impulse.

Im 20. Jh. waren die gemeinsamen Themen aller Richtungen: das Kastensystem, die Unberührbaren, Probleme der Frauen, Prostitution, orthodoxe Dogmatik, Aberglaube, politische Ungerechtigkeit, Kolonialisierung u. a. Das erwachende politische Bewußtsein drängte zu neuen Ausdrucksformen. Die meisten der zwischen 1935 und 1947 aufgeführten ind. Dramen waren Einakter und wurden von Studenten in kleinen Sälen oder in Klassenzimmern inszeniert, da viele Theaterhäuser in Kinos umfunktioniert wurden. – Das Amateurtheater wurde allmählich organisiert. In Bengalore wurde die Amateur Dramatic Association (ADA) gegründet. Viele von Ibsens Dramen wurden von der ADA übersetzt und aufgeführt.

Indian Peoples' Theatre (IPT): Das IPT war die erste allind. Theater-Organisation; sie existierte nicht lange, aber ihr Beitrag war für die ind.

Theaterentwicklung bedeutend. Durch sie wurden Schriftsteller wie Khwaja Ahemed Abbas und Manmath Ray, der Schauspieler und Produzent Shombhu Mitra berühmt. Das IPT reiste von Ort zu Ort, inszenierte Einakter, Dramen und Balletts und verhalf dem Theater wieder zu Ansehen.

Indian National Theatre (INT): Unter Führung von Kamaladevi Cattopadhyaya wurde das INT gegr. Es führte Stücke in vielen Sprachen, einschließlich der Minderheitensprachen, in Bombay auf. Das INT besaß viele Theaterhäuser in Andhra, Karnataka, Bombay, Gujarat u. a. und versuchte, das Berufstheater wiederzubeleben. Dank des Einflusses des IPT und des INT wurde die Qualität der Texte, der Regie und der Inszenierungen rasch verbessert. Sombhu Mitra (in Kalkutta) und Satyadev Dube (in Bombay) gaben dem Theater neue Impulse.

Das indische Theater nach 1947

Nach 1947 wurden zwei allind. Organisationen gegründet: Saṅgīt Nāṭak Academy (SNA) und National School of Drama (NSD).

SNA und NSD: Die SNA (1953) wurde mit Unterstützung der Regierung zum Zentrum der darstellenden Künste Indiens; 1959 entstand das erste Nationaltheater, die NSD in Delhi. Dies sollte Ausbildungszentrum sowie Forschungsinstitut für Theaterwissenschaft sein.

Die NSD übte einen großen Einfluß im Norden aus und bereicherte das Hindi-Theater, welches früher kaum Bedeutung hatte. Sie entdeckte und förderte Schauspieler, Schriftsteller und Regisseure, die heute überall in Indien hohes Ansehen genießen wie z. B. Sombhu Mitra, Utpal Datt (*1929), Badal Sirker (*1925) aus Bengalen, Tendulkar (*1928), Khanolkar (1930–76), Alekar (*1949) aus Maharashtra, Girish Karnad, Lankesh aus Karnataka und Mohan Rakesh aus der Hindi-Region. Die NSD förderte auch Übertragungen von Dramen ausländischer Autoren wie Brecht, Dürrenmatt, Ibsen, Ionesco, Beckett, Tschechow in Hindi und anderen indischen Sprachen.

Ebrahim Alkazi (*1925), selbst ein brillanter Schauspieler, Regisseur und Bühnenbildner, trat 1962 die Stelle des Direktors der NSD an. Er ließ fünf Theater bauen, zog es allerdings vor, neun Monate im Jahr im Freien zu spielen. Seine größte Leistung war die Umwandlung einer alten halbverfallenen Festung in das großartige Purana Qila-Theater. Er verarbeitete viele regional-traditionelle Formen des Volkstheaters und nutzte sie in neuer Funktion. Jährlich wurden sanskrit., moderne ind., asiat. sowie europ. Dramen aufgeführt. Als Alkazi 1977 sein Amt niederlegte, übernahm B. V. Karanth (*1929) die NSD. Er widmete seine Aufmerksamkeit hauptsächlich der Organisation von Workshops und Theaterfestivals. Bestimmend wurde seine Auseinandersetzung mit den traditionellen Theaterformen wie Kathakali und Yakṣagāna sowie Tanzformen wie

440 Indisches Theater

Bhavāi und Kutiyaṭṭam; damit belebte er die Theaterbewegung bes. in Karnataka.

Aus der politischen Befreiungsbewegung entstand die Indian People's Theatre Association (IPTA), von der sich aber bedeutende Mitglieder wie Sombhu Mitra oder Utpal Datt bald trennten. Manoranjan Bhattacharya (1889–1954), Sombhu Mitra und Gangadas Basu (1910–71) gründeten eine neue Gruppe, Bahurupi, in Bengalen und etablierten dort einen realistischen Stil auf der Bühne.

In den 50er Jahren erlebte das Marathi-Theater eine neue Blüte mit der Gründung von Gruppen wie Raṅgayan in Bombay und die Progressive Dramatic Association in Pune. P. K. Atre und P. L. Deshpande (*1919) schrieben für diese Theater humorvolle Satiren; Vasant Kanetkar bearbeitete historische Themen, und Vijay Tendulkar setzte sich mit sozialen Problemen auseinander.

Als Vater des neuind. Balletts wird Udayshankar angesehen, obwohl schon Rabindranath Tagore Nṛtta-Rūpaka (= Balletts) verfaßt und aufgeführt hatte. Außerdem sind Darpaṇa von Mrinalini Sarabhai und Nṛtta-Darpaṇ von Krishnan Kutti bekannte Ballettgruppen.

Zu dieser Zeit entstanden auch viele Laiengruppen. Das ind. National-Theater und Vidya Bhavan (Bombay) förderten insbesondere das moderne experimentelle Theater in Maharashtra. Im Chabildas-Movement (1975) organisierte sich das experimentelle Theater. Durch Verzicht auf Bühne und Kulissen und mit billigen Eintrittskarten wurde versucht, die Kluft zwischen Schauspielern und Publikum zu überbrücken. Anfang der 70er Jahre schuf die Theatre Academy (Pune) unter Regie von Jabbar Patel und Alekar einen neuen Stil für die Marathi-Bühne: ausgiebiger Gebrauch volkstümlicher Elemente, Tanz und Gesang. Badal Sirkar gründete 1967 in Kalkutta eine sog. «alternative Gruppe»: Śatābdi; sie war um eine Synthese des von Europa beeinflußten städtischen und des einheimischen ländlichen Theaters bemüht.

Straßen- und Zimmertheater mit Stücken zu aktuellen Themen, aufgeführt mit Trommeln, Zimbeln, Gedichten und improvisierten Dialogen werden immer beliebter. Eine Theatergruppe aus Bombay, das Navanir-māṇ, organisierte zwei Nāṭya-Jatrās, Festivals für Straßentheater, im Oktober 1984 und April 1985. Daran nahmen u. a. Gruppen aus Andhra, Punjab und Maharashtra teil. Das Thema der zweiten Nāṭya-Jatrā waren Frauenprobleme: die soziale Stellung der Frau, das Problem der Mitgift, Vergewaltigung, Gleichberechtigung usw.

In der letzten Zeit haben sich auch in Parsi, Urdu, Punjabi, Telugu, Kannada und Tamil neue Theatergruppen etabliert. Im östlichen Indien aber dominiert das bengalische Theater mit seinem politischen Engagement. Hauptzentrum der Aktivitäten im Norden ist Delhi; im Westen ist Maharashtra, bekannt für sozialkritisches und experimentelles Theater.

Im Süden steht nach wie vor das traditionelle Tanztheater im Vordergrund.

Anand, Mulk Raj: The Indian Theatre. London o. J.; Rangacharya, Adya: The Indian Theatre. New Delhi 1971; Gupta, Chandra Bhan: The Indian Theatre. Banaras 1954; Joshi, P. A.: Bharatīya Lōkanātya. Pune 1980; Bhatkal, G. R. (ed.): The Marathi Theatre. Bombay 1961; Kale, K. N./Kulkarni, V. L./Dhavate, V. R. (eds.): Marāthi Raṅgabhūmī: Marāthi Nāṭak. Bombay 1971; Nadkarni, Dnyaneshwar: New Directions in Marathi Theatre; Naik, Bapurao: Origin of Marāthi Theatre, New Delhi 1964; Das Gupta Hemendra Nath: The Indian Stage. Bde. 1, 2, 3, Kalkutta 1944; Gargi Balawant: Raṅgamañcha. Delhi 1968; Theatre Centre, India (ed.): Theatre in India. New Delhi o. J.; Zeitschriften: Enact, New Delhi, Bharatashastra, Bombay.

Neeti A. Badwe

Inspizient

Spielwart, der hinter den Kulissen steht und für den reibungslosen technischen Ablauf der Vorstellung verantwortlich ist. Er kontrolliert den Bühnenaufbau, gibt das Zeichen zum Auftritt, zum Vorhangziehen, für plötzliche Geräuscheffekte usw.

Bernard Poloni

Inszenierung

(→ Regie, → Regisseur, → Theatertheorie) Die I. ist ein relativ neuer Begriff, der in der 1. Hälfte des 19. Jh. entstanden ist mit dem Hervortreten von ‹Intendanten-Dramaturgen› als Gesamtverantwortlichen für Schauspiel und künstlerische Darbietung. Bis dahin hatten → Inspizient oder → Prinzipal lediglich Ordnungsfunktionen.

1. Funktionen der I.: Nach André Veinstein sind zwei Begriffsbestimmungen möglich, eine aus der Sicht des Publikums, die andere aus der der Spezialisten: «Im breiteren Sinne bezeichnet der Begriff I. die Gesamtheit der Mittel szenischer Interpretation: Bühnenbild, Beleuchtung, Musik und Schauspielweise... Im engeren Sinne die Tätigkeit, welche darin besteht, die verschiedenen Elemente der szenischen Interpretation eines Bühnenwerks in einer bestimmten Spielzeit und einem bestimmten Spielraum zu gestalten.» Insofern sind vier Hauptfunktionen der I. zu unterscheiden:

Raum: Die I. besteht darin, die dramatische Schreibweise eines Texts in die szenische Schreibweise umzusetzen. «Die Kunst der I. ist die

442 Inszenierung

Kunst, das im Raum zu entwerfen, was der Dramatiker nur in der Zeit entwerfen konnte» (Appia). Die I. als Gestaltung des Texts durch Schauspieler und szenischen Raum zielt darauf ab, die Textpartitur szenisch so geeignet wie möglich zu konkretisieren, und ist deshalb, nach Artaud, «in einem Stück der echt und spezifisch theatralische Teil des Schauspiels».

Koordination: Die verschiedenen Komponenten einer Aufführung, die meist mehreren mitarbeitenden Künstlern obliegen (Dramaturg, Musiker, Bühnenbildner etc.), werden zusammengebracht und koordiniert durch den →Regisseur. Sei es, um eine integrierte Einheit zu erzielen (→Gesamtkunstwerk), oder ein Ganzes, worin jede Teil-Kunst ihre Selbständigkeit bewahrt (Brecht), der Regisseur hat die Aufgabe, über den Zusammenhang der einzelnen szenischen Elemente, also deren globalen Sinn, zu entscheiden. Diese Arbeit des Koordinierens besteht in der Erklärung und dem Kommentar der →Fabel mit Hilfe aller Ausdrucksmittel der →Bühne. Die I. muß ein organisches Gesamtsystem bilden, worin jedes Einzelne sich in das Ganze integriert, worin alles seine Funktion in der Gesamtkonzeption hat. So Jacques Copeau: «Unter I. verstehen wir den Entwurf einer dramatischen Handlung. Das ist die Gesamtheit der Bewegungen, Gesten, Haltungen, die Harmonie der Mienenspiele, der Stimmen, des Schweigens; es ist die Totalität des szenischen Schauspiels, einem Denken entsprungen, das sie entwirft, regelt und harmonisiert. Der Regisseur erfindet und gestaltet zwischen den Figuren jenes geheime und doch sichtbare Band..., ohne das ein Drama, wenn auch noch so hervorragend interpretiert, das Beste seiner Wirkung einbüßt.»

Sinngestaltung: Für Stanislawski heißt die Gestaltung einer I., den tieferen Sinn des dramatischen Texts materiell als augenscheinlich erscheinen zu lassen. Dazu verfügt die I. über alle szenischen (Bühnenform, Beleuchtung, Kostüme etc.) und Spielmittel (Schauspielkunst, Körperlichkeit, Gestik). Die I. betrifft zugleich das Milieu, in dem die Schauspieler sich bewegen und deren psychologische und gestische Interpretation eines Texts oder Buchs, einer Textinterpretation im Handeln.

Schauspielerleitung: I. ist vorwiegend auch die praktische Arbeit mit den Schauspielern, Stückanalyse und genaue Anweisungen zur Gestik, zu den Verlagerungen, dem Rhythmus und der Phrasierung des zu sprechenden Texts. Das Studium der Figur, ihrer Motivierungen, ihrer Innerlichkeit wird gemeinsam vom →Dramaturgen und vom Regisseur geleistet; danach gilt es, die der Interpretation der Rolle angemessensten Ausdrucksmittel zu finden, wobei der Grundgestus (Brecht) des Stücks wie die Abfolge der verschiedenen Gesten der Schauspieler zu berücksichtigen sind.

2. Probleme der I.: Die Erscheinung des →Regisseurs in der Entwicklung des Theaters kennzeichnet eine neue Haltung gegenüber dem Text; dieser galt lange als der Ort einer einzigen möglichen Interpretation, die aufzuspüren war. Heute dagegen ist der Text eine Aufforderung, seine mehrschichtigen, oft auch widersprüchlichen Bedeutungen ausfindig zu machen, eine neue Interpretation durch eine originelle I. zu provozieren. Sinn der Theaterkunst ist fortan sowohl in der Form und der dramatischen und szenischen Struktur als auch im Text zu suchen. Der Regisseur steht nicht außerhalb des Werks, er wird zur Grundkomponente der theatralischen Darbietung: der notwendigen Vermittlung zwischen Text und Schauspiel, insofern als beides sich bedingt.

Die Alternative, die noch heute von manchen Regisseuren gesehen wird, den Text oder die Aufführung zu ‹spielen›, ist verfehlt; denn im Sinne der Theatralisierung enthält jeder Text den Entwurf seiner Aufführung, wobei nur der Grad der Theatralisierung des Texts auf der Bühne veränderbar ist. Die I. gilt heute als umfassender Diskurs mittels der Aktion und Interaktion der szenischen Systeme, worin der Text nur eine – freilich grundlegende – Komponente darstellt. Seine wesentlichen Ausdrucksmittel sind:
– die Bühnenanweisungen als szenischer Kommentar zur Realisation;
– der Text selbst, der über Ort/Ablauf der Handlung, Figurenposition etc. sowie Bühnenkonventionen, Wirklichkeitskonzept der Darstellung, Sensibilität der Epoche für Zeit und Raum eine Art elementares I.-Schema enthält;
– der entscheidende Eingriff des Regisseurs: Wenn auch im Regiebuch festgehalten, ist er nur schwer von der Aufführung zu trennen. Diese Metasprache des Regisseurs, die völlig in der Darstellung von Handlung und Figuren aufgeht, erscheint wohl am eindeutigsten in der modernen → Szenographie;
– das bildliche und unbewußte Denken der Künstler: Der Regisseur spielt die Rolle des Mediums zwischen dramatischer und szenischer Sprache und versucht, mittels Imaginationen und Visionen sowie der körperlich-seelischen Ausdruckskunst der Schauspieler den Innenraum nach außen zu drängen. Die wirkliche Bühne wäre demzufolge auch Projektion der ‹anderen Bühne›.

Bablet, D.: La mise en scène contemporaine (1887–1914). Paris 1968; ders.: Les révolutions scéniques au XXe siècle. Paris 1975; Dhomme, S.: La mise en scène d'Antoine à Brecht. Paris 1959; Dietrich, M.: Regie in Dokumentation, Forschung und Lehre. Salzburg 1975; Dort, B.: Théâtre réel. Paris 1971; Jacquot, J./Veinstein, A.: La mise en scène des œuvres du passé. Paris 1957; Langer, S.: Feeling and Form. New York 1953; Pandolfi, V.: Regia e registi nel teatro moderno. Capelli 1961; Pavis, P.: Dictionnaire du théâtre. Paris 1980; ders.: Voix et images de la scène. Lille 1985; Schwarz, H.: Regie, Idee und Praxis moderner Theaterarbeit. Bonn 1974; Veinstein, A.: La mise en scène théâtrale et sa condition esthétique. Paris 1955; Wills, J. R.: The Director in a Changing Time. Palo Alto 1976.

Patrice Pavis

Inszenierungsanalyse

Bezeichnung für 1. Verfahren, die auf allgemeine Aussagen über Merkmale von Inszenierungen und die Methoden zu (objektivierender) Analyse dieser Merkmale zielen; 2. konkrete Beschreibungen und Analysen von Inszenierungen.

Zu 1: Als Inszenierung (→Theatertheorie) betrachtet man einerseits nur das, was auf der Bühne aufgeführt wird. Andererseits ist es methodisch sinnvoll, zwischen den Theatermachern, der Inszenierung (Aufführung) und den Zuschauern (Rezipienten) zu unterscheiden. Steinbeck (1970) hat einige methodische und systematische Konsequenzen einer solchen triadischen Betrachtungsweise ausgearbeitet. In bezug auf die Quellenproblematik der historischen Theaterforschung unterscheidet er die intendierte, die reale und die vermeinte Bühnengestalt. So ist eine Skizze der Dekoration eine Quelle der intendierten Bühnengestalt, ein Dekorationsstück ein Teil der realen Bühnengestalt und die Idee der Rezipienten über die gesehene Dekoration ein Aspekt der vermeinten Bühnengestalt. Folglich kann sich die I. auf den Produktionsprozeß (z. B. die Intentionen der Theatermacher), auf die Inszenierungsmerkmale sowie auf die Rezeption durch die Zuschauer beziehen. Neben dieser Auffassung kann theatralische Kommunikation auch weiter gefaßt werden, wenn z. B. die Produktionsbedingungen in die Analysen einbezogen werden (z. B. Subventionspolitik). – Zur Methodologie dazu: Van Kesteren, 1981; Übersicht von Konzepten und Theorien: Pavis 1980; Carlson 1984.

Ein Problem bezüglich der I. ist, daß viele Arbeiten wenig konsequent zwischen der Analyse einer Inszenierung und der Analyse des Dramentextes unterscheiden. Verwirrend in der neueren semiotisch orientierten Forschung ist dabei die Bezeichnung der Aufführung als Text. De Marinis (1978) verteidigt die Auffassung, daß die I. sich distanzieren solle vom Studium des Texts als Grundlage für die Aufführung: Analysen der Beziehungen zwischen Dramentext und Aufführung bei Hogendoorn (1976) und Serpieri (1978). Ersterer arbeitet Simultanität und Multimedialität als Kriterium der Aufführung heraus. Berücsichtigt man die Unterschiede zwischen Dramentext und Inszenierung, so können jedoch viele Verfahren der Dramenanalyse mutatis mutandis auch für die I. angewendet werden. Dem Produktions- wie dem Rezeptionsprozeß wurde bislang in der Forschung relativ wenig Aufmerksamkeit geschenkt. Untersuchungen zum Produktionsprozeß beziehen sich vor allem auf Interpretationsprobleme (Hansen en Bormann 1969; Perdue 1975) und die Zusammenarbeit Schauspieler/Regisseur (Anderson 1975; Trauth 1975; Ruble 1975). Quantitativ-methodische Beiträge zur Rezeptionsforschung: Schälzky 1980 und Tinchon 1977; allgemein theoretische: Tindemans 1977, 1979; Eschbach 1979. Eine Übersicht der Methoden und Resultate der empirischen Rezeptionsforschung: Schoenmakers 1983.

Die Theatersemiotik hat sich vor allem mit allgemeinen theoretischen Fragen bezüglich der Inszenierung beschäftigt: Welches sind die Basismerkmale einer Inszenierung? Welche Materialien können im Theater als Zeichenträger funktionieren? Was sind die typischen Merkmale der Zeichen im Theater, die typischen Codes des Theaters? Was ist die kleinste Zeicheneinheit? – Ostension und Deixis gelten als Basismerkmale der Zeichen einer Inszenierung (Eco 1976; Elam 1980). Ostension ist die Bezeichnung für das Zeigen von ‹etwas› in einer kommunikativen Situation (anstatt dies sprachlich zu benennen). Das Zeigen von ‹etwas› in einer theatralischen Situation bewirkt, daß dieses ‹etwas› vom Rezipienten als Zeichen aufgefaßt wird. Ostension impliziert Deixis, den Akt des Zeigens. Es sind die Handlungen und die Sprache, womit die dramatis personae ihre Relation zu den anderen Figuren, zu den Objekten und zum Raum andeuten. Verbale Deixis bedeutet, daß die Interpretation oder der Referent der Wörter nur von der Situation her erkannt werden kann (wie ‹du›, ‹dort›, ‹ich› usw.). Mit Ostension als Basismerkmal ist die Bedeutung von Raum und Zeit verbunden, das hic et nunc, wo Handlungen gezeigt werden. – Analysevorschläge für Raum: Pavis 1980; Übersfeld 1981, 52ff; für Zeit: Pavis 1980; Elam 1980, 117ff; Übersfeld 1981, 239ff.

Dank der Ostension können die meisten Materialien der Wirklichkeit im Theater als Zeichenträger fungieren. Kowzan (1975, 206) klassifiziert sie in einem Schema auf Grund verschiedener Gesichtspunkte: akustisch/visuell; Zeit/Raum, schauspielerabhängig/nichtschauspielerabhängig; artikulierte Laute (Sprache, Redestil)/körperlicher Ausdruck (Mimik, Gestik, Motorik)/äußerliche Merkmale des Schauspielers (Maske, Haartracht, Kostüm)/szenischer Aufbau (Requisiten, Dekoration, Beleuchtung)/nicht artikulierte Laute (Musik, Geräusche). Pfisters (1977, 27) Klassifikation orientiert sich an Kanal, Code-typ, Sender und Informationsvergabe (durativ oder nicht durativ). Eine Variante beider Klassifikationen bei Fischer-Lichte (1983, I, 28) mit einem ausführlichen Kommentar. Solche Klassifikationsschemata gestatten die Charakterisierung des Zeichengebrauchs eines Regisseurs, einer Gruppe, einer Epoche usw. Als mögliche Relationen zwischen sprachlichen und außersprachlichen Zeichen nennt Pfister (1977, 73ff) Identität, Diskrepanz und Komplementarität. Diese Konzepte können auch für die Analyse der Relationen zwischen allen genannten Zeichenkategorien angewendet werden.

Mit den spezifischen Merkmalen der theatralischen Zeichen haben sich die Prager Strukturalisten (Bogatyrev, Zich, Honzl; siehe Matejka und Titunik 1976) beschäftigt. Als typisch für das theatrale Zeichen gelten

446 Inszenierungsanalyse

sein Zeichen-vom-Zeichen-Charakter und seine Mobilität. Mit Zeichen-vom-Zeichen meint man, daß das Theater oft nur die Abbildung von Objekten und Handlungen zeigt, die selbst wieder als potentielle Zeichen funktionieren: ein Stück Glas als Zeichen für Diamant, der seinerseits das Zeichen ‹Königtum› oder ‹Reichtum› erzeugen kann. Laut Fischer-Lichte ist dieser Zeichen-vom-Zeichen-Charakter nicht typisch theatral. Auch andere Kunstformen kennen dieses Phänomen. Charakteristisch wäre eher: «Jedes beliebige, in einer Kultur als Zeichen fungierende Objekt vermag ohne jegliche materielle Veränderung als theatralisches Zeichen für dasjenige Zeichen, das es selbst darstellt, zu fungieren» (1983, I, 181).

Mobilität bedeutet, daß während einer Aufführung die gleichen Zeichenträger verschiedene Bedeutungen (Interpretanten) erzeugen können. Zwei Holzstücke, quer aufeinanderliegend, können z. B. als Schwert gebraucht, aber auch als ein Kreuz aufgefaßt werden. Die Mobilität kann sich beziehen auf das Phänomen, daß derselbe Zeichenträger in verschiedenen Kontexten verschiedene Bedeutungen erhält, oder auf das Phänomen, daß die gleiche Bedeutung von verschiedenen Zeichenträgern erzeugt werden kann, z. B. die Bedeutung ‹heiß› durch Beleuchtung, Kleidung, Wörter usw.

Im Theater können alle Codes der Wirklichkeit wirksam sein. Daneben gibt es typische theatrale Codes oder Subcodes, wie Make-up-Konventionen, Sprechkonventionen (→Bühnensprache) usw. (siehe Elam 1980, 52 ff). Als einen sehr spezifischen, nur dem Theater eigenen Code nennt Fischer-Lichte (I, 21) den internen Code des Theaters, der regelt, welche Zeichen gebraucht werden können in welchen Kombinationen und mit welchen Bedeutungen.

Analog zur Sprachwissenschaft wurden viele Versuche unternommen (Kowzan 1968; Corvin 1971), eine Inszenierung in kleinste Bedeutungseinheiten zu unterteilen (siehe Elam, 46 ff; Fischer-Lichte, 183 ff). Das Scheitern dieser Versuche schreibt man der falschen Analogie mit den Objekten der Linguistik zu (Elam 1980, 46 ff); gerade das Fehlen von homogenen Einheiten sieht Fischer-Lichte als typisch für das Theater (1983, I, 183 ff) an.

Neben den genannten Analysemöglichkeiten der gebrauchten Zeichen und ihren Merkmalen sind Analysemethoden vorgestellt worden für (u. a.) die Interrelationen der Momente einer Inszenierung in ihrem Zusammenhang; den Spannungsaufbau; die Figurenkonfigurationen einer Inszenierung und die Kräfte in der fiktionalen Welt; die Mikroanalyse der Dialoge.

Van der Kun (1970) beschreibt die Analyse der Teile oder Momente einer Inszenierung in ihren Interrelationen. Zentral in seiner Theorie ist der Begriff ‹Aktionsmoment›. Ein solches Moment wirkt dank seiner Beziehungen zu anderen Momenten einer Aufführung z. B. spannend oder rührend. Derartige Relationen können in bezug auf Handlungen der Vergangenheit (retrospektiv), der Gegenwart (simultan) oder der Zukunft (prospektiv) in der Aufführung auftreten. Auch können sie sich auf Elemente des Weltbilds der Zuschauer beziehen. Solche Relationen führen zu graphischen Darstellungen, die ein Bild vermitteln, wie Teilmomente mit der gesamten Aufführung zusammenhängen.

Beckermann (1970) analysiert den Spannungsaufbau kleinerer Einheiten von Texten oder Aufführungen mit Hilfe eines Konfliktmodells. Sein Begriff ‹Segment› bezeichnet eine Einheit mit Spannungszu- und abnahme. Der Spannungsaufbau bis zum Höhepunkt (Crux) entsteht, indem Intentionen (projects) einer Figur einem Widerstand (resistance) begegnen (oft die konfliktauslösende Intention einer anderen Figur).

Souriau (1950) strebte eine Analyse an, die weiter geht als eine Analyse der Konfiguration der Figuren. Er versucht, jene Kräfte in der dramatischen Welt zu analysieren, welche die Handlungen einer Situation bestimmen. Er unterscheidet sechs «Kräfte» in der dramatischen Szene: 1. die thematische Kraft, das Subjekt, das handelt; 2. den Wert, dem das Subjekt nachstrebt; 3. den Empfänger des Werts; 4. den Antagonisten als Rivalen von (1); 5. den Schiedsrichter; 6. den Helfer. Nicht alle Kräfte brauchen immer zugleich anwesend sein. Ebensowenig vertreten Figuren immer die gleiche Kraft oder nur eine. Mit Hilfe dieser Kräfte (Aktanten) wäre es – laut Souriau – möglich, alle dramatischen Situationen zu analysieren und zu charakterisieren. Pavis (1976, 87ff) reduziert dieses aktantielle Modell auf vier Kräfte (ohne 2 und 3). Dieses Modell ähnelt somit den Kategorien der klassischen Dramaturgie: Protagonist, Antagonist und Tritagonist (Verhagen 1963), wenn diese nicht als Figuren, sondern als Kräfte interpretiert werden. Analysen und Interpretationen mit Hilfe aktantieller Modelle in: Übersfeld 1982, 53ff.

In einer Mikroanalyse der einzelnen Dialoge analysiert H. Schmid (1973) den dialogischen Bedeutungsaufbau. Nicht die einzelne Replik, sondern die Replik zusammen mit der Gegenreplik als Aktions- und Reaktionsschema gilt als kleinste Analyseeinheit. Elam (1980, 184ff) schlägt eine Mikroanalyse, basierend auf deiktischen Elementen und aktivierten Kommunikationskanälen, vor. In bezug auf diese verschiedenen Analyseansätze stellen sich folgende grundlegende Fragen: Wie ist es möglich, die Folgerungen intersubjektiv zu machen, namentlich in bezug auf die erzeugte Spannung und Bedeutung oder Interpretation? Inwieweit können Aussagen gemacht werden über die theatralische Kommunikation, d. h. die Spannung und Bedeutung, welche die Rezipienten einer Inszenierung zuordnen?

Zu 2: Analysen und Beschreibungen von Inszenierungen sind zu unterscheiden nach allgemeinen Arbeiten über Produktionsmerkmale einer

448 Inszenierungsanalyse

Periode oder einer Gruppe von Inszenierungen (z. B. die «Theatre Production Studies», editiert durch John Russel Brown). Auch in diesen Arbeiten werden dem Produktionsprozeß und der Rezeption relativ wenig Aufmerksamkeit geschenkt (Ausnahmen z. B. Brauneck 1974; Selbourne 1982: über Peter Brooks *A Midsummer Night's Dream*; Coppieters, 1977: über die Rezeption der *People Show* 1964). Unterlagen, die für die Rekonstruktion des Produktionsprozesses relevant sind, wie z. B. Passows Ausgabe von Max Reinhardts Regiebuch zu *Faust I*, stehen kaum zur Verfügung. Über Inszenierungen und ihre Interpretation liegen dagegen viele Publikationen vor. Wichtig ist die konsequent inszenierungsbezogene Reihe von Bablet und Jacquot: *Les voies de la création théâtrale*.

Anderson, R. G.: A Pilot Investigation Concerning the Use of Videotape Recording in Improving Actor-Director Communications during the Rehearsal Period. Diss. Univ. of Missouri 1975; Beckerman, B.: Dynamics of Drama, Theory and Method of Analysis. New York 1970; Brauneck, M.: Literatur und Öffentlichkeit im ausgehenden 19. Jh. Stuttgart 1974; Carlson, M.: Theories of the Theatre. A Historical and Critical Survey, from the Greeks to the Present. Ithaca/London 1984; Coppieters, F.: Towards a Performance Theory of Environmental Theatre. Diss. Antwerpen 1977; Corvin, M.: A Propos des spectacles de R. Wilson: essai de lecture sémiotique. Cahiers Renaud-Barrault 77 (1971), S. 90–111; Eco, U.: Semiotics of Theatrical Performance. The Drama Review 21 (1977), 107–117; Elam, K.: The Semiotics of Theatre and Drama. London 1980; Eschbach, A.: Pragmasemiotik und Theater. Tübingen 1979; Fischer-Lichte, E.: Semiotik des Theaters. 3 Bde. Tübingen 1983; Hansen, B./Bormann, E.: A New Look at the Semantic Differential. Speech Monographs 36 (1969), 2, 163–171; Hogendoorn, W.: Lezen en zien spelen. Diss. Leiden 1976; Kesteren, A. van: Theaterwetenschap. Methodologie voor een jonge wetenschap. Diss. Antwerpen 1981, Kesteren, A. van/Schmid, H. (Hg.): Moderne Dramentheorie, Kronberg/Ts. 1975; Kowzan, T.: Littérature et Spectacle. Den Haag etc. 1975; Kun, J. I. M. van der: Handelingsaspecten in het drama. (Diss. Nijmegen 1938) Amsterdam 1970; Marinis, M. de: Lo spettacolo come testo (I). Versus 1978, 66–104; Matejka, L./Titunik, I. (ed.): Semiotics of Art: Prague School Contributions. Cambridge (Mass.) 1976; Passow, W.: Max Reinhardts Regiebuch zu Faust I. 2 Bde. München 1971; Pavis, P.: Problèmes de semiologie théâtrale. Montreal 1976; ders.: Voix et images de la scène. Lille 1985; Perdue, M. F. R.: The Influence of the Director on Cast and Audience Perception of the Message of a Play as Measured by Paired Comparison Scaling. Diss. Pennsylvania State Univ. 1975; Pfister, M.: Das Drama. Theorie und Analyse. München 1977; Ruble, R. M.: Performer Descriptions of stressed rehearsal Conditions Created by an Authoritarian and a Libertian Direction Method. Diss. Bowling Green 1975; Schälzky, H.: Empirisch-quantitative Methoden in der Theaterwissenschaft. München 1980; Schmid, H.: Strukturalistische Dramentheorie. Semantische Analyse von Čechows *Ivanov* und *Der Kirschgarten*. Kronberg/Ts. 1973; Schmid, H./van Kesteren, A.: Semiotics of Drama and Theatre. Amsterdam/Philadelphia 1984; Schoenmakers, H.: Zeven manieren om de zevende hemel te bezoeken. (Diss. Antwerpen) Amsterdam 1983; Selbourne, D.: The Making of a Midsummer Night's Dream. London 1982; Serpieri, A. et al., Come communica il teatro: dal testo alla scena. Milano 1978; Souriau, E.: Les deux cent mille situations dramatiques. Paris 1950; Steinbeck, D.: Einleitung in die Theorie und Systematik der Theaterwissenschaft. Berlin 1971; Tinchon, H. J.: Experimentelle Wirkungsforschung im Bereich der Massenmedien. Wien 1977; Tindemans, C.: The Theatre Public. A Semiotic Approach (Das Theater und sein Publikum). Wien 1977, 32–42; ders.: De voorstellingsanalyse. Enkele (voorzichtige) methodologische openingen. Scenarium, 3 (1979), 56–67; Trauth, S. M.: An Investigation of the Effects of the Director's System of Communication on Actor Inventiveness and the Rehearsal atmosphere. Diss. Bowling Green 1975; Übersfeld, A.: Lire le Théâtre. Paris 1982; Verhagen, B.: Dramaturgie. (2e dr. bezorgd door W. Ph. Pos.) Amsterdam 1963; Bablet, D./Jacquot, J. (ed.): les voies de la création théâtrale. Paris 1970–83 (11 Bde.).

Henri Schoenmakers

Intendant

(→Theatersystem, →Hoftheater, →Deutscher Bühnenverein) Der I. ist der künstlerische Leiter eines Theaters der öffentlichen Hand. Ihm obliegt im Regelfall neben der künstlerischen auch die wirtschaftliche Leitung des Theaters im Rahmen der von dem Rechtsträger vorgegebenen Geschäftsanweisung. Er vertritt – unbeschadet der Repräsentation durch den Rechtsträger – das Theater in der Öffentlichkeit. Für den Bühnenleiter eines →Privattheaters hat sich der Begriff des Direktors eingeprägt. Der I. wird von dem Rechtsträger des Theaters eingestellt. Auf Grund des I.-Vertrags ist ihm die Leitung des Theaters übertragen. Im Rahmen dieser Tätigkeit obliegen ihm u. a. folgende Aufgaben:
▸ Gestaltung des Spielplans: Mit der Gestaltung und Durchführung des Spielplans verwirklicht sich der künstlerische Auftrag eines I. In ihm spiegelt sich sein künstlerisches Konzept wider.
▸ Einstellung und Entlassung von Bühnenmitgliedern sowie des nichtkünstlerischen Personals: Diese Aufgaben dienen der bzw. ermöglichen ebenfalls erst die Durchsetzung seines künstlerischen Konzepts. Deshalb ist der Wechsel eines I. häufig mit einem Auswechseln des künstlerischen Personals verbunden. Viele I. umgeben sich mit einer festen Gruppe, die sie dann ‹mitbringen›.
▸ Verteilung der Rollen, der Regieaufträge, die Regie und bühnenbildnerischen Aufgaben sowie sonstige künstlerische Aufgaben.
    Im Einzelfall ist der I. auch für den Verwaltungsbereich des Theaters verantwortlich. Er wird diese Aufgabe jedoch an einen Verwaltungsdirektor bzw. Verwaltungsleiter delegieren, der von dem Rechtsträger für das Theater eingestellt wird. Teilweise sehen die Theater-Verfassungen jedoch vor, daß neben dem I. ein kaufmännischer Direktor gleichberechtigt und zum Teil künstlerisch mitverantwortlich eingesetzt ist. Diese

450 Intendant

Verfassung befindet sich in der Regel bei Theatern, die in der Form einer privatrechtlichen Person (GmbH) organisiert sind. Dem I. sind alle Bühnenmitglieder und das gesamte techn. und Verwaltungspersonal unterstellt und unterliegen seinen Weisungen. Damit stellt sich der I. praktisch als Arbeitgeber der am Theater Beschäftigten dar, obwohl diese ihre Verträge mit dem Rechtsträger abschließen und der I. hierbei den Rechtsträger vertritt. Im Theateraufbau nimmt der I. eine Sonderstellung ein: einerseits übt er gegenüber den an einem Theater Beschäftigten Arbeitgeberfunktion aus, andererseits wird er von dem jeweiligen Rechtsträger befristet eingestellt. – Die I. bilden auf Grund ihrer Sonderstellung eine eigene Gruppe im →Deutschen Bühnenverein.

Die Stellung des I. ist in den 70er Jahren zunehmend in Frage gestellt. Es wurde eine Mitbestimmung der Bühnenkünstler an der Spielplangestaltung sowie der Rollenbesetzung und der Einstellung von Bühnenmitgliedern gefordert. Diese Forderungen wurden – abgesehen von Einzelfällen (z. B. Kiel, Berlin, Frankfurt/M.) – nicht realisiert. Nach wie vor obliegt dem I. die alleinige Verantwortung für das Theater.

Historische Entwicklung
Erst im Zusammenhang mit der Errichtung stehender Bühnen taucht der Begriff des I. auf. Er entstammt urspr. dem frz. feudalen Verwaltungssystem. Die Übernahme dieses Verwaltungsbegriffs auf das Theaterwesen ergab sich, als während des 18. Jh. die adligen Höfe stehende Theater gründeten. Das Amt des I., das urspr. nur ein Nebenamt war, avancierte im 19. Jh. zur selbständigen Hofcharge, was bedeutet, daß sie nur noch dem hohen Adel vorbehalten und von Verdiensten – meist auf militärischem Gebiet – abhängig war. Diese Hof-I., denen urspr. rein administrative Befugnisse zustanden, zogen immer mehr künstlerische Kompetenzen an sich. In den sog. Stadttheatern zeichnet sich eine andere Entwicklung ab: Der von der Stadt eingesetzte I. hat nur künstlerische Aufgaben, während die administrativen und finanziellen Fragen dem städtischen Komitee oblagen. In den 20er Jahren konsolidierte sich im Sprachgebrauch der Begriff des I. für den künstlerischen und verwaltungsmäßigen Leiter eines Staats- bzw. Stadttheaters. In der Zeit nach Erlaß des Reichskulturkammergesetzes vom 22.9.1933 blieb diese Bezeichnung für den künstlerischen und verwaltungsmäßigen Leiter eines Theaters der Öffentlichkeit erhalten. Dieser Sprachgebrauch dauert fort.

Ballettintendanz/intendant
Die Einrichtung selbständiger Ballettintendanzen an Mehrspartenhäusern stellt im deutschsprachigen Raum eine neue Entwicklung dar. Künstlerisch und bis zu einem gewissen Grad auch wirtschaftlich und organisatorisch ist damit eine weitgehende Unabhängigkeit der Tanz-

ensembles von den Operndirektoren bzw. -intendanten verbunden, denen die Ballettdirektoren gewöhnlich unterstellt sind. Die Ballettintendanz bilden in der Regel ein künstlerisch verantwortlicher Choreograph (meist zugleich Chefchoreograph des Ensembles) und ein Verwaltungsleiter (Betriebsdirektor). Die Aufgaben des Ballettintendanten in der Sparte Tanz entsprechen denen des Opern- bzw. Schauspielintendanten (Hamburg, Frankfurt/Main).

Däubler, W. Die betriebsverfassungsrechtliche Sonderstellung von Bühnenbetrieben. In: Bühnengenossenschaft 12 (1980), S. 6–9; Dünnwald, R.: Die Rechtsstellung des Theaterintendanten. Diss. Köln 1964; Kunig, P.: Bühnenleiter und Kunstfreiheitsgarantie. In: Die öffentliche Verwaltung 1982, S. 765 ff.

Roswitha Körner / Horst Vollmer

Intermezzo

Intermède; →Entremés, Intromesi, Intromessa, →Zwischenspiele. Fester theatralischer Gattungsbegriff. Eigenständige dramatische Kurzform. Einschübe zur Ausfüllung von →Zwischenakten. Drameneinlagen vom 15. bis 17. Jh. Zunächst kein Zusammenhang, erst allmählich Vereinigung zu eigenständiger dramatischer Spielfolge.

Entwicklung aus sechs künstlerischen Gestaltungsformen: antiken Chören, span. →Entreméses, engl. →Interludes, frz. →Farcen, dem Volkslied und dem Rüpelspiel. Elemente: Tänze, Pantomimen, akrobatische Vorführungen, Chöre, Musikstücke, Rezitationen, Singspiele mythologischen Charakters, pompös ausgestattete Ballette, burleske Typenstücke mit erotischer Komponente, phantasievolle Aufzüge und Feuerwerke.

Junk, V.: Handbuch des Tanzes. Hildesheim/New York 1977; Pirrotta, N.: Intermedium. In: Blume, F. (Hg.): Musik in Geschichte und Gegenwart. Bd. VI. Sp. 1310–1326. Kassel 1960; Riemann, H./Gurlitt, W.: Interludium und Intermedium. In: Riemann Musiklexikon. Sachteil. Mainz 1967, S. 407–408.

Helga Ettl

Internationale Kulturfabrik Kampnagel

Hamburger Theaterzentrum (ehemaliges Eisenwerk) für experimentelle, avantgardistische Richtungen des →Freien Theaters, das sich zu einem der bedeutendsten seiner Art in Deutschland entwickelt hat. Seit 1986 findet in der I. K. K. mit staatlicher Unterstützung (ca. 3,5 Mio. DM jährlich) kontinuierliche Theaterarbeit statt. Das Zentrum verfügt über vier Bühnenräume, die gelegentlich von den Staatstheatern genutzt werden, zahlreiche Probenräume, eine Ausstellungshalle, eine Galerie («KX») und ein malerisch-morbides Außengelände, das zu experimentellen Out-door-Performances anregt. Jährlich werden mit wechselnden Hamburger Theatermachern ca. zehn Eigenproduktionen erarbeitet. Internationale Gastspiele (Schwerpunkt Tanztheater) geben einen Überblick über aktuelle Entwicklungen der Freien Theaterszene.

Leitung 1986–89: Hannah Hurtzig und Mücke Quinckhardt; seit 1990: Hans Man in't Veld (ehemals →Het Werktheater) und Wolfgang Kremer.

Seit 1984 findet auf dem Gelände jährlich das «Internationale Sommertheater Festival» statt, das mit wechselnden thematischen Schwerpunkten einen Überblick über Entwicklungen des Avantgardetheaters gibt und sich zum größten und bedeutendsten seiner Art in Deutschland entwickelt hat. Seit 1987 gibt es einmal pro Jahr ein Kabarettfestival, seit 1990 Internationale Tanztheaterwochen; seit Januar 1992 arbeitet dort auch das «JAK» (Jugendtheater auf Kampnagel).

Deutsches Schauspielhaus Hamburg (Hg.): Spielorte. Hamburg 1984; Zentrum für Theaterforschung der Universität Hamburg: Theaterstadt Hamburg. Reinbek 1989, S. 213–215; Schindler, C.: Kampnagelfabrik Hamburg. Die Suche nach nicht-traditionellen Spielstätten als Ausdruck ästhetischer und struktureller Veränderungen am Theater. Magisterarbeit, Universität Hamburg 1991 (unveröffentl.)

Annette Waldmann

Intimes Theater

Bezeichnung für eine sich um die Jahrhundertwende in verschiedenen Ländern Europas entwickelnde neue Form des Theaters – in architektonischer, dramatisch-dramaturgischer und schauspielerischer Hinsicht. Zu den Vorläufern gehören Antoines →Théâtre Libre, die sich anschließende Bewegung der →Freien Bühnen und Lugné-Poës →Théâtre de l'Œuvre. 1895 entstand ein erstes I.T. in München, 1906 mit anderem Namen, aber ähnlicher Zielsetzung, Max Reinhardts Kammerspiele in Berlin. Am bekanntesten und wohl auch einflußreichsten ist das am 26.11.1907 in Stockholm mit seinem Kammerspiel *Der Scheiterhaufen* eröffnete I.T. A. Strindbergs, das er mit A. Falck gründete. Was Strindberg unter I.T. verstand, bezog sich auf alle am theatralischen Vorgang Beteiligten. Ein kleines Theater sollte die Möglichkeit direkten Kontakts zwischen Bühne und Publikum ermöglichen, zugleich aber verhindern, daß zur Füllung eines großen Hauses dem Massengeschmack Zugeständnisse gemacht werden müßten. Kleine Form auch bei den neu zu schreibenden Stücken, Verzicht auf äußere Handlung und große Besetzung, Verzicht auch auf naturalistische Bühnenausstattung, an deren Stelle stilisierte, symbolhafte Requisiten treten sollten (→Symbolistisches Theater). Auch die Schauspieler sollten eine neue, intime Art der Darstellung entwickeln, die ohne Effekte und Virtuosentum vor allem suggestiv und andeutend wirken sollte. Trotz Erfolgen beim Publikum und später auch bei der Kritik mußte das I. T. vor allem aus finanziellen Gründen bereits am 11.12.1910 geschlossen werden. Hinzu kam der Bruch Strindbergs mit seinem Partner Falck. – Bereits die zeitgenössischen Gegner der neuen Form bekämpften das I. T. als Ausdruck eines elitären Ästhetizismus, beklagten seine programmatische Absage an die Massenwirksamkeit und die soziale Funktion des Theaters.

Trotz seiner kurzen Lebensdauer übte das I. T. Strindbergs bis in die Gegenwart hinein großen Einfluß aus, besonders seine entsprechenden dramaturgischen Vorstellungen. Ihre Wirkungen reichen bis zu Ionesco, Adamov und Beckett.

Delius, A.: Intimes Theater. Kronberg/Ts. 1976; Miller, A. J.: The Independent Theatre in Europe, 1887 to the Present. New York 1931; Strindberg, A.: Über Drama und Theater. Hg. v. M. Kesting u. V. Arpe. Köln 1966.

Wolfgang Beck

Intrige

(Lat. intricare = verwickeln; ital. intrigo; frz. intrigue) Im Deutschen oft enger verwendet als im Ital. und Frz. im Sinne von Verwicklungen, Kabalen, Ränken, daher häufiger Gebrauch in der Komödie, bes. der sog. ‹Intrigenkomödie›, frz. ‹comédie d'intrigue›: Die durch den Intriganten eingefädelte Verwicklung mit Wiederholungseffekten und Theaterstreichen ist darin die Grundlage der Komik nebst der Endbereinigung. In der Tragödie führt die I. absichtlich oder ironisch den Untergang des Helden herbei, so in Shakespeares *Othello* (1605) die Listen des Jago, in Schillers *Don Carlos* (1787) die gutgemeinte I. des Posa. – Im Frz. gilt die I. seit der Klassik als die äußere, sichtbare Entwicklung des Geschehens bei strenger Kausalität der Abfolge. Nach Marmontel ist «die I. eine Kette, von der jedes Ereignis ein Glied sein muß» (1787). Für A. Simon kann es so formuliert werden: «Die I. ist der Gegenstand des Stücks, das Spiel der Umstände, der Knoten der Ereignisse. Die Handlung ist die tiefere Dynamik dieses Gegenstands» (1970). Insofern entspricht die I. eher dem engl. ‹plot›.

Knorr, H.: Wesen u. Funktion des Intriganten. Diss. Erlangen 1951; Pavis, P.: Dictionnaire du théâtre. Paris 1980; Simon, A.: Dictionnaire du théâtre français contemporain. Paris 1970.

Gérard Schneilin

Irish Dramatic Movement

Literarische Bewegung, die seit den 80er Jahren des 19. Jh. als Teil der nationalen ‹Irish Renaissance› bemüht war, eine eigenständige irische Theaterkultur zu etablieren. Neben der parlamentarischen ‹Home Rule›-Bewegung und der 1893 von Douglas Hyde (1862–1946) gegr. Gaelic League gehörte die I. D. M. zu den bedeutendsten Faktoren bei der Herausbildung einer irischen Identität. Gefördert werden sollten Dramen, die einem irischen Publikum irische Sujets präsentierten, wobei häufig auf irisch-keltische Mythen rekurriert wurde. Diese romantische Rückbesinnung war jedoch nicht Selbstzweck, sondern sollte das Bewußtsein eigener Traditionen einer als fremd und aufgezwungen empfundenen Kultur, der engl., entgegensetzen.

1899 gründeten William Butler Yeats (1865–1939), George Moore (1852–1933), Edward Martyn (1859–1924) und Lady Augusta Gregory (1852–1932) das Irish Literary Theatre in Dublin. Der gleiche Personenkreis gründete im Jahre 1901 The Irish National Theatre Society, aus der 1904 in Zusammenarbeit mit den Schauspielern William (1872–1949) und Frank Fay (1873–1931) das → Abbey Theatre hervorging.

Zu den wichtigsten Dramen, die unter dem Einfluß der I. D. M. entstanden sind, gehören *Cathleen Ni Houlihan* (1902) von Yeats und Lady Gregory, Yeats' *Countess Cathleen* (1899) sowie die Hauptwerke von John Millington Synge (1871–1909), *The Playboy of the Western World* (1907) und *Deirdre of the Sorrows* (1910).

Ellis-Fermor, U.: The Irish Dramatic Movement. London 1977; Fallis, R.: The Irish Renaissance. Dublin 1978; Völker, K.: Yeats und Synge. Velber 1972.

Werner Bleike

Ironie

(Griech.: ‹euronia› = Verschleierung) Doppelbödigkeit eines Texts mit offensichtlicher und tieferer, oft gegensätzlicher Bedeutung. – 1. Allgemein ein Mittel der Komik des Autors und seiner Personen, bes. in → Komödie, → Tragikomödie und anderen komischen Gattungen. – 2. Dramatische I. ist als Strukturelement an Situation und Kommunikation gebunden; sie besteht darin, daß Autor und Zuschauer mehr wissen als die Personen (bes. die Hauptfigur) oder gewisse Figuren mehr als andere (Seher, Sprecher). Insofern wirkt sie verfremdend. – 3. Die tragische I. besteht darin, daß der Held in seiner Verblendung und Hybris Sinn und Zweck seiner Handlungen mißversteht und statt der erwähnten Lösung des Konflikts seinen eigenen Untergang herbeiführt. Sie wird durch die Peripetie ausgedrückt und ist mit der dramatischen I. insofern verbunden, als die Wahrnehmung des Sinns beim Helden und beim Publikum sich nicht deckt.

Berühmtestes Beispiel der dramatischen und tragischen I. ist *Oedipus Rex* (nach 429 v. Chr.) von Sophokles (497/96–406 v. Chr.).

Behler, E.: Der Ursprung des Begriffs der tragischen Ironie. In: Arcadia 5 (1970), 2; ders.: Klassische Ironie – Romantische Ironie – Tragische Ironie. Darmstadt 1972; Booth, W.: The Rhetoric of Irony. Chicago 1974; Schäfer, A. (Hg.): Ironie und Dichtung. München 1970; Sharpe, R. B.: Irony in the Drama. Chapel Hill 1959; States, B. O.: Irony and Drama. Ithaca 1971.

Patrice Pavis

Isshin-denshin

‹Von Herz zu Herz›, urspr. die direkte, unmittelbare Unterweisung des Schülers durch seinen Lehrmeister im Buddhismus bezeichnend, hat als durchgehendes Prinzip jap. Traditionsweitergabe auch im Bereich der Theaterkultur Auswirkungen gehabt. Zum ersten wirkte diese Traditionsart schulbildend und ließ, verstärkt durch das familiare Prinzip in kunstausübenden Berufen, das gerade bei den lange Zeit sozial verachteten, eine gesellschaftliche Rand- und Sondergruppe bildenden Schauspielern (überlebens)notwendig war, in den bekannten Theaterformen Schauspielerfamilien entstehen und somit Vererbung und Überlieferung zu Pfeilern vormoderner Schauspielkunst werden. – Im →Nô sind es die fünf traditionell die *shitekata*-Hauptrollen stellenden Familien Kanze, Hoshô, Komparu, Kongô und Kita sowie die als ‹3 Fächer› bezeichneten Familien der Nebenspieler, der Musiker und der *kyôgen*-Komödianten. Im *kabuki* werden in den sechs bis sieben Schauspielerdynastien, die heute auf eine dreihundertjährige Tradition zurückblicken, Vornamen und Beinamen berühmter Schulahnen und Darsteller von Generation zu Generation vererbt und damit die z. T. allerdings nur durch Adoption zu sichernde Erbfolge auch nach außen demonstriert. Zum zweiten schlägt sich dieses Tradierungsprinzip in der textlichen Grundlage der genannten Bühnenkünste nieder: Ausgearbeitete Bühnenbücher (*daihon, shôhon*) mit genauem Text und detaillierten Regieanweisungen sind bei den die unmittelbare direkte Unterweisung bevorzugenden Theaterformen nicht so notwendig, wurden erst relativ spät verfaßt und dem familienexklusiven Prinzip entsprechend geheim überliefert.

Roland Schneider

İstanbul Şehir Tiyatrosu

(Stadttheater Istanbul) Das İŞT geht zurück auf das erste türk. Theater, Dârülbedayi, das 1913 bis 1914 unter Mithilfe des Franzosen André Antoine (→ Théâtre Libre) gegründet wurde. Vorher gab es nur Theater, die von Angehörigen ethnischer Minderheiten, vor allem Armeniern, geleitet wurden; diese führten Werke in ihrer eigenen und in türk. Sprache auf. Auch die Schauspieler des Dârülbedayi waren anfangs zum großen Teil Armenier, Juden oder Griechen, die ersten Türkinnen traten erst 1918 auf. In der Frühzeit dieses Theaters wurden nur Übersetzungen gespielt, die auch nach der ersten Aufführung eines türk. Werks (1917) in der Überzahl blieben. Lange Zeit wurde ein Stück nur zwei- bis siebenmal aufgeführt; erst nachdem der Regisseur Muhsin Ertuğrul zum Direktor berufen wurde (1927), steigerte sich die Zahl der Aufführungen. Im Jahre 1934 wurde der Name in İŞT geändert. Seit dieser Zeit wurden verstärkt Werke türk. Autoren in den Spielplan aufgenommen. Die Besucherzahlen stiegen kontinuierlich. Heute spielt das İŞT regelmäßig auf drei Bühnen und besuchsweise in den verschiedenen Stadtteilen. In den Sommermonaten finden in der Burg Rumelihisarı Freilichtaufführungen statt. Neben diesem kommunalen Theater gibt es in Istanbul zahlreiche private Theater.

Maren Fittschen

ITI

Internationales Theater-Institut. – Ziel der Institution ist die Förderung des kulturellen Austauschs zwischen den Völkern, die Mitteilung von Erfahrungen aus dem Bereich des Theaters. 1948 in Prag gegr., befindet sich das Zentralbüro heute in Paris, es veranstaltet Kolloquien, Tagungen und Theaterfestivals, so seit 1954 das → Theater der Nationen; ein bes. Schwerpunkt ist die Förderung und der Austausch mit Theater-Kulturen der Dritten Welt. Das ITI ist Mitglied der UNESCO und gibt die zweisprachige Zeitschrift «Le Théâtre dans le Monde»/«World Theatre» heraus.

Es gibt über 60 nationale Zentren, das Zentrum Bundesrepublik Deutschland des Internationalen Theaterinstituts e. V. hat seinen Sitz in Berlin, veranstaltet allein oder in Zusammenarbeit mit anderen nationalen Zentren Workshops und Seminare, Theateraustausch mit anderen Ländern, berät staatliche Stellen in Theaterfragen und stellt eine Bibliothek mit Schriften der ausländischen ITI-Zentren und Fachliteratur zur Verfügung. Außerdem informiert Berlin über das deutschsprachige Theaterleben mit schriftlichen Veröffentlichungen und in anderen Medien (z. B. Video).

Genossenschaft Deutscher Bühnenangehöriger (Hg.): Deutsches Bühnenjahrbuch 1985. Hamburg 1984.

Ute Hagel

Jahreszeitenspiele

Im slaw.-dt. Grenzgebiet hatte sich der Brauch des Winteraustreibens eingebürgert, eine Tradition, die auch in anderen Teilen Europas in verschiedensten Formen lebendig war oder noch ist. Eine Strohpuppe, ein wilder Mann wird ausgetrieben, getötet, verbrannt. Doch hat sich dieser Brauch gewöhnlich nicht zum Drama verdichtet. Die Urform des Neidhartspiels: das Suchen nach dem Veilchen, erster Text 14. Jh., hat den Charakter eines Frühlingsspiels. Doch entwickelte sich dieser Stoff sehr rasch zu einer umfassenden →Farce und verlor so den jahreszeitlichen Charakter. Ein anderes J. ist ein Schweizer Mai-Herbst-Spiel aus dem 14. Jh. Eine Aufführung ist jedoch mehr als zweifelhaft. Dagegen wurde ein Tiroler Dokument desselben Stoffs wirklich auf der ortlosen Bühne der →Fastnachtsspiele dargeboten (→Mittelalter/Drama und Theater des Mittelalters).

Catholy, E.: Das Fastnachtspiel des Spätmittelalters (Hermaea 8). Tübingen 1961; Christ-Kutter, F.: Frühe Schweizerspiele (Altdt. Übungstexte 19). Bern 1963; Dörrer, A.: «Jahreszeitenspiele». In: Verfasserlexikon V, S. 437–443.

Wolfgang F. Michael

Japanisches Theater

Auch in Japan sind Tanz, Gesang und pantomimische Darstellung, Grundelemente der Schaukunst, in ihren Anfängen eng mit kultischen Handlungen verbunden gewesen. Sowohl die frühesten greifbaren Tanzformen, die *kagura*, als auch der in den Mythen geschilderte Tanz der

Göttin Uzume, mit dem die Sonne(ngottheit) aus dem Dunkel gelockt wird, weisen auf den Zusammenhang zu sog. *tamafuri*-Beschwörungen hin, mit denen man die lebenspendende Ursubstanz (*tama*) zur Materialisierung im menschlichen Körper bewegen wollte. Andere frühgeschichtliche Formen wie die Tänze *yamato-mai* und *ta-mai* entsprangen dem Kult um die Reisfeldbestellung und überlebten in zeremonialisierter Form im höfischen Reisweihe-Ritus.

Seit mit der Einführung des Buddhismus ab dem 5. Jh. über Korea oder auch direkt von China eine starke Rezeption chinesischer Kultur einsetzte, wurden jene autochthonen Formen durch vom Festland einfließende Formen modifiziert und bereichert, aber auch überdeckt und verdrängt. Im 7. Jh. brachten koreanische Einwanderer das ‹chinesische› *gigaku* mit, eine Art musikbegleitete Prozessionsmaskerade, an deren Ende Einzeltänze und pantomimische Gruppendarbietungen standen. Die Herkunft dieser Schaukunstform ist wohl in Zentral- oder Vorderasien zu suchen, von wo sie ab dem 3. Jh. nach China eingeflossen war. Das ab dem 8. Jh. nach Japan eingeführte *bugaku*, musikalische Stücke und Gruppentänze mit teils tungusisch-koreanischen, teils indisch-chinesischen Elementen, wurde bald Mittelpunkt höfischer Zeremonialmusik.

Für die Ausbildung späterer jap. Theaterformen, auch des →Nô, sollte jedoch der Einfluß des in mehreren Wellen nach Japan gelangenden chinesischen *san-yüeh* entscheidender sein. *San-yüeh*, jap. *sangaku* bzw. bald, noch stärker japonisiert, *sarugaku* ausgesprochen, war Sammelbezeichnung für eine Vielzahl von (Volks-)Schaukünsten, die neben Akrobatik und Zaubertricks auch tänzerisch-musikalische, pantomimische und wahrscheinlich auch dramatische Elemente enthielten. Das von professionellen sarugaku-Spielern bei Hoffesten oder von Laienspielern, den Höflingen, nach Banketten aufgeführte sarugaku scheint neben akrobatischen auch komische Elemente enthalten zu haben, ebenso wie das ab dem 10. Jh. sporadisch, ab dem 11. Jh. häufig in den Quellen erwähnte Volks-sarugaku, das an den großen Schreinfesten in Kyôto und Nara zahlreiche Zuschauer fand. Berichten in zeitgenössischen Tagebüchern oder im *Unshû-shôsoku* (Briefsteller; um 1050) zufolge beinhaltete dieses Volks-sarugaku bereits kürzere Szenen mit geschlossener Handlung und Dialog, was von Fujiwara Akihiras (989–1066) verfaßten *Shin-sarugaku-ki* (‹Bericht über das Neue Sarugaku›; um 1030) indirekt bestätigt wird.

Träger dieses sarugaku waren die sog. *sarugaku-hôshi* (sarugaku-‹Mönche›), eine der zahlreichen Gruppen der *zôgeisha* genannten Wanderkünstler, die sich seit dem Beginn des 11. Jh. in steuerfreien Sondersiedlungen (*sanjo*) bei Tempeln und Schreinen ansiedelten und für die Gestaltung der Feste verantwortlich waren. Diese sanjo-Sondersiedlungen und die von ihnen getragenen Feste wurden so Ausgangspunkt und

Nô: Maske einer alten Frau in einer Aufführung des Nô-Nationaltheaters Tokio (DG)

PLAN OF NŌ STAGE

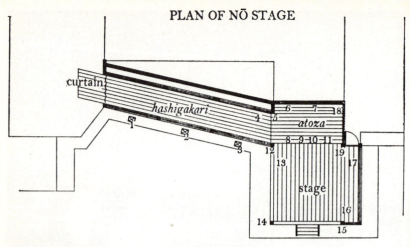

1. third pine
2. second pine
3. first pine
4. Kyōgen performer's seat
5. Kyōgen pillar
6. *kōken*'s seat
7. *kagami ita*
8. *taiko* player's seat
9. *ōkawa* player's seat
10. *kozutsumi* player's seat
11. flutist's seat
12. *shite* pillar
13. *shite* performer's seat
14. "eye-fixing" pillar
15. *waki* pillar
16. *waki* performer's seat
17. seats for the chorus
18. *kirido*
19. flute pillar

Grundriß einer Nô-Bühne (TS)

Szene einer Nô-Aufführung: Geistererscheinung (TS)

Chujo-Maske. Tanz (hayamai) in einer Nô-Aufführung; im Hintergrund der Chor (KH)

Szene aus einer Kabuki-Aufführung (FM)

Szene aus einer Jôruri-(Bunraku-)Aufführung (FM)

Bühnentechnische Anweisung für eine Geistererscheinung
durch Hängevorrichtungen (TS)

Performance der Butoh-Gruppe «Byakko-sha» (JA)

Nukleus einer Vielzahl mittelalterlicher Schaukunstformen: *shushi*-(‹Magier›-)Meister, ehemals Exorzisten und Heilpraktiker, gestalteten urspr. buddhistische Stoffe zu einem weltlichen Unterhaltungsspiel um, an dem Sänger, Instrumentalisten und Tänzer mitwirkten. Bei dem *shira-byôshi* und ihrer Nachfolgekunst, *kusemai*, trugen Männergruppen zum Tanz halbreligiöse legendenhafte Stoffe vor, Frauengruppen zumeist Lieder – Künste, aus denen sich dann im späten Mittelalter auch die vom Schwertadel geschätzte Tanz- und Rezitationsbühnenkunst der *kôwaka* herausbildete. Neben sog. glück- und segenerflehenden Tänzen, *ennen-mai* und *senzumanzai*, profitierten jedoch auch jene beiden Gattungen mittelalterlicher Theaterkunst von der kreativen, künstlerischen Austausch evozierenden Atmosphäre der sanjo und ihres Umfelds, die bald am höchsten geschätzt wurden, das *dengaku* und das Nô. Das *dengaku*, wörtl. ‹Feldspiel›, hat seinen Ursprung in kultischen Spielen und Festen um das Umsetzen der jungen Reispflanzen in das Wasserfeld. Diese ‹Feld-Feste› (*ta-asobi*), erweitert um unterhaltende Teile, wurden schon in der Heian-Zeit (794–1192) oft zu reinen Schauvorführungen, getragen von professionellen Spielern, wohl aus dem sanjo-Bereich, die sich ab der Mitte des 12. Jh. in gildenähnlichen Gruppen (*za*) organisierten. Während der Kamakura-Epoche (1192–1333) erreichte das dengaku durch Hereinnahme von dramatischen Elementen und durch begabte Künstler, die z. T. auch Lehrer der Nô-Meister waren, außerordentliche Popularität, die es sich jedoch bald mit dem Sarugaku-Nô teilen mußte, das es schließlich in der Muromachi-Epoche (1333–1573) in der Gunst des (adligen) Publikums ablöste.

Ein Zweig des sarugaku hatte sich bis zum 14. Jh. in Kontakt und Austausch mit dem dengaku, durch die neue Organisationsform der za sowie durch erhöhten Einbezug von Tanz und Gesang in sein Repertoire vom Volks-sarugaku emanzipiert und war, wie die zeitgenössische Bezeichnung ab Ende des 13. Jh. belegt, zum ‹Kunst-sarugaku›, *sarugaku (no) nô*, geworden, als das es unter den Großmeistern Kan'ami (1333–84) und dessen Sohn Zeami (1363–1445) die Protektion des hohen Schwertadels fand und durch Aufnahme und künstlerische Umsetzung der vom Zen geprägten ästhetischen Normen seines neuen Publikums zu dem noch heute geschätzten lyrischen Tanzdrama →Nô wurde, begleitet durch die die komischen Elemente der sarugaku-Tradition fortführende prosaischheitere Kunst der →*kyôgen*-Possenspiele. – Die Neuzeit, die Tokugawa-Epoche (1600–1867), erlebte zwei miteinander konkurrierende Schaukunstformen, das *jôruri*-Puppenspiel und das →kabuki-Theater.

Seine Ende des 16. Jh. anzusetzende Entstehung verdankt das →*jôruri*, inzwischen häufiger →*bunraku* genannt, dem Zusammenspiel dreier Künste: der Rezitation der populären Liebesgeschichte um die Prinzessin Jôruri, der *samisen*-(Lauten-)Musik und dem Puppenspiel, seine Blüte

460 Japanisches Theater

wurde durch das Zusammenwirken zweier Künstlerpersönlichkeiten, des Rezitators Takemoto Gidayu (1651–1714) und Japans berühmtesten Dramatikers Chikamatsu Monzaemon (1653–1725), eingeleitet und dauerte über eineinhalb Jh. an. Seine ‹historischen Dramen› (*jidaimono*), mehr noch seine ‹bürgerlichen Tragödien› (*sewamono*), die, oft in Verarbeitung aktueller Ereignisse, den Konflikt zwischen sozialer Verpflichtung (*giri*) und natürlichen Gefühlen (*ninjô*) dramatisierten, trafen den Geschmack des nun bürgerlich-städtischen Publikums. Das *kabuki*, das seinen Ursprung in um die Wende zum 17. Jh. von wandernden Schreintänzerinnen vorgeführten Tanzspielen hatte, entwickelte sich über das sog. Frauen-kabuki (*onna-kabuki*) und dessen Nachfolgekunst, das Knaben-kabuki (*wakashû-kabuki*) – beides waren revueartige, stark erotisch gefärbte Shows, die bald behördlicherseits verboten wurden – in der zweiten Hälfte des 17. Jh. zum ‹Männer-kabuki›. Seine erste Blüte, eingeleitet durch eine Weiterentwicklung des dramatischen Elements sowie durch das Auftreten erster großer, meist schul- und traditionsbildender Schauspieler, liegt in der Genroku-Epoche (1688–1703), in der in den drei städtischen Zentren – Edo, Osaka, Kyôto – eine urbane Theaterkultur entstand, die viele Bereiche städtischen Lebens (Mode, Kunst) prägen sollte. Die befruchtende Konkurrenz des *jôruri*-Puppentheaters verlangte den Schauspielern und der Bühnentechnik Höchstleistungen ab, die dem kabuki von einer zweiten Hochblüte Ende des 18. Jh. bis zur Meiji-Restauration (1868) die Gunst des Publikums sicherte.

Japans Konfrontation mit dem Westen in der Meiji-Restauration war für die gesamte Theaterszene folgenreich: Das Nô, über Jahrhunderte ars reservata des Schwertadels, verlor nach dessen Entmachtung seine Mäzene, einzelne Schulen gingen unter, andere öffneten sich der Ausbildung von (zahlenden) Laienspielern. Das höfische *bugaku* wurde zum festen Bestandteil offizieller Staatszeremonien aufgewertet. Das kabuki wurde von einer europaorientierten Kulturpolitik als unzeitgemäß und als vulgär kritisiert, mußte sich einschneidende Veränderungen gefallen lassen, wurde nun als ‹alte Schule› (*kyûha*) bezeichnet.

In bewußter Abgrenzung zu dieser entstand das →*shimpa* (‹Neue Schule›), das in den 80er Jahren des 19. Jh. als politisch engagiertes Theater begann, sich (nach einer Periode des Reportagetheaters) ab Beginn des 20. Jh. vornehmlich der Dramatisierung populärer Romane zuwandte. – Sein Konkurrent, das *shingeki* (‹Neues Theater›), bevorzugte seit seiner Entstehung im 1. Jahrzehnt unseres Jh. stets westliche Stücke, spielte ab der Taishô-Zeit (1912–26) allerdings auch moderne jap. Dramatiker. In der Nachkriegszeit litt es teilweise unter der dogmatischen Festlegung auf den realistischen Stil und verlor Teile seines experimentellen Engagements an das neue Untergrundtheater (→*angura*).

Im heutigen Japan existieren, nachdem Nô und kabuki ihre Schwierigkeiten überwunden haben, stets vor vollen Häusern spielen und zu (subventionierten) Kulturgütern geworden sind, alt und neu nebeneinander, das aristokratische Tanzdrama des Mittelalters und das bürgerliche Theater der Neuzeit neben den beiden modernen Schulen und den verschiedenen Spielarten des Untergrund- und Situationstheaters.

Barth, J.: Japans Schaukunst im Wandel der Zeiten. Wiesbaden 1972; Blau, H.: Sarugaku und Shushi. Wiesbaden 1966; Bohner, H.: Nô. Einführung. Tôkyô 1959; Ernst, E.: The Kabuki Theatre. New York 1956; Inoura, Y.: A History of Japanese Theatre I. Tôkyô 1971; Kawatake, T.: A History of Japanese Theatre II. Tôkyô 1971; Muccioli, M.: Il teatro giapponese. Milano 1962; Scott, A. C.: The Puppet Theatre of Japan. Rutland 1963.

Roland Schneider

Jaunatnes Teātris Riga

Das Jugendtheater Riga, gegr. 1941, spielt auf zwei Bühnen in Lettisch und Russisch (unterschiedliches Repertoire) Märchen, nationale Dramatik und Werke der Weltliteratur (1988 *Lolitá* von V. Nabokov) für Kinder, Jugendliche und Erwachsene. Neben P. Petersons und U. Pucitis prägt v. a. Adolf Šapiro (*1939) den Stil des J. T. (ab 1964 Chefregisseur und Intendant), leitet auch die Nachwuchsausbildung am Theater (Theorieunterricht im Konservatorium). Bemerkenswerte Aufführungen mit intellektuellem Zugriff, souveräner Beherrschung der Ausdrucksmittel (Artistik, Tanz, Gesang), reicher Psychologisierung, gestisch-realistischer Spielweise (Verfremdung und Einfühlung): 1981 *Peer Gynt*, 1982 *Der Waldschrat* von A. Tschechow, 1985 *Furcht und Elend des Dritten Reiches* (Gastspiele in Berlin, München), *Prinz von Homburg* (Titelrolle A. Shukow). Bevorzugt werden existentielle Fragen, ausgehend von der Individualität der Figuren.

Elke Wiegand

Jaunimo Teatras Vilnius

Staatliches Jugendtheater Vilnius, gegr. 1966. Im Repertoire litauische Dramatiker (S. Šaltenis), Dramen der Weltliteratur (1966 *Romeo und Julia*), moderne westeurop. und politisch-brisante russ. Autoren (J. Schwarz: *Der Drache*; *Der nackte König*). Künstlerische Leiter: 1965–68 A. Ragauskaitė, 1968–74 V. Čibiras, 1974–88 D. Tamuteviciutė; seit 1988 Eimuntas Nekrošius (*1952), Schüler von A. Gontscharow am →GITIS (1973–78). International gefeierte Inszenierungen (Son-

462 Jesuitentheater

derpreis BITEF-22) von Nekrošius prägen das J. T. schon seit 1980: *Die Katze vor der Tür* von Šaltenis/Kanovičius; Quadrat; 1981 *Pirosmani, Pirosmani...*; 1982 *Liebe und Tod in Verona*, Rockoper nach Shakespeare; 1986 *Onkel Wanja*; 1991 *Die Nase* nach Gogol. Er, den A. Miller ein Genie nannte, gestaltet in poetischen Metaphern und surrealistischer Bildersprache zentrale Themen wie Einsamkeit, Erniedrigung, Tod, Liebe, Schöpfertum. Synthese von Tradition und Modernität, Theatralität und Schlichtheit, großem Entwurf und Blick für Details. N.: «Für mich sollte eine Aufführung wie ein Gedicht geboren werden, das nicht vorausgesehen und von langer Hand geplant werden kann.» Bühnenbildnerin: Nadeshda Gultiajewa. Ab 1984 zahlreiche Auslandsgastspiele.

Elke Wiegand

Jesuitentheater

Das erste Ereignis des J. war die Aufführung des *Euripus* (1549) des Löwener Minoriten Levinus Brechtus 1555 in Wien. Das Theater der Jesuiten (1534 Ordensgründung zu Paris, 1540 vom Papst Paul III. bestätigt) blieb lange die bei weitem verbreitetste Theaterform im ganzen süd- bzw. südostdt., z. T. auch rheinischen Raum. Geburtsort und tragende Institution des (neulat.) J. war die Schule mit ihren peripheren Organisationen, den Akademien, zu denen nur die besten Schüler Zugang hatten, sowie den auch literarisch orientierten Marianischen Kongregationen. Neben der Poesie und den Affixiones (Chronogramme, Monogramme, Embleme usw.) gehörten die dramatischen Spiele zum festen Bestandteil des Erziehungssystems. Weit davon entfernt, sich auf tradierte Formen des religiösen Theaters zu beschränken, die kaum über das Niveau der Rezitation hinausgingen, ließen die Lehrer kleinere Stücke (actiunculae) und Dialoge (das →Schuldrama im engeren Sinne), zugleich ganze drei- oder fünfaktige Stücke, Komödien, Tragödien und nicht näher definierte Schauspiele zuerst am Anfang, dann am Ende (Preisverteilung) des Schuljahrs (ludi autumnales, Herbstaufführungen) einstudieren und aufführen. Auch zu festlichen Anlässen wie Kirchenweihungen, Heiligsprechungen, Translationen von Gebeinen, Besuchen von hohen kirchlichen und weltlichen Würdenträgern wurde gespielt. Aus der manchenorts engen Zusammenarbeit mit den Höfen läßt sich die nicht geringe Zahl der Gelegenheitsstücke (in Frankreich auch Ballette, s. Claude François Menestrier 1631–1705) erklären, die dem Gattungssystem der Casualpoesie entsprechend Geburten, Vermählungen, militärische Siege theatralisch feierten. Wurden solche Darbietungen – den Schul- und Fastnachtsspielen ähnlich – nicht wiederholt, so gelangten die Herbstdramen zwei- oder dreimal vor einem jeweils anderen geladenen Festpublikum externer Besucher zur Aufführung.

In einer Zeit, die auf Disziplinierung im Staat und restlose Eliminierung der volkstümlichen Belustigungen zielte, trachtete das J. danach, der Schaulust der Bevölkerung kompensatorisch zu genügen. Infolge der sich zuspitzenden konfessionellen Spannungen wurde es zum Instrument der sich etablierenden gegenreformatorischen Territorialmacht. Seine Aufgabe bestand deswegen auch darin, ein möglichst viele Schichten umfassendes Publikum anzusprechen, was dem theatralischen Element nur dienlich sein konnte. Die öffentlichen Vorstellungen zeichneten sich durch ein Gepränge aus, von dem wir uns heute kein rechtes Bild machen können und das auch sehr unterschiedlich gewesen sein mag. Fest steht jedenfalls, daß sich die Jesuiten immer aller ihnen zur Verfügung stehenden Mittel der Theatertechnik bedienten. →Simultan- und Kulissenbühne, Himmel und Hölle veranschaulichende Vertikalität, Stürme und Gewitter, Flugmaschinen und Wolken, auf denen Allegorien, Götter, Heilige, Engel thronten: Das gesamte Instrumentarium der spätmittelalterlichen und barocken Dramaturgie wurde zum Zweck der Relaxatio und vor allem der Catechisatio bemüht. Blieb die Zahl der Schauspieler verhältnismäßig gering – normalerweise waren nicht mehr als 10 bis 20 dramatis personae am Geschehen beteiligt –, so stieg die der Statisten häufig über 50. In den im Freien gegebenen Schauspielen ging sie sogar in die Hunderte. Lieder, Chöre und Musikbegleitung unter gelegentlicher Mitwirkung berühmter Komponisten (so Roland de Lassus/Orlando di Lasso in München) wurden bei den großen Aufführungen eingesetzt.

Für das damit verbundene lehrhafte Moment sorgten →Prologe, Epiloge und Chöre, die ab 1600 ausnahmslos in lat. Sprache abgefaßt wurden. Einziges Zugeständnis an die offensichtlich zahlreichen Lateinunkundigen waren die sog. →Periochen, kurze zweisprachige Inhaltsangaben, die an die Zuschauer verteilt wurden. Der 1597 in München anläßlich der Aufführung des *Triumphs des Heiligen Erzengels Michael* eingeführte Usus hielt sich überall bis zur Aufhebung (1773). Die damit erreichte Internationalität gibt von den Verbindungen zwischen den wichtigsten europ. Ländern Rechenschaft, wobei die Wahl der rezipierten ausländischen Werke und Autoren weitestgehend von der konfessionellen Orthodoxie abhing.

Hielt sich das Gros der Theaterdichter, die der Abfassung von Dramen als einer der ihnen von den Ordensstatuten auferlegten vielfachen Verpflichtungen nicht unbedingt gewachsen waren, an bewährte, Wirksamkeit und Erfolg garantierende Rezepte, dann träumte mancher Talentiertere davon, als ein Terentius oder Seneca christianus anerkannt zu werden. Gerade diesen auf das Dichterische Wert legenden Autoren schien eine Klärung ihrer poetisch-poetologischen Positionen notwendig.

464 Jesuitentheater

So ist es nicht verwunderlich, daß wir den Jesuiten, denen die ital. Aristoteles-Kommentare bekannt waren, die erste Poetik auf dt. Boden zu verdanken haben (*Poeticarum Institutionum Libri Tres*, Ingolstadt 1594, des Jakob Pontanus, 1542–1626). Am einflußreichsten waren aber A. Donatis (1584–1640) *Ars poetica* (Rom 1631), T. Galluzzis (1574–1649) *Commentarii tres* (Rom 1621), V. Guiniggis (1601–53) *Poesis... dramatica* (Antwerpen 1634), F. Strades (1572–1649) *Prolusiones poeticae* (Rom 1617) sowie die *Palaestra eloquentiae ligatae* (Köln 1657) des auch in protestantischen Kreisen hochgeschätzten Rheinländers J. Masen (1606–81). Unter den Deutschen taten sich Franz Neumayr (1697–1765: *Idea Foeseos*, Ingolstadt 1751), Ignaz Weitenauer (1709–83: *Ars Poëtica*, Augsburg und Freiburg i. B. 1757) und Anton Claus (1691–1754: Anmerkungen zu seinen 1741 in Augsburg herausgegebenen *Tragoediae ludis autumnalibus datae*) hervor. An all diesen Texten läßt sich keine genaue Definition des Jesuitendramas ablesen. Einzig und allein in Hinsicht auf das →Märtyrerdrama, dessen Rechtfertigung und Implikationen, herrschte eine gemeinsame Meinung. Von einer grundsätzlichen Ablehnung der aristotelischen Forderung nach mittleren Charakteren ausgehend, befürworteten die Theoretiker das Exemplarische, notfalls Extreme, wobei die die Handlung bewertenden Chöre zur identifizierenden oder distanzierenden Beurteilung einluden. Die imitatio Christi, deren bewunderungswürdigster Exponent ihnen zufolge eben der Märtyrer war, galt ihnen als das Vorbild des gottgefälligen Lebens, folglich als das nicht zu übertreffende Modell christlicher Dramatik. Immer ging es um Liebe zur Tugend und Haß gegen das Laster, Anregung zur praxis pietatis, Kampf im Dienste des vom Tridentinum verkündeten Lehrgebäudes der Mutter-Kirche, deren Vermittlungsrolle ununterbrochen in Erinnerung gebracht wurde, schließlich um das Bündnis mit den führenden politischen Kräften unter strengster Beachtung des Primats des Papstes in spiritualibus. Der poeta im Jesuiten war vom monachus nicht zu trennen. Dies läßt sich u. a. in der stets präsenten transzendentalen Dimension des Gezeigten beobachten, ebenso unmißverständlich in der nicht zu übersehenden Neigung, ‹Fälle› zu präsentieren. Der Autor ist Deuter, Mahner und nicht zuletzt Richter. Er wird nie müde, daran zu erinnern, daß der Mensch den Anfeindungen von Caro, Mundus und Satan ausgesetzt ist, denen er nur mit Hilfe der ihm von der allein seligmachenden Kirche verliehenen Waffen – Sakramente, Prozessionen, Wallfahrten, Gebete, Kirchenbesuch usw. – zu widerstehen vermag. Zwar wurden die kriegerischen Erfolge Ludwigs XIV. in Paris und nach 1685 in Straßburg mit überschwenglichem Lob begrüßt, das Reich der habsburgischen Kaiser vom Südtiroler Nikolaus Avancini (1611–86) und dessen Nachfolgern als Antizipation von Gottes Reich gepriesen; dennoch entsprach solche Zuversicht nicht der Grundstimmung. So einmalig Jakob Bidermanns

(1577–1639) Einsiedler- und Märtyrerdramen, in denen der Mensch in seiner nackten Kreatürlichkeit und Schwäche geschildert wird, auch sein mögen, sie geben doch wie alle Jesuitendramen zu verstehen, daß Vollkommenheit auf Erden unmöglich ist. Die zur Statik neigenden Fest- und Weihespiele sind Projektionen einer Vision, die auf die nie zu erreichende Koinzidenz von irdisch-menschlicher Wirklichkeit und göttlicher Schöpfung schließen läßt. Allen opernhaften Elementen zum Trotz (Wiener *ludi caesarei*) ist die auf Scheinkonflikten beruhende Handlung nicht frei von Gravitas. Alles steht unter dem Zeichen der Hinfälligkeit, überall herrscht der Gegensatz zwischen Diesseits und Jenseits, Unbeständigkeit und Dauer, Zeit und Ewigkeit. Die vom Ordensgründer empfohlene Anwendung der Sinne («applicatio sensuum») liegt dem Prinzip der Visualisierung zugrunde, deren Bedeutung für die Entstehung des Theaters selbst nicht hoch genug veranschlagt werden kann, konzentriert sich aber vorwiegend auf die sinnliche Vergegenwärtigung des Lebens und Leidens Christi.

Das Quasi-Monopol, das sich die Jesuiten in manchen Regionen (Polen, Belgien, den der Macht der Habsburger unterstehenden Gebieten, Bayern) im Bereich des Unterrichts erkämpft hatten, sicherte ihnen eine ebensowenig angefochtene Vormachtstellung in dem des Theaters. Selbst im 18. Jh. wurden sie von den immer ungünstiger werdenden historischen Bedingungen zumindest äußerlich kaum berührt. Jahrhundertelang war dieses Theater ‹die Schule der kath. Welt›, zumal es das Benediktiner- und Piaristendrama – und nicht nur in der Anfangsphase – entscheidend beeinflußte und zur Legitimation des Theaters innerhalb der ganzen Kirche beitrug.

Schwächen, die teils von objektiv zeitbedingten Faktoren herrühren, teils dem System selbst zuzuschreiben sind, wird man leicht registrieren können. Das streng hierarchische System, der ständige Ortswechsel der Patres, der durch zu viele Aufgaben bewirkte Zeitdruck gaben den meisten Jesuiten fast nie die Möglichkeit, in ihrer musischen Betätigung einen eigenen Stil zu entwickeln. Was die Jesuiten schrieben, schrieben sie als Teil einer Institution, deren Interessen sie zu vertreten hatten. Bei allem Einverständnis mit den Zielen der katholischen Herrscher mußten sich die Autoren Eingriffe in die Wahl und Gestaltung der Stoffe seitens der Auftraggeber gefallen lassen. Beträchtliche Unterschiede lassen sich zwischen den einzelnen Bühnen feststellen, deren Folgen nicht nur techn. Art waren. Auch das starre Festhalten am Latein wirkte sich in der 2. Hälfte des 17. Jh. auf die Bedeutung des J. in Hinsicht auf die profane Literatur negativ aus. Die dt. Dramatiker Gryphius, Birken, Anton Ulrich, von Braunschweig, Haugwitz, Hallmann, Lohenstein haben gewiß von den Jesuiten gelernt. Das von ihnen praktizierte barocke Schauspiel und →Trauerspiel emanzipierte sich aber bald von diesen Modellen zu-

466 Jesuitentheater

gunsten einer deutschsprachig-nationalen Literatur. Auch der Bruch zwischen Barock und Aufklärung ändert nichts an der Tatsache, daß das Drama der Jesuiten immer mehr an Bedeutung verlor, selbst dort, wo es eine führende Position gehabt hatte wie in Österreich, wo die ital. Oper zum aristokratischen Genre kat'exochen geworden war. Die Erneuerungsbestrebungen im 18. Jh. in München (Corneille-Nachahmung) blieben am Rande des literarischen Lebens. Volkssprache und Latein, Kunstwille und intendierte Wirkung in der Tradition der Erbauungsliteratur, subjektiver Gestaltungswille und kollektive Belange kollidierten immer mehr, und für derartige Probleme hatte die Ordensleitung keine Lösung parat. Auf die Herausforderungen der anbrechenden neuen Zeit – Absolutismus, aufgeklärter Despotismus, das Ich als Movens der denkenden und dichterischen Aktivität – wußten die Jesuiten keine Antwort. In die Defensive gedrängt, vermochten sie nur das zu wiederholen, was sie früher gesagt hatten. Ihre Bühne mußte sich wieder mit dem engen Raum der Schule abfinden, dem sie einst entkommen war, überlebte sich unverstanden und verspottet (Nicolai), ein Relikt aus entschwundenen Zeiten. Ist das Ende der dramatischen Tätigkeit des Ordens auf politische, d. h. außerliterarische Ursachen zurückzuführen, so fällt es nicht von ungefähr mit dem endgültigen Sieg der hartnäckig verworfenen, schließlich jedoch stärkeren Tendenz zur Verselbständigung der Kunst zusammen. Das Theater der Jesuiten ist ein wichtiges Bindeglied zwischen Humanistendrama und barockem bzw. klassizistischem Trauerspiel. Kulturgeschichtlich gesehen ist es als eine – allerdings höchst bedeutende – Erscheinungsform des vorindividuellen Zeitalters anzusehen.

d'Amico, S. (Hg.): Enciclopedia dello spettacolo, 5, Sp. 1159–77; s. u. Gesuiti, teatro dei. Rom 1962; Boogerd, L. van den: Het Jezuïtendrama in de Nederlanden. Groningen 1961; Boysse, E.: Le théâtre des Jésuites. Paris 1880; Flemming, W.: Geschichte des Jesuitentheaters in den Landen dt. Zunge. Berlin 1923; Garcia-Soriano, J.: El teatro universitario y humanistico en España. Toledo 1945; Griffin, N.: Jesuit School Drama. A Checklist of Critical Literature. London 1976 (= Research Bibliographies and Checklists 12); Müller, J.: Das Jesuitendrama in den Ländern dt. Zunge vom Anfang bis zum Hochbarock. 2 Bde. Augsburg 1930; Sommervogel, C.: Bibliothèque de la Compagnie de Jésus. Brüssel/Paris 1890–1900; Szarota, E. M.: Das Jesuitendrama im dt. Sprachgebiet. Eine Periochenedition, 4 Bde. München 1973–87; Valentin, J.-M.: Le théâtre des jésuites dans les pays de langue allemande (1554–1680). Salut des âme et ordre des cités, 3 Bde. Bern 1978; Valentin, J.-M.: Le théâtre des Jésuites dans les pays de langue allemande. Répertoire bibliographique des pièces représentées et des documents conservés (1555–1773), 2 Bde. Stuttgart 1983–84.

Jean-Marie Valentin

Jeune Premier

→ Rollenfach und Bezeichnung für einen Darstellertyp, v. a. im frz. Theater – z. B. Rodrigue in *Le Cid* (1636) von Pierre Corneille (1606–84) oder *Romeo* bei William Shakespeare (1564–1616). Er vereinigt eine schlanke, mehr als mittelgroße Gestalt, ein ausdrucksvolles, männlichschönes Gesicht und eine tragende Stimme mit innerem Feuer, Tiefe des Gefühls und der Fähigkeit, alle Empfindungen, von der zartesten Liebesregung bis zum Zornausbruch, auszudrücken. Der J. P. verbindet in einer Person Wesenszüge des Helden und des Liebhabers (dt.: «erster Liebhaber», «jugendlicher Liebhaber» oder «erster jugendlicher Liebhaber»). Markantester Darsteller solcher J. P.-Rollen in Theater und Film in der Nachkriegszeit war Gérard Philipe (1922–59).

Bernard Poloni

Jiddisches Theater

Unter Jiddisch versteht man «die Sprache, deren sich die nicht-assimilierten… mittel- und osteuropäischen Juden im Alltagsleben… bedienen» (Beranek). Es ist eine «Nahsprache» des Deutschen, hervorgegangen aus mittelhochdt. Dialekten. Die im 14./15. Jh. vertriebenen dt. Juden nahmen sie mit nach Osteuropa, wo sie sich durch Aufnahme vor allem hebräischer und slawischer Elemente eigenständig weiterentwickelte. Da nach orthodoxer Ansicht Hebräisch lediglich für religiöse Zwecke benutzt werden durfte, gewann das Jiddische als Umgangssprache große Bedeutung.

Jüdisches Theater hat keine Tradition. Die Zerstreuung der Juden in viele Länder, ihre unterdrückte Lage, vor allem religiöse Gründe verhinderten seine Entwicklung – in Hebräisch wie in Jiddisch. Die einzig tolerierte Form szenischer Darbietung war bis ins 19. Jh. das «Purimspiel», das an die alttestamentarische Erzählung von Haman erinnert, der die Juden vernichten wollte, und an ihre Rettung durch Ester. Seit dem 16. Jh. wurden in Verbindung mit Liedern und komischen Szenen die auf biblischen (selten auf weltlichen) Stoffen basierenden «Purimspiele» aufgeführt.

Die Autoren der ersten jiddischen Dramen seit Ende des 18. Jh. waren Vertreter der jüdischen Aufklärung, der «Haskalah», deren Ziel es war, die Juden Osteuropas an die moderne Zeit heranzuführen. Aber erst in der zweiten Hälfte des 19. Jh. wurde das Jiddische Literatursprache. In dieser Zeit entwickelte sich aus bestehenden Traditionen eine Gruppe volkstümlicher und sozialkritischer Berufsunterhalter, die «Broder sin-

468 Jiddisches Theater

ger» (Sänger aus Brody, der Stadt, aus der die ersten bekannten Sänger dieser Art stammten). Sie stellten einen Großteil der ersten Schauspieler des j. T. Unter ihrem Einfluß begann der «Vater des j. T.», Abraham Goldfaden, 1867 im rumänischen Jassy einfache Stücke mit Musik zu schreiben. Waren sie anfangs bloße Szenarien, die Platz für Improvisation ließen, so wurden sie später ausgearbeiteter und in sich schlüssiger. Seine ersten Erfolge riefen eine Vielzahl anderer Gruppen ins Leben, deren Zusammensetzung, Lebensdauer und Repertoire sich nur selten exakt verfolgen lassen.

Von Beginn an hatte das j. T. mit Widerständen zu kämpfen. Religiös begründete Ablehnung gehörte hierzu wie der Mangel an Stücken, an Schauspielern und einem Publikum, das bereit und in der Lage war, das entstehende Theater zu unterstützen – finanziell und ideell. Hinzu kamen immer neue staatliche Repressionen, die zur Massenemigration osteurop. Juden und dadurch zur Internationalisierung des Jiddischen führten. Bevorzugtes Ziel der Einwanderung waren die USA, wo vor allem in New York die jüdische Bevölkerung sprunghaft anstieg. Theater hatte für die Neueinwanderer in vieler Hinsicht Bedeutung, es vermittelte Heimatgefühle und trug dazu bei, sich in der neuen Umgebung zurechtzufinden. Da die ersten Theatergruppen keine festen Häuser und nur ein begrenztes Publikum hatten, waren sie gezwungen, dessen Bedürfnissen nach Sentimentalität und heimatlicher Musik nachzukommen und in extrem kurzen Abständen neue Produktionen zu erstellen. Dies führte zu fabrikmäßiger Herstellung mehr oder weniger zusammenhangloser Stücke, von Gegnern mit dem Sammelnamen «shund» bezeichnet. Eine Änderung trat erst ein, als mit Jakob Gordins Stücken Realismus in Sprache, Handlung und Charakterzeichnung Eingang ins j. T. fand. Er hatte vor der Jahrhundertwende bestimmenden Einfluß auf das j. T. in der ganzen Welt. Auch die «Mutter des j. T.», Rachel Ester Kaminska, wurde mit Aufführungen seiner Stücke über Polen hinaus berühmt. Neben Gordin traten weitere Autoren mit literarischem Anspruch bzw. wurden nun auch Stücke aufgeführt, die vordem kein Publikum gefunden hatten. Das j. T. in Europa und den USA bemühte sich in den ersten beiden Jahrzehnten des 20. Jh. um die Überwindung des kommerziell erstarrten Theaterbetriebs. Beeinflußt vor allem vom Moskauer Künstlertheater (→MChAT), entstanden zahlreiche jiddische Theatergruppen, die sich diesen Bestrebungen widmeten. Seit 1916 arbeitete die schnell berühmt gewordene «Wilna-Truppe» professionell, die einen flexiblen Realismus vertrat und die Geschlossenheit der Ensembleleistung betonte. Wohl ihr größter Erfolg war die UA der jiddischen Fassung von An-Skis *Der Dibbuk* 1920, des Stücks, dessen Inszenierung auch →«Habima» berühmt machte. Nach einer Europatournee bereiste die Gruppe 1924 die USA, wo sie sich spaltete.

In Rußland wurde nach der Oktoberrevolution auch das j. T. (wie das anderer Minderheiten) subventioniert. Das bedeutendste russ. Ensemble war das 1919 gegr. Moskauer Jiddische Staatliche Künstlertheater (GO-SET), dessen Leitung Alexander Granowski (1890–1936) übertragen wurde, der 1929 von einer Europatournee nicht in die Sowjetunion zurückkehrte. Sein Nachfolger wurde S. M. Michoëls (1890–1948). Beim Beginn des dt. Überfalls auf die Sowjetunion befand sich GOSET auf einer Tournee; erst nach Kriegsende kehrten die verbliebenen Schauspieler nach Moskau zurück. Den stalinistischen Repressalien fielen der Leiter und viele Mitglieder zum Opfer. Antisemitismus, Kosmopolitismuskampagne und entzogene Subventionen führten 1952 zur Schließung des GOSET.

Im gleichen Zeitraum wie in Osteuropa wurden in den USA die ersten jiddischen Künstlertheater gegründet. Auch hier waren es vor allem Amateurgruppen, die sich bereits 1917 landesweit organisierten. Zu den bekanntesten Gruppen gehören die bis in die Gegenwart spielende, 1915 gegr. «Folksbiene» und das Arbeitertheater «Artef», das von 1925 bis 1953 bestand. Professionelle Künstlertheater erlebten meist nur wenige Spielzeiten, nur das von Maurice Schwartz 1918 gegr. «Yiddish Art Theater» konnte sich bis 1950 halten. Vor allem die Veränderung des Publikums beeinflußte das j. T. in den USA. Während sich durch Assimilation und Fluktuation die potentielle Zuschauerzahl verringerte, blieben wegen der restriktiv gehandhabten Gesetze neue Einwanderungswellen jiddischsprechender Juden aus.

In Osteuropa erschwerten zur gleichen Zeit andere Probleme die Arbeit des j. T.: Antisemitismus, Massenarbeitslosigkeit von Juden, staatliche Repressionen. Trotzdem wurde weiter Theater gespielt, u. a. von dem 1921 von Ida Kaminska und ihrem Mann gegründeten «Warschauer Jiddischen Künstlertheater», das 1928 aufgeben mußte und 1938/39 erneut zu arbeiten begann. In Wilna entstand ein Museum für das j. T., das während des Kriegs zerstört wurde. Seit 1926 gab es in Łódź, seit 1934 in Warschau ein jiddisches Marionettentheater. Als neues Genre wurde die «kleynkunst» ausgebildet, satirisch-politische Kabarett-Revuen.

Mit dem Beginn des 2. Weltkriegs, der Errichtung von Ghettos und KZs fanden all diese Bemühungen ein brutales Ende. Aber auch im Ghetto (→Ghettotheater), ja sogar noch im Angesicht der Gaskammern wurde Theater gespielt (→Theater in den Konzentrationslagern). Theater hatte hier wieder ganz unmittelbare Funktionen, als Ablenkung vom Grauen, das Publikum und Schauspieler umgab, und als Bestätigung kultureller Identität und Selbstachtung. Ähnliches gilt für die Theateraufführungen, die unmittelbar nach der Befreiung in den Lagern und KZs von den nun «Displaced Persons» genannten ehem. Gefangenen durchgeführt wurden. Zwischen 1945 und 1949 spielten mindestens sechs Grup-

470 Jiddisches Theater

pen. 1947 wurde in München sogar eine eigene Organisation gegründet. Wenigstens erwähnt werden sollen das «Münchner Jiddische Theater», das von 1946 bis 1949 bestand, und das 1946 gegründete «Musikalische Jiddische Kleinkunst Kollektiv».

Die fast völlige Vernichtung des jiddischsprechenden osteuropäischen Judentums, die Zerstreuung der Überlebenden in alle Welt hat das j. T. nicht nur seiner Schauspieler, sondern vor allem seiner Zuschauer beraubt. Dennoch setzten sofort nach Kriegsende Bemühungen um einen neuen Anfang ein. In Polen spielte bereits 1944 wieder eine Truppe in den befreiten Gebieten, nach Kriegsende wurde das Jiddische Staatstheater gegründet, als dessen künstlerische Leiterin Ida Kaminska berufen wurde und das 1955 ein eigenes Haus in Warschau beziehen konnte, das heute als Staatliches Jüdisches Theater «E. R. Kamińska» von Szymon Szurmiej geleitet wird. In Rumänien wurden 1948 in Bukarest und 1949 in Jassy mit staatlicher Unterstützung j. T. gegründet und 1958 das Staatliche Jiddische Theater in Bukarest. Weder in der Sowjetunion noch in Westeuropa gab es nach dem Krieg noch professionelle j. T. von nennenswerter Zahl. In den USA leiden Zuschauer und Schauspieler unter Überalterung; Amateurgruppen und bemühte Neuansätze werden diesen Prozeß wohl nicht aufhalten können. Auch in Israel hat das j. T. keine neue Heimat gefunden. Jiddisch galt als die Sprache des Ghettos, der Vergangenheit. Viele Neueinwanderer verstanden es nicht. Um Hebräisch als Staatssprache durchzusetzen, wurde Jiddisch lange Jahre hindurch abgelehnt. Erst in den letzten Jahren hat sich hier etwas verändert. 1975 wurde mit staatlicher Förderung das Jiddische Künstlertheater gegründet, ein Jahr später in Jerusalem eine internationale Konferenz über die jiddische Kultur abgehalten. In den USA fand im Juni 1980 das «First Annual Jewish Theatre Festival» statt.

Akhtsik yor jidish teater in Rumenia 1876–1956. Bukarest 1956; Alexander Granach und das jiddische Theater des Ostens. Berlin 1971; Besedy o teatral'nom iskusstve (S. Michoëls). In: Teatr (Moskau) 1990, Nr. 4; Buloff, J.: From the Old Marketplace. Cambridge, Mass. 1991; Goren, B.: Di geshikhte fun yidishn teater. 2 Bde. New York 1923; Lifson, D. S.: The Yiddish Theatre in America. Cranbury 1965; Liptzin, S.: A History of Yiddish Literature. Middle Village 1972; Perlmutter, S./Mestel, Y. (Hg.): Yidishe dramaturgn un kompositors. New York 1952; Picon-Vallin, B.: Le théâtre juif soviétique pendant les années vingt. Lausanne 1973; Sandrow, N.: Vagabond Stars. A World History of Yiddish Theater. New York u. a. 1977; Shatsky, Y.: Arkhiv far der geshikhte fun yidishn teater un drame. New York 1930; Shayn, Y.: Arum Moskver Yidishn Teater. Paris 1964; Turkow-Grudberg, Y.: Yidish teater in Poylen. Warschau 1951; Zylbercweig, Z.: Hantbukh fun yidishn teater. Mexico City 1970; ders.: Lexikon fun yidishn teater. 5 Bde. New York/Mexico City 1931–67.

Wolfgang Beck

Jôruri (oder Bunraku)

Das jap. →Puppentheater. Es entstand im 16. Jh. und besteht aus den drei Elementen des Puppenspiels, der Textrezitation (*jôruri*; ein einzelner Sprecher übernimmt sämtliche Rede- und Erzählparts, was eine so fulminante physische Anstrengung bedeutet, daß die Rezitatoren in der Regel alle 30 Minuten wechseln) und der shamisen-Musikbegleitung (shamisen: ein in der 2. Hälfte des 16. Jh. aus China über die Ryûkyû-Inseln nach Japan gelangtes 3-Saiten-Instrument, das mit einem großen Plektron – bachi – geschlagen wird und einen spröden, bei hartem Anschlag aber auch sehr mächtigen Klang hat. Der Resonanzkörper ist in der Regel mit Hunde- oder Katzenhaut bespannt). Schon Texte des 11. Jh. berichten über nomadisierende Puppenspieler (*kairaishi, kugutsu-mawashi*), die von der Darstellung von Puppentänzen, Taschenspielereien, Jagd und Prostitution lebten. Puppen wurde schon im altjap. Glauben eine apotropäische Kraft zugeschrieben; im Shintô-Kult vertraten sie die Gottheiten. Schon im 19. Jh. wurde hierin der Ursprung des Puppenspiels gesehen. Wahrscheinlich ist es aber kontinentaler Herkunft, entwickelte sich in Japan jedoch von einem Kult zu einer Kunst. Ein Teil der kairaishi-Gruppen wurde seit dem 13. Jh. seßhaft und siedelte sich hauptsächlich in der Nähe von Schreinen und Tempeln an, von wo sie aber immer noch und oft über Land zogen und in einem vor die Brust gehängten Holzkasten, der ‹Bühne›, Nô-Adaptationen u. ä. vorführten. Anfang des 17. Jh. gingen Puppenspieler der Provinz Settsu dazu über, das Geschehen der populären biwa-begleiteten (biwa: chinesische Laute) jôruri-Balladen synchron mit Puppen darzustellen. Verschiedentliche Erwähnungen des ningyô-jôruri (Puppen-jôruri) dokumentieren, daß sich diese neue Schaukunstform schon um 1615 durchgesetzt hatte. Bald danach schon verlagerte sich das Zentrum des Puppenspiels aus Kamigata (Kyôto-Osaka-Gegend) ins neue, gewaltig aufstrebende Edo (heute Tôkyô). Die urspr. primitiven Puppen (*deku* oder *deku-bô*; ein Ton- oder Holzkopf, von dem die Kleider herunterhingen) und die Ausstattungen der Bühne und des Theaters wurden so schnell verfeinert und üppig, daß schon 1635 der berühmte aus Kamigata stammende Puppenmeister Satsuma Jôun (1593–1672; Vertreter des als hart und männlich geltenden *kô*-Stils, der sich zumeist Heldengeschichten zum Thema nahm; im Gegensatz dazu stand der ‹weiche› *nan*-Stil) vorübergehend wegen Zurschaustellung übermäßigen Luxus ins Gefängnis geworfen wurde. Eine wichtige Zäsur für die Entwicklung des Puppentheaters bedeutete der Großbrand von 1657 in Edo, der die Hälfte der Stadt zerstörte. Das Zentrum des Puppenspiels verlagerte sich zurück nach Kamigata. Die Zusammenarbeit des Puppenspielers Takamoto Gidayû (1651–1714) und des Theaterunternehmers Takeda Izumo (1691–1756) mit dem größten Dramatiker jener

Zeit, Chikamatsu Monzaemon (1653–1724), am Puppentheater Takemoto-za in Osaka führte zur Glanzzeit des jôruri-Puppenspiels. Das historische Schauspiel *Kokusenya kassen*, der ‹Kampf des Coxinga›, wurde
1715 zu einem der größten Erfolge in der Geschichte des Puppentheaters.
(Bald wurde auch dieses Stück, wie viele andere jôruri, von den → kabuki-
Theatern adaptiert und nachgespielt.)

Das Takemoto-za stand in einem heißen Konkurrenzkampf mit einem
anderen, in vieler Hinsicht ebenbürtigen Puppentheater in Osaka, dem
Toyotake-za (1703 von Wakadayû, 1651–1714, gegründet). Während der
2. Hälfte des 18. Jh. ebbte die Popularität des jôruri nach und nach ab, ein
Puppentheater in Osaka nach dem anderen schloß seine Pforten, und ein
Teil der Sänger und Spieler wanderte nach Edo ab, wo das jôruri zwar
überleben konnte, aber ein bei weitem weniger spektakuläres Dasein fristete als in Osaka. Bedeutendster jôruri-Autor in Edo war der genial-
extravagante Hiraga Gennai (1728–79). Die Technik der Puppenführung
und die Rezitation hatte um 1800 ihren Endpunkt erreicht. Auch das Repertoire erfuhr nach diesem Datum keine bedeutende Erweiterung mehr.
Unter dem Namen bunraku (von Uemura Bunrakuken I, der 1871 in
Osaka ein Puppentheater errichtete, das Bunraku-za) hat sich das jôruri
bis in unsere Tage erhalten; im 20. Jh. war es immer wieder vom Aussterben bedroht, aber das im Jahre 1984 mit großem Aufwand errichtete und
reich und mit modernster Technik ausgestattete Bunraku-Theater in
Osaka mag als manifester Beweis dafür gelten, daß das jôruri – vorläufig –
seine Krisen überwunden hat.

Zu Technik und Darstellung: Hauptrollen darstellende Puppen werden von drei Spielern geführt, Nebenrollen darstellende nur von einem.
Die männlichen Puppen sind ca. 1,20 m groß, die weiblichen wesentlich
kleiner und leichter. Der Hauptspieler (*omozukai*) bewegt Kopf, Rumpf
und rechten Arm, der 1. Nebenspieler (*hidarizukai*, ‹Linksspieler›) bewegt den linken Arm und der 2. Nebenspieler (*ashizukai*, ‹Fußbeweger›)
die Beine der Puppe. Die Gesichter der beiden Nebenspieler sind unter
einer schwarzen Kapuze verborgen. Es gibt ungefähr 30 verschiedene
Handtypen, unter denen einige alle fünf Finger, ja sogar alle drei Finger-
gelenke bewegen können. Auch die Köpfe sind oft Meisterwerke der
Schnitzkunst und der Mechanik (mechanische Puppen waren im 15. Jh.
aus China bekannt geworden, später brachten christliche Missionare mechanisches Spielzeug ins Land); viele können Augen, Lider, Brauen und
(allerdings nur die männlichen Puppen) den Mund bewegen; selbst das
Problem der Wunderheilung eines Pockennarbigen wurde ‹technisch› gelöst. Die Ausbildung der Puppenspieler dauerte Jahrzehnte, und von der
Rezitationstechnik wird behauptet, daß nur derjenige, der von Kindheit
an mit der jôruri-Musik und den jôruri-Texten vertraut ist, hoffen kann,
sie zu meistern.

Nicht nur die zur Aufführung gebrachten Genres, sondern auch die Darstellungstechniken des bunraku haben eine große Ähnlichkeit mit denen des kabuki (kabuki und bunraku stritten durch die Jahrhunderte permanent um die Gunst des Publikums. Zeitweise galt das bunraku als die glaubwürdigere, realistischere Kunst, so daß die kabuki-Schauspieler bei den Puppen in die Lehre gehen mußten!); wie im kabuki besteht auch das bunraku-Spiel aus einer Sequenz festgelegter furi (konventionalisierte Stilisierungen alltäglicher Bewegungen) und kata (Ausdrucks- und Bewegungsmuster), mit denen – quasi komprimiert – gesteigerte Gefühlsbewegungen dargestellt werden, die jeweiligen Höhepunkte rhythmischer Bewegungsphasen.

Barth, J.: Japans Schaukunst im Wandel der Zeiten. Wiesbaden 1972; Keene, D.: Bunraku. The Art of the Japanese Puppet Theatre. Tôkyô 1965; Ortolani, B.: Das japanische Theater. In: Kindermann, H. (Hg.): Fernöstliches Theater. Stuttgart 1966.

Peter Pörtner

Jüdisch-politisches Kabarett

Das j.-p. K. wurde 1927 in Wien von Oskar Teller, Victor Schlesinger und Fritz Stöckler gegründet. Es war zionistisch ausgerichtet, wandte sich gegen jede Assimilation der Juden und lehnte sozialistische wie klerikalkonservative Politik ab. Gespielt wurde hauptsächlich vor den zionistischen Gruppen Wiens. Die Texte stammten u. a. von den Gründern, die gemeinsam unter dem Pseudonym ‹Victor Berossi› schrieben. Nach der Besetzung Österreichs wurde es von Teller in New York unter dem Namen «Die Arche» noch eine Zeitlang weitergeführt. Gespielt wurden Texte von Friedrich Torberg, Fritz Grünbaum, Hugo F. Koenigsgarten u. a.

Budzinski, K.: Pfeffer ins Getriebe. München 1982; Greul, H.: Bretter, die die Zeit bedeuten. Köln/Berlin 1967 (erw. Ausg., 2. Bde. München 1971); Weys, R.: Cabaret und Kabarett in Wien. Wien 1970.

Wolfgang Beck

Juese / lianpu (Chin. Rollenfächer / Masken)

Eine einfache Typisierung der Rollen läßt sich bereits in den burlesken «Adjutanten-Spielen» (canjun xi) der Tang-Zeit (618–907) nachweisen, einer Vorform des eigentlichen Theaters. Durch die Rolle werden Typ und gewisse Charaktereigenschaften der dargestellten Person angedeu-

474 Juese / lianpu (Chin. Rollenfächer / Masken)

tet; aus der Rolle ist auch bereits ersichtlich, auf welcher der vier Darstellungsformen (changgong: «Gesang»; zuogong: «Gestik»; nianbai: «Sprechen»; wuda: «Akrobatik») das Schwergewicht liegt. Es gibt in den diversen Formen des Theaters (→Pekingoper, →Lokales Theater) verschiedene Weisen der Rolleneinteilung. Die am weitesten verbreitete sieht vier Haupt-Rollenfächer vor, innerhalb deren es wiederum eine weitgehende Spezialisierung gibt:

1. sheng (männliche Rolle). Entsprechend einer groben Einteilung der Stücke in bürgerliche (wenxi) und militärische Dramen (wuxi) ist auch das sheng-Rollenfach weiter unterteilt in (1.1) bürgerlicher oder ziviler (wensheng) und (1.2) militärischer sheng (wu sheng). Bei den (1.1) wensheng gibt es (1.1.1) ältere Männer (laosheng, je nach Alter mit weißem oder schwarzem Bart; Hauptausdrucksmittel sind mit natürlicher, fast dem europ. Bariton entsprechender Stimme gesungene lange Arien) und junge Männer (xiaosheng), meist vornehme, seltener aus kleinen Verhältnissen stammende, stets aber vielversprechende Jünglinge, junge Liebhaber, das Idealbild des jungen Mannes verkörpernd. Der xiaosheng ist die wohl schwierigste Rolle im chin. Theater, und gute xiaosheng sind sehr selten; er spricht mit natürlicher Stimme, singt aber in einem schwer zu erlernenden Falsett; in seiner Stimme wie in seinem gesamten Auftreten verbindet er höfliche Zurückhaltung, Kultiviertheit und Männlichkeit. Der (1.2) wusheng ist ebenfalls unterteilt in (1.2.1) ältere (wu laosheng, meist ein General mit vier Fahnen auf dem Rücken, die Größe seines Heeres symbolisierend) und (1.2.2) jüngere Krieger (wu xiaosheng). Eine prägnante Untergruppe des letztgenannten Faches sind die «Krieger mit kurzem Rock und Waffen» (duanda), welche nie singen, selten sprechen, sondern nur akrobatische Kampfszenen vorführen.

2. dan (weibliche Rolle). Bis ins 20. Jh. wurden weibliche Rollen von Männern gespielt, die ein großes Raffinement entwickelt hatten, weibliche Wesensmerkmale in der dem chin. Theater eigenen konzentrierten Weise interpretierend darzustellen. Die dan-Rolle wird unterteilt in: (2.1) laodan (ältere Frau), die mit einer natürlichen Stimme singt, gebeugt, meist auf einen Stock gestützt, geht; (2.2) qingyi, der Typ des jungen schönen Mädchens, der treuen Frau oder gehorsamen Tochter, also der Idealtyp der chin. Frau, die sich durch elegante und äußerst zurückhaltende Gestik auszeichnet und sich hauptsächlich in langen Arien ausdrückt; (2.3) huadan (Blumenmädchen), die lebenslustige, verführerische, kokette junge Frau und femme fatale, oft eine Kurtisane; (2.4) daoma dan (Frau mit Säbel und Pferd), ein waffengewandtes junges Mädchen mit akrobatischen Fähigkeiten; (2.5) caidan (bunte Frau), komische Rolle, oft auch intrigante Frau, verschlagene Dienerin oder Heiratsvermittlerin.

3. jing (auch hualian: «bemaltes Gesicht» genannt), das Rollenfach mit

Juese / lianpu (Chin. Rollenfächer / Masken) **475**

der auffälligen Gesichtsbemalung (lianpu) und dem breitesten Spektrum an Charakteren. Das Äußere und das Auftreten des jing muß besonders ehrfurchtgebietend und einschüchternd sein; von seiner Stimme wird erwartet, daß «das Theater noch drei Tage nach dem Auftritt widerhallt»; er hat also ein starkes, volles, dabei etwas nasales Organ. Die Gesichtsmasken werden aus sieben Grundfarben gebildet, durch die jeweils bestimmte Charaktereigenschaften symbolisiert werden: Rot zeigt einen mutigen, impulsiven und loyalen Menschen; Weiß ist die Farbe des listigen, verräterischen Schurken; eine überwiegend schwarze Maske weist auf einen offenen, ehrlichen und gerechten Menschen; durch Violett wird Verschlossenheit, Zurückhaltung bei gleichzeitiger Loyalität gezeigt; ein wilder, rauher, schlauer Charakter, dem indessen Loyalität und Pflichtgefühl nicht fremd sind, wird durch eine überwiegend blaue Maske ausgedrückt; auf einen vorausschauenden intelligenten Geist, der zugleich gerissen und schlau ist, weist die Farbe Gelb hin; Grün schließlich zeigt einen hinterhältigen Ränkeschmied. Eine Person wird durch die Kombination dieser Grundfarben (hinzu kommen Gold und Silber in der Regel bei übernatürlichen Wesen) charakterisiert, wobei auch eine Rolle spielt, in welcher Gesichtspartie die eine oder andere Farbe überwiegt. Dafür gibt es für jede Rolle bestimmte Konventionen, in deren Rahmen aber jeder Darsteller Wert darauf legt, durch eigene Varianten seine persönliche Interpretation der Rolle zu betonen.

4. chou (komische Rolle, Clown). Der chou ist kenntlich an dem runden oder eckigen weißen Fleck um Nase und Augen. Manchmal wird er in der Rolleneinteilung auch an erster Stelle genannt, denn der Kaiser Xuanzong der Tang-Dynastie, ein Ahnherr und Schutzpatron des Theaters (→Chinesisches Theater; →Liyuan), soll chou-Rollen gespielt haben. Auf diese Überlieferung ist auch ein weiterer Brauch zurückzuführen, nach dem kein Schauspieler vor dem chou mit dem Schminken beginnen durfte. Der chou hat kaum Gesangspartien, sondern meist in einfacher Umgangssprache gesprochenen Text.

In aller Regel hat sich ein Schauspieler entsprechend der Besonderheiten seiner Stimme, seines Aussehens und Körperbaus seit seiner frühen Ausbildung auf eines der vier Rollenfächer spezialisiert. Innerhalb eines Fachs kann er die Rolle wechseln; z. B. von qingyi zu huadan, von wusheng zu laosheng etc.; von einem bedeutenden Schauspieler wird sogar erwartet, daß er verschiedene Rollen spielen kann, nie jedoch außerhalb seines Rollenfachs.

Chang Pe-chin: Chinese Opera and Painted Face, Taipei 1969; Qi Rushan: Xiju juese mingci kao. In: Qi Rushan quanji. Taipei 1964, Bd. 2; Zhongguo da baike quanshu, xiqu quyi. Beijing / Shanghai 1983.

Bernd Eberstein

476 Jugendtheater (in den Niederlanden)

Jugendtheater (in den Niederlanden)

Das J. hat sich in den Niederlanden seit der Theaterrevolution der «Aktion Tomaat» 1969 schnell entwickelt. 1985 zählt das J. ungefähr 200 Gruppen, die teils mit, teils ohne öffentliche Subventionen arbeiten. Viele haben sich aus emanzipatorischen Jugendgruppen der 60er Jahre entwickelt. Houtman (1978) teilt das J. in drei Gruppen ein: 1. das gesellschaftlich-kritische J., das mittels Kontrasten oder einfacher Gegenüberstellungen zwischen Mann/Frau, Arbeiter/Herr eine kritische gesellschaftliche Haltung erzeugen will (*Tejater Teneeter*, Nijmegen); 2. das sozial-emanzipatorische J., das das Kind und dessen Umgebung als Thematik wählt (*Wederzijds*, Amsterdam); 3. das traditionelle J. mit dem Ziel, die Kinder mittels Märchen und/oder Abenteuergeschichten zu unterhalten (*Amsteltoneel*).

In den letzten Jahren tendiert man dazu, weniger explizit pädagogisch zu arbeiten. Der Phantasie der Kinder wird mehr Aufmerksamkeit geschenkt, mit mehr Spielraum für eigene Interpretation und Aktivierung der eigenen Erfahrungen.

Seit 1981 existiert die Organisation «De Bundeling» (Das Bundel), die die Interessen der Jugendgruppen vertritt und für eine bessere Subventionspolitik in bezug auf das J. agiert. Die Organisation «De Krakeling» fördert die Aufführungen von J. und organisiert Workshops für Jugendliche.

Dieho, B. (u. a.): Theater op de bres. Amsterdam 1979; Jeugd en Samenleving 7/8 (1981), Themanummer Kindertheater; Rijswoudt, C. van: Van Theorie naar Praktijk. Het subsidiebeleid ten aanzien van Kindertheater 1969–1983 (Unpubl. Magisterarbeit Institut voor Theaterwissenschaft). Amsterdam 1984; Speltribune 4 (1980), Themanummer Kindertheater; Toneel Teatraal 2 (1971), Themanummer Kindertheater.

Carin van Rijswoudt

Kabarett (Cabaret)

(Frz. Schenke, Restaurant, aber auch in Fächer eingeteilte Speiseschüssel; möglicherweise nach dem span. ‹caba retta›, bunte Schüssel) Bezeichnung für eine kleine Bühne und die dort gebotene Form des Unterhaltungstheaters, die in der Regel aus einer durch Conférencen zusammengehaltenen Folge von Sketchen, Liedern, Parodien u. ä. besteht, in denen in literarischer oder/und kritisch-satirischer Form politische und gesellschaftliche Zustände glossiert werden.

Seit der Entstehung des K. wird nicht nur über die ‹richtige› Schreibweise gestritten, sondern auch über seine Inhalte und die Form ihrer

Kabarett(Cabaret) **477**

Darbietung. Während man heute unter «Cabaret» eher die literarisch bestimmte Unterhaltungsform versteht, wird «K.» vor allem als Bezeichnung für die politisch-satirische Form benutzt, hat sich im deutschsprachigen Raum aber auch als Gattungsbezeichnung durchgesetzt. Gattungstheoretische Bestimmungen sind beim K. schwierig, da es besonders sensibel gegenüber gesellschaftlichen Veränderungen ist, auf die es rascher und konsequenter reagieren muß als das Theater. Es ist in hohem Maße abhängig von seinem Publikum und muß sich auf dessen Bedürfnisse einstellen – auch da, wo es sie kritisiert. Das Fehlen einer durchgehenden Handlung bringt das K. formal in die Nähe der →Revue, des →Varietés. Anders als diese wendet es sich nicht in erster Linie an die Sinne, sondern an den Verstand des Zuschauers. Der weitgehende Verzicht auf illusionserzeugende Mittel und damit das ausschließliche Angewiesensein auf Sprache verhindert weitgehend die Internationalität des K. In einem anderen Sinne als die übrigen Formen des Theaters ist K. eine ‹transitorische› Kunst. Wiederaufnahmen früherer Nummern und Pointen sind kaum möglich, schon wegen des schnellen Veraltens aktueller Anspielungen. K., speziell das politische, ist «Spiel mit dem erworbenen Wissenszusammenhang des Publikums» (Henningsen). Dieses ‹Wissen› ist nicht in sich geschlossen, es weist Brüche auf, Tabus und Verdrängungen schließen die Lücken nur scheinbar. Hier hat das K. die Möglichkeit, mit seinen Mitteln (Travestie, Parodie, Karikatur u. a.) beim Publikum Bewußtseinsprozesse auszulösen.

Als ‹Geburtstag› des K. gilt der 18. 11. 1881, an dem Rodolphe Salis das →«Chat Noir» in Paris eröffnete. Natürlich gab es Vorläufer, Traditionen, die aufgegriffen und integriert wurden. Vor allem die in Frankreich weit zurückreichende Tradition des polemisch-satirischen und sozialkritischen Chansons ist hier zu nennen. Der Erfolg der ersten ‹Cabarets› hatte internationale Ausstrahlung. Den für die weitere Entwicklung bestimmendsten Einfluß übten sie in Deutschland aus. Durch Gastspiele hatte man die Möglichkeiten des neuen Genres selbst sehen können. Literarische Anregungen kamen hinzu, vor allem durch die Romane Holger Drachmans (*Forskrevet*, dt. «Verschrieben», 1892) und Otto Julius Bierbaums (*Stilpe*, 1897).

1901 wurden die ersten dt. K. gegründet: Ernst von Wolzogens →«Überbrettl» in Berlin und →«Die Elf Scharfrichter» in München. Wichtig ist an ihnen vor allem, daß sie zahlreiche Nachahmer hervorriefen, die das Genre in Europa etablieren halfen. In Holland, Norwegen, Dänemark wurden in den folgenden Jahren ebenso K. gegründet wie in Österreich, Ungarn, Polen und Rußland. Längerfristig und auf breiter Grundlage konnte sich das K. aber vor allem im deutschsprachigen Raum durchsetzen. Nach der Gründung der Weimarer Republik und der Aufhebung der Zensur entwickelte sich verstärkt das, was wir heute unter

478 Kabarett (Cabaret)

politisch-satirischem K. verstehen. Spätestens nach der Inflation setzte der Wandel des Publikumsgeschmacks dieser Entwicklung ein vorläufiges Ende. Unterhaltung wurde bevorzugt, die K.-Revuen bestimmten für einige Jahre das Bild. Im Gegensatz zu dieser Tendenz wurde das K. von politisch linker Seite als Medium der Aufklärung und Agitation erkannt. Aus den Sprechchorgruppen der KPD entstanden Spielgruppen wie «Das rote Sprachrohr», «Die Nieter», «Die Roten Blusen», deren Aufführungen Mittel der Revue und des K. verbanden.

In den meisten übrigen Ländern blühte die literarische Form des K. Erst in den letzten Jahren der Weimarer Republik trat in Deutschland wieder verstärkt politisches K. hervor, das nach der Machtübergabe an die Nationalsozialisten ein schnelles Ende fand. Die meisten Kabarettisten wurden ins Exil getrieben oder ermordet. Unter dem Eindruck der faschistischen Diktatur in Deutschland und des Austrofaschismus im eigenen Land setzte im österr. K. eine Politisierung ein, die es auch zahlreichen exilierten Kabarettisten ermöglichte, bis zur Besetzung Österreichs weiterzuarbeiten. Während des Exils gewann das K. für die Betroffenen eine wichtige Funktion zur Selbstverständigung, als eine der wenigen Möglichkeiten, sich kritisch artikulieren zu können und um über Radio auf die dt. Bevölkerung einzuwirken (→Exiltheater). Von Shanghai bis London, von Paris bis Jerusalem gab es eine Vielzahl von K.-Abenden, von denen zumeist wenig überliefert ist. Der Gemeinplatz, daß es dem K. in schlechten Zeiten gutgeht, bewies seine relative Gültigkeit in den von Deutschland besetzten Ländern. In Skandinavien gewannen plötzlich sogar die Märchen H. C. Andersens politische Brisanz, in der Résistance wurde das frz. Chanson wieder politisch. In all diesen Ländern diente das K. der Stärkung des nationalen Selbstbehauptungswillens.

In den ersten Jahren nach Ende des 2. Weltkriegs gab es fast überall eine (zumeist kurze) K.-Renaissance. Die Euphorie der ersten Jahre ging schnell verloren. In der Bundesrepublik konnten sich wenige K. etablieren. Kaum hatten sie sich durchgesetzt und erreichten u. a. durch das Fernsehen ein Millionenpublikum, erlahmte häufig der kritische Eifer. Aus Gründen der Breitenwirkung verzichtete man auf kritische Schärfe, wurde ‹populärer› – gelegentlich ohne zu merken, daß man an Wirksamkeit verlor, was man an Beifall gewann. Bereits zu Beginn der 60er Jahre entstanden eine Reihe von K., die von einem neuen Verständnis aus politisch-aktuelles K. voll satirischer Schärfe machten. Auch von ihnen gaben die meisten nach wenigen Jahren auf. Seit den 70er Jahren macht sich ein neuer Trend bemerkbar. Zum einen die Zunahme von Solokabarettisten, zum anderen entdecken in den Medien unzureichend repräsentierte gesellschaftliche Gruppen wie Frauen oder die ‹alternative Szene› die Möglichkeiten des K. zur Artikulation ihrer Interessen und als Mittel der Selbstverständigung.

Kabarett(Cabaret) **479**

In der DDR entstanden nach kurzlebigen Versuchen in der Nachkriegszeit seit den 50er Jahren (1953 →Die Distel, Berlin; 1954 →Die Pfeffermühle, Leipzig; 1955 Die Herkuleskeule, Dresden) wichtige K.-Ensembles, die rasch starke und dauerhafte Resonanz fanden; in den 80er Jahren existierten (neben einigen hundert zum Teil sehr leistungsfähigen Amateur-Ensembles) elf professionelle K. in den wichtigen größeren Städten Ostdeutschlands. Neben untauglichen Versuchen ‹positiver Satire› und durch die Feindbilder des kalten Krieges geprägter Kritik am westlichen Imperialismus wirkten diese K. zunächst vorwiegend durch humorvolle Darstellung alltäglicher und lokaler Probleme. Bald wagten sie sich aber auch an grundsätzlichere Erscheinungen staatlicher Bürokratie, Mängel sozialistischer Planwirtschaft und sogar einige Tabu-Themen (wie die rhetorischen Zerrbilder in den DDR-Medien oder die Allmacht der DM als ‹zweiter Währung›) heran. Der Vorzug staatlicher Subventionierung, der relativ große Ensembles (bis zu zehn Kabarettisten) und langfristig aufgebautes Repertoire gestattete, wurde durch den Nachteil eingeschränkter Aktualität und strenger Kontrolle kompensiert. Nicht selten mußten Programme wegen allzu deutlicher Kritik abgesetzt oder überarbeitet werden; die Bewertungsmaßstäbe der lokalen Behörden gingen dabei oft weit auseinander. Improvisation war generell nur in engsten Grenzen möglich. Andererseits erfüllte K. – in kleinen Spielstätten, abgeschirmt von der Massenwirksamkeit der Medien – eine bewußt tolerierte Ventilfunktion: Dem öffentlichen Lachen wurden jene Probleme ausgeliefert, die jedem Zuschauer bekannt waren, aber sonst nicht diskutiert werden konnten. Die stärksten Wirkungen hatte K. in vom Publikum sensibel aufgenommenen Andeutungen, Metaphern, Tonfällen und Gesten. In den 70er und 80er Jahren waren viele K.-Programme (z. B. die Texte von P. Ensikat und W. Schaller) revueartig mit durchgehender Handlung konzipiert; sie wurden oft von anderen K. und selbst Theatern nachgespielt. Nach Ende der DDR haben die ostdeutschen K. ihre Privilegien, als einzige Institutionen gesellschaftliche Mißstände öffentlich angreifen und unter sicheren materiellen Bedingungen arbeiten zu können, eingebüßt. Obgleich noch unsicher über ihre neue Funktion und ihre Spielräume in der Marktwirtschaft, genießen die meisten alten und einige neuentstandene K. hohe Akzeptanz beim Publikum.

Seit Beginn der Geschichte des K. verfolgt die jeweilige Staatsmacht argwöhnisch seine Entwicklung. Zensur begleitete es zu allen Zeiten, nicht nur unter diktatorischen Herrschaftsformen. Offene Beschränkungen findet man heute kaum noch, sie sind ersetzt durch ‹strukturelle Zensur›. Bestimmte Kabarettisten werden systematisch von den Medien ferngehalten, bereits fertiggestellte Aufnahmen werden nicht gesendet, unliebsame Äußerungen durch ‹Tonstörungen› unterbrochen oder – wie der Südwestfunk an den Leiter der Frankfurter →«Schmiere», Rudolf

Rolfs, schrieb: «Wir zensieren natürlich nicht. Allerdings die Auswahl der Texte müssen Sie uns überlassen.» (→ABC, →Das Bügelbrett, →Der Blaue Vogel, →Cabaret Voltaire, →Chat Noir, →Cornichon, →Die Distel, →Die Drei Tornados, →Die Elf Scharfrichter, →Floh de Cologne, →Jüdisch-politisches Kabarett, →Kabarett der Komiker, →Die Katakombe, →Die Kleine Freiheit, →Das Kom(m)ödchen, →Das Laterndl, →Lieber Augustin, →Literatur am Naschmarkt, →Le Mirliton, →Münchner Lach- und Schießgesellschaft, →(Münchner) Rationaltheater, →Die Pfeffermühle, →Das Politische Kabarett, →Reichskabarett, →Schall und Rauch, →Die Schaubude, →Die Schmiere, →Simplicissimus, →Theater der Prominenten, →Überbrettl)

Appignanesi, L.: Das Kabarett. Stuttgart 1976; Budzinski, K.: Das Kabarett. Düsseldorf 1985; ders.: Pfeffer ins Getriebe. München 1982; ders.: Wer lacht denn da? Braunschweig 1989; Ewers, H. H.: Das Cabaret. Berlin/Leipzig 1904; Fleischer, M.: Eine Theorie des Kabaretts. Bochum 1989; Gebhardt, H. (Hg.): Kabarett heute. Berlin 1987; Greul, H.: Bretter, die die Zeit bedeuten. Köln/Berlin 1967 (erw. in 2 Bden. München 1971); Heinrich-Jost, I.: Hungrige Pegasusse. Berlin (1984); Henningsen, J.: Theorie des Kabaretts. Ratingen 1967; Hippen, R.: «Sich fügen – heißt lügen». Mainz 1981; ders.: Kabarettgeschichte-n. 25 Bde. (geplant). Zürich 1986ff (*noch im Ersch.*); Hösch, R.: Kabarett von gestern und heute. 2 Bde. Berlin 1967–72; Hoffmann, G.: Das politische Kabarett als geschichtliche Quelle. Frankfurt/M. 1976; Kamp, J. E. van de: Mens, durf te leven! Grote Figuren uit het cabaret in en om Amsterdam tot 1940. Amsterdam 1978; Keiser, C.: Herrliche Zeiten – 1916–1976. 60 Jahre Cabaret in der Schweiz. Bern 1976; Kühn, V.: Das Kabarett der frühen Jahre. Berlin 1984; ders. (Hg.): Kleinkunststücke. Bd. 1ff Weinheim/Berlin 1987ff (*noch im Ersch.*); Otto, R., W. Rösler: Kabarettgeschichte. Berlin 1981; Pelzer, J.: Criticism through mockery. Satirical Concepts and Functional Problems in West German Kabarett. Diss. Madison 1981; Reisner, I.: Kabarett als Werkstatt des Theaters. 2 Bde. Diss. Wien 1961; Rösler, W. (Hg.): Geh ma halt a bisserl unter. Kabarett in Wien von den Anfängen bis heute. Berlin 1991; Segel, H. B.: Turn-of-the-Century Cabaret. New York 1987; Van Sweringen, B. T.: Kabarettist an der Front des kalten Krieges. Günter Neumann und das politische Kabarett in der Programmgestaltung des Radios im amerikanischen Sektor Berlins (RIAS). Passau 1989; Veigl, H.: Lachen im Keller. Kabarett und Kleinkunst in Wien. Wien 1986; Weihermüller, M.: Discographie der deutschen Kleinkunst. 2 Bde. Bonn 1991; Weys, R.: Cabaret und Kabarett in Wien. Wien 1970; Wittlin, J. (Hg.): Warschau, abends um halb zehn. Polnisches Kabarett. Berlin 1979; Zivier, G., H. Kotschenreuther, V. Ludwig: Kabarett mit K. Berlin 1974.

Wolfgang Beck/Manfred Pauli

Kabarett der Komiker

Berliner Kabarett, am 1.12.1924 von dem Schauspieler und Conférencier Kurt Robitschek mit Paul Morgan, Max Adalbert und Max Hansen eröffnet. In der Mischung aus Kabarett, Theater und Varieté entsprach das

«KadeKo» dem Trend der Zeit. Nach mehrfachem Umzug eröffnete das K.d.K. am 19. 9. 1928 im eigenen Haus. Hier wurde 1932 die erste «Kabarett-Oper» aufgeführt: *Rufen Sie Herrn Plim!* (Text: Robitschek/Marcellus Schiffer, Musik: Mischa Spoliansky). Bekannte Regisseure wie Jürgen Fehling inszenierten hier Tschechow und Kisch, berühmte Berliner Schauspieler traten ebenso auf wie internationale Gäste (z. B. Yvette Guilbert, Jacques Tati). Seine Bedeutung erhielt das K.d.K. durch die zeitkritischen Conférencen fast aller bedeutenden →Conférenciers der Zeit. Nach der Machtübergabe an die Nationalsozialisten und der Emigration K. Robitscheks und einer Reihe seiner Mitarbeiter leitete zuerst Hanns Schindler, dann Willi Schaeffers das K.d.K. Ihm gelang es durch Verzicht auf jede Art von Kritik, das K.d.K. bis zur allg. Schließung der Theater 1944 geöffnet zu halten. – Robitschek konnte den Spielbetrieb in New York noch bis nach 1945 aufrechterhalten. Vor ausverkauften Häusern mit vorwiegend älteren Emigranten spielte er vor allem Lach-Programme. Antifaschistische Satiren waren nur in geringem Umfang vertreten. – Nach Kriegsende eröffnete Schaeffers das K.d.K. erneut und machte Kleinkunst, nicht mehr Kabarett – ebensowenig wie der Klavierhumorist Klaus Günter Neumann, der 1965 ein K.d.K. in West-Berlin eröffnete.

Budzinski, K.: Pfeffer ins Getriebe. München 1982; Günther, E.: Geschichte des Varietés. Berlin ²1981; PEM (d. i. P. E. Marcus): Heimweh nach dem Kurfürstendamm. Berlin 1952; Schaeffers, W.: Tingeltangel – Ein Leben für die Kleinkunst. Hamburg 1959; Zivier, G./Kotschenreuther, H./Ludwig, V.: Kabarett mit K. Berlin 1974.

Wolfgang Beck/Jan Hans

Kabuki

Jap. Theaterform. – Die sog. bürgerliche Schaukunst der Edo-Zeit (1600–1868); vereint Schauspiel, Tanz und Musik; repräsentative Kunstform der *chônin*-Kultur, der Kultur der Städter und Kaufleute, die sich in ihrer Neigung zu Farbenpracht, Luxus und Exeggeration nicht wenig von den stilleren, mehr aristokratischen traditionellen Kunstformen Japans (→Nô) unterscheidet. Doch zollten auch die chônin dem überlieferten japanischen Geschmack Tribut, indem sie den Begriff des *iki* oder *sui*, der höchst verfeinerten, kennerhaften (ja fast dandyhaften) Eleganz zu einer zentralen Kategorie ihres ästhetischen Empfindens machten; ‹iki› war es, was der Welt des Freudenviertels (Yoshiwara) und des kabuki ihren faszinierenden Reiz verlieh. In seiner 300jährigen wechselvollen Entwicklung, während der sich die noch heute (und in zunehmendem Maße) in

482 Kabuki

aller Welt bekannte Form des Männer-kabuki herausschälte, war es immer wieder und über lange Perioden den Repressionen der Zentralregierung (Shôgunat) ausgesetzt, der es als Welt der Übertretung, der Prostitution, der Homosexualität, der Verschwendung stets verdächtig war. Kabuki hat sich der Überlieferung nach aus den von zeitgenössischen Volksliedern begleiteten Tänzen einer Tempeltänzerin mit dem Namen Izumo no Okuni entwickelt, die um das Jahr 1600 in Kyôto aufgetreten sein soll. Später haben Frauengruppen Tanzspiele aufgeführt, die *onna-kabuki* (Frauen-kabuki) oder *kabuki-odori* (kabuki-Tanz) genannt wurden. Damals spielten die Frauen auch die männlichen Rollen. Männer sorgten nur für komische Einlagen, bis die Regierung, weil sie die Sittlichkeit nicht gern gefährdet sah, 1629 das Frauen-kabuki verbot. Das Jünglings-kabuki (*wakashû-kabuki*), das an dessen Stelle trat, scheint die Sittlichkeit nicht minder bedroht zu haben und wurde 1652 ebenfalls verboten. Es wurde vom kabuki der Männer, der ‹Kerle› (‹*yarô*›*-kabuki*), abgelöst. Im Gegensatz zu den Anfängen wurden ab jetzt sämtliche Rollen, auch die der Frauen, von Männern gespielt. (Die Schauspieler, die sich auf Frauenrollen spezialisieren, werden im Kabuki *onnagata* genannt; *tachiyaku*, eigtl. ‹stehender Spieler› – was urspr. für Schauspieler im allgemeinen gebraucht wurde, weil diese im Gegensatz zu den Musikern standen –, bezeichnet seit der Verselbständigung der Frauendarstellung als eigenes Fach nur noch Männerdarsteller.) Tatsache ist, daß das kabuki sich erst von dieser Zeit an zu einer wirklichen Bühnenkunst entwickelte – freilich nicht, weil es nun ganz in den Händen der Männer lag, sondern weil es die Bedürfnisse spiegeln und auf die Bedürfnisse antworten mußte, mit denen die sich gewaltig entwickelnde städtische Bevölkerung es konfrontierte. (In der Frühzeit des kabuki improvisierten die Schauspieler ihre Texte weitgehend, nur Spielhandlung und wichtige Textpassagen wurden fixiert; erst seit 1680 erschienen die Namen der Schreiber auf den Programmzetteln – *banzuke* – oder in publizierten Lesefassungen.) Der Gipfel der Entwicklung, die die Klasse der *chônin* zu den wichtigsten Kulturträgern und -förderern des Landes machte, bildet die Ära Genroku (*nengo*, ‹Jahresdevise› der Jahre 1688–1703), zugleich auch – selbstverständlich geradezu – eine Blütezeit des kabuki. Um die Schauspieler wurde ein veritabler Starkult getrieben. Die Größten ihres Faches, wie Ichikawa Danjurô (1660–1703), Nakamura Shichisaburô (1662–1708), Sakata Tôjurô (1647–1709) oder der vielgepriesene Frauendarsteller Yoshizawa Ayame (1673–1729), galten als Autoritäten in Fragen der Mode und des guten Geschmacks. Die onnagata dienten den Kurtisanen der Freudenviertel als Vorbild weiblicher Eleganz und Delikatesse. Dennoch verhinderte das Zwielichtige ihres Standes eine volle gesellschaftliche Anerkennung; auch in, gerade in Japan repräsentierten die Schauspieler die Demimonde; die Glücklichsten unter ihnen blieben Outlaws mit Privilegien.

Die kabuki-Stücke lassen sich in drei Kategorien einteilen: 1. die *jidai-mono* (‹historische Dramen›), 2. die *sewamono* (‹bürgerliche Dramen›), 3. die *shosagoto* (tanzorientiertes kabuki). Die *jidaimono* behandelten historische Themen, ohne jedoch auf Geschichtstreue Wert zu legen; im Gegenteil, oft wurde bewußte Geschichtsklitterung getrieben, um unter der Maske historischer Personen oder Motive Zeitgenössisches auf die Bühne zu bringen, was unverstellt zu tun verboten war. Die *sewamono* kamen erst in der Genroku-Periode auf; es ist nicht abwegig, in ihnen das japanische Gegenstück zum ‹bürgerlichen Trauerspiel› zu sehen. Zentrales Thema der sewamono ist die dilemmatische Kollision von Liebe/Neigung und Pflicht, von *ninjô* und *giri* (oft Bearbeitungen aktueller, dem Publikum wohlvertrauter Stoffe oder Vorkommnisse); auch die über gut und böse erhabene Macht des Geldes wird thematisiert. Den ‹bürgerlich›-tragischen Helden bleibt dabei zumeist nur der Tod. Konfliktlösung durch Verschwinden. Der Doppelselbstmord der Liebenden (*shinjû*) ist ein so häufiges Motiv, daß man hier fast von einem eigenen Genre sprechen könnte. Die *shosagoto* sind durchchoreographierte Tanzstücke, nicht selten Adaptationen bekannter Nô-Vorlagen, in ihrer Funktion nicht unvergleichbar den großen Koloraturarien der europ. Oper; sie geben dem Schauspieler Gelegenheit, alle Register seiner Kunst zu ziehen und sie – gleichsam en bloc – dem Urteil des Publikums zu präsentieren.

Insgesamt läßt sich behaupten, daß, obgleich das kabuki Momente eines ‹Gesamtkunstwerks› enthält, das kunstentscheidende Element im kabuki das des theatralischen und sprachlichen Gestaltungsausdrucks ist. Tendenziell wenigstens verliert die Sprache ihren Mitteilungs-, ja Zeichencharakter, oder versucht, nur noch Zeichen ihrer selbst zu sein. Die Sprache des kabuki, das *serifu*, ist nahe dem Schrei, dem Schluchzen, dem Wimmern, kurz: dem Naturlaut, paradoxerweise trotz der nicht geringen Stilisierung und artifiziellen Reduktion. Das Geschehen in einem kabuki-Stück darf Brüche und Inkonsequenzen aufweisen, die psychologische Zeichnung darf grob und skizzenhaft sein (oft ist sie jedoch, bes. in den Werken Chikamatsu Monzaemons, 1653–1724, bis ins feinste durchgeführt); wesentlich ist, daß die Handlung immer wieder einen Vorwand für die Darstellung menschlicher ‹Ursituationen› bietet: Haß, Liebe, Eifersucht, Angst, Freude, Überraschung, Trauer, Zorn und Rührung. An diesen Stellen kommt das kabuki ‹zu sich›, die Zeit wird ignoriert, die Szene erstarrt zu einem stehenden Bild (*mie*), und das Publikum ruft: ‹mattemashita!› – ‹Darauf haben wir gewartet!›

Seine zweite und eigentliche Glanzzeit erlebt das kabuki in den Jahren zwischen 1780 und 1830, nachdem der berühmte Dramatiker Namiki Shôzô (1730–73) unter anderem durch die Erfindung einer Vorform der Drehbühne (1758) und der Einführung von Versenkungs- und Hebungsapparaturen die Bühnentechnik entscheidend verbessert hatte. Danach setzte eine Periode der Dekadenz ein, die nichtsdestoweniger (den Niedergang der Shôgunatsregierung auf vermittelte Weise spiegelnd) neue Genres hervorbrachte – wie die sog. *kizewamono* (Unterweltsstücke), deren bekanntestes das Drama *Yotsuya Kaidan* von Tsuruya Namboku IV ist, ein Grusel- und Gespensterstück, das auch heute noch seine Wirkung nicht verfehlt (nicht zuletzt wegen seiner frappierenden ‹Modernität›). Der letzte der großen kabuki-Klassiker war Kawatake Mokuami (1816–87), der über 300 Stücke schrieb, in denen häufig die dunklen, unberechenbaren, ‹bösen› Seiten der menschlichen Natur zum Thema erhoben werden. Sie bezeugen das Ende einer langen Epoche und den verwirrenden (geradezu katastrophischen) Einbruch einer neuen Zeit. Nach einer Übergangsphase, die zum Teil groteske Versuche einer Europäisierung brachte (z. B. *zangirimono*: die Schauspieler traten mit europ. kurzem Haarschnitt auf), wird das kabuki heute wieder mehr als erhaltungswürdiges Kulturgut betrachtet, das die Funktion der Verlebendigung vergangener Werte erfüllt.

Barth, J.: Japans Schaukunst im Wandel der Zeiten. Wiesbaden 1972; Leims, Th. (Hg.): European Writing on Japanese Theatre. Wien/Köln 1991; ders.: Die Entstehung des Kabuki. Leiden 1990; Nakamura, M.: Kabuki. Tokio/New York 1990; Ortolani, B.: Das japanische Theater. In: Kindermann, H. (Hg.): Fernöstliches Theater. Stuttgart 1966; ders.: Das Kabukitheater. Kulturgeschichte der Anfänge. Tôkyô 1964; Senzoku, T.: Kabuki. Das Theater des altjapanischen Bürgertums. Tôkyô 1964.

Peter Pörtner

Kamishibai

Jap., wörtl. →Papiertheater – Nachfolger der schon während der Edo-Zeit (1600–1868) in Japan bekannten Laterna magica (*utsushi-e*, ‹projizierte Bilder›); entstand in der Mitte der Meiji-Zeit (1868–1912), urspr. wurden dabei etwa 25 cm große, an Stäben befestigte Papierfiguren vor einem bemalten Hintergrund bewegt. Später wurde diese Art Spiel in einem Zelt gezeigt, bes. bei religiösen Festen und Volksbelustigungen. Der beliebteste Stoff war das *Saiyûki*, eine phantastische Geschichte aus dem alten China. Bis zum Beginn der Shôwa-Zeit (seit 1926) hatte das kamishibai eine außerordentliche Popularität erreicht. In den 30er Jahren entwickelte sich eine neue Art des Spiels, bei dem die Geschichte auf eine Serie von Bilderbogen gezeichnet war, die (nach Art der Moritatensänger) in einem Kasten gezeigt wurden. Dieser neue Typ des kamishibai vertrieb das ältere Papierpuppenspiel bald völlig und erlangte eine ungeheure Ausbreitung, bes. unter den sozial schwächer Gestellten in den Vorstadtvierteln. Die militaristische Regierung setzte das kamishibai in der zweiten Hälfte der 30er Jahre zu propagandistisch-edukativen Zwekken ein. Nach dem Krieg erlebte das kamishibai dank seiner Einfachheit eine neue Blüte, und 1949 wurden in Japan etwa 50 000 kamishibai-Spieler gezählt. Der Konkurrenz des Fernsehens konnte es allerdings nicht standhalten; seit 1960 werden keine neuen Bildserien mehr produziert. Viele kamishibai-Maler verlegten sich auf das Malen von Comic strips (*manga*), ein Genre, das bis in die neueste Zeit in Japan nichts von seiner exzessiven Popularität eingebüßt hat.

Peter Pörtner

Kammerschauspieler

Ehrentitel, der an hervorragende Schauspieler früher von Fürsten, heute von staatlichen oder städtischen Behörden verliehen wird.

Bernard Poloni

Kammerspiel

Die Bezeichnung K. umschreibt den dramaturgischen Bau von Stücken, die wenige Personen und wenige Schauplätze, meist Innenräume, haben. Auch die Figurenkonflikte werden ‹innen›, psychologisch facettenreich motiviert und nicht in plakativ-großräumigen Aktionen ausgetragen. A. Strindberg verwendete den Ausdruck K. erstmals 1907 für Stücke, die er für das →Intime Theater Stockholm geschrieben hatte (*Wetterleuchten, Brandstätten, Scheiterhaufen*). Gleichzeitig bürgerte sich ‹K.› als Kennzeichnung für Theatergebäude ein, die nur einen geringen Abstand zwischen Bühne und Zuschauerplätzen haben. Die von Max Reinhardt dem «Deutschen Theater» angefügten «Kammerspiele», 1906 mit Ibsens *Gespenster* eröffnet, waren die erste deutsche Bühne, die auch architektonisch die trennende Rampe aufzuheben suchten. In diesen Theatern können die Schauspieler mit feinsten sprachlichen und gestischen Nuancen ihre Rollen gestalten – wie es die Dramen A. Strindbergs, A. Schnitzlers, M. Maeterlincks, F. Wedekinds und anderer Autoren vorsehen. Sie enthüllen häufig hinter der Fassade gutbürgerlicher Ordnung die seelische Not und die Lebenslüge der Figuren. In der Gegenwart entstehen nur noch wenige Theatertexte, die als K. bezeichnet werden könnten.

Delius, A.: Intimes Theater. Untersuchungen zur Programmatik und Dramaturgie einer bevorzugten Theaterform der Jahrhundertwende. Kronberg 1976.

Roland Dreßler

Kampfbühne

Von Lothar Schreyer (1886–1966) in Hamburg 1919 gegr. Bis 1921 Aufführungen expressionistischer Theater-Gesamtkunstwerke. K. ist nach der →Sturmbühne wichtigstes expressionistisches Experimentiertheater. Prinzipien von Schreyers Bühnenkunstwerk: Einheit von Form, Farbe, Bewegung und Ton. Der «Spielgang» wird best. durch Klangsprechen, Farbkomposition der Masken und der Bewegung. Zwischen Oktober 1919 und Frühsommer 1921 Erarbeitung von acht Inszenierungen: August Stramms *Haidebraut* und *Kräfte*; Krippenspiel nach einem alten Text von 1589; Friedrich Hölderlins *Der Tod des Empedokles* (2. Fassung); Lothar Schreyers *Kreuzigung, Mann, Kindersterben*; Herwarth Waldens *Spiel an der Liebe, Sünde*. Die Aufführungen fanden statt in der Kunstgewerbeschule Hamburg.

Pirsich, V.: Der Sturm. Herzberg 1985; Wasserka, I.: Die Sturm- und Kampfbühne. Kunsttheorie und szenische Wirklichkeit im expressionistischen Theater Lothar Schreyers. Diss. Wien 1965.

Ingeborg Janich

Karagiozis

Hauptheld des neugriech. →Schattentheaters, welchem diese volkstümliche Kunstform insgesamt ihren Namen entliehen hat. Die Hauptfigur stammt nach wichtigen Modifikationen vom →Karagöz, dem entsprechenden Helden des türkischen Schattentheaters. Aufführungen des letzteren waren wahrscheinlich einigen Bevölkerungsschichten griech. Abstammung im Osmanischen Reich bereits am Ende des 18. und zu Beginn des 19. Jh. bekannt. Dennoch fällt die älteste bezeugte öffentliche K.-Vorstellung in einer griech. Stadt erst in die Zeit nach der Gründung des neugriech. Königreichs (1832) in den August 1841. In den folgenden Jahren scheint das Schattenspiel sich in den Gleisen der traditionellen osmanischen Vorbilder, aber in griech. Sprache von griechischsprachigen Karagiozisspielern aufgeführt, zu entwickeln. Das türk. Repertoire gerät jedoch mit seiner bezeichnenden Obszönität des Dialogs wie auch der Handlung mit den europäischen Sitten und Werten der neugebildeten Bürgerklasse in Konflikt, so daß diese eine Reihe von polizeilichen Verboten erwirkt. Ein Aufschwung erfolgt erst wieder in den 80er Jahren des 19. Jh., als es einer Truppe von K.-Spielern (Leitung: Dimitris Sardunis, Pseud. Mimaros) gelang, das Repertoire sowie die Figuren der zeitgenössischen kulturellen Situation anzupassen. Den beiden Hauptfiguren, die das griech. Schattentheater vom osmanischen ererbt hat, d. h. dem erfinderischen, hungerleidenden Proletarier K. und dem knechtischen, kompromißbereiten Kleinbürger Chatziavatis, werden neue, aus der griech. Volkskultur abgeleitete Standardtypen hinzugefügt: der ungeschlachte Viehzüchter Barbajorgos, der verwestlichte Protz Sior Dionysios von den Ionischen Inseln, der gewalttätige albanische Söldner Veligekas, Vertreter der Willkür der Staatsmacht, der feige Raufbold Stavrakas u. a.

Die Popularität dieser volkstümlichen Unterhaltung während der ersten Jahrzehnte des 20. Jh. war offenbar darin begründet, daß sie die Selbstentfremdung und die Ängste der breiten Masse des Volks in einer schwierigen Übergangsperiode der Geschichte des Landes authentisch widerspiegelt. Nach 1919 beginnt man, mehrere Stücke des ‹klassischen› K.-Repertoires (weitgehend mündliche Überlieferung) niederzuschreiben und in Groschenheften oder im Rahmen gelehrter Versuche zum Studium des Phänomens zu veröffentlichen.

Chatzipantazis, Th.: I isvoli tu Karagiozi stin Athina tu 1890 (Das Eindringen des Karagiozis in Athen 1890). Athen 1984; Danforth, L. M.: Tradition and Change in Greek Shadow Theater. In: Journal of American Folklore 96, N. 381. July/September 1983; G. M. Siphakis: I paradosiaki dramaturgia tu Karagiozi (Die traditionelle Dramaturgie des Karagiozis). Athen 1984; Kiurtsakis, J.: Prophoriki paradosi ke omadiki dimiurgia, to paradigma tu Karagiozi (Mündliche Überlieferung und Gruppenschöpfung. Das Beispiel Karagiozis). Athen 1983; Puchner, W.: Das neugriechische Schattentheater Karagiozis. München 1975; Rosenthal-Kamarinea, I.: Hauptformen des griechischen Theaters und ihre Entwicklung. In: Kultur im Migrationsprozeß. Hg. von M. Fehr. Berlin 1982, S. 97–112; Yayannos, A. u. a.: The World of Karaghiozis. Athen 1976 u. 1977.

Thodoros Chatzipantazis

Karagöz

Das türkische →Schattentheater erhielt seinen Namen von seinem Helden K. (= Schwarzauge). K. ist kahl, hat einen schwarzen Bart und eine überdimensionale linke Hand, mit der er Ohrfeigen verteilt. Möglicherweise war er ursprünglich Zigeuner. Er gilt als ungebildet, ist grob im Ausdruck, aber mit Mutterwitz und Bauernschläue gesegnet. Die Figuren des K.-Spiels sind flach, ca. 40 cm hoch, aus transparentem, bemaltem Kamelleder. Die einzelnen Körperteile sind an zwei bis drei Punkten beweglich verbunden, so daß sie getrennt bewegt werden können. Am Hals ist das Loch für den Führungsstab, K. hat ein zweites Loch in seiner linken Hand. Mit dem Stab preßt der Spieler (karagözcü, früher auch: hayalci) die Figuren gegen die 1 m × 1,60 m große Leinwand, die von hinten angestrahlt wird. Die einzelnen Teile der K.-Aufführung und ihre Abfolge sind festgelegt: giriş (Einführung), muhavere (Dialog), fasıl (Handlung), bitiş (Schluß). Vor der Einführung ist eine unbewegliche Figur (gösterme), z. B. ein Baum oder ein Haus, auf der Leinwand zu sehen, die keinen Bezug zum folgenden Stück haben muß. Im ‹giriş› grüßt *Hacivat*, der oberflächlich gebildete Gegenspieler des K., Gott durch die Wendung ‹Hay Hak›, spricht ein Ghasel über die Vergänglichkeit der Welt und beschreibt seinen Wunsch nach einem Gesprächspartner. Der Teil ‹muhavere› beginnt, indem K. von rechts oben auf die Bühne springt. Der folgende Dialog ist voll von Mißverständnissen, da beide Figuren eigene Gesprächsebenen benutzen: K.' Sprache ist derb und voll obszöner Anspielungen, Hacivats geziert und mit Fremdwörtern durchsetzt. Dieser Teil kann Anspielungen auf Tagesereignisse enthalten und ist daher bei jeder Aufführung unterschiedlich lang. Er endet mit einer Prügelei. Von der nun folgenden Handlung leitet sich der Name des Stücks ab, z. B. ‹Die Reise nach Yalova›, ‹K. als Schreiber›. In die Rahmenhandlung eingebettet – meist nimmt K. durch Vermittlung des Hacivat eine Arbeit auf, für die er denkbar ungeeignet ist –, treten nacheinander Figuren auf, die stereotypisch verschiedene soziale und ethnische Bevölkerungsgruppen darstellen: *Perser, Kurde, Lase, Jude, Grieche, Franke* (= Europäer), die Frau (*Zenne*), der Süchtige (*Tiryaki*), der Zwerg *Beberuhi* u. a. Die Imitation der verschiedenen Sprechweisen erfordert ein hohes Maß an Können vom Spieler, daneben muß er über großes manuelles Geschick verfügen. Nachdem K. in Einzelszenen mit jeder Figur Wortgefechte, die oft mit Prügelei enden, geführt hat, greift zum Schluß der Wächter *Tuzsuz Ali Bekir* ein. Das fasıl kann durch die Anzahl der Szenen beliebig lang gestaltet werden. Im Schlußteil entschuldigen sich K. und Hacivat für sprachliche Mängel und kündigen Titel, Ort und Zeit der nächsten Aufführung an.

Man vermutet, daß das Schattentheater zur Zeit seiner größten Erfolge, im 18. und 19. Jh., neben dem Ziel der allgemeinen Volksbelustigung auch satirisch die Politik des Reichs und – in der Person des K. – den Unmut des Volks darstellen wollte. Das Repertoire eines karagözcü mußte früher mindestens 28 Stücke umfassen, damit er in jeder Nacht des Fastenmonats Ramadan eines aufführen konnte; daneben waren K.-Aufführungen besonders bei Beschneidungsfeiern beliebt. Im Zuge der Hinwendung an das europäische Theater in der 2. Hälfte des 19. Jh. verlor K. an Bedeutung. Erst seit den 60er Jahren dieses Jh. ist eine allmähliche Neubesinnung auf diese Theaterform zu bemerken, wozu auch die Verbreitung durch das Fernsehen beiträgt.

Kudret, C.: Karagöz, 3 Bde. Ankara 1968; Ritter, H.: Karagös. Türkische Schattenspiele, 2 Bde. Istanbul 1941; Tietze, A.: The Turkish Shadow Theater and the Puppet Collection of the L. A. Mayer Memorial Foundation. Berlin 1977.

Maren Fittschen

Kasperletheater

In direkter Anlehnung an den barocken →Hanswurst kreierte der Komiker Laroche um 1770 die komische Figur des Kasper(-l; -le) als Spaßmacher des Wiener Vorstadttheaters (→Alt-Wiener Volksstück). Weitere Bezüge zum Harlekin der →Commedia dell'arte. Im 19. Jh. wurde K. eine volkstümliche Form des →Handpuppenspiels mit der derben, witzigen, prügelnden, stets die Oberhand behaltenden K.-Puppe im Zentrum. Die Spielorte, meist Jahrmärkte, das spezifische Publikum (Kinder) und eine allseitige Verbreitung trugen zur starken Regionalisierung der hauptsächlich mündlich tradierten Kasperliaden bei. Mit Beginn des 20. Jh. mit wechselnder Intensität an Schulen und Kindergärten zu pädagogischen Zwecken eingesetzt (→Puppentheater, →Marionettentheater).

Eichler, F.: Das Wesen des Handpuppen- und Marionettenspiels. Emsdetten 1949; Miller, N./Riha, K.: Kasperletheater für Erwachsene. Frankfurt/M. 1978; Rabe, E.: Kasper Putschenelle. Hamburg 1924.

Erich Krieger

Kata

Ausdrucks- und Bewegungsfiguren im →Nô, →*kyôgen*, →*kabuki*, die als Grundelemente der gesamten schauspielerischen Darstellung fungieren und jede Aktion des Spielers als stilisierte Momentaufnahme eines Bewegungsablaufs oder als komprimierte Symbole eines Gemütszustands strukturierend bestimmen.

Roland Schneider

Die Katakombe

Im Keller des «Vereins Berliner Künstler» eröffnete am 16. 10. 1929 Werner Finck mit Hans Deppe, R. A. Stemmle u. a. das Kabarett K., das sich bald zu einem der führenden politisch-literarischen Ensembles Berlins entwickelte – nicht zuletzt dank der Mitwirkung politisch so engagierter Künstler wie Ernst Busch, Hanns Eisler und Kate Kühl. Chansons, Parodien, literarisch-politische Sketche, parodistische Tänze und Pantomimen wurden durch Fincks Conférencen verbunden. Nach einem Jahr kam es zum Bruch, die politisch engagierten Künstler schieden aus. Finck und der neu hinzugekommene Rudolf Platte zogen mit einer neuen Gruppe in ein neues Domizil. Die K. wurde weniger kämpferisch, weniger politisch.

Nach Beginn der faschistischen Herrschaft konnte die K. noch weiterspielen. Ein eher unverbindliches Programm verband nun die Conférencen Fincks, der seinen stotternden, die Pointe unausgesprochen lassenden Stil bis zur Perfektion ausbilden konnte. Am 10. 5. 1935 schließlich wurden «Tingeltangel» und K. geschlossen, Finck u. a. Mitglieder des Ensembles in «Schutzhaft» ins KZ Esterwegen verschleppt und – wohl einmalig im faschistischen Deutschland – nach ihrer Freilassung von einem Gericht freigesprochen. Während Finck in Haft war, hatten einige Mitglieder der Gruppe versucht, mit reduziertem Programm weiterzuspielen (der Name K. war verboten), aber ohne Erfolg. – Finck gründete nach dem Krieg mit der «Mausefalle» 1946 in Stuttgart, 1951 in Hamburg, eher kurzlebige Kabaretts und trat danach hauptsächlich als Solist auf.

Budzinski, K.: Wer lacht denn da? Braunschweig 1989; Finck, W.: Alter Narr, was nun? München 1972; ders.: Witz als Schicksal, Schicksal als Witz. Hamburg 1966; Heiber, H.: Die Katakombe wird geschlossen. München 1966; Hösch, R.: Kabarett von gestern und heute. 2 Bde. Berlin 1967–72.

Wolfgang Beck

Katarimono-Rezitationskunst

Katari-gei (‹Erzähl›-Kunst), aus der altjap. Tradition der professionellen Geschichte[n]erzähler (*kataribe*) stammend und bis zum angehenden Mittelalter in unterschiedlichen Ausprägungen – Predigtvorträge, Kriegs- und Heldenerzählungen, Bildererklärer – in weiten Teilen die mündliche Literatur bestimmend, ist gewöhnlich integraler Bestandteil in bekannten jap. Schaukunstformen wie →Nô, *bunraku* oder →*kabuki*, gewinnt jedoch gelegentlich auch Eigenständigkeit als Bühnenkunstform wie in den spätmittelalterlichen *kôwaka-mai*, die – ihrem Publikum, den Samurai, entsprechend – Heldengeschichten vortragen, oder in der neuzeitlichen *rakugo*-Monologkunst, die in ihren Vorläufern, den professionellen Vorlesern, bis in das 17. Jh. zurückreicht und auf Wortwitz und Sprach- wie Sprechziel zielend Alltagsstoffe vorträgt und schließlich in die kabarettartige *yose*-Alleinunterhalterkunst mündet.

Roland Schneider

Kathak

(Kathak = Geschichtenerzähler) Eine Tanzform aus dem Norden Indiens (→ Indisches Theater). Der K.-Stil ist in Kostüm und Technik von islamischen Stilelementen mit geprägt worden. Die Tänzer treten in weitschwingenden Pluderhosen auf. Die K.-Spiele greifen inhaltlich auf Krishna-Mythen zurück. Im Gegensatz zum → Bharata Natyam charakterisieren den K. weiträumige Schritte, rasche Drehungen und Wirbelbewegungen. Beine haben exponierte Bedeutung, werden mit Hunderten von Glöckchen besetzt. Waden- und Fußknöchel dienen als Rhythmus- und Klanginstrumente. Zwei Elemente tragen den K.-Stil: Ausdrucksfähigkeit und virtuose Fußarbeit. Der K.-Tänzer agiert in aufrechter, entspannter Körperhaltung, zeigt hohe Vibrationsfähigkeit und flexible Fußtechnik. Im Gegensatz zum → Kathakali-Theater setzt er den ganzen Fuß auf. Die künstlerische Aussagekraft des K. wird in hohem Maße von der Improvisationskraft des Tänzers und Spielers geprägt. – 711 n. Chr.: erste Araber in Nordindien. Auseinandersetzung mit der angestammten Kultur. Minarette und Moscheen in Delhi. Sultane, Khane, Mogule, Nawabs und Rajas ziehen ind. Handwerker und Künstler an ihre Höfe. Indisch bleiben die Epen und Mythen der Rezitationen, die getanzten Volksschauspiele und der Tempeltanz. Bereits nach 1700 im Königreich Madluya Pradesh und in Benares Renaissance der K.-Pflege durch Janki Prasad und seine Brüder. Da der Punjab und Kashmir erst 1850 von den Briten erobert worden sind, konnten Forscher in diesen Regionen Indiens die höchsten Verfeinerungen des K.-Stils auffinden. Die Brahmanin Menaka (1899–1947) tritt um 1920 als erste Solotänzerin des K. auf. 1926 tanzte sie in einer Aufführung vor der Pawlowa. Die Menaka gründet eine Tanzgruppe, die den K. und andere ind. Folklore pflegt (1936 Europa-Tournee, 1938 Tanzschule in Khandala/Bombay). Der keralische Dichter Menon (1878–1958) setzt sich mit Verve für das K.-Tanztheater ein. Aufbau des ersten modernen Instituts zur Pflege von Tanz, Musik und Dichtung in Keralien (1930).

Balakrishna, M.: Classical Indian Dance. Calcutta 1967; Ghvnani, E.: The Dance in India. Bombay 1970; Rebling, E.: Die Tanzkunst Indiens. Wilhelmshaven 1982.

Helga Ettl

Kathakali

(Katha = Erzählung; Kali = Tanzschauspiel) Das Tanztheater Keralas. Im K. wird der Bhagavati-Mythos getanzt. Charakteristika des K. sind: ausgeprägte Mimik und Gestik; imitative und symbolische Bedeutungsgehalte; Nritta (festlicher, heiterer, ausschmückender Tanz) und Nritya (erzählender Tanz, ohne gesprochenes Wort); Einheit von Gesang, Instrumentalspiel, Poesie und tänzerischer Darstellung; Ästhetik der Bhavas (Emotionen des Mimen) und Rasas (Stimmungen, die durch Bhavas beim Zuschauer ausgelöst werden). Diese Ästhetik wird getragen durch acht Spezifika: auffallend große Kopfbedeckungen; weiße Kostüme; kunstvolle Maskierungen; Farbsymbolik der Gesichter; Eckigkeit der Armbewegungen; akrobatische Körperhaltung; Leidenschaftlichkeit des dramatischen Gefühlsausdrucks; spannungsreiche Kampfszenen. – Die Mythen zu Ehren der Erdmutter stehen im Zentrum der theatralischen Darbietungen des Bhagavati-Mythos (Kämpfe der großen Urmutter Kali oder Bhagavati gegen das Böse). 175 n. Chr. entsteht das *Tamil*-Epos; 1652 das Tanzspiel *Krishnanattam* (noch in Sanskrit); 1658 in der Sprache des Volkes (Malayalam) das *Ramanattam*. Es ist der unmittelbare Vorläufer des heutigen K. Die Tänzer treten ohne Maske auf, deshalb ausgeprägte Mimik, Gesichter geschminkt. Zahlreiche Hastas (Hand- und Fingerhaltungen). Alle Künstler treten im K. zu einem Gesamtkunstwerk zusammen. Rabindranath Tagores aufklärende Arbeit führt in den 20er Jahren zu einer Renaissance der klassischen Tradition Indiens. Neben Tagore: Vallathol N. Menon (1878–1958, Dichter und Friedenskämpfer) und Rukmini Devi. Mit dem Kerala Kalamandalam (gegründet 1930 als Zentrum für Keralische Kunst und Kultur) wird die Wiedergeburt des K. gesichert (→ Ritualtänze; → Indisches Theater).

Daniélou, A./Vatsyayan, K.: Kathakali. Indisches Tanztheater. Hg. vom Internationalen Institut für Vergleichende Musikstudien und Dokumentationen. Berlin 1972; Srinivasan, R.: Kathakali, das Tanzdrama aus Kerala. In: Beiträge zur Musikwissenschaft. Sonderheft: Indien, Jg. 8, H. 2. Berlin 1966.

Helga Ettl

Katharsis

Aristoteles (*Poetik* 1449 b 27 f) bestimmt die Wirkung der Tragödie als K. (‹Reinigung›), d. h. als reinigende Befreiung von den bei der Betrachtung der tragischen Ereignisse erregten Affekten → Furcht und Mitleid. K. bedeutet dabei nicht, wie seit Lessing in immer neuen Variationen behauptet, die moralisch-ethische Läuterung und Besserung des Zuschauers als

Folge einer endgültigen oder zeitweiligen Befreiung von schädlichen Affekten oder ihrer Reduzierung und Reinigung, sondern, in der kultischmedizinischen Bedeutung des Wortes ‹Purgierung›, Ausscheidung der im Verlauf der Aufführung erregten tragischen Affekte. Diese Purgierung ist mit dem Gefühl einer befreienden Erleichterung verbunden, die nach Aristoteles das der Tragödie eigentümliche Vergnügen ist.

Schadewaldt, W.: Furcht und Mitleid? (1955). In: ders. Hellas und Hesperien. Zürich/Stuttgart 1970, S. 194–236; Fuhrmann, M.: Einführung in die antike Dichtungstheorie. Darmstadt 1973, S. 94–98.

Bernd Seidensticker

Katona József Szinház (Budapest)

Das Katona-József-Theater (1951–82 Kammerbühne des →Nemzeti Szinház) wurde 1982 von Gábor Zsámbéki (* 1943; 1974–78 Direktor des →Csiky Gergely Szinház) und Gábor Székely aus Szolnok, die 1978–82 als leitende Regisseure am →Nemzeti Szinház waren und einen Teil des Ensembles, u. a. Tamás Major (1910–85) und Hilda Gobbi (1913–88), mitnahmen, gegründet (1982 *Waldschrat* von Tschechow, R.: G. Zsámbéki), zur besten ungar. Bühne entwickelt und zu Weltruhm geführt. Gastspiele in aller Welt, Preise des BITEF (1984 *König Ubu*, R.: G. Zsámbéki) und des Pariser Théâtre de l'Europe (1990 *Platonow*, R.: Tamás Ascher). Ensemblespiel führender Darsteller Ungarns (u. a. P. Blaskó, J. Básti, D. Udvaros, M. Töröcsik); der konkreten Realität und dem Publikum verpflichtet. Psychologisch-realistische Spielweise, offen für Elemente der Avantgarde und Experimente; Erneuerung der ungar. Schauspielkunst. Maximale literarische Ansprüche (klassische und moderne Werke der Weltliteratur), Zusammenarbeit mit ungar. Autoren (György Spiró: *Der Impostor*, 1983; *Hühnerköppe*, 1986; R.: beide G. Zsámbéki), Gleichwertigkeit von Text, Regie und Schauspieler. Ständiger Gastregisseur T. Ascher (1986 *Drei Schwestern*; 1987 *Drei Mädchen in Blau* von L. Petruschewskaja). 1992 Studiobühne.

Elke Wiegand

Kindertheater/Jugendtheater

K. im eigentlichen Sinne ist das (professionelle) Theater für Kinder, bei dem Kinder primär zuschauend tätig sind, zuweilen auch mitreden (vor allem im →Puppenspiel), manchmal auch mitspielen (Sonderform Mitspiel). Das ‹pädagogische K.› (engl. Theatre in Education) versteht sich als Bereich der Spiel-, Theater-, Interaktionspädagogik; die Aufführung für Kinder ist ein Baustein im Gesamtzusammenhang von Vor- und Nachbereitung und eigenen Spielversuchen; verbunden wird die Aufführung mit Lernprozessen und Projekten. Kinder meint in diesem Zusammenhang alle Nichterwachsenen; bei genauerer Bestimmung werden K. und Jugendtheater unterschieden.

Drei verwandte Erscheinungen werden, nur z. T. berechtigt, ebenfalls mit der Bezeichnung K. belegt: 1. das spontane Rollen- und Interaktionsspiel des Kindes. Die Möglichkeit dazu wird von Kindern im Alter von zwei bis drei Jahren entdeckt; soweit Zeugnisse vorhanden sind, geschieht das ausnahmslos. Die weitere Entwicklung und Formung ist in den einzelnen Kulturen unterschiedlich. Theater kann von Kindern spontan erfunden werden als ein wiederholendes Zeigen mit Bezug auf einen Adressaten (Publikum); kindliches Spiel bzw. Verhalten kann durch Beobachtetwerden von außen zum Zeigen gemacht werden und nimmt dann Züge des Schau-spielens an (in diesen beiden Entwicklungen werden Ursprünge des Theaters wiederholt). Kinder können Theater aber auch spielerisch nachahmen. Dann entwickelt sich ein familien- oder nachbarschaftsgebundenes Spiel vor Zuschauern (mit Eintrittsgeld, Plakaten usw.; Zuschauer können auch Puppen sein), bei dem ‹Theater› so gespielt wird wie ‹Kaufmann› oder ‹Schule›. – 2. Das didaktisch angeleitete Rollen- und Interaktionsspiel (engl. creative drama; frz., ital., österr. Animation), dessen pädagogische Bedeutung in der Schule wie außerhalb mehr und mehr erkannt wird. – 3. Das Theater von Kindern, das sich entweder prozeßhaft und nicht im vorhinein geplant aus den Rollenspielversuchen entwickelt oder produktorientiert angezielt, auch leistungsorientiert eingedrillt wird. Das Theater von Kindern ist traditionell im Brauchtum vorhanden, wird pädagogisch und zur Repräsentation in der Schule, im Geschäftstheater kommerziell genutzt.

Im Theater sind Kinder und Jugendliche bis ins 19. Jh. hinein selbstverständliche Mitdarsteller und Mitzuschauer; nur selten werden sie von besonderen, häufig kultisch bedingten Formen ausgeschlossen (eher Mädchen als Knaben), entwickeln und übernehmen aber auch eigene Formen. Im völkerkundlich erschließbaren, vorliterarischen «Urtheater hat jeder das Recht, mimische Spiele darzustellen: Männer und Frauen, Burschen und Mädchen dürfen mitspielen»; doch ordnen die Alten schon «Übungsspiele an und lassen die Jungen so lange probieren, bis sie das mimische Handwerk beherrschen» (Eberle, 1955). Erst mit geschlechtlicher, sozialer, altersmäßiger Differenzierung treten Sonderformen auf; vor allem mit der Jugend- und Knabenweihe sind viele Formen eines Theaters für und von Nichterwachsenen verbunden. – Im Volksschauspiel «wird man das Gesamtvolk als die tragende Gemeinschaft im allge-

Kindertheater/Jugendtheater 495

meinen ansprechen müssen», doch sind die ausübenden Gemeinschaften häufig besondere Gruppen, darunter Burschenschaften (Stubenspiel), Schüler (Umzugsspiel), Kinder (verstärkt in Grenz- und Außengebieten). «Die führende Rolle von Älteren, welche diese Burschengruppen wieder leiteten, anlernten, darf dabei auch nicht übersehen werden» (Schmidt, 1962).

In den →Wanderbühnen und stehenden Theatern des 17. bis 19. Jh. spielen (Schauspieler-)Kinder selbstverständlich mit (Kinderrollen in rührenden Familienszenen, Statisten in der Oper, Zwerge, Genien usw.). Immer wieder gab es auch reine, sogenannte K., in denen geschäftstüchtige Prinzipale ihre «kleinen Affen» (Lessing) zur Schau stellten (nach 1740 Nicolini, nach 1760 F. Berner, 1815–21 Kinderballett Horschelt in Wien). Neben diesen weithin öffentlich bekanntgewordenen Truppen gibt es das Spiel im häuslichen Kreis der Liebhaber- und Familientheater. Dorthin hatte sich das Schultheater nach seiner großen Zeit zurückgezogen, getragen von den dt. Familien-, schließlich Kinderzeitschriften (nach engl. Muster; die beliebteste der «Kinderfreund» von Chr. F. Weiße 1775–82). Die moralisierend-nüchternen Stückchen sind dramatische Beweisführungen von Vernünftigkeit und Nützlichkeit in alltäglichen Szenen. Sie werden, entsprechend dem Gesellschaftstheater der Erwachsenen, meist in der Familie, durchaus aber auch für eine beschränkte Öffentlichkeit gespielt. Bis heute gibt es kaum eine Kinderballettschule, die nicht wenigstens einmal im Jahr zu einer Aufführung einlädt; auch im 18. Jh. wurde K. häufig als «Theater-Pflanzschule» legitimiert und mit Residenztheatern verbunden. Für die Entwicklung zum Weihnachtsmärchen werden im 19. Jh. wichtig die Kinderballette der K. Lanner in Hamburg (1863), Kinderaufführungen in Wien (1855 und ab 1862), insbesondere die Kinderkomödie von Görner (1806–84) ab 1854. Dieser verbindet Barocktraditionen des phantastischen und zauberischen Theaters (in der verbürgerlichten Form der Pariser Féerie und des Wiener Zauberspiels von Stranitzky bis Raimund) mit der Handlung bekannter Volksmärchen und schafft so mit mancherlei Elementen aus Oper (*Zauberflöte*) und Ballett (Ausstattungsballett) den Typ des (von ihm nicht so genannten) Weihnachtsmärchens, das bis in die Gegenwart hinein die Pflichtübung etablierter Theater bleibt: Aufführung in der Weihnachtszeit, Ausstattung, Märcheninhalt, Bezug auf Weihnachten zumindest im Schlußbild (Apotheose), erste Regieaufgabe für Anfänger. Dieses Weihnachtsmärchen ist die Antwort auf den allmählichen Ausschluß der Kinder aus dem Erwachsenentheater (auf Breslauer Theaterzetteln wird Kindern unter vier Jahren der Besuch verweigert; Iffland schließt in Berlin die noch nicht Sechsjährigen aus). Der vorweihnachtliche Kassenschlager wird zunächst von primär geschäftlich interessierten Privattheatern, ab 1880 auch von Staatstheatern aufgenommen.

Trotz der sich verstärkenden Proteste entwickelt sich erst im 20. Jh. ein anderes K. In Moskau gründet N. Saz (* 1903) 1918 ein K., das als «Zentrales Theater für Kinder» imponierend ausgebaut wird und später Modell ist für das K. der Volksdemokratien (straffe zentrale Leitung und Planung, hochqualifizierte Mitarbeiter, Theaterpädagogen, enge Zusammenarbeit mit der Schule, genaue Altersdifferenzierung, politisch bestimmter Spielplan). Weitere Gründungen: 1921 in New York durch C. T. Major; 1927 das Scottish Children Theatre durch B. Waddell; 1929 in Paris das Théâtre de l'Oncle Sébastien durch L. Chancerel; 1931 das Skoletheatret in Oslo; 1934 das Theater der Jugend in Wien; 1945 in Holland das Ballett für Kinder Scapino; 1965 in Moskau die erste Oper für Kinder (ebenfalls durch N. Saz). In Deutschland deutet sich eine Modernisierung in Stil und Inhalt erst kurz vor 1933 an (Brecht, Weill, Hindemith, Dessau, Kästner, Forster); erst 1948 (Nürnberg) bzw. 1953 (Dortmund) gelingt Stadttheatern die Einrichtung eines ständigen Theaters der Jugend. Aber noch 1955 formuliert H. Tornau in ihrer Dissertation: «Im großen und ganzen muß man doch sämtliche Reformversuche am Weihnachtsmärchen als gescheitert betrachten.» Erst ab 1966 wird eine grundlegende Veränderung von den Autoren des K. im Berliner →«Reichskabarett», später →Grips, begonnen. Sie stellen sich dem politisch-pädagogischen Anspruch des Theaters, durchdringen immer genauer die gegenwärtige Realität von Kindern und Erwachsenen, werden vielfach (auch im Ausland) nachgespielt und regen eine Fülle von Neugründungen an. M. Schedlers «Sieben Thesen zum Theater für sehr junge Zuschauer» (Theater heute, 1969), die K.-Tagung in Marl (1970), das K.-Festival und die Fachtagung der Akademie der Künste Berlin (1971) und gleichartige Bestrebungen der Spielpädagogik führen zu einer intensiven öffentlichen Diskussion, die sich auch auf die etablierten Erwachsenentheater auswirkt (Denkschrift des dt. Bühnenvereins 1971) und zu einer kräftigen Entwicklung des emanzipatorischen K. in den 70er Jahren führt, während in der Gegenwart kommerzielle Interessen, Märchen und Unterhaltung wieder an Ansehen gewinnen. – Diese Bemerkung gilt nicht für das Jugendtheater im engeren Sinne.

Die DDR-Kulturpolitik schenkte dem professionellen K. große Aufmerksamkeit, da sie es als Instrument der «sozialistischen Bewußtseinsbildung» verstand. In der Anfangsphase bestimmte dabei das sowjetische Vorbild auch die starke pädagogische Orientierung. Dem 1946 eröffneten «Theater der Jungen Welt» in Leipzig folgten weitere K. in Dresden, Ost-Berlin, Halle und Magdeburg mit erheblicher personeller und materieller Ausstattung. Zudem verpflichtete das Ministerium für Kultur auch die «Erwachsenentheater», regelmäßig Inszenierungen für unterschiedliche Altersgruppen ins Repertoire zu nehmen. In den 50er und 60er Jahren beherrschten sog. Besserungsstücke die Bühnen, in denen ein Außenseiter geläutert ins Kollektiv zurückkehrt. Diese Geschichten, oft im schulischen Alltag angesiedelt, waren einem Erziehungsprogramm verpflichtet, das das Kind als einen noch unentwickelten Erwachsenen begriff, der in die Gesellschaft hineinsozialisiert werden müsse. Individualität und altersgemäße Eigenheiten wurden eher unterdrückt als ermutigt. Existentielle Konflikte, z. B. auf politischem oder sexuellem Gebiet, blieben unausgesprochen. Mit der Inszenierung von Klassikern oder der Adaption klassischer Dramen – wie einer banalen Musical-Fassung von Shakespeares *Was ihr wollt* – sollten die jungen Zuschauer jedoch auch für das ‹eigentliche› Theater sensibilisiert werden. Die Zuschauer der untersten Altersgruppe sahen Märchen-Dramatisierungen, in denen von ihrer widerspruchsreichen Realität nicht oder nur metaphorisch die Rede war. Bis in die 70er Jahre spiegelte das K. eine heile Welt, wenngleich oft in künstlerisch beeindruckenden Inszenierungen, die den Spielcharakter der Theaterkunst betonten (z. B. Regisseur Horst Hawemann am Ostberliner Theater der Freundschaft). Diese besondere Ästhetik und die günstigen Arbeitsbedingungen sicherten dem K. der DDR weltweite Beachtung. An der Entwicklung des emanzipatorischen K. waren die Bühnen der DDR jedoch kaum noch beteiligt, weil der mündige Zuschauer nicht ins Konzept der staatlich verordneten Pädagogik paßte. Dennoch gab es auch schon vor 1989 engagierte Versuche (z. B. am Dresdner Theater der Jungen Generation), im Widerspruch zur Bildungspolitik den persönlichen Anspruch auf individuelle Lebensgestaltung zu ermuntern.

Bauer, K. W.: Emanzipatorisches K. München 1980; Dieke, G.: Die Blütezeit des K. Emsdetten 1934; Eberle, O.: Cenalora. Leben, Glaube, Tanz und Theater der Urvölker. Olten 1955; Hoffmann, Chr.: Theater für junge Zuschauer. Berlin (DDR) 1976; dies.: Kinder- und Jugendtheater der Welt. Berlin (DDR) 1984; Jahnke, M.: Von der Komödie für Kinder zum Weihnachtsmärchen. Meisenheim 1977; Klewitz, M./Nickel, H.-W.: K. und Interaktionspädagogik. Stuttgart 1972; Laturell, V. D.: Theater und Jugend. Eine Zusammenstellung aus 500 Jahren Münchner Theatergeschichte. München 1970; Saz, N.: Kinder im Theater. Erinnerungen. Berlin (DDR) 1966; Schedler, M.: Kindertheater. Geschichte, Modelle, Projekte. Frankfurt/M. 1972; ders.: Schlachtet die blauen Elefanten. Bemerkungen über das Kinderstück. Weinheim/Basel 1973; Schmidt, L.: Das dt. Volksschauspiel. Berlin 1962; Schneider, R./Schorno, P.: Handbuch des Kindertheaters. Basel 1984; Schneider, W.: Kindertheater nach 1968. Köln 1984; Tornau, H.: Die Entstehung und Entwicklung des Weihnachtsmärchens auf der dt. Bühne. Diss. Köln 1955.

Hans-Wolfgang Nickel/Roland Dreßler

Kirow-Theater

(Leningradski gosudarstwennyj akademitscheski teatr opery i baleta imeni S. Kirowa) Eines der ältesten russ. Musiktheater in Leningrad; Opern- und Ballettaufführungen schon im 18. Jh., UA von M. I. Glinkas (1804–57) *Iwan Susanin* (1936), *Ruslan und Ludmilla* (1842). In den 60er Jahren des 19. Jh. – das Theater heißt von jetzt an Mariinski – orientieren sich K. N. Ljadow (Chefdirigent 1850–69) und E. F. Naprawnik (Chefdirigent 1869–1916) an den Komponisten des «Mächtigen Häufleins», die nationale Elemente in der russ. Musik betonen, aber auch an den sog. Westlern wie P. I. Tschaikowsky (1840–93), S. I. Tanejew (1856–1915), an Verdi und Wagner. Um die Jahrhundertwende singt F. I. Schaljapin (1873–1938) am K. 1920 Umbenennung in «Staatliches akademisches Opern- und Ballett-Theater». Mit den Aufführungen des Strawinsky-Balletts *Pulcinella* (1926) und der Komischen Oper *Die Liebe zu den drei Orangen* von Prokofieff (1926) sowie des *Boris Godunow* in der Originalfassung (1928) noch einmal eine bedeutende künstlerische Entwicklung in der Geschichte des Theaters (→ St. Petersburger Ballett).

Bogdanov-Berezovskij, V.: Leningradskij gosudarstvennyj akademičeskij ordena Lenina teatr opery i baleta im. S. Kirova. Leningrad 1959; Glinka, M. I.: Pis'ma i dokumenty. Leningrad 1953; Teljakovskij, V. A.: Vospominanija. 1898–1917. Petrograd 1924.

Annelore Engel-Braunschmidt

Klassik

Das klassische Theater ist zeitlich und räumlich begrenzt. Ausgangs- und für viele Höhepunkt der K. ist das Theater der Antike (→ Antikes Theater), vor allem Griechenlands. In Anlehnung an die Antike entwickelt sich in Europa zwischen dem 16. und dem 18. bis zum frühen 19. Jh. eine zweite Phase der K. Das ital. Cinquecento (→ Rinascimento) war in Theorie und Praxis grundlegend und wegweisend für das neue klassische Theater; von da aus breitete sich der Einfluß aus auf die frz. K. im 17./18. Jh., dann die dt. K. um 1800. Das engl. und span. Theater hatten ihre Höhepunkte im → Elisabethanischen Theater und im → Siglo d'oro, die trotz gewisser Einwirkungen aus der Antike und dem Cinquecento eher in den Rahmen des europ. → Barocktheaters gehören. Ausläufer der frz. K. sind im engl. Restaurationstheater, vor allem bei John Dryden (1631–1700: *Essay of Dramatic Poesie*, 1668; *All for Love*, 1678) und Thomas Otway (1652–85: *Venise Preserved*, 1682, adapt. von H. v. Hofmannsthal: *Das gerettete Venedig*, 1905); ebenso im ital. Theater des 18. Jh. bei Vittorio

Graf Alfieri für die Tragödie (1749–1803: *Oreste*, 1776–78; *Filippo*, 1775–81; *Saul*, 1782–84; *Mirra*, 1784–86) und für die Komödie Carlo Goldoni (1707–93: *Il Servitore di due Patroni*, 1746; *La Locandiera*, 1753; *Il Rusthegi*, 1760, u. a.), welcher die →Commedia dell'arte im Geiste Molières erneuerte; späteste Äußerungen der klassischen Theorie in Deutschland (bereits epigonal) bei Gustav Freytag (1816–95) mit dessen kanonischem Regelbuch *Die Technik des Dramas* (1863). Zu den Erneuerungsversuchen im 20. Jh.: →Tragödie.

Frz. Klassik: K. bezeichnet in Frankreich die Blütezeit des Theaters im 17. und z. T. 18. Jh., 1630–1760, mit den Autoren Pierre Corneille (1606 bis 84), Molière (1622–73), Racine (1639–99), Marivaux (1688–1763), Voltaire (1694–1778) und einer Vielzahl großer Schauspieler. Die 1680 gegr. und immer noch bespielte →Comédie Française in Paris bewahrt Bühnentradition und Repertoire der K. Dieses Theater ist zu charakterisieren durch seine außerordentlich treue Bezugnahme auf Aristoteles (384–322 v. Chr.: *Poetik*) und Horaz (65–8 v. Chr.: *Ars poetica*); es akzeptiert die von den antiken Autoren auferlegten Normen und Zielsetzungen für das Theater (→Antikes Theater). Die Lehre von der Läuterung der Leidenschaften (→Katharsis), die Aristoteles für die →Tragödie formuliert hatte, und die von Horaz aufgestellte Regel, das Angenehme mit dem Nützlichen zu verbinden, bilden die Grundlagen klassischer Dramentheorie in Frankreich, teils erweitert, durchweg aber systematisiert: *Poétique* (1640) von La Mesnardière (1610–63), *La Pratique du théâtre* (1657) von Abbé d'Aubignac (1604–76), *L'Art poétique* (1674) von Nicolas Boileau (1636–1711), *Eléments de littérature* (1787) von J. F. Marmontel (1723–99). Die *Poetices libri* (1561) des J. C. Scaliger (1484–1558), noch ganz aus dem Geiste der Renaissance verfaßt, waren die unmittelbaren Vorlagen der frz. Klassizisten.

Für das Theater waren Fragen der Poetik oft ein Element der Aktualität, ja der Mode. Erfolgsstücke lösen einen ‹Streit› aus (*Le Cid*, 1637; *L'Ecole des Femmes* von Molière, 1663; *Tartuffe*, 1664; *Don Juan*, 1665; *Andromaque* von Racine, 1667), der nicht nur der Engherzigkeit weniger erfolgreicher Rivalen zuzuschreiben ist, auch das (gebildete) Publikum möchte verstehen, was es bewundert. Die Dramatiker liefern selbst sorgfältige Erklärungen ihrer Dichtkunst: *Examens* von Corneille, *Préfaces* von Racine und vor allem Molières *Trois discours sur le poème dramatique*, 1660. Einige Autoren wie Molière (*La Critique de ‹ L'Ecole des Femmes›*, 1663) gehen soweit, daß sie aus diesen techn. Themen ein theatralisches Zwischenspiel machen. Noch vor Boileau ist Jean Chapelain (1595–1674), Theoretiker der klassischen Dramaturgie (*Lettre à Godeau sur la règle des vingt-quatre heures*, 1630, und *Sentiments de l'Académie française sur ‹Le Cid›*, 1637), eines der ersten Mitglieder der Académie

500 Klassik

française. Chapelain hat K. so definiert: 1. die Regeln des Anstands und der Wahrscheinlichkeit sind für die gesamte klassische Literatur verbindlich; 2. speziell für das Theater gilt als oberstes Gesetz die Wahrung der →drei Einheiten.

Anderthalb Jh. lang wurde Europa durch dieses Theater fasziniert, und zwar weder als bloße Wiedergeburt der Antike noch als Akkumulation nur techn. Leistungen, sondern vor allem, weil es eine ideale Welt widerspiegelte... Wie es seine Repräsentanten konzipiert hatten, war diese in erster Linie zur Ergötzung einer gesellschaftlichen Elite entwickelte Kunst in wenigen Jahren derart universell geworden, daß sie offenbar auch andere gesellschaftliche Gruppen fesselte. Richelieu, nach ihm Mazarin (1602–61), Ludwig XIV. (1638–1715) und unter ihm J. B. Colbert (1619–83) mit seinem Mitarbeiter Charles Perrault (1628–1703) haben nacheinander eine Art amtliches und nicht ganz uneigennütziges Mäzenat gepflegt, um die Schriftsteller an den königlichen Hof zu binden. Ludwig XV. (1710–74) und Ludwig XVI. (1754–93) gelang dies immer weniger. Allein die Hauptstadt des Königreichs gab den Ton der Eleganz an, aber die ‹Stadt› durfte im 17. Jh. keinen anderen Geschmack haben als den des ‹Hofes›, der aufgehört hatte, der private Kreis eines üppigen Feudalherrn zu sein, der eine Art gesellschaftlicher Mikrokosmos geworden war, in dem sich die lebendigen Kräfte der Nation versammelten (→Höfisches Theater).

Die Protagonisten dieses Theaters verkörperten den Typ des ‹honnête homme›, den die frz. Kultur des 17. bis 18. Jh. feierte, mit seinem Willen, in der Gemeinschaft mit anderen zu leben, seiner Sorge, zwischen den verschiedenen gesellschaftlichen Schichten Beziehungen herzustellen. Blaise Pascal (1623–62) und Ritter de Méré (1607–84) haben als große Anhänger der ‹honnêteté› unterstrichen, daß das Beispiel mehr taugt als das Studium der Regeln, wenn es heißt zu lernen, gut zu sprechen und recht zu denken. Das klassische Theater hat lange Zeit diese Beispielfunktion erfüllt. Es diente weder als Tribüne eines Philosophen noch einer besonderen Politik. Der Cartesianismus, das Freidenkertum, später die Aufklärung haben es nur oberflächlich berührt. Selbst die Monarchie wird nie vorbehaltlos gerühmt; dieses Theater respektierte auch unter dem Befehl der Obrigkeit die Werte der Einzigartigkeit und die Rechte des Individuums. Der ‹honnête homme› ist gleichzeitig jemand, der in sich etwas Heroisches bewahrt, dessen Energie jederzeit geweckt werden kann. Mit einer reservierten, aber echten Sympathie bedachten daher die Zuschauer die sublimen Verhaltensweisen und extremen Entscheidungen der tragischen Helden und selbst die unannehmbaren Wahnvorstellungen der großen ‹ridicules› von Molière. Man hält dem Schriftsteller die Fähigkeit zugute, die Grenzen des Menschseins zu zeigen, alle Antriebe spielen zu lassen. Das klassische Theater spiegelt eine Gesellschaft

wider, in deren Werthicrarchie die Werte des Lebens in guter Gesellschaft die erste Stelle einnahmen, die aber nicht für so naiv gehalten werden wollte, daß man ihr verbergen könnte, daß hinter dieser so geschätzten und zu konsolidierenden Fassade sich der Mensch mit Gewalt und
Begierde verbarg.

Dt. Klassik: Im wesentlichen gilt auch für die dt. K. die Verbundenheit mit
der antiken Tradition sowie die Ausarbeitung einer bestimmten Poetik.
Nur ist die Bewegung, verglichen mit der frz., in Zeit, Raum, Autoren-
zahl und -produktion weit eingeschränkter, von Goethes ital. Reise
(1786) bis etwa zu seinem *Faust I* (1808). Zentrum der dt. K. war Weimar,
mit Versailles/Paris allerdings kaum vergleichbar; Hölderlin war auch
geographisch isoliert. Die Theaterproduktion umfaßt hauptsächlich das
Werk Johann Wolfgang Goethes (1749–1832; *Iphigenie auf Tauris*, 1779;
Torquato Tasso, 1790; *Die natürliche Tochter*, 1803; *Faust 1 und 2*), das
von Friedrich Schiller (1759–1805; *Wallenstein*-Trilogie, 1798–99; *Maria
Stuart*, 1800–01; *Die Jungfrau von Orléans*, 1801; *Die Braut von Messina*
1802–03; *Wilhelm Tell*, 1804) sowie von Friedrich Hölderlin (1770–1843)
das *Empedokles*-Fragment (1802) und die Sophokles-Übertragungen
Ödipus und *Antigone* (1804). Auch typologisch konzentrieren sich die
Autoren vornehmlich auf die Tragödie; klassische Komödien wie im frz.
und ital. Theater gibt es nicht.
   Stofflich sind bei weitem nicht alle Stücke mit der Antike verbunden:
Iphigenie, z. T. Szenen des *Faust, Die Braut von Messina* und das spär-
liche Bühnenwerk Hölderlins. Jedoch steht die gesamte dt. K. in einer
andauernden Auseinandersetzung mit den Kunstidealen der Antike und
der frz. K. (vgl. der Einfluß Racines auf Goethes *Tasso*). Niederschlag
findet diese Auseinandersetzung in zahlreichen theoretischen Abhandlungen: bei Goethe (die Gespräche über Drama und Theater in *Wilhelm
Meisters Lehrjahren* 1795–96, die Essays *Shakespeare und kein Ende*,
1813–16, und *Nachlese zu Aristoteles' Poetik*, 1827, sowie die *Ecker-
mann-Gespräche*), bei Schiller (*Über den Grund des Vergnügens an tragischen Gegenständen, Über die tragische Kunst*, beide 1792; *Über Anmut
und Würde, Über das Pathetische*, 1793; Vorrede zur *Braut von Messina:
Über den Gebrauch des Chors in der Tragödie*); auch der gemeinsame
Traktat *Über epische und dramatische Dichtung* (1797) sowie der reichhaltige Briefwechsel der beiden Dichter; bei Hölderlin der *Grund zum
Empedokles*, die *Anmerkungen zur Antigone* sowie die *Philosophischen
Schriften*.
   Gemeinsame Grundgedanken der K.: Maß und Form, Humanität als
allg. menschliche, die Gesellschaft durchdringende Kraft, Darstellung
der sittlichen Werte, Tendenz zur Idealität und zum Symbolhaften. We-
sentlich sind auch die Reflexionen über die Schicksalhaftigkeit der

502 Klassik»

menschlichen Existenz, die Unausgleichbarkeit des Tragischen und die versöhnende Macht der →Katharsis, die über die Rührung zu erzielen ist. Auch formal sind in den klassischen Werken Goethes und Schillers Gemeinsamkeiten (Dramaturgie, Sprachform) festzustellen, obwohl Schillers Stücke nie wie z. B. Goethes *Natürliche Tochter* in äußerster Typisierung und Stilisierung, gleichsam als Ende der klassischen Tragödie in Europa, gestaltet sind. Beide halten sich weitgehend an die analytische Technik der sophokleischen Tragödie und die Grundregeln der aristotelischen Poetik (vor allem die Einheit der Handlung).

Das Werk Hölderlins weicht von der eher ‹apollinischen› Position Goethes und von Schillers ethisch-ästhetischem Konzept ab, die beide weniger als Nachahmung antiker Themen und Formen, sondern vielmehr als Neuformung und Aneignung aus dem Geiste zeitgenössischer Ideen (z. B. Kantsche Philosophie) angesehen werden müssen. Hölderlins Reflexion der griech. Geisteswelt verkennt zwar die Distanz zwischen Antike und dem 18./19. Jh. nicht; jedoch in seiner theologischen Auffassung des Tragischen als ‹Gottesgeschehen›, dem Dichten über Götternähe und -ferne, Gott- und Menschsein, der Übertragung der altgriech. Formen und Verse kommt er wohl Sophokles näher als jeder andere Tragiker des neuklassischen Theaters.

Insgesamt liegt der K. in Deutschland die Idee einer ästhetisch-moralischen Bildung zugrunde, in deren Mittelpunkt das klassische Humanitätsideal steht. Diesem weitgespannten Ideenwerk entsprach freilich in keiner Weise ein gesellschaftlich-kulturelles Umfeld, das vergleichbar wäre mit der Situation in Frankreich. Für das Theater vermochte das von Goethe (seit 1790) geleitete Weimarer Hoftheater nicht annähernd die normbildende Funktion zu übernehmen, die die Comédie Française für Frankreich innehatte. Dennoch ist die Auseinandersetzung mit dem klassischen Drama auch im deutschsprachigen Theater eine permanente Herausforderung bis in die heutige Zeit (→Antikenrezeption). – Klassische Stücke führen auch im 20. Jh. die Statistiken der Spielpläne an.

Adam, A.: Histoire de la littérature française au XVIIe siècle, 5 Bde. Paris 1948–56; Adorno, Th. W.: Zum Klassizismus von Goethes Iphigenie. In: Gesammelte Schriften, XI 499. Frankfurt/M. 1974; Borchmeyer, D.: Tragödie und Öffentlichkeit. München 1973; Bruford, W. H.: Kultur und Gesellschaft im klassischen Weimar 1775–1806. Göttingen 1966; Bürger, Chr.: Der Ursprung der bürgerlichen Institution Kunst im höfischen Weimar. Frankfurt/M. 1977; Burger, H. O. (Hg.): Begriffsbestimmung der Klassik und des Klassischen. Darmstadt 1972; Kapp, V.: Die Idealisierung der höfischen Welt im klassischen Drama. In: Brochmeier, P./Wetzel, H.: Französische Literatur in Einzeldarstellungen, Bd. 1. Stuttgart 1981; Lancaster H. C.: A History of French Dramatic Literature in the 17th Century, 9 Vols. Baltimore 1929–42; ders.: French Tragedy in the Time of Louis XV and Voltaire 1715–74. Baltimore 1950; ders.: French Tragedy in the Reign of Louis XVI and the Early Years of the French Revolution 1774–92. Baltimore 1953; Matzat, W.: Dramenstruktur und Zuschauerrolle. Theater in der frz. Klassik. München 1982; Müller, J.: Goethes Dramentheorie. In: Grimm, R. (Hg.): Deutsche Dramentheorien I. Frankfurt/M. 1971; Rasch, W.: Goethes Torquato Tasso. Stuttgart 1954; Reiss, T. J.: Toward Dramatic Illusion: Theatrical Technique from Hardy to Horace. Newhaven 1971; Scherer, J.: La dramaturgie classique en France. Paris 1955; der.: Racine et/ou la cérémonie. Paris 1982; Schmidt, J. (Hg.): Über Hölderlin. Frankfurt/M. 1970; Staiger, E.: Schiller. Zürich 1967; Steiner, G.: Antigones. New York 1984; Truchet, J.: La tragédie classique en France. Paris 1975.

Gérard Schneilin / Roger Zuber

«Kleine Bühne» des Freien Deutschen Kulturbundes (London)

Obwohl Großbritannien das Zufluchtsland einer Reihe prominenter Bühnenkünstler war (Elisabeth Bergner, Lucie Mannheim, Grete Mosheim, Ernst Deutsch, Paul Grätz, Oskar Homolka, Fritz Kortner, Konrad Veidt), gab es erst nach der Massenflucht aus Österreich und der Tschechoslowakei deutschsprachiges Exiltheater in London. Die «Kleine Bühne» mit ihrem Leiter Erich Freund und ihren Textern Egon Larsen und Fritz Gottfurcht spielte vor allem politisch-satirische Revuen. Die Nummernprogramme mit abwechselnd dt. und engl. Beiträgen, an denen gelegentlich auch engl. Schauspieler mitwirkten, waren eine ideale Form, um auf aktuelle politische Themen und Fragen des Exilalltags mit künstlerisch-theatralischen Mitteln zu reagieren.

Leske, B./Reinisch, M.: Der Freie Deutsche Kulturbund. In: Exil in der Tschechoslowakei, in Großbritannien, Skandinavien und Palästina. Leipzig 1980.

Jan Hans

Die Kleine Freiheit

Als Trude Kolman (urspr. Gertrud Kohlmann) am 25.1.1951 in München ihr Kabarett K. F. vorstellte, hatte sie bereits langjährige einschlägige Erfahrungen gesammelt, in Berlin vor und nach der Machtübergabe an die Nationalsozialisten sowie im Wiener Exil, von wo aus sie über Paris nach London fliehen konnte. An der K. F. nahm ein Großteil der ehem. Mitarbeiter der →«Schaubude» teil, vom Autor Erich Kästner bis zu den Schauspielern Ursula Herking und Bum Krüger. Als die K. F. ihre Arbeit begann, waren die euphorischen Hoffnungen der unmittelbaren Nachkriegszeit bereits geschwunden, die ‹große Freiheit› war es nicht geworden. So fanden sich von Anfang an resignative Töne in den Programmen,

504   Kleines Dramatisches Theater (Sankt Petersburg) ⎯⎯⎯⎯⎯⎯⎯⎯⎯⎯⎯⎯⎯⎯⎯⎯

die treffende Satire verbanden mit literarischem Niveau und perfekter theatralischer Umsetzung. Auch hier gab es →Mittelstücke, deren Aufnahme Kolmans Intention eines satirischen Zeittheaters entgegenkam. – Mitte der 50er Jahre zogen sich Kästner und Gilbert zurück, Kabarett-Revuen und zeitkritisches Theater traten an die Stelle satirisch-politischen Kabaretts. Nach seiner Rückkehr aus der Emigration schloß sich Friedrich Hollaender der K. F. an, für die er 1957 bis 1961 vier erfolgreiche ‹Revuetten› schuf.

Budzinski, K.: Die öffentlichen Spaßmacher. München 1966; ders.: Wer lacht denn da? Braunschweig 1989; Greul, H.: Bretter, die die Zeit bedeuten. Köln/Berlin 1967 (erw. Ausg., 2 Bde. München 1971); Kolman, T. (Hg.): Münchner Kleine Freiheit. München 1960; Zivier, G./Kotschenreuther, H./Ludwig, V.: Kabarett mit K. Berlin 1974.

Wolfgang Beck

Kleines Dramatisches Theater (Sankt Petersburg)

(Malyj dramatičeskij teatr). 1911–14 spielen in dem Gebäude des K. D. T. nacheinander sechs verschiedene Theater. 1944 wird das Kleine Dramatische Theater gegründet, das wegen fehlender Programmatik zunächst unbedeutend bleibt. Ab 1966 interessante Aufführungen durch J. Schiffner (Adaption der Poetik des epischen Theaters; Brecht). Profilgewinn erst mit J. Padwe, Towstonogow-Schüler, der 1974–83 das Theater leitet (Zusammenarbeit mit jungen Dramatikern). Ab 1974 inszeniert Lew Dodin (*1944) am K. D. T. K. Čapek, T. Williams, A. Wolodin, *Leb und vergiß nicht* nach V. Rasputin, 1980 *Das Haus* nach dem Roman von F. Abramow (1920–83) und führt ab 1983 als Chefregisseur das K. D. T. zu internationalem Erfolg: *Brüder und Schwestern* 1985 (nach dem Roman F. Abramows), *Herr der Fliegen* 1986 (nach Golding), *Gaudeamus* 1990 (nach S. Kaledins Roman *Baubataillon*). Durch Authentizität der Darstellung Bestärkung des Menschlichen im Menschen; Theatralität, Bilder, Hyperbeln entstehen aus der schauspielerischen Analyse des konkreten Vorgangs. Für Dodin muß eine Aufführung nicht konstruiert, sondern geboren werden; Zentrum ist der Schauspieler, in dem der Regisseur «stirbt».

Elke Wiegand

Kleines Organon für das Theater

Bertolt Brechts Grundlagentext «für das Theater des wissenschaftlichen Zeitalters» ist Weiterführung und Bilanz seiner Geanken über →episches Theater und nichtaristotelische Dramaturgie, während eines Zwischenaufenthalts in Zürich im Sommer 1948 entstanden. Kernstück der «Schriften zum Theater», 1949 erstmals gedruckt in der Zeitschrift «Sinn und Form», 1. Sonderheft Bertolt Brecht, 1953 in den «Versuchen» (H. 12), 1964 in Bd. 7 der «Schriften zum Theater» mit «Nachträgen» (1952–54). Formale Anlehnung an Francis Bacons (1561–1626) antiaristotelische Schrift *Novum Organum, sive indicia vera de interpretatione naturae* (1621). Methodisch will Brecht mit dem K. O. für die Dramatik durchsetzen, was Bacon für die Naturwissenschaft erreicht hat (induktive Methode, experimentelles Vorgehen, «Wissen ist Macht»). Weitere Quellen: Denis Diderot (1713–84), vor allem dessen *Paradoxe sur le comédien* (1773), sowie der Briefwechsel zwischen Goethe und Schiller (in erster Linie die Teile über Fragen des Epischen und Dramatischen).

Im *Arbeitsjournal* notierte Brecht am 18. 8. 1948: «mehr oder weniger fertig mit KLEINES ORGANON FÜR DAS THEATER; es ist eine kurze zusammenfassung des MESSINGKAUFS. hauptthese: daß ein bestimmtes lernen das wichtigste vergnügen unseres zeitalters ist, so daß es in unserm theater eine große stellung einnehmen muß. auf diese weise konnte ich das theater als ein ästhetisches unternehmen behandeln, was es mir leichter macht, die diversen neuerungen zu beschreiben» (2, 835). Demzufolge ist das K. O. ein Konzentrat aus dem Fragment gebliebenen Großprojekt in Dialogform *Der Messingkauf* (1939–40, veröff. 1963). Im Gegensatz zu früheren Bekundungen erklärt Brecht hier das Theater wieder zum Ort der Unterhaltung (Kritik am «Kulinarischen» unterbleibt). Tatsächlich handelt es sich jedoch nur um eine Akzentverschiebung: Statt vom «Lehrtheater» zu sprechen, bezeichnet der Stückeschreiber «die besondere Sittlichkeit» als Möglichkeit des «Genießens». →Einfühlung wird weiterhin abgelehnt. Brecht macht es sich zur theatralischen Aufgabe, die naturwissenschaftlichen Kenntnisse von der Veränderbarkeit der Welt im Sinne von Marx und Engels auf die Gesellschaft anzuwenden (politische Wirkungsästhetik). In 77 Paragraphen, samt Vorrede und Schlußwendung, faßt das K. O. die Grundprinzipien der Brechtschen Theaterkonzeption zusammen («Umrisse einer denkbaren Ästhetik»). – Das Ganze zielt auf Erzeugung einer «kritischen haltung gegenüber der gesellschaftlichen welt». Methodischer Zentralbegriff ist die →Verfremdung (§ 42). Sie beeinflußt die Arbeit des Schauspielers (§ 47 ff) ebenso wie die Situation des Publikums (§ 35 und 67). Grundsätzlich fordert Brecht für das Theater «Experimentierbedingungen» (§ 52), den «allgemeinen Gestus des Zeigens» (§ 71) und – mit Nachdruck – ästhetisch ver-

506 Kokette

mitteltes Vergnügen (§ 66 und 75). Dem alten Begriff des «epischen Theaters» substituiert er die Bezeichnung «Theater des wissenschaftlichen Zeitalters», die er dann in den 50er Jahren durch den Begriff des «dialektischen Theaters» ersetzt (vgl. «Nachträge zum K.O.»). Das K.O. ist nicht nur die erste philosophische Grundlegung der Verfremdung, sondern überhaupt ‹das› theoretische Grundlagenwerk des Brecht-Theaters. Für den Stückeschreiber war der Text wohl in erster Linie gedacht als Orientierungsschrift für die Durchsetzung seiner Methode nach der Rückkehr aus dem Exil. Auf dieser Basis erarbeitete er dann seine Modellinszenierungen (→Modellaufführung) mit dem →Berliner Ensemble.

Grimm, R.: Vom Novum Organum zum Kleinen Organon. Gedanken zur Verfremdung. In: Das Ärgernis Brecht. Hg. v. W. Jäggi/H. Oesch (= Theater unserer Zeit 1). Basel 1961, S. 45–70; Hill, Cl.: Bertolt Brecht (= UTB 694). München 1978, S. 159f; Klotz, V.: Bertolt Brecht. Versuch über das Werk. Bad Homburg v. d. H. ³1967, S. 119ff; Knopf, J.: Brecht-Handbuch. Theater. Eine Ästhetik der Widersprüche. Stuttgart 1980, S. 458–460.

Theo Buck

Kokette

(Frz.: coquette) Weibliches Rollenfach v. a. im frz. klassischen Theater. Die K. ist eine junge, mondäne Frau, die sich durch Schönheit und Vermögen auszeichnet, den Männern gefällt und von ihnen umworben wird. Wortwitzig und schlagfertig, leichtsinnig und frivol brilliert sie durch ihre lebhafte, aber eher oberflächliche Intelligenz und ihre Anmut. Zwar beleidigt oder verletzt sie gar manchen Verehrer, doch mehr aus Leichtsinn als aus böser Absicht. Archetypische K.-Gestalt ist Célimène, die ‹grande coquette› aus Molières (1622–73) *Le Misanthrope* (1666), deren Name heute zur Bezeichnung einer jungen, reizvoll verlockenden Frau verwendet wird, die mit den Männern spielt, ohne ihnen je nachzugeben. Eine Variante der K. ist die ‹coquette vertueuse›, die tugendhafte K., etwa die Comtesse Almaviva in Beaumarchais' (1732–99) *Le Mariage de Figaro* (1874), die lediglich in der Absicht, ihren Mann zurückzugewinnen, ihr Spielchen mit dem Pagen treibt, sich also der Koketterie nur als Mittel zum Zweck bedient. Die K. lebt in abgewandelter Form im Theater des 19. Jh. als →Salondame weiter.

Bernard Poloni

Komidylle (Komeidyllion)

Besondere Form sittenbeschreibender Musikkomödie, die auf der griech. Bühne während der 90er Jahre des 19. Jh. gespielt wurde (→ Komödie). Ihr Ursprung ist zum einen auf die → Vaudeville-Vorstellungen zurückzuführen, die frz. Ensembles auf der Durchreise in der griech. Hauptstadt nach 1871 mit großem Erfolg gaben, zum anderen auf die neuen Anreize, welche die volkskundlichen Interessen der sog. literarischen Generation von 1880 den griech. Künstlern vermittelten. Im Rahmen dieser Impulse entfernt sich das Athener Theater nach 1889 vom ausländischen Repertoire und den einheimischen historischen Dramen und experimentiert mit den Lokalidiomen und Volkstrachten sowie den traditionellen Sitten der Landbevölkerung unter Einbeziehung von heiteren Liedern und Tänzen.

Das Stück, das diese Bewegung initiierte und das Vorbild aller nachherigen ähnlichen Versuche abgab, war *I Tychi tis Marulas* (Das Glück der Marula) von Dimitrios Koromilas (1850–98), eine Komödie, die sich mit dem Leben der Diener provinzieller Abstammung in einem Athener Herrenhaus befaßte. In den unmittelbar folgenden Jahren errangen die Stücke von Dimitrios Kokkos (1856–91) *O Barbalinardos i to Telos tis Marulas* (Onkel Linardos oder Marulas Ende, 1890), *I Lyra tu Jeronikola* (Die Lyra des alten Nikolas, 1891) und *O Kapetan-Jakumis* (Käpt'n Jakumis, 1892) sowie das Stück *I Nyfi tis Kuburis* (Die Braut von Salamis, 1895) des hervorragendsten Komödianten der Zeit, Evangelos Pantopulos (1860–1913), große Erfolge. In allen diesen und weiteren Komödien waren Hauptfiguren: Angehörige der arbeitenden Klasse von Athen (kleine Modistinnen, Maurer, Kohlenträger, Seeleute) und ihre Verwandten vom Dorf, die in die Stadt kommen, um jene zu besuchen, und nach einer Reihe komischer Abenteuer die Kluft zwischen ihren eigenen traditionellen Sitten und denen der nach westeuropäischer Art lebenden Bürgerschicht entdecken. Der Grund für den großen kommerziellen Erfolg, den die K. erfuhr, ist offenbar in ihrer – wenn auch recht äußerlichen und oberflächlich behandelten – Verbindung mit dem wichtigsten sozialen Problem dieser Zeit zu suchen, d. h. der Verwestlichung und dem sprunghaften Verfall des herkömmlichen Lebensstils.

Die kurze Blüte der K. führte das neugriech. Theater immerhin zu einer neuen Entwicklungsphase. Sie verhalf zum erstenmal den einheimischen Berufstheatertruppen im Bewußtsein des bürgerlichen Publikums zum Durchbruch, welche seit den 60er Jahren des 19. Jh. vergeblich eine Anerkennung erstrebt hatten.

Chatzipantazis, Th.: To Komeidyllio, 2 Bde. Athen 1981; Sideris, J.: To Komeidyllio 1888–1896. Athen 1933; Valsa, M.: Le Théâtre grec moderne de 1453 à 1900. Berlin 1960.

Thodoros Chatzipantazis

Komiker

Allgemein Schauspieler, der komische Rollen spielt. Unterschied zu: →Komische Person, deren Komik bereits durch Kostüm, Maske und Auftreten vorgegeben ist. Charakter-K.: z. B. der jugendliche Komiker, die komische Alte usw.

Horst Schumacher

Komische Person

Seit der Antike in vielfacher Gestalt auftretende feststehende Bühnenfigur, dient dem derben Vergnügen des Zuschauers und wendet sich häufig direkt an das Publikum, das Theatergeschehen und sich selbst kommentierend. Typische Eigenschaften sind Freß-, Sauf-, Prahl-, Spott- und Geschlechtslust, Tölpelhaftigkeit und mitunter gerissenes Intrigantentum, Räsonierbedürfnis. Erstes Auftreten im antiken →Mimus, dann im mittelalterlichen geistlichen Drama der geprellte Teufel, der Salbenkrämer-Knecht Rubin. Im Spätbarock die außerhalb der Ereignisse stehende kommentierende Person, im →Elisabethanischen Theater der →Clown, im dt. Theater →Pickelhering, Hanswurst, Staberl, Thaddädl. Im →Alt-Wiener Volksstück unter Raimund (1790–1836) und Nestroy (1801–62) wird die k. P. eine komische Charakterrolle. Im frz. Theater wurde der →Arlecchino der ital. →Commedia dell'arte übernommen. Seit dem 19. Jh. hat sich die k. P. als Clown auch außerhalb des Theaters im →Zirkus einen Platz erobert.

Catholy, E.: Komische Person und dramatische Wirklichkeit. In: Festschrift Helmut de Boor. Tübingen 1966, S. 193–208; Kindermann, H.: Die Commedia dell'arte und das Volkstheater. Wien 1938.

Horst Schumacher

Komissarshewskaja-Theater

Von Vera Fjodorowna Komissarshewskaja (1864–1910) 1904 in Petersburg gegr. Theater («Dramatisches Theater»), das die auch als ‹russ. Duse› bezeichnete Schauspielerin bis 1909 leitete. Hier setzte die künstlerische Erneuerung – und Europäisierung – des vorrevolutionären russ. Theaters ein, indem die Komissarshewskaja W. E. Meyerhold (1874–1940), F. F. Komissarshewski (1882–1954), N. N. Jewreinow (1879–1953) zur Mitarbeit heranzog (in der Saison 1906/07 trat A. Ja. Tairow als Schauspieler am K. auf). Hatte sie anfangs noch die Hauptwerke des modernen Theaters (Ibsen, Strindberg, Hauptmann, Gorki, dessen *Sommergäste* 1905 verboten wurden) bevorzugt, so trat mit dem Engagement Meyerholds (1906, 1907 bereits Bruch) der zeitkritische Aspekt gegenüber einem offen symbolistischen zurück: Mit der Inszenierung von A. Bloks *Schaubude* (1906, *Balagantschik*), L. Andrejews *Leben des Menschen* (1907) präsentierte das Theater die dichterische russ. Avantgarde. Während das Publikum darauf mit Befremden reagierte, war – dank der mitreißenden Schauspielkunst der Komissarshewskaja – Maeterlincks *Schwester Beatrice, Pelleas und Melisande* ein einhelliger Erfolg.

Mit ihrem Bruder Fjodor gewann die Komissarshewskaja 1906 einen Regisseur, der zwar in der Praxis noch unerfahren, theoretisch jedoch interessant war und aus der Zusammenarbeit mit Meyerhold und Jewreinow Ideen für sein Totaltheater, seinen alle Künste beherrschenden Universalschauspieler bezog. Darüber hinaus nahm Fjodor Einflüsse von Stanislawski und Craig auf. Er emigrierte 1919 nach England, ging 1939 in die USA; er gehört zu den Begründern des modernen →Regietheaters in Rußland wie im Westen.

Der experimentierfreudige, anfänglich einer stilisierenden Richtung huldigende Jewreinow wechselte vom Alten (Starinnyj) Theater in Petersburg, das er zum Zwecke der Rekonstruktion frz. Stücke des Mittelalters und der span. Renaissance selbst mitbegründet hatte, 1908 an das K. Seine Inszenierung von O. Wildes *Salome* (1909) wurde von der Zensur verboten. 1925 emigrierte er nach Frankreich und widmete sich dort überwiegend der Theorie und Geschichte des Theaters. – Nach dem Tod der Komissarshewskaja (1910) löste sich das Ensemble des K. auf. Das jetzige Staatl. Theater «V. F. Komissarshewskaja» in Petersburg ist das 1942 gegr. «Blockade-Theater».

Kryžickij, S.: Režisserskie portrety. Moskva/Leningrad 1928; Rybakova, Ju.: Komissarževskaja. Leningrad 1971; Sbornik pamjati V. F. Komissarževskoj. Sankt Petersburg 1911; Tal'nikov, D.: Komissarževskaja. Moskva/Leningrad 1939.

Annelore Engel-Braunschmidt/Red.

Das Kom(m)ödchen

Eines der bedeutendsten Kabarettensembles der BRD. Nachdem es einige Zeit an dem Kabarett eines Freundes («Die Wäscheleine») mitgearbeitet hatte, gründete das Ehepaar Kay und Lore Lorentz ein eigenes Kabarett, das am 29.3.1947 als «Kleine Literaten-, Maler- und Schauspielerbühne» eröffnet wurde. War man anfangs in Ausstattung und Präsentation noch abhängig von berühmten Vorbildern, so fand man doch bald einen eigenen Stil: eine Mischung von anspielungsreichen Texten, die präzise Satire verbanden mit gefälliger, harmlos erscheinender Form. Anfang der 50er Jahre kamen mit Dr. Eckart Hachfeld und Martin Morlock zwei profilierte Autoren hinzu, die literarisches Niveau und Konkretheit der Satire positiv beeinflußten. Ein schauspielerisch perfektes Ensemble lieferte sanft beißende Satire mit Widerhaken für ein vorwiegend bildungsbürgerliches Publikum. Gesellschaftlich längst etabliert und akzeptiert, bezog das K. 1967 ein neues Haus. Schon bald sah man sich von seiten der ‹Studentenbewegung› und der von ihr beeinflußten neuen linken Kabarettgruppen als systemstabilisierend kritisiert, mit dem Regierungsantritt der sozialliberalen Koalition in Bonn eines wichtigen Ziels für die Satire beraubt. Auch das K. benötigte einige Jahre, um mit einem veränderten Ensemble einen Neuansatz für die eigene Arbeit zu finden. Durchgreifende Änderungen des Programms und seiner Präsentation blieben allerdings aus. Inzwischen hat sich Lore Lorentz weitgehend zurückgezogen. Noch immer aber ist das K. nicht nur eines der bekanntesten Kabaretts Deutschlands, sondern auch ‹Sprungbrett› für zahlreiche junge Kabarettisten, die hier den Durchbruch schaffen.

Berger, M.: Kabarett nach vorn. Berlin 1966; Budzinski, K.: Die Muse mit der scharfen Zunge. München 1961; ders.: Pfeffer ins Getriebe. München 1982; ders.: So weit die scharfe Zunge reicht. München 1964; ders.: Die öffentlichen Spaßmacher. München 1966; ders. (Hg.): Vorsicht, die Mandoline ist geladen. Frankfurt/M. 1970; ders.: Wer lacht denn da? Braunschweig 1989; Greul, H.: Bretter, die die Zeit bedeuten. Köln/Berlin 1967 (erw. Ausg., 2 Bde. München 1971); Hösch, R.: Kabarett von gestern und heute. 2 Bde. Berlin 1967–72; Lorentz, K.: Das Kom(m)ödchen-Buch. Düsseldorf 1955; Otto, R./Rösler, W.: Kabarettgeschichte. Berlin ²1981; Zivier, G./Kotschenreuther, H./Ludwig, V.: Kabarett mit K. Berlin 1974.

Wolfgang Beck

Kommos

Griech.; Bezeichnung für einen streng ritualisierten, ekstatischen Trauer- und Klagegesang; in der Tragödie nach Aristoteles (*Poetik* 1452 b 24 f) ganz oder zum großen Teil gesungener Klage-Dialog zwischen Schauspielern und Chor (vgl. z. B. Aischylos' *Choephoren* 306 ff).

Popp, H.: Das Amoibaion. In: W. Jens (Hg.): Die Bauformen der griech. Tragödie. Poetica Beiheft 6. München 1971, S. 221–275.

Bernd Seidensticker

Komödie

(Griech. komedia = Ritualchöre und Spottgesänge beim Dionysoskult) Die wohl dauerhafteste und formenreichste Gattung im westlichen Theater von der Antike bis heute, jedoch schwer eindeutig zu definieren, wenn auch deren Geschichte leicht zu verfolgen ist. K. im weitesten Sinne heißt oft Theater überhaupt, Stück, Aufführung, Truppe, Gebäude, Theaterkunst. Im engeren Sinne bedeutet K. seit der →Renaissance in der nacharistotelischen Tradition ein Stück, welches sich in der Gattungshierarchie nach oben von der →Tragödie, nach unten von der →Farce unterscheidet. Insofern behandelt die K. auf spezifische Art ‹niedrigere Charaktere›, konkrete, unheroische Menschen mit alltäglichen Problemen und Konflikten. Der Bereich der K. ist allmählich auf die Lebenswelt der Stadt und Vorstadt beschränkt worden (die dörfliche Welt der Bauern blieb eher →Schwank und →Posse vorbehalten), auf Alltagsfiguren, Heiterkeit sowie eine praktische Moral zur anständigen Lebensführung. Versuche, genaue Regeln, eine bestimmte Dramaturgie der K. zu erstellen, scheitern oft gerade an der Mehrschichtigkeit und Freiheit einer Gattung, deren Hauptcharakter das Spiel in all seinen Nuancen ist. Selbst die ausschließliche Identifikation mit dem Komischen ist angefochten, gibt es doch eine intensive Beschäftigung der Autoren und der Forschung mit dem Begriff der ‹ernsten K.›. Die Komödienproblematik ist allerdings untrennbar mit jenem Zentralbegriff und dem des Lachens verbunden.

Historisch gesehen ist zuerst die Relativität der K. und des Komischen zu betonen: Sie schwanken zwischen Erweiterung und Verengung der Begriffe und Effekte, mit erheblichen Differenzen zwischen Kulturen und Epochen. Allerdings gibt es gemeinsame Effekte, Figuren, Situationen und Formen. Grundlegender ist in der Geschichte der K. der Widerspruch zwischen den volkstümlichen Tendenzen der Gattung und den literarischen Ambitionen der Autoren und Theoretiker, der etwa von den Anfängen bis ins 19. Jh. vorherrscht.

512 Komödie

Im Theater der Antike entwickelt sich die K. aus den ursprünglichen populären Formen bis zu Höhepunkten der literarischen und gesellschaftlichen K., dann zurück zum Volkstheater: in Athen, von Dionysosfesten und Farcen zu Aristophanes (um 450–388 v. Chr.) und Menander (um 342–292 v. Chr.) und späterem Volkstheater; in Rom, von volkstümlichen Tänzen, Satiren und Pantomimen zu Plautus (um 250–184 v. Chr.) und Terenz (um 190–159 v. Chr.), zurück zu den →atellanes. Die volkstümlichen Formen des komischen Spiels verdrängen bis zur Renaissance die literarische K.: →Farcen, →Sotien und →Moralitäten beherrschen die primitiven Bühnen und dienen dem →Mysterienspiel höchstens als Zwischenbelustigung. Erst im ital. Theater des Cinquecento (→Rinascimento) entwickelt sich die Zweispurigkeit von Volkstheater und literarischer K., die sich bis ins 19. Jh. hält: Gegen die volkstümlichen Stücke des Ruzzante (1502–43) setzt sich die ‹commedia sostenuta›, die Literatur-K. von Lodovico Ariosto (1474–1533), Pietro Aretino (1492–1556) und Nicolo Machiavelli (1469–1527) durch; erst nach dem Triumph der →Commedia erudita kann sich die populäre →Commedia dell'arte entfalten. In Imitation des antiken Theaters versuchen die Theoretiker, die Theatergattungen mit strengen Regeln zu bestimmen und zu trennen: so die Italiener Castelvetro, Robertello und Minturno, vor allem der Franzose Julius Caesar Scaliger (*Poetices*, 1561) und die Theoretiker des →Jesuitentheaters. Hier entstand die Definition der K. als mittlere Gattung zwischen Tragödie und Farce. Die Regeln geben zwar der K. Halt und Stellenwert; jedoch entwickelt sich das literarische komische Theater in der Folge der ital. Renaissance zuerst als Kombination verschiedenartiger Bauformen und Effekte: vor allem im →Barocktheater der ersten Hälfte des 17. Jh., in der span. →comedia und im engl. →Elisabethanischen Theater, so einerseits bei Pedro Calderón de la Barca (1600–81) und Felix Lope de Vega Carpio (1562–1635), andererseits bei William Shakespeare (1564–1616), Ben Jonson (1572–1637), Thomas Middleton (1570–1627), Francis Beaumont (1584–1616) und John Fletcher (1579–1625). Auch wenn nachher zur Zeit der →Klassik und Postklassik bes. unter dem Einfluß von Nicolas Boileau (1636–1711: *L'Art poétique*, 1674) die Regeln der literarischen K. im Sinne der Einheit, Schicklichkeit und Wahrhaftigkeit kodifiziert worden sind, sind doch die Meisterwerke der ‹hohen K.› meist synkretistische Stücke, wo alle Quellen, auch des Volkstheaters, sinn- und kunstvoll verarbeitet sind: so bei den beiden größten Autoren des 17. und 18. Jh., Molière (1622–73) und Carlo Goldoni (1707–93).

Im 18. Jh. tritt das komische Theater aus gesellschaftspolitischen und literarischen Gründen in eine Krise; die K. überlebt nur als literarisches Autorentheater bei Goldoni und Pierre Marivaux (1688–1763; *Le Jeu de l'amour et du hasard*, 1730), wobei letzterer das Spiegelbild als Bauform und die subtile Sprachkomik innovativ einführt (‹marivaudage›). In der

Komödie 513

2. Hälfte des Jh. triumphiert dann als ‹ernste K.› das →bürgerliche Trauerspiel und das komische Schauspiel bei Denis Diderot (1713–84) und Gotthold Ephraim Lessing (1729–81). Die Krise dauert im 19. Jh. an; die K. versandet als geschliffenes, gutgemachtes Stück meist im Konformismus der sog. bürgerlichen K. (s. vor allem in Frankreich Eugène Scribe, 1791–1861) und weicht den Erfolgen des →Melodramas und des →Vaudeville, oder sie versteigt sich im literarischen Formalismus des →romantischen Lustspiels. Ausnahmen sind die populäre Tradition des →Alt-Wiener Volksstücks (Ferdinand Raimund, 1790–1836; Johann Nestroy, 1801–62) und der kritische Sittenrealismus der Russen Nikolai Gogol (1809–52: *Der Revisor*, 1836) und Alexander Ostrowski (1823–86).

Die Renaissance der K. erfolgt Ende des 19. Jh. und im 20. Jh. bis heute, wobei sich der Begriff der K. so ausbreitet, daß er sich mit dem des →Dramas und der →Tragikomödie überschneidet. Die Erneuerung entsteht zugleich aus dem Zugriff bei Autoren und Regisseuren zu neuen gesellschaftlichen und dramaturgischen Motiven und Mitteln und zu allen Elementen der Überlieferung, inkl. des asiatischen Theaters, des →Marionettentheaters und des →Zirkus. Wesentliche Richtungen sind
– unter dem Einfluß des realistischen und des naturalistischen Theaters die sozial-kritische K., so Gerhart Hauptmann (1862–1946: *Der Biberpelz*, 1893), George Bernard Shaw (1856–1950: *Mensch und Übermensch*, 1903; *Pygmalion*, 1912), Wladimir Majakowski (1893–1930: *Die Wanze*, 1928), Bertolt Brecht (1898–1956: *Herr Puntila und sein Knecht Matti*, 1940), Sean O'Casey (1884–1960);
– die allegorisch-phantastische K. mit realistisch-burleskem Einschlag, z. B. in Frankreich Paul Claudel (1868–1955: *Protée*, 1913), in Belgien Fernand Crommelynk (1885–1970: *Le cocu magnifique*, 1920) und Michel de Ghelderode (1898–1962: *Fêtes d'enfer*, 1929), in Italien Luigi Pirandello (1867–1936);
– die poetisch-lyrische K. in der Nachfolge der Symbolisten, so die Iren John Millington Synge (1871–1909) und William Butler Yeats (1865–1939), der Anglo-Amerikaner T. S. Eliot (1888–1965), der Franco-Libanese Georges Schehadé (1910–89);
– endlich die originellste und aggressivste Form im 20. Jh., im Sinne des ‹Anti-Theaters› oft ‹Anti-K.› genannt, mit eindeutig tragikomischen Ansätzen: etwa bei dem Vorgänger der Form Alfred Jarry (1873–1907: *Ubu roi*, 1896), den frz. Surrealisten und den Dadaisten, ihren Nachfolgern Eugène Ionesco (*1912), dem Polen Witold Gombrowicz (1904–69) oder Samuel Beckett (1906–89). Hier sprengt die K. im →Absurden und →Grotesken die tradierten Kategorien der Dramaturgie (Handlung, Figuren, Sprache, Logik).

Die Weitschweifigkeit der Geschichte der K. erklärt die Schwierigkeit, eine kohärente Poetik zu entwickeln. Einige wesentliche Faktoren dieser

514 Komödie

komplexen Problematik sind: Relativität; Vielzahl; Widersprüchlichkeit der Motive, Typen, Effekte und Bauformen; Probleme der zur K. und Komik gehörenden Sonderformen wie Humor, Ironie, Satire, Witz, →Burleske, →Groteske, →Parodie u. a.; Anzahl der Unter- oder Nebengattungen wie →Farce, →Schwank, →Posse und die vielen Komposita der K. (z. B. →Rührstück, →Intrigenk., →Comedy of Manners, →Comedy of Humours etc.); Relation zur →Tragödie und Tragik, vor allem zur →Tragikomödie; letzten Endes die Tendenz der K., alle Normen und Regeln zu zerstören im Sinne einer totalen Freiheit des Spiels, was die Versuche einer einfachen Wesensbestimmung fast unmöglich macht. Darum soll weniger auf die Typenkonstellation oder die zahlreichen Motive und Bauformen hingewiesen werden als auf zwei wesentliche Punkte: die Grundstruktur der K. und die Theorien des Komischen.

Die Struktur des Komischen kann mit Hegel (*Ästhetik*) wie die des Tragischen als dreipolig verstanden werden: Im Spannungsverhältnis zwischen dem Absoluten und den Repräsentanten des Subjekts und des Objekts kennzeichnet diese Struktur, daß, vom sinngebenden Absoluten gerechtfertigt, die Gesellschaft und ihre Vertreter ordnungssteuernd und ideologiesetzend wirken. Die lachende Kritik bezieht sich auf das ‹komische› Subjekt, das außerhalb der Norm geraten ist. Nur, «das Lustspiel ist fromm» (Max Frisch, *Tagebuch*), es glaubt an eine metaphysische oder gesellschaftliche Ordnung: Die ausschweifende Figur wird am Ende geheilt, gebessert, die Harmonie lächelnd wiederhergestellt. Umgekehrt kann das Subjekt sinnvoll sein und die heruntergekommene Gesellschaft als veränderungsbedürftig erscheinen. In beiden Fällen ist das Ende gut: «Happy-End, durchschaut und trotzdem verteidigt» (Ernst Bloch, *Prinzip Hoffnung*). Darum ist die →Handlung der K. oft dreisträngig: Harmonie am Anfang – gestörtes Gleichgewicht – Wiederherstellung der Harmonie. Erst im 19. und 20. Jh. ersetzt oft ein negativer Schluß den früheren positiven: offen, kreisförmig oder parodistisch. Hier nähert sich die K. der →Tragikomödie.

Ohne ein Grad von Komik kommt die K. selten aus, selbst in der ‹ernsten K.›. Auch hier sind die Theorien zahlreich; genannt seien: die Überlegenheitstheorie (Thomas Hobbes, 1588–1679; Justus Möser, 1720–94), die Kontrast- oder Inkongruenztheorie (Immanuel Kant, 1724–1804), die historisch fundierten Theorien Hegels und Marx' (Komik des historischen Verfalls, K. als Anachronismus: Ereignis einmal als Tragödie, dann K.), die psychoanalytische Theorie Sigmund Freuds (1856–1939, Entspannungs- und Entlastungsfunktion der K.), die Theorie von Henri Bergson (1859–1941, Objektivität der komischen Haltung, Komik als soziale Funktion, Strukturanalyse) etc. Komik und K. zeigen kritisch gesellschaftliche Mißverhältnisse multiperspektivistisch zum Zweck der Lösung durch das Lachen.

Abirached, R.: Artikel ‹comédie›. In: Encyclopedia universalis. Paris 1985; Arntzen, H.: Die ernste Komödie. München 1968; ders. (Hg.): Komödiensprache. Beiträge zum dt. Lustspiel zwischen dem 17. und 20. Jh. Münster 1988; Catholy, E.: Das dt. Lustspiel. Stuttgart 1969; Bergson, H.: Le rire. Paris 1940; Fock, R.: Grundlegung der Ästhetik des Komischen. Diss. Wien 1986; Freud, S.: Der Witz und seine Beziehung zum Unbewußten. Frankfurt/M. 1969 u. ö.; Frye, N.: Analyse der Literaturkritik. Stuttgart 1964; Greiner, B.: Die Komödie. Tübingen 1992; Grimm, R./Berghahn, K. (Hg.): Wesen und Formen des Komischen im Drama. Darmstadt 1975; Haida, P.: Komödie um 1900. München 1973; Hinck, W.: Die dt. Komödie. Düsseldorf 1977; ders./Grimm, R.: Zwischen Satire und Utopie. Frankfurt/M. 1982; Martini, F.: Lustspiele – und das Lustspiel. Stuttgart 1974; Mauron, Ch.: Psychocritique du genre comique. Paris 1964; Preisendanz, W.: Das Komische, das Lachen. In: Ritter, J./Gründer, K.: Historisches Wörterbuch der Philosophie. Darmstadt 1976; ders./Warning, R.: Das Komische. München 1976; Sareil, J.: L'écriture comique. Paris 1984; Steffen, H. (Hg.): Das dt. Lustspiel I–II. Göttingen 1968; Voltz, P.: La comédie. Paris 1964; Wagner, H. (Hg.): Absurda comica. Studien zur dt. Komödie des 16. und 17. Jh. Amsterdam 1988.

Gérard Schneilin

Komos

Griech.; ausgelassener, feucht-fröhlicher (privater oder offizieller) Umzug zum Abschluß eines Festes oder Symposions durch Dorf oder Stadt; ein K. hat wohl auch den ersten Tag der ‹Großen Dionysien› beschlossen (→ Antikes Theater). Der Name ‹Komödie› verweist auf die Entstehung der Gattung aus solchen kōmoi.

Pickard-Cambridge, A. W.: Dithyramb, Tragedy, and Comedy. Oxford ²1962 (rev. T. B. L. Webster), p. 133–162.

Bernd Seidensticker

Komparse

(Ital. comparire = erscheinen) Teilnehmer an Massenszenen ohne eigenen Namen und ohne Rollentext. Die Gesamtheit der K., deren Auftreten und Anordnung in Massenszenen heißt Komparserie. Anders als bei den → Statisten besteht an großen Bühnen die Komparserie aus einem festen Schauspielerchor, während sie an kleineren Bühnen vom Opernchor gestellt wird. Seit dem epochemachenden Auftreten der → Meininger ist die Aufgabe der K. viel bedeutender geworden als früher. Sie sollen durch stummes Spiel in die Handlung eingreifen und die Illusion verstärken, so z. B. in der Apfelschußszene in Friedrich Schillers (1757–1805) *Wilhelm Tell* (1804) oder die Forumsszene in William

Shakespeares (1564–1616) *Julius Caesar* (1599). Heute wird das Wort K. v. a. beim Film benutzt, während das Wort →Statist beim Theater vorherrscht.

Bernard Poloni

Kom-Teatteri

(KOM-Theater) Ende der 60er Jahre entstand in Finnland eine Gruppentheaterbewegung (→Freies Theater) als Protest der jungen Theatermacher gegen die institutionellen Theater. Absichten der Gruppentheater waren: die Demokratisierung der Theaterkunst und das Theater dorthin zu bringen, wo bislang aus wirtschaftlichen, sozialen und geographischen Gründen diese Kunstform unerreichbar geblieben war. Das KOM-Theater ist von diesen Gruppen eine der ältesten und die künstlerisch interessanteste. Es begann als schwedischsprachige Gruppe 1969 unter der Leitung von Kaisa Korhonen, wurde aber schon im darauffolgenden Jahr finnischsprachig. Das Programmgerüst des KOM-Theaters bilden zeitgenössische finnische Stücke; viele junge Schriftsteller sind Mitglieder der Gruppe gewesen. KOM benutzt in den Inszenierungen Musik und visuelle Effekte in vielseitiger Weise. Zu Beginn war das Repertoire von KOM stark politisch; mit der Zeit ist der Schwerpunkt mehr auf künstlerische Ziele übergegangen, ohne dabei die gesellschaftlichen Ausgangspunkte zu vergessen. – Verantwortlich für die künstlerische Leitung des Theaters waren u. a. der Komponist Kaj Chydenius, die Regisseure Pekka Milonoff und Kalle Holmberg sowie die Schriftstellerin Pirkko Saisio.

Anneli Suur-Kujala

Konflikt

(Lat. conflictus = Zusammenstoß) Der K. ist von der Antike bis zum idealistischen und später dem realistischen Theater der Kern der Handlung, die spezifische Ausdrucksform von Spiel und Gegenspiel. Hegel zufolge beruht das Handeln notwendigerweise auf der Kollision gleichberechtigter sittlicher Charaktere und Mächte, was zu Aktionen und Reaktionen führt. Genauso unausweichlich wie die Austragung des K. ist aber auch seine Lösung im Gefühl der Versöhnung. Das Tragische (→Tragödie) besteht in dieser Bipolarität, beruht «auf der Anschauung solch eines K. und dessen Lösung» (*Ästhetik*, 1835). Die marxistische Ästhetik sieht seit der Sickingen-Debatte zwischen Marx/Engels und Lassalle 1859 den K. als in den geschichtlichen Widersprüchen und deren gesellschaftlicher Auflösung begründet. Dadurch wird der dramatische K. zum Träger des Ideengehalts eines jeden Dramas, zugleich zum Organisationsprinzip der Fabel, Figurenkonstellation und Konstruktion eines Stücks. Der K. ist also Kern der materialistischen Dialektik.

Insofern als philosophische, geschichtliche oder psychologische Mächte und Kräfte im Widerstreit dramatisch von repräsentativen Figuren verkörpert werden, ist der K. an die Darstellung des handelnden Helden und seines oder seiner Widersacher, der →Prota- und Antagonisten, gebunden. Die idealistische und materialistische Dramatik verlangen beide den Gebrauch aller szenischen Mittel zur Realisierung des K. Wo K. zur Konfliktlosigkeit wird, Aktion zur Inaktion, Handlung zur ‹Ersatzhandlung›, wie in der modernen Tragikomödie und im →absurden Theater, verschwindet die Darstellung des dramatischen K. zugunsten anderer Bauformen.

Hegel, F.: Ästhetik. Frankfurt/M. 1970; Marx, K./Engels, F.: Über Kunst und Literatur. Berlin 1967; Szondi, P.: Versuch über das Tragische. Frankfurt/M. 1961.

Gérard Schneilin

Den Kongelige Ballet

Kontinuierliche zweihundertjährige Ballett-Tradition, die mit der Eröffnung des Königlichen Theaters in Kopenhagen 1748 beginnt. Von der Mitte des 16. Jh. an fördert der Hof Aufführungen von Balletten. Französische und dänische Ballettmeister entwickeln das hohe technische und künstlerische Niveau der Hoftänzer. 1771 wird von Pierre Laurent eine der Oper angegliederte Ballettschule gegründet. 1775 bis 1816 kommt Vincenzo Galeotti (1733–1816) als Tänzer, Ballettmeister und Choreograph nach Kopenhagen; er kreiert 50 Ballette. *Die Launen des Cupido und des Ballettmeisters* (1786) gehört zu den ältesten, teilweise erhaltenen Choreographien. Ihr einzigartiges Profil erhält die Kompanie jedoch durch August Bournonville (1805–79). Er übernimmt 1829 die Ballettdirektion und entwickelt in Kopenhagen auf der Grundlage der klassisch-frz. Schule die Bournonville-Technik, die als dän. Stil in die Ballettgeschichte eingeht. Seine Technik konzentriert sich speziell auf die männlichen Tänzer, die von Bournonville nach Jahrzehnten vorrangiger Ballerinenkunst wieder in adäquate Aufgaben eingewiesen werden: schnelle Drehungen, größtmögliche Sprungkraft, Virtuosität, mimische und dramatische Gestaltungsfähigkeit, Freude und Lebendigkeit. 1864 reformiert Bournonville das Schulsystem nach frz. Vorbild. 1836 choreographiert er *La Sylphide* (nach Filippo Taglioni, 1777–1871). Das Ballett wird heute weltweit in der Bournonville-Version getanzt. Weitere Choreographien: *Napoli* (1842); *Die Kirmes zu Brügge* (1851) nach flämischen Gemälden; *Eine Volkssage* (1854) nach einem Märchen von Andersen und *Fern von Dänemark* (1860). Hans Beck (1861–1952) setzt von 1894 bis 1915 die Pflege des Bournonville-Repertoires fort. Nach Beck bleiben bis 1930 die Leistungen durchschnittlich. Erst mit Harald Lander (1905–71) gewinnt das dänische Ensemble erneut Standfestigkeit und internationale Anerkennung. Landers *Etudes* (1948) sind ein Höhepunkt unter den Neuproduktionen. Ab 1951 wechseln die Direktorate.

Seit 1985 ist Frank Andersen künstlerischer Direktor des Kgl. Dänischen Balletts.

Eine aufsehenerregende Neugestaltung bedeuteten die Kompositionen von Flemming Flindt, der 1966–77 Ballettmeister war. Vor allem seine Choreographien von Ionescos Werken (z. B. *Jeu de Massacre*, 1972) überzeugten durch ihre künstlerische Kühnheit, Originalität und Qualität. Sein moderner Tanzstil und die spektakulären Tanzeinlagen fanden ein breites Publikum. Danach gewannen die Bournonville-Werke wieder an Bedeutung, was sich u. a. auf dem großen Bournonville-Festival 1979 zeigte. Durch das Festival und spätere Gastspiele im Ausland gewann das DKB erneut internationales Interesse. In den letzten Jahren hat das DKB angefangen, seine elitäre Position zu durchbrechen. Das geschieht z. T. durch Öffentlichkeitsarbeit und den Versuch, in den Sommermonaten den Schauplatz von der Bühne auf die Straße zu verlegen. Für ein ernstzunehmendes und hochqualifiziertes Ensemble wie das DKB erscheint es notwendig und unumgänglich, sich ständig mit neuen Stilarten auseinanderzusetzen und das Repertoire mit aktuellen internationalen und dän. Werken zu erweitern. Die größte Herausforderung bleibt jedoch, an der Bournonville-Tradition festzuhalten, sie zu erneuern und weiterzuentwickeln. Sie bildet das Fundament für die Schulung am Königlichen Theater, die den Tänzern und dem DKB ihre besondere Profilierung und Position in der internationalen Ballettgeschichte gegeben hat, was durch das Bournonville-Festival 1992 bestätigt wurde.

Aschengreen, F.: Perspektiv på Bournonville. Kopenhagen 1980; ders.: Balletbogen. Kopenhagen 1982; ders.: Balletten børn. Kopenhagen 1986; ders.: Jean Cocteau and The Dance. Kopenhagen 1986; Bournonville, A.: Mit Theaterliv 1848–77. 3 Bde. Kopenhagen 1865ff; Clarke, M./Clement, C.: Tänzer. Köln 1985; Fredericia, A.: Auguste Bournonville. Kopenhagen 1979; Hallar, M./Scavenius, A. (Hg.): Bournonvilleana. Kopenhagen 1992; Jacobsen, S. Kragh/Krogh, T.: Den kongelige danske Ballet. Kopenhagen 1952; Næslund, E.: Skandivanien. In: Regnitz, H./Koegler, H. (Hg.): Ballett 1984. Zürich 1984, S. 101f; Rebling, E.: Ballett – gestern und heute. Berlin 1957.

Patricia Stöckemann / Else Kjær

Det Kongelige Teater

Das Königliche Theater, dän. Nationalbühne für Schauspiel, Oper und Ballett (→Den Kongelige Ballet), besteht seit 1747 im Tjærehuset, Kopenhagen, wo es 1748 von König Frederik V. mit einem Neubau gegründet wurde. Das K. T. wurde von 1750 bis 1770 durch die Stadt, von 1770 bis 1848 vom dän. König und ab 1849 vom Staat verwaltet und finanziert. Um 1830 umgebaut, 1872 abgerissen, wurde 1874 das jetzige K. T. eröffnet, das 1931 um die Schauspielbühne Nye Scene, 1970 durch die Intimbühne Comediehuset und später Gråbrødrescenen erweitert wurde. Das K. T. untersteht heute dem dän. Kultusministerium (erhält 50 Prozent aller staatlichen Theatersubventionen in Dänemark); es wurde 1983 bis 1985 modernisiert. Von den Anfängen bis heute werden überwiegend Schauspiele und Komödien aufgeführt; wie die staatlich subventionierten Landesteilbühnen in Kopenhagen (elf Privattheater), Århus und Ålborg ist auch das K. T. gesetzlich verpflichtet, Werke von dän. Dramatikern besonders zu berücksichtigen. Dem K. T. war von 1886 bis 1968 eine Schauspielschule angegliedert (heute Statens Teaterskole).

Voraussetzung für die dän. Theatertradition ist die Eröffnung 1722 von Lille Grønnegadeteatret, das ein königliches Privileg erhielt, Aufführungen in dän. Sprache zu veranstalten, um ein größeres Publikum für das Theater zu gewinnen. Für diese erste dän. Schaubühne, bestehend aus frz. Schauspielern und dän. Studenten unter der Leitung von René Magnon de Montaigu, schrieb der junge Universitätsprofessor Ludvig Holberg (1684–1754) innerhalb von sechs Jahren 27 Komödien. Beeinflußt von Molière, →Commedia dell'arte und der klassischen Komödie zeichnet sich Holberg durch eine erstaunliche Kreativität aus, die es dem Lille Grønnegadeteatret ermöglichte, bereits im Eröffnungsjahr ein selbständiges dän. Repertoire zu spielen. 1728 wurde es aus finanziellen Gründen geschlossen. Während der Regierungszeit (1730–46) des pietistischen Königs Christian VI. bestand ein Verbot für die Aufführung von Komödien; zur gleichen Zeit wurden Holbergs Komödien erfolgreich in Deutschland aufgeführt. Ein paar Jahrzehnte war das Repertoire des K. T. jedoch von frz. Singspielen geprägt, erst in den 1770er Jahren fanden neue dän./norw. Dramatiker Zugang zur Bühne. Die wachsende Vorliebe des Publikums für das sentimentale, kleinbürgerliche Drama bewirkte jedoch, daß Iffland und Kotzebue zunehmend das Repertoire dominierten. Anfang des 19. Jh. wurden vor allem nationalromantische Tragödien von Adam Oehlenschläger (1779–1850) aufgeführt.

1825 präsentierte Johan Ludvig Heiberg (1791–1860) sein erstes →Vaudeville, das vom Publikum sehr positiv aufgenommen wurde. Dieser

Erfolg bildete den Auftakt für die zweite Blüte der dän. Nationalbühne. Heiberg suchte als Zensor, Kritiker, Übersetzer und Schriftsteller den Geschmack des dän. Publikums zu bilden. Andere dän. Autoren schrieben ebenfalls Vaudevilles (u. a. Hans Chr. Andersen, T. Overskou, H. Hertz und J. C. Hostrup), zu deren Publikumserfolg vor allem die elegante Musik beitrug.

Als erster Regisseur am K. T. wurde 1858 der erfolgreiche Schauspieler F. Høedt angestellt; seine Ernennung löste heftige Debatten aus über die Kompetenzen eines Regisseurs. Høedts psychologische Regieführung stellt einen entscheidenden Bruch mit älteren dän. Theaterkonventionen dar; Bühnenbilder, Arrangement und Requisiten wurden zur Personencharakteristik eingesetzt. Diese wirklichkeitsnahe Gesamtgestaltung stieß jedoch bei vielen auf Ablehnung, weil sie als derb und unschön galt. Schließlich aber machte Høedts Arbeitsmethode doch Schule und setzte sich im → naturalistischen Theater allgemein durch, etwa gleichzeitig mit der Eröffnung des neuen Hauses (1874). Eingang ins Repertoire des K. T. fanden nun die Norweger H. Ibsen und B. Bjørnson, zusammen mit den dän. Dramatikern H. Drachmann, E. Brandes, G. Esmann, O. Bentzon und H. Nathansen. Die zentrale Gestalt als Regisseur wurde W. Bloch, dessen Inszenierungen sowohl des klassischen als des modernen Repertoires eine Tradition begründeten, die das Nationaltheater bis weit ins 20. Jh. geprägt hat.

Mit dem Theatergesetz von 1889 wurde das Schauspielprivileg des K. T. von 1750 aufgehoben und damit die Lage der zahlreichen Privattheater erheblich verbessert. Ernsthafte Konkurrenz zum K. T. bildeten u. a. Dagmarteatret und Folketeatret mit einem modernen naturalistischen Repertoire. In den ersten Jahrzehnten des 20. Jh. stagnierte das K. T., neue Stücke wurden im Repertoire kaum berücksichtigt, der spätnaturalistische Stil wurde beibehalten. Experimente und Stilerneuerungen blieben weitgehend den Privattheatern vorbehalten. Erst mit H. Gabrielsen als Regisseur wurden ernsthafte Versuche unternommen, mit der Blochschen Tradition zu brechen und das Theater zu re-theatralisieren.

Eine zentrale Gestalt der 30er und 40er Jahre war Kaj Munk (1898–1944) mit seinen hist. Dramen, die jedoch weder hinsichtlich Form noch Inhalt eine Erneuerung mit sich brachten. Dies bewirkten erst ab 1930 die komisch-satirischen Dramen von C. E. Soya (1896–1983) und die poetisch-satirischen gesellschaftskritischen Stücke von Kjeld Abell (1901–61).

Eine formale Erneuerung bedeutete die Rezeption von Brechts → epischem Theater und des → absurden Theaters der Franzosen. Bereits in den 30er Jahren wurde Brecht am K. T. aufgeführt. Erfolg hatten seine Stücke aber nur in Riddersalen und Arbejdernes Teater, zu denen Brecht persönliche Kontakte hatte. Die Brechtsche Technik war dem eher konventionellen Schauspielstil, der am K. T. gelehrt und gepflegt wurde, fremd. Erst einer neuen Generation von Regisseuren (Sam Besekow, Søren Melson, Palle Kjærulff-Schmidt) gelang es, einen neuen Aufführungsstil durchzusetzen. – Wichtigster Vermittler des modernen dän. Dramas der 60er und 70er Jahre am K. T. war der Regisseur Carlo M. Pedersen. Dramen von Klaus Rifbjerg und Ernst Bruun Olsen wurden große Publikumserfolge.

Trotz Aufforderungen vom K. T. an dän. Dramatiker, für die Nationalbühne zu schreiben, sind neue Tendenzen und Entwicklungen des modernen dän. Dramas eher an den Landesteilbühnen, u. a. Cafeteatret, Folketeatret, Gladsaxe-Teater und Århus-Teater, sichtbar. Die gesetzliche Verpflichtung für das K. T., «ohne Einseitigkeit die besten dramatischen Arbeiten sowohl von älteren als auch von jüngeren, namentlich dänischen Schriftstellern und Komponisten aufzuführen», bedeutet für das K. T. eine gewisse Einschränkung in seiner Repertoirepolitik.

Ende der 80er Jahre wurde das Ensemble drastisch verkleinert. Das hing zum einen mit der finanziellen Lage des Theaters zusammen, bedeutete aber andererseits eine größere Flexibilität in der Planung des Repertoires, das auf Kosten der Klassiker radikal erneuert wurde.

Hansen, P.: Den danske Skueplads. Bd. 1–2. København 1889–93; Jensen, A. E.: Studier over europæisk drama i Danmark 1722–1770. Bd. 1–2. Kbh. 1968; Krogh, T.: Teatret på Kgs. Nytorv 1748–1948. Kbh. 1948; Leicht, G./Hallar, M.: Det kgl. teaters Repertoire 1889–1975. Kbh. 1975; Ludvigsen, Chr.: Moderne teaterproblemer. Kbh. 1964; Neiiendam, R.: Det kongelige Teaters Historie 1874–90. Bd. 1–5. Kbh. 1919–30; Overskou, T.: Den danske Skueplads. Bd. 1–7. Kbh. 1854–76; Schyberg, F.: Dansk Teaterkritik indtil 1914. Kbh. 1937; Teatervidenskabelige studier. Bd. 1 ff. Kbh. 1976.

Else Kjær

Konstruktivismus und Theater

Als K. wird eine Richtung in der bildenden Kunst bezeichnet, die zuerst in Rußland unmittelbar vor und nach der Revolution von 1917, dann auch in anderen Ländern Europas in unterschiedlicher Ausprägung und Intensität in Erscheinung trat. An die Stelle der schöpferischen Komposition, die in der Individualität des Künstlers begründet ist, setzte sie die Konstruktion des Materials. In der Sowjetunion hat sich der K. in Zusammenhang mit der von Boris Arwatow konzipierten ‹Produktionskunst› von den ‹Staffeleikünstlern› (Kasimir Malewitsch, Wassily Kandinsky) getrennt und der (dreidimensionalen) Gestaltung von Modellen für die neue Industriekultur zugewandt, die dem zurückgebliebenen Agrarland den Anschluß an den technischen und ökonomischen Standard West-

522   Konstruktivismus und Theater

europas und der Vereinigten Staaten bringen sollte. Die ‹Maschinen-kunst› entwickelte sich (Naum Gabo, Antoine Pevsner, Alexander Archipenko); Wladimir Tatlin, der später auch für das Theater gearbeitet hat, konstruierte ein ‹Monument für die III. Internationale›, ein Gerüst aus Metall und Glas mit rotierenden Raumkörpern, das als Versammlungsstätte und Informationszentrum dienen sollte. Wie so viele andere Entwürfe wurde auch dieser nicht realisiert. El Lissitzky, der dann im deutschen Exil aus dem Geist des K. seine ‹Elektro-mechanische Schau› *Sieg über die Sonne* als ein konsequent →Mechanisches Theater konzipierte, hat das als Grund für die Hinwendung vieler Architekten und Bildhauer zum Theater genannt.

Nachdem er schon vor der Revolution mit Künstlern der Avantgarde gearbeitet hatte, verpflichtete Alexander Tairow (1885–1950) u. a. die Konstruktivisten Georgi Jakulow (1884–1928), Alexandra Exter (1882–1949) sowie die Brüder Wladimir (1899–1933) und Georgi Stenberg (1900–1983) als Bühnenbildner an sein ganz am Prinzip der ästhetischen Autonomie gegenüber der Wirklichkeit orientiertes Moskauer ‹Kammertheater›. Die wichtigsten Inszenierungen waren: *Gewitter* von A. N. Ostrowski (1922), *Der Mann der Donnerstag war*, nach K. E. Chesterton (1923) und *Die heilige Johanna* von Shaw (1924).

Auch Wsewolod Emiljewitsch Meyerhold (1874–1940) hat in mehreren Inszenierungen (*Tarelkins Tod* von Suchowo-Kobelyn, 1922; *Die Erde bäumt sich* von Marcel Martinet, 1923; *D. E. – Her mit Europa* nach Motiven von Ilja Ehrenburg und Bernhard Keller, 1924; *Ich will ein Kind haben* von Sergej Tretjakow, Projekt 1928) konstruktivistische Grundsätze realisiert sowie eine Reihe weiterwirkender Neuerungen eingeführt wie die Filmprojektion auf der Bühne, den Einsatz von Motorrädern und Autos, die Durchdringung von Zuschauerraum und Bühne oder die Verwendung von bewegten Wänden, die das blitzschnelle Arrangieren immer neuer Schauplätze ermöglichte.

Das eindrucksvollste Beispiel des Bühnenkonstruktivismus war Meyerholds Inszenierung der Farce *Der großmütige Hahnrei* von Fernand Crommelynck (1922), für die Ljubow Popowa (1889–1924) ein Holzgerüst baute mit Treppen, Stegen, Schwungrädern und (als Anspielung auf den flämischen Schauplatz des Stückes) Windmühlenflügeln, die sich im Takt der Leidenschaften der Hauptfigur bewegten. Auf dieser als ihre ‹Werkbank› verstandenen Bühne traten die Schauspieler ungeschminkt und in einheitlicher ‹Produktionskleidung› auf, d. h. in blauen Overalls; so waren sie gezwungen, mit ihrem Körper auszudrücken, was sonst Kostüm und Maske schaffen. Meyerhold entwickelte auch eine Bewegungsform, die unter dem Stichwort →Biomechanik Grundsätze des K. realisiert und insofern eine Parallele zur Bühnengestaltung darstellt.

Arvatov, B.: Kunst und Produktion. München 1972; Die Maler und das Theater im 20. Jahrhundert – Ausstellungskatalog. Frankfurt/M. 1986; Meyerhold, W. E.: Schriften. Berlin 1979; Raumkonzepte. Konstruktivistische Tendenzen in Bühnen- und Bildkunst 1910–1930. Frankfurt/M. 1986; Tairow, A.: Das entfesselte Theater. Potsdam 1923/Köln 1964.

Peter Simhandl

Kontamination

Der Begriff (lat. ‹contaminare›: berühren, antasten, beflecken) bezeichnet das von den röm. Komödienschreibern bei der kreativen Rezeption der griech. Originale häufig angewandte Verfahren, entweder eine Szene aus einer anderen griech. Komödie in das bearbeitete Stück einzuarbeiten oder verschiedene griech. Originale miteinander zu kombinieren.

Gaiser, K.: Zur Eigenart der röm. Komödie. In: Aufstieg und Niedergang der röm. Welt I 2 (1972), S. 1058–1066.

Bernd Seidensticker

Konversationsstück

Das K. ist ein leichteres Schauspiel oder Lustspiel, das in den höheren Gesellschaftskreisen spielt, im Ton der Konversation, der geistreichen Unterhaltung gehalten wird und in dem der witzige, pointierte Dialog wichtiger ist als die meist schablonenhafte Fabel und die ebenso oberflächlich gezeichneten Charaktere. Milieugebundene Standardthemen des K. sind z. B. das Frauenstimmrecht, die freie Liebe, die Mesalliance oder der Sozialismus. Das K. beherrscht weitgehend die europ., v. a. die engl. und die frz. Theaterproduktion in der zweiten Hälfte des 19. Jh. und um die Jahrhundertwende, während in Deutschland das Fehlen einer monolithischen bürgerlichen Gesellschaft eine ähnliche Entfaltung nicht erlaubte. Als «Rettungsversuch des Dramas durch die Rettung des Dialogs, der allerdings zur bloßen Konversation wird» (Peter Szondi), ist das K. im Grunde genommen eine unbeabsichtigte Karikatur des klassischen Dramas in der Form des ‹well made play› bzw. der ‹pièce bien faite›. Doch – anders als im Drama – fehlt dem K. jeder Anspruch auf Absolutheit: Seine Typologie ist keine innerdramatische, sondern eine rein gesellschaftlich bedingte; seine Handlung wird von unerwarteten, unmotivierten, von außen her in das Stück hereinbrechenden Ereignissen vorangetrieben. – Hauptautoren von K. in diesem Sinn sind in Frankreich Eugène Scribe (1791–1861), Victorien Sardou (1831–1908), Sacha Guitry (1885 bis 1957), in Großbritannien Oscar Wilde (1856–1900), George Bernard Shaw (1863–1950), Thomas Stearns Eliot (1888–1965). Eine Verwandlung und Vertiefung erfährt das K. mit Hugo von Hofmannsthals (1874–1929) *Der Schwierige* (1921) bzw. mit Samuel Becketts (1906–89) *Warten auf Godot* (1953), in dem die Reduktion des Dramas auf unterhaltende Konversation thematisiert wird und in das absolut Negative, in das Sinnlos-Automatische des Zwiegesprächs und die Unerfülltheit der dramatischen Form mündet.

Bernard Poloni

Kordax

Ausgelassen fröhlicher und obszöner Einzel- oder Gruppentanz, der für die griech. Komödie und den Mimus charakteristisch war.

Bernd Seidensticker

Koryphaios

Bezeichnung des Chorführers im antiken Drama, der den →Chor leitet und in Sprechszenen stellvertretend für den Chor mit den Schauspielern spricht.

Bernd Seidensticker

Kostümbildner

Der K. entwirft in Absprache mit dem Bühnenbildner und dem Regisseur Kleidung und Zubehör für die Darsteller bei Bühne, Film und Fernsehen. Er ordnet sich dabei in das Konzept der Inszenierung ein. In der Regel enthält jede Entwurfsskizze des K. (Figurine) Angaben über Farbe, Schnitt, Material und Dekor; sie muß dem Gewandmeister Vorstellung und Idee des K. klar vermitteln. Die Wurzeln des Berufs sind verzweigt und vielfältig. So haben im Laufe der Geschichte Dichter, Maler, Architekten, Schneider, Fürsten, Schauspieler, Bühnenbildner und Regisseure die Kostümgestaltung zwischen traditionellem und revolutionärem Geist beeinflußt. Eine eigenständige Ausbildung zum K. hat sich erst in diesem Jh. herausgebildet. Sie umfaßt heute – mit unterschiedlicher Gewichtung an den einzelnen Schulen – einen theoretisch-wissenschaftlichen Teil

(Dramaturgie, Kultur-, Theater-, Kostümgeschichte, Psychologie, Soziologie, Farb-, Material-, Schnittkunde); einen künstlerisch-gestalterischen Teil (Zeichnen, Malen, Modellieren, Darstellungstechniken, Fotografie, Lichtdesign); einen techn.-praktischen Teil (Entwurfsumsetzung, Modellbau).

Dorothea Dieren

Kothurn

Spezifischer Schuh der antiken Tragödie; weicher, weiter, niedriger Stiefel mit schnabelartiger Spitze, der in klassischer Zeit eine flache Sohle hatte. Erst im Hellenismus beginnt, in Zusammenhang mit der →Proskenium-Hochbühne und der →Onkos-Maske, die Erhöhung der Sohle, eine Entwicklung, die schließlich in röm. Zeit zu dem beinahe stelzenartigen bis zu 20 cm hohen K. führt, der lange Zeit zu Unrecht als Schuh der klassischen griech. Tragödie gegolten hat. Das Mißverständnis hat zu schwerwiegenden Fehlschlüssen über die Schauspielkunst des 5. Jh. geführt.

Simon E.: Das antike Theater. Heidelberg 1972, S. 23f.

Bernd Seidensticker

Kreolengroteske

Volkstümliches Theater am La Plata von den 20er Jahren bis etwa 1950. Wiederbelebungstendenzen in der Gegenwart. Hauptvertreter Armando Discépolo (1887–1971) u. a. «Die Personen der Stücke demonstrieren nicht mehr die Rationalität einer Fabel, sondern sie verkriechen sich in die Winkel ihrer Enttäuschungen, ihres Einverständnisses, die von der Gesellschaft geforderten Anpassungen nicht verwirklichen zu können» (Reichardt, S. 86).

Kaiser-Lenoir, C.: El grotesco criollo: estilo teatral de una época. La Habana 1977; Reichardt, D.: Tango. Verweigerung und Trauer. Kontexte und Texte. Frankfurt/M. 1981 (^{2}1984).

Martin Franzbach

Kriminalstück

Das K., das zum →Unterhaltungstheater gehört, ist in der Regel die Adaptation für die Bühne von Kriminalromanen. Meistens schildert das K. die Ermittlung und die Festnahme des Täters aus der Sicht des Detektivs. Einst im →Boulevardtheater stark vertreten – größter Dauererfolg ist dabei Agatha Christies (1890–1976) *The Mousetrap*, seit 1956 in London jahrzehntelang ununterbrochen aufgeführt –, hat es inzwischen Rundfunk und Fernsehen erobert, v. a. als Serie nach gleichem Muster.

August, E.: Dramaturgie des Kriminalstücks. Diss. Berlin 1966.

Bernard Poloni

Krippenspiel

Mittelpunkt des religiösen Weihnachtsspiels (ab 10. Jh.). Daneben Hirten-, Dreikönigs- und Prophetenspiele. Das K. vereinigt diese speziellen Formen in einem geschlossenen Weihnachtsdrama um die Geburt Jesu Christi. Im Mittelalter zunächst von fahrenden Gruppen dargestellt (auch als →Puppentheater), wurde das K. bald Domäne des lokalen →Laienspiels. Stark regional beeinflußt, oft in direktem Bezug zur handwerklichen Krippenkultur (z. B. Oberösterreich). Wird heute noch von der kath. Kirche bei Gemeindeweihnachtsfeiern gepflegt.

Jungbauer, A.: Das Weihnachtsspiel des Böhmerwaldes (1911); Pailler, W.: Weihnachtslieder und Krippenspiele aus Oberösterreich und Tirol. Niederwalluf 1971; Schmidt, L.: Formprobleme der deutschen Weihnachtsspiele. Emsdetten 1937.

Erich Krieger

Kukla oyunu

Türk. Puppentheater. Je nach Art der Puppe (kukla) werden unterschieden (→Puppentheater): 1. el k.sı, 2. ipli k., 3. iskemle k.sı, 4. araba k.sı, 5. dev. k.

1. Kopf und Hände der ‹el k.sı› (Handpuppe) bestehen aus Pappmaché oder Holz, der Köper wird durch die Bekleidung gebildet. Der Puppenspieler (k.cı) läßt die Figuren agieren, indem er den Kopf der k. mit seinem Zeigefinger, die Arme mit Daumen und Mittelfinger bewegt. Die stereotypen Hauptfiguren des K. o. sind *İhtiyar*, ein alter, reicher Mann, und sein Diener *İbiş* (vgl. *Hacivat* und *Karagöz*; *Pişekâr* und *Kavuklu* im

Kukla oyunu 527

(→Ortaoyunu). Andere Namen für İbiş sind *Sadık* (Treuer), *Uşak* (Diener) oder *Komik*. Seine Sprache ist ungehobelt, manchmal anzüglich, aber immer witzig; er mißversteht oft die anderen Personen, was zu mancherlei Wortspielerei führt. Andere Stereotypen sind das Liebespaar *Genç kız* (junges Mädchen) und *Sirar* (jugendlicher Liebhaber) sowie ihre Gegenspieler *Tiran* oder *Hain* (Schlechter) und *Cadaloz* (Megäre); alle Figuren können auch persönliche Namen erhalten. Daneben treten Vertreter verschiedener Ethnien oder sozialer Gruppen in typischer Kleidung und mit ihrer jeweils typischen Sprache auf. Die Wirkung der Aufführung beruht auf Wortwitz und dem ‹taklit›, der Imitation verschiedener Sprechweisen durch den k.cı. Unerläßlich sind darüber hinaus Prügelszenen. Themen des K. o. sind dem →Karagöz-Spiel entlehnte Handlungen oder Räuber- und Liebesgeschichten, die volkstümlichen Erzählungen nachgebildet sind. Schriftlich fixierte K. o. existieren auch heute kaum; der k.cı kennt den Inhalt des Stücks und den Gang der Handlung, der Wortlaut wird während der Aufführung und im Hinblick auf die Zuhörerschaft improvisiert. Musik taucht nur als Gesang der Dialekttypen auf. – Die Bühne des K. o. ähnelt mit Vorhang und Kulisse der des →Kasperle-Theaters. – Auf einigen Dörfern Anatoliens findet sich eine Version des Handpuppen-Spiels, bei welchem der k.cı im Liegen drei Puppen durch seine beiden Hände und ein Knie bewegt. Bis vor kurzem wurde das K. o. kaum noch aufgeführt, heute ist ansatzweise eine Neubelebung erkennbar.

2. Die ‹ipli k.› (→Marionette) ist eine an Fäden bewegte Ganzkörperpuppe. Sie wurde vermutlich im 19. Jh. aus Europa importiert; nach dem Engländer Thomas Holden, der mit großem Erfolg an Istanbuler Theatern Puppenspiele vorführte, heißt sie auch ‹holden k.sı›. Die Typen und Stücke entsprechen denen des Handpuppen-Spiels. Heute ebenfalls sehr selten.

3. Nur noch aus der Literatur bekannt sind die drei anderen K. o.-Arten: Beim Puppenkasten (iskemle k.sı = Schemelpuppe) tanzen zwei bis vier Puppen auf einem Kasten, indem sie durch seitlich angebrachte Fäden bewegt werden. Es sind dies der Fischer Yani, der Nichtsnutz Panayot und die Mädchen Katinga und Rabia, alles nichttürkische Namen. Diese Form des K. o. wurde fast ausschließlich von Zigeunern vorgeführt und war auch auf dem Balkan sowie in Nordafrika bekannt.

4./5. An Festtagen waren im 17. bis 19. Jh. bei Straßenumzügen Wagen mit Puppen, die sich durch das Rollen der Räder bewegten (araba k.sı), und Riesenpuppen (dev k.) zu sehen. Diese waren übermannsgroße Figuren, in die ein Mann schlüpfte und die oft zwei Gesichter oder zwei Köpfe hatten und im Arm eine weitere Puppe trugen. Über ihre Bedeutung ist nichts bekannt.

528 Kulissenbühne

And, M.: A History of Theatre and Popular Entertainment in Turkey. Ankara 1963; ders.: Geleneksel Türk Tiyatrosu – Kukla, Karagöz, Ortaoyunu. Ankara 1969; Spies, O.: Türkisches Puppentheater. Versuch einer Geschichte des Puppentheaters im Morgenland. Emsdetten 1959.

Maren Fittschen

Kulissenbühne

Die K.- oder Gassenbühne wurde erstmalig 1618 im neu erbauten →Teatro Farnese in Parma durch Giovanni Battista Aleotti als Dekorationssystem genutzt. Die Kulissen sind mit Leinwand oder Papier bespannte Holzrahmen, die paarweise auf der rechten und linken Seite der →Bühne angeordnet und nach hinten gestaffelt eine Tiefenwirkung des →Bühnenbildes ermöglichen. Der hintere Abschluß erfolgt durch einen Prospekt, die Kulissen werden horizontal als oberer Abschluß durch →Soffitten verbunden. Das Bühnensystem besteht vereinfacht aus hintereinander gestaffelten und kleiner werdenden Rahmen. Auf diese Bildebenen wird das Bühnenbild perspektivisch aufgelöst. Die Wirkung der Außen- und Innenräume wird durch den bewußten Einsatz ‹falscher› Perspektiven erhöht. Voraussetzung für diese Art von Dekoration sind tiefe Bühnenräume, Distanz des Zuschauers zur Spielfläche und strikte Trennung von Bühnen- und Zuschauerbereich.

Die K. entfaltet ihre illusionäre Wirkung natürlich nur für die Zuschauer, die im Umfeld der zentralen Mittelachse und nicht zu hoch über Bühnenniveau sitzen. Alle anderen Zuschauerpositionen müssen sich mit Teilillusionen bzw. Unzulänglichkeiten durch verzerrte Einblicke begnügen. Die Darstellung durch den Schauspieler oder Sänger kann sich in der K. bis zu dem Punkt in die Tiefe entwickeln, an dem der Darsteller in den optischen Konflikt mit der Maßstäblichkeit des Perspektivbilds gerät. Aus dem Freiraum zwischen den Kulissen, den Gassen, tritt der Darsteller auf, bzw. aus den Gassen heraus wurden die Kulissenteile durch Kerzen, Öl- oder Gasleuchten erhellt. Durch einen zentralen Seilantrieb können Kulissenpaare gegenläufig bewegt und damit schnellere Bildwechsel herbeigeführt werden. Die perspektivische Wirkung wird durch ein leichtes Ansteigen (1–4%) des Bühnenbodens (Bühnenfall) verstärkt. Die K. ist das bestimmende Dekorationssystem in den europ. Theatern bis ca. 1880, als sich mehr und mehr die plastischen, dreidimensionalen Bühnenaufbauten und der Stahlbau mit neuen bühnentechn. Verwandlungssystemen an den Theatern durchsetzten. – Ein vollständig erhaltenes Kulissensystem mit Antriebsgeräten aus Holz und Tauen ist u. a. im →Drottningholmer Schloßtheater (Schweden) noch heute in Funktion zu besichtigen.

Braulich, H. / Hamann, E. O.: Beiträge zur Geschichte der Theatertechnik. III. Teil. Berlin 1980; Schubert, O.: Das Bühnenbild. München 1955; Unruh, W.: Theatertechnik. Berlin 1969.

Horst Birr

Kulturpolitik und Theater (BRD / DDR)

(→Theatersystem, →Nationaltheater, →Volksbühne) Die Bundesrepublik steht in der Tradition der Kulturstaatidee. Obwohl das Grundgesetz keine ausdrückliche Regelung enthält, wird die Förderung und Erhaltung des kulturellen Lebens als staatliche Aufgabe angesehen, Art. 5 GG schützt den Wirk- und Werkbereich künstlerischer Tätigkeit. Die Kulturpolitik ist in erster Linie eine kommunalpolitische Angelegenheit. 1979 fielen 50 Prozent aller kulturellen Ausgaben auf die Kommunen, während die Länder mit 47 und der Bund lediglich mit 2,7 Prozent beteiligt waren, wobei zu berücksichtigen ist, daß kompetenzrechtlich der Bund nur für auswärtige Kulturangelegenheiten zuständig ist. Das Theater nimmt den zentralen Bereich in der Kulturpolitik ein.

In der DDR wurde Kulturpolitik als Förderung und Schutz der «sozialistischen Kultur, die dem Frieden, dem Humanismus und der sozialistischen Gesellschaft dient» und als Kampf gegen «die imperialistische Unkultur, die der psychologischen Kriegführung und der Herabwürdigung des Menschen dient» (Artikel 18 der Verfassung der DDR von 1974) inhaltlich definiert und durch das Ministerium für Kultur und die Kulturabteilung des ZK der SED zentralistisch gelenkt. Obwohl die meisten Theater administrativ den Räten der Bezirke, der Kreise oder der Städte unterstanden, war der reale Einfluß der Kommunen gering. Die Finanzierung der Theater erfolgte auf der Grundlage zentraler Pläne aus dem Staatshaushalt. Im Kulturetat stand Theater (1988 mit 17,2 %) an erster Stelle vor Kultur- und Klubhäusern (12,9 %) und Museen (11,9 %).

Die Kulturpolitik bzw. Kulturarbeit der Städte und Kommunen orientiert sich an den Empfehlungen des Dt. Städtetags. Dieser ist die Dachorganisation der kreisfreien und eines Teils der kreisangehörigen Städte und Städteverbände in der Bundesrepublik (Sitz in Köln). Er vertritt die dt. Städte gegenüber den Regierungen und Parlamenten. Einschneidende Bedeutung hatten die Empfehlungen des Dt. Städtetags aus dem Jahr 1971 und 1973, in dem die Stadt als Ort der Sozialisation, Kommunikation und Kreativität verstanden wird. Kultur habe einen dreifachen Auftrag: Förderung der Kommunikation, Schaffung von Spielräumen als Gegengewicht zu den Zwängen des Lebens und die Herausforderung zur Reflexion. Damit ist der Kulturbegriff um seine soziale Dimension erweitert worden. Auf diesem Hintergrund wird nunmehr die Ansicht vertreten, daß «aus dem demokratischen Gleichheitsgrundsatz, dem Recht auf freie Entfaltung und der Kunstfreiheit folgt, daß allen Schichten der Bevölkerung eine kommunikative und nicht einseitig reglementierte Teilhabe am Kulturgeschehen zu ermöglichen ist». Die Kulturpolitik sei also ein Verfassungsauftrag. Unter dem Schlagwort «Kultur für alle» (Hilmar Hoffmann) wird die Demokratisierung der Kultur verlangt, quasi eine Forderung nach kultureller Infrastruktur erhoben. Diese fruchtbare Diskussion der kulturpolitischen Verantwortlichen darf jedoch nicht darüber hinwegtäuschen, daß die kulturellen Ausgaben nach wie vor unter dem Aspekt der Standortfragen und des Freizeitwertes einer Stadt als Investitionsförderungsmittel gesehen werden. Die kulturpolitische Diskussion hat für den Theaterbereich dazu geführt, daß auch alternative Gruppen (→ Freies Theater) als förderungswürdig angesehen werden. Diese Förderung ist jedoch im Verhältnis zum etablierten Theaterwesen verschwindend gering.

Grabbe, J.: Kommunale Kulturfinanzierung und Kulturpolitik. In: Der Städtetag 10 (1982), S. 652 ff; Hoffmann, H.: Perspektiven der kommunalen Kulturpolitik. Frankfurt/M. 1974; Köhler, F. H.: Zur Entwicklung kommunaler Kulturausgaben 1975 bis 1979. In: Verwaltungsschau 1981, S. 303 ff; Neue Schriften des Dt. Städtetags 29 (1973); Pappermann, E.: Grundzüge eines kommunalen Kulturverfassungsrechts. In: Dt. Verwaltungsblatt 1980, S. 701 ff; Schwencke (Hg.): Plädoyer für eine neue Kulturpolitik. Heidelberg 1979; ders.: Kultur für alle. Frankfurt/M. 1981.

Roswitha Körner/Manfred Pauli

Kunqu

Das kunqu (chin. «Kunshan-Oper») entstand um die Mitte des 16. Jh. in Kunshan, Provinz Jiangsu. Seine Entstehung ist eng mit dem Namen des Musikers und Sängers Wei Liangfu verknüpft, über den sonst kaum etwas bekannt ist. Zunächst war es einfach ein Musikstil, auf der Basis des in Kunshan selbst verbreiteten Melodienkanons (Kunshanqiang) komponiert aus Elementen mehrerer südlicher Stile, wie des Yiyangqiang aus Jiangxi, des Yuyaoqiang und des Haiyanqiang aus dem nördlichen Zhejiang (→ difang xi, Lokales Theater) sowie aus dem auf das Yuan-Drama (→ zaju) zurückgehenden Nördlichen Musikstil (beiqu). Ein anderer Name für das K. war «mit Wasser polierte Musik» (Shuimodiao), womit die stilistischen Besonderheiten des kunqu angedeutet werden: weich, melismatisch, gefühlvoll, verfeinert, geprägt durch den klagenden Klang der Bambusflöte (qudi) als charakteristischem Begleitinstrument. Allg. werden im kunqu fast nur Blasinstrumente benutzt, im Unterschied zur

Kunqu 531

→Pekingoper mit ihren schrilleren Saiteninstrumenten. Das kunqu stellt also eine Verschmelzung nördlicher Melodien, die sich für heroische, lebhafte Szenen eigneten, und südlicher Melodien, geeignet für kontemplative oder romantische Szenen, dar, wobei ein deutliches Übergewicht beim südlichen Kanon liegt.

Der Dramatiker Liang Chenyu (ca. 1520–ca. 93) trug ebenfalls viel zur Verbreitung des kunqu bei, vor allem durch sein Drama *Huanshaji* («Die Seidenwäscherin»), eine Schilderung der Liebe zwischen dem Staatsmann Fan Li und der chin. Helena, Xi Shi, im 5. Jh. v. Chr. Das Drama, welches als erstes auf der Kunshan-Musik basierte, war so erfolgreich, daß sich mit ihm das kunqu schnell durchsetzte, das traditionelle zaju und →chuanqi verdrängte und für die kommenden zwei Jh. das Theaterleben Chinas beherrschte. Fast alle bedeutenden Dramen des 17. und 18. Jh. wurden als kunqu geschrieben, so Tang Xianzus (1550–1617) *Mudanting* («Der Päonien-Pavillon»), Kong Shangrens (1648–1718) *Taohuashan* («Der Pfirsichblüten-Fächer») und Hong Shengs (1645–1704) *Changshengdian* («Der Palast des ewigen Lebens»). Die Stücke des kunqu waren ebenso wie die seines Vorläufers, des chuanqi, in der Regel sehr lang, oft nicht unter 40 bis 50 Szenen; ihre Aufführung erstreckte sich daher vielfach über mehrere Abende. Später wurden meist nur einzelne besonders beliebte Szenen gespielt.

Das kunqu war das kultivierte literarische Theater der gebildeten Elite. Die strenge Regelhaftigkeit der Musik und der Sprache sowie die komplexe Darstellungstechnik machten es zu einer der schwierigsten Theaterformen für den Schauspieler wie für den Zuschauer. Das kunqu verbreitete sich über ganz China, sein Zentrum blieb jedoch das wirtschaftlich und kulturell führende Mittelchina, besonders die Stadt Suzhou, neben Peking die kulturelle Hauptstadt. Aus dieser Gegend stammten auch die meisten Dramatiker und Schauspieler des kunqu.

Der Niedergang des kunqu setzte im 19. Jh. ein. Ein Grund war das Entstehen zahlreicher lokaler und regionaler Theaterstile (→difang xi), die an Popularität gewannen und das kunqu zurückdrängten. Einen schweren Schlag erhielt das kunqu infolge der Verwüstungen, die in Mittelchina durch die Taiping-Rebellion (1850–64) verursacht wurden und durch die auch Suzhou in Mitleidenschaft gezogen worden war. Anfang des 20. Jh. gab es nur noch wenige kunqu-Truppen. Als verbreitete Theaterform war die →Pekingoper an die Stelle des kunqu getreten. Erst nach der Gründung der Volksrepublik China 1949 wurden Versuche unternommen, dem kunqu neues Leben einzuhauchen. Das traditionelle kunqu-Stück *Shiwu guan* («Fünfzehn Geldschnüre»), ein Kriminalstück um die ungerechtfertigte Verurteilung eines Liebespaares und dessen Befreiung durch einen weisen Richter, wurde zu einem der populärsten Stücke der 50er und 60er Jahre. 1956 und 1985 wurden in Shanghai Festspiele des kunqu veranstaltet, zu denen jeweils die bekanntesten Schauspieler und neugegründeten Gruppen zusammengeholt wurden. Trotz dieser Bemühungen indes gehört das kunqu heute zu den Formen des Musiktheaters, die besonders stark unter schwindenden Zuschauerzahlen zu leiden haben.

Hung, Josephine Huang: Ming Drama. Taipei 1966; Tsiang Un-kai: K'ouen K'iu, Le théâtre chinois ancien. Paris 1932; Yao Hsin-nung: The Rise and Fall of the K'un Ch'ü (Quisan Drama). In: T'ien Hsia Monthly II, 1 (Jan. 1936), 63–84.

Bernd Eberstein

Kunstfach / Rollenfach

Mit dem Begriff K. wird in dem Dienstvertrag, den ein Bühnenkünstler mit einem öffentlich-rechtlichen oder privaten Theater abschließt, das Rollengebiet angegeben, zu dessen Übernahme er sich vertraglich verpflichtet. Rechtlich bedeutet diese tarifvertraglich vorgeschriebene Angabe im Vertrag zum einen den Schutz der Bühnenmitglieder vor der Übernahme einer seinem vertraglichen Rollengebiet fernliegenden Aufgabe. Zum anderen wird mit dieser Angabe der Beschäftigungsanspruch (→Schauspieler) des Bühnenmitglieds konkretisiert. Die Institution der K.-Bezeichnung geht von einem Theaterverständnis aus, wonach bestimmte Typen, Charaktere und Gestalten in den aufgeführten Theaterstücken häufiger vorkommen (vgl. z. B. die Definition des Bühnenoberschiedsgerichts: «Typen von menschlichen Charakteren und Typen von menschlichen Gestalten, die in den jeweils aufgeführten Werken häufiger vorkommen und daher Aufgabegebiete zu verzeichnen vermögen»). Die Fachbezeichnung entstammt der →Commedia dell'arte, die auf dem Prinzip des Spiels verschiedener feststehender Rollen bzw. Typen beruhte. Diese Vorstellung mag auch teilweise auf die Bühnenliteratur des 18./19. Jh. zutreffen. Nach dem allg. Theaterlexikon von R. Blum, K. Herlos-Herloßsohn und H. Marggraff (1840) gibt es folgende Fächer: für Männer: Erste Rolle, Helden, Charakterrolle, Erster Liebhaber und jugendlicher Held, →Bonvivants, Chevaliers und Gecken, Intriganten, Bösewichter, Verräter, Mantellrollen, Vertraute, Pfiffige, Bediente, röm. Rollen, Aushilfsrollen; für Frauen: Heldenmütter, Erste Heldinnen und Liebhaberinnen, →Koketten und muntere Liebhaberinnen, Soubretten oder Kammermädchen, komische Alte, Zweite und Dritte Liebhaberinnen, Aushilfsrollen. Von der gegenwärtigen Dramaturgie sind diese Vorstellungen jedoch überholt. Dies führt zu Problemen bei der Abfassung von Schauspielerverträgen. Deshalb wird teilweise versucht, zumindest den Umfang des Rollengebiets nach ‹kleiner›, ‹mittlerer› oder ‹großer› Rolle festzulegen. – Auf Grund der stimmlichen Vorgaben bereitet die Umschreibung des K. im Musiktheaterbereich keine größeren Schwierigkeiten.

Diebold, B.: Das Rollenfach im dt. Theaterbetrieb des 18. Jh. 1913; Greiffenhagen, G.: Zur Problematik der Kunstfachbezeichnung im Bühnenrecht. In: UFITA 1975.

Roswitha Körner

Kyôgen

Die *kyôgen*-‹Possenspiele›, noch heute lebendiger Bestandteil jap. Theaterkultur, blicken als komische Interludien zwischen zwei →Nô-Spielen auf etwa 600 Jahre ununterbrochene Aufführungstradition zurück. Der Ursprung dieser wörtlich ‹verrückte Worte› bedeutenden Komödien ist in den vom Hofadligen Fujiware no Akihira (989–1066) in seinem *Shinsarugaku-ki* (1030) beschriebenen Burlesken der *sarugaku*-Volksschaukunstformen zu suchen. Gegenüber anderen sarugaku-Formen wie dem Nô, das sich durch Hereinnahme von Tanz und Gesang zum lyrischen Tanzdrama wandelte, setzte das kyôgen auf dialog- und handlungsorientierte realistische Darstellung und Komik und konnte sich so als selbständiges Possenspiel etablieren. Diese Selbständigkeit wird jedoch durch seine enge Bindung an das Nô-Theater relativiert: kyôgen wird, vergleichbar dem griech. Satyrspiel, als entspannendes Element zwischen den ernsten Nô-Spielen aufgeführt und ist dem Nô-Ideal des *yûgen*, der ‹reizvollen Anmut›, verpflichtet, das alles Vulgäre von der Bühne verbannt (und somit auch dem Realismus oft Grenzen setzt). Kyôgen-Spieler waren ferner während der ganzen Muromachi-Zeit (1333–1573) stets Mitglieder von Nô-Schulen, bevor sich Anfang der Neuzeit die drei kyôgen-Schulen Okura, Izumi und Sagi etablierten, von denen die beiden erstgenannten noch heute existieren. (Die Sagi-Schule erlosch Anfang unseres Jh.) – Das kyôgen-Repertoire umfaßt gegenwärtig etwa 200 Stücke, deren Texte, die *daihon*-‹Bühnenbücher›, im 16./17. Jh. niedergeschrieben, in den einzelnen Schulen geheim überliefert wurden und authentischer sind als die aus Aufführungsaufzeichnungen entstandenen sog. *kyôgenki*-Versionen.

Thematisch werden die Stücke, die komische Situationen des (mittelalterlichen) Alltags darstellen, meist nach den Hauptpersonen der Handlung benannt: glückverheißende Götterstücke, Stücke, die große (*daimyô*) oder kleine (*shômyô*) Feudalfürsten durch deren bauernschlaue Diener Taró-kaja und Jirô-kaja übertölpelt sehen, Stücke, die Schwächen oder ‹Pech› von Mitgliedern sozialer Gruppen wie den *yamabushi*-Exorzisten, dem *shukke*-Klerus, der blinden *zatô*-Rezitatoren schildern, Possen um die Suche eines Ehepartners (*muko-iri-mono*) oder um den Alltagszwist zwischen Mann und Frau. Gespielt wird auf der Bühne des →Nô; wie im Nô treten ein Hauptspieler (*shite*) und ein Nebenspieler, im kyôgen *ado* genannt, auf – nur selten weitere Personen. Auch das kyôgen kennt nur männliche Darsteller, kennt Masken, verwendet deren Typen – Frau, Dämon, Gott, Tier – allerdings seltener. Bei den Großrequisiten herrscht die gleiche Andeutung und Symbolisierung wie im Nô, die Kleinrequisiten sind dagegen realistisch. Die Sprache ist weitgehend die Umgangssprache des späten Mittelalters, die Aktionen der Spieler wie im Nô durch eine Vielzahl von *kata*-Grundmustern bestimmt. In seinen besten Stücken stößt kyôgen zur Sozialkritik vor, in den meisten Spielen bleibt es jedoch auf der Ebene eines auf Wortwitz und Situationskomik beruhenden, dialog- und handlungsorientierten Typentheaters stehen.

Beaujard, A.: Le Théâtre comique des Japonais. Paris 1937; Kato, H.: Kyôgen, ein Beitrag zur Funktion dieses Genres. Diss. Wien 1976; Kenny, D.: A Guide to Kyôgen. Tôkyô 1968.

Roland Schneider

Labanschulen

Der Tänzer, Tanz-Pädagoge und Tanztheoretiker Rudolf von Laban (1879–1959; →Ausdruckstanz), ein lebhafter Geist, vehement, spontan, bildet zu Beginn dieses Jh. einen Brennpunkt des freien Tanzes in Deutschland. Laban erkundet zunächst die Gesetzmäßigkeiten des Tanzes. Den Kern seiner Tanztheorie bildet die Schwungskala, die Gliederung des dreidimensionalen Raums in zwölf Bewegungsrichtungen. Zentrum dieses Raums ist der Tänzer, der in der Begegnung mit dem Raum zu vielen Raumformen und Ausdrucksgebärden geführt wird. Alle L. basieren auf dieser Tanztheorie. 1910 erste Ausbildungsstätte München; in den Sommermonaten 1913 und 1914 auf dem Monte Verità/Ascona, der ein Treffpunkt aller Reformer zu Beginn des Jh. war. Mary Wigman (1886–1973; →Ausdruckstanz), Gertrud Leistikow (1885–1948) und Suzanne Perrottet (1889–1983) zählen zu den Assistentinnen Labans. Sie bauen auf Labans Lehre auf und eröffnen nach dem 1. Weltkrieg Schulen in Dresden, Amsterdam, Den Haag und Genf. 1914 bis 1918 unterrichtet Laban in Ascona und Zürich. Stuttgart und Mannheim sind Hauptwirkungsstätten des Pädagogen in den Nachkriegsjahren. In Stuttgart tritt 1920 K. Jooss (1901–79; →Ballets Jooss, →Ausdruckstanz) in den Schülerkreis ein. Labans chorische Reigenfolge *Der schwingende Tempel*, 1922 unter freiem Himmel erarbeitet, entsteht in Gleschendorf/Lübekker Bucht. In Hamburg eröffnet Laban kurz darauf eine Zentralschule. Die speziellen räumlichen Gegebenheiten des kleinen Saals im Zoologischen Garten und in der Ernst-Merck-Halle führen zur Kammertanzbühne und zu Choreographien von Bewegungschören. Laban bildet Laien- und professionelle Tänzer für große chorische Spiele und den Kammertanz heran. 1924: Tanzdrama *Agamemnon*, angeregt durch Noverres Ballett-Pantomime *Der gerächte Agamemnon* (1771, Wien; →ballet d'action). Dramatisch-antinomisch agieren Chorblöcke. 1925 bis 1934 löst Albrecht Knust (1896–1978) den Lehrer in der Leitung der Hamburger Labanschule ab. Laban gründet 1925 in Würzburg ein Choreographisches Institut, das er 1927 nach Berlin verlegt. Schülerin von Knust und Laban ist Lola Rogge (1908–90). Sie führt nach Knusts Berufung an die Folkwang-Schule Essen die Hamburger Tanzinstitution 1934 als Lola-Rogge-Schule weiter. Labans Hamburger Modellarbeit wird wegweisend für die Gründung weiterer Labanschulen im In- und Ausland: Berlin (H. Feist), Lübeck (S. Pander Gellmitz), Münster (K. Jooss), Frankfurt (S. Bodmer, L. Müller), Stuttgart (E. Walcher), Zürich (S. Perrottet), Bern (E. Sauerbeck), Basel (K. Wulff) und Budapest (E. Török). 1937/38 verläßt Laban als Pazifist und Sozialist Deutschland und emigriert nach England, wo er sich mit K. Jooss, Sigurd Leeder (1902–81) und Lisa Ullmann (1907–85) zusammenschließt. Die nach Laban benannten deutschen Schulen werden ab 1937/38 geschlossen oder unter verändertem Namen weitergeführt. In England Vertiefung der Bewegungsstudien. Die Ergebnisse werden für die Praxis der Tanzerziehung, der Therapie und der Arbeitspsychologie nutzbar gemacht. Mit Lisa Ullmann 1946 Eröffnung des Art of Movement Studio in Manchester, das 1953 nach Addlestone verlegt, später der University of London als Laban Centre for Movement and Dance angegliedert wird. Die Grundlagenarbeit zur Erstellung einer Tanz-Schrift (→Tanznotationen) entwickeln K. Jooss und A. Knust weiter. 1940 Dance Notation Bureau, New York. – Publikationen Labans: *Die Welt des Tänzers* (1920); *Choreographie* (1926); *Schrifttanz: Methodik, Orthographie, Erläuterungen* (1928); *Ein Leben für den Tanz* (1935); *Der moderne Ausdruckstanz* (1981, dt. Ausg.); *Kunst der Bewegung* (1988).

Lämmel, R.: Der Moderne Tanz. Berlin o. J.; Maack, R.: Tanz in Hamburg. Hamburg 1975; Peters, K.: Brennpunkt Laban. In: Die Tanzarchiv-Reihe 19–20, S. 30–34. Köln 1979.

Patricia Stöckemann

Laboratoire de Théâtre Art et Action

Forschungs- und Spielstätte für experimentelles Theater in Paris von 1911 bis 1951, zunächst als Art et Liberté. Abseits des kommerziellen Theaterbetriebs gegründet und geleitet von dem Architekten Edouard Autant (1872–1964) und seiner Frau, der Schauspielerin Louise Lara (1876 bis 1952). Produktivste Periode: 1917 bis 1939; insgesamt fanden 402 Aufführungen von 112 Werken statt. Die kostenlosen Theaterabende wurden i. d. R. von Amateurschauspielern bestritten. Zu den wichtigsten Mitarbeitern gehörten die Maler Valmier und Le Fauconnet sowie Akakia-Viala, Claude Autant-Lara, Vera Idelson, Marie-Louise van Veen (Dekoration und Regie). A. e. A. gliederte seine Arbeit in 1. Théâtre Choréique (poetisches Sprech- und Musiktheater), 2. Comédie Spontanée (aktualisierte Technik der Commedia dell'arte), 3. Théâtre du Livre (Dramatisierung von Romanen), 4. Théâtre Universitaire (szenische Umsetzung von philosophischen Schriften), 5. Théâtre de Chambre. Im Repertoire schwerpunktmäßig Werke der Surrealisten und Futuristen, viele Erstaufführungen, u. a. Marinetti, Corra, Settimelli, Pratella (*Teatro Futurista Sintetico*, 1918; *Une Nuit au Luxembourg*, 1922), Wyspianski (*Les Noces*, 1923), Ribemont-Dessaignes (*L'Empereur de Chine*, 1925), Vasari (*L'Angoisse des Machines*, 1927). Geprägt von den Ideen Alfred Jarrys und Gordon Craigs, verwendete man symbolische und geometrisch-abstrakte Dekorationen, Masken, verzichtete auf komplexe Technik, experimentierte mit der Simultanbühne, versuchte, Farben, Töne und Wörter einander zuzuordnen. Besonderes Interesse auch an Theaterarchitektur. 1937 entstand der Entwurf eines Raumtheaters (Théâtre de l'Espace), der jedoch nicht die Zustimmung der Behörden fand. In dem Bemühen um neue Konzeptionen und Erfahrungen war A. e. A. allen anderen Avantgarde-Theatern in Frankreich voraus. Der Nachlaß befindet sich in der Bibliothèque Nationale de l'Arsenal, Paris.

Corvin, M.: Le Laboratoire de Théâtre Art et Action. Lille 1973.

Barbara Müller-Wesemann

Lafayette Players

Eröffnet 1915 im New Lincoln Theatre, New York, mit der Farce *The Girl at the Foot*. Als man von der Gründerin Anita Bush verlangte, sie solle der Gruppe den Namen ‹Lincoln Players› geben, wechselte sie zu dem zweiten Theaterhaus der Zeit, das für ein überwiegend schwarzes Publikum bereitstand, dem Lafayette Theatre. Hier gab es, noch im gleichen Jahr, das Debüt mit *Across the Footlights*. Die L. P. sandten auch bald Gruppen auf Tournee, und gleichsam Niederlassungen wurden 1916 in Chicago und Washington D. C. etabliert. Erst infolge der Weltwirtschaftskrise mußten die L. P. 1932 ihre Arbeit einstellen. Durch ihre jahrelange ununterbrochene Produktion schufen die L. P. wesentliche Voraussetzungen für ein Umdenken in der kulturellen Öffentlichkeit hinsichtlich der kontinuierlichen Beschäftigung schwarzer Kulturschaffender im Theaterbereich. Ihre erfolgreichsten Inszenierungen schlossen diejenigen weißer Dramatiker von Rang wie O'Neill und William Inge ein. Auch Dubose Heywoods *Porgy*, die Vorlage zu Gershwins späterer Volksoper, wurde von den L. P. gezeigt. Eine Wiederbelebung der L. P. gab es von 1967 bis 1972 als The New Lafayette Theatre mit Robert Macbeth als künstlerischem Leiter und Ed Bullins als ‹playwright in residence›.

Thompson, M. F.: The Lafayette Players, 1917–32. In Hill, E. (ed.): The Theater of Black Americans. Vol. II. New York 1980, p. 13–32; Bullins, E. (ed.): The New Lafayette Theatre Presents: Plays with Aesthetic Comments by Six Playwrights. New York 1974.

Dieter Herms

Laienspiel

Der Begriff L. bezeichnet eine konkrete historische Erscheinungsform des Theaters jugendbewegter Gruppen im 20. Jh.; er sollte nicht verwendet werden als Sammelbegriff für das nichtprofessionelle Theater insgesamt. L. in diesem Sinne entstand im engen Zusammenhang mit der Jugendbewegung und der musischen Erziehung der neuen Schule nach 1900 im deutschsprachigen Raum. Es setzte sich scharf ab gegen das professionelle Theater wie gegen das Vereinstheater (→Liebhabertheater), entwickelte eigene Spielformen und eine eigene Textwelt. Es bestimmte in den 20er Jahren weithin die großen Bühnenverbände, wurde 1933 abgeschnitten oder übernommen, wirkte aber nach 1945 weiter bis in die Gegenwart hinein, in der es von Spielpädagogik und Amateurtheater abgelöst wird; damit war eine dt. Sonderentwicklung beendet.

L. darf nicht als einheitliche Theaterbewegung angesehen werden. Auch ist bisher nicht empirisch überprüft, wer wann was vor wem wie spielte. So sind wir einerseits auf die gedruckten Spieltexte der vielen L.-Verlage angewiesen, andererseits auf die programmatischen Deklarationen (vor allem in vielen kleinen Zeitschriften); aus ihnen hat P. Wolfersdorf die Ästhetik der großen Gruppierungen des L. zu erschließen versucht.

Von Beginn an sind zumindest vier Quellen wirksam: 1. die naiven Berichtspiele der Wandergruppen mit ‹Szenen aus ihrem Fahrtenleben› (erste Gruppen 1896 in Berlin-Steglitz); 2. die Theatralisierung der Jugendbewegung insgesamt (Kluft, Lager, Lagerfeuer, Horde, Nest, Thing) mit den Wunschrollen Scholar, Vagant, Ritter, Landsknecht (1913 Treffen auf dem Hohen Meißner); 3. das in reflektiertem Gegensatz zum professionellen Theater entstandene Schulspiel Martin Luserkes (*1888; ab 1906 im Landerziehungsheim Wickersdorf); 4. die halbprofessionellen Wandertruppen (G. Haass-Berkow ab 1914 mit dem *Oberuferer Christgeburtsspiel*, M. Gümbel-Seiling ab 1916 mit dem *Redentiner Osterspiel*; H. Holtorf und W. Blachetta ab 1920). Dazu kommt die Freilichtbühnenbewegung (1907 Gründung des Harzer Bergtheaters). Geprägt wird die neuromantische, antibürgerliche Suche der bürgerlichen Jugendlichen von der Sehnsucht nach einfacher, naturverbundener Gemeinschaft, nach sozialer Gerechtigkeit und wahrhafter Frömmigkeit. Sie fliehen aus der Industriegesellschaft zu bäuerlicher Dorfkultur und altem Volksgut in Lied, Tanz, Spiel, Brauchtum, Sage, Märchen, Legende; Individualität, Erlebnis, Gefühl, Charakter stehen gegen Intellektualismus und rezeptiven Enzyklopädismus. Wie in der pädagogischen Bewegung insgesamt sollen die menschlichen, künstlerischen, geselligen, gemeinschaftsbildenden Kräfte der Persönlichkeit entfaltet werden; das schließt sozial- und gesellschaftskritische Ansätze (die in den sozialistisch-marxistischen Gruppen ausgearbeitet wurden) und völkisch-nationale Akzente ein; sie führen einen Teil der L.-Bewegung folgerichtig in die NS-Spielscharen.

Der Spielstil zeichnete sich aus durch (oftmals dogmatischen) Verzicht auf Vorhang und Kulisse, durch einfache, starkfarbige Gewänder (Spielkleid, nicht Kostüm!), durch sparsame Gestik und die Suche nach laiengeeigneten Spieltexten. Man wollte künden, wirken und erziehen; man erstrebte die innere Verbundenheit einer echten Gemeinschaft Spieler–Zuschauer in der Erbauung des weihevollen Festes. Gegen professionelles und Vereinstheater gewandt, suchte man die «eigene Gebärde» (R. Mirbt, 1896–1975), forderte Spieltexte «von wesentlichem und wirkendem Gehalt», die «in ihrer Ausdrucksform dem Spielgestaltungsvermögen der Ausführenden entsprechen» (I. Gentges, *1900); das waren in der Gruppe selbsterarbeitete Texte wie Rückgriffe in die Theatergeschichte (Geistliche Spiele, H. Sachs; bei Luserke auch Shakespeare; Dramatisierungen von Märchen usw.).

Nach 1945 wurde die L.-Bewegung in den Westzonen, später in der Bundesrepublik noch einmal bestimmend. Geblieben waren von ihr vor allem die ‹Laienspiele›, d. h. von Verlagen herausgegebene Texte, die entgegen dem ursprünglichen Gedanken mehr und mehr ‹nachinszeniert› wurden. Das protestierende und sich auf sich selbst besinnende Spiel der Laien verkam zum fremdbestimmten und vergangenheitsverhafteten Expertenspiel. Nur mühsam befreiten sich jüngere Gruppen von dem ‹verpflichtenden Kanon› der etablierten Texte und der tradierten Spielweise. Sie griffen wieder zu Texten und Ausdrucksformen des professionellen Theaters (vor allem den absurden Experimentierstücken), schrieben im Zuge der schärferen Politisierung ab Ende der 60er Jahre wieder selbst, näherten sich stärker spielpädagogischen Formen und ersetzten folgerichtig das Wort L. mehr und mehr durch Spiel und (Amateur-) Theater.

Brix, G.: Wesen, Gestaltung und Wert der jugendlichen Laienspielbewegung in den Jahren der Wirrnis von 1918–33. Diss. 1937; Bonn, F.: Jugend und Theater. Emsdetten 1939; Beitl, R. (Hg.): Taschenbuch für Laienspieler. Berlin 1928; Frantzen, P.: L. in der Weimarer Zeit. Eine Dokumentation. Recklinghausen 1969; Gentges, I.: Das Laienspielbuch (Hg. zus. mit R. Leibrandt, R. Mirbt und B. Sasowski). Berlin 1929; Gerst, W. C. (Hg.): Gemeinschaftsbühne und Jugendbewegung. Frankfurt/M. ²1924; Kaiser, H. (Hg.): L. und Amateurtheater seit 1945. Eine Dokumentation. Recklinghausen 1972; Lebede, H.: Jugend und Bühne (Hg. zus. mit L. Pallat). Breslau 1924; Meissner, K.: Das L. und seine Bedeutung für die Erziehung (Diss. 1950); Mirbt, R.: Von der eigenen Gebärde. Ein L.-Buch in 26 Beispielen. München 1951; ders.: L. und Laientheater. Vorträge und Aufsätze aus den Jahren 1923–59 (1960); Nickel, H.-W.: L. In: Lexikon der Kinder- und Jugendliteratur. Weinheim; Sasowski, B. (Hg.): Das Buch von Fest und Feier. Berlin 1929; Vesper, W. (Hg.): Deutsche Jugend. 1934; Wolfersdorf, P.: Stilformen des L. Eine historisch-kritische Dramaturgie. Braunschweig 1962.

Hans-Wolfgang Nickel

Landesbühne

Im Unterschied zu den →Stadt- und Staatstheatern haben die L. den besonderen kulturpolitischen Auftrag zur flächendeckenden Bespielung in Gebieten, in denen kein öffentliches Theater ansässig ist. Mehr als die Hälfte der Vorstellungen werden außerhalb des Sitzortes gespielt (Abstecherbetrieb). Die Rechtsträgerschaft liegt zum Teil beim jeweiligen Bundesland (unter besonderer Beteiligung der bespielten Gemeinden und des Sitzortes). Teilweise haben sich mehrere Städte und Gebietskörperschaften zum Zweck der Unterhaltung des Theaterbetriebs als Rechtsträger zusammengeschlossen (teilweise auch als Städtebundtheater bezeichnet). Diese Aufgabenstellung bringt Besonderheiten im Arbeits- und Produktionsprozeß mit sich, z. B. Verringerung der täglichen Probenzeiten durch die Fahrten zu den Abstecherorten, ständiges Einstellen auf neue Bühnenraum- und Bühnenakustikverhältnisse; letzteres gilt für die Darsteller wie auch hinsichtlich der Gestaltung und Einrichtung des Bühnenbildes. Die inhaltliche Arbeit der L. hat sich auf die unterschiedlichen Besucherstrukturen an den verschiedenen Spielorten einzustellen. So bil-

540 Landestheater Linz

det u. a. das Kinder- und Jugendtheater einen Schwerpunkt im Theaterprogramm. Die L. konkurrieren in der Publikumsgunst mit den Tourneetheatern, die ohne eine entsprechende inhaltliche Theaterarbeit mit Erfolgsstücken, besetzt mit Stars aus Film und Fernsehen, ebenfalls durch die Lande reisen. – Die L. sind überwiegend im deutschen Bühnenverein zusammengeschlossen und bilden zum Zwecke ihrer Interessenvertretung eine eigene Gruppe.

Mitglieder der Landesbühnengruppe im Deutschen Bühnenverein, Bundesverband deutscher Theater:

Grenzlandtheater des Kreises Aachen; Vorpommersche Landesbühne, Anklam; Badische Landesbühne Bruchsal; Westfälisches Landestheater (WLT), Castrop-Rauxel; Landestheater Detmold; Landestheater Burghofbühne im Kreis Wesel, Dinslaken; Landesbühne Sachsen, Dresden-Radebeul; Landesbühne Sachsen-Anhalt, Lutherstadt Eisleben; Württembergische Landesbühne Esslingen; Landesbühne Hannover; Städtebundtheater Hof; Nordhessisches Landestheater Marburg; Landestheater Schwaben (LTS), Memmingen; Rheinisches Landestheater Neuss e. V.; Landestheater Mecklenburg Neustrelitz; Landesbühne Rheinland-Pfalz, Neuwied; Mecklenburgisches Landestheater, Parchim; Bühnen der Stadt Quedlinburg; Thüringer Landestheater Rudolstadt; Schleswig-Holsteinisches Landestheater und Sinfonieorchester, Schleswig; Uckermärkische Bühnen, Schwedt; Landestheater Sachsen-Anhalt Nord, Stendal; Landestheater Württemberg-Hohenzollern (LTT), Tübingen; Landesbühne Niedersachsen Nord, Wilhelmshaven; Mitteldeutsches Landestheater, Wittenberg/Bernburg, Theater Zeitz.

Landesbühnengruppe im Deutschen Bühnenverein, Bundesverband deutscher Theater (Hg.): Landesbühnen-Journal Spielzeit 1992/93.

Roswitha Körner/Red.

Landestheater Linz

Festliche Spiele werden im Linzer Schloß vor den Kaisern Friedrich III. und Maximilian I. aufgeführt. Pflege des lateinischen →Schulspiels, →Jesuitentheater. Wandertruppen treten in der ständischen Reitschule und im Ballhaus auf der Promenade auf. Erstes Theatergebäude: ein umgebauter Speicher auf der Donaulände (1752–86). Aufführungen im Redoutensaal. 1803 Eröffnung des neuerbauten «Landständischen Theaters» an der Promenade. 1955–58 Umbau durch Clemens Holzmeister: Neubau der «Kammerspiele» (421 Plätze), Umbau des «Großen Hauses» (756 Plätze). 1973 Eröffnung der Studiobühne «Theaterkeller Ursulinerhof». – L. L. hat Dreispartenbetrieb, die heterogene Publikumsstruktur bedingt ein großes Stückeangebot, derzeit ca. 30 Produktionen im Jahr. Pflege der modernen Oper, zahlreiche österr. und deutschsprachige Erstaufführungen im Schauspiel. Gut organisiertes Abonnementsystem (ca. 15 000 Abonnenten). Schwerpunkt Jugendarbeit (eigenes Jugendteam seit 1974). Die «Linzer Theaterzeitung» erscheint monatlich seit 1956. Als Theaterorchester steht dem L. L. das Bruckner-Orchester (100 Musiker) zur Verfügung. Intendant: Dr. Roman Zeilinger.

Pfeffer, F.: Das Linzer Landestheater 1803–1925. Diss. Wien 1926; Wimmer, H.: Das Linzer Landestheater 1803–1958. Linz 1958; 150 Jahre Landestheater Linz. Festnummer d. Zeitschrift Oberösterreich Heft 3/4, Winter 1953/54.

Friedrich Wagner/Red.

Lateinamerikanisches Theater

Das Kulturleben in der Kolonialzeit strahlte größtenteils von den Vizekönigshöfen (Lima, Buenos Aires, Bogotá, México) an der Peripherie aus und orientierte sich an den europäischen Metropolen (Madrid und Lissabon). Erst nach den Unabhängigkeitskriegen und der Herausbildung der über 20 Nationalstaaten (1810–26) begannen eine stärkere Öffnung zu anderen Kulturkreisen, ein umfassenderer Verschmelzungsprozeß und die Herausbildung eines eigenständigen nationalen Theaters, das freilich immer noch bei hohen Analphabetenraten und wirtschaftlicher Unterentwicklung einer Bildungselite in den Städten vorbehalten blieb. Die Mexikanische Revolution (1910–17) markiert für Lateinamerika den Aufbruch der Massen mit ihren Forderungen nach einer Verbesserung der wirtschaftlichen und sozialen Lage, die auch eng an die Forderung nach Bildung für alle gebunden war. Seitdem hat sich in Lateinamerika ein reiches Theaterleben entwickelt, das längst die Städte und die festen Plätze verlassen hat und eine wichtige Rolle bei den Prozessen der Bewußtseinsveränderung, aber auch als reines Unterhaltungselement spielt. Auch das kulturelle Erbe Europas und Nordamerikas wird weiterhin gepflegt, wogegen das L. T. in Europa meist nur durch Emigranten aus der lateinamerikanischen Theaterszene zur Kenntnis genommen zu werden pflegt.

Wenn man den span. Kolonialchronisten und archäologischen Funden vertrauen kann, waren die szenischen Darstellungen der vorkolumbischen Indianer vor allem religiös und rituell orientiert, durch rhythmische Tanzelemente charakterisiert. Trotz der späteren Mischung mit christlichen Zutaten läßt sich aus Form und Inhalt mittelamerikanischer Tänze noch heute auf ursprüngliche theatralische Ausdrucksformen schließen. Das heroische Tanzdrama *Der Mann von Rabinal Achí* z. B. ist nach der oralen Tradition der Quiché-Indianer in Guatemala über verschiedene Stufen rekonstruiert und erst im 19. Jh. veröffentlicht worden. In einem dialogisierten Szenenquartett wurde der Kampf zwischen einem Krieger von Rabinal und einem Quiché mit Opferausgang dramatisiert.

542 Lateinamerikanisches Theater

Es scheint, als ob das →Missionstheater der Jesuiten an die autochthonen indianischen Traditionen angeknüpft hätte. Denn schon in dem Schuldrama und den geistlichen Festspielen (→Auto Sacramentales) gelang es den Jesuiten, profanes und eucharistisches Gedankengut miteinander zu verschmelzen. Bei der engen Einheit zwischen Staat und Kirche fiel die Indoktrinierung der Indianer über das Medium Theater um so leichter, als die Eroberung Amerikas (Conquista) ideologisch sich als Fortführung des jahrhundertelangen Kampfes (Reconquista) gegen die ‹ungläubigen› Araber auf der Iberischen Halbinsel darstellte. Teufel, Fegefeuer und Vorhölle verbanden sich mit der Furcht der Indianer vor Zauberern, Geistern und Dämonen zu einem wirkungsvollen Disziplinierungsinstrument. Die mittelalterliche span. Tradition der ‹Tänze der Araber und Christen› wurde auf die Unterwerfung der indianischen Völker übertragen.

Neben diesen primitiven, stark schematisierten Theaterformen blühten in den größeren Städten – entsprechend der Theaterkultur in den europäischen Metropolen – in Theaterhäusern oder auf Bühnen in den Hinterhöfen von Häuserblocks (→Corrales) alle Arten volkstümlicher Dramatik. Trotz dieser Vielfalt zogen es in der ‹Neuen Welt› geborene Dramatiker wie Juan Ruiz de Alarcón y Mendoza (1581?, México–1639, Madrid) immer wieder vor, ihr Glück im Gefolge von Calderón und Lope de Vega in Madrid zu versuchen. Eher dramatisierten span. Autoren Ereignisse der Eroberung Amerikas für ein staunendes span. Publikum, als daß weiße oder kreolische Dramatiker an einem eigenständigen amerikanischen Theater arbeiteten. Der Dramenimport aus Spanien und später aus dem Frankreich Corneilles, Molières, Racines überwog allemal die einheimische Produktion. Neben der Palast- und Corralbühne gab es das öffentliche Komödienhaus und die Klosterbühne. In Brasilien zeigten sich seit etwa 1770 Anfänge eines Singspiel- und Operntheaters. Im allgemeinen überflügelte das geistliche Theater das weltliche, obwohl die→Loas, →Sainetes und→Entremeses des→Género Chico – kurzweilige Einakter mit Alltagsstoffen – beim Publikum am beliebtesten waren. Mit Sor Juana Inés de la Cruz (1648–95) drangen die in Mexiko geschriebenen geistlichen Festspiele und Lustspiele nach Calderónscher Manier auch nach Europa.

Erst mit der Unabhängigkeitsbewegung zu Beginn des 19. Jh. änderten sich die Stoffe (die jetzt realitätsbezogener und gesellschaftskritischer wurden) und die Funktion der Institution Theater, das vor allem im La Plata-Becken mit den großen europäischen Einwanderungswellen des 19. Jh. sich dem ganzen Reichtum der Weltliteratur öffnete. Im Verbund mit der Musik und dem Roman wurden Gattungsgrenzen überschritten, wie beim →Gauchotheater Ende des 19. Jh. am La Plata, das unter Einbezug argentin. Tänze (Pericón, Milonga, Payada) und Pantomime über die regionalen Grenzen hinaus in ganz Lateinamerika bekannt wurde. –

Als Spanien die letzten überseeischen Kolonien (Kuba, Puerto Rico,

«El cantar de los cantares». R: B. Bert. Grupo teatro Itaca, Mexiko 1989 (OP)

«Paso de dos» (E. Pavlovsky). R: L. Yusem. Teatro Babilonia de Buenos Aires, 1990 (AB)

«Macunaima». Grupo Teatro Macunaima. Teatro São Paulo, 1978 (FP)

Philippinen) im span.-kuban.-nordamerik. Krieg (1895–98) verlor, spiegelte auch das L. T. mit der Fülle gastspielender ausländischer Impresarios und Ensembles diese Frühphase des Kulturimperialismus wider, der bis zum heutigen Tage (mit Ausnahme Kubas und Nicaraguas) das L. T. weitgehend zur Exporthalde nordamerik. und europ. Theaterprodukte machte. Wenn an dieser Stelle mit den Namen von Dramenautoren gegeizt wird, so bedeutet das einmal die Kapitulation vor der schieren Fülle, zum anderen die Schwierigkeit, aus soviel künstlerischem Mittelmaß, aus Nachahmung und Pastiche herausragende Schriftsteller hervorzuheben.

Neben der Weltwirtschaftskrise 1929/30 und der Phase der Importsubstitution, mit dem Aufschwung der Gewerkschaften, Kulturgruppen, Arbeiterzirkel, Theatervereinigungen und Experimentierbühnen bildeten sich neue vielfältige Ausdrucksformen des Theaters, das sich seitdem in zwei Richtungen entwickelte: in ein nach wirtschaftlicher Unabhängigkeit strebendes politisch engagiertes Kollektivtheater und in ein an traditionellen Mustern orientiertes kommerzialisiertes Theater mit Festbühnen in den großen Städten. Das gesellschaftskritische Kollektivtheater knüpfte an die Theorien von Konstantin S. Stanislawski, Erwin Piscator, Bertolt Brecht, Antonin Artaud u. a. an, die neben der Aktualisierung der Klassiker das Theater als Waffe im Klassenkampf schmiedeten. Ein Teil dieser Theoretiker und Autoren versuchte später, in der Emigration in den USA in «dramatic workshops» zusammen mit fortschrittlichen nordamerik. Dramatikern (z. B. Arthur Miller, Tennessee Williams) einigen Einfluß auf das zeitgenössische Theater zu nehmen. Vor allem jüdische und deutsche Emigranten arbeiteten an der Vermittlung des progressiven europ. und nordamerik. Theatererbes mit. In Brasilien fanden sich schon nach der avantgardistischen «Woche der modernen Kunst» (1922) Ansätze zu einem bewußt nationalen Theater.

Jetzt treffen wir auch auf Dramatiker unter den berühmteren lateinamerik. Autoren. Pablo Neruda, Eduardo Mallea, Julio Cortázar, Augusto Roa Bastos, Jorge Icaza, Raquel de Queiroz u. a. Wegen der Konkurrenz durch die Massenmedien muß auch in Lateinamerika das Theater mehr Phantasie aufwenden, um den Zuschauer anzulocken.

Angesichts der Fülle der Tendenzen, Themen und Experimente kann hier nur an einigen Beispielen die Problematik des lateinamerik. Gegenwartstheaters etwa seit dem Ende des 2. Weltkriegs aufgezeigt werden. Im Zusammenhang mit dem Ringen um eine nationale Volkskultur, welche die Masse des größtenteils analphabetischen und um seine Existenz kämpfenden Volkes erreichen sollte, ist der Brasilianer Augusto Boal (* 1931) mit seinem Teatro Arena, 1956 in São Paulo gegründet, am weitesten gegangen. Von der konsequenten Ausbildung der Schauspieler bis zur Gestaltung der Inszenierung arbeitete das Kollektiv an neuen Formen, Stilen und Stoffen, die in Zusammenarbeit mit den Zuschauern selbst entstanden. Was Paulo Freire mit seiner «Erziehung zur Befreiung» im besten aufklärerischen Sinne intendierte (den Menschen dazu zu bringen, sich seines Verstandes ohne Anleitung eines anderen zu bedienen), versuchte Boal mit seinem → «Theater der Unterdrückten». Ausgehend vom Rundbautheater ging Boal bald zu flexibleren Formen des Theaters über (→ Unsichtbares Theater, Forum-, Statuen-, Zeitungstheater), bei denen die Akteure wie zufällig als Straßenpassanten in öffentlichen Verkehrsmitteln, in Restaurants, in Hotels, bei Vorträgen usw. durch Diskutieren und Agieren den Zuschauer unbewußt zum Engagement und ‹Mitspielen› verführen wollten. Der Bewußtseinsprozeß sollte dabei über die Aktivierung der unterdrückten Phantasie und Spontaneität gehen. Wie politisch gefährlich dieses Theater und die daran anschließenden Diskussionen waren, zeigen die Verhaftung, Folterung und Ausweisung Boals 1971. Erst nach der Demokratisierung der Verhältnisse in Brasilien konnte Boal in den 80er Jahren seine Formen, um Erfahrungen im Exil bereichert, auch in seiner Heimat weiterentwickeln.

Ähnliche Erfahrungen machten die unabhängigen Theatergruppen in anderen Ländern Lateinamerikas (am bedeutendsten «El Galpón», Uruguay, das kolumbianische «Teatro Experimental de Cali», das argentinische «Libre Teatro Libre», der «Grupo de Teatro Ollantay», Ecuador, «La Candelaria» aus Kolumbien, «Rajatablas» aus Venezuela, «Cuatrotablas» aus Peru u. a.), die von der Phase des Kalten Kriegs über brutale Militärdiktaturen bis zu den restaurativ-repressiven Regierungsformen unserer Tage zur spärlichen Gegenöffentlichkeit in ihren Ländern gehörten, wenn sie nicht emigrieren mußten, weil sie in ihren Stücken Ausbeutung und Elend anprangerten. Bei einer Zuspitzung der Klassenkämpfe wie im Chile der «Unidad Popular» (1970–73) nahm das Theater eine wichtige Rolle wahr, die sich sogar als Überlebensstrategie in den Konzentrationslagern der faschistischen Junta bewährte, wo das Theater im Untergrund vielen Gefangenen Mut zusprach.

Eine Sonderentwicklung nahm das Theater auf Kuba. Hier wurden nach dem Sieg der Revolution 1959 Voraussetzungen geschaffen, die das Theater für Minoritäten ein für allemal der Vergangenheit angehören ließen. Ein Netz von Hoch- und Fachschulen für Schauspieler, Regisseure, Bühnentechniker und Theaterinstrukteure entstand, und jedermann konnte gratis nicht nur zuschauen, sondern auch in den zahlreichen Laiengruppen aktiv Theater spielen. Generell läßt sich sagen, daß im heutigen Kuba die Bühne das Szenarium par excellence ist, auf dem mit der bürgerlichen Vergangenheit abgerechnet, aber auch konstruktive Kritik an eigenen Mißständen (Machismo, Schwarzhandel, Aberglauben, Familienprobleme u. a.) geübt wird. Gruppen wie das «Politische Theater Bertolt Brecht», das → «Teatro Escambray», die Pantomime oder die «Theatergemeinschaft» von Santiago sind auch im Ausland durch ihre Tourneen bekannt. – Zum L. T. muß schließlich auch das →«Teatro Campesino» gerechnet werden, das, 1965 als Landarbeitertheater von Luis Valdéz gegründet, in den USA einen schwierigen Kurs zwischen Mythos, Anpassung und Rebellion steuert.

Die Konkurrenzsituation mit den Massenmedien, der Kaufkraftverlust des Bürgertums, der Funktionswandel kultureller Werte u. a. Faktoren belasten auch die gegenwärtige Situation des Theaters in den Metropolen Lateinamerikas. Beim Paradigmenwechsel zum postmodernen Theater blicken die Bühnenautoren und Regisseure immer noch stärker auf Stanislawski und Meyerhold als auf ihre eigene Experimentiercourage. Als Beispiele können die Performances des Chilenen Alberto Kurapel und sein plurimediales Theater, aber auch die «Karnevalisierung» (Bachtin) des Theaters durch Ramón Griffero oder die Mythenzerstörung der antiken Tragödie durch den Mexikaner Luis de Tavira gelten. In diese Reihe gehört auch das avantgardistische Theater von Marco Antonio de la Parra, in dem Marx und Freud auf der Bühne dialogisieren.

Adler, H.: Politisches Theater in Lateinamerika. Von der Mythologie über die Mission zur kollektiven Identität. Berlin 1982; ders. (Hg.): Theater in Lateinamerika. Ein Handbuch. Berlin 1991; Blanco, R.: Von Apu Ollantay bis Brecht. Theater als Waffe im Klassenkampf Lateinamerikas. Berlin 1983; Boal, A.: Theater der Unterdrückten. Frankfurt/M. 1979; Bravo-Elizondo, P.: El teatro hispanoamericano de crítica social. Madrid 1975; Dauster, F. N.: Historia del teatro hispanoamericano. Siglos XIX y XX. México ²1973; Garzón Céspedes, F. (ed.): El teatro latinoamericano de creación colectiva. La Habana 1978; Gutiérrez, S. (ed.): Teatro popular y cambio social en América Latina. Panorama de una experiencia. Costa Rica 1979; Luzuriaga, G. (ed.): Popular Theater for Social Change in Latin America. Essays in Spanish and English. Los Angeles 1978; Lyday, L. F./Woodyard, G. W. (eds.): Dramatists in Revolt. The New Latin American Theater. Austin/London 1976; Menéndez Quiroa, L. (ed.): Hacia un nuevo teatro latinoamericano. Teoría y metodología del arte escénico. San Salvador 1977; Saz, A. del: Teatro social hispanoamericano. Barcelona 1967; Solórzano, C.: Teatro latinoamericano en el siglo XX. México 1964 (Colección Pormaca. 10). (Zeitschrift) Conjunto. Teatro Latinoamericano. La Habana.

Martin Franzbach

Laterna Magica

Theater in Prag, in dem seit 1959/60 Stücke verschiedener Art in einer Mischung von Schattenspiel, Ballett, Schauspiel und Pantomime gespielt werden. Mit Hilfe von Projektionen, wechselnden Beleuchtungseffekten und musikalischer Begleitung werden in der Mischung verschiedener theatralischer Genres reizvolle und überraschende Wirkungen erzielt.

Wolfgang Beck

Das Laterndl (London)

Das von Martin Miller gegr. Emigrantenensemble, an dem vor allem Schauspieler und Texter aktiv waren, die bis 1938 an den Wiener Kleinkunstbühnen → «Lieber Augustin» und → «Literatur am Naschmarkt» gearbeitet hatten (später kam auch Erich Fried dazu), präsentierte zwischen 1939 und 1945 – von einer internierungsbedingten Pause abgesehen – kontinuierlich österr. Literatur in London. Im Programm wechselten Revuen, Kabarett und Unterhaltungstheater (Schnitzler, Molnar, Goetz, Wildgans) einander ab.

Jan Hans

Laufendes Band

Obwohl bereits 1906 erstmalig bei einer Opernaufführung verwendet, ist der Einsatz von Laufbändern auf der Bühne unmittelbar mit dem Namen Piscator (1893–1966) und dessen *Schwejk*-Inszenierung (1928) verbunden. Um zu zeigen, daß Schwejk, obwohl ständig in Bewegung, nicht von der Stelle kommt, ließ man zwei 17 Meter lange und fünf Tonnen schwere Rollbänder auf die Vorführungsfläche montieren. Auf eine Leinwand projiziert, zogen wechselnde Spielorte und Figuren an dem Hauptdarsteller vorüber. Technisch unausgereift, erwiesen sich die Rollbänder als äußerst geräuschvoll. Dennoch waren die ‹laufenden Bänder› von nun an aus der Bühnenapparatur Erwin Piscators nicht mehr wegzudenken: Bei der Eröffnungsinszenierung der zweiten Piscatorbühne (Walter Mehring, 1896–1982: *Der Kaufmann von Berlin*, 1929) fanden sie als Teil einer komplexen technischen Bühnenkonstruktion erneut Verwendung.

Knellessen, F. W.: Agitation auf der Bühne. Emsdetten 1970, S. 146–153; Piscator, E.: Das politische Theater (1929). Reinbek bei Hamburg 1963, S. 136–139 u. 179–195.

Carl Wege

League of Workers' Theatre

Erste Dachorganisation aller → Arbeitertheater in den USA, 1932 gegr. und 1935 umbenannt in New Theatre League. Sie koordinierte bis zu 100 Agitpropgruppen mit dem Ziel, die Idee des Klassenkampfes durch Theater zu verbreiten. Sie übernahm die Zeitschrift «Workers' Theatre» und veranstaltete sog. Theatre Nights, Arbeitertheater-Festivals in New

York, in denen sich die bekannteren Agitpropgruppen mit ihren besten Produktionen vorstellten. Zu diesen gehörten u. a. A. Amith und E. Kazan, *Dimitroff* (1934); C. Odets, *Waiting for Lefty* (1935); P. Green, *Hymn to the Rising Sun* (1936); B. Bengal, *Plant in the Sun* (1937). Im Zusammenhang des allgemeinen Niedergangs des Arbeitertheaters in der ausgehenden ‹roten Dekade› stellte auch die New Theatre League 1941 ihre Arbeit ein.

Dieter Herms

Lebende Bilder

Im Gegensatz zur bewegten Szene und zum effektsuchenden Gruppenbild (Tableau) die statische Darstellung von Szenen aus Mythologie, Geschichte, Bibel, Heiligenlegende durch lebende Personen. Auch Werke der bildenden Kunst oder allegorische Themen wurden so von gleichsam stumm erstarrten Personengruppen nachgestellt. Schon in der klassischen Antike üblich, sehr häufig in mittelalterlichen Krippenszenen und Passionsspielen, desgleichen bei barocken Umzügen. Im 18. Jh. hat die frz. Prinzenerzieherin Gräfin Stéphanie-Félicité de Genlis (1746 bis 1830) in ihren Theaterstücken für die höfische Jugend die l. B. wieder populär gemacht, deren Verwendung in den *Attitüden* bei Lady Emma Hamilton (1765–1815) als mimische Solo- oder Gruppendarstellung Goethe beeinflußte: Bilderszenen am Weimarer Hof und Beschreibung in den *Wahlverwandtschaften*. Weite Verbreitung fanden die l. B. in der zweiten Hälfte des 19. Jh. in der Darstellung gestellter (Schlacht-)Szenen bei Feierlichkeiten von Kriegervereinen und vaterländischen Gesellschaften; aber auch von sozialdemokratischen Theatervereinen wurden l. B. politischen Inhalts bei Parteiveranstaltungen inszeniert (Umgehung der Zensur). Heute fortentwickelt als Schlußbilder von Revuen: Folies-Bergère, Moulin Rouge, Paradis Latin, Lido; auch in Fastnachts- und Karnevalsumzügen (auf Wagen).

Holmström, K. Gram: Monodrama, Attitudes, Tableaux vivants. Stockholm 1967.

Horst Schumacher

Lehrstück

Der Begriff des L. und die ihm zugehörigen szenischen Arbeitsformen sind wesentlich mit dem Namen Bertolt Brechts verbunden. Brechts Beschäftigung mit dem L. setzt etwa um 1928 ein und schlägt sich nieder in einer Reihe von kurzen Stücken, die sich in der Dramaturgie, der Personenzeichnung, der Sprachbehandlung deutlich abheben von den übrigen Stücken: *Flug der Lindberghs* (1929, seit 1949 *Der Ozeanflug*), das *Badener Lehrstück vom Einverständnis* (1929), *Der Jasager* (1930) bzw. *Der Jasager und Der Neinsager* (1931), *Die Maßnahme* (1930), *Die Ausnahme und die Regel* (1930/31 bzw. 1937), *Die Horatier und die Kuriatier* (1934). Sie schlägt sich weiter nieder in einer Reihe von L.-Veranstaltungen in Zusammenarbeit mit Schülern, Lehrern, pädagogischen Institutionen, Arbeiterchören, Schauspielern und Musikern und schließlich in einer Reihe von Stückfragmenten sowie in einem Komplex theoretischer, zum großen Teil fragmentarischer Texte zur Theorie des Lehrstücks. – Die Flucht Brechts aus Deutschland (1933) beendet die praktische Beschäftigung mit dem L., während die theoretische weiterläuft – der wichtigste zusammenhängende Beitrag stammt aus dem Jahr 1937.

Die von Brecht selbst durchgeführten oder angeregten Praxisversuche fanden jeweils unter sehr verschiedenen Bedingungen statt. Der *Flug der Lindberghs* und das *Badener Lehrstück vom Einverständnis* etwa wurden im Rahmen der Baden-Badener Kammermusik (1929) aufgeführt. Ebenso wurde die Aufführung der *Maßnahme* in der Berliner Philharmonie (1930) vor allem als Beispiel einer neuen Arbeitermusik-Kultur aufgenommen. In bezug auf die Schule war die praktische Erprobung des *Jasagers* Brechts gewichtigster L.-Versuch.

Es sind verschiedene Faktoren, die das L. zu einem Instrument der Untersuchung machen:

– Die Aufhebung des Systems Spieler und Zuschauer: Das L. entwickelt Formen, die die bisherigen Zuschauer an Handlungsformen beteiligen.
– Die Nachahmung und Kritik vorgegebener Muster: Der Text des L. stellt das Modell her, das zum Gegenstand und zugleich Mittel der Untersuchung gesellschaftlicher Zusammenhänge wird.
– Die epische Spielweise: «Das Studium des V-Effektes ist unerläßlich.» Wichtig wird zudem phasenweise die (unterbrochene) Einfühlung in Menschen, Handlungsweisen, Haltungen und Situationen.
– Die Kommentare: Dies sind zunächst eher theoretische Texte (Lesekommentare), Lehrtexte, die den L. beigegeben sind. Unter Kommentar kann weiter verstanden werden «die Gesamtheit aller theatralischen Mittel mit kommentierender bzw. die Handlung unterbrechender Funktion (wie z. B. Film), die bereits Piscator als ‹Kommentar› bezeichnet hat» (Steinweg 1972, S. 105).

– Die Kontrolle der Apparate: Unter den Begriff Apparat fallen bei Brecht sowohl technische Apparate wie Filmgeräte, Projektionsapparate, mechanische Musik als auch gesellschaftliche Institutionen, z. B. der Rundfunk (als Gerät wie als Institution), schließlich auch der «Kollektive Apparat», der durch das L. «organisiert» wird. Neben der Kontrolle über die (technischen) Apparate spielt im L. die Kontrolle durch die Apparate eine Rolle.

Inzwischen gibt es eine Reihe von Versuchen, die sich in unterschiedlichster Weise dem L.-Komplex genähert haben. Eine theatrale Lernform mit spezifischen Verfahrensweisen zeichnet sich ab. Generell umreißt sie eine Theaterarbeit zwischen den drei Spannungspunkten Ästhetische Praxis – Politische Praxis – Kollektive Praxis/Gruppenpraxis.

Wesentliche Praxiselemente und Verfahrensweisen der L.-Arbeit sind, soweit sie auf Brecht zurückweisen, unmittelbar aus den Handlungsformen der *Straßenszene* abzuleiten. Es sind dies vor allem:

– Kopie und Variante: Die Darstellungen von Haltungen und Vorgängen müssen so deutlich ausgeformt sein, daß sie von jedem Mitspieler in ihrem Kern übernommen und in einem weiteren Schritt kontrolliert abgewandelt werden können.

– Gestische Analyse: Ein Vorgang wird unterteilt in Einzelvorgänge, in denen jeweils ein eindeutiger Einzelgestus sichtbar wird.

– Handlungsbilder: Dieser Begriff meint die Konzentration bestimmter wichtiger Handlungselemente in einer geschlossenen Form oder einem geschlossenen Formelement des Theatervorgangs.

– Szenische Situationsanalyse: Dieses Verfahren greift bestimmte herausragende Situationen heraus, die Gelenkstellen der Handlung, und entfaltet sie in Varianten unter jeweils veränderten Handlungsbedingungen. Hier setzt das ‹soziologische Experiment› an. Als direktes Vorbild bei Brecht kann die Umarbeitung des ursprünglichen Stückes *Der Jasager* zu dem Doppelstück *Der Jasager und Der Neinsager* gelten.

– Parallelszenen: Dieses Verfahren ist unter verschiedenen Aspekten von Brecht selbst entwickelt worden, vor allem in seinen Übungsstücken für Schauspieler. Für die L.-Arbeit sind sie ein Mittel, die Metapher des L. auf die Erfahrungs- und Vorstellungswelt der Spieler zu beziehen. Sie können darüber hinaus als Kontrastszenen, als Aktualisierungen, als Einblendungen von Assoziationen erscheinen.

Die Richtungen, in denen sich die Beschäftigung mit dem L. schließlich über Brecht hinaus weiterentwickelt hat, lassen sich nicht exakt voneinander absetzen; doch sind verschiedene Akzentuierungen auszumachen, die sich zugleich an bestimmten pädagogischen Arbeitsfeldern festmachen lassen. Die Versuche der Einmaligen Theatergruppe, *Die Ausnahme und die Regel* in der Beziehungsstruktur von Clowns zu interpretieren, fanden ihre Fortsetzung zum Teil als Theaterarbeit im Rahmen kultureller Lebenszusammenhänge unter Einbeziehung wiederentdeckter Elemente des Volkstheaters und der Volkskultur. L.-Arbeit kann weiter als exemplarischer Fall einer Lernform Theater vor allem im schulischen Bereich gelten. Dahinter stehen Versuche, Theaterarbeit und projektorientiertes Lernen in komplexer Weise miteinander zu verbinden.

Die breiteste L.-Praxis hat sich inzwischen in den Hochschulen entwickelt, und zwar unter den verschiedensten Aspekten und aus den unterschiedlichsten Motivationen heraus. Hier hat sich auch verhältnismäßig schnell der Prozeß einer Integration aller möglichen Spiel- und Theaterverfahren in die L.-Tätigkeit vollzogen. L.-Arbeit hat sich damit zu einem komplexen Verfahren der Spiel- und Theaterpädagogik entwickelt.

AG Außerschulische Bildung/Praml, W. u. a.: Modellprojekt «Zwischen Weltfirma und Dorf» – Ein Abschlußbericht. Frankfurt-Höchst o. J. (1982); Binnerts, P. u. a.: Die Ausnahme und die Regel. Ein Versuch mit dem Lehrstück von Bertolt Brecht. Berlin 1977; Koch, G./Steinweg R./Vaßen, F. (Hg.): Asoziales Theater, Erfahrungen durch Lehrstücke: Spielversuche und Anstiftung zur Praxis. Köln 1984; Richard, J.: Brechts ‹Lehrstücktheater und Lernen in der Schule›. In: Steinweg, R. (Hg.): Auf Anregung Bertolt Brechts. Frankfurt/M. 1978; Bitter, H. M.: Auf dem Weg zum Lehrstück in der Schule. In: Steinweg, R. (Hg.): Auf Anregung Bertolt Brechts. Frankfurt/M. 1978; ders.: Ausgangspunkt: Brecht, Versuche zum Lehrstück. Recklinghausen 1980; ders.: Berliner Lehrstückgut, der «Ozeanflug» mit Hauptschülern. In: Koch/Steinweg/Vaßen (Hg.): Asoziales Theater. Erfahrungen durch Lehrstücke, Spielversuche und Anstiftung zur Praxis. Köln 1984; Steinweg, R.: Das Lehrstück – ein Modell des sozialistischen Theaters. In: alternative 78/79 (1971); dies.: Das Lehrstück. Brechts Theorie einer politisch-ästhetischen Erziehung. Stuttgart 1972; dies. (Hg.): Brechts Modell der Lehrstücke. Zeugnisse, Diskussion, Erfahrungen. Frankfurt/M. 1976; dies. (Hg.): Auf Anregung Bertolt Brechts: Lehrstücke mit Schülern, Arbeitern, Theaterleuten. Frankfurt/M. 1978; Szondi, P.: Bertolt Brecht, Der Jasager und Der Neinsager. Vorlagen, Fassungen und Materialien. Frankfurt/M. 1966. – Eine vollständige Zusammenstellung der Literatur zum Lehrstückproblem findet sich in Koch/Steinweg/Vaßen 1984. Unveröffentlichte Literatur ist nahezu vollständig im Lehrstück-Archiv an der Universität Hannover einzusehen.

Hans Martin Ritter

Leibeigenentheater

Privates Adelstheater in Rußland, vom Gutsherrn aus leibeigenen Bauern zusammengestellt. Ende des 17. Jh. aufgekommen; bestand bis zur Aufhebung der Leibeigenschaft (1861). Am verbreitetsten (mehr als 170 L.) um die Wende vom 18. zum 19. Jh. Von Bedeutung für die Entwicklung des Theaters in Rußland waren die acht L. der Grafen Scheremetjew, das L. des Fürsten N. B. Jussupow, das L. des Grafen R. Woronzow.

Die L. sorgten nicht nur in Städten, sondern auch in der Provinz für die Verbreitung der Theaterkunst; sie waren überdies eine der Quellen, aus denen die Berufstheater sich speisten.

Dynnik, T.: Krepostnye aktery. Moskva 1927; dies.: Krepostnoj teatr. Moskva/Leningrad 1933; Šamurina, Z.: Krepostnye teatry. Moskva 1923.

Annelore Engel-Braunschmidt

Leipziger Theater

Mehrere Spielstätten (Schauspielhaus mit 797 Plätzen, Kellertheater mit 100 Plätzen, Neue Szene mit ca. 100 Plätzen, Rangfoyer). – Traditionsreiche Theaterstadt (seit Spätmittelalter), 1731 Beginn des deutschen Dramas mit der UA des *Sterbenden Cato* von Johann Christoph Gottsched (1700–66) durch die Truppe der «Neuberin» (d. i. Caroline Neuber, 1697–1760), 1766 Eröffnung Stadttheater, wichtigste Direktoren: 1775–77 Abel Seyler (1730–1800), 1818–28 Friedrich Theodor von Küstner (1784–1864), der 1817 das Stadttheater etablierte, 1869–70 Heinrich Laube (1806–84), 1870–76 Friedrich Haase (1825–1911), 1912–18 Max Martersteig (1853–1921), 1919–29 Alwin Kronacher, der das Alte Theater leitete und zu Viehweg am Schauspielhaus in produktivem Spannungsverhältnis stand, UA von Jahnns *Richard III* (1922), Brechts *Baal* (1923), und Tollers *Hinkemann* (1923), 1932–47 Hans Schüler, 1947–50 Max Krüger, 1950–54 Max Burghardt (1893–1977), 1954–58 Johannes Arpe (1897–1962), 1958–89 Karl Kayser (*1914). Kayser hat viele repräsentative Klassiker-Inszenierungen (vor allem Schiller) am L. T. inszeniert, die von einem traditionalistischen Theaterverständnis getragen wurden. 1990 hat sich das Leipziger «Theaterkombinat» aufgelöst, das Sprechtheater arbeitet in den o. g. Spielstätten als «Leipziger Schauspiel» unter Intendant Wolfgang Hauswald. Er setzt auf einen behutsamen, aber konsequenten Wandel der Theaterästhetik, die in der Ära Kayser zu Rhetorik und Naturalismus tendierte. Das Leipziger Schauspiel war 1991 erstmals Gastgeber der «euroscene», des «Festivals der europäischen Avantgarde». Eine Fortsetzung dieser west-osteuropäischen «Theatermesse» ist vorgesehen.

Eckard, F.: Das Leipziger Stadttheater unter C. Christian Schmidt. 1959; Funke, Ch./Hoffmann-Ostwald, D./Otto, H.-G.: Theater-Bilanz. Berlin (DDR) 1971, S. 242–244; Pietzsch, I.: Werkstatt Theater. Berlin (DDR) 1975, S. 68–75; Schulze, F.: 100 Jahre Leipziger Stadttheater. Leipzig 1917; Leipziger Bühnen. Leipzig 1956.

Andreas Roßmann/Roland Dreßler

Lesedrama

Das Wort L. (auch Buchdrama) bezeichnet ein Werk mit den äußeren Formmerkmalen eines Dramas, das aber nicht für die Bühne bestimmt ist bzw. auf technische und personelle Aufführbarkeit keine Rücksicht zu nehmen scheint. L. entstehen zum Teil aus dem Verzicht auf dramaturgische Informsetzung, so z. B. bei Seneca (4?–65 v. Chr.), bei dem die Textrezitation Vorrangstellung einnimmt, oder bei den Humanisten, die Platos (429–347 v. Chr.) Dialoge nachahmen; zum Teil aus der Nachahmung bestehender Theaterformen ohne Kenntnis der entsprechenden Bühnentechnik, wenn z. B. Sturm-und-Drang-Autoren Shakespeares (1564–1616) Szenentechnik nachahmen, ohne die Bühnentechnik der Elisabethanischen Zeit zu kennen. Die technische Perfektionierung und Entwicklung ermöglicht manchmal auch die Bühnenaufführung von Stücken, die urspr. als L. angesehen wurden, z. B. Christian Dietrich Grabbes (1801–36) *Napoleon oder die hundert Tage* (1831) oder Paul Claudels (1868–1955) *Der seidene Schuh* (1924). Neuerdings werden wieder bewußt und gezielt L. geschrieben, etwa von Rolf Hochhuth (*1931) mit Werken wie *Der Stellvertreter* (1963) oder *Die Soldaten* (1967), die zwar für die Bühne konzipiert sind, jedoch erst durch die Lektüre der beigefügten umfangreichen Dokumentation tiefer auf den Leser wirken.

Bernard Poloni

Libretto

(Diminutiv zu ital. libro; also kleines Buch) 1. Seit dem 18. Jh. ein in kleinem Format oder als Heft publiziertes Textbuch zu musikalischen Bühnenwerken; 2. im übertragenen Sinne der Text der musikalisch-dramatischen Werke selbst; 3. das Szenarium von Balletten und Pantomimen. Dieses von einem Librettisten konzipierte Szenarium reicht für eine Ballettgestaltung ebensowenig aus wie das Filmszenarium für einen Film. Ballette und Pantomimen bedürfen bei der Neuschöpfung der →Minutage.

Abert, A.: Libretto. In: Blume, F. (Hg.): Musik in Geschichte und Gegenwart. Bd. VII. Sp. 708–727. Kassel 1960; Riemann, H./Gurlitt, W.: Riemann Musiklexikon. Sachteil, S. 519–522. Mainz 1967.

Helga Ettl

Lieber Augustin

Name zweier Wiener Kabaretts, der in beiden Fällen auf den legenden-umwobenen Volkssänger der Pestzeit (1679) zurückgeht, Symbol des Willens zum Überleben auch unter ungünstigen Umständen.

1. Am 16. 11. 1901 eröffnete der Schriftsteller und Kritiker Felix Salten das «Jung-Wiener Theater zum Lieben Augustin», vom Programm eher ein literarisches Varieté als ein Kabarett – im ganzen eine wenig erfolgreiche Kopie des Wolzogenschen → «Überbrettl».

2. Die Schauspielerin Stella Kadmon eröffnete am 7. 11. 1931 ihren L. A., in dem – im Gegensatz zum sonst in Wien üblichen Stil – Zeitkritik, Satire und Parodie geboten wurden. War im Anfang Peter Hammerschlag fast alleiniger Autor, so kamen später F. Eckardt und die aus Deutschland emigrierten H. F. Koenigsgarten und G. H. Mostar hinzu und durch sie längere Szenen und → Mittelstücke, bis die Besetzung Österreichs 1938 auch diesem Kabarett ein Ende setzte. Kadmon mußte ins Exil nach Palästina gehen, wo sie in Tel Aviv das kurzlebige «Cabaret Papillon» gründete und später vor allem Vortragsabende gab. – Am 1. 6. 1945 wurde der L. A. von F. Eckardt wiedereröffnet, später von C. Merz geleitet, bis 1947 Stella Kadmon aus dem Exil zurückkehrte. Nach zwei Kabarett-Programmen wandelte sie den L. A. um in das «Theater der Courage», das sie über 30 Jahre leitete und in dem zahlreiche Ur- und Erstaufführungen moderner Dramatik stattfanden.

Bolbecher, S.: Vom «Lieben Augustin» zum «Theater der Courage». In: Die Welt des Jura Soyfer. Wien 1991; Hakel, H.: Wiennärrische Welt. Wien 1961; ders.: Wigl-Wogl. Wien 1962; Hammerschlag, P.: Der Mond schlägt grad halb acht. Wien/Hamburg 1972; Joukhadar, M.: «Theater der Courage». Diss. Wien 1980; Reisner, I.: Kabarett als Werkstatt des Theaters. Diss. Wien 1961; Rösler, W. (Hg.): Geh ma halt a bisserl unter. Berlin 1991; Veigl, H.: Lachen im Keller. Wien 1986; Weys, R.: Cabaret und Kabarett in Wien. Wien 1970.

Wolfgang Beck

Liebhaber

1. Dilettant, Laie, Amateur; entsprechend → L.-Theater oder L.-Bühne das Theater privater Gruppen seit dem 18. Jh., z. B. das L.-Theater am Weimarer Hof (1775–84), an dem Goethe als Schauspieler, Autor und Regisseur mitwirkte; das Düsseldorfer L.-Theater unter Karl Immermann (1828). 2. → Rollenfach: jugendlicher, sentimentaler, komischer, tragischer usw. L.

Horst Schumacher

Liebhabertheater

Theateraufführungen von Laien im 18. und 19. Jh. Im höfischen Bereich die Einstudierung und Aufführung von Schäferspielen, Opern, Operetten, Balletten, Schattenspielen, Zauber- und Puppenspielen, Maskeraden u. a. Alle Rollen, oft auch die Musikbegleitung, wurden von den adeligen Mitgliedern des jeweiligen Hofes übernommen. Diese Veranstaltungen dienten ausschließlich dem Amüsement des Hofes und seiner Gäste. Eine besondere Rolle nimmt das von Goethe 1776 am Weimarer Hof eingerichtete L. ein; dem Weimarer Vorbild folgten die Höfe in Kassel, Meiningen, Gotha, Darmstadt und Karlsruhe.

Im nichthöfischen Bereich wird das L., das sich auch Dilettantentheater nennt, vom Bürgertum in den Städten getragen (→ Amateurtheater). In den Anfängen noch beschränkt auf die Darstellung biblischer Stoffe und auf Motive der Historie, entwickelt es sich zu einem reinen → Unterhaltungstheater mit Schwerpunkt auf Lustspielen, Schwänken und kleinen dramatischen Szenen, die im Familienkreis oder vor geladenen Gästen gezeigt werden. Die strenge Abgrenzung dieser Theaterform zum Berufsschauspiel wird in der ebenfalls gebräuchlichen (historischen) Bezeichnung ‹Privattheater› deutlich. Mit der immer größeren Beliebtheit des Dilettantentheaters ging auch eine Diskussion um seine Berechtigung einher. Schon früh wurde die Gefahr einer Selbstüberschätzung seiner Betreiber erkannt und in einer Vielzahl von Anleitungs- und Lehrbüchern seine Möglichkeiten und Grenzen beschrieben. Es wurde ihm zugestanden, zur «Unterhaltung, Anregung und Erheiterung kleinerer Kreise» zu dienen. Wie das erfolgreich durchzuführen sei, erklärten Bücher wie *Das Liebhaber-Theater wie es sein soll!*, *Dilettantentheater für Damen* und *Katechismus für Liebhaber-Bühnen und Anfänger in der Darstellungskunst*. Ende des 19. Jh. verstärkte sich die Entwicklung hin zur Gründung von Theatervereinen, die nicht mehr in ‹jedem beliebigen größeren Zimmer› spielen konnten und eine größere Öffentlichkeit suchten. Sie schlossen sich 1893 in einer Dachorganisation zusammen (→ Bund Deutscher Amateurtheater).

Falck, R.: Zur Geschichte des Liebhabertheaters. Berlin 1887; Sichardt, G.: Das Weimarer Liebhabertheater unter Goethes Leitung. Weimar 1957.

Ute Hagel

Lilla Teatern

(Kleines Theater) In Finnland sind insgesamt fünf schwedischsprachige Berufstheater tätig: das Schwedische Theater in Helsinki, als schwedischsprachige Nationalbühne, das Schwedische Theater von Åbo, das Wasa Theater in Vaasa und das Schultheater sowie das Kleine Theater in Helsinki. Das 1940 gegründete Kleine Theater ist von diesen Theatern das originellste. Anfangs arbeitete es im wesentlichen als kleine Revuebühne. Erst als im Jahr 1955 Vivica Bandler die Leitung übernahm, entwickelte es sich zu der radikalsten Avantgarde-Bühne der nordischen Länder. Ausländische Regisseure und Bühnenbildner gastierten am L. T., das viele Gastspielreisen durch Europa unternahm. 1967 wurden die Schauspieler Lasse Pöysti und Birgitta Ulfsson Leiter des Theaters; sie bauten das Programm hauptsächlich auf eigenen Produktionen auf. Schwedischsprachigen Dramatikern wurden aktuelle Stücke in Auftrag gegeben, die jeweils in enger Zusammenarbeit mit der Schauspieltruppe entstanden. Oft waren diese Stücke gesellschaftskritisch; zur Tagespolitik wurde mit spontan entstandenen Kabarett-Programmen Stellung genommen. Mit Asko Sarkola als Intendanten nahm der Anteil an Klassikern im Programm zu, aber auch an aktuellen Interpretationen. Heute spielt die Bühne sowohl auf schwedisch als auch auf finnisch. – 1985 erhielt das L. T. die Auszeichnung des europäischen Rates.

Anneli Suur-Kujala

Literatur am Naschmarkt

Wie die als Freiluftkabarett gegründete «Stachelbeere» ging auch die L. a. N. aus dem «Bund junger Autoren Österreichs» hervor. Wenige Monate nach der Konkurrentin wurde sie am 3. 11. 1933 eröffnet, so genannt nach den Intentionen ihrer Gründer (F. W. Stein, R. Weys u. a.) und der Lage ihres Auftrittsorts. Von Anfang an wurde in der L. a. N. das Schwergewicht auf szenische Texte gelegt, dominierte hier das ‹Theater›. Schon bald bildeten die in der L. a. N. entwickelten →Mittelstücke das von normalem Nummernkabarett umrahmte Rückgrat des Programms. Zu den Autoren gehörten u. a. R. Weys, H. Weigel, F. Torberg und J. Soyfer. Man spielte nicht nur Bearbeitungen und selbstgeschriebene Mittelstücke, sondern auch Einakter von Nestroy, Offenbach und (als dt. Erstaufführung) Th. Wilders *The Long Christmas Dinner*. Ihren Höhepunkt erlebte die L. a. N. in der Saison 1936/37, in der zeitweilig drei Ensembles spielten, eines im Stammhaus, je eines auf Tournee durch die Tschechoslowakei und Österreich. Nach dem ‹Anschluß› Österreichs wurden alle Kabaretts verboten bzw. lösten sich selbst auf.

Das Mitglied der L. a. N., A. Müller-Reitzner, erhielt als Parteimitglied der NSDAP im Spätherbst 1938 den offiziellen Auftrag, ein linientreues Kabarett zu gründen. Mit den nach Emigration und Verhaftungen verbliebenen Autoren und Kabarettisten der L. a. N. eröffnete er am 29. 1. 1939 das «Wiener Werkel», das trotz zahlreicher Schwierigkeiten bis zur allg. Schließung der Theater 1944 bestand und in versteckter Form immer wieder Kritik an der Politik der Nationalsozialisten übte. – Im Juni 1945 nahm das «Wiener Werkel» als «Literatur im Moulin Rouge» den Betrieb wieder auf, mußte aber wegen fehlenden Publikumsinteresses bereits am 20. 1. 1946 endgültig schließen.

Hakel, H.: Wiennärrische Welt. Wien 1961; ders. (Hg.): Wigl-Wogl. Wien 1962; Kühn, V. (Hg.): Deutschlands Erwachen. Berlin 1989; Lang, M.: Kleinkunst im Widerstand. Das Wiener Werkel. Diss. Wien 1967; Reisner, I.: Kabarett als Werkstatt des Theaters. Diss. Wien 1961; Rösler, W. (Hg.): Geh ma halt a bisserl unter. Berlin 1991; Veigl, Hans: Lachen im Keller. Wien 1986; Weigel H.: Gerichtstag vor 49 Leuten. Graz 1981; Weys, R.: Cabaret und Kabarett in Wien. Wien 1970; ders.: Literatur am Naschmarkt. Wien 1947.

Wolfgang Beck

Little Theatre Movement

Entstanden um 1910 in den USA als Versuch einer Antwort auf den kommerziellen Theaterbetrieb. Die L. T. M. bestand zunächst nur aus kleinen → Amateurtheatergruppen, die Werke von geistiger und ästhetischer Relevanz bei gleichzeitigen Experimenten mit neuen Techniken anboten. Wichtige Impulse gingen von Maeterlinck, Meyerhold, Rouché und anderen Praktikern und Theoretikern des europ. Experimentiertheaters aus. Bei zunehmender Professionalisierung und regionaler Ausdifferenzierung in drei Grundtypen (Art Theatres in den Großstädten, Community Theatres in Kleinstädten und College Theatres an den Hochschulen) entstanden häufig unüberwindliche Finanzierungsschwierigkeiten, die rasch zur Schließung oder zur Absorption durch das Kommerztheater führten. Seinen Höhepunkt erreichte die L. T. M. mit den → Provincetown Players und den → Washington Square Players. Bevor die L. T. M. erst 1915 New York erreichte, waren freie «Art Theatres» in Boston und Chicago entstanden: Hull House Players, Robertson Players (beide 1907); Toy Theatre, Chicago Little Theatre (beide 1912). Die 1910 gegr. «Drama League of America», die 1925 in eine «National Theatre Conference» überging, bildete das theoretische und organisatorische Dach. Die wichtigsten Universitätstheater waren die Dakota Players (Prof. F. Koch, 1906); Wisconsin Players (T. H. Dickinson, 1911) und vor allem «47 Workshop» (G. P. Baker, Harvard University, 1912). Baker gründete

1925 das Yale University Theatre. Er hatte grundsätzlichen Anteil an der Verankerung der Ausbildung professioneller Theaterschaffender (Regisseure, Dramaturgen, Schauspieler etc.) in den Drama Departments der Universitäten. Die wichtigsten Community Theatres, die heute noch bestehen, sind das Cleveland Playhouse (1917) und die Pasadena Community Playhouse Association (1918). Zwischen 1910 und 1929 gab es ca. 1000 nichtkommerzielle Theater innerhalb der L. T. M. Diejenigen, die als professionelle Theater überlebten, waren New Yorker «Art Theatres» wie z. B. Neighborhood Playhouse, Equity Players, Civic Repertory Theatre. Das wesentliche Ziel der L. T. M., künstlerisch relevantes Theater dezentral, d. h. außerhalb New Yorks, zu etablieren, war mißlungen.

Downer, A.: Fifty Years of American Drama, 1900–50. Chicago 1951; Fröhlich, P.: Das nichtkommerzielle amerik. Theater. Rheinfelden 1974; Gagey, E. M.: Revolution in American Drama. New York 1948.

Dieter Herms

Living Newspaper

Wichtigste Form des Agitproptheaters in den USA der 1930er Jahre, gleichsam mit Notwendigkeit aus der sozialen Krise der ‹Great Depression› entwickelt. Das L. N. bestand aus einer episodisch strukturierten Szenenfolge, die – zumeist kollektiv erarbeitet – aktuelle politische Probleme und ihre soziohistorischen Hintergründe behandelte, unter künstlerischem Einsatz von Musik, Film, Radio, Schattenspielen etc. Der Name L. N. bedeutete jedoch auch die Verlebendigung von Zeitungskommentaren, Statistiken, Reden etc. Im Rahmen des → Federal Theatre gab es 1936 bis 1939 sieben ‹Ausgaben› des L. N. Bereits die ersten, unter dem Titel *Ethiopia* als dokumentarische → Montage der Vorgänge in Abessinien konzipiert, wurden staatlich untersagt, da Mussolini und Haile Selassie darin auftraten. Die wichtigsten anderen, *Triple – A Plowed Under, Injunction Granted, One Third of a Nation*, behandelten soziale Probleme in den USA. Neben einem Repertoire in New York wurde das L. N. auch als Genre eingesetzt in politischen Auseinandersetzungen, z. B. ‹Strike Marches On› bei der Fabrikbesetzung von General Motors in Flint, Michigan, durch die neu gegründete Gegengewerkschaft CIO.

Bültemann, U.: Produktion und Aufführung des Living Newspaper ‹Strike Marches On›. In: Gulliver 4 (1978), 140–146; Goldman, A.: Life and Death of the Living Newspaper Unit. In: Theatre Quarterly 3 (1973), 69–89; McDermott, D.: The Living Newspaper as a Dramatic Form. In: Modern Drama 8 (1965), 82–94.

Dieter Herms

Living Theatre

Eines der am längsten bestehenden US-Theater überhaupt, das von 1951 bis 1985 (mit Unterbrechungen) noch unter Leitung der beiden Gründer Julian Beck (1925–85) und Judith Malina (*1926) funktioniert und arbeitet. Bis 1963 produzierte das L. T. in verschiedenen Häusern der Off-Broadway-Szene New Yorks; die wichtigste Inszenierung dieser Phase war *The Brig* von K. Brown, durch die der autoritäre Charakter der US-Gesellschaft entlarvt wurde. Gefängnis und Gewalt erscheinen als zentrale Metaphern eines repressiven Systems, das die Menschen in Opfer und Exekutierer aufteilt. Die bedeutsamsten Produktionen entstanden 1963 bis 1968 in Europa: *Mysteries and Smaller Pieces* (insgesamt 265mal aufgeführt), *Frankenstein, Antigone, Paradise Now*. In ihnen wurde die Zusammenführung der Beckschen pazifistisch-anarchistischen Grundhaltung mit der Artaudschen Konzeption des Theaters der Armut als immer wieder variierte Auflösung der Grenzen zwischen Theater und Leben, Fiktion und Realität, Ästhetik und Politik praktiziert und zelebriert. Eine siebenmonatige Tournee der USA mit allen vier Produktionen 1968 brachte auch den Durchbruch des L. T. an der ‹Heimatfront› und ein partielles Einmünden in die dortigen Oppositionsbewegungen als →Guerilla- und →Straßentheater.

Der Aufenthalt des L. T. in Brasilien 1969 bis 1971 resulierte in mehreren Szenen und Bestandteilen des projektierten Zyklus *The Legacy of Cain*, Variationen zum Gewalt-Thema. Fortgesetzt wurde die Arbeit am Zyklus in Pittsburgh 1974 bis 1975, wo ein Stipendium der Mellon-Stiftung auch eine gewisse ökonomische Basis schuf. Sicherlich unter dem Einfluß von Einsichten in die Mechanismen des Stahlimperiums entstanden hier: *Six Public Acts to Transmute Violence into Concord: Tampering with the Master/Slave System: Ceremonies* und *Processions: Changing Pittsburgh: Prologue to the Legacy of Cain* und *The Money Tower* (beide 1975). Die wichtigste Produktion einer Phase, da man auf mehreren europ. Festivals gastierte (1976–78), war *Prometheus*, die Version und Vision des L. T. von Kreativität und Revolution.

Ende 1983 kehrte die Truppe nach New York zurück und stieß mit den Inszenierungen *Masse Mensch* (E. Toller), *The Yellow Methuselah* und *The Archeology of Sleep* bei Publikum und Kritikern auf Unverständnis. Erst das 1986 als Hommage an den ein Jahr zuvor verstorbenen Julian Beck veranstaltete *Restrospectacle*, ein Zusammenschnitt aus Inszenierungen der 35jährigen Geschichte des L. T., war erfolgreich und förderte die Bildung eines neuen Ensembles. 1989 ließ sich das L. T. in New York wieder in einem festen Haus nieder und spielte u. a. *German Requiem* (Eric Bentley), *The Body of God, Tumult* und *I and I* (Lasker-Schüler).

Beeinflußt von Meyerhold, Piscator, Artaud und Brecht sowie von nachhaltigem Einfluß auf Gruppen wie das →Bread and Puppet Theatre und das Firehouse Theatre in den USA, Orbe-Récherche théâtrale und Théâtre du chêne noir in Frankreich, CAST und Red Ladder Theatre in England, kann das L. T. gleichwohl keinem bestimmten Typus zugerechnet werden. Seine Techniken umfaßten annähernd alles, was das alternative Theater der letzten 40 Jahre kennzeichnet: Collage, Montage, Improvisation, physische Einbeziehung des Publikums, Prozession, mystische Kommunikation, Happening, politisches Theater, Straßentheater, Guerillatheater, Environmental Theatre. Alle Formen trugen bei zu jener Einheit von «life, revolution and theatre» mit dem Ziel eines «unconditional NO to the present society» (J. Beck, 1968). In welchem Ausmaß das L. T. in der Tat die Kreise der Herrschenden störte, zeigen die nicht mehr zu zählenden Verhaftungen, Prozesse und Verurteilungen Becks und Malinas und anderer Akteure. Das L. T. gab Anlaß zu zahlreichen Neugründungen und Abspaltungen in Europa und beiden Amerikas. Es ist das internationalste US-Theater der Neuzeit, wobei neben São Paulo vor allem Rom, Paris (bzw. Avignon) und West-Berlin als wichtige Stationen außerhalb der USA gelten müssen.

Bartolucci, G.: The Living Theatre. Roma 1970; Beck, J.: The Life of the Theatre. San Francisco 1972; Biner, P.: Le Living Theatre. Lausanne 1968; Brown, K. H.: The Brig. With an Essay on the Living Theatre by Julian Beck and Director's Notes by Judith Malina. New York 1965; Kothes, M. M.: Guerilla Theater. Tübingen 1990; Malina, J./Beck, J.: Paradise Now. New York 1971; Neff, R.: The Living Theatre: USA. New York 1970; Rostagno, A./Beck, J./Malina, J. (Hg.): We, The Living Theatre. New York 1970; Shank, T.: American Alternative Theatre. London 1982.

Uschi Bauer/Dieter Herms

Liyuan (Birnengarten)

Traditionelle Bezeichnung für das chin. Musiktheater (→Chin. Theater). Auf Veranlassung des musikliebenden und -kundigen Kaisers Xuanzong (reg. 712–56) der Tang-Dynastie wurde in der Hauptstadt Chang'an, dem heutigen Xi'an, eine Schule zur Ausbildung von Musikern und Tänzern eingerichtet. Als Ort wurde ein Campus des Namens «Birnengarten» gewählt. Der Kaiser selbst besuchte diese Schule mehrmals und unterzog die Schüler einer Prüfung. Schon bald wurde der Name liyuan auch für andere Institutionen des Unterhaltungsgewerbes verwendet. Später wurde der Name auf die Schauspieler übertragen, die sich seitdem «Jünger des Birnengartens» (l. zidi) nannten. Wie das Leben des Kaisers Xuanzong insgesamt, wurde auch die Gründung der Musikschule im liyuan Gegenstand der Legendenbildung. So erzählte man sich, daß der Kaiser eine Reise unternahm, um seine zum Mond entflogene Lieblingskonkubine Yang Guifei zurückzuholen. Auf dem Mond, im Jadepalast, hörte er ein so herrliches Orchester, daß er beschloß, ein solches auch in seinem eigenen Palast einzurichten. – Kaiser Xuanzong wurde später als Ahnherr und Schutzgott der Schauspieler verehrt. Seine Liebe zu Yang Guifei war Thema mehrerer bedeutender Dramen.

Ren Bantang: Tang xinong. Shanghai 1984, S. 1111–1152.

Bernd Eberstein

Loa

Prolog zur →Comedia des klassischen span. Theaters, seit Juan del Encina (1469?–1529?). Im 17. Jh. auch im religiösen Theater mit allegorischem Charakter vor dem →Auto Sacramental.

Flecniakoska, J.-L.: La ‹Loa› comme source pour la connaissance des rapports troupe-public. In: Dramaturgie et Société. Paris (1968), pp. 111–116.

Martin Franzbach

Lokalposse

Die L. ist die heitere Form des Lokalstücks, d. h. eines realistisch gehaltenen →Volksstücks, das mittels meist typisierter Personen die Eigentümlichkeiten einer Stadt, seltener einer Gegend, auf der Bühne darstellt – etwa die lokale Mundart, lokale Sitten, Lebensformen und Verhältnisse. Neben der rein komischen bzw. parodierenden L. sind auch das moralisch unterweisende Sittenstück und das sozialkritisch orientierte →Volksstück zu erwähnen. Die aus Italien – mit landschaftlich gebundenen Sondertypen im Zusammenhang mit der →Commedia dell'arte – über Frankreich, v. a. mit der Pariser L. in den dt. Sprachraum gekommene L. hat sich hier in einzelnen Zentren, meist Großstädten, etabliert. So entwickelt sich in der zweiten Hälfte des 18. Jh. die Wiener L. mit den →lustigen Personen Thaddädl und Rochus Pumpernickel, mit Emanuel Schikaneders (1751–1812) Dummem Anton, Josef Anton Stranitzkys (1676–1726) Hanswurst, Johann Joseph Laroches (1745–1806) Kasperl oder Adolf Bäuerles (1786–1859) Staberl. Ihren Höhepunkt stellen die →Possen Johann Nepomuk Nestroys (1801–62) dar. Weitere wichtige Zentren sind Berlin mit dem Berliner Lokalstück seit dem 19. Jh. – Karl von Holtei (1798–1880), Adolf Glassbrenner (1810–76); München mit den L. von

Ludwig Thoma (1867–1921) bzw. Bayern, wo die L. als Dialektposse fortlebt und von Laienbühnen, z. B. dem ‹Bauerntheater› in Regensburg, aufgeführt wird; Hamburg (v. a. ‹Ohnsorg-Theater›), wo Formen der satirischen L. und der sozialen Satire nebeneinander bestehen; Frankfurt und Darmstadt mit Ernst Niebergalls (1815–1843) Charakterkomödien (*Der Datterich*, 1841) und schließlich das Elsaß, in dem seit Georg Daniel Arnolfs (1780–1829) *Pfingstmontag* (1816) ein reges lokales Mundarttheater gepflegt wird.

Klotz, V.: Bürgerliches Lachtheater. München 1980.

Bernard Poloni

London Contemporary Dance School

R. Howard (* 1924) holt 1963 die Graham Company nach England. 1966 gründet er die L. C. D. S, aus der ein Jahr später das London Contemporary Dance Theatre hervorgeht. Die Direktion übernimmt R. Cohan (* 1925). Cohans Versuch, die Graham-Technik für Europa zu adaptieren, führt zur Eingliederung des Graham-Stils in das europäische Tanztheater. Ausbildungsprogramm: Certificate-Kurs und ab 1982 für qualifizierte Tänzer mit Universitätsreife der Degree-Kurs. Die L. C. D. S. ist eines der ersten westeuropäischen Ausbildungsinstitute, das den Schwerpunkt seiner Arbeit auf die Tanzerziehung an Hochschulen und Volkshochschulen legt. Jeder erfolgreiche Absolvent des Degree-Kurses schließt mit dem Bachelor of Arts in Contemporary Dance ab.

Wohlfahrt, H. Th.: Die London Contemporary Dance School. In: Ballett-Journal/ Das Tanzarchiv 2 (1984), S. 36–39.

Patricia Stöckemann

Long-Run-System

Engl. Bezeichnung für einen Serienspielplan an Stelle eines wechselnden →Repertoires (→en suite). Eingeführt und durchgesetzt Mitte des 19. Jh. durch Charles Kean im Londoner Princess Theatre. Sowohl die anderen Londoner Bühnen als auch Provinztheater gingen zu diesem System über, was dazu führte, daß Experimente weitgehend unmöglich wurden, neue Schauspieler und Regisseure kaum noch Arbeitsmöglichkeiten bekamen und frühes Star-System sich ausbildete.

Wolfgang Beck

Lord Chamberlain

Der L. C. war ursprünglich ein wichtiger Funktionsträger am brit. Königshof (→Theaterzensur). Zur Zeit der Tudor- und Stuartmonarchie (16. und 17. Jh.) war er durch das ihm unterstellte Amt des ‹Master of the Revels› für die Unterhaltung am Hof zuständig, was Maskenspiele und dramatische Aufführungen einschloß. Zu seinen Aufgaben zählte auch die Zulassung sämtlicher Theaterstücke zur Aufführung und Drucklegung. 1737 wurde dem L. C. direkt die Kontrolle über die Bühnen im Bereich der City of Westminster, also dem westlichen Zentrum Londons, übertragen. Durch die Lizenzverordnung (Licensing Act) von 1737 und durch das Theatergesetz von 1843 wurde er ermächtigt, alle Dramen zu zensieren, die als verleumderisch, obszön, blasphemisch oder zum Aufruhr gegen Krone und Staatskirche beitragend angesehen wurden. Tatsächlich kam es von Anfang an immer wieder zu Fällen politischer Zensur. Lösten Henry Fieldings politische Satiren im frühen 18. Jh. die Zensurgesetzgebung aus, so unterdrückte der L. C. im Gefolge der Frz. Revolution gesellschaftskritische Stücke, und noch in den 60er Jahren des 20. Jh. kam es zu teils moralisch, teils politisch motivierten Verbotsfällen, z. B. bei Edward Bonds *Early Morning* (1967). Nach langem Widerstand vieler Theaterschaffender und etlichen Skandalen wurde auf Grund eines Parlamentsbeschlusses die Zensurfunktion des L. C. abgeschafft, was besonders für das entstehende Alternativtheater eine befreiende Wirkung hatte.

Bentley, G.: The Profession of Dramatist in Shakespeare's Time, 1590–1642. Princeton 1971; Conolly, L. W.: The Censorship of English Drama 1737–1824. San Marino (Cal.) 1976; Klotz, G.: Alternativen im britischen Drama der Gegenwart. Berlin 1978.

J. Lawrence Guntner

Luisenburg-Festspiele

Auf einer 700 m hoch gelegenen Freilichtbühne im Fichtelgebirge, nahe bei der fränkischen Stadt Wunsiedel, finden von Ende Mai bis Mitte August die L. statt. Schon im 17. und 18. Jh. wurden in dem mittelalterlichen Los- oder Luchsburg genannten Felsenlabyrinth Schüleraufführungen veranstaltet; sie gilt als das älteste →Naturtheater in Deutschland. Am Beginn des 19. Jh. wurde die Ruine nach Preußens Königin Luise benannt. Der Münchner Generalintendant Ritter von Possart löste 1914 die Heimatspiele durch Berufstheater, die Künstlerspiele, ab. Heute kommen namhafte Schauspieler zum Sommertheater nach Wunsiedel. Die erfolgreiche Praxis der Stückauswahl hält sich an Klassiker wie Goethe, Shakespeare und Kleist, die in volkstümlicher Manier gespielt werden, daneben die klassisch gewordenen zeitgenössischen Autoren wie Sartre, Dürrenmatt und Brecht, umgeben von heiteren süddt.-österr. Theaterstücken. Intendant: Prof. Hans Peter Doll.

An eine natürliche, von Felsen und Bäumen abgeschlossene Bühne schließt sich eine ovale Zuschauerarena an, die, 1970 neu konstruiert, mit einem Regendach versehen, ca. 1800 Zuschauer aufnimmt.

Ute Hagel / Red.

Lustige Person

Die L. P. ist eine typisierte komische Bühnenfigur, die seit der Antike in verschiedenen historischen und lokalen Varianten immer wieder im europ. Theater vorkommt. Sie hat stets eine doppelte Funktion: einerseits soll sie durch Aussehen, Gestik und Wortwitz das Publikum belustigen, andererseits ist sie als antithetische Parallelfigur zum Helden ein Element der Relativierung des Geschehens auf der Bühne, der Durchbrechung der Illusion auch, indem sie sich oft direkt ans Publikum wendet (→aparte, Beiseitesprechen). Die typischen Züge der L. P., die meist als Lieblingsfigur des breiten Publikums auch nach dessen Lieblingsessen genannt wird, sind Gefräßigkeit, zügelloser sexueller Appetit, Tölpelhaftigkeit, verbunden mit Prahlsucht, Gerissenheit, Possenreißerei und Spottlust, zusammen mit einem lächerlichen Räsonierbedürfnis. Oft kennzeichnen sich die nationalen Varianten der L. P. auch durch eine groteske Vergröberung und komische Übertreibung der typischen Eigenschaften des entsprechenden Landes. Die antike Komödie, z. B. bei Aristophanes (455–386 v. Chr.) in Griechenland, Plautus (250–184 v. Chr.) und Terenz (185?–160 v. Chr.) in Rom, und der →Mimus kennen bereits feste, typisierte L. P., v. a. im Sklaven und →Diener; das Mittelalter seinerseits kennt die ersten L. P. des dt. Theaters mit dem Salbenkrämer-Gehilfen Rubin im Passionsspiel und dem geprellten Teufel im geistlichen Drama, während das →Fastnachtsspiel der frühneuhochdeutschen Zeit diese Tradition mit dem Typ des grobianischen, zugleich listigen und tölpelhaften Bauern, etwa bei Hans Folz (1479–um 1510), Hans Rosenplüt (um 1400–70) und Hans Sachs (1494–1576), fortsetzt. Mit dem Aufkommen der Wandertruppen im 16./17. Jh. diversifiziert sich der Typ der L. P. in Europa; in Italien sind es die landschaftlich gebundenen Figuren der →Commedia dell'arte wie Arlecchino, der Dottore oder Pantalone, die die span. Szene mit der Gestalt des Gracioso, die frz. bei Molière (1622–73) sowie mit den Figuren →Harlequin, Jean Potage (= Hans

564 Lustspiel

Suppe) und dem um 1815 in Lyon entstandenen →Guignol beeinflussen; in England sind es der Narr im →Elisabethanischen Theater, wo er bei William Shakespeare (1564–1616) die dramatische Funktion des antiken Chors übernimmt, in den →Haupt- und Staatsaktionen der Folgezeit dagegen anti-tragisch wirkt, und der von Robert Reynolds 1618 geschaffene →Pickelhering der →Englischen Komödianten. Ähnliche L. P. entstehen dann auch im dt.-sprachigen Raum, etwa der um 1700 von Joseph Anton Stranitzky (1676–1726) neu belebte →Hanswurst, der als Kasperl bzw. als verwandte Gestalt bei Ferdinand Raimund (1790–1836), Johann Nepomuk Nestroy (1801–62) oder Ludwig Anzengruber (1839–89) auf der Salzburger und Wiener Bühne fortleben sollte. Johann Christoph Gottsched (1700–66) indessen bekämpft in Deutschland die L. P. unnachgiebig, weil sie die Einheit und Wirkung des ernsten Dramas sprenge; 1737 wird sie von Friederike Caroline Neuber (1697–1760) in einem in Leipzig aufgeführten feierlichen allegorischen Vorspiel von der Bühne verbannt. Auch die Berechtigung von Rolle und Funktion der L. P. durch Gotthold Ephraim Lessing (1729–81) in der *Hamburgischen Dramaturgie* (1767–69), Justus Möser (1720–94) und den jungen Johann Wolfgang Goethe (1749–1832) konnte die Verbannung von der nord- und mitteldeutschen Bühne nicht wettmachen, während sich die L. P. in Österreich und im süddt. Raum als Staberl oder Thaddädl behauptet und manchmal sogar zum echten Charakter wird. In neuerer Zeit bleibt die L. P. die Kernfigur des Dialektstücks und lebt außerhalb des Theaters im →Zirkus als →Clown weiter. Gleichzeitig erfährt sie als Schwejk eine Umwandlung ihrer Funktion, die parallel zur Umwandlung der gesamttheatralischen Perspektive verläuft.

Höllerer, W.: Zwischen Klassik und Moderne. Stuttgart 1958; Rommel, O.: Die Alt-Wiener Volkskomödie. Wien 1952.

Bernard Poloni

Lustspiel

1. Dt. Begriff, weitgehend Synonym für →Komödie. 2. Ausschließlich bei gewissen dt. Theoretikern wird zwischen L. und Komödie unterschieden. August Wilhelm Schlegel (1767–1845) behauptet in den Wiener *Vorlesungen über dramatische Kunst und Literatur* (1808), die Tragödie spiele in einer idealistischen, die Komödie in einer phantastischen, das L. in einer wahrscheinlichen Welt (von der Neuen attischen Komödie an). Für Otto Rommel ist die Komödie satirisch konzentriert auf die dem Lachen ausgesetzte ‹komische Gestalt›; das L. werde mittels des Humors in ‹heitere Gelöstheit› gerückt. Diese Unterscheidung hat sich weder in der

Forschung noch in der komischen Produktion durchzusetzen vermocht. Im Ausland gibt es sie nicht.

Grimm, R./Bergmann, K. (Hg.): Wesen und Formen des Komischen im Drama. Darmstadt 1975; Schrimpf, H.J.: Komödie und Lustspiel. In: Zs. f. dt. Phil. 97/1978, Sonderheft: Festgabe für B. v. Wiese, S. 152–182.

Gérard Schneilin

Lyceum Theatre

Londoner Theater, von James Payne 1765 für die Society of Artists erbaut. 1794 richtete Dr. Samuel Arnold das Haus für den Gebrauch als Konzert- und Ausstellungshalle ein. So fand im Lyceum u. a. die erste Ausstellung der Wachsfiguren Madame Tussauds statt (1802). Für das Jahr 1805 ist gesichert, daß zwei Theater existierten und auch bespielt wurden. 1809 ging das Theater an Samuel Arnold, den Sohn Dr. Arnolds, der die Genehmigung erhielt, das ‹Lyceum› im Sommer als Opernhaus zu betreiben. Nachdem das ‹Drury Lane Theatre› abgebrannt war, spielte dessen Ensemble von 1809 bis 1812 im ‹Lyceum›. War das Haus 1792 in Programmzetteln als ‹Theatrical Saloon, Lyceum›, betitelt worden, so wird es 1810 zum erstenmal ‹Theatre Royal, Lyceum› genannt. Das Programm bestand zu dieser Zeit aus →Ballad Operas, →Musicals und →Melodramen. Umbau 1816. Das ‹Lyceum› war das erste Londoner Theater, das für die Bühne Gasbeleuchtung benutzte (ab August 1817). 1830 brannte das Haus nieder. Es wurde 1834 wieder aufgebaut und im selben Jahr neu eröffnet. In den folgenden Jahrzehnten wurde das Theater u. a. von Madame Vestris mit ihrer Truppe, Kate Bateman und Ellen Terry, der Mutter Edward Gordon Craigs, bespielt. – Anfang des 20. Jh. wurde das Haus kurzfristig als Music-Hall benutzt, bis 1907 Smith und Carpenter das ‹Lyceum› übernahmen und mit ihren Shakespeare-Inszenierungen überaus erfolgreich waren. Danach führten die Melvilles das Theater (ab 1909), die eine neue, sehr erfolgreiche Tradition begründeten, welche 30 Jahre anhielt. Die letzten Vorstellungen fanden vom 28. Juni bis 1. Juli 1939 statt (*Hamlet* mit John Gielgud in der Titelrolle). Heute dient das L. als Tanzpalast.

Frenzel, H. A.: Geschichte des Theaters. München 1979; Rosenfeld, S.: Early Lyceum Theatres. In: Theatre Notebook, Vol. XVIII (1964); The Oxford Companion to the Theatre. Ed. by Ph. Hartnell. London/New York/Toronto 1951.

Elke Kehr

566   La Maddalena

La Maddalena

Teil eines 1973 gegründeten feministischen Kulturzentrums in Rom und bisher das einzige ital. Theater, das ausschließlich von Frauen kollektiv geleitet, betrieben und verwaltet wird. Arbeitsbereiche des Kollektivs: Aufarbeitung der Geschichte der Unterdrückung der Frau in Vergangenheit und Gegenwart; Entwicklung einer autonomen weiblichen Sprache, die nicht durch die Erfahrungen der Männer geprägt ist (→ Frauentheater). L. M. versteht sich als offener Workshop, in dem Frauen ihre theatralischen Fähigkeiten erproben können. Es gibt kein festes Ensemble, sondern einzelne Produktionsgruppen. Die ersten Arbeiten des Kollektivs hatten stark didaktischen Charakter und behandelten die üblichen Fragen feministischer Diskussion: die Rolle der Frau in der Gesellschaft, Partnerschaftsproblematik, Frauen im Beruf, Funktion der Familie, Abtreibung, Prostitution. Eine zweite Arbeitsphase bildete die verstärkte Beschäftigung mit dem Medium Theater. Es folgte eine Neuinterpretation von Klassikern aus feministischer Sicht.

Elke Kehr

Magyar Népi Szinház

Traditionsreichste und populärste Form des ung. Theaters, die als Ausdruck der nationalen Gedanken- und Gefühlswelt gilt; Wandlungen extrem unterworfen, von seinem nationalen und volkstümlichen Ursprung nie zu trennen. Erste Spuren im 16. und 17. Jh. in → Zwischenspielen von → Schuldramen und in der Sprachgestaltung der siebenbürgischen → Mysterienspiele von Csiksomlyó (1721–74). Mit *Tempeföi* (1793) und *Frau Karnyó* (1799) ist Mihály Csokonai-Vitéz (1773–1805) Hauptvertreter innerhalb des → Schultheaters. In der Wanderbühnenphase (1790–1837) spielt Literatur eine untergeordnete Rolle, es schlägt das Volkstümliche in der Aufführungspraxis, darstellerisch und vor allem musikalisch durch; bahnbrechende Inszenierungen dieser Richtung: *A kérök* (Die Freier, 1819) und *Csalódások* (Enttäuschungen, 1829) von Károly Kisfaludy (1788–1830), der als Begründer des ungarischen Lustspiels gilt. Die theatrale Konzeption des → Volksstücks schuf jedoch Ede Szigligeti (1814–78). Aufführungszahlen bis 1867 belegen durchschlagenden Erfolg: *Szökött katona* (Deserteur, 1843) 98mal, *Két pisztoly* (Zwei Pistolen, 1844) 78mal, *Csikós* (Tschikosch, 1847) 93mal. Wiens Einfluß ist zwar zu spüren, nationale Originalität herrscht jedoch vor; besonders beliebt sind die Volksliedeinlagen. Das Volksstück erhält ein eigenes Haus 1875 durch die Gründung des Népszinház (Volkstheater), wo es durch die

Erfolge der Sängerin und Schauspielerin Lujza Blaha (1850–1926) zur vollen Blüte kommt. Sie regt die Entstehung zahlreicher Stücke dieses Genres an; am erfolgreichsten sind Ede Tóth (1844–76) und Ferenc Csepreghy (1842–80). Musterbeispiel für den Blahaschen ‹Stil› *A falu rossza* (Der Dorflump, 1875), dieses Stück wird 1500mal gespielt, es vermischt realistische und märchenhafte Elemente. Aus dieser Entwicklung tritt das Märchen als Singspiel auf den Plan und hat mit *János vitéz* (Johann, der Held, 1904, Sujet: Petöfi, Musik: Pongrác Kacsóh, 1873–1924) den größten Erfolg in der ungarischen Theatergeschichte. Kacsóhs Musik vermochte freilich nicht richtungsbestimmend für die in aller Welt beliebte ungarische Operette zu werden; Einflüsse sind erst später bei Zoltán Kodály (1882–1967) mit *Háry János* (Johann Hary, 1926) und *Székelyfonó* (Spinnstube, 1933) zu erkennen. Die Episodisten der Blahaschen Volksstücke entpuppten sich als Vorläufer der Volksstücke realistischer, ja naturalistischer Prägung. In Géza Gárdonyis (1863–1922) *A bor* (Der Wein, 1901) betreten zum erstenmal realistische Bauern die ungarische Bühne. In den Stücken von Zsigmond Móricz (1879–1942) kommt der realistisch-volkstümliche Stil zu seinem Höhepunkt. Eine neue Qualität erhält in diesen Stücken das Gesellschaftskritische: *Sári biró* (Richter Charlotte, 1909), *Úri muri* (Herrengelage, 1929), *Kismadár* (Vögelchen, 1940). Einen besonderen Beitrag zum Volksstück leistet Áron Tamási (1897–1966), dessen Stücke durch Elemente des Mythischen, Feenhaften und Lyrischen charakterisiert sind: *Enekes madár* (Der singende Vogel, 1934), *Csalóka szivárvány* (Trügerischer Regenbogen, 1942), *Boldog nyárfalevél* (Glückliches Pappelblatt, 1961). Nach 1945 wird das Volksstück verpönt, ja verachtet. Erst mit *Tóték* (Die Tóts, 1967) gelangt das Volksstück wieder zu neuem Durchbruch. Dabei distanziert sich der Autor István Örkény (1912–80) durch eine Bühnenpersiflage in dem Stück ‹Dorflump› (1965) scharf von der Blahaschen Prägung des Volksstücks.

Sándor Gulyás

Maison de la Culture

Ein Rundschreiben eines Abteilungsleiters für Theaterfragen im frz. Kulturministerium, Biasini, propagierte zuerst die Gründung von Kulturhäusern (M. d. l. C.) in den frz. Provinzstädten, die wegen jahrhundertelanger zentralistischer Entwicklung weitgehend ‹kulturelle Wüste› (désert culturel) waren. Die M. d. l. C. sollten die Kultur allen Bevölkerungsschichten zugänglich machen, ein Ort der Begegnung mit Theater- und Konzertsälen, Ausstellungsräumen, Bibliotheken (und nur vereinzelt Volkshochschuleinrichtungen) sein. Das Theater stand von Anfang an im

Vordergrund der Arbeit; der Theatersaal bildete den baulichen Mittelpunkt der meisten M. d. l. C., deren Leitung fast immer ein Theatermann hatte und hat. Die rein auf das Bühnenschaffen ausgerichtete praktische Arbeit der M. d. l. C. wird vor allem von bildenden Künstlern stark kritisiert. – 1963 eröffneten die ersten M. d. l. C. in Le Havre, Caen, Bourges. Nach und nach kamen Amiens, Thonon, Grenoble, Firminy, Saint-Etienne, Créteil hinzu. Die meisten M. d. l. C. wurden in der Amtszeit des gaullistischen Kulturministers und Schriftstellers André Malraux gegründet, dem die Idee der M. d. l. C. daher oft fälschlich zugeschrieben wird. Neben dem Umbau bestehender Gebäude wurden neue M. d. l. C. von berühmten Architekten errichtet: in Firminy von Le Corbusier, in Grenoble von Wogenscky-Polieri. In Paris selbst gibt es kein M. d. l. C. genanntes Haus, sondern Centres Culturels oder Maisons des Jeunes et de la Culture.

Das Budget der M. d. l. C. wird je zur Hälfte vom Staat und von der Gemeinde getragen. Während der Staat den Leitern der M. d. l. C. im allgemeinen freie Hand läßt, versucht die Gemeinde, auf die Programmgestaltung Einfluß zu nehmen, was vor allem im Mai 1968 im Rahmen der Studentenrevolte zu auch an die Öffentlichkeit getragenen Konflikten führte. – Das eigentliche Ziel der M. d. l. C., die Provinz kulturell zu beleben, ist nur begrenzt erreicht worden. Die örtliche Arbeiterbevölkerung in die ‹Kulturtempel› oder ‹Kulturpaläste› zu ziehen, gelang kaum. Die Benutzer sind hauptsächlich studentische Jugend, Intellektuelle und Bildungsbürgertum.

Horst Schumacher

Mai-Tanzformen

Die mit *mai* bezeichneten jap. Tänze werden gewöhnlich als von professionellen Tänzern vorgeführte Tanzkünste den *odori* genannten, von Laien, oft zum eigenen Vergnügen, getanzten Tänzen gegenübergestellt. – Der Beginn der M. führt zurück zu archaischen, mit dem Shintô-Kult zusammenhängenden Tänzen; die weitere Geschichte sieht M. in viele der etablierten Theaterformen wie →Nô und →*kabuki* als einen Bestandteil neben dramaturgischen und musikalischen Elementen integriert, kennt aber auch selbständige Bühnentanzkunst.

Als früheste ist das sog. *kagura*, Japans ältester Ritualtanz, zu nennen, das nach Anfängen, die in Beschwörungsriten liegen, ab der Jahrhundertwende in seiner höfischen Form (*mikagura*) zu Ehren der Sonnengöttin, in seinen ländlichen Formen (*satokagura*) auch zu Ehren anderer shintoistischer Gottheiten, ursprünglich von Tänzerinnen, später von Shintô-

Priestern aufgeführt wurde. Kontinentalen Ursprungs ist das bis ins 7. Jh. zurückreichende *bugaku*, orchesterbegleitete Tänze, die mit ihrer Bühne und in ihrer dreiteiligen (*jo – ha – kyû*) Struktur spätere Theaterformen wie das Nô beeinflußten sowie bis zum Mittelalter viele autochthone jap. Tanzformen aufsogen und überdeckten.

Im frühen Mittelalter, als die Zeit des Schwertadels angebrochen war, traten neue Tänze auf die Bühne: Der *shirabyôshi*-Tanz, urspr. von männlichen Tempelbediensteten tänzerisch gestaltete Legenden, wurde hauptsächlich in seiner späteren Form populär, in der Tänzerinnen in Männerkleidern abbildungsfreie, stark rhythmisch betonte Tänze vorführten. Die Nachfolgekunst, der *kusemai* (‹nicht regelhafter Tanz›), der in Teilen später in das Nô aufgenommen wurde, hatte seine Blüte in der Namboku-Zeit (1336–92), teilte sich in Männer-, Frauen- und Knabentanz, war in der Regel Einzeltanz und wurde vom Vortrag religiöser Legenden oder Liedchen begleitet, ein Element, dessen Verstärkung seine Nachfolgekunst, die vom Schwertadel geschätzten *kôwaka-mai*-‹Tänze›, im 16. Jh. den Übergang von Tanzkunst zu →*katarimono*-Rezitationskunst vollziehen ließ.

Aus der Vielzahl mittelalterlicher Bühnentanzformen, die glückverheißende, segenbringende Funktionen hatten, ragt vor allem der *ennen-mai* (‹Lebensverlängerungstanz›) heraus, der sich ab der Mitte des 12. Jh. zur Unterhaltungskunst wandelte und in seinen beiden Typen den *ôfuryô* und *kofuryû* dem Nô ähnliche dramaturgische und strukturelle Elemente zeigt. Von ähnlich segenbringender Funktion waren die *okina*-Tänze, später traditionelle Eröffnungstänze des Nô-Programms, die für das Land Frieden, für das Volk Wohlergehen sichern sollten.

Spätestens das ausgehende Mittelalter sieht die meisten der genannten Tänze des *mai*-Typs in populäre Theaterformen integriert; das neuzeitliche Theater schöpft vielfach daneben aus der *odori*-Richtung der Tänze, und erst die Moderne läßt entweder in den Westen entlehnten Formen (Revue, Ballett) oder in den auch aus traditionellen Quellen schöpfenden Ausdruckstänzen der jüngsten Zeit (z. B. →*butô*) Tanz als eigenständiger Bühnenkunstform angemessenen Raum.

Ashira, H.: The Japanese Dance. Tôkyô 1965; Barth, J.: Japans Schaukunst im Wandel der Zeiten. Wiesbaden 1972; Wolz, C.: Bugaku, Japanese Court Dance. Providence 1971.

Roland Schneider

Majakowski-Theater (Moskau)

(Moskovskij akademičeskij teatr im. Vl. Majakovskogo) Eines der ersten Schauspielhäuser der Sowjetzeit, 1922 eröffnet, hieß bis 1943 «Theater der Revolution», 1943 «Moskauer Dramentheater», erhielt 1954 den Namen Majakowskis, seit 1964 Akademisch. – Unter der künstlerischen Leitung von Meyerhold (1922–24) konstruktivistische Inszenierungen von Tollers *Die Maschinenstürmer* und *Masse Mensch*; mit der Steigerung exzentrischer Kunstgriffe zu symbolhafter Verallgemeinerung in Ostrowskis *Ein einträglicher Posten* (1923) gewinnt ein klassisches Drama auf exemplarische Weise zeitgenössische Aktualität. Mitte der 20er Jahre Hinwendung zu zeitgenössischen sowj. Stücken: *Echo* von Bill-Bjelozerkowski (1924), *Eine Torte aus Luft* von Romaschow (1926), *Der Mann mit der Aktentasche* (1928) von Fajko. Als Höhepunkt galten die Inszenierungen von N. F. Pogodins (1900–62) Dramen über den soz. Aufbau *Das Poem von der Axt* (1931), *Mein Freund* (1932), *Nach dem Ball* (1934) durch A. D. Popow (1892–1961), der das M. T. 1930–35 leitete. Mit seinem Konzept vom «denkenden Schauspieler» strebt er nach einer Verbindung der Erfahrungen Stanislawskis und Wachtangows. Der Weggang Popows bedingt den Verlust klarer Konzeptionen.

Nach der Rückkehr des Theaters aus der Evakuierung 1943 übernimmt N. P. Ochlopkow (1900–67) die Leitung. Der Poetik Majakowskis folgend, betont er staatsbürgerliche Thematik, revolutionäres Pathos und Monumentalität der Gestalten und sucht die künstlerischen Verfahren Meyerholds, Wachtangows und Stanislawskis fruchtbar zu machen. Er bevorzugt heroische Stoffe sowohl im zeitgenössischen sowj. als auch im klassischen Drama: Fadejew *Die junge Garde* (1947), Gorki *Die Mutter* (1948), Arbusow *Irkutsker Geschichte* (1960); Ostrowski *Das Gewitter* (1953), Shakespeare *Hamlet* (1954), Brecht *Mutter Courage und ihre Kinder* (1960). Später verfolgt er die Idee eines synthetischen Theaters mit Elementen des Volkstheaters (etwa des jap.), der Pantomime und des Balletts, mit Chor und Orchester – paradigmatisch die Aufführung der *Medea* des Euripides (1961) –, pflegt die Veränderbarkeit der Bühne, direktes Spiel, Fehlen der vierten Wand und besteht bei aller Monumentalität der Figuren auf differenzierter psychologischer Nuancierung. Seit 1967 prägt A. Gontscharow (*1918) als Chefregisseur das Profil des M. T.: russ. Klassik; M. Bulgakows *Flucht*; sowj./russ. Gegenwartsdramatik; Dramatisierungen von Leskow (1979 *Lady Macbeth von Mzensk*) und Gorki (1981 *Klim Samgin*).

Alpers, B.: Teatr Revoljucii. Moskva 1928; Očerki istorii russkogo sovetskogo dramatičeskogo teatra. Bd. 1ff. Moskva 1954ff.

Annelore Engel-Braunschmidt / Elke Wiegand

Malersaal

Theaterwerkstätte, in der die Dekorationsteile gewöhnlich unter Bühnenlichtverhältnissen bemalt und von oben (Brücke) aus der Distanz betrachtet werden können.

Erich Krieger

Maly Theater (Moskau)

(Kleines Theater, Gosudarstvennyj akademičeskij Malyj teatr) Ältestes russ. Schauspieltheater in Moskau; erhielt seine Bezeichnung 1924 beim Einzug in das eigene Gebäude am heutigen Theaterplatz im Unterschied zum benachbarten «Bolschoi», dem Oper und Ballett vorbehaltenen «Großen Theater». 1776 aus der Schauspielertruppe der Moskauer Universität hervorgegangen, spielte das Ensemble des M. T. unter dem Einfluß des russ. Aufklärers N. I. Nowikow neben Werken westeurop. Autoren (Molière, Voltaire, Lessing) Stücke der einheimischen (D. I. Fonwisin, A. O. Ablesimow, J. B. Knjashnin), trat von Anfang an für realistische und progressive Tendenzen ein und verband im 19. Jh. auf eindrucksvolle Weise russ. Dramatik und Schauspielkunst. Mit A. S. Gribojedows Komödie *Verstand schafft Leiden* (erste vollständige Aufführung 1831) und N. V. Gogols *Revisor* (1836) gelangten die besten russ. Dramatiker, mit P. S. Motschalow (1800–48) und M. S. Stschepkin (1788–1863) die besten russ. Schauspieler der 1. Hälfte des 19. Jh. auf die Bühne; die demokratisch gesinnte Kritik, vor allem W. G. Belinski, beförderte alle Bestrebungen, Repertoire und Schauspielkunst zu verbessern.

Mit den Befreiungsbewegungen der 60er Jahre des 19. Jh. erlebt das M. T. eine neue Entwicklungsphase: Die Bühne wird beherrscht von den Dramen A. N. Ostrowskis (1823–86) mit ihren Angriffen auf die Rückständigkeit vor allem der russ. Kaufmannschaft (das M. T. bringt alle seine Stücke – es sind 47 – zur UA), die Kritik von den gesellschaftlichen und ästhetischen Ansichten der Sozialrevolutionäre N. G. Tschernyschewski und N. A. Dobroljubow. Fonwisins Komödien erleben Neuinszenierungen, in das Repertoire aufgenommen werden A. S. Puschkins kleine Tragödien, Dramen von I. S. Turgenjew und A. W. Suchowo-Kobylin, von Lessing, Goethe, Shakespeare, Gutzkows *Uriel Acosta*. Unter den Schauspielern ragt P. M. Sadowski heraus, die zentralen Frauenrollen verkörpert G. N. Fedotowa. Um die Jahrhundertwende prägen A. P. Lenski, A. I. Jushin, die Tragödin M. N. Jermolowa die Schauspielkunst.

Unter dem Druck der reaktionären Politik in den 80er und 90er Jahren des 19. Jh. setzt ein Rückzug in die Klassik ein; von zeitgenössischen russ. Werken werden L. N. Tolstois *Früchte der Aufklärung* (1891) und *Die Macht der Finsternis* (1895) uraufgeführt. Tschechows und Gorkis Stücke gehen andernorts über die Bühne. Vom symbolistischen Theater bleibt das M. T. fast unberührt; die Bühnenreformen am Ende des 19. und Beginn des 20. Jh. gehen vom →Moskauer Künstlertheater aus. Erst nach der Revolution tritt eine Wiederbelebung ein: Das M. T. präsentiert Revolutionsthematik (*Oliver Cromwell*, von A. W. Lunatscharski, 1921) in Werken sowj. Dramatiker; großen Erfolg hat *Ljubow Jarowaja* von K. A. Trenjow (1926). Jetzt gelingen auch Inszenierungen von Dramen Gorkis (bes. *Barbaren*, 1941). Die realistischen Prinzipien (Betonung der ideellen und sozial bedeutungsvollen Komponente in der Kunst, lebendiges vollblütiges Spiel), wie sie seit den Anfängen des M. T. mit den Namen Stschepkin und Motschalow verbunden sind, gehen mühelos in die sog. Methode des sozialistischen Realismus über.

Nach dem XX. Parteitag (1956) Inszenierung kritischer Gegenwartsstücke von V. Rosow, S. Aljoschin u. a. Russ. und internat. Klassik inszenieren ab 1962 J. R. Simonow, B. Rawenskich (1973 A. K. Tolstois *Zar Fjodor Ioannowitsch* mit I. Smoktunowski) und sehr interessant Leonid Hejfez (* 1934, Schüler von M. Knebel und A. D. Popow): 1971 *Kretschinskis Hochzeit*; 1972 *Vor Sonnenaufgang* mit M. Zarjow (1903-87), der seit 1950 Direktor des M. T. war; 1977 *Verschwörung des Fiesco zu Genua*. Gegenwärtige Leitung: Juri Solomin. Die Stschepkin-Schule des M. T. bildet in nationalen Studios Nachwuchs aus, u. a. für das Theater der Sowjetdeutschen.

Zograf, N. G.: Malyj teatr vtoroj poloviny XIX v. Moskva 1960; ders.: Malyj teatr v konce XIX – načale XX veka. Moskva 1966; Malyj teatr. 1824–1974. Tom I. 1824–1917. Moska 1978.

Annelore Engel-Braunschmidt/Elke Wiegand

La Mama Experimental Theatre Club

Als ‹Cafe La Mama› im Herbst 1961 von der Schwarzamerikanerin Ellen Stewart mit einer Boutique und Ausstellung eröffnet; nach dem Vorbild des Caffe Cino ab Juni 1962 Uraufführungen junger Autoren. Nach langwierigen Querelen mit Polizei und Lizenzbehörden, mehrfacher Schließung und Umzug schließlich 1964 auf der Basis eines Privatclubs mit dem Namen L. reorganisiert. War das →Open Theatre die wichtigste Erscheinung des →Off-Off-Broadway im Hinblick auf Improvisationstechniken und Werkstattmethoden, so gebührt dem L. das Verdienst, durch Tourneen und internationale Workshops diese Arbeitsformen verbreitet zu haben. Bereits 1965 gab es mit einem Repertoire von 21 Stücken (u. a. von Paul Foster, Leonard Melfi, Sam Shepard, Jean-Claude van Itallie, Lanford Wilson) eine Tournee nach Paris und Kopenhagen. Eine weitere Europareise 1967 (BRD, Niederlande, Dänemark, Schweden, Großbritannien, Italien) brachte schließlich Anerkennung durch Kulturstiftungen in den USA (National Endowment for the Arts, Ford Foundation), wodurch der internationale Workshop ‹La Mama Plexus› ermöglicht wurde. L. expandierte: 1971 gab es zwei eigene Theaterhäuser in New York, und 1973 waren vom L. ca. 450 Inszenierungen von rund 300 jungen Autoren gezeigt worden. Im Verlauf der 70er Jahre gab es zeitweilig Schwesterunternehmungen des L. in Amsterdam, Bogotá, London, Melbourne, München, Paris, Tokio, Toronto.

Fröhlich, P.: Das nichtkommerzielle amerik. Theater. Rheinfelden 1974; Heilmeyer, J./Fröhlich, P.: Now. Theater der Erfahrung. Köln 1971; Orzel, N./Smith, M. (eds.): Eight Plays from Off-Off-Broadway. New York 1966.

Dieter Herms

Manipuri

Das klassische Tanztheater in Manipur (→ Indisches Theater). Die Renaissance des M. ist dem bengalischen Poeten Rabindranath Tagore (1861–1941) zu danken. Er verpflichtet als Tanzmeister an seine Schule in Santiniketan/Kalkutta 1918 den Guru Buddhimantra Sinha, 1926 Nabba Kumar. Kumar knüpft an uralte tanztheatralische Volksschauspiele an, aber er säkularisiert den M. 1926 und 1930 Neubelebung in ganz Indien. – Das M.-Tanztheater kennt kein solistisches Repertoire. Alle Soli sind in Tanzduette oder Tanzensembles eingebettet. Jede Tanzgruppe bildet ein Kollektiv, das auf Improvisationen verzichten muß. Der Bewegungsduktus des M. lebt nicht von der strengen Klarheit des → Bharata Natyam, nicht von den rechtwinklig ausgerichteten Bewegungsführungen des → Kathakali und auch nicht von der Brillanz des → Kathak. Er ist im M., auf dem Schlangenkult fußend, fließend, anmutig und bewegt, folgt einer feinfühligen Poesie und wirkt durch seine starke Originalität. Das älteste Tanztheater des M., der Lai Haraoba, vereint zwei differente künstlerische Entwicklungen: urgesellschaftliches und vorhinduistisches Brauchtum und klassisches Tanzschauspiel. Im Lai Haraoba schließen sich an die getanzte Kosmogonie vielfältige Berufs- und Arbeitstänze an (→ Ritualtänze).

Balakrishna, M.: Classical Indian Dance. Calcutta 1967; Bhavnani, E.: The Dance in India. Bombay 1970; Ghosh, S.: Tagore and Manipuri Dances. Marg. Publications. Teil 5. In: Classical and Folk Dances of India. 6 Teile. Bombay 1963; Rebling, E.: Die Tanzkunst Indiens. Wilhelmshaven 1982.

Helga Ettl

Mantel- und Degenstück

(Span.: comedia en capa y espada) Im Gegensatz zur ‹comedia de ruido› ist das M. ein nach der typischen Kleidung – Mantel und Degen – der in ihr auftretenden Gesellschaftsschichten – niederer Adel und oberes Bürgertum – benanntes Intrigenstück in Versen, das auf einer quasi nackten Bühne aufgeführt wird. Kern der Handlung ist meistens ein durch Zufall oder gesellschaftliche Konventionen, bei denen der Ehrbegriff im Mittelpunkt steht, verhinderter Heiratsplan eines oder zweier Paare. Die Handlung führt durch eine Reihe von Mißverständnissen und Verwechslungen zum glücklichen Ausgang, während eine Parallelhandlung unter den Bediensteten für Belustigung und Erheiterung sorgt. Die Blütezeit des M. liegt im sog. Goldenen Zeitalter (→Comedia) mit Pedro Calderón de la Barca (1600–81), Tirso de Molina (1583–1648) und v. a. Lope de Vega (1562–1635), der in seinem *Arte nuovo de hacer comedias* (1609) die Verstypen für traurige (dècimas), erzählende (romance) bzw. Liebesszenen (redondillas) festlegt. Das M. lebt im 18. und 19. Jh. mit dem →Melodram und dem Schauerdrama in abgewandelter Form wieder auf.

Bernard Poloni

Märchendrama

Bühnenstück, dessen Handlung und Dramaturgie konsequent einer Märchenwelt zugeordnet ist. Dabei kann die ganze Handlung erfunden, einzelne Motive bekannten Märchen, Legenden oder Sagen entnommen sein oder das ganze Stück auf Volks- oder Kunstmärchen beruhen. Märchenformen gibt es auch in anderen theatralischen Genres, dem →Ballett und der Oper ebenso wie in der →Pantomime und dem Singspiel. Eine Untergruppe des M. bildet die Féerie, die bühnentechnisch zumeist aufwendige Darstellung einer Feengeschichte, die seit der entsprechenden literarischen Mode des 17. Jh. bis weit ins 19. Jh. hinein sich großer Beliebtheit erfreute. Als Autoren sind Gozzi und Lesage ebenso zu nennen wie Raimund und Nestroy, der Schöpfer von Feenpantomimen J. G. Debureau ebenso wie der Musiker J. Offenbach. Ende des 19. Jh. fanden Féerien vorübergehend auch Eingang im →Zirkus und der →Revue.

Das eigentlichc M. erlebte den Höhepunkt seiner Wirkung in der Romantik (→Romantisches Theater) und den verschiedenen nach- und neuromantischen Strömungen im Europa des 19. Jh. Nicht nur Märchendichter wie H. C. Andersen schrieben M., sondern auch Schriftsteller wie Ibsen und Strindberg. Die Darstellung der Märchenwelt kann dabei ihren Sinn in sich selbst tragen, sie kann zur Gegenwelt der Realität stilisiert werden (z. B. bei G. Hauptmann) oder – parodistisch – zur Gesellschafts- und Literaturkritik dienen (z. B. L. Tieck, *Der gestiefelte Kater*, J. L. Schwarz, *Der Drache*).

Abgesehen von wenigen zum klassischen Repertoire gehörenden Stücken taucht das M. heute in der Regel nur noch als Kinderstück, als Weihnachtsmärchen zum finanziellen Ausgleich des Theateretats im Spielplan der Bühnen auf.

Kober, M.: Das deutsche Märchendrama. Frankfurt/M. 1925 (Reprint Hildesheim 1973); Tornau, H.: Die Entstehung und Entwicklung des Weihnachtsmärchens auf der deutschen Bühne. Köln 1955.

Wolfgang Beck

Marionette

Figur des →Puppentheaters; Gliederpuppe, die mit Hilfe von Fäden, die zumeist in einem Führungskreuz zusammengefaßt sind, vom Spieler von oben dirigiert wird. Die Etymologie des Namens ist unsicher. Vielleicht abgeleitet von einem mittelalterlichen Narren oder dem «Marotte» genannten Zepter des Narren, erscheint auch die Herleitung von der «Mariole» genannten Figur der Maria im mittelalterlichen Krippenspiel oder aus dem frz. Schäferspiel *Jeu de Robin et Marion* (13. Jh.) möglich. Im Französischen bedeutet «marionnette» jede Art theatralisch genutzter Puppe.

Die Herkunft der M. ist umstritten, ihre Entstehung in Indien oder Persien bzw. China ist nicht gesichert. Umstritten ist auch, ob erhaltene Gliederpuppen aus dem Griechenland des 5. Jh. v. Chr. Theaterpuppen waren oder als Kinderspielzeug dienten. Bereits seit dem Mittelalter sind M. in Europa bekannt. Seit dem 16. Jh. durchzogen M.-Bühnen ganz Europa. Auch auf normalen Wanderbühnen wurden in Notzeiten oder als Nachspiel M. benutzt. Dank der besonderen Beweglichkeit der M. und der damit verbundenen darstellerischen Möglichkeiten wurde sie bis in die Gegenwart vor allem zur Nachahmung des Personentheaters genutzt. Im 18. Jh. wurde die M. auch als höfischer Zeitvertreib beliebt. Das moderne M.-Theater wurde begründet durch J. L. Schmid, der 1858 in München ein M.-Theater gründete, für das Franz Graf Pocci über 50 Stücke schrieb. 1900 errichtete die Stadt München das erste feste Haus für das Spiel mit M. Im 20. Jh. wurde die M. dank der Bemühungen von Autoren und bildenden Künstlern die bevorzugte Figur des künstlerisch bestimmten Puppenspiels.

Batek, O.: Marionetten – Stab-, Draht- und Fadenpuppen. o. O. 1980; Baty, G./Chavance, R.: Histoire des marionnettes. Paris 1959; Chesnais, J.: Histoire Générale des Marionnettes. Paris 1947; Foulquié, Ph. (Hg.): Les théâtres de marionnettes en France. Lyon 1985; Humbert, R.: La vie des marionnettes. Paris 1987; Kraus, G.: Das kleine Welttheater. München u. a. 1988; La marionnette et la société. Charleville-Mézières 1990; Leydi, R./Mezzanotte Leydi, R.: Marionette e burattini. Mailand 1958; Meilink, W.: Bibliografie van het Poppenspel. Amsterdam 1965; Mignon, P.-L./Mohr, J.: Marionettentheater. Lausanne 1963; Sandig, H.: Die Ausdrucksmöglichkeiten der Marionetten und ihre dramaturgischen Konsequenzen. Diss. München 1958; Simmen, R.: Marionetten aus aller Welt. Eltville 1978; Wittkop-Menardeau, G.: Von Puppen und Marionetten. Zürich 1962.

Wolfgang Beck

Marketing im Theater

Marketing als ein Ansatz marktorientierten Denkens und Handelns bedeutet Planung, Abstimmung und Kontrolle sämtlicher auf den Markt ausgerichteten Aktivitäten. Als Unternehmensphilosophie ursprünglich im kommerziellen Bereich entwickelt (Profit-Marketing), wird Marketing heute zunehmend auch von öffentlichen Dienstleistungsbetrieben genutzt (Nonprofit-Marketing).

Die Anwendung eines Marketing-Konzepts im Theater bedeutet nicht die Anbiederung an ein möglichst breites Publikum unter Preisgabe der besonderen künstlerischen Ziele. M. i. T. versteht sich vielmehr als ein Prozeß, der die Ziele des jeweiligen Hauses (u. a. künstlerische Freiräume, optimale Platzausnutzung, gesicherte Finanzierung) mit den Bedürfnissen seines Publikums (u. a. Unterhaltung, Bildung, Geselligkeit) in Einklang bringen soll. Ein Marketing-Konzept zielt auch nicht primär auf die quantitative Ausweitung von Maßnahmen der Öffentlichkeitsarbeit und der Werbung, wie sie seit den 60er Jahren in vielfältiger Weise genutzt werden, sondern bietet die Grundlagen für den strategischen Einsatz und die Kontrolle solcher Aktivitäten. Die Planung und Umsetzung eines ganzheitlichen Marketing-Konzepts im Theater fällt nicht allein in den Verantwortungsbereich der Abteilung Kommunikation, sondern betrifft die Mitarbeiter an der Kasse ebenso wie das technische Personal und kann ohne die Unterstützung der künstlerischen und kaufmännischen Leitung praktisch nicht funktionieren. Folgende Prinzipien gilt es, in diesem Prozeß zu beachten:

1. Ausgangspunkt für ein Marketing-Programm ist die Untersuchung und Bewertung des Ist-Zustands eines Theaters. Eine solche Situationsanalyse schließt das Budget und das Publikum sowie das gesamte Produkt des Hauses ein, d. h. Ensemble, Programm, Räume, Mitarbeiter, Corporate Identity, Corporate Design, Corporate Communications, Image etc. Sie beschreibt zugleich seine Stärken und Schwächen und die Chancen und Gefahren, denen es ausgesetzt ist. 2. Auf die Situationsanalyse folgt die Formulierung von Zielen, ohne die weder vorhandene Ressourcen optimal genutzt noch der tatsächliche Erfolg gemessen werden können. Neben künstlerischen Zielen spricht man von Marketing-Zielen, die z. B. Verkaufszahlen, Zielgruppen, Imageveränderungen betreffen. 3. Die Zielgruppen des Theaters werden definiert und nach soziodemographischen und psychographischen Kriterien voneinander abgegrenzt (Marktsegmentierung). Gemeint sind damit neben dem realen und potentiellen Publikum die öffentlichen Geldgeber und privaten Sponsoren, ferner die Medien, die Vertreter der Schulen, Besucherorganisationen etc. als Multiplikatoren. 4. Vor dem Hintergrund der Ziele und bei optimaler Nutzung der Ressourcen werden Strategien festgelegt und in einem kleinschrittigen Maßnahmenplan konkretisiert. In einem Marketing-Mix werden unter Berücksichtigung der Interessen und Bedürfnisse der verschiedenen Adressaten Angebotspakete zusammengestellt und den Zielgruppen zugeordnet (Positionierung). 5. Mit Hilfe einer kontinuierlichen Erfolgskontrolle läßt sich feststellen, ob die gefällten Entscheidungen den erwarteten Erfolg tatsächlich gebracht haben bzw. wo Korrekturen notwendig sind.

Hilger, H.: Marketing für öffentliche Theaterbetriebe. Frankfurt/M. u. a. 1985; Kommunale Gemeinschaftsstelle für Verwaltungsvereinfachung: Die Museen. Besucherorientierung und Wirtschaftlichkeit. Köln 1989; dies.: Führung und Steuerung des Theaters. Köln 1989; Kotler, P.: Marketing für Nonprofit-Organisationen. Stuttgart 1978; Müller-Wesemann, B.: Marketing im Theater. Hg. vom Zentrum für Theaterforschung der Universität Hamburg und dem Deutschen Bühnenverein e. V. 1992; Roth, P.: Kultursponsoring. Meinungen, Chancen und Probleme, Konzepte, Beispiele. Landsberg 1989.

Barbara Müller-Wesemann

Märtyrerdrama

Einer der zwei Haupttypen des →barocken Trauerspiels, welches sich aufteilen ließe in die eher aristotelische Vanitas- und Fortuna-Tragödie, die Greuel, Laster- und Leidenschaftsstücke, die Tragödie des Tyrannen und des Fürstensturzes und das mehr platonische M. Dies hat seine Quellen im Theater des Mittelalters (→Mittelalter) sowie im Cinquecento (→Ri-

578 Märtyrerdrama

nascimento), seine Höhepunkte im 17. Jh. in der Nachfolge des →Schuldramas und der Heiligen- und Eremitenstücke des →Jesuitentheaters, vor allem beim Niederländer Jost van den Vondel (1587–1679: *Maegden*, 1639; *Maria Stuart*, 1646), bei Andreas Gryphius (1616–64: *Catharina von Georgien*, 1657: *Leo Arminius*, 1650 und *Papinianus*, 1659, als Mischformen) und in der frz. →Klassik bei Pierre Corneille (1606–84: *Polyeucte*, 1641). Im erbaulichen Tugend- und Lasterschema der Barocktragödie und im heilsgeschichtlichen Rahmen des damaligen Glaubens entwickelt sich als M. die physische Vernichtung einer unschuldigen christlichen Herrschergestalt, welche gerade im Untergang die Kardinaltugenden von Beständigkeit, Großmut, Klugheit und Vernunft illustrieren. Der moralisch-religiöse Triumph im ewigen Heil nach der Bewährungsprobe macht allerdings das M. untragisch; sein Effekt ist, in der Reinigung der Furcht und dem Glauben Trost zu finden.

Literarisch hat das M. als solche nur ein kurzes Leben, bis etwa Ende des 17. Jh. Umgestaltete Formen im Sinne des dt. Idealismus sind zu finden bei Friedrich Schiller (1759–1805: *Maria Stuart*, UA 1800; als Mischform *Die Jungfrau von Orleans*, UA 1801) sowie in gewissen Erlösungsstücken der dt. Romantik (→Romantisches Theater), so bei Ludwig Tieck (1773–1853: *Leben und Tod der heiligen Genoveva*, 1800) oder Zacharias Werner (1768–1823). Im 20. Jh. in Anlehnung an das span. Goldene Zeitalter (→Comedia), bes. Calderón, Höhepunkte des heilsgeschichtlichen M. bei Paul Claudel (1868–1955: *Partage de midi*, 1906: *Le soulier de satin*, 1930) und Hugo v. Hofmannsthal (1874–1929: *Der Turm*, 1926). Parodierte Form im Sinne der marxistischen Umfunktionierung bei Bertolt Brecht (1898–1956: *Die heilige Johanna der Schlachthöfe*, 1929–30). Mustergültiges zeitgenössisches Beispiel in der Tradition des Nachvollzugs der Passion Christi und der Schillerschen Läuterungstragödie, verbunden mit tragisch-kritischer Darstellung der geistigen Problematik des christlichen Widerstands gegen das NS-Regime, bei Rolf Hochhuth (*1931) in *Der Stellvertreter* (1963).

Alexander, R. J.: Das dt. Barockdrama. Stuttgart 1984; Bray, R.: La formation de la doctrine classique en France. Paris 1951; Benjamin, W.: Ursprung des dt. Trauerspiels. Frankfurt/M. 1964; Lindenberger, H.: Historical Drama. Chicago 1975; Neuss, R.: Tugend und Toleranz. Bonn 1989; Rehm, W.: Götterstille und Göttertrauer. München 1951; Schings, H.-J.: Consolatio tragoediae. In: Grimm R. (Hg.): Deutsche Dramentheorien I. Frankfurt/M. 1971.

Gérard Schneilin

Maschinenkomödie

Form des →Alt-Wiener Volksstücks im 18. Jh. Weiterentwicklung der Bernardoniade, benannt nach Bernardon (Johann Joseph Felix von Kurz, 1717–84, österr. Stegreifschauspieler, Dramatiker und Prinzipal). Extemporierte Zauberburleske. Elemente der M.: Maschinerie der Barockoper, →Feuerwerke, Wasser, Arien, Verkleidungen; →Pantomime und Operette als Einschübe. Vorlagen: antike Stoffe, allegorische Vorstellungswelt der Festzüge, →Jesuitentheater, Barockoper, frz. klassische Tragödien, frz. und ital. Komödien, zeitgenössische Literatur und Dramatik. Die Komik der M. resultiert aus der Hilflosigkeit des überheblichen Individuums gegenüber irrationalen Mächten und aus der Verwirrung des Ich-Gefühls der Protagonisten. Stücke: *Die Reise des Bernardon aus der Höllen, Der aufs neue begeisterte und belebte Bernardon, Der neue Krumme Teufel, Bernardon der dumme Nachfolger des Dr. Faustus* u. v. a.

Gregor, J.: Weltgeschichte des Theaters. Zürich 1933; Rommel, O.: Die Alt-Wiener Volkskomödie. Wien 1952; ders.: Die Maschinenkomödie. Leipzig 1935.

Ingeborg Janich

The Mask

Theaterzeitschrift, 1908 von Edward Gordon Craig (1872–1966) in Florenz gegründet, existierte (mit Unterbrechungen von 1916–18 und von 1919–23) bis zum Jahre 1929. Mitarbeiter waren außer Craig, der unter mehr als 60 Pseudonymen, deren bekanntestes ‹J. S.› (für John Semar) war, für die Zeitschrift schrieb, Gino Ducci und Dorothy Nevile Lees. Im März 1908 erschien die erste Ausgabe in engl. Sprache, zunächst als Monatszeitschrift, ab 1909 als Vierteljahrsheft, 1918/19 als Monatsschrift, 1923 als Jahresband und von Januar 1924 bis Oktober 1929 regelmäßig als Vierteljahrsschrift. Die Auflage betrug etwa 1000 Exemplare. Verbreitung in aller Welt. – In Th. M. definierte Craig seine Theatertheorie. Der Rückgriff auf die Vergangenheit geschah dabei im Hinblick auf eine Definition eines ‹Theaters der Zukunft›. Craig orientierte sich vor allem an der →Commedia dell'arte, der Sacra Rappresentazione, an den theoretischen Schriften von Serlio, Riccoboni und Gozzi und an den außereurop. ethnischen Theaterformen, z. B. dem asiat. Theater. Häufig erschienen im Th. M. Auszüge aus Texten von Plato, Aristoteles, Goethe, Nietzsche, Tolstoi, Shakespeare u. a. ‹The Mask› hatte einen außerordentlich großen Einfluß auf die Künstler jener Epoche und wirkte formbildend auf die Theaterentwicklung der 20er und 30er Jahre.

Bablet, D.: Edward Gordon Craig. Paris 1962; Craig, E.: Gordon Craig. The Story of his Life. London 1968.

Elke Kehr

Maske / Maskentheater

Das Gesicht des Toten ist starr, ohne Mimik; dies ist die erste und tiefverwurzelte M.-Erfahrung der Menschheit. Vor mehr als 20000 Jahren erkannten die Jäger die täuschende Wirkung der Maskerade mit Tierfellen und Schädelknochen, die Tarn-M. Erste M.-Tänze und schamanistische Rituale sind aus dieser Zeit durch Höhlenzeichnungen bekannt. Schädelknochen von Verstorbenen blieben über deren Tod hinaus erhalten. Jeder Mensch wußte, daß die M. des Todes direkt unter seiner Haut liegt.

Das Vorstellungsvermögen über die eigene Person hinaus führte zu Gedanken(spielen), zu einfachsten Mythologien, später zu Religionen und liegt heute im Bereich von Fantasy und Science-fiction. Wesentlich in allem ist die Tragik des Sterbens, der Erstarrung des Gesichts. Die Schädelknochen dienten in vielen Kulturen als Grundlage für M. Die goldenen Totenmasken aus den Gräbern von Mykenae (16. Jh. v. u. Z.) schützten das Antlitz des Toten, zeigten aber gleichzeitig die individuellen Züge und sollten die Persönlichkeit erkennbar erhalten.

Heute lernt der aufgeklärte Mensch, sein Leben wie ein Schauspiel zu erleben, seine Rollen in der Gesellschaft richtig zu spielen; dazu bedient er sich verschiedener Attribute der Maskerade: Schminke, Sonnenbrille, Frisur, Mode. Die Alltags-M. ist Gesellschaftsspiel, und das alltägliche Theater mit M. bietet Ersatzwirklichkeit, doppelte Realität – die Grundbedingung jeden Theaters. Die Angst vor dem Tode wird aufgelöst in der Faszination des M.-Spiels.

M. des Theaters: Mit der Entstehung des klassischen griech. Theaters (→Antikes Theater) als Kunstform entwickelte sich die Theater-M. →Tragödien wurden mit M. gespielt, die nicht wesentlich größer als das menschliche Gesicht waren, mit gefühlsbetontem Ausdruck; überliefert sind nach Polydeukes (2. Jh. u. Z.) 28 verschiedene Typen: alte und junge Männer, Sklaven und Frauen. In der →Komödie wurde mit übertrieben großen Gesichts-M. gespielt, grotesk stilisiert; es gab mindestens 44 unterscheidbare und dem Publikum bekannte Typen. Die M. erlaubten den Darstellern (nur Männer) den glaubwürdigen und schnellen Wechsel in die verschiedenen Rollen.

Ein neuer Impuls des theatralischen M.-Spiels kam im 16. Jh. durch die →Commedia dell'arte in Italien auf, der sich bald auch über Frankreich (Molière) nach England (Shakespeare) ausbreitete. Bestimmte Men-

Maske/Maskentheater 581

schentypen wurden ohne gefühlsmäßigen Ausdruck in den M.-Formen charakterisiert. Da es sich um Halb-M. handelte, konnten die Schauspieler durch →Mimik der unteren Gesichtshälfte die jeweiligen Stimmungen und Gefühle der dargestellten Personen ergänzend zur Sprache zum Ausdruck bringen. Die heute gebräuchlichste M. ist die Schmink-M., ggf. ergänzt durch Teilplastiken oder plastische Veränderungen des Schauspielergesichts. Typisierung wird durch entsprechende Frisuren, symbolisierende Farbgebung bzw. stilisierende Linienführung betont.

Das bürgerliche Theater des 19. Jh. stellte den individuellen Menschen dar, den vielschichtig variierenden Ausdruck der Gefühle, konnte somit die M. nicht gebrauchen. Gegen die allzu beliebige Mimik und Gebärdensprache richtete sich die Forderung Gordon Craigs, den Schauspieler abzuschaffen und die →Über-Marionette zu entwickeln; er schreibt in seinem Essay *Das Theater der Zukunft* (1907): «...daß die Maske das einzig richtige Mittel ist, den seelischen Ausdruck im Gesichtsausdruck Gestalt werden zu lassen.»

In der neueren Theatergeschichte sind nur die sog. Alltags-M. hinzugekommen; bezeichnenderweise muß ein Filmschauspieler als bestes Beispiel genannt werden: das zum Lachen unfähige, dem Ausdruck persönlicher Gefühle völlig verschlossene Gesicht des Buster Keaton. Andere Stars sind eher durch maskenhaft verfestigte, klischeehaft erstarrte Gesichter bekannt. Das ‹verdeckte Theater› benutzte die Alltags-M.

Der Betrachter oder Zuschauer sollte sich darüber klar sein, daß sich hinter jeder M. ein durch ihren Ausdruck versteckter Anteil des persönlichen Charakters oder Gefühls des M.-Trägers verbirgt. Es soll nicht unerwähnt bleiben, daß es im Theater auch vehemente Gegner jeden M.-Spiels gibt, z. B. Jerzy Grotowski (Polen, *1933).

Im Bereich des dt. →Ausdruckstanzes, vor allem von Mary Wigman und Harald Kreutzberg, wurden M. schon in den 20er Jahren vielfach eingesetzt. Etienne Decroux (Frankreich) betonte die Ausdruckskraft des Körpers, indem er seinen Kopf, sein Gesicht mit einem Tuch verhüllte. Der Effekt der Verhüllung wurde mit Hilfe der sog. Neutral-M. (ohne Ausdruck von Gefühlen in der M.-Form) verstärkt und ist in der Mimenausbildung heute nicht mehr wegzudenken. Um so widersprüchlicher erscheint die Hervorhebung des Gesichts durch die weiße Schmink-M. bei den meist schwarz kostümierten Pantomimen.

Erst die Inszenierungen des ital. Regisseurs Giorgio Strehler am →Piccolo Teatro di Milano brachten in den 50er Jahren eine Wiederbelebung der Commedia-M. Bert Brecht sieht für mehrere Stücke die Verwendung von M. vor, z. B. in *Der Kaukasische Kreidekreis*. Eine der bekanntesten Theater-M. der Gegenwart ist die Schmink-M. des Mephisto von Gustaf Gründgens (1899–1963) aus der Verfilmung seiner *Faust*-Inszenierung von 1956.

582 Maske/Maskentheater

Einen beispielhaften Impuls für die neue Arbeit mit M. im Theater setzte das →Bread and Puppet Theatre von Peter Schumann (*1934) aus New York/Vermont mit seinen Straßentheateraufführungen und Theaterinszenierungen seit Mitte der 60er Jahre. Nachfolger sind heute einige freie Theatergruppen wie Baufirma Meißel und Co. (Frankfurt) oder Dagol-Masken, Rituale, Stille (Berlin). Neue Impulse bringen in Polen die Scena plastyczna KUL (Lublin), in Schweden Jordcirkus (Stockholm). – Vorbehalte der Schauspieler stehen der Arbeit mit Gesichts-M. an den staatlichen Bühnen oft entgegen. Nur wenige Inszenierungen haben mehr als lokales/momentanes Interesse gefunden: *Peer Gynt* (Schaubühne am Halleschen Ufer, Berlin, 1972) oder *Ödipus* (Schauspielhaus Köln, 1984). Neben dem Versuch, historische Quellen der europäischen Theatertradition wieder zu erschließen, wird die Faszination der Arbeit mit M. heute im wesentlichen aus außereuropäischen Kulturen oder Theaterformen abgeleitet, z. B. →Théâtre du Soleil (Paris). Unter der Bezeichnung Ethno-Theater verbreitete sich seit Beginn der 80er Jahre ein neuer Kulturimperialismus; u. a. werden M. verschiedenster Herkunft beliebig mit Kostümen, Tanzformen, Musik und mythologischen Inhalten vermischt und als Theatervorstellungen angeboten.

M.-Spiel ist immer (auch) Theater. Der Ausdruck des M.-Gesichts bildet eine Einheit mit dem entsprechenden Kostüm und wird zur ganzen Gestalt durch entsprechende Haltung und Bewegung. Das Spiel hat nur Bedeutung, wenn damit die neue Gestalt glaubwürdig wird. M.-Spiel als Darstellung einer neuen Persönlichkeit, eines anderen Charakters muß so weit von gewöhnlicher Handlung entfernt sein wie der Ausdruck des M.-Gesichts vom normalen Gesicht des Menschen. Andernfalls versteckt die M. nur den Spieler und wird zur Illustration des Textes. Ein Dämon, ein dämonischer Charakter, eine dämonisierte Person darf nicht gutmütig sein – oder es muß so überzeugend gegen das Vorurteil/Klischee gespielt werden, daß diese Verwandlung zum eigentlichen Inhalt wird. Stilisierte oder abstrakte M.-Formen brauchen entsprechend vereinfachte Bewegungsformen. Überflüssige Bewegungen und mehrere Handlungen gleichzeitig sollten vermieden werden. Die Faszination der M. wirkt nur, solange das Spiel lebendig bleibt. Es gibt nur zwei Regeln: Eine M. kann nicht träumen, und: eine M. blickt immer in Richtung ihrer Nasenspitze. Ausnahmen sind die meisten Commedia-M. sowie M., deren Augenöffnungen so gestaltet sind, daß die Augen des Darstellers gleichzeitig die Augen der M. sind.

M.-Bau: In den meisten Traditionen werden M. aus Holz geschnitzt. Die klassischen griech. M. wurden (vermutlich) aus stuckiertem Leinen auf ein Tonmodell kaschiert. Die M. der Commedia dell'arte werden aus Leder über ein Holzmodell geformt, M. können aus Blech sein (Ritterhelme, Schandmasken), aus verschiedenem Material geflochten, aus Pa-

Maske / Maskentheater 583

pier gcfaltet, aus weicheren Materialien modelliert und gehärtet werden. Um zu einer persönlichen Ausdrucksform zu gelangen, kann ein Modell aus Töpferton geformt werden; dieses Material bietet die größten Freiheiten der Gestaltung. Auf dieses Modell kann die spätere M. kaschiert werden, z. B. aus Packpapier mit Hilfe von Tapetenkleister, aus Mullbinden mit Holzleim, aus kunststoffbeschichtetem Gewebe mit Lösungsmittel. Um Feinheiten und Glätte der Oberfläche möglichst genau zu erhalten, kann vom Tonmodell ein Gipsabdruck abgenommen werden und das Material der M. in diese Negativform eingelegt, eingepreßt, eingegossen (Gummimilch) werden.

M.-Formen: es ist zu unterscheiden: Halb-M.: z. B. die Commedia-M. – Gesichts-M. bedecken nur das Gesicht des Spielers, wollen meist durch den Gesichtsausdruck wirken, gleichgültig, ob es menschlich ist oder tierhaft, ein Phantasiewesen oder eine Karikatur. – Ganzkopf-M. werden als volle Kopfform erarbeitet und über den Kopf des Spielers gestülpt (auch Stülp-M. genannt), liegen oft auf den Schultern auf oder werden durch Einlagen mit dem Kopf des Spielers verbunden. – Aufsatz-M. werden auf oder über dem Kopf des Spielers befestigt; sie vergrößern die Gestalt und haben oft übermenschliche Bedeutung.

M.-Bildner: Je nach Vorbildung gibt es in der BRD eine zwei- bzw. dreijährige Ausbildung an größeren Theatern, Opern, TV-Anstalten. Die praktischen Ausbildungsinhalte sind vom Berufsverband vorgeschrieben und werden für die Abschlußprüfung vorausgesetzt. Theoretische Kenntnisse in Theatergeschichte, Stilkunde etc. sind selbständig zu erarbeiten. Zum Vergleich: In der DDR erfolgte die Ausbildung als dreijähriges Fachschulstudium mit den Schwerpunkten handwerkliches Können, künstlerisch-ästhetisches Empfinden sowie theoretisches Wissen. In Schweden gibt es eine dreijährige Hochschulausbildung, wofür bereits eine qualifizierte Vorbildung verlangt wird. Die Aufnahmeprüfung (nur alle zwei Jahre) dauert dort eine ganze Woche – in der BRD dauert die Abschlußprüfung drei Tage.

Bihalji-Merin, O.: Masken der Welt. Gütersloh 1970; Caillois, R.: Die Spiele und die Menschen. Stuttgart 1960; Corson, R.: Stage Makeup. New Jersey 1975; Craig, E. G.: Über die Kunst des Theaters. Berlin 1969; Ebeling, I.: Masken und Maskierung. Köln 1984; Gregor, J.: Die Masken der Erde. München 1936; Kachler, K. G.: Über das Wesen und Wirken der Theatermaske. In: Antaios, Bd. XI. Stuttgart 1970, S. 192–208; Melchinger, S.: Das Theater der Tragödie. München 1974; Sheleen, L.: Théâtre pour devenir autre. Paris 1983; Sorell, W.: The other face – the mask in the arts. London 1973; Schweeger-Hefel, A.: Masken und Schauspiel bei fremden Völkern. Wien 1955; Young, D.: Theaterwerkstatt. Maskenbildnerei und Schminken. Augsburg 1988.

Uwe Krieger

Maskentänze

(Arab.: maskarat = verkleidete Person, Possenreißer – Verspottung; mlat.: masca; span.: máscara; ital.: maschera; frz.: masque = künstliche Hohlgesichtsform; aber auch Verkleidung, kostümierte Person, falscher Schein) Die →Maske ist ein theatralisches Mittel zur Verstärkung des mimischen Ausdrucks und zur Unterstützung der imaginativen Darstellungsmöglichkeiten.

▸ *Naturvölker:* Für die Naturvölker muß der Kontakt zu den übernatürlichen Kräften die höchste Absicherung ihrer Lebenskräfte bedeutet haben. Die Maske allein erlaubte den Umgang mit der Großen Macht. Jede Maske weitete das Selbst aus. Anfangs waren nur Schmink- und Farbmasken üblich, später gelang es, Masken aus den Knochen von Tierschädeln zum Überstülpen zuzurichten. Schließlich gab es Masken aus Holz, Leder, Metall oder aus Stoff. Die Maske ist mit dem Haarteil eng verbunden. Als M. sind Tier-, Jagd-, Initiations- und Erntetänze in die Kosmologien und Mythologien der Völker eingebaut worden. Bei den Kalabari in Nigeria besaß die Maske die Macht, zum Wohle aller Zurückgebliebenen zu wirken. Bei den M. durfte kein Flecken Haut den Menschen verraten. Die Yorubas betonten vor dem Tanz den Akt der Einkleidung. Er wurde von Priestern durch Inkantationen und Tieropfer vollzogen. Damit wurde das Maskenkleid als göttlich ausgewiesen. Seine Berührung führte zum Tod. Die Ijimere tragen beim M. zwei Kleider übereinander und einen prunkvollen Königsmantel, die capa africana. Der Höhepunkt des M. wird durch kunstvolle Capa-Spiele im großen alaba gestaltet mit hinreißenden Drehungen, Schwüngen, Positionen und Raumformationen. Der Erdmutter «onile» zu Ehren führen die gelede ein großes Maskenspiel auf. In ihm tritt die Erdmutter sowohl als aya (= Hexe) als auch als onile (= Segensspenderin) auf. Dramaturgisch existieren vier Spielteile. Die Bewegungsmuster des Tanzes weisen auf die Geschlechterrollen hin. Die männliche gelede-Maske verkörpert Kraft, Geschicklichkeit und Freiheit im Stampfen, in Sprüngen und Wendungen, die den Körper nahezu wie ein Segel im Winde erscheinen lassen. Als weibliche Maske tanzen die Männer mit dem Rücken zum Zuschauerkreis. Der weibliche Solo-gelede lebt von rapiden Stakkato-Bewegungen, was zum Fußtrommeln führt, und von einer Fersen-Zehen-Technik, ähnlich dem plantatacón in Andalusien. Die Ladakh-Tänzer der Himachal Pradesh verkörpern im M. den Sieg der guten Geister über die bösen. Zu den →Chhao-Tänzen (grundsätzlich M.) gehören der Ozean-Tanz und der kolam thullar, der den Mythos der Bhagavatis (Erdmutter) szenisch ausspielt. Phantastisch bemalte Masken aus Holz und Palmblättern bilden riesige Kopfbedeckungen. Die Farben Weiß, Gelb, Grün, Rot und Schwarz dienen neben sehr differenten Mustern der Symbolisierung. See-

Maskentänze 585

muscheln stellen die Zahnreihen, fächerförmige Pfauenfedern die Kopf-
zier. Aus dem 7. und 8. Jh. stammen die noch ohne Bühne auskommen-
den Maskenspiele Japans, die «Gagaku-Maskenspiele». Das Gagaku-
Theater beginnt mit dem Aufzug der Tänzer und Musikanten, an den sich
die pantomimischen Darbietungen der grotesk maskierten Mimen anschließen, die auch phallische Szenen eingliedern.

▸ *Antike:* In Griechenland (→ Antikes Theater) werden die M. auf den
Dionysoskult (→ Dionysien) zurückgeführt. Der eigentliche Schöpfer der
künstlerisch geformten farbigen Masken war Aischylos. Er nutzte die
Maske nicht als kultische Insignie, sondern strebte in dramatischem Spiel
den weithin erkennbaren theatralischen Gesichtsausdruck an. Das → Satyrspiel kennt Masken mit grotesken Wulstlippen, Tierohren und aufge-
stülpten Nasen. Das griech. Maskenarsenal zählte zur Zeit Menanders im
4. Jh. 44 Maskentypen auf. In Rom durften bis zum 1. Jh. von Berufsschauspielern keine Masken getragen werden, sie waren Unfreie. Die
→ Atellana als derb volkstümliches Stegreifspiel kennzeichnet vier feststehende Grotesk-Maskentypen.

▸ *Mittelalter:* Die Mimen Roms retten mit dem Tanz und den Pantomimen das Theater und damit auch die M. in das Mittelalter hinüber. Wie
die Mimen selbst, so treiben auch die M. im frühen Mittelalter ihr Wesen
im volkstümlichen → Brauchtum, in → Mysterienspielen und Prozessionen, etwa in den Charivari. Der Begriff Charivari bezeichnet im Mittelalter einen Aufzug von lärmenden Masken, Tänzern und Trommlern. Bauern und Bürger tragen im Zug Teufels- und Tierköpfe und verunsichern
als Ungetüme und Dämonen das ansonsten wohlgeordnete Leben der
Mitbürger. Als «Buffonis» schließen sie sich zumeist den in die Stadt ein-
ziehenden Komödianten an. Von den Umzügen aus wandern die Masken
in das Kirchen- und auf das Marktplatztheater. Der Adel maskiert sich
auf seinen Schwertleiten, Banketten, Turnieren und anderen Festen.
Zum kunstvoll gestalteten theatralischen Schau- und Tanzspiel entwikkelt sich das Treiben der M. in den Prozessionen und → Trionfi der Renaissance und des Barock. Vom 14. Jh. an kennt Frankreich Maskeraden
als simple Vorformen des späteren → Ballet de Cour. Im Juni 1564 zieht
ein Maskenzug des Cesare Negri durch Mailand. Auf 25 Karren und Wagen verkörpern die Masken allegorisch alle Regungen der Seele. Aus dem
Jahr 1664 ist das Versailler Gartenfest als Maskerade überliefert. Der
Barock unterscheidet «Mascarades à grand spectacle», die Auffahrt fest-
lich geschmückter Wagen, und «Mascarades du palais», auf denen Tänze
und Rezitationen einander abwechseln. Als Verschmelzung beider Formen entstehen zu Heinrichs IV. Zeit die Ballets-Mascarades als vierteilige
dramaturgische Gestaltungen. Die engl. → «Masques» sind eine Form der
Kurzweil bei Hofe. 1634 entwickelt Ben Jonson die → Anti-Masques
(→ Ritualtänze; → Mysterienspiele; → Totentänze).

Berger, R.: African Dance. Wilhelmshaven 1984; Ferguson, L.: Some early masks and Morris dances. In: Modern Psychology 24 (1926); Johannsmeier, R.: Spielmann, Schalk und Scharlatan. Reinbek bei Hamburg 1984; Rebling, E.: Die Tanzkunst Indiens. Wilhelmshaven 1982; Weege, F.: Der Tanz in der Antike. Hildesheim 1976.

Helga Ettl

Masque

Aristokratische Form der dramatischen Unterhaltung mit einer Blütezeit am engl. Hof unter Jakob I. und Karl I. (1603–42). Gekennzeichnet durch Musik, Tanz und aufwendige Ausstattung. Häufig wurden die Zuschauer(innen) als Tänzer(innen) in die höfischen Inszenierungen einbezogen. Ursprung im Folkritual, in dem maskierte oder verkleidete Gäste dem Edelmann Geschenke überreichten, der sich dem feierlichen Abschlußtanz anschloß. Unter Ben Jonson (1572–1637) und dem Architekten und Bühnenbildner Inigo Jones (1573–1652) erreichte das M. seine Vollendung (*Oberon, the Fairy Prince*, 1611). 1609 führte Jonson die ante-masque mit *The Mask of Queens* ein, die dem eigentlichen Maskenspiel vorausging und einen Kontrast zu ihr bildete, z. B. durch groteske Tänze. Als die Repräsentationsfunktion der M. immer deutlicher in den Vordergrund rückte, bes. nach dem Rücktritt von Ben Jonson (1634), verlor die Form an dramatischer Substanz. Sie wurde nach der Restauration der brit. Monarchie (1660) nicht wieder aufgenommen, beeinflußte aber die Entwicklung der Oper und die des Balletts in England und bereitete die Einführung der aus Italien kommenden Perspektivkulissen vor.

Lindley, D. (Hg.): The Court Masque. Manchester 1984; Orgel, S.: The Jonsonian Masque. Cambridge (Mass.) 1965; Orgel, S./Strong, R.: Inigo Jones: The Theatre of the Stuart Court. 2 Vols. Berkeley 1973; Welsford, E.: The Court Masque. A Study in the Relationship between Poetry and the Revels. Cambridge 1927 (repr. 1962).

J. Lawrence Guntner

Massenregie

M. ist eine Methode zur Gestaltung des Bühnengeschehens in Theaterformen und Inszenierungen, in denen ‹das Volk› oder ‹die Menge› durch eine Vielzahl von Darstellern repräsentiert wird; durch Gruppenbilder und -bewegungen, durch chorisches Singen, Sprechen, Schreien und durch kollektive Gestik sollen (mehr oder weniger kalkuliert) bestimmte emotionale Wirkungen erzielt werden; die Zuschauer sollen zu einer Einheit zusammengeschmolzen, seelisch ergriffen und erhoben, möglichst weitgehend in den Bann der theatralen Aktion gezogen werden. – M. gab es im religiösen Theater des Spätmittelalters (→Mittelalter/Drama und Theater des Mittelalters), insbesondere bei den mehrtägigen Aufführungen von Passionsspielen auf Marktplätzen, im Ordenstheater und in den Huldigungsspielen des →Barocktheaters, bei den historisierenden Klassikeraufführungen der →Meininger im letzten Viertel des vorigen Jh. sowie vor allem dann bei Max Reinhardt in den mit Hunderten von Statisten in Großräumen erstellten Produktionen wie *König Ödipus* von Sophokles (1910 in der Musikfesthalle München, dann im Zirkus Schumann in Berlin, 1911 im Zirkus Busch in Wien), der religiösen Pantomime *Das Mirakel* nach einem Szenarium von Paul Vollmoeller (ab 1914 in Berlin, Wien, Budapest, London, New York) und des *Danton* von Romain Rolland (Großes Schauspielhaus Berlin, 1919). Auch im →Massentheater nach der Russ. Revolution und bei den Festspielen der dt. Gewerkschaften 1920 bis 1924 in Leipzig spielte die M. eine große Rolle.

Peter Simhandl

Massentheater

Diese durch die große, manchmal in die Tausende gehende Zahl von Darstellern und Zuschauern sowie durch die Tendenz zu ihrer oft pseudoreligiösen Vereinigung im Sinne einer übergeordneten Idee charakterisierte Erscheinungsform von Theater begegnet schon in den Konzeptionen einiger Theaterreformer nach der Jahrhundertwende (z. B. bei Adolphe Appia und Georg Fuchs), in der Praxis aber erst im Jahre 1920 in der Sowjetunion als Mittel zur Ausgestaltung der Festtage des ‹Roten Kalenders›, zwischen 1920 und 1924 (*Mysterium der befreiten Arbeit, Zur Weltkommune, Die Erstürmung des Winterpalais*), dann in den Massenfestspielen der Gewerkschaften in Leipzig (*Spartakus, Der arme Konrad*, und nach Szenarien von Ernst Toller: *Bilder aus der Französischen Revolution, Krieg und Frieden, Das Erwachen*), in den Jahren um 1930 als Teil sozialdemokratischer Sportfeste und schließlich im →Thingspiel der Nationalsozialisten. Wichtige Elemente des M. sind die rhythmische Bewegung von Menschenblöcken, der Sprechchor, die Musik, die nur durch wenige Bauelemente veränderte Architektur der Plätze oder Stadien und das Licht der Scheinwerfer.

Eichberg, H. u. a.: Massenspiele. Stuttgart 1977; Paech, J.: Das Theater der russ. Revolution. Kronberg/Ts. 1974.

Peter Simhandl

Maxim-Gorki-Theater (Berlin)

Unter den Linden/Am Kastanienwäldchen. Zwei Spielstätten (Maxim-Gorki-Theater mit 445 Plätzen, Studiobühne mit 120 Plätzen), Gebäude der ehemaligen Berliner Singakademie, erbaut 1823 bis 1827 nach Entwürfen von Schinkel, Intendant seit 1968: Albert Hetterle (*1918). – Eröffnung 1952, hervorgegangen aus dem von Robert Trösch (*1911) seit 1947 geleiteten «Neuen Theater» und dem von Maxim Vallentin (*1904) seit 1949 geleiteten «Jungen Ensemble», der auch bis 1968 Intendant des M. war.

Das M. ist der Schauspieltradition von Konstantin Sergejewitsch Stanislawski (1863–1938) verpflichtet, neben dem Werk Gorkis führte es vor allem zeitgenössische Stücke aus der Sowjetunion, daneben auch aus anderen ‹Bruderländern› und der DDR auf, von letzteren z. B. *Lohndrükker* und *Die Korrektur* (1958) von Heiner Müller (*1929), später mehrere von Reiner Kerndl (*1928, zeitweise Hausautor), Claus Hammel (1932–90), Rudi Strahl (*1931, zeitweise Hausautor), Jürgen Groß (*1946, zeitweise Hausautor). In den 80er Jahren artikulierte das M. in besonderer Weise – durch Aufführungen sowjetischer «Perestroika»-Stücke von Schatrow, Gelmann u. a., durch aktuelle Sichten auf bisher kaum gespielte westeuropäische Dramatik, durch die gleichsam programmatische Inszenierung von Volker Brauns *Übergangsgesellschaft*, 1988 – das immer dringender werdende Bedürfnis nach Veränderungen in der DDR-Gesellschaft. Wichtige Regisseure der 60er Jahre waren Hans Dieter Mäde (*1930) und Horst Schönemann (*1927), später haben neben Hetterle vor allem Rolf Winkelgrund (*1936) (u. a. *Einer flog über das Kuckucksnest*, 1982, Vitracs *Victor*, 1988) und Thomas Langhoff (*1938) (u. a. *Drei Schwestern*, 1979, *Sommernachtstraum*, 1980, *Mein Kampf* von Tabori, 1989) das künstlerische Profil des M. bestimmt.

Funke, Ch./Kranz, D.: Theaterstadt Berlin. Berlin (DDR) 1978, S. 99–112; Funke, Ch./Hoffmann-Ostwald, D./Otto, H.-G.: Theater-Bilanz. Berlin (DDR) 1971, S. 76–79; Möckel, M. (Hg.): Das Maxim Gorki Theater 1952–1972. Berlin (DDR) 1972; Pietzsch, I.: Werkstatt Theater. Berlin (DDR) 1975, S. 88–96; Kranz, D.: Berliner Theater. Berlin 1990.

Andreas Roßmann/Manfred Pauli

Max-Reinhardt-Seminar

«Die vollkommene Meisterung des Handwerks, die souveräne Beherrschung des Wortes und der Stimme, die gründliche musikalische, rhythmische, tänzerische, sportliche, ja sogar akrobatische und die gesangliche

Ausbildung wird in Zukunft vom Schauspieler verlangt werden.» Mit diesen Worten eröffnete Max Reinhardt (1873–1943) 1929 in Wien seine Schauspielschule. – «Abteilung für Schauspiel und Regie» an der Wiener Hochschule für Musik und Darstellende Kunst lautet der offizielle Name des Seminars heute. Angeboten wird eine je vierjährige Schauspiel- oder Regieausbildung; pro Jahrgang werden nach einer Aufnahmeprüfung ca. 15 Schüler übernommen, in der Sparte Regie fünf bis sechs. Schauspiel- und Regieschüler haben die Möglichkeit, durch die Erarbeitung der jährlichen Schulproduktionen praktische Theater- und Aufführungserfahrungen zu machen: Im Schönbrunner Schloßthea- ter (1747 eröffnet, ältestes noch in Betrieb befindliches Wiener Ba- rocktheater, 450 Zuschauer), moderne Studiobühne (ab Oktober 1992), Gastspiele im In- und Ausland (u. a. Berlin, Hamburg, Bratislava, Paris, Sydney). Lehrkörper: ca. 42 Professoren und Lehrbeauftragte (Mitglie- der verschiedener Wiener Bühnen und international renommierte Thea- terleute wie Heiner Müller, Feruccio Soleri, Josef Svoboda, Giorgio Strehler, Oleg Tabakov).

Holasek, H. P.: Das Max Reinhardt Seminar. Diss. Wien 1967; Schwarz, H.: Max Reinhardt und das Wiener Seminar. Wien 1973.

Ute Hagel / Ingeborg Janich

MChAT

(Moskovskij chudožestvennyj akademičeskij teatr im. M. Gor'kogo) Moskauer Künstlertheater; urspr. MChT (Moskovskij chudožestvennyj teatr), 1920 mit dem Zusatz «akademisches» versehen. 1898 von K. S. Stanislawski (1863–1938) und W. I. Nemirowitsch-Dantschenko (1858–1943) als privates Bühnenunternehmen gegr. mit dem erklärten Ziel, ein für alle Bevölkerungsschichten zugängliches Theater zu schaf- fen. Dem «hohen Stil» des →Hoftheaters und dem kommerziellen Thea- ter wollte Stanislawski ein «Theater der Wahrheit und der Kunst» entge- genstellen. Inspiriert durch Aufführungen der →Meininger, führte er um- fassende Reformen durch, wobei der authentischen Darstellung der Rol- len, der schauspielerischen Harmonie des Ensembles sowie einer mög- lichst naturgetreuen Dekoration besondere Bedeutung zukam.

Zur Eröffnung des Künstlertheaters am 14. Oktober 1898 wurde mit großem Erfolg das historische Drama *Zar Fjodor Ioannowitsch* von A. K. Tolstoi gespielt. Weltruhm erlangte das Theater durch die Aufführung der *Möwe* von A. P. Tschechow (1860–1904), die als zweite Premiere am 17. Dezember 1898 stattfand. Ein Jahr zuvor war das Stück im Peters- burger Alexandrinski-(heute →Puschkin-)Theater durchgefallen. Mit der

590 MChAT

Moskauer Aufführung wurde die stilisierte schwebende Möwe zum Emblem des M.; sie ist es bis heute.

Den Intentionen der beiden Gründer des Künstlertheaters, die zugleich – bis 1938 – seine Leiter waren, kamen bes. die Dramen Tschechows entgegen. Die erfolgreichen Inszenierungen von *Onkel Wanja* (1899), *Drei Schwestern* (1901), *Der Kirschgarten* (1904) brachten dem Theater die Benennung «Haus Tschechows» ein. Für die frühen Dramen Gorkis, *Nachtasyl* (1902), *Die Kleinbürger* (1902), *Kinder der Sonne* (1905) wandten sich die Schauspieler von dem verfeinerten Lyrismus der Tschechow-Stücke ab und einem von sozialem Pathos getragenen Ton zu. Nach Stanislawski war Gorki der Initiator und Schöpfer der gesellschaftspolitischen Linie am M. Auf dieser Linie lagen auch die Inszenierungen von Hauptmanns *Fuhrmann Henschel* (1899), *Einsame Menschen* (1899), *Michael Kramer* (1901), von Ibsens *Hedda Gabler* (1899), *Die Wildente* (1901), *Die Stützen der Gesellschaft* (1903), bis vor dem Hintergrund der revolutionären Unruhen ab 1905 die Zensur diese Art Dramen aus dem Repertoire verbannte. Danach bestimmten der Kulturpessimismus der Symbolisten, Stücke von Maeterlinck, L. Andrejew den Spielplan.

Zwischen 1906 und 1917 erstreckt sich für Stanislawski eine Experimentierphase. Neue Regieverfahren ermöglichen gelungene Inszenierungen u. a. der bis dahin kaum beachteten Dramen I. S. Turgenjews (1818–83) *Ein Monat auf dem Lande* (1909), *Der Kostgänger, Wo es dünn ist, reißt es auch, Die Provinzlerin* (alle 1912). Zusammen mit L. A. Sulershizki legt Stanislawski den Grund für sein System im Ersten Studio des M., das 1913 eröffnet wird. G. Craig rückt mit seiner *Hamlet*-Inszenierung 1911 das M. an die Spitze der avantgardistischen Theater. Eine Erneuerung und Erweiterung erfahren die bühnenbildnerischen Prinzipien, indem Künstler wie M. W. Dobushinski, N. K. Rörich, A. N. Benois, B. M. Kustodiew herangezogen werden. Dennoch lösen sich viele Schüler Stanislawskis, vor allem Meyerhold und Wachtangow, mit radikaleren Programmen vom Künstlertheater. Es galt als überlebt. Die Oktoberrevolution beschleunigte diese Entwicklung. Nach der Revolution jedoch wurde ihm der Titel «akademisches Theater» verliehen, galt es als Repräsentant des sozialistischen Realismus. 1932 gab man ihm den Namen Maxim Gorki.

Unter den veränderten gesellschaftlichen Bedingungen und auf Grund der künstlerischen Erfahrungen der Vergangenheit suchte das M. Zugang zur zeitgenössischen sowj. Dramatik. Es folgen Aufführungen von M. A. Bulgakow *Die Tage der Turbins* (1926), W. W. Iwanow *Panzerzug 14–67* (1927), L. M. Leonow *Untilowsk* (1929). Gleichzeitig werden russ. und westeurop. Dramen neu interpretiert. 1920 war das – von Wachtangow geleitete – 3., 1921 das 4. Studio gegründet worden.

Pflegestätte großer Schauspielkunst, u. a. O. L. Knipper-Tschechowa

(1868–1959), das Ideal der Stanislawski-Schule, die subtilste Verkörperung Tschechowscher Gestalten; W. I. Katschalow (1875–1948); in der zweiten Generation O. N. Androwskaja (1898–1975), N. P. Batschalow (1899–1937); später u. a. A. N. Gribow (1902–1977).

Mehrfach Auslandsgastspiele, u. a. 1906 in Deutschland, 1922 bis 1924 in Deutschland, der Tschechoslowakei, Frankreich, Jugoslawien, USA, 1937 Paris.

Im 2. Weltkrieg Evakuierung. Auch nach 1945 viele Auslandsgastspiele des MChAT, das weiterhin als erste Bühne des Landes gilt, obwohl sich hier auch nach dem ‹Tauwetter› die allgemeinen Erstarrungstendenzen des sowj. Theatersystems besonders kraß auswirken (Überalterung und künstler. Niedergang des Ensembles, Manifestierung von Führungspositionen, kaum Chancen für den Nachwuchs). In der Krisensituation des MChAT 1970 übernimmt O. N. Jefremow (1927) vom «Sowremennik» die Leitung, bildet ein neues Repertoire (russ. Klassik und zeitgenössische Dramatik von Rostschin, Gelman, Schatrow, Wampilow, Petruschewskaja), arbeitet mit Gastregisseuren, engagiert begabte Schauspieler (Kaljagin, Tabakow, Smoktunowski, Wertinskaja, Sawwina). Ernste Konflikte zwischen den Protagonisten der 158köpfigen Truppe führen 1987 zur generellen Neustrukturierung als «Vereinigung Künstlertheater» mit zwei selbständigen Theatern, Studio-Schule und Museen. 1990 endgültige Aufspaltung in ein MChAT «M. Gorki» (Leitung T. W. Doronina, zunächst im 1973 erbauten Riesenhaus am Twerskoi Boulevard, dann in der Moskwin-Str.) und ein MChAT «A. P. Tschechow», das O. N. Jefremow im 1987 wiedereröffneten alten Gebäude (Jugendstil) leitet.

Markow, P. A./Čuškin, N.: Moskovskij Chudožestvennyj teatr. 1898–1948. Moskva 1950; Moskovskij Chudožestvennyj teatr. 1898–1938. Bibliografičeskij ukazatel'. Sost. A. Aganbekjan. Moskva/Leningrad 1939; Moskovskij Chudožestvennyj teatr v illjustracijach i dokumentach. 1898–1938. Moskva 1938; Moskovskij Chudožestvennyj teatr v illjustracijach i dokumentach. 1939–43. Moskva 1945; Moskovskij Chudožestvennyj teatr v sovetskuju epochu. Moskva 1962, ²1974; Sobolev, Ju. V.: Moskovskij Chudožestvennyj teatr. Moskva/Leningrad 1938. Makkin, A.: Golosa Rossii (MChT 1898–1988). In: Teatr (Moskva) 1988, Nr. 10.

Annelore Engel-Braunschmidt/Elke Wiegand

Mechane

Theatermaschine des griech. Theaters, mit deren Hilfe Personen, besonders Götter, durch die Luft auf die Bühne oder das Bühnendach transportiert werden konnten. Aussehen und Technik der M. sind unklar; aus dem 2. Namen der M. (Geranos: Kran, Kranich) darf man schließen, daß

es sich um eine Art Kran handelte, der über das Bühnenhaus hereinge-
schwenkt wurde; S. Melchinger vermutet, daß er mit einer Art Gondel
versehen war. Die M. diente vor allem für die Epiphanie des nach ihr
benannten →Deus ex machina, daneben für alle Arten von mythischen
Luftdurchquerungen und ihre Parodierung in der Komödie.

Seit wann die M. den Dramatikern zur Verfügung stand, ist umstritten.
Daß es die spektakuläre Theatermaschine aber bereits im 5. Jh. gab, kann
angesichts ihrer Parodierung durch Aristophanes nicht bezweifelt werden. Für Aischylos ist sie nicht zu sichern; Sophokles scheint sie vermieden zu haben; offenbar hat erst Euripides vollen Gebrauch von ihr gemacht.

Arnott, P.: Greek Scenic Conventions in the Fifth Century. Oxford 1962, p. 72 bis
78; Blume, H.-D.: Einführung in das antike Theaterwesen. Darmstadt 1978,
S. 69–72; Melchinger, S.: Das Theater der Tragödie. München 1974, S. 195 bis
200.

Bernd Seidensticker

Mechanisches Theater

Als M. T. bezeichnet man eine bestimmte Form des →Puppentheaters,
bei der die menschliche Kraft als Bewegungselement weitgehend oder
völlig ausgeschaltet ist; in seiner Tradition bis in die Renaissance zurück-
reichend, erlebte das M. T. als Vergnügen des Adels wie als Volksbelustigung auf Jahrmärkten im 18. und 19. Jh. seine Blüte; besonders beliebt
waren Darbietungen artistischer Szenen sowie des Weihnachtsgesche-
hens (‹Krippentheater›).

Der Begriff M. T. ist aber auch im Zusammenhang der Entwicklung im
20. Jh. für Darstellungen gebräuchlich, bei denen der Mensch als Akteur
durch Objekte ersetzt ist, die wirklich maschinell-mechanisch oder auch
durch verdeckt agierende Menschen, also pseudo-mechanisch, bewegt
werden. Schon im Zuge der antinaturalistischen →Theaterreform um
1900 forderte Edward Gordon Craig die Ablösung des Schauspielers
durch die →Über-Marionette und den Umbau des Theaters in ein mechanisches Instrument. Was bei Craig noch eine recht allgemeine Utopie
blieb, haben die Künstler des →Futuristischen Theaters in ihren Manifesten genauer beschrieben und in ‹Mechanischen Balletten› und ‹Dramen
der Gegenstände› praktisch realisiert. Das Theater als eine ‹Maschine zur
Erzeugung von Gefühlen› – diese Vorstellung der Futuristen wirkte tendenziell im →Konstruktivismus des nachrevolutionären Theaters in der
Sowjetunion nach, in El Lissitzkys Entwurf einer zentral gesteuerten
‹elektro-mechanischen Schau› nach der ‹futuristischen› Oper *Sieg über*

die Sonne von Alexej Krutschonych und M. W. Matjuschin, in den Bühnenmanifesten des Malers Fernand Léger, der die ‹anthropozentrische Schaustellung› mechanisch ‹erneuern› wollte, in Kurt Schwitters' Projekt der →Merzbühne sowie in der theoretischen und praktischen Bühnenarbeit am Bauhaus. Die Betonung der mechanischen Aspekte des Körpers und die Annäherung des Menschen an die scheinbar mechanisch funktionierende Kunstfigur durch Umkleidung mit starren ‹Kostümbauten› sind vor allem für die Experimente von Oskar Schlemmer, dem Leiter der ‹Bühnenwerkstatt› am Bauhaus, charakteristisch. Mit seinen ‹Figuralen Kabinetten›, in denen geometrische und gegenständliche Formen teilweise über ein Triebrad, teilweise durch unsichtbare Helfer bewegt wurden, schuf Schlemmer auch Beispiele für ein M. T. In dieser Richtung folgten ihm seine Schüler mit mechanischen Bewegungsfolgen abstrahiert-menschlicher oder ungegenständlicher Spielkörper; eine davon trug den treffenden Titel *Der Mann am Schaltbrett*. Auf diese Funktion reduziert begegnet der Mensch auch in der von Schlemmers Bauhaus-Kollegen Laszlo Moholy-Nagy konzipierten *Mechanischen Exzentrik*, einer Synthese der Darstellungselemente Form, Licht, Farbe, Bewegung, Ton und Geruch in einem ‹Aktionsvorgang›, der ganz den Forderungen einer bis ins letzte beherrschenden Bühnenorganisation entspricht. Von Bauhaus-Ideen ist schließlich auch Wassily Kandinskys Programm einer abstrakten →Bühnensynthese und dessen Realisierung in der Produktion *Bilder einer Ausstellung* geprägt, die als künstlerischer Höhepunkt der in Erscheinungen wie der ‹Laterna magica› oder verschiedenen Formen des ‹Multi-Media-Theaters› nach dem 2. Weltkrieg weitergeführten Entwicklung gelten kann.

Brauneck, M.: Theater im 20. Jh. Reinbek bei Hamburg 1982; Die Maler und das Theater im 20. Jh. – Ausstellungskatalog. Frankfurt/M. 1986; Raumkonzepte. Konstruktivistische Tendenzen in Bühnen- und Bildkunst 1910–1930. Frankfurt/M. 1986.

Peter Simhandl

Mecklenburgisches Staatstheater Schwerin

1836 «Großherzogliches Hoftheater», niedergebrannt 1882. Großes Haus mit 680 Plätzen 1883–86 erbaut, Kammerbühne mit ca. 200 Plätzen. Intendant Mario Krüger. – Teil des M. S. Sch. ist die «Fritz-Reuter-Bühne» (ein niederdeutsches Ensemble mit Abstechern in die Mecklenburger Region) und ein «Figurentheater». – Seit 1974, da Christoph Schroth (*1937) das Ensemble als Schauspieldirektor (und zeitweilig als Intendant) leitete, verschaffte es sich weit über sein Spielgebiet hinaus

594 Meddah

Beachtung. Besonders die zupackenden und bildkräftigen (freilich auch verflachenden) Klassiker-Inszenierungen Schroths (u. a. 1979 *Faust I/II* an einem Abend, 1984 *Demetrius/Dimitri* von F. Schiller/V. Braun, 1989 *Wilhelm Tell*) enthielten verdeckte Kritik an der DDR-Gesellschaft – ebenso auch die «Schweriner Entdeckungen», vielteilige Projekte in verschiedenen Theaterräumen, die das Schweriner Schauspiel bisweilen zur ‹ersten Adresse› des DDR-Theaters machten. Publikumszuspruch und fachliche Anerkennung liefen nicht auseinander. Schroth und seine künstlerischen Mitarbeiter haben 1989 das M. S. Sch. verlassen.

Pietzsch, I.: Werkstatt Theater. Berlin 1975, S. 122–128; Ullrich, R.: Schweriner Entdeckungen. Berlin 1986.

Roland Dreßler

Meddah

Mimischer Erzählkünstler, arab.: maddāḥ (Lobredner). Im arabischen Raum pries der M. ursprünglich das Lob des Propheten und seiner Familie, später das der Könige und Helden der Volkserzählungen. In der Türkei entwickelte sich daraus eine eigene theatralische Kunstgattung. Die Themen – bevorzugt komische Situationen – wurden dem Alltagsleben entnommen und enthielten nicht selten Kritik an den herrschenden sozialen und politischen Mißständen. Vorherrschende Erzählform war der Dialog. Die Kunst des M. beruhte vor allem auf dem *taklit*, der Imitation aller in seiner Geschichte vorkommenden Personen in Gestik, Mimik und Sprache und der Nachahmung von Tierstimmen und Geräuschen. Reiche Gelegenheit dazu boten die Sprechweisen der nichttürkischen Minderheiten des Osmanischen Reichs, z. B. Jude, Perser, Grieche, Armenier, aber auch die Gelehrtensprache und Frauenstimmen gehörten zum Repertoire des M., ebenso typische Lieder verschiedener Bevölkerungsgruppen. Unentbehrliche Requisiten waren ein Stock, dessen Klopfen den Beginn anzeigte, und ein Tuch, das der M. über einer Schulter trug, wenn er es nicht als Turban oder Kopftuch zur Charakterisierung seiner Gestalten um den Kopf wand oder sich mit ihm den Schweiß abwischte.

Der häufigste Vortragsort eines M. waren Kaffeehäuser, doch konnte er auch zu privaten Feiern eingeladen werden. Er bot eine beliebte Unterhaltungsform an den Abenden des Fastenmonats Ramadan. Heute ist der Beruf des M. weitgehend verschwunden. Es gibt vereinzelt Bemühungen, die vorwiegend mündlich tradierten Geschichten aufzuschreiben und den Beruf des M. in seiner ursprünglichen Form wiederzubeleben.

Nutku, Ö.: Meddahlık ve Meddah Hikâyeleri. Ankara o. J.; Uplegger, H.: Das Volksschauspiel. In: Philologiae Turcicae Fundamenta. Wiesbaden 1965.

Maren Fittschen

Die Meininger

Bezeichnung für das Ensemble des Hoftheaters Meiningen unter Leitung des Herzogs Georg II. von Sachsen-Meiningen. – Gegründet hatte das am 17. 12. 1831 eröffnete Hoftheater Herzog Bernhard II. Nachdem er 1866 zugunsten seines Sohnes abgedankt hatte, begann dieser mit dem Aufbau eines reinen Schauspielensembles. Ziel seiner Bemühungen war ein Mustertheater. Georg II. war kein bewußter Theatertheoretiker, bei seinen Reformbemühungen ging er wesentlich vom malerischen Eindruck aus. Seit 1870 leitete er die Bühne selbst, der von 1868 bis 1870 Friedrich von Bodenstedt als Intendant vorgestanden hatte. Georg II. setzte den malerischen Historismus konsequent auf der Bühne durch. Seine Reformbemühungen waren gekennzeichnet von größtmöglicher historischer Treue, die Authentizität des Textes ebenso betreffend wie die bis ins Detail gehende Festlegung des Kostüms, der Dekoration und des Bühnenbilds, das zugunsten plastischer Entwürfe weitgehend auf gemalte Kulissen verzichtete. Kennzeichnend für die Inszenierungen Georgs II. war die Massenregie, deren choreographischer Charakter sich deutlich gegen die bisherige Tradition absetzte, die vor allem das statische Element betonte. Das Schwergewicht der Bemühungen lag auf dem Zusammenwirken der einzelnen Elemente zu einem ‹Gesamtkunstwerk›. In bewußter Abkehr vom üblichen System reisender Virtuosen bildete Georg II. ein Ensemble, in dem auch ‹Stars› jederzeit Statistenrollen übernehmen mußten. Der ursprünglich als Charakterkomiker engagierte Ludwig Chronegk setzte als Regisseur die Ideen des Herzogs auf der Bühne um. Sein Anteil an der Entwicklung und dem Ruf der M. wird gelegentlich unterschätzt.

Nach intensiver Vorbereitung unternahmen die M. seit 1874 Tourneen durch ganz Europa. Am 1. 5. 1874 gaben sie in Berlin ihr erstes Gastspiel, am 1. 7. 1890 in Odessa ihr letztes. In den 16 Jahren, in denen sie reisten, besuchten sie bei 81 Gastspielen insgesamt 38 Städte und gaben 2591 Vorstellungen. Sie beeinflußten die Theaterentwicklung in ganz Europa und den USA; Regisseure und Theaterleiter wie Otto Brahm, André Antoine und Konstantin Stanislawski (→ Stanislawski-System) empfingen durch sie wichtige Anstöße für ihre eigene Arbeit, die in allen Fällen den Historismus der M. produktiv weiterentwickelte.

Ihre Bedeutung für die Entwicklung des Theaters liegt im Bestehen auf

596 Melodrama

historischer Genauigkeit in allen Bereichen, im Spiel mit der →Vierten Wand wie in der Betonung des Ensemblespiels, vor allem aber in der Herausbildung des Regietheaters im modernen Sinne. Vieles von dem, was die M. propagierten, war nicht nur ihr Werk, hatte Vorläufer und Begleiter. Ihr Verdienst – und ihre Grenze – lag in der Rigorosität, mit der sie ihre Ideen durchsetzten. Manches davon blieb äußerlich, neigte zur Übertreibung; dennoch kann man ihnen selbst den Vorwurf der ‹Meiningerei› kaum machen. Auch ihr Ruf leidet indessen unter den Übertreibungen der Nachahmer.

Grube, M.: Geschichte der Meininger. Stuttgart/Berlin/Leipzig 1926; Hahm, Th.: Die Gastspiele des Meininger Hoftheaters im Urteil der Zeitgenossen unter besonderer Berücksichtigung der Gastspiele in Berlin und Wien. Diss. Köln 1970; Hoffmeier, D.: Die Meininger – Streitfall und Leitbild. Diss. Berlin 1988; Jansen, M.: Meiningertum und Meiningerei. Eine Untersuchung über die Aus- und Nachwirkungen der Meininger Theaterreform. Diss. Berlin 1948; Osborne, J. (Hg.): Die Meininger. Texte zur Rezeption. Tübingen 1980; ders.: The Meiningen Court Theatre 1866–1890. Cambridge 1988; Richard, P.: Chronik sämtlicher Gastspiele des herzoglich Sachsen-Meiningschen Hoftheaters (1874 bis 1890). Leipzig 1891.

Wolfgang Beck

Melodrama

M. (griech. melos = Lied und Drama = Handlung) bezeichnet ursprünglich im Italien des 17. Jh. ein vollständig gesungenes musikalisches Drama, später in Frankreich seit dem *Pygmalion* (1775) von Jean-Jacques Rousseau (1712–78) einen kurzen Monolog, musikalisch untermalt und pantomimisch expressiv. In der Folge entwickelte sich daraus die Zwischengattung, welche seit 1800 als M. bezeichnet wird.

Das M. entstand mit dem Riesenerfolg des Stücks *Coelina ou l'Enfant du mystère* (1800) von René-Charles Guilbert de Pixérécourt (1773–1844; 2275 Aufführungen). Historisch gesehen ist das M. trotz abschätziger Werturteile die Theaterform des 19. Jh.; sie überdauert kaum die Jahrhundertwende. Bei den drei frz. Autoren des *Traité du mélodrame* (1817; gez.: A!A!A! = Abel Hugo, Armand Malitourne und Jean Adler) ist zu lesen: «Die Zeit Ludwigs XIV. war die der Poesie und der Redekunst, das XVIII. Jh. die der Philosophie und der Vernunft, das XIX. Jh. die der Chemie und des M.» Räumlich entstand und entwickelte sich das M. in Frankreich und breitete sich bald in Übersetzungen und Originalwerken in der ganzen Welt aus, vor allem in Großbritannien und in den USA. Das M. hatte seine eigenen Autoren, seine Theater, Schauspieler, Regisseure, sein Publikum und auch seine eigene poetische Form.

Melodrama 597

In vielem hat das frz. Genre im 19. Jh. als modellhaft und wegweisend gewirkt. Es ist aber nicht einheitlich, bes. was Motive und Inhalte betrifft. Zur Revolutionszeit entstanden, war es beeinflußt von Schillers Erstlingsdrama *Die Räuber* (1792) und den Rührstücken und Sittengemälden August Kotzebues (1761–1819), bes. *Menschenhaß und Reue* (UA 1787), durch die Tradition des →bürgerlichen Trauerspiels, vor allem von Michel-Jean Sedaine (1719–97), und auch durch die engl. Schauerromane von Horace Walpole (1717–97) und Ann Radcliffe (1764–1823). Diese Verquickung von volkstümlichen Romanen und überlieferten, z. T. überholten dramatischen Formen (Pixérécourt bezog sich ausdrücklich auf gewisse Regeln der klassischen →Tragödie) ist wesentlich für die Gattung. Wichtig aber war in dieser Entstehungsphase besonders die wenn auch zwiespältige ideologische Zielsetzung: für Charles Nodier war das M. eine Schule des Volkes, «die Moralität der Revolution», im Grunde das Volkstheater als moralische Anstalt. Statt der Kirche wird das Theater zur Kanzel und der Schreiber von Melodramen zum Volkstribunen, und zwar unter der Doppelherrschaft der Vorsehung und des Gesetzes. Neben Pixérécourt waren die wichtigsten frz. Autoren dieser ersten, ‹klassischen› Phase des M. Louis Caigniez (1762–1842) und Jean Cuvelier de Trye (1766–1824), Caigniez' *La Pie voleuse* (Die diebische Elster, 1815) war ein Riesenerfolg, wie auch die musikalische Adaptation *La Gazza Ladra* (1817) von Gioacchino Rossini (1792–1868). – Die 2. Phase des frz. M. ist die romantische (1823–48). Sie setzt ein mit einem großen Erfolg, *L'Auberge des Adrets* (1823) von drei wenig profilierten Autoren (B. Antier, A. Lacoste, Alex. Chapponier), worin die mythische Figur des edlen Räubers, Robert Macaire, die wohl berühmteste des M. überhaupt, geschaffen wurde. Kennzeichnend für diese Periode ist eine Verquickung des M. und des romantischen Dramas, die allerdings eine Unterscheidung nicht leicht macht. Stücke von Victor Hugo (1802–85) wie *Inez de Castro* (1819) oder *Lucrezia Borgia* (1833) und bes. von Alexandre Dumas Vater (1802–70), so *La Tour de Nesles* (1832) und *Richard Darlington* (1831), galten für die damalige Kritik als M. Die größten Autoren der Zeit im spezifischen Bereich des M. waren aber: Victor Ducange (1783–1833) mit *Thérèse ou l'Orpheline de Genève* (1820), *La Fiancée de Lamermoor* (1828, später: Oper von Gaetano Donizetti, 1797–1848, *Lucia di Lammermoor*, 1835) und *Trente ans ou la vie d'un joueur* (1831); Frédéric Soulié (1800–47) mit sozialkritischen M. wie *L'Ouvrier* (1840) oder *La Closerie des Genêts* (1846), einem der großen Bühnenerfolge des Jh.; Adolphe Dennery (1811–99) mit *La Dame de Saint-Tropez* (1844), *Marie-Jeanne ou la Femme du peuple* (1845) und am Ende seines Lebens dem überwältigenden Bühnenerfolg *Les Deux Orphelines* (1874); endlich Auguste Anicet-Bourgeois (1806–71), neben Dennery der wohl geschickteste Handwerker des M., Autor u. a. von *Le*

598 Melodrama

Docteur noir (1846), *La Mendiante* (1852), *L'Aveugle* (1857). – Die dritte und letzte große Phase des M. in Frankreich, auch die verschiedenartigste, lag zwischen dem Second Empire und dem 1. Weltkrieg (1848–1914). Jean-Marie Thomasseau unterscheidet vier Grundkategorien in der reichhaltigen Produktion: das militärische, patriotische und historische M. mit zwei Stücken als Höhepunkt, *Le Bossu* (1862) von Paul Féval (1817–87) und Auguste Anicet-Bourgeois sowie *La Bouquetière des Innocents* (1862); das naturalistische Sittenmelodrama mit z. B. *L'Etrangère* (1876) von Alexandre Dumas Sohn (1824–95) oder *La Fille des chiffoniers* (1861) von A. Anicet-Bourgeois und Dugué; das Abenteuer- und Forschermelodrama mit großartigen Regietricks, so *Les Pirates de la Savane* (1859) von Anicet-Bourgeois; endlich das Kriminal- und Justizmelodrama, worin sich bes. zwei Autoren hervortaten: Xavier de Montépin (1823–1902) mit einem der Meisterwerke des M. *La Porteuse de pain* (1889) und dem techn. raffinierten Krimi *La Policière* (1890); Pierre Decourcelle (1856–1926), bekannt vor allem für die oft gespielten M. *Gigolette* (1893), *Les Deux Gosses* (1896) und *La Môme aux beaux yeux* (1906). – Charakteristisch für die Produktion von M. war die Adaptation populärer Volksromane für die Bühne, welche oft zu den größten Theatererfolgen wurden; so *Les Mystêres de Paris* (1842–43) und *Le Juif errant* (1844) von Eugène Sue (1804–57); *Les Misérables* (1862) von Victor Hugo; *Le Maître de Forges* (1883) von Georges Ohnet (1848–1918); *Rocambole* (1884) von Pierre Alexis Ponson du Terrail (1829–71); *Le Tour du Monde en 80 jours* (1874) von Jules Verne (1828–1905).

Sowohl die Übersetzung der frz. Meisterdramen wie die Adaptation frz. und engl./amerik. Romane waren ausschlaggebend für den Triumph des M. auf den Bühnen Großbritanniens und der USA im 19. Jh. Ein erster Erfolg war Thomas Holcrofts (1745–1809) Übersetzung von Pixérécourts *Coelina, A Tale of Mystery* (1802). Wenn auch vor allem die frz. M. die Londoner Bühnen beherrschten, so kamen doch einige einheimische Autoren zum Erfolg. So nach Holcroft William Thomas Moncrieff (1794–1857) mit seinem Triumph *The Rajah's Daughter* (1823), der anonyme Autor des Erfolgsstücks *Maria Marten or the Murder in the Barn* (1830), Douglas Jerrold (1803–57) mit sozialkritischen M. wie *Martha Willis, the Servant Maid* (1831), Wilkie Collins (1824–89) mit seinen Kriminalmelodramen. Einer der Höhepunkte dieser Produktion war *The Silver King* (1882) von Henry Arthur Jones (1851–1929) und Henry Herman, sonst Autoren von realistischen Sittendramen. Als der wohl beste Könner dieses Genres galt Henry Irving (1838–1905); neben zahlreichen Adaptationen frz. M. inszenierte und spielte er die großen Shakespeare-Stücke – ein Zeichen für die Verquickung der Gattungen auf den damaligen Londoner Bühnen. Auch hier Dramatisierungen von bekannten Romanen, besonders von Charles Dickens (1812–70) und Sir Walter

Melodrama 599

Scott (1771–1832). Der im 19. Jh. meistadaptierte Roman war wohl Dikkens' *Oliver Twist*. – Auch der erste bekannte amerik. Autor von M., John Howard Payne (1791–1852), begann mit Übersetzungen aus dem Frz. Der berühmteste Autor und Schauspieler von M. auf den angelsächsischen Bühnen, Dionysius Lardner Boucicault (1822–90), schrieb irische M. wie *The Shaughraun* (1874) oder *The Colleen Bawn* (1860), Stücke über den amerik. Bürgerkrieg wie *Belle Lamar* (1874) und *The Octoroon, of Life in Louisiana* (1859), wo unter der Idee des Rassenfriedens generöse Porträts von weißen ‹Cavaliers› und schwarzen Sklaven gestaltet sind. Insofern als in den USA die politischen Ereignisse unmittelbar auf der Bühne dramatisiert wurden, spielte dort das M. wie in Frankreich eine didaktische Rolle: Das berühmteste amerik. M. ist die Adaptation des Romans von Harriet Beecher Stowe (1811–96) durch George L. Aiken (1830–76): *Uncle Tom's Cabin* (1853); es wirkte sich nachdrücklich auf das Rassenproblem in den USA aus und stellt somit die gesellschaftliche Funktion des M. im 19. Jh. unter Beweis. – In Amerika dauerte die Produktion von erfolgreichen M. länger an als in Europa. Noch am Anfang des 20. Jh. waren George M. Cohan (1878–1942) oder Bayard Veiller (1871–1943) und Elmer Rice (1892–1967) auf diesem Feld aktiv, bes. im Bereich des Kriminal- und Justizmelodramas, so Veillers *Within the Law* (1912), *The Thirteenth Chair* (1917) und *The Trial of Mary Duggan* (1928) oder Rices *On Trial* (1914) mit Rückblendetechnik aus dem Film.

Im deutschsprachigen Raum hat sich ein eigenständiges M. nie durchsetzen können. Dafür sind gattungstheoretische, ideologische und dramaturgische Probleme verantwortlich. Das M. konkurriert mit dem →bürgerlichen Trauerspiel, der →Schicksalstragödie und dem Sittendrama sowie dem →Rührstück; die dt. Kritiker und Autoren haben sich infolgedessen nie so für das M. eingesetzt wie die Franzosen; auch fehlten die nötigen Volksbühnen. In Frankreich, England und den USA hatte das M. seine Bühnenketten, seine Schauspieler, sein klassengemischtes Publikum. In Paris eroberte das M. von Anfang an das →Boulevardtheater: so das Boulevard du Temple, als Boulevard du Crime bekannt. In London spielte das M. im Covent Garden und im Drury Lane, in New York auf dem →Broadway. Auf allen Bühnen Europas und Amerikas gastierten mit den Erfolgsstücken die Schauspieler, die oft im M. ihre Lehre und ihr Debüt gemacht hatten. Frédérick Lemaître (1800–76), der in der Rolle des Robert Macaire glänzte, Sarah Bernhardt (1845–1923), Marie Dorval (1798–1849), Rachel (1820–58), Charles Fechter (1824–79), Charles Kean (1811–68) u. a.

Der Erfolg des M. ist weitgehend auf die Poetik dieser Zwischengattung zurückzuführen. Gibt es auch keine ‹Ars poetica› des Genres trotz der Versuche Pixérécourts und Nodiers, so hat es doch seine eigene Ziel-

600 Melodrama

setzung und daher seine Struktur, Figurenkonstellation und Thematik. Es gibt eine Ästhetik, eine Dramaturgie des M. mit ihren nationalen Merkmalen.

Ziel des M. ist die dramatische Darstellung einer Spannung zwischen der tugendhaften Unschuld und dem schuldhaften Laster, eines manichäischen Konflikts zwischen Gut und Böse, wobei der Ausgang, ob glücklich oder unglücklich, jedenfalls beim Zuschauer die Bewunderung für Tugend und Unschuld sowie Abscheu, wenn auch nicht ohne eine gewisse zweideutige Faszination, für das Übel weckt. Strukturell findet dieser Konflikt seinen Ausdruck in einem typischen Raster mit möglichen Varianten. Die Gesamtstruktur besteht aus drei Grundphasen: einer Eingangssituation der Harmonie, wo üblicherweise in geschlossenem Raum, Garten, Haus, Laube, die noch unbedrohte Unschuld gehegt ist; hierin wird dann die Unschuld aufgestöbert, gefährdet, verjagt hin zu Orten, wo das Böse waltet: Wald, Wirtshaus, Irrweg; am Ende wird die frühere Gesellschaft der Unschuld und Tugend wiederhergestellt als Rückkehr der Harmonie. Die Intrige wird also vorangetrieben durch eine Kette von Topoi, welche grundlegend sind für das Genre: Verfolgung/Fall/Wiedererkenntnis/Rettung, oft thematisch verklammert im Liebesmotiv. Wie in der →Schicksalstragödie, nur mit anderer Zielsetzung, da ja die Fatalität meist der gütigen Vorsehung weicht, drückt sich diese Verkettung durch eine Reihe von Zeichen aus – Kreuz, Blitz, Dolch, Schwur etc.

Träger dieser Intrige sind schematisch geordnete, typisierte Figuren: die beiden Grundgestalten des M., Gut und Böse verkörpernd, die Unschuld, üblicherweise repräsentiert durch Frau/Mädchen/Kind, verfolgt durch den Schurken, erstere meist passiv, ein Opfer, letzterer aktiv, die Intrige antreibend, als finsterer Intrigant. Dazwischen, unerläßlich für ein gemischtes Genre, die komische Figur, deren Funktion es ist, die Spannung aufzulockern. Daneben die Komparsen, je nach der Reichhaltigkeit der Intrige, meist Vater als →Père noble oder Mutter, dann eine geheimnisvolle, allmächtige Figur als →Deus ex machina, dazu Tiere zwecks Anreiz zum Spektakel. In der Relation dieser Figuren mit- und gegeneinander herrscht keinerlei psychologische Kausalität: Held(in) und Schurke sind nicht psychisch motiviert, Gut und Böse nicht gerechtfertigt; sie sind einfach da, als zeitliche Wesenheiten, gegebene Komponenten einer manichäisch gesehenen Weltordnung. Darum hat der Zuschauer auch den Eindruck trotz der Zeitsprünge und Raumveränderungen, daß sich das M. im Zeit- und Raumlosen abspielt.

Insofern ist das M. keineswegs ein Ort der Analyse; es wird nichts erwiesen, es wird nur etwas vorgezeigt, mit allen möglichen Sinneseindrücken massiv dargestellt. Im M. wird dem Publikum eine Anhäufung von Peripetien und Theaterstreichen vorgeführt, die oft in Bildern kulminiert, worin alle Formen des Visuellen und des Auditiven (Dekor, Kostüm, Ballett, Pantomine, Musik, Lärm etc.) zusammenstreben. Nicht von ungefähr gelten die Autoren von M. oft als die ersten bedeutenden Regisseure, vereinigten sie doch in ihrer Person oft die Funktion des Dramaturgen, des Bühnenbildners und gar des Musikers – daher auch im M. die emphatische Sprache sowie der übertrieben expressionistische Stil der Schauspielweise. In diesem hyperbolischen Zeichenspiel wird nichts verdrängt, ist alles hyperpathetisch als Folge einer «Ästhetik des Staunens».

Das M. ist heute als Theaterform von den Bühnen fast völlig verschwunden. Einige wollen den Grund dafür in der Ideologie sehen: «Das M.», schrieb Louis Althusser, «ist veraltet; die Mythen und Almosen, die es ans Volk austeilte, sind heute anders organisiert, und raffinierter.» Gewiß, zu bestimmten Zeiten mochte man meinen, es sei für Adel und Bürgertum ein Mittel gewesen, das Volk am moralischen Gängelband zu halten. Doch hat es auch als echtes Volkstheater fortschrittliche Gedanken zum Ausdruck gebracht und dank seines ungeheuren Erfolgs im 19. Jh. in der Gesellschaft verbreitet. Für andere sind die Didaskalien zu genau, dem kreativen Regisseur zu wenig Spielraum lassend. Und doch sah Antoine Artaud (1896–1948) in seinem Programm des 1. Manifests zum *Theater der Grausamkeit* (1932) «ein oder mehrere M. der Romantik» vor, «in denen die Unwahrscheinlichkeit zu einem aktiven und konkreten poetischen Element werden wird». Der Grund für das Verschwinden des M. von den Bühnen ist wohl eher darin zu suchen, daß es sich in andere, neuere Kunstformen übertragen ließ: Der Film, historisch der expressionistische, genremäßig der Wildwest- oder der Spionagefilm hat mit noch größerer visueller Suggestionskraft Themen, Figuren und Topoi des M. übernommen; darum sind viele der großen Triumphe des M. wiederholt verfilmt worden. Diese Effekte finden sich in gesteigerter Form auch im Fernsehspiel, insbesondere der Serie, wieder; ein eklatantes Beispiel ist *Dallas*.

A!A!A!: Traité du mélodrame. Paris 1817; Bentley, E.: The Life of the Drama. New York 1964; Booth, M. R.: English Melodrama. London 1965; Brooks, P.: Une esthétique de l'étonnement – le mélodrame. In: Poétique 19/1974; La Revue des Sciences Humaines. Lille 162/1976; Thomasseau, J.-M.: Le mélodrame. Paris 1984.

Gérard Schneilin

Merzbühne

Parallel zu seiner Merzdichtung, zur Merzmalerei und zu seinem Merzbau hat Kurt Schwitters (1887–1948), der als Ein-Mann-Unternehmen ‹Dada Hannover› verkörpert, auch eine M. entworfen. Das Wort

602 Merzbühne

‹Merz›, das ihm beim Herstellen eines Klebebildes von einer Anzeige der Kom*merz*- und Privatbank übriggeblieben ist, steht für das Gestaltungsprinzip des Künstlers: das Zusammenfügen fertiger Teile – in der Dichtung sind es Sätze aus Zeitungen, Katalogen, Gesprächen, in den Bild-Collagen und im Merzbau gefundene Gegenstände – zu neuen ästhetischen Realitäten. Nach diesem Grundatz soll auch das Kunstwerk der M. gestaltet sein. In dem ‹an alle Bühnen der Welt› gerichteten Manifest *Ich fordere die Merzbühne* von 1919 schreibt Schwitters: «Man setze riesenhafte Flächen, erfasse sie bis zur gedachten Unendlichkeit, bemäntele sie mit Farbe, verschiebe sie drohend und zerwölbe ihre glatte Schamigkeit... Dann nehme man Räder und Achsen, bäume sie auf und lasse sie singen (Wasserriesenüberständer). Achsen tanzen miterrad rollen Kugeln Faß. Zahnräder wittern Zähne, finden eine Nähmaschine, welche gähnt... Menschen selbst können auch verwendet werden... Und nun beginnt die Glut musikalischer Durchtränkung. Orgeln hinter der Bühne singen und sagen ‹Fütt Fütt›» (Schwitters, Bd. 5, S. 40f). Was von diesen Vorstellungen ernst gemeint ist, was als Parodie auf das wortschöpferische Pathos des →Expressionistischen Theaters und den Maschinenkult des →Konstruktivismus und des →Futuristischen Theaters, läßt sich nicht eindeutig feststellen. Jedenfalls verlangt Schwitters, daß die Materialien nicht logisch in ihren alltäglichen Beziehungen, sondern innerhalb der Logik des Kunstwerks zu verwenden sind. Damit befindet er sich in Übereinstimmung mit dem →Dadaistischen Theater, überschreitet aber dessen Horizont, wenn er die Zerstörung der Logik nur als Vorausbedingung für einen neuen künstlerischen Aufbau sieht.

In dem aus Gegenständen und Vorgängen der zeitgenössischen Realität collagierten Geschehen der M. soll sich nach Schwitters die Idee des Gesamtkunstwerks verwirklichen; ‹alle Faktoren› müssen miteinander verschmelzen; der Text darf nicht Grundlage, sondern muß ‹Bestandteil› der Aufführung sein. Schwitters plädiert für die spontane Veränderung des Bühnengeschehens durch die Zuschauerreaktionen; Protest und Störung sollen vorausgeplant und integriert werden. Mit dieser dadaistischen Idee nimmt er Prinzipien des →Happenings der 60er Jahre vorweg, dessen dt. Hauptvertreter Wolf Vostell sich ausdrücklich auf ihn berufen hat.

Ab 1923 arbeitete Schwitters am Projekt einer ‹Normalbühne Merz›, die mit der M. nicht die geringste Ähnlichkeit hat. An die Stelle des Traums von der Konfrontation aller Materialien und der Verschmelzung aller Künste im Gesamtkunstwerk tritt jetzt ein von Einfachheit und Abstraktion bestimmtes Programm. Die Normalbühne verwendet nur einfache Formen (Gerade, Ebene, Würfel, Kreis, Kugel) und wenige Farben (Schwarz, Grau, Weiß, Rot), ist einfach konstruiert und in den Maßen normiert. Ungefähr gleichzeitig mit dem Umschwenken von der dadaistischen Utopie der M. zu der abstrakt-konstruktivistischen Normalbühne ändert Schwitters auch den Stil seiner Versuche im Drama. An Stelle dadaistischer Minidramen schrieb er jetzt ein stilisiertes *Schattenspiel* mit Personifikationen abstrakter Begriffe. Ab 1924 entstanden dann seine größeren Stücke, in denen meist Alltagssituationen absurd-grotesk zugespitzt erscheinen. Das bekannteste, der als Opernlibretto konzipierte *Zusammenstoß*, wurde 1976 uraufgeführt.

Lach, F.: Der Merz-Künstler Kurt Schwitters. Köln 1971; Schwitters, K.: Das literarische Werk. Bd. 4: Schauspiele und Szenen. Köln 1977; ders.: Das literarische Werk, Bd. 5: Manifeste und kritische Prosa. Köln 1981.

Peter Simhandl

Meta Theater

Das 1979 von der Tänzerin Ulrike Döpfer und dem Architekten Axel Tangerding entworfene und gegründete Werkhaus Moosach an der Peripherie Münchens dient mit einer variabel bespielbaren Hallenkonstruktion als Sitz des M. T. In Kontakt mit dem Theaterlaboratorium J. Grotowskis und der Auseinandersetzung mit vornehmlich asiatischen Theaterformen (→Nô-Spiel) bemüht sich eine internationale Gruppe von Schauspielern, Tänzern, Regisseuren, Musikern und bildenden Künstlern um eine Theaterform, in der Dichtung, Bewegung, Ritual, Raumskulpturen und Instrumentalmusik verschmelzen und auf ihre Grundessenzen reduziert werden. Die Produktionen des M. T. wurden bei zahlreichen Gastspielen im In- und Ausland vorgestellt. Daneben gastieren (und unterrichten) im M. T. außereuropäische Schauspielgruppen und Künstler wie die Foo Hsing →Pekingopern-Truppe aus Taipei (1988), die Bunya-und-Noroma-Puppenspieler von der japanischen Insel Sado (1989), die Yoruba-Bata-Truppe aus Nigeria (1991) oder der Nô-Meister Akira Matsui der Kita-Schule Tokyo (1992). – Wichtigste Arbeiten: *Flechtungen – der Fall Partzifall* (1979); *Grid* (1982); *Über den Berg kommen* (1984, Nô-Adaption); *Drei Frauen in Gelb* (1986); *Im Gefolge fallender Blüten* (1987); *Kantan-Trilogie* (1989, Nô- und Kyôgen-Adaptionen).

Meta Theater. Moosach 1992; Müller, U.: Parzival 1980 – Auf der Bühne, im Fernsehen und im Film. In: Kühnel, J. u. a. (Hg.): Mittelalter-Rezeption II. Göppingen 1982.

Irene Wegner

The Method

Dieser international gebräuchliche Fachterminus bezeichnet eine in der
→Theaterpädagogik weitverbreitete Methode des Darstellens, die von
dem amerikanischen Schauspiellehrer Lee Strasberg (1901–82) in den
30er und 40er Jahren entwickelt und in dem 1947 gegründeten →‹Actor's
Studio› in New York, einer Fortbildungsstätte für Schauspieler, erprobt
worden ist. Fundament ist das methodisch-didaktische ‹System› einer
Schauspielkunst des ‹geistig-seelischen Naturalismus›, das von Konstantin Sergejewitsch Stanislawski (→Stanislawski-System) zwischen 1910 und
1938 in immer neuen Varianten formuliert und in seiner Tätigkeit als
Schauspieler und Regisseur am Moskauer Künstlertheater (→MChAT)
überprüft worden ist. Strasberg hat – neben der Grundforderung nach
‹glaubwürdiger› Darstellung durch rollenadäquates eigenes Erleben des
Schauspielers – vor allem jene von Stanislawski unter dem Begriff
‹Psychotechnik› zusammengefaßten Methoden übernommen, die für
dessen erste Arbeitsphase (bis ca. 1925) charakteristisch sind; die spätere
‹Theorie der physischen Handlungen› mit ihrer Priorität beim Herstellen
des ‹Körperlebens› der Figur wurde kaum rezipiert. Im Zentrum der M.
steht das Bemühen um die Aktivierung des ‹affektiven Gedächtnisses›,
das sowohl das ‹sensorische Gedächtnis› als auch das ‹emotionale Gedächtnis› umfaßt; durch das Erinnern an die sinnlich wahrnehmbaren
Umstände eines Erlebnisses aus der eigenen Biographie (‹sensorische Erzählung›) sollen sich auch die ursprünglich damit verbundenen Gefühle
wieder einstellen. Ein entsprechendes Training, vorbereitet durch Übungen zur Entspannung (‹Stuhl-Entspannung›), zur Konzentration (Arbeit
mit vorgestellten Objekten) und zur Veräußerung von Gefühlen (‹Song
and Dance-Übung›), führt zu einer allgemeinen Sensibilisierung für die
eigenen psychischen und physischen Prozesse sowie für die der Rolle, zur
Entwicklung der darstellerischen Kreativität und zur Entfaltung der (besonders auch für den Filmschauspieler wichtigen) Fähigkeit, die Umrisse
einer Figur ‹auf Abruf› mit eigenem Erleben zu füllen. Diese (auch für
nichtnaturalistische Erscheinungsformen der Schauspielkunst wichtigen)
Qualitäten bringt der Schauspieler in seine Arbeit an der Rolle ein. Auch
dafür adaptiert Strasberg Vorschläge von Stanislawski, wie etwa die analytische und dabei Vorstellungen und Emotionen stimulierende Aufbe-
reitung der Rolle durch die vier ‹W-Fragen› (Wer bin ich? Wo befinde ich
mich? Was mache ich dort? Was ist vorher geschehen?) und die improvi-
satorische Erkundung des Vorfeldes und des Umfeldes der darzustellenden Aktion.

Schauspielhaus Bochum (Hg.): Lee Strasberg – Schauspieler-Seminar. Bochum 1983; Strasberg, L.: Ein Traum von Leidenschaft. München 1989; ders.: Schauspielen und das Training des Schauspielers. Berlin 1988.

Peter Simhandl

Meyerhold-Methode

Wenn B. Brecht (1898–1956) in einer (undatierten) Äußerung die «Fortschrittlichkeit der M.» definiert, so erweckt er damit den Eindruck, Meyerhold habe, wie er selbst, ein ausgearbeitetes theoretisches Werk geschaffen. Das aber ist nicht der Fall. Keine dieser Theorien kann, einzeln betrachtet, als M. bezeichnet werden; zwar lassen sich methodische Konstanten beobachten, aber nur die Theaterarbeit insgesamt verdient diese Bezeichnung. Die überlieferten Aufsätze, Reden, Interviews, Gespräche mit Schauspielern, bezogen auf aktuelle Situationen, bedürfen jeweils der Erläuterung.

Wsewolod Emiljewitsch Meyerhold (1874–1940) hatte als Schauspieler begonnen und zwischen den Tätigkeiten eines Akteurs, Theaterleiters und Regisseurs gewechselt (→Komissarshewskaja-, →Puschkin-Theater), ehe er 1920 auf Wunsch Lunatscharskis zum Leiter der Theaterabteilung des Kommissariats für Volksbildung (Narkompros) in Moskau ernannt wurde und den →Theateroktober proklamierte. Um diese Zeit verfügte Meyerhold «über immense Theatererfahrung, über ein ungeheures Arsenal theatralischer Ausdrucksmittel, die er virtuos zu handhaben» verstand (R. Tietze). Der Bruch zum Illusionstheater ist endgültig vollzogen, sein in den Jahren 1905/06 in Opposition zum →Moskauer Künstlertheater entwickeltes Konzept eines (eigen-)bedingten (uslovnyj) Theaters ist identisch geworden mit seiner Person. →Stanislawskis psychotechn. System, in dem der Schauspieler durch aufrichtiges Erleben der dargestellten Situation die Emotion des Zuschauers affizieren soll, stellte Meyerhold sein Konzept eines antinaturalistischen, theatralisierten Theaters entgegen, das mit den «theatralischen Primärelementen Maske, Geste, Bewegung und Intrige» arbeitet und für das er den Begriff «uslovnyj» von V. Brjusow übernahm. Theatralität konnte Meyerhold an Jewreinows Altem Theater (→Komissarshewskaja-Theater), dem russ. Jahrmarktstheater (→Balagan), an der →Commedia dell'arte und dem traditionellen fernöstlichen Theater studieren; seinen Intentionen kam 1906 A. Bloks Drama *Die Schaubude* (Balagantschik) auf ideale Weise entgegen: Neben anderen illusionszerstörenden Momenten hatte Blok die Person eines ‹Autors› eingeführt, die in direkter Publikumsanrede die Handlung kommentierte. Meyerhold schätzte die technifizierte Bühne als ‹natür-

606 Meyerhold-Methode

licher› ein als die naturalistischen Dekorationen des Stanislawski-Theaters. Weitere Merkmale seines bedingten Theaters waren die Aufhebung der Rampe, die Annäherung der Theateraktion an den Tanz (Bedeutung der Körpersprache), die an den Zuschauer gerichtete Aufforderung zum Mitmachen, Mitdenken.

Die Theatralisierung des Theaters, das Sichtbarmachen theatermäßiger Elemente, die den Betrachter ständig daran erinnern, daß er sich im Theater befindet und daß der Schauspieler eine Rolle spielt, übte Meyerhold in seinem Studio (1913–18 Meyerhold-Studio, als Erstes Theater der RSFSR erneut von Meyerhold übernommen) nach einem aus Gymnastik, Akrobatik, Tanz, Pantomime u. a. gemischten Trainingsprogramm (→Biomechanik). 1922 führte er die neue Ausdruckssprache, in der Emotionen in Bewegung umgesetzt sind, in der Aufführung von Crommelyncks Farce *Der großmütige Hahnrei* erstmalig der Öffentlichkeit vor. Er inszeniert Agitationsstücke, testet, unbeirrt von sozioökonomischen Wandlungen (NEP), seine Kunstmittel. Episierung des Dramas (Prinzip der epischen Reihung selbständiger Szeneneinheiten), Filmisierung des Theaters (Projektion revolutionärer Losungen auf Leinwand, Scheinwerfer), Typisierung der Personen zu ‹sozialen Masken› schaffen Distanz zwischen dargestellter Handlung und Rezipient, aktivieren politisches Bewußtsein, geben dem Theater eine gesellschaftliche Funktion.

Die neuen Theorien erlauben es dem Avantgardisten Meyerhold auch, sich dem klassischen Erbe zuzuwenden. Inszenierungen von Ostrowskis *Wald* (1924, anfänglich in 33 Episoden unterteilt) und Gogols *Revisor* (1926) waren Höhepunkte Meyerholdscher Theaterarbeit. Um 1930 büßt Meyerhold die Rolle als Führer der revolutionären Theateravantgarde ein; später wird ihm «Formalismus» vorgeworfen, sein Theater 1938 geschlossen, er selbst 1939 verhaftet. – Im Prozeß der Theaterarbeit war Meyerhold ein glänzender Improvisator, ein «Poet» des Theaters, der die ästhetische Zeichenfunktion in den Vordergrund stellte. Seine Anregungen für die moderne Regie sind noch nicht ausgeschöpft, obwohl manche seiner Experimente als überholt gelten können.

Alpers, B. V.: Teatr social'noj maski. Moskva/Leningrad 1931; Braun, E.: The Theatre of Meyerhold. New York 1979; Hoover, M. L.: Meyerhold and his set designers. New York u. a. 1988; Mailand-Hansen, C.: Mejerchol'ds Theaterästhetik in den 1920er Jahren. Kopenhagen 1980; Mejerchol'd, V. È.: Perepiska. Moskva 1976; Mejerchol'd, V. È.: Stat'i, pis'ma, reči, besedy. Teil 1: 1891–1917. Teil 2: 1917–39. Hg. von A. V. Fevral'skij/B. I. Rostockij u. a., Moskva 1968; Meyerhold, W.: Schriften. Bd. 1–2. Berlin 1979; Paech, J.: Das Theater der russ. Revolution. Theorie und Praxis des proletarisch-kulturrevolutionären Theaters in Rußland 1917 bis 1924. Kronberg/Ts. 1974; «Revizor» v Teatre im. Vs. Mejerchol'da. Sbornik statej. Leningrad 1927; Rudnickij, K.: Režisser Mejerchol'd. Moskva 1969; ders.: Mejerchol'd. Moskva 1981; Schwarz, W. F.: Zur Diachronie der uslovnost' im Spannungsfeld von Drama und Theater (Von Puškin zu Majakovskij). Theoretische Grundlegung. In: Slavisches Spektrum. Festschrift für Maximilian Braun zum 80. Geburtstag. Wiesbaden 1983, S. 463–71; Tietze, R. (Hg.): Vsevolod Meyerhold. Theaterarbeit 1917–1930. München 1974; Tvorčeskoe nasledie V. È. Mejerchol'da. Moskva 1978; Zolotnikkij, D.: Zori teatral'nogo oktjabrja. Leningrad 1976; ders.: Budni i prazdniki teatral'nogo oktjabrja. Leningrad 1978.

Annelore Engel-Braunschmidt

Mickerytheater

Das M. ist die wichtigste internationale Theaterinstitution in den Niederlanden, die vornehmlich alternative oder freie ausländische Theateraufführungen präsentiert (→Freies Theater). M. wurde 1965 durch Ritsaert ten Cate gegründet. Anfänglich war es nicht nur ein Theater, sondern auch eine Galerie, ein Verlag für bibliophile Bücher, ein Designbüro usw. – M. wollte dem niederl. Theater neue Impulse geben, weil die Theatersituation als stagnierend erfahren wurde. Die erste Aufführung war ein Stück von Johnny Speight (1965, Regie: John van de Rest). Ein Erfolg in der gleichen Saison war die Aufführung von Jean Genets *Les Bonnes*, wobei die drei Frauenrollen von männlichen Schauspielern gespielt wurden. Seit 1965 organisiert M. Aufführungen ausländischer Gruppen. Allgemeines Ziel ist es, Theateraktivitäten zu ermöglichen und zu stimulieren, die anderswo nicht stattfinden (können). Dazu werden ausländische Gruppen eingeladen, die neue Entwicklungen am Rande des offiziellen Theaters zeigen. Gruppen, die M. als typische Vertreter bestimmter Richtungen betrachtet, werden öfters vorgestellt, damit ihre Entwicklung verfolgt werden kann. Solche ‹Hausgruppen› sind z. B.: Traverse Theatre (R. Jim Haynes, Edinburgh), →La Mama (New York), →The Pip Simmons Theatre Group (London). →Tenjo Sajiki (Shuji Terayama, Tokio), The People Show (London).

Fünf Jahre war M. ein Privatunternehmen, finanziert von Ritsaert ten Cate. 1970 bekam er einen Zuschuß vom Kulturministerium. Im gleichen Jahr zog das Theater von Loenersloot nach Amsterdam, wo M. seitdem in einem alten Kino etabliert ist. Der Theaterraum des M. hat keine Bühne und keine feste Trennung von Zuschauerraum und Spielplatz. Auf diese Weise wurde eine wichtige Bedingung für räumliche Experimente und für Neuentwicklungen bezüglich des Verhältnisses Zuschauerraum/Spielplatz erfüllt. Gerade die oben genannten ‹Hausgruppen› des M. haben diese räumlichen Möglichkeiten stets optimal genutzt.

Neue Entwicklungen werden auch stimuliert durch die Produktion von eigenen Projekten. Das erste war *Fairground* (1975). Dabei wurden als typische Merkmale der M.-Projekte die Untersuchungen der Beziehung Zuschauer/Inszenierung, das Verhältnis Theater/Realität, und der Relation von Theater/audiovisuelle Medien eingeführt. Spektakulär bei dieser Produktion war, daß zum erstenmal die M.-Kästen gebraucht wurden, d. h., die Zuschauer bekamen Plätze in drei Kästen, die mittels eines Luftkissensystems durch den Theaterraum schwebten. Auf diese Weise sahen die Zuschauer nicht nur verschiedene Szenen an verschiedenen Stellen, sondern auch Szenen in anderen Reihenfolgen. Es wurden verschiedene Projekte mit diesen Kästen realisiert: *Cloud Cuckooland* (1978, mit Tenjo Sajiki), *Outside* (1979), *Fairground '84* (1984). In der Saison 1984/85 liegt der Akzent M. auf der Relation Theater/Video oder Fernsehen. Dabei arbeitet man mit dem Videozentrum Montevideo zusammen. Ein erstes Projekt aus dieser Reihe war *The Ballista* (1984, mit Pip Simmons).

Hollenberg, I./Klinkenberg, R.: Mickery in Amsterdam. De geschiedenis van januari 1972 tot juni 1979 met een analyse van de voorstellingen. 2 Bde. Amsterdam 1980 (Mickery Dossier 1); The Masque of the Red Death, The Pip Simmons Theatre Group deel I. Amsterdam 1980 (Mickery Dossier 4); Schoenmakers, H.: Cloud Cuckooland, deel 2. Een Mickeryproject in samenwerking met de groep Tenjo Sajiki, Tolio: een studie naar de reacties van het publiek. Amsterdam 1979 (Mickery Dossier 6); Towards a Nuclear Future, The Pip Simmons Theatre Group deel II. Amsterdam 1980 (Mickery Dossier 4).

Henri Schoenmakers

Mime

Seit dem 18. Jh. im dt. Sprachraum benutzte Bezeichnung für den Schauspieler. Auch Darsteller des antiken →Mimus. Oft auch herabsetzend wegen des übertrieben Schauspielerhaft-Theatralischen mancher Darsteller. Frz. und engl. wird Mime oft mit Pantomime gleichgesetzt.

Horst Schumacher

Mimesis

Grundkonzept der antiken Ästhetik (lat.: imitatio); die Bedeutungsbreite des Wortes reicht von kopierender Abbildung bis zu freier schöpferischer Nachahmung. Aristoteles entwirft in den ersten drei Kapiteln der *Poetik* ein System der mimetischen, d. h. die Wirklichkeit abbildenden Künste, zu denen neben der Literatur auch Musik und Tanz sowie Malerei und Plastik zählen; im Theaterbereich sind folglich Dichter und Schauspieler, Choreuten und Musiker mimetische Künstler.

Fuhrmann, M.: Einführung in die antike Dichtungstheorie. Darmstadt 1973; Gebauer, G./Wulf, Ch.: Mimesis. Reinbek 1992.

Bernd Seidensticker

Mimik

(Griech.) In der Physiologie die verschiedenen Formen des menschlichen Gesichts durch das ‹Mienenspiel›, d. h. durch Muskelbewegung bzw. die bleibende ‹mimische Spur› durch häufige Wiederholung ein und derselben Bewegung (fröhlich-ausgeglichener, trauriger, distanzierter, aggressiver usw. Gesichtsausdruck) (→Nonverbale Kommunikation). In der Schauspielkunst wird die M. von →Geste und Gebärde (Gebärdensprache) wie Vortrag unterschieden, sowohl begleitend zum vorgetragenen Text oder selbständig im (stummen) →Pantomimenspiel. Fixierung der M. zur größeren Publikumswirksamkeit durch Benutzung von →Masken (→Commedia dell'arte u. a.).

Heikertinger, F.: Das Rätsel der Mimik und seine Lösung. 1954.

Horst Schumacher

Mimodrama

(Griech.) Drama, das ohne Worte, nur durch Pantomimen, mitunter mit Musikbegleitung aufgeführt wird; auch stumm gespielte Teile eines Dramas, z. B. bei Arrabal, Artaud, Beckett, Cocteau, Handke (*Das Mündel will Vormund sein*, 1969) und Ionesco.

Horst Schumacher

Mimus

(Lat. Lehnwort, griech.: mimos, Nachahmung) Antikes volkstümlich-burleskes Stegreifspiel (→Stegreiftheater), in dem die Darsteller den Text weitgehend improvisierten (in der Regel waren wohl, wie in der →Commedia dell'arte, nur Handlungsgerüst und Regiekonzept schriftlich fixiert); Gesang und Tanz, Clownerien und Akrobatik spielten eine wesentliche Rolle. Aus dieser Natur der Gattung erklärt sich, daß wir nur wenige Spielfabeln und Szenen kennen und keinen einzigen wirklich aufgeführten M. als vollständigen Text besitzen. Der M., der letztlich auf einfache Formen mimetischen Tanzes und komischer Nachahmung zurückgeht, hat sich als subliterarische Volksbelustigung immer neben der Tragödie und Komödie gehalten und nach deren ‹Ende› (d. h. in Griechenland seit dem 3. Jh. v. Chr., in Rom seit dem 1. Jh. v. Chr.) die Bühnen der griech. und röm. Welt immer stärker beherrscht. Der bis in die Spätantike außerordentlich populäre M. hat in vielfacher und im einzelnen nicht leicht zu rekonstruierender Weise (wie die manche Gemeinsamkeiten aufweisende →Atellana) auf populäre komische Spielformen des Mittelalters und der frühen Neuzeit eingewirkt (auf den türk. →Karagöz ebenso wie auf die →Commedia dell'arte). Gespielt wurde der M. in seiner Blütezeit auf der großen →Proskeniumsbühne der Kaiserzeit ohne besondere Dekoration; den Bühnenhintergrund bildete ein zweigeteilter Vorhang (siparium), hinter dem die Mimen auf ihren Auftritt warteten. Die Stücke waren kurz (ca. 1–1½ Std.); den Stoff bildeten Szenen aus dem Alltagsleben der unteren Gesellschaftsschichten, mit Vorliebe erotisch-obszönen Charakters; dabei ist interessant, daß beim M. im Unterschied zu allen anderen dramatischen Gattungen der Antike Frauenrollen von Frauen gespielt wurden, die sich am Ende der Vorstellung dem Publikum nackt präsentierten; es wurde ohne Masken gespielt; das Kostüm war, passend zum Sujet, ein stilisiertes Alltagskostüm. In Analogie zum Satyrspiel wurde der M. auch als komisches Nachspiel (Exodium) für Tragödienaufführungen verwendet.

Rieks, R.: Mimus und Atellane. In: E. Lefèvre (Hg.): Das röm. Drama. Darmstadt 1978, S. 348–377; Wiemken, H.: Der Mimus. In: G. A. Seeck (Hg.): Das griech. Drama. Darmstadt 1979, S. 401–433.

Bernd Seidensticker

Minimal Dance

M. D. ist ein in den 50er/60er Jahren des 20. Jh. durch die Choreographen der Post Modern Dance-Generation (→Post Modern Dance) geborener Bewegungsduktus, der sich unter dem Einfluß asiatischer Kunstpflege als meditativer Tanz herausgebildet hat. Der M. D. stützt sich auf kleinste Bewegungselemente, wiederholt diese monoton, bildet Varianten und zielt auf Versenkung. Die Choreographen verzichten auf Handlung; sie konzentrieren sich geistig und körperlich mit hypnotischer Intensität auf Bewegungseinheiten. Bewegungsreduktionen sollen den Betrachtenden auf Grund der Entlastung aller Wahrnehmungsqualitäten zu gesteigerten Erfahrungsperspektiven hinführen. Der Lebende soll vom Begriff der Zeit befreit werden und die Länge seiner Wahrnehmung als einen maßlosen Maßstab empfinden lernen. W. Sorell sagt der Minimal Art Entwicklungsmöglichkeiten voraus, weil ihre geistigen Gehalte einen Weg zurück zum Ritual freilegen. Vertreter: M. Cunningham (*1919), T. Brown (*1936), Y. Rainer (*1934), M. Monk (*1943), T. Tharp (*1942), L. Childs (*1940), L. Dean (*1945) (→Tanztheater).

Friedl. P./Klett, R.: Neues US-Tanztheater. In: Theater heute 7 (1982); Hanraths, M./Winkels, H. (Hg.): Tanz-Legenden. Frankfurt/M. 1984; Schmidt, J.: Der Vater der neuen Tanzkunst. In: Ballett International 5 (1983), S. 20–21; ders.: Die Enkelinnen tanzen sich frei. In: Ballett International 1 (1983), S. 12–15; Sorell, W.: Der Tanz als Spiegel der Zeit. Wilhelmshaven 1985, S. 404, 410.

Patricia Stöckemann

Minstrel Show

Erste überhaupt auf nordamerik. Boden entwickelte Theaterform im 19. Jh., gespielt von schwarz geschminkten Weißen, die Burlesken, Sketches, Tänze und sentimentale Lieder aufführten, wobei Fiedel, Banjo und Tamburin eingesetzt wurden. Frühestes Beispiel: *Virginia Minstrels* (seit 1843). Die M. S. perpetuierte in grober Verzerrung jenen Stereotyp des Sklaven als unbekümmerten, stets tanzenden und lustigen Clown, der bereits auf der Großplantage die Gäste des Sklavenhalters zu unterhalten hatte. Als die Schwarzamerikaner ab 1865 selbst die M. S. zu übernehmen begannen, hatte sich der Stereotyp zu sehr verfestigt, um nennenswerte Korrekturen zuzulassen. Die wichtigste ausschließlich schwarze Gruppe: die «Georgia Minstrels» (seit 1865). Wenngleich häufig in den Händen weißer Unterhaltungsmanager als reaktionäres Propagandainstrument mißbraucht, bot die M. S. den Rahmen für musikalische und tänzerische Kreativität der Schwarzen. So wie die Traditionen des Negro Spirituals und der schwarzen Arbeitslieder in die M. S. eingingen, gingen Blues, Charleston, Boogie Woogie, Jitterbug etc. daraus hervor.

Ihde, H.: Von der Plantage zum schwarzen Ghetto. Leipzig 1975; Toll, R. C.: Blacking Up. The Minstrel Show in Nineteenth-Century America. New York 1974; Traylor, E. W.: Two Afro-American Contributions to Dramatic Form. In: E. Hill (ed.): The Theatre of Black Americans I. Englewood Cliffs 1980, p. 45–60; Wittke, C.: Tambo and Bones – A History of the America Minstrel Stage. Durham 1930.

Dieter Herms

Minutage

Ein neu zu erstellendes Tanzdrama geht von einem Stoff aus. Der Stoff oder Plot müssen für ein Ballett notwendig zunächst als geraffte, aber szenisch noch ungegliederte Inhalts- und Handlungsverlaufsform, als Ballett-Exposé niedergeschrieben und vom Choreographen in ein Szenarium umgewandelt werden. Das Szenarium legt Szenenfolgen und -gestaltungen vor. Fast gleichzeitig mit diesem Szenarium entsteht die M.; denn die endgültige Szenenaufteilung eines Tanzdramas bedarf des unmittelbaren Denkens in Tanzgestaltungs- und Tanzbewegungsformen. – Die M. dient dem Komponisten als Richtlinie für seine Gestaltungen. Sie darf von ihm nur in Absprache und Beratung mit dem Choreographen variiert werden. Die gesamte Voraussetzung für den Erfolg des Tanztheaters liegt somit, anders als in der Oper, nicht beim Komponisten, sondern einzig beim Choreographen. Die M. enthält neben den exakten Szeneneinteilungen mit allen Ab- und Auftritten und dem Szenenverlauf in Solo-, Ensemble- und Gruppentätigkeit reguläre Kompositionsanweisungen für diffizilste Zeitdauern (in Minuten und Sekunden) und Metren, Vorgaben zum Charakter der Musik, Skizzierungen zu Raumabgrenzungen und -formationen, zu Bewegungsführungen und -duktus. Verbunden damit werden Vorschläge zu Instrumentalbesetzungen und Hinweise auf Anforderungsgrenzen. Notwendig werden in der M. Markierungen von Bildwechseln und evtl. Raum- und Dekorationsansprüchen. Die M. beweist, daß das Ballett in erster Linie als dramatische Form verstanden werden will, in der alle Künste synergetisch zusammenfinden. Erfinder der M. und damit Wegbereiter des echten Tanztheaters war Charles-Louis Didelot (1767–1836) (→Ballet héroïque-pantomime).

Henze, H. W.: Undine. München 1959.

Helga Ettl

Le Mirliton

(Frz. ‹die Rohrflöte›) 1885 von dem Chansonnier Aristide Bruant in den früheren Räumen des →«Chat Noir» gegründetes Cabaret, in dem er seine sozialanklägerischen, im Pariser Argot geschriebenen «chansons réalistes» vortrug. Als Werbung erschien in unregelmäßigen Abständen eine ebenfalls M. genannte Zeitschrift. Bruants Darstellungsmanier sowie die Aggressivität seiner Behandlung des Publikums machten paradoxerweise den Erfolg bei seinen (groß-)bürgerlichen Zuschauern aus. Er wurde Mode, als gesellschaftlicher ‹Exotismus› gefeiert, als Chansonnier und Dichter anerkannt und vereinnahmt. Der finanzielle Erfolg seiner

Auftritte ermöglichte ihm bereits 1895 den Rückzug auf ein Landgut. Nach seinem Ausscheiden wurde M. in «Cabaret Aristide Bruant» umbenannt, ohne indessen an die früheren Erfolge anknüpfen zu können.

Angelis, R. de: Storia del café-chantant. Mailand 1946; Bruant, A.: Chansons. 2 Bde. Ahrensburg 1965–66; Carco, F.: La Belle Époque au temps de Bruant. Paris 1954; Knapp, B. L.: Le Mirliton. Paris 1968; Méténier, O.: Le chansonnier populaire Aristide Bruant. Paris 1895; Oberthur, M.: Cafés and Cabarets of Montmartre. Salt Lake City 1984; Segel, H. B.: Turn-of-the-Century Cabaret. New York 1987; Valbel, H. (ed.): Les chansonniers et les cabarets artistiques de Paris. Paris 1895; Zévaès, A.: Aristide Bruant. Paris 1943.

Wolfgang Beck

Missionsschauspiel

Ideologisches Instrument der Missionare, das christliche Gedankengut dramaturgisch im Dienste der Einheitsziele von Staat und Kirche bei der Kolonisierung Lateinamerikas einzusetzen.

Im span. und port. Kolonialbereich wurden die religiösen Theaterformen und Themen der Metropolen geschickt mit autochthonen indianischen Traditionen vermischt: Herodes (72 v. Chr.–4 v. Chr.) wurde z. B. zu einem aztekischen Herrscher; seine Priester und sein Hof ähnelten der Hierarchie Moctezumas II. (um 1466–1520).

Adler, H.: Politisches Theater in Lateinamerika. Berlin 1982; Brinckmann, B.: Quellenkritische Untersuchungen zum mexikan. Missionsschauspiel (1533–1732). Gießen 1970.

Martin Franzbach

Mitspiel(theater)

Theater hat durch die Besonderheit des lebendig anwesenden Publikums immer M.-Charakter; im literarisch bestimmten Autorentheater wurde dieser Charakter freilich zurückgedrängt. Im Gegenzug entwickelten sich besondere Formen vor allem im Bereich des Kindertheaters, die bewußt und intendiert das Mitspielen (Mitdenken, Mitentscheiden, Mitplanen) der Zuschauer wollen. M. reicht vom Husten und Klatschen über Zwischenrufe (etwa beim Puppentheater), Dialoge mit dem Kasper (oder einer anderen Kontaktfigur), wirklicher Mitgestaltung (dem eigentlichen M.) bis zur Spielstunde (die nicht mehr den Schauspieler, nur noch den Spielleiter kennt) bzw. zum freien Spiel ohne Publikum und Spielleiter.

Erste Versuche macht N. Saz im sowj. Kindertheater (das Spielstück) schon 1924. P. Pörtner (*1925) entwickelt M.-Stücke für Erwachsene (*Scherenschnitte*, 1963); A. Boal (*1931) läßt im Forum-Theater (→ Theater der Unterdrückten), angeregt durch P. Freires Pädagogik der Unterdrückten, Zuschauer unterschiedliche Lösungsmöglichkeiten eines Konflikts als Vorgriff auf künftige Realität durchspielen; seit 1978 leitet er in Paris das Centre d'étude et de diffusion des techniques actives d'expression. M. im Kindertheater ist meist ein Theater für kleine Gruppen (Mini-, Monodramen; Theater im Schulhaus, Zürich; → Animationstheater wie die engl. → Theatre in Education-Gruppen; Stücke des Modellversuchs Künstler und Schüler in der BRD und West-Berlin), doch gibt es auch Versuche mit Hunderten von Mitspielern (Fest im Märkischen Viertel; M.-Aktionen des Kindertheaters Birne auf ev. Kirchentagen).

Boal, A.: Theater der Unterdrückten, Frankfurt/M. 1979; Dörger, D.: Mini- und Mono-Dramen. Eine Anleitung zu theatralen Kleinformen. Wilhelmshaven 1985; Pörtner, P.: Spontanes Theater. Köln 1972; O'Toole, J.: Theatre in Education. New objectives for Theatre – New Techniques in Education. London 1976.

Hans-Wolfgang Nickel

Mittelalter / Drama und Theater des Mittelalters

‹Geburt aus dem Geiste der Musik› gilt auch für das Theater des Mittelalters. Aus den Melismen in der Liturgie des Gottesdiensts erwuchsen als mnemotechn. Hilfsmittel die sog. Tropen, die der komplizierten Tonfolge bes. bei dem Halleluja unterlegt wurden. Die für die Weiterentwicklung fruchtbarste Trope wurde in der Messe des Ostersonntags gesungen. Der dialogische Charakter dieser Trope aus dem 9. Jh. deutet auf seine dramatischen Möglichkeiten. Doch erst als diese Trope von der Messe gelöst auf den Abschluß der morgendlichen Matutin übernommen wurde, konnte sich eigentliches Drama bilden. Das älteste Dokument dafür ist die *Regularis Concordia* aus dem 10. Jh. Hier stellen vier Geistliche mitten im Gottesdienst und als Teil desselben den Engel und die drei Marien am Grabe dar. In der Kleidung, Requisit, Gestik wird versucht, das Geschehen zu verlebendigen, zum Drama, zum Theater vorzustoßen. Dieses Benediktiner Regelbuch war maßgeblich nicht nur für die engl. Benediktinerklöster; auch auf dem Kontinent dürfte dieses Vorbild eingewirkt haben. Diese Visitatio, wie sie genannt wird, umschließt nach dem biblischen Bericht den Besuch der Marien am Grabe, den Lauf der Apostel Petrus und Johannes zum Grab, die Erscheinung Christi vor Maria Magdalena. Der Text beruht völlig auf liturgischer Sprache, wird noch während des Gottesdiensts vorgetragen, wird gesungen.

Man hat diese Formen Osterfeiern genannt im Unterschied zu einer umfangreicheren Form, die spätestens im 13. Jh. auftaucht, die man →Osterspiel nennt. Vier dieser lateinischen Osterspiele sind ganz oder als Fragment erhalten. Auf Bitte der Juden um Bewachung des Grabs werden Wächter ans Grab geschickt, die später, als sie die Auferstehung vermelden, von den Juden bestochen werden. Die Marien kaufen ihre Salben, bevor sie zum Grab gehen. Eines dieser lateinischen Spiele schließt sogar mit dem zweimaligen Erscheinen Christi vor den Jüngern. Man hat diese Trennung zwischen lateinischer Feier und lateinischem Spiel darum vollziehen wollen, weil man nicht glauben konnte, daß diese umfangreicheren Dokumente noch innerhalb der Kirche, noch als Teil des Gottesdiensts gebraucht wurden. Doch gerade bei dem umfangreichsten, dem von Tours heißt es: «sinistra parte ecclesie stans.» Ein anderes Dokument, das von Klosterneuburg, setzt ein: «Cantatis Matutinis in die Pasche.» Also wie die Feiern wurde auch dieses Spiel zu Ende der Matutin aufgeführt. Zudem stimmt der Wortlaut weitgehend mit dem der Feiern überein. Es scheint also die Unterscheidung Feier – Spiel um so weniger sinnvoll, als schon das erste Dokument, die *Regularis Concordia*, im Charakter durchaus dramatisch wirkt.

Höhepunkt des Geschehens zur Osterzeit bleibt freilich die Passion Christi, die später in den Volkssprachen so wichtig werden sollte. In lateinischer Sprache sind drei Texte überliefert. Schon aus früher Zeit (12. Jh.) ist ein fragmentarischer Text aus der monastischen Metropole Monte Cassino in Süditalien erhalten. Doch ein weiteres Fragment aus Sulmona, eine deutliche Ergänzung dieser Tradition, erweist, daß dieses Drama das gesamte Ostergeschehen umfaßte.

Die beiden anderen Texte, beide in der Handschriftensammlung der *Carmina Burana*, behandeln zwar nur die eigentliche Passion, aber der kürzere endet mit der Anweisung: «et ita inchoatur ludus de resurrectione.» Also muß dieser Ludus nach der Matutin im Rahmen der Kirche dargebracht worden sein. Auch das zweite umfangreichere Spiel muß im gottesdienstlichen Rahmen aufgeführt worden sein. Von Maria heißt es «per horam quiescat sedendo». Also wird das Spiel sehr passend bei der Marienklage durch die Hora, wahrscheinlich die Matutin, unterbrochen.

Zu diesen Phänomenen der Osterzeit und offensichtlich mit diesen als Vorbild formen sich auch zur Weihnachtszeit dramatische Nuclei. Diese freilich sind weit geringer an Zahl. Die Verkündigung Mariae, die Verkündigung an die Hirten und ihre Anbetung, der Mord der Unschuldigen, der Zug der drei Könige, das Zeugnis der Propheten für das Kommen des Heilands werden dargeboten. Bei den letzten beiden Stoffen zeigt sich schon die Möglichkeit zu bewegungshafter Entwicklung. Alle diese Elemente werden zusammengefaßt in dem großartigen *Benediktbeurer Weihnachtsspiel*, auch dieses noch in der Kirche. «In fronte ecclesiae» kann nur bedeuten am Westende der Kirche, denn Aaron bringt einen Zweig «que super altare floruit».

Überblicken wir die Dokumente, so finden wir bei aller Vielfalt eine Einheit in der Darstellungsform. Sie ergibt sich auch aus dem Zusammenhang mit dem Gottesdienst. Die Kirche ist der Raum; der Altar im Osten der Kirche gestaltet sich zum Brennpunkt der Handlung. Der Blick nach Osten, nach dem heiligen Land, war schließlich immer schon ein Grundsymbol christlicher Doktrin. Der Altar, oft ein Behälter von Reliquien, dient zunächst als Grab Christi, wenn auch später oft bes. Grabstrukturen, «sepulcra», gewöhnlich am Ostende der Kirche, errichtet wurden. Der Altar dient auch als Krippe, obwohl diese später oft an anderen Stellen der Kirche aufgestellt wurde. Zunächst ist also ein Gegenüber zu denken zwischen der darstellenden Geistlichkeit im Chor oder der Vierung und der schauenden Gemeinde. Aber diese Scheidung wird in späteren Dokumenten durchbrochen. In der St. Blasienkirche in Braunschweig z. B. konzentrierte sich die Darstellung zunächst im Chor oder am Ostende des Schiffs. Aber in späteren Dokumenten durchzieht Maria Magdalena die ganze Länge des Schiffs auf der Suche nach dem Heiland.

Andere Dokumente zeigen die Ausdehnung über den Gesamtraum der Kirche noch deutlicher. Bei dem Dreikönigsspiel von Fleury ist die Krippe am Westende der Kirche aufgestellt. Die drei Könige treffen sich vor dem Hauptaltar im Chor. Am «hostium chori» befragen sie die Umstehenden («astantes»). Dann ziehen sie zu Herodes etwa am Ostende des Schiffs und weiter zur Krippe, später auf anderem Wege (hinter dem Thron des Herodes?) wieder zurück. Dieses Dokument ist bedeutungsvoll für ein weiteres Phänomen: Mit der Ausdehnung durch die ganze Kirche wird die gesamte Gemeinde zum Mitspielen gebracht. Gleich zu Anfang heißt es: «subito omnis multitudo cum Angelo dicat.» Später laden die Hirten «populum circumstantem adorandum Infantem». Wie schon erwähnt, befragten die Könige die Umstehenden. Die Darstellung wird hier in exemplarischer Form zum Wiedererleben der heiligen Begebenheiten.

Neben diesen mehr oder weniger traditionsgebundenen Spielen ragen schon in früher Zeit Sonderdokumente aus dem Gesamtbild hervor. Durchaus einzigartig, ohne Vorläufer oder Nachfolger, behandelt der *Tegernseer Ludus de Antichristo* das Weltende. Nachdem der Kaiser sich das gesamte Christentum unterworfen hat, gewinnt der Antichrist durch Gewalt, Bestechung und List die Weltherrschaft, bis schließlich seine Herrschaft zusammenbricht. Im Osten (der Kirche?) ist das heilige Land, im Süden sind die Könige von Babylon und Griechenland, im Westen der Kaiser, der König von Frankreich, der Papst und die Kirche. Der Norden ist also für die Zuschauer vorbehalten. In wuchtiger, grandioser Sprache und stolz in nationalem Bewußtsein rollt das Drama ab.

«Das Martyrium der hl. Apollonia». Szene nach einem Mysterienspiel. Miniatur aus dem «Livre d'Heure von Etienne Chevalier»; um 1450 (TS)

Gesamtansicht der Passionsspielbühne von Valenciennes, 1547.
Miniatur aus «Mystère de la Passion» (TS)

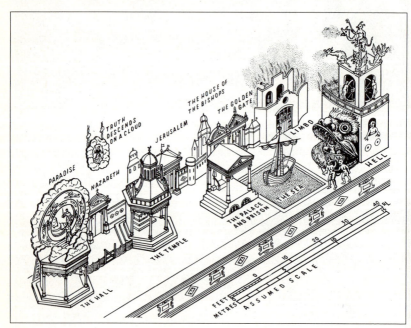

Rekonstruktion des Bühnenplans des «Mystère de la Passion» von Valenciennes (TS)

Spielszenen aus dem «Mystère de la Passion», 2. Tag (TS)

10. Tag (TS)

16. Tag (TS)

Corpus Christi-Spiel. Wagenbühnenaufführung in Coventry
(Rekonstruktion von Leacroft) (TS)

«Weingartenspiel». Figurine:
«Satan», Allegorie des Neides (TS)

«Weingartenspiel». Szenarium:
«Höllenrachen» (TS)

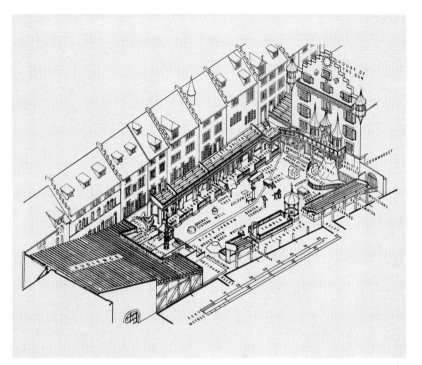

Rekonstruktion der Bühne des Luzerner Passionsspiels von 1583, basierend auf Cysats Bühnenplan für den ersten Tag (TS)

Szenarium einer Fastnachtsspiel-Aufführung. Federzeichnung von Edlibach (TS)

Rekonstruktion von F. Brunelleschis «Himmelfahrt» in Santa Maria del Carmine, 1439 (TS)

Andere Themen außerhalb liturgischer Tradition finden gelegentlich dramatische Behandlung: verschiedene Legenden um den heiligen Nikolaus, die Auferweckung Lazari, St. Pauli Bekehrung, die weisen und törichten Jungfrauen und aus dem Alten Testament Daniel. Zwei wichtige Beobachtungen drängen sich hier auf. Alle Dokumente enden mit einem Te Deum oder anderer Formulierung, die den Anschluß an den Gottesdienst erweisen, einige haben sogar Hinweise auf das Kircheninnere. Außerdem sind sie verknüpft mit best. Klöstern wie das Spielbuch von Fleury oder mit Persönlichkeiten wie Hilarius. Hier liegen also spezielle Arbeiten aus Klosterschulen vor; Hilarius, ein Schüler Abälards, ist einer der ersten wandernden Kleriker.

Aus früher Zeit schon, aus dem 12. Jh., ist der erste Text in Volkssprache überliefert, der *Jeu d'Adam*, vermutlich aus der Normandie. Er umfaßt Sündenfall, Kain und Abel, eine Prophetenszene. Er wurde auf Gerüsten vor der Kirche aufgeführt; doch kam Gott aus der Kirche, in die er auch wieder abtrat. Die genaue Bühnenform läßt sich nicht mehr rekonstruieren. Der biblische Stoff, der Rückhalt an der Kirche, die Nutzung des kirchlichen Chors, lateinische Bühnenanweisungen verraten den Zusammenhang mit der Tradition.

Anschluß an den Gottesdienst ist erwiesen für *Les Trois Maries*, eine frz. Adaption des Ostergeschehens, oder für *La Seinte Res*, das wohl aus England stammt. Auch der erste bekannte Dramatiker in der Volkssprache wirkte noch am Ende des 12. Jh.: Jean Bodel in Arras. Seine außerordentlich lebendige Behandlung einer Nikolaus-Legende zeigt, wie das dürre Gerippe des lat. Dramas in ein blutvolles Bild des Alltagslebens gewandelt werden kann. Frankreich war überhaupt reich an Einzelleistungen. Erwähnt sei nur noch Adam de la Halle, der weniger als 100 Jahre nach Jean Bodel in seinem *Jeu de la feuillée* oder seinem *Robin et Marion* – rein weltliche Spiele, arm an Handlung, aber reich an Lebensbeschreibung – die dramatischen Fähigkeiten eines Trouvère zeigt.

So bedeutungsvoll diese Einzelleistungen sein mögen, wird sonderbarerweise in Frankreich keine Brücke sichtbar von dem frühen so lebendigen klösterlich liturgischen Theaterleben und den großen zyklischen Darstellungen des späteren Mittelalters. Im Spätmittelalter ersteht freilich eine andere Welt. Auch dann sind Einzelautoren am Werk. Wie im Frühmittelalter ist der Stoff biblisch oder mindestens religiös. Aber statt des Mikrokosmos eines Einzelstoffs stehen umfassende dramatische Epen da, die das gesamte christliche Geschehen von der Schöpfung bis zum Weltende mit allem Detail in mehreren Tagewerken abhandeln. Wo früher der kleine Kreis der Klosterkirche den Anforderungen des Spiels genügte, bewegt sich nun auf weitem Platz eine ganze städtische Gemeinschaft, vielleicht noch immer überwacht und angespornt von einem Geistlichen oder von einem Vertreter des Rats. Dieses Zusammenwirken aber

618 Mittelalter / Drama und Theater des Mittelalters

macht die Darstellungen zu wirklichen Volksschauspielen. Die bedeutendsten Dokumente sind *La Passion du Palatinus*, *La Passion d'Autun*, *La Passion de Semur*, *La Passion d'Arras*, *La Passion de Greban*, *La Passion de Jean Michel*. Daneben gibt es noch eine Anzahl von Mirakel-Stücken, die sich bes. in der Sammlung *Les Miracles de Notre Dame* erhalten haben. Endlich besitzt die Bibliothek Ste. Geneviève zahlreiche Heiligen- und Märtyrerdramen.

Auch in England klafft eine Lücke zwischen wenigen frühen liturgischen Denkmälern und den späten umfassenden Fronleichnamszyklen in der Volkssprache. Ist es der Sprachenwirrwarr zwischen Frz. und Engl., der hindernd auf die dramatischen Bemühungen einwirkte? Eine Höllenfahrt (*Harrowing of Hell*) aus dem 13. Jh. ist der früheste engl. Text. Die Fronleichnamszyklen sind erst aus der zweiten Hälfte des 14. Jh. sicher belegt. Texte sind erhalten aus Cornwall, Chester, York, Wakefield (*Towneley Play*), Lincoln (*Ludus Coventriae*). Alle Dokumente sind mit dem Fronleichnamsfest verbunden (→ Moralität).

Auch in Italien bilden sich Sondertraditionen. Zwar hat sich in Cividale aus früher Zeit ein umfassender Zyklus erhalten, der Leben und Leiden Christi umfaßt. Doch das charakteristisch italienische Drama zeigt andere Gestalten. Aus der Flagellantenbewegung entstehen geistliche Lieder, die Lauden. Als sich die Flagellanten zu festen Organisationen konsolidiert hatten, erwuchsen aus einigen der dialogischen Lauden einfache dramatische Darbietungen, die oft zu fester Tradition wurden. Auch aus der Predigt konnten szenische Darbietungen erwachsen. Man versuchte nämlich die Leiden Christi durch lebende Bilder bes. eindrücklich zu vergegenwärtigen. Diese sog. Devotionen gingen aber selten über → lebende Bilder oder → Pantomine hinaus. Schließlich entstehen gegen Ende des 15. Jh., bes. in Florenz, geistliche Schaustellungen, Repräsentationen, die von Knaben vorgeführt wurden.

Einzig in Deutschland läßt sich ein fortlaufendes Band von den lat. Kirchenspielen zu dt. Volksdramen in rohen Umrissen erkennen. Aus dem 13. Jh., gleichzeitig mit den lat. Spielen der Benediktbeurer Sammlung, ist das erste Osterspiel, freilich nur als Fragment, überliefert. Dieses Spiel aus Muri in der Nordschweiz enthält zwar wesentlich dieselben Szenen, wie sie früher oder später zur Tradition gehörten; doch geben viele Einzelheiten dem Dokument einen eigentümlich wirksamen Ausdruck. Mehrere der anderen Osterspiele, ein bis zwei Jahrhunderte später, sind reich an übermütigen, unzweideutigen Einlagen. Oft sind Übereinstimmungen zwischen diesen Spielen gerade nur in diesen Einlagen zu finden. Zudem sind die Handschriften dieser Spiele an Plätzen weit von ihren durch den Dialekt gegebenen Entstehungsorten überliefert. Man hatte früher angenommen, daß Spielleute, Vaganten die Träger gewesen sein müssen, die den festen Rahmen der kirchlichen lat. Tradition mit ihren leichten Eingebungen gesprengt hätten. Dem ist neuerdings widersprochen worden, ohne jedoch einen Gegenbeweis zu erbringen. Später bildeten sich neue Traditionen, doch erst nachdem das Bürgertum in das Theaterleben eingriff. Überlieferung und Texte sind aus drei Zentren erhalten, aus Frankfurt am Main, Tirol, Luzern. Alle drei Spieltraditionen begannen als Osterspiele, Frankfurt im 13. Jh., Tirol spätestens im 14. Jh., Luzern erst im 15. Jh. In Frankfurt z. B. kann man verfolgen, wie ein frühes Osterspiel noch ganz in der einfachen Gestalt der frühen Zeit sich ausweitete zu einem zweitägigen Zyklus (Frankfurter Dirigierrolle, frühes 14. Jh.) und dann weiter an Umfang und Detail gewann (Spiele aus dem 15. und 16. Jh.), bis dann die Reformation dieser Entwicklung ein Ende setzt. In Luzern dagegen wird noch das ganze 16. Jh. gespielt, und sein Ableger Villingen lebt noch weiter bis ins 17. Jh., freilich gespeist von neuen Ideen. Daneben bestanden auch in Deutschland vereinzelt →Fronleichnamsprozessionsspiele.

Aebischer, P. (Hg.): Le Mystère d'Adam (= Textes Littéraires Français 99). Genf 1964; Creizenach, W.: Geschichte des neueren Dramas. Halle 1911; Frank, G.: The Medieval French Drama. Oxford 1954; Fricker, R.: Das ältere engl. Schauspiel. Bern 1975; Michael, W. F.: Das deutsche Drama des Mittelalters (= Grundriß der germanischen Philologie 20). Berlin 1971; ders.: Frühformen der dt. Bühne (= Schriften der Gesellschaft für Theatergeschichte 62). Berlin 1963; Petersen, G.: Aufführungen und Bühnenplan des älteren Frankfurter Passionsspiels. In: ZfdA LIX (1921–22), S. 83–126; Ranke, F.: Das Osterspiel von Muri. Aarau 1944; Sievers, E.: Die lat. liturgischen Osterspiele der Stiftskirche St. Blasien zu Braunschweig (Diss. Würzburg 1935). Berlin 1936; Young, K.: The Drama of the Medieval Church. 2 Vols. Oxford 1933.

Wolfgang F. Michael

Mittelstück

Literarische Form speziell des österr. Kabaretts. In der Regel einaktiges Stück von mehreren Szenen, das – thematisch und formal unabhängig – in der Mitte des übrigen Programms steht. Als erstes M. wurde das von R. Weys in Anlehnung an die Alt-Wiener Märchenposse *Der letzte Zwanziger* von N. J. Kola geschriebene Stück *Die Metamorphosen des Herrn Knöllerl* in der →«Literatur am Naschmarkt» aufgeführt.

Das M. entsprach der dort angestrebten Mischform von Kabarett und Theater und setzte sich in den meisten österr. Kabaretts durch. Häufig angelehnt an Volksstücke des 19. Jh., wurden auch eigene Stücke von bis zu 50 Minuten Spieldauer geschrieben. Am bekanntesten wurden die M. von Jura Soyfer, u. a. *Der Lechner-Edi schaut ins Paradies, Vineta.*

Hakel, H.: Wiennärrische Welt. Wien 1961; ders. (Hg.): Wigl-Wogl. Wien 1962; Hösch, R.: Kabarett von gestern und heute. 2 Bde. Berlin 1967–72; Reisner, I.: Kabarett als Werkstatt des Theaters. Diss. Wien 1961; Rösler, W. (Hg.): Geh ma halt a bisserl unter. Berlin 1991; Soyfer, J.: Das Gesamtwerk. Wien u. a. 1980; Veigl, H.: Lachen im Keller. Wien 1986; Weigel, H.: Gerichtstag vor 49 Leuten. Graz 1981; Weys, R.: Cabaret und Kabarett in Wien. Wien 1970; ders.: Literatur am Naschmarkt. Wien 1947; ders.: Wien bleibt Wien, und das geschieht ihm ganz recht. Wien 1974.

Wolfgang Beck

Modellaufführung

Der von Bertolt Brecht (1898–1956) geprägte Begriff bezeichnet eine Aufführung, die durch zahlreiche Fotos, eingehende Beschreibungen und Regieanweisungen in einem Modellbuch festgehalten wird. Das Modellbuch wird als Ausgangspunkt für andere Inszenierungen desselben Stückes vorgeschlagen. Es enthält üblicherweise einen genauen Schnitt von Handlung und Szenen in Aktionsmomente, Bemerkungen zu den Hauptfragen der Rollengestaltung (Haltungen, Gesten, Gruppierungen), aber auch Anweisungen zu Kostüm, Maske, Dekoration und Requisiten. Jede ‹knechtische› Benutzung eines Modells wurde von Brecht freilich abgelehnt: «Modelle zu benutzen ist so eine eigene Kunst; soundso viel davon ist zu erlernen. Weder die Absicht, die Vorlage genau zu treffen, noch die Absicht, sie schnell zu verlassen, ist das richtige ... Am besten ist es, wenn man sie verändert.»

Für die Herstellung von Modellbüchern war das →Berliner Ensemble verantwortlich, welches in diesem Sinne den Band *Theaterarbeit* (1952) veröffentlichte. Das «Antigonemodell», zusammen mit Caspar Neher 1948 erarbeitet, bleibt für den Typus der M. repräsentativ. Diese für Brecht kennzeichnende Arbeitsweise fand keine wesentliche Fortführung. Als ein ähnlicher Versuch, ein Theaterstück dem Publikum und besonders Spielleiter und Schauspielern präzise darzulegen, könnte Dürrenmatts *Der Mitmacher. Ein Komplex. Text der Komödie. Dramaturgie. Erfahrungen. Berichte. Erzählungen* (1976) angesehen werden. Es drückt sich darin jedoch nicht das Ergebnis kollektiver Arbeit aus, sondern vielmehr der Wunsch des Autors, sich ‹falsche Darstellungen› zu ersparen.

Brecht, B.: Schriften zum Theater. Frankfurt/M. 1981; Jacquot, J. (ed.): Les voies de la création théâtrale. Paris 1970; Weigel, H./Berliner Ensemble (Hg.): Theaterarbeit. Berlin 1952.

Adriana Hass

Modern Dance

Parallel zum dt. →Ausdruckstanz entwickelt sich in Amerika der M. D., dessen Bewegungssprache ein neues Körperbewußtsein ankündigt. Ursache: Auflehnung gegen Moralvorstellungen, instinktive Abwehr der zunehmenden Technisierung und der damit verbundenen Deprivation des Individuums. Der M. D. insgesamt entfaltet seine Ausstrahlungskraft vorrangig durch die kreative Fähigkeit markanter Frauen, die in ihrem Körperausdruck Identität und Selbstbehauptung nach außen tragen wollen. – Isadora Duncan (1877–1927; →Ausdruckstanz) und Loie Fuller (1862–1928) finden als Pionierinnen zunächst nur in Europa Anerkennung. Ihre völlig veränderte, nach Auffassung der Duncan auf die Antike zurückgreifende Körpersprache basiert auf den Erkenntnissen von François Delsarte (1811–71), der in seinen umfangreichen Analysen menschlicher Gebärden Korrelationen zwischen seelischen Antrieben und motorischen Reaktionen aufzuzeigen versucht. Delsartes Ausdruckslehre wird in den USA zur Basis einer Tanz- und Schauspieltheorie, die auf die Identität von Emotionen, Kognitionen und deren Bewegungsartikulationen (→Ballet d'action) drängt. Die Duncan z. B. strebt unaufhörlich nach einer der momentanen Seelenlage adäquaten Totalgebärde. – Die Amerikanerin Ruth St. Denis (1878–1968) akzentuiert bereits ab 1915 östliche Tanzstile (Indien, Ägypten), allerdings ohne exakte Kenntnis der entsprechenden Tanztechnik. So vermag sie das Wesen des östlichen und des antik-klassischen Tanzes nicht zu durchdringen. Adaptiert werden von ihr Posen, Bewegungsformen und Handgesten. R. St. Denis versteht wie Laban, Wigman und Duncan ihren Tanz als neue Körperreligion. Gemeinsam mit ihrem Mann Ted Shawn (1891–1972) gründet sie 1915 in Los Angeles die Denishawn-Schule, die eine Tanztruppe ausbildet. Als weitere Protagonistinnen des M. D. gelten Doris Humphrey (1895–1958) und Martha Graham (1894–1991). – Doris Humphrey, Tänzerin, Choreographin und Pädagogin, gehört von 1917 bis 1928 zur Denishawn-Truppe. Der bloße Eklektizismus der St. Denis in der Gestaltung östlicher Themen stößt sie ab. Sie wünscht, sich in eigenständiger Weise mit zeitgenössischen Fragestellungen tänzerisch auseinanderzusetzen. Ihr Bemühen führt zu einer originalen Tanztechnik, deren Kerntheorie die motorischen Prozesse des Abfallens (fall) vom und des Zurückkehrens (recovery) zum Gleichgewicht bilden. Humphreys Theorie geht von den Spontanbewegungen des Körpers aus und verzichtet auf jeden klassischen Bewegungscode. Ausgangsgebärde aller tänzerischen Bewegungen wird für sie das Gehen. Humphrey gründet 1928 in New York ein Tanzstudio. – Martha Graham, von 1916 bis 1923 in der Denishawn-Schule und -Truppe, entwickelt nach einer Begegnung mit Mary Wigman auf Grund des Studiums der Ausdrucksformen und der Fotos von

622 Monodie

M. Wigman die Graham-Technik. Die Tanzarbeit der Graham kreist um die Aufarbeitung und Lösung der eigenen psychischen Konflikte. Grahams Technik basiert in der Bewegungsführung auf dem Wechsel von Contraction (Zusammenziehen) und Release (Entspannen). Der Rücken und das Becken bilden das Ursprungs- und Führungsfeld aller Bewegungen, sie sind die Stützpfeiler einer jeden Körperhaltung. Nach Graham ist eine Haltung in einer speziellen Situation zu einem bestimmten Zeitpunkt dann organisch angemessen zu nennen, wenn die Situation spontan im Ausdruck aufgeht. Die Graham-Technik stellt eine eigenständige Tanztechnik neben der klassischen Ballettechnik dar (→ Post Modern Dance).

Anderson, J.: Wider die Zwänge öder Gewöhnlichkeit. In: Ballett (Jahrbuch) 1977, S. 52–55; Liechtenhan, R.: Vom Tanz zum Ballett. Stuttgart/Zürich o. J.; Schmidt-Garre, H.: Ballett. Vom Sonnenkönig bis Balanchine. Hannover 1966; Stüber; W.: Geschichte des Modern Dance. Wilhelmshaven 1984.

Patricia Stöckemann

Monodie

Das Wort M. bezeichnet einen unbegleiteten bzw. durch Instrumentalbegleitung mit gleicher Melodieführung verstärkten Sologesang. Die M. hat ihren Ursprung in Griechenland, etwa in den Tragödien Euripides' (480–406 v. Chr.), in denen mit den Chorliedern, Kommoi und Amoibaia kontrastierende, durch Flöte oder Zitherspiel begleitete Arien der Schauspieler die dramatischen Höhepunkte untermalen. Später wurde die M. in die römischen Theaterstücke übernommen und lebte weiter im Volksgesang. Seit dem 17. Jh. erscheint die M. auch in der Oper, und zwar als Arie, bei der die musikalische Begleitung vor der menschlichen Stimme in den Hintergrund tritt.

Bernard Poloni

Monodrama

Das M. ist ein für einen einzigen handelnden und sprechenden Darsteller und evtl. stumme Nebenrollen konzipiertes Theaterstück. Oft werden Text und Handlung durch Musikbegleitung oder Einsatz techn. Medien (Fernsehen, Telefon, Plattenspieler, Bilderprojektion usw.) untermalt bzw. dramaturgisch verstärkt. Das bereits im antiken Theater, etwa bei Aischylos (525–456 v. Chr.) vertretene M. erlebt eine erste Blüte im 18. Jh., v. a. in den Jahren 1770 bis 1785, in Frankreich und in Deutsch-

E. M. Shawn. «Adlertanz» in dem Tanzdrama «Feather of Dawn», 1923 (WSt)

M. Graham. «Lamentation», 1930 (SS)

D. Humphrey. «Dionysiaques», 1932 (EM)

land – etwa bei Jean-Jacques Rousseau (1712–78: *Pygmalion*, 1770) oder Johann Wolfgang von Goethe (1749–1832: *Proserpina*, 1776). Das M. setzt damals neue dramaturgische Akzente und entspringt dem Wunsch, die Innenwelt der Seele zu ergründen und aufzudecken. Das M. führt somit zur Betonung der lyrischen Momente im Drama, wobei die Intensität der seelischen Vorgänge durch äußere Elemente stilistischer (Anakoluthe, Hyperbolik, Ausrufe), spielerischer (Pantomime) oder technischer (Musikbegleitung) Natur noch betont werden. Mit der Zeit wird aber das M. zu oberflächlichem Sprachspiel. Monotonie der Thematik, Überspitzung der Rhetorik, auch die Neigung mancher Schauspieler zu glanzvollen Soloauftritten, bei denen die Virtuosität das Dramatisch-Lyrische verdrängte, ließen das M. ins Klischeehafte verfallen. Das 19. Jh. kannte dann nur noch epigonale Nachahmer und Parodisten dieser Gattung. Erst das 20. Jh. brachte eine Wiederbelebung des M., doch unter veränderten Voraussetzungen und mit anderen Zielen. Die Tendenz im M. ist nun, parallel zur Gesamtentwicklung in der Literatur, die Reduktion der Bühnenwelt bei Inszenierung, Personen und Text, die offene Frage nach der Identität des einzelnen bei wachsendem Mißtrauen gegenüber der Sprache, der Möglichkeit der zwischenmenschlichen Kommunikation. So gestaltet nun das M. diese Sprachskepsis, diese Auflösung des Ichs auf der Bühne. Die Sprache wird zum mechanischen Sprechen, die seelische Innenwelt wird zum Schauplatz eines Geschehens, das ständig im Zeichen des Todes steht, die Bühne wird zur Negation der Bühne. Die Musikbegleitung wird ebenfalls durch verschiedene Erscheinungsformen der Maschine ersetzt – so bei Arnolt Bronnen (1895–1959: *Ostpolzug*, 1926), bei Jean Cocteau (1889–1963: *La voix humaine*, 1930), bei Samuel Beckett (1906–89: *Das letzte Band*, 1958), bei Peter Hacks (*1928: *Ein Gespräch im Hause Stein über den abwesenden Herrn von Goethe*, 1976) oder bei Thomas Bernhard (*1931: *Der Präsident*, 1976; *Minetti*, 1977). Diese Entwicklung des M. im 20. Jh. kulminiert in *Wunschkonzert* (1972) von Franz Xaver Kroetz (*1946), das eine einzige stumme Person inszeniert, die zum Schluß Selbstmord begeht.

Demmer, S.: Untersuchungen zu Form und Geschichte des Monodramas. Köln/ Wien 1982.
Bernard Poloni

Monolog

(Griech. monos = allein, loges = Rede) Im Gegensatz zum →Dialog Selbstgespräch. Auf dem Theater vorgetragener Diskurs, und zwar von einer einzelnen Person, die von der Anwesenheit anderer mitspielender Figuren keine Notiz nimmt. Dabei wird in Szenen mit mehreren Personen

624 Monolog

der Unterschied zwischen M. und Beiseitesprechen, →Aparte/aside relevant. – Im Gegensatz zum Dialog ist der M. hauptsächlich auf die sprechende Person bezogen; es gibt eine einzige Referenzebene, er fordert keine Gegenrede, ist aber desto nachhaltiger an das Publikum gerichtet. Vom Sprachlichen her charakterisiert den M. ein totales Fehlen metalinguistischer Elemente, dagegen aber eine Häufigkeit von Ausrufungsformen.

Eine präzise Bestimmung des M. ist schwierig, da sie nach verschiedenen Kriterien herausgearbeitet werden kann. Nach einem situativen Kriterium beispielsweise, in dem die Einsamkeit des Sprechers, der seine Replik als Selbstgespräch an kein Gegenüber auf der Bühne richtet, wären längere Botenberichte oder eine große Rede keine M., da sie ja an Figuren auf der Bühne oder an das Publikum gerichtet sind. Nach einem strukturellen Kriterium, das den Umfang und den in sich geschlossenen Zusammenhang einer Replik berücksichtigt, würde es sich bei diesen jedoch um M. handeln, da sie in sich geschlossene Solo-Reden größeren Umfangs sind (Pfister, 1977). In diesem Kontext wird der begriffliche Unterschied der angelsächsischen Fachterminologie zwischen «Soliloquy» und M. besonders einleuchtend: «Der M. unterscheidet sich vom Dialog durch seine Länge und relative Vollständigkeit und vom Soliloquy durch die Tatsache, daß er sich an jemanden wendet. Das Soliloquium wird von einer Person gesprochen, die allein ist oder so tut, als ob sie allein wäre. Es ist eine Art, mit sich selbst zu sprechen...» (Dictionary of World Literature, S. 272).

Theatergeschichtlich war der M. am Anfang. Er beruht primär auf einer der Grundbedingungen der Existenz der Theaterform: der Konvention. Dem Kommunikationsbedürfnis des menschlichen Wesens entsprungen, ist der M. in der griech. Tragödie (→Antikes Theater) zum Grundbestandteil geworden. Erst durch das Eingreifen des Chors unterbrochen, wird er dann durch Aischylos und Sophokles zur hohen Reife entwickelt. Mit Euripides wurde der M. zum Stilmittel der Tragödie erhoben durch den →Prolog. Da der M. auf Konvention beruht, kann ein Darsteller während des Vortrags nicht nur eine, sondern mehrere Personen interpretieren. Dies eröffnet die Möglichkeit – ähnlich dem Dialog –, aktionale und nichtaktionale M. zu unterscheiden. Strikte Abgrenzungen sind jedoch auch hier nicht zu treffen. Aktionale M., in denen sich beim Sprechen Handlung als Situationsveränderung vollzieht, entsprechen eher der antiken und klassischen Tragödie, der geschlossenen Form des Dramas, denjenigen Strukturen also, die einer straffen Tektonik verpflichtet sind. Bisweilen findet sich der aktionale M. in Begriffsbildungen wie ‹Konflikt-M.›, ‹Planungs-M.›, ‹Entscheidungs-M.›, die ihn eigentlich in seiner Komplexität begrenzen, wieder. Der dramatische, innerlich kämpfende Kern dieser M.-Art bleibt unverändert: das Individuum in

Monolog 625

Auseinandersetzung mit mehreren Handlungsmöglichkeiten, die es zum Treffen einer Wahl und zum Handeln treiben. Was verwandelt wird, ist die Tektonik, die Ausdrucksweise. Die hier besprochene M.-Art ist gekennzeichnet durch einen symmetrischen Aufbau, eine klare Entwicklung der Für- und Gegenargumente und ein logisches Vorwärtsschreiten, das zur Entschlußfassung und zur →Handlung führt. Der Eindruck rationaler Distanz sowie inhaltlicher und formaler Geschlossenheit wird erweckt. Die Konvention überwiegt. Parallel dazu gibt es den selteneren M. in der offenen Form des Dramas, der in kurzen, abgehackten Sätzen eine Folge oft logisch unzusammenhängender Gefühle und Gedanken wiedergibt, z. B. die Woyzeck-M. in der Szene «Freies Feld» in Büchners *Woyzeck* (1835).

Der nichtaktionale M. unterscheidet sich vom aktionalen M. dadurch, daß er eine Handlung vermittelt, aber kein situationsveränderndes Handeln in sich trägt. Seine Hauptfunktionen sind Information und Kommentar. Diese M.-Art hat eine lange und ununterbrochene Tradition. Im antiken Prolog einsetzend, von der späteren röm. Komödie aufgegriffen, fand er in den →Mysterienspielen des Mittelalters eine Fortführung und gleichzeitig eine neue Form: in der Anrufung. Diese M.-Art nähert sich am meisten dem Bericht und der Erzählung. Das →Renaissancetheater kultiviert ebenfalls den M., der im 17. Jh. besonders vom span. Theater als «soliloquios» neu geprägt wurde.

Da das Vortragen und Interpretieren des M. für den Schauspieler immer eine Bewährungsprobe bedeutet, gleichzeitig ihm aber die Gelegenheit bietet, als Protagonist, als Solospieler aufzutreten, wird er auch im →Straßen- und Markttheater verwendet, so im frz. →Théâtre de la Foire und im →viktorianischen Theater. Im →Varietétheater und in den →Music Halls gilt er bis heute als Schlüsselelement der Vorstellung, in diesem Sinne auch die heutigen One-Man-Shows im Theater und Fernsehen.

Die Vielfalt der Funktionen, die der M. im Laufe der Jh. zu erfüllen vermag – Expositions-M., Brücken- oder Übergangs-M., Binnen-M., lyrischer M. in Klassik und Romantik, häufig auch im Drama des Expressionismus; Reflexions-M. u. a. –, erklärt die lange Dauer dieses recht unrealistisch und artifiziell wirkenden Bühnenmittels. Anstöße zu einer Dialogisierung des M. kamen durch die den M. ersetzenden Dialoge mit →Vertrauten. Der Drang nach →Mimesis führte im Realismus (→Realistisches Theater) und besonders im Naturalismus (→Naturalistisches Theater) zu einem starken Zurücktreten des M. Ibsen als Hauptvertreter des psychologischen Theaters rühmte sich, das Kunststück vollbracht zu haben, in *Brand* (1866) ganz ohne die Konvention des M. ausgekommen zu sein. Strindberg rehabilitiert den M. bald darauf im Vorwort zu *Fräulein Julie* (1888), indem er ihn als motivierte, sich aus der Situation ergebende Ausdrucksform postuliert.

626 Montage

Um die große Bedeutung, die im Drama des 20. Jh. dem M. zukommt, verstehen zu können, sind wichtige Entwicklungen der M.-Form zu beachten. Die zahlreichen →Monodramen, die eigentlich gleichzeitig M.-Stücke sind und sich über das ganze 20. Jh. (bes. nach 1945) verstreuen, sind Manifestationen gestörter Kommunikation, von Isolation und Entfremdung des Individuums. Wo der Dialog versagt, wo seine Überlebenskraft als künstlerische Ausdrucksform unzureichend wird, regiert der M. die Szene. Jean Cocteau, *La voix humaine* (1930), Samuel Beckett, *Das letzte Band* (1959) und *Ein Stück Monolog* (1983), E. Ionesco, *Der neue Mieter* (1965), P. Handke, *Kaspar* (1968), Kroetz, *Wunschkonzert* (1972), verweisen auf die Infragestellung des M.; Pantomime, Objekt-Symbolik und außersprachliche theatralische Zeichen ersetzen ihn.

Klotz, V.: Geschlossene und offene Form im Drama. München 1980; von Matt, P.: Der Monolog. In: Keller, W. (Hg.): Beiträge zur Poetik des Dramas. Darmstadt 1976; Mukarovsky, J.: Dialog und Monolog. Frankfurt/M. 1967; Pfister, M.: Das Drama. München 1977; Scherer, J.: La dramaturgie classique en France. Paris 1950; Szondi, P.: Theorie des modernen Dramas. Frankfurt/M. 1963.

Adriana Hass

Montage

(Frz.: Zusammenfügen, -bauen) Paradigmatisches Verfahren der Moderne, um sprachlich, stilistisch, inhaltlich unterschiedliche oder heterogene Teile eines Kunstwerks zusammenzufügen (→Collage). – Den Gipfel ihrer Bedeutsamkeit erreicht die M. in den historischen Avantgarde-Bewegungen der ersten Jahrzehnte des 20. Jh. (→Dadaistisches Theater, →Surrealistisches Theater, →Futuristisches Theater, →Konstruktivismus und Theater) und dem damals neuen Medium Film. Da die Erscheinungsformen der bürgerlichen Welt nach der industriellen Revolution nicht mehr als anschauliche Totalität darstellbar und überkommene mimetische Verfahren angesichts dieser Realität obsolet schienen, suchte die M. die Grenzen und Rangunterschiede zwischen künstlerischen Kategorien zu überwinden und alle möglichen Formen und Stoffe miteinander in Kommunikation treten zu lassen. Die so gewonnene formale Beweglichkeit ließ die Realität als Vorratskammer, als potentiellen Rohstoff erscheinen und eröffnete die Chance der Multimaterialität, der Bedeutungsmultivalenz, einer Mischung der Realitätsgrade und Wirklichkeitsschichten eines Kunstwerks.

Sergej Eisenstein (1898–1948) setzte an die Stelle des abbildend-erzählenden Theaters mit seiner illusionistischen, raum-zeitlich linearen Widerspiegelung der Ereignisse die M. der Attraktionen (1923), die Aneinanderreihung von selbständigen Elementen, die auf die Psyche des Publikums einwirken sollten im Sinne eines bestimmten thematischen Endeffekts. Die distinkten Elemente der M., die stimulierenden Attraktionen, zielen auf eine Emotionalisierung des Zuschauers. Dieses Konzept der M. isolierter Einheiten im Theater nahm Eisenstein auch zur Grundlage seiner M. im Film, die im Aufeinanderprall zweier begrenzter Abbildungseinheiten, zweier Einstellungen, die Assoziation in Richtung eines intendierten Sinns lenken will. Die M. ist jetzt nicht eine bloße Summe von Teilelementen, sondern ergibt als dialektisches Produkt einen neuen Bedeutungszusammenhang.

Als Organisationsprinzip der Aneinanderreihung einzelner Szenen eines Dramas ist die M. von der Klassik bis zur Moderne zu finden: die Staccato-Struktur in den Dramen Shakespeares (1564–1616), die sprunghaft Kurzszene an Kurzszene reiht und damit schroffste Gegensätzlichkeiten der Stimmung oder der Weltsicht in unmittelbar antithetische Berührung bringt, weist ebenso ein M.-Verfahren auf wie z. B. die *Trilogie des Wiedersehens* (1976) von Botho Strauß (*1944), in der die kaleidoskopische Abfolge von 47 kurzen Einzelszenen, den Momentaufnahmen oder Einstellungen eines Films gleich, durch harte Blackouts oder weiche Blenden voneinander abgetrennt sind.

Jürgens-Kirchhoff, A.: Technik und Tendenz der Montage in der bildenden Kunst des 20. Jahrhunderts. Lahn/Gießen 1978; Lindner, B./Schlichting, H. B.: Die Destruktion der Bilder; Differenzierungen im Montagebegriff. In: Montage/Avantgarde. Alternative 122/23. Berlin 1978, S. 209–224; Bürger, P.: Theorie der Avantgarde. Frankfurt/M. 1974; Schlegel, H.-J. (Hg.): Sergej M. Eisenstein 1. München 1974.

Ulrich Stein

Moralitäten

Allegorische Spiele des späten Mittelalters. Die Handlung bestand aus dem Kampf zwischen personifizierten Abstraktionen, z. B. Gnade und Gerechtigkeit, gegen Neid und Gier im Leben des Menschen. Im Gegensatz zu den →Mysterienspielen, die in Zyklen und von Laien aufgeführt wurden, wurden M. als Einzelstücke vornehmlich von Berufsschauspielern gespielt. Durch Charakterdoubling konnten sie auch von einer kleinen Anzahl von Schauspielern aufgeführt werden. M. behandelten hauptsächlich drei Bereiche: die ‹ars moriendi› (Totentanz), das Streitgespräch zwischen den Tugenden und vor allem den Kampf zwischen Laster und Tugenden um die Seele des Menschen. M. bereits 1378 erwähnt (*Pater Noster Play* in York). Die älteste Handschrift (*The Pride of Life*) stammt von 1400 bis 1425. Die beliebteste englische M. war Mankind (ca.

628 Moriske / Moreske / Moresca / Morris dance

1471). M. waren wandlungsfähiger als die Mysterienspiele und paßten sich der veränderten historischen und dramatischen Umwelt an. Realistische und komische Elemente wurden aufgenommen, verkörperte Abstraktionen wie Mankind wurden zu konkreten, erkennbaren Figuren, und das Ringen der Tugenden und Laster wurde mit dem Bezug zu Gegenwartsleben durchsetzt.

Habicht, W.: Studien zur Dramenform vor Shakespeare. Heidelberg 1968; Happé, P.: Song in Morality Plays and Interludes. Lancaster 1991; Potter, P.: The English Morality Play. London 1975; Wickham, G.: Early English Stages: 1300 to 1660. Rev. Ed. Vol. 1. London 1980.

J. Lawrence Guntner

Moriske / Moreske / Moresca / Morris dance

Getanzte Chronik der unaufhörlichen Kämpfe zwischen den Christen und Ungläubigen. In der Renaissance beliebtester Gesellschaftstanz und als solcher stets → Waffentanz. Für alle Hoffestlichkeiten vor dem → Ballet de Cour Höhepunkt des Festes. – Morisco = ein nach der Rückeroberung Spaniens durch den Cid im Lande verbliebener und bekehrter Maure. Moriscos = die christianisierte arabische Bevölkerung. Moresca = ursprünglich ein orientalisch «heidnischer» Fruchtbarkeitstanz, der später zum historisch gebundenen dramatischen Schau- und Maskentanzspiel ausgebaut wird. Spielleute begleiten das Tanzspiel. In der volkstümlichen M. tanzen junge Leute auf Dorf- oder Ortsplätzen das Spiel, dessen Mittelpunkt der Mattucino bildet, der in phantasievoller Kleidung mit Schellen behangen auftritt. Der Mattucino, in den meisten M. mit geschwärztem Gesicht (ein Mohr), und die Ritter fechten. Der Narr (Mohr) stirbt. Ein → Divertissement folgt. Früh entwickelt die Choreographie komplizierte Tanz-, Wende- und Drehfiguren, gewagte Degenstöße und Sprünge über den Degen. Die M. endet in der Schlußformation mit der Rosa: Alle Tänzer treten zusammen und werfen den Mattucino in die Luft. In der emanzipierten M. treten nur sechs bis acht Tänzer als Ritter und eine Dame neben dem Mattucino auf. Auf den Balearen wird aus dem Narren ein Teufel. An die Stelle des Ritterkorps treten Pferdeattrappen. Mit den Pferdetänzen hat die M. einen ethnologisch bekannten Tanztyp eingebunden. Umgekehrt verselbständigt sich dieses Tanzspielelement in den Roßtänzen, → Turnieren, → Roßballetten Europas. – Der *morris dance* Englands zentriert die «Mayde Maryan». Die Figur des Mattucino erhält im morris dance an ihrer gehörnten Mütze Eselsohren und reitet auf einem Zepter. Häufig spricht der Narr in England das Publikum als ‹Erklärer› der → «dumb show» an. Belgien und Rumänien kennen zwei M.-Varianten. Bis in die Neuzeit hinein feiert ein Spiel in Tollo/Abruzzen den Seesieg bei Lepanto (1571) über die Türken in Form der M.

Böhme, F. M.: Geschichte des Tanzes in Deutschland. Leipzig 1886; Engel, H.: Moresca, Moriskentänze. In: Blume, F. (Hg.): Musik in Geschichte und Gegenwart. Bd. IX. Sp. 575–579. Kassel 1960; Junk, V.: Handbuch des Tanzes. Nachdruck Hildesheim/New York 1977; Nettl. P.: Exotik in früherer Zeit. In: Musica XIV (1960). Kassel/Basel, S. 215.

Helga Ettl

Moritat

(Etymologie umstritten; möglicherweise von Rotwelsch ‹more› = Lärm, Furcht, oder vom mittellat. ‹moritates› bzw. dem frz. ‹moralitée› oder durch Zerdehnung aus ‹Mordtat› abgeleitet.) Heute meist allg. für die öffentlich vorgetragenen Lieder des →Bänkelsangs benutzter Begriff, in der Forschung uneinheitlich gebraucht. Während die einen M. – entsprechend dem Auftauchen des Begriffs um 1850 – lediglich zur Bezeichnung des parodistischen Bänkelsangs des 19. und 20. Jh. verwenden möchten (Petzoldt), benutzen ihn andere als allg. Bezeichnung für «die in Verbindung mit einer Bilddemonstration gesungene Wunder- und Schauermär» (Riedel).

Böhme, G.: Bänkelsängermoritaten, vornehmlich solche zu Anfang des 19. Jahrhunderts. Diss. (masch.) München 1920; Braungart, W. (Hg.): Bänkelsang. Stuttgart 1985; Janda, E./Nötzoldt, F.: Die Moritat vom Bänkelsang oder Das Lied der Straße. München 1959; Petzoldt, L.: Bänkelsang. Stuttgart 1974; Riedel, K. V.: Der Bänkelsang. Hamburg 1963; Riha, K.: Moritat, Bänkelsang, Protestballade. Königstein/Ts. ²1979; Schilder Bilder Moritaten. Berlin 1987 [Katalog]; Sternitzke, E.: Der stilisierte Bänkelsang. Diss. Marburg 1933.

Wolfgang Beck

Moskauer Staatliches Kammertheater

(Gosudarstvennyj Moskowskij Kamernyj teatr) 1914 von A. J. Tairow (1885–1950) zusammen mit Alice Koonen (1889–1974) und einer Gruppe junger Schauspieler gegr., am 12. Dez. 1914 mit dem altind. Mysterienspiel *Śakuntalā* von Kālidāsa eröffnet. Der Inszenierungsstil wandte sich programmatisch ebenso gegen den psychologisierenden Naturalismus Stanislawskis wie gegen die Technifizierung und Stilisierung des Theaters durch Meyerhold, obgleich Tairow mit dem letzten Vorstellungen vom universalen Schauspieler gemeinsam hatte. Meyerholds Regie-Experimente hatte Tairow bereits 1906/07 kennengelernt, als er im →Komissarshewskaja-Theater in A. Bloks *Balagantschik* als Schauspieler auftrat. «Synthetisches Theater», das alle Theatergattungen (Oper, Operette, Ballett, Sprechtheater, Pantomime) vereinen sollte, forderte K. A. Mardshanischwili (= Mardshanow, 1872–1933), dessen Freiem Theater Tairow sich 1913 anschloß und wo er die Pantomime *Der Schleier der Pierrette* (nach A. Schnitzler, *Der Schleier der Beatrice*) inszenierte (1913; 1916 Neuinszenierung am M. S. K.).

Die Suche nach der «reinen Theatralität» ließ das M. S. K. zur Zeit der sowj. Kulturrevolution als Inbegriff bourgeoiser Theaterkultur erscheinen; Anstoß erregte Tairows Auffassung, die reale Bühnenemotion habe ihre Säfte «nicht aus dem wirklichen Leben... zu ziehen, sondern aus dem erschaffenen Leben jenes szenischen Gebildes, das der Schauspieler aus dem Zauberreich der Phantasie zu schöpferischem Dasein erweckt» (→ *Das entfesselte Theater*, S. 69). Dem Vorwurf, sein Theater sei reaktionär, versuchte Tairow mit dem Entwurf eines «strukturellen» an Stelle eines «sozialistischen» Realismus zu begegnen und die Realität als Stimulans für den Schauspieler anzuerkennen. Allein solange sein Programm das synthetische Theater blieb, er die hohe Tragödie mit Buffonade und Operette mischte, wurde sein Stil als abstrakt empfunden.

Kunstgriffe der Show, der Operette vereinen sich in der Aufführung von Brechts/Weills *Dreigroschenoper*, der ersten Verkörperung eines Brecht-Dramas auf einer sowj. Bühne (1930); aber erst 1933 erfährt ein sowj. dramatisches Werk eine gültige Inszenierung am M. S. K., die *Optimistische Tragödie* von W. W. Wischnewski. Erfolgreich ist 1940 das nach Flauberts gleichnamigem Roman konzipierte Schauspiel *Madame Bovary* mit A. Koonen, der bedeutendsten Protagonistin des Tairow-Theaters, als Emma. 1949 wurde Tairow, der das M. S. K. bis dahin leitete, im Kontext der Kampagne gegen den Kosmopolitismus früherer Fehler (Inszenierung von M. Bulgakows *Purpurinsel*, die 1929 verboten wurde) und neuer Verfehlungen (Westtrend, Formalismus, Ästhetizismus) bezichtigt und abgesetzt. Schließung des M. S. K. 1950.

Deržavin, K.: Kniga o Kamernom teatre. 1914–34. Leningrad 1934; Kamernyj teatr. Stat'i i zametki, vospominanija. Moskva 1934; Očerki istorii russkogo sovetskogo dramatičeskogo teatra. Bd. 2–3. Moskva 1960–61 (Kapitel «Moskovskie teatry»); Tairow, A.: Das entfesselte Theater. Leipzig/Weimar 1980; Rudnickij, K.: Aleksandr Tairow – konec puti. In: Teatral'naja žizn' (Moskva) 1988, Nr. 21; Litavrina, M.: Vysšaja mera ili drama iz-za ostrova. In: Teatral' naja žizn' 1989, Nr. 16 u. 17.

Annelore Engel-Braunschmidt/Elke Wiegand

Mudra

Sanskrit: Finger- und Handhaltung von symbolischer Bedeutung in buddhistischen und hinduistischen Kulturen (→Indisches Theater). M. nennt Maurice Béjart (*1924 oder 1927) seine 1970 in Brüssel gegründete, dem →Ballet du XXe Siècle zugeordnete Tanzschule. Der Ausbildungsgang strebt eine totale Schauspielausbildung des Tänzers an, der dazu befähigt werden muß, sich in Stimme und Bewegung ganzheitlich auszudrücken. Béjart will Menschen ausbilden, die auch zu tanzen verstehen, nicht aber Tänzer, denen das Menschsein überlassen bleibt. 1977 entsteht in Dakar (Senegal) eine Zweigstelle: die Mudra-Afrique. Die künstlerische Leitung dieser Institution übernimmt Germaine Acogny. In Dakar wollen Acogny und Béjart ein afrik. Tanzvokabular ausformen, das den tänzerischen Begabungen Afrikas ein euro-afrikanisches Kulturleben erlaubt. Auch im Senegal sollen die Tänzer zu «Interprêtes du spectacle» werden. Der Tanzpublizist Berger lehnt die angestrebte Synthese zweier entgegengesetzter Körperstile ab, Béjart argumentiert dementgegen: Keine Tradition dürfe zum schlummernden See werden. Nicht für die Reinerhaltung einer Ethnie tritt Béjart ein, wohl aber für deren Fortentwicklung und damit für die Entfaltungsmöglichkeiten und Neuschöpfungen von Tanzstilen. Die markanten Bewegungsstrukturen des afrikanischen Tanzes sollen nach Béjart das bisherige Gebärden-Repertoire beleben und variieren.

Der Mudra-Schule Brüssel wird 1981 von der Universität Paris/Sorbonne die Praxisausbildung der Doktoranden für den Studiengang Tanz anvertraut.

Béjart, M.: Ein Augenblick in der Haut eines anderen. München 1980; Berger, R.: African Dance. Wilhelmshaven 1984; Wangenheim, A.v.: Mudra-Afrique – Symbolsprache der Gesten. In: Ballett-Journal/Das Tanzarchiv III (1981), S. 56–58.

Patricia Stöckemann

Mülheimer Theatertage

Seit 1976 jährliches Theatertreffen im Mai in Mülheim an der Ruhr. Förderung des jeweils neuen deutschsprachigen Dramas mit dem Ziel, unter sechs bis sieben ausgesuchten Stücken, die in den vorangegangenen zwölf Monaten uraufgeführt wurden, eines als das beste der Saison mit dem «Mülheimer Dramatikerpreis» in Höhe von 10 000 DM auszuzeichnen. Preisträger: Franz Xaver Kroetz (1976), Gerlind Reinshagen (1977), Martin Sperr (1978), Heiner Müller (1979), Ernst Jandl (1980), Peter Greiner (1981), Botho Strauß (1982), George Tabori (1983 und 1990),

Lukas B. Suter (1984), Klaus Pohl (1985), Herbert Achternbusch (1986), Volker Ludwig (1987), Rainald Goetz (1988), Tankred Dorst (1989).

Schulze-Reimpell, W. (Hg): stücke '76–'90. Köln 1991.

Werner Schulze-Reimpell / Red.

Mummers' Play

Populärform des Dramas aus dem engl. Mittelalter, aufgeführt von maskierten oder verkleideten → Laienspielern, vor allem zu Weihnachten, um den Tod des alten und die Wiedergeburt des neuen Jahres zu feiern. Ursprung im Fruchtbarkeitsritus; beeinflußte das mittelalterliche Drama. Das M. P., wie es heute noch gelegentlich aufgeführt wird, stammt vom St. George Play ab, das den Kampf zwischen St. George und dem türkischen Ritter darstellt. St. George unterliegt zunächst, wird aber vom herbeigeholten Doktor geheilt oder vom Tod erweckt. Zum Schluß wenden sich die Spieler an das Publikum, und eine Kollekte wird gesammelt.

Brody, A.: The English Mummers and Their Plays: Traces of Ancient Mystery. London 1969; Wickham, G.: Early English Stages: 1300 to 1660. Rev. Ed. Vol. 1. London 1980.

J. Lawrence Guntner

Münchener Künstlertheater

Reformbühne Anfang des 20. Jh. 1907 Verein M. K. gegr.; Georg Fuchs (1868–1949) Schriftführer und Dramaturg im künstlerischen Beirat, Journalist und Theatertheoretiker, Reformideen: Abschaffung der Rampe («transorchestrale Einheit»), Amphitheater (mit abschließender Logenreihe), Ablehnung des Naturalismus und des Illusionismus auf der Bühne, Rückbesinnung auf Urformen der Schauspielkunst, auf Tanz und rhythmische Bewegung, Erneuerung des Theaterspiels als Kulthandlung. Zusammenarbeit mit dem Maler Fritz Erler. – Das M. K. wurde von dem Architekten Max Littmann erbaut, typisch ist seine → Reliefbühne. Eröffnungsvorstellung mit *Faust I* (17. 5. 1908). Spielplan: Shakespeare, Kotzebue, Ruederer, Gryphius, Cervantes und Fuchs (*Tanzlegendchen*). 1909 Auflösung des Vereins M. K., Theater an Max Reinhardt verpachtet. Georg Fuchs war Theaterleiter ohne Einfluß auf die künstlerische Führung; 1911–13 waren Pächter der Drei-Masken-Verlag und der Dramaturg Georg Fuchs; Spielplangestaltung ohne Verwirklichung der Reformideen. 1914 Schließung des M. K.

Brauneck, M.: Theater im 20. Jh. Programmschriften, Stilperioden, Reformmodelle. Reinbek bei Hamburg 1982; Fuchs, G.: Die Revolution des Theaters. München/Leipzig 1909; ders.: Die Schaubühne der Zukunft. Berlin/Leipzig o. J. (Das Theater, Bd. XV); Prütting, L.: Die Revolution des Theaters. Studien über Georg Fuchs. München 1971 (Münchener Beiträge zur Theaterwissenschaft, Bd. 2).

Ingeborg Janich

(Münchner) Kammerspiele

Bedeutendste Münchner Sprechbühne. Zwei Spielstätten: Schauspielhaus (einziges erhaltenes Jugendstiltheater Deutschlands, 1900/01 erbaut von Heilmann & Littmann, Innenarchitekt: Prof. Richard Riemerschmied, 1970–72 originalgetreu restauriert), Werkraum (seit 1957, Neues Werkraumtheater seit 1961, Umbau 1983); angeschlossen Theater der Jugend in der Schauburg (seit 1977) und Otto Falckenberg-Schule (Fachakademie für Darstellende Kunst der Landeshauptstadt München). 1911 als Privattheater unter dem Namen «Münchner Lustspielhaus» in der Augustenstraße von Dr. Eugen Robert (1877–1944) gegründet, seit 1912 Name M. K., 1926 Umzug in das Schauspielhaus in der Maximilianstraße, seit 1939 städtisches Eigentum. – 1911–13 Direktion Eugen Robert, 1913–16 Erich Ziegel (1876–1950), 1916/17 Hermann Sinsheimer (1884–1950), 1917–44 Otto Falckenberg (1873–1947), 1945–47 Intendanz Erich Engel (1891–1966), 1947–63 Hans Schweikart (1895–1975), 1963–72 August Everding (*1929), 1973–83 Hans Reinhard Müller (1922–89), seit 1983 Dieter Dorn (*1935).

Seit Falckenberg Pflegestätte des zeitgenössischen Dramas. Mitarbeiter Falckenbergs: Lion Feuchtwanger (1884–1958), Bert Brecht (1898–1956), Caspar Neher (1897–1962); Regisseure: Erich Engel, Erwin Piscator (1893–1966), später Friedrich Domin (1902–1961), Heinz Dieter Kenter (1896–1984), Karl Heinz Martin (1886–1948), Ausstattungschef Otto Reigbert (1890–1957). Unter Hans Schweikart Spielplan der Humanität, Stücke von Bert Brecht, Friedrich Dürrenmatt (1921–90), Peter Hacks (*1928); Ausstattungschef Wolfgang Znamenacek (1913–53), später Jörg Zimmermann, Inszenierungen Fritz Kortners (1892–1970), Leopold Lindtbergs (1902–84), Leonard Steckels (1901–71). Mitarbeiter August Everdings: Ivan Nagel (Dramaturgie), Dieter Giesing (Oberspielleiter). UA von Peter Weiss (1916–82) und Heinar Kipphardt (1922–82), erste Inszenierungen von Peter Stein (*1937). Unter Hans Reinhard Müller im Spielplan: Tankred Dorst, Botho Strauß, Heiner Müller, Thomas Brasch; Inszenierungen von Johannes Schaaf, Dieter Dorn, Harald Clemen, Ernst Wendt (1937–86), Adolf Dresen, Benno Besson, Thomas Langhoff, Robert Wilson.

634 Münchner Lach- und Schießgesellschaft

1978–81 kontinuierliche Arbeit von George Tabori: Unter Dieter Dorn Theater «der sinnlichen Aufklärung». Inszenierungen von Alexander Lang; Jürgen Rose Berater der Theaterleitung (Ausstattung).

Petzet, W.: Theater. Die M. K. 1911–72. München 1973; Müller, H.-R./Dorn, D./Wendt, E.: Theater für München. Ein Arbeitsbuch der Kammerspiele 1973–83. München 1983.

Ingeborg Janich

Münchner Lach- und Schießgesellschaft

Eines der bekanntesten Kabarettensembles der BRD, entstanden auf einem Faschingsfest (17.2.1955). Der Erfolg der ersten Vorstellung führte zu weiteren unregelmäßigen Aufführungen unter dem Gruppennamen «Die Namenlosen», zu denen bereits Dieter Hildebrandt und der Texter Klaus Peter Schreiner gehörten. Schon Ende 1955 konnten sie in ein eigenes Domizil umziehen. Als Manager und Regisseur kam der Sportreporter Sammy Drechsel (†1986) hinzu. Nach einer Spaltung der Gruppe vervollständigten eine Reihe von Profikabarettisten das Ensemble, das Ende 1956 zum erstenmal unter neuem Namen auftrat.

In relativ kurzer Zeit setzten sie sich dank ihres Könnens und engagierter Texte durch. Fernsehübertragungen ihrer Programme trugen zu ihrer Beliebtheit bei, führten aber allmählich auch zu einer Veränderung von Stil und Inhalt. Zugunsten angestrebter Breitenwirkung verzichteten sie gelegentlich auf aktuelle Polemik und aggressive Schärfe. Dennoch weigerte sich der Bayrische Rundfunk bereits 1966, ihre Programme in Zukunft live auszustrahlen. Mit dem Beginn der sozialliberalen Koalition in Bonn (1969) sahen sie – wie viele andere Kabarettisten – ihre Existenzberechtigung gefährdet, schien doch erreicht, wofür sie jahrelang gestritten hatten. 1972 schieden die bisherigen Mitglieder der Gruppe aus und gingen zum Theater oder Fernsehen bzw. arbeiteten als Solokabarettisten weiter (D. Hildebrandt). Nach einer Pause begann die M. L. u. S. 1976 in wechselnder Besetzung wieder zu spielen – mit wachsendem Erfolg. Zu den bisherigen Textern kamen neue hinzu, auf diese Weise Kontinuität und innovative Elemente verbindend.

Budzinski, K.: Pfeffer ins Getriebe. München 1982; ders.: Die öffentlichen Spaßmacher. München 1966; ders.: Wer lacht denn da? Braunschweig 1989; Hildebrandt, D.: Was bleibt mir übrig. München 1986; Pelzer, J.: Criticism through Mockery. Diss. Madison 1981; Schreiner, K.P.: Die Zeit spielt mit. München 1976.

Wolfgang Beck

(Münchner) Rationaltheater

Am 28.1.1965 eröffneten der Diplomsoziologe Rainer Uthoff, der Student Ekkehard Kühn und der Schauspieler Horst A. Reichel in dessen «Theater 44» mit dem Programm «Henkerswahlzeit» das M. R. Seit 1968 ist Uthoff alleiniger Leiter des sich seit der Gründung als ‹Dokumentationskabarett› verstehenden Unternehmens, das von Anfang an Bild- und Tondokumente in sein Programm einbezog. Inhaltlich kompromißlos, versuchte das M. R. schon frühzeitig, nicht reines Nummernkabarett zu machen, sondern themenzentriert zu arbeiten und über die Kritik an individuellen Erscheinungen zu einer grundlegenden Analyse der gesellschaftlichen Verhältnisse zu gelangen. Versuche in den 60er Jahren, durch Texte bekannter Literaten das Kabarett zu verändern, erwiesen sich rasch als nicht tragfähig. 1969 begann «Knast – 1. deutsches Sing-Sing-Spiel» die Reihe der einem Thema gewidmeten Programme, die mit «Bonn Hur» (1970), «Wer beschiß Salvatore G.?» (1971), «Vom Säugling zum Bückling» und «Tagesshow mit Kommentar und Meckerkarte» (1974) fortgesetzt wurden. Als das nur noch R. genannte Kabarett 1975 nach Schwabing umzog, hatte es über 60 Strafverfahren gewonnen, die von seiner Kritik Betroffene gegen es angestrengt hatten. Mit der «1. deutschen Bon(n)zenschau» (1976) kehrte das R. zum Nummernkabarett zurück. Der Versuch der Etablierung eines Frauenkabaretts scheiterte 1979. 1982 gab Uthoff das Ensemblekabarett auf und spielte seither «Uthoffs Tagesschau» mit jeweiligen Aktualisierungen. Anläßlich des 50. Jahrestags der Machtübergabe an die Nationalsozialisten spielte das R. Anfang 1983 «Wenn wir wüßten, was der Adolf mit uns vorhat». Gastspiele und Theateraufführungen ergänzen heute das Programm, das wesentlich themenzentriert ist.

Budzinski, K.: Das Kabarett. 100 Jahre literarische Zeitkritik – gesprochen – gesungen – gespielt. Düsseldorf 1985; ders.: Pfeffer ins Getriebe. München 1982; ders.: Wer lacht denn da? Braunschweig 1989; Greul, H.: Bretter, die die Zeit bedeuten. Köln/Berlin 1967 (erw. Ausg., 2 Bde. München 1971).

Wolfgang Beck

Münchner Volkstheater GmbH

Kommunales Theater. Wiedereröffnung 1983 im umgebauten Theater in der Briennerstraße (erbaut 1955). Knüpft an Tradition des Volkstheaters im süddeutsch-österr. Raum an, Spielplan: klassische Autoren der süddeutsch-österr. Dialektliteratur (Ferdinand Raimund, Johann Nestroy, Ludwig Anzengruber, Ludwig Thoma, Franz Molnar, Ödön von Horváth, Marie-Luise Fleißer, Karl Valentin, Karl Schönherr u. a.), daneben Stücke aus der großen außerdt. Volkstheatertradition (z. B. Marcel Pagnol, Sean O'Casey, Edoardo de Filippo) und Zusammenarbeit mit zeitgenössischen Autoren. 1983–88 Intendant Jörg-Dieter Haas, seit 1988 Intendantin Ruth Drexel (*1930).

Geschichte des Münchner Volkstheaters. Hg. anläßlich der Wiedereröffnung am 24. November 1983.

Ingeborg Janich

Muou xi / Kuilei xi (Chin. Puppentheater)

Wenn man von Legenden absieht, läßt sich das Puppentheater erstmals im 2. Jh. n. Chr. nachweisen. Zur Song-Zeit (960–1279) erlebte es zugleich mit dem Theater infolge der Entwicklung urbaner Kultur einen raschen Aufschwung. Seitdem ist es überall in China sehr beliebt. Heute sind drei Formen des Puppentheaters verbreitet, das Spiel mit Stab-, Hand- und Fadenpuppen. Verbreitet war das sog. Tragstangen-Theater (piandan xi): Ein Puppenspieler trug die gesamte Ausrüstung – vor allem die aus einem Holzkasten bestehende Bühne und die Puppen – an den beiden Enden einer Stange über der Schulter und zog so von Dorf zu Dorf. Für eine Aufführung brauchte er nur die Stange im Boden zu verankern, den Kasten an ihrem oberen Ende zu befestigen und konnte mit dem Spiel beginnen. – Historisch sind noch weitere Formen des Puppentheaters überliefert: die pyrotechnische Puppe (yaofa kuilei), welche offenbar durch eine Art Feuerwerkskörper bewegt wurde, und die Wasserpuppe (shui kuilei), welche auf einem mit Wasser gefüllten Boot mittels eines hydraulischen Mechanismus in Bewegung gesetzt wurde. Schließlich ist noch die «Puppe aus Fleisch» (rou kuilei) zu nennen, eine fast absurde Entwicklung des Puppentheaters, Verbindung zwischen diesem und dem eigentlichen Theater: Mehrere Kinder wurden von jeweils einem Mann auf der Schulter getragen und bewegten sich zu Musik und Gesang wie Puppen, deren Bewegungen ihrerseits ja bereits menschliche Bewegungen imitierten.

Liu Mau-Tsai: Puppenspiel und Schattentheater unter der Sung-Dynastie. In: Oriens Extremus, XII. Jahrgang, Heft 2 (Dez. 1967), S. 129–142; Obraztsov, Sergei V.: The Chinese Puppet Theatre. London 1961; Dolby, W.: The Origins of Chinese Puppetry. In: Bulletin of the School of Oriental and African Studies 41 (1978), 97–120; Sun Kaidi: Kuilei xi kaoyuan. Shanghai 1953.

Bernd Eberstein

Music Hall

Die M. H. war in Großbritannien von ca. 1850 bis 1920 eine populäre Form der Freizeitunterhaltung brit. Kleinbürger und Arbeiter oder auch deren Schauplatz. Sie entstand aus der traditionellen Wirtshausunterhaltung und war die britische Variante des kontinentalen → Varietés. Das Programm der M. H. bestand aus einer losen Abfolge von Songs und kurzen Sketchen verschiedener bekannter Komiker («comic turns»), z. T. auch aus akrobatischen Einlagen, Ballett und Tiernummern. Nach dem Herauswachsen aus den Kneipen und dem Bau eigener Gebäude wurde die M. H. zu einer Familienunterhaltung mit teils konservativer, oft auch rebellischer Grundtendenz. Seit dem Ende des 19. Jh. unterlag die M. H. immer stärker kommerziellen Interessen und wurde zu einer Keimstelle der beginnenden Unterhaltungsindustrie. Durch die bis heute bekannten Songs und ihre Stars wirkte die M. H. bewußtseinsprägend; Marie Lloyd (1870–1922), Gus Elen (1862–1940), Dan Leno (1860–1904), Vesta Tilley (1864–1952), Albert Chevalier (1851–1923), Little Tich (1868–1928), Harry Lauder (1870–1950), George Formby (1905–61) u. a. m. Die Paradigmen der M. H. – wiederkehrende Motive, Charaktertypen, schlagfertiger, oft entlarvender Witz – teilten sich im 20. Jh. den neuen Massenkommunikationsmedien und auch dem engl. Drama mit. Die M. H. selbst hat sich jedoch trotz zahlreicher Wiederbelebungsversuche nach 1920 nicht gegen die stärker privatisierenden Medien der Massenunterhaltung behaupten können.

Bailey, P. (Hg.): Music Hall. Philadelphia 1986; Cheshire, D. F.: Music Hall in Britain. Newton Abbot 1974; Schneider, U.: Die Londoner Music Halls und ihre Songs 1850–1920. Tübingen 1984; Senelick, L./Cheshire, D. F./Schneider, U.: British Music Hall 1840–1923: A Bibliography and Guide to Sources, with a Supplement on European Music Hall. Hamden (Conn.) 1981.

Bernd-Peter Lange

Mysterienspiel

Als Mysterien gelten Geheimkulte, die ohne Tanzszenen, bis zur Trance führend, nicht denkbar sind. M. in Griechenland nutzen der Orpheus-, Apollo-, Athene-, Hera- und Dionysos-Kult (→ Antikes Theater). – Das Mittelalter entfaltet vom 13. Jh. an antike und christliche Thematiken in M. Alle durch Religion und Politik, auch Kriege veranlaßten Sorgen der Bevölkerung klingen im M. an. Der Tanz in Form der «balli» oder «balletti» belebt die Spiele, die zunächst in der Kirche und danach vor der Kirche aufgeführt werden. Dramatischer Kern aller M. ist die Dichoto-

638 **Mysterienspiel** (Spanien) ⸻

mie zwischen Gut und Böse. Der Tanz, der im 13. Jh. im katholischen Glaubensraum bereits offiziell aus der Kirche verbannt worden war, erobert sich im M. erneut den Altarraum, in dem das Heer der Bösen, Luzifer und seine Gesellen, tanzen, zuweilen auch die Vertreter des guten Prinzips, etwa Engel oder Jungfrauen. Dramaturgisch verfolgt die Gotik im M. den chorischen Gedanken. Chöre der Apostel, Engel, Heiligen, der törichten und klugen Jungfrauen, der Juden, Wächter, Knechte und nicht zuletzt der Teufel agieren. Die Bühne fehlt fast immer. Erst spät werden auf Plätzen schachtelartige Bühnen gebaut, von denen ein Steg zum Kirchenportal führt. Die Spieler ziehen wie bei der →Moresca mit Dekorations- und Requisitenkarren tanzend, singend und spielend durch die Straßen bis zum Kirchplatz. Die ältesten M. mit Dialogen und Balletten sind aus Italien überliefert (14. Jh.: *Die Erschaffung Adams* und *Die Vertreibung aus dem Paradies*), aus Österreich das *Wiener Spiel*. In ihm tanzen die Wächter am Grabe, die Juden vor Pilatus, die Knechte springen, und die Teufel treiben beides. Den ebenfalls tanzenden Rittern tritt eine Prozession von sieben Engeln entgegen. In der Vorhölle werden die Ankömmlinge in eine Schlachtenszene verwickelt (→Waffentänze). Aus der Kirche vertrieben, werden die M. als volkstümliche Spiele dreister. Im Redentiner Auferstehungsspiel (1464) bildet zum Beispiel eine eigenständige Tanzpantomime, ein Teufelsballett in Form der →Moreske, den Beschluß. Satanas schleppt zum Gaudium der Gläubigen einen Geistlichen herbei, der eine Frühmette verschlafen hat. Im Frankfurter Passionsspiel (1493) begrüßt Maria Magdalena ihre Gesellen mit einem Solotanz und -lied. Das Aachener Passionsspiel (1501) überrascht mit zwei Tanzduetten: zwischen Maria Magdalena und einem Kriegsgesellen sowie zwischen Marias Diener und einem Satyr, einem Teufelsdämon. Die zur Spätgotik gehörende Roheit entfaltet sich voll im Tanz der Juden unter dem Kreuz von Golgatha. Beliebte Protagonistin für M. ist neben Maria Magdalena die Tochter des Herodes, Salome. →Ritualtänze (Religiöse Tänze); →Mysterienspiel (Spanien); →Mystery Play.

Gregor, J.: Kulturgeschichte des Balletts. Zürich o. J./Wien 1944; Johannsmeier, R.: Spielmann, Schalk und Scharlatan. Reinbek bei Hamburg 1984.

Helga Ettl

Mysterienspiel (Spanien)

Im mittelalterlichen Spanien dramatische Inszenierungen, die ihre Stoffe aus dem Alten und Neuen Testament, aus Heiligenviten usw. bezogen. Überliefert ist das Fragment eines geistlichen Spiels von 147 Versen, dem *Auto de los Reyes Magos* (Dreikönigsspiel, Manuskript Wende 12./

13. Jh.). Dazu traten im 15. Jh. die Passions- und Krippenspiele von Gómez Manrique (1412?–90?). Aus der Zeit um 1492 ist mit dem *Misterio de Elche* ein anonymes katalanisches Mysterienspiel erhalten, das noch heute aufgeführt wird.

Studervant, W.: The Misterio de los Reyes Magos: Its Position in the Development of the Mediaeval Legend of the Three Kings. Baltimore 1927.

Martin Franzbach

Mystery Play

Frühe, mittelalterliche dramatische Form (→Mittelalter/Drama und Theater des Mittelalters, →Mysterienspiel) mit dem Versuch, die Ereignisse der Bibel einem Laienpublikum plastisch und eindrucksvoll darzustellen. Ursprung im lat. religiösen Drama des Mittelalters, im Ritual der Kirche, im Folkpageantry und der spontanen volkstümlichen Feier religiöser Feste. Die M. P. werden unter dem Begriff ‹miracle plays› subsumiert, obwohl im engeren Sinne unterschieden wird zwischen M. P., die ein biblisches Thema, und ‹miracle plays›, die ein nichtbiblisches Thema, vornehmlich Heiligenlegenden oder die Wunder heiliger Reliquien behandeln. M. P. wurden in großen Zyklen (bis über 40 Stücke) zum Corpus Christi (Fronleichnam) aufgeführt. Die Zyklen wurden nach den Spielorten benannt: Beverley, Chester, York, Coventry, Wakefield (auch Towneley genannt). M. P. werden ab 1376 in York erwähnt, könnten bereits früher existiert haben. (Ab 1318 wird Corpus Christi in ganz England gefeiert.) Die M. P. wurden auf fahrbaren Bühnen, →Pageants genannt, von Laiendarstellern gespielt (Mitglieder der Handwerkszünfte oder der ‹secular clergy›). Die M. P. behandeln drei thematische Schwerpunkte aus der Bibel: das Alte Testament (Schöpfungsgeschichte, der Sündenfall, die Propheten), das Neue Testament (die Verkündigung, die Geburt Christi, Besuch der Hirten und der Heiligen Drei Könige, Jesus im Tempel) und der Tod und Wiederauferstehung Christi (von der Passion bis zu Pfingsten). Im 15. Jh. verstärkt realistische und komische Elemente festzustellen (s. «Secunda Pastorum» in dem Wakefield-Zyklus). Trotz größter Beliebtheit wurden die M. P. nach der Reformation (1534) von der anglikanischen Staatskirche unterdrückt.

Diller, H.-J.: Redeformen des englischen Mysterienspiels. München 1973; Mills, D./McDonald, P.: The Drama of Religious Ceremonial. In: The Revels History of English Drama. Vol. 1. London 1983, p. 67–121; Nelson, A.: The Medieval English Stage: Corpus Christi Pageant and Plays. Chicago 1974; Wickham, G.: Early English Stages: 1300–1600. Rev. Ed. Vol. 1. London 1980.

J. Lawrence Guntner

Mythos

(Griech. = Wort, Rede, Erzählung) Erzählung von Göttern, Halbgöttern, sagenhaften Vorfahren; Bericht von Anfang und Ursprung der Welt, ihren Machtstrukturen und Ordnungsverhältnissen in Bildern und Geschehensabläufen. M. bedeutet im engsten Sinn religiös verbindliche Göttergeschichte, weiter gefaßt auch von Heroen und exemplarischen Figuren. Theater hat mit Faust, Don Juan, Hamlet u. a. solche exemplarischen quasi-mythischen Figuren dem Phantasierepertoire zugeführt.

Im weitesten Sinn ist M. jede Überlieferung, die es mit numinosen Kräften zu tun hat, kollektive Phantasien aller Art, Idealbilder, Utopien. Für die Theaterwissenschaft relevant ist das theatertheoretische Problem des Ursprungs des Theaters, des möglichen Zusammenhangs zwischen Theater, →Ritual, M. durch anthropologische Konstanten (Spiel, Maskerade, Karneval, Mimesis).

Seit den 70er Jahren beeinflußt anthropologische Forschung die Theatertheorie. Peter Brook (*1925), Eugenio Barba (*1936), Richard Schechner (*1934) analysieren Rituale, um ein ‹interkulturelles› Theater zu befördern. So behauptet Schechner (1985) für Rituale in Neu-Guinea einen fließenden Übergang zwischen rituellem «social drama» und «aesthetic drama». Zentriert um den Begriff der →Performance, entsteht ein Theaterbegriff, der zwischen realen Tätigkeiten und ästhetischem Tun ein breites Feld ritualisierter Handlungen erfaßt. Problematisch bleibt freilich die Übertragung ritualisierter Ansätze auf hochentwickelte Industriekultur, in der der Glaube an die Wirksamkeit symbolischer Handlungen weithin fehlt. Dennoch zeigt die Basisdefinition des mythischen Rituals (Verkörperung bedeutungsvoller Gesten vor einem Publikum zu bestimmten ausgezeichneten Zeitpunkten an ebenfalls klar ausgesonderten Orten) die Nähe zum Theater.

Theatertheorie mit Akzent auf Ritual und M. geht vor allem in den USA einher mit Theorie der Postmoderne, transhistorischer Auffassung des (gesellschaftlichen) Lebens insgesamt vom Imponiergehabe und Parade der Tiere über Magie bis zu Gottesdiensten, Festen, Zeremonien und Umgangsformen als rituell. Während solche Verallgemeinerung fragwürdig wird, bleibt die Analyse der mythisch-rituellen Basis einzelner Aspekte des Theaters und des Dramas fruchtbar. Nicht nur die →Tragödie, sondern auch die →Komödie steht seit der Antike in Beziehung zum M. So entstand die Komödie aus Fruchtbarkeitsriten (Gelegenheit zu obszönen Späßen). Noch in späteren Komödien scheint mythischer Ursprung (Verwandlung, Verkleidung, Transformation der Natur im Jahreslauf, ‹Maskerade› der Jahreszeiten) durch.

Barber, C. L.: Shakespeare's Festive Comedy. Princeton 1959; Benjamin, W.: Ursprung des dt. Trauerspiels. Frankfurt/M. 1963; Bohrer, K. H.: Mythos und Moderne. Frankfurt/M. 1984; Grimes, R. L.: Beginnings in Ritual Studies. Washington 1982; Lindenberger, H.: Historical Drama. Chicago/London 1975; Schechner, R.: Between Theatre and Anthropology. Philadelphia 1985; Vernant, J.-P./Vidal-Naquet, P.: Mythe et tragédie en Grèce ancienne. Paris 1973.

Hans-Thies Lehmann

Nachspiel

Kurzes, meist einaktiges Spiel nach dem Abschluß eines längeren Stücks gespielt, meist ohne direkten inhaltlichen Bezug dazu, bes. häufig komisches Spiel nach dem ernsten Stück im Sinne und in der Tradition des →antiken Theaters, wo das →Satyrspiel am Ende der Tragödientrilogie aufgeführt wurde. – So das römische Exodium, die niederl. Kluchten, im →Elisabethanischen Theater die ‹jigs› (ital., frz. gigue = Tanzform), Possen mit Tanz, Gesang und derben Späßen nach den Hauptstücken, nach der →Haupt- und Staatsaktion die Hanswurstspiele. Diese zur heiteren Auflockerung des Publikums vorgesehenen N. wurden gegen Ende des 18. Jh. aus Geschmacksgründen vom bürgerlichen Theater zugunsten des feierlichen →Vorspiels aufgegeben.

Das N. erscheint im Theater des 20. Jh., bes. im zeitgenössischen, wieder in doppelter Form:

– wie der →Epilog und mit denselben Funktionen als abschließender Teil eines Stücks, z. T. handlungsdeutend und schließend, so in Brechts *Herr Puntila und sein Knecht Matti* (1949 UA) und *Der kaukasische Kreidekreis* (1954) mit Bezug auf den Prolog;

– als autonomes, allerdings thematisch auf die Handlung des Stücks bezogenes Spiel, so Max Frischs (1911–91) *Nachspiel zu Biedermann und die Brandstifter* (1958), wo eben als Lehre zu diesem ‹Lehrstück ohne Lehre› auf die Unbelehrbarkeit der Menschen angespielt wird. – Im außerdeutschen Sprachbereich entspricht der Begriff N. weitgehend dem des Epilogs.

Gérard Schneilin

Naive

(Frz. = unbefangen, natürlich) Weibliches →Rollenfach für junge Schauspielerinnen, entspricht der frz. ‹ingénue› – z. B. Silvia in Pierre de Marivaux' (1688–1763) *La double inconstance* (1723), Ondine in Jean Giraudoux' (1882–1944) gleichnamigem Stück (1939) oder Käthchen in Heinrich von Kleists (1777–1811) *Käthchen von Heilbronn* (1810). Typische Wesenszüge der N. sind eine arglose, unverstellte und anspruchslose Seele, natürliche, ungekünstelte Empfindungen und Gedanken, die ohne Rücksicht auf das sog. ‹Schickliche› geäußert werden. Gegen Ende des 18. Jh. war die N., sozusagen das genaue Gegenteil der →Soubrette, besonders beliebt. War diese aufgeweckt, witzig und kokett, so wirkte die N. durch ihre Ahnungslosigkeit und Unbefangenheit, ihre unschuldige Treuherzigkeit rührend. Sie kam nach Deutschland als ‹Agnese› nach der Agnes aus Molières (1622–73) *Ecole des femmes* (1662). Mit der Zeit entwickelte sie sich zu einer ‹heroischen› oder ‹pathetischen› N. (frz. ‹ingénue héroïque› et ‹pathétique›), weil sie jeden metaphysischen Wissens entbehrt, ähnlich manchen naiven Männerfiguren wie z. B. der Woyzeck (1836) Georg Büchners (1813–37) oder Schwejk in Jaroslav Hašeks (1883–1923) *Die Abenteuer des braven Soldaten Schwejk* (1921–23). Eine überzeugend wirkende Darstellung der klassischen N. ist heute auf der Bühne sehr schwierig, da sie der modernen Bewußtseinslage kaum noch entspricht.

Bernard Poloni

Nancy

Die Theaterfestspiele von N. gehen zurück auf Jack Lang (*1939), der Professor für öffentliches Recht an der Universität N. war, bevor er 1981 von Staatspräsident François Mitterrand als Kulturminister in die neue Regierung berufen wurde. Lang gründete 1958 mit Edouard Guibert eine Studentenbühne in N. und 1962 die internationalen Festspiele der Studententheater (Festival international de théâtre universitaire). 1964 treten in N. → Bread and Puppet und das →Teatro Campesino auf. 1967 werden auch nichtstudentische Theater zugelassen. 1969 Umbenennung in Welttheater-Festspiele (Festival mondial de N.). 1976 offizielle Leitung durch Lew Bogdan, obwohl Lang weiter der Geist der Festspiele von N. bleibt. Als ‹rote Bretter› (tréteaux rouges) bezeichnet, gelten die Festspiele von N. als Domäne der Linken. – Hauptziele: Wiederaufführung vergessener Stücke der klassischen Literatur; Förderung unbekannter Autoren; Kolloquien und Ausstellungen über das Theaterschaffen, Aufführung politischer Tendenzstücke durch Truppen aus Lateinamerika und Afrika sowie starke Vertretung osteuropäischer Ensembles.

Horst Schumacher

Nanxi

Das nanxi («Südliches Theater») gilt als die früheste Form des eigentlichen Theaters in China. Es entwickelte sich während der Song-Dynastie (960 bis 1279) unter Verwendung der in Südchina verbreiteten Melodien (nanqu), während sich im Norden das →zaju und das yuanben entwickelten. Da es seinen Ursprung in der Hafenstadt Wenzhou/Provinz Zhejiang hatte, hieß es auch Wenzhou zaju oder Yongjia zaju (nach einem anderen Namen für Wenzhou). Auch die Bezeichnung xiwen («Theatertext») war für das nanxi gebräuchlich. Die begrifflichen Schwierigkeiten werden weiter dadurch verstärkt, daß der Begriff nanxi später auch als generelle Bezeichnung für die südlichen Theaterstile, besonders das →chuanqi der Ming-Zeit, gebraucht wurde.

Wegen der nur bruchstückhaft erhaltenen Informationen können wir uns lediglich ein ungefähres Bild des songzeitlichen nanxi machen. Uns sind etwa 170 Titel von Stücken bekannt; vollständig erhalten aber sind nur drei von urspr. 33 Stücken, welche in die Yongle-Enzyklopädie (*Yongle dadian*) von 1408 aufgenommen wurden. Einige andere Stücke des nanxi sind uns nur in späteren mingzeitlichen Fassungen erhalten. Nach dem erhaltenen Material zu urteilen, waren die nanxi von sehr unterschiedlicher Länge und nicht in Akte oder Bilder unterteilt. Sie werden durch eine «Themenangabe» (timu) eingeleitet, einen Vierzeiler, welcher bereits den Inhalt des Stücks ganz kurz zusammenfaßt. Zuerst tritt der mo (männliche Nebenrolle) auf, äußert sich zu allg. Themen wie der Vergänglichkeit der Jugend und streitet mit den Schauspielern hinter der Bühne darüber, welches Stück zur Aufführung kommen soll. Dann faßt er in einer oder zwei Arien noch einmal den Inhalt des Stücks, auf das sie sich geeinigt haben, zusammen. Erst danach tritt der sheng (männliche Hauptrolle) auf, und das Stück beginnt. Andere Rollenfächer des nanxi sind dan (weibliche Rolle), wai (verschiedene Nebenrollen), chou (Clown) und jing (negativer Charakter).

Das nanxi der Song-Zeit war immer volkstümlicher, teilweise auch derber und in der Sprache einfacher und kunstloser als das nördliche Drama. In seinen Inhalten war es oft recht kritisch, so daß es sich mehrfach mit behördlichen Verboten auseinanderzusetzen hatte. Aus diesen Gründen galt es den Gebildeten als besonders vulgäre Form einer ohnehin wenig geachteten Kunst. Es wurde daher mit Mißachtung und i. d. R. mit Schweigen bedacht, weswegen unsere Kenntnisse heute so spärlich sind. Erst im 20. Jh. begann man, sich ernsthaft mit dem nanxi zu befassen.

Um die Mitte des 14. Jh. erlebte das nanxi eine erneute Blüte, nunmehr unter dem Einfluß des →zaju seiner derben Ursprünglichkeit entkleidet und zu einer kultivierten, auch dem konfuzianisch Gebildeten akzeptablen Theaterform weiterentwickelt. Das aus dem nanxi hervorgehende

644 Národní Divadlo (Prag)

→chuanqi kündigte sich bereits an. Als Höhepunkt der nanxi-Literatur dieser Zeit gilt «Die Laute» (*Pipa ji*) von Gao Ming (ca. 1301–ca. 70).

Zhao Jingshen: Song Yuan xiwen benshi. Shanghai 1934; Idema, W./West, S. H.: Chinese Theater 1100–1450. A Source Book. Wiesbaden 1982; Zbikowski, T.: Early Nan-hsi Plays of the Southern Sung Period. Warsaw 1974.

Bernd Eberstein

Národní Divadlo (Prag)

Prager Nationaltheater. Mit dem Verlust der Eigenstaatlichkeit der Tschechoslowakei im Jahre 1621 ging der Verlust der Schriftsprache einher, die nur noch durch die Bibel und durch das →Laientheater bewahrt wurde. Theater wurde zunächst in dt. Sprache gespielt. Erst 1786 erfolgte die erste Theateraufführung in tschech. Sprache (am ‹Nostitz-Theater› in Prag); ebenfalls 1786 wurde das ‹K. u. k. Vaterländische Theater› gegründet, im Volksmund ‹die Bude› genannt. – Erste Bestrebungen zu einem →Nationaltheater gingen von dem Dramatiker und Schauspieler Kajetán Tyl (1808–56) aus, der in Zusammenarbeit mit dem Dichter Havlíček das Programm des neuen N. plante. Bereits in den 50er Jahren des 19. Jh. wurden Geldsammlungen für das N. veranstaltet; allerdings konnte man nach dem Revolutionsjahr 1848 nicht an den Bau eines großen, repräsentativen Hauses denken und schuf deshalb 1862 zunächst das kleine Interimstheater, das dann volle 20 Jahre bestand. Es gelang dem tschech. Theater in dieser Zeit nicht, einen eigenständigen Stil zu entwickeln; auch war das schauspielerische Niveau des Sprechtheaters erschreckend niedrig. Ein höheres künstlerisches Niveau erreichte die Oper, besonders unter Bedřich Smetana (1824–84), der sie seit 1866 leitete. 1881 wurde endlich das N. eröffnet; der Bau brannte jedoch kurz nach seiner Eröffnung ab. Man begann sofort mit dem Neubau und feierte bereits 1883 die Wiedereröffnung des Hauses mit einer Aufführung von Smetanas *Libuša*. Internationale Aufmerksamkeit errang das N. 1892 bei seinem Wiener Gastspiel mit Smetanas *Verkaufter Braut*. Der Anschluß an das europ. Theater gelang jedoch erst unter Karel Kavarovič (1862–1920) als Leiter der Oper und Jaroslav Kvapil (1868–1950) als Leiter des Schauspiels, in deren Spielplan die neuen europ. Dramatiker und Komponisten aufgenommen wurden. Bis heute liegt der Schwerpunkt der künstlerischen Arbeit im Bereich der Oper, wobei Smetana, Dvořak und Janaček einen festen Platz im Repertoire des Hauses einnehmen.

Es gibt am P. N. feste Ensembles für Oper, Ballett und Schauspiel. Unter dem Oberbegriff N. D. werden ab 1. 4. 1992 drei Bühnen zusammengefaßt: das «Nationaltheater an der Moldau» (nach gründlicher Restaurierung zur 100-Jahr-Feier 1983 wiedereröffnet), das Stavovské Divadlo (Ständetheater, zwischenzeitlich als Tyl-Theater geführt), das nach langjähriger Rekonstruktion 1991 mit *Don Giovanni* (hier auch uraufgeführt) in der Regie von D. Radok wiedereröffnet wurde, und das Kolowrat (Studiobühne). Die seit 1983 zum N. D. gehörende Nová Scena (Neue Bühne) wurde an die →Laterna magica verpachtet, das Smetana-Theater (ehem. Deutsches Theater), der Oper und dem Ballett verpflichtet, zur Staatsoper erklärt. Generalintendant 1983–89 Komponist Paur, ab 1991 der Theaterwissenschaftler Jindřich Černý. Schauspieldirektoren 1987–89 Milan Lukeš, seit 1989 der Regisseur Ivan Rajmont. Die Oper leitet Eva Hermannová.

Kindermann, H.: Theatergeschichte Europas, Bd. X, Naturalismus und Impressionismus (3. Teil). Salzburg 1974; Lukavský, R.: Herecký styl Národního divadla, in: České divadlo Bd. 8, hrsg. v. Divadelní ústav. Praha 1983; Hilmera, J.: Stavovské národu! O tom, je se Stavovské Divadlo stalo součástí Divadla Národního. Praha 1991.

Elke Kehr / Elke Wiegand

Narodnija teatar «Ivan Vazov» (Sofia)

(Nationaltheater «Iwan Wasow»). Die Entstehung des bulgarischen Theaters ist eng mit der nationalen Wiedergeburt nach 500 Jahren osmanischer Fremdherrschaft verbunden; daher auch seine aufklärerisch-patriotische Funktion, die lange bestimmend bleibt. 1881 wird in Plowdiw die erste professionelle Theatergruppe gegründet, aus der 1904 das «Bulgarische Nationaltheater» hervorgeht. Im Repertoire Weltdramatik (v. a. Ibsen) und bulg. Autoren (Straschimorow); revolutionierend 1919/20 Geo Milews expressionistische Inszenierungen. N. O. Massalitinow (1880–1961) vom →MChAT führt 1925–44 das →Stanislawski-System ein. Der Spielstil des N. (naturgetreue Darstellung mit Hang zur pathetisch-romantischen Überhöhung) bleibt bis in die 50er Jahre für das bulg. Theater bestimmend. Nach 1945 wirken am N. B. Danowski (Verdienst um Durchsetzung Brechts), Kristju Mirski (literarisch-poetisches Theater), Filip Filipow (historisierende Methode), der 1957–64 Direktor des N. ist (1970–75 A. Getman, gegenwärtig: W. Stefanow). Ende der 50er, v. a. in den 70er/80er Jahren Reformierung des Regiestils in Bulgarien; die wichtigsten Regisseure des Landes wie A. Schopow, I. Dobtschew, E. Chalatschew, M. Mladenowa, Krikor Asarjan, Leon Daniel und Willi Zankow inszenieren heute ständig oder als Gäste am N.

Elke Wiegand

Narr

Bedeutung und Wesen: Der Narr, gleich welchen Typs, in welchen Kontinenten und Zeiten, ist als Figur entweder in eigener Person antinomisch angelegt oder tritt von vornherein in zwei und mehr wesensmäßig differenten Figuren auf. Der Herkunft nach sind Narren kosmische Urwesen göttlich-tierischer Natur. Zum einen behindern Defekte ihres Wesens- und Verhaltensrepertoires sie derart, daß sie zwangsläufig unangepaßt und isoliert auf ihre Umwelt reagieren müssen, dem Menschen also in jeder Hinsicht unterlegen sind; zum anderen besitzen sie in ihrer locker gewitzten und beträchtlichen Lernfähigkeit eine den Menschen übertreffende Bewußtseinsentwicklung. In der Figur des Narren manifestieren sich inferiore menschliche Eigenschaften, die offenbar für fortgeschrittene Gesellschaften keinesfalls verlorengehen dürfen. So erlebt der Archetyp des Narren über Jahrhunderte hinweg seine Wiedergeburten in sich wandelnden, für die jeweilige Zeit stets typischen Projektionen. Da widersprüchlich angelegt, verdeutlicht das Handeln des Narren absurde Gegensätze, erregt Gelächter und Ironie, bewirkt Entlastung, weckt Hoffnungen; der Narr ist auch ‹Delight-maker› (Freuden- und Lichtbringer). Zugleich verkörpert er jedes nur denkbare Mißlingen, torkelt ahnungslos in geradezu widersinnige und von vornherein aussichtslose Situationen, ohne in ihnen unterzugehen. Er konfrontiert den Menschen mit seinem Selbst, hält ihm den Spiegel vor. Die Narrenfigur ist Träger eminent menschlicher Bedürfnisse; daher seine Einwirkungs- und Machtposition im Ritual, in Tempel- und Kirchenbezirken, bei Stammesfürsten, an fernöstlichen und westlichen Höfen, auf den Brettern der Spielbuden und Theater, inmitten der Volkstumulte, der →Happenings, der Feste und Feiern, in literarischen und bildnerischen Darstellungen. Der Narr tritt urig und sensibel auf, zotig und verträumt, als total mißglückte Existenz, der nur ein Zufall auf die Beine helfen kann, und als integrierend Einfluß nehmender, gewitzter, aber auch boshafter Ränkeschmied. Und stets ist er ‹Schausteller›, also von vornherein auf ein Publikum aus. Neben den mythologischen Spielen und dem Volkstheater, in denen er furchtlos heilige oder profane zeremonielle und politische Zustände mit ausgereiftem Humor karikiert, erobert er modifiziert das Leben der Höfe, dort ebenfalls Normen ironisierend und verspottend. An diesem Platz gewinnt er Züge des Alten Weisen hinzu. Er wird als nach außen projizierte Figur der Mann des Dialogs, der Korrektor und Alleinunterhalter, oft der gefürchtete Spötter. Als Schausteller und Fahrender, dann Schauspieler und Künstler besteigt er die Bühnen des Welttheaters, irrt weiter durch Volksspektakel, wandelt sich zum Zirkus- und Filmclown. Der Narr als hemmungsloser Individualist fordert die Menschen schlicht auf, mit sich selbst fertig zu werden. Als Symbol vermittelt er die Einsicht, daß menschlicher Gewinn im Verzicht liegt, daß Tragik sich stets mit einer Spreu Glück mischt. In diesem Spektrum präsentiert sich der Narr als eine höchst aktive Figur, die die Bedeutsamkeit des Handelns aufdeckt. Den Kampf, von politischer Sprengkraft getragen, führt er gegen Erstarrung und Vergessen. Um in allen Aufgaben agierend überzeugen zu können, braucht der närrische Schausteller einen akrobatisch durchtrainierten Körper, pantomimische und tänzerische Ausbildung, vielfache instrumentale Fertigkeiten, muß er Sänger und Schauspieler sein und nicht zuletzt ein mit dem Alltag und den politischen Konstellationen zutiefst vertrauter und gescheiter Kopf.

Bekleidung und Embleme sind die ältesten Signale des Narrentums. 1. Kopfbedeckungen: Der Spitz- oder Zuckerstockhut des →Pulcinella ist beim Koshare der Tehua-Indianer bereits in einer Spitzmütze aus getrockneten Kornblättern oder auch Federn vorgebildet; Ägypter tragen sehr hohe Schilfmützen oder Spitzmützen mit hängendem Zipfel wie der Jan Posset der englischen Fastnachts- und Volksspiele, der Kasper Larifari des Puppentheaters. Neben dem Spitzhut die Tellermütze des →Pierrot und →Brighella, der schwarze Zweispitz mit aufgeschlagener und geteilter Krempe (Hörner markierend) des →Arlecchino. Der Harlekin heute trägt den Spitzhut. Der Krempenhut stammt vom →Zanni. – 2. Embleme der Kopfbedeckungen sind prachtvolle Hahnen- oder gar Pfauenfedern (→Zanni, →Pickelhering, →Hanswurst, Narr der Hutler, François Fratellini); daneben Fuchs- oder Hasenschwänze (Zottler). – 3. Die Maske: vielfach grotesk und übergroß, oft mit Perücken oder ganzem Maskenkleid verbunden – Japan, Gagaku-Spiele; →Chhao-Tänze Indiens u. a.; Afrika, die Masken der →Atellana, die schrecklich zerzausten Tiermasken der Charivari; der Zani und seine Kumpane (ausgeprägte Langnasen); Arlecchino; im Volksbrauch die Narren unter den Perchten, Zottlern, Hutlern. Im Spiel auf der abendländischen Bühne und an den Höfen vermindern sich die clownesken Gesichtsverkleidungen; üblich werden schwarze Halbmasken aus Stoff (Brighella, Pierrot) oder Bemalungen. Die Weißclowns treten mit weiß geschminkten Gesichtern auf, der englische Pickelhering und der dumme August mit grotesk bemalten. Unförmige Nasen und aufgeworfene Lippen bleiben Überreste der Tiermasken (→Maskentänze; →Ritualtänze). – 4. Um die Gestik zu bereichern, das Schwingen, Wedeln, Zuschlagen und Abwehren betonen zu können, tragen die Narren Zweige (Ägypten), Peitschen, Stäbe (Hermes, Merkur, Perchten, Zottler), Holzlatten (Zani), Pritschen (Pulcinella und Kasper, Pierrot und Harlekin), Holzschwerter (Narr im Mysterienspiel, Mattucino der Moriske), eine ausgestopfte Tuchballenwurst (Wurstl der Pinzgauer Perchten), ein rotweißes Bauerntuch (Hanswurst und Wurstl der Imsterer Schemen). – 5. Die Körperbekleidung entwickelt sich entsprechend der zwiefachen Natur nach zwei Richtungen: a) Von

648 Narr

der wild zerzausten Tierfigurine aus Fell, Fransen, Federn bis hin zum Lumpen- und Flickenkleid, das im 16. Jh. dann zum wohlgeordneten Harlekin-Rhomben-Dress in Rot-Gelb-Grün, bei Zirkus- und Filmclowns zum tragikomisch wirkenden, abgetragenen Anzugensemble der kleinen Leute wird. Der Hanswurst trägt ein aufgeputztes Alltagsgewand. b) Weit umhüllendes, zweiteiliges, leicht flatterndes Gewand, entweder uni weiß oder wie in der Commedia, noch auf die Dienerstellung verweisend, weiß mit grünen Querstreifen, bald aus ärmlichem, bald aus kostbarem Material.

Narrentypen und ihr Sujet. 1. Rituelle Clowns: Sanskrit: nrtù = Narr und Tänzer. Die Zusammengehörigkeit von Theater, Tanz, Musik, Sprache und Akrobatik prägt alle närrischen Personen in den Heiligen Spielen Asiens, der Südsee, den indianischen und afrikanischen Regionen. Der Mutwillige karikiert im Zeremoniell die Mitwirkenden und erschreckt die Zuschauer. Die Chühü'Wimkya der Hopi (Indianer) z. B. entstellen geheiligte Rituale zur Burleske, indem sie mitten in die Zelebration der Kachinas (Götter der Fruchtbarkeit) hineinplatzen, von Dächern in die Feierlichkeit herabrutschen, verzückt auf Pferdeattrappen dahergaloppieren und lautstark die Lieder der Kachinas nachäffen. Sie tanzen und springen, täuschen Stürze vor, lenken die Andächtigen auf Grund ihrer Kunststücke vom Spiel ab und bringen sie zum Lachen. Beachtlicherweise tauschen am Ende des Auftritts die Kachinas mit ihnen Geschenke aus. Der Chühü'Wimkya stemmt sich gegen die Permanenz des Gebundenseins. Kushilavas (Narren des indischen Mythenkreises) flechten zu diesem Zweck ironisch-witzige extemporierte Anspielungen auf kritikwürdige, hochgestellte Persönlichkeiten in den Spieltext. Als Narrenpaare treten u. a. auf: Penasar und Kartala (Sanskrit-Dramen); Wen ch'ou und Wu ch'ou in chinesischen Volksspielen. 2. Antike (→Antikes Theater): Hermes-Mythos; Groteskfiguren der Aristophanes-Komödien. Keine spezielle Benennung. – Rom differenziert in der →Atellana der dorischen Mimen (3. Jh. v. Chr.) vier Typen: Der spritzige Dasseus steht neben dem unbeholfenen Maccus, der bullenäugige Prahler Bucco neben dem greisen Pappus. Die Ludi plebei ergötzen mit Stupidus und Sannio, dem Dummkopf. Stupidus bläst eine meterlange Posaune. 3. Mittelalter (→Mittelalter/Drama und Theater des Mittelalters): Im großen Straßentreiben der «Charivari» (Umzüge lärmender Masken) ist der «Wilde Mann», der Waldläufer, mit dämonisch grotesken Zügen Anführer aller Hellequins. Neben ihm stolpert die «Struwelfratze» mit Riesenmaske. Hellequin, dann Herlequin, ist im 12. Jh. noch ein Gattungsname für sehr verschiedene Grotesktypen. – Im Zentrum der →Moriske springt mit geschwärztem Gesicht der erschlagene und wieder auferstehende «Mattucino». Auf den Spielbuden treibt in den Krämerszenen der «Rubin» gerissene Possen als Diener des Medicus. – Die Beschreibungen der kirchlichen und später profanen Narrenfeste, zu denen Priester und Schüler, als Äbte und Bischöfe verkleidet, im Altarraum die Narrenpeitsche schwingen dürfen, lassen rebellische Kräfte ahnen, die einmal im Jahr die Nivellierung der Standesunterschiede durchsetzen (Korrektive gegen Korruptionen). Der Country Jokel narrt das englische Volk in sakralen und profanen Volksspielen. Scharlachrote Nase, dämonische Züge. – Frankreich kennt vor dem Herlequin den Jean Potage; auf russischen Jahrmärkten tanzen Petruschka und Duratschek; in Ungarn prahlt der Háry János. 4. Neuzeit 16. bis 18. Jh.: S. Brants *Narrenschiff* (1494), Th. Murners *Narrenbeschwörung* (1550) sowie Eulenspiegel, Bertoldo und Skogin, Schelme je eines deutschen, italienischen und englischen Volksbuches, leiten die Narrenära ein. Hans Sachs: drei Fastnachtsspiele 1531/57/68; der Hofnarr des Ahasver in zwei Estherdramen (1536/59). – W. Shakespeare: Probstein in *Wie es Euch gefällt!* (1599/1600): Pförtner im *Macbeth* (1600); Totengräber im *Hamlet* (1600/02); Edgar im *King Lear* (1605/06); Caliban und die Spaßmacher im *Sturm* (1610/11). →Commedia dell'arte: etwa ab 1550 Venedig und Lombardei. Erste Periode: die Zani (bergamaskische Bauern). Typ 1: fett, plump, behäbig; Typ 2: der Arlecchino: witzig, ironisch und traurig zugleich. Der erste Zani wird zum Brighella. – Pulcinella (= junger Truthahn): rüpelhaft, hämisch, unbeholfen, oft boshaft, in Neapel heimisch. Pierrot vervollständigt neben der derben, gesund denkenden, stets heiter aufgelegten Zagna, Franceschina, in Frankreich später Colombina, das Gauklerquintett. – Die englische Wanderbühne des John Greene erfindet den Pickelhering (= in Salzbrühe eingelegter Hering), die Robert-Brown-Truppe den Jan Posset; Frankreich den Jean Potage (Hans Supp). – Wiener Stegreifspiele und Zauberpossen entwerfen lokal gefärbte Figuren, an erster Stelle den Hans Wurst – Hanswurst, Salzburger Bauer; später, bei sich verstärkender Kritikfunktion auch Diener oder Handwerker (Schöpfung J. A. Stranitzkys, 1676–1726). Nach J. Chr. Gottscheds (1700–66) aufklärerischem Kampf (1730) und der Caroline Neuberin (1697–1760, bedeutendste Leiterin einer deutschen Wanderbühne) Bemühen um das Bildungstheater (1737 Leipzig: symbolische Verbannung des Hanswurst) und dem Hanswurst-Streit in Wien (Verbot des Extemporierens auf Bühnen 1770) agieren im Theater am Kärntnertor der von Kurz (1717–83) ins Rollenfach eingebrachte Bernardon (barocke Zauberelemente und Commedia dell'arte-Spiel), der Leopold und Lipperl, Henzlers Tiroler Wastl, der Staberl und schließlich als literarisch fixierter Rollenträger der dumme, gutmütige Thaddädl. – Als Wurstl lebt die Wiener Figur im Brauchtum (→Brauchtumstänze) der Perchten-, Schemen- und Hutlerläufe; in der Schweiz im Blätzle Bua; im Rheingau unter den Gecken. 19. Jh.: Volksspiele bei F. Raimund (1790–1836) *Der Barometermacher auf der Zauberinsel* (1823). J. N. Nestroy (1801–62) *Der böse Geist Lum-*

pazivagabundus (1833) und *Einen Jux will er sich machen* (1842). G. Büchner (1810–37) *Leonce und Lena* (1836, aufgeführt 1911). 20. Jh.: G. Hauptmann (1862–1946) *Schluck und Jau* (1895); *Der Narr in Christo* (1907/10). Fr. Wedekind (1864–1918) *König Nicolo* (1902). E. Toller (1893–1939) *Hoppla, wir leben!* (1927). J. Priestley (1894–1984) *Tale the Foot Away* (1954). B. Brecht (1898–1956) *Mutter Courage* (1941); *Herr Puntila und sein Knecht Matti* (1949); *Der kaukasische Kreidekreis* (1954); *Der aufhaltsame Aufstieg des Arturo Ui* (1958). S. Beckett (1906–89) *Warten auf Godot* (1953). F. Dürrenmatt (1921–90) *Die Physiker* (1962). Zirkus: die Grimaldis, Fratellinis, Tom Belling, Auriol, Rivel und Grock u. a. Fratellini-Typen sind François: der Weißclown, eleganter Akrobat; Paul: stolpert auf der ständigen Suche nach der Hibiskusblüte durch die Arena; Albert: der Stupidus im angegrauten Mantel mit langer roter Nase – ein kleiner, vom Leben betrogener Mann, der die magischen Wirkungen der Gegenstände bestaunt. Film: Vorrangig Engländer und Amerikaner: Danny Kaye, Buster Keaton, Pat und Patachon, Charlie Chaplin, Stan Laurel, Oliver Hardy, Woody Allen. Aus Frankreich stammen die Brüder Lumière, Jean-Louis Barrault, der Baptiste aus *Les enfants du Paradis*, und die Bip-Figur des Marcel Marceau.

Barloewen, C. v.: Clown, zur Phänomenologie des Stolperns. Königstein/Taunus 1981; Johannsmeier, R.: Spielmann, Schalk und Scharlatan: Die Welt als Karneval. Volkskultur im späten Mittelalter. Reinbek bei Hamburg 1984; Jung, C. G.: Zur Psychologie der Tricksterfigur. In: Jung, C. G.: Die Archetypen und das kollektive Unbewußte. Ges. Werke. Bd. IX/1. Hg. von Jung-Merker, L./Olten, E. R. Freiburg/Breisgau 1976, S. 273–290; Meyer, W.: Werden und Wesen des Wiener Hanswursts. Diss. phil. Leipzig 1931; Spörri, R.: Die Commedia dell'arte und ihre Figuren. Hg. von R. Simmen. Zürich 1963; Usinger, F.: Die geistige Figur des Clowns in unserer Zeit. In: Akademie der Wissenschaften und der Literatur. Jg. 1964. Nr. 2. Wiesbaden 1964.

Helga Ettl

Het Nationale Ballet (Amsterdam)

1961 formiert sich die Kompanie aus dem 1959 gegründeten Amsterdam Ballet des M. ter Weeme und dem bereits seit 1954 bestehenden Het Nederlands Ballet von S. Gaskell (1904–74). Anfangs leiten S. Gaskell und M. ter Weeme das H. N. B. gemeinsam. In der Folgezeit übernimmt Gaskell bis 1969 die Direktion. Den Tänzer und Choreographen Rudi van Dantzig (*1933) beruft das H. N. B. 1967 zum künstlerischen Direktor. Weitere Hauschoreographen: der ehemalige Direktor und Mitbegründer des →Nederlands Dans Theater Hans van Manen (*1932) und der Tänzer und Designer Toer von Schayk (*1936). Neben Neuproduktionen des

Choreographen-Triumvirats erarbeitet das H. N. B. klassisch-romantische Ballette, Diaghilew-Kreationen, Standardwerke des modernen Repertoires und ausgewählte Stücke des →Modern Dance. In den letzten Jahren wurden Tänzer der Truppe zu eigener Choreographie ermutigt. Das umfassende, facettenreiche Repertoire des H. N. B. weist Vielseitigkeit, hohes Niveau und Engagement aus. Die drei Choreographen konnten deshalb Anfang der 60er Jahre, in einem Land ohne Ballettgeschichte, neue und internationale Maßstäbe setzen. – Van Manen: Gegner von Handlungsballetten und psychologischen Interpretationen. Tanz darf nicht mit Literatur gleichgesetzt werden. Visualisierung von Musik. Klare Strukturen (*Twilight*, 1972; *Adagio Hammerklavier*, 1973; *Live*, 1979). – Van Dantzig: Form und Struktur unbedeutend. Er thematisiert Umweltverschmutzung, Atomwaffen, Hunger, Diskriminierungen (*Monument for a Dead Boy*, 1965; *Moments*, 1968; *Epitaph*, 1969; *Painted Birds*, 1971; *Life*, 1979). – Van Schayk ist zugleich Bildhauer und Bühnenbildner. Sein Opus tritt zeitkritisch auf. Antikriegsballette: *Triptychon Pyrrhic Dances I, II* und *III* (1974–80).

Schaik, E. v.: Das niederländische Dilemma: Individuum oder Instrument? In: Ballett International 4 (1982), S. 38–40; ders.: Report: Niederlande. In: Ballett International 12 (1983), S. 49; Interview mit Rudi van Dantzig von Helmut Scheier. In: Ballett International 6–7 (1984), S. 35–39.

Patricia Stöckemann

Nationale Scene i Bergen

Um 1780 bis 1830 waren in den größeren Städten Norwegens private amateurdramatische Gesellschaften tätig, die von Patriziern und Handelsleuten getragen und organisiert wurden. Diese Gesellschaften hatten einen außerordentlich geschlossenen Charakter, die Aufführungen waren i. d. R. nur Mitgliedern zugänglich, die ausschließlich einem ökonomisch unabhängigen Personenkreis angehörten. Solche Aufführungen wurden mit großzügigem Aufwand durchgeführt und erreichten ein hohes künstlerisches Niveau.

Die 1794 gegründete Dramaturgische Gesellschaft in Bergen errichtete 1800 das Comoediehus, allg. die ‹Komödie› genannt, das bis 1909 als Theater genutzt wurde. Das Gebäude wurde im 2. Weltkrieg zerstört.

1850 wurde Ole Bulls Norske Teater gegründet, 1852–1857 war Henrik Ibsen (1828–1906) als Regisseur dort tätig, 1857 bis 1859 gefolgt von Bjørnsterne Bjørnson (1832–1910). 1863 ging Det Norske Teatret in Konkurs, 1872 wurde N. S. gegründet. – In den 1870er Jahren wurden Stücke der nationalnorw. Opposition in stärkerem Maße auf das Pro-

652 Nationaltheater

gramm gesetzt; Gunnar Heiberg (1857–1929) zeichnete sich während seiner Tätigkeit als Intendant des Theaters 1884 bis 1888 durch einen realistischen und oppositionellen Inszenierungsstil aus. – 1909 wurde der Spielbetrieb im Neubau des Theaters fortgesetzt. Seit 1876 wurden Stücke von über hundert norwegischen Dramatikern aufgeführt.

Blanc, T.: Norges første nationale Scene (Bergen 1850–63). Et bidrag til den norske dramatiske Kunsts Historie. Kristiania 1884; Bull, M.: Minder fra Bergens første nationale Scene. Bergen 1905. Wiers-Jenssen, H./Lorentzen, B. (Hg.): Det første norske teater. Bergen 1949; Nygaard, K./Eiliv, E.: Den Nationale Scene 1931–1976. Oslo 1977; Poulson, A.: Komediebakken og Engen. Femti års teatererindringer. Oslo 1932.

Martin Kolberg

Nationaltheater

Pflegestätte nationaler Dramatik und Schauspielkunst (→Neuzeit/Theater der Neuzeit). Der N.-Gedanke setzte sich in Deutschland in der zweiten Hälfte des 18. Jh. durch. Ziel ist die Ausbildung einer nationalen Theaterkultur bürgerlichen Zuschnitts. Das Theater (als «moralische Anstalt») sollte die Einheit der Nation, die «ästhetische Erziehung» die moralische befördern; gegen die höfische Theaterkultur gerichtetes bürgerlich-emanzipatorisches Reformprogramm im Dienste der Aufklärungsideale.

Gegenpol zur bürgerlichen N.-Bewegung ist der N.-Gedanke, wie er in Frankreich zur Gründung eines Staatstheaters führte (Théâtre Français, später als →Comédie Française); Vorbild für das N. in Deutschland sind die Reformideen von Johann Elias Schlegel (*Gedanken zur Aufnahme des dän. Theaters*, 1764). Erster fehlgeschlagener Versuch eines dt. N.: 1767–69 die Hamburger Entreprise, Direktion Johann Friedrich Löwen (1727–71), Dramaturg Gotthold Ephraim Lessing (1729–81), kaufmännischer Leiter Abel Seyler (1730–1800); Schauspieler: Konrad Ekhof (1720–78), Konrad E. A. Ackermann (1712–71), Friederike Hensel (1738–89). 1776 wird das →Burgtheater Wien von Kaiser Joseph II. zum N. ernannt; 1779 Gründung des N. Mannheim (Leitung Wolfgang Heribert Reichsfreiherr v. Dalberg, 1750–1806) durch Karl Theodor Kurfürst v. d. Pfalz. 1786 wird das Berliner Hoftheater zum N. erklärt unter Carl Theophil Döbbelin (1727–93) und August Wilhelm Iffland (1759–1814). Das Weimarer Hoftheater, ab 1791 unter Leitung Goethes und Mitarbeit Schillers, wird erst 1919 in Deutsches N. umbenannt. Im Laufe des 19. Jh. verbindet sich der →Festspielgedanke mit der N.-Idee; Repräsentanten dieser Bewegung: Franz Frhr. von Dingelstedt (1814–81), Karl Leberecht Immermann (1796–1840), Philipp Eduard Devrient (1801–77), Richard Wagner (1813–83). Gründungen von N. erfolgen auch in Nord- und Osteuropa: 1748 Kopenhagen, Leitung Ludwig Holberg (1684–1754), 1779 Warschau, Teatr Narodowy (N.), Prager N. (Graf Franz Anton v. Nostitz-Rhineck), 1792 Holztheater in Ofen (Ungarn), 1808–12 Ungarisches N. unter Leitung von Karl v. Vida in Pest; weitere N. in Belgrad, Zagreb, Oslo. – In der Schweiz gibt es im 18. und 19. Jh. nationale Landschaftstheater der Helvetischen Bewegung und Volksfesttradition, die ebenfalls im Dienst der Verbreitung nationalen Gedankenguts stehen. Im 20. Jh.: →National Theatre London, 1962 von Sir Laurence Olivier gegr.

Archer, W./Granville Barker, H.: A National Theatre. Scheme & Estimates. London 1907; Devrient, E.: Das N. des neuen Deutschlands. Eine Reformschrift. Neu hg. v. d. Genossenschaft Deutscher Bühnenangehöriger. Berlin 1919; Hammer, K. (Hg.): Dramaturgische Schriften des 18. Jh. Berlin (DDR) 1968; Petersen, J.: Das dt. N. Leipzig/Berlin 1919 (Zeitschrift f. d. dt. Unterricht: 14. Ergänzungsheft); Stadler, E.: Das neuere Freilichttheater in Europa und Amerika, II. Die Entstehung des nationalen Landschaftstheaters in der Schweiz. Einsiedeln 1953.

Ingeborg Janich

National Theatre

Nach vielen Entwürfen eines brit. → Nationaltheaters, u. a. dem von David Garrick (1717–79) und dem von Edward Bulwer-Lytton (1803–73), entstand erst 1963 eine N. T. Company unter Vorsitz von Laurence Olivier (1907–89). Nachdem das Ensemble des N. T. zunächst im Londoner →Old Vic spielte, bezog es nach dessen Fertigstellung 1976 das neuerbaute N. T. am südlichen Themseufer in London. Das N. T. ist die eine Hälfte eines wirklichen brit. Nationaltheaters, denn Shakespeare als Herzstück der engl. Theatertradition wird vom zweiten großen subventionierten Theaterensemble, der →Royal Shakespeare Company, aufgeführt, nachdem Pläne eines einzigen N. T. gescheitert waren. Das heutige N. T. an der Waterloo Bridge ist ein Monumentalbau von Denys Lasdun und umfaßt drei Bühnen (in der Reihenfolge der Größe: das Olivier Theatre, das Lyttelton und das Cottesloe Theatre).

Cook, J.: The National Theatre. London 1976; Elsom, J./Tomalin, N.: The History of the National Theatre. London 1978.

Bernd-Peter Lange

Nationaltheatret i Oslo

1870 wurde die dramatische Gesellschaft in Christiania (Oslo) gegründet, ein geschlossener Kreis aus Angehörigen des saturierten Bürgertums, der das Laientheater auf hohem Niveau betrieb. Vor und nach der Loslösung Norwegens von Dänemark und dem Beginn der Personalunion mit Schweden 1814 gab es auf politischem wie sprachlich-kulturellem Gebiet Versuche der Schaffung einer Eigenständigkeit Norwegens. Die Problematik der Schaffung eines N. ist in diesem Zusammenhang zu sehen. – Johan Peter Strömberg (1772–1834) versuchte als erster, ein N. zu gründen (Eröffnung 1827; fiel 1835 dem Feuer zum Opfer). Die Tätigkeit dieses Theaters wurde 1837 bis 1899 im Gebäude am Bankplass als Christianiatheater fortgesetzt.

Um 1845 erfaßte die nationale Bewegung Norwegens in stärkerem Maße Literatur und Kunst. Zu Beginn der 50er Jahre hatten u. a. Handwerker ein Amateurtheater geschaffen, dessen Einnahmen zur Unterstützung der inhaftierten Vertreter der Thraniterbewegung (der norw. Arbeiterbewegung) verwendet wurden. Das Interesse der Unterschicht Christianias an der Theaterkunst führte maßgeblich zur Erfüllung des in der Stadt allgemein gehegten Wunsches nach der Errichtung einer stärker von norw. Bühnensprache und Dramatik geprägten Bühne. Am 11. Okt. 1852 eröffnete Christiania norske dramatiske Skole das Theater in der Møllergade. Sprache und Repertoire des Christianiatheaters blieben hingegen wesentlich länger dem von Johan Ludvig Heiberg (1791–1860) geprägten dän. Geschmack verhaftet und verharrte in der Tradition Adam Gottlob Oehlenschlägers (1779–1850). Zu Beginn der 60er Jahre zwang die Rezession die beiden Theater zum Zusammenschluß; gleichzeitig wurde der dän. Einfluß zurückgedrängt.

Nach den Konkursen der norw. Theater in Bergen und Trondhjem war das Christianiatheater spätestens von 1865 an für mehrere Jahre einzige feste Bühne in Norwegen. Bjørnsterne Bjørnson (1832–1910) war 1865 bis 1867 Regisseur. Ludvig Josephson (1832–99) inszenierte 1873 als erster *Peer Gynt* mit der Musik Edvard Griegs (1843–1907). Das Feuer von 1877 brachte starke Zerstörungen, ein Wiederaufbau war jedoch möglich. Bjørnsterne Bjørnsons Sohn Bjørn Bjørnson (1859–1942) trug 1884 bis 1891 zur Modernisierung des Christianiatheaters bei; er hatte in Wien und Meiningen wertvolle Erfahrungen gesammelt. 1878 bis 1899 war Hans Ludvig Schrøder (1836–1902) Intendant des Theaters. Schrøders Konservativismus wird in der Literatur kontrovers diskutiert; bezeichnend ist hier der lange schwelende Streit um Ibsens Drama *Die Gespenster*.

1899 wurde der Betrieb als N. in der Stortingsgate fortgesetzt. Während Bjørn Bjørnsons Chefperiode 1899 bis 1907 standen Aufführungen der norw. Klassiker im Mittelpunkt. Danach wurden in stärkerem Maße Schauspieler mit der Regie beauftragt, die später auch Intendanten wurden. Auf diese Weise trat die moderne norwegische und ausländische Dramatik in den Vordergrund. Anton Rønneberg, der 1930 bis 1933 Intendant war, lieferte wertvolle Beiträge zur Geschichte des norw. Theaters. – Während der dt. Besetzung wurde der Theaterbetrieb in starkem Maße boykottiert, etliche Schauspieler flohen nach Schweden. Nach dem Krieg setzte das N. seine Tätigkeit als Oslos Hauptbühne fort. 1963 wurde eine Nebenszene eröffnet.

Anker, Ø.: Johann Peter Strömberg. Mannen bak det første offentlige teater i Norge. Oslo 1958; Blanc, T.: Christiania Theaters Historie 1827–1877. Kria 1899; Røine, E.: Vandring i Nationaltheatret. Oslo 1967; Rønneberg, A.: Nationaltheatret 1949–1974. Oslo 1974; Wiers-Jenssen, H.: Nationaltheatret gjennem 25 aar, 1899–1924. Kria 1924.

Martin Kolberg

Naturalistisches Theater

Der Naturalismus behauptet sich zwischen 1880 und 1900 als gesamteuropäisches Phänomen. Als Literatur des positiven Zeitalters strebt er eine wissenschaftlich exakte Darstellung der Wirklichkeit an: Es gilt, das Mittel des Experiments auf die Literatur zu übertragen und den Menschen in seinem Milieu darzustellen, wobei man alle physischen und sozialen Komponenten, die ihn mitbestimmen können, in die Analyse einbezieht. Für Zola ist die Kunst «ein Stück Natur, gesehen durch ein Temperament»; Arno Holz formuliert strenger: «Die Kunst hat die Tendenz, wieder die Natur zu sein. Sie wird sie nach Maßgabe ihrer jeweiligen Reproduktionsbedingungen und deren Handhabung» oder «Kunst = Natur – x». Ziel der literarischen Arbeit ist also, die Erscheinungen der Wirklichkeit möglichst deckungsgleich wiederzugeben und den Faktor x, die künstlerische Subjektivität und die Unvollkommenheit der künstlerischen Mittel, möglichst gering zu halten. Daher resultiert bei den Naturalisten ein gewisses Mißtrauen gegenüber Intuition und Phantasie und die Betonung des wissenschaftlich gesammelten Tatsachenmaterials: Man greift auf die vorhandene Dokumentation zurück, verschafft sich aber auch Eindrücke vor Ort. Literatur soll zum Protokoll (Zola) werden.

Dieser Wille, Natürliches darzustellen, führt in der Wahl von Stoffen und Gestalten zur Ablehnung des Außergewöhnlichen und des ‹edlen Helden›. Es wird ‹Normalität› gesucht, was die Tradition als das Häßliche und Niedere verwirft. Dirnen, Alkoholiker, Geisteskranke, die unteren sozialen Schichten werden Gegenstand der Darstellung. Das Proletariat als die Klasse, die das industrielle Zeitalter am besten vertritt, ist nun der literarischen Gestaltung würdig. Der angestrebten wissenschaftlichen Objektivität in der Schilderung einer unverhüllten Wirklichkeit wird aber nicht Genüge geleistet. Die Darstellung bekommt meist einen eindeutig pessimistischen Zug, der sich durch den Einfluß des im Positivismus herrschenden Determinismus erklären läßt.

Auf dramatischem Gebiet charakterisiert sich zuerst der Naturalismus durch seine Kritik des bürgerlichen Theaters der Zeit. Im Namen der Wahrheit verurteilt Zola das «pièce bien faite», weil in ihm der Akzent nur auf die Handlung gelegt werde. Das naturalistische Drama hingegen hat laut Arno Holz «vor allem Charaktere zu zeichnen. Die Handlung ist nur Mittel». Die verwickelte, sorgfältig zusammengefügte, aber realitätsferne Intrige des bürgerlichen Dramas wird zugunsten der Gestaltung eines fait divers aufgegeben. Es gilt auch hier, den Menschen in seinem Milieu darzustellen. Dieses wird dramaturgisch zuerst durch den Handlungsraum veranschaulicht – daher die Bedeutung der äußerst genauen Bühnenanweisungen, die zur Charakterisierung der Gestalten dienen, und das Einsetzen aller illusionistischen Kunstmittel der Bühnenbildner zur Heraufbeschwörung einer milieugetreuen Stimmung. Die Sprache wird im selben Sinne behandelt: Jede Gestalt spricht die Sprache ihrer sozialen Schicht – daher meistens das Vorherrschen der Umgangssprache und der Dialekte im dt. naturalistischen Drama, selbst wenn diese oft in stilisierter Form wiedergegeben werden. Die exakte Wirklichkeitsgestaltung führt zur Nachahmung des Stammelns und Stotterns, zum Gebrauch von Anakoluthen und grammatikalisch falschen Redewendungen, zur Vermeidung des unnatürlich wirkenden Monologs und zur Einführung des sog. ‹Sekundenstils›, der den Dialog ständig durch die entsprechenden Regieanweisungen unterbricht, um die kleinsten Bewegungen und Geräusche in peinlich genauer Abfolge wiederzugeben. Aus Wahrscheinlichkeitsgründen werden Ort- und Zeiteinheiten bewahrt und eine geringe Personenzahl vorgezogen. Jedoch wird die geschlossene Form aufgehoben insofern, als man auf die Einteilung des Akts in kurze, genau abgegrenzte Szenen verzichtet und das Drama lieber in breiten Stimmungsbildern gestaltet. Insgesamt erscheint das naturalistische Drama als eine besonders ausgeprägte Form des illusionistischen Theaters: Dem Zuschauer soll eine streng mimetische Wiedergabe des wirklichen Lebens vorgestellt werden; es gilt, in ihm den Eindruck zu erzeugen, er wohne einem der Realität abgelauschten Schauspiel gleichsam heimlich bei (→ Vierte Wand). In diesem Vorherrschen des schildernden Moments kann aber eine Schwäche der naturalistischen Dramatik erkannt werden: Es birgt in sich die Gefahr einer Vernachlässigung des eigentlichen Dramas (vgl. die Vorliebe des Naturalisten für das analytische Drama, das durch den geringen Handlungsandrang eine umständlichere Milieuschil-

Naturalistisches Theater   657

derung und Darstellung der Personen ermöglicht). Es führt auch zum epischen Theater: verkapptes ep. Ich, ep. Distanzierung in der Person des ‹Fremden›, Bericht, Beschreibung, Revue, statische Szenenreihe durchbrechen die dramatische Spannung.

Das frz. Drama des Naturalismus illustriert diesen Einfluß des Epischen in aller Deutlichkeit: Die Stücke von Zola (1840–1902: *L'Assomoir*, 1879; *Germinal*, 1888) und Goncourt (1822–76: *Germinie Lacerteux*, 1888) sind meistens nur Bühnenbearbeitungen von Romanen, die nach einem kurzen Erfolg in Vergessenheit gerieten. Nur das Werk von Henry Becque (1837–99) hat sich auf der Bühne gehalten; obwohl er sich als Erbe der Klassiker betrachtete, weisen seine düsteren Milieuschilderungen (*Die Raben*, 1882; *Die Pariserin*, 1885) viele gemeinsame Züge mit dem Naturalismus auf. Von europ. Bedeutung waren die Inszenierungen von Antoine (1858–1953), der 1887 das →Théâtre Libre gründete und die Deutschen (Brahms →Freie Bühne in Berlin) sowie die Engländer (Breins Independant Theater in London) entscheidend beeinflußte.

Die eigentlichen dramatischen Hauptwerke des Naturalismus sind in den dt. und nordeurop. Literaturen zu finden. An der Grenze zwischen Realismus und Naturalismus steht der norwegische Dramatiker Henrik Ibsen (1828–1906), der in den Dramen seiner Reife (*Stützen der Gesellschaft*, 1877; *Nora*, 1877; *Gespenster*, 1882; *Hedda Gabler*, 1889) die von ‹Lebenslüge› und Menschenhaß beherrschte bürgerliche Gesellschaft seiner Zeit darstellt. Dank seiner ‹analytischen› Dramaturgie, die sich vom ursprünglichen Einfluß des «pièce bien faite» befreit und zu einer persönlichen, straff komponierten, monologfreien Form gefunden hat, deckt er ihre Fehler, ihr Versagen in der Vergangenheit und ihre ererbten Belastungen auf. Sein Werk, das in England einen andauernden Erfolg genießt, fand auch ein starkes Echo in Deutschland. Konsequent naturalistisch sind die Dramen von Arno Holz (1863–1929) und Johannes Schlaf (1862–1941) gebaut: *Papa Hamlet*, 1889, und *Die Familie Selicke*, 1892, wo alle Prinzipien naturalistischer Gestaltung verwirklicht werden (radikale Verkürzung der Handlung, Prinzip der Heldenlosigkeit, Aneinanderreihung von Szenen ohne Handlung usw.). Literarisch bedeutender ist Gerhart Hauptmann (1862–1946), mit den Dramen *Vor Sonnenaufgang* (1889), *Die Weber* (1892–93), *Der Biberpelz* (1893), *Der rote Hahn* (1901), *Fuhrmann Henschel* (1903), *Rose Bernd* (1903), *Die Ratten* (1911). Seine Stücke weisen eine Tendenz zur Episierung, zum «offenen Schluß» auf, aber es vollzieht sich in ihnen eine Überwindung des strengen Naturalismus durch subtile Charaktergestaltung. Im sozialen Drama *Die Weber* tritt zum erstenmal das Proletariat als kollektiver Protagonist auf, und *Der Biberpelz* ist eines der seltenen gelungenen Beispiele einer naturalistischen Komödie. – Im Vorwort zu *Fräulein Julie* (1889), das mit *Der Vater* (1887) und *Totentanz* (1907) zu August Strindbergs Hauptwerken zählt, definiert der schwedische Dramatiker (1849–1912) die Prinzipien für das naturalistische Drama, die er in diesem Stück befolgen will: Die «unregelmäßig arbeitenden Gehirne» der Figuren entwickeln einen ins Ausweglose führenden, ständig unterbrochenen Dialog. Die Charaktere, die als Komplex zahlreicher verschiedener Eigenschaften konzipiert werden, sind den Gesetzen der Vererbung und des Milieus unterworfen. Strindbergs Beschäftigung mit der sozialistischen Theorie findet in seinen Dramen ihren Niederschlag: Auffassung, daß die Zukunft den unteren Klassen gehört; der als Gesetz des Kapitalismus erkannte soziale Kampf ‹aller gegen alle› wird in den Bereich menschlichen Zusammenlebens verlegt: Darstellung der brutalen Selbstbehauptung des Bourgeois, Geschlechterkämpfe, Entlarvung des Destruktiven im Menschen. In seinem Spätwerk findet der Dramatiker über den Naturalismus hinaus zu Ausdrucksformen, die das →symbolistische, ja das →expressionistische Theater beeinflussen.

Eine solche Entwicklung sowie die G. Hauptmanns weist auf die Grenzen des Naturalismus hin, der nach der Jahrhundertwende als organisierte Strömung verschwindet, obwohl er die weitere Entwicklung der dramatischen Literatur z. T. immer noch beeinflußt. So weisen im Werk des nordamerik. Dramatikers Eugene O'Neill (1888–1956) Stücke wie *Bound East for Cardiff* (1916), *Beyond the Horizont* (1920), *Anna Christie* (1921) naturalistische Züge auf: milieuechte Schilderung der Seeleute oder der amerik. Bauern; Themen wie Alkoholismus und Prostitution usw. – Am produktivsten war die kritische Auseinandersetzung Bertolt Brechts (1898–1956) mit der naturalistischen Ästhetik; sein →episches Theater stellt die dialektische Überwindung des Naturalismus dar. Auch bei Maxim Gorki (1868–1936) geht die naturalistische Theorie in einer sozialistischen Auffassung des Realismus auf. Schließlich könnte man in bestimmten Strömungen der Filmkunst einen Einfluß der naturalistischen Dramaturgie entdecken (vgl. Renoirs *Toni*, 1935, oder die neurealistische Schule, →Verismus).

Brands, H. G.: Theorie und Stil des konsequenten Naturalismus. 1978; Brauneck, M.: Literatur und Öffentlichkeit. Studien zur Rezeption des naturalistischen Theaters in Deutschland. Stuttgart 1974; Cogny, P.: Le naturalisme. Paris 1968; Hamann, R./Hermand, J.: Naturalismus. Berlin-Ost 1968; Hilscher, E.: Gerhart Hauptmann. Berlin 1969; Hoefert, S.: Das Drama des Naturalismus. Stuttgart 1968; Mahal, E.: Naturalismus. München 1975; Osborne, J.: The Naturalist Drama in Germany. Manchester 1971; Schulz, G.: Zur Theorie des Dramas im dt. Naturalismus. In: Grimm, R. (Hg.): Deutsche Dramentheorien. Bd. II. Frankfurt/M. 1971; Szondi, P.: Theorie des modernen Dramas. Frankfurt/M. 1956; Zola, E.: Le Naturalisme au théâtre. Paris 1881.

Alain Muzelle

Naturtheater

Sonderform des →Freilichttheaters. Theaterform in freier Natur (Wald-gelände, Steinbruch) oder unter freiem Himmel (Burgruine, freier Marktplatz, Platz vor Architekturfassaden, geschlossener Hof etc.) unter Einbeziehung und Mitwirkung der umgebenden Natur und Naturstim-mung seit 2. Hälfte des 18. Jh. Einfluß J. J. Rousseaus und engl. Natur-und Landschaftsdichter. Früheste Aufführungen in Deutschland und Frankreich (Inszenierungen Goethes: 1780 Ettersburger Wald, 1782 Schloßpark von Tiefurt). 19. Jh.: nationale Akzente, Tell-Spiele in der Schweiz, Passionsspiele in Oberammergau, historische Heimatspiele im bayerisch-fränkischen Raum; in Frankreich: röm. Theater in Orange ab 1869; 20. Jh.: Deutschland: Gründung des Harzer Bergtheaters bei Thale (Ernst Wachler, 1903); Drittes Reich: neue Phase der N.-Bewegung durch Ausbau der N. und Bau von →Thingstätten; Amerika: Amphithea-ter von Point Loma (Kalifornien 1901), Red Rock Theatre (Denver, Col.). N. sind heute meist sommerliche Festspielbühnen: u. a. Avignon (→Festival d'Avignon), Palasthof; Domfestspiele Bad Gandersheim, Schloßfestspiele Heidelberg, Stiftsruine →Bad Hersfeld, Komödienspiele Schloß Porcia (Spittal/Drau), Salzburg (→Salzburger Festspiele), *Jeder-mann*-Aufführungen am Domplatz (seit 1920), Freilichtspiele Schwä-bisch Hall (seit 1925), Bergwaldtheater Weißenburg/Bayern, →Luisen-burg-Festspiele Wunsiedel; Waldbühne Zoppot (Gdansk).

Schöpel, B.: Naturtheater. Studien zum Theater unter freiem Himmel in Südwest-deutschland. Tübingen 1965 (Volksleben, Bd. 9); Stadler, E.: Das neuere Frei-lichttheater in Europa und Amerika. 1. Grundbegriffe. Einsiedeln 1951 (19. Jb. d. Schweizer. Ges. f. Theaterkultur). 2. Die Entstehung des Nationalen Landschafts-theaters in der Schweiz. Einsiedeln 1953 (21. Jb. d. Schweizer. Ges. f. Theaterkul-tur).

Ingeborg Janich

Nederduytsche Academie

Anfang des 17. Jh. gab es in Amsterdam zwei Rederijker-Gesellschaften (Rhetoriker), die Theateraufführungen veranstalteten. Im Jahre 1617 gründete Samuel Coster (1579–1665) eine dritte Gesellschaft in einem Gebäude an der Keizersgracht, die N. A. Diese Gesellschaft wurde von Literaten und Schauspielern gebildet, und es wurde vor einem zahlenden Publikum gespielt. Die Einnahmen wurden großenteils dem Burgerwees-huis (Waisenhaus) zugewiesen. 1622 verkaufte Coster die N. A. an das Waisenhaus. Dieses beauftragte eine konkurrierende Rederijker-Gesell-schaft, die sog. Brabantse Kamer, mit der Betreuung der Theaterauffüh-

660 Nederlands Dans Theater

rungen. Die Kamer führte eine Art Abonnentensystem ein; auch die Schauspieler wurden bezahlt. Im Jahre 1632 zwangen die Stadtbehörden die letzte selbständig auftretende Gesellschaft zur Fusion, so daß es nur noch eine Theatergesellschaft gab: die Amsterdamsche Kamer. Spielplatz blieb die N. A., bis Jacob von Campen 1637 die →Amsterdamsche Schouwburg baute. Der Raum des Theaters war 22 m lang, 17 m breit und ca. 8,5 m hoch; nur an der Rückwand gab es eine Galerie. Die Bühne war offen, ohne Vorhang. In der Mitte der Hinterwand gab es ein großes Kompartiment, flankiert von zwei Bühneneingängen im Monumentalstil. Dieses Kompartiment war mit Vorhängen abzuschließen. Auffällig war eine Wand aus Drehschirmen (aus Tuch), die zweiseitig bemalt werden konnte, so daß die Illusion einer Landschaft oder eines Gebäudes vermittelt werden konnte. Man benutzte dieses Kompartiment für Tableaux-vivants, aber auch für Spektakelszenen, z. B. Krönungsszenen, Schlachtszenen u. ä. An beiden Bühnenseiten gab es zwei weitere Eingänge, die zu kleineren Kompartimenten verwendet werden konnten. Die Bühne war auch mit einem «hemelwerck» versehen, einem Lift in Form einer Wolke, der vom Bühnenboden zum Bühnenstock hinauf- und hinunterfuhr. Der Gesamteindruck dieser Bühne war der einer durch Kompartimente zusammengeschlossenen →Simultanbühne mit einer deutlichen Trennung von Schauspielern und Zuschauern, wobei die nicht auftretenden Spieler sich unsichtbar für das Publikum hinter der Bühne aufhielten. In der N. A. wurden die Theaterstücke der Rederijker aufgeführt, unter denen so bekannte Autoren wie Coster, Pieter Cornelisz Hooft (1581–1647) und Joost van den Vondel (1587–1679) waren.

Hummelen, W. M. H.: Amsterdams Toneel in het begin van de Gouden Eeuw. s'Gravenhage 1982; Worp, J. A.: Geschiedenis van den Amsterdamschen Schouwburg 1496–1772. Uitgegeven met aanvullingen tot 1872 door Dr. J. F. M. Sterck. Amsterdam 1920.

Wil Hildebrand

Nederlands Dans Theater

Rasend schnelle, energie- und emotionsgeladene Bewegungsabläufe, hohes tänzerisches Niveau und ausgereifter, empfindsamer Stil zeichnen heute das N. D. T. aus, das seit 1975 unter Jiři Kylián (*1947) arbeitet. Seit den 60er Jahren zählt es zu den interessanten und wegweisenden Kompanien. 1959 hat sich das Ensemble unter der Leitung von B. Harkarvy (*1930) als Splittertruppe des Het Nederlands Ballet formiert (→Het Nationale Ballet). – Die Tanzgruppe sucht neue Ausdrucksmöglichkeiten, setzt sich mit Zeitstilen auseinander und kreiert auf die Individualitäten der Tänzer zugeschnittene Ballette. Es entstehen Zimmerballette, Gestaltungen für kleine Tanzensembles, die auf Soli- und Corpsdifferenzierungen verzichten. 1960 übernimmt Hans van Manen (*1932) das künstlerische Direktoriat. Van Manens tänzerische Innovationen gliedern alltägliche Bewegungsabläufe ein und stellen sie in einen oft humorvollen, trockenen Kontext, der sich auf schlichte Mittel, eine Vielfalt von Gestaltungsideen und geschlossene Formen stützt. Die Stilbesonderheiten faszinieren und regen das dt. →Tanztheater an. Neben van Manen choreographiert von 1962 bis 1970 G. Tetley (*1926). Das Ausscheiden beider Choreographen 1970 führt in eine Krise, die durch die Einstellung Kyliáns überwunden wird.

Im Januar 1991 ruft Kylián das Nederlands Dans Theater 3 (NDT 3) ins Leben, das – mit Gérard Lemaître als Projektleiter – den älteren, reifen, über vierzigjährigen Tänzer in den Mittelpunkt stellt. Projektweise sollen Stücke mit unterschiedlicher Besetzung und verschiedenen Choreographen erarbeitet werden. Bedingung des Unternehmens: nach einer Reihe von Aufführungen ist das Projekt beendet, die Stücke gehen in kein Repertoire ein.

Luuk, U. (Text): Nederlands Dans Theater. Augsburg 1981; Schaik, E. v.: Neue Wege und Spuren. 25 Jahre N. D. T. In: Ballett International 4 (1984), S. 27–31; ders.: Hans van Manen. Bewegung und Form. Interview. In: Ballett International 1 (1984), S. 21–23.

Patricia Stöckemann

Negro Ensemble Company

Gegr. 1967, entwickelte sich die N. E. C. unter der künstlerischen Leitung des Dramatikers Douglas Turner Ward und mit Unterstützungsgeldern aus der Ford Foundation rasch zum Mittelpunkt des →schwarzamerik. Theaters in New York. Außer einer Serie erfolgreicher Inszenierungen leistete sie auch durch die Einrichtung von Kursen und Workshops einen Beitrag zur Ausbildung afroamerik. Theaterschaffender. Der politische Anspruch der N. E. C. war ein gemäßigter; neben dem ‹theatre of black experience› sollte auch weltliterarisch bedeutsame Dramatik zur Aufführung kommen. De facto waren dies lediglich der *Lusitanische Popanz* von Peter Weiss und *Kongi Harvest* des Afrikaners Wole Soyinka. Nach Europatourneen mit Dramen von Joseph Walker und Turner Ward selbst (1968–70) waren die erfolgreichsten Inszenierungen der N. E. C.: Walkers *River Niger* und Leslie Lees *First Breeze of Summer* (1972–75), die jeweils an den Broadway und ins Fernsehen übernommen wurden. Workshops und Festivals machten die N. E. C. zu einem nationalen

Zentrum schwarzamerik. Theaters, wo viele spätere Stars entscheidende Elemente ihrer Ausbildung erhielten. Nationale und internationale Tourneen (neben Europa z. B. Australien und Virgin Islands) ließen die N. E. C. zum bedeutendsten schwarzamerik. Theater der 70er Jahre avancieren.

Dieter Herms

Nelson-Revue

N.-R. ist die Bezeichnung für ein «kabarettistisches Gesamtkunstwerk» (PEM), die von Rudolf Nelson in den 20er Jahren in Berlin ausgebildete Form der Kammer-Revue (→Revue). – Nelson, eigentlich Rudolf Lewysohn, geboren am 8. 4. 1878 in Berlin, verließ nicht nur seinen Beruf als kaufmännischer Angestellter, sondern brach auch seine musikalische Ausbildung ab, um sich als musikalischer Begleiter an Kleinkunstbühnen zu versuchen. 1904 eröffnete er mit Paul Schneider-Duncker den «Roland von Berlin», in dem mit pikanten Texten und spritziger Musik ein feudales Publikum unterhalten wurde. Nach der Trennung von Schneider-Duncker (1907) eröffnete Nelson das →«Chat Noir», das er bis 1914 leitete. Er bot seinem exklusiven Publikum ein literarisch-musikalisches Kabarett. In den folgenden Jahren schrieb er zusätzlich die Musik zu mehreren Revuen des Metropol-Theaters, einige Operetten und eröffnete das Metropol-Kabarett. Seine eigene Form fand er schließlich, nachdem er 1919 «Nelsons Künstlerspiele» gegründet hatte, 1920 bereits in «Nelson-Theater» umbenannt. Er verließ das Nummernkabarett zugunsten einer kleinen kabarettistischen Revue, in der Aktualität ohne Gesellschaftskritik sich verband mit luxuriös-raffinierter Ausstattung – zusammengehalten durch die von Nelson unermüdlich ge- und erfundenen Melodien. In den 20er Jahren schrieb er rund 30 dieser Revuen. Die zumeist eher harmlosen Texte standen im Gegensatz zu den eher satirisch-zeitkritischen ‹Revuetten› seines Konkurrenten Friedrich Hollaender.

Nach der Machtübernahme der Nationalsozialisten wurde die N.-R. nach Wien verpflichtet. Von den österr. Faschisten wurde jedoch nach kurzer Zeit die Absetzung erzwungen, die N.-R. floh in die Schweiz. 1934, bei einem Gastspiel in Zürich, engagierte der Holländer Louis Davids die N.-R. nach Amsterdam. In 14tägigem Wechsel brachte er bis 1940 annähernd 100 Programme heraus. Seine Textautoren waren sein Sohn Herbert und Emmerich Bernauer, seine wichtigsten Darsteller: Dora Paulsen, Max Ehrlich, Kurt Gerron, Eva Busch und Karl Farkas. Hauptwirkungsstätte war das Kabarett-Theater «La Gaîté» in Amsterdam, in den Sommermonaten gastierte die Truppe in Scheveningen.

Nach der Besetzung der Niederlande gelang es Nelson zusammen mit Dora Paulsen unterzutauchen. – 1949 kam Nelson das erste Mal wieder nach Deutschland und Berlin, wo er sich in der Folgezeit öfter zu Gastspielen aufhielt, sich schließlich niederließ und am 5. 2. 1960 starb. Sein Sohn Herbert Nelson setzt zusammen mit seiner Frau Eva die Arbeit seines Vaters fort und tritt mit eigenen Kabarettprogrammen vor allem in den USA auf.

Budzinski, K.: Pfeffer ins Getriebe. München 1982; Günther, E.: Geschichte des Varietés. Berlin ²1981; Jameson, E.: Am Flügel: Rudolf Nelson. Berlin 1967; Kothes, F.-P.: Die theatralische Revue in Berlin und Wien 1900–1938. Wilhelmshaven 1977; Kühn, V.: Das Kabarett der frühen Jahre. Berlin 1984; Nelson, R.: Nacht der Nächte – Revue meines Lebens. Berlin o. J.; PEM (d. i. P. E. Marcus): Heimweh nach dem Kurfürstendamm. Berlin 1952.

Wolfgang Beck / Jan Hans

Nemzeti Szinház (Budapest)

Das Nationaltheater, gegr. 1837, ging aus dem Kampf für die nationale Unabhängigkeit Ungarns ab Ende des 18. Jh. hervor (erstes ungar. Ensemble 1790 unter László Kelemen). Da der Bau ohne Hilfe des Hofes oder Staats zustande kam, lebt es in dem ungarischen Kulturbewußtsein als Symbol der politischen und geistigen Unabhängigkeit. Seit 1840 Staatstheater, gilt es als Förderungsanstalt der nationalen Dramatik und Pflegestätte der nationalen →Klassik. Das Ensemble bildet stets eine Elite von Schauspielern, die sich durch künstlerische Vorbildlichkeit und nationale Originalität auszeichnen. Unter seinem ersten Direktor, dem Kritiker József Bajza (1837/38), noch Sprech- und Operntheater, wurde es zur Geburtsstätte der ersten echt ungarischen Theatergattung, des →Volksstücks durch Ede Szigligeti (auch als Direktor 1873–78 tätig), sowie der nationalen Oper unter dem Dirigenten und Komponisten Ferenc Erkel (1810–93). 1875 verselbständigt sich das Volksstück, 1884 die Oper; sie bekamen eigene Häuser. Erste Blütezeit unter der Direktion von Ede Paulay (1878–94), der als Regisseur diesem Metier künstlerische Geltung verschaffte. Intensive Klassikerpflege durch den Aufstieg der großen Tragödin Mari Jászai (1850–1926). Uraufführungen nationaler Klassiker: Mihály Vörösmartys *Csongor und Tünde* (1879) und Imre Madáchs *Die Tragödie des Menschen* (1883). 1913 wird der Bau abgerissen, das Ensemble zieht in das Gebäude des Volkstheaters (Népszinház) um, später (1966) nochmals in das des Ungarischen Theaters (Magyar Szinház). Zweite Blütezeit unter Sándor Hevesis Direktionszeit (1922–32). Groß angelegte Shakespeare-, Molière- und Ibsen-Zyklen sowie ungar. Volksstückserien. Eröffnung der Kammerspiele 1922. Zusammenarbeit mit dem wichtigsten Autor der Epoche, Zsigmond Móricz, und Serien-

664 Neue Medien und Theater

erfolge durch seine Stücke. 1935 bis 1944 ist Antal Németh Direktor des →Nationaltheaters, dem es gelang, die geistige Unabhängigkeit – trotz Nazieinflusses – weitgehend zu bewahren. Bedeutende Regieleistungen, Uraufführungen für die Zeit weltanschaulich aussagekräftiger Autoren. 1949 Verstaatlichung des ungar. Theaterwesens. Tamás Major (1910–85) übernimmt die Direktion (1945–62) und prägt zusammen mit linksorientierten Theaterleuten (Endre Gellért, 1914–60; Endre Marton) aus der Vorkriegszeit und dem Untergrund ein neues Profil auch in der Spielweise (→Stanislawski-System). Die Bemühungen Majors (auch Anhänger Brechts und Meyerholds) um Reform des Regie- und Spielstils u. a. mit Stücken von Brecht und P. Weiss führen zur inneren Polarisierung des Ensembles. Wie zuvor mit T. Major ist das N. S. 1978–82 künstlerisch führend durch die Arbeiten der Chefregisseure Gábor Székély (*1944) und Gábor Zsámbéki (*1943; vom →Csiky Gergely Szinház): *Dantons Tod*; *Emigranten* von Mrozek/*Die Küche* von Wesker; *Heinrich IV*. Ihr neues Theaterkonzept können sie aber erst ab 1982 im →Katona József Szinház (1951–82 Kammerbühne des N. S.) realisieren. Glanzpunkte setzte auch der hochbegabte Imre Csiszár (Intendant ab 1989); wurde 1991 durch das Kulturministerium abgelöst.

P.-Kádár, J.: A Nemzeti Szinház 100 éves története (Die Geschichte des 100jährigen Nationaltheaters). Budapest 1940; Székely, G. (Hg.): A Nemzeti Szinház (Das Nationaltheater). Budapest 1965; Szekér, L.: A Nemzeti Szinház 150 éve. Budapest 1987.

Sándor Gulyás / Elke Wiegand

Neue Medien und Theater

Die seit Beginn der 80er Jahre in der Bundesrepublik kontrovers geführte Diskussion über die unter dem Begriff ‹Neue Medien› zusammengefaßten neuen Kommunikationstechnologien wie Btx, Bildtelefon, Teletex, Telefax, Video, Bildplatte sowie Kabel- und Satellitenfernsehen ist sehr bald auch von den Theatern aufgenommen worden. Von Interesse sind dabei vor allem die vier letztgenannten N. M. (→Fernsehen und Theater, →Film und Theater).

Die Diskussion um das Verhältnis der Theater zu den neuen Aufzeichnungs- und Übertragungsmedien setzte in einer Situation ein, in der die Popularisierung des Mediums Video und die technische Ausreifung der Bildplatte sowie vor allem die Ausweitung der Fernsehkapazitäten im Zuge der breit angelegten Verkabelung die Medienlandschaft tiefgreifend zu verändern begannen. Sie wurde durch eine gewisse Furcht vor der Konkurrenz motiviert, die den Theatern aus einer Vielzahl neuer Fernsehprogramme und einem dadurch möglicherweise veränderten Freizeitverhalten des Publikums zu erwachsen droht. Allerdings befinden sich diejenigen, die eine Beteiligung der Theater an den N. M. strikt ablehnen – etwa weil sie eine Mittäterschaft der Theater «an der Verblödung der Nation, der Verkümmerung des kommunikativen Umgangs» (A. Petersen, Intendant des Nationaltheaters Mannheim) befürchten –, deutlich in der Minderheit.

Darüber jedoch, wie die N. M. im Interesse der Theater zu nutzen sind, gehen die Meinungen weit auseinander. Zum Teil werden die neuen Produktions- und Distributionsmöglichkeiten als Chance für die Theater begriffen, sich aus der ‹Abhängigkeit› des öffentlich-rechtlichen Fernsehens zu lösen und die audiovisuelle Verwertung ihrer Produktionen in Eigenregie vorzunehmen. Im Mittelpunkt solcher Überlegungen stehen selbstproduzierte Theateraufzeichnungen, die den privaten Veranstaltern des Kabelfernsehens oder auf dem Video- und Bildplattenmarkt zum Verkauf angeboten werden sollen. Zur konkreten Umsetzung dieses Konzeptes wird nach einer Idee des Münchner Generalintendanten A. Everding z. Z. vom → Deutschen Bühnenverein ein sog. Medien-Pool erprobt, in dem neun Theater gemeinsam ihre audiovisuellen Produktionen vermarkten (dazu gehören u. a. Schaubühne Berlin, Residenztheater München, Staatstheater Stuttgart, Schauspielhaus Bochum). Als praktisches Vorbild könnte dabei das «Pilotprojekt» des Stadttheaters Ingolstadt dienen, das ebenfalls dem Pool angehört: Bei kommunaler Vorfinanzierung wurde dort eine vielbeachtete *Faust*-Inszenierung unter Federführung des Theaters von einer privaten Video-Firma aufgezeichnet. Diese relativ preiswerte Aufzeichnung konnte an einen der Betreiber des Kabelpilotprojekts München mit Gewinn verkauft werden. Die Befürworter solcher Konzepte begründen sie zum einen mit der Aussicht auf zusätzliche Einnahmen, zum anderen mit dem Argument der Demokratisierung: Hochsubventionierte Theater- und Operninszenierungen könnten so einem Massenpublikum zugänglich gemacht werden, dem sie bisher vorenthalten blieben.

Kritiker solcher Überlegungen bezweifeln nicht nur deren Realisierbarkeit, sie bemängeln vor allem deren künstlerische und kulturpolitische Konsequenzen. Dabei zeichnen sich vier Problemkomplexe ab:

1. Die Frage nach der Finanzierung von Theateraufzeichnungen (Kosten zwischen 50 000 und 100 000 DM) ist weitgehend ungeklärt. Insbesondere ist dabei die angespannte Haushaltslage der Rechtsträger der Theater, vor allem der Kommunen, zu berücksichtigen. Die Erfahrungen des Stadttheaters Ingolstadt können auf Grund ihrer Einmaligkeit nicht verallgemeinert werden. Wenn andere Theater dem Beispiel folgen und somit als Konkurrenten auf dem privaten Medienmarkt auftreten, werden die Einnahmen sinken.

2. Ebenso ungeklärt sind die tariflichen Regelungen der Leistungsschutzrechte des künstlerischen Theaterpersonals und die verlagsrechtlichen Fragen.

3. Der von Optimisten prognostizierte Bedarf an Theateraufzeichnungen ist zu bezweifeln. Das Zuschauerinteresse an kulturellen Darbietungen im Fernsehen bzw. auf Videokassetten ist relativ gering und wird auch aller Voraussicht nach nicht steigen. Es ist daher zu befürchten, daß durch die zwangsläufige Fixierung der privaten Fernsehanbieter auf hohe Einschaltquoten lediglich die ‹populären› Theaterformen auf ein nennenswertes Interesse stoßen werden. Das vielbeschworene amerik. Vorbild legt die Vermutung nahe, daß lediglich konventionelle Inszenierungen mit hochkarätiger Besetzung eine Chance auf dem privaten Medienmarkt haben. Dies gilt verstärkt für den Bereich des Musiktheaters. Dagegen steht zu befürchten, daß experimentellen und künstlerisch ambitionierten Produktionen der Zugang zu den N. M. verwehrt bleibt. Gegen die Einrichtung eines subventionierten ‹Kulturkanals›, in dem sie ihren Platz hätten, spricht nach Ansicht des Dt. Städtetages, daß die Kultur damit endgültig in die ‹Gettosituation› des Minderheitenprogramms gedrängt würde.

4. Die Ausstrahlung repräsentativer, überregional bedeutsamer Theateraufzeichnungen scheint nicht nur wenig geeignet, den Theatern ‹vor Ort› neue Zuschauer zu gewinnen; sie widerspricht auch einer Kulturpolitik, die die Bürger innerhalb ihres sozialen Bezugsraums zu kultureller Partizipation anregen will und die von dieser Warte das Theater vor allem als Ort der Interaktion von Spiel und Zuschauer begreift. Ein solches Selbstverständnis prägt auch die Haltung einer Mehrzahl von befragten Intendanten und Dramaturgen dt. Theater. Eine vom Bundesinnenministerium im Auftrag gegebene Studie empfiehlt den Theatern vor diesem Hintergrund, sich «in einer sich schnell verändernden Medienlandschaft als *Gegensatz* zu den reproduzierenden Medien (zu) profilieren».

In der bereits zitierten Rundfrage unter Theatermachern wird die Nutzung der N. M. von vielen Skeptikern nicht grundsätzlich ausgeschlossen. Sie sehen die Möglichkeiten jedoch eher im Bereich der Werbung und Öffentlichkeitsarbeit. Das Spektrum reicht von Spielplaninformationen durch Btx über Theater-Werbespots an öffentlichen Plätzen bis hin zu einer intensivierten Kulturberichterstattung (Proben- und Werkstattberichte, Direktübertragungen) innerhalb der neuen lokalen Kabelkanäle. – Einen beachtenswerten Weg zur Nutzung des N. M. Video zeigt die Zusammenarbeit des Schauspielhauses Nürnberg mit der Medienwerkstatt Franken auf. Dort wurden zu einzelnen Inszenierungen (*Die Physiker, Nicht Fisch, nicht Fleisch, Bruder Eichmann*) Videobänder hergestellt, die sowohl die Entstehung einer Aufführung

Neue Medien und Theater 667

als auch den dramaturgischen Hintergrund der Stücke thematisierten. Diese «Video-Programmhefte» stießen vor allem an Schulen auf große Resonanz.

In Österreich ist zur medialen Auswertung von Produktionen der Bundestheater 1981 die «Teletheater Videofilm-Produktions- und Vertriebsgesellschaft mbH» gegründet worden. Die Teletheater GmbH verwertet im wesentlichen Produktionen des Musiktheaters. In der Schweiz steht man den N. M. bisher skeptisch gegenüber. Der Gründung einer entsprechenden Verwertungsinstitution stehen u. a. Schwierigkeiten entgegen, die sich aus der Viersprachigkeit der Schweiz ergeben.

In diesem Zusammenhang sei auf die Medienpraxis in den Niederlanden hingewiesen. Die Auseinandersetzung mit den N. M., insbesondere dem Kabelfernsehen, begann dort wesentlich früher. Das Niederländische Theaterinstitut (Amsterdam), zu 100 Prozent vom Staat subventioniert, hat die Aufgabe, niederländische Theaterproduktionen zu archivieren. Darüber hinaus beteiligt es sich an Produktionen von Theateraufzeichnungen für mehrere Fernsehsender, wobei es als Ko- bzw. als alleiniger Produzent fungiert. Den Sendern steht ein einmaliges Senderecht zu, die weitere Verwertung übernimmt das Theaterinstitut. Der Ertrag aus Video-Verleih, Video-Verkauf, Wiederholungssendungen etc. wird zwischen den Theatergruppen und dem Institut geteilt. Die Leistungsschutzrechte liegen – so ein Entwurf – bei den Theatergruppen. Da diese verpflichtet sind, ihre Produktionen einem möglichst großen Publikum zugänglich zu machen, wenn sie subventioniert werden, haben sie den indirekten Auftrag, ihre Produktionen der medialen Verwertung zur Verfügung zu stellen.

Neue Medien – Herausforderung für das Theater. In: Dt. Bühne 7 (1983), S. 12 ff; Theater-TV: Ein weltweites Geschäft? In: Dt. Bühne 1 (1984), S. 8 ff; Saurer Regen oder Besinnung auf das Eigentümliche des Theaters. In: Dt. Bühne 6 (1984), S. 9 ff. Everding-Interview. In: Dt. Bühne 9 (1984), S. 23 ff. Bericht von der Medientagung des Nordwestdeutschen Landesverbands der Dt. Bühnenvereins. In: Dt. Bühne 7 (1984), S. 16 ff. – Herdlein, H.: Medienverwirrung. In: bühnengenossenschaft 11 (1984), S. 4; Korte, W. B.: Neue Medien und Informationstechnologien-Auswirkungen in Kunst- und Kulturbereich. In: Rundfunk und Fernsehen 1 (1985), S. 21 ff; ders.: Der Bühnenkünstler im Zwielicht des Medienpools. In: bühnengenossenschaft 12 (1985), S. 10 ff; Riepenhausen, B.: Bühne im Bildschirm. In: bühnengenossenschaft 5 (1983), S. 11; Girth, P.: Videooper-Rechtsfragen des zeitgenössischen Musikbetriebes. In: Film und Recht 1984, S. 19 ff.

Peter Kelting / Roswitha Körner

Neue Sachlichkeit

Nachdem die humanistischen Ideale vom ‹Guten, Wahren und Schönen› im 1. Weltkrieg ihr Debakel erlebt hatten und der expressionistische Traum vom ‹neuen Menschen› unter die Stiefel der Noske-Truppen geraten war, zeigte sich ein Teil der Bürger und Intellektuellen geneigt, auf den ‹Boden der Tatsachen› zurückzukehren. Als die idealistischen Maskeraden verbraucht waren, wurde das Bürgertum ‹sachlich› und wandte sich verstärkt «der Herstellung von Zahnpasta» zu (Alfred Döblin). Eine Kunstausstellung verhalf dem Begriff N. S. – der bereits seit längerem in der Luft gelegen hatte – 1925 zum endgültigen Durchbruch. Zunächst auf dem Gebiet der darstellenden Künste eingeführt, wurde der Begriff schon bald auf andere Bereiche der Ästhetik übertragen. Gegen Ende der 20er Jahre bezeichnete N. S. sowohl eine vom Bauhaus-Produkt bis zur Zeitoper reichende Kunst‹richtung› als auch eine zeitgemäß desillusionierte Lebenshaltung.

Für das Theater nach 1925 bedeutete N. S.: die Revolution, die auf der Straße mißlang, wurde jetzt auch auf der Bühne abgesetzt. Die Welt ‹wie sie ist› sollte gezeigt werden. Das Einverständnis mit der modernen Industriegesellschaft trat an die Stelle der expressionistischen Revolte gegen Technik und Großstadt. So wurde Bertolt Brecht (1898–1956), Autor von *Mann ist Mann* (1926), von der sachlichen Theaterkritik als erster deutscher Bühnendichter gepriesen, «der die Mechanik des Maschinenzeitalters weder feiert noch angreift sondern selbstverständlich nimmt» (Herbert Ihering). «An die Stelle des Kunstwerks» sollte sich – so das neue Ästhetikideal – «die Sache selbst, der authentische Gegenstand schieben» (Wilhelm Michel). Das schreibende Subjekt hatte hinter dem darzustellenden Objekt zu verschwinden: das fiktional-ästhetische Element der Bühnenkunst hinter dem faktisch-materialen. Statt wie in früheren Zeiten aus dem Innenleben zu schöpfen, Kunstfiguren ‹zu erfinden› und Phantasiewelten zu entwerfen, waren die Vertreter der N. S. entschlossen, sich an die sichtbare, von jedermann ‹überprüfbare› Außenwelt zu halten. Sachkompetenz statt Imagination: nachweisbare Tatsachen und wissenschaftliche Erkenntnisse sollten die Grundlagen einer neuen Ästhetik des 20. Jh. bilden. Gegenüber dem Theaterpublikum hatten sich die Autoren darauf zu beschränken, das Material zu liefern – Deutung und Auswertung des Bühnenstoffs blieb dagegen den Rezipienten vorbehalten. Allerdings wurde dieses ‹Programm› in seiner idealtypischen Radikalität von keinem der sachlichen Autoren je auch nur annähernd in die ästhetische Praxis umgesetzt.

Neue Stoffe aus Politik und Wirtschaft eroberten die Bühne, ohne daß sogleich eine materialadäquate Darstellungsform gefunden wurde. «Das Petroleum sträubt sich», einem Wort Brechts zufolge, «gegen die fünf

Neue Sachlichkeit 669

Akte», dennoch widerstanden die sachlichen Autoren keineswegs der Versuchung, die neuen Stoffkomplexe erneut in traditionelle Dramenformen zu zwängen. (Vgl. dazu Lion Feuchtwangers, 1884–1958, *Die Petroleuminseln* [1927] und Leo Lanias, 1896–1961, *Konjunktur* [1928]. Brechts *Weizen*, 1928 für die Piscatorbühne angekündigt, wies über Feuchtwangers und Lanias Versuche hinaus, blieb jedoch bezeichnenderweise Fragment.)

Der militärische Sieg der anglo-amerik. Truppen an der Westfront erwies sich als Sieg auf der ganzen Linie. Mitte der 20er Jahre machten sich die Amerikaner auf, die Bühnen Berlins zu erobern: «Sie entsandten einige Divisionen von Romanschriftstellern, eine zusammengesetzte Brigade dramatischer Autoren und ein Kampfgeschwader von Filmstars. Und in weniger als einem halben Jahr wurde das künstlerische Berlin dem Erdboden gleichgemacht» (Otto Alfred Palitzsch). Die dt. Autoren folgten dem Zug der Zeit und schrieben «angelsächsische Stücke» (L. Feuchtwanger, 1927). Das Ende der abendländischen Kultur schien gekommen: Jazz, Boxsport und Tanzrevuen drangen in die ehrwürdigen Musentempel – und fanden ihren Widerhall im Theaterstück der N. S. Bei der Berliner Premiere der *Petroleuminseln* (L. Feuchtwanger) spielte eine Jazzband vor den Kulissen eines Autorennens. Ein Conférencier forderte das Publikum auf, «scharf zuzuschauen, bis der Kampf sich klärt». Man sprach angelsächsisch unterkühlt, fast beiläufig, ohne jede Emphase. Genaue Orts- und Zeitangaben (wie *Kalkutta, 4. Mai* – so der Titel eines weiteren «angelsächsischen Stücks von L. Feuchtwanger») signalisierten, daß man nicht daran dachte, sich lange mit ‹Theorie› aufzuhalten, sondern fest entschlossen war, sogleich zur Sache zu kommen. Statt des kategorischen Imperativs dienten jetzt Statistiken und andere empirisch ermittelte Erfahrungswerte als Richtlinien menschlichen Handelns. Durch den Verfall der ewigen Werte ‹freischwebend› geworden, fanden die sachlichen Bühnenhelden in materiellem Genuß, fortwährender Betriebsamkeit und erstklassigen Geschäftsabschlüssen ihre Selbsterfüllung. Die neusachliche Dramatik ersetzte die Leitbilder der Vorkriegszeit, den Bohemien und die einsame Künstlernatur, durch den realitätstüchtigen Zyniker des 20. Jh.

Giesing, M. u. a.: Fetisch ‹Technik› – Die Gesellschaft auf dem Theater der ‹Neusachlichkeit›. In: Weimarer Republik, Ausstellungskatalog. Berlin ³1977, S. 783–822; Koebner, T.: Das Drama der Neuen Sachlichkeit und die Krise des Liberalismus. In: Rothe, W. (Hg.): Die deutsche Literatur der Weimarer Republik. Stuttgart 1974, S. 19–46; Lethen, H.: Neue Sachlichkeit 1924–32. Stuttgart ²1975; Sloterdijk, P.: Kritik der zynischen Vernunft. Frankfurt/M. 1983, bes. Bd. 2, S. 777–920.

Carl Wege

Neues Theater Halle

Das Gebäude war 1891 als repräsentative Vergnügungsstätte im Stadtzentrum eröffnet worden («Kaisersäle»), dann mehrfach umgebaut und schließlich in einem desolaten Zustand. Dadurch erhielten Hallische Schauspieler die Möglichkeit, sich außerhalb staatlicher Planung und Förderung einen eigenen Theaterraum zu schaffen. 1981 wurde das provisorisch eingerichtete N. T. H. zunächst als zweite Bühne des Landestheaters H. eröffnet, seitdem in fortwährenden Um- und Ausbauten zu einem multidisponiblen Bühnenraum mit 460 Zuschauerplätzen erweitert. – Seit 1991 als Sprechtheater selbständig, bildet es das Kernstück einer «Kulturinsel», zu der ein auch im Winter bespieltes Hoftheater, Literaturcafé, Galerie und Theaterkneipe gehören. Weitere Räume für kulturelle Kommunikation werden derzeit vom Ensemble unter dem engagierten Intendanten P. Sodann (*1936) ausgebaut. Der Spielplan verbindet Unterhaltung mit hohem ästhetischen Anspruch, Clownerien und weltliterarische Dramatik. Das N. T. H. greift einen Teil jenes Hallischen Theaterprogramms auf, das zwischen 1966 und 1972 auf das DDR-Theater starken Einfluß ausgeübt hatte. Intendant G. Wolfram (1922–91) und Regisseur H. Schönemann (*1927) waren angetreten, Widersprüche der realsozialistischen Gesellschaft auf der Bühne zu veröffentlichen und so eine (begrenzte) Demokratisierung des Systems anzuregen (u. a. Uraufführung der Dramatisierung von H. Kants Roman *Die Aula* und U. Plenzdorfs *Die neuen Leiden des jungen W.*).

Funke, Ch.: Der Regisseur Horst Schönemann. Ein Beitrag zur Geschichte des Theaters in der DDR. Berlin 1971; Halle-Information (Hg.): Kleine hallesche Theatergeschichte. Halle 1990.

Roland Dreßler

Neuzeit / Theater der Neuzeit

1. «When looking toward the past creates a new view of the future, reconstruction fulfills the goals of the avant-garde» (M. Kirby): Genau dieser Umschlag von Rekonstruktion (der Antike) in Innovation ereignet sich zu Beginn des *neuzeitlichen Theaters*, mit einer Verspätung freilich gegenüber anderen Künsten, die für die soziale, publikumsabhängige Kunst des Theaters typisch ist. Während das Italien der Renaissance «das Zeitalter der Theologie schon hinter sich» (de Sanctis) hat und die Literatur ihren Inhalt dem Spiel der Einbildungskraft, dem Kult der Form unterwirft, findet die um eine «Wiederherstellung der Herrschaft des Geistes» ringende dt. Renaissancekultur vor lauter sittlich-religiösem Eifer nicht zur

Form. Auch Frankreich öffnet sich nur zögernd den neuen Impulsen, favorisiert noch bis ins 17. Jh. hinein die mittelalterliche Überlieferung von →Mysterienspiel (das um 1550 ausläuft), Moralité, vor allem aber der populären →Farce, einem satirischen Spiegel der Alltagswelt, als Substrat einer weithin säkularisierten Theaterlust.

Um den langwierigen Prozeß der Ablösung des mittelalterlichen durch ein neuzeitliches Theater an einem Datum festzumachen (→Renaissancetheater): zwei Ereignisse des Jahres 1486 erhellen das Dunkel um das antike Theater, der erste Druck von Vitruvs *De architectura*, des um 30 v. Chr. entstandenen Quellenwerks auch zum spätantiken Theaterbau, und erste Aufführungen der röm. Komödiendichter Plautus und Terenz in Rom und Ferrara. Dort freilich signalisiert schon die Verwendung einer ital. Übersetzung der *Zwillinge* die Überlagerung des humanistischen Interesses an einer getreuen Rekonstruktion durch ein ganz aktuelles Theaterinteresse, das sich nicht zuletzt im Prunk der Kostüme und Schaueffekte manifestiert. Intermedien zwischen den einzelnen Akten, in denen sich der Sinnenzauber von Musik, Tanz und Pantomine frei entfalten kann, lassen den humanistischen Ansatz in Ferrara bald in Vergessenheit geraten. Anders in Rom, wo es dem berühmten Humanisten Pomponius Laetus (1427–97) und seinen Schülern um authentische Wiedergabe der röm. Komödien (bald auch der *Phaedra* Senecas) geht, obschon seine Gönner – wie der Kardinal Riario – ihm die Errichtung eines vitruvianischen Theaters noch verweigern. Während man in Ferrara den Einheitsschauplatz der →Terenzbühne – Häuserzeile mit mehreren Türen zur Straße hin – noch in fünf plastische ‹Häuser› nach Art der mittelalterlichen Mansionen auflöst, bleibt in Rom, wo man 1513 auf einer Bühne von 31 m Breite und 6,7 m Tiefe spielt, die durch eine repräsentative Schauwand abgeschlossen wird, die Konstanz der Raumfunktion durchgehend gewahrt. Die Illustrationen der Lyoner Terenzausgabe (1493) des Niederländers Jodocus Badius, der vermutlich auch bei Pomponius studierte, dürften ein ziemlich getreues Abbild der röm. Humanistenbühne vermitteln, während in den ersten dt. Terenzausgaben wie der Ulmer oder der Straßburger (1496) die Häuser noch in der Art eines Marktplatzes so angeordnet sind, daß sich die Darsteller nicht vor, sondern zwischen ihnen bewegen.

Wie sich die Autorität Vitruvs auch im Theaterbau durchsetzt, bezeugt noch heute das von Andrea Palladio (1508–80) entworfene →‹Teatro Olimpico› in Vicenza (1584) – sieht man einmal davon ab, daß aus perspektivischen Gründen das Halbrund von Amphitheater und Orchestra zum Halboval abgeflacht ist. Der flächige Charakter der 25 m breiten, aber nur 6 m tiefen Bühne wird noch betont durch die mächtige Höhe der Szenenwand, die mit ihrem stark überhöhten Mittelportal jenseits ihrer szenischen Funktion auch eine architektonische, der Festlichkeit des Zuschauerraums korrespondierende Wirkung anstrebt und damit beide Bereiche einem gemeinsamen höfisch-gesellschaftlichen Realitätskreis zuordnet. Das dramatische Geschehen vollzieht sich noch nicht hinter einer imaginären Wand, sondern in der Welt der Zuschauer. Blickt man freilich durch die Portale der rückwärtigen Schauwand, fällt der Blick auf perspektivisch angeordnete Straßen, die das Teatro Olimpico zum Exempel einer andernorts zur gleichen Zeit schon weit vorangeschrittenen Entwicklung machen, die von der idealistischen Humanistenbühne (→ Humanismus/Drama und Theater des Humanismus) zur illusionistischen Renaissancebühne führt. In ihr setzt sich fort, was um die Mitte des 15. Jh. mit dem →Straßentheater der →Trionfi, der Nachbildung altröm. Triumphzüge, und den allegorisch-mythologischen Festspielen begonnen hatte: eine Lust am betörenden Schein prunkvoller Bilder und Kostüme, am beziehungsreichen Maskenspiel, das in den mythologischen Gottheiten den Veranstaltern des Festes huldigt. Kein Geringerer als Leonardo da Vinci ist unter denen, die sich 1490 an einem Festspiel zur Hochzeit des Herzogs von Mailand *Die Huldigung der 7 Planeten* beteiligen – mit einer Drehbühne, die den Szenenwechsel bei offener Bühne erlaubt.

Denkt man sich den Mittelbogen, die Porta Regia, von Vicenza so verbreitert, daß er die ganze Bühne überspannt, gewinnt man eine Vorstellung von jener frühen Bildbühne, die die erste Aufführung einer ital. Komödie, der *Cassaria* des Ludovico Ariosto (1474–1533) 1508 in Ferrara, auch zu einem theatergeschichtlichen Ereignis macht. Wer immer der erste war, der in diesen Jahren das Bild einer Stadt oder einer idyllischen Landschaft in perspektivischen Dekorationen auf die Bühne zauberte, Baldassare Peruzzi (1481–1536), der 1514 die röm. Premiere von Bibbienas (1470–1520) *Calandria* ausstattete, oder ein anderer – sein Vorbild macht so rasch Schule, daß Sebastiano Serlio (1475–1554) die Entwicklung von Theaterbau und perspektivischer Winkelrahmenbühne (so benannt nach den beiden mit bemalter Leinwand bespannten Holzrahmen, die im stumpfen Winkel zusammenstoßen, eine Seite dem Zuschauer, die andere der Bühnenmitte zukehrend) in seiner *Architettura* von 1545 abschließend zusammenfassen kann. Gespielt wird auf einem nur 2,5 m tiefen Podium vor der 6 m tiefen Hinterbühne, die nicht in das Spiel einbezogen werden kann und meist durch einen gemalten Prospekt beschlossen wird. Zu ebener Erde bilden →Proszenium und →Orchestra eine Zwischenzone. Die drei Musterentwürfe Serlios für Tragödie, Komödie und Satyrspiel verdeutlichen, daß noch nicht das Streben nach dem stückbezogenen Milieu, sondern – in formaler Abwandlung einiger weniger Bildtypen – die Freude an Schönheit und Mannigfaltigkeit des Bildes dominiert.

Gegen Ende des Jh. gewinnen die frontalen Gebilde an Zahl und Tiefe, die noch verstärkt wird durch einen neuen Bühnentypus, der die vorderen

Häuser bis an den Bühnenrand vorzieht. Die Trennung von Spiel- und Bildbühne wird aufgehoben durch einen Rahmen, der beide Bereiche umspannt.

Schon um 1530 hat sich der Typus einer ital. Komödie konsolidiert, die als Commedia erudita (gelehrte Komödie) ihre Abhängigkeit vom röm. Vorbild, die Nachahmung überlieferter antiker Standes- und Charaktertypen, Verwicklungen und Intrigen im Namen trägt und nur selten – wie in Niccolò Machiavellis (1469–1527) *Mandragola* (UA Florenz 1520) – aktuelle, in zeitgenössischen Charakteren angelegte Probleme behandelt. Um so bemerkenswerter die ersten Schritte zur Aktualisierung der festen Typen wie des miles gloriosus, der als Soldat der span. Besatzungsmacht auftritt (wie der Pedant als Dottore), aber erst in der Commedia dell'arte als Capitano zur stehenden Figur wird.

2. Die → *Commedia dell'arte* ist aber primär nicht eine Weiterentwicklung der Commedia erudita, sondern der vitale Protest der sich rasch ausbreitenden Berufsschauspieler gegen die Sterilität des akademisch-literarischen Theaters, inspiriert eher von der venezianischen Volkskomödie, die in dem Paduaner Angelo Beolco, genannt Ruzzante (1502–42), einem Schauspieler, der sich seine burlesk-realistischen Stücke selbst schrieb und schon 1529 Schauspielerinnen beschäftigte, ihren überragenden Meister fand.

Eine verblüffende Ähnlichkeit der Commedia dell'arte mit dem antiken → Mimus, insbesondere der → Atellana, der Stegreifposse der Osker mit ihren vier stehenden Typen – dem Freßsack (Maccus), dem Buckligen (Dossenus), dem Alten (Pappus) und der Tierimitation (Bucco) –, nährt den Verdacht, daß der Mimus – als menschliche Uranlage verstanden oder als historische, vom Christentum in den Untergrund verdrängte Erscheinung – die Gunst der Stunde zur glorreichen Auferstehung nutzt. Das geschieht um die Jahrhundertmitte nicht weit von Atella bei Neapel, wo eine komische Figur auftaucht, die man mit Maccus anreden möchte, wenn sie nicht Pulcinella hieße. Rasch formiert sich die Konkurrenz, etwa in dem Lastträger Zanne aus Bergamo, der meist zu zweit auftritt (die aktive Komik des Spaßmachers gegen die passive des Tölpels ausspielend) und es gegen Ende des Jh. zu den berühmten Namen Arlecchino und Brighella gebracht hat. Um den aktiven Narren, den Drahtzieher (mit der Tiermaske) gruppiert sich ein Ensemble, das die passive, die Charakterkomik vertritt: Pantalone, der geizige, mißtrauische Alte, der schusselige Dottore, der bramarbasierende Capitano, dazu die Verliebten und allerlei Randfiguren, nicht zu vergessen die gewitzte Partnerin des Arlecchino, Colombina. Die beiden Pfeiler der Commedia dell'arte stützen sich gegenseitig: Nur der auf einen einzigen, grotesk übersteigerten Typus fixierte Akteur kann – am roten Faden eines Szenariums (Canevas), ausgerüstet mit einem Vorrat an Einfällen (Concetti) und mimisch-

674 Neuzeit / Theater der Neuzeit

artistischen Effekten (Lazzi) – ‹improvisieren›, als Virtuose der verbalen wie der ‹körperlichen Beredsamkeit›.

Ein sozialkritischer Realitätsbezug der frühen Commedia dell'arte verliert sich, je mehr ihre Figuren sich zu ‹selbstherrlichen Potenzen› auswachsen, die nicht mehr auf die Realität, sondern den eigenen Fundus rekurrieren und «nicht auf dem Umweg über das Leben, sondern durch sich selbst Glauben erzwingen» (Kommerell). Bei solcher Stärke des Theaters wird die Bühne, ein einfaches Brettergerüst auf dem Markt oder im Saal, ohne oder mit einfachen Dekorationen (Vorhängen), unwesentlich.

3. Das dt. Echo auf die Errungenschaften der ital. Renaissance ist schwach und zwiespältig, während der ital. Humanismus nördlich der Alpen immerhin ein Form- und Bildungsbewußtsein weckt, das freilich bald in den Strudel der Glaubenskämpfe hineingezogen wird und sich unter Vernachlässigung kultureller Reformziele zur pädagogischen Bewegung im Dienste bürgerlicher Stadtkultur verengt. Terenz-Aufführungen in den Lateinschulen folgen keinem musischen Impuls, sondern fördern die (lutherische) Sittenlehre sowie die sprachliche und körperliche Gewandtheit der Schüler.

Stärker noch erweist sich das deutschsprachige Drama, das sich zumal in der Schweiz und im Elsaß seinen mittelalterlichen Stil lange bewahrt (die berühmteste Inszenierung des Luzerner Osterspiels findet 1583 statt), als Vehikel stadtbürgerlicher Gesinnung. Die Parabel vom verlorenen Sohn wird zum Ventil eines sittlichen Rigorismus, den nur die Fastnacht für einen flüchtigen Moment dispensiert.

Anders in den *Niederlanden*. Dort verbindet sich im Theater der Rederijker (Rhetoriker) ein in langer Moralitäten-Tradition bewährtes sittliches Engagement mit einem ästhetischen Eifer, der sich an humanistischer Form- und Sprachkultur, nicht minder aber am dekorativen Prunk der Trionfi, der gerade in den Niederlanden zu hoher Blüte gediehenen Kultur der höfischen Feste und Einzüge orientiert. Die Festwagen und die nicht selten mehrstöckigen Schaugerüste an Straßen und Plätzen mit biblischen, mythologischen und allegorischen Szenen und Tableaux schlagen eine direkte Brücke zu den → Vertooninge, den lebenden Bildern auf der Bühne der Rederijker. Beim mehrtägigen Landjuweel (Theaterwettbewerb über ein vorgegebenes Thema), an dem sich 1561 in Antwerpen 14 R-Kammern aus dem ganzen Land beteiligen, stehen neben dem allegorischen Preisspiel (Sinnspiel) immer auch kürzere, possenhafte Stücke im Programm, das mit einem – gemessen an den Darbietungen der Zünfte, Gilden etc. in den Nachbarländern – beispiellosem Aufwand an Menschen, künstlerischem Schmuck in Wort und Bild inszeniert wird und immer auch Reichtum und Bildungsstolz der großbürgerlichen Veranstalter demonstriert. Für die in die Handlung ‹eingeblendeten› (den mittelalterlichen Präfigurationen vergleichbaren) Vertooninge haben die Rederijker in der rückwärtigen Bühnenfront eigene Schauplätze eingerichtet, die bei Bedarf durch Öffnen des Vorhangs ein neues biblisches oder mythologisches ‹Zitat› präsentieren. Die tonangebende Kunst im Land, die Malerei, spielt stumm (oder von einem Sprecher kommentiert) auch auf dem Theater eine Hauptrolle.

Die dt. Antwort auf den Anbruch der Neuzeit, die einseitige Fixierung des Dramas auf den Glaubensstreit, die Rückkehr auch des Humanistendramas zu biblischen Stoffen, bremst auch die Entwicklung neuer Bühnenformen. Fast unbeachtet, unverstanden bleibt die Terenz- oder Badezellenbühne. Schule aber macht die Heidelberger UA des neolat. *Henno* von Johannes Reuchlin (1497) mit der Ablösung des mittelalterlichen Simultan- durch das Sukzessionsprinzip, das den Orts- und Szenenwechsel durch das Abtreten der Darsteller und eine gesprochene Ortsangabe (auf neutraler Bühne) zu Beginn der folgenden Szene bewerkstelligt.

Von dieser Neuerung profitiert nicht zuletzt das anspruchslose dt. →Fastnachtsspiel, das in der Frühzeit des Hans Sachs (1494–1576) noch mit der ‹ortlosen Stubenbühne› operiert («die Szene ist das Theater», mit Lessing zu reden), bis Sachs 1531 an einer Bearbeitung des *Henno* die Technik der neutralen Verwandlungsbühne erlernt. Sie erlaubt es ihm, wahre Berge von Stoff, von bewegter Handlung auf die leere Bühne zu schaufeln, auf Kosten freilich seiner eigentlichen Begabung für das realistische Detail. Im schroffen Gegensatz zur Fülle der Stoffe, Themen, Schauplätze: die Monotonie ihrer Gestaltung, die kaum einen Unterschied macht, ob ein Bauer über ein verlorenes Kalb klagt oder Tristan über Isolde. Wenn Sachs bei der Aufführung seiner Meistersingerdramen schon die von manchen Forschern behauptete Gliederung des Podiums in Vor- und Hinterbühne (für Innenszenen) einführte, wie sie um 1573 der elsässische Pfarrer Johann Rasser auf einer Schulbühne in Ensisheim praktizierte, wäre er ein früher Exponent jener realistischen Tendenzen, die das wechselnde Milieu durch bewegliche Requisiten, feste oder gemalte Türen, Vorhänge u. a. m. zu konkretisieren suchen.

4. →*Elisabethanisches Theater:* Daß die erste große Blütezeit eines neuzeitlichen Theaters an den Namen einer Herrscherin geknüpft ist, soll uns nicht an den literarischen Beitrag Elisabeths, die erste engl. Übersetzung einer lat. Tragödie, sondern an die weltpolitische Dimension dieses Vorgangs erinnern, der sich unter ihrer Herrschaft (1558–1603), die England zur Weltmacht aufsteigen läßt, und unter dem Protektorat des Hofes, der die führenden Truppen gegen die Schikanen der puritanischen Stadtbehörden abschirmt, ereignet. Auch als Vermittler zwischen den Humanisten und dem aufstrebenden Bürgertum spielt der Hof eine wichtige Rolle, während der neue Stand des Berufsschauspielers sich schon durch sein wechselndes Publikum, den Hof und das Volk, auf einen Ausgleich zwi-

676 Neuzeit/Theater der Neuzeit

schen der volkstümlichen Überlieferung und den humanistischen Errungenschaften in Form und Sprache verwiesen sieht.

Grundpfeiler dieses ersten Theaters aus dem Geist der Neuzeit: die Entdeckung des tragischen Individuums und die der nationalen Geschichte. Während der antike Held «als tragischer Held immer der gleiche» (Benjamin) war, ist die Tragödie Shakespeares (1564–1616) nicht Verhandlung über den Menschen, sondern Handlung, Schau-Spiel, Enthüllung des Lebens ganz als sinnliche Wirklichkeit, als atemberaubend, im kunstvollen Wechselspiel von Aktion und Reaktion Zeit und Raum durcheilende Begebenheit. Goethe attestiert Shakespeare «die erste große Verknüpfung des Wollens (das im modernen ‹sogenannten Drama› dominiere) und (des die antike Tragödie beherrschenden) Sollens im individuellen Charakter.» Die Mehrdeutigkeit, die der Person – als wollender Mensch und sollender Charakter – zuwächst, erzwingt eine neue Konzeption des Dramas, die (so Herder) nicht auf das «Eine der Handlung», sondern «auf das Ganze eines Ereignisses» hinarbeitet, nicht analytische Stringenz intendiert, sondern die Intensität und Dynamik des sich exponierenden Lebens.

Schon die erste engl. Blankvers-Tragödie, der *Gorboduc* (1560), behandelt einen sagenhaften Stoff aus der engl. Vorgeschichte, wenngleich nahezu statisch im rhetorischen Stil des Seneca: als eine handlungsarme Demonstration humanistischer Wortkunst in Nachbildung der tradierten Redetypen wie Klage-, Fluch- oder Preisrede. Wie wurde aus diesem Gefüge blockartig aneinandergereihter Monologe die kunstvoll verschlungene, in exzentrischen Situationen und grausigen Effekten schwelgende Handlung schon eines Thomas Kyd (1558–94, *Spanische Tragödie* um 1586)? Die Berufsschauspieler haben – als Auftraggeber oder Stückeschreiber – das Heft in die Hand genommen, und schon Kyd schreibt mit dem Blick auf ihre (am Publikum getesteten) Forderungen, im Einklang wiederum mit Seneca und einem Katharsis-Verständnis, das durch die Häufung des Schrecklichen an den Anblick des Leids gewöhnen und zur Gelassenheit erziehen will. Bei Kyd, vor allem bei Christopher Marlowe (1564–93) verschmelzen rhetorisches Drama und Handlungsdrama, erhält die rhetorische Tragödie ihren Helden in Gestalt des selbstherrlichen Tatmenschen jenseits von Gut und Böse. Sein schrankenloser Individualismus freilich kann Shakespeares letztes Wort nicht sein, so sehr *Richard III.*, die Inkarnation des Bösen, die zugrunde geht, ohne zu bereuen, Marlowes Helden noch nahesteht.

Kontinentale Einflüsse, insbesondere die pastorale Mode, beeinflussen auch die zunächst aus volkstümlichen Spielformen wie der Moralität oder dem Interludium gespeiste Komödie. Meister des preziös-verschnörkelten →Schäferspiels, das bei Hofe zunächst ein Privileg der halbwüchsigen Chorknaben war, ist John Lyly (um 1554–1606). Halb fasziniert, halb amüsiert von Lylys verstiegener Wortakrobatik, hat Shakespeare sie in seiner Komödie *Verlorene Liebesmüh* teils imitiert, teils parodiert. Lylys Figuren haben nur eine Zunge, Shakespeare gibt den seinen ein Gesicht und eine Seele, ohne sie aus dem luftigen Zwischenreich von Poesie und Narretei in eine verifizierbare Wirklichkeit hinabzustoßen.

Die ersten festen Theatergebäude vor den Toren Londons (1576 «The Theatre») erinnern in Form und Anlage noch an die Behelfsbühnen in rechteckig angelegten, mit Galerien zum Hof versehenen Gasthäusern bzw. Tierkampfarenen. Bei den sechs bis 1600 noch folgenden Bauten – darunter der «Globus» (→Globe) der Brüder Burbage (1599), zu dessen Teilhabern auch Shakespeare zählt – sollte sich die Grundform nur unwesentlich ändern: ein kreisähnliches Vieleck mit Galerien, einem nicht überdachten Hof (dem Stehparkett: pit), dem teilüberdachten, ca. 100 qm großen rechteckigen Podium und dem in Höhe und Ausdehnung von Mal zu Mal aufwendigeren tiring-house (Bühnenhaus), das eine (vermutlich) wenig benutzte Hinterbühne (inner-stage) für überraschende discoveries, eine Oberbühne und in der Dachhütte eine komplizierte Maschinerie enthält. Durch eine große und mehrere kleine Versenkungen auf der Vorderbühne können Darsteller verschwinden, aber auch Requisiten und Versatzstücke (ein Grabstein, eine Rednertribüne) auf die ca. 1,20 m hohe Plattform gehoben werden. Zur Hauptsache aber ist die Zeit- und Ortsbestimmung Sache des Worts, der ‹gesprochenen Kulissen›, auf die sich Shakespeare so meisterhaft versteht.

Sprachlich-dramaturgische Stilelemente wie →Prolog und Epilog, Rede, Lied oder Chorus gelangen auf einer drei-, wo nicht allseitig von Zuschauern umgebenen Raumbühne, die den Schauplatz nach Belieben konkretisieren, aber auch (etwa im Monolog oder Beiseite) wieder neutralisieren kann, erst in bestimmten räumlichen Positionen zur Wirkung: Je näher zum Publikum ein Passus gesprochen wird, desto unzweideutiger versteht er sich als ‹epische› Information, als spöttischer oder skeptischer Kommentar an die Adresse der Zuschauer. Die Mittel, mit denen eine Figur sich aus der Gesprächssituation löst und den Publikumsbezug verstärkt (Wortspiel, Anachronismus etc.), lassen sich überwiegend auf die Randzone der elisabethanischen Bühne als den Zwischenbereich von Fiktion und Wirklichkeit lokalisieren, der insbesondere den «fools», Dienern und kleinen Leuten vorbehalten ist.

Bestanden die frühen →Wandertruppen meist nur aus vier Männern und einem Knaben (für alle Frauenrollen), so zählen die führenden Truppen um die Jahrhundertwende an die 30 Mitarbeiter: acht bis zwölf der Truppe als Teilhaber fest verbundene Schauspieler, etliche angestellte Akteure, die Lehrlinge (Frauenrollen), dazu Musiker und Hilfskräfte. Der Truppe des →Lord Chamberlain, der auch Shakespeare angehört,

678 Neuzeit / Theater der Neuzeit

gelingt es in den späten 90er Jahren, die → Admirals-Truppe im Ansehen (und in der Zahl der Aufführungen bei Hofe) zu überflügeln. Seit 1603 darf sie sich «King's men» nennen. Für die Wintermonate steht ihr seit 1608 im Blackfriars auch ein überdachtes Theater zur Verfügung (das freilich nur einen Bruchteil der mehr als 2000 Zuschauer faßt, die man für die «public theatres» errechnete). In den «private theatres», vor allem aber den höfischen Aufführungen (Bankettsaal von Whitehall) beginnt schon zu Lebzeiten Shakespeares die Unterwanderung der elisabethanischen Bühne durch die perspektivische Bildbühne, die Inigo Jones (1573–1652) als Schüler Palladios aus Italien einführte, in Zusammenarbeit zunächst mit dem Dramatiker Ben Jonson (1572–1637), der zu spät erkannte: «O Schaueffekte! Mächtige Schaueffekte! Die Beredsamkeit der Maskenspiele! Was brauchen wir Prosa oder Verse oder Sinn, um eure Unsterblichkeit auszudrücken?» Mit der Schließung aller Theater durch die Puritaner endet im Jahr 1642 eine große Epoche.

5. Auch in *Spanien* geht das *Siglo de Oro* (→ Comedia), die etwa zeitgleich mit dem elisabethanischen Theater einsetzende nationale Blütezeit, ziemlich abrupt – mit dem Tode Philipps IV. (1665) – zu Ende, umspannt aber immerhin ein volles Jh. Unübersehbar die Parallelen zwischen dem → Volkstheater hier und da – bei gänzlich konträren politisch-sozialen Vorzeichen: In einer Epoche der verlorenen Schlachten und Illusionen, des unaufhaltsamen Verfalls einer Weltmacht sonnt sich das Theater (und das span. Selbstbewußtsein) in Glanz und Größe einer ritterlich-heroischen Welt, die der span. Roman – Ideal und Wirklichkeit ironisch konfrontierend – bereits als leere Maskerade entlarvt. Eine ganze Nation ist dem Phantasieersatz Theater verfallen, an die 300 Truppen spielen um 1730, aber über die erste Stufe der anfangs provisorischen, dann fest installierten Podiumbühne in den Höfen der Wirtshäuser gelangt man (anders als in London) nur wenig hinaus: Eine Oberbühne (lo alto del teatro) kommt als Nebenbühne hinzu, eine Versenkung, Versatzstücke, Vorhänge, einfache Dekorationen und (wie in London kostbarster Besitz einer Truppe) ein aufwendiger Kostümfundus. Die Zuschauer dieser → Corrales genannten Theater sitzen auf Bänken unmittelbar vor der Bühne, auf seitlichen und rückwärtigen Tribünen und Galerien, das große Mittelfeld aber gehört den berüchtigten ‹mosqueteros›, deren keineswegs immer spontane Beifalls- oder Mißfallenskundgebungen über Erfolg oder Niederlage entscheiden. Frauen müssen bes. Eingänge und ‹cazuelas› benutzen. Besitzer oder Pächter der Corrales sind die geistlichen Bruderschaften, die aus ihrem Einnahme-Anteil ihre Spitäler betreiben, bis die Stadt Madrid (nach dem Vorbild Sevillas) 1638 das lukrative Geschäft in eigene Regie übernimmt. Gespielt wird wie in London am frühen Nachmittag. Ein Auftrittsverbot für Frauen (1596) kann sich nicht durchsetzen.

Wie die christliche Welt- und Heilsordnung in Spanien über alle geistigen Impulse von Renaissance und Humanismus triumphierte, so ist auch die einfache Form der span. →Comedia kaum Gegenstand theoretischer Debatten und schon bei Lope de Vega (1562–1635), der an die 1500 Theaterstücke aus dem Ärmel schüttelte, weitgehend fixiert. Die Einteilung in drei «jornadas» (Akte), die Mischung von Komik und Tragik, die Mißachtung der klassizistischen Einheiten von Zeit und Ort finden wir in allen Spielarten der Comedia, deren bekannteste das von Lope bevorzugte →Mantel- und Degenstück (comedia de capa y espada) ist. Zwischen den einzelnen Akten gibt man Zwischenspiele (→entremés), selbständige kleine Stücke mit Musik und Tanz, und Romanzen.

Auf dem Wege von Lope de Vega über Tirso de Molina (1584–1648) zu Pedro Calderón de la Barca (1600–81) gewinnt die Comedia an psychologischer Tiefenschärfe – auf Kosten ihrer szenischen Turbulenz. Das barock-kath. Weltbild, das die Welt als Theater und das Theater als Spiegel der Welt begreift, findet bei Calderón seinen reinsten Ausdruck.

Theater aber ist nicht nur Comedia, auch die Feste der Kirche und des Hofs drängen in diesem Jh. zum Theater. Als Calderón 1635 zum Leiter des Hoftheaters von Buen Retiro und königlichen Dramatiker ernannt wird, obliegt es ihm, die geistlichen Schauspiele (→autos sacramentales) zu schreiben, die alljährlich zum Fronleichnamstag mit großem szenischen Aufwand arrangiert werden. Die Ausrichtung auf das Wunder der Eucharistie, die Erlösung des sündhaften Menschen durch Brot und Wein als Christi Leib und Blut, charakterisiert die autos als Werkzeug der Gegenreformation. Da nur theologisch versierte Zuschauer das komplexe System der Glaubensbegriffe zu entschlüsseln vermögen, werden die andern durch ein beispielloses Aufgebot an himmlischen und höllischen Geistern, an Flugmaschinen und Verwandlungen entschädigt. Die Bühne (im Freien) ist eine Kombination von festem Gerüst und beweglichen Wagen (carros), die von drei Seiten an das Podium herangefahren werden. Ital. Künstler wie Cosme Lotti setzen (seit 1626) auch am Hof Philipps IV. (der mit der Schaupielerin Maria Calderona liiert war) die Perspektivbühne durch – zur Enttäuschung Lopes: «Meine Verse waren das wenigste», weil der Sinnenzauber das Wort überwucherte.

6. Die Polarität von paganer Weltlust und christlichem Stoizismus, ja weltflüchtiger Askese – als den alternativen Antworten auf das blinde Walten der Fortuna – prägt die barocke Signatur auch des mitteleurop. Theaters im 17. Jh. Hier Theater als Zierspiegel absolutistischer Macht, als festlich-repräsentativer Triumph des schönen Scheins über die fatale, in Spiel und Zeremoniell kunstvoll überhöhte Kreatürlichkeit – dort Theater als christliches Gleichnis vom trügerischen Glanz aller Macht und Schönheit (→Jesuitentheater, protestantisches →Schultheater). In

680 Neuzeit / Theater der Neuzeit

gebührender Distanz zu beiden das →Volkstheater der Wandertruppen (→Wanderbühne), die ausufernde Tragikomik der →Haupt- und Staatsaktionen.

Italiens Beitrag: die →Kulissenbühne und die Oper. Dem barocken Lebensgefühl, das sich wieder irrationalen Mächten ausgeliefert weiß, entspricht die Aufsprengung der Bühne in die Höhe und vor allem die Tiefe des Raums. Aus der Horizontalbühne wird eine Vertikalbühne, auf der göttliche, allegorische und mythologische Erscheinungen einen regen Luftverkehr unterhalten; die Querachse des Spiels wird abgelöst durch die Tiefenachse.

Mit einer Reihe glanzvoller Feste wird das Florenz der Medici im letzten Drittel des 16. Jh. zur Hauptstadt des manieristischen Theaters, das mit der Wiederentdeckung der durch Vitruv überlieferten →Periakten- oder →Telaribühne die statischen Bilder laufen lehrt. Spätestens für die Festlichkeiten von 1568, die Baldassare Lanci da Urbino leitete, ist die Verwendung von dreikantigen, um ihre Achse drehbaren, mit auswechselbaren Dekorationen bespannten Prismen erwiesen. Der Meister der Periaktenbühne und des manieristischen Theaters ist Bernardo Buontalenti (1536–1608), sein Meisterwerk: die vier Wochen währenden Hochzeitsfeierlichkeiten von 1589, die die Palette festlicher Spiele, Turniere, Maskenzüge um die neuen Elemente Wasser und Feuer bereichern – ein nächtliches →Wassertheater, das den Hof des Palazzo Pitti für ein Seegefecht zwischen Türken und Christen in ein Riesenbassin verwandelt, und eine brennende Stadt in einem der Intermedien, deren Verwandlungszauber im Verein mit Musik und Tanz die jeweilige Komödie zum bloßen Rahmen degradiert. Auch die Unterwelt mit Drachen und flammenspeienden Furien fehlt nicht. Als Figurine – in der Rolle des Arion – ist auch Jacopo Peri (1561–1633) überliefert, der wenig später mit seiner *Dafne* (1594) die erste (pastorale) Oper komponiert. Schon Buontalenti und sein Schüler Giulio Parigi achten auf strenge Symmetrie der beiden die Tiefenachse flankierenden Periaktenreihen. Der gemalte, die Spielbühne abschließende Prospekt riegelt die Tiefenachse nicht mehr ab, sondern setzt sie fort.

Zwei Theater, die Giovan Battista Aleotti (1546–1636) in Ferrara (1606) und Parma (1619) erbaut – das berühmte →Teatro Farnese, das erst 1944 durch Bomben weitgehend zerstört wurde –, bringen die Dynamisierung und Vertiefung der Szene zu einem ersten Abschluß – durch das neue Verwandlungssystem der Kulissen, flächiger bemalter Rahmen, die von einem beweglichen Schlitten auf der Unterbühne gehalten und in der Regel paarweise so miteinander verbunden sind, daß die zurückgleitende →Kulisse (von frz. couler = gleiten) die korrespondierende automatisch vorzieht. Der Abschluß des Bilds nach oben erfolgt durch die ebenfalls (in der Oberbühne) beweglichen →Soffitten. Die Bühne gewinnt erheblich

Neuzeit / Theater der Neuzeit   681

an praktikabler Tiefe, muß diese also nicht mehr primär durch die Künste der Perspektive vortäuschen. Da die Vertiefung der Bühne eine Verkürzung des (amphitheatralischen) Zuschauerraums gebietet, drängt Aleotti diesen in der Weise zusammen, daß er die hinteren Plätze in ein zweites und drittes (mit Rang und Logen versehenes) Stockwerk verlegt. Das Parterre kann auch als zweite Bühne benutzt oder mit der Kulissenbühne zu einem Gesamtschauplatz verschmolzen werden, der zur Eröffnung (1628) u. a. ein →Roßballett mit einer Seeschlacht kombiniert, wie das auf höfischen Festen (z. B. 1616 in Florenz) nicht mehr ungewöhnlich war. Als 1637 die *Pratica di fabricar scene...* des Nicola Sabbattini (1574–1654) erscheint, ist die Kulissenbühne nahezu ausgereift, und auch die höfischen Theaterbauten – wie das Wiener Opernhaus von 1667 – orientieren sich nun an Aleotti.

Der erste große Virtuose des neuen Instruments aber ist Giacomo Torelli (1608–78), der 1642 mit der Inszenierung der Oper *La Finta Pazza* die Hauptstadt der neuen Kunstform Oper, Venedig (wo dem ersten Opernhaus von 1637 bis zum Ende des Jh. neun weitere folgen), und ab 1645 auch den frz. Königshof erobert. Typisch für Torelli und vorbildlich für seine Nachfolger: die Aufgliederung der zentralen (auf den Herrscher in Parkett oder Loge zulaufenden) Bildachse in zwei oder drei Tiefenfluchten.

Mit Ludovico Burnacini (1636–1707), dem überragenden Repräsentanten der hochbarocken Bühnenarchitektur, der von 1652 bis 1707 an der Wiener Hofoper tätig ist, verlagert sich der künstlerische Schwerpunkt nach Wien. Die ausschweifende, vom Betrachter kaum verifizierbare Fülle malerisch-architektonischer Schnörkel steht im schroffen Kontrast zur strengen Linienführung Torellis, die über das architektonisch Realisierbare nie hinausgeht. Neu gegenüber der zweigeteilten Bühne Torellis ist ihre Dreiteilung in zwei praktikable Zonen mit je fünf Kulissenpaaren und einen unbegehbaren Schauraum mit dem Prospekt.

Unter den wenigen nichtital. Bühnengestaltern von Rang seien herausgehoben Joh. Oswald Harms (1643–1708), der anfangs in Dresden, dann an den führenden Häusern der dt. Oper in Braunschweig und Hamburg (erste Bürgeroper nach venezianischem Vorbild 1678–1738) tätig ist, und der Franzose Jean Bérain (1638–1711), der die Abkehr der frz. Opernbühne vom ital. Vorbild einleitet mit Räumen von klassizistischer Klarheit auf einer deutlich abgeflachten, in der Tiefe verriegelten Bühne. Um so reicher, schöner, phantasievoller auch bei ihm (wie bei Shakespeare und den Spaniern) die Kostüme – als Elemente nicht der Dekoration, sondern der bewegten Darstellung.

Ein wichtiger Schritt hin zum Guckkasten, zur Trennung der Raumsysteme Bühne und Zuschauerraum – die freilich durch den architektonischen Charakter auch der Dekoration noch verklammert bleiben – vollzieht sich zu Beginn des 18. Jh. entweder durch eine seitliche Verschiebung der Raumachse oder aber ihre Drehung um 45 Grad, die eine Diagonal- statt der Zentralperspektive ergibt. In beiden Fällen bekommt der einsehbare Bühnenraum den Charakter eines unvollständigen, zufälligen Ausschnitts. Bei Giuseppe Galli-Bibiena (1696–1757) führt die neue (seinem Vater Ferdinando zugeschriebene) Achsenordnung durch Anwendung eines spitzeren Winkels zur Auflösung jeder überschaubaren Raumordnung. Im Bühnenportal überschneiden sich zwei unterschiedliche Raumsysteme: «Der Zuschauer blickt in eine andere Welt, von der das Bühnenbild einen scheinbar zufälligen Ausschnitt bildet» (D. Frey). Haltung und Bewegung der Darsteller sind auf der barocken Opernbühne geprägt durch die Positionen und Pas des frz. Balletts, das höfische Zeremoniell und eine ausladende, im Körpergleichgewicht kunstvoll ausbalancierte Gebärdensprache.

7. Die Geschichte des gegenreformatorischen *Ordenstheaters* umfaßt ca. zwei Jh. – von der ersten großen Aufführung der Jesuiten in Wien 1555 bis zum Verbot weiterer Aufführungen durch Maria Theresia 1768. Neben den Jesuiten entfalten zumal die Benediktiner (mit den Schwerpunkten Salzburg und Kremsmünster) eine reiche Spielpraxis. An poln. oder ung. Jesuitengymnasien wird auch in der Landessprache gespielt, generell aber ist gerade das Festhalten am lat. Text der Motor einer konsequenten, im Zusammenwirken der Farben, Klänge und Maschinenkünste mit der Oper wetteifernden Theatralisierung des geistlichen Dramas im Dienst der propaganda fidei. An die Stelle großer Freilichtaufführungen tritt um die Jahrhundertwende mit der Errichtung fester (Aula-)Bühnen ein im Kollegienkalender verankerter Theaterbetrieb, der in der öffentlichen «Schlußkomödie» gipfelt, für die der Leiter der obersten Klasse, der rhetorica, als Autor und Regisseur verantwortlich ist. Nach dem hochbarocken Schema eröffnen eine musikalische Einleitung und eine pantomimische oder getanzte Inhaltsvorschau (scena muta) das Spiel, das jeden Akt mit einer allegorischen Szene beschließt, aber auch zwischen den Akten mit Interludien und Balletten aufwartet. Schon Jakob Bidermann (1578–1639), dessen Comico-Tragoedia vom hoffärtigen, verdammten und bekehrten Gelehrten *Cenodoxus* (1609) die Entwicklung krönt, arbeitet mit einem sehr beweglichen Bühnentypus (mit symmetrisch zweigeteilter Hinterbühne). Im regelmäßigen Wechsel von kurzer und tiefer (durch einen Mittelvorhang verschließbarer) Bühne verwandelt auch Nicolaus Avancini (1612–86) in seiner vom Hof finanzierten Wiener Aufführung der *Pietas victrix* (1659) die Szenerie, nun aber bereits auf einer perfekten Kulissenbühne, auf der er alle Register seiner mehr inszenatorischen als literarischen Virtuosität ziehen kann.

Auf seinem Höhepunkt in den 60er Jahren des 17. Jh. verfügt auch das *protestantische → Schultheater* in Schlesien (Breslau und an den Höfen der

Neuzeit / Theater der Neuzeit   **683**

Piasten) über die zweiteilige Kulissenbühne, die im Wechsel von Vorder-
und Hinterbühne (die durch den «Schnurrahmen» des Mittelprospekts
separiert werden) bespielt wird. Der Primat des Wortes, die Sprachkraft
eines Andreas Gryphius (1616–64) zumal, die der starren Form des
Alexandriner-Dramas das Äußerste an lyrischer Bewegtheit abgewinnt,
wie auch die bescheideneren Mittel der Veranstalter setzen der Ver-
operung enge Grenzen, so sehr dann auch bei Daniel Casper von Lohenstein (1635–83) und Johann Christian Hallmann (1640–1704) die flim-
mernde Metaphorik des Wortes zur Entgrenzung in Klang und Farben
tendiert und die Sprache «von innen aus zur Oper drängt als der irrationalen Ausdrucksform ihres... antithetischen Lebensgefühls» (P. Hanka-
mer). Das höfisch-weltliche Ethos, nach dem die Zeit nun verlangt, ist –
in der Musik schon ästhetische Realität – noch nicht sagbar.

   8. *Berufskomödianten.* Die ersten engl. Komödianten (sechs Mann und
ein Knabe), die 1586 am Hof von Kopenhagen und danach in kursächsi-
chem Dienst auftreten, werden im Kostgeldregister als Instrumentisten
und Springer geführt und bedienen sich weniger ihrer Muttersprache als
der übernationalen Sprachen Musik und Artistik. An ihrer Spitze: William Kempe (†1603), nachmals Clown der Truppe Shakespeares. Aber
auch als dann größere Truppen aufkreuzen wie die Robert Brownes, die
1592 zur Frankfurter Messe u. a. Stücke von (nach) Marlowe aufführt, hat
das elisabethanische Drama keine reale Chance, dem landessprachlichen
Theater neue Maßstäbe zu setzen, da umgekehrt sprachlicher und geistiger Horizont des Publikums zur Skelettierung der Texte (von ohnehin
fragwürdiger Authentizität) auf den nackten Stoff, die vergröberte
Aktion und die bald ausufernden Aktivitäten des Spaßmachers nötigen.
Dabei verwildern die komischen Rollen zu festen, an den Akteur gebundenen komischen Typen – wie dem Pickelhering Robert Reynolds, der
1628 Brownes Nachfolger John Green ablöst und in seinem Repertoire
bereits die Verdrängung engl. Stücke durch die europ. Schäfermode und
höfisch-galante Stoffe romanischer Herkunft dokumentiert. Um überall
‹anzukommen›, muß der wandernde Pickelhering gesichtslos bleiben,
kann er – im Unterschied zum österr. Hanswurst – nirgends Wurzeln
schlagen und zur Persönlichkeit ausreifen.

   Schon um die Jahrhundertwende wird die engl. schrittweise durch die
dt. Sprache verdrängt, und auch der Nachwuchs rekrutiert sich zunehmend aus einheimischen Kräften, darunter nach dem 30jährigen Krieg
auch die ersten Schauspielerinnen und zahlreiche Studenten. Die Truppe
des Carl Andreas Paulsen spielt nach der Jahrhundertmitte nicht nur
Faust und *Hamlet* und die Haupt- und Staatsaktionen span. Ursprungs,
sondern auch zwei Komödien Molières, sein Schwiegersohn, der Magister Johannes Velten (1640–92), auch einen *Papinian* nach Gryphius.
Seßhaft wird das Berufstheater in den Niederlanden schon 1638 in De

Amsterdamsche Stadsschouwburg, die mit der Alexandriner-Tragödie *Gysbreght van Aemstel* des auch für Gryphius vorbildlichen Joost van den Vondel (1587–1679) eröffnet wird. Als die Truppe des Joh. Christian Kunst 1702 den russ. Hof mit dem westeurop. Theater bekannt macht, läßt ihr Peter I. in Moskau ein eigenes Komödienhaus errichten.

Die Bühne der Wandertruppen gleicht sich im 17. Jh. zunächst der durch die Mittelgardine zweigeteilten Schulbühne an. Wo ein höfischer Gastgeber oder eine Stadt schon über ein entsprechend eingerichtetes Theater verfügt, spielt man gelegentlich auch auf der Kulissenbühne – bis dann 1711 der Wiener Josef Stranitzky als erster Prinzipal in einem für die Oper errichteten Theater (am Kärntnertor) seßhaft wird.

9. *Französische Klassik.* Das Zusammenwirken aller Künste bei den höfischen Theaterfesten von Paris und Versailles – wie den mehrtägigen «Plaisirs de l'isle enchantée» von 1664 – markiert einen Höhepunkt barocker Festkultur, das frz. Theater aber hat sich dem barocken Dualismus nach kurzer Übergangsphase (die in den Komödien Corneilles noch durchscheint) verweigert. Die Tragödienhelden Pierre Corneilles (1606–84) erheben sich über das bange Gefühl der Nichtigkeit und Vergänglichkeit aller irdischen Dinge zu jener Selbstbeherrschung, die sie auch zu Herren ihres Schicksals macht. Ein Sinn für Maß und Form läßt sie nach einem weltlichen Ethos streben, das den sinnlichen mit dem sittlichen Menschen versöhnt und sich insbesondere den staatlichen und gesellschaftlichen Ordnungen verpflichtet weiß. Die Möglichkeit tragischer Konflikte ist damit nicht aufgehoben, sondern erstmals seit Shakespeare zurückgewonnen – bei Corneille vornehmlich durch eine Skala der Tugenden, auf der die politische der privaten Moral übergeordnet ist, bei Jean Racine (1639–99) durch die Aufwertung der tragischen Leidenschaft, die nicht nur als Bedrohung des sittlichen Seins, sondern auch als Steigerung der Persönlichkeit erscheint. Wo aber der Mensch, der sich im Wort des Dichters offenbart, als das einzige Wunder verstanden wird, ist auch der barocke Maschinen- und Kulissenzauber entbehrlich. Das Festhalten an den ‹Regeln› des Aristoteles wie der Einheit von Ort und Zeit (mit der sich Corneille freilich ähnlich schwertut wie mit der Forderung nach dem ‹mittleren Mann› als Held der Tragödie oder einem ‹Schuld›-Begriff, der die Tat der Erkenntnis vorausgehen läßt) ist nicht Pedanterie, sondern Medium der Konzentration. Der Zuschauer ist nicht aufgerufen, sich mit Personen oder Ereignissen zu identifizieren, sondern wird durch die hochstilisierte Form, Schmuck und Pathos der Rede wie der Gewänder auf Distanz gehalten, damit er sich ganz auf das Für und Wider der Argumente konzentriere.

Corneilles wichtigster Vorgänger, der Schauspieler Alexandre Hardy (1570–1632), schlägt als Stückeschreiber von span. Fruchtbarkeit mit seiner Universalgattung der «tragi-comédie» noch allen Regeln ein Schnippchen. Er schreibt schon für die Comédiens du Roi in Paris, die 1629 unter dem Komiker Gros-Guillaume im →Hôtel de Bourgogne seßhaft werden. Als Corneille sich der Bühne zuwendet, hat Paris bereits ein zweites Theater, das →Théâtre du Marais. Beide haben einen schweren Stand gegenüber den Italienern, die schon um 1570 (Truppe der Gelosi unter Flaminio Scala) die Commedia dell'arte nach Frankreich gebracht hatten und in den 50er Jahren mit der «Ancienne troupe de la Comédie Italienne», der u. a. der berühmte Scaramouche Tiberio Fiorilli (1608?–94) und der Arlecchino Domenico Biancolelli (Dominique) angehören, im Petit-Bourbon Fuß fassen. Seit 1658 spielen die Italiener und die aus der Provinz zugewanderte Truppe Molières abwechselnd unter einem Dach, dem des Petit-Bourbon zunächst, seit 1661 bis zum Tod Molières (1622–73) im Palais Royal. Damit kommt es zu einer in Europa einzigartigen Symbiose, von der Molière als stückeschreibender Schauspieler nachhaltig profitiert, seit den 80er Jahren aber auch das bis dahin ganz auf die artistische Bravour der Körpersprache abgestellte Spiel der Italiener, das mit Szenen und Liedern in frz. Sprache auch der polemisch-satirischen Wortkomik eine angemessene Rolle zuweist. Damit beginnt eine Entwicklung vom puren Spiel zur literarischen Komödie, die durch die Ausweisung der Italiener 1697 (nach einem faux pas gegenüber der allgewaltigen Mme de Maintenon) nur unterbrochen wird. Denn als sie 1716 (unter Luigi Riccoboni und Dominique d. J.) wieder in das →Hôtel de Bourgogne zurückkehren, verstärken sie – schon um sich der neuen Konkurrenz der Forains, des Jahrmarkttheaters, zu erwehren, das seinerseits die →Commedia dell'arte-Tradition trotz immer neuer Verbote lebendig erhalten hatte – den literarischen Anspruch: Kein Geringerer als Pierre de Marivaux (1688–1763) liefert ihnen seit 1720 maßgeschneiderte (auf die Stars der Truppe zugeschnittene) Stücke.

Er verfährt damit nach dem Vorbild Molières, der aus dem Schauspielerpotential seiner Truppe und den überlieferten Typen insbesondere der Commedia dell'arte, die er aktualisierte und vertiefte – ohne die Dominanz eines hervorstechenden Wesenszuges aufzuheben –, eine neue Charakterkomödie schuf. Daß allenfalls sechs seiner 32 Stücke die Bedingungen der haute comédie erfüllen und Molière sich namentlich in der neuen Gattung der (höfischen) Ballettkomödie alle erdenklichen dramaturgischen Freiheiten leistet, unterstreicht, wie sehr er seine Stücke als szenische Partituren, nicht als literarische Texte verstand.

Nach dem Tod Molières wird seine Truppe mit der des Théâtre Marais im Hôtel Guénégaud vereinigt und 1680 auch mit der Truppe des Bourgogne. Aus drei Theatern wird eines: die →Comédie Française, das Théâtre Français. Eigentlicher Gewinner der Kurskorrektur aber ist Jean-Baptiste Lully (1632–87), der sich 1672 für seine Académie Royale de Musique das Opernprivileg verschafft und nach dem Tod Molières ins

Palais Royale einzieht. Lullys «tragédie lyrique» und die →«opéra-ballet» obsiegen als frz. Alternative über die ital. Oper. Aber die Geschichte hat ein Nachspiel: Die comédie en Vaudeville, eine pantomimische Komödie mit Gesang, die von den Forains als ein Akt der Notwehr gegen das ihnen auferlegte Sprechverbot erfunden worden war, mausert sich im 18. Jh. zur opéra comique, der Charles-Simon Favart (1710–92) schließlich ein eigenes Haus einrichtet. Sein Erfolg und der denkwürdige Triumph der *Serva padrona* Pergolesis (1710–36) in Paris 1752, der das Ende der heroischen «tragédie lyrique» besiegelt, sind so überwältigend, daß sich auch das théâtre italien (→Comédie Italienne) auf die neue Art von Musiktheater umstellt und 1762 mit der Truppe Favarts fusioniert. Selbst Carlo Goldoni (1707–93), dem in seiner Pariser Zeit ein Platz im Spielplan reserviert bleibt, kann dieses Einmünden der Commedia dell'arte in ein burleskes Musiktheater nicht mehr aufhalten. Er selbst freilich hatte der Commedia dell'arte auf seine, sprich: die Molièresche Weise ein Ende bereitet (nach hartem Kampf gegen seinen konservativen Widersacher Carlo Gozzi, 1720–1806), indem er die mittlerweile doch etwas vergreisten Theatertypen mit der venezianischen Wirklichkeit konfrontierte. Die Wirkungen Molières erreichen auch den hohen Norden, wo 1722 das neue dän. Theater in Kopenhagen mit seinem *Geizigen* eröffnet wird und Ludvig Holberg (1684–1754) mit 26 Komödien innerhalb von fünf Jahren in dieser Spur bleibt.

10. Vom *Klassizismus* zum *bürgerlichen Illusionismus*: Voltaire (François-Marie Arouet, 1694–1778), ein Mann der Tradition in der Liebe zur großen Form, ein Vorkämpfer des Neuen als Oberhaupt der europ. Aufklärung, in deren Dienst die Schaubühne zur Kritik an Religion, Staat und Gesellschaft aufgerufen ist, kann den Untergang der haute tragédie in Rückzugsgefechten gegen die Schau- und Spielgattungen (Oper, →Vaudeville, komische Oper), schließlich auch die neuen bürgerlich-sentimentalen Gattungen (comédie larmoyante, →bürgerliches Trauerspiel), denen seine Moral des Verstehens und Verzeihens Vorschub leistet, allenfalls verzögern. Den entscheidenden Schritt zum bürgerlichen Schauspiel, die volle Legitimation des bürgerlichen Alltags als Gegenstand des Dramas (im genre sérieux als ‹bürgerliches Familiengemälde›, mit tragischem Ausgang als tragédie domestique), leistet Denis Diderot (1713–84). Von Gotthold Ephraim Lessing (1729–81) verehrt, stößt er mit dem Postulat einer nicht mehr auf den individuellen Charakter, sondern den sozialen Standort eines Menschen («les conditions») ausgerichteten Komödie auf dessen Widerspruch, da die Fixierung auf die ‹Verhältnisse› die Forderung an den autonomen einzelnen, sich selbst zu ‹bessern› und andere durch sein Beispiel zu überzeugen, relativieren könnte. Statt einer Stufenleiter, die vom Typischen der Komödie zum Individuellen der Tragödie führt, propagiert Lessing eine Annäherung

der Gattungen unter dem Aspekt einer für alle verbindlichen, vom Charakter zu erbringenden ‹Allgemeinheit› (Nachvollziehbarkeit).

Zur Erweiterung ihres klassizistischen Formenkanons, insbesondere größerer, die ‹Schönheit› freilich nicht verletzender Natürlichkeit sieht sich auch die Schauspielkunst gedrängt, in den historisch-theoretischen Schriften der in Paris wirkenden Luigi Riccoboni (1677–1753), seines Sohnes Francesco (1707–72) u. a. Dabei verlagert sich der ästhetische Bezugspunkt von der Klang und Rhythmus regulierenden Formensprache der Musik zur Augenkunst der Malerei, ihrer Zeichen- und Gebärdensprache wie ihrer kompositorischen Symbolik, die eine wahre Manie sog. →lebender Bilder entfesselt, in denen die Bewegung zum Akt- oder Szenenschluß zum kunstvoll arrangierten Tableau erstarrt, das bis hin zu Schiller oft mit einer resümierenden Sentenz verknüpft ist.

Heftig umstritten in diesem Kontext die ‹Sensibilitätsfrage›, ob der Schauspieler in seiner Rolle aufgehen oder sie innerlich unbewegt aus dem erlernten Wissen um die äußeren Zeichen seelischer Vorgänge gestalten solle. Da er zur urspr. Sprache der (oft stummen, pantomimischen) Natur zurückfinden müsse und überdies mit sittlichen Forderungen nur überzeugen könne, solange er sich mit ihnen identifiziert, plädiert Diderot in den *Unterhaltungen über den Natürlichen Sohn* (1757) für eine intuitive, den Mechanismus der Regeln negierende Kunst, 20 Jahre später aber, im *Paradox über den Schauspieler*, für den seine Sensibilität beherrschenden, die Wesensverwirklichung nicht seines Ego, sondern einer Rolle anstrebenden Schauspieler, der die immer unvollkommene Natur zur Schönheit und Wahrheit der Kunst vollendet und stets die rechte Wirkung auf den Zuschauer im Auge behält. Lessing glaubt, an Diderot anknüpfend, daß sich der Mechanismus von Affekt und sprachlich-körperlichem Ausdruck bei einem Schauspieler, der die äußeren Zeichen halbwegs beherrscht, auch umkehren lasse und dann auch solche Veränderungen bewirken könne, die (wie die blitzenden Augen, die schwellenden Muskeln des Zornigen) nicht unserm Willen unterliegen. An der Comédie Française blockieren das Festhalten am barocken Kostüm – das erst bei Lekain (eig. Cain, Henri-Louis, 1729–78) und der Clairon (eig. Léris de La Tude, Claire, 1723–1803) durch annähernd historische Kostüme verdrängt wird – oder gar die erst nach der Jahrhundertmitte abgestellte Unsitte, Zuschauer auf der Bühne Platz nehmen zu lassen, alle Reformtendenzen.

Englands Beitrag zum Theater der bürgerlichen Aufklärung, die Begründung der rührseligen Komödie durch Richard Steele (1671–1729) u. a. und des bürgerlichen Trauerspiels durch George Lillo (1693–1739) mit dem *Kaufmann von London* (1731), findet auf dem Kontinent mehr Widerhall als im Lande, wo das Theater – auf dem Fundament einer breiten Tradition von Shakespeare bis zur aristokratisch-frivolen «Comedy of

Manners» der Restaurationszeit, von der Pantomime bis zum Vaudeville (herausragend die *Bettleroper*, 1728, eine «ballad-opera» von John Gay, 1685–1732) – mehr und mehr vom äußeren Aufwand und dem Wettstreit der namhaften Schauspieler geprägt wird. Unter ihnen erobert sich der bei aller Verwandlungsfähigkeit atemberaubend ‹natürliche› David Garrick (1717–79, von 1747 bis 1776 auch Mitinhaber und Direktor des →Drury Lane Theatre), «Mensch unter Marionetten», die unumstrittene Spitzenposition. Dem Kontinent voraus ist England indes nicht nur in der Vielfalt theatralischer Vergnügungen, sondern auch in der wachsenden Entfremdung von Literatur und Theater, dem Abwandern der großen Schriftsteller und des anspruchsvolleren Publikums zum realistischen Roman.

11. Mit einer strengen Literarisierung und Sozialisierung, die ihm der Leipziger Literaturpapst Johann Christoph Gottsched (1700–66) verordnet, begibt sich das dt. Theater um 1730 in die Schule des frz. Klassizismus. Das Bündnis, von dem sich Gottsched ein Instrument zur Popularisierung der sittlichen und kulturpatriotischen Ziele der Aufklärung, die andere Seite, vertreten insbesondere durch die Neubersche Truppe (1727–50), künstlerische Seriosität (spektakuläres Symbol: die Verbannung des Harlekin) und bürgerliche Reputation verspricht, hält nicht lange, ist aber nach Goethes Urteil überaus folgenschwer: Das dt. Theater erkauft seinen sozialen Aufstieg, die Ein-bürgerung, mit der Verbürgerlichung, mit einem faden, seine vitalen Kräfte lähmenden Konformismus. Verhängnisvoll schon die Schwerpunktverlagerung aus dem südlichen Deutschland, wo das Theater «eigentlich zu Hause war», in den protestantischen Norden, wo der Widerstand der Geistlichkeit «die Freunde der Bühne (nötigte), diese der höhern Sinnlichkeit eigentlich nur gewidmete Anstalt für eine sittliche auszugeben» (*Dt. Theater*, 1813). Daß die «Gottschedische Mittelmäßigkeit» sich in eine «vielleicht nie zu zerstörende Mittelmäßigkeit des dt. Theaters» perpetuierte, das Theater zur Kanzel verkümmerte, hat es selbst zu verantworten – allen voran seine stilprägenden Protagonisten Konrad Ekhof (1720–78, 1753 Gründer der ersten Schauspiel-Akademie innerhalb der Schönemannschen Gesellschaft), Friedrich Ludwig Schröder (1744–1816) und August Wilhelm Iffland (1759–1815), die «das Gefühl ihrer Würde auch auf dem Theater nicht aufgeben konnten» und eine penetrante Sentimentalität, eine «An- und Ausgleichung aller Stände und Beschäftigungen» inaugurierten, die das Theater nicht mehr auskurierte. – Daß Lessing, der auf dem Vergnügen insistierte (als «unzertrennlich» vom «Nutzen» des Trauerspiels wie der Komödie), mit der *Minna von Barnhelm* (1767) den Blick über den bürgerlich-literarischen Horizont hinaus «in eine höhere, bedeutendere Welt» eröffnete und dem Theater einen «spezifisch temporären Gehalt» zurückgab, hat Goethe rühmend betont. Das Scheitern der

Nationaltheater-Idee in Hamburg (1767–69) – wo weder die Forderung nach materieller noch die nach geistiger, durch die Person des Leiters garantierter Unabhängigkeit eingelöst wurde, aber auch der Egoismus der Schauspieler und das Desinteresse des Publikums bewiesen, daß «wir Deutsche noch keine Nation sind» – wirft auch Lessing, den kritischen Dramaturgen der «Entreprise», zurück. Mit dem wirkungsästhetischen (die Mittel des Dramatikers aus dem Zweck des Dramas ableitenden) Zugriff seiner *Hamburgischen Dramaturgie* entthront er die klassizistischen Franzosen, ebnet er Shakespeare den Weg und entwickelt er eine auf «Einfühlung» basierende Theatertheorie, die das Mitleid des Zuschauers als eigentliches medium humanitatis apologisiert: «Der mitleidigste Mensch ist der beste Mensch, zu allen gesellschaftlichen Tugenden... der aufgelegteste.»

«Wir haben Schauspieler, aber keine Schauspielkunst.» Ekhof, den ‹Denkschauspieler›, der die Kunst auf die Höhe der Wissenschaft heben möchte, die nichts dem Zufall oder der Willkür überläßt, der aber am Ideal einer durch Schönheit geadelten Natur festhält und die gestischen Schablonen und Posituren der frz. Schule nur vorsichtig verabschiedet, bewundert Lessing als Meister der Rede, der den Primat des Wortes im ernsten Schauspiel erneuert. Mustergültig die «Mischung von Feuer und Kälte», mit der Ekhof allgemeine Reflexionen und Sentenzen aus dem Spiel erst separiert, dann wieder mit ihm verknüpft. Friedrich Ludwig Schröder, der über Tanz und Pantomime zur Schauspielkunst findet, überträgt die realistischen Ansätze bei Ekhof auch auf den mimisch-gestischen Ausdruck und wird zwei Jahre nach dem Ende des Nationaltheaters (1771) im gleichen Theater am Gänsemarkt zum legitimen Testamentsvollstrecker der →*Hamburgischen Dramaturgie* – mit neuen denkwürdigen Shakespeare-Premieren, der Absage an die Franzosen und dem Eintreten für die dt. Stürmer und Dränger Goethe, Klinger, Wagner, Lenz. Daß er in den 80er Jahren (auch als Autor) auf die von Goethe beklagte allg. Linie selbstgefälliger bürgerlicher Familiengemälde einschwenkt, bezeugt eine nicht bloß vom Publikum erzwungene Anpassung des zum wohlhabenden Bürger avancierten Direktors.

Die Konsolidierung des Theaterbetriebs in festen Häusern, die Rangerhöhung und den raschen sozialen Aufstieg der führenden Schauspieler symbolisiert nicht zuletzt die Errichtung höfischer →Nationaltheater in Wien (Burgtheater 1776), Mannheim (1778), Berlin (1786), gleichzeitig auch in Warschau (1779). Schiller wagt es 1784, Lessings Hamburger Fazit umzukehren: «Wenn wir es erlebten, eine Nationalbühne zu haben, so würden wir auch eine Nation.» Immun gegen die aufklärerischen Reformbestrebungen bleibt nur das Wiener Volkstheater, das unter Josef Stranitzky (1676–1726), dem Schöpfer des →Hanswurst, schon 1711 im Theater beim Kärntnertor seßhaft wird. Unter seinen Nachfolgern Gott-

690   Neuzeit / Theater der Neuzeit

fried Prehauser (1699–1769) und Felix Kurz-Bernardon (1711–84) wird aus der vom Hanswurst unterminierten →Haupt- und Staatsaktion barocken Zuschnitts die anzügliche Stegreifburleske mit Gesang und die mit allem techn. Zauber der Barockoper brillierende →Maschinenkomödie, ehe der Wiener Wortführer des regelmäßigen Theaters, Josef von Sonnenfels, 1769 ein Verbot des →Stegreiftheaters erwirkt. Zu dieser Zeit aber hat Philip Hafner (1735–64) dem Volkstheater mit der →Wiener Lokalposse schon einen neuen Weg gewiesen, auf dem es unwiderstehlich seinem Höhepunkt unter Ferdinand Raimund (1790–1836) und Johann Nestroy (1801–62) entgegenstrebt.

12. Als Johann Wolfgang Goethe 1791 zum Leiter des neuen Weimarer Hoftheaters ernannt wird, ist sein Theaterinteresse nahezu erloschen. Friedrich Schiller belebt es wieder, ermutigt ihn, gegen das Theater der Kotzebue und Iffland – die in den 26 Jahren der Direktion Goethes 35 Prozent der Schauspiel-Aufführungen bestreiten – Modelle eines in Repertoire und Spielweise von Grund auf anderen Theaters gemeinsam zu entwickeln. Widerstand erwächst nicht nur aus der Provinzialität des Ortes (Weimar ist ein Nest mit 6000 Einwohnern), der Schauspieler und des Publikums, sondern vor allem aus der Schwierigkeit, einen an (antiker) Kunst und Literatur entwickelten ‹Stil›-Begriff nachträglich auf das Theater zu übertragen. Von Shakespeare, dem Idol des jungen Goethe, der ihn freilich nie (oder erst im hohen Alter) für einen Theaterdichter hielt und in Weimar nur entstellt zu Wort kommen läßt (Spielplananteil zwei Prozent, während Goethe und Schiller insgesamt noch 21 Prozent erreichen), führt der Weg zurück nach Hellas. Anregungen liefert auch das ital. Volkstheater, das Frauenrollen durch Männer darstellen läßt, die also nicht sich selbst spielen, sondern ein Kunstprodukt darbieten, das auch die Zuschauer stets als Kunst genießen, in einer «Art von selbstbewußter Illusion». Vorbildlich ferner die «gegenwärtige frz. tragische Bühne», die nach Wilhelm von Humboldts von Goethe publiziertem Bericht nicht auf den Darsteller abgestellt ist, der eine Rolle spielt, sondern auf den Deklamator, der für den Verzicht auf den immer charakteristischen (= subjektiven) Mimus durch die Melodie und den rhythmischen Fluß seiner Verse, durch malerische Attitüden und schöne Tableaus entschädigt und sich damit einem Ganzen einfügt, in dem Wort und Bild, Sinn und Symbol sich zur Identität des Wahren und Schönen verbinden. Jede rollenhaft individualisierende Darstellung müßte einen klassischen Text von der höchsten Stufe der Kunst, dem «Stil», auf die der «Manier» zurückstufen (auf der das Objektive noch mit dem Subjektiven verschmolzen, das Wesen der Dinge durch den Geist des Künstlers verdeckt ist). So ist es nur konsequent, wenn Goethe die Bühne «als ein figurenloses Tableau» versteht, «worin der Schauspieler die Staffage macht».

Die Kalamität des Lavierens zwischen den Stilen illustriert Goethes

Billigung zweier unterschiedlicher Sprechstile (in den *Regeln für Schauspieler*), der eigentlich klassischen «Rezitation», die den Zuschauer immer fühlen läßt, «daß hier von einem dritten Objekt die Rede ist», und der – den «Stil»-Abstand aufhebenden – «Deklamation», der rollenbezogenen, individuell gefärbten Vortragsweise, bei der der Schauspieler «jede leidenschaftliche Regung als wirklich gegenwärtig mitzuempfinden» scheint. Hier ist die Rücksichtnahme auf Schiller, seine aktionsreichen, psychologisch differenzierten Dramen evident, die anders nicht spielbar wären. Auch in der Körpersprache und der Bewegung im Raum (bevorzugt: die Diagonale) ist jeder Illusionismus – «als wenn kein Dritter dabei wäre» – strikt untersagt. «Haltung und Bewegung der Hände und Arme» orientieren sich an Maß und Symmetrie antiker Statuen, wobei sich die «obere Hälfte der Arme» (im Gegensatz zu den ausladenden Gebärden des Barock) nun an den Leib schmiegen und «in einem viel geringeren Grade bewegen (soll) als die untere Hälfte».

Um die poetische Freiheit dem Stoff gegenüber, die schon durch die sinnliche Präsenz einer dramatischen Handlung gefährdet ist, kreist auch die dramaturgische Diskussion zwischen Goethe und Schiller, die auf eine Episierung der Tragödie auf Kosten des Dramatischen hinausläuft, mit der sich Schiller freilich schwertut. Auch der Vers, der alle Charaktere und Situationen «nach einem Gesetz behandelt», leistet nicht, was sich Schiller verspricht: daß er alles «Charakteristisch-Verschiedene» in die Dimension des Allgemeinen emporhebe. So geht er denn, da auch die «euripidische (analytische) Methode» in der *Maria Stuart* (1802) nicht zum Ziel führt, in der *Braut von Messina* (1803) noch einen Schritt weiter: Er setzt auf den → Chor als «lebendige Mauer», mit der sich die Tragödie von der Wirklichkeit abschließt. Annähernd realisiert aber ist das klassische Stilideal am ehesten in Goethes Trauerspiel *Die natürliche Tochter* (1803), in der alles Vorganghafte, Zufällige, Individuelle zur transparenten Form, zu einem «Stil der lebendigen Standbilder» (Kurt May) überhöht ist. – Angemerkt sei, daß Goethe im Lustspiel, das in Weimar freilich keine große Rolle spielte, dem Schauspieler alle Fesseln löst und ihm das ganze (de facto eher spärlich ausgebildete) Register derbkomischer Wirkungsmittel anempfiehlt. Stilisierung also auch hier – nicht ins Schöne und Allgemeine, sondern ins Groteske, mit dem Blick auf die hierzulande freilich unerreichbare Commedia dell'arte.

Daß es Goethe gelang, einige Schauspieler «an ein gebundenes, kunstreicheres Spiel zu gewöhnen», wurde erkauft mit der Farblosigkeit des Ensembles. Der Tod Schillers besiegelt das Scheitern des Weimarer Experiments. Das klassische dt. Theater bleibt – anders als das in London, Madrid, Paris – ein lokales Ereignis, ja, eine interne, folgenlose Veranstaltung im Hause der Literatur, über die das Theater der Iffland und Konsorten zur Tagesordnung schreitet. Die «jungen Männer von Geist und Talent», die (so Goethe «bekümmert» an Kleist) «auf ein Theater warten, welches da kommen soll» – die Kleist, Büchner, Grabbe haben das Nachsehen.

13. Das 19. Jh.: Auf dem Weg zum Guckkasten, der dem Zuschauer eine in sich abgeschlossene Welt vortäuscht, behauptet das klassizistische Bühnenbild einen letzten ‹Kunst›-Vorbehalt im Sinne der «selbstbewußten Illusion» Goethes. Einerseits fordert auch Karl Friedrich Schinkel (1781–1841), der Meister dieser Ära, eine getreue Nachbildung historischer Architektur, ja sogar von Natur und Pflanzenwelt, andererseits gewinnt er durch den gemalten «symbolischen Hintergrund», der die tiefgestaffelte barocke Scheinarchitektur ablöst, eine reliefartige Spielfläche parallel zur Rampe, die in Schinkels Berliner Nationaltheater (1817) als neutrales, von Säulen eingefaßtes Proszenium eine Zwischenzone bildet, in der sich die beiden Welten von Zuschauer und Bühne überschneiden. Gegen die «Trödelbühne» des Guckkastens, die zur Abdankung der Phantasie führen müsse, setzt er auf die Klarheit, Schönheit und Symbolkraft der künstlerischen Komposition, die indes von kommerzialisierten Historismus der Dekorationsateliers schnell veräußerlicht wird. So gewinnt die flache Reliefbühne alsbald wieder an räumlicher Tiefe: Sie füllt sich mit Baum und Strauch, Möbeln und Requisiten, aber auch Treppen, Brücken etc., die der sich formierenden Regiekunst ein erstes Betätigungsfeld eröffnen. Seit dem Ende des 18. Jh. setzt sich, zuerst in London und Paris, um die Jahrhundertmitte auch auf der dt. Bühne die geschlossene Zimmerdekoration (mit Türen, Wänden, Möbeln statt des rückwärtigen Prospekts), seit den 20er Jahren die Gasbeleuchtung durch. Erst in diesem Guckkasten – der schließlich die Verdunkelung des Zuschauerraums erzwingt – wird ein intimeres Ensemblespiel oder jener zwanglose Konversationston möglich, den Laube am Wiener Burgtheater durchsetzt.

Die Blütezeit des Wiener Theaters ist eine Blüte von Volkstheater, das in den Schauspieler-Dichtern Raimund und Nestroy kulminiert, und →Burgtheater, das es unter Josef Schreyvogel (1814–32) und Heinrich Laube (1849–67) versteht, aus literarischer Not (die durch eine strenge Zensur noch verschärft wird) szenische Tugenden zu entwickeln: die des Zusammenwirkens bedeutender Schauspieler in einem Ensemble, das den Klassikern – die Schreyvogel in den Mittelpunkt rückt, als der erste halbwegs unabhängig praktizierende Dramaturg des dt. Theaters – nicht minder gerecht wird als der Konfektionsware (überwiegend frz. Provenienz), der Laube auf spartanisch einfacher Bühne seine besondere, ganz auf darstellerische Subtilität und Homogenie bedachte Sorgfalt widmet. So standhaft Laube an Schauspielern festhält, die das Publikum nicht gleich annimmt, so konformistisch trennt er sich von Autoren wie Shakespeare oder Goethe, die dem «weiter und feiner ausgebildeten» Ge-

Neuzeit / Theater der Neuzeit 693

schmack der Gegenwart nicht mehr entsprechen. Laube realisiert noch
einmal die Einheit von Werkstil und Darstellungsstil – aber eben im Sou-
terrain des Theaters. Als er seinen Hut nehmen muß, hat auch das Wiener
Volkstheater sich bereits in das Talmi-Wienertum der Operette zersetzt.
Ludwig Anzengruber (1839–89), der es auf den Boden der Wirklichkeit
zurückführen möchte, findet kein Publikum mehr.

Die Kommerzialisierung und Nivellierung des Theaters im scharfen
Konkurrenzkampf um die Publikumsgunst (= Marktposition) und damit
verbunden die Dominanz des Virtuosentums, die Emanzipation vom literarischen Drama hin zu spektakulären Mischformen mit Musik, Tanz und
Pantomime (bis hin zu zirzensischen Spezialitäten wie dem Hippodrama),
ein ausschweifender Historismus und die Verwilderung der Publikumssit-
ten und -ansprüche – diese Tendenzen prägen das engl. und frz. Theater
stärker noch als das auf gewisse Bildungspflichten vereidigte dt. Theater.
Aber während die Deutschen im idealistischen Bildungstheater (der
Schiller-Epigonen) einen Selbstbetrug kultivieren, mit dem sie sich die
Wirklichkeit vom Leibe halten, bewahren sich das engl. und frz. Theater
im Wandel der Moden die eigene Physiognomie und eine frappierende
Vitalität. – Die Aufhebung des Lizenzsystems (Paris erstmals 1791, Lon-
den seit 1843) bringt das ruhmreiche Théâtre Français (Comédie Française) im dritten, dem romantischen Jahrzehnt – das mit der Orthodoxie
der Regeln und Gattungen bricht – in arge Bedrängnis und läßt in London
die durch Neubauten auf 3600 bzw. 3000 Plätze erweiterten Lizenztheater
Drury Lane und →Covent Garden nach der Jahrhundertmitte einer mobi-
leren Konkurrenz erliegen. Das Théâtre Français verdankt seine Rettung
1838 einer jungen Tragödin, der Rachel (Elisa Rachel Félix, 1821–58),
während die Romantiker in Frédérick Lemaître (1800–76) das einzigartige Genie der schöpferischen Improvisation verehren, das (nach Balzac) aus dem schlechtesten Stück der Welt noch «eine rasende Sensation»
macht. Faszinierend aus dt. Sicht schon in den 30er Jahren das frz. Ensemblespiel – das Resultat von bis zu 60 Proben (während man in
Deutschland, so E. Devrient, «die schwierigsten Stücke mit 3 bis 4 Proben auf die Bühne bringt»), das sich in langen Aufführungsserien aus-
zahlt.

Auch in London geht man, nachdem Shakespeares *Heinrich VIII.* in
der Inszenierung von Charles Kean (1811–68) 1855 mehr als 100 Aufführungen en suite erreichte, zum →Long-Run-System über, das die Auflösung fester Ensembles (stock-companies), aber auch den Zerfall des (nicht
mehr konkurrenzfähigen) Provinztheaters zur Folge hat. Der kritische
Theodor Fontane rühmt die Shakespeare-Inszenierungen Samuel Phelps
(1804–78) im «Sadlers-Wells-Theater», einer «kleinen Musterbühne»,
die jenen «Sinn für das Ganze» hat, der den dt. Hoftheatern abgeht, während er gegen die berühmten Shakespeare-Inszenierungen Keans, deren

694 Neuzeit / Theater der Neuzeit

Aufwand und kulturhistorische Akribie nicht zuletzt den Meininger Herzog Georg II. begeisterte, da protestiert, wo die «Verkeanisierung» Shakespeares alles Leichte und Phantastische, etwa im *Wintermärchen*, «ins schwerfällig Philisterhafte» veräußerlicht.

In Deutschland gibt es kein romantisches, kein biedermeierliches oder jungdt. Theater (obschon nach dem Scheitern der März-Revolution 1848 die vormals jungdt. Autoren Laube und Dingelstadt als Burgtheater-Direktoren Karriere machen) und debütiert zwischen 1852 (*Maria Magdalene* von F. Hebbel) und 1889 (*Vor Sonnenaufgang* von G. Hauptmann) kein dt. Drama von literarischem Rang auf der Bühne. Gegen den Strom (der selbstgefälligen Mittelmäßigkeit, der Hahnenkämpfe um die Publikumsgunst) schwimmen nur einzelne wie Karl Immermann (1796–1840), dessen Düsseldorfer «Mustervorstellungen» (1833–37) gegen «die Dämonen des Gespreizten, Rhetorischen oder der hohlen Handwerksmäßigkeit» auf das konzertante Ensemble setzen wie auf die Konkordanz von Werk- und Aufführungsstil (Skakespeares *Was ihr wollt* 1840 auf einer Kreuzung von elisabethanischer Raum- und klassizistischer Reliefbühne).

Richard Wagners (1813–83) Vorstellungen vom →Gesamtkunstwerk münden konsequent in die Errichtung eines Festspielhauses mit versenktem Orchester und amphitheatralisch ansteigendem Zuschauerraum (Bayreuth 1876, nach Ideen G. Sempers).

Konsequent verfährt auch Georg II., Herzog von Sachsen-Meiningen (1826–1914), ein Schüler des Historienmalers Wilhelm von Kaulbach, bei der Umsetzung des malerischen in einen szenischen Historismus, der über die Keansche «Echtheit» der (von Georg selbst entworfenen) Dekorationen und Kostüme, der Stoffe und Materialien hinaus auch in der räumlichen Komposition den noch fehlenden Schritt zur dynamischen Massenszene im ‹realistischen› Raum vollzieht, indem er das halbrunde symmetrische Tableau durch kleine, bewegliche Gruppierungen auf ‹gebautem›, durch Treppen und Podeste gegliederten Bühnenboden ersetzt. Den Triumph einer in Sprache und Gebärde noch völlig epigonalen, in monatelangen Proben erarbeiteten Ensemblekunst konnten die →Meininger von 1874 bis 1890 auf Gastspielreisen in alle Welt durch entsprechende Aufführungsserien (allein 330mal *Julius Cäsar*) auch ökonomisch untermauern.

Von den Meiningern fasziniert, überträgt André Antoine (1858 bis 1943), ein theaterbesessener Laie, Gründer des →Théâtre Libre in Paris 1887, ihre Methode auf «la vie toute crue» des naturalistischen Dramas. Auch Otto Brahm (1856–1912, von Haus aus Kritiker) will als Leiter der Berliner →Freien Bühne (1889) unter Verzicht auf allen schönen Schein, ja alles Theatralische schlechthin, jene alltägliche soziale Wirklichkeit reproduzieren, die in Meiningen noch ausgesperrt war. Brahm

Neuzeit / Theater der Neuzeit   **695**

stützt sich nicht (wie anfangs Antoine und Stanislawski) auf das Potential «unverdorbener» Laien, sondern auf Mitstreiter vom Rang Rudolf Rittners (1869–1943) oder Else Lehmanns (1866–1940), die als «Menschendarsteller» (A. Kerr: «Dieses Haus ist kein Theater, sondern ein Menschenhaus») ein neues Ethos praktizieren: die Polarität von Hingabe bis zur Selbstentäußerung und Selbstverwirklichung in der Aneignung einer dramatis persona. Da dieses Prinzip Schauspieler voraussetzt, die «reicher» sind, als es die Rolle verlangt, die einen «Überschuß» (S. Jacobsohn) einbringen, der sich dem Publikum als Siegel der Authentizität unmittelbar einprägt, ist auch das Ende des Brahm-Ensembles vorgezeichnet: der Rückzug aus täglicher professioneller Selbstentblößung ins Privatleben (Rittner) oder die Sezession (A. Bassermann). Deren produktives Haupt: der junge Max Reinhardt (1873–1943), der die kreative Phantasie und Verwandlungskraft des Schauspielers rehabilitiert und revitalisiert. Als inoffizieller Regisseur übt Brahm – in den Probenpausen – angewandte Theaterkritik: Indem er Differenzen zwischen Rolle und Darsteller präzisiert, vermittelt er zwischen zwei Individualitäten, auf daß sie zu einem Dritten verschmelzen (das sich mithin bei Umbesetzungen verändert). Finden müssen die Darsteller den Weg dahin selbst. Da Brahm mit Hirn und Gehör inszeniert, alle optischen Reize aber – darin ein Anti-Meininger – nicht minder verachtet als jede darstellerische Virtuosität, hat er (so Jacobsohn) «zeitlebens nur ein Halbtheater geführt».

So ist denn nicht Brahm, sondern Konstantin Stanislawski (1863–1938, 1888 Mitbegründer der Gesellschaft für Kunst und Literatur, 1898 des «Moskauer Künstlertheaters») der Vollender des illusionistischen Theaters, das im Zusammenklang aller szenischen Wirkungsmittel alle Sinne des Zuschauers anspricht. Bei Stanislawski sieht G. Hauptmann 1906 erstmals verwirklicht, was er für seine Stücke immer erträumte: «ein einfaches, tiefes, gehaltvolles Spiel ... ohne jede theatralische Vergewaltigung und Konvention.»

14. Schon vor der Jahrhundertwende aber signalisieren Stücke und Aufführungen (von H. v. Hofmannsthal, F. Wedekind, A. Jarry, G. B. Shaw u. a.), aber auch Manifeste (A. Appias *Die Musik und die Inszenierung*, 1899) den Anbruch der *Moderne*, die Inanspruchnahme des Theaters für eine neue Literatur wie auch die Forderung nach seiner Befreiung vom Joch der Literatur. Mit der Zersplitterung der Avantgarde in Literatur und Kunst, der Simultaneität divergierender Stile und Tendenzen, vor allem der Entdeckung seiner eigenen Historizität, die, banal gesagt, *Julius Cäsar* nicht mehr als «römisches», sondern elisabethanisches Drama ausweist, erschließen sich dem Theater ungeahnte Freiräume, nicht nur im Rückgriff auf verschüttete Traditionen des Volkstheaters (Commedia dell'arte etc.), sondern bald auch in der Erweiterung des Horizonts auf fremde Kulturen wie das fernöstliche Theater (als einer ge-

stisch hochentwickelten Alternative zum verbalisierten und ‹privatisierten› westlichen Theater). Zum eigentlichen Urheber des Theaterkunstwerks avanciert nun erst der bis dahin eher handwerklich arrangierende Regisseur als der produktive Koordinator der neuen Freiheiten und Konzepte.

Sein erster genialer Prototyp – auch in der rastlosen Expansivkraft, die vom Drehbühnenzauber des *Sommernachtstraums* (1905) bis zur Stilbühne, vom Kammerspiel bis zum Massenspektakel in der Arena («Großes Schauspielhaus»), von der avantgardistischen Experimentierbühne («Das junge Deutschland») bis zum kirchlichen Weihespiel und den kulturpatriotischen → Salzburger Festspielen immer neue szenische Provinzen erobert – heißt Max Reinhardt.

Kindermann, H.: Theatergeschichte Europas. Bd. 1–10. Salzburg 1957 ff (mit ausführlichen bibliographischen Hinweisen).

Diedrich Diederichsen

New Playwrights' Theatre

Gegr. 1927 von u.a. John Dos Passos (1896–1970), Michael Gold (1893–1967) und John Howard Lawson (1895–1981). Den Millionendollar-Movies Hollywoods und den «smarten Immobilienmaklern, die den Broadway regieren», wollte man das Konzept eines «revolutionären, experimentellen, futuristischen» Theaters entgegensetzen (Dos Passos). Mit den Einflüssen des sowj. Konstruktivismus und Futurismus verschmolzen diejenigen des dt. Expressionismus und des populären Massentheaters der USA. Die wichtigsten Inszenierungen (1929 wurde das N.P.T. bereits wieder eingestellt) waren: Dos Passos, *Airways Inc.*, M. Gold, *Hoboken Blues*; Lawson, *The International*; Upton Sinclair, *Singing Jailbirds*. Das N.P.T. war neben der ‹Proletbühne› das einzige progressive Theater der ‹goldenen zwanziger Jahre› in den USA. Seine Rolle als Wegbereiter der ‹roten Dekade›, der demokratisch-sozialistischen Kultur der 30er Jahre, muß als hoch veranschlagt werden.

Fröhlich, P.: Das nichtkommerzielle amerik. Theater. Rheinfelden 1974; Knox, G. A./Stahl, H. M.: Dos Passos and the Revolting Playwrights. Uppsala 1964.

Dieter Herms

New York City Ballet

Die USA, die für ihr N. Y. C. B. George Balanchine (1904–83), den letzten Choreographen der →Ballets Russes de Serge Diaghilev gewinnen konnten, sind mit dieser größten und für Amerika charakteristischsten Ballett-Kompanie zum Auffangbecken und Abbild der geistigen Traditionen von vorrangig drei Kontinenten (Amerika, Europa, Afrika) geworden. Das N. Y. C. B. hat in präziser und kontinuierlicher Arbeit bei stetem Ausbau seines Bewegungsrepertoires die Stoffe und Ausdrucksgebärden der Zeiten ertanzt und gestaltet. Die Magie der Frühzeiten wird gehaltlich in Ballettkreationen ebenso bewältigt wie Mythen, Epen und Mysterien, Märchen, Legenden und Sagenstoffe der unterschiedlichsten Länder. Die Tanzdramen des N. Y. C. B. vergegenwärtigen Personalporträts, Regional- und Epochenstudien, interpretieren beeindruckend Urprobleme der Menschheit. Der Kreis dieser im Tanztheater zur Gegenwart werdenden Tragödien und Komödien wird erweitert durch →Sinfonische Ballette, Alltagsszenen, lyrische Bilder, das pulsierende Leben der ‹Staaten›, Strebungen, Ängste, Bedrohungen, abstrakt-formal ästhetische Gebärden- und Formationsspiele, Clownerien und Burlesken, Gesellschaftsspiele und Technikversionen. Diese Vielfalt der Aussagebefähigung und Weltverarbeitung lebt im Namen des N. Y. C. B. Mit ihm erobert das Tanztheater den ihm gebührenden Rang neben Musik, Malerei und Architektur zurück und strahlt auf ästhetische Prozesse allgemein aus, die das Profil der Zeit, ihre Gestaltungskräfte und Aussageweisen mitbestimmen. →Ausdruckstanz, →Modern Dance, Jazz Dance, African Form, Musical-Technik, Kubismus, Pantomime, Bewegungschor und den American way of life verknüpft Balanchine mit den Urformen der klassisch-romantischen Ballettsprache. Diesem unermüdlichen Arbeiter erschließen sich die variablen Bereiche, weil er sein monumentales Œuvre nicht im abstrakten Raum eines freien Componere ansiedelt, sondern als Tanzschöpfer und Tanzerzieher gemeinsam mit und für die Ausbildung seiner Kompanie gestaltet. Eine erstaunliche Musikalität, die Urbeziehung zum Tempo, die Erfassung der Senkrechten im Raum als der langen, offenen Linie des Körpers, der malerisch geschulte Blick, der das Kostüm reduziert und in den Farben und Schnittformen der bloßen Trikots Wirkungsträger erkennt, der Chagall verwandte Sinn für Urbilder, aber auch für deren letztes Maß – das sind die Idiome, die die Choreographien Balanchines und seiner Kompanie auszeichnen und ihn und das Ballett zur Geburt und zur Verwirklichung eines neuen Stils führen, dem *Neoklassizismus*, in dem sich alle Bewegungserfahrungen der Tanztechniken, des Tanzens und Choreographierens verdichten.

Mit der →School of American Ballet hat Balanchine sein Werk 1934 zunächst von der Basis her fundiert; denn ein künstlerisch ausgereiftes

698 Niederdeutsches Theater

Tanzensemble, in dem nahezu jeder Tänzer Solist ist, kann nur in einer angemessenen Tanzausbildungsstätte nach diffizilsten Methoden herangebildet werden. 1935 wird das American Ballet zusammengestellt. In der 1946 gegründeten Ballet Society bewähren sich dann bereits die Jahre ungestörter kontinuierlicher Ausbildung auf Grund minuziöser Lehrplanentwürfe.

Die Ballet Society leitet als Generaldirektor L. Kirstein (*1907). Als künstlerischer Direktor und Kodirektor stehen ihr Balanchine und J. Robbins (*1918) vor. Die Eingliederung der Ballet Society in das New York City Center for Music and Drama und damit auch die Umbenennung der Ballet Society in N. Y. C. B. ist dem großartigen Wurf des *Orpheus*-Balletts 1948 zu danken, einem Meisterwerk der Zusammenarbeit von Balanchine und Strawinsky. Balanchine reinigt die klassizistisch verfehlte Schlußvariante Glucks und gibt dem Orpheus-Mythos seine markante Härte zurück. *Orpheus* entfaltet seine nachhaltige Wirkung gerade durch den Abstrich aller Umhüllung, durch die Beschränkung auf den mythologischen Kern. Strawinsky folgt dieser Inspiration, der Minutage Balanchines, mit einer Musik, die gleichermaßen das eherne Gerüst des Stoffs in scharfen Konturen vorgibt. Die Reduktion auf das Einfache im Zusammenspiel aller an der Aufführung beteiligten Künstler führt zu einer in der Ballettgeschichte modellhaften, geschlossenen Werkgestalt. – Auf das Drängen von Balanchine und Kirstein wird für das N. Y. C. B. 1964 das New York State Theatre im Lincoln Center for Performing Arts erbaut.

Koegler, H.: Balanchine und das moderne Ballett. Velber 1964; ders.: George Balanchine. Tribut an den großen Choreographen. In: Ballett International 9 (1983), S. 9–13; Schmidt-Garre, H.: Ballett. Vom Sonnenkönig bis Balanchine. Hannover 1966; Wendland, J.: «Mozart der Choreographen». Zum Tod von George Balanchine. In: Ballett-Journal/Das Tanzarchiv 3 (1983), S. 8–13.

Patricia Stöckemann

Niederdeutsches Theater

Bis zum programmatischen Neueinsatz zu Beginn des 20. Jh. tritt niederdt. Theater zumeist in subliterarischen Genres und Typen auf. In den Zwischenspielen des 17. Jh. wird in einzelnen niederdt. sprechenden Figuren ‹dörperliche Tumbheit› verspottet. An frz. und ital. Vorbildern ist die Hamburger Barockoper (1678–1728) orientiert, deren nicht handlungsintegrierte niederdt. Arien und Couplets Vorläufer einer trivialliterarischen ‹Liedermode› sind. Seit Mitte des 18. Jh. gelangt in Hamburg die plattdt. Lokalposse zur Blüte. Nach 1848 wird Plattdt. zur Literatur-

Niederdeutsches Theater   699

sprache aufgewertet. Mit der kulturpessimistischen Sozialutopie des ‹Rembrandt.› Julius Langbehn (1851–1907) gewinnt das Plattdt. dann politisch-ästhetische Funktionen. So schreibt unter Einfluß der Heimatkunstbewegung Fritz Stavenhagen (1876–1906) u. a. die plattdt. Dramen *Der Lotse* (UA 1901), *Mudder Mews* (UA 1905) und *De düütsche Michel* (UA 1907). Hier wie auch in den Spielen nachfolgender Autoren suggeriert der plattdt. Dialekt der Figuren elitäre Volkseigenart. Initiator und strategischer Förderer ist Richard Ohnsorg (1876–1947), der mit dem niederdt. Drama das kleinbürgerlich-proletarische Publikum ‹völkisch› erziehen will. Ohnsorg gründet 1902 ein Laientheater, das 1921 in ‹Niederdeutsche Bühne Hamburg› umbenannt wird. Hiervon angeregt, bilden sich Anfang der 20er Jahre über 30 ‹Speeldeelen›, die sich zum Niederdeutschen Bühnenbund zusammenschließen. Im Zeitraum von 1920 bis 1930 gelangen knapp 200 plattdt. Schauspiele zur Uraufführung, rund 55 Autoren schreiben für das niederdt. Theater, das in der Weimarer Republik zu einer Schaltstelle wird. Mit seiner Führeridolatrie und seinem ‹Stammeskunst›-Mythos agitiert niederdt. Theater gegen den vorgeblich‹autoritätslosen› Parteienstaat. Die stereotypen Handlungs- und Figurenschemata können sich nach 1933 nahezu nahtlos ins faschistische Kulturprogramm einpassen. Viele Stücke sind der Blut-und-Boden-Ideologie verpflichtet. In Bruno Peyns (1887–1970) Kammerspiel *Lüchtfuer* (UA 1931) verübt ein durch Unfall zeugungsunfähiger Leuchtturmwärter Selbstmord, damit seine Frau an der Seite eines Freundes ihre ‹Mutterpflicht› erfüllen kann. Evident ist das faschistische Ideologem: Mit der Erniedrigung der Frau zum Zuchttier korrespondiert die Phantasie, die sie zum Objekt männlicher Verfügungsgewalt macht. August Hinrichs (1879–1956) Thingspiel *De Stedinge* (UA 1934) wird auf einer Kultstätte bei Oldenburg zwischen 1934 und 1937 vor über 30000 Zuschauern mehrfach aufgeführt. In Hamburg erhält die niederdt. Bühne 1936 eine eigene Spielstätte, wird – mit wachsenden Subventionen – zum einzigen plattdt. Berufstheater und trägt seit 1946 den Namen des Gründers. Ein dem ‹völkischen› Heroismus komplementärer ästhetischer Faktor des niederdt. Theaters ist eine zum besonderen Dialektmerkmal deformierte Komik: Die strikte Ahndung von Regelverletzungen und Ausbruchsversuchen gehört von Anfang an zur Effektdramaturgie des plattdt. Lachtheaters. Seit 1954 sind die Aufführungen des Ohnsorg-Theaters im Fernsehen ein Segment der Unterhaltungsindustrie. Gegenwärtig führen in Norddeutschland ca. 200 Amateurtheater und Spielgruppen plattdt. Schauspiele auf. 31 niederdt. Laientheater sind in zwei regionalen Bühnenbünden organisiert. In der Folge des ‹Medienwechsels› der Mundart zur Literatur- und Bühnensprache hat sich das Plattdt. auf dem niederdt. Theater von der Alltagssprache immer weiter entfernt. Die Versatzstücke aus anachronistischen Handlungen und komischen Worthülsen befriedi-

gen vor allem das Unterhaltungsbegehren der Zuschauer. Wegen des Miß-
verhältnisses von Spielbetrieb und Stückangebot ergänzt hoch- und fremdsprachige Boulevardliteratur das Repertoire: Indiz einer Krise, weil niederdt. Theater nicht länger politisch-idealistisch zu begründen ist. Es hat
nach 1945 lediglich kleinbürgerliche Normen festschreiben können.

Bichel, U.: Drama. In: G. Cordes/D. Möhn (Hg.): Handbuch zur niederdeutschen Sprach- und Literaturwissenschaft. Berlin 1983, S. 391–411; Lesle, U.-Th.:
80 Jahre Ohnsorg-Theater oder: Der mühsame Versuch, plattdeutsches Volkstheater ernst zu nehmen. In: TheaterZeitSchrift 8 (1984), S. 104–111; ders.:
Schwank. In: G. Cordes/D. Möhn (Hg.): Handbuch zur niederdeutschen Sprach-
und Literaturwissenschaft. Berlin 1983, S. 508–535; ders.: Von ‹völkischer Not›
zum Literaturtrost. Ein Beitrag zur Geschichte des niederdeutschen Theaters.
Diss. phil. Hamburg 1985; Richardt, G.: Zu Entwicklungstendenzen der niederdeutschen Bühnenliteratur in der DDR bis 1952/53. Mit einem Überblick bis Mitte
der sechziger Jahre. Diss. Rostock 1988.

Ulf-Thomas Lesle

Nô

Das Nô, Japans lyrisches Tanzdrama, ein komplexes Gesamtkunstwerk
aus dramatischer Dichtung, Gesang, Tanz und Musik, in dessen hoher
Stilisierung und weihevoller Stimmung ein halbes Jt. zurückreichende
Aufführungstradition nahezu unverändert bewahrt wurde, ist in seiner
heutigen Form Endprodukt eines künstlerischen Entwicklungsprozesses,
der im 13. Jh. einsetzt und um die Mitte des 15. Jh. weitgehend abgeschlossen ist. Während dieses Entwicklungsprozesses gelingt es einem der
vielen Zweige der *sarugaku* genannten (Volks-)Schaukunstformen des
frühen → jap. Theaters, sich von diesen anderen Formen zu emanzipieren,
zum sog. Kunst-sarugaku (*sarugaku [no] nô*) zu werden und sich schließlich zur noch heute geschätzten Form des ‹klassischen› Nô-Theaters zu
vervollkommnen. Entscheidend für diese Emanzipation waren mehrere
Faktoren: Die in dem *sarugaku* der Kamakura-Zeit (1192–1333) übliche
Form der dialogbegleiteten realistischen (sog. *monomane-*)Darstellung
wurde stilisiert und durch Einbezug von in Japans Theaterkunst traditionell höher geachteten tänzerischen und gesanglichen Elementen bereichert. Die Loslösung von Tempel- und Schreinfesten, der Hauptdomäne
frühmittelalterlicher Schaukunst, und die Hinwendung zu einem neuen
Publikum, dem (hohen) Schwertadel, führte zu einer Übernahme von
dessen durch den Zen-Buddhismus geprägten ästhetischen Normen, die
Inhalt, Stil und Selbstverständnis der neuen Kunst bestimmten. Hinzu
kam schließlich das Wirken genialer Künstlerpersönlichkeiten, die wie
Kan'ami (1333–84) den Gesangstil, damit auch Teile der Nô-Struktur

reformierten oder, wie sein noch berühmterer Sohn Zeami (1363–1443), in zahlreichen kunsttheoretischen Schriften die noch heute gültigen Prinzipien der Nô-Kunst formulierten: statt realistischer Abbildung der Wirklichkeit die stilisierte Darstellung des inneren Wesens; Formans dieser Darstellung ist das Ideal des *yûgen*, der ‹vornehmen Anmut› bei höchster Ausdruckstiefe, gekrönt durch *hana*, die ‹Blüte›, die ebenso für die künstlerische Vollkommenheit des ‹Nicht-(mehr-)Spielens› steht wie für ästhetische Gipfelpunkte der als ideal geltenden sog. ‹reizvollen› (*omoshiroshi*) und ‹überraschend Freude erweckenden› (*mezurashi*) Darstellungskunst.

Spätere Nô-Meister wie Zenchiku (1405–70), der das zenbuddhistische Element in der Kunsttheorie noch stärker betonte, oder Nobumitsu (1435–1516), der, selbst ein berühmter *waki*-(Nebenrollen-)Darsteller, durch Ausgestaltung der *waki*-Parte eine höhere Dramatisierung zwischenmenschlicher Konflikte erreichte, haben Akzente gesetzt, haben die durch Zeamis Werk in Kunsttheorie, Aufführungspraxis und innerer Einstellung des Spielers vorgegebenen Einsichten vertieft oder komplementiert, ohne an dem seit Zeami bis heute geltenden Grundkanon ästhetischer, aber auch praxis-, d. h. spielbezogener Normen zu rütteln.

Das Nô-Repertoire, das früher wohl etwa 3000 Stücke umfaßte, heute nur mehr aus einem Kanon von über 200 Stücken besteht, bezieht seine Stoffe aus literarischen Werken der Heian- (794–1192) und der Kamakura-Zeit (1192–1333) sowie aus Sagen und Legenden von meist buddhistischer Provenienz. Verfaßt wurden die relativ kurzen, als Libretto für die Aufführung konzipierten Stücke (unterschiedlichen literarischen Niveaus) überwiegend von den Nô-Schauspielern selbst; die Hälfte des gegenwärtigen Kanons stammt von Zeami. Das Repertoire wird neben anderen Einteilungen – z. B. *geki-nô* (‹dramatisches Nô›), versus *furyû-nô* (‹Tanz-Nô›) oder *genzai-nô* (‹Gegenwarts-Nô›), in dem ein Mensch die Hauptrolle spielt, versus *mugen-nô* (‹Traumbild-Nô›), in dem Gottheiten, Geister sich in einer traumhaften Erfahrung offenbaren – traditionell in fünf Gruppen von Spieltypen gegliedert, die sich hinsichtlich ihrer Stellung in der Programmabfolge und ihrer Thematik unterscheiden. Das aus fünf Stücken, die aus je einer anderen Gruppe gewählt werden, bestehende Programm, dem der segenbringende okina-Tanz vorangestellt wird und das durch die heiter-prosaischen Komplemente der Nô-Spiele, die sog. →*kyôgen*-Possenspiele unterbrochen wird, beginnt mit einem segenverheißenden ‹Götter-N.› (*kami-nô*), an das sich ein Stück aus der Gruppe der ‹Rachegeister›-(*shura*-)Spiele anschließt, das von Befriedung und ‹Erlösung› dieser Geister, meist toter Krieger, erzählt. In den Drittspielen, Stücken mit stark lyrischem Duktus, deren Inhalt oft Liebesbeziehungen sind, stehen Frauen – im Nô stets von männlichen Schauspielern gespielt, was die Bezeichnung *katsura-mono* (‹Perückenstücke›) für diesen Spieltyp erklärt – im Mittelpunkt. Für die inhaltlich stark heterogene Gruppe der Viertspiele gelten neben den *genzai-nô* die sog. *monogurui-mono*, die ‹Stücke der Rasenden›, als repräsentativ, in denen durch schwere Schicksalsschläge getroffene Frauengestalten vor Schmerz dem Wahnsinn anheimfallen. Das Programm wird durch die *kiri-mono*, (‹Schlußstücke›) beendet, in denen Dämonen und Geister auftreten.

Dieses normalerweise aus fünf Stücken bestehende, heute jedoch oft gekürzte Programm ist dreigeteilt in folgender (aus dem altjap. *bugaku*-Tanzspiel übernommener) Gliederung: *jo* (‹Einleitung›), *ha* (dreiteiliger ‹Hauptteil›) und *kyû* (‹Schluß›), eine Einteilung, die auch im Einzel-Nô wiederkehrt und dort dem dramaturgisch bedingten Zweieraufbau mit zwei Aufzügen (*maeba, nochiba*) in je fünf Abschnitten unterlegt ist.

Die librettoartigen Nô-Texte werden neben dem Chor von Hauptspielern (*shite*) und Nebenspielern (*waki*), denen gelegentlich noch ein ‹Begleiter› (*tsure*) beigegeben wird, in rollencharakterisierender Stimmlage im Rezitativ (*kotoba*) oder Gesang (*fushi*) vorgetragen. Die aus der buddhistischen Liturgiemusik (*shômyô*) stammende Melodik des Gesangs kennt nur acht Melodieformen, das aus Flöte, Großtrommel und zwei Hüfttrommeln bestehende Orchester gibt das metrische Gerüst. Grundprinzipien der Darstellung wie der Ausstattung sind Schlichtheit und Stilisierung.

Eine quadratische, 35 qm große, überdachte Bühne, nahezu unverändert seit dem 15. Jh., mit ständig gleichem Bühnenbild, gemalter Kiefer und gemaltem Bambus, begrenzt von vier Eckpfeilern, die dramaturgische Funktionen haben, gleichzeitig den durch die Maske im Sichtfeld eingeengten Spielern Orientierungshilfe geben. Ein Steg, auf dem der Auftritt der Spieler beginnt, eine Hinterbühne für das Orchester und die Künstlergarderobe. Ähnlich sparsam die Requisiten, selten gebracht und von hoher Stilisierung: vier Stangen eine Hütte, ein Blumengesteck ein Garten, der Fächer bald Flügel, bald Wasser symbolisierend. – Der Aufführungsstil, getragen von Andeutung, Stilisierung und Symbolisierung, zielt auf das Wesentliche. Jede Aktion des Spielers, auch der – überwiegend abbildungsfreie – Tanz, ist durch eine feste Zahl von Ausdrucks- und Bewegungsfiguren (*kata*) vorgeschrieben und festgesetzt, Sememe der Nô-Kunst: unterschiedliche Fußstellung charakterisiert die Rolle der Frau, des Kriegers, des Dämonen, ein Heben der Hand vor die Augen bedeutet Weinen, ein Drehen des Kopfes gilt als Suchen. Die Gesichtsmasken tragen keine individuellen Züge, sind Frau, Krieger, Geist, ihre ‹Neutralität› wird vom Spieler extensiv genutzt, sparsame Bewegungen nutzen das Spiel von Licht und Schatten aus, verleihen der starren Maske Leben und eine Ausdruckskraft, die zum integralen Bestandteil des aus Wort und Musik, Tanz und Spiel lebenden Kunstwerks N. wird.

Barth, J.: Japans Schaukunst im Wandel der Zeiten. Wiesbaden 1972; Benl, O.: Seami Matokiyo und der Geist des Nô-Schauspiels. Wiesbaden 1953; Blassen, W.: Die Bewegungseinheiten (KATA) des japanischen No-Spiels. Bochum 1987; Bohner, H.: Gestalten und Quellen des Nô. Tôkyô/Osaka 1955; ders.: Nô. Die einzelnen Nô. Tôkyô 1956; Gellner, W.: Die Kostüme des Nô-Theaters. Stuttgart 1990; Goff, J.: Noh Drama and The Tale of Genji. Princeton 1991; Hesse, E. (Hg.): No – vom Genius Japans. Zürich 1990; Zobel, G.: Nô-Theater. Tôkyô 1987.

Roland Schneider

Nonverbale Kommunikation / Körperkommunikation

Unter n. K. im weiteren Sinne werden all jene Verhaltensphänomene zusammengefaßt, die neben und außerhalb der verbalen Äußerungen in den situativ gebundenen Face-to-face-Interaktionen eine kommunikative Rolle spielen. Damit sind in der Regel auch die vokalen Produktionen gemeint, die nicht entsprechend dem Regelsystem einer bestimmten Einzelsprache produziert werden – etwa nichtlexikalisierte und nichtmorphemisierte Vokalisationen (Husten, Keuchen, Lachen, Stöhnen etc.) sowie die stimmlich artikulatorischen Eigenschaften der eigentlich verbalen Produktion (Stimmlage, Lautstärke, Sprechgeschwindigkeit, Rhythmus). Von dieser paraverbalen Kommunikation kann man die Körperkommunikation abgrenzen.

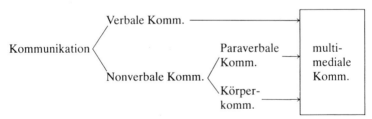

Insgesamt ereignet sich menschliche Kommunikation stets als multimediale Kommunikation, die sich – gleichzeitig – in den drei grundsätzlichen Medien, der verbalen, der paraverbalen und der Körperkommunikation konstituiert. Unter Körperkommunikation (oder nonverbaler Kommunikation im engeren Sinne) versteht man zum einen sowohl alle körperlichen Aktivitäten (Bewegungsfolgen, Haltungen, Zustände) wie auch die äußere Erscheinung (Kleidung, Schmuck, Haartracht) jeweils einer Person, zum anderen das wechselweise Einspielen von räumlichen Distanzen, von Formen der Körperorientierung und des unmittelbaren Körperkontakts zwischen zwei oder mehr Personen. Im einzelnen wird unterschieden in:

704 Nonverbale Kommunikation / Körperkommunikation

► Mimik: Signalwirkung haben im menschlichen Gesicht vor allem der Stirn-, Augen- und Mundbereich. Mimische Signale wirken besonders im Nahbereich. Auf größere Distanzen können die oft feinen Unterschiede im Ausdruck nicht mehr eindeutig unterschieden werden.

► Blickkontakt: Die Augen selbst haben auf Grund der speziellen Anatomie (dunkle Pupille vor hellem Hintergrund) auch einen visuellen Signalcharakter. Dabei spielen das Öffnen und Schließen der Lider, die Blickrichtung und -dauer sowie der Öffnungsgrad der Pupillen eine Rolle. Augensignale wirken im Intim-, Nah- und mittleren Fernbereich.

► Gestik: Auf Grund der dem Menschen möglichen (anatomisch bedingten) großen Freiheit der vorderen Extremitäten ergibt sich ein breiter Spielraum kommunikativ relevanter Gesten. Die hinteren Extremitäten haben dagegen nur geringe kommunikative Bedeutung, da sie zumeist funktional (für die Fortbewegung) eingesetzt werden. Ausnahmen sind Fuß- und Beingesten beim Sitzen.

► Körperhaltung: Damit sind Kopf- und Rumpfhaltungen, deren relationale Lage zueinander sowie Bewegungen des ganzen Kopfes oder Rumpfes gemeint. Signalwirkung hat darüber hinaus auch der Muskeltonus (Spannung der Muskeln). Gestik und Körperhaltung wirken sowohl im Intim- und Nahbereich wie auch im mittleren und weiten Fernbereich. Der Muskeltonus spielt vor allem im Intimbereich bei Körperkontakt oder unmittelbarer Nähe eine Rolle.

► Proxemik: Signalwirkung haben die räumlichen Abstände wie die spezielle Orientierung der Partner zueinander (Distanz, Zuwenden/Abwenden). Personelle Abstände differieren von Kultur zu Kultur. Grundsätzlich aber läßt sich das Raumverhalten in vier immer wieder feststellbare Zonen aufgliedern – Intimbereich, Nahbereich, Ambivalenz- (mittlerer) und Distanzbereich (weiter Fernbereich).

► Äußere Erscheinung: Kommunikative Wirkung kommt neben diesen motorischen Signalen auch dem Stil der jeweiligen Kleidung zu, ebenso dem auswechselbaren oder körpergebundenen Schmuck (Tätowierung), der Haartracht, bestimmten Körperbemalungen sowie Gegenständen, die mitgeführt werden oder mit denen man sich umgibt (Handtasche, Speer, Auto oder Wohnsitz). Äußere Erscheinung wie Kulturgegenstände wirken in allen Distanzbereichen.

Hinsichtlich ihres kommunikativen Funktionierens unterscheiden sich verbale und n. K. grundsätzlich voneinander. Verbale Kommunikation ist eine symbolhafte Kommunikation. Sie manifestiert sich als interaktive Sinnkonstituierung über konventionell festgelegte, diskrete Elemente (Phonem, Morphem, Lexem) sowie deren hierarchische Kombinationen (Satz, Text, Gespräch). N. K. dagegen ist eine indikatorische Signalkommunikation. Sie funktioniert über analoge Ausdrucksakte (Tonhöhenverlauf, Handbewegungen) und ist Anzeichen innerer Befindlichkeiten oder interpersoneller Einstellungen. Allerdings gibt es auch nonverbale Verhaltenselemente mit rein konventioneller Symbolbedeutung – sogenannte Embleme – sowie vollständige nonverbale Zeichensysteme mit Grammatik – etwa die Gebärdensprache Gehörloser. Dies trifft für die n. K., speziell die Körperkommunikation, jedoch nicht zu. Von daher sollte man den Ausdruck ‹Körpersprache› vermeiden. Die einzelnen Verhaltenselemente der Körperkommunikation lassen sich weder eindeutig lexikalisieren noch werden sie nach Regeln produziert, die denen der natürlichen Einzelsprachen entsprechen. Erst die verschiedenen Kontextzusammenhänge wie räumlicher und institutioneller Rahmen, mit der je spezifischen interpersonellen Beziehung (Situationskontext), der engere und weitere Handlungs- und Interaktionszusammenhang (Handlungskontext) sowie die Relation zu den übrigen verbalen und nonverbalen Teilakten im multimedialen Kommunikationsakt (Gestaltkontext) erlauben Aussagen über die besondere kommunikative Funktion eines bestimmten nonverbalen Verhaltenselements. So kann das ‹Hochziehen der Schultern› relativ zu den drei genannten Kontexten verschiedenes bedeuten: Ausdruck des Erschreckens oder Frierens, Submissionssignal zur Beschwichtigung oder emblematische Geste des Nichtwissens oder Nichtkönnens.

In diesem Sinne kann n. K. grundsätzlich als bloße epiphänomenale (physiologische) Begleiterscheinung emotionaler Zustände (Zittern, Schwitzen, motorische Unruhe), als ritualisierter Ausdrucksakt innerer Haltungen oder interpersoneller Einstellungen (sich in die Brust werfen, sich ducken) oder als symbolisches Emblem mit bestimmter Bedeutung (einen Vogel zeigen) auftreten. Epiphänomenale Verhaltensformen sind unmittelbar als Anzeichen innerer Zustände verstehbar, da sie auf angeborenen Verhaltensmechanismen beruhen. Ritualisierte Ausdrucksakte sind ebenfalls universal verstehbar, da sie als stammesgeschichtliche Anpassungen des Menschen in seinem Verhaltensrepertoire verankert, häufig dann allerdings kulturell überformt und spezifisch ausgeprägt sind. Sie dienen vor allem der Beziehungskommunikation. In ihnen läßt sich eine auf der gesamten Welt auftretende ‹hoch–tief›- und ‹rechts–links›-Symbolik nachweisen, in der sich die beiden zentralen Dimensionen interpersonellen Verhaltens, ‹dominant–submissiv› und ‹distanziert–intim›, ausdrücken (vgl. ‹eine hochgestellte Persönlichkeit› oder ‹jemanden links liegenlassen›). Embleme schließlich sind lediglich im Rahmen spezieller kultureller und subkultureller Standards verständlich. Verschiedene Theaterformen wie etwa das japanische →Kabuki-Theater, die →Peking-Oper, das klassische →antike Theater oder auch die →Pantomime machen unterschiedlichen Gebrauch von diesen Verhaltenselementen. Gerade das ostasiatische Theater ist gekennzeichnet durch eine Vielzahl emblematischer Verhaltenselemente, die den artifiziellen und professionellen

706 Nonverbale Kommunikation/Körperkommunikation

Charakter dieser Kunstformen ausmachen, wodurch sie für Europäer schwer zugänglich sind.

Von besonderer Bedeutung sind die verschiedenen Möglichkeiten des Zusammenspiels von verbaler und Körperkommunikation. Im Prinzip lassen sich drei mögliche Formen des Zusammenwirkens nennen. Das nonverbale Verhalten kann äquivalent (gleichsinnig/gleichbedeutend), komplementär (ergänzend) oder aber konträr (widersprechend) zum verbalen Verhalten sein.

Im einzelnen wird unterschieden in:

▸ Substitution: Dies ist ein Spezial- und Extremfall eines komplementären Zusammenwirkens, bei dem – etwa im Falle von Emblemen – das nonverbale Verhalten vollständig das verbale ersetzt.

▸ Amplifikation: Damit ist ein äquivalent-komplementäres Zusammenwirken im Sinne von Betonung, Illustration und Verdeutlichung des verbalen durch das nonverbale Verhalten gemeint.

▸ Kontradiktion: Hier handelt es sich um einen auch als ‹Kanaldiskrepanz› bezeichneten Widerspruch von verbalem und nonverbalem Verhalten.

▸ Modifikation: Dabei liegt ein komplementärer Zusammenhang von verbalem und nonverbalem Verhalten vor, bei dem das nonverbale Verhalten das verbale abschwächt und modifiziert, ohne ihm allerdings ganz zu widersprechen (etwa Ironiesignale).

Auch wenn dem Menschen ein reiches Repertoire an nonverbalen Signalen zur Verfügung steht, so ist der Bedeutungsumfang n. K. gegenüber der verbalen Kommunikation, in der letztlich die gesamte innere und äußere Welt thematisiert werden kann, grundsätzlich auf den Bereich der Beziehungskommunikation und der Interaktionsorganisation beschränkt.

Argyle, M.: Körpersprache und Kommunikation. Paderborn 1979 (engl. Original 1975); Birdwhistell, R. L.: Introduction to Kinesics: An Annoted System for Analysis of Body Motion and Gesture. Washington 1952; Eibl-Eibesfeldt, I.: Die Biologie des menschlichen Verhaltens. Grundriß der Humanethologie. München/Zürich 1984; Espenschied, R.: Das Ausdrucksbild der Emotionen. München/Basel 1985; Hall, E. T.: The Hidden Dimension. New York 1966; Molcho, S.: Körpersprache. München 1983; Posner, R./Reinecke, H.-P. (Hg.): Zeichenprozesse. Semiotische Forschung in den Einzelwissenschaften. Wiesbaden 1977; Sager, S. F.: Sprache und Beziehung. Linguistische Untersuchungen zum Zusammenhang von sprachlicher Kommunikation und zwischenmenschlicher Beziehung. Tübingen 1981; Scheflen, A. E.: Körpersprache und soziale Ordnung. Kommunikation als Verhaltenskontrolle. Stuttgart 1976 (engl. Original 1972); Scherer, K. R./Wallbott, H. G. (Hg.): Nonverbale Kommunikation: Forschungsberichte zum Interaktionsverhalten. Weinheim/Basel 1979.

Sven Frederik Sager

Norddeutsches Theatertreffen

Seit 1971 jährlich, seit 1983 zweijährlich in wechselnden Theaterstädten der norddt. Küstenländer, finanziert aus Überschüssen des Norddeutschen Werbefernsehens. Initiative des Deutschen Bühnenvereins, Landesverband Nordwest, und des NDR mit dem Ziel einer Kooperation von Theater und Fernsehen. Zunächst Verpflichtung des NDR-Fernsehens, vier von einer Jury ausgewählte Aufführungen aufzuzeichnen und zu senden. Seit 1974 ist dem Fernsehen überlassen, ob eine Aufführung aufgezeichnet wird und welche. Sendungen von Szenenausschnitten und Features über die Arbeit der beteiligten Bühnen. Die Jury verleiht bis zu sechs Geldpreise für «bemerkenswerte oder förderungswürdige» künstlerische Einzelleistungen oder Ensembles. Seit 1977 thematische Vorgaben, deren Berücksichtigung Voraussetzung für die Teilnahme ist. Ergänzung durch Gastspiele ausländischer Bühnen, auch alternativer Theater, Workshops, Fortbildungsveranstaltungen für Mitglieder der norddt. Bühnen.

Schulze-Reimpell, W.: Norddeutsches Theatertreffen 1971–1980. Hamburg 1980.

Werner Schulze-Reimpell

Norske Teatret i Oslo

Im 19. Jh. waren mehrere Versuche unternommen worden, die Selbständigkeit der norwegischen Kultur auch am Theater zu fördern. Folgende Gründungen fester Bühnen sind Ausdruck dieser Bemühungen: Det Norske Teater bzw. Den Nationale Scene Bergen (1850–63 bzw. 1872 ff), Kristiania Norske Teatret (1852–63) und Trondhjems Norske Teatret (1861–65). 1899 wurde in Christiania Det Norske Spellaget mit der Zielsetzung der stärkeren Förderung nationaler Dramatik gegründet, das hieraus entstandene N. T. stand von seiner ersten Saison (1913) an im Zentrum der Auseinandersetzungen um die Sprachfrage; während der in dieser Saison erfolgten Aufführung von Holbergs *Jeppe på Bjerget* in nynorsker Umarbeitung kam es zu handgreiflichen Auseinandersetzungen im Theatersaal. – Im Spannungsfeld der Auseinandersetzungen um die Sprachfrage erreichte das Theater ein hohes künstlerisches Niveau. Das 1914 aufgeführte Stück *Der Lehrer* von Arne Garborg (1851–1924) wurde auch im nichtskandin. Ausland zur Kenntnis genommen. Tolstoi und O'Neill wurden aufgeführt, auch das Stück *Daurgardsfolket* des dän. Romanschriftstellers Martin Andersen-Nexö (1869–1954). Hans Jacob Nielsen inszenierte 1948 eine *Peer Gynt*-Aufführung, der eine völlig neue ‹antiromantische› Deutung des Stücks zugrunde lag.

Ein eigenes Gebäude erhielt N. T. erst 1946; das ehem. Gebäude des Casino-Theaters in der Stortingsgate wurde übernommen. Im September 1985 erfolgte der Umzug in ein neues Gebäude in der Kristian IV gate. Hierbei handelt es sich um das größte Theatergebäude Skandinaviens; die Hauptszene umfaßt 800 Sitzplätze, die Nebenszene 200.

Dalgaard, O.: Det Norske Teatret 1913–1953. Oslo 1953; Sletbak, N.: Det Norske Teatret femti år, 1913–1963. Oslo 1963; Kiran, H.: Scenekunst. Til Det Norske Teatret 1913–1963. Oslo 1963.

Martin Kolberg

La Nuova Scena

Die 1968 von Dario Fo gegründete Theatergruppe ist die Nachfolge-truppe der →Compagnia Dario Fo. Mit der Gründung von N. S. zog sich Fo vom Publikum des sog. aufgeklärten Bürgertums und vom subventio-nierten Theater zurück und spielte seine Stücke fortan in Vorstädten, Arbeitersiedlungen, Fabriken, Gefängnissen und Gewerkschaftssälen. N. S. arbeitete als freie Gruppe und spielte ausschließlich für die ARCI, einer von der PCI gegründeten gewerkschaftlichen Kulturorganisation. Die Gruppe verstand sich als Kollektiv, dessen Ziel es war, jene politi-schen Prozesse in Gang zu setzen, die die Arbeiterklasse an die Macht bringen sollten. Stücke aus dieser Zeit sind u. a. *Grande pantomima con bandiere e pupazzi piccoli e medi*, 1968; *Ci ragiono e canto, No. 2*, 1969; *Legami pure che tanto io spacco tutto lo stesso*, 1969 – und vor allem *Mistero Buffo*, 1969, Fos bisher erfolgreichstes Stück, das Ergebnis langjäh-riger Beschäftigung mit der Volkskultur. – 1970 kommt es über Fos Aus-einandersetzung mit der offiziellen Kulturpolitik der PCI zum Bruch, das Kollektiv spaltet sich, Fo, Rame und der radikalere Teil von N. S. grün-den im Oktober 1970 das Theaterkollektiv →La Comune.

Fo, D.: Dario Fo parla di Dario Fo. Cosenza 1977; Jungblut, H.: Das politische Theater Dario Fos. Frankfurt/M. 1978.

Elke Kehr

Oberammergauer Passionsspiel

In dem oberbayerischen Dorf wird seit 1634 (fast) alle zehn Jahre ein →Passionsspiel aufgeführt; Anlaß: die Einhaltung des Gelübdes, das die Oberammergauer Bürger nach der Überwindung der 1633 wütenden Pest abgelegt hatten. Dieser Zehnjahresrhythmus wurde nur wenige Male un-terbrochen oder verschoben: 1770, 1815, 1870, 1920, 1930 und 1984.

Oberammergauer Passionsspiel 709

Zwischen Mai und September jeder Spielperiode finden ca. 100 Aufführungen statt. Jede Aufführung dauert vom Morgen bis zum Abend; umrahmt von Orchester und Chören mit der Musik von Rochus Dedler zeigten 1984 1700 Darsteller das Passionsspiel nach dem Text von Joseph Alois Daisenberger. Die Spieler sind ausschließlich Laiendarsteller aus dem Ort. Sie werden zwei Jahre vor Beginn der Aufführung vom Passionsspielkomitee in geheimer Wahl aus den Reihen der spielberechtigten Oberammergauer Bürger gewählt. Im Laufe der Entwicklung der Spiele trat neben die kirchliche immer mehr die finanzielle und touristische Bedeutung dieser Veranstaltung.

Unbekannt ist, welcher Text der ersten Aufführung von 1634 zugrunde lag; das älteste erhaltene Spielbuch stammt von Georg Kaiser aus dem Jahre 1662. 1674 erweitert (vermutlich) Michael Eyrl den Text mit Auszügen eines aus dem Anfang des 17. Jh. von Johann Aelbl verfaßten Passionsspiels. Ab 1680 wurde das Spiel auf die zehner Jahre verlegt.

Die Spiele fanden bis 1674 vermutlich in der alten Pfarrkirche statt; um die Wende zum 18. Jh. wurde die Veranstaltung wahrscheinlich ins Freie verlegt. Ferdinand Rosner verfaßte 1750 ein barockes Reimspiel mit dem Titel *Bitterneß Leyden, Obsiegender Todt, und Glorreiche Auferstehung des Eingefleischten Sohn Gottes einer christlichen Versammlung vorgestellt.* Er betont darin deutlich, daß die Judenschaft nur ein zufälliger Erfüllungsgehilfe Satans ist, indem er das Böse personifiziert auftreten läßt, und daß damit jeder Christ als Sünder schuldig ist an den Leiden Jesu. 1780 erfolgt eine Bearbeitung des Rosner-Textes im ‹Stil der Zeit› von Peter Magnus Knipfelberger. Den endgültigen Abschied vom barocken Spiel Rosners bedeutet der 1811 von Othmar Weiß in neuhochdeutscher Prosa verfaßte Text *Das große Versöhnungsopfer auf Golgatha.* Die wichtigste inhaltliche Veränderung: nicht mehr das Böse an sich, sondern die Juden werden für Christi Tod verantwortlich gemacht. Gespielt wurde inzwischen auf einer zentralperspektivisch angelegten Kulissenbühne, deren Grundstruktur bis in die 80er Jahre erhalten blieb.

Die Bearbeitung des Oberammergauer Pfarrers Joseph Alois Daisenberger von 1860, «entsprechend dem Antikenbild der Jahrhundertmitte, die die Figur Christi mit ihrem ‹Nazarenertum› zeigt», ist auch die Grundlage des heutigen Passionsspiels. Dieser Text wurde ab 1950 und besonders 1970 und 1980 stark angegriffen, da er «in seinem Kern auf der jüdischen Kollektivschuld aufbaut». 1977 wurde das von Alois Fink als *Nova Passio* verfaßte Stück, das sich stark an den Rosner-Text anlehnte, probeaufgeführt; es konnte sich jedoch nicht durchsetzen. 1980 und 1984 wurde eine wenig veränderte Daisenberger-Fassung gespielt.

1880 bis 1900 wurden nach Plänen des Architekten Carl Lautenschläger Bühne und Zuschauerraum neu gestaltet. Dieser Umbau wurde jedoch nur vier Spielperioden bespielt. Die heutige Bühne beruht hauptsächlich auf dem Neubau von 1928/29, der den ‹Freilichtcharakter der Anlage völlig bewahrt›. Die ganze Spielfläche wird vom Tageslicht erhellt, auch die Mittelbühne, die durch Glasdach und durchsichtige Wände geschützt ist. Die gesamte Szenerie wird durch eine aufwendige Unterbodenmaschinerie beschickt. Der überdachte Zuschauerraum faßt heute etwa 4700 Besucher.

Fink, R./Schwarzer, H.: Die ewige Passion. Düsseldorf/Wien 1970; Jaron, N./Rudin, B.: Das Oberammergauer Passionsspiel. Dortmund 1984; Rappmannsberger, F. J.: Oberammergau. München 1960.

Ute Hagel

Odeion

(Griech. ôdé, der Gesang; lat. Odeum) Kleines ‹Theater› mit rechteckigem Grundriß und Dach (in Rom deshalb auch ‹theatrum tectum› genannt); eine Art Konzerthalle, die vor allem für musikalische Darbietungen und Wettbewerbe, seit der röm. Kaiserzeit auch für Deklamationen, Rezitationen und öffentliche Vorträge benutzt wurde. Vorbild für Form und Lage (oft in Verbindung mit einem großen Freilichttheater) war das O., das Perikles (ca. 440 v. Chr.) direkt östlich neben dem → Dionysostheater errichten ließ (und in dem vielleicht auch Theaterproben stattfanden).

Bieber, M.: The History of the Greek and Roman Theatre. Princeton [2]1961, p. 174–177, 220–222.

Bernd Seidensticker

Odin Teatret

Dän. Theater, 1964 in Oslo von dem Grotowski-Schüler Eugenio Barba (* 1936) gegründet, übersiedelte 1966 nach Holstebro, wo ihm Räumlichkeiten und finanzielle Unterstützung von Staat und Gemeinde zugesichert wurden. Das O. T. gehört zu der Gruppe von 24 Gemeindetheatern, die regelmäßig auch vom Staat subventioniert werden. 1984 wurden die vielfältigen Aktivitäten des O. T. umstrukturiert. Unter dem Namen Nordisk Teaterlaboratorium arbeiten das O. T., O. T. Verlag, O. T.-Film, Farfa und ISTA, International School of Theatre Anthropolgy. – Ziel des O. T. ist es, die Kunst des Schauspielers durch experimentelle Arbeit (interkulturellen Austausch, Rezeption ethnischer Theatertraditionen u. a.) zu erforschen, neue Methoden der Theaterpädagogik zu entwickeln und die gewonnenen Erfahrungen in Aufführungen zu prüfen, die in Dänemark und besonders im Ausland große Aufmerksamkeit erregt haben. O. T. veranstaltet Seminare und Gastspiele und publiziert theatertheoretische Arbeiten. 1980 gründet E. Barba die ISTA, ein interdisziplinäres Theaterforschungslabor, das regelmäßig Seminare anbietet. Das O. T. hat ital. (u. a. das Teatro Potlach in Fara Sabine, das Teatro Tascabile in Bergamo) und lateinamerikanische Theater beeinflußt und in Dänemark u. a. das Tukaq Theater (in Fjaltring 1975 gegründet), dessen Vorstellungen Stoffe aus grönländischen Mythen und Sagen gestalten. Durch die Erforschung eines emotionalen visuellen Theaters, dessen Vorstellungen – einige in Zusammenarbeit mit dän. Schriftstellern – dem Rituellen nahekommen, soll versucht werden, die Trennung von Kunst und Leben aufzuheben und eine existentielle Haltung zum Ausdruck zu bringen. Das O. T. ist die international bekannteste dän. Experimentalbühne, die über drei Jahrzehnte hinweg ihren besonderen Arbeits- und Spielstil auf kreative und faszinierende Art beibehalten und weiterentwickelt hat.

Wichtigste Produktionen: *Ornitofilene* (1965–66), *Kaspariana* (1967 bis 68), *Min Far Hus* (1972–74), *Come! And the Day will be Ours* (1976–80), *Millionen Marco* (1979), *Brechts Aske 2* (1982–84), *Anabasis* (1982–84), *Oxyrhyncus Evangeliet* (1985–87), *Judith* (ab 1987), *Talabot* (1988–91), *Memoria* (ab 1990), *Itsi-Bitsi* (1991), *The Castle of Holstebro* (ab 1991).

Barba, E.: Modsætningernes spil. Kopenhagen 1980; ders.: Il Brecht dell' Odin. Mailand 1981; ders.: Bemerkungen zum Schweigen der Schrift. Köln 1983; ders.: Jenseits der schwimmenden Inseln. Reinbek 1985; ders.: Anatomie de l'acteur. Lectoure 1985; ders.: The Dilated Body. Rom 1985; ders.: De flydende øer. Kopenhagen 1989; ders.: Viaggi con l'Odin. Mexico 1990; ders.: The Secret Art of the Performer. London 1992; Berg, M.: Treklang. Kopenhagen 1986; Christoffersen, E. E.: Skuespillerens vandring. Århus 1989; Teatrets Teori og Teknikk. Holstebro 1966–73; Breve til Min Fars Hus. Holstebro 1974; Il Libro dell' Odin. Holstebro 1978; Vor by igåridagimorgen. Holstebro 1989; Le théâtre qui danse. Lectoure 1989; Dictionary of Theatre Anthropology. London/New York 1991.

Else Kjær/Red.

Odissi

Regionalstil des ind. Unionsstaates Orissa (→Indisches Theater). Mitte der 50er Jahre als selbständiger Stil entdeckt. O. meidet Trennung von Nritta (festlicher, heiterer Tanz) und Nritya (erzählender Tanz). Allgemein ist das O.-Tanzspiel ein einziger langer Tanz aus fünf bis sieben Teilen. Das Charakteristikum des O.-Stils sind Hüftbewegungen. Sprache: Oriya. – Seit dem 8. Jh. Tanzspiele der Maharis in der Tanzhalle und im Heiligtum. Priester des O.-Kultes sind ausschließlich Brahmanen. Skulpturen überliefern mehr als 200 Tanzhaltungen. Jagannath, der Herr des Weltalls, steht im Mittelpunkt des *Gita-Govinda*-Tanzspiels, das bis heute zu Puri im Jagannath-Tempel aufgeführt wird. Zu Ehren Jagannaths werden 62 Festlichkeiten gefeiert. Höhepunkt des O.-Tanzes ist das Frühlingsfest, das Chandra Jatra. – Der O. kennt sechs Fußpositionen (die Pada Bhedas), Grundformen des Sitzens und Gehens (Belis), Drehungen (Bhramaris) und leichte Sprünge im Sitzen, in der Halbhocke und im Stand (die Utplavanas). Mit den Hacken werden komplizierte Rhythmen geschlagen. Der O. blieb von allen moslemischen, persischen und arabischen Einflüssen frei (→ Ritualtänze).

Gargi, B.: Theater und Tanz in Indien. Berlin 1960; Kothari, S.: Odissi Dance. In: Quarterly Journal. Vol. III. Nr. 2 (1974); Rebling, E.: Die Tanzkunst Indiens. Wilhelmshaven 1982.

Helga Ettl

Off-Off-Broadway

Vierte, alternative, im wesentlichen nichtkommerzielle Theaterbewegung in den USA, nach dem → Little Theatre Movement, dem → Arbeitertheater der ‹roten Dekade› und dem Off-Broadway. Die doppelte Vorsilbe impliziert, daß man sich auf zweifache Weise räumlich und konzeptionell distanziert; von der lediglich auf Profite ausgerichteten Unterhaltungsindustrie des Broadway sowie von der dem Broadway immer ähnlicher werdenden Institution des Off-Broadway. Das Off-Broadway, ein Theater ‹abseits› des Broadway, konstituierte sich zuerst im Sommer 1947 am Cherry Lane Theatre und Provincetown Playhouse. Es hatte kein spezifisches künstlerisches oder politisches Konzept und machte in der Regel keinen Hehl daraus, sich als Sprungbrett zum Broadway oder zu anderen Formen der besser bezahlten professionellen Bühne zu begreifen. Seine bekanntesten Beispiele: Artist's Theatre, Phoenix Theatre, Playwrights Unit und Circle in the Square. Die letztgenannte, von dem Panamesen José Quintero begründete Einrichtung zeigt, wie mit qualitativ hochstehenden Inszenierungen ‹moderner Klassiker› (O'Neill, Tennessee Williams, Thornton Wilder) die Achtung der Pressekritik und das Interesse von Zuschauerschichten erreicht wurden, denen das Broadwayangebot intellektuell zu anspruchslos war.

Wie alle drei voraufgegangenen Bewegungen des alternativen Theaters blieb auch das O.-O.-B. im wesentlichen auf die Innenstadt New Yorks beschränkt. Vom Off-Broadway unterschied es sich im Ansatz dadurch,

daß in Cafés, Kirchen, abgetakelten Warenhäusern und auf Speicher-
böden (‹lofts›) ein oft nur für 10 bis 30 Zuschauer Platz bietendes, häufig
politisch motiviertes, immer stark experimentierendes ritualisiertes
Theater von Amateuren angeboten wurde, die sich programmatisch ge-
gen den Broadway absetzten. Das O.-O.-B. war in der Sprachgebung und
im Selbstverständnis oft mit dem ‹Underground Theatre› synonym. Die
Rubrik O.-O.-B. wurde seit November 1960 regelmäßig im Kulturteil der
«Village Voice» verwendet, nachdem Douglas Watt den Begriff in einer
Kritik der Tageszeitung Daily News (24.5.1958) eingeführt hatte. Michael Smith ordnete die ‹Take 3›-Inszenierung von Jarrys *König Ubu*
(September 1960) als Beginn des O.-O.-B. ein, da hier «Imagination die
Profitorientierung ersetzt habe». Das O.-O.-B. ließ sich allgemein durch
folgende Merkmale kennzeichnen: nichtkommerzielle Orientierung;
Amateurstatus der Mitarbeiter; Kollektivproduktionen; Bereitschaft
eines zahlenmäßig überschaubaren Publikums, an kollektiven Erfahrungen teilzunehmen; Entwicklung multimedialer Formen: Film, Happening, Tanz. Allen Experimenten gemeinsam war die Ablehnung der
‹plastic-media-controlled-society›.

Das erste O.-O.-B.-Theater war das Caffe Cino des Italieners Joe
Cino (eröffnet Dezember 1958). Kunstausstellungen und Dichterlesungen führten ab Sommer 1959 zu einer Tradition allwöchentlicher Erstaufführungen junger Autoren. Auf diese Weise wurden Werke fast aller
Dramatiker, die im nachhinein als die wichtigsten O.-O.-B.-Autoren bewertet wurden, im Caffe Cino inszeniert: Paul Foster, Robert Heide,
William Hoffman, Sam Shepard, Lanford Wilson u. a. Joe Cino, der
lediglich das Café betrieb und sich nicht in die Inhalte der Theaterarbeit
einmischte, verübte 1967 Selbstmord. Das Caffe Cino wurde daraufhin
geschlossen. Weitere bedeutsame O.-O.-B.-Theater waren: Cafe La
Mama (→La Mama Experimental Theatre Club); Judson Poets' Theatre
(Al Carmines, 1961, Judson Church); →Open Theatre; Theatre Genesis
(Michael Allen, Ralph Cook, 1964, St. Mark's in-the Bouwerie Church);
Playhouse of the Ridiculous (John Vaccarao, 1965, Studio Coda Gallery,
Tenth St.). Die in diesen Einrichtungen mit häufig wechselnden Besetzungen und unter dem Zuspruch stark schwankender Zuschauermengen
bis in die 70er Jahre hinein agierenden Gruppen waren einerseits dem
klassischen und modernen europ. Theater gegenüber aufgeschlossen
(Shakespeare, O'Casey, Brecht, absurdes Theater) und brachten andererseits nach und nach alle wichtigen jungen US-Autoren auf die Bühne,
neben den genannten: Leonard Melfi, Lawrence Ferlinghetti, Murray
Mednick, Ronald Tavel, Rochelle Owens, Israel Horowith, Jean-Claude
van Itallie. Brachte die geringe Beachtung der Inszenierung durch die
bürgerliche Kritik einerseits Isolation und eine gewisse Normierung
durch das Exzentrische mit sich, so nahmen sich doch in den frühen 70er

714 Old Vic (Theatre)

Jahren führende Verlagshäuser (Bobbs-Merrill; Dell; Bantam; Hill and Wang, E. P. Dutton etc.) der Texte an und brachten sie in preisgünstigen Taschenbuchausgaben heraus. Indem beispielsweise →Bread and Puppet, →Living Theatre und →Performance Group als teilweise am O.-O.-B. zugehörig betrachtet werden können, kommt dieser Bewegung das Verdienst zu, für die 60er Jahre einen lockeren institutionellen und konzeptionellen Rahmen bereitgestellt zu haben für die Realisierung bedeutsamer und vielfältiger innovativer Theaterströmungen in den USA der Nachkriegszeit.

Bock, H./Wertheim, A. (eds.): Contemporary American Drama. München 1981; Fröhlich, P.: Das nichtkommerzielle amerik. Theater. Rheinfelden 1974; Heilmeyer, J./Fröhlich, P.: Now. Theater der Erfahrung. Köln 1971; Grabes, H. (Hg.): Das amerik. Drama der Gegenwart. Kronberg 1976; Parone, E. (ed.): New Theatre for Now. New York 1971; Roose-Evans, J.: Experimental Theatre. New York 1970; Orzel, N./Smith, M. (eds.): Eight Plays from Off-Off-Broadway. New York 1966; Schroeder, J. (ed.): The New Underground Theatre. New York 1968; Smith, M. (ed.): The Best of Off-Off-Broadway. New York 1969.

Dieter Herms

Old Vic (Theatre)

1816 gegr. Londoner Theater, zunächst unter dem Namen Royal Coburg, 1833 als Royal Victoria, bald Old Vic genannt. Aufführungsstätte für →viktorianische →Melodramen und andere Formen volkstümlicher Unterhaltung. Seit 1900 auch Opernaufführungen. Unter Lilian Baylis (1874–1937) seit 1914 Shakespeareinszenierungen – deren einziges Londoner Zentrum nach dem 1. Weltkrieg. Nach Zerstörung 1941 Wiedereröffnung 1950; bis 1963 Aufführungen des gesamten Zyklus von Shakespeares Dramen. Von 1963 bis 1976 vorübergehend Sitz des →National Theatre, in dem neben Shakespeare verstärkt das brit. Gegenwartsdrama gepflegt wurde. Seit Fertigstellung des National Theatre-Komplexes an der Themse nur noch sporadisch in Betrieb.

Dent, E. J.: A Theatre for Everybody. The Story of the Old Vic and Sadler's Wells. London 1945; Hamilton, C./Baylis, L.: The Old Vic. London 1926.

Bernd-Peter Lange

Onafhankelijk Toneel

Gegründet 1972 in Amsterdam als Kollektiv von Schauspielern und bildenden Künstlern. O. T. versteht sich als eine ständige Werkstatt für die Entwicklung neuer Theaterformen, neuer Produktionsmethoden und ist speziell mit der Untersuchung der Beziehung zwischen Theater- und anderen Kunstformen befaßt. Außer Texterfassungen für die eigenen Inszenierungen werden auch Gemälde, Plakate, Environments und Objekte produziert. Diese spielen zusammen mit Tanz und Bewegung eine wichtige Rolle in den Aufführungen. O. T. spielt auf kleineren Bühnen, auf der Straße, in Zelten usw. – Nach einigen Projekten über Majakowski wurde O. T. bekannt durch die Aufführung einer Serie von sieben klassischen Dramen unter dem Titel «de Favorieten».

In Gertrude Steins *A Circular Play* (1979) wurde Kubismus in Wort und Bewegung übersetzt. Bei Gorkis *Sommergäste* (1980) war die Wahl des Spielorts thematisch; es wurde mitten im Sommer in den Räumen und Gärten einer alten verfallenen Villa auf einem Landgut in der Residenz Den Haag gespielt. Aus subventionstechnischen Motiven hat 1983 einer der wichtigsten Initiatoren von O. T., der Regisseur und Schauspieler Jan Joris Lammers (* 1942) die neue Gruppe «Maatschappij Discordia» gegründet; sie arbeitet vornehmlich mit fertigen Dramentexten (Handke, Thomas Bernhard, Klassiker), während O. T. mit Mirjam Koen (* 1948) und Gerrit Timmers (* 1948) sich weiter auf die Synthese von Theater/Tanz/Bildende Kunst konzentriert.

Léon van der Sanden

Onkos

Charakteristikum der hellenistischen →Maske, von den Römern übernommen; bogenförmiger Haaraufsatz über der Stirn, der zusammen mit dem seitlich lang und üppig herabfallenden Haar, der weiten Öffnung des Mundes und einer gewisen Starre den Masken eine stark pathetische Expressivität verleiht.

Bernd Seidensticker

Ontological-Hysteric Theatre

Phänomen des US-Theaters, das ausschließlich mit der Person Richard Foremans verbunden ist. Er gründete 1968 die Gruppe O.-H. T., um seine Szenenfolgen zu produzieren, die mit dem Problem des Bewußtseins und der Struktur von Bewußtsein befaßt sind. Sie basieren auf Notizen und Diagrammen, ständig im Wandel begriffenen Texten des Autors, ebenso wie Bewußtsein nach der Vorstellung Foremans in permanentem Themenwechsel, in Unterbrechung und Wiederbeginn besteht. Ekstatik und Hysterie drücken sich in der theatralischen Umsetzung solcher Bewußtseinsprozesse in der Kontrolle ‹gefrorener› Bewegungen aus, so daß die Elemente der Szenenfolgen als statisch erstarrte Seinsweisen wahrgenommen werden können, unterstützt durch gezielt eingesetzte Toneffekte, die oft in ihrer Schrillheit die Schmerzschwelle überschreiten: Die Zuschauer sollen sich ihrer ‹Wahrnehmungsfunktion› bewußt werden. Solche Inszenierungen waren: *Total Recall* (1970); *Pandering to the Masses. A Misrepresentation* (1975); *Le Livre des Splendeurs* (1976); *Penguin Touquet* (1981).

Davy, K. (ed.): Richard Foreman. Plays and Manifestos. New York 1976; Shank, T.: American Alternative Theatre. London 1982.

Dieter Herms

Open Theatre

Konzeptionell wichtigste Gruppe des Off-Off-Broadway, gegr. 1963 von Joseph Chaikin (* 1935). Die Bedeutung des O. T. besteht in einer durchweg politischen Bewußtseinslage, der Hervorbringung junger Autoren und Autorinnen (Megan Terry und Jean-Claude van Itallie) und der Erarbeitung best. Improvisationstechniken, der sog. ‹transformations›. Diese Übungen, beginnend beispielsweise mit einer Darstellung alter Frauen, übergehend zu Kinderspielen, dann zu kämpfenden Männern, sollen Realität sukzessive zerstören, ersetzen und damit in Frage stellen. Eine Collage im Transformationsstil war Megan Terrys politische Rockoper *Viet Rock* (1966), einer der wichtigsten Kulturbeiträge gegen den Vietnamkrieg. *The Serpent* (1967) und *Terminal* (1969), letzteres auf einer ausgedehnten Europatournee gezeigt, behandelt die Themen Gewalt und Tod. *The Mutation Show* (1971, beeinflußt vom Leben Kaspar Hausers) und *Nightwalk* (1973) waren die letzten Produktionen, ehe das O. T. 1973 seine Arbeit einstellte. In seinen psychophysischen Praktiken ähnelte das O. T. dem Theaterlabor Grotowskis (→ Armes Theater). Bis heute benutzen Schauspielschulen der USA die Improvisationsübungen des O. T. zu

Ausbildungszwecken. Neben Grotowski waren Brecht, Artaud (→Theater der Grausamkeit), das →Living Theatre (dessen Mitglied Chaikin zuvor gewesen war) und Peter Brook von Einfluß für die Herausbildung des charakteristischen Spielstils des O. T.

Chaikin, J.: The Presence of the Actor; Notes on the Open Theater, Disguises, Acting, and Repression. New York 1972; Malpede, K. (ed.): Three Works by the Open Theatre (Terminal, The Mutation Show, Nightwalk). New York 1974; Pasolli, R.: A Book on the Open Theatre. New York 1970; Shank, T.: American Alternative Theatre. London 1982.

Dieter Herms

Opéra-ballet

André Campra (1660–1744), provençalischer Komponist, erweitert die Tanznummer in der Oper und entwickelt so aus den bisherigen Opernaufführungen heraus die Gattung des O.-b., in der kompositorisch und dramatisch Tanz und Gesang als gleichberechtigte Künste behandelt werden. Die dramatische Form ermöglicht den Entwurf eines nur knappen Handlungsgerüsts, das den Einbau von →Divertissements und Entrées erlaubt. 1697 wird Campras *L'Europe galante* uraufgeführt, ein O.-b., das über seine Gattung hinaus auch durch Titel und Stil berühmt geworden ist. Anschauungen über Galanterie und geistvolle Caprice haben das Rokoko eingeleitet. Meister des O.-b. nach Campra ist Jean Ph. Rameau (1683–1764) mit seinen *Les Indes galantes*. In dem magischen Blumenballett hat Marie Sallé (1707–56) die Rose getanzt. Sie galt als heroischdramatische Primaballerina, die in besonderem Maße durch Ausdrucksbefähigung und Beseelung bezaubern konnte (→Ballet héroïque-pantomime).

Gregor, J.: Kulturgeschichte des Balletts. Zürich o. J. / Wien 1944; Reyna, F.: Das Buch vom Ballett. Paris 1955; Riemann, H. / Gurlitt, W.: Opéra-ballet. In: Riemann, H.: Musik Lexikon. Sachteil. S. 663. Kassel 1967; Schmidt-Garre, H.: Ballett. Vom Sonnenkönig bis Balanchine. Hannover 1966.

Helga Ettl

Orgien Mysterien Theater

Das O. M. T. ist eine von Hermann Nitsch (* 1938) aus der Aktionsmalerei entwickelte Form des Theaters. Vom Informel (auch: Tachismus) beeinflußt, realisierte Nitsch ab 1960 «Schüttbilder», wobei neben Farbe auch Blut, Gedärm und Tierkadaver benutzt wurden. 1962 kommt es mit

718   Ortaoyunu

Otto Mühl und Adolf Frohner zu einer ersten Aktion (Einmauerungsaktion mit *Selbsterhebung in den Doktorstand*; Manifest: *Die Blutorgel*) (→Happening). Die erste Idee (1957) des O. M. T. entwickelt sich zu «Abreaktionsspielen», einem «Theater ohne Worte» mit «Zerreißungs- und Grundexzessen, Lärmmusik», Essen und Trinken und anderen Sinneserlebnissen sowie einer synästhetischen Aufführung, deren Komposition durch Partituren genauestens festgelegt ist. Teile des auf sechs Tage projektierten «Existenzfestes» wurden bisher weltweit in über 80 Aktionen – die längste dauerte drei Tage (Prinzendorf, 1984) – aufgeführt. Das O. M. T. als eine Form des Gesamtkunstwerks schließt die Zyklen der Natur (Tages- und Jahreszeiten, Leben und Sterben) ein.

Nitsch, H.: Das O. M. T. Darmstadt 1969; ders.: Das O. M. T. Bd. II Neapel 1976; ders.: das orgien mysterien theater 1960–1983. Eindhoven 1983 (van Abbemuseum Eindhoven); Projekt Prinzendorf. Kulturhaus der Stadt Graz. Graz 1981.

Johannes Lothar Schröder

Ortaoyunu

‹Spiel der Mitte›, türk. Form des Stegreiftheaters. Nur die Reihenfolge der Teile: giriş (Prolog), muhavere (Dialog), fasıl (Handlung), bitiş (Epilog) und bestimmte Wendungen für Prolog und Epilog sind festgelegt sowie der Gang der Handlung in groben Umrissen fixiert, ansonsten handeln und sprechen die Spieler frei. Dadurch bleibt Raum für Anspielungen auf Tagesereignisse und für Improvisation, Situationskomik und Wortspiele, worauf Reiz und Wirkung des O. beruhen. Hauptdarsteller sind die Spielleiter *Pişekâr*, angetan mit pelzbesetztem Kaftan und spitzem Turban, in der Hand die Rassel ‹pastal› oder ‹şakşak›, und sein Gegenspieler *Kavuklu* mit Kaftan und rundem Turban. Dieser ist gewitzt, gibt sich aber oft tölpelhaft und mißversteht bewußt seine Mitspieler. Ihm folgt als Diener oder Sohn der *Kavuklu arkası*, ein Zwerg oder Buckliger. Die anderen Schauspieler erscheinen erst im Handlungsteil. Pişekâr verschafft Kavuklu eine Wohnung oder Arbeit, wodurch dieser mit Vertretern verschiedener Volksgruppen zusammentrifft und dabei allerhand Unheil anrichtet. Nacheinander treten Nachbarn oder Kunden auf und karikieren im Gespräch mit Kavuklu die typischen Charakterzüge und Sprechweisen der Minderheiten im Osmanischen Reich wie *Jude, Armenier, Grieche* oder der Bevölkerungsgruppen, die als besonders einfältig (*Kastamonulu*) oder tapfer gelten (*Zeybek*). Die Frau (*Zenne*) wurde früher stets von einem Mann dargestellt. Jedem der Stereotypen ist eine Melodie zugeordnet, die seinen Auftritt ankündigt. Die Musiker (Trommel und Oboe, manchmal auch weitere Instrumente) sitzen gut sichtbar an der Schmalseite des Platzes und sind in das Spiel integriert. Gespielt wird auf einem runden oder ovalen Platz inmitten der Zuschauer, daher der Name ‹Spiel der Mitte›. Während der Aufführung umrunden die Schauspieler langsam den Platz, so daß sie von allen Zuschauern gleichermaßen gesehen werden. Die Bühnendekoration besteht aus *dükkân* und *Yenidünya.* Dükkân sind ein ca. 1 m hoher Paravent mit zwei Flügeln und ein Schemel; er dient als Geschäftsraum jeder Art. Yenidünya, ein hoher Paravent mit drei bis vier Flügeln, stellt jedes in dem Stück benötigte Gebäude, ein Haus, Badehaus o. ä., dar; meist ist er von allen Seiten einsehbar. Das O. oder Vorformen waren vermutlich seit dem 13. Jh. bei den anatolischen Türken bekannt. Mitte des 19. Jh. begann mit der Hinwendung zum europäischen Theater der Niedergang des O., das als primitiv und rückständig galt. Seit kurzem sind verstärkt das Bemühen um eine Förderung des O. und Vorschläge zu seiner Aktualisierung zu erkennen.

Kudret, C.: Ortaoyunu. Ankara 1973.

Maren Fittschen

Österreichische Bühne (The Austrian Theatre) (New York)

Die von Ernst Lothar in New York gegr. Bühne, zu deren Ensemble eine Reihe bekannter Schauspieler des Wiener →Burgtheaters gehörte (u. a. Adrienne Gessner, Oscar Karlweis, Arnold Korff, Eduard Wengraf), brachte es auf fünf Inszenierungen, bevor sie – wie alle vergleichbaren Exiltheater-Versuche in New York – aus wirtschaftlichen Gründen zum Aufgeben gezwungen war.

Jan Hans

Osterspiele

Das O., hervorgegangen aus der Urzelle des geistlichen Dramas (→Mittelalter/Drama und Theater des Mittelalters), der *Visitatio Sepulcri*, umfaßt Szenen wie: Salbenkauf der Marien, Auferstehung, Besuch der Marien am Grab, Lauf der Jünger, Gang nach Emmaus, Himmelfahrt. Die ersten Dokumente sind noch ganz oder großenteils in lat. Sprache geschrieben: Tours, Klosterneuburg, Benediktbeuern. Im 14. Jh. erscheinen sie in den Volkssprachen. Diese Spiele zeigen deutlich Übereinstimmungen. Nur das früheste dt. Spiel (Muri, 13. Jh.) und das späte Spiel von Redentin zeigen andere Charakteristika. Das sog. *Innsbrucker Osterspiel* (14. Jh.) aus Thüringen gilt als Urform oder der Urform nahestehend. Mit diesem Spiel beginnt eine eigentümliche Entwicklung. Die meisten Spiele fügen nun grobe, oft obszöne weltliche (weitgehend standardisierte) Szenen ein. Die meisten Handschriften dieser O. wurden an Orten gefunden, die weit entfernt von ihren durch den Dialekt nachgewiesenen Entstehungsorten liegen. Eine feste lokale Tradition ließ sich bei diesen Spielen nicht erweisen. Diese Phänomene führten die Forschung dazu, einen Einfluß der Vaganten oder der Klosterschüler zu vermuten. Das ist neuerdings – jedoch ohne Gegenbeweise – bestritten worden.

Michael, W. F.: Fahrendes Volk und mittelalterliches Drama. In: Kleine Schriften der Gesellschaft für Theatergeschichte XVII (1960), S. 3–8; Rueff, H.: Das rheinische Osterspiel der Berliner Handschrift (= Abhandlungen der Gesellschaft der Wissenschaften zu Göttingen phil. hist. Klasse nF 18). Berlin 1925; Young, K.: The Drama of the Medieval Church. Oxford 1933.

Wolfgang F. Michael

Otto-Falckenberg-Schule

Der Schauspieler und Regisseur Otto Falckenberg (1873–1947) wollte in seiner Schule dem «jungen Menschen das zunächst durchaus ungeklärte und unerkennbare Wesen des Theaters, genau gesprochen des Schauspielers... deuten, einsichtig... machen und zum Erlebnis... bringen!» (1944). Für ihn war das gründliche Erlernen des technischen Handwerkzeugs des Schauspielers Teil einer ‹organischen› Darstellung. – Die O., gegr. 1947 in München, war bis September 1982 Berufsfachschule, seitdem ist sie Fachakademie für darstellende Kunst. Angeboten wird eine vierjährige Schauspiel- bzw. Regieausbildung. Die Verbindung zu den →Münchner Kammerspielen ermöglicht es den Schülern, schon während der Ausbildung an einem Theater auftreten zu können. Schulleitung: Jörg Hube.

Falckenberg, O.: Mein Leben – Mein Theater. München 1944.

Ute Hagel

Outrieren

(Frz. ‹outrer› = übertreiben) Die unangemessene Darstellung einer Rolle durch übertriebenes Spiel. O. kann durch das Bemühen eines Schauspielers entstehen, seiner (kleinen) Rolle Bedeutung zu geben (→Chargieren), kann aber auch bewußt eingesetztes Stilmittel eines Inszenierungskonzeptes sein.

Wolfgang Beck

Pageant

P. bezeichnet sowohl die fahrbaren Plattformbühnen, auf denen die mittelalterlichen →Mystery Plays aufgeführt worden sind, als auch die Spiele selbst. Das P. bestand aus einer Bühne auf einem Karren mit vier bis sechs Rädern (Wagenbühne/Carros). Es wurde entweder zu verschiedenen Spielstätten in der Corpus Christi-Prozession (→Fronleichnam) gezogen, wo eine Episode aus dem Mysterienzyklus gespielt wurde, oder die P. wurden in einem großen Kreis aufgestellt («staging in the round»), z. B. vor der Kirche, und die Zuschauer wanderten von einem P. zum nächsten. Regieanweisungen sagen, daß auch auf der Straße vor und um das P. gespielt wurde. Von einer bestimmten Zunft für eine Szene oder Episode gebaut, zeigte ein P. häufig die Eigenschaften der Zunft; z. B. wurde das P. für das Spiel von Noah und seiner widerspenstigen Frau von der Zunft der Fischhändler gebaut. Der Ursprung, die Chronologie und die Verbreitung der Spielzyklen, die auf den P. aufgeführt worden sind, sind noch relativ unbekannt und umstritten. Corpus Christi wird ab 1318 in ganz England gefeiert, aber →Mysterienspiele auf P. werden erst 1377 in Beverley erwähnt. Von einigen Bühnenhistorikern werden die P. sogar als Vorbild für die Plattformbühne der öffentlichen →Elisabethanischen Theater (→Shakespearebühne) angesehen.

Cawley, A.: The Staging of Medieval Drama. In: The Revels History of Drama in English. Vol. 1. London 1983, p. 1–66; Nelson, A.: The Medieval English Stage: Corpus Christi Pageants and Plays. Chicago 1974; Southern, R.: The Medieval Theatre in the Round: A Study of the Staging of The Castle of Perseverance and Related Matters. London 1975; Wickham, G.: Early English Stages 1300 to 1660. Vol. 1. London 1980.

J. Lawrence Guntner

Palliata

Lat. Adjektiv, zu ergänzen ‹fabula›; Gattungsbezeichnung für die röm. Komödien, denen eine griech. Vorlage zugrunde liegt (alle Stücke des Plautus und Terenz); gebildet ist der Begriff nach dem für diese dramatische Gattung charakteristischen Kostümstück, dem ‹pallium› (lat. Name für das griech. Himation), einem weiten überwurfartigen griech. Obergewand.

Blänsdorf, J.: Plautus, S. 135–222, und Juhnke, H.: Terenz, S. 223–307. In: E. Lefèvre (Hg.): Das röm. Drama. Darmstadt 1978.

Bernd Seidensticker

Pantomime

(Pantomimos = griech. alles nachahmend) Darstellung einer Szene oder Handlung durch Gebärden, Mienenspiel und Tanz mit oder ohne Masken unter Verzicht auf das Wort; Bezeichnung für Gattung und Ausübende. Blütezeiten: römische Kaiserzeit, 16. Jh., frühes 19. Jh. Theorien über Ursprung: 1. P. als Form der röm. Kaiserzeit (getrennt vom p. Tanz) seit 22 v. Chr., P. begleitet von Sänger oder Chor und Orchester, kostbare Kostüme, Masken (Augenspiel), Masken- und Kostümwechsel; Pylades aus Kilikien (Tragödien-P., Lehrbuch über P.) und Bathyllus aus Alexandria (wollüstige mythologische Liebes-P., auch parodistisch), zuerst gemeinsame P.-Theater und Schulen, später getrennt. 2. P.-Entwicklung aus mimischen, kultischen und sportlichen (Waffen-)Tänzen; Ursprung orgiastischer Feste der Ptolemäerzeit in Ägypten (Osiris-Mysterien), Dionysoskult. Mimische Monologe (cantica), begleitet von Flöte oder Orchester und Chor. P. trägt Maske. P.-Tänze bereits im Urtheater (Tier-P.), altägypt., babylon., ind. kultischen Festen, fernöstl. Theater (→Peking-Oper, Volkstheater). Telestes (Tanzlehrer Aischylos', 5. Jh. v. Chr.) zum erstenmal alleinige mimische Darstellung einer Komödie, Fingerspiel, Begleitung: Chor oder Sänger. P. mit kultischen, mythologischen, tragisch-literarischen, aber auch aktuellen Stoffen. Verbreitung im ganzen griech. Sprachraum, Ägypten und Syrien (Heimat berühmter P.); Italien: röm. Zeit: p. Tänze als Einlagen zwischen Akten der Tragödien und Komödien, →Atellanenspiele. Seit Augustus beherrscht P. die Bühnen des röm. Imperiums. Es gibt Pantomimendynastien. Gesellschaftliche Stellung der P.: in Griechenland hoch angesehen, in Rom eher mißachtet (personae inhonestae), da meist Sklaven oder Freigelassene; Ausnahmen waren Günstlinge der Caesaren und vornehmer Römer. Förderer und berühmte P.: Augustus – Pylades, Bathyllus, Hylas, Nomios, Pierus; Caligula, Claudius – Mnester; Nero – Paris d. Ä.; Domitian – Paris d. J.; Traian – Pylades d. J.; unter den Antoninen Palastschulen für P. und staatliche Truppen in Rom und den Provinzen; seit dem 1. Jh. n. Chr. auch Auftreten von Frauen; berühmte Pantomiminnen waren: Helladia («Hosenrollen»), Rhodoclea (5. Jh. n. Chr.), Theodora (508–548, Gattin Kaiser Justinians), Anthusa (9. Jh.); 352 n. Chr. gibt es angeblich 3000 Pantomiminnen in Rom. Nach Untergang Westroms Weiterbestehen der P. in Konstantinopel. Berühmte P. der Spätzeit: Karamallos, Chrysomallos, Helladios, Margarites. Gegner der P.: u. a. Valentinianus, Valens, Theodosius, Justinian und die Kirchenväter. Als Kunstform ist die P. in dieser Zeit verschwunden. Kontinuität der mimischen Überlieferung ist umstritten. P.-Elemente in christlichen Passionsspielen und Moralitäten. Im Mittelalter: Gaukler und Jokulatoren. In der Renaissance: Wiederbelebung in der →Commedia dell'arte, →Wander-

Pantomime 723

bühnen – p. Einlagen. Wende 17./18. Jh. Versuch der Erneuerung in England und Frankreich. Jahrmarktstheater (Volkstheater), Paris Märkte von Saint-Germain und Saint-Laurent, später Boulevard du Temple (Théâtre de Funambules). Berühmter P. Jean Gaspard Deburau (1796–1846), gen. Baptiste, stumme Rolle des Pierrot, höchste Blüte der p. Technik, konventionelle dramatische Handlung. Unter seinen Nachfolgern (Sohn Charles, Paul Legrand) geht die Reinheit der P. verloren, Fortsetzung im → Zirkus (→ Clowns). England: Jahrmärkte (St. Bartholomäus – Theater Lee, Jahrmarkt von Greenwich): P. Einlagen in Umzugspausen. John Rich, gen. Lun (gest. 1761), berühmter engl. P. und stummer Harlekin. Harlekin und Gesellen Helden der engl. P. Coventgarden Theatre und Saddler's Wells Theatre. Joe Grimaldi (1778–1837), erster Clown. Pferde-P. 20. Jh.: Einfluß der → Theaterreform E. G. Craigs, J. B. Wachtangows und A. Tairows. P.-Inszenierungen W. Meyerholds (Ps. Doktor Dapertutto, u. a. nach Schnitzlers *Schleier der Pierette*, 1910/11), G. Craig: *The Masque of Hunger* (P. 1903). Moderne P. Verbindung von Künstlichkeit der Form und Naivität des Bildhaften. Etienne Decroux (1898–1991) Schüler von Jacques Coupeau und Charles Dullin (1885–1949). Schöpfer der modernen P.-Technik und -Sprache. «Mime pure». Abstrakte Marionette. «Kunst, sich mit dem ganzen Körper auszudrücken und mit der umgebenden Welt zu identifizieren.» Gesicht: neutrale Maske. Reduzierung der Rolle der Hände. Verzicht auf Dekoration, Kostüm, Requisite und Musik. Eigene Schule in Paris mit Sohn Maximilian. Schüler: Elyane Guyon, Catherine Toth, Jean-Louis Barrault (* 1911): P., später Schauspieler, Regisseur und Theaterleiter; Marcel Marceau (* 1923): P., Weiterentwicklung der Sprache von Decroux, Figur des Bip, Mimodramen nach literarischen Vorbildern (→ Commedia dell'arte, jap. Nô-Spiele, Nestroy und Gogol), u. a. *Le manteau*, 1951, *Le duel dans les ténèbres, Pierrot de Montmartre*, 1952, *Les trois paruques*, 1953, *Le 14 Juillet*, 1956, *Le petit cirque*, 1958, *Les masques,* 1959; Jean Soubeyran: P., spielte mit M. Marceau, später mit dt.-frz. Truppe hauptsächlich in Deutschland. Grotesk-satirisches Talent. Sozialkritische → Mimodramen. Film *Der junge Engländer*. Palucca-Schule Dresden, Komische Oper Berlin (W. Felsenstein), später Choreograph an Theatern. Lehrbuch der Pantomime. Jacques Lecoq (* 1921), P. von Decroux beeinflußt. Seit 1956 zweijährige Mimenkurse in Paris. Geht von formalistischen Leitsätzen des reinen Mimus ab. Bereichert P.sprache durch Klang, Farbe, Licht. Psycholog. Situationen. Zeitgenössische Vertreter: Henryk Tomaszewski (* 1924), poln. P., gründet 1956 das P.-Studio in Wrocław, 1958 umbenannt in P.-Theater Wrocław, ab 1959 staatliches Th. Experimentelles Bewegungstheater. Eigene Symbolsprache, absurde Elemente. Abendfüllende Mimodramen: *Das Labyrinth, Fausts Höllenfahrt, Gilgamesch* u. a. Ladislav Fialka (* 1931), tschech. P. Gründete

1958 Theater am Geländer in Prag. Solo-P. und Theater-P. mit Ensemble. Ziel: synthetisches P.-Theater, tragische und komische Elemente, traditionelle Stoffe der P. Wolfram Mehring, frz. P., arbeitete bei Decroux, gründete zusammen mit Grillon Théâtre franco-allemand, später → «Théâtre de la Mandragore». 1963 Eröffnung der Mimenschule «Le Mandragore». ‹Mimenspectacle›: *Leonce und Lena, Woyzeck* u. a. Samy Molcho (* 1936), österr. P. israel. Herkunft, entwickelt individuellen Stil aus Elementen des → Kabuki und der europ. P. Solo-Abende. Prof. am Reinhardt-Seminar. Dimitri (* 1935), Schweizer P., Clown, Schüler von Decroux. 1971 Gründung seines eigenen Theaters in Verscio (Tessin). Teatro Dimitri, einziges Th. des Kanton Tessin mit ständiger Truppe und regelmäßigen Veranstaltungen aller Sparten (P., Tanz, Clownerien, Musik, Kabarett). 1975 angeschlossen Scuola Teatro Dimitri, in der grundlegende Disziplinen des Theaterberufs gelehrt werden. Seit 1978 Compagnia Teatro Dimitri. P.-Theater Kefka, Köln. 1974 von Milan Sládek gegr.

Bartussek, W.: P. und darstellendes Spiel. Mainz 1990; Falckenberg, B./Titt, G.: Die Kunst der P. Köln 1987; Frow, G.: «Oh, Yes It Is». A History of P. London 1985; Hausbrandt, A.: Das P.-Theater Tomaszewskis. Warszawa 1975; Hera, J.: Der verzauberte Palast. Aus der Geschichte der P. Berlin 1981; Lecoq, J. (Hg.): Le théâtre du geste. Mimes et acteurs. Paris 1987; Meffert, B.: Welt der P. Berlin 1984; Meyer, F. (Hg.): Milan Sladek. P.-Theater. Köln 1985; Simon, K. G.: P. Ursprung. Wesen. Möglichkeiten. München 1960; Soubeyran, J.: Die wortlose Sprache. Lehrbuch der P. Velber o. J.; Theater und Schule Dimitri. Bern 1985; Zwiefka, H. J.: Pantomime. Moers 1987.

Ingeborg Janich

Pantomimeteatret

Dän. → Freilichttheater im Tivoli, Kopenhagen, 1874 gegründet. P. ist einmalig in der europ. Theatergeschichte durch sein Repertoire, das aus klassischen Pantomimen und Balletts im → Commedia dell'arte-Stil besteht. Diese Tradition fand Zugang zum dän. Publikum vor allem durch die Künstlerfamilien Casorti und Price Anfang des 19. Jh. Kennzeichnend für diesen ital./engl. Stil, an dem das P. bis heute ungebrochen festhält, ist: Bühnenaufbau im Stil des 18. Jh., keine sprachlichen Mittel, vereinfachte Personenkonstellation, überirdische Figuren und Schlußapotheose. Pantomimenaufführungen gibt es seit der Eröffnung im Tivoli 1843.

Dybroe, M.: Pantomimeteatret og dets publikum. Kongerslev 1978; Engberg, H.: Pantomimeteatret. København 1959; Krogh, T.: Forudsætninger for den Casortiske Pantomime. Kbh. 1936.

Else Kjær

Papiertheater

Die wohl jüngste Form des Puppentheaters, bekannt und beliebt seit dem 19. Jh., da erst die Erfindung der Lithographie seine massenhafte Verbreitung ermöglichte. Vervielfältigte Ausschneidebögen bildeten die Grundlage für den Eigenbau des P. und seiner flachen Figuren, die mit Hilfe von Stäben bewegt werden konnten. Das P. diente in der Regel zum häuslichen Nachspielen von Theateraufführungen, es gab spezielle Ausschneidebögen für beliebte Theaterstücke (→Kamishibai).

Batchelder, M.: The Puppet-Theatre-Handbook. London 1948; Böhmer, G.: Puppentheater. München 1969; Ransome, G. G.: Puppets and Shadows. A Bibliography. Boston 1931; Schneider, I.: Puppen- und Schattenspiele in der Romantik. Diss. Wien 1920; Schreiner, K.: Puppen & Theater. Köln 1980; Zeitzle, A.: Die Texthefte des Papiertheaters. Diss. Stuttgart 1990; Zwiauer, H.: Papiertheater. Wien 1987.

Wolfgang Beck

Parabase

Standardszene der griech. ‹Alten Komödie› (5. Jh.); in der Regel dramatisch und thematisch ohne Zusammenhang mit der Handlung, die für ca. 100 Verse ‹suspendiert› ist. In der P. legt der Chor Kostüm und →Maske ab und wendet sich, bei leerer Bühne, direkt an das Publikum; im ersten Teil der zweiteiligen Komposition ‹spricht› der Dichter durch den Chorführer (Rezitativ zur Flöte) in eigener Sache (über sich und seine Dichtung, über Rivalen und Kritiker); im zweiten Teil folgen meist Hymnen an Götter und moralisch-didaktische oder politische Ratschläge, Kritik und Spötteleien; die archaisch strenge Bauform löst sich in den späteren Komödien des Aristophanes auf, und die P. verschwindet schließlich ganz.

Gelzer, Th.: Aristophanes. In: G. A. Seeck (Hg.): Das griech. Drama. Darmstadt 1979, S. 279f.

Bernd Seidensticker

Parabelstück

Die Parabel ist eine gleichnishafte Erzählung, eine Kurzform des Epischen. In ihr wird in lehrhafter Absicht ein allgemeiner theologischer, philosophischer, sittlich-politischer oder -sozialer Sachverhalt in ein einprägsames Bild übertragen, wobei die genaue Ausdeutbarkeit des Bildes wesentlich ist. Parabeln erscheinen auch als Elemente in der Struktur eines Stücks; z. B. die Ringparabel in G. E. Lessings *Nathan der Weise* (1783), die ‹Kästchenszene› in Shakespeares *Kaufmann von Venedig* (1577–79) und adaptiert in Brechts *Herr Puntila und sein Knecht Matti* (1940), die Parabel vom Magen und den Gliedern in Shakespeare/Brechts *Coriolan* (1577–79; 1952–53). – Das P. ist die Ausdehnung und Einbeziehung des Parabolischen auf ein Stück als Ganzes sowie die einzelnen Bauformen der dramatischen Struktur. In Anlehnung an die Lehrstücke des 16. und 17. Jh. und bes. die Aufklärungsparabeln hat Bertolt Brecht die Parabel oft zum dialektischen Kernstück seines Stücks gemacht. Nach Klaus-Detlev Müller sind es vier Merkmale, die das →Brecht-Theater und die Parabel vergleichbar gestalten: 1. der durchgängige Bezug zur außerästhetischen Wirklichkeit; 2. die Verbindlichkeit einer Lehre, die Wissen begründet; 3. die Verfremdungstechnik; 4. die epische Darbietungsweise. ‹Ideenverkörpernde› P. sind in Brechts Werk vor allem *Mann ist Mann* (1926), *Die Rundköpfe und die Spitzköpfe* (1936), *Das Verhör des Lukullus* (1939), *Der aufhaltsame Aufstieg des Arturo Ui* (1958), *Der gute Mensch von Sezuan* (1943), *Turandot* (1954); jedoch tragen auch seine anderen Stücke fast immer parabolische Züge.

Auch Paul Claudel (1868–1955) schrieb aus christlicher Sicht P. Es ging darum, das Übersinnliche in lehrhafter Absicht sinnlich, d. h. bildhaft zu gestalten und zu kommentieren aus der Sicht des Gläubig-Wissenden, so in *Le Soulier de satin ou le pire n'est pas toujours sûr* (1919–24), *Le Livre de Christophe Colomb* (1930, vertont von Darius Milhaud), *La Sagesse ou la Parabole du festin* (1949).

Neben der Lehrparabel, die auf einem festen, objektiven Standpunkt des Autors fußt, wird in der Forschung die ‹schwebende Parabel› unterschieden; sie bewegt sich nicht mehr in einem präzis bestimmbaren weltanschaulichen System und läßt keine Lösung mehr zu, da der Autor meist auch nicht an Sinn und Veränderbarkeit der Welt glaubt. Es gibt Parabeln für die dunkle Rätselhaftigkeit der Welt, so im →absurden Theater, nach dem Motto von Wolfgang Hildesheimer (1916–91): «Jedes absurde Theaterstück ist eine Parabel!» (*Erlanger Rede über das Absurde Theater*, 1960). Insofern können auch die Stücke von Beckett und Ionesco als P. einer unverständlichen Welt interpretiert werden. Der profilierteste Vertreter des P. neben Brecht ist Max Frisch (1911–91). Mit ihm geht aber auch das P. im deutschsprachigen Theater mit Ausnahme des nachbrechtschen sozialistischen P. (Peter Hacks, * 1928; Hartmut Lange, * 1937; Erwin Strittmatter, * 1912) zu Ende. Nach *Biedermann und die Brandstifter* (1958), einem ‹Lehrstück ohne Lehre›, und *Andorra* (1961) gibt Frisch das Genre des P. auf: «...habe ich ein zunehmendes Unbehagen an der Parabel. Die Parabel tendiert zum Quod erat demonstrandum, sie impliziert Lehre... Die Parabel geht meistens auf.» Frisch gibt zu, er habe sie nur gewählt, «um dem Imitiertheater zu entgehen» (*Dramaturgisches. Ein Briefwechsel mit W. Höllerer*, 1969). Auch der Engländer John Arden (* 1930) geht denselben Weg nach *Sergeant Musgrave's Dance* (1959), einer ‹unhistorischen Parabel›. Im Theater hat sich trotz dramatischer Erfolge der nichtdidaktischen P. nur die Form der Lehrparabel behauptet.

Brettschneider, W.: Die moderne dt. Parabel. Berlin 1971; Hinck, W.: Das moderne Drama in Deutschland. Göttingen 1973; Kaufmann, H.: Bertolt Brecht – Geschichtsdrama und Parabelstück. Berlin 1962; Müller, K.-D.: Das Ei des Kolumbus? In: Keller, W. (Hg.): Beiträge zur Poetik des Dramas. Darmstadt 1976.

Gérard Schneilin

Parachoregema

Im griech. Theater Bezeichnung der zusätzlich, d. h. zu den vom Staat bezahlten Schauspielern, benötigten Personen für kleine Nebenrollen (z. B. Pylades in den aischyleischen *Choephoren*) sowie alle Arten von Statisten; die Finanzierung mußte wohl zusätzlich zu den Kosten für den Chor vom Choregen übernommen werden.

Melchinger, S.: Das Theater der Tragödie. München 1974, S. 170–185.

Bernd Seidensticker

Paraskenien

Teil des griech. Theaterbaus; an beiden Enden des Bühnenhauses ca. 5 m vorspringende Seitenflügel von ca. 6–7 m Breite, wohl in Form offener Säulenhallen, die das architektonische Problem der toten Zwickel zwischen der kreisrunden Orchestra und dem rechteckigen Bühnengebäude befriedigend lösten, die Bühne an den Seiten optisch begrenzten und die Akustik verbesserten; P. sind erst für das Steintheater des Lykurg (ca. 340 v. Chr.) gesichert, lassen sich jedoch mit guten Argumenten bereits für das perikleische Theater des 5. Jh. erschließen (→ Antikes Theater).

Bernd Seidensticker

Paraszenien

Das Wort P. bezeichnet im antiken Theater zwei im rechten Winkel angesetzte Seitengebäude, die zu den Zuschauern vortreten, die Flügel des Königspalasts darstellen und gleichzeitig als Aufenthaltsort für alle Mitwirkenden und als Aufbewahrungsstätte für Kostüme, Masken und Maschinen dienen.

Bernard Poloni

Parkett

(Frz. ‹parquet›) Ursprünglich bestimmte Art des Fußbodenbelags, dann an der (Pariser) Börse Raum für die Wertpapiermakler, im frz. Gericht Raum für Richter und Staatsanwaltschaft; im Theater die Sitzplätze im Saal (unten) zum Unterschied von Balkon und Logen. Das Theater-P. wird im heutigen Frz. in der Regel ‹orchestre› oder ‹parterre› genannt.

Horst Schumacher

Parodie

(Griech. parodia = Gegengesang) Zur Gattung der Satire gehörend, ist die P. ein Stück oder eine Reihe von Bauformen in einem Stück, welche einen gegebenen anderen Text mit Hilfe von verschiedenartigen komischen Effekten kritisch herabsetzt. Die Grenzen der P. mit der →Travestie und der →Burleske sind fließend und in der Forschung ungenau abgesteckt; auch geographische Verschiedenheiten sind häufig verwirrend. Eine Definition, der zufolge die Travestie die Erscheinungsfolgen modifiziere, die P. aber den Inhalt, ist z. T. historisch begründet, in der heutigen Sicht allerdings einengend.

Die P. entstand in Griechenland, so Aristoteles, bei Hegemon von Thasos (5. Jh. v. Chr.) als Gegenstück und heiterer Ausklang zu den Tragödien. Der größte griech. Vertreter dieser Kunst machte die P. auch selbständig: Aristophanes (450/445 – ca. 388 v. Chr.) parodiert in den *Fröschen* (405) Aischylos und Euripides. In der Folge, vom Mittelalter bis heute, wurden beide Formtendenzen weitergeführt. Zu den größten Parodisten gehören u. a. Shakespeare, Johann Nepomuk Nestroy (1801 – 62), der Hebbel und Richard Wagner verspottete; in der komischen Oper Offenbach (1819 – 80), der in *Orpheus in der Unterwelt* (1858) und in *Die schöne Helena* (1860) die antike Mythologie durch Anhäufung von Anachronismen lächerlich macht.

Im heutigen Theater ist die P. bes. häufig als werkimmanente Bauform verwendet mit mehrfachen Funktionen. Einmal werden die überlieferten Formen als Ganzes oder in Teilaspekten zerstört und zugleich zu Komponenten von neuen Formen gemacht, so als P. von Shakespeares *Macbeth* (1605 etwa) die Tragikomödie *Macbett* (1972) von Eugène Ionesco (* 1912); so die ‹Komödien› *Romulus der Große* (1949) und *Der Besuch der alten Dame* (1956) von Friedrich Dürrenmatt (1921–90) oder das komische Lehrstück *Biedermann und die Brandstifter* (1958) von Max Frisch (1911–91), worin Bauformen der antiken Tragödie mit neuen Inhalten aus der heutigen bürgerlichen Ideologie gefüllt und dadurch kritisch umfunktioniert sind. Bes. eindeutig ist andererseits der Gebrauch der P. als Gesellschaftssatire bei Brecht, so die P. von Shakespeares *Richard III.* und Goethes *Faust I.* in *Der aufhaltsame Aufstieg des Arturo Ui* (1941).

Wesentlich in der parodistischen Verzerrung ist nach Auffassung der russ. Formalisten und nach Theodor W. Adorno die gleichzeitige Zerstörung und Erneuerung einer Form. Insofern ist die P. ein innovierendes Mittel. Der frühere Text wird in der dialektischen Struktur der P. bewahrt; die Umfunktionierung ist nur als ironische Relation zum Original möglich, es wird zugleich kritisch erneuert und konserviert.

Heidsieck, A.: Die Travestie des Tragischen im dt. Drama. In: Sander, V. (Hg.): Tragik und Tragödie. Darmstadt 1971; Hein, J.: Parodien des Wiener Volkstheaters. Stuttgart 1986; Highet, G.: Anatomy of Satire. New York 1962; Karrer, W.: Parodie, Travestie, Pastiche. München 1977; Ronge, P.: Polemik, Parodie und Satire bei Ionesco. Bad Homburg 1967; Verweyen, Th./Witting, G.: Die Parodie in der neueren deutschen Literatur. Darmstadt 1979; Weisstein, U.: Parody, Travesty, and Burlesque. Bloomington 1966.

Gérard Schneilin

Parodos

1. Teil des griech. →Theaterbaus; Bezeichnung der beiden seitlichen Zugänge in die Orchestra (und zum Zuschauerraum); durch die P. zog der Chor ein und wieder aus. Zunächst traten so auch die Schauspieler auf; nach Errichtung eines Bühnenhauses nur noch die aus größerer Entfernung kommenden Personen. Nach einer vielleicht bereits im 5. Jh., sicher in der ‹Neuen Komödie› gültigen Konvention, die sich im Dionysostheater an den natürlichen geographischen Gegebenheiten orientierte, bedeutet wohl a) Auftritt von rechts (vom Zuschauer aus): vom Hafen, b) Auftritt von links: aus der Stadt, vom Markt. Bei Plautus und Terenz ist

730 Passionsspiele

es dagegen anscheinend genau umgckchrt gewesen. – 2. Bezeichnung für das Einzugslied des Chors in die Orchestra.

Bernd Seidensticker

Passionsspiele

P. (→Mittelalter/Drama und Theater des Mittelalters) sind vor allem in Deutschland und Frankreich überliefert. Dort haben wir Kunde von ihnen seit dem Spätmittelalter, wo sie als ausgeprägte Form vor uns stehen. Gewöhnlich kennen wir auch deren Autoren. In Deutschland dagegen haben wir anonyme Traditionen, die über Jahrhunderte nachweisbar und über ganze Landschaften verstreut sind: Frankfurt und das ganze hessische Gebiet vom 13. bis ins 16. Jh., Tirol, Luzern und Villingen im 15. und 16. Jh. Die Beteiligung aller Bevölkerungsschichten macht sie zu Volksdramen. Bühnenform ist die ausgedehnte →Simultanbühne (→Oberammergau).

Bergmann, R.: Katalog der deutschsprachigen geistlichen Spiele und Marienklagen des Mittelalters. München 1986; Frank, G.: The Medieval French Drama. Oxford 1954; Henker, M. (Hg.): Hört, seht, weint und liebt. Passionsspiele im alpenländischen Raum. München 1990; Michael, W.F.: Frühformen der deutschen Bühne. Berlin 1963; Neumann, B.: Geistliches Schauspiel im Zeugnis der Zeit. München/Zürich 1987; Petersen, J.: Aufführung und Bühnenplan des älteren Frankfurter Passionsspiels. In: ZdA LIX (1921/22), S. 83–126.

Wolfgang F. Michael

Paterson Pageant

Einmalige Aufführung eines →Massentheaters im Madison Square Garden, New York, am 7.6.1913. Dieses von dem progressiven Journalisten John Reed (1887–1920) mit streikenden Textilarbeitern/innen organisierte Schauspiel sollte den von der anarcho-syndikalistischen Gewerkschaft Industrial Workers of the World im Zentrum der Textilindustrie von Paterson, New Jersey, durchgeführten Streik dokumentieren und weiter mobilisieren. Wesentliche Phasen des realen Geschehens wurden nachgestellt und dramatisch verdichtet: die Arbeitsniederlegung, die Streikpostenketten, Polizeigewalt, Ermordung und Begräbnis von Valentino Modestino, Massenversammlungen, die Evakuierung der Kinder, die politischen Reden der IWW-Führer Elizabeth Gurley Flynn, Carlo Tresca und William D. Haywood. Das P.P. sollte über den konkreten Anlaß hinaus die historische Dimension des Klassenkampfes verbildlichen. Wichtige Elemente der Proletkult- und Agitprop-Dramatik der 1920er und 30er Jahre scheinen im P. P. vorweggenommen.

Kornbluh, J. L. (ed.): Rebel Voices. An IWW Anthology. Ann Arbor 1964, p. 197–226.

Dieter Herms

Pathos

(Griech.: Leid, Leidenschaft, Ergriffensein) Auf der Bühne gesteigerter, geballter Ausdruck in Rede, Schrei und Gestik einwirkend auf ein Gegenüber, sei es Antagonist oder Zuschauer/-hörer. Negativ im Sinne von ‹hohlem, leerem P.›, Schwulst, phrasenhafte Deklamation, übertriebene, outrierte Spielweise, im →Melodrama oder der →Parodie vorherrschend. In der →antiken Tragödie gilt P. als dramatische Darstellung des physischen und seelischen Schmerzes des Helden, nach Aristoteles durch die bewegte Rede (Rhetorik) und die vorwärtstreibende →Handlung (Poetik) beim Zuschauer Furcht und Mitleid bewirkend. Zu Höhepunkten kommt es im →Elisabethanischen Theater, vor allem bei Shakespeare, und in der frz. und dt. →Klassik sowie im →bürgerlichen Trauerspiel (Theorie bei Lessing und Diderot). Es kommt hier zur Psychologisierung und Moralisierung des Effekts im Rahmen des Idealismus, so bei Friedrich Schiller (1759–1805) in den Abhandlungen *Vom Erhabenen* und *Über das Pathetische* (1793), zugleich die philosophische Begründung und dramatische Ausformung des P.: Tragische Kunst gilt als ‹Darstellung der leidenden Natur› und zugleich als ‹Darstellung des moralischen Widerstands gegen das Leiden›, insofern gleichermaßen ästhetisch und ethisch, sinnlich und übersinnlich. Das P. wirkt also handlungsfördernd und erzielt beim Zuschauer das Mitleiden. Dieselbe Definition findet sich in Hegels *Ästhetik* als ‹objektives P.›, später im Naturalismus (→Naturalistisches Theater) vor allem mimisch-gestisch als Ausdruck der leidenden Opfer; im Expressionismus (→Expressionistisches Theater) übersteigerter pathetischer Stil im Wandlungs- und Verkündigungsdrama als Rede, Schrei und Geste. Auch im sowj. Revolutionstheater, z. B. bei Maxim Gorki (1868–1936), als Ausdruck der Rolle des Helden und der Subjektivität im Geschichtsprozeß. Bei Brecht wird das P. mit ‹Vorsicht› gebraucht, jedoch nicht ausgeschaltet. In gewissen Formen des ironischen Theaters (romantische Komödie, modernes ‹Antitheater›, zeitgenössische ‹Komödie›) oft Umfunktionierung zum Antipathos als Verfremdungseffekt.

Berghahn, K. L.: Das Pathetischerhabene. In: Grimm, R. (Hg.): Deutsche Dramentheorien, Bd. I. Frankfurt/M. 1971; de Romilly, J.: L'evolution du pathétique d'Eschyle à Euripide. Paris 1961; Staiger, E.: Poetik. Zürich 1946.

Gérard Schneilin

Pekingoper

Die P. (jingxi, wörtl. «hauptstädtisches Theater») ist der am weitesten verbreitete und populärste Stil des chin. Musiktheaters. Im Westen wird sie fälschlicherweise oft mit diesem gleichgesetzt; tatsächlich ist sie nur ein Stil unter vielen. Die Geburtsstunde der P. schlug 1790, als aus Anlaß des Geburtstags des Kaisers Qianlong (reg. 1736–96) Theatergruppen aus der Provinz Anhui nach Peking kamen. Dort war bis dahin unter den Gebildeten das →kunqu und im Volk das yiyangqiang beliebt (→difang xi, Lokales Theater). Bereits 20 Jahre später wurde das Theaterleben in Peking durch vier Anhui-Truppen beherrscht, welche ihre hervorragende Bedeutung während des ganzen 19. Jh. beibehielten. Sie brachten zwei Musikstile nach Peking, deren Verbindung eine wesentliche Voraussetzung für das Entstehen der P. war: das melancholische erhuang und das lebhafte xipi. Entsprechend der Bedeutung dieser beiden Musikstile wurde die P. auch vielfach Pihuang genannt. Die Musik der P. wird geprägt durch Streich- und Schlaginstrumente, im Gegensatz zum kunqu, dessen Musik durch Blasinstrumente gespielt wird.

Von Anfang an war die P. nicht wie das klassische Theater (→zaju) der Yuan-Zeit oder auch das →chuanqi und das kunqu durch seine Stücke und Autoren bestimmt, sondern durch die Bühne und die Schauspieler. Meist tritt für das Publikum der Inhalt des Stücks, welcher ohnehin i. d. R. genau bekannt ist, in den Hintergrund zugunsten der Darstellungskunst des Schauspielers; nicht das Wort, sondern Gesang, Tanz, Akrobatik, Mimik und besondere Gestik sind der P. wesentlich. Die P. ist reines Bühnentheater, nicht literarisches Drama. Dementsprechend ist die Sprache der P. viel einfacher und die Prosodie der Verse viel weniger streng als beispielsweise im kunqu.

Im 19. Jh. war die P. vor allem durch einige Darsteller des →Rollenfachs «älterer Mann» (laosheng) geprägt. Die bedeutendsten waren Cheng Changgeng (1812–80) und sein Schüler Tan Xinpei (1847–1917). Sie stellten die großen Kaiser, Staatsmänner und Generäle der chin. Geschichte dar, vielfach in Stücken über Episoden aus der Zeit der Drei Reiche (3. Jh.), der chin. Helden-Ära. Diese inhaltliche Ausrichtung der P. kann durchaus als Ausdruck aufkeimender patriotischer Gefühle in weiten Teilen der Bevölkerung gewertet werden, die sich in einer Zeit zunehmender Bedrohung durch europ. Mächte der großen Persönlichkeiten der eigenen Geschichte entsann. Die P., die uns auf den ersten Blick dem Alltag und der Gegenwart so weit entrückt erscheint, war tatsächlich mit der sozialen und politischen Gegenwart stets eng verbunden. In der zweiten Hälfte des 19. Jh. breitete sich die P. in ganz China aus. Zweites Zentrum neben Peking wurde Shanghai, wo sich ein besonderer Stil entwickelte: reichere, zuweilen geradezu verschwenderische Ausstattung, Verwendung von Kulissen. Man sprach daher von der orthodoxen hauptstädtischen Schule (jingpai) und der freieren Shanghaier Schule (haipai) der P. Im 20. Jh. waren es neben weiteren großen laosheng-Darstellern vor allem Darsteller der Rolle junger Frauen (dan), die in der P. hervortraten. Das mag z. T. daran gelegen haben, daß die Rolle der Frau generell ein vieldiskutiertes Thema war. Auch hatte die P. einen hohen Grad der techn. Perfektion und künstlerischen Verfeinerung erreicht, so daß ein kultiviertes und kundiges Publikum einen besonderen Reiz bei der gekonnten Darstellung einer Frauenrolle durch einen Mann empfand. Vor allen Dingen aber war es der bekannteste Schauspieler der P., der auf diese Entwicklung Einfluß nahm, der große Frauendarsteller Mei Lanfang (1894–1961). Er war für fast fünf Jahrzehnte der unangefochtene Star der P.; er trug durch seine Auslandsreisen maßgeblich dazu bei, daß die P. auch in Europa und Amerika bekannt wurde.

Nach dem Sieg der Revolution 1949 wurde die Situation für die P. schwieriger, besonders weil von politischer Seite Erwartungen bezüglich einer bestimmten thematischen Ausrichtung an sie herangetragen wurden. Stücke, die mit den Wertmaßstäben der Kommunistischen Partei nicht übereinstimmten, mußten geändert werden oder wurden verboten. Ein Ausdruck dieser Entwicklung war die lange und bis heute nicht abgeschlossene Diskussion über die sog. Gegenwartsstücke, Stücke also, in denen Themen und Menschen der Gegenwart auf die Bühne gebracht werden. Diese Forderung führte schließlich dazu, daß während der Kulturrevolution 1966 bis 1976 nur noch Gegenwartsstücke aufgeführt wurden. Heute allerdings dominiert wieder das traditionelle Repertoire die Bühne der P.

Cheng, J.: Gesichter der Peking-Oper. Hamburg 1990; Gissenweher, M./Sieckmeyer, J.: Peking-Oper. Schaffhausen u. a. 1987; Mackerras, C.: The Rise of the Peking Opera 1770–1870, Social Aspects of the Theatre in Modern China. Oxford 1972; Mackerras, C.: The Chinese Theatre in Modern Times – From 1840 to the Present Day. London 1975; Scott, A. C.: The Classical Theatre of China. London 1957; Scott, A. C.: Mei Lan-fang, Leader of the Pear Garden. Hongkong 1959; Wu Zuguang, Huang Zuolin, Mei Shaowu: Peking Opera and Mei Lanfang. Beijing 1981.

Bernd Eberstein

Père noble

Männliches → Rollenfach, bezeichnet eine ältere Vaterfigur, in der sich tiefer Ernst mit Autorität vereinigt – z. B. der alte Horace in Pierre Corneilles (1606–84) *Horace* (1640) oder Attinghausen in Friedrich Schillers (1759–1805) *Wilhelm Tell* (1804). Der P. n. vereinigt in sich Strenge der Gefühle und der Sprache, eine Neigung zum Moralisieren und meist schablonenhafte, nuancenlose psychologische Vorstellungen, die sehr an die römische ‹patria potestas› erinnern; gerührt ist er nur, wenn die Ehre des Vaterlandes auf dem Spiel steht.

Bernard Poloni

Performance

Der engl. Begriff bedeutet Vorführung, Aufführung, Darstellung und betrifft nicht nur theatralische und musikalische Aufführungen, sondern bezeichnet auch die Leistungsfähigkeit eines Menschen oder einer Maschine (high performance technology). Mit P. klassifiziert man seit den 60er Jahren die Arbeiten von Künstlern, die sich mit darstellenden Experimenten mit und ohne Publikum beschäftigen. Ziel dieser Verfahren ist nicht mehr das Kunstobjekt, sondern der Prozeß. Dabei werden die Grenzen der theoretisch und ästhetisch definierten Kunstgattungen sowie die Künstlerrolle in Frage gestellt und überschritten. Wie die Ausdrucksformen sind auch die Begriffe aus verschiedenen Bereichen der Kunst und des Lebens übertragen worden. Üblich sind: Aktion, Aktionismus, Aktionskunst, Activity, Aufführungskünste, Body Art (Körperkunst), Demonstration, Event, → Happening, Live Art, Non Static Art, Piece (Stück). Die Vielfalt der Begriffe erklärt sich aus der heterogenen historischen Entwicklung der P. und den unterschiedlichen Richtungen in der Kunstkritik und der Theoriebildung. Die Begriffe werden oft unbedacht als Synonyme verwendet. Obwohl die Kunstgeschichte ephemere Werke vieler Künstler kennt, geht man im 20. Jh. namentlich von den ital. und russ. Futuristen, den Dadaisten, Surrealisten und Bauhauskünstlern aus, um eine Geschichte der P. zu fundieren. Bestimmende außerkünstlerische Einflüsse kommen aus der Ethnologie (Schamanismus), Mythologie, Psychologie, Theologie (Zen-Buddhismus), der technologischen Entwicklung (Atombombe, Kommunikationsmittel), den Kriegen in der Dritten Welt, den Protest- und Bürgerrechtsbewegungen, dem Zirkus und der Akrobatik. Maßgebliche Motoren der Entwicklung der P. sind Künstler, deren Arbeiten und Rolle sich aus der ästhetischen und institutionellen Festlegung gelöst haben, oder Außenseiter neben der Kunstszene: Theater (A. Artaud, A. Jarry); Tanz (I. Duncan, Rudolf v. Laban, S. Diaghilew, M. Cunningham); Musik (E. Satie, L. Russolo, J. Cage); Malerei (M. Duchamp, J. Pollock); Skulptur (J. Beuys); Architektur (V. Tatlin, Luftarchitektur von Y. Klein und W. Ruhnau); Literatur (J.-K. Huysmans, F. Kafka, K. Schwitters); Film (‹Expanded Cinema›); Video (N. J. Paik); Sport (A. Cravan, Boxer). – Im individuellen Schaffen eines Künstlers sind P. nicht von ausschließlicher und durchgehender Bedeutung; P. kennzeichnen Phasen persönlichen und gesellschaftlichen Umbruchs. Neben der intermediären Ausdrucksform einzelner stehen Kollaborationen, die Spezialisten wie Choreographen, Musiker, Komponisten, Tänzer und bildende Künstler zur Realisierung eines Stücks vereinen.

Battcock, G./Nickas, R.: The Art of P. New York 1984; Bronson A. A./Gale, P.: P. by Artists, Toronto 1979; Goldberg, R.: P. London 1979; Melzer, A.: Latest Rage The Big Drum. Dada & Surrealist, P. Ann Arbor 1976, [2] 1980; Kirby, M.: Futurist P. New York 1971; Aufsätze und Dokumentationen in: Kunstforum International, Bde. 13 (1975), 24 (1977), 27 (1978), 32 (1979), 58 (1983); «High Performance» (Los Angeles) und «Performance» (London) – beide Zeitschriften erscheinen seit 1978.

Johannes Lothar Schröder

Performance Group

Gegr. 1967 in New York von Richard Schechner (* 1934) mit u. a. dem Ziel, auf der Grundlage der Prinzipien des → Environmental Theatre die Normen und Masken des Alltagslebens zu durchbrechen. Die Darsteller/innen sollen verwunden und verwundbar sein. Die erste Produktion der P. G., *Dionysus in 69*, stand unter dem Einfluß Grotowskis (→ Armes Theater) und basierte in seinen Textelementen auf den Dramen Euripides'. *Makbeth* (1969) verknüpft die Shakespeare-Vorlage mit dem Faschismus; *Commune* (1970/71) verbindet die Ermordung Sharon Tates mit dem Massaker von My Lai. Spätere Inszenierungen Schechners versuchten, die Methoden des Environmental Theatre auch auf das moderne Drama Jean Genets, Sam Shepards oder Ted Hughes' anzuwenden. Schechner gab 1980 die Leitung der P. G. auf, die sich daraufhin in Wooster Group umbenannte. Die P. G. hat mit einiger professioneller Überzeugungskraft ein Konzept realisiert, wonach sich Theater in ganzheitlichen Räumen vollzieht, nicht fragmentiert durch geltende Konventionen.

Schechner, R.: Essays on Performance Theory 1970–76. New York 1977; ders.: Makbeth – After Shakespeare. Schulenburg (Tx.) 1978; ders. und Performance Group: Dionysus in 69. New York 1970; Shank, T.: American Alternative Theatre. London 1982.

Dieter Herms

Periakten

Teil der Bühnenausstattung des hellenistischen Theaters; zwei prismenförmige, drehbare, auf allen drei Seiten bemalte Ständer. Zeitpunkt der Einführung (nicht vor der hell. Zeit), Standort (wahrscheinlich an den →Parodoi) und Funktion (Anzeige des Szenenwechsels durch Drehung zu einem anderen, den neuen Schauplatz zeigenden Bild oder Anzeige der Herkunft der durch die jeweilige →Parodos auftretenden Person) sind unsicher. Die P. wurden im 16. Jh. wieder aufgenommen – zuerst in Italien durch Bernado Buontalenti (1536–1608) in Florenz, dann auch durch Josef Furttenbach (1591–1667) mit seiner in Ulm gebauten und im *Mannhaften Kunstspiegel* (1603) beschriebenen Telari-Bühne; zur gleichen Zeit wird diese Bühnentechnik durch Jean Dubreuil, 1602–70, und Maciej Sarbiewski, 1595–1640, auch in Frankreich und Polen verbreitet. Da die P. urspr. für nur drei Bühnenbilder vorgesehen waren, wurden sie später mit übereinandergelegten Stoffbahnen ausgestattet, die bei Szenenwechsel aufgerollt werden konnten. Doch wurden die unpraktischen und unhandlichen P. bald zugunsten selbständig aufgestellter Kulissen aufgegeben, und zwar durch Gian Battista Aleotti (1546–1636) und vor allem Giacomo Torelli (1608–78) im Novissimo Theater in Venedig 1641.

Beare, W.: The Roman Stage. London ²1955, p. 238–245; Jungmaier, C.: Periakten im griech.-röm. Theater. Diss. Wien 1972.

Bernard Poloni / Bernd Seidensticker

Perioche

Griech.: das Ganze, der Inhalt (→Jesuitentheater). Seit Ende des 16. Jh. ausführliches gedrucktes Programm für die lat. Aufführungen der Jesuitenkollegs und anderer Ordens-Schultheater. Verfaßt vom Choragus in lat. oder Landessprache oder zweisprachig. Auflage ca. 200 Exemplare. P. oder Synopsen enthalten Titel, Widmung, Namen der veranstaltenden Klasse, zu deren Gunsten die Prämien verteilt werden, Datum der Aufführung, Argumentum (meist wörtliches Zitat aus der für die Handlung benützten Quelle), Inhaltsangabe, Szenarium und Verzeichnis der Mitwirkenden. Erstmalig in dieser Form: Jesuitenaufführung *Der Triumph des Heiligen Michael* (München 1597).

Drozd, K. W.: Schul- und Ordenstheater am Collegium S. J. Klagenfurt (1604–1773). Klagenfurt 1965; Ebeling, F. W.: Prospekte [Periochen] zu Schulkomödien. In: Serapeum 23 (1862), S. 168–176; 28 (1867), S. 117–140; Kindermann, H.: Das Theater der Barockzeit. Salzburg 1959; Weller, E.: Die Leistungen der

Jesuiten auf dem Gebiet der dramatischen Kunst. Bibliographisch dargestellt. In: Serapeum 25 (1864) und 27 (1866).

Ingeborg Janich

Person

Aus dem Lat. persona = Maske, später auch Rolle, abgeleiteter Begriff. Auftretende fiktive Person, auch Charakter, Figur, Gestalt genannt. P. ist eine vom Dramatiker erfundene Figur, gleichzeitig aber auch vom Schauspieler verkörperte, gespielte, dargestellte Figur. Wie in kommunizierenden Röhren stehen Autor und Schauspieler (dabei, mit variabler Wirkung, Regisseur, Dekoration, Kostüm und Maske) innerhalb des schöpferischen Prozesses der Gestaltung dramat. P.

Um einen Überblick, aber auch eine nähere Bestimmung zu erhalten, bedarf die Vielzahl und Mannigfaltigkeit dramatischer P. einer Typologie. So unterscheiden sich z. B. die P. des geschlossenen von denen des offenen Dramas durch folgende Kennzeichen: Die P. des geschlossenen Dramas, d. h. hauptsächlich die →dramatis personae der antiken Trag., der frz. tragédie classique und der klassischen Tragödien, entstammen der Geschichte und dem Mythos. Den Regeln der Antike entsprechend, gehören die P. der →Tragödie dem hohen gesellschaftlichen Stand an, die der →Komödie aber den niederen Ständen. Da sie als überzeitlich und auf den Gipfeln der sozialen Hierarchie stehend gedacht sind, tragen sie in sich die totale Verflechtung zwischen Individuum und Funktion, zwischen Mensch und Rolle. Daher ihr Herausgehobensein, das ihnen die Würde der Tragik verleiht, sie aber in einer gewissen Einseitigkeit verkapselt. Sie sind statisch, machen im Laufe der Tragödie keine Entwicklung durch, bleiben Träger der Idee, die den Kern ihres Wesens ausmacht. Ihrer besonderen Stellung völlig bewußt, verbergen sie ihre privat-persönlichen Eigenschaften unter der ihnen zugeteilten Repräsentanzfunktion. Sie stehen dem traditionellen Begriff des Helden bzw. der Heldin (positiv oder negativ) am nächsten, da sie als ideale Menschentypen aufgefaßt werden. Als solche sind sie keineswegs charakterlich ‹plastisch›, sondern eher ‹flächig›. Eine P. kann mehrere Rollen spielen, aber kaum mehreren Ideen/Idealen entsprechen. Dazu die aufschlußreiche Aussage Schillers: «Auch die tragischen P. selbst bedürfen dieses Anhalts, dieser Ruhe, um sich zu sammeln; denn sie sind keine wirklichen Wesen, die bloß der Gewalt des Moments gehorchen und bloß ein Individuum darstellen, sondern ideale P. und Repräsentanten ihrer Gattung, die das Tiefe der Menschheit aussprechen» (*Über den Gebrauch des Chors in der Tragödie*). Einer geordneten Welt angehörend, wissen sie

738 Person

Ordnung in die Emotion zu bringen und mit Besonnenheit ihr Schicksal zu erfüllen: Sie stehen in einem geschlossenen, an P. nie zahlreichen Handlungskreis. Aus ihrer starren, präzisen Konfiguration entlassen, würden sie ihren Sinn, ihre Rolle, verlieren.

Im Gegensatz dazu stehen die P. des ‹offenen Dramas›. Sie entspringen keiner geordneten, einheitlichen Welt, sondern einer, die durch Vielheit gekennzeichnet ist. Vielheit der Handlung, des Raums, der Zeitqualität; das offene Drama kennzeichnet eine große Anzahl von P. nach dem Prinzip, das Ganze in Ausschnitten zu zeigen. Die P. des offenen Dramas werden weder zeitlich noch sozial aus der Normalebene herausgehoben. Sie können allen Ständen angehören, besitzen weder Größe noch Besonnenheit, sind eher Vertreter einer eingeschränkten Mündigkeit; sie sind infolgedessen ‹dynamische› Figuren, die unter dem Einfluß der Umwelt, ihrer eigenen Triebe und Affekte, die unerwartetsten Wandlungen vollziehen. Ihr Verhalten ist fast nie voraussehbar, ist bedingt von vielfachen Determinanten. Worin sie wirklich eingebunden sind, ist das Aktuelle, ihr betontes Hier-und-Jetzt-Sein. Daraus ergibt sich im modernen Drama auch die Krise der dramatischen P. (Identitätsverlust).

Es gibt noch weitere mögliche Typologien der P. Erwähnenswert die Triade: Personifikation – Typ – Individuum. Am abstraktesten ist die Personifikation, die sich im mittelalterlichen →Moralitätendrama und in den →barocken geistlichen Spielen der Jesuiten als dominante Form der Figurenkonzeption offenbart. Die P. geht darin in der Funktion völlig auf. Sie ist Teil eines allegorischen Systems. Der Typ stellt eine weitere Etappe dar. Er ist reicher aufgebaut, verkörpert nicht nur eine einzige Eigenschaft, sondern einen Komplex soziologischer und psychologischer Merkmale. Hier findet die weite Skala von →Rollenfächern, von Shakespeare und →der Commedia dell'arte über die →Klassik und das →Volkstheater bis zum heutigen →Boulevardtheater ihre Vertreter. Das moderne Theater weist eine besondere Vorliebe für Typen auf. Sie tragen meistens keine Namen mehr, ihre Identität geht langsam verloren, sie agieren nur noch als Vertreter bestimmter sozialer Kategorien: Arzt, Bauer, Vater, Sohn, Richter, Arme, Reiche, Jedermann usw. Das Individuum als Spielart der P. dominiert die Dramaturgie des Naturalismus, verbirgt aber trotz aller Lebenswahrscheinlichkeit und Realitätstreue die Absicht, das Einmalige und Unwiederholbare hervorzubringen. – Im Brecht-Theater Gespaltenheit der P. oder Aufspaltung der Figuren (Shen-Te/Shui-Ta, Puntila, P. Mauler) als Zeichen der gesellschaftlichen Widersprüche.

Die immer heftigere Ablehnung des Realismus auf der Bühne im 20. Jh. führt zu einer noch stärkeren Infragestellung der P. als fiktiver Figur. Dennoch: «Die Krise der P. ist nur Zeichen und Bedingung ihrer Vitalität» (Abirached).

Abirached, R.: La crise du personnage dans le théâtre moderne. Paris 1978; Ducrot, O./Todorov, T.: Dictionnaire encyclopédique des Sciences du langage. Paris 1972; Kesting, M.: Der Abbau der Persönlichkeit. In: Keller, W. (Hg.): Beiträge zur Poetik des Dramas. Darmstadt 1976; Mittenzwei, W.: Gestaltung und Gestalten im modernen Drama. Berlin (Ost)/Weimar 1965. Pfister, M.: Das Drama. München 1977; Polheim, K. K.: Die dramatische Konfiguration. In: Keller, W. (Hg.): Beiträge zur Poetik des Dramas. Darmstadt 1976.

Adriana Hass

Petruschka

Russ. →Puppentheater und Hauptfigur (offensichtlich auf die ital. →Pulcinella zurückgehend) in demselben. Schon im 17. Jh. nachgewiesen, im 19. und noch Anfang des 20. Jh. populär.

Cechnovicer, O./Eremin, I.: Teatr Petruški. Moskva/Leningrad 1927; Kelly, C.: Petruska. Cambridge/New York 1990.

Annelore Engel-Braunschmidt

Die Pfeffermühle

Leipzig: Am 23. 4. 1954 begann die Geschichte der «Leipziger P.» als zweitem professionellem Kabarett der DDR. Bis heute wurden über 60 Programme aufgeführt; neben satirisch-aktuellen auch die Tradition des Kabaretts pflegende Vorstellungen. Trotz der Verleihung des Kunstpreises der Stadt (1966) waren Funktionäre nur selten mit der P. zufrieden, die die gewünschte «positive» Kritik vermissen ließ (so wurde 1964 der künstlerische Leiter Edgar Külow abgelöst).

Die P. konnte sich als Aushängeschild der Messestadt (wie auch die «academixer», 1978 aus einem Studentenkabarett entstanden) manches an Satire und Kritik erlauben, was sonst in der DDR nur schwierig durchzusetzen war. Dennoch waren ihre Möglichkeiten eingeschränkt – u. a. durch vorherige Programmabnahme, durch genehmigungspflichtige ‹Improvisation›. Dabei trat auch in der DDR mehr und mehr ‹strukturelle› Zensur an die Stelle offener Beschränkungen. Leiter der P. ist seit mehr als einem Jahrzehnt der Autor und Kabaretthistoriker Rainer Otto. Als einziges Kabarett der DDR konnte die P. in den 80er Jahren Auslandsgastspiele durchführen. Seit dem Ende der DDR ermöglichen Doppelinszenierungen des aktuellen Programms Gastspielreisen und den regelmäßigen Spielbetrieb. Gegenwärtig ist die P. noch eine kommunale (und damit subventionierte) Einrichtung; über Privatisierungspläne ist noch nicht entschieden.

München/Zürich: Die erste Vorstellung der von Erika Mann gegründeten P. (der sie auch als Texterin, Darstellerin, Conférencier, Direktor und Organisator diente) fand noch in Deutschland statt: am 1. 1. 1933 in der Münchner «Bonbonniere». Die Exil-Karriere des Kabaretts begann am 1. 10. 1933 im Hotel «Hirschen» in der Nähe von Zürich. Von hier aus unternahm die P. bis 1937 Gastspielreisen in die Tschechoslowakei, nach Holland, Belgien und Luxemburg. Zum Ensemble gehörten u. a. Therese Giehse, der Komponist Magnus Henning und die Grotesktänzerin Lotte Goslar. Nach einem von Schweizer Nationalisten im Zürcher Kursaal inszenierten Krawall verabschiedete der Kantonatsrat eine «Lex Pfeffermühle»: Ausländischen Kabaretts mit politischer Tendenz wurde fürderhin das Auftreten in Zürich untersagt. Andere Kantone schlossen sich dieser Verfügung an. Bis zu ihrem Verbot hatte die Gruppe in der Schweiz mehr als tausend Vorstellungen gegeben. Eine im Winter 1936/37 in die USA unternommene Gastspielreise wurde zu einem Mißerfolg: die Form der Kleinkunst war in den USA traditionslos und stieß auf Unverständnis.

Budzinski, K.: Pfeffer ins Getriebe. München 1982; Gebhardt, H. (Hg.): Kabarett heute. Berlin 1987; Hösch, R.: Kabarett von gestern und heute. 2 Bde. Berlin 1967–1972; Keiser-Hayne, H.: Beteiligt euch, es geht um die Erde. Erika Mann und ihr politisches Kabarett die «Pfeffermühle» 1933–1937. München 1990; Otto, R./Rösler, W.: Kabarettgeschichte. Berlin [2]1981; Otto, R.: Pfeffermüllereien. Berlin 1975; ders. (Hg.): 15 Jahre Leipziger Pfeffermühle. Leipzig 1969; «Scharfe Sachen». Texte des Leipziger Kabarett «Die P.». Leipzig 1957.

Wolfgang Beck/Jan Hans

Phlyakenposse

Unterital.-griech. volkstümliche →‹Komödie›; ursprünglich subliterarisch, improvisiert; erst um 300 v. Chr. durch Rhinton v. Syrakus zur Literaturform gemacht. Zahlreiche Vasenbilder (Phlyakenvasen) erlauben gewisse Schlüsse auf Themen und Motive, Bühne, Kostüme und Ausstattung; besonders beliebt waren offenbar (besonders bei Rhinton) Mythentravestie und Tragödienparodie.

Gigante, M.: Rintone e il teatro in Magna Grecia. Neapel 1971; Trendall, A. D.: Phlyax Vases. BICS Suppl. 19, London 1967.

Bernd Seidensticker

Piaoyou (Laienschauspieler)

In allen Stilen des traditionellen →chin. Theaters hatten seit jeher Laiendarsteller (→Laienspiel) eine große Bedeutung. Das mag bei einer derart schwierigen und hinsichtlich ihrer darstellerischen Mittel komplexen Theaterform zunächst überraschend erscheinen; es kann aber gewiß als Zeichen einer außerordentlichen Beliebtheit des Theaters gewertet werden. Die Laien gründeten eigene Ausbildungs- und Übungsstätten (piaofang). Nicht selten engagierten sie bekannte professionelle Schauspieler als Lehrer. Natürlich war die Ausbildung der Laien nicht so streng wie das jahrelange intensive Training der Berufsschauspieler; fehlende Strenge und Intensität indessen wurden kompensiert durch Enthusiasmus, nicht selten auch durch hohe Begabung. – Das Laientheater stellte überdies ein wichtiges Reservoir für den Stand der professionellen Schauspieler dar, da nicht wenige Laiendarsteller «ins Meer hinabstiegen» (xia hai), das heißt, die Schauspielerei zu ihrem Beruf machten. Einige der großen Schauspieler des 19. und 20. Jh. hatten als Laien zum Theater gefunden (Wang Xiaonong, Liu Housheng, Sun Juxian, Yu Zhenfei u. a.).

Bernd Eberstein

Piccolo Teatro di Milano

Das P. T. M. wurde als erstes →Teatro Stabile am 14. Mai 1947 von Giorgio Strehler (* 1921) und Paolo Grassi (* 1919) in einem Mailänder Kino gegründet. Das Theater wurde mit *Nachtasyl* von Gorki eröffnet. Im Repertoire der ersten Jahre Stücke von Shakespeare und Goldoni; später inszenierte man auch Tschechow und Brecht. Ziel der Gründer war es, ein →Volkstheater zu schaffen, das einer proletarischen, antielitären Kultur dienen sollte. Erstmals wurde hier Theaterpolitik unter Heranziehung der Stadtverwaltung und anderer politischer Organe praktiziert, um das Theater jedem Bürger zugänglich zu machen.

Am dramaturgischen Konzept des P. T. hat sich seit seiner Gründung kaum etwas geändert. Das Programm soll nicht dem Vergnügen einer Klasse, sondern dem Interesse der Nation dienen. Deshalb wird eine systematische Darbietung grundlegender Themen des ital. Dramas und des Welttheaters versucht. Nicht alle Inszenierungen waren populär, denn Strehler lehnte jede nur publikumswirksame Volkstümlichkeit ab und bestand darauf, die intellektuelle Komplexität seiner Stücke zu wahren. 1968 verließ Strehler vorübergehend das P. T., kehrte jedoch 1972, als Grassi, der inzwischen das Theater allein geleitet hatte, zum Leiter der

742   Pip Simmons Theatre Group

Mailänder Scala berufen wurde, wieder ans P. T. zurück. – Inzwischen hat das Theater eine zweite Spielstätte, das Teatro Lirico. Ein Neubau ist inzwischen bezogen.

Elke Kehr

Pip Simmons Theatre Group

Alternative Theatergruppe, 1969 aus Jim Haynes Drury Lane Arts Lab hervorgegangen. 1973 aufgelöst, 1974 neugegründet, spielt seither überwiegend im → Mickery Theatre, Amsterdam. Mit ihrem experimentellen, surrealistischen Stil und dem Einsatz multimedialer Techniken gehört die Gruppe zur → Avantgarde des → Fringe Theatre. – Durch ihre Teilnahme am Hamburger Welt-Theater-Festival 1979 wurde die Gruppe international bekannt. Zu ihren bedeutendsten Produktionen gehören *Superman* (1969), *Do It!* (1971), *The George Jackson Black and White Minstrel Show* (1973), *An die Musik* (1975) sowie Adaptionen von Shakespeares *The Tempest* (1977), Büchners *Woyzeck* (1977) und Zamyatins *We* (1979).

Ansorge, P.: Disrupting the Spectacle: Five Years of Experiment and Fringe Theatre in Britain. London 1975; Craig, S. (ed.): Dreams and Deconstructions. Alternative Theatre in Britain. Ambergate 1980; Itzin, C.: Stages in the Revolution. Political Theatre in Britain since 1968. London 1980.

Werner Bleike

Pirandellismus

Der in Agrigent geborene Luigi Pirandello (1867–1936) verfaßte in 45 Jahren seiner Schriftstellerlaufbahn neben zahlreichen anderen Werken rund 40 Theaterstücke, die ihn weltberühmt machten und auf welche sich der Begriff P. in erster Linie bezieht. – Pirandello beginnt mit der Nachahmung und Übernahme der bürgerlichen Komödie, wobei er jedoch unerwartete Intrigen entwickelt bzw. die Strukturen des Theaters seiner Zeit ins Gegenteil verkehrt, z. B. *Così è se vi pare* (1917, dt. «So ist es wie Sie meinen»). Zwischen 1920 und 1930 schreibt er eine Reihe von Stükken, die eine revolutionäre Dramaturgie begründen, in der die Korrosion der hergebrachten dramatischen Formen und die Problematik des psychologischen Relativismus wie der gesellschaftlichen Determiniertheit im Konflikt mit dem inneren Gefühl zusammenkommen. *Sei personaggi in cerca d'autore* (1921, dt. «Sechs Personen suchen einen Autor») markiert die Geburt des großen Pirandellischen Theaters und den Beginn seines Weltruhms. Auf der ersten Ebene handelt es sich um ein weinerliches Melodrama: Eine entzweite Familie findet sich in einer neuen Zerreißprobe, nachdem Vater und Schwiegertochter einander an einem verrufenen Ort wiederbegegnet sind. Die zweite Ebene ist die tragische Projektion dieser Personen (ersten Grades) in ‹Personen› (zweiten Grades): Der Vater will seine Schwäche überwinden, in der ihn seine Schwiegertochter belassen möchte, die hierin im stillen eine Rechtfertigung für ihren eigenen Lebenswandel sieht. Mutter und Sohn spielen ihre ablehnende Haltung aus, und zwei Kinder, die kein Wort sagen, stellen den Todesinstinkt dar, den jede der anderen Personen in einer jeweils verschiedenen Logik auf die Bühne bringt. In der Konfrontation mit diesem Melodrama und mit dieser Tragödie läuft die flüchtige Komödie der Schauspieler ab, die zugleich – dank ihrer Funktion – als einzige imstande sind, diese Geschichte ‹wiederaufzunehmen› und weiterzuführen, und vollkommen außerstande, den Einsatz zu verstehen und in den intimen Dramenkern der Protagonisten einzudringen. Zu der Trilogie des «Theaters im Theater» gehören noch die Stücke *Ciascuno a suo modo* (1924, dt. «Jeder nach seiner Art») und *Questa sera si recita a soggetto* (1930, dt. «Heute abend wird aus dem Stegreif gespielt»).

Der Begriff P. deckt ein Netz von nicht systematisch miteinander verbundenen Begriffen ab: Humor, überspannte Logik, Leidenschaft für kommentative Beweisführung, die auf die Demontage der Gesellschaftskomödie und der Mythomanie angewendet werden; sie lassen so in der Automatik des Alltäglichen Unbewußtes, Schuld, Absurdes zusammenlaufen und bringen gemeinsam die Sinnlosigkeit der Existenz und die bedingte Willkür des ‹Theaters› an den Tag.

Pirandello hat den theoretischen Niederschlag seiner Lebensphilosophie *umorismo* genannt: das ‹Gefühl vom Gegenteil›, die zugleich traumhafte und schmerzliche Erkenntnis, daß statt des Seins genau das Gegenteil: der Schein anzutreffen ist (eine schrecklich geschminkte alte Frau statt würdig zurückhaltender Akzeptanz des Alters). Der nicht im Objekt, sondern im Subjekt zu findende *umorismo* ist eine Konstruktion von ‹Gegenteilen›, wobei der Geist seine Ungeheuer durch perverse Dialektik hervorbringt. Hieraus ergibt sich die Bedeutung der ‹Räsoneure›, Kommentatoren, Zuschauer von Amts wegen, Spielleiter, die sie ‹verstanden› haben, Regisseure anderer wie der eigenen Person, die das Gewissen des Werks sind, die Dynamik der Rede und der Situation.

P. läßt sich so charakterisieren, daß in diesem Werk eine triviale, wiedererkennbare, beruhigende Tradition (gleichzeitig Vaudeville und ein bestimmtes Italienbild) mit Zersetzungsfermenten koexistieren und aufeinanderwirken, die den Zuschauer ständig vor die Frage stellen, ob er einer (realistischen) Darstellung ersten Grades beiwohnt oder einer Darstellung zweiten Grades (teilweise parodistisch und also ironisch) oder

negativ einer Dialektik der Absetzung der ‹Wirklichkeit› und ihrer überkommenen Bilder. Die Theatertechnik hat also eine präzise ideologische
Bedeutung: Korruption und Korrosion der Gesellschaft werden analy-
tisch dargestellt durch den Abbau im Akt der sie vorführenden Kunstfor-
men. Die große menschliche Komödie des Menschen (Molière), dann
Komödie der sozialen Beziehungen geworden (Goldoni), degradiert zur
Sittenkomödie im Boulevardtheater, endet hier als Komödie/Tragödie
der Tragödie/Komödie: Die Lebenstragik ist Theaterkomik, aber das
Drama der Aufführung ist eine Tragödie. Der P. ist zusammengefaßt die
Erfindung einer Dramaturgie mit bescheidenen Tricks im Dienst des
Kontrasts zwischen triumphierender Mittelmäßigkeit und sublimer Pa-
thetik.

Borlenghi, A.: Pirandello o dell'ambiguità. Padua 1968; Büdel, O.: Pirandello.
London 1966; Ferrante, L.: Pirandello. Florenz 1958; Genot, G.: Pirandello. Paris
1970; Lugnani, L.: Pirandello, Letterature e Teatro. Florenz 1970.

Gérard Genot

Piscatorbühne

Eindeutig für die Sache des Proletariats Partei zu ergreifen, war Erwin
Piscators (1893–1966) politisch-ästhetisches Programm. 1924 als Regisseur an die Berliner Volksbühne berufen, geriet er durch seine politisch-
agitatorischen Inszenierungen schon bald in Widerspruch zum neutralisti-
schen Kurs des Bühnenvorstands. Man trennte sich. Ein großindustrieller
Mäzen verhalf Piscator 1927 zu einem eigenen Theater im Berliner Westen: der ersten P. Damit war die materielle Voraussetzung gegeben, eine
eigenständige Theaterarbeit zu entwickeln. Sowohl die Bühnen- als auch
die Dramenform war von Grund auf zu revolutionieren, um zu einer dem
Zeitalter der Wissenschaft und Technik adäquaten Bühnenästhetik zu gelangen – ein Vorhaben, das von Beginn an von Kompromissen begleitet
war: Statt eine von Walter Gropius (1883–1969) konzipierte «Theatermaschine» (→Totaltheater) in Betrieb nehmen zu können, mußten Piscator und seine Mitarbeiter mit einer traditionellen Guckkastenbühne –
dem Theater am Nollendorfplatz – vorliebnehmen. Trotz beschränkter
räumlicher Möglichkeiten entwickelte Piscator dennoch binnen kurzer
Zeit Bühnenformen, die in die Theatergeschichte eingingen: die →Eta-
genbühne, die →Segment-Globus-Bühne. Bei der Dramenfassung von
Hašeks *Schwejk* (1928) kamen →laufende Bänder zum Einsatz.
    Die neuen Stücke, die Piscator an seiner Bühne inszenieren wollte,
waren noch nicht vorhanden; also sah man sich gezwungen, auf konventionell gebaute Dramen zurückzugreifen. Diese Dramen dienten dem Regis-

Piscatorbühne 745

seur als Rohmaterial – sie waren nach politisch-dramaturgischen Gesichtspunkten neu zu organisieren. Von zwei ‹Fronten› aus unternahm Piscator den Versuch, die traditionelle Dramenform zu sprengen: 1. durch ‹Episierung› des Bühnenstoffs, d. h. «Ausweitung der Handlung und Aufhellung ihrer Hintergründe, also Fortführung des Stückes über den Rahmen des nur Dramatischen hinaus»; 2. durch Auflösung der ‹in sich geschlossenen› Dramenhandlung in revueartige ‹Einzelnummern›. Film und Filmprojektionen erweiterten die szenische Handlung ins Historisch-Dokumentarische, so durch Verwendung von Fotomaterial über den 1. Weltkrieg in der Polit-Revue *Trotz alledem!* (1925). – Die Theaterproduktionen der P. waren Ergebnis eines kollektiven Inszenierungsprozesses; sie entstanden in enger Zusammenarbeit von Regie, Bühnenmusik, -technik, dem Schauspielerensemble und einem Autorenteam, das Piscator bei der Auswahl und Bearbeitung der Theaterstoffe behilflich war.

1927 ins Leben gerufen, war die P. bereits ein Jahr später bankrott. Die Übernahme eines weiteren Theaters hatte sich als geschäftliche Fehlkalkulation erwiesen. Ein zweiter Versuch (1929) verlief ebenfalls wenig erfolgreich. Das Dilemma der P. bestand darin, dem Programm nach ein proletarisches Massenpublikum ansprechen zu wollen, de facto aber zur Finanzierung der aufwendigen Theaterproduktionen auf das zahlungskräftige Publikum des Berliner Westens angewiesen zu sein.

Nach der Auflösung der zweiten P. schloß sich ein Teil des Schauspielerensembles zum Piscator-Kollektiv zusammen. Der Regisseur der großen Formen und aufwendigen Mittel kehrte zu seinen Anfängen zurück und erwies sich als ein Theatermann, der trotz äußerst beschränkter finanzieller Möglichkeiten dennoch in der Lage war, mit seinen politisch-agitatorischen Inszenierungen in die Klassenkämpfe der Weimarer Republik einzugreifen.

Boeser, K./Vatková, R. (Hg.): Erwin Piscator. Eine Arbeitsbiographie. 2 Bde. Berlin 1987; Haarmann, H.: Erwin Piscator und die Schicksale der Berliner Dramaturgie. München 1991; Innes, C. D.: Erwin Piscator's Political Theatre, Cambridge 1972; Knellessen, F. W.: Agitation auf der Bühne. Emsdetten 1970, S. 76–188; Mac Alpine, S.: Visual aids in the production of the first Piscator-Bühne 1927. Frankfurt/M. 1990; Piscator, E.: Das politische Theater. Berlin 1929. Von Felix Gasbarra bearbeitete Neuausgabe. Reinbek bei Hamburg 1963; ders.: Schriften. 2 Bde. Berlin (DDR) 1968; ders.: Theater, Film, Politik. Ausgewählte Schriften. Berlin (DDR) 1980; ders.: Zeittheater. Reinbek bei Hamburg 1986; Weisstein, U.: Soziologische Dramaturgie und politisches Theater. In: Reinhold Grimm (Hg.): Deutsche Dramentheorien II. Wiesbaden [3]1981, S. 181–207; Willett, J.: Erwin Piscator. Die Eröffnung des politischen Zeitalters auf dem Theater. Frankfurt/M. 1982.

Carl Wege

Plakat / Theaterplakat

Die typischen Attribute, die dem Medium P. im allg. zuerkannt werden, wie auffällig, groß, bunt, werbewirksam, kaufanregend u. ä., lassen sich auf den Bereich des Theater-P. nicht ohne weiteres übertragen. «Das Hauptproblem, das als unlösbarer Widerspruch hinter allen Theaterplakatentwürfen lauert, ist, ob es sich um ein Werbemittel oder um ein eigenständiges Kunstwerk handelt...» (August, 1976). Aber auch für die Theater sind P. ein Instrument ihrer ‹Öffentlichkeitsarbeit›, sie müssen erkennen lassen, wofür sie stehen – nicht nur für sich selbst, sondern für eine best. Inszenierung oder ein best. Theater. Sie werden vom Passanten fast automatisch mit Werbeplakaten verglichen, so daß die graphische Qualität und der drucktechn. Aufwand gewissen Ansprüchen genügen müssen. Trotzdem läßt sich eine Tendenz zum ‹künstlerischen›, ‹geschmacksbildenden› P. absehen; neben Graphik-Designern stammen immer mehr P.-Entwürfe von freien Malern, Bildhauern oder Bühnenbildnern, die in erster Linie ihre Idee und Interpretation eines Theaterstücks in ein Bild, eine Graphik, eine Fotografie oder Collage umsetzen und erst an zweiter Stelle an die Werbewirksamkeit bzw. -möglichkeit denken.

August, E. C.: Kunst, die keiner anschaut? In: Theater heute 8 (1976), S. 21–23; Doll, H. P.: Stuttgarter Theaterplakate 1972–85. Münster 1984; Loeffler, P.: Schweizer Theaterplakate 1906–1925. Basel/Boston 1988; Mellinghoff, F. (Hg.): Plakatanschlag für Friedrich Schiller. Dortmund 1980; Rademacher, H.: Theaterplakate. Berlin 1987.

Ute Hagel

Das Politische Kabarett

1927 in Wien von Ludwig Wagner und Victor Grünbaum als sozialdemokratisches Wahlkampfkabarett gegründet. Mitwirkende waren ausschließlich Laien, zumeist sozialdemokratische Studenten. Das P. K. trat verstärkt vor und in Wahlkämpfen auf. Der bedeutendste Autor, der aus dieser Gruppe hervorging, war Jura Soyfer. Da sich die satirisch-politischen Programme eindeutig gegen Klerikalismus und Austrofaschismus richteten, wurde das P. K. zusammen mit der SPÖ verboten. Die letzten Vorstellungen fanden im Wahlkampf 1932 statt. Nach dem Krieg gab es weitere Versuche eines sozialdemokratischen politischen Kabaretts. 1946 wurde von Amateuren «Der rote Hund» als Wanderkabarett gegründet, und 1949 zogen die von Berufsschauspielern gebildeten «Wiener Spatzen» mit zwei Programmen durch ganz Österreich. Fortsetzungen fanden diese Bemühungen nicht.

Eiselt-Weltmann, S.: Das «Politische Kabarett» und die «Roten Spieler».
Diss. Wien 1987; Reisner, I.: Kabarett als Werkstatt des Theaters. Diss. Wien
1961; Scheu, F.: Humor als Waffe. Politisches Kabarett in der ersten Republik.
Wien/München/Zürich 1977; Soyfer, J.: Das Gesamtwerk. Hg. von H. Jarka.
Wien/München/Zürich 1980; Weys, R.: Cabaret und Kabarett in Wien. Wien
1970.

Wolfgang Beck

Politisches Theater

Der Begriff ist erst seit Erwin Piscators 1929 erschienenem Buch *Das
politische Theater* gängig geworden, die Sache jedoch ist so alt wie das
Medium selbst. Seit der griech. Antike hat sich das Theater immer wieder mit den Problemen des Zusammenlebens in der Gemeinschaft beschäftigt, Kritik an den herrschenden politischen Zuständen geübt, für
bestimmte Standpunkte Agitation und Propaganda betrieben. Von den
Tragödien des Aischylos und Sophokles, von den Komödien des Aristophanes über die Historien von Shakespeare, die Stücke von Schiller
und Beaumarchais, über *Dantons Tod* von Büchner und *Napoleon oder
die hundert Tage* von Grabbe führt die Reihe der Stücke mit eindeutig
politischer Intention bis in unser Jh., bis zu der Dramatik von Brecht,
zu den Stücken von Sartre und Camus, von Max Frisch, Peter Weiss,
Rolf Hochhuth oder Heinar Kipphardt. Ob mit einem Drama direkt
politische Absichten verbunden sind oder nicht, seine Wirkung bezieht
sich jedenfalls auf den Menschen als Totalität von Individuum und
Gemeinschaftswesen und ist insofern immer auch eine politische.
Trotzdem haben – seit Kant das ‹interesselose Wohlgefallen› als Wirkungsweise der Kunst postulierte – viele Dramatiker die politische Dimension ihrer Werke und des Theaters überhaupt bestritten. Goethe
etwa grenzte den politischen Bereich scharf von dem autonom gedachten Bezirk des ‹Edlen, Guten und Schönen› ab und begründete damit
eine Denkrichtung, die im 19. und 20. Jh. zu Vorbehalten gegen politische Motive und vor allem gegen Tendenz in der Kunst führte. Exemplarisch wurde die Abstinenz von Politik nach 1960 im Zusammenhang
der Programmatik des absurden Theaters von Eugène Ionesco vertreten, der in radikaler Opposition zu Brechts epischem Theater darauf
insistiert, daß ‹das Menschliche› über ‹dem Sozialen› steht und das
politische Engagement im Theater den Menschen von seinem eigentlichen Wesen entfremdet.

Seine konsequenteste Ausformung findet das P. T. nach der Oktoberrevolution von 1917 in der Sowjetunion als Mittel zum Aufbau der er-
strebten neuen Gesellschaft sowie zwischen den beiden Weltkriegen in

748 Politisches Theater

Deutschland als Lehr- und Agitationstheater im Interesse des Proletariats. Im russ. Revolutionstheater wirkt sich eine als ‹Proletkult› bezeichnete Kulturpolitik aus, die von der Überzeugung ausging, daß eine eigenständig proletarische Kultur geschaffen werden müsse, getragen nicht von bürgerlichen Spezialisten, sondern von werktätigen Laien. Im Zusammenhang des von Wsewolod Meyerhold als Leiter der Theaterabteilung des Volkskommissariats für Bildungswesen propagierten → ‹Theateroktobers› entstanden die Aufführungen des → Massentheaters sowie vielfache Aktivitäten von Laiengruppen in Wohnbezirken und Fabriken. Aus den ‹Werkstätten›, die zur politischen und künstlerischen Weiterbildung der Laiendarsteller gegründet wurden, entwickelten sich bald die dann doch wieder von Berufskünstlern getragenen Institutionen, in denen vor allem Meyerhold und der dann als Filmregisseur zu Weltruhm gelangte Sergej Eisenstein, beeinflußt von Ideen des → Konstruktivismus, ein P. T. zu realisieren suchten, das als Vorbild für ein richtiges Verhalten im Alltagsleben, vor allem in der Produktion dienen sollte (Theater als ‹Fabrik des qualifizierten Menschen›).

In Deutschland hat Erwin Piscator (1893–1966) nahezu unabhängig von der Entwicklung in der Sowjetunion zu ähnlichen Formen des P. T. gefunden. In seiner ersten Schaffensperiode (1920/21) erprobte er in Berlin ein von Arbeiterschauspielern getragenes → Proletarisches Theater. Auf der Basis parteilicher Stücke von Maxim Gorki, Upton Sinclair, Franz Jung und einer eigenen Szenenfolge *Gegen den weißen Schrecken – Für Sowjetrußland* sowie einer einfachen, typisierenden Spielweise wurde für ein halbes Jahr – dann wurde das Unternehmen polizeilich verboten – zum erstenmal in Deutschland der Gedanke der proletarischen Agitation konsequent mit dem Medium Theater verbunden. (Bei den vorausgehenden Versuchen blieb die Politik entweder an der Peripherie, wie beim sozialdemokratischen → Arbeitertheater der Vorkriegszeit, oder die proletarischen Zuschauer wurden mit den bürgerlichen Kulturwerten vertraut gemacht, wie es bei den Aktivitäten der → Volksbühne der Fall war.) In seiner zweiten Arbeitsetappe schuf Piscator mit der *Revue Roter Rummel* (1924), einer Folge von Sketches, Couplets, Rezitationen und Demonstrationen von Arbeitersportlern, sowie mit dem historischen Bilderbogen über den 1. Weltkrieg *Trotz alledem* (1925) die Grundmodelle des Agitprop-Theaters, das – getragen im wesentlichen von der KPD – in der zweiten Hälfte der 20er Jahre relativ große Bedeutung erlangte; im Jahr 1929 spielten in Deutschland 300 Truppen, die insgesamt 3,5 Millionen Zuschauer erreichten. Piscators dritte Station war das Berufstheater; nach Gastinszenierungen an der Volksbühne und am Berliner Staatstheater (*Fahnen* und *Sturmflut* von Alfons Paquet, 1924 und 1926; *Nachtasyl* von Gorki, 1926; Schillers *Räuber*, 1926; *Gewitter über Gottland* von Ehm Welk, 1927) gründete er

– nachdem sich Walter Gropius' Entwurf für ein →Totaltheater aus finanziellen Gründen nicht realisieren ließ – in dem bestehenden Theater am Nollendorfplatz die erste →Piscator-Bühne, die nach Produktionen von Ernst Tollers *Hoppla, wir leben* (1927), Alexej Tolstois *Rasputin* (1928) und Jaroslav Hašeks *Der brave Soldat Schwejk* (1928) aus finanziellen Gründen aufgeben mußte. Als ein weiterer Versuch zur Etablierung einer Piscator-Bühne mißlingt (einzige Inszenierung: Walter Mehrings *Kaufmann von Berlin*, 1929), gründet Piscator 1930 – durchaus in Übereinstimmung mit der Kulturpolitik der KPD, die zu der Zeit im Sinne der Gewinnung bürgerlicher Schichten zu einer ‹Volksfront› die Aufführung eher argumentierender, geschlossener Stücke (z. B. von Friedrich Wolf und Gustav von Wangenheim) durch Kollektive (arbeitsloser) Schauspieler fördert – mit einigen seiner Darsteller das Piscator-Kollektiv (→Piscator-Bühne) und inszeniert in diesem Rahmen Carl Credés *§ 218 – Frauen in Not, Des Kaisers Kuli* von Theodor Plivier und Friedrich Wolfs *Tai Yang erwacht* (1930/31).

Nebens Brechts →epischem Theater und dessen →Lehrstück sind die Inszenierungen Piscators der wichtigste Beitrag zum P. T. in den 20er Jahren. Brecht und Piscator stimmen darin überein, daß Theater die Welt nicht nur widerspiegeln darf, sondern durch Aufzeigen der sozialen Gesetzmäßigkeiten einen Beitrag zu ihrer Veränderung im Sinne der marxistischen Zielsetzung leisten muß. Während Brecht dafür eine neue, die Vorgänge der Realität ‹verfremdende› Dramaturgie und Spielweise entwickelt, will Piscator mit Hilfe von einmontierten Dokumenten und einer aufwendigen Maschinerie (Foto- und Filmprojektionen, Etagenbühne, laufende Bänder) in seinem (schon vor Brecht als ‹episch› konzipierten und auch so bezeichneten) Theater das Geschehen zwischen den Individuen einbetten in das gesellschaftlich-politische Umfeld (‹Soziologische Dramaturgie›) und so das Verständnis und die agitatorische Wirkung bei seinem – allerdings im wesentlichen nicht proletarischen, sondern bürgerlichen – Publikum steigern.

Auch nach der Rückkehr aus der Emigration hatte Piscator erheblichen Anteil an der Entwicklung des P. T. Als Intendant der →Freien Volksbühne in West-Berlin von 1962 bis 1966 verhalf er den wichtigsten Stücken des →dokumentarischen Theaters zur Uraufführung: Rolf Hochhuths *Der Stellvertreter* (1963), Heinar Kipphardts *In der Sache J. Robert Oppenheimer* (1964) und Peter Weiss' *Die Ermittlung* (1965). Während hier die politische Komponente in erster Linie in Gehalt und Intention der Stücke liegt, wirkte sich die allgemeine Politisierung der Kultur in den späten 60er und in den frühen 70er Jahren vor allem auf die Bedingungen der Theaterarbeit aus (Mitbestimmung, Kollektivregie, Gründung ‹Freier Gruppen›) sowie auf die kritisch-politische Konzeptionierung von Klassiker-Inszenierungen. Die Wiederaufnahme von Formen des Agitprop-Theaters der 20er Jahre im ‹Straßentheater› und die Rezeption außereurop. Formen des P. T. wie etwa Auguste Boals → Theater der Unterdrückten blieben nur vorübergehende Erscheinungen.

Brauneck, M.: Theater im 20. Jh. Reinbek bei Hamburg 1982; Fiebach, J.: Von Craig bis Brecht. Berlin 1975; Hoffmann, L./Hoffmann-Ostwald, D.: Dt. Arbeitertheater 1918–33, Bde. 1 und 2. Berlin 1972; Ismayr, W.: Das politische Theater in Westdeutschland. Meisenheim/Glan 1977; Melchinger, S.: Geschichte des politischen Theaters. Velber 1971; Paech, J.: Das Theater der russ. Revolution. Kronberg/Ts. 1974; Piscator, E.: Schriften, Bd. 1 und 2. Berlin (DDR) 1968; Weber, R.: Proletarisches Theater und revolutionäre Arbeiterbewegung. Köln 1976.

Peter Simhandl

Politisches Volkstheater (USA)

Unter P. V. wird eine Sonderform des kritisch-alternativen Theaters verstanden, die international z. B. das Theater Dario Fos (Italien), → Théâtre du Soleil (Frankreich), die Gruppe → 7 : 84 (England) oder → Gripstheater (BRD) einschließt. In den USA zählen zum P. V. → The San Francisco Mime Troupe, → Bread and Puppet Theatre, → Teatro Campesino, New York Street Theatre Caravan. Das P. V. spielt kaum Stücke fremder Autoren/innen nach, sondern zeichnet sich durch eigenwillige Bearbeitungen und originale Kollektivproduktionen aus. Das P. V. ist aus den vielfältigen Strömungen des → Straßen- und Agitationstheaters der 1960er Jahre entstanden, wobei es auch dem Agitprop und → Arbeitertheater der 1920/30er Jahre wichtige Impulse verdankt.

Organisatorisch sind die Gruppen des P. V. dem → freien Theater zuzurechnen. Sie arbeiten nach dem ‹nonprofit›-Prinzip, werden als solche häufig von staatlichen Instanzen anerkannt, wenden sich auch ideologisch und künstlerisch gegen das kommerzielle Theater. Verantwortlichkeiten und künstlerischer Einsatz sind häufig von der Rotation bestimmt. Zwar greifen die Gruppen des P. V. oft Themen der Geschichte der Arbeiterbewegung auf (San Francisco Mime Troupe: *False Promises*; New York Street Th. Caravan: *Sacco and Vanzetti*; *The Molly McGuires*), doch sprengen ihre künstlerischen Formen und Darstellungsmittel den Rahmen, der vom Agitprop- und epischen Theater bereitgestellt wird.

Ein spezifisches Merkmal des P. V. ist die Rezeption von Genres und Versatzstücken populärer Massenkultur, Unterhaltung und Illusionsindustrie, wobei unter Aufrechterhaltung und Intensivierung des Unterhaltungselements die zumeist unpolitischen oder gar reaktionären Inhalte ausgetauscht werden. Das P. V. funktioniert also jene überlieferten Gattungen und Formen um, setzt sie strategisch ein, um die eigenen aufklärerischen und agitatorischen Aussagen zu transportieren. Beispiele sind zunächst Gattungen der erstkulturellen Theatertradition selbst, →Commedia dell'arte, →Melodrama, →Minstrel Show, darüber hinaus Formen der Konsumkunst wie Agententhriller, Detektivroman, Comic strip, Erfolgsschlager. Die Stücke des P. V. sind häufig satirische →Musicals. Ziel solcher Wirkungsästhetik ist, ein am bürgerlichen Bildungstheater nicht partizipierendes Publikum im Sinn einer gegenkulturellen Blockbildung gleichzeitig zu unterhalten und zu informieren, zur Strukturierung seines eigenen Lebenszusammenhangs anzuleiten und zu ermutigen.

Heilmeyer, J./Fröhlich, P.: Now. Theater der Erfahrung. Material zur neuen amerik. Theaterbewegung. Köln 1971; Herms, D.: Agitprop USA. Zur Theorie und Strategie des politisch-emanzipatorischen Theaters in Amerika seit 1960. Kronberg 1973; Herms, D./Paul, A.: Politisches Volkstheater der Gegenwart. Berlin 1981; Shank, T.: American Alternative Theatre. London 1982.

Dieter Herms

Posse

Als P. werden verschiedene Formen des volkstümlichen komischen Theaters bezeichnet, die sich durch größere Bedeutung des Stoffs vor der reinen Form (besondere Bedeutung hat die Improvisation), einfachen linearen Handlungsablauf, oberflächliche Situations- oder Typenkomik und in den meisten Fällen Verzicht auf jede moralische Unterweisung des Zuschauers kennzeichnen. Die P. organisiert sich meistens um eine lokale →lustige Person, die durch Kleidung, Sprache, Benehmen bzw. durch die Konfliktsituationen, in die sie gerät, zum Lachen anregt. Bei Gelegenheit, etwa im Deutschland der ersten Hälfte des 19. Jh., kann die P. aber auch gegenwärtige politisch und sozial motivierte Erschütterungen einer Gesellschaft ironisch thematisieren bzw. entlarven. Eine Sonderform der P. bildet die speziell an eine Stadt oder eine Landschaft gebundene →Lokalposse. – Vorläufer der P. sind der antike →Mimus, die →Atellane und die →Commedia dell'arte in Italien, die →Fastnachtsspiele in Deutschland, die holländischen Kluchten und das Singspiel der →Englischen Komödianten. Die dt. Bezeichnung Posse für ähnliche kurze und derbe Nachspiele der Wanderbühnen wird zum erstenmal im 17. Jh. belegt, und zwar im Stückverzeichnis der Truppe vom Meister Velten, das für das Jahr 1679 die Aufführung der P. *Von Münch* und *Pickelhäring* aufweist. Als Johann Christoph Gottscheds (1700–66) Theaterreform P. und lustige Personen von der Bühne verbannte, lebte in Deutschland die Gattung in Übersetzungen frz. komischer Einakter weiter, in deren Tradition einzelne dt. P. um die Jahrhundertwende mit August von Kotzebue (1761–1819) bzw. in der ersten Hälfte des 19. Jh.

mit Ernst Raupach (1784–1852) und Heinrich Laube (1806–84) stehen. Danach kommt die P. zu vollem Glanz und erreicht anerkannten literarischen Wert, vor allem mit dem Aufblühen des →Wiener Volkstheaters unter Ferdinand Raimund (1791–1836) und Johann Nepomuk Nestroy (1801–62).

Klotz, W.: Bürgerliches Lachtheater. München 1980.

Bernard Poloni

Post Modern Dance

Der P. M. D. tritt als Bewegung gegen die etablierte Generation des →Modern Dance und deren Ästhetik auf. Die Amerikaner Merce Cunningham (*1919) und Alwin Nikolais (*1912), in der Tradition des Modern Dance und →Ausdruckstanzes aufgewachsen, signalisieren in ihren Choreographien Qualitäten eines neuen Stils und führen den Modern Dance in den P. M. D. über.

Merce Cunningham wird 1940 Tänzer in der Kompanie von Martha Graham (1894–1991; →Modern Dance). Bereits fünf Jahre später befreit er sich vom Graham-Stil, weil er dessen Tanzbewegungen weder als Ausdruck der Psyche noch als Träger von Gedanken und Ideen nachempfinden kann. Cunningham postuliert, daß Bewegungen keine Bedeutungsträger im freien Spiel der Bewegungskräfte sind. Bewegungen verdeutlichen nicht, sie wollen in seinen Choreographien einzig figural verstanden werden. Insofern lehnt er jeden geschlossenen Handlungsverlauf ab. Das Bewegungsrepertoire des P. M. D. strebt danach, die Fülle der menschlichen Bewegungsmöglichkeiten, der Gebärdensprache im weitesten Sinne einzubringen. Cunninghams Tanzkreationen zeichnen sich durch diffizile Aktionen und Posen aus, die ein hohes technisches Niveau beim Tänzer voraussetzen. Musik und Bühnenbild entstehen im Entwicklungsakt unabhängig vom Bewegungsentwurf. Zwischen den Künstlern M. Cunningham, John Cage und Robert Rauschenberg, die mehrere Werke als Choreograph, Musiker und Bühnenbildner gestalten, werden ausschließlich die Zeitspannen abgesprochen, innerhalb deren ein Ereignis in Szene gesetzt werden soll. Die Aufführungsstruktur belebt dementsprechend ein Zufallsmoment. Die Tanzinnovationen der drei genannten Künstler beschleunigen neben schöpferischen Impulsen anderer Kunstsparten den Ausbau der intermediären multimedialen Theater-Formen →Happening, →Performance Art. Jeder der drei Künstler dringt für sich, trotz der letztendlich synkretistischen Absicht, auf die Autonomie seiner Kunstrichtung im Gesamtkunstwerk. So überraschen die Gestaltungen des P. M. D. neben veränderten Bewegungsmustern auch

Y. Rainer in «Trio A», 1982

Szene aus «Summerspace» von M. Cunningham, 1958. Bühne: R. Rauschenberg (RR)

A. Nikolais: «Imago», 1963

Post Modern Dance 753

durch ein neugefaßtes Raum-, Zeit- und Strukturverständnis. Die Aufführungsräume beschränken sich nicht auf herkömmliche Bühnen; es werden vielmehr Sportplätze, Museen, Kunsthallen und öffentliche Plätze zu bevorzugten Spielstätten. Ein Sich-zur-Schau-Stellen an alltäglichen Orten bezeugt den Willen, Kunst und Leben ineinanderfließen zu lassen. Das Zeitgefühl der getanzten Schaustücke drängt zu Simultanaktionen auf einer Aufführungsfläche. Der Zuschauer soll wie im Leben gezwungen werden, Ereignisse willkürlich zu selektieren. Mit Cunningham setzen sich nahezu alle Tänzer der jüngsten Generation auseinander.

Alwin Nikolais, Choreograph, Musiker, Bildhauer, Maler in eins, kreiert ein Tanztheater, das die Komponenten Bewegung, Zeit, Raum, Klang und Farbe zu einem theatralischen Spiel zusammenführt. Nikolais' anthropologisches Weltbild sieht den Menschen als Glied inmitten der Bewegungen und Entfaltungen des Kosmos. Dementsprechend erleben die Zuschauer in seinen tanztheatralischen Aufführungen Konzeptionen, in denen Strukturen von und in Welt schaubar gemacht werden. Subtile Lichtregie, den Körper verdeckende, aber in keiner Weise starr hemmende, sondern von ihm zu steuernde dehnbare und anschmiegsame Ganzmasken unterstützen und beleben die fließenden und auch erstarrenden Bewegungsinspirationen der Tänzer. Skulpturale Positionen, sphärische Aktionen und deren unentwegt sich abwandelnde Gesetzmäßigkeiten werden im Tanz ebenso darstellbar wie das In- und Aufeinanderbezogensein der Teile eines jeden Organismus. Nikolais regt seine Tänzer zu abstrakten Bewegungen an, er schließt Elemente des klassischen Tanzes nicht aus. Der Gebärdensprache kommt Nikolais' musikalisches Componere entgegen, das etwa Beschleunigungen, Filterungen, Zerstückelungen strukturell einzubringen vermag.

1962 bis 1966 New Yorker Judson Memorial Church (Greenwich Village), ein Zentrum für junge amerikanische Choreographen und Tänzer in der Gefolgschaft des P.M.D. Für alle Judson Dance Theatre-Choreographen ist der Tanz wie für Cunningham absolutes kinetisches Ereignis. – Yvonne Rainer (* 1934), Trisha Brown (* 1936) und Lucinca Childs manifestieren die Ästhetik des →Minimal Dance, die die 60er Jahre in den USA bestimmt und auf dem europ. Kontinent erst ab 1980 ein interessiertes Publikum gewinnt. – Meredith Monk (* 1943) und Kenneth King (* 1948) wenden sich von der Minimal Art ab und gestalten expressiv ‹epische Opern› und ‹lebendiges Kino›. Bewegungen, Gesang, Sprache und Video verflechten sich zu einem polyästhetischen, gesamttheatralischen Schaustück. Diese Schaustücke zählen zur Avantgarde des amerikanischen experimentellen Theaters (→Tanztheater).

Fischer, E. E.: Tanzend nach den Wurzeln suchen. In: Ballett International 12 (1983), S. 32–37; Kneiss, U.: Aspekte bzw. Perspektiven des Post Modern Dance.

Diss. Wien 1986; Kostelnatz, R.: American Imaginations. Berlin 1983; Schmidt, J.: Der Vater der neuen Tanzkunst. In: Ballett International 5 (1983), S. 20–22; Stüber, W. J.: Geschichte des Modern Dance. Wilhelmshaven 1984.

Patricia Stöckemann

Praetexta

Lat. Adjektiv, zu ergänzen ‹fabula›; Gattungsbezeichnung für röm. Tragödien mit nationalröm. Stoff; so genannt nach dem Kostüm der Helden, der toga praetexta, der mit einem Purpurstreifen geschmückten Toga der hohen röm. Beamten. Schöpfer der Gattung war Naevius (270–201 v. Chr.), erhalten ist lediglich das pseudo-senecanische historische Trauerspiel *Octavia*.

Schmidt, P. L.: Die Poetisierung und Mythisierung der Geschichte in der Tragödie ‹Octavia›. In: W. Haase (Hg.): Aufstieg und Niedergang der röm. Welt 32.2. Berlin/New York 1985, S. 1421–1453.

Bernd Seidensticker

Premiere

(Frz. *première* – erste) Erste Aufführung einer Theaterproduktion vor der Öffentlichkeit, die sich neben dem geladenen Publikum (Presse, Prominenz, Politik, Honoratioren) durch einen traditionell konstanten Zuschauerkreis (P.-Publikum) ausweist. Der Erfolg der P. und die Resonanz von seiten der →Theaterkritik bestimmen häufig weitere Zuschauerzahlen und damit die Laufzeit der →Inszenierung.

Monika Sandhack

Prinzipal

Das aus dem Frz. übernommene Wort bezeichnete im 17. und im frühen 18. Jh. in Deutschland den Leiter der damals entstehenden Berufsschauspielertruppen (→Theatersystem). Er war zugleich Inhaber der nötigen Privilegien, Besitzer des theatralischen Apparats (Kostüm und Dekorationsfundus), regelte die gesamte Aktivität der Truppe und war nicht selten zugleich der erste Schauspieler – er wurde daher auch Komödiantenmeister genannt.

Bernard Poloni

Privattheater

Im Gegensatz zum öffentlich-rechtlichen Theater befindet sich ein P. ganz oder überwiegend in privatem Besitz (→ Theatersystem). Soweit ein privates Theater eine eigene Spielstätte besitzt und dramatische, musikalische oder choreographische Bühnenwerke aufführt, kann es Mitglied im → DBV werden. P. erhalten z. T. öffentliche Zuschüsse.

Roswitha Körner

Proben

Vorbereitung einer Theateraufführung unter Leitung des → Regisseurs in schematischer, im einzelnen jedoch variierender Abfolge: Nach Abschluß der Konzeptionsphase (Erwerb der Aufführungsrechte, dramaturgische Bearbeitung der Spielvorlage, regieliche Besprechungen zwischen Regisseur, Theaterleitung, Ausstatter und Schauspieler) beginnen die P. im dt. Theater mit der Lesung des Textes in verteilten Rollen nach Besetzungsplan, dabei erste Annäherung an das Stück. Auf die Lese-P. folgt die (heute seltene) Stell-P. mit Festlegung der wichtigsten Gänge sowie Auf- und Abtritte. Noch zuvor oder bald darauf findet die erste techn. P. (Bau-P.) mit provisorischen Aufbauten (möglichst maßstabsgetreu) statt zur weiteren Disposition der Bühnentechnik und Werkstätten. Alle sich daran anschließenden P. heißen Stück-P. (bzw. Bühnen-P., sobald sie auf der Hauptbühne erfolgen), in denen die → Inszenierung in allen Einzelheiten erarbeitet wird. Diese längste Phase der P. mündet in erste Versuche zum Durchlauf der gesamten → Aufführung, die auf Dauer, Rhythmus, Proportionen und Geschlossenheit hin überprüft wird. Zwischengeschaltet werden in der Schlußphase jeweils Dekorations-, Beleuchtungs- und Kostüm-P., um das Bühnenbild techn. einzurichten, die Lichtwechsel festzulegen und die Kostüme anzupassen. Der → General-P., die vor der → Premiere unter Aufführungsbedingungen abläuft und öffentlich sein kann, gehen Haupt-P. mit Originalkostümen und -dekorationen voraus. Außerdem kennt das Theater Wiederaufnahme-P. (sofern eine Aufführung nach längerer Pause erneut angesetzt wird), Umbesetzungs- oder Einweisungs-P. (wenn eine Rolle von einem anderen Schauspieler übernommen wird), Verständigungs-P. zur Anpassung an veränderte Bühnenverhältnisse bei Gastspielen; ferner Tanz- und Musik-P.

Die P.-Zeit, im 19. Jh. kaum mehr als eine Woche, verlängerte sich mit den Anfängen des → Regietheaters (bei den → Meiningern sowie am Moskauer Künstlertheater [→ MChAT] unter Leitung Stanislawskis Ausdehnung auf mehrere Monate, davon mehrwöchige Lese-P.). Im deutschsprachigen Theater setzte sich nach 1945 ein Minimum von drei bis sechs Wochen durch. Die P.-Zeit beträgt heute an großen Häusern zumeist acht bis zehn Wochen und länger.

Monika Sandhack

Programmheft

Eine von der →Dramaturgie erstellte Broschüre für Theaterbesucher mit Informationen zu einer →Inszenierung, meist ergänzt durch lose eingelegte Besetzungszettel (Stücktitel, Autor, Namen aller Beteiligten, Datum, Dauer der Veranstaltung). – Die P., im 20. Jh. (in Deutschland erstmals am 30. August 1884 im Schiller-Theater Berlin) entwickelt aus den →Theaterzetteln, sind nach Ländern und an einzelnen Theatern sehr unterschiedlich in Form, Farbe, Umfang und Qualität. Sie enthalten u. a. Einführungen in das Werk mit Textauszügen, Sach- und Assoziationsmaterial, Essays zu Stück und Autor, Probenskizzen, Bühnenbild- und Kostümentwürfe, Fotos der Mitwirkenden, Theaternachrichten, Spielplanvorschauen; daneben Anzeigen, die zusätzliche Einnahmen garantieren. Ende der 60er Jahre an deutschsprachigen Theatern Tendenz zu materialreichen P.-Büchern als Foren, auf denen Theaterarbeit dargestellt und diskutiert wird mit Publikum und Kritik (vorbildlich Schauspielhaus Stuttgart und später Bochum, Schaubühne am Halleschen Ufer/ Lehniner Platz in Berlin).

Kressin, H.: Die Entwicklung des Theater-P. in Deutschland von 1894–1941. Ein publizistisches Mittel im Dienst des Theaters. Diss. Berlin 1968.

Monika Sandhack

Proletarisch-revolutionäres Theater

Die Novemberrevolution scheiterte, aber sie öffnete die Augen für das Revolutionäre: Für klassenbewußte Dramatiker, Schauspieler und Regisseure gab es nach 1918/19 kein Zurück mehr zu der politisch unverbindlichen Arbeiterbildungskultur der Vorkriegszeit. Probleme des Klassenkampfs sollten von jetzt an das Bühnengeschehen bestimmen. In Anlehnung an das russische Vorbild und zugleich im Widerspruch zu der (zunächst noch an konventionellen Ästhetikwerten orientierten) KPD-Politik entwickelte sich jenseits der traditionellen Arbeitertheaterorganisationen (→Volksbühne) eine genuin proletarische Kultur (‹Proletkult›). Am Anfang dieser Entwicklung stand das Massenspektakel (verbunden mit einem kollektiven Solidaritätserlebnis): 900 Laienschauspieler und 50 000 Zuschauer wirkten mit, als 1920 bei den Leipziger Festspielen Szenen aus dem römischen Spartakusaufstand zur Aufführung kamen. Sprechchöre übernahmen Funktionen, die im bürgerlichen Theater Individualdarstellern zukamen. Wichtige Impulse für die proletarische Theaterbewegung gingen von den Polit-Revuen Erwin Piscators (1893–1966) und der Agitprop-Truppe →Blaue Blusen aus. Nach einem Gastspiel der sowj. Blauen Blusen (1927) formierten sich in Deutschland ähnliche Gruppen (Das rote Sprachrohr u. a.). Die personenarme Kurzszene trat in der zweiten Hälfte der 20er Jahre an die Stelle des aufwendigen Massendramas. Direkte Publikumsansprache, kabarettartige Situationskomik und argumentativer Schlagabtausch zwischen ‹dem› Proletarier und ‹dem› Bourgeois bildeten die Grundelemente der Agitprop-Dramatik. Gespielt werden konnte – dank eines Minimums an Requisite – zu jeder Zeit, an jedem Ort; bevorzugte Spielorte waren Straße und Hinterhof.

Hoffmann, L. / Hoffmann-Ostwald, D.: Deutsches Arbeitertheater 1918–33. Eine Dokumentation, 2. Bde. Berlin (DDR) [2]1972; Hoffmann, L.: Das Theater des sowjetischen und des deutschen Proletkult 1917–1922. Diss. Berlin 1988; Knellessen, W. F.: Agitation auf der Bühne. Emsdetten 1970; Lacis, A.: Revolutionär von Beruf. München 1971, S. 81 ff; Pfützner, K.: Das revolutionäre Arbeitertheater in Deutschland 1918–33. In: Schriften zur Theaterwissenschaft, Bd. 1. Leipzig 1959, S. 375–493; Trommler, F.: Das politisch-revolutionäre Theater. In: Rothe, W. (Hg.): Die deutsche Literatur in der Weimarer Republik. Stuttgart 1974, S. 77–113.

Carl Wege

Prolog

(Griech. prologos = Vorrede) Begrüßungs- oder Einführungsrede in die Handlung durch den Chor, einen oder mehrere Sprecher, Schauspieler, Direktor; im mittelalterlichen geistlichen Drama: praecursor (lat.: Vorläufer, Bekanntgeber), im →Fastnachtsspiel: Einschreier, heute: Ansager, Registrator, Sprecher. Bauform des Theaters von der Antike über Mittelalter und Klassik bis zu den heutigen Anti-Illusionsstücken, besonders im →epischen oder →dokumentarischen Theater.

Der P., der sich von der →Exposition unterscheidet, ist durch einige Hauptfunktionen gekennzeichnet: 1. dient der Ankündigung, Erläuterung oder Ausdeutung eines Stücks als Anfangsteil oder eigenständiges Schauspiel in Reduktion (insofern gleicht er dem Vorspiel); 2. als perspektivenverändernde Bauform ermöglicht er dem Zuschauer Identifikation und Verfremdung inner- und außerhalb der Handlung; 3. als progressiver Übergang aus der Wirklichkeit ins Spiel ermöglicht er in Analogie mit dem Roman die theaterspezifische auktoriale Reflexion über das Werk bei Einbeziehung des Zuschauers (vgl. Goethe *Faust I*, ‹Prolog im Himmel› mit Gespräch zwischen Autor, Direktor, Schauspielern und Publikum). Insofern spielt er eine bedeutende Rolle in der dramaturgischen Kommunikationsstruktur; 4. spielt er im heutigen Theater durch Anrede an den Zuschauer eine teils informative, teils kritische Rolle; 5. ist er in Relation mit dem →Epilog oder den Bildern des Stücks Teil der internen Handlungsdialektik.

Banerjee, N.: Der Prolog im Drama der dt. Klassik. 1970; Jens, W.: Die Bauformen der griech. Tragödie. München 1971; Pavis, P.: Dictionnaire du Théâtre. Paris 1980.

Gérard Schneilin

Proskēnion / Proszenium

Die hellenistische Hochbühne (wörtlich: etwas, das vor der Skēnē errichtet ist), eine drei bis vier Meter hohe, auf einem von Säulen getragenen Unterbau ruhende Bühne, die dem unteren Teil des Bühnengebäudes vorgeblendet war (zur Ausschmückung →Skēnographie).

Bernd Seidensticker

Protagonist

Im griech. Theater der 1. Schauspieler (entsprechend heißen der 2. und 3. Schauspieler Deuteragonist und Tritagonist); der P. engagierte die beiden anderen Schauspieler, nahm als einziger der drei am Schauspielerwettbewerb (→Agon) teil und wurde in den Urkunden dramatischer Aufführungen gleichberechtigt neben dem Namen des Dichters und des →Choregen verewigt.

Pickard-Cambridge, A. W.: The Dramatic Festivals of Athens. Oxford [2]1968 (rev. J. Gould and D. M. Lewis), p. 132–135.

Bernd Seidensticker

Provincetown Players

Zuerst in Cape Cod (Mass.) als Sommertheater, dann im New Yorker Greenwich Village etablierten sich die P. P. als wichtigste Gruppe des → Little Theatre Movement (1915). Der Aufstieg des bedeutendsten Dramatikers der USA, Eugene O'Neill (1888–1953), ist untrennbar mit der Entwicklung der P. P. verknüpft. Bis zur Spielzeit 1920/21 wurden praktisch alle Uraufführungen seiner Einakter von den P. P. gegeben. Die erste Premiere eines abendfüllenden Dramas von O'Neill, *Emperor Jones*, fand 1920 mit dem schwarzen Schauspieler Charles Gilpin in der Titelrolle statt. In den 1920er Jahren wurden die P. P. unter der Leitung eines Triumvirats, dem auch O'Neill angehörte, in «Experimental Theatre» umbenannt. Im Dezember 1929 löste sich das Experimental Theatre als unmittelbare Folge des New Yorker Börsenkrachs auf.

Deutsch, H./Hanau, S.: The Provincetown – A Story of the Theatre. New York 1931; Fröhlich, P.: Das nichtkommerzielle amerik. Theater. Rheinfelden 1974.

Dieter Herms

Psychodrama

J. L. Moreno (1892–1974), Wiener Arzt, Künstler, Schriftsteller, schuf in den 20er Jahren das P. aus Beobachtungen des spontanen Kinderspiels, Elementen des Stegreiftheaters und einer Neuformulierung des Kathartischen. Beeinflußt von Henri Bergsons Theorie einer universalen schöpferischen Spontaneität, suchte Moreno nach einem Theater spontan-kreativer Begegnung. Théâtre Impromptu, jeder ist Autor, Schauspieler, Zuschauer: durch die Aufhebung der Trennung von Sein und Schein, Realität und Abbildung im Augenblick des Stegreifs wird eine im Alltag nicht erfahrbare Intensität des Erlebens bereitgestellt, eine Teilhabe am göttlichen Prinzip des Schöpferischen. Starke Affinität Morenos zum religiös-magischen Ursprung des Theaters als archaisches → Ritual, in dem die mythische Einheit noch gewahrt ist wie bei afroamerikanischen Riten und bestimmten indianischen Kulten. Moreno gelang die Weiterentwicklung des → Stegreiftheaters zum P. durch eine Erweiterung des Katharsisbegriffs. → Katharsis, d. h. im aristotelischen Theater die reinigende Wirkung des Tragischen auf den Zuschauer, der, am Scheitern des Helden leidend, sich von eigener Zerrissenheit befreit. Im P. vollzieht sich das kathartische Drama zunächst im Protagonisten selbst; in der Dramatisierung vergangener Lebenssituationen kann der Protagonist die im Kontext dieser Erfahrungen abgespaltenen Gefühle wiedererleben, dadurch sein Rollenrepertoire erweitern, spontan-kreativ handeln lernen, auch durch

760 Psychodrama

Einsicht in die lebensgeschichtlichen Zusammenhänge. Die Gruppe, dem antiken Chor verwandt, dynamisiert durch Übernahme unterschiedlicher Rollen wie Doppelgänger, Antagonist, Hilfs-Ich diesen Verwandlungsprozeß, erblickt im Spiegel seines Repräsentanten das eigene Selbst, die eigene Verwandlung. P. ist immer auch Soziometrie, Gruppenpsychotherapie (→Theatertherapie).

Schon vor Moreno war die therapeutische Wirkung des Theaters bekannt. So finden wir P.-Rollentausch bei Aristophanes' (445–380 v. Chr.) *Die Wespen*, 422 v. Chr.; Stegreifepisoden, improvisiertes Rollenspiel in Marivaux' (1688–1763) *Les acteurs de bonne foi*, 1757. P.-Ansätze auch im Bereich der Medizin; bereits in der Antike Falldarstellungen, z. B. bei Galenus, 199 v. Chr.; Freuds Studie über den therapeutischen Effekt bei *Psychopathologischen Charakteren auf der Bühne* (1905/06). Sandor Ferenczis Arbeit mit psychoanalytischem Rollenspiel 1919/33 wird Grundlage des «Therapeutischen Theaters», das V. Iljine, zunächst in Anlehnung an Schauspielmethoden K. S. Stanislawskis (1863–1938), in Moskau 1906/15 weiterentwickelt, ab 1928 in Paris, beeinflußt von Morenos Spontaneitätstheorie. Gleichzeitig theatrotherapeutische Versuche, d. h. soziokulturelle Arbeit mit Mitteln des Theaters; berühmtes Beispiel Marquis de Sades (1740–1814) Tanz- und Theaterfeste mit Beteiligung von Anstaltsinsassen und Mitgliedern der kleinen Pariser Theater im Hospiz von Charenton, in dem er selbst interniert war, 1808 bis 1813, dem Jahr des Aufführungsverbots durch die Regierung. Im Zusammenhang mit der Antipsychiatriebewegung kollektive Theaterinszenierungen von psychisch Kranken, eingeladenen Künstlern, Pflegepersonal verbunden mit animatorischen Mitspielaktionen im Stadtteil, z. B. 1973 das Projekt «Marco Cavallo», das Blaue Pferd als Symbol eines Lebens ohne Mauern in der Psychiatrie von Triest (Leitung Franco Bassaglia).

Heute ist das P., das Moreno in New York (1925–1974) zu einer komplexen soziometrischen Gruppentherapie weiterentwickelte, eine bedeutende dramatherapeutische Methode mit großem Einfluß auf eine Vielzahl neu entstandener Therapieformen; das Analytische P. ab 1955 in Frankreich, 1976 Gestaltdrama Fritz Perls', die Encounter-Bewegung und die Transaktionsanalyse Bernes. P. hat sich an Schulen, Krankenhäusern, im Strafvollzug der USA und in Frankreich durchgesetzt; in der Bundesrepublik, 1955 erstmals vorgestellt, wächst seine Bedeutung. Fritz Perls hatte am Moreno-Institut (New York) studiert wie auch Elia Kazan und Lee Strasberg (→The Method), die Gründer und Leiter des die Methoden Stanislawskis (→Stanislawski-System) fortführenden →Actor's Studio (New York).

Dieser weite Aktionsradius des P. in Alltagskultur, Therapie, Theater sowie als gruppendynamisches Instrumentarium für sozialpsychologische Feldforschung, soziotherapeutische Projekte, zeigt seine Vielfältigkeit und methodische Flexibilität, die bedeutende Theaterregisseure unserer Zeit zu nutzen gewußt haben, wie Pina Bausch (* 1940), George Tabori (* 1914), auch das →Living Theatre, das →Squat Theatre und zahlreiche Gruppen des →Open Theatre in New York, aber auch die breite soziokulturelle Bewegung der Animation Culturelle in Frankreich.

Burkart, V.: Befreiung durch Aktionen. Wien 1972; Feldhendler, D.: Psychodrama und Theater der Unterdrückten. Frankfurt/M. 1987; Marschall, B.: «Ich bin der Mythe». Von der Stegreifbühne zum Psychodrama Jakob Levy Morenos. Wien u. a. 1988; Moreno, J. L.: Der Königsroman. Potsdam 1923; ders.: Das Stegreiftheater. Potsdam 1924; ders.: Who Shall Survive? Beacon House 1953; ders.: Gruppenpsychotherapie und Psychodrama. Stuttgart 1959; Petzold, H.: Angewandtes Psychodrama. In: Therapie, Pädagogik, Theater und Wirtschaft. Paderborn 1972; Leutz, G.: Psychodrama, Theorie und Praxis. New York 1974.

Barbara Rüster

Publikum

Das P. als Gemeinschaft der Zuschauer ist die Voraussetzung für den theatralischen Wirkungsprozeß. Zwischen Theater als Spiel und dem P. als Zuschauern besteht eine dialektische Beziehung. Theater ist stets Spiel vor Zuschauern, erst in der Spannung von Spielen zu Zuschauen ereignet sich die Theaterhandlung. In der Theatergeschichte wandeln sich vielfach soziale Struktur und die Form der kommunikativen Beteiligung des P.; der Grundbezug von Spiel und Zuschauen blieb davon unberührt (→Antikes Theater, →Japanisches Theater, →Chinesisches Theater, →Indisches Theater, →Afrikanisches Theater, →Mittelalter/Drama und Theater des Mittelalters, →Neuzeit/Theater der Neuzeit, →20. Jh./ Theater im 20. Jh., →Höfisches Theater, →Schultheater, →Jesuitentheater, →Volkstheater, →Arbeitertheater, →Kindertheater, →Frauentheater, →Volksbühne, →Theatertheorie).

Die gegenwärtige Struktur der öffentlich-rechtlichen und der privaten Theater in Deutschland (BRD) ist nach wie vor als bürgerlich zu bezeichnen. Aus einer wohl als repräsentativ anzusehenden Untersuchung der Hamburger Bürgerschaft von 1975/76 ergibt sich folgendes Bild: 46,1 % Beamte, 48,3 % Angestellte, 42,7 % Selbständige, 19 % Arbeiter und 21,5 % Auszubildende. Dabei ist zu berücksichtigen, daß nur 5 bis (max.) 10 % der Bewohner der Bundesrepublik ins Theater gehen. Im übrigen hat der Theaterbesuch eine rückläufige Tendenz: Während 1965/66 noch etwa 20 Mio. Besucher registriert werden konnten, hat sich die Besucherzahl auf 18,3 Mio. (Stand 1987/88) eingependelt. Für die privaten Theater liegen die Besucherzahlen bei etwa 5,4 Mio. Das Besucherinteresse verteilt sich auf folgende Sparten: Schauspiel 35,4 %, Oper 27,4 %, Ope-

762 Pulpitum

rette 8,1%, Ballett 8,2%, Kinder- und Jugendtheater 9,3%, Musical 7,5%, Konzert 4,1%.

Zuschauergruppen, denen der Zugang zum kulturellen Leben aus den verschiedensten Gründen erschwert ist, an das Theater heranzuführen, bemüht sich vor allem das → Freie Theater; aber auch die etablierten Bühnen versuchen zunehmend, z. B. durch die Nutzung unkonventioneller Spielorte, neue Publikumsschichten zu erreichen. Eine wesentliche Rolle in diesem Zusammenhang spielen die kulturpolitischen Bemühungen um eine Dezentralisierung des kulturellen Angebots der Städte und die kulturelle Versorgung der Provinz.

Beckerman, B.: Theatrical Presentation. New York 1990; Bennett, S.: Theatre Audiences. New York 1990; Descotes, J.: Le public de théâtre et son histoire. Paris 1964; Kindermann, H.: Die Funktion des Publikums im Theater, Wien 1971; ders.: Die Karikatur als Quelle der Publikumsforschung. Wien 1975; ders.: Das Theaterpublikum. 3 Bde. in 4. Salzburg 1979–86; Pavis, P.: Semiotik der Theaterrezeption. Tübingen 1988; Schölling, T.: Das gesellige Vergnügen Theater. Diss. Berlin 1987; Stuke, F. R. (Hg.): Theater und Öffentlichkeit. Münster 1989; Das Theater und sein Publikum. Wien 1977.

Roswitha Körner/Red.

Pulpitum

Lat. Bezeichnung für Bühne; daneben auch scaena.

Puppentheater

Entweder stumme, mit Musik untermalte oder mit menschlichen Stimmen unterlegte Form des Theaters, bei der an die Stelle von Menschen zwei- bzw. drei dimensionale Figuren treten, die auf verschiedene Weise von den Spielern bewegt werden können. Da ‹Puppe› (von lat. ‹pupa› = Mädchen, Puppe) nur plastische Figuren bezeichnet, wird in der Forschung zunehmend der Terminus «Figurentheater» verwandt. Material, Art der Figuren und ihrer Führung haben zu verschiedenen Klassifizierungsversuchen geführt wie Spiel mit plastischen Figuren (→ Handpuppe, → Stab- oder Stockpuppe, → Marionette) oder Spiel mit zweidimensionalen Figuren (→ Schatten-, Schemen-, Silhouettentheater, → Papiertheater, → Mechanisches Theater). Überschneidungen sind dabei nicht zu vermeiden.

Zeit und Ort der Entstehung des P. liegen im dunkeln. Anzunehmen ist jedoch, daß die einzelnen Formen zu verschiedenen Zeiten an unter-

Puppentheater 763

schiedlichen Orten entstanden sind, gegenseitige Beeinflussungen sind schwierig zu belegen. Bereits antike Zeugnisse unterrichten uns vom Bestehen des P. in Griechenland und Rom. Da es lange Zeit hindurch zur Imitation des Personentheaters benutzt wurde, besann man sich auf die spezifischen Möglichkeiten des P. in Europa erst seit der Mitte des 19. Jh. Neuerdings wird es zunehmend auch im pädagogischen und psychotherapeutischen Bereich eingesetzt (→Maskentheater). Künstlichkeit und notwendige Stilisierung der Puppe ermöglicht es z. B., einzelne Wesenszüge des Menschen hervorzuheben und so über eine permanente ‹Verfremdung› des theatralischen Geschehens im P. erfahrbar zu machen. Seine Blütezeit erlebte das P. im 18. und 19. Jh., als auch Schriftsteller wie Goethe und Kleist sich mit ihm zu beschäftigen begannen. Das moderne Theater hat das P. in seinen verschiedenen Ausprägungen auf vielfache Weise beeinflußt. Hingewiesen werden soll dabei nur auf die Benutzung überdimensionierter Puppen beim amerik. →Bread and Puppet Theatre, die Experimente mit Figuren in den Kabaretts →«Chat Noir», →«Schall und Rauch» und →«Die Elf Scharfrichter».

Andererseits hat das moderne P. zahlreiche Anregungen durch das Theater empfangen und weiter ausgebildet. Bemühungen von Bühnenbildnern und -reformern wie Appia und Craig sind zu erwähnen wie die Versuche mit Puppen am Bauhaus. Autoren wie Bernus, Čapek und Pocci, bildende Künstler wie Klee, Schlemmer, Kandinsky und Klimt haben zur Erneuerung und eigenständigen Entwicklung des modernen P. ebenso beigetragen wie Puppenspieler (P. Brann, M. Jacob, A. Aicher, J. Skupa und S. Obraszow). Besonders gefördert wurde das P. in den ehemaligen sozialistischen Staaten, wo neben der Gründung staatlicher Bühnen auch Fachausbildungen für Puppenspieler durchgeführt wurden. Wie sich das P. in diesen Ländern bzw. ihren ‹Nachfolgestaaten› entwickelt, bleibt abzuwarten.

In der DDR gab es zeitweilig mehr als zwölf P., die entweder als selbständige Sparte einem Theater angeschlossen waren oder über ein eigenes, technisch meist gut ausgerüstetes Haus und ein größeres Ensemble verfügten. Diese staatliche Förderung wurde zunächst durch das sowjetische Vorbild angeregt, dessen P. sich in opulenten Spielstätten und vor einem großen Publikum präsentierte. In der DDR entstanden P.ensembles mit strikter Spezialisierung (Regisseur, Ausstatter, Dramaturg usw.); gleichzeitig wurden die kleinen, privat geführten Wandertruppen ausgeschaltet. Obgleich es gerade auf ostdeutschem Gebiet noch nach 1945 eine lebendige Tradition des P. gab, meist als Familienunternehmen über Generationen geführt, konnten nur wenige dem Druck der Verstaatlichung ausweichen. Sie blieben über Jahrzehnte die einzigen Privattheater der DDR. – Die arbeitsteilige Professionalisierung der Puppenspieler erlaubte ein anspruchsvolles Repertoire. So konnten auch Stücke

764 Puppentheater

ohne parodistischen Ulk und dramaturgische Abstriche inszeniert werden, die herkömmlich dem ‹Menschentheater› vorbehalten sind (Strindbergs *Fräulein Julie* oder Brechts *Furcht und Elend des Dritten Reiches*). Seit etwa 1980 gab es auch private Einzelspieler, die fast vergessene Techniken oder in Deutschland wenig bekannte Formen des P. ausprobierten und so zur künstlerischen Herausforderung für das institutionalisierte P. wurden.

Während in Asien Puppenspieler eine sozial geachtete Stellung hatten, waren es in Europa seit dem Mittelalter vor allem Schausteller und wandernde Schauspieler, die das P. prägten. Ihre gesellschaftliche Außenseiterstellung führte auch zur Abwertung des P. Wie die übrigen Bereiche der →Schaustellerei (aber auch des Theaters) unterlagen auch die P. zahlreichen Verboten und Zensurmaßnahmen. Aktuelle Anspielungen boten dabei ebenso Anlässe für staatliches Eingreifen wie der angeblich fehlende moralische und belehrende Gehalt des P.

Gegenwärtig sind die Puppenspieler in nationalen (wie «Deutscher Bund für Puppenspiele», 1928 bis 1933, Neugründung 1948) und internationalen Vereinigungen (UNIMA, gegr. 1929, neugegr. 1957) organisiert. Es existieren in zahlreichen Ländern Publikationsorgane für Fragen des P. sowie spezielle Forschungseinrichtungen (wie seit 1949 das «Deutsche Institut für Puppenspiel») und Spezialsammlungen (u. a. in Moskau, Dresden, Lyon, Detroit und München) (→Handpuppe, →Jôruri, →Kukla oyunu, →Marionette, →Muou xi/Kuilei xi, →Papiertheater, →Schattentheater/Schementheater/Silhouettentheater, →Stabpuppe/Stockpuppe, →Über-Marionette, →UNIMA).

Batchelder, M.: The Puppet-Theatre-Handbook. London 1948; Baty, G./Chavance, R.: Histoire des marionnettes. Paris 1959; Benegal, S. u. a. (eds.): Puppet Theatre Around the World. Neu-Delhi 1960; Boehn, M. v.: Puppen und Puppenspiele. 2 Bde. München 1929; Bohlmeier, G.: Puppenspiel 1933–1945 in Deutschland. Bochum 1985; Jeanne, P.: Bibliographie des marionnettes. Paris 1926; Kipsch, W. (Hg.): Bemerkungen zum Puppenspiel. Frankfurt/M. 1992; Knoedgen, W.: Das unmögliche Theater. Stuttgart 1990; Leydi, R./Mezzanotte Leydi, R.: Marionette e burattini. Mailand 1958; Maindron, E.: Marionnettes et Guignols. Paris 1900; McPharlin, P.: The Puppet Theatre in America. New York [2]1969; Mehnert, M.: Entwicklungstendenzen des Puppentheaters der DDR seit den 70er Jahren. Diss. Berlin 1990; Meilink, W.: Bibliografie van het Poppenspel. Amsterdam 1965; Philpott, A.: Dictionary of Puppetry. London 1969; Puppentheater in Österreich. Wien 1987; Purschke, H. R.: Die Entwicklung des Puppenspiels in den klassischen Ursprungsländern Europas. Frankfurt/M. 1984; ders.: Die Puppenspieltraditionen Europas. Deutschsprachige Gebiete. Bochum 1986; Ransome, G. G.: Puppets and Shadows. A Bibliography. Boston 1931; Schreiner, K.: Puppen & Theater. Köln 1980; Speaight, G.: The History of the English Puppet Theatre. London [2]1992; Technau, S. (Hg.): Zu Besuch in der Kasperbude. Frankfurt/M. 1992; Till, W.: Puppentheater. München 1986; Wegner, M. (Hg.): Die Spiele der Puppe. Köln 1989; Weinkauff, G.: Der Rote Kasper.

Das Figurentheater in der pädagogisch-kulturellen Praxis der deutschen und österreichischen Arbeiterbewegung von 1918–1933. Bochum 1982; Die Welt des Puppenspiels. Berlin 1989; Wittkop-Menardeau, G.: Von Puppen und Marionetten. Zürich 1962.

Wolfgang Beck / Roland Dreßler

Puschkin-Theater (Sankt Petersburg)

(Peterburgskij gosudarstvennyj akademičeskij teatr dramy im. A. S. Puškina) Petersburg, von 1832 bis 1920 Alexandrinski-Theater (nach der Gemahlin Nikolais I., Alexandra Fjodorowna); ältestes russ. Dramentheater, 1756 gegründet. Der erste Direktor war der russ. klassizistische Dichter A. P. Sumarokow (1717–77); die Truppe wurde vom ‹Vater› des russischen Theaters F. G. Wolkow (1729–63) geleitet. Das 1832 bezogene neue Gebäude von K. I. Rossi gehört zu den besten architektonischen Schöpfungen des russ. Klassizismus. Im 19. Jh. neben dem →Maly Theater in Moskau Zentrum des russ. Bühnenrealismus; Aufführungen von Gribojedow *Verstand schafft Leiden* (1831), Gogol *Der Revisor* (1836), Ostrowski *Das Gewitter* (1859). Hervorragend unter den Schauspielern A. E. Martynow.

1896 bis 1904 spielte Vera Komissarshewskaja (1864–1910), die dann ihr eigenes Theater eröffnete, im Alexandrinski-Theater, 1908 bis 1917 führte Meyerhold dort Regie; aber die modernistischen Strömungen um die Wende 19./20. Jh. fanden im kaiserlichen Theater keinen Nährboden. Nach der Oktoberrevolution verhalf der Kommissar für Volksbildung, A. W. Lunatscharski, dem Theater zu politischem wie künstlerischem Fortbestehen; 1920 wurde sein *Faust*-Drama dort aufgeführt. 1937, aus Anlaß des 100. Todestags des Dichters, erhielt das Theater den Namen A. S. Puschkins.

Das Repertoire berücksichtigt klassische russ. sowie sowj. und westeurop. Dramen; ein Ereignis war 1955 die innovative Inszenierung der *Optimistischen Tragödie* von W. W. Wischnewski (1900–51) durch G. A. Towstonogow (1915–89), der epische Breite mit erregend lyrisch-heroischem Erzählen verband. Künstlerischer Leiter 1938–66 L. Wiwjen; gegenwärtig: I. O. Gorbatschow.

Al'tšuller, A. Ja.: K istorii akademičeskogo teatra dramy im. A. S. Puškina. In: Učenye zapiski gosudarstvennogo naučno-issledovatel'skogo instituta teatra i muzyki. T. 1. Leningrad 1958; Jur'ev, Ju.: Zapiski. T. 1–2. Leningrad/Moskva 1963; Karatygin, P. A.: Zapiski. T. 1–2. Leningrad 1929–30; Sto let. Aleksandrinskij teatr-teatr Gosdramy (1832–1932). Leningrad 1932.

Annelore Engel-Braunschmidt / Red.

Quyi (Kleine Theaterformen des chin. Theaters)

Unter dem Begriff quyi («Gesangskunst») werden die einfachen und populären Formen darstellender Kunst und der Unterhaltung zusammengefaßt, in denen Geschichten oder Dialoge mit gestischen, mimischen, sprachlichen und musikalischen Mitteln vorgetragen werden. Wegen ihrer Einfachheit können sie überall und bei jeder Gelegenheit ohne weitere Vorbereitung dargeboten werden, auf Straßen, Plätzen, bei Feiern, Versammlungen, privaten Veranstaltungen etc. Sie sind daher in ganz China außerordentlich verbreitet und beliebt. I. d. R. werden sie von einem oder zwei Darstellern vorgebracht; im Falle eines Darstellers übernimmt dieser im Laufe der Erzählung vielfach mehrere Rollen. – Wie das Theater zeichnen sich auch die quyi durch eine außerordentliche Formenvielfalt aus. Nach einer in jüngster Zeit angestellten Untersuchung gibt es etwa 340 regionale und lokale Formen der quyi. Gemäß den Besonderheiten ihrer Vortragsweise lassen sich die meisten auf vier Grundformen zurückführen:

1. «Geschichten zur Trommel» (guqu, guci). Von Nordchina ausgehend, breiteten sie sich seit der Ming-Zeit (1368–1644) in ganz China aus und bildeten zahlreiche regionale Stile wie die «Blumentrommel-Geschichten» (Huaguci) und «Fischtrommel-Geschichten» (Yugu ci) in Zentralchina oder die «Geschichten zur großen Trommel» (Dagu shu) im Norden. Im Rhythmus der meist siebensilbigen Verse wird der Vortrag entweder vom Vortragenden selbst oder von einem Begleiter auf einer Trommel bzw. auch auf einer dreisaitigen Zither (sanxian) untermalt und akzentuiert.

2. «Erläuterte Geschichten» (pingshu, pinghua, pingci, pingtan). Seit dem Beginn der Qing-Dynastie (1644–1911) vor allem in Nordchina verbreitet. Auch diese Erzählform bildete viele regionale Stile, meist nach dem Ort ihres Entstehens benannt wie die Yangzhou pingshu, Suzhou pingshu, Sichuan pinshu etc. Sie werden von einem Darsteller vorgetragen. Dieser hält das sog. «Aufmunterungs-Holz» (xingmu) in der Hand, einen kleinen Holzstab, den er auf den Tisch schlägt, um die Aufmerksamkeit der Zuhörer auf sich zu lenken und um die Erzählung zu unterstreichen. Es gibt auch Formen, die zur Instrumentenbegleitung gesungen werden wie die tanci in der Gegend um Suzhou, vorgetragen zur dreisaitigen Zither (sanxian) oder zur chin. Gitarre (pipa).

3. «Wechselgespräche» (xiangsheng). Auch sie sind urspr. in Nordchina entstanden, haben aber Verbreitung im ganzen Land gefunden. Sie sind hervorgegangen aus Erzählungen witziger Geschichten, aber auch aus Formen der Nachahmung von Geräuschen, Stimmen und Tierlauten, die hinter einer Trennwand vorgetragen wurden. Heute stellen die xiangsheng einen komischen, satirischen Dialog dar mit folgenden vier

Mitteln der Darstellung: Erzählung (shuo) von Witzen, Rätseln und Wortspielen; Nachahmung (xue) von Tierlauten, Stimmen, Geräuschen, aber auch von äußeren Eigentümlichkeiten von Menschen etc.; sich gegenseitig zum Lachen bringen (dou); Singen (chang) von Spottversen. Es gibt drei verschiedene Formen des xiangsheng: der von einem einzelnen Darsteller vorgetragene Solo-xiangsheng (dankou xiangsheng); das von zwei Darstellern vorgetragene Wechselgespräch (duikou xiangsheng), die verbreitetste Form; und der von drei oder mehr Darstellern gespielte Gruppenxiangsheng (qunkou xiangsheng).

4. «Erzählung im schnellen Takt» (kuaiban shu), vor allem in Nordchina verbreitet. Es sind gereimte Geschichten, deren Vortrag vom Erzähler mit rhythmischen Schlägen zweier Bambusklappern begleitet wird. Eine Variante sind die «Erzählungen im schnellen Takt aus Shandong» (Shandong kuaishu), die zwar in der Provinz Shandong entstanden, heute aber ebenfalls in ganz Nordchina verbreitet sind; in ihnen werden Kupferklappern verwendet.

Der Inhalt der in den kleinen Theaterformen vorgetragenen Geschichten war traditionell vielfach bestimmt durch die Heldenerzählungen aus der Zeit der Drei Reiche (3. Jh.), durch die Gestalten aus dem Roman *Shuihu zhuan* («Die Räuber vom Liangshan Moor») oder durch die Abenteuer des Affen Sun Wukong aus dem Roman *Xiyou ji* («Die Reise nach Westen»). Die Geschichten sind bis heute beliebt; aber sehr viel stärker als das eigentliche Theater standen die Kleinen Theaterformen immer auch neuen Themen und Erzählungen aus dem Alltagsleben offen.

Fu Xihua: Quyi luncong. Shanghai 1953; Hrdlicka, Z.: Old Chinese Ballads to the Accompaniment of the Big Drum. In: Archiv Orientální XXV, 1 (1957), 83–143; Pimpaneau, J.: Chanteurs conteurs bateleurs – littérature orale et spectacles populaires en Chine. Paris 1977; Prusek, J.: Die Chui-tsi-shu, erzählende Volksgesänge aus Honan. In: Asiatica, Festschrift Friedrich Weller. Leipzig 1954, S. 453–483; Walls, J. W.: Kuaibanshu: Elements of the Fast Clappertale. In: Chinoperl Papers 7 (1977), 60–91; Zhao Jingshen: Quyi congtan. Beijing 1982; Zhongguo da baike quanshu, xiqu quyi. Beijing/Shanghai 1983.

Bernd Eberstein

Rachetragödie

Die R. war eine der Hauptformen der → elisabethanischen Dramenliteratur. Tragödie, in der das Motiv der Rache Stoff und Handlungsgerüst, der Rächer den dramatischen Protagonisten darstellt. In der Renaissance durch den Einfluß Senecas (4 v. Chr. – 65) und von Garnier, weniger von Calderón, nach England vermittelt. Blütezeit etwa 1580 bis 1630. Die erste bekannte R. in England war *Gorboduc* (1561) von Thomas Norton

768 Radioteatret

(1532–84) und Thomas Sackville (1536–1608). Die bekannteste elisabeth. R. war *The Spanish Tragedy* (ca. 1586) von Thomas Kyd (1558–94) mit genrespezifischen Elementen wie dem Motiv der Rache für den Tod eines ermordeten Sohnes, Geistererscheinungen, Wahnsinn, melodramatischer Bühnensprache und hochstilisierter Rhetorik. Kyd beeinflußte unmittelbar Shakespeares Hamlet, evtl. über einen nicht überlieferten *Ur-Hamlet*, aber schon *Titus Andronicus* (1594) war eine R. Andere Typen der R. verfaßten zur Zeit Shakespeares und später Christopher Marlowe (1564–1593) in *The Jew of Malta* (ca. 1592); John Marston (1576–1634) mit *Antonio's Revenge* (1600) und *The Malcontent* (1604), Henry Chettle (ca. 1560–1607) in *Hoffman* (1602), Cyril Tourneur (ca. 1570/80–1616) in *The Revenger's Tragedy* (1607) sowie *The Atheist's Tragedy* (1611), George Chapman (ca. 1560–1634) mit *The Revenge of Bussy D'Ambois* (1607), John Webster (ca. 1580–1638) in *The White Devil* (1612), Thomas Middleton (1580–1627) und William Rowley (ca. 1585–1626) mit *The Changeling* (1622). Nach 1600 nahmen in der R. die dekadent übersteigerten Züge der Rache allmählich überhand: Mord, Korruption und Perversionen erschienen in grotesker Ausprägung. Nach 1642 Abbruch der Tradition. In späteren Epochen nur gelegentlich Wiederaufnahmen der R., meist jedoch eher durch ein Nachwirken des Rachemotivs denn als Fortsetzung der elisabethanischen Tragödienform im engl. Sinne, so z. B. in der Romantik in Percy Bysshe Shelleys (1792–1822) Lesedrama *The Cenci* (1819), auch in Victor Hugos *Hernani* (1830) und *Ruy Blas* (1838). Im 20. Jh. Nachklänge bei Arthur Miller in *A View from the Bridge* (1955) und David Rudkin in *Afore Night Come* (1962).

Bowers, F. T.: Elizabethan Revenge Tragedy 1587–1642. Princeton 1959; Clemen, W.: Die Tragödie vor Shakespeare. Heidelberg 1955.

Bernd-Peter Lange

Radioteatret

Die Medien der skandin. Länder zeichnen sich durch ein vergleichsweise großes Angebot an im Kulturbereich anzusiedelnden Produktionen aus. So strahlte z. B. Norsk Rikskringkasting bereits kurz nach seiner Entstehung eine Reihe kaum für das Radio bearbeiteter Dramen Ibsens und Bjørnsons aus: Auch in Dänemark waren von der ersten Stunde des Rundfunks an Theaterleute dabei, die ersten kamen vom Königlichen Theater und vom Dagmartheater.

Das skandin. R. stand zunächst unter dem Einfluß der jeweiligen alteingesessenen Bühnen. Unter dem Einfluß von Otto Rung (*1874) strahlte der Vorläufer von Danmarks Radio bereits 1925 drei mit der Besetzung des Königlichen Theaters inszenierte Dramen aus, nämlich *Nein* von Johann Ludvig Heiberg (1791–1860), *Henrik und Pernille* von Ludvig Holberg (1684–1754) und *Die Schule der Frauen* von Jean Baptiste Molière (1622–73). Das skandin. R. beeinflußte auch Bühne und Bühnendichtung. In diesem Zusammenhang sind z. B. die norweg. Dichter Finn Havrevold und Tormod Skagestad (*1920) zu erwähnen. Skagestad wurde u. a. Intendant von Det Norske Teater in Oslo, wo er die ‹nynorske› Dichtung förderte. Einer der wenigen Dichter, die mit der eigentlichen radiophonischen Theaterform, dem Hörspiel, wirklich zu experimentieren wagten, war der Däne Hans Christian Branner (1903–66). Seine Radiodramatik macht den größten Teil seines Gesamtwerks aus. Etliche skandin. Dichter unternahmen im Rahmen des R. nur vereinzelte Versuche oder lehnten es sogar vollständig ab wie z. B. Kjeld Abell (1901–61). – Vor dem Aufkommen des TV-Theaters wurde das skandin. R. häufig lediglich als unfertiges Kunstmedium betrachtet, während es sich danach stets bemühen mußte, durch hohes künstlerisches Niveau aus dem Schatten des TV-Theaters herauszutreten.

Anker, L.: Scenekunsten i Norge fra fortid til nutid. Oslo 1968; Franzén, N.: Hört och sett – Radio och television. Stockholm 1975; Nørgaard, F.: Radioteater. Musik. TV-teater. De musiske udsendelser DR 1925–1975. København 1975.

Martin Kolberg

Rangtheater

Das R. ist der Standardbautyp des 17. bis 19. Jh. in Europa. Bis zu sechs Ränge (Galerien) können übereinander gestaffelt werden (Teatro alla Scala, 1778, Mailand). Diese bes. Anordnung der Zuschauer soll sich aus den barocken Festen und Turnieren, denen man aus Fenstern, Arkadenumgängen und von Balkonen der angrenzenden Gebäude zusah, herausgebildet haben. Die Ränge sind in den Hoftheatern in abgeschlossene Logen für vier bis acht Zuschauer unterteilt. Die prächtig ausgestaltete Hofloge im ersten Rang ist der wahre Mittel- und Bezugspunkt des Zuschauerraums. Der Vorteil des R. liegt darin, daß eine größere Anzahl von Zuschauern in kurzer Distanz zur Bühne angeordnet werden kann. Die reich ornamentierte Rangverkleidung bewirkt die Brechung des Schalls und damit eine Verbesserung der Hörsamkeit. Die Nachteile liegen in der schlechten Bühneneinsicht der seitlichen Logen und der höheren Ränge. So gibt es zur Verbesserung dieses Mangels die unterschiedlichsten Grundrißlösungen (U-Form, Glockenform, Eiform, Hufeisenform, Tennisschlägerform, Ellipse, Flaschenform).

Die Kritik am R.-System entzündet sich im 19. Jh. vor allem an der sozialen Schichtung der Zuschauer nach Rängen. Im ‹Olymp›, dem obersten Rang, versammelten sich auf billigen Stehplätzen diejenigen, die gesellschaftlich die niedrigste Stufe einnahmen. Mit der Übernahme der Hoftheater in die bürgerliche Regie verfeinerte sich das R. bzw. paßte sich den neuen gesellschaftlichen Umgangsformen an. Die Logenwände wurden niedriger oder entfielen, die Zahl der Ränge verringerte sich, die seitlichen Ränge wurden verkürzt und tragende Stützen durch Kragträger ersetzt. – Im modernen → Theaterbau bilden die stützenfreien Ränge amphitheatralische Sitzplatzebenen, die notwendig werden, um bei größerer Zuschauerzahl die Sichtentfernung zur Bühne nicht zu groß werden zu lassen (→ Freie Volksbühne, Berlin, 1963).

Baur-Heinhold, M.: Theater des Barock. München 1966; Zielske, H.: Deutsche Theaterbauten bis zum 2. Weltkrieg. Berlin 1971.

Horst Birr

Raslila

Neben dem Lai Haraoba sind die Choloms und Raslilas für den → Manipuri typisch. Dem vishnuitischen Reformkönig Charairongba (1697 bis 1709) gelang der Ausbau Manipurs zu einem Zentralreich mit der Metropole Imphal. Charairongbas Tochter Lairobi tanzte als Radha (Gattin Krishnas) 1769 in der ersten Raslila-Aufführung. Das R.-Tanz-Schauspiel ist ein religiöses Zeremoniell. Die Tänzer der R. tragen auch heute noch als charakteristisches Kostüm bodenlange Reifröcke mit gestreiftem Rand. Für R.-Aufführungen wurden früher im Tempelbezirk kreisrunde, von zwölf Säulen umgrenzte bühnenartige Schauplätze errichtet. Gespielt wurde vom Sonnenuntergang bis zur Morgenröte. Jedes Tanzspiel war dramaturgisch in 14 bis 18 Szenen gegliedert. Protagonist aller R. ist Krishna (→ Manipuri; → Ritualtänze).

Rebling, E.: Die Tanzkunst Indiens. Wilhelmshaven 1982; Rischbieter, H. (Hg.): Theater-Lexikon. Stichwort: Indisches Theater. Sp. 668–672. Schwäbisch Hall 1983.

Helga Ettl

Räsoneur

(Frz. raisonneur = Klugschwätzer) Männliches → Rollenfach, in der Regel eine ältere Nebenfigur – Vater, Oheim –, die die Handlung der anderen Figuren kommentierend beobachtet und charakterisiert, ihre Lage und ihr Benehmen erläutert und ggf. motiviert und sich dabei oft als Sprachrohr des Autors oder der Gesellschaft direkt an die Zuschauer wendet.

Bernard Poloni

Realistisches Theater

R. T. zielt ab auf die objektiv-getreue Wiedergabe der ‹Realität› auf der Bühne. Diese Wirklichkeit wird im engeren Sinne verstanden als geschichtliche und gesellschaftliche Umwelt. Im breiteren Sinne ist die Frage der Verarbeitung der Realität, die Interpretation der Wirklichkeit durch dramatische Darstellung oder Nachahmung (Mimesis) ein Grundproblem des Theaters seit Aristoteles, die sich auch heute jedem Dramaturgen weiterhin stellt.

Im eigentlichen historischen und engeren Rahmen ist das r. T. dasjenige der Zeit des ‹bürgerlichen Realismus› (ca. zwischen 1848 und 1880). Diese Periode kennzeichnet sich durch die totale Vorherrschaft der Erzählkunst und vor allem des Romans in ganz Europa. Über die Theorie des Dramas wird zwar reflektiert – mit zwiespältigem Erfolg, vor allem in Deutschland –; die Praxis des Dramas jedoch bleibt unfruchtbar, höchstens epigonal.

Paradoxerweise wird in Theorie und Praxis von Shakespeare als Modell des realistischen Dramas ausgegangen, im Gegensatz zu einem als Idealisten verschrienen Schiller. Man kehrt aber dann in der Praxis noch mehr als in der Theorie zu klassischen Maßstäben zurück; darin liegt das Scheitern des Theaters im Realismus. Otto Ludwig (1813–65) will in seinen *Shakespeare-Studien* (1851–65) den ‹poetischen Realismus› als Kompromißlösung zwischen dem ‹realistischen› Shakespearedrama und der idealistischen frz. klassischen Tragödie einfordern. Gustav Freytag (1816–95) unternimmt in der *Technik des Dramas* (1863) eine pragmatische Sammlung von dramaturgischen Rezepten und Regeln, die zur Kanonisierung der überlieferten aristotelischen Theaterauffassung führt: Der angebliche Realist schreibt die letzte umfassende Abhandlung über die → klassische Tragödie.

Realistische Stücke gibt es desgleichen vor oder nach der Zeit des bürgerlichen Realismus, so in Deutschland im Werk Georg Büchners

772 Realistisches Theater

(1813–37: *Dantons Tod*, 1835; *Woyzeck*, 1835–36) und Christian Dietrich Grabbes (1801–36: *Napoleon oder die Hundert Tage*, 1831; *Hannibal*, 1835), die aber erst zur Zeit des Naturalismus entdeckt und aufgeführt wurden. Hier entsteht in Anlehnung an Shakespeare und den → Sturm und Drang historisches und soziales Volkstheater mit individuellen und Massenszenen in neuartiger dramatisch-epischer Form. Friedrich Hebbel (1813–63: *Maria Magdalene*, 1844; *Agnes Bernauer*, 1852), ein Außenseiter zur Zeit des Realismus, scheitert letzten Endes ideologisch und formal in seiner dramatischen Verwirklichung der Problematik Hegels; charakteristisch für den bürgerlichen Realismus ist er nicht. Im Grunde entsprechen erst die Stücke des Naturalismus (→ Naturalistisches Theater), vor allem Henrik Ibsens (1828–1906), dem, was ein r. T. hätte sein können, d. h. eine kritische Darstellung des bürgerlichen Zeitalters mit seiner Problematik und seinen Widersprüchen. Deswegen überschneiden sich in der Forschung manchmal gewisse Analysen des realistischen und des naturalistischen Theaters.

Zur Zeit des bürgerlichen Realismus entsteht auch der ‹sozialistische Realismus›, Anlaß war die sog. ‹Sickingen-Debatte› zwischen Ferdinand Lassalle (1825–64), dem Autor des historischen Dramas *Franz von Sikkingen* (1858), und Karl Marx und Friedrich Engels im Jahre 1859. Oberflächlich verdankt Marx dem bürgerlichen Realismus gewisse Merkmale, insbesondere das Kanonisieren der klassischen Literatur. Wichtiger aber sind zwei Grundzüge: einmal in der Tradition der realistischen Autoren seit Büchner und Grabbe die Chiffre Shakespeare. Marx an Lassalle: «Du hättest dann von selbst mehr Shakespearisieren müssen, während ich Dir das Schillern, das Verwandeln von Individuen in bloße Sprachrören des Zeitgeistes als bedeutendsten Fehler anrechne.» Sodann die Grundlage des sozialistischen Realismus: Die Darstellung der Revolution habe nicht von oben herab im Charakter eines einzigen, zu früh gekommenen Helden zu erfolgen. Wichtig sei vielmehr die Dramatisierung der objektiven Klassengegensätze und historischen Widersprüche, der Kämpfe und Bewußtwerdung der Massen sowie die Betonung in der Tragik des Zuspätkommens, des Untergangs von Helden der vergangenen Werte, der bestehenden Ordnung. Diese Ideologie sowie gewisse Gedanken zur offenen, shakespearisierenden Form wurden von Brecht übernommen wie auch von den sowj. Autoren des 20. Jh. Auch da spricht man von r. T. Anknüpfend an die Tradition des bürgerlichen Realismus und des Naturalismus vom → Sturm und Drang bis Gerhart Hauptmann, will Brecht den sozialistischen Realismus sehen als ‹kämpferisch›, ‹historisch›, das Typische, ‹historisch Bedeutsame› darstellend, die gesellschaftlichen Widersprüche auf Veränderungen hin repräsentierend, ‹human›, mit realistischer Einstellung zum Publikum, auf → Verfremdung statt → Einfühlung abzielend. Diese Definition des Realismus darf für das gesamte Theater des Sozialismus gelten, wenn auch die stalinistische Variante durch Überbetonung des Nationalismus und des einseitig positiv und optimistisch gezeichneten Helden stark davon abfiel.

Auch die angelsächsische Forschung spricht im 20. Jh. intensiv von r. T. als Nachfolge des bürgerlichen Realismus und des Naturalismus. Als Vorgänger gelten Henrik Ibsen und Anton Tschechow sowie deren Aufführungen im →MChAT durch Konstantin Stanislawski (1863–1938) und Wladimir J. Nemirowitsch-Dantschenko (1858–1943). Realistisch im Sinne der wirklichkeitsnahen Milieuschilderung bis zum Sozialkritischen, einer epischen Verfremdungstechnik in Regie und Schauspielweise, der Übernahme von volkstümlichen Elementen in Stoff und Sprache ist zuerst die irische Theaterbewegung des →Abbey Theatre mit John Millington Synge (1871–1909: *The Playboy of the Western World*, 1907) und Sean O'Casey (1880–1964: *Juno and the Paycock*, 1924; *The Plough and the Stars*, 1926). In den USA zeigt sich r. T. im →Group Theatre und im →Actors' Studio unter Regie von Lee Strasberg (1901–82) und Elia Kazan (1909–85): zuerst Stücke marxistischen Einflusses mit Mischung von expressionistischen und realistischen Agitprop-Elementen von Clifford Odets (1906–63: *Waiting for Lefty*, 1935; *Golden Boy*, 1937); eher volkstümlich und populistisch bei William Saroyan (1908–81: *The Time of Your Life*, 1939), vor allem aber in Stücken von Eugene O'Neill (1888–1953: *Long Day's Journey into Night*, 1939–41, UA 1956; *A Moon for the Misbegotten*, 1941–43, UA 1947), Tennessee Williams (1914–83: *A Streetcar named Desire*, 1947; *Cat on a Hot Tin Roof*, 1955) – hier mit realistisch-psychoanalytischer Darstellung des amerik. Südens; Arthur Miller (*1915: *Death of a Salesman*, 1949; *A View from the Bridge*, 1955) mit sozialer Analyse und tragischer Darstellung des Durchschnittsmenschen. Später Volksstücke mit Beschreibung der Alltagsexistenz des kleinen Mannes bei Paddy Chayefsky (1923–81: *Marty*, 1953). In England Neorealismus in den 50er und 60er Jahren, oft als ‹Waschküchentheater› abgetan, auch ‹Zorniges Theater› genannt im Anklang an das ausschlaggebende Stück von John Osborne (*1929) *Look back in Anger* (1956): heftige Auseinandersetzung im Dialekt einer Unterschicht-Figur gegen Konventionen und soziale Ungerechtigkeiten der britischen Gesellschaft. Anschließend vor allem Arnold Wesker (*1932) mit Darstellung einer Familie vom Land in *Roots* (1959) und Edward Bond (*1935) mit dem brutalen Porträt von Jugendlichen aus der Unterschicht in *Saved* (1965). In Frankreich realistische Tendenz im →‹Théâtre du quotidien›; im deutschsprachigen Theater neben den Stücken des →epischen Theaters hauptsächlich die zeitgenössischen →Volksstücke.

Brecht, B.: Schriften zur Literatur und Kunst 2. In: Gesammelte Werke, Bd. 19. Frankfurt/M. 1967; Hayman, R.: The Set-up: An Anatomy of British Theatre

774 Rechts und links auf dem Theater

Today. London 1973; Lukács, G.: Deutsche Realisten des 19. Jh. Berlin 1953; ders.: Probleme des Realismus. Berlin 1955; Martini, F.: Deutsche Literatur im bürgerlichen Realismus (1848–98). Stuttgart 1964; Schanze, H.: Theorie des Dramas im bürgerlichen Realismus. In: Grimm, R. (Hg.): Deutsche Dramentheorien II. Frankfurt/M. 1973; ders.: Drama im bürgerlichen Realismus. Frankfurt/M. 1973; Styan, J. L.: Modern Drama in Theory and Practice 1: Realism and Naturalism. Cambridge 1981; Taylor, J. R.: Anger and After: A Guide to the New British Drama. London 1962; ders.: The Second Wave: British Drama of the Sixties. London 1978; Weales, G.: American Drama since World War II. New York 1962; ders.: The Jumping Off Place: American Drama in the Sixties. New York 1969.

Gérard Schneilin

Rechts und links auf dem Theater

Hatte im antiken Theater der Auftritt von rechts oder links noch inhaltliche Bedeutung (von rechts = Ferne, von links = Heimat), so ist es heute eine vor allem formale Bestimmung. Entsprechende Angaben in Stücktexten beziehen sich auf den Blickwinkel vom Zuschauer aus.

Wolfgang Beck

Reduta

Redoute, Warschau; 1919 bis 1939, gegründet von M. Limanowski und J. Osterwa (1885–1947, Schauspieler, Regisseur, Pädagoge, Anhänger des psychologischen Realismus). Avantgardistisches Theater, entwickelte neue Formen und Methoden der Schauspielerarbeit. 1919 bis 1924 als Theaterlaboratorium und Schauspielerkommune ohne kommerzielle Ziele betrieben. Ausschließlich poln. Dramatik (22 Premieren, 1700 Aufführungen). Das künstlerische Konzept steht dem → Stanislawski-System nahe. 1922 entstand das Instytut Reduty (Redoute-Institut), eine eigene Schauspielschule. 1925 bis 1930 nach Wilna und Grodno verlegt. Großangelegte Gastspieltourneen. Nach der Rückkehr nach Warschau auf die Kammerspielarbeit beschränkt. Von der R. führt ein direkter Weg zu den Experimenten anderer poln. Theaterlaboratorien und zur Arbeit von J. Grotowski (→ Armes Theater).

Slawomir Tryc

Reformation / Drama und Theater der Reformation

Im Rückblick hat man von der Reformationszeit in England den Eindruck, als strebte man auf Shakespeare zu. Wie theologisch in der Bibelübersetzung Wittenberg das Vorbild war, so übernahm John Bale das lat. Kampfdrama aus dem Wittenberger Kreis; er übertrug den *Pammachius* des Naogeorg ins Engl. In seinem eigenen Drama erscheint die Titelfigur Kynge Johan wie der Kaiser Julian im *Pammachius* als ein Opfer der bösen Geistlichkeit. Neben Bale wirkt als protestantischer Tendenzdramatiker, freilich in lat. Sprache, Georgius Buchanan mit seinem *Baptistes* und seinem *Jephtes*, die ihrerseits in Deutschland übernommen wurden. In der Abhängigkeit von humanistischen Formen bleiben diese Dramen wesentlich rezitierend, sie dringen nicht zur Handlung, zum Theater durch. Neben Schulen und Universitäten, wo kleine anspruchslose Stücke an der Tagesordnung waren, entstehen Wandertruppen, die Vorstufe zu den festen Theatern der Shakespeare-Zeit. Ihr Repertoire besteht vornehmlich aus →Interludien mit mehr Gepränge als Handlung. Der Einfluß Senecas führt dann zu wirklichen Tragödien wie dem an *Lear* gemahnenden *Gorboduc* von Thomas Sackville. Jedoch bleibt diesem und ähnlichen blutrünstigen Dramen unter dem Einfluß Senecas ein stark rhetorisches Element.

Auch in Frankreich wirkte die Antike maßgeblich nach, doch weniger Seneca als die Griechen. Jodelle, Jean de la Péruse und Jacques Grévin aus dem Kreis der Plejade ahmen in ihren meist der Antike entnommenen Stoffen vor allem sophokleische Form nach. Auch hier siegt wesentlich Rhetorik über dramatische Wirkung.

Neben dem Rederijkerdramen mit Prangstücken aus Allegorie und Legende entwickelte sich in den Niederlanden ein beachtliches lat. Humanistendrama. Cornelius Crocus, ein strikter Terenzianer, begrenzt in seinem *Joseph* alles Geschehen auf eine Örtlichkeit. Auch Macropedius, ein Bewunderer Reuchlins, beschränkt sich in seinem *Asotus* (Verlorenen Sohn) auf einen Schauplatz. In seinen recht groben Schwänken erweitert er den Bühnenplatz. Doch sein bestes Werk, *Hecastus* (Jedermann), gewinnt durch die Einheit des Ortes eine außerordentlich scharfe Kontur. Gnaphaeus erweitert in seinem *Acolastus* (Verlorenen Sohn) sehr geschickt die Einortbühne des Terenz, die Vaterhaus und Fremde umfassen kann.

Vielgestaltiger und reicher entwickelte sich das Drama in dem Geburtsland der Reformation. In Thüringen vor allem bilden sich aus einer Synthese aus humanistischer Begrenzung und religiösem Stoff kurze meist dtspr. Dramen aus dem Alten Testament und der Gleichniswelt. Die Passion, das Leiden Christi, war durch das Machtwort Luthers als dramatischer Stoff tabu. Schulmeister wie Greff, Voith, Knaust und manche andere schmiedeten ihre Knüttelversdramen. Paul Rebhun sucht eine entscheidende Reform der Metrik. Er experimentiert mit den verschiedensten Rhythmen, doch müssen dabei Versbetonung und Sinnbetonung immer zusammenfallen. Der lat. dichtende Thomas Naogeorgus überragt alle in leidenschaftlicher protestantischer Tendenz. In seinem grandiosen Frühwerk *Pammachius* wird der jahrhundertelange Kampf zwischen Papst und Kaiser in vier Akte zusammengedrängt.

In der Schweiz und im Elsaß wandelt sich das Volksdrama des Mittelalters in große protestantische Bürgermassendramen in Bern, Zürich, Biel und kath. Dramen in Luzern, Solothurn, Fribourg. Vielfach zweitägige Werke behandeln ungefähr alle Themen der biblischen Geschichte auf weiter Simultanbühne. Auch vor der Passion schreckt man nicht zurück. Rüte, Ruoff, Funckelin im protestantischen Lager, Aal, Bletz, Salat, Cysat im kath. verbinden mittelalterliche Formen mit den neuen techn. Mitteln. Daneben entwickelt sich im Süden, in Basel, Augsburg und Straßburg, ein humanistisches Drama und Theater. Das Werk von Sixt Birck entwickelt sich in Basel von urspr. reinem Rezitationsdrama in frühhumanistischem Stil zu kompakter wirklich dramatischer Form in seiner *Susanna* und seiner *Judith*. Als Rektor der Augsburger Lateinschule wendet er dieselbe Form in seinen lat. Dramen an. Der Kreis von Lehrern und Schülern um ihn übernimmt diesen Theaterstil weitgehend. Mit einfachsten Mitteln werden zwei oder drei Örtlichkeiten nebeneinander aufgebaut. Um keine Innenräume zeigen zu müssen, spricht man aus den Fenstern der Häuser. Das Straßburger Akademietheater konzentriert sich dagegen vollkommen auf antike Werke. Neben Plautus und Terenz werden griech. Tragödien aufgeführt. Doch im Gegensatz zu Birck mit seiner Theaterlust will Johannes Sturm, der Rektor der Straßburger Schule, in seinen Theateraufführungen vor allem das reine, klassische Latein und Griechisch üben lassen.

Am großartigsten beherrscht Hans Sachs den Theaterapparat. Er folgt zwar Reuchlin, den er übersetzte, in den Anwendung der → Sukzessionsbühne, aber er übernimmt auch Elemente der → Simultanbühne. Seit 1550 spielt er in Sälen mit Podien und hinterem Abschluß. Schiffe fahren an dieses Podium heran. Aus einer Versenkung kommt der wiedererweckte Lazarus, steigen Tote herauf. Doch wird die Szenerie manchmal auch nur im Dialog angedeutet.

Creizenach, W.: Geschichte des neueren Dramas. Bd. II. Halle 1918; Fricker, R.: Das ältere engl. Schauspiel. Bern 1975; Michael, W. F.: Frühformen der dt. Bühne (Schriften der Gesellschaft für Theatergeschichte 62). Berlin 1963; ders.: Das dt. Drama der Reformationszeit. Bern 1984.

Wolfgang F. Michael

Regie

(Fr. *régie* – Verwaltung, Leitung) R. umfaßt den Aufgabenbereich des →Regisseurs und damit die Einrichtung, Einstudierung und künstlerische Leitung einer →Inszenierung. Die Zielvorstellungen der R. können verschieden sein; sie reichen von Versuchen einer originalgetreuen Interpretation über die Umsetzung der vom Autor festgelegten Möglichkeiten bis hin zur kritischen Auslegung eines Werks nach ausgewählten Gesichtspunkten, ja zur freien Produktion, für die der Text nur mehr Ausgangspunkt ist (→Regietheater). Der Interpretationsvielfalt steht bei neuzeitlichen Werken das Urheberrecht entgegen, das bei einschneidenden Änderungen in Text und Struktur des Stücks die Zustimmung des Autors verlangt.

In der Antike wurde R. zumeist vom Autor ausgeübt, der sich für die Einstudierung der Chöre verantwortlich zeigte. Das R.-Interesse richtete sich weniger auf das Spiel der Darsteller, zumal der Dichter häufig selbst agierte. Sofern er nicht R. führte, wurde ein professioneller Chorleiter (Didaskalos) engagiert. Chor-R. dagegen bedeutete keine künstlerische Arbeit, sondern die finanzielle und materielle Ausstattung der Chöre, die ausgewählten Privatleuten (Choregen) oblag.

Im Theater des Mittelalters fielen dem sog. Spielordner (zunächst Priester, im →Jesuitentheater Pädagogen) R.-Aufgaben zu, indem er Arrangement, Szenenablauf und Sprachgestaltung überwachte. Das Barocktheater kannte R. auf Grund hochentwickelter Bühnentechnik und stilbewußter Aufführungen in Form einer Spielleitung (der Position des heutigen Inspizienten vergleichbar).

Mit dem Aufkommen wandernder Schauspieltruppen übernahmen →Prinzipale (Caroline Neuber, 1697–1760; Konrad Ekhof, 1720–78; Fr. Ludwig Schröder, 1744–1816), in der Regel erste Schauspieler, neben organisatorischen Aufgaben die künstlerische Leitung, beschränkt jedoch auf szenische Anordnungen und Stückauswahl; ihr Einfluß wirkte sich mehr auf Disziplin und Bildungsniveau der Darsteller aus.

Seit Etablierung fester Theater trat R. als eigene Gestaltungsinstanz deutlich hervor. Den Anfang machte Goethe am Weimarer Hoftheater, gefolgt u. a. von Joseph Schreyvogel (1768–1832) und später Heinrich Laube (1806–84) in Wien, Ernst August Klingemann (1777–1831) in Braunschweig, Karl L. Immermann (1796–1840) in Düsseldorf, Eduard Devrient (1801–77) in Karlsruhe, Franz von Dingelstedt (1814–81) in München, Weimar und Wien. In diesen frühen, eher dramaturgischen R.-Versuchen zeichneten sich Ansätze zu intensiver Probenarbeit und einheitlicher Spielführung ab. Als erster verantwortlicher Regisseur nach heutigen Maßstäben gilt Georg II. von Meiningen (1826–1914), der die Aufführung eines Stücks von der Bearbeitung über technische Proben bis

778 Regie

hin zur schauspielerischen Gestaltung leitete, zudem die Entwicklung und Ausbildung des Ensembles (→Meininger) vorantrieb. Nach seinem Vorbild setzte sich R. auf der Bühne mit Hilfe naturgetreuer Wiedergabe von Wirklichkeit durch. Neue techn. Möglichkeiten und die für den Naturalismus (→Naturalistisches Theater) notwendige analytische Durchdringung der Rollen samt Textdeutung, auch die Umsetzung wissenschaftlicher Erkenntnisse in die Praxis verliehen der R. seit etwa 1900 zusätzliche Bedeutung. In Frankreich schloß sich André Antoine (1858–1943) mit seinem →Théâtre libre dem R.-Stil der Meininger an. Konstantin S. Stanislawski (1863–1938) verfeinerte am Moskauer Künstlertheater (→MChAT) den naturalistischen R.-Ansatz und erreichte einen bis dahin ungekannten Grad an illusionistischer Perfektion: Äußere und innere Vorgänge der Darstellung wurden bei der Suche nach Natürlichkeit und Wahrhaftigkeit der Empfindung in Einklang gebracht, jegliche Theaterwirkung vermieden, zudem das Ensemblespiel hervorgehoben. Damit wurde der R. eine weitere wichtige Aufgabe zugewiesen. Mit Otto Brahm (1856–1912), der nicht R. führte, sondern die Schauspieler durch Beratung und Kritik beeinflußte, vollzog sich in Deutschland zunächst an der Freien Bühne, später am Dt. Theater Berlin die Entwicklung zur naturalistischen Inszenierungstechnik, die bald an ihre Grenzen stieß. Die Überwindung des Naturalismus kündigte sich in den Inszenierungen Max Reinhardts (1873–1943) durch übersteigert realistisches Spiel und effektvolle Bühnenbilder an. Tendenzen zu individueller R.-Führung, getragen von Phantasie und schöpferischer Kraft, waren offensichtlich. R. war zum Instrument geworden, mit dem die Ausarbeitung individueller Zielsetzungen gelang. Die Auflösung des illusionistischen Theaters begann mit dem Expressionismus (→Expressionistisches Theater), der die R. in formaler, stilistischer Hinsicht bereicherte, zugleich ihre Position als Ziel und Form bestimmendes, zentrales Moment der theatralischen Aktion stärkte. Leopold Jessner (1878–1945) suchte für klassische Dramen nach neuen, schlichten Ausdrucksformen, um sich der Stückidee anzunähern. Jacques Copeau (1879–1949) wollte auf dem Wege größtmöglicher Einfachheit in szenischer Gestaltung bis zum Kern der Dichtung vordringen. Freien Umgang mit der literarischen Textvorlage übten die sowj. Revolutionsregisseure: Wsewolod E. Meyerhold (1874–1942) führte das filmische Montageprinzip für seine Aufführungen ein und ordnete die schauspielerischen Auftritte einem festen R.-Konzept unter, das sich an dem Sinnbild des techn. Zeitalters orientierte; Alexander I. Tairow (1885–1950) und Jewgeni B. Wachtangow (1883 bis 1922) gaben dem Schauspiel seine freie Entfaltung zurück und behaupteten Theater als Kontrast zur Wirklichkeit. Erwin Piscator (1893–1966) verdichtete R. unter Hinzunahme aufwendiger Bühnenmaschinerie und dokumentarischen Materials zur politisch-agitatorischen

B. Brecht: «Mutter Courage und ihre Kinder». R: B. Brecht u. E. Engel.
B: T. Otto u. H. Kilger. Berliner Ensemble 1949 (BE)

B. Brecht: «Die Mutter». R: B. Brecht: B: C. Neher. Berliner Ensemble 1951 (BE)

B. Brecht: «Der Brotladen». R: M. Karge u. M. Langhoff. B: K. v. Appen.
Berliner Ensemble 1967 (BE)

W. Shakespeare: «Maß für Maß». R: P. Zadek. B: W. Minks. Bremen 1967 (GV)

B. Brecht: «Leben des Galilei». R: G. Strehler. B: L. Damiani.
Piccolo Teatro di Milano 1963 (PTM)

A. Tschechow: «Der Kirschgarten». R: G. Strehler. B: L. Damiani.
Piccolo Teatro di Milano 1974 (PTM)

«Min Fars Hus». R: E. Barba. Odin Teatret Holstebro 1972 (RPa)

S. J. Witkiewicz: «Kurka Wodna». R: T. Kantor. Cricot 2. Krakau 1967

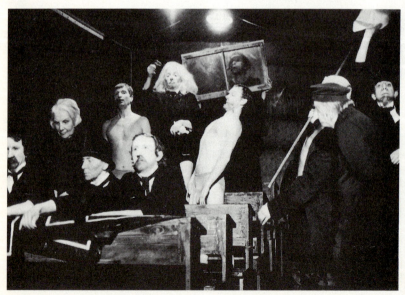

«Die tote Klasse». R: T. Kantor. Cricot 2. Krakau 1975 (GK)

Sophokles/H. Müller: «Philoctetes». R: H. Lietzau. B: J. Rose.
Deutsches Schauspielhaus Hamburg 1968 (RG)

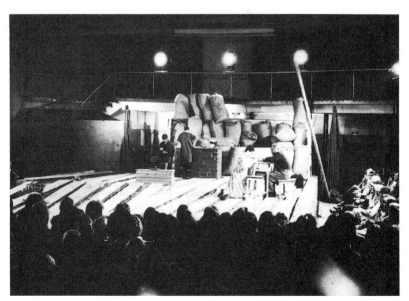

F. X. Kroetz: «Stallerhof». R: U. Heising. Deutsches Schauspielhaus Hamburg 1973 (JB)

M. Fleißer: «Fegefeuer in Ingolstadt». R: P. Stein. B: K.-E. Herrmann.
Schaubühne Berlin 1972 (JB)

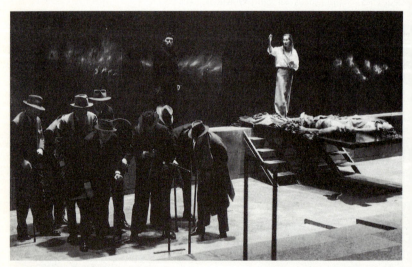

Aischylos: «Orestie». R: P. Stein. B: K.-E. Herrmann. Schaubühne Berlin 1980 (RW)

Aischylos: «Orestie». R: L. Ronconi. Venedig 1972 (CB)

T. Dorst: «Toller». R: P. Chèreau. B: R. Peduzzi. Villeurbanne 1973 (MN)

H. Müller: «Zement».
R: R. Berghaus. Berlin
(DDR) 1973 (MSt)

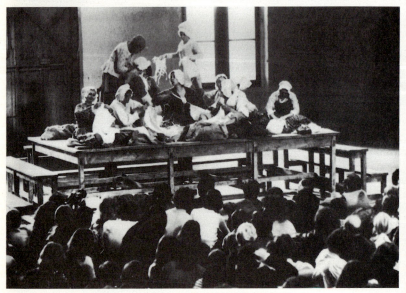

«1793». R: A. Mnouchkine. Théâtre du Soleil. Vincennes 1973 (MB)

W. Shakespeare: «Heinrich IV.». R: A. Mnouchkine. Théâtre du Soleil.
Vincennes 1984 (Mg)

W. Shakespeare: «A Midsummer Night's Dream». R: P. Brook.
Royal Shakespeare Company 1970 (DF)

«Mahabharata». R: P. Brook. CIRT. Paris 1985 (PR)

W. Shakespeare: «Timon von Athen». R: P. Brook. CIRT. Paris 1974 (BH)

«A letter for Queen Victoria». R: R. Wilson. New York 1974 (MBi)

Aussage. Mit Bertolt Brechts (1898–1956) →epischem Theater, das auf gesellschaftliche Erfahrungen antwortete, erreichte R. durch demonstrierendes und aufklärendes Spiel auf der Bühne einen bes. Stellenwert. Die Abkehr von der Illusion und die Hinwendung zur Aktualität zog eine Reihe unterschiedlicher Entwicklungen nach sich, wie sie von Jürgen Fehling (1885–1968), Heinz Hilpert (1890–1967), Gustaf Gründgens (1899–1963), Erich Engel (1891–1966), Lothar Müthel (1896–1965), Hans Schweikart (1895–1975), Karl-Heinz Martin (1888–1948) u. a. aufgenommen und fortgeführt wurden bis hin zu einer kritisch einsetzenden, alle Stilrichtungen umfassenden R. Durch Verwendung vielfältigster Elemente (Farbe, Licht, Geräusch, Musik, Tanz, Pantomime) öffneten sich der R. neue, keinem Stil mehr verpflichtete Interpretations-, Formungs- und Darstellungstechniken, die sich produktiv vor allem an best. Ensembles auswirkten (→Berliner Ensemble, →Piccolo teatro, →Schaubühne am Halleschen Ufer/Lehniner Platz, →Théâtre du Soleil, →Taganka Theater). R. war und ist damit an die Leistung und formale Entscheidung des Regisseurs bzw. R.-Teams gebunden (zunächst B. Barlog, O. F. Schuh, L. Lindtberg, F. Kortner, K.-H. Stroux; gegenwärtig R. Noelte, P. Palitzsch, P. Zadek, K. M. Grüber, P. Stein, C. Peymann, L. Bondy u. a. m.).

Die Abwehr tradierter Form- und Wertvorstellungen stand im Zuge politischer Aufbruchsstimmung aus den 60er Jahren am Anfang der neueren R.-Entwicklung, die sich mit dem Zerfall der Protestbewegung in viele Facetten, in subjektive Sehweisen zerlegte. Diese Auflösung verbindlicher Interpretations- und Darstellungsmuster birgt jedoch neben neuen Perspektiven und Einsichten die Gefahr hektischer Neuerungsversuche und kurzlebiger Modetrends in sich. In jüngster Zeit dagegen sind R.-Versuche in Richtung einer Konzentration auf das Werk, auf die Struktur des Textes zu beobachten.

Brauneck, M.: Klassiker der Schauspielregie. Reinbek 1988; Dhomme, S.: La mise en scène contemporaine d'André Antoine à Bertolt Brecht. Paris 1959; Dietrich, M. (Hg.): R. in Dokumentation, Forschung und Lehre. Salzburg 1975; Gortschakow, N.: R.-Unterricht bei Stanislawski. Berlin 1959; Ihering, H.: R. Berlin 1943; Kathrein, K.: Entwicklungsgeschichte der R.-Praxis von Ekhof bis Georg von Meiningen. Diss. Wien 1964; Löffler, P.: R. In: M. Hürlimann (Hg.): Atlantisbuch des Theaters. Zürich 1966, S. 325–330; Melchinger, U.: Zur Geschichte der R. In: M. Hürlimann, a. a. O., S. 331–340; Neumann, K.: Typologie der R. Diss. München 1955; Schwarz, H.: R. Idee und Praxis moderner Theaterarbeit. Bremen 1965; Winds, A.: Geschichte der R. Berlin/Leipzig 1925.

Monika Sandhack

Regietheater

R. weist im weiteren Sinne auf ein erkennbares Konzept durch Regieführung hin, meint im besonderen jedoch die Methode der Anpassung eines dramatischen Werks an das Regieinteresse, vor allem die Dominanz von Inhalten und Theorien, Bild- und Materialentwürfen gegenüber den individuellen Darstellungsweisen des Schauspielers.

Begründet durch die Forderung des Naturalismus (→Naturalistisches Theater) nach Herstellung einer naturgetreuen Wirklichkeit auf der Bühne, entfaltete sich das R. zu Beginn des 20. Jh. durch Befreiung von der Literatur. Zugleich konstituierte sich das Theater als autonome Kunstform: Nicht mehr der Dramatiker, sondern der Regisseur galt als eigentlicher Schöpfer des Kunstwerks. Durch den seit den 20er Jahren dieses Jh. bestimmenden Wirkungs- und Verbrauchswert des Theaters hat sich das Regieinteresse vom Kunst- auf den Zeitwert verschoben. Auf der Suche nach neuen Erkenntnis- wie Darstellungsmöglichkeiten mit den Mitteln des Theaters ist Regie von der bloßen Rekonstruktion eines Textes zu dessen Veränderung durch Interpretation übergegangen. R. ist, so gesehen, Interpretationstheater, das an der Erkenntnis der Gegenwart mit zeitgenössischen Stücken ebenso arbeitet wie mit tradierten Werken, die es auf neue Perspektiven hin zu befragen gilt: «Regie geht, wo sie sich als Zeitgenossenschaft versteht, von neuen Fragen aus. Der Prozeß, in dem Regie sich mit Hilfe der Darsteller verwirklicht, ist die Interpretation. Interpretation ist aber nun nicht mehr verstanden als Nachzeichnung, als Intonieren, Einfühlen, Ausarbeiten des Vorgefundenen, sondern als Herausziehen dessen, was uns angeht; als Ermittlung einer Erkenntnis und deren Darstellung durch einen szenisch denkenden Intellekt» (Rühle, S. 101). Der Regisseur ist also nicht nur «Nachzeichner» und «Interpret», sondern zugleich Erprober, Entdecker und Erfinder (ders., S. 117); seine Position (wie die des Dramaturgen und Ausstatters) erfährt eine deutliche Aufwertung. R. ersetzt damit nicht das dramatische Werk, es weist auf dieses selbst zurück. Der freie Umgang mit Stücken und die Überwindung konventioneller Spielformen haben der Regie nur allzuoft den (nicht immer unberechtigten) Vorwurf der Untreue am Werk, der Formzerstörung eingetragen.

Melchinger, S.: Stück und Regie. In: Dt. Sektion des Internationalen Theater-Instituts e. V. (Hg.): Internationales Colloquium 70. Regie. Essen 1970, S. 21–34; Rühle, G.: Anarchie in der Regie? Frankfurt/M. 1982.

Monika Sandhack

Regisseur

(Frz. – Verwalter) Der Titel wurde vermutlich erstmals 1771 von dem Schauspieler Stephanie d. Ä. am Wiener Burgtheater geführt, später in den Mannheimer Theaterprotokollen (1785) für Inspizientendienste eingesetzt. – Der R. ist heute für die szenisch-künstlerische Realisation einer → Inszenierung verantwortlich und koordiniert als deren Leiter die mit dem jeweiligen Projekt anfallenden Arbeiten: Dazu gehören in der Vorbereitungsphase Lektüre, Bearbeitung und Analyse des Stücks (in der Regel zusammen mit dem → Dramaturgen), Konzeption des Bühnenbildes und Wahl der Kostüme, Requisiten etc. in Absprache mit Ausstattern und der techn. Leitung, Gespräche mit der Intendanz und den Schauspielern über Rollenbesetzungen (einige R. ziehen es vor, das Ensemble an den konzeptionellen Entwürfen zu beteiligen). Aus den Vorbesprechungen entwickelt sich ein vom Regieteam (R., Regieassistent, Produktionsdramaturg, Bühnen- und Kostümbildner) erstelltes vorläufiges Inszenierungskonzept. Mit den → Proben beginnt die eigentliche Inszenierungstätigkeit, in deren Zentrum die Arbeit mit den Schauspielern, die Gestaltung und Einstudierung ihrer Rollen steht (Wort- und Bewegungsregie), daneben die Anlage und Leitung der einzelnen Szenen (Ensemblespiel, Szenenregie) sowie die Einrichtung der Technik (Licht, Bühnenmechanik, Projektionen, Geräusche, Musik). Die Überwachung der → Aufführung während der laufenden → Spielzeit wird zumeist nicht vom R. geleistet, sondern einem Regieassistenten bzw. Abend-R. überlassen. – Zur historischen Entwicklung des Berufsbildes → Regie.

Bergmann, G. M.: Der Eintritt des Berufs-R. in die deutschsprachige Bühne. In: Maske und Kothurn 12 (1966), S. 63–92; Foerster, P. v.: Das Urheberrecht des Theater-R. Berlin 1973; Legband, P.: Der R. Hamburg 1947.

Monika Sandhack

Reichsdramaturg

Die → Reichstheaterkammer beschließt 1933 die Einsetzung eines R.: «Es ist die Aufgabe des Reichsdramaturgen, die Anwendung der nationalsozialistischen kulturellen Grundsätze in der deutschen Theaterwelt durchzuführen»; d. h. vor allem Ausschaltung der politisch u. rassisch verfolgten Theaterschaffenden. Propagandaminister J. Goebbels ernennt 1934 Rainer Schlösser für diese Position; dieser war seit 1931 kulturpolitischer Schriftleiter beim «Völkischen Beobachter» und wird 1935 Leiter der Theaterabteilung im Propagandaministerium.

782 Reichskabarett

Drewniak, B.: Das Theater im NS-Staat. Düsseldorf 1983; Wulf, J.: Theater und Film im Dritten Reich. Gütersloh 1964.

Ute Hagel

Reichskabarett

1965 gründeten die Schauspieler und Kabarettisten Doris Bierett, Siegrid Hackenberg, Dieter Kursawe, Alexander Welbat, Peter Herzog und der Autor Volker Ludwig (eigentlich Eckart Hachfeld jun.) das R. in Berlin, das im gleichen Jahr mit dem Programm «Kein schöner Land» eröffnete. 1966 zog es in ein eigenes Haus und begann Programme mit übergreifender Thematik zu entwickeln, so u. a. «Bombenstimmung» (seit 1966), ein ‹Lehrstück› über den Zusammenhang von Kapitalismus und Krieg. Ihr vielleicht bestes und alle Möglichkeiten politischen Kabaretts ausschöpfendes Programm war: «Der Guerilla läßt grüßen» (Mai 1968); mit dem Programm «Rettet Berlin!» hörte das R. 1971 auf zu bestehen (→ Grips Theater). – 1983 gründete Ludwig im Probenraum des «Grips-Theaters» ein neues Kabarett, das «Institut für Lebensmut», das bereits im folgenden Jahr sein Ende fand.

Budzinski, K.: Das Kabarett. 100 Jahre literarische Zeitkritik – gesprochen – gesungen – gespielt. Düsseldorf 1985; ders.: Pfeffer ins Getriebe. München 1982; ders.: Wer lacht denn da? Braunschweig 1989; Greul, H.: Bretter, die die Zeit bedeuten. Köln/Berlin 1967 (erw. Ausg., 2 Bde. München 1971).

Wolfgang Beck

Reichstheaterkammer

Das im September 1933 von der NS-Regierung verabschiedete Reichskulturkammergesetz schrieb eine Gliederung des kulturellen Lebens in Deutschland vor. Der Reichskulturkammer (RKK), Leitung J. Goebbels, waren sieben Einzelkammern untergeordnet, u. a. die Reichstheaterkammer (RTK), diese wiederum war ab 1936 in sieben Abteilungen gegliedert; die Theater-Abteilung des Propagandaministeriums hatte die Aufsicht über die RTK. Ihr mußten die Spitzenverbände des dt. Theaters beitreten: → Deutscher Bühnen-Verein, → Genossenschaft Deutscher Bühnenangehöriger, Vereinigung der künstlerischen Bühnenvorstände, Deutscher Chorsängerverband und Tänzerbund, Vereinigung der Bühnenverleger, Verband dt. Berufsmusiker. Nur Mitglieder der RTK waren berechtigt, in ihrem Beruf tätig zu sein, Ausschlüsse waren einem Berufsverbot gleichzusetzen. – Als erster Präsident der RTK wurde von Goebbels Otto Laubinger, als sein Stellvertreter Werner Krauß (beide Schauspieler) ernannt.

Drewniak, B.: Das Theater im NS-Staat. Düsseldorf 1983; Wulf, J.: Theater und Film im Dritten Reich. Gütersloh 1964.

Ute Hagel

Reinhardt-Bühnen

Zusammenfassung der privatwirtschaftlich geführten Theater, die unter direkter künstlerischer und finanzieller Leitung Max Reinhardts (1873–1943) standen. Stets war der Theatermann R. auch gleichzeitig Theaterorganisator und Theaterunternehmer (→Salzburger Festspiele). Die meisten seiner Häuser wurden für seine Zwecke um- bzw. neugebaut; daraus resultierten zahlreiche bühnenbauliche und inszenatorische Neuerungen (z. B. stetig gekrümmter Rundhorizont, Lichtdekorationen, →Arenabühne etc.).

Die wichtigsten R.-B.: Berlin: 1902: Kabarett →«Schall und Rauch» (später Kleines Theater). 1903: Neues Theater am Schiffbauerdamm. 1905: →Deutsches Theater mit Kammerspielen. Ab 1911 Organisierung der R.-B. in Form eines Theaterkonzerns. 1915 bis 1918 Übernahme der →Volksbühne am Bülowplatz in Pacht. 1919: Nach Umbau Eröffnung des →Großen Schauspielhauses (ehem. Zirkus Schumann) mit fast 5000 Plätzen. 1924: Komödie am Kurfürstendamm. Bis 1930/31 Kauf weiterer Berliner Theater; schließlich standen in Berlin elf Theater mit über 10000 Sitzplätzen unter direktem Einfluß von Max Reinhardt. Wien: 1923: →Theater in der Josefstadt. 1928: Schönbrunner Schloßtheater (Schauspieler- und Regisseurseminar, →Max-Reinhardt-Seminar).

1933 übereignete Max Reinhardt, durch die Machtübernahme der Nationalsozialisten gezwungen, das Deutsche Theater mit den Kammerspielen «dem deutschen Volke». In der Emigration in den USA gelang es Max Reinhardt nicht mehr, als Regisseur oder Theaterleiter Fuß zu fassen.

Braulich, H.: Max Reinhardt. Theater zwischen Traum und Wirklichkeit. Berlin 1966; Huesmann, H.: Welttheater Reinhardt, Bauten, Spielstätten, Inszenierungen. München 1983.

Erich Krieger

Renaissancetheater

Das R. ist gewissermaßen die ‹Werkstatt›, in der im 16. Jh. die Voraussetzungen des modernen europ. Theaters geschaffen werden; dazu gehören: die literarisch-dramatische Produktion, die Neudefinierung und Festlegung der Regeln der späteren →klassischen Dramaturgie, die Entwicklung von Genres (vor allem für das komische Theater), die Einrichtung der modernen →Szenographie, die Gestaltung eines neuartigen →Theaterbaus sowie die schrittweise Professionalisierung der Theaterarbeit. – Mittelpunkt und Ursprung des R. ist das ital. Cinquecento (→Rinascimento). Nicht nur die →Antikenrezeption, die Gestaltung der Regeln und Formen von →Tragödie, →Tragikomödie, →Komödie und →Schäferspiel, die Geburt des Humanistentheaters (Humanismus/Drama und Theater des Humanismus), die Entwicklung des →höfischen Theaters und der →Trionfi gingen von dort aus, sondern auch die Entwicklung des Theaterbaus, der →Szenographie, von →Bühnenbild, →Regie und →Schauspielkunst.

Übernahme des Regelwerks des ital. R. in ganz Westeuropa: in England (*Gorboduc*, 1561 von Thomas Norton, 1532–84, und Thomas Sackville, 1536–1608), Frankreich (*Cléopâtre captive*, 1552, von Jodelle, 1532–73, und *Les Juives*, 1583, von Robert Garnier, 1544–90) und Spanien, dann aber Eigenständigkeit in der jeweiligen Entwicklung des Theaters in Spanien (→Siglo de Oro), etwas später auch in England im →Elisabethanischen Theater; im deutschsprachigen Raum Meistersang, →Schuldrama, →Jesuitentheater und auch →höfisches Theater, die Rederijkers in den Niederlanden.

Borcherdt, H. H.: Das europ. Theater im Mittelalter und in der Renaissance. Berlin 1935, Neudr. 1969; Jacquot, J.: Les Fêtes de la Renaissance. Paris 1956–60; ders. (ed.): Le lieu théâtral à la Renaissance. Paris 1964; Kernodle, G. R.: From Art to Theatre, Form and Convention in the Renaissance. London 1947; Lebègue, R.: La tragédie française de la Renaissance. Paris 1954; Mulryne, J. R./Shewring, M. (Hg.): Theatre of the English and Italian Renaissance. New York 1991.

Gérard Schneilin

Repertoire

Gesamtheit der auf dem →Spielplan einstudierten und jederzeit abrufbaren Stücke eines Theaters, das (im Gegensatz zur En-suite-Bühne mit Serien-Aufführungen) über ein fest engagiertes →Ensemble verfügen muß.

Monika Sandhack

Replik 785

Repertory Theatre

Bis ins späte 19. Jh. hinein sind Repertoiretheater kontinentaleurop. Prägung in England unbekannt. Das Bestreben, die Theaterlandschaft außerhalb Londons zu beleben, führt zu Beginn des 20. Jh. zur Ausbreitung der R. T.-Movement. Dem Londoner Star-System sollte in den Provinzstädten ein an regionalen Interessen und Traditionen orientiertes Theater entgegengesetzt werden. Das Gaiety Theatre, Manchester, 1907 von Annie Horniman (1860–1937), mit Henry Arthur Jones eine treibende Kraft der Bewegung, erworben, war das erste engl. Repertoiretheater. Bald darauf folgten weitere, etwa in Liverpool (1911) und Birmingham (1913). Der Begriff des R. T. erfährt hier eine Modifikation insofern, als die ‹regional reps› einen wöchentlichen, zweiwöchentlichen, bisweilen gar monatlichen Programmwechsel vornehmen.

Die Konkurrenz durch Film und Fernsehen führte Mitte des Jahrhunderts zur Schließung von ca. 150 R. T. Der Niedergang wird durch den Beschluß des Arts Council gebremst, bis zu 50 Prozent der Neu- und Umbaukosten für Theater zu übernehmen. So entstehen zwischen 1958 und 1976 über fünfzig neue ‹regional reps›, von denen einige eine wichtige innovative Rolle im zeitgenössischen engl. Theater spielen. Das Old Vic, Bristol, das Belgrade, Coventry, bes. aber die ‹reps› in Newcastle, Hull und Stoke-on-Trent haben in den 60er und 70er Jahren ein wirkungsvolles Gegengewicht zur traditionellen Theaterhochburg London geschaffen.

Kosok, H. et al.: Drama und Theater im England des 20. Jahrhunderts. Düsseldorf 1980; Rowell, G./Jackson, A.: The Repertory Movement. A History of Regional Theatre in Britain. London 1984; Thomsen, Ch. W.: Das englische Theater der Gegenwart. Düsseldorf 1980.

Werner Bleike

Replik

(Frz. réplique) Erwiderung, bei der der Angegriffene die Argumente des Gegners benutzt und sie zu seiner eigenen Rechtfertigung verwendet. Dramaturgisch gesehen geht die R. im dramatischen Theater mit einer Frage-Antwort-Dialektik einher, die die Handlung vorantreibt.

Bernard Poloni

Reprise

(Frz. reprise) Wiederaufnahme eines Repertoirestücks, das längere Zeit nicht gespielt wurde, in den Spielplan.

Manfred Brauneck

Requisiten

Alle beweglichen Gegenstände (einschließlich Speisen und Getränke), die die Darsteller für ihr Spiel auf der Bühne brauchen. Zuständig für die Auswahl (in Absprache mit dem Regisseur bzw. dem Bühnenbildner) und die Bereitstellung der R. für die jeweilige Aufführung ist der Requisiteur.

Manfred Brauneck

Restaurationstheater

Das R. knüpfte bei der Tradition des → elisabethanischen Theaters an, führte jedoch Neuerungen ein: Schauspielerinnen, Guckkastenbühne, ein in Logen (box), Parterre (pit) und Galerien (galleries) gegliederter Zuschauerraum, bewegliche Kulissen und aufwendige Dekorationen. Nachdem zunächst mit der kulturellen Hegemonie der Aristokratie libertinistische, polemisch antipuritanische Tendenzen im Theaterbetrieb herrschten, öffnete sich allmählich das R. immer mehr bürgerlichen Publikumsschichten. Sittenreform und Wegfall von Aufführungsmonopolen sorgten um 1700 für das Ende des R.

Avery, E. L./Scouten, A. H.: The London Stage 1660–1700. A Critical Introduction. Carbondale/Edwardsville 1968; Brunkhorst, M.: Drama und Theater der Restaurationszeit. Heidelberg 1985; Jones, M./Southern, R.: Theatres and Actors. In: Loftis, J./Southern, R./Scouten, A. H./Jones, M. (eds.): The Revels History of Drama in English, V: 1660–1750. London 1976, p. 81–157.

Bernd-Peter Lange

Revue

(Frz. ‹la revue› = Übersicht, Aufzählung, Rundschau) R. bedeutet: 1. die lose Aneinanderreihung verschiedener, untereinander nicht oder nur mittelbar zusammenhängender Szenen, die als stilistisches Mittel in allen Formen des Theaters benutzt wird; 2. eine eigenständige Form des Theaters, die in der Verknüpfung verschiedener Stilmittel sich von anderen theatralischen Formen unterscheidet. Sie ist «ein synthetisches Genre» (Kothes). Die Benutzung des Begriffs R. in Zusammensetzungen wie Kabarett-R. oder R.-Film deutet auf begriffliche Unsicherheiten und eine Vermischung der o. a. Bedeutungsebenen.

Historisch lassen sich hauptsächlich zwei Formen der R. unterscheiden, die aktuelle (zumeist satirische) R. und die das visuelle Moment betonende Ausstattungs-R. Beide Arten sind gekennzeichnet durch die Reihung von →Sketchen, Musik- und Tanznummern, deren einziger Zusammenhalt in einer losen Rahmenhandlung besteht bzw. durch einen →Conférencier hergestellt wird. In der R. sind Elemente verschiedener Unterhaltungsgenres zusammengeflossen, die Übergänge zum →Varieté oder zum →Kabarett sind fließend. Die älteste R. im Sinne der o. a. Definition bildet die «R. de fin d'année» Frankreichs. In ihr wurden in einzelnen Nummern die politischen und gesellschaftlichen Ereignisse des jeweils vergangenen Jahres satirisch glossiert. Schauelemente wie Ballett und Gesang wurden in die lockere Szenenfolge integriert. Das wachsende Bedürfnis des Bürgertums nach bloßer Unterhaltung führte gegen Ende des 19. Jh. zum Verzicht auf Aktualität und zur Betonung des Visuellen.

Primär diese Form wirkte auf die Entwicklung der R. in Deutschland und Österreich ein, ebenso auf England und die USA. Dabei führten unterschiedliche Traditionen und die Veränderungen des Publikumsgeschmacks zu eigenständigen Entwicklungen. Während die Ausstattungs-R. («R. à grand spectacle») sich in Frankreich bis heute behaupten konnte, veränderte sich in den anderen Ländern die R. und ging schließlich in anderen Formen auf. Wurde in den USA lange Zeit hindurch eine Mittelform zwischen R. und Varieté gepflegt, so führte die Entwicklung dort zum Musical und unter Benutzung des neuen Mediums Film zum R.-Film, zum Filmmusical. In Großbritannien war vor allem die Kammer-R. («Intimate R.») beliebt, die schon von ihren räumlichen Möglichkeiten her auf großen Aufwand verzichten mußte. →Music Hall und Varieté nahmen Elemente der R. auf und integrierten sie.

Im dt. Sprachraum gewann die R. erst in diesem Jh. an Bedeutung. Den Beginn machte auch hier die Jahres-R., die von 1903 bis 1914 im Berliner Metropoltheater nach frz. Vorbild aufgeführt wurde, selbst Vorbild werdend für ähnliche Versuche in Wien. Anders als in Paris wurde jeder satirisch-kritische Unterton wegen der Zensur und des großbürger-

788 Revue

lichen bis adligen Publikums vermieden. Diese konservative Haltung verstärkte sich noch in den Revuen der Kriegszeit. Ebenso verlief die Entwicklung in Wien, wo von Anfang an mehr (Lokal-)Patriotisches im Vordergrund gestanden hatte. Nach Ende des 1. Weltkriegs war die Jahres-R. Vergangenheit. An ihre Stelle trat die Ausstattungs-R., in der Musik und Tanz das Wort ersetzten. Bereits in den 20er Jahren gewannen kleinere Formen an Bedeutung, die Kammer-R., die Kabarett-R., deren Hauptvertreter Rudolf Nelson (→Nelson-Revue) und Friedrich Hollaender waren. Auch in Österreich begann die R. zur gleichen Zeit ihren Siegeszug, hier mit dem Markenzeichen «Wiener R.». Sie war inhaltlich unverbindlich, konnte nie den Einfluß der Operette verleugnen und erwarb sich so «einen Ehrenplatz in der Geschichte des theatralischen Kitsches» (Günther). Die Nationalsozialisten trieben zahlreiche Autoren und Komponisten von R. ins Exil oder brachten sie um, gleichzeitig führte ihr Interesse an der ablenkenden Funktion der R. zu einer neuen Blüte speziell der unpolitischen «Wiener R.». Nach dem Krieg war die große Zeit der R. vorbei. Neue Medien, neue Unterhaltungsgenres, ein veränderter Publikumsgeschmack trugen dazu nicht unerheblich bei.

Die Form der R. mit ihrer mehr oder weniger unverbundenen Aufeinanderfolge von Nummern, mit der Mischung verschiedener Genres zu einem neuen Ganzen hatte seit den 20er Jahren immer wieder Einfluß auf das sich als politisch verstehende Theater. Nur hingewiesen werden kann hier auf die von Erwin Piscator (mit Felix Gasbarra) geschriebene und inszenierte *Revue Roter Rummel*, die als Auftragsarbeit für die KPD am 22. 11. 1924 Premiere hatte (→Proletarisch-revolutionäres Theater). In ihr verband Piscator Formelemente der R. mit denen des Varietés und Kabaretts, benutzte zusätzlich Filmeinspielungen und die Musik als dramaturgisches Mittel. Der große (wenn auch nicht finanzielle) Erfolg ließ Piscator noch verschiedentlich auf diese Form zurückgreifen (*Trotz alledem!*, 1925; Tollers *Hoppla, wir leben*, 1927). Sie hatte vor allem aber einen auslösenden Effekt auf das →Agitproptheater. Aber auch Autoren wie Brecht, Wolf und Wangenheim, Majakowski oder der Regisseur Meyerhold nahmen Einflüsse vor allem der politisch-satirischen Revue auf. – Mit der Entwicklung des politischen Theaters in den 60er Jahren übte die R. noch einmal verstärkt Einfluß auf Theatermacher aus, u. a. auf Joan Littlewoods *Oh, what a lovely war!*, Peter Brooks *US*, Wilfried Minks' *Gewidmet: Friedrich dem Großen*. Aber auch als Mittel zur Wiedergewinnung theatralischer Unmittelbarkeit wurden Elemente der R. eingesetzt, etwa in Jean-Louis Barraults *Rabelais* oder Ariane Mnouchkines *1789*. Hinzuweisen bleibt auf die Versuche Peter Zadeks, Romanvorlagen für das Theater in R.form spielbar zu machen (Falladas *Kleiner Mann, was nun* 1972, H. Manns *Professor Unrat* als *Der Blaue Engel* 1974 und 1992).

Aulnet, H.: Le Music-Hall moderne. Paris 1936; Bang-Hansen, O.: Chat Noir og Norsk Revy. Oslo 1961; Baral, R.: Revue. New York ²1970; Damase, J.: Les Folies du Music-Hall. Paris 1960; Dreyfus, R.: Petite Histoire de la Revue de Fin d'Année. Paris 1909; Falconi, D./Frattini, A.: Guida alla rivista e all'operetta. Mailand 1953; Günther, E.: Geschichte des Varietés. Berlin ²1981; Hasche, Ch.: Bürgerliche Revue und «Roter Rummel». Diss. Berlin 1980; Jacques-Charles: Cent ans de Music-Hall. Genf/Paris 1956; Jansen, W.: Glanzrevuen der 20er Jahre. Berlin 1987; Kothes, F.-P.: Die theatralische Revue in Berlin und Wien 1900-1938. Wilhelmshaven 1977; Mander, R./Mitchenson, J.: British Music-Hall. London 1965; Wem gehört die Welt – Kunst und Gesellschaft in der Weimarer Republik. Berlin 1977.

Wolfgang Beck

Rhetorik

Wie die Stilistik die Kunst des Schreibens, ist die R. die Kunst des Redens als natürliche Begabung, als Beredsamkeit oder als Regelwerk, als ästhetisch-pragmatische Formenlehre. Als Theorie der Redekunst besteht die R. seit dem 5. Jh. v. Chr. Aus Sizilien nach Athen brachte damals Gorgias ein entwickeltes Modell, dessen Kategorien und Exempel die Volks-, Gerichts- und Festreden nicht nur bei den Meistern dieser Gattungen (Demosthenes in der politischen und Lysias in der juristischen Gattung, Isokrates im Panegyrikos und Platon im philosophischen Dialog) prägten, sondern auch den Adressaten durchaus geläufig waren; die formalen Ansprüche der etwa durch Aristoteles' R.-Lehrbuch ausgebildeten Griechen stellten zunehmend statt künstlerische künstliche Ansprüche an die Redner, Dichter und Literaten im allg. Die modischen Konventionen der R. führten zum Verlust von Natürlichkeit und Spontaneität, letztlich von Qualität. Dieser Niedergang der R. verlieh dem Eigenschaftswort rhetorisch die Konnotation des Artefaktes, z. B. bei der rhetorischen Frage (bei der entweder die Antwort bekannt ist oder keine Antwort zu erwarten ist).

Nichtsdestoweniger gelangte die R. bei den Römern zu neuer Blüte, zumal die politische Verfassung zeitweilig den Volkstribunen Macht in die Hand spielte, etwa Gaius Gracchus, den noch Cicero drei Generationen später für den größten Redner Roms hielt. Von Cicero selber sind in großem Umfang Reden und Betrachtungen über das Reden erhalten. Einen bleibenden Einfluß sicherte der klassischen röm. R. der Verfasser und Lehrer der Methode, *de institutione oratoria*, Quintilian, ein Jh. nach Cicero.

Im Mittelalter wurde die R. zur wichtigsten Disziplin unter den Artes liberales des Triviums neben Grammatik und Dialektik, welches mit dem Quadrivium (Arithmetik, Geometrie, Astronomie und Musik) zur allge-

790 Rhetorik

meinbildenden Propädeutik von Theologie, Juristerei und Medizin gehörte. Diese Entwicklung verwischte die Grenzen der R., zumal ihre psycho-pragmatischen Gesetzmäßigkeiten auch in der schriftlichen Kommunikation herrschen, etwa in der Briefkunst, im Lehrbuch oder im Zeitungswesen. Die bloße Opposition von ‹mündlich› und ‹schriftlich› bzw. ‹gesprochen› und ‹geschrieben› ist zu dürftig, wie etwa Theorie und Praxis der Vorlesung zeigen. Zumindest wären zu unterscheiden: gesprochene mündliche, gesprochene schriftliche, geschriebene mündliche und geschriebene schriftliche Sprache. Das aufgeführte Theaterstück fiele in die erste Sparte. Offenkundig wäre diese Sparte – wie die drei anderen – vorsichtig zu unterteilen, denn eine Theateraufführung verlangt nicht unbedingt Unmittelbarkeit und scheitert nicht notwendigerweise an gebundener Sprache.

Wie auf jede Blütezeit der R. folgte eine Abstinenzperiode: Die Renaissance hatte für die Figurenklischees, Verbrämungen und rituellen Anspielungen wenig übrig. In den anschließenden verschiedenen europ. Bildungswelten spielte die R. eine ungleiche Rolle; der Norden mißtraut ihr, während die Anrainer des Mittelmeers sie weiterhin pflegen.

Nach dieser auseinanderstrebenden Entwicklung steht die R. heutzutage in einem stark konvergierenden Prozeß, weniger unter dem Einfluß des Films als unter dem des Fernsehens, insbesondere der politischen Debatten und der Werbesendungen. Im Fernsehen wird bes. deutlich, daß sich R. nicht auf Wortstellung und Tonführung beschränkt. Die kritischen Jahre nach dem Stummfilm zeigen, wie sensibel das Verhältnis von Gestik und Sprache ist. Über die Gestik kann aber der Autor nur in sehr beschränktem Maße verfügen. Eine spezifische Theater-R. hat Gestik und Inszenierung einzuschließen, darf aber darüber den Vorrang der Rede nicht vergessen. Die Sprache des Theaters unterscheidet sich von den klassischen drei Hauptgattungen der Rede, daß sie zwei Adressaten hat, den fiktiven, den Rollenpartner und den realen, das Publikum, und dabei so beschaffen ist, daß es den Anschein hat, als sei der Partner auf der Bühne die Zielperson und das Publikum nur unbekannter Zeuge oder unerkannter Mitwisser; dies gilt sogar in den Extremfällen des Monologs und der R. zweiten Grades beim Theater im Theater.

Die R. bleibt auch in der Welt des Theaters die zielbewußte und gekonnte Gestaltung als Wortwahl und Wortfolge. Unter den vier Ursachen «warum der Dichter die Wortfolge ändert», nämlich «den Ausdruck der Leidenschaft verstärken, etwas erwarten lassen, Unvermutetes sagen und dem Perioden gewisse kleine Nebenschönheiten geben, wodurch er etwa mehr Wohlklang, oder leichtere und freyere Wendungen bekommt» (Klopstock), spielen die beiden mittleren die größte Rolle in der Theater-R., weil sie den doppelten Effekt der Identifikation und der Distanz von Zuschauer und Publikum verstärken, auch wenn Schauspieler erst vom

Parkett auf die Bühne steigen oder sogar bis zum Ende im Saal bleiben. Die Ergründung der pejorativen Abdrift des Eigenschaftswortes ‹theatralisch› bestätigt diese Ambivalenz der spezifischen Theater-R. Im eigentlichen Sinne ist theatralisch, was das Theater betrifft oder zu ihm gehört, z. B. ein bühnengerechter Einfall. Im übertragenen Sinne deutet dieses Wort auf Unangemessenes, Übertriebenes, Geziertes und Gespreiztes. Dieser Eindruck entsteht meistens, wenn so gesprochen wird, als sei eigentlich ein Dritter der Angesprochene, aber kein Dritter da und man selber der Zweite ist, der Gesprächspartner, auf dessen Wellenlänge – auch das ist eine rhetorische Figur – der Redner, mehr oder minder bewußt, sich nicht eingestellt hat.

Barner, W.: Barockrhetorik. Tübingen 1970; Barthes, R.: Littérature et société. Bruxelles 1967; Blaß, F.: Attische Beredsamkeit I–III. Leipzig 1887–98; Dockhorn, K.: Macht und Wirkung der Rhetorik. Bad Homburg 1948; ders.: Die antike Rhetorik als Quelle des vorromantischen Irrationalismus in Literatur- und Geistesgeschichte. Göttingen 1949; Fey, G.: Die Antike in der modernen Rhetorik. Stuttgart 1979; Gerber, G.: Die Sprache als Kunst. Darmstadt 1961; Kennedy, A. K.: Dramatic Dialogue. Cambridge 1983; Kopperschmidt, J.: Allgemeine Rhetorik. Stuttgart 1973; Larthomas, P.: Le langage dramatique. Paris 1980; Lausberg, H.: Handbuch der literarischen Rhetorik. München 1973; Plett, H. F.: Einführung in die rhetorische Textanalyse. Hamburg 1975; ders. (Hg.): Rhetorik. München 1976; Todorov, T.: Théories du symbole. Paris 1977; Ueding, G.: Einführung in die Rhetorik. Stuttgart 1976.

Jean-Marie Zemb

Rinascimento / Cinquecento

Das moderne europ. Theater entsteht im Italien des 15. und 16. Jh. durch das Zusammentreffen mehrerer Einflußgrößen: 1. ein aus den mittelalterlichen liturgischen Spielen abgeleitetes religiöses Theater, aus dem über die ‹lauda drammatica› (in Umbrien entstanden) die florentiner ‹Sacra rappresentazione› des 15. Jh. wurde, wo sakrale Inhalte mit dem weltlich-komischen Realismus zusammentreffen; 2. im Zeitalter des Humanismus die Wiederentdeckung des antiken Theaters und antiker Kultur; 3. die mit dem Aufschwung der Fürstenhöfe verbundene Entwicklung der Hoffeste, die mehr und mehr die bevorzugten Orte einer Theatralisierung der Macht werden, wobei das Theater notwendigerweise ein integrierender Bestandteil ist. – Die Theateraufführung ist ein Bestandteil einer Politik der Repräsentation und setzt sich nicht nur als kulturelle, gesellschaftliche und ideologische Erscheinung durch, wobei die wirkliche Bühne immer eine symbolische, imaginäre Bühne verbirgt, die sich auf die Gesellschaft der Epoche, auf ihre Institutionen und Wertvorstellungen be-

792 Rinascimento/Cinquecento

zieht. So beschränkt sich das ital. Theater des R. trotz gewisser Anzeichen nicht darauf, das →antike griech. oder lat. Theater nachzuahmen oder im besten Sinne wiedererstehen zu lassen. Es handelt sich buchstäblich um eine Wieder-Erfindung des Theaters als gesellschaftliche Erfahrung, und zwar der Theateraufführung mit allen ihren Aspekten (sowohl textuell wie szenisch und musikalisch), besonders aber um die Genese aller Theatergattungen und -formen, die in der Folge Europa erobern sollten: →Komödie (und →Commedia dell'arte), →Tragödie, →Tragikomödie, →Schäferspiel, →Melodrama u. a.

Die →Komödie

Von der *Philologia* (vor 1336) von Francesco Petrarca (1304–74) bis zum Anbruch des 16. Jh. sind die in Italien geschriebenen Komödien (etwa 30) lat. Komödien, Werke von Humanisten wie *Paulus* (um 1390) von Pietro Paolo Vergerio (1370–1444), *Philodoxus* (1426) von Leon Battista Alberti (1404–72) oder *Chrysis* (1444) von Enea Silvio Piccolomini (1405–64), der später Papst wurde unter dem Namen Pius II. Die erste in der ‹Vulgär›-Sprache geschriebene Komödie, *Li sei contenti* von Galeotto Del Caretto (um 1455–1530), ist 1499 verfaßt worden. Als erste ‹gelehrte› oder ‹regelentsprechende› ital. Komödie betrachtet man im allg. *Cassaria* (1508) von Ludovico Ariosto (1474–1533), dem späteren Autor des *Orlando furioso* (1516).

Ferrara, die Heimat Ariosts, feiert die Wiedergeburt des →antiken Theaters am glänzendsten, wenn auch nach den ersten ital. Ausgaben von Plautus (1472) und Terenz (1473) Komödienaufführungen dieser beiden lat. Autoren in anderen Städten stattfanden (Florenz, Rom). Ab 1486, dem Jahr der *Menaechmi*-Premiere, nehmen die Aufführungen der lat. Komödien beim Karneval und anderen prachtvollen Festen am Hof der Herzöge von Este zu. An die Stelle der lat. Texte treten nach und nach ital. Übersetzungen. Der junge Ariost, der selbst in einigen lat. Stücken gespielt hatte, schreibt nach *Cassaria* vier weitere Komödien: *Suppositi* (1509), *Negromante* (1519), *Lena* (1527) und *Scolastica* (unvollendet). Ariost ging von einer streng die Personen, Situationen und dramaturgische Struktur der lat. Stücke imitierenden Komödie aus, emanzipierte sich aber nach und nach von seinen Vorbildern unter prinzipieller Beibehaltung der Regeln. Wenige Jahre später entstehen einige der besten Komödien des ital. R.: *Calandria* (1513) des späteren Kardinals Bibbiena (1470–1520), phantasievolle, prall-sinnliche Nachempfindung der *Menaechmi* von Plautus, und besonders *Mandragola* (1518) von Machiavelli (1469–1527), worin unvermeidliche Reminiszenzen der lat. Komödie und des *Decamerone* einer sehr persönlichen Gestaltung einer von niedrigen Instinkten beherrschten und den Machenschaften großer Betrüger ausgelieferten Menschheit nicht im Wege stehen. Zwischen 1520 und

Kostümzeichnung von Leonardo da Vinci (TS)

Szenarium eines Triumphzugs: «Triumph der Keuschheit» von J. Sellaio, um 1480/90 (TS)

Plastische «Stehende Bilder» im Stil der Sacra Rappresentazioni. Pietà von N. dall'Arca. Bologna 1463 (TS)

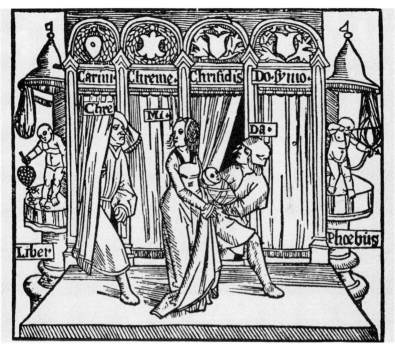

Terenzbühne mit Komödienszene (TS)

Ansicht einer tragischen Bühne von Bramante (oder Umkreis). Kupferstich, um 1500 (TS)

Bühne des Teatro Olimpico in Vicenza; Entwurf: A. Palladio, 1585 (TS)

«Inferno». Bühnengestaltung von B. Buontalenti für ein Intermezzo (TS)

«Naumachia» im Hof des Palazzo Pitti, 1592, anläßlich einer Medici-Hochzeit.
Entwurf des Szenariums: B. Buontalenti (TS)

Skizze für ein Bühnenkostüm («Muse») von G. Vasari, 1566 (TS)

Rinascimento/Cinquecento   793

1530 treten zwei der vielleicht begabtesten komischen Autoren des 16. Jh. auf: Angelo Beolco (1496/1502?–1542), ein eher unter dem Namen Ruzante bekannter Schauspieler und Autor (so genannt nach der Person, deren Rolle er gewöhnlich auf der Bühne spielte), und Pietro Aretino (1492–1556), dessen Ruhm sich mehr auf seine eher pornographischen Werke und seine Tätigkeit als Meistersänger stützt als auf sein keineswegs unbedeutendes theatralisches Werk. Ruzante widmet von *Pastoral* (1518–20) bis *Anconitana* (1534–35) seine bedeutendsten Theaterwerke der liebevollen Schilderung der bäuerlichen Welt; er entmythisiert die Verfeinerungen der toskanischen Sprache durch die Ausdrucksstärke des Paduaner Dialekts und kontrastiert die eitle Abstraktion der großen Ideale der Zeit durch die instinktive Natürlichkeit seiner armen Helden und die Trivialität des Wirklichen. Aretino dagegen gestaltet mit einem ganz anderen formellen Repertoire, aber mit ähnlichem Schwung, von seinen ersten beiden Stücken (*Cortigiana*, 1525/34; *Marescalo*, 1526/34) an das Leben des Hofes.

In Siena setzen sich zwei verschiedene Theatertypen durch: das der Pre-Rozzi, dann der Rozzi, deren Autoren-Schauspieler Handwerker sind, die gern gegen die Bauern in ihren Stücken sticheln; schließlich das sozial und kulturell höherstehende, aus der Akademie der Intronati hervorgegangene Theater, repräsentiert durch *Gl'Ingannati* (vor 1537), *Amor costanta* (1536) von Alessandro Piccolomini (1508–78) und *La Pellegrina* (1564) von Scipione Bargagli (1537–86). In Venedig erscheint *La Veniexiana* (1536/37), eine anonyme Komödie, die zu den köstlichsten der Epoche gehört.

Ungefähr die Hälfte der etwas über 200 erhalten gebliebenen Komödien des 16. Jh. wurden nach 1560 verfaßt, was beweist, daß der Aufstieg der Gattung durch den verstärkten politischen, religiösen und kulturellen Absolutismus zur Zeit der Gegenreformation nicht gebremst worden ist. Die Qualität entspricht jedoch nicht entfernt der Quantität. Das einzige große Komödienwerk ist *Candelaio* (1582) von Giordano Bruno (1548–1600): ein leidenschaftliches dialogisiertes Pamphlet, Zerrspiegel einer zu Ende gehenden Epoche. – Schließlich muß ein Typ der Komödie genannt werden, der um die Mitte des 16. Jh. entstand und dann eine große Rolle im ital. und europ. Theater der folgenden Jh. spielen sollte: die → Commedia dell'arte.

Die → Tragödie

Wesentlich ist hier die → Antikenrezeption (Aristoteles, Epiktet, Seneca), verbunden mit christlichem Moralismus, sowie einer Reflexion über Sinn und Form der Tragödie bei den großen Theoretikern, welche das Theater nachhaltig beeinflussen sollten: Robortello, Minturno, Castelvetzo u. a. Die ‹Wiedergeburt› der ital. Tragödie ist, selbst wenn sie einen großen

794 Rinascimento / Cinquecento

Einfluß auf die europ. Tragädie gehabt hat, weit davon entfernt, den Komödien vergleichbare Meisterwerke hervorgebracht zu haben. 1515 schreibt dann Giangiorgio Trissino (1478–1550), ein überzeugter Hellenist und Aristoteles-Anhänger, seine erste wirkliche Tragödie: die *Sofonisba*, Aischylos und Sophokles nachahmend. Diese Nachahmung der griech. Tragödie hat in der Geschichte der Tragödie und des Aristotelismus eine bedeutende Rolle gespielt durch die leidenschaftliche Erörterung, die sie in gelehrten Kreisen hervorrief. Erst mit der Wiederentdeckung und Auslegung der *Poetik* des Aristoteles erfährt die Gattung ihren eigentlichen Aufschwung. Sperone Speroni liest 1542 seinen Kollegen der Akademie der Infiammati in Padua die *Canace* vor, worin er die nach seiner Ansicht wesentlichen Elemente der antiken Tragödie, Peripetie und Katharsis, wieder zu Ehren kommen läßt. Bemerkenswert sind die Tragödien von G. B. Giraldi Cinzio (1504–73) aus Ferrara, wo die streng moralistische Deutung der aristotelischen Katharsis eine besondere Form annimmt. In Reaktion auf die Nüchternheit der in der Nachahmung der Griechen stehenden Tragödien erzielt Giraldi einen großen Erfolg mit seinem Stück *Orbecche* (1541, die erste auf die Bühne gebrachte ital. Tragödie), das vom heftigen und leidenschaftlichen Theater Senecas inspiriert ist. Die kathartische Gewalt (→Katharsis) dieser ersten ‹Metzelei› der modernen Tragödienliteratur – fünf Tote – stützt sich auf eine heilsame Erschütterung des Zuschauers. Giraldi ist mit seinen in einem Zeitraum von weniger als zehn Jahren geschriebenen Tragödien der ‹Erfinder› der Schauertragödie geworden.

Das →Schäferspiel

Seit den Humanisten des 15. Jh. und der *Arcadia* (um 1485/1504), in der Jacopo Sannazaro (um 1456–1530) seine Sehnsucht nach einer Welt der Idylle ausgedrückt hatte, war die Vorliebe für die Schäferliteratur in Italien lebendig geblieben. Die eigentliche Geburtsstunde des Schäferspiels schlägt wie für Tragödie und Komödie in Ferrara: *Egle* (1545) von Giraldi Cinzio, ein Satyrspiel, das der eigentlichen Schäferthematik fernsteht, aber für die Struktur der Gattung wegweisend ist; *Il Sacrificio* (1554) von Agostino Reccari (†1590), einem echten Prototyp der Gattung; *Aminta* von Torquato Tasso und *Il Pastor fido* (1581/90) von Giambattista Guarini (1538–1612). Die beiden letztgenannten Stücke sind unbestrittene Meisterwerke ihrer Gattung und werden häufig nachgeahmt. Die Faszination, die sie besonders auf die Librettisten ganz Europas ausübten, erklärt sich wohl nicht nur allein durch ihren literarischen Wert, sondern auch durch ihre Vereinigung von Poesie und Musik, womit sie den Ursprung der Oper bilden. *Aminta* dürfte das erste Stück sein, das durchlaufende Musikbegleitung hatte und so der Vereinigung von Text und Musik in den ersten ital. →Melodramen noch vorausging, aus denen sich die

Oper entwickeln sollte: *La Dafne* (1594) und *Euridice* (1600) von Iacopo Peri (1561–1633), *Amfiparnaso* (1594) von Crazio Vecchi (1550–1605) und der berühmte *Orfeo* von Claudio Monteverdi (1567–1643).

Baratto, M.: La Commedia del Cinquecento. Vicenza 1975; Borsellino, N./Mercuri, R.: Il Theatro del Cinquecento. Bari 1973; Buck, A.: Italienische Dichtungslehren vom Mittelalter bis zum Ausgang der Renaissance. Tübingen 1952; Fagiolo, M.: La Scenografia, delle sacre rappresentazione al futorismo. Florenz 1973; Fontana, A.: La Scena. In: Storia d'Italia I; I caratteri originali. Turin 1972; Neri, F.: La Tragedia italiana del Cinquecento. Florenz 1904 (Neudruck Turin 1971); Pinelli, A.: I Teatri. Florenz 1973; Stäuble, A.: La commedia umanistica del Quattrocento. Florenz 1968; Toffanin, G.: Il cinquecento. Mailand 1950; Weinberg, B.: A History of Literary Criticism in the Italian Renaissance. 2 Bde. Chicago/Toronto 1961; Zorzi, L.: Il Teatro e la città. Turin 1977.

Paul Larrivaille

Ritual

(Lat. ritualis = dem ritus ‹feierlicher, festgelegter religiöser Brauch› entsprechend) (→Ritualtänze). Im Zusammenhang mit der Theorie vom Ursprung des europäischen Dramas aus dem Kultus werden insbesondere für die griech. →Tragödie (→Antikes Theater) bestimmte kultische Elemente oder Riten angegeben, die einen wesenhaften Zusammenhang mit einem bestimmten Ritual beweisen sollen. Als Beispiel diene der vielleicht eindrucksvollste und nachhaltigste Versuch von G. Murray, der erstmals 1912 und danach wiederholt die These aufgestellt hat, die Tragödie sei die Fortentwicklung des Frühlingsrituals des Vegetationsgottes Dionysos (→Dionysien). Murray versuchte sogar, entscheidende Teile dieses dionysischen Frühlingsrituals, das für ihn identisch mit dem →Dithyrambos war, auszumachen und in den Tragödien wiederzufinden. Es sollte einen →Agon des Jahres gegen seinen Feind geben, einen Teil über die Leidensgeschichte des Jahresdämons: seine rituelle Tötung, einen Botenbericht darüber, eine Totenklage ebenso wie die Wiederfindung, Wiederbelebung und Verherrlichung des Getöteten. Es läßt sich nicht allzuschwer erweisen, daß dieses Schema ebensowenig für die Tragödie verwertbar ist, wie es einen aus ethnologischen Beobachtungen und spekulativen Ideologien hergestellten Anachronismus in die Vergangenheit darstellt. Obgleich man des weiteren unterscheiden kann zwischen solchen derartigen Versuchen, die die Tragödie kaum tangieren, und anderen, die inhaltlich wie formal enger mit der Tragödie zu verbinden sind und stärker auch antike Quellen berücksichtigen wie die Ursprungstheorie aus dem Ritual der Totenklage, gemeinsam aber ist allen Ritualtheorien, daß sie das Wesentliche des dramatischen Geschehens im religiösen

Ritual, im ‹dromenon› (griech. ‹heilige› Handlung) sehen wollen. Mit zunehmender Kritik werden zwar unhaltbare konkrete Parallelen und Analogien aufgegeben, aber man besteht weiter darauf, hinter dem Erscheinungsbild des tragischen Spiels sei ein möglicherweise blutiges Ritual. So vertritt noch jüngst W. Burkert, die Tragödie sei eigentlich ein Menschenopfer; über Euripides (480–406 v. Chr.) meint er, dieser finde schließlich zurück zur «tragischen Grundsituation...., die sich noch immer im Menschenopfer darstellt», und dem von ihm festgestellten «Aufbruch des Individualismus» in der athenischen Gesellschaft des 6. Jh. v. Chr. «erscheint... im Spiegel des Mythos (d. i. in der Tragödie, d. Verf.) seine unheimliche kollektive Kompensation: das Menschenopfer». Die offenbare Faszination, die Tragödie im Grunde als ein Menschenopfer zu verstehen, mag daran liegen, daß man sich den Mythos, den Inhalt des Dramas, letztlich doch nur unter der ‹höheren Weihe› des Rituals vorstellen kann, ganz im Sinne der Ritualtheorie von W. R. Smith, J. E. Harrison und J. G. Frazer. Eine tiefwurzelnde Vorliebe für das Primitive als das vermeintlich Wesentliche und für die ‹Tat› im Ritual setzt sich fort in dem nicht mehr reflektierten methodischen Irrtum, die Totalität des Religiösen in den Einrichtungen der primitiven Gesellschaften gebiete den Schluß, künftige Errungenschaften des Menschen seien, falls sie auch nur keimhaft in den vorwiegend religiösen primitiven Formen auszumachen sind, im Wesen religiös.

Im Ergebnis werden die Konturen zwischen Ritual und Drama verwischt. Während das Ritual als ‹dromenon› das Ereignis vollzieht: der Kampf, das einander Jagen, Töten, Zerstückeln, das Wiedererwecken und Auferstehen eines Gottes oder eines Dämonen, wird im Ritual im einzelnen handgreiflich von den maskierten Akteuren als von den Dämonen ‹Ergriffenen› vollzogen; das Ritualdrama macht das Geschehen im Vollzug zum präsentischen Ereignis; in der griech. Tragödie hingegen findet all dies in diesem Sinne nicht mehr statt. Der Handlungsbegriff des Dramas ist ein grundsätzlich anderer als der des Rituals. Die handgreiflichen Ereignisse werden in der Regel von der Bühne verbannt. In den erhaltenen griech. Tragödien findet das «Geschehen grauenhafter, blutiger, entsetzlicher Natur» nicht auf der Bühne statt. Soweit die Taten nicht vor der Zeit des Dramas liegen, werden sie in den «hinterszenischen Raum verlegt» (Joerden). Abgesehen von der Verbannung solcher Taten, die das Ritual bevorzugt, werden alle Handlungen nicht als solche dargestellt, sondern der argumentative Diskurs über sie.

Im Berichten, Diskutieren, im Nachdenken und Äußern von Gefühlen über die Ereignisse, im Planen, Verabreden und Prophezeien von ihnen wird ihre Ablehnung oder ihre Notwendigkeit, ihre Wünschbarkeit oder ihre Verwerflichkeit, ihr Preis oder ihr Tadel im Medium der Sprache dargestellt. Die Handlung des Dramas ist diese Sprache. Die Geschehnisse werden in ihrem Für und Wider gemessen an subjektiven und kollektiven, an sozialen, an politischen und auch an religiösen Wertvorstellungen, an etablierten Werten, an Urteilen, die auch noch unsrer Reflexion standhalten, ebenso wie an gesellschaftlich oder historisch bedingten Vorurteilen. Es ist, als seien die in Rede stehenden Taten und Leiden der Menschen der Anlaß, das Drama ihrer Begründung durch die Handelnden vorzuführen.

Burkert, W.: Homo necans. Berlin 1972; ders.: Mythos und Mythologie. In: Die Welt der Antike. Bd. 1. Berlin o. J.; Joerden, K.: Zur Bedeutung des Außer- und Hinterszenischen. In: Die Bauformen der griechischen Tragödie. Hg. von W. Jens. München 1971; Lesky, A.: Die tragische Dichtung der Hellenen. Göttingen [3] 1972; Maertens, J.-Th.: Ritanalyses. Montbonnot 1987; Murray, G.: Excursus on the Ritual Forms preserved in Greek Tragedy. In: Harrison, J. E.: Themis. A Study of the social origins of Greek religion. Cambridge [2] 1928; Pickard-Cambridge, A.: Dithyramb, Tragedy and Comedy. Oxford 1927; Schechner, R.: Between Theater & Anthropology. Philadelphia 1985; ders./Appel, W. (Hg.): By Means of Performance. Intercultural Studies of Theatre and Ritual. Cambridge 1990; ders.: Theater-Anthropologie. Spiel und Ritual im Kulturvergleich. Reinbek 1990; Turner, V.: Vom Ritual zum Theater. Frankfurt/M. u. a. 1989.

Franzjosef Schuh

Ritualtänze

Magische Denk- und Verhaltensweisen sind ahistorisch. Ihre Ausprägungen, Verdichtungen und ihre Durchschlagkraft wirken von Kultur zu Kultur und von Epoche zu Epoche verschieden. Ritualtänze (→Ritual) können dementsprechend ihrem Gehalt nach keineswegs als nur archaisch-ethnologische Tänze gelten. Die geistigen Inbilder aller magischen und auch mythologischen Tanzspiele leben in den Kulturen der Kontinente in unterschiedlichsten Formen bis zur Gegenwart fort. Der Begriff Ritualtanz vertritt Tanzspiele, die streng in Kulte eingebunden sind. Mit diesen Tanzspielen begegnen wir der Urform des Theaters überhaupt. Kulte ohne Tanz, Darstellung, Gesang, Instrumentalspiel, Sprache, vom Ruf bis zur Rezitation, sind nicht denkbar. Alle Künste in ihren Urformen werden in den magischen Aktionen synergetisch auf das Ziel hin ausgerichtet, verzweifelte Schwäche gegenüber den Mächten der Natur oder gegenüber äußeren Feinden zu überwinden und übergroße Faszinationen zu verarbeiten. Die Menschen müssen ihr Selbst übersteigen oder zumindest ausweiten; sie wollen die im Leben erfahrenen Mächte im Kultspiel erreichen und binden, ja in den Ritualaktionen einwirkend unterstützen. In so hoher Absicht werden Rituale zu Fest- und Spielzeiten. Sie führen zu ersten Lebensverlaufsstrukturen, den Festkalendern. In Festen mar-

798 Ritualtänze

(A. Magische Tänze; B. Mythologische Tänze; C. Religiöse Tänze)
I. Theogonien/Kosmogonien

A. 1. Kosmologische Tänze
2. Astraltänze
3. Tänze zu Ehren der Großen Mutter
4. des Großen Vaters
5. Göttermythen
6. Götterlegenden
7. Dichotomie Licht – Dunkel
8. Heilige Hochzeit
9. Gottessohn – die Eingeburt

B. siehe I. A. 1–7

C. siehe I. A. 1–9
10. Leben Jesu
11. Leiden Jesu
12. Alttestamentliche Themenkreise
13. Offenbarungsgeschehen
14. Marienfeste
15. Feste der jüdischen Religion

II. Jahreskreis/Natur

A. 1. Sonnentänze
2. Wetterkatastrophen
3. Große Fluten
4. Regenzeiten
5. Schneeschmelze

6. Trockenzeiten
7. Wildtierzüge
8. Vogelflüge
9. Fischschwärme
10. Fruchtbarkeit

B. siehe II. A. 1–10

C. siehe II. A. 1–10

III. Monatsfolge/Tageslauf

A. 1. Jahreszeiten
2. Sonnentänze
3. Mondtänze

4. Tag- und Nachtfolge
5. Ernte
6. Beruf

B. siehe III. A. 1–6

C. siehe III. A. 1–6

IV. Stammes-/Völkerleben

A. 1. Bandstiftung
2. Jagd (Tier- und Maskentänze)
3. Krieg (Waffen-, Stock- und Schwerttänze)

B. IV. A. 1–3
4. Heldenmythen
5. Gesetzgebungsmythen

C. 6. Advent
7. Weihnacht
8. Ostern
9. Pfingsten
10. Heiligenfeste
11. Kirchweih
12. Maurenkriege
13. Türkenkriege

V. Menschenleben

A. 1. Initiation
2. Hochzeit
3. Geburt
4. Heil- und Medizintänze
5. Leichen- und Totentänze
6. Inzest

7. Bruderhaß
8. Hybris
9. Ritual- und Rechtsverletzung

C. 10. Glaubenskonflikt
11. Teufelspakt
12. Märtyrerschicksal

B. siehe V. A. 1–5

Ritualtänze 799

kierte Ereignisse stiften eine aus der Vergangenheit her in der Erinnerung festgemachte Gegenwart. Die Zeit schwingt von Zeitmal zu Zeitmal, von Fest zu Fest. – Die frz. Felshöhlen von Tuc d'Audoubert und Trois Frères überliefern als Felsbildkunst der Eiszeit bereits Tiertänze, vom Magier geleitet, die von Kühn auf mindestens 15 000 v. Chr., von Gregor für die afrikanischen Höhlenmalereien von Tel Issaghen / Fezzan auf das 12. bis 6. Jahrtausend v. Chr. datiert werden. Offenbar ist alle Felsbildkunst religiöse Kunst; insofern sind alle Ritualtänze religiöse Tänze. Die aufgefundenen Höhlen sind kultische Plätze, an denen sich erstes magisch-kultisches Theater ereignete. In großen Beschwörungsriten leben Tanz und Darstellung als Aktion und Schaustellung zugleich. Der Mensch hat sich von allem Anfang an neben der Wirklichkeitswelt seiner Krisen- und Schreckenszeiten eine Wesenswelt aufgebaut, in der er die emotionalen Erregungen und Bilder seines Inneren nach außen tragen und Wirklichkeit bezwingen kann. Das räumlich begrenzte Leben eines jeden ethnologischen Volks kennt eine hohe Anzahl von einschneidenden Ereignissen: die Jahreszeiten, die Perioden der großen Schneeschmelzen, Überschwemmungen, Regenzeiten und Ernten, die mit dem Jahreslauf verbundenen Züge, Flüge und Schwärme der Tiere. Und das Menschenleben selbst wird durch die Kulminationspunkte seiner Stammes- und Völkergeschichte und durch die kritischen Phasen seiner eigenen Lebensentfaltung geprägt. Die Ausführungen verdeutlichen, daß magisch-mythische Tänze symbolische und sinnbildliche Tänze sein müssen. Der sinnbildliche Tanz kann für die Darstellung seiner Inbilder pantomimische Mittel nutzen.

Die Tänze aller *Religions- und Heldenmythologien* bauen grundsätzlich auf den Gehaltskreisen der magischen Tänze auf. Als Tanzanlässe neu zu berücksichtigen sind Heldenmythen und Gesetzgebungen (IV. B. 4 und 5). – Die kritischen Phasen des menschlichen Lebenslaufs unter V., die ‹rites de passages›, erweitern sich um die mythologisch gestalteten Urkonflikte des Menschen: Inzest, Bruderhaß, Hybris, Ritual- und Rechtsverletzungen (V. B. 6–9).

Die *religiösen Tanzspiele* entwachsen wiederum den überlieferten Mythen und auch noch den Magien. Insofern sind weder historisch noch gehaltlich mythologische und religiöse Tänze gegeneinander abzugrenzen. Als religiöse Tänze beziehen wir hier nur die des christlichen Tanzes ein. Der Themenblock unter I. C. nimmt Spiele zur Passion, zur Auferstehung, zum Offenbarungsgeschehen, zu alttestamentlichen Themenkreisen und zum Leben der Maria auf. – In den Zyklus des Völkerlebens werden christliche Feste eingebunden: Advent, Weihnacht, Ostern, Pfingsten, Heiligenfeste, Kirchweihen etc. (IV. C. 6–11). Den Ausbau religiöser Tanzspiele gestatten die Kämpfe in den Mauren- und Türkenkriegen (IV. C. 12 und 13). Glaubenskonflikte, der Teufelspakt und Märtyrerschicksale bereichern Tanzkomplex V (V. C. 10–12).

800 Rolle

Das Christentum hat in den ersten Jahrhunderten Tänze unbefangen in seine *Liturgien* eingegliedert und somit bruchlos altes religiöses Geistesgut synthetisiert und tradiert. Den historischen Quellen nach fördert Gregorius Thaumaturgos in der Diözese am Pontus im 3. Jh. die Einführung von Tanzspielen und heiligen Pantomimen in den Ritus. Das Christentum ist zunächst durchaus eine Religion des Tanzes. Doch glaubt die Kirche, sich in der Liturgie gegenüber den tänzerischen Religionen der Antike, des Orients und des Nordens vehement abgrenzen zu müssen, um liturgischen Vermischungen auszuweichen. So nimmt die christliche Kirche Roms den Kampf gegen den Tanz auf. Synodalbeschlüsse und Kampfschriften gegen das Tanzen vom 6. bis zum 17. Jh. belegen dies. Die Verbote richten sich seit dem 6. Jh. nach Berichten in Strafbüchern vorrangig gegen das Tragen von Tiermasken (→Tiertänze). Geistliche tanzen und singen jedoch weiterhin ihre Lobeshymnen in der Messe. Sie erfassen die Hände der Meßknaben und umschreiten im feierlichen ‹Reigen› den Hochaltar. In Prozessionen werden Tanzspiele der Kleriker speziell hinter den Madonnenstatuen zelebriert. 1682 tanzt der Bischof von St. Martial im Gottesdienst und in der Prozession die Pilota. In Andalusien sind die Kirchenreigen aus dem Gottesdienst bis heute nicht fortzudenken. Nachdem der Tanz aus den Gotteshäusern auswandern mußte, wird ihm im Gegensatz zum Drama nun auch der Kirchplatz versperrt. Das Tanzspiel erobert sich daraufhin zunächst als chorisches Ballett und dann solistisch die →Mysterienspiele. Alle magisch-heiligen Tänze aber werden in starker Reduktion in das Brauchtum des Volks abgedrängt (→Brauchtumstänze).

Gennep, A. v.: Les rites de passage. Paris 1909; Gregor, J.: Kulturgeschichte des Balletts. Zürich o. J. / Wien 1944; Günther, D.: Der Tanz als Bewegungsphänomen. Hamburg 1962; Kühn, H.: Die Felsbilder Europas. Stuttgart 1952; Wosien, M.-G.: Sacred dance. Encounter with gods. London 1974.

Helga Ettl

Rolle

Das Wort R. (→Kunstfach) wird vom lat. ‹rotula› (‹Rädchen›; in der mlat. Kanzleisprache ‹Schriftrolle›, ‹Urkunde›) abgeleitet; um 1400 ins Deutsche entlehnt aus dem Französischen (rôle). Erst seit Ende des 16. Jh. bezeichnet R. den Anteil eines Schauspielers am Spiel, der in der Regel auf einen handlichen Papierstreifen geschrieben wurde, der bei den Proben so abgerollt wurde, daß nur der jeweils zu sprechende Text sichtbar war; erstmals 1598 in Amsterdam, Gryphius übernimmt 1663 diese Praxis in Schlesien (vgl. Kluge, Etym. Wörterbuch).

Eine R. im Theater zu spielen, bedeutet nach heutigem Verständnis Verwandlung in einen anderen Charakter, aber nicht bis zur Selbstaufgabe; Distanz zum eigenen Ich und der Mut, sich zu produzieren, bleiben erhalten. Die Erarbeitung der R. ist für den Schauspieler ein schwieriger Prozeß. Sobald er die Bühne betritt, muß er wissen, daß er nicht mehr als er selbst dort steht, sondern in der zu verkörpernden R. Es ist schwierig, das Gefühl zu beschreiben, welches den Schauspieler befällt, wenn er den Einstieg in die R. versucht. Er probiert aus in dauernder Anspannung, versucht diese oder jene Geste, überprüft sie, ob sie zu der zu verkörpernden R. paßt. Er probiert verschiedene Tonfälle aus und wiederholt dabei immer wieder seinen Text. Es ist möglich, daß ein Schauspieler den Zugang zu einer R. nie findet, daß ihm dabei auch der Regisseur nicht helfen kann. – Das Verhältnis Schauspieler – Rolle wird in der Theatertheorie unterschiedlich bestimmt: →Stanislawski-System, →Meyerhold-Methode, →Verfremdungseffekt, →Armes Theater, →Theater der Grausamkeit, →The Method, →Theaterpädagogik, →Psychodrama.

Der R.-Begriff wird auch in der Sozialpsychologie und der Soziologie zur Beschreibung von Interaktionsstrukturen benutzt; dem liegt die Annahme analoger Strukturen von Theaterhandlung und Alltagskommunikation zugrunde. Diese Analogievorstellung von Theater und Leben, vermittelt über den R.-Begriff, führt in ihrer metaphysisch-religiösen Andeutung zur Idee vom Welttheater (→Theatrum Mundi; →Barocktheater).

Barrault, J.-L.: Mein Leben mit dem Theater. Köln 1967; Berger, P. L./Luckmann, Th.: Die gesellschaftliche Konstruktion der Wirklichkeit. Frankfurt/M. 1970; Brecht, B.: Schriften zum Theater. Bde. 1–7. Frankfurt/M. 1963; Burzynski, T./ Osinski, Z.: Das Theater Laboratorium Grotowskis. Warszawa 1979; Dreitzel, H. P.: Die gesellschaftlichen Leiden und das Leiden an der Gesellschaft. Stuttgart 1972; Goffman, E.: Wir alle spielen Theater. München 1969; Huizinga, J.: Homo ludens. Reinbek bei Hamburg 1956; Langer, G.: Die Rolle in Gesellschaft und Theater. Oberwil bei Zug 1980; Moreno, J. L.: Das Stegreiftheater. Potsdam o. J.; Stanislawski, K. S.: Die Arbeit des Schauspielers an sich selbst. Berlin 1963.

Günter Langer/Red.

Romantisches Theater

Die Romantik als künstlerische, geistige Strömung entsteht in Abkehr vom Rationalismus der Spätaufklärung und entwickelt sich in Europa von den 90er Jahren des 18. bis zu den ausgehenden 40er Jahren des 19. Jh. Wegen der Vielseitigkeit, ja Gegensätzlichkeit ihrer Werke entzieht sie sich jeder näheren einheitlichen Definition, um so mehr, als sie nicht zugleich in allen Ländern ihre Blütezeit erlebt: Während sie z. B. in

802 Romantisches Theater

Deutschland 1820 bereits ihren Höhepunkt überschritten hat, behauptet sie sich erst nachher in Frankreich und Spanien als organisierte Bewegung. Obwohl sie als gesamteurop. ästhetische Revolution allen literarischen Gattungen ihr eigenes Gepräge verleiht, leistet die Romantik hauptsächlich nur in zwei Ländern Wesentliches im Bereich der Dramentheorie und der dramatischen Produktion: in Deutschland und Frankreich.

Ausgangspunkt der dt. Dramentheorie sind die kunstkritischen Schriften der Brüder Schlegel: Friedrich Schlegel (1772–1829), der in seinen *Kritischen Fragmenten* (1797–1800) und im *Gespräch über die Poesie* (1800) das romantische Programm verkündet, und August Wilhelm (1767–1845), dessen Berliner *Vorlesungen über schöne Literatur und Kunst* (1801–04) und vor allem Wiener *Vorlesungen über dramatische Kunst und Literatur* (1808) europ. Berühmtheit erlangten. Während Friedrich Schlegels Begriff der Universalpoesie auf dem dramatischen Gebiet in Abkehr von Antike und Klassik zur Einführung einer Mischform führt, wo die Verschmelzung verschiedener literarischer Gattungen angestrebt wird und Vers und Prosa einander ablösen, münden August Wilhelm Schlegels geistesgeschichtliche Betrachtungen in eine Theorie der Tragikomödie als der dem Zeitgeist am besten entsprechenden dramatischen Form. Damit stimmt er mit Schelling (1775–1854) überein, der 1802 in seiner *Vorlesung über die Philosophie der Kunst* schreibt, «daß die Mischung des Entgegengesetzten, also vorzüglich des Tragischen und des Komischen selbst, als Prinzip dem modernen Drama liegt». Diese Tragikomödie Schlegelscher Prägung soll zugleich episch sein und sich um eine Neubelebung der Lyrik, insbesondere durch die Wiedereinführung des Chors, bemühen. August Wilhelm Schlegel fordert außerdem, daß natürliche Stoffe in historischen Schauspielen vorrangig behandelt werden, wobei er sich von seinem Bruder trennt, der für die Schaffung eines mythologischen Dramas eingetreten war. Beide Brüder vereinigen sich wieder im Preisen Shakespeares, den sie als den typischsten Vertreter der Moderne betrachten. August Wilhelm Schlegels Bewunderung gilt auch den romanischen Literaturen – vgl. Calderón (1600–81), in dessen religiös gegründeten Schauspielen er den tiefsten Ausdruck der menschlichen Erlösung erkennen will. An diesen Stücken bewährt er seine Übersetzungskunst; seine höchste Leistung in dieser Hinsicht bleibt aber seine Shakespeare-Übertragung, eine Aufgabe, die er zuerst allein, später mit Ludwig Tieck (1773–1853) und dessen Tochter Dorothea löst; diese Übersetzung wird heute noch wegen ihrer sprachlichen Schönheit am meisten gespielt. – Wichtig für die spätere Entwicklung der frz. romantischen Dramentheorie ist sein in den Wiener Vorlesungen geführter Angriff gegen die Ästhetik des frz. klass. Theaters: Er kritisiert das strenge Einhalten von Ort- und Zeiteinheit, den Gebrauch von kalten, in Alexandriner gefaßten Tiraden, die konventionelle Rolle der Vertrauten, die systematische Wahl von antiken Stoffen.

Diese Kritik, die für dt. Leser nichts Neues enthielt (→Sturm und Drang), wurde in Frankreich durch Mme de Staël (1766–1817) popularisiert. Sie ließ die Vorlesungen Schlegels 1814 ins Frz. übertragen; der Einfluß seiner Thesen ist in ihrem Buch *Von Deutschland* (1810) besonders spürbar: Gegenüberstellung von Antike und Moderne, Definition der modernen, d. h. romantischen Kunst als christlich-natürliche Dichtung, Hinweis auf die Meisterwerke der nordeurop. Literatur – Shakespeare, Goethe, Schiller, die dt. Romantik. So leitet sie die frz. theoretische Auseinandersetzung um das Drama ein, die sich hauptsächlich in den 20er Jahren entfalten wird. Es geht dabei vor allem um drei Hauptprobleme: die Kritik der →drei Einheiten, die Debatte um das Versdrama, die Vermischung der dramatischen Gattungen. Da klassizistische Dramatiker wie Casimir Delavigne (1793–1843) Gestalten und Ereignisse der frz. Geschichte schon zum Thema ihrer Tragödien gemacht haben, rückt die Frage der Wahl moderner Stoffe nicht in den Mittelpunkt der Auseinandersetzung. Zu erwähnen sind polemische Werke wie der unter dem Einfluß des vom ital. Dichter Manzoni (1785–1873) veröffentlichte *Brief über die Einheiten* (1820) entstandene Essay von Stendhal (1783–1842) *Racine und Shakespeare* (1823–25) («Was ist romantische Tragödie? Ich antworte kühn: es ist eine Prosatragödie, die sich über mehrere Monate erstreckt und in verschiedenen Orten spielt.») und der *Brief an Lord**** (1829), den Alfred de Vigny (1797–1863) programmatisch seiner Übersetzung des *Othello* voranstellt. Jedoch formuliert Victor Hugo (1802–1885) im Vorwort zum Stück *Cromwell* (1827) die frz. Theorie des romantischen Dramas am einprägsamsten. Die dramatische Form der Gegenwart sei eine Mischform: «Wir sind auf dem poetischen Höhepunkt der modernen Zeit angekommen. Shakespeare ist das Drama; und das Drama, das im selben Atemzug das Groteske und das Erhabene, das Schreckliche und das Possenhafte, die Tragödie und die Komödie, verschmilzt, ist das Kennzeichen... der Literatur der Gegenwart.» Dies entspricht dem modernen Weltgefühl, das durch die christliche Lehre geprägt wird. «An dem Tage, da das Christentum zum Menschen sagte: ‹Du bist zweierlei›..., entstand das Drama.» Zur realitätsgerechten Schilderung des Menschen, in dem sich also der Körper, dem Groteskes und Komisches anhaften, mit einer erhabenen, tragischen Seele vereint, ist die Überwindung der klassischen Trennung von Komödie und Tragödie notwendig: so entsteht ein tragikomisches Drama, in dem komischer Körper und tragische Seele immer gleichzeitig dargestellt werden. Derselbe Wahrheitsanspruch führt zur Nichtbeachtung der Einheiten des Orts und der Zeit. Es geht aber nicht um eine flache Wiedergabe der Wirklichkeit: Die Kunst ist zwar Spiegel der Natur, aber einer verdichteten, gesteigerten. Die romantische Dramaturgie braucht also nicht alltägliche Gestalten und Ereignisse, sondern außergewöhnliche

Taten und Helden, beeindruckende Vertreter des Menschheitsschicksals, Wortführer des Dichters, der durch sie einen dreifachen, natürlichen, menschlichen und sozialen Auftrag erfüllt. So bekommt das Drama einen glühend lyrischen Charakter, weshalb Hugo Stendhals Theorie des Prosa-schauspiels verwirft: Verteidigung des Alexandriners, den es nur durch eine neue rhythmische Gestaltung beweglicher und lebendiger zu machen gilt. Das frz. Drama erhebt auch den Anspruch, alle Gattungen in sich einzuschließen; so weist es auch epische Züge auf (vgl. die Bedeutung der eingehenden Bühnenanweisungen).

Die dramatische Produktion der dt. Romantik entspricht nicht den Erwartungen ihrer Theoretiker. Es wurde kein bedeutsames tragikomisches Werk verfaßt. Die konsequente Anwendung der ästhetischen Grundsätze Friedrich Schlegels führte zur Verletzung dramatischer Gesetzmäßigkeiten: Es entstanden unaufführbare →Lesedramen, aus losen chronologisch angeordneten Episoden bestehend, die nur von der Hauptgestalt zusammengehalten werden, so daß der dramatische Konflikt zur Biographie erweitert wird. Außerdem führen die zahlreichen Nebenhandlungen zum Anwachsen des Stücks. – Diese Vorliebe für das Lesestück läßt sich z. T. auch durch die der Romantik nicht gerade freundliche Gesinnung erklären, die in den dt. Theatern der Zeit herrschte: In Weimar dominierte der klassische Geschmack, und Iffland (1759–1814), Direktor des Berliner Kgl. Neuen Theaters, ließ fast nur Zugstücke und Werke der Klassiker – insbesondere Schillers – aufführen. – Bahnbrecher war Tieck; er schrieb Werke wie *Leben und Tod der heiligen Genoveva* (1800) und *Kaiser Oktavianus* (1804), die ersten christlichen historisierenden Schauspiele der Romantik. Diese Dramen wurden zum Vorbild für die historischen Schauspiele von Achim von Arnim (1781–1831), Joseph von Eichendorff (1788–1857) und Friedrich de La Motte Fouqué (1777–1843).

Von größerer Bedeutung ist die romantische Komödie, eine Gattung, die von Tieck geschaffen wurde (*Der gestiefelte Kater*, 1797; *Die verkehrte Welt*, 1800) und die auch Clemens Brentano (1778–1842) illustrierte (*Ponce de Leon*, 1804). In ihr waltet die romantische Ironie als formgebende Instanz: Hauptanliegen des Dramatikers ist ein Spiel mit der Theaterillusion, mit dem Spiel, also eine Form der Poesie. Im besten und bis heute immer noch aufgeführten Stück *Der gestiefelte Kater* wird das Publikum selbst zum Akteur, Autor und Hanswurst treten auf, es wird im Durcheinander über Rollen, Illusion und Nicht-Illusion geredet. Die verschiedensten Formen der Illusionsbrechungen werden verwendet, manche Erfindungen scheinen das epische Drama (→Episches Theater) anzukündigen. Mit *Leonce und Lena* (1836) schreibt Georg Büchner (1813–37) das letzte romantische Lustspiel, das zugleich die Gattung kritisch überwindet: parodistische Auflösung der romantischen Formelemente, romantische Ironie wird für die sozialkritische Satire genutzt. Erst in der Zeit der Hoch- und Spätromantik entstanden wieder dramatische Werke, die den Regeln des bühnengerechten Aufbaus folgten. Zacharias Werner (1768–1823) schuf 1810 mit seinem Einakter *Der 24. Februar* die erste →Schicksalstragödie, eine romantische Modegattung, der selbst Franz Grillparzer (1791–1872) in seinem Erstling *Die Ahnfrau* (1817) Tribut zollte. Auffälligerweise gehört der einzige große Dramatiker der romantischen Epoche, Heinrich von Kleist (1776–1811), nicht zur romantischen Schule. Zwar ist der Einfluß der romantischen Weltanschauung in seinem Werk spürbar – die Thematik der *Familie Schroffenstein* (1803) ist mit der der Schauerromantik verwandt; die tragikomische Fassung von Molières *Amphitryon* (1807), wo außerdem die antike Fabel mit christlichen Motiven verbunden wird, begeisterte den romantischen Theoretiker Adam Müller (1779–1829); die *Hermannsschlacht* (1808) darf als Beitrag zum romantischen Nationaldrama betrachtet werden; die mittelalterliche Märchenwelt des *Käthchen von Heilbronn* (1810), selbst wenn das Stück die Ritterdramen parodiert, ist ohne die Romantik kaum vorstellbar. Jedoch weicht Kleists Ästhetik von der romantischen entschieden ab: Er versucht nicht, wie es Schlegel verlangt, die drei Hauptarten der Poesie zu verschmelzen; es geht ihm um die Gestaltung der rein dramatischen Form, wodurch er sich eher den Klassikern nähert: *Penthesilea* (1808), *Prinz Friedrich von Homburg* (1811).

Auch das frz. Theater der Romantik erfüllte nicht die hohen Ansprüche seiner Theoretiker. Seine Produktionen wurden von drei Faktoren mitbestimmt: die Fortschritte der Dekoration (vgl. die Entdeckung des Dioramas durch Daguerre), der Einfluß von erfolgreichen Schauspielern, wie Frédérick Lemaître (1800–76), die ihre Auffassung eines effektvollen Schauspiels geltend zu machen wußten, der Triumph des →Melodramas in den Pariser Boulevardtheatern. So entfaltete sich das romantische Drama zum Illusionstheater, in dem eine ereignisreiche und bunte Handlung mit vielen Überraschungseffekten, die Vorliebe für wirkungsvolle Szenen mit Lokalkolorit, die Neigung zum gefühlvoll predigenden Ton und zu großen, vereinfachenden Kontrasten sowie die Pantomime vorherrschten. Behandelt wurden vor allem historische Themen, insbesondere aus der frz. und ital. Renaissance. Prosper Mérimée (1803–70), indem er 1825 das *Theater der Clara Gazul* veröffentlichte, wo sich der Einfluß des Calderón spürbar macht, kündigte das Anheben einer neuen Epoche an. Diese begann eigentlich 1829, als Dumas sein historisches Drama *Heinrich der Dritte und sein Hof* an der Comédie Française, der Hochburg der Klassiker, aufführen ließ, gipfelte 1830 mit der Uraufführung von Hugos lyrischem Drama *Hernani* auf derselben Bühne, wobei es zu einer regelrechten Theaterschlacht zwischen Klassikern und Romantikern kam und letztere einen eklatanten Sieg errangen, und 1838 mit *Ruy*

Blas, dem Meisterwerk Hugos, das die Verschmelzung des Erhabenen und des Grotesken am Schicksal des Titelhelden darstellt, und sie endete 1843 mit dem Mißerfolg von Hugos *Burggrafen*. Erst später aber – manche sogar um die Jahrhundertwende – wurden die besten frz. Dramen der Romantik auf die Bühne gebracht: Alfred de Musset (1810–57), nachdem sein Erstling *Die venetianische Nacht* (1830) durchgefallen war, schrieb nämlich seine dramatischen Werke nur für den Druck. Es entstanden eine Reihe von Komödien, wo das Tragische im Hintergrund lauert – *Zwischen Lipp' und Kelchesrand* (1832), *Die Launen der Marianne* (1833), *Man spielt nicht mit der Liebe* (1834) und *Lorenzaccio* (1834), das einzige bedeutende historische Drama der frz. Romantik. Musset entfernt sich vom Melodrama, nähert sich seinem Vorbild Shakespeare, indem er die Kunst der Psychologie und des Individualisierens mit der Darstellung einer ganzen Epoche, der florentinischen Renaissance, souverän verbindet.

Insgesamt ist also das romantische Drama vor allem geistes- und literaturgeschichtlich bedeutend, da nur wenige Stücke heute noch im Spielplan der Theater stehen. Jedoch haben sich romantische Bühnenwerke anderer Art erfolgreich erhalten, besonders im Bereich von Oper und Ballett.

Arntzen, H.: Die ernste Komödie. München 1968; Descotes, M.: Le drame romantique et ses grands créateurs. Paris 1955; Guthke, K. S.: Die moderne Tragikomödie. Theorie und Gestalt. Göttingen 1968; Kluge, G.: Spiel und Witz im romantischen Lustspiel. Diss. Köln 1963; Korff, H. A.: Geist der Goethezeit. Bde. III und IV. Berlin 1949, 1953; Lefebvre, H.: Musset. Paris 1970; Schmidt, P.: Romantisches Drama. In: Grimm, R. (Hg.): Deutsche Dramentheorien I. Frankfurt/M. 1971; Strohschneider-Kohrs, I.: Die romantische Ironie. In: Die dt. Romantik. Göttingen 1978; Übersfeld, A.: Le Roi et le Bouffon. Paris 1974.

Alain Muzelle

Roßballett

Den Ursprung aller Roßballette bilden die mittelalterlichen →Turniere. Ihr kriegerisch-kämpferischer Geist wird theatralisiert. Jenseits dieser Entwicklung finden sich Roßtänze in sakralen und profanen Schautänzen aller Kontinente, vor allem in Indien, Afrika, Südamerika. Vom 17. Jh. an ist das R. nur noch eine von Pferden und Reitern ausgeführte ‹hohe Reitkunst›. Zu den berühmtesten Aufführungen von R. zählen: 1606 das *Ballet à cheval des quattre Elements* zu Paris und 1608 der Florentiner *Ballo di persone a cavallo*. Auf dem großen Karneval von Cosimo II. in Florenz wird ein →Trionfo zu Fuß und zu Pferde ausgeführt, der *Guerra de'Amore* (1615). Dieser vorwiegend militärische Festzug zieht in ein riesiges Oval ein, das von Tribünen umstanden ist. Zunächst fechten Ritter zu Fuß, von Reitern flankiert. Dann reitet man eine Quadrille, für die der Architekt 16 Figuren als Bodenchoreographie gezeichnet hat. In die Geschichte geht auch das Pariser Karussell von 1662 ein (500 Darsteller zu 20 Gruppen). Zweifellos das prächtigste aller equestrischen Ballette choreographiert der Wiener Hof 1666 zur Hochzeit Leopolds I. (1658–1705): *La contessa dell' asia e dell' acqua.* 1667 wird zu dem Jahr des Wiener R. (1500 Darsteller). Zunächst umfahren Festwagen das Rund. Als Wolkenballett senkt sich mit Hilfe einer Maschinerie der «Tempel der Ewigkeit» herab. Eine kriegerische Gruppe von 8 Trabanten, 16 Reitknechten und 12 Trompetern trabt in das Spielzentrum ein. Ihr folgt auf seinem Leibroß Speranza, in prächtigem Kostüm und mit weißblauem Federbusch, der regierende Monarch Leopold I.

Biehn, H.: Feste und Feiern im alten Europa. München o. J.; Gregor, J.: Kulturgeschichte des Balletts. Zürich o. J./Wien 1944; le Menestrier, P. J.: Des Ballets anciens et modernes selon les Règles du Théâtre. Paris 1981, S. 231–232.

Helga Ettl

Rote Grütze (Berlin)

Wichtiges →Kinder- und Jugendtheater der emotionalen Betroffenheit, entstand 1972 aus dem →Grips Theater. – In kollektiver Arbeit und langwierigen Proben- und Selbsterfahrungsprozessen entstanden bisher Stücke zum Thema Liebe, Sexualität, Drogen (das Kinderstück *Darüber spricht man nicht* mit starken →Mitspielelementen 1973; die Jugendstücke *Was heißt hier Liebe?*, 1976, *Mensch ich lieb dich doch*, 1980; das Kinderstück *Nippes und Stulle spielen den Froschkönig*, 1985).

Franke, H.: Ohne mich fehlt mir was. München 1982.

Hans-Wolfgang Nickel

Royal Academy of Dramatic Art

Meist zu R. A. D. A. abgekürzt. Eine der führenden brit. Schulen für Schauspiel und Bühnentechnik. 1904 von Beerbohm Tree in London gegr. Ausbildungsstätte vieler bekannter Schauspieler/innen. Bes. auf klassische Sprechausbildung spezialisiert. Die R. A. besitzt mit dem Vanbrugh Theatre im Zentrum Londons eine feste Bühne für Amateuraufführungen.

Bernd-Peter Lange

Royal Ballet

Das Sadler's Wells Ballet erhält 1956 durch königliches Dekret den Titel Royal Ballet. Die Initiative zu der mit dem Ernennungsakt realisierten engl. Ballett-Tradition geht auf Ninette de Valois (*1898) und Lillian Baylis (1874–1937) zurück. Die Valois hat u. a. bei Cecchetti (1850–1928) studiert und in der Diaghilew-Kompanie getanzt (→Ballets Russes). 1926 gelingt ihr die Gründung der Academy of Choreographic Art in London. L. Baylis, Direktorin des Old Vic Theatre, engagiert die Valois als Bewegungspädagogin für Schauspieler. 1931 siedelt N. de Valois mit ihren Schülern in das neu erbaute Sadler's Wells Theatre über. Aufführungen der Kompanie finden zunächst im →Old Vic und im Sadler's Wells Theatre statt, später nur im Sadler's Wells Theatre mit der Kompanie-Bezeichnung Sadler's Wells Ballet. Die Valois fördert die Begabung junger Talente und erkennt F. Ashtons choreographisches Genie. Ashton (1904–1988) wird ab 1935 Chefchoreograph für das noch Vic-Wells-Ballet, 1952 Associate Director und 1963 Nachfolger der Valois, die sich fortan den Ausbildungsgängen der →Royal Ballet School zuwendet. Nachfolgedirektoren Ashtons sind ab 1970 MacMillan, ab 1977 N. Morrice, ab 1986/87 Anthony Dowell.

Beaumont, C.: Complete Book of Ballets. London 1951; Clarke, M.: The Sadler's Wells Ballet. London 1958; Koegler, H./Günther, H.: Reclams Ballettlexikon. Stuttgart 1984.

Patricia Stöckemann

Royal Ballet School (London)

Die R. B. S. ist Zentralschule der Royal Academy of Dancing, einer engl. Organisation zur Förderung von geschultem Tänzer- und Tanzlehrernachwuchs. Sie ist aus der von Ninette de Valois (*1898) 1926 gegründeten Academy of Choreographic Art und der daraus 1931 entstandenen Sadler's Wells School (→Royal Ballet) hervorgegangen. 1947 wird die Umorganisation der Schule nach dem Vorbild der Petersburger Ballettschule (→St. Petersburger Ballett) eingeleitet. – Die R. B. S. gliedert sich in «Lower» und «Upper School». Seit 1955 ist die Lower School sowohl Internats- als auch Tagesschule in White Lodge/Richmond Park, London. Alle Mädchen und Jungen von 11 bis 16 Jahren erhalten in einer zur R. B. S. gehörenden Schule regulären allgemeinbildenden Unterricht mit dem Lehrstoff der Realschule. Ältere Schüler und bereits graduierte Absolventen besuchen eine staatliche Upper School in der Talgarth Road. Die Ausbildung zielt auf Allgemeinbildung, künstlerisches und historisches Verständnis, Formgefühl und Geschmack, tänzerische Qualifikationen, Bühnen- und Ensembleerfahrung.

Calouste Gulbenkian Foundation (ed.): Dance Education and Training in Britain. London 1980; Niehaus, M.: Ballettfaszination. München 1978; Wohlfahrt, H. Th.: Ausbildung an der Royal Academy of Dancing. In: Ballett-Journal / Das Tanzarchiv 1 (1984), S. 42–43.

Patricia Stöckemann

Royal Court Theatre

Bekanntes Londoner Theater am Sloane Square, Chelsea. Gegr. 1871, Neubau 1888, 1932 Kino, 1940 ausgebombt, 1952 als Theater wiedereröffnet. Seit 1956 Sitz der English Stage Company, bis 1965 unter dem künstlerischen Leiter George Devine. Neben der →Royal Shakespeare Company und dem →National Theatre wichtigstes brit. Subventionstheater, speziell für den Bereich des zeitgenössischen Dramas. Bis heute einflußreichste Bühne der Theateravantgarde und des →experimentellen Theaters. →Absurdes Theater, →episches Theater, Drama der →Angry Young Men, →politisches und feministisches Alternativtheater sind vom R. C. T. einem vorwiegend intellektuellen bürgerlichen Publikum zugänglich gemacht worden. Daneben auch Klassikeraufführungen und ehrgeizige Neuinszenierungen vergessener Stücke. Die English Stage Company fördert bes. junge Autoren und ihre Erstlingswerke, darunter z. B. John Osborne (* 1929), John Arden (* 1930), Edward Bond (* 1934), Harold Pinter (* 1930), Howard Brenton (* 1942), Caryl Churchill (* 1939). Neuerdings Schaffung der im jährlichen Wechsel besetzten Stelle eines ‹resident playwright›. Die Studiobühne des R. C. T. Upstairs ergänzt das Repertoire. Neue Stücke werden jeweils im Programmheft abgedruckt und in Zusammenarbeit mit dem wichtigsten brit. Theaterverlag Methuen vertrieben.

Browne, T. W.: Playwrights' Theatre. The English Stage Company at the Royal Court Theatre. London 1975; Doty, G. A./Harbin, B. J. (Hg.): Inside the Royal Court Theatre, 1956–1981. o. O. 1990; Findlater, R. (ed.): At the Royal Court. Twenty Five Years of the English Stage Company. London 1981.

Bernd-Peter Lange

Royal Shakespeare Company

1960 unter diesem Namen von Peter Hall (*1930) begründetes Ensemble. Mitdirektoren bald Peggy Ashcroft (*1907) und Peter Brook (*1925). Die R. S. C. führt Shakespeares Dramen, aber auch andere Klassiker auf. Das hochsubventionierte Ensemble beschäftigt in seinen Theatern in Stratford-upon-Avon und London (dort zunächst im Aldwych Theatre, seit 1983 im neuerbauten Barbican Arts Centre in der City) eine große Anzahl Schauspieler mit festem Vertrag, für einzelne Aufführungen auch bekannte Gastschauspieler. Die Inszenierungen wechseln zwischen Stratford und London und werden oft auf internationalen Tourneen gezeigt. Dabei liegt der Schwerpunkt in Stratford bei Shakespeare-Aufführungen, in London bei anderen brit. und europ. Klassikern, auch der Moderne, letztere z. T. auf den Studiobühnen The Other Place (Stratford) und Warehouse (London).

Beauman, S.: The Royal Shakespeare Company: A History of Ten Decades. London 1982; Chambers, C.: Other Spaces. New Theatre and the RSC. London 1980; Lahrmann, H.: Shakespeare-Inszenierungen in England. Die R. S. C. (1960 bis 1982). Frankfurt/M. u. a. 1988; Thomsen, C. W.: Das englische Theater der Gegenwart. Düsseldorf 1980.

Bernd-Peter Lange

Ruhrfestspiele

Festspielhaus, Theater im Depot Recklinghausen. Für spontane Hilfe der Bergarbeiter, die mit Sonderschichten im Winter 1946 Kohle für die Hamburger Theater förderten, bedankten sich diese in Recklinghausen («Kunst für Kohle»). Seit 1947 mehrwöchige Festspiele, getragen vom Dt. Gewerkschaftsbund und der Stadt Recklinghausen. 1947 bis 1951 künstlerischer Leiter Dr. Karl Pempelfort (1901–75), 1951 bis 1965 Otto Burrmeister (1899–1966). Überwiegend Klassiker-Inszenierungen mit eigens engagierten renommierten Darstellern und Regisseuren. Zunehmende Kritik an eher routinierten Aufführungen ohne Innovationskraft im überdimensionierten, poesiefeindlichen Festspielhaus (1966). 1981 neues Konzept mit einem ständigen Ensemble. Seitdem Ausweitung der Aktivitäten auf das ganze Jahr in alternativer Spielstätte und außerhalb Recklinghausens (Gewerkschaftshäuser, Betriebe). Spielplan parteilich politisch im Sinne der Gewerkschaftsziele, künstlerisch oft unbefriedigend. Versuche mit neuem Agitprop-Stil in kleinen, selbstentwickelten Stücken des Ensembles. Festspielleitung und Geschäftsführung Hansgünther Heyme (*1935).

Gelsing, W.: Otto Burrmeisters Volkstheaterideal. Diss. Bochum 1975; Limbach, A.: Ruhrfestspiele. Diss. Köln 1967.

Werner Schulze-Reimpell / Red.

Rührstück

Das R. ist eine Trivialisierung des bürgerlichen Theaters mit versöhnlichem Ausgang. Das R. bezweckt nicht nur die Erschütterung des Zuschauers wie etwa das klassische →Trauerspiel, sondern letzten Endes dessen durch Heiterkeit und guten Ausgang hervorgerufene Erleichterung und Belehrung. Die Entstehung und die Ausbreitung des R. erklären sich durch das Hochkommen des Bürgertums mit seinen übertriebenen Idealen von Tugend und Edelmut und durch den Wandel der moralischen und philosophischen Vorstellungen im 18. Jh. Die Aufklärung betrachtet den Menschen als grundsätzlich gut und verbesserbar. So setzt sich das R. zum Ziel, den Zuschauer nicht mehr nur zu belustigen, sondern zu rühren, appelliert an seine Gefühle, um ihn auf gefällige, milde Weise am Beispiel derer zu erbauen, die durch Zufall, durch die Begebenheiten des Lebens vom Weg der wahren Tugend abkommen, zu ihm aber zurückfinden; das R. kann somit als eine Variante der →Tragikomödie angesehen werden, die von der Komödie die bürgerlichen Typen und Charaktere übernimmt, von der Tragödie aber den pathetischen Handlungsablauf.

Vorläufer des R. ist in Frankreich die ‹comédie larmoyante› eines Pierre Claude Nivelle de la Chaussée (1692–1754) bzw. Voltaire (1694 bis 1778) mit *L'enfant prodigue* (1736) und *Nanine* (1749), in England die aus dem Familienstück hervorgegangene →‹sentimental comedy› eines Richard Steele (1672–1729) oder Colley Cibber (1671–1757). In Deutschland folgen dann das weinerliche Lustspiel von Christian Fürchtegott Gellert (1715–69), Johann Elias Schlegel (1719–49) oder Christian Felix Weiße (1726–1804) mit dessen Adaptation von *Romeo und Julia*. Selbst Gotthold Ephraim Lessing (1729–81) fordert in der *Theatralischen Bibliothek* (1754) von der Komödie nicht nur Heiterkeit, sondern auch Rührung, was er am Beispiel seines Stücks *Minna von Barnhelm* (1767) demonstriert. Danach fällt das R. ab und wird oft zur trivialen Parodie großer tragischer Themen der Weltliteratur, etwa von Othello, Hamlet, King Lear, bei Heinrich Leopold Wagner (1747–79) und Friedrich Ludwig Schröder (1744–1819). Mit August Wilhelm Iffland (1759–1814) und August von Kotzebue (1761–1819) erfährt das R. hierauf eine neue Blütezeit; Kotzebues Werke werden sogar in England und Amerika zu →Melodramen umgearbeitet. Trotz aller Kritik und Angriffe durch Johann

Wolfgang von Goethe (1749–1832), Friedrich Schiller (1759–1805) oder Ludwig Tieck (1773–1853) behauptet sich das R. auf der dt. Bühne am Ende des 18. Jh. und am Anfang des 19. Jh. (allein zwischen 1781 und 1814 entstehen 63 R.) und übertrifft an Erfolg und Popularität die Werke der Klassiker. Noch im 19. Jh. werden mit großem Erfolg R. von Charlotte Birch-Pfeiffer (1800–68) und Roderich Benedix (1811–73) geschrieben und aufgeführt, und gegen Ende des Jh. nimmt sogar noch Hermann Sudermann (1857–1928) Elemente des R. in seine naturalistischen Dramen auf.

Glaser, A.: Das bürgerliche Rührstück. Stuttgart 1969; Guthke, K. S.: Das bürgerliche Drama des 18. und frühen 19. Jh. In: Hinck, W. (Hg.): Handbuch des deutschen Dramas. Düsseldorf 1980.

Bernard Poloni

Sadir Natya

Einziges solistisches Genre des →Bharata Natyam im Südosten Indiens; reinste Form; Solotanz. Nur von nicht brahmanischen Frauen getanzt: Devadasis (Tempeltänzerinnen), Rajadasis (Tänzerinnen an Höfen), Nattuvanars (Tanz-Lehrmeister). Die Tänzerinnen fungieren zugleich als Erzählerinnen. Es musizieren: 1 Saiteninstrumentalist oder 1 Flötist und 1 Mridanga-Trommler. Heute hat sich eine sechsteilige dramatische Grundform herausgebildet. Tanzspiele zu Ehren Shivas.

Rebling, E.: Die Tanzkunst Indiens. Wilhelmshaven 1982, S. 130–136.

Helga Ettl

Sainete

Beliebte dramatische Kurzform (→Einakter) im spanischsprachigen Bereich mit burlesken Volkstypen seit dem 16. Jh. Hauptvertreter im 18. Jh.: Ramón de la Cruz (1731–94), der rund 300 dieser Dialog-Einakter verfaßte. Die damalige Madrider Hofgesellschaft ist dort anschaulich abkonterfeit.

Hamilton, A.: A Study of Spanish manners, 1750–1800, from the Plays of Ramón de la Cruz. Urbana (Ill.) 1926.

Martin Franzbach

Salondame

Weibliches →Rollenfach. Die S. charakterisiert sich durch elegante Erscheinung und Sprechweise. Vereinzelt vertreten im klassischen Repertoire – z. B. Célimène in Molières (1622–73) *Le Misanthrope* (1666) –, ist das Fach der S. besonders in den frz. Salonstücken des 19. Jh. weit verbreitet. Im 20. Jh. macht dann der Film aus dieser eleganten, schönen, mit den Gefühlen spielenden S. die ‹femme fatale› bzw. den ‹Vamp›.

Bernard Poloni

Salzburger Festspiele

Vorläufer waren die Mozartfeste im 19. Jh. 1917 Gründung einer Festspielhausgemeinde u. a. durch Max Reinhardt (1873–1943), Hugo von Hofmannsthal (1874–1929), Hermann Bahr (1863–1934) und Richard Strauss (1864–1949). Festspiele seit 1920 unter Einbeziehung der Stadt als Szenerie. Ziel: «musikalisch theatralische Festspiele in Salzburg zu veranstalten, das heißt: uralt Lebendiges aufs neue lebendig machen… an sinnfällig auserlesener Stätte» (Hofmannsthal). Eröffnung mit *Jedermann* von Hofmannsthal, seitdem in Anlehnung an die Inszenierung von Reinhardt ständig im Repertoire. 1922 *Salzburger Großes Welttheater* von Hofmannsthal in der Kollegienkirche (Regie: Reinhardt). Mozartpflege als Schwerpunkt. 1926 (Kleines) Festspielhaus, →Felsenreitschule. 1960 Großes Festspielhaus (2371 Plätze), 30 Meter Portalöffnung für große Opern. Nach 1945 Wiederbelebung der 1938 unterbrochenen Tradition, u. a. durch Gottfried von Einem (* 1918). Herausragende Mozart-Inszenierungen durch Oscar Fritz Schuh (1904–85) – Salzburger Mozart-Stil. Zahlreiche Opernuraufführungen. – 1960 Präsident Bernhard Paumgartner (1887–1971), bestimmender Einfluß von Karl Böhm (1894–1982) und Herbert von Karajan (1908–89). Seit 1974 mehrere UA von Stücken Thomas Bernhards. Erweiterung der Festspiele durch Fest in Hellbrunn und von Schuh initiiertes «Salzburger Straßentheater». Seit 1967 Salzburger Osterfestspiele durch H. v. Karajan (Konzert und Oper). Ab 1992 Direktorium Dr. Heinrich Wiesmüller, Präsident; Dr. Gerard Mortier, Intendant; Prof. Dr. Hans Landesmann, Kaufm. Leiter; Leiter des Schauspiels: Peter Stein. Neue Akzente und Leitlinien.

Kaut, J.: Festspiele in Salzburg. Salzburg 1965, 1970, 1973; Schuh, O. F.: Salzburger Dramaturgie. Salzburg 1969.

Werner Schulze-Reimpell / Red.

San Francisco Mime Troupe

Wichtigste Gruppe des modernen →politischen Volkstheaters in den USA. Gegr. von R. G. Davis 1959 als «Mime Studio and Troupe» mit dem Ziel, gegen den bürgerlichen und kommerziellen Theaterbetrieb experimentell Pantomime, Tanz, Jazz und absurdes Worttheater zu kombinieren. Seit 1962 erkämpfte sich die S. F. M. T. das Recht der freien Aufführung in den Parks und adaptierte die Commedia dell'arte in amerik. Verhältnisse. Mit den politischen Oppositionsströmungen der 1960er Jahre entwickelte Davis das →Guerilla Theatre und funktionierte Formen der →Minstrel Show und des →Melodramas für Theateragitation um. Die S. F. M. T. trennte sich 1970 von ihrem Direktor Davis und suchte den Weg zum ethnisch gemischten multinationalen Kollektiv. Wurden zuvor meist Dramenvorlagen bearbeitet, gilt seit 1970 das Prinzip der kollektiven Eigenproduktion, wofür die ‹Hausautorin› Joan Holden häufig das Skript liefert. Der Typus des komplexen politischen Volkstheaters, der Musicalelemente, Tänze, die Rezeption von massenkulturellen Trivialformen wie Thriller, Comic strip etc. mit einer gewichtigen politischen Aussage integriert, wurde durch *The Dragon Lady's Revenge* (1971) zum erstenmal erreicht, ein Stück über den Drogenimperialismus der USA in Südostasien. Weitere wichtige Stationen: *Frijoles* (Welternährungskrise, 1974); *False Promises* (Anti-Bicentennial, 1976); *Hotel Universe* (Hausbesetzungsproblematik, 1977); *Last Tango* (Mittelamerika, 1981); *Factperson/Factwino-Trilogie* (Reagan, Moral Majority und Aufrüstung, 1980–85); *Steeltown* (Fabrikstillegung, Jubiläumsinszenierung, 1984); *The Mozamgola Caper* (Drittweltverschuldung, 1986); *Ripped van Winkle* (Yuppiesierung der 68er Generation. Kanalisierung des Drogenhandels in die Ghettos, 1988); *Seeing Double* (Palästinenserfrage, 1989); *Rats* (Verelendung in den USA, 1990); *Uncle Tom's Cabin* (nach alter Bühnenfassung des Romans von H. Beecher-Stowe, 1990); *Back to Normal* (Golfkrieg, 1991).

Neben einer regelmäßigen Freiluftsaison als Straßen- und Parktheater in der Bay Area (San Francisco und Umgebung) führt die S. F. M. T. ausgedehnte US-Tourneen durch, 1977, 1980, 1981, 1985 auch solche nach Europa; als erste US-Truppe 1979 in Kuba und 1985 beim Festival des politischen Liedes in der DDR. Die S. F. M. T. erhielt zahlreiche Ehrenpreise und Auszeichnungen, ohne nennenswerte finanzielle Einnahmen, und wird nach wie vor kaum subventioniert. Sie verbindet auf unnachahmliche Weise Spaß und Politik, wobei die Wirkungsästhetik auf ‹befreiendes Gelächter›, auf die ‹Lust am Verändern› abzielt.

Burger, G.: Die San Francisco Mime Troupe und Peter Schumanns Bread and Puppet Theatre. Zwei komplementäre Modelle aufklärerischen Theaters. Diss.

St. Petersburger Ballett **815**

Bremen 1992; Burger, G./Herms, D.: Ein Vierteljahrhundert San Francisco
Mime Troupe. Berlin 1984; Davis, R. G.: The San Francisco Mime Troupe – The
First Ten Years. Palo Alto 1975; Herms, D.: Agitprop USA. Kronberg 1973;
Herms, D./Paul, A.: Politisches Volkstheater der Gegenwart. Berlin 1981;
Shank, T.: American Alternative Theatre. London 1982; The San Francisco Mime
Troupe: By Popular Demand – Plays and Other Works. San Francisco 1980.

Dieter Herms / Uschi Bauer

St. Petersburger Ballett

1742 Opernhaus Petersburg – 1757 Großes Kaiserliches Theater für Oper
und Ballett Petersburg – 1917 Staatliches Marinski-Theater Leningrad –
1920 Staatlich Akademisches Theater für Oper und Ballett =
G. A. T. O. P. (russ. Abkürzung) – 1935 Leningrader Akademisches
Theater für Oper und Ballett S. M. Kirow.

1738 erste Tanzschule Rußlands; Leitung: J. B. Landé. Neben und
nach ihm wirken die Reformchoreographen Fr. Hilverding (1710–68;
→Ballet héroïque-pantomime) und Gasparo Angiolini (1723–96). Den
Ausbau des tänzerischen Niveaus dankt die Ballett-Institution Didelot
(1767–1837). Er dringt auf eine Ausbildungserweiterung von zwei auf
drei Jahre, führt mimischen Unterricht ein und fordert musikalische
Grundstudien. Didelot fügt Noverres Reformideen (→Ballet d'action)
entscheidende dramaturgische Ansätze hinzu (→Ballet héroïque-pantomime). Puschkin schreibt, daß in Didelots Tanzschöpfungen mehr Poesie
zu finden ist als in der gesamten französischen Literatur. 1847: Marius
Petipa (1818–1910) «premier danseur», 1862 Ballettmeister. In fünf
Jahrzehnten 50 Ballette, 17 ältere Choreographien, 35 Opern. Petipa
zentriert die Ballerina als Protagonistin. Romantische Sujets. Keine
Charakterentwicklung, aber exzellente tänzerische Raum- und Bewe-
gungsformationen. Viele Werke Petipas gelten heute international als
klassisches Repertoire, vor allem: *Dornröschen, Nußknacker, Schwanensee.* – Nächste umfassende tanzpädagogische Leistung: Enrico Cecchetti
(1850–1928). Cecchetti unterschreibt 1879 seinen Vertrag mit dem Großen Haus und wird 1892 Lehrer der angegliederten Schule. Diaghilew
gewinnt ihn 1910 für seine →Ballets Russes. Wandel des choreographischen Stils durch Aufbegehren der Nachwuchstalente noch vor Petipas
Rücktritt. Fokin (1880–1942) fixiert bereits 1904 Reformideen, die ener-
gisch auf eine dramatisch-stilistische Einheit von Musik, Tanz, Dekor und
Libretto dringen. Erst als Chefchoreograph Diaghilews (1909) kann Fokin seine Vorstellungen, auch die zum choreo-sinfonischen Ballett, realisieren.

Nach der Oktoberrevolution 1917: Sorge um Arbeitsplätze, Angst vor

816 St. Petersburger Ballett

Hunger und Typhus. Von 165 Ballettmitgliedern emigrieren 34 Künstler, unter ihnen alle Spitzenballerinen, Startänzer und die Reformchoreographen Fokin und Romanow; 23 Tänzer ziehen in ungefährdete Provinzen, 11 sterben. Lopuchow treibt die Ausbildung des begabten Nachwuchses voran. Die Beschlüsse der «Petrograder Konferenz aller Tanzpädagogen» 1918 (→ Bolschoi-Ballett) und staatliche Unterstützung ermöglichen einen vehementen Aufbau. Bereits 1921 studieren an der Akademie des G. A. T. O. P. 350 Kinder und Jugendliche. Nach kurzer Stagnation und nach der Konstitution eines Theaterkollektivs erarbeitet die reorganisierte Kompanie traditionsbewußt zunächst das Petipa-Repertoire. Die nachrevolutionäre sowjetische Ballettgeschichte durchlebt von 1918 bis 1985 drei Entwicklungsphasen.

1. Reorganisation und Integration: Phase der Stilreform und -ausweitung; Ära der Experimente; Stilmannigfaltigkeit. a) Bewußte Traditionseroberung, -vertiefung und Neuinszenierungen des klassischen Repertoires; national-regionale Ansätze, die zur Systematisierung des Charaktertanzes führen und den Volkstanz der Republiken in das Tanztheater einbeziehen. b) Arbeiten der Modernisten: Konstruktivismus, Maschinismus, Expressivität, absoluter Tanz, statische Studien, Alltagsbewegungen, Clownerien, Akrobatik, Kunstsynkretismus, Streben nach Integration von Tanz und Pantomime. c) Das Sinfonische Ballett: Den Grundstein zum Sinfonischen Ballett hatten bereits Petipa und Iwanow (1834–1901) gelegt. Fokin in Petersburg und Gorski in Moskau entwerfen choreo-sinfonische Dichtungen. Lopuchow begründet nach der Revolution die Theorie des → Sinfonischen Balletts und prägt den Begriff. In der Praxis erfüllt er seine Forderungen mit *Die Erhabenheit des Weltalls*, Musik: 4. Sinfonie von Beethoven. Balanchine assistiert (→ New York City Ballet). Erst zehn Jahre später, 1933, nach der Aufführung von *Choreartium* (4. Sinfonie von Brahms) durch Massine in Paris, setzt der Gattungsbegriff sich im westeuropäischen Ballettschaffen durch. – 2. Das → Choreodrama integriert die Solisten in die Kompanie, verselbständigt Chorszenen und nutzt sie zu vehement-dramatischen Volksszenen. Die Aktionen des Chors weiten sich zu Monumentalgemälden aus, die zwangsläufig die psychologische Führung der Figuren vernachlässigen. Pantomimische Szenen dominant. – 3. In den 1950er und 60er Jahren setzen sich junge Choreographen mit dem tänzerischen Poem durch (Grigorowitsch). Die Ballettdirektoren treten gegen das Choreodrama auf, das die ureigene Aussage des Tanzes nicht mehr berücksichtigt und freiwillig dramatische Möglichkeiten aufgibt. Der Ausgleich zwischen Tanz und Pantomime wird gesichert. Solotänzer und Corps de ballet werden psychologisch intensiv geführt. Das Balletttheater der GUS vertritt heute den ‹Modernen Realismus›, der dank der Arbeit des → Bolschoi-Balletts und der Republikzentren einen Reichtum an Stilen vorzuweisen

hat. Moderner Realismus: ein Tanztheater, das die Zeit und den Menschen in komplizierten dialektischen Wechselbeziehungen poetisch widerspiegelt, nicht aber naturalistisch abbildet (Grigorowitsch).

In der gesamten nachrevolutionären Zeit war das Kirow-Ballett, das 1991 in St. Petersburger Ballett umbenannt wurde, unflexibler als das Bolschoi-Ballett in Moskau, neigte weniger zu Experimenten, drang mehr auf Absicherung. Trotz der erreichten Standardaufführungen fand die Kompanie bisher keine Choreographenpersönlichkeit, die – gleich Grigorowitsch in Moskau – durch Reformen, Elan und persönlichen Führungsstil das Ensemble zu einer festen Truppe hätte zusammenschließen können.

Ballett-Journal/Das Tanzarchiv: Leningrad – 200 Jahre Kirow-Ballett. Dezember 1983, S. 44–47; Grigorowitsch, J.: Synthese der Traditionen. In: Die Welt des Tanzes in Selbstzeugnissen. Hg. von L. Wolgina und U. Pietzsch. Wilhelmshaven, 2 (1979), S. 310–321; Lupochow, F.: Nach dem großen Oktober. In: Die Welt des Tanzes in Selbstzeugnissen. Hg. von L. Wolgina und U. Pietzsch. Wilhelmshaven, 2 (1979), S. 93–125; Rebling, E.: Ballett – gestern und heute. Berlin 1957; Schmidt-Garre, H.: Ballett. Vom Sonnenkönig bis Balanchine. Hannover 1966.

Patricia Stöckemann

Satyrspiel

Komisches griech. Drama (→ Komödie), das seinen Namen von den den → Chor bildenden Satyrn hat. Entstehung und Frühgeschichte sind eng mit der → Tragödie verbunden (und ähnlich unklar und umstritten); auch in der Blütezeit des attischen Dramas gibt es vielfache Gemeinsamkeiten und Verbindungen zwischen den beiden ungleichen Schwestern: Im dramatischen Wettbewerb der ‹Großen → Dionysien› sind immer drei Tragödien und ein S. zu einer → Tetralogie verbunden; sie haben dieselben Autoren, verwenden dieselben Schauspieler, denselben Chor und, wenigstens teilweise, dieselben Kostüme und Requisiten (→ Antikes Theater); in Bauform und dramatischer Struktur besteht kein wesentlicher Unterschied (das S. ist kürzer und einfacher und arbeitet mit einem deutlich kleineren und stärker typisierten Figurenarsenal). Sprache und Metrik sind bei allen Differenzen in Stilhöhe und Strenge doch eng verwandt; ihre Stoffe nehmen beide aus der griech. Mythologie. Dabei ist das klassische S., soweit wir sehen können, nicht, wie immer wieder behauptet wird, Mythosparodie oder -travestie und auch nicht Tragödienparodie. Gestaltet werden vielmehr aus dem reichen Reservoir des Mythos heitere oder doch unproblematische, oft märchenhafte Stoffe. – Der genaue Zeitpunkt und die Gründe für die obligatorische Verbindung von Tragödie und S. sind ungeklärt. Die auch aus dem Theater anderer Zeiten und

Kulturen bekannte Verbindung von tragisch-ernstem und ausgelassenheiterem Spiel dient wohl in erster Linie der emotionalen Erleichterung (comic relief).

Seidensticker, B.: Das Satyrspiel. In: G. A. Seeck (Hg.): Das griech. Drama. Darmstadt 1979, S. 204–257.

Bernd Seidensticker

Schäferspiel

Das S. (ital. pastorale; engl. pastoral drama; frz. pastorale dramatique), eine höfische Gattung, entwickelte sich vor allem in Italien im Zeitalter der Renaissance, danach an den Höfen Europas, hauptsächlich in Frankreich und England sowie mit weniger Durchschlagskraft im dt. Adel und Großbürgertum. Die Form ist gattungsmäßig schwer zu definieren, überschneidet sich doch das Schäferdrama mit Schäferkomödien und -tragikomödien.

In Nachahmung der Antike – bes. Theokrits *Idyllen* (3. Jh. v. Chr.) und Vergils (70–12 v. Chr.) *Eklogen* – entstand das ital. Schäferspiel aus drei Formen, der dialogisierten Ekloge der höfischen Feste, dem höfischen mythologischen Drama sowie deren burlesken →Parodie, dem Hirtenschwank. Als erstes ital. Schäferspiel gilt Agostino de' Beccaris *Il sacrificio* (1554), seine Höhepunkte erreichte es mit Torquato Tassos (1544–95) *Aminta* (1573) und Giovanni Battista Guarinis (1538–1612) Tragikomödie *Il pastor fido* (1583). Von Italien aus breitete sich die Form mit Hilfe von erfolgreichen Übersetzungen der ital. Meisterwerke im 16. und 17. Jh. in ganz Europa aus: zuerst in England, mit u. a. 1584 John Lylys (1554?–1606) *Galathea* und George Peeles (1558?–1597?) *Arraignment of Paris*, dann u. a. John Fletchers (1579–1625) Meisterwerk *The Faithful Shepherdess* (1610). Höhepunkte sind Shakespeares *As you like it* (Wie es euch gefällt, 1599?), *Comus* (1634) von John Milton (1608–74) und das letzte, unvollendete Stück von Benjamin Jonson (1572–1637), *The Sad Shepherd* (1641 post.); in England widmeten sich also die literarischen Größen der Zeit dieser Form. In Frankreich wirkte parallel zum ital. Einfluß die Schäferromanze *L'Astrée* (1607–28) von Honoré d'Urfé (1567–1625) sowie die Diskussion um die Erstellung der klassischen Regeln. Als die besten und erfolgreichsten Spiele gelten hier *Les Bergeries* (1625) von Racan (1589–1670) und bes. Jean Mairets (1604–1686) *Sylvie* (1628) und *Silvanire* (1629). In Deutschland waren vor allem die Übertragungen bemerkenswert. Von den dramatischen Spielen ist bes. von Andreas Gryphius (1616–64) die Doppelkomödie *Das verliebte Gespenst* und *Die geliebte Dornrose* (1660) bekannt, wo sich in ital. Manier Schäferlustspiel und Bauernposse zur Kontrastierung ‹hoher› und ‹niederer› Liebe ineinander verschränken.

Nimmt man Abstand von gewissen nationalen Merkmalen, welche allerdings historisch nicht ohne Bedeutung sind, so bilden die S. im wesentlichen einen gemeinsamen Typus. Im Mittelpunkt ist als Intrige eine Art Liebesreigen: Die Liebespaare, meist Schäfer und Schäferinnen, finden, trennen und finden sich am Ende zurück zu einer neuen Liebesordnung, die harmonischer wirkt als der Anfangszustand. Unvorbereitetes und Abenteuerliches ist ausgeschlossen in einem streng geometrischen dramatisch-elegischen Spiel. Die bald freundliche, bald feindliche Natur dient den Liebesspielen der Hirten und Hirtinnen als Rahmen.

Jedoch ist diese Natur nicht nur Konvention: Ob Arkadien oder Sizilien, ob Wald oder Gebirge, ist sie mythisch erhöht zur Utopie eines goldenen, harmonischen Zeitalters, wo sich die zwar elementare, doch kulturell geordnete Naturexistenz der Künstlichkeit des Hoflebens oder der Nüchternheit und Härte des Alltags widersetzt. Dazu gesellt sich das barocke Spiel und Widerspiel von Sein und Schein, worin sich der Mensch nur im Verstellen, in der Vergänglichkeit, in der Beweglichkeit flüchtig erfassen läßt.

Wenn auch das Schäferspiel als solches spätestens Mitte des 17. Jh. verschwand, war sein Einfluß wesentlich. Dank seiner musikalischen Einlagen, Ballette und Chöre hat es entscheidend zur Geburt der Oper beigetragen, vor allem in Italien bei Metastasio (1698–1782). Im Theater hat diese Untergattung in Italien und Frankreich fruchtbare dramaturgische Diskussionen ausgelöst, die für die klassischen Theorien wegweisend waren. Und Bauformen aus dem S. sind überall bis ins 18. Jh. hinein von den bedeutendsten Autoren übernommen worden. Bei Shakespeare finden sich neben *As you like it* auch pastorale Elemente in *The Two Gentlemen of Verona, Love Labour's Lost* (1594–95), *A Midsummer Night's Dream* (1595–96) sowie *Much Ado About Nothing* und *Twelfth Night* (1598 bis 1600). In Frankreich hat es die Komödien von Corneille (1606–84), Racine (1639–99), Molière (1622–73) und Marivaux (1688–1763) nachhaltig beeinflußt. Goethe schrieb noch 1767 sein Alexandrinenspiel *Die Laune des Verliebten*, und in Schillers Schauspiel *Wilhelm Tell* (UA 1804) sind noch Nachwirkungen zu finden.

Effe, B.: Schäferspiel. Die Genese einer literarischen Gattung. 1977; Rousset, J.: La littérature de l'âge baroque en France. Paris 1954; Vosskamp, W. (Hg.): Schäferdichtung. Bonn 1977.

Gérard Schneilin

Schall und Rauch

Das Kabarett S. u. R. entstand aus dem Berliner Künstlerkreis «Die Brille», dem u. a. Max Reinhardt, Friedrich Kayßler und Christian Morgenstern angehörten. Silvester 1900 waren sie mit einem parodistischen *Jahrhundertwende-Weihenachtsspiel* so erfolgreich an die Öffentlichkeit getreten, daß weitere Vorstellungen folgten, meist zu wohltätigen Zwecken. Daraufhin plante man regelmäßige Auftritte, den Streit um den Namen beendete ein Hinweis auf Goethes «Name ist Schall und Rauch». Als «Kleines Theater (S. u. R.)» fand am 9. 10. 1901 die offizielle Premiere statt. Erfolg hatte man vor allem mit literarischen Parodien. Zeitkritische Bemerkungen fanden sich allenfalls in Zwischenspielen, die Theaterzensur verhinderte jede Kritik. Die Folge war, daß man sich mehr und mehr auf Chansons, Rezitationen und Parodien beschränken mußte. Gerade dafür aber war das notwendige Publikum nicht vorhanden. So wurde seit dem 25. 9. 1902 S. u. R. als reine Schauspielbühne von Reinhardt weitergeführt.

Eine nur wenige Jahre dauernde Wiederauferstehung fand S. u. R., als Reinhardt im umgebauten Zirkus Schumann das «Große Schauspielhaus» (→ Reinhardt-Bühnen) eröffnete. In den umgebauten Kellerräumen (1100 Plätze) wurde am 8. 12. 1919 S. u. R. mehr als literarisches Theater denn als Kabarett wieder begonnen. Zentraler Bestandteil jeden Programms sollte eine Parodie auf das im Großen Schauspielhaus gespielte Stück sein. Chansons, Rezitationen, Puppenspiele sowie der erste in einem Kabarett gezeigte Karikaturfilm (von Walter Trier) ergänzten das Programm. Auch der Kreis Berliner Dadaisten und Expressionisten fand hier eine Öffentlichkeit; Klabund und Walter Mehring, George Grosz und John Heartfield gehörten ebenso zu den Mitarbeitern wie Gustav von Wangenheim. Mit dem Rückzug Reinhardts aus dem Großen Schauspielhaus fand auch S. u. R. sein Ende, wenn es auch bis 1924 und der Übernahme des Hauses durch Erik Charell und seine Groß-Revuen als reines Unterhaltungskabarett ein kümmerliches Dasein fristete. Auch dem Versuch von F. Markiewicz, 1945 ein verkleinertes S. u. R. zu etablieren, war kein dauernder Erfolg beschieden.

Budzinski, K.: Pfeffer ins Getriebe. München 1982; Hösch, R.: Kabarett von gestern und heute. 2 Bde. Berlin 1967–72; Kühn, V.: Das Kabarett der frühen Jahre. Berlin 1984; PEM (d. i. P. E. Marcus): Heimweh nach dem Kurfürstendamm. Berlin 1952; Reinhardt, M.: Schall und Rauch. Berlin/Leipzig 1901; Segel, H. B.: Turn-of-the-Century Cabaret. New York 1987; Sprengel, P. (Hg.): Schall und Rauch: Erlaubtes und Verbotenes. Berlin 1991.

Wolfgang Beck

Schattentheater / Schementheater / Silhouettentheater

Formen des →Puppentheaters, bei denen flache Figuren von unten oder der Seite hinter einer beleuchteten Leinwand geführt werden. Je nach Material und Herstellung sind dabei verschiedene Arten zu unterscheiden. Die Figuren des Schattentheaters werden aus lichtundurchlässigem Material (vor allem Leder) gefertigt, Schemenfiguren aus transparentem Material, das Licht auch durch die Figuren scheinen läßt. Silhouetten sind in der Regel aus festem Papier oder Pappe gefertigte Scherenschnitte.

Das S. ist besonders beliebt in Asien, wo es zu höchster Perfektion entwickelt wurde. Es stammt aus dem magisch-religiösen Bereich, ist urspr. Ahnendienst. Schriftliche Quellen belegen das S. seit dem 11. Jh. In China (→Chinesisches Theater) nach der Legende im 2. Jh. v. Chr. entstanden, läßt es sich erst seit der Sung-Periode (11. Jh.) nachweisen. Zu den traditionellen Stoffen gehören buddhistische und taoistische Legenden ebenso wie Episoden der chinesischen Geschichte. Frühzeitig wohl auch schon von wandernden Schaustellern gezeigt, die aktuelle Bezüge in ihre Darstellungen einfließen ließen, spielte das S. eine wichtige Rolle im sozialen Gefüge. Für Indien (→Indisches Theater) ist es zweifelsfrei belegt erst seit dem 13. Jh., wobei die Texte zumeist auf hinduistischen Epen basieren, die auch eine wichtige Grundlage für das indonesische S. spielen, das vor allem auf Java und Bali zu finden ist. Neben den hinduistischen war das indonesische S. vor allem islamischen Einflüssen ausgesetzt, die sich auf das Repertoire und die Gestaltung der Figuren auswirkten. In Thailand wird seit dem 15. Jh. S. gezeigt, dessen Besonderheit es ist, daß auch vor dem beleuchteten Schirm gespielt wird.

Die ältesten erhaltenen Texte des S. stammen aus Ägypten, wo es seit dem 13. Jh. nachgewiesen ist. Relativ stabile Traditionslinien führen bis ins 19. Jh., als das alte S. ausstarb, später unter türk. Einfluß noch einmal wiederbelebt wurde, ohne sich auf Dauer durchsetzen zu können. Im Gegensatz zu den traditionell religiös bestimmten ostasiat. Formen hat das türk. S. (→Karagöz) weltliche, komische Inhalte; seit dem 16. Jh. war es im ganzen türk. Reich bekannt. In Europa ist das S. seit dem 17. Jh. bekannt, konnte sich aber gegenüber den anderen Formen des Puppenspiels nie durchsetzen. Im ersten Kabarett, dem 1881 gegr. →«Chat Noir», wurde S. erfolgreich aufgeführt und des öfteren nachgeahmt. Der aus dem George-Kreis stammende Alexander von Bernus versuchte in den von ihm initiierten «Schwabinger Schattenspielen» (1906–09) vergeblich die Durchsetzung des S. Seit 1919 experimentierte die Filmemacherin Lotte Reiniger mit Scherenschnitten, die sie zur Herstellung ganzer Silhouettenfilme benutzte, die sie zu einer Pionierin des modernen Puppenfilms werden ließen (→Karagiozis, →Yingxi).

Amtmann, P. (Hg.): Puppen, Schatten, Masken. München 1986; Batchelder, M.:
The Puppet-Theatre-Handbook. London 1948; Blackham, O.: Shadow Puppets.
London 1960; Bobber, H. L. u. a.: Türkisches Schattentheater Karagöz. Frank-
furt/M. 1983; Böhmer, G.: Puppentheater. München 1969; Böhmer, G./Selt-
mann, F./Wilhelm, C.: Asiatische Schattenspiele. Berlin 1969; Boehn, M. v.:
Puppen und Puppenspiele. München 1929; Bordat, D./Boucrot, F.: Les
Théâtres d'ombres. Paris 1956; Bührmann, M.: Das farbige Schattenspiel. Bern
1955; Damianakos, S. (ed.): Théâtres d'ombres. Charleville 1986; Goslings,
B. M.: De wajang op Java en Bali. Amsterdam 1939; Hirth, F.: Das Schattenspiel
der Chinesen. Budapest 1900; Hoenerbach, W.: Das nordafrikanische Schatten-
theater. Mainz 1959; Höpfner, G.: Südostasiatische Schattenspiele. Berlin 1967;
Horsten, E.: Beiträge zur Erforschung des Javanischen Schattentheaters. Diss.
Wien 1963; Jacob, G.: Geschichte des Schattentheaters. Hannover 1925; ders. und
H. Jensen: Das chinesische Schattentheater. Stuttgart 1933; dies. und H. Losch:
Das indische Schattentheater. Stuttgart 1931; Jeanne, P.: Bibliographie des ma-
rionnettes. Paris 1926; Kaminski, G./Unterrieder, E.: Der Zauber des bunten
Schattens. Chinesisches Schattenspiel einst und jetzt. Klagenfurt 1988; Keeler,
W.: Javanese Shadow Plays, Javanese Selves. Princeton 1987; Meilink, W.: Bi-
bliografie van het Poppenspel. Amsterdam 1965; Mellema, R. L.: Wayang pup-
pets. Amsterdam 1954; Nold, W. (Hg.): Handbuch Puppenspiel, Figurentheater.
Frankfurt/M. 1979; Philpott, A.: Dictionary of Puppetry. London 1969; Raab,
A.: Das europäische Schattenspiel. Donauwörth 1970; Ransome, G. G.: Puppets
and Shadows. A Bibliography. Boston 1931; Rosenberg, K.: Die traditionellen
Theaterformen Thailands von den Anfängen bis in die Regierungszeit Rama's VI.
Diss. Hamburg 1970; Schneider, I.: Puppen- und Schattenspiel in der Romantik.
Diss. Wien 1920; Schreiner, K.: Puppen & Theater. Köln 1980; Scott-Kemball, J.:
Javanese Shadow Puppets. London 1970; Siyavuşgil, S. E.: Karagöz. Istanbul
1961; Spies, O.: Türkisches Puppentheater. Emsdetten 1959; Wilpert, C. B.:
Schattentheater. Hamburg ^{2}1974.

Wolfgang Beck

Die Schaubude

Am 15. 8. 1945 fand die ‹Test›-Premiere des Kabaretts S. in den damals
als amerik. Soldatenkino dienenden Münchner Kammerspielen statt.
Hausautor war Erich Kästner, als Conférenciers fungierten Hellmuth
Krüger und Walther Kiaulehn, zu den Schauspielern gehörten später so
bekannte Namen wie Ursula Herking, Karl Schönböck, Karl John, Bum
Krüger und Siegfried Lowitz. Am 21. 4. 1946 fand die Premiere im endgültigen Domizil statt – mit rund 700 Plätzen ein für Kabaretts ungewöhnlich großer Raum. Bei der in der unmittelbaren Nachkriegszeit verbreiteten Hoffnung auf demokratische Erneuerung sollte auch das Kabarett zur
moralischen Aufarbeitung der faschistischen Vergangenheit beitragen.
So waren vor allem zeitbezogene Texte in Chansons, Szenen und Parodien für die literarisch niveauvollen Programme der S. bestimmend. Die

Währungsreform 1948 in den Westzonen brachte die S. wie viele andere Kabaretts in finanzielle Schwierigkeiten, deren Folgen sie Anfang 1949 zum Aufgeben zwangen.

Budzinski, K.: Pfeffer ins Getriebe. München 1982; ders.: Wer lacht denn da? Braunschweig 1989; Greul, H.: Bretter, die die Zeit bedeuten. Köln/Berlin 1967 (erw. Ausg., 2 Bde. München 1971); Otto, R./Rösler, W.: Kabarettgeschichte. Berlin 1981; Zivier, G./Kotschenreuther, H./Ludwig, V.: Kabarett mit K. Berlin 1974.

Wolfgang Beck

Schaubühne am Lehniner Platz / Schaubühne am Halleschen Ufer

Gegründet 1962 in Berlin unter dem Namen Schaubühne am Halleschen Ufer von Leni Langenscheidt, Waltraud Mau, Jürgen Schitthelm, Klaus Weiffenbach. Eröffnungsinszenierung: *Das Testament des Hundes oder Die Geschichte der Barmherzigen* von Ariano Suassuna (Regie: Konrad Swinarski, 1929–75). – Privattheater, bis 1970 ohne festes Ensemble; seit August 1970 Ensembletheater unter künstlerischer Leitung von Peter Stein (*1937), Geschäftsführer: Schitthelm und Weiffenbach. – Peter Stein gab bereits mit seiner ersten Inszenierung – *Gerettet* von Edward Bond (München, 1967) – «das überraschendste Debüt eines Regisseurs am dt. Theater nach dem Krieg» (Iden, S. 17). Von Fritz Kortner (1892–1970), bei dem er an den Münchner Kammerspielen assistiert hatte, übernahm Stein die Genauigkeit und Differenziertheit des Spiels, das Interesse an Sprache als Ansatzpunkt jeder Inszenierung. Diese Arbeitsweise prägte deutlich die Aufführung des Goetheschen *Tasso* (Bremen, 1969). Stein verschärfte durch raffiniert übersteigerte Ästhetik den im Stück angelegten Widerspruch zwischen Macht und Kunst, stellte Parallelen zur Gegenwart durch immanente Kritik am Kunstwerk her: Die Abhängigkeit des Künstlers – Tasso als unfreiwilliger «Emotionalclown» (Stein) in Diensten der höfischen Gesellschaft – handelte ebenso von der Abhängigkeit ihrer Produzenten. Aus den Widersprüchen zwischen Zwängen des Stadttheaters und Arbeitswünschen der Gruppe um Peter Stein, die sich in München formiert (1967: Bonds *Gerettet*, 1968: Brechts *Im Dickicht der Städte, Vietnam-Diskurs* von P. Weiss), über das Bremer Theater (1968: Schillers *Kabale und Liebe*, 1969: Goethes *Tasso*) und Zürcher Schauspielhaus (1969: Bonds *Early Morning*, O'Caseys *Kikeriki*, 1970: Middleton & Rowleys *Changeling*) vergrößert und gefestigt hatte, zog man die Konsequenz und suchte nach einem eigenen Ort kontinuierlicher Zusammenarbeit. Pläne für ein Mitbestimmung erprobendes

824 Schaubühne am Lehniner Platz / Schaubühne am Halleschen Ufer _____

Theatermodell in Frankfurt zerschlugen sich. In dieser Situation nahmen Stein und seine Schauspieler das Angebot des Berliner Senats an, die Schaubühne am Halleschen Ufer zum 1. August 1970 zu beziehen. Subventioniert mit einem Etat von lediglich 1,8 Mill. Mark, sollte ein Kollektiv-Theater betrieben werden, über dessen Spielplan-, Besetzungs-, Engagements- und Gagenfragen in der Vollversammlung aller am Theater Beschäftigten entschieden wurde. Die künstlerische Leitung oblag einem Direktorium, dem zunächst die beiden Geschäftsführer Schitthelm und Weiffenbach (nicht abwählbar), die Regisseure Peter Stein und Claus Peymann sowie der Dramaturg Dieter Sturm angehörten. – Als Konsequenz aus den Politisierungsprozessen der 60er Jahre wirkte die Gründung der S. auf andere Theater jedoch nicht durch Neuerungen im institutionellen Bereich, sondern durch den beispielhaften Maßstab ihrer Inszenierungsarbeit: längere, umfassende Informations- und Diskussionsvorarbeiten des ganzen Ensembles; genaue Aufzeichnung und damit bessere Überprüfbarkeit der Probenprozesse; ständige Infragestellung der eigenen Methoden und Ziele. Daß die S. diese Techniken ausbildete und prägte, ist vor allem dem Einfluß der Dramaturgen Dieter Sturm und (vorübergehend) Botho Strauß zuzuschreiben. – Thematisch an kollektiven Arbeitsformen anknüpfend, eröffnete die S. mit Brechts *Die Mutter* (Titelrolle: Therese Giehse) unter Regie von P. Stein. In den folgenden Jahren entwickelte sich die S. zu einer international führenden Bühne der zeitgenössischen Theaterkunst und trug zur Erkundung neuer, geistiger Theaterräume und Spielformen bei. Wesentlichen Anteil daran hatten die Inszenierungen Peter Steins, von denen richtungweisende Impulse auf die übrige Theaterlandschaft ausgingen (u. a. 1971: *Peer Gynt*; 1972: *Prinz Fr. v. Homburg, Fegefeuer in Ingolstadt*; 1974: *Sommergäste*; 1976: *Shakespeares Memory*; 1978: *Trilogie des Wiedersehens, Groß und klein*; 1980: *Orestie*; 1984: *Drei Schwestern, Der Park*); daneben die mit verletzlicher Phantasie ausgestatteten, düsteren Visionen seines Antipoden Klaus Michael Grüber (1972: *Geschichten aus dem Wiener Wald*; 1974: *Die Bakchen*; 1975: *Empedokles*; 1977: *Winterreise*; 1982: *Hamlet*; 1984: *An der großen Straße*; 1985: *König Lear*) und – in jüngerer Zeit – die Arbeiten Luc Bondys (1976: *Die Wupper*; 1977: *Man spielt nicht mit der Liebe*; 1982: *Kalldewey, Farce*; 1985: *Triumph der Liebe*). Die S. ist so vor allem das Ergebnis der dort arbeitenden Regisseure, gestärkt durch die Dramaturgie, doch mehr noch ist sie das Ergebnis der Arbeit einer Gruppe von Schauspielern, die in kritischer Auseinandersetzung die an sie herangetragenen (theoretischen wie praktischen) Ansprüche erfüllen. Die Überprüfung der Möglichkeiten von Theater und seiner spezifischen Mittel blieb neben dem Zweifel an gesellschaftlichen Erneuerungsprozessen die Grundlage der Inszenierungsarbeit. Theater wird in diesem Sinne nicht verstanden als Widerspruch, der sich gegen die Gesellschaft richtet, sondern Widerspruch als Moment, das dem Theater strukturell zugehört. Es ist die Leistung der S., diesen Gedanken in unterschiedlichen Stoffen herausgearbeitet und neu formuliert zu haben. – Im September 1981 erfolgte der Umzug des Theaters in den Mendelssohn-Bau am Kurfürstendamm: ehemals ein Groß-Kino, nun ein unendlich variabler, nach Bedarf in drei Säle unterteilbarer Riesenbau ohne feste Raum- und Sitzanordnung. Im August 1985 Wechsel der bisherigen künstlerischen Leitung: An die Stelle Peter Steins als zentraler Bestimmungs- und Integrationsfigur traten Luc Bondy (bis 1988), Christoph Leimbacher und Dieter Sturm; dazu ab 1988 Jürgen Gosch, ab 1989 Wolfgang Wiens und ab 1992 Andrea Breth.

Canaris, V. (Hg.): B. Brecht. Regiebuch der S.-Inszenierungen. Frankfurt/M. 1971; ders. (Hg.): Goethe u. a.: T. Tasso. Regiebuch der Bremer Inszenierung. Frankfurt/M. 1970; Fiebach, J./Schramm, H. (Hg.): Schaubühne am Halleschen Ufer. In: Kreativität und Dialog. Theaterversuche der 70er Jahre in Westeuropa. Berlin 1983, S. 147–267; Iden, P.: Die Schaubühne am Halleschen Ufer 1970–1979. München/Wien 1979; Patterson, M.: Peter Stein. Germany's leading theatre director. London 1980; Sandmeyer, P.: Voraussetzungen und Möglichkeiten kollektiven Berufstheaters in Deutschland. Diss. Berlin 1973; Schaubühne am Halleschen Ufer (Hg.): Peer Gynt. Ein Schauspiel aus dem 19. Jh. Dok. Berlin 1971.

Monika Sandhack/Red.

Schauspiel

1. Aufführung von Theaterstücken vor Publikum (→Theatertheorie). 2. Im dt. Sprachgebrauch: Bezeichnung für →Drama (→Dramentheorie) als Ober- und Sammelbegriff für alle Gattungen und Untergattungen desselben. 3. Ebenfalls im dt. Sprachgebiet: Begriff für Gattung, die sich von →Tragödie und →Komödie unterscheidet, allerdings auch unterschieden zu Mittelgattungen wie →Tragikomödie oder →bürgerliches Trauerspiel, welche eher der dem ‹genus mediocre› der traditionellen Rhetorik entsprechen. Also ein ernstes, gehobenes Stück, ohne komische Einschläge, zwar zuweilen tragisch angelegt, jedoch bei Aufhebung des üblichen tragischen Ausgangs. Die großen Beispiele sind u. a. zwischen Aufklärung und Romantik zu finden, der humanistischen Komponente des dt. Idealismus entsprechend, so Lessings *Nathan der Weise* (1779), obgleich vom Autor «ein dramatisches Gedicht» genannt, Schillers *Wilhelm Tell* (UA 1804) und Kleists *Prinz Friedrich von Homburg* (1821 post.). Goethe nannte *Götz von Berlichingen* (1773), *Iphigenie auf Tauris* (1779) und *Torquato Tasso* (1789) Schauspiele – die heutigen Interpreten reagieren da anders –, *Clavigo* (1774), *Stella* (1776) und *Egmont* (UA 1796) hinge-

gen ‹Trauerspiele›, wohl aus seinem eigenen Verständnis von Tragik und Tragödie heraus. In heutiger Sicht wird z. B. *Tasso* als Tragödie verstanden. Im engl. und frz. Sprachbereich gelten Schauspiele durchgehend als Dramen oder Tragödien, läßt doch die frz. Klassik z. B. optimistische Tragödienschlüsse zu, so Corneilles *Horace* (1640), *Cinna* (1642) und *Nicomède* (1651) oder Racines *Bérénice* (1670), mit Einfluß auf Goethes *Tasso*.

Gérard Schneilin

Schauspieler

Wie kein anderer Stand hat der S. um seine Stellung in der Gesellschaft kämpfen müssen. Noch heute ist sein Sozialprestige höchst ambivalent und seine soziale Lage durch eine Reihe von Sonderregelungen bestimmt, die vor allem aus der Eigenart des Arbeitsplatzes Theater resultieren.

Arbeitsrechtliche Situation (insbes. für die BRD)
Zunächst besteht die Möglichkeit, daß sich der S. durch ein festes Engagement an ein Theater bindet, nämlich einen Spielzeitvertrag abschließt. Anders als im übrigen Arbeitsleben ist es im Theaterbereich zulässig – und auch der Regelfall –, auf Spielzeitdauer befristete Arbeitsverträge abzuschließen. Rechtliche Grundlage hierfür ist der zwischen der →Genossenschaft Deutscher Bühnenangehöriger und dem →Deutschen Bühnenverein abgeschlossene Tarifvertrag «Normalvertrag-Solo» und der Tarifvertrag über die Nichtverlängerungsmitteilung. Nach diesen tarifvertraglichen Regelungen endet ein Engagement nicht durch Kündigung (Ausnahme: Möglichkeit der fristlosen Kündigung), sondern durch Zeitablauf. Das Arbeitsverhältnis verlängert sich automatisch zu denselben Vertragsbedingungen um eine weitere Spielzeit, falls nicht zuvor eine der beiden Vertragsparteien (Theaterunternehmer oder Bühnenmitglied) innerhalb bestimmter Fristen schriftlich mitgeteilt hat, daß das Vertragsverhältnis nicht verlängert werden soll (sog. Nichtverlängerungsmitteilung). Je nach Dauer der Betriebszugehörigkeit muß zu Anfang der zu beendenden Spielzeit oder sogar zu Ende der vorangegangenen Spielzeit diese Nichtverlängerungsmitteilung erfolgen. Nach 15 Jahren Zugehörigkeit kann nur noch eine Änderung der Beschäftigung, nicht mehr jedoch eine Beendigung des Arbeitsverhältnisses erfolgen. Dieses Zeitvertragssystem ist nicht unumstritten. Die Schauspielervertretung rügt es als unsozial und nicht mehr zeitgerecht. Der BVD, unterstützt von der Rechtsprechung des Bundesarbeitsgerichts, rechtfertigt dieses System jedoch

damit, daß das Theater flexibel auf das Publikumsbedürfnis nach Abwechslung zu reagieren habe, daß es unmöglich sei, in einem Gerichtsverfahren die Gründe für die Notwendigkeit der Beendigung eines Dienstvertrages zu prüfen. Das Problem des Zeitvertrags ergibt sich aus der sozialen Überlegung, daß Arbeitsverhältnisse grundsätzlich unbefristet sein sollten und nur in den im Kündigungsschutzgesetz näher geregelten Fällen beendigt werden können. Das Kündigungsschutzgesetz soll die aus sachlichen Gründen erforderlichen Beendigungen einem gerichtlichen Kontrollverfahren unterziehen. Dieses Gesetz berücksichtigt jedoch nicht die besondere Situation eines Theaterbetriebs. Denn die Gründe, die zu einer Beendigung eines Engagements führen, sind künstlerischer Natur und nicht justitiabel. Das Grundgesetz hat in Art. 5 die Freiheit der Kunst postuliert. Mit Art. 5 GG wäre es unvereinbar, die künstlerischen Überlegungen einer gerichtlichen Kontrolle zu unterziehen. Die sozialen Ungerechtigkeiten, die zwangsläufig mit der Beendigung eines Arbeitsverhältnisses verbunden sind, müssen mit anderen Mitteln aufgefangen werden. Die Tarifvertragsparteien haben einen Anfang bereits dadurch gemacht, daß der Tarifvertrag über die Mitteilungspflicht Abfindungen für diejenigen vorsieht, die infolge eines Intendantenwechsels ausscheiden mußten und in der ersten Spielzeit nach dem Intendantenwechsel nicht in einem Arbeitsverhältnis stehen.

Das Arbeitsverhältnis eines Bühnenmitglieds unterscheidet sich noch durch weitere Besonderheiten vom allg. Arbeitsleben: Nach den tarifvertraglichen Bestimmungen hat ein Bühnenkünstler grundsätzlich einen Anspruch auf angemessene Beschäftigung. Dies bedeutet, daß er mit zwei Fachrollen (→ Kunstfach) pro Spielzeit einzusetzen ist. Der Bühnenkünstler hat für jede Ortsabwesenheit vorher einen Urlaub zu beantragen (Residenzpflicht), der allerdings nicht mit dem Anspruch auf Erholungsurlaub verrechnet werden kann. Diese Regelung bezweckt, daß bei einer etwaigen Vorstellungsänderung der Spielbetrieb sichergestellt ist. Die Vergütung der Künstler wird frei ausgehandelt. Über den Anpassungsrahmentarifvertrag für öffentlich-rechtlich getragene Bühnen folgt eine Anbindung an die Tariferhöhungen des öffentlich-rechtlichen Dienstes. Das Vergütungssystem stellt ferner auf den Status eines Theaters als Staats-, Stadt- oder Landestheaters ab. An den privaten Bühnen werden die Gagen frei ausgehandelt, hierfür haben sich bestimmte Gagensätze eingespielt. Eine weitere Besonderheit ist die Geltung der Bühnenschiedsgerichtsbarkeit für Rechtsstreitigkeiten aus dem Dienstverhältnis.

Neben den festangestellten Bühnenmitgliedern arbeiten viele Bühnenkünstler als sog. freie Künstler. Diese sind meist nur für ein best. Stück oder für einen Teil der Spielzeit vertraglich an ein Theater gebunden. Ihre Stellung läßt sich mit der eines Freiberuflichen vergleichen.

Ausbildung

Der Zugang zur Bühne und zum Engagement ist frei. Für den Abschluß eines Vertrags ist nicht der Nachweis eines Diploms, Zeugnisses o. a. erforderlich, es zählt allein das Können. Anders als beispielsweise in der ehemaligen DDR gibt es auch kein Ausbildungsmonopol des Staats. Die Ausbildung (→Schauspielschulen, →Theaterpädagogik) erfolgt über staatliche Hochschulen und Konservatorien. Daneben haben sich verschiedene private Ausbildungsstätten etabliert, die nicht unter staatlicher Aufsicht stehen. Den seit den Anfangszeiten des →Dt. Bühnenvereins und der →Genossenschaft Dt. Bühnenangehöriger angeprangerten Mißständen der fehlenden staatlichen Aufsicht im Schauspielausbildungswesen versuchen sie durch die Einrichtung der Paritätischen Prüfungskommission entgegenzuwirken.

Soziale Situation

In keinem anderen Berufszweig ist die Arbeitslosigkeit so groß wie bei den S., insbes. bei den Schauspielerinnen. Einer großen Anzahl an Interessenten stehen relativ wenig Arbeitsstellen gegenüber. Dies führt dazu, daß viele S. in verwandte Bereiche wie Synchronsprechen, Hörspiel etc. abwandern oder Nebenberufe ergreifen, die nichts mit dem Theater zu tun haben.

Für die Arbeitsvermittlung ist – wie für alle Bereiche – die Bundesanstalt für Arbeit monopolisiert. Die Vermittlung erfolgt über die zentrale Bühnen-, Fernseh- und Filmvermittlung (ZBF) der Bundesanstalt für Arbeit (Generalagentur Frankfurt/M., Agenturen in Hamburg, München, Leipzig und Berlin). Daneben gibt es einige von der Bundesanstalt für Arbeit zugelassene Privatvermittler. Die Bundesanstalt für Arbeit veranstaltet z. T. für arbeitslose Bühnenkünstler Fortbildungskurse, um ihre Vermittelbarkeit zu erhalten. Gerade für den Bühnenkünstler kommt es darauf an, sein Können durch ständige Aufführungspraxis unter Beweis zu stellen bzw. zu entwickeln. Nur durch öffentliches Auftreten kann er auch eine gewisse Bekanntheit erwerben.

Die Alters- und Krankheitsvorsorge erfolgt über die Pflichtversicherung der Bayerischen Versicherungskammer, die allerdings nur für fest engagierte Bühnenkünstler, nicht jedoch für die freien Künstler gilt. Ein weiterer gesetzlicher Beitrag für die soziale Absicherung der Künstler soll das Künstlersozialversicherungsgesetz bringen, das das Prinzip der Pflichtversicherung für alle künstlerisch Tätigen verwirklichen sollte.

Stellung in der Gesellschaft

Das Verhältnis der Gesellschaft zum S., Sänger, Tänzer, Musiker etc. war durch die Geschichte hindurch immer zwiespältig. Waren der Spitzenstar oder die Primadonna verherrlichte Idole, so war der unbekannte Bühnenkünstler immer suspekt. Bis ins 19. Jh. hinein wurde ihm sogar die Beerdigung auf dem Friedhof verweigert. Auch heute ist das Verhältnis der Öffentlichkeit zu den Bühnenkünstlern nicht ungetrübt. Die Künstlerenquete aus dem Jahre 1974 gibt hierüber Auskunft: Die Attraktivität künstlerischer Berufe insgesamt hängt von dem Bildungsgrad der Befragten ab. Das Bildungsniveau spielt ebenfalls bei dem grundsätzlichen Interesse für ‹Kunst› eine Rolle. Es ist auch im letzten Drittel des 20. Jh. immer noch – oder erst recht – suspekt, sein Leben ‹spielend› zu verbringen. Solange die Aufgabe der Kunst – dies gilt insbesondere für das Theater – nach der Einschätzung der Befragten «entspannen, unterhalten» (59% der Befragten), «Schönes, Ästhetisches herstellen» (52%), «die Umwelt menschlicher, schöner gestalten» soll (40%) und lediglich ein knappes Drittel der Befragten der Kunst auch Funktionen wie «neue Denkweisen und eigene Phantasien entwickeln helfen» zuordnen, wird sich die Stellung der Bühnenkünstler in einer an Leistung orientierten Gesellschaft nicht ändern.

Bender, W. F. (Hg.): Schauspielkunst im 18. Jh. Stuttgart 1992; Boner, G.: Schauspielkunst. Zürich/Stuttgart 1988; Brückner, G.: Die rechtliche Stellung der Bühnenkünstler in geschichtlicher Entwicklung. Diss. Greifswald 1930; Bühnen- und Musikrecht. Hg. vom Dt. Bühnenverein. Darmstadt o. J.; Crisolli, J./Randohr, L.: Das Tarifrecht im öffentlichen Dienst. Bd. 4. München 1984; Doll, H.-P. (Hg.): Mein erstes Engagement. Stuttgart 1988; Ebert, G.: Der Schauspieler. Berlin 1991; Fohrbeck, K./Wiesand, A. J.: Der Künstlerreport. Darmstadt/Neuwied 1972; Fohrbeck, K./Wiesand, A. J./Woltereck, F.: Arbeitnehmer oder Unternehmer. Zur Rechtssituation der Kulturberufe. Berlin o. J.; Geitner, U. (Hg.): Schauspielerinnen. Bielefeld 1988; Leppin, H.: Histrionen. Bonn 1992; Möhrmann, R. (Hg.): Die Schauspielerin. Frankfurt/M. 1989; Schmitt, P.: Schauspieler und Theaterbetrieb. Tübingen 1990.

Roswitha Körner/Red.

Schauspielhaus Bochum

Schauspielhaus, Kammerspiele, Theater unten. 1915 Theaterbau für Gastspiele. 1919 Ensemble, Schauspieltheater, Intendant Dr. Saladin Schmitt (1883–1951) bis 1949, formstrenges, heraldisches Stiltheater, Klassikerpflege in Zyklen (Shakespeare, Schiller, Kleist, Hebbel, Grabbe u. a.). 1944 Zerstörung des Schauspielhauses, Wiederaufbau 1953 und 1966 (Kammerspiele). 1949 bis 1972 Intendant Hans Schalla (1904–83), temporeiches, brillantes Regietheater, konsequente Ensemblepolitik, Fortsetzung der Shakespearepflege, Auslandsgastspiele. 1972 bis 1977 Intendant Peter Zadek (*1926), regionsbezogenes Volkstheater, provozierende Shakespeare-Inszenierungen, literarische Revuen, Schauspielerprojekte; Hausautor Tankred Dorst (*1925). 1979 bis 1986 Intendant Claus Peymann (*1937) innerhalb eines Leitungsteams, Vergegenwärtigung der Klassiker als Zeitgenossen, Einsatz für neue dt. Stücke, führendes Uraufführungstheater, Auslandsgastspiele. Ab 1986 Intendant Frank-Patrick Steckel (*1943).

Beil, H. (Hg.): Das Bochumer Ensemble. Ein dt. Stadttheater 1979–1986. Königstein/Ts. 1986; Bochumer Aspekte 69. Bochum 1969; Doll, P.: Hans Schalla. Bochum 1983.

Werner Schulze-Reimpell

Schauspielhaus Chemnitz

1838 eröffnet, wurde das Schauspielhaus 1862 in städtische Regie übernommen und 1863–65 umgebaut. 1906–09 Errichtung des später als Opernhaus genutzten Neuen Stadttheaters, 1925 Umbau des inzwischen ‹Alten Theaters› zum Schauspielhaus. Intendant 1912–30 Richard Tauber, der von Hans Hartmann abgelöst wurde. Karl-Heinz Stein, 1933 der «erste Intendant im neuen Reich», wurde 1934 von Walther Pottschau, dieser 1937/38 von Hermann Schaffner ersetzt. Im März 1945 wurden die Theater zerstört. Nach Kriegsende spielte das Schauspiel im ausgebauten Saal eines Altersheims. 1976 durch einen Brand weitgehend zerstört, wurde es 1980 wiedereröffnet (419 Plätze). Einen überregionalen Ruf genießt die Oper, an der unter Operndirektor Carl Riha u. a. 1962–66 Harry Kupfer tätig war. Das Opernhaus wird seit 1988 mit großem Aufwand renoviert und soll Ende 1992 neu eröffnet werden. Intendanten der Chemnitzer Theater (bzw. 1953–90 Karl-Marx-Stadt) waren Karl Görs, Oskar Kaesler, Paul-Herbert Freyer und (1961–66) Hans Dieter Mäde. Nachfolger wurde Gerhard Meyer, der 1990 in den Ruhestand trat und von Jörg Liljeberg (1990–92) abgelöst wurde. Schauspieldirektor blieb Hartwig Albiro. – Während des Bestehens der DDR Bemühungen um die DDR-Gegenwartsdramatik. So UA der Stücke *Das Lied meines Weges* (1969), *Prognose* (1971), *Van Gogh* (1973) von Alfred Matusche (1909–73), *Hinze und Kunze* (1973) und *Tinka* (1976) von Volker Braun (*1939), *Denkmal* (1983) von Jürgen Groß, *Hauptbahnhof* (1990) von Michael Peschke. Die Chemnitzer Bühnen waren für viele Künstler das ‹Sprungbrett› auf dem Weg zu den Berliner Bühnen.

Funke, Ch. u. a. (Hg.): Theater-Bilanz 1945–1969. Berlin 1971; Hundert Jahre Chemnitzer Schauspielhaus 1838–1938. Chemnitz 1938; Müller, H. (Hg.): Festschrift zur Eröffnung des Opernhauses am 26. und 27. Mai 1951 (Chemnitz 1951).

Andreas Roßmann / Wolfgang Beck

Schauspiel Köln / Oper der Stadt Köln

Schauspielhaus, Kammerspiele, Schlosserei; Oper der Stadt Köln. Anfänge mit Passionsspiel und Jesuitentheater. 1767 hölzerner Theaterbau für reisende Truppen. 1782, 1829, 1862, 1872 Neubauten, 1902 Opernhaus. 1905 bis 1911 Intendant Max Martersteig (1853–1926), 1925 bis 1926 Ernst Hardt (1876–1947). Im Krieg Theater zerstört. Neubau 1957 (Oper), 1962 (Schauspielhaus). 1947 bis 1959 Intendant Herbert Maisch (1890–1974), 1959 bis 1963 Oscar Fritz Schuh (1904–85), 1968 bis 1975 Claus Helmut Drese (*1924), Schauspieldirektor Hansgünther Heyme (*1935). 1975 Trennung von Oper und Schauspiel. Oper: Intendant Dr. Michael Hampe (*1935). Schauspiel: 1975 bis 1979 Intendant Heyme, Schauspieldirektor Roberto Ciulli (*1934), 1979 bis 1985 Intendant Jürgen Flimm (*1941), ab 1985 Dr. Klaus Pierwoß (*1942), Schauspieldirektor Horst Siede (*1936) und Alexander v. Maravić, seit 1990 Günter Krämer Intendant. Seit Ende der 60er Jahre überregional beachtetes Schauspiel.

Flimm, J.: ... Zum Augenblicke sagen, verweile doch! Köln 1985; Schmidt, J.: Elf Jahre Schauspiel Köln. Köln 1979.

Werner Schulze-Reimpell / Red.

Schauspielschulen

Die Ausbildung der Berufsschauspieler in Schulen ist erst seit der Indienstnahme des Theaters durch das Bürgertum als notwendig erachtet worden. Vorher wurden die nötigen Fähigkeiten direkt in der Spielpraxis erworben, manchmal unter der Betreuung eines erfahrenen Schauspielers oder des Prinzipals der Truppe. Die im bürgerlichen Theater geforderte Analyse, Interpretation und glaubwürdige Darstellung differenzierter Rollengebilde wirft methodische Fragen auf, die bis heute in der →Theaterpädagogik diskutiert werden. Bei dem schon 1753/54 von Konrad Ekhof (1720–78), dem bedeutendsten dt. Schauspieler der Zeit, unternommenen Versuch, innerhalb der sich ‹Schönemannsche Gesellschaft› nennenden Wandertruppe eine ‹Schauspieler-Akademie› einzurichten, war die inhaltliche Komplizierung des Darstellungsprozesses noch ein Nebenmotiv; eine größere Rolle spielte die sittliche Bildung als Voraussetzung für die Emanzipation des Berufsstandes. Auch in den ersten tatsächlich als Ausbildungsstätten konzipierten, zwischen 1770 und 1780 eingerichteten S. (Sonderklasse der Militärschule Stuttgart, Schule am Hoftheater Mannheim, Privatschule von Johann H. F. Müller in Wien) nahm die Erziehung zum ‹gesitteten Betragen› breiten Raum ein.

Mit der Neugründung von Stadttheatern, initiiert und getragen vom wirtschaftlich und politisch konsolidierten Bürgertum, wächst in der zweiten Hälfte des 19. Jh. der Bedarf an Darstellern; gleichzeitig wird der Beruf des Schauspielers, dessen Sozialprestige erheblich gestiegen ist, zum ‹Traumberuf›, auch in zahlungskräftigen Schichten. So etabliert sich die Privatausbildung – teils durch erfolgreiche, teils durch gescheiterte Schauspieler – als einträgliches Gewerbe. Eine Steigerung des Niveaus bringen die um 1905 in Zusammenhang mit renommierten Theatern gegründeten Schulen in Düsseldorf (Louise Dumont/Gustav Lindemann), Köln (Max Martersteig) und Berlin (Max Reinhardt). Im Laufe der nächsten Jahrzehnte wird ein Teil der S. verstaatlicht (meist in Verbindung mit Hochschulen für Musik). Die Ausbildung auf privater Basis und die in Verbindung mit Theatern laufen aber weiter.

Dieser Struktur entspricht auch heute noch die Schauspielerausbildung im deutschsprachigen Raum. Neben den vierzehn staatlichen und städtischen Schulen (Berlin, Bochum, Essen, Frankfurt/M., Hamburg, Hannover, München, Saarbrücken, Stuttgart, Wien, Graz, Salzburg, Zürich und Bern), von denen zwei in Verbindung mit einem Theater stehen (Otto-Falckenberg-Schule München, Westfälische Schauspielschule Bochum), gibt es ca. 25 Privatschulen und eine kaum überschaubare Zahl von Privatlehrern. Eine seit Mitte der 70er Jahre relevante Sonderform der Ausbildung ist die durch Workshops, wie sie als Bestandteil der alternativen Theaterszene mit unterschiedlicher Ausrichtung und Qualität in den Großstädten angeboten werden. Die staatlichen und städtischen Schulen, an denen hauptberufliche Theaterpädagogen wie auch Praktiker (Schauspieler und Regisseure) lehren, nehmen unter ihren Bewerbern eine strenge Auslese nach Begabung und berufsspezifischen Anlagen vor. In einem in der Regel vierjährigen Studium konfrontieren sie ihre Schüler mit einem breit gefächerten Angebot von Gruppen- und Einzelunterrichten, die sich auf die Bereiche Improvisation und Darstellung, Körper und Bewegung, Stimme und Sprechen, Theaterkunde und Dramaturgie verteilen. Teilweise werden die Lehrveranstaltungen in Form eines fächerintegrierten Projektstudiums mit dem Ziel öffentlicher Aufführungen durchgeführt. Die Ausbildung endet mit einem ‹Bühnenreifeprüfung› genannten Abschlußexamen.

In der DDR erfolgte Schauspielerausbildung nahezu ausschließlich an staatlichen Instituten mit Hochschulstatus in vierjährigem Studium: an der Hochschule für Schauspielkunst «Ernst Busch» Berlin (mit einer Filiale in Rostock), dem Fachbereich Schauspiel an der Theaterhochschule «Hans Otto» Leipzig (wo eine kombinierte Hochschul-/Theaterstudio-Ausbildung praktiziert wird; ab 1992 ist eine Fusion mit der Leipziger Musikhochschule beabsichtigt) und dem Fachbereich Schauspiel an der Hochschule für Film und Fernsehen «Konrad Wolf» in Potsdam-Babelsberg. Der künstlerisch-technische Standard der Ausbildung an den S. der DDR war hoch; zu den anerkannten Leistungen gehörten neben Praxisbezogenheit Bemühungen um Systematisierung in der Schauspielpädagogik.

Ebert, G./Penka, R. (Hg.): Schauspielen. Handbuch der Schauspielerausbildung. Berlin 1991; Lackner, P.: Schauspielerausbildung an den öffentl. Theaterschulen der Bundesrepublik Deutschland. Frankfurt/M. u. a. 1985; Schauspielerausbildung an der Theaterhochschule in Leipzig. In: Wiss. Beiträge d. Theaterhochschule Leipzig 2/1990; Waller, M. (Hg.): Handbuch für Schauspieler und Theatergruppen. München 1988; Wardetzky, D.: Über die Tätigkeit des Schauspielers. 2 Tle. Potsdam-Babelsberg 1985.

Peter Simhandl/Manfred Pauli

Schausteller

Als S. werden heute Einzelpersonen oder Familien bezeichnet, die als Mitglieder des ambulanten Gewerbes mit eigenen Schaubuden, Belustigungs-, Schieß-, Warenausspielungs- und Fahrgeschäften sowie mit mobilen Gaststätten Volksfeste aller Art bereisen. Der Begriff S., seit dem frühen 19. Jh. belegt, konnte sich erst gegen Ende des Jh. allg. durchsetzen. – S. im heutigen Sinne unterscheiden sich vom →Fahrenden Volk, dem sie historisch zuzurechnen sind, vor allem dadurch, daß sie in der Regel einen festen Wohnort haben und nur während der Geschäftssaison reisen. Wenn auch einzelne Genres der Schaustellerei älter sind, haben sich die meisten ihrer Geschäfte in heutiger Form erst im 19. Jh. entwikkelt und durchgesetzt. Ältere Formen wie Schaubuden, in denen Akrobatik, Zauberei, Abnormitäten und Kuriositäten usw. gezeigt wurden, haben an Bedeutung verloren, seit ihre Darbietungen im späten 19. Jh. in →Zirkus und →Varieté integriert wurden.

S. litten und leiden – wie alle Fahrenden – bis in die Gegenwart unter gesellschaftlicher Mißachtung und Benachteiligung. Seit Ende des 19. Jh. (1884 «Erster Congress Deutscher Schausteller») sind die S. auf nationaler und internationaler Ebene organisiert. In der BRD im am 13. 1. 1950 gegr. «Deutschen Schaustellerbund» (Mitglied der «Europäischen Schausteller-Union») und in der «Hauptvereinigung des ambulanten Gewerbes und der Schausteller in Deutschland e. V.» (Mitglied der «Union Européenne des Commerçants ambulants et Industriels Forains»). In verschiedenen Ländern besitzen die S. eigene Fachzeitschriften für ihre Belange, so in der BRD z. B. «Der Komet», der seit dem 15. 8. 1883 erscheint.

834 Schautanz

Arnold, H.: Vaganten, Komödianten, Fieranten und Briganten. Stuttgart 1958; Faber, M.: Schausteller. Bonn 1981; Garnier, J.: Forains d'hier et d'aujourd'hui. Orléans 1968; Jay, R.: Sauschlau & feuerfest. Menschen, Tiere, Sensationen des Showbusiness. Offenbach 1988; Saltarino (d. i. H. W. Otto): Fahrend Volk. Leipzig 1895 (Nachdruck Berlin 1978); Scheugl, H.: Showfreaks & Monster. Köln 1974; Schwäke, H. S.: Lang war der Weg... Die Geschichte der Gründung des DSB, aufgezeichnet nach authentischen Unterlagen. Herford o. J.

Wolfgang Beck

Schautanz

S. bezeichnet ein auf Zuschauer bezogenes Tanzereignis, unabhängig von Gattung, Form, Stil und Art der tänzerischen Darbietung. S. hat es auf allen Stufen der Kultur und an allen Orten gegeben, von magisch-mythologischen, religiösen und Brauchtumstänzen über Prozessionen und Zirkusaufzüge bis hin zu barocken Hoffestlichkeiten, vom Volks- und Gesellschaftstanz bis zur Kunstform des Balletts in allen Stilen.

Patricia Stöckemann

Schicksalstragödie

Im weiteren Sinne des Wortes wird als S. jedes Theaterstück verstanden, in dem eine übermächtige Größe (Gewalt, Kraft, Schicksal) in das menschliche Handeln eingreift und es in ihrem Sinne gegen die Intention der Protagonisten fügt. Es wird bes. auf die griech. Tragödie verwiesen (→ Antikes Theater), wo übergeordnete Mächte – Götter, daimôn, Moira – jegliches menschliche Handeln auszuschalten scheinen – in diesem Sinne später auch auf die → klassische frz. und dt. Tragödie, bes. am Falle von Schillers *Braut von Messina* (UA 1803). Diese interpretative Bezeichnung zieht die Tragödie zu einem gewissen Fatalismus hin. Sie neigt auch zur Redundanz: Wird nur der Schicksalsbegriff darin isoliert betrachtet, könnte jede Tragödie als Schicksalstragödie verstanden werden. Eine solche allzu breite Interpretation verkennt aber in der griech. Tragödie die grundlegende Doppelkausalität des Geschehens: Die Verwirklichung eines göttlichen Urteils kommt immer durch den menschlichen Willen, es geschieht nichts, ohne daß der Mensch darein verwickelt wäre. Das Fatum klammert die menschliche Verantwortung nie aus. Auch begründet es gerade im Scheitern des Menschen seine Größe, selbst im *Oedipus Rex* des Sophokles, worin oft das Modell des antiken fatalistischen Stücks gesehen wird. In der klass. Tragödie geht dann eine solche Interpretation an der dialektischen Relation zwischen transzendenter Macht und menschlicher Freiheit vorbei.

Der Begriff des Schicksalsdramas oder der S. sollte vielmehr in einem engeren Sinne gebraucht werden, wobei allerdings auf gewisse Einflüsse der antiken und klass. Tragödie sowie des →bürgerlichen Trauerspiels (George Lillo: *Fatal Curiosity*, 1737) verwiesen werden kann. Dieses Genre läßt sich dann trotz seines heterogenen Charakters historisch in die Romantik einordnen und formal auf ein einheitliches Grundschema beziehen. Historisch entstand diese Untergattung wohl in der dt. Frühromantik und entwickelte sich zeitlich und räumlich in engstem Rahmen: etwa bis 1845 im deutschsprachigen Theater. Später, so bei Ibsen (1828–1906) oder Gerhart Hauptmann (1862–1946), kann man nur noch von flüchtigen Einflüssen sprechen. Und im engl. oder frz. Theater ist zur selben Zeit von ‹drama› und ‹genre sombre› (finsteres Genre), ‹drame noir› (schwarzes Drama) oder gar →Melodrama die Rede; den Begriff S. jedoch gibt es dort nicht.

In der dt. Romantik ist der Gattungstypus vom Ursprung an geprägt. Im zweiaktigen Trauerspiel *Der Abschied* (1792) des jungen Ludwig Tieck (1773–1853) und in dessen Tragödie *Karl von Berneck* (1795) hat man es mit einer radikalen Verstofflichung und Verdinglichung, einer oft unbekannten Schicksalskraft zu tun, welche den passiven Menschen zum Spielball einer grausamen Mechanik entmächtigt. Die Verdinglichung hat schon Tieck als Wesensmerkmal dieser Art Dramatik bestätigt. Sie repräsentiert einmal das Ausgeliefertsein des Menschen an ein undurchschaubares Fatum; zum anderen ist sie das Symbol für einen psychologischen und sozialen Determinismus, der später im →Naturalismus breiter ausgeformt wird, die ‹Melancholie› des Helden mit Bezug auf Vererbung und Milieu. Jedenfalls wird in einer solchen Dramatik der Mensch zum Objekt scheinbar sinnloser Kräfte, was ihr im Unterschied zur antiken und klass. Tragödie etwas Nihilistisches verleiht.

Trotz des hintergründigen Verweises auf eine christliche Heilsordnung steht dieser objektivistische Fatalismus auch im Mittelpunkt des Stücks, für welches Gervinus die Bezeichnung S. geprägt hat: Zacharias Werners (1768–1823) →Einakter *Der 24. Februar* (1809). Familienfluch, unheilkündende Vögel und tödliches Messer verdinglichen auch hier ein Schicksal, welches in seiner chronologischen Fixierung an ein bestimmtes Datum zugleich quantitativ konkretisiert und vom Sinne her abstrahiert wird. Immerhin gibt der Bezug auf Gott dem Stück Werners eine Tiefenschicht, die seinen Epigonen gänzlich abgeht. *Der 29. Februar* (1812) und *Die Schuld* (1812) von Adolf Müllner (1774–1829), *Das Bild* (1819) und *Der Leuchtturm* (1819) Ernst von Houwalds (1778–1845), *Der Müller und sein Kind* (1835) von Ernst Raupach (1784–1852) sind solche Riesenerfolge einer Gebrauchsdramatik, welche nur noch aus Tricks, Schauer-

836 Schmidt Theater-Varieté-Kneipe / Schmidts Tivoli

effekten und verwässerten Hinweisen auf die Vorsehung bestand. Auch Karl Gutzkow (1811–78) vermag mit seinem Drama *Der 13. November* (1845) die heruntergekommene Form nicht mehr zu beleben. Sie bestand weiter in den Gespensterstücken des → Wiener Volkstheaters.

Im Grunde konnte sich das Genre nach Tieck und Werner nur auf zwei Arten behaupten: einmal da, wo sich gewisse Bauformen des verdinglichten Fatalismus mit anderen weltanschaulichen und strukturellen Elementen vermischten, die größeren Autoren eigen sind – so in Grillparzers Erstlingswerk *Die Ahnfrau* (1816), wo neben dem Geschlechterfluch und dem Dolchmotiv eine für jene österr. Dramatik charakteristische Religiosität barocker und bes. Calderónscher Prägung mitschwingt. So auch in Christian Dietrich Grabbes (1801–36) Erstling *Herzog Theodor von Gothland* (1821), wo Bauformen der S. das Trauerspiel des Weltschmerzes und der Verzweiflung nur oberflächlich tragen. Auch Otto Ludwigs (1813–65) Trauerspiel *Der Erbförster* (1853) ist vor allem ein → realistisches Drama. Die andere Art des Überlebens, die aber schon von dem Überholtsein des Genres zeugt, ist die → Parodie. *Die verhängnisvolle Gabel* (1826) August Graf von Platens (1796–1835) ist ein frühes Beispiel dafür. Parodistische Meisterstücke sind vor allem die der Wiener Volksstückschreiber; man denke an den 3. Akt von Nestroys (1801–62) Posse *Der Zerrissene* (1844), in der nicht nur Weltschmerz und Zerrissenheit, sondern die ‹ganze praktische Romantik› der Schicksals- und Schauerstücke (Beil, Eule, Gespenst, unterirdischer Gang, Falltür, Doppelgänger, Schuld etc.) verlacht sind.

Bauer, R. u. a. (Hg.): Inevitabilis vis fatorum. Der Triumph des Schicksalsdramas auf der europäischen Bühne um 1800. Bern u. a. 1990; Kraft, H.: Schicksalsdrama. Göttingen 1974; Thiergard, U.: Schicksalstragödie als Schauerliteratur. Diss. Göttingen 1957; Ziegler, Kl.: Das dt. Drama der Neuzeit. In: Stammler, W. (Hg.): Deutsche Philologie im Aufriß, II. Berlin 1966, S. 2278–2287.

Gérard Schneilin

Schmidt Theater-Varieté-Kneipe / Schmidts Tivoli

«Familie Schmidt», eine der bekanntesten freien Gruppen Hamburgs, bekannt für politisch engagiertes, tabubrechendes, grelles Schwulentheater, eröffnete 1988 ein eigenes, 250 Plätze umfassendes Theater auf der Reeperbahn: das S. T.-V.-K. Als konzeptioneller Gegenpart zur → Internationalen Kulturfabrik Kampnagel stehen hier populäre Theaterformen, → Revue, → Varieté, Travestie, poetische Kleinkunst, → Kabarett, Musikshows und Musicals auf dem Programm. Höhepunkt ist die jeweils samstags stattfindende «Schmidt-Show», die von den Protagonisten des

Hauses, Corny Littmann (alias Herr Schmidt), Ernie Reinhardt (alias Alt-Diva Lilo Wanders) und Jutta Wübbe (alias Marlene Jaschke) als anarchische Karikatur auf TV-Shows inszeniert wird. Das Theater erhält keine staatlichen Zuschüsse und finanziert sich allein über Gastronomie und Spielbetrieb. 1991 eröffnete die Gruppe ebenfalls auf der Reeperbahn ein weiteres Haus, «Schmidts Tivoli», einen prunkvoll restaurierten, denkmalgeschützten Gründerzeitpalast, in dem bei gleichem Programmschwerpunkt vor größerem Publikum (700 Plätze) aufwendigere Produktionen gezeigt werden können.

Annette Waldmann

Die Schmiere

Die sich selbst provozierend als «das schlechteste Theater der Welt» bezeichnende S. ist in vielfacher Hinsicht eines der ungewöhnlichsten Kabaretts der Bundesrepublik. Gründer und Spiritus rector der S. ist Rudolf Rolfs, der sich nach fast vier Jahrzehnten im Juni 1989 zurückzog. In Frankfurt/Main gegr. und am 9. 9. 1950 in Bad Vilbel mit dem Programm «Für Menschen und Rindvieh» eröffnet, hat die S. bis heute die wohl niedrigsten Eintrittspreise eines institutionalisierten Kabaretts – bemerkenswert auch deshalb, weil staatliche Subventionen programmatisch abgelehnt werden. Es ist das einzige Kabarett der BRD, das ein festes Repertoire hat und mehrere Programme abwechselnd spielt, von denen einige seit Jahrzehnten – mit aktuellen Einschüben – auf dem Spielplan stehen. So wurde *Die tote Ratte in der Limonadenflasche* seit dem 1. 5. 1958 über 600mal aufgeführt, *Sie sind ein Ferkel, Exzellenz* sogar weit über 700mal seit 1965. Seit der Gründung wurden rund 50 Programme aufgeführt; als neuestes: *Heute günstig: Bratwurst mit Laufmasche.*

Budzinski, K.: Das Kabarett. 100 Jahre literarische Zeitkritik – gesprochen – gesungen – gespielt. Düsseldorf 1985; ders.: Pfeffer ins Getriebe. München 1982; ders.: Die öffentlichen Spaßmacher. München 1966; ders.: Wer lacht denn da? Braunschweig 1989; Greul, H.: Bretter, die die Zeit bedeuten. Köln/Berlin 1967 (erw. Ausg., 2 Bde. München 1971); Rolfs, R.: Die Schmiere, das schlechteste Theater der Welt. 9 Bde. Frankfurt/M. 1955–63; ders.: Das Abenteuer «Schmiere». Waldacker 1985.

Wolfgang Beck

Schminke

Mittel zum Färben der Haut, Lippen, Augenbrauen und Wimpern, neben Sprache, →Gestik und →Ausstattung ein Element der Schauspielkunst (→Bühnenkostüm). Die S. soll zunächst einem durch die Bühnenbeleuchtung verursachten Verblassen des Teints entgegenwirken, führt allerdings dabei durch Verdeckung etwaiger ‹Schönheitsfehler› oder Alterserscheinungen im Gesicht zu einer Vereinheitlichung der Physiognomie. Dieser Effekt kann bewußt angestrebt werden, um im Gegensatz zum Starprinzip bzw. zum individuellen Helden den Eindruck der anonymen Masse und des kollektiven Helden auf der Bühne zu erwecken. Diese Entwicklung im Gebrauch der Schminke geht mit einer Gesamtentwicklung der Theater- und Schauspielerauffassung im 20. Jh. einher. War früher der physische Typ des Schauspielers entscheidend für dessen Fixierung auf ein bestimmtes →Rollenfach – was im →Boulevardtheater noch weitgehend der Fall ist –, so wird heute dem Temperament des Schauspielers größerer Wert beigemessen, wobei die S. eine Anpassung der Physiognomie an die individualisierte Rolle erlaubt. Rolle und Funktion der S. sind dann von denen der →Maske kaum noch unterscheidbar, v. a. da, wo die bewußt dick aufgetragene, übertreibende S. das Gesicht in eine lebende, quasi typisierte Maske verwandelt (etwa in Inszenierungsarten wie der des Kollektivs «Rote Rübe» in München oder beim →Clown im →Zirkus). Gebraucht wird heute oft auch die Kombination Schminke/Maske.

Carson, R.: Stage Make-up. New York 1961; Pirchan, E.: Maskemachen und Schminke. Wien 1951; Vitaly, G.: Maquillage de théâtre. Paris 1955.

Bernard Poloni

School of American Ballet (New York)

Die S. o. A. B. bildet seit 1934 den Tänzernachwuchs des →New York City Ballet heran. Als Lincoln Kirstein (* 1907) George Balanchine (1904–83) 1934 aus Frankreich nach Amerika holt, um mit ihm in Hartford/Connecticut eine Tanzausbildungsstätte, die S. o. A. B., zu gründen, war er von der Idee besessen, daß Balanchine einen spezifisch amerikanischen Ballettstil werde kreieren können. Der russ. Tänzer und Choreograph G. Balanchine realisiert diesen berechtigten Wunsch des künstlerisch autonom werdenden amerikanischen Kontinents. Doch er drängt aus Hartford in die Metropole der USA. 1935 zieht die Schule von Hartford nach New York und stellt sich im gleichen Jahr mit ihrer Kompanie vor, dem American Ballet. 1970 erhält die S. o. A. B. eine ihr adäquate

Wirkungsstätte im Lincoln Center. Kinder-, Anfänger- und Fortgeschrittenenklassen werden dank der pädagogischen Erfahrung Balanchines nach eigenständig von ihm ausgearbeiteten Lehrplänen unterrichtet, in die musikalische Ausbildungsfächer integriert worden sind.

Niehaus, M.: Ballettfaszination. München 1978; Schmidt-Garre, H.: Ballett. Vom Sonnenkönig bis Balanchine. Hannover 1966.

Patricia Stöckemann

Schuldrama

Das S. nutzt die pädagogischen Möglichkeiten des Rollenspiels als Methode sprachlichen und sozialen Lernens. Der innerhalb eines bestimmten schulischen Erziehungssystems zweckbedingte Charakter dieser der Gebrauchs- und Gelegenheitsliteratur zuzuordnenden Textsorte sowie der doppelte Produktions- (Autor/Lehrer – Darsteller/Schüler) und der doppelte Rezeptionsvorgang (Darsteller/Schüler – Eltern bzw. Schulherren) sind konstitutiv für die Schuldramatik. Die interne Funktion (praktische rhetorische Übung und Belehrung im inhaltlichen Sinne) wird im Rahmen der ‹Lust›- und ‹Nutz›-Perspektive ergänzt durch die externe Funktion der Selbstdarstellung gegenüber Elternschaft und Schulträger.

Das als Frucht des Humanismus in der Nachahmung von Terenz und Plautus entstandene S. zehrt von der städtischen Theaterfreudigkeit an den aus dem Mittelalter überkommenen →Fastnachts- und geistlichen Spielen. Vom Humanistendrama (→Humanismus/Drama und Theater des Humanismus) übernahm es die feste textliche Grundlage, die auf das Wort konzentrierte Aufführungspraxis mit der sich allmählich durchsetzenden Struktur Prolog, Argumentum, in Akte und Szenen eingeteilter Text und Epilog sowie die ‹Terenzbühne› mit ihrer Rückwand aus einzelnen Zellen für die verschiedenen dargestellten Personen. Als fester, den Unterricht ergänzender Bestandteil, als Übung in der lat. Konversation und im freien und sicheren öffentlichen Auftreten und sozialen Verhalten, als den allg. Studieneifer fördernedes Mittel der moralischen Belehrung sowie als Leistungsnachweis der Schule gegenüber Eltern und Schulbehörde wurde das S. in den Ordnungen der Lateinschulen fixiert. In diesem Sinne von Luther und Melanchthon befürwortet und gefördert, wurde es im Zeitalter der konfessionellen Auseinandersetzungen besonders im Stammland der Reformation zur Waffe in der religiösen Polemik, zum Mittel der Verkündigung und der Seelsorge im Dienste der ‹propaganda fides› und zu einem Element des Kommunikations- und Handlungsfeldes der ‹reformatorischen Öffentlichkeit›. Die durch die Konfessionalisierung des S. bewirkte Kanalisierung der dem weltanschaulichen

840 Schuldrama

Zweck untergeordneten künstlerischen Gestaltung half bei der Überwindung antiker Vorbilder und förderte eine aktualisierende Öffnung für zeitgenössische Konflikte, die über die moralisierende Intention hinausging und für ein erweitertes Publikum zugeschnitten war. So wurde die mit einem Quasi-Monopol ausgestattete, den Schulherren unterstehende Schulbühne als dem direkten kirchlichen Zugriff entglittenes Laientheater zum determinierenden Element der Sonderentwicklung des dt. Theaters des 16. Jh. Im Mutterland der Reformation bestimmten die ständige Nähe der Andersgläubigen und die zentrale Stellung der Schule mit der Rhetorik als instrumenteller Disziplin den schöpferischen Vorgang.

Bei aller Vielfalt der dramatischen Strukturen lassen sich die S. auf die Grundmodelle der →Moralität und des allegorischen Spiels (z. B. ‹Jedermannsspiele›) des protestantischen Bibeldramas zurückführen. Der Jedermann-Stoff wurde von Christian Ischyrius reformationsfeindlich im *Homulus* (1536), von Georg Macropedius (1475–1558) im *Hecastus* (1539), von Thomas Naogeorg (um 1500–63) als Illustration der lutherischen Rechtfertigungslehre gegen die Werkgerechtigkeit im *Mercator* (1540) behandelt. Besondere Fülle bietet, mit zuweilen ungeklärtem Verhältnis des Autorenabhängigkeitsverhältnisses, das Bibeldrama als Erbe des mittelalterlichen geistlichen Spiels, mit Präfigurativcharakter der zur Heilsgeschichte parallelen Handlungen und der vertrauten Stoffe wegen auch dem lateinunkundigen Publikum zugänglich. Es gab viele Stoffe aus dem Alten Testament. Aus dem Neuen Testament – Luther riet von Passionsdarstellungen ab, die mehr das Mitleid als den Glauben förderten – werden häufig die Gleichnisse unter Einbezug alltäglicher Situationen dargestellt. Oft nachgeahmtes Vorbild ist das unpolemische S. *Acolastus* (1529) des Niederländers Gulielmus Gnaphäus (1493–1568). Der ebenfalls von Macropedius (*Azotus*, 1510) und Burkard Waldis (um 1490–1556: *De parabell vam verlorn Szohn*, 1527) behandelte Stoff bot die sinnfälligste Darstellung der evangelischen Lehre von der Rechtfertigung. Weltliche Stoffe aus Sage und Geschichte des Altertums werden zuweilen christlich überformt und zeitgeschichtliches Geschehen z. T. stark polemisch geprägt (so Johannes Agricola, 1492–1566: *Tragedia Johannis Hus*, 1537). In Naogeorgs Kampfdrama (in S.-Form) gegen den Papst als Antichrist *Pammachius* (1538, vier dt. Übersetzungen), einer Art zeitgeschichtlichem Mysterium, verlebendigen spannungsvolle dramatische Abläufe Lehrhaftigkeit und Polemik sowie die ursprünglich personifizierten Abstrakta als Träger der Handlung. In Stücken mit Bezug auf Schul- und Studentenleben und schwankartigen Motiven (Macropedius: *Rebelles*, 1535, *Petriscus*, 1536; Christoph Stymmelius, 1525–88: *Studentes*, 1549) wird die lat. Humanistentradition Johann Reuchlins (1455–1522: *Henno*, 1497) und Jakob Wimphelings (1450–1528: *Stylpho*, 1480) wieder aufgegriffen.

Schuldrama 841

Eine besondere Ausprägung und Sonderstellung erfuhr das lat. S. in Straßburg, ein Verdienst des Rektors des ev. Gymnasiums, des humanistischen Pädagogen Johannes Sturm, der den Vorrang antiker Dramen und Stoffe im Repertoire gegen den Vorwurf, zuwenig Bibeldramen aufzuführen, verteidigte (1565) und den humanistischen Geist stärker als den protestantischen betonte. Gereimte dt. Inhaltsangaben, dt. Argumente, zuweilen Übersetzungen (z. B. von Wolfhart Spangenberg) für die lateinunkundigen Zuschauer, deren Andrang (schätzungsweise bis zu 2000) die Verlegung der Aufführungen in den Gymnasiumshof erforderte, ihre Fortführung nach der Erhebung der Schule zur Akademie (Akademietheater) und das Weiterleben der Sturmschen Tradition unter Caspar Brülow (1585–1627) sind charakteristisch für diese Straßburger Ausprägung einer Alternative zur Berufsdramatik.

Die Schule als Aufführungsort bedingt die einfache Ausstattung (Straßburg ist hier Ausnahme), die allmähliche Beschränkung der Aufführungsdauer, die Ausmerzung des moralisch allzu Anstößigen und die komischen Einschübe aus Schul- und Studentenleben. Das Deklamatorische, nicht die schauspielerische Leistung, prägt die Darstellungsart.

Der allmähliche Übergang zum Deutschen (als Zwischenformen: dt. Prolog, dt. Inhaltsangabe vor jedem Akt, dt. Zwischenspiel im lat. Text, Übersetzung lat. Stücke) erfolgte besonders beim Bibeldrama (Greff, 1534), ließ zwar den Zweck der Übung im Lateinischen entfallen, änderte jedoch zunächst den Grundcharakter des S. nicht (Luther und Melanchthon als ‹Praeceptor Germaniae› blieben Kronzeugen). In etlichen Schulordnungen blieb das dt. S. verpönt. Zuweilen wurde, nach der lat. Schulaufführung, das Stück dt. auf dem Rathaus oder dem Markt wiederholt. Mit der Volkssprache drangen aber volkstümliche Elemente ins S., Grenzen zum Bürgerspiel wurden verwischt, Handwerksgesellen traten neben Schülern auf: Das zur Mischgattung gewordene S. (z. B. Frischlins *Frau Wendelgart*, 1579: Synthese aus lat. S. und dt. Volksschauspiel mit Stoff aus der heimatlichen Geschichte) verlor allmählich die durch den pädagogischen Zweck verliehene Stileinheit. Das dt. S. breitete sich von Sachsen aus mit Paul Rebhuhn (1505–46): *Ein Geistlich spiel von der Gotfurchtigen vnd keuschen Frawen Susannen* (1535), *Ein Hochzeitspil auff die Hochzeit zu Cana* (1538) als klassischem Vertreter der protestantischen S. (metrische Neuerungen, ausgeprägter humanistischer Formwille mit Streben nach der geschlossenen Form der Antike). In Zusammenhang mit dem Bibeldrama steht eine Weiterentwicklung der →Terenzbühne mit bespielbaren Innenräumen auf der Hinterbühne. Landschaftliche Varianten des S. sind z. T. auf Substratunterschiede in der Tradition zurückzuführen.

Das S. lebte in der Zeit der Gegenreformation weiter, indem es sich – mit abgeschwächter konfessioneller Akzentuierung: Das protestantische

842 Schuldrama

S. wird zum Drama an protestantischen Schulen – dem Bildungsauftrag der protestantischen Gymnasien anpaßte, redegewandte, wohlerzogene, ‹politische› junge Leute für Beamtenlaufbahnen heranzuziehen. Der Einschnitt des 30jährigen Krieges, die Konkurrenz der engl. Berufskomödianten und der dt. Wandertruppen, die Operneinflüsse, Kulissenbühne und Theatermaschinerie (z. B. in Zittau und Breslau), die Entfaltung des →Jesuitentheaters, das Verdrängen der Bibeldramen durch →Haupt- und Staatsaktionen oder barocke zeitgeschichtliche Allegorien verändern Bedeutung, Stil, Inhalt und Existenzbedingung des S. Die als ‹schlesische Kunstdramen› eingestuften Werke von Gryphius und Lohenstein wurden z. T. für die Breslauer Schulbühnen geschrieben, wo die Tradition des S. mit Johann Christian Hallmann (1645–1706) und Elias Major (1588–1669) weiterlebte. In Leipzig verbanden sich S. und Bandenstück. Johann Sebastian Mitternacht (1613–79) und Christian Zeidler (1643–1707) stellten das S. in den Dienst der Absolutismuskritik.

Das S. erlebte eine bedeutsame Nachblüte mit dem Zittauer Rektor und Lohenstein-Gegner Christian Weise (1642–1708), der jährlich für den Schulgebrauch ein Lustspiel, ein biblisches und ein historisches Stück verfaßte (55 Stücke, z. B. *Trauerspiel von dem neapolitanischen Hauptrebellen Masaniello*, 1682). Als Vertreter des frühaufklärerischen Bildungsideals strebte er für seine Zöglinge den «Weg zur galanten Manier in unserer dt. Sprache», die «freimütige und höfliche» Rede, «politische» Erziehung, praktische Gelehrsamkeit und Urteilsfähigkeit an. Mit seiner zum Realistischen tendierenden Darstellungsweise, der Benutzung der lustigen Figur als kritischem Kommentator und seiner Offenheit für die Anregungen anderer Genres durchbrach er ständische Eingrenzung und Vorschriften über Darsteller-, Akten- und Szenenzahl sowie sprachliche Normen und lieferte dadurch einen Ansatzpunkt für das bürgerliche Drama. Das von der pietistisch geprägten Pädagogik inspirierte Verbot von Schulaufführungen Anfang des 18. Jh. in Preußen, Sachsen und anderen Territorien traf eine Gattung, die weitgehend ihren Platz neben Wanderbühne, Hoftheater und lokaler berufsständischer Theaterpflege eingebüßt hatte. Vertreter des S. in Frankreich sind Muret und Beza (*Abraham sacrifiant*, Genf 1550), in Schottland Buchanan (*Jephte*, 1557).

Creizenach, W.: Geschichte des neueren Dramas. 2 Bde. Halle 1918–23; Kaiser, M: Mitternacht–Zeidler–Weise. Das protestantische Schultheater nach 1648 im Kampf gegen höfische Kultur und absolutistisches Regiment. Göttingen 1972; Kaulfuß-Diesch, C.: Schuldrama. In: RL der dt. Literaturgeschichte. Hg. von P. Merker/W. Stammler. III. Bd. Berlin 1928/29, S. 194–201; Maaßen, J.: Drama und Theater der Humanistenschulen in Deutschland. Augsburg 1929; Michael, W. F.: Frühformen der dt. Bühne. Berlin 1963; Riesel, E.: Das neulat. Drama der Protestanten in Deutschland vom Augsburger Religionsfrieden bis zum Dreißigjährigen Krieg. Diss. Wien 1929; Schmidt, E.: Die Bühnenverhältnisse des dt.

Schuldramas und seiner volkstümlichen Ableger im 16. Jh. Berlin 1903; Stammler, W.: Von der Mystik zum Barock 1400–1600. Stuttgart ²1950; Tarot, R.: Schuldrama und Jesuitentheater. In: Handbuch des dt. Dramas. Hg. von W. Hinck. Düsseldorf 1980, S. 35–47; Zeller, K.: Pädagogik und Drama. Untersuchungen zur Schulcomödie Christian Weises. Tübingen 1980.

Frédéric Hartweg

Schulspiel

S. heißt die Arbeit mit Formen von Spiel und Theater innerhalb von Schulfächern, in eigenen S.-Stunden, in Arbeitsgemeinschaften und Projektgruppen, in vortherapeutischen Spielgruppen. Dabei geht es sowohl um die Vermittlung von Sachinhalten wie um Selbst-, Fremd- und Gruppenerfahrung (also um soziales Lernen oder Verhaltenslernen) und immer um die eigene Betroffenheit des Spielers, der innerhalb des Spiels selbsttätig und selbstbestimmt handelt (handeln darf). S. als umfassende Bezeichnung schließt →Schultheater ein.

Hans-Wolfgang Nickel

Schultheater

Unter S. läßt sich seit dem Mittelalter die Entwicklung, Erprobung, Einstudierung und Aufführung dramatischer Werke mit Schülern und durch Schüler unter Anleitung von Lehrern verstehen; es schließt Formen des Kabaretts, des Pantomimen-, Figuren-, Maskentheaters, auch der Schuloper, des Tanzes, der Rezitation, des Sprechchors, schließlich des Hörspiels, Films und Videofilms ein, soweit sich die Institution Schule ihrer annimmt. In der Gegenwart ist das S. nur ein Teil des umfassenden Lernbereichs ‹Schulspiel› (Spiel- und Theaterpädagogik).

S. hat eine wechselvolle Geschichte; neben langen Perioden, in denen Schulen hier nur sporadisch aktiv wurden, neben solchen mit umfassendem Anspruch an die Theaterarbeit (die dann als fester Teil und Medium des sozialen Lernens verstanden wurde) stehen solche, in denen S. auf begrenztes ästhetisches Tun reduziert war. Im Mittelalter waren Zöglinge von Kloster- und Lateinschulen, Vaganten und später Studenten selbstverständliche Mitwirkende im religiösen wie im weltlichen Theater. Besondere Funktionen übernahmen Schüler in den Heischebräuchen, bei den Narrenfesten, in der parodierenden Liturgie des Knabenbischof. Neben diesen praktischen theatralischen bzw. vortheatralischen Aktivitäten blieb die Rhetorik, als Kunst der öffentlichen Rede in der Antike Teil der

844 Schultheater

Allgemeinbildung und zu einem umfassenden Lehrgebiet ausgearbeitet, auch im Mittelalter verpflichtend als eine der sieben ‹artes liberales›, oft in zentraler Stellung innerhalb des Triviums. Ähnlich bestimmend blieben im sich langsam formierenden europ. Schulwesen die antiken Dramen (insbes. Seneca, Terenz, Plautus) als Lesedramen und Stilmuster.

Von höchster Bedeutung sowohl für die allg. Theatergeschichte wie für das Schulwesen wurde das S. der beginnenden Neuzeit, das sog. →Schuldrama. Auf Anregung von Luther und Melanchthon wird in evangelischen Schulen allerorten gespielt; Zentrum wird Straßburg unter Joh. Sturm (Gründung 1538). Dem protestantischen S. folgten die katholischen Orden, insbesondere das →Jesuitentheater, dessen Blütezeit etwa 1550–1650 war.

Im Verlauf des 18. und 19. Jh. rückte das S. mehr und mehr aus dem Zentrum des öffentlichen Interesses in eine Randstellung. Ursache sind weniger die Verbote als das sich ausbreitende Berufstheater. S. blieb jedoch üblich. Zudem gab es von den Schulen mancherlei Verbindungen mit dem Dilettantentheater, den Theatervereinen, der kleinstädtischen Geselligkeit. So traf der Neubeginn des →‹Laienspiels› im 20. Jh. nicht auf ein völliges Vakuum. Ende der Weimarer Republik suchten auch politisch bewußte Autoren den Zugang zur Schule (Brecht mit seinen Lehrstück-Versuchen um 1930, Hindemith), ehe der NS-Staat die positive Entwicklung unterbrach.

Nach 1945 begann das S. mit den alten Stücken und den alten Anschauungen der Zeit vor 1933. Erst allmählich gelang unter dem Begriff →Amateurtheater die Lösung vom Laienspiel, die Annäherung an das professionelle Theater; mit der Entwicklung des Schulspiels kam es mehr und mehr auch zu selbstgeschriebenen oder montierten Stücken. In jüngster Zeit wird ‹Darstellendes Spiel› innerhalb des Curriculums an gymnasialen Oberstufen angeboten, teilweise auch in der Sekundarstufe; Arbeitsgemeinschaften S. gibt es an vielen Schulen. Theaterinteressierte Lehrer sind in der BAG (Bundesarbeitsgemeinschaft Spiel in der Schule) zusammengeschlossen. Vom S. gibt gibt es zahlreiche Verbindungslinien zum Schulspiel, das als der umfassendere Zusammenhang auch nicht zuschauerbezogene Körper-, Interaktions- und Rollenspiele einbezieht.

Amersdorffer, H.: Schulbühnen und Puppenspiel. Berlin 1958; Müller, R. (Hg.): Spiel und Theater als kreativer Prozeß. Berlin 1972; Nickel, H.-W.: Spiel-, Theater-, Interaktionspädagogik. Recklinghausen 1976; Stadler, E. (Hg.): Schweizer Schultheater 1946–66. Bern 1967.

Hans-Wolfgang Nickel

Schurke

(Frz. traître) Der S. ist als antithetische Parallelfigur zum positiven Helden der Kristallisationspunkt aller moralischen und physischen Laster. Vor allem in zwei Arten von Theaterstücken spielt er eine Zentralrolle. Er ist einerseits die Verkörperung des Listigen und des Bösen im →Melodrama. Der jede Menschlichkeit entbehrende S. ist einer der vier Haupttypen des Melodramas neben dem →Jeune Premier oder jungen Helden, dem reinen, ahnungslosen jungen Mädchen und einer grotesken, dem Narren nahestehenden Gestalt; er verfolgt, verrät, quält ohne Bedenken und Nuancen und geht meistens am Ende des Stücks unter, löst dadurch beim Zuschauer zuerst Grauen, dann ein Gefühl der Erleichterung aus. Anderseits ist der S. als ‹traître›, Verräter, ein entscheidend wichtiges Strukturelement des klassischen Dramas: Als perverse Gegengestalt zum Helden vernichtet er jede heroische Harmonie; er wirkt um so mehr in diesem Sinn, als er das Vertrauen des Helden gewonnen hat, zu einem festen Bestandteil von dessen Person geworden ist, die ihm innewohnende Versuchung und die sich daraus ergebende Gefahr verkörpert. Vollkommenste S.-Figur in diesem Sinn ist wohl Jago, negatives Double von Othello bei William Shakespeare (1564–1616).

Bernard Poloni

Schwank

(Mhd. swanc = lustiger Einfall) Der Begriff S., der im Mittelalter und in der frühneuhochdeutschen Zeit eine meist knappe, scherzhafte Erzählung in Vers oder Prosa bezeichnet, wird seit Ende des 19. Jh. auch zur Kennzeichnung lustiger Schauspiele mit Situations- und Typenkomik verwendet. Anders als die oft bis zur totalen Verspottung alles Irdischen gehende →Posse oder die →Komödie versucht der S., die dargestellte Torheit der Personen durch Klugheit zu schlagen, und beabsichtigt dabei v. a., wenn nicht gar ausschließlich, die Belustigung der Zuschauer durch Situationskomik und Pointe ohne rührende Effekte, ohne Pathos, ohne ‹tiefere Bedeutung›. Stark typisierte Personen aus dem realistisch geschilderten bürgerlichen Milieu geraten unwillkürlich und wiederholt in komische Situationen, die auf Überraschung, Verwechslung und Mißverständnis beruhen, ohne je auf Daseinsproblematik und -kritik, Sozialkritik oder psychologische Vertiefung abzuzielen. Als typisch bürgerliche Theaterform vermeidet dabei der S. im Unterschied zur →Lokalposse jede ausgeprägte Bindung an eine bestimmte Stadt oder Landschaft. Seine Themen sind aus dem bürgerlichen Alltag mit seinen Tücken entnommen und beziehen sich oft auf Lebens- und Sprachbereiche, die sonst auf der Szene und im Leben tabu sind, etwa die Zote oder den Ehekonflikt. Mit dem durch die Weltwirtschaftskrise und die darauffolgende Entwicklung in Deutschland herbeigeführten Niedergang des in den Gründerjahren hochgekommenen Bürgertums einerseits und mit der Fortentwicklung der Dramaturgie im Bereich des Komischen anderseits überlebt sich auch die Schwankliteratur in Deutschland.

Klotz, V.: Bürgerliches Lachtheater. München 1980; Wilms, B.: Der Schwank. Diss. Berlin 1969.

Bernard Poloni

Schwarzamerikanisches Theater / Black Theatre

Unbeschadet des Umstands, daß die erste offizielle Bühne, die African Company (gegr. von Mr. Brown 1821), 1823 dessen *King Shotaway* als erstes Negerstück der USA aufführte, entwickelte sich das Theater der Afrikaner auf amerik. Boden als massenhafte Praxis aus den improvisierten Laien- und Volkskunstdarbietungen auf den Sklavenplantagen, einer Unterhaltungskultur, die gleichermaßen das Lied, die Instrumentalmusik, Tänze, Burlesken und Sketche als verbal transportierte Anteile einschloß. Da das Theater des weißen Nordamerikas im 18. und 19. Jh. wesentlich die Bräuche des jeweiligen europ. Herkunftslandes kopierte, ist das S. T., in der Form der →Minstrel Show freilich umgehend den urspr. Produzenten entwendet, das erste originäre Theater der USA überhaupt. Arbeitslied und Negro Spiritual gingen darin ebenso ein wie tänzerische Elemente und Musikinstrumente der afrik. Tradition (Banjo, Tamburin). Die Tradition schwarzen Shakespeare-Theaters begann mit der Astor Place Coloured Tragedy Company in den 1870er Jahren. B. J. Ford und J. A. Arneux waren die führenden Shakespeare-Darsteller zweier Jahrzehnte. Die Minstrel Show büßte an Popularität ein mit dem Aufkommen der Ragtime Musicals um die Jahrhundertwende, z. B. *In Dahomey* (1902) von Paul L. Dunbar. Den entscheidenden ersten Ansatz eines sozialkritischen S. T. bildete das Massenschauspiel *The Star of Ethiopia* (1913), geschrieben und organisiert von William E. B. DuBois, das in New York ein Publikum von 30000 Menschen erreichte. Seine Einflüsse werden am ehesten aufgenommen in der wichtigsten und langlebigsten Gruppe des S. T., den →Lafayette Players (1915–32) und in einigen anderen Versuchen, in der Phase der ‹Harlem Renaissance› seriöses S. T. in New York aufzubauen (Krigwa Players 1926; Harlem Experimental Theatre 1928; Harlem Suitcase Theatre 1937; Rose McClendon Players 1938; American Negro Theatre, 1940). Bedeutsam sind überdies der Durch-

Schwarzamerikanisches Theater / Black Theatre 847

bruch schwarzer Akteure in weißen progressiven Gruppen (z. B. Charles Gilpin als *Emperor Jones* 1920, Paul Robeson in der Hauptrolle von *All God's Chillun Got Wings* 1924, beide Stücke von O'Neill und von den →Provincetown Players aufgeführt) und die Einrichtung der ‹Negro units›, schwarzamerik. Abteilungen des →Federal Theatre Project (1935–39). Während sich das S. T. des Nordens somit ganz auf New York konzentrierte, sollte eine 1930 gegr. Negro Inter-Collegiate Drama Association der Förderung von S. T. im Süden der USA, ausgehend von den Colleges und Universitäten, dienen.

Unbeschadet aller Versuche vor 1950, ein kritisches nationales ethnisches Theater der Afroamerikaner in Harlem zu etablieren, gab es die großen Erfolge des S. T., freilich meistens als Musical und unter weißer Regie, am Broadway, wobei *A Trip to Coontown* (1898) und *The Sons of Ham* (1900) am Anfang dieser Entwicklung stehen. Langston Hughes' *Mulatto* (1935) und die Dramatisierung des Romans von Richard Wrights *Native Son* (1941) markieren gewisse Höhepunkte einer auch anspruchsvolleren schwarzen Dramatik am Broadway. Ein großer Erfolg war schwarzen Tourneetheatern seit der zweiten Hälfte der 30er Jahre mit der Volksoper *Porgy and Bess* beschieden, vertont von George Gershwin.

Die Civil Rights-Bewegung der 50er und 60er Jahre und nachfolgende unterschiedlichste politische Gruppierungen fanden einen vielfältigen Niederschlag im kulturellen Sektor, u. a. repräsentiert durch das ‹Black Arts Movement› und die Formulierung einer ‹Black Aesthetic›. Das S. T. nahm an dieser Entwicklung teil. Häufig betrieben die herausragenden Dramatiker eine Zeitlang ihre eigene Bühne, so im Süden John O'Neal das →Free Southern Theater, in New York Douglas T. Ward die →Negro Ensemble Company und Ed Bullins das New Lafayette; Versuch einer Anknüpfung an die berühmten →Lafayette Players. Der Lyriker und Dramatiker Amiri Baraka (vormals LeRoi Jones) verfügte über das Spirit House in Newark, New Jersey. Marksteine schwarzer Dramatik setzte das Greenwich Mews Theatre, New York, mit zwei Inszenierungen der 50er Jahre: William Branch, *In Splendid Error*, ein großangelegtes schwarzamerik. Geschichtsdrama, kontrastiert die historischen Figuren Frederick Douglass und John Brown im Kontext des Harper Ferry-Vorfalls. Loften Mitchell, *A Land Beyond the River*, thematisiert die Rassentrennung im Schulsektor.

Laut Baraka und Bullins best. zwei Hauptmerkmale die vielfältige kritische Dramenproduktion der 60er und 70er Jahre, die sich – über die gesamten USA verteilt – in rund 40 Theatergruppen, mehr oder weniger professionell und kaum von Stiftungsgeldern unterstützt, vollzieht: das Theater der schwarzen Erfahrung und das Theater der Revolution. Die Stücke der Baraka, Bullins, Davis, Mitchell, Hansberry, Kennedy, Harrison, Mackey, Milner, Greaves, Caldwell, O'Neal, Ward u. a. zeigen

848 Segment-Globus-Bühne

einerseits die Lebensverhältnisse der Schwarzen in den USA wahrheitsgetreu auf und deuten andererseits die Bedingungen oder Möglichkeiten der Veränderung dieser Verhältnisse an. Die politischen Bewegungen seit Civil Rights haben zweifelsfrei der schwarzen Dramatik und Theaterarbeit Originalität, Selbstbewußtsein und Würde verliehen. Neben präziserer politischer Aussagekraft erleben viele dieser Inszenierungen eine Renaissance afrik. Kulturtraditionen und verdichten häufig die originär amerik. Musiktraditionen des Jazz und Blues. Ein primär kommunales Ritualtheater war auch das 1968 in Harlem von Anne Teer gegr. National Black Theatre, das Stücke von Carlton Molette, Paul C. Harrison u. a. herausbrachte.

Der in den 70er Jahren beobachtbare Rückgang experimenteller Gruppen korreliert mit einem neuerlichen Durchbruch des schwarzen Musicals am → Broadway: *Purlie*; *Raisin*; *Bubbling Brown Sugar*; *The Wiz*; *Don't Bother Me I Can't Hope*; *Your Arms Too Short to Box With God* und *Timbuktu!*. Damit wurde dieser schon länger moribunden Institution der weißamerik. Amüsierindustrie neues Leben eingehaucht. Ebenfalls während der 80erJahre richtete das New Yorker Shakespeare Public Theatre schwarzamerik. und spanischsprechende Tourneegruppen ein.

Arata, E./Rotoli, N.: Black American Playwrights, 1800 to the Present. Metuchen 1976; Bullins, E. (ed.): New Plays from the Black Theatre. New York 1979; Couch, W. (ed): New Black Playwrights. New York 1970; Grabes, H. (Hg.): Das amerikanische Drama der Gegenwart. Kronberg 1976; Herms, D./Witzel, B.: Von James Baldwin zum Free Southern Theater. Positionen schwarzamerik. Dramatik im soziokulturellen Kontext der USA. Bremen 1979; Hill, E. (ed.): The Theatre of Black Americans. 2 Bde. Englewood Cliffs 1980; Isaacs, E. J. R.: The Negro in the American Theatre. New York 1947; King, W./Milner, R. (ed.): Black Drama Anthology. New York 1971; Manske, R.: Black Theater der 80er Jahre in New York City. Diss. Frankfurt/M. 1989; Mitchell, L.: Black Drama. The Story of the American Negro in the Theatre. New York 1967; Ostrow, E. J. (ed.): Center Stage. An Anthology of Twenty-One Contemporary Black-American Plays. Urbana 1991; Riley, C.: On Black Theatre. In: Gayle, A. (ed.): The Black Aesthetic. New York 1971, p. 295–311.

Dieter Herms

Segment-Globus-Bühne

Die Globusbühne stammt aus dem reichhaltigen Formenarsenal Wsewolod Meyerholds. In Deutschland wurde dieser Bühnenaufbau erstmalig bei Erwin Piscators *Rasputin*-Inszenierung (1927) verwendet. Bei der S.-G.-B. handelt es sich um eine drehbare, dreidimensionale Halbkugel (den Erdball symbolisierend), die sich an verschiedenen Stellen aufklappen läßt und so den Blick auf wechselnde Räume und Szenen freigibt. Im geschlossenen Zustand auf einer Drehbühne kreisend, diente sie bei der *Rasputin*-Aufführung zugleich als (gewölbte) Projektionsfläche für Dokumentarfilmaufnahmen.

Knellessen, F. W.: Agitation auf der Bühne. Emsdetten 1970, S. 133–146; Piscator, E.: Das politische Theater (1929). Reinbek bei Hamburg 1963, S. 160–178.

Carl Wege

Sentenz

Spruch, der nach dem lat. Vorbild einen allgemeingültigen abstrakten Gedanken ausdrückt, ein moralisches, politisches, psychologisches Gesetz formuliert. Formal gesehen charakterisiert sich die S. durch ihre Knappheit, dank welcher sie sich leicht aus ihrem Kontext herauslösen kann, um sich dem Gedächtnis einzuprägen. In der dramatischen Dichtung ist sie ein typisches Merkmal der klassischen geschlossenen Form, die ja das Normative, das stets Gültige heraushebt und den Einzelfall als besondere Verkörperung einer allgemeinen Idee betrachtet. Durch den Gebrauch der S. ordnet sich die dramatische Gestalt dem Überindividuellen unter. Die S. wird im frz. Theater des 17. Jh. häufig verwendet, wo sie, da sie meist eine einzige Zeile einnimmt, eine besonders einprägsame Form bekommt. «A vaincre sans pèril on triomphe sans gloire» (Pierre Corneille, 1606–84). Die dramatischen Werke der Weimarer Klassiker sind auch reich an sentenziösen Versen. «Der Starke ist am mächtigsten allein» (Schiller, 1759–1805). Auch wesentlich in der dt. Barockdramaturgie als Elemente des Stückebaus («des Trauerspiels Grundseulen», Georg Ph. Harsdörffer, 1648) und dialogische Teile des Rededuells (→ Stichomythie).

Scherer, J.: La dramaturgie classique en France. Paris 1983; Schöne, A.: Emblematik und Drama im Zeitalter des Barock. München 1964.

Alain Muzelle

Sentimental Comedy

Die S. C. war eine neue Form der → Komödie im frühen 18. Jh., eine empfindsame Alternative zur vorangehenden libertinistischen → Restaurationskomödie. Ihr Ursprung, etwa bei Colley Cibber (1671–1757) und Richard Steele (1672–1729), stand im Zusammenhang mit der Sitten- und Theaterreform nach der «Glorreichen Revolution» von 1689. Die in der S. c. teilweise auf Kosten des Komischen vertretenen bürgerlichen

850   Sentimentale

Tugenden entsprachen denen der gleichzeitigen moralischen Wochenschriften, und Steele, der Herausgeber des *Tatler*, war ihr wichtigster Repräsentant (als Hauptwerk des Genres gilt *The Conscious Lovers*, 1722). Nach Steele ging die S. C., analog zur frz. comédie larmoyante, immer mehr ins bürgerliche → Rührstück über, besonders in den Komödien von Hugh Kelly (1739–77) und Richard Cumberland (1732–1811). Daher im späteren 18. Jh. selbst bei empfindsamen Autoren wie Oliver Goldsmith (1728–74) und bei Richard Brinsley Sheridan (1751–1816) eine Gegenreaktion. Goldsmith stellte der S. C. als «weeping comedy» seine Idee der «laughing comedy» gegenüber. Seitdem sind Aufführungen der S. C. selten.

Barkhausen, J.: Die Vernunft des Sentimentalismus. Untersuchungen zur Entstehung der Empfindsamkeit und empfindsamen Komödie in England. Tübingen 1983; Sherbo, A.: English Sentimental Drama. East Lansing 1957.

Bernd-Peter Lange

Sentimentale

Weibliches → Rollenfach. Das über das Engl. aus dem Frz. entlehnte Wort bezeichnet ein jugendlich gefühlvolles Mädchen – bzw. die Darstellung einer solchen Rolle –, dessen Empfindsamkeit aber, anders als bei der → Naiven, bewußt und überlegend ist – z. B. Olivia in William Shakespeares (1564–1616) *Was ihr wollt* (1599).

Bernard Poloni

7:84 Theatre Company

Theatergruppe, 1971 von dem engl. Dramatiker John McGrath (*1935) gegr., der auch die überwiegende Zahl der aufgeführten Stücke verfaßt. Der Name der Gruppe verdankt sich einer Statistik aus dem Jahr 1966, nach der die sieben Prozent der brit. Bevölkerung 84 Prozent des nationalen Reichtums gehören. Seit 1973 gibt es zwei unabhängig voneinander arbeitende Ensembles in England und Schottland.

7:84 versteht sich als politische Gruppe, die mit ihrer Arbeit die Perspektive einer sozialistischen Umgestaltung der Gesellschaft zu fördern sucht. Als einer der wenigen Gruppen des → alternativen Theaters gelang es ihr, den Anspruch einzulösen, einem Arbeiterpublikum Theater nahezubringen, das in Form und Inhalt dessen politischen Interessen und kulturellen Traditionen entspricht.

Besonders erfolgreich war dabei die Produktion von McGrath' *The Cheviot, The Stag and the Black, Black Oil* (1973), einem Stück über die Geschichte Schottlands von den Einhegungen der Highlands bis zum Nordseeöl, mit dem 7:84 (Scotland) eine ausgedehnte Tournee durch entlegene Gebiete des Hochlands und der Inseln unternahm. Zu den bekanntesten Produktionen von 7:84 (England) gehören *The Ballygombeen Bequest* (1972) von John Arden (*1930) und Margaretta D'Arcy (*1934), *Trees in the Wind* (1971), *Lay Off* (1975), *Yobbo Nowt* (1975) und *Bitter Apples* (1979), alle von McGrath geschrieben. Die engl. Gruppe löste sich 1983 auf. 7:84 (Scotland) spielt seit dieser Zeit auch in England, bes. im Londoner Half Moon Theatre.

Itzin, C.: British Alternative Theatre Directory 1984/85. Eastbourne 1985; Klotz, G.: Britische Dramatiker der Gegenwart. Berlin (DDR) 1982; McGrath, J.: A Good Night Out. Popular Theatre: Audience, Class and Form. London 1981.

Werner Bleike

Shaffytheater

In einem gemieteten Saal an der Keizersgracht in Amsterdam initiierte Steve Austen 1968 die ersten Aufführungen. Als erstes wurde eine Kabarettaufführung des niederl. Schauspielers/Sängers Ramses Shaffy organisiert, dessen Namen das Theater trägt. Ziel von Austen war es, Theaterinitiativen zu präsentieren, die in der offiziellen Theater- und Musiklandschaft nicht realisiert werden konnten (→Freies Theater, →Fringe, →Mickerytheater). Subventioniert vom Kulturministerium, von der Provinz und von der Stadt, bietet S. Aufführungsmöglichkeiten für finanziell schwache Gruppen, die aber wichtig für die Entwicklung des Theaters sind. S. präsentiert nicht nur Aufführungen, es produziert Aufführungen auch mittels Aufträgen an Theatermacher, von denen man interessante Produkte erwarten kann. In der ersten Saison wurden 62 Aufführungen von sieben verschiedenen Produktionen gegeben. Diese Anzahl steigerte sich, als das ganze Gebäude mit mehreren Sälen in Betrieb genommen wurde. So gab es 1976/77 752 Aufführungen von 107 Gruppen in 128 verschiedenen Produktionen, und 1981/82 805 Aufführungen von 139 Gruppen in 174 verschiedenen Produktionen.

Im Laufe der Zeit wurden neue Initiativen entwickelt und unterschiedliche Theaterformen akzentuiert: Seit 1970/71 u. a. Nachtvorstellungen und Kindertheater (Kaktus), Musikabende (Boy Edgar); seit 1976/77 werden relativ viele Pantomimen-Aufführungen präsentiert (Will Spoor) und neue Entwicklungen auf dem Gebiet des Tanzes gezeigt und gefördert (Krisztina de Chatel, Stichting Dansproduktie, Ton Lutgerink). Daneben wurde mit Filmaktivitäten begonnen. Die Förderung des Zusammengehens verschiedener Disziplinen oder der Kombination von Podestkünsten mit anderen Kunstformen läuft wie ein roter Faden durch das Programm des S.

S. erreicht ein junges Publikum auch außerhalb von Amsterdam durch Aufführungen in vielen anderen kleinen Theatern (Circuit). Dieser Teil der Aktivitäten wurde so umfangreich, daß sie die Stiftung Theater Netwerk Nederland 1981 übernahm. Eine andere international bekannte Initiative ist das → Festival of Fools, das 1975 zum erstenmal vom S. organisiert wurde. In der Saison 1978/79, als S. zehn Jahre existierte, wurde ein Kolloquium über «Entwicklungen in den Podiumkünsten und praktisches Theatermanagement» organisiert.

Mostart, P./van Vliet, A.: Vijftien jaar Shaffytheater (unpubl. Magisterarbeit, Institut für Theaterwissenschaft). Amsterdam 1985.

Henri Schoenmakers

Shakespearebühne

(→ Bühne) Ein relativ großes, rundes oder achteckiges, z. T. überdachtes Fachwerkgebäude für Freiluft-(outdoor-)Aufführungen. Eine Plattformbühne ragte in den stuhl- oder banklosen Hof (yard) hinein, der von zwei- oder dreistöckigen überdachten Galerien umschlossen war. Die Bühnenhinterwand bestand aus einer Wand mit Eingängen links und rechts, darüber eine Oberbühne oder Galerie für Musiker, Szenen (Zinnen- oder Balkonszenen) oder Zuschauer. Möglicherweise befand sich eine Innenbühne unter der Galerie zwischen den Eingängen. Hinter der Bühnenwand war der Umkleideraum (tiring house) für die Schauspieler. Die Vorderbühne war überdacht und wahrscheinlich mit Sternen bemalt (heavens). Über dem Dach befand sich ein Raum, von dem aus die Bühnenhandwerker Maschinen bedienen konnten, um einen Schauspieler oder eine Kulisse hinunterzulassen oder hochzuziehen. Vom Fenster oder Balkon im Raum konnte ein Trompeter das Signal zum Beginn des Stücks blasen. Darüber war ein Fahnenmast, um den Einwohnern Londons zu zeigen, daß gespielt wurde. (Die öffentlichen Theater lagen außerhalb der damaligen Stadtgrenzen Londons.) Unter der Vorderbühne befand sich ein Zwischenraum (hell), aus dem Geister oder Teufel durch eine Klapptür auf die Bühne steigen konnten. Der Raum konnte auch als Grab (s. *Hamlet*) oder Hexenküche (s. *Macbeth*) dienen. Die Zuschauer standen im Hof (groundlings) vor und um die Vorderbühne herum oder auf den Galerien. Einige saßen auf Stühlen oder Bänken auf den Galerien oder sogar auf der Bühne. Die erste öffentliche Bühne The

wan Theatre. London 1596: Bühne mit Zuschauerrängen (TS)

Bühne des «Red Bull Playhouse» mit Figuren aus den Erfolgsstücken der Zeit (TS)

Theatre wurde 1576 von James Burbage errichtet. Die berühmteste Bühne war →The Globe, wo Shakespeares Truppe gespielt hat. Die S. wurde von einem heterogenen, hauptsächlich nichtaristokratischen Publikum besucht (→Elisabethanisches Theater). In The Swan sollen bis zu 3000 Zuschauer Platz gefunden haben. Unter den sieben öffentlichen Bühnen zu Shakespeares Lebzeiten gehörten The Theatre 1576–98), The Globe (1599–1619), The Swan (1595-ca. 1637) und The Rose (ca. 1587–1605) zu den bekanntesten.

Beckermann, B.: Shakespeare at the Globe, 1599–1609. New York 1962; Castrop, H.: Das elisabethanische Theater. In: I. Schabert (Hg.): Das Shakespeare-Handbuch. Stuttgart 1972, S. 73–125; Chambers, E.: The Elizabethan Stage. 4 Vols. London 1923; Gurr, A.: The Shakespearean Stage, 1574–1642. Cambridge 1970; Harbage, A.: Shakespeare and the Rival Traditions. Repr. Bloomington 1970; Hodges, W.: The Globe Restored: A Study of the Elizabethan Theatre. London 1968; Hosley, R.: The Playhouses. In: J. Barroll et al. (eds.): The Revels History of Drama in English. Vol. 3. London 1973, p. 119–236; Southern, R.: The Open Stage, London 1953; Wickham, G.: Early English Stages 1300 to 1660. Rev. Ed. Vol. 2. London 1980.

J. Lawrence Guntner

Shimpa

Jap., ‹Neue Schule›. – Name einer Bewegung, die versuchte, in Japan ein modernes Theater nach europ. Muster aufzubauen. Sein Gründer Sudô Sadanori (1867–1907) war Mitglied der damals oppositionellen liberalen Partei (*jiyû-tô*); er betrachtete das Theater als ein Forum für die Verbreitung liberaler Ideen, als Medium politischer Propaganda. Eine umfassende ‹theatralische› Idee fehlte ihm – wie dem *shimpa* überhaupt. Die von ihm begründete Gesellschaft für die Reform des Theaters (man mußte u. a. auch für die Wiederzulassung weiblicher Darsteller eintreten) sorgte für manchen öffentlichen Skandal. Geradezu revolutionär war, daß Sudôs Truppe aus Amateurschauspielern bestand; bisher hatte man in Japan nur Berufsschauspieler gekannt, die nach einem strengen Familiensystem organisiert waren. Sudô versuchte zwar, dem herrschenden →*kabuki* zeitgenössisches →‹avantgardistisches› Theater entgegenzusetzen, übernahm dabei aber doch manche Elemente der traditionellen japanischen Schaukunst. (Im Gegensatz zum kabuki sprach man allerdings mit natürlicher Stimme und verzichtete weitgehend auf Tanz und Musik.) Künstlerisch hatten seine Aufführungen kein hohes Niveau, aber das Flair des Neuen reizte die Neugierde des Publikums.

Ein zweiter wichtiger shimpa-Pionier war Kawakami Otojirô (1864–1911); er besaß ein großes satirisches Talent und eine unermüd-

854 Shingeki

liche Tatkraft. In seinem turbulenten und an Mißerfolgen reichen Leben soll er über 180mal verhaftet worden sein. Nach einer Europareise überraschte er die Japaner mit Bühnentricks und neuen Beleuchtungssystemen, die er mitgebracht hatte. Während des Kriegs gegen China brachte er (in fast operettenhaften Inszenierungen) Kriegsreportagen und Kriegsdramen auf die Bühne. Bei einer *Hamlet*-Aufführung ließ er Hamlet auf einem Fahrrad über das →*hanamichi* auftreten. Eine bedeutsamere Leistung Kawakamis war die Gründung einer Kaiserlichen Schule für Schauspielerinnen.

Trotz aller Unsicherheiten (und Absurditäten) entwickelte die Neue-Schule-Bewegung im Gegenzug gegen das Traditionell-Erstarrte, Formelhafte der überlieferten Theaterformen nach und nach einen eigenen Stil und konnte zwischen 1904 und 1909 (auch bedingt durch eine interne Krise der kabuki-Bühne nach dem Tod dreier ihrer bedeutendsten Schauspieler) große Erfolge verzeichnen. Wirkliche Meisterwerke hat das shimpa nicht hervorgebracht; das Repertoire dieser Zeit umfaßte im wesentlichen Kriegsreportagen (jetzt über den Krieg gegen Rußland), Kriminal- und Rührstücke, später Bearbeitungen von Zeitungsromanen. Eine starke Konkurrenz bedeutete 1910 das →*shingeki*, das ‹Neue Theater›, das auf die klassisch-japanische Tradition völlig Verzicht zu leisten versuchte. – 1924 publizierte Ii Yôhô (1871–1932), eine der hervorragendsten Figuren der shimpa-Bewegung, unter dem Titel *Nihon no engeki no setsu* seine Vorstellungen über das Wesen des Theaters.

Nach dem 2. Weltkrieg ist es zu einem Volkstheater mit wieder stark kabukiähnlichen Zügen umfunktioniert worden, was zwar sein Überleben garantiert, zugleich aber auch das Wort shimpa zu einem Decknamen für Rührseligkeit und Melodramatik gemacht hat.

Barth, J.: Japans Schaukunst im Wandel der Zeiten. Wiesbaden 1972; Ortolani, B.: Das japanische Theater. In: Kindermann, H. (Hg.): Fernöstliches Theater. Stuttgart 1966.

Peter Pörtner

Shingeki

Jap., ‹Neues Theater›. – Sammelbegriff für die nach der Meiji-Restauration (1867/68) in Japan einsetzenden Versuche, ein den tiefgreifenden Umwälzungen im geistigen und sozialen Bereich entsprechendes neues Theater nach westlichen Vorbildern zu entwickeln. Zwei der wesentlichsten Punkte seines Programms waren: die Kriegserklärung an das →*kabuki* und das Credo, daß das Theater ein Ort intellektueller Auseinandersetzung zu sein habe. Die Pioniere des *shingeki* hatten sich intensiv und

Shingeki 855

umfassend mit der traditionellen und zeitgenössischen Kultur des Westens beschäftigt und erreichten in ihren programmatischen Schriften ein hohes theoretisches Niveau – vor allem der (Shakespeare-)Übersetzer, Dramatiker, Regisseur und Universitätsprofessor Tsubouchi Shôyô (1859–1935), der auf die Entwicklung des modernen japanischen Theaters und des modernen japanischen Romans einen prägenden Einfluß ausübte.

Die erste Periode, in der fast ausschließlich europ. Stücke aufgeführt wurden, dauerte etwa bis 1923. (Die Zeit von 1898 bis 1908 wird wegen des auffälligen Vorherrschens von Ibsen-Inszenierungen auch Ibsen-Ära genannt.) Als repräsentativ für die in dieser Periode entstandenen Theaterstücke kann Kurata Hyakuzôs religiöses Drama *Shukke to sono deshi* (‹Der Mönch und sein Schüler›) von 1916 genannt werden. – Trotz des Bekenntnisses gegen die Tradition war die Aufführungspraxis dieser Zeit noch sehr stark vom kabuki geprägt (Sprechen mit gepreßter Stimme, Falsett-Artikulation, schematische Gebärden und Schritte).

Mit der Errichtung des Tsukiji-Theaters (1924) und nachdem einige der shingeki-Pioniere Europareisen absolviert hatten, wobei sie Reinhardt und Stanislawski begegnet waren, begann die zweite, sog. ‹experimentelle Periode› (1924–29), die eigentliche Blütezeit des shingeki, gefördert durch den Mäzen und Regisseur Graf Hijikata. Das Tsukiji-Theater war das erste auch westlich organisierte Theater Japans, in dem der Regisseur an die Stelle des ehemaligen Truppendirektors (zagashira) getreten war. Auch der Bühnenapparat und die gesamte Theaterausstattung entsprach zum erstenmal westlichem Niveau. In den ersten drei Jahren des Theaters wurden nur westliche, danach auch moderne japanische Autoren aufgeführt. Eng verknüpft mit der ‹experimentellen› Epoche des shingeki ist der Name Osanai Kaoru (1881–1928). Nach seinem Tod (kurz nach der Rückkehr aus Rußland, wo er im Moskauer Künstlertheater sein Ideal gleichsam in Aktion hatte erleben dürfen) begann die dritte Phase des shingeki, die des sozialkritischen, sog. ‹proletarischen› Dramas, dessen künstlerischer Wert allerdings immer umstritten war. Das Werk *Die Straße ohne Sonne* (1929) nach einem Roman von Tokunaga Sunao (1899–1958) gilt als typisches Beispiel dieses Genres. Überflüssig zu erwähnen, daß auch das ‹proletarische› Theater der politischen Gleichschaltung in den 30er Jahren, die jegliche nichtaffirmative Kreativität zum Erliegen brachte, zum Opfer fiel.

Unmittelbar nach dem 2. Weltkrieg versuchte das Shinkyô gekidan an die sozialkritische Tradition anzuknüpfen, wurde aber sehr bald ebenfalls Opfer der politischen Verhältnisse, die jetzt von der amerikanischen Besatzungsmacht diktiert wurden. Erfolgreicher waren die politisch ‹Unabhängigen›, das literarische und künstlerische Moment betonenden shingeki-Gruppen wie «Kumo» (Die Wolke, um Fukuda Tsuneari),

«Haiyû-za» (Das Schauspieler-Theater, um Senda Koreya) und «Mingei» (Das Volkstheater).

Ortolani, B.: Shingeki, The Maturing New Drama of Japan. In: Roggendorf, J. (ed.): Studies in Japanese Culture. Tôkyô 1963; Shimomura, N.: Shingeki. Tôkyô 1956.

Peter Pörtner

Simplicissimus

1. Als am 1.5.1903 die ehem. Kellnerin Kathi Kobus ihr eigenes Lokal «Zur neuen Dichtelei» eröffnete, wurde ein Kabarett quasi gegen den Willen der Besitzerin begründet. Nach juristischen Streitigkeiten wegen des Namens benannte sie ihr Lokal nach der gleichnamigen satirischen Zeitschrift. Kabarett im Sinne regelmäßigen Spielbetriebs war nicht beabsichtigt, jeder Gast konnte etwas vortragen. Zu denjenigen, die dem S. sein Gesicht gaben, gehörten L. Scharf, E. Mühsam und als Hausdichter Hans Bötticher, der sich ab 1919 Ringelnatz nannte. Vor dem 1. Weltkrieg kamen J. R. Becher, Klabund und H. Ball hinzu. Bereits nach dem 1. Weltkrieg lebte der S. hauptsächlich von seiner eigenen Legende. Nach dem Tode von K. Kobus 1929 hatte er verschiedene Besitzer. Er bestand bis zum Ende des 2. Weltkriegs, 1946 wurde er sogar noch einmal wiederbelebt und besteht bis heute als Gaststätte weiter.

2. Der Wiener S., als «Simpl» längst eine legendäre Institution, hat seinen Namen zwar von seinem Münchner Namensvetter entlehnt, im übrigen aber nur wenig mit ihm gemeinsam. Das «Bierkabarett S.» wurde am 25.10.1912 als Brettl mit Restaurationsbetrieb eröffnet. Von Anfang arbeitete man mit fest engagierten Kräften, schnellem Programmwechsel, vermied politische Satire und orientierte sich an unterhaltender Kleinkunst. Zu einem nicht unbeträchtlichen Teil lebte der S. vom Können seiner Conférenciers, zu denen mit F. Grünbaum, L. Békeffy und K. Farkas bedeutende Vertreter des Berufs gehörten. 1927 wurde hier die sog. «Doppelconférence» (→ Conférence) erfunden. Mit Kurzrevuen hatte der S. Anfang der 30er Jahre das ihm angemessene Genre gefunden. Nach der Besetzung Österreichs bot der S. verstärkt seichte Unterhaltung. Seine wichtigsten Kräfte mußten ins Exil gehen (z. B. K. Farkas) oder wurden, wie F. Grünbaum, von den Nazis ermordet. Bereits im Juni 1945 wurde der S. wiedereröffnet, gewann jedoch erst mit der Rückkehr K. Farkas' aus den USA wieder an Bedeutung. Seit seinem Tode 1971 lebt der S., das älteste bestehende Kabarett, nur noch als Legende seiner selbst.

Bötticher, H.: Simplicissimus, Künstlerkneipe und Kathi Kobus. München 1925/
26; Farkas, K.: Ins eigene Nest. Wien 1988; Haback, E. M.: Der Wiener Simplicissimus 1912 bis 1974. Diss. Wien 1977; Kühn, V.: Das Kabarett der frühen Jahre.
Berlin 1984; Rösler, W. (Hg.): Geh ma halt a bisserl unter. Berlin 1991; Simplicissimus – Künstlerkneipe. München 1932; Veigl, H.: Lachen im Keller. Wien 1986;
Weys, R.: Cabaret und Kabarett in Wien. Wien 1970.

Wolfgang Beck

Simultanbühne

Die S. ist die fast ausschließliche Bühnenform des mittelalterlichen Dramas (→Mittelalter/Drama und Theater des Mittelalters). Die ganze im
Drama dargestellte Welt, selbst Himmel und Hölle, wird nebeneinander
aufgebaut. Dabei nutzt man eine symbolische Anordnung. Der Himmel
wird gewöhnlich am Ostende des Spielraums angesetzt; der Blick nach
Osten ist der Blick nach dem Heiligen Land. Die Hölle sollte demnach im
Westen sein usw. Doch aus pragmatischen Gründen folgte man diesem
Schema selten in allen Einzelheiten. Alle Mitspieler sind von Anfang bis
zu Ende auf der Bühne anwesend. Es gibt kein Auftreten und Abtreten.
Die Toten kommen in den Himmel oder in die Hölle, die Mitspieler haben eine Mansion, ein Häuschen, das zur besseren Sicht nur aus Pfosten
und Dach besteht. Einige dieser Mansionen, bes. der Himmel (gewöhnlich der Balkon eines Hauses), können durch Vorhänge abgeschlossen
werden. Der Höllenrachen, meist als Rachen eines Ungeheuers gestaltet,
bleibt geschlossen und erlaubt keinen Einblick ins Innere.

Michael, W. F.: Frühformen der dt. Bühne (Schriften der Gesellschaft für Theatergeschichte 62). Berlin 1963.

Wolfgang F. Michael

Simultantheater

Theaterform, deren Hauptaussage wesentlich durch das Prinzip der Simultaneität (Gleichzeitigkeit) bestimmt wird. Nicht jedes Theater, das
auf einer →Simultanbühne stattfindet, ist S. Über der formalen Gleichzeitigkeit einer zwei- oder mehrteiligen Simultanbühne steht beim S. die
Einheit der Idee. Im S. des Mittelalters (→Mysterien-, →Passions-, Le-
gendenspiele) z. B. bildet die gleichzeitige szenische Präsenz von Weltge-
schehen, Hölle und Himmel die Ganzheit des christlichen Kosmos ab; die
Spielhandlung wird aus dieser Sicht reflektiert und bewertet. Erreicht
werden soll dadurch die Identifikation des Zuschauers mit der christ-

858 Sinfonisches Ballett

lichen Weltordnung. Die Simultanbühne des S. kann auch Parallel- oder Kontrasthandlungen zeigen; die gedankliche Sinnfälligkeit der simultanen Bezüge gründet in der Einheit der Idee des Stücks.

Elisabeth Scherf

Sinfonisches Ballett

Das S. B. hat die dramaturgischen Möglichkeiten des Tanztheaters, und zwar von chorischen Massenszenen bis zu Ensembleszenen, von realistischen bis zu absoluten oder gar abstrakten Tanzgestaltungen hin erweitert. Der Choreograph erwirbt im S. B. die Freiheit, unabhängig von Gehalten und Symbolismen einzig in Raum- und Zeitstrukturen zu denken. Die Körpersprache kann im S. B. die Musik interpretieren, dialogisieren und konstrastieren. Außerhalb der musikalischen und tänzerischen Logik liegende Gesetze sind nicht zu beachten. Dennoch unterlegen Choreographen ihren Entwürfen vielfach einen Handlungsverlauf oder eine philosophisch-anthropologische Idee. Neben sinfonischen Kompositionen werden auch Kammer- und Solomusik ausgewählt: Etuden, Präludien, Nocturnes, Quartette etc.

Geschichte: Salvatore Vigano (1769–1821, →Ballet héroïque-pantomime), Wegbereiter des Choreodramas. *Die Geschöpfe des Prometheus* zur Musik von Beethoven. Verzicht auf pantomimisches Beiwerk. – Isadora Duncan (1877–1927, →Ausdruckstanz) tanzt 1908 in New York zur 8. Sinfonie von Beethoven. – Michail Fokin (1880–1942, →Bolschoi-Ballett) programmiert die dramatisch-stilistische Einheit der Künste im Tanz-Opus. Fokin und Gorski (1871–1924) entwerfen choreo-sinfonische Dichtungen. – 1915 A. Gorski: 5. Sinfonie von Glasunow. – Lopuchow (1886–1973, →St. Petersburger Ballett) entwickelt Theorie und Begriff des S. B. 1923 Tanzsinfonie *Die Erhabenheit des Weltalls*; Balanchine assistiert. – Massine: 1933 *Choreartium* (4. Sinfonie von Brahms). 1933 *Les Présages* (Tschaikowskys *Symphonie pathétique*). 1936 die *Symphonie fantastique* von Berlioz. – George Balanchine (1904–83, →New York City Ballet): 1952 *Scotch Symphony* (Mendelssohn-Bartholdy). 1954 *Opus 34* (Schönberg). 1955 *Pas de dix* (Glasunow). 1956 *Allegro brillante* (Tschaikowsky). 1963 *Movements for Piano and Orchestra* (Strawinsky) u. a. Balanchine meidet jeden Inhalt. Raum, Kostüm, Dekor betonen die frei sich entfaltende Formenwelt als Raumspiel. – J. Cranko (1927–73): 1950 *The Witch* (Ravel, Klavierkonzert G-Dur). 1961 *Katalyse* (Schostakowitsch, Konzert für Klavier und Trompete). 1966 *Brandenburgische Konzerte Nr. 2 und 4* (Bach). 1966 *Konzert für Flöte und Harfe* (Mozart). 1968 *Begegnungen in drei Farben* (Strawinsky, Konzert für Klavier und Blasorchester) u. a. Gegenwärtig setzen M. Béjart (→ Ballet du XXe Siècle), J. Neumeier (Zyklus nach Mahler-Sinfonien) und J. Grigorowitsch (→ Bolschoi-Ballett) Schwerpunkte im Choreographieren von S. B.

Chujoy, A.: Sinfonisches Ballett. In: Programmheft der Hamburger Staatsoper zur Dritten Sinfonie von Gustav Mahler in der Choreographie von John Neumeier. Uraufführung; Fokin, M.: Brief an die Londoner Times vom 6.7.1914; Grigorowitsch, J.: Synthese der Traditionen. In: Die Welt des Tanzes in Selbstzeugnissen. Hg. von Wolgina, L./Pietsch, U. Wilhelmshaven ²1979, S. 310–321; Liechtenhan, R.: Vom Ballett zum Tanz. Stuttgart/Zürich o. J.

Helga Ettl

Skēnographie

‹Bühnenmalerei› im antiken Theater; laut Aristoteles (*Poetik* 1449 a 18) von Sophokles erfunden (Aischylos hat sie am Ende seines Lebens noch übernommen); das, was die Griechen S. nannten, ist nicht etwa naturalistische Kulissenmalerei, d. h. Darstellung des jeweiligen Schauplatzes, sondern perspektivische Architekturmalerei. Die vier Stücke einer → Tetralogie bzw. die fünf Komödien (→ Antikes Theater) spielten also wahrscheinlich vor der Einheitskulisse entweder eines Palasts (Tragödie) oder eines bis dreier Stadthäuser (Komödie). Gemalt wurde auf die gewiß mehrteilige vordere Verkleidung des Bühnenhauses. Der Grad des Realismus und die Möglichkeiten zur Variation (innerhalb eines Stücks, zwischen Stücken) ist umstritten. Echte Kulissenmalerei ist erst für das hellenistische Theater nachweisbar: Jetzt wurden zwischen den Säulen, die die hohe Bühne (→ Proskenion) trugen, auswechselbare Holzbilder (Pinakes) aufgestellt und die Fassade des Bühnenhauses durch (in der Regel) drei große Öffnungen, die sogenannten ‹Thyromata›, architektonisch gegliedert, in die (wie in Wechselrahmen) Bühnenbilder eingehängt werden konnten. Da diese offenbar immer wieder verwendet wurden, können auch sie keine individuellen Bühnenbilder gewesen sein. Wir müssen mit konventionellen Dekorationen rechnen, wie sie von dem röm. Architekten Vitruv für die tragische, die komische und die Satyrspielbühne beschrieben worden sind (Vitruv, 7 praef. 11).

Simon, E.: Das antike Theater. Heidelberg 1972, S. 31–40; Blume, H.-D.: Einführung in das antike Theaterwesen. Darmstadt 1978, S. 60–66.

Bernd Seidensticker

Sketch

(Engl. ‹Skizze›) Ein aus einer oder mehreren Szenen bestehendes ‹Kurz-drama› mit häufig ironisch-witzigem Inhalt, wenigen Personen und einer durchgehenden Handlung, die zumeist in einer überraschenden Schluß-pointe (‹black out›) gipfelt. Es ist eine sowohl im Theater wie in der →Re-vue und vor allem im →Kabarett beliebte Form.

Wolfgang Beck

Škola dramatičeskogo iskusstva (Moskau)

(Schule der dramatischen Kunst). Im Kontext der Studio-Theater-Bewe-gung 1986 gegr. und geleitet von Anatoli Wassiljew (*1942), der zuvor am →MChAT, →Taganka-Theater, Stanislawski-Theater und in Rostow vielbeachtete Inszenierungen machte: 1978 *Wassa Shelesnowa* (Erste Variante), 1979 *Die erwachsene Tochter eines jungen Mannes*, 1985/86 *Cerceau* (beide von V. Slawkin). Die S.D.K. ist das erste staatliche Thea-terstudio mit Vertragssystem. Auseinandersetzung mit russ. Theatertra-ditionen (A. Tschechow, M. Tschechow, Ethik Stanislawskis, →Stanis-lawski-System). Ensemble «Gleichgesinnter» (Ästhetik, künstlerische Weltsicht, Akzeptanz der Spielregeln). Achtung vor dem Text als Haupt-quelle der Aufführung schließt improvisatorisches Theater nicht aus. 1987 *Sechs Personen suchen einen Autor*. Viele Schüler, Förderung junger Regisseure; Stanislawski-Seminare in Berlin, zahlreiche Auslandsgast-spiele (BRD, BITEF 1987).

Elke Wiegand

Skomorochen

(Skomorochi) Mittelalterliche russ. Spielleute, die als Musikanten, Sän-ger, Tänzer und Komödianten zugleich auftraten. Erste Erwähnung 1068, Blütezeit 15. bis 17. Jh., zu Zünften (70–100 Personen) zusammen-geschlossen, von der Kirche bekämpft. Starke Improvisation, Bezug zum Alltagsgeschehen, Einbeziehung des Zuschauers. Im 19. und Anfang des 20. Jh. von Einfluß auf Schaubude (→Balagan) und Puppentheater.

Belkin, A. A.: Russkie skomorochi. Moskva 1975

Annelore Engel-Braunschmidt

Slovenské Narodné Divadlo (Bratislava)

Das Slowakische Nationaltheater, gegr. 1920 (vorher nur Laientheater in der Slowakei), entstand mit Unterstützung des tschech. Theaters; erste Aufführungen in Tschechisch. Zum SND gehören Oper, Ballett und Schauspiel. 1932–39 ein tschech. und ein slowak. Schauspielensemble; erste Berufsschauspieler: O. Borodáčová, J. Kello und Janko Borodáč, der mit Inszenierungen klassischer slowak. Literatur auf nationale Authentizität orientierte. Ján Jamnicky begründet eine wichtige Traditionslinie (Synthese expressiver und poetischer Ausdrucksmittel), die J. Budský und K. L. Zacher nach 1944 fortsetzen. Aus dem SND geht 1946 die Nová Scena hervor, 1955 neues Gebäude, 1961 Kammerbühne Malá Sena. Inszenierungen slowak. Autoren (P. O. Hviezdoslav, I. Bukovčan, J. Solovič, P. Karvaš), russ. und Weltdramatik durch T. Rakovsky, M. Pietor, P. Haspra, P. Mikulik. Bedeutung für die Entwicklung des Theaternetzes in der Slowakei.

Elke Wiegand

Snake Theatre

Bekanntestes Beispiel des →Environmental Theatre an der Westküste der USA. Gegr. 1972 von Laura Farabough und Christopher Hardman, ist es in einem allgemeinen Sinn zugleich mythologisch und politisch. Die bekanntesten Produktionen sind *Somewhere in the Pacific* (1978), *24th Hour Cafe* (1978), *Auto* (1979) und *Ride Hard/Die Fast* (1980).

Dieter Herms

Soffitten

(Ital. soffitto = Zimmerdecke) Bemalte, senkrecht gestaffelt hängende, zumeist auch mit eigener Beleuchtung versehene Leinwandbahnen, die bei der →Kulissenbühne die obere Bühnenöffnung verdecken und einen illusionistischen Raumabschluß vortäuschen.

Manfred Brauneck

Sotie

(Frz. sot = Narr) Die vermutlich in der →Basoche entstandene S. ist ein satirisch-possenhaftes frz. Bühnenstück in Versen aus der zweiten Hälfte des 15. und dem 16. Jh. Anders als die etwas kürzere →Farce bringt die S. vor allem stark typisierte Gestalten auf die Bühne – die den Narren des dt. →Fastnachtsspiels ähnlichen und mit denselben Attributen (zweifarbiges Kostüm, Narrenkappe, Narrenkolben) ausgestatteten ‹sots› und die ‹gallans› – und daneben einzelne allegorische Figuren, die sie in die Nähe der →Moralitäten rücken. Die S. soll nicht nur durch Sprachspiele und buntes Treiben auf der Bühne Heiterkeit und Lachen beim Publikum erregen (‹sotie-parade› und ‹sotie-rébus›); sie will vielmehr durch das Mittel der fingierten Narretei das Unheil und Verderben versprechende Fehlverhalten aller Gesellschaftsgruppen kritisieren und aufdecken. Sie nimmt so die Form der eine Gerichtsverhandlung karikierenden und mehr politisch polemisierenden ‹sotie-jugement› an (*Sotie du roy des sotz*; *Jeu du prince des sots et de la mère Sotte*: Pierre Gringoire, 1475–1558); oder die etwas komplexere und abstraktere Form der an die Moralität grenzenden ‹sotie-action›, welche über die Kritik an präzisen Mißständen hinaus allgemeinere, weltanschauliche Themen aufgreift.

Aubailly, J. C.: Le monologue, le dialogue et la Sotie, essai sur quelques genres dramatiques de la fin du Moyen Age et du début du XVIème Siècle. Paris 1975; Goth, B.: Untersuchungen zur Gattungsgeschichte der Sotie. München 1967.

Bernard Poloni

Soubrette

Komisches weibliches →Rollenfach der Kammermädchen und Zofen in →Komödie, Oper und Operette. Die S. ist in allen ihren Varianten eine Bedienstete eines Herrn bzw. einer Herrin und somit eine Parallelgestalt zum →Diener. Durch ihr kühnes Auftreten, ihren Intrigengeist, ihr lebendiges, temperamentvolles Herumwirbeln auf der Bühne bringt sie des öfteren die Handlung in Gang. Die S. des westeurop., v. a. des frz. und dt. Theaters findet ihren Ursprung in der ‹serva› der →Commedia dell'arte, etwa Fantesca oder Servetta. Das Fach wird dann ins span. Theater übernommen, etwa bei Miguel de Cervantes Saavedra (1547–1616) oder im 18. Jh. José de Cañizares (1676–1750), vor allem ins frz. komische Theater, wo es eine bedeutende Entwicklung erfährt. Bei Molière (1622–73) ist sie noch eine einfache bäuerliche Dienerin (‹servante›) – etwa Dorine in *Tartuffe* (1669). Mit Dancourt (1661–1725) und Alain-René Lesage (1668–1747) wird sie zur Kammerzofe (‹suivante›), einem jungen Mädchen aus der Stadt, das zugleich gewitzt und ehrgeizig ist. Den Höhepunkt der Entwicklung stellt die S. bei Pierre de Marivaux (1688–1763) und Pierre Caron de Beaumarchais (1732–99) dar – etwa Lisette in *Das Spiel von Liebe und Zufall* (1730) und v. a. Suzanne in *Figaros Hochzeit* (1784). Hier ist sie eine lebensfrohe, kokettierende und intrigierende, aber auch tugendhafte Kammerzofe, die entscheidend zur Demaskierung von Lug und Trug beiträgt. In Deutschland hat sich die S. seit Franziska in Gotthold Ephraim Lessings (1719–81) *Minna von Barnhelm* (1767) immer mehr zur munteren Liebhaberin gewandelt, die weniger kokett und berechnend ist als vielmehr ehrlich-gemütvoll und liebenswürdig. Mit dem Ende des 18. Jh. gewinnt dann die →Naive immer mehr an Beliebtheit und löst die S. als ihr genaues Gegenteil ab. Ähnliches geschieht im frz. Theater mit der weinerlichen Zofe der ‹comédie larmoyante› bzw. der ‹femme de chambre› im →Vaudeville und Théâtre de Boulevard. Echte S. in der Nachfolge der Commedia dell'arte und Molières sind nur noch im Wiener Volkstheater (→Alt-Wiener Volksstück) anzutreffen. Anzumerken ist noch, daß sich im heutigen Sprachgebrauch das Wort S. zunehmend auf Oper und Operette beschränkt.

Aziza, C./Olivieri, R./Stick, R.: Dictionnaire des types et caractères littéraires. Paris 1978; Ribaric/Demers, M.: Le valet et la soubrette de Molière à la Révolution. Paris 1970.

Bernard Poloni

Souffleur

(Frz. ‹Einflüsterer/Zuflüsterer›) Person, die aus dem verdeckten →S.-Kasten vorn in der Bühnenmitte unterhalb der Rampe den Schauspielern den Text ihrer Rolle durch leises Mitsprechen einhilft und so das Steckenbleiben (sog. Hänger) verhindert. Wegen der höheren Stimmlage wird die weibliche Souffleuse bevorzugt.

Horst Schumacher

Souffleurkasten

Verdeckter, oft versenkter oder versenkbarer Aufsatz auf dem Bühnenboden, zumeist vorn in der Mitte der Rampe, in dem der →Souffleur sich aufhält. Im modernen Theater kaum noch in der Form vorhanden. Traditionell kastenförmig, aber auch in Muschelform oder überhaupt vom Zuschauerraum nicht erkennbar. Zugang von der Unterbühne oder – falls der Souffleur in den Kulissen sitzt – von der Seite her.

Horst Schumacher

Soufflierbuch

Textbuch des →Souffleurs, das neben dem Wortlaut des Stücks Striche, Vorhangzeichen und andere Hinweise enthält. Bei nie gedruckten Stücken und kleinen Truppen gibt es manchmal nur noch das S. als erhaltene Textquelle. Name und persönliche Anmerkungen des Souffleurs, Requisitenverzeichnis, Sichtvermerke der Zensurbehörde u. a. machen das S. theatergeschichtlich interessant.

Horst Schumacher

Spatz und Co

Wichtiges Schweizer →Kinder- und Jugendtheater seit 1976, entwickelt meist eigene, realitäts- und problembezogene Stücke zusammen mit den jeweiligen Zielgruppen; begann 1979 mit dem alljährlichen Schweizer Kinder- und Jugendtheatertreffen; Materialienhefte, theaterpädagogische Vor- und Nacharbeit zu den Aufführungen.

Hans-Wolfgang Nickel

Spiel

Die Welt als S. – diesen Gedanken formuliert frühes antikes Philosophieren schon bei Heraklit: «Die Lebenszeit ist ein Knabe, der spielt, hin und her die Brettsteine setzt: Knabenregiment.» In dieser Denktradition steht Platons Wort vom Menschen als «Spielzeug Gottes», aufgenommen als Forderung in den ‹Gesetzen›: «Jeder, Mann oder Frau, muß dahin streben und die schönsten Spiele zum wahren Wert seines Lebens machen» (*Nomoi* 803 BC). Der Gedanke wirkt nach bei Plotin (Spiel als theoria, als seliges Anschauen Gottes, als sympathisches Mitspiel der Menschen) und bei den Kirchenvätern: «Denn der erhabene Logos – er spielt. Mit buntesten Bildern schmückt er, wie's ihm gefällt, auf jegliche Weise den Kosmos» (Gregor von Naszianz).

Erschrecken gegenüber der Grenzenlosigkeit des Lebens («Alles ist in

Spiel 865

Bewegung und nichts bleibt stehen», Heraklit; «Doch wie einen Zug im Brettspiel das Leben zu wiederholen, das gibt es nicht», Antiphon) führt zur Besinnung auf die Möglichkeiten des menschlichen Spiels (als Fest, als Ritus, als Besinnung, als theoria, als Theater und eben als Spiel): Heraustreten aus dem Kontinuum Wirklichkeit in eine Welt mit eigenen Gesetzen (bei König Pelasgos etwa aus den «Schutzflehenden» des Aischylos Eintreten in den Spielraum des Denkens) und Rückkehr in die Wirklichkeit mit Ergebnissen aus diesem frei geschaffenen Zwischenraum. Zweierlei also ist Spiel den Griechen: Weltgesetz und Freiraum des Menschen.

In der Folgezeit verkommt dieses Denken zur bloßen Metapher; Theater wird zum Paradigma: «Die ganze Welt ist Bühne / und Fraun und Männer, alle spielen mit» (Jacques in *Wie es euch gefällt*). Was in Schillers Spieltheorie noch umfassend anthropologisch gedeutet wird, reduziert sich auf Kinderspiel (Rousseau, Pestalozzi, Fröbel), das möglichst auf ein Prinzip zurückgeführt wird (von Spencer auf Kraftüberschuß, von Lange und Hall auf Trieb und Rekapitulation von Kultur, von Carr und Groos auf Katharsis, von Lazarus auf Erholung, von der Pädagogischen Bewegung auf Schöpfertum). Auch in der Gegenwart bleiben pädagogisch-psychologische Spieltheorien trotz allmählicher Ausweitung begrenzt (vor allem auf die kognitive Entwicklung bei Piaget in Entwicklungspsychologie und Lernforschung, auf Rollenspiel in Sozialpsychologie und Gruppenforschung, auf die Beziehung zur Arbeit in der sowj. Psychologie, auf innerpsychische Verarbeitung in der Psychoanalyse).

Wichtigere Erkenntnisse, die als Bausteine zu einer neuen Gesamtsicht die Rückkehr zu dem antiken Gedanken (Spiel als Weltgesetz) gestatten, kommen aus der mathematischen Spieltheorie (der Theorie strategischer, d. h. vom Verhalten der Spieler abhängiger Spiele), der Evolutionstheorie (die Entstehung der Arten betreffend), der Atomphysik (mit der Heisenbergschen Unschärfebeziehung), der Molekularbiologie, der «Ökologie des Geistes» (Bateson).

In besonderer Weise gestaltet sich das Spiel zwischen Welt und Lebewesen, wenn das Lebewesen sich ein Bild der Welt schafft und auf Grund dieses Bildes handelt. Beim Menschen wird der Weg von der Information zum Verhalten durch Sprache, Weltanschauung, Kultur, individuelle Erfahrung, Mitteilung usw. gebrochen. Bateson bezeichnet es als eine «sehr wichtige Stufe in dieser Entwicklung» der Kommunikation, «wenn der Organismus allmählich aufhört, ganz ‹automatisch› auf die Stimmungs-Zeichen eines anderen zu reagieren, und fähig wird, das Zeichen als ein Signal zu erkennen», d. h. als interpretationsbedürftig und interpretationsfähig. Damit aber bringen sich beide Interaktionspartner in die Kommunikation ein und gestalten sie gemeinsam. «Auf der menschlichen Ebene führt dies zu einer unermeßlichen Vielfalt von Komplikatio-

866 Spielpädagogik

nen und Verdrehungen im Bereich von Spiel, Phantasie und Kunst» (Bateson). Zusätzlich zum (unbewußten) Spiel der Welt entwickelt der Mensch also mehr und mehr ihre Vielfalt durch eigene Spiele. Ein spezifisches Spiel, das wir mit der Welt und miteinander spielen, ist das Theater; andere sind Sprachen, Wissenschaften, Theorien. Im Theater formulieren wir Bilder der Wirklichkeit (zufällig, geschichtlich, frei), auf die die Wirklichkeit (regelgemäß, gesetzlich) antwortet im Dialog zwischen dem Möglichen und dem Wirklichen – freilich nicht ohne sich durch unsere Bilder zu verändern. Darin liegt die Verantwortung, die wir mehr und mehr übernehmen (müssen), wohl wissend, daß unsere Freiheit von heute uns Regeln für das Morgen setzt – damit Zukunftsbewußtsein und Verantwortungskraft von uns fordernd. – Umfassend philosophisch reflektiert wird dieser Zusammenhang von Axelos in seinem Hauptwerk *Das Spiel der Welt*: «Die großen Mächte bilden eine fortlaufende Totalität, ohne Zentrum oder Brennpunkt, Ursprung oder Motor, Quelle oder Kern, Grund oder Prinzip, die das Spiel ihrer Struktur begrenzte. Dieses Nicht-Zentrum – nicht existierend oder nicht nachweisbar, wenn die Frage nach dieser Formulierung erfolgt – ist kein Mangel oder Verlust, sondern das Spiel selbst, das auch die Suche nach dem Zentrum spielt.»

Axelos, K.: Das Spiel der Welt (Le jeu du monde. Paris 1969). 2 Bde. Wuppertal 1972; Bateson, G.: Ökologie des Geistes, darin: Eine Theorie des Spiels und der Phantasie. Frankfurt/M. 1981 (Steps to an Ecology of Mind, 1972); Diels, H.: Die Fragmente der Vorsokratiker. Reinbek bei Hamburg 1957; Eigen, M./Winkler, R.: Das Spiel. Naturgesetze steuern den Zufall. München 1975; Flitner, A.: Spielen–Lernen. Praxis und Deutung des Kinderspiels. München 1972; Jacob, F.: Das Spiel der Möglichkeiten. Von der offenen Geschichte des Lebens. München 1983 (Le jeu des possibles, Paris 1981); Nestle, W.: Die Vorsokratiker. Köln 1956.

Hans-Wolfgang Nickel

Spielpädagogik

S. (→Theaterpädagogik) ist die Bezeichnung für einen neuen, umfassenden, professionellen Handlungs-, Forschungs-, Lehr- und Lernbereich, der sich nach 1945 zunächst in England und USA, dann in anderen europ. Ländern ausbildete. S. in diesem umfassenden Sinn umgreift eine Fülle von Spielformen: Körperspiele, Materialspiele (bis hin zum Figuren- und Maskentheater), Interaktionsspiele, rhetorische Spiele, gruppendynamische Spiele, Rollenspiele, Lehr- und Lernstück (im Anschluß an Brecht), Theater (aktiv als Spieler, Autor, Regisseur), professionelles Theater (kommunikativ als Zuschauer), Fest. Der Gebrauch dieser Spielformen reicht von momentanen Einschüben in der Schulstunde wie in der Gruppenarbeit bis zu langfristigen fächerübergreifenden Vorhaben (Fest,

Spielpädagogik 867

Theater). Unterscheiden lassen sich bei allen Formen Übungen (streng durch Regeln bestimmt, meist stark vom Spielleiter geführt und korrigiert), Spiele (freie Entwicklungen innerhalb der bestimmenden Regeln), →Improvisationen (noch weniger festgelegte Entwicklung von einer gegebenen Grundlage aus oder zu einem gegebenen Ziel hin), Ereignisse (weitgehend unbestimmt in Ausgangspunkt, Verlauf, Endpunkt).

Sobald nicht die Gesamtgruppe miteinander spielt oder simultan alle Kleingruppen nebeneinander, wird der Vorführcharakter des Spiels mehr oder weniger stark bewußt; er kann angestrebt und zum Theater vor Publikum entwickelt werden.

Charakteristisch für die S. ist die Person des Spielleiters (drama teacher, Animator). Zwar waren und sind in allen Gesellschaften Spiele üblich; einzelne Spiele (zum Zeitvertreib, zur Erholung oder zur Pflege der Geselligkeit, als didaktische Hilfe oder als Prinzip in der Schule) sind ohne Ausbildung möglich und brauchen keinen professionellen Spielleiter. Die grundlegende Erhaltung der Spielfähigkeit des Kindes bzw. ihre Wiederherstellung und Entwicklung zu reflektierendem, verantwortetem Spiel braucht pädagogisch intendierten und didaktisch strukturierten Umgang mit Formen von S. und Theater, also den ausgebildeten Spielleiter. Er hat es gelernt, eine gezielte Abfolge von Übungen, Spielen, Improvisationen, Ereignissen, Vorführungen, Beratungen, Gesprächen, Erkundungen, Unterweisungen als Training für die Spielgruppe und schließlich mit der Spielgruppe zu entwickeln. Spiel und Theater sind in diesem Verständnis keine isolierten Ereignisse, sondern stehen in einem vielfach sprachlich vermittelten Zusammenhang sozialer Wirklichkeit: Erkundung, Spielaufgabe (Spielregel), Planung, Spiel (Spielhandlung), Nachbereitung, häufig erneute Planung, erneutes Spiel, möglichst Transfer. In dieser Einbindung erweisen sich Spiel und Theater als projektverwandt. Zusätzlich zu den Charakteristika des Projektunterrichts erscheinen der starke Bezug zur Körperlichkeit des Spielers und der durchgängige, nicht nur inhaltliche Bezug zu Fragen von Ich/Gruppe/Gesellschaft, der zu gemeinsamer Planung von Spielleiter/Spielgruppe und schließlich zur Selbstverantwortung der Spielgruppe führen muß.

S. in diesem Sinne ist also nicht nur ein weiteres Kunstfach, das zum Theater führen soll wie eine traditionelle Musikerziehung zum Konzert; S. als eigener Lernbereich weiß sich insbesondere dem sozialen Lernen verpflichtet und versteht sich als Regulativ zur gegenwärtigen Pädagogik; sie macht den vernachlässigten Bereich der sozialen Erfahrung, damit den Spieler selbst zum zentralen ‹Gegenstand›.

Von den möglichen Spielformen der S. wurden in der BRD bisher nur jeweils Teilbereiche genutzt; auch muß ihre Verankerung im Curriculum der allgemeinbildenden Schule noch erreicht werden. – Die Entwicklung der S. und ihre Bezeichnung in den europ. Ländern ist unterschiedlich:

868 Spielplan

→Animation (frz., ital., auch in Österreich), creative drama, educational drama, drama (so auch in Holland), expression corporelle, expression dramatique, jeux dramatiques, jeu scolaire, expressie door woord en gebaar (Holland), Darstellendes Spiel (Grundkurse in der gymnasialen Oberstufe), Freizeitpädagogik, Interaktionspädagogik, →Schulspiel (Lehr- und Prüfungsfach an der Hochschule der Künste Berlin; Freigegenstand in den österr. Schulen; Wahlpflichtkurse in der Sek. I), Spiel und Arbeit (Fachhochschulen), Spiel/Musik/Tanz (Sporthochschule Köln mit einer eigenen Spielleiterausbildung), Theaterpädagogik (Ausbildungsrichtung an der Schauspielakademie Zürich, der Hochschule Hildesheim), Spiel- und Theaterpädagogik (Studienrichtung am gleichnamigen Institut der Hochschule der Künste Berlin). Diese Bezeichnungen benennen die Mittel (Spiel, Theater, Darstellung, Drama, Körper), formulieren Ziele (Interaktionslernen, Spielen, Theater machen und verstehen), beziehen sich auf unterschiedliche Institutionen (Schule, Theater, Freizeit); sie meinen jeweils einen Lernbereich mit umfassendem Anspruch.

Der isolierte Begriff →‹Theaterpädagogik› kann in eingeschränktem Sinn auch die spezielle Berufsausbildung für Theatermacher bezeichnen (also die Tätigkeit von Schauspielschulen, Regieseminaren, Bühnenbildklassen). Theaterpädagogik wird ebenfalls gebraucht als Bezeichnung für die Erziehung des Zuschauers, also für eine allgemeine Einführung in die Kunstform ‹Theater›, entweder nur verbal-belehrend oder kreativ, unter Einbeziehung eigener Spielversuche. Theaterpädagogik in diesem Sinne gibt es an einigen Theatern; in der Schule ist sie, soweit überhaupt erkennbar vorhanden, oft mit den Fächern Deutsch, Kunst oder Musik verbunden. In beiden Fällen läßt sich Theaterpädagogik als ein Teilbereich der S. verstehen.

Baer, U.: Wörterbuch der Spielpädagogik. Basel 1981; Broich, J.: Spiel- und Theaterpädagogik. Systematischer Literaturnachweis. BIB-report, Beiheft 18, 1981 (Interaktionspädagogik, Bd. IV); Kreuzer, K.-J. (Hg.): Handbuch der Spielpädagogik, Bde. 1–4. Düsseldorf 1983f; Nickel, H.W.: Spiel, Theater-, Interaktionspädagogik. Recklinghausen 1977 (Hilfen für Spielleiter 16); Ziegenspeck, J.: Spielen in der Schule. Sachstandsbericht und systematischer Literaturnachweis. BIB-report, Beiheft 13, 1980 (Interaktionspädagogik, Bd. I).

Hans-Wolfgang Nickel

Spielplan

Zusammenstellung der im Laufe einer oder mehrerer →Spielzeiten neu zu inszenierenden Stücke, bei →Repertoiretheater auch die bereits einstudierten und lediglich wiederaufgenommenen Werke. Inhaltliches Konzept und zeitliche Disposition erarbeitet in der Regel die →Dramaturgie in Absprache mit der Theaterleitung. Nach ihrem Entwurf werden Schauspieler verpflichtet, Regie und Rollen vergeben, Produktionskosten berechnet. Als S. gilt ferner die Liste der wöchentlich bzw. monatlich angesetzten →Aufführungen.

Monika Sandhack

Spielzeit

Zeit kontinuierlichen (meist abendlichen) Spielbetriebs, im deutschsprachigen Theater in der Regel vom Spät- bis zum Frühsommer des nächsten Jahres, dazwischen Theaterferien (ca. sechs Wochen). – Im ital. Theater des 17./18. Jh. beschränkte sich die S. der Oper auf den Karneval. Im Theater des 19. Jh. dauerte die S. einer (meist wandernden) Truppe zwei bis drei Monate, häufig auf Herbst und Frühjahr festgelegt, allenfalls ergänzt durch Sommer-S. in Badeorten. Heute richten sich alle stehenden Theater nach dem ganzjährigen Spielrhythmus.

Monika Sandhack

Sprechchor

Im 19. Jh. übernahmen die sozialdemokratischen Arbeiterbildungsvereine das chorische Deklamieren von Gedichten aus der bürgerlichen Tradition, jedoch kaum zum Zweck der Agitation und Propaganda. In der Weimarer Republik entwickelte sich der S. zu einem wesentlichen künstlerischen Ausdrucksmittel der organisierten Arbeiterbewegung. Unter Gustav von Wangenheim (1895–1975) führte 1923 der Zentrale S. der KPD Groß-Berlin dessen Werk *Chor der Arbeit* auf, in dem er der gewohnten expressiv-pathetischen Rezitation dialogische und satirische Stilmittel mit aktuellen Bezügen entgegenstellte. Dramatische Wirkung wurde mit sprachlichen Mitteln (Gegeneinander verschiedener Stimmen, Pausen, Dämpfungen, Verstärkungen, Rhythmik etc.) erzielt, unterstützt durch plakative Symbole und Zeichen. In den ersten Jahren der Herrschaft des Nationalsozialismus wurde der S. als entscheidender dramaturgischer Baustein in die von der SA getragene →Thingspielbewegung übernommen.

Hoffmann-Ostwald, D./Hoffmann, L. (Hg.): Deutsches Arbeitertheater 1918–1933. Berlin 1972; Menz, E.: Sprechchor und Aufmarsch. In: Denkler, H./

Prümm, K. (Hg.): Die deutsche Literatur im Dritten Reich. Stuttgart 1976; Sprang, K.: Der Sprechchor und seine Bedeutung für die Gedichtbehandlung. Breslau 1927.

Erich Krieger

Squat Theatre

Ungarische Exilgruppe in den USA (New York seit 1977), die von 1969 bis 1972 im Kassák-Kulturhaus, Budapest, und zwischen 1973 und 1976 in Polen und Westeuropa spielte, unter Leitung von Peter Halász und Anna Koós. Die bekanntesten Inszenierungen sind *Pig, Child, Fire!* (1977) und *Andy Warhol's Last Love* (1978). Abgesehen von verlesenen Textpassagen aus z. B. Dostojewski oder Artaud, von z. B. überspielten Tonbändern mit Text und Stimme Ulrike Meinhofs, enthalten die S. T.-Produktionen keine Dialoge. Die Stücke bestehen aus Zeichen und Aktionen. Parallelen ergeben sich zu Richard Foremans Theaterstil (→Ontological-Hysteric Theatre) ebenso wie demjenigen des →Environmental Theatre. Für das S. T. sind Theater und Lebensrealität verschmolzen.

Shank, T.: American Alternative Theatre. London 1982.

Dieter Herms

Staatliche Schauspielbühnen Berlin

Schillertheater, Schloßparktheater, Schillertheater Werkstatt. 1945 Beginn städtischen Theaters in den unzerstörten Gebäuden des Schloßparktheaters unter Leitung von Boleslaw Barlog (*1906) und des Hebbeltheaters unter Karl Heinz Martin (1888–1948). Klassische Stücke und Autoren der 30er und 40er Jahre akzentuieren die Spielpläne. Jürgen Fehling (1885–1968), Karl Heinz Stroux (1908–85), Walter Felsenstein (1901–75), Fritz Kortner (1892–1970), Rudolf Noelte (*1921) inszenieren neben Barlog und Martin. 1951 Eröffnung des wiederaufgebauten Schillertheaters, das 1908 gegründet und 1935 bis 1944 von dem Schauspieler Heinrich George (1893–1946) geleitet wurde. Organisatorische Verbindung mit dem Schloßparktheater als Kleinem Haus. Hebbeltheater wird an wechselnde Privattheaterdirektoren verpachtet oder dient als Ausweichquartier der Staatsbühnen. – 1951 bis 1972 Intendant Boleslaw Barlog, Oberspielleiter bis 1955 Karl Heinz Stroux, 1972 bis 1980 Hans Lietzau (1913–91), 1980 bis 1985 Boy Gobert (1925–86), 1985 bis 1990 Heribert Sasse (*1945). 1990–93 Alfred Kirchner, Alexander Lang, Vera Sturm und Volkmar Clauß. – Zunehmend schwindende Ausstrahlung, ohne Innovationsimpulse. Vernachlässigung des deutschsprachigen Gegenwartsdramas.

Reichardt, H. J. u. a.: 25 Jahre Theater in Berlin. Berlin 1972.

Werner Schulze-Reimpell / Red.

Staatsschauspiel Dresden

Nachdem 1985 die Staatsoper in die wiederaufgebaute Semper-Oper zog, erfolgte die organisatorisch-administrative Trennung. Das S. D. verfügt nun über zwei ständige Spielstätten, das Schauspielhaus mit 909 Plätzen (eröffnet 1913, zerstört 1945, wiederaufgebaut 1948, zuletzt 1990 erheblich modernisiert) und das Kleine Haus mit 532 Plätzen, sowie einige Werkstattbühnen. – Traditionsreiche Theaterstadt, Wandertruppen, 1647 Schloßtheater, 1696 französisches Schauspielhaus, 1700–33 festes Ensemble, 1755 Komödienhaus, von 1835 bis 1841 etablierte Ludwig Tieck (1773–1853) literarisches Repertoire mit Kleist, Calderón und – vor allem – Shakespeare. 1841 Theaterumbau Hofoper durch Gottfried Semper, nach Brand 1878 wiederaufgebaut, 1873 königliches Schauspielhaus. Wichtige Bühne des Expressionismus: 1916 UA *Der Sohn* von Walter Hasenclever (1890–1940), 1917 DEA *Mörder, Hoffnung der Frauen* von Oskar Kokoschka (1886–1980). – Intendanten u. a.: 1947–50 Karl von Appen (1900–81), 1950–51 Martin Hellberg (* 1905), 1966–72 Hans-Dieter Mäde (* 1930). Gerhard Wolfram (1922–91), zuvor Intendanz am → Deutschen Theater Berlin, übernahm 1984 das S. D., das er zur führenden Sprechbühne der DDR-Provinz machte. Dabei förderte er mit den Chefregisseuren Horst Schönemann (* 1927) und den Regisseuren Klaus-Dieter Kirst (* 1941) und Wolfgang Engel (* 1945) ausgeprägt unterschiedliche Handschriften in einem Ensemble. Besonders die Klassikinszenierungen Engels (u. a. *Penthesilea*, *Nibelungen* und *Faust I / II*), die prononciert gegenwärtiges Zeitgefühl ansprachen, sicherten dem S. D. internationale Beachtung. Wolfram und sein Chefdramaturg Dieter Görne, seit 1990 Intendant des S. D., setzten auch Inszenierungen durch, die der DDR-Kulturpolitik nicht genehm waren, z. B. *Die Umsiedlerin* (1985) von Heiner Müller (* 1929) oder die UA *Die Ritter der Tafelrunde* (1989) von Christoph Hein (* 1944).

Funke, Ch. / Hoffmann-Osterwald, D. / Otto, H.-G. (Hg.): Theater-Bilanz. Berlin (DDR) 1971, S. 202–203; Hellberg, M.: Im Wirbel der Wahrheit. Berlin (DDR) 1978; Pietzsch, I.: Werkstatt Theater. Berlin (DDR) 1975, S. 53–59 und 88–96; Proeßl, R.: Geschichte des Hoftheaters in Dresden. Dresden 1878; 300 Jahre Staatstheater Dresden. Dresden 1966.

Andreas Roßmann / Roland Dreßler

Staatstheater Stuttgart

Opernhaus, Schauspielhaus, Kammertheater. Vorgänger: Hoftheater seit dem 16. Jh., Humanistendrama um Nikodemus Frischlin (1547–90). Im 17. Jh. Beschränkung auf Oper und Ballett, Ende 18. Jh. auch Schauspiel. 1787 Christian Daniel Schubart (1739–91) Theater- und Musikdirektor (Hofdichter). 1846 bis 1951 Franz (von) Dingelstedt (1814–81). 1902 Brand des Hoftheaters, 1912 Neubau durch Max Littmann (1862–1931), der auch das Münchner Prinzregententheater, das Berliner Schillertheater, die Weimarer Bühne u. a. baute. Eröffnung mit UA *Der Bürger als Edelmann* (Hofmannsthal/R. Strauss), Regie Max Reinhardt (1873–1943). 1919 Staatstheater. Schauspielhaus im Krieg zerstört (wiederaufgebaut). Opernhaus 1984 restauriert. 1949 bis 1972 Intendanz Walter Erich Schäfer (1901–84), 1985 Wolfgang Gönnenwein. Schauspieldirektoren: 1950–58 Paul Hoffmann (1902–90), 1958–63 Günther Lüders (1906–75), 1965–72 Peter Palitzsch (*1918), 1975–1979 Claus Peymann (*1937), 1979–85 Hansgünther Heyme (*1935), 1985–88 Ivan Nagel (*1931), seit 1988 Jürgen Bosse, ab 1993 Friedrich Schirmer. Operndirektoren: 1970–74 Wolfgang Windgassen (1914–74).

Die Oper fand in den 60er Jahren Beachtung durch Inszenierungen von Wieland Wagner (1917–1966) als «Winter-Bayreuth». Das Schauspiel gewann unter Palitzsch und Peymann überregionales Renommee.

Stuttgarter Ballett

Höhepunkte des Bühnentanzes erlebt Stuttgart bereits 1759–66 unter J.-G. Noverre (1727–1810; →Ballet d'action) und 1824–28 unter F. Taglioni (1777–1871; →Ballet de l'Opéra de Paris; Ballet Blanc). Nicholas Beriozoff (*1906) schafft 1958–61 die Voraussetzungen für das heutige S. Als dessen Gründer gilt John Cranko (1927–73), Direktor von 1961 bis zu seinem Tod 1973. Nachfolger sind 1974–76 Glen Tetley (*1926; →Nederlands Dans Theater) und seither Marcia Haydée (*1937). Cranko verschafft dem S. als erster deutscher Ballettkompanie internationale Bedeutung. Als Förderer zahlreicher Tänzer- und Choreographenpersönlichkeiten (u. a. M. Haydée, Egon Madsen, Birgit Keil, Richard Cragun, Heinz Clauss, John Neumeier, Jiri Kylián) legt er den Grundstein für den dauerhaften Bestand des Ensembles und beeinflußt maßgeblich die Entwicklung des Ballettschaffens in der Bundesrepublik Deutschland. Vorbildhaft für andere Institute in der damaligen Bundesrepublik wirkt der von Cranko und der Ballettmeisterin Anne Woolliams (*1926) betriebene Ausbau der angeschlossenen Ballettschule (seit 1973: John-Cranko-Schule) zu einer professionellen Tänzerakademie. Direktoren nach Woolliams sind von 1976–90 H. Clauss (*1935) und seither Alex Ursuliak (*1937).

Zu Crankos Arbeiten gehören Neuschöpfungen abendfüllender Ballette (*Onegin, Der Widerspenstigen Zähmung*), klassisch-romantische und neuere Handlungsballette wie *Schwanensee* und *Romeo und Julia* sowie zahlreiche einaktige erzählende und abstrakte Choreographien. Charakteristisch für Cranko sind dramatische, bisweilen akrobatische Pas de deux in neoklassizistischem Stil. Nach Glen Tetley leitet Marcia Haydée das Ensemble «im Geiste John Crankos». Haydée präsentiert gezielt Nachwuchschoreographen wie Uwe Scholz (* 1958) und William Forsythe (* 1949; → Ballett Frankfurt), in jüngerer Zeit Daniela Kurz (* 1966) und Renato Zanella (* 1961). Ohne Chefchoreograph verstärkt die Kompanie darüber hinaus die Zusammenarbeit mit Gästen wie J. Neumeier (* 1942; → Hamburg Ballett), Maurice Béjart (* 1927; → Ballet du XXe Siècle), J. Kylián (* 1947; → Nederlands Dans Theater) und Hans van Manen (* 1932; → Nederlands Dans Theater, Het Nationale Ballet). Mit Haydées eigenen Inszenierungen (*Dornröschen* 1987, *Giselle* 1989) nimmt die Bedeutung der großen Cranko-Ballette im Repertoire des Stuttgarter Balletts ab.

Doll, H.-P.: Stuttgarter Theaterarbeit 1972–85. Stuttgart 1985; Finsterer, A.: Festschrift des Württ. Staatstheaters. Stuttgart 1962; John-Cranko-Gesellschaft (Hg.): Stuttgarter Ballett Annual. Stuttgart 1978ff; Percival, J.: John Cranko. Stuttgart/Zürich 1985; Regitz, H. (Hg.): Tanz in Deutschland. Berlin 1984; Waidelich, J. D.: Vom Stuttgarter Hoftheater zum Württembergischen Staatstheater. Diss. München 1957.

Werner Schulze-Reimpell/Horst Vollmer/Red.

Stabpuppe/Stockpuppe

Puppenart, die vom Spieler von unten oder der Seite mit Stäben und zusätzlichen mechanischen Vorrichtungen bewegt wird. – Die S. hat lange Tradition in Ostasien, wo sie für eigene theatralische Veranstaltungen benutzt wird, teilweise aber auch im Zusammenhang mit Aufführungen des → Schattentheaters steht. In Europa waren bis ins 20. Jh. die Stockpuppen als volkstümliche Abart bekannt. Angeblich nach belgischen Vorbildern gründete der Kölner Schneidermeister Christoph Winter 1802 das «Kreppchen», das als «Kölner Hänneschen» bis heute in einem eigenen Theater gespielt wird. Die Figuren dieses Theaters, die relativ unbeweglich sind, sitzen auf einer bis zum Boden reichenden Holzstange und werden über eine darin eingelassene Eisenstange geführt. – Nach javanischen Vorbildern schuf der Wiener Künstler Richard Teschner S., mit denen er seit 1912 öffentlich auftrat.

874   Die Stachelschweine

Amtmann, P. (Hg.): Puppen, Schatten, Masken. München 1966; Batchelder, M.: The Puppet-Theatre-Handbook. London 1948; Batek, O.: Marionetten-, Stab-, Draht- und Fadenpuppen. Ravensburg 1980; Böhmer, G.: Puppentheater. München 1969; Boehn, M. v.: Puppen und Puppenspiele. 2 Bde. München 1929; Fettig, H.: Hand- und Stabpuppen. Stuttgart 1970; «Hänneschen läßt die Puppen tanzen». Köln 1976; Philpott, A.: Dictionary of Puppetry. London 1969; Schreiner, K.: Puppen & Theater. Köln 1980.

Wolfgang Beck

Die Stachelschweine

Im Berliner Jazzkeller «Die Badewanne» begann 1949 als Einlage zwischen Publikumstanz das Kabarett S., das bis heute eine Berliner Institution darstellt. Mitte der 50er Jahre hatte es sich durchgesetzt, mit Texten u. a. von R. Ulrich und Thierry, dem die Gruppe ihren Namen verdankt, mit Regisseuren wie Wolfgang Neuss und Egon Monk. – Anfangs noch um differenzierte Satire bemüht, die sich wohltuend fernhielt vom sterilen Antikommunismus etwa der «Insulaner», markierte die Verleihung des Berliner Kunstpreises 1957 einen Wendepunkt in ihrer Entwicklung. Ihre wachsende Popularität, die Ausstrahlung ihrer Programme im Fernsehen führte sie zum Bemühen um möglichst große Breitenwirkung, was zunehmend auf Kosten des intellektuellen Niveaus und der kritischen Potenz ging. Der Umzug im Juni 1965 ins «Europa-Center» machte ihre Programme (inzwischen über 50) zwar technisch immer perfekter und aufwendiger, die Texte jedoch verließen seither nur noch selten das Niveau unreflektierten Amüsements und der Klamotte. Ob und wie sich die im vereinigten Berlin schärfer gewordene Konkurrenz auf ihre Programme auswirken wird, bleibt abzuwarten.

Budzinski, K.: Pfeffer ins Getriebe. München 1982; ders.: Die öffentlichen Spaßmacher. München 1966; ders.: Wer lacht denn da? Braunschweig 1989; Greul, H.: Bretter, die die Zeit bedeuten. Köln/Berlin 1967 (erw. Ausg., 2 Bde. München 1971); Lenk, E. (Hg.): Die Badewanne. Berlin 1991; Tschechne, W.: Ich hab' noch meine Schnauze in Berlin. Hannover 1967; Ulrich, R./Herbst, J.: Erinnern Sie sich noch? Berlin 1954; dies./Thierry: Die Stachelschweine. Berlin 1956; Ulrich, R.: Es sollte alles ganz anders werden. Frankfurt/M. 1990.

Wolfgang Beck

Städtische Bühnen Frankfurt

Schauspielhaus, Kammertheater. 1788 bis 1791 Nationaltheater. Im 19. Jh. Vereinigte Stadttheater als Aktiengesellschaft mit städtischem Zuschuß (Altes Schauspielhaus, Neues Schauspielhaus, Opernhaus mit zusammen mehr als 4000 Plätzen). Städtische Bühnen, 1951 bis 1968 Intendant Harry Buckwitz (1904–88), konsequente Brecht-Pflege gegen politischen Widerstand. 1963 Neubau Schauspielhaus und Kammertheater neben der Oper («Theaterinsel»). 1972 organisatorische Trennung von Oper und Schauspiel. Oper: 1972 bis 1977 Intendant (und GMD) Christoph von Dohnanyi (*1929), 1977 bis 1987 GMD Michael Gielen (*1927), 1987–90 Intendant und GMD Gary Bertini (*1927), ab 1991 Prof. Hans Peter Doll. 1972 bis 1980 Mitbestimmungsmodell im Schauspiel, dreiköpfiges Direktorium mit einem vom Ensemble gewählten (wechselnden) Mitglied, von der Stadt bestimmter Direktor Peter Palitzsch (*1918), Regisseur Hans Neuenfels (*1941). Engagiertes sozialkritisches Theater. 1981 bis 1985 Intendant Adolf Dresen (*1935), 1985 bis 1990 Dr. Günther Rühle (*1924), ab 1990 Prof. Hans Peter Doll, ab 1991 Schauspielintendant Prof. Peter Eschberg.

Heym, H.: Frankfurt und sein Theater. Frankfurt/M. 1963; Kirschner, J.: Was wird aus dem Theater? Die Diskussion um das Frankfurter Schauspiel 1945–51. Frankfurt/M. 1989; Loschütz, G./Laube, H.: War da was? Frankfurt/M. 1980; Mohr, A. R.: Das Frankfurter Schauspiel 1929–1944. Frankfurt/M. 1974.

Werner Schulze-Reimpell/Red.

Stadttheater

Nach der Satzung des →Deutschen Bühnenvereins gehören dazu jene Theater, die von einer oder mehreren Gemeinden bzw. von einer juristischen Person, die ganz oder überwiegend von diesen Körperschaften getragen wird, unterhalten werden (→Theatersystem). Die S. bilden eine Gruppe im DBV (vertr. mit 6 Mitgliedern im Verwaltungsrat). Mit dem Begriff des S. wird allgemein auch das öffentlich getragene Theater mit seinem spezifischen Inszenierungsstil und Besucherstrukturen umschrieben.

Spielplatz 1. Jahrbuch für Theater 71/72. Hg. v. K. Braun und K. Volker. Berlin 1972, S. 27–41.

Roswitha Körner

Stadttheater Basel

Stadttheater, Komödie. 1834 Theaterbau durch Aktiengesellschaft, zunächst verpachtet. Seit 1919 Oberspielleiter, 1925–32 Direktor Oskar Wälterlin (1895–1961), Regisseur Walter Felsenstein (1901–75). Einsatz für den jungen Friedrich Dürrenmatt (1921–90) durch Ernst Ginsberg (1904–64). 1968–75 Direktor Werner Düggelin (*1928), Dürrenmatt zeitweise künstlerischer Beirat und Regisseur. UA von Dürrenmatt-Bearbeitungen (*König Johann*, *Play Strindberg*). Förderung junger Autoren wie Dieter Forte (*1935) und Heinrich Henkel (*1937). 1975–78 Direktor der vormalige Oberspielleiter Hans Hollmann (*1933). 1978–88 Direktor Horst Statkus, 1988–93 Frank Baumbauer.

Ende der 20er Jahre beginnt die Pflege des Bühnentanzes am S. B. Ballettmeister sind u. a. 1928–30 Rosalia Chladek (*1905) und 1945–51 Heinz Rosen (1908–72). Seine erste Blüte erlebt das S. B. 1955–67 unter Wazlaw Orlikowsky (*1921), der das klassisch-romantische Repertoire des 19. Jh. sowie zahlreiche zeitgenössische (Handlungs-)Ballette erarbeitet. Nach einer Übergangszeit mit rasch wechselnden Chefchoreographen (u. a. 1970–73 Pavel Smok, *1927) wird 1973 Heinz Spoerli (*1941) Direktor des B. (bis 1991; seither Ballettdirektor der Deutschen Oper am Rhein Düsseldorf-Duisburg). Er führt die Kompanie, unterstützt von dem Ballettmeister Peter Appel (*1933), an die Spitze des schweizerischen Bühnentanzschaffens. Spoerli pflegt einen sich am Werk George Balanchines orientierenden neoklassizistischen Tanzstil. Zu seinen Arbeiten gehören zeitgemäße Interpretationen traditioneller Werke (wie *Giselle*, *Nußknacker*, *La Fille mal gardée*, *Schwanensee*, *Romeo und Julia*), aber auch die UA *John Falstaff* (Musik: Thomas Jahn) und Henzes *Orpheus* sowie zahlreiche, meist handlungslose Kurzballette oft zu Kompositionen des 20. Jh. Durch seine ebenso künstlerisch ambitionierte wie publikumswirksame Repertoiregestaltung gewinnt Spoerli breite Zuschauerkreise. Seit 1991 leitet Youri Vàmos (*1946) das Ballett.

Ashoss, B.: Das Basler Theater unter W. Düggelin. Diss. Wien 1977; Eckert, H.: Heinz Spoerlis Basler Ballett. Basel 1991; Flury, Ph./Kaufmann, P.: Heinz Spoerli – Ballett-Faszination. Zürich 1983; Pastori, J.-P.: Tanz und Ballett in der Schweiz. Zürich 1985; Schmassmann, M.: Das Basler Stadttheater. Diss. Wien 1970.

Werner Schulze-Reimpell/Horst Vollmer/Red.

Ständeklausel

Klausel der Renaissance- und Barockpoetik, wonach die Tragödie nur vom Schicksal der Könige, Fürsten und Vertreter höherer Stände handeln darf, während Personen aus den niederen Ständen, insbesondere die Bürger, nur in der Komödie als Hauptgestalten auftreten dürfen. Diese Forderung, Ausdruck einer absolutistischen Haltung, wird von den Theoretikern der Zeit dadurch legitimiert, daß die bürgerliche Lebensform der für die Tragödie notwendigen Erhabenheit und Würde ermangele und nur die hohe soziale Stellung des Helden die überzeugende Darstellung der tragischen Fallhöhe ermögliche. Mit dem Sieg des →Bürgerlichen Trauerspiels erfolgte eine Überwindung der S.

Alexander, R.: Das dt. Barockdrama. Stuttgart 1984; Daunicht, R.: Die Entstehung des bürgerlichen Trauerspiels in Deutschland. Berlin 1965; Schings, H.-J.: Consolatio Tragoediae. In: Grimm, R. (Hg.): Deutsche Dramentheorien I. Frankfurt/M. 1971; Szondi, P.: Die Theorie des bürgerlichen Trauerspiels. Frankfurt/M. 1973.

Alain Muzelle

Stanislawski-System

Eine vergleichende Analyse der →Biomechanik Meyerholds und der Methode der «physischen Handlung» Stanislawskis würde unzweifelhaft Gemeinsamkeiten zutage fördern und die Auffassung von Stanislawski und Meyerhold als unversöhnlichen Gegnern widerlegen. Meyerhold hat seinen Lehrer Konstantin Sergejewitsch Stanislawski (1863–1938), mit dem er 40 Jahre in aktiver Wechselbeziehung stand, zeit seines Lebens – selbst während des →Theateroktobers – verehrt: «Konstantin Sergejewitsch und ich suchen in der Kunst dasselbe; nur geht er vom Inneren zum Äußeren und gehe ich vom Äußeren zum Inneren» (Zit. bei Fevral'skij: Stanislavskij i Mejerchol'd, S. 291.) (→Theaterpädagogik).

Stanislawski war ein großer Pädagoge, Erfinder, Künstler, reich an Initiativen, mit dem fast alle Innovationen des modernen russ. Theaters verbunden sind. Er war der erste russ. Regisseur, der seine Arbeit auf eine wissenschaftliche Grundlage stellte. Sein ‹System› ist die Summe seiner Erfahrungen in der künstlerischen Praxis. Theorie und Methodik legte er in verschiedenen Publikationen nieder. Herauszubilden begann Stanislawski seine Theorie in der «Moskauer Gesellschaft für Kunst und Literatur», die er 1888 zusammen mit A. A. Fedotow (1863–1909) gründete; entscheidend war 1898 die Gründung des Moskauer Künstlertheaters (→MChAT) zusammen mit W. I. Nemirowitsch-Dantschenko (1858–1943), der Dramaturgie und geschäftliche Leitung übernahm. Sta-

878 Stanislawski-System

nislawskis Konzept der Anfangsphase sah eine illusionistische Reproduktion der Lebenswirklichkeit auf der Bühne vor (Einfluß des dt. und frz. Naturalismus; Moskauer Gastspiel der →Meininger 1890). Künstlerische «Wahrheit» bedeutete Detailtreue, für die Lokalstudien als sinnvoll erachtet wurden (der Bühnenbildner einer *Othello*-Inszenierung z. B. wurde nach Zypern entsandt). Diese «Wahrheit» sollte jedoch nicht den Ruhm des Regisseurs oder das Startum beim Schauspieler befördern, sondern verstand sich gesellschaftspolitisch als Dienst am Volk.

Stanislawski hat nie Wirklichkeitsabklatsch gefordert, immer aber künstlerische Überzeugung auf der Bühne. Zu diesem Zweck verlangte er vor allem Wahrheit beim Schauspieler. Ließ sich die Physis studieren und trainieren, mußte solches auch im Bereich der Psyche möglich sein. Stanislawskis Methode der Psychotechnik, geboren aus dem Nachdenken über das Geheimnis des schauspielerischen Erfolgs, sollte es dem Künstler ermöglichen, «in sich jenes Selbstgefühl wachzurufen, bei dem die Intuition am leichtesten über ihn kommt». Die Theorie von der «produktiven Einfühlung», wie sie Stanislawski an Inszenierungen von Dramen Tschechows und Gorkis entwickelte, basierte auf der Überzeugung, daß der Schauspieler seine Rolle «nicht durch zufällige Inspiration» gestalte, sondern «durch eine ganze Reihe von Inspirationen, die auf den Proben hervorgerufen und fixiert und im Moment des Schaffens dank der affektiven Erinnerung wiederholt werden». Stanislawskis methodische Prinzipien sind die Reproduktion von Empfindungen aus dem «affektiven Gedächtnis», schöpferische Phantasie und genaue Kenntnis der Umwelt der Rollenfigur. Um die Vorstellungs- und Handlungskraft des Schauspielers zu aktivieren, entwickelte er ein System von Konzentrations- und Imaginationsübungen. Der Darsteller solle sich sagen: «Mir sind die Dinge nicht wichtig, sondern das, was ich tun, wie ich mich in dieser oder jener Erscheinung verhalten würde – *wenn* alles, was mich auf der Bühne umgibt, Wahrheit *wäre*. Ich begriff, daß die schöpferische Arbeit in dem Augenblick beginnt, wenn in der Seele und Phantasie des Schauspielers das magische schöpferische ‹wenn-wäre› auftaucht» (Theorie des «Wenn–Wäre»/«Als ob»).

Die Perfektion, zu der Stanislawski mit seiner Konzeption des psychologischen, illusionistischen Einfühlungstheaters um 1905/06 gelangt war, führte in eine Krise, aus der er sich durch die Beschäftigung mit Entwicklungen im westeurop. Theater (1905/06 Deutschlandtournee, Begegnung mit Max Reinhardt) zu befreien suchte. Die zweite Krise drohte bei Ausbruch der Oktoberrevolution. Stanislawski galt als Repräsentant ‹bürgerlich-subjektivistischer› Kunst, sein Theater lief Gefahr, geschlossen zu werden. 1922 bis 1924 begaben sich Regisseur und Ensemble auf eine zweijährige Gastspielreise durch Europa und die USA. Danach war Stanislawski aus gesundheitlichen Gründen nicht mehr unmittelbar an der Leitung des Theaters beteiligt.

Nun richtete der Theoretiker Stanislawski seine Bemühungen vor allem auf den Ausbau seines Systems der «schöpferischen Phantasie» (der Pädagoge Stanislawski hatte bereits vier Schauspielstudios gegr. – das erste 1913, das vierte 1922 –, in denen nach seiner Methode unterrichtet wurde). Der anfänglich geforderten «Logik der Gefühle» zog er Ende der 20er Jahre eine «Logik der Handlung» vor, die sich überdies auf eine materialistische Grundlage stellen ließ. Schlüsselbegriffe in Stanislawskis neuem Konzept sind «physische Handlung» und «Überaufgabe». Wenn der Schauspieler eine konkrete Vorstellung von der Rollengestalt besitzt, ihre Lebensumstände, ihre Verhaltensweisen erarbeitet und sich in die Psyche der Bühnengestalt eingefühlt hat, stellt sich nach Stanislawskis Überzeugung die richtige «physische Handlung» von selbst ein. Ein Zerfall der Bühnenhandlung in Einzelhandlungen wird durch Beachtung der «Überaufgabe» vermieden, d. i. die Kenntnis von der Idee des Stücks, dem Anliegen des Autors, die leitende Idee der Inszenierung.

Die wesentliche wirkungsgeschichtliche Bedeutung Stanislawskis liegt in der Schaffung eines methodischen Systems der Schauspielkunst, der Psychotechnik.

Stanislavskij, K. S.: Stat'i. Reči. Besedy. Pis'ma. Moskva 1953; ders.: Sobranie sočinenij v 8 tomach. Moskva 1954–61. *In dt. Sprache:* Stanislawski, K.: Das Geheimnis des schauspielerischen Erfolgs. Übers. von A. von Meyenburg. Zürich 1938; Ethik. Berlin 1950; Mein Leben in der Kunst. Berlin 1951; Die Arbeit des Schauspielers an der Rolle. Hg. v. G. W. Kristi. Berlin 1955; Theater. Regie und Schauspieler. Hamburg 1958; Die Arbeit des Schauspielers an sich selbst. Bd. 1–2. Berlin 1961–63; Briefe 1886–1938. Berlin 1975. – Brauneck, M.: Theater im 20. Jahrhundert. Programmschriften, Stilperioden, Reformmodelle. Reinbek bei Hamburg 1982; Cole, T. (Hg.): Acting. A Handbook of the Stanislawski-Method. London/New York 1955; Fevral'skij, A.: Stanislavskij i Mejerchol'd. In: Tarusskie stranicy. Literaturno-chudožestvennyj sbornik. Kaluga 1961, 289–91; Prokofjew, W.: K. S. Stanislawskij und seine Theorie der schauspielerischen Erziehung. In: Stanislawski, K. S.: Theater. Regie und Schauspieler. Hamburg 1958, 131–59; Stroeva, M. N.: Režisserskie iskanija Stanislavskogo 1898–1917, Moskva 1973; 1917–38, Moskva 1977.

Annelore Engel-Braunschmidt

Stanze

(Ital. stanza, frz. stances) Die S. ist urspr. eine ital. Strophenform aus acht weiblichen Elfsilbern (Endecasillabi) mit dem Reimschema ab ab ab ac. Diese auch als Oktave oder Ottaverine bezeichnete S. wird gegen Ende des 13. Jh. erstmals als Versmaß in der ital. erzählerischen Dichtung benutzt und dann zur herrschenden, in der Hochrenaissance gar zur obligaten Form in der Epik. Im 14. und 15. Jh. wird die S. auch von der Lyrik

880 Stasimon

und vom Drama übernommen. In der klassischen Dramaturgie – als ‹stances› in Frankreich v. a. in den Jahren 1630 bis 1660 – bezeichnet der Begriff S. eine Reihe von regelmäßigen Strophen mit einheitlichem Reim- und Rhythmusschema, die von einer in der Regel allein auf der Bühne stehenden Person vorgetragen werden. Jede Strophe endet pointiert und entspricht einer Etappe im verinnerlichten Nachsinnen dieser Person. Die S. erfüllt einerseits eine stilistische Funktion als ‹Gedicht im Gedicht›, andererseits eine dramaturgische Funktion durch die gegenseitige Einwirkung der Lage der Person auf ihre Rede und der Rhetorik auf ihre Entscheidungen und Taten.

Scherer, J.: La dramaturgie classique en France. Paris 1950.

Bernard Poloni

Stasimon

‹Standlied› des →Chors in der griech. →Tragödie; alle Chorlieder mit Ausnahme der →Parodos. Die Bezeichnung S. bedeutet nicht etwa, daß der Chor während des Vortrags unbeweglich an seinem Platz stehen bleibt, sondern wohl – im Unterschied zum Parodos, dem Einzugslied – nun an seinem eigentlichen Standort, in der Orchestra, singt und tanzt.

Dale, A. M.: Stasimon and Hyporcheme (1950). In: ders.: Collected Papers. Cambridge 1969, p. 34–40.

Bernd Seidensticker

Stationendrama

Als eine bestimmte Erscheinungsweise des ‹Dramas der offenen Form›, das im Gegensatz zu dem linear und final gebauten, meist in Akte gegliederten ‹Drama der geschlossenen Form› aus einer lockeren Reihung von Einzelszenen besteht, ist das S. durch das Vorhandensein einer zentralen durchgehenden Figur charakterisiert. Seine Bauweise begegnet bereits im mittelalterlichen →Passionsspiel und im barocken →Märtyrerdrama. Gegen Ende des vorigen Jh. wird sie von August Strindberg (1849–1918) zur Darstellung der Lebensreise seiner Helden genutzt (*Glücks-Peters Reise*, 1881/82, und *Die Schlüssel des Himmelreichs*, 1891/92). Doch erst in seiner Trilogie *Nach Damaskus* (1897–1904) bezeichnet Strindberg die einzelnen Episoden ausdrücklich als ‹Stationen› und stellt damit die Assoziation zur Passion Christi her. Auf Strindberg berufen sich programmatisch die Dramatiker des →Expressionistischen Theaters, die in ihren

S. (z. B. Georg Kaisers *Von morgens bis mitternachts*, 1912; Hanns Johsts *Der junge Mensch*, 1916; Ernst Tollers *Die Wandlung*, 1919; Friedrich Wolfs *Der Unbedingte*, 1921) den Leidensweg und die ‹Wandlung› ihrer Helden darstellen, mit denen sie sich meist in hohem Maße identifizieren. Die übrigen Figuren sind dabei oft nur Projektionen der inneren Wirklichkeiten des Protagonisten. Auf Grund der Dominanz des ‹Dichter-Helden› kommt es im S. kaum zur Entwicklung eines Konflikts zwischen den Figuren; es herrscht vielmehr das Prinzip der Beschreibung von Zuständen, was eine grundsätzliche Ent-Spannung des dramatischen Geschehens zur Folge hat.

Stefanek, P.: Zur Dramaturgie des Stationendramas. In: Keller, W. (Hg.): Beiträge zur Poetik des Dramas. Darmstadt 1976, S. 382–404.

Peter Simhandl

Statist

(Aus lat. stare = stehen) Darsteller stummer Nebenrollen, der nur dazustehen oder vorgeschriebene Bewegungen zu tun hat. Die S. unterstehen einem Statistenchef und bilden in personenreichen Inszenierungen mit den ‹Edelstatisten›, die einen Satz zu sprechen haben, die Statisterie. Die S. werden in der Regel, anders als die →Komparsen, von der Straße herbeigeholt und füllen nur die Szene, ohne sie zu beleben. Heute wird das Wort S. vorwiegend in der Theatersprache verwendet, das Wort →Komparse dagegen eher beim Film.

Bernard Poloni

Stegreiftheater

Das Spiel aus dem Stegreif oder das S. entsteht fast ohne Vorbereitung (→Improvisation) im Prozeß des Spielens. Stegreif (mhd.) bedeutet Steigbügel; das Bild: der reitende Bote verläßt nicht den Steigbügel nach Übergabe der Botschaft, sondern er reitet unverzüglich mit erhaltener Antwort zurück. – J. L. Moreno hat in seinem 1921 in Wien gegründeten S. wesentliche Erkenntnisse zur Therapieform des →Psychodramas gewonnen. Zur Geschichte des S. →Commedia dell'arte, →Mimus.

Moreno, J. L.: Das Stegreiftheater. Berlin 1923; Scherf, E.: Aus dem Stegreif. In: Kursbuch 34. Berlin 1973.

Elisabeth Scherf

Stehendes Theater

Bezeichnung für ein in einem nur dem Theater gewidmeten Gebäude spielendes, längere Zeit an einem Ort bleibendes Ensemble mit festem Engagement. Gegenbegriff zu den →Wanderbühnen, die nur kurzzeitig an einem Ort verweilten, dort entweder Säle mieteten für ihre Aufführungen oder selbst eine eigene ‹Bude› aufschlugen, auf der sie spielten. Heute bezeichnet S. T. auch den Gegensatz zum →Tourneetheater. – Im Deutschland des 18. Jh. war der Begriff eng verbunden mit der Idee eines →Nationaltheaters. Entsprechend den jeweiligen historischen Bedingungen verlief die Herausbildung S. T. in den verschiedenen Ländern unterschiedlich, sowohl was die zeitliche Abfolge wie die Intensität der Entwicklung betraf.

Wolfgang Beck

steirischer herbst

Österreich. Avantgarde-Festival mit Schwerpunkt auf dem musikalischen Sektor. Findet seit 1968 jährlich in den Monaten September, Oktober und November in Graz statt. Träger: Land Steiermark, Stadt Graz, Österr. Rundfunk Landesstudio Steiermark, Vereinigte Bühnen Graz und private Institutionen. Intendant: Horst Gerhard Haberl. Theater (Oper, Schauspiel, Ballett, Kabarett), Musikprotokoll (Konzerte), Bildende Kunst (Dreiländerbiennale trigon, Ausstellungen, Installationen, Performance, Kunstpreis), Symposien (Steirische Akademie, Literatursymposion, Musiksymposion, Trigonsymposion, Architektursymposion). Lesungen, Hörspiele, Workshops, Grazer Filmtage, Fernsehtage, Open House (für die Jugend, auch Untergrundkunst).

Zahlreiche Uraufführungen österr. und deutschspr. Dramatiker: u. a. Ödön von Horváth: *Zur schönen Aussicht* (1969); Gerhard Roth: *Lichtenberg* (1973), *Sehnsucht* (1977), *Dämmerung* (1978), *Erinnerungen an die Menschheit* (1985); Ernst Jandl: *Die Humanisten* (1976), *Aus der Fremde* (1979); Elfriede Jelinek: *Was geschah, nachdem Nora ihren Mann verlassen hatte oder Stützen der Gesellschaften* (1979); Felix Mitterer: *Veränderungen* (Gastspiel des Theaters in der Josefstadt, 1980); Peter Turrini: *Josef und Maria* (Gastspiel des Volkstheaters Wien, 1980); Herbert Achternbusch: *Mein Herbert* (1983); Heiner Müller: *Bildbeschreibung* (1985); Ursula Voss/George Tabori: *Masada* (Coproduktion mit dem Theater der Kreis, 1988); Botho Strauß: *Angelas Kleider* (1991).

Kaufmann, P. (Hg.): 20 Jahre steirischer herbst. Wien/Darmstadt 1988.

Ingeborg Janich

Stella Kultur Management

Private Holdinggesellschaft für Ensuite-Musicalproduktionen (Stella Theaterproduktions GmbH, Stella Opernveranstaltungs GmbH, Stella Musical Veranstaltungs GmbH). Drei Spielstätten: Operettenhaus, Hamburg (erbaut 1948/50, renoviert 1979/80), Musical *Cats* von Andrew Lloyd Webber seit 1986; Neue Flora, Hamburg (erbaut 1989/90), Musical *Das Phantom der Oper* von Andrew Lloyd Webber seit 1990; Starlighttheater, Bochum (erbaut 1988, Arenaform), Musical *Starlight Express* seit 1988.

Ingeborg Janich

Stichomythie

Die S. ist ursprünglich ein Dialog, wo jede Replik sich nur über eine Zeile erstreckt und inhaltlich in Gegensatz zur vorangegangenen steht. Die Replik kann auch einen Doppelvers – Distichomythie –, in weniger strengen Varianten sogar einen Vierzeiler einnehmen oder auf eine Halbzeile reduziert werden – Hemis. Durch diese schnelle Abwechslung von Rede und Gegenrede eignet sich die S. für die Darstellung von Konfliktsituationen und heftigen Auseinandersetzungen. Der Dialog in der S. entwickelt sich gewöhnlich zum Rededuell: Die Sprache wird zur Waffe, womit es den Gegner zu kontern und zu überwinden gilt. Der höchst rhetorische Charakter der S. wird durch den häufigen Gebrauch der →Sentenz und der Anaklasis (Wiederaufnahme desselben Wortes durch den 2. Gespächspartner) unterstrichen. Die S. ist im griech. Drama in den Tragödien des Seneca (4 v. Chr.–65 n. Chr.), im Renaissance- und Barocktheater beliebte Dialogform; sie wird von den frz. und dt. Klassikern und später noch – meistens in antikisierender Absicht – verwendet.

Jens, W.: Die Stichomythie in der frühen griech. Tragödie. München 1955; Scherer, J.: La Dramaturgie classique en France. Paris 1983.

Alain Muzelle

Stilbühne

Bühnenausstattung und -bau aus der Zeit kurz vor und nach der Jahrhundertwende, entstanden im Umfeld der antinaturalistischen, symbolistischen Kunstbewegung. Wichtigste Exponenten in Deutschland (→Theaterreform) waren Georg Fuchs (1868–1949) und das → Münchener Künstlertheater sowie Peter Behrens (1868–1940); in Frankreich der Lyriker Paul Fort (1872–1960) mit dem Théâtre de l'Art und sein Nachfolger Lugné-Poë am → Théâtre de l'Œuvre; in Rußland vor allem Meyerhold; in England E. G. Craig (→ Über-Marionette).

Höhepunkte waren die Aufführungen der Stücke der Symbolisten wie Maeterlinck, Ibsen, Strindberg, Claudel, Alexander Blok (1880–1921) und die Mitarbeit bekannter Maler wie die ‹Nabis› bei Paul Fort (Sérusier, Bonnard, Vuillard) und Lugné-Poë, für den auch E. Munch und Toulouse-Lautrec malten, oder bei Meyerhold und Stanislawski V. E. Egorov und A. Golovin. Charakteristisch für die S. ist die Vorherrschaft des Worts und des sprechenden Schauspielers, unterstützt durch mildfarbige Vorhänge, stilisierte Versatzstücke und erlesene Gegenstände mit symbolischer Bedeutung. Es ging um diskrete Evokation, Schattierungen, Nuancen, Suggestion durch Farben und Beleuchtung, subtile Korrespondenzen zwischen verschiedenen künstlerischen Eindrücken und Effekten. Allerdings bei Lugné-Poë (Jarrys *Ubu-Roi*, 1896) und den Russen (Meyerholds Inszenierung von Bloks *Balaganchik*, 1906) auch manchmal kritische Verzerrung des Ästhetizismus ins → Groteske. – Die S. war eine wichtige Phase der Retheatralisierung, wegweisend für das → theatralische Theater und die Theaterarbeit der Maler der Ecole de Paris.

Bablet, D.: La mise en scène contemporaine 1887–1914. Brüssel 1968; ders.: Les révolutions scéniques du XXe siècle. Paris 1975; Brauneck, M.: Theater im 20. Jh. Reinbek bei Hamburg 1982.

Gérard Schneilin

Straßentheater

(→ Politisches Volkstheater [USA], → Arbeitertheater, → Politisches Theater, → Freies Theater) Eine Form des Theaters, die ihre Gegensätzlichkeit zum «Theater Theater» (P. Handke) mit dem Verweis auf den anderen Spielort manifestiert. Insbesondere politische Theatergruppen haben sich Form und Bezeichnung des Straßentheaters für ihre kritisch oppositionellen Interessen zu eigen gemacht.

Formen des S. existierten in Deutschland schon während der Weimarer Republik im Zusammenhang mit der Arbeiterbewegung. Damals schlossen sich sozialistische und kommunistische Arbeiter nach sowj. Vorbild (→ Theateroktober, → Blaue Blusen) zu Theatergruppen zusammen, spielten Sketches sowie längere Agitationsstücke auf der Straße und bei

Versammlungen. Bekannte Agitpropgruppen waren Rotes Sprachrohr, Rote Revue und Truppe 31. Auch die happeningartigen Aktionen im Rahmen der Protestbewegung gegen die Remilitarisierung der BRD von 1954 bis 1957 und die Sprechwerk-Aufführungen der Naturfreunde- und Gewerkschaftsjugend sowie die Songgruppen der Ostermärsche (ab 1960/61) sind zu den Vorläufern des S. in der BRD zu rechnen.

Die S. der 67/68er-Bewegung hatten ein eindeutiges Aufklärungsinteresse. Sie verstanden sich als Alternative zum traditionellen Theater. Ästhetische Fragen waren dem S. unwichtig, ja eher verpönt, gar tabuisiert. Die Gruppen spielten kurze, aktualitätsbezogene, selbstgeschriebene Szenen und Stücke. Oft wurde für eine bestimmte Demonstration oder Aktion eine Szene entwickelt, die dann nur einmal zur Aufführung kam. Die Stilmittel waren zumeist recht puritanisch gehalten, die Sprache oft abstrakt und plakativ. Wesentliche Inspirationen gingen von US-amerikan. S.-Gruppen aus, insbesondere von →Bread and Puppet, →San Francisco Mime Troupe und dem →Teatro Campesino. Die meisten bundesdeutschen S. übernahmen aber nicht den szenischen Reichtum der amerikan. S.; sie hatten nur zu einem geringen Teil Interesse an der Entwicklung ihres theatralen Stils. Kulturkritische Reflexion mündete in aller Regel in undialektischer Negation: «Weg mit der Kunst», «ästhetische Formen sind nur kulinarisch» (Westberliner Sozialistisches Straßentheater) waren die einschlägigen Parolen.

In den 70er Jahren verlor das S. in der BRD seine ausschließliche Abhängigkeit vom Primat der Politik. Intensivere Auseinandersetzungen mit Theaterästhetik und Spielpädagogik hatten die Entwicklung neuer Formen des S. zur Folge: Prozessionen, Maskenspiele, Zirkusnummern, Mitmachaktionen. Das politische S. ist seither nur eine Form unter anderen und prägt keinesfalls mehr das Bild der gesamten S.-Szene.

Hüfner, A.: Straßentheater. Frankfurt/M. 1970; Streettheatre versus Festival. Wien/Köln 1989.

Georg Stenzaly

Stratford-upon-Avon

Ort in der mittelenglischen Grafschaft Warwickshire, in dem William Shakespeare geboren wurde, seine letzten Jahre verbrachte und starb. 1769 veranstaltete David Garrick (1717–79) das erste Sommerfestival. 1879 wurde das erste Theater auf dem Standort des jetzigen Schauspielhauses eröffnet und ein einwöchiges Dramenfestival im Sommer begonnen. 1932 wurde das Shakespeare Memorial Theatre (heute Royal Shakespeare Theatre) eröffnet. 1960 wurde die →Royal Shakespeare Company unter der Leitung von Peter Hall mit Sitz in S. und London gegründet (RSC).

J. Lawrence Guntner

Striptease

(Engl. to strip = abstreifen, entkleiden, ausziehen; to tease = aufreizen, plagen) Varieté- oder Kabarett-Nummer, wobei meist eine einzige Person sich unter Musikbegleitung langsam und schrittweise entkleidet; ursprünglich nur Frauen-, mit dem Schwulen- und Transvestiten-Kabarett auch Männer-S. – Der Ursprung des S. ist umstritten. Vorläufer in der amerik. →Burleske (burlesque), einem nur Männern vorbehaltenen Komödien- und Sex-Entertainment. Erfinder der volkstümlich als ‹Beine-Schau› (leg show oder burleycue) bezeichneten abendfüllenden burleycue comedy (mit Bloßstellung ‹verborgener weiblicher Reize›/‹woman's hidden charms› und einem ‹hootchy-kootchy› genannten Bauchtanz als Zusatzattraktion) war Michael Bennett Leavitt (1843–1933). Eigentliche Entstehung des S. wohl durch die Trapezkünstlerin Charmian, die bei einer Vorführung unabsichtlich ihr Trikot verlor. Um 1920 S. am New Yorker Broadway durch Gypsy Rose Lee als Revue-Element ausgebildet. S. gehört heute in den Show-Nummern der Nachtlokale zur Routine.

Barthes, R.: In: Mythologies. Paris 1957; Bell, L.: Strip-tease as a National Art. In: American Mercury 1965; Chevalier, D.: Métaphysique du strip-tease. Paris 1960.

Horst Schumacher

Studententheater

Seit dem frühen 15. Jh. wird an Universitäten Theater gespielt (→Schultheater, →Humanismus/Drama und Theater des Humanismus). Die verschiedenen Formen von S. heute unterscheiden sich vor allem durch die Beziehung der Spielgruppen zur Universität. Eine Form ist das Theaterspiel, das fest an bestimmte universitäre Ausbildungsgänge gebunden ist: z.B. Theatergruppen an theaterwissenschaftlichen Instituten, die die theoretisch erworbenen Kenntnisse praktisch erproben wollen oder in Vergessenheit geratene bzw. noch unbekannte Stücke aufführen; vor allem aber Theateraufführungen von Studenten an Hochschulen für Darstellende Kunst, die unmittelbarer Teil des Ausbildungsbetriebs sind (z. B. als Abschlußprüfungen).

Eine andere Form ist das Theaterspiel von Studenten aus den unterschiedlichsten Fachbereichen, deren Bezug zur Universität sich meist nur auf die Benutzung von deren Räumen beschränkt. Diese Form von S. kam insbesondere in den Jahren nach 1945 auf; charakteristisch war die Beschäftigung mit Klassikern und literarischen Raritäten, die Auseinandersetzung mit dem amerik., engl. und frz. Nachkriegstheater und mit dem absurden Theater. Direkte Kontakte zu ausländischen S. ermöglichten die jährlichen internationalen Treffen: ab 1949 die Internationale Theaterwoche in Erlangen, ab 1952 das Festival Internazionale del Teatro Universitario in Parma. Die experimentelle Dramatik (Beckett, Adamov, Ionesco) prägt das S. besonders in der Mitte der 60er Jahre. Ende der 60er Jahre erfolgt eine Politisierung des S. in unmittelbarem Zusammenhang mit der sog. Studentenbewegung und der außerparlamentarischen Opposition (→Straßentheater). Um der Einengung ihres Wirkungskreises durch die Bindung an die Universität zu entgehen, engagieren sich in den 70er Jahren immer mehr S. außerhalb der Universitäten bei den sog. Freien Gruppen (→Freies Theater). Die Entwicklung führte zu einer völligen Loslösung aus dem akademischen Umfeld. Heute existieren an bundesdt. Universitäten kaum noch S., allenfalls im Zusammenhang mit fremdsprachlichem Unterricht.

Das amerik. College-Theatre nimmt innerhalb des S. eine Sonderposition ein. An den Drama Departments mancher Universitäten kann ein akademischer Abschluß (bachelor of arts) erreicht werden; die Ausbildung ist generell durch eine enge Verbindung von theoretischer und praktischer Arbeit geprägt. Die Studenten arbeiten an den in der Regel gutausgestatteten Campus-Theatern quasi unter professionellen Bedingungen. Neben dem festen Lehrkörper werden regelmäßig renommierte Künstler als Lehrer eingeladen. Diese Campus-Theater sind in vielen Städten der USA die eigentlichen Träger des lokalen theater-kulturellen Lebens: als Träger bzw. Initiatoren von Festspielen und Sommerkursen und vor allem mit dem regelmäßigen Angebot ihrer Aufführungen. Seit 1969 gibt es das American College Theatre Festival.

Auch in England spielt die Theaterarbeit studentischer Clubs eine wichtige Rolle für den Nachwuchs in den Theaterberufen. 1885 bereits wurde die Oxford University Dramatic Society (OUDS) gegründet, aus der zahlreiche bedeutende Schauspieler und Regisseure hervorgegangen sind. Gespielt wird vor allem Shakespeare, oft unter Mitarbeit professioneller Regisseure.

Eine besondere Bedeutung hat das S. in Polen. Als ‹Barometer der gesellschaftlichen Stimmung› spielt das S. seit 1955/56 bis heute die Rolle

888 Studententheater

einer dritten Kraft in der polnischen Kultur. Finanziell u. a. durch Studentenorganisationen und Hochschulen unterstützt, konzentriert es sich in den Studentenklubs (nur wenige verfügen über eigene Räume); einige (z. B. «Kalambur» – Wrocław, «Teatr STU» – Kraków) sind vielseitig aktiv: Bilder- und Fotogalerien, literarische und musikalische Aktivitäten, eigene Cafés, Verlagstätigkeit. Gesamtzahl: ca. 100; Hauptzentren: Kraków, Wrocław, Warszawa, Poznań, Łódź. Verschiedenartige Ausdrucksformen: politisches Kabarett, «Theater der Poesie», Pantomime (Warszawa, Łódź, Szczecin, Wrocław – «Gest», gegr. 1962). Instrumental- und Experimentaltheater. In der zweiten Hälfte der 70er Jahre sind fünf Studententheater zu Berufstheatern geworden (vom Staat finanziert; Externenprüfungen der Schauspieler), wobei sie sich jedoch eine gewisse programmatische Unabhängigkeit erhalten haben.

Die erste Hälfte der 60er Jahre ist – trotz einer schnellen quantitativen Entwicklung der Studententheater – durch ihre geringere gesellschaftliche Resonanz gekennzeichnet. Auf der Suche nach neuen Formen konzentrieren sich die Gruppen auf ästhetische Experimente, wobei die gegenwärtige Lyrik zum wichtigsten Bühnenstoff wurde. Im Repertoire dominieren mehr illustrative als kreative Formen. Ende der 60er Jahre wird die politische, ästhetische und Repertoirekrise an den Theatern immer sichtbarer. Die durch die Ereignisse von 1970 verursachte Erschütterung hatte zur Folge, daß das Studententheater (auch ‹politisches›, ‹offenes›, ‹unabhängiges› bzw. junges Theater genannt) den Charakter einer Bewegung anzunehmen beginnt. In den Theatern setzt man sich mit der aktuellen Politik und der poln. Geschichte auseinander, sucht nach eigener Identität, kämpft um einen neuen Menschen. Im Vordergrund stehen experimentelle Theater; eine entscheidende Rolle spielt dabei das Theater-Laboratorium von Jerzy Grotowski (→Armes Theater).

Die ausschlaggebenden Gruppen zu dieser Zeit waren: «Teatr STU» in Kraków (gegr. 1966, ab 1975 professionell). Gründer, Regisseur, Intendant: Krzysztof Jasiński (*1943), über 70 Premieren, paratheatralische Vorstellungen, Werkstätte, Zuschauerraum (ab 1976) 220 Plätze, drei Zelte (600–1200 Plätze), Bildergalerie, Café. Teilnahme an ca. 100 In- und Auslandsfestivals (u. a. vielmals in der BRD), zahlreiche internationale Preise. Im Repertoire u. a. Ionesco, Cocteau, Picasso, Eliot, Joyce. Sein Weg führte von der Diagnose der sozial-politischen Situation (die Aufführung *Spadanie* 1971 eröffnete eine neue Epoche in der Entwicklung des poln. Studententheaters) und der Zerschlagung von Nationalmythen (*Sennik polski*, 1971) bis hin zum Aufgreifen universeller, philosophischer Probleme (Freiheit, Wahrheit). – «Teatr 77» in Łódź (gegr. 1970), mehrere Bühnen: Drama, Poesie, Kabarett, Pantomime. Zyklus: *Koło czy tryptyk*, 1971; *Pasja*, 1972; *Retrospektywa*, 1973 (u. a. Venedig,

Nancy). «Teatr Ósmego Dnia» (gegr. 1964 als Studententheater, seit 1979 professionell). Über 40 Premieren (u. a. England, Italien). Experimentelles Theater; in der ersten Periode Inszenierung von Stücken (u. a. poln. Erstaufführung von Weiss' *Marat/Sade*). Knüpft an das →Theater der Grausamkeit von Artaud und an Erfahrungen von Grotowski an. Konsequent realisiertes Prinzip der kollektiven Arbeit. Höchst metaphorisierte Theatersprache, einfache Mittel, intensive emotionelle Spannung, «Poetik des Geschreis». In den 70er Jahren u. a. Verwertung eigener Texte und Fragmente aus der Literatur (Dostojewski, Lenin, Camus, Faulkner, Eliot, Barańczak).

Zu Höhepunkten im kulturellen Studentenleben wurden Festivals verschiedener Art (in den 70er Jahren etwa 20 jährlich), vor allem in Łódź und Wrocław. Die durch das Zentrum des Offenen Theaters «Kalambur» veranstalteten Internationalen Festivals des Offenen Theaters (1967–75, alle zwei Jahre) waren – neben dem Festival in →Nancy – die größte Präsentation der Theateravantgarde Europas und gleichzeitig die einzige in den sozialistischen Ländern. An fünf Festivals beteiligten sich über 100 Theater aus 24 Ländern, darunter →Bread and Puppet Theatre, →Odin Teatret und →Tenjo Sajiki von Shuji Terayama. Der Direktor der Festivals war Bogusław Litwiniec, Regisseur, Schauspieler, Gründer und langjähriger Intendant des Theaters «Kalambur». In einer veränderten Form wurden die Festivals des Offenen Theaters ab 1978 fortgesetzt. – Ośrodek Teatru Otwartego «Kalambur» (gegr. 1957, seit 1979 professionell); über 60 Premieren; paratheatralische Vorstellungen, vielmals im Ausland (auch in der BRD). Führendes Studententheater seit den 60er Jahren. Verschiedene Inspirationsquellen: politisches Kabarett, avantgardistische Einakter, Dokumentarstücke, u. a. Stücke von Borchert, Frisch und Kroetz. Bahnbrechende Aufführung *Szewcy* von S. I. Witkiewicz (90 Aufführungen); eigene Form im poetischen Theater gefunden: *Futurystykon* (1967) und *W rytmie siońca* (1970) – Synthese des politisch und moralisch engagierten Theaters. Seit einigen Jahren hauptsächlich Stücke für Kinder. Besonders aktiv als Künstlerklub: Café, Bildergalerie, Kabarett, Verlagstätigkeit; lädt polnische und ausländische Theater ein.

Ein großer Teil der ‹offenen Theater› war in den 70er Jahren mit dem sog. Paratheater, dem Wander-, Straßentheater, verbunden, wo es zu einer interdisziplinären Zusammenarbeit von bildender Kunst, Musik, Pantomime und Theater kam. Hauptrepräsentanten dieser Entwicklung sind das «Teatr Ósmego Dnia», «Teatr STU», «Teatr 77» und «Akademia Ruchu» in Warszawa (gegr. 1973 von Wojciech Krukowski): happeningartige Aktivitäten bis hin zum Straßentheater. Vorherrschend ist die dynamische Körperplastik, die sich in die soziale Wirklichkeit einmengt und nur selten durch das Wort unterstützt wird; Prinzip der kollektiven

890 Studio

Kreation. Ende der 70er Jahre wurde das ‹offene Theater› zu einem Teil der offiziellen Kultur, viele Gruppen gerieten in die existentiell-moralistische Rhetorik ohne größere Resonanz. Andererseits bilden sich neue Gruppen im Lande und beleben die Szene Anfang der 80er Jahre. Lublin wird ein neues Zentrum des ‹offenen Theaters› (Teatr Provisorium; Scena Plastyczna der Katholischen Universität; «Gardźienice»), das in der gegenwärtigen ökonomischen und allgemeinen Sinnkrise des poln. Theaters keine Nachfolger hat.

Banachowska, K. (u. a.): Ośrodek Teatru Otwartego Kalambur. Warszawa 1982; Chudziński, E./Nyczek, T. (Red.): Teatr STU. Warszawa 1982; Drawicz, A. (u. a.): Teatry studenckie w Polsce. Warszawa 1968; Nyczek, T.: Pełnym głosem. Teatry studenckie w Polsce 1970–75. Kraków 1980; Renk, H. E.: Zwischen Theorie und Praxis. In: Theater heute 10/1985; Sztuka Otwarta (Hg.): AOT Kalambur. Wrocław. Bd. 1: Teatr a poezja 1975; Bd. 2: Wspólnota – kreacja – teatr 1977; Bd. 3: Parateatr 1980; Bd. 4: Parateatr II 1982.

Ute Hagel / Slawomir Tryc / Elke Wiegand

Studio

(Ital. Atelier, Arbeitszimmer) Als Studio- oder Werkstatt-Theater konzipierte Versuchsbühne, oft als ‹Kleines Haus› einem größeren Theater angeschlossen, spielt vor weniger Zuschauern und bevorzugt avantgardistische Stücke. Die ersten Studio-Theater befanden sich am Moskauer Künstlertheater (→MChAT) unter Konstantin Sergejewitsch Stanislawski (1863–1938), und zwar das erste unter Leopold Antonowitsch Sulerschitzki (1872–1916) 1913, das zweite 1916, das dritte 1920 unter Jewgeni Bogrationowitsch Wachtangow (1883–1922) und das vierte 1922, aus dem die →Habima entstand.

Horst Schumacher

Studio 1934

Kennzeichen des Arbeitsstils der im März 1934 von Hedda Zinner in Prag gegr. Emigrantengruppe war der bes. Einsatz vokaler und musikalischer Elemente, der wie in einem Orchester erfolgte – eine Kunstform, die ohne Requisiten, Dekoration und Kostüme auskam, die Kollektivität förderte und durch die Voiceband-Experimente des tschech. Theatermannes František Burian angeregt war. Zum Kern der Gruppe gehörten neben Hedda Zinner die Texter Fritz Erpenbeck und Erich Freund sowie der Pianist Rolf Jacoby. Bis zum Sommer 1935 brachte die Gruppe vier vielbeachtete Programme heraus, die eine Mischung aus Kabarett, Kantate, Rezitation und Schauspiel mit deutlich politischen Akzenten darstellten.

Jan Hans

Studio-Theater-Bewegung

Die S.-T.-B. in der GUS/UdSSR seit der 2. Hälfte der 80er Jahre ist als Demokratisierungs- und Erneuerungsbewegung im Theater verbunden mit dem gesellschaftlichen Umbruch und dessen Vorbereitung, knüpft im Anspruch (ideell und organisatorisch) an ähnliche Trends in den 20er und 50/60er Jahren an. Neben Studio-Theatern im Amateurbereich (oft auf hohem Niveau) ist sie auf professioneller Ebene der Versuch, Raum für ästhetische Experimente, die in den Strukturen der ‹steinernen› Theater nicht möglich waren, zu schaffen, dem Nachwuchs rechtzeitig eine Chance zu geben, auch neue Theater zu gründen (→Škola Dramatičeskogo iskusstva). Mit der Perestroika ab 1985/86 Legalisierung von im Untergrund existierenden Theatergruppen und Entstehung neuer («Terra mobile», St. Petersburg). Inszenierungen von vergessener/verbotener Dramatik (Oberiuten) der 20er Jahre, westeurop. Absurder, zeitgenössischer Autoren, auch Experimente mit der Klassik (Studio «Tschjot-Netschet»; Studio «Tschelowek»; Theaterstudio «Am Nikita-Tor»; «Studio-Theater von O. Tabakow»; Jugend-Theaterstudio «Na Krasnoi Presne»). In Moskau z. Z. mehr als 200 Studios, die Mehrzahl künstlerisch unbedeutend wegen fehlender Programmatik für das ‹andere Theater›, mangelnder Beherrschung entsprechender Ausdrucksmittel. Unter dem ökonomischen Druck der Selbstfinanzierung Kommerzialisierungstendenzen. Der Russische Theaterverband unterstützt mit der VOTM (Allrussische Vereinigung «Kreative Werkstätten») innovative Studios in Moskau, Petersburg, Woronesh u. a.

Elke Wiegand

Stummes Spiel

Mimisch-gestisches Spiel eines Schauspielers zum Ausdruck seiner Gefühle während der Zeit, in der er auf der Bühne ist, aber keinen Text zu sprechen hat. Das s. S. gewann größere Bedeutung erst im 18. Jh., seit vor allem in den bürgerlichen Schauspielen detaillierte Bühnenanweisungen Mienenspiel und Gestik der Schauspieler als Ausdrucksmittel in die Aufführung einzubeziehen begannen. – Vor der Entwicklung des s. S. vermittelten die Schauspieler im Drama und der Oper häufig durch ‹Beiseitesprechen› (→Aparte) dem Zuschauer ihre Gefühle und Meinungen während der Zeit, in der sie keinen Rollentext hatten.

Wolfgang Beck

Sturmbühne

Von Herwarth Walden (eig. Georg Levin, 1878–1941) und Lothar Schreyer (1886–1966) im September 1917 in Berlin gegr. Die S. ist neben der →«Kampfbühne» wichtigstes expressionistisches Experimentiertheater. 1918 auch Zeitschrift S. (Mitarbeiter u. a. Walter Mehring, Kurt Schwitters). Es war der Versuch der Entwicklung eines expressionistischen Theaters als Einheit von Wortkunstwerk, Bewegungskunstwerk und Werk der bildenden Kunst. Einzige Aufführung der S.: August Stramms *Sancta Susanna* (1918). – Die Zeitschrift «Der Sturm» (1910 bis 32), der Sturm-Verlag, die Kunstabende, die Kunstschule (ab 1916) und die Galerie «Sturm» (1912–28) waren Foren des Frühexpressionismus, Kubismus und Futurismus in Deutschland. Waldens «Wortkunsttheorie» gilt als Zusammenfassung der Ästhetik des «Sturm».

Pirsich, V.: Der Sturm. Herzberg 1985; Wasserka, I.: Die Sturm- und Kampfbühne. Kunsttheorie und szenische Wirklichkeit im expressionistischen Theater Lothar Schreyers. Diss. Wien 1965.

Ingeborg Janich

Sturm und Drang / Theater des Sturm und Drang

Von F. M. Klingers gleichnamigem Drama (urspr. Titel: *Wirrwarr*, 1776) Ende des 19. Jh. übernommene Bezeichnung für die dt. Literaturepoche zwischen 1769 und 1785/86. Sie ist in ihrer Bedeutung, ihrer genauen zeitlichen Einordnung und der Abgrenzung von anderen Epochen bis heute umstritten. Ihr Beginn wird zumeist mit Herders *Journal meiner Reise im Jahre 1769* angesetzt, ihr Ausklang mit dem Ende von Schillers Mannheimer Zeit (1785) und dem Beginn von Goethes ital. Reise (1786). S. u. D. ist eine auf den deutschsprachigen Raum beschränkte Erscheinung der Literatur, die in den übrigen europ. Ländern keine Entsprechung hatte und auch auf die anderen Künste nur geringen Einfluß ausübte. Er ist eine zeitlich begrenzte Erscheinung im Jh. der Aufklärung, deren Postulate er zugleich aufnimmt, weiterführt und kritisiert.

Während sich in den meisten europ. Ländern die Aufklärung entfaltete und die gesellschaftliche Krise einer Revolution entgegendrängte, fand im Heiligen Römischen Reich Deutscher Nation die Revolution in der Literatur statt, erklärlich aus seiner historischen und sozioökonomischen Sonderentwicklung. Forderungen wurden erhoben, die für die Entwicklung der dt. Literatur und Ästhetik entscheidende Bedeutung gewannen: Die bereits in der Aufklärung angelegte und geäußerte Sozialkritik wurde verschärft, das selbstschöpferische Genie trat an die Stelle des nach vorgegebenen Regeln arbeitenden Dichters, die Rechte des Individuums gegenüber der abstrakten Ratio und ‹Vernünftigkeit› der Aufklärung wurden angemeldet, Kunst sollte nicht mehr Zwecken gehorchen, die außer ihr lagen, sondern ‹autonom› sein (was nicht mit dem ‹L'art pour l'art› der Jahrhundertwende verwechselt werden darf). Die Stürmer und Dränger, zu denen Herder, Lenz, Wagner, Klinger ebenso gehörten wie der junge Goethe und der frühe Schiller, lehnten die Theorie, Kunst sei lediglich Naturnachahmung, ebenso ab wie die überkommene normative Gattungspoetik – was nicht heißt (wie ihnen oft vorgeworfen wurde), sie seien grundsätzlich gegen jede Art von Regeln für die Kunst gewesen. Das Drama war für sie die wichtigste Dichtungsgattung. Dennoch gibt es keine in sich geschlossene Dramaturgie des S. u. D., der die Werke aller Autoren untergeordnet werden könnten.

Die dramaturgischen Neuansätze des S. u. D. grenzen sich ab von der klassizistischen frz. Tragödie (ähnlich wie bereits Lessing) und beziehen sich statt dessen auf das ‹Genie› Shakespeare. Hinzu kommt der Einfluß der Franzosen Diderot und Mercier. Grundlegend für ihre Definition der Kunst und des Künstlers war der Engländer Shaftesbury, der den Dichter als «zweiten Schöpfer» bezeichnet hatte. Dieser Ansatz ermöglichte es den Stürmern und Drängern, von der Nachahmungstheorie abzurücken, Kunst als Neuschöpfung zu begreifen und zugleich den genialen Künstler von der Herrschaft vorgegebener Regeln zu befreien. Trotz dieser gemeinsamen Grundanschauungen gibt es unterschiedliche Akzentuierungen in den poetologischen Auffassungen der Stürmer und Dränger. Tendierte Herder etwa dazu, das Drama zur Dichtung schlechthin auszuweiten, ohne dabei Rücksicht auf das eigentlich Theatralische zu nehmen, so blieb J. M. R. Lenz in seinen *Anmerkungen übers Theater* (entworfen 1771, überarbeitet veröff. 1774) sehr viel näher an der Realität des damaligen Theaters. Sein pessimistischer Blick auf die Gegenwart erlaubte es Lenz, aktuelle Entwicklungen des Theaters scharfsichtig zu analysieren; tastend und zögernd waren hingegen seine Versuche, das angestrebte Drama der Zukunft zu beschreiben. Auch ihm ging es – wie Lessing – um Aufklärung mittels des Theaters. Er mißtraute jedoch der unmittelbaren Wirkung von Furcht und Mitleid auf den Zuschauer und der Umsetzung dieser Affekte in allg. Menschlichkeit. Dem unbeeinflußbaren Fatum der antiken griech. Tragödie stellte Lenz die gesellschaftliche Determinierung des individuellen Schicksals gegenüber, der Schicksals- die Charaktertragödie. Im Gegensatz zu Lessing galt für Lenz nicht mehr das →bürgerliche Trauerspiel als das seiner Zeit angemessene Genre, sondern die Komödie, in der es nicht mehr um das Auslachen individuellen Fehlverhaltens geht, sondern um die durch Komik mögliche Kritik an den Verhältnissen («Komödie ist Gemälde der menschlichen Gesellschaft, und wenn die ernsthaft wird, kann das Gemälde nicht lachend werden»). In seinen Bemühungen um das Theater als Medium gesellschaftlicher Kritik und aufklärerischer Bemühung griff Lenz auch auf die bereits von Lessing u. a. propagierte →Nationaltheateridee zurück.

Auch der junge Schiller nahm diesen Gedanken in seinem Aufsatz über *Die Schaubühne als eine moralische Anstalt betrachtet* (1784) auf, der 1785 unter dem weniger programmatisch klingenden Titel «Was kann eine gute stehende Schaubühne eigentlich wirken?» veröffentlicht wurde. In Umkehrung des pessimistischen Fazits Lessings, ohne eine Nation gebe es auch kein Nationaltheater, betonte Schiller: «Wenn wir es erlebten, eine Nationalbühne zu haben, so würden wir auch eine Nation.» Das Theater war für Schiller am Ende seiner ersten Schaffensperiode «mehr als jede andere öffentliche Anstalt des Staats eine Schule der praktischen Weisheit, ein Wegweiser durch das bürgerliche Leben», der Ort, wo die Gerechtigkeit geübt wurde, die die Realität nur zu oft versagte. – Auch diese Einschätzung des Theaters und seiner Möglichkeiten blieb Utopie, genauso wie die Dramen der Stürmer und Dränger und ihre theoretischen Äußerungen Zeugnisse eines ‹notwendigen› Scheiterns sind: Das theatralisch umgesetzte Ungenügen am «tintenklecksenden Säculum» (Schiller) konnte die Verhältnisse in Deutschland nicht ändern.

Arntzen, H.: Die ernste Komödie. München 1968; Guthke, K. S.: Das deutsche bürgerliche Trauerspiel. Stuttgart 1972; Hammer, K. (Hg.): Dramaturgische Schriften des 18. Jahrhunderts. Berlin 1968; Hinck, W. (Hg.): Sturm und Drang. Kronberg/Ts. 1978; ders.: Sturm und Drang. Frankfurt/M. 1989; Huyssen, A.: Drama des Sturm und Drang. München 1980; Martini, F.: Die Poetik des Sturm und Drang. Versuch einer Zusammenfassung. In: Grimm, R. (Hg.): Deutsche Dramentheorien. Bd. I. Wiesbaden ³1980, S. 123–156; Mattenklott, G./Scherpe, K. R. (Hg.): Literatur der bürgerlichen Emanzipation im 18. Jahrhundert. Kronberg/Ts. 1973; Müller, P. (Hg.): Sturm und Drang. Weltanschauliche und ästhetische Schriften. 2 Bde. Berlin/Weimar 1978; Nicolai, H. (Hg.): Sturm und Drang. Dichtungen und theoretische Texte. 2 Bde. München 1971; Nivelle, A.: Kunst- und Dichtungstheorien zwischen Aufklärung und Klassik. Berlin 1960; Szondi, P.: Die Theorie des bürgerlichen Trauerspiels im 18. Jahrhundert. Hg. von G. Mattenklott. Frankfurt/M. 1973; Wacker, M. (Hg.): Sturm und Drang. Darmstadt 1985.

Wolfgang Beck

Sukzessionsbühne

Die S., wohl von Reuchlin im *Henno* eingeführt, deutet Ortswechsel dadurch an, daß die Darsteller abtreten und, wenn nötig, wieder auftreten. Oft bezeichnet der Dialog oder Monolog die Örtlichkeit. Hans Sachs wußte meisterhaft durch den Dialog eine ganze Szenerie zu imaginieren.

Michael, W. F.: Frühformen der dt. Bühne (Schriften der Gesellschaft für Theatergeschichte 62). Berlin 1963.

Wolfgang F. Michael

Suomen Kansallisteatteri (Finnisches Nationaltheater)

Das erste finnischsprachige Berufstheater wurde im Jahre 1872 gegründet. Seine Wurzeln lagen im finnischen Volkstheater; zu seiner Entstehung trug wesentlich der Kampf um die Durchsetzung der finnischen Sprache bei (gegenüber der Vorherrschaft des Schwedischen). Das Nationaltheater (mit dem damaligen Namen Finnisches Theater) begann als Volksbühne. Es trat auf Tourneen in allen Teilen des großen, dünnbesiedelten Landes auf. Der erste Intendant dieses Theaters war Kaarlo Bergbom, der als Regisseur besonders von den Ideen der →Meininger beeinflußt war. Kaarlo Bergbom spornte die einheimischen Schriftsteller dazu an, Stücke für das Nationaltheater zu schreiben. Die meisten Schauspiele des finnischen Nationalschriftstellers Aleksis Kivi sowie die Dramen der großen Realistin der finnischen Literatur Minna Canth wurden unter Bergboms Zeit uraufgeführt. – Zu den bedeutenden Spielzeiten des Theaters gehört die Intendanz von Eino Kalima von 1917 bis 1950; Kalima führte die Stanislawski-Methode in Finnland ein (richtungweisende Tschechow-Inszenierungen). Unter Arvi Kivimaa (1950–74) wurden engere Kontakte mit Westeuropa geknüpft. Kivimaa nahm die wichtigsten modernen Autoren in seinem Spielplan auf, von wo aus sie ihren Weg zu den anderen Theatern des Landes fanden (z. B. Anouilh, Sartre, Beckett). – Heute bietet das Nationaltheater einen breitgefächerten Spielplan auf drei Bühnen an, der aus einheimischen und ausländischen Klassikern sowie modernen Stücken besteht.

Anneli Suur-Kujala

Surrealistisches Theater

Die Bedeutung des s. T. liegt in der mit größter Radikalität betriebenen experimentellen Erprobung aller Bühnenmittel (→Dadaistisches Theater). Noch kategorischer als der Dadaismus anerkennt von 1922 an der Surrealismus nur die Autonomie des Textes und verweigert grundsätzlich jegliche Gattungsunterscheidung. André Breton (1896–1966) bezeichnet im *1. Manifest des Surrealismus* (1924) die Sprache als Schlüssel zur surrealistischen Tätigkeit, was die Anerkennung des gesprochenen Theaters impliziert: «Am besten passen sich die sprachlichen Formen des Surrealismus an den Dialog an.» Wesentlich dabei ist, daß die Sprache der Bühne die Befreiung von gesellschaftlichen Zwängen ermöglicht. Das Theater gilt den Surrealisten also nur als ein Mittel, eine Technik. Breton hat das Theater nie als ein wesentliches Medium der surrealistischen Aktivitäten betrachtet; er hat es sogar im *Point du jour* (1934) total verurteilt. Darum konnte das große s. T., das von Antonin Artaud (1896–1948) und Roger Vitrac (1899–1952), für Breton nur eines von Abweichlern oder Gegnern sein (→Theater der Grausamkeit).

Eine Unterscheidung zwischen dadaistischem Theater und s. T. ist weitgehend künstlich, von den Daten und den Sympathien der beteiligten Autoren abgeleitet. Ihre philosophische und dramaturgische Haltung ist im Grunde dieselbe: Es geht darum, den gesellschaftlichen Rahmen des Stücks zu sprengen, Raum, Zeit, Intrige und Personen, um mittels der Sprache und des Schauspiels eine poetische Tiefenströmung freizulegen, welche das Publikum mitreißt.

Läßt man die älteren Texte des Douanier Rousseau (1844–1910) beiseite, so ist das erste Stück, worauf Dadaismus und Surrealismus sich beziehen, *Ubu roi* von Alfred Jarry (1873–1907), am 10. Dez. 1896 im →Théâtre de l'Œuvre uraufgeführt. Im närrisch-grotesken Spiel werden in diesem symbolistischen Drama alle überlieferten Bühnenkonventionen zerstört. Trotz der verwirrenden Bedeutung seines moralischen Inhalts ist das Stück *Les Mamelles de Tirésias* (1917) von Guillaume Apollinaire (1880–1918) ein zweiter Schritt zu einem neuen, von jedem Realismus befreiten Theaterstil. *Le Piège de Méduse* (1913) von Erik Satie (1866–1925), eine aggressiv-komische Skizze, ist wohl die erste Erscheinung des dadaistischen Theaters. Der bedeutendste Autor dieser Bewegung ist jedoch T. Tzara: In *La Première aventure céleste de Monsieur Antipyrine* (1916) wird die Zerstörung der Sprache zur Poesie des Wahnsinns; wie auch *Cœur à gaz* (1921) löste es erhebliche Skandale aus.

Diejenigen, die später zu den Hauptvertretern des Surrealismus werden sollten, schrieben am Anfang ihrer Karriere meist gemeinschaftlich kurze Stücke, Collagen zusammenhangloser Traumbilder: *S'il vous plaît* und *Vous m'oublierez* (1920) von André Breton und Philippe Soupault,

Comme il fait beau! (1923) von Breton, Robert Desnos (1900–45) und Benjamin Péret (1899–1959) sind Experimente, die Traumwelt auf die Bühne zu bringen. Die dramatischen Versuche von Louis Aragon (1897–1984) hatten damals eine größere Wirkung; besonders der surrealistische Prolog seines tragischen → Vaudevilles *L'Armoire à glace un beau soir* (1923), ebenso *Au pied du mur* (1925) mit absurden Dialogen, ähnlich den Stücken von Ionesco. 1927 veröffentlichen Aragon und Breton gemeinsam *Le Trésor des Jésuites* mit Elementen der Film- und Feuilletontechnik der Zeit.

Die bedeutenden Theaterautoren des Surrealismus sind aber außerhalb der Bewegung um Breton zu suchen. Zuerst Artaud und Vitrac – nach kurzer Zugehörigkeit zur Gruppe der Surrealisten von Breton ausgeschlossen –, sodann Autoren und Regisseure in der Folge Jarrys und Apollinaires: Jean Cocteau (1889–1963) mit *Les Mariés de la Tour Eiffel* (1921); *Locus Solus* (1922) und *La Poussière des soleils* (1927) von Raymond Roussel (1877–1933). Nach dem 2. Weltkrieg sind noch zu nennen Julien Gracq (*1910: *Le Roi pêcheur*, 1949), Georges Schéhadé (1910–89: *Monsieur Bob'le*, 1951) sowie die Vertreter des → Absurden Theaters; z. B. Ionesco. 1962 zog dieser folgendes Fazit aus dem Surrealismus: «Auch der Surrealismus ist nichts Neues… Was wollte der Surrealismus: freimachen? Liebe und Traum… Die surrealistische Revolution war, wie jede, eine Rückkehr, eine Rückgabe, der Ausdruck notwendiger Lebens- und Geistesbedürfnisse» (*Expérience du théâtre*).

Béhar, H.: Le théâtre dada et surréaliste. Paris 1979; Bürger, P.: Der französische Surrealismus. Wiesbaden 1971; Grimm, J.: Das avantgardistische Theater Frankreichs, 1895–1930. München 1982; Nadeau, M.: Geschichte des Surrealismus. Reinbek bei Hamburg 1965; Rubin, W. S.: Dadaismus. Stuttgart 1978; ders.: Surrealismus. Stuttgart 1979; Waldberg, P.: Der Surrealismus. Köln 1972.

Michel Autrand

Symbolistisches Theater

Das s. T. versuchte, in der zweiten Hälfte d. 19. Jh. einsetzend, die Tradition des klassisch-romantischen Theaters zu erneuern. Nicht nur sind die Übergänge vom Symbolismus zum Surrealismus (→ Surrealistisches Theater), selbst zum → Absurden Theater fließend, sondern auch die Grenzen zwischen Naturalismus und Symbolismus sind weniger scharf, als in der Regel dargestellt. Nicht von ungefähr haben die bedeutendsten Naturalisten symbolistische Phasen in ihrer Entwicklung oder solche Elemente in ihren Stücken, so Henrik Ibsen, August Strindberg, Gerhart Hauptmann oder Anton Tschechow. Das s. T. ist äußerst vielschichtig, mit anderen ästhetischen Bewegungen verzweigt und in ganz Europa verbreitet.

898 Symbolistisches Theater

Chronologisch entsteht, nach Vorstufen im Werk Richard Wagners (1813–83), der Symbolismus vor allem in Frankreich, wo er seine reinste Form findet, und später, mit dem Naturalismus vermischt, in Skandinavien. In Frankreich ist Gustave Flauberts (1821–80) *La Tentation de Saint-Antoine* (1874) das erste symbolistische Meisterwerk, welches Philippe de Villiers de l'Isle-Adam (1838–89) und den jungen Paul Claudel (1868–1955) inspirierte. Der Symbolismus wird dann vorrangig zu einer lyrischen Bewegung (Jean Moréas, 1856–1910; Emile Verhaeren, 1855–1916; Jules Laforgue, 1860–87, u. a.). Allerdings war Stéphane Mallarmé (1842–98), der bedeutendste Autor des Symbolismus, in seinen Rezensionen auch einer der wichtigsten Theatertheoretiker dieser Bewegung. Seine Notizen über Richard Wagner, den Tanz, die Schauspieler, das Publikum, sind die wohl entschiedenste Ablehnung des Bühnenrealismus zugunsten der Idee eines idealen, bis heute noch nicht verwirklichten Theaters. Zwei andere, weniger ambitiöse Texte sind *Le Trésor des humbles* von Maurice Maeterlinck (1862–1949) und das Vorwort zu seiner Theaterausgabe von 1896 sowie das zum *Théâtre de l'âme* von Edouard Schuré (1900). In all diesen Texten wird durch die Rückkehr zur antiken Tragödie und zu Shakespeare, durch den Wagnerkult und die Bewunderung des *Axël* (1885) von Villiers de l'Isle-Adam gegen die moralischen und soziologischen Analysen der herrschenden Klasse jener Zeit der Primat der ‹metaphysischen Suche› behauptet, welche allein Text und Schauspiel ihre Tiefe und Schönheit verleiht. In der Suche nach dem Sakralen im Theater – wenn auch mystisch verhüllt in den Stücken Maeterlincks oder grob und grotesk bei Jarry – liegt der überhöhte, elitäre geistige Anspruch dieser Bewegung, die in ihrer Zeit auf die Ablehnung des Publikums stieß, die Theaterentwicklungen im 20. Jh. jedoch nachhaltig beeinflußte: Man wollte ‹poésie pure›, ‹théâtre pur›.

Die wichtigsten Regisseure für das s. T. waren der Schweizer Adolphe Appia (1862–1928: *La mise en scène du drame wagnérien*, 1895; *Die Musik und die Inszenierung*, 1899; berühmte Wagner-Inszenierungen mit Verschmelzung von Musik, architektonischer Stilisierung, rhythmischer Gestik und bes. Lichteffekten); der Engländer Gordon Craig (1872 bis 1966: *On the Art of the Theatre*, 1905 und 1911; *Towards a New Theatre*, 1913; *Puppets and Poets*, 1921; vor allem Bühnentheoretiker mit nur fünf Inszenierungen: Gesamtkunstwerk betont durch Gestik, Rhythmus, Tanz; Theorie der →Übermarionette; Idee des ‹théâtre pur›); die Franzosen Paul Fort (1872–1960, Begründer 1890 des ‹Théâtre mixte›, dann ‹Théâtre d'art›) und vor allem Lugné-Poë (1869–1940) im →Théâtre de l'Œuvre. In diesem Theater wurden bis zur Schließung 1899 die Meisterwerke der ersten Phase des Symbolismus aufgeführt, nach Villiers *Axël* besonders die Stücke Maeterlincks *La Princesse Maleine* (1889), *L'Intruse* und *Les Aveugles* (1890), *Pelléas et Mélisande* (1893, 1902 von

Debussy vertont), *Intérieur* (1894), gekennzeichnet durch die wilde, bewußt unvollendete rhythmische Musikalität der Rede, die Symbolik der Bilder und die Todesatmosphäre. In diesen ‹statischen Dramen› weicht die Handlung der Situationsdramatik. Passive Gestalten harren ihres unvermeidlichen Schicksals und kommentieren ihre desolate Lage in chorischen Repliken. Es finden sich Ansatzpunkte zu Beckett und Ionesco. – Die zweite Phase des frz. s. T. ist beherrscht vom jungen Paul Claudel (1868–1955). Während der ersten Phase nicht aufgeführt, haben sich diese Stücke ab 1912/14 bis heute durchgesetzt als Höhepunkte s. T.: *Tête d'Or* (1890, erst 1959 im Théâtre de France von Barrault uraufgeführt), *La Ville* (1893 und 1901), *La Jeune fille Violaine* (1892/1901), *Le Repos du septième jour* (1896). Claudel ist der einzige frz. Dramatiker, der den Grundsätzen des Symbolismus treu blieb; auch in *Partage de midi* (1906), im gigantischen *Soulier de satin* (1929) oder den kleineren Dramen mit Musik und Tanz wie *Le Livre de Christophe Colomb* (1929), *Jeanne au bûcher* (1938) und *L'Histoire de Tobie et de Sara* (1942) sind die Ideen Mallarmés lebendig, in der mystischen Suche nach dem Sakralen, im Ritual-Lyrischen, im Sinn fürs Experimentieren, in der Bühnenfreiheit und der Betonung des Musikalischen selbst im Diskurs.

Ein anderer symbolischer Impuls ging paradoxerweise von den Naturalisten (→Naturalistisches Theater) aus, so bei Henrik Ibsen (1828–1906), der besonders in seinem Alterswerk die realistischen Handlungen symbolisch überhöhte: *Die Wildente* (1884), *Rosmersholm* (1886), *Die Frau vom Meer* (1888), *Hedda Gabler* (1890), *Baumeister Solness* (1892) und *John Gabriel Borkmann* (1896). Ebenso in August Strindbergs (1849–1912) Altersdramen *Damaskus*-Trilogie (um 1900), *Traumspiel* (1901), *Totentanz* (1905), *Gespenstersonate* (1907) u. a., in denen die Alogik der Traumstruktur, die Repräsentation der Ich-Spaltung, die Über-Ich/Ich/Es-Analyse, die Seelenerforschung und -darstellung sowie Dekoration, Entleerung der Bühne und Funktion des Requisits als Mitspieler der Figur sich ständig überschneiden mit symbolischen Forderungen und Themen.

Von den Franzosen und Skandinaviern aus, doch auch aus altgriech. und orient. Quellen sowie der christlichen Tradition breitete sich der Symbolismus auf fast alle großen Theater der Welt aus, oft in Verquikkung mit anderen Theaterbewegungen und Dramaturgien: z. B. im deutschsprachigen Theater die halb naturalistischen, halb symbolischen Traumvisionen Gerhart Hauptmanns (1862–1946) in *Hanneles Himmelfahrt* (1893), *Die versunkene Glocke* (1896), *Und Pippa tanzt* (1906). In Österreich verbindet Hugo von Hofmannsthal (1874–1929) seine Symboltheorie (*Gespräch über Gedichte*, 1903) und seine Auffassung der Poesie (*Poesie und Leben*, 1897: Gesamtanspruch der Kunst, Seelenhaftigkeit, Geist, Musik und Tanz) mit dem Schaffen ‹lyrischer Dramen› wie

900 Symbolistisches Theater ⎯⎯⎯⎯⎯⎯⎯⎯⎯⎯⎯⎯⎯⎯⎯⎯⎯⎯⎯⎯⎯⎯

Der Tor und der Tod (1894), *Das kleine Welttheater* (1897) und *Der Kaiser und die Hexe* (1897) u. a., der Bearbeitung von griech. Tragödien (*Elektra*, 1903; *Ödipus und die Sphinx*, 1905, Regie Max Reinhardt) und engl. Dramen (*Das gerettete Venedig*, 1905, nach Otway, Regie G. Craig). – Maeterlincks Einfluß drang bis nach Rußland, wo Leonid Andrejew (1871–1919) allegorisch-mystische Dramen schrieb, welche von den großen realistischen Regisseuren wie Meyerhold, Stanislawski und Nemirowitsch-Dantschenko in Petersburg und Moskau inszeniert wurden: *Zu den Sternen* (1905), *Das Leben des Menschen* (1907), *Anathema* (1909). – Im angelsächsischen Theater setzt dieser Einfluß mit dem Werk Oscar Wildes (1854–1900) ein: *Salome*, ein Traumspiel mit Farbsymbolik und Ritualmomenten (1893, inszeniert von Lugné-Poë und in Berlin von Max Reinhardt, vertont 1905 von Richard Strauss). John M. Synge (1871–1909) schrieb das symbolistische Stück *Riders to the Sea* (1904). Im Werk des Iren William Butler Yeats (1865–1939) wirken neben Mallarmé und Maeterlinck auch die Mystik Jakob Böhmes und Swedenborgs, die irische Mythologie, das japanische →Nô-Theater sowie die Theaterreformideen Gordon Craigs: so *The Land of Heart's Desire* (1894), *On Baile's Strand* (1904) und die *Four Plays for Dancers* (1916–17), bes. *At the Hawk's Well*, worin Musik, Masken, Tanz und Vers im Sinne des Nô verschmolzen sind. Bei Thomas S. Eliot (1888–1965) ist die symbolische Form von *Murder in the Cathedral* (1935) aus dem Ritual der Messe abgeleitet: Der überwältigende Effekt des Stücks resultiert aus der Übereinstimmung der dramatischen Handlung mit der religiösen symbolischen Bedeutung und der Struktur des Stücks. – In Italien schrieb Gabriele d'Annunzio (1863–1938) unter dem Einfluß von Wagner, Nietzsche und Maeterlinck symbolistische Dramen als Reaktion auf den →Verismus: *Sogno di un mattino di primavera* (1897), *La Città morta* (1898), *La Gioconda* (1899), *La Figlia di Jorio* (1904), *Le Martyre de Saint-Sébastien* (1911, vertont von Debussy). Auch im Theater Pirandellos und im →Pirandellismus sind symbolische Elemente zu finden. – Der Spanier Federico García Lorca (1898–1936), dessen Ursprünge im Surrealismus liegen, steht mit seinen Stücken ebenfalls in der symbolistischen Bewegung: die span. Motive in *Bodas de sangre* (1933), *Yerma* (1934) und *La casa de Bernardo Alba* (1936) sind in ihrer Verschmelzung von Poesie, Musik, Licht und Farben dem Theater von Appia und Craig verpflichtet. Auch hier findet sich allerdings ein Nebeneinander von Symbolismus und Realismus: «Das Theater ohne Gefühl für den sozialen Puls, ohne historischen Puls, das Drama des Volks, ohne die echten Farben der Landschaft... darf sich nicht Theater nennen» (Nachwort zu *Yerma*).

Das s. T. ist durch seine Ambitionen, Innovationen und Experimente die wohl bedeutendste Revolution im westlichen Theater seit der Ära der Klassik und Romantik; in ihm haben alle Neuentwicklungen von Regie, Theatertheorie, Schauspielkunst und Dramatik im 20. Jh. ihre Wurzeln.

Anderson, D. L.: Symbolism – A Bibliography of Symbolism as an International and Multi-Disciplinary Movement. New York 1975; Chiari, J.: The Contemporary French Theatre – The Flight from Naturalism. New York 1958; Got, M.: Théâtre et symbolisme. Paris 1955; Henderson, J. A.: The First Avant-garde. London/Toronto 1971; Robichez, J.: Le symbolisme au théâtre. Paris 1957; Styan, J. L.: Modern drama in theory and practice 2: Symbolism, Surrealism and the Absurd. Cambridge 1981; Wilson, E.: Axel's Castle. A Study in the Imaginative Literature of 1870–1930. London 1931.

Michel Autrand / Gérard Schneilin

Szenographie

(→Bühnenbild) Die skênographia ist im klassischen Griechenland die Kunst, das Theater zu schmücken, und der malerische Dekor. In der Renaissance ist die Szenographie die Technik, eine Leinwand im Hintergrund der Bühne perspektivisch zu bemalen. Im modernen Sinn ist es die Wissenschaft und Organisation der Bühne und des Bühnenraums. S. entsteht auch durch Bedeutungsübertragung des Bühnenbilds selbst, das sich aus der Arbeit des Szenographen ergibt. Heute drängt sich dieser Begriff auf und tritt an die Stelle des Bühnenbilds, um die Vorstellung von Ausschmückung zu überwinden, die sich noch oft mit dem überholten Konzept des Theaters als Dekoration verbindet. Die S. bringt den Anspruch zur Geltung, eine Kunst im dreidimensionalen Raum zu sein (der als vierte Dimension die Zeit hinzuzufügen wäre) und nicht mehr eine Bildkunst der bemalten Leinwand, womit sich das Theater bis zum Naturalismus (→Naturalistisches Theater) lange begnügt hat. Die Bühne will nicht länger als die Materialisierung fragwürdiger Szenenangaben gelten; sie lehnt es ab, die Rolle einer ‹bloßen Figurantin› für einen vorhandenen und bindenden Text zu spielen (→Inszenierung, →Theatertheorie, →Inszenierungsanalyse).

Wenn das Bühnenbild im zweidimensionalen Raum angesiedelt ist, der durch die bemalte Leinwand dargestellt wird, ist die S. eine Kunst im dreidimensionalen Raum. Sie entspricht dem Übergang von der Malerei zur Bildhauerkunst oder Architektur. Diese ‹Mutation› der szenographischen Funktion ist mit der Entwicklung der Dramaturgie verbunden und entspricht ebenso einer autonomen Entwicklung der Bühnenästhetik wie einem tiefgreifenden Wandel des Textverständnisses und der Textdarstellung auf der Bühne. Man hat lange geglaubt, daß das Bühnenbild die wahrscheinlichen und idealen Raumkoordinaten des Texts wiederzuge-

902 Szenographie

ben habe, genauso wie sie der Autor bei der Niederschrift seines Stücks vorgesehen hatte: Die S. bestand darin, dem Zuschauer die Mittel an die Hand zu geben, einen allgemeinen neutralen Ort (Palast, Platz) zu lokalisieren und wiederzuerkennen, der auf alle Situationen paßt und geeignet ist, den ewigen Menschen abstrakt zu situieren, unabhängig von seinen ethnischen oder sozialen Wurzeln. Heute dagegen versteht sich die S. nicht mehr als ideale und eindeutige Illustration eines dramatischen Texts, sondern als Einrichtung, den Text und das menschliche Handeln zu erhellen (und nicht mehr zu illustrieren), eine Aussage-Situation darzustellen (und nicht mehr einen festen Ort) und den Sinn der Inszenierung im Austausch zwischen Raum und Text anzusiedeln. Die S. ist auch das Ergebnis einer semiologischen Konzeption der Inszenierung: In-Einklang-Bringen der verschiedenen szenischen Materialien, Interdependenz dieser Systeme, insbesondere von Bild und Text; Suche nach der möglichst produktiven und nicht nach der ‹idealen› oder ‹getreuen› Aussagesituation, um den dramatischen Text zu lesen und ihn mit anderen Theaterpraktiken zu verbinden. ‹Szeno-graphieren› bedeutet, ein Spiel von Verbindungen und Proportionen zwischen Text- und Bühnenraum herzustellen, d. h. jedes System ‹für sich› und in Zusammenhang mit dem anderen in einer Serie von Übereinkünften und Verschiebungen zu strukturieren.

In seiner neuen Machtfülle ist sich der Szenograph seiner Autonomie und der Originalität seines Beitrags zur Verwirklichung einer Aufführung bewußt. Früher war er eine untergeordnete Person, die nur den Hintergrund der Bühne zu malen hatte, und zwar zur größeren Ausstrahlung des Schauspielers und Regisseurs. Heute hat er die Aufgabe, die Raumdimension total zu gestalten: szenisch, szenographisch und theatralisch. Der Rahmen für seine Tätigkeit wird immer größer: die Bühne und ihre Einteilung, die Beziehung zwischen Bühne und Zuschauerraum, die Einbindung des Zuschauerraums in das Theatergebäude und das soziale Umfeld, die unmittelbare Umgebung des Bühnenraums und des Theaters. Diese verantwortliche Übernahme der Raumvolumen verleitet den Szenographen manchmal dazu, die gesamte Inszenierungsarbeit zu seinen Gunsten umzufunktionieren; dies ist der Fall, wenn der Bühnenraum nur ein Vorwand für eine Ausstellung von Bildern ist oder ein Formenexperiment mit Volumen und Farben. Berühmte Maler – wie Picasso oder Matisse – hat diese Ausdrucksform ihrer Werke gereizt. Die Versuchung des Ästhetizismus in einem von sich aus schon schönen Bühnendekor bleibt groß, trotz der Warnungen der Regisseure, das Bühnenbild auf seine ihm gemäße Proportionen reduzieren zu wollen und den Szenographen für die Miterarbeitung am Sinn einer Aufführung zu gewinnen suchen.

Trotz der Vielfalt zeitgenössischer Experimente der S. kann man einige Tendenzen ausmachen:

▸ Brechung der frontalen Gegenüberstellung und des ‹Guckkastens› ital. Art, um die Bühne zum Zuschauerraum zu öffnen, den Zuschauer näher an die Handlung heranzuführen. Die Bühne à l'italienne wird in der Tat heute als unzeitgemäß, hierarchisierend und auf einer distanzierten und illusionistischen Auffassung beruhend empfunden. Ihre Ablehnung schließt jedoch ihre Wiederbelebung nicht aus; als Experiment mit dem Ort der Illusion, der Phantasie und der allseitig eingesetzten Maschinerie. Die Umkehrung ist vollständig, der Guckkasten ital. Art ist nicht mehr der Zufluchtsort des Wahrscheinlichen, sondern der Bezugspunkt der Enttäuschung und der Phantasievorstellung.

▸ Öffnung des Raums und Vervielfachung der Blickpunkte, um die einheitliche und bildliche Wahrnehmung zu relativieren, indem die Zuschauer rund um das Theatergeschehen oder manchmal ins Theatergeschehen gesetzt werden.

▸ Anordnung der S. nach den Bedürfnissen des Schauspielers und für ein spezifisches dramaturgisches Vorhaben.

▸ Restrukturierung des Bühnenbilds, indem fallweise Raum, Gegenstand oder Kostüme im Vordergrund stehen: Begriffe, die über die erstarrte Vision einer auszustattenden Fläche hinausgehen.

▸ Entmaterialisierung der Szene. Dank der Verwendung leichter und mobil einsetzbarer Werkstoffe wird die Bühne wie ein Zubehör und eine ‹Verlängerung› des Schauspielers benutzt. Beleuchtung und Scheinwerferorgeln modellieren im Dunkel der Bühne jeden beliebigen Ort und jede beliebige Stimmung.

Die Szene ist in all ihren zeitgenössischen Anwendungen nicht mehr zwangsmäßig Bestandteil der gemalten Dekoration von einst, sondern dynamisches und Viel-Funktionen-Element der Theateraufführung.

Literaturhinweise: →Bühnenbild, →Inszenierung, →Inszenierungsanalyse.

Patrice Pavis

Tableau

(Frz. = Bild, Gemälde) Das Wort T. bezeichnet in Anlehnung an die Malerei ein durch Gruppierungen und Figuren der Schauspieler oder Tänzer auf der Bühne in quasi erstarrtem Zustand entstehendes Bild. Ausgangspunkt des T. war das Theater des Mittelalters, wo es, ähnlich wie später in der Barockoper, im Jesuitentheater, im →Zauber- und Märchenspiel vor allem als Schlußbild einer Aufführung, als →Apotheose im Sinne einer Erhebung von Personen und Helden in himmlische Sphäre gebräuchlich war. Im klassischen Theater nimmt das T. die Form einer effektvollen Schlußstellung am Ende einer Szene oder eines Akts an, die dann durch den Haupt- oder Zwischenvorhang den Blicken des Publikums entzogen wird (*Wallensteins Tod*, 1799, III, 23; *Maria Stuart*, 1800, II, 9; *Wilhelm Tell*, 1804, V, 2). Mit dem 18. Jh. gewinnt aber das T. eine andere dramaturgische Funktion und wird an Stelle des →Akts zu einem Strukturelement des Theaterstücks. Anders als der →Akt, der einer Erzählphase bzw. einer Phase im Handlungsablauf entspricht, bildet das T. eine thematische Einheit. Diese Funktion des T. geht mit einer Episierung des Theaters einher, die vor dem durchgehenden dramatischen Ablauf die visuell prägnante Darstellung einzelner Momente bevorzugt, wobei sich Sinn und Zweck dieser neuen Dramaturgie, die von Denis Diderot (1713–84) über Jacob Michael Reinhold Lenz (1751–92), Georg Büchner (1813–37), Alfred de Musset (1810–57) und Frank Wedekind (1864–1918) bis Bertolt Brecht (1898–1956) reicht, mit der Zeit ändern. Diderot z. B. bezweckt dadurch eine harmonische Synthese von Bewegung, dramatischer Verdichtung und Handlung (siehe den Artikel «Composition» in der *Encyclopédie*, 1751–72). Bei Brecht dagegen ist das T. ein typisches, doch unvollständiges Fragment, das der kritischen und nachvollziehenden Perspektive des Zuschauers bedarf; jedes T. ist ein in sich geschlossenes, vom nächsten scharf getrenntes dramaturgisches Ganzes, ohne jedoch für sich allein eine Bedeutungseinheit zu werden, was den Zuschauer zum kritischen Vergleich der T. miteinander anregen soll.

Szondi, P.: ‹Tableau und coup de théâtre›. In: ders.: Lektüren und Lektionen. Frankfurt/M. 1973.

Bernard Poloni

Taʿziya

Schiitisches →Passionsspiel. Das T. gehört neben Prozessionen und Predigten zu den alljährlich anläßlich des Todes von Husain stattfindenden Trauerfeierlichkeiten. Der Enkel des Propheten – und für die Schiiten der rechtmäßige Nachfolger – fiel in der Schlacht bei Kerbelāʾ am 10. Muharram 680; dadurch erlangte sein Widersacher Yazid die Kalifenwürde.

Vom 1. bis 10. Muharram werden in schiitischen Städten täglich Prozessionen durchgeführt, in denen bereits die Schauspieler des anschließenden T. mitgehen. Das T. ist ein Zyklus von über 50 Szenen, die zum Teil nur in losem Zusammenhang zur Tragödie des Husain stehen (Abraham opfert Isaak, Joseph im Brunnen), zum Teil Ereignisse des Frühislam und die Vorgeschichte der Schlacht von Kerbelāʾ darstellen. Höhepunkt ist die Wiedergabe der Schlacht, wobei der Schlußkampf mit dem Tode Husains häufig weggelassen wird, um Ausschreitungen der erregten Zuschauer gegen die Darsteller der feindlichen Personen zu verhindern. Die

Aufführungen dauern etwa zwei Stunden. Sie finden im Freien oder in einem mit schwarzen Tüchern ausgeschlagenen Raum statt; die Zuschauer sitzen im Kreis um die Bühne herum. Als Requisiten dienen ein Bottich mit Wasser zur Darstellung des Euphrat und gehacktes Stroh als Wüstensand. Die ausschließlich männlichen Schauspieler sind in der Regel Laien.

Die Texte des T., vorwiegend gebundene Rede, sind schriftlich fixiert, die Verfasser unbekannt. Die Auswahl der Szenen und die Aufeinanderfolge ist dem Regissseur überlassen. In der vorliegenden Form ist das T. in Persien seit dem Anfang des 19. Jh. bekannt, seit die Dynastie der Safawiden an die Macht gelangte und die Schia zur Staatsreligion erhob. T.-Aufführungen wurden 1927 verboten, seit Gründung der Islamischen Republik Iran (1979) werden sie jedoch wieder gefördert. Auch unter den Schiiten im Irak, in Indien (dort seit 1934 verboten) und im Libanon ist das T. verbreitet.

al-Haidari, I.: Zur Soziologie des schiitischen Chiliasmus. Ein Beitrag zur Erforschung des irakischen Passionsspiels. Freiburg 1979; Monchi-Zadeh, D.: Taᶜziya. Das persische Passionsspiel. Stockholm 1967; Müller, H.: Studien zum persischen Passionsspiel. Freiburg 1966.

Maren Fittschen

Taganka-Theater / Theater an der Taganka (Moskau)

(Moskovskij teatr dramy i komedii na Taganke). Nach dem 2. Weltkrieg in Moskau gegründetes Theater. 1964 Neugründung durch Juri Ljubimow (* 1917). Erste Aufführung: 1964 Brechts *Der gute Mensch von Sezuan* mit Absolventen der Stschukin-Schule des →Wachtangow-Theaters. Das T. T. wird zur experimentierfreudigsten und mutigsten Bühne des Landes; erlangt internationale Anerkennung, Gastspiele in Westeuropa aber erst ab 1977. Ljubimow ist als Regisseur der Idee des totalen Spiels verpflichtet; weitgehend Regie-Theater (Meyerhold, Wachtangow). Drei Grundlinien: 1. B. Brecht (*Sezuan*, *Galilei*, *Turandot*), ferner zahlreiche eigene Dramatisierungen russ. Prosa (1977 *Meister und Margarita* nach M. Bulgakow; 1978 Dostojewskis *Schuld und Sühne*), die die Brechtsche Ästhetik realisieren; 2. Kompositionen aus Lyrik und biographischem Material zum Thema Dichter / Künstler – Theater / Gesellschaft (A. Wosnessenski, W. Majakowski, A. Puschkin, Wladimir Wyssozki); 3. Klassik: *Hamlet* mit dem Protagonisten und Dichter-Sänger W. Wyssozki (1938–80) in der Titelrolle; Molière, Ostrowski, Puschkin. Seit 1980 zunehmend politische Angriffe auf das T. T. und Ljubimow, der 1984 ausgebürgert wird und bis 1988 in Westeuropa und Israel inszeniert (auch im

906 Tampereen Työväen Teatteri

Musiktheater). 1984–87 glücklose Leitung des T.T. durch A. Efros (1925–87); bis 1990 leitet N. Gubenko (1964–70 Schauspieler am T.T.) und engagiert sich für Ljubimows endgültige Rückkehr (1989). 1988 rekonstruiert L. seine verbotenen Inszenierungen *Wladimir Wyssozki* (1981), *Der Lebendige* nach B. Moshajew (1969), *Boris Godunow* von Puschkin (1983); er inszeniert Puschkins *Kleine Tragödien* und Erdmans *Selbstmörder*, übernimmt 1990/91 wieder das Ensemble, kann jedoch nicht an die einstigen Erfolge als Regisseur und Theaterleiter anknüpfen.

Lioubimov, Y.: Le feu sacré. Paris 1985; Zingerman, B.: Zametki o Ljubimove (vremja-xudožnik-obraz). In: Teatr (Moskva) 1991, Nr. 1.

Elke Wiegand

Tampereen Työväen Teatteri

Das ‹Arbeitertheater von Tampere› hat eine einzigartige Stellung im finnischen Theaterleben. Seine Tätigkeit begann im Rahmen des Vergnügungsausschusses im Arbeiterverband als Schauspielclub auf Amateurbasis. Offiziell wurde das Theater 1901 gegründet. Tilda Vuori war die erste langjährige Leiterin des Theaters von 1906 bis 1917. Die professionelle Entwicklung des Theaters begann jedoch erst unter Kosti Elo (1919–40). Er brachte in erster Linie Elemente des dt. Expressionismus auf die Bühne. Antimilitaristische und gesellschaftlich Stellung nehmende Stücke entsprachen dem Geist der Arbeiterbewegung. Aus wirtschaftlichen Gründen war jedoch das Spektrum des Repertoires breit, es umfaßte Musiktheater und besonders die vom einheimischen Publikum bevorzugten Volksstücke. In den Jahren 1943 bis 1964 war Eino Salmelainen Intendant des Theaters. Seine Regiekunst hatte einen umwälzenden Einfluß auf das gesamte finnische Theater. Er befreite die Darstellungsweise von den traditionellen Klischees, achtete besonders auf die psychologische Genauigkeit der Schauspielerarbeit, interessierte sich für die aktuelle Dramatik (Brecht, Anouilh, Sartre, Camus, Frisch) und schuf eine fruchtbare Zusammenarbeit mit den finnischen Dramatikern. Nach Salmelainen wirkten als künstlerische Leiter des Theaters u. a. Eugen Terttula, Kai Savola und Lasse Pöysti. – 1985 wurde ein neues Theatergebäude fertiggestellt, das von den Architekten Marjatta und Martti Jaatinen entworfen wurde. Als einziges finn. Arbeitertheater erhält das Arbeitertheater von Tampere finanzielle Unterstützung durch den Staat.

Anneli Suur-Kujala

Tanz

▶ *Zur Begriffsgeschichte:* ahd.: saizôn, abgeleitet aus dem Lat. saltare (= tanzen und springen), got. laikan (= springen, spielen, hüpfen, tanzen). Spiel, Melodie, Gesang, Tanzlied. – Der sprachliche Rückgriff verdeutlicht, daß Bewegungs-, Spiel-, Gesangs- und Musizierformen im Bedeutungsfeld des Wortes zusammengezogen werden, was, vorausgreifend, den späteren Nachweis der Synthese im Kunstbereich Tanz vorbereitet. Die Quellen des Minnesanges ab ca. 1200 weisen den gesprungenen Reigen des Volks als saltatio, den nur getretenen, geschrittenen höfischen Reigen dagegen als chorea-ballatio aus. Erstmals werden demnach im burgundischen Raum die späteren und bis heute differenten Tanzformen ‹Ballett› und ‹Tanzen› unterschieden. Die ehemals auf Grund der Bewegungsformen Springen und Schreiten als Stilformen der Choreographie und zugleich Musik vollzogenen Abgrenzungen kennzeichnen die heutigen Stilunterschiede nicht mehr.

▶ *Wortbedeutungen:* Der Begriff Tanz tritt in fünf Bedeutungsversionen auf: 1. Das Nomen benennt einen Kunstbereich, den Tanz. Der Spartenbegriff umfaßt alle denkbaren tänzerischen Ereignisse gleich welcher Tanzform, -klasse, -gattung, -art, welcher Choreographie, klanglichen Gestalt, Inszenierung, Funktion, gesellschaftlichen Bezogenheit, gleich an welchem Zeit- und Standort. Unterhalb dieser Bereichskategorie bilden das Tanztheater und der Gesellige Tanz die beiden markant zu differenzierenden Teilbereiche des Kunstfeldes Tanz. 2. Die Kategorie kennzeichnet einen historisch- und ethnologisch-regional gebundenen, choreographisch, musikalisch und inszenatorisch unverkennbaren Tanztyp (etwa den Branle, Czardasz, Bolero, die Rumba etc.). 3. Der Terminus wird für eine Kompositionsgattung eingesetzt, welche die unter zwei charakterisierten Tanztypen als Modell auswählt, aber im Kompositionsakt stilisiert (Suiten, Konzertwalzer). 4. Der Begriff wird für Tanzveranstaltungen, Tanzfeste genutzt und meint darüber hinaus 5. das Tanzgeschehen selbst.

▶ *Tanz* als Kennzeichnung des Kunstbereichs umspannt die Teilbereiche Tanztheater und Geselliger Tanz, die Gebiete Kultisch-rituelles Tanztheater = A , Profanes Tanztheater = B , Ballett = C , Tanztheater der Gegenwart = D , Tanz im Musiktheater = E ; das Gebiet Geselliger Tanz = F , Schultanz = G und Behindertentanz = H , deren Klassen (Siglen I, II etc.) und Gattungen, als Arten die jeweiligen Nummern, Szenen, Ensembleformen des Tanztheaters und die Tanztypen und -weisen (vgl. hierzu das Schema auf S. 909). Im Vergleich zu den Teilbereichskategorien Tanztheater, Schautanz und der Gebietskategorie Ballett ist ‹Tanz› die am weitesten ausgreifende und alle anderen Erscheinungsformen tänzerischer Natur umfassende Bezeichnung.

908 Tanz

▶ Der Begriff *Schautheater* ist dem Begriff des Tanztheaters nicht gleichzuordnen; er greift vielmehr vom Tanztheater auf die Veranstaltungsformen des Geselligen Tanzes über. Nahezu jede Klasse des Geselligen Tanzes (A B) beschreibt Tanzvollzüge, in denen die Tänzer keineswegs nur agieren, um Geselligkeit zu pflegen, ein Hobby zu betreiben, einer Liebhaberei nachzugehen. Die Klassen weisen vielmehr Tanzformen aus, die auch als Tanzkunst beansprucht werden, teils aus musikalischer Kennerschaft, teils im Willen, Körperkunst zu üben. Die Tanzenden gestalten Vorführungen, Schauveranstaltungen für Publikum. Dennoch ist ‹Schautanz› kein Tanztheater. Ihm fehlt der dramatische Aufriß und die bewußt gestaltete geschlossene Form.

▶ Das *Ballett* ist als Gebiet wiederum nur eine Gestaltungsform des Tanztheaters, die auf den abendländischen Raum von ca. 1550 bis heute eingeschränkt werden kann. Die *Gita Govinda* Indiens (→Odissi) und das →Kagura-Tanzspiel Japans gelten als Tanztheater oder als Tanztheaterspiele. Bei Ausweitung des Ballettbegriffs könnten beide Tanzspiele mit gutem Recht als Ballett aufgefaßt werden, was hier um der historisch-regionalen Differenzierung willen vermieden wird.

▶ Der *Gesellige Tanz*, dessen Gebiete, Klassen, Gattungen etc. bisher international übergreifend nicht systematisiert wurden, umfaßt die Techniken und Formen von Tanztypen oder Tanzstilen, die sowohl einen charakteristischen Bewegungs- als auch Musik- und Inszenierungsstil ausbilden und sich darüber hinaus im Brauchtum auch zu Spielgestaltungen ausweiten können. Die Grenzen zwischen dem Geselligen Tanz und dem Schautanz, aber auch dem Tanztheater sind also fließend.

▶ Alle weiteren Ausführungen wenden sich ausschließlich dem *Tanztheater* zu und beschreiben die Gesetze der Kunstsparte Tanz: Das Tanztheater ist von Anfang an Aufführungstheater, das sich an Zuschauende und Teilhabende wendet. Die heiligen Tanzspiele der Urgesellschaft z. B. werden ohne Zweifel in der Absicht vollzogen, durch magisch-mythologische Beschwörung Wiedergeburt und Segenspendung zu erwirken. Trotz dieser Funktion sind der das Spiel leitende und tanzende Schamane und alle am Ritual Teilhabenden sich der Fiktion bewußt, in die sie eintreten. Niemals verläßt sie im Trancetanz die Wahrnehmungskraft (z. B. Voodoo). Der Magier steuert und gestaltet das große Spiel tanztechnisch und inszenatorisch kunstvoll. Bewegungen, Schritte und Raumgliederungen bleiben den Gesetzen des Rituals streng unterworfen.

1. Das Tanztheater gewinnt durch die *Symbiose* der Gesetzmäßigkeiten vierer Kunstbereiche seine einmalige charakteristische Gestalt und Wirkkraft. Zu spannungsvollem Zusammenklang werden verbunden: die Bewegungskunst (auch Körper- oder Gebärdenkunst), die Musik, die Inszenierungskunst und die dramatische Gestaltung. Da jeder Einzelbereich durch grundlegende Faktoren, durch spezielle Parameter bestimmt

Tanz 909

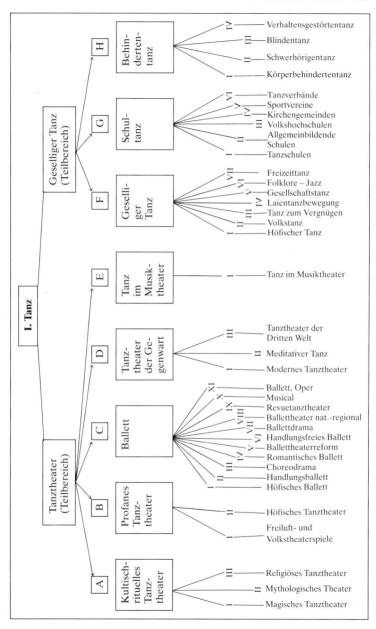

II. Tanz

Parameterbereich Bewegung

1. Attitüden
Motionen als Bewegungen am Ort, im Stand, im Moment des Sprungs, der Drehung

2. Aktionen
Lokomotionen sind Fortbewegungen. Sie durchmessen, gliedern und erobern die Tanzräume.

3. Positionen
Frontbestimmungen in Richtung auf den Tanztrainer, Partner, das Ensemble, die Gruppe, das Publikum oder Medien

4. Gruppierungen
Solo, Paar (Tanzduett, Pas de deux); Ensembles; Corps de Ballet oder Tanzgruppe – die Anzahl der Tanzenden

5. Richtungs- und Abgrenzungsformationen
Raumwege als Bodenlinien oder Höhenbewegungen mit Hilfe von Bühnenaufbauten oder Flugapparaturen

6. Raumgliederungsformen
Bodenflächenbildungen und Raumkörperformen, erzeugt durch die Par. 1–5, Medien, Beleuchtung, Farbgebung

Parameterbereich Musik

1. Klangstärke
Grade
Stufen
Evolutionen

2. Klangzeit
Tempo
Metrum
Rhythmus

3. Klangfarbe
Instrumentation
Verzierungstechniken
Spieltechniken

4. Klanghöhe
Tonhöhenanordnungen im Zeitverlauf (Melos), in Klanghöhenschichtungen (Setzweisen)

Parameterbereich Inszenierung

1. Personalregie
Choreograph
Tänzer
Beleuchter

2. Raumregie
Choreograph
Bühnenbildner
Maler
Plastiker
Architekt
Beleuchter

3. Maskenregie
Choreograph
Bühnenbildner
Maler
Plastiker
Maskenspezialist

4. Lichtregie
Choreograph
Beleuchter

5. Kostümregie
Choreograph
Kostümbildner

wird, stellt sich das Tanztheater in seinen Ausdrucks- und Darstellungsbestrebungen als vieldimensionales Interaktionsgefüge dar, dessen Lebendigkeit und energetische Impulse aus den Interdependenzen und Spontaneitäten, aus den physisch-sensorischen und -motorischen Gegebenheiten und Übertragungen, den geistigen Imaginationen erwachsen. Am mehrkanaligen Kommunikationssystem sind die Zuschauer ebenso beteiligt wie die Akteure und Konzipienten. Handwerklich-technische und künstlerische Bedingungen und Aktionen vernetzen sich.

2. Jeder der unter II A (= Bewegungskunst) (vgl. Schema auf S. 910) kurz charakterisierten Parameter $\boxed{A}$ 1 bis 6 dringt auf Raumgestaltung. Tanz ohne Raum- und zugleich Formstreben gleitet in bloßes Bewegungsspiel ab. Die *Tanzbewegungen*, in tanztheoretischer Differenzierung die 7. Bewegungsform neben den Brauch- (= Alltagsformen), Arbeits-, Sport- und Akrobatikformen, den Spiel- und pantomimischen Formen, sind durch den Zug in die Weite und Höhe der Räume und durch die gebundenen dynamisch ineinanderfließenden oder auch eckig sich auseinander entfaltenden und zyklisch kombinierten Bewegungslinien charakterisiert. Tanzbewegungen erschöpfen sich nicht im Erleben und Zum-Ausdruck-Bringen eines individuellen Bewegungsdrangs, sondern kennzeichnen simultan zur Bewegungsausführung Atem-, Körper-, Aufführungs- und genetisch erworbene Lebensräume und erschließen im Ausdrucksempfinden wirksam werdende kosmische Räume. Deshalb setzt der Tanzende sogar zum ‹Flug› an (Ballets volants bei Didelot, 1767–1837; →Ballet héroïque-pantomime; Flugapparate der Renaissance und des Barock; das Flugtheater der ital. Futuristen: Fedele Azari 1918). Neben dem Raumbezug reizt den Körper das Spiel mit der erlebten und absoluten Zeit, das von den Agierenden und dem Publikum erfahren wird. Ein leistungsfähiger Tänzer zeichnet sich durch die Befähigung aus, extrem verlangsamte oder beschleunigte Tempi bei gleicher Bewegungsqualität durchhalten zu können – und dies nicht nur in technisch-sportlicher Absicht, sondern vorrangig in dem nahezu als Spiel empfundenen Zeiterlebnis. Im Drang dieses Raumgestaltungs- und -durchmessungswillens tritt die Tanzkunst in Korrelation zur Inszenierungskunst, die den Tanzraum bereitet, tanzangemessen gestaltet und demgemäß erst spezielle Bewegungskompositionen ermöglicht oder sogar kreiert – etwa wenn ein ganzes Corps de Ballet sich tanzend in den großen Maschen eines senkrecht über die volle Breite der Bühne herabgelassenen Netzes bewegt (M. Béjart – Bayreuth 1961, *Tannhäuser*, I. Akt) oder über ausgedehnt spiegelnde Treppen als Tableau tanzt.

3. Im Bereiche der →Zeit ist die Bewegungskunst der *Musik* (II B) verschwistert. Beide Künste sind an die Zeit gekettet und erfahren in der Auseinandersetzung mit ihr nachdrückliche Gestaltungsqualitäten. Im Tanz reagiert der Körper spontan auf ein von der Musik angeschlagenes

912 Tanz

Metrum. In gleichem Maß aber wird sich ein improvisierendes Instrumentalensemble metrisch an die Körper- und Raumbewegungen der Tänzer binden. In der Rhythmenfolge, einem Teilgebiet des Parameters B 2, können beide Künste, gestützt auf vorgegebene oder sich herausbildende Tempi und Metren, total unabhängig und frei verfahren. Bereits im musikalischen Klangfeld eröffnen sich im dreidimensionalen Spannungsnetz von Tempo, Metrum und Rhythmus ungeahnt interessante und wirkungsvolle Gestaltungsmöglichkeiten beim Komponieren. Wenn dieses Klangnetz sich mit den Tanzgesetzlichkeiten verknüpft, ereignen sich in hohem Maße komplexe, motivierende, Eindrücke erzeugende und Reaktionen auslösende Prozesse, auf die der abendländische Tanz sich kaum konzentriert. Im afrikanischen Tanzgeschehen (→ Afrikanisches Theater) integriert sich der Körper des Tänzers bewußt als Klangquelle in das musikalische Ensemblespiel und erzeugt im Sichtfeld der Zuschauer durch die Kontrapunktierung mit dem Klangfeld einen polyphonen Akt. Im Tanztheater sollte dementsprechend Musik nicht als ‹Begleitung› aufgefaßt werden. Ballettkompositionen und Choreographieentwürfe (→ Minutage) berücksichtigen dieses Ineinanderspiel der Künste bereits im Konzept, legen es fest und bereiten es vor, damit sich am Aufführungsabend ‹Tanztheater› ereignen kann. Die letzten Ausführungen verdeutlichen, daß die zuweilen geführten Diskussionen zur Fragestellung Tanz mit oder ohne Musik auf Mißverständnissen beruhen. Sie leben von einer zu engen Vorstellung über das, was Musik real ist. Die tänzerische Bewegung bedarf im Gegensatz zur pantomimischen (→ Pantomime), die auf Stille hin gestalten kann und soll, des umhüllenden und vermittelnden Klangraums. Erst der Klang bindet letzte mangelnde Bewegungsanschlüsse oder überbrückt ästhetisch bewegungsmäßig bewußt geplante Brüche oder Einschnitte. Auch die Generalpausen der Musik sind tanzwirksam. Die Musik selbst ist eine seit den Uranfängen in Raum und Zeit von bewußten Sinneswahrnehmungen geführte und von Sinneseindrücken geleitete und somit geordnete Setzung und Kombination von Schallereignissen, die durch eine Fülle denkbarer Klangquellen erzeugt werden können. Die erste Klasse aller möglichen Klangquellen in der Systematik der Musikinstrumente ist die der körpereigenen Instrumente, also Füße, Hacken, Fersen, Fußspitzen – Finger, Hände und Arme in Gegen- und Aufschlagtechniken auf Brustkorb, Bauchregion, Pelvis, Oberschenkel, Knie und Fußsohlen. Im Sitz- und Hocktanz schlagen die Gesäßbacken auf die Bodenfläche. Die ersten Barfußtänzer des Ausdruckstanzes, die ohne Musik tanzen wollten, konnten gar nicht anders, als in der Vehemenz ihrer Bewegungen gleich den Afrikanern mit blanken Füßen in komplizierten, den Ausdruck spiegelnden Rhythmen den Boden zu schlagen. Indische Tänzer vermögen noch heute, Rhythmen zu treten, die kaum ein europäischer Schlagzeuger realisieren kann. Die rhythmischen Elemente in der Musik stellen gestaltete Zeitgliederungen dar. Das Zapateado der andalusischen Flamencotänzer (mit dem Torero-Absatz geleistete Hacken-Fersen-Spitzen-Schlagtechnik) reißt in den Konzertarenen der Welt große Zuhörerkreise zu Beifallsstürmen hin. Rhythmus und Tempo, eingefügt in das Metrum, sind ein entscheidender Teilbereich des musikalischen Parameterfeldes = B 2. Aufbauend auf den Zeitkonstruktionen mischen sich die Klangfarbenprozesse = B 3 mit Klangstärken = B 1 und Klanghöhenprozessen = B 4.

Neben dem vorgestellten körpereigenen Schlagwerk kann die Tanzpartitur die ‹Timbres› der Geräusch- und Stimmcollagen bis zur Reduktion auf Elemente nutzen, Sprachspiele und Sprechchöre, Vokalisen, Gesänge und Vokalensembles, mechanische und elektronische Klänge auswählen und mit den traditionellen Schlag-, Blas- und Saiteninstrumenten instrumentieren. Welches Klangnaturell ein Ballett-Opus der Moderne oder ferner Ethnien auch auszeichnen mag, welchen Bewegungsstil die Choreographie auch ansetzt, die Tanzenden werden in ihrer ‹Hörbarkeit›, ob gegen oder im Einklang mit der Musik, zum Miterzeuger im Klangkörper. Die Musik ihrerseits stellt sich, zuweilen sogar in unerhörter Eigendisziplin, auf die Körperkunst und deren physische Begrenzungen ein. Das trifft bereits auf den Kompositionsakt zu, in noch höherem Maße aber auf die Realisation. Der Dirigent des Tanztheaters darf nicht ‹seine› Tempoauffassungen einschlagen, wenn die Choreographie diesen widerspricht, wenn ein Tänzer evtl. erschöpft oder aber in bester Form ist. Der musikalische Leiter der Aufführung muß vielmehr mit allen Instrumentalisten das Tanzgeschehen tragen. Insofern ist keineswegs jeder Dirigent zum Ballettkapellmeister geeignet. Tonbandeinspielungen sind, der künstlerisch-musikalischen Interpretation entgegengesetzt, für jede Kompanie eine Notlösung aus Kosten- oder Raumgründen. Die bloße Reproduktion der Musik verhindert letztendlich den spontanen Realisationsakt aller Beteiligten, auch den der Zuschauer. Vom Charisma eines befähigten Dirigenten und Orchesters empfängt der Tänzer nicht selten Ausstrahlungen, die seine Ausdruckskraft und seinen Bewegungsschwung steigern. Als Komponist z. B. hat nie ein anderer die Gesetze des Tanzes intensiver beherrscht und ist der Ausdrucksindividualität der Tänzer einfühlsamer gefolgt als Igor Strawinsky (→Ballets Russes de Serge Diaghilev; →New York City Ballet). Er half den Idealfall des Tanztheaters erfüllen, indem er auf eine Kompanie zu komponierte und deren Befähigung in kaum vorstellbarem Maße herausforderte (*Le Sacre du Printemps*, 1912).

4. Tanztheater ereignet sich nicht im total leeren Raum. Bei gewollt frei lagernder Bühne werden Raumvorstellungen durch wechselnde Tanzbewegungsfelder, Lichtkegel und Farbfilter erzeugt. Allgemein vollziehen sich Tanzereignisse im Eingestimmt- und Ausgerichtetsein auf Bühnen-

elemente und Requisiten. – Die *Inszenierung* (= II C) verstärkt, beschleunigt, malt psychische Motivationen aus, unterstützt sie durch Symbole oder hemmt Willensstrebungen, sorgt für Überraschungen, markiert den Kunststil und ermöglicht durch Handwerk und Technik künstlerische Sujetvorgaben, Szenenabfolgen, Höhendifferenzen. Die Arbeit der Regie richtet sich auf die Darsteller, im Tanztheater auf die Tänzer, den Raum, die Beleuchtung, die Maske und das Kostüm. Diese Gestaltungsfaktoren unterliegen neben handwerklich-technischen Vorbedingungen den Gesetzmäßigkeiten der Malerei, Plastik und Architektur und erzielen auch die Wirkung dieser Künste, deren Vertreter sich deshalb an exzeptionellen Inszenierungen der Tanztheatergeschichte beteiligen: 1917 *Parade*, P. Picasso; 1919 *Der Dreispitz*, P. Picasso; 1920 *Pulcinella*, P. Picasso; 1920 *Le Chant du Rossignol*, H. Matisse; 1924 *Le Train Bleu*, P. Picasso (Vorhang); 1945 *Der Feuervogel*, M. Chagall. (→Ballets Russes de Serge Diaghilev).

▶ *Funktionen und Wirkungsweisen:* Tanz als kulturelle Aktivität, als repräsentative Objektivation einer Kultur erfüllt im personalen und sozialen Bereich die gleichen Funktionen wie jede andere Kunstsparte. Was den Tanz in seiner Wirkungsweise von anderen Sparten unterscheidet, ist die Körperlichkeit der Kunstmaterie, die das Tanz- mit dem Sprechtheater teilt, weniger mit dem Musiktheater, das über seine musikalischen Strukturen hinaus dramatische Gesetze nur teilweise erfüllen kann. Die zeitliche Länge der Arien z. B. verhindert das Ausspielen der Situation körperdramatisch. Die Lebensvollzüge erfahren Verinnerlichungen, die dem Zuschauer vorrangig musikalisch übermittelt werden. – Neben der Körperlichkeit als Qualität werden die Theaterformen durch die Mehrkanaligkeit des Sender-Empfänger-Systems charakterisiert, das über die komplexen Motalitätsakte hinaus, die somästhetisch empfangen werden (das haptische, taktile, kinästhetische Sinnesfeld und der Gleichgewichtssinn verarbeiten die Eindrücke), die verbal- und klangauditive und visuell-wahrnehmende Auffassung anspricht. Jeder Kanal erläutert und erweitert die durch einen anderen Kanal vermittelten Informationen. Ein wechselseitiges Aufdecken und Verdeutlichen setzt ein. Das Nichterfassen einer Aktionsphase über einen kürzeren Zeitraum hin behindert die Erschließung des sinnvoll vorgegebenen Zusammenhangs nicht. Die Vielfalt der Komponenten auf mehreren Erscheinungs- und Zeichenebenen bewirkt erhöhte sensitive Perzeption, aber auch eine verinnerlichte gesamtmotorische Präsenz.

Das erlebte Theatergeschehen setzt den Zuschauer instand, ohne die Zwischenschaltung kognitiver Prozesse Konflikte, Erfahrungen, Beglückungen spontan-körperlich erfassen zu können. Gegebenheiten und Einsichten drängen sich abrupt auf und ‹er›füllen den Mitvollziehenden. Selbstverständlich korrespondieren geistige Einordnungsprozesse; nur müssen diese reaktiv-geistigen Operationen zum Zeitpunkt des Vollzugs nicht bewußt werden.

Die acht aufgeführten Funktionen sind in der Geschichte des Tanzes von allem Anfang an gegeben (→Ritualtanz) und werden genutzt. Die Breite des Funktionsverständnisses war und ist auch heute kaum an spezielle Bewegungs- und Darstellungsformen gebunden, an bildhafte oder ebenbildliche, sinnbildliche oder symbolische, absolute oder abstrakte Darstellungsweisen. Wohl aber sind Tänzer und Zuschauer durch historische und ethno-regionale Bewegungs- und Ausdrucksgebärden geprägt. Dieses Grundbewegungsrepertoire einer Ethnie kann aber, je nach geistiger Offenheit und Bewegungsfreude, beliebig erweitert werden.

Als erste Funktion des Tanzes gilt die Nachahmung (III A), die auf seiten des Tanzenden einen extrovertierten Charakter und dementsprechende Verhaltensweisen impliziert. Der nachahmende und abbildende Tänzer gewinnt seine Gestaltungskraft aus der intensiven Beobachtung der Außenwelt. Während der Aufarbeitung vertiefen seelisch-geistiges Erleben und Reifungsprozesse die Eindrücke. Insofern ist die Abbildungsfunktion eng mit dem Sublimierungsbestreben (III B) verknüpft, das sich auf Introversion gründet und im Tanzakt in seinen Willensbekundungen nach außen tritt. Das Abbildungsbedürfnis erwächst aus der Not, Angst zu bewältigen, und aus der Erfahrung, Freude und Beglückung als ‹Zufall› erwarten zu müssen. Aus den Erfahrungen eines Lebenswegs erwächst auch die Ausdrucksfunktion des Tanzes (III C), die Bekenntnisse verbildlicht und objektiviert. Ob Abbildung, Sublimierung oder Ausdruck, unter welche bewußte oder unbewußte Absicht das Tanz-

---

III. Funktionen des Tanztheaters

A. Abbildung — *B. Sublimierung* — *C. Ausdruck*
Nachahmung — Emotionsbewältigung — Bekenntnis

D. Erkenntnisinstrument — *E. Identitätsfindung*
Auseinandersetzung mit Welt — Ich-Ausbau
Aufbau von Weltbildern — Selbstdarstellung

F. Ästhetisches Erleben
Phantasie-Konzepte
Entlastung
Freistellung von Welt

G. Erziehungsinstrument — *H. Bandstiftung*
Mittel der Akkulturation — Mittel der Begegnung
Weitergabe aller ‹Patterns of Culture› — Begründung von Einvernehmen

drama sich auch stellen mag, es vermittelt Einsicht in Welt und arbeitet Welt auf (III D). Der Tanz ist Erkenntnisinstrument und klärt Lebenspositionen, indem er den Ausbau einer Weltansicht (Weltanschauung) erleichtert. Für die Person bedeutet dieses Vorgegebensein, daß sie sich in tänzerischen Akten ausbauen und Identität erwerben kann (III E). Seit den Urgesellschaften und bis in die Stadien der Kulturvölker hinein war der Tanz Erziehungsmittel (III G). Im großen Tanztheater erwarben die Aufwachsenden und so die Stämme und Völker unentbehrliche Verhaltensweisen, das gesamte System der ‹Patterns of Culture›. Der Tanz ist demnach Vorausnahme und Einübungsinstrument. Die Zivilisationsgesellschaften kennen in Breite keine verpflichtenden Tanzspiele mehr und haben mit ihnen ihr wirksamstes Lehr- und Lernsystem aufgegeben und verloren. Verhaltenserwerb und Vorübung, die Erweiterung des Vorstellungsrepertoires überhaupt, erfolgen in modernen Kulturstaaten, wenn tänzerische Ausdrucksweisen genutzt werden, nahezu ausschließlich in geselligen Tanzformen, für eine Minderheit darüber hinaus in perzeptiven Erlebnissen von Tanztheater. Dieses Vertrautsein nur einer Minderheit mit tänzerischen Realisationen bedeutet Spontaneitätsverlust; denn kein Theatererleben ersetzt den selbsttätigen Aktionsvollzug.

Im Bereich der bandstiftenden Funktion (III H) wird seit ca. 20 Jahren in breiten gesellschaftlichen Zonen das aktive Tanzen neu belebt durch Studenten- und Schüleraustausch, Begegnungen auf Reisen, Jugendlager, Volkstanzfestivals, Tanzkurse, Sport- und Gemeindegruppen, Schul-, Eltern- und Amateurkreise, öffentliche Veranstaltungen, Fernsehsendungen und Tanzfilme. Immer eindeutiger wird die Einsicht vertreten, daß sich fremde Kulturen über nonverbale Kunstsparten am ehesten erschließen lassen. Der Wille, am tänzerischen Gestalten außereuropäischer Kontinente teilzuhaben und auf diesem Wege Empathie auszubauen, begegnet uns heute bei Menschen in allen Ländern. Die Bereitschaft, Lebensstile akzeptieren und verstehen zu wollen, hat zum Ansteigen des Tanztheaterinteresses gerade in der jungen Generation geführt. Es wird deutlich, daß in jeder Evolution auch die künstlerisch-schöpferische Phantasie des Menschen am Werk ist. Die Erfahrung wächst, daß jede neu erworbene Verhaltensweise die menschliche Anpassungsbefähigung verbreitert, so daß die Chancen zu überleben wachsen. – In der gleichzeitigen Präsenz aller Funktionsansätze und auf Grund der vorausgegebenen Vielfalt der Einwirkungsfelder, Handlungsaspekte und Farbigkeiten des Sich-in-Szene-Setzens vermittelt das Tanztheater einen einmaligen und nur von ihm zu empfangenden ästhetischen Genuß (III F). Im tänzerischen Ereignis gelingt den Vollziehenden und den mit ihnen Erlebenden die totale Freistellung aus allen Zwängen des ‹Alltäglichen›. Räumliche Weiten bewahren den genießenden Menschen vor Zugriffen, Gestalt gewordene Strukturen fordern zum Verweilen auf. Die

Phantasie entdeckt ihre Möglichkeiten und vergnügt sich in Entwürfen und Vorgriffen, im Anblick von ‹Kunstgebilden der echten Art›. Das Selbst verharrt in einer einmaligen Gegenwart und stellt sich in diesem Wagnis, transzendierend, gegen die Geschichte.

Brauneck, M.: Theater im 20. Jahrhundert. Programmschriften, Stilperioden, Reformmodelle. Reinbek bei Hamburg 1982; Feldmann, F.: Der Tanzbegriff in seiner Schichtung. In: Die Musik in Geschichte und Gegenwart. Stichwort Tanz. Bd. XIII. Sp. 89–91. Kassel/Basel 1966; Günther, D.: Der Tanz als Bewegungsphänomen. Wesen und Werden. Reinbek bei Hamburg 1962; Hickmann, H.: Vor- und Frühgeschichte, Altorientalische Hochkultur. In: Die Musik in Geschichte und Gegenwart. Stichwort Tanz. Bd. XIII. Sp. 91–95. Kassel/Basel 1966; Nettl, P.: Ballett. In: Die Musik in Geschichte und Gegenwart. Bd. I. Sp. 1169–1181. Kassel/Basel 1949–51.

Helga Ettl

Tanzarchive/-museen/-bibliotheken

T. dienen der systematischen Sammlung, Erfassung und Ordnung von Tanzcodierungssystemen, Tanzpublikationen (schöngeistiger und wissenschaftlicher Literatur in Buchform, Vorträgen, Referaten, Manuskripten zu Rundfunk- und Fernsehaufzeichnungen, Fachzeitschriften, Zeitschriften und Presseartikeln, Rezensionen), Aufführungsmitschnitten und Spezialfilmaufzeichnungen sowie Bildmaterialien. T. konzentrieren ihre Systematisierung entweder auf einen Teilbereich der Tanzwissenschaft, Tanztheorie oder -praxis (Ethnien, Regionen, Kompanien, Stile), oder sie haben sich für eine Dokumentation zum Phänomen Tanz allgemein entschieden.

Ägypten: Kairo: Cairo Ballet Institute (Ballett, Tanz; Bücher, Programme, Zeitschriften). – *Australien:* Flemington: The Australian Archives of the Dance (Tanz; Bücher, Zeitschriften, Skizzen, Plakate, Programme, Fotos, Filme). – *BRD:* Köln: Das Tanzarchiv (Ballett, Tanz, Festspiele, Mimenspiel, Marionetten, Varieté, Bewegung, Bilder, Radio, Fernsehen, Folklore; Bücher, Rezensionen, Manuskripte, Skizzen, Drucke, Fotos, Programme, Zeitungsausschnitte, Schallplatten). – Ehemalige *DDR:* Leipzig: Akademie der Künste der DDR – Tanzarchiv (Monographien, Zeitschriften, Librettos zu Balletten, Schallplatten, Fotos). – *Indien:* Seraikella: The Palace Collection of the Maharajah. Patna: Nritya Kala Mandir. New Delhi: Sangeet Natak Akademi (Academy of Dance, Drama and Music). Jaipur: Bharatiya Lok Kala Mandal. Cuttack: Kala Vikas Kendra. Ahmedabad: Darpana. – *Israel:* Tel Aviv: Central Library for Music and Dance (Oper, Ballett, Tanz, Festspiele, Feiern, Mimenspiel, Varieté, Cabaret, Folklore). – *Italien:* Genzano: Centro Documentazione Danza (1985 Eröffnung des ersten Nationalen Zentrums für Tanzdokumentation; Konzentration zunächst auf Etablierung einer Bibliothek, Videothek und Sammlung aller Materialien, die mit Tanz zu tun haben). – *Kanada:* Toronto: The National Ballet of Canada Archives (Ballett, Tanz; Bü-

918 Tanzfestspiele / Wettbewerbe

cher, Geschäftsbücher, Zeitschriften, Skizzen, Drucke, Plakate, Programme, Zeitungsausschnitte, Fotos). – *Mexiko:* Mexiko: CID-Danza INBA (Centro de Informacion y Documentation de la Danza; 1983 gegr.; setzt sich zur Aufgabe, alles was mit Tanz zu tun hat, zu sammeln, zu erforschen, zu dokumentieren, zu organisieren, zu erhalten und zu archivieren). – *Niederlande:* Den Haag: Bibliotheek en Documentatie Centrum van Het Centraal Dansberaad (Ballett, Tanz, Folklore; Bücher, Zeitschriften, Manuskripte, Drucke, Skizzen, Programme, Zeitungsausschnitte, Filme). – 1985 kam es in den Niederlanden zur Gründung des «Nederlands Instituut voor de Dans», einer Organisation, die als zentrale Informationsstelle dienen wird und den Tanz in Holland auf vielfache Weise fördern und unterstützen will. – *Schweden:* Stockholm: Dansmuseet (1953 im Königl. Theater in Stockholm eröffnet; 1981 erhält das Dansmuseet einen eigenen Gebäudekomplex im Stockholmer Diplomatenviertel; Sammlung von Tanzgegenständen aus aller Welt). – *UdSSR:* Leningrad: Museum attached to the Leningrad State, Academic Maly Theatre of Opera and Ballet (Musical, Ballett, Tanz; Plakate, Tonaufzeichnungen, Filme, Skizzen, Programme, Fotos, Zeitungsausschnitte). Perm: Perm Museum of the Tchaikovsky Academic Theatre of Opera and Ballet (Musical, Ballett, Tanz). Moskau: Museum of the State Academic Bolshoi Theatre (Musical, Ballett, Tanz; Manuskripte, Skizzen, Plakate, Programme, Fotos, Bücher, Schallplatten, Filme, Erinnerungsstücke). Nowosibirsk: Novosibirsk State Museum of the Academic Theatre of Opera and Ballet (Musical, Ballett, Tanz; Manuskripte, Plakate, Programme, Skizzen, Erinnerungsstücke). – *USA:* New York: New York Public Library, Dance Collection (Ballett, Tanz; Bücher, Zeitschriften, Manuskripte, Programme, Plakate, Designs, Drucke, Fotos, Zeitungsausschnitte, Filme, Tonaufzeichnungen, Erinnerungsstücke). – *Jugoslawien:* Belgrad: Institute of Musicology (Oper, Ballett, Tanz, Folklore).

Quellen: Brinson, P.: Background to European ballet. Leyden 1966; Veinstein, A./Golding, A. S. (Hg.): Bibliothèque et Musées des Arts du Spectacle dans le Monde. Paris 1984; Koegler, H./Günther, H.: Reclams Ballettlexikon. Stuttgart 1984; Regitz, H./Koegler, H.: Ballett 1985. Zürich 1985; CID-Danza/Mexikos Tanzarchiv. In: Ballet International 5 (1985), S. 43. Dokumentationszentrum für Tanz in Italien. In: Ballett International 10 (1985), S. 41.

Patricia Stöckemann

Tanzfestspiele / Wettbewerbe

Tanzfestspiele und -wettbewerbe sind in regelmäßigen Abständen veranstaltete Tanztage/Tanzwochen oder einmalig stattfindende Ereignisse auf nationaler oder internationaler Ebene, die dem Tanzinteressierten Einblick in das Repertoire der geladenen Kompanien und Vergleichsmöglichkeiten zur Beurteilung der gegenwärtigen transkulturellen Tanzsituation vermitteln. – Wettbewerbe entscheiden über das tänzerische bzw. choreographische Niveau der Teilnehmer und der vorgestellten Kreationen. Preisverteilungen sind oft mit Ausbildungsstipendien und Gastengagements verbunden.

Patricia Stöckemann

Tanznotationen

T. stellen Versuche dar, tänzerische Bewegungsabläufe zu codifizieren. Im abendländischen Kulturkreis sind seit dem 15. Jh. Tanzaufzeichnungssysteme entworfen worden, die sich nach differenten Notierungsmethoden ordnen lassen, aber selten in der ‹reinen› Form erscheinen.

1. Wortkürzel (= Abkürzungen = Tanzschrittsammlungen für Tanzschrittbezeichnungen). Wortkürzelnotationen benennen Bewegungen, beschreiben sie aber nicht. Sie beschränken sich auf ein begrenztes, exakt bestimmbares Bewegungsrepertoire. Sobald Bewegungen vom standardisierten, traditionellen Vokabular abweichen, muß die Notation auf weitere Hilfsmittel zurückgreifen. Quellen: Mitte des 15. Jh. zwei span. und zwei burgundische Manuskripte. – 1588 Thoinot Arbeaus *Orchésographie* (Abb. 1) (Wortkürzelnotation und exakte Beschreibung).

2. Bodenpläne und Bodenwege: Erfassung der Raumaufteilung und der Raumwege. Zur genaueren Beschreibung wird zusätzlich die Wortkürzelmethode herangezogen. Bodenwegnotierungen setzen ein codifiziertes oder tradiertes Schrittmaterial voraus. Quellen: 1700 Auger Feuillets *Choréographie* (Abb. 2) (Bodenwegschrift, ergänzt durch zusätzliche Zeichen für den Charakter und die Modalität der Schrittausführung; Codierung des Tänzer-Raum-Verhältnisses).

3. Strichfiguren: Sie bilden den Tänzer, seine Positionen und Stellungen in der Abfolge von Tanzphasen und -elementen ab (quasi Dia-Serie). Quellen: 1852 Artur Saint-Léons *Sténographie* (Abb. 3) (erster ausgearbeiteter Strichfigurencode, eingefügt in ein Liniensystem zur Fixierung einzelner Körperteile).

1887 Friedrich A. Zorns *Grammatik der Tanzkunst* (Abb. 4) (Weiterentwicklung des Systems von Saint-Léon).

1956 Rudolf und Joan Benesh' *Benesh Movement Notation* (Abb. 5) (Strichfiguren und 5-Linien-System. Obwohl sich das System schwerpunktmäßig auf die klassisch engl. Schule des →Royal Ballet konzentriert, ist der Code auf alle Bewegungsstile und jede Aktionsform übertragbar; Institut für Benesh-Notation).

4. Musiknoten: Sie sind in ein Liniensystem eingetragene Noten als Bewegungszeichen, die Tanzbewegungen oder den Raum und die Zeit in einem erfassen. – 1855 Bernhard Klemms *Katechismus der Tanzkunst* – 1892 Vladimir Stepanovs *Alphabet des Mouvements du Corps Humain* (Benutzung eines 9-Linien-Systems zur Differenzierung der Körperteile. Ab 1890 in den Lehrplan der Kaiserlichen Ballettschule zu Petersburg aufgenommen). – 1964 Charles McCraws *Scoréography* (Abb. 6) (die Bewegungsanalyse von Laban wird einbezogen).

5. Abstrakte Zeichen: Elemente eines spekulativ konzipierten Codes,

920 Tanznotationen

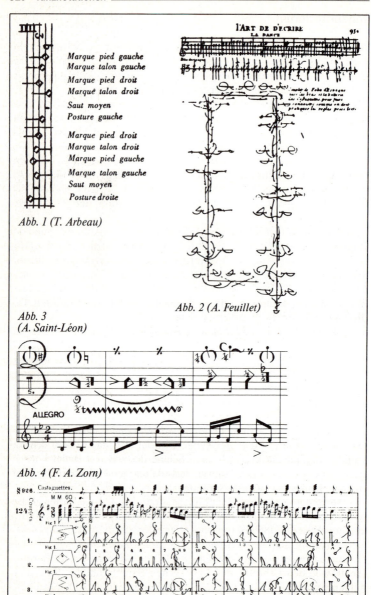

Abb. 1 (T. Arbeau)

Marque pied gauche
Marque talon gauche
Marque pied droit
Marqué talon droit
Saut moyen
Posture gauche

Marque pied droit
Marque talon droit
Marque pied gauche
Marque talon gauche
Saut moyen
Posture droite

Abb. 2 (A. Feuillet)

Abb. 3 (A. Saint-Léon)

Abb. 4 (F. A. Zorn)

Tanznotationen 921

Abb. 5 (R. und J. Benesh)

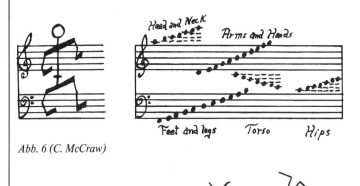

Abb. 6 (C. McCraw)

Abb. 7 (F. Delsarte)

922 Tanznotationen

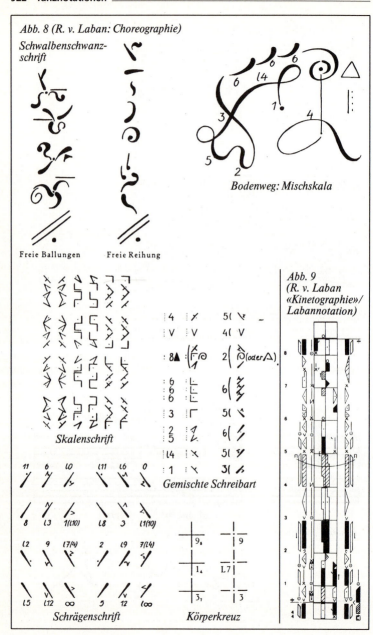

Abb. 8 (R. v. Laban: Choreographie)

Schwalbenschwanz-schrift

Bodenweg: Mischskala

Freie Ballungen   Freie Reihung

Skalenschrift

Gemischte Schreibart

Schrägenschrift   *Körperkreuz*

Abb. 9 (R. v. Laban «Kinetographie»/Labannotation)

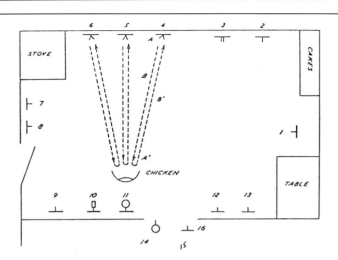

Abb. 10a (G. Kurath, Zusammenhängender Grundentwurf 1960)

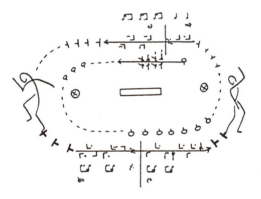

Abb. 10b (G. Kurath, Federtanz 1964)

T_1	5	lean more right
	6	nglereg left
	7	kipat both sampur, gedrug right
	+	seblak both sampur
	8	nyatok both sampur

Abb. 11 (S. Woodard-Notation)

924 Tanznotationen

dessen Zeichenklassen nicht aus realen Bewegungsverläufen abgeleitet werden können. – 1985 François Delsartes Bewegungsschrift (Abb. 7) (Delsarte entwickelt das Bewegungssystem auf der Basis seiner philosophischen Gedankengänge).

1926 Rudolf von Laban: *Choréographie* (Abb. 8); weiterentwickelte Fassung: *Kinetographie/Labannotation* (Abb. 9). (Tanzaufzeichnungssystem auf der Basis von Bewegungsabläufen, nicht Positionen. Die Symbole vereinen Richtungs- und Zeitangaben. Die Trennung von Körperraum und Tanzraum wird ausgeschlossen. Als eines der umfassendsten Systeme ist die Kinetographie auf alle Bewegungsstile und -typen anwendbar. Zentrum der Labannotation ab 1946: Dance Notation Bureau, New York.)

1958 Noa Eshkol/Abraham Wachmann: *Mouvement Notation* (Versuch, die Mechanik der Entstehung von Bewegungen zu notieren).

Codierungssysteme der Tanzethnologie

Alan Lomax, Irmgard Bartenieff, Forrestine Paulay: «Choreometrics Project»: In Anlehnung an die Effort-Shape-Theorie von Laban erfassen die Autoren Bewegungsqualitäten, die Rückschlüsse auf den Tanzstil erlauben.

Gertrude Kurath (Abb. 10a, b). Bewegung und Musik werden in differenten Zeichen nebeneinander abgebildet: Strichfiguren, Symbole und Termini der Labannotation, Musiknotation, geometrische Zeichen. *Strukturalistisch-linguistische Modelle:*

Alice Singer (1974), David Williams (1978), Yoshihiko Ikegami (1971), Stephanie Woodard (1976) (Abb. 11): Tiefenstrukturen werden im Code als Oberflächenstrukturen erfaßt. Verwendung von Buchstaben und mathematischen Zeichen sowie der Labannotation.

György Martin und Ernö Pesovár (1961): *A structural analysis of Hungarian folk dance.* Grundlegung der osteuropäischen Volkstanzforschung. Klassifikationssystem: Elemente – Zellen – Prozeß, Motive – Phrasen, Sektion, Design. Verwendung von Buchstaben und mathematischen Zeichen.

				Prozesse		
Phrase:	A	B	C	z. B.:	$\dfrac{A}{abba}$ =	$\dfrac{\text{Phrase}}{\text{Motiv}}$
Motiv:	a	b	c			
Zelle:	ȧ	ƀ	ȼ	oder:	$\dfrac{a}{\text{ȧ ƀ}}$ =	$\dfrac{\text{Motiv}}{\text{Zelle}}$
Element:	α	β	γ			
				oder:	$\dfrac{\text{ȧ}}{\alpha\ \beta\ \gamma}$ =	$\dfrac{\text{Zelle}}{\text{Element}}$

Adrienne Kaeppler differenziert für die Erfassung von Tanzstrukturen fünf Ebenen: 1. Dance Genres = Tanztypen. Tanztypen insgesamt stellen jeweils differente, identische oder partielle Motive zusammen. 2. Motive = Kombinationen von Morphokinemen, die umgangssprachlich als Tanzbewegungen verbalisiert werden. 3. Morphokineme beziehen sich auf eindeutig abzugrenzende, durch Anfang und Ende gekennzeichnete Bewegungen der Hände, Arme, Finger, Beine, Füße, des Kopfes und anderer Körperteile. 4. Kineme = Bewegungen und Stellungen, die Grundeinheiten darstellen, aus denen sich alle denkbaren Bewegungsfolgen und -schichtungen zusammensetzen lassen. 5. Allokineme = Partialeinheiten der Kineme und deren Varianten. – Inventarisierung durch Labannotation u. a.

Archbult, S.: Labannotation. In: Ballett International 6–7 (1985), S. 21–23; Jeschke, C.: Tanzschriften. Ihre Geschichte und Methode. Bad Reichenhall 1983; Weidig, J.: Tanz-Ethnologie. Ahrensburg 1984; Wendland, J.: Eine autorisierte Tanzschrift muß komplex sein. In: Das Tanzarchiv, Heft 7, Dezember 1971, S. 197–200.

Patricia Stöckemann

Tanztheater

1. Bezeichnung für Tanzgruppen in der BRD ab 1972. 2. Vom Ende der 70er Jahre an trifft der Begriff als stilistischer Gattungsbegriff eindeutig spezielle Formen und Gestaltungsweisen der Tanzkunst. Gerhard Bohner (1936–92) wählt die Titulatur T. erstmalig 1972 zur Kennzeichnung seiner Darmstädter Kompanie. 1973 übernimmt Pina Bausch (* 1940) das Ballett der Städtischen Bühnen Wuppertal als →Wuppertaler Tanztheater, Jahre später Reinhild Hoffmann (* 1943) mit G. Bohner das →Bremer Tanztheater. Zu welchem Zeitpunkt und an welchem Orte das Nomen T. sich dann als Gattungs- und Stilbegriff für die Produktionen von Tanztheatergruppen durchsetzen konnte, kann auf Grund der fehlenden Theater- und Tanzforschungen nicht ausgewiesen werden. Als markante Stilmerkmale der modernsten experimentell-ästhetisch-tänzerischen Ausdrucksformen sind herauszustellen: Montage- und Verfremdungstechniken, die Auffassung eines ‹work in progress›, die multimedialen Vernetzungen, der Bezug zur Gegenwart und zu Alltagsproblemen, die bewußt angestrebte Subjektbezogenheit der Thematiken und die Absage an jede vorgegebene tanztechnische Codifizierung. Das Wuppertaler Tanztheater unter P. Bausch wird durch die Nutzung und Herausstellung dieser Charakteristika zum Prototyp all der in der Folge entstehenden T.-Varianten. P. Bausch gestaltet in der Absicht, die theatralisch-dramatur-

926 Tanztheater

gische Seite des Tanzes auszuformen. So greift sie Konzeptionen des →«Theaters der Grausamkeit» von Artaud, des →«armen Theaters» von Grotowski und des →Happenings auf. – Das T. bettet, wie schon so oft in seiner mehrtausendjährigen Tanzgeschichte, sein ureigenes Medium, die Gebärdensprache, in polyästhetische Ausdrucksformen ein. Es nutzt unter speziellen Zielsetzungen die experimentell-dramaturgischen, skulpturalen, filmischen und klanglichen Künste. Die Plakatierung T. steht für die grundsätzlichen und energischen Bestrebungen der jungen dt. Choreographen, die sich von traditioneller Ballettästhetik distanzieren wollen. In der Konfrontation finden die Choreographen der Moderne zu Konzeptionen eines theatralischen Tanzes, der neoexpressionistische Züge trägt.

Im Jahre 1961 wird die «Internationale Sommerakademie des Tanzes» von Krefeld nach Köln verlegt. Gastdozenten aus aller Welt bestimmen jetzt das Kursprogramm. Wenige Jahre später werden ausländische Kompanien (Cunningham, van Manen, Ailey) zu Gastspielen eingeladen. Die Innovationen und der Verve, den diese internationalen Tänzerpersönlichkeiten der dt. Ballettszene zutragen, beunruhigen die stagnierenden inländischen Tanzensembles und führen sie zu mutigeren, der Zeit angemessenen, phantasievollen Neuansätzen. Die Ergebnisse gewinnen auf dem 1968 von der Sommerakademie veranstalteten Choreographen-Wettbewerb erstmals Form und Anerkennung. Die Kölner Wettbewerbe bieten in allen folgenden Jahren jungen experimentierfreudigen Nachwuchskräften die Chance, sich offiziell zu profilieren.

Die Nachwuchstalente J. Ulrich (*1944), H. Baumann (*1939), J. Burth (*1944) und G. Veredon (*1943) übernehmen in Köln 1971/72 die Ballettdirektion der Kölner Bühnen. Das bisher ausschließlich klassisch geschulte Kölner Opernballett wird zu einem kollektiv geführten modernen Tanzensemble, das offiziell den Namen Tanz-Forum der Bühnen der Stadt Köln erhält. Die Zielsetzungen des Choreographen-Kollektivs verzichten auf traditionelle hierarchische Ballettstrukturen, auf die Dominanz der klassischen Tanztechnik und richten ihre Trainingsarbeit auf die Graham-Technik aus (→Modern Dance). Die allgemeinen politischen Demokratisierungs- und Emanzipationsbestrebungen der 60er Jahre werden ernst genommen. Experimentelle Arbeiten, die auf Zufall und Improvisation vertrauen, tasten sich an ein zeitgenössisches Tanztheater heran. Man strebt nach Austausch und nach partnerschaftlichem Werkschaffen mit außerdeutschen Choreographen, etwa Ch. Bruce (*1945), G. Tetley (*1926) und H. v. Manen (*1932; →Nederlands Dans Theater). Doch auch die Pflege der ehemals von K. Jooss kreierten Ballette (→Ballets Jooss) repräsentiert den Ausdrucks- und Gestaltungswillen des Tanz-Forums, das zum markanten Experimentierfeld des dt. T. aufsteigt. Als Öffentlichkeitsarbeit, in Hin-

Tanztheater 927

wendung zu einem breiten Publikum, veranstaltet das Tanz-Forum Matineen, Einführungsveranstaltungen, Workshops, lecture demonstrations, Diskussionen.

Nach seiner erfolgreichen Arbeit in Köln übernimmt Hans Kresnik (*1939; →Bremer Tanztheater) in der Spielzeit 1968/69 als Ballettmeister und Choreograph die Bremer Ballettkompanie. Dort lösen seine politisch akzentuierten Tanzschöpfungen beim bisher an Märchenballette gewöhnten Abonnentenpublikum Entrüstung und Empörung aus. Kresnik gewinnt jedoch junge studentische Zuschauerkreise. So wird sein Versuch, tagespolitische Ereignisse im Tanz zu thematisieren, schließlich als Pionierarbeit begrüßt. Seine Choreographien erschöpfen sich zunächst in Demonstrationen des vordergründig Wirklichen. Kresniks erste gesellschaftskritische Produktion *Paradies?* (1968) prangert die Bonner Notstandsgesetze und das Attentat auf den Apo-Führer Rudi Dutschke an. Immer extremer sind seitdem seine bewegten Bilder geworden, die komplizierte Machtverhältnisse und ihre Ursachen herausstellen. Doch hat sich Kresniks Interesse sehr bald von den konkret politischen Themen, die er in loser Bilderfolge, revueartig und in einer Mischung aus Agitprop und Popästhetik auf die Bühne bringt, abgewandt. Statt dessen setzt er sich anhand von Einzelbiographien oder literarischen Stoffen mit den Mythen unserer Gesellschaft auseinander und erzielt durch die Konzentration auf die dramaturgische Vorlage eine formale Verdichtung seiner Stücke. Gerhard Bohner (Schüler von Mary Wigman; →Ausdruckstanz) beginnt seine choreographische Laufbahn in den 60er Jahren in Berlin, veranstaltet 1967 an der Berliner Akademie der Künste seinen ersten eigenen Ballettabend und gewinnt auf dem Kölner Choreographenwettbewerb den zweiten Preis. Als Choreograph nach Darmstadt berufen (1972–75), bemüht sich Bohner dort, Tanz-Reformideen zu realisieren, die die Zielsetzungen des Kölner Tanz-Forums überschreiten. Die Balletthierarchie wird abgebaut, öffentliche Proben, Matineen und Diskussionen finden statt, die den Zuschauer zu engagierter kreativer Mitarbeit hinführen wollen. Die Idee von gemeinsamen Tanzschöpfungen scheitert an den Tänzern, die dem hohe Ansprüche stellenden choreographischen Arbeitseinsatz nicht gewachsen sind. 1977 zeichnen sich in Bohners Stücken Fragestellungen zum Thema Mensch und Raum ab, die zur Rekonstruktion des *Triadischen Balletts* von O. Schlemmer (→Bauhaustänze) führen. Mit Reinhild Hoffmann teilt Bohner für die Jahre 1978 bis 1981 die Leitung des Bremer Tanztheaters. Ab 1981 arbeitet er, bis zu seinem Tod, als freier Choreograph.

Reinhild Hoffmann, Schülerin von K. Jooss (→Ballets Jooss, →Ausdruckstanz), tanzt noch unter der Leitung von Pina Bausch Ende der 60er Jahre im Folkwangballett (→Folkwang-Tanzstudio). In den 70er Jahren entwirft sie Choreographien für eigene Soloauftritte, übernimmt

928 Tanztheater

1978–86 die Leitung des →Bremer Tanztheaters, zeitweise zusammen mit Gerhard Bohner, und geht dann als Choreographin ans Schauspielhaus Bochum. Tanz bleibt für Reinhild Hoffmann, im Gegensatz zu Pina Bausch, durchgängiges Ausdruckselement. Aus weiblicher Sichtweise heraus beleuchtet sie speziell die psychischen Ursachen von menschlichen Verhaltensweisen, etwa Ängsten, Sehnsüchten und Zwängen. Ihre Stücke kreisen häufig um vorgegebene Themen wie *Könige und Königinnen*, *Callas* oder *Verreist*. Assoziative Bilderfolgen ersetzen eine durchgängige Handlung. Requisiten, Kostümierungen, Bildmotive, szenische Metaphern sind in einen eher ikonographischen denn inhaltlichen Zusammenhang eingebunden. Eine starke Ästhetisierung der Bewegungsabläufe unterscheidet sie von dem direkten Bewegungseinsatz einer Pina Bausch, mit der sie bis Mitte der 80er Jahre zu den bedeutendsten Vertreterinnen des bundesdt. T. zählte.

Als Choreographin und Solotänzerin gehört auch Susanne Linke (*1944) zu den Protagonistinnen des T. Sie absolviert noch bei Mary Wigman in Berlin die dreijährige Ausbildung und studiert im Anschluß daran, 1967, an der Folkwangschule in Essen. Sie wird Tänzerin in dem von Pina Bausch geleiteten →Folkwang-Tanzstudio, dem sie 1975–77 gemeinsam mit Reinhild Hoffmann vorsteht und für das sie auch in den folgenden Jahren so maßgebliche Choreographien wie *Frauenballett* oder *Wir können nicht alle nur Schwäne sein* kreiert. Vorbilder für die Solotänzerin Susanne Linke sind Mary Wigman und Dore Hoyer (→Ausdruckstanz). Die Suche nach dem wahren Ausdruck, die eigene Person durch den Körper sprechen zu lassen, in tänzerischer Bewegung etwas mitzuteilen, sind Aspekte, die den Tanz der Linke auszeichnen und ihn in die Tradition des dt. Ausdruckstanzes stellen.

Inspiriert von den Vorkämpfern des bundesdt. T., formieren sich ab ca. 1970 nahezu ausschließlich von Frauen geprägte frei arbeitende Gruppen in der BRD. Sie erproben die Spielformen des T. Im Gegensatz zur expressiv-mystischen und auch euphorischen Gebärdensprache des →Ausdruckstanzes und seiner Laienchöre (→Bewegungschor) thematisieren die Tanztheater-Choreographen der Off-Szene Auseinandersetzungen mit der Realität, arbeiten am alltäglichen Bewegungsrepertoire und an dessen konventionellen Alltagserfahrungen. Sie stellen nüchtern vor oder psychologisieren Gehalt und Anlage der Tanzstücke. Zu den mittlerweile renommiertesten Gruppen der zweiten Tanztheatergeneration gehört die 1979 gegründete Laokoon Dance Group unter der Leitung von Rosamund Gilmore. Tanz im konventionellen Sinn ist in ihren Stücken nicht mehr anzutreffen. Darauf deutet bereits das seit 1984 fein durchgestrichene «Dance» im Namen hin und die Reduzierung auf die Ensemblebezeichnung Laokoon seit 1992. Ihre choreographische Inspiration findet die Choreographin im Menschlichen, in der Psyche,

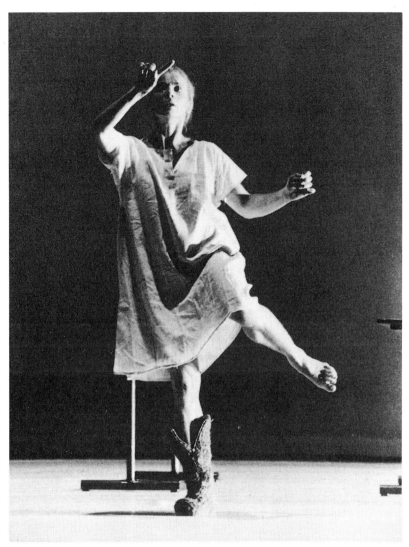

S. Linke: «Schritte verfolgen» (GW)

R. Hoffmann: «Könige und Königinnen». Bremer Tanztheater, 1982

P. Bausch: «Blaubart». Wuppertaler Tanztheater, 1977 (GW)

J. Kresnik: «Macbeth». Heidelberg 1988 (GA)

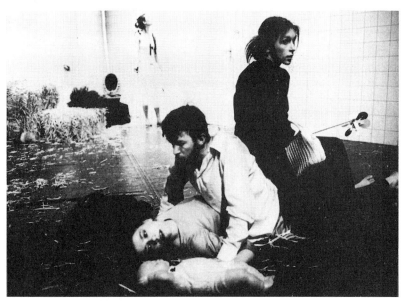

R. Gilmore: «Locus». Laokoon Dance Group, 1984 (Kr)

G. Bohner: «Zwei leben zwei Leben», 1988 (GW)

M. Béjart: «Die Stühle» (nach E. Ionescu). Hamburg 1988 (Ki)

W. Forsythe: «LDC». Frankfurt 1985 (GW)

J. Kresnik: «Ulrike Meinhof». Bremen 1990

den Gefühlen, den Einflüssen der Gesellschaft auf das Individuum. Ihre Bewegungssprache ist direkt, gibt den körperlichen Ausdruck der Empfindungen und Erfahrungen unmittelbar wieder. Jede Geste ist auf ihren Aussagewert hin überprüft, keine Bewegung vollzieht sich um ihrer selbst willen. Kompromißlos und radikal durchbricht die Gilmore in Stücken wie *Egmont*, *Blaubart*, *Winter ade*, *h-moll-Messe* die Fassade des bloßen Scheins und dringt vor bis auf die Grundfesten menschlicher Existenz.

Das Tanzschaffen der ehemaligen DDR verbindet den sowj.-realistischen und klassischen Stil mit Formen des «Neuen Künstlerischen Tanzes» der 1902 geborenen Gret Palucca (→Ausdruckstanz; Palucca-Schule, Dresden). Im Gegensatz zum T. der ursprünglichen BRD, das sich von der klassischen Tanztechnik abwendet, pflegt das T. der ehemaligen DDR die von der Tradition erworbenen und überlieferten Erfahrungen, ohne auf ein experimentelles T. mit dem Ziel der Gesellschaftsformung und -ausdeutung zu verzichten. Die Freistellung einer experimentierfreudigen Off-Szene entfällt. Nicht primär die Frage nach Stilmitteln und Techniken, sondern nach dem Sinn des Bühnengeschehens, nicht Radikalität als Ausdruck gegen bestehende ästhetische Werte und konventionelle Gesellschaftsnormen, sondern Einflußnahme in Form eines realitätsbezogenen gesellschaftsorientierten Handlungsvollzugs im tanzkünstlerischen Kontext bilden Ansatz und Ziel des T. in der ehemaligen DDR. In diesem Sinn arbeiten Tom Schilling (* 1928; ab 1965 →Ballett der Komischen Oper Berlin) und Harald Wandtke (* 1939; 1980–91 Chefchoreograph der Dresdner Staatsoper). Kammertanzabende bieten den Ensembletänzern Wandtkes Gelegenheit, ihre gesellschaftlichen Ambitionen in Choreographien umzusetzen. An den «Improvisationsabenden» (Palucca-Tradition) wirken neben den Tänzern Sänger, Instrumentalisten und Schauspieler mit. Nach entsprechenden ästhetischen Gesichtspunkten entwarfen Dietmar Seyffert (* 1943) am Leipziger Opernhaus und Hermann Rudolph (* 1935) am Theater Karl-Marx-Stadt, heute Chemnitz, ihre Choreographien. Mit der politischen Wende 1989 ist das Theater- und Tanzschaffen in den neuen Bundesländern in eine Phase des Umbruchs und der Desorientierung getreten. Die Palucca-Schülerin Arila Siegert (* 1953), die bereits vor dem Zusammenschluß beider deutscher Staaten mit eigenwilligen, am westdeutschen T. orientierten Abenden und Rekonstruktionen von Werken Dore Hoyers sowie der Ausdruckstänzerin Marianne Vogelsang an die Öffentlichkeit getreten ist, hat es derzeit – auch als Gruppenchoreographin – schwer, sich mit ihren Stücken in der vielfältigen, konkurrenzstarken Tanzlandschaft zu behaupten. Versuche, ein T. nach westlicher Prägung zu etablieren, unternimmt Irina Pauls derzeit am Schauspielhaus in Leipzig. Ballettdirektor der Kompanie der Oper Leip-

930 Tanztheater

zig ist seit 1991 der aus Hessen stammende Uwe Scholz (*1958), der zuvor die Geschicke des Züricher Balletts lenkte. An der Semperoper Dresden hat Johannes Bönig (*1960) 1991 die Leitung des Ballettensembles übernommen. Er war bis dahin in der freien Szene Hollands tätig und versucht jetzt, als Choreograph eines klassisch ausgerichteten Ensembles neue Akzente zu setzen. Bereits die Namensgebung Tanzbühne Dresden deutet auf ein modern ambitioniertes Tanztheaterschaffen hin.

Die stilistische Vielfalt des aktuellen internationalen Tanzgeschehens kann gegenwärtig nur in groben Tendenzen markiert werden. Der weitreichende Einfluß des amerik. →Post Modern Dance ist unverkennbar. Bewegungen werden weiterhin als kinetisches Ereignis, als Spiel der Kräfte, als schlichte Präsentation der menschlichen Bewegungsmöglichkeiten verstanden. Auch der «New Dance», die jüngste amerik. Entwicklungsform des →Post Modern Dance, spürt in seinen Entwürfen dem Bewegungsgeschehen nach und gestaltet absolut. Technische Brillanz, Virtuosität und präzis strukturierte Bewegungsverläufe bestimmen nach jener reduktiven Phase in den 60er Jahren (→Minimal Dance) die neuen Tanzgestaltungen. Sowohl den Vertretern der postmodernen als auch denen der jüngsten Generation gelingen nach kontinuierlich vorangetriebenen Bewegungsexperimenten vielfältige Stilvarianten: Y. Rainer, T. Brown, L. Childs, K. King, L. Dean (→Post Modern Dance, Minimal Dance). Molissa Fenley (*1954): fließende energiegeladene Bewegungsfolgen; durchstrukturierte Kompositionen, teilweise ohne Musik; Dana Reitz: Auseinandersetzung mit der chin. Bewegungskunst Tai Chi. Minimal-Ästhetik (→Minimal Dance), z. T. ohne Musik; Charles Moulton: tänzerische Bewegungsspiele auf der Basis sportlicher, athletischer und akrobatischer Lokomotionen; Bill T. Jones: subsumiert sämtliche Stile der Tanzgeschichte: Klassik, Modern Dance, Breakdance, Rock 'n' Roll usw.; Eiko & Koma sind 1976 aus Japan nach New York übergesiedelt und nutzen Elemente des →Butô. Sie gestalten spannungsgeladene, minimal sich verändernde, zeitlupenhaft geführte Bewegungen; immense Körperbeherrschung, Rückgriff auf archaische Rituale; die Kanadierin Karole Armitage: Entwicklung einer kantigen, harten, der Punk-Rock-Musik unterworfenen Bewegungssprache, die auf der Grundlage der klassischen Tanz- und Cunningham-Technik aufbaut.

Frankreich, ein Land mit 400jähriger Tanztradition (→Ballet de l'Opéra de Paris, →Ballet d'action, →Comédie-ballet), stellt ab 1968 seine traditionelle Tanzästhetik in bezug auf gegenwartsbezogene Aussageformen in Frage. Die Niederlassung der Amerikaner Carolyn Carlson und Alwin Nikolais (→Post Modern Dance) in Frankreich lösen starkes Interesse an Tanzkursen im modernen Stil aus. Nach einer Adaptionsphase entwerfen frz. Choreographen einen eigenwillig gestalteten Stil. Ab 1980 gelingen auch Gegenentwürfe zum bundesdeutschen Tanztheater. Jean-Claude Galotta, 1979 «Compagnie Emile Dubois»: Cunningham-Stil (→Post Modern Dance), Verfremdung klassischer Tanzelemente durch Alltagsgesten und -bewegungen; Galotta koppelt Bewegungsabläufe an Handlungsmotive; Maguy Marin: ehemalige Zusammenarbeit mit Carolyn Carlson, «Compagnie Maguy Marin»: schlichteste Bewegungsvollzüge (Setzen, Sich-Legen, Rollen, Aufstehen), exaktes Timing, mummenschanzartig verfremdete Körper, die die pessimistische Sichtweise der Beckettschen Weltauslegung interpretieren (*May B*); Régine Chopinot, 1978 «Compagnie du Grèbe»: Gehalte und Bewegungsausführungen werden der Alltagswirklichkeit entlehnt, kurze choreographische Szenen, humorvoll, optimistisch (*Via*); Karine Saporta (span. Abstammung) entwickelt eine eigenständige Körperschulung (Lockerung, Konzentration, Atemtechnik, Energie- und Ausdauertraining). Gehalte: das Aufspüren von Beweggründen menschlicher Träume, Gedanken, Ängste; Marc Tompkins: Männerkompanie aus Tänzern, Pantomimen und Schauspielern; hohes darstellerisches Niveau, Verbindung von Komik und Tragik; Diaprojektionen, Bühnenbilder und die Klangwelt sollen in Synthese mit absurden Körperbewegungen, Verrenkungen, Grimassen geometrisch wirkende Formen erzeugen (*Trahisons-Men*). Dominique Bagouet: eigene Kompanie seit 1980. Seine Choreographien leben in Strenge und Präzision aus der theatralischen Spannung der Dimensionen Musik–Kostüm–Beleuchtung–Bewegung (*Désert d'Amour*).

Im Spannungsfeld der Pole →Post Modern Dance (New Dance) und →Tanztheater, zu deren Aktualisierung die zunehmende Zahl der internationalen Festspiele, Workshops, Kongresse und Gastspielreisen der Choreographen beitragen, siedeln sich die vielfältigen Erscheinungsformen des internationalen T. an. Sie zeichnen sich durch z. T. unvereinbare Ansätze und individuelle Gestaltungsweisen aus, die auf unterschiedlichen Tanzstilen beruhen und auch tanzfremde Techniken und Bewegungskonzepte einbeziehen: Kampfsportarten, ostasiatische Bewegungsformen und Meditationspraktiken, akrobatische, sportive und pantomimische Elemente, Disco-, Rock-, Punkart, Breakdance oder →Butô. Verallgemeinernd läßt sich feststellen, daß die Bewegungssprache des zeitgenössischen T. durch hohes technisches Niveau, ungeheure Dynamik, immer rasanter werdende Bewegungsabläufe und Tempi geprägt ist und vielfach an die schnellen Schnittfolgen von Videoclips erinnert. Vertreter dieser Richtung sind die kanadische Gruppe LaLaLa Human Steps und der Belgier Wim Vandekeybus mit ihrem furios-virtuosen, akrobatischen Stil. Demgegenüber steht die auf Langsamkeit zielende Richtung des →Butô. Ein T. ganz eigener Prägung schaffen Grenzgänger wie der Japaner Saburo Teshigawara, der als Bildhauer begann und über das Interesse am menschlichen Körper zum Tanz und zur Choreographie kam, sowie der aus Ungarn stammende und in Frankreich lebende Josef Nadj, der ebenfalls über die Bildende Kunst und die Musik zum Theater und schließlich zum Bewegungstheater gelangte. Zu den bemerkenswerten Choreographen in jüngster Zeit gehört die Belgierin Anne Teresa De Keersmaeker mit ihrer Gruppe Rosas. Sie verwendet in ihren klar strukturierten Choreographien mit Vorliebe live gespielte moderne Musik, die sie direkt mit expressiven tänzerischen Abläufen konfrontiert. Diese Namen stehen nur als Beispiele für die stilistisch vielfältigen tanztheatralen Richtungen, die unter dem Terminus T. subsumiert werden.

Brunel, L.: Experimenteller Tanz. In: Ballett International 5 (1982), S. 26–27; Garske, R.: a) Ballett DDR, b) Deutsche Staatsoper Berlin – Egon Bischoff (Interview), c) Oper Leipzig – Dietmar Seyffert (Interview), d) Staatstheater Dresden – Harald Wandtke (Interview). In: Ballett International 2 (1984), S. 6–23; Koegler, H./Günther, H.: Reclams Ballettlexikon. Stuttgart 1984; Köllinger, B.: Tanztheater. Berlin (DDR) 1983; Pszkowska, A.: Butô-Tanz. München 1983; Regitz, H. (Hg.): Tanz in Deutschland. Berlin 1984; Schaik, E. v.: Report Niederlande (Butô). In: Ballett International 10 (1983), S. 41; Schlicher, S.: Tanztheater. Traditionen und Freiheiten. Reinbek 1987; Schmidt, J.: a) Die Enkelinnen tanzen sich frei. In: Ballett International 1 (1983), S. 12–15; b) Wie sie sich bewegen und was sie bewegt. In: Ballett International 6–7 (1982), S. 6–10; c) Tanzwunder. In: Westermann Monatshefte. Januar 1985, S. 6–18; Servos, N.: a) Das arme Tanztheater. In: Ballett International 3 (1983), S. 44–45; 5 (1983), S. 40–41; 6 (1983), S. 34–37; b) Tanz und Emanzipation. In: Ballett International 1 (1982), S. 51–56; c) Tendenzen des intern. Tanztheaters. In: Ballett International 1 (1985), S. 6–13; Siegel, M. B.: New Dance in Amerika. In: Ballett International 1 (1982), S. 80–83; Vaughan, D.: Vom Modern Dance zur Postmoderne. In: Ballett International 5 (1982), S. 20–22; Welzien, L.: In Trance ist kein Gefühl tabu. Butô, oder japan. experimentelles Tanztheater. In: Theater heute 2 (1981), S. 24–25.

Patricia Stöckemann

Tanztheater der Komischen Oper Berlin

Die Kompanie besteht seit 1965. Sie wird von Tom Schilling (*1928) – 1956–64 Ballettdirektor der Semperoper Dresden – aufgebaut und seither künstlerisch geleitet. Als Ko-Direktor fungiert 1974–91 Bernd Köllinger (*1944; Librettist zahlreicher Schilling-Choreographien), seit 1992 Doris Laine (*1931). Neben dem →Ballett der Deutschen Staatsoper Berlin entwickelt sich das T. zur namhaftesten Ballettkompanie in der Deutschen Demokratischen Republik. – Den Titel Tanztheater erhält das klassische Ensemble in Anlehnung an den von Walter Felsenstein (1901–75; seit 1947 Intendant der Komischen Oper) geprägten Musiktheater-Begriff. Ziel ist die Entwicklung einer eigenständigen Form des (erzählenden) Tanzes, dem Schilling «die Stilmittel und Ausdrucksformen des Modernen Tanzes, des Balletts, der Folklore, der Pantomime und der Bewegung an sich» zuordnet (→Tanztheater). Im Repertoire des T. überwiegen Schillings eigene Arbeiten, zu denen zahlreiche abstrakte sowie einaktige und abendfüllende dramatische Ballette gehören. Werke des traditionellen Ballettrepertoires (*Cinderella, Romeo und Julia, Schwanensee*) inszeniert er auf der Grundlage stark veränderter Libretti. Außerdem adaptiert er bspw. Goethes *Wahlverwandtschaften* und Offenbachs *Hoffmanns Erzählungen* für die Tanzbühne. Gastchoreographen des T. sind u. a. Harald Wandtke (*1939), Arila Siegert (*1953; →Tanztheater), Birgit Scherzer (*1955) und Dietmar Seyffert (*1943).

Köllinger, B.: Tanztheater. Berlin 1983; Fritzsche, D.: Die sowjetische Ballettkunst wirkte befruchtend – Anmerkungen zum Ballett in der DDR. In: Regitz, H. (Hg.): Tanz in Deutschland – Ballett seit 1945. Berlin 1984.

Horst Vollmer

Teatr Dramatyczny (Warschau)

Dramatisches Theater. Drei Bühnen; zwölfmal im Monat tritt hier das →Teatr Narodowy auf. Repertoire: hauptsächlich poln. Gegenwartsstücke. Das T. D. entstand 1955 durch Umgestaltung des ehemaligen Teatr Wojska Polskiego (Theater des Polnischen Heeres, gegr. 1943, 1945–49 in Łódź, gilt als die interessanteste poln. Bühne jener Zeit; Intendant 1946–49 L. Schiller; Teatr im. W. Bogusławskiego). Als T. D. seit 1957 wird es unter der Leitung von M. Meller (1955–62) die führende poln. Bühne (als Regisseure u. a. L. René, K. Swinarski und L. Zamkow; als Bühnenbildner u. a. J. Kosiński, auch A. Sadowski und W. Daszewski). In dieser Zeit entwickelt das T. D. neue Formen der Dramaturgie und Theaterästhetik in Polen. 41 Premieren, zahlreiche Erstaufführungen, u. a. Brecht (Welturaufführung von *Schweyk im Zweiten Weltkrieg*, 1957), westliche und poln. Stücke der Gegenwart (Anouilh, Ionesco, Beckett, Sartre, Dürrenmatt, Mrożek, Gombrowicz, Witkiewicz). In den 60er Jahren wurden neben zeitgenössischen auch klassische Stücke inszeniert; in den 70er Jahren (Intendant G. Holoubek 1972–82; als Regisseure L. René und J. Jarocki) Schwerpunkt auf der Dramatik des 20. Jh. Das T. D. war Organisator der bekannten Warschauer Theatertreffen. In den 80er Jahren Umwandlung in Teatr Rzespopolita (Theater der Republik) – Bühne für Gastspiele. 1991 Verpachtung an W. Kubiak; 1992 Witkiewicz' *Schuster* (Regie: M. Prus).

Slawomir Tryc/Elke Wiegand

Teatr im. J. Słowackiego (Krakau)

Słowacki-Theater, Krakau. Im Repertoire vor allem das nationale poln. Drama. Zwei Bühnen: Teatr im. J. Słowackiego und Teatr Miniatura. Gegründet 1893 als Teatr Miejski (Stadttheater), die heutige Benennung seit 1909. In der Periode des sog. Jungen Polens (1890–1918) war das T. Sł. eine der bedeutendsten polnischsprachigen Bühnen; Uraufführungen der Werke der poln. Romantik (Intendanten: T. Pawlikowski, J. Kotarbiński, L. Solski). Zusammenarbeit mit dem neben den Romantikern wichtigsten poln. Dramenautor, Maler und Theaterreformer S. Wyspiański (1869–1907). Die künstlerisch produktivste Periode in der Zwischenkriegszeit (1918–39) unter der Leitung von T. Trzciński (1918–26 und 1929–32): u. a. poln. Dramatik und ausländische Autoren (Pirandello, Kaiser, Wedekind). Unter der Intendanz von J. Osterwa (1932–35) Schwerpunkt auf poln. Klassik. K. Frycz (1935–39, auch 1945–46) wird der Schöpfer des modernen poln. Bühnenbildes. Ab 1940 ist das T. Sł. das dt. Stadttheater des Generalgouvernements. Wiedereröffnet als T. Sł. im Febr. 1945. 1946 bis 1954 Zusammenschluß mit dem →Teatr Stary, bis 1949 städtisches, dann staatliches Theater. In den ersten Jahren poln. und ausländische Klassik (Shakespeare, Molière, Shaw, de Vega); Erfolge waren oft mit hervorragenden Schauspielern verbunden (M. Ćwiklińska, L. Solski, J. Leszczyński, J. Osterwa). Ende der 50er Jahre bedeutende Inszenierungen auch des modernen westlichen Schauspiels (Miller, Cocteau, Dürrenmatt u. a.), in den 60er Jahren auch O'Neill, Sartre und Brecht neben poln. Autoren. – Enge Zusammenarbeit mit den Vertretern der sog. Krakauer Schule, der radikalsten Strömung im poln. Bühnenbild (A. Majewski, A. Cybulski, W. Krakowski, L. u. J. Skarżyński). Künstlerische Leitung 1973–92 Jerzy Krasowski (* 1925), der dann das →Teatr Narodowy übernimmt; gegenwärtig: J. Goliński.

Slawomir Tryc / Red.

Teatr Narodowy (Warschau)

National-Theater. Eröffnet am 19. 11. 1765 im Opernhaus als das erste poln. Berufstheater. Ständiger Sitz in Teatr Wielki seit 1833 (erbaut 1825–33; drei Ensembles: Oper, Ballett, Drama – genannt nach dem Saal «Rozmaitości»). 1833 bis 1915 WTR (Warschauer Regierungstheater) genannt, unter russ. Verwaltung; offizieller Name (Theater und Saal in Teatr Wielki) seit 1924. 1928 bis 1939 Filiale Teatr Nowy (Neues Theater). 1939 abgebrannt. Wiederaufgebaut 1949 bis 1965, Eröffnungsaufführung am 13. 12. 1949. In den Jahren 1954 bis 1957 mit dem Teatr

Współczesny zusammengeschlossen. In den Jahren 1783 bis 1814 (mit Unterbrechungen) unter der Leitung von W. Bogusławski (1755–1829), Theaterdirektor (auch in Wilna und Lwow), Schauspieler, Regisseur, Mitbegründer des poln. Openntheaters. Propagierte vor allem eine Nationaldramaturgie (→Nationaltheater), aber auch Shakespeare, Molière, Schiller, Lessing, Corneille im Repertoire. Nach der Teilung Polens der wichtigste Hort der poln. Kultur und Sprache. In der zweiten Hälfte des 19. Jh. erlebte das T. N. die sog. «Epoche der Stars» (H. Modrzejewska/ Modjeska, W. Rapacki, B. Leszczyński u. a.). In der Zwischenkriegszeit trotz einiger wichtiger Aufführungen im Schatten des →Teatr Polski. In der Nachkriegszeit lange keine Stabilität in der Leitung des Hauses und seiner programmatischen Ausrichtung; bemüht um den Aufbau eines Repertoires, das die gesamte poln. Nationaldramatik umfassen sollte und Einrichtung einer eigenen Inszenierungswerkstatt. Als Mitarbeiter die Regisseure: L. Schiller, W. Horzyca, E. Axer, K. Dejmek, B. Korzeniewski, A. Hanuszkiewicz, K. Swinarski; die Bühnenbildner: W. Daszewski, J. Kosiński, A. Stopka; die Schauspieler: J. Woszczerowicz, K. Opaliński, T. Łomnicki, T. Kurnakowicz, I. Eichlerówna, G. Holoubek, B. Krafftówna, W. Łuczycka, H. Mikołajska, A. Szczepkowski, Z. Kucówna, D. Olbrychski, S. Zaczyk, J. Kobuszewski. Die interessantesten Perioden unter der Leitung von K. Dejmek (1962–68, mit bedeutenden Inszenierungen des altpoln. Dramas) und A. Hanuszkiewicz (1969–82, mit Klassikerinszenierungen). Nachdem am 9. 3. 1985 in der Direktionszeit von J. Krasowski und K. Skuszanka (1982–90) die Bühne im Teatr Wielki (Großes Theater) abgebrannt war, zunächst Aufführungen im Teatr Mały (Kleines Theater, Nebenbühne des T. N. seit 1973) und im →Teatr Dramatyczny, dann Einstellung des Spielbetriebs, Auflösung des Ensembles und Gründung des Instituts zur Vorbereitung der Wiedereröffnung des T. N. etwa um die Jahrtausendwende.

Grodzicki, A.: Regisseure des polnischen Theaters. Warszawa 1979.

Slawomir Tryc / Elke Wiegand

Teatr Nowy (Łódź)

Neues Theater, Łódź: zwei Bühnen; gegründet 1949 von einer Gruppe junger Absolventen der Theaterhochschule unter Leitung von K. Dejmek (Intendant 1949–61 und 1975–80). In den ersten Jahren spiegelte das Repertoire die aktuellen politischen und gesellschaftlichen Probleme wider im Stil eines dogmatischen sozialistischen Realismus, sog. Produktionsdramen. In der zweiten Hälfte der 50er Jahre →politisches Theater mit starkem Engagement für gesellschaftliche Erneuerungsbestrebungen. Inszenierungen der poln. Klassik und des altpoln. Dramas. In der zweiten Hälfte der 70er Jahre vor allem moralisch und politisch engagierte Stücke. Prominente Mitarbeiter die Regisseure: J. Warmiński und B. Korzeniewski.

Slawomir Tryc

Teatro Arena

Von Augusto Boal (* 1931) in São Paulo 1956 gegründetes Volkstheater, das in Dörfern und Slums vor Analphabeten aufgeführt wurde. Die in Kollektivarbeit verfaßten Agitationsstücke breiteten sich rasch aus, fanden in ganz Lateinamerika Nachahmer und wurden vor allem durch die folgenden Diskussionen für die Regierung so brisant, daß Boal 1971 verhaftet, gefoltert und ausgewiesen wurde. Die Grundideen des T. A. leben vielfach im lateinamerikanischen und in abgewandelter Form im europäischen Kollektiv- und →Straßentheater fort.

Boal, A.: Theater der Unterdrückten. Frankfurt/M. 1979; Driskell, Ch. B.: The Teatro de Arena of São Paulo: An innovative professional theater for the people. In: G. Luzuriaga (ed.): Popular Theater for Social Change in Latin America. Los Angeles 1978, pp. 270–280.

Martin Franzbach

Teatro Campesino

Gegr. 1965 im Kontext eines Landarbeiterstreiks in Delano (Kalifornien). Luis Valdez (* 1940) inszenierte mit Farmarbeitern kurze Sketches (actos), die unmittelbar im Streikgeschehen eingesetzt wurden, und trug entscheidend dazu bei, daß die Gewerkschaft United Farmworkers' Union entstand und nach und nach von den landwirtschaftlichen Großkonzernen als Tarifpartner akzeptiert wurde. Die ‹actos› dramatisierten mit komischen und satirischen Mitteln zunächst nur die soziale Lage der ‹campesinos› (*Two Faces of the Boss*), später die Probleme und Lebensbedingungen der Mexikaner in den USA (Chicanos) schlechthin (*Los Vendidos*) oder auch internationale Fragen (*Vietnam Campesino*). Mit der kulturnationalistischen Orientierung des Chicano Movements entwickelte Valdez seit 1969 den ‹mito›, eine Theaterform, die thematisch wie bildlich die Mythen der Chicanos vermitteln soll, d. h. ihre vorkolumbianische indianische Vergangenheit. Zugleich kam es zur Rezeption und Adaption des ‹corrido›, der mexikan. Volksballade aus den Grenzgebie-

Teatro Cooperativo 937

ten. Die Inhalte der Balladen bildeten einen historisch vertiefenden ‹laufenden Kommentar› zum Handlungsgeschehen, die musikalische Form ermöglichte die ständige Präsenz einer Musikgruppe auf der Bühne. Der gleichzeitig entwickelte ‹historical cycle of San Juan Bautista› enthält neben *La Pastorela* und *Va Virgen del Tepeyac* auch *Rose of the Rancho*, eine Bearbeitung eines Broadway-Dramas von David Belasco (1906). Besonders gelungene Verklammerungen von ‹acto›, ‹mito›, ‹corrido› und ‹Historia› sind die Produktionen *La carpa de los rascuachis* (1972–76) und *Fin del mundo* (1975–80), beide auch auf Europatourneen (1978 bzw. 1980) gezeigt. – Seit 1890 gab das T. C. den Status eines kontinuierlich arbeitenden Kollektivs auf und beschränkte sich darauf, als Produktionsgesellschaft im eigenen Theaterhaus von San Juan Bautista mit jeweils neu verpflichtetem Ensemble eine Reihe von Inszenierungen herauszubringen, z. B. *Soldier Boy* (1982), *Bandido* (1983), *Corridos* (1983/84).

Herms, D.: Luis Valdez – Chicano Dramatist. An Introduction and an Interview. In: Bock, H./Wertheim, A. (Hg.): Essays on Contemporary American Drama. München 1981, S. 257–78; ders.: Die zeitgenössische Literatur der Chicanos (1959–1988). Frankfurt/M. 1990, S. 53–89; ders.: Zwischen Mythos, Anpassung und Rebellion. El Teatro Campesino 1978. In: ders./Paul, A.: Politisches Volkstheater der Gegenwart. Berlin 1981, S. 81–99; Rahner, Ch.: Chicano-Theater zwischen Agitprop und Broadway. Die Entwicklung des Teatro Campesino (1965–1985). Tübingen 1991; Valdez, L.: Actos. Fresno 1971.

Dieter Herms

Teatro Cooperativo

Theaterunternehmen auf genossenschaftlicher Basis, sie unterstehen den für Genossenschaften geltenden ital. Gesetzen. T. C. werden von einem Verwaltungsrat geleitet, dessen Mitglieder jedes Jahr neu gewählt werden. Mitglied kann jedermann werden. Die T. C. tragen sich in der Regel selbst, und zwar durch die Beiträge der Genossenschaftler und durch die Einnahmen aus den Vorstellungen. Nur einige wenige der knapp 400 genossenschaftlich organisierten Theater Italiens erhalten staatliche Subventionen.

Elke Kehr

Teatro de Creación Colectiva

Vorherrschende Form des →politischen Theaters in Lateinamerika (→Lateinamerikanisches Theater), das in (teilw.) Zusammenarbeit mit dem Zuschauer Stoffe und Techniken erarbeitet, Überlebenshilfe gibt und zur Bewußtseinsveränderung beizutragen versucht. Auf Tourneen im Ausland werden die Probleme der Unterprivilegierten konkret verdeutlicht. Anknüpfend an die Theorien von Konstantin S. Stanislawski, Bertolt Brecht, Antonin Artaud u. a. versuchen diese Gruppen, im Sinne einer Gegenöffentlichkeit – in Militärdiktaturen oft unter Lebensgefahr – Informationen und Zusammenhänge weiterzugeben. Auf internationalen Festivals oder Wettbewerben wurden eine Reihe gemeinsamer Merkmale und Zielsetzungen, aber auch Unterschiede je nach regionalen, publikumssoziologischen, historischen o. a. Voraussetzungen deutlich. Bekannte Ensembles: Libre Teatro Libre (Argentinien), Grupo de Teatro Ollantay (Ecuador), →Teatro Experimental de Cali, ‹La Candelaria› (Kolumbien), →Teatro Escambray (Kuba), Cuatrotablas (Peru), Colectivo Nacional de Teatro (Puerto Rico), Rajatablas (Venezuela) u. v. a.

Adler, H.: Politisches Theater in Lateinamerika. Von der Mythologie über die Mission zur kollektiven Identität. Berlin 1982; Garzón Céspedes, F. (ed.): El teatro latinoamericano de creación colectiva. La Habana 1978; Gutiérrez, S. (ed.): Teatro popular y cambio social en América Latina. Panorama de una experiencia. Costa Rica 1979; Luzuriaga, G.: Popular Theater for Social Change in Latin America. Essays in Spanish and English. Los Angeles 1978; Lyday, L. F./Woodyard, G. W. (eds.): Dramatists in Revolt. The new Latin American Theater. Austin/London 1976; Menéndez Quiroa, L. (ed.): Hacia un nuevo teatro latinoamericano. Teoría y metodología del arte escénico. San Salvador 1977.

Martin Franzbach

Teatro degli Independenti

Auch Teatro Sperimentale degli Independenti; 1922 von Anton Giulio Bragaglia (1890–1960) gegründet. Der unterirdische Theatersaal selbst war eine futuristisch ausgeschmückte antike Basilika. Die Räume des Theaters wurden nicht nur als Ausstellungsräume und Schauspielräume verwendet, es fanden dort auch Künstlerkabaretts und Tanzveranstaltungen statt.

Das T. I. war praktisch das erste →Teatro Stabile und Bragaglia der erste Regisseur, der in Italien Strindberg und Wedekind aufführte. Daneben galt sein Interesse den jungen ital. Autoren, besonders den Futuristen (→Futuristisches Theater). Zu seinen Mitarbeitern gehörten die futuristischen Szenographen Marchi, Prampolini, Pannaggi, Paldini, Fornari, Valente. Regie führte in der Regel Bragaglia selbst. Zusammen mit seinen Brüdern Carlo und Arturo entwickelte Bragaglia ein Programm, das auf eine Gesamtharmonie der modernen Kunst hinzielte. Grundlegende Reformen der Bühnentechnik trugen dazu bei, alles Theatralische auf derselben künstlerischen Ebene zu vereinigen, d. h., Bragaglia konzipierte ein Theater, das Regisseur, Bühnenbildner und Schauspieler denselben künstlerischen Stellenwert zuweist.

In seiner programmatischen Schrift *Del teatro teatrale* (1927) entwickelt Bragaglia eine Synthese von spontanem Improvisationstheater und szenographischen Experimenten. Die Theaterszene wird architektonisch aufgefaßt. Es gibt keine Kulissen, sondern ‹szenoplastische› Lösungen. Die von Appia beeinflußte Lichtregie Bragaglias gilt als bahnbrechend und wegweisend für die Beleuchtungstechnik. Ein weiteres Ausdrucksmittel waren ‹mobile Masken› aus Kautschuk, die in sechs gleichzeitig spielbereiten Szenenarrangements in, neben, über und unter der Bühne einsatzbereit waren. Bragaglia inszenierte u. a. Jarry (*Ubu*, 1926), Apollinaire (*Les Mamelles de Tiresias*, 1927), Ghelderode (*La Morte del dottore Faust*, 1928), aber auch Strindberg, Pirandello, Sternheim, Shaw, Schnitzler. – 1931 mußte das T. I. aus finanziellen Gründen geschlossen werden (→Teatro dell'arti).

Die Premiere, 1. Oktoberheft 1925.

Elke Kehr

Teatro de la Esperanza

Begann als Teatro Mecha 1969 in Santa Barbara, Kalifornien, umbenannt in T. d. l. E. 1971 unter Leitung von Jorge A. Huerta (* 1942). Bedeutendstes →Chicano Theater nach dem →Teatro Campesino und einzige kontinuierlich arbeitende professionelle Theatergruppe der Chicanos in den USA der Gegenwart. Wichtigste Inszenierungen: *Guadalupe* (1974), Dramatisierung von Civil Rights-Verletzungen gegenüber Chicanos in einer Nachbarstadt; *La victima* (1976), eine marxistisch inspirierte Einwanderersaga; *Octopus* (1981), das nach dem gleichnamigen Roman von Frank Norris diese Tiermetapher für den weißamerik. Monopolkapitalismus verwendet; *La loteria de pasiones* (1983), komödiantische, rein spanischsprachige Behandlung dieses erregenden zentralamerik. Volksglücksspiels. 1987 als ‹work-in-progress›: *Teo's Final Spin*; das Werk behandelt, über die Chicanoperspektive hinausgehend, das US-Engagement in Zentralamerika.

Herms, D.: Die zeitgenössische Literatur der Chicanos (1959–1988). Frankfurt/M. 1990, S. 90–96; Huerta, J. A. (Hg.): El Teatro de la Esperanza. Goleta 1973; ders.: Chicano Theater. Themes and Forms. Ypsilanti 1983.

Uschi Bauer / Dieter Herms

Teatro dell'arti

Nachdem sein →Teatro degli Independenti 1931 aus finanziellen Gründen geschlossen werden mußte, initiierte Bragaglia 1937 die Gründung des T. d. a. innerhalb der 1935 errichteten Staatlichen Akademie der Schauspielkunst in Rom. Er leitete das Theater bis 1943 und führte hier das künstlerische Konzept des Teatro degli Independenti weiter. Für das T. d. a. entwickelte er einen Spielplan des modernen Welttheaters mit Stücken von O'Neill, O'Casey, Wilder und Salacrou.

1951 von dem Schauspieler Vittorio Gassman und dem Dramaturgen und Autor Luigi Squarzina (beide Jahrgang 1922) wiedergegründet. Gassman wollte das Theater popularisieren. Unter dieser Prämisse wurde auch das Repertoire des T. d. a. (klassische und moderne Stücke) gestaltet. Ein eindrucksvoller Erfolg war die Inszenierung des *Hamlet* 1952. Gassmans Verdienst ist es, mit dieser und anderen Inszenierungen das Interesse des ital. Publikums am Sprechtheater geweckt zu haben. – Gassman leitete das Theater bis 1953. Auch danach setzte er seine Bemühungen um eine Popularisierung des Theaters fort, so mit dem Zelttheater Teatro Populare Italiano, mit dem er 1960/61 mit einer Inszenierung von Manzonis *Adelchi* Italien bereiste. 1963 trat seine Truppe in London auf mit einer Produktion *The Heroes*, die aus Auszügen aus seinem Repertoire bestand.

Elke Kehr

Teatro Escambray

(→Lateinamerikanisches Theater) Kuban. Kollektivtheater, 1968 von Sergio Corrieri (*1931) in der Sierra del Escambray, einem bes. rückständigen Gebiet, gegründet. Ziel: aus dem Theater ein wirksames Instrument im Kampf gegen die Unterentwicklung zu machen. Die heute über 50 Akteure fügten sich dem Rhythmus der Bauern ein, lernten deren Probleme kennen, diskutierten und probten mit Laien zusammen ihr Material. Themen: Machismo, Schwarzhandel, Aberglauben, Familienprobleme u. a.

Das auch im Ausland (Tournee BRD März 1984) bekannte Theater ist vor einer reichen kulturellen Infrastruktur von Hoch- und Fachschulen für Schauspieler, Regisseure, Bühnentechniker und einer alphabetisierten Bevölkerung nach 1959 zu sehen.

Ende der 80er Jahre zeigten sich Auflösungserscheinungen, die nicht zuletzt mit der Übernahme hoher politischer Ämter durch den Direktor S. Corrieri zusammenhingen.

Adler, H.: Politisches Theater in Lateinamerika. Berlin 1982; Leal, R. (ed.): Teatro Escambray. La Habana 1978; Séjourné, L.: Teatro Escambray: una experiencia. La Habana 1977.

Martin Franzbach

Teatro Experimental de Cali

Von Enrique Buenaventura 1957 gegründetes kolumbian. Theaterkollektiv (urspr. Theaterschule seit 1955), das seine Themen vor allem der Slum- und Landbevölkerung nahebringt, z. B. die Geschichte von Streiks und staatlicher Repression, die Ausbeutungsmethoden der United Fruit Company usw.

Fuentes, V.: La creación colectiva del Teatro Experimental de Cali. In: G. Luzuriaga (ed.): Popular Theater for Social Change in Latin America. Los Angeles 1978, pp. 338–348.

Martin Franzbach

Teatro Farnese

Papst Paul III. erhob 1545 Parma zum Herzogtum und verlieh es als erblichen Besitz unter päpstlicher Lehnshoheit seinem natürlichen Sohn Pier Luigi Farnese (1520–86). Aus dieser Zeit stammt der unvollendete, 1583 begonnene Palazzo Pilotta mit dem aus Holz erbauten T. F. Das Theater ist das Werk des aus Ferrara stammenden Architekten Giovan Battista Aleotti, genannt L'Argenta (1546–1636), erbaut im Auftrag von Ranucci I. in den Jahren 1618 und 1619, aber erst eingeweiht zur Hochzeit von Odoardo mit Margherita de Medici 1628; im 2. Weltkrieg (1944) durch Fliegerbomben zerstört. Das T. F. in Parma war in vieler Hinsicht ein Novum: Vergrößerung des Zuschauerraums, nachdem das Hoftheater für ein zahlendes Publikum zugänglich gemacht worden war; Logenhaus mit Rängen, wodurch die Trennung der Zuschauer nach Rang und Würden möglich wurde: Diese Theaterform fand, besonders durch die aus dem Geist des Barock entstandene Oper, in ganz Europa Nachahmung.

942 Teatro Goldoni

Vom kriegszerstörten T. F. sind noch die Mauern und Zwischenwände erhalten. Das Theatergebäude war 87,22 m lang, 32,15 m breit und 22,67 m hoch; die Bühne hatte 40 m Tiefe und 12 m Breite. Die U- oder Hufeisenform der Zuschaueranordnung ist klar zu erkennen.

Guerrieri, G./Povoledo, E.: Il secolo dell' invenzione teatrale. Katalog. Mailand 1951; Tintelnot, H.: Barocktheater und Barockkunst. Berlin 1939.

Horst Schumacher

Teatro Goldoni

Als großherzogliches →Hoftheater in Florenz von Luigi Gargani erbaut, sollte in unmittelbarer Nähe der Residenz der Großherzöge von Toskana als dekoratives Theater mit anschließender Arena dienen und durch eine Fülle von Verbindungssälen die Begegnung von Künstlern, Intellektuellen und Hofgesellschaft erleichtern. Eröffnung am 7.4.1817 mit *Il Burbero benefico* und *La Figlia mal custodita* von Carlo Goldoni (1707–93). Die Arena wurde 1818 dem Publikum geöffnet und bot 1500 Personen Platz (das eigentliche Theater bis zu 1600). Im 19. Jh. hauptsächlich Repertoire-Theater, 1860 bis 1870 als Gastspieltheater für die besten ital. Bühnen erster Höhepunkt. 1908 wurde die Arena Goldoni von Edward Gordon Craig (1872–1966) zum Zentrum seiner Arbeit für die Erneuerung des Theaters erhoben. In Florenz begründete Craig 1908 die (bis 1929 erscheinende) Zeitschrift *The Mask*. 1913 begann in der Arena G. die Gordon Craig School als Schauspielschule, die vor allem – Theaterforschung und Theaterpraxis eng verbindende – Theaterwerkstatt war und Craigs Theaterideen (→Über-Marionette) weiterentwickeln und erproben sollte; wurde 1917 nach Requirierung der Arena G. durch die Militärbehörden geschlossen. Endgültige Schließung des T. G. 1925.

Bablet, D.: Edward Gordon Craig. Köln/Berlin 1965; Craig, E. G.: Index to the Story of my Life. London 1957; Kreidt, D.: Kunsttheorie der Inszenierung. Zur Kritik der ästhetischen Konzeption Adolphe Appias und Edward Gordon Craigs. Diss. FU Berlin 1968.

Horst Schumacher

Teatro Immagine

Mitte der 60er Jahre von dem ital. Schauspieler und Regisseur Mario Ricci (*1928) und den Malern Santaro und Frasca in Rom gegründet. Das T. I. proklamiert die Autonomie aller Ausdrucksmittel; Filmeinblendungen, Verzerrungen, musikalische und textliche Zitate ergänzen den schauspielerischen Ausdrucksbereich. Der Schauspieler selbst ist ein Ausdrucksmittel unter anderen gleichberechtigten. Die theaterkonzeptionellen Ideen von Grotowski (→ Armes Theater) und Wilson werden in der Arbeitsweise des T. I. verwertet.

Quadri, F.: L'avanguardia teatrale in Italia (Materiali 1960–76). Turin 1977.

Elke Kehr

Teatro Independiente

Alternative zur kommerziellen Theaterstruktur in Spanien, die vor allem in der Endphase des Franquismus (1965–75) politische Bedeutung gewann. Unter ständigen Repressionen und Zensureingriffen fristete dieses Untergrundtheater sein Leben, bis die veränderten politischen Bedingungen und die materiellen Zwänge die Kollektive zur Auflösung veranlaßten.

Wellwarth, G. E.: Spanish Underground Drama. Teatro español underground. Madrid 1978.

Martin Franzbach

Teatro Olimpico

Wie die anderen Bauten von Andrea Palladio (1508–80) in seiner Geburtsstadt Vicenza zeigt das T. O. bahnbrechende Neugestaltung der auf antiker Grundform beruhenden Theaterarchitektur (→ Theaterbau). Die ganzheitliche Auffassung der klassischen Baukunst ist hier im Sinne der Renaissance mit zeitgemäßen Aufgaben in Einklang gebracht. Die als Scenae frons reich gegliederte Bühne mit drei Toren und Blick auf dahinterliegendes Gassengewirr liegt zu Füßen eines halbrunden, steil ansteigenden Zuschauerraums. Beispielgebend für die Theaterarchitektur der Renaissance und teilweise auch des Barock. Das 1580 bis 1585 erbaute T. O. wurde von Palladios Sohn Scilla und dem aus Vicenza gebürtigen venezianischen Baumeister Vincenzo Scamozzi (1552–1616) fertiggestellt.

Barbieri, F./Cevese, R./Magagnato, L.: Guida di Vicenza. 1953ff; ders.: Teatri italiani del cinquecento. Venedig 1954; Werner, E.: Theatergebäude. Bd. I: Geschichtliche Entwicklung. Berlin 1954.

Horst Schumacher

Teatro San Ferdinando

Das im 18. Jh. auf private Initiative in Neapel errichtete Theater diente im 19. Jh. als Opern- und Schauspielhaus mit volkstümlichem Repertoire. Um 1930 umgebaut und als Teatro Impero wiedereröffnet, 1943 durch Fliegerbomben zerstört. Nach Wiederaufbau durch Eduardo De Filippo 1954 Neueröffnung und Sitz seines napolitanischen Dialekttheaters (→ Volkstheater) bzw. der von ihm geleiteten Truppe La Scarpettiana.

Viviani, V.: Piccola Storia del San Ferdinando. Neapel 1954.

Horst Schumacher

Teatro stabile

Ital. Bezeichnung für Schauspielerensemble mit eigenem ‹festen› Theatergebäude. Auch verwendet für Truppe mit festem Standort und vorzugsweiser Bespielung von auswärtigen Häusern («Ballett du XXe siècle» von Maurice Béjart; Städtebundtheater in der Schweiz, Gastspieltheater in der Bundesrepublik). Die Hoftheater, Stadttheater und Staatstheater sind T. s., deren Träger ein Fürstenhof bzw. eine Gebietskörperschaft ist. Zu Beginn des 20. Jh. sind T. s. Träger einer Bewegung des experimentellen Theaters: z. B. das → Théâtre-Libre in Frankreich, die → Freie Bühne Otto Brahms in Berlin, die → Provincetown Players. Mit dem Aufkommen der Regie verbanden viele Theaterleiter ihren Namen mit dem ihres ‹festen› Hauses, z. B. → Théâtre du Vieux-Colombier von Cocteau, → Théâtre de l'Œuvre von Lugné-Poë, die → Piscator-Bühne Erwin Piscators. In den Jahren nach dem 2. Weltkrieg sind Avantgarde-Theater wie → Piccolo Teatro di Milano und → Berliner Ensemble Bertolt Brechts T. s. Experimentiertheater ohne Subventionen öffentlicher Träger als T. s. zu führen, scheitert oft aus ökonomischen Gründen.

Camilleri, A.: I Teatri stabili in Italia. Bologna 1959.

Horst Schumacher

Teatro Umoristico

Unter dem Namen T. U. bildeten die drei Geschwister, Schauspieler und Stückeschreiber Titina (*1898), Eduardo (1900–84) und Peppino (*1903) De Filippo 1932 eine Truppe im Teatro Sannazaro in Neapel, bekannt als compania del T. U. ‹I de Filippo›. Damit hatten sich die schon 1929 gemeinsam auftretenden und gelegentlich selbstverfaßte Stücke aufführenden Geschwister selbständig gemacht. Unter Eduardos Leitung bereisten sie ganz Italien und wurden als Erneuerer des napolitanischen Mundarttheaters berühmt.

Magliulo, G.: De Filippo. 1960; Repaci, L.: Umorismo tragico dei De Filippo. 1940.

Horst Schumacher

Teatr Polski (Warschau)

Polnisches Theater. Intendant: K. Dejmek (* 1924) seit 1981, Regisseure: J. Bratkowski, J. Rakowiecki; Bühnenbildner: K. Pankiewicz, Ł. Kossakowska u. a. Zwei Bühnen: Teatr Polski und Teatr Kameralny (Kammertheater). Im Repertoire hauptsächlich poln. Dramatik. – Gegründet 1913 (oft als Geburtsstunde des modernen poln. Theaters bezeichnet), derzeit das bühnentechnisch modernste poln. Theater (Drehbühne). 1918 bis 1939 auch das Teatr Mały (Kleines Theater) angeschlossen. In der Zwischenkriegszeit (1918–39) geleitet von A. Szyfman (1882–1967), auch 1946 bis 1949 und 1955 bis 1957. Das erfolgreichste Theater jener Zeit mit einem hervorragenden Ensemble (Regisseure: L. Schiller, A. Węgierko, A. Zelwerowicz). Vielfältiges Repertoire: außer der poln. Klassik auch Shakespeare, Molière, Shaw u. a. Ab 1940 als dt. Theater der Stadt Warschau geführt. Nach 1945 das einzige unversehrt gebliebene Theater Warschaus; wiedereröffnet 1946. Ende der 60er Jahre (Intendant Jerzy Kreczmar †) vor allem Klassik, seit den 70er Jahren besonders poln. Gegenwartsdramatik.

Slawomir Tryc

Teatr Rapsodyczny

Rhapsodisches Theater, Krakau, gegründet 1941 von M. Kotlarczyk (1908–78) als Theater im Untergrund. 1941 bis 1945 sieben Premieren, 22 Aufführungen; bestand mit Unterbrechung (1953–1957) bis 1967. Hauptsächlich Inszenierungen bedeutender Stücke der Weltliteratur und selten aufgeführter Bühnenwerke. Einfache Inszenierungsform, dem Wort untergeordnet; oft musikalisch illustriert.

Malak, T.: «Polska będzie, Lolusiu...». In: Teatr (Warszawa) 1991, Nr. 11.

Slawomir Tryc

Teatr Stary (Krakau)

Altes Theater. Vier Bühnen: Teatr Stary, Teatr Kameralny (Kammertheater), Sala H. Modrezejewskiej (Modrzejewska-Saal), «Przy ulicy Sławkowskiej 14» (In der Sławkowska-Straße 14). Umfangreiches Repertoire: von den poln. Autoren und Weltliteratur bis hin zum zeitgenössischen Drama. In den letzten Jahren u. a. Dostojewski, Norwid, Sophokles, Calderón. Das T. S. entstand 1781, seit 1799 am Szczepański-Platz (außer 1830–43; abwechselnd poln. und dt. Aufführungen). Bedeutender künstlerischer Aufschwung 1871 bis 1885 unter der Leitung von S. Koźmian (1836–1922) mit Aufführungen u. a. von Stücken von Fredro, Schiller, Goethe (*Faust*, 1869) und Shakespeare; hohes Niveau der Schauspielkunst. Die Hauptprinzipien der sog. «Krakauer Schule von S. Koźmian» waren: individuelle Gestaltung der Rolle, Kollektivarbeit in den Proben, Anerkennung der schöpferischen Rolle des Regisseurs. 1893 geschlossen und umgebaut, seit 1906 als Konzertsaal genutzt; wiedereröffnet 1945 mit Werken poln. zeitgenössischer Autoren (viele Debüts, hauptsächlich Kammerschauspiele). Auch während des Zusammenschlusses mit dem →Teatr im. J. Słowackiego (1946–54) nahm das T. S. eine künstlerische Sonderstellung ein. In der zweiten Hälfte der 50er Jahre und Anfang der 60er Jahre unter der Intendanz von W. Krzemiński (1957–63) neue Repertoirestruktur, poln. Stücke, aber auch Shaw, Lorca, Ibsen, Williams, Zuckmayer. Unter der Leitung von Z. Hübner (1963–69) eine neue Etappe: im Repertoire vor allem Klassik in individueller, schöpferischer Interpretation und moderne poln. Autoren. Auch unter der Leitung von J. P. Gawlik (1970–81), Stanisław Radwan (Komponist des T. S.) und gegenwärtig Tadeusz Bradecki (Autor und Regisseur), die die Programmatik fortsetzen, bleibt das T. S. die führende poln. Bühne mit großem Erfolg auch im Ausland. Den hohen Rang verleihen ihm v. a. die Regisseure Konrad Swinarski (1929–75), Jerzy Jarocki (*1929), Andrzej Wajda (auch L. Zamkow, J. Szajna, J. Grotowski, J. Grzegorzewski u. a.).

Sławomir Tryc/Elke Wiegand

Teatr Współczesny (Warschau)

Zeitgenössisches Theater; Schwerpunkt des Repertoires zeitgenössische Dramatik. Gegründet 1945 in Łódź als Teatr Kameralny (Kammertheater), 1949 nach Warschau verlegt und umbenannt in T. W. 1954 bis 1957 mit dem →Teatr Narodowy zusammengeschlossen. Hohes künstlerisches Niveau, konsequenter Stil durch E. Axer (*1917) geprägt (1945–48 Kointendant, 1948–81 Intendant), inszenierte die meisten der Aufführungen selbst; reflektierende, intellektuell-psychologische Kammerstücke mit großer Präzision in der Dialogführung, kollektive Arbeitsformen. Bereits während der Łódź-Periode eine der interessantesten Bühnen in Polen (u. a. engl. und amerik. Dramatik: Shaw, Priestley, Williams). In der ersten Hälfte der 50er Jahre vor allem poln. Gegenwartsdramatik. Nach 1957 (*Warten auf Godot*) an der Spitze der poln. Theater, zusammen mit dem →Teatr Dramatyczny und dem Teatr Ateneum (Warschau). Hauptsächlich westliche Autoren im Repertoire (Brecht, Wilder, Osborne, Ionesco, Weiss, Frisch), aber auch poln. (u. a. Mrożek) Dramatiker. In den 80er Jahren u. a. Gombrowicz, Tschechow, Camus. Als Mitarbeiter die Regisseure: J. Kreczmar, A. Bardini, Z. Hübner, K. Swinarski (1929–75), als Bühnenbildner: O. Axer, W. Daszewski, K. Kosiński und die Schauspieler: H. Borowski, J. Englert, I. Eichlerówna, Jan Kreczmar, A. Łapicki, T. Łomnicki, R. Hanin, M. Komorowska, B. Krafftówna, A. Śląska, Cz. Wołłejko, Z. Zapasiewicz. Seit 1982 Intendant: Maciej Englert, Schüler von E. Axer.

Slawomir Tryc

Teichoskopie

Dramaturgisches Hilfsmittel, das mit dem →Botenbericht verwandt ist und sich doch von ihm unterscheidet: Während der Botenbericht dramatisch undarstellbare Ereignisse verkündet, die bereits vergangen sind, dient die T. dazu, für die Entwicklung der Handlung wichtige Ereignisse, die außerhalb der Bühne stattfinden, zugleich von einer Gestalt erzählen zu lassen, die auf der Bühne steht und von einer erhöhten Stelle aus – Wachturm, Hügel – das Schauspiel verfolgt, das die anderen Personen und das Publikum nicht sehen können. Im Vergleich zum Botenbericht hat die T. den Vorteil, daß sie durch die Gleichzeitigkeit vom Geschehen und dessen Bericht diesem eine gesteigerte dramatische Spannung und Lebendigkeit verleiht.

Das Wort T. («Mauerschau»), das dem Griech. entnommen ist, spielt ursprünglich auf eine Szene im 3. Gesang der *Ilias* von Homer (8. Jh. v. Chr.) an, wo Helena Priamos und den Troern von der Stadtmauer aus die griech. Fürsten schildert. In der modernen Zeit gilt Shakespeare (1564–1616) auch hier als Vorbild (vgl. *Julius Caesar* V, 3; 1599). In Deutschland wird die T. hauptsächlich von den Dramatikern der Goethezeit verwendet (vgl. u. a. *Der Prinz von Homburg* II, 2, 1811, von Heinrich von Kleist, 1776–1811).

Klotz, V.: Geschlossene und offene Form im dt. Drama. Stuttgart 1960; Weltmann, L.: Die ‹verdeckte Handlung› bei Kleist. Diss. Freiburg 1924.

Alain Muzelle

Teichtheater

Form des →Gartentheaters. Prunkvolle Opernaufführungen auch bei künstlichem Licht auf Verwandlungsbühnen unter Einbeziehung des Wassers. Frühestes Beispiel eines T.: im Rahmen der Hoffeste des span. Königs Philipp V. Theater auf einer Barke im Garten von Buen Retiro (1640); ‹Plaisirs de l'Ile enchantée›, Versailles (1664); kaiserlicher Hof in Wien; Laxenburg (1679) und Favorita (ab 1699), Dekorationen von Ludovico Burnacini (1636–1707) und Giuseppe Galli-Bibiena (1696–1757); Hochzeit Karl IV., Barcelona, Ausstattung Ferdinando Galli-Bibiena (1657–1743); T. von Lazienki in Warschau (1792).

Baur-Heinhold, M.: Theater des Barock. Festliches Bühnenspiel im 17. und 18. Jh. München 1966; Meyer, R.: Hecken- und Gartentheater in Deutschland im 17. und 18. Jh. Emsdetten 1934; Schlick, J.: Wasserfeste und Teichtheater des Barock. Diss. phil. Kiel 1962/63.

Ingeborg Janich

Terenzbühne

Die Antike, bes. die röm. Komödie, beschränkte die gesamte Handlung auf einen Ort, einen Platz, an den die Häuser der handelnden Personen angrenzten. Weitere Bühnenzugänge führten in die Stadt bzw. in die Ferne. Dieses Einortdrama wurde von den Humanisten durch einfache Häuserrahmen dargestellt. Von der →Simultanbühne unterscheidet sich diese Bühnenform nicht nur durch die örtliche Begrenzung, sondern die Darsteller traten auf und gingen ab. Die sog. erweiterte T. zieht diesen einen Ort so weit auseinander, daß er z. B. im *Acolastus* (dem «Verlorenen Sohn» des Gnaphaeus) Heimat und Fremde einschließen kann. Doch bleibt noch immer stoffliche und örtliche Begrenzung. Man vermeidet Innenräume. Ein Abschluß erlaubt den Darstellern, aufzutreten und abzutreten.

Michael, W. F.: Frühformen der dt. Bühne (Schriften der Gesellschaft für Theatergeschichte 62). Berlin 1963.

Wolfgang F. Michael

Tetralogie

Bezeichnung für die Kombination von drei Tragödien (Trilogie) mit einem Satyrspiel, die jeder der drei zum tragischen Wettbewerb an den großen Dionysien zugelassenen Dichter (→ Antikes Theater) produzieren mußte; Aischylos gilt als Schöpfer und Meister der Inhaltstrilogie bzw. -tetralogie, in der die drei Tragödien bzw. alle vier Stücke in einem stofflichen und thematischen Zusammenhang stehen; nach Aischylos sind Inhaltstrilogien nur noch vereinzelt, Inhaltstetralogien nicht sicher nachweisbar.

Bernd Seidensticker

Thalia Theater (Hamburg)

Staatstheater mit zwei Spielstätten: T. (erbaut 1911/12 von der Architektengemeinschaft Kallmorgen und Lundt, Bühnenhaus und Zuschauerraum im 2. Weltkrieg zerstört, Wiederaufbau 1956 durch Werner Kallmorgen jun. Gelungene Verbindung von Elementen des späten Jugendstils und Klassizismus und nüchterner modernistischer Formensprache der 50er Jahre), TiK (Thalia in der Kunsthalle, seit 1972). 1843 von Chéri Maurice (i. e. Charles Schwartzenberger, 1805–96) am Pferdemarkt (heute Gerhart-Hauptmann-Platz) gegründet, 1912 Neubau auf der gegenüberliegenden Platzseite. Direktion Chéri Maurice 1843–85 und 1893/94; 1847 und 1849–54 vereinigt mit dem Stadttheater, Spielplan: Lustspiele, später auch Konzession für Schauspiele, T. damals «Burg des Nordens» genannt; 1885–87 Doppeldirektion Gustav Maurice und Stadttheaterdirektor Pollini (i. e. Bernhard Pohl, 1836–97), 1887–93 Direktion Gustav Maurice; 1894–97 Direktion Pollini; 1898–1904 Doppeldirektion Franz Bittong (1842–1904, seit 1876 Oberspielleiter des T.) und Max Bachur (Kaufmännischer Direktor, 1845–1920); 1904–14 Direktion Max Bachur, 1904–15 Oberspielleiter Leopold Jeßner (1878–1945), begründete mit seinen Wedekind-Inszenierungen seinen antinaturalistischen Regiestil der ideellen Expression; 1915–31 Direktion Hermann Röbbeling (1875–1949), von 1928–31 vereinigt mit dem Deutschen Schauspielhaus; 1932 kommissarische Leitung Friedrich Lobe; 1932–34 Direktion Erich Ziegel (1876–1950); 1934–42 Direktion Paul Mundorf (1903–76), 1934/35 Mitdirektor Erich Kühn, ab 1935 Ernst Leudesdorff (1885–1954), 1937 wird das T. vom Staat übernommen. 1942–45 Direktion Robert Meyn (1896–1972), ab 1943 Zweigstelle Thalia-Kammerspiele in der Hartungstraße; August bis November 1945 vereintes Ensemble aus Deutschem Schauspielhaus und T. unter der Lei-

950 Theater

tung von Rudolf Külüs (1901–75). Ab Dezember 1945 ist das T. wieder selbständig, Intendant bis 1964 Willy Maertens (1893–1967), bis zum Wiederaufbau Behelfsbühne im Zuschauerraum, eine Ausweichspielstätte ist das Haus Schlankreye, Spielplan: Boulevard-Klassiker, klassische Komödien, zeitgenössische Amerikaner (A. Miller, T. Williams, Th. Wilder); 1964–69 Intendanz Dr. Kurt Raeck (1903–81), Schauspielertheater, Erweiterung des Spielplans: Shakespeare, ernste Klassik, klassische Moderne, bestbesuchtes Theater der Bundesrepublik; 1969–80 Intendant Boy Gobert (1925–86), führt die Linie Kurt Raecks fort, Spielplan: neben Komödien klassisches Schauspiel und kritisches Zeitstück, zahlreiche Erstaufführungen, u. a. englischer Autoren (T. Stoppard, H. Pinter), Inszenierungen von Hans Hollmann, Hans Neuenfels, Karlheinz Stroux, Hans Schweikart, Boleslaw Barlog, ab 1973 Jürgen Flimm als Oberspielleiter engagiert; 1980–85 Intendant Peter Striebeck (* 1938); seit 1985 Intendant Jürgen Flimm (* 1941), Literaturtheater, Spielplan: Klassik, literarisch anspruchsvolle Unterhaltung und Förderung der zeitgenössischen Dramatik, u. a. durch einen zeitweiligen Hausautor (Klaus Pohl), Inszenierungen u. a. von Ruth Berghaus, Jürgen Gosch, Alexander Lang, Katharina Thalbach, Robert Wilson; Bühnenbildner: Rolf Glittenberg, Erich Wonder; richtungweisende theaterpädagogische Arbeit (Thalia-Treff: theoretische und praktische Kurse für Jugendliche), Zusammenarbeit mit der Universität Hamburg (Studiengang Schauspieltheater-Regie).

Greeven, E. A.: 110 Jahre Thalia Theater 1843–1953. Hamburg 1953; Blasche, G. / Witt, E.: Hamburger Thalia Theater. Boy Gobert. Hamburg 1980; Theaterstadt Hamburg. Hg. Zentrum für Theaterforschung. Reinbek 1989.

Ingeborg Janich

Theater

(Griech. theatron = Raum zum Schauen) 1. Urspr. techn. Begriff für den Zuschauerteil des →antiken T., dann für den gesamten →T.-Bau; 2. veraltet nach frz. Vorbild, dramatisches Werk (‹Das T. des Herrn Diderot›); 3. der T.-Betrieb, das gesamte T.-Wesen, ein Mikrokosmos, in dem sich fast alle ‹realen› Berufe und Tätigkeiten noch einmal finden; 4. im Alltag: ‹T. oder Szenen machen› für übertriebenes, leidenschaftliches und / oder auf Effekt bedachtes Verhalten; 5. T. im Sinne von künstlerischer Praxis, zu der die Minimalelemente Spieler, Rolle, Zuschauer sowie die zeit-räumliche Einheit von Rollenspiel und Zuschauen gehören. Diese Kombination ermöglicht die spezifische Kommunikation, die T. von anderen Kunstformen trennt. Hinzu kommen in der Regel (doch nicht notwendig) eine breite Skala möglicher T.-Zeichen: Stimme, →Gestik, Mimik, Kostüm, →Maske, Bewegungen beim Schauspieler; Raumgestaltung, Lichteinsatz, Musik, Geräusche usw. Die T.-Semiotik analysiert und klassifiziert diese Zeichen (→T.-Theorie).

Der Ursprung des T. liegt in kultisch-rituellen Handlungen und Tänzen (Kult, →Tanz), in denen der Mensch sich numinosen Wesen mimetisch anverwandelt. Den meisten neueren T.-Formen ist gemeinsam, daß sie die Rolle des literarischen Texts zugunsten der spezifischen →Theatralität einschränken. T. ist heute nicht mehr vorrangig definiert als dienende Kunst, die das Drama nur szenisch realisieren soll, sondern autonome Kunstform als Inszenierungskunst.

Beim heutigen T. sind folgende Unterscheidungen nach verschiedenen Kriterien zu treffen: 1. nach Status der Beteiligten: Professionelles T./ →Amateur-T. Im griech. Altertum standen Dramatiker und Schauspieler in hohem Ansehen, nahmen T. als Amateure wahr. Erst im Hellenismus einsetzende Professionalisierung. →Commedia dell'arte (= Metier) benennt sich so zur Abgrenzung gegen «dilettanti». Das →höfische T., anfangs von adligen Amateuren getragen, im 18. und 19. Jh. noch vielfach Liebhaber-T. bei Adel und Bürgertum. Seit dem 17. Jh. verbreitet sich das Berufsschauspielertum (→Englische Komödianten); in Deutschland erhielt Magister Velten 1685 als erster eine feste Besoldung; Laienspiel in der Jugendbewegung (Gruppenerlebnis im Vordergrund); heute vielfach Freie Gruppen (→Freies Theater), in denen Amateure und professionell ausgebildete Schauspieler zusammenwirken. Erst im 20. Jh. Schauspielschulen, vorher Lernen bei einem älteren Schauspieler. Professionalisierung des T. in den USA und England stärker als in Deutschland (Tradition des Bildungs-T., Subventionen). 2. nach Art der Finanzierung: frei finanziertes kommerzielles T., meist mit zugkräftigem Gaststar. Kennzeichen: Orientierung am Erfolg (→Unterhaltungs-T.), meist geringer künstlerischer Anspruch: →Schul- und Universitäts-T., auch T. von Verbänden, von den jeweiligen Institutionen mit deren Geldmitteln unterhalten; freie Gruppen, mit öffentlichen Mitteln gefördert; subventioniertes T., also →Stadt- und →Staats-T., →Landesbühnen und sog. →Privat-T., die erhebliche finanzielle Förderung erhalten. In diesen Fällen Mischfinanzierung durch Bund, Länder und Gemeinden. Eigentliches Staats-T. gibt es z. B. in Frankreich, das mit →Comédie Française (gegr. 1680) auch das älteste Staats-T. besitzt (→Theatersystem). 3. nach Spektrum unterscheidet man Schauspielhaus, Opernhaus, reines →Tanz-T. und Ballett und Mehrspartenhaus, in der Regel mit Schauspiel, Oper, Operette, Ballett. 4. nach dem angesprochenen Publikum (damit verbunden thematischer Schwerpunkt): →Kinder-T., →Jugend-T., →Frauen-T., →Arbeiter-T., →Volks-T. Hierher auch der Begriff Bildungs-T., das sich ans Bildungsbürgertum wendet.

Während die häufig getroffene Unterscheidung von Provinz-T. und T. der Metropole (oder «führenden» T.) unklar zwischen Kategorie Spielort und der der Qualität schwankt, ist sinnvoller, 5. die Unterscheidung nach Zwecken (Motiven, Intentionen) in: →politisches T. (z. B. →Straßen-T., →Proletarisch-revolutionäres T.); pädagogisches T. (z. B. Kinder-T.); kommerzielles T. (z. B. →Tournee-T.); →experimentelles (avantgardistisches) T. (mit primär künstlerischen Zwecken); therapeutisches T. (z. B. Gefängnis-T.); →Boulevard-(Unterhaltungs-)T. Diese Kategorien bezeichnen jeweils den dominanten Zweck, schließen Überschneidungen nicht aus. Ein ästhetisch experimentelles T. mag politische, ein kommerzielles T. auch künstlerische Zwecke verfolgen. 6. Unterscheidung nach der Art der Zusammenarbeit: vom kurzlebigen Workshop-T. über die mehr oder minder stabile Freie Gruppe zum wechselnden oder festen →Ensemble und schließlich dem T. als Lebensform (→Living Theatre, T.-Laboratorium von Jerzy Grotowski, *1933, →Odin Teatret).

Hinzu kommen eine Reihe von Sonderformen, die unter den Begriff T. fallen: →Kabarett, →Revue, Show, →Musical, →Café-T., →erotisches T., →Varieté, →Puppen-T., →Schatten-T. Solange die genannten Grundelemente (Spieler, Rolle, Zuschauer, zeit-räumliche Einheit des Vorgangs) gegeben sind, erfüllen all diese Formen den Begriff T.

Hans-Thies Lehmann

Theater am Schiffbauerdamm (Berlin)

Erbaut ca. 1890 (Architekt: Simon) mit 684 Plätzen, seit 1954 Domizil des →Berliner Ensembles. Künstlerisch bedeutend vor allem von 1928 bis 1931 unter der Leitung von Ernst Josef Aufricht (1898–1971), einem der letzten Privattheaterdirektoren mit Mut zu finanziellem und literarisch-politischem Risiko, der dort am 31. 8. 1928 mit *Die Dreigroschenoper* von Bertolt Brecht (1898–1956) und Kurt Weill (1900–50), Regie: Erich Engel (1891–1966), Bühne: Caspar Neher (1897–1962), eröffnete und damit einen Welterfolg auf den Weg brachte. Weitere, z. T. wichtige Uraufführungen kritischer Stücke folgten: 1929 *Giftgas über Berlin* von Peter Martin Lampel (1894–1965), das nach der Premiere, einer geschlossenen Vorstellung, verboten wurde, *Pioniere in Ingolstadt* von Marieluise Fleißer (1901–74), Regie: Brecht (anonym), Bühne: Neher, *Happy End* von Dorothy Lane (d. i. Elisabeth Hauptmann, 1897–1973)/Brecht/Weill; 1930 *Feuer aus den Kesseln* von Ernst Toller (1893–1939); 1931 *Jud Süß* von Paul Kornfeld (1889–1942), Regie: Leopold Jessner (1878–1945), und *Italienische Nacht* von Ödön von Horváth (1901–38), Regie: Francesco von Mendelssohn. Neben führenden Regisseuren der Zeit, darunter auch Karl Heinz Martin (1886–1948), engagierte der ‹rote Direktor› viele namhafte Schauspieler, so Roma Bahn (1897–1975), Lotte Lenya (1900–81), Carola Neher (1900–42), Ernst Deutsch (1890–1963), Heinrich George (1893–1946), Heinrich Gretler (1897–1977), Gustaf Gründgens (1899–1963), Albert Hoerrmann (1899–1980), Theo Lingen (1903–78), Rudolf Platte (1904–84), Erich Ponto (1884–1957), Heinz Rühmann (* 1902), Heinz Schweikart (1895–1980). – Nach dem Krieg übernahm zunächst (1945/46) Rudolf Platte, anschließend (1946 bis 1950) Fritz Wisten (1890–1962) die Intendanz, der ein literarisch-komödiantisches Repertoire aufbaute, aber auch neue Parteidramatik, z. B. von Hedda Zinner (* 1907), uraufführte. 1950 fusionierte das Ensemble mit jenem der →Volksbühne, die bis zur Wiedereröffnung ihres alten Hauses am Luxemburg-(vormals Bülow-)Platz 1954 das T. a. S. bespielte und es dann für das →Berliner Ensemble freimachte.

Aufricht, E. J.: Erzähle damit Du Dein Recht erweist. Berlin 1966, S. 60–133; Goertz, H./Weyl, R. (Hg.): Komödiantisches Theater: Fritz Wisten und sein Ensemble. Berlin (DDR) 1957.

Andreas Roßmann

Theater am Turm – TAT (Frankfurt)

1953 gegründet als Landesbühne Rhein-Main in Nachfolge des Rhein-Mainischen Verbandstheaters. Rechtsträger Frankfurter Bund für Volksbildung. 1965 bis 1969 Regisseur Claus Peymann (* 1937), Dramaturg Wolfgang Wiens (* 1941), realistisches kritisches Volkstheater, 1966 Debüt des Dramatikers Peter Handke (* 1942), zahlreiche Handke-UA. 1971 Aufgabe des Landesbühnenstatus, nur auf Frankfurt bezogene Aufführungen. Mitbestimmung (TAT-Modell). 1974 bis 1975 Intendant Rainer Werner Fassbinder (1945–82), 1975 Hermann Treusch (* 1937), Umwandlung in Kinder- und Jugendtheater. 1980 ohne Ensemble, Probenort und Spielstätte für freie Gruppen, Gastspiele, Direktion Peter Hahn (* 1941). 1985 Christoph Vitali (* 1940), Modifizierung des Konzepts zu mehr Eigenproduktionen, experimentelles Theater.

Werner Schulze-Reimpell

Theater an der Ruhr im Raffelbergpark

1980 von Roberto Ciulli und Dr. Helmut Schäfer als «Alternative zu herkömmlichen deutschen Theaterstrukturen» gegründet. Theatermodell, bei dem «Qualität der künstlerischen Arbeit auch Maßstab für Technik» ist und «Vorrang vor gewerkschaftlicher Einschränkung durch starre Arbeitszeitregelung» hat. Kein eigenes Haus, Spielstätten: ehemaliger Kursaal im Raffelbergpark und Stadthalle Mülheim, Gastspiele im In- und Ausland. Mobile städtische Bühne, nicht im Dt. Bühnenverein, Gesellschaftsform: GmbH, Gesellschafter: Stadt Mülheim, Roberto Ciulli und Dr. Helmut Schäfer. – Ensemble: 15 Schauspielerinnen und Schauspieler, 14 Mitarbeiter Technik/Werkstätten, vier Verwaltungsangestellte. Pro Jahr werden zwei neue Inszenierungen erarbeitet; langjähriges Repertoire: Shakespeare, Antike, zeitgenössische Dramatik. Seit 1986 (Tod von Gordana Kosanović, 1935–86) Neuaufbau des Spielplans. Das T. ist eine multikulturelle Institution – es arbeitet mit dem Türkischen Nationaltheater zusammen und ist gleichzeitig der Sitz des Roma-Theater Pralipe (aus Skopje, Jugoslawien, vertrieben). Das T. wurde 1987/88 zum Theater des Jahres gewählt. Der Förderverein vergibt alle zwei Jahre den Gordana Kosanović-Schauspielpreis abwechselnd an dt. und jugosl. Schauspieler (1. Preisträger war 1987 Ulrich Wildgruber).

Dr. Roberto Ciulli (* 1934 in Mailand), Philosophie-Studium in Mailand und Pavia, 1960–62 Gründung und Leitung des Zelttheaters «Il Globo» am Stadtrand von Mailand, 1965–73 Regisseur am Deutschen Theater Göttingen, 1974–77 Gastregisseur an der Freien Volksbühne und am Schiller-Theater Berlin, 1979–81 Regisseur am Düsseldorfer Schauspielhaus (Ciulli/Schäfer *Alkestis* nach Euripides, dafür 1. Publikumspreis des 14. BITEF-Festivals in Belgrad), 1980 T., 1981 Gastinszenierungen in Belgrad und Stuttgart. Auszeichnungen: 1988 Kritikerpreis für Theater vom Verband der dt. Kritiker e. V., 1989 Preis für die beste Regie für *Kaspar* im Rahmen des 23. BITEF-Festivals Belgrad, 1990 «Orden der jugosl. Fahne mit goldenem Kreuz» für besondere Verdienste um die kulturellen Beziehungen zwischen der BRD und Jugoslawien sowie den Orden «Mérite en Faveur de la Culture Polonaise» für besondere Verdienste um die poln. Kultur. – Für Roberto Ciulli ist eine Inszenierung ein fortwährender Prozeß. Auch nach der Premiere sind noch Veränderungen und Neufassungen möglich.

Die Theatervisionen des Roberto Ciulli. Bruchstücke. Essen 1991; Wolf, E.: Das Abendland versuchen. Theater an der Ruhr/Mülheim. Köln 1991

Ingeborg Janich

Theater auf dem Theater

Dramaturgisches Gestaltungsmittel, das der Tradition des Spiels im Spiel entspricht: Eine Theateraufführung spielt als Szene in einem Theaterstück; Beispiele in Shakespeares *Hamlet* und im *Sommernachtstraum*. Als Stilmittel romantischer Ironie (→Romantisches Theater) eingesetzt: Ludwig Tieck im *Gestiefelten Kater*, Verwirrspiel mit den beiden Realitätsebenen («das Schauspiel eines Schauspiels», Schlegel), als ironische Brechung der Realität. Bemerkenswerterweise erlebte Tiecks *Gestiefelter Kater* einen Bühnenerfolg erst durch die Inszenierung Jürgen Fehlings 1921, dem Erscheinungsjahr von Pirandellos *Sechs Personen suchen einen Autor*, dem bekanntesten Stück des modernen Theaters (→Pirandellismus), das das T. a. d. T. zum Konstruktionsprinzip seiner Fabel macht. Ebenso im zeitgenössischen Theater das Stück *Marat/Sade* von Peter Weiss (UA 1964, Regie K. Swinarski).

Kokott, J. H.: Das Theater auf dem Theater im Drama der Neuzeit. Diss. Köln 1968; Nelson, J. R.: Play within a Play. London 1958.

Adriana Hass

Theaterausstellungen

Internationale Ausstellung für Musik und Theaterwesen, Wien 1892: erster Versuch einer groß angelegten internationalen T.

Erste deutsche T., Berlin 1910 in Ausstellungshallen am Zoologischen Garten. Bestandsaufnahme des deutschsprachigen Theaters mit einem Ausstellungstheater (ausgestattet mit den damals neuesten Errungenschaften der Technik). Veranstalter: Gesellschaft für Theatergeschichte, Leitung: Dr. Heinrich Stümcke.

Moderne Theaterkunst, 13. Ausstellung des Freien Bundes in der Kunsthalle Mannheim, Jan./Febr. 1913, Leitung: Dr. Friedrich Wichert. Keine historische Abteilung, Überblick über modernes Bühnenbild, Figurinen, Theaterarchitektur, Theaterplakate und →Marionettentheater. Katalogbeiträge von Peter Behrens, Adolphe Appia, Edward G. Craig u. a.

Theaterkunst-Ausstellung Kunstgewerbemuseum Zürich 1914, Leitung Alfred Altheer. Mittelpunkt: Präsentation von E. G. Craig und A. Appia, Hauptgewicht auf Schweizer Künstlern.

Internationale Ausstellung neuer Theatertechnik: 1924 anläßlich des Musik- und Theaterfestes der Stadt Wien in den Sälen des Konzerthauses, Konzept Friedrich Kiesler (1890–1965, Maler, Architekt, Bühnenbildner). Übersicht über die Erneuerung des Theaters aus der Sicht der Kubisten (Entwürfe für das →Ballett Suédois und →Ballet Russe der frz.

956 Theaterausstellungen _____

Maler/innen Georges Braque, Jean Hugo, Fernand Léger, Irène Lagut, Marie Laurencin, Hélène Perdriat; Würfelbühne von Hans Fritz), Futuristen (F. T. Marinetti, Enrico Prampolini), Konstruktivisten (J. B. Wachtangow, A. Tairow, Forregger; L. Moholy-Nagy, →Merz-Bühne v. K. Schwitters) und Expressionisten (Lothar Schreyers ekstatische Theaterpartituren, groteske Figurinen von George Grosz, abstrakt-mechanische Entwürfe Oskar Schlemmers, phantastisch-expressives Architekturmodell für das Salzburger Festspielhaus von Kurt Poelzig). Katalog nach damalig neuesten typographischen Prinzipien gestaltete Dokumentation der europ. Theateravantgarde. Mittelpunkt der Ausstellung: Kieslers ‹Railwaytheater›: freischwebende Raumbühne des Theaters der Zeit, Zuschauerraum kreist in schleifenden Bewegungen um den sphärischen Bühnenkern. Andere Raumbühnen: ‹Ringtheater› Oskar Strnads, ‹Rundtheater› von Harry Täuber, Kuppelbau des ‹Theaters ohne Zuschauer› (von Rudolf Hönigsfeld entworfen für das →‹Stegreiftheater› von Dr. Jacob Moreno-Levy), ‹Theaterprojekt› von Wilhelm Treichlinger und Fritz Rosenbaum und ‹Volkshaus der Kunst› von Walter Neuzil, Franz Löwitsch und Rudolf Scherer (Gemeinnützige Kunst-Konsumgenossenschaft). – Leger- und Träger-System richtungweisend für Ausstellungsarchitektur.

Deutsche T. Magdeburg 1927. Künstler. Gestaltung: Prof. Albinmüller (Darmstadt). «Spiegelt das einigermaßen vollständige Bild vom Werden und Sein des dt. Theaters.» Kein historisches Museum, sondern Schau des damaligen bühnenbildnerischen Schaffens, Jury (Victor Barnowsky, Emil Pirchan, Otto Reigbert u. a.), außerhalb des Spruchs der Jury: Staatstheater, Bauhaus Dessau u. a. Kunstakademien und -gewerbeschulen, Publikumsverbände, Organisationen. Sonder-Ausstellung: Theater und Film, Theater und Rundfunk, Theater und Lautforschung. Experimentierbühne. Katalog und Zeitschrift «Die vierte Wand» (Schriftleitung Paul Merbach).

Theaterkunst-Ausstellung Kunstgewerbemuseum Zürich 1931; internationale Schau nach sachlichen Gesichtspunkten gegliedert: Stilbühne, realistische und konstruktivistische Bühne, szenischer Expressionismus und abstraktes Bühnenbild.

Internationale Ausstellung für Theaterkunst, Wien 1936. Überblick über damaligen Stand der Theaterkunst und der Randgebiete künstlerischer Film, orientalisches Theater, Maskenkunst, Puppentheater.

Europ. T. Wien 1955. Wissenschaftliche Leitung und Katalog: Franz Hadamowsky und Heinz Kindermann, künstlerische Gestaltung: Clemens Holzmeister, Stephan Hlawa, Gottfried Neumann-Spallart. Entwicklung des europ. Theaters von der griech. Antike bis zur Gegenwart; Leihgeber: Museen, Sammlungen, Bibliotheken und Theater aus 21 europ. Ländern.

Theaterausstellungen 957

Ausstellung Theaterbau, Mathildenhöhe zu Darmstadt anläßlich des V. Darmstädter Gesprächs «Theater» 1955. Ausstellungsleitung: Dr. Hans Werner Hegemann, Frankfurt/M., Gestaltung: Roman Clemens, Zürich. Komitee «Darmstädter Gespräche»: u. a. Gustav Rudolf Sellner, Ernst Schröder. «Versuch, sichtbare Darstellung sowohl der vorhandenen als auch der sich anbahnenden Möglichkeiten im Theaterbau zu bieten» für Bauherrn, Architekten und interessiertes Publikum. Wesentliche Stationen der Theaterarchitektur von europ. Anfängen bis zur Gegenwart.

Expressionismus. Literatur und Kunst 1910–1923. Eine Ausstellung des Deutschen Literaturarchivs im Schiller-Nationalmuseum Marbach a. N. 1960. Ausstellung und Katalog: Paul Raabe, H. L. Greve und Ingrid Grüninger.

T. «Die Bühne als Form – Internationale Schauspielszene seit 1945», Berlin, Akademie der Künste 1971. Ausstellungskonzept: Willi Schmidt, Ralph Wünsche, Katalog: Dietrich Gronau, Walter Huder, W. Schmidt, R. Wünsche. Überblick über internationale vorwiegend europ. Theaterarbeit nach 1945 unter Mitarbeit und Beratung von Theaterleuten und -wissenschaftlern aus Westeuropa. Nach Berlin in Paris, Rom, Athen und Zürich.

Theater im Exil 1933–45 (→ Exiltheater). Akademie der Künste, Berlin 1973. Ausstellung, Konferenz und Filmretrospektive anläßlich der Eröffnung des Ludwig-Berger-Archivs, Ernst-Deutsch-Archivs, Fritz-Kortner-Archivs, Leonard-Steckel-Archivs und der Sammlung Theater im Exil. Ausstellung und Katalog: Walter Huder.

Theater in der Weimarer Republik. Ausstellung vom Kunstamt Kreuzberg und des Instituts für Theaterwissenschaft der Universität Köln, Berlin 1977. Ausstellung und Katalog: Günter Erken, Dieter Ruckhaberle u. a.

Der Hang zum Gesamtkunstwerk. Europ. Utopien seit 1800. Kunsthaus Zürich, Städtische Kunsthalle und Kunstverein für die Rheinlande und Westfalen Düsseldorf, Museum moderner Kunst, Museum des 20. Jh. Wien, Orangerie des Schlosses Charlottenburg Berlin 1983/84. Ausstellung und Katalog: Harald Szeemann.

Kataloge: Die Bühne als Form – Internationale Schauspielszene seit 1945. Berlin 1971; Glossy, K. (Hg.): Fachkatalog der Abteilung für Deutsches Drama und Theater. Internationale Ausstellung für Musik und Theaterwesen. Wien 1892; Hadamowsky, F./Kindermann, H.: Europ. T.-A. Wien 1955; Huder, W.: Theater im Exil 1933–45. Berlin 1973; Internationale Ausstellung für Theaterkunst. Wien 1936; Kiesler, F. (Hg.): Internationale Ausstellung neuer Theatertechnik. Wien 1924; Moderne Theaterkunst. Mannheim 1913; Raabe, P./Greve, H. L./Grüninger, I.: Expressionismus 1910–23. München 1960; Rapp, F. (Hg.): Dt. T.-A. Magdeburg 1927; Szeemann, H.: Der Hang zum Gesamtkunstwerk. Europ. Utopien seit 1800. Aarau/Frankfurt 1983; Theater in der Weimarer Republik. Hg. v. Kunstamt Kreuzberg und dem Institut für Theaterwissenschaft der Universität Köln. Berlin 1977; Theaterkunst-Ausstellungen Zürich 1914 und 31.

Ingeborg Janich

Theaterbau

Die Entwurfsaufgabe für einen Theaterneubau und die bei der Planung zu beachtenden Besonderheiten lassen sich heute etwa so beschreiben: Gesucht ist der Entwurf eines vielfach gegliederten Baukörpers als Ort des künstlerischen Schaffens und ständigen Zeigens der besonderen Kunstform Theater. Dieses ‹Gesamtkunstwerk› Theater vereint in sich eine Vielzahl von Einzelkünsten: die darstellende Kunst, den Tanz, den Gesang, die Musik, die Malerei, die Plastik und die Lichtkunst. Sie werden sicht- und hörbar im Laufe eines flüchtigen, einmaligen Theaterabends. Jede der Kunstgattungen nimmt teil am Gelingen der Aufführung und stellt seine eigenen räumlichen und techn. Forderungen an den Architekten. Raum, Zeit und Mensch wandeln und verwandeln sich ständig auf der Bühne, teils durch die Mittel des Darstellers, teils durch großen bühnentechn. bzw. lichttechn. Aufwand (→ Bühnentechnik). Herzstück des Theaters ist die → Bühne als statischer, endlicher Raum mit der Potenz zu unendlichen Möglichkeiten. Auf und vor ihr sollte aber weiterhin der Mensch das Maß der Dinge sein, z. B. bei der Frage, wie gut oder schlecht sieht und hört der Zuschauer die Ereignisse und im besonderen den Darsteller auf der Bühne, und bei welcher Größenordnung wird die Zahl der Zuschauer zur anonymen Masse bzw. zur Zuschauergemeinschaft. Kann das Zuordnungsverhältnis von Darsteller und Zuschauer durch eine bes. Anordnung die Aussagen des Theaterstücks verstärken oder auch abschwächen? Da aber das Theater letztlich in den Köpfen der Zuschauer stattfindet, stellt sich die Frage nach dem Einfluß der Raumform und -gestalt bei diesem Vorgang.

Das Theatergebäude ist aber auch gleichzeitig Arbeitsplatz (→ Betriebsorganisation des Theaters) je nach Spielgattung für bis zu 200 unterschiedliche Theaterberufe, die mehrheitlich nicht künstlerisch arbeiten, sondern das Theater auf der Ebene von Organisation, Verwaltung, Handwerk und Technik begleiten. Die Anforderungen hierbei an die Qualität des Arbeitsplatzes sind die gleichen wie diejenigen in der Industrie und Verwaltung.

Aus der Art der betrieblichen Führung als Repertoiretheater (→ Repertoire) und aus der Kunstgattung, die das Theater pflegt, haben sich spezielle Raum- und Funktionsprogramme entwickelt, die in Deutschland

Theaterbau 959

bei Architekturwettbewerben in jeweils gering veränderter Form als Grundlage des Entwurfs immer wieder genommen werden. Vereinfacht gliedert sich danach der T. in folgende Raumbereiche: 1. Eingangsbereich und Foyer; 2. Zuschauerraum; 3. Bühne; 4. Werkstätten und Magazine; 5. Verwaltung.

Die funktionale Zuordnung der Raumbereiche zueinander ist bestimmt durch die Betriebsstruktur und die hier ablaufenden Arbeitsprozesse, der Verknüpfung bzw. Trennung von Bereichen aus Gründen von Störung und Sicherheit. Ein besonderer Aspekt beim T. ist hierbei die Frage der Verkehrsführung sowohl zum Gebäude als auch im Theater selbst. Der Zuschauerraum wird in einem kurzen Zeitraum von einer großen Zahl von Besuchern gefüllt bzw. nach der Vorstellung oder im Fall eines Brandes schnell entleert. Die Verkehrswege sollen einerseits ins Freie führen und übersichtlich sein, andererseits stellen Verkehrsflächen wie Foyer und Treppenanlagen einen gestalterischen Höhepunkt im Gesamtentwurf dar. Hier gilt es sich zu entscheiden zwischen der Ökonomie der Wege und dem Anspruch, diesen Räumen eine zeitgemäße Funktion im Sinne eines Begegnungsraums für die Zuschauer zu geben. Noch komplexer ist die Verkehrsführung von Personen und Material auf und hinter der Bühne. Die ständige Verwandlung des Spielorts ist oft gebunden an den Transport von gewichtigen Dekorationsteilen und speziell in der Oper an die Fluktuation vieler Darsteller zur und von der Bühne weg. Kurze und überschneidungsfreie Wege sind Voraussetzung für das Gelingen eines Theaterabends.

Die Bühne mit ihren Verwandlungsmaschinen wie Drehscheibe, Versenkungen, Hebevorrichtungen, Transportwagen ist kein ungefährlicher Arbeitsplatz, was die Zahl der Unfälle und hier bes. die der Theaterbrände in den letzten Jh. beweist. Die sich daraus entwickelten gesetzlichen Sicherheitsvorschriften bestimmen die Gestaltung des modernen T. in Fragen der Wahl der Baustoffe, Verkehrsführung, der Teilung des Baus in Brandabschnitte, der Anordnung der Zuschauer zur Bühne, der Art und Gestaltung der Spielfläche in einem so starken Maße, daß der Architekt in seiner Arbeit auf reine Gestaltungsfragen und das Problem der Integration des T. in bestehende Bebauung reduziert wird. Da der T. als öffentliche kulturelle Einrichtung eine bes. Bauaufgabe in der Stadt- und Architekturgeschichte darstellt, rückt die Frage der architektonischen Handschrift bzw. Gestaltungstheorie bei der Entscheidung in Architekturwettbewerben, in der Architekturkritik und auch in der öffentlichen Meinung in den Vordergrund. Dem Architekten steht als Vorbild eine gradlinig verlaufende Entwicklungsgeschichte des T. gegenüber. Das reicht vom antiken →Amphitheater über barockes →Hoftheater, bürgerliches Stadt- und →Staatstheater bis hin zu neusten Formen der für Theaterzwecke modifizierten Fabrikhallen. Eine Beschreibung der

960 Theaterbau

T.-Geschichte ist ohne die Analyse des Umfelds wie Gesellschafts- und Kultursystem, Stand und Bedeutung der Theaterkunst in der jeweiligen Epoche, Trägerschaft, Publikumsstruktur, Entwicklung der Baukunst unvollständig.

Die Entwicklungsgeschichte der baulichen Anlage beginnt bei den frühen Formen des minoischen Theaters auf Kreta und Lemnos (3. und 2. Jahrtausend v. Chr.). Lineare oder abgewinkelt ansteigende Treppenanlagen mit davor liegendem Spielplatz nach Südwesten oder Südosten ausgerichtet sind Stein gewordenes Zeugnis von der einfachen gegenüberliegenden Zuordnungsmöglichkeit von Zuschauer und Spieler. Die Theateranlage war unmittelbarer Teil der Stadt. – Das klassische griech. Theater (→ Antikes Theater), seit 500 v. Chr. in ein festes Bühnensystem geformt, hat seine Wurzeln in kultischen Tänzen und Gesängen zu Ehren des Fruchtbarkeitsgottes Dionysos. Das erste architektonische Element war der kreisrunde Tanzplatz (Orchestra) mit einem Opferaltar in der Mitte. Am Rand stand ein Garderobenzelt, das in der folgenden Entwicklung zum steinernen Bühnenhaus (Skene) wurde. Die Zuschauer versammelten sich, wie auch in anderen Kulturkreisen, ringförmig zu diesem rituellen Ereignis um die Orchestra. Die für ein Theater riesige Anzahl von 17000 Zuschauern im Dionysostheater um 330 v. Chr. und die topographische Hangsituation an der Akropolis ließ zwangsläufig die ringförmig ansteigende Sitzordnung entstehen. Die einzelnen Sitzreihen, die im Dreiviertelkreis die Orchestra umgaben, waren ähnlich wie in Sportarenen stark überhöht, d. h., die Höhenunterschiede der einzelnen Sitzflächen lagen bei ca. 40 cm. Die Sicht der Zuschauer auf den Darsteller war dadurch optimal; aber je weiter und damit höher er sich von der Orchestra mit einem Durchmesser von ca. 20 m entfernte, desto mehr kam er in eine sog. Aufsichtssituation, d. h., der Darsteller verkürzte sich in seiner sichtbaren Körpergröße. Der Schauspieler mußte sich diesen Umständen durch Vergrößerung seiner Figur (Kothura), durch große Gebärde und → Maske, durch modulierte Sprache und Bewegung anpassen.

Der Zuschauer sah neben dem Spiel über das Skenegebäude hinweg in die freie Naturlandschaft; die Veränderungen des Himmels, des Lichts und der Schatten waren Teil des Spiels. Die Natur als Ort der Götter war ständig anwesend. Das Sitzen in der Form eines Amphitheaters ermöglichte es, daß sich die Zuschauer selber untereinander sehen konnten, wodurch sich leichter das Gefühl einer Zuschauergemeinschaft herstellte. Die sehr gute Akustik bei Entfernungen bis zu 60 m vom Rand der Orchestra ergab sich durch die Trichterform der Anlage und die Aufwinde am Hang. Das Bühnenhaus wurde im weiteren Verlauf nach Einführung von Einzelsprechern, die dem Chor gegenüberstanden, verfeinert und ausgebaut. Das Gebäude erhielt einen erhöhten Vorbau (→ Proszenium) mit einer einfachen Theatermaschinerie für bes. Götterauftritte. Drei Tore führten in das Innere des Gebäudes und bezeichneten Innenräume bzw. Auftrittsorte. Der klassische griech. T. ist Vorbild bei der Planung vieler Idealentwürfe und auch realisierter T.

Das Modell des griech. Theaters wurde von der Siegermacht Rom in der Bauform des röm.-hellenistischen Theaters, jedoch nicht in den Inhalten des Spiels übernommen. Das Publikum saß in unterschiedlichen Sitzkategorien nach der Klassenstruktur der röm. Gesellschaft. Die halbkreisförmige Orchestra wurde Sitzplatz für Ehrengäste und Senatoren und somit Teil der Zuschaueranlage. Die mehr linear und reliefartig ausgerichtete Spielweise bedingte die Vergrößerung der vor dem Bühnenhaus liegenden Spielfläche (pulpitum). Den Abschluß bildete eine reich ornamentierte und mehrstöckige Repräsentativfassade (scenae frons) mit drei Toren als Auftrittsmöglichkeit. Vor dieser Fassade erschien das Spiel der Schauspieler klein und unbedeutend. Zuschauertribüne und Bühnenhaus wurden zu einem geschlossenen Theatergebäude zusammengefügt. Die Überdeckung des Zuschauerraums konnte mit einem Stoffsegel, das mit Wasser und wohlriechenden Essenzen besprüht wurde, erfolgen. Rampen- und Zwischenvorhänge (→Theatervorhang) lassen auf dekorative Veränderungen und auf entsprechende techn. Mittel wie Bühnenwagen und gemalte Dekorationswände schließen. Die Leistung der röm. Baukunst bestand darin, daß die Theater nicht nur an Berghängen errichtet wurden, sondern auf Grund der Entwicklung der aus Einzelmauerwerkssteinen zusammengefügten Gewölbearchitektur an jeder beliebigen Stelle der Stadt ihren Standort finden konnten. Die Lage der griech. Theater war gebunden an die Örtlichkeit einer Kultstätte. Das röm. Theater hat keinen bes. markanten Standort.

Das röm.-hellenistische Theater und seine im Verlauf von ca. 400 Jahren geschaffenen Bauten haben die nachfolgende Entwicklung in der →Renaissance und dem →Barock nachhaltig beeinflußt. Die Überlieferung der alten Formen erfolgte durch die 1414 wiederentdeckten Schriften des röm. Baumeisters Vitruv (88–26 v. Chr.), der im fünften Band seiner Schrift *De architectura* ausführlich das antike Theater beschreibt.

In der Zeit des Mittelalters (→Mittelalter/Drama und Theater des Mittelalters) wurde kein eigenständiger, fester T.-Typ entwickelt. Was überliefert ist, sind auf Zeit hergestellte Buden, plastische Bilder, Holztribünen, Dekorationswagen, Bretterbühnen für die verschiedenen Formen des Sakralen Theaters (Krippenspiele, →Passionsspiele, →Mysterienspiele). Zunächst fand die Darstellung biblischer Stoffe an verschiedenen Orten des Kirchenraums (Altar, Chor, Lettner) statt. Die drastische Darstellung verdrängte jedoch diese Spiele aus dem Kirchenraum, und es kam zur Entwicklung verschiedener Spielformen im Freien, vor den Kirchen, auf Marktplätzen, im Stadtraum. Die →Simultanbühne, am Beispiel der 25 Tage dauernden Passionsspiele von Valenciennes (1547), war

962 Theaterbau

eine langgestreckte Bühnenanlage, auf der Orte irdischer und symbolischer Art (Himmel, Hölle, Palast des Pilatus) als plastische Dekoration aufgebaut waren. Die Zuschauer saßen dem Spielort linear gegenüber und wanderten im Lauf der Passionsgeschichte längs den Spielorten. Bei den Passionsspielen in Villingen (1600) umringten die Gläubigen als Mitleidende die einzelnen Schauplätze. Der Leidensweg Christi wurde vom Zuschauer auch als Weg zurückgelegt. Neben den kirchlichen Spielen entwickelte sich ein weltliches Volkstheater. Gespielt wurde dabei auf einer einfachen hochgestellten Bretterbühne mit Vorhang als Abschluß und Auftrittsmöglichkeit. Die Zuschauer standen im Dreiviertelrund und sahen hinauf zu den Schauspielern, sie hatten eine sog. Untersicht. Der Kontakt zu den Schauspielern war unmittelbar, da über das Leben selber verhandelt wurde. – Diese provisorischen Theaterformen sind in jüngster Zeit wieder in den Innenstädten anzutreffen. Mit der Veränderung des Stadtkerns zur Monofunktion von Handel und Verwaltung sollen →Straßentheatergruppen, Gaukler, bildende Künstler, Musiker das urbane Leben zurückbringen.

Die T.-Entwicklung im elisabethanischen Zeitalter (→Elisabethanisches Theater) ist von besonderer Bedeutung, da das dramatische Werk Shakespeares, das heute einen so hohen Anteil an den Spielplänen der Theater hat, in vollkommen anders gearteten Theaterräumen, wie wir sie heute vorfinden, aufgeführt wurde. Es handelt sich um die Epoche des engl. Theaters in der Regierungszeit Elisabeths I. (1558–1603). Das Theater war ein Ort der lebhaften politischen und sittlichen Auseinandersetzung. Die kommerziell geführten Unternehmen wurden von allen Ständen besucht. Das literarisch und politisch interessierte Bürgertum saß auf drei übereinanderliegenden Rängen, die in einer Kreisform einen offenen Hof bildeten. Die Hoffläche, in die sich die Bühne hineinschob, war der Platz für das niedere Volk, das stehend den unmittelbarsten Kontakt mit den Schauspielern hatte. Die Adligen saßen in Logen neben der Bühne und zeigten sich wie in den folgenden Epochen in ihrer Selbstinszenierung. Die Bühne selber war von einer Dachkonstruktion überspannt, die von zwei Säulen getragen wurde. Das Dach war Wetterschutz, aber auch symbolisch Himmel. Durch Luken konnten Geister herabschweben und Versatzstücke heraufgezogen werden. Das Bühnenhaus hinter der vorgeschobenen Spielfläche hatte in sich mehrere Spielebenen. Die erste Galerie wurde als Innenraum, erhöhter Stadtplatz und als Balkon, die zweite Galerie als Spielort des Orchesters genutzt. Auf der Bühne selber fanden alle Außenszenen statt. Die neutrale Bühne bekam ihre örtliche Bedeutung durch das gesprochene Wort, das ergänzt wurde von unproportionalen, vereinfachten Versatzstücken wie Berg, Stadttor, Höhle. Der Gang der Handlung mußte nicht durch langwierige Umbauten unterbrochen werden, die frei verfügbaren Spielräume erlaubten ra-

Theaterbau 963

sche Orts- und Szenenwechsel. Trotz der hohen Zuschauerzahl von 2000 Personen muß die Atmosphäre sehr intim und lebendig gewesen sein. Das Theater als öffentlicher Platz der Auseinandersetzung mobilisierte die Phantasie der Zuschauer gerade auch durch den reduzierten Einsatz von bildnerischen Mitteln. Beispielhafte Bauten waren das Swan Theatre (1594) und das →Globe Theatre (1599). – Das elisabethanische T.-Modell hat vor allem in angelsächsischen Ländern in der Neuzeit Pate für Neubauplanungen (Chinchester Festival Theatre, 1962) gestanden.

Der Ausgangspunkt für die auch heute noch gültige Form des T. liegt in Italien, in den noch zu besichtigenden Renaissance-Baudenkmälern des →Teatro Olimpico in Vicenza und des →Teatro Farnese (1628) in Parma (→Neuzeit/Theater der Neuzeit). 1584 nach den Plänen von Andrea Palladio (1508–80) erbaut, war das Teatro Olimpico der Rekonstruktionsversuch eines antiken Theaters für Aufführungen der griech. und röm. Theaterliteratur. Die Quellen dieser Rekonstruktion waren die 1414 wiedergefundene Schrift Vitruvs *De architectura* und die vorgefundenen Theaterruinen. Die Elemente des spätröm. Theaters sind in abgewandelter Form zitiert wie die dreizehn steil ansteigenden Zuschauerreihen, die aber nicht in einer Kreisform ausgebildet sind, sondern eine Halbellipse als Grundriß bilden. Die Zuschauertribüne wird oben von einer Säulenreihe begrenzt. Die Orchestra, hier der Platz für die Musiker, bildet einen breiten Graben zur 25 m breiten und 6 m tiefen Bühne, die von einer dreitürigen reich gegliederten Architekturfassade abgeschlossen wird. Durch die drei Öffnungen geht der Blick auf plastisch ausgebildete Straßenzüge, deren Häuser sich nach hinten perspektivisch verkleinern. Da das Theater sich in einem geschlossenen Raum befindet, ist zu vermuten, daß durch diese Scheinarchitektur, durch die Bemalung der Zuschauerraumdecke als Himmel und die allg. Gestaltung der Wände als Außenfassade der Eindruck erweckt werden soll, als befände sich der Zuschauer im Freien. Die langgestreckte Bühne fördert ein reliefartiges Spiel, der Zuschauer bewahrt dazu einen abwägenden kritischen Abstand. Die mittlere Tür der Palastarchitektur ist wesentlich größer im Vergleich zu den röm. Vorbildern. Daraus wird die These abgeleitet, daß sich hiermit das Bühnenportal des barocken Guckkastentheaters ankündigt. Die Vorläufer des Teatro Olimpico waren provisorische Gerüstbauten im Hof- oder Festsaal eines Palasts, die nach Erfüllung ihres einmaligen Zwecks wieder abgerissen wurden. Sebastiano Serlio (1475–1552) entwickelte 1540 hierfür einen Bauplan, bei dem der Zuschauerraum dem röm. Vorbild entsprach. Die Bühne selber war ein langgestreckter 1,10 m hoher Vorbau, hinter dem je nach Stück (Tragödie, Komödie, Satire) ein nicht begehbares, perspektivisch verkürztes, gestaffeltes Hintergrundbild (Winkelrahmenbühne) aufgebaut wurde. Der optische Eindruck von Bühnentiefe wurde durch die aufkommende Kunst der Perspektivmalerei bewirkt.

Die bildnerische Illusion hielt Einzug ins Theater. Bisher konnten räumliche bzw. bildnerische Veränderungen nur von Stück zu Stück vorgenommen werden. Durch die Anforderung aber, innerhalb eines Stückverlaufs verschiedene Spielorte bildnerisch sichtbar zu machen, kam es zu verschiedenen Erfindungen von beweglichen Dekorationen. Das System, das sich bis in unser Jh. durchgesetzt hat, ist die Veränderung des Bühnenbilds durch die hintereinander gestaffelte →Kulissenbühne. Die Spielfläche teilte sich demzufolge in zwei ca. gleich große Bereiche: Spielbühne und Bildbühne. Neben der horizontal verlaufenden Verwandlungstechnik entwickelte sich im Barock eine vertikal gerichtete Hub- und Senktechnik für Dekorationsteile und Darsteller. Eine Erläuterung bühnentechn. Effekte verfaßte Nicola Sabbattini 1639 in dem Buch *Practica di fabricar scene*. Um die Wirkung der Perspektivbühne zu steigern und die Sicht der Zuschauer im Parkett zu verbessern, wurde die Bühne um zwei bis vier Prozent nach vorn geneigt (Bühnenfall).

Das →Teatro Farnese im herzoglichen Schloß zu Parma ist der Ausgangspunkt für den höfischen und bürgerlichen T. der kommenden Jh. Bühne und Zuschauerraum wurden durch den bes. architektonisch gestalteten ‹Bilderrahmen› und das davor plazierte Orchester der neu entwickelten Kunstform Oper getrennt. Die Unmittelbarkeit der Zwiesprache des Darstellers mit dem Zuschauer war schon auf Grund der Entfernungen nicht möglich und nicht gewollt. Die Perspektivbühne definierte sich als ideales Gegenbild zu der Welt der nur noch Zuschauenden. Die Manipulations- und Verwandlungstechnik gab dem Darsteller wenig Gelegenheit, davor zu bestehen. Die U-Form der Zuschauertribüne im Teatro Farnese, dessen Grundform sich aus dem griech. Stadion ableitete, wiederholte sich in der Entwicklung in ausgeklügelten Varianten. Der freie, ebene Raum vor der Bühne verwies auf andere Nutzungsformen wie höfische Feste, Sport- und Kampfspiele. In diesen Fällen wurde die Bühne wieder in den Gesamtraum integriert. Der Theaterraum als Teil der höfischen Kultur (→Höfisches Theater, →Barocktheater) war Ort der Selbstdarstellung mittels Darstellung. Diesem besonderen Anlaß der Selbstfeier mußte der Theaterraum als Ganzes entsprechen. Die teilweise ausufernde und monumentale Scheinarchitektur des Zuschauerraums wurde im Bühnenbild fortgesetzt. Die Oper, die sich auch aus dem Rekonstruktionsversuch antiken Theaters, bei dem man annahm, daß die Texte gesungen wurden, entwickelte, setzte sich als neue Kunstgattung für das Fest- und Repräsentationsbedürfnis der europ. Fürstenhäuser durch. Die Theater waren umgebaute Ball- und Redoutensäle und somit Teil des Schloßkomplexes. Dem in Holz konstruierten teatrum folgte bald ein eigenständiger T. Parallel dazu entwickelten sich öffentliche Theater in den Stadtrepubliken Italiens wie das Teatro Cassiano 1637 in Venedig. Diese Unternehmungen waren auf eigene Einnahmen angewie-

Theaterbau 965

sen, mußten somit die Anzahl der zahlenden Gäste erhöhen. Die Größenordnung von notwendigen 1500 bis 2000 Plätzen führte zu der bekannten Form der Ränge (→ Rangtheater), die sich zuerst parallel zu den Saalwänden an drei Seiten rechtwinklig übereinander staffelten.

Der höfisch-öffentliche T. blieb in seiner Grundstruktur Vorbild und Muster, als zu Beginn des 19. Jh. die Trägerschaft in die Hände des erstarkten Bildungsbürgertums ging. Es kam zur Gründung von privatwirtschaftlichen Kapitalgesellschaften, sog. Theateraktivvereinen, die sich für den Betrieb des Theaterwesens verantwortlich zeigten und in zunehmendem Maße auch als Bauherrn auftraten. Die Grundform des frz. Ranglogentheaters war bis in das 20. Jh. der gebräuchliche Typ. Die Unterschiede lagen in dem Aufwand der eingesetzten Mittel und in der Größenordnung, ob für Oper oder Schauspiel konzipiert. Aufgewertet wurden die Eingangshallen, Treppenanlagen und die Foyers als Treffpunkt zur Selbstdarstellung des emanzipierten Bürgertums. Das Theater wurde zu einer außerordentlichen Bauaufgabe im Klassizismus, so daß sich Architekten wie Karl Friedrich Schinkel (Schauspielhaus Berlin, 1818) und Gottfried Semper (Hoftheater Dresden, 1841; Staatsoper Dresden, 1871) langfristig theoretisch und praktisch mit dem T. beschäftigten. Ausgehend von dramaturgischen Analysen (Lessing, Goethe) reiften neue T.-Konzepte. Die neue Dramentechnik, geprägt von der Auflösung der Einheit von Zeit, Ort und Handlung, forderte nicht mehr die Vortäuschung der Wirklichkeit, sondern mehr einen symbolhaften Bühnenraum, ähnlich dem Shakespeare-Theater, bei dem sich die Phantasie des Zuschauers entzünden konnte (→ Stilbühne). Der Spielraum des Darstellers als feststehende maßstäbliche Architektur sollte so nah wie möglich zum Zuschauer hin geordnet werden. Der Ort der Handlung deutete sich in veränderbaren Hintergrundprospekten an. Den Übergang vom Handlungsraum zum bildnerischen Definitionsraum leisten architektonische Elemente wie Mauern, Treppenanlagen, Geländer. Schinkel konnte diese Ideen weniger in Bauvorhaben als in seiner Tätigkeit als Bühnenbildner in Berlin umsetzen. Eine noch grundlegendere Kritik formulierte sich in den Reformbestrebungen, das Ranglogentheater mit seinen unterschiedlichen Platzgattungen durch die ‹demokratische› Form des antiken Runds zu ersetzen. Unterschiedliche Ansätze gab es in der Festlegung der Übergangszone von Zuschauerraum und Bühne. Richard Wagner (1818–83) ging in seinen Reformvorschlägen von den Anforderungen des Musikdramas aus, das in seinem Verständnis von gesellschaftlichen Momenten frei gehalten werden sollte. Der Zuschauer habe sich ausschließlich auf das Geschehen der Bühne zu konzentrieren, sich selbst und die Bezüge zur Realität zu vergessen und einzutauchen in die vollkommene Illusion. Gottfried Semper (1803–79) entwickelte 1865 im Entwurf für ein Festspielhaus in München einen Idealplan, der sich erst 1875 im Bau

966 Theaterbau

des Bayreuther Festspielhauses durch den Architekten Otto Brückwald realisieren konnte. Das antike Rund reduzierte sich auf die Kreissegmentform des steil ansteigenden Zuschauerraums, die eine ungehinderte Sicht und Hörsamkeit auf die Bühne hin ermöglichte. Das Orchester wurde in dem neutralen, räumlich undefinierten Zwischenraum (‹mystischer Abgrund›) unsichtbar abgesenkt. Die seitlichen Wände des Zuschauerraums formten sich aus querstehenden ‹Kulissenmauern›, die den Blick des Zuschauers ohne Unterbrechung durch einen Portalrahmen auf die Bühne führten. Die Einführung der Verdunklung des Zuschauerraums war ein weiterer konsequenter Schritt in dem Konzept Wagners zu einem Gesamtkunstwerk. – 1901 schuf der Architekt Max Littmann mit dem Prinzregententheater in München eine Kopie des Zuschauerraums nach Bayreuther Vorbild.

Ein anderer Ansatz zu Reformen im T. lag in der Entwicklung der Volkstheateridee (→ Volksbühne), d. h., das Theater sollte als Bildungsmittel breiteren und anderen Bevölkerungsschichten zugänglich gemacht werden. Als die angemessene demokratische Form des Zuschauerraums galt auch hier das ranglose Amphitheater. Im Schiller-Theater Berlin verwirklichten Max Littmann und Jacob Heilmann 1907 diese Idee des keilförmig ansteigenden Parketts. Die Lösung wurde etwas getrübt durch das Hinzufügen eines aus Platzgründen notwendigen Rangs. Dieses Modell des ‹zweirangigen Amphitheaters› wird Vorbild für viele Theaterneubauten nach dem 2. Weltkrieg.

Zwei Daten sind für die Weiterentwicklung von bes. Bedeutung. 1871 wurde durch Erlaß der Gewerbefreiheit im Dt. Reich jedem Unternehmer möglich, ein Theater auf eigenes Risiko zu betreiben bzw. zu bauen. Die Folge war eine Flut von Betriebsgründungen auf der Basis von Gewinn und damit verbunden der Ausbeutung des Schauspielerstands. Nach einer Phase der Stabilisierung solider Theaterunternehmen kam es zu einer regen Bautätigkeit, den Gründerjahren des T. Hinzu kam, daß sich in den Provinzstädten die Meinung durchsetzte, daß zum Grundbestand einer Stadt ein Theater gehöre. Unter dem Berufsstand der Architekten bildete sich eine Generation von T.-Fachleuten heraus. Ihre bekanntesten Vertreter sind Heinrich Seeling (1852–1932, zwölf Bauten), Bernhard Sehring (1855–1941, fünf Bauten), Martin Dülfer (1859–1942), Max Littmann (1862–1911, elf Bauten), Karl Moritz (1863–1943) und die Architektengemeinschaft Ferdinand Fellner (1847–1916) und Herrmann Helmer (1849–1919) mit 47 Bauten in Europa.

Die Formensprache war einheitlich; sie bediente sich historischer Stile, glitt aber im Zuschauerraum zuweilen in den ‹Karussellbarock› ab. Es herrschten die Farben Rot und Gold vor, und die Bauelemente waren nicht nur aus akustischen Gründen reich mit Stuck verziert. Mit Manfred und Gottfried Semper (Dresdner Opernhäuser) setzte sich die Auffas-

Theaterbau 967

sung durch, daß die äußere Form des T. sich auf seine innere Funktion beziehen muß. Zuschauer- und Bühnenhaus wurden in Form und architektonischen Details voneinander abgesetzt. Das Theater erhielt im Stadtraum seinen bes. zentralen Standort, seine Bedeutung wurde durch die tempelartige Eingangsgestaltung und den hoch aufragenden Bühnenturm verstärkt. Der Funktionalismus wurde 1889 mit dem Erlaß der Preußischen Polizeiverordnung zum beherrschenden Gestaltungsprinzip. Veranlaßt durch zahllose Theaterbrände mit katastrophalen Folgen – wie beim Brand des Wiener Ringtheaters im Jahr 1881 mit 450 Toten –, wurden nunmehr bei Theaterneubauten zahlreiche Sicherheitsauflagen vorgeschrieben, die wesentlichen Einfluß auf die Gestaltung des Gesamtkörpers hatten. Bei den Auflagen für den Zuschauerraum wurde von einem Prototyp des Rangtheaters ausgegangen. Mindest- und Höchstabmessungen, drei Ränge als Maximum, Art der Zuschauerverteilung, exakte Festlegung der Verkehrswege, Fassungsvermögen, zulässige Baustoffe waren Determinanten, die die Entwurfsmöglichkeiten für den Architekten einschränkten. Ebenso exakt wurden Auflagen für die Bühne mit obligatorischem Bühnenturm gegeben. Der Bau wurde in Brandabschnitte geteilt, wobei die Trennung zwischen Bühne und Zuschauerraum durch einen notwendigen →eisernen Vorhang als Guckkastenbühne für zukünftige Bauten vorgeschrieben wurde. Die Polizeiverordnung bewirkte die nach außen sichtbare Gliederung des Baukörpers in Eingangs-Foyer-Bereich, Zuschauerhaus, Bühnenhaus und Arbeits-Verwaltungs-Trakt. Die Nachteile des Rangtheaters, d. h. schlechte Sicht von den Seiten und von den höheren Rängen, wurden in der Weise verbessert, daß man sich auf zwei Ränge beschränkte, indem man den ersten Rang mit Verzicht auf die Proszeniumslogen bis unmittelbar an das Portal führte und den zweiten Rang auf den hinteren Bereich verkürzte.

Eine wesentliche Veränderung fand zum Ende des 19. Jh. weniger im Zuschauerraum als vielmehr in der techn. und räumlichen Ausstattung der Bühne statt. Die gesetzliche Einführung des Stahlbaus und die Entwicklung neuer Antriebstechniken hatte eine Reihe von bühnentechn. Erfindungen zur Folge wie Drehscheibe bzw. Drehbühne, Versenkungen, großflächige Transportwagen und Zuganlagen. Diese Maschinentheater waren notwendig geworden, da das perspektivisch gestaffelte Kulissenbild langsam abgelöst wurde durch die Entwicklung vollplastischer Realräume. Dementsprechend wurden Schwerlasttransportsysteme aus anderen industriellen Bereichen in das Theater übertragen. Die Bühnen mußten folgerichtig nach drei Seiten durch Neben- bzw. Hinterbühnen erweitert werden, um fertig aufgebaute Bühnenbilder hereinfahren zu können. Ebenfalls Einzug in das Theater hielt die elektrische Beleuchtung (→Bühnenbeleuchtung), die mit ihren Möglichkeiten das Theater aus der Dämmerung des Kerzenlichts entließ. Wo in der Kulissenbühne

968 Theaterbau

Licht und Schatten noch gemalt werden mußte, da bestand nun die Möglichkeit des elektrischen Zauberns von Taglicht, Nachtdämmerung und des Spektrums farbigen Lichts.

Zwei Gegenpositionen zur barocken Illusionsbühne konnten sich zu Beginn des 20. Jh. baulich formulieren. In dem →Münchner Künstlertheater, 1908 von Max Littmann erbaut und von Georg Fuchs theoretisch konzipiert, wurde auf die Tiefenbühne zugunsten einer breiten Reliefbühne verzichtet. Diese Raumausbildung erschien für den menschlichen Körper in Verbindung mit einer einfachen symbolhaften Dekoration günstig. Dem Reliefspiel gegenüber saß der Zuschauer in einem rechteckigen, steil ansteigenden ‹Hörsaal›. Das Münchner Künstlertheater vereinigte in sich die gestalterische Beschränkung auf die wesentlichen Raumbestandteile und die Erkenntnis, daß die hauptsächliche Wirkung vom Schauspieler ausgeht, der mit seinem Körper überschwengliche Spannungen mit der Absicht erregt, die Zuschauer in denselben Zustand zu versetzen. Bühne und Zuschauerraum werden zu einer Einheit. Die Vereinigung von Zuschauer und Schauspieler in einem gemeinsamen Raum war auch der Anlaß für den Umbau des Zirkus Schumann 1919 durch Hans Poelzig zum →Großen Schauspielhaus in Berlin. Das Inszenierungskonzept von Max Reinhardt für ein →Massentheater sah vor, daß sich 3500 Zuschauer wie im Zirkus um eine weit in den Zuschauerraum hineinragende Spielfläche gruppierten. Angeschlossen war ein voll techn. ausgerüsteter Bühnenraum, der durch ein mobiles Wandsystem nach Bedarf abgetrennt werden konnte.

In den 20er Jahren fand die Reform des T. wesentlich in den Köpfen und auf dem Papier von Architekten statt. Ausgangspunkte waren u. a. die politischen und sozialen Veränderungen nach 1918, die vom Theater eine Stellungnahme zu den gesellschaftlichen Veränderungen forderten (Brecht, Piscator), das Bekenntnis zum Volks- und Massentheater mit den antiken T.-Vorbildern. Die Architekten wurden aber auch in Versuchung geführt durch die sprunghafte Entwicklung der Technik, die es erlaubte, durch Stahlkonstruktion ‹unendlich› erscheinende Raumgebilde zu planen oder durch Licht, Projektion und Film den Zuschauer total in den Bann des Spiels zu ziehen. Die Technik wurde zum sichtbaren dramaturgischen Element und Teil der Architektur. Der Totalraum sollte vor allem flexibel für bekannte und noch zu findende Theaterformen sein; denn auch die darstellenden Künste befanden sich zur gleichen Zeit auf dem Weg des experimentellen Erforschens neuer Theaterformen – Schlemmer (→Bauhausbühne), Meyerhold (→Biomechanik), Tairow, Kandinsky (→Bühnensynthese). Die entwickeltste Lösung dieser Suche nach dem neuen Theaterraum findet sich in dem Entwurf für ein →Totaltheater (1926/27) von Walter Gropius in Zusammenarbeit mit Erwin Piscator. Das Konzept sieht sowohl die Möglichkeit des Guckkastentheaters

Theaterbau 969

als auch der Ring- und Arenabühne vor. Die vorgesehene Bühnentechnik war in ihrer Größe und Vielfältigkeit vergleichbar mit den großen Maschinentheatern der Zeit. Das ‹Aufrollen neuer Inhalte› durch den massiven Einsatz von Theatertechnik war eine Hoffnung, die sich in der neueren Theatergeschichte nicht hat einlösen können.

Im Nationalsozialismus wurden für die sog. Massen- und Volkstheaterbewegung →Freilichttheater und Thing-Theater (→Thingspiel) entworfen, die wiederum die antiken Vorbilder zitierten. Die T.-Tätigkeit beschränkte sich ansonsten auf zwei Neubauten in Dessau und Saarbrükken, auf die Umgestaltung verschiedener Zuschauerräume in Art der Herrschaftsarchitektur, auf den Ausbau der bühnentechn. Anlagen sowie auf den obligatorischen Einbau der Führerloge (Schiller-Theater Berlin). Das gleichgeschaltete dt. Theaterwesen wurde Mittel für den NS-Propagandaapparat (→Völkische Dramaturgie).

Von den 147 Spielstätten, die sich vor dem Krieg auf dem Gebiet der BRD und West-Berlins befanden, wurden vor allem in den Großstädten ca. 70 Theatergebäude zerbombt. Die Sehnsucht nach Theater konnte nicht zerstört werden, was sich in der Gründung von ungezählten behelfsmäßigen Spielstätten in Kinos, Turnhallen und Gaststätten manifestierte. Die Zeit der improvisierten Kleinstbühne war zwar nur kurz bemessen, aber durch die erzwungene Primitivität und den idealistischen Einsatz gab es Anstöße zu neuen regielichen und szenischen Lösungen. Relativ schnell, so 1948 beim Staatstheater Braunschweig, setzte die Phase der Wiederherstellung zerstörter Theatergebäude ein.

Mit der Gründung der Bundesrepublik 1949 und der Integration in das westliche Wirtschaftssystem (Marshallplan) begann die Zeit des ökonomischen Aufschwungs und des Wiederaufbaus der Städte und Gemeinden. Das Grundgesetz geht bei der Verteilung der staatlichen, öffentlichen Aufgaben davon aus, daß der Kulturbereich wie Bildung, Förderung der Künste und der Musik, Theater, Museen, Volksbildung und Heimatpflege Angelegenheit der Bundesländer, Städte und Gemeinden sei. Besonders den Städten und Gemeinden kommt als freiwillige Leistung die Förderung und Finanzierung des Theaters zu (→Kulturpolitik und Theater). Diese Unterstützung soll sich hauptsächlich auf den materiellen Schutz beziehen und keinen Einfluß nehmen auf die künstlerische Arbeit. Die Trägerschaft der Theater liegt in der Mehrheit dezentral in der Regie der öffentlichen Hand und in geringem Umfang in den Händen privater Unternehmer. Die Rechtsformen sind vielfältig und reichen vom Theater als Eigenbetrieb der öffentlichen Verwaltung bis hin zu der privatrechtlichen Form einer Gesellschaft mit beschränkter Haftung (GmbH) (→Theatersystem). Die Erstellung des T. als auch das Aufbringen laufender Betriebskosten erfolgt i. d. R. über eine Mischfinanzierung aus Mitteln der örtlichen Gemeinde, Gemeindezusammenschlüssen (→Landesbühne) und der Bundesländerhaushalte. Überschlägig geht man davon aus, daß ein Drittel der Baukosten jährlich als Unterhaltungskosten anzusetzen sind. Das Theater wird begriffen als eine von der Allgemeinheit getragene und nicht auf Gewinn gerichtete Institution, die für ein anonymes Publikum das Kulturerbe pflegt und neuen Formen des Theaters den Weg bereitet.

Mit dem Aufbau des von Georg Laves errichteten klassizistischen Opernhauses Hannover durch die Architekten Werner Kallmorgen und Klaus Hoffmann begann 1950 eine Phase der Rekonstruktion bzw. Neugestaltung historischer Bausubstanz. Das Opernhaus Hannover ist ein gelungenes Beispiel für die Verschmelzung traditioneller Formen mit der Sachlichkeit neuer Architektur. Wie bei vielen Bauten dieser Art wurde die Stuckpracht als unzeitgemäßes Symbol abgeschlagen und durch eine nüchterne Formensprache ersetzt. Diese Eingriffe bewirkten teilweise wie beim Stuttgarter Opernhaus eine nachhaltige Verschlechterung der Akustik, was wiederum 30 Jahre später ein Grund für die detailgenaue Wiederherstellung der urspr. Fassung ist. Die heute aktuellen Aspekte des Denkmalschutzes hatten in den 50er Jahren aus Gründen der fehlenden finanziellen Mittel und der Suche nach einer neuen zeitgemäßen Architektursprache keine Bedeutung.

Die weiteren Theaterwiederaufbauten (z. B. Schiller-Theater Berlin 1951, Opernhaus Frankfurt 1951, →Schauspielhaus Bochum 1953, Staatsoper Hamburg 1955, Cuvilliés-Theater München 1958) sind eine Mischung aus erhalten gebliebenen Teilen des Vorkriegsbaus und neuen Aus- und Anbauten. Die Hamburgische Staatsoper (Gerhard Weber) war für die folgende Phase der Theaterneubauten durch die Lösung der Ranggliederung und der transparenten Außenfassade beispielgebend. Um 1700 Zuschauer auf vorgegebenem eingeengtem Baugrund Platz geben zu können, sieht der Entwurf vier übereinanderliegende Ränge vor. Um die sonst übliche schlechte Sicht zu vermeiden, werden die seitlichen Rangplätze in logenähnlichen Platzgruppen zusammengefaßt und als auskragende Balkone zur Bühne hin gerichtet. Diese gestaffelten ‹Schlitten› werden Vorbild für fast alle Nachkriegs-Rangtheater. Ein weiteres signifikantes Element ist die Auflösung der Straßen- und Foyerfront in eine Glasfassade, die optisch und programmatisch die Verbindung von Kultur- und Alltagswelt herstellen soll. Diese beschriebenen architektonischen Lösungen sind kennzeichnend für die bescheidenen Versuche, sich in der Baugestaltung von den klassischen Vorbildern zu lösen. Allgemein wurde jedoch an der Rekonstruktion der historischen Form des Guckkastentheaters festgehalten, der hochmechanisierten Bühnenanlage, der Anordnung der Hauptbauteile in ein festgefügtes Schema, an dem äußeren monumentalen Erscheinungsbild und an einem repräsentativen, festlichen Gestaltungskanon, der sich jedoch bescheidener Mittel bedient.

Theaterbau 971

Im T. wird sichtbar, daß der Neubeginn 1945 mehr die Fortschreibung der Organisations- und Produktionsform des Theaters um die Jahrhundertwende ist. Die Bestimmungsgrößen auch für die funktionelle und gestalterische Ausformung waren und sind der diffus formulierte gesellschaftliche Auftrag an die Theater, die hieraus abgeleitete Verpflichtung zum Repertoire-Spielplan meist noch in mehreren Sparten und die Entwicklung der Bühnenbildkunst zu plastischen Szenenaufbauten, aus der sich das System der dt. →Bühnentechnik entwickelt hat.

Je nach Größenordnung der Stadt oder Gemeinde, den finanziellen und politischen (kulturpolitischen) Verhältnissen und dem gewählten Theatermodell formten sich in den folgenden drei Jahrzehnten spezifische T.-Typen und verwandte Kulturbauten mit Theatereinrichtungen heraus.

Das sind zusammengefaßt:

1. Monofunktionales Opern- oder Schauspielhaus, teils ergänzt um ein Studio oder Kammerspiel; dieser von einer Theatersparte genutzte Gebäudetyp findet nur in den Großstädten sein Publikum (z. B. Staatsoper Hamburg, →Freie Volksbühne Berlin).

2. Mehrspartenbetrieb mit einer großen Bühne für Oper, Ballett und großes Schauspiel und einem kleinen Haus, Studio oder Kammerspiel, zusammengefaßt in einem Haus oder in einem Gebäudekomplex. Die Untergrenze der Leistungsfähigkeit für Drei- bzw. Vierspartenbetrieb liegt bei einer Gemeindegröße von 200 000 Einwohnern, unterhalb dieser Zahl sind nur noch Schauspielensembles existenzfähig (z. B. Mannheimer Nationaltheater).

3. Gastspieltheater ohne ein eigenes Theaterensemble in mittleren und kleineren Gemeinden, die so beschaffen sein müssen, daß sie Gastspiele (private →Tourneetheater, Landesbühnen) aller Sparten ermöglichen sollen. Der Baukörper verkleinert sich hier durch den Wegfall des aufwendigen Werkstatt- und Verwaltungstrakts (z. B. Theater der Stadt Wolfsburg).

4. Kulturelle Zentren und Mehrzweckbauten mit einem größeren Versammlungsraum, der neben Kongressen, Ausstellungen und Unterhaltungsveranstaltungen auch Theateraufführungen ermöglichen soll (z. B. Festhalle der Stadt Unna).

5. Kongreßzentren ebenso wie die kulturellen Mehrzweckbauten mit einem breiten Spektrum von Veranstaltungsformen geplant und für Theaterzwecke mit einer Bühnenanlage ausgestattet (z. B. ICC-Berlin).

6. Offene Spielräume sind ehem. Kinos, Fabrikhallen, Filmstudios, Ausstellungs- und Lagerhallen, die als Alternative je nach Inszenierungskonzept zu einem neuen Theaterraum umgestaltet werden (z. B. Kampnagel-Fabrik Hamburg).

7. Theaterbau in seiner kleinsten Ausformung als Teil einer pädago-

972 Theaterbau

gischen oder sozial-kulturellen Einrichtung wie Aula und Turnhalle in Schulbauten, Versammlungsraum mit Bühne in Jugend- und Nachbarschaftsheimen.

8. Freilichttheater (z. B. Freilichtbühne in der Stiftsruine →Bad Hersfeld).

Die Zahl (ca. 190) der nach dem Krieg wieder aufgebauten bzw. neu errichteten Theater in der Bundesrepublik, gemessen an der Bevölkerungszahl, ist in keinem anderen Land der Welt erreicht worden. Die überregionale Verteilung entspricht der traditionell dezentralisierten Theaterstruktur. Die Theaterzentren sind Berlin, Hamburg und München und die Ballungszentren längs des Rheins. In dem restlichen ländlichen Raum besteht eine Unterversorgung; weniger als ein Drittel der Gesamtbevölkerung wohnt in Städten, die ein eigenes Theater betreiben. Die kleinen und mittleren Gemeinden können durch Errichtung eines Gastspielhauses an die mobile Theaterversorgung durch private Tourneetheater-Unternehmen und die Landesbühnen angeschlossen werden. Dem konventionellen Kulturverständnis entsprechend liegen die Theatergebäude i. d. R. im Kerngebiet (historischer Kern) einer Stadt. In dem Standort ‹repräsentativer Platz› oder auch Park manifestiert sich die Vorstellung von einem Theater als etwas Besonderem, das sich von der profanen, städtischen Umgebung abzuheben hat.

Mit der Eröffnung des Stadttheaters in Münster (Deilmann, von Hausen, Rave und Ruhnau) 1956 und ein Jahr später des Nationaltheaters Mannheim (Weber) begann ein Boom von Theaterneubauten, der sich über ca. 15 Jahre erstreckte und mit der Fertigstellung des Theaters der Stadt Wolfsburg (Scharoun) 1972 endete. Die Bauten in Münster und Mannheim sind gut vergleichbar, da die Ausgangssituation eine ähnliche und typische ist. Die Einwohnerzahl in beiden Fällen liegt zwischen 250 000 und 300 000. Die Ensembles bestehen jeweils aus mehreren Sparten (Oper, Ballett, Schauspiel), was sich in Schaffung eines Großen und eines Kleinen Hauses (Zwillingsbau) niederschlägt. Die Platzzahlen liegen in Mannheim (1200/500–700) im Vergleich zu Münster (955/320) höher, da das Publikumseinzugsgebiet in Mannheim wesentlich größer ist. Im Baukörper in Münster stellen sich die unterschiedlichen Funktionen übersichtlich erkennbar dar. Das Foyer öffnet sich durch Glaswände nach allen Seiten; bis auf den Bühnenbereich ist der rechte Winkel, bezeichnend für eine Kategorie von T. dieser Zeit, aus dem Entwurf verbannt, der schwarz gehaltene Zuschauerraum mit amphitheatralischem Parkett und drei Rängen wirkt intim. Der Bau erscheint wider alle Tendenzen der funktionalen Nachkriegsarchitektur als durchgestaltete Architekturplastik. Dazu ganz im Gegensatz der streng kubische, nach außen hin verschlossene, solitäre Baukörper in Mannheim. Wie aus den Wettbewerbsunterlagen hervorgeht, orientiert er sich in seiner klassischen Strenge an dem Wettbewerbsbeitrag von Mies van der Rohe, der wie in der realisierten Nationalgalerie in Berlin vorschlägt, das gesamte Innere durch allseitige Glaswände zu zeigen und den Zuschauerraum selbst durch Tageslicht zu erhellen. Beiden Bauten ist gemeinsam, daß sich in den Kleinen Häusern der Wunsch nach Veränderbarkeit des theatralen Raums je nach Stück und Konzeption realisieren kann. – 30 Jahre nach dem Entwurf des Totaltheaters konnte Piscator das Kleine Haus in Mannheim mit Schillers *Räubern* in einem gesamt bespielten Raum mit einer Hauptspielfläche, die auf zwei Seiten von Zuschauern umgeben war, eröffnen.

Die sparsame techn. Einrichtung und der hohe personelle Aufwand für den Umbau von einer Theaterform zur anderen ließ im Repertoirebetrieb eine intensive Nutzung der neuen Möglichkeiten nicht zu. Experimentelle Studios als Einraumtheater mit mobiler Bestuhlung und wechselnden Szenenflächen wurden in Ergänzung zu konventionellen neuen Großen Häusern 1959 im Stadttheater Gelsenkirchen (von Hansen, Rave, Ruhnau), 1969 im Schauspielhaus Düsseldorf (Pfau) und im Stadttheater Ulm (Schäfer) realisiert. Architektonische Variabilität, Polyvalenz und Flexibilität, bedingt durch Hubpodien, lose Bestuhlung und Bestuhlungswagen, Schiebewände, offene Beleuchtungsstege und techn. Decke, sind die Mittel für die Schaffung der drei unterschiedlichen Theaterräume: axiale Rahmenbühne, gegenüber von zwei Publikumsgruppen und Arenabühne. Die Raumdramaturgie in diesen Versuchsstudios geht von der Aufhebung der Rampe als notwendige Trennungslinie bzw. vierte Wand der realistischen und naturalistischen Dramatik des 19. Jh. aus. Sie stellt den Schauspieler im wahrsten Sinne des Wortes wieder in den urspr. Mittelpunkt der aus dem Dunkel befreiten Zuschauermenge. Sowohl der Schauspieler, dem jetzt der Rückzugs- und Deckungsbereich der Dekoration genommen ist, als auch der Zuschauer, der in Teilen seine Anonymität verliert, müssen sich aus gewohntem Verhaltensmuster lösen. Der Schauspieler hat seine reliefartige Spielweise aufzugeben zugunsten eines körperlichen Gestus, die verkürzte Distanz zum Spiel rückt auch den Zuschauer geistig näher an das Geschehen.

In keinem anderen Zeitabschnitt der dt. Geschichte wurden so viele neue Theater gebaut wie in den 60er Jahren. Es waren sowohl repräsentative Bauten wie die Deutsche Oper Berlin (Bornemann 1961), die Staatsoper München (Graupner, Fischer 1963) und die für Kulturbauten beispielhafte Philharmonie Berlin (Scharoun 1963) als auch die große Zahl der Mehrspartentheater in mittleren Großstädten wie Bonn, Ingolstadt, Wuppertal, Düsseldorf und Ulm. Für die planenden Architekten ist der jeweilige Theaterentwurf i. d. R. eine einmalige Bauaufgabe. Da der künftige Nutzer des Theaters im Entwurfsprozeß meist nicht vertreten und der Bauherr (Politiker, Kulturdezernent, Bau- und Verwaltungs-

974 Theaterbau

fachleute) ein widersprüchlicher und diffuser Partner sein kann, entwickelt der Architekt sein Konzept auf bekannten, konventionellen Mustern. Er wird in den tradierten Theatervorstellungen von den beratenden Theateringenieuren unterstützt. Außer G. Graupner, der als Spezialist sieben T. verwirklichen konnte, haben wenige ein zweites Mal ein Theater entworfen bzw. erstellt. Eine architektonisch beispielhafte Lösung ist in diesem Zeitraum nicht entwickelt worden. Große Hoffnungen liegen in der Realisierung des Entwurfs für das Opernhaus in Essen, dessen Wettbewerb Alvar Aalto 1959 gewonnen hatte. (*Red.*: Fertiggestellt 1988.)

Zusammenfassend zeichnet sich über diese Phase folgendes Bild. In der Fülle der Theaterneubauten entwickeln sich nur wenige Neuansätze (Kleines Haus Düsseldorf, Podium Ulm), die das vorherrschende Muster erweitern und verändern. Die Tendenz geht zur Optimierung der axialen Rahmenbühne, was sich in vielfältigen Verbesserungen und Details ausdrückt. Das alte Rangsystem wird aufgelöst zu hörsaalähnlichen sechseckigen Zuschauerräumen, in denen alle Plätze annähernd den gleichen Sitz- und Sichtkomfort haben sollen. Ziel ist die ausschließliche Konzentration der Zuschauer auf das Bühnengeschehen und das Ausschalten aller diesen Vorgang störenden Faktoren. Im Gegensatz zu den Hoftheatern ist der Kontakt unter den Zuschauern nicht erwünscht bzw. soll funktionell getrennt davon in der weitläufigen Foyerlandschaft durch welchen Umstand auch immer stattfinden. Das Parkett-Theater als Symbol der sozialen Einheit der Zuschauer dokumentiert sich stellvertretend im Schauspielhaus Düsseldorf (Bernhard M. Pfau 1969). Die 1030 Zuschauer sitzen in einem leicht ansteigenden Muschelgewölbe. Das Fehlen eines Rangs führt folglich zu einer größeren Distanz zur Bühne für das letzte Drittel der Zuschauer. Der Übergang vom Zuschauerraum zur Bühne ist typisch gelöst. Der Bühnenrahmen wird optisch nicht mehr betont, der Übergang und die Anpassung an das Bühnenbild werden durch ein mobiles Wandsystem so fließend wie möglich gestaltet. Zuschauerraum und Portalzone werden zwecks Unauffälligkeit in dunklen Edelhölzern bzw. Farben gehalten. Die Variabilität der Portal- und Vorbühnenzone ist der wesentliche Beitrag in dieser Phase der T.-Entwicklung. Die Portalzone kann je nach Stück und Sparte durch fahr- und klappbare Elemente und Hubpodien in ihrer Größe und Erweiterung in den Zuschauerraum angepaßt werden. Die Reformen zielen auf die Überwindung der architektonischen Trennungslinie, die angeblich eine Barriere zwischen Schauspieler und Zuschauer bildet. Das Schauspielhaus Düsseldorf ist auch ein gutes Beispiel für die Optimierungsbestrebungen im Bühnenbereich und der bühnentechn. Einrichtungen als Resultat der steigenden Ansprüche an die Qualität und Dimension der Dekoration. Die Bühnenfläche wird um Neben- und Seitenbühnen erweitert und mit einer aufwendigen Transporttechnik versehen. Die Fläche der Nebenräume nimmt durch den Ausbau der Magazine, Werkstätten und Verwaltung ständig zu. In ihrer äußeren Gestalt entwickeln sich die Neubauten weg von der funktionalen Gliederung hin zur Architekturplastik nach der individuellen Handschrift des Architekten. Der für die Bühne bestimmende rechte Winkel wird in Schiefwinkligkeit, Asymmetrie und Kurven aufgelöst. Der Bühnenturm entwickelt sich entweder zur alles überspannenden Haube, oder der Baukubus wird in Kleinteiligkeit aufgelöst. Die Innengestaltung, orientiert am Prinzip der sparsamen Festlichkeit und Repräsentation, entspricht in der Wahl der Materialien, dem Schmuck und der Lichtgestaltung dem Ideal der gemessenen, ordentlichen Feierlichkeit. Die monofunktionalen Kultureinrichtungen lassen dann auch nur im wesentlichen die eine Theaterform unter vielen zu, für die sie gebaut worden sind.

Die Unzufriedenheit der Schauspieler nicht nur über die Theaterarchitektur, sondern im bes. über die gesellschaftliche Funktion und Art der staatlichen Theaterbetriebe ließ stilbildende Theaterereignisse – →Living Theatre, Jerzy Grotowski (→Armes Theater), Orlando Furioso – in Fabriken, Sportarenen und Messehallen entstehen. Die bildenden Künste auf dem Weg der Grenzüberschreitungen nutzten die Mittel des Theaters in Happenings und Performances auf öffentlichen Plätzen. Die Konvention, was Theater sei und in welchem Rahmen es stattzufinden habe, ist Anfang der 70er Jahre, verursacht durch Wirtschaftskrise, Studentenrevolte, Krise der Städte, aufgehoben worden. Das Theater war gezwungen, sich neu zu orientieren, d. h. neue Spielformen für ein breites Publikum in Parteilichkeit zu den Vorgängen in der Gesellschaft zu entwickeln (→Freies Theater).

Der Auszug aus den in der Stadtstruktur isoliert liegenden Stadt- und Staatstheatern in Industrie- und Zweckbauten lag nahe. Diese durch Zweckmäßigkeit und Arbeit geprägten Hallen stellen in vielerlei Beziehung eine Alternative zu den anonymen Glas- und Betonarchitekturen dar. Es fehlt die saubere, bürgerliche Festlichkeit. Die starke optische Eigenwirkung und der zu jeder Veränderung mögliche Großraum läßt neue Bühnenformen und eine andere Bildsprache zu. Der Zuschauer sieht die Spuren des Arbeitsprozesses. Die Art und Weise des Theatermachens wird ihm nicht verheimlicht. Das Suchen nach neuen Theaterräumen hat seine Vorbilder z. B. in dem Roundhouse, einem ehem. Lokomotivschuppen in London, in den experimentellen Universitätstheatern der Vereinigten Staaten und in der →Cartoucherie, einer alten Munitionsfabrik in der Nähe von Paris.

Die Neu- und Umgestaltung des Theaterraums als Teil des Inszenierungskonzepts ist an der Schaubühne am Halleschen Ufer in Berlin zu einer eigenen Bühnenbildkunstform entwickelt worden. Von 1970 an über den Zeitraum von zehn Jahren wurde der einfache Vortrags- und Versammlungsraum ohne Bühnenturm und bühnentechn. Einrichtungen nach allen nur erdenklichen Varianten der Theaterformen, Zuordnungsmöglichkeiten der Zuschauer, Materialeigenschaften der Dekoration etc. ausgelotet. Der Gesamtraum wird zu einem wesentlichen Wirkungsfaktor, die Festlegung der Anordnung der Zuschauer zum Spiel wird Teil der Regie. Das Bühnenbild beschränkt sich nicht nur auf die Spielfläche, sondern umspannt den Gesamtraum als Environment; Ortswechsel im Stück sind nicht ‹Bilderwechsel›, sondern tatsächlicher Ortswechsel im Raum durch den Schauspieler oder den Zuschauer. Eine Steigerung in der Aneignung neuer Räume für das Theater ist das Suchen nach dem für das Stück geeigneten Spielort, vergleichbar mit der Drehortsuche beim Film. So wurden durch die Schaubühne u. a. ein Filmstudio, ein ehem. Hotel und das Olympiastadion als Ort theatralischer Ereignisse bestimmt. Die Mühen und Kosten waren bei den oben beschriebenen Raumvariationen so hoch und der Grad der Etablierung und Wertigkeit der Schaubühne in der Berliner Kulturpolitik so fortgeschritten, daß der Bau eines neuen Theaters für die Zwecke dieser anderen Theaterkonzeption reif war.

1981 wurde das umgebaute Filmtheater «Universum» (Erich Mendelsohn 1927) als →Schaubühne am Lehniner Platz eröffnet. Das Ergebnis ist eine neue Kategorie von T., die sich aus den Raumerfahrungen zu einer Konzeption des neutralen Theatermehrzweckraums verdichtete. Mittelpunkt ist ein elementarisierter Grundraum, der sich in drei akustisch isolierte Einzelräume teilen läßt, um auch parallellaufende Produktionen zu ermöglichen. Der Boden läßt sich durch 76 hydraulisch angetriebene Scherenhubpodien in eine Grobtopographie für die erwünschte Theaterform staffeln. Ein traditioneller Bühnenturm fehlt; statt dessen ist der obere Raumabschluß als techn. Gitterrostdecke zur Befestigung der Beleuchtungsgeräte und Punktzüge ausgebildet. Der Wunsch nach einem entmaterialisierten, dunklen Einheitsraum mit der Möglichkeit zur Herstellung der überlieferten, aber auch neuen Bühnenformen ist erreicht.

In der neueren T.-Planung hat sich das Modell des unbestimmten Grundraums in der Stadthalle Unna (Brandt/Böttcher) und im Kammertheater Stuttgart als Teil der Staatsgalerie (James Stirling 1983) realisiert. Den derzeitigen Höhepunkt bildet die Planung für die Opéra de la Bastille (Carlos Ott) in Paris, die am 14. Juli 1989 zum 200. Jahrestag der Stürmung und Zerstörung der Bastille eröffnet wurde. Unter einem Dach vereinen sich ein Opernhaus für 2700 Zuschauer und ein Mehrzweckraum (salle modulable). Das Große Haus als Rangtheater, das, durch den Ausbau des Bühnenbereichs zu zehn Nebenbühnen auf zwei Ebenen, 450 täglich wechselnde Vorstellungen im Jahr zu erschwinglichen Eintrittspreisen (Volksoper) ermöglichen soll, ist das letzte Stadium der Optimierungsversuche des barocken Guckkastentheaters. Der Salle Modulable ist die Weiterentwicklung des Schaubühnen-Modells, da unterschiedliche Topographien des Bodens und auch der Decke möglich sind; für die klassischen Formen des Theaters ist darüber hinaus eine feste, ansteigende Zuschauertribüne und ein Bühnenturm zum Einheitsraum addierbar.

Auch dieses Beispiel zeigt, daß die Theaterneubauten der letzten 30 Jahre zu keinen großen architektonischen Lösungen führten. Um so weniger erstaunlich oder verdächtig ist die verstärkte Entwicklung der letzten Jahre in allen europ. Ländern, ob Ost oder West, daß Theater-Kulturdenkmäler mit erheblichen finanziellen Mitteln restauriert und aufpoliert werden. Beispiele hierfür sind das Deutsche Schauspielhaus in Hamburg oder das Hessische Staatstheater Wiesbaden.

Bablet, D./Jacquot, J. (Hg.): Le lieu théâtral dans la société moderne. Paris 1963; Badenhausen, R./Zielske, H. (Hg.): Bühnenformen – Bühnenräume – Bühnendekorationen. Beiträge zur Entwicklung des Spielorts. Berlin 1974; Bentham, F.: New Theatres in Britain. London: Rank Strand Electric 1970 (= A TABS Publication); Braun, K. u. a.: Mobiler Spielraum – Theater der Zukunft. Frankfurt/M. 1970; Deutsche Theatertechnische Gesellschaft (Hg.): Theaterszene. Theaterbau. 1971–1975. Eine Dokumentation des Theaters in der Bundesrepublik Deutschland. Hamburg o. J. [1975]; Deutsche Sektion des Internationalen Theaterinstituts (Hg.): Unsere Theaterneubauten nach 1945. Berlin o. J. [1967]; Fischer, M. F. (Hg.): Historische Theater in Deutschland. Teil 1: Westliche Bundesländer. Hannover 1991; Gabler, W.: Der Zuschauerraum des Theaters. Leipzig 1935; Graubner, G.: Theaterbau-Aufgabe und Planung. München 1968; Hoffmann, H.-Chr.: Die Theaterbauten von Fellner und Helmer. München 1966; ders.: Theater und Oper in der deutschen Stadt. In: Die deutsche Stadt im 19. Jahrhundert. München 1974; International Federation for Theatre Research/Fédération internationale pour la recherche théâtrale: Theatre Space/Der Raum des Theaters. Eine Untersuchung der Wechselwirkungen zwischen Raum, Technik, Spiel und Gesellschaft. Beiträge zum Kongreß. Hg. von Heinrich Huesmann (English Version/Deutsche Fassung). München 1977; Izenour, G. C.: Theater Design. New York 1977; Job, H./Ostertag, R.: Theater für morgen. Stuttgart 1969 (= Projekt-Bücher 8); Kallmorgen, W.: Theater heute. Darmstadt 1955; Kindermann, H.: Bühne und Zuschauerraum. Ihre Zuordnung seit der griechischen Antike. Graz/Köln 1963; Leacroft, R. u. H.: Theatre and Play house. London/New York 1984; Les lieux du spectacle. L'architecture d'aujourd'hui, No. 199. Paris, Octobre 1978; Pausch, R.: Theaterbau in der BRD. Zur Ideologiekritik des monofunktionalen Theaterbaus seit 1945. Berlin (Publikationsstelle der TU) 1974 (= Diss. Phil. Köln 1973); Ruhnau, W.: Versammlungsstätten. Gütersloh 1969 (= DBZ-Baufachbücher 6); Schmidt, D. N. (Hg.): Das Theater von Alvar Aalto in Essen. Essen 1988; Schubert, H.: Moderner Theaterbau. Internationale Situation. Dokumentation. Projekte. Bühnentechnik. Stuttgart/Bern 1971; Silvermann, M.: Contemporary Theatre Architecture (1946–1966). New York (The New York Public Library) 1965; Storck, G.: Probleme des modernen Bauens und die Theaterarchitektur des 20. Jahrhunderts in Deutschland. (Diss. Phil.) Bonn 1971; Theatermuseum Mün-

978 Theater der Freien Hansestadt Bremen

chen: Theaterbau in der Bundesrepublik Deutschland. Ausstellung und Katalog: Eckehart Nölle. München 1977; Werner, E.: Theatergebäude. 1. Band. Geschichtliche Entwicklung. Berlin 1954; Wild, F. (Red.): Mehrzweckgebäude für gesellschaftliche Funktionen. Film – Konzert – Vortrag – Diskussion – Spiel – Theater. München 1970 (= Entwurf und Planung, Heft 6); Zielske, H.: Deutsche Theaterbauten bis zum 2. Weltkrieg. Typologisch-historische Dokumentation einer Baugattung. Berlin 1971 (= Schriften der Gesellschaft für Theatergeschichte 65).

Horst Birr

Theater der Freien Hansestadt Bremen

Theater am Goetheplatz, Schauspielhaus, Concordia. 1782 erstes Theatergebäude. 1843 Neubau. 1883 bis 1885 Angelo Neumann (1838–1910) artistischer Leiter. 1944 zerstört, Wiederaufbau 1950, Schauspielhaus 1985. 1962 bis 1973 Intendant Kurt Hübner (* 1916), Entwicklung des «Bremer Stils», prägend für das Theater der 70er Jahre (Peter Zadek, Wilfried Minks, Rainer Werner Fassbinder, Klaus Michael Grüber). → Bremer Tanztheater: 1968 bis 1978 Hans Kresnik, 1978 bis 1986 Reinhild Hoffmann, 1986 bis 1989 Rotraut de Neve und Heidrun Vielhauer, seit 1989 wieder Johann Kresnik. 1985 bis 1992 Intendant Tobias Richter (* 1953). Ab 1992/93 Generalintendant Hansgünther Heyme.

Büthe, O.: Theater und Schauspielkunst in Bremen seit der Goethezeit, Diss. Mainz 1967; Mauer, B./Krauss, B.: Spielräume – Arbeitsergebnisse – Theater Bremen 1962–1973. Bremen 1973.

Werner Schulze-Reimpell/Red.

Theater der Grausamkeit

Zentraler Begriff der Theaterprogrammatik von Antonin Artaud (1896–1948), der nach schwerer psychischer Erkrankung mit 25 Jahren zum erstenmal im Theater auftritt unter der Regie von Lugné-Poë (1869–1940), dann Firmin Gémier (1869–1933), Georges Pitoëff (1884–1939) und vor allem Charles Dullin (1885–1949). Artaud wird auch bekannt als Lyriker. Von André Breton (1896–1966) zuerst gepriesen, dann heftig abgelehnt, da er in der surrealistischen Revolution nur «eine Wandlung der inneren Zustände des Wesens» sehen wollte, bleibt er trotzdem dem Geist des Surrealismus sehr nahe und gründet 1926 mit Robert Aron und Roger Vitrac das → Théâtre Alfred Jarry; vier Vorstellungen fanden statt mit nur je ein bis zwei Aufführungen; auf dem Programm standen Stücke der drei Gründer, darunter *Les Mystères de*

l'amour (1927) und _Victor_ (1928) von Vitrac, aber auch der 3. Akt von
Paul Claudels _Le Partage de midi_ (1906) und August Strindbergs _Traum-_
spiel (1907). Das Experiment scheiterte an der schwachen Resonanz und
an Finanzschwierigkeiten. Mit Müh und Not konnte Artaud 1935 für 14
Tage seine Adaption _Les Cenci_ nach Stendhal und Shelley aufführen, in
der er die Hauptrolle spielte. Es war die erste Realisation der Idee des
«Theaters der Grausamkeit», jedoch erneut ein Mißerfolg. Artaud reiste
nach Mexiko und experimentierte mit Drogen. Danach vermochte er
(nach längerem Aufenthalt in einer Heilanstalt und infolge einer Krebs-
erkrankung) bis zu seinem Tod keine öffentliche Rolle mehr zu spielen.
Seine Bedeutung gründet in seiner legendären Persönlichkeit, Inbegriff
kompromißloser Künstlerschaft und Theaterbesessenheit. Seine Vorstellungen über Theatertheorie und Regie sind in der Essaysammlung _Das_
Theater und sein Double (1938) vereinigt.

Ausgangspunkt ist für Artaud die radikale Ablehnung des überlieferten Theaters insgesamt, aller üblichen Auffassungen von Raum, Zeit,
Psychologie und aller Konventionen des Theaters seiner Zeit. Im Gegensatz dazu beschwört er ein magisches und metaphysisches Theater
(letzteres ist für ihn eines der Synonyme für T. d. G.), wobei er seine Inspirationen in den Riten primitiver Kulte oder des orientalischen Theaters sucht, z. B. in den Tänzen Balis oder Mexikos. Artaud fordert ein
Theater der Körperlichkeit, des Leibs, als dessen unmittelbarer Ausfluß
ihm auch die Sprache gilt, vor jeder Begrifflichkeit: «eine neue Körpersprache, aus Zeichen bestehend, nicht mehr aus Wörtern». Als ‹Meister
sakraler Zeremonien›, ‹einmaliger Schöpfer› ordnet der Regisseur diese
neue Körper- und Raumsprache in strengem Diskurs an zum «Aufglü-
hen» der großen metaphysischen Erfahrungen, des Werdens, des
Schicksals, des Chaos. Grausamkeit ist in Artauds Theater nicht unbedingt Gewalt und Blut, eher Lebenskraft, Hellsicht, unerträgliche
Strenge. Das straff geregelte Schauspiel erscheint dann dem Zuschauer
als faszinierend mächtiger «Traumniederschlag». Mit äußerster Kraft
will er ein Gesamtschauspiel auf die Bühne bringen, unter Einbeziehung
aller außersprachlichen Ausdrucks- und Darstellungsmittel, «Musik,
Tanz, Plastik, Pantomime, Mimik, Gestik, Architektur, Licht und Dekor.» Ergebnis soll für Schauspieler und den Zuschauer ein Theater der
Selbsterkenntnis sein, der ‹grausamen Heilung›, eine Art Neugeburt des
Lebens durch das Theater.

Die Rückkehr zum reinen, totalen Theater, die Suche nach einer echten Spezifität der Theatersprache, die Forderung nach der Autonomie
des Schauspiels vom literarischen Text hat Artaud gemein mit Adolphe
Appia, Edward Gordon Craig oder auch Wsewolod Meyerhold. Artauds
Eigenart besteht darin, daß er sein Leben, seinen Körper, sein Schreiben
zum Ausübungsort seiner Gedanken gemacht hat und darin zu einer Art

Märtyrerfigur geworden ist. Indem er das Theater als echte Existenzerfahrung versteht, nicht als ästhetisches Unternehmen oder als Kunstwerk, unterscheidet er sich von allen anderen Theatertheoretikern. Die Ideen Artauds gingen ein in die Theaterarbeit von Jean-Louis Barrault, Roger Blin, des →Living Theatre, Jerzy Grotowskis (* 1933) und Peter Brooks (* 1925). – Philosophen des Strukturalismus wie Jacques Derrida haben in seinem Werk einen der drei großen Versuche dieser Zeit, neben denen von Lévinas und Bataille, sehen wollen, sich der alten Metaphysik zu entziehen. Auch wird betont, daß er als erster praktisch und theoretisch Ermittlungen der Psychiatrie, Anthropologie und der Linguistik für das Theater verwertet hat. Er ist zu einer der Grundfiguren des heutigen Theaters geworden, der Antipode zu Brechts Aufklärungstheater schlechthin.

Charbonnier, G.: Essai sur Antonin Artaud. Paris 1959; Derrida, J.: L'Ecriture et la différence. Paris 1967 (dt.: Die Schrift und die Differenz. Frankfurt/M. 1976); Durozoi, G.: Artaud, l'aliénation et la folie. Paris 1972; Grimm, J.: Das avantgardistische Theater Frankreichs, 1895–1930. 1982; Gouhier, H.: Antonin Artaud et l'essence du théâtre. Paris 1975; Kapralik, E.: Antonin Artaud 1896–1948. 1977; Kaschel, G.: Text, Körper und Choreographie. Frankfurt/M. 1981; Virmaux, A.: Antonin Artaud et le théâtre. Paris 1970; Virmaux, O. und A.: Artaud, bilan critique. Paris 1980.

Michel Autrand

Theater Der Kreis (Wien)

Von George Tabori 1986–90 geleitetes Theaterzentrum im Wiener Schauspielhaus mit offenen Workshops für Schauspielerinnen und Schauspieler im A&A (Actors and actresses) Studio. Als Theaterlabor ohne Produktionszwang und Gegenmodell zum ‹Staatstheater-Luxus› gegründet. Entwickeln zeitkritische und wirklichkeitsnahe Theaterexperimente mit Hilfe der gruppentherapeutischen Methode. Das Publikum wird in die Gruppe einbezogen. Tabori arbeitet mit assoziativen Bildern aus dem Unbewußten. Ein zentrales Thema ist die Selbsterforschung in Verbindung mit der Doppelproblematik in der Passion der Juden (Qual der Opfer und Scham der Überlebenden). – Wechselndes Ensemble; Gruppenmitglieder sind u. a. Therese Affolter, Angelica Domröse, Silvia Fenz, Ursula Höpfner, Isabel Karajan, Leslie Malton, Hildegard Schmahl, Michael Degen, Rainer Frieb, Detlef Jacobsen, Hilmar Thate, Vitus Zeplichal; Musik: Stanley Walden; Bühnenraum: Andreas Szalla; Co-Regisseur: Martin Fried. Eröffnung am 5. 5. 1987 mit O'Neill *Der Eismann kommt* (Regie: M. Fried). Inszenierungen von George Tabori: u. a. G. Salvatore *Stalin* (Publikumspreis der Mülheimer Theatertage

1988), Th. Brasch *Frauen. Krieg. Lustspiel* (UA, Coproduktion mit den Wiener Festwochen und den Bregenzer Festspielen; Kainz-Medaillen 1987/88 für Regie an G. Tabori und für die Darstellung der Klara an A. Domröse); *Lears Schatten* nach Shakespeare (UA, Coproduktion mit den Bregenzer Festspielen), Shakespeare *Hamlet* (Coproduktion mit den Wiener Festwochen), 1989/90. Neben Tätigkeit im T. Regiearbeiten am →Burgtheater: u. a. *Weisman und Rotgesicht* (UA, Mülheimer Dramatikerpreis), 1990.

Ingeborg Janich

Theater der Nationen (Théâtre des Nations)

Internationales Theaterfestival, das 1954 im Rahmen des 6. Weltkongresses des Internationalen Theater-Instituts der UNESCO (→ITI) in Paris durchgeführt wurde. Leitung: A.-M. Julien und Claude Planson. Es fand zunächst jeden Sommer für sechs bis zwölf Wochen mit staatlicher und städtischer Unterstützung in Paris statt. 1957 wurde es institutionalisiert und von 1965 bis 1968 sowie 1972 von Jean-Louis Barrault geleitet. Nach mehrjähriger Unterbrechung wird es seit 1975 auf Vorschlag des ITI jeweils in einem anderen Land ausgerichtet: Warschau (1975), Belgrad (1976), Paris (1977), Caracas (1978), Hamburg (1979), Amsterdam (1980), Venedig (1981), Sofia (1982), Nancy (1984), Baltimore, San Francisco (1986). – Das T. d. N. ermöglichte erstmals in der Theatergeschichte das Zusammentreffen westlicher mit asiatischer, afrikanischer und südamerikanischer Theaterkunst. Sein Verdienst ist es daher auch, bedeutende Truppen aus aller Welt überregional bekannt gemacht zu haben, u. a. das →Berliner Ensemble, die →Royal Shakespeare Company, das →Piccolo Teatro di Milano sowie die →Peking-Oper.

Barbara Müller-Wesemann

Theater der Prominenten

Die Kabarett-Revue unter der Leitung von Willi Rosen beschäftigte fast nur Schauspieler und Kabarettisten, die schon vor 1933 auf dt. Bühnen und durch Filme auch im Ausland bekannt waren: Siegfried Arno, Otto Wallburg, Szöke Szakall, Max Ehrlich. Die Texte für die mit jährlich vier bis fünf Revuen ab 1937 in den Niederlanden gastierende Truppe stammten ebenso wie die Kompositionen fast ausschließlich von Rosen. – Nach der dt. Besetzung wurden Rosen und Ehrlich in das Lager Westerbork eingeliefert, das für 100 000 von den 140 000 jüdischen Einwohnern der Niederlande letzte Durchgangsstation in die Gaskammern von Ausch-witz, Bergen-Belsen, Maidanek oder Theresienstadt wurde. Bis zu ihrem eigenen Abtransport nach Theresienstadt unterhielten sie hier ein Lager-Kabarett (→Theater in den Konzentrationslagern).

Jan Hans

Theater der Unterdrückten

Theoretisch und praktisch vielerprobtes Volkstheater (später auch Thea-ter der Befreiung genannt), das Augusto Boal (*1931) mit vielfältigen Formen und Inhalten (z. B. Unsichtbares Theater, Forum-, Statuen-, Zeitungstheater) seit 1956 (zuerst im →Teatro Arena, São Paulo) bis zu seiner Ausweisung aus Brasilien 1971, danach in Lateinamerika, USA, Europa (u. a. in zahlreichen Workshops) entwickelt hat (→Lateinameri-kanisches Theater). Anknüpfend an Konstantin S. Stanislawski, Bertolt Brecht u. a. steht das Engagement des Zuschauers gegen äußere und in-nere Zwänge im Mittelpunkt. Anders als Brecht will Boal das Theater aber nicht in den Dienst der Revolution stellen, sondern es als General-probe zum Bestandteil der Revolution selbst machen. Im Idealfall führen diese Gedanken zum Entwurf von Handlungsmodellen, die jedoch in den hochindustrialisierten Gesellschaftsformen des Kapitalismus anders als in den Ländern der ‹Dritten Welt› mangels Erprobung zu Frustrationen führen können.

Boal, A.: Theater der Unterdrückten. Frankfurt/M. 1979; Pörtl, K.: Revolution und Untergang im lateinamerikanischen Gegenwartstheater: Boals Theater der Befreiung und Wolffs Theater der Angst. In: Iberoamericana 8 (1979), S. 23–43; Thorau, H.: Augusto Boals Theater der Unterdrückten in Theorie und Praxis. Rheinfelden 1982.

Martin Franzbach

Theater der Welt

Pendant zum →«Theater der Nationen» des Internationalen Theaterinsti-tuts (→ITI), veranstaltet vom Zentrum Bundesrepublik des ITI und je-weils einer Stadt, finanziert aus kommunalen, Landes- und Bundesmit-teln. Gegründet auf Anregung des Bundes nach der starken Resonanz des «Theaters der Nationen» 1979 in Hamburg. Erstmals 1981 in Köln, 1985 in Frankfurt/M., 1987 Stuttgart, 1989 Hamburg, 1991 Essen, 1993 München. – Versuch, über neue Tendenzen, Spielweisen und ästhetische Innovationen im Welttheater zu informieren. Starke Berücksichtigung des außereurop. Theaters, dem als exemplarisch geltende Inszenierungen aus der Bundesrepublik Deutschland konfrontiert werden. Beschränkung auf Schauspiel, Tanztheater und Performance.

Werner Schulze-Reimpell / Red.

Theaterfotografie

Zwei Richtungen: 1. Dokumentarfotografie. Fotografische Abbildung (Szenen- und Rollenfotos) einer Inszenierung, die Gegebenheiten und Atmosphäre möglichst authentisch aus dem Spielverlauf heraus aufgenommen wiedergibt. 2. Porträtfotografie (Rolle und Zivil) und gestellte Szenenfotos.

Die frühesten Theaterfotos entstanden als Zivil- und Rollenporträts von darstellenden Künstlern in Fotoateliers in den 50er Jahren des 19. Jh., z. B. in denen der frz. Künstlerfotografen, u. a. Gaspard-Félix Tournachon, genannt Nadar (1820–1910), in Paris oder der Münchner Fotografen Franz Hanfstaengel (1804–77) und Joseph Albert (1825–80) und im Hofatelier Elvira. Für Dokumentarfotos fehlten damals sowohl in den Theatern (mangelhafte Beleuchtung) als auch bei den Fotografen die technischen Voraussetzungen. Die frühesten dokumentarischen Ansätze lassen sich in zivilen Gruppen- und Rollenfotos in den 60er Jahren des 19. Jh. nachweisen, seit der zweiten Hälfte der 70er Jahre des 19. Jh. wurden in gut ausgestatteten Fotoateliers Inszenierungsmomente mit Versatzstücken, Requisiten und Prospekten nachgestellt. Frühe Inszenierungsdokumentationen des deutschsprachigen Raums stammen von Joseph Albert, der 1871 die Oberammergauer Passionsspiele (Szenenfotos) und 1876 bei den Bayreuther Festspielen Porträts sämtlicher Haupt- und Nebendarsteller fotografierte. Mit der Einführung der elektrischen Bühnenbeleuchtung Ende der 80er Jahre des 19. Jh. und durch Erfindungen im Bereich der Kameratechnik und des Negativmaterials waren die technischen Voraussetzungen für Szenenfotos in geschlossenen Theaterräumen gegeben. Durch das Verfahren der Autotypie wurde die Veröffentlichung von T. in Zeitschriften möglich, 1903 Gründung der Zeitschrift «Das Theater» in Berlin, die bis 1942 erschien. Seit der Jahrhundertwende existieren nachgestellte Szenen- und Gruppenaufnahmen und Bühnenbildfotos. Dokumentarische Szenenfotos (Momentaufnahmen während der Aufführung aus dem Spielablauf heraus ohne zusätzliche Ausleuchtung) sind erst seit den 20er Jahren möglich nach der Entwicklung der Ermanox-Kamera und der Leica. Nach

984 Theaterfotografie

Einführung der Postkarte (1865 in Deutschland, 1872 in Frankreich) überwiegen bis zum Beginn des 2. Weltkriegs Porträts von Bühnenkünstlern. Um die Jahrhundertwende änderte sich der Stil bei den Zivil- und Rollenporträts: Die aufwendigen Prospekte und Versatzstücke werden durch einen neutralen Hintergrund ersetzt. Etwa um diese Zeit kann man die Spaltung der T. in Dokumentar- und Porträtfotografie feststellen. Mitte der 20er Jahre war der Beruf des Theaterfotografen etabliert als Ausbildungsberuf des Handwerks, aber auch freiberuflicher Fotograf mit Fachhochschulabschluß oder Bildjournalist. Kommerzielle Grundlagen bilden theaterintern die Programmheft- und Aushangfotos, Pressefotos und Porträts für die darstellenden Künstler und ihre Fans.

Seit Anfang der 20er Jahre wurden neue Anforderungen an die T. gestellt durch die Entwicklung des Regietheaters. Die Dokumentation von Bühnenbild, Situations- und Bewegungsregie und gestellte Szenenfotos verdrängen die Rollenporträts der Fotoateliers. Die journalistische Momentfotografie setzt sich aber erst nach dem 2. Weltkrieg endgültig durch (eine bestimmte Situation soll möglichst unbemerkt aufgenommen und authentisch wiedergegeben werden). Dokumentation und Nutzung der T. für den Probenprozeß wird z. B. beim Berliner Ensemble durch die Modellbücher der Inszenierungen (Fotos Ruth Berlau) ermöglicht.

Fotografinnen und Fotografen im dt. Sprachraum: Clärchen und Hermann Baus (Köln, Hamburg), Lotte Bermbach (Düsseldorf), Ruth Berlau (Zusammenarbeit mit B. Brecht), Rudolf Betz (1907–70, München), Helmut Blattner (Berlin), Dr. Walter Boje (Hamburg), Jean-Marie Bottequin (Belgien, München), Hans Böhm (Berlin, Wien), Ralf Brinkhoff (Hamburg), Ilse Buhs und Jürgen Remmler (Berlin), Hans-Ludwig Böhme (Dresden), Rosemarie Clausen (1907–90, Berlin, Hamburg), Chargesheimer (1924–72, Köln), Michael Dannemann (Düsseldorf), Klaus Dierig (München), Mara Eggert (Mannheim, Frankfurt), Atelier Ellinger (Salzburg), Siegfried Enkelmann (Tanz- und Ballettfotografie), Atelier Fayer (Wien), Trude Fleischmann (1895–1990, Wien, New York), Gertrud Fuld (München), Germin (Hamburg), Roswitha Hecke (Bremen, Bochum, Hamburg/Peter Zadek), Elisabeth Henrichs (Hamburg), Oliver Herrmann (Berlin), Hans Holdt (München), Wilfried Hösl (München), Heinz Köster (Berlin), Rolf Löckmann (Wuppertal), Pit Ludwig (Darmstadt), Hans Meyer-Veden (Hamburg), Stefan Odry (Köln), Barbara Pflaum (Wien), Fritz Peyer (Hamburg), Wilfried Rabanus (München), Willy Saeger (1901–85, Berlin), Ingeborg Sello (Hamburg), Kurt Saurin-Sorani (1909–77, Wuppertal), Gisela Scheidler (Berlin), Peter Schnetz (Basel), Daisy Steinberg (Recklinghausen, Bonn), Hildegard Steinmetz (München), Oda Sternberg (München), Sabine Toepffer (München), Abisag Tüllmann (Frankfurt), Liselotte Strelow (Düsseldorf, Berlin), Ruth Walz (Berlin), Ruth Wilhelmi (1904–77, Berlin), Madeleine Winkler-Betzendahl (Stuttgart, Berlin), Fritz Wolle (Hamburg, Bremen), Günter Wolfson (Hamburg), Hilde Zeman (Heidelberg, München), Axel Zeininger (Wien), Leonard Zubler (Zürich).

Balk, Cl.: Theaterfotografie. Eine Darstellung ihrer Geschichte anhand der Sammlung des Deutschen Theatermuseums. München 1989.

Ingeborg Janich

Theatergesetz

Begrifflich versteht man unter einem T. ein Gesetz, das die wesentlichen Rechtsfragen des Theaters regelt. Die Forderung nach einem T. ist alt, wenn auch jede Epoche diesen Begriff anders definierte. Im 18. Jh. (vgl. Ekhofs Bemühungen) sollte es die soziale Not der Schauspieler lindern helfen, in späterer Zeit sollte es umfassend die Beziehung des Theaters zum Staat sowie alle sonstigen Fragen regeln (Arbeitsrecht, Urheberrecht etc.). Als ein erstes T. mag das Stein-Hardenbergsche Theaterstatut von 1808 gelten, danach sollte das Theater als öffentliche Anstalt dem Ministerium für Kultur und Bildung unterstellt werden. Allerdings wurde das Statut nie in Kraft gesetzt. Im Vormärz und in der Zeit der Gründung des Bühnenvereins (→ Deutscher Bühnenverein) strebte man an, das Theater, seinem Bildungsauftrag entsprechend, der staatlichen Aufsicht zu unterstellen. 1848 wurde ein T. für Preußen erarbeitet, das jedoch wieder in den Archiven verschwand. 1858 beschloß der Bühnenverein, beim Dt. Bundestag und den verschiedenen Regierungen vorstellig zu werden, um ein «Allg. Theatergesetz» zu verabschieden, das «die Verhältnisse des Theaters zum öffentlichen Leben, zum Staat, zur Gesellschaft, die Bedingung einer Theaterkommission, die Abgrenzung des Ressorts der verschiedenen Theater in ein und derselben Stadt und alle dahin einschlagenden Fragen» regeln sollte. Auch diese Initiative führte nicht zur Verabschiedung eines T. Erst 1909, nachdem zwischen Bühnenverein und Bühnengenossenschaft die Verhandlungen über verschiedene Fragen gescheitert waren, ergriff die dt. Reichsregierung die Initiative, die wegen des Kriegs und des folgenden Zusammenbruchs jedoch nicht verwirklicht wurde. Eine quasi-gesetzliche Regelung wurde 1924 mit der Allgemeinverbindlichkeitserklärung des zwischen dem DBV und der Bühnengenossenschaft vereinbarten Normalvertrags erreicht; allerdings regelt dieser Tarifvertrag nur das Verhältnis zwischen dem Bühnenmitglied und dem Bühnenunternehmer. Ein T. wurde erst in der NS-Zeit erlassen: Am 15.5.1934 wurde das Reichstheatergesetz verabschiedet. Es hat jedoch wenig mit den bisher mit einem T. verbundenen Vorstellungen zu tun; mit ihm wurde das bisherige Theatersystem gleichgeschaltet. Sowohl die privaten als auch die öffentlichen Theater, die bisher der Kompetenz der jeweiligen Kulturministerien unterlagen, wurden dem Reichspropagandaministerium unterstellt. Die Gewerbefreiheit für den Theaterbereich wurde aufgehoben und die Eröffnung eines Theaters von einer Konzession abhängig gemacht. Dem Reichspropagandaminister oblag ferner die Bestätigung der Anstellungsverhältnisse der Bühnenvorstände, Intendanten; ferner konnte er Aufführungen untersagen bzw. absetzen. Eine weitere Kontrolle des Theaterwesens erfolgte über den →Reichsdramaturgen Schlösser, dem alle Spielpläne zur Genehmigung vorgelegt werden mußten, ferner über die Institution der →Reichstheaterkammer, Teil der Reichskulturkammer, deren Präsident Reichspropagandaminister Goebbels war.

Die bundesrepublikanische Rechtsordnung enthält kein T.; die Regelung der theaterspezifischen Rechtsverhältnisse ergibt sich aus dem Grundgesetz sowie den allg. Gesetzen. Bedeutsam ist in diesem Zusammenhang die in Art. 5 Abs. 3 GG garantierte Freiheit der Kunst. Diese grundgesetzliche Bestimmung führt im Einzelfall jedoch nur zu einer Gesetzauslegung, die versucht, der Besonderheit des Theaters gerecht zu werden.

Drewniak, B.: Das Theater im NS-Staat. Düsseldorf 1984; Erbel, G.: Inhalt und Auswirkung der verfassungsrechtlichen Kunstfreiheitsgarantie. Berlin 1966; Götz von Olenhusen, A.: Handbuch des Medienrechts, Tl. 2. 2 Bde. Freiburg 1988; Klein, W.: Der Preußische Staat und das Theater im Jahre 1848. Berlin 1924; Schrieber/Metten-Lollatz: Das Recht der Reichskulturkammer. 2 Bde. Berlin 1943.

Roswitha Körner

Theater in den Konzentrationslagern

Zu fast allen größeren nationalsozialistischen Konzentrationslagern liegen Berichte über theatralische Darbietungen vor. Aufgeführt wurden zumeist Programme und Stücke, die auf die Situation der Häftlinge direkt oder indirekt Bezug nahmen; zu einem großen Teil entstanden die Texte in den Lagern selbst. Soweit Theaterarbeit nicht reine SS-Auftragsleistung war, enthielt sie immer auch die Möglichkeit zur Demonstration der eigenen Ungebrochenheit; durch Rückgriff auf die kulturelle und politische Tradition ließen sich gegen alle Erniedrigungen kollektiv Selbstbewußtsein wiederherstellen und Überlebenswille mobilisieren. Dies geschah vor allem durch Kleinformen wie Rezitation, Couplets, Sketche u. ä., die nur einen minimalen technischen Aufwand erforderten; heimlich in den Lagerbaracken, aber auch vor der SS wurden Programme aufgeführt, die an die Intentionen des politischen Kabaretts und der Arbeiterkulturbewegung anknüpften. Wichtige Mittel dieser Revuen wie auch der größeren Stücke waren satirische Anspielung und Analogie; das Medium Theater bot zudem die Möglichkeit, den satirisch-ironischen Effekt auch durch die schauspielerische Präsentation eines vom Wortlaut her unverfänglichen

Textes zu erzeugen (z. B. *Schreckenstein* von R. Kalmar, E. Geschonneck und V. Matejka in Dachau 1943). Theaterarbeit in den KZs war immer mit Lebensgefahr für die aufführenden Häftlinge verbunden; nicht zuletzt deshalb sind nur wenige längere Texte überliefert. Die Rekonstruktion bleibt weitgehend auf die Berichte der Überlebenden angewiesen.

Goldfarb, A.: Theatre and Drama and the Nazi Concentration Camps. Diss. City University of New York, 1978, p. 25–47; Naumann, U.: Zwischen Tränen und Gelächter. Satirische Faschismuskritik 1933 bis 1945. Köln 1983, S. 216–227; Schneider, W.: Kunst hinter Stacheldraht. Leipzig [2]1976.

Rolf D. Krause

Theater in der Josefstadt (Wien)

Das T. i. d. J. (eröffnet 1788) ist das größte österr. Privattheater mit drei bespielten Bühnen: die Hauptbühne im 7. Wiener Gemeindebezirk, die dem Theater den Namen gab, mit 774 Plätzen, die Kammerspiele im Stadtzentrum mit 528 Plätzen und dem Rabenhof (Werkraumtheater und Probebühne, 300 Plätze). Das T. i. d. J. versteht sich als ‹moderne Kammerbühne›, deren Spielplan sich aus Boulevardstücken, Volksstücken, klassischen Problemstücken (des 20. Jh.) und gelegentlich Klassikern zusammensetzt. Subventioniert wird das T. i. d. J. durch Stadt Wien und österr. Staat.

«Mit den besten Lustspielen, Opern, Balletts und Pantomimen» wollte der Gründer des T. i. d. J., Karl Mayer, sein Publikum unterhalten. Nach mehrmaligem Pächter- und Besitzerwechsel wird das renovierte Haus 1822 wiedereröffnet. Gespielt werden heitere und ernste Volksstücke, Zauberspiele, Melodramen, Lustspiele und Pantomimen. Unter der Direktion von Johann August Stöger beginnt eine massive Förderung der Oper (ab 1832), die als Gattung den Spielplan bis Mitte der 50er Jahre bestimmt. Als 1889 Josef Jarno die Direktion übernimmt (bis 1923), führt er das moderne literarische Theater ein: Neben qualitativ hochwertigen Boulevardstücken ruft er die Tradition der ‹Literarischen Matineen› ins Leben. 1923/24 wird das Haus von dem Wiener Architekten Prof. Carl Witzmann umgebaut nach den Vorstellungen Max Reinhardts im Stil des Teatro Fenice in Venedig. Am 1. 4. 1924 Eröffnung mit Goldonis *Diener zweier Herren*. Reinhardt gibt dem Ensemble die Bezeichnung «Die Schauspieler im Theater in der Josefstadt unter Führung von Max Reinhardt». Dieses Motto zeigt sein Programm bezüglich seiner Arbeit mit den Schauspielern. In der Zeit von 1924 bis 1937 hat Reinhardt in 27 Inszenierungen selber Regie geführt; als er im September 1925 die Leitung seiner Berliner Bühnen wieder übernimmt, vertritt ihn Emil Geyer. 1933 übergibt er die Direk-

988 Theaterkritik

tion an Otto Ludwig Preminger, ab 1935 versucht Ernst Lothar mit einem «Spielplan der Dichtung» Stücke mit humanistischem Charakter durchzusetzen. Nach der endgültigen Übersiedlung Reinhardts in die USA übernimmt Heinz Hilpert die Direktion des T. i. d. J.

Nach dem 2. Weltkrieg bereits am 1. 5. 1945 Fortsetzung des Spielbetriebs; am 8. 6. ist die offizielle Eröffnungspremiere des Direktoriums Rudolf Steinboeck mit einem «Europäischen Einakterabend» (Tschechow, Courteline, Nestroy). «... Reinhardt hat Problemtheater und Boulevardtheater, neben sparsamer Klassikerpflege, vom Schauspieler aus inszeniert und, in die höchste Form des Komödiantischen gehoben, als Programm dargeboten. Genauso ist es seit 1945 geblieben...» (Kindermann, 1963). Dieser Tradition fühlten sich auch die folgenden Direktorien verpflichtet. Direktoren nach 1945: 1945–53 Rudolf Steinboeck (*1908), 1953–58 (gem. mit Franz Stoß) und 1977–84 Ernst Haeussermann (1916–84), 1958–77 Franz Stoß, 1984–87 Heinrich Kraus, 1986 designiert Boy Gobert (1925–86), seit Anfang 1988 Otto Schenk und Robert Jungbluth. Berühmte Josefstädter: Hugo Thimig (1854–1944), Helene Thimig (1889–1974), Hermann Thimig (1890–1982), Hans Thimig (1900–91), Adrienne Gessner (1896–1987), Hans Moser (1880–1964), Ernst Deutsch (1890–1969), Fritz Kortner (1892–1970), Leopold Rudolf (1911–78), Vilma Degischer, Hilde Krahl, Christine Ostermayer, Elfriede Ott, Hans Holt, Guido Wieland.

Bauer, A.: Das Theater in der Josefstadt zu Wien. Wien/München 1957; Bauer, A./Kropatschek, G.: 200 Jahre Theater in der Josefstadt. Wien/München 1988; Gregor, J.: Das Theater in der Wiener Josefstadt. Wien 1924; 175 Jahre Theater in der Josefstadt. 1788–1963. Wien 1963; Kindermann, H.: 175 Jahre Theater in der Josefstadt. In: 175 Jahre Theater in der Josefstadt. 1788–1963. Wien 1963; Klingenbeck, F. (Hg.): Max Reinhardts Theater in der Josefstadt. Salzburg 1972.

Ute Hagel/Red.

Theaterkritik

Teil der literarischen Kritik, jedoch umfassender, weil von einem Ereignis abgeleitet, das nahezu alle Künste in einen Zusammenhang gegenseitiger Reflexion und Kommentierung bringt; beschreibender, interpretierender, einordnender und wertender, auch glossierender Bericht über einen abgeschlossenen, nur bedingt wiederholbaren Vorgang auf der Bühne nach subjektiven Kriterien für Presse, Funk oder Fernsehen (veröff. Meinung). Erläuterung und Darstellung sowohl der literarischen Vorlage, der Absicht des Autors, als auch der theatralischen Realisierung und deren Absicht. Journalistische Tätigkeit und deren Gesetzen unterworfen (meist vorgegebene Länge des Berichts), adressiert an Laien und Fachleute, darum Bemühen um substantiiert verständlichen, möglichst ‹feuilletonistischen› Stil ohne wissenschaftlichen Anspruch; Niveau der Argumentation abhängig vom intellektuellen Level des auftraggebenden Organs. Von unbestreitbarem, aber oft überschätztem Einfluß auf Karrieren, Besucherzahlen der Theater und Erfolg von Theaterstücken. Kunstrichterfunktion, in der Wirkung abhängig vom Renommee des Theaterkritikers und des Publikationsorgans. Voraussetzung ist keine spezielle Ausbildung, aber Kenntnis der Produktionsweisen des Theaters und Information über Tendenzen und Innovationen des Theaters allgemein und in den verschiedenen Zentren. Problem und steter Vorwurf ist die Frage nach den Kriterien eines Urteils. Sie können immer nur jeweils neu aus der Differenz von Absicht und Ausführung, Anspruch und Ergebnis nach eigener Sicht und (auch weltanschaulicher) Überzeugung des Kritikers vom ‹Richtigen›, seiner Erwartung an das Theater, die sich auch in Forderungen an die Bühne artikuliert, gewonnen werden.

Die T. entwickelte sich mit der Bildung einer kritischen Öffentlichkeit durch die Presse im 18. Jh. in Deutschland. Als erster Theaterkritiker gilt G. E. Lessing (1729–81). Obwohl Angestellter des Hamburger Nationaltheaters, informierte er nicht nur über die Absichten der Bühne und erörterte grundsätzliche ästhetische Fragen, sondern besprach auch die Aufführungen kritisch (→Hamburgische Dramaturgie). Die Beurteilung schauspielerischer Leistungen mußte er allerdings nach einem eher wohlwollenden, höflich umschriebenen Einwand gegen eine Darstellerin aufgeben. Ständige T. seit Ende des 18. Jh. Häufig journalistisches Forum von Dichtern zur Propagierung ästhetischer Programme. Wichtiger Einfluß von Ludwig Tieck (1773–1853) auf die romantische Auffassung des Theaters und der Schauspielkunst («Dresdner Abendzeitung»). Politisch-gesellschaftlich orientierte T. durch Ludwig Börne (1786–1837); literarische Feuilletons als T. in Korrespondentenberichten Heinrich Heines (1797–1856) aus Paris; Wortführer des «Jungen Deutschland» (auch in eigener Sache) Heinrich Laube (1806–84). Problematisch die Entwicklung der «Nachtkritik», oft undifferenziert polemisch (Moritz Saphir, 1795–1858).

Beginn einer Spezialisierung in Schauspiel- oder Opern-/Ballett-Kritik: 1870 bis 1890 schrieb Theodor Fontane (1819–98) für die Berliner «Vossische Zeitung» T. mit bescheidenem Dafürhalten ohne Besserwisserei, kritisch gegen «pietätvoll-verlogene» Hoftheater-Inszenierungen und aufgeschlossen für das Neue (Naturalisten), wie auch der Kritiker und spätere Theaterleiter Otto Brahm (1856–1912). In den ersten Jahrzehnten des 20. Jh. in Berlin neben Siegfried Jacobsohn (1881–1926) und Julius Bab (1880–1955) Antipoden Alfred Kerr (1867–1948), der in expressionistischem Telegrammstil aphoristisch pointierte, manchmal ge-

990 Theaterkritik

reimte T. von unerbittlicher Subjektivität und Schärfe im «Berliner Tageblatt» schrieb und Kritik als Kunst gesehen wissen wollte, und Herbert Ihering (1888–1977), der weniger für die Zeitungsleser als für die Theaterleute schrieb, sich gegen das Kommerztheater wandte und sich im «Berliner Börsen-Courier» vehement für Ernst Barlach (1870–1938) und den jungen Brecht (1898–1956) einsetzte sowie für den Regisseur Erwin Piscator (1893–1966). Ihering postulierte: «Die Fähigkeit eines Kritikers beweist sich darin, mit seinen kritischen Argumenten den Regisseur zu überzeugen, ihn zu befruchten, damit er für seine nächste Arbeit daraus Nutzen ziehen kann.» In Wien wesentlich Karl Kraus (1874–1936). In Frankfurt/M. Bernhard Diebold (1886–1945). – Im «Dritten Reich» wurde T. durch «Kunstbetrachtung» ersetzt.

Nach 1945 mit dem Verlust der Theaterhauptstadt auch Dezentralisierung der T. von Einfluß. Wesentliche Impulse der deutschsprachigen T. gingen und gehen aus von Benjamin Henrichs, Georg Hensel, Peter Iden, Joachim Kaiser, Hellmuth Karasek, Walter Karsch, Heinz Klunker, Friedrich Luft, Siegfried Melchinger, Hennig Rischbieter, Günther Rühle, Jochen Schmidt, Albert Schulze Vellinghaus, in Österreich Hilde Spiel, in der Schweiz Elisabeth Brock-Sulzer.

In der DDR war die fachlich autorisierte Theaterkritik vor allem in der seit 1946 erscheinenden Zeitschrift «Theater der Zeit» versammelt. In den 50er Jahren unterstützten viele Kritiker die dogmatische Kulturpolitik der DDR, indem sie die Inszenierungen an einem (sehr eng gefaßten) Realismus-Begriff maßen (z. B. Fritz Erpenbeck, der die sog. spätbürgerliche Moderne ablehnte und Brechts künstlerische Einbürgerung behinderte). Als sich auf den Bühnen allmählich auch Dramaturgien und Spielweisen entwickelten, die nicht ins tradierte Spieler-Gegenspieler-Modell paßten, folgte die T. zeitversetzt diesem Wandel. Seit den 70er Jahren unterstützten viele Kritiker künstlerisch innovative, auch politisch von der DDR-Staatsräson abweichende Inszenierungen. (Beispiele: Martin Linzer, Friedrich Dieckmann u. a.). Darum gehörten behördliche Eingriffe in die T. ins Tagesgeschäft der Redaktionen. Diese Praxis förderte eine eher bedächtige, verhüllende Schreibweise, die mehr auf die subtile Spiegelung künstlerischer Leistungen als auf subjektiv zuspitzende Polemik setzte. Methodische Grundlage bildete dabei für viele Kritiker (wie Ch. Funke oder I. Pietzsch) Brechts Vorschlag zur Beschreibung schauspielerischer Vorgänge, wie sie im Handbuch «Theaterarbeit. 6 Aufführungen des Berliner Ensembles» exemplarisch dargestellt sind.

Hamm, P. (Hg.): Kritik von wem, für wen, wie 1968; Hensel, G.: Anmaßungen der Theaterkritik. Darmstadt 1968; Jánosi, A.-M.: Theaterkritiker als Theaterschriftsteller. Journalismus und Theater in Wien von der Jahrhundertwende bis 1933. Diss. Wien 1987; Krechel, U.: Information und Wertung. Diss. Köln 1972; Melchinger, S.: Keine Maßstäbe? Zürich 1959; Meier, P.: «Schlagt ihn tot, den

Hund! Er ist ein Rezensent.» Theater- und Literaturkritik. Gümlingen/Bonn 1987; Michael, F.: Die Anfänge der T. in Deutschland. 1905.

Werner Schulze-Reimpell/Roland Dreßler

Theater-Manufaktur Berlin

Freie Gruppe in Berlin (West), gegründet 1972 von zehn Wiener und westdeutschen Schauspielern um Otto Zonschitz (*1939), Ilse Scheer (*1936) und den Musiker Rudolf Stodola (*1946). Ihre Produktionsstätte war bis 1982 eine ehemalige Schokoladenfabrik in Neukölln, seitdem im alten Haus der →Schaubühne am Lehniner Platz. – Die T. versteht sich als politisches Volkstheater-Kollektiv, das in seinen, meist von Zonschitz verfaßten und inszenierten Stücken historisch-dokumentarisches Material (von den deutschen Bauernkriegen bis zum südamerikanischen Befreiungskampf) aufarbeitet und revueartig-lehrstückhaft präsentiert. Wichtigste Produktionen: *1848* (1973), *Johann Faustus* (1977), Libretto der unvertonten Oper von Hanns Eisler (1898–1962), dessen Uraufführung Zonschitz schon 1974 am Landestheater Tübingen besorgt hatte; *Das Richtfest* (Auftragsarbeit für die Ruhrfestspiele Recklinghausen und die Berliner Festwochen 1978); *Murieta* nach Pablo Neruda (Auftragsarbeit für die Württembergischen Staatstheater Stuttgart 1979). Auch Inszenierungen von Stücken Brechts, Peter Weiss' und Nestroys; Kabarett-Programme und Liederabende. Seit dem Umzug ins Haus am Halleschen Ufer tritt die T. künstlerisch auf der Stelle. Viele Gastspiele im In- und Ausland, 1979 Kulturpreis des DGB.

Andreas Roßmann

Theateroktober

Von W. E. Meyerhold, 1920/21 Leiter der Theaterabteilung (russ. Teatral'nyj otdel = TEO) des Kommissariats für Volksbildung, proklamierte Umgestaltung des Theaters im Gefolge der Oktoberrevolution. Hauptgedanken: 1. Errichtung eines Systems führender Theater im ganzen Land; 2. Politisierung der Theaterprogramme; 3. Einrichtung von Bildungsinstitutionen zum Zwecke der Erarbeitung und Vermittlung neuer ideologischer Formen; 4. Kampf gegen die professionellen bürgerlichen Theater, die eine den Ideen des Kommunismus feindliche Gesellschaftsordnung propagierten. – Ästhetische Aufgaben in Regie, Darstellung, Bühnenbild treten zurück zugunsten von →Agitprop, der

Sichtbarmachung von Konstruktionslinien, einem «offenen Theater»: «Keine Pausen, kein Psychologisieren und kein ‹Erleben› auf der Bühne und bei der Erarbeitung der Rolle. Das ist unsere Maxime. Viel Licht, Freude, Wucht und Schwungkraft, unbeschwertes Schöpfertum, Miteinbeziehen des Publikums in die Handlung – das ist unser Programm» (Meyerhold 1920). Klassische Stücke dienten nur noch als «Kanevas» für «szenische Konstruktionen», Anregungen kamen vom Laientheater (Arbeiter, Soldaten), inszeniert wurden Massenspektakel wie *Sturm auf das Winterpalais* (1920), gesucht waren neue Stücke im Sinne von Agitationsschauspielen für die Sache der proletarischen Revolution.

Programmatischen Charakter hatten die Inszenierungen von W. W. Majakowskis *Mysterium buffo* (1918), von E. Verhaerens sozialutopischem Drama *Die Morgenröte* (1920). Zeigte sich an ihnen, daß die Literatur imstande war, Theater zu schaffen, so galt umgekehrt von nun an, daß auch das Theater Literatur schaffen konnte: W. N. Bill-Bjelozerkowski, K. A. Trenjow, S. M. Tretjakow, W. W. Majakowski, W. W. Wischnewski vertreten die neue sowj. Dramatik. Die Auseinandersetzungen um die Regie finden zwischen Meyerhold, Stanislawski, Tairow (psychologisch-naturalistische Darstellung), → Wachtangow (Wegfall der «vierten Wand»), Ochlopkow, Popow statt.

Die anfängliche Dynamik des sowj. Theaters ist durch Stalinherrschaft und Weltkrieg in eine Stagnation geraten, aus der sie sich erst allmählich wieder löste. Die Innovationen der 20er Jahre haben im Westen weitreichendere Folgen gehabt als in der Sowjetunion, wo sie jedoch gleichfalls nicht verdrängt werden konnten (zu nennen sind die Regisseure G. Towstonogow, Ju. Ljubimow, A. Efros, B. Lwow-Anochin).

Hoffmann, L. / Wardetzky, D. (Hg.): Meyerhold, W. E. / Tairow, A. I. / Wachtangow, Je. B.: Theateroktober. Leipzig 1967; Mailand-Hansen, C.: Mejerhol'ds Theaterästhetik in den 1920er Jahren. Kopenhagen 1980; Rudnickij, K.: Mejerchol'd. Moskva 1981; Tietze, R. (Hg.): Vsevolod Meyerhold. Theaterarbeit 1917–30. München 1974; Zolotnickij, D.: Zori teatral'nogo oktjabrja. Leningrad 1976; ders.: Budni i prazdniki teatral'nogo oktjabrja. Leningrad 1978.

Annelore Engel-Braunschmidt

Theaterpädagogik

T. (→ Spielpädagogik) ist ein integrierter Teil der Spiel-, Theater- und Interaktionserziehung. T. im engeren Sinne meint die Vermittlungsbemühungen der allgemeinbildenden Schule und des professionellen Theaters insbesondere gegenüber jüngeren Besuchern, die über den Besuch der Aufführung hinausgehen; in ihren Formen ist diese T. mit den Formen der Spiel- und Theaterpädagogik weitgehend identisch. T. meint weiter die künstlerische Ausbildung zum professionellen Theater, zum Beruf des Regisseurs, des Bühnen- und Kostümbildners und insbesondere des Schauspielers.

Über die Frage, wie die Qualifikationen zum Regisseur pädagogisch zu vermitteln sind, gehen die Meinungen weit auseinander. Im westlichen deutschsprachigen Raum gibt es Ausbildungsgänge in Form von ‹Regieklassen› an Schauspielabteilungen von Musikhochschulen in Wien, Graz, Salzburg und Essen. Neue Studiengänge für Schauspielregie wurden in Hamburg und München eingerichtet; sie werden von den Universitäten in Verbindung mit den Staatstheatern durchgeführt. Überlegungen zu einer institutionalisierten Regieausbildung als Aufbaustudium (nach Schauspiel oder Theaterwissenschaft) oder im Rahmen einer ‹Theaterakademie› werden seit einigen Jahren an mehreren Orten angestellt. Ein ausformuliertes pädagogisches Konzept gibt es dafür ebensowenig wie für die heute dominierende Ausbildung von Regisseuren als Assistenten direkt am Theater. In dieser Funktion erwerben auch die Bühnen- und Kostümbildner einen Teil ihrer Berufsqualifikation, nachdem sie in der Regel an einer Hochschule für bildende Künste meist in einem engen Meister-Schüler-Verhältnis studiert haben.

Von einer T. im Sinne einer überindividuell gültigen Konzeption kann lediglich in bezug auf die Schauspielerausbildung (→ Schauspielschulen) gesprochen werden. Ihre heutige Erscheinung gründet in der schauspielmethodischen Problematik des frühen bürgerlichen Dramas und Theaters. Während in den vorhergehenden Epochen die kaum hinterfragte Weitergabe des handwerklichen Instrumentariums in der praktischen Arbeit selbst die Regel war, wird mit der (von Diderot und Lessing zuerst aufgestellten) Forderung nach Illusionierung des Zuschauers und – damit in Zusammenhang – der psychologischen Ausdifferenzierung der Figuren das Verhältnis zwischen Schauspieler und Rolle problematisch. Im Sinne einer glaubwürdigen Darstellung muß der Schauspieler nun einerseits die Rolle, andererseits seine eigene psycho-physische Disposition analysieren und beide in Relation setzen. Wie das zu geschehen hat, wird zur zentralen Frage der Schauspieltheorie und dann der Schauspielmethodik und -pädagogik. Schon um die Mitte des 18. Jh. stehen sich die Befürworter zweier unterschiedlicher Standpunkte gegenüber. Die einen fordern vom Schauspieler absolute Bewußtheit und keinerlei Gefühl (‹Bewußtseinstheorie›, von Diderot und Francesco Riccoboni vertreten), die anderen das Ausfüllen der Rolle mit eigenem Erleben, ohne jedes Kontrollbewußtsein (‹Selbsttäuschungstheorie›, vertreten von Raimond de St. Albin). Daß beide Ansätze, in dieser Radikalität vertreten, nicht realisierbar sind, liegt auf der Hand. In der Praxis setzt sich das schauspielerische Handeln immer aus einer einfühlend-miterlebenden und einer demonstrierend-kontrollierenden Komponente zusammen.

994 Theaterpädagogik

In erster Linie auf die Schulung der Fähigkeit zur Einfühlung zielt das bisher umfassendste schauspielpädagogische Konzept, das von Konstantin Sergejewitsch Stanislawski (1863–1938) ca. 1910 in enger Verbindung zu seiner Arbeit als Schauspieler und Regisseur am ‹Moskauer Künstlertheater› entwickelte ‹System› ab (→Stanislawski-System). Ausgehend vom allgemeinen Programm eines ‹geistig-seelischen Naturalismus› und dessen Grundforderung nach glaubwürdiger Darstellung, umfaßt es einen ‹Psychotechnik› genannten Komplex von Gedanken und Übungen zur Aktivierung der ‹inneren Komponenten› des Schauspielers sowie eine ab ca. 1925 entstandene, als ‹Theorie der physischen Handlungen› bezeichnete Methodik der auf genauer Stück- und Rollenanalyse beruhenden Schaffung des ‹Körperlebens› der Figur. Je nach Aufgabe, Situation und individueller Disposition – so der Vorschlag von Stanislawski in der letzten Fassung seines immer wieder variierten ‹Systems› – soll der Schauspieler von der intellektuell bestimmten Handlungsabsicht, von der Aktivierung des Gefühls oder vom logischen Vollzug der Handlung in ihrer physischen Dimension ausgehen. Die methodisch-pädagogische Konzeption von Stanislawski und ihre Adaption durch Lee Strasberg in →The Method sind bis heute das Kernstück der T., wie sie in den →Schauspielschulen Anwendung findet. Die von Bertolt Brecht entwickelten Methoden, die auf eine Stärkung der demonstrativen Komponente des schauspielerischen Handelns durch die Nachahmung des in der Umwelt Beobachteten und durch die Parteinahme zum Verhalten der Figur hinzielen, werden heute nicht als Alternative, sondern als wichtige Ergänzungen zum Stanislawski-System berücksichtigt. In den westlichen Ländern sind jüngst auch Methoden und Techniken des →Armen Theaters von Jerzy Grotowski zum Bestandteil der T. geworden. Meist abgelöst von der dahinterstehenden Theaterideologie werden manchmal auch Ansätze fernöstlicher Theaterformen in die T. integriert. Bezugsfelder sind auch die allgemeine Körperbildung (Gymnastik, Bioenergetik), der Kampfsport (Aikido, Fechten), die Akrobatik, die Atemschulung und Sprecherziehung sowie die Literaturwissenschaft (Dramenanalyse).

Brecht, B.: Schriften zum Theater. Frankfurt/M. 1963; Ebert, G./Penka, R. (Hg.): Handbuch Schauspielen. Berlin 1981; Handeln und Betrachten. Materialien zu einer Theorie der Spiel- und Theaterpädagogik. Berlin 1985; Klöden, G. v.: Grundlagen der Schauspielkunst. Velber 1967; Ritter, H. M. (Hg.): Spiel- und Theaterpädagogik. Berlin 1990; Stanislawski, K. S.: Die Arbeit des Schauspielers an sich selbst. Bd. 1 und 2. Berlin 1961 und 1963; ders.: Die Arbeit des Schauspielers an der Rolle. Berlin 1965.

Peter Simhandl

Theaterreform um 1900

Die als T. bezeichnete Erscheinung, deren Hauptvertreter als Programmatiker und Regisseure Adolphe Appia (1862–1928), Edward Gordon Craig (1872–1966), Peter Behrens (1868–1940), Georg Fuchs (1868–1949), Wsewolod Emiljewitsch Meyerhold (1874–1940) und Jacques Copeau (1879–1949) waren, ist ein wichtiger Wendepunkt der Theatergeschichte: Das Illusionsprinzip, wie es das Theater seit seiner Indienstnahme durch das Bürgertum beherrschte, und der Naturalismus als seine konsequenteste Ausformung werden radikal in Frage gestellt. Mit der Abkehr der ‹kulturtragenden Schichten› von der als immer bedrohlicher empfundenen industriellen Massengesellschaft und ihrem wachsenden Konfliktpotential entfällt die Motivation zu ihrer detailgenauen Nachahmung auf der Bühne. Die Reformer opponieren gegen die ‹Rationalität› des →naturalistischen Theaters und gegen seinen ‹Nützlichkeitsstandpunkt›; die Darstellung des sozialen Elends und die damit verbundene Mitleidshaltung lehnen sie ab. Das Theater soll nach Ansicht der Reformer nicht wie im Naturalismus (→Naturalistisches Theater) die empirisch faßbare Wirklichkeit widerspiegeln, sondern Symbole finden für die dahinter verborgenen ‹ewigen Wesenheiten› wie Ruhe, Harmonie und Schönheit. Mit der Beschwörung solcher Werte wird die Theaterkunst für breite Schichten des gehobenen Bürgertums und der Aristokratie zu einem Ort der Flucht aus der als unerträglich empfundenen Realität. Entsprechend Friedrich Nietzsches Postulat, daß das Dasein und die Welt nur als ästhetische Phänomene gerechtfertigt sind, wird das ‹Reich des Schönen› als die eigentliche Wirklichkeit aufgefaßt und das Kunstwerk zum Modell des Lebens erhoben. Ausgehend von der ‹Parole Individualität›, die sie ebenfalls von Friedrich Nietzsche übernehmen, setzen die Theaterreformer den subjektiven künstlerischen Ausdruck als neues Ideal an die Stelle des Objektivitätsstrebens der Naturalisten. Das Theaterkunstwerk soll allein die Visionen und Träume seines Schöpfers spiegeln. Die einzelne Künstlerpersönlichkeit muß deshalb die uneingeschränkte Verfügungsgewalt über alle ihr zu Gebote stehenden Kunstmittel besitzen. In der Konzeption von Adolphe Appia ist es der Autor des fiktiven ‹Wort-Ton-Dramas›, der durch die Musik die Bewegung des Darstellers und über diese wieder die Struktur des mit geometrischen Körpern ausgestatteten ‹Rhythmischen Raums› bestimmt; bei Gordon Craig dagegen ist der Regisseur der Schöpfer des Theaterkunstwerks, der alle Mittel in die Hand bekommt, indem ihm gestattet wird, das Drama auf die ihm wesentlich erscheinende ‹zentrale Idee› zu reduzieren, den Schauspieler nach dem Ideal der →Über-Marionette zu seinem Exekutivorgan zu machen und das Bühnenbild schließlich entsprechend seiner Vision selbst zu gestalten.

Die Entlastung der Theaterkunst vom Zwang zur ‹lebensechten› Darstellung hat zur Institutionalisierung des Regisseurs als schöpferischem Künstler geführt, der sich autonom verhält nicht nur zur Realität (‹Theatralisierung des Theaters› ist ein wichtiges Stichwort der T.), sondern auch zur dramatischen Literatur, zu der er nun nicht mehr eine ‹dienende› Haltung einnimmt, sondern eine interpretierende, die er einfach als ‹Material› benutzt. Die kreative Energie des Regisseurs wird befördert durch die Wiederentdeckung von Ausdrucksmitteln wie Musik und Tanz, Pantomime und Maskenspiel, Clownerie und Akrobatik. Formen des nichtillusionistischen Volkstheaters wie der →Commedia dell'arte, der mittelalterlichen frz. Farce, des russ. Jahrmarkttheaters gewinnen Vorbildfunktion. Das künstlich-spielhafte Moment von Theater erfährt eine umfassende Renaissance in den konzeptionellen Überlegungen von Gordon Craig sowie in der vorrevolutionären Theaterarbeit von Meyerhold und bei Copeau.

Parallel dazu zeigt sich innerhalb der T. ein starkes Bemühen um die Wiedergewinnung der mythisch-kultischen Dimension von Theater (in erster Linie bei Appia, Behrens, Fuchs). Unter Berufung auf das Theater der Antike und das geistliche Spiel des Mittelalters konzipieren und veranstalten die Theaterreformer oft als →Massentheater gedachte, religiös akzentuierte →Festspiele, die als Bestandteil einer umfassenden Reform der Lebenskultur sowie als Alternative zum kommerzialisierten Routine-Theater verstanden werden. Wichtig ist ihre gemeinschaftsbildende Funktion; in einer ‹rauschhaften› Kommunikation sollen Darsteller und Zuschauer zu einer Einheit verschmelzen und dabei eine seelische Reinigung erfahren. Als Bedingung dafür werden einerseits eine metrisch-stilisierte Sprechweise und eine statuarische oder rhythmisch-tänzerische Bewegungsform angesehen, andererseits eine neue Architektur, bei der die seichte Relief-Bühne (→‹Stilbühne›) und der Zuschauerraum – etwa durch den ‹Blumensteg› des japanischen Theaters – miteinander verbunden werden und die Rampe, die den Reformern geradezu als Symbol für das naturalistische Theater gilt, aufgehoben ist.

Appia, A.: Die Musik und die Inscenierung. München 1899; Balme, Ch. (Hg.): Das Theater von morgen. Texte zur deutschen Theaterreform (1870–1920). Würzburg 1988; Behrens, P.: Feste des Lebens und der Kunst. Leipzig 1900; Brauneck, M.: Theater im 20. Jh. Reinbek bei Hamburg 1982; Copeau, J.: Registres I. Appels. Paris 1974; Craig, E. G.: Über die Kunst des Theaters. Berlin 1969; Fiebach, J.: Von Craig bis Brecht. Berlin 1975; Fuchs, G.: Die Schaubühne der Zukunft. Berlin/Leipzig o. J.; Meyerhold, W. E.: Schriften. Berlin 1979; Simhandl, P.: Konzeptionelle Grundlagen des heutigen Theaters. Berlin 1985.

Peter Simhandl

Theatersammlung / -museum / -archiv

T. ist zumeist gleichzeitig Bibliothek, Archiv und Museum. Planmäßige Sammlung und Archivierung von Primär- und Sekundärliteratur (Bücher, Zeitschriften, Stücktexte, Manuskripte, Programmhefte, Aufführungskritiken, Zeitungsausschnitte), Handschriften, Briefen, Bildern, Dias, Aufführungsfotos, Plakaten, Bühnenbildmodellen, Entwürfen, Zeichnungen, Kostümentwürfen, Tonträgern etc. Viele T. sind zusammengeschlossen in der Société Internationale des Bibliothèques et Musées des Arts du Spectacle (SIBMAS).

Wichtige T.: Institut für Theaterwissenschaft der Freien Universität Berlin (gegr. 1948 von Prof. H. Knudsen, aufgebaut auf der theaterhistorischen Sammlung W. Unruh); Archive, Sammlungen und Bibliotheken der Akademie der Künste, Berlin, und Archive der ehem. Akademie der Künste der DDR (u. a. Sammlung zum deutschen Exil, Tanzarchiv Leipzig, Personenarchive Bertolt Brecht, Erich Engel, Walter Felsenstein, Herbert Ihering, Ernst Legal, Hans Otto, Gustav von Wangenheim, Friedrich Wolf); Brecht-Zentrum, Berlin; Zentrum für Theaterdokumentation und -information Berlin (bes. Inszenierungsdok. seit 1967); Märkisches Museum Berlin, Abt. Berliner Theater- und Literaturgeschichte; Theaterbibliothek «Die Möwe», Berlin; Dumont-Lindemann-Archiv, Theatermuseum der Landeshauptstadt Düsseldorf (1933 gegr. von Gustav Lindemann, u. a. Nachlässe Gustaf Gründgens und Paul Henckels, Material Ära Stroux); Staatl. Kunstsammlungen Dresden, Puppentheatersammlung (Geschichte des Puppenspiels in Deutschland, bes. Sachsen); Stadt- und Universitätsbibliothek Frankfurt/M., Abteilung Musik, Theater und Medien, Sammlung Friedrich Nicolas Manskopf (Überregionale Sammlung der gesamten theater- und medienwissenschaftlichen Literatur des In- und Auslands für die Bundesrepublik Deutschland im Auftrag der Dt. Forschungsgemeinschaft. Zentrale Sammlung deutschsprachiger Bühnenmanuskripte); Museum der Stadt Gotha, Abt. Musik/Theater (mit Ekhof-Theater); Theatersammlung der Freien und Hansestadt Hamburg (gegr. 1940, Schwerpunkt hamburgische Theatergeschichte); Theatermuseum, verbunden mit dem Institut für Theater-, Film- und Fernsehwissenschaft der Universität Köln, Schloß Wahn (1919 gegr. von C. Niessen); Lessing-Museum Kamenz; Theaterhochschule «Hans Otto» Leipzig, Hochschulbibliothek und -archiv; Staatl. Museen Meiningen, Theatermuseum; Dt. Theatermuseum (früher Clara-Ziegler-Stiftung), München (eröffnet 1910, Sammlungen zur Theatergeschichte aller Völker und Zeiten); Neuberin-Museum Reichenbach/Vogtland; Stiftung Weimarer Klassik, Zentralbibliothek der dt. Klassik, Shakespeare-Bibliothek, «Faust»-Sammlung; Österreichisches Theatermuseum, eröffnet 1991, hervorgegangen aus der Theatersammlung der Österr. Nationalbibliothek (1922 gegr., Dokumentation des österr., deutschsprachigen und Welttheaters, Nachlässe bedeutender österr. Theaterleute); Institut für Theaterwissenschaft an der Universität Wien (1943 gegr. von H. Kindermann, seit 1955 Herausgabe der Zeitschrift «Maske und Kothurn. Internationale Beiträge zur Theaterwissenschaft»); Theaterhistorisches Museum Christiansborg, Kopenhagen (1912 gegr.); Bibliothek und Archiv des Nederlands Theater Instituut, Amsterdam; Bibliothèque Nationale Departements, Bibliothèque de l'Arsenal, Paris (gegr. im 18. Jh. von Marquis de Paulmy d'Argenson, seit 1797 öffentliche Bibliothek); Victoria and Albert Museum-Theatre Museum, London (gegr. 1974,

998 Theaterskandal

diverse Einzelsammlungen, auch ital. und frz. Theater des 18. und 19. Jh.); Biblioteca e raccolta teatrale del Burcardo, Rom (gegr. 1931, Sammlung der S.I.A.E., d. i.: Società Italiana degli Autori ed Editori); Museo teatrale alla Scala, Milano (seit 1913 Museum, seit 1954 Bibliothek, Schwerpunkt u. a. Commedia dell'arte); Schweizerische Theatersammlung, Bern (Nachlaß Adolphe Appia); Zentrales Staatliches Theatermuseum «Bachruschin», Moskau (1894 gegr.); Staatliche Theaterbibliothek «Lunatschcharski», Leningrad (1756 gegr., u. a. Zensurarchiv); New York Public Library, Billy Rose Theatre Collection (1931 eingerichtet, seit 1965 Teil des Lincoln Center for the Performing Arts).

Archive, Bibliotheken, Museen ... zum Bereich «Darstellende Künste» in der Bundesrepublik Deutschland. (Erlangen 1992); Veinstein, A./Golding, A. S. (Hg.): Bibliothèques et musées des arts du spectacle dans le monde. Paris 1985; Theatersammlungen in der Bundesrepublik Deutschland und Berlin (West). Berlin 1985

Ingeborg Janich/Manfred Pauli

Theaterskandal

Als der «Verein Freie Bühne» (→Freie Bühne) 1889 das erste Stück G. Hauptmanns *Vor Sonnenaufgang* aufführte, erlebte das wilhelminische Berlin seinen ersten großen Theaterskandal. Befürworter und Gegner der Aufführung lieferten sich heftige Wortgefechte, und auf dem Höhepunkt der Auseinandersetzungen warf ein bekannter Berliner Arzt eine mitgebrachte Geburtszange als Ausdruck seines Protestes auf die Bühne. Sowohl die Vorgänge im Parkett als auch die sich anschließenden Debatten um das soziale Drama Hauptmanns lassen diese Uraufführung als prototypischen Theaterskandal erscheinen. Die realistische Darstellung sozialen Elends enttäuschte die normative Erwartungshaltung eines Publikums, das eher an harmlose Possen gewöhnt war, und erschütterte den gesellschaftlichen Konsens über die Mittel und die Funktion des Theaters vor der Jahrhundertwende. Die Überschreitung dieses Konsenses ist eines der Strukturprinzipien des T. Allzu minuziöser Realismus ebenso wie die Darstellung von Gewalt und Sexualität oder vermeintliche Blasphemie auf der Bühne sind jene Tabus, an deren Durchbrechung sich immer wieder Skandale entzündeten. Wie die gesellschaftlichen unterliegen aber auch die theatralischen Tabus dem historischen Wandel. An welchen Themen sich die Gemüter bis zum Skandal erhitzen, ist an den jeweiligen Stand der theatralischen Konvention gebunden. Die Schocks, die der Naturalismus (→Naturalistisches Theater) um 1890 noch auslöste, gehörten zehn Jahre später bereits zum Repertoire dt. Bühnen.

Die Enttabuisierung, die Zumutung des Außerordentlichen, das die Skandale auslöst, geht meist von theatralischen Innovationen aus, deren Protagonisten jenen Konsens in Frage stellen. Vom Naturalismus über das →Zeitstück der 20er Jahre und das →Absurde Theater Becketts,

Ionescos u. a. bis hin zu den Provokationen des sog. →Regietheaters um 1970: Die Erweiterung und Neubestimmung des auf dem Theater Möglichen wurde nicht selten durch handfeste Theaterskandale eingeleitet. Je erstarrter die jeweiligen historischen Strukturen des Theaters sind, desto skandalöser müssen solche Innovationen dem Publikum erscheinen.

Das Kommunikationssystem Theater ist auf Grund seiner hochgradigen Ritualisierung besonders störanfällig gegenüber ‹aggressivem spektatorischen Konfliktverhalten›, das als Reaktion der ‹Ärgernis nehmenden› Zuschauer den Theaterskandal ausmacht. Der Verletzung des Tabus durch die Theatermacher steht der Bruch der kommunikativen Konvention durch zumindest einen Teil des Publikums gegenüber. Die Skandalierer durchbrechen – sei es durch massenhaften Exodus, begleitet von lautstarken Mißfallenskundgebungen, sei es durch handgreifliche Angriffe – ihre durch ritualisierte Reaktionsformen gekennzeichnete Zuschauerrolle. Sie versuchen, die Akteure auf der Bühne an der Wahrnehmung ihrer Rolle zu hindern und den nicht skandalierenden Teil des Publikums in ihre Empörung einzubeziehen.

Im außertheatralischen Raum findet der Skandal seine Fortsetzung, indem sich die Skandalierer an andere Institutionen wenden mit der Absicht, das Theater durch Druck von außen zu zwingen, die Aufführung abzusetzen. Statt die Zensurbehörde einzuschalten oder wie die Gegner des Naturalismus die Gerichte zu bemühen, nutzen sie heute vielmehr die wachsende Macht der Medien; die publizistische Resonanz, die sie finden, entscheidet über das Ausmaß eines Skandals. Besonders deutlich wurde diese Wechselwirkung zwischen in- und externer Öffentlichkeit bei den Vorfällen um *Der Müll, die Stadt und der Tod* von R. W. Fassbinder in Frankfurt, wo die Premiere durch eine Bühnenbesetzung von Mitgliedern der Jüdischen Gemeinde verhindert wurde. Die Aufführung war bereits im Vorfeld publizistisch skandaliert worden. Nach der verhinderten Premiere wuchs der öffentliche Widerstand gegen das als antisemitisch inkriminierte Stück derart, daß es auf lange Sicht unspielbar zu sein scheint.

Das Wissen um diese Funktionsmechanismen erlaubt es den Theatermachern, Skandale ‹herzustellen› und zu provozieren. So machten die ital. Futuristen (→Futuristisches Theater) und die Dadaisten (→Dadaistisches Theater) die Provokation des Publikums in ihren theatralischen Aktionen selbst zum Thema, der Skandal wurde zur rituellen Kunsthandlung erklärt. Das Ende der Skandalfähigkeit des Theaters ist allerdings in einem Moment erreicht, in dem das Publikum den Skandal als Bestandteil seiner Erwartungshaltung antizipiert hat.

Brauneck, M.: Theater im 20. Jh. Reinbek bei Hamburg 1982; Hensel, G.: Theaterskandale und andere Anlässe zum Vergnügen. Stuttgart 1983; Laermann, K.: Die gräßliche Bescherung. Anatomie des politischen Skandals. In: Kursbuch 77. Berlin 1984; Lichtenstein, H. (Hg.): Die Fassbinder-Kontroverse oder Das Ende

1000 Theatersystem (im deutschsprachigen Raum) ────────────────

der Schonzeit. Königstein/Ts. 1986; Paul, A.: Aggressive Tendenzen des Theaterpublikums. Diss. München 1969; Rühle, G.: Anarchie in der Regie? Frankfurt/
M. 1982.

Peter Kelting

Theatersystem (im deutschsprachigen Raum)

Die Struktur des bundesrepublikanischen Theatersystems
Das gegenwärtige Theater der Bundesrepublik stellt sich als ein im we-
sentlichen von staatlicher Beteiligung geprägtes System dar. Dieses in
den letzten drei Jh. stetig gewachsene T. läßt sich einteilen in
– die Theater der öffentlichen Hand,
– Privattheater,
– die sog. Freien Gruppen.
Das Deutsche Bühnenjahrbuch 1990 verzeichnet: 37 Staatstheater, 86
Stadttheater (einschl. Kreis/Land/Bund und/oder GmbH als Rechtsträger), 21 Landestheater, 6 Städtebundtheater, 79 Privattheater, 70
Tourneetheater.
Als *Theater der öffentlichen Hand* werden die Theater bezeichnet, deren Rechtsträger eine staatliche Körperschaft ist. Je nach Art der Rechtsträgerschaft handelt es sich um ein Staatstheater, ein Stadttheater oder
eine Landesbühne.
Die von der öffentlichen Hand getragenen Theater treten in verschiedenen Rechtsformen auf. Die häufigste Form ist der *Regiebetrieb*. Hierbei ist das Theater als Teil des Kulturamts/Referats in die städtische Verwaltung eingegliedert. Diese Rechtsform hat zur Konsequenz, daß die
Finanzierung nach den Grundsätzen des öffentlich-rechtlichen Haus-
haltswesens und der Kameralistik abgewickelt wird. Das jeweilige
Stadtparlament verabschiedet im Rahmen des Gesamtetats auch den
Theateretat. Über die Etathoheit übt es faktisch eine Kontrolle über das
Theater aus (etwa in der Frage der Bewilligung eines Nachtragshaushal-
tes, z. T. kann der Intendant Verträge nur bis zu einer bestimmten Höhe
allein unterzeichnen). Insb. gegenüber dem Kulturausschuß ist die Lei-
tung eines Regiebetriebs Rechenschaft schuldig. Von den öffentlichen
Theatern werden mehr als die Hälfte als Regiebetriebe bzw. Eigenbe-
triebe geführt.
Daneben werden die Theater der öffentlichen Hand als juristisch selbständige Institute in Form einer juristischen Person des Privatrechts oder
des öffentlichen Rechts geführt, nämlich als Anstalt des öffentlichen
Rechts, als Zweckverband, als GmbH und als eingetragener Verein.
Trotz dieser Form bleibt die öffentliche Hand der Rechtsträger. Diese

Theatersystem (im deutschsprachigen Raum) **1001**

Form führt jedoch zu einer organisatorischen Selbständigkeit, die öffentliche Hand ist lediglich Aufsichtsbehörde. Gleichwohl unterliegt das Theater der Aufsicht des Rechnungshofs. Auch der Etat wird von dem jeweiligen Stadtparlament verabschiedet und kontrolliert.

Je nach Größe des Hauses verfügt das Theater über eine oder mehrere Sparten, nämlich Schauspiel, Oper, Ballett. Teilweise unterhält die öffentliche Hand für jede Gattung ein organisatorisch selbständiges Theater.

Das T. der BRD wird ferner durch *private Theater* geprägt. Im Gegensatz zu den Theatern der öffentlichen Hand verdanken diese ihre Gründung einer Privatinitiative und befinden sich in Privatbesitz. Aufgrund der Bestimmungen der Gewerbeordnung (vgl. §33a) können Theater ohne besondere Erlaubnis errichtet werden (vgl. §33a Gewerbeordnung, der darauf abstellt, daß es sich um theatralische Vorstellungen mit «höherem Interesse der Kunst» handelt). Die Privattheater sind wirtschaftlich selbständig; sie treten meist in der Form einer GmbH oder eines eingetragenen Vereins auf. Z. T. erhalten sie staatliche Zuschüsse. Die privaten Theaterunternehmer bilden eine eigene Gruppe im →Dt. Bühnenverein (DBV). Über die Mitgliedschaft im DBV unterliegen die Privattheater teilweise der Tarifbindung (z. B. NV-Solo, →Schauspieler). Die wirtschaftliche Eigenverantwortung sowie andere Produktionsverhältnisse führen zu bes. Strukturen: In den meisten Fällen spielen die Privattheater en suite, d. h., es wird ein Stück ausschließlich eine Zeitlang gespielt. Die Privattheater beschäftigen auch keine festen Ensembles, sondern binden jeweils für die Dauer eines Stücks ein Schauspielerensemble an ihr Haus. Vielfach werden Stars, die aus Film und Fernsehen bekannt sind, als Zugnummer für ein Stück engagiert.

Als Privattheater sind auch die sog. *Tourneetheater* konzipiert, die im Gegensatz zu den Privattheatern keine feste Spielstätte haben, sondern durch die Bundesrepublik und das dtspr. Ausland mit einem oder mehreren Stücken reisen und es in den verschiedensten, für Theateraufführungen geeigneten Räumlichkeiten wie Schulaulen, Stadthallen, Mehrzweckhallen o. ä. aufführen. Die Tourneetheater haben ebenfalls kein festes Ensemble. Sie sind jedoch nicht im Dt. Bühnenverein organisiert; zu der Privattheatergruppe gehören nur die Theater, die ein stehendes Unternehmen, d. h. ein festes Haus bespielen. Es gibt derzeit 42 Tourneetheaterunternehmen, die insb. für die Landesbühnen eine starke Konkurrenz darstellen.

Das T. wird seit einiger Zeit durch eine weitere Gruppe von Theatern geprägt, die allerdings nur aus systematischen Gründen zusammenfaßbar ist, die sog. *Freie Gruppe*. Diese Freien Gruppen (→Freies Theater) sind Zusammenschlüsse von Schauspielern, Bühnenhandwerkern usw. ohne einen mit dem herkömmlichen Staatstheater vergleichbaren organisatori-

1002 Theatersystem (im deutschsprachigen Raum)

schen Apparat. Die Freien Gruppen bilden keine einheitliche Gruppe; einziges gemeinsames Kennzeichen ist die bewußte Abwendung vom staatlichen Theater in ästhetischer wie auch in organisatorischer Hinsicht. Die Freien Gruppen erhalten seit einiger Zeit teilweise staatliche Zuschüsse, allerdings in relativ geringer Höhe (z. B. Hamburg: DM 400000 bei einem Gesamtetat für Theater von rund 117 Mill. [1984]). Die Vergabe erfolgt nach unterschiedlichen Kriterien (z. T. wählt ein von Theaterfachleuten besetzter Ausschuß die zu bezuschussende Gruppe aus).

Geschichte
Das T. der Bundesrepublik (und z. T. auch im dtspr. Ausland) ist das Ergebnis einer langen Entwicklung, die etwa in der zweiten Hälfte des 17. Jh. ihren Anfang nahm. Das Theater, das zunächst nur den Gebildeten und die Kirche interessierte, wurde gegen Ende des 17. Jh. Bestandteil des gesellschaftlichen und des höfischen Lebens.

Die Einbeziehung des Theaters in das Staatswesen erfolgte in zwei Phasen: Die Höfe stellten einen Prinzipal und seine Truppe an, wobei die Schauspieler z. T. höfische Titel («Cammerlacquayen») erhielten. Diese höfische Anstellung bedeutete jedoch lediglich eine vorübergehende soziale Sicherung. Der Tod des Landesherrn, der die Truppe engagiert hatte, beendete oft die Anstellung (vgl. etwa die Anstellung der Truppe von Velthen am sächsischen Hof). Teilweise erhielt die Prinzipalschaft Zuschüsse (vgl. Schönemannsche Truppe in Mecklenburg).

▸ Der zweite Schritt auf dem Weg zum staatlich getragenen Theater erfolgte im 18. Jh. mit der Einrichtung sog. →Hoftheater. Diese Phase wird durch die organisatorische Einbindung einer Schauspielergesellschaft in den Hofapparat eines Landesherrn gekennzeichnet. Das Theater wird unter Verantwortung eines Hofintendanten (→Intendant) in eigener Regie betrieben. Damit entwickelte sich zugleich das stehende Theater, zunächst jedoch als höfische Angelegenheit. Diese Entwicklung wird teils vom aufklärerischen Zeitgeist getragen (vgl. Gellert 1751: «Das Theater müßte auf öffentliche Kosten erhalten werden»), teils erfolgt die Gründung der Hoftheater aus repräsentativen Gründen. Die erste bedeutende Hoftheatergründung – abgesehen von der Episode des Engagements der Velthenschen Gesellschaft am sächsischen Hof in Dresden 1685 bis 1691 als Hofbedienstete – erfolgte in Wien. In Wien wird 1776 von Kaiser Joseph II. das deutsche Schauspiel als Hof- und Nationaltheater «zur Verbreitung des guten Geschmacks, zur Veredelung der Sitten» aus der Taufe gehoben.

Weitere Hoftheatergründungen in Deutschland: 1775 Gotha, 1777 Mannheim, 1778 München, 1786 Berlin, 1788 Mainz, 1797 Kassel, 1791 Weimar, 1795 Dessau, 1801 Stuttgart, 1814 Dresden.

Neben der Gründung der Hoftheater prägt die Entstehung der sog.

Stadttheater das dt. Theaterwesen des 18. Jh. In den reichsunmittelbaren Städten wurden Nationaltheater gegr. und den umherziehenden Schauspielergesellschaften/Prinzipalschaften zur Verfügung gestellt. Dieses Stadttheaterwesen war ein reines Unternehmertheater; der Prinzipal trug die gesamte finanzielle und künstlerische Verantwortung. Eine finanzielle Beteiligung der Stadt erfolgte kaum, allenfalls wurden die Gebäude pachtfrei, Wasser und Heizung etc. kostenlos zur Verfügung gestellt. Das Stadttheaterwesen entwickelte sich langfristig zum sog. Geschäftstheater: Wo das Gebäude an den Meistbietenden verpachtet wurde, wo überhaupt die Stadt sich an den Einnahmen beteiligte, überlagerte bald das finanzielle Kalkül alle künstlerischen Überlegungen. Die Vergabe erfolgt ohne jeden Nachweis der Befähigung oder finanzieller Sicherheiten. Vielfach besaßen die zahlreich entstehenden Stadttheater nicht die notwendigen finanziellen Voraussetzungen, so daß es sehr oft zum Bankrott kam und immer wieder Schauspieler brotlos wurden. Die Folge war eine große Zahl arbeitsloser Schauspieler, das soziale Prestige des Theaters sank immer mehr. Unter Hinweis auf die Bildungsaufgabe des Theaters wurden Reformen gefordert. Die Stein-Hardenbergschen Reformen sahen beispielsweise ein Statut vor, wonach das Theater zu den Anstalten gehöre, die Einfluß auf die allg. Bildung haben und deshalb dem Ministerium für Unterricht und Kultus zu unterstellen sei (1808 Königsberger Königliches Publikandum). Diese Reform wurde allerdings nie verwirklicht, in der Verfassung rangierte das Theater nach wie vor als öffentliche Anstalt «zur Bequemlichkeit und zum Vergnügen». Demzufolge wurde es – mit Ausnahme der Hoftheater – der Polizei unterstellt, das Hoftheater blieb dem Einfluß des Hofs ausgeliefert. Zwar erkannte man die Bildungsfunktion des Theaters an, aber gerade deshalb wurde sie nicht einem künstlerischen Direktor allein übertragen, sondern sollte unter Aufsicht eines erfahrenen Hofbeamten oder verdienten Adligen gestellt sein.

Die Entwicklung in den anderen dt. Staaten war nicht anders. Von seiten der beteiligten Künstler wurde dieser Zustand kritisiert. Es wurde die Verabschiedung eines →Theatergesetzes gefordert: Es sollten in allererster Linie die sozialen Belange der Bühnenkünstler geregelt werden, aber auch das Verhältnis zwischen Theaterwesen und Staat. Die Initiative zur Verbesserung der «dt. Theaterzustände» ging von der Direktorenseite aus. Die Abhängigkeit insb. der Stadttheater vom geschäftlichen Erfolg führte zu dem sog. Vertragsunwesen, gegen das sich die dt. Theaterleiter mit der Gründung eines Kartellverbands, →dem Dt. Bühnenverein, zu wehren versuchten. Bühnenverein und später auch die GDBA forderten dringend die Verabschiedung eines →Theatergesetzes, das grundlegende Fragen wie die Zulassung von Theatern, die Regelung der Rechtsbeziehung zwischen Theatern und Schauspielern, das Ausbildungswesen, die soziale Absicherung (Alter, Krankheit etc.) sowie Fra-

1004 Theatersystem (im deutschsprachigen Raum)

gen der →Theaterzensur regeln sollte. 1909 setzte der Dt. Reichstag endlich eine Kommission zur Erstellung einer gesetzlichen Regelung ein. Bevor es jedoch zu einer Verabschiedung durch den Reichstag kam, brach der 1. Weltkrieg aus.

Das bestehende T. hatte sich jedoch schon so weit gefestigt, daß nach dem Zusammenbruch 1918 die Hoftheater von den Ländern als Rechtsnachfolger der Landesherrn übernommen wurden. Eine Veränderung ergab sich bei den Stadttheatern. In den 20er Jahren erfolgte eine Kommunalisierung der Stadttheater. Während 1914 von 418 Theatern nur zehn in städtischer Eigenregie geführt wurden, war 1932 die Zahl der Regiebetriebe auf 147 angestiegen. Die Ursachen hierzu lagen z. T. in dem außergewöhnlich hohen Publikumsinteresse. Die Kommunalisierung ist jedoch auch auf dem Hintergrund der Kulturtheaterbewegung zu verstehen. Bereits der Bühnenverein hatte die staatliche Verantwortung für das Theater und eine dementsprechende Neuordnung des Hof- und Stadttheaterwesens gefordert. Mit der Einführung der Gewerbefreiheit 1869 kam es zu einer raschen Vermehrung der Theater, die in der Folgezeit wieder zusammenbrachen. Mit dieser «Theater-Gewerbefreiheit» verbreitete sich das Geschäftstheaterwesen weiter, das mit einem künstlerisch minderwertigen Theater einherging. Diesem künstlerischen Verfall und dem sozialen Elend der Schauspieler sagte die GDBA den Kampf an. Sie forderte den gemeinwirtschaftlichen Betrieb der Theater durch die Kommunen, wobei sich ihre Forderungen insbesondere auf die Pachtbühnen der Provinz bezogen. Auch der Bühnenverein erhob 1913 die Forderung nach Unterstützung der Privattheater und nach Übernahme in staatliche Regie. Gegen die vom Reichsminister des Innern 1920 vorgeschlagene Kommunalisierung der Theater wandte die Sozialisierungskommission ein, daß dies wohl geeignet sei, um Auswüchse zu beseitigen, «andererseits bietet die Kommunalisierung... die große Gefahr, daß aus politischen, konfessionellen Gründen u. ä. Rücksichten auch künstlerisch wertvolle Betriebe geschlossen werden könnten». Gleichwohl nahm die Kommunalisierung des Theaterwesens ihren Lauf.

Diese Entwicklung wird 1933/34 durch die nationalsozialistische Machtergreifung in eine andere Richtung gedrängt. Mit der Errichtung der →Reichstheaterkammer (1933) wurden alle Bühnenschaffenden gleichgeschaltet und zu Zwangsmitgliedern. GDBA und Bühnenverein wurden nach Erlaß des Reichstheatergesetzes vom 15. Mai 1934 im September 1934 zwangsweise aufgelöst. Das Reichstheatergesetz unterstellte alle im Reichsgebiet bestehenden Theater «hinsichtlich der Erfüllung ihrer Kulturaufgabe» der Führung des Reichsministers für Volksaufklärung und Propaganda (§ 1). Dieses Gesetz galt ohne Einschränkung für öffentliche und private Theater, die Gewerbefreiheit wurde aufgehoben. Der Reichsminister für Volksaufklärung kontrollierte die Anstellung und

Theatersystem (im deutschsprachigen Raum) **1005**

Entlassung von Bühnenleitern, Intendanten, Theaterdirektoren, Kapellmeistern und Oberspielleitern. Für die preußischen Staatstheater hatte sich Göring als Ministerpräsident die Oberaufsicht verschafft, so daß ihm insb. die Berliner Staatstheater unterstanden (→Theatergesetz, →Theaterzensur).

Devrient, E.: Geschichte der dt. Schauspielkunst. Berlin 1848; Drewniak, B.: Das Theater im NS-Staat. Düsseldorf 1984; Hofmann, J.: Kritisches Handbuch des westdt. Theaters. Berlin 1981; Hohenemser, P.: Verteilungswirkungen staatlicher Theaterfinanzierung. Frankfurt/M. 1984; Lenk, W.: Das kommunale Theater. Diss. 1933; Seelig, L.: Geschäftstheater oder Kulturtheater. Berlin 1919; Wolf, A.: Der Entwurf eines Reichstheatergesetzes. Berlin 1913.

Die Stellung des Theaters in der Bundesrepublik

Das T. der Bundesrepublik hat seine letzte Prägung in der Zeit der Weimarer Republik erhalten. Mit der Übernahme der Hoftheater durch die Landesherren als staatliche Theater und die Übernahme vieler Stadttheater in städtische Regie wurde die öffentliche Aufgabe des Theaters anerkannt und die Theater der Zuständigkeit der Kultusministerien zugewiesen. Nach dem Zusammenbruch des 3. Reichs knüpfte man bei der Wiedereinrichtung des Theaterwesens an die Situation vor 1933 an. Die beteiligten Verbände →DBV, →GDBA etc. sorgten dafür, daß die bisher erzielten tariflichen Regelungen wieder Geltung erhielten. Das Grundgesetz sieht eine föderative Bundesstaatlichkeit vor, in der den Ländern die Kulturhoheit zugewiesen ist. Aus dem Grundrecht des Art. 5 folgt die grundsätzliche Entscheidung zum bundesrepublikanischen Kulturstaat. Das verfassungsrechtliche System der Bundesrepublik enthält jedoch keine Regelung, die die Unterhaltung des Theaters zu einer staatlichen Aufgabe macht, ein Zustand, der sich bei den Etatberatungen auswirkt. In Zeiten finanzieller Knappheit wird erfahrungsgemäß zuerst am Theater-Etat eingespart. Die Verfassung der Bundesrepublik sieht kein Kulturmonopol des Staates vor. Vielmehr ist es im Rahmen der gewerberechtlichen Bestimmung jedermann ohne staatliche Genehmigung möglich, ein Theater zu gründen, sofern «ein höheres Interesse der Kunst oder Wissenschaft dabei obwaltet». Faktisch ist das bundesrepublikanische T. jedoch ein vom Staat – sei es in eigener Regie, sei es durch seine Zuschüsse – getragenes Wesen. Gleichwohl gibt es keine umfassende Regelung der theaterspezifischen Rechtsfragen. Im Rahmen der grundgesetzlich abgesicherten Tarifautonomie handeln die beteiligten Verbände (DBV sowie die Arbeitnehmervereinigungen) die arbeitsrechtlichen Vereinbarungen aus. Anders als im 19. Jh. gelten jedoch auch zugunsten der am Theater arbeitenden Beschäftigten die sozialrechtlichen Errungenschaften. Die Kunstfreiheitsgarantie erlaubt allerdings in Einzelfällen Einschränkungen (z. B. Problematik der befristeten Verträge, →Schau-

1006 Theatersystem (im deutschsprachigen Raum) ─────────────

spieler). Auf dem Hintergrund der wettbewerbsrechtlichen Bestimmungen hat der DBV mit den Verlagen und Verwertungsgesellschaften unverbindliche Rahmenbestimmungen für das Verhältnis Autor/Bühne getroffen. Auch im Ausbildungswesen versuchen die Bühnengewerkschaften und der DBV, über die gemeinsame Einrichtung der Paritätischen Prüfungskommission den Gefahren des nicht staatlich geregelten Ausbildungswesens entgegenzuwirken.

Das T. der Bundesrepublik wird durch ein Spannungsverhältnis zwischen Theater und Staat geprägt, das sich aus der Rechtsträgerschaft und der staatlichen Subventionierung zwangsläufig ergibt. Bei den in eigener Regie getragenen Theatern haben die staatlichen Aufsichtsgremien (Kulturausschuß, Kulturreferat usw.) die Kompetenz über die Besetzung der Intendanz und damit die Möglichkeit, die künstlerische und politische Richtung des Theaters zu bestimmen. Die Intendantenbestellung ist deshalb immer ein Politikum. Vereinzelt ist vom Rechtsträger versucht worden, die Anstellung als Intendant von «sozialer Akzeptanz» abhängig zu machen (vgl. Vertragsverlängerung des Intendanten Brecht in Essen 1982) oder an ein Konzept der «Ausgewogenheit» (Berufung des Generalintendanten in Oldenburg 1984) anzubinden. Weitere Einflußmöglichkeiten eröffnen sich über den jeweiligen Intendantenvertrag und die Dienstanweisungen. Soweit diese vorsehen, daß der Intendant den Spielplan vorzulegen hat oder den Kulturausschuß unterrichten muß, können sich auch darüber ständige Abhängigkeiten ergeben. Selbst die privaten Theater, die staatliche Zuschüsse erhalten, können sich einer Abhängigkeit nicht erwehren. Das Subventionswesen ist nicht gesetzlich geregelt, sondern steht im staatlichen Ermessen. Über diesen Regelungszusammenhang hat der Staat Einflußmöglichkeiten. Mit der Bereitstellung finanzieller Mittel erhebt der Staat Ansprüche gegen das Theater. Die künstlerische Freiheit ist zwar im Grundgesetz verankert, aber in der Praxis wird immer wieder mit dem Hinweis auf die Zuwendung staatlicher Mittel eine Unterordnung des Theaters unter staatliche Interessen gefordert (vgl. die Rede des Hamburger Bürgermeisters bei der Eröffnung des Dt. Schauspielhauses in Hamburg, Herbst 1984. In: Theater heute 11 [1984], S. 3 ff). Inhaltliche Korrekturversuche des Rechtsträgers werden z. T. mit der kulturpolitischen Verantwortung des Kulturausschusses zu rechtfertigen versucht.

Fuchs, H. J.: Theater als Dienstleistungsorganisation. Frankfurt/M. 1988; Hohenemser, P.: Verteilungswirkungen staatlicher Theaterfinanzierung. Frankfurt/M. 1984; Kunig, P.: Bühnenleiter und Kunstfreiheit. In: Die öffentl. Verwaltung 1982, S. 765 ff; Revermann, K. H.: Die Grenzen der Zensur. In: Theater heute 5 (1971), S. 1 ff.

Theatersystem (im deutschsprachigen Raum) **1007**

Publikum und Bundesorganisationen
(→Besucherorganisationen, →Publikum)
Ein weiterer, das bundesdeutsche T. prägender Faktor ist das organisierte Publikum. Da die öffentlichen Theater nicht vollständig vom Rechtsträger finanziert werden, sondern sich im Rahmen des vom Rechtsträger vorgegebenen →Einnahmesolls selbst tragen müssen, erlangt das Publikum, insb. das organisierte, eine beherrschende Funktion. Etwa 30 Prozent der Karten werden über Abonnements vergeben, 25 Prozent über Besucherorganisationen verkauft, so daß lediglich die Hälfte der Karten in den sog. freien Verkauf gelangen. Hieraus wird klar, daß bei der Spielplangestaltung zwecks Einhaltung des Einnahmesolls entsprechende Rücksichten genommen werden müssen. Die künstlerische Qualität eines Hauses wird vielfach an der Platzausnutzungsquote gemessen. Die →Besucherorganisationen fordern – insbesondere im Zusammenhang mit der allg. Mitbestimmungsdiskussion der 70er Jahre – eine weitgehende Mitsprache bei der Wahl des Intendanten, Spielplangestaltung usw. So soll z. B. im Aufsichtsgremium der öffentlichen Theater auch ein Vertreter der Besucherorganisation mit einem Stimmrecht vertreten sein. Dies ist z. T. bereits erreicht. Aber auch ohne Stimmrecht im Aufsichtsgremium ergibt sich über die Abnahme von Theaterkarten durch die Besucherorganisation ein starker Einfluß.

Daiber, H.: Das Publikum und seine Vereine. In: Theater heute 3 (1962).

Das Theatersystem der Deutschen Demokratischen Republik (1949–90)

Statistische Angaben zum Theatersystem in der DDR 1990 (nach Statistischem Jahrbuch und «Ensembles der DDR». Hg. von DTO): 59 Theater-Institutionen (Staats-, Landes-, Kreis- und Stadttheater, davon 35 Mehrspartentheater und 4 Kindertheater); 194 Theatergebäude (Spielstätten).

In der Nachkriegszeit wurden auf dem Territorium der späteren DDR mehr als 90 Theater wiedereröffnet oder neugegründet, teils in kommunaler, teils in privater Trägerschaft; bis 1950 waren dann fast alle in öffentlichen Besitz überführt. Für das T. in den Anfangsjahren der DDR war einerseits die Weiterführung bürgerlicher Traditionen (nicht des proletarisch-revolutionären Theaters der 20er/30er Jahre) mit dem dominierenden Typus des mehrspartigen Stadttheaters charakteristisch, andererseits die ideelle und institutionelle Erneuerung aus dem Geist des Antifaschismus (geprägt durch ehemals Verfolgte wie Bertolt Brecht, Wolfgang Langhoff, Maxim Vallentin, Gustav von Wangenheim oder Fritz Wisten); Theaterneugründungen wie das →Berliner Ensemble, das →Maxim-Gorki-Theater Berlin oder die nach sowjetischem Vorbild konzipierten →Kindertheater stehen für diese Erneuerung, die in den 50er und 60er Jahren starke internationale Beachtung fand.

1008 Theatersystem (im deutschsprachigen Raum)

Die Theater der DDR waren einer strikten Anleitung und Kontrolle durch die Regierung (bis 1954 Staatliche Kommission für Kunstangelegenheiten, danach Ministerium für Kultur) unterstellt; nachgeordnete Einrichtungen wie die Direktion für Theater und Orchester (anstelle früherer Theateragenturen für die berufliche Lenkung und Vermittlung der Künstler, die «Kaderpolitik», verantwortlich) und die Direktion für das Bühnenrepertoire (die die Theater bei der Spielplanung beriet und vor der die Spielpläne jährlich «verteidigt» werden mußten) sicherten den umfassenden zentralistischen Einfluß auf Künstler und Theater. Das →Deutsche Theater, das →Berliner Ensemble und die Deutsche Staatsoper Berlin unterstanden als Staatstheater unmittelbar der Regierung; alle anderen Bühnen waren den Räten der Bezirke, Kreise oder Städte zugeordnet, unterlagen also einer zweiten, dezentralen Anleitung. Die SED, die sich als ideologisch und auch kulturpolitisch führende Kraft der Gesellschaft verstand, hat nicht selten (auf Plenartagungen des Zentralkomitees) Theater, Künstler oder einzelne Inszenierungen scharfer Kritik unterzogen, oft mit der Konsequenz des Verbots von Aufführungen oder der Ablösung von Intendanten. In Organisationen wie der Gewerkschaft Kunst (in der Nachfolge der Genossenschaft Deutscher Bühnenangehöriger) und dem →Verband der Theaterschaffenden (seit 1966) fand Interessenvertretung, Erfahrungsaustausch und Weiterbildung, aber auch politisch-ideologische Einflußnahme durch Staat und Partei statt. Mit relativ hohen Subventionen konnten in der DDR ein dichtes Netz von Theatern (1990 noch 59 selbständige Institutionen, davon 35 Mehrsparten-Theater) erhalten und sehr niedrige Eintrittspreise gewährleistet werden. Arbeitsrechtlich waren die Theaterleute seit 1978 (durch Arbeitsgesetzbuch und Rahmenkollektivvertrag) allen anderen Beschäftigten in der DDR gleichgestellt: d. h. unbefristete Arbeitsverträge, Kündigung nur bei nachgewiesener Nichteignung oder groben Disziplinverstößen. Praktisch hat diese sehr weitgehende soziale Sicherung zu Verkrustungen und Überalterungen vieler Ensembles geführt. Die restriktive Kulturpolitik gab Freien Gruppen im T. der DDR sehr wenig Raum; Experimente und alternative Kunstbemühungen konnten sich nur innerhalb der Institutionen oder in Bindung an Klubhäuser oder Organisationen (z. B. den Jugendverband FDJ) vollziehen; dabei erfreuten sich besonders seit den 80er Jahren kleine kommunikationsintensive Theaterräume wachsender Beliebtheit beim Publikum.

Die Ausbildung für die künstlerischen Theaterberufe erfolgte in der DDR prinzipiell in staatlichen Hoch- und Fachschulen (Sonderregelungen waren Ausbildungsverträge an Theatern mit staatlicher Abschlußprüfung); der DDR-Theaternachwuchs galt international als vorzüglich ausgebildet (→Schauspielschulen). Der Theaterbesuch in Ostdeutschland erfolgte überwiegend durch Vermittlung von Besucherorganisationen: 1946–53 durch die Volksbühne, danach durch von den Theatern und den

Gewerkschaften (FDGB) gemeinsam getragenen Abonnements (den sogenannten Betriebs-Anrechten, auch anderen speziellen Anrechts-Formen). In den 80er Jahren profiliert sich Theater in der DDR mehr und mehr als Stätte kritischer ästhetischer und gesellschaftlicher Diskurse (teilweise als Ersatz für sonst nicht vorhandene Öffentlichkeit; nicht zufällig haben Theaterleute großen Anteil an der politischen Wende 1989 – z. B. als Veranstalter der legendären Protestdemonstration am 4. 11. 89 auf dem Berliner Alexanderplatz).

Mit dem Anschluß Ostdeutschlands an die BRD werden die föderalen Strukturen und tarifrechtlichen Grundlagen des bundesdeutschen T. übernommen; erheblicher Personalabbau und drastische Einschnitte in das Theater-Netz sind absehbar.

Mittenzwei, W. (Hg.): Theater in der Zeitenwende. Berlin 1972; Funke, Ch./ Hoffmann-Ostwald, D./Otto, H.-G.: Theater-Bilanz. Berlin 1971; Schriften zum Theater (über 200 Einzelhefte). Hg. vom Verband der Theaterschaffenden.

Theater in Österreich und in der Schweiz

Österreich

Das österr. T. ist ebenfalls ein im wesentlichen staatlich getragenes System aus Stadt- und Landestheater sowie Privattheatern. Eine Besonderheit stellt das Bundestheaterwesen dar: Die Bundesregierung in der Kompetenz des Bundesministers für Unterricht und Kunst unterhält die im Bundesverband zusammengeschlossenen Bundestheater (→Burgtheater, Staatsoper, Volksoper), alle in Wien ansässig.

Die Stadt- und Landestheater sind im «Theatererhalterverband österr. Bundesländer und Städte» zusammengeschlossen, während der Wiener Bühnenverein der Zusammenschluß der Bundestheater und aller Wiener Theater mit mindestens zwanzig ganzjährig engagierten Bühnenkünstlern (z. Zt. sieben Privattheater) ist. Im Gegensatz zum bundesrepublikanischen System ist die Gründung eines Theaterbetriebs konzessionspflichtig. Der jeweilige Landeshauptmann entscheidet nach einer strengen Bedarfsprüfung, ob ein neues Theater zugelassen wird.

Der Theaterbetrieb läuft im wesentlichen ganzjährig mit einer zweimonatigen Sommerpause. In der Sommersaison werden in Wien sowie in der Republik Sommertheater bzw. Sommerfestspiele veranstaltet, die von hoher touristischer Attraktivität sind.

Das Einnahmesoll der öffentlich getragenen Theater liegt etwa bei 20 Prozent, während dies je nach Einzelfall bei den privaten Theatern z. T. wesentlich höher liegt. Die Eintrittspreise liegen über dem bundesdt. Durchschnittswert. Die Platzausnutzung bei den Bundestheatern stellt sich wie folgt dar: Staatsoper 84,5 %, Burgtheater 72,1 %, Volksoper 85,6 % (Österr. Bundestheaterverband, Bericht 89/90).

1010 Theatersystem (im deutschsprachigen Raum) ⎯⎯⎯⎯⎯⎯⎯⎯⎯⎯⎯⎯

Österreich steht ebenso wie die Bundesrepublik Deutschland in der Tradition der *Kulturstaatsidee*. Art. 17, 17 a Staatsgrundgesetz schützt die Freiheit des Wirk- und Werkbereichs künstlerischer Tätigkeit. Auch die österr. Verfassung sieht – abgesehen von der Kompetenzzuweisung für die Bundestheater – keinen ausdrücklichen Kulturförderungsauftrag des Staats vor. Die Förderung der Theater, insb. der Bundestheater, erfolgt in Österreich über alle kulturpolitischen und traditionellen Überlegungen hinaus auch aus touristischen und volkswirtschaftlichen Gründen.

Das *Rechtsverhältnis* zwischen dem Bühnenmitglied und dem Theater regelt sich nach dem Schauspielergesetz, das erstmals 1922 erlassen wurde. Das Bundesgesetz über den Bühnendienstvertrag sieht in § 29 die Befristung des Dienstverhältnisses vor.

Kapfer, H.: Schauspielergesetz. Wien 1974; Revermann, K. H.: Die typisch österr. Lösung. In: Dt. Bühne 4 (1985), S. 39 ff; Österr. Bundestheaterverband, Bericht 1989/90.

Schweiz

Das schweizerische T. hat, anders als in Deutschland und Österreich, seinen Ursprung nicht im feudalen → Hoftheaterwesen, sondern beruht auf privaten Gründungen. Dieser Umstand prägt das heutige Bild: Von den neunzehn Berufstheatern (elf in der dtspr. Schweiz und acht in der frz. Schweiz) haben alle mit Ausnahme des Stadttheaters Luzern private Rechtsträger (als Aktiengesellschaften, Genossenschaften, Stiftungen, Vereine). Die Theater erhalten jeweils erneut zu beantragende Subventionen, die etwa zu 70 bis 80 Prozent den Theateretat decken; im übrigen tragen die Theater das wirtschaftliche Risiko selbst. Die Theaterlandschaft ist ferner davon geprägt, daß die Schweiz von vier Kultursprachen beherrscht wird. Das Theaterleben spielt sich im wesentlichen in der dtspr. und der frzspr. Schweiz ab.

Aufgrund seiner privaten Tradition hat das Theater noch nicht seine Anerkennung als ‹*öffentliche Aufgabe*› gefunden. Die öffentlichen Zuschüsse fließen recht knapp, wobei zu beobachten ist, daß politischer Druck auf die Spielplangestaltung ausgeübt wird. Als Ausdruck eines gewandelten kulturpolitischen Verständnisses mag die 1975 erfolgte Verselbständigung des Bundesamts für Kulturpflege (Bern) angesehen werden, das ehemals dem Bundesinnenministerium untergeordnet war. Dieses Amt soll kulturpolitische Grundsatzentscheidungen vorbereiten sowie in der allg. Förderung des kulturellen Verständnisses der Öffentlichkeit dienen. Im Rahmen einer Kulturinitiative wurde 1980 gefordert, daß der Bund 1 Prozent seiner Finanzausgaben für kulturelle Zwecke ausgeben solle, verbunden mit der verfassungsmäßigen Absicherung der Pflicht zur Förderung kulturellen Schaffens. Die gegenwärtige Situation der kulturellen Szene der Schweiz ist geprägt von einem Kampf der Theater und alternativen Gruppen (Rock- und Pop-Gruppen, Animations- und Agitationstheatergruppen) um die spärlichen staatlichen Subventionen für kulturelle Aufgaben, was in Einzelfällen zu Kürzungen des Theateretats geführt hat.

Die *Bühnen* der dtspr. und frzspr. Schweiz sind im Schweizer Bühnenverband organisiert, während die Bühnenkünstler im Schweizer Bühnenkünstlerverband (dtspr. Schweiz) und im Syndicat Suisseromand du Spectacle (beide unter dem Dachverband des Verbandes des Personals des öffentlichen Dienstes) vereinigt sind. Der Schweizer Bühnenverband ist Mitglied der internationalen Arbeitsgemeinschaft dtspr. Theater (Bern), der sowohl der Dt. Bühnenverein als auch die österr. Verbände angehören. Die Arbeitgeber- und Arbeitnehmervereinigung handeln im Rahmen ihrer begrenzten Kompetenzen für Solopersonal, Chor und Ballett Gesamtverträge aus, während alle übrigen Vertragsverhältnisse (Musiker, Bühnentechniker etc.) jeweils in örtlichen Sondervereinbarungen geregelt werden. Das künstlerische Personal ist ebenfalls auf Zeitvertragsbasis engagiert. Die Nichtverlängerungsmitteilungen werden zum 31. Januar (im 1. Vertragsjahr) bzw. zum 30. November ausgesprochen; allerdings muß der Intendant vorher das Bühnenmitglied nachweislich in zwei repräsentativen Rollen gesehen haben. Rechtsstreitigkeiten werden unter Verzicht auf den ordentlichen Rechtsweg vor den Bühnenschiedsgerichten ausgetragen, die allerdings – im Gegensatz zur regen Tätigkeit der bundesdeutschen Schiedsgerichte – in den letzten Jahren relativ selten angerufen worden sind.

Theater in der Schweiz. Hg. von K. G. Kachler u. Benz-Bürger. Zürich 1977; Szene Schweiz. Jährl. erscheinende Dokumentation des Theaterlebens. Hg. von der Schweizer Gesellschaft für Theaterkultur. Weitere Nachweise in «Szene Schweiz» 8 (1980/81); Revermann, K. H.: Kampf an der Kasse. In: Dt. Bühne 6 (1985), S. 40ff; Zörner, W.: Finanziell leicht verwundbar. In: Dt. Bühne 9 (1981), S. 12ff.

Roswitha Körner / Manfred Pauli

Theatertheorie

Frühformen der T. finden sich schon in der Antike (→ Antikes Theater). Platon (429 v. Chr. – 347 v. Chr.) trifft Unterscheidung zwischen nachahmender Darstellung (Schauspiel) = Mimesis und Erzählung (Lyrik) = Dihegesis sowie Verbindung beider (Epos, in dem Bericht/Dihegesis und direkte Rede/Mimesis miteinander abwechseln). Platon betont im Rahmen der Dichterschelte Gefahren der Mimesis im Theater; sie führe durch Angleichung ans Dargestellte zu Amoral, Krankheit, Wahnsinn, Verweiblichung, sei nach Möglichkeit einzuschränken (*Politeia*

1012 Theatertheorie

392d–398b). Aristoteles (384 v. Chr.–322 v. Chr.) dagegen geht von ungefährlichem Vergnügen des Menschen an Darstellung aus. Seine *Poetik* ist die erste → Dramentheorie, zugleich T.: Die Tragödie soll Furcht (Phobos) und Mitleid, Schaudern (Eleos) hervorrufen, dadurch Reinigung (Katharsis) von solchen Affekten (oder solcher Affekte) bewirken. Die theatralen Elemente behandelt Aristoteles unter dem Begriff Opsis (etwa = ‹Inszenierung›), hält sie aber für untergeordnet dem dramatischen Text gegenüber, dessen Wirkung auch ohne Theater zustande käme. Überhaupt ist T. bis zum 20. Jh. vorwiegend → Dramentheorie und -poetik. Eigentliche T. hat zum Gegenstand: die Beschreibung der Institution → Theater; Ursprung und historisch wechselnde Funktionsbestimmungen des Theaters im kulturellen und gesellschaftlichen Kontext; Produktion und Rezeption des Theaters als semiotische Praxis und Kommunikationsprozeß sowie als Teil einer allg. Kultursemiotik; Entwicklung angemessener Beschreibungs- und Deutungsmethoden der Aufführung; Abgrenzung und Vergleich des Theaters mit benachbarten ästhetischen Praxisformen; Bestimmung der → Theatralität im engeren Sinn; allg. Theaterästhetik, Theaterkonzeptionen.

1. Ursprung: Theater beruht urspr. auf Mimesis (griech. mimeisthai = tänzerisch darstellen). Im magisch-rituellen Zauber macht sich der Mensch Göttern, Dämonen, numinosen Wesen, Tieren gleich, wobei Maske, Kostüm, Requisiten, tranceartige Zustände der ‹Verwandlung› vorkommen. Solch rituelles Rollenspiel (auch → Urtheater, aber besser, weil unmißverständlich: Vorform des Theaters) wird unterschieden vom eigentlichen Theater, von dem erst bei vorwiegend ästhetischer statt religiöser Beteiligung der Zuschauer gesprochen werden kann. In Europa (Griechenland) Herkunft des Theaters aus dem religiösen Agon zu Ehren der Götter, Zusammenhang mit dem Dionysos-Kult. Aus Chorgesang mit zwei Halbchören Entwicklung des Vorsängers (Hypokrites), dann eines zweiten und dritten Akteurs, die sich aus dem Chor lösen. Nur in Griechenland entwickelt sich aus dem religiösen Spiel die ästhetisch autonome Kunstform Theater. Die Wortbedeutung von mimeisthai spricht gegen verkürzende Auffassung der Mimesis als Nachahmung, die im Gefolge der Rezeption der *Poetik* des Aristoteles herrschend wurde. Im 20. Jh. häufige Versuche – vor allem: Antonin Artaud (1896–1948) –, das psychologische Theater durch Rückkehr zu rituellen Ursprüngen zu beleben. Richard Schechner zieht Parallelen zwischen Theater der ‹Primitiven› und den therapeutisch intendierten Theaterformen von Jerzy Grotowski (* 1933), Joseph Chaikin (*1935), Peter Brook (* 1925); parareligiöse, therapeutische Kommunikationsversuche auch im → «Living Theatre».

2. T. hat die unterschiedlichen gesellschaftlichen Funktionen des Theaters einschließlich der Abwehr aller Funktionalisierung zu untersuchen.

Theatertheorie 1013

So steht das antike Theater im Zentrum der athenischen Polis, dient ihr als Selbstdarstellung, Ort der Selbstvergewisserung und gemeinsamer Bewußtwerdung über die drängenden Probleme des rechtlichen, politischen und religiösen Lebens. Zwar wird im Mittelalter (Theater im Dienst der Kirche) eine quasi-kultische Funktion erreicht; doch die Natur der christlichen Religion (Entwertung der sinnlichen Wirklichkeit) läßt nicht zu, daß Theater mehr sein darf als dienende Illustration, Mittel der Belehrung. Die Wiederkehr einer gesellschaftlich verbindenden Funktion des Theaters wie im antiken Athen ist seither der rote Faden zahlreicher T. und Utopien geblieben. In der →Renaissance entsteht die Oper aus den Versuchen einer Wiederbelebung der antiken Theaterverhältnisse; Denis Diderot (1713–84) und Louis-Sébastien Mercier (1740–1814) wünschen sich im 18. Jh. Massenspektakel zur Beförderung bürgerlicher Tugenden, entwerfen nach dem Vorbild der Antike die Utopie bürgerlicher Theatralik, die «Wahrheiten durch den elektrischen Schlag des Gefühls» (Diderot) vermitteln soll; Friedrich Nietzsche entwirft im Spiegel der Antike, wo er das Ineinander von Apollinischem und Dionysischem realisiert glaubt, die Utopie einer Zivilisation nach dem Vorbild einer dionysisch-tragischen Kunst, die die Unterwerfung des Lebens unter die verselbständigte Theorie (das Sokratische) rückgängig machen könnte; Richard Wagner (1813–83) versucht, durch den Rückgriff auf nordische Mythologie die auf dem antiken Mythos basierende Tragödie der Griechen in neuer Form zu begründen, um Theater als Ort nationaler und weltbürgerlicher Vereinigung wiederzugewinnen. Aber eine schon an den Äußerlichkeiten von Bühne und Theaterbau abzulesende Trennung von Spiel und Publikum macht seit der Renaissance Theater als vereinigendes Erlebnis obsolet. Mit der Bühne ‹à l'italienne› und dem Proszeniumsrahmen wird die im Klassizismus vollendete scharfe Absonderung der Bühne vom Zuschauerraum eingeführt.

Die →Klassik bildet die erste geschlossene, logisch durchgebildete T. aus: ein Regelsystem, das im Zug der mit der Renaissance (seit 1540) einsetzenden Aristoteles-Entdeckung mit Umdeutung der *Poetik* vom Deskriptiven zum Präskriptiven einen dramatischen und theatralen Normenkodex aufstellt: Wahrscheinlichkeit, Vernunft, Schicklichkeit in Stoffwahl, Sprache und Darstellung; gehobene Verssprache; strenge Beachtung der Einheit von Zeit, Ort und Handlung. Im 17. und 18. Jh. ist Theater wesentlich Repräsentation, idealisierender Spiegel der höfischen Gesellschaft (→Höfisches Theater), während im 18. und 19. Jh., zunächst neben dem höfischen, das bürgerliche Theater entsteht, das zwar auch bürgerlicher Repräsentation dient, jedoch eine soziologische und funktionelle Umdefinition des Theaters vornimmt: Theater als «moralische Anstalt» mit der neuen Funktion einer erstmalig der Unterhaltung eines breiten, anonymen Publikums gewidmeten Institution. Im 20. Jh. steht T.

1014 Theatertheorie

vor dem Problem, daß der Massenkonsum von reproduzierten Schrift- und Bildwerken, das Aufkommen von Film und Fernsehen und die Entstehung einer «Kulturindustrie» (Adorno) die Existenzgrundlagen des Theaters verändert haben. Theater der Moderne und Postmoderne verweigert sich – von signifikanten Ausnahmen abgesehen (Bertolt Brecht, 1898–1956) – weithin einer politischen Funktionsbestimmung, versteht sich vielmehr als Ort des Experiments, wo in der Tradition des Modernismus Möglichkeiten des Zeichengebrauchs erkundet werden. Soziologisch ergibt sich für das Theater durch die Konkurrenz zum massenhaft reproduzierten und konsumierten Produkt der Filmindustrie und der elektronischen Unterhaltungsmedien, daß seine gesellschaftliche Funktion ein relativ begrenztes Publikum betrifft. Die Unmöglichkeit massenhafter Wirksamkeit (aber umgekehrt auch die Entlastung von diesem Zwang, der auf das Niveau der aufwendigen Filmproduktionen drückt) erlaubt es dem Theater, Ort komplexer ästhetisch-gesellschaftlicher Reflexion zu sein und sich auf den Kern ureigenster Merkmale zu besinnen, der von anderen Medien nicht einzuholen ist: die Lebendigkeit des Hier und Jetzt, in dem Produktion/Emission und Rezeption der Zeichen zusammenfallen, die körperliche Kopräsenz von Akteuren und Zuschauern, die eine einzigartige sinnlich-intellektuelle Erfahrung ermöglicht (→ Theatralität).

3. Schwierig ist eine Minimaldefinition des Theaters als kulturell-ästhetische Zeichenpraxis, weil einerseits Sozialpsychologie und Soziologie die ‹theatralischen› Aspekte auch der nichtästhetischen Alltagskommunikation immer besser erforscht haben, andererseits das Theater der Moderne die klassischen Definitionen sprengt durch Formen wie → Happening, → «unsichtbares Theater», street art, → Performance usw.

Der Grundvorgang, eine Rolle zu übernehmen, ein ‹Als-ob›-Verhalten zu üben, ist aller Kommunikation in wechselndem Grad immanent. «Taking the role of the other» (Mead) ist als mentale Voraussetzung personaler Interaktion erkannt worden. Geht man den Formen nach, die die «presentation of self» im Alltagsleben annimmt, so kommt man zu der Feststellung Erving Goffmans: «All the world is not, of course, a stage, but the crucial ways in which it isn't are not easy to specify.» Psychoanalyse und die Dekonstruktion der um den Wahrheitsbegriff zentrierten Denkkategorien der europ. Tradition haben die Grenze zwischen ‹spontanem› und ‹inszeniertem› Verhalten neu problematisiert, die Kunstentwicklung selbst läßt kaum mehr eine scharfe Distinktion zwischen ästhetischer und nichtästhetischer Praxis zu: menschliche Sexualität erweist sich z. T. als gebunden an theatralische Inszenierungen, regelrechte Szenarios als Ermöglichungsbedingung von Lust; Übergang zwischen sexuellem und ästhetischem Verhalten auch im → erotischen Theater.

Unter dem Gesichtspunkt → «performance» sind zahlreiche Aspekte des Alltags partiell dem Theater analog: Sportveranstaltungen, bei denen der Schauwert das sportliche Duell mitbestimmt oder außer Kraft setzt (Schau-Ringen); Phänomene wie rekonstruierte Dörfer aus früheren Jahrhunderten, in denen von Spielern die Rollen von Menschen früherer Jahrhunderte bis ins Detail übernommen werden (Plymouth, Mass., in USA); im Zuge des Tourismus auf Bestellung vorgeführte religiöse Zeremonien (Indonesien); Theaterformen, die Alltagsvorgänge und ahnungslos zu Mitspielern werdende Passanten integrieren (Squat-Theater, New York), ließen in den 70er Jahren gerade den Grenzbereich zwischen Theater im herkömmlichen Sinn und anderen Kunst- und Verhaltensformen ins Zentrum des Interesses rücken.

Als umfassende Formel für Theater bietet sich an: «S spielt R für Z», mindestens ein *S*pieler spielt vor einem oder mehreren *Z*uschauern eine *R*olle – und zwar in ein und derselben Zeit/Ort-Einheit. Theater in diesem weiten Sinn umfaßt die mehr oder minder bewußt gestaltete Alltagsszene, die Übernahme einer Rolle z. B. bei einem Bewerbungsgespräch, das gezielte demonstrierende Vorspielen im Alltag (Brechts «Straßenszene», an der er das →«epische Theater» demonstriert); →Aktionskunst aller Art, insoweit die beteiligten Künstler nicht spontan agieren, sondern eine geplante Aktion ausführen und insofern eine Rolle spielen; schließlich die ‹normalen› Theaterformen, also: Darstellung fiktiver Figuren durch Schauspieler, (gewöhnlich) unter Einsatz einer breiten Skala von Theaterzeichen. – An zwei Theaterformen, dem →Lehrstück, das nach Brechts Konzeption nicht für Zuschauer, sondern für die Agierenden gespielt wird, und am →«unsichtbaren Theater» (Augusto Boal, * 1931), wo die Zuschauer Zuschauer sind, ohne es zu wissen, wird deutlich, daß Theater in best. Fällen auch ohne die subjektiv bewußte Verabredung zustande kommen kann, daß einige die Rolle der Zuschauer übernehmen. Entweder können sie – wie bei Boals politischen Szenen – durch eine vorgetäuschte, scheinbar spontan entstandene Situation nur objektiv Zuschauer sein, oder es gibt – wie beim Lehrstück – nur eine theoretische Spaltung der Beteiligten in Akteur und Lernenden (Zuschauer). Nicht ausgeschlossen sind aus der Definition «S spielt R für Z» →Puppen- und →Marionettentheater, denn auch der unsichtbare Puppenspieler spielt durch Bewegungen und Stimme ‹Rollen› mit Hilfe der Puppen. Ausgeschlossen sind dagegen Grenzphänomene wie «Theater der Gegenstände» (→Bauhausbühne) oder reine Raum-Inszenierung, z. B. *Rudi* (Berlin 1979) von Klaus Michael Grüber (* 1942) und dem Bühnenbildner Erich Wonder (* 1944) – Formen, die im Grenzbereich zur bildenden Kunst (Installation, Environment) angesiedelt sind.

Von der Filmvorführung (→Film und Theater) unterscheidet sich Theater durch die Einheit von Spielraum und Zuschauerraum, während das Kino einen realen mit einem imaginären Raum verbindet sowie durch

1016 Theatertheorie

größere Freiheit der Rezeption. Die Ästhetik des Films ist durch die unbewußte Lenkung und Manipulation des Blicks und speziell der Raumerfahrung gekennzeichnet, während die Theaterästhetik durch die sinnlich-konkrete Präsenz der Zeichen ‹gebrochen› ist, weniger Faszination und traumähnliche Identifikation hervorruft, sondern einen höheren Grad von Bewußtsein impliziert (damit sind keine Werturteile gegeben, sondern unterschiedliche Bedingungen der ästhetischen Kommunikation benannt); ferner durch die Zentrierung auf den Menschen. Die ‹Sprache› der Dinge im Film geht zwar auch bis zu einem gewissen Grad in Theaterästhetik ein; doch steht hier, anders als im Film, wo z. B. durch Großaufnahmen Details ‹sprechend› werden, letztlich die menschliche Person, der menschliche Körper im Zentrum.

4. Eine besondere Schwierigkeit der T. besteht in der Flüchtigkeit des Gegenstands. Anders als bei Text und fixiertem Film ist die Aufführung nicht nur nachträglich kaum zu rekonstruieren und zudem jeden Abend anders, sondern als Gebilde insgesamt stets nur ‹intendiert›. Ihre Hermeneutik muß sich bereits als Ausgangsmaterial auf eine Fiktion stützen: die von Publikumsreaktionen unabhängige, von Dispositionen der Akteure unbeeinflußte idealtypische Gesamtheit der Textur aus Theaterzeichen. Glücklicherweise gibt es deren außerordentlich viele und von Schwankungen z. T. hochgradig unabhängige, so daß die von Theaterpraktikern gern (und was ihr Erleben angeht, auch mit Recht) übertriebene Unterschiedlichkeit verschiedener Realisationen der ‹gleichen› Inszenierung sich weit genug relativiert, um eine kritische wissenschaftliche Analyse des Gegenstands zu erlauben. – Eine andere Schwierigkeit der T. stellt sich mit der Analyse der Rezeption. Die Aufnahme durch den Zuschauer stellt keine neutrale Rezeption der Zeichen dar, sondern schließt eine gewisse Identifikation ein, Mimesis geschieht bei Produktion und Rezeption.

Man unterscheidet die Gesamtheit der theatralischen Zeichen in ihrer wechselseitigen Verknüpfung als Inszenierungs- oder Aufführungstext von der meist gegebenen literarischen Vorlage, dem dramatischen Text. Das Theater als Aufführungstext integriert den dramatischen Text als eine Zeichendimension unter anderen. Was auf der Bühne bzw. in dem ästhetisch strukturierten Spielraum geschieht/erscheint, ist durch die Tatsache des ‹Rahmens› Theater notwendigerweise ästhetisiert. Ob Menschen, Gegenstände, Kleider, Licht, Geräusche, Musik, Raumverhältnisse, Zeitrhythmen oder Bewegungsarten – alles, einschließlich der ohnehin als Zeichen organisierten Sprache, wird im Theater zum Zeichen. (Ein Stuhl ist in der Spielsituation kein Stuhl, sondern – z. B. – Zeichen für Stuhl.)

Ähnlich wie für die Theorie des Films besteht für die T. das Problem, wohl einen Text oder Syntagmen aus Zeichen konstatieren zu können, aber keine feststehenden kleinsten Einheiten. Das macht die Rede von einem theatralen Code problematisch. In aller Regel definieren Inszenierungen den größten Teil ihres Zeichenrepertoires aktuell, gültig nur für die gegebene Inszenierung. Eine best. Figurenkonstellation z. B. gewinnt in einem Fall signifikanten Status, bleibt in einem anderen bloß äußerliches Arrangement. Daher ist die Analyse des Zeichenprozesses Theater notwendig an Interpretation und Reflexion verwiesen, an Hermeneutik, die ästhetische und historische, im weitesten Sinn reflektierende Auslegung der Aufführung als Kunst. Verselbständigte Semiotik ergibt lediglich eine Vielzahl relevanter (und irrelevanter) Data, sie benötigt die hermeneutische Anstrengung, um über Verfahren, Voraussetzungen und Kriterien der Strukturbildung und Relevanzzuschreibung Rechenschaft abzulegen.

5. All dies vorausgesetzt, lassen sich verschiedene Ebenen von Zeichen nach ihrer Materialität differenzieren: beim Spieler linguistische, paralinguistische, mimische, gestische, proxemische Zeichen; optische Zeichen wie Kostüme, Maske, Requisiten, Raumgestaltung, Dekoration, Licht; akustische Zeichen wie Geräusch und Musik. Ebenso wie Sprache kennt der Inszenierungstext Redundanzen, schon dadurch, daß fast jede Bedeutung durch mehrere Zeichen ausdrückbar ist, Bedrohung etwa durch linguistische («Achtung!»), paralinguistische (angsterfüllte Tonlage), visuelle (Schatten ziehen auf) oder akustische Zeichen (Lärm, Donner). Die Vielfalt der potentiell ästhetisch-wirksamen Systeme, die in ihrer mehr oder weniger vollständigen Verbindung die Gesamtheit des Theaters ausmachen, hat zu unterschiedlichen Theorien über ihr Zusammenwirken geführt. Die eine Linie sieht im Zusammenwirken und Zusammenstimmen der Zeichenebenen die besondere Qualität des Theaters (→Gesamtkunstwerk). Dagegen steht die Auffassung Brechts, der den produktiven Widerspruch, wie überhaupt für die künstlerische Arbeit, so auch für das Gegen- statt Miteinander der Zeichenebenen favorisiert: «So seien all die Schwesterkünste der Schauspielkunst hier geladen, nicht um ein ‹Gesamtkunstwerk› herzustellen ... sondern ... ihr Verkehr miteinander besteht darin, daß sie sich gegenseitig verfremden.» In der avantgardistischen Ästhetik etwa von Gertrude Stein (1847–1946) und Robert Wilson (* 1941) wiederum steht das Nebeneinander der Theaterelemente im Vordergrund, eine bewußt angestrebte Disparatheit, die auf eine Schulung der einzelnen Sinne abzielt, die, auf sich selbst gestellt, neue Schärfe der Wahrnehmung erreichen sollen. Beeinflußt von Stein und der Kategorie des «landscape play» ist neben Richard Foreman vor allem Robert Wilson, dessen schwer deutbares Bildertheater in keine der großen Linien einzupassen ist und weiterhin Herausforderung für die T. bleibt.

6. Das 20. Jh.: Ist es, seit normative Ästhetik unmöglich wurde, die

Aufgabe von Theorie nicht, den Künsten Vorschriften zu machen, sondern das künstlerisch Produzierte auf den Begriff zu bringen, so gilt dies in besonderem Maß von der T., da seit dem Ende des 19. Jh. fast jedes Jahrzehnt neue, erweiterte Grenzen des Theaters bringt. Mit dem Naturalismus (→ Naturalistisches Theater) ging eine jahrhundertelange vom Nachahmungspostulat beherrschte Epoche des Theaters zu Ende und machte (ähnlich wie in anderen Künsten) einer fortwährenden Suche nach neuen Darstellungsformen Platz (Moderne). Zuvor aber erwuchs aus der konsequenten Zuspitzung des Naturalismus noch die T. von Konstantin S. → Stanislawski (1863–1938), der die theatralische Illusion durch systematische Ausbildung des Schauspielers zu Konzentration und ‹produktiver Einfühlung› in die gestaltete Figur vervollkommnete. Alle erneuernden T. im 20. Jh. setzten sich von → Stanislawski ab, da sein Name unlösbar mit dem psychologischen Illusionstheater verbunden war, das in allen Theaterrevolutionen, dem epischen Theater ebenso wie dem absurden, dem heiligen oder dem Anti-Theater Ziel des Angriffs wurde.

Betrachtet man die modernen Gegenentwürfe, so ist keine scharfe Grenze zu ziehen zwischen der wissenschaftlichen T. und den Konzeptionen einflußreicher Theaterpraktiker, da beide sich gegenseitig beeinflußt haben. Die Grundlagen der heutigen T. werden durch die Namen Artaud und Brecht bezeichnet. Das → «Theater der Grausamkeit» formulierte den radikalen Bruch mit dem Theater der Repräsentation, der Wiederholung, der bloßen Verdopplung des fleischlosen Worts durch traditionelle «mise en scène». Statt dessen verlangt Artaud ein autonomes Theater, in dem das Wort wieder Geste wird, das Unaussprechliche der Körperlichkeit zu seinem Recht kommt, eine Bühnentextur aus Licht, Klang, Schrei, Geste, Bewegung, Rhythmus entsteht. Dieses nicht ästhetisch-kontemplative Theater soll auf die Nerven der Zuschauer wirken und durch Emanzipation des verschütteten Gefühls für die lebendige, freie Kreativität, ja Gottgleichheit des Menschen die erstarrte abendländische Zivilisation bekriegen.

Vorläufer der neuen T. ist bereits Alfred Jarry (1873–1907), dann die futuristische Ästhetik der Montage und Simultanität (assoziative Verknüpfung statt logischer Abfolge) sowie theatrale Aktionen (Dada, Surrealisten), die zum → Happening führen. Von Futurismus und → Konstruktivismus her ist aber auch die Idee des abstrakten Theaters inspiriert. «Theater der Gegenstände», «Theater der Farben», futuristisches Lufttheater, sind Brücke zur T. des Bauhauses. Theater soll – weitgehend ohne menschliche Akteure – aus den technifizierten Bühnenelementen und ihrem Spiel entstehen (Übergang zu bildender Kunst). Ablösung der herkömmlichen Dekorationsbühne durch szenisch gestalteten Raum gab es schon in der antinaturalistischen Ästhetik von Adolphe Appia (1862–1928) und Edward Gordon Craig (1872–1966). Fließende Über-

Theatertherapie 1019

gänge zwischen Theaterästhetik des Futurismus, Dada, Surrealismus, Konstruktivismus. Im Bauhaus ebenfalls Anknüpfung an Idee des Gesamtkunstwerks. Artauds radikale T. und die Entwürfe der Bauhaus-Künstler, Konstruktivisten und Surrealisten wirken bis heute bei fast allen Schöpfern und Theoretikern des avantgardistischen Theaters nach.

Die Gegenposition zu Artaud, doch in der Absicht mit diesem vereint, durch Theater die bürgerliche Gesellschaft und Zivilisation zu erschüttern, ist die T. von Bertolt Brecht (1898–1956). Zentrale Kategorien sind →«episches Theater» und «Verfremdung». Anknüpfend an die philosophische Kategorie der Entfremdung wird diese verstanden als Dreischritt von Verstehen – Nichtverstehen – Verstehen. Den gezeigten Vorgängen wird das Einleuchtende genommen durch →Verfremdungseffekte (V-Effekte): Historisieren, zitierende Sprechweise; Unterbrechung durch Erzählungen, Lieder, Titel; Zeigetechnik. Der Zuschauer wird nicht durch Illusion getäuscht, bleibt sich der Theatersituation bewußt. Dramaturgie der →«Einfühlung» wird aufgegeben als der Rationalität des «wissenschaftlichen Zeitalters» nicht adäquat. Kritik an Gesellschaft und Verhalten wird möglich durch Theater, das mittels kritischer Distanz des Zuschauers Alternativen denkbar bleiben läßt; Vorgang nicht als Schicksal (‹Nicht-Sondern›-Technik). Soziale Bedeutung individuellen Verhaltens wird durch «Gestus» gezeigt. Brechts T. setzt bei der lehrhaften →Parabel an, der Akzent liegt auf Fabel, nicht Charakter. Undifferenzierte Inanspruchnahme Brechts für platte Didaxe führte seit den 70er Jahren zu deutlichem Nachlassen des Interesses der Theatermacher an Brecht, in dessen T. Raum für Emotionen, Subjektivität, Mehrdeutigkeit vermißt wird. Exakte Neulektüre der Texte (eher als der T. selbst) würde verschüttete Facetten von Brechts Konzeptionen sichtbar machen, die bis in die 70er Jahre von unermeßlichem Einfluß auf Theorie und Praxis des internationalen Theaters waren. Auch in der wissenschaftlichen T. haben seine Thesen tiefe Spuren hinterlassen. Eigene Erwähnung verdient Brechts Theorie des →Lehrstücks, das als offen strukturiertes Dispositiv unterschiedlichen politisch-theatralen Gebrauch ermöglicht.

Eine relativ junge Entwicklung der T. ist die Theater-Anthropologie. Ebenfalls auf Inspiration Artauds fußend, der sich bereits auf orientalisches Theater als Vorbild berief, haben Theaterleute wie Grotowski, Brook, Eugenio Barba (*1936) oder Suzuki Tadashi Versuche unternommen, eine universelle Theatersprache durch interkulturellen Austausch zwischen westlichen und östlichen Theaterformen zu entwickeln, besonders durch neue Art des Schauspielertrainings, im Unterschied von der psychologischen Ausbildung mit Schwerpunkt auf körperlicher Selbstwahrnehmung, Atmung, universalen Basisgesten. Hier berühren sich T. und Anthropologie, da in Ritual, Performance und Theater universal gültige, jedenfalls brauchbare Darstellungs- und Verhaltensbausteine ge-

1020 Theatertheorie

sucht werden. Z. B. das ind. →Kathakali, jap. →Nô-Theater und deren streng formalisierte Ausbildungsmethoden wurden von Barba und Grotowski studiert und hatten Folgen für Grotowskis Theaterlaboratorium, seine «paratheatralischen Experimente» seit 1969 und das seit einigen Jahren in den USA betriebene Projekt des «objektiven Theaters», das R. Schechner als Synthesis zu den Antithesen «Armes Theater» und «Paratheater» ansieht. Mit ähnlichen Zielen betreibt Barba seine Internationale Schule für Theater-Anthropologie (ISTA), in der Lehrer u. a. aus Japan, Bali, Indien, China, Peru, Europa zusammenkommen, nicht um eine synkretistische Mischung, sondern gemeinsame Grundelemente des Theaters zu finden. «Theater-Anthropologie untersucht das sozio-kulturelle und physiologische Verhalten des Menschen in einer Performance-Situation» (Barba, 1982).

Adorno, T. W.: Ästhetische Theorie. Frankfurt/M. 1970; ders./Horkheimer, M.: Dialektik der Aufklärung. Amsterdam 1947; Artaud, A.: Le théâtre et son double. Paris 1964; Barba, E.: Jenseits der schwimmenden Inseln. Reinbek 1985; Blau, H.: Blooded Thought. Occasions on Theatre. New York 1982; Derrida, J.: De la grammatologie. Paris 1967; ders.: Die Schrift und die Differenz. Frankfurt/M. 1976; Fischer-Lichte, E.: Semiotik des Theaters. Tübingen 1983; Goffman, E.: The Presentation of Self in Everyday Life. New York 1959; Kristeva, J.: La révolution du langage poétique. Paris 1974; Lehmann, G. K.: Phantasie und künstlerische Arbeit. Berlin/Weimar 1976; Mead, G. H.: Mind, Self and Society. University of Chicago Press 1970; Metz; C.: Le signifiant imaginaire. Paris 1977; Pavis, P.: Voix et images de la scène. Lille ²1985; Schechner, R.: Between Theatre and Anthropology. Philadelphia 1985; Steinbeck, D.: Einleitung in die Theorie und Systematik der Theaterwissenschaft. Berlin 1970; Steinweg, R. (Hg.): Auf Anregung Bertolt Brechts: Lehrstücke mit Schülern, Arbeitern, Theaterleuten. Frankfurt/M. 1978; Turner, V.: The Ritual Process. Cornell University Press 1982; Vernant, J.-P./Vidal-Naquet, P.: Mythe et tragédie en grèce ancienne. Paris 1973; Szondi, P.: Theorie des modernen Dramas. Frankfurt/M. 1963.

Hans-Thies Lehmann

Theatertherapie

Trainingstechniken des Theaters, besonders des experimentellen, sollen das ästhetische Material, den eigenen Körper, die Stimme und die Sinne wach und in Bewegung halten. Einige dieser Methoden können bei psychisch oder körperlich behinderten oder kranken Menschen emanzipatorische und heilende Schritte initiieren.

Eine therapeutische Theaterarbeit gibt Sinn im Rollenspiel, im Psychodrama, in Bewegungstherapie, in Projektarbeit in entsprechenden Institutionen. Dabei besteht ein Unterschied zwischen der laienspielhaften Theaterarbeit mit therapeutischer Wirkung in sozial betreuten Gruppen

und den Therapieformen z. B. des Psychodramas, in denen die Bewältigung psychischer Konflikte sich theatraler Mittel bedient.

Der künstlerischen und therapeutischen Arbeit mit dem eigenen Körper haben sich besonders gewidmet J. Grotowski, der den eigentherapeu-
tischen Wert als ‹Abfallprodukt› in der Theaterarbeit erkennt; R. v.
Laban, durch den in England intensive Forschung in der Bewegungstherapie eingeleitet wurde; M. Feldenkrais, der einen harmonischen Bewe-
gungsablauf des menschlichen Körpers entwickelt hat; V. N. Iljine, der
schon zu Anfang dieses Jahrhunderts über Theater u. a. mit alten Menschen gearbeitet hat (Petzold); die anthroposophische → Eurythmie.

Brook, P.: Der leere Raum. Berlin 1983; Feldenkrais, M.: Bewußtheit durch Bewegung. Frankfurt/M. 1978; Grotowski, J.: Für ein armes Theater. Hannover
1969; Laban, R. v.: Der moderne Ausdruckstanz in der Erziehung. Wilhelmshaven 1981; Petzold, H. (Hg.): Psychotherapie und Körperdynamik. Paderborn
1977; Petzold, H. (Hg.): Dramatische Therapie. Stuttgart 1982; Sennett, R.: Verfall und Ende des öffentlichen Lebens. Die Tyrannei der Intimität. Frankfurt/M.
1983.

Hinnerk Peitmann / Red.

Theater und Philharmonie Essen GmbH

Stadttheater. Musiktheater im Aalto-Theater (Eröffnung 1988), erbaut
nach den preisgekrönten Entwürfen von Alvar Aalto (1898–1976).
Sprechtheater: Spielstätten: Grillo-Theater (Raumtheater, 300 bis 500
Plätze, erbaut 1892, Umbau 1988–90, Architekt Werner Rhunau), Studio im Grillo-Theater (Raumtheater), Casa Nova I und II. Stadttheater
(Stiftung des Industriellen Friedrich Grillo) eröffnet am 16.9.1892,
1892–94 erster Pächter und Direktor Albert Berthold (1841–1926). Unter Intendant Hans Gelling (1858–1911) von 1904 bis 1907 Theater-
Union mit Dortmund. Intendant Georg Hartmann (1862–1936) letzter
Pächter des Essener Theaters. 1912 wird das T. in städtische Verwaltung
übernommen. 1912–18 Intendant Dr. Johannes Maurach (1883–1951).
1921–30 Intendant Stanislaus Fuchs (1864–1942): während seiner
Intendanz Caspar Neher und später Hein Heckroth (1901–70) Ausstattungsleiter, Hannes Küpper Dramaturg und Herausgeber der Theaterzeitschrift «Der Scheinwerfer», Herbert Waniek Leiter des Schauspiels, Kurt Jooss Leiter der Tanzgruppe. 1940–58 Intendant Dr. Karl
Bauer (1900–82); Inszenierungen von Gustav Rudolf Sellner und Erwin
Piscator, Bühnenbildner Alfred Siercke (1910–85) und Fritz Brauer
(1911–84), zahlreiche Ur- und Erstaufführungen. 1958–67 Generalintendant Dr. Erich Schumacher (1908–86): Inszenierungen u. a. von Erwin Piscator, Harry Buckwitz und Adolf Rott, Chefdramaturgin Dr. Ilka

1022 Theatervorhang

Boll, Bühnenbildner u. a. Teo Otto, Jean-Pierre Ponnelle, Hein Heckroth; Hauptakzente des Spielplanes neben Klassikern auf zeitgenössischen Dramatikern; «Szenische Werkstatt Essen» diente der Förderung der zeitgenössischen dt. Dramatik. 1978–83 Intendant Ulrich Brecht. 1985–92 Schauspieldirektor Hansgünther Heyme (*1935): Macht gesellschaftskritisches politisches Theater in der Nachfolge Erwin Piscators; sieht Theater als «aufklärerische Anstalt» im Sinne Schillers, hält sich an dessen Forderung, «durch Spiel ein Mensch zu werden»; kommentiert die Gegenwart mit manipulierten klassischen Texten. Ab 1993 Schauspieldirektor Jürgen Bosse.

Feldens, F.: 75 Jahre Städtische Bühnen Essen. Geschichte des Essener Theaters 1892–1967. Essen 1967. Theater in Essen 1974–1978. Eine Dokumentation. Wuppertal o. J.

Ingeborg Janich

Theatervorhang

Vorhangsysteme neuzeitlicher Bühnen bestehen in erster Linie aus einem Hauptvorhang, meist einem geteilten, nach beiden Seiten hin beweglichen, raffbaren Stoffvorhang, seltener einer bemalten Leinwandfläche, die nach Art der Prospekte (→Kulisse) aufgezogen wird, einem Deck- oder Schallvorhang, der hinter dem Hauptvorhang verläuft und dazu dient, den Lärm von Bühnenumbauten zu dämpfen, und schließlich dem feuerpolizeilich vorgeschriebenen →‹Eisernen Vorhang› (in Deutschland seit 1889 obligatorisch, zuerst 1782 in Lyon verwendet).

Man unterscheidet die Vorhangformen nach ihrer Position, die sie im Bühnenraum einnehmen, und/oder ihrer Verwendung innerhalb der Aufführung. Der Hauptvorhang (identisch mit dem Vordervorhang) hängt vor der Bühne und trennt die Welt des Spiels vom Raum der Zuschauer; der Zwischenvorhang hängt zwischen Vorder- und Hinterbühne und gliedert den Bühnenraum; der Hintergrundvorhang bildet den Abschluß der Bühne; Teilvorhänge verhüllen/enthüllen gelegentlich Teile der Bühne, Nischen, Zelte, Türeingänge usw.; der Verwandlungsvorhang tritt in Funktion, wenn innerhalb des Spiels die Bühne verändert wird.

Die älteste Form des Theatervorhangs ist der Auftrittsvorhang, der von den Schauspielern beim Auftritt benutzt wird. Die Melanesier und Aborigines benutzen für kultische Veranstaltungen eine Wand, den Zeremonialschirm, hinter der sich die Geister bis zu ihrem Auftritt verbergen können. Die ostasiatischen Völker gestalten die Grenze zwischen Diesseits und Jenseits, die erste Begegnung mit dem Außerirdischen, statt dessen mit einem Auftrittsvorhang, der zudem Neugierde und Spannung erzeugt, die Gemütsverfassung des Protagonisten und in Japan den Rang des Spielers andeutet. Dabei benutzt man Teilvorhänge in Japan und China. In Indien (→Indisches Theater) war der Auftrittsvorhang beim Volkstheater ein Hintervorhang, aber im klassischen Theater wurden die ersten Teile hinter einem Zwischenvorhang gespielt, um die Götter und Dämonen zu befrieden. Das jap. →Kabuki-Theater (→Japanisches Theater) kennt seit der Mitte des 17. Jh. neben dem Auftrittsvorhang den Hauptvorhang, außerdem den Akt- und Verwandlungsvorhang, Hintervorhänge und den Enthüllungsvorhang.

Die Geschichte des T. im westeurop. Bereich beginnt im kaiserlichen Rom (→Antikes Theater); das griech., hellenistische und vorhellenistische Theater des 4. bis 1. Jh. v. Chr. kennt keine T., wie archäologische Untersuchungen nachweisen. Im röm. Theater nimmt man seit Mitte des 1. Jh. v. Chr. die Verwendung eines Vordervorhangs an: das ‹aulaeum›. Der Vordervorhang wurde erst notwendig, als nicht mehr Dieseits und Jenseits, sondern Bühnenwelt und Alltagswelt getrennt werden mußten. Ursprünglich im Bereich der Mimenaufführungen als Hintergrund- und Auftrittsvorhang angesiedelt, ist das ‹siparium› die zweite Vorhangform der Römer. Im Laufe der Zeit werden die unterschiedlichen Bezeichnungen aber austauschbar.

Die mittelalterliche →Simultanbühne kennt wiederum keinen Hauptvorhang, sondern benutzte kleinere Teilvorhänge zur Ver- und Enthüllung einzelner Handlungsorte. Im 16. Jh. benötigte die Perspektivbühne den Vordervorhang, um den Zuschauer zu Beginn des Spiels durch sein Öffnen zu überraschen und in eine Scheinwelt zu versetzen. Die ital. Verwandlungs- und →Kulissenbühne und damit der Hauptvorhang kommt durch die höfischen Opern- und Ballettaufführungen in den deutschsprachigen Raum (etwa seit 1519); die Jesuitenbühne (→Jesuitentheater) entwickelte sich parallel zu den Hoftheatern und benutzte den Hauptvorhang in gleicher Weise. Das protestantische →Schultheater und später die →Wanderbühnen übernahmen seine Form. Im Volkstheater des deutschsprachigen Raums ist der Hauptvorhang seit 1637 nachgewiesen, nach dem 30jährigen Krieg ist er die Regel. Im 18. Jh. wird der Hauptvorhang dann auch für die Bezeichnung der Aktschlüsse eingesetzt. Im 20. Jh. erhält der T. zu seinen Grundfunktionen Unterteilung, Verhüllung und Enthüllung weitere dramaturgische Funktionen, ändert sein Aussehen (z. B. die halbhohe Brecht-Gardine) und seinen Zweck. Eine Konsequenz aus der Durchsetzung des antiillusionistischen Theaters ist der völlige Wegfall des T. Der vielfältige Gebrauch des T. im gegenwärtigen Theater entspricht der Vielfalt der theaterästhetischen Formen.

Seit der Renaissance wurden Haupt- und/oder Vordervorhang oft auch als Gemälde gestaltet mit allegorischen und mythologischen Szenen. Der Vorhang prägte die ‹Stimmung› im Zuschauerraum eines Theaters und wurde von den Theaterarchitekten als Stilmittel eingesetzt. Mit der

Abkehr vom Illusionismus im 20. Jh. werden einfache Stoff- oder Samt-vorhänge (meist rote) den kunstvollen Gemälde- und Draperie-Vorhän-gen vorgezogen. – Eine Sonderform, die schon im 17. Jh. nachgewiesen ist, bleibt allerdings erhalten, der sog. Stückvorhang, d. i. ein Vorhang, der, meist von bekannten Künstlern entworfen (in der Moderne z. B. von Picasso und Dalí), nur für eine bestimmte Inszenierung benutzt wird (→Japanisches Theater, →Chinesisches Theater).

Bachler, K.: Gemalte Theatervorhänge in Deutschland und Österreich. München 1972; Radke-Stegh, M.: Der Theatervorhang. Meisenheim am Glan 1978.

Wim J. M. Achten / Ute Hagel

theaterwerkstatt hannover

Älteste freie Gruppe der Stadt Hannover. 1975 gegründet, Schwerpunkte Eigenproduktionen zu aktuellen Themen in Zusammenarbeit mit Auto-ren und Komponisten; v. a. Kinder- und Jugendtheater, daneben auch Animation, theatralische Forschung und Weiterbildung. Seit 1977 feste Spielstätte im Pavillon am Raschplatz. Aufgrund unzureichender Finan-zierung Spielbetrieb zum 31. 12. 1991 eingestellt. Ab August 1992 Wie-deraufnahme der Arbeit mit neuen strukturellen und künstlerischen Schwerpunkten (einzelne Großprojekte) unter der künstlerischen Lei-tung von Martina v. Boxen.

Ingeborg Janich

Theaterwissenschaft

T. ist als eigenständige Wissenschaft eine relativ junge Disziplin. Sie um-faßt alle Bereiche, die in irgendeiner Form mit dem Theater im allg. und der speziellen Aufführung in Verbindung stehen, die in ihrer nicht iden-tisch wiederholbaren Einmaligkeit nur rekonstruiert werden kann, da sie keine manifesten Untersuchungsgegenstände hinterläßt. – Vereinfacht lassen sich zwei hauptsächliche Forschungsgebiete der T. unterscheiden: 1. Theatergeschichte, die Inszenierungs- und Lokaltheatergeschichte, aber auch die historische Entwicklung einzelner Bereiche wie Bühnen-bild, Regie usw. umfaßt; 2. systematische T., die sich mit phänomenolo-gischen, morphologischen und ästhetischen Problemen des Theaters als kultureller Äußerung beschäftigt. Hierzu gehören u. a. auch Theaterkri-tik, Publikumsforschung, Wirkungsgeschichte und Schauspielkunst.

T. als wissenschaftliche Disziplin entwickelte sich erst im 20. Jh. und

Theaterwissenschaft **1025**

hat sich bis heute noch nicht unangefochten durchsetzen können. Ansätze gab es in Deutschland bereits im 18. (Gottsched, Lessing, J. J. Engel), verstärkt im 19. Jh. (Tieck, Laube, Prutz, Mundt, E. Devrient, Chr. Birch u. a.). Erste programmatisch theaterwissenschaftliche Arbeiten entstanden aber erst Ende des vorigen Jh. innerhalb der Literaturwissenschaft. Zwar hatte bereits 1846 Th. Mundt an der Berliner Universität eine theaterwissenschaftliche Vorlesung angekündigt («Dramaturgia seu historica ac theoria artis dramaticae et scenicae apud populos recentiores»), doch waren es bis zum Ende des Jh. vor allem ‹Fachfremde›, Historiker und Altphilologen, die als erste T. an dt. Hochschulen betrieben, ohne daß dafür der Begriff zur Verfügung gestanden hätte. Für die Herausbildung des Fachs wichtiger als jene doch eher vereinzelten Bemühungen war der unablässige Einsatz des Berliner Literaturwissenschaftlers M. Hermann seit der Jahrhundertwende. 1919 legte er eine Denkschrift über die Notwendigkeit eines theaterwissenschaftlichen Instituts vor, die 1923 zur entsprechenden Gründung an der Berliner Universität führte. Kennzeichnend für das Mißtrauen gegenüber der neuen Disziplin war die Unterstellung des selbständigen Instituts unter den Ordinarius für Literaturwissenschaft, die bis 1944 beibehalten wurde. Auch an anderen Universitäten bemühten sich Dozenten um Etablierung und Anerkennung der T., so etwa Julius Petersen in Frankfurt und später in Berlin, vor allem aber Artur Kutscher, der seit 1909/10 an der Münchener Universität regelmäßig über theaterwissenschaftliche Fragestellungen las. Der seit 1921/22 als Lektor an der Universität Köln lehrende Carl Niessen erhielt 1929 die erste Professur für T. in Deutschland. 1926 wurde in München das «Institut für Theaterkunde» gegründet, dem 1943 das «Zentralinstitut für T.» in Wien (H. Kindermann) und die Errichtung einer Professur in Berlin folgten, auf die der ehem. Lektor H. Knudsen berufen wurde.

In Deutschland kann T. gegenwärtig an den Universitäten bzw. Hochschulen in Berlin (Freie Univ., Humboldt-Univ.), Bochum, Erlangen, Frankfurt a. M., Gießen, Göttingen, Hildesheim, Köln, Leipzig (Theaterhochschule «Hans Otto», ab 1992/93 auch Univ.), Marburg und München studiert werden. Im deutschsprachigen Raum kommen die Universitäten Bern und Wien hinzu. Daß die T. auch international noch um Anerkennung kämpfen muß, zeigt z. B. die Errichtung entsprechender Institute in Dänemark, Italien und den Niederlanden erst lange nach dem Ende des 2. Weltkriegs. Anders sieht die Tradition aus in Frankreich, wo seit 1896 an der Sorbonne T. unterrichtet wurde, und den USA, wo G. P. Baker seit 1895 über T. las und an zahlreichen Universitäten sog. «Drama Departments» eingerichtet wurden.

In engem Zusammenhang mit der Etablierung der neuen Wissenschaft stand die Gründung von Theatergesellschaften, Spezialmuseen und die Veranstaltung entsprechender Ausstellungen. Bereits 1894 wurde in

1026 Theaterwissenschaft

Moskau die «Rußkoe Teatralnoe Obsčestvo» gegr., 1901 in Paris die «Société de l'histoire du théâtre», 1902 die «Gesellschaft für Theatergeschichte» in Berlin. Gründungen in zahlreichen anderen Ländern folgten, im deutschsprachigen Raum etwa die «Gesellschaft für schweizerische Theaterkultur» (1927) und die «Gesellschaft für Wiener Theaterforschung» (1942). Auf internationaler Ebene kamen 1945 die «International Society for Theatre Research», seit 1955 die «Fédération Internationale pour la Recherche Théâtrale» hinzu, vor allem das 1948 in Prag begründete «Internationale Theater-Institut» (→ITI), eine Unterorganisation der UNESCO. – Aus dem 1866 eingerichteten Archiv der Pariser Oper entwickelte sich das erste →Theatermuseum der Welt. 1909 wurde die theaterwissenschaftliche Abteilung des Londoner «Victoria and Albert Museum» eröffnet, 1913 das Mailänder «Museo Teatrale alla Scala», 1922 die Theatersammlung der Österreichischen Nationalbibliothek und das Stockholmer Drottningholm-Museum. Weitere wichtige Einrichtungen dieser Art sind das Theaterhistorische Museum Kopenhagen, die Schweizerische Theatersammlung in Bern und seit 1932 die «Theatre Collection» der New Yorker Public Library. In Deutschland wurde 1910 mit dem Aufbau des Münchener Theatermuseums begonnen. Hinzu kam 1929 das Museum der Preußischen Staatstheater sowie durch die Initiative Carl Niessens eine umfangreiche Sammlung in Köln, die sich heute in Schloß Wahn befindet. Wichtige Sammlungen befinden sich außerdem in Berlin und Hamburg («Theatersammlung»). Gab es bei der Pariser Weltausstellung von 1878 bereits eine Sonderabteilung für das Theater, so fand die erste «Internationale Ausstellung für Musik und Theater» in Wien statt, der 1910 eine erste dt. Theaterausstellung in Berlin, 1927 eine weitere in Magdeburg folgten. 1955 wurde in Wien die umfassende «Europäische Theaterausstellung» durchgeführt.

In ihrer relativ kurzen Fachgeschichte hatte die T. besonders in Deutschland erhebliche Probleme neben der Begründung ihres Fachgebiets mit der Entwicklung einer eigenen Methodik. Die ‹Gründerväter› der T. und die folgende Generation verzichteten weitgehend auf gegenstandskonstitutive methodische Reflexionen zugunsten der immerzu erneuten Abgrenzung vor allem von der Literaturwissenschaft. Hinzu trat als Problem seit Beginn der Fachgebiete der «Januskopf» (Steinbeck) der T., das Bemühen um wissenschaftlichen Freiraum und theaterpraktische Bedeutung – bei gleichzeitigem programmatischen Verzicht auf eine spezialisierte Ausbildung. Die Berufung auf den ‹Theaterabend› als Zentrum theaterwissenschaftlicher Bemühung und auf ‹Urphänomene› des Theaters wie den «Mimus» führte durch die ahistorische Betrachtungsweise in Verbindung mit einem vordergründigen ‹Autonomiebegriff› vom Theater zur besonderen Anfälligkeit der T. für wissenschaftsfremde Manipulationen.

Theaterwissenschaft 1027

Neben dem bis heute erhobenen Vorwurf eines selbstgenügsamen Positivismus war eine der Folgen dieser Ansätze die reibungslose und z. T. begrüßte Integration der T. in den dt. Faschismus. An die Stelle des von den Nationalsozialisten zwangspensionierten Max Herrmann rückte der vormalige Kritiker des «Völkischen Beobachters» und Lektor für T., H. Knudsen, der noch Anfang der 70er Jahre die methodischen Ansätze seines Vorgängers pries, ohne seines grauenvollen Todes im KZ Theresienstadt zu gedenken. Kindermann, Niessen und zur Nedden gehörten zu frühen Befürwortern des NS. Daß die meisten dieser Wissenschaftler nach dem Ende des 2. Weltkriegs nahezu bruchlos wieder in die Universitäten integriert wurden und das Fach bis fast in die Gegenwart hinein dominierten, trug zweifelsohne dazu bei, daß eine kritische Fachgeschichte bis heute allenfalls ansatzweise vorliegt.

Immer noch bestimmt die «Existenzangst der Anfänge» (Steinbeck) in nicht unerheblichem Maße die T. im deutschsprachigen Raum. Eingefordert seit längerem, durchgeführt erst in Ansätzen, wäre für die T. eine kritische Selbstreflexion nötig – auch unter Einbeziehung historisch-materialistischer Ansätze, wie sie in der DDR versucht wurden. Sie müßte sich selbst als geschichtlich und gesellschaftlich integrierte Wissenschaft begreifen, um dann über die Erweiterung ihres Untersuchungsgegenstandes durch die Massenmedien (Rundfunk, Film, Fernsehen, Video) und ihrer Untersuchungsperspektiven zu einer angemessenen Grundlegung des Fachs zu gelangen und zur Ausbildung einer übergreifenden Medienästhetik.

Eberle, O.: Theaterschule und Theaterwissenschaft. Elgg 1945; Fiebach, J./ Münz, R.: Thesen zu theoretisch-methodischen Fragen der Theatergeschichtsschreibung. In: Wiss. Zs. d. Humboldt-Univ. Berlin, Ges.-sprachwiss. Reihe 23 (1974); Haarmann, H.: Theater und Geschichte. Gießen 1974; Hadamczik, D. (Hg.): Theater... der Nachwelt unverloren. Berlin 1987; Hoerstel, K./Schlenker, J.: Verzeichnis der Hochschulschriften. Diplom- und Staatsexamensarbeiten der DDR zum Drama und Theater (1949 bis 1970). Berlin 1973; Klier, H. (Hg.): Theaterwissenschaft im deutschsprachigen Raum. Darmstadt 1981; Knudsen, H.: Methodik der Theaterwissenschaft. Stuttgart u. a. 1971; ders.: Theaterwissenschaft. Werden und Wertung einer Universitätsdisziplin. Berlin/Hamburg/Stuttgart 1950; Kutscher, A.: Grundriß der Theaterwissenschaft. München [2]1949; Meier, M./Roessler, P./Scheit, G.: Theaterwissenschaft und Faschismus. (Wien 1981); Möhrmann, R. (Hg.): Theaterwissenschaft heute. Berlin 1990; Niessen, C.: Handbuch der Theaterwissenschaft. Bd. 1, Teil 1–3. Emsdetten 1949–58; Rojek, H. J.: Bibliographie der deutschsprachigen Hochschulschriften zur Theaterwissenschaft, 1953 bis 1960. Berlin 1962; Schäfer, R.: Ästhetisches Handeln als Kategorie einer interdisziplinären Theaterwissenschaft. Aachen 1988; Schumacher, E.: Theaterkritik und Theaterwissenschaft. Berlin 1986; Schwanbeck, G.: Bibliographie der deutschsprachigen Hochschulschriften zur Theaterwissenschaft von 1885 bis 1952. Berlin 1956; Steinbeck, D.: Einführung in die Theorie und Systematik der Theaterwissenschaft. Berlin 1970; Székessny, G.: Kritik der Theaterwissenschaft. Diss. München 1955; Veinstein, A. (ed.): Bibliothèques et musées des arts du spectacle dans le monde. Paris 1968; Wille, F.: Abduktive Erklärungsnetze. Zur Theorie theaterwissenschaftlicher Aufführungsanalyse. Frankfurt/M. u. a. 1991.

Wolfgang Beck

Theaterzensur

Zensur ist der (hoheitliche) Versuch, Kunst zu regulieren. Sie setzt die Beherrschung eines Machtapparats oder zumindest ein Abhängigkeitsverhältnis voraus. – Eine Zensur des Theaters findet statt, seitdem es Theater gibt. Bereits von der Theaterpraxis der Antike berichtet Plato, daß Stücke vor ihrer ersten Aufführung einer amtlichen Prüfung unterzogen wurden. Die Gesetzgebung des Lykurg sah eine Bestrafung der Schauspieler vor, die während der Aufführung vom klassischen Text abwichen. Solange Theater in der Form der kirchlichen Mysterienspiele erfolgte, übte die Kirche faktisch dadurch Zensur aus, daß die Aufführung unter ihrer Aufsicht erfolgte. Erst als das Theater an die Öffentlichkeit trat, wurde von seiten des Staates versucht, das Aufführungswesen zu kontrollieren. Die Überwachung erfolgte zwar nicht immer unter dem Begriff der ‹Zensur›, jedoch konnte durch das Privilegienwesen (→ Theatersystem, → Intendant) letztlich auch eine Art der Zensur ausgeübt werden. Erstmals unter Maria Theresia wurde eine Zensurbehörde eingesetzt, die jedoch nicht auf politischem Gebiet tätig werden sollte, sondern den Auftrag hatte, «Unsinn und Gemeinheit» von der Bühne zu verbannen, um dem moralischen Anspruch des Theaters gerecht zu werden (1751). Als einer der Zensoren war Joseph von Sonnenfels (1733–1817) tätig, der vehement gegen die vulgären → Hanswurstiaden kämpfte (1786). In Frankreich läßt sich Zensur als politische Institution bis auf das Jahr 1477 zurückverfolgen, in dem das Parlament Aufführungen von seiner Genehmigung abhängig machte. Die Frz. Revolution schaffte zunächst einmal die T. ab, ordnete jedoch gleichfalls an, daß jedes Theater dreimal in der Woche je eines der Dramen *Brutus, Wilhelm Tell, Gaius Gracchus* oder ein ähnliches, die Revolution verherrlichendes Werk aufführen sollte. 1806 wurde offiziell die T. wieder eingeführt. In Deutschland hatte sich in der Zuständigkeit der Polizei die T. entwickelt. Mit Circular-Rescript vom 16. März 1820 wurde ausdrücklich die T. eingeführt. Die Revolution von 1848 führte vorübergehend zu einer Abschaffung der T., da sie mit dem Grundsatz der öffentlichen Redefreiheit unvereinbar sei (so die amtliche Begründung). 1851 wurde sie jedoch bereits durch die Berliner Theaterverordnung, die bald überall nachgeahmt wurde, wieder eingeführt. Diese Verordnung blieb Rechtsgrundlage bis zum Wirksamwerden der Weimarer Reichsverfassung. Die Institution der Zensur im vorigen Jh. rechtfertigte sich mit dem Hinweis auf Abwehr möglicher Gefahren. Kriterium war ferner das Ehrgefühl bzw. sittliche Gefühl, das nicht verletzt werden dürfe. So wurde beispielsweise der *Prinz von Homburg* erst zehn Jahre nach dem Tod des Dichters aufgeführt, weil es für unerträglich gehalten wurde, die «unmännliche Verzweiflung» eines preußischen Heerführers am Abend vor seinem Tod zu zeigen. Praktisch sahen die Theaterverordnungen vor, daß der Theaterunternehmer das Textbuch zur Genehmigung «zeitig» vorher vorlegen mußte. Ein Verstoß gegen diese Vorlagenpflicht sowie das Abweichen (Extemporieren) von der genehmigten Vorlage während der Aufführung wurde mit Geldstrafe oder sogar dem Entzug der Theaterkonzession bestraft. Die Zensurbestimmungen galten nicht für die Hoftheater. Diese unterlagen jedoch faktisch durch ihre unmittelbare Einbeziehung in den Hof und der Leitung durch einen Hofintendanten einer staatlichen Überwachung, die eine polizeiliche Zensur überflüssig machte. In Österreich sollte die Zensur verhüten, daß politische, religiöse oder soziale Einrichtungen auf der Bühne dargestellt werden. Die Zensur führte damit zu merkwürdigen Auswüchsen: Um beispielsweise Schillers *Jungfrau von Orleans* burgtheaterfähig zu machen, wurde die Geliebte des Königs zu seiner legal angetrauten Ehefrau gemacht, in *Kabale und Liebe* wurde aus dem Präsidentenvater ein «Onkel» gemacht. Das nationalsozialistische Regime führte mit dem Reichstheatergesetz (1934) wieder die T. ein. Gemäß § 5 RTG konnte der Minister für Propaganda und Volksaufklärung zur «Erfüllung der Kulturaufgabe des Theaters» Aufführungen verbieten (→ Theatergesetz). Mit der Institution des → Reichsdramaturgen (offiziell ab 1.1.1934 im Amt) wurde eine Zensurbehörde geschaffen, der alle Spielpläne zur Genehmigung vorzulegen waren. Darüber hinaus entschied er über die «Unbedenklichkeit» von Theaterstücken im Sinne der nationalsozialistischen Dramaturgie.

Für die Bundesrepublik Deutschland sieht das Grundgesetz in Art. 5 Abs. 1 Satz 3 vor, daß eine Zensur nicht «stattfindet». Aber auch in der Verfassung der DDR war Zensur nicht vorgesehen; allerdings gab das inhaltlich bestimmte Gebot zu Förderung und Schutz der «sozialistischen Nationalkultur» und zum Kampf gegen «imperialistische Unkultur» (Artikel 18 der Verfassung von 1974) die Handhabe für staatliche Kontrollen und Verbote; tatsächlich begutachtete das Ministerium für Kultur (und die ihm unterstellte Direktion für das Bühnenrepertoire) alle Theaterspielpläne; Uraufführungen und DDR-Erstaufführungen bedurften generell (wie auch literarische Erstveröffentlichungen) der Genehmigung durch den Kulturminister.

Juristisch ist zwischen der sog. Vorzensur und Nachzensur zu differenzieren. Mit der sog. Vorzensur wird die Veröffentlichung einer Meinungsäußerung von voriger staatlicher Genehmigung abhängig gemacht, während man unter einer Nachzensur die nachträgliche Sanktion versteht. Das Grundgesetz verbietet lediglich die sog. Vorzensur, was letztlich wieder die Zensurfreiheit beschränkt. Im übrigen gilt die Zensurfreiheit des Grundgesetzes nur im Verhältnis zwischen Staat und Bürger. Dies folgt aus dem Charakter der Grundrechte als Abwehrrechte des Bürgers gegenüber staatlichem Handeln.

Unabhängig von staatlichen Eingriffen ergeben sich aber aus den Abhängigkeiten, in denen das Theater steht, zensurgleiche Folgen:

1. Zensurgleiche Eingriffe können sich über die finanzielle Abhängigkeit des Theaters vom Staat ergeben. Man vergleiche etwa die Feststellungen des Bayerischen Obersten Rechnungshofes, der 1977 durch Androhung von Subventionsentzug folgendes feststellte: «Die Spielpläne und Konzertprogramme enthalten seit etlichen Jahren einen weit größeren Anteil moderner Werke. Sie führen im Ergebnis dazu, daß die erheblichen Subventionen am breiten Publikum vorbeigeleitet werden... Wir halten daher eine publikumsorientierte Änderung der künftigen Spiel- und Konzertpläne für unerläßlich.»

2. Auch über die Bestellung eines Intendanten kann faktisch Zensur ausgeübt werden; so kann eine Vertragsverlängerung unterbleiben, weil der Spielplan politisch nicht akzeptiert wird.

3. Kraft seines Direktionsrechts bzw. seiner Verantwortung kann ein Intendant zensorisch wirken, indem er bestimmte Stücke nicht aufführen läßt bzw. bestimmte Regiekonzepte nicht zuläßt.

4. Zensorische Wirkung üben u. U. auch die Theaterorganisationen aus, indem sie es in der Hand haben, bestimmte Aufführungen durch die Nichtaufnahme in ihr Programm zu fördern bzw. zu boykottieren.

5. Auch andere gesellschaftliche Zusammenhänge können faktisch eine Zensur darstellen, beispielsweise öffentliche Reaktionen, die u. U. zu administrativen Beschlüssen führen. So führte die Reaktion der kath. Kirche und ihrer Presse gegen ein Stück der Gruppe →«Rote Grütze» im Jahre 1976 zu dem sog. «Rote-Grütze-Erlaß», der den Besuch der Aufführung von der Zustimmung der Eltern abhängig machte.

Borower; D. C.: Theater und Politik. Die Wiener Theaterzensur im politischen und sozialen Kontext der Jahre 1893 bis 1914. Diss. Wien 1988; Brauneck, M.: Literatur und Öffentlichkeit im ausgehenden 19. Jh. Stuttgart 1974; Clare, J.: «Art Made Tongue-Tied by Authority»: Elizabethan and Jacobean Dramatic Censorship. New York 1990; «Der Freiheit eine Gasse». Dokumentation zur Zensur im Theater. Initiative für die Freiheit der Theaterarbeit 1978. Offenbach; Devrient, E.: Die Geschichte der Dt. Schauspielkunst. 2 Bde. Berlin 1848; Goldstein, R. J.: Political Censorship of Arts and the Press in Nineteenth-Century Europe. Basingstoke 1989; Kienzle, M./Mende, D.: Zensur in der Bundesrepublik 1980. München; Klein, W.: Der Preußische Staat und das Theater im Jahre 1848. Berlin 1924; Knies, W.: Schranken der Kunstfreiheit als verfassungsrechtliche

Problematik. München 1967; Leiss, L.: Kunst und Konflikt. In: Opet, O. (Hg.): Theaterrecht. Berlin 1897, S. 132 ff; Sommer, M.: Zur Geschichte der Theaterzensur. Diss. Berlin 1945 (unveröff.).

Roswitha Körner

Theaterzettel

Seit dem 15. Jh. bezeugte Einzelblätter mit Angaben zu einer Theateraufführung (handschriftlich erstmals 1466 mit →Ankündigung eines Passionsspiels in Hamburg, gedruckt erstmals 1520 für eine Aufführung in Rostock; beide enthielten Inhalt, Ort und Zeitpunkt der Aufführung). Das geistliche Schultheater des 16. und 17. Jh. gab Veranstaltungen zweisprachig (lat./dt.) durch sog. Synopsen und Periochen bekannt, verwies neben Inhalt auf Zweck und Ziel der Darstellung; das →Barocktheater pries zudem Schaueffekte an. Gegen Ende des 17. Jh. setzte sich eine einheitliche Form durch: Genehmigung des jeweiligen Fürsten als erste Mitteilung, ihr folgten Truppe, Stücktitel und Aufführungstermin, Handlungsverlauf in ausschmückender Sprache, Orts- und Zeitangabe. Seit Mitte des 18. bis ins 19. Jh. hinein wurden die vom Leiter oder Dichter der Truppe verfaßten T. in privaten und öffentlichen Häusern verteilt. Außer dem Namen des Prinzipals wurden jetzt ggf. der Autor bzw. Bearbeiter des Stücks und dessen literarische Form angegeben, ferner die Figuren und erstmalig die Namen der Darsteller, daneben der Eintrittspreis. Die Hof- und Stadttheater des 19. Jh. führten diese Tradition fort. Die Nennung des Regisseurs auf dem T. erfolgte vereinzelt ab 1820, regelmäßig erst ab 1880 (ebenso die wöchentliche Ankündigung des →Spielplans auf großformatigen Theaterplakaten als Ergänzung des T.). Ein größeres Bedürfnis nach Information, Analyse und Kommentaren führte seit 1900 (insbesondere durch die Volksbühnenbewegung) zur Ausweitung des T. zum →Programmheft.

Eder, R.: T. Dortmund 1980; Hänsel, J.-R.: Geschichte des T. und seine Wirkung in der Öffentlichkeit. Diss. Berlin 1962; Hagemann, C.: Geschichte des T. Diss. Heidelberg 1901; Pies, E.: Einem hocherfreuten Publikum. Hamburg/Düsseldorf 1973.

Monika Sandhack

Theatralisches Theater

Künstlerische Tendenz zur Erneuerung des Theaters nach der Jahrhundertwende (→Stilbühne, →Theaterreform), welche sich gegen das →Illusionstheater, den akademischen Realismus und die Milieuschilderungen des Naturalismus (→Naturalistisches Theater) wandte, um der Retheatralisierung willen (Georg Fuchs, 1868–1949: *Die Schaubühne der Zukunft*, 1904; *Die Revolution des Theaters*, 1909). Bedeutende Vertreter dieser Haltung sind in Rußland Wsewolod E. Meyerhold (1874–1940), Jewgeni B. Wachtangow (1883–1922) und Alexander J. Tairow (1885–1950) sowie vor allem in Frankreich Jacques Copeau (1879–1949: *Essai de rénovation dramatique*, 1913). Das Theatralische dieses ‹neuen Theaters› (E. Gordon Craig) wird gesucht in einer Rückkehr zu den großen Theaterformen der Vergangenheit (→Antikes Theater, →Mittelalter/Drama und Theater des Mittelalters, →Elisabethanisches Theater, →Commedia dell'arte) und außereurop. Kulturen. Wesentlich darin sind für Meyerhold und Copeau die Betonung der szenischen Arbeit des Regisseurs und der Schauspieler sowie die Vorherrschaft des Spielerischen, daher vor allem die Bewunderung für die Commedia dell'arte mit ihrer ‹volkstümlichen Einfachheit› (Copeau), ihrer Stegreiftechnik, der Verwendung der Akrobatik und der →Farce. Angestrebt wurde ein Theater der ‹nackten Bretter› (Copeau), worin die Bühne, bar jeden unnützen Dekors, dem Autor und dem Schauspieler zurückgegeben werden sollte: Die Bühne ist das ‹Instrument des Dramatikers›, ‹der Ort des Dramas, nicht des Bildes und der Maschinerie›. In diesem Sinne waren die Inszenierungen Copeaus im →Théâtre du Vieux Colombier angelegt; Einfluß auf die Künstler des →Cartel, bes. seinen Schüler Louis Jouvet (1887–1951).

Bablet, D.: La mise en scène contemporaine 1887–1914. Brüssel 1968; ders.: Copeau et le théâtre théatral. In: Maske und Kothurn 15/1, 1969; Kurtz, M.: Jacques Copeau. Biographie d'un théâtre. Paris 1950.

Gérard Schneilin

Theatralität

Bezeichnung für das dem Theaterprozeß im Unterschied zum (dramatischen) Text, aber auch zu reproduzierenden Künsten Spezifische: die kombinierte Vielfalt unterschiedlicher Zeichensysteme wie Licht, Klang, Körperlichkeit, Raum in der konkreten Aufführungssituation einerseits; die dem Theater allein wesentliche zeit-räumliche Einheit von Emission und Rezeption der Zeichen im Hier und Jetzt der Aufführung andererseits. T. bezieht sich auf den gesamten Inszenierungstext minus den dra-

matischen oder sonstigen vorgegebenen linguistischen Text. Die Inszenierung bestimmt auch das vorgegebene Textmaterial: Durch Stimmart,
Sprechweise, Lautstärke, Tempo, räumliche Disposition werden die
sprachlichen Zeichen modifiziert, ergänzt, gedeutet. Der Begriff T. zielt
auf Inszenierung als umfassende autonome Kunstpraxis im Gegensatz zur
traditionellen Auffassung des Theaters als mise en scène des Dramas,
dem die Inszenierung gerecht werden müßte. Theater nimmt aber notwendigerweise nicht die ganze Fülle des Textes auf (es muß sich für best.
Auslegungen entscheiden, also andere mögliche unterdrücken), ergänzt
andererseits unvermeidlich den Text durch Hinzufügen neuer Elemente.

Der Begriff T. erfaßt auch, daß Theater nicht nur der vorgeführte Vorgang ist, sondern auch die spezifisch organisierte Interaktion zwischen
Theatervorgang und Publikum einschließt. Diese kann mit Bezug auf
Zeitdauer, Raum, psychologische Struktur, Art und Umfang des Körperkontakts unterschiedlich ausfallen; daher umfaßt Theater neben dem
dramatischen oder sonstigen Text und dem umfassenden Inszenierungstext als drittes Niveau den «performance»-Text» (Richard
Schechner). Nicht erst in radikalen Formen des Environment-Theaters,
sondern schon im Gefolge von Antonin Artaud (1896–1948) ist T.
Schlagwort gegen ‹literarische›, logozentrische Dramaturgie, für die
Schaffung eines nicht primär auf Sinn und Bedeutung orientierten sinn-
lich-körperlichen Theaterstils, für Autonomie der Theaterkunst mit Einbeziehung aller denkbaren sinnlichen Momente (Musik, Schrei, Lichtregie, Tanz usw.), um die Herrschaft der abstrakten, reproduzierenden
Wortkultur im Theater zu brechen.

Hans-Thies Lehmann

The Theatre

‹The Theatre› war das erste feste Londoner Theatergebäude und wurde
1576 durch James Burbage (ca. 1566–1636) errichtet. Es war ein offener
Holzbau, außerhalb der Stadt im Norden gelegen. Der Zuschauerraum
bestand aus drei übereinanderliegenden Galerien, deren oberste gedeckt
war. An einer Seite befand sich das schmale Bühnenhaus mit allen notwendigen Räumen für die Schauspieler. Die von Säulenstümpfen getragene Spielfläche ragte weit in den Hof hinein. Die Hinterbühne war von
zwei Säulen flankiert, zwischen denen die Bühne bis zur Höhe der ersten
Galerie emporstieg. An dieser Stelle trug das Bühnenhaus eine Reihe von
Balkonen. Der mittlere Balkon diente als Oberbühne, die übrigen waren
der Musikkapelle und vornehmen Besuchern vorbehalten. Der Spielplan
des ‹Theatre› sah neben Fechtkämpfen und artistischen Darbietungen

1034 Théâtre Antoine

auch Schauspielaufführungen der →Chamberlain's Men vor. – Als im Jahre 1597 nach Ablauf der Mietzeit der Grundeigentümer den Abriß des Hauses verfügte, transportierte man das Bauholz über die Themse und erbaute aus diesem Holz das →Globe.

Chambers, E. K.: The Elizabethan Stage. 1951; Frenzel, H. A.: Geschichte des Theaters. München 1979; Lawrence, W. J.: The Elizabethan Playhouse. 1912; Stamm, R.: Geschichte des Engl. Theaters. 1951.

Elke Kehr

Théâtre Alfred Jarry

1926 gegründet von Antonin Artaud (1896–1948), Roger Vitrac (1899–1952) und Robert Aron; 1927 erste Vorstellung; 1929 bereits wieder geschlossen. Inszeniert wurden u. a. 2 Stücke von Vitrac, dem Fortsetzer des surrealistischen Theaters unter dem Einfluß von Alfred Jarry, darunter *Victor ou les enfants au pouvoir* (dt. «Victor oder Die Kinder an der Macht»). Artaud versuchte, im T. A. J. seine Ideen als Theatertheoretiker zu verwirklichen: Totaltheater in der Überwindung von jeder Trennung zwischen Bühne und Zuschauerraum; Akzentuierung von Gestik, Mimik, Rhythmus und Bewegung (→Theater der Grausamkeit).

Horst Schumacher

Théâtre Antoine

In Paris gelegenes Theater, von 1896 bis 1906 die erste reguläre ständige Spielstätte für André Antoine (1858–1943) und sein →Théâtre-Libre, bevor er 1906 (bis 1914) die Leitung des Théâtre de l'Odéon übernahm. Das T. A. beherbergte die verschiedensten Truppen. 1937 – zur Zeit des Spanischen Bürgerkriegs – erzielte Jean-Louis Barrault hier seinen Durchbruch als Regisseur mit der historischen Tragödie *Numencia* von Cervantes. Bekanntes Uraufführungstheater (1948 *Die schmutzigen Hände*, 1951 *Der Teufel und der liebe Gott* von Jean-Paul Sartre).

Antoine, A.: Mes souvenirs sur le Théâtre Antoine et sur l'Odéon. Paris 1928.

Horst Schumacher

Théâtre de Gennevilliers

1964 von Bernard Sobel (1936 in Paris-Belleville als Bernard Rothstein geboren) gegründetes Theaterensemble im Arbeiterviertel Gennevilliers im Norden von Paris. Sobel ist Lizentiat der Germanistik der Pariser Sorbonne und entdeckte als Mitglied einer frz. kommunistischen Studentendelegation bei den Weltjugendfestspielen im seinerzeitigen Ostberlin die Arbeit des Berliner Ensembles. Er bewirbt sich um ein Stipendium der DDR und bleibt schließlich vier Jahre beim Berliner Ensemble, wird Regieassistent von Brecht und Helene Weigel und arbeitet im Kollektiv mit Benno Besson, Manfred Wekwerth, Peter Palitzsch. Nach seiner Rückkehr nach Paris arbeitet Sobel unter Jean Vilar im →Théâtre National Populaire, ist Mitbegründer des Théâtre Gérard Philipe in der kommunistisch regierten Stadt Saint-Denis nördlich Paris. 1964 erhält Sobel vom Bürgermeister von Gennevilliers das Angebot, in der «salle des Grésillons», wo 1951 Mutter Courage aufgeführt worden war, ein ständiges Theater aufzubauen.

Zahlreiche Inszenierungen von Brecht, Shakespeare, Ostrowski, Heiner Müller, Kleist, Marlowe, Adaptierungen für die Bühne nach Thomas Mann (*Mario und der Zauberer*), Heinrich Mann (*Madame Legros*), Isaak Babel (*Maria*) haben das – 1982 zum Centre Dramatique National erhobene – TdG zu einer Experimentierwerkstatt des modernen Theaters gemacht, das nach Sobels Meinung in den Arbeitervorstädten, wo die Ungleichheit im Zugang zu jeder Form von Bildung am spürbarsten ist, seine eigentliche Wirkung als Teil des Lebens (partie de la vie) und nicht nur Dekor (décor) entfaltet, ein Theater der Widersprüche im Herzen der Stadt (au cœur de la cité).

Temkine, R.: Mettre en scène au présent. V. Bernard Sobel. La Cité – L'Age d'homme. Paris 1979; de La Coste, P.: Bernard Sobel, théâtre de contradiction. In: L'Express, Juni 1991.

Horst Schumacher

Théâtre de la Foire

(Frz. ‹Jahrmarkttheater›) Auf den Pariser Vorstadtjahrmärkten Saint-Germain und Saint-Laurent von 1661 (Théâtre de Mademoiselle) bzw. 1664 (Théâtre de la Troupe du Dauphin) bis 1786 etablierte Bühnen mit meist ‹stummen Stücken› (pièces à la muette), deren Handlung von →Couplets unterbrochen bzw. kommentiert wurde, wobei der pantomimisch den Sinn der Worte hervorhebende Harlekin (harlequin) die Zuschauer zum Mitsingen animierte. Alain René Lesage (1668–1747)

1036 Théâtre de la Mandragore

machte die ‹stummen Stücke› zu oft beißenden Satiren, in denen auch die Aufführungen der Comédie Française parodiert wurden.

1714 wurden die bekanntesten T.d.l.F. zur ‹Komischen Oper› (Opéra-Comique), die 1762 mit der sog. →Comédie Italienne vereinigt wurde.

Horst Schumacher

Théâtre de la Mandragore

Das ‹Mandragolatheater› wurde 1958 von Wolfram Mehring (*1930 Münster) als dt.-frz. Avantgardetruppe gegründet, die zunächst in dt. und frz. Sprache vor studentischem Publikum im Deutschen Haus (Heinrich-Heine-Haus) der Internationalen Pariser Studentenwohnstadt (Cité Universitaire) die *Goldtopfkomödie* von Plautus und Büchners *Leonce und Lena* und ab 1964 im →‹Théâtre du Vieux Colombier› u. a. *Woyzeck* von Georg Büchner, *Von morgens bis mitternachts* von Georg Kaiser, *Scherz, Satire, Ironie und tiefere Bedeutung* von Grabbe aufführte. Die Inszenierungen im Rahmen des gleichzeitig 1958 von Mehring begründeten →Centre international de Recherches Théâtrales/Scéniques setzten die Idee vom «totalen Schauspieler» um: Betonung der Körpersprache, Spiel mit Masken. Seit Mitte der 60er Jahre zahlreiche Gastspiele und Gastinszenierungen. Symbiose westlicher, fernöstlicher, indischer und afrikanischer Theatertraditionen in den jüngsten Inszenierungen in außereuropäischen Sprachen.

Horst Schumacher

Théâtre de l'Atelier

1822 für →Vaudeville-Theater erbaut. Diente zeitweilig als Kino. 1923 von dem Schauspieler und Regisseur Charles Dullin (1885–1949) neu eröffnet und bis 1941 geleitet. Eine Schauspielschule war angeschlossen. Dullin bestand auf dem Werkstattcharakter der Aufführungen, sah Theaterarbeit als kollektive Erfahrung, räumte Improvisationen viel Platz ein. Das Repertoire umfaßte Klassiker (Aristophanes, Shakespeare, Ben Jonson, Molière) wie auch zeitgenössische Dramatiker (Achard, Cocteau, Salacrou, Vitrac). Viele berühmte Theaterleute gingen aus dem A. hervor: Jean-Louis Barrault, Etienne Décroux, Jean Marais, Marcel Marceau, Jean Vilar. Von 1941 bis 1973 übernahm André Barsacq (1909–73) die Leitung. Schwerpunkte: Anouilh, Claudel, Dürrenmatt, Konstruktivismus. Seit 1976 unter der Direktion von Pierre Franck.

Arnaud, L.: Charles Dullin. Paris 1952; Dullin, Ch.: Souvenirs et notes de travail d'un acteur. Paris 1946.

Barbara Müller-Wesemann

Théâtre de l'Europe

Im September 1983 nahm auf Initiative des frz. Kulturministers Jack Lang im Pariser → Théâtre de l'Odéon ein europäisches Theater seine Arbeit unter der Leitung von Giorgio Strehler auf, der damit – nach Gastspielen mit dem → Piccolo Teatro di Milano und einer Gastinszenierung der *Sommergäste* von Maxim Gorki an der → Comédie Française – zum erstenmal vertraglich fest an Paris gebunden werden konnte. Das Odéontheater sollte zwar das zweite Haus der Comédie Française bleiben, aber sechs Monate im Jahr ausschließlich als «frz. Institution für Europa» (Strehler) europäische Theaterpräsenz und -kontinuität sichern, nicht nur gelegentlich und zufällig Festspiele oder internationale Theater-Treffen in der Art des → Théâtre des Nations veranstalten. Neben Gastspielen waren daher Eigenproduktionen das Fernziel, die sich zunächst – wie eine Strehlersche Neuinszenierung von Shakespeares *Sturm* für das Odéon, aber von der Truppe des Piccolo Teatro auf ital. einstudiert – ausschließlich durch die Etikettierung von herkömmlichen Gastspielen unterscheiden. Jährlich bisher vier bis sechs – meist fremdsprachige – Aufführungen ausländischer Ensembles. Sprachrohr des T. d. l'E. ist die Vierteljahreszeitschrift *Théâtre en Europe* (n° 1, Januar 1984).

Die Grundkonzeption des T. d. l'E. hat sich nicht geändert, seit das Théâtre de l'Odéon ausschließlich (seit März 1990) als Europa-Theater fungiert und Lluis Pasqual für zunächst drei Jahre die Leitung übernahm. Strehler steht dem T. d. l'E. weiter als Regisseur für Eigeninszenierungen in frz. Sprache zur Verfügung und hat den Vorsitz des durch Entscheidung des frz. Kulturministers Jack Lang mit Sitz im Théâtre de l'Odéon gegründeten Europäischen Theaterverbandes (Union des Théâtres de l'Europe). Die zwölf Mitgliedsbühnen sind neben dem Odéon-Théâtre de l'Europe das Piccolo Teatro, Teatro d'Europa in Mailand, das Teatro Lliure in Barcelona, Kungliga Dramatiska Teatern in Stockholm, Royal National Theatre in London, Royal Shakespeare Company in London, Düsseldorfer Schauspielhaus, Deutsches Theater und Kammerspiele in Berlin, Berliner Ensemble, Katona József Szinház in Budapest, Bulandra Theater in Bukarest und Maly Theater in Sankt Petersburg.

Horst Schumacher

Théâtre de l'Œuvre

Entstand 1892 unter der Leitung des Schauspielers und Regisseurs Aurélien Lugné-Poë (1869–1940) in unmittelbarer Nachfolge des symbolistischen Théâtre de l'Art (Paul Fort). Ablehnung des Boulevard-Theaters der Belle Époque sowie des Naturalismus Antoines, Vorliebe für Symbolismus (Maeterlincks *Pelléas et Mélisande*, UA 1893). Auf dem Spielplan standen Werke von Ibsen, Strindberg, Gorki und Kaiser. Die Uraufführung von A. Jarrys *Ubu Roi* (1896) verursachte einen der größten Skandale der Theatergeschichte. Zahlreichen noch unbekannten Dramatikern wurden hier erste Aufführungsmöglichkeiten geboten: Anouilh, Claudel, Crommelynck, Rolland, Salacrou. 1932 gab Lugné-Poë die Leitung an L. Beer ab, 1944 folgte R. Rouleau, seit 1961 Direktion G. Herbert.

Lugné-Poë, A.: Acrobaties. Paris 1931; Robichez, J.: Lugné-Poë. Paris 1955.

Barbara Müller-Wesemann

Théâtre des Amandiers

Westlich Paris in Nanterre gelegenes Theater, gehört mit dem Théâtre de la Commune d'Aubervilliers und dem Théâtre Gérard Philipe in Saint-Denis zu den bekanntesten Pariser Vorstadt-Bühnen. Entstand aus dem Festival de Nanterre, das 1965 erstmals in einem Zirkuszelt stattfand, 1966 in die Universität Nanterre verlegt wurde. 1971 als Centre Dramatique National de Nanterre staatliche Anerkennung und Förderung aus Haushaltsmitteln. 1976 Einweihung des Kulturhauses (Maison de la Culture) als Sitz des Theaters. 1982 Umbenennung in T. d. A. (‹Mandelbaumtheater›), Leitung Patrice Chéreau und Catherine Tasca, Verpflichtung des Regisseurs Alain Combrecque, der Luc Bondy – mit einer aufsehenerregenden Inszenierung des Schnitzler-Stücks *Das weite Land* – und André Engel (Direktor des Straßburger Nationaltheaters Théâtre National de Strasbourg/TNS) – mit einer Bühnenbearbeitung des Céline-Romans *Reise ans Ende der Nacht* (Voyage au Bout de la Nuit) – als Gastregisseure heranzog. Auch Filmatelier, Schauspielschule (Leitung Pierre Romans) verbunden mit Studium der Theaterwissenschaft an der Universität Nanterre. – Seit 1990 leitet Jean Pierre Vincent (* 1942), der seine Theaterlaufbahn in der Compagnie Patrice Chéreau (1965–68) begonnen hatte, das T. d. A.

Dossier «Patrice Chéreau à Nanterre». In: Le Monde, 25. 11. 1982.

Horst Schumacher

Théâtre des Bouffes du Nord

Im Norden des Pariser Stadtgebiets gelegenes Theater; gegen Ende des 19. Jh. gegründet als Nachahmung der Bouffes Parisiens, die Jacques Offenbach (1819–80) 1855 eröffnet hatte. Das Theater im Prunk- und Plüschstil der Belle Époque hatte seine Glanzzeit um die Jahrhundertwende als Music Hall sowie unter der Leitung von Aurélien Lugné-Poë (1869–1940), der hier Maeterlincks Märchendrama *Pelleas und Melisande* und verschiedene Ibsen-Stücke aufführte. Das lange unbenutzte und zum Abbruch bestimmte Theater wurde 1974 für Peter Brook und seine Mitarbeiterin Micheline Rozan Basis des bisher notdürftig untergebrachten Studienzentrums Centre International de Recherche Théâtrales (CIRT, seit 1979 →Centre International de la Création Théâtrale, CICT). Wiedereröffnung mit einer frz. Fassung von Shakespeares *Timon von Athen* im kaum restaurierten Theatersaal; der Plüsch war entfernt, die Zwischenwände waren niedergerissen worden, die Mauern weiß gestrichen, die hufeisenförmig angeordneten Zuschauersitzreihen erinnerten noch an das frühere Theater, während die Bühne ein offener freier Raum wurde. In dieser Umgebung ohne Bühnenmaschinerie soll die Direktheit des Theaters auf die Zuschauer wirken. Weitere Aufführungen: 1975 *Les Iks*, 1977 *Ubu aux Bouffes* nach Alfred Jarrys *Ubu Roi*, 1978 *Antonius und Kleopatra* und *Maß für Maß* von Shakespeare, 1979 *L'Os* von Birago Diop, 1981 Tschechows *Kirschgarten, La Tragédie de Carmen*, 1985 die Neun-Stunden-Dramatisierung des Sanskrit-Versepos *Mahabharata*.

C. N. R. S.: Peter Brook. Paris 1985 (= Les voies de la création théâtrale); Croydon, Margaret: The Center. A narrative. o. O. (1980).

Horst Schumacher

Théâtre du Marais

1634 von Montdory eröffnet. Geht offenbar auf das Théâtre de l'Hôtel d'Argent zurück, das Pierre Venier, Vater der ersten namentlich bekannten frz. Schauspielerin, mit seiner Truppe bezog, als das →Hôtel de Bourgogne im Besitz der Confrérie de la Passion das einzige ständige Schauspielhaus war. Die Konkurrenz des T. d. M. brachte das Hôtel de Bourgogne 1634, 1641 und 1647 in ernste Schwierigkeiten. Durch königliche Anordnung wurden Schauspieler des T. d. M. an das Hôtel de Bourgogne versetzt. – Uraufführungen vieler Dramen von Pierre Corneille: *La Place royale, Médée, L'Illusion comique, Le Cid, Horace, Cinna, Polyeucte, La Mort de Pompée, Le Menteur, La Suite du Menteur, Rodogune, Théodore.* 1673 Zusammenschluß mit der Truppe Molières auf kö-

1040 Théâtre du Quotidien

nigliche Verordnung: erste gemeinsame Aufführung im Théâtre Guénégaud. Dort wurde 1680 – durch Fusion mit der Truppe des Hôtel de Bourgogne – die →Comédie Française geschaffen.

Deierkauf-Holsboer, S. W.: Le Théâtre du Marais. 2 Bde. Paris 1954–58.

Horst Schumaher

Théâtre du Quotidien

Unter dem Einfluß des angelsächsischen Realismus der Amerikaner
Paddy Chayefsky (1923–81: *Marty*, 1953) oder David Mamet (*1947:
American Buffalo, 1977), der Engländer Arnold Wesker (*1932: *Roots*,
1959), Edward Bond (*1935: *Saved*, 1965) und des zeitgenössischen dt.
→Volksstücks, besonders von Franz-Xaver Kroetz (*1946), entwickelt
sich in Frankreich Mitte der 70er Jahre eine neue Art dramatischer Produktion. Sie basiert auf der fast klinischen, mikroskopischen Darstellung
des Alltagslebens, vor allem des Lebens der Kleinbürger und der sozialen
Außenseiter. – So bei Jean-Paul Wenzel (*1947) in *Loin d'Hagondange*
(1974) das traurige Leben eines Rentnerehepaars oder in *Dimanche*
(1974) von Michel Deutsch (*1948) Leben und Tod einer jungen Arbeite-
rin. Der interessanteste Vertreter der Bewegung des T.d.Q. ist Michel
Vinaver (*1927): *Iphigénie hôtel* (1963), *Théâtre de chambre* (1978) und
Les travaux et les jours (1979) verklären mit Humor und der Genauigkeit
der Alltagssprache die Banalität der kleinbürgerlichen Existenz.

Sarrazac, J.-P.: L'Avenir du drame. Lausanne 1981; Vinaver, M.: Ecrits sur le
théâtre. Lausanne 1982.

Jean-Pierre Sarrazac

Théâtre du Soleil

Seit 1964 bestehende Theaterkooperative (gleiches Gehalt für alle), gegründet und geleitet von der frz. Regisseurin Ariane Mnouchkine
(*1939). Seit 1970 auf dem Gelände einer ehem. Munitionsfabrik in Vincennes bei Paris (→Cartoucherie) ansässig. Erste Produktionen: Gorkis
Die Kleinbürger (1964/65) und *Capitaine Fracasse* nach Gautier (1965/
66). Weskers *Die Küche* wurde 1968 in bestreikten Fabriken gespielt.
Weitere erfolgreiche Inszenierungen (Eigenproduktionen): *1789* (1970),
1793 (1973); *L'Age d'or* (1975), *Mephisto* nach Klaus Mann (1979). Zwei
Filme in der Regie von Mnouchkine: *1789* (1974) und *Molière* (1977).
Von einem urspr. sechsteilig geplanten Shakespeare-Zyklus wurden bis-

lang drei Teile realisiert: *Richard II.*. (1981), *Was ihr wollt* (1982), *Heinrich IV.*, 1. Teil (1984). 1991 Inszenierung der *Orestie* von Aischylos. Die Produktionen des T.d.S. entstehen in monatelanger gemeinsamer Arbeit. Intensives Körpertraining, Artistik und Improvisation sind wesentlicher Bestandteil der Proben. Einbeziehung von Techniken der Commedia dell'arte, des Volks- und Marionettentheaters; im Shakespeare-Zyklus Verfremdung durch Kostüme und Musik nach jap. und ind. Vorbild, Spiel auf mehreren Bühnen und Laufstegen, Verzicht auf Dekorationen, Theater als Ort der kritischen Reflexion von Vergangenheit und Gegenwart.

Penchenat, Cl.: La vie d'une troupe: Le Théâtre du Soleil. In: Couty, D./Rey, A. (eds.): Le Théâtre. Paris 1980, pp. 210–225; Simon, A.: Le Théâtre du Soleil. In: T.E. Théâtre en Europe 3 (1984), pp. 77–116; Seym, S.: Das Théâtre du Soleil. Stuttgart 1992.

Barbara Müller-Wesemann

Théâtre du Vieux-Colombier

Pariser Theater, 1913 gegründet und bis 1924 geleitet von dem Schauspieler und Regisseur Jacques Copeau (1879–1949). In Opposition zum naturalistischen Theater verwarf Copeau jeglichen szenischen Illusionismus ebenso wie den akademischen Stil der Comédie Française. Seine schmucklose Einheitsbühne (tréteau nu) entsprach dem Wunsch, die ‹Wahrheit› und die ‹Schönheit› der Dichtung in den Mittelpunkt des Theatergeschehens zu rücken. Das Augenmerk richtete sich auf Sprache, Gestik und Mimik, Licht und sparsame, symbolische Dekoration. Schwerpunkte des Repertoires waren Molière und Shakespeare sowie zeitgenössische Autoren: Claudels *Der Tausch* (UA 1914), Shakespeares *Was ihr wollt* (1914), Mussets *Die Launen der Marianne* (1918), Maeterlincks *Pelléas und Mélisande* (1919), Molières *Der Misanthrop* (1919) – die drei letztgenannten Inszenierungen als Gastspiele in New York –, Gides *Saul* (UA 1922), Gozzis *Turandot* (1923). Die dem V.C. angegliederte Schauspielschule verlangte von ihren Schülern intensives Körpertraining (Tanz, Pantomime, Nô, Commedia dell'arte), totale Unterordnung unter das dichterische Werk, Verzicht auf persönliche Ambitionen und Starkult. Aus der Schule gingen u.a. hervor: Louis Jouvet, Charles Dullin, Jean Dasté. In seinen Reformbemühungen war das V.C. wegweisend für das moderne frz. Theater. Nach Copeaus Rückzug in die Bourgogne (1924) richteten sich dort zeitweilig die Compagnie des Quinze und G. Pitoëff ein. 1944 war es Uraufführungsort für Sartres *Huis Clos*. Das V.C. ist seit vielen Jahren geschlossen. 1962–70 hatte der dt. Regisseur

Wolfram Mehring (*1930) im V. C. seine Theaterwerkstatt →Théâtre de la Mondragore und das Forschungszentrum →Centre de Recherches Théâtrales / Scéniques eingerichtet, um in Weiterentwicklung der Ideen von Etienne Décroux seine Konzeption vom «totalen Schauspieler» zu verwirklichen.

Borgal, C.: Jacques Copeau. Paris 1960; Kurtz, M.: Jacques Copeau. Biographie d'un théâtre. Paris 1950.

Barbara Müller-Wesemann / Horst Schumacher

Theatre Guild

Wichtige alternative Theaterunternehmung in den USA, die in den 1920er und 30er Jahren die Brücke schlug zwischen dem →Little Theatre Movement vor Beginn und während des 1. Weltkriegs einerseits, dem Off-Broadway Theatre nach dem 2. Weltkrieg andererseits. Die T. G. wurde 1918 von ehemaligen Mitgliedern der →Washington Square Players gegr. Sie baute ein erfolgreiches Abonnementssystem auf, das zehn Jahre später allein in New York 23000 Abonnenten aufwies und schon 1925 ermöglichte, das eigene Theaterhaus, Guild Theatre in der 52. Straße nahe dem Broadway, glanzvoll mit Shaws *Caesar and Cleopatra* zu eröffnen. Mehrere Tourneegruppen bespielten regelmäßig Baltimore, Boston, Chicago, Cleveland, Philadelphia, Pittsburgh und andere Großstädte. Zwar entging die T. G. in ihrer organisatorischen und ökonomischen Struktur nicht immer der Verführung, teilweise die Profitorientierung des →Broadway zu übernehmen, zeichnete sich diesem gegenüber jedoch durch ein weitgehend erhalten gebliebenes Repertoiresystem und die Auswahl relevanter inländischer und internationaler sowie auch klassischer Dramatik aus. Nach den →Provincetown Players brachte die T. G. ab 1928 viele Uraufführungen O'Neills heraus. Die T. G. war das ausschließliche Einfallstor der Dramen von G. B. Shaw in den USA. Unter den Klassikern wurden Ben Jonsons *Volpone* und Goethes *Faust* gegeben; *Masse-Mensch* von E. Toller und *Brülle, China* von S. M. Tretjakow erlebten ihre Uraufführungen in den USA im Guild Theatre. Ibsen, Claudel, Ernö Vaida, Rolland, Philip Barry vervollständigten das internationale Repertoire der T. G. In der ‹roten Dekade› wurden die sozialkritischen Dramen von Rice, Lawson und Maxwell Anderson gespielt; 1934 kam John Wexleys Dramatisierung der ‹Scottsboro Nine›-Anklage, *They Shall Not Die*, heraus. Der T. G. gebührt das entscheidende Verdienst, sich zwei Jahrzehnte lang im nicht leicht zu bestimmenden Zwischenraum von Broadway und sozial engagiertem Theater erfolgreich behauptet zu haben.

Clurman, H.: The Naked Image – Observations on the Modern Theatre. New York 1966; Eaton, W. P.: The Theatre Guild – The First Ten Years. New York 1929; Fröhlich, P.: Das nichtkommerzielle amerik. Theater. Rheinfelden 1974; Himelstein, M.: Drama Was a Weapon – the Left Theatre in New York 1929–41. New Brunswick 1963.

Dieter Herms

Theatre in Education (T. i. E.)

Vor allem in Großbritannien stark verbreitete Form von → Kinder- und Jugendtheatern, die mobil insbesondere in Schulen spielen und ihre Aufführungen durch aktive Formen von Vor- und Nachbereitung ergänzen. Ähnlich das Theater im Schulhaus (Zürich, Bern), die Spielwerkstatt (Berlin), auch → Mitspielformen des Modellversuchs «Künstler und Schüler».

Dörger, D.: Mini- und Monodramen. Wilhelmshaven 1985.

Hans-Wolfgang Nickel

Théâtre-Libre

André Antoine (1858–1943), Schauspieler, Regisseur, Theaterleiter und Theaterkritiker, hatte schon als Angestellter einer Pariser Gasgesellschaft eine Amateurtruppe aufgebaut, die unter dem Namen T.-L. in der Passage de l'Elysée-Montmartre von 1887 bis 1894 untergekommen war. Wegbereiter des modernen Theaters. Bekämpfung des eingefahrenen, eintönigen Klassiker-Repertoires der → Comédie Française und der seichten Erfolgsstücke in der Art von Alexandre Dumas d. J. durch provozierende Inszenierungen. Verwirklichung eines naturalistischen Theaters im Sinne Emile Zolas, dem Freund und Förderer von Antoine. Statt gemalter Dekorationen minuziös nach der Realität kopierte plastische Bühnenbauten, statt ‹theatralischer› Gesten ‹natürliche› Bewegung der Schauspieler. – Einen ‹realistischen› Shakespeare vermochte Antoine in der frz. Literatur nicht zu entdecken. An die Stelle frz. Autoren wie Zola, Balzac, Henri Becque, Maupassant traten daher bald Hauptwerke der naturalistischen Weltdramatik, die das T.-L. frz. erstaufführte: *Die Macht der Finsternis* von Tolstoi (1888), *Wenn wir Toten erwachen* und *Die Wildente* von Ibsen (1890/91), Strindbergs *Fräulein Julie* (1893); *Die Weber* von Gerhart Hauptmann (1893, im gleichen Jahr wie die Berliner Uraufführung). Finanzieller Zusammenbruch des T.-L. 1894. 1896 bis 1906 setzte Antoine seine Arbeit im → Théâtre Antoine fort, 1906 bis 1914 leitete er das → Théâtre de l'Odéon. Wiederaufnahme der erfolgreichen Dramen aus der Zeit des T.-L.; daneben machte Antoine als erster bedeutender frz. Shakespeare-Regisseur *König Lear, Julius Cäsar, Coriolanus, Romeo und Julia* in Frankreich heimisch. Überschuldet, zog sich Antoine als Theaterleiter 1914 zurück und wirkte drei Jahrzehnte als Kritiker. Die Gründung der → Freien Bühne 1889 in Berlin und des → Independent Theatre 1891 in London sind ohne das T.-L. nicht zu denken. Der von Antoine propagierte Realismus wirkte auf Stanislawski und Brecht.

Antoine, A.: Mes souvenirs sur le Théâtre-Libre. Paris 1921 (dt. 1960); ders.: Mes Souvenirs sur le Théâtre Antoine et sur l'Odéon. Paris 1928; Kovacevic, M.: La Vie, l'œuvre, l'influence et le prestige d'Antoine. Paris 1941; Roussou, M.: André Antoine. Paris 1954; Veinstein, A.: Du Théâtre Libre au Théâtre Louis Jouvet. Paris 1955.

Horst Schumacher

Théâtre National de Chaillot (TNC)

Seit 1973 Name des im Chaillotpalast (an der Stelle des zur Pariser Weltausstellung 1937 abgerissenen Palais du Trocadéro) untergebrachten Staatstheaters, nachdem der ursprüngliche Name → Théâtre National Populaire dem seinerzeit von Patrice Chéreau und Roger Planchon geleiteten Theater in Villeurbanne gegeben worden war. Der erste Intendant des T. N. C., Jack Lang, wollte ein Experimentiertheater und eine Begegnungsstätte zur Formerneuerung schaffen. Mit der Integrierung eines Kindertheaters (Théâtre National des Enfants, TNE) zugleich Jugendbühne für engagierte, antiautoritäre Stücke. Seit 1981 leitete Antoine Vitez das T. N. C., zu dem Großes Haus Grand Théâtre Salle Jean Vilar, Kleines Haus Théâtre Gémier sowie die Foyerbühne Grand Foyer gehören.

Mit der Übernahme des TNC durch Jérôme Savary 1988 wurde die Spielzeit auf zehn Monate verlängert, die Schauspielschule Ecole du TNC weiter ausgebaut und nach dt. Vorbild eine Reihe von Arbeitsstipendien für Nachwuchsdramatiker (bourses d'auteurs) gestiftet. Eine steigende Zahl von Inszenierungen sind internationale Koproduktionen (z. B. *Artagnan* mit dem Berliner Schiller-Theater).

Horst Schumacher

Théâtre National de l'Odéon

Frz. Staatstheater in Paris. Geht zurück auf ein königliches Patent vom 10.8.1779, worin Ludwig XVI. die Errichtung eines Theaters im lat. Viertel und in unmittelbarer Nähe des Palais du Luxembourg für die Comédie Française beschließt. Einweihung 1782 (1900 Plätze, darunter im Orchester – für die damalige Zeit ungewöhnlich – Sitzplätze im Parkett) unter dem Namen Théâtre Français. Erster großer Erfolg mit *Figaros Hochzeit* (1785) von Beaumarchais (1732–99). Im 19. Jh. Aufführungen von Opern, romantischen, dann realistischen Stücken, z. T. anspruchsvolle Unterhaltungsstücke und →Melodramen: Rossini, Musset, Dumas d. Ä. u. a. Höhepunkte des O. zu Beginn des 20. Jh.: 1906 bis 1914 mit André Antoine, ehemaliger Direktor des →Théâtre-Libre; 1922 bis 1933 mit Firmin Gémier (1869–1933), der das Repertoire des zweiten Hauses der Comédie Française um Erfolgskomödien bereicherte. Von 1946 bis 1959 hieß das O. amtlich Salle Luxembourg, während das Stammhaus der Comédie Française in der rue Richelieu Salle Richelieu genannt wurde. 1.9.1959 Verselbständigung des O. als Théâtre de France unter Leitung von Jean-Louis Barrault: Einweihung 21.10.1959 mit *Tête d'or* (dt. «Goldhaupt») von Paul Claudel. Zehn Jahre hindurch entwickelte Barrault gemeinsam mit Madeleine Renaud einen der interessantesten Spielpläne in der frz. Theaterlandschaft: Ur- und Erstaufführungen zeitgenössischer Dramatik (Ionesco, Billetdoux, Duras, Albee, Beckett, Genet u. a.), Wiederaufnahmen (Giraudoux, Pirandello, Claudel, Anouilh) und Klassiker. Gleichzeitig empfing Barrault im O. auch das →Théâtre des Nations mit – meist fremdsprachigen – Aufführungen ausländischer Ensembles. 1967 wurde im Gebäude des O. ein Studiotheater, Le petit Odéon, mit 110 Sitzplätzen und einer 10-qm-Bühne eingerichtet. Barrault mußte 1968 die Leitung des O. aufgeben, nachdem Studenten während der Mairevolte 1968 sein Theater mehrere Wochen besetzt gehalten hatten. Seit 1971 heißt das O. wieder T. N. O. Nach Pierre Dux und Jacques Toja wurde 1983 François Barachin Intendant, gleichzeitig Ernennung von Giorgio Strehler zum Leiter des im O. residierenden →Théâtre de l'Europe.

Im März 1990 übernahm Lluis Pasqual die Leitung des nun ausschließlich als Europa-Theater genutzten Odéon-Théâtre de l'Europe, während Giorgio Strehler – neben seiner Tätigkeit am Piccolo Teatro – die Präsidentschaft des neugegründeten, im Odéon residierenden, Verbandes Europäischer Theater (Union des Théâtres de l'Europe) übertragen wurde.

Cahiers de le Compagnie Madeleine Renaud – Jean-Louis Barrault. Paris 1946ff.

Horst Schumacher

Théâtre National Populaire (T. N. P.)

Gegründet 1920 in Paris im für die Weltausstellung 1878 errichteten Palais du Trocadéro von Firmin Gémier (1869–1933), der ein wirkliches Volkstheater schaffen wollte, aber wegen ungenügender Mittel gezwungen war, Gastspiele anderer staatlicher Bühnen – Opéra, opéra-comique, Comédie Française, Odéon – zu bringen. Mit der Errichtung des Palais de Chaillot auf den Fundamenten des abgerissenen Trocadéro zur Weltausstellung 1937 stand ein Theatersaal mit 3000 Sitzplätzen zur Verfügung, in dem die Arbeit des T. N. P. im März 1939 mit Molières *Le Bourgeois Gentilhomme* (Der Bürger als Edelmann) wieder aufgenommen wurde. 1940 bis 1951 unter Pierre Aldebert Inszenierung großer Freilichtaufführungen wie *Le Vray mystère de la Passion* auf dem Vorplatz von Notre-Dame. 1951 übernahm Jean Vilar (1912–71) die Leitung und spielte, solange das Palais de Chaillot noch von den Vereinten Nationen benutzt wurde, in den Pariser Arbeitervorstädten, vielleicht inspiriert von den 1947 gegründeten Ruhrfestspielen in Recklinghausen. Berühmte Aufführungen: *Le Cid* von Corneille, Kleists *Prinz von Homburg* (mit Gérard Philipe), Brechts *Mutter Courage*. Die Verwirklichung einer Idee der Volksbühne als *service public* führt nach der Rückkehr des T. N. P. ins Chaillot-Gebäude zu einschneidenden praktischen Neuerungen: Einlaß 18.45 Uhr mit ‹accueil en musique› (musikalische Einstimmung) und Möglichkeit zur Einnahme preiswerter Mahlzeiten, damit Arbeiter und Angestellte unmittelbar vom Arbeitsplatz ins Theater kommen konnten. Spielbeginn 20.15 Uhr, eine Stunde früher als in allen anderen Theatern, Trinkgeldverbot, kostenlose Garderobe. Vilar wollte Familienfestatmosphäre schaffen und gleichzeitig Respekt vor dem Bühnenwerk, daher pünktlicher Spielbeginn und Schließung des Zuschauerraums, so daß Zuspätkommende bis zur Pause warten mußten. Besondere Abonnementsformen und Besucherorganisationen und regelmäßige Diskussionsrunden mit Schauspielern und Regisseuren sicherten ein praktisch immer vollbesetztes Haus. Am Ende der Spielzeit begab sich das gesamte T. N. P.-Ensemble nach Avignon, wo Vilar auch nach der Niederlegung der Intendanz des T. N. P. die Festspielleitung behielt. 1963 bis 1967 leitete Georges Wilson das T. N. P. und erweiterte es durch einen zweiten Saal Salle Gémier mit 500 Plätzen, der 1967 mit Stücken von Kateb Yacine und Tankred Dorst eingeweiht wurde. 1973 wurde die Bezeichnung T. N. P. dem Théâtre de la Cité de Villeurbanne bei Lyon (Leitung: Roger Planchon) übertragen. Das Haus im Chaillotpalast heißt seitdem Théâtre National de Chaillot, das sein erster Intendant Jack Lang zu einem interdisziplinären Gestaltungszentrum ausbauen wollte und dem er ein Kindertheater, Théâtre National des Enfants, angliederte. 1981 wurde Antoine Vitez Direktor des T. N. C.

Seit 1989 leitet Jérôme Savary (*1942), der Begründer des →Grand Magic Circus, das T.N.P.

Vilar, J.: De la Tradition théâtrale. Paris 1955; ders.: Le Théâtre service public. Paris 1975. S. auch die Zeitschrift des T.N.P.: Bsef. Paris 1951–71.

Horst Schumacher

Theatre of Images

Robert Wilson (*1941 in Waco, Texas) ist mit seinen rätselhaften, surrealen Bilderwelten (theater of images), die aus vollkommener Lichtregie («Ich male mit Licht im Raum wie der Maler mit Farben auf der Leinwand») und unerschöpflich scheinender Phantasie leben, einer der mit Abstand originellsten und wichtigsten Theatermacher der letzten Jahrzehnte. Seine zugleich monumentalen und minimalistischen Bildfolgen mit oft quälend langsamen Bühnenvorgängen und ‹formalistischem› Design verzichten auf jede traditionelle Dramaturgie, stellen eine ‹Dekonstruktion› der dramatischen Grundelemente Person, Zeit, Raum, Handlung dar (postdramatisches Theater). Licht, Requisiten und Schauspielerbewegungen unterliegen strengster Geometrisierung, Wilsons Theaterpraxis ist ‹architektonisch›. Äußerste Zeitdehnung macht Zeitlichkeit als solche zur sinnlichen Erfahrung; der Raum wird segmentiert; Stimmen sind durch subtile Tontechnik von Figuren getrennt; Repetition, Musikalität, Rhythmus von Sprache, Licht, Körpern, Dingen tritt an die Stelle unmittelbar einsichtigen Zusammenhangs; der Text kennt kaum Kohärenz, wird als lediglich ein Element des Repertoires neben anderen benutzt; Verweise, Zitate, Assoziationen, Bezugnahmen auf gesellschaftliche, politische Realität und theatralische Normen eröffnen Assoziationsraum, der auf Realität nur anspielt, sie nicht abspiegelt; die über den ganzen Theaterraum verteilten Stimmen erzeugen Klangraum; traumartige Qualität der Bilder wird verstärkt durch Ausblenden der Emotionen.

Wilsons Dekonstruktionstheater läßt Herkunft aus therapeutischer Praxis erkennen, seine Sprach- und Tanzübungen (Entspannung, «taking time») mit gehirngeschädigten Kindern in der von ihm in New York 1969 gegr. Byrd Hoffman Foundation. Künstlerische Traditionslinien sind Idee des Gesamtkunstwerks, Surrealismus, Bauhaus-Design und -Bühne, Umfeld der New Yorker Theateravantgarde der 60er Jahre; Zusammenarbeit mit dem Komponisten Phil Glass und der Tänzerin Lucinda Childs. Bedeutende Produktionen Wilsons (nach Anfängen der 60er Jahre) sind u. a.: *The Life and Times of Sigmund Freud* (1969); *Deafman Glance* (1970), das als Gastspiel 1971 in Frankreich, Italien, Holland

1048   Theatre Union

Wilsons Ruhm in Europa begründete (wo er bis heute weit bessere Resonanz und Arbeitsmöglichkeiten findet als in den USA); *The Life and Times of Josef Stalin* (1973); *A Letter for Queen Victoria* (1974); *Einstein on the Beach* (1976), eine Oper in Zusammenarbeit mit Philip Glass, ein Höhepunkt von Wilsons Schaffen: *I was sitting on my patio* (1977); *Death, Destruction and Detroit* (1979); *The Golden Windows* (1982); *The Civil Wars* (1984), bislang Fragment gebliebenes, weltweites Großprojekt, urspr. für die Olympischen Spiele 1984 in Los Angeles geplant. Weitere Produktionen sind u. a.: *Medea* (1984); *Knee-Plays* (1985); *Hamletmaschine* (H. Müller, 1986); *Quartett* (H. Müller), *Parzival* (T. Dorst), *Death, Destruction & Death II* (1987); *Le Martyre de Saint Sébastien* (C. Debussy, Ballett), *Cosmopolitan Greetings, The Forest* (1988); *Orlando, Schwanengesang* (A. Tschechow, 1989); *The Black Rider: The Casting of the Magic Bullets, König Lear* (1990); *Alice* (1992).

Brecht, S.: The Theatre of Visions: Robert Wilson, New York 1978; Lehmann, H.-T.: Robert Wilson, Szenograph. In: Merkur 7 (1985); Quadri, F.: Il teatro di Robert Wilson. Robert Wilson. From a Theater of Images. Catalogue (The Contemporay Arts Center Cincinnati, Ohio) 1980; Robert Wilson's Vision. Boston, New York 1991; Shyer, L.: Robert Wilson and his Collaborators. New York 1989.

Hans-Thies Lehmann

Theatre Union

Gegr. 1933 mit der Aufgabe, dem →Broadway vergleichbare professionelle Aufführungen abendfüllender Stücke zu zeigen, die gleichwohl ‹vom Standpunkt der Interessen der Arbeiterklasse› geschrieben waren. Die Eintrittspreise sollten für Arbeiter erschwinglich sein. Die T. U. mietete das Civic Repertory Theatre, richtete ein Abonnementssystem ein und schuf sich ein Stammpublikum von Arbeitern, Angestellten und Intellektuellen. In den drei Spielzeiten 1933 bis 1935 erreichte sie mit u. a. Brechts *Mutter*, Sklars und Maltz' *Peace on Earth*, Sklars und Peters *Stevedore*, Beins *Let Freedom Ring* ingesamt 500000 Zuschauer und war damit die erfolgreichste Institution eines politisch-emanzipatorischen Theaters in den USA der 30er Jahre. Das beste Stück der T. U., J. H. Lawsons'*Marching Song*, dessen Inszenierung in das Nora Bayes Theatre am Broadway verlegt wurde, um bürgerlich-progressive Mittelschichten anzusprechen, wurde zu ihrem letzten Projekt. Die Auflösung 1937 war außer durch finanzielle Schwierigkeiten auch durch die politischen Auseinandersetzungen bedingt, die die kommunistische Bewegung der USA auf Grund der stalinistischen Säuberungen erschütterten.

Dieter Herms

Theatre Workshop

1945 gegr. Theaterkollektiv – zu den Gründungsmitgliedern gehörten u. a. Joan Littlewood (* 1914), Ewan McColl und Gerald Raffles – in der Tradition der linken Theaterbewegung der 30er Jahre (→ Arbeitertheater). Nach längerer Tourneearbeit, vor allem in den nordengl. Industriegebieten, übernahm T. W. 1953 das Theatre Royal im Ostlondoner Arbeiterbezirk Stratford. Es nahm sich vor allem der Pflege des sozialistischen und populären Theaters an im programmatischen Versuch, das Theaterpublikum in den Bereich der Arbeiterklasse auszudehnen. Hierin war es nur begrenzt erfolgreich, dagegen sehr einflußreich in der Vermittlung Brechts in England. Weltruhm erlangten bes. die Inszenierungen der Stücke Brendan Behans (1922–64) und von Shelagh Delaneys (* 1939) *A Taste of Honey* (1958), später auch der satirischen Antikriegsrevue *Oh, What a Loveley War* (1963), die auf eine internationale Tournee ging. Nach dem Ausscheiden Littlewoods kam 1964 das Ende des T. W.; das Theater in East Stratford blieb jedoch mit Unterbrechungen bis heute in Betrieb.

Goorney, H.: The Theatre Workshop Story. London 1981; Taylor, J. R.; Anger and After. A Guide to the New British Drama. Harmondsworth 1966.

Bernd-Peter Lange

Theatromanie

Theaterleidenschaft im weiteren Sinne. Im engeren Sinne Bezeichnung für den hohen Stellenwert des Theaters in der deutschen Klassik und Romantik. Beispiele dafür sind die Theaterromane, in denen junge, idealistische Menschen die Lösung ihrer persönlichen Konflikte vom Theater erwarten: bei Goethe (*Wilhelm Meisters theatralische Sendung*, 1777–85, bzw. *Wilhelm Meister*, 1795–96), Jean Paul (*Titan*, 1800–03); Karl Philipp Moritz (*Anton Reiser*, 1785–90).

Horst Schumacher

Théatron Technis (Athen)

(Theater der Kunst). Die bedeutendste griech. Theatereinrichtung der Nachkriegszeit, 1942 vom Regisseur Karolos Kun in Athen gegründet. Dieser hatte seine Karriere mit Amateurvorstellungen ein Jahrzehnt zuvor angefangen und es geschafft, dem einheimischen kulturellen Leben

1050 Théatron Technis (Athen)

mit der Bildung einer Art Vorläufertruppe, der →«Volksbühne», in den
Jahren 1934 bis 1936 einen neuen Impuls zu geben; bei deren Aufführungen hatte er versucht, Elemente der volkstümlichen Kunst zur Interpretation traditioneller Stücke zu verwerten. Das T. begann aber mit Stücken
von Ibsen, Pirandello und Bernard Shaw. Diese Prioritäten haben sein
Repertoire bis 1950 geprägt, erweitert um Theaterstücke von russ.
(Tschechow und Gorki), amerik. (O'Neill, Williams und Miller) und
span. Autoren (Lorca). 1954 erwirbt das Ensemble sein eigenes Theater
in einem kleinen unterirdischen Rundbau. Einen großen Teil seines Repertoires nehmen nun zeitgenössische amerik. Autoren ein, deren Stücke
den Schauspielern dabei helfen, einen psychographischen Realismus in
ihren Vorstellungen zu entwickeln, der bis zu jener Zeit der griech.
Bühne unbekannt war. Diese Tendenz wird nach 1957 durch Aufführungen von Bertolt Brechts Stücken und nach 1960 durch Übernahme von
Stücken des Theaters des Absurden (namentlich Ionesco und Pinter) aus-
geglichen. Die wichtigsten Beiträge des T. d. K. zur kulturellen Entwicklung Griechenlands waren aber vor allem sein Experimentieren auf dem
Gebiet des Wiederauflebens des antiken Dramas, insbesondere der ari-
stophanischen Komödie, sowie die Förderung einer Reihe von jungen
griech. Autoren. Mit den Aufführungen der Stücke von Aristophanes
(*Plutos*, 1957; *Vögel*, 1959; *Frösche*, 1966; *Lysistrate*, 1969; *Acharner*,
1976; *Friede*, 1977; *Thesmophoriazusen*, 1985) ist es Karolos Kun gelungen, mit modernen szenischen Mitteln den lyrischen Charakter sowie den
unverwüstlichen volkstümlichen Humor des altgriech. Dichters zum erstenmal wiederzugeben – eine Errungenschaft, die nach erfolgreichen
Aufführungen der Truppe in Paris (1962, 1965), London (1964, 1965,
1967) und anderen europäischen Städten (München, Venedig, Zürich
usw.) weltweite Anerkennung gefunden hat.

Obwohl andererseits die Förderung und das Bekanntmachen junger
griech. Autoren (Jakovos Kambanellis, Dimitris Kechaidis, Lula Ana-
gnostaki, Jorgos Armenis u. a.) keine Entwicklung mit gesamteurop. Resonanz gewesen sein dürfte, hat sie doch die griech. Bühne von der Vorherrschaft des ausländischen Repertoires befreit und ihr geholfen, nach
1965 einen eigenen Charakter herauszubilden. Diese Autoren sowie eine
beträchtliche Anzahl von Schauspielern, die in der Schule des T. d. K. ausgebildet wurden, haben heute seinen Geist und seine Ideale aus dessen
Theatersaal in andere Räume weitergetragen.

Thodoros Chatzipantazis

Theatrum mundi

Lat.: Theater der Welt, dt. auch →Welttheater. Entspricht der Weltanschauung, in der das ganze Welttreiben ein vorüberziehendes Schauspiel ist und infolgedessen jedes menschliche Wesen seine ihm vom Schicksal (in der Antike) oder vom Gott (im christl. Theater) auferlegte Rolle zu spielen hat, bis der Tod sie ihm abnimmt. Diese weitgefaßte Metapher ist ein traditionelles Motiv, ein «theozentrisches Gleichnis» (Curtius) seit der Antike (vorherrschend bei den Stoikern und Skeptikern, aber auch bei Marcus Aurelius, Plato, Seneca, Augustinus) und dem Mittelalter (im christlichen geistlichen Drama, in den →Mysterienspielen), gewinnt eine besondere Bedeutung bei allen großen Dichtern und Dramatikern der Spätrenaissance und des →Barocktheaters: bei den Vertretern des span. «siglo d'oro»: Lope de Vega, Francisco de Quevedo y Villegas und großartig bei Calderón in *Das große Welttheater* (1675). Auch bei Shakespeare ist diese Weltanschauung tief verankert; sie wird von seinen Gestalten besonders in ihren Reflexionsmonologen zum Ausdruck gebracht (Jacques, der Melancholiker, aus *Wie es euch gefällt*, II, 7, oder *Macbeth*, V, 5).

Goethe zeigt sich diesem traditionellen Motiv ebenso verpflichtet, da er seinem *Faust* den «Prolog im Himmel» vorsetzt. Das Drama beginnt eigentlich im «Himmel», und die Rollen werden vom «Herrn» erteilt. Im 19. Jh. ist die Metapher vom T. m. vor allem bei den Romantikern sehr beliebt; man findet sie aber auch in G. Büchners *Dantons Tod* (1835) als grundlegende Weltanschauung und neu variiert von Madach in der *Tragödie des Menschen* (1860). 1888/91 setzt Arthur Schnitzler vor seinen Zyklus *Anatol* eine Einleitung, die diese Weltanschauung hochpreist, und bald danach gibt H. v. Hofmannsthal mit dem Stück *Das Kleine W.* (1897) und *Das Salzburger Große W.* (UA 1922, Regie Max Reinhardt) die aufschlußreichsten Beispiele für die Tragweite dieses Motivs. In tragikomischer Sicht heute auch bei Friedrich Dürrenmatt, also parodistisch, ‹Komödie als Welttheater›.

Curtius, C. R.: Europäische Literatur und lateinisches Mittelalter. Bern/München 1948; Dürrenmatt, F.: Theater – Schriften und Reden II. Zürich 1972; Warnke, J. F.: The World as Theatre. New York 1969.

Adriana Hass

Theorikon

Griech.: ‹Schaugeld›; ein Tagegeld in Höhe von zwei Obolen, das in Athen den Armen aus einem besonderen staatlichen Fonds für den Besuch der Aufführungen an den Staatsfesten gezahlt wurde; zunächst wohl nur für die ‹Großen Dionysien›, dann für immer mehr Feste. Der Zeitpunkt der Einführung des T. ist umstritten; Ende des 4. Jh. wurde es wieder abgeschafft.

Pickard-Cambridge, A. W.: The Dramatic Festivals of Athens. Oxford ²1968 (rev. J. Gould and D. M. Lewis), p. 265–270; Kob, F.: Polis und Theater. In: G. A. Seeck: Das griech. Theater. Darmstadt 1979, S. 520–522.

Bernd Seidensticker

Thespis

Attischer Tragiker, mit dessen Namen die erste staatliche Tragödienaufführung an den von dem Tyrannen Peisistratos neugeordneten ‹Großen →Dionysien› 536/33 v. Chr. verbunden ist. In zahlreichen antiken Zeugnissen gilt T. als ‹Schöpfer der →Tragödie›; ihm wird die Einführung des ersten Schauspielers, der Maske sowie des →Prologs und der Rhesis (d. h. der längeren Sprechpartie) zugeschrieben. Die späte Nachricht vom ‹T.-Karren› (nur bei Horaz, *Ars Poetica* 276), bei dem man an eine im Wagen herumziehende Wandertruppe gedacht hat, verdient kein Vertrauen.

Lesky, A.: Die tragische Dichtung der Hellenen. Göttingen ³1972, S. 49–56.

Bernd Seidensticker

Thingspiel

Das T. (Thing – altfries., altsächs., gehegtes Gericht, Gerichtssache, Volksversammlung) sollte als neues «nationales Bekenntnistheater» «Mittelpunkt des gesellschaftlich-festlichen, national-politischen und künstlerischen Lebens der einzelnen Städte» werden (Brenner, 1963). Bereits 1933 begann man mit einer großangelegten Kampagne für diese Theaterform zu werben, ohne noch die entsprechenden Aufführungsstätten und Stücke zu haben. Im folgenden Jahr wurde ein Architektenwettbewerb zur Planung der Spielstätten ausgeschrieben, und im Juni 1934 wird in Brandenbergen bei Halle die erste T.-Stätte eröffnet. Zwar werden für die Spielzeit 1934/35 offiziell 58000 Besucher angegeben, doch schon Ende 1935 geht diese Bewegung aus Mangel an geeigneten Stükken, auf Grund techn. Schwierigkeiten (bedingt durch die Großanlagen) und das Desinteresse des Publikums zu Ende. 1937 erklärt J. Goebbels die T. für nicht mehr ‹reichswichtig›.

Die bis dahin ca. 40 fertiggestellten T.-Stätten waren auf ‹historisch geweihtem Boden›, bei Hünengräbern, Ruinen, Kampfplätzen u. ä. gebaut worden: in Annaberg, Bad Schmiedeberg, Eichstätt und Koblenz z. B. Ihre architektonische Gliederung war immer gleich: eine in drei Spielebenen aufgeteilte Segmentbühne, umgeben von amphitheatralisch angeordneten Zuschauerreihen, durch die, konzentrisch-symmetrisch angelegt, die Zugänge zur Bühne führten. Die Aufgabe dieses Theaters im ‹erzieherischen› Sinne war es, das ‹Erlebnis der Volksgemeinschaft› in einer politischen Kultfeier zu zelebrieren. Dazu bediente man sich dramaturgischer und theatraler Elemente aus mittelalterlichen →Mysterienspielen (→Massentheater) und aus den aus Sport und Kampf entwickelten Stadionspielen. Das Motiv der Erlösung wurde von ersteren übernommen, der effektvolle Ablauf von letzterem. Am Beginn standen Chorspiele wie die *Düsseldorfer Passion* von P. Beyer, schließlich wurden mehr aktuelle politische Bezüge eingearbeitet und in Form eines Aufmarschtheaters dargestellt, das geprägt war von Massenszenen, Gesang, Echoeffekten, Glocken- und Fanfarenklängen, Fahnen, Emblemen und Uniformen, wie z. B. die *Deutsche Passion 1933* von R. Euringer.

Braumüller, W.: Freilicht- und Thingspiel. Berlin 1935; Brenner, H.: Die Kunstpolitik des Nationalsozialismus. Reinbek 1963; Reichl, J.: Das Thingspiel. Frankfurt/M. 1988; Schöpel, B.: Naturtheater. Tübingen 1965.

Ute Hagel

Tirade

Eine T. ist eine längere, in sich geschlossene →Replik. Sie ist meistens eine rhetorische Konstruktion aus Aussage, Frage und Argument. In der klassischen Dramaturgie wird jede T. quasi zur lyrischen Einlage im Text, die mit den anderen T. thematisch und poetisch korrespondiert. Sie stellt einen Gegensatz zum schnellen Wortwechsel, etwa zur →Stichomythie, und zum affektbeladenen Ausruf dar.

Scherer, J.: La dramaturgie classique en France. Paris 1950.

Bernard Poloni

Togata

Lat. Adjektiv, zu ergänzen ‹fabula›; Gattungsbezeichnung für die röm. Komödien, die nicht Bearbeitung griech. Vorlagen sind, sondern einen Stoff des ital.-röm. Alltagslebens zum Gegenstand haben und folglich, im Gegensatz zur → Palliata, im röm. Kostüm, der Toga, gespielt wurden.

Bernd Seidensticker

Totaltheater

Für die experimentierfreudige → Piscatorbühne entwarf der Architekt Walter Gropius (1883–1969) 1927 eine raum- und lichttechnisch hochentwickelte Theatermaschinerie – T. genannt. Jedoch wurde das Projekt aus finanziellen Gründen nie realisiert. Gropius' Theaterbaukonstruktion lag die Vorstellung zugrunde, durch «Mobilisierung aller räumlichen Mittel» sowohl die Distanz zwischen Schauspieler und Publikum als auch die Differenzierung in verschiedenen Zuschauer‹klassen› (‹Rangordnung›) aufzuheben. Der Konzeption nach handelte es sich bei dem T. um ein egalitäres Massentheater, das 2000 Besuchern Platz bieten sollte. Für die Inszenierungen boten sich mehrere, z. T. variable Spielflächen an: 1. die Rundbühne und 2. die Vorbühne, die sich 3. durch Drehung um 180 Grad in eine allseitig von Zuschauern umgebene Rundarena verwandeln ließ. Die Deckenkuppel und die Seitenwände konnten als Projektionsflächen für Filmaufnahmen genutzt werden. – Die Begriffe T. und ‹totales Theater› sind deutlich voneinander zu trennen: Verstanden Gropius und Piscator (1893–1966) unter T. eine Architekturform, so verbirgt sich hinter der Bezeichnung totales Theater «die Idee von der Entfesselung der gesamten darstellenden Künste» (Gesamtkunstwerk).

Gropius, W.: Theaterbau (1934). Wiederveröffentlicht in: Brauneck, M. (Hg.): Theater im 20. Jahrhundert, Reinbek bei Hamburg 1982, S. 161–169; Piscator, E.: Totaltheater und totales Theater (1966). In: ders.: Theater, Film, Politik. Berlin 1980, S. 439–441; Woll, St.: Das Totaltheater. Ein Projekt von Walter Gropius und Erwin Piscator. Berlin 1985 (= Schriften der Gesellschaft für Theatergeschichte, Bd. 68).

Carl Wege

Totentanz

T. durchziehen die Zeiten. Im Ritualtanz des Todes verbinden sich die Leichenkulte mit erotischen Elementen und Initiationsriten. In Kamerun z. B. wirbeln die Totentänzer ihre Lendentücher in die Höhe, um das Glied freizulegen. In Karelien werfen im Stamme der Yarps die Frauen beim Tode junger Männer die Grasröcke ungestüm in die Höhe. – Im 3. Jahrtausend wurden beim T. in Ägypten ebenso wie beim Lebenszauber Weitschritt und Beinwurf geübt. Für die Initiation und für das Aus-dem-Leben-Scheiden gilt, daß der Mensch sich im Zustand des Ausgereiftseins mit transzendenten Dimensionen konfrontieren muß. So wollten die Naturvölker Seelen in die jenseitige Welt geleiten, aber auch deren Erdenplatz magisch absichern. Deshalb verbanden Medizinmänner Tieropfer, Dankgebete und Tänze zu einer großen Schaustellung. Die Totentänzer trugen Masken und suchten, mit deren Hilfe in Vorstellungen über das Besessensein vom Geist des Toten einzudringen (Yoruba).

In Ägypten stellten die T. eine Sonderform der →Trionfi dar. Man tanzte im Leichenzug in langen, oft offen getragenen Gewändern, Zweige schwingend, und man tanzte an der Gruft. Die Männer trugen im Tanz spitze Schilfmützen, die Frauen klatschten. Die Grabtänze wurden vielfach von Zwergen ausgeführt, z. T. von afrikanischen Pygmäen. – In Rom tanzten Etrusker im Leichenzug, und zwar die Sikinnis des →Satyrspiels. Die Verstorbenen wurden im T. mit Maske und in Verkleidung verkörpert. Die Träger dieser Rollen trieben allerlei Scherz, indem sie den Toten imitierten und karikierten. In Vespasians Leichenprozession wurde dessen Geist karikiert, berichtet Sueton. Kunstreiter, die Desaltores, erheiterten die staunenden Zuschauer und die Begleiter des Leichenzugs. Hinter den Desaltores sprang, burlesk gekleidet, eine harlekinartige Figur drein, sogar in buntem Lappenkleid mit hoher Mütze, was an den ägyptischen Schilfaufputz denken läßt. Doch nicht allein die Etrusker mischten Spaßmacher und→Narren in den Totenzug ein. – In Tibet traten neben zwei Totenkopfträgern mit Gerippen auch zwei Spaßmacher auf. Tod und Narrentum verbündeten sich gleichfalls im Skalptanz der Cheyenne. Die Clowns trugen dort die Kleider der Erschlagenen. Die bizarre Idee tanzender Totengerippe pflegte auch Rom. In Orissa trugen die Totentänzer der Leichenprozessionen die Werkzeuge, Kleider und Gebrauchsgegenstände des Verstorbenen auf dem Kopf wie später auch im europäischen Mittelalter. – Beispiel für einen Leichenzug als lineares Ballett im Mittelalter ist das Totenfest Karls V. in Brüssel (1558). Die Prozessionsform wurde dort dramatisch phantasievoll gegliedert, etwa durch das Ehrenpferd des Toten, die Standarte, ein ungeheures Schiff mit Allegorien, die die guten Eigenschaften des Verewigten abbildeten. Geschwungene Standarten belebten die Bewegungsvollzüge.

1056 Tourneetheater

Die ursprünglichste Tanzformation des T. war die Kreisform, deren Zentrum die Leiche, den Scheiterhaufen oder Kleiderreste des Toten bildeten. Schamanen, Medizinmänner, Trommler, Tierfiguren und Masken umtanzten den Kreismittelpunkt. Auf den Färöer und dem dänischen Festland wurde der Sarg noch bis 1930 darstellend umtanzt. Auf Borneo umrundete ein Tänzer achtmal jenen Baum, der zum Sarg ausgewählt und gehöhlt werden sollte.

Das große Spiel des *Todesreigens*, nach dem spanischen T.-Gericht *Danza General de la muerta*, stammt aus dem 14. Jh. In ihm tanzt der Tod erstmals mit zwei Jungfrauen und danach mit 30 weltlichen und geistlichen Standespersonen den Reigen. Den Tod als Tänzer überliefern etruskische Grabplatten. 1376 gestaltet Frankreich den «Danse macabre» literarisch und bildlich. Die T.-Sitte in Europa stammt aus den Pestzeiten des 14. Jh. T.-Spiele sind in Kärnten bekannt. Das Kinderspiel vom «Schwarzen Mann» ist eine Reduktion des «Danse macabre». – Moderne Varianten: *Der grüne Tisch*, 1932 (Jooss, Musik: F. Cohen); *Das Totenmal*, 1930; *Totenklage*, 1936 (Wigman); *El Penitente*, 1940 (Graham); *Coro di morti*, 1942 (A. de Milloss, Musik: G. Petrassi); *Le jeune homme et la Mort*, 1946 (R. Petit); *La Valse*, 1951 (Balanchine, Musik: Ravel); *La Danse des morts*, 1954 (Lola Rogge, Musik: W. Kraft).

Biehn, H.: Feste und Feiern im alten Europa. München o. J.; Rebling, E.: Die Tanzkunst Indiens. Wilhelmshaven 1982; Rosenfeld, H.: Der mittelalterliche Totentanz. München 1948; Sachs, C.: Weltgeschichte des Tanzes. Berlin 1933; Seelmann, W.: Die Totentänze des Mittelalters. Norden 1893.

Helga Ettl

Tourneetheater

Privatwirtschaftlich arbeitende, nichtsubventionierte Theaterunternehmen ohne festes Ensemble und Spielstätte. T. gleichen die Defizite bei der Bespielung von Städten ohne Theater und in der Provinz aus, stehen aber auch in starker Konkurrenz zu den ebenfalls mobilen → Landesbühnen. Aus ökonomischen Gründen meist geringe Risikobereitschaft bei der Spielplangestaltung: vornehmlich Klassiker, bewährte Dramen der Moderne, → Boulevard, gängiges Musiktheater. Oft stehen ein oder mehrere publikumswirksame Stars im Mittelpunkt eines sonst zweitklassigen Ensembles. Gelegentlich aber auch hervorragende Produktionen gerade auf Grund von Starbesetzungen. Im deutschsprachigen Raum bestreiten derzeit ca. 50 Unternehmen pro Spielzeit etwa 4800 Schauspiel- und 900 Musiktheaterabende. Seit einiger Zeit versuchen die in der Interessengemeinschaft der Städte mit Theatergastspielen (INTHEGA) zusammengeschlossenen Städte, Einfluß auf die Spielplangestaltung der T. zu gewinnen, um die Einbindung der Produktionen in regionale und kommunale Kulturplanungen zu erleichtern.

Mykenae Theater-Korrespondenz, Nr. 9. Darmstadt 1984; Pierwoß, K.: Kritische Aspekte zum Tourneetheater. In: Bühnengenossenschaft 3 (1975); S. 12–17; Theater als Produkt der Marktwirtschaft. In: Die Deutsche Bühne 11 (1980).

Erich Krieger

Tragikomödie

Die T. ist zwar eine dramatische Form von langer Tradition, jedoch bis heute noch nicht eindeutig definiert. Es sind zwei wesentliche, im Grunde unterschiedliche Entwicklungstendenzen der T. festzustellen, so daß von zwei verschiedenen, historisch abgegrenzten Formen gesprochen werden kann: 1. einer ursprünglichen T. von der Antike bis zum 18. Jh. und 2. einer modernen seit Mitte des 18. Jh. bis heute.

1. Der Römer Titus Maccius Plautus (ca. 250–184 v. Chr.) gilt als der erste, der im Prolog zu *Amphitryon* (191) das Wort T. im Sinne einer Mischform gebrauchte. In der Folge, im Theater der Renaissance, des Barock und der Frühklassik, sind vier Typen dieser Mischform von → Tragödie und → Komödie zu unterscheiden (K. S. Guthke): Stücke mit gemischtem Personal; Stücke mit vermischtem Stil, Elementen aus Tragödie und Komödie; Dramen, wo ernste und lächerliche Elemente nebeneinanderstehen; ernste, sogar tragisch angelegte Stücke mit gutem Schluß. Ausgangspunkt dieser Entwicklung war die ital. Renaissance, vor allem bei Giambattista Girardi, ‹Il Cinthio› (1504–73), sowie Giovanni Battista Guarini (1538–1612) mit seinem → Schäferspiel *Il Pastor fido* (1589) und der Abhandlung *Compendio della poesia tragicomica* (1601). In Spanien gilt als wesentliche T. *La Celestina* oder die T. von *Calisto und Melibea* (1499–1502), Fernando de Rojas (1465–1541) zugeschrieben; die Mischformen waren aber vor allem im Rahmen der → comedia und im Werke des Lope de Vega (1562–1635) zahlreich. Im engl. → Elisabethanischen Theater gibt es tragikomische Elemente in Komödien und Schäferspielen Shakespeares, die großen Exponenten der T. sind jedoch John Fletcher (1579–1625) und Francis Beaumont (1584–1616), die oft als Koautoren auftraten, z. B. *Philaster* (1610), *The Maid's Tragedy* (1611) oder *The Scornful Lady* (1613). Als Theoretiker der Form tat sich später John Dryden (1631–1700) hervor, bes. im *Essay of Dramatic Poesy* (1668). Begründer der frz. T. ist Alexandre Hardy (15?–1632), der Autor von etwa 300 solcher Stücke, so *La force du sang* (1626) und *Elmire* (1628). In seiner Folge sind im Rahmen der frz. Klassik zu nennen: Jean de Rotrou

1058 Tragikomödie

(1609–50: *Laure persécutée*, 1637–39), Georges de Scudéry (1601–67: *L'Amour tyrannique*, 1638–39), Jean Mairet (1604–86: *Virginie*, 1635) und Philippe Quinault (1635–88: *Stratonice*, 1660). Als das Meisterwerk der frz. T. gilt *Le Cid* (1637) von Pierre Corneille (1605–84).

Kann für diese Mischform eine gemeinsame Poetik ermittelt werden? Neben den allg. Merkmalen des →Barocktheaters und der Vorklassik (Bestreben, auf Empfindung und Phantasie des Zuschauers einzuwirken; Vorliebe für gewaltsame Handlung, außergewöhnliche Situationen und Theaterstreiche, für Finten und Verkleidung, Hyperbolik und Pointe) sind auch sehr spezifische Eigenschaften zu finden: 1. ein glückliches Ende nach heftigen Konflikten mit tragischen Untertönen; 2. gemischtes Personal mit obligaten Funktionen, d. h. Hauptfiguren standesgemäß höheren Ranges; 3. Vermischung von Tragik und Komik, auch da je nach sozialem Rang der Figuren: nur die höheren Ränge sind meist in ernste Konflikte verwickelt, auch hat das Komische eine untergeordnete, spannungslockernde Funktion; 4. behandelt wird nicht Größe und Fall der Fürsten, sondern die Privatsphäre und -intrige, selbst im Geschichtlichen. In dieser ‹additiven› Spielart tendieren die Bauformen zum Neben- oder Gegeneinander.

2. Dagegen ist die moderne Form nicht eine additive, sondern eine ‹synthetische›, beruhend auf der ‹Identität der Gegensätze› (Goethe). In Theorie und Praxis setzt sie ein in der Mitte des 18. Jh., entwickelt sich im Laufe des 19. und bestätigt sich dann im 20. Jh. als die wesentliche Formtendenz mit dem →epischen Theater.

Hatte das dt. Theater mit der alten Form der T. wenig zu tun, so ist sein Beitrag zu Entstehung und Entwicklung der modernen grundlegend. Als Begründer der modernen T. gilt der Sturm und Drang-Autor Jakob Michael Reinhold Lenz (1751–92) in Theorie (*Anmerkungen über das Theater*, 1774; *Pandaemonium Germanicum*, 1775) und Praxis (*Der Hofmeister*, 1774; *Der neue Menoza*, 1775; *Die Soldaten*, 1776). Seine Wirkung setzt allerdings erst später ein. Die erste wichtige Phase in der Geschichte der modernen T. ist das 19. Jh. mit dem doppelten Höhepunkt der Romantik und des Naturalismus. Eine theoretische Basis ist hauptsächlich bei den Philosophen des dt. Idealismus zu finden, so bei Friedrich Schlegel (1772–1829: *Über das Studium der griech. Poesie*, 1797), Adam Müller (1779–1829: *Vorlesungen über dramatische Kunst*, 1806) und in Hegels *Ästhetik* (1835): «Die tiefere Vermittlung ... der tragischen und komischen Auffassung zu einem neuen Ganzen besteht nicht im Nebeneinander oder Umschlagen dieser Gegensätze, sondern in ihrer sich wechselseitig abstumpfenden Ausgleichung.» Zusammenfassend für diese Wertschätzung der T. Friedrich Schelling (1775–1854: *Philosophie der Kunst*, 1802–03): «... daß die Mischung des Entgegengesetzten, also vorzüglich des Tragischen und Komischen selbst, als Prinzip dem modernen Drama

Tragikomödie 1059

zugrunde liegt.» Dramaturgisch dann wird die T. eindeutig bestimmt als die eigentliche Theaterform der Zeit in der →frz. Romantik, s. vor allem Victor Hugo (1802–85: *Vorwort zu Cromwell*, 1827). Als wichtigste T. sind zu nennen: Hugos *Hernani* (1830) und *Ruy Blas* (1838), Alfred de Mussets *Lorenzaccio* (1834) und in Deutschland Heinrich von Kleists (1777–1811) *Amphitryon* (1807). Tragikomische Einschläge haben die Stücke von Georg Büchner (1813–37) und Christian Dietrich Grabbe (1801–36), bei letzterem die T. *Don Juan und Faust* (1828). Als Ausklang dieser Phase im Realismus sind gewisse Stücke Friedrich Hebbels (1813–63) zu verstehen, bes. als Anwendung der Theorien Hegels, so *Ein Trauerspiel in Sizilien* mit einem bedeutenden Vorwort über die Dramaturgie der T. (1851). Der Naturalismus repräsentiert den Ausklang der T. im 19. Jh. und den Übergang zur T. im 20. Jh. Im skandin. Theater ist hier grundlegend das Werk Henrik Ibsens (1828–1906), bes. *Die Wildente* (1885). Im dt. Theater ist Gerhart Hauptmann (1862–1946) der namhafteste Exponent dieser Gattung: *Der rote Hahn* (1901), *Peter Brauer* (1908–10) und vor allem *Die Ratten* (1911). Im russ. Theater die T. Anton Tschechows (1860–1904) *Die Möwe* (1896), *Onkel Wanja* (1896), *Drei Schwestern* (1901) und *Der Kirschgarten* (1904).

In der Folge sind in der ersten Hälfte des 20. Jh. wesentlich für die Entwicklung der T. der Ire Sean O'Casey (1880–1964) mit *Juno and the Paycock* (1924) und *The Plough and the Stars* (1926) sowie der Italiener Luigi Pirandello (1867–1936) mit *Sei personaggi in cerca d'autore* (1921) und *Enrico IV* (1922). Der dt. Expressionismus weist in vielen Stücken eine Tendenz zur T. auf, so bei Carl Sternheim (1878–1942: *Die Hose*, 1911; *Bürger Schippel*, 1913), Georg Kaiser (1878–1945: *Von morgens bis mitternachts*, 1916; *Kanzlist Kreher*, 1922). Im Welttheater nach dem 2. Weltkrieg ist die T. zu einer Konstante geworden. Bei drei der größten Autoren ist die T. die fast ausschließliche Form: Samuel Beckett (1906–89) mit *Warten auf Godot* (1953) oder *Das Endspiel* (UA 1957); Eugène Ionesco (* 1912) mit *La cantatrice chauve* (1950), *Les Chaises* (1952) oder *Rhinocéros* (1959); Friedrich Dürrenmatt (1921–90) mit *Romulus der Große* (1949), *Der Besuch der alten Dame* (1956); *Die Physiker* (1962). Die zwei letzteren liefern auch wesentliche Beiträge zur Dramaturgie der T.: Ionescos *Notes et contre-notes* (1962) und Dürrenmatts *Theater-Schriften und -Reden* (I, 1966; II, 1972). Das moderne →Volksstück ist stark beeinflußt von der T., so Ödön v. Horváth (1901–38: *Geschichten aus dem Wiener Wald*, 1931) oder Wolfgang Bauer (* 1941). Im angelsächsischen Theater ist die T. heute wohl die weitverbreitetste Form: so in England Harold Pinter (* 1930) mit *The Caretaker* (1960) oder *Old Times* (1971); Edward Bond (* 1934) Mit *Early Morning* (1968) oder *Lear* (1971); Tom Stoppard mit *Rosencrantz and Guildenstern are dead* (1966); in den USA Edward Albee (* 1928) mit *The Zoo Story* (1959), *The*

1060 Tragikomödie

American Dream (1961), *Who's Afraid of Virginia Woolf* (1962) oder Sam Shephard (*1943) mit *Fool for Love* (1983). Es seien noch genannt in Deutschland Martin Walser (*1927) mit *Eiche und Angora* (1962) und dem Essay *Imitation oder Realismus* (1964) sowie Botho Strauß (*1944) mit *Groß und klein* (1978) und *Kalldewey* (1982), der Spanier Fernando Arrabal (*1932) mit *Le Grand Cérémonial* (1963), der Pole Slawomir Mrožek (*1930) mit *Tango* (1965), *Der Buckel* (1975), der Tscheche Václav Havel (*1936) mit *Vernissage* (1975).

Trotz zahlreicher Überschneidungen zwischen T., →Komödie, →Drama oder →Farce (manche Autoren, so Dürrenmatt oder Ionesco, nennen ihre T. Komödien) gibt es eine Poetik dieser modernen T. Grundlegend dafür ist eine perspektivistische Veränderung des Verhältnisses zwischen Tragik und Komik: das tragikomische Theater gilt als die heute mögliche Tragödie bzw. Komödie, welche sich somit beide in dieser neuen Formsynthese aufheben, in einer Art «dialektischen Spannung» (Ionesco). Aus dem Spannungsbezug zwischen Tragik und Komik, Lachen und Grauen entsteht die T. Die Gesamtform ist über drei Grundaspekte erfaßbar: Vision, Struktur und Bauformen. 1. Die tragikomische Vision ist kennzeichnend durch eine metaphysische Auseinandersetzung in ‹ontologischer Leere› (Ionesco): so das Werk Becketts; durch den Kampf des Einzelmenschen gegen eine Gesellschaft, die zur anonymen, sinnlosen Mechanik herabgesunken ist, in einer Art Apokalypse, die menschlichen Ursprungs ist; endlich durch eine klischeehafte, uneigentliche Sprache, in welcher der einzelne bis zur Selbstentfremdung zugerichtet wird oder zur Sprachlosigkeit erstarrt. 2. Für die Struktur der T. ist schon prägnant die Hebbelsche Umformung des tragischen Systems Hegels: Nur noch das Subjekt bewahrt Sinn und Berechtigung, das Objekt ist sinnlos, das Absolute desakralisiert, degradiert und pervertiert; darum kann Dürrenmatt in seiner T. *Der Besuch der alten Dame* behaupten, Ills «Tod ist sinnvoll und sinnlos zugleich». 3. Zur Darstellung dieses besonderen Spannungsverhältnisses hat sich ein System von eigenen Bauformen entwickelt, welche einmal in der Beziehung von Intrige und Charakter besteht, zum anderen in der eigenartigen Kombination von vier Grundelementen, →Parodie, Paradox, Ambivalenz und →Groteske. – Das so vermittelte Weltbild ohne versöhnenden tragischen Schluß oder komischen Triumph ergibt in kritischer Form eine Dramaturgie des Zweifels, der Unlust, des Unbehagens – dem existentiellen Grundgefühl unserer Zeit angepaßt.

Brauneck, M./Schneilin, G. (Hg.): Drama und Theater. Bamberg 1986; Guichemerre, R.: La tragicomédie. Paris 1981; Guthke, K. S.: Geschichte und Poetik der dt. Tragikomödie. Göttingen 1961; ders.: Die moderne Tragikomödie. Göttingen 1968; Herrick, M. T.: Tragicomedy. Its Origin and Development in Italy, France and England. Urbana 1955; Kott, J.: Shakespeare heute. München 1980; Styan,

J.L.: The Dark Comedy. The Development of Modern Comic Tragedy. Cambridge 1962.

Gérard Schneilin

Tragödie

(Griech.: Bocksgesang, →Antikes Theater) Im Gegensatz zur Komödie, die von der Antike bis heute in verschiedensten Ausformungen existiert und sozial wie kulturell unbegrenzt variabel erscheint, ist die T. eine streng gegliederte Gattung, welche sich nur zu bestimmten Zeiten in der Geschichte hat entfalten können.

In der Theatergeschichte des Westens hat es bisher nur zwei Perioden gegeben, in denen die T. als Theatergattung vorherrschte: das →Antike Theater, vor allem Griechenlands von Aischylos (525–456 v. Chr.) bis Euripides (um 480–406 v. Chr.) mit einem Nachspiel in Rom bei Seneca (um 4 v. Chr.–65 n. Chr.), sodann in Westeuropa mit der relativ kurzen Periode vom →Renaissancetheater über das Goldene Zeitalter Spaniens (→Comedia) und das engl. →Elisabethanische Theater bis zur frz. und dt. →Klassik. Die antike T. hatte in der Praxis der großen Tragiker und in der *Poetik* des Aristoteles (384–322 v. Chr.; ca. 330) ihre eigenen Motive, Formen und Regeln. Diese sind während des zweiten Höhepunkts der T. zuerst von den Theoretikern des Humanismus, dann von den Autoren imitiert, adaptiert und kodifiziert worden – so in der Theorie vor allem wegweisend die Poetiken der ital. Renaissance (Robortello, Castelvetro, Riccoboni u. a.), die *Poetices* des Franzosen Julius Caesar Scaliger (1484–1558), später die *Ars Poetica* des Alexander Donatus (1631), die Schriften der beiden Niederländer Gerardus Vossius und Daniel Heinsius, in Deutschland Martin Opitz (1597–1639: *Buch von der dt. Poeterey*, 1624), Nicolas Boileau (1636–1711: *Art poétique*, 1674) in Frankreich, endlich in England Sir Philip Sidney (1554–86: *Defence of Poesie*, 1581), Thomas Rymer (1641–1713), John Dryden (1631–1700: *Essay of Dramatic Poesy*, 1668). Höhepunkte der T. in Italien bei Giambattisto Giraldi Cinthio (1504–73), in Spanien bei Pedro Calderón de la Barca (1600–81), im Elisabethanischen Theater bei Christopher Marlowe (1564–93) und in den großen T. Shakespeares, im dt. Barocktrauerspiel bei Andreas Gryphius (1616–64) und Daniel Casper von Lohenstein (1635–83), dann in der frz. und dt. Klassik bei Pierre Corneille (1606–84) und Jean Racine (1639–99), Johann Wolfgang v. Goethe (1749–1832), Friedrich von Schiller (1759–1805) und Friedrich Hölderlin (1770–1843). In der Folge setzt das Epigonentum ein, sowohl bei Vittorio Alfieri (1749–1803) als bei Voltaire (1694–1778) oder auch bei Friedrich Hebbel

1062 Tragödie

(1813–63), der vielleicht am besten das Auseinanderklaffen von Inhalt und Form in der späten T. exemplifiziert. Der Ausnahmefall ist in der dt. Romantik Heinrich Kleist (1777–1811), bei dem wohl die T. zum letztenmal kulminiert. Das späte 19. und bes. das 20. Jh. versuchen, die T. neu zu gestalten, ohne allerdings dieses Ziel zu erreichen.

Poetologisch haben die T. des westlichen Theaters trotz Abweichungen und -zweigungen der Regeln und Vorschriften, der Themen und Bauformen wesentliche Grundmerkmale gemein. In der Nachahmung der Antike unter Anwendung der aristotelischen Poetik stehen im Mittelpunkt die →Mimesis und die →Katharsis als Folge von Furcht und Mitleid. Die Gattungstheorie fordert die strenge Trennung der Gattungen, wobei die T. auf der höchsten Stufe steht. Die Grundregeln der Wahrscheinlichkeit, der Schicklichkeit und des Dekorums haben zur Folge die Regel der →drei Einheiten sowie die →Ständeklausel. Daraus entsteht das besondere Formgefüge dieses Identifikationstheaters. Philosophisch liegt ihm der Glaube an Vernünftigkeit und Gesetzlichkeit der Welt zugrunde: eine Ordnung und Harmonie, die, dem menschlichen Verstand zugänglich, vollständig in der Sprache aufgeht und sich darin offenbart. Im Primat der Sprache drückt sich der humanistische Grundsatz aus, wonach das Wort sich vollständig mit dem Gedanken deckt, Wesen und Bezug von Mensch, Welt und Gott klar zum Ausdruck bringen kann – daher, im Unterschied zu →Komödie oder Drama, der durchgehende hohe Sprachstil, die kohärente Verssprache (Alexandriner in der romantischen T. und im dt. barocken Trauerspiel, Blankvers im Elisabethanischen Theater, iambischer Pentameter im dt. klassischen Trauerspiel). Die Identifikation vollzieht sich dramaturgisch innerhalb eines streng rationalistisch-deterministischen Kausalitätsrahmens: lückenlose Fabel, einheitliche, zielstrebige →Handlung, Lösung des Konflikts und Wiederherstellung der Harmonie, Vereinheitlichung von Raum und Zeit, strenge funktionale Gliederung der fünf Akte mit szenischer Steigerung (I Exposition – II Konfliktaufbau – III Kollision – IV Retardierung und Beschleunigung – V Katastrophe und Versöhnung), Figurenkonstellation mit klaren Gegenspielerpositionen.

Die innere Spannung dieses äußeren Formgefüges ist im Tragischen zu finden. Es ist im →Antiken Theater mehr metaphysisch-mythisch begründet, später eher moralisch. Trotz zahlreicher, oft widersprüchlicher Definitionsversuche ist das Tragische strukturell bestimmbar als schicksalsbedingter, unausweichlicher und unlösbarer Wertekonflikt zwischen zwei sinnvoll gleichberechtigten Repräsentanten, wobei der meist notwendige Untergang des schuldigen Einzelhelden als Bestätigung der sinngebenden, übergeordneten Macht galt. (T. ohne Sühne- und Opfertod sind z. B. Corneilles *Horace*, 1640, *Cinna*, 1642; Racines *Bérénice*, 1670; Goethes *Iphigenie*, 1787; *Torquato Tasso*, 1789.) Auch gilt das Tragische seit

Tragödie 1063

den Griechen als Grenzsituation, wobei das Übertreten der Grenze als schuldhaft empfunden und bestraft wird.

Wegen der Gleichberechtigung der antagonistischen Mächte beruht die T. auf Spannung und Ambivalenz. Im →Drama oder →Melodrama ist nur einer der beiden Gegenspieler berechtigt; in der T. geht der Riß durch beide Repräsentanten, jeder hat zugleich recht und unrecht.

Dadurch erklären sich die relative Seltenheit der T. in der Theatergeschichte und die Schwierigkeit einer Wiedergeburt heute. Die T. ist in ihren zwei Hauptphasen entstanden zu Zeiten des Umbruchs: jeweils im Übergang von einer kosmischen Weltauffassung, in der das Göttliche und Sakrale die Welt durchdringen, zu einer Weltsicht, die die individuellen Werte der Vernunft und des Einzelwillens zur Geltung bringt. Daher die Spannung, der Streit, die Ambivalenz und schließlich der Ausgleich der Werte. Darum die Unmöglichkeit einer christlichen T. Taucht das Tragische nur als Unwissen oder momentane Verzweiflung innerhalb einer als gültig gehaltenen göttlichen Ordnung auf, so ergibt sich, wie im Mittelalter oder im span. Barock, das →Mysterienspiel, jedoch keine T. Desgleichen im Theater des 20. Jh., wenn versucht wird, T. mit christlichen mythischen Inhalten zu schreiben – so bei Hugo von Hofmannsthal (1874–1929) die Allegorien *Jedermann* (1911) oder *Das Salzburger große Welttheater* (1922); so die Märtyrerstücke im 20. Jh., die Varianten der → Märtyrertragödien des Barock sind: etwa in England T. S. Eliots *Murder in the Cathedral* (1888–1965; 1935) oder in Frankreich *Port-Royal* (1954) von Henri de Montherlant (1896–1972), *Dialogues des Carmélites* (1949) von Georges Bernanos (1888–1948); so vor allem das Werk Paul Claudels (1868–1955), dessen Stücke von *Le Partage de midi* bis zu *Le soulier de satin* (1906–25) immer wieder zeigen, wie das Tragische zurückweicht vor der göttlichen Gnade und der Vorsehung. Ausnahmen in dieser Entwicklung sind etwa Hofmannsthals T. *Der Turm* (1925) oder *Der Stellvertreter* (1963) von Rolf Hochhuth (*1931); darin droht vor den apokalyptischen Verbrechen der Zeit der christliche Glaube zu zerbrechen, so daß Zweifel und Verzweiflung die tragische Ambivalenz ermöglichen.

Wesentlich für die T. im 20. Jh. ist die Neubearbeitung in Gehalt und Form der antiken Mythen: Neuaufführungen (in Deutschland und Österreich von Max Reinhardt und Leopold Jessner bis Peter Stein), Übersetzungen und Bearbeitungen (→Antikenrezeption); T.-form mit neu interpretierten Mythen – so im deutschsprachigen Theater Hofmannsthals Adaptation *König Ödipus* (1905) und seine T. *Elektra* (1903) und *Ödipus und die Sphinx* (1905); Brechts *Antigone* nach der Hölderlin-Version des Sophokles (1947); später Peter Hacks (*1928) mit *Amphitryon* (1967), *Prexaspes* (1968), *Omphale* (1969) und Heiner Müllers Stücke *Philoktet* (1965), *Herakles 5* (1966), *Ödipus, Tyrann* (1966), *Prometheus* (1967), *Horatier* (1969), *Zement* (1973), *Medeaspiel* (1974). In England z. B. die

1064 Tragödie

Übersetzungen von William B. Yeats (1865–1939) und die Versuche von T. S. Eliot (1888–1965), so *The Family Reunion* (1939, nach der *Oresteia* des Aischylos). In Frankreich mit alter und ununterbrochener Antikentradition: Jean Cocteaus (1889–1963) Bearbeitungen (*Antigone*, 1928; *Oedipus Rex* 1927) und Travestien (*La machine infernale*, 1934); *Ödipus und Orpheus* (1926); Jean Giraudoux' (1882–1944) *La guerre de Troie n'aura pas lieu* (1935), *Electra* (1937); Jean Anouilhs (*1910) *Eurydice* (1942) und *Antigone* (1943); Jean-Paul Sartres (1905–80) *Les Mouches* (1943). In den USA Robinson Jeffers (1887–1962) mit *Medea* (1947) und *The Cretan Woman* (1954) und besonders Eugene O' Neills (1888–1953) *Mourning becomes Electra* (1931). Psychoanalyse, Existenzphilosophie, Marxismus versuchen die antiken Mythen neu zu interpretieren und die Form der T. wiederzubeleben. Die Erneuerung des Theaters im 20. Jh. vollzieht sich freilich weniger über Rekonstruktion oder Adaption der T. als in Entwicklungen der →Komödie, der →Tragikomödie, des →Volksstücks und des→epischen Theaters.

In all diesen Versuchen manifestiert sich eine intensive philosophische Suche nach dem Tragischen in der modernen Welt, von Hegel und Schopenhauer über Nietzsche, Scheler, Lukács, Unamuno, Heidegger, Jaspers u. a. Tragik ist heute freilich weniger in der T. manifest als paradoxerweise in der Spannung mit dem Komischen in der Tragikomödie Becketts oder Dürrenmatts.

Bonnard, A.: La tragédie et l'homme. Neuchâtel 1951; Brauneck, M. / Schneilin, G. (Hg.): Drama und Theater. Bamberg 1986; Camus, A.: Conférence prononcée à Athènes sur l'avenir de la tragédie. In: Théâtre, récits, nouvelles. Paris 1963; Domenach, J.-M.: Le retour du tragique. Paris 1967; Jacquot, J. (Hg.): Le théâtre tragique. Paris 1965; Jens, W. (Hg.): Die Bauformen der griech. Tagödie. München 1971; Kommerell, M.: Lessing und Aristoteles. Frankfurt/M. 1940; Lancaster, H. C.: A History of French dramatic Literature in the 17th century. Baltimore 1929–42; Lesky, A.: Die griech. Tragödie. Stuttgart 1938; Klotz, V.: Geschlossene und offene Form im Drama. München 1960; Mann, O.: Poetik der Tragödie. Bern 1958; Omesco, I.: La métamorphose de la tragédie. Paris 1978; Sander, V. (Hg.): Tragik und Tragödie. Darmstadt 1971; Scherer, J.: La dramaturgie classique en France. Paris 1950; Steiner, G.: Der Tod der Tragödie. München/Wien 1962; Szondi, P.: Theorie des modernen Dramas. Frankfurt/M. 1956; ders.: Versuch über das Tragische. Frankfurt/M. 1961; Truchet, J.: La tragédie classique en France. Paris 1975; Vernant, J.-P. / Vidal-Naquet, P.: Mythe et tragédie en Grèce ancienne. Paris 1972; Wagner, H.: Ästhetik der Tragödie von Aristoteles bis Schiller. Würzburg 1987.

Gérard Schneilin

TRAM

(Abk. für *Teatr rabotschej molodjoshi* – Theater der Arbeiterjugend) Mitte der 20er Jahre in der UdSSR aus Zirkeln der Arbeiterlaienkunst entstanden, getragen vom Komsomol, breitete sich schnell über das ganze Land aus: um 1932 ca. 25 000 Mitglieder, Mitte der 30er Jahre 70 000. Hatte seinen Ursprung im Leningrader T.; war das erste professionelle Arbeiterjugendtheater, das die gesamte T.-Bewegung prägte: «Das Theater der Arbeiterjugend wollte mit den Kräften jugendlicher Schauspieler Jugendstücke für ein jugendliches Publikum spielen» (Lunatscharski). Stand im Mittelpunkt der Diskussionen um das neue sozialistische Theater, zielte mit politischer Agitation auf den sozialistischen Aufbau. Verwendete künstlerische Mittel, die der «Lebenden Zeitung», den → Blauen Blusen, nahestanden, beeinflußt vom Proletkult, von Meyerhold (Musik, sportliche Anlagen, direkte Hinwendung zum Publikum). Verschmolz Mitte der 30er Jahre verschiedentlich mit anderen Theatern (in Leningrad 1936 mit dem Roten Theater, aus dem später das Staatliche Leningrader Lenin-Komsomol-Theater hervorging) oder zerfiel.

Lunačarskij, A. V.: TRAM. In: ders., Sobranie sočinenij. T. 3. Moskva 1964, S. 396–401; Zograf, N. G.: Teatral'naja samodejatel'nost'. Očerki istorii russkogo sovetskogo dramaturgičeskogo teatra. T. I. Moskva 1954, S. 467–478.

Annelore Engel-Braunschmidt

Trauerspiel

Seit dem 17. Jh. im dt. Sprachraum übliche Bezeichnung für → Tragödie. Wie für → Komödie, → Lustspiel besteht diese Unterscheidung nicht in anderen Sprach- und Theaterkulturen. Theoretisch werden jedoch Unterscheidungen von T. und Tragödie in der Forschung diskutiert. So verbindet für das ‹barocke T.› Walter Benjamin den Begriff ‹Tragödie› mit Mythos und Opfer und bezieht ihn auf die griech. Tragödie; dagegen sei mit T. Geschichte verbunden, teils mit Heilsgeschichte, teils mit säkularisierter Geschichte, mit didaktischer Moralität und psychologisierter Tragik (→ bürgerliches Trauerspiel, → Märtyrerdrama).

Benjamin, W.: Ursprung des dt. Trauerspiels. Frankfurt/M. 1963; Guthke, K. S.: Das dt. bürgerliche Trauerspiel. Stuttgart 1980.

Gérard Schneilin

Traumspiel

Abschluß und Höhepunkt der von A. Strindberg unmittelbar nach dem Ende der *Inferno*-Krise geschriebenen Dramen – von spezifischer dramaturgischer Struktur. *Ett drömspel* (geschr. 1901, 1902 veröff.) ist der Versuch Strindbergs, seine zentralen Themen in neuer theatralischer Form zusammenfassend darzustellen in dem Bemühen, «die unzusammenhängende, aber scheinbar logische Form des Traumes nachzuahmen» (Strindberg). Über das Stück hinaus wichtig ist die in ihm vorgenommene Aufhebung der drei Einheiten von Zeit, Ort und Handlung, die Abwendung von der naturalistischen Dramaturgie, der kontrapunktische Aufbau im Sinne einer polyphonen Symphonie. Revolutionierend war die Abwendung von der Illusionsbühne, die stilisierende, symbolische Benutzung von Requisiten (→Symbolistisches Theater). Zur bleibenden Bedeutung des T. trägt neben dem Verzicht auf die seit der Renaissance für das europ. Theater konstitutiven drei Einheiten vor allem die psychoanalytische Demontage des Individuums bei, das – als Fiktion entlarvt – in viele Facetten aufgespalten wird. – Der Einfluß des T. reicht weit in die Theaterentwicklung des 20. Jh.; bei den Expressionisten (→Expressionistisches Theater) zeigt er sich ebenso wie bei den Surrealisten (→Surrealistisches Theater) und den Vertretern des →absurden Theaters, bei Artaud und Adamov, bei Ionesco und Beckett ebenso wie bei Brecht.

Müssener, H.: August Strindberg, «Ein Traumspiel». Meisenheim 1965; Paul, F.: August Strindberg. Stuttgart 1979; Szondi, P.: Theorie des modernen Dramas. Frankfurt/M. [7]1970; Taub, H.: Strindberg als Traumdichter. Göteborg 1935.

Wolfgang Beck

Travestie

(Ital. travestire = verkleiden) Die Grenzen zwischen T., Parodie und im Frz. und Engl. →Burleske sind fließend und daher theoretisch nicht eindeutig bestimmbar. Etwas forciert wird oft behauptet, die T. verspotte ein Stück durch Über- oder Unterbetonung der Erscheinungsformen (Sprache, Umwelt, Bauformen), während die →Parodie bei Bewahrung der Formen den Inhalt kritisch verändere. Musterbeispiele im deutschsprachigen Theater sind die T. Nestroys (1801–62), so die T. von Friedrich Hebbels (1813–63) *Judith* (1841), *Judith und Holofernes* (1849).

Literatur: → Parodie.

Gérard Schneilin

Tribüne für Freie Deutsche Literatur und Kunst in Amerika

Kundgebungen, Lese-, Rezitations- und Liederabende bildeten das Programm der 1941 von Brecht, Bruckner, Feuchtwanger, Graf, Herzfelde, Heym, Heinrich Mann, Viertel u. a. als Nachfolgeorganisation des 1940 aufgelösten «Schutzverbandes Deutsch-Amerikanischer Schriftsteller» gegr. «Tribüne». Im Februar 1942 gab die Organisation Bruckners *Rassen*, das bis dahin in New York nur in einer Amateuraufführung zu sehen gewesen war, in einer Leseaufführung. Im Mai 1942 brachte die «Tribüne» fünf Szenen aus Brechts *Furcht und Elend des Dritten Reiches*, das in New York erst nach Kriegsende in einer professionellen englischsprachigen Produktion lief.

Jan Hans

Trionfi

Der T. der Renaissance leiten sich ab aus den →Mysterienspielen, Legenden und Maskeraden des Mittelalters, haben ihr Vorbild aber bereits in den Prozessionen Ägyptens und der Antike und den Triumphzügen Roms. Nach Appian tanzen beim Trionfo des Lucius Aemilius Paullus 17 n. Chr. etruskische Ludiones und Histriones hinter den Liktoren, vor dem Feldherrn, nur mit Leibgurt und goldener Stirnbinde. Der Anführer aller Tänzer tritt wie der Triumphator im Prunkgewand auf. Einer der Tänzer trägt als Spaßmacher und Karikaturist ein herabwallendes Purpurkleid mit goldenen Halsketten und Armringen, vollführt aber lächerliche Gebärden und verspottet im Sieger den möglichen künftigen Besiegten. Für die T. werden prunkvolle Wagen und Karren ausgestattet, auf denen Mimen im Maskenspiel agieren. Neben den Wagen schreiten, laufen, hüpfen und springen Vorläufer, Begleiter und Nachfolger. Getanzt wird auf den Wagen, wie etwa 1579 bei der Hochzeit des Francesco di Medici. Der Triumphzug stellt sich als fahrendes Theater dar, in das schon früh →Intermezzi eingebaut werden. Der Umzug hält auf freien Plätzen an. Gesänge, Tänze, Rezitationen finden als Tanzpantomimen am Ort vor günstig gelegenen Zuschauertribünen im stillstehenden Zuge statt. Der geplante Kreuzzug gegen die Türken wird Anlaß für einen Trionfo, das große Fasanenfest von 1454. Freiwillige sollen für die Rückeroberung Konstantinopels angeworben werden. Dieser Triumphzug findet bereits in der geschlossenen Runde, in einem Speisesaal statt. Völlig anders gestaltet ist der Brautzug Maximilians I. mit Bianca M. Sforza von Mailand 1493. In ihn sind alle Umzüge der Zeiten integriert, von den Panathenäen, über Roms T. bis zu den kultischen Prozessionen des Christentums. Bedeutende Maler haben die Festwagen und Triumphbögen ausgestaltet. Bereits im Trionfo des Alfons von Neapel (1443), der sich als ‹Triumphator› feiern ließ, drängt Florenz zur Wiederbelebung des antiken Schautanzes: 60 junge Florentiner fechten die Pyrrhiche (→ Waffentänze); Fußsoldaten treiben Mummenschanz. Auf Scheinpferden kämpfen sie – vorausziehend – gegen die Türken. – 1506, nach der Eroberung von Bologna, läßt Julius II. vier der zwölf Triumphwagen mit ehemals frommen Darstellungen durch römisch-historische ersetzen. 1551 veranstaltet Heinrich II. in Rouen einen dramatisch-szenisch choreographierten Zug, diesmal mit Tanzpantomimen zu Lande und zu Wasser. Schwärme von Meeresgottheiten – auf Delphinen reitend – begleiten als ‹Triumphwagen› Neptuns ein Schiff. Zwei weitere gerüstete Schiffe liefern sich eine Schlacht. Zu Lande führt der Trionfo in ein Brasilianerdorf, in dem Speer- und Bogenspiele vorgeführt werden. 1616 durchzieht Stuttgart ein Umzug in 14 Szenen, der auf 92 Kupferstichtafeln noch heute bewundert werden kann (Römerzug, Naturgottheiten, mythologische Szenen, Heiligenlegenden, Jagdszenen; als komische Figuren: große Teufel, auf Widdern reitend; danach ein Schlittenzug mit den Allegorien der Zeiten, Stunden und Gestirne; im großen Schlußballett werden schließlich alle Berufe mit ihren speziellen Tätigkeiten konterfeit. Beim kurfürstlich bayrischen Freudenfest (1662) tanzen Affen im Zug ein Fackelballett.

Die Form der T. drängt auf Grund ihrer Struktur zum Verfall wegen des fehlenden Zentrums und wegen der Überfülle der Szenenfolge. Die größten Choreographen der T. suchten vor der Stagnation Abhilfe im ‹Ringelrennen›. Aus dieser Zentrierung der Darbietungen entwickelt sich später das zyklische Ballett. Die Wurzel dieser Gattung ist allen voran der Trionfo zu Fuß und zu Pferd, das → Roßballett. Nachfahren der T. sind Blumenkorsos und Karnevalszüge (→ Brauchtumstänze; → Ritualtänze).

Biehn, H.: Feste und Feiern im alten Europa. München o. J.; Gregor, J.: Kulturgeschichte des Balletts. Zürich o. J. / Wien 1944; Reyna, F.: Das Buch vom Ballett (Des Origines du Ballet). Paris 1955; Weege, F.: Der Tanz in der Antike. Hildesheim 1976.

Helga Ettl

Truppe

Das Wort T. bezeichnet in der Regel eine feste, stabile Gruppe von Schauspielern und anderen Mitarbeitern, die von einem oder mehreren von ihnen geleitet wird; in neuerer Zeit kann der Leiter auch der Regisseur sein. Diese T. wird von Fall zu Fall bzw. von Spielzeit zu Spielzeit durch weitere Engagements ergänzt. Urspr. wurden neben T. auch die beiden Begriffe Bande und Gesellschaft verwendet, wobei die allmähliche inhaltliche Abwertung eines Worts zum Rückgriff auf das nächste führt. Als z. B. das Wort Bande als für die Bezeichnung Schauspieler «von besseren Sitten und Fähigkeiten zu niedrig» (Adelung) empfunden wurde, wurde es durch das Wort T. ersetzt. Als dann dieses Wort wiederum vorwiegend auf umherziehende Gruppen von Schauspielern und Spielleuten angewendet wurde, wurde für rechtliche, oft an ein festes Theater gebundene Schauspieler der Begriff Gesellschaft verwendet. In den Anfangszeiten des Berufstheaters waren die Schauspieler sehr selten seßhaft, die T. also die gängige Organisationsform, angefangen mit den T. der →Commedia dell'arte in Italien, mit den →Englischen und Holländischen Komödianten in Deutschland, die ab Mitte des 17. Jh. von dt. T. abgelöst wurden und mit den fahrenden Spielleuten in Frankreich; sie spielten in rasch aufgeschlagenen Schaubuden und Marktplätzen oder Festwiesen, mußten oft improvisieren und kannten also weder geschlossenen Raum noch streng fixierten Text. Danach etablierten sich allmählich feste, seßhafte T. bzw. Gesellschaften, urspr. auch ‹stehende Bühnen› genannt, die nach und nach die Wandertruppen verdrängten – so die ‹teatri stabili› in Italien, die 1660 gegründete →‹Comédie Française› in Frankreich, die Hof- und Residenztheater des 18. Jh. in Deutschland. Heute sind echte Wanderbühnen und -truppen in Deutschland und Frankreich mit der Dezentralisierung in der Theaterorganisation – siehe die Stadttheater in Deutschland, die ‹centres dramatiques› in Frankreich – eine Seltenheit geworden; bedeutender ist ihre Rolle in England und in den USA geblieben. Das Wort T. wird demgemäß v. a. als Bezeichnung für die sog. Freien Truppen (→Freies Theater, Gruppentheater) gebraucht; weniger geläufig für →Tourneetheater wie z. B. die aus der Schweiz stammende Gruppe Der Grüne Wagen. Für feste Bühnen dagegen hat sich die Bezeichnung →Ensemble durchgesetzt, während sich der Begriff Kompanie, wohl unter Einfluß des engl. ‹company›, vorwiegend auf Ballettkompanien bezieht.

Bernard Poloni

Turniere

Als Mittelpunkt der großen Hoffeste im Mittelalter hatten die T. die Funktion, ritterlichen Geist zu pflegen und moralische Haltung zu fördern. Vom Pfingstfest zu Mainz an (1184) sind alle T. theatralische Schauspiele. In mittelalterlicher allegorischer Verkleidung wird zum Beispiel

1070 Typenkomödie

das T. zur Hochzeit Karls des Kühnen 1468 ausgestattet. Zwerg und Riese reiten in Brügge ein. Die heilige Gudula führt ein Untier durch die Straßen. Fackelträger folgen den Rittern. Auch als Exoten verkleidete Rittergruppen werden zum festen Bestandteil der gerittenen und getanzten T., später der → Roßballette; → Waffentänze; → Prozessionen.

Gregor, J.: Kulturgeschichte des Balletts. Zürich o.J./Wien 1944; Schmidt-Garre, H.: Ballett. Vom Sonnenkönig bis Balanchine. Hannover 1966.

Helga Ettl

Typenkomödie

Älteste Komödienform, deren komische Wirkung nicht aus der Verwicklung in Situationen wie in der Situationskomödie oder aus der überspitzten Darstellung eines Charakters wie in der → Charakterkomödie herrührt, sondern aus dem Handeln bestimmter Figuren mit pointierten, überindividuellen Merkmalen soziologischer bzw. psychologischer Natur – etwa der geizige oder der lüsterne Alte, der Pedant, der junge Liebhaber, der Medikus usw. Die Tendenz zur Typisierung ist in jedem komischen volkstümlichen Theater vorhanden. Der erste bedeutende literarische Beleg der T. geht auf die griech. Neue Komödie (→ Antikes Theater) zurück; sie nimmt dann über Plautus (250–184 v. Chr.) und Terenz (185?–160 v. Chr.) Einfluß auf die Komödienliteratur des Abendlands, vorwiegend in Italien mit der → Commedia dell'arte, und entwickelt sich mit Carlo Gozzi (1720–1806), Carlo Goldoni (1707–93) und Molière (1622–73) nach und nach zur Charakterkomödie weiter. Die T. lebt heute im Volks- bzw. Dialekttheater weiter.

Literatur: → Komödie.

Bernard Poloni

Überbrettl

Dem Ü. (das seinen Namen einer Analogiebildung zu Nietzsches ‹Übermenschen› verdankt) gebührt der Ruhm, das erste deutschsprachige Kabarett gewesen zu sein. Initiator und Gründer war Ernst von Wolzogen, Verfasser humoristischer Romane und Leiter des «Akademisch-Dramatischen Vereins» in München.

Mit 10000 Mark geliehenem Kapital begann das «Bunte Theater (Ü.)» nach nächtlicher Voraufführung am 18.1.1901 in der 650 Plätze umfassenden «Secessionsbühne» in Berlin sein kurzes Dasein. Das Programm umfaßte Pantomimen, Schattenspiele, Chansons, Rezitationen und Parodien. Wenn auch die Eröffnung möglicherweise nur zufällig mit dem 30. Jahrestag der Reichsgründung und dem 200. Geburtstag der preußischen Monarchie zusammenfiel, so hatte das Datum doch symptomatischen Charakter. Politische Satire, soziale Anklage lagen Wolzogen fern. Alle trotzdem noch verbliebenen Reste von Satire unterband die Präventivzensur des kaiserlichen Deutschland. Der große Erfolg führte zu einer Fülle von Nachahmungen und veranlaßte Wolzogen zu einer Deutschlandtournee. Als das Ü. nach Berlin zurückkehrte, hatte sich der verbliebene Rest des Ensembles selbständig gemacht, der Besitzer der «Secessionsbühne» ein eigenes «Buntes Brettl» eröffnet. Wolzogen ging erneut auf Tournee und eröffnete am 28. 11. 1901 ein rund 1000 Plätze umfassendes eigenes Haus, in dem kurzzeitig L. Thoma als Dramaturg arbeitete. Wolzogen hatte sich mit Geldgebern verbinden müssen, die zunehmend Einfluß auf das Programm nahmen und ihn im Februar 1902 als Leiter ‹beurlaubten›, bis er im Juni öffentlich zurücktrat. M. Zickel übernahm zuerst mit M. Salzer, später mit E. Paetel die Leitung des Ü., dessen Programm sich immer mehr reinem Theater näherte, bis Ende Dezember 1902 der «Bunte Teil» des Programms, der allein noch kabarettistische Texte enthalten hatte, endgültig wegfiel.

Bab, J.: Die Berliner Boheme. Berlin/Leipzig (um 1906); Budzinski, K.: Pfeffer ins Getriebe. München 1982; Greul, H.: Bretter, die die Zeit bedeuten. Köln/Bonn 1967 (erw. Ausg., 2 Bde. München 1971); Hösch, R.: Kabarett von gestern und heute. Berlin 1967–72; Jansen, W.: Das Varieté. Berlin 1990; König, E.: Das Überbrettl Ernst von Wolzogens und die Berliner Überbrettl-Bewegung. 2 Bde. Diss. Kiel 1956; Kühn, V.: Das Kabarett der frühen Jahre. Berlin 1984; Segel, H. B.: Turn-of-the-Century Cabaret. New York 1987; Wolzogen, E. v.: Wie ich mich ums Leben brachte. Braunschweig 1922.

Wolfgang Beck

Über-Marionette

Der von Edward Gordon Craig (1872–1966) im Rahmen seines Beitrags zur →Theaterreform um 1900 geprägte Begriff, der zum erstenmal 1907 in dem Manifest *Der Schauspieler und die Ü.-M.* auftaucht, bezeichnet das Ideal einer Bühnenfigur, das sich nicht am ‹Menschen aus Fleisch und Blut›, sondern an der unbelebten Gestalt orientiert. Weil der Regisseur im Sinne der ästhetischen Perfektion seines Werks nur mit den Materialien arbeiten kann, die planbar und verfügbar sind, der Mensch aber mit Eigenwillen begabt, Sklave seiner Gefühle, dem Zufall ausgeliefert ist, muß er als Darsteller die Bühne räumen und durch die absolut manipulierbare Ü. ersetzt werden. Mit dem Schauspieler wird auch der Realismus als ‹plumpe Nachbildung des Lebens› von der Bühne verbannt. Die Ü. leitet ihre Gestalt nicht aus der ‹lebendigen Natur› ab; in ihrer ‹reinen Künstlichkeit› ist sie vielmehr ein ‹Abkömmling der Steinbilder in den alten Tempeln›, ein Symbol ewiger Wesenheiten wie Kraft, Ruhe und Harmonie; ihre Schönheit ist ‹dem Tode ähnlich und strahlt doch lebendigen Geist aus›. In dem von Craig utopisch entworfenen ‹Theater der Zukunft› soll die Ü. tatsächlich den Schauspieler ersetzen; im Reformkonzept für das bestehende Theater dagegen ist sie das Ideal, nach dem sich der Schauspieler bilden soll. Statt des Überschwangs der Gefühle fordert Craig den disziplinierten, rein technischen Gebrauch der Mittel, statt des natürlichen Erlebens die künstliche Gestaltung der Figur, und zwar genau entsprechend den Vorstellungen des Regisseurs.

Craig, E. G.: Über die Kunst des Theaters. Berlin 1969.

Peter Simhandl

Underground Theatre

Der Begriff erfuhr eine Inflation im Kontext der oft diffusen anarchistisch-oppositionellen Strömungen in den USA der 1960er Jahre, aber auch außerhalb der USA. Wie selbstverständlich sprach man vom Underground-Film und von der Underground-Zeitung, also auch vom U. T. De facto war U. T. im großen und ganzen synonym mit →Off-Off-Broadway. So lautet der Untertitel einer Dramenanthologie *The New Underground Theatre: Eight Plays from Off Off-Broadway*. In seinem Selbstverständnis definiert sich das U. T. durch die totale Ablehnung der herrschenden gesellschaftlichen Normen und die zugleich radikale Negation der klassischen Definitionen des Theaters. – U. T. erzeuge nicht Furcht und Mitleid, erziehe, inspiriere oder erhebe nicht und sei weder philosophisch noch ästhetisch. Man könnte diejenigen Theaterstücke im engeren Sinn als U. T. bezeichnen, die eine militant politische Aussage mit extrem obszönem Gebrauch der Sexualität in Sprache und szenischer Bildlichkeit verkoppeln und dadurch bei ihrer Aufführung einen Skandal (durch polizeiliches Verbot etc.) hervorriefen, z. B.: Tuli Kupferberg, *Ficknam* und Lennox Raphael, *Che!*

Nyssen, U. (Hg.): Radikales Theater. Köln 1969; Raphael, L.: Che! New York 1969; Schroeder, R. J. (ed.): The New Underground Theatre. New York 1968.

Dieter Herms

UNIMA

(Union Internationale des Marionnettes; seit 1969: Union Internationale de la Marionette) Wesentlich auf Initiative frz., dt. und tschechosl. Puppenspieler am 20.5.1929 in Prag gegr. internationale Vereinigung der Puppenspieler. Nach dem 2. Weltkrieg wurde sie in Prag 1957 neu gegründet. Seit 1960 ist die U. ordentliches Mitglied des Internationalen Theater-Instituts (→ITI) der UNESCO. – Nahmen am ersten Kongreß 1929 Puppenspieler aus elf Nationen teil, so gehören der U. heute über 50 Nationen an. Sie ist in nationale Sektionen gegliedert, die über die ganze Welt verteilt sind. Sie hält regelmäßig Kongresse ab, veranstaltet Festivals und Ausstellungen, veröffentlicht Publikationen zu Geschichte und Theorie des Puppenspiels.

Puppentheater International. 50 Jahre UNIMA. Berlin 1980.

Wolfgang Beck

Unity Theatre

1936 in London gegr. →Amateurtheater, das aus den dem Workers' Theatre Movement (WTM) zugehörigen Rebel Players hervorging (→Arbeitertheater/Volksbühne). Seit 1937 feste Spielstätte in der Goldington Street im Londoner Arbeiterviertel St. Pancras. – Von Beginn an der Communist Party, dem linken Flügel der Labour Party und anderen politischen Kräften, die eine Volksfront anstrebten, eng verbunden, war es das Ziel des U. T., Theater für Arbeiter zu machen. Wesentliches Vehikel hierfür war die ‹affiliated membership›, die kollektive Mitgliedschaft ganzer Körperschaften, was die Eintrittspreise bzw. Beiträge drastisch senkte.

Das U. T. machte die in den USA äußerst beliebte Form der →Living Newspaper in England bekannt. Herbert Marshall, neben André van Gyseghem und John Allen einer der wichtigsten (professionellen) Regisseure des U. T., führte bereits bei seiner ersten Inszenierung, Clifford Odets *Waiting for Lefty* (1936), Stanislawskis Method Acting ein. In den Jahren nach dem 2. Weltkrieg konnte das U. T. zunächst an seine Vorkriegserfolge anknüpfen. Seit Ende der 60er Jahre wurde das Selbstverständnis als →Arbeitertheater aufgegeben. Prominenteste Abspaltung vom U. T. ist die Alternativtheater-Gruppe CAST (Cartoon Archetypal Slogan Theatre).

Craig, S. (ed.): Dreams and Deconstructions. Alternative Theatre in Britain. Ambergate 1980; Lehberger, R.: Das sozialistische Theater in England 1934 bis zum

1074 University Wits

Ausbruch des Zweiten Weltkriegs. Frankfurt/M. 1977; Page, M.: The Early Years at Unity. In: Theatre Quarterly 1 (1971), pp. 60–65.

Werner Bleike

University Wits

Eine Gruppe von akademisch gebildeten Schriftstellern, die zwischen 1585 und 1592 durch ihre Pamphlete, Prosaromanzen und Dramen einen großen Einfluß auf die Entwicklung der engl. Literatur, vor allem auf das Drama, ausübten. Zu den U. W. gehörten Thomas Nashe (1567–ca. 1601), Robert Greene (ca. 1560–92), Thomas Lodge (1558–1625), George Peele (1557–96) und Thomas Kyd (1558–94). Wegen ihrer klassisch-humanistischen Vorbildung zählen Christopher Marlowe (1564–93) und John Lyly (1554–1606) ebenfalls dazu. Kyd mit *The Spanish Tragedy* (ca. 1587) und Marlowe mit *Tamburlaine* (1587/88) befreiten die Tragödie von der Einengung klassischer Vorbilder. Marlowes «mighty line» entwickelte den Blankvers entscheidend weiter und ebnete den Weg für Shakespeare. In seinen Lustspielen machte John Lyly die Prosa zu einem nuancierten Ausdrucksmedium der Komödie. Die U. W. führten auch Dramenformen ein, die später von Shakespeare und anderen weiterentwickelt wurden: die Rachetragödie (*The Spanish Tragedy*), die Tragödie der großen Persönlichkeit (Marlowes *Tamburlaine, Dr. Faustus*, ca. 1592), das Historienspiel (Marlowes *Edward II.*, 1592), die höfische Komödie (John Lyly, *Campaspe*, 1583/84), *Edymion* (1588) und die romantic comedy: Robert Greene, *Friar Bacon and Friar Bungay* (ca. 1589), George Peele, *The Old Wives Tale* (ca. 1590). Trotz ihrer enormen literarischen Produktivität und ihrer engagierten Teilnahme an literarischen Auseinandersetzungen blieb den U. W. außer Marlowe und Lyly der erhoffte Ruhm versagt. In *A Groatsworth of Wit bought with a Million of Repentance* (1592) beklagt sich Robert Greene über seine mangelnde Anerkennung; gleichzeitig warnt er seine Genossen vor einem gewissen «Shake-scene». Es ist die erste Erwähnung von Shakespeare als Dramatiker.

Brown, J./Harris, B.: Elizabethan Theatre. Stratford-upon-Avon Studies IX. London 1966; Clemen, W.: Die englische Tragödie vor Shakespeare. Heidelberg 1955; Kernan, A.: The Plays and Playwrights. In: J. Barroll et al. (eds.): The Revels History of Drama in English. III. London 1975, p. 237–360.

J. Lawrence Guntner

Unsichtbares Theater

Technik des →‹Theaters der Unterdrückten› von Augusto Boal (*1931), bei der die Akteure wie zufällig als Straßenpassanten in öffentlichen Verkehrsmitteln, in Restaurants, in Hotels, bei Vorträgen usw. ins Diskutieren und Agieren kommen, um den Zuschauer unbewußt zum Engagement und ‹Mitspielen› zu verführen. Das U. T. will Unterdrückung und verlorene Spontaneität sichtbar machen und zur Befreiung des Menschen von äußeren und inneren Zwängen beitragen.

Boal, A.: Theater der Unterdrückten. Frankfurt/M. 1979.

Martin Franzbach

Unterhaltungstheater

Zweck des U. ist ausschließlich die Unterhaltung, d. h. die Zerstreuung des Zuschauers ohne Anspruch auf Erbauung oder Belehrung. Die unterhaltende Funktion ist immer eine Aufgabe des Theaters, insbes. des komischen Theaters gewesen, z. B. der →Farce im ausgehenden Mittelalter, der →Commedia dell'arte, der leichten →Komödie (Molière: «die gebildeten Leute zum Lachen zu bringen») und des →Melodramas. Doch wird speziell seit der Mitte des 19. Jh. mit U. der Gegensatz zu intellektuell anspruchsvollem, kritschem Theater gemeint. U. wird gleichbedeutend verstanden mit →Boulevardtheater und →Vaudeville; seine beliebtesten Stoffe sind meist erotischer Natur; es will den Zuschauer durch politische, philosophische oder religiöse Thematik weder schockieren noch beunruhigen. In neuerer Zeit wird das U. u. a. in den →En-suite-Theatern gepflegt, hat aber in Film und Fernsehen als Unterhaltungsmedien (mit ähnlichen Genres im Fernsehspiel und in den Serien) mit größerer Schlagkraft und breiterem Publikum eine übermächtige Konkurrenz bekommen.

Bernard Poloni

Urtheater

Das U. (→Ritual) müßte durch eine vergleichende Untersuchung von Kinderspiel, Tierspiel, prähistorischen Funden und heute noch (möglichst unbeeinflußt) lebenden Naturvölkern erschlossen werden; ethnologische Literatur wäre mit Vorsicht heranzuziehen, desgleichen Material über die Vorgeschichte des Theaters der Hochkulturen. – Den ersten um-

1076 Varieté

fassenden und bis heute einzigen Versuch einer Darstellung hat Eberle 1954 unternommen, gestützt auf völkerkundliche Arbeiten (überwiegend vor 1940 publiziert, beruhend auf Expeditionen zumeist vor dem 1. Weltkrieg). Er stellt den Gebrauch von Masken, Kostümen, Requisiten, Dekorationen und Musik fest; Rollendarstellungen lassen sich erkennen (häufig Naturkräfte, Götter, Dämonen, Tiere). Fruchtbarkeit und Initiation, Jagd und Ernte, Jahreslauf und Naturgeschichte werden ‹dargestellt›, im Ritus kultisch vollzogen; Erziehung, Therapie, kultisches Ritual und Theater lassen sich noch kaum voneinander scheiden; es gibt keine durchgehende Trennung von Spielern und Zuschauern, alle ‹wirken› mit. Tanz, Gesang, Musik sind integriert. Steigerungen bis hin zu Rausch und Besessenheit sind möglich.

Eberle, O.: Cenalora. Leben, Glaube, Tanz und Theater der Urvölker. Olten 1954.

Hans-Wolfgang Nickel

Varieté

(Frz., Verschiedenheit, Abweichung, Abwechslung) Form des →Unterhaltungstheaters, das aus der losen Aneinanderreihung einzelner Sprech-, Musik- und Tanznummern besteht, verbunden mit Akrobatik und Dressur, zusammengehalten in der Regel durch einen →Conférencier. Zugleich ist V. die Bezeichnung für einen Gebäudetyp, in dem entsprechende Darbietungen gezeigt werden. Eine exakte Definition und Abgrenzung von benachbarten theatralischen Formen ist schwierig. Wie die →Revue ist das V. ein synthetisches Genre, dessen Entwicklung in den einzelnen Ländern von unterschiedlichen Traditionen beeinflußt wurde. V. ist Unterhaltung für ein Massenpublikum und als solche unmittelbar abhängig von Veränderungen des Geschmacks und der ästhetischen Normen.

V. ist eine Entwicklung des bürgerlichen Zeitalters, gefördert durch das Unterhaltungsbedürfnis des mittleren und Kleinbürgertums. Nicht ohne Grund entstand es zuerst in den neuen industriellen Zentren. Wichtige Frühformen des V. sind seit der zweiten Hälfte des 18. Jh. die engl. «Pub- and Saloon-Theatres», in denen vor allem Sänger und Komiker auftraten, und unabhängig davon die «Cafés chantants» bzw. «Cafés concerts» im Frankreich des 19. Jh. Im deutschsprachigen Raum waren es neben den «Polkakneipen» (mit Sängern und Tänzern) und den Singspielhallen (in denen Gesang und Tanz dominierten) die Spezialitätentheater (in denen Akrobatik und Magie hinzukamen), aus denen das V. hervorging. Während hier die Artistik an Bedeutung gewann, wurde in

Varieté 1077

Österreich mehr das musikalische Element betont. In den USA wurden weitgehend europ. Formen übernommen und mit eigenen Entwicklungen wie →«Minstrel-Show», «Extravaganza» und «Burlesque» verbunden. In Rußland gewann das V. erst um die Jahrhundertwende unter frz. Einfluß an Bedeutung, wurde dann während und nach der Oktoberrevolution längere Zeit als bürgerlich-dekadent abgelehnt und erst nach dem 2. Weltkrieg weiterentwickelt.

Bei allen unterschiedlichen nationalen Traditionen lassen sich – mit zeitlichen Verschiebungen – gemeinsame Entwicklungslinien feststellen. War das V. zu Beginn in den meisten Ländern mehr eine ‹Zugabe› zur Gastronomie und beschränkte sich sein Programm weitgehend auf musikalische und tänzerische Darbietungen und komische Einlagen, so erlebte es in der Zeit um die Jahrhundertwende seinen Höhepunkt. Besonders in Deutschland bildete sich der ‹internationale Varietéstil› heraus, der lange Jahre bestimmend wurde. Seine Kennzeichen waren präziser und rascher Nummern- und Programmwechsel bei starker Betonung des artistischen Elements. Verbunden war diese Entwicklung mit konsequenter Kapitalisierung des V.-Geschäfts, dem Entstehen großer V.-Gebäude und der Bildung von internationalen, kartellähnlichen V.-Gesellschaften sowie der raschen Herausbildung des Agentenwesens. Bereits nach dem 1. Weltkrieg mußte sich das V. des Films erwehren. In allen Ländern entstanden Kino-V., in denen Filme und V.-Nummern gezeigt wurden.

In Deutschland wurden nach der Machtübergabe an die Nationalsozialisten auch die Artisten «gleichgeschaltet» und das V. verstärkt in Tourneen der «NS-Gemeinschaft Kraft durch Freude» bzw. während des Kriegs zur Truppenbetreuung eingesetzt.

In den meisten Ländern erlebte das V. in allen seinen Formen nach Ende des 2. Weltkriegs eine kurze Blüte, bevor in der Konkurrenz mit dem Fernsehen, der Schallplattenindustrie und (seit den 50er Jahren) mit dem →Striptease die meisten großen V. schließen mußten. Als allg. Trend ist heute die Bevorzugung kleinerer Formen und musikalischer Genres zu beobachten sowie international ein Ansteigen des Tournee-V. – In der ganzen Welt haben die meisten Länder mehr oder weniger freiwillig den europ. bzw. amerik. V.-Stil übernommen, wobei in Afrika und Südamerika gelegentlich Versuche zu verzeichnen sind, eigene nationale Formen zu entwickeln (→Friedrichstadt-Palast, →Hansatheater, →Wintergarten).

Berg, R.: Varieté. Hannover 1988; Bost, P.: Le cirque et le music-hall. Paris 1931; Damase, J.: Les Folies du Music-Hall. Paris 1960; Fargue, L.-P.: Music-Hall. Paris 1948; Gobbers, E.: Artisten. Düsseldorf 1949; Günther, E.: Geschichte des Varietés. Berlin ²1981; Hakel, H. (Hg.): Wigl-Wogl. Wien 1962; Jacques, Charles: Cent ans de Music-Hall. Genf/Paris 1956; Jansen, W.: Das Varieté. Berlin 1990; Mander, R./Mitchenson, J.: British Music Hall. London 1965; Moeller van den Bruck, A.: Der neue Humor-Varietéstil. Berlin/Leipzig 1902; ders: Das Varieté.

1078 Vaudeville

Berlin 1902; Moulin, J.-P./Kindler, E.: Eintritt frei – Varieté. Lausanne 1963;
Norman, R.: Das lustvolle Leben der Kabarettisten und Artisten. Pirmasens o. J.;
PEM (d. i. P. E. Marcus): Heimweh nach dem Kurfürstendamm. Berlin 1952; Pütz,
K. H. (Hg.): . . . und abends in die Scala. Berlin 1991; Ramo, L.: Storia del varietà.
Mailand 1956; Saltarino (d. i. H.-W. Otto): Das Artistentum und seine Geschichte.
Leipzig 1910; ders.: Fahrend Volk. Leipzig 1895 (Nachdruck Berlin 1978);
Uwarowa, J. (Hg.): Russkaja sowjetskaja estrada 1917–1929. Moskau 1976; dies.
(Hg.): Russkaja sowjetskaja estrada 1930–1945. Moskau 1977; Winkler, G. (Hg.):
Unterhaltungskunst A–Z. Berlin 1978.

Wolfgang Beck

Vaudeville

V. war urspr. die Bezeichnung für heitere, oft satirische Gassenhauer und
Volkslieder; das Wort wurde vom ‹Val de Vire› (dt. ‹Tal de Vire›) in der
Normandie abgeleitet, wo der frz. Volksdichter Olivier Basselin am Anfang des 15. Jh. solche Texte, die meist gegen die engl. Besatzer gerichtet
waren, verfaßte. Danach bezeichnete das Wort V. im 16./17. Jh. Nachahmungen dieser ersten Texte bzw. volkstümliche Trink- und Spottlieder
mit schlichter Melodie. Noch in diesem Sinn benutzt Nicolas Boileau
(1636–1711) das Wort in seinem *Art poétique* (1674). Später vollzieht sich
ein Bedeutungswandel, V. bezeichnet zuerst eine leichte Komödie mit
spottenden Liedeinlagen, die – anders als die Couplets der Operette –
vom Publikum mitgesungen wurden. Diese für Frankreich typischen ‹pièces en vaudeville› wurden in den Vorstadttheatern von Paris aufgeführt,
da sie vom Monopolrecht der →Comédie Française nicht betroffen waren, und können als Vorstufe der komischen Oper betrachtet werden;
namhafte Autoren sind Alain-René Lesage (1668–1747), Louis Fuzelier
(1672–1752), Alexis Piron (1689–1733), Charles Simon Favart
(1710–92), Jacques Autreu (1657–1745). Mit der Zeit treten Text und
Handlung immer mehr in den Vordergrund, während die Liedeinlagen
nur noch am Ende der Auftritte bzw. der Aufzüge beibehalten werden.
1792 gründet Pierre Barré (1750–1832) das erste Vaudevilletheater in der
Rue de Chartres und verfaßt zusammen mit Radet (1751–1831) und Des-
fontaines (1733–1835) zahlreiche solche V. – etwa *Arlequin afficheur, Le
mariage de Scarron, René le Sage* oder *Gaspard l'Avisé*. Nach 1815 übernimmt Antoine Désaugiers (1772–1827) die Leitung des Theaters, verfaßt selbst manche V. und führt auch Werke des wohl berühmtesten V.-
Autors der ersten Hälfte des 19. Jh. auf, nämlich Eugène Scribe
(1791–1861), der in seiner Antrittsrede zur →Comédie Française diese
V.-Gattung verteidigte (*Une nuit de la garde nationale*, 1815; *Michel et
Christine, Le Vieux Garçon, Le Colonel* usw.). In der zweiten Hälfte des

Verband der Theaterschaffenden der DDR 1079

19. Jh. erfährt das V. unter dem Second Empire seine eigentliche Glanzzeit mit den Werken von Eugène-Marin Labiche (1815–88), der zusammen mit seinen Mitarbeitern 168 Stücke, darunter mehr als 100 Comédie-V., geschrieben hat (*Le chapeau de paille d'Italie,* 1851; *Le voyage de Monsieur Perrichon,* 1860; *La cagnotte,* 1864). Letzter namhafter Verfasser von V., die das typische Dreieckverhältnis in Szene setzen, ist dann um die Jahrhundertwende Georges Feydeau (1862–1921). Heute bezeichnet das Wort V. allg. eine Gesangsposse, während in England und Amerika der Begriff etwa gleichbedeutend mit →Kabarett ist.

Gidel, A.: Vaudeville. In: de Beaumarchais, J.-P. / Couty, D. / Rev, A.: Dictionnaire des littératures de langue française. Paris 1984; ders: Le vaudeville. Paris 1986.

Bernard Poloni

Verband der Theaterschaffenden der DDR

1966 gegr. Organisation für künstlerisch, wissenschaftlich, politisch und publizistisch tätige Theaterleute. Zentrales Anliegen war das Bemühen um ständige Niveauhebung sozialistisch-realistischen Theaterschaffens sämtlicher Sparten durch Kolloquien, Seminare, Tagungen, Förderungen und Mitarbeit in politischen und Verwaltungsorganen. Darüber hinaus Veranstalter von Workshops (Werkstattage des DDR-Schauspiels, des Kindertheaters, der jungen Theaterschaffenden) und Weiterbildungsveranstaltungen (z. B. Erich-Engel-Seminar für Schauspieler und Regisseure), Herausgeber der Zeitschrift «Theater der Zeit» und einer Schriftenreihe «Material zum Theater» (mehr als 200 Hefte), Herstellung und Verleih von Inszenierungsdokumentationen und gezielte Förderung von Öffentlichkeitsarbeit. Pflege enger internationaler Beziehungen, insbesondere zu Theaterverbänden der ehemals sozialistischen Länder. Präsidenten waren 1966–84 Wolfgang Heinz (1900–84) und 1984–89 Hans-Peter Minetti (* 1926). Nach einem letzten (außerordentlichen) Kongreß im Januar 1990 beschloß der provisorische Vorstand des V. d. T. Ende 1990 die Selbstauflösung.

Erich Krieger / Manfred Pauli

Verband Deutscher Freilichtbühnen e. V. (VDF)

Zusammenschluß nichtprofessioneller Theater, 55 Mitgliederbühnen. Geschäftsstelle in Hamm. Der VDF ist Mitglied des BDAT.

Zeitschrift: Die Freilichtbühne.

Hans-Wolfgang Nickel

Vereinigte Bühnen Graz

Graz verfügt über zwei Theater: das Opernhaus (1271 Sitzplätze) und das Schauspielhaus (576 Sitzplätze). Das Schauspielhaus, 1776 errichtet, diente bis zur Erbauung des Opernhauses auch dem musikalischen Genre. Mitte des vorigen Jh. kam das Stadttheater, auch ‹Thalia› genannt, hinzu, das hauptsächlich circensische Volksbelustigungen zeigte. Neben diesem Vergnügungstheater wurde 1899 schließlich das Opernhaus errichtet. Hinter fast unveränderter Fassade mußte das Schauspielhaus zweimal wieder aufgebaut werden: 1823 nach einem verheerenden Brand und 1964 nach einer kriegsbedingten Verfallsperiode. Das Opernhaus überstand den Krieg nahezu unbeschadet. Ab 1983 wurde es grundlegend restauriert und der gesamte Bühnenraum mit modernster Theatertechnik ausgerüstet; in Zuschauerraum und Foyer versuchte man den Originalzustand des Erbauungsjahres wiederherzustellen.

Die V. B. verfügen über zahlreiche Nebenspielstätten: die Studiobühne (300 Sitzplätze), das Theater im Malersaal (240 Sitzplätze), den Redoutensaal (200 Sitzplätze) und die Probebühne (180 Sitzplätze). Die Grazer Oper zeichnete sich in den letzten Jahren unter der Intendanz von Carl Nemeth, der die Vereinigten Bühnen seit 1972 leitet, international durch Produktionen selten gespielter Werke aus. Die Zusammenarbeit mit dem Avantgardefestival →‹steirischer herbst› führte bei Oper und Schauspiel, seit 1976 unter der Direktion von Rainer Hauer, zu zahlreichen Ur- und Erstaufführungen. Intendant seit 1990 Dr. Gerhard Brunner.

Birgit Amlinger/Red.

Verfremdung, Verfremdungseffekt (V-Effekt)

V. ist ein küsntlerisches Verfahren der Illusionsdurchbrechung in der Darstellung. Allerdings fehlte vor Bertolt Brecht (1898–1956) ein einheitlicher Begriff dafür, so daß derartige Phänomene einerseits unter Ironie, →Groteske, Satire, →Parodie, Witz u. ä. m. rubriziert wurden, ande-

Verfremdung, Verfremdungseffekt (V-Effekt)   1081

rerseits unter Metaphorik, Emblematik, Allegorie, Symbolik oder auch Hermetik und Manierismus. Die Skala der Techniken der V. reicht von Trivialformen wie →Bänkelsang, Jahrmarktsplärrer und →Moritat bis zur hochartifiziellen Aufsprengung fiktionaler Totalitätsbilder (etwa in der barocken Emblematik oder in den Deformationen der Abbildungskonvention durch Kubismus, Expressionismus und Surrealismus). Wesenselement der V. ist durchweg die daraus resultierende Aufschließkraft und Verständnishilfe bei Zerstörung der konventionellen Sichtweisen. Den Gegensatz dazu bildet das auf Identifikation, Einfühlung und Illusionierung angelegte autonome Kunstwerk. – Als literaturtheoretischer Begriff findet sich die V. im russ. Formalismus, vor allem bei Viktor Schklowski (*Die Kunst als Verfahren*, 1916), und zwar als Gegensatz zu in sich geschlossenen, mimetischen Realitätsbildern («neues Sehen» statt konventionelles «Wiedererkennen»).

Brecht entwickelte im Verlauf der 30er Jahre den Begriff der V. als nachträgliche Zentralkategorie seines →«epischen Theaters». Sicher verwertete er dabei Anregungen von Hegel, Marx, möglicherweise auch von Bacon, Galilei, Diderot, Schklowski und besonders Sergej Tretjakow (1892–1939). Doch dürften hauptsächlich theatergeschichtliche Traditionen wie →Prolog, →Chor, →Epilog, Beiseitesprechen, Musikuntermalung, Simultanbühne usw., vor allem auch das ostasiatische Theater und das Volkstheater, Anregungen vermittelt haben. Wie stets verfuhr Brecht dabei eklektisch. Entscheidend ist seine Bestimmung der V. als dialektische Erkenntnis in der Weise, daß Vertrautes in einem fremden, fragwürdigen Licht erscheint und danach neu gesehen wird. V. ist gewissermaßen die Dialektik des ‹Durchblicks› (vermeintliches Verstehen von Altbekanntem – Nicht-mehr-Verstehen – neues, wirkliches Verstehen). Brecht dehnt sodann – und das ist völlig neu – den dialektischen Erkenntnisprozeß von der künstlerischen Produktion auf die Rezeption durch das Publikum aus mit dem Ziel politischer Wirkung.

Mittel zur Herbeiführung der V. ist der V.-Effekt («V-Effekt»). Er kann definiert werden als künstlerisches Verfahren zur Aufdeckung der gesellschaftlichen Widersprüche (dialektisierte Vermittlung und Rezeption). V.-Effekte bestimmen im selben Maße Sprachform, Dialogführung und Dramenbau (in Gestalt einer strikt auktorial bestimmten Kommentarebene im Stück) wie dann auch die Spielweise der Schauspieler oder die Elemente der →Inszenierung (Bühnenbild, Musik, Beleuchtung, Projektionen, Choreographie, Kostüme, Masken).

Mit ihrer Verbindung ästhetischer, philosophischer, gesellschaftlicher und politischer Belange bilden V. und V.-Effekt den methodischen Kern von Theorie und Praxis der Theaterarbeit Brechts. Fast alle ‹Öffnungs›-Tendenzen des modernen Dramas und Theaters basieren auf der produktiven Auseinandersetzung mit den V.-Praktiken des Brecht-Theaters.

1082 Verismus

Die verfremdende Spielweise charakterisiert heute, allen Unterschieden zum Trotz, die Inszenierungspraxis der meisten Regisseure des Welttheaters. Diese Vorliebe erklärt sich offenbar dadurch, daß die V. der theatralischen Produktion den ‹impliziten Zuschauer› beschert.

Brecht, B.: Schriften zum Theater. Hg. v. S. Unseld (= Bibliothek Suhrkamp 41). Frankfurt/M. 1957; Brüggemann, H.: Literarische Technik und soziale Revolution. Versuche über das Verhältnis von Kunstproduktion, Marxismus und literarischer Tradition in den theoretischen Schriften Bertolt Brechts (= das neue buch 33). Reinbek bei Hamburg 1973, S. 139–164, 250–258; Grimm, R.: Vom Novum Organum zum Kleinen Organon. Gedanken zur Verfremdung. In: Das Ärgernis Brecht. Hg. v. W. Jäggi/H. Oesch. Basel 1961, S. 45–70; ders.: Der katholische Einstein. Brechts Dramen- und Theatertheorie. In: Brechts Dramen. Neue Interpretationen. Hg. v. W. Hinderer. Stuttgart 1984, S. 11–32; Knopf, J.: Brecht-Handbuch: Theater. Eine Ästhetik der Widersprüche. Stuttgart 1980, S. 378–402.

Theo Buck

Verismus

(Ital. verità = Wahrheit) Ital. literarische und musikalische Bewegung von Ende 19. bis Anfang 20. Jh., dem →Naturalismus nahe. Historisch entstand der V. 1884 mit der UA der *Cavalleria Rusticana* von Giovanni Verga (1840–1922), dem wichtigsten Vertreter der Bewegung, in Reaktion gegen das bürgerliche epigonale und melodramatische Theater. Drei Hauptrichtungen sind zu unterscheiden:
– am ursprünglichsten die sizil. Dramen von Giovanni Verga (*La Lupa*, 1896) und Luigi Capuana (1839–1915: *L'aria del continente*, 1915), realistisch-soziale Darstellungen des Lebens und der Leidenschaften der sizil. Landbevölkerung;
– der Mailänder bürgerliche V. von Giuseppe Giacosa (1847–1906: *Tristi Amori*, 1890), Marco Praga (1862–1929: *Le Vergini*, 1889), Camillo Antona-Traversi (1857–1934: *Le Rozeno*, 1891): kritisches Bild der bürgerlichen Moral bei Brandmarkung der Relation Geld – Liebe – Macht;
– die Mailänder proletarischen Dialektdramen von Carlo Bertolazzi (1870–1916: *El nost Milan*, 1893) mit Darstellung der Existenz der Großstadtarbeiter im Stil des europ. Naturalismus.
Ästhetisch beruht der V. auf der Aufgabe aller künstlichen Spielkonventionen (Monologe, Tiraden, Vertraute, Chor etc.) zugunsten einer wirklichkeitsgetreuen Milieuschilderung bei starker Betonung des Regionalismus sowie der Herausstellung der deterministischen Faktoren in der Land- und Stadtexistenz der Sozialschichten.
Berühmtester Aspekt des V. ist die musikalische Erneuerung der ital.

Oper, weitgehend mit Libretti der veristischen Schriftsteller: so *Cavalleria rusticana* (1890) von Pietro Mascagni (1863–1945), *Pagliacci* (1892) von Ruggiero Leoncavallo (1858–1919) und bes. die Werke Giacomo Puccinis (1858–1924), *La Bohème* (1896), *La Tosca* (1900).

d'Amico, S. (ed.): Enciclopedia dello Spettacolo. Rom 1962 (Artikel: Verismo); Pandolfi, V.: La missione del naturalismo nel teatro italiano. In: Il Dramma. Turin 1956. Nr. 234; Ulivi, F.: La letteratura verista. Turin 1972.

Gérard Schneilin

Versatzstück

(Auch ‹Versetzstück›, ‹Setzstück›) Teil der Bühnendekoration. Die kleineren, leicht ‹versetzbaren›, beweglichen Dekorationselemente, die von Bühnenarbeitern auf die Bühne gestellt werden. Geländer, Treppenverkleidungen, Bäume, Büsche, Zäune, Mauern, Felsen, Brunnen. Zu unterscheiden von den Hängestücken, die vom Schnürboden herabhängen.

Horst Schumacher

Versdrama

Drama in Versen, d. h. in gebundener Sprache, gewann in Gegenbewegung zum seit dem 18. Jh. vordringenden Drama in Prosa, das dann im naturalistischen Milieustück einen Höhepunkt erreichte, um die Jahrhundertwende (1900) größere Bedeutung. Beispiele: Hugo von Hofmannsthal, *Der Tor und der Tod* (1893); Gerhart Hauptmann, *Die versunkene Glocke* (1896); Franz Werfel, *Die Troerinnen* (1915); in der außerdeutschen Literatur bei Gabriele d'Annunzio, Maurice Maeterlinck, W. B. Yeats, T. S. Eliot, Ezra Pound, Christopher Fry, Archibald MacLeish u. a.

Donoghue, D.: The Third Voice. Princeton 1959; Peacock, R.: The Poet in the Theatre. London 1946.

Horst Schumacher

Vertooningen

Eigentlich heißt das niederl. Wort «verto(o)ning» einfach Vorführung, bzw. Aufführung. Zur Zeit der → Rederijker-Kammern, besonders im 15. und 16. Jh., sind V. stumme Darstellungen, die als → Zwischenspiele in den von den Rederijkern aufgeführten Sinnspielen oder Moralitäten eingefügt wurden. – Die Rederijker gaben ihre Vorführungen bei diversen Gelegenheiten. Sie organisierten Wettkämpfe (Landjuwelen und Haagspelen) und auch lokale Festivitäten. Bei Fürsteneinzügen u. ä. arbeiteten sie mit der Lukasgilde der bildenden Künstler zusammen, um Prozessionen, → lebende Bilder und → Pantomimen zu gestalten. Auf Wagen oder großen Gerüsten wurden Bilder, Gemälde und komplette → lebende Bilder aufgestellt, meistens historische und biblische Szenen sowie Vorstellungen von antiken Helden.

Das Rederijker-Drama besteht aus einer Montage selbständiger Szenen. Es gibt keine Akte. Zur Abwechslung und um das Spiel zu verdeutlichen, wurden V. (oder tog[h]en) eingefügt. Es konnte sich dabei auch nur um einzelne Figuren handeln (etwa Christus am Kreuz) oder – besonders im 16. Jh. – um lebende Bilder aus der christlichen Vorstellungswelt oder dem antiken Mythos, die als Parallelen zu den Allegorien des Dramas (Symbolfunktion) angelegt waren. Die V. sind im Hintergrund des Podiums oder an den Seiten situiert, wahrscheinlich in Nischen, die mit einem Vorhang verschlossen waren. Abbildungen von Bühnenbildentwürfen aus Gent (1539) und Antwerpen (1561) zeigen eine Hintergrund-Dekoration mit einem Bühnenobergeschoß für lebende Bilder. Dies ist wahrscheinlich eine idealtypische Vorstellung. Die Figuren trugen oft eine Banderole mit ihrem Namen oder ihrer Bedeutung und blieben völlig stumm; bisweilen wurde ein Kommentar gesprochen, begleitet von Musik und Gesang.

Kindermann, H.: Theatergeschichte Europas, II. Salzburg [1]1959 ([2]1966), S. 226–242; Mak, J. J.: De rederijkers. Amsterdam 1944, S. 66–68; Worp, J. A.: Geschiedenis van het drama en van het tooneel in Nederland, I. Groningen 1904, S. 126–132, 174–181.

Marjoke de Roos

Vertrauter

Der V. (frz./engl.: confident) ist ein → Rollenfach des frz. klassischen Theaters, das auch von der dt. Klassik übernommen wurde. Er ist keine selbständige Person, sondern gibt dem Helden die Gelegenheit, seine Pläne und Gedanken zu äußern, ist also quasi ein Teil des Helden. Oft sind die Dialoge zwischen Helden und V. im Grunde nur auf zwei Gesprächspartner aufgeteilte Monologe, die den Zwiespalt und den inneren Kampf in Seele und Bewußtsein des Helden veranschaulichen. Der V., der dabei die Rolle des antiken Chors übernimmt und ähnlich wie dieser eine gemäßigte, vernünftige, exemplarische Weltauffassung vertritt, sagt nichts, was nicht auch im Innern des Helden lebte; beim Entscheidungsmonolog z. B. vertritt der V. den einen von zwei antagonistischen Standpunkten und bringt dadurch den Helden dazu, seinen eigenen Standpunkt zu verdeutlichen und zu vertiefen. Dadurch bringt er auch den Helden und den ihm innewohnenden tragischen Konflikt zur Geltung. Der V. ist also einerseits ein Double des Helden, dessen Vertrauen er genießt – und dies schon seit der epischen Tradition der Antike (siehe Achilles und Patrokles, Orest und Pylades bei Homer, Nisus und Euryalus bei Vergil) bzw. in der Epik des Mittelalters (siehe Roland und Olivier in *Rolands Lied*). Aber der V. ist andererseits auch ein Realitätsprinzip; da er in keinem tragischen Konflikt verfangen ist, weiß er um praktische Lösungen und Auswege, während der Held zwangsläufig seinem Verderben, seinem Fall zustrebt: Pylades, der ‹traute Freund›, kann Orest aus seinem tragischen Zwiespalt nicht heraushelfen, ebensowenig Philippe Strozzi Lorenzaccio im gleichnamigen Stück von Alfred de Musset (1810–57); in *Phèdre* (1677) von Jean Racine (1639–99) empfiehlt Oenone praktische, vom Lebenswillen getragene Lösungen, die Phèdre jedoch zurückweist. Entschlossen ergibt sie sich dem Tod als schicksalhafter Sühne. Jeder Versuch der V., um Helden und Zuschauer aus der tragischen Sphäre zu entfernen, zu der sie die Ohnmacht des Helden immer wieder zurückführt, muß scheitern. Mit dem Niedergang der Tragik und der →Tragödie, mit dem Niedergang des tragischen Helden geht zwangsläufig auch der V., anders als sein Pendant in der →Komödie, der →Diener, unter.

Schérer, J.: La dramaturgie classique en France. Paris 1955.

Bernard Poloni

Videotanz

Videotanz ist eine junge Kunstgestaltung, die sich in Europa Anfang der 80er Jahre zuerst in Frankreich entwickelte. Gemeint sind Choreographien, die speziell für die Kamera, speziell für das filmische Medium geschaffen werden. Diesen Werken steht keine Bühnenchoreographie voran, sondern der Tanz entsteht in einem Konzept für die Kamera. Die zweidimensionale filmische Abbildung gegenüber dem dreidimensionalen Bühnenraum wird von den Filmemachern und Choreographen berücksichtigt und neue Formen der Interaktion von Tanz und Kamera entwickelt. Je nach Dominanz der beiden kooperierenden Künste reicht das Spektrum von der Neuinszenierung einer Choreographie dank einer mobilen Kamera draußen in Stadt oder Natur bis hin zu durchkonstruierten Konzepten der Bildbearbeitung, in denen Schnitt, Montage und filmische Effekte überwiegen.

Die Begegnung beider Künste datiert bereits auf den Beginn der Filmgeschichte. Filmpioniere wie Thomas Edison oder Georges Méliès versuchten, Tanzbewegung im bewegten Bild einzufangen. Einerseits entwickelte sich in der Filmkunst eine dokumentarische Linie, andererseits entstanden Fiktion und Experimentalfilme. Beide Stränge finden sich auch in den dem Film folgenden technischen Errungenschaften Fernsehen und Video, wobei das Medium Fernsehen Experimenten gegenüber bisher eher zurückhaltend ist. Statt dessen finden sich im Programmschema Studioaufzeichnungen von einigen Bühnenwerken sowie Choreographenporträts.

Eigentliche Vaterfigur des Videotanzes ist der Amerikaner Merce Cunningham (→Post Modern Dance). Als Choreograph bereits prägende Persönlichkeit der amerikanischen Avantgarde, schuf er zusammen mit dem Filmemacher Charles Atlas sowie mit dem Pionier der Videokunst Nam June Paik Choreographien speziell für die Kamera und erforschte die unterschiedliche Wirkungsweise tänzerischer Bewegung im Bild im Gegensatz zur Bühne. Eine Ausnahme auf europäischem Boden bildeten Anfang der 70er Jahre mehrere Werke der schwedischen Choreographin Birgit Cullberg (→Cullbergballetten) für das Fernsehen. Sie nutzte den kleinen Bildschirm als Bühne und ließ ihre Tänzerinnen und Tänzer vor elektronisch gestanzten Hintergründen im Raum schweben. Während in den Vereinigten Staaten schon zur Zeit der Blüte des Experimentalfilms nach dem 2. Weltkrieg Begriffe wie ‹Film-dance›, ‹Cine-dance› oder ‹Choreo-cinema› in dieser Disziplin eingeführt wurden, etablierte sich der Begriff ‹Videodance›, ‹Videodanse› bzw. ‹V.› in Europa erst mit der Vermarktung des Videomediums als Sammelbezeichnung kreativer Verbindungen von Tanz und Film bzw. Video.

Claudia Rosiny

Vierte Wand

Die naturalistische Dramentheorie verlangt, daß die Seite der Bühne, die im Theater zum Zuschauerraum hin offen bleibt, quasi als v. W. behandelt wird; d. h. man spielt, ohne das Publikum direkt zu beachten und vermittelt diesem den Eindruck, einem der Realität entnommenen

Schauspiel gleichsam heimlich beizuwohnen (→Naturalistisches Theater, →Illusionstheater).

Alain Muzelle

Vigszinház (Budapest)

Anders als das ung. Nationaltheater ist das Lustspieltheater keine Anstalt der nationalen Bewegung, sondern reines Geschäftstheater. Seine Gründung (1896) ist aus der Entwicklung Budapests zur Großstadt hervorgegangen; Theater des Bürgertums, ohne je auf Lokaltheaterniveau abzusinken. Durch geschicktes Finanzgebaren von Gábor Faludi (1846–1932) ermöglicht, entfaltet sich rasch ein Theaterstil, der zuerst durch seine Novität, später durch seinen gehobenen Unterhaltungscharakter anzieht. Das künstlerische Profil wird durch den Regisseur Mór Ditrói (1851–1945) geprägt: Bevorzugung der Konversation in der Sprachgestaltung, genaues Ensemblespiel, Tempo, Unmittelbarkeit und Realismus im Arrangement und im Bühnenbild. Führende Schauspieler-Mitgestalter: Gyula Hegedüs (1870–1931) und Irén Varsányi (1878–1932). Als tragende Grundlage des Programms gilt das zeitgenössische französische Lustspiel, vertreten z. B. durch Flers und Caillavet, Bisson u. a. Vorliebe für das Frivole, Modische, Elegante und Exklusive. Sehr früh zeichnet sich schon die Tendenz ab, diesem Stil aus Eigenem, Heimatlichem und Lokalem zu entsprechen, was das Lustspieltheater zur Geburtsstätte des modernen ungarischen Dramas werden läßt. Bereits 1902 kündigt das Theater einen Dramenzyklus für 100 Abende von Werken ungarischer Autoren an. Die Uraufführung *Az ördög* (Der Teufel, 1907) markiert den epochemachenden Wendepunkt. Die Stücke von Ferenc Molnár (1878–1952), *Liliom* (1910), Schwan (1920), Spiel im Schloß (1926), aber auch von Ferenc Herczeg (1863–1954) und Sándor Hunyadi (1890–1942) bilden weiterhin die Basis des Programms. Durch Molnár entstehen die sog. Exportstücke des Lustspieltheaters, die ständig auf den Bühnen des Welttheaters gespielt werden. Das Lustspieltheater ist auch die geistige Heimstatt des ungarischen Bühnennaturalismus, vor allem durch Sándor Bródy (1863–1924), dessen *A dada* (die Amme, 1902) und *A tanitónö* (Die Lehrerin, 1908) brisante gesellschaftskritische Aussagen beinhaltet. Durch Ankauf von Aktien übernimmt 1921 der Amerikaner Ben Blumenthal das Theater, die künstlerische Leitung geht in die Hand des Regisseurs Dániel Jób (1880–1955) über. Der Bau wird 1945 durch Bomben zerstört, das V. spielt bis 1949 in einem ehemaligen Kino, dann wird sein Ensemble aufgelöst. 1951 Wiederaufbau als Theater der ungar. Volksarmee, 1960 Rückbenennung in V., 1967 Kammerbühne im Pesti Szinház mit Akzent auf Förderung neuer ungar. Dramatik (I. Örkény, 1912–80:

1088   Viktorianisches Theater

Katzenspiel, Blutsverwandte, Pisti im Blutgewitter). Zoltán Varkony (1912–79) prägt 1963–79 das Profil des V. (Unterhaltung im besten Sinne). In den 70er Jahren auch Musicals (fiktiver Report über ein amerik. Pop-Festival) in der Regie László Martons, der heute das V. leitet.

Berczeli, A. Károlyné: A Vigszinház müsora 1896/1949 (Programm des Lustspieltheaters 1896/1949). Budapest 1960; Magyar, B.: A Vigszinház története (Die Geschichte des Lustspieltheaters). Budapest 1979.

Sándor Gulyás / Elke Wiegand

Viktorianisches Theater

Die viktorianische Zeit (i. e. S. 1837–1901, oft mit dem 19. Jh. gleichgesetzt) war eine der theaterhistorischen Blütezeiten Großbritanniens. Während die im 18. Jh. entscheidende aristokratische Patronage des Theaters verfiel und sich die gesellschaftlichen Oberschichten allmählich vom Theater abwandten, kam es zu einer starken Expansion des Theaterbetriebs, speziell in London, ab Ende des 19. Jh. auch in den neuen industriellen Ballungszentren. Das Theaterpublikum dehnte sich in kleinbürgerliche, z. T. auch proletarische Schichten aus. Es entstanden große neue Theaterbauten, z. T. voller Prunk, von denen etliche erhalten sind. Das Repertoire des V. T. stützt sich einerseits auf die brit. Klassiker, speziell auf Shakespeare, andererseits auf neu entstehende oder traditionelle populäre dramatische Genres wie die Burleske, die Farce oder das Melodrama, auch die Oper und das Ballett. Das V. T. wurde vor allem von großen Schauspielern geprägt, die zugleich Intendantenfunktionen hatten: etwa William Charles Macready (1793–1873), Samuel Phelps (1804–78), Charles Kean (1811–68) und Henry Irving (1838–1905). Der Einfluß der Dramatiker und der Regie blieb dagegen gering; auch kam es zu keiner überdauernden dramatischen Produktion. Zu den größten vikt. Theatern zählten die zu Beginn des 19. Jh. neu erbauten →Drury Lane Theatre und das →Covent Garden Theatre, die jeweils über 3000 Plätze aufwiesen, zu den traditionellen kleineren das King's Theatre und das Little Theatre, Haymarket, auch das Royalty Theatre. Außerhalb des Londoner Zentrums entstanden neue, riesige Bauten: das Pavillon, Whitechapel, das Grecian Theatre, das Surrey Theatre, das Lyceum, das Adelphi, das St. James Theatre. Bis in die Gegenwart am bekanntesten blieb das Royal Victoria, 1816 errichtet und bald →Old Vic genannt. Seit Mitte des 19. Jh. setzte sich im V. T. ein naturalistisch bestimmter Theaterstil durch, dem die einzige für das 20. Jh. bedeutsame Eigenprägung des vikt. Dramas entsprach: das sog. «well-made-play», etwa in Dion Boucicaults (1820–90) tragikomischen Problemstücken.

Kosok, H.: Drama und Theater im 19. Jh. In: Nünning, J. (Hg.): Das engl. Drama. Darmstadt 1973, S. 349–402; Richards, K./Thomson, P. (Hg.): Nineteenth Century British Theatre. London 1971; Rowell, G.: The Victorian Theatre 1792–1914. A Survey. Cambridge ²1978; Southern, R.: The Victorian Theatre: A Pictorial Survey. Newton Abbott 1970.

Bernd-Peter Lange

Viktor Kingissepa nim. Tallinna Riiklik Akademiline Draamateater

Das Tallinner Dramentheater (1940 Staatliches, 1957 Akademisches, ab 1957 Namensgebung Viktor Kingissepp) wurde 1916 von Schülern Karl Mennings (1874–1941) gegründet, der 1906 das erste Berufstheater Estlands «Vanemuine» in Tartu schuf. 1870 gilt als Geburtsjahr des estn. Theaters, das eng mit der Nationalbewegung verbunden war und bis 1906 in Laienzirkeln gepflegt wurde. Das T. D. orientierte sich an Max Reinhardt, O. Brahm, A. Antoine und K. Stanislawski, spielte Hauptmann, Ibsen, Tolstoi, Sudermann und estn. kritische Realisten (A. Kitzberg, *Im Wirbelsturm*). 1920 bringt Paul Sepp (1885–1943) Erfahrungen des →MChAT und W. Meyerholds ein. Aufführungen impressionistischer und symbolistischer Stücke (L. Andrejew, E. Toller), estn. Autoren (A. Tammsaare) und Weltdramatik. 1940 Umzug ins Tallinner Deutsche Theater, 1948/49 Reorganisation und Erweiterung des Ensembles. Künstlerische Leiter: 1952–70 I. Tammur, 1970–76 Voldemar Panso (1920–77; Schüler von M. Knebel), der dem →Stanislawski-System und Brecht verpflichtet ist (frühe Brecht-Inszenierung in der UdSSR 1958 *Puntila*; 1970 *Hamlet*; 1975 *Richard III.*). Seit 1977 leitet der Schauspieler und Regisseur Mikk Mikkiver das T. D. und setzt das Erbe seines Lehrers fort. Auslandsgastspiele u. a. in Finnland, BRD.

Elke Wiegand

Virtuose

V. bezeichnet allgemein einen Meister seines Fachs, einen hervorragenden Interpreten. Der Begriff gehört eigentlich der musikalischen Fachsprache an und wurde im 18. Jh. aus dem Ital. übernommen. Im Theater haftet dem Wort V. eine leicht pejorative Bedeutung an im Sinne einer zu äußerlichen, auf unmittelbaren Effekt zielenden Betonung der schauspielerischen Mittel. Der Begriff V. wurde vor allem für die ital. Schauspieler benutzt, die gegen Ende des 19. Jh. durch Europa reisten wie Adélaide

Ristori (1821–1906), Ermete Zacconi (1857–1948) und Ermete Novelli (1851–1919). Da ihr Spiel von keiner echten Dramatik getragen war und sie oft im Star-System des 19. Jh. befangen waren, wirkte ihre Kunst recht oberflächlich. Die Spielart der V., die auf sorgfältiger Beobachtung und Detailgenauigkeit beruhte, bereitete jedoch das Theater eines André Antoine (1857–1943) oder → Stanislawski (1863–1938) im 20. Jh. vor.

Bernard Poloni

Völkische Dramaturgie

Von 1933 bis zum Ende des NS-Staats bestand in Deutschland die Einrichtung des → Reichsdramaturgen. Alle Theater mußten ihre Spielpläne von ihm genehmigen lassen. Ziel war die völkisch-nationale Umgestaltung und Neuorganisation des gesamten Theaterwesens zu einem wirkungsvollen Propagandainstrument: einer ‹völkischen› Anstalt, die die Vollendung der → Nationaltheateridee sein sollte, dt. Theater sollte «das nationalste Theater der Welt» (Best, 1940) werden. Richtlinie aller dramaturgischen Überlegungen war die weltanschauliche Ausrichtung, d. h. die nationalsozialistische Ideologie. Ihre ‹Grundgesetze› sollten «die Gesetze einer alten Ästhetik... zerbrechen» (Best, 1940). Die Begriffe ‹Blut› und ‹Rasse› wurden auch für den Bereich des Theaters als ‹lebensnotwendige› Bewertungskriterien eingeführt: «der rassische Wert wird auch den Bühnenkünstler des deutschen Nationaltheaters mitbestimmen» (Best, 1940). Für den Autor eines Theaterstücks reichten nicht mehr Kunst und Können aus, er mußte «eben Nationalsozialist sein, der sich auf die Dramaturgie der völkischen Eigenart versteht..., der Dichter, Kamerad dem Staatsmann!» (Best, 1940). Die Schwierigkeit aber bestand darin, daß es neue Schriftsteller von Format, die diesen ideologischen Ansprüchen gerecht wurden, kaum gab. So bestanden die Spielpläne dann häufig aus jenen ‹alten› Stücken, die die Zensur noch erlaubte: ausgewählte Klassiker, dt. Unterhaltungsstücke, Blut-und-Boden-Dramen, ‹völkische Zeitdramatik› und Geschichtsdramen.

Best, W.: Völkische Dramaturgie. Würzburg/Aumühle 1940; Drewniak, B.: Das Theater im NS-Staat. Düsseldorf 1983; Dussel, K.: Ein neues, ein heroisches Theater? Bonn 1988.

Ute Hagel

Volksbühne

Nach Aufhebung des Sozialistengesetzes 1890 als Freie V. in Berlin gegründet, hervorgegangen aus dem Kampf um die Überwindung des bürgerlichen Bildungsmonopols; genossenschaftliche Organisation überwiegend proletarischer Theaterbesucher. Geringfügige Mitgliedsbeiträge berechtigten zum Besuch einer Vorstellung pro Monat. Überwindung der Klassengesellschaft im Zuschauerraum: keine Preisabstufungen, Verlosung der Plätze bzw. Platzvergabe nach dem Rotationsprinzip. Gespielt wurde an Sonntagnachmittagen in gemieteten Theatern mit wechselnden Schauspielern. Zur Aufführung kamen neben klassischen Dramen Werke naturalistischer Autoren. Erste Inszenierung (1890) *Stützen der Gesellschaft* von Henrik Ibsen (1828–1906). 1893 Uraufführung von Gerhart Hauptmanns (1862–1946) *Die Weber*. Von Anfang an Kontroverse um den politischen Kurs der V.-Bewegung. Auf der einen Seite stand Franz Mehring (1846–1919, Leiter der Freien V. 1892–96), der Kunst als Instrument im Emanzipationskampf des Proletariats begriff. Auf der anderen Seite stand Bruno Wille (1860–1928, Leiter der Freien V. bis 1892), der – jenseits aller Klassenkämpfe – in der V. eine politisch neutrale ‹volkspädagogische› Bildungseinrichtung sah («Die Kunst dem Volke», kulturelle Erziehung der Massen). Nach Auseinandersetzungen um die Organisationsstruktur (Wille widersetzte sich der Forderung, den Mitgliedern Einfluß auf die künstlerische Leitung der V. zu gewähren) 1892 Abspaltung der Wille-Fraktion, Gründung der Neuen Freien V. Zählte die Neue Freie V. 1885 1500 Mitglieder (Freie V.: 8000), so waren es 1911 50000 (Freie V. 17000). Nach Ablösung Mehrings im Vorstand der Freien V. nivellierten sich die Gegensätze zwischen den beiden Theaterorganisationen. Beseelt von dem gleichen apolitischen Bildungsideal, stand einer Wiedervereinigung nichts mehr im Wege. 1913 Kartellbildung, 1920 organisatorischer Zusammenschluß zur Berliner V. e. V. Nach dem 1. Weltkrieg Ausdehnung der V.-Organisation auf das gesamte Reichsgebiet. 1920 Gründung des Verbands der Dt. V.-Vereine, der 1927 263 Ortsvereine mit insgesamt 540000 Mitgliedern umfaßte.

Seit 1914 verfügte die V. über ein eigenes Theater am Bülowplatz in Berlin. 1. Direktor: Emil Lessing (1857–1921), gefolgt von Max Reinhardt (1873–1943, Direktor von 1915–18). Stand E. Lessing noch in der Tradition des naturalistischen Theaters, so gab es zwischen der Bühnenästhetik M. Reinhardts und den Zielen der V.-Bewegung keinerlei Berührungspunkte mehr. Mit Reinhardt suchte die V. Anschluß an die bürgerliche Theaterentwicklung. Weitere Direktoren: Friedrich Kayßler (1874–1945, Direktor bis 1923), Fritz Holl (1883–1942, Direktor bis 1928), Heinrich Neft (1868–1944, Direktor bis 1929). Erwin Piscator (1893–1966), 1924 zum Regisseur an die V. berufen, geriet durch seine

1092 Volksbühne

politisch-agitatorischen Inszenierungen in Konflikt mit dem Bühnenvorstand. An *Gewitter über Gottland* (1927, von Ehm Welk, 1884–1966), einem Schauspiel, bei dem Piscator einen Seeräuber des Mittelalters als Revolutionshelden des 20. Jh. auftreten ließ, schieden sich die Geister: Piscator verließ 1927 die V. Zugleich formierte sich in den Reihen der V.-Jugend – den «Sonderabteilungen» – der Widerstand gegen die von Siegfried Nestriepke (1885–1963) betriebene Verbandspolitik. Die Umwandlung des ‹Konsumvereins› in ein ‹Kampftheater› wurde gefordert. 1930 Auflösung des Arbeitsausschusses der ‹Sonderabteilung›. Die ‹Politisierung› der V. war jedoch nicht aufzuhalten: Mit Karlheinz Martin (1886–1948) gewann die V. 1929 einen Intendanten, der →Zeitstücke inszenieren ließ. Auf Martin folgte 1932 Heinz Hilpert (1890–1967, Direktor bis 1934). 1933 ‹Gleichschaltung› der V. durch die Nazis. Das Theater am Bülowplatz, seit 1937 in staatlicher Hand, wurde im 2. Weltkrieg zerstört. 1947 Neugründung als Bund Dt. V. in der SBZ und 1948 als Verband der Dt. V.-Vereine in Westdeutschland.

Obgleich die Orts- und Landesverbände in der DDR rasch Mitglieder gewannen, wurde die V. 1953 liquidiert, begründet mit der Kulturverantwortung der einheitlichen Gewerkschaftsorganisation FDGB. Die in den Betrieben verankerten Gewerkschaftsbüros sollten Kartenvertrieb und Kunstpropaganda übernehmen. Hintergrund der V.-Auflösung war ihre sozialdemokratische Vereinstradition, die der SED-Strategie widersprach. In Westdeutschland entwickelte sich die V. rasch zu einer einflußreichen Besucherorganisation.

1948 Übernahme des Theaters am Kurfürstendamm als «Haus der Freien Volksbühne» in West-Berlin. 1963 Eröffnung eines neuerbauten Theaters in West-Berlin (→Freie Volksbühne Berlin). 1. Direktor: E. Piscator, 1962–66. Piscator verhalf während dieser Zeit dem →Dokumentardrama zum Durchbruch. 1963 zählte der V.-Verband 430000 Mitglieder (höchste Mitgliederzahl nach dem 2. Weltkrieg), 1984 waren es 250000. Die V. versteht sich als Alternative zum kommerziellen Kulturbetrieb; unter der Devise «Theater für alle» will sie kulturell ‹Unterprivilegierten› einen ‹zweiten Bildungsweg› zur Bühnenkunst eröffnen.

Braulich, H.: Die Volksbühne. Berlin (DDR) 1976; Chung, H.-B.: Die Kunst dem Volke oder dem Proletariat? Die Geschichte der Freien Volksbühnenbewegung in Berlin 1890–1914. Frankfurt/M. u.a. 1989; Gärtner, M.: Verband der deutschen Volksbühnen-Vereine. Düsseldorf 1978; Ihering, H.: Der Volksbühnenverrat (1928). In: ders.: Der Kampf ums Theater. Berlin (DDR) 1974, S. 246–258; Pforte, D. (Hg.): Freie Volksbühne Berlin. 1890 bis 1990. Berlin 1990; Schwerd, A.: Zwischen Sozialdemokratie und Kommunismus. Zur Geschichte der Volksbühne 1918–1933. Wiesbaden 1975.

Carl Wege / Roland Dreßler

Volksbühne Berlin

Theater am Luxemburg-(vormals Bülow-)Platz, 1913/14 nach Entwürfen von Oskar Kaufmann (1873–1956) mit drei Rängen und ca. 2000 Plätzen erbaut, im 2. Weltkrieg zerstört und 1952–54 wiederaufgebaut. Als städtisches Theater untersteht die V. (noch) dem Berliner Senat (vorher dem Magistrat von Berlin, DDR); zwei Spielstätten (das große Haus mit 926 Plätzen, das Theater im 3. Stock mit ca. 100 Plätzen). Intendant wird 1992 (nach einem zweijährigen Interregnum) Frank Castorf (* 1951). Eröffnet 1914 von der Arbeiter-Besucherorganisation →Freie V. (gegr. 1890), wurde das Haus 1915 bis 1918 an das Ensemble Max Reinhardts (1873–1943, →Deutsches Theater) vermietet, 1918 bis 1923 folgte Friedrich Kayßler (1874–1945) und 1923–29 Fritz Holl als Direktor; wichtigste künstlerische Kraft Mitte der 20er Jahre aber war der Regisseur Erwin Piscator (1893–1966), dessen von revolutionärem Impetus geprägte politisch-dokumentarische Produktionen 1927 zum spektakulären Bruch mit dem (sozialdemokratischen) Vorstand führten; 1929–32 leitete Karl-Heinz Martin (1888–1948) die V. (größter Erfolg 1931: *Liliom* mit Hans Albers, 1892–1960). 1933 wird die V. von den Nationalsozialisten zum «Theater am Horst-Wessel-Platz» gleichgeschaltet und dem Reichspropagandaministerium unterstellt, 1939 wurde Eugen Klöpfer (1886–1950) Intendant, der 1938 den Auftrag auf Auflösung der V. stellte, dem 1939 von Goebbels entsprochen wurde.

Das Haus, im Krieg zerstört, wurde 1954 wiedereröffnet, die V.-Besucherorganisation war 1953 vom FDGB («Freier Deutscher Gewerkschaftsbund» der DDR) übernommen worden, 1954 bis 1962 war Fritz Wisten (1890–1962, zuvor am →Theater am Schiffbauerdamm) Intendant, der mit *Wilhelm Tell* eröffnete, einen volkstümlich-komödiantischen Spielplan (Nestroy, Goldoni, Hauptmann, Tolstoi, Thoma) mit Klassikern und neueren sozialkritischen Werken (z. B. U. Becher, J. P. Sartre) sowie zeitgenössischen sowjet. und DDR-Stücken (drei UA von Hedda Zinner, * 1907) ergänzte. 1963 bis 1965 war Wolfgang Heinz (1900–84; →Deutsches Theater), 1965 bis 1968 Karl Holán (* 1926) Intendant, 1969 wurde der Brecht-Schüler Benno Besson (* 1922; →Berliner Ensemble, →Deutsches Theater) zunächst künstlerischer Oberleiter, 1974 Intendant der V., die unter ihm aus dem Schatten des Deutschen Theaters und des →Berliner Ensembles trat und zum lebendigsten, auch einflußreichsten DDR-Theater der 70er Jahre wurde.

Besson bemühte sich erfolgreich um neue Zuschauerschichten; mit zwei «Spektakeln» (1973 und 1974), auf denen fünf Volksstücke bzw. acht DDR-Gegenwartsstücke an einem Abend (neben- und hintereinander) gezeigt wurden, machte er die V. zu einem Mittelpunkt der Öffentlichkeit. Als Regisseur konzentrierte er sich auf Stücke von Gozzi

(1713–86), Molière (1622–73) und Shakespeare (1564–1616), doch erlaubten ihm die Brecht-Erben (→Berliner Ensemble) nur einmal, seine Beschäftigung mit Brecht (*Der gute Mensch von Sezuan*, 1971) fortzusetzen. Um so entschiedener führte er seine (am Deutschen Theater begonnene) Zusammenarbeit mit Peter Hacks (*1928) und Heiner Müller (*1929) weiter, dessen Stücke (*Weiberkomödie*, 1971; *Die Bauern*, 1976; *Der Bau*, 1980) vor allem Fritz Marquardt (*1928) inszenierte; daneben förderte er junge Dramatiker wie Christoph Hein (*1944, 1973–78 Hausautor) und vor allem das Regie-Duo Manfred Karge (*1938)/Matthias Langhoff (*1941; →Berliner Ensemble). Seit der Abberufung Bessons, der die DDR nach über 25 Jahren Theaterarbeit verließ, gravierende künstlerische Qualitätsverluste während der Intendanz von Fritz Rödel (*1930) 1978 bis 1990. Aus dem Durchschnitt konventioneller Inszenierungen (Hauptmanns *Biberpelz* mit Marianne Wünscher in der Hauptrolle, Regie: Helmut Straßburger, *1930/Ernstgeorg Hering, *1942, war das Erfolgsstück der 80er Jahre) ragten einzelne Produktionen markant heraus, so *Leonce und Lena* (1978), Regie: Jürgen Gosch (*1943, seit 1980 in der BRD); *Der Bau* (1980), Regie: Marquardt; *Macbeth* (1982) von Heiner Müller (nach Shakespeare), Regie: Müller; *Der Meister und Margarita* nach Bulgakow (1980), Regie: Siegfried Höchst (1939–91), oder Schillers *Räuber* in der Inszenierung von Frank Castorf; im 3. Stock: *Die Frauen von Troja* (1980), Regie: Bernd Renne (*1943); *Der Auftrag* (1980), Regie: Müller/ Ginka Tscholakowa (*1945); *Das trunkene Schiff* von Paul Zech, Regie: Castorf.

Funke, Ch./Kranz, D.: Theaterstadt Berlin. Berlin (DDR) 1978, S. 113–129; Funke, Ch./Hoffmann-Ostwald, D./Otto, H.-G. (Hg.): Theater-Bilanz. Berlin (DDR) 1971, S. 85–87; Pietzsch, I.: Werkstatt Theater. Berlin (DDR) 1975, S. 97–103; Klunker, H.: Zeitstücke und Zeitgenossen: Gegenwartstheater in der DDR. München ²1975, S. 114–163; Wardetzky, J.: Theaterpolitik im faschistischen Deutschland. Berlin (DDR) 1983; Kranz, D.: Berliner Theater. Berlin 1990.

Andreas Roßmann/Manfred Pauli

Volksschauspiel

Im Unterschied zu dem Terminus →Volksstück für eine auf unterhaltende Wirksamkeit bei einem breiten Publikum zielende Dramatik (trivial-klischeehaft oder sozialkritisch-emanzipatorisch), im Unterschied aber auch zu dem für die verschiedensten Formen des Theaters für das Volk (entweder in Sinne der Gesamtbevölkerung oder der Unter- und Mittelschichten), über das Volk, vom Volk und im Interesse des Volkes gebräuchlichen Begriff Volkstheater, meint V. diejenigen Formen des nichtprofessionellen Theaters, die im Rahmen der überlieferten Ordnun-

Volksschauspiel 1095

gen der Volkskultur stehen und in ihren tradierten Formen zur brauchtümlichen Ausgestaltung weltlicher und religiöser Terminfeste dienen. Als Volk im Sinne der Trägerschicht des V. wird seit der Romantik, als sich das Wort einzubürgern begann, in erster Linie die ländlich-bäuerliche Bevölkerung angesehen. Über die Frage, ob die religiösen Aufführungen der Städtebürger im mittelalterlichen Theater (→Mittelalter/ Drama und Theater des Mittelalters) dem V. zuzurechnen sind, gehen die Meinungen auseinander. Das städtische →Fastnachtsspiel und das →Schulspiel innerhalb des →Renaissancetheaters sowie das Ordensdrama des →Barocktheaters gehören nicht zum V., wenn auch viele Verbindungen dahin existieren. Texte und Aufführungsformen aus diesen Bereichen wurden zum Bestandteil der Volkskultur und als solche jahrhundertelang tradiert. Dabei haben Einzelpersönlichkeiten (Pfarrer, Schulmeister, aber auch bäuerliche Spielführer) sowie bestimmte Berufsgruppen (wie etwa die Bergknappen oder die Salzschiffer mit ihrem halbprofessionellen Theaterwesen) eine wichtige Funktion ausgeübt. Als Ausführende des V. begegnen meist die Angehörigen der dörflichen Burschenschaften, manchmal – im Endstadium der Überlieferung – auch Kinder; Frauen waren lange Zeit ausgeschlossen. Die Zuschauer gehörten in der Regel derselben überschaubaren Gemeinschaft an wie die Spieler; erst seit der Jahrhundertwende zogen manche Aufführungen eine große Zahl außenstehender Besucher an (z. B. die Passionsspiele in Erl oder →Oberammergau). Damit änderte sich ihre Funktion; das V. wurde mancherorts zur ‹Folklore›.

Die Erscheinungsformen des V. innerhalb des dt. Sprachraums wurden nach kulturgeographischen Gesichtspunkten geordnet (‹Volksschauspiellandschaften›) sowie nach Aufführungsweisen und Stoffbereichen gegliedert. Die ortsfesten Spielbräuche und die Umzugsspiele, die wiederum von den größeren Prozessionsspielen (z. B. zu Fronleichnam) zu unterscheiden sind, haben ihren Ursprung oft im Rüge- und Heischebrauchtum; im Zentrum der als Streit oder als Aneinanderreihung verschiedener Spielelemente aufgebauten Kurzszenen zwischen pflanzen-, tier-, menschen- oder symbolgestaltig maskierten Figuren steht die Aktion; meist kommen sie mit einigen Textformeln aus. Heute noch lebendige Beispiele dafür sind etwa das Sternsingen, das Begraben der Fastnacht, das Einholen, Setzen und Umschneiden von Maibäumen und Hochzeitsbäumen. – Im ‹Stubenspiel› gewinnt das spielhafte Brauchtum einen längeren festgelegten Text, eine in stilisierten Bewegungs- und Sprechformen fixierte Spielweise und die Bauern- oder Wirtsstube als Spielraum mit einer dreiseitig von Zuschauern umgebenen neutralen, meist nur mit wenigen Symbolrequisiten ausgestatteten Spielfläche. In dieser Form wurden bis in unsere Zeit vor allem Spiele aus dem Weihnachtsfestkreis (Hirtenspiel, Paradeisspiel) aufgeführt. Seit Beginn unse-

1096 Volksstück

res Jh. ist allerdings eine deutliche Tendenz zum Übergang auf die Guckkastenbühne festzustellen. – Das ‹Bühnenspiel› wird mit den überlieferten Formen des Freilichtspiels zur Kategorie des Großspiels zusammengefaßt. Das. V. kennt außer den Stoffen, die mit den weltlichen und
geistlichen Festen des Jahreslaufs in Zusammenhang stehen, eine Fülle
von dramatisierten Erzählstoffen; Heiligenlegenden, Volksbücher, Märchen und Ritterromane sind die Quellen. In stofflicher Hinsicht bestehen
enge Beziehungen zum →Puppentheater, das aber hauptsächlich doch
professionell oder halbprofessionell betrieben wird.

Schmidt, L.: Das deutsche Volksschauspiel. Berlin 1962.

Peter Simhandl

Volksstück

Dem *modernen* V. liegt die Auseinandersetzung mit dem →Alt-Wiener
V. im ausklingenden 19. und im 20. Jh. zugrunde. Als Volkstheater bleibt
es zugleich Theater über das Volk und für das Volk mit dem Ziel, die
mittleren und unteren Schichten der Bevölkerung in einer ihnen verständlichen Form zu unterhalten und aufzuklären. Insofern bedarf das V.
der Identifikation zwischen Adressaten und Bühnenpersonal, in den dargestellten Problemkreisen und in der verwandten Bühnensprache. Daß
diese Auffassung der Bühne heute zu volkstümlichen Irrwegen, z. B.
kommerziellen Dialekt- und Unterhaltungsbühnen (vgl. das Hamburger
‹Ohnsorgtheater›, die Kölner ‹Millowitschbühne›, der Müncher ‹Komö-
dienstadl› u. a.) führen mußte, welche Volkstümlichkeit mit anspruchs-
loser Unterhaltung und →Boulevardtheater gleichsetzen, täuscht nicht
über den experimentellen, ja engagierten Charakter moderner Volkstheater hinweg. Auf Grund einer zunehmenden Problematisierung des
Begriffs ‹Volk› schließen die beiden überlieferten Hauptintentionen des
V., Unterhaltung und Belehrung, einander immer mehr aus.

Aus dem Niedergang des Alt-Wiener V. heraus gelangt die Gattung
nahezu unverändert ins 20. Jh., insbesondere mit Ludwig Anzengrubers
(1839–89) V. und bäuerlichen Heimatkomödien (*Der Pfarrer von Kirch-
feld*, 1871; *Der Meineidbauer*, 1871). Unter Einfluß eines märchenhaften
Schicksals neigen alle Konfrontationen dazu, ein gutes und versöhnliches
Ende zu erfahren. Dabei knüpft Anzengruber durch das Verlegen der
Handlung in einen engen dörflichen oder familiären Kreis sowie durch
das Einmontieren von Couplets und das Verwenden eines naturalistisch
gefärbten Dialekts an bewährte Muster an. Das V. dient nun der Entlarvung christlicher Heuchelei und der Glorifizierung der naturnahen, unverfälschten Ehrlichkeit im Sinne Feuerbachs, dem Aufzeigen Gottes in

Volksstück 1097

jedem einfachen, guten Menschen. Einen Schritt weiter in der metaphysischen Dimension geht Ludwig Thoma (1867–1921), der die Begriffe des Tragischen und des Volkstümlichen aneinanderrückt und somit eine Kluft überbrückt, deren Ursprung der Gegensatz zwischen adeliger tragischer Form und niederem bürgerlichen Lustspiel bildet. Das Tragische des V. *Magdalena* (1912) – wegen seines Ausgangs auch ‹bayerische Emilia Galotti› genannt – gründet im unerbittlichen Normensystem einer oberbayerischen Landgemeinschaft, das jeden Ausbruchsversuch mit dem Tod bzw. Freitod bestraft. Indem das V. die Erstarrung des Volks als leeren Moralkodex aufzeigt, verlagert es die Auseinandersetzung zwischen Gut und Böse in die Sphäre des Volkstümlichen selbst. Eine ähnliche Verschiebung erfährt die naturalistisch stilisierte Mundart als Sprache ‹für› das Volk, Notbehelf zur Überwindung der Distanz zwischen ‹Volksschriftsteller› und Volk. Im Aufzeigen einer gesellschaftlichen Determination des Menschen und in der Infragestellung eines Dialekts, der seine – noch bei Raimund und Nestroy intakte – volkstümliche Ursprünglichkeit eingebüßt hat, zeichnen sich zwei bedeutsame Aspekte der V.-Renaissance in den 20er Jahren ab.

Geradezu anachronistisch erscheint in diesem Kontext das Werk Carl Zuckmayers (1896–1977), dessen V. (*Der fröhliche Weinberg*, 1925; *Der Hauptmann von Köpenick*, 1931) die heile Welt des Volks heraufbeschwören. Die komödienhafte Auflösung aller Gegensätze in Happy-End und festlichem Gesang dient dem Preisen der natürlichen Einfalt, inneren Weisheit und vitalen Kraft des einfachen Menschen aus dem Volk. Zuckmayers V. fallen mit dem Ende einer unproblematischen Gattung zusammen. Die ‹Erneuerung› des V. durch das Dreigestirn Fleißer – Horváth – Brecht setzt neue Schwerpunkte, die um soziale Alienation, Kommunikationslosigkeit, ja Sprachlosigkeit kreisen. Dabei erfährt das V. auch eine formelle Umgestaltung: Eine episierende Dramaturgie verzichtet sowohl auf eine einheitliche, durchgehende Handlung zugunsten von einzelnen, aneinandergereihten Tableaus und Bildern als auch auf die Illusion einer heilen Welt im obligaten guten Ende. Das V. dient nicht mehr wie einst im ‹Besserungsstück› der bloßen Bestätigung einer etablierten Ordnung, sondern wendet sich als Dramaturgie des Publikums an einen aktiven bzw. kritischen Zuschauer. In ihren V. schildert die Ingolstädterin Marieluise Fleißer (1901–74) die Atmosphäre einer bayerischen Kleinstadt im Stil der ‹Neuen Sachlichkeit›. Selbst private, zwischenmenschliche Beziehungen verraten die Nachwirkungen gesellschaftlichen Zwangs und sozialer Zurichtung, auf die letztlich das Ausbleiben des guten Endes in *Pioniere in Ingolstadt* (1928) als stumme Anprangerung einer unveränderbaren Hierarchie zurückzuführen ist. Die Zurücknahme des zeitlosen Mythos von der Innigkeit und Gemüthaftigkeit des ‹Volks› in der modernen, von historischen und ökonomischen Fakten bedingten

1098 Volksstück

Welt strebt auch der Österreicher Ödön von Horváth (1901–38) an, durch ‹Zerstörung› und ‹Erneuerung› des alten V. zugleich. Horváths V. (*Geschichten aus dem Wiener Wald*, 1931; *Kasimir und Karoline*, 1932) schildern im ‹Mittelstand›, dem von der Proletarisierung bedrohten Kleinbürgertum, den für die heutige Zeit repräsentativen gesellschaftlichen Menschentypus, dessen Spießertum gleichzeitig durch Musik, Klischees und Kitsch herbeizitiert und als falsches Bewußtsein demaskiert wird. Der ‹Bildungsjargon›, ein Gemisch von leeren Floskeln und uneigentlichen Sprachfetzen, hat den Dialekt verdrängt; die von Sprachlosigkeit bedrohten Figuren erfahren ein tragikomisches Schicksal, welches das Theater Horváths vollends in die Nähe des →absurden Theaters rückt. Horváths V. knüpfen zudem an Nestroy an, indem sie durch Umkehrung eines Wertesystems konsequent auf die Desillusionierung des Publikums zielen. Als durchweg problematische Gattung versteht auch Bert Brecht (1898–1956) das V.; in seiner Absage an «krudes und anspruchsloses Theater» führt Brecht in seinen V. *Herr Puntila und sein Knecht Matti* (1940), z. T. auch in *Schweyk im 2. Weltkrieg* (1944) – nach der Vorlage Jaroslav Hašeks (1883–1923) – die Tradition des historischen V. unter Einarbeitung eigener dramatischer Theorien fort. Brechts V. streben auf der theoretischen Grundlage des Essays *Volkstümlichkeit und Realismus* (1938) als Kunst für die breiten, fortschrittlichen Volksmassen nach dem Aufzeigen wesentlicher sozialer Abhängigkeiten und geschichtlicher Prozesse in volkstümlich einfacher, abstrakt ‹stilisierter› Form. Dabei kann das gute Ende – wie im offenen Schluß des *Puntila* – nur als Appell an die Veränderung der Wirklichkeit durch die neuen Schichten des aufgeklärten Volks, d. h. das Proletariat, in Aussicht gestellt werden. Spätestens mit Brecht wird das V. unter starker Abgrenzung von einer ‹völkischen› Ideologie zur Reflexion über soziale Mißstände, ja über den Begriff des Volks selbst. Das erneuerte V., dessen Blütezeit nach Mitte der 60er Jahre eintritt, ist nicht mehr ohne historisch-kritische Betrachtung des Volks denkbar.

Die Horváth- und Fleißer-Renaissance nach 1965 geht mit einer regen V.-Produktion einher, sei es als sozialkritisches ‹Anti-Theater› Rainer Werner Fassbinders (1946–82) mit *Katzelmacher* (1968) oder als Dialektstück mit *Rozznjogd* (1971) des heimatlich provokativen Peter Turrini (*1944). Turrinis Vorbild in Sachen Mundarttheater, Hans Carl Artmann (*1921), prägt auch weitere Mitglieder der sog. ‹Grazer Gruppe› wie Wolfgang Bauer (*1941), dessen V. *Party for six* (1967), *Magic Afternoon* (1968/69) den Soziolekt der jungen Generation und moderne Kommunikationsprobleme kritisch beleuchten. Martin Sperr (*1944) untersucht in seiner ‹bayerischen Trilogie› *Jagdszenen aus Niederbayern* (1965), *Landshuter Erzählungen* (1967), *Münchner Freiheit* (1971) die moralische, gesellschaftliche und ökonomische Grundlage der Nachkriegszeit, wobei Sperrs V. z. T. Standpunkte der ‹außerparlamentarischen Opposition› vertreten. Deutlich unter dem Einfluß Brechts steht der im hessischen Stadtjargon schreibende Wolfgang Deichsel (* 1936), etwa mit *Bleiwe Losse* (1971). Zwischen seinen beiden Lehrmeistern Horváth und Brecht und somit am Scheideweg modernen Volkstheaters steht die herausragende Persönlichkeit des Franz Xaver Kroetz (* 1946). In seiner ersten Schaffensperiode führt Kroetz die sprachliche Reduktion im Sinne Horváths konsequent weiter, indem er seinen Figuren selbst den prekären Boden des kleinbürgerlichen ‹Bildungsjargons› entzieht: In *Wildwechsel, Heimarbeit, Männersache* (alle 1970), *Stallerhof, Geisterbahn* (1971), z. T. auch in *Oberösterreich* (1972) scheitert das Bewußtsein stets an Welt und Sprache, Sprachlosigkeit und totale Kommunikationsunfähigkeit schwinden nach *Das Nest* (1975), wo Kroetz' Figuren ihre Probleme und gesellschaftliche Lage durchschauen und – in der Mundart ‹gebrochen› – artikulieren können. Kroetz' innerer Zwiespalt, sein Pendeln zwischen der Horváthschen Hervorhebung der Sprachlosigkeit in den unteren Schichten des Volks und dem Brechtschen Appell an gesellschaftliche Veränderung durch sprachüberlegene Räsoneure aus dem Proletariat entspricht als Paradigma dem Schwanken moderner Theaterautoren zwischen der Ionesco / Beckett- und der Brecht-Nachfolge, zwischen ‹absurdem› und ‹epischem› Theater. Indem das moderne V. über jeden Unterhaltungsgehalt hinaus sich als Spiegelbild sozialer Zurichtung, aber auch als kritische Reflexion über Wesen und Lage des Volks neue dramaturgische Instrumente aneignet und erarbeitet, wird allen Kontroversen zum Trotz das V. zu einem vollwertigen Bestandteil zeitgenössischen Theaters überhaupt.

Aust, H. / Haida, P. / Hein, J.: Volksstück. München 1989; Brauneck, M. / Schneilin, G. (Hg.): Drama und Theater. Bamberg 1986; Hein, J. (Hg.): Theater und Gesellschaft. Das Volksstück im 19. und 20. Jh. Düsseldorf 1973; Klotz, V.: Dramaturgie des Publikums. München 1976; Motekat, H.: Das «Neue Volksstück». In: H. M.: Das zeitgen. dt. Drama. Stuttgart / Berlin 1977; Müller, G.: Das Volksstück von Raimund bis Kroetz. München 1979; Schiffermüller, I.: Die Erneuerung des Volksstücks in den 60er Jahren. Diss. Innsbruck 1980; Schmitz, Th.: Volksstück. Stuttgart 1990.

Jean-Marie Winkler

Volkstheater Rostock

Gegründet 1895; Großes Haus mit 587 Plätzen, daneben mehrere kleine Spielstätten, auch in Warnemünde, Abstecher in Wismar und Güstrow. Die in der DDR einstmals renommierte Freilichtbühne Ralswiek / Rügen (1959 UA *Klaus Störtebeker*) soll, unter anderer Trägerschaft, wieder bespielt werden. Intendant 1952–85 (außer 1970–72) Hanns Anselm Perten (1917–85), 1986–90 Ekkehard Prophet (*1936), seit 1990 Bernd Renne (*1943). – 1751 «Comödienhaus» im Palaisgebäude, 1786 Neues Theaterhaus, niedergebrannt 1880, Stadttheater am Steintor 1895, zerstört 1942, seitdem ehemalige «Philharmonie» als Großes Haus, 1975 bis 1979 rekonstruiert. – Etwa 200 Ur- und Erstaufführungen seit 1952, darunter mehr Stücke aus dem Westen als jede andere DDR-Bühne, so *Marat/ Sade* (1964), *Die Ermittlung* (1965), *Gesang vom lusitanischen Popanz* (1967), *Vietnam-Diskurs* (1968), *Hölderlin* (1973) von Peter Weiss (1916–82), *Lysistrate und die Nato* (1975), *Tod eines Jägers* (1977), *Juristen* (1980), *Ärztinnen* (1981) und *Judith* (1985) von Rolf Hochhuth (*1931), aber auch Max Frisch (1911–91), Martin Walser (*1927), Eugene O'Neill (1888–1953), Tennessee Williams (1914–83) u. a. Diese Weltoffenheit im Repertoire, die sich auch durch die zeitweilige Aufnahme einer chilenischen Exiltheater-Gruppe ins V. R. ausdrückte, erkaufte Intendant Perten durch seine extrem enge Bindung an die DDR-Kulturpolitik. Die internationale Aufmerksamkeit für das Rostocker Schauspiel war größer als seine regionale Akzeptanz. Intendant Renne setzt nun auf stärkeren Publikumszuspruch durch unterhaltsames Theater.

Institut für Gesellschaftswissenschaften beim ZK der SED (Hg.): Theater in der Zeitenwende. Zur Geschichte des Dramas und des Schauspieltheaters in der DDR 1945–1968. 2 Bde. Berlin 1972; Funke, Ch. / Hoffmann-Ostwald, D. / Otto, H.-G. (Hg.): Theater-Bilanz. Berlin (DDR) 1971, S. 275–278; Pietzsch, I.: Werkstatt Theater. Berlin (DDR) 1975, S. 104–113; Klunker H.: Zeitstücke und Zeitgenossen. Gegenwartstheater in der DDR. München ²1975, S. 245–273.

Andreas Roßmann / Roland Dreßler

Volkstheater Wien

1889 bis 1945 Deutsches Volkstheater, ab 1945 Volkstheater. Gründung durch den «Laube-Verein» (Verbindung von Schriftstellern und Freunden des 1884 abgebrannten Wiener Stadttheaters), der am 25. Mai 1886 beschloß, ein «deutsches Volksschauspielhaus mit sehr billigen Eintrittspreisen in Wien zu begründen». Das Konzept war, im Gegensatz zum höfischen Theater und zur seichten Unterhaltung anderer Wiener Bühnen, aktuelle Zeitstücke, Volksstücke, Klassiker und österr. Dramatik für ein großes Publikum zu spielen. – Die Baupläne stammen von den Theaterarchitekten Ferdinand Fellner und Hermann Helmer. März 1888: Baubeginn. 14. September 1889: Schlußsteinlegung und Eröffnung mit Uraufführung von Anzengrubers *Der Fleck auf der Ehr'*. Wichtige Inszenierungen: 1890 Ludwig Anzengruber: *Das vierte Gebot* (Protest der Kirche gegen Aufführung), 1891 Henrik Ibsen: *Die Wildente* (ÖE), 1900

Volkstheater Wien 1101

Hermann Bahr: *Wienerinnen* (UA) – beide Inszenierungen lösten Theaterskandale aus, 1902 H. Ibsen: *Peer Gynt* (DE), 1910 Karl Schönherr: *Glaube und Heimat* (UA), 1918 Arthur Schnitzler: *Professor Bernhardi* und 1929 *Im Spiel der Sommerlüfte* (UA), 1930 Ferdinand Bruckner: *Elisabeth von England* (UA). Bedeutende Schauspieler im V. waren: Adele Sandrock, Helene Odilon, Annie Rosar, Hansi Niese; Alexander Girardi, Max Pallenberg, Raoul Aslan, Alexander Moissi, Hans Moser, Albert Bassermann, Karl Skraup.

Während der nationalsozialistischen Okkupation Österreichs zu einem «Kraft-durch-Freude-Theater» umgebaut. Gegen Ende des 2. Weltkriegs schwer beschädigt. Vorerst nur Instandsetzungsarbeiten. 18. 6. 1945 Eröffnung. 1948 Umwandlung in eine GmbH und Gründung der Volkstheatergemeinde durch den Österr. Gewerkschaftsbund. Inszenierungen: 1948 Ödön von Horváth: *Geschichten aus dem Wienerwald* (ÖE) – Theaterskandal. Unter L. Epp (1952–68) österr. Erstaufführung zeitgenössischer Literatur: z. B. 1953 Albert Camus: *Der Belagerungszustand*, 1956 Friedrich Dürrenmatt: *Der Besuch der alten Dame*, 1961 Jean Genet: *Der Balkon*, 1962 Max Frisch: *Andorra*; 1963 Aufhebung des Brecht-Boykotts in Wien durch *Mutter Courage und ihre Kinder*, 1964 Rolf Hochhuth: *Der Stellvertreter* (ÖE). Unter G. Manker (1969–79) exemplarische Nestroy-Inszenierungen und Schnitzler-Pflege, 1971 *Zug der Schatten* (UA), Uraufführungen junger österr. Autoren: z. B. 1969 Wolfgang Bauer: *Change*, und 1971 *Silvester oder Das Massaker im Hotel Sacher*, 1972 Peter Turrini: *Sauschlachten*. Unter P. Blaha spielte das V. zeitbezogene, fortschrittliche und auf die Zukunft orientierte Stücke, die Stellung beziehen und Gesinnung zeigen. Politisches Theater über aktuelles Zeitgeschehen und Zeitgeschichte (Frieden, Antifaschismus, Gleichberechtigung): z. B. 1983 Friedrich Wolf: *Die Matrosen von Cattaro*, 1985 Joshua Sobol: *Ghetto* (ÖE); ebenso Stücke, die Probleme behandeln, mit denen die Menschen zu leben haben: 1985/86 H. Ibsen: *Ein Volksfeind*, J. Savary: *Weihnachten an der Front*, F. Hochwälder: *Der Himbeerpflücker*; daneben Volksstücke und Possen von Nestroy bis Heinz R. Unger (1985 *Zwölfeläuten*). Unter Emmy Werner Rückkehr zum Repertoiretheater. Motto der ersten Spielzeit: Anpassung und Ungehorsam.

Eine besondere Initiative ist seit 1954 das «Volkstheater in den Außenbezirken». Diese Tournee bringt das V. regelmäßig in die Außenbezirke Wiens, wo die Mehrheit der arbeitenden Bevölkerung wohnt. Mittlerweile zu einem fixen Bestandteil des kulturellen Lebens in Wien geworden. 1981 Gründung des «V.-Studio». In Eigenverantwortung leitet das Ensemble des V. eine kleine Bühne, die sich der Gegenwartsdramatik widmet. 1984 Eröffnung der Schauspielschule im V. Unter Blaha Beginn der Reihe «V.-extra» (über den üblichen Theaterbetrieb hinausreichende Veranstaltungen) (→ Volksbühne).

1102 Vorspiel

Intendanten und ihre Direktionszeit: Emmerich von Bukovics (1889–1905), Adolf Weise (1905–16), Karl Wallner (1916–18), Alfred Bernau (1918–24), Rudolf Beer (1924–32), Rolf Jahn (1932–38), Walter Bruno Iltz (1938–44), Rolf Jahn (Juni 1945), Günther Haenel (Juli 1945–48), Paul Barnay (1948–52), Leon Epp (1952–68), Gustav Manker (1969–79), 1979–87 Paul Blaha, seit 1988 Emmy Werner.

Applaus. 25 Jahre Volkstheater in den Außenbezirken. AK-Begegnungen. Hg. v. Kammer für Arbeiter und Angestellte für Wien. Wien 1979; Das neue Volkstheater. Festschrift. Wien/München 1981; Das Wiener «Volkstheater» 1889–1966. In: «Maske und Kothurn». Vierteljahresschrift für Theaterwissenschaft. Hg. v. Inst. f. Theaterwissenschaft an der Univ. Wien. 13. Jg. (1967), H. 4; Teichgräber, A.: Das «Deutsche» Volkstheater und sein Publikum Wien 1889–1964. Ein theaterwissenschaftlicher Beitrag zur Morphologie des Publikums an Hand der Spielplananalyse eines kontinuierlich geführten Wiener Theaters. Diss. phil. Wien 1965; Schreyner, E.: 100 Jahre Volkstheater. Wien/München 1989.

Erna Wipplinger/Red.

Vorspiel

1. Kurzes, einaktiges Gelegenheitsstück anläßlich von Festlichkeiten im →höfischen Theater oder Hoftheater (vgl. Goethe: *Vorspiel zur Eröffnung des Weimarischen Theaters am 19. September 1807*). 2. Kurze Szenenfolge oder Szene eines umfassenderen Dramas; ergänzt dann die Exposition, unterscheidet sich vom →Prolog, →Zwischenspiel oder →Epilog durch dramatische Darstellung von Tatsachen und Begebenheiten, die das Stück ergänzen, deuten, kritisch beleuchten. Beispiele sind: Schillers *Wallensteins Lager* (UA 1798) als ausführliche, episch breit angelegte Darstellung der historischen Verhältnisse zum Verständnis von *Die Piccolomini* und *Wallensteins Tod* ((UA 1799); als Rahmenhandlung das Vorspiel zu Brechts *Der kaukasische Kreidekreis* (1944ff), den Streit zweier georgischer Kolchosen um ein Tal vorführend, in dialektischer Beziehung zur Kreidekreis-Parabel, welche in der Folge entwickelt wird. 3. Oft auch gleichbedeutend mit Prolog, besonders in der außerdt. Dramaturgie, wo sprachlich oft nur ein Wort zur Verfügung steht (z. B. engl. oder frz.).

Gérard Schneilin

Vorstellung

Urspr. an die Arbeit des Schauspielers angelehnt (eine Figur vorstellen, d. h. sie zu imaginieren, abzubilden und vorzuführen), heute in der Regel gleichbedeutend mit →Aufführung. Das Ergebnis einer →Inszenierung wird in Form der Aufführung vorgestellt und ist gebunden an die individuellen Leistungen der Schauspieler ebenso wie an Publikumshaltungen und -erwartungen, die zusammen das Transitorische, Nichtwiederholbare jeder V. ausmachen.

Monika Sandhack

Wachtangow-Theater (Moskau)

(Gosudarstvennyj akademičeskij teatr im. Evg. Vachtangova) In Moskau 1921 gegr., hervorgegangen aus dem Schauspielstudio, das Jewgeni Bagrationowitsch Wachtangow (1883–1922) seit 1913 geleitet hatte und das 1920 bis 1924 als 3. Studio dem Moskauer Künstlertheater (→MChAT) eingegliedert war. Wachtangow, einer der bedeutendsten Schüler Stanislawskis, lehrte nach dessen ‹System› und bildete zusammen mit Meyerhold und Tairow das Dreiergestirn des →Theateroktobers. Er bejahte die Oktoberrevolution, betonte die Einheit des Künstlers mit dem Volk (Verzicht auf die →«vierte Wand» im Theater), die Gegenwartsbezogenheit des Stücks, die Verbindung theatralischer Mittel mit erlebten Gefühlen, die besondere Bedeutung äußerer Ausdrucksmittel wie Rhythmik, Gestik, Plastizität, das Primat der Phantasie, den Kampf gegen Naturalismus und modernistische Plattheit. Letztlich suchte er eine Synthese von →Stanislawski-System und →Meyerhold-Methode, von psychologischen und konstruktivistischen Verfahren. – Das sowj. Drama wurde erst nach Wachtangows frühem Tod Grundlage des Repertoires (L. Sejfullina *Wirineja*, 1925; L. Leonow *Die Dachse*, 1927; Ju. Olescha *Die Verschwörung der Gefühle*, 1929; Zusammenarbeit mit Gorki 1932). Wachtangow hatte mit Maeterlinck *Der blaue Vogel* (1921), mit Einaktern von Tschechow begonnen, mit C. Gozzi *Prinzessin Turandot* (1922) aufgehört. Erneuerung der Inszenierung 1963 (noch heute im Spielplan) durch R. N. Simonow (1899–1968), der seit 1920 Schauspieler am W. T., später auch Chefregisseur und Intendant war. Auch Jewgeni R. Simonow (*1925) pflegte 1958–89 die Tradition des Theatergründers. 1989 übernimmt Michail M. Uljanow (*1927), langjährig Schauspieler im Ensemble, die künstlerische Leitung und gibt jungen Regisseuren die Chance zum Debüt (P. Fomenko, G. Tschernjachowski, A. Kaz). Dem Theater ist die Stschukin-Schauspielschule angegliedert.

1104 Wandertänze

Hoffmann, L./Wardetzky, D. (Hg.): Wsewolod E. Meyerhold. Aexander I. Tairow. Jewgeni B. Wachtangow. Theateroktober. Beiträge zur Entwicklung des sowj. Theaters. Frankfurt/M. 1972; Očerki istorii russkogo sovetskogo dramatičeskogo teatra. Bd. 1–2. Moskva 1954–60; Simonow, R.: S Vachtangovym. Moskva 1959.

Annelore Engel-Braunschmidt/Elke Wiegand

Waffentänze

Mit dem Zerfall der Urgesellschaft und dem Aufbau erster militärischer Demokratien werden Verteidigung und Angriff organisiert, Körper der Kämpfer gestählt, schnelle Aktions- und Reaktionsfähigkeit trainiert. Völkergruppen tanzen, wie vor der Jagd (→Jagdtänze), magische, aufrüttelnde und einende W., die diffizile akrobatische Künste ausbilden. Getanzt wird mit Speeren, Pfeil und Bogen, Stöcken, später Schwertern. Homer beschreibt Schwerttänze, in denen mit außerordentlichem Geschick das Untertauchen und Überspringen der Waffe geübt wird. Noch heute spielen die Banri Kampfszenen, in denen sie, zu Boden fallend und auf dem Rücken liegend, kunstvoll fechten. Dhuliyas/Assam wirbeln während des Schwerterschwingens Schüsseln durch die Luft, ja tanzen sogar auf Stelzen. Bei den Bodo-Kachari/Assam tanzen Frauen mit je zwei Schwertern. Ganz Südamerika, besonders Brasilien, liebt die Macalele als Schwert- oder Stocktanz (→Rituáltänze).

Gregor, J.: Kulturgeschichte des Balletts. Zürich o. J./Wien 1944; Rebling, E.: Die Tanzkunst Indiens. Wilhelmshaven 1982; Sachs, C.: Weltgeschichte des Tanzes. Berlin 1933.

Helga Ettl

Wanderbühne

Die W. war die übliche Theaterform während der Anfänge des Berufstheaters in Europa (→Neuzeit/Theater der Neuzeit; →Commedia dell'arte). Die dt. W. geht in ihren Ursprüngen zurück auf engl. und holl. Komödianten, die im 16. und 17. Jh. den deutschsprachigen Raum bespielten. Zwar hatte es auch hier zu allen Zeiten wandernde Sänger, Akrobaten, Tierbändiger etc. gegeben (Vaganten, →Schauspieler), auch schauspielende Truppen waren nicht unbekannt; zu einem eigenständigen dt. Berufstheater war es jedoch nicht gekommen.

Nach ersten Besuchen auf dem Kontinent (Ende des 16. Jh.) nahmen engl. Truppen (→Elisabethanisches Theater) Anfang des 17. Jh. auch dt.

Wanderbühne 1105

Mitglieder auf und brachten ihnen das Schauspielerhandwerk bei. Allmählich kam es auch zur Benutzung der dt. Sprache; Mitte des 17. Jh. schließlich bildeten sich rein dt. Truppen, die sich aber häufig noch als «Englische Komödianten» bezeichneten, da dieser Name eine gewisse Werbewirksamkeit (Professionalität, spektakulärer Aufführungsstil, Repertoire) barg. Ab etwa 1650 gab es dt. →Prinzipale wie den Magister Johannes Velten (u. a. deshalb bedeutsam, weil er als erster in Deutschland Schauspielerinnen beschäftigte), Andreas Elenson, Johann Christian Kunst; erste Prinzipalinnen waren Maria Ursula Hofmann, Katharina Elisabeth Velten und Sophie Julie Elenson. Die Anzahl der Schauspieler einer Truppe betrug zunächst 14 bis 18. Einzelne besonders erfolgreiche Ensembles arbeiteten in späterer Zeit mit einer größeren Anzahl von Mitgliedern. Man kann aber davon ausgehen, daß im Durchschnitt fünf Männer und drei Frauen für Trauer- und Lustspiel zugleich engagiert wurden, dazu nochmals je zwei für das Lustspiel sowie einige Episodenspieler. Technisches Personal gab es in der Regel nicht; jedoch beschäftigten einige Truppen einen Schneider oder einen Maschinisten, da Kostüme und Requisiten neben den Rollenbüchern das wichtigste Besitztum der W. darstellten und entsprechend gepflegt wurden.

Das Repertoire der W. war begrenzt. Neben den kurzen einaktigen →Zwischen- und Nachspielen (→Pickelhering) wurden vor allem Stücke von George Peele, Thomas Kyd, Shakespeare, Marlowe und Massinger, seit Mitte des Jh. auch von Molière, Racine und Corneille und Stücke des ital. und span. Barocktheaters – in der Regel in äußerst fragwürdigen, oft verballhornenden Übersetzungen – gespielt. Ein umfangreicheres Repertoire war allerdings auch nicht erforderlich, da die Truppen den gesamten deutschsprachigen Raum bespielten und die einzelnen Städte deshalb nur in größeren Zeitabständen frequentiert wurden. Der Darstellungsstil der Wandertruppen zeichnete sich durch drastische Verdeutlichung (pathetische Sprache, gravitätische Gebärden) und reiche Kostümausstattung aus. Musik, Tanz und Akrobatik ergänzten die Darbietungen. Es ist ein deutliches Stilgefälle zu verzeichnen zwischen jenen Prinzipalen, die ihr künstlerischer Ehrgeiz zu durchdachten schauspielerischen und dramaturgischen Konzeptionen führte, und jenen, die aus wirtschaftlicher Notwendigkeit auf solche Feinheiten wenig Rücksicht nehmen konnten und lediglich dem Publikumsgeschmack zu entsprechen trachteten.

Die wirtschaftliche Lage auch der größten und renommiertesten Wandertruppen war durchaus ungesichert. Höfische Engagements waren zunächst noch selten, nur einzelne Vorstellungen bei Hofe sind häufiger bezeugt. Die meisten Prinzipale versuchten, ein Patent als Hofkomödiant zu erlangen, das ihnen zwar nicht Lohn und Brot bei Hofe sicherte, sie aber im Herrschaftsbereich des betreffenden Fürsten zur Berufsausübung berechtigte und oft die Erlangung der Spielerlaubnis durch den Rat der

1106   Wanderbühne

Stadt erleichterte. Die wenigen Schauspieler, die als →Hofschauspieler angestellt wurden, erhielten wie alle Hofbeamten Bestallungsdekrete, die sie zu Dienst-, Residenz- und Treuepflicht verpflichteten.

Viele Wanderschauspieler übten einen mit ihrer Wandertätigkeit leicht zu vereinbarenden Zweitberuf aus wie Zahnreißer, Pferdehändler oder Bruchschneider, eine Notwendigkeit, die sich aus ihrer ungesicherten wirtschaftlichen Situation ergab. Bedingt durch die Ausgaben während der Wanderschaft, wenn nicht oder nur selten gespielt werden konnte, und durch die Auflagen der Stadträte, welche in der Regel die Höhe der Eintrittspreise, die Steuern (meist ein Viertel der Einnahmen), das Repertoire und die Tage und Tageszeiten, an denen gespielt werden durfte (d. h. normalerweise außerhalb der kirchlichen Feiertage und der üblichen Gottesdienstzeiten), festlegten, war der Lohn der Wanderschauspieler äußerst gering. Wenigen gelang der Wechsel in einen bürgerlichen Beruf am Ende ihrer Bühnenlaufbahn. Ein energischer Versuch, Arbeitsbedingungen und -prinzipien festzulegen, wurde in Deutschland erst 1753 von Konrad Ekhof (1720–78) unternommen. Seine «Verfassung» enthielt 24 Artikel und behandelte vor allem die Vorgehensweise beim Erarbeiten der Stücke, das Verhalten der Schauspieler als Truppenmitglieder, in der Öffentlichkeit und bei der Arbeit. Ekhof gehört bereits zu einer neuen Generation von Wanderschauspielern, zu der auch Caroline Neuber (1697–1760), Konrad Ernst Ackermann (1712–71), Johann Friedrich Schönemann (1704–82) und Friedrich Ludwig Schröder (1744–1816) zählen. Sie alle waren Prinzipale, die sich allmählich aus der Tradition der alten W. lösten und sowohl künstlerische als auch soziale Verbesserungen anstrebten (→Nationaltheater). Als erste hatte sich Caroline Neuber um eine Verbesserung des Publikumsgeschmacks und um die Aufführung von Stücken dt. Autoren verdient gemacht. Ihr Werk wurde von Schönemann, der etwa zehn Jahre ihrer Truppe angehörte, fortgesetzt. Auch Friedrich Ludwig Schröder, einer der wenigen Prinzipale, die es durch ihre Arbeit zu bescheidenem Wohlstand brachten, setzte sich verstärkt für die jungen dt. Autoren ein. Schröder und Ekhof waren auch die ersten, die eine fundierte Ausbildung der Schauspieler und eine Sicherung ihrer sozialen Stellung anstrebten. So gründete Ekhof 1753 eine Akademie für Schauspieler, die – obgleich nicht von langer Dauer – den ersten Versuch darstellte, die Schauspielerausbildung zu organisieren. Schröder machte sich um die Einrichtung einer Pensionsanstalt für Schauspieler verdient. Der wichtigste Punkt der in dieser Zeit entwickelten programmatischen Ansätze zu einer Reform des Theaters war jedoch der allen Prinzipalen gemeinsame Wunsch nach einem eigenen Theater (→Stehendes Theater), einem Haus, das ihnen kontinuierliche Arbeit ermöglichen sollte. Das erste größere Privattheater wurde schließlich 1755 in Königsberg von Konrad Ackermann errichtet. Dieses

Haus hatte ca. 800 Plätze; es wurde jedoch nur etwa ein Jahr lang bespielt, dann zwangen Kriegswirren Ackermann zu erneuter Wanderschaft.

Wanderbühnen hielten sich noch bis Ende des 19. Jh. Eine Ausnahme bildet Böhmen; hier spielten noch zu Beginn dieses Jh. Wandertruppen, selbst nach dem 2. Weltkrieg, wenn auch aus anderen Motivationen heraus (es ging jetzt vor allem darum, auch die Zuschauer in entlegenen Gebieten zu erreichen), wurde diese Tradition wieder aufgenommen. In gewisser Weise setzen heute die →Landesbühnen die Wanderbühnentradition fort, ebenso in jüngster Zeit die Zelttheater (→Freies Theater), die so neue Publikumsschichten erschließen wollen.

Baesecke, Anna: Das Schauspiel der engl. Komödianten in Deutschland. Halle 1935; Bolte, J.: Von Wanderkomödianten und Handwerker-Spielen des 17. und 18. Jh. In: Sitz. Ber. der Preuß. Akad. d. Wiss., phil.-hist. Klasse XIX. 1934; Brauneck, M. (Hg.): Spieltexte der Wanderbühne. Bd. I–IV. Berlin 1970 ff; Creizenach, W.: Die Schauspiele der engl. Komödianten, Kürschners Deutsche Nationalliteratur, Bd. 23. Berlin/Stuttgart, o. J.; Flemming, W.: Das Schauspiel der Wanderbühne. In: Deutsche Literatur in Entwicklungsreihen, Reihe Barockdrama, Bd. III. Leipzig 1931; Frenzel, H. A.: Geschichte des Theaters. München 1979; Heine, C.: Das Schauspiel der dt. Wanderbühne vor Gottsched. 1889; Herz, E.: Engl. Schauspieler und engl. Schauspiel zur Zeit Shakespeares in Deutschland. In: Theatergeschichtliche Forschungen, Bd. 18. Hamburg 1903; Maas, H.: Äußere Geschichte der engl. Theatertruppen in dem Zeitraum von 1559–1642. Leipzig/London 1907; Wanderbühne. Theaterkunst als fahrendes Gewerbe. Berlin 1988.

Elke Kehr

Washington Square Players

Wichtigste Theatergruppe des →Little Theatre Movement nach den →Provincetown Players. Gegr. 1915, spielten die W. S. P. insgesamt 62 Einakter und sechs abendfüllende Stücke europ. und amerik. Autoren bis zu ihrer Schließung 1918, zunächst im Bandbox Theatre, dann in The Comedy, New York. Früher als die Provincetown Players zahlten die W. S. P. Gagen und waren auch einer Expansion des Theaterunternehmens gegenüber offen. Sie gingen 1918 in die →Theatre Guild über.

Dieter Herms

Welttheater

→Theatrum mundi und analog zu dem von Goethe geprägten Begriff «Weltliteratur» im Sinne von Gemeingut der Menschheit, von Universalität und Internationalismus, geläufig gewordener Ausdruck in der Theaterwissenschaft. Das Entstehen des →ITI (1948) und seines Festivals →«Theater der Nationen» stellen die konkrete organisatorische Verwirklichung dieses wichtigen Theaterbegriffs dar.

Melchinger, S.: Das moderne Welttheater. München 1963; Rischbieter, H./Melchinger, S.: Welttheater. Braunschweig 1962.

Adriana Hass

Werkstatt

(Engl. workshop; frz. atelier, stage; zuweilen auch Laboratorium) Eine insbesondere im Bereich der Spiel- und Theaterpädagogik, die bisher kaum über institutionalisierte Ausbildungsgänge verfügt, übliche Form zumeist praktischer Aus- und Weiterbildung; auch eine der gegenwärtigen Freizeitgesellschaft entsprechende Form von Freizeitgestaltung mit kreativer Eigentätigkeit und erfahrungsbestimmtem Lernen (von Handwerk, Kunst und Selbsterfahrung über Hobbyurlaub und Unterhaltung bis zum Sektentum). Vorformen sind die freien Schauspiel-, Atem-, Bewegungskurse seit der Jahrhundertwende, Seminare zur politischen Bildung (vor allem nach 1945); heute vielfach in Jugendbildungsstätten (z. B. Jugendhof Scheersberg mit der Internationalen Theater-W. seit 1969), wichtige Finanzierungsquelle für freischaffende Künstler und Freie Gruppen.

Hans-Wolfgang Nickel

Het Werkteater

1970 gegr. kollektives Gruppentheater mit Sitz in Amsterdam (→Freies Theater), entstanden im Zusammenhang mit der politisch-künstlerischen Protestbewegung der 60er Jahre gegen das bürgerlich-etablierte Theater. Die W.-Mitglieder suchten nach neuen, eigenen theatralischen Ausdrucksformen, verstanden sich nicht als Produktions-, sondern als Forschungsgruppe, als Laboratorium. In kollektiver Arbeitsform entwickeln sie ihre Stücke über Improvisationen selbst. Ihr Engagement gilt vor allem der Problematik sozialer Randgruppen und Minderheiten. Arbeitsgrundlage sind genaue literarische Recherchen, besonders aber Gespräche und Diskussionen mit den Betroffenen. Gespielt wird meist in Alltagskleidung mit wenigen Requisiten, an verschiedenen Orten, der Problematik entsprechend, in Gefängnissen, Krankenhäusern, Jugendheimen, psychiatrischen Kliniken oder in ihrem eigenen Haus am Kattegat. Im Sommer zieht das W. mit einem Zelt durch das Land. Diese sog. Sommerprojekte behandeln in satirischer Form bestimmte Aspekte des niederländischen Zusammenlebens. Clownerie, Slapstick, Akrobatik, Gesang, Musik sind seine Elemente. In den letzten Jahren zeichnet sich immer stärker die Tendenz ab, in kleinen Gruppen von zwei bis drei Schauspielern eigene Probleme und Erfahrungen in Projekte umzusetzen oder auch literarische Stoffe zu bearbeiten. 1984 fand das W. als Gruppentheater sein Ende.

Wichtige Produktionen: *Toestanden*, das erste größere Projekt, schildert die Zustände in psychiatrischen Anstalten (1972); *Misdaad*, ein Projekt über Kriminalität (1973); *Avondrood* (Abendrot) zeigt das Zusammenleben in einem Altenheim (1974); *Feest voor Nico* (1974); *Niet Thuis*, über Heimkinder (1975); *Hallo Medemens* (1976); *Als de dood* und *Je moet ermee leven*, zwei Stücke über Sterben und Sterbensbegleitung in Krankenhäusern (1977); *Een zwoele zomeravond* (1978); *Zus of Zo*, behandelt Probleme der Homosexualität (1979); *Oom Wanja (Onkel Wanja*, Tschechow 1979); *Bosch en Lucht* (Waldeslust), erzählt zwei Geschichten; behinderte Kinder in ihrem Heim Waldeslust – eine holländische Touristengruppe im sonnigen Spanien (1980); *De Huisbewaarder* (Der Hausmeister, Pinter 1981); *U bent mijn Moeder* (Du bist meine Mutter); Joop Admiraal spricht von seiner Mutter, indem er sich in sie verwandelt (1981); *Die Möwe* (Tschechow 1983); *Adio* (1984); *Die Krönung der Poppea* (Monteverdi 1985).

Ogden; D. H.: Performance Dynamics and the Amsterdam Werkteater. Berkeley 1987.

Petra Lüdeke/Red.

West End

Sammelbegriff für die über 40 kommerziell betriebenen Theater des Londoner Westens (zwischen Covent Garden und Mayfair). Zentrum ist die Shaftesbury Avenue mit ihren zahlreichen Privattheatern. W. E. als Begriff für ein auf Vermarktung bedachtes Unterhaltungstheater wird oft abwertend gebraucht, ist aber dennoch ein Zielpunkt vieler Autoren und Inszenierungen des Subventions- und Alternativtheaters. Die Theater des W. E. sind fast sämtlich fest in der Hand weniger Konzerne in der Vergnügungsindustrie und stehen unter großem Konkurrenzdruck. Sie bieten ein breites Spektrum von billigen Revuen bis hin zu ambitionierteren Aufführungen gegenwärtiger Dramatiker. Bekannteste Theater des W. E.: →Drury Lane, Wyndhams, Adelphi, Albery, Apollo, Comedey, Lyric, Mayfair, Haymarket, Piccadilly, Phoenix, St. Martins's Strand, Shaftesbury, Palace, Westminster, Windmill.

Hayman, R.: The Set Up. An Anatomy of the English Theatre Today. London 1973; Martin, R.: Hinter den Kulissen. Einige erfolgsbedingende Faktoren des engl. Theaters: Geld, Macht und Subvention. In: Fehse, K.-D./Platz, N. (Hg.): Das zeitgenössische engl. Drama. Einführung, Interpretation, Dokumentation. Frankfurt/M. 1975, S. 11–24; Thomsen, C. W.: Das englische Theater der Gegenwart. Düsseldorf 1980.

Bernd-Peter Lange

Wintergarten

Der Berliner W., lange Jahre eines der führenden →Varietés der Welt, verdankt seinen Namen einem wirklichen Wintergarten im 1880 eröffneten Central-Hotel. Aus ihm wurde jedoch schon bald ein Ballsaal, in dem gelegentlich auch Künstler auftraten. Die erste Varietévorstellung fand wahrscheinlich am 10. 9. 1886 statt. Die nächste belegbare Vorstellung am 17. 9. 1887 enthielt nur Gesangsvorträge und Musikdarbietungen, noch keine Artistik. In wenigen Jahren verschaffte sich der W. durch die Attraktivität seiner Darbietungen internationales Ansehen. Zu ihnen gehörten die damals überaus beliebten «Five Sisters Barrison» (an denen sich ein jahrelang andauernder Skandal entzündete), die Chansonnette Yvette Guilbert, die Tänzerinnen Saharet, La Belle Otero und Olga Desmond ebenso wie Spitzenleistungen der Artistik. Die Varieténummer *Das Bioskop* vom 1. 11. 1895 war die erste öffentliche Filmvorführung der Welt.

Umfangreiche Umbauten erweiterten 1900 und 1928 die techn. Möglichkeiten des W. Die Varietékrise während des 1. Weltkriegs meisterte der W. ebenso wie die Wandlungen des Publikumsgeschmacks – durch die Aufnahme von Ballett- und Revueeinlagen und den Rückgriff auf bewährte Stars wie den Coupletsänger Otto Reutter. Am 21. 6. 1944 setzten Bomben der Existenz des W., der bis zuletzt am traditionellen Nummernprogramm festgehalten hatte, endgültig ein Ende.

Festschrift 40 Jahre Wintergarten. Berlin 1928; Festschrift 50 Jahre Wintergarten. Berlin 1938 (Nachdruck 1975); Gobbers, E.: Artisten. Düsseldorf 1949; Günther, E.: Geschichte des Varietés, Berlin [2]1981; Jansen, W.: Das Varieté. Berlin 1990; K(üsshauer), W.: Wintergarten, 1887–1900–1925. Berlin (1925); Moulin, J.-P./ Kindler, E.: Eintritt frei – Varieté. Lausanne 1963; PEM (d.i.P. E. Marcus): Heimweh nach dem Kurfürstendamm. Berlin 1952.

Wolfgang Beck

Workers' Laboratory Theatre

Gegr. 1930 im Rahmen eines Workers' International Relief Program, 1934 umbenannt in «Theatre of Action». Das W.L.T. umfaßte die Unterabteilung «Theatre Collective» (1932–36) und «Shock Troupe» (1933ff). Das W.L.T. war ein kommunistisch orientiertes Arbeitertheater, seit 1934 zunehmend professionalisiert. Zunächst trat es nur auf politischen Versammlungen und Kundgebungen auf und unterstützte die Ausführungen kommunistischer Redner durch Agitpropszenen wie *Unemployed, The Sell Out, The Great Show*. Von 1933 bis 1936 spielte das W.L.T. auf professioneller Basis in angemieteten Theaterhäusern Einakter von u.a. G. Nowikow, P. Martin und M. Blankfort.

Dieter Herms

Wuppertaler Bühnen

Opernhaus, Schauspielhaus. 1806 Bau des ersten Elberfelder Theaters. 1919 nach vielen gescheiterten Theatergründungen Zusammenschluß der Bühnen beider Städte zu «Vereinigten Stadttheatern Barmen-Elberfeld». 1929 nach Fusion beider Städte «Städtische Bühnen Wuppertal». 1933 bis 1941 Intendant Dr. Günther Stark (1889–1970). Alle Bühnenhäuser im Krieg zerstört. 1950 bis 1955 Fusion der Stadttheater Wuppertal und Solingen. 1956 Neueröffnung des Opernhauses, 1966 neues Schauspielhaus, eröffnet durch eine Rede von Heinrich Böll (1917–85). 1958 bis 1964 Intendant Dr. Grischa Barfuß (*1917), 1964 bis 1975 Arno Wüstenhöfer (*1920). – Operndirektor 1965 bis 1975 Kurt Horres (*1932), Ballettdirektorin seit 1973 Pina Bausch (*1940). 1979 bis 1983 Intendant Dr. Hellmuth Matiasek (*1931), 1983 bis 1988 Jürgen Fabritius (*1941); seit 1988 Holk Freytag.

Werner Schulze-Reimpell

Wuppertaler Tanztheater

Pina Bausch (*1940), ehemalige Folkwangschülerin und seit 1969 Leiterin des Essener →Folkwang-Tanzstudios, übernimmt in der Spielzeit 1973/74 die Direktion der Ballettabteilung an den Wuppertaler Bühnen. Die Tänzer ihres Essener Ensembles und ihrer Wuppertaler Balletttruppe vereinigen sich zum W.T. Gemeinsam mit dem W.T. erarbeitet Pina Bausch neue ästhetische Ausdrucksformen, die heute zum Inbegriff

1112 Wuppertaler Tanztheater

für das →Tanztheater geworden sind und die gesamte Tanz- und Ballettlandschaft nachhaltig beeinflussen. Lose gereihte Bilder aus Ablichtungen des Lebens erinnern bei P. Bausch an dadaistische Stilelemente und an →Collagentheater. Kein dramatischer Handlungsfaden faßt die sich gegenseitig erklärenden und widersprechenden oder die sich einander ausschließenden und z. T. parallel verlaufenden Szenen- und Bühnenbilder zu einem kausal-logischen Verlaufsganzen zusammen. P. Bauschs Theater der Bruchstücke und Ausschnitte spielt gegen alle Seh- und Hörgewohnheiten der traditionellen Ballettbesucher an und irritiert rational-analytische Betrachtungsweisen; es fordert dementgegen ein breites emotionales Sich-Einlassen auf Bilder. Wie Brecht (→Verfremdungseffekt) löst auch P. Bausch Verhaltensweisen aus dem üblichen Kontext heraus, um sie in einen neuen Sinnzusammenhang einzugliedern. Die Verfremdungstechnik hebt die Eindeutigkeit der eingefahrenen Verhaltensmuster auf und stellt sie in Frage. Die erzielte Wirkung ist ein Ergebnis aufspringender Assoziationen und Emotionen. – P. Bauschs Theater kann keiner Tanzgattung im herkömmlichen Sinne zugeordnet werden. Die Choreographin arbeitet mit Hilfe aller theatralischen Mittel aus dem Bereich des Films, des Musik- und Sprechtheaters und der Performance Art. Die Körpersprache des W. T. befreit sich von jedem festgelegten Bewegungskodex und bezieht die Sprech- und Singstimme als Träger für bestimmte Aussageintentionen ein. Die Tänzer des Bausch-Ensembles werden direkt am Schöpfungsprozeß einer Arbeit beteiligt, die mit dem Aufführungsdatum nicht etwa abgeschlossen ist, sondern als work in progress Fortführung fordert. Improvisationen und Assoziationen sind von P. Bausch genutzte Techniken. Die Tänzer ihrer Kompanie bringen ihre Persönlichkeiten bis zur völligen Selbstentäußerung in den choreographischen Entstehungsvorgang ein. Ein Auszug aus R. Hoghes Probentagebuch gibt Einblick: «Sich auf die Knie des Partners stellen, sie niederdrücken auf den Boden – ‹C'est bien pour toi›. Ein paar Takte auf dem Klavier spielen und flirten... Fallen üben. Körperteile freilegen und berühren. Arm, Fuß, Hand, Nacken, Wade, Bauch, Schulter, Rücken, Po entblößen und vorsichtig an den Arm, den Fuß, den Nacken, die Wade, den Bauch, die Schulter, den Rücken, den Po des Partners halten. Den entblößten Körperteil wieder verdecken. Einen neuen Berührungspunkt suchen.» Pina Bauschs Arbeit ist wie die des →Modern Dance für das feministische Theater wegweisend geworden, hat aber darüber hinaus die gesamte Theaterszene innovativ beeinflußt.

Hanraths U./Winkels H. (Hg.): Tanz-Legenden. Frankfurt/M. 1984; Hoge, R./ Weiss, V.: Bandoneon – Für was kann Tango alles gut sein? Darmstadt 1981; Müller, H.: Offenheit aus Überzeugung. In: Regitz, H. (Hg.): Tanz in Deutschland. Ballett seit 1945. Berlin 1984; ders.: Pina Bausch, Wuppertaler Tanztheater. Köln 1979; Servos, N.: Das neue Tanztheater. In: Theater heute 6 (1985), S. 1–15.

Patricia Stöckemann

Yingxi (Chin. Schattentheater)

Die erste quellenmäßig gesicherte Erwähnung einer Darstellung mit Schattenpuppen legt nahe, daß diese Form der Darstellung – ähnlich wie das Puppentheater – aus dem Totenkult hervorging. 121 v. Chr. soll sich Kaiser Wu der Han-Dynastie von einem Magier seine verstorbene Lieblingsfrau als Schattenriß auf einem beleuchteten Vorhang vor Augen geführt lassen haben. Ein Schattentheater im eigentlichen Sinne indes ist erst aus dem 11. Jh. belegt, aus der Song-Zeit also (960–1279), einer Zeit allg. Aufschwungs populärer Kunstformen. Seitdem werden die Puppen aus Papier, meist jedoch aus Leder geschnitten; ist das Leder dünn genug, läßt es sich darüber hinaus einfärben, so daß auch Farbeffekte zu erzielen sind. Die Figuren sind i. d. R. im Profil geschnitten. Eine aparte Entwicklung ebenfalls zur Song-Zeit war das Große Schattentheater (da yingxi), in dem anstatt ausgeschnittener Figuren lebendige Menschen hinter einer Leinwand als Schattenfiguren auftraten. – Ähnlich wie beim Theater haben sich auch beim Schattentheater regionale Stile entwickelt, deren bekannteste diejenigen aus Peking und aus der Provinz Sichuan waren, deren Hauptunterschied darin bestand, daß die Figuren aus Sichuan größer waren als die aus Peking. Meistens spielen drei bis acht Schattenspieler, Amateure oder professionelle Darsteller, in einer Gruppe zusammen, begleitet von einem kleinen Orchester. Die gesamte Aufführungsweise weist eine gewisse Nähe zum eigentlichen Theater auf. So gibt es wie bei diesem die vier Rollentypen (sheng: «männliche Rolle», dan: «weibliche Rolle»; jing: «geschminkte Rolle»; chou: «komische Rolle») mit zahlreichen Untergliederungen. Auch die Stücke behandeln vielfach die gleichen Stoffe wie die Theaterstücke, religiöse, mythologische oder historische, die der populären Erzählliteratur entnommen sind.

Broman, S.: Chinese Shadow Theatre. Stockholm 1981; Jacob B./Jensen, H.: Das chinesische Schattentheater. Stuttgart 1933; Wimsatt, G. B.: Chinese Shadow Shows. Cambridge (Mass.) 1936.

Bernd Eberstein

Yûgen

Jap., ‹vornehme Anmut›, ‹charme subtil›. Ein schon um die Zeitenwende in China entstandener Begriff, der sich aber erst in Japan zu einer ästhetischen Kategorie entwickelte, mit dem – mehr oder minder entsprechend seiner urspr. Bedeutung des Unbestimmt-Vagen – eine geheimnisvolle, am Kosmischen (im Sinne des Taoismus) teilhabende, zugleich aber elegant-verfeinerte Schönheit und deren betörend-schmerzliche Wirkung auf die menschliche Psyche bezeichnet wird. – Im Laufe der Geschichte wurden verschiedene Seiten des *yûgen* betont: die stille Schönheit (bei Shunzei), die Eleganz (bei Shôtetsu und Zeami), die elegante Schlichtheit (bei Shinkei und Zenchiku). – In bezug auf den Aufführungsstil des →Nô vermerkt Zeami in seinem *Kakyô* («Blumenspiegel»): «tadu utsukushiku nyûwa naru tei, yûgen no hontai nari» («Der Stil reiner Schönheit und Milde, das ist die Essenz von yûgen»).

Hisamatsu, S.: The Vocabulary of Japanese Literary Aesthetics. Tôkyô 1963.

Peter Pörtner

Zaju

Das zaju («vermischtes Theater»), entstanden während der Song-Zeit (960–1279), war das klassische chin. Theater, dessen Blütezeit während der Yuan-Dynastie (1271–1368) lag. Aus Nordchina stammend, verwendete es den nördlichen Melodienkanon (beiqu). Klassisch ist es aus zwei Gründen zu nennen: Es stellt den ersten literarischen Höhepunkt des chin. Theaters dar, und es zeichnet sich durch formale Strenge aus. Vier formale Besonderheiten sind hervorzuheben:
1. Ein zaju hat fast immer vier Akte (zhe), außerdem ein Vor- oder Zwischenspiel (xiezi). 2. Die Auswahl der Arienmelodien (qu) folgte strengen Regeln; so hatten alle Melodien eines Akts die gleiche Tonart. 3. Die Verse aller Arien in einem Akt haben den gleichen Endreim. 4. Alle Arien werden von einem Schauspieler, dem Hauptdarsteller, gesungen.

Die Homogenität der Endreime und der Tonart innerhalb eines Akts gab jedem Akt ein starkes Eigengewicht. Das wird durch andere formale Mittel noch verstärkt, so durch einleitende Verse am Anfang und durch zusammenfassende Verse am Ende eines Aktes sowie durch die Tatsache, daß eine in einem Akt neu auftretende Rolle sich wieder vorstellt, auch wenn das in einem früheren Akt bereits geschehen ist. Daher wurden nicht selten einzelne Akte aus dem Gesamtgeschehen herausgelöst und für sich aufgeführt.

Heute sind noch 160 bis 170 zaju aus der Yuan-Zeit erhalten, gesammelt und 1616 herausgegeben in *Yuanqu xuan* (Ausgewählte Yuan-Dramen) von Zang Maoxun sowie in der 1959 von Sui Shusen in Peking herausgegebenen Fortsetzung zu diesem Werk, welche Stücke enthält, die erst in den letzten Jahrzehnten gefunden worden waren.

Als die bedeutendsten Dramatiker des zaju gelten die «Vier Großen des Yuan-Dramas» (Yuanqu si dajia): 1. Guan Hanqing (ca. 1220 bis ca.1305). Er gilt allg. als größter Yuan-Dramatiker; mit Sicherheit war er der fruchtbarste: Er schrieb etwa 60 Dramen, von denen allerdings nur 17 bis 18 erhalten sind. Als sein wichtigstes Stück wird *Dou E yuan* («Die ungerechte Bestrafung der Dou E») angesehen. Dou E, Muster einer selbstlosen Tochter und treuen Ehefrau, wird durch eine Intrige des Mordes bezichtigt und hingerichtet. Nach ihrem Tod wird durch einen gerechten Beamten und Richter – ihren eigenen Vater – ihr Fall wieder aufgerollt, und die Schuldigen werden bestraft. 2. Bai Pu (1226–ca. 1306) schrieb *Wutong yu* («Regen auf dem Paulonia-Baum»), ein Stück über ein immer wiederkehrendes beliebtes Sujet der chin. Literatur, die Liebe zwischen dem Tang-Kaiser Minghuang und seiner Konkubine Yang Guifei. 3. Ma Zhiyuans (um 1280) bekanntes Drama ist *Hangong qiu* («Herbst im Han-Palast»), ein Stück über den Konflikt zwischen Liebe und Staatsräson: Kaiser Yuan der Späteren Han-Dynastie (25–220) sieht sich gezwungen, seine Lieblingskonkubine Wang Zhaojun dem Hunnen-Khan zur Frau zu geben. 4. Zheng Guangzu (ca. 1260–ca. 1320) trat vor allem mit dem Stück *Qiannü li hun* («Qiannüs Seele wandert umher») hervor. – Diesen vier Dramatikern ist Wang Shifu (Ende 13. Jh.) an die Seite zu stellen, der das bekannteste Liebesdrama der chin. Theaterliteratur geschrieben hat, *Xixiang ji* («Das Westzimmer»).

Viele Stücke dieser und anderer Dramatiker des zaju blieben bis in die jüngste Zeit populär, und ihre Stoffe wurden in andere Formen des Theaters übertragen.

Zu Beginn der Ming-Zeit wurde das zaju als verbreitete Theaterform vom freieren →chuanqi abgelöst. Nur noch wenige Dramatiker schrieben zaju, unter ihnen besonders Zhu Youdun (1379–1439) und Zhu Quan (1378–1448), deren Dramen sich indes nicht mehr so streng an die klassischen Regeln hielten.

Crump, J. I.: Chinese Theater in the Days of Kublai Khan. Tucson (Ariz.) 1980; Shih Chung-wen: The Golden Age of Chinese Drama: Yüan Tsa-chü. Princeton 1976.

Bernd Eberstein

1116 Zarzuela

Zarzuela

Span. Singspiel (nach dem früheren Königspalast genannt), das im Rahmen des →‹Género Chico› (dram. Kurzgattung) vor allem im 19. und 20. Jh. großen Aufschwung nahm und mit den aufwendigsten Revuen und Musicals konkurrierte. Bekanntester Librettist war Ricardo de la Vega (1839–1910) mit *La verbena de la paloma* (1894) in bisher über 20 000 Aufführungen.

El Libro de la Zarzuela. Madrid (usw.) 1982; Mindlin, R.: Die Zarzuela. Das span. Singspiel im 19. und 20. Jh. Zürich 1965.

Martin Franzbach

Zauberstück

Als besondere Form des →Alt-Wiener Volksstücks, deren Entwicklung ihren Höhepunkt Anfang des 19. Jh. erreichte, verbindet das Z. volkstümliche und märchenhafte Elemente. Zauberer, Feen, Geister und personifizierte Allegorien bevölkern zwischen Himmel und Erde ein übernatürliches Reich mit z. T. echt bürgerlich-menschlichen Gepflogenheiten und können durch ihr Eingreifen nach Belieben irdisch-menschliche Geschicke lenken oder beeinflussen. Als Vorbilder und Ansatzpunkte dienen u. a. barocke →Mysterienspiele, Stegreifhandlungen der →Commedia dell'arte, Motive aus frz. Märchen – z. B. aus Perraults *Contes de ma mère l'Oye* –, arab. Erzählungen wie die *1001 Nacht* (Übers. Galland) und Bestandteile volkstümlichen Aberglaubens. Ziel des Z. ist sowohl die Flucht in die märchenhaften Sphären der Phantasieliteratur als auch das Aufzeigen sittlicher Werte im Sinne des ‹Besserungsstücks›. Nicht selten bieten Feen und Zauberer als nichtirdische Wesen Anlaß zu mittelbarer gesellschaftlicher Kritik unter Umgehung der amtlichen Zensur. Die Gattung des Z. erfährt mannigfaltige Wandlungen, die von der reinen Maschinenkomödie des Joseph von Kurz (1717–84) über die ‹Zauberburleske› bei Philipp Hafner (1735–64) bis zum ‹Singspiel› und zur ‹Zauberoper› *Die Zauberflöte* (1791) von Emanuel Schikaneder (1751–1812) mit Musik von Mozart reichen. Die ‹Großen Drei›, Joseph Alois Gleich (1722–1841), Karl Meisl (1775–1853), Adolf Bäuerle (1786–1856), verknüpfen in ihren ‹Zauberpossen› und ‹parodistischen Zauberspielen› märchenhafte Zauberelemente mit satirisch-komischen Komponenten der →Lokalposse, wobei sie endgültig Z. und ‹Besserungsstück› gleichsetzen. Diese Synthese führt Ferdinand Raimund (1790–1836) in seinen ‹Original-Zauberspielen› (*Das Mädchen aus der Feenwelt oder der Bauer als Millionär*, 1826); *Der Alpenkönig und der Menschenfeind*, 1828; *Der*

Verschwender, 1834) zur literarischen Vollendung. Das Z. wird durch Johann Nepomuk Nestroy (1801–62) in *Der böse Geist Lumpazivagabundus oder das liederliche Kleeblatt* (1833) als Illusionstheater in Frage gestellt und bleibt fortan nur noch in vereinzelten parodistischen Anspielungen (vgl. den ‹Zauberkönig› in den *Geschichten aus dem Wiener Wald*, 1931, des Ödön von Horváth, 1901–38) erhalten.

Rommel, O.: Die Alt-Wiener Volkskomödie. Wien 1952.

Jean-Marie Winkler

Zeit

In der Welt des Theaters verbindet sich, wie in der Geschichte, die sog. objektive oder physikalische Z. mit der subjektiven oder psychologischen Z. Nichtumkehrbarkeit und Nichtwiederholbarkeit gehören eigentlich zur objektiven Z.; im Z.-Erlebnis und im Z.-Bewußtsein werden Kontinuität und Homogenität des Nacheinanders bzw. Aufeinanderfolgens von Ereignissen durch sprunghaft gleitende Scheidung aufgehoben. Als Raum des Denkens und als Raum des Handelns fällt das Momentane oft auseinander. Im Unterschied zum Film kann das Theater wegen seiner Sprachgebundenheit die Gesetze der Wahrnehmung der Z. nicht durch Z.-Lupen- oder Z.-Raffereffekte übertreten. Ein Naturgesetz ist allerdings die berühmte dritte Einheit nicht, nämlich der Ablauf einer geschlossenen Handlung an einem gleichbleibenden Schauplatz innerhalb eines «Sonnentags» (Aristoteles). Ist die relative Geschlossenheit eines Geschehens eine wesentliche Forderung der Dramaturgie, so erlaubt die Bühnentechnik verdeckte oder offene Ortswechsel und, damit verbunden, Z.-Sprünge, die sich nicht an die Regel der summarischen 24 Stunden halten. Die Vorstellung von Z. und Raum als die Erfahrung erst ermöglichenden reinen Anschauungsformen und damit als vorgegebenen Kategorien der Eingrenzung und Gliederung der dramaturgischen Darstellung waren der Antike fremd. Wie Platon verstand Aristoteles die Z. als Reflexion einer meßbaren Änderung von Bestehendem und unterwarf die Konvention der Z.-Einheit der zentralen Forderung nach Handlungseinheit. Strenge, Lockerung, Regelwidrigkeit und scheinbare Regellosigkeit – sowohl in der Praxis als auch in der zeitlich meistens erst nachfolgenden Theorie – lassen sich denn auch als Sekundärmerkmale von Neuerungen und Schulen verstehen: Renaissance, Klassik, Romantik, Expressionismus und andere Formwelten entwickeln in ihrem Theater spezifische Temporalitäten. Sollen perfekte Illusion oder Identifikation angestrebt werden, oder sollen Distanz und Verfremdung einen nachhaltigeren Tiefgang garantieren? In jedem Fall werden temporale Gesetz-

1118 Zeit

mäßigkeiten gelten, aber immer als relative Konsequenz von primären Inhalts- und Darstellungsforderungen.

Unter allen literarischen Gattungen zeichnet sich das Drama (Theater) durch das Privileg des Dichters (Regisseurs) aus, den zeitlichen Ablauf des Stücks zu bestimmen, von Eingriffen der Inszenierung und des Vortrags abgesehen. Der Zuschauer kann weder unterbrechen noch beschleunigen oder bremsen. Sein Rezeptionsvermögen ist jedoch nicht beliebig. So ist denn eine Z.-Einheit auch in einem anderen, trivialeren Sinne zu verstehen: fünf Akte in zwei Stunden, drei Einakter in der gleichen Z., eine Tetralogie in einer Festwoche als Verbindung von drei Tragödien mit einem Satyrspiel, Pausen oder nicht, gar mit Zwischenspielen oder Büfett usw., das sind vor allem temporal relevante Aspekte von formalen Entscheidungen. Allen Konzeptionen bzw. Realisationen gemeinsam sind jedoch die Vergegenwärtigung der Vergangenheit in Erinnerung, Erzählung oder Bericht und die Vergegenwärtigung der offenen Zukunft in Wunsch- und Alpträumen, Planung, Komplott, Wahrsagung und bes. Vorwissen der Zuschauer, etwa eines Verrats oder einer Entdeckung. Wer die Z. nicht beherrscht, dem läuft die Handlung auseinander.

Was jedoch der Theaterdichter nicht beherrschen kann, erst recht nicht in den extremen Formen des Trauerspiels und des Lustspiels, ist die objektive menschliche Z. als Schicksal; die scheinbare Überwindung jenes Unüberwindbaren würde jedem Stück den innersten Wert nehmen, der – immanent oder/und transzendent – noch tiefer als die Handlung anzusetzen ist: der Zeitenlauf und ein Schicksal, das sich unweigerlich und unaufhaltsam vom Anfang bis zum Ende ereignet. Die Handlung selber erscheint als ein Versuch, den Ablauf der Ereignisse zu beeinflussen und wenigstens eine annehmbare Harmonie oder Gemeinsamkeit zu erwirken und so das Fatum durch Ratio zu zähmen. In allen Mythologien erscheint die souveräne Z. unter zwei Gesichtern: die unbarmherzige Stetigkeit des ewigen, zyklischen Laufs, dem nichts enteilen kann (Kronos), und der günstige Augenblick, der immer schon vorbei ist, die Gelegenheit, deren Schopf in der Hand behält, wer ihn fassen wollte (Kairos). Die Verbindung beider Gesetzlichkeiten in den Formprinzipien der Tragödie und der Komödie ist nicht die gleiche; während im Tragischen Kronos zum Zuträger des Kairos wird, fällt in der Komik dem Kairos immer wieder die Aufgabe der Huldigung an den Kronos zu: In beiden enthüllen alle Coups de théâtre nur Unabänderliches, sei es Natur, sei es Schicksal; die Überraschungen führen zur verhüllenden Enthüllung der Z. als des eigentlichen Gegenstands des Dramas.

Doležel, L.: A Scheme of Narrative Time. In: Matejka, L./Titunik, I. R.: Semiotics of Art. Cambridge 1977; Grebeníčková, R.: Die Zeit im Drama. In: Orientace

V 2 (1970); Herrnstein Smith, B: Poetic Closure. Chigaco 1970; Hirt, E.: Das Formgesetz der epischen, dramatischen und lyrischen Dichtung. Leipzig 1923; Klotz V.: Geschlossene und offene Form im Drama. München 1960; Linke, F. H.: Dramaturgie der Zeit. Freiburg i. Br. 1977; Meyerhoff, H.: Time in Literature. Berkeley 1955; Petsch, R.: Wesen und Formen des Dramas. Halle/S. 1945; Pfister, M.: Das Drama. München 1977; Pütz, P.: Die Zeit im Drama. Göttingen 1970; Sinclair, L.: Time and the Drama. In: Explorations 6 (1956).

Jean-Marie Zemb

Zeitstück

Der Krieg von 1914–1918 und die darauf folgende Revolution hatten das politische Bewußtsein geschärft. Zu Beginn der 20er Jahre gab es für Schriftsteller und Publikum kein Zurück mehr zur apolitischen Kunstidylle der Vorkriegszeit. Die Zuschauer wollten sich ‹stellen› lassen, und die Autoren entzogen sich nicht länger ihrer gesellschaftlichen Verantwortung. ‹Zeitgemäß› schreiben hieß Themen wie «Napoleon, Pythagoras oder Werthers Leiden» zu vermeiden (Fred Hildenbrandt) und sich statt dessen den Fragen der Gegenwart zuzuwenden. Das Z. entstand aus der Kritik an den zeitlos-überzeitlichen Problemstellungen des traditionellen Bühnenwerks.

Der Enthüllungsjournalismus eines Egon Erwin Kisch stand Pate, als das politische Z. aus der Taufe gehoben wurde. Ähnlich wie bei der literarischen Reportage wurden jetzt auch auf den Theaterbühnen der Weimarer Republik konkrete gesellschaftliche Mißstände aufgedeckt und öffentlich zur Diskussion gestellt. Bevorzugte Themen waren Abtreibung, Kriegsgefahr, Probleme der Jugend und Jugenderziehung, Todesstrafe und Justizwillkür. Am individuellen Fallbeispiel wurden gesellschaftliche Zusammenhänge sichtbar gemacht. Bevorzugter Handlungsort war der Gerichtssaal, ein Ort, an dem man Unrecht sprach – doch noch ehe die hohen Richter ihr Fehlurteil verkünden konnten, erstatten die Zeitautoren Gegenanzeige und verwandelten die Gerichtsszene in ein Tribunal gegen Klassenjustiz und bürgerliche Doppelmoral. Man saß über die kapitalistische Gesellschaft zu Gericht. Erwin Piscator (1893–1966) verstand es, in *§218* (1929, von Carl Credé) die Aburteilung einer Proletarierfrau in eine Art Volksabstimmung gegen den Abtreibungsparagraphen umzufunktionieren. Ziel war die Überwindung gesellschaftlicher Bedingungen, die zu individuellen Tragödien führen. Obwohl gelegentlich auf das Niveau des Milieustücks abgleitend, unterschied sich das politische Z. deutlich vom naturalistischen Drama des 19. Jh. Nicht Not und Verzweiflung standen am Ende der Vorführung, sondern die Aufforderung, sich zu entscheiden. Der moralische Impetus des Zeittheaters

1120 Zeitungstheater

war aktivistisch. Durch ‹Entfesselung der Tatsachen› appellierte der Zeitautor an den räsonierenden Bürger, sich für die Änderung der gezeigten Zustände einzusetzen, nicht immer ohne Erfolg: Der Aufführung von Peter Martin Lampels (1894–1965) *Revolte im Erziehungshaus* (1928) folgten Reformen in den Verwahrungsanstalten. Geschrieben aus aktuellem Anlaß, waren die Z. für den sofortigen Gebrauch bestimmt. Man sprach daher auch von ‹Gebrauchskunst›. War das Ziel erreicht, verlor das Stück seine Daseinsberechtigung.

Bot die liberale Verfassung der Weimarer Gesellschaft einerseits die Voraussetzung dafür, bestimmte Themenbereiche zu enttabuisieren (wie Sexualfragen; vgl. dazu Ferdinand Bruckners, 1891–1958, *Krankheit der Jugend*, 1926), so dokumentierten andererseits Zensurmaßnahmen gegen Lampels *Giftgas über Berlin* (1929) die unverändert gesellschaftspolitische Brisanz so mancher offenen Staatsgeheimnisse: In Lampels *Giftgas* ging es um die heimliche Wiederaufrüstung der Reichswehr. Mit Beginn der 30er Jahre verlor das Z. rasch an Bedeutung. Zum einen war jetzt wieder Weltanschauungstheater gefragt, nicht aber Kritik an Einzelphänomenen; zum anderen nahm mit Beginn der Weltwirtschaftskrise das unpolitische Unterhaltungstheater einen erneuten Aufschwung.

Hermand, J./Trommler, F.: Die Kultur der Weimarer Republik. München 1978, S. 246–256; Ihering, H.: Zeittheater. In: Glaeser, E. (Hg.): Fazit. Hamburg 1929, S. 261–286; Rühle, G.: Das Zeitstück (1967). In: ders.: Theater in unserer Zeit, Frankfurt/M. [2]1980, S. 82–118; Schneider, H.: Das Zeitstück. Probleme der Justiz. In: Weimarer Republik, Ausstellungskatalog. Berlin [3]1977, S. 835–842.

Carl Wege

Zeitungstheater

Erste Techniken des → ‹Theaters der Unterdrückten›, die Augusto Boal (*1931) mit seinen Mitarbeitern Ende der 60er Jahre entwickelte. Ein Akteur liest auf der Straße Zeitungsberichte vor, versucht durch Kontrastierung, Rhythmus, Pantomime, Pointen u. a. dem Zuhörer Widersprüche bewußt zu machen und die sog. ‹Objektivität› der Presse zu entlarven.

Boal, A.: Theater der Unterdrückten. Frankfurt/M. 1979.

Martin Franzbach

Zentralverband Schweizer Volkstheater (ZSV)

Entspricht dem →BDAT. Fast 200 Mitgliedervereine; 1983/84 brachten sie nahezu 1300 Aufführungen mit 320000 Zuschauern.

Monatszeitschrift: Theaterzytig.

Hans-Wolfgang Nickel

Zimmertheater

In der Notlage nach dem 2. Weltkrieg in Deutschland und Österreich entstandene Form des Theaters auf kleinstem Raum, sozusagen Miniatur-Kammertheater, weil die Theatergebäude z. T. zerstört waren oder wegen Kohlemangels nicht beheizt werden konnten. Weniger als 100 Zuschauerplätze, sehr kleine Bühne, vorwiegend Aufführung von Stücken mit wenigen Personen, oft auch als Experimentierbühne. Erste Z. 1945 in Düsseldorf, Hamburg (Theater im Zimmer), Bremen. In Wien in der Form des Kellertheaters.

Horst Schumacher

Zirkus

(Nach lat. ‹circus›, griech. ‹kírkos›, der Kreis) Bezeichnung für ein Gebäude (zumeist ein Zelt), in dem Darbietungen von Akrobaten, Clowns, Dressuren u. a. gezeigt werden, sowie für das Programm als Ganzes. Bei kaum einer anderen theatralischen Form ist wie beim Z. die Entwicklung eines bestimmten Gebäudetyps und einer Bühnenform derart unmittelbar mit der Entwicklung des Programms verbunden. Z. ist eine synthetische Form, die Zusammenstellung unabhängiger und in sich geschlossener Darbietungen zu einem neuen Ganzen. Die einzelnen Nummern des Z. haben eine lange, bis in die Antike reichende Tradition; neu ist am Z. ihre nach kompositorischen Gesichtspunkten geordnete Zusammenstellung, der Verzicht auf jede Form von Wettkampf. Dies verbietet es, den modernen Z. als Nachfolger der antiken «circenses» anzusehen. Von Einfluß auf den Z. waren indessen die→Schaustellerei, die Vorführungen auf Jahrmärkten (→Fahrendes Volk).

Als im 18. Jh. die Jahrmärkte ihre Bedeutung verloren, mußten sich auch die Schausteller neue Arbeitsfelder suchen, u. a. im entstehenden Z. Der ehem. Soldat Philipp Astley eröffnete 1772 in London eine «riding-school», die er später überdachen ließ. Sein «amphitheatre» gilt als das erste Z.-Gebäude der Welt. Es enthielt bereits die runde Manege, bis heute unverzichtbarer Bestandteil jedes Z. Die Form ergab sich zwangsläufig, da nur auf einer runden Bahn Akrobatik auf dem Pferd möglich ist. Das Pferd aber dominierte im frühen Z., entsprechend den Interessen des meist der Oberschicht angehörenden Publikums. Zwar zeigte auch Astley in London wie in seinem am 7. 7. 1782 in Paris eröffneten ‹Amphitheater› Seiltänzer, Athleten, Abnormitäten und heroische Pantomimen, im wesentlichen aber nur als Pausenfüller. Als er 1793 wegen der Revolutionskriege Paris verlassen mußte, übernahm der Artist Antoine Franconi das Haus, bis er am 28. 12. 1807 den «Cirque olympique» eröffnete. Ein Dekret Napoleons, das die Bezeichnung ‹Theater› für die Aufführung von Raritäten und Kuriositäten verbot, hatte die Aufgabe der Bezeichnung ‹Amphitheater› erzwungen. Der Vorliebe der Zeit für Antikes entsprechend, benannte Franconi sein neues Haus um, dessen Erfolg Z. rasch zur allg. benutzten Gattungsbezeichnung machte. – Der Einfluß des Theaters auf die neue Kunstform führte zum Einbau immer größerer Bühnen, zusätzlich zur Manege. Dadurch konnten immer aufwendigere Zirkuspantomimen gezeigt werden, die trotz ihres Namens keineswegs stumm zu sein brauchten.

Für lange Zeit blieb der frz. Z. unerreichtes Vorbild für die Unternehmungen in den übrigen Ländern Europas. Nach 1830 hatte eine Verschiebung der Publikumsstruktur zugunsten des mittleren und Kleinbürgertums eingesetzt, dessen Interesse an Pferden geringer, an Unterhaltung aber größer war als das des bisherigen. So wurden allmählich neue Genres in den Z. aufgenommen. Hierzu gehört u. a. der Clown, der im Z. als Allround-Artist begann und dessen Funktion die des Pausenfüllers war. Vor allem in Deutschland, wo der Z. von Anfang an ein bürgerliches Vergnügen gewesen war, setzte nach 1840 eine Entwicklung ein, die gekennzeichnet ist durch die Differenzierung bestehender und die Aufnahme neuer Genres. Der sich entfaltende amerik. Z. mit dem Streben nach Spitzenleistungen und möglichst raschem Ortswechsel (Benutzung der Eisenbahn) beeinflußte in der zweiten Hälfte des 19. Jh. zunehmend den europ. Z. Hatte man sich im frz. Z. bemüht, den einzelnen Trick in eine Handlung einzubauen, so wurde er jetzt Selbstzweck. Die Pferdedarbietungen verloren endgültig ihre Bedeutung, andere Genres traten gleichberechtigt hinzu, die Clownerie, Parterre- und Luftakrobatik, Jonglerie und seit Mitte des 19. Jh. die Raubtierdressur.

Beibehalten wurde bis zum Jahrhundertende die Zirkuspantomime. Unter dem Einfluß von Buffalo Bills «Wild West Circus» wurden auch Messerwerfer und Kunstschützen in den Z. integriert sowie als letztes Genre die Zauberei. Anders als im amerik. Z. hatte in Europa das Zeigen von menschlichen und tierischen Abnormitäten, die sog. «Side-Show», immer nur untergeordnete Bedeutung. Hier waren wichtiger sog. «Völkerschauen», die Gruppen von Eingeborenen aus den Kolonien als Attraktion vorführten. Die Weiterentwicklung des Z. führte auch zu veränderten Arbeitsformen. Die Entwicklung einzelner Nummern an Stelle der Ensembleleistung, die Konkurrenz der → Varietés führten zu einem immer rascheren Wechsel des Programms. Z. wurde mehr und mehr eine Geldanlage, die sich möglichst schnell amortisieren mußte.

In Europa behinderten vor allem die beiden Weltkriege die kontinuierliche Weiterentwicklung des Z., in Deutschland kam hinzu die Vertreibung und Ermordung zahlreicher Artisten in der Zeit der faschistischen Herrschaft. Qualitative Veränderungen erlebte der Z. in dieser Zeit nur in der Sowjetunion, wo man nach der Oktoberrevolution sehr schnell die wichtige Rolle erkannte, die der Z. für die Unterhaltung und Beeinflussung des Publikums bot. Während in den sozialistischen Ländern vor allem staatliche Z.-Unternehmen bestanden und der Nachwuchs auf staatlichen Fachschulen ausgebildet wurde (bei heute zumeist ungesicherter Zukunft), nahm die Zahl selbständiger Unternehmen in Westeuropa und Amerika ständig ab. – Zu erwähnen bleiben noch Versuche, die alten Traditionen des Z. wiederzubeleben. 1974 wurde in Paris von der traditionsreichen Artistenfamilie Gruss der «Cirque Gruss à l'ancienne» gegr., in dem nur klassische Z.-Nummern gezeigt werden. 1976 wurde von Bernhard Paul der Z. «Roncalli» gegr., der sich zum Ziel gesetzt hat, die Poesie in den Z. zurückzubringen. Der unerwartete Erfolg gab dem Experiment recht. Zahlreiche Nachahmungen entstanden, und auch traditionelle Z.-Unternehmen streben inzwischen etwas Ähnliches an.

Adrian: Histoire illustrée des cirques parisiens d'hier et d'aujourd'hui. Paris 1957; Artisten. Berlin 1986 (Katalog); Barloewen, C. v.: Clowns. Königstein 1981; Bemmann, H. (Hg.): Die Artisten. Berlin 1965; Berger, R./Winkler, D.: Künstler, Clowns und Akrobaten. Berlin 1983; Bogdan, R.: Freak Show. Chicago 1988; Bose, G./Brinkmann, E.: Circus. Berlin 1978; Christl., O.: Zirkushistorische Forschungsarbeit in Europa und Amerika. Linz 1961; Clement, H./Jando, D.: The Great Circus Parade. Milwaukee 1989; Coutet, A.: La vie du cirque. Grenoble, Paris 1948; Culhane, J.: The American Circus. New York 1990; Durant, J. und A.: Pictorial History of the American Circus. New York 1962; Eberstaller, G.: Zirkus und Varieté in Wien. Wien 1974; Günther E./Winkler, D.: Zirkusgeschichte. Berlin 1986; Halperson, J.: Das Buch vom Zirkus. Düsseldorf 1926; Jando, D.: Histoire mondiale du cirque. Paris 1977; Jay, R.: Sauschlau & feuerfest. Menschen, Tiere, Sensationen des Showbusiness. Offenbach 1988; Johnson, W.: Zauber der Manege? Hamburg 1992; Kiphard, E. J.: Die Akrobatik und ihr Training. Essen 1961; Klünner, H.-W.: Zirkusstadt Berlin. Berlin (1986); Krause, G.: Die Schönheit in der Zirkuskunst. Berlin 1969; Kusnezow, J.: Der Zirkus der Welt (mit einem ergänzenden Teil von E. Günther und G. Krause). Berlin 1970; Lehmann, A.: Unsterblicher Zirkus. Leipzig 1939; Mannix, D. P.: Freaks. San Francisco 1990; May Chappin, E.: The Circus from Rome to Ringling. New York 1963; Merkert, J. (Hg.): Zirkus, Circus, Cirque. Berlin 1978; Peuchmaurd, J.: Eintritt frei – Zirkus. Lausanne 1963; Rausser, F./Platz, H. P.: Cirque – Zirkus – Circo.

Lausanne 1975; Scheugl, H.: Showfreaks & Monster. Köln 1974; Schulz, K./Ehlert, H.: Das Circus Lexikon. Nördlingen 1988; Sluis, F. van: Circus in Europa. Bussum 1966; Thétard, H.: La merveilleuse historie du cirque. 2. Bde. Paris 1947; Toole-Stott, R.: Circus and the Allied Arts. A World Bibliography. 5 Bde. Liverpool 1957–92; Wilsmann, A. Ch.: Die zersägte Jungfrau. Kleine Kulturgeschichte der Zauberkunst. Berlin 1938; Ziethen, K.-H.: Die Kunst der Jonglerie. Berlin 1988.

Wolfgang Beck

Zürcher Schauspielhaus

Privattheater, 1890 erbaut; bis 1921 im Verband des Stadttheaters, 1921–1926 Direktion Franz Wenzler, ab 1926 Direktion Ferdinand Rieser; Ausbau des Innenraums und des Bühnenhauses. Wurde nach der Machtübergabe in Deutschland zum Sammelbecken bedeutender exilierter Schauspieler und Regisseure und avancierte in den Jahren 1933 bis 1945 zur bedeutendsten deutschsprachigen Bühne außerhalb des Reichs, an der viele im Exil entstandene Stücke ihre Erstaufführung erlebten. Bühnenkünstler von unterschiedlicher politischer und weltanschaulicher Gesinnung (u. a. die Schauspieler Therese Giehse, Maria Becker, Sybille Binder, Ernst Ginsberg, Wolfgang Heinz, Kurt Hirschfeld, Kurt Horwitz, Erwin Kalser, Wolfgang Langhoff, Karl Paryla, Leonard Steckel; die Regisseure Gustav Hartung und Leopold Lindtberg; der Bühnenbildner Teo Otto) fanden sich zu einem antifaschistischen Ensemble von seltener Geschlossenheit zusammen, das seinen gemeinsamen Nenner in einem zeit- und gesellschaftskritischen Theater fand. Als Rieser 1938 das Theater verkaufte, machten sich die Nazis Hoffnungen, das verhaßte Emigranten-Ensemble zerschlagen zu können. Durch die Intervention des Schweizer Sozialdemokraten Emil Oprecht – der sich bereits als Verleger um die Verbreitung der Exilliteratur verdient gemacht hatte – gelang es, der Pfauenbühne eine neue finanzielle Basis zu schaffen. Neuer Direktor wurde Oskar Wälterlin, der – bei einer Neuinszenierung pro Woche – einen wesentlich an Klassikeraufführungen orientierten Spielplan konzipierte. Die ‹großen Dramen› Brechts (*Mutter Courage und ihre Kinder, Leben des Galilei, Der gute Mensch von Sezuan*) erlebten hier ihre Uraufführung. Weitere wichtige Erstaufführungen sind: Else Lasker-Schülers *Arthur Aronymus und seine Väter*, Georg Kaisers *Soldat Tanaka* und *Floß der Medusa*, Zuckmayers *Bellmann* und *Des Teufels General*, Bruckners *Denn seine Zeit ist kurz*. Die Feindschaft der Nationalsozialisten hatte sich das Zürcher Schauspielhaus bereits 1933/34 mit den Inszenierungen von Bruckners *Rassen* und Wolfs *Professor Mamlock* zugezogen. – Die Bedeutung des Z. S. liegt in der Bewahrung von künstlerischen und darstellerischen Traditionen der 20er Jahre und Strömungen der Moderne, von denen das dt. Theater in der Zeit des Faschismus abgeschnitten war.

Direktoren nach 1945: bis 1961 Oskar Wälterlin (1895–1961); 1961–64 Kurt Hirschfeld (1902–64), 1965–68 Leopold Lindtberg (1902–84), 1969/70 Dr. Peter Löffler, 1970–78 Harry Buckwitz, 1978–82 Gerhard Klingenberg, 1982–89 Gerd Heinz, 1989–92 Achim Benning, 1992–95 Gerd Leo Kuck. – Der Spielplan Hirschfelds war richtungweisend für das Nachkriegstheater des dt. Sprachraums; UA von Max Frisch und Friedrich Dürrenmatt.

Aller Tage Abend. Eine Rückschau. Schauspielhaus Zürich 1982–1989. Zürich 1989; Bachmann, D./Schneider, R. (Hg.): Das verschonte Haus. Das Zürcher Schauspielhaus im 2. Weltkrieg. Zürich 1987; Dumont, H.: Das Zürcher Schauspielhaus von 1921–1938. Lausanne 1973; Fluchtpunkt Zürich. Nürnberg/Zürich 1987; Jauslin, Ch./Naef, L. (Hg.): Ausgangspunkt Schweiz–Nachwirkungen des Exiltheaters. Willisau 1989; Mittenzwei, W.: Das Zürcher Schauspielhaus 1933–45. Berlin 1979; Schauspielhaus Zürich 1938–1958. Zürich 1958; Schweizer Theaterbuch. Zürich 1964.

Jan Hans/Ingeborg Janich

20. Jahrhundert/Drama und Theater im 20. Jahrhundert

(→Theaterreform, →Stilbühne, →Symbolistisches Theater, →Expressionismus, →Futuristisches Theater, →Konstruktivismus und Theater, →Dramentheorie, →Episches Theater, →Dokumentartheater, →Szenographie, →Theaterbau, →Theatersystem, →Theatertheorie, →Freies Theater)

In der Auseinandersetzung mit dem Theater im 20. Jh. ist die Rede einerseits vom ‹Tod der Tragödie› (G. Steiner), von der ‹Krise des Dramas› (P. Szondi), andererseits von ‹Rückkehr des Tragischen› (J. M. Domenach) und der ‹Erneuerung des Theaters› (J.-P. Sartre). Diese scheinbar widersprüchlichen Aussagen verweisen auf das Spannungsfeld des Theaters heute zwischen Tradition und Erneuerung. Diese Situation ist charakterisiert nicht nur durch die Vielfalt der Bewegungen, Gruppen und Autoren in allen Ländern, sondern auch durch die Vermehrung und Diversifizierung der institutionellen Struktur des Theaters, die Wandlung des Schauspielerstatus und das Experimentieren mit neuen Schauspieltechniken, vor allem aber den neuen Stellenwert von →Regie und →Szenographie. Das Theater hat fortan nicht mehr, wie noch im 19. Jh., Text und Intention des Autors so adäquat wie möglich umzusetzen, sondern die Inszenierung emanzipiert sich vom Autor des literarischen Werks, erhebt Anspruch auf einen eigenen künstlerischen Status. Elemente an-

1126 20. Jahrhundert / Drama und Theater im 20. Jahrhundert

derer Theaterkulturen und Bereiche (→Kabarett, →Music Hall, →Revue, →Zirkus) werden in die Ästhetik des modernen Theaters integriert.

Formgeschichtlich und typologisch zeichnen sich im Theater des 20. Jh. zwei große einander gleich- und entgegenlaufende Entwicklungslinien ab: einerseits die Übernahme und Fortführung der überlieferten →Tragödienform, andererseits Versuche, neue Formen aus tradierten Einzelelementen zu erarbeiten, was Sartre mit dem Sammelbegriff des ‹kritischen Theaters› umschreibt und sich in zwei Tendenzen aufspalten läßt, das →epische und das →tragikomische Theater.

1. Weiterführung der Tradition im Theater des 20. Jh.
Die Bindung an die überlieferte Tragödienform, der Versuch ihrer Wiederbelebung und Weiterführung im 20. Jh. ist um so überraschender, als am Ende des 19. Jh. bedeutende Theaterautoren des Naturalismus (→Naturalistisches Theater) und Symbolismus (→Symbolistisches Theater) den Weg zu einer neuen Dramatik angebahnt hatten: so Henrik Ibsen (1828–1906), August Strindberg (1849–1912), Gerhart Hauptmann (1862–1946), Anton Tschechow (1860–1904) und Alfred Jarry (1873–1907). Trotz dieser Neuansätze bleibt die Auseinandersetzung mit der →Tragödie und dem →Tragischen, wie gebrochen auch immer, zentrales Thema des theatralischen Diskurses auch am Beginn des 20. Jh., wesentlich ausgetragen in Autorenrezeption: Neuinszenierungen antiker Stücke – in Deutschland von Max Reinhardt (1873–1943) bis Peter Stein (*1937) –, Übersetzungen und Adaptationen von Hofmannsthal oder Paul Claudel bis Brecht und Heiner Müller sind eine Konstante im Theater des 20. Jh. Selbst in Stücken des →epischen oder →tragikomischen Theaters oder in der →Komödie spielt diese Auseinandersetzung eine wesentliche Rolle. Es wird vor allem darauf abgezielt, die antiken Motive und Fabeln mit modernen Inhalten aufzufüllen, sie aus neuer Sicht – psychoanalytischer oder philosophischer – zu interpretieren. Diese Tendenz charakterisiert bes. das frz. Theater bis in die 50er Jahre hinein; André Gide (1869–1951), Jean Cocteau (1889–1963), Jean Giraudoux (1882–1944), J.-P. Sartre (1905–80). u. a., gleichermaßen aber auch die dt., engl. oder amerik. Dramatik: T. S. Eliots (1888–1965) *The Family Reunion* (1939) geht auf die *Oresteia* des Aischylos zurück; Eugene O'Neills (1888–1953) *Mourning becomes Electra* (1931) vermischt die Atridenfabel, den amerik. Bürgerkrieg und Freudsche Begriffe. Oft versinkt allerdings in solchen Adaptionsversuchen das Tragische in Banalisierung, Ironisierung, Desakralisierung, jedenfalls in der →Parodie. Selbstkritisch schrieb dazu T. S. Eliot: «Es war nicht möglich, aus den Furien griechische Göttinnen oder moderne Gespenster zu machen. Doch ist ihr Scheitern ganz einfach ein Symptom dafür, wie man notgedrungen scheitern muß, will man Modernes und Antikes zusammenfü-

gen.» Zwei dieser Versuche halten dagegen im Verschleiß der Mythen stand, die *Antigone* von Jean Anouilh (*1910: 1943), worin die antike Maske zum wahren Gesicht der Zeit wurde im Konflikt zwischen Aufstand und Gewalt des damals besetzten Frankreich, und die Versuche von Heiner Müller (*1929: *Philoktet*, 1965; *Herakles* 5, 1966; *Ödipus Tyrann*, 1966; *Prometheus*, 1967; *Medeaspiel*, 1974): Im Marxschen Sinne wird die geschichtliche Tragik zur Komik, die Tragödie zum parabolischen Modell, im Sinne der sozialistischen Utopie zur ‹Farce›.

Allein der christliche Mythos vermag im 20. Jh. die tragische Spannung noch aufrechtzuerhalten, etwa im *Turm* von Hugo von Hofmannsthal (1874–1929: 1926), worin die tragische Struktur von Calderóns *Das Leben, ein Traum* (1600–81; UA 1635) durch die Vorahnung des Faschismus neu gedeutet wird. Oder auch in Rolf Hochhuths *Stellvertreter* (*1931: 1963), ein Stück, in dem der christliche Glaube vor der Ungeheuerlichkeit der Nazi-Greuel auf die Zerreißprobe gestellt ist. Demgegenüber sind die aus christlicher Glaubensüberzeugung verfaßten Tragödien von Georges Bernanos (1888–1948: *Dialogues des Carmélites*, 1952), Henri de Monthérlant (1896–1972: *Port-Royal*, 1954) und vor allem Paul Claudel (1868–1955: *Le Partage de midi* bis *Le soulier de satin*, 1906–25) im Grunde Anti-Tragödien, die Sinnfrage ist hier nie grundsätzlich zur Disposition gestellt.

2. Die Erneuerung des Theaters im 20. Jh.

Wesentlich für die Entwicklung des Theaters im 20. Jh. ist allerdings weniger dieser Rückgriff auf die Tradition, als vielmehr die Suche nach neuen theatralischen Formen und Sprachen, welche die gegenwärtigen Probleme und Konflikte angemessen zum Ausdruck bringen. Viele Autoren, so verschiedenartig ihre Ideologien und Dramaturgien auch sein mögen, sind sich in der Absage an die überlieferte Form des →Illusionstheaters einig. Die Grundtendenzen dieser gemeinsamen Haltung sind etwa so zu bestimmen: Absage an →Mimesis und →Katharsis, →Imitation und →Identifikation dadurch, daß in diese neue Theaterkunst ‹die reflektierende Haltung des Künstlers ihr gegenüber› (Sartre), eine ‹kritische Haltung› (Brecht) integriert ist; der Gebrauch aller Ausdrucksmittel und Genres ohne Trennung oder Hierarchismus, je nach Zweck und Ziel des Autors. Dies impliziert auch ein Inventar aller verfügbaren bühnentechn. Mittel, deren Aufnahme, Kombination, Ausbau und Umgestaltung im Rahmen einer experimentierfreundlichen, offenen, kritischen Haltung. Schließlich die Aufgabe des Tragischen als zentraler theatraler Wirkungsintention zugunsten anderer Affekte. Bei aller Vielfalt der Formen und theatralischen Lösungsversuche ist diese Entwicklung in zwei mehrschichtigen, zugleich widersprüchlichen und konvergierenden Haupttendenzen darstellbar.

1128   20. Jahrhundert / Drama und Theater im 20. Jahrhundert

→ *Episches Theater:* Die Episierung des westlichen Theaters setzt Ende des 19. Jh. mit dem Naturalismus ein, der mit seinen Bauformen und seiner Sprachbehandlung nicht nur die entscheidende Vorstufe für das epische Theater Brechts darstellt, sondern auch die angelsächsischen Autoren des Realismus (→ Realistisches Theater) nach 1945 und die zeitgenössischen Volksstückschreiber entscheidend beeinflußt hat; auch die Amerikaner Tennessee Williams (1914–83: *Endstation Sehnsucht,* 1947) und Arthur Miller (* 1915: *Der Tod des Handlungsreisenden,* 1949) oder Englands ‹zornige junge Männer›, John Osborne (* 1929: *Blick zurück im Zorn,* 1956) oder Arnold Wesker (* 1932: *Roots / Tag für Tag,* 1959) sowie Martin Sperr (* 1944) und Franz Xaver Kroetz (* 1946) stehen in seiner Nachfolge. Im wesentlichen aber entwickelt sich das epische Theater in zwei oft gemeinsam verlaufenden, wenn auch getrennt zu sehenden Richtungen: zum einen unter dem Einfluß von Erwin Piscator (1893 bis 966) das dt. und amerik. → Zeitstück der 20er bis 30er Jahre, zumeist marxistischer Prägung, das in den 60er Jahren im → Dokumentartheater weitergeführt wird, sodann in der wohl umfassendsten Systematisierung des → epischen Theaters durch Bertolt Brecht, samt den sich darauf berufenden Nachfolgern.

Brecht hat das epische Theater als Produkt einer philosophischen, ideologischen und ästhetischen Reflexion entwickelt und in praktischer Theaterarbeit erprobt. Diese im 20. Jh. einmalige Synthese von Theorie und Praxis hat das gesamte zeitgenössische Theater entscheidend beeinflußt, insofern als diese kritische Experimentaldramatik ideologieentlarvend, emanzipatorisch, didaktisch und unterhaltend zugleich ist. Die dramatischen Modelle der marxistischen Utopie, die auf der Bühne erstellt werden, verweisen auf eine über- und durchschaubare, abbildbare und veränderbare Welt, welche bar jeglicher tragischen Perspektive ist. Für viele Autoren, Regisseure und Schauspieler wegweisend ist die Technik der → Verfremdung. Höhepunkte dieser Entwicklung sind die Stücke: *Mutter Courage und ihre Kinder* (1938 / 1939), *Leben des Galilei* (1938 / 39 – 1945 / 46 – 1955), *Herr Puntila und sein Knecht Matti* (1940), *Der gute Mensch von Sezuan* (1938 / 42); *Der kaukasische Kreidekreis* (1943 / 54). – Nachahmungen, aber auch Weiterentwicklungen des Brechttheaters in der DDR bei Peter Hacks (* 1928), Hartmut Lange (* 1937) und Heiner Müller (* 1929), in Frankreich beim reifen Sartre (*Nekrassov,* 1955; *Les séquestrés d'Altona,* 1959) oder, vermischt mit neuen Kommunikationsstrukturen, bei Armand Gatti (* 1924: *Chant public devant deux chaises électriques,* 1966). Der Versuch einer Synthese von epischem Theater und Artauds Vision eines → Theaters der Grausamkeit liegt dem Ritualtheater Jean Genets (1910–86) zugrunde: *Les Bonnes* (1947), *Le Balcon* (1957), *Les Nègres* (1959), *Les Paravents* (1961); ebenso dem *Marat / Sade* (1964) von Peter Weiss (1916–82), alles Stücke, in denen sich die Genauigkeit

20. Jahrhundert / Drama und Theater im 20. Jahrhundert **1129**

einer Brechtschen Parabel mit der Magie Artauds verbindet. Verwendung der parabolischen Form bei Ablehnung der marxistischen Ideologie findet sich bei Max Frisch (1911–91: *Biedermann und die Brandstifter*, 1958; *Andorra*, 1961) oder dem Engländer John Arden (*1930: *Sergeant Musgrave's Dance*, 1959): Nicht die kritische Haltung wird in Frage gestellt, sondern der optimistische Glaube an die Abbildbarkeit und Veränderbarkeit der Welt. Ähnliche kritische Vorbehalte formulieren Martin Walser (*1927: *Imitation oder Realismus*, 1964) und Peter Handke (*1942). Die Einsicht in die Komplexität und Undurchsichtigkeit einer widerspruchsvollen, ambivalenten Wirklichkeit führen zur Ablehnung nicht mehr glaubhafter Utopien und zur Infragestellung zu einschichtiger Geschichtskonstruktionen. Am schärfsten wohl die Verurteilung dieser Art des realistischen Theaters bei Theodor W. Adorno als Vorwurf gegenüber dem →Dokumentartheater: «Überall wird personalisiert, um anonyme Zusammenhänge, die ... nicht länger durchschaubar sind und deren Höllenkälte das verängstigte Bewußtsein nicht mehr ertragen kann, lebendigen Menschen zuzurechnen ... Die Absurdität des Realen drängt auf eine Form, welche die realistische Fassade zerschlägt.» Nach der Vorherrschaft des epischen Theaters zwischen 1930 und 60/70 tritt eine andere Dramaturgie wieder in den Vordergrund, welche der neuen Ratlosigkeit und Skepsis Rechnung trägt.

Komisches und →tragikomisches Theater: Auch hier geht es um kritisches Theater. In neuartiger Sicht vermischen sich im tragikomischen Theater Strukturen und Formen der Komödie und der Tragikomödie, Einsichten des Naturalismus, des Expressionismus, Dadaismus und des Surrealismus, des →Pirandellismus, des sog. →Absurden Theaters und der →Groteske, welche zeitlich parallel zum epischen Theater und sich gelegentlich auch überschneidend mit ihm das Theater im 20. Jh. durchziehen.

Viele der maßgeblichen Autoren des Theaters im 20. Jh. gehören bei aller Verschiedenartigkeit dieser Strömung an oder stehen ihr nahe: von den Naturalisten Henrik Ibsen, Gerhart Hauptmann und Anton Tschechow, über die dt. Expressionisten Carl Sternheim (1878–1942) und Georg Kaiser (1878–1945), den Iren Sean O'Casey (1880–1964), den Italiener Luigi Pirandello (1867–1936), den österr. Volksstückautor Ödön von Horváth (1901–38) bis zu den bedeutenden Zeitgenossen: das erste große Dreigestirn der Tragikomödie nach 1945, Samuel Beckett (1906–89), Eugène Ionesco (*1912), Friedrich Dürrenmatt (1921–90), sodann die Engländer Harold Pinter (*1930), Edward Bond (*1934) und Tom Stoppard (*1937), die Amerikaner Edward Albee (*1928) und Sam Shephard (*1943), der Spanier Fernando Arrabal (*1932), der Pole Slawomir Mrožek (*1930), der Tscheche Václav Havel (*1936); im deutschsprachigen Theater stehen dieser Richtung nahe u. a. Botho Strauß

(*1944) und Peter Handke (*1942). Es ist ein Theater der Unsicherheit, eine Dramaturgie des Zweifels, die den Zuschauer ohne Denkhilfe läßt.

Neben den hier skizzierten Grundtendenzen des Theaters im 20. Jh., die sich in der Auseinandersetzung mit der Theaterliteratur ausgebildet haben, existiert eine Vielfalt →experimenteller Theaterformen, die sich vor allem in zwei Grenzbereichen darstellt; als →Tanztheater und als →Performance (→Aktionskunst, →Happening; →Dramentheorie, →Theatertheorie).

Adorno, Th. W.: Versuch, das Endspiel zu verstehen. In: Noten zur Literatur II. Frankfurt/M. 1961; Arnold, H. L./Buck, Th. (Hg.): Positionen des Dramas. München 1977; Brauneck, M. (Hg.): Das dt. Drama vom Expressionismus bis zur Gegenwart. Bamberg 1970; ders.: Theater im 20. Jh. Reinbek bei Hamburg 1982; ders./Schneilin, G.: Theater und Drama. Bamberg 1986; Domenach, J.-M.: Le retour du tragique. Paris 1967; Downer, A. S.: Fifty Years of American Drama 1900–50. Chicago 1951; Guicharnaud, J.: Modern French Theatre from Giraudoux to Genet. New Haven 1967; Hayman, R.: Theatre and Anti-Theatre – New Movements since Beckett. New York 1979; Hinck, W.: Das moderne Drama in Deutschland. Göttingen 1973; Jacquart, E.: Le théâtre de dérision. Paris 1974; Jacquot, J. (ed.): Le théâtre moderne. Paris 1958–67; Karasek, H.: Dramatik in der Bundesrepublik seit 1945. In: Lattmann, D. (Hg.): Die Literatur der Bundesrepublik Deutschland. München 1973; Klotz, V.: Dramaturgie des Publikums. München 1976; Mennemeier, F. N.: Modernes dt. Drama. München 1973; Sartre, J.-P.: Un théâtre de situations. Paris 1973; Sokel, W.: The Writer in Extremis. Stanford 1959; Steiner, G.: Der Tod der Tragödie. München/Wien 1962; Styan, J. L. Modern drama in theory and practice 1–3. Cambridge 1983; Szondi, P.: Theorie des modernen Dramas. Frankfurt/M. 1956; Wendt, E.: Moderne Dramaturgie. Frankfurt/M. 1974.

Gérard Schneilin

Zwischenakt

Das Wort Z. bezeichnet eigentlich die Pause zwischen den →Akten eines Dramas. Während die Aufführungen v. a. von volkstümlichen Schauspielern urspr. durch Einlagen aller Art, sog. →Zwischenspiele oder Intermezzi, häufiger unterbrochen wurden, beschränkten sich diese Einlagen mit dem Hochkommen der humanistischen Poetik und ihrer Forderung nach strikter Einhaltung der →drei Einheiten von Handlung, Ort und Zeit auf die Pausen zwischen den Akten und gewannen teilweise eine umfangreiche Dimension (Musik, Chor, Ballett, Feuerwerk und Massenaufzüge in der Barockzeit). Sie sollten das Publikum vom Dekorationswechsel auf der Bühne ablenken und es inzwischen unterhalten. Die Modernisierung der Bühnentechnik – z. B. die Drehbühne –, die einen raschen Kulissenwechsel ermöglicht, und die Prinzipien der neuen Dramaturgie haben heutzutage zu äußerster Reduktion – kurze Musikeinlage – bzw. zur Aufgabe des Z. geführt. Auf frz. bezeichnet ‹entracte› sogar nur noch die Pause zum Foyerbesuch in Theater und Oper.

Bernard Poloni

Zwischenspiel

Ein Z. ist ein kurzes dramatisches Spiel, eine heitere oder komische Einlage, oft begleitet von Musik und Tanz, innerhalb der Haupthandlung zu bes. Anlaß (als Kommentar, Kontrast oder Parallelaktion), später vor allem zur Unterhaltung des Publikums während des Szenenwechsels. Ausgangspunkt des Z. ist das antike Theater. Die griech. → Komödie kennt die → Parabase, die mit der Zeit nach dem ersten epeisodion vorverlegt und zu einer launig-ernsten Ansprache – bzw. Gesang des Chors – ohne direkten Zusammenhang mit der Handlung wird; die griech. → Tragödie kennt die → stasimata, die ebenfalls vom Chor zwischen den epeisodia gesungen wurden und sich bei Agathon (um 400 v. Chr.) zu reinen musikalischen Choreinlagen ohne Bezug zur Handlung entwickelten. Das röm. Theater setzt diese Tradition mit → Mimus und → Pantomime fort. Von da aus nahm das Z. in den verschiedenen Ländern mit ihren theatralischen Besonderheiten unterschiedliche Formen an. Die profanen Schauspiele sowie die → Mysterienspiele des Mittelalters pflegen Einlagen aller Art: Tänze, Pantomime einerseits, Psalmen und religiöse Gesänge, Teufels- oder Mirakelszenen anderseits, in denen die Musik eine wichtige Rolle spielte und aus denen sich die → Intermezzi des ital. Theaters im 16. Jh. herausentwickelten. Diese beschränkten sich bald unter Einfluß der Humanisten auf die → Zwischenakt-Pausen, waren anfangs nur Madrigale oder madrigalähnliche Stücke, erweiterten sich dann zu ganzen Musikstücken, komischen Chor- bzw. Singspielen, reichlich ausgestatteten Balletten bzw. in der Barockzeit zu Feuerwerkszenen mit Massenaufzügen. Wiesen die Intermezzi urspr. kaum einen thematischen oder logischen Zusammenhang untereinander bzw. zur Handlung des Dramas auf, so gewannen sie nach und nach thematische Kontinuität, verselbständigten sich und gingen in das Genre der ‹opera buffa› oder der komischen Oper über. – In Frankreich erfährt das Z. eine ähnliche Entwicklung als intermède im 17. und 18. Jh., sei es als Choreinlage bei Etienne Jodelle (1532–73) und bei Jean Racine (1639–99) in *Esther* (1689) und *Athalie* (1691), sei es als komische Einlage mit Musik und Tanz bei Molière (1622–73), etwa in *Le bourgeois gentilhomme* (1670) *Monsieur de Porceaugnac* (1669) oder *Le malade imaginaire* (1673). Im 18. Jh. empfiehlt Denis Diderot (1713–84) mimische ‹jeux entractes› als Zwi-

1132 Zwischenspiel

schenakteinlagen, und Beaumarchais (1732–99) versucht sich darin, doch werden sie vom Théâtre Français nie akzeptiert. Jean-Jacques Rousseau (1712–78) seinerseits schreibt musikalische Z., z. B. in *Le devin du village* (1752); schließlich werden die Z. in die ‹opéra bouffe› eingehen.

In Deutschland behalten die Z. mehr den Charakter von reinen Einlagen, etwa als komische Einlage um die Person von Pickelhering oder Hanswurst bzw. als Balletteinlage im seriösen Drama, ohne sich je zu einer eigenständigen Form weiterzuentwickeln. Die interludes des engl. Theaters entstehen und entwickeln sich unabhängig von der ital. Tradition; es sind urspr. kurze Sketche und Szenen zur Unterhaltung und Belustigung der Zuschauer bei höfischen Festen und Umzügen, dann selbständige Teile eines Festprogramms, in denen allegorische Gestalten in Szene gesetzt werden; mit Henry Medwall (1462?–nach 1500: *Fulgens and Lucres*, 1495) und v. a. mit John Heywood (1497?–1580: *The play of the Weather*, 1533; *The four p's,* 1545) erreicht das engl. ‹interlude› seine Blütezeit, wird dann immer differenzierter und strenger nach Akten und Szenen, Haupt- und Nebenfiguren gegliedert und führt letztlich zum eigentlichen Drama. In Spanien schließlich nimmt das Z. als Einlage bei Festlichkeiten, später, im 17. Jh., eine lustige, nicht selten gar grobianische Einlage zwischen den Akten eines Dramas ohne Zusammenhang mit dessen Inhalt; literarischen Rang erreicht das → ‹entremés› bei den großen Autoren des sog. ‹Goldenen Zeitalters›.

Bernard Poloni

Literaturhinweise **1133**

Allgemeine Bibliographien

Annotated Bibliography of New Publications in the Performing Arts. New York 1970 ff (ersch. alle 3 Monate).

Arnott, J. F., J. W. Robinson: English Theatrical Literature. 1559–1900. A Bibliography. London 1970.

ASSITEJ-Katalog. Ein Verzeichnis der aktuellen Angebote von Theatern und Theaterverlagen für Kinder und Jugendliche. Duisburg u. a. 1983 ff.

Bibliographie des Musikschrifttums. Leipzig 1936–41, Frankfurt/M. 1950 ff (ersch. zweijährl.).

Bibliographies and Indexes in the Performing Arts. Westport 1984 ff (ersch. unregelmäßig).

Bramwell, R. (Hg.): Bibliography of Selected Plays for Performance to & by Children. London o. J.

Breed, P. F., F. M. Sniderman (Hg.): Dramatic criticism index. Detroit 1972.

Brockett, O. G., S. L. Becker, D. C. Bryant: A bibliographical guide to research in speech and dramatic art. Glenview 1963.

Bryan, G. B.: Stage Deaths. A Biographical Guide to International Theatrical Obituaries, 1850 to 1990. 2 Bde. Westport 1991.

Bryan, G. B.: Stage Lives. A Bibliography and Index to Theatrical Biographies in English. O. O. 1985.

Cavanagh, J.: British Theatre. A Bibliography 1901 to 1985. Mottisfont 1989.

Collins, A., A. Seelen: Published Plays and Books on every Aspect of the Theatre. 2 Bde. New York 1967.

Deutsches Bühnen-Jahrbuch. Bd. 1 ff Berlin, Hamburg 1889 ff [1890–1914 u. d. T.: Neuer Theater-Almanach].

Dictionnaire des hommes de théâtre français contemporains. T. 1 ff. Paris 1967 ff.

Hadamowsky, F.: Bücherkunde deutschsprachiger Theaterliteratur. 2 Tle. in 3 Bdn. Wien u. a. 1982–88.

Heidtmann, F., P. S. Ulrich: Wie finde ich film- und theaterwissenschaftliche Literatur? Berlin [2]1988.

Hoerstel, K., I. Schlenker: Verzeichnis der Hochschulschriften, Diplom- und Staatsarbeiten der DDR zum Drama und Theater (1949–1970). Berlin 1973.

The International Bibliography of Theatre 1982 ff. New York 1984 ff.

Lederer, H.: Handbook of East German Drama 1945–1985. New York u. a. 1987.

Litto, F. M.: American dissertations on drama and the theatre. Kent 1969.

Lowe, C. J.: A guide to reference and bibliography for theatre research. Columbus 1971.

Newman, R.: Annotated Bibliography of New Publications in the Performing Arts. 3 Bde. New York 1972.

Possemiers, J.: International Bibliography. Theatre and Youth. Paris o. J.

Ransome, G. G.: Puppets and shadows. A Bibliography. Boston 1931.

Rojek, H. J.: Bibliographie der deutschsprachigen Hochschulschriften zur Theaterwissenschaft von 1953 bis 1960. Berlin 1962.

1134 Literaturhinweise

Schaal, R.: Verzeichnis deutschsprachiger und musikwissenschaftlicher Dissertationen 1861–1960. Kassel 1963.

Schindler, O. G.: Theaterliteratur. Wien ^{2}1978.

Schoolcraft, R. N.: Performing Arts Books in Print. New York 1973.

Schuster, R. S.: Gedruckte Spielplanverzeichnisse stehender deutscher Bühnen im Ausgang des 18. Jahrhunderts bis 1896. Eine kritische Bibliographie. Frankfurt/M. 1985.

Schwanbeck, G.: Bibliographie der deutschsprachigen Hochschulschriften zur Theaterwissenschaft von 1885–1952. Berlin 1956.

Slevin, G.: Drama in Education: a Bibliography. London 1971.

Stagecraft and Theatre: a Bibliography. London 1965.

Stratman, C. J.: Bibliography of Medieval Drama. 2 Bde. New York ^{2}1972.

Teatro. Bibliografia. Madrid 1961.

Theater heute. Jahrbuch. Velber 1960ff.

Trussler, S. (Hg.): Theatre facts supplement. Bibliography series. Nr. 1ff London, Los Angeles 1975ff.

Ulrich, P. S.: Theater, Tanz und Musik im Deutschen Bühnenjahrbuch. Ein Fundstellennachweis. 2 Bde. u. 1 Nachtragsbd. Berlin 1985ff.

Van Tassel, W. H. Theory and Practice in Theatre for Children. An annotated bibliography. Diss. Univ. of Denver 1969.

Veinstein, A. (Hg.): Catalogue des films sur le théâtre et l'art du mime. Paris 1965.

Whalon, M. K.: Performing Arts research. Detroit 1976.

Wolf, M. (Bearb.): Bibliographie Darstellende Kunst und Musik. 3 Bde. München 1991.

Wormser, O.: Le théâtre et l'enseignement. Bibliographie commentée. Paris 1953.

Enzyklopädien, Lexika, Schauspielführer

Allgayer, W. (Hg.): Dramenlexikon. 2 Bde. Köln, Berlin 1958–60.

Arpe, V.: Knaurs Schauspielführer. München, Zürich (neu bearb.) 1979.

Banham, M. (Hg.): The Cambridge Guide to World Theatre. Cambridge 1988.

Berger, K. H., K. Böttcher, L. Hoffmann, M. Naumann: Schauspielführer. 3 Bde. in 6. Berlin 1975.

Bordman, G.: The Oxford Companian to American Theatre. New York 1984.

Bremser, M. (Hg.): International Dictionary of Ballet. London 1991.

Couty, D., Rey, A.: Le Théâtre. Paris 1980.

Crampton, E.: Handbook of Theatre. London 1973.

Dictionnaire des personnages dramatiques et littéraires de tous les temps et de tous les pays. Paris 1960.

Dieterich, G.: Pequeño diccionario del teatro mundial. Madrid 1974.

Dramenlexikon. Hg. Deutsches Theatermuseum. Jahrband 1985ff. München 1986ff.

Emmel, F.: rororo-Schauspielführer. Reinbek ^{3}1970.

Enciclopedia dello spettacolo. 9 Bde. Rom 1954–62. Aggiornamento 1955–65. Rom 1966. Appendice di aggiornamento: Cinema. Rom 1963. Indice repertorio. Rom 1969.

Encyclopédie du théâtre contemporain. 2 Bde. Paris 1957–59.

Literaturhinweise 1135

Gassner, J., E. Quinn (Hg.): The Reader's Encyclopedia of World Drama. London 1970.

Gregor, J. [ab Bd. 7: Dietrich, M.] (Hg.): Der Schauspielführer. Bd. 1 ff. Stuttgart 1953 ff.

Hensel, G.: Spielplan. Schauspielführer von der Antike bis zur Gegenwart. Frankfurt/M., Berlin 1986.

Kathrein, K.: rororo Schauspielführer. Reinbek (29.–33. Tsd.) 1991.

Kienzle, S.: Schauspielführer der Gegenwart. Stuttgart 5 1990.

Kosch, W. (ab Bd. 3: I. Bigler-Marschall): Deutsches Theater-Lexikon. Bd. 1 ff. Klagenfurt u. a.; Bern 1953 ff [*noch im Ersch.*]

Kröjer, M. [d. i. Collet, P.]: Theater A–Z. Antwerpen 1959.

Lounsbury, W. C.: Theatre backstage from A to Z. Seattle (neu bearb.) 1973.

McGraw-Hill Encyclopedia of world drama. 4 Bde. New York 1872.

Pavis, P.: Dictionnaire du théâtre. Paris 1980.

Rischbieter, H. (Hg.): Theater-Lexikon. Zürich u. a. 1983.

Schneider, O.: Tanz-Lexikon. Wien, Mainz 1985.

Teatral'naja enciclopedija. 5 Bde. Moskau 1961–67.

El teatro. Enciclopedia del arte escenico. Barcelona 1958.

Trilse, Ch. u. a.: Theaterlexikon. Berlin 2 1978.

Who's who in the arts. Hg. O. J. Groeg. 2 Bde. Ottobrunn 1975.

Who's who in the theatre. London 16 1977.

Winkler, G. (Hg.): Unterhaltungskunst A–Z. Berlin 1978.

Theaterzeitschriften

ASSITEJ. Publikationsorgan der Internationalen Assoziation für Kinder- und Jugendtheater. Sek. BRD. Stuttgart 1970 ff.

L'avant-scène. Journal du théâtre. Paris 1950 ff.

ballett international (vormals: Ballett-Info). Köln 1982 ff.

British theatre review. Eastbourne 1973 ff.

Die Bühne. Wien 1958 ff.

Die Bühnengenossenschaft. Amtliches Organ der Genossenschaft Deutscher Bühnenangehöriger. Hamburg 1949 ff.

Bühnenkunst. Sprache, Musik, Bewegung. Stuttgart 1987 ff.

Bühnentechnische Rundschau. Zeitschrift für Theatertechnik. Berlin 1907 ff.

Bühne und Parkett. Hg. Verband der dt. Volksbühnenvereine. Berlin 1972 ff.

Dance magazine. New York 1926 ff.

Die deutsche Bühne. Monatsschrift des deutschen Bühnenvereins. Köln 1909 ff.

Drama in Education. London 1972 ff.

The drama review (vormals: Tulane drama review). New York 1955 ff.

Drama. Hg. The British Drama League. London 1919 ff.

Forum Modernes Theater. Tübingen 1986 ff.

Interscena. Revue für Szenographie und Theatertechnik. Hg. Institut für Szenographie. Prag 1967 ff.

Maske und Kothurn. Hg. Institut für Theaterwissenschaft an der Universität Wien. Wien 1955 ff.

Medienwissenschaft. Zeitschrift für Rezensionen über Veröffentlichungen zu sämtlichen Medien. Marburg 1987 ff.

Modern drama. Toronto 1958 ff.

1136 Literaturhinweise

Musikbühne. Berlin 1974 ff.

Opera news. New York 1937 ff.

Opernwelt. Die deutsche Opernzeitschrift. Velber 1960 ff.

Performing Arts. Journal. New York 1977 ff.

Plays and Players. London 1953 ff.

Puppenspiel Information. Hg. Verband Deutscher Puppentheater. Wuppertal 1974 ff.

Revue de la Société du théâtre. Paris 1948 ff.

Schweizerische Theaterzeitung. Elgg 1946 ff.

Sipario. Rivista di teatro, scenografia, cinema, balletto, tv. Mailand 1946 ff.

Der Spielplan. Die monatliche Theatervorschau. Braunschweig 1953 ff.

Spiel & Bühne. Hg. Bund Deutscher Amateurtheater. Heidenheim.

Tanzdrama. Hg. Mary Wigman Gesellschaft. Köln 1987 ff.

Teatervetenskap. Informationsskrift fran Institutionen för Teater- och filmvetenshap vid Stockholms Universitet. Stockholm 1969 ff.

Teatr. Moskau 1937 ff.

Theater heute. Velber 1960 ff.

Theater der Zeit. Blätter für Bühne, Film und Musik. Berlin 1946–92.

TheaterZeitSchrift. Beiträge zu Theater, Medien, Kulturpolitik. Hg. Verein zur Erforschung theatraler Verkehrsformen. Berlin 1982 ff.

Theatre. The American Theatre. Hg. The International Theatre Institute of the United States. New York 1969 ff.

Le Théâtre en Pologne. Bulletin mensuel du Centre Polonais de l'Institut International du Théâtre. Warschau 1958 ff.

Theatre design and technology. Journal of the Institute for Theatre Technology. Pittsburgh / Penn. 1965 ff.

Theatre quarterly. London 1971 ff.

Theatre research international. Hg. International Federation for Theatre Research. London 1958 ff.

Theatre studies. The Journal of the Ohio State University Theatre Research Institute. Columbus / Ohio 1954 ff.

Toneel Theatraal. Amsterdam (1990 = 111. Jg.).

Travail théâtral. Lausanne 1970 ff.

Variety. New York 1905 ff.

Lexika der Theatersprache

Giteau, C.: Dictionnaire des arts du spectacle. Paris 1970.

Granville, W.: The theatre dictionary. Westport 1970.

Mara, Th.: The Language of Ballet. Cleveland 1966.

Mehlin, U. H.: Die Fachsprache des Theaters. Düsseldorf 1969.

Philpott, A.: Dictionary of Puppetry. London 1969.

Rae, K., R. Southern (Hg.): Lexique international de termes techniques de théâtre en huit langues. New York 1959.

Rohr, U.: Der Theaterjargon. Berlin 1952.

Schneider, G.: Probensprache der Oper. Tübingen 1983.

Sergel, S. L.: The Language of show biz. Chicago 1973.

Trapido, J. (Hg.): An International Dictionary of Theatre Language. Westport, London 1985.

Literaturhinweise   **1137**

Überblicksdarstellungen

Adler, H. (Hg.): Theater in Lateinamerika. Ein Handbuch. Berlin 1991.

Altman, G., R. Freund, K. Macgowan, W. Melnitz: A Pictorial History of World Theatre. o. O. 1953.

Bablet, D. u. J. Jacquot (Hg.): Les Voies de la création théâtrale. Bd. 1 ff. Paris 1970 ff.

Batchelder, M.: The puppet-theatre-handbook. London 1948.

Berthold, M.: Weltgeschichte des Theaters. Stuttgart 1968.

Dubech, L.: Histoire générale illustrée du théâtre. 5 Bde. Paris 1931–34.

Dumar, G.: Histoire des Spectacles. Paris 1965.

Etherton, M.: The Development of African Drama. London 1982.

Fiocco, A.: Teatro Universale dal Naturalismo ai giorni nostri. Bologna 1963.

Fischer-Lichte, E.: Geschichte des Dramas. 2 Bde. Tübingen 1990.

Freedley, G., J. A. Reeves: A History of the Theatre. New York [3] 1968.

Frenzel, H. A.: Geschichte des Theaters. Daten und Dokumente 1470–1890. München [2] 1984.

Frischauer, P. (Hg.): Die Welt der Bühne als Bühne der Welt. 2 Bde. Hamburg 1967.

Gascoigne, B.: World Theatre. London 1968.

Ghilardi, F.: Storia del teatro. Mailand 1961.

Gregor, J.: Weltgeschichte des Theaters. Zürich 1933.

Hoyo, A. del: Teatro mundial. Madrid 1955.

Hürlimann, M. (Hg.): Das Atlantisbuch des Theaters. Zürich, Freiburg 1966.

Kindermann, H. (Hg.): Fernöstliches Theater. Stuttgart 1966.

Kindermann, H.: Theatergeschichte Europas. 10 Bde. Salzburg 1957–1974.

Londré, F. H.: The History of World Theatre. From the English Restoration to the Present. New York 1991.

Moussinac, L.: Le théâtre des origines à nos jours. Paris 1957.

Nicoll, A.: World Drama from Aeschylus to Anouilh. London 1949.

Niculescu, M. u. a. (Hg.): Puppentheater der Welt. Berlin 1966.

Pandolfi, V.: Il teatro drammatico di tutto il mondo dalle origini a oggi. 2 Bde. Rom 1959.

Pignarre, R.: Geschichte des Theaters. Hamburg 1960.

Rischbieter, H., J. Berg: Welttheater. Braunschweig [3] 1985.

Wilson, G. B.: Three Hundred Years of American Drama and Theatre. Englewood Cliffs 1973.

Abkürzungen der Fotonachweise

AB (Andrés Barragán), BE (Berliner Ensemble), BH (B. Heyliges), BM (British Museum), BN (Bishu Nandi), CB (Claude Bricage), DF (David Farrell), DG (Denis Gontard), EM (Edward Moeller), FM (Fred Mayer), FP (Festival of Perth), GA (G. Amos), GK (Günther K. Kühnel), GV (Günter Vierow), GW (Gert Weigelt), IB (Ilse Buhs), ITO (Indian Tourism Office, New Delhi), JA (Jun Abe), KH (Kanedo Hiroshi), Ki (Kilian), Kr (Kranl), LR (Lola Rogge), MB (Michel Berger), MBi (Michel Biannoulatos), Mg (Magnum), MN (Marcello Norberth), MSt (Maria Steinfeld), OP (Oscar Pugliese), PR (Pablo Reinoso), PTM (Piccolo Teatro di Milano), RC (Rosemarie Clausen), RP (Photo Renger-Patzsch), RPa (Roald Pay), RR (Richard Rutledge), RW (Ruth Walz), SNA (Sangeet Natak Academi, New Delhi), SP (Sebastian Papa), SS (Soichi Sunami), Th (Photo Thiele), TS (Hamburger Theatersammlung), WSt (White Studios, N.Y.)